Theoretical **Models** and **Processes** of Reading

Fifth Edition

Robert B. Ruddell
University of California at Berkeley

Norman J. Unrau
California State University,
Los Angeles

EDITORS

INTERNATIONAL
Reading Association
800 BARKSDALE ROAD, PO BOX 8139
NEWARK, DE 19714-8139, USA
www.reading.org

Director of Publications   Joan M. Irwin
Editorial Director, Books and Special Projects   Matthew W. Baker
Managing Editor   Shannon Benner
Permissions Editor   Janet S. Parrack
Acquisitions and Communications Coordinator   Corinne M. Mooney
Associate Editor, Books and Special Projects   Sara J. Murphy
Assistant Editor   Charlene M. Nichols
Administrative Assistant   Michele Jester
Senior Editorial Assistant   Tyanna L. Collins
Production Department Manager   Iona Muscella
Supervisor, Electronic Publishing   Anette Schütz
Senior Electronic Publishing Specialist   Cheryl J. Strum
Electronic Publishing Specialist   R. Lynn Harrison
Proofreader   Elizabeth C. Hunt

Project Editors   Matthew W. Baker and Shannon Benner

Cover Design   eureka

Library of Congress Cataloging-in-Publication Data
Theoretical models and processes of reading / Robert B. Ruddell, Norman J. Unrau, editors.--5th ed.
    p. cm.
 ISBN 0-87207-502-8 (pbk.) — ISBN 0-87207-503-6 (supplementary CD)
 1. Reading. 2. Reading—Research.   I. Ruddell, Robert B.   II. Unrau Norman.
 LB1050.T48 2004
 428.4--dc22

                                                        2004001313

Dedicated to pioneering
and contemporary reading researchers
who have made a difference.

Contents

Section Three

Models of Reading and Writing Processes

Section Four

Literacy's New Horizons: An Emerging Agenda for Tomorrow's Research and Practice

Preface

Welcome to the world of reading and literacy research. We (Robert Ruddell and Norman Unrau) invite you to join us in the exciting exploration and understanding of the reading process—the process that pioneer reading theoretician Edmund Burke Huey called "the most intricate workings of the human mind...and the most remarkable specific performance that civilization has learned in all its history" (1908/1968, p. 6). Although this is the fifth edition of *Theoretical Models and Processes of Reading* (TMPR5), you will find that 70% of the selections in this volume have not appeared in earlier editions. A compact disc (CD) supplements the book and contains selections from current research, as well as classics from previous editions of TMPR, to enrich and support the TMPR5 selections contained here.

Our specific goals in this preface are

- to briefly explain the overall purposes that guided the selection of pieces for TMPR5,

- to share a brief background on the past editions of TMPR (1970, 1976, 1985, 1994) leading to the present fifth edition,

- to identify the specific criteria used in selecting individual pieces for this volume and to provide a brief glimpse into the content of TMPR5, and

- to acknowledge those individuals who assisted us in the development of TMPR5.

Purposes of This Volume

We thoroughly searched the past and most current theory and research literature to identify pieces that could be used to develop

- an in-depth knowledge and understanding of the most current reading and literacy research,

- an understanding of a wide range of research designs and their application to expanding the literacy knowledge base,

- a precise understanding of a wide range of theoretical models and cognitive processes,

- the ability to critically evaluate and critique a wide range of reading and literacy research,

- the ability to assess a wide range of literacy theories reflected in various theoretical models, and

- an understanding of reading and literacy research and the ability to use and apply this knowledge base in generating new research and informing instructional decision making.

A Brief Background on *Theoretical Models and Processes of Reading*

The first edition of TMPR grew from a symposium presented at the 14th Annual Convention of the International Reading Association held in Kansas City, Missouri, in 1969. Harry Singer, University of California, Riverside, and Robert Ruddell, University of California, Berkeley, had discussed the idea that a published book might grow from invited speakers' high-quality research presentations at the convention. But, central to this idea was the creation of a volume to honor Professor Jack Holmes, University of California, Berkeley, who passed away in 1968. Holmes had been Singer's doctoral advisor and mentor and Ruddell's former senior colleague at Berkeley.

This collection of papers, edited by Singer and Ruddell, was published in 1970 as the first edition of TMPR. The book contained two major parts. The first part contained six papers and reactions, which came directly from the symposium and dealt with linguistic, perceptual, and cognitive components of the reading process. Contributors to this part included S. Jay Samuels, Joanna Williams, George Spache, Russell Stauffer, Roy Kress, and Albert Kingston.

The second part of the volume included nine selected articles that developed theoretical models of the reading process, including Jack Holmes's Substrata-Factor Theory, Kenneth Goodman's "psycholinguistic guessing game," Richard Venezky and Robert Calfee's reading competency model, and Eleanor Gibson's classic article on learning to read.

That first volume, 348 pages in length, was used immediately and widely in graduate reading programs across the United States.

The second edition, published in 1976, was approximately 75% new and more than twice as long (768 pages) as the first edition. Several new ideas for TMPR2 had come out of the editors' preplanning discussions—either in Harry's home in Riverside or Bob's study in Berkeley. For example, the editors decided to provide focusing questions at the beginning of each section and to include research articles that would illustrate various research traditions. This volume was dedicated to those researchers whose work contributed to an understanding of the reading process.

This 1976 volume had four sections:

- "Introduction," which highlighted pioneers in reading research and the nature of the reading process
- "Processes of Reading," which contained subsections on language, visual processing, perception, word recognition, cognition, affect, and cultural interaction;
- "Models," which included pieces based on psycholinguistics (Ruddell and Goodman), information processing (including Gough and Anderson), developmental differences (Holmes and Singer), and affect (Mathewson); and
- "Teaching and Research Issues," with pieces by Harry Singer, Richard Venezky and colleagues, George Miller, and Irene Athey, which focused on teaching, modeling, text comprehension, and developmental processes, respectively.

The third edition of TMPR, again edited by Singer and Ruddell, was published in 1985 and was dedicated to professors, researchers, and graduate students who formulate theories of reading and literacy, test hypotheses, and generate new knowledge in the field. The four main sections of this 976-page volume were "Historical Changes in Reading," "Processes of Reading," "Models of Reading," and "Teaching and Research Issues," which, while similar in topic to the 1976 edition, were comprised of more than 70% new selections.

Examination of the third edition's content quickly reveals the impact of theory and research from literacy's allied disciplines, ranging from cognitive psychology with emphasis on schema theory and metacognition to sociolinguistics emphasizing greater concern for cultural and ethnic diversity in literacy learning. New to that volume, each "Processes of Reading" section included at least one research exemplar article to complement each major theory piece.

The fourth edition of TMPR, published in 1994, was dedicated to a consummate theory builder and researcher of reading processes—the late Harry Singer (1925–1988).

This fourth edition, like its predecessors, had grown in length (1,296 pages), but also like previous editions, the majority of the content provided new frameworks and insights (more than 80% of the selected articles had not appeared in earlier volumes). This volume also retained four main themes of earlier editions: "Historical Changes in Reading: Researchers and Their Research," "Processes of Reading and Literacy," "Models of Reading and Literacy Processes," and "New Paradigms: Theory, Research, and Curriculum."

The selections found in these four sections of the fourth edition reflected a knowledge explosion in our field over the previous 10 years—new and revised theoretical perspectives, new paradigms, use of multiple research stances, and new research findings.

It is interesting to note that the International Reading Association has sold more than 46,000 copies of the first four editions of TMPR.

Selection Criteria and Content of the Fifth Edition

We, the editors, have spent many hours discussing the structure and content of the present volume. We searched widely for new works to account for the many developments over the last 10 years that have had or will continue to have impact on the literacy field. We also have identified new pieces to fill gaps, eliminated pieces that did not fit, and negotiated about the inclusion of many high-quality theory and research pieces.

The criteria used to guide our selection process consisted of the following:

- The pieces for each of the four sections must represent the very best scholarship in the field.

- Final selections for Section One ("Perspectives on Literacy Research and Its Application: Viewing the Past, Envisioning the Future") and Section Four ("Literacy's New Horizons: An Emerging Agenda for Tomorrow's Research and Practice") must be well conceptualized, reflect a historical perspective identifying key changes in the literacy field, and identify new and promising directions for research and practice.

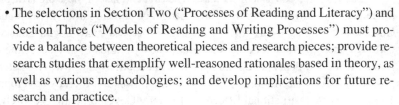

- The selections in Section Two ("Processes of Reading and Literacy") and Section Three ("Models of Reading and Writing Processes") must provide a balance between theoretical pieces and research pieces; provide research studies that exemplify well-reasoned rationales based in theory, as well as various methodologies; and develop implications for future research and practice.

- To the greatest possible extent, research selections need to provide a clear theory-based rationale, connect to a well-constructed research design, formulate logical conclusions and implications that advance the literacy field, and be readable and accessible to graduate students and professionals alike.

While selected pieces from past TMPR editions were retained, major emphasis was placed on the inclusion of recent works that reflect new and promising directions in the field. Fortunately, the CD that supplements TMPR5 has enabled us to include a number of other TMPR classics, as well as a number of recent research pieces that could not be included in TMPR5 because of space limitations.

When we began our work on this edition, Matt Baker, IRA's Editorial Director of Books and Special Projects, asked that we develop a series of questions related to the book and to solicit suggestions from professors and instructors from various universities around the world who had used TMPR4 and previous editions. This survey produced a number of excellent suggestions, many of which have been incorporated into TMPR5. For example, you will find a special emphasis on second-language learning, critical literacy, and delayed or struggling readers, as well as a new section on instructional effects on literacy achievement. The survey responses also influenced the design of Questions for Reflection to account for the integration of research, theory, and practice.

And now, we will shift our attention to a brief peek at the contents of TMPR5. The four major sections of the text parallel those of earlier editions, but close examination reveals a number of distinctive changes.

Section One contextualizes TMPR5 in today's rapidly changing literacy world. For example, the opening conversational piece between Richard Allington and Anne McGill-Franzen identifies key trends and influences in literacy instruction ranging from national assessment to school reform. Patricia Alexander and Emily Fox's work provides important historical insights into literacy research and practice over the past 50 years. Their discussion explores five eras, ranging from the "Era of Conditioned Learning" in the 1950s and early 1960s to the present "Era of Engaged Learning." Each of the five eras identifies key factors that have influenced change in research and practice. The importance of literacy policy and policy research on teaching and learning is highlighted in the contribution from Sheila Valencia and Karen Wixson.

Section Two consists of six parts. The first and last of these areas differ significantly from TMPR4. The first part, "Language and Cognition in Sociocultural Contexts," combines the TMPR4 "Language Processes" and "Social Context and Culture" areas. New selections include those by James Paul Gee, Anne Haas Dyson, Robert Jiménez, and Patton Tabors and Catherine Snow. A greater emphasis has been placed on the role of sociocognition and literacy development. The sixth part, "Instructional Effects on Literacy Development," is entirely new and focuses on the role of teaching and tutoring in literacy development. Works found in this section include those by Robert Ruddell, Rachel Brown and her colleagues, Judith Langer, and Jill Fitzgerald.

The remaining four parts in this section provide a virtual catalog of key factors influencing the acquisition and development of reading processes. For example, Part 2, "Foundations for Literacy Development," provides insight into the development of literate registers (Cox, Fang, & Otto), learning to read words (Juel & Minden-Cupp), phases of word learning with implications for delayed and disabled readers (Ehri & McCormick), texts for beginning readers (Hiebert & Martin), the importance of fluency (Kuhn & Stahl), Matthew effects in reading (Stanovich), and patterns in reading disability (Spear-Swerling).

The three remaining parts emphasize comprehension, metacognition, and reader response and engagement. We provide a mix between the classics and the new in Part 3, "Comprehension Development From Words to Worlds." For example, we have retained Richard Anderson's classic piece on schema theory with John Bransford's response, provided Rand Spiro's latest work on adaptive flexibility, and included a research agenda for improving reading comprehension from the RAND Reading Study Group. Part 4, "Extending Comprehension Through Metacognition," introduces two new pieces, one by Douglas Hacker on self-regulated comprehension and a second by Bonnie Meyer and Leonard Poon on text structure, while retaining the classic Brown, Palincsar, and Armbruster work. The topic of Part 5, "Reader Response, Motivation, and Engagement," has experienced a major research thrust during the past decade. The five selections in this part introduce the reader to leading researchers: Lee Galda and Richard Beach, Donna Alvermann and her colleagues, Joyce Many, John Guthrie and his colleagues, and Robert Ruddell and Norman Unrau.

Section Three of the volume contains a wide range of models that represent markedly different reading and writing theories. We have retained a number of the cognitive-processing models that appeared in previous editions because of their sound rationale and robust nature. From a historical perspective we may view these models as representing different waves of theory development. These extend from S. Jay Samuels, through David Rumelhart, and more recently Marilyn Jager Adams. New to the cognitive-processing focus are models by Marcel Adam Just and Patricia Carpenter, Paul van den Broek and his colleagues, and Walter Kintsch. Mark Sadoski and Allan Paivio have updated their dual coding model, and we have included the new framework for understanding cognition and affect in writing by John Hayes. Louise Rosenblatt's transactional theory model has been retained as has Grover Mathewson's attitude-influence model and Robert Ruddell and Norman Unrau's sociocognitive-based reading-as-a-meaning-construction-process model.

Section Four contains five selections that are all new to TMPR5. Each piece focuses on a different part of the literacy spectrum of the future. The piece by Deborah Dillon and her colleagues calls for a move away from narrow paradigm conflicts and political agendas to a pragmatic approach that allows us to focus our attention on pressing problems that demand solutions if we are to provide a sound knowledge base for literacy growth. Also included is a second selection from the RAND Reading Study Group that offers a blueprint for a well-reasoned agenda to increase understanding of complex reading comprehension processes and for implementing this knowledge base in practice. A vision of a theory of new literacies is developed in the piece by Donald Leu and his colleagues, who emphasize that the protean nature of electronic communication ensures that this form of literacy will remain in constant change. The challenge to literacy educators in using electronic communication is directly confronted in this work. Lorrie Shepard's work develops a historical framework contrasting assessment models in the form of the behaviorist-scientific measurement model and the social-constructivist model. She too challenges educators to examine the purpose of assessment and how purpose is related to desired student outcomes. The last selection in TMPR5 is by Claude Goldenberg, who not only reviews an extensive body of research on literacy learning for low-income children but also presents high-priority implications for instruction and research that are designed to increase literacy development for these children.

We have developed Questions for Reflection for each of the four sections. Our questions are designed to

- encourage readers to link and integrate knowledge across theory, model, and research articles;
- help readers connect knowledge from selections to the reader's professional life;
- assist readers in transforming their current knowledge base through discussion and deeper thinking about the readings;
- prompt (re)considerations of selections in order to get at the "bigger picture"; and
- require summaries and applications of key ideas to classroom reading instruction.

The CD developed for use with TMPR5 provides supporting articles targeted to each of the four sections of the text. For example, the first section is supported by two pieces from TMPR3 (a chapter on pioneers in reading research by Constance McCullough and a review of landmarks in reading research by Harry Singer) and two pieces from TMPR4 (one on reading pioneers and contemporaries by Harold Herber and the other a 30-year literacy journey by P. David Pearson and Diane Stephens).

TMPR5 identifies a number of essential factors that are critical to our continued progress in helping individuals learn to read and comprehend language. We have made significant strides toward that goal, and so we must continue in our efforts as teachers, graduate students, and researchers.

Acknowledgments

As we conclude this preface, we would like to acknowledge and recognize a number of individuals who have assisted us in this demanding effort. First, we wish to thank each of the literacy researchers and theory builders who contributed work and provided permission to use their work in TMPR5. Second, we express our appreciation to those professors and instructors who responded to our questionnaire and expressed their informed opinions and needs that contributed to our selection process for TMPR5. Third, special appreciation is given to the library assistance of Phyllis J. Hallam, Research Associate at the University of California, Berkeley, and Suzanne McEvoy, Research Associate at California State University, Los Angeles, and a graduate student working toward her Ph.D. in Educational Studies at Claremont Graduate University. We would especially like to thank Sandra McCormick, Professor Emeritus, The Ohio State University, for her "close read," research insight, and editorial suggestions for several of the pieces.

We also want to acknowledge the caring and creative encouragement of our families as this edition evolved. To Bob's wife, Sandy, and her thoughtfulness, trust, and patience go heartfelt thanks and admiration. To Norm's wife, Cherene, and her listening ear go volumes of appreciation compressed into these brief words of warm thanksgiving.

Last, and certainly not least, is our appreciation for a number of individuals at IRA headquarters. First among these is Matt Baker, Editorial Director of Books and Special Projects. Matt has provided constant support and encouragement during this edition's evolution. His survey idea has contributed strong field presence to our selection process, and his openness to new ideas, such as the CD that accompanies TMPR5, is greatly appreciated. We also thank Joan Irwin, Director of Publications, who has had an influential hand in supporting this and previous editions of TMPR. We also appreciate the important contribution of the following members of the Publications Division, all of whom worked in some capacity on this book: Shannon Benner, Tyanna Collins, Elizabeth Hunt, Michele Jester, Corinne Mooney, Sara Murphy, Iona Muscella, Charlene Nichols, Janet Parrack, Anette Schuetz, and Cheryl Strum.

Finally, we would like to thank Executive Director Alan Farstrup and the members of the IRA Board of Directors for their support in making this fifth edition of *Theoretical Models and Processes of Reading* possible.

Robert B. Ruddell
Norman J. Unrau

Reference

Huey, E.B. (1968). *The psychology and pedagogy of reading.* Cambridge, MA: MIT Press. (Original work published 1908)

About the Editors

Robert B. Ruddell

Robert B. Ruddell is Professor Emeritus in the Language and Literacy, Society and Culture Faculty Group at the University of California at Berkeley. He has taught teacher credential and graduate courses in reading and language development and was the Director of the Advanced Reading-Language Leadership Program.

Bob began his teaching career at the age of 18 in a one-room country school in the Allegheny Mountains of West Virginia, has taught at all grade levels, and served as a supervisor of reading in a Pennsylvania county schools office. He has mixed his work in public schools with his university teaching and research and has worked with teachers in schools ranging from inner-city to rural areas. He has lectured and conducted workshops for teachers in each of the 50 states of the United States and with teachers in Australia, Canada, England, Germany, Ivory Coast, and Sweden.

Bob is the recipient of the International Reading Association's William S. Gray Citation of Merit, an award that recognizes lifetime achievement and leadership contributions to the field of reading and literacy development. He also received the Oscar S. Causey Research Award from the National Reading Conference in recognition of his research on influential literacy teachers and was awarded the California Reading Hall of Fame "Crystal Apple" teaching award. He is a member of and has been president of the Reading Hall of Fame and has served on the IRA Board of Directors and the California Reading and Literature Project Board.

Bob is the author of *Teaching Children to Read and Write: Becoming an Effective Literacy Teacher* (Allyn & Bacon) and four other college texts. His articles have appeared in *The Reading Teacher* and *Language Arts* as well as in a variety of research journals and yearbooks. His research and teaching interests are focused on the development of comprehension and critical thinking, reader engagement and motivation, and the study of influential teachers.

He received his M.A. degree from West Virginia University and George Peabody College for Teachers and his doctorate from Indiana University.

Bob and his wife, Sandy, enjoy travel throughout the United States and abroad. He also delights in reading suspense and mystery novels and in playing golf.

Norman J. Unrau

Norman J. Unrau is a Professor at California State University, Los Angeles, in the Division of Curriculum and Instruction, where he teaches courses on literacy, cognition, and learning in credential and M.A. programs. He also serves as Coordinator of the M.A. in Education program with a focus on middle and high school curriculum and instruction, and he facilitates M.A. candidates' pursuit of certification by the National Board for Professional Teaching Standards. For several years, he served as a university coach to develop literacy and learning in a large urban middle school in the Los Angeles Unified School District.

Norm completed his master's degree at Columbia University's Teachers College. After 3 years of teaching at Goddard College in Vermont, he migrated to California, where he taught high school English and social studies for nearly 25 years. He completed his doctorate in education at the University of California at Berkeley's Graduate School of Education. His work at Berkeley focused on cognition in reading and writing.

Norm has served as editor of the International Reading Association's *Journal of Adolescent & Adult Literacy*. He is the author of *Content Area Reading and Writing: Fostering Literacies in Middle and High School Cultures* (Merrill/Prentice Hall) and *Thoughtful Teachers, Thoughtful Learners: A Guide to Helping Adolescents Think Critically* (Pippin). For *Literacy in America: An Encyclopedia of History, Theory, and Practice* (ABC-CLIO), he wrote "Models of the Reading Process." He has also published articles on reading, writing, critical thinking, assessment, motivation, and graduate programs in education that have appeared in the *Journal of Adolescent & Adult Literacy, Teacher Education Quarterly, Issues in Teacher Education*, and other professional journals.

When not teaching, writing, or reading, Norm enjoys music. His wife, Cherene, is a piano teacher. Norm also plays tennis, bicycles, swims, hikes, and runs.

Contributors

Marilyn Jager Adams
Soliloquy Learning
Cambridge, Massachusetts, USA

Patricia A. Alexander
University of Maryland
College Park, Maryland, USA

Richard L. Allington
University of Florida
Gainesville, Florida, USA

Donna E. Alvermann
University of Georgia
Athens, Georgia, USA

Daniel K. Anderson
Grinnell Regional
    Medical Center
Grinnell, Iowa, USA

Richard C. Anderson
University of Illinois at Urbana-
    Champaign
Champaign, Illinois, USA

Bonnie B. Armbruster
University of Illinois at Urbana-
    Champaign
Champaign, Illinois, USA

Richard Beach
University of Minnesota
Minneapolis, Minnesota, USA

John D. Bransford
University of Washington
Seattle, Washington, USA

Ann L. Brown
University of California, Berkeley
Berkeley, California, USA
(Deceased)

Rachel Brown
Syracuse University
Syracuse, New York, USA

Dana W. Cammack
Teachers College, Columbia
    University
New York, New York, USA

Patricia A. Carpenter
Carnegie Mellon University
Pittsburgh, Pennsylvania, USA

Courtney B. Cazden
Harvard Graduate School
    of Education
Cambridge, Massachusetts, USA

Julie L. Coiro
University of Connecticut
Storrs, Connecticut, USA

Nathalie Coté
Belmont Abbey College
Belmont, North Carolina, USA

Richard L. Coulson
Southern Illinois University
Carbondale, Illinois, USA

Beverly E. Cox
Purdue University
West Lafayette, Indiana, USA

Kathleen E. Cox
University of Maryland
College Park, Maryland, USA

Deborah R. Dillon
University of Minnesota
Minneapolis, Minnesota, USA

Anne Haas Dyson
Michigan State University
East Lansing, Michigan, USA

Linnea C. Ehri
Graduate Center of the City
    University of New York
New York, New York, USA

Zhihui Fang
University of Florida
Gainesville, Florida

Paul J. Feltovich
Institute for Human and Machine
    Cognition
Pensacola, Florida, USA

Jill Fitzgerald
University of North Carolina
    at Chapel Hill
Chapel Hill, North Carolina, USA

Ellice A. Forman
University of Pittsburgh
Pittsburgh, Pennsylvania, USA

Emily Fox
University of Maryland
College Park, Maryland, USA

Ronald Fyfe
Fyfe & Mitchell Ltd.
Aberdeen, Scotland, United Kingdom

Lee Galda
University of Minnesota
Minneapolis, Minnesota, USA

James Paul Gee
University of Wisconsin-Madison
Madison, Wisconsin, USA

Claude Goldenberg
California State University, Long
    Beach
Long Beach, California, USA

Susan R. Goldman
University of Illinois at Chicago
Chicago, Illinois, USA

Kenneth S. Goodman
University of Arizona
Tucson, Arizona, USA
(Emeritus)

Yetta M. Goodman
University of Arizona
Tucson, Arizona, USA
(Emeritus)

Philip B. Gough
University of Texas
Austin, Texas, USA

Colin Green
The George Washington University
Washington, DC, USA

John T. Guthrie
University of Maryland
College Park, Maryland, USA

Douglas J. Hacker
University of Utah
Salt Lake City, Utah, USA

M.A.K. Halliday
University of Sydney
New South Wales, Sydney, Australia
(Emeritus)

John R. Hayes
Carnegie Mellon University
Pittsburgh, Pennsylvania, USA

Shirley Brice Heath
Stanford University
Stanford, California, USA

Elizabeth E. Heilman
Michigan State University
East Lansing, Michigan, USA

Elfrieda H. Hiebert
University of California, Berkeley
Berkeley, California, USA

Glynda Hull
University of California, Berkeley
Berkeley, California, USA

Robert T. Jiménez
University of Illinois at Urbana-
   Champaign
Champaign, Illinois, USA

Connie Juel
Stanford University
Stanford, California, USA

Marcel Adam Just
Carnegie Mellon University
Pittsburgh, Pennsylvania, USA

Walter Kintsch
University of Colorado
Boulder, Colorado, USA

Charles K. Kinzer
Teachers College, Columbia
   University
New York, New York, USA

Melanie R. Kuhn
Rutgers, The State University of New
   Jersey
New Brunswick, New Jersey, USA

Judith A. Langer
University at Albany
Albany, New York, USA

Donald J. Leu, Jr.
University of Connecticut
Storrs, Connecticut, USA

Geoffrey Lewis
University of Aberdeen
Aberdeen, Scotland, United Kingdom

Tracy Linderholm
University of Florida
Gainesville, Florida, USA

Joyce E. Many
Georgia State University
Atlanta, Georgia, USA

Leigh Ann Martin
University of Michigan
Ann Arbor, Michigan, USA

Grover C. Mathewson
Florida International University
Miami, Florida, USA
(Deceased)

Sandra McCormick
The Ohio State University
Columbus, Ohio, USA
(Emeritus)

Anne McGill-Franzen
University of Florida
Gainesville, Florida, USA

Jamie L. Metsala
University of Maryland
College Park, Maryland, USA

Bonnie J.F. Meyer
Pennsylvania State University
University Park, Pennsylvania, USA

Cecilia Minden-Cupp
Harvard Graduate School
of Education
Cambridge, Massachusetts, USA

Evelyn Mitchell
Fyfe & Mitchell Ltd.
Aberdeen, Scotland, United Kingdom

William E. Nagy
Seattle Pacific University
Seattle, Washington, USA

David G. O'Brien
University of Minnesota
Minneapolis, Minnesota, USA

Beverly White Otto
Northeastern Illinois University
Chicago, Illinois, USA

Allan Paivio
University of Western Ontario
London, Ontario, Canada
(Emeritus)

Annemarie Sullivan Palincsar
University of Michigan
Ann Arbor, Michigan, USA

Leonard W. Poon
University of Georgia
Athens, Georgia, USA

Michael Pressley
Michigan State University
East Lansing, Michigan, USA

RAND Reading Study Group
Santa Monica, California, USA

Mike Rose
University of California
Los Angeles, California, USA

Louise M. Rosenblatt
New York University
New York, New York, USA
(Emeritus)

Robert B. Ruddell
University of California, Berkeley
Berkeley, California, USA
(Emeritus)

David E. Rumelhart
Stanford University
Stanford, California, USA

Mark Sadoski
Texas A&M University
College Station, Texas, USA

S. Jay Samuels
University of Minnesota
Minneapolis, Minnesota, USA

Ted Schuder
Cooperative Educational
Service Agency 10
Chippewa Falls, Wisconsin, USA
(Emeritus)

Judith A. Scott
University of California, Santa Cruz
Santa Cruz, California, USA

Lorrie A. Shepard
University of Colorado at Boulder
Boulder, Colorado, USA

Catherine E. Snow
Harvard University
Cambridge, Massachusetts, USA

Louise Spear-Swerling
Southern Connecticut State
    University
New Haven, Connecticut, USA

Rand J. Spiro
Michigan State University
East Lansing, Michigan, USA

Steven A. Stahl
University of Illinois at Urbana-
    Champaign
Champaign, Illinois, USA

Keith E. Stanovich
University of Toronto
Toronto, Ontario, Canada

Patton O. Tabors
Harvard Graduate School
    of Education
Cambridge, Massachusetts, USA

Yuhtsuen Tzeng
National Chung Cheng University
Chia-Yi, Taiwan, Republic of China

Norman J. Unrau
California State University, Los
    Angeles
Los Angeles, California, USA

Sheila W. Valencia
University of Washington
Seattle, Washington, USA

Paul van den Broek
University of Minnesota
Minneapolis, Minnesota, USA

Peggy Van Meter
Pennsylvania State University
University Park, Pennsylvania, USA

Allan Wigfield
University of Maryland
College Park, Maryland, USA

Joseph M. Wisenbaker
University of Georgia
Athens, Georgia, USA

Karen K. Wixson
University of Michigan
Ann Arbor, Michigan, USA

Josephine P. Young
Arizona State University
Tempe, Arizona, USA

Michael Young
Southern Illinois University
Carbondale, Illinois, USA

Perspectives on Literacy Research and Its Application: Viewing the Past, Envisioning the Future

Introduction

Our intent in Section One is to provide accessible and vibrant articles that enable you to enter conversations about what has affected literacy research and instruction in the past and will without doubt continue to exercise effects in the future. The three articles serve as lenses to look on three separate but interacting spheres: connections between applied research and informed decision making, perspectives of research and theory over the past 50 years, and the influence of policy on both research and instruction. In coming years, this last sphere of policy may well be an exceptionally powerful influence on not only the selection of research topics and methodologies but also on classroom practices.

Where were we? Where are we? Where are we going? These questions guide Richard Allington and Anne McGill-Franzen's piece "Looking Back, Looking Forward: A Conversation About Teaching Reading in the 21st Century" (#1) that begins this section. These two literacy researchers discuss what has troubled them during the recent past and what they have learned from their work with perplexing aspects of literacy. They identify several issues that captured the attention of researchers and educators for significant periods of time: the literacy needs of children from low-income families, accountability programs, tensions between quality of instruction and quality of curriculum materials, disabled and struggling readers, and direct instruction. The authors then explore the future of literacy education, focusing their discussion on school reform (How should schools change?), intervention programs (What programs, if any, work and why?), technology (What role will it play in children's learning to read?), and school quality (How can poor children succeed in good schools?).

More answers to the questions of where we were and hints of where we are going come from Patricia Alexander and Emily Fox, who provide us with "A Historical Perspective on Reading Research and Practice" (#2). In their article, the authors survey the past 50 years of reading history and identify five perspectives on learning beginning with the "Era of Conditioned Learning" in the 1950s and progressing to our current "Era of Engaged Learning" that commenced in the mid-1990s and continues into the present. The authors then distill lessons learned from those 50 years. Their review of 50 years of reading research and instruction magnifies and clarifies factors, such as trends in research, that have guided and shaped the identity and evolution of the field of reading.

In their article, "Literacy Policy and Policy Research That Make a Difference" (#3), Sheila Valencia and Karen Wixson contribute a base of historical understandings about policy, standards, assessment, and instruction. That base could be used to induce and/or inform generalizations, patterns, insights, research recommendations, and professional positions. Further, the base should enable the members of the educational community to adopt a stronger, more constructive role as shapers of policy rather than to serve primarily as recipients of policies they are expected to put into action.

These literacy issues of yesterday and tomorrow are never far from this edition's immediate, central concerns about the vitality and value of literacy research and practice today. Perhaps it will come as no surprise to discover that the first and last sections of this volume address many of the same issues that puzzle and perplex teachers, researchers, administrators, policymakers, and parents. But between the reverberations created by the beginning and the end, we have all the rich research, theory, and practice that fill the middle. Section Two provides a spectrum of studies that are focused on literacy processes and that, like tributaries, often contribute to the oceans of knowledge that have been synthesized into the reading and other literacy models presented in Section Three.

Questions for Reflection

1. What major changes in reading instruction and reading research have occurred over the past 50 years? What were the influences that produced these changes? (#1—Allington & McGill-Franzen; #2—Alexander & Fox; #3—Valencia & Wixson)

2. How has the conception of the reading process changed over the past 50 years? (#2—Alexander & Fox)

3. Which literacy leaders have been instrumental in changing our conceptions of the reading process in recent years and what ideas did they develop that contribute to our conceptualizations? (#1—Allington & McGill-Franzen; #2—Alexander & Fox; #3—Valencia & Wixson)

4. What specific change or changes in reading research and/or practice have you observed personally? What contributed to the change(s) you identified?

5. Rather than simply being recipients of policy change, what action could literacy educators initiate for shaping literacy policies to improve reading and literacy development? (#1—Allington & McGill-Franzen; #2—Alexander & Fox; #3—Valencia & Wixon)

6. Provide an example of a local, state, or national policy that has affected literacy instruction in your classroom or school district. Describe its implementation and the policy's effects. What research base supports this policy? What aspects of the policy's implementation were effective and which could have been improved?

Supplementary CD Selections

CD 1.1 McCullough, C.M. (1985). Pioneers of research in reading. In H. Singer & R.B. Ruddell (Eds.), *Theoretical models and processes of reading* (3rd ed., pp. 2–7). Newark, DE: International Reading Association.

CD 1.2 Singer, H. (1985). A century of landmarks in reading research. In H. Singer & R.B. Ruddell (Eds.), *Theoretical models and processes of reading* (3rd ed., pp. 8–20). Newark, DE: International Reading Association.

CD 1.3 Herber, H.L. (1994). Professional connections: Pioneers and contemporaries in reading. In R.B. Ruddell, M.R. Ruddell, & H. Singer (Eds.), *Theoretical models and processes of reading* (4th ed., pp. 4–21). Newark, DE: International Reading Association.

CD 1.4 Pearson, P.D., & Stephens, D. (1994). Learning about literacy: A 30-year journey. In R.B. Ruddell, M.R. Ruddell, & H. Singer (Eds.), *Theoretical models and processes of reading* (4th ed., pp. 22–42). Newark, DE: International Reading Association.

1

Looking Back, Looking Forward: A Conversation About Teaching Reading in the 21st Century

Richard L. Allington and Anne McGill-Franzen

Turn-of-the-century prognosticating about schooling seems to fall into two broad categories: wildly optimistic or cautiously pessimistic. Perhaps this is because the evaluations of both historical progress and the current state of affairs in schooling also seem to fall into similar categories. The media, for instance, have largely portrayed public schooling in the United States as an outright failure, not only over the past decade (Berliner & Biddle, 1996; Bracey, 1997) but also historically (Rothstein, 1998). Politicians and policymakers have both fed the media and echoed their criticisms. We believe the current public discourse around schooling reflects that of the past. Even Dewey (1968), at the turn of the last century, called for a vastly different education than the norm of factory-like schools that were more frightening than the sweatshops of the day. To be blunt, there is a similar perception about contemporary schools: Public education has failed and drastic change is needed. This perception is even more true, it seems, when the topics of literacy teaching and learning are the focus.

With this context as a backdrop we initiated a discussion of schooling in the United States—particularly literacy teaching and learning—past, present, and, of course, future.

Looking Back

AMF: What have we accomplished since John Dewey called for progressive education?

RLA: As we entered the 20th century, schools in the United States were just coming to grips with compulsory public education. Child labor laws had been enacted and enforced only recently, and compulsory attendance was spotty, especially in the most rural regions of the nation. The city school systems

From *Reading Research Quarterly*, *35*, 136–153. Copyright © 2000 by the International Reading Association.

and the one-room country school provided most children with access to schooling through eighth grade most commonly, but only a few students, and then mostly males, attended school beyond this point. In 1890, for example, fewer than 10% of students were enrolled in secondary schools, and an even smaller percentage of females was enrolled. However, there was a rapid acceleration in high school attendance, and by 1920 universal high school education was required in most states. Nonetheless, two thirds of those who entered high school failed to graduate (Rothstein, 1998).

In addition, the turn of the century marked the emergence of the scientific method as the modern way to solve social problems. There is a familiar ring to much of the educational rhetoric of that era—one that echoes in the rhetoric emanating from the Business Council today. For instance, Elwood Cubberly (1908), then dean of Stanford University's education school, wrote of schools as

> factories in which the raw materials (students) are to be shaped and fashioned into products to meet the various demands of life. The specifications for manufacturing come from the demands of 20th century civilization, and it is the business of schools to build its pupils to the specifications laid down. (pp. 49–52)

Cubberly went on to note that the United States was engaged in a global competition where more highly skilled workers were needed, and, therefore, schooling had to improve. Needed improvements were to be drawn from scientific analyses including time-activity studies and standardized assessments to estimate both the intellectual capacity of students and the effectiveness of teachers. An educational bureaucracy with more centralized and more vigorous control of curriculum and assessment was proposed to manage the new, more efficient methods of schooling. Dissemination of the new science of reading instruction was to be accomplished through the application of the new scientific findings to textbook design, including far more detailed manuals for teachers (Shannon, 1989). Does any of this sound familiar?

AMF: Amazingly familiar. As you said, scientific study was applied to reading within the first few decades of the 20th century, and yet, just a few years ago, the profession felt the need to establish a journal and conference named *Scientific Studies of Reading*, lest we reading people forget our roots in scientific inquiry.

Beginning in 1915, there were recommendations for effective reading instruction offered by a handful of education and psychology professors in the yearbooks of the National Society for the Study of Education. The research of William S. Gray and E.L. Thorndike, for example, was used to design graded reading materials using controlled vocabulary, surely one of the most important developments in the teaching of reading in the 20th century. Concerns about substantial failure in learning to read prompted these new designs for beginning reading materials. For instance, from the late 1920s to the early 1960s, fewer and fewer unique words were introduced in the primary readers, leading some advocates to decry the whole-word method as overly simplistic and limiting to children's reading development (McGill-Franzen, 1993; Smith, 1934/1965).

Nonetheless, in terms of reading curriculum, the controlled-vocabulary basal reader dominated from 1930 to the late 1980s. The directed-reading activity emerged as the dominant instructional activity; seatwork, using the ubiquitous workbook, became another. Matching children with graded books at a level appropriate to their development became a central, if often ignored, tenet of reading instruction. Betts (1949) promoted informal oral reading criteria for placing students with texts at their independent or instructional reading levels, thus creating an instructional framework that endures to this day. Students were organized into three groups for reading instruction. According to the differentiated educational experiences plan, a scientific idea of this time (Allington, 1991), pacing through the curriculum was based on some estimate of each group's capacity for learning. There were other schemes—such as the Joplin, Missouri, plan—that grouped children by reading achievement, regardless of age, for their reading lessons, an arrangement that is gaining in popularity today.

During the 1920s and 1930s reading instruction shifted from a heavy reliance on oral recitation to an emphasis on silent reading and comprehension (Allington, 1984). As for the reading curriculum, most commercial basals offered a blend of whole-word and phonics lessons. Basal readers now emphasized childhood experiences more than moral tales and offered less visibly patriotic content in the upper grades (Smith, 1934/1965). There were challenges to the existing order, from both advocates of more child-centered pedagogies and advocates of a return to traditional education (Spring, 1989). By midcentury, Flesch (1955) popularized the call for a greater emphasis on phonics, and Bloomfield and Barnhart (1962) created readers consistent with linguistic theory of the time; but it was the Dick and Jane reader that prevailed (Langer & Allington, 1992), at least until recently.

RLA: Even as the design of reading lessons was drawn from the increasing array of scientific experiments on reading acquisition in the 1930s and 1940s, the popular press rarely wearied of accusing education of replacing basic skills teaching with "fad and fancy" (Rothstein, 1998, p. 16). This seems a central theme in U.S. education—no matter what the actual circumstances, the press finds fault with current instructional practice. If instruction is innovative, the press finds faddism; if instruction is basic, the press finds stagnation.

AMF: In many respects, by 1930 modern schooling, the experience so familiar to all of us, was largely in place. In other words, age/grade groupings were common wherever the number of students was sufficient, graded curriculum materials and achievements were standardized nationally through textbook and test publishers, and centralized educational bureaucracies had developed at state, county, and city levels. Of course, schools were still legally segregated by race in many states and were commonly segregated by social class.

RLA: Progressive reformers of the era characterized schooling as stulti-fyingly uninteresting as well as hardly fostering the goals of a just and democratic society (Luke, 1988). At the same time, conservative critics regularly decried the "slipping standards" and the "rising numbers of illiterates" while calling for a return to traditional schooling (Rothstein, 1998, pp. 10–16). The nation's future often was seen as imperiled because our schools were simply not preparing suf-ficiently skilled workers, scientists, and scholars. This occurred as the United States emerged as a world power both militarily and economically.

In fact, throughout the 1930s, 1940s, and 1950s there were relatively con-sistent complaints about U.S. schools and one reform plan followed another (Cuban, 1990; Rothstein, 1998; Tyack & Cuban, 1995). The 1957 launch of the Russian space satellite, Sputnik, accelerated demands for education reform—demands that schools become more academically challenging. Education was touted as a national defense issue, and, for the first time, the calls for reform im-plicated a substantive role for the federal government (Dow, 1991). But it was, perhaps, the Supreme Court's 1954 *Brown v. Board of Education of Topeka* de-cision (Winston, 1996), undoing the separate but equal doctrine that had al-lowed racially segregated schooling, that would lead most immediately to U.S. federal involvement in education.

AMF: In the 1960s, the U.S. federal government began to fund education programs to improve schools, particularly schools that were recently desegre-gated. The National Defense Education Act of 1959 (NDEA) added guidance counselors, primarily to better identify the intellectually gifted students who were seen as needing an accelerated education to advance rocket science in the United States, and funded the education of teachers to work specifically in low-income communities. I had an NDEA fellowship to attend the University of Pittsburgh [Pennsylvania] for a master's in reading education. Without that support in the late 1960s, I would not have become a teacher. What about you?

RLA: Well, I became an elementary school teacher in 1968. My under-graduate education was funded, in part, by an NDEA loan. But, because I taught in a high-concentration, low-income, rural school, 20% of my debt was forgiv-en each year. In the end, then, I did not have to pay any of that money back. I think I would have still become a teacher without that program, but it did make teaching more attractive, especially in a high-poverty elementary school.

AMF: The Civil Rights Act of 1964 made possible the Elementary and Secondary Education Act of 1965 (ESEA) and federal intervention in local schools. The ESEA was supposed to provide funding for a variety of initiatives, but primarily funding to improve the educational programs of economically dis-advantaged children and youth (McGill-Franzen, 1994). The ESEA also provid-ed funding for an enormous expansion of university-based reading teacher education programs.

RLA: Yes. In fact, the reading profession owes much debt to the ESEA. It was that Act that literally institutionalized reading teachers into the educational workforce. A working premise of ESEA was that adding specially trained reading teachers to schools with many disadvantaged children would improve the quality of classroom reading in those schools. Unfortunately, most reading teachers employed under Title I (called Chapter 1 initially) of the ESEA were simply given a room down the hall where they worked with groups of eligible students (Allington, 1986). There was little evidence that the Title I programs had any substantive positive effects on the quality of classroom instruction, and many have noted problematic impacts of the ESEA.

Head Start, first funded through the Office of Economic Opportunity in 1965, and the Bilingual Education Act of 1968, the Education of Handicapped Children Act of 1975, and ESEA all were federal efforts to foster access to improved education for historically underserved populations of students. At least one of these federal educational initiatives was operating in every U.S. school district by 1976. Thus, federal influence on education was increasing even though education had been viewed historically as a state responsibility and, therefore, no concern of the federal government.

AMF: But federal intervention was motivated by growing evidence that schools served only some students well. The Coleman report (1966) was a wake-up call to U.S. educators: Schools served only to perpetuate the social and economic inequality of society at large; schools did not make a difference in the lives of children from low-income and minority families. The large gap in achievement between minority and white students provided the impetus to try to level the playing field for children disadvantaged by poverty.

In 1967, as a first-year teacher—a junior high teacher in a large, recalcitrant city school district in the southern United States—I witnessed the educational travesty that racial isolation wrought. The junior high student body was entirely minority and poor. I was the school's first reading teacher, hired with Title I money. I taught there for three years. During each of five daily class periods, I had 20 students, a reduction of at least 15 or 20 students from the usual size of an English class. Each quarter the students changed, so no student ever had two quarters of remediation. Because I was the only reading teacher the school had ever had, and because the need was so great, I taught hundreds of students in my three years. None of my seventh graders could read beyond a primer level when they arrived; many could not read at all. One young man proudly showed me what he had been taught in nine years of school: to write his name without copying the label his mother taped to his pencil.

I believe Title I was needed and is still needed. Title I is, in theory, generous, smart policy and a remarkable achievement of federal intervention. Unfortunately, an emphasis on compliance produced unforeseen negative consequences in the implementation of Title I.

RLA: The basic design of these federal initiatives created a second educational system within schools, especially schools with many poor children. In most schools the federal programs were administratively, and often instructionally, separate from the general education program and less effective than had been hoped (Allington, 1994). Timar (1994) succinctly summarized this problem:

> Title I shaped behavior in schools in several unintended ways that, in the long term, inhibited organizational effectiveness.... The program developed its own culture, one that favored uniformity and procedural regularity over innovation, experimentation, and the exercise of professional judgment. Schools could be sanctioned for not following the rules, but they could not be legally sanctioned for failing to teach students. (p. 53)

I would argue that the ESEA policy logic was well crafted but that the implementation went awry. This was a massive program of national scale implemented by trial and error. In fact, most of the highly criticized, red-tape regulatory aspects of Title I evolved after it was clear that many local education agencies were not spending the new federal money on the intended recipients. It is usually quite easy to criticize programs after the fact, but developing ideal social or educational programs that solve the intended problems is a complex undertaking, especially because policy is invariably distorted as it trickles from Washington, D.C., to the state capitals, to districts, and then to schools and classrooms.

AMF: The uniformly disappointing results of the national evaluations of Title I and Head Start (e.g., Austin, Rogers, & Walbesser, 1972; Carter, 1984; Zigler & Muenchow, 1992) sorely tested the heart and will of the people in the United States to continue to support the antipoverty educational programs' legislation of the 1960s.

RLA: Yes, but those disappointing results may have been due to an unbounded optimism that infected many reformers during the 1960s. Zigler and Muenchow (1992) noted, "Some of the hopes of the mid-1960s were naive; some led to inflated promises that no social program could possibly deliver" (p. 1). Title I, for instance, provided a few hundred dollars extra per participating child, and there were always more nonparticipating eligible children than there were participants. The situation has been the same for the Head Start program. Nonetheless, the first large-scale study of Title I–sustained effects (Carter, 1984) suggested that the program had little long-term impact on student reading achievement. But this study showed that early-grades interventions seemed to produce reliably better results than later-grades designs. This finding initiated a shift in Title I policy. For the first 20 years of the program, Title I remediation typically did not begin until third grade or later. As Carter (1984) pointed out, Title I often offered too little, too late. This view was more recently echoed by Puma and his colleagues (1997) in the second longitudinal evaluation of Title I: "The level of instructional assistance Title

I students generally received was in stark contrast to their levels of educational need" (p. iii). Title I has been a large and unwieldy program that has never been adequately funded to achieve the substantial and optimistic goals set for it.

AMF: Nonetheless, the steady and even slightly improving achievement of economically disadvantaged students is testimony to Title I effects. After all, the proportion of school-age children from low-income families increased dramatically between 1960 and 1990, so making even a stable achievement pattern across this period is something of an accomplishment (Grissmer, Kirby, Berends, & Williamson, 1994).

RLA: I agree. Given the track record schools have with children from low-income families and the increased proportion of those children in the school population—almost a 50% rise in 30 years—the relatively small improvements in reading achievement on the National Assessment of Educational Progress (NAEP) over the past 30 years (National Center for Education Statistics, 1998) might be considered an accomplishment. But more on this later.

So, as school systems have struggled to educate increasing proportions of the student population to ever-higher levels of achievement, public concerns about the actual educational attainment levels of graduates seem to have burgeoned. A new era of school accountability was ushered in when minimum competency testing was implemented within a decade (1970–1980) across the United States (Heubert & Hauser, 1999). High school graduation tests were instituted that typically required demonstration of some minimal level of proficiency in the basic skills, with a particular focus on basic reading proficiency. But most states also implemented earlier levels of minimal competency testing in reading, commonly at third and sixth grade. These tests gradually became high-stakes assessments as state education agencies began releasing school performances to the media and identifying blue-ribbon schools and underperforming schools—schools where the proportion of children failing to meet the imposed standard exceeded state benchmarks (Airasian, 1988).

Performance on the minimal competency assessments was most often unsatisfactory in schools enrolling many children from low-income families, even though the achievement levels set on these tests were, in fact, quite minimal levels of proficiency. Nonetheless, every year there were a number of schools that failed to achieve the state minimum standard, and the schools were then targeted for state-sponsored improvement plans. This pattern was repeated in state after state.

AMF: Similarly, the federal government initiated the NAEP in 1971 to monitor student achievement in the basic skills. Across the numerous administrations of the NAEP, and across the various state testing programs, student reading achievement performances gradually improved (Berliner & Biddle, 1996). At the same time, the source of the improved performances, especially the reports of dramatic improvements in achievement in some districts in a very short time, was questioned. For instance, our study of the unintended effects of educational reform (Allington & McGill-Franzen, 1992) demonstrated that, in several of the school districts we studied, virtually all the improvement in reported performance on state tests over a decade could be accounted for by the increased incidence of retention in grade and increased identification of students as disabled. Retention artificially enhanced reported scores, as low-achieving students were held out of the testing for an additional year of schooling and the performances of students with disabilities, if they sat for the exams, were not included on school reports. Haladyna, Nolan, and Haas (1991) reported that substantial test preparation, much of it deemed unethical, existed in schools with the goal of enhancing test performances. Similarly, outright falsification of test performances have been reported in the media too commonly (McGill-Franzen & Allington, 1993). Such concerns are once again being raised in districts across the United States.

RLA: Concern about the low demands of minimum competency tests was one of the reasons national standards and a national test were proposed in the 1990s. This was a proposed level of federal involvement that would have been unthinkable when Title I was created. I think it was with the release of two federal reports in the early 1980s—*A Nation at Risk* (National Commission on Educational Excellence, 1983) and *Becoming a Nation of Readers* (Anderson, Hiebert, Scott, & Wilkinson, 1985)—that it became clear to me that there were plans for even greater federal involvement in education, despite the mixed results of Title I and other federal programs. Along came the first national education summit (Finn, 1991), where the widely implemented minimum competency goals were vociferously derided and a call for world class standards emerged. But the push for federal education standards did not fare well, so federal funds were allocated to support the development of new state standards and assessments of those standards if a state wished to continue receiving federal education funding. The NAEP achievement reporting was altered with absolute proficiency levels established for the first time (Rothman, 1995). Achievement of these new proficiency levels was what was to be reported to the public.

Not surprisingly, the new NAEP proficiency levels were at some variance with actual student performance, and thus the NAEP results became evidence that schools in the United States were failing to educate children sufficiently well. Never mind that the reading achievement of 9-year-olds in the United States on the NAEP kept creeping upward. Never mind that U.S. 9-year-olds outperformed 9-year-olds in 29 of the 32 industrialized nations in recent international literacy comparisons (Elley, 1992). Failure of students to achieve the new NAEP proficiency benchmarks has been used as evidence of the need for fundamental changes to the structure and governance of education in the United States (Bennett et al., 1998) and for changes in reading instructional methods (e.g., Sweet, 1997).

AMF: But Dick, reading methods have changed, and changed again, over the past few decades. Although the controlled-vocabulary basal reading series had remarkable longevity, it was seriously challenged, first by skills-mastery curriculum models and materials in the 1960s and 1970s, then by schema theory and the emphasis on comprehension during the early 1980s. This was followed by a shift toward implementing literature-based instruction, process approaches to writing, and integrated language arts in the late 1980s and early 1990s. This is not to say that basal readers disappeared from U.S. classrooms during that time—they did not (Canney, 1993; Strickland, Walmsley, Bronk, & Weiss, 1994). Rather, commercial basal reading materials changed and, in many classrooms, became but one component of the reading curriculum. Trade book reading and writing both became more prominent (Allington, Guice, Michelson, Baker, & Li, 1996; Knapp, 1995). In some schools basals did disappear from classrooms in the late 1980s and early 1990s, although this was far from a universal experience. Now, I would say that we have gone full circle, with vocabulary control, especially the decodability of words presented (Allington & Woodside-Jiron, 1998b), dominating commercial reading materials and skills mastery emphasized once again.

RLA: But even though the nature of the reading curriculum has shifted over time, elementary school children's reading achievement in the United States has remained quite stable over the past 30 years.

AMF: Are you saying that curriculum materials have nothing to do with achievement?

RLA: Basically, yes. I think this was, in fact, the most important message of the First-Grade Studies (Bond & Dykstra, 1967):

> Future research might well center on teacher and learning situations rather than method and materials. The tremendous range among classrooms within any method points out the importance of elements in the learning situation over and above the methods employed.... Children learn to read by a variety of materials and methods. (p. 67)

The most important variable in teaching reading, I believe, is the quality of classroom reading instruction, and that seems largely independent of the nature of the curriculum materials. It amazes me that it is only recently that we have begun to estimate the impact of access to high-quality teaching. What amazes me more is the incredible impact of access to good classroom teachers. In their study, Bembry, Jordan, Gomez, Anderson, and Mendro (1998) reported enormous differences (e.g., 35+ percentile ranks) in reading achievement for children who spent three years with more effective teachers (upper 40% in achievement gains) compared to children who spent three years with less effective teachers (bottom 40%). Sanders (1998) reported similar differences in patterns of achievement among children whose teachers varied in their instructional effectiveness.

In our recent study of exemplary first-grade teachers (Pressley et al., 1999), there were large effects for exemplary teachers on the achievement of the lowest achieving children. What is interesting is that the teachers Bembry and her colleagues (1998) studied were from a single school district with a common curriculum plan, whereas the exemplary teachers we studied were located in a dozen school districts in five states—the epitome, perhaps, of curriculum materials' variation. I cannot think of better demonstrations of the impotence of curriculum materials.

That said, let me make one more comment: I do think easy access to a rich array of well-designed curriculum materials can make good teaching more likely. Our exemplary teachers routinely used multiple curriculum materials. But I think that was because they viewed their job primarily as teaching children and not as teaching curriculum material. If we take this idea of the importance of children's access to high-quality teachers seriously, I think it suggests a quite different approach to better meeting the needs of children who find learning to read more difficult. That is, we would concentrate more on improving classroom instruction and worry less about special programs and curriculum materials.

AMF: On the topic of special programs, the National Center for Education Statistics (1998) recently reported surprisingly that the majority of personnel in U.S. elementary schools are persons other than classroom teachers. Thus, I would argue that one primary shift that has been accomplished in the latter half of the 20th century is the enormous expansion of remedial and special education, such that nonclassroom teaching personnel, many supported with federal funding, have become a dominant presence in elementary schools. Certainly, the number of children identified as learning disabled (LD) in reading has skyrocketed, a phenomenon that has attracted little notice within the reading profession (McGill-Franzen, 1987) but prompted the recently well-publicized National Institute of Child Health and Human Development (NICHD) research agenda (Lyon, 1995) and the publication of *Preventing Reading Difficulties in Young Children* (Snow, Burns, & Griffin, 1998), a synthesis of research and policy recommendations for beginning reading instruction by the National Research Council.

RLA: Yes, but it remains unclear to me just how research on children with learning disabilities informs us about improving beginning reading for most children.

AMF: The research on learning disabilities is relevant to reading instruction if you believe, as I do, that classification of any child as learning disabled is a socially and politically negotiated process based, at least in part, on family and school resources for intensive instruction for struggling readers, and the public reckoning brought to bear on individual teachers and individual schools for low reading test scores. A combination of these elements, I believe, sustains the erroneous belief that high percentages of young, struggling readers learn differently than their peers and cannot be expected to make average progress or participate in the public accountability stream.

Although struggling readers often confront a host of challenges beyond the quality of their reading instruction, I submit that knowledgeable and caring teachers can teach every child to read, and indeed they hold themselves accountable for doing so. Such teachers know reading development, but they also know the children they teach—not only where each child falls along a continuum of literacy development but also how each child functions as a person within particular family and community contexts. Most important, such teachers do not teach from within a rigid pedagogy—whether so-called constructivist or traditional—they teach from what children need to know. Currently, research in the field of learning disabilities has helped inform teaching and learning of children with diverse abilities and achievement levels, demonstrating that focused reading instruction enables the majority of children who might otherwise be considered learning disabled to achieve levels and at average rates (e.g., Vellutino et al., 1996).

RLA: I don't disagree generally, but there is a widely disseminated misinterpretation of much of the LD intervention work—reporting that such research supports a relatively narrow and rigid pedagogy for beginning reading for all children (e.g., Moats, 1998; Sweet, 1997). Although NICHD officials have discounted these misinterpretations (Fletcher & Lyon, 1998), we still see state policies being enacted based on them (e.g., Allington & Woodside-Jiron, 1998a, 1998b). Let me revise my earlier point: I worry that too much emphasis is being placed on a small subset of reading research, no matter how powerful the findings (Pressley & Allington, 1999). We are better served by attempting to incorporate those studies into the larger set of studies of reading acquisition and effective instruction.

Moving on, I think federal education policy is now shifting based on a recognition of the failure of 30 years of special programs largely segregated from the core curriculum and the general education classroom. Federal program regulations have begun emphasizing in-classroom service models instead of pull-out programs, instruction on the core curriculum rather than on a separate and specialized curriculum, collaboration among general education and special programs personnel, professional development to build school capacity to better serve disadvantaged children, and outside-of-school programs, summer school, and extended day programs (Allington & McGill-Franzen, 1995; National Commission on Time and Learning, 1994).

In addition, the new state standards-setting process and the development of new assessments to measure achievement of those standards, along with new accountability measures for schools where achievement is low, all occupied much of the professional and policy debate in the 1990s (McGill-Franzen, 2000). There is, of course, a link between the recent emphasis on extending school time and these new standards. As the National Commission on Time and Learning (1994) so succinctly put it, "For the past 150 years, American public schools have held time constant and let learning vary.... Holding all students to the same high standards means that some students will need more time" (pp. 1–3).

Coupled with these developments is the widespread public and political support for ending social promotion and not promoting children to the next grade until they have mastered grade-level standards. But such calls are hardly new; they have echoed across the century, and the extra time interventions offered today have been the prescription offered before (Rothstein, 1998).

To me, the recent charges of faddism run rampant in U.S. education and the calls for a return to the basics, especially a return to an emphasis on phonics as the solution to the perceived ills of elementary school reading instruction (Learning First Alliance, 1998), sound substantially like the earlier calls throughout the 20th century. Likewise, the calls for relying on research—or someone's interpretation of some of the research—to solve the educational challenges echoed across the 20th century. It was the research of the 1970s and 1980s that led us away from controlled-vocabulary texts and phonics skill-and-drill programs—the same research that targeted reasons for students' poor comprehension as the major focus for research at the federally funded Center for the Study of Reading at the University of Illinois.

AMF: Throughout the recent history of education whenever there has been a sharp political shift to the left, there has been almost immediately a pull toward the right, so that the center regains equilibrium. I think that the same forces operate in teaching reading. Our exemplary California teachers, who are informants in a cross-state policy study, insist that they knew right away that phonics was missing from the 1987 literature framework for teaching English language arts:

> When we adopted 9 years ago, our previous basal program was more a whole language program, influenced by the state framework. But many teachers in California quickly became aware that the programs were missing a lot of pieces.... We were in the middle of the whole language movement that emphasized literature and deemphasized phonics. We were still teaching phonics, but the programs we adopted didn't have any explicit phonics instruction in them, so the teachers were sort of grabbing what they could because they knew it was important. (McGill-Franzen, Woodside-Jiron, Machado, & Veltema, 1998, p. 10)

Our California respondents in this same policy study did not object to more emphasis on the code in their reading instruction and, in fact, reported more of a phonics emphasis in their practice; rather, they objected to the legislative mandate that they do so.

> The way the legislation is written, it is addressing the areas of need in California and we as educators need to [be accountable in] each of those areas. However, when the legislation gets into telling us how to address those areas, then, because it is written by legislators, not educators, it loses its power. (McGill-Franzen et al., 1998, p. 11)

Exemplary teachers saw the legislative detail as a rebuke to their professionalism, a breach in the contract between them and the community that they as teachers would know how to do the right thing.

Likewise, the emphasis on 1970s skill-and-drill in Head Start and kindergarten classrooms brought about the shrill denouncement of any literacy instruction at all from the National Association for the Education of Young Children (NAEYC) in the 1980s, thus banishing print from classrooms for disadvantaged children for at least a decade, including the innocuous alphabet song (McGill-Franzen, 1993). In the process, research was produced (and published) by progressives that suggested that children taught reading by direct instruction were more likely to become juvenile delinquents (Schweinhart & Weikart, 1998). I believe that the emotionality of the current debate over direct instruction and phonics has its roots in these excesses of the past. It is not far-fetched to speculate, for example, that children from low-income families need direct instruction in phonemic elements of the English language precisely because their experiences in preschool, and even in kindergarten, have been bereft of any such attention. What do you think of my theory?

RLA: Well, the problem for me is this: What do you mean by direct instruction? I think the Sacks and Mergendoller (1997) and the Purcell-Gates, McIntyre, and Freppon (1995) studies, among others, suggest that children from low-income families benefit more from rich language and literacy environments than they do from traditional skills classrooms. But I think that the whole language teachers in the studies often did offer direct instruction in phonemic awareness and letter–sound relationships; they just did not offer the sort of instruction that most people would label direct instruction. Let me ask you, was the instruction offered by the books and the teachers in our Philadelphia kindergarten study direct instruction (McGill-Franzen, Allington, Yokoi, & Brooks, 1999/2000)? There were no teaching scripts. There were no drills, no stack of worksheets, no phonics wall charts.

AMF: Direct instruction does not necessarily mean instruction that is highly scripted in terms of teacher prompts and student response, although I suppose it could be. The defining feature of direction instruction, in my view, is that it is explicit. I am not sure what you mean by drills and worksheets, but I sense that these are code words for bad things. If *drills* is a code name for practice, then yes, practice should follow explicit teaching, and in those kindergarten classes, practice did follow. Remember the word banks? I don't know what to say about worksheets. I have seen worksheet tasks that I liked and others that I didn't like. A task does not have to appear in a worksheet format to be bad, and all worksheet tasks are not bad. I do remember some worksheets in the Philadelphia study kindergarten classes. As for phonics charts, if you are referring to "*a* is for *apple*" charts, then they were indeed on the walls of the kindergartens we observed. Whether anyone used these charts is another question. Why would they, with their word wall in place? I would say that word walls (Cunningham, 1995), with both high-frequency words and common spelling patterns represented there, are a more transparent medium for gaining knowledge of the orthography and more useful for explicit instruction than phonics wall charts.

RLA: Perhaps I have conceded the definition of the term *direct instruction* to those folks who create and market commercial materials that are highly scripted—materials considered teacher proofed. Kameenui, Simmons, Chard, and Dickson (1997) even argued that "the way the information is packaged before teacher delivery" (p. 67) is one of the defining characteristics of direct instruction. I do think instruction often needs to be explicit, to use Duffy's term (Duffy, Roehler, & Rackliffe, 1986). But part of the expertise of effective teachers is knowing what to be explicit about and when. As for skills and worksheets, what I was attempting to emphasize was an enormously reduced role of decontextualized drill and practice today compared to historical practices—especially compared to reading curricula from the 1960s and 1970s.

In fact, in the Philadelphia project (McGill-Franzen et al., 1999/2000), the experimental group of teachers learned how to be explicit while reading a story to kindergarten children, while composing a morning message and modeling sound stretching in front of those children, and so on. But they were not given packages of isolated skills with scripts to follow in introducing those scripts to children. Nonetheless, there does seem to be a consensus that explicitness is necessary for instruction to be effective. Perhaps this is one of the key issues for the 21st century—what to be explicit about and when and how.

One way of thinking about commercial curriculum materials would be to evaluate what features of print and texts they identify as needing explicit instructional attention. The decodable text issue, for instance, seems but a shift in which text features are targeted for explicit attention. But, again, the shift toward more attention to vocabulary control, in this case attention to the relationship of the word structure and the decoding skills children have acquired, seems a response to the basal publishers' recent lack of concern about the type and numbers of unique words that children encountered in beginning reading materials. In other words, many classroom teachers noted the difficulty that beginning readers had when they encountered so many new words of so many different sorts in the literature-based basals or trade book collections (Hoffman et al., 1998).

AMF: Although you refer to curriculum as the materials (or textbooks) of instruction, the curriculum that matters, in my view, is the enacted curriculum. Earlier you emphasized the role of the teacher in the enacted curriculum, but the teacher is only one part, albeit an essential part, of the total context. As Ball and Cohen (1996) and others have pointed out, the enacted curriculum is co-constructed by students and the knowledge they bring to the classroom, by teachers and their understandings, as well as by the materials teachers and students use (Barr, 1975; Weber, 1970). I do not believe that teachers have to create their own curriculum rather than use commercial materials to be considered exemplary. We have been socialized into thinking that commercial curriculum materials are not as effective as curriculum materials that teachers themselves develop. To construct, say, a first- or a third-grade reading curriculum from scratch would require heroic efforts on the part of teachers—I believe you refer to such teachers as Joan of Arc teachers. On the other hand, commercial curriculum materials rarely offer opportunities for teachers to extend their learning beyond implementation of the particular materials at hand, say, for example, with examples of student work or the understandings that underpin such work. However, Reading Recovery does: Teachers build a theory of learning based on the student's response to particular materials. Although many have decried commercial reading materials as deskilling teaching and teachers (Goodman, Shannon, Freeman, & Murphy, 1988), these ubiquitous materials may, in the future, be reconceptualized (and redesigned) as educative for teaching practice as well as for student learning:

> Teachers could be engaged with curriculum materials in ways that generated learning if the materials were integrated into a program of professional development aimed at improving their capacity to teach. In that case, well-designed materials could be a resource for teachers' learning. (Ball & Cohen, 1996, p. 8)

Teachers often are knowledgeable and discriminating users of commercial curriculum, and I think that is just what we found in our California policy study. The teacher I quote in the following excerpt was representative of exemplary teachers there in that she understood reading development, the possibilities of the commercial curriculum materials, and the needs of the children she taught in particular:

> When we adopted [a basal reading program], we did not adopt it as our complete reading program, we adopted it as our shared reading program, which is whole-class instruction and direct instruction of skills. Then we put in guided reading separate from the basal, with leveled texts, and [we also put in separately] literature discussion groups with books that are at whatever level the kids are, and [we also put in] the writing piece. If we hadn't done this, we would be back to the stage where we've got a ton of kids that can't read the [grade level] basal. The way we have it structured [now] we've got leveled books in place for kids who can't read at grade level, so they will receive guided reading instruction with books appropriate to their level. (McGill-Franzen et al., 1998, p. 12)

RLA: I don't really disagree with you on this. The key is how commercial materials are used. The problem, as I see it, is that too often just following the reading series becomes the standard practice in schools where a basal is uniformly adopted; that is, the reading series dominates the instructional time. But no basal series contains enough reading material to produce high-achieving readers. A basal can be useful as a general framework, say, for use on Monday and Tuesday, but when the basal lessons become the total reading program, achievement suffers. I mean, how can anyone justify spending five days on a single 20-minute story or excerpt? If the basal enhances the likelihood of routinization instruction, if it fosters unresponsive and unreflective teaching, if it rest amount of reading and writing that children do, then it creates more problems than it solves. But this is not a new concern, as Betts (1949) noted:

> In some schools instructional materials are limited almost exclusively to basic textbooks in reading, science, and other areas. These basic textbooks are often misused. At each grade level the book carrying that grade level designation is used as the prescription for undifferentiated, mass instruction of all the children in the class.
>
> At the other extreme are schools that attempt to rule out basic textbooks. In these situations, conditions can be equally frustrating for both teacher and pupils. Teachers can be overworked by attempting to devise study materials. Children can be frustrated in their efforts to deal with materials of unsuitable readability.
>
> The methods of using instructional materials is a crucial factor in adjusting instruction to individual needs. (p. 268)

As I noted earlier, I think our most effective teachers teach children, not materials. They may use commercial materials regularly, but they do not use them slavishly. They use an array of curriculum materials and instructional strategies. Our most effective teachers are curriculum problem solvers, and, often, the commercial materials are part of the solution.

AMF: Schools and programs and reading lessons may change, but when teachers plunge into the risky business of change, there is no guarantee that instruction will improve (Elmore, Peterson, & McCarthy, 1996).

RLA: True, change is not always productive (Elmore et al., 1996), nor is the process predictable (Johnston, Allington, Guice, & Brooks, 1998). Nevertheless, schools and curriculum are always changing.

Looking Forward

AMF: So let's talk about the schools of the future. I think that currently, as has been the case historically, there is no clear agreement on just how schools should change.

RLA: Well, in fact, Tyack and Cuban (1995) have argued that reforms are often stifled because they violate the grammar of schooling:

> Most Americans have been to school and know what a "real school" is like. Congruence with that cultural template has helped maintain the legitimacy of the institution in the minds of the public. But when schooling departed too much from the consensual model of a real school, failed to match the grammar of schooling, trouble often ensued. (p. 9)

If Cuban (1990) is correct, we can expect that although some aspects of schooling will change rather rapidly, the nature of classrooms may not be so easily altered. That is, although classrooms today certainly look different than they looked at the turn of the last century, evidence suggests that the initiate-reply-evaluate (IRE) pattern of classroom discourse dominated then and dominates today. The question, though, is why some would end the dominance of the IRE while others insist on its merits. In some senses, this difference alone accounts for much of the rancor between traditionalists and reformers today.

AMF: Well, Dick, any question today about discourse is loaded. It is loaded because, to me, talk about discourse has often sounded fatalistic: You are born into a discourse community and there you stay forever. Instead, I like the way Applebee (1996) situates discourse within the disciplines. This approach separates talk about language use from race and social class issues and puts it in the context of disciplinary knowledge, knowledge that is taught and learned in the classroom. Each disciplinary community privileges ways of thinking, talking, and writing, and each discourse community has its own traditions and, I imagine, reforms. I see the central issue here as one of access to the discourse, not one necessarily of discourse structures, like IRE. So I would pose the question as, How can we teach all students to become participants in the discourse, say of English language arts, so that they not only understand the discourse, but can transform it? Appropriate teaching strategies are those that make the process of disciplinary thinking, talking, and writing transparent to the learner and engage the learner in knowing. The work of Judith Langer (1995) suggests important ways teachers can scaffold students' understandings of literature, and, of course, chief among these strategies is discussion. Through discussion, teachers can help students move between the text and the interpretation, between literature and their lives. As you suggest, Dick, it is difficult for many to give up the traditional IRE pattern of classroom lessons; Langer tells inservice teachers that it is like getting new bones.

However, it is worth the effort: Martin Nystrand (1997) found that a single instance of a teacher building on a student response during a class period correlated with measurable achievement gains for students in that class. Although Nystrand studied secondary classrooms, other researchers at the Center for English Learning and Achievement are currently looking at the qualitative dimensions of discourse within exemplary classrooms with integrated curricula. The benefits of teaching strategies that honor multiple perspectives and make the process of understanding transparent have already been documented (Goatley, Brock, & Raphael, 1995; McGill-Franzen & Lanford, 1994).

RLA: It seems obvious to me that these more complicated patterns of classroom discourse relate to the new thoughtful literacy standards that have been put in place. But we have only scant research available on the sorts of instructional environments that foster achievement of those standards. In other words, almost all the available research estimated achievement using the older basic skills assessments—even the reliable, replicable research that is so much talked about these days. Enriching our understanding about the nature of curriculum instruction that fosters achievement of the new standards would seem a worthy focus of the next generation of researchers.

But the new standards implicate another important facet of schooling: educating those children who have historically found it difficult to keep pace with their peers when offered schooling of similar quantity and quality. Alan Odden (1997) explained the problem in economic terms:

> The current standards-based reform goal is to raise achievement of 75% or more of the students to the level currently attained by only 25% (NAEP proficient level).... This goal—a 100–200% increase in results—represents a quantum, not just a marginal, improvement in school performance. (p. 4)

For schools to achieve this sort of improvement represents, perhaps, the greatest challenge to the ingenuity of educators in the United States. No longer will a third or more of the students be allowed to lag in development, completing 10 or 13 years of schooling with minimal academic proficiencies. Even historically underachieving students will achieve at substantially higher levels. Or at least that is the current stance of educational policymakers. It is the children of the poor who currently are most likely to fail to achieve current standards in U.S. schools. Poor children are dramatically overrepresented in special education programs (Wagner, 1995), and they are also the target population of the federal Title I program. They are the children most likely to be retained in grade and to leave school without a diploma. Because children of color are three times as likely to live in homes with family incomes below the federal poverty line, they are disproportionately represented in the ranks of children having difficulty.

AMF: And poor children and children of color are most likely to be penalized under the new standards movement. As Ron Wolk (1998), the former editor of *Education Week*, said in a commentary, education policy is on a "collision course with reality" (p. 48). Students from low-income communities have been unlikely to meet the historical minimal standards, so how can these same students be expected to meet even higher expectations for achievement? Further, we are holding students accountable for a thinking curriculum without having put in place a pedagogy that will enable such learning.

RLA: A carrot-and-stick approach seems to be the prevailing policy.

AMF: I understand the stick: accountability in the form of public scorn and public takeover of low-performing schools. Improving such schools is an undeniable moral imperative, a Deweyan challenge from the turn of last century—we must offer all children the schools we want for our own.

Beleaguered teachers and administrators are desperate for programs that work, to use a current phrase. I guess the carrot offered to struggling school administrators and teachers is a loosely defined research base for choosing one program or set of materials over another, and, unfortunately, we researchers have gotten into down-and-dirty mudslinging to support these district shopping trips.

It should come as no surprise that faithful implementation of a coherent instructional program, such as that of Success for All (SFA), where none existed before, will improve reading achievement. Bob Slavin wrote in an evaluation of the IBM Write to Read program (1991) that when a program is compared with nothing, the intervention program will post better results.

RLA: Ah, but the question: Is SFA a carrot that actually improves achievement? Or, more accurately, considering the financial investment, is SFA a cost-effective way to improve achievement? I think the answer is probably not. Venezky's (1998) analysis addressed the question that way. It is true that children attending SFA schools read a bit better, relatively, than the kids in the control schools, but their achievement remained incredibly low in absolute standards (about 2.5 years below grade level at the end of elementary school). Personally, I don't think Slavin's genius is in curriculum design. Rather, what he understood and what the initial SFA design achieved was a restructuring of resources so that tutoring, parent involvement, and increased reading instructional time were accomplished in schools where most of the children desperately needed access to more and better teaching. The mistake Slavin made, I think, is that he came to depend increasingly on materials to teach, and the SFA effort became increasingly standardized so that local adaptations were discouraged.

But I do agree with you that many teachers, many administrators, and the American Federation of Teachers (AFT) all seem to see SFA and some other programs as a carrot. But I don't think this is because they believe that these programs will actually raise achievement. Instead, these supposedly proven programs will be the new fall guys—something else to blame for the failure to educate disadvantaged children. After these programs are implemented, continuing school failure can be blamed on the program because it was supposedly a program that worked. Accepting mandates for implementing proven programs will provide teachers and administrators with an alternative defense. In essence what the AFT seems to be saying is "Sure you tell us what to do—minute by minute, day by day, and we will do it. But then don't blame us if we follow orders and implement these programs and achievement fails to improve. We did what we were told. It must be that the programs were badly designed or these kids just cannot learn."

AMF: I am not that skeptical of the AFT. I understand that schoolwide curriculum reform, like SFA, is a preferable alternative, in the AFT's view, to state or city takeover of low-performing schools and the bad publicity and loss of confidence that attend the teaching profession whenever this happens. I submit that when programs that work have improved achievement in low-performing schools, there was no coherent reading program to speak of and little professional development for teachers prior to the new program implementation. At least SFA and other such programs give teachers a running start: SFA provides the curriculum materials and actually supports teachers in curriculum implementatio

The bleak scenario that you described earlier could happen, but it is as likely that an explicitly scripted program would work, as DISTAR has at Wesley Elementary in Houston, Texas, despite demoralized teachers and against all odds (Palmaffy, 1998). In this scenario, student learning would transform teacher and community expectations, as it has at Wesley. Although highly structured reading programs are surely not the ideal—expert teachers are the ideal—if these approaches support some teachers in some contexts, and children learn to read, why are we throwing mud on them? Children cannot wait—they must learn to read with the teachers they have.

RLA: There just is no consistent evidence such programs do work, and the little research available has not been conducted by disinterested parties (Stahl, Duffy-Hester, & Stahl, 1998). I am not surprised when someone, somewhere manages to implement a program—any program—successfully. Virtually every curriculum approach used in the First-Grade Studies worked in some classrooms (Bond & Dykstra, 1967). But every program studied did not work well in some classrooms. I am not advocating the slinging of mud, but I am saying that the evidence suggests that more expert teachers get better results than the inexpert ones and that those who would suggest that teacher-proofed materials are the new panacea are simply wrong. I am more convinced than ever that instead of offering packaged programs, we need to concentrate our efforts on enhancing the expertise of teachers. Perhaps Robert Rothman (1995) said it most succinctly: "It's the classroom, stupid" (p. 174).

There seems to be growing recognition, among some policymakers, that it is teachers who teach, not materials. Thus, there are calls, like the following one from the National Commission on Teaching and America's Future:

> What teachers know and understand about content and students shapes how judiciously they select from texts and other materials and how effectively they present material in class. Their skill in assessing their students' progress also depends upon how deeply they understand learning, and how well they can interpret students' discussions and written work. No other intervention can make the difference that a knowledgeable, skillful teacher can make in the learning process. (Darling-Hammond, 1997, p. 8)

In an ideal world, in the schools I would design for the 21st century, all teachers would be more expert and have more authority to act on that expertise. They also would work in school environments that were well designed to support this work. That is, schools would have a rich supply of materials for teachers to select for instructional use. School days would be less fragmented and provide teachers and students with long blocks of uninterrupted time for reading and writing activity, time to do the work of schooling. Schools would be collegial places where the professional staff worked with one another to develop their expertise and improve their teaching.

AMF: I hope that as the SFA developers learn more about teachers' understandings of the curriculum materials and students' responses there will be more opportunities for teachers' learning beyond SFA.

RLA: Well, if I had to select a school design from the catalog of school reform efforts currently operating across the United States, I would choose the Basic School (Boyer, 1995) and the Learning Network school designs (Herzog, 1997), blending the two together. In both cases there is a general framework that can guide school reform. But in both cases the reforms are developed more from inside than imposed from outside. In both cases teacher inquiry is an important component of how change proceeds, as is collegial conversation and professional problem solving. In both cases the focus is on improving instruction by fostering teacher development. This approach, of course, seems risky to many policymakers because it acknowledges the importance and expertise of those who work daily with children and turns decision making largely over to the teachers. This exemplifies what Rowan (1990) called a commitment strategy to reform as opposed to a control strategy (where you tell people exactly what to do). He traces the pillar-to-post swings of policymakers between commitment (e.g., site-based management) and control (e.g., mandates for daily phonemic awareness lessons) over the past several decades. I do think that the sorts of schools we will have in 21st century will depend largely on whether policymakers decide to invest in fostering commitment to reform as opposed to trying simply to mandate it.

For instance, right now, the new standards movement seems designed to redefine the nature of academic work, and that seems to me another area of contention in educational reform. The debate was perhaps best characterized by a candidate for the post of state superintendent of instruction, who, in criticizing the state social studies standards, vowed that if elected, kids would learn important facts— like the capitals of the 50 states. She was not elected, however. Nonetheless, there are influential figures, E.D. Hirsch (1996) comes to mind, who advocate the teaching of facts for item-based learning goals. Conversely, there are folks who advocate for inquiry-based education and downplay the importance of facts.

AMF: Linda Darling-Hammond, whom you quoted earlier, has said that the reforms of the last millennium, although almost indistinguishable from those of the present in the emphasis on thoughtful literacy, failed to survive because teachers of that era were not prepared to teach within a constructivist pedagogy that holds the academic curriculum and the needs of learners in equal sway. Even now, lest history repeat itself, Darling-Hammond (1996) warned us to consider the complex pedagogy teachers need to meet the goals of the new standards movement: "[Curriculum reformers] fail to consider that teachers teach from what they understand and believe about learning, what they know how to do, and what their environments will allow" (p. 9). Enacting change is complex, and there are few absolutes. Teachers need support, and the kind of support depends on what they know and understand and believe, and on the context of their practice.

RLA: Agreed. Now, this might be a good point to raise the issue of the potential role of technology in learning to read. Having lived through an era of unfulfilled predictions as to how first television and then videotape recordings were going to transform curriculum and instruction, I cannot help but be pessimistic about the influence of new technology on schooling, especially on classroom lessons. I suppose that if an inquiry-based education becomes the preferred curriculum model, then the Internet might play some substantial role. I can almost imagine classroom-based tailored testing on computers much like the recent versions of the Graduate Record Examination. I don't think computer technology will have much impact until workstations are built right into student desks. At that point, however, the computer might become a substitute for the textbook and the worksheet, and then the dominant pattern of instruction could continue. But I'm not sure if that should be seen as progress.

AMF: Right now I see technology as another way to privilege those who have and to disadvantage those who have not. The issue is access. I am thinking here of out-of-school use: roaming the Internet at home, e-mailing friends, practicing for college entrance exams, composing and revising homework assignments, doing phonics. Of course, we all say that technology has enormous potential—it does, but for whom? Before Bill Gates finishes the wiring of community libraries, perhaps he could find a way to build and wire a library in one of the many low-income communities without one, and for those low-income communities with libraries, find a way to keep them open more than two or three hours a day.

RLA: The polls show public support for increasing access to technology in schools, so maybe the current inequities will diminish. But the polls indicate an increasing approval for another educational reform: privatization of public education through vouchers and charter schools. I worry that such reforms may result in a balkanization of not only schools but also society in the United States. We haven't really discussed the contribution public education has made to the civil nature of this melting pot of a nation.

I worry because I think we are already too stratified on economic factors and because the trend toward greater income separation between high- and low-income families has been accelerating. Although our schools are too economically and racially segregated, I do think the notion of the *common school* experience is a useful ideal for public education.

AMF: Well, Dick, the common school experience seems like just another word for the same-old view of the world that most of us experienced in school. And communities and the schools within are already balkanized. Fortunately for us and our children, the schools in our community are good ones. Bethlehem Central High School was ranked by *Newsweek* (Mathews, 1998) as one of the 100 best public high schools in the United States; the elementary schools in our community have been similarly honored. U.S. public elementary and secondary schools in middle class communities are excellent, better than private schools, and possibly the best public schools in the world. A related article in the same issue of *Newsweek* said that the most successful schools in large urban areas are frequently parochial, and these schools are not effective because of the religious connection, but because of their smaller size, the strong sense of community, the shared values of high academic goals, and the expectation of service to the neighborhood community.

These are the schools we, as a society, should want for all children. I have to believe these are the schools that the National Congress for Public Education celebrated last year in Washington, DC.

Unfortunately, other public schools in the United States, those serving children from impoverished communities, are rarely as good as schools in middle class communities. Why should poor children be trapped in bad schools? It seems to me that those who inveigh against charter schools or tutoring vouchers for poor families are not supporting children, but rather a principle (that of public education as a common good). Forgive me for saying this, but it seems racist and elitist to support public school policies that deny poor and minority children an education comparable to that of middle class children. School choice will be the civil rights issue of the millennium. For a civil society, it matters not at all that the society is diverse, only that it be just and accord all its children the same opportunities to learn.

RLA: I agree with your argument up to the point where you decide that a common public education is an unsalvageable ideal. The reason that the achievement gaps between more and less advantaged children have been narrowing is that we have actually made some progress in reducing the discrepancies you rightly denounce. But I worry also that schools are being saddled with a baggage not of their making—a baggage they cannot and should not have to carry alone. Coles (1998) noted that politicians are cheered by educators' endless rancorous debates about the one best way to teach beginning reading because, in his view, that debate allows them to continue to ignore the larger and more expensive-to-implement social factors that contribute to the likelihood of children's school success.

I was stunned by the implications of a recent large-scale longitudinal study of more and less advantaged children (Entwisle, Alexander, & Olson, 1997). The researchers found that the achievement gap at sixth grade—almost three years' difference—between these two groups of children could be accounted for by the achievement differences children arrived at school with and by accumulated summer reading loss! By assessing achievement twice a year, the researchers demonstrated that learning across the school year was comparable for the two groups of children. Schools did not help the disadvantaged children catch up, but when the children were in school they fell no further behind either. Entwisle and her colleagues concluded,

Of the many ways to improve the school climate in poor neighborhoods, the main one is to correct the mistaken but politically correct perception that these elementary schools are falling down on the job. (p. 164)

They also argued for substantial investments in urban community development—development of opportunities for poor children to have a childhood more like those middle class children have outside of school. I am quite sure they would support your call for better-stocked, better-staffed, and more accessible public libraries in economically disadvantaged communities. However, vouchers and charter schools seem like the perfect political solution—you just move the same money around a bit and continue to blame the teachers, the unions, and the parents when things just get worse for the most vulnerable children and their families.

AMF: I am not persuaded by Entwisle and colleagues. I believe that schools can and must make a difference in the lives of all children, and if the schools we have do not support and inspire children from poor communities to be all they can be, then as educators, we have a moral imperative to create schools that do.

RLA: So I guess the answer to what sort of schools will we have in the 21st century can be best stated as "It will depend." It will depend on the decisions we as a society make about what it means to teach and what it means to learn and to be literate, and whether schools are seen as important in achieving the ideals of a just, democratic society.

AMF: Indeed.

Acknowledgments

The preparation of this article was supported in part by funding under the Educational Research and Development Program (Grant No. R117G10015) as administered by the Office of Educational Research and Improvement, U.S. Department of Education. The article reflects the interpretations and opinions of the authors and does not necessarily reflect the positions or policies of the sponsoring agency.

References

Airasian, P.W. (1988). Symbolic validation: The case of state-mandated, high-stakes testing. *Educational Evaluation and Policy Analysis, 10,* 301–313.

Allington, R.L. (1984). Oral reading. In P.D. Pearson, R. Barr, M.L. Kamil, & P. Mosenthal (Eds.), *Handbook of reading research* (pp. 829–864). New York: Longman.

Allington, R.L. (1986). Policy constraints and effective compensatory reading instruction: A review. In J.V. Hoffman (Ed.), *Effective teaching of reading: Research and practice* (pp. 261–289). Newark, DE: International Reading Association.

Allington, R.L. (1991). The legacy of "slow it down and make it more concrete." In J. Zutell & S. McCormick (Eds.), *Learner factors/teacher factors: Issues in literacy research and instruction* (40th yearbook of the National Reading Conference, pp. 19–30). Chicago: National Reading Conference.

Allington, R.L. (1994). What's special about special programs for children who find learning to read difficult? *Journal of Reading Behavior, 26,* 1–21.

Allington, R.L., Guice, S., Michelson, N., Baker, K., & Li, S. (1996). Literature-based curriculum in high-poverty schools. In M.F. Graves,

P. van den Broek, & B.M. Taylor (Eds.), *The first R: Every child's right to read* (pp. 73–96). New York: Teachers College Press; Newark, DE: International Reading Association.

Allington, R.L., & McGill-Franzen, A. (1992). Unintended effects of educational reform in New York State. *Educational Policy, 6,* 396–413.

Allington, R.L., & McGill-Franzen, A. (1995). Individual planning. In M. Wang & M. Reynolds (Eds.), *Handbook of special and remedial education* (pp. 5–35). New York: Pergamon.

Allington, R.L., & Woodside-Jiron, H. (1998a). "30 years of research...": When is a research summary not a research summary? In K. Goodman (Ed.), *In defense of good teaching: What teachers need to know about the reading wars* (pp. 143–157). York, ME: Stenhouse.

Allington, R.L., & Woodside-Jiron, H. (1998b). Decodable texts in beginning reading: Are mandates based on research? *ERS Spectrum, 16,* 3–11.

Anderson, R.C., Hiebert, E.H., Scott, J.A., & Wilkinson, I. (1985). *Becoming a nation of readers: The report of the Commission on Reading.* Washington, DC: National Institute of Education.

Applebee, A.N. (1996). *Curriculum as conversation: Transforming traditions of teaching and learning.* Chicago: University of Chicago Press.

Austin, G.R., Rogers, B.G., & Walbesser, H.H. (1972). The effectiveness of compensatory education: A review of the research. *Review of Educational Research, 42,* 171–182.

Ball, D., & Cohen, D. (1996). Reform by the book: What is—or might be—the role of curriculum materials in teacher learning and instructional reform? *Educational Researcher, 25*(9), 6–8, 14.

Barr, R. (1975). The effect of instruction on pupil reading strategies. *Reading Research Quarterly, 10,* 555–582.

Bembry, K.L., Jordan, H.R., Gomez, E., Anderson, M., & Mendro, R.L. (1998, April). *Policy implications of long-term teacher effects on student achievement.* Paper presented at annual meeting of the American Educational Research Association, San Diego, CA.

Bennett, W.J., Fair, W., Finn, C.E., Flake, F., Hirsch, E.D., Marshall, W., et al. (1998, July–August). A nation still at risk. *Policy Review,* pp. 2–9.

Berliner, D.C., & Biddle, B.J. (1996). *The manufactured crisis: Myths, fraud, and the attack on America's public schools.* White Plains, NY: Longman.

Betts, E.M. (1949). Adjusting instruction to individual needs. In N.B. Henry (Ed.), *Reading in the elementary school* (48th yearbook of the National Society for the Study of Education: Part II, pp. 266–283). Chicago: University of Chicago Press.

Bloomfield, L., & Barnhart, C. (1962). *Let's read, a linguistic approach.* Detroit, MI: Wayne State University Press.

Bond, G.L., & Dykstra, R. (1967). The cooperative research program in first-grade reading instruction. *Reading Research Quarterly, 2,* 5–142.

Boyer, E.L. (1995). *The basic school: A community for learning.* Princeton, NJ: Carnegie Foundation for the Advancement of Teaching.

Bracey, G.W. (1997). *Setting the record straight: Responses to misconceptions about public education in the United States.* Alexandria, VA: Association for Supervision and Curriculum Development.

Canney, G. (1993). Teachers' preferences for reading materials. *Reading Improvement, 30,* 238–245.

Carter, L. (1984). The sustaining effects study of compensatory and elementary education. *Educational Researcher, 12*(4), 4–13.

Coleman, J.S., Campbell, E., Hobson, C., McPortland, J., Mood, A., Weingeld, F., et al. (1966). *Equality of educational opportunity.* Washington, DC: U.S. Government Printing Office.

Coles, G. (1998). *Reading lessons: The debate over literacy.* New York: Hill & Wang.

Cuban, L. (1990). Reforming again, again, and again. *Educational Researcher, 19*(1), 3–13.

Cubberly, E.P. (1908). *Changing conceptions of education.* Cambridge, MA: Houghton Mifflin.

Cunningham, P.M. (1995). *Phonics they use: Words for reading and writing.* New York: HarperCollins.

Darling-Hammond, L. (1996). The right to learn and the advancement of teaching: Research, policy, and practice for democratic education. *Educational Researcher, 25*(6), 5–17.

Darling-Hammond, L. (1997). *Doing what matters most: Investing in quality teaching.* New York: National Commission on Teaching and America's Future.

Dewey, J. (1968). *The school and society*. Chicago: University of Chicago Press.

Dow, P.B. (1991). *Schoolhouse politics: Lessons from the Sputnik era*. Cambridge, MA: Harvard University Press.

Duffy, G., Roehler, L., & Rackliffe, G. (1986). How teachers' instructional talk influences student understanding of lesson content. *The Elementary School Journal, 87*, 3–16.

Elley, W.B. (1992). *How in the world do students read? IEA study of reading literacy*. The Hague, the Netherlands: International Association for the Evaluation of Educational Achievement.

Elmore, R.F., Peterson, P.L., & McCarthy, S.J. (1996). *Restructuring in the classroom: Teaching, learning, and school organization*. San Francisco: Jossey-Bass.

Entwisle, D.R., Alexander, K.L., & Olson, L.S. (1997). *Children, schools, and inequality*. Boulder, CO: Westview.

Finn, C.E. (1991). *We must take charge: Our schools and our future*. New York: Free Press.

Flesch, R. (1955). *Why Johnny can't read and what you can do about it*. New York: Harper & Row.

Fletcher, J., & Lyon, G.R. (1998). Reading: A research-based approach. In W. Evers (Ed.), *What's gone wrong in America's classrooms?* Stanford, CA: Hoover Institute Press.

Goatley, V.J., Brock, C.H., & Raphael, T.E. (1995). Diverse learners participating in regular education 'Book Clubs.' *Reading Research Quarterly, 30*, 352–380.

Goodman, K.S., Shannon, P., Freeman, Y., & Murphy, S. (1988). *Report card on basal readers*. Katonah, NY: Richard C. Owen.

Grissmer, D.W., Kirby, S.N., Berends, M., & Williamson, S. (1994). *Student achievement and the changing American family*. Santa Monica, CA: RAND Institute on Education and Training.

Haladyna, T.H., Nolan, S.B., & Haas, N.S. (1991). Raising standardized achievement test scores and the origins of test score pollution. *Educational Researcher, 20*(5), 2–7.

Herzog, M. (Ed.). (1997). *Inside Learning Network schools*. Katonah, NY: Richard C. Owen.

Heubert, J., & Hauser, R. (1999). *High stakes: Testing for tracking, promotion and graduation*. Washington, DC: National Academy Press.

Hirsch, E.D. (1996). *The schools we need and why we don't have them*. New York: Doubleday.

Hoffman, J.V., McCarthy, S.J., Elliott, B., Bayles, D., Price, D., Ferree, A., et al. (1998). The literature-based basals in first-grade classrooms: Savior, satan, or same-old, same-old? *Reading Research Quarterly, 33*, 168–197.

Johnston, P., Allington, R.L., Guice, S., & Brooks, G.W. (1998). Small change: A multilevel study of the implementation of literature-based instruction. *Peabody Journal of Education, 73*, 81–103.

Kameenui, E.J., Simmons, D.C., Chard, D., & Dickson, S. (1997). Direct-instruction reading. In S.A. Stahl & D. Hayes (Eds.), *Instructional models in reading* (pp. 59–84). Mahwah, NJ: Erlbaum.

Knapp, M.S. (1995). *Teaching for meaning in high-poverty classrooms*. New York: Teachers College Press.

Langer, J.A. (1995). *Envisioning literature: Literary understanding and literature instruction*. New York: Teachers College Press; Newark, DE: International Reading Association.

Langer, J.A., & Allington, R.L. (1992). Curriculum research in writing and reading. In P.W. Jackson (Ed.), *Handbook of research on curriculum* (pp. 687–725). New York: Macmillan.

Learning First Alliance. (1998, Spring/Summer). Every child reading. *American Educator, 22*, 52–60.

Luke, A. (1988). *Literacy, textbook, and ideology: Postwar literacy instruction and the mythology of Dick and Jane*. New York: Falmer.

Lyon, R. (1995). Research initiatives in learning disabilities: Contributions from scientists supported by the National Institute of Child Health and Development (Supplement No. 1). *Journal of Child Neurology, 10*, S20–S126.

Mathews, J. (1998, March 30). 100 high schools that work. *Newsweek*, pp. 52–56.

McGill-Franzen, A. (1987). Failure to learn to read: Formulating a policy problem. *Reading Research Quarterly, 22*, 475–490.

McGill-Franzen, A.M. (1993). *Shaping the preschool agenda: Early literacy, public policy and professional beliefs*. Albany: State University of New York Press.

McGill-Franzen, A.M. (1994). Is there accountability for learning and belief in children's potential? In E.H. Hiebert & B.M. Taylor (Eds.), *Getting reading right from the start: Effective early literacy interventions* (pp. 13–35). Boston: Allyn & Bacon.

McGill-Franzen, A. (2000). Policy and instruction: What is the relationship? In M.L. Kamil, P.B. Mosenthal, P.D. Pearson, & R. Barr (Eds.), *Handbook of reading research* (Vol. 3, pp. 889–908). Mahwah, NJ: Erlbaum.

McGill-Franzen, A., & Allington, R.L. (1993). Flunk 'em or get them classified: The contamination of primary grade accountability data. *Educational Researcher, 22*(1), 19–22.

McGill-Franzen, A., Allington, R.L., Yokoi, L., & Brooks, G. (1999/2000). Putting books in the room seems necessary but not sufficient. *Journal of Educational Research, 93*, 67–74

McGill-Franzen, A.M., & Lanford, C. (1994). Exposing the edge of the preschool curriculum: Teachers' talk about text and children's literary understandings. *Language Arts, 71*, 264–273.

McGill-Franzen, A., Woodside-Jiron, H., Machado, V., & Veltema, J. (1998, December). *A study of state education policymaking and implementation in English language arts curriculum and assessment in four states*. Paper presented at the National Reading Conference, Austin, TX.

Moats, L. (1998, Spring/Summer). Teaching decoding. *American Educator, 22*, 42–49, 95–96.

National Center for Education Statistics. (1998, December). Long-term trends in student reading performance. *NAEP Facts, 3*(1), 1–3.

National Commission on Educational Excellence. (1983). *A nation at risk*. Washington, DC: U.S. Government Printing Office.

National Education Commission on Time and Learning. (1994). *Prisoners of time*. Washington, DC: U.S. Government Printing Office.

Nystrand, M. (1997). *Opening dialogue: Understanding the dynamics of language and learning in the English classroom*. New York: Teachers College Press.

Odden, A. (1997). Raising performance levels without increasing funding. *School Business Affairs, 14*, 4–12.

Palmaffy, T. (1998, January/February). No excuses. *Policy Review*, pp. 18–25.

Pressley, M., & Allington, R.L. (1999). What should reading instructional research be the research of? *Issues in Education, 5*, 1–35.

Pressley, M., Wharton-McDonald, R., Allington, R.L., Block, C.C., Morrow, L.M., Tracey, D., et al. (1999). *The nature of effective first-grade literacy instruction* (Research Report No. 11007). Albany, NY: National Research Center on English Learning and Achievement.

Puma, M.J., Karweit, N., Price, C., Ricciuti, A., Thompson, W., & Vaden-Kiernan, M. (1997). *Prospects: Final report on student outcomes*. Washington, DC: U.S. Department of Education, Planning and Evaluation Services.

Purcell-Gates, V., McIntyre, E., & Freppon, P. (1995). Learning written storybook language in school. *American Educational Research Journal, 32*, 659–685.

Rothman, R. (1995). *Measuring up: Standards, assessment, and school reform*. San Francisco: Jossey-Bass.

Rothstein, R. (1998). *The way we were? The myths and realities of America's student achievement*. New York: Century Foundation Press.

Rowan, B. (1990). Commitment and control: Alternative strategies for the organizational design of schools. In C.B. Cazden (Ed.), *Review of research in education* (pp. 353–389). Washington DC: American Educational Research Association.

Sacks, C.H., & Mergendoller, J.R. (1997). The relationship between teachers' theoretical orientation toward reading and student outcomes in kindergarten children with different initial reading abilities. *American Educational Research Journal, 34*, 721–740.

Sanders, W.L. (1998, December). Value-added assessment: A method for measuring the effects of the system, school and teacher on the rate of student academic progress. *School Administrator, 55*(11) [Online]. Retrieved from http://www.aasa.org/SA/dec9801.htm

Schweinhart, L.J., & Weikart, D.P. (1998). Why curriculum matters in early childhood education. *Educational Leadership, 55*(2), 57–60.

Shannon, P. (1989). *Broken promises: Reading instruction in twentieth-century America*. Granby, MA: Bergin & Garvey.

Slavin, R.E. (1991). Reading effects of IBM's "Write to read" program: A review of evaluations. *Education Evaluation and Policy Analysis, 13*, 1–11.

Smith, N.B. (1965). *American reading instruction*. Newark, DE: International Reading Association. (Original work published 1934)

Snow, C., Burns, S., & Griffin, P. (Eds.). (1998). *Preventing reading difficulties in young children*. Washington, DC: National Academy Press.

Spring, J. (1989). *The sorting machine revisited*. New York: Longman.

Stahl, S.A., Duffy-Hester, A., & Stahl, K.A.D. (1998). Everything you wanted to know about phonics (but were afraid to ask). *Reading Research Quarterly, 33*, 338–355.

Strickland, D.S., Walmsley, S.A., Bronk, G., & Weiss, K. (1994). *School book clubs and literacy development: A descriptive study* (Report Series 2.22). Albany: State University of New York at Albany.

Sweet, R.W. (1997, May/June). Don't read, don't tell: Clinton's phony war on illiteracy. *Policy Review*, pp. 38–42.

Timar, T. (1994). Federal education policy and practice: Building organizational capacity through Chapter 1. *Educational Evaluation and Policy Analysis, 16*, 51–66.

Tyack, D., & Cuban, L. (1995). *Tinkering toward Utopia: A century of public school reform*. Cambridge, MA: Harvard University Press.

Vellutino, F., Scanlon, D., Sipay, E., Small, S., Pratt, A., Chen, R., et al. (1996). Cognitive profiles of difficult-to-remediate and readily remediated poor readers: Early intervention as a vehicle for distinguishing between cognitive and experiential deficits as basic causes of specific reading disability. *Journal of Educational Psychology, 88*, 601–638.

Venezky, R.L. (1998). An alternative perspective on Success for All. In K.K. Wong (Ed.), *Advances in educational policy* (Vol. 4, pp. 145–165). Stamford, CT: JAI Press.

Wagner, M. (1995). *The contribution of poverty and ethnic background to the participation of secondary school students in special education*. Menlo Park, CA: SRI International.

Weber, R.M. (1970). A linguistic analysis of first grade reading errors. *Reading Research Quarterly, 5*, 427–451.

Winston, J.A. (1996). Fulfilling the promise of Brown. In E.C. Lagemann & L.P. Miller (Eds.), *Brown v. Board of Education: The challenge for today's schools* (pp. 157–166). New York: Teachers College Press.

Wolk, R. (1998, December 9). Education's high-stakes gamble. *Education Week*, p. 48.

Zigler, E., & Muenchow, S. (1992). *Head Start: The inside story of America's most successful educational experiment*. New York: Basic Books.

2

A Historical Perspective on Reading Research and Practice

Patricia A. Alexander and Emily Fox

At the time the International Reading Association was created in 1956, the reading research community was poised at a new juncture in its history (Monaghan & Saul, 1987). The efforts of researchers during this period gave rise to extensive literature on learners and the learning process that remains an enduring legacy for the domain of reading. Yet, this was not the only period of significant change the reading community has experienced in the past 50 years. In fact, reading has periodically responded to internal and external forces resulting in both gradual and dramatic transformations to the domain—transformations that have altered reading study and practice. Our purpose here is to position those transformations within a historical framework. As with others (e.g., VanSledright, 2002), we hold that such a historical perspective allows for reasoned reflection and a certain wisdom that can be easily lost when one is immersed in ongoing study and practice. That is because a historical perspective broadens the vista on reading and adds a critical dimension to the analysis of present-day events and issues.

To capture this historical perspective, we survey eras in reading research and practice that have unfolded in the past 50 years and that symbolize alternative perspectives on learners and learning. For each era, we describe certain internal and external conditions that helped to frame that period, as well as the views and principles of learning that are characteristic of that era. Moreover, we explore both the prevailing views of learning within those periods and rival stances that existed as educational undercurrents. To bring this historical vista into focus, we highlight exemplary and prototypic works that encapsulate the issues and concerns of the time. Of course, we recognize that the boundaries and distinctions we draw between these eras are approximations of permeable and overlapping periods of reading research and practice. Nonetheless, these eras remain a useful platform from which the subsequent contributions in this volume can be explored.

The Era of Conditioned Learning (1950–1965)

The Conditions for Change

As early as the first decades of the 20th century, during the nascence of psychology, the processes of reading were already of passing interest to educational researchers (e.g., Buswell, 1922; Huey, 1908; Thorndike, 1917). However, it was not until much later in that century that reading became a recognized field of study with systematic programs of research aimed at ascertaining its fundamental nature and the processes of its acquisition. Although reading had long been a basic component of formal schooling in the United States, there was little concerted effort to marry research knowledge and instructional practice until much later in the 20th century. Instigation for that marked change came as a result of a confluence of social, educational, political, and economic factors during the 1950s.

The postwar United States was a fertile ground for transformations in reading research and practice for several reasons. For one, the high birth rate during and immediately following World War II resulted in record numbers of children entering the public school system (Ganley, Lyons, & Sewall, 1993). This baby boom contributed to both quantitative and qualitative changes to the school population. One of the qualitative changes was a seeming rise in the number of children experiencing difficulties in learning to read. Such reading problems, although nothing new to teachers, took on particular significance in the age of Sputnik, as America's ability to compete globally became a defining issue (Allington & McGill-Franzen, 2000, see #1 this volume). The outcome was a growing public pressure on the educational community to find an answer to the "problem" of reading acquisition.

One of the groundbreaking but controversial publications of this period was *Why Johnny Can't Read—And What You Can Do About It* by Rudolf Flesch (1955). This book exemplified a growing interest in reading research and its relevance to educational practice (Ruddell, 2002). In arguments reminiscent of contemporary debates, Flesch attacked the prevailing look-say method of reading instruction as a contributor to the reading problems experienced by many U.S. students. As the basis for his attack, Flesch referenced research that established the effectiveness of phonics-based techniques over those that relied on a whole-word approach. Before long, books such as *The New Fun With Dick and Jane* (Gray, Artley, & Arbuthnot, 1951), with their look-say approach, gave way to controlled vocabulary readers and synthetic phonics drill and practice in such approaches as the *Lippincott Basic Reading Program*, *Reading With Phonics*, and *Phonetic Keys to Reading* (Chall, 1967).

The burgeoning interest in finding an answer to children's reading problems interfaced with psychological research in the guise of Skinnerian behaviorism, the prevailing research orientation at the time (Goetz, Alexander, & Ash, 1992). With its promise of bringing a scientific perspective to the reading "problem," behaviorism seemed suited to the task at hand (Glaser, 1978). In effect, it was time to turn the attention of the research community to the fundamental task of learning to read and apply the same principles of analysis that explained and controlled the behavior of animals in the laboratory to children's language learning. Such an analysis would presumably result in pedagogical techniques based on an understanding of the physiological and environmental underpinnings of human behavior (Glaser, 1978).

Based on this perspective, the processes and skills involved in learning to read could be clearly defined and broken down into their constituent parts. Those constituent parts could then be practiced and reinforced in a systematic and orderly fashion during classroom instruction (Pearson & Stephens, 1994). With this analytic view, there was a growing tendency for problems in the reading act to be looked on as deficiencies in need of remediation, just as physical ailments require medical remedies. Indeed, it was a medical metaphor of reading, with its diagnosis, prescription, and remediation, that came to the foreground in the 1950s. Moreover, despite the claims of some within the reading research community that little of significance occurred in reading until the 1960s (Weaver & Kintsch, 1991), the continued influence of behaviorism on educational practice remains evident today.

Guiding View

Because of the prevailing influences of behavioristic theory in educational research and practice, reading during this period was conceptualized as conditioned behavior, and just another process susceptible to programming. The Skinnerian or strict behaviorist perspective was that learning should not be conceived as growth or development, but rather as acquiring behaviors as a result of certain environmental contingencies. As Skinner (1974) stated,

> Everyone has suffered, and unfortunately is continuing to suffer, from mentalistic theories of learning in education.... The point of education can be stated in behavioral terms: a teacher arranges contingencies under which the student acquires behavior which will be useful to him under other contingencies later on.... Education covers the behavior of a child or person over many years, and the principles of developmentalism are therefore particularly troublesome. (pp. 202–203)

In this theoretical orientation, learning resulted from the repeated and controlled stimulation from the environment that came to elicit a predictable response from the individual. This repeated pairing of stimulus and response, often linked with the application of carefully chosen rewards and punishments, led to the habituation of the reading act. For example, the child presented with the symbols C-A-T immediately produces the desired word, *cat*, seemingly without cognitive involvement.

The philosophical grounds for this stance lay in the works of the empiricist David Hume (1777/1963) and his narrow conception of knowledge as perception and learning as habituated association (Strike, 1974). The investigation of academic learning, thus, involved identification of the requisite desired behaviors and determination of the environmental conditions (i.e., training) that produced them. Depending on how strictly the behaviorist paradigm was followed, hypotheses and conclusions were more or less restricted to discussion of observable behaviors and the environmental stimuli that preceded them (Strike, 1974).

The task for this generation of reading researchers, therefore, was to untangle the chained links of behavior involved in reading so that learners could be trained in each component skill. The act of reading consisted of the competent and properly sequenced performance of that chain of discrete skills. Research was additionally concerned with the structuring and control of materials effective in the delivery of environmental stimulation and practice opportunities (Glaser, 1978; Monaghan & Saul, 1987). There was also a concomitant interest in the identification and remediation of problems in skill acquisition, which would require even finer-grained analysis of the appropriate behaviors so that skill training could proceed in the smallest of increments (Glaser, 1978).

Resulting Principles

Out of the labors of the reading researchers of this era came a body of literature on the multitude of subskills required for reading. The interest in the study of the components of reading processes was exemplified by such efforts as the interdisciplinary studies at Cornell University that became the Project Literacy program (Levin, 1965; Venezky, 1984). As a result of the behaviorist emphasis on studying observable behavior, there was a particular focus on reading as a perceptual activity. Such perceptual activities included the identification of visual signals; the translation of these signals into sounds; and assembly of these sounds into words, phrases, and sentences (Pearson & Stephens, 1994). Phonics instruction came to be seen as part of the logical groundwork for beginning to read (Chall, 1967, 1995) and had the desirable attribute of being eminently trainable. The counterpart of this emphasis on skills was an interest in developing and validating diagnostic instruments and remedial techniques (Smith & Keogh, 1962). Where there were problems in skill acquisition, the solution was likely to be an individually paced training program (Glaser, 1978).

Rival Views of Learner and Learning Process

Although the behaviorist perspective dominated the psychological research of the time, alternative theories of human learning operated beneath the surface. The legacy of William James (1890) endured in the notion that human thought mattered in human action and that introspection and self-questioning were effective tools for uncovering those thoughts. According to James (1890), reading would be best described as mindful habit. As such, reading would be best examined through a psychological lens via introspection rather than through the behaviorists' physiological lens of observation of measurable behaviors. From such mental inspection, hypotheses as to the nature of reading could be forged (Jenkinson, 1969). This approach stood directly against the behaviorist antagonism to "mentalism" and insistence on observation of overt behavior only. When researchers addressed questions about the reasoning involved in reading, they leaned toward a Jamesian stance, and away from strict behaviorism (Alexander, 2003).

From another angle, the reductionist aspect of behaviorism—with its intended training program of bottom-up assembly of linked sets of behaviors to create a coherent activity such as learning to read—stood in opposition to Gestalt theory (Wertheimer, 1945/1959). For Gestalt theory, understanding phenomena as wholes was essential and could never be achieved by concatenation of individual facts, skills, or observations (Wulf, 1922/1938). Although explanation of perceptual processes occupied much of the attention of Gestalt theorists, their focus was on the phenomenon as a whole rather than on its elements. Human beings brought to the tasks of perception the propensity and ability to synthesize and make coherent sense out of their perceptual data. Such coherence and sense could not be achieved by assembly alone. The top-down perspective of the holistic Gestalt modality was evident in the orientation to reading development held by those Chall (1967) identified as "linguistic" proponents, who emphasized whole-word recognition, the importance of context in comprehension and word identification, and the consideration of reading as a unique human activity with its own definitive characteristics.

The Era of Natural Learning (1966–1975)

The Conditions for Change

By the mid-1960s, there was already a general unrest in the reading community with the precepts of Skinnerian behaviorism (Ryle, 1949) and with the conceptualization of reading as discrete skills passively drilled and practiced until reflexively demonstrated. Several factors served to hasten the transition in research on the learner and the learning process. One of those factors was an increased interest in internal mental structures and processes sparked by advances in neurology and artificial intelligence (Ericsson & Smith, 1991). Both of these movements turned attention back inside the human mind and away from the environment.

Another factor in this theoretical transformation was the fact that the dissatisfaction with behaviorism as an explanatory system was shared by diverse segments of the educational research community whose views on many other issues were frequently at odds (Pearson & Stephens, 1994). In the mid-1960s, a U.S. federally funded nationwide cooperative research venture, the First Grade Studies (Bond & Dykstra, 1967), brought together researchers on 27 different reading projects in a systematic comparison of various approaches to instruction in beginning reading. The attention of researchers in a wide range of disciplines had been drawn to the investigation of the reading process, the effect of which was an interdisciplinary perspective on the nature of reading and the teaching of reading that remains a hallmark of the field.

Two communities of theorists and researchers were especially influential in setting the stage for this period of reading research, linguists and psycholinguists. On the one hand, linguists following in the tradition of Chomsky (1957, 2002) held to a less environmentally driven and more hard-wired view of language acquisition, and hence of reading. Psycholinguistic researchers, on the other hand, felt that the attention to discrete aspects of reading advocated in behaviorism destroyed the natural communicative power and inherent aesthetic of reading (Goodman & Goodman, 1980; Smith, 1973, 1978). Given these circumstances, the stage was set for a new era of reading research.

Guiding View

In this new era of reading research, the conceptualization that served as the formative stance was of learning as a natural process. Language, as with other innate human capacities, was to be developed through meaningful use, not practiced to the point of mindless reaction, as behaviorists proposed. This notion of "hard-wired" capacities blended the explanatory language of physiology and psychology (Chomsky, 1965). It was assumed that human beings were biologically programmed to acquire language under favorable conditions. This programming involved the existence of mental structures designed to perform the complex task of assimilating and integrating the particular linguistic cues provided by a given language community (Chomsky, 1975).

Such a view of the language learner was strongly influenced by the writings of linguist Noam Chomsky (e.g., 1998, 2002) and marked a dramatic shift from the behaviorist view of learning as conditioning. In his classic volume *Syntactic Structures*, Chomsky (1957) helped establish the field of generative grammar, which focused on the assumed innate mental structures that allowed for language use. Chomsky argued that it was critical to separate human mental competencies from subsequent performance, an argument that distinguished him from the majority of linguists of the time concerned with the performance end of language (i.e., transformational grammar). In framing his theory, Chomsky was influenced by the emerging research in neuroscience and cognitive science (Baars, 1986). He saw unquestionable relations between the universality of neurological structures and the universality of grammatical structures. His assertion was that humans emerge from the womb with a preexisting template that guides language use. "Languaging" was thus perceived to unfold naturally, to follow a developmental trajectory, and to involve not just the action of the environment on the individual but also the individual's contribution in the form of a predisposition or innate capacity (Chomsky 1957, 1998). This shift in the view of language acquisition from conditioned behavior to natural process inevitably reverberated in the reading research community in the form of psycholinguistics (Goodman, 1965;

Smith, 1973). As with the generative grammarians, psycholinguists argued that because all human languages follow similar production rules, the capacity for language must be built-in. Psycholinguists carried this assumption beyond oral language into print or reading. They also focused on semantics and how meaning is acquired, represented, and used during the process of reading. Consequently, learning to read, the written counterpart of acquiring an oral language, came to be viewed as an inherent ability, rather than a reflective act involving the laborious acquisition of a set of skills (Harste, Burke, & Woodward, 1984). Just as children came to understand the spoken language of their surrounding community (Halliday, 1969), they would come to understand its written language given enough exposure in meaningful situations (Goodman & Goodman, 1980).

While generative grammarians and psycholinguists sought for the universals underlying human language acquisition and use, others during this time period became interested in the interaction of language as a system and language in its particular social uses. Sociolinguistic investigations such as those of Labov (1966) and Shuy (1968) began to explore variations in everyday language use and the relationship of those variations to social roles (Labov, 1972). The contrast between the everyday language of children growing up in different social settings and the language demanded in an educational setting began to surface as an issue for educational research and practice (Labov, 1971; Shuy, 1969).

Resulting Principles

With the view that language development was a native capacity of human beings, significant changes occurred not only in perceptions of the nature of reading but also in the position of reading relative to other language processes and in preferred modes of diagnosis and instruction. Specifically, because the premise underlying this "natural" movement was that language had a natural and rule-governed structure, it became essential to unite all manner of language acquisition and use. To assume that the process of acquiring and using written language was somehow unique from that of speaking or listening would be disruptive to the theoretical premises on which this perspective was founded. Thus, in this period and for subsequent eras of reading research, we see a tendency toward the aggregation of the language arts into the unified field of literacy (Halliday & Hasan, 1976).

Concurrent with this new view of reading as natural process, investigations into the inferred mental structures and processes of reading in relation to performance took shape. For one, the learner was cast in the role of an active participant, a constructor of meaning who used many forms of information to arrive at comprehension (Halliday, 1969). Learning to read was not so much a matter of being taught, but a matter of arriving at facility as a result of a predisposition to seek understanding within a language-rich environment.

For another, reading diagnosis within this period was less about isolating and correcting problems in the underlying skills of reading than it was about understanding how readers arrived at their alternative interpretations of written text (Clay, 1967, 1976). Unlike the diagnostic studies of the preceding period (Christenson & Barney, 1969; Smith & Keogh, 1962; Snyder & Freud, 1967), this new model of diagnosis did not focus on identifying and eradicating the source of readers' errors. Rather, the goal was to ascertain how the unexpected responses readers produced were reflective of their attempts at meaning-making (Goodman & Goodman, 1980). The groundbreaking work by Goodman and colleagues on miscue analysis was prototypic of this reconceptualization occurring in reading diagnosis (e.g., Goodman, 1965).

Rival Views of Learner and Learning Process

It is interesting that some of the very conditions that sparked the "reading as natural process" movement helped to establish a rival view of reading that came to dominate in the subsequent decade (Fodor, 1964; Fodor, Miller, & Langendoen, 1980). Specifically, a number of individuals invested in cognitive science and artificial intelligence were equally fascinated with the internal structures and processes of the human mind, as were generative grammarians and psycholinguists. However, for these researchers, the focus was more on how those processes and procedures could be best represented symbolically and transferred into computer programs that could approximate human performance (Fodor, 2001). In effect, these individuals were interested in creating "intelligent machines" that mimicked the problem solving of intelligent humans (Alexander, 2003).

What was significant about this alternative view of learners and learning was the lack of any presumption that the mental structures and processes being uncovered via neuroscience meant that resulting performance was somehow innate or hard-wired. To the contrary, the variability in human performance these researchers observed and documented suggested that seeming similarities in human language processes were likely the result of acquired or learned knowledge and processes combined with innate mental capabilities. This seemed especially true for written language, which required the manipulation of a symbolic system not required in oral communication or in other problem-solving domains, such as history or biology (Chi, Glaser, & Farr, 1988).

Although human neurology had a role to play, it was not as a regulator of language use. Within this rival group, there was a growing interest in text-based performance because of the opportunity it provided to investigate the subtle and not-so-subtle differences between experts and novices in terms of their memory, recall, and problem-solving approaches. The level of detail required to approximate even the simplest of human actions resulted in a growing appreciation for the power of individual differences and for the degree to which the specific domain of study and the task altered mental processes (Chase & Simon, 1973). For example, researchers of this period found chess to be an excellent venue for study because it is a game with a rigid and limited rule structure. Yet, there were clearly those who excelled at this mental game. Researchers studied the knowledge and processes of expert chess players to understand how experts visualize tasks, anticipate the moves of their opponents, and act to counter those moves. From this vantage point, any attempt to unify all forms of language acquisition and performance would be discounted within the rival group. Rather, reading as the processing of written text needed to be examined in its own right and not subsumed under the process of acquiring and using oral language.

The Era of Information Processing (1976–1985)

The Conditions for Change

By the mid-1970s, the reading research community again was poised for theoretical transformation. Conditions for that change included the growing attention to the structure and processes of the human mind and increased U.S. federal funding for basic reading research (Alexander, 1998a). The effects of these converging conditions were the creation of research centers dedicated to reading research and, concomitantly, a significant influx of theorists and researchers into the reading community whose interests were more in basic than applied research and whose roots were primarily in cognitive psychology (Pearson & Stephens, 1994). The interdisciplinary character of these centers, most notably the Center for the Study of Reading at the University of Illinois at Urbana-Champaign, involved individuals from psychology and reading-related fields such as English, literature, communications, and writing.

Given their more basic research agenda and their strong cognitive roots, these alliances forwarded a perspective on reading that deviated markedly from the orientation that had dominated. Specifically, this new perspective held little regard for the innateness or naturalness of reading and little interest in the amalgamation of literacy fields. As would be expected, some within the reading research community felt uneasy about this basic research emphasis, arguing that it had the "deleterious" effects of "squeezing out" reading educators and undervaluing instructional practice (Vacca & Vacca, 1983, p. 383).

Guiding View

On the basis of research published between 1976 and 1985, it was cognitive psychology, and more specifically information-processing theory, that dominated the domain of reading (Anderson, 1977). However, a psycholinguistic undercurrent remained evident during this period and gained momentum as new constituents joined the reading community. Even given the continuing presence of psycholinguistics, this remained the era of cognitive psychology characterized by unprecedented research on knowledge, especially the construct of prior knowledge (Alexander, 1998a). Much of this knowledge research was influenced by the philosophy of Immanuel Kant (1787/1963). Kantian philosophy was significant for its distinction between the sensible world and the intelligible world as varied sources of human knowledge.

> By "sensible world" [Kant] meant the world as perceived by the senses; he would later call this also the phenomenal world, or world of appearances. By "intelligible world" he meant the world as conceived by the intellect or reason.... Here Kant already laid down his basic theses: that space and time are not objective or sensible objects, but are forms of perception inherent in the nature and structure of the mind; and that the mind is no passive recipient and product of sensations, but is an active agent—with inherent modes and laws of operation—for transforming sensations into ideas. (Durant & Durant, 1967, p. 534)

Thus, this new generation of reading researchers searched for general processes or "laws" that explained human language as an interaction between symbol system and mind. With the burgeoning studies in expert/novice differences and artificial intelligence (Chi, Feltovich, & Glaser, 1981; Ericsson & Smith, 1991; Schank & Abelson, 1977), the medical metaphor of diagnosis, prescription, and remediation that reigned in the 1950s and the learning-as-natural metaphor of the 1960s were replaced with a mechanistic information-processing metaphor (Reynolds, Sinatra, & Jetton, 1996). Text-based learning was about knowledge, which was organized and stored within the individual mind, and resulted from the input, interpretation, organization, retention, and output of information from the individual's environment (Samuels & Kamil, 1984).

Resulting Principles

As noted, the construct of prior knowledge and its potent influence on students' text-based learning were enduring legacies of this era (Alexander, 1998a; Alexander & Murphy, 1998). Specifically, the readers' knowledge base was shown to be *powerful*, *pervasive*, *individualistic*, and *modifiable*. Prior knowledge was linked to individuals' perspectives on what they read or heard (Pichert & Anderson, 1977), their allocation of attention (Anderson, Pichert, & Shirey, 1983), and their interpretations and recall of written text (Bransford & Franks, 1972; Lipson, 1983). In addition, significant associations were established between readers' existing knowledge and their subsequent reading performance (Stanovich, 1986, see #17 this volume), comprehension (Alvermann, Smith, & Readence, 1985), memory (Anderson, Reynolds, Schallert, & Goetz, 1977), and strategic processing (Alexander & Judy, 1988; Garner, 1987).

Because of the primacy of reading-specific studies during this period, there arose an extensive literature on text-based factors, particularly in relation to comprehension. Writings on story grammar, text cohesion, text structure, and text genres proliferated (Armbruster, 1984; Kintsch & van Dijk, 1978; Mandl, Stein, & Trabasso, 1984; Meyer, 1975; Taylor & Beach, 1984). Further, in parallel with the focuses within the broader cognitive field, reading theorists and researchers investigated the organization of knowledge in the mind (Anderson, 1977; Rumelhart, 1980) and how that organization distinguished novice readers from more expert readers (Allington, 1980; August, Flavell, & Clift, 1984; Lundeberg, 1987; Paris & Myers, 1981).

The information-processing research of this period resulted in a multitude of cognition-related constructs. Of the many constructs articulated in this decade, schema theory remains one of the most potent legacies of the time. In fact, Baldwin et al. (1992) described schema theory as "one of the hottest topics in the history of NRC [National Reading Conference]" (p. 507). The theoretical construct of schemata—what Rumelhart (1980) called the building blocks of cognition, drew explicitly from the philosophy of Kant (Anderson et al., 1977) and embodied the power, pervasiveness, individuality, and modifiability of knowledge previously mentioned. Even those forwarding alternative explanations for the structure of human knowledge and the processing of information have had to counter the tenets of schema theory and the body of supporting evidence (Sadoski, Paivio, & Goetz, 1991).

One of the distinguishing characteristics of this research period was its focus on the individual mind. Such an individualistic perspective was understandable for several reasons. First, the computer-based guiding view that shaped this era was fundamentally a model of individual knowledge acquisition and use. There was little, if any, consideration of sociocultural or contextual influences on the processing of linguistic information. Second, the research studies generated during this period strongly supported individualistic interpretations of written text. In effect, any presumption that only one interpretation would result from reading text was empirically disputed (Brewer, 1980).

Finally, the research activities of this period demonstrated that students' knowledge could be significantly modified through direct intervention, training, or explicit instruction (Paris & Winograd, 1990; Pressley, Goodchild, Fleet, Zajchowski, & Evans, 1989; Weinstein, Goetz, & Alexander, 1988). This body of strategy research highlighted the modifiability of individuals' knowledge bases and their approaches to information processing. These studies targeted a spectrum of general text-processing strategies, including summarization, mapping, self-questioning, and predicting (Brown, Campione, & Day, 1981; Hansen, 1981; Raphael & Wonnacott, 1985; Tierney, Readence, & Dishner, 1990). There also was consideration of instructional environments and pedagogical techniques that contributed to improved comprehension of text (Duffy, Roehler, Meloth, & Vavrus, 1986; Pearson, 1984; Pressley, Lysynchuk, D'Ailly, Smith, & Cake, 1989).

Rival Views of Learner and Learning Process

Among the most vocal critics of the information-processing approach to reading research were those who held to a more naturalistic and holistic view of reading (e.g., Smith, 1985). Many of the psycholinguists who had fueled the "natural" movement were significant forces in this rival perspective. However, there were several important distinctions between this iteration of the natural movement and its predecessor. For one, there was a shift away from the neurological or physiological arguments central to that earlier period and more concern for naturalism in the materials and procedures used to teach reading. One reason for this shift in emphasis was the new alliances that invigorated this alternative view. Specifically, there was an influx of literature and writing researchers into the reading community who were more interested in the unity within the language arts than in any potential dissimilarities. The expanding literature on the common bases of reading and writing was indicative of this integrated view (Spivey & King, 1989; Tierney, Soter, O'Flahavan, & McGinley, 1989), as were the studies on discussion (Alvermann & Hayes, 1989; Bloome & Green, 1984; Heath, 1982).

Characteristic of this rival view was an increased concern for the aesthetic of reading over the rational (Rosenblatt, 1978/1994). One outcome of this philosophical reorientation was a rather negative attitude toward knowledge as the "residue" of information getting or fact-finding (Rosenblatt, 1978/1994, p. 23). This unfavorable view of knowledge as information getting is well represented in the writings of Louise Rosenblatt, especially her classic treatise *The Reader, the Text, and the Poem: The Transactional Theory of the Literary Work* (1978/1994). With her writings, Rosenblatt framed several decades of literacy research around the notion of reader stances or responses to text (e.g., Britton, 1982; Cox & Many, 1992; Fish, 1980).

Rosenblatt contended that, depending on the goal of the learner and the instructor, an individual's response to a literary work falls along a continuum from an efferent to an aesthetic stance. Those assuming a more efferent stance seek to uncover the "truths" voiced by some invisible or anonymous author.

> In nonaesthetic reading, the reader's attention is focused primarily on what will remain as the residue *after* the reading—the information to be acquired, the logical solution to a problem, the actions to be carried out. As the reader responds to the printed words or symbols, his attention is directed outward so to speak, toward concepts to be retained, ideas to be tested, actions to be performed after the reading. (Rosenblatt, 1978/1994, p. 23)

By contrast, readers holding to an aesthetic stance focus on the literary experience and allow themselves to discover the pleasure and beauty of the story.

> In aesthetic reading, in contrast, the reader's primary concern is with what happens *during* the actual reading event.... *In aesthetic reading, the reader's attention is centered directly on what he is living through during his relationship with that particular text* [author's emphasis]. (Rosenblatt, 1978/1994, pp. 24–25)

This contrast between the aesthetic and efferent stances Rosenblatt described had the effect of casting learning from text, central to the information-processing orientation, in an unfavorable light and countered the seemingly analytic, less-personal perspective of reading forwarded by cognitive researchers (Benton, 1983; Britton, 1982; Rosenblatt, 1938/1995). In effect, the goal was to lose oneself *in* the text and not specifically to learn *from* it. For those who espoused this goal, a "learning-from-text" perspective transformed a natural literary, aesthetic experience into an unnatural, overly analytic act.

The Era of Sociocultural Learning (1986–1995)

The Conditions for Change

Moving into the mid-1980s, there were indications that the reading community was positioned for further change. The explanatory adequacy of the computer metaphor that had guided the information-processing–based research of the previous decade was perceived as diminishing, even by those in the field of artificial intelligence who had fostered this metaphor (Anderson, Reder, & Simon, 1996). For instance, within cognitive psychology, the earlier information-processing approach was replaced by a constructivist theory that acknowledged learning as individualistic and rejected the mechanistic and computer-like aspects of learning implicit in this stance (Reynolds et al., 1996).

This shift in emphasis may have come to pass as the applications of the information-processing approach in such areas as expert systems development and classroom training programs were seen to have less than ideal outcomes. The expert systems that were designed to imitate human decision-making processes (e.g., Clancey, 1983) did not always live up to their claims (Chipman, 1993). In the realm of reading education, the application of information-processing theory in cognitive training programs also proved less promising than anticipated, which engendered doubt as to the feasibility of these training approaches (Harris, 1996). Many students failed to benefit from the explicit instruction in strategies or components of reading that was intended to improve their text-based learning. For some students, there were no improvements produced by this instruction, while for others, the benefits did not endure or transfer (Paris, Wasik, & Turner, 1991). Although the prior era of information-processing researchers had embraced general "laws" of text processing, these laws did not appear to account for the behaviors and results seen in specific applications, such as with particular populations, types of textual materials, and in variable classroom conditions (Paris, Wasik, & Turner, 1991).

A further force for change was the increased influence of alternative perspectives and research traditions speaking from outside the realm of cognitive psychology. Writings in social and cultural anthropology, such as the works of

Vygotsky (1934/1986), Lave (1988), and others (Heath, 1983; Rogoff, 1990), provided a new viewpoint for literacy researchers, as well as those in the larger educational research community. These writings sparked a growing acceptance in the literacy community of the ethnographic and qualitative modes of inquiry advocated in social and cultural anthropology. Along with these modes of inquiry came the practice of studying literacy with naturally occurring texts in natural settings, such as classrooms, homes, and workplaces (Anderson, Wilson, & Fielding, 1988). These new approaches brought the methodology of literacy research more in line with the holistic and aesthetic school of thought. Reflecting this shift in emphasis, the *Journal of Reading Behavior* became first the *Journal of Reading Behavior: Journal of Literacy* in 1991 and then the *Journal of Literacy Research* in 1996. This shows that the behavioral orientation toward reading of the 1950s and 1960s, reflected in the title of this journal of the National Reading Conference for many years thereafter, was fully abandoned in favor of a more integrated designation in the early 1990s.

An additional impetus to change was the development of a systematic attitude of distrust or devaluing of formal knowledge, and of the traditional mode of scientific inquiry. It might be said that the outcome of learning came to be less important than the learning process (Sfard, 1998). The goal of learning was no longer seen as the development of an individually held body of knowledge, but rather the creation of a mutual understanding arising in the social interaction of particular individuals in a particular context at a particular time. At the extremes of the research community, were those who portrayed the knowledge gained in school settings as an oppressive tool of political and cultural authorities seeking to maintain their dominance over the disempowered (McLaren, 1998). At another extreme were those who characterized schooled knowledge as the currently agreed-on interpretation of a reality that was essentially unknowable and unverifiable (von Glaserfeld, 1991). A common thread in these theoretical movements active during this time, such as critical theory, postmodernism, and radical constructivism, was the denial of privileged status to formal or schooled knowledge (Gee, 1989; Woods & Murphy, 2002). This multitude of divergent voices and interacting factors pushed research on learning toward a new stage in its development.

Guiding View

As a result of the aforementioned forces, group orientations came to replace the earlier focus on individualistic learning and instruction seen in the prior era (Alexander, Murphy, & Woods, 1996). Literacy research now sought to capture the shared understanding of the *many*, rather than the private knowledge of the *one*. From detection of the universal laws of learning, the goal became the description of the "ways of knowing" unique to particular social, cultural, and educational groups. The adoption of social and cultural perspectives on literacy learning inspired broader acceptance and exploration of the shared literacy experiences advocated in the aesthetic stance of the prior era. The dominant perspective during this time became the view of learning as a sociocultural, collaborative experience (Alexander, 1996; Reynolds et al., 1996), and of the learner as a member of a learning community (Brown & Campione, 1990). The widespread popularity of such concepts as cognitive apprenticeship, shared cognition, and social constructivism during this time period are evidence of the power of this view.

Resulting Principles

In this era of literacy research, the ongoing movement was toward increased sophistication of the conception of knowledge. Reviews of the knowledge terms used by literacy researchers and in broader educational contexts (Alexander, Schallert, & Hare, 1991; de Jong & Ferguson-Hessler, 1996; Greene & Ackerman, 1995) revealed that literacy involved a multitude of "knowledges." Knowledge was not a singular construct, but existed in diverse forms and interactive dimensions (Paris, Lipson, & Wixson, 1983; Prawat, 1989). These various knowledges had to be coordinated or reconciled in the performance of any nontrivial literacy act.

A primary locus for this adaptive activity was in the reconciliation of schooled and unschooled knowledge (Gardner, 1991). Students arrive at school with an extensive prior body of conceptual knowledge guiding their understanding and use of language. This unschooled knowledge (also known as *informal knowledge* or *spontaneous concepts*) could differ markedly in character from more formally acquired school knowledge (i.e., *scientific concepts*) (Alexander, 1992; Vygotsky, 1934/1978). Research in the field of conceptual change and misconceptions showed that this unschooled knowledge could be a more salient factor in students' learning from texts than their formally acquired knowledge (Alexander, 1998c; Guzzetti & Hynd, 1998; Vosniadou, 1994). The relative dominance of informal knowledge over formal understandings could be because what is learned in a school setting appears of limited relevance and therefore limited value to students (Alexander & Dochy, 1995; Cognition and Technology Group at Vanderbilt, 1990; Whitehead, 1929/1957). Unschooled knowledge might also possess a concrete and personal referent lacking in much of school learning (Alexander, Murphy, & Woods, 1996).

Beyond the recognition of knowledge's multiple forms, there was a growing awareness that one's knowledge was not always a positive force in subsequent learning and development. One's existing knowledge could impede or interfere with future learning in the form of misconceptions or barriers to conceptual change (Chinn & Brewer, 1993; Perkins & Simmons, 1988; Roth, 1985). Research on persuasion also provided insight into the possible negative role of preexisting knowledge (Alexander, Murphy, Buehl, & Sperl, 1997; Chambliss, 1995; Garner & Hansis, 1994). Specifically, those who approached arguments and evidence presented in text with little relevant knowledge or with a strong opinion proved more resistant to the authors' persuasive message.

Besides these investigations of the complexity of knowledge, research on knowledge and learning in this era also turned to investigation of the conditionality of knowledge. Conditionality of knowledge could arise from domain-specificity or task-specificity, as well as from social or contextual factors. The new awareness of the salience of social and contextual contributions to learning was evident in the proliferation of such terms as *learning communities* (Brown & Campione, 1990), *socially shared cognition* (Resnick, Levine, & Teasley, 1980), *distributed cognition* (Salomon, 1993), *shared expertise* (Brown & Palincsar, 1989), *guided participation* (Rogoff, 1990), *situated action* (Greeno & Moore, 1993), and *anchored instruction* (Cognition and Technology Group at Vanderbilt, 1990). Most members of the literacy research community agreed that schooling, at least, was a social and cultural phenomenon, along with its resultant knowledge (e.g., Cognition and Technology Group at Vanderbilt, 1996; Lave, 1988; Rogoff, 1990). Schools clearly functioned as social institutions centered around the interactions of students and teachers. Designed to serve socially contrived goals, schools operated as unique socially sanctioned contexts in which students were to build the requisite knowledge base for our postindustrialized societies (e.g., Perret-Claremont, Perre, & Bell, 1980).

Certain researchers made the sociocultural nature of schools and classrooms the focus of their efforts, developing instructional procedures that engendered optimal social interchanges in the classroom (e.g., Bereiter & Scardamalia, 1989; Collins, Brown, & Newman, 1989; Palincsar & Brown, 1984). In these approaches, teachers played the essential role of facilitator or guide (Rogoff & Gauvain, 1986; Vygotsky, 1934/1986), with the scaffolding provided by the teacher diminishing in proportion to the students' increasing knowledge, interest, and strategic abilities in a particular area (e.g., Alexander, 1997b; Brown & Palincsar, 1989), so that students could develop self-direction and autonomy (Deci & Ryan, 1991).

Conditionality came into play as well in investigations of possible domain-specificity of knowledge and learning. Domains made up the realm of academic learning and provided the settings against which choices of vocation and avocation were framed (Alexander, 1998b). The question of the possible relationship of these domains to some objective reality remained (Bereiter, 1994; Matthews, 1994). Nonetheless, these domains differed significantly from one another (Spiro, Feltovich, Jacobson, & Coulson, 1992; Spiro & Jehng, 1990), with these differences strongly affecting the inscription, perception, communication, and learning of the associated knowledge in such domains (Alexander, 1998b; Nolen, Johnson-Crowley, & Wineburg, 1994; Stahl, Hynd, Glynn, & Carr, 1996). One attempt to characterize this diversity was the use of the term *structuredness*, involving the grouping of problems typical of the domain in terms of their form and content or in having an optimal algorithmic or heuristic solution strategy (Frederiksen, 1984).

Some of these domain differences would no doubt seem obvious from even a superficial comparison of such representative texts as a mathematics textbook or a historical account (Ball, 1993; Putnam, Heaton, Prawat, & Remillard, 1992; VanSledright, 1996). Other differences were more deeply imprinted in the beliefs of students and teachers about the domain itself, and also about their own competencies in that domain (Alexander & Dochy, 1995; Pajares, 1992). What it meant to *know* mathematics versus history or what doing well required in literature versus science was seen to differ (Matthews, 1994; Wineburg, 1996). These differences arose from beliefs about the epistemological characteristics of different domains, including the certainty of their central concepts or fundamental principles (Schommer, 1990, 1993).

Because domains vary in significant ways, it was logical for researchers to assume that students' knowledge, strategic thinking, and motivations would likewise vary along domain lines (Alexander, 1997b; Murphy & Woods, 1996). This meant that a global label such as "good" or "poor" student would be perceived as too general and in need of qualification. The critical question was "good at what or poor at what"? Such domain-specific or task-specific qualification of student ability added to the conditionality of learning.

Rival Views of Learner and Learning Process

In this era, what characterized rival theories of learning were not dichotomous viewpoints on the nature of literacy, such as the earlier split along the dimension of rational versus aesthetic. During this period, predominant and rival views were in agreement on the value of considering social and contextual forces in literacy. The distinction between the predominant and rival stance came in the relative importance attached to the context or to social interactions. Specifically, for certain segments of this community, the situated character or social nature of knowledge and knowing became the central focus (Sfard, 1998).

Research on situativity or situated action (e.g., Greeno & the Middle School Mathematics Through Applications Project Group, 1998; Greeno & Moore, 1993) was grounded in the perceptual investigations of Gibson (1966), and in the symbolic-processing theory developed by researchers in artificial intelligence and technology (Greeno & Moore, 1993). From this foundation, researchers evolved an emphasis on the learning affordances offered in the conditions of the immediate learning environment and saw knowledge as nontransferable between situations or contexts (Sfard, 1998). Within this perspective, learning could not be separated from the situation in which it occurred, so that knowledge came to reside in the context itself, rather than in the individual learners. From the standpoint of human interactions, as well, certain sociocultural researchers came to the position that knowledge was not merely shaped or colored by social experiences and interactions, but actually existed in those interchanges rather than in individual minds (Sfard, 1998). For those holding to this view, knowledge would be present when students are socially engaged in discussion or collaborative-learning activities. With these varied sociocultural perspectives on literacy came a radical shift from the prior era's location of knowledge in the mind and emphasis on individuality of knowledge and the process of knowing.

The Era of Engaged Learning (1996–Present)

The Conditions for Change

As the 1990s wound down, there were forces at work that boded a change in the way learners and learning were perceived and studied within the literacy community. Those forces led to changing perceptions of text, readers, and the reading process. Prior to this period, texts were generally defined as printed materials (e.g., books or magazines) read in linear fashion (Wade & Moje, 2000). Further, readers targeted in the research were most often young children acquiring the ability to decode and comprehend written language or older students struggling with the demands of traditional text-based learning (Hiebert & Taylor, 2000; Pigott & Barr, 2000). Moreover, outside the concern for readers' efferent or aesthetic response to literature or the creation of a stimulating print-rich learning environment, there was little regard for motivation in the form of readers' goals, interests, and involvement in the learning experience (Oldfather & Wigfield, 1996). However, several conditions conspired to change these "typical" perceptions of text, reader, and reading, ushering in the current era of reading research.

First, with the growing presence of hypermedia and hypertext, the reading community began to consider the nature and form of these nonlinear and less traditional forms of text on students' learning (Alexander, Kulikowich, & Jetton, 1994; Bolter, 1991). The term *nonlinear text* refers to discourse accompanied by a database management system that guides or prompts readers to other informational sites and sources (Gillingham, Young, & Kulikowich, 1994). This influx of hypermedia and hypertext became coupled with an increased attention to classroom discourse and its role in students' academic development (Alvermann, Commeyras, Young, Randall, & Hinson, 1997). Researchers considered the form and content of that discourse and its relation to reading performance, as well as to subject-matter learning (Jetton & Alexander, 1998). Collectively, the interest in hypermedia and classroom discourse extended notions of text to both traditional and alternative forms (Alexander & Jetton, 2003).

Second, during this time, the rich and impressive body of literature on motivation that had formed over the past several decades found its way into the reading community (Guthrie & Wigfield, 2000). This infusion of motivation research led to the consideration of such critical factors as learners' interest, goals, self-efficacy beliefs, as well as their self-regulation and active participation in reading and text-based learning (Almasi, McKeown, & Beck, 1996; Ames, 1992; Hidi, 1990; Schallert, Meyer, & Fowler, 1995; Schraw, Bruning, & Svoboda, 1995; Turner, 1995). One of the characteristics of this motivational research was its social cognitive perspective on student learning (Pintrich & Schunk, 2001). In other words, these motivational factors were not considered in isolation but were studied in relation to other factors such as students' knowledge, strategic abilities, sociocultural background, and features of the learning context. The result of this infusion of motivation theory and research into the reading literature was a reconceptualization of the student as engaged or motivated reader (Guthrie & Wigfield, 2000). This motivational focus was especially apparent in the research and publications of the National Reading Research Center funded by the Department of Education.

Finally, for many reasons, including a deepening understanding of human development, the increased longevity of the population, and the mounting demands of functioning within a postindustrial, information-technological age, the literacy community's view of reading shifted (Alexander, Murphy, & Woods, 1996; Reinking, McKenna, Labbo, & Kieffer 1998). Throughout the previous eras of reading research, activities, debates, and stances revolved primarily around the acquisition of reading processes and whether reading could best be understood as a discrete set of skills or as a more natural unfolding of competence fostered by meaningful, aesthetic engagement. What has become apparent, however, is that neither orientation toward reading effectively captures the complexity of reading or recognizes the changing nature of reading as individuals continue their academic development (Alexander, 2003). In other words, it has become increasingly more difficult to ignore that reading is a domain that relates not only to the young or struggling reader but also to readers of all abilities and ages. Further, reading extends beyond the initial phase of acquisition and across the lifespan as readers engage in a range of reading-related, goal-directed activities. Current initiatives directed toward adolescent and adult readers are evidence of the expanded view of reading (RAND Reading Study Group, 2002, see #27 and #53 this volume; National Institute of Child Health and Human Development [NICHD], 2000). Thus, earlier dichotomization of reading into "learning to read" and "reading to learn" stages (Chall, 1995) is shifting to a more integrated and developmental perspective.

Guiding View

Putting a label on an ongoing era is certainly a risky venture, given that hindsight is far more acute. However, as this latest decade of reading research draws to a close, we believe that it can be aptly described as the Era of Engaged Learning. The label "engaged" captures several of the aforementioned forces that are shaping perceptions of reading and informing research in that domain. For one, it acknowledges that reading is not confined to traditional print materials but extends to the texts students encounter daily, including the nonlinear, interactive, dynamic, and visually complex materials conveyed via audiovisual media (Alexander & Jetton, 2003). It also entails the discussions that occur around both traditional and alternative texts (Alvermann et al., 1997; Wade, Thompson, & Watkins, 1994).

Of course, our present understanding of how students learn by means of alternative forms of text remains emergent (Alexander, Graham, & Harris, 1998; Wade & Moje, 2000). If our history in dealing with other forms of nonprint modes of communication (e.g., television) is any indication, we have a great deal to learn about the potentials of alternative, nonlinear media (Neuman, 1988). For example, as these alternative forms of text become more prevalent, literacy researchers and practitioners may need to reconsider fundamental concepts such as learning, memory, and strategic processing (Bolter, 1991; Garner & Gillingham, 1996; Goldman, 1996; Salomon, Perkins, & Globerson, 1991). Further, practitioners will need to examine how pedagogical techniques and learning environments can be adapted to assist not only readers who struggle with traditional text but also those who get lost in hyperspace (Alexander, Kulikowich, & Jetton, 1994; Reinking et al., 1998).

Engagement also pertains directly to students' meaningful and goal-directed participation in text-based learning. While the philosophical writings of Skinner, Chomsky, Kant, and Vygotsky were central to prior eras of reading research, the writings of John Dewey (e.g., 1910/1991, 1913) have been key to this era. Dewey's notions of experiential learning and interest are evident in the conceptions of engagement framed within the burgeoning motivation research and have resulted in a unification of once oppositional stances. In this most recent era of literacy research, the learner is conceptualized as a motivated knowledge seeker (Alexander, 1997a). This perception differs from the Kantian distinction (1787/1963) between the sensible and the intelligible world inherent in information-processing theory and the efferent/aesthetic distinction underlying the psycholinguistic perspective of reading (Goodman & Goodman, 1980; Rosenblatt, 1938/1995). Specifically, it is assumed that a search for understanding or the act of learning via text involves the integration of cognitive and motivational forces.

The research on reader engagement further establishes that learners are more than passive receptacles of information (Guthrie & Wigfield, 2000). They are active and willful participants in the construction of knowledge (Alexander, 1997a; Reed & Schallert, 1993; Reed, Schallert, & Goetz, 1993). However, the picture of engagement emerging during this decade deviates from prior sociocultural interpretation in terms of the focus on the individual learner within the educational environment (Alexander & Murphy, 1999). In particular, while the learner still resides and operates within a sociocultural context, attention again is turned to the individual working to create a personally meaningful and socially valuable body of knowledge. Thus, the portrait of the engaged reader framed by the research has both individualistic and collective dimensions, a reconciliation of information-processing and sociocultural perspectives of past decades (Guthrie, McGough, Bennett, & Rice, 1996; Guthrie, Van Meter, et al., 1996).

A further consequence of this view of the learner as actively engaged in the process of learning has been a rekindled interest in strategic processing. In contrast to the habituated skills of earlier eras, the effective use of strategies is understood to require reflection, choice, and deliberate execution on the part of the learner (Alexander, Graham, & Harris, 1998). Strategy use by its nature calls for engaged learners who are willing to put forth effort, and who can knowledgeably respond to the demands of a particular situation. The body of literature on learning strategies, particularly reading comprehension, has grown in recent years in response to this new view of the engaged learner (Pressley, 2002).

Finally, the view of learners as actively engaged allows for a developmental perspective on reading. Developmentally, individuals are continually in the process of learning to read and have a direct role to play in their literacy. From this vantage point, students are not complete as readers when they can demonstrate basic linguistic skills or fluency in reading. Rather, they continue to grow as readers as their linguistic knowledge, subject-matter knowledge, strategic capabilities, and their motivations expand and mature (Alexander, 1997b). This developmental perspective on reading extends concern beyond the early elementary years into adolescence and adulthood.

We see this developmental orientation toward reading in recent reports and the activities of the Center for the Improvement of Early Reading Achievement (CIERA). For example, in its summary report titled *Partnership for Reading: Adolescent Literacy—Research Informing Practice: A Series of Workshops*, The Partnership for Reading (National Institute for Literacy, 2002) identified development as a superordinate principle for organizing the research agenda on adolescent literacy. Similarly, the RAND Reading Study Group (2002), in its publication *Reading for Understanding: Toward an R&D Program in Reading Comprehension*, describes learning to read well as "a long-term developmental process" (p. xiii) and recognizes the need for research that "will contribute to better theories of reading development" (p. 29).

Resulting Principles

Several principles appear to guide the current decade of reading research. One of those principles pertains to the complexity and multidimensional nature of reading. Specifically, notions that reading is cognitive, aesthetic, *or* sociocultural in nature are set aside. Instead, all these forces are actively and interactively involved in reading development (Alexander & Jetton, 2000). For example, there is a significant relationship between learners' knowledge and their interests (Alexander, Jetton, & Kulikowich, 1995; Csikszentmihalyi, 1990). Similarly, encountering personally relevant texts promotes deeper student engagement in their learning (Guthrie & Wigfield, 2000).

Another guiding principle of this era is that students encounter a range of textual materials, both traditional and alternative, that should be reflected in the learning environment (Wade & Moje, 2000). Although their views on the merits of technology differ, educational researchers acknowledge that technology has transformed learning and teaching (Cuban, 1993; Postman, 1993; Scardamalia, Bereiter, McLean, Swallow, & Woodruff, 1989). Today's K–12 students in postindustrial societies have never experienced a world without computer-based technologies. They regularly surf the Web, send e-mail, and use instant messaging—acts that have changed the face of information processing and human communication (Alexander & Knight, 1993; Garner & Gillingham, 1996). This technological revolution has produced an unimaginable proliferation of information sources and text types. This proliferation further complicates perceptions of reading and places new demands on today's readers (Gillingham et al., 1994). For instance, effective readers must become capable of assessing credibility, identifying possible biases, analyzing persuasive or literary techniques, and locating and selecting optimal sources. However, these new technologies also may hold promise for reading in what Reinking et al. (1998) call a post-typographic world.

Because reading is multidimensional in character, with significant relations among readers' knowledge, strategic processing, and motivation, simple models or theories based on a "learning to read" and "reading to learn" distinction need to be supplanted with more complex, reciprocal models of reading development (Alexander, 2003). Specifically, investigation of the initial stages of reading acquisition should not be isolated from the issues emerging when comprehension of texts becomes the focus. This requires a genuinely developmental theory of reading, spanning preliteracy reading readiness to proficient adult reading. This developmental vision of reading was reflected in the report of the RAND Reading Study Group (2002, see #27 and #53 this volume):

> a vision of proficient readers who are capable of acquiring new knowledge and understanding new concepts, are capable of applying textual information appropriately, and are capable of being engaged in the reading process and reflecting on what is read. (p. xiii)

Rival Views of Learner and Learning Process

In this era, the views in the literacy research community of the learner as a motivated, engaged knowledge-seeker and of the learning process as developmental and anchored in a sociocultural context stand in sharp contrast to a trend that has been gaining momentum over the past several decades. We have chosen to label this rival perspective as learning as reconditioning. The choice of the term *reconditioning* signals several significant features of this rival undercurrent. First, as in the early conditioning period, this rival stance is invested in the identification, teaching, and remediation of the subskills or components underlying reading acquisition (e.g., Foorman, Francis, Fletcher, Schatschneider, & Mehta, 1998). In addition, the emphasis in this rival orientation is on beginning or struggling readers who have yet to master these reading fundamentals.

Unlike the earlier Era of Conditioned Learning, the current concentration on reading subskills and components is less driven by theory than by other forces. One of the forces is the drive toward accountability, primarily in the form of high-stakes testing, and the drive for national standards (Paris & Urdan, 2000). From the stance of learning as engagement, assessments that foster knowledge-seeking around challenging, valuable, and meaningful problems and issues would be warranted (American Psychological Association Presidential Task Force on Psychology in Education, 1993). However, such problems are not readily measurable or as predictive of reading difficulties in the early years. Moreover, the effort to institute national standards that seemingly prescribe the content and skills learners should have acquired at given points in their school careers thus constrains the views of learners and learning (Paris & Urdan, 2000).

Another difference between the conditioning and reconditioning perspectives is the alliances each represents. Specifically, the present investment in basic skills and components of reading has gained support from researchers in special education and others who work with struggling readers (Foorman et al., 1998; Torgesen, 1998, 1999). These researchers have been joined by those engaged in neuroscience. In particular, advancements in neuroimaging techniques have allowed researchers to examine the neurological structures and processes of struggling readers or readers with special needs (Shaywitz et al., 2000). On the basis of such neuroimaging studies, still in a formative stage, researchers have attempted to pinpoint the specific neurobiological or physiological patterns related to specific reading outcomes or documented conditions (Pugh et al., 1997; Shaywitz, Fletcher, Holahan, & Shaywitz, 1992).

Emergent Premises: Lessons of the Past 50 Years

In this overview of the past 50 years of reading research, our discussion has been anchored by the conception of the learner and learning process underlying the approach to reading research in a given time period. Investigations of learning are, of necessity, situated in the context of a particular slant on the nature of the learner and on how learning occurs. Identifying that context allows the essential character of the research endeavors in different time periods and from different theoretical orientations to emerge from the myriad of studies and reported findings.

As we look across the eras of reading research on learners and learning and consider the characteristics and guiding principles unique to each, we cannot help but recognize that there are patterns evident in the fabric of that literature on learners and learning that bind those eras together. Those patterns—what we refer to as the emergent premises—are among the most important lessons to be derived from this historical analysis.

• Membership within the reading community is flexible and alters the basic identity of that community and its orientation toward research and practice. Characterizing the prototypic reading researcher would be a difficult task. That is because the membership of the reading community has remained in flux. Over the past 50 years, those considered to be among the leading reading researchers have ranged from reading specialists to psycholinguists, from literature researchers to cognitive scientists, and from special educators to generative grammarians. Because of the interdisciplinary and fluid nature of the reading community, the issues and perspectives on research and practice forwarded by its members have similarly been interdisciplinary and fluid in nature. If one were interested in predicting the future of reading research, it would be wise to look carefully at community demographics. Who is being drawn to the reading field and what special orientations, interests, and methodologies do they bring into this community of practice?

• Prevailing trends within the research literature reflect the influence of sociopolitical forces *outside* the reading community. While forces within the reading community, such as its membership, have been influential in shaping the eras of reading research, forces outside the community also have served as change agents. Consider the transformational effect of baby boomers and Sputnik on reading research and practice in the 1950s and 1960s, for example, or the impact that significant governmental funding for cognitive research had on the reading research agenda in the 1970s and 1980s. Further, as with the broader educational community, the reading community has not been immune to the effects of technology or the accountability movement, nor has its members been oblivious to the needs of the linguistically and culturally diverse students populating U.S. classrooms in increasing numbers. Such sociopolitical influences combine with forces within the reading community to transform the reading landscape and give each era of research its distinctive character (Valencia & Wixson, 2001, see #3 this volume). What is not clear in this historical analysis is the degree to which the reading community is proactive or reactive in relation to such powerful external forces.

• There is a recurrence of issues and approaches to reading research and practice across the decades. The ebb and flow of reform movements have been well documented in the educational literature (Alexander, Murphy, & Woods, 1996). This iterative reform pattern also is evident in the reading research literature in terms of perspectives on learners and learning. Perhaps the most obvious recurrence is the shifting emphasis on whole-word or phonetic instructional approaches. Despite periodic calls for balanced or integrated programs of research and practice in the literature (Stahl & Miller, 1989), the debate over the "right" or "most effective" approach continues unabated (Goodman, 1996). Other such recurring themes in the extant literature include more individualistic or more social emphases, variable interest in the use of controlled vocabulary readers or "authentic" literature (Rosenblatt, 1978/1994), and the valuing or devaluing of knowledge (Alexander, 1998a).

It would seem that knowledge of reading's history might serve to temper some of the unabashed support for particular new reform efforts that are, in actuality, iterations or reincarnations of past reading approaches with qualified or questionable records of success. At the very least, such a historical perspective would remind us that many current initiatives have legacies that deserve consideration.

• The history of reading research reveals a shifting emphasis on the physiological, psychological, and the sociological. While reading always involves physiological, psychological, and sociological dimensions, each era weighs these dimensions differently. When we look across the eras of reading research described in this article, it becomes apparent that each is distinguished by the relative weight placed on body, mind, or society when understanding the nature of learners and learning. In effect, while reading invariably entails human physiology, psychological processing, and social engagement, it is these factors' relative importance that becomes a defining feature for each era. For example, physiology, which focuses on the biological, chemical, and neurological dimensions of human performance, was clearly present in the behavioral orientations of Skinner and others, where reading was a conditioned response. The physiological perspective was evident again in the Chomskian views of language as a "hard-wired" capacity, and more recently in the growing interest in neurological structures and reading performance.

Psychological orientations, which deal with the mental processes of the mind, were most apparent in the Era of Information Processing. This orientation continues in the studies of expertise, motivation, and learner development. Here, the focus is squarely on process and functioning—the mental software—rather than on the physical or neurochemical structures—the mental hardware—from which these processes and functions may arise.

Finally, throughout reading history there have been periods in which the concern has not been centered on the individual student or his or her mental structures or processes. Rather, the focus has been on the student in relation to others (human-to-human interactions) or the learning of groups who share history (e.g., gender or ethnic groups) or geography (e.g., classroom communities). We see this sociological framework clearly in the rising interest in sociocultural perspectives and in research on cooperative or collaborative learning.

To understand the history of reading research, we need to appreciate the impact of these varied perspectives on learner and learning that become mirrored in the research questions posed, the methodologies applied, and the interpretations made. Indeed, the tensions felt within and across each of the eras described in this article arise, in part, because of the contrasting perspectives held by segments of the reading community.

Yet, as we stated, reading is invariably physiological, psychological, *and* sociological, suggesting the need for an integrated orientation. Reading invariably involves the physical, from the appropriation of visual stimuli through the neurological processing of those stimuli. Moreover, reading embraces the psychological in terms of the interpretation, storage, and retrieval of text; the formulation of goals and expression of interests; and much more. Finally, reading is sociological in that it involves intra- and interindividual communication through linguistic media that are themselves socioculturally influenced. Therefore, a meaningful integration of these orientations will require a broad, yet fine-grained view of reading that can incorporate information about brain structures and mental activities into an account of individual and social behavior.

• The cycle of changes observed in the history of reading research involves developmental maturation of the field. The movement from era to era in the past 50 years has represented an overall positive trend. Comparing the respective views of the learner and learning process of each era, we see that they have become progressively more sophisticated and also more inclusive. Each succeeding generation of researchers has investigated a wider range of phenomena, and often at a greater level of complexity. Similarly, the recurrence of themes has functioned iteratively, not merely reiteratively, in that the terms of the debate have been redefined and expanded as dictated by the prevailing perspective on learners and learning. Evidence that the field is not merely changing but maturing can be found in the broadening membership in the reading research community and the wide acceptance of multidisciplinary techniques and forms of inquiry.

• Without an overarching, developmental theory of reading, differential perspectives on research and practice may be judged as conflicting rather than complementary. Despite the promising activities of the last era, reading researchers still have not produced a well-accepted developmental theory that looks broadly at the nature of reading across the lifespan. The barriers to such a "grand" theory have been many, including the continuing focus on early reading, especially phonics and phonological awareness; difficulties in assessing deep and complex processes; the requirement of interdisciplinary cooperation; and more (Alexander, 2003; Ruddell, 2002).

In the absence of such a grand theory, it is highly likely that overly simplistic models or rival "camps" will continue to characterize the decades of reading. For example, across these eras, it has been commonplace to conceptualize the stages of reading under the banners of "learning to read" and "reading to learn" (Chall, 1995). However, more recent research makes it evident that these two hypothesized "stages" are, in fact, inextricably intertwined throughout reading development (Alexander, 2003). Even as readers begin to unravel the mysteries of language, they are constructing their knowledge base. Simultaneously, as readers pursue knowledge in academic domains, they are building a richer understanding of language.

A unifying theory of reading development would supersede such overly simplistic stage theories, just as it would potentially illustrate how the seemingly conflicting or rival views of reading we have described herein are complementary parts of a complex whole. Thus, it is not whether whole-word or phonics is "right" or "effective," but when, for whom, and for what the value of a whole-word or phonics-based approach can be substantiated. Perhaps, if current trends continue, the reading research community will achieve the developmental orientation that has eluded it for so long.

Concluding Thoughts

Our purpose in this historical analysis of the past 50 years of reading research is to provide readers a lens through which to view current theory and practice. Such a retrospective comes with no assurances. Historical analysis, after all, is an interpretative science. However, a glance backward at where reading research has been may serve to remind us that today's research and practice are a legacy with roots that reach into the past. Moreover, by paying our respects to that past, we may better understand the activities of the present and envision the paths for reading research that lie ahead.

References

*indicates that article is included on TMPR5 supplementary CD.

Alexander, P.A. (1992). Domain knowledge: Evolving themes and emerging concerns. *Educational Psychologist, 27*(1), 33–51.

Alexander, P.A. (1996). The past, present, and future of knowledge research: A reexamination of the role of knowledge in learning and instruction [Editor's notes]. *Educational Psychologist, 31*, 89–92.

Alexander, P.A. (1997a). Knowledge-seeking and self-schema: A case for the motivational dimensions of exposition [Special issue]. *Educational Psychologist, 32*(2), 83–94.

Alexander, P.A. (1997b). Mapping the multidimensional nature of domain learning: The interplay of cognitive, motivational, and strategic forces. In M.L. Maehr & P.R. Pintrich (Eds.), *Advances in motivation and achievement* (Vol. 10, pp. 213–250). Greenwich, CT: JAI Press.

Alexander, P.A. (1998a). Knowledge and literacy: A transgenerational perspective. In T. Shanahan & F.V. Rodriguez-Brown (Eds.),

National Reading Conference yearbook 47 (pp. 22–43). Chicago: National Reading Conference.

Alexander, P.A. (1998b). The nature of disciplinary and domain learning: The knowledge, interest, and strategic dimensions of learning from subject-matter text. In C. Hynd (Ed.), *Learning from text across conceptual domains* (pp. 263–287). Mahwah, NJ: Erlbaum.

Alexander, P.A. (1998c). Positioning conceptual change within a model of domain literacy. In B. Guzzetti & C. Hynd (Eds.), *Perspectives on conceptual change: Multiple ways to understand knowing and learning in a complex world* (pp. 55–76). Mahwah, NJ: Erlbaum.

Alexander, P.A. (2003). Profiling the developing reader: The interplay of knowledge, interest, and strategic processing. In D.L. Schallert, C.M. Fairbanks, J. Worthy, B. Maloch, & J.V. Hoffman (Eds.), *52nd yearbook of the National Reading Conference* (pp. 47–65). Oak Creek, WI: National Reading Conference.

Alexander, P.A., & Dochy, F.J.R.C. (1995). Conceptions of knowledge and beliefs: A comparison across varying cultural and educational communities. *American Educational Research Journal, 32*(2), 413–442.

Alexander, P.A., Graham, S., & Harris, K.R. (1998). A perspective on strategy research: Progress and prospects. *Educational Psychology Review, 10*(2), 129–154.

Alexander, P.A., & Jetton, T.L. (2000). Learning from text: A multidimensional and developmental perspective. In M.L. Kamil, P.B. Mosenthal, P.D. Pearson, & R. Barr (Eds.), *Handbook of reading research* (Vol. 3, pp. 285–310). Mahwah, NJ: Erlbaum.

Alexander, P.A., & Jetton, T.L. (2003). Learning from traditional and alternative texts: New conceptualization for an information age. In A.C. Graesser, M.A. Gernsbacher, & S.R. Goldman (Eds.), *Handbook of discourse processes* (pp. 199–241). Mahwah, NJ: Erlbaum.

Alexander, P.A., Jetton, T.L., & Kulikowich, J.M. (1995). Interrelationship of knowledge, interest, and recall: Assessing a model of domain learning. *Journal of Educational Psychology, 87*(4), 559–575.

Alexander, P.A., & Judy, J.E. (1988). The interaction of domain-specific and strategic knowledge in academic performance. *Review of Educational Research, 58*(4), 375–404.

Alexander, P.A., & Knight, S.L. (1993). Dimensions of the interplay between learning and teaching. *Educational Forum, 57*(3), 232–245.

Alexander, P.A., Kulikowich, J.M., & Jetton, T.L. (1994). The role of subject-matter knowledge and interest in the processing of linear and nonlinear texts. *Review of Educational Research, 64*(2), 201–252.

Alexander, P.A., & Murphy, P.K. (1998). The research base for APA's learner-centered principles. In N.M. Lambert & B.L. McCombs (Eds.), *Issues in school reform: A sampler of psychological perspectives on learner-centered schools* (pp. 25–60). Washington, DC: American Psychological Association.

Alexander, P.A., & Murphy, P.K. (1999). Learner profiles: Valuing individual differences within classroom communities. In P.L. Ackerman, P.C. Kyllonen, & P.D. Roberts (Eds.), *The future of learning and individual differences research: Processes, traits, and content* (pp. 413–431). Washington, DC: American Psychological Association.

Alexander, P.A., Murphy, P.K., Buehl, M.M., & Sperl, C.T. (1997, December). *The influence of prior knowledge, beliefs, and interest in learning from persuasive text.* Paper presented at the annual meeting of the National Reading Conference, Scottsdale, AZ.

Alexander, P.A., Murphy, P.K., & Woods, B.S. (1996). Of squalls and fathoms: Navigating the seas of educational innovation. *Educational Researcher, 25*(3), 31–36, 39.

Alexander, P.A., Schallert, D.L., & Hare, V.C. (1991). Coming to terms: How researchers in learning and literacy talk about knowledge. *Review of Educational Research, 61*(3), 315–343.

Allington, R.L. (1980). Teacher interruption behaviors during primary-grade oral reading. *Journal of Educational Psychology, 71*(3), 371–377.

Allington, R.L., & McGill-Franzen, A. (2000). Looking back, looking forward: A conversation about teaching reading in the 21st century. *Reading Research Quarterly, 35*, 136–153.

Almasi, J.F., McKeown, M.G., & Beck, I.L. (1996). The nature of engaged reading in classroom discussions of literature. *Journal of Literacy Research, 28*(1), 107–146.

Alvermann, D.E., Commeyras, M., Young, J.P., Randall, S., & Hinson, D. (1997). Interrupting gendered discursive practices in classroom talk about texts: Easy to think about, difficult to do. *Journal of Literacy Research, 29*(1), 73–104.

Alvermann, D.E., & Hayes, D.A. (1989). Classroom discussion of content area reading assignments: An intervention study. *Reading Research Quarterly, 24*, 305–335.

Alvermann, D.E., Smith, L.C., & Readence, J.E. (1985). Prior knowledge activation and the comprehension of compatible and incompatible text. *Reading Research Quarterly, 20*, 420–436.

American Psychological Association Presidential Task Force on Psychology in Education. (1993). *Learner-centered psychological principles: Guidelines for school redesign and reform.* Washington, DC: American Psychological Association.

Ames, C. (1992). Classrooms: Goals, structures, and student motivation. *Journal of Educational Psychology, 84*(3), 261–271.

Anderson, J.R., Reder, L.M., & Simon, H.A. (1996). Situated learning and education. *Educational Researcher, 25*(4), 5–11.

Anderson, R.C. (1977). The notion of schemata and the educational enterprise. In R.C. Anderson, R.J. Spiro, & W.E. Montague (Eds.), *Schooling and the acquisition of knowledge* (pp. 415–431). Hillsdale, NJ: Erlbaum.

Anderson, R.C., Pichert, J.W., & Shirey, L.L. (1983). Effects of reader's schema at different points in time. *Journal of Educational Psychology, 75*, 271–279.

Anderson, R.C., Reynolds, R.E., Schallert, D.L., & Goetz, E.T. (1977). Frameworks for comprehending discourse. *American Educational Research Journal, 14*(4), 367–381.

Anderson, R.C., Wilson, P.T., & Fielding , L.G. (1988). Growth in reading and how children spend their time outside of school. *Reading Research Quarterly, 23*, 285–303.

Armbruster, B.B. (1984). The problem of "inconsiderate texts." In G.G. Duffy, L.R. Roehler, & J. Mason (Eds.), *Comprehension instruction: Perspectives and suggestions* (pp. 202–217). New York: Longman.

August, D.L., Flavell, J.H., & Clift, R. (1984). Comparison of comprehension monitoring of skilled and less skilled readers. *Reading Research Quarterly, 20*, 39–53.

Baars, B.J. (1986). *The cognitive revolution in psychology.* New York: Guilford.

Baldwin, R.S., Readence, J.E., Schumm, J.S., Konopak, J.P., Konopak, B.C., & Klingner, J.K. (1992). Forty years of NRC publications: 1952–1991. *Journal of Reading Behavior, 24*(4), 505–532.

Ball, D.L. (1993). With an eye on the mathematical horizon: Dilemmas of teaching elementary school mathematics. *The Elementary School Journal, 93*(4), 373–397.

Benton, M.G. (1983). Secondary worlds. *Journal of Research and Development in Education, 16*(3), 68–75.

Bereiter, C. (1994). Constructivism, socioculturalism, and Popper's World 3. *Educational Researcher, 23*(7), 21–23.

Bereiter, C., & Scardamalia, M. (1989). Intentional learning as a goal of instruction. In L.B. Resnick (Ed.), *Knowing, learning, and instruction: Essays in honor of Robert Glaser* (pp. 361–392). Hillsdale, NJ: Erlbaum.

Bloome, D., & Green, J. (1984). Directions in the sociolinguistic study of reading. In P.D. Pearson, R. Barr, M.L. Kamil, & P.

Mosenthal (Eds.), *Handbook of reading research* (pp. 395–422). New York: Longman.

Bolter, J.D. (1991). *The writing space: The computer, hypertext, and the history of writing.* Hillsdale, NJ: Erlbaum.

Bond, G.L., & Dykstra, R. (1967). The cooperative research program in first-grade reading instruction. *Reading Research Quarterly, 2*, 5–142.

Bransford, J.D., & Franks, J.J. (1972). The abstraction of linguistic ideas. *Cognitive Psychology, 2*, 331–350.

Brewer, W.F. (1980). Literary theory, rhetoric, and stylistics: Implications for psychology. In R.J. Spiro, B.C. Bruce, & W.F. Brewer, (Eds.), *Theoretical issues in reading comprehension: Perspectives from cognitive psychology, linguistics, artificial intelligence, and education.* (pp. 221–243). Hillsdale, NJ: Erlbaum.

Britton, J.N. (1982). *Prospect and retrospect.* Montclair, NJ: Boynton/Cook.

Brown, A.L., & Campione, J.C. (1990). Communities of learning and thinking: Or, a context by any other name. *Human Development, 21*, 108–125.

Brown, A.L., Campione, J.C., & Day, J.D. (1981). Learning to learn: On training students to learn from text. *Educational Researcher, 10*(2), 14–21.

Brown, A.L., & Palincsar, A.S. (1989). Guided, cooperative learning and individual knowledge acquisition. In L.B. Resnick (Ed.), *Knowing, learning, and instruction: Essays in honor of Robert Glaser* (pp. 393–451). Hillsdale, NJ: Erlbaum.

Buswell, G.T. (1922). *Fundamental reading habits: A study of their development* (Supplementary Educational Monographs, No. 21). Chicago: University of Chicago Press.

Chall, J.S. (1967). *Learning to read: The great debate.* New York: McGraw-Hill.

Chall, J.S. (1995). *Stages of reading development* (2nd ed.). New York: Wadsworth.

Chambliss, M.J. (1995). Text cues and strategies successful readers use to construct the gist of lengthy written arguments. *Reading Research Quarterly, 30*, 778–807.

Chase, W.G., & Simon, H.A. (1973). Perception in chess. *Cognitive Psychology, 4*, 55–81.

Chi, M.T.H., Feltovich, P., & Glaser, R. (1981). Categorization and representation of physics problems by experts and novices. *Cognitive Science, 5*, 121–152.

Chi, M.T.H., Glaser, R., & Farr, M. (1988). *The nature of expertise*. Hillsdale, NJ: Erlbaum.

Chinn, C.A., & Brewer, W.F. (1993). The role of anomalous data in knowledge acquisition: A theoretical framework and implications for science instruction. *Review of Educational Research, 63*, 1–49.

Chipman, S.F. (1993). Gazing once more into the silicon chip: Who's revolutionary now? In S.P. Lajoie & S.J. Derry (Eds.), *Computers as cognitive tools* (pp. 341–367). Mahwah, NJ: Erlbaum.

Chomsky, N. (1957). *Syntactic structures*. New York: Mouton de Gruyter.

Chomsky, N. (1965). *Aspects of the theory of syntax*. Cambridge, MA: MIT Press.

Chomsky, N. (1975). *Reflections on language*. New York: Pantheon Books.

Chomsky, N. (1998). *On language: Chomsky's classic works: Language and responsibility and reflections on language in one volume*. New York: New Press.

Chomsky, N. (2002). *On nature and language*. New York: Cambridge University Press.

Christenson, A., & Barney, L. (1969). Oral reading errors among intermediate children. *Education, 89*, 307–311.

Clancey, W.J. (1983). The epistemology of a rule-based expert system: A framework for explanation. *Artificial Intelligence, 20*(3), 215–252.

Clay, M.M. (1967). The reading behavior of five-year-old children: A research report. *New Zealand Journal of Educational Studies, 2*, 11–31.

Clay, M.M. (1976). *Young fluent readers: What can they teach us?* London: Heinemann.

Cognition and Technology Group at Vanderbilt. (1990). Anchored instruction and its relationship to situated cognition. *Educational Researcher, 19*(6), 2–10.

Cognition and Technology Group at Vanderbilt. (1996). Looking at technology in context: A framework for understanding technology and education research. In D.C. Berliner & R.C. Calfee (Eds.), *Handbook of educational psychology* (pp. 807–840). New York: Macmillan.

Collins, A., Brown, J.S., & Newman, S.E. (1989). Cognitive apprenticeships: Teaching the crafts of reading, writing, and mathematics. In L.B. Resnick (Ed.), *Knowing, learning, and instruction: Essays in honor of Robert Glaser* (pp. 453–494). Hillsdale, NJ: Erlbaum.

Cox, C., & Many, J.E. (1992). Toward an understanding of the aesthetic response to literature. *Language Arts, 69*(1), 28–33.

Csikszentmihalyi, M. (1990). *Flow: The psychology of optimal experience*. New York: Cambridge University Press.

Cuban, L. (1993). *How teachers taught: Constancy and change in American classrooms, 1890–1990*. New York: Teachers College Press.

Deci, E.L., & Ryan, R.M. (1991). A motivational approach to self: Integration in personality. In R. Dienstbier (Ed.), *Nebraska symposium on motivation: Perspectives on motivation* (Vol. 38, pp. 237–288). Lincoln: University of Nebraska Press.

de Jong, T., & Ferguson-Hessler, M.G.M. (1996). Types and qualities of knowledge. *Educational Psychologist, 31*, 105–113.

Dewey, J. (1991). *How we think*. Buffalo, NY: Prometheus Books. (Original work published 1910)

Dewey, J. (1913). *Interest and effort in education*. Boston: Riverside.

Duffy, G.G., Roehler, L.R., Meloth, M.S., & Vavrus, L.G. (1986). Conceptualizing instructional explanation. *Teaching and Teacher Education, 2*(3), 197–214.

Durant, W., & Durant, A. (1967). *Rosseau and revolution: The story of civilization, Part X*. New York: Simon & Schuster.

Ericsson, K.A., & Smith, J. (1991). *Toward a general theory of expertise: Prospects and limits*. New York: Cambridge University Press.

Fish, S. (1980). *Is there a text in this class? The authority of interpretive communities*. Cambridge, MA: Harvard University Press.

Flesch, R. (1955). *Why Johnny can't read—And what you can do about it*. New York: Harper & Brothers.

Fodor, J.A. (1964). *The structure of language: Readings in the philosophy of language*. New York: Prentice-Hall.

Fodor, J.A. (2001). *The mind doesn't work that way: The scope and limits of computational psychology*. Cambridge, MA: MIT Press.

Fodor, J.A. (with Katz, J.J., Langendoen, D.T., & Miller, G.A., Eds.). (1980). *The language of thought*. Cambridge, MA: Harvard University Press.

Foorman, B.R., Francis, D.J., Fletcher, J.M., Mehta, P., & Schatschneider, C. (1998). The role of instruction in learning to read: Preventing reading failure in at-risk children.

Journal of Educational Psychology, 90(1), 37–55.

Frederiksen, N. (1984). Implications of cognitive theory for instruction in problem solving. *Review of Educational Research, 54*(3), 363–407.

Ganley, A.C., Lyons, T.T., & Sewall, G.T. (1993). *The U.S.A. since 1945: After Hiroshima* (3rd ed.). White Plains, NY: Longman.

Gardner, H. (1991). *The unschooled mind: How children think and how schools should teach.* New York: Basic Books.

Garner, R. (1987). *Metacognition and reading comprehension.* Norwood, NJ: Ablex.

Garner, R., & Gillingham, M.G. (1996). *Internet communication in six classrooms: Conversations across time, space, and culture.* Mahwah, NJ: Erlbaum.

Garner, R., & Hansis, R. (1994). Literacy practices outside of school: Adults' beliefs and their responses to "street texts." In R. Garner & P.A. Alexander (Eds.), *Beliefs about text and instruction with text* (pp. 57–73). Hillsdale, NJ: Erlbaum.

Gee, J.P. (1989). Literacy, discourse, and linguistics: Essays by James Paul Gee [Special issue]. *Journal of Education, 171*(1), 1–176.

Gibson, J.J. (1966). *The senses considered as perceptual systems.* Boston: Houghton-Mifflin.

Gillingham, M.G., Young, M.F., & Kulikowich, J.M. (1994). Do teachers consider nonlinear text to be text? In R. Garner & P.A. Alexander (Eds.), *Beliefs about text and instruction with text* (pp. 201–219). Hillsdale, NJ: Erlbaum.

Glaser, R. (1978). The contributions of B.F. Skinner to education and some counterinfluences. In P. Suppes (Ed.), *Impact of research on education: Some case studies* (pp. 199–265). Washington, DC: National Academy of Education.

Goetz, E.T., Alexander, P.A., & Ash, M.J. (1992). *Educational psychology: A classroom perspective.* Columbus, OH: Merrill.

Goldman, S.R. (1996). Reading, writing, and learning in hypermedia environments. In H. van Oostendorp & S. de Mul (Eds.), *Cognitive aspects of electronic text processing* (pp. 7–42). Norwood, NJ: Ablex.

Goodman, K.S. (1965). A linguistic study of cues and miscues in reading. *Elementary English, 42,* 639–643.

Goodman, K.S. (1996). *On reading.* Portsmouth, NH: Heinemann.

Goodman, K.S., & Goodman, Y.M. (1980). Learning to read is natural. In L.B. Resnick & P.A. Weaver (Eds.), *Theory and practice of early reading* (Vol. 1, pp. 137–154). Hillsdale, NJ: Erlbaum.

Gray, W.S., Artley, A.S., & Arbuthnot, M.H. (1951). *The new fun with Dick and Jane.* Chicago: Scott, Foresman.

Greene, S., & Ackerman, J.M. (1995). Expanding the constructivist metaphor: A rhetorical perspective on literacy research and practice. *Review of Educational Research, 65*(4), 383–420.

Greeno, J.G., & the Middle School Mathematics Through Applications Project Group. (1998). The situativity of knowing, learning, and research. *American Psychologist, 53*(1), 5–26.

Greeno, J.G., & Moore, J.L. (1993). Situativity and symbols: Response to Vera and Simon. *Cognitive Science, 17,* 49–59.

Guthrie, J.T., McGough, K., Bennett, L., & Rice, M.E. (1996). Concept-oriented reading instruction: An integrated curriculum to develop motivations and strategies for reading. In L. Baker, P. Afflerbach, & D. Reinking (Eds.), *Developing engaged readers in school and home communities* (pp. 165–190). Mahwah, NJ: Erlbaum.

Guthrie, J.T., Van Meter, P., McCann, A., Wigfield, A., Bennett, L., Poundstone, C., et al. (1996). Growth of literacy engagement: Changes in motivations and strategies during concept-oriented reading instruction. *Reading Research Quarterly, 31,* 306–332.

Guthrie, J.T., & Wigfield, A. (2000). Engagement and motivation in reading. In M.L. Kamil, P.B. Mosenthal, P.D. Pearson, & R. Barr (Eds.), *Handbook of reading research* (Vol. 3, pp. 403–422). Mahwah, NJ: Erlbaum.

Guzzetti, B., & Hynd, C. (1998). *Perspectives on conceptual change: Multiple ways to understand knowing and learning in a complex world.* Mahwah, NJ: Erlbaum.

Halliday, M.A.K. (1969). Relevant models of language. *Educational Review, 22*(1), 26–37.

Halliday, M.A.K., & Hasan, R. (1976). *Cohesion in English.* London: Longman.

Hansen, J. (1981). The effects of inference training and practice on young children's reading comprehension. *Reading Research Quarterly, 16,* 391–417.

Harris, K.R. (1996, April). *The state of strategy research: Is this old territory or are there new frontiers?* Panel discussion presented at the annual meeting of the American Educational Research Association, New York.

Harste, J.C., Burke, C., & Woodward, V.A. (1984). *Language stories and literacy lessons*. Portsmouth, NH: Heinemann.

Heath, S.B. (1982). What no bedtime story means: Narrative skills at home and school. *Language in Society, 11*(1), 49–76.

Heath, S.B. (1983). *Ways with words: Language, life, and work in communities and classrooms*. New York: Cambridge University Press.

Hidi, S. (1990). Interest and its contribution as a mental resource for learning. *Review of Educational Research, 60*(4), 549–571.

Hiebert, E.H., & Taylor, B.M. (2000). Beginning reading instruction: Research on early interventions. In M.L. Kamil, P.B. Mosenthal, P.D. Pearson, & R. Barr (Eds.), *Handbook of reading research* (Vol. 3, pp. 455–482). Mahwah, NJ: Erlbaum.

Huey, E.B. (1908). *The psychology and pedagogy of reading*. New York: Macmillan.

Hume, D. (1963). *An enquiry concerning human understanding and selections from a treatise of human nature*. La Salle, IL: Open Court. (Original work published 1777)

James, W. (1890). *Principles of psychology* (Vols. 1 & 2). New York: Holt.

Jenkinson, M.D. (1969). Sources of knowledge for theories of reading. *Journal of Reading Behavior, 1*, 11–29.

Jetton, T.L., & Alexander, P.A. (1998, April). *Teachers' views of discussion: Issues of control, time, and ability*. Paper presented at the annual meeting of the American Educational Research Association, San Diego.

Kant, I. (1963). *Critique of pure reason* (N. Kemp Smith, Trans.) London: Macmillan (Original work published 1787)

Kintsch, W., & van Dijk, T.A. (1978). Toward a model of text comprehension and production. *Psychological Review, 85*, 363–394.

Labov, W. (1966). *The social stratification of English in New York City*. Washington, DC: Center for Applied Linguistics.

Labov, W. (1971). Systematically misleading data from test questions. *Urban Review, 9*(3), 146–170.

Labov, W. (1972). *Sociolinguistic patterns*. Philadelphia: University of Pennsylvania Press.

Lave, J. (1988). *Cognition and practice: Mind, mathematics, and culture*. Cambridge, UK: Cambridge University Press.

Levin, H. (Ed.). (1965). *Planning for a reading research program*. Ithaca, NY: Cornell University.

Lipson, M.Y. (1983). The influence of religious affiliation on children's memory for text information. *Reading Research Quarterly, 18*, 448–457.

Lundeberg, M. (1987). Metacognitive aspects of reading comprehension: Studying understanding in legal case analysis. *Reading Research Quarterly, 22*, 407–432.

Mandl, H., Stein, N.L., & Trabasso, T. (1984). *Learning and comprehension of text*. Hillsdale, NJ: Erlbaum.

Matthews, M.R. (1994). *Science teaching: The role of history and philosophy of science*. New York: Routledge.

McLaren, P. (1998). *Life in schools: An introduction to critical pedagogy in the foundations of education* (3rd ed.). New York: Longman.

Meyer, B.J.F. (1975). *The organization of prose and its effects on memory*. Amsterdam: North-Holland.

Monaghan, E.J., & Saul, E.W. (1987). The reader, the scribe, the thinker: A critical look at the history of American reading and writing instruction. In T.S. Popkewitz (Ed.), *The information of school subjects: The struggle for creating an American institution* (pp. 85–122). Philadelphia: Falmer.

Murphy, P.K., & Woods, B.S. (1996). Situating knowledge in learning and instruction. *Educational Psychologist, 31*(2), 141–145.

National Institute for Literacy. (2002). *The Partnership for Reading: Adolescent literacy (Research informing practice: A series of workshops)*. Washington, DC: Author. Retrieved October 10, 2003, from http://novel.nifl.gov/partnershipforreading/adolescent/summary.html

National Institute of Child Health and Human Development. (2000). *Report of the National Reading Panel. Teaching children to read: An evidence-based assessment of the scientific research literature on reading and its implications for reading instruction* (NIH Publication No. 00-4769). Washington, DC: U.S. Government Printing Office. Retrieved October 10, 2003, from http://www.nichd.nih.gov/publications/pubskey.cfm?from=nrp

Neuman, S.B. (1988). The displacement effect: Assessing the relation between television viewing and reading performance. *Reading Research Quarterly, 23*, 414–440.

Nolen, S.B., Johnson-Crowley, N., & Wineburg, S.S. (1994). Who is this "I" person, anyway? The presence of a visible author in statistical text. In R. Garner & P.A. Alexander (Eds.), *Beliefs about text and instruction with text* (pp. 41–55). Hillsdale, NJ: Erlbaum.

Oldfather, P., & Wigfield, A. (1996). Children's motivations to read. In L. Baker, P. Afflerbach, & D. Reinking (Eds.), *Developing engaged readers in school and home communities* (pp. 89–113). Mahwah, NJ: Erlbaum.

Pajares, M. F. (1992). Teachers' beliefs and educational research: Cleaning up a messy construct. *Review of Educational Research*, 62(3), 307–332.

Palincsar, A.S., & Brown, A.L. (1984). Reciprocal teaching of comprehension-fostering and monitoring activities. *Cognition and Instruction*, 2, 117–175.

* Paris, S.G., Lipson, M.Y., & Wixson, K.K. (1983). Becoming a strategic reader. *Contemporary Educational Psychology*, 8, 293–316.

Paris, S.G., & Myers, M. II (1981). Comprehension monitoring, memory, and study strategies of good and poor readers. *Journal of Reading Behavior*, 13(1), 5–22.

Paris, S.G., & Urdan, T. (2000). Policies and practices of high-stakes testing that influence teachers and schools. *Issues in Education*, 6(1/2), 83–107.

Paris, S.G., Wasik, B.A., & Turner, J.C. (1991). The development of strategic readers. In R. Barr, M.L. Kamil, P. Mosenthal, & P.D. Pearson (Eds.), *Handbook of reading research* (Vol. 2, pp. 609–640). White Plains, NY: Longman.

Paris, S.G., & Winograd, P. (1990). How metacognition can promote academic learning and instruction. In B.F. Jones & L. Idol (Eds.), *Dimensions of thinking and cognitive instruction* (pp. 15–51). Hillsdale, NJ: Erlbaum.

Pearson, P.D. (1984). Direct explicit teaching of reading comprehension. In G.G. Duffy, L.R. Roehler, & J. Mason (Eds.), *Comprehension instruction: Perspectives and suggestions* (pp. 222–233). New York: Longman.

* Pearson, P.D., & Stephens, D. (1994). Learning about literacy: A 30-year journey. In R.B. Ruddell, M.R. Ruddell, & H. Singer (Eds.), *Theoretical models and processes of reading* (4th ed., pp. 22–42). Newark, DE: International Reading Association.

Perkins, D.N., & Simmons, R. (1988). Patterns of misunderstanding: An integrative model for science, math, and programming. *Review of Educational Research*, 58(3), 303–326.

Perret-Claremont, A., Perret, J., & Bell, N. (1980). The social construction of meaning and cognitive activity in elementary school children. In L.B. Resnick, J.M. Levine, & S.D. Teasley (Eds.), *Perspectives on socially shared cognition* (pp. 41–62). Washington, DC: American Psychological Association.

Pichert, J.W., & Anderson, R.C. (1977). Taking different perspectives on a story. *Journal of Educational Psychology*, 69, 309–315.

Pigott, T.D., & Barr, R. (2000). Designing programmatic interventions. In M.L. Kamil, P.B. Mosenthal, P.D. Pearson, & R. Barr (Eds.), *Handbook of reading research* (Vol. 3, pp. 99–108). Mahwah, NJ: Erlbaum.

Pintrich, P.R., & Schunk, D.H. (2001). *Motivation in education: Theory, research, and applications* (2nd ed.). Englewood Cliffs, NJ: Prentice Hall.

Postman, N. (1993). *Technopoly: The surrender of culture to technology*. New York: Vintage Books.

Prawat, R.S. (1989). Promoting access to knowledge, strategy, and disposition in students: A research synthesis. *Review of Educational Research*, 59(1), 1–41.

Pressley, M. (2002). Comprehension strategies instruction: A turn-of-the-century report. In C.C. Block & M. Pressley (Eds.), *Comprehension instruction: Research-based best practices* (pp. 11–27). New York: Guilford.

Pressley, M., Goodchild, F., Fleet, J., Zajchowski, R., & Evans, E.D. (1989). The challenges of classroom strategy instruction. *The Elementary School Journal*, 89(3), 301–342.

Pressley, M., Lysynchuk, L.M., D'Ailly, H., Smith, M., & Cake, H. (1989). A methodological analysis of experimental studies of comprehension strategy instruction. *Reading Research Quarterly*, 24, 458–470.

Pugh K.R., Shaywitz B.A., Shaywitz, S.E, Shankweiler, D.P., Katz, L., Fletcher, J.M., et al. (1997). Predicting reading performance from neuroimaging profiles: The cerebral basis of phonological effects in printed word identification. *Journal of Experimental Psychology: Human Perception and Performance*, 23, 299–318.

Putnam, R.T., Heaton, R.M., Prawat, R.S., & Remillard, J. (1992). Teaching mathematics for understanding: Discussing case studies of four fifth-grade teachers. *The Elementary School Journal, 93*(2), 213–228.

RAND Reading Study Group. (2002). *Reading for understanding: Toward an R&D program in reading comprehension.* Santa Monica, CA: RAND.

Raphael, T.E., & Wonnacott, C.A. (1985). Heightening fourth-grade students' sensitivity to sources of information for answering comprehension questions. *Reading Research Quarterly, 20*, 282–296.

Reed, J.H., & Schallert, D.L. (1993). The nature of involvement in academic discourse tasks. *Journal of Educational Psychology, 85*(2), 253–266.

Reed, J.H., Schallert, D.L., & Goetz, E.T. (1993, April). *Interest happens but involvement takes effort: Distinguishing between two constructs in academic discourse tasks.* Paper presented at the annual meeting of the American Educational Research Association, Atlanta, GA.

Reinking, D., McKenna, M.C., Labbo, L.D., & Kieffer, R.D. (1998). *Handbook of literacy and technology: Transformations in a post-typographic world.* Mahwah, NJ: Erlbaum.

Resnick, L.B., Levine, J.M., & Teasley, S.D. (1980). *Perspectives on socially shared cognition.* Washington, DC: American Psychological Association.

Reynolds, R.E., Sinatra, G.M., & Jetton, T.L. (1996). Views of knowledge acquisition and representation: A continuum from experience centered to mind centered. *Educational Psychologist, 31*, 93–104.

Rogoff, B. (1990). *Apprenticeship in thinking: Cognitive development in social context.* New York: Oxford University Press.

Rogoff, B., & Gauvain, M. (1986). A method for the analysis of patterns illustrated with data on mother-child instructional interaction. In J. Valsiner (Ed.), *The individual subject and scientific psychology: Perspectives on individual differences* (pp. 261–290). New York: Plenum.

Rosenblatt, L.M. (1994). *The reader, the text, the poem: The transactional theory of the literary work.* Carbondale: Southern Illinois University Press. (Original work published 1978)

Rosenblatt, L.M. (1995). *Literature as exploration.* New York: Modern Language Association. (Original work published 1938)

Roth, K.J. (1985). Developing meaningful conceptual understanding in science. In B.F.

Jones & L. Idol (Eds.), *Dimensions of thinking and cognitive instruction* (pp. 139–175). Hillsdale, NJ: Erlbaum.

Ruddell, R.B. (2002). *Teaching children to read and write: Becoming an effective literacy teacher* (3rd ed.). Boston: Allyn & Bacon.

Rumelhart, D.E. (1980). Schemata: The building blocks of cognition. In R.J. Spiro, B.C. Bruce, & W.F. Brewer. (Eds.), *Theoretical issues in reading comprehension: Perspectives from cognitive psychology, linguistics, artificial intelligence, and education* (pp. 33–58). Hillsdale, NJ: Erlbaum.

Ryle, G. (1949). *The concept of mind.* London: Hutchinson.

Sadoski, M., Paivio, A., & Goetz, E.T. (1991). Commentary: A critique of schema theory in reading and a dual coding alternative. *Reading Research Quarterly, 26*, 463–484.

Salomon, G. (1993). *Distributed cognitions: Psychological and educational considerations.* Cambridge, UK: Cambridge University Press.

Salomon, G., Perkins, D.N., & Globerson, T. (1991). Partners in cognition: Extending human intelligence with intelligent technologies. *Educational Researcher, 20*(3), 2–9.

Samuels, S.J., & Kamil, M.L. (1984). Models of the reading process. In P.D. Pearson, R. Barr, M.L. Kamil, & P. Mosenthal (Eds.), *Handbook of reading research* (pp. 185–224). New York: Longman.

Scardamalia, M., Bereiter, C., McLean, R.S., Swallow, J., & Woodruff, E. (1989). Computer-supported intentional learning environments. *Journal of Educational Computing Research, 5*(1), 51–68.

Schallert, D.L., Meyer, D.K., & Fowler, L.A. (1995). The nature of engagement when reading in and out of one's discipline. In K.A. Hinchman, D.J. Leu, & C.K. Kinzer (Eds.), *Perspectives on literacy research and practice* (44th yearbook of the National Reading Conference, pp. 119–125). Chicago: National Reading Conference.

Schank, R.C., & Abelson, R.P. (1977). *Scripts, plans, goals, and understanding: An inquiry into human knowledge structures.* Hillsdale, NJ: Erlbaum.

Schommer, M. (1990). Effects of beliefs about the nature of knowledge on comprehension. *Journal of Educational Psychology, 82*(3), 498–504.

Schommer, M. (1993). Epistemological development and academic performance among secondary students. *Journal of Educational Psychology*, *85*(3), 406–411.

Schraw, G., Bruning, R., & Svoboda, C. (1995). Sources of situational interest. *Journal of Reading Behavior*, *27*(1), 1–17.

Sfard, A. (1998). On two metaphors for learning and the dangers of choosing just one. *Educational Researcher*, *27*(2), 4–13.

Shaywitz, B.A., Fletcher, J.M., Holahan, J.M., & Shaywitz, S.E. (1992). Discrepancy compared to low achievement definitions of reading disability: Results from the Connecticut Longitudinal Study. *Journal of Learning Disabilities*, *25*(10), 639–648.

Shaywitz, B.A., Pugh, K.R., Jenner, A.R., Fulbright, R.K., Fletcher, J.M., Gore, J.C., et al. (2000). The neurobiology of reading and reading disability (dyslexia). In M.L. Kamil, P.B. Mosenthal, P.D. Pearson, & R. Barr (Eds.), *Handbook of reading research* (Vol. 3, pp. 229–249). Mahwah, NJ: Erlbaum.

Shuy, R.W. (1968). Detroit speech: Careless, awkward, and inconsistent, or systematic, graceful, and regular? *Elementary English*, *45*(5), 565–569.

Shuy, R.W. (1969). Some considerations for developing beginning reading materials for ghetto children. *Journal of Reading Behavior*, *1*(2), 33–43.

Skinner, B.F. (1974). *About behaviorism.* New York: Vintage Books.

Smith, C.E., & Keogh, B.K. (1962). The group Bender-Gestalt as a reading readiness screening instrument. *Perceptual and Motor Skills*, *15*, 639–645.

Smith, F. (1973). *Psycholinguistics and reading.* New York: Holt, Rinehart & Winston.

Smith, F. (1978). *Understanding reading: A psycholinguistic analysis of reading and learning to read.* (2nd ed.). New York: Holt, Rinehart & Winston.

Smith, F. (1985). A metaphor for literacy: Creating worlds or shunting information? In D.R. Olson, N. Torrance, & A. Hildyard (Eds.), *Literacy, language, and learning: The nature and consequences of reading and writing* (pp. 1–39). Hillsdale, NJ: Erlbaum.

Snyder, R.T., & Freud, S.L. (1967). Reading readiness and its relation to maturational unreadiness as measured by the spiral aftereffect and other visual-perceptual techniques. *Perceptual and Motor Skills*, *25*, 841–854.

Spiro, R.J., Feltovich, P.J., Jacobson, M.J., & Coulson, R.L. (1992). Cognitive flexibility, constructivism, and hypertext: Random access instruction for advanced knowledge acquisition in ill-structured domains. In T.M. Duffy & D.H. Jonassen (Eds.), *Constructivism and the technology of instruction: A conversation* (pp. 57–75). Cambridge, UK: Cambridge University Press.

Spiro, R.J., & Jehng, J.C. (1990). Cognitive flexibility and hypertext: Theory and technology for the nonlinear and multidimensional traversal of complex subject matter. In D. Nix & R.J. Spiro (Eds.), *Cognition, education, and multimedia: Exploring ideas in high technology* (pp. 163–205). Hillsdale, NJ: Erlbaum.

Spivey, N.N., & King, J.R. (1989). Readers as writers composing from sources. *Reading Research Quarterly*, *24*, 7–26.

Stahl, S.A., Hynd, C.R, Glynn, S.M., & Carr, M. (1996). Beyond reading to learn: Developing content and disciplinary knowledge through texts. In L. Baker, P. Afflerbach, & D. Reinking (Eds.), *Developing engaged readers in school and home communities* (pp. 139–163). Mahwah, NJ: Erlbaum.

Stahl, S.A., & Miller, P.D. (1989). Whole language and language experience approaches for beginning reading: A quantitative research synthesis. *Review of Educational Research*, *59*, 87–116.

Stanovich, K.E. (1986). Matthew effects in reading: Some consequences of individual differences in the acquisition of literacy. *Reading Research Quarterly*, *21*, 360–407.

Strike, K.A. (1974). On the expressive potential of behaviorist language. *American Educational Research Journal*, *11*(2), 103–120.

Taylor, B.M., & Beach, R.W. (1984). The effects of text structure instruction on middle-grade students' comprehension and production of expository text. *Reading Research Quarterly*, *19*, 134–146.

Thorndike, E.L. (1917). Reading as reasoning: A study of mistakes in paragraph reading. *Journal of Educational Psychology*, *8*(6), 323–332.

Tierney, R.J., Readence, J.E., & Dishner, E.K. (1990). *Reading strategies and practices* (3rd ed.). Boston: Allyn & Bacon.

Tierney, R.J., Soter, A., O'Flahavan, J.F., & McGinley, W. (1989). The effects of reading and writing upon thinking critically. *Reading Research Quarterly*, *24*, 134–173.

Torgesen, J.K. (1998). Instructional interventions for children with reading disabilities. In B.K. Shapiro, P.J. Accardo, & A.J. Capute

(Eds.), *Specific reading disability: A view of the spectrum* (pp. 197–200). Parkton, MD: York.

Torgesen, J.K. (1999). Reading disabilities. In R. Gallimore, L.P. Bernheimer, D.L. MacMillan, D.L. Speece, & S. Vaughn (Eds.), *Developmental perspectives on children with high incidence disabilities: Papers in honor of Barbara K. Keogh* (pp. 157–182). Mahwah, NJ: Erlbaum.

Turner, J.C. (1995). The influence of classroom contexts on young children's motivation for literacy. *Reading Research Quarterly, 30,* 410–441.

Vacca, R.T., & Vacca, J.L. (1983). Two less than fortunate consequences of reading research in the 1970's (Guest editorial). *Reading Research Quarterly, 18,* 382–383.

Valencia, S.W., & Wixson, K.K. (2001). Literacy policy and policy research that make a difference. In J.V. Hoffman, D.L. Schallert, C.M. Fairbanks, J. Worthy, & B. Maloch (Eds.), *Fiftieth yearbook of the National Reading Conference* (pp. 21–43). Chicago: National Reading Conference.

VanSledright, B. (2002). *In search of America's past: Learning to read history in elementary school.* New York: Teachers College Press.

VanSledright, B.A. (1996). Closing the gap between school and disciplinary history? Historian as high school history teacher. In J. Brophy (Ed.), *Advances in research on teaching* (Vol. 6, pp. 257–289) Greenwich, CT: JAI Press.

Venezsky, R.L. (1984). The history of reading research. In P.D. Pearson, R. Barr, M.L. Kamil, & P. Mosenthal (Eds.), *Handbook of reading research* (pp. 3–38). New York: Longman.

von Glaserfeld, E. (1991). *Radical constructivism in mathematics education.* Dordrecht, Netherlands: Kluwer.

Vosniadou, S. (1994). Capturing and modeling the process of conceptual change. *Learning and Instruction, 4,* 45–69.

Vygotsky, L.S. (1978). *Mind in society: The development of higher psychological processes* (M. Cole, V. John-Steiner, S. Scribner, & E. Souberman, Eds. & Trans.). Cambridge, MA: Harvard University Press. (Original work published 1934)

Vygotsky, L.S. (1986). *Thought and language* (A. Kozalin, Trans.). Cambridge, MA: MIT Press. (Original work published 1934)

Wade, S.E., & Moje, E. (2000). The role of text in classroom learning. In M.L. Kamil, P.B. Mosenthal, P.D. Pearson, & R. Barr (Eds.), *Handbook of reading research* (Vol. 3, pp. 609–627). Mahwah, NJ: Erlbaum.

Wade, S.E., Thompson, A., & Watkins, W. (1994). The role of belief systems in authors' and readers' constructions of texts. In R. Garner & P.A. Alexander (Eds.), *Beliefs about text and instruction with text* (pp. 265–193). Hillsdale, NJ: Erlbaum.

Weaver, C.A., & Kintsch, W. (1991). Expository text. In R. Barr, M.L. Kamil, P. Mosenthal, & P.D. Pearson (Eds.), *Handbook of reading research* (Vol. 2, pp. 230–245). White Plains, NY: Longman.

Weinstein, C.E., Goetz, E.T., & Alexander, P.A. (Eds.). (1988). *Learning and study strategies: Issues in assessment, instruction, and evaluation.* San Diego, CA: Academic Press.

Wertheimer, M. (1959). *Productive thinking.* New York: Harper & Row. (Original work published 1945)

Whitehead, A.N. (1957). *The aims of education and other essays.* New York: Macmillan. (Original work published 1929)

Wineburg, S.S. (1996). The psychology of learning and teaching history. In D.C. Berliner & R.C. Calfee (Eds.), *The handbook of educational psychology* (pp. 423–437). New York: Simon Schuster Macmillan.

Woods, B.S., & Murphy, P.K. (2002). Thickening the discussion: Inspecting constructivist theories of knowledge through a Jamesian lens. *Educational Theory, 52*(1), 43–59.

Wulf, F. (1938). Tendencies in figural variation. In W.D. Ellis (Ed. & Trans.), *A source book of Gestalt psychology* (condensed) (pp. 136–148). New York: Routledge & Kegan Paul. (Original work published 1922)

3

Literacy Policy and Policy
Research That Make
a Difference

Sheila W. Valencia and Karen K. Wixson

We wrote this review while our country was in the throes of one of the most controversial presidential elections in our history. Although the outcome was unknown on December 2, 2000, what was certain, even on that date, was that education and education policy were at the top of both candidates' agendas. Whereas policy research dating back to the 1970s demonstrated that "policy can't mandate what matters" (McLaughlin, 1990), such findings have not shaken policymakers' determination to instigate more and more educational policies. In fact, today 49 of 50 states have adopted content standards in reading and writing, 48 of 50 have enacted policies on statewide testing (Education Week, 2000), and the number of phonics bills introduced annually increased 900% between 1994 and 1997 (Patterson, 2000). But what do we really know about the effect of literacy policies and what do we know about the kind of policy research that has been conducted?

That was our assignment for this year's review of research—policy. Although at first glance, this one-word topic seems fairly proscribed, anyone who does policy-related research or reads in it or simply lives in our current educational environment knows this is no small domain. So, in preparation for this review, our first job was to understand and narrow our focus—what is included in policy research, what piece of it should we address, what sources should we use. We begin with a quick sense of the terrain to situate this review in the larger context.

Review Parameters: Dimensions and Sources

Dimensions

Policies vary along several dimensions. First, they vary in terms of *locus of authority*—where a policy originates or who has the real authority over it. So, policies related to national testing such as National Assessment of Educational Progress (NAEP) or special programs such as Title I and special education have their origin and are monitored at the federal level. However, for the most part, states have been the center of educational policymaking over the past two decades, since we have had a focus on standards (Linn, 2000; McGill-Franzen, 2000). Add to these policies on standards and assessment, state policies on teacher quality, class size, bilingual education, restructuring, and resource allocation and the power of states is clear. And here, at the state level, is where the pressure point—high stakes—is usually found. There are also policies at the district and classroom levels. At these levels, state policies often get translated into specific policies that influence daily classroom life—mandated curriculum, retention, professional development, special services, and policies on grading and grouping, just to name a few.

Second, policies also differ in *scope*—how far-reaching or ambitious they are. Some policies are fairly narrow, targeting a particular practice, program, or resource allocation, such as implementing new assessments or establishing cut scores for special programs. Others are broader and much more complex, with a systemic focus (Smith & O'Day, 1991), such as the reform package in Kentucky in which school organization, new content standards and assessments, professional development, governance, and finance are all included. The point of systemic reform is to create a coherent set of efforts rather than a series of discrete unrelated policies and actions.

Finally, policies differ in terms of their *focus*—what they target. For example, policies may focus on graduation requirements, organizational issues, specific groups of students, or curriculum. Amazingly, studies show that although the majority of reform efforts are proposed to improve student learning and teaching, most policies do not focus on the classroom. In fact, a study of more than 1,500 schools districts found that fewer than 50% had policies focused on both curricular content and teaching (Shields & Knapp, 1997).

Obviously the policy landscape is vast and varied, requiring us to set some parameters for this review. We decided to focus on what McLaughlin (1992) describes as a generation of research on reform that began in the 1980s; it is focused on ambitious standards and has as its goal improved teaching practice. These policies vary in scope (some narrow, some complex) but for the most part they reside at the state level. As a result, the slice we cut for this review is standards-oriented state policies. We will not review specific policies related to Title I or special education—for those we refer you to McGill-Franzen's excellent chapter in the *Handbook of Reading Research* (McGill-Franzen, 2000). We focus here on literacy policies that target the broader population. And, we will not deal with the question of whether research *should* influence policy or the process of policymaking. These topics we leave to our braver colleagues and to different venues.

Sources

With regard to our sources, we did not use stories or newspaper clippings for this review. We relied on published pieces including books, articles, conceptual pieces, and technical reports from research projects and centers. As a result, we do not deal with some of the "hottest" issues of the hour—the so-called Texas "miracle" (Haney, 2000; Hoffman, Assaf, & Paris, 2000), the impact of Proposition 227 (bilingual education in California), or the new literacy policies in California. There is simply not yet enough high-quality research available on these policies. And, as these new hot topics suggest, the policy ground has shifted and *is* shifting as we speak. Our review therefore is not only retrospective, as all reviews are, but it reflects policies that may now look quite different even though many of the studies we cite are from the last several years. This is simply the nature of a review and the nature of educational policy in this age of reform.

We begin with a brief review of the findings and the nature of current literacy policy research—a kind of survey of what we know and the kind of research we have. From there, we offer a model for thinking about policy research that is informed by the research. Then, we present two case studies compiled from the research to support this new and, we believe, useful model for us as literacy researchers and educators. These cases and this model lead to policies that can make a difference and to insights into how to improve literacy policy research.

Overview of Research

This review is informed by an analysis of approximately 50 policies studies related to literacy standards and assessment that we conducted for the *Handbook of Reading Research* (see Valencia & Wixson, 2000, for a complete list of studies reviewed). We begin here because standards and assessment are a major thrust of many state policies from this generation of reform. What did we find?

First, at a kind of metalevel, we found that it mattered whether the researchers were grounded in policy, measurement, or literacy. They targeted different audiences for their work and typically did not publish in the same places (see Table 1). Even their bibliographic citations had little overlap. In addition, they had different research questions, conceptual frameworks, methodologies, and perspectives on literacy. In our view, these are important differences because they ultimately shape what we learn from the research, limit the possibility of learning across perspectives, and influence policy.

Policy researchers, for example, typically focus on broad reforms involving standards, reorganization, governance, and the like; literacy is simply one of the subject areas of the reforms they study. In fact, we found it difficult to identify policy studies that had enough information on literacy issues to include in our review. When they did, we often had to search to find the portions that were related to reading and writing. Policy researchers' questions typically focused on

TABLE 1
Sources of Literacy Policy Research

Policy
    Educational Policy
    Educational Evaluation and Policy Analysis
    National Center for Research on Evaluation, Standards, and Student Testing (CRESST)
    Consortium on Policy Research in Education (CPRE)
    American Educational Research Journal

Assessment
    Applied Measurement in Education
    Educational Assessment
    Educational Measurement: Issues and Practice
    National Center for Research on Evaluation, Standards, and Student Testing (CRESST)
    RAND

Literacy
    National Reading Conference Yearbook
    Reading Research Quarterly
    The Elementary School Journal
    National Reading Research Center (NRRC)
    Educational Assessment
    Language Arts

the system, and their data were gathered through surveys and interviews. When they focused on teachers, it was typically through self-reports of their practices rather than observations of classroom practice. That said, however, there is a new group of policy researchers who are more focused on subject-specific issues and classroom instruction than we have typically seen in the past. We return to these researchers and their work later.

Measurement researchers, as we might expect, were most interested in the assessment components of reform and were particularly concerned with validity issues and with the psychometric qualities of new assessments that are needed for accountability and policy. For the most part, they relied on statistical analysis and, to some extent, self-reports, interviews, and artifacts to address their questions.

Literacy researchers generally asked questions about instruction and learning in relation to literacy research and theory. For example, do new standards and assessments result in better reading and writing instruction? Are reforms consistent with sound research and theory on literacy learning? Just as literacy was the vehicle for many policy studies, rather than a targeted area of study, policy was the vehicle for many literacy studies. Literacy researchers typically looked closely at actual classroom teaching practices and evidence of student learning, but for the most part they did not explore the policy context in any systematic or in-depth way. Policy provided the backdrop to their literacy research.

Looking beneath orientation and focus at the specific content of these studies, we found that, in general, policies that are focused on literacy standards and assessment *do* have an influence on teachers' beliefs and practices. However, the influence is not always in the expected or the desired direction. The effects of policies are mediated by a large number of factors such as teachers' knowledge, beliefs, and existing practices; the economic, social, philosophical, and political conditions of the school or district; the stakes attached to the policy; the specificity of the policy; and the quality of the support provided to teachers and administrators. It also appears that policy by itself is not sufficient to promote desired change; simply implementing new assessments or creating new standards does not ensure improved teaching or learning. What is less clear, however, is just what it would take to improve teaching and learning. Although several studies suggest that discipline-specific professional development is important for policy to have the desired effect, we do not know much about successful professional development processes or the quality of these processes.

In sum, these studies suggest the need for more coordinated research on policy issues. There appears to be a trade-off between understanding the broader context of policy and specific understanding of how factors mediate its enactment in classrooms. These studies also clearly suggest the need to address specific subject-matter issues. There seems to be an almost tacit assumption among many policy and measurement researchers that whatever holds true for one subject matter will likely be the case for others.

As we broadened our search for this review beyond policy studies concerned with standards and assessment, we found converging evidence of the need for research to address two areas: (1) specific subject matter in policy research and (2) the tension between policy research viewed from the national, state, or district levels (what we label the "global view") and policy viewed from classrooms (what we label the "local view").

Most of us are well aware of the important role of subject matter in teaching and learning from the work of Schwab (1964) and Shulman (1987). However, several studies support the need to take on subject matter more directly in policy research. One is a case study by Spillane (2000) in which he tracked a teacher's response to both literacy and mathematics reform. Although this teacher was eager to improve her practice in both subjects and was in a supportive environment for learning, there were substantial differences in what and how she taught across subjects. Spillane posits that this teacher brought different resources—different understandings, dispositions, and commitments—to the reform in math and reading, and thus she experienced very different opportunities to learn about her own practice. Two other studies, one by Willingham and Cole (as cited in Linn, 2000) and the other by Linn (2000), demonstrated significant differences across achievement test scores and subtests scores in different subject areas, adding a psychometric perspective to the subject matter argument. In other words, subject area matters in policy work.

As to the tension between global-level and local-level views of policy, we can go back as early as the 1980s (i.e., Elmore & McLaughlin, 1988; Sabatier & Mazmanian, 1980) to note that

> Change is ultimately the problem of the smallest unit. At each point in the policy process, a policy is transformed as individuals interpret and respond to it. What actually is delivered or provided under the aegis of a policy depends finally on the individual at the end of the line. (McLaughlin, 1987, p. 174)

Although there seems to be widespread acknowledgment that teachers play a critical role in enacting policy, much of the policy research has continued to focus on the inputs (i.e., the various policies) and the expected outcomes, or outputs, leaving the working space between them unexplored. When that space is explored, it is often through analysis of surface features such as teacher qualifications, school structure, or time spent on particular activities. We argue that researchers must do a better job finding out what is going on inside that space, inside the "black box," where the effects of policy are studied in terms of the *quality* of teaching and learning (see Figure 1).

We cannot continue to expect that inputs alone will stimulate change or continue to generate more policies, whatever they may be (e.g., class size, restructuring, teacher qualification, curriculum) and expect they will make a difference. The research reviewed above suggests policies cannot stand alone nor are they enacted in a vacuum. Teachers and administrators are not simply conduits for policy.

FIGURE 1

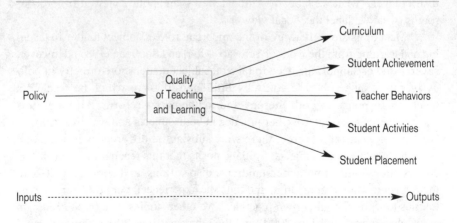

Similarly, we cannot continue to focus only on outputs as the indicators of change, such as student achievement, numbers of students graduating, teacher knowledge, curriculum alignment, or even teacher behaviors such as topics covered, time spent teaching, or self-reported teaching strategies. They are important to be sure, but to focus solely on these would be missing how real improvement in learning is created. We offer three arguments and sample studies to support why it is problematic to judge policy efficacy by focusing only on outputs.

Focus on High-Stakes Test Scores

We have a great deal of evidence dating back 10 to 15 years that points to the negative consequences of high-stakes testing: narrowing of the curriculum, overemphasis on basic skills, excessive time spent on test preparation, exclusion of low-achieving or special education students from testing (Allington & McGill-Franzen, 1992; Nolen, Haladyna, & Hass, 1992; Resnick & Resnick, 1992; Shepard, 1991). More recently, Linn (2000) identified new evidence that test scores may not reflect true student learning. Looking at state test scores over 12 years, he found that results can give an inflated impression of true performance when the same test has been in place for a number of years. Specifically, he found that performance appeared to be increasing when the same form of the test was used over time, but when the test form was changed, student performance dropped off significantly when judged by comparable national norms. Interestingly, just 2 years after the new form was implemented, there was a sharp increase in student performance, a clear demonstration of teaching to a particular test rather than teaching for genuine learning.

Linn (2000) also found that different cut-scores, or performance standards, can send mixed messages about performance. For example, he demonstrated that the percentage of students passing state assessments was substantially higher than the percentage of students scoring at the proficient level on the fourth-grade NAEP reading test. For example, 88% of Wisconsin students met the state standard in reading but only 35% scored at the proficient level on NAEP. Although the state standard was intended to identify students who may need remediation and the NAEP standard was intended to represent "solid academic performance," which are very different standards, it is obvious that we would draw different inferences about the quality of student learning from each test. This pattern of differences across tests has been replicated recently in a high-profile study of test scores in Texas. Klein, Hamilton, McCaffrey, and Stecher (2000) found that reading gains on the Texas Assessment of Academic Skills (TASS) were several times greater than they were on NAEP. Just what do these tests measure and what do their results mean? However, beyond these problems of validity and generalizability, which certainly merit attention, is the added problem that scores do not reveal what is happening in classrooms to produce the scores. Essentially, a focus on outputs distracts us from looking at the quality of teaching and learning.

Focus on Change

A second reason to question outputs is the tendency of policymakers to focus on change—for example a change in the curriculum covered, or time students spend on particular tasks, or even teachers' instructional practices such as working with small groups. Change is not necessarily improvement. It can be a sign of "instability, indecision or lack of vision" (Shields & Knapp, 1997). Conversely, lack of change may not be a sign of poor-quality teaching or learning.

A good example of danger of focusing on change is found in research conducted in Vermont by Lipson, Mosenthal, and colleagues, who examined instructional quality under Vermont's state portfolio policy (Lipson & Mosenthal, 1997; Lipson, Mosenthal, & Mekkelsen, 1996; Mosenthal, Lipson, Mekkelsen, Daniels, & Jiron, 1996). Their classroom observations revealed that some teachers, those who had already used process writing and portfolios, changed little under the new portfolio policy; they did not need to change in order to align their practices with the new policy. On the other hand, they argue that what might appear to be fairly small changes (e.g., students developing ownership in writing) set the stage for more profound changes in instruction over time; that a small change may be quite significant.

Sometimes changes appear more meaningful than they are. For example, a longitudinal study of restructuring carried out by the Consortium for Policy Research in Education (CPRE) (Elmore, Peterson, & McCarthy, 1996) found that although all the teachers and administrators in restructured schools had complied with policies and had changed school structures (i.e., grouping practices, more professional development, shared decision making), classroom observations revealed these changes had little relationship to changes in teaching practices. And several other studies (Cohen & Ball, 1990a; Heaton, 1993; Mayer, 1999) have demonstrated that even teachers' self-reports of change in teaching practices are often at odds with their observed epistemological stances and actual instructional practices. Note that in all these studies, the researchers had to go beyond tallies of time or activities or even self-reports to get at the quality of teaching. They had to go into the classrooms and they had to bring subject matter expertise to their analyses.

The Moral Imperative

A third reason for caution in using outputs is put forward by Black and William (1998a, 1998b). Using their research on classroom assessment in England and an extensive review of related research, they assert that the prime locus for raising achievement is the classroom. They argue that it is strange and simply unfair to leave the workings inside the black box entirely up to teachers on their own. In fact, their work demonstrates that teachers who are supported in learning how to use classroom assessment to make instructional decisions and to provide feedback to their students actually produce significant gains on traditional achievement tests, especially for their low-achieving students. This call to help teachers focus on the quality of instruction, what we name here the "moral imperative," is also recommended by the National Research Council report on Title I Testing and Assessment (Elmore & Rothman, 1999). The report cites several studies that question the effectiveness of policy focused only on standards, assessment, and accountability. They argue that policies must be tied directly to building the capacity of teachers and administrators to improve instruction. The National Commission on Teaching and America's Future (Darling-Hammond, 1997) draws a similar conclusion.

Beyond the Black Box

If our argument for focusing on the black box, on the quality of teaching and learning, seems rather obvious, as it must to those who work in classrooms, let us assure you that it is not obvious to many who do policy research. For example, among the articles we read for this review was a summary of research on new Title I programs that focused on achievement test scores, characteristics of the schools and districts, and organizational structures. Of the 13 studies in this summary, only 2 actually looked at instruction. In another study, researchers asked various people to evaluate test items as a way to judge the quality of what was taught in schools. Clearly, looking inside the black box is not common practice in policy research. It takes time and subject matter expertise, and it is difficult to do on a large scale or under tightly controlled experimental conditions.

Perhaps one of the first close looks inside the black box in our field came with Richard Allington's seminal work on the quality of instruction for Title I students, which called into question the traditional reliance on compliance with the rules and regulations as a measure of effectiveness. Instead, he looked at the quality of the instruction these students received and, as we all know, he found that instruction lacking (Allington, 1983; Allington & McGill-Franzen, 1989; Allington, Stuetzel, Shake, & Lamarche, 1986).

But we do not want to stop here. We want to go further to suggest that looking inside the black box, at the quality of teaching and learning, is not enough. We must look at the contexts in which the teaching and learning exist—the policy environments that surround and filter influences on teaching and learning. This is how we can bridge the divide between the global and local perspectives and between generic and subject-specific teaching and learning that we identified at the beginning of this review.

To make this point, we rely on a model developed by Michael Knapp and colleagues at the Center for the Study of Teaching and Policy at the University of Washington (Center for the Study of Teaching and Policy, 2000) and recent research that has informed the model (see Figure 2). This graphic, which we have adapted, places the black box of "quality of teaching and learning" in the context

FIGURE 2
The Quality of Teaching and Learning in Context

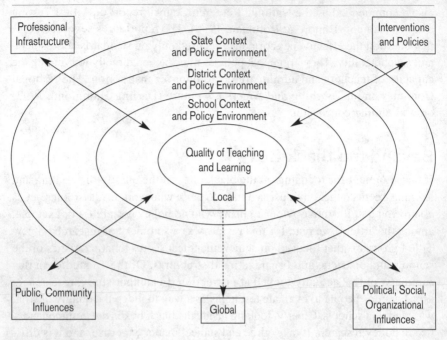

From Center for the Study of Teaching and Policy, University of Washington.

of conditions and forces that have the most potential to influence what happens in the classroom. Classrooms reside in schools, which reside in districts, which reside in states. Note the term *policy environment*, which connotes the array of policies past and present, the contexts from which those policies emerge, the coherence of the policies, and responses to those policies that all come together to create a policy environment. The model also reminds us that policy passes through many filters on its way to the classroom, all of which can have a significant influence on the quality of teaching and learning. Policy is not simply handed over; it is shaped by the events, conditions, and players inside and outside the classroom. Furthermore, the filters are bidirectional and interactive. For example, teachers shape how policies are defined in schools, and districts influence state and community perceptions and support for new initiatives; ultimately practice influences policy itself (Cohen & Ball, 1990b). Taken together, these contexts can support or undermine the policy goals. Consequently, what we need in order to understand the effects of policy is research that considers these contexts, that tries to understand the influence of these conditions and interactions among them on the quality of teaching and learning.

This model reflects much of the research we have reviewed so far. But it is especially influenced by the work of two groups: (1) David Cohen, Deborah Ball, and their colleagues and former students (e.g., Cohen & Ball, 1990a, 1990b; Cohen & Barnes, 1993; Cohen & Hill, 2000; Jennings, 1996; Spillane, 1998) and (2) Michael Knapp and his associates (Knapp & Associates, 1995; Knapp, Bamburg, Ferguson, & Hill, 1998). In general, these researchers have merged policy and subject matter expertise, the global and local, to study teaching quality. Their work also reminds us of the reciprocal relationship between policy and teaching—that teachers are at once the targets and agents of change.

A little thought experiment might illuminate how this model can enhance research on the relationship between policy and the quality of teaching and learning. Imagine research on a first-grade class-size reduction policy aimed at improving reading achievement. Regardless of whether the outputs indicated that student reading achievement improved or declined, we would need to ask questions like the following to judge the effectiveness of the policy: What does reading instruction look like in these classrooms—the materials, curriculum, pedagogy, classroom organization, and instructional discourse? What do we know about the qualifications and background of the teachers—certified, previous experience at primary grades, beliefs about reading instruction, and knowledge? What kind of professional development was provided at the state, district, and school levels? What do we know about the curriculum being implemented (e.g., type, mandated or self-selected)? What about teachers' role in selecting the curriculum? What kinds of assessments are in place—high-stakes tests, portfolios, and so on?

With the review of research and this conceptual model as background, we now move to two case studies compiled from research representing a variety of levels, from a more global to a more local perspective. Research at the more global end of the continuum is usually focused more on policy questions than on subject matter analyses and rarely includes classroom observation. Research in the middle of this continuum often reflects a combined interest in policy and subject matter issues and often includes some level of classroom observation. Research at the more local end of the continuum is typically more concerned with subject matter issues than general policy questions and relies heavily on classroom observation.

We examined the literature representing a number of state and district policy contexts before finding two that had a relatively full complement of studies spanning the global-local continuum. The states we selected for our case studies are Michigan and Kentucky. The policy contexts investigated in these two states are also distinct enough to provide some interesting contrasts. As each case study unfolds, what appears are some instances in which difficulties in interpretation arise because research does not situate itself in both local and global contexts. In other instances, there are studies that try to understand the constellation of influences that converge on policy implementation.

Before presenting the case studies, a few caveats are in order. First, when a full range of research is available for a particular policy context, it is likely the policy context has been in place for some period of time. As a result, the policy contexts studied in Michigan and Kentucky are not necessarily those that are currently in place. A related issue is that the layering of studies from the most global to the most local does not always reflect the chronology of findings within a particular policy context. For that reason, it is important to attend closely to the time frames in which data were collected. Finally, as literacy policy researchers who have worked in Michigan, we want to make clear that our only role in the research reviewed here was as informants.

Case Study 1: Michigan

We begin our case study of Michigan with a description of the policy environment at the time of the research we review. According to Goertz, Floden, and O'Day (1995), three key factors characterized the policy context in Michigan at that time: (1) local educators' desire to redirect reading curriculum away from basic skills to higher-order processes, (2) state government's desire to make the education community more accountable, and (3) the historical use of organizations outside the state department of education to communicate and implement reform efforts.

The literacy policy context was framed by Michigan's Essential Goals and Objectives in reading and state assessments derived from these objectives. The reading objectives in place at the time of the research presented here were developed jointly between the state and the Michigan Reading Association (MRA) and adopted by the state in 1986. These objectives reflected a "new" vision of reading that was emerging from the professional community at that time, one that recognized comprehension as the ultimate goal of reading and characterized the reading process as interactive, constructive, and dynamic.

Although the education profession in Michigan played a major role in defining the content of the state's standards and assessments, those outside the profession determined which policies should drive education reform and in what direction. For two decades, Michigan used a low-stakes assessment based on the Essential Goals and Objectives to communicate content standards and to encourage changes in local curriculum. This approach of "friendly persuasion" fit the state's strong tradition of control but did not produce the type of workforce Michigan businesses needed.

Responding to calls from the business community and the governor for greater accountability in education, the legislature enacted Public Act 25 (PA 25) of 1990 requiring local school boards to prepare and distribute annual education reports. PA 25 also called for voluntary implementation of the state model core curriculum and required districts to report on the status of their curriculum compared to the state's model core. In the year following the passage of PA 25, the legislature called for a high-stakes high school graduation test. Although school improvement plans were to include professional development, there were no specific state policies on professional development for reading.

More Global Emphasis

We begin our review of research with a large-scale policy study by Goertz et al. (1995) that looked at reading in Michigan and writing in two other states. The stated purposes for this study included examining district, school, and teacher responses to state reform policies in a small number of reforming schools and districts, and studying the capacity of the educational system to support education reform. The findings are based on data gathered from interviews and surveys conducted in 1993–1994 in actively reforming elementary and middle schools located in three states—California, Michigan, and Vermont. Although we can distill information about language arts from this report, it is important to remember that it is about systemic reform, not about language arts per se.

The portion of the study dealing directly with language arts reform in Michigan examines the degree to which teachers' reports on their instruction were consistent with explicit or implicit curriculum recommendations in state policies such as the model core curriculum and state assessments. The data indicate that Michigan teachers emphasized content matching the "meaning-centered" view of Michigan's Essential Goals and Objectives in Reading (1986). For example, both elementary and middle school teachers in the study indicated that they spent over 3 hours per week on comprehension strategies and having students respond to what they read, and barely over 30 minutes per week on basic skills, such as phonics and word recognition. They also indicated spending the largest amount of time in whole-class activities. In addition, both elementary and middle school teachers spent close to 50% of their instructional time using literature trade books and no more than about a third of their time with reading basals. Goertz et al. concluded that the call for school districts to incorporate state goals and objectives in their own curriculum led the two districts in this study to review, revise, and/or develop their curricula, and the impending requirement that students pass a test for a state-endorsed diploma made the state assessments a more important aspect of teachers' professional lives.

However, a closer look at the two elementary schools in Michigan revealed important similarities and differences with the general findings. Although both schools described their reading instruction as shifting from decoding to understanding, teachers in School #2 indicated that they relied far more heavily on their literature-based reading series than did teachers in School #1, who reported using other instructional materials such as trade books, book clubs, and subject area reading an average of 80% of the time. Also, teachers in School #1 reported that half of their instructional time was spent with students working in pairs or doing individual work, whereas teachers in School #2 reported spending two thirds of their time in whole-class lessons and discussion.

What is important here are the differences between the aggregated data and what was learned upon closer examination of the individual schools. No doubt, these differences are what led Goertz et al. to conclude that when state policy instruments send messages that are in line with what educators are hearing from other sources, they can be used to inform changes in instruction. Although teachers indicated that they had been influenced by state policy instruments such as curriculum and assessments, these state influences were by no means the only, or even the most important, influences on practice. Teachers reported that their own knowledge and beliefs about the subject matter and their students, for example, generally had a larger influence than state policies.

A second global study by Spillane (1996) provides further evidence that state policies play out differently in different educational contexts; however, in this study, the emphasis is on districts instead of schools. Using interviews to examine the impact of Michigan reading policy on both an urban and a suburban district, Spillane found that the suburban district used the revision of the state reading test as a lever to move in a different direction from the basic skills orientation of the central administrators. In contrast, the state's reading policy did not figure prominently in the reading program developed in the urban district. For example, a new basal reading program was mandated accompanied by a traditional workbook that provided students with drill in reading skills. Administrators made no effort to revise district policy on student assessment despite significant revisions of the state's reading test.

Combining Global and Local Emphases

A study by Standerford (1997) represents another layer of investigation and highlights the tensions between classroom and district practice within Michigan's policy context. She studied two small districts from 1988 until 1991. Both districts formed reading curriculum committees in an effort to interpret the state reading policy and design an official district response. To understand what happened in these districts, Standerford observed both the curriculum committees and the classroom practices of the teachers on these committees.

Standerford's results indicated that the district rules, objectives, players, audiences, and time frames made participation in the district effort quite separate from both state policy and from the classroom changes that individual teachers were making. Districts' responses to state reading reform appeared to be focused primarily on compliance with little attention to the substance of the policy. In contrast, the teachers made changes in their classroom practice based on their individual professional development activities, but were often unsure just how those changes fit with the state policy.

Standerford concluded that state and district policies had influenced the teachers' efforts by making them aware that changes were expected in reading instruction, but had not made clear for the teachers what those instructional changes were, nor offered much support for their efforts to figure that out for themselves. As teachers learned more about the new ideas, they gradually changed the enacted curriculum in their classrooms. Yet, those instructional changes were minimally represented in the written curriculum that they produced as members of the district committees because their roles and objectives were defined differently at the district and classroom levels.

More Local Emphasis

Research by Jennings (1996) and Spillane and Jennings (1997) moves even closer to the local end of the continuum. Looking at nine second- and fifth-grade teachers in the suburban district Spillane (1996) reported on previously, Spillane and Jennings (1997) found that the extent to which teachers' practices reflected the district's literacy initiative depended on how well the reforms were elaborated by the district.

Initial data analysis suggested significant uniformity in language arts practice among the nine classrooms and offered striking evidence that the district's proposals for language arts reform were finding their way into practice. For example, they found that all nine teachers were using literature-based reading programs and trade books, engaging in activities such as writers workshop, and focusing on comprehension over skills-based instruction. However, closer inspection of the observation data suggested differences across classrooms that were not captured by their analytical framework. This led Spillane and Jennings to a revised analytical frame focused on classroom tasks and discourse patterns that revealed important "below the surface" differences in pedagogy. Comparing results using the two analytical frameworks, Spillane and Jennings showed that it is relatively easy to arrive at very different conclusions about the extent to which reforms calling for more ambitious pedagogy have permeated practice.

Jennings (1996) also conducted an in-depth case study of three Michigan teachers, one of whom taught in the suburban school reported on previously. Jennings found that the ideas and practices the teachers brought to their learning influenced how and what they learned from the policy. However, she also noted the complexity of figuring out teachers' prior knowledge as well as how it shaped their learning. For example, two of the teachers brought ideas about reading and reading practices consistent with the reform, yet they learned very different things because they had different dispositions toward the policy. One of the two brought an eagerness to see the policy as something from which to learn and, as a result, did learn new ideas from it. The other did not learn because she was reluctant to see the policy as something from which she could learn rather than a reinforcement of what she already knew.

Spillane and Jennings (1997) argue that if reforms are meant to help all students encounter language arts in a more demanding and authentic manner, then policy analysts cannot rely solely on indicators such as the materials and the activities teachers use. We would add that to be able to explore these issues effectively, one must understand a great deal about the subject matter that is the focus of the reform. Spillane and Jennings have amassed a great deal of knowledge about language arts and language arts instruction over their years of studying language arts reform. We believe that without this knowledge, they might never have even seen the differences that led them to develop new analytical frameworks or to probe teachers' understandings and ultimately to uncover important differences in teachers' learning and classroom practice.

What have we learned through the juxtaposition of studies, from global to local, about the impact of Michigan reading reform in a relatively low-stakes policy environment? Aggregated data from teacher surveys suggest alignment of practice with state policy. However, a closer look at districts, schools, and classrooms reveals important differences in practices. Although the policy clearly had an impact on districts, the response varied from substantive change consistent with the policy, to superficial compliance, to staying the course. Furthermore, teachers' practices within these districts also varied ranging from practices that were surprisingly more consistent with the intent of the state policy than was their district's response, to superficial changes that did not reflect the true intent of the policy. From the more local perspective, these studies suggest that reading policy and recommended curriculum were not uniformly implemented in Michigan, a finding that may have been influenced by the low-stakes nature of the situation and the lack of attention to professional development in the policies. Although districts seemed to have the potential to mediate teachers' practices, they were not automatically influential or helpful; when district response was congruent with state policy and when districts worked to elaborate policy, practice was more likely to be positively influenced. Although there is a relatively full complement of studies in Michigan across layers of investigation, there is also a serious lack of information on how the various responses to the policy affected student learning.

Case Study 2: Kentucky

Now we turn to Kentucky, a state with a very different policy context. In what has become a historic decision, the Kentucky Supreme Court ruled in June 1989 that the public school system was "unconstitutional" because every child in Kentucky was not being provided with an equal opportunity for an adequate education. As a result, the court ordered the state to establish a more equitable system and to monitor it on a continuing basis. The Kentucky Education Reform Act (KERA) of 1990 resulted from this court decision.

KERA represents one of the most comprehensive pieces of educational reform legislation ever enacted in the United States. It was designed to change the state's entire educational system and address nearly every aspect of public education including administration, governance and finance, school organization, accountability, professional development, curriculum, and assessment. The areas that have received the most research attention, at least with regard to literacy practices, are assessment and professional development.

As part of its charge to enact KERA, the Kentucky Department of Education (KDE) developed a multifaceted professional development program to help schools and teachers achieve the reform goals. In 1994, the legislature allocated 65% of all state professional development funds directly to schools. The KDE also developed a new statewide assessment system known as the Kentucky Instructional Results Information System (KIRIS). KIRIS, which has recently been reenvisioned as the Commonwealth Accountability Testing System (CATS), was designed to be both performance based and high stakes and included yearlong portfolios in mathematics and writing. KIRIS assessments were aggregated to determine a school score, which in turn became part of an accountability index used to determine how much gain a school needed to receive cash rewards and avoid state sanctions. The emphasis placed on the accountability index led many to equate KIRIS more with accountability than with performance-based assessment, and, in time, blur the distinctions between KIRIS and KERA that were clear in the early 1990s.

More Global Emphasis

Koretz and his colleagues (Koretz, Barron, Mitchell, & Stecher, 1996) used telephone and written surveys to examine the influence of KIRIS assessments; information about language arts is embedded in the responses of the elementary teachers in this study. The teachers reported that they supported the new assessments and even changed some of their practices such as spending more time on writing, although they felt that more specific curriculum frameworks would be helpful. On the negative side, however, they reported spending considerable time in test preparation activities and a tendency to deemphasize untested material, and they did not support the use of test results for accountability. In addition, teachers' expectations rose for high-achieving students rather than low-achieving students, and they credited student gains to specific test practice and test familiarity rather than to true improvements in capabilities. So, we learn that the assessment policy was having both positive and negative influence on teachers.

A more recent CRESST/RAND study by Stecher, Barron, Kaganoff, and Goodwin (1998) provides more of a subject-matter emphasis, but still focuses primarily on general policy questions. Reporting on the results of a 1996–1997 survey, this research was designed to examine contrasts between practices that were consistent with Kentucky's view of standards-based education and practices that were consistent with traditional views of education. Responses left little doubt that KERA and KIRIS had effects on writing curriculum and instruction in Kentucky. Writing teachers aligned themselves philosophically with the standards-based approach but continued to combine traditional and standards-based practices. Another interesting finding was that Kentucky teachers rated professional development highly and felt well prepared to teach most aspects of writing.

Stecher et al. (1998) observed that despite the alignment among the standards, KIRIS assessments, state curriculum materials, and training opportunities, there were few associations between KIRIS gains and reported classroom practices. They concluded there was "no convincing evidence that a particular set of actions or policies would produce higher scores. If there is such a pattern it would appear to include both standards-based and traditional approaches" (p. 85). The authors were disappointed not to have found stronger links between reported practices and student performance. They speculated that perhaps Kentucky educators have not found a practice or constellation of practices that consistently promotes higher achievement.

Another global study by McDonnell and Choisser (1997) used interviews and teachers' assignments instead of self-reports as a measure of teaching practice in social studies, math, and language arts; they produced results similar to the Stecher et al. (1998) study. The McDonnell study found that teachers had added new instructional strategies such as having students work in groups, but that they were still using traditional approaches as well and had not fundamentally changed the depth and sophistication of the content they were teaching. For example, few of the teachers' assignments included the state learning goals that stress thinking critically, developing solutions to complex problems, and organizing information to understand concepts.

Combining Global and Local Emphases

In contrast to the previous group of studies, Bridge (1994) combined an emphasis on general policy issues with an emphasis on literacy instruction by examining the reading and language arts instruction in Kentucky's newly mandated primary schools. A structured observation guide was used to determine the extent to which teachers' practices reflected the literacy practices recommended by the KDE. The results supported the Stecher and McDonnell global findings that teachers were using a combination of newly recommended and traditional practices, and they add important detail about teachers' instructional practices in reading and language arts. For example, a finding that teachers combined traditional approaches with newer ones was supported by observational information such as

> In one classroom in which the observer reported that there were about 3,000 books, the teacher had children complete skills charts together and dictate sentences with "T" words. At the same time, children were working on a project related to the Caldecott books.

What is clear from this example is that, as in the Michigan research, the schemes used for analysis and observation, and researchers' definitions of traditional and reform-oriented practices, have a significant impact on the findings and conclusions.

Although in a subsequent classroom study Bridge, Compton-Hall, and Cantrell (1997) found changes in the amount and quality of writing activities compared with a 1982 study, the authors were reluctant to attribute the changes to the reform because most teachers had learned a great deal about process writing in the ensuing 13 years. The results of these two studies leave unclear the impact of the policy on classroom literacy practice.

More Local Emphasis

The last set of studies provides more of a local perspective on literacy practices within the content of the Kentucky reforms. Callahan (1997) conducted an ethnographic case study of a high school English department faced with implementing state portfolios in 1992–1993, the second year of the mandate. This research demonstrates how local context interacted with the state's emphasis on accountability to work against fulfilling the intent of the mandate to both improve teaching and learning and hold schools accountable for student learning.

Unlike some other districts where the responsibility for enacting the portfolio mandate was shared among teachers and administrators, the principal of this high school charged the English department with this task. This decision, combined with the fact that this was the school's first experience with portfolios, led the English teachers to perceive the portfolio as a test of their competence as a department and of the reputation of the school. Individually, the English teachers acknowledged that they were asking for more and different kinds of writing from their students than they had in the past and were using scoring criteria to discuss writing with their students. In addition, as a department, they recognized that *all* students needed the opportunity to write personal narratives, stories, and poems and were exploring ways to provide these opportunities. The portfolio mandate was not, however, creating the kind of classroom writing experiences envisioned by KDE in which students are engaged in a continual process of goal setting, writing, self-reflection, and portfolio assessment. In focusing on the portfolio content and scoring requirements, the English teachers were responding to KDE's emphasis on these features and their principal's decision to give them the responsibility for this visible element of their school's accountability score. Their individual classroom practices were not under scrutiny, but their ability to follow the portfolio content requirements and scoring guide was. Consequently, teachers put their energy into the visible, procedural elements of the high-stakes assessment rather than deeper-level changes in instruction.

Finally, focusing on exemplary case studies in the larger, multiyear CRESST/RAND study by Stecher et al. (1998), Borko, Elliott, and Uchiyama (1999) concluded that the case study schools and teachers provided "existence proof" that Kentucky's approach to professional development can provide the resources needed to support statewide, standards-based educational reform. Nevertheless, Wolf and McIver's (1999) brief case study of Mr. Bass, an exemplary seventh-grade writing teacher in one of the case study schools, revealed that the basic tension between best practices in the classroom and preparing students for the demands of externally mandated portfolios still existed 5 years after Callahan gathered her data. This comment from Mr. Bass clearly illustrates this problem:

> I'm responsible for the on demand. I'm responsible for the open response. I'm responsible for the portfolio. And doggone it, there are times that—Boy, this is really strange. Because of KERA, I changed my style of teaching to a more workshop-oriented approach. But because of KIRIS testing, I'm not allowed to truly implement that approach. (p. 406)

The juxtaposition of studies focused on different levels of analysis offers insight into the impact of KERA and KIRIS on writing instruction. Within this relatively high-stakes policy context, the research suggests that state policy had an impact at both the school and teacher levels, but not always in ways researchers judged to be consistent with the reform. For example, several studies suggest that although there was change, teachers were not yet "up to speed" in their instructional practices; they combined traditional and reform-based strategies.

The combination of high stakes and an extensive professional development program from the state was likely responsible for the greater impact on teachers in Kentucky than in Michigan. Yet, the collective evidence suggests that the dual goals of the reform for accountability and for improving teaching and learning often worked at odds with each other. Overall, as in Michigan, there was little research on the relation between teachers' practices and student learning; unlike the Michigan case, however, we know little about the district role in the Kentucky reform.

Conclusions and Implications

We focus our conclusions and implications on both what we have learned about literacy policies that are likely to make a difference and what we have learned about the nature of the research.

The literature reviewed here suggests that to be effective, literacy policies need to address several issues. First, policies must be educative (Cohen & Barnes, 1993); that is, they must take into account the learning required of enactors. Policies must be more than mandates; they must attend to the new learning required by people and systems at all levels. Second, policies must also include provisions for in-depth professional development for teachers and administrators that are coordinated at the state level. This means partnering with local educational agencies to ensure the funding, support materials, and guidance needed for local level enactors at district, school, and classroom levels. Finally, policies must also address the problem of developing accountability systems that do not interfere with desired improvements in teaching and learning. Such systems will most likely involve multiple indicators of achievement and shared responsibility for data collection at classroom, school, district, state, and national levels.

This review also provides some insights into the nature of literacy policy research. The most obvious conclusion is that literacy policy research needs to use a layered approach of complementary studies conducted at all levels, from global to local, within the policy environment. At the same time, such studies should incorporate multiple perspectives, including those of both policy and literacy researchers. If we only have aggregated data, it is clear that we can be misled about the impact of state policy—in either direction. Alternatively, if we only have classroom observation data, we cannot understand the relations between state policy and responses at the district, school, and teacher levels.

The nature of more global research demands that teaching practice be evaluated in terms of self-reports or other proxies for teaching without situating them within the contexts of the classroom, school, and district. From the classroom-based studies we gain much needed detail about what it is teachers are doing within the larger contexts of their classrooms and schools. Looking across the continuum of studies raises questions about researchers' expectations with regard to literacy instruction and the validity/utility of the schemes used to characterize teaching practices or their proxies. It is questionable that counting up instances of somewhat discrete entities representing either more or less desirable practice can tell us much about the effectiveness of the policy in improving teaching and learning. The whole of teaching practice may be more than the sum of its parts.

Literacy policy research needs to probe deeply into the relations among particular classroom contexts, teacher practices, and specific types of student learning rather than simply focusing on test scores or aggregated data. Consequently, it is essential to address what counts as quality teaching and learning in literacy. This review revealed the lack of consensus, even among literacy researchers, as to what constitutes quality or aligned literacy teaching and learning and, as a result, it raises questions about the ways researchers evaluate practice. This is a problem that needs to be dealt with directly and systematically within the literacy domain or it will continue to undermine our ability to say much of anything that is meaningful about the impact of policy on literacy teaching and learning. In our view, the more detailed the research data, the more likely we are to be able to judge for ourselves other researchers' conclusions.

Clearly, finding ways to understand the effects of literacy policy is not simple. We owe it to ourselves and to our students not to oversimplify the questions or answers. Ultimately if we take this difficult road we can discover literacy policy and policy research that make a difference.

References

Allington, R.L. (1983). The reading instruction provided readers of differing ability. *The Elementary School Journal, 83,* 548–559.

Allington, R.L., & McGill-Franzen, A. (1989). School response to reading failure: Chapter 1 and special education students in grades 2, 4, and 8. *The Elementary School Journal, 89,* 529–542.

Allington, R.L., & McGill-Franzen, A. (1992). Does high stakes testing improve school effectiveness? *Spectrum, 10,* 3–12.

Allington, R.L., Stuetzel, H., Shake, M.C., & Lamarche, S. (1986). What is remedial reading? A descriptive study. *Reading Research and Instruction, 26,* 15–30.

Black, P., & William, D. (1998a). Assessment and classroom learning. *Assessment in Education, 5*(1), 7–74.

Black, P., & William, D. (1998b). Inside the black box: Raising standards through classroom assessment. *Phi Delta Kappan, 80,* 139–148.

Borko, H., Elliott, R., & Uchiyama, K. (1999). *Professional development: A key to Kentucky's reform effort* (CSE Tech. Rep. No. 512). Los Angeles: National Center for Research on Evaluation, Standards, and Student Testing, University of California.

Bridge, C.A. (1994). Implementing large scale change in literacy instruction. In C.K. Kinzer & D.J. Leu (Eds.), *Multidimensional aspects of literacy research, theory, and practice* (43rd yearbook of the National Reading Conference, pp. 257–265). Chicago: National Reading Conference.

Bridge, C.A., Compton-Hall, M., & Cantrell, S.C. (1997). Classroom writing practices revisited: The effects of statewide reform on writing instruction. *The Elementary School Journal, 98,* 151–170.

Callahan, S. (1997). Tests worth taking? Using portfolios for accountability in Kentucky. *Research in the Teaching of English, 31,* 295–336.

Center for the Study of Teaching and Policy. (2000). *Mid-term review materials.* University of Washington: Author.

Cohen, D.K., & Ball, D.L. (1990a) Policy and practice: An overview. *Educational Evaluation and Policy Analysis, 12,* 347–353.

Cohen, D.K., & Ball, D.L. (1990b). Relations between policy and practice: A commentary. *Educational Evaluation and Policy Analysis, 12,* 249–256.

Cohen, D.K., & Barnes, C.A. (1993). Pedagogy and policy. In D.K. Cohen, M.W. McLaughlin, & J.E. Talbert (Eds.), *Teaching for understanding: Challenges for policy and practice* (pp. 207–239). San Francisco: Jossey-Bass.

Cohen D.K., & Hill, H.C. (2000). Instructional policy and classroom performance: The mathematics reform in California. *Teachers College Record, 102,* 294–343.

Darling-Hammond, L. (1997). *Doing what matters most: Investing in quality teaching.* New York: National Commission on Teaching and America's Future.

Education Week. (2000). Quality Counts 2000. *Education Week, 19*(18), 72–75.

Elmore, R.F., & McLaughlin, M.W. (1988). *Steady work: Policy, practice, and the reform of American education.* Santa Monica, CA: RAND.

Elmore, R.F., Peterson, P.L., & McCarthy, S.J. (1996). *Restructuring in the classroom: Teaching, learning, and school organization.* San Francisco: Jossey-Bass.

Elmore, R.F., & Rothman, R. (Eds.). (1999). *Testing, teaching, and learning: A guide for states and school districts.* Washington, DC: National Academy Press.

Goertz, M.E., Floden, R.E., & O'Day, J. (1995). *Studies of education reform: Systemic reform (Vol. 1): Findings and conclusions.* New Brunswick, NJ: Consortium for Policy Research in Education, Rutgers University.

Haney, W. (2000). The myth of the Texas miracle in education. *Education Policy Analysis and Archives, 8*(42). Available: http://epaa.asu/epaa/v8n41

Heaton, R. (1993). Who is minding the mathematics content? A case study of a fifth-grade teacher. *The Elementary School Journal, 93,* 153–162.

Hoffman, J.V., Assaf, L.C., & Paris, S.G. (2000). High-stakes testing in reading: Today in Texas, tomorrow? *The Reading Teacher, 54,* 482–499.

Jennings, N.E. (1996). *Interpreting policy in real classrooms: Case studies of state reform and teacher practice.* New York: Teachers College Press.

Klein, S.P., Hamilton, L.S., McCaffrey, D.F., & Stecher, B.M. (2000). What do test scores in Texas tell us? *Educational Policy Analysis Archives, 8*(49). Available: http://epaa.asu/epaa/v8n49

Knapp, M.S., & Associates. (1995). *Teaching for meaning in high-poverty classrooms.* New York: Teachers College Press.

Knapp, M.S., Bamburg, J.D., Ferguson, M.C., & Hill, P.T. (1998). Converging reforms and the working lives of frontline professionals in schools. *Educational Policy, 12,* 397–418.

Koretz, D.M., Baron, S., Mitchell, K.J., & Stecher, B.M. (1996). *Perceived effects of the Kentucky Instructional Results Information System (KIRIS).* Santa Monica, CA: RAND.

Linn, R.L. (2000). Assessments and accountability. *Educational Researcher, 29*(2), 4–16.

Lipson, M.Y., & Mosenthal, J. (1997, April). *The differential impact of Vermont's writing portfolio assessment on classroom instruction.* Paper presented at the annual meeting of the American Educational Research Association, Chicago.

Lipson, M.Y., Mosenthal, J.H., & Mekkelsen, J. (1996, December). *A close look at teacher change: What gets influenced, who changes and why.* Paper presented at the annual meeting of the National Reading Conference, Charleston, SC.

Mayer, D.P. (1999). Measuring instructional practice: Can policymakers trust survey data? *Educational Evaluation and Policy Analysis, 1,* 29–45.

McDonnell, L., & Choisser, C. (1997). *Testing and teaching: Local implementation of new state assessments.* Los Angeles: National Center for Research on Evaluation, Standards, and Student Testing, University of California.

McGill-Franzen, A. (2000). Policy and instruction: What is the relationship? In M.L. Kamil, P.B. Mosenthal, P.D. Pearson, & R. Barr (Eds.), *Handbook of reading research* (Vol. 3, pp. 889–908). Mahwah, NJ: Erlbaum.

McLaughlin, M.W. (1987). Learning from experience: Lessons from policy implementation. *Educational Evaluation and Policy Analysis, 9,* 171–178.

McLaughlin, M.W. (1990). The RAND change agent study revisited: Macro perspectives and micro realities. *Educational Research, 19,* 11–16.

McLaughlin, M.W. (1992). Educational policy: Impact on practice. In M. Aiken (Ed.), *American Educational Research Association encyclopedia of educational research* (pp. 375–382). New York: Macmillan.

Mosenthal, J., Lipson, M.Y., Mekkelsen, J., Daniels, P., & Jiron, H.W. (1996). The mean-ing and use of portfolios in different literacy contexts: Making sense of the Vermont Assessment Program. In D.J. Leu, C.K. Kinzer, & K.A. Hinchman (Eds.), *Literacies for the 21st century* (45th yearbook of the National Reading Conference, pp. 113–123). Chicago: National Reading Conference.

Nolen, S.B., Haladyna, T.M., & Haas, N.S. (1992). Uses and abuses of achievement test scores. *Educational Measurement: Issues and Practice, 11*(2), 9–15.

Patterson, F.R.A. (2000). The politics of phonics. *Journal of Curriculum and Supervision, 15,* 179–211.

Resnick, L.B., & Resnick, D.L. (1992). Assessing the thinking curriculum: New tools for educational reform. In B.R. Gifford & M.C. O'Connor (Eds.), *Future assessments: Changing views of aptitude, achievement, and instruction* (pp. 37–75). Boston: Kluwer.

Sabatier, P., & Mazmanian, D. (1980). The implementation of public policy: A framework of analysis. *Policy Studies Journal, 8,* 538–560.

Schwab, J.J. (1964). Structure of the disciplines: Meanings and significances. In G.W. Ford & L. Pugno (Eds.), *The structure of knowledge and the curriculum* (pp. 6–30). Chicago: Rand McNally.

Shepard, L.A. (1991). Will national tests improve student learning? *Phi Delta Kappan, 72,* 232–238.

Shields, P.M., & Knapp, M.S. (1997). The promise and limits of school-based reform: A national snapshot. *Phi Delta Kappan, 79,* 288–294.

Shulman, L.S. (1987). Knowledge and teaching: Foundations of the new reform. *Harvard Educational Review, 57,* 1–20.

Smith, M., & O'Day, J. (1991). Systemic school reform. In S.H. Fuhrman & B. Malen (Eds.), *The politics of curriculum and testing* (pp. 233–268). Bristol, PA: Falmer.

Spillane, J.P. (1996). School districts matter: Local educational authorities and state instructional policy. *Educational Policy, 10,* 63–87.

Spillane, J.P. (1998). State policy and the non-monolithic nature of the local school district: Organizational and professional considerations. *American Educational Research Journal, 35,* 33–63.

Spillane, J.P. (2000). A fifth-grade teacher's reconstruction of mathematics and literacy teaching: Exploring interactions among identity, learning, and subject matter. *The Elementary School Journal, 100,* 307–330.

Spillane, J.P., & Jennings, N.E. (1997). Aligned instructional policy and ambitious pedagogy: Exploring instructional reform from the classroom perspective. *Teachers College Record, 98,* 449–481.

Standerford, N.S. (1997). Reforming reading instruction on multiple levels: Interrelations and disconnections across the state, district, and classroom levels. *Educational Policy, 111,* 58–91.

Stecher, B.M., Baron, S., Kaganoff, T., & Goodwin, J. (1998). *The effects of standards-based assessment on classroom practices: Results of the 1996–97 RAND survey of Kentucky teachers of mathematics and writing* (CSE Tech. Rep. No. 482). Los Angeles: National Center for Research on Evaluation, Standards, and Student Testing, University of California.

Valencia, S.W., & Wixson, K.K. (2000). Policy-oriented research on literacy standards and assessment. In M.L. Kamil, P.B. Mosenthal, P.D. Pearson, & R. Barr (Eds.), *Handbook of reading research* (Vol. 3, pp. 909–935). Mahwah, NJ: Erlbaum.

Wolf, S.A., & McIver, M.C. (1999). When process becomes policy: The paradox of Kentucky state reform for exemplary teachers of writing. *Phi Delta Kappan, 80,* 401–406.

Section Two

Processes of Reading and Literacy

Introduction

This section includes a spectrum of articles providing a foundation in socially embedded language and cognitive processes upon which readers build knowledge, skills, and strategies. Knowing all young readers do not stay on the road to proficient reading, we include articles addressing the problems that throw some readers off the road. However, most emergent readers evolve through identifiable phases of reading growth, acquire word knowledge, develop comprehension, and become self-regulating as they gain metacognitive skills. All of these aspects of a reader's growth are explored in these articles. But that is not the end of the story. Because the ways readers respond to and engage with texts vary widely, we include articles exploring response and engagement. Furthermore, engaged, responsive teachers using effective instructional strategies can have profound, enduring effects on children's development as readers, including those who struggle to master the process. Here we provide an overview of each part's content and contribution to our understanding of reading processes. Questions for Reflection and a list of supplementary CD articles follow each part's overview.

Part 1: Language and Cognition in Sociocultural Contexts

For this introductory section on literacy processes, we selected articles that reflect a sociolinguistic base from which reading emerges and the subsequent effects of that base on reading. We sought perspectives that went beyond reading solely as a network of cognitive processes to a view of reading as a sequence of meaning-construction events capable of defining us, others, and our world. James Paul Gee's article "Reading as Situated Language: A Sociocognitive Perspective" (#4) adopts the view that reading is far more than processing skills; it is a process embedded in a context of social interaction and culture. As children learn social languages—such as the language of rap, street gangs, classrooms, or law—they also are socialized into Discourses, which Gee also calls "communities of practice" or "identity kits." While socialized into Discourses, children build cultural models that inform Discourse members of what is linguistically normal behavior for that community. This framework establishes a reader's world and suggests that the reader's work in that world is to gain a critical consciousness of how he or she is defined by texts. In what some educators refer to as "literacy for new times" (Luke, 1995), readers can use the tools of critical literacy to liberate themselves from a subjectivity defined by texts.

Acknowledging that meanings are socially constructed, M.A.K. Halliday looks closely at a child's developing discourse skills in language. Through "The

Place of Dialogue in Children's Construction of Meaning" (#5), he shows us how a Discourse, in Gee's sense, contributes to a child's grasp of language and formation of personal identity.

Anne Haas Dyson, like Halliday, listened closely to the talk of children, observed how they used speech, and found how a child's inner speech revealed the development of writing within a social context. In "Writing and the Sea of Voices: Oral Language In, Around, and About Writing" (#6), Dyson helps us hear a young writer's talk that mediates many of the writing processes. Many of those processes, such as planning, monitoring, and evaluating, are explained later in Section Three of this volume, where John Hayes describes his model of writing (#49). However, Dyson shows us how "scaffolding" with more able writers, like their teachers, enables children to acquire self-regulating processes through interaction in Vygotsky's "zone of proximal development," a critical developmental gap between what a young writer can accomplish alone and what he or she could accomplish with the guidance of a more expert writer.

In "Exploring Vygotskian Perspectives in Education: The Cognitive Value of Peer Interaction" (#7), Ellice Forman and Courtney Cazden reveal how adult–child interactions differ from child–child interactions in school settings and so emphasize the importance of providing children with classroom interactions, such as peer tutoring and collaborative work. Those forms of peer exchange provide opportunities to practice questioning and direction-giving, language activities young children rarely perform in school-situated child–teacher transactions.

The next two articles in this part of Section Two demonstrate the intersubjective defining powers of language. In *Ways With Words*, Shirley Brice Heath (1983) describes the ways language shaped intersubjective experience among black working-class families in Trackton, one of two adjacent Appalachian communities that she investigated. In "The Children of Trackton's Children: Spoken and Written Language in Social Change" (#8), Heath shows us how transitioning from an Appalachian culture to an urban culture changes the forms and functions of language. As communities dissolved and moved from town to city, she witnessed shifts in the meanings of cultural membership, in the process of language socialization, and in social values and beliefs.

In "Literacy and the Identity Development of Latina/o Students" (#9), Robert Jiménez describes his investigation of the interaction between literacy and identity. Like Heath, Jiménez focuses on the interplay between language, social practice, and presentation of self. Jiménez found that students' bilingual language and literacy influenced their identities while their identities influenced their literacy development. Among the trends identified were the functions of English and Spanish literacy in their lives and the importance of literacy in interpersonal relationships.

In "Young Bilingual Children and Early Literacy Development" (#10), Patton Tabors and Catherine Snow examine the language skills of children exposed to second languages (usually English) in early childhood, under what conditions children develop biliteracy, and the degree to which development of English takes away time essential to the growth of the child's home language. The research findings these authors use to frame the complex picture of bilingual children's multiple pathways to acquiring English and to the fate of their home language could clearly help educators design appropriate programs serving bilingual children. With states legislating or using the referendum process to enact literacy programs affecting bilingual children in schools, the framework these authors construct also should be read by state policymakers and citizens alike. The decisions of policymakers in government offices and of citizens in the voting booth shape cultures and their newer citizens' sense of self.

The shaping influence of culture and language that a reader brings to a text is described vividly in Glynda Hull and Mike Rose's "'This Wooden Shack Place': The Logic of an Unconventional Reading" (#11). These authors reveal their readiness to revisit their own interpretations of texts after hearing alternative understandings that a minority college freshman constructs following his reading of a poem.

As a group, these articles demonstrate how literacy development is embedded in social and cultural contexts whose influence persists from a child's earliest moments of language acquisition, throughout the self-shaping school years, and well into adult life in college and the workplace. As we move toward a closer inspection of cognitive processes, including phonological processing, word recognition, fluency, comprehension, and metacognition, we suggest keeping in mind that each phase of reading growth and each instant of reading occur within a social and cultural theater that contributes to every child's role and sense of reality.

Questions for Reflection

1. What is meant by the term *critical literacy*? How can educators use the "tools of critical literacy" to help readers free themselves from a cultural model projected by texts? (#4—Gee; #6—Dyson)

2. How does a Discourse (note the capital *D*) contribute to a student's grasp of language and the formation of personal identity? (#4—Gee)

3. Explain how language and literacy influence a student's identity, and, in turn, further literacy development. (#4—Gee; #5—Halliday; #9—Jiménez; #10—Tabors & Snow; #11—Hull & Rose)

4. How does talk serve to mediate reading and writing in young children? How do peer "scaffolding" and peer tutoring facilitate development of self-regulating processes in the young reader and writer? Use your readings to support your answer. (#4—Gee; #6—Dyson; #7—Forman & Cazden)

5. What is meant by the "zone of proximal development"? What factors influence a student's learning in this "zone"? (#7—Forman & Cazden)

6. How does the social and cultural context of the classroom affect students' literacy development? In what ways can you influence this context to enhance your students' reading and writing growth? (#4—Gee; #6—Dyson; #9—Jiménez; #10—Tabors & Snow; #11—Hull & Rose)

Supplementary CD Selections

CD 2.1 Carroll, J.B. (1985). The nature of the reading process. In H. Singer & R.B. Ruddell (Eds.), *Theoretical models and processes of reading* (3rd ed., pp. 25–34). Newark, DE: International Reading Association.

CD 2.2 Dyson, A.H. (1999). Coach Bombay's kids learn to write: Children's appropriation of media material for school literacy. *Research in the Teaching of English, 33*(4), 367–402.

CD 2.3 Guzzetti, B.J., Young, J.P., Gritsavage, M.M., Fyfe, L.M., & Hardenbrook, M. (2002). Studies on gender and discussion. In *Reading, writing, and talking gender in literacy learning* (pp. 15–44). Newark, DE: International Reading Association; Chicago: National Reading Conference.

CD 2.4 Jiménez, R.T., García, G.E., & Pearson, P.D. (1996). The reading strategies of bilingual Latina/o students who are successful English readers: Opportunities and obstacles. *Reading Research Quarterly, 31*, 90–112.

CD 2.5 Kamhi-Stein, L.D. (1998). Profiles of underprepared second-language readers. *Journal of Adolescent & Adult Literacy, 41*, 610–619.

CD 2.6 Love, K., & Hamston, J. (2001). Out of the mouths of boys: A profile of boys committed to reading. *The Australian Journal of Language and Literacy, 24*(1), 31–48.

CD 2.7 Moll, L.C. (1994). Literacy research in community and classrooms: A sociocultural approach. In R.B. Ruddell, M.R. Ruddell, & H. Singer (Eds.), *Theoretical models and processes of reading* (4th ed., pp. 179–207). Newark, DE: International Reading Association.

CD 2.8 Rogers-Zegarra, N., & Singer, H. (1985). Anglo and Chicano comprehension of ethnic stories. In H. Singer & R.B. Ruddell (Eds.), *Theoretical models and processes of reading* (3rd ed., pp. 611–617). Newark, DE: International Reading Association.

Additional Recommended Reading

Luke, A., & Freebody, P. (1997). Shaping the social practices of reading. In S. Muspratt, A. Luke, & P. Freebody (Eds.), *Constructing critical literacies: Teaching and learning textual practice* (pp. 185–225). Cresskill, NJ: Hampton Press.

Part 2: Foundations for Literacy Development

The chapters in this part progress from preschool children's acquisition of a literate register through word learning and into fluency. With heightened concern in this edition about individual differences in reading acquisition, we include pieces that address the long-term consequences to readers going "off track" in their progress toward proficiency.

Focusing on emergent literacy, Beverly Cox, Zhihui Fang, and Beverly White Otto examine when and how children develop knowledge of a literate register and relationships between its acquisition and social-economic factors ("Preschoolers' Developing Ownership of the Literate Register," #12). The authors' search for indicators of cohesion in oral and written texts produced by children in different contexts yields important findings that enlarge our understanding of emergent literacy development, connections between writing and the reading process, and the influence of economic factors on literacy acquisition.

How do children learn to read words, and what instructional strategies are most effective? Those questions guided Connie Juel and Cecilia Minden-Cupp's research reported in "Learning to Read Words: Linguistic Units and Instructional Strategies" (#13). The authors found that in real classrooms, differential instruction addressing a range of emergent readers' needs made significant differences in facilitating children's progress. Children beginning first grade with low literacy levels received phonics instruction while higher-range readers engaged in different activities, such as discussion of texts and their structure.

In "Phases of Word Learning: Implications for Instruction With Delayed and Disabled Readers" (#14), Linnea Ehri and Sandra McCormick describe five phases and their accompanying reading behaviors. These phases progress from "pre-alphabetic," so called because these children do not use alphabetic knowledge to read words, to "automatic," in which readers manifest proficient word reading. The authors also provide instructional practices that contribute to delayed and disabled readers' growth in each phase as they learn new strategies to decipher words.

Building on research related to children's word learning, Elfrieda Hiebert and Leigh Ann Martin examine what research has to say about the effects of different types of texts on emergent readers. In "The Texts of Beginning Reading Instruction" (#15), the authors also explore several dimensions of text evaluation, including the number of unique words in a text and how engaging it is, as well as the kinds of contributions these dimensions make to a child's reading acquisition.

Struggling, increasingly impoverished, or disabled readers form the focus of the next three articles in Part 2. The authors of these articles investigate the following issues:

- Fluency, including its successful and delayed development (Melanie Kuhn and Steven Stahl's "Fluency: A Review of Developmental and Remedial Practices" [#16])

- The Matthew effects, or the theory that while those rich in literacy skills become richer, the poor drop further behind (Keith Stanovich's "Matthew Effects in Reading: Some Consequences of Individual Differences in the Acquisition of Literacy" [#17])

- Causes of, preventive measures for, and interventions benefiting students with reading disabilities and other reading problems (Louise Spear-Swerling's "A Road Map for Understanding Reading Disability and Other Reading Problems: Origins, Prevention, and Intervention" [#18])

This set of articles takes us into the heart of today's debates over causes both biological and environmental of reading disability, methods of categorizing reading problems, the long-term effects of low literacy levels that begin early in life, and the value of various interventions that could benefit those afflicted with reading problems of various magnitudes.

Questions for Reflection

1. What linguistic and sociological variables are related to language and reading acquisition? How is a child's literate register related to early reading and literacy development? (#12—Cox et al.)

2. What linguistic and graphic units possess psychological reality in the word-identification process? What learning strategies enhance children's reading growth? (#13—Juel & Minden-Cupp; #14—Ehri & McCormick)

3. What is meant by "phases of word learning"? How do these phases help us understand "off track" reading of delayed and disabled readers? How can an understanding of these phases be of value in creating instructional intervention for off-track readers and avoid long-term effects of low literacy levels? (#14—Ehri & McCormick; #18—Spear-Swerling)

4. What factors affect text difficulty and, therefore, influence the reading acquisition process for children? (#15—Hiebert & Martin; #18—Spear-Swerling)

5. What is meant by "Matthew effects in reading"? What is the genesis of the notion of "Matthew effects"? What role does reading fluency play in creating such effects? (#16—Kuhn & Stahl; #17—Stanovich; #18—Spear-Swerling)

6. Develop a summary of those foundational factors you believe to be of critical importance in early literacy instruction. Use the readings to support your ideas. (articles #12 through #18)

Supplementary CD Selections

CD 2.9 Ehri, L.C. (1994). Development of the ability to read words: Update. In R.B. Ruddell, M.R. Ruddell, & H. Singer (Eds.), *Theoretical models and processes of reading* (4th ed., pp. 323–358). Newark, DE: International Reading Association.

CD 2.10 Ehri, L.C., Nunes, S.R., Willows, D.M., Schuster, B.V., Yaghoub-Zadeh, Z., & Shanahan, T. (2001). Phonemic awareness instruction helps children learn to read: Evidence from the National Reading Panel's meta-analysis. *Reading Research Quarterly, 36*, 250–287.

CD 2.11 Goodman, K.S. (1976). Reading: A psycholinguistic guessing game. In H. Singer & R.B. Ruddell (Eds.), *Theoretical models and processes of reading* (2nd ed., pp. 497–508). Newark, DE: International Reading Association.

CD 2.12 McCormick, S. (1994). A nonreader becomes a reader: A case study of literacy acquisition by a severely disabled reader. *Reading Research Quarterly, 29*, 157–176.

CD 2.13 Purcell-Gates, V. (1996). Stories, coupons, and the *TV Guide*: Relationships between home literacy experiences and emergent literacy knowledge. *Reading Research Quarterly, 31*, 406–428.

CD 2.14 Ruddell, R.B. (1976). Language acquisition and the reading process. In H. Singer & R.B. Ruddell (Eds.), *Theoretical models and processes of reading* (2nd ed., pp. 22–38). Newark, DE: International Reading Association.

CD 2.15 Samuels, S.J. (1976). Modes of word recognition. In H. Singer & R.B. Ruddell (Eds.), *Theoretical models and processes of reading* (2nd ed., pp. 270–282). Newark, DE: International Reading Association.

CD 2.16 Smolkin, L.B., & Donovan, C.A. (2000). *The contexts of comprehension: Information book read alouds and comprehension acquisition* (CIERA Report No. 2-009). Ann Arbor, MI: University of Michigan, Center for the Improvement of Early Reading Achievement.

CD 2.17 Sulzby, E. (1994). Children's emergent reading of favorite storybooks: A developmental study. In R.B. Ruddell, M.R. Ruddell, & H. Singer (Eds.), *Theoretical models and processes of reading* (4th ed., pp. 244–280). Newark, DE: International Reading Association.

CD 2.18 Swanborn, M.S.L., & de Glopper, K. (1999). Incidental word learning while reading: A meta-analysis. *Review of Educational Research*, *69*(3), 261–285.

CD 2.19 Wardhaugh, R. (1976). Theories of language acquisition in relation to beginning reading instruction. In H. Singer & R.B. Ruddell (Eds.), *Theoretical models and processes of reading* (2nd ed., pp. 42–66). Newark, DE: International Reading Association.

Additional Recommended Readings

Gibson, E. (1985). Trends in perceptual development: Implications for the reading process. In H. Singer & R.B. Ruddell (Eds.), *Theoretical models and processes of reading* (3rd ed., pp. 144–173). Newark, DE: International Reading Association.

O'Connor, R.E., Bell, K.M., Harty, K.R., Larkin, L.K., Sackor, S.M., & Zigmond, N. (2002). Teaching reading to poor readers in the intermediate grades: A comparison of text difficulty. *Journal of Educational Psychology*, *94*(3), 474–485.

Tzeng, O.J.L., & Wang, W. (1985). The first two Rs: The way different languages reduce speech to script affects how visual information is processed in the brain. In H. Singer & R.B. Ruddell (Eds.), *Theoretical models and processes of reading* (3rd ed., pp. 209–221). Newark, DE: International Reading Association.

Part 3: Comprehension Development From Words to Worlds

The nine articles that compose this, the largest part of the section on reading and literacy processes, extend from a review of vocabulary processes to an extensive research agenda that cuts deeply into perplexing and troubling aspects of comprehension. Many of the entries between these end pieces are classics that enrich our understanding of schema theory, an evolved set of integrated assumptions about how our minds organize memories and how those memories, when activated, shape the meanings we construct as we read. Even though some of these pieces were originally published 20 or more years ago, they afford a rich grounding in research and theory applicable to literacy studies today.

In "Vocabulary Processes" (#19), William Nagy and Judith Scott provide a comprehensive review of vocabulary acquisition processes. Their interest lies in answering two related questions: How do children add words to their reading and writing vocabularies, and how do they learn the meanings of new words? The authors reveal to us the complexities of word knowledge and the value of meta-linguistic awareness in learning words.

The next five articles explore the forms and functions of background knowledge, including the effects of contexts and word knowledge on miscues. Richard Anderson's classic piece "Role of the Reader's Schema in Comprehension, Learning, and Memory" (#20) explains schema theory, provides examples of evidence supporting the theory, and makes recommendations for the theory's application to classroom instruction. John Bransford, in "Schema Activation and Schema Acquisition: Comments on Richard C. Anderson's Remarks" (#21), elaborates on Anderson's main points, clarifying differences between schema activation and schema construction, and clarifying the impact of knowledge structures on comprehension while reading. Yetta and Kenneth Goodman ("To Err Is Human: Learning About Language Processes by Analyzing Miscues" [#22]) develop the role of schema in meaning construction through their exploration of miscue analysis. Arguing that there is nothing random about miscues, the Goodmans explain the role of schema-forming miscues as a kind of struggle toward accommodation of new information and schema-driven miscues as those reflecting assimilation of either old or new information into a preexisting schema. A reader's linguistic and conceptual schematic background manifests itself in both miscues and in the reader's conceptual understanding of texts.

In "Cognitive Flexibility Theory: Advanced Knowledge Acquisition in Ill-Structured Domains" (#23), Rand Spiro and his colleagues explore the learning of complex concepts and identify cognitive elements that interfere with advanced learning. The outgrowth of that exploration is cognitive flexibility theory, a view of cognition that emphasizes multiple representations of concepts, multiple linkages between knowledge structures, and the promotion of schema assembly rather than the activation of schema as prepacked, monolithic units of knowledge in memory. For learning in ill-structured domains where we encounter sometimes overwhelming complexity, such as learning to read or teaching reading, Spiro's theory, along with its situation-specific orientation, is a remarkably insightful and organic accommodation to earlier, more mechanistic views of schema form and function. In a follow-up to his earlier work, Spiro applies the concept of "principled pluralism" to both teaching and learning to read ("Principled Pluralism for Adaptive Flexibility in Teaching and Learning to Read" [#24]). While the "pluralism" part of the title refers to assembling multiple perspectives from prior knowledge, its "principled" nature derives from assembling aspects applicable to a specific and current situation and setting the less important aspects aside.

Nathalie Coté and Susan Goldman, in "Building Representations of Informational Text: Evidence From Children's Think-Aloud Protocols" (#25), tackle the challenge of describing how learners construct coherent representations of instructional text material. The authors use think-alouds to enable them to look more closely at children's cognitive activities while they develop and update mental representations of content area texts. The authors found that readers used many processing strategies to build a coherent situation model that went beyond the text base. Building on Kintsch's "construction-integration" model of reading (Section Three, #46), the work of these authors raises and addresses a specific comprehension question: How do learners deal with constraints imposed by a text's content and structure while processing activated prior knowledge?

How early adolescent learners process texts while conducting a research investigation is the focus of a naturalistic study conducted by Joyce Many and her colleagues titled "Traversing the Topical Landscape: Exploring Students' Self-Directed Reading–Writing–Research Processes" (#26). The authors uncovered several major task impressions while observing students' composing-from-sources processes, including accumulating, transferring, and transforming information. Students who viewed research as transforming information were also most likely to adopt multiple perspectives of the topics they investigated.

Culminating and concluding this set of articles focused on aspects of comprehension is the RAND Reading Study Group's "A Research Agenda for Improving Reading Comprehension" (#27). This piece provides a summary of what we know and what we need to know about four critical domains of comprehension: instruction, teacher preparation, teacher professional development, and comprehension assessment. The research agenda concludes with a review of key issues pressing for attention.

Questions for Reflection

1. What are the key factors that influence the acquisition of vocabulary? How are the meanings of new words acquired? (#19—Nagy & Scott)

2. What is meant by the term *schema*? How do students acquire a new schema? Why is this information critical to understanding comprehension instruction? (#20—Anderson; #21—Bransford)

3. How does a schema-forming miscue differ from a schema-driven miscue? How can this differentiation be of value in understanding the way in which children process text? (#22—Goodman & Goodman)

4. How does cognitive flexibility theory differ from schema theory? How is it similar? Explain how the concept of "cognitive flexibility" is related to the concept of "principled pluralism." How can the concepts of cognitive flexibility and principled pluralism be applied to understanding comprehension processing of difficult content area text? (#20—Anderson; #21—Bransford; #23—Spiro et al.; #24—Spiro)

5. How do students activate text-related prior knowledge while constructing and integrating meaning from difficult text? (#25—Coté & Goldman) How does a student's stance toward composing a text influence the composing process and the final composition (consider *accumulating, transferring, transforming*)? In addition to the Many et al. article (#26), use the readings on schema theory (#20—Anderson; #21—Bransford), cognitive flexibility theory (#23—Spiro et al.), and principled pluralism (#24—Spiro) in your response.

6. How do Anderson's (#20), Bransford's (#21), and Spiro's (#23, #24) explanations of how schema function help explain differences in the performance of students writing research papers in the Many et al. research (#26)?

7. What comprehension domain addressed in the RAND Reading Study Group (#27) (instruction, teacher preparation, professional development, or comprehension assessment) do you believe to be most important? Why? Identify one problem within the domains of either instruction or comprehension assessment that you would like to research. Outline a study that would provide empirically based knowledge about the problem you have selected. Use information from the readings in this section to support your approach to the problem. (articles #19 through #27) (Note: The domains of teacher preparation and professional development will be addressed in Part 6: Instructional Effects on Literacy Development.)

Supplementary CD Selections

CD 2.20 Anderson, R.C., & Freebody, P. (1985). Vocabulary knowledge. In H. Singer & R.B. Ruddell (Eds.), *Theoretical models and processes of reading* (3rd ed., pp. 343–371). Newark, DE: International Reading Association.

CD 2.21 Gersten, R., Fuchs, L.S., Williams, J.P., & Baker, S. (2001). Teaching reading comprehension strategies to students with learning disabilities: A review of research. *Review of Educational Research, 71*(2), 279–320.

CD 2.22 Hartman, D.K. (1995). Eight readers reading: The intertextual links of proficient readers reading multiple passages. *Reading Research Quarterly, 30*, 520–561.

CD 2.23 Hochberg, J., & Brooks, V. (1976). Reading as an intentional behavior. In H. Singer & R.B. Ruddell (Eds.), *Theoretical models and processes of reading* (2nd ed., pp. 242–251). Newark, DE: International Reading Association.

CD 2.24 Many, J.E. (2002). An exhibition and analysis of verbal tapestries: Understanding how scaffolding is woven into the fabric of instructional conversations. *Reading Research Quarterly, 37*, 376–407.

CD 2.25 McCormick, S. (1992). Disabled readers' erroneous responses to inferential comprehension questions: Description and analysis. *Reading Research Quarterly, 27*, 55–77.

CD 2.26 Palincsar, A.S., & Magnusson, S.J. (2000). *The interplay of firsthand and text-based investigations in science education* (CIERA Report No. 2-007). Ann Arbor, MI: University of Michigan, Center for the Improvement of Early Reading Achievement.

CD 2.27 Pearson, P.D., & Camperell, K. (1994). Comprehension of text structures. In R.B. Ruddell, M.R. Ruddell, & H. Singer (Eds.), *Theoretical models and processes of reading* (4th ed., pp. 448–468). Newark, DE: International Reading Association.

CD 2.28 Stauffer, R.G. (1970). Reading as cognitive functioning. In H. Singer & R.B. Ruddell (Eds.), *Theoretical models and processes of reading* (pp. 124–141). Newark, DE: International Reading Association.

CD 2.29 Taylor, B.M. (1985). Good and poor readers' recall of familiar and unfamiliar text. In H. Singer & R.B. Ruddell (Eds.), *Theoretical models and processes of reading* (3rd ed., pp. 494–500). Newark, DE: International Reading Association.

Additional Recommended Readings

Bower, G.H., Black, J.B., & Turner, T.J. (1985). Scripts in memory for text. In H. Singer & R.B. Ruddell (Eds.), *Theoretical models and processes of reading* (3rd ed., pp. 434–476). Newark, DE: International Reading Association.

Cunningham, A.E., & Stanovich, K.E. (1998). What reading does for the mind. *American Educator, 22*(1 & 2), 8–15.

Van Dijk, T.A., & Kintsch, W. (1985). Cognitive psychology and discourse: Recalling and summarizing stories. In H. Singer & R.B. Ruddell (Eds.), *Theoretical models and processes of reading* (3rd ed., pp. 794–812). Newark, DE: International Reading Association.

Part 4: Extending Comprehension Through Metacognition

Basic to the concept of metacognition is thinking about one's own thinking. Metacognitive thoughts arise from reflection on our internal representations of reality or on cognitive processes related to constructing knowledge or solving problems, including processes like reading. The articles included in this part present a model of self-regulated reading and the study of two strategies to promote it: reciprocal teaching and training in text structure recognition.

When reviewing articles on metacognition for this edition, we were surprised to discover a rather interesting trend. For an ERIC search covering the period from 1978 through 1984, a 7-year interval, 127 articles appeared in response to a search using the keyword *metacognition*. For the 9-year period from 1985 through 1993, 439 articles appeared. And for the 9 years since the publication of the previous edition of this book in 1994 up to and including 2002, 236 articles appeared. The hey-day of metacognitive research may have come and gone. However, many researchers believe, as do we, that much remains to be learned about metacognitive processes. Certainly, research on metacognition remains germane to our deeper understanding of reading comprehension and to its improvement.

The first article in this section, "Self-Regulated Comprehension During Normal Reading" (#28) by Douglas Hacker, addresses metacognition in reading. After clarifying the language used to describe the regulation of reading, Hacker presents a cognitive–metacognitive model of self-regulated comprehension. He identifies the components involved in the process and how they work. He then discusses the process of self-regulation in meaning-making while reading, a process that could be described as the metacognitive monitoring and controlling of cognition.

Developing more self-regulated readers able to improve their comprehension was the goal of Ann Brown and her colleagues in their early work on reciprocal teaching. Their article "Instructing Comprehension-Fostering Activities in Interactive Learning Situations" (#29) describes the structure of reciprocal teaching they used in several initial training studies to determine the effectiveness of the method. Four integrated activities or skills (summarizing, questioning, clarifying, and predicting) were selected for training adequate decoders who were poor comprehenders. Since their early endeavors to evaluate reciprocal teaching's effects, especially on struggling readers, the method has proliferated into classrooms across the United States.

Bonnie Meyer and her colleagues have been studying the impact of text structure knowledge on comprehension for more than 20 years. In "Effects of Structure Strategy Training and Signaling on Recall of Text" (#30), she and Leonard Poon found that readers receiving strategy training in text structure, including use of signal words, such as *because* in a problem/solution writing plan, remembered more information and recalled more key ideas compared to untrained readers. Trained readers transferred what they had learned to improving recall of everyday texts, such as newspaper articles and other forms of exposition.

All of these articles related to the application of strategic thinking to one's reading processes or evolving text representation reveal positive effects on comprehension, including a deeper understanding of a text and its improved recall.

Questions for Reflection

1. What is meant by the term *metacognition*? Using Hacker's cognitive–metacognitive model (#28), explain the cognitive and metacognitive components that are involved in the metacognitive process. Which of these components are you aware of using as you read easy text? Difficult text? (#28–Hacker)

2. How can self-regulation during meaning construction be taught? Use information from articles in this section to support your response. (#28–Hacker; #29–Brown et al.; #30–Meyer & Poon)

3. Briefly describe the structure and nature of reciprocal teaching. Why is this instructional strategy promising, especially for struggling readers, as a method of developing comprehension and more self-regulated reading? (#28–Hacker; #29–Brown et al.)

4. Does metacognitive ability change as students progress through the grades? Why or why not? What research supports your belief? (#29–Brown et al.; #30–Meyer & Poon)

5. How is text-structure knowledge related to self-regulated reading? Explain how a reader's awareness of the meanings of signal words, such as *because*, might affect comprehension and recall of text content. (#30–Meyer & Poon)

Supplementary CD Selections

CD 2.30 Cox, B.E. (1994). Young children's regulatory talk: Evidence of emerging metacognitive control over literary products and processes. In R.B. Ruddell,

M.R. Ruddell, & H. Singer (Eds.), *Theoretical models and processes of reading* (4th ed., pp. 733–756). Newark, DE: International Reading Association.

CD 2.31 Garner, R. (1994). Metacognition and executive control. In R.B. Ruddell, M.R. Ruddell, & H. Singer (Eds.), *Theoretical models and processes of reading* (4th ed., pp. 715–732). Newark, DE: International Reading Association.

CD 2.32 Yopp, H.K., & Singer, H. (1994). Toward an interactive reading instructional model: Explanation of activation of linguistic awareness and metalinguistic ability in learning to read. In R.B. Ruddell, M.R. Ruddell, & H. Singer (Eds.), *Theoretical models and processes of reading* (4th ed., pp. 381–390). Newark, DE: International Reading Association.

Additional Recommended Reading

Prawat, R.S. (1989). Promoting access to knowledge, strategy, and disposition in students: A research synthesis. *Review of Educational Research, 59*(1), 1–41.

Part 5: Reader Response, Motivation, and Engagement

In this part, we include studies addressing response to texts and literacy engagement for different purposes and with varying effects. All reflect concerns about reader motivation, an often neglected but integral dimension of the reading process. Comprehension and learning from texts are highly dependent on a reader's level of engagement.

In "Response to Literature as a Cultural Activity" (#31), Lee Galda and Richard Beach review the evolution of research on response, looking at texts, readers, and contexts. Noting the inseparability of these elements, the authors suggest that future research will focus on sociocultural perspectives of response. Mirroring the widening sociocultural contexts of reading addressed earlier in this volume (#4—Gee; #5—Halliday; #8—Heath; #12—Cox et al.), including the power of texts to define readers and the effects of social class on the interpretation of texts, Galda and Beach encourage teachers to help their students reflect on their construction of text worlds as bridges to participation in real, lived worlds. By engaging in critical reflection, students become empowered to understand their lived worlds and to transform them.

Reflecting aspects of critical literacy and its influence on literacy studies, Donna Alvermann and her colleagues reveal the shaping effects on response to texts of institutions and social contexts ("Adolescents' Perceptions and Negotiations of Literacy Practices in After-School Read and Talk Clubs" [#32]). Framing literacy as critical social practices, the authors analyze the discourse of a group of adolescents talking in an out-of-school setting about books they have read. Released from more defined roles of school-sanctioned responses, students tried out new positions. Participants in the read and talk clubs became more aware of the power of social institutions, like schools, to shape or guide response to texts and of the need to provide students with access to freer forums for deeper response to and exploration of texts, authorities' role in shaping discourse about them, and students' personal worlds.

Exploring aspects of Louise Rosenblatt's transactional theory of reading (Section Three, #48), Joyce Many investigates "The Effect of Reader Stance on Students' Personal Understanding of Literature" (#33). In this creative study, Many makes important discoveries about the impact on depth of understanding and recall of narrative texts when adolescent students adopt an aesthetic stance. The implications for teaching literature in school classrooms are intriguing and may challenge more traditional efferent-oriented pedagogy.

During the 1990s and into this decade, John Guthrie, Allan Wigfield, and their colleagues have made substantial contributions to our growing understanding of literacy engagement and its components. In "Motivational and Cognitive Predictors of Text Comprehension and Reading Amount" (#34), Guthrie, Wigfield, and colleagues describe the multiple pathways through which motivational variables contribute to reading achievement and text comprehension. They report results of their studies with elementary, middle, and high school students, studies showing that reading amount predicted comprehension and motivation predicted reading amount.

In "The Role of Responsive Teaching in Focusing Reader Intention and Developing Reader Motivation" (#35), we (Ruddell & Unrau) synthesized an abundance of research on motivation and identified factors critical to both a student's and her teacher's motivational system. Using the eye as a metaphor for focusing motivation, we arrayed factors feeding a central intention of a reader to engage in reading or a teacher to engage in literacy instruction. Many of the variables moving an individual to engage in a literacy event relate to that individual's beliefs about herself, whether those beliefs are about her identity, self-efficacy, or the value of undertaking a learning or teaching task. But beyond beliefs, task engagement resources, including a reader's text-processing powers or a teacher's instructional design skills, also impact engagement.

The need for research that will enable us to understand more deeply the motivational elements that move students and their teachers to engage successfully in literacy events cannot be overestimated. Our knowledge is quite limited; our need to learn more is vast. As Alexander and Fox (Section One, #2) point out in their historical perspective on reading research and practice, we are now living in the "Era of Engaged Learning." These authors point out that, in the mid-1990s, a flood of research on motivation found its way into the literacy community, partly through the work of the National Reading Research Center at the University of

Maryland and the University of Georgia. This led to reconceptualizing students as engaged readers who bring to reading not only their cognitive capacities and skills but also individual identities and entire cultural worlds that affect attunement with school and its own educational and social world. Sometimes worlds collide; sometimes they orbit in harmony. We need to know more to amplify moments of attunement and to deepen engagement of both students and their teachers.

Questions for Reflection

1. What is meant by the terms *reader response*, *motivation*, and *engagement*? How are these concepts related? (#31—Galda & Beach)

2. How is the sociocultural context of the classroom related to a student's response, motivation, and engagement? Consider the work of Galda and Beach (#31), Gee (#4), Dyson (#6), Heath (#8), Jiménez (#9), Tabors and Snow (#10), Hull and Rose (#11), and Cox et al. (#12) in supporting your answer. How does the "culture" of a low-achieving reading group differ from the "culture" of a high-achieving reading group?

3. What is meant by the statement "By engaging in critical reflection, students become empowered to understand their lived worlds and to transform them"? (#31—Galda & Beach; #32—Alvermann et al.; #35—Ruddell & Unrau)

4. How do social institutions, such as schools, influence students' response to text? What effect does reader stance have on personal understandings and interpretations of literature? (#32—Alvermann et al.; #33—Many)

5. Explain how reader motivation might influence the volume of reading a student engages in and how amount of reading might, in turn, affect comprehension growth. Use your reading to support your response. (#34—Guthrie et al.)

6. What variables motivate and focus a reader's intention to engage in reading or any literacy event? (#35—Ruddell & Unrau) What task-engagement resources can teachers use to motivate and focus a reader's intention?

7. Why do you think that Alexander and Fox have identified the present era of reading research and practice as the "Era of Engaged Learning"? (#2—Alexander & Fox)

Supplementary CD Selections

CD 2.33 Athey, I. (1985). Reading research in the affective domain. In H. Singer & R.B. Ruddell (Eds.), *Theoretical models and processes of reading* (3rd ed., pp. 527–557). Newark, DE: International Reading Association.

CD 2.34 Athey, I., & Holmes, J.A. (1976). Reading success and personality characteristics in junior high school students. In H. Singer & R.B. Ruddell (Eds.), *Theoretical models and processes of reading* (2nd ed., pp. 381–388). Newark, DE: International Reading Association.

CD 2.35 Baker, L., & Wigfield, A. (1999). Dimensions of children's motivation for reading and their relations to reading activity and reading achievement. *Reading Research Quarterly, 34*, 452–477.

CD 2.36 Fecho, B. (2001). "Why are you doing this?": Acknowledging and transcending threat in a critical inquiry classroom. *Research in the Teaching of English, 36*(1), 9–37.

CD 2.37 Gee, J.P. (2000). Teenagers in new times: A new literacy studies perspective. *Journal of Adolescent & Adult Literacy, 43*, 412–420.

CD 2.38 McKenna, M.C., Kear, D.J., & Ellsworth, R.A. (1995). Children's attitudes toward reading: A national survey. *Reading Research Quarterly, 30*, 934–956.

CD 2.39 Squire, J.R. (1994). Research in reader response, naturally interdisciplinary. In R.B. Ruddell, M.R. Ruddell, & H. Singer (Eds.), *Theoretical models and processes of reading* (4th ed., pp. 637–652). Newark, DE: International Reading Association.

CD 2.40 Wade, S.E., Buxton, W.M., & Kelly, M. (1999). Using think-alouds to examine reader-text interest. *Reading Research Quarterly, 34*, 194–216.

CD 2.41 Wigfield, A. (1997). Children's motivations for reading and reading engagement. In J.T. Guthrie & A. Wigfield (Eds.), *Reading engagement: Motivating readers through integrated instruction* (pp. 14–33). Newark, DE: International Reading Association.

CD 2.42 Young, J.P. (2000). Boy talk: Critical literacy and masculinities. *Reading Research Quarterly, 35*, 312–337.

Additional Recommended Readings

Beach, R., Appleman, D., & Dorsey, S. (1994). Adolescents' uses of intertextual links to understand literature. In R.B. Ruddell, M.R. Ruddell, & H. Singer (Eds.), *Theoretical models and processes of reading* (4th ed., pp. 695–714). Newark, DE: International Reading Association.

Wigfield, A., & Guthrie, J.T. (1997). Relations of children's motivation for reading to the amount and breadth of their reading. *Journal of Educational Psychology*, *89*(3), 420–432.

Part 6: Instructional Effects on Literacy Development

This part is an innovation with the fifth edition. Several readers of earlier editions and professionals who responded to our questionnaire requested applications of research and theory to practice. In response, we include articles on influential teaching, transactional strategies instruction, the characteristics of instruction in "beating the odds" schools, and the potential of trained college students to help children learn to read.

In the first article, "Researching the Influential Literacy Teacher: Characteristics, Beliefs, Strategies, and New Research Directions" (#36), Robert Ruddell builds a theoretical base for his work on influential teachers, sketches a research-based portrait of these masterful teachers, explores factors shaping their teaching style, explains strategies they use, and provides implications for instruction and research that could deepen our knowledge of teacher effectiveness.

Citing reciprocal teaching (#29) as an example of multiple-strategies reading instruction, Rachel Brown and colleagues introduce their model of transactional strategies instruction ("A Quasi-Experimental Validation of Transactional Strategies Instruction With Low-Achieving Second-Grade Readers" [#37]). The authors explain their approach is "transactional" because readers are encouraged to transact with texts, consonant with Rosenblatt's theory (#48), and because they transact meanings with other readers in small groups. The specific transactional strategies instruction program evaluated in this piece was Students Achieving Independent Learning (SAIL). The authors found clear evidence that SAIL increased elementary students' awareness and use of strategies, their acquisition of information from texts, and their scores on standardized tests of reading.

While transactional strategies instruction worked with elementary students, what facilitates students' superior literacy achievement in middle schools and high schools, especially in low-income communities? That's the question Judith Langer answers in "Beating the Odds: Teaching Middle and High School Students to Read and Write Well" (#38), for which she received IRA's 2003 Albert Harris Award (given for work that makes an outstanding contribution to the prevention and/or assessment of reading and learning disabilities). In these beating-the-odds schools, Langer found six well-integrated features that distinguished higher-performing from more typically performing schools. Meaningful and successful learning in beating-the-odds classrooms that Langer studied arose from teachers whose instruction was based on (a) the overt teaching of enabling strategies to carry out reading, writing, and thinking tasks; (b) the systematic use of separated, simulated, and integrated skill instruction; (c) the creation of overt connections between new knowledge across lessons, classes, grades, and even communities; (d) the belief that achieving a learning goal is not an end point but an opportunity to extend and deepen understanding; (e) the notion that students collaborate in classrooms to gain depth and complexity of understanding; and (f) integrating test preparation into regular lessons. These beating-the-odds teachers serving low-income communities appear to operate on a common principle: We learn best while engaged in activities that are personally and socially meaningful.

Jill Fitzgerald poses a research question that serves as her article's title: "Can Minimally Trained College Student Volunteers Help Young At-Risk Children to Read Better?" (#39). To summarize her study in a word: Yes. However, there is much more to the story's plot than that answer. First, the gains for at-risk children who received high-level tutoring (i.e., two 40-minute sessions for 25 weeks) were a substantial 1.19 grade levels. Second, the largest impact was on reading words. And third, growth patterns in reading were different for low-gain and high-gain children. For a 6-month intervention program, the treatment group gains for reading level in terms of effect size were impressive.

(For more on tutoring as a means of helping low-achieving elementary school students, see Goldenberg, Section Four, #56.)

Questions for Reflection

1. How do high and low achievers perceive their influential teachers? What shared beliefs about teaching are held by those teachers? How do highly influential teachers' meaning construction, meaning negotiation, and reader motivation strategies differ from those of less influential teachers? What is the nature of the meaning negotiation process used by the influential teacher? (#36—Ruddell)

2. What is a *transactional instructional strategy*? What is the theory base that underlies this strategy? What instructional gains were made by students using the SAIL strategy? How would you explain these gains in terms of the theory base of the study? (#37—Brown et al.)

3. What features appeared in the instruction of the higher-performing teachers in the "beating the odds" schools? Based on the study, how would you explain the success of the beating-the-odds schools from a sociocultural theory perspective? (#38—Langer)

4. How do you explain the instructional effectiveness of the minimally trained college students in the Fitzgerald study on instructional reading level and the ability of the at-risk readers to read words?

What future research is needed to better understand the use and effectiveness of tutors in working with at-risk students? (#39– Fitzgerald)

5. Return to the RAND Reading Study Group work (#27) and reexamine the domains of teacher preparation and teacher professional development in relation to comprehension instruction. Select a specific area from one of these two domains and briefly discuss how you would design a research study that would add to our teacher preparation or professional development knowledge base.

Supplementary CD Selections

CD 2.43 Armbruster, B.B., Anderson, T.H., & Ostertag, J. (1987). Does text structure/summarization instruction facilitate learning from expository text? *Reading Research Quarterly, 22,* 331–346.

CD 2.44 Dole, J.A., Brown, K.J., & Trathen, W. (1996). The effects of strategy instruction on the comprehension performance of at-risk students. *Reading Research Quarterly, 31,* 62–88.

CD 2.45 Jordan, G.E., Snow, C.E., & Porche, M.V. (2000). Project EASE: The effect of a family literacy project on kindergarten students' early literacy skills. *Reading Research Quarterly, 35,* 524–546.

CD 2.46 Mathes, P.G., Howard, J.K., Allen, S.H., & Fuchs, D. (1998). Peer-assisted learning strategies for first-grade readers: Responding to the needs of diverse learners. *Reading Research Quarterly, 33,* 62–94.

CD 2.47 O'Donnell-Allen, C. (2001). Teaching with a questioning mind: The development of a teacher research group into a discourse community. *Research in the Teaching of English, 36*(2), 161–211.

CD 2.48 Paris, S.G., Lipson, M.Y., & Wixson, K.K. (1994). Becoming a strategic reader. In R.B. Ruddell, M.R. Ruddell, & H. Singer (Eds.), *Theoretical models and processes of reading* (4th ed., pp. 788–810). Newark, DE: International Reading Association.

CD 2.49 Pressley, M., El-Dinary, P.B., Gaskins, I., Schuder, T., Bergman, J.L., Almasi, J., & Brown, R. (1992). Beyond direct explanation: Transactional instruction of reading comprehension strategies. *The Elementary School Journal, 92*(5), 513–555.

CD 2.50 Ruddell, R.B. (1994). The development of children's comprehension and motivation during storybook discussion. In R.B. Ruddell, M.R. Ruddell,

& H. Singer (Eds.), *Theoretical models and processes of reading* (4th ed., pp. 281–296). Newark, DE: International Reading Association.

CD 2.51 Spivey, N.N., & King, J.R. (1994). Readers as writers composing from sources. In R.B. Ruddell, M.R. Ruddell, & H. Singer (Eds.), *Theoretical models and processes of reading* (4th ed., pp. 668–694). Newark, DE: International Reading Association.

Additional Recommended Readings

Langer, J.A. (2000). Excellence in English in middle and high school: How teachers' professional lives support student achievement. *American Educational Research Journal, 37*(2), 397–439.

Morrow, L.M., & Young, J. (1997). A family literacy program connecting school and home: Effects on attitude, motivation, and literacy achievement. *Journal of Educational Psychology, 89*(4), 736–742.

Wharton-McDonald, R., Pressley, M., & Hampston, J.M. (1998). Literacy instruction in nine first-grade classrooms: Teacher characteristics and student achievement. *The Elementary School Journal, 99*(2), 101–128.

References

Heath, S.B. (1983). *Ways with words: Language, life, and work in communities and classrooms.* Cambridge, UK: Cambridge University Press.

Luke, A. (1995). When basic skills and information processing just aren't enough: Rethinking reading in new times. *Teachers College Record, 97*(1), 95–115.

4

Reading as Situated Language: A Sociocognitive Perspective

James Paul Gee

My main goal here is to situate reading within a broad perspective that integrates work on cognition, language, social interaction, society, and culture. In light of recent reports on reading (National Institute of Child Health and Human Development, 2000; Snow, Burns, & Griffin, 1998) that have tended to treat reading quite narrowly in terms of psycholinguistic processing skills, I argue that such a broad perspective on reading is essential if we are to speak to issues of access and equity in schools and workplaces. I also argue that reading and writing cannot be separated from speaking, listening, and interacting, on the one hand, or using language to think about and act on the world, on the other. Thus, it is necessary to start with a viewpoint on language (oral and written) itself, a viewpoint that ties language to embodied action in the material and social world.

I have organized this article into four parts. First, I develop a viewpoint on language that stresses the connections among language, embodied experience, and situated action and interaction in the world. In the second part, I argue that what is relevant to learning literacy is not English in general, but specific varieties of English that I call "social languages." I then go on to discuss notions related to the idea of social languages, specifically Discourses (with a capital *D*) and their connections to socially situated identities and cultural models. In the third part, I show the relevance of the earlier sections to the development of literacy in early childhood through a specific example. Finally, I close the article with a discussion of the importance of language abilities (construed in a specific way) to learning to read.

A Viewpoint on Language

It is often claimed that the primary function of human language is to convey information, but I believe this is not true. Human languages are used for a wide

From *Journal of Adolescent & Adult Literacy*, 44, 714–725. Copyright © 2001 by the International Reading Association.

array of functions, including but by no means limited to conveying information (Halliday, 1994). I will argue here that human language has two primary functions through which it is best studied and analyzed. I would state these functions as follows: to scaffold the performance of action in the world, including social activities and interactions; to scaffold human affiliation in cultures and social groups and institutions through creating and enticing others to take certain perspectives on experience. *Action* is the most important word in the first statement; *perspectives* is the most important word in the second. I will discuss each of these two functions in turn.

Situated Action

Traditional approaches to language have tended to look at it as a closed system (for discussion, see Clancey, 1997). Any piece of language is treated as representation (re-presenting) of some information. On the traditional view, what it means to comprehend a piece of language is to be able to translate it into some equivalent representational system, either other language (one's own words) or some mental language or language of thought that mimics the structure of natural languages (e.g., is couched in terms of logical propositions).

However, there are a variety of perspectives today on language that tie its comprehension much more closely to experience of and action in the world. For example, consider these two remarks from work in cognitive psychology: "comprehension is grounded in perceptual simulations that prepare agents for situated action" (Barsalou, 1999a, p. 77); "to a particular person, the meaning of an object, event, or sentence is what that person can do with the object, event, or sentence" (Glenberg, 1997, p. 3).

These two quotes are from work that is part of a family of related viewpoints. For want of a better name, we might call the family "situated cognition studies" (e.g., Barsalou, 1999a, 1999b; Brown, Collins, & Dugid, 1989; Clancey, 1997; Clark, 1997; Engeström, Miettinen, & Punamäki, 1999; Gee, 1992; Glenberg, 1997; Glenberg & Robertson, 1999; Hutchins, 1995; Latour, 1999; Lave, 1996; Lave & Wenger, 1991; Wenger, 1998). While there are differences among the members of the family (alternative theories about situated cognition), they share the viewpoint that meaning in language is not some abstract propositional representation that resembles a verbal language. Rather, meaning in language is tied to people's experiences of situated action in the material and social world. Furthermore, these experiences (perceptions, feelings, actions, and interactions) are stored in the mind or brain, not in terms of propositions or language but in something like dynamic images tied to perception both of the world and of our own bodies, internal states, and feelings: "Increasing evidence suggests that perceptual simulation is indeed central to comprehension" (Barsalou, 1999a, p. 74).

It is almost as if we videotape our experiences as we are having them, create a library of such videotapes, edit them to make some prototypical tapes (or set of typical instances), but stand ever ready to add new tapes to our library. We reedit the tapes based on new experiences or draw out of the library less typical tapes when the need arises. As we face new situations or new texts we run our tapes—perhaps a prototypical one, or a set of typical ones, or a set of contrasting ones, or a less typical one, whatever the case may be. We do this to apply our old experiences to our new experience and to aid us in making, editing, and storing the videotape that will capture this new experience, integrate it into our library, and allow us to make sense of it (both while we are having it and afterward).

These videotapes are what we think with and through. They are what we use to give meaning to our experiences in the world. They are what we use to give meaning to words and sentences. But they are not language or *in* language (not even in propositions). Furthermore, because they are representations of experience (including feelings, attitudes, embodied positions, and various sorts of foregrounds and backgrounds of attention), they are not just information or facts. Rather, they are value-laden, perspective-taking movies in the mind. Of course, talking about videotapes in the mind is a metaphor that, like all metaphors, is incorrect if pushed too far (see Barsalou, 1999b, for how the metaphor can be cashed out and corrected by a consideration of a more neurally realistic framework for "perception in the mind").

On this account, the meanings of words, phrases, and sentences are always situated, that is, customized to our actual contexts (Gee, 1999a). Here context means not just the words, deeds, and things that surround our words or deeds, but also our purposes, values, and intended courses of action and interaction. We bring out of our store of videotapes those that are most relevant to understanding our current context or those that allow us to create and construe that context in a certain way. We can see this in even so trivial an example as the following: If you hear "The coffee spilled, go get the mop," you run a quite different set of images (that is, assemble a quite different situated meaning) than when you hear "The coffee spilled, go get a broom."

On this account, too, the meaning of a word (the way in which we give it meaning in a particular context) is not different than the meaning of an experience, object, or tool in the world (i.e., in terms of the way in which we give the experience, object, or tool meaning):

> The meaning of the glass to you, at that particular moment, is in terms of the actions available. The meaning of the glass changes when different constraints on action are combined. For example, in a noisy room, the glass may become a mechanism for capturing attention (by tapping it with a spoon), rather than a mechanism for quenching thirst. (Glenberg, 1997, p. 41)

While Glenberg here is talking about the meaning of the glass as an object in one's specific experience of the world at a given time and place, he could just as well be talking about the meaning of the word *glass* in one's specific experience of a piece of talk or written text at a given time and place. The meaning of the word *glass* in a given piece of talk or text would be given by running a simulation (a videotape) of how the glass fits into courses of action being built up in the theater of our minds. These courses of action are based on how we understand all the other words and goings on in the world that surrounds the word *glass* as we read it: "[T]he embodied models constructed to understand language are the same as those that underlie comprehension of the natural environment" (Glenberg, 1997, p. 17).

If embodied action and social activity are crucially connected to the situated meanings oral or written language convey, then reading instruction must move well beyond relations internal to texts. Reading instruction must be rooted in the connections of texts to engagement in and simulations of actions, activities, and interactions—to real and imagined material and social worlds.

Perspective-Taking

Let me now turn to the second function of language already mentioned. Consider, in this regard, the following quote from Tomasello (1999):

> [T]he perspectivial nature of linguistic symbols, and the use of linguistic symbols in discourse interaction in which different perspectives are explicitly contrasted and shared, provide the raw material out of which the children of all cultures construct the flexible and multi-perspectival—perhaps even dialogical—cognitive representations that give human cognition much of its awesome and unique power. (p. 163)

Let's briefly unpack what this means. From the point of view of the model Tomasello was developing, the words and grammar of a human language exist to allow people to take and communicate alternative perspectives on experience (see also Hanks, 1996). That is, words and grammar exist to give people alternative ways to view one and the same state of affairs. Language is not about conveying neutral or objective information; rather, it is about communicating perspectives on experience and action in the world, often in contrast to alternative and competing perspectives: "We may then say that linguistic symbols are social conventions for inducing others to construe, or take a perspective on, some experiential situation" (Tomasello, 1999, p. 118).

Let me give some examples of what it means to say that words and grammar are not primarily about giving and getting information but are, rather, about giving and getting different perspectives on experience. I open Microsoft's website: Is it selling its products, marketing them, or underpricing them against the competition? Are products I can download from the site without paying for them free, or are they being exchanged for having bought other Microsoft products (e.g., Windows), or are there strings attached? Note also how metaphors (like "strings attached") add greatly to, and are a central part of, the perspective-taking we can do. If I use the grammatical construction "Microsoft's new operating system is loaded with bugs," I take a perspective in which Microsoft is less agentive and responsible than if I use the grammatical construction "Microsoft has loaded its new operating system with bugs."

Here is another example: Do I say that a child who is using multiple cues to give meaning to a written text (i.e., using some decoding along with picture and context cues) is reading, or do I say (as some of the pro-phonics people do) that she is not really reading, but engaged in emergent literacy? (For those latter people, the child is only really reading when she is decoding all the words in the text and not using nondecoding cues for word recognition.) In this case, contending camps actually fight over what perspective on experience the term *reading* or *really reading* ought to name. In the end, the point is that no wording is ever neutral or just "the facts." All wordings—given the very nature of language— are perspectives on experience that comport with competing perspectives in the grammar of the language and in actual social interactions.

How do children learn how words and grammar line up to express particular perspectives on experience? Here, interactive, intersubjective dialogue with more advanced peers and adults appears to be crucial. In such dialogue, children come to see, from time to time, that others have taken a different perspective on what is being talked about than they themselves have. At a certain developmental level, children have the capacity to distance themselves from their own perspectives and (internally) simulate the perspectives the other person is taking, thereby coming to see how words and grammar come to express those perspectives (in contrast to the way in which different words and grammatical constructions express competing perspectives).

Later, in other interactions, or when thinking, the child can rerun such simulations and imitate the perspective-taking the more advanced peer or adult has done by using certain sorts of words and grammar. Through such simulations and imitative learning, children learn to use the symbolic means that other persons have used to share attention with them: "In imitatively learning a linguistic symbol from other persons in this way, I internalize not only their communicative intention (their intention to get me to share their attention) but also the specific perspective they have taken" (Tomasello, 1999, p. 128).

Tomasello (1999) also pointed out—in line with my previous discussion that the world and texts are assigned meanings in the same way—that children come to use objects in the world as symbols at the same time (or with just a bit of a time lag) as they come to use linguistic symbols as perspective-taking devices on the world. Furthermore, they learn to use objects as symbols (to assign them different meanings encoding specific perspectives in different contexts) in the same way they learn to use linguistic symbols. In both cases, the child simulates in his head and later imitates in his words and deeds the perspectives his interlocutor must be taking on a given situation by using certain words and certain forms of grammar or by treating certain objects in certain ways. Thus, meaning for words, grammar, and objects comes out of intersubjective dialogue and interaction: "[H]uman symbols [are] inherently social, intersubjective, and perspectival" (Tomasello, 1999, p. 131).

If value-laden perspectives on experience are connected to the situated meanings oral or written language convey, then, once again, we have an argument that reading instruction must move well beyond relations internal to texts. Reading instruction must be rooted in the taking and imagining of diverse perspectives on real and imagined material and social worlds. The moral of both the functions of language that we have discussed is this: Our ways with words (oral or written) are of the same nature as our ways with ways of understanding and acting on the material and social world. In a quite empirical sense, the moral is one Freire (1995) taught us long ago: Reading the word and reading the world are, at a deep level, integrally connected—indeed, at a deep level, they are one and the same process.

Social Languages

The perspective taken thus far on language is misleading in one respect. It misses the core fact that any human language is not one general thing (like English), but composed of a great variety of different styles, registers, or social languages. Different patterns of vocabulary, syntax (sentence structure), and discourse connectors (devices that connect sentences together to make a whole integrated text) constitute different social languages, each of which is connected to specific sorts of social activities and to a specific socially situated identity (Gee, 1999a). We recognize different social languages by recognizing these patterns (in much the way we recognize a face through recognizing a certain characteristic patterning of facial features).

As an example, consider the following, taken from a school science textbook: "1. The destruction of a land surface by the combined effects of abrasion and removal of weathered material by transporting agents is called erosion.... The production of rock waste by mechanical processes and chemical changes is called weathering" (Martin, 1990, p. 93).

A whole bevy of grammatical design features mark these sentences as part of a distinctive social language. Some of these features are heavy subjects (e.g., "The production of rock waste by mechanical processes and chemical changes"); processes and actions named by nouns or nominalizations, rather than verbs (e.g., "production"); passive main verbs ("is called") and passives inside nominalizations (e.g., "production...by mechanical processes"); modifiers that are more "contentful" than the nouns they modify (e.g., "transporting agents"); and complex embedding (e.g., "weathered material by transporting agents" is a nominalization embedded inside "the combined effects of...," and this more complex nominalization is embedded inside a yet larger nominalization, "the destruction of...").

This style of language also incorporates a great many distinctive discourse markers, that is, linguistic features that characterize larger stretches of text and give them unity and coherence as a certain type of text or genre. For example, the genre here is explanatory definition, and it is characterized by classificatory language of a certain sort. Such language leads adept readers to form a classificatory scheme in their heads something like this: There are two kinds of change (erosion and weathering) and two kinds of weathering (mechanical and chemical).

This mapping from elements of vocabulary, syntax, and discourse to a specific style of language used in characteristic social activities is just as much a part of reading and writing as is the phonics (sound-to-letter) mapping. In fact, more people fail to become successful school-based, academic, or work-related readers or writers because of failing to master this sort of mapping than the phonics one.

There are a great many different social languages—for example, the language of medicine, literature, street gangs, sociology, law, rap, or informal dinnertime talk among friends (who belong to distinctive cultures or social groups). To know any specific social language is to know how its characteristic design features are combined to carry out one or more specific social activities. It is to know, as well, how its characteristic lexical and grammatical design features are used to enact a particular socially situated identity, that is, being, at a given time and place, a lawyer, a gang member, a politician, a literary humanist, a "bench chemist," a radical feminist, an everyday person, or whatever. To know a particular social language is either to be able to "do" a particular identity, using that social language, or to be able to recognize such an identity, when we do not want to or cannot actively participate.

Let me give two further examples of social languages at work. First, I'll use an example I've used in this journal before. It's about a young woman telling the same story to her parents and to her boyfriend (*JAAL*, February 2000; Gee, 1996). To her parents at dinner she says, "Well, when I thought about it, I don't know, it seemed to me that Gregory should be considered the most offensive character." But to her boyfriend later she says, "What an ass that guy was, you know, her boyfriend." In the first case, the young woman is taking on the identity of an educated and dutiful daughter engaged in the social activity of reporting to her parents her viewpoints on what she has learned in school. In the second case, she is taking on the identity of a girlfriend engaged in the social activity of bonding with her boyfriend.

Here is a second example from Myers (1990, p. 150): A biologist wrote in a professional science journal, "Experiments show that *Heliconius* butterflies are less likely to oviposit on host plants that possess eggs or egg-like structures." Writing about the same thing in a popular science magazine, the same biologist wrote, "*Heliconius* butterflies lay their eggs on *Passiflora* vines. In defense the vines seem to have evolved fake eggs that make it look to the butterflies as if eggs have already been laid on them." In the first case, the biologist is taking on the identity of professional scientist engaged in the social activity of making experimental and theoretical claims (note, for instance, the subject "Experiments") to professional peers. In the second case, the biologist is taking on the identity of a popularizer or scientific journalist engaged in the social activity of telling the educated public a factual story about plants and animals (note, for instance, the subjects "butterflies" and "vines").

Now here is the bite of social languages and genres: When we talk about social languages and genres, oral and written language are inextricably mixed. Some social languages are written; some are spoken. Some have both spoken and written versions; written and spoken versions are often mixed and integrated within specific social practices. Furthermore, social languages are always integrally connected to the characteristic social activities (embodied action and interaction in the world), value-laden perspectives, and socially situated identities of particular groups of people or communities of practice. If discussions about reading are not about social languages (and thus, too, about embodied action and interaction in the world, value-laden perspectives, and socially situated identities), then they are not, in reality, about reading as a semiotic meaning-making process (and it is hard to know what reading is if it is not this).

Here is another part of the bite of talk about social languages and genres. Both inside and outside school, most social languages and genres are clearly not acquired by direct instruction. While some forms of (appropriately timed) scaffolding, modeling, and instructional guidance by mentors appear to be important, immersion in meaningful practice is essential. Social languages and genres are acquired by processes of socialization, an issue to which I will turn below.

It is inevitable, I would think, that someone at this point is going to object that social languages are really about the later stages of the acquisition of literacy. It will be pointed out that the current reading debates are almost always about small children and the earlier stages of reading. What, it will be asked, has all this talk of social languages got to do with early literacy? My answer is, everything. Social languages (and their connections to action, perspectives, and identities) are no less relevant to the first stages of learning to read than they are to the later ones (and there are not so much stages here as the same things going on over time at ever-deeper and more complex levels). However, before I turn to the relevance of social languages to early childhood at the end of this article, I need to develop briefly a few more theoretical notions related to social languages.

Discourses

I said earlier that social languages are acquired by socialization. But now we must ask, socialization into what? When people learn new social languages and genres—

at the level of being able to produce them and not just consume them—they are being socialized into what I will call Discourses with a big *D* (I use discourse with a little *d* to mean just language in use, Gee, 1996, 1999a; see also Clark, 1996). Even when people learn a new social language or genre only to consume (interpret) but not produce it, they are learning to recognize a new Discourse. Related but somewhat different terms others have used to capture some of what I am trying to capture with the term *Discourses* are communities of practice (Wenger, 1998), actor–actant networks (Latour, 1987, 1991), and activity systems (Engeström et al., 1999; Leont'ev, 1978).

Discourses always involve language (i.e., they recruit specific social languages), but they always involve more than language as well. Social languages are embedded within Discourses and only have relevance and meaning within them. A Discourse integrates ways of talking, listening, writing, reading, acting, interacting, believing, valuing, and feeling (and using various objects, symbols, images, tools, and technologies) in the service of enacting meaningful socially situated identities and activities. Being-doing a certain sort of physicist, gang member, feminist, first-grade child in Ms. Smith's room, special ed (SPED) student, regular at the local bar, or gifted upper middle class child engaged in emergent literacy are all Discourses.

We can think of Discourses as identity kits. It's almost as if you get a toolkit full of specific devices (i.e., ways with words, deeds, thoughts, values, actions, interactions, objects, tools, and technologies) in terms of which you can enact a specific identity and engage in specific activities associated with that identity. For example, think of what devices (e.g., in words, deeds, clothes, objects, attitudes) you would get in a Sherlock Holmes identity kit (e.g., you do not get a "Say No to Drugs" bumper sticker in this kit; you do get both a pipe and lots of logic). The Doctor Watson identity kit is different. And we can think of the Sherlock Holmes identity kit (Discourse) and the Doctor Watson identity kit (Discourse) as themselves parts of a yet larger Discourse, the Holmes–Watson Discourse, because Watson is part of Holmes's identity kit and Holmes is part of Watson's. Discourse can be embedded one inside another.

One Discourse can mix or blend two others. For example, Gallas (1994) created a sharing-time Discourse (a way of being a recognizable sharer in her classroom) that mixed Anglo and African American styles. Discourses can be related to each other in relationships of alignment or tension. For example, Scollon and Scollon (1981) have pointed out that school-based Discourses that incorporate essayist practices and values conflict with the values, attitudes, and ways with words embedded in some Native American home and community-based Discourses (i.e., ways of being a Native American of a certain sort). These latter Discourses value communicating only when the sender knows the receiver of the communication and his or her context and do not value the sorts of fictionalizing (generalizing) of sender and receiver that essayist practices involve.

Cultural Models

Within their socialization into Discourses (and we are all socialized into a great many across our lifetimes), people acquire cultural models (D'Andrade & Strauss, 1992; Gee, 1999a; Holland & Quinn, 1987; Shore, 1996; Strauss & Quinn, 1997). Cultural models are everyday theories (i.e., story lines, images, schemas, metaphors, and models) about the world that people socialized into a given Discourse share. Cultural models tell people what is typical or normal from the perspective of a particular Discourse (or a related or aligned set of Discourses).

For example, certain types of middle class people in the United States hold a cultural model of child development that goes something like this (Harkness, Super, & Keefer, 1992): A child is born dependent on her parents and grows up by going through (often disruptive) stages toward greater and greater independence (and independence is a high value for this group of people). This cultural model plays a central role in this group's Discourse of parent–child relations (i.e., enacting and recognizing identities as parents and children).

On the other hand, certain sorts of working class families (Philipsen, 1975) hold a cultural model of child development that goes something like this: A child is born unsocialized and with tendencies to be selfish. The child needs discipline from the home to learn to be a cooperative social member of the family (a high value of this group of people). This cultural model plays a central role in this group's Discourse of parent–child relations.

These different cultural models, connected to different (partially) class-based Discourses of parenting, are not true or false. Rather, they focus on different aspects of childhood and development. Cultural models define for people in a Discourse what counts as normal and natural and what counts as inappropriate and deviant. They are, of course, thereby thoroughly value laden.

Cultural models come out of and, in turn, inform the social practices in which people in a Discourse engage. Cultural models are stored in people's minds (by no means always consciously), though they are supplemented and instantiated in the objects, texts, and practices that are part and parcel of the Discourse. For example, many guidebooks supplement and instantiate the above middle class cultural model of childhood and stages. On the other hand, many religious materials supplement and instantiate the above working-class model of childhood.

Figure 1 summarizes the discussion so far, defining all the theoretical tools and showing how they are all related to one another.

Early Literacy as Socioculturally Situated Practice

I turn now to a specific example involving early literacy from my own research. I do this both to give a more extended example of the perspective I have developed so far and to show the relevance of this perspective to early childhood and the earliest stages of the acquisition of literacy. The event is this: An upper middle class, highly educated father approaches his 3-year-old (3:10) son, who is sitting at the kitchen table. The child is using an activity book in which each page contains a picture with a missing piece. A question is printed under the picture. The child uses a "magic pen" to rub the missing piece and "magically" uncovers the rest of the picture. The part of the picture that is uncovered is an image that constitutes the answer to the question at the bottom of the page, though, of course, the child must put this answer into words.

In the specific case I want to discuss here, the overt part of the picture was the top half of the bodies of Donald and Daisy Duck. The question printed at the bottom of the page was "In what are Donald and Daisy riding?" (Note the social language in which this question is written. It is not the more vernacular form: "What are Donald and Daisy riding in?") The child used his pen to uncover an old-fashioned Model T sort of car with an open top. Donald and Daisy turn out to be sitting in the car.

The father, seeing the child engaged in this activity, asks him, after he has uncovered the car, to read the question printed below the picture. Notice that the father has not asked the child to give the answer to the question, which is a different activity. The father is confident the child can answer the question and has a different purpose here. It is to engage in an indirect reading lesson, though one of a special and specific sort.

The father is aware that the child, while he knows the names of the letters of the alphabet and can recognize many of them in words, cannot decode print.

He is also aware that the child has on several previous occasions, in the midst of various literacy-related activities, said that he is "learning to read." However, in yet other activities, at other times, the child has said that he "cannot read" and thereafter seemed more reluctant to engage in his otherwise proactive stance toward texts. This has concerned the father, who values the child's active engagement with texts and the child's belief, expressed in some contexts and not others, that he is not just learning to read, but is in fact "a reader."

We might say that the father is operating with a however tacit theory (cultural model) that a child's assuming a certain identity ("I am a reader") facilitates the acquisition of that identity and its concomitant skills. I believe this sort of model is fairly common in certain sorts of families. Parents co-construct an identity with a child (attribute, and get the child to believe in, a certain competence) before the child can actually fully carry out all the skills associated with this identity (competence before performance).

So, the father has asked the child to read the printed question below the picture of Donald and Daisy Duck sitting in the newly uncovered car. Below, I give the printed version of the question and what the child offered as his "reading" of the question:

Printed version: In what are Donald and Daisy riding?

Child's reading: What is Donald and Daisy riding on?

After the child uttered the above sentence, he said, "See, I told you I was learning to read." He seems to be well aware of the father's purposes. The child, the father, the words, and the book are all here in sync to pull off a specific practice, and this is a form of instruction, but it's a form that is typical of what goes on inside socialization processes.

The father and son have taken an activity that is for the child now a virtual genre—namely, uncovering a piece of a picture and on the basis of it answering a question—and incorporated it into a different metalevel activity. That is, the father and son use the original activity not in and for itself but as a platform with which to discuss reading or, perhaps better put, to co-construct a cultural model of what reading is. The father's question and the son's final response ("See, I told you I was learning to read") clearly indicate that they are seeking to demonstrate to and for each other that the child can read.

Figure 2, which will inform my discussion that follows, (partially) analyzes this event in terms of the theoretical notions we have developed above.

From a developmental point of view, then, what is going on here? Nothing so general as acquiring literacy. Rather, something much more specific is going on. First, the child is acquiring, amidst immersion and adult guidance, a piece of a particular type of social language. The question he has to form—and he very well knows this—has to be a classificatory question. It cannot be, for instance, a

FIGURE 2
Partial Analysis of a Literacy Event

Text	=	Written:	In what are Donald and Daisy riding?
		Read:	What is Donald and Daisy riding on?
		Remark:	See, I told you I was learning to read.
Social language	=	Classificatory question	
Genre	=	Uncover the piece of the picture, form a classificatory question to which the picture is an answer, and give the answer	
Cultural model	=	Reading is the proactive production of appropriate styles of language (e.g., here a classificatory question) and their concomitant meanings in conjunction with print	
Discourse (identity)	=	Emergent reader of a certain type (filtering school-aligned practice into primary Discourse)	

narrative-based question (e.g., something like "What are Donald and Daisy doing?" or "Where are Donald and Daisy going?"). Classificatory questions (and related syntactic and discourse resources) are a common part of many school-based (and academic) social languages, especially those associated with non-literary content areas (e.g., the sciences).

The acquisition of this piece of a social language is, in this case, scaffolded by a genre the child has acquired, namely to uncover the piece of the picture, form a classificatory question to which the picture is an answer (when the parent isn't there to read the question for the child), and give the answer. This genre bears a good deal of similarity to a number of different nonnarrative language and action genres (routines) used in the early years of school.

Finally, in regard to social languages, note that the child's question is uttered in a more vernacular style than the printed question. So syntactically it is, in one sense, in the wrong style. However, from a discourse perspective (in terms of the function its syntax carries out), it is in just the right style (i.e., it is a classificatory question). It is a mainstay of child language development that the acquisition of a function often precedes acquisition of a fully correct form (in the sense of contextually appropriate, not necessarily in the sense of grammatically correct).

In addition to acquiring a specific piece of certain sorts of social languages, the child is also, as part and parcel of the activity, acquiring different cultural models. One of these is a cultural model about what reading is. The model is something like this: Reading is not primarily letter-by-letter decoding but the proactive production of appropriate styles of language (e.g., here a classificatory question) and their concomitant meanings in conjunction with print. This is a model that the father (at some level quite consciously) wants the child to adopt, both to sustain the child's interest in becoming a reader and to counteract the child's claims, in other contexts, that he can't read. Of course, the child's claim that he can't read in those other contexts reflects that, in other activities, he is acquiring a different cultural model of reading, namely one something like this: Reading is primarily the ability to decode letters and words, and one is not a reader if meaning is not primarily driven from decoding print. As his socialization proceeds, the child will acquire yet other cultural models of reading (or extend and deepen ones already acquired).

The genres, social languages, and cultural models present in this interaction between father and son existed, of course, in conjunction with ways of thinking, valuing, feeling, acting, and interacting and in conjunction with various mediating objects (e.g., the book and the "magic pen"), images (the pictures of Donald, Daisy, and the car), sites (kitchen table), and times (morning as father was about to go to work). In and through the social practices that recruit these genres, social language, and cultural models, the 3-year-old is acquiring a Discourse. The father and the child are co-constructing the child as a reader (and, indeed, a person) of a particular type, that is, one who takes reading to be the proactive production of appropriate styles of language and meanings in conjunction with print. This socially situated identity involves a self-orientation as active producer (not just consumer) of appropriate meanings in conjunction with print—meanings that, in this case, turn out to be school and academically related.

However, this Discourse is not unrelated to other Discourses the child is or will be acquiring. I have repeatedly pointed out how the social language, genre, and cultural models involved in this social practice are in full alignment with some of the social languages, genres, cultural models, and social practices the child will confront in the early years of school (here construing schooling in fairly traditional terms).

At the same time, this engagement between father and child, beyond being a moment in the production of the Discourse of a certain type of reader, is also a moment in the child's acquisition of what I call his primary Discourse. The child's primary Discourse is the ways with words, objects, and deeds that are associated with his primary sense of self formed in and through his (most certainly class-based) primary socialization within the family (or other culturally relevant primary socializing group) as a "person like us." In this case, the child is learning that "people like us" are "readers like this."

Now consider what it means that the child's acquisition of the reader Discourse (being-doing a certain type of reader) is simultaneously aligned with (traditional) school-based Discourses and part of his acquisition of his primary Discourse. This ties school-related values, attitudes, and ways with words, at a specific and not some general level, to his primary sense of self and belonging. This will almost certainly affect how the child reacts to, and resonates with, school-based ways with words and things.

Reading and Early Language Abilities

Many of the recent reading reports (e.g., see Gee, 1999b; National Institute of Child Health and Human Development, 2000; Snow, Burns, & Griffin, 1998) have stressed that there is significant correlation between early phonological awareness and later success in learning to read and, thus, called for early phonemic awareness training in schools and early sustained and overt instruction on phonics. However, some of these reports are aware that a good many other things, besides early phonological awareness, correlate with successfully learning to read in the early years of school. It turns out, for instance, that the correlation between early language abilities and later success in reading is just as large as, if not larger than, the correlation between early phonological awareness and success in reading. Indeed, as one might suspect, early language abilities and early phonological awareness are themselves correlated (Snow et al., 1998):

> [P]erformance on phonological awareness tasks by preschoolers was highly correlated with general language ability. Moreover it was measures of semantic and syntactic skills, rather than speech discrimination and articulation, that predicted phonological awareness differences. (p. 53)

> What is most striking about the results of the preceding studies is the power of early preschool language to predict reading three to five years later. (pp. 107–108)

> On average, phonological awareness ($r = 46$) has been about as strong a predictor of future reading as memory for sentences and stories, confrontation naming, and general language measures. (p. 112)

So what are these early language abilities that seem so important for later success in school? According to the National Research Council's report (Snow et al., 1998), they are things like vocabulary—receptive vocabulary, but more especially expressive vocabulary—the ability to recall and comprehend sentences and stories, and the ability to engage in verbal interactions. Furthermore, I think that research has made it fairly clear what causes such verbal abilities. What appears to cause enhanced school-based verbal abilities are family, community, and school language environments in which children interact intensively with adults and more advanced peers and experience cognitively challenging talk and texts on sustained topics and in different genres of oral and written language.

However, the correlation between language abilities and success in learning to read (and in school generally) hides an important reality. Almost all children—including poor children—have impressive language abilities. The vast majority of children enter school with large vocabularies, complex grammar, and deep understandings of experiences and stories. It has been decades since anyone believed that poor and minority children entered school with "no language" (Gee, 1996; Labov, 1972).

The verbal abilities that children who fail in school lack are not just some general set of such abilities, but rather specific verbal abilities tied to specific school-based practices and school-based genres of oral and written language of just the sort I looked at in the earlier example of the 3-year-old making up a classificatory question. This 3-year-old will have been exposed to a great number of such specific, but quite diverse, practices, each offering protoforms of later school-based and academic social languages and genres. These protoforms, always embedded in specific social practices connected to specific socially situated identities (and useless when not so embedded), are the stuff from which success in school-based and academic reading flows. These are the sorts of protoforms that must be delivered to all children—amidst ample practice within socialization in specific Discourses—if we are to have true access and equity for all children.

References

Barsalou, L.W. (1999a). Language comprehension: Archival memory or preparation for situated action. *Discourse Processes, 28,* 61–80.

Barsalou, L.W. (1999b). Perceptual symbol systems. *Behavioral and Brain Sciences, 22,* 577–660.

Brown, A.L., Collins, A., & Dugid, P. (1989). Situated cognition and the culture of learning. *Educational Researcher, 18,* 32–42.

Clancey, W.J. (1997). *Situated cognition: On human knowledge and computer representations.* Cambridge, UK: Cambridge University Press.

Clark, A. (1997). *Being there: Putting brain, body, and world together again.* Cambridge, MA: MIT Press.

Clark, H.H. (1996). *Using language.* Cambridge, UK: Cambridge University Press.

D'Andrade, R., & Strauss, C. (Eds.). (1992). *Human motives and cultural models.* Cambridge, UK: Cambridge University Press.

Engeström, Y., Miettinen, R., & Punamaki, R. (Eds.). (1999). *Perspectives on activity theory.* Cambridge, UK: Cambridge University Press.

Freire, P. (1995). *The pedagogy of the oppressed.* New York: Continuum.

Gallas, K. (1994). *The languages of learning: How children talk, write, dance, draw, and sing their understanding of the world.* New York: Teachers College Press.

Gee, J.P. (1992). *The social mind: Language, ideology, and social practice.* New York: Bergin & Garvey.

Gee, J.P. (1996). *Social linguistics and literacies: Ideology in Discourses* (2nd ed.). London: Taylor & Francis.

Gee, J.P. (1999a). *An introduction to discourse analysis: Theory and method.* London: Routledge.

Gee, J.P. (1999b). Reading and the New Literacy Studies: Reframing the National Academy of Sciences report on reading. *Journal of Literacy Research, 31,* 355–374.

Glenberg, A.M. (1997). What is memory for? *Behavioral and Brain Sciences, 20,* 1–55.

Glenberg, A.M., & Robertson, D.A. (1999). Indexical understanding of instructions. *Discourse Processes, 28,* 1–26.

Halliday, M.A.K. (1994). *Functional grammar* (2nd ed.). London: Edward Arnold.

Hanks, W.F. (1996). *Language and communicative practices.* Boulder, CO: Westview.

Harkness, S., Super, C., & Keefer, C.H. (1992). Learning to be an American parent: How cultural models gain directive force. In R. D'Andrade & C. Strauss (Eds.), *Human motives and cultural models* (pp. 163–178). Cambridge, UK: Cambridge University Press.

Holland, D., & Quinn, N. (Eds.). (1987). *Cultural models in language and thought.* Cambridge, UK: Cambridge University Press.

Hutchins, E. (1995). *Cognition in the wild.* Cambridge, MA: MIT Press.

Labov, W. (1972). *Language in the inner city.* Philadelphia: University of Pennsylvania Press.

Latour, B. (1987). *Science in action.* Cambridge, MA: Harvard University Press.

Latour, B. (1991). *We have never been modern.* Cambridge, MA: Harvard University Press.

Latour, B. (1999). *Pandora's hope: Essays on the reality of science studies.* Cambridge, MA: Harvard University Press.

Lave, J. (1996). Teaching, as learning, in practice. *Mind, Culture, and Activity, 3,* 149–164.

Lave, J., & Wenger, E. (1991). *Situated learning: Legitimate peripheral participation.* New York: Cambridge University Press.

Leont'ev, A.N. (1978). *Activity, consciousness, and personality.* Englewood Cliffs, NJ: Prentice-Hall.

Martin, J.R. (1990). Literacy in science: Learning to handle text as technology. In F. Christe (Ed.), *Literacy for a changing world* (pp. 79–117). Melbourne, NSW, Australia: Australian Council for Educational Research.

Myers, G. (1990). *Writing biology: Texts in the social construction of scientific knowledge.* Madison: University of Wisconsin Press.

National Institute of Child Health and Human Development. (2000). *Report of the National Reading Panel. Teaching children to read: An evidence-based assessment of the scientific research literature on reading and its implications for reading instruction* (NIH Publication No. 00-4769). Washington, DC: U.S. Government Printing Office. Available: www.nationalreadingpanel.org

Philipsen, G. (1975). Speaking "like a man" in Teamsterville: Culture patterns of role enactment in an urban neighborhood. *Quarterly Journal of Speech, 61,* 26–39.

Scollon, R., & Scollon, S.W. (1981). *Narrative, literacy, and face in interethnic communication.* Norwood, NJ: Ablex.

Shore, B. (1996). *Culture in mind: Cognition, culture, and the problem of meaning.* New York: Oxford University Press.

Snow, C.E., Burns, M.S., & Griffin, P. (Eds.). (1998). *Preventing reading difficulties in young children.* Washington, DC: National Academy Press.

Strauss, C., & Quinn, N. (1997). *A cognitive theory of cultural meaning.* Cambridge, UK: Cambridge University Press.

Tomasello, M. (1999). *The cultural origins of human cognition.* Cambridge, MA: Harvard University Press.

Wenger, E. (1998). *Communities of practice: Learning, meaning, and identity.* Cambridge, UK: Cambridge University Press.

5

The Place of Dialogue in Children's Construction of Meaning

M.A.K. Halliday

Meaning as a Social Phenomenon

Much of the discussion of children's language development in the last quarter of a century, especially in educational contexts, has been permeated by a particular ideological construction of childhood. This view combines individualism, romanticism, and what Martin calls "childism": the Disneyfied vision of a child that is constructed in the media and in certain kinds of "kiddie lit."[1] Each child is presented as a freestanding autonomous being, and learning consists in releasing and bringing into flower the latent awareness that is already there in the bud. This is the view that was embodied in the "creativity" and "personal growth" models of education by James Britton, John Dixon, and David Holbrook in Great Britain; and more recently, from another standpoint, in the United States in Donald Graves's conception of children's writing as a process and of their text as property to be individually owned.[2] It has been supported theoretically first by Chomskyan innatism and later by cognitive science models that interpret learning as the acquisition of ready-made information by some kind of independent processing device (cf. Kintsch, 1988).

What these various discourses have in common is that they are all essentially antisocial—or perhaps "asocial," to be more accurate. In this they contrast with interpretations of development and learning that would make reference to Vygotsky, to Bernstein, and, in linguistics, to the functional, social-semantic tradition that derives from European scholarship, especially the Prague and London schools, from glossematics, and from the American anthropological linguists.[3] In this view, meaning is a social and cultural phenomenon and all construction of meaning is a social process. We can use the term *intersubjective* for it provided we do not take this to imply that the "subject" comes into existence first and then proceeds to interact with other subjects. There is no subject until construed by social meaning-making practices (see Thibault, 1990).

Developmental Stages

In studying child language development some 20 years ago I was struck by how clearly this social-semantic perspective stands out once you observe how children begin to communicate—especially if you observe it from birth and in a natural form, without eliciting or experimenting and without using too many technical aids. These practices tend to obscure the social nature of semiotic development, whereas the traditional diary method of child language studies brings it out. In this context, some fairly clearly defined developmental stages seemed to me to emerge:[4]

1. presymbolic ("primary intersubjectivity"), typically birth to 0;5

1 to 2. transition stage, typically 0;5 to 0;8

2. symbolic—protolinguistic ("secondary intersubjectivity"), typically 0;8 to 1;4

2 to 3. transition stage, typically 1;4 to 2;0

3. symbolic—linguistic, typically 2;0 and on

Because I was focusing specifically on the development of language, I concentrated on the last three, referring to them as "phases":

2. symbolic—protolinguistic = Phase 1, "protolanguage"

2 to 3. transition = Phase II, "transition"

3. symbolic—linguistic = Phase III, "language"

Since then detailed studies of early language development have been carried out in comparable terms, based on intensive observation of children in their homes, by Clare Painter and by Jane Oldenburg; and Qiu Shijin has observed a population of Chinese children living in Shanghai, over a short period but covering different ages within the range. All have used the same theoretical framework for their interpretations (see Oldenburg, 1990; Painter, 1984; Qiu, 1985).

From the beginning of life a child's acts of meaning are joint constructions, dialogically enacted between himself and some "significant other" by reference to whom he is achieving a personal identity. Colwyn Trevarthen documented this process for the presymbolic stage many years ago when he showed that a newborn infant within 2 or 3 weeks of birth takes part in exchanging attention.[5] This exchange of attention is the beginning of language. It has no "content" in the adult sense, but it has meaning. For the child, the meaning is "we are together and in communication; there is a 'you'—and a 'me.'" "You" and "me" are, of course, mutually defining; neither can exist without the other. I shall not dwell on this stage here, but I have found it fascinating to take part in, and have been amazed by, the semogenic potential of these early microencounters. They are not entirely without content, as a matter of fact, but there is as yet no *systematic* construing of experience.

When the child begins to control his material environment, typically at about 4 to 5 months, he begins the transition to *systematic* symbolic construction. He can reach out and grasp an object that is in view; this coincides with his first *symbolic* encounter with the environment, which takes the form of an act of meaning that is something like "that's interesting!—what is it?" This introduces a "third person" into the protoconversation alongside the "you" and the "me." The act itself may take any accessible form (my own subject Nigel produced a high-pitched squeak)—anything that can engage the child and the other in shared attention to some third party. This third party, which is construed as "neither you nor me," is typically not, in fact, an object but a happening—a commotion of some kind like a sudden noise or a bright light coming into the child's attention. But the act of meaning is clearly *addressed*; the meaning is jointly constructed, and the material phenomenon is construed as experience only through the shared act of exchanging a symbol. The mother, of course, or whoever is sharing in the act, responds in her own tongue; she says, "Yes, those were pigeons," or "That's a bus," or "See, they've put the lights on." But the semogenic process is dialogic, in two distinct respects: on the one hand *interpersonally*, in that the two acts define each other as question and answer, and on the other hand *experientially*, in that some kind of perturbation in the environment is construed dialogically as a phenomenon of experience. In other words, it is through language that this "third party" acquires the status of reality.

The child is also at the same time construing his own body; the first *symbolic* construction of self versus environment coincides more or less with the first construction of this same opposition in *material* terms. What is "out there" is what can be grasped, "grasping" being both a material process and a process of consciousness. But it has to be actively explored on both these planes, and the transition to the systematic symbolic stage, that of the protolanguage, takes place only after the child has learned that he can detach himself from the material environment (by rolling over). This protolanguage phase, that of "secondary intersubjectivity," is then reached, typically at somewhere between 7 and 10 months of age, through a change in both forms of his dialogue with the environment. On the one hand, in his *bodily* engagement the child learns to propel himself from one place to another by some form of crawling. He now has the freedom of space-time; and at the same time he achieves the semiotic freedom of construing meanings into systems—that is, on both planes he achieves paradigmatic choice. This choice of meaning is the essential characteristic of protolanguage.

Protolanguage is the form of language that we humans share with what we think of as the "higher" mammals: mainly primates and cetaceans, but it also appears in our two most favored pets, cats and dogs, at least when they interact with us. All these are, of course, different languages, but all have the same formal structure, as systems of simple signs. In the process of his symbolic activity, the child construes meaning into *systems*, and the systems are functional in different contexts—I referred to these as "microfunctions" in my analysis. The process is, of course, dialogic; the others share in construing the meaning potential. In this protolinguistic phase we can see clearly how meaning is created at the point of impact of the material and the conscious, in the dialectic engagement between these two domains of experience. Consider a typical protolinguistic dialogue such as the following:

> [Mother is holding child in her lap, throwing his toy rabbit in the air and catching it. The child is watching attentively.]
>
> Child: [ə̃ə̃]
>
> Mother: There he goes!
>
> Child: [ə̃ə̃ə̃]
>
> Mother: Oh, you want me to throw him up again, do you? All right. There he goes!
>
> Child: [loudly] [m̃n̂g]
>
> Mother: No, that's enough. Let's find something else to do.

Here the material processes taking place in space-time (the mother throwing up the rabbit and catching it) impact on the conscious processes whereby both parties are attending, with shared positive affect, both to the other and to the third party, the rabbit-commotion. It is the interpenetration of these two that generates a *meaning*, such as "that's fun; I want you to do it again," and also a contrasting meaning of "I *insist* that you do it again!" These evolve dialogically as part of a shared *system* of meanings in different microcontexts, which includes others such as "I want/don't want that object," "let's be (you and me) together/let's attend to this (third party) together," "I like/am curious about that," and so on.

It is in protolanguage, then, that the activity of *meaning* comes to be construed in the form of a system, such that there is an ongoing dialectic relationship between the *system* and the *instance*. The system is the potential for generating instances, and by the same token each new instance perturbs the system.[6] The system is a dynamic open system, metastable in character, that persists only through constantly changing in interaction with its environment, because the material conditions that engender it are never totally identical. (We may note that this impacting of the conscious with the material takes place at both "ends" of the symbolic process, the semantic and the phonetic, so that the system is evolving at both these interfaces, both in the construction of content and in the construction of expression. In the latter, the material conditions are those of the child's own body, his physiological potential—which also, of course, is constantly changing.)

The second major transition is that from protolanguage into language—into the distinctively human semiotic that is not, as far as we know, shared by other species. In the course of this transition the resource for making meaning is further transformed, this time into a system of another, significantly different kind. In the context of overall development, while protolanguage goes with crawling, language goes with walking, and both these activities are carried out by specialized organs—mouth and legs—leaving arms and hands free for other purposes. But the criterial, and critical, difference between protolanguage and language is that language is *stratified*; that is, it has a *grammar*. A grammar (strictly, "lexicogrammar"—syntax, vocabulary, morphology if any) is a purely symbolic system that is introduced "in between" the content and the expression; that is, it is a distinct level of semiotic organization located between the two material interfaces. Unlike a protolanguage, a language cannot be described as a system of signs; it is a system based on the more complex principle of *realization*, which cannot be reduced to pairs of *signifiant/signifié*. The grammar thus does not interface directly with either material environment. But at the same time it is not neutral between the two; it is biased toward the content plane. The grammar is a "natural" grammar which has evolved as the primary means for construing experience and enacting social processes—still, of course, in dialogic contexts.

Only a system that is stratified in this way can construe meaning in the form of "information"—as a specifically linguistic commodity that can be *exchanged*, on the model of the exchange of goods and services that evolves with protolanguage. Without a grammar there can be no information. Once a grammar has evolved, I can tell you things and we can argue about them. The critical final step leading to the joint construction of information is the complex one of *arguing about*: the combination of mood with transitivity, in grammatical terms. But the child cannot reach this point in one giant leap. Let us try to enumerate the main steps in his progress.

Dialogic Construction of Meaning

It seems that children have a favorite strategy for achieving the transition from child tongue to mother tongue. It may be universal, or some aspects of it may be, and it may well have been the course taken by language in its evolution. The grammar makes it possible to construe experience, through the system of transitivity and its lexical counterpart in naming.[7] But at the same time, because the grammar is a purely abstract system at one remove from the material interfaces it also makes it possible simultaneously to construe two contrasting dialogic modes (when they become grammaticalized we know them as "moods"): the imperative, or "pragmatic" mode, meaning "this is how things *should* be; you bring them about!" and the declarative, or "mathetic" mode, meaning "this is how things *are*; you can check whether you agree." Early examples of pragmatic utterances from my records were

1. water ón (turn the water on!), squeeze órange (squeeze an orange!)
   get dówn (I want to get down!), play tráin (let's play with the train!)

All had rising tone and demanded a response. Contrast these with mathetic utterances such as the following, all on a falling tone:

2. big bàll (that's a big ball), new rècord (here's a new record)
   red sweàter (I've got my red sweater), two hàmmer (I'm holding two hammers)

These were from 1;7. A later example (1;9) shows the two modes in syntagmatic sequence:

3. no room walk on wàll...walk on óther wall (there's no room to walk on [this] wall; I want to walk on the other wall!)

The three English-speaking children who were recorded intensively by natural language diaries all made this distinction systematically as the primary semantic option in the protolanguage-language transition. All three expressed it prosodically, by intonation and/or voice quality, and in all three the pragmatic was the marked option. The Chinese-speaking children also made it and also expressed it prosodically; however, there were not enough data to establish the markedness pattern.[8]

The pragmatic is a demand for goods and services; it seeks a response, in the form of action, and the "others" involved in the dialogue recognize and construe it as such (unconsciously, of course). That does not mean that they always accede to the request; but they show that they have gotten the message, and in that respect "no" is as effective as "yes." Gradually, during the course of the transition, the pragmatic evolves into a demand for information; thus ontogenetically (and perhaps also phylogenetically) the interrogative, although in the adult grammar it pairs with the declarative, is derived by splitting off from the imperative—a demand for action becomes a demand for verbal action. The mathetic, on the other hand, does not demand any action. What it does do is invite confirmation: "Yes, that's a big ball," "It's not a big ball; it's a little ball," "It's not a ball; it's a melon," and so on. And here an important question arises: What is the essential condition for entering into a dialogue of this kind, in which one interactant corroborates, or disputes, what the other one has just said? It is that the experience must have been *shared*. You cannot corroborate or dispute what happened unless you also were there to see it.

Thus the basic form of information is *turning shared experience into meaning*: that is, telling someone something that they already know. I can construe an experience semiotically, and offer the construction to you, provided I know that you have shared the experience; and you then share in construing it. Thus the construction is again dialogic: Meaning is created by the impact between a material phenomenon and the shared processes of consciousness of those who participated in it.

Every parent is familiar with the situation in which his or her child is asked to give information to someone about an experience that person has not shared, and the child is unable to do it. Mother has taken the child to the zoo; when she comes home she says, "Tell Daddy what you saw at the zoo today." Daddy is attending, but the child cannot oblige—either he remains silent, or he turns back to Mummy and tells her. Why? Because she was the one with whom he shared the experience. How can he tell Daddy about it, when Daddy wasn't there?

Conversation, then, evolves as the joint construal of shared experience, whereby phenomena that are accessible to the consciousness of both parties—things both can see, events both have experienced—are turned dialogically into meanings. This is how conversation begins and how it continues for a child until he is well on the way from protolanguage to mother tongue. No doubt conversation continued in that way for many generations in the history of the human species, before its further potential was taken up. But the potential is there once the *system* of meaning-making is in place; this is what enables the listener to construe phenomena that only the speaker has actually witnessed. And in the course of time each child makes this same discovery: that language can *create* information—it can take the place of shared experience. It is not necessary for the listener to have been there and seen the thing too; the experience can be *reconstrued* out of the language. This is such a major discovery that Nigel, at least, consistently used a different grammar for the two situations: He had one form for "I'm telling you something we shared," which was his original context for giving information, and another form for "I'm telling you something that happened, even though you weren't there to see it." This grammatical distinction is not made in the adult language, so after a few months Nigel gave it up. We do not distinguish between telling people what (we think) they know and telling them what (we think) they don't know; the declarative covers both. But at the same time, we do not stop using language in the earlier way. In communication models the concept of information is usually taken to imply that knowledge is being transmitted from a knower to a nonknower: "I know something that you don't know; I 'mean' it, and as a result you now know it." Where this happens, language is operating as a surrogate for shared experience—a way of sharing semiotically what has not been shared materially. Prototypically this is monologic, because only the knower takes part in transforming it into meaning. But it is mainly in rather specialized uses of language, like an academic lecture, that information is constructed and imparted in this monologic way. Most of the time when we are in the indicative mood we are construing meanings interactively on the basis of shared experience. The prototypical form of this process is the dialogic one, in which the construction proceeds by argument. Arguing is the shared construction of experiential meaning; it occupies the space from consensus to conflict, and interactants will typically move between the two as they extend their dialogue into conversation.[9]

In *Learning How to Mean* I give an example of the joint construction of *narrative* in a dialogue between Nigel and his parents when Nigel was 1;8. Nigel had been taken to the zoo and had picked up a lid from a plastic cup that he was clutching in one hand while stroking a goat with the other hand. The goat started to eat the lid; the keeper intervened, saying that the goat shouldn't eat the lid— it wasn't good for it. Some hours later, back home, Nigel recalled the incident:

Nigel: try eat lìd

Father: What tried to eat the lid?

Nigel: [repeating] try eat lìd

Father: What tried to eat the lid?

Nigel: goàt...man said nò...goat try eat lìd...man said nò

A few hours later again Nigel returned to the story, this time with his mother:

Nigel: goat try eat lìd...man said nò

Mother: Why did the man say no?

Nigel: goat shòuldn't eat lid...[shaking his head] goòdfor it

Mother: The goat shouldn't eat the lid; it's not good for it.

Nigel: goat try eat lìd...man said nò...goat shòuldn't eat lid...[shaking head] goòdfor it

We tend to think of narrative and dialogue as opposed forms of discourse, but this type of text suggests that in its early development narrative itself is dialogic. The material experience had been shared between child and parents; the child then takes the initiative in verbalizing it so that it becomes part of a shared construction of reality. The parents join in, their turns taking the form of questions, but these are not simply interpersonal prompts—because they are *wh*-type questions, they contain experiential information: "What tried to eat the lid?" says, "There was a doer [grammatically, an actor]; you identify it"; "Why did the man say no?" says, "There was a reason [grammatically, some expression of cause]; you identify it." Thus there is joint participation in the construing of this experience.

We may compare this with the sequence of texts shown in the figure below, taken from the record of conversations over a period of about eight months, when Nigel was between 2;10 and 3;6. These are not narratives of events, but rather the ongoing construction of a general concept, in this case that of "cats." The child is older now, and in these instances he is asking the questions; many of these are yes/no questions, but there are also *wh*-type questions of "how?" and "why?" In both types, of course, the child is also *contributing* information:

"Do cats like meat/bones/marrow?"—constructing and testing out a taxonomy of potential foods.

"How do the cat's claws come out?"—they come out and go in again.

"Does it go with [i.e., walk on] its claws?"—they come out and go in in different contexts and functions.

The Construction of "Cats" (Nigel From 2;10 to 3;6)

Text A1: Nigel at 2;10;22

Nigel: And you [that is, "I"] saw a cat in Chania Falls.
Mother: Yes, you saw a cat in Chania Falls.
Nigel: And you picked the cat up. Mummy, do cats like meat?
Mother: Yes, they do.
Nigel: Do cats like bones? Do cats like marrow?

Text A2: Nigel at 2;10;26

Nigel: Can I stroke the cat? You ["I"] want to stroke the cat...you want to scratch it...it's drinking its milk...it's moving its tail out...it's moving its tail outside...it's scratching...it's putting its tail up...what's this?
Mother: I don't know; I suppose it's its elbow.
Nigel: It's waggling its tail...it's lapping it with its tongue...you can go near its elbow...you *can* go near its elbow...but you can't go too near its face...because it thinks you might take away its milk...it was just a bit frightened...it thought that you might take away its milk...has it finished its milk?

Text A3: Nigel at 2;11;5

Nigel: [thinking about "The House That Jack Built"] What is a rat?
Father: It's a sort of big mouse.
Nigel: Does the rat go when the cat has killed it?
Father: No, it doesn't go any more then.
Nigel: Why did the cat kill the rat?
Father: Cats do kill rats.
Nigel: Why do they?
Father: [formula] You'll have to wait to understand that till you're a bit bigger.
Nigel: No, I can understand it now.
Father: Well, cats just like to eat rats and mice.
Nigel: Why do they like to eat them?
Father: They just do.

(continued)

Text A4: Nigel at 2;11;15

Nigel: Why did the cat go out? Mummy, why did the cat go out?
Mother: It gets fed up, having its tail squashed.

Text A5: Nigel at 3;0;26

Nigel: How do the cat's claws come out?
Father: They come out from inside its paws. Look, I'll show you.
Nigel: Does it go with its claws?
Father: Not if it's going along the ground.
Nigel: And not if it's climbing up a tree.
Father: Yes, if it's climbing up a tree it does go with its claws.

Text A6: Nigel at 3;2;7

Nigel: Will the cat eat the grape?
Father: I don't think so. Cats like things that go, not things that grow.

Text A7: Nigel at 3;5;12

Nigel: Cats have no else to stop you from trossing them...cats have no other way to stop children
          from hitting them...so they bite. Cat, don't go away! When I come back I'll tell you a story. [He
          does so.]

Text A8: Nigel at 3;6;12

Nigel: Can I give the cat some artichoke?
Mother: Well, she won't like it.
Nigel: Cats like things that go; they don't like things that grow.

Text A9: Nigel at 3;6;14

Nigel: I wish I was a puppet so that I could go out into the snow in the night. Do puppets like going
          out into the snow?
Father: I don't know. I don't think they mind.
Nigel: Do cats like going out in the snow?
Father: Cats don't like snow.
Nigel: Do they die? [He knows that some plants do.]
Father: No, they don't die; they just don't like it.
Nigel: Why don't puppets mind snow?
Father: Well [hesitating]...puppets aren't people.
Nigel: Yes, but...cats also aren't people.
Father: No, but cats are alive; they go. Puppets don't go.
Nigel: Puppets do go.
Father: Yes, but you have to make them go; like trains.
Nigel: Trains have wheels. Puppets have legs.
Father: Yes, they have legs; but the legs don't go all by themselves. You have to make them go.

From M.A.K. Halliday (1984b)

But the conversations achieve much more than that. Experientially, for example, the dialogue constructs the general taxonomy of plants and animals ("things that grow" versus "things that go"); compare the complex argument around a four-way distinction of cats, puppets, people, and trains at 3;6. Interpersonally, it evolves into a dynamic modeling of question, answer, challenge, contradiction, and the like that is the essential component of the resources out of which all conversation is constructed.

I have given various examples elsewhere from my own records (cf. Halliday, 1978); many more will be found in the writings of Oldenburg and Painter, as well as throughout the now extensive literature on child language (but note that very little of this takes any account of protolanguage). It is instructive both to examine single instances and to track conversational motifs through time, as in the cat extracts just cited. For example, in wondering how Nigel had construed his experience of time and space I was able to put together conversational fragments extending over several years, while Joy Phillips, from intensive study of the earlier data, showed how he had developed the fundamental semantic strategies of comparison and contrast. And the extraordinarily rich body of natural conversation between mothers and their children of 3;6 to 4;0 that Ruqaiya Hasan has assembled, which is reported on briefly in her paper given at the conference "Analisi del Dialogo," Bologna, May 2–5, 1990, adds a significant new dimension to our understanding of the development of dialogue. In all these early discourses we see clearly how the text interacts with its environment, such that meaning is created at the intersection of two contradictions: the experiential one, between the material and the conscious modes of experience, and the interpersonal one, between the different personal histories of the interactants taking part. Thus from the ontogenesis of conversation we can gain insight into human learning and human understanding.

Notes

[1] This ideology is particularly characteristic of what has been called the "manipulative capitalist" society. See Martin (1989, especially Chapter 4, *passim*).

[2] See, for example, Dixon (1967), Graves (1983). For an excellent critique, see Rothery (1990, chapter titled "The Pedagogies of Traditional School Grammar: Creativity, Personal Growth, and Process"); see also Rothery (1996).

[3] Among contemporary linguists an outstanding contributor to the development of this tradition is Claude Hagège. See, for example, Hagège (1985).

[4] The initial interpretation of my observations is contained in Halliday (1975). The data to age 2;7 is available in Halliday (1984b). See also Bullowa (1979).

[5] Colwyn Trevarthen's important work in this field is presented in a number of his papers; see especially (1979) and (1980). For his work on the protolanguage phase, see (1978). Bruner's work provides a valuable general theoretical underpinning from a psychological standpoint; compare Bruner (1977).

[6] Contrast genetically transmitted communication systems (like the dances of bees), where instances do not perturb the system. This fundamental feature of semiotic systems is obscured in adult

language by the massive quantitative effects to which it contributes (cf. Halliday, 1987), but it is seen very clearly at the protolanguage phase of development.

For language as a dynamic open system, see Lemke's articles "Towards a Model of the Instructional Process," "The Formal Analysis of Instruction," and "Action, Context, and Meaning," in Lemke (1984).

[7] Naming (lexicalized denotation) and transitivity are the cornerstones of the potential of language for construing experience (the experiential metafunction, in the terms of systemic theory). They were first explicitly linked in this way by Mathesius; see, for example, (1936). For naming in the development of conversation, see Halliday (1984a).

[8] It may seem surprising that, with children learning a tone language, a major distinction such as this could be realized by intonation. In fact, of course, Chinese uses intonation (grammatical tone) as well as lexical tone; but this is irrelevant. The protolanguage is "child tongue," not mother tongue; you cannot tell, when a child is speaking protolanguage, what language his mother tongue is going to be, and although by the time children introduce this distinction they are already launched into the mother tongue, this particular contrast is still their own invention.

In some instances, in fact, their system runs counter to the pattern of the mother tongue. Thus in Nigel's grammar proto-imperatives, being pragmatic, were rising in tone, whereas in English the informal imperative is typically falling; while when he first used dependent clauses, which have no macrofunction, he gave them the unmarked (falling) tone. Thus when, at just under 1;9, he said, "When New-World finish, song about bús!" ("When the *New World* [symphony] is finished, sing me the song about a bus"), the first clause was falling and the second rising, whereas in adult English the tones would have been the other way around.

[9] From her study of long conversations among groups of adults, Suzanne Eggins postulates that it is in fact the periodicity of consensus and conflict that is the major factor in keeping conversations going. See Eggins (1990).

References

Bruner, J.S. (1977). Early social interaction and language acquisition. In H.R. Shaffer (Ed.), *Studies in mother-infant interaction*. London: Academic.

Bullowa, M. (1979). Infants as conversational partners. In T. Myers (Ed.), *The development of conversation and discourse*. Edinburgh, Scotland: Edinburgh University Press.

Dixon, J. (1967). *Growth through English*. Oxford, UK: Oxford University Press.

Eggins, S. (1990). *Keeping the conversation going: A systemic-functional analysis of conversational structure in casual sustained talk*. Doctoral dissertation, University of Sydney, Australia.

Graves, D.H. (1983). *Writing: Teachers and children at work*. Portsmouth, NH: Heinemann.

Hagège, C. (1985). *L'homme de paroles: contribution linguistique aux sciences humaines*. Paris: Fayard.

Halliday, M.A.K. (1975). *Learning how to mean: Explorations in the development of language*. London: Edward Arnold.

Halliday, M.A.K. (1978). Meaning and the construction of reality in early childhood. In H.L. Pick, Jr., & E. Saltzman (Eds.), *Modes of perceiving and processing of information*. Hillsdale, NJ: Erlbaum.

Halliday, M.A.K. (1984a). Language as code and language as behaviour: A systemic-functional interpretation of the nature and ontogenesis of dialogue. In R.P. Fawcett et al. (Eds.), *The semiotics of culture and language* (Vol. 1). London: Frances Pinter.

Halliday, M.A.K. (1984b). *Listening to Nigel: Conversations of a very small child*. Sydney: University of Sydney, Linguistics Department.

Halliday, M.A.K. (1987). Language and the order of nature. In N. Fabb et al. (Eds.), *The linguistics of writing*. Manchester, UK: Manchester University Press.

Kintsch, W. (1988). The role of knowledge in discourse comprehension: A construction-integration model. *Psychological Review*, 95(2).

Lemke, J.L. (1984). *Semiotics and education*. Toronto: Victoria College, University of Toronto.

Martin, J.R. (1989). *Factual writing: Exploring and challenging social reality*. Oxford, UK: Oxford University Press.

Mathesius, V. (1936). On some problems of the systematic analysis of grammar. *Travaux du Cercle Linguistique de Prague, 6.*

Oldenburg, J. (1990). Learning the language and learning through language in early childhood. In M.A.K. Halliday, J. Gibbons, & H. Nicholas (Eds.), *Learning, keeping and using language: Selected papers from the Eighth World Congress of Applied Linguistics.* Amsterdam: Benjamins.

Painter, C. (1984). *Into the mother tongue: A case study of early language development.* London: Frances Pinter.

Qiu, S. (1985). Transition period in Chinese language development. *Australian Review of Applied Linguistics, 8*(1).

Rothery, J. (1990). *"Story" writing in primary school: Assessing narrative type genres.* Doctoral dissertation, University of Sydney, Australia.

Rothery, J. (1996). Making changes: Developing an educational linguistics. In R. Hasan & G. Williams (Eds.), *Literacy in society.* London: Longman.

Thibault, P.J. (1990). *Social semiotics as praxis: Test, social meaning making and Nabokov's "Ada."* Minneapolis: University of Minnesota Press.

Trevarthen, C. (1978). Secondary intersubjectivity: Confidence, confiding and acts of meaning in the first year. In A. Lock (Ed.), *Action, gesture and symbol: The emergence of language.* London: Academic.

Trevarthen, C. (1979). Communication and co-operation in early infancy: A description of primary intersubjectivity. In M. Bullowa (Ed.), *Before speech: The beginning of interpersonal communication.* Cambridge, UK: Cambridge University Press.

Trevarthen, C. (1980). The foundations of intersubjectivity: Development of interpersonal and cooperative understanding in infants. In D. Olson (Ed.), *The social foundations of language and thought: Essays in honor of Jerome S. Bruner.* New York: Norton.

6

Writing and the Sea of Voices: Oral Language In, Around, and About Writing

Anne Haas Dyson

I learned that
space is a good place
to be if I lovd [lived]
in that place I would
died Srey [Sorry] Ms. Rita
Oh Precious
You DoNe iT
Srey [Sorry] Boys AND girls

O n its own, isolated on an expanse of paper, the above text makes little
sense. To construct that sense, readers would no doubt be helped if I provided the "sea of talk" on which the writing floated. That metaphor of
the sea of talk was suggested by James Britton more than 25 years ago. In his
words,

> All that the children write, your response [as educator] to what they write, their
> response to each other, all this takes place afloat upon a sea of talk. Talk is what
> provides the links between you and them and what they write, between what they
> have written and each other. (1970, p. 29)

That is, children, like the author of the "Precious" text above, generate their ideas
and sustain their written voices through talk with others.

In the years since Britton offered his metaphor, researchers have worked to
understand more fully the relation between talk and writing. Paradoxically,
through these efforts, child writers have become more firmly anchored to sociocultural contexts, and the sea of talk has been channeled carefully—grounded,
in fact, within dyadic encounters, literacy events, and cultural practices.

From Indrisano, R., & Squire, J.R. (Eds.), *Perspectives on Writing: Research, Theory, and Practice* (pp. 45–65). Copyright © 2000 by the International Reading Association.

And yet, the notion of floating writing that so captured Britton's imagination is making a comeback, although the sea is no longer so tranquil. In its recent manifestations, writing does not so much float on a sea of talk as mediate a sea of voices; the individual writer is not only supported by, but also struggling against, the currents of the never-ending human conversation.

In this piece I consider the transformations of Britton's sea of talk. In order to keep afloat myself, I will take along with me 6-year-old Denise, the playful author who, quite literally, raised her oral and written voice to a space child named Precious.

The Solidification of the Sea: Functions, Dyads, and Events

My decision to ground this discussion not only in theoretical constructs, but also in data excerpts from an ongoing study involving Denise, reflects a major theoretical and methodological turn in language studies. That turn, beginning most notably in the late 1960s, was away from the study of language as an abstraction and toward consideration of everyday speech—and writing—as concrete "utterances" (Bakhtin, 1986).

The reasons given for this turn are complex and diverse, among them new technological possibilities (particularly the tape recorder) and new theoretical challenges as well. For example, in response to Chomskian generative grammar based on edited written sentences, some socially oriented linguists analyzed the messiness of conversational speech (Chafe, 1982), while others offered performance rules for speech in diverse cultural contexts (Hymes, 1972); developmentally oriented linguists explored how young children acquired complex linguistic rules (Brown, 1973), and suggested functional needs that organized biological possibilities for language (Halliday, 1973).

This observational turn in language studies yielded rich concepts for analytically examining the sea of talk and, more specifically, for studying how speech functioned during composing and how that functioning was linked to social relationships and cultural life. These efforts added theoretical layers of grounded, useful detail for language arts researchers and educators.

The Functions of Talk: Listening to the Young

Influenced by those who documented the functions of children's speech, like Halliday (1973) and Tough (1977), researchers developed coding schemes to describe the functions of speech during early writing (e.g., Dyson, 1983; Graves, 1979). Although older children and adults may write silently, young children, still developing the use of inner speech (Vygotsky, 1962), are typically quite audible writers. To illustrate, following is an excerpt from the child talk that accompanied the "Precious" text:

[Denise and Vanessa, both first graders, are sitting side by side, working on their "What I Learned About Space" pieces. They are to proceed quietly, because their teacher, Rita, is working intently with the rest of the class. Denise has written "I learned," apologized (in writing) for using the word died (a word Vanessa said she was not supposed to be using), and now focuses on Precious, the space robot she made.]

Denise: I'm gonna write, "Oh Precious." Precious, she got on my nerves.... "Oh Precious. You done it. You done it. Oh Precious, you done it." I would say it in a mean voice. "OH PRECIOUS! YOU DONE IT! I'm GONNA [unclear] YOU! YOU DONE IT!"

Vanessa: Write it in big ol' letters!

Denise: [does so and then reads] "OH PRECIOUS! YOU DONE IT!"

Rita: Denise! Be quiet!

[Denise looks startled, mildly embarrassed, and then smiles and writes Sre (sorry) boys and girls (i.e., sorry I disturbed you).]

As Denise composes, her talk reveals and sustains the social relationships within which writing takes shape; in this case those relationships involve Denise with her space child, her best friend, her teacher, and her class. Moreover, her talk serves as a kind of "recruiting area" (Britton, 1970, p. 29) for the representational aspects of writing, and also as a regulator, helping her (and others) plan, encode, monitor, orchestrate, and evaluate her written efforts:

"I'm gonna write, 'Oh Precious,'" Denise planned.

"Write it in big ol' letters," suggested Vanessa, who had some notion of how to encode spoken meanness in written graphics.

Talk's self-regulatory function—its role in helping individuals control and organize their own behavior (Vygotsky, 1962)—has received much research attention. Children less sophisticated than Denise may use print as a kind of prop (Dyson, 1983)—an interesting phenomenon to be explored, talked about (for instance, "This is my Mama's name"), and used in varied kinds of social, often playful activity (such as playing post office or school).

As they gain a functional understanding of print as a means of recalling instead of only representing messages (Luria, 1983), children's speech both reveals and supports their efforts to act on this understanding. From early attempts to differentiate one squiggle—or one letter—from another by more familiar means (color, shape, size, physical context), children may turn their attention to sound itself (Clay, 1975; Ferreiro & Teberosky, 1982; Read, 1986). Their speech thus becomes raw material and a tool with which to manipulate this material

(Dyson, 1983). Child observers thus can hear the more spontaneous activity of speaking literally becoming the more "volitional" (Vygotsky, 1962; 1987, p. 204), more deliberate, act of rendering meaning through drawing speech.

In the following excerpt, also of Denise and her friend Vanessa, the use of speech to manipulate speech is very evident:

[Denise is writing about her Thanksgiving Day, but she is struggling with the spelling of that holiday.]

Vanessa: You don't gotta spell the whole thing, just sound it out like you can, girl.... 'Cause that word...is long.

[Denise, however, finds the word displayed in the classroom. She then uses self-regulatory speech, orally rereading, monitoring, and planning her words.]

Denise: "For Thanksgiving" [reading], I [writing] had, went [planning]... How do you spell *went*?

Vanessa: W—[pauses, walks to a pocket-chart word bank and brings back *want* for her friend]

Denise: Read the back [of the card].

Vanessa: "I want a red pencil" [reading]—oh, that's *want*. [Retrieves another card.] This has got to be it.

Denise: That's *with*.

Vanessa: Where is *went*?

Denise: I just got to sound it out! I just got to sound it out!

[Denise does so, listening to the sounds as she pronounces the word slowly. She continues on, writing "for Thanksgiving I wet (went) to Hace hez (Chucky Cheese)," sounding out the name of that restaurant with Vanessa's help, and then she adds "and I sow (saw)."]

Denise: I just gotta put one thing and you know what it's gonna be!

Vanessa: My name, or your name, [and] I love you....

[Denise gives Vanessa her writing book so that Vanessa can write her own name.]

Denise: If you sign Wenona [another child's name] I'm gonna be mad at you.

Vanessa: OK.

A logical question raised by Denise's speech is, How do children learn to use oral language in these ways? The answer to this question helps solidify those seaworthy links between writers and others and to organize these links into patterns of talk.

Dyads: Scaffolding Reflective Behavior

Inspired both by a newly available book of Vygotskian theory (Vygotsky, 1934/1978) and based on research on parent/child interaction in language learning (e.g., Cross, 1975), in the 1980s researchers added to a focus on students and their texts a consideration of dyadic encounters between students and teachers about their texts.

From this perspective, children's self-regulatory speech during writing is linked to the responsive, regulating talk of adult guides or other experts. During writing, these guides "loan" children their consciousness about language and language use (Bruner, 1986, p. 175); they thus negotiate the developmental gap—the "zone of proximal development" (Vygotsky, 1934/1978, p. 84)—helping children to choose, encode, and reflect on their written choices. In pedagogical discussions of writing, there are many visions of children as "apprentice" journalists, novel writers, and researchers, getting responsive help from adults and from each other as well (e.g., Graves, 1983; Rogoff, 1994).

In these "scaffolding" interactions, teachers, like their caregiver counterparts (Ninio & Bruner, 1978), orally support children's language. Scaffolding is central to an oft-recommended instructional activity—"writing conferences." In these conferences, teachers respond to child writers in ways that they hope children will respond, in time, to their own and each other's written efforts. Building from the pedagogical work of Graves (1983), Sowers suggested that such conferences revolve around "versions of reflect (what was it [the reported experience] really like?), expand (what else is important to add [to your text about that experience]?), and select (what is most important?)" (1982, p. 87; 1985).

Denise's teacher, Rita, responded to her children and their writing both individually as they wrote and in whole-class sharing sessions. Her responses to children grappling with encoding are reflected quite clearly in the earlier interactions of Vanessa and Denise (for example, their trips to check the word bank, their admonishments to sound out words as best they could). Rita also responded to her children with queries about text clarity and informativeness, and she encouraged her children to talk to each other in this way. For example, Rita instructed her class, "If you just say to me, 'Oh yeah, I love the holidays; I had a good time,' I'm gonna come back to you and ask, 'What was a good time?' You can do that for each other."

Despite the usefulness of the scaffolding metaphor, and its predictable routines and contingent responses, thoughtful observers questioned the heavy emphasis on dyadic scaffolds. After all, unlike the middle class caregivers and their singular charges studied in language-development research, teachers have 20 to 30 children or more, and those children do not necessarily share sociocultural background with their teachers. What kinds of assumptions about teacher-student relationships and about textual structures and functions undergird the recommended talk during conferences? Do all students share these assumptions? Are there other kinds of helpful teacher-student talk about writing (Delpit, 1988; Gray, 1987; Reyes, 1991; Walker, 1992)? What about the children themselves—do they help each other only by revoicing their teachers' words (Daiute, 1989; Dyson, 1989)?

To address these questions, researchers and educators needed to step back from those dyadic encounters between teachers and children and to allow both teachers and children complex histories and roles in diverse institutions (families, classrooms, schools, communities). In the 1980s and 1990s, this stepping back was aided by Vygotskian interpretations that stress the sociocultural nature of intellectual thought and, moreover, by ethnographic perspectives on language and literacy in communities and, particularly, by the construct of the event.

Events: Supporting Community Participation

Like all oral interaction, the responsive talk of guiding teachers is itself organized within, and constitutive of, social activity or "events." In fact, as Barton (1994) points out, activities involving oral language provide the context for most instances of print use: "Even in the most seemingly literate of environments, such as a court of law, a schoolroom, or a university office, most of the conventions of how to act and what to do [with and through texts] are passed on orally" (p. 90). Informal interactions, collaborative work sessions, and formal meetings are all occasions for the generation, development, presentation, and revision of ideas encoded in diverse media, including print—and they are also occasions that reveal and sustain participants' social relationships.

These occasions for use of and talk about print—whether in family or government agency—are literacy events (Basso, 1974; Heath, 1983). Like speech events (Hymes, 1972), *literacy events* are energized by particular purposes, characterized by certain ways of relating to other participants, and marked by expected moods, possible and anticipated oral interactions, and also by expected text topics and structures. Many scholars have investigated the diverse ways in which such events are organized within the interactional patterns and cultural values—the events—of everyday life (e.g., Heath, 1983; Philips, 1975).

Learning Within Events. The shift from dyadic encounters to literacy events entails a rethinking of oral/written configurations and their relationship to learning to write. In *dyadic instructional encounters*, social relationships are primarily helpful ones, in which more expert others (or perhaps collaborative peers) help learners write; the goal is that the learner internalizes the oral guidance so that gradually those others can withdraw.

In *events*, there may be many participants with diverse roles, not all of which are explicitly helpful. In fact, even the most expert writers are not necessarily aware of the assumptions about purposes, relationships, and structural features that guide their efforts (Applebee, 1996; Freedman & Medway, 1994). Further, social participants in events do not disappear and leave writers "alone";

rather, over time social relationships change, as do the nature of the learner's participation and perhaps the nature of the event itself.

From this perspective, learning to produce different kinds of texts or genres requires many opportunities to participate orally in the social spheres—the interrelated literacy events—within which such genres matter, and learning itself can happen in many ways: listening to and observing others talk about and use text, receiving explicit instruction, engaging in the event alongside more expert and responsive others, and gaining feedback from participants (who are not necessarily helpers) in an audience role.

Ethnographic researchers have illustrated the oral and written configurations—the complex events—within which people use, and learn to use, print. For example, in many cultural contexts, children may collaborate orally to compose a written letter with their parents. However, across letter-writing events, literacy expertise may be distributed quite differently among child and adult participants because of their respective knowledge of written graphics, genre conventions, audience expectations, and linguistic code (control over a standard language). These differences may engender nontraditional family dynamics (for instance, children guiding adults), thus, they may have ramifications for both social and language learning (Schieffelin & Cochran-Smith, 1984; Vasquez, Pease-Alvarez, & Shannon, 1994).

A related illustration is provided by Kalman's (1996) study of the work life of Mexican scribes. The scribes earn their livelihood composing letters for clients who come to them for assistance in varied legal, workplace, and family matters. Because the distribution of relevant expertise varies between scribes and clients, the scribes' composing events entail complex oral negotiating. In Kalman's words, "Any use of writing and written texts implies understanding how convention, purpose, knowledge, and power are negotiated to produce a particular piece of writing" (p. 215). Moreover, given new social circumstances for writing such as new institutional contexts or new relationships, any "expert" can become a "novice."

Classroom Events. Classrooms, too, are kinds of communities within which conventions, purposes, knowledge, and power are negotiated. In these communities, suggest Moll and Whitmore (1993), the basic organizational unit for learning is not the dyadic zone of proximal development but the "collective" zone, formulated by diverse events in varied units of study. Participating in this zone entails the interactive use of both oral and written language to make decisions about topics for study, resources to consult, and issues to analyze, as well as more text-focused decisions involving planning, encoding, and evaluating text.

Children's talk about and use of text is guided, then, not only by scaffolding interactions but also by their evolving understanding of event purposes, social relations, and textual expectations—understanding gained from and negotiated by oral participation. Over school years, as the curriculum differentiates into disciplines, children's participation in literacy events and their associated genres becomes a means for participation in and development of disciplinary knowledge (Applebee, 1996; Freedman & Medway, 1994).

Some researchers have focused attention on the interplay between the nature of teacher-organized talk, teacher-student relationships, and student writing (e.g., Applebee, 1996; Gutierrez, 1992; Losey, 1997; Nystrand, 1996; Sperling & Woodlief, 1997). A consistent finding of such work is that the "default" teacher-student interaction pattern, to use Cazden's term (1988, p. 53), predominates in classrooms, providing minimal support for student composing. As Cazden discusses, to enact this familiar interactional rhythm, teachers ask testing questions, students provide minimal responses, and teachers evaluate those responses. This interactional mode is very well suited to "assembling factual information" that can be provided in "short answers" (p. 50)—but not well suited to interactively guided composing in which ideas are exchanged, elaborated, and integrated.

For example, Gutierrez (1992) examined composing lessons in elementary classrooms serving primarily immigrant Latino children. Although all classrooms offered writing opportunities to children, the way those opportunities were realized varied strikingly, and an important factor in that variation was the nature of classroom talk. In classrooms in which talk about writing was predominantly teacher controlled (with the teacher giving directions, asking known information questions, and evaluating student understanding of *the* way to do a task), students had limited opportunities to generate or elaborate their ideas; to draw from their own experiences and linguistic resources; to adopt the multiple roles of author, reader, and critic; or even to grasp the purpose of a writing task. For instance, teaching children "brainstorming" as a singular task to be done "correctly" may allow them little sense of what they are doing, or why, or how, as a purpose-driven, socially organized event, brainstorming might be linked to other events in some larger endeavor.

Although they did not use words like "collective zones" or "literacy events," members of an urban teachers' study group (Dyson, with Bennett et al., 1997)—all experienced primary teachers—described and enacted such zones and events. The teachers valued highly social activities allowing child participants many potential avenues to negotiate social participation and symbol use in classroom settings. For example, in her second-grade classroom, teacher Jill Walker orchestrated a series of events involving Arnold Lobel's well-known characters Frog and Toad. In one event, the children chose partners, play-acted a Frog and Toad story, and wrote improvised lines. They negotiated character roles, generated dialogue, reflected on (and argued about) chosen dialogue lines and potential spellings, studied books to see how to format dialogue, and watched the clock so that they did not "squabble" over whose turn it was to type on the classroom computer. Although Jill's interactions with her students scaffolded their efforts, so too did the children's own interactions and their understanding of the familiar activity of role-play. (For extended discussions of play and writing, see Daiute, 1989, 1993.)

I will now return to Denise's space text. As composer, Denise was supported in part by her understanding of familiar classroom reporting activities. For example, she and her classmates made use of the teacher-modeled opening line "I learned that" when they planned what they would tell their parents about space and also when they reported to each other facts they had learned recently—both oral events linked to the assigned written report. Still, this description of classroom events does not adequately account for Denise's text, which flows over the boundaries of those official events. A more adequate account requires some theoretical wave-making in this too peaceful sea of talk.

Making Waves: Unofficial Events and Critical Practices

At this point, Britton's fluid sea of talk may seem quite organized: Writers' talk is channeled by functional use and dyadic encounters within literacy events, which are interrelated within institutional, including disciplinary, contexts. And yet, that sea of talk is not, in fact, so easily contained. In any institution, talk mediates participants' social and cultural identities that are not subsumed by—and potentially in conflict with—social roles in officially sanctioned events. By examining unofficial events and considering critical practices, I begin to make some waves in that peaceful sea.

Unofficial Events: Complicating Agendas

There are always official, as well as unofficial, networks of social organization (Goffman, 1963). In classroom communities, children simultaneously participate in official and unofficial events (for instance, those governed by their relationships with other children). Moreover, their interactions in these events are shaped by the repertoire of genres or familiar ways of using language they bring from other institutions, including their homes, churches, the popular media, and the local peer cultures themselves (Dyson, 1989, 1993; Gilmore, 1983; Heath, 1983; Sola & Bennett, 1985).

For example, readers may recall Denise's and Vanessa's shared assumption that Denise would write Vanessa's name and "I love you"—certainly not an official expectation of a student's essay about "My Thanksgiving," but very much an unofficial expectation of these best friends and "fake sisters." Moreover, if Denise had violated those expectations, Vanessa—not her teacher, Rita—would have corrected her.

In an urban arts magnet school, I examined the role of unofficial relationships and peer talk in children's literacy learning (Dyson, 1989). Children's earliest "texts" were woven through the use of many available symbolic resources or media; their talk and drawing carried much of the functional work of representing, reflecting on, and sharing texts. Influenced by official writing events (and official expectations) for writing, the children's social, playful, and reflective talk about each other's drawing began to engulf their writing as well, helping print become a legitimate object of attention.

Moreover, peer relationships themselves—linked to the values and concerns of unofficial worlds—began to be mediated through writing. Children began to use peers as characters in their stories and to plan to include certain words or actions to amuse or tease them. Like Denise and Vanessa, they began to manipulate the elements (and thereby the words) of written language in order to manipulate the oral responses of others to their efforts.

Such anticipated responses, and the oral interaction through which they are realized, may conflict with the dominant interactional patterns of official school events, as illustrated in another urban study site (Dyson, 1993). Consistent with a Bakhtinian perspective, the social responses anticipated and desired were an integral aspect of the genres—or types of textual "utterances" (Bakhtin, 1986, p. 60)— the children composed. For example, sometimes the focal children (in this study, all African American) recalled experiences watching popular media stories or listed well-known celebrities; the desired social response seemed to be "Oh yeah, I saw that [know that] too." Often these were not texts that lent themselves well to conference-type oral "reflection," or "expansion," because recalling a shared experience—not explicitly communicating a unique experience—was the goal.

The children also composed artful stories, frequently drawing from their oral expressive resources (that is, features of verbal art, which highlight the musical and image-creating properties of language; see Tannen, 1989). Even first graders initiated revisions of these texts; familiarity with popular genres often guided their efforts to make words rhyme, phrases rhythmic, dialogue fast-paced, and images funny. Given their anticipation of a performance, with its associated pleasures, given and received, children might take help from those in "collaborator" or "teacher" roles, but not from those regarded as "audience" (event roles often combined in writing pedagogy).

Educators, like all language users, are not always aware of their own assumptions about appropriate social roles and textual structures in literacy events. The diversity of children's social agendas underscores the importance of careful teacher observation of peer talk during composing time. In his study in an urban site serving mainly Chinese American and immigrant students, Lee (1997) provides a clear illustration of this need. He reveals how low peer status could severely limit immigrant children's access to peer assistance (including help with translating) and, more generally, to the social guidance and social energy peer talk potentially provides.

Further, the diversity of child agendas also suggests the need for teacher-student discourse that allows space for and expects student elaboration and explanation of their own work. Such discourse helps teachers enact "permeable" curricula in which they allow for students' social and linguistic knowledge, for class members to learn from each other, and for their own "loaning of consciousness" to their students; in this loaning, teachers provide vocabulary and analytic talk that allows unexpected knowledge and unanticipated agendas consideration in the classroom "collective zone" (Dyson, 1993).

Unanticipated agendas provide insight into the social, developmental, and textual sense of Denise's writing that opens this piece. As she was completing a textual world, she also was participating in different social worlds, themselves linked to different aspects of her sociocultural identity; for example, she was a student saying "what she learned," an irritated mother of her robot child "Precious" (and Vanessa's playful sister), and a dutiful child and a polite human being, apologizing for forgetting where she was. Thus, her text mediated—provided a substantive form for, but also shaped—her actions in diverse official and unofficial spheres, with their respective space and time dimensions and textual resources. Denise appropriated "I learned that" from the official world, "YOU DONE IT!" from unofficial ones, and the conversational "sorrys" from general conventions of politeness in and out of school. The resulting oral and written excursions into varied space and time structures (unexpected shifts of tense and author stance) are common in young children's writing (Dyson, 1989); they reflect the multiple textual and social worlds negotiated in a composing act.

This attention to Denise orienting and reorienting herself in a swirling sea of talk—swallowing its words, becoming a part of the sea even as she moves within it—prepares the way for the final construct to be considered herein, that of critical practices.

Critical Practice: Questioning Agendas

As the language philosopher Bakhtin explains, the words we appropriate as our own—those we swallow, so to speak—always "taste" of the situational and relational contexts in which they were learned (1981, p. 293). Thus, learning social roles, cultural values, and power relations is an integral aspect of learning language, oral or written. The very words, genres, and vernaculars that allow us to express ourselves also express us—they position us in a social and political world. For example, Denise's word *precious* was resisted by the boys with whom she and Vanessa were supposed to design a planet. "Every planet name [the girls] came up with had *precious* in it," said Samuel, one of the boys in the class, in explaining his group's failure to collaborate.

The dyadic scaffolds and interactive events within which children learn to compose do not necessarily help them reflect on ideological assumptions (such as perceptions of "girl words"). For some scholars, the word *practice*, in contrast to the word *event*, highlights the ideological aspects of literacy use (see especially Street, 1995). *Critical literacy* practices involve talk that helps participants reflect on given words—and potentially change their ways of acting on and with those words in given social worlds.

Building on the critical pedagogy of Freire (1970), literacy educators in diverse settings have studied the kinds of interactions that support such reflection. During traditional writing conference events, interaction is organized around individuals and their writing; response flows between teacher and/or peers on the one hand and the writer on the other. During critical literacy practices, the interactional dynamic is different. Writer, teacher, peers—all may respond to each other. Points of difference and agreement are viewed not only as developmental gaps in writing skill, but also as potential sociopolitical gaps to be articulated and examined.

For example, in an urban primary school, teacher Kristin Stringfield promoted critical reflection through an Author's Theater activity in which children acted out their composed texts (studied in Dyson, 1997). Many of these texts were based on the popular media, especially superhero stories, whose ideologically charged content such as gender roles and physical power generated many sociopolitical gaps. For example, children's different perceptions of who could be a superhero or a victim, or even of the value of superhero stories themselves, were initially visible in children's giggles, sour faces, scrunched noses, and cries of "that's not fair," in response to a peer's Author's Theater presentation. By helping the children articulate these views—by lending them her own analytic vocabulary for comparing texts—Stringfield helped the children link interrelated issues of gender, race, and power to authors' decisions about details of character and plot— that is, about how they would revoice words appropriated from the media.

In related work, Moss (1989) describes her efforts to help secondary students articulate their pleasures in and reservations about what she terms the "un/popular" fictions of teenage romance stories and comic book adventures; in so doing, she reveals the complex authorial processes—decisions about the portrayal of love, power, and gender roles—that lie behind a seemingly simplistic text. And, in a powerful piece, poet June Jordan (1988) describes her African American college students' talk about writing—especially their talk about the kind of talk in writing—as she helped them "separate themselves from their own activity [their own speech]" and to reflect on the "historical dimensions" of the negative evaluations they had appropriated uncritically about African American vernaculars (Freire, 1970, p. 80). (For a moving analysis of critical literacy as enacted in an adult women's writing group, see Heller, 1997.)

The message undergirding these educators' critical practices is that appropriating words, stories, genres, and linguistic codes involves more than being situationally appropriate or communicatively competent in language events (Hymes, 1972). The appropriation of words and the deliberate decision to use them or not in particular ways involves decisions about being itself, about who authors want to be as they orient themselves among others in a sea of voices. Becoming aware of how textual options link to social and ideological alternatives is dependent on interaction with others positioned differently in the sea.

The Sea of Voices

The scholarship reviewed in this piece initially makes Britton's sea of talk more socially organized and then disrupts that order, providing more interactional cross-currents, more ideological waves. As Britton anticipated, the social relationships—the dyadic links and interactive events—realized through talk allow writers a sense of direction and purpose, as well as supportive others to help them on their way. However, those helpful relationships, steeped in societal beliefs and values, also channel writing in ways that may constrain us as members of a particular gender, ethnic group, social class, discipline, or other constructed category. And yet, it is in the socially lively, sometimes turbulent, sea of voices that new discursive routes may form as old ones come together, move apart, or intertwine in fresh ways (for an interesting discussion of this idea, see Gilyard, 1996).

Further, writers do more than recruit ideas from that sea—they swallow its very words. Indeed, for Bakhtin (1986, p. 62), most written genres have been formed by "absorb[ing] and digest[ing]" simpler, usually oral, genres such as dialogue. Thus, our written voices are quite literally linked to the oral voices of others. Sometimes our appropriated words slip away from us, not because of a writing skill problem per se, but because of our socio-ideological positioning—we may not anticipate the meanings others may find in our words.

For young children, the social, ideological, and textual complexities of the sea of voices can result in awkward texts, such as Denise's space report. But, on occasion, when given time and ideological space (for instance, different perspectives or orientations to subject matter) and the support of at least some familiar social waters (such as events), even the youngest of writers can position themselves quite skillfully amid the sea. To illustrate, I offer, in closing, another of Denise's texts, this one written during a study unit about freedom and slavery.

The freedom and slavery unit is a regular one in local schools—I have witnessed many such units. But Rita's was different in its fullness of voices—voices singing, orating, reading, and in dialogue, often accompanied by, guided by, or stimulated by written texts. For example, she consulted an adult's reference book about the African American artist Jacob Lawrence as she showed the children slides of his well-known paintings of Harriet Tubman's life. She interwove commentary on Lawrence's artistic style with a telling of Tubman's own story as imagined by the artist. Lawrence is famous for his drawing of hands, Rita told them, and Harriet Tubman had strong hands. Because of her strength, Tubman had to chop wood, haul water, and plow, but "she was not gonna give in," even though, as Rita told her students, she would be beaten if she were caught running away.

Before, during, and after the study of Lawrence and his paintings, Rita played and taught the children the words to Pete Seeger's version of "Follow the Drinking Gourd"; she also played albums by, shared a video about, and discussed the artistic skill of the vocal group Sweet Honey in the Rock: "Do you want your freedom?" one of the group sings. "Oh yeah," echo the other singers, joined by the voices of Rita and the children.

In small collaborative groups, the children discussed and made posters about what freedom and slavery meant, historically and in their own lives. Denise, who is African American, told her group that she had been a slave for 3 months. "I'm just playing," she told me later when I asked her about it—a serious kind of play in which one imagines a different self, takes a different angle on a word and a world.

With the rest of the class, Denise listened to (and chose to read with Vanessa) Faith Ringgold's *Aunt Harriet and the Underground Railroad* (1992), whose own text appropriates songs and, moreover, features a young girl like Denise who finds contemporary meaning in historical time. Denise also memorized Eloise Greenfield's (1978) poem about Harriet Tubman, which, as Rita pointed out, uses a kind of written talk to "break the rules" about how written language is supposed to sound—and rule breaking is sometimes a good thing to do:

> Harriet Tubman...
>
> Didn't come in this world to be no slave
> And wasn't going to stay one either....
>
> She ran to the woods and she ran through the woods
> With the slave catchers right behind her
>
> And she kept on going 'til she got to the North
> Where those mean men couldn't find her
>
> Nineteen times she went back South
> To get the three hundred others
> She ran for her freedom nineteen times...

All this singing, poem reciting, picture drawing, story reading, and talking created a collective zone of voices down, around, and about writing. Children who were African American, Asian American, and European American could position themselves differently in their own writing of texts—as sharers of facts, commentators on social evils, or storytellers—and in those stories they could be distant narrators or first-person participants.

In her own story, Denise began as a third-person narrator but, through dialogue, also became a first-person participant. As her story illustrates, she had not only learned from and with other voices, she also had appropriated those other voices to express herself. In reading her text, readers may hear echoes of many others, among them Ringgold, Greenfield, Seeger, her teacher Rita, and Denise herself.

> Aunt Harriet wasnt a slave
> for Log. She was born a
> Slave. She ran back to
> sav 300 PePal. She said

We Are going To be free.
But I will follow The Drinking GorD North.
We did it Said HarrieT
yes yes yes yes yes yes
But WhaT if he beats us?
Cit [Can't.] We are SafE now.

It was speech that linked Denise's spoken words to her written ones, in all the texts shared herein. It was speech too—in the form of social dialogue—that invited her into the literate activities of her classroom worlds, be they official or unofficial. It was and is critical dialogue that will help Denise understand the literary, social, and political ramifications of her chosen genres, plots, characters, and words. And, of course, it is the words themselves—with their complex links to a diversity of sources, oral and written, and to a diversity of perspectives—that will keep her, us, and all our students active forces in the dialogic currents of the times.

References

Applebee, A. (1996). *Curriculum as conversation: Transforming traditions of teaching and learning*. Chicago: University of Chicago Press.

Bakhtin, M. (1981). Discourse in the novel. In C. Emerson & M. Holquist (Eds.), *The dialogic imagination: Four essays by M. Bakhtin* (pp. 259–422). Austin: University of Texas Press.

Bakhtin, M. (1986). *Speech genres and other late essays*. Austin: University of Texas Press.

Barton, D. (1994). *Literacy: An introduction to the ecology of written language*. London: Blackwell.

Basso, K. (1974). The ethnography of writing. In R. Bauman & J. Sherzer (Eds.), *Explorations in the ethnography of speaking* (pp. 425–432). Cambridge, UK: Cambridge University Press.

Britton, J. (1970). *Language and learning*. Harmondsworth, Middlesex, UK: Penguin.

Brown, R. (1973). *A first language: The early stages*. Cambridge, MA: Harvard University Press.

Bruner, J. (1986). *Actual minds, possible worlds*. Cambridge, MA: Harvard University Press.

Cazden, C. (1988). *Classroom discourse: The language of teaching and learning*. Portsmouth, NH: Heinemann.

Chafe, W. (1982). Integration and involvement in speaking, writing, and oral literature. In D. Tannen (Ed.), *Spoken and written language: Exploring orality and literacy* (pp. 35–53). Norwood, NJ: Ablex.

Clay, M. (1975). *What did I write?* Auckland, NZ: Heinemann.

Cross, T. (1975). *Some relationships between mothers and linguistic levels in accelerated children* (Papers and reports on child language development, Vol. 10). Stanford, CA: Stanford University.

Daiute, C. (1989). Play as thought: Thinking strategies of young writers. *Harvard Educational Review, 59*, 1–23.

Daiute, C. (Ed.). (1993). *The development of literacy through social interaction*. San Francisco: Jossey-Bass.

Delpit, L. (1988). The silenced dialogue: Power and pedagogy in educating other people's children. *Harvard Educational Review, 58*, 280–298.

Dyson, A.H. (1983). The role of oral language in early writing processes. *Research in the Teaching of English, 17*, 1–30.

Dyson, A.H. (1989). *Multiple worlds of child writers: Friends learning to write*. New York: Teachers College Press.

Dyson, A.H. (1993). *Social worlds of children learning to write in an urban primary school*. New York: Teachers College Press.

Dyson, A.H. (1997). *Writing superheroes: Contemporary childhood, popular culture, and classroom literacy*. New York: Teachers College Press.

Dyson, A.H. (with A. Bennett, W. Brooks, J. Garcia, C. Howard-McBride, J. Malekzadeh, C. Pancho, et al.). (1997). *What differences does difference make? Teacher perspectives on diversity, literacy, and the urban primary school*. Urbana, IL: National Council of Teachers of English.

Ferreiro, E., & Teberosky, A. (1982). *Literacy before schooling*. Portsmouth, NH: Heinemann.

Freedman, A., & Medway, P. (Eds.). (1994). *Learning and teaching genre*. Portsmouth, NH: Boynton/Cook.

Freire, P. (1970). *Pedagogy of the oppressed*. New York: Continuum.

Gilmore, P. (1983). Spelling "Mississippi": Recontextualizing a literacy-related speech event. *Anthropology & Education Quarterly, 14*, 235–256.

Gilyard, K. (1996). *Let's flip the script: An African American discourse on language, literature, and learning*. Detroit, MI: Wayne State University Press.

Goffman, E. (1961). *Asylums: Essays on the social situation of mental patients and other inmates*. Chicago: Aldine Press.

Graves, D. (1979). Let children show us how to help them write. *Visible Language, 13*, 16–28.

Graves, D.H. (1983). *Writing: Teachers and children at work*. Portsmouth, NH: Heinemann.

Gray, B. (1987). How natural is "natural" language teaching: Employing wholistic methodology in the classroom. *Australian Journal of Early Childhood, 12*, 3–19.

Greenfield, E. (1978). *Honey I love*. New York: Harper & Row.

Guttierez, K. (1992). A comparison of instructional contexts in writing process classrooms with Latino children. *Education in Urban Society, 24*, 244–262.

Halliday, M. (1973). *Explorations in the functions of language*. London: Edward Arnold.

Heath, S.B. (1983). *Ways with words: Language, life and work in communities and classrooms*. Cambridge, UK: Cambridge University Press.

Heller, C. (1997). *Until we are strong together*. New York: Teachers College Press.

Hymes, D. (1972). Models of the interaction of language and social life. In J.J. Gumperz & D. Hymes (Eds.), *Directions in sociolinguistics* (pp. 35–71). New York: Holt, Rinehart & Winston.

Jordan, J. (1988). Nobody means more to me than you and the future life of Willie Jordan. *Harvard Educational Review, 58*, 363–374.

Kalman, J. (1996). Joint composition: The collaborative letter writing of a scribe and his client in Mexico. *Written Communication, 13*, 190–220.

Lee, P. (1997). *Constructing social and linguistic identities: Exploring competence, social goals, and peer interactions within the writing curriculum of a 4th grade ESL classroom*. Unpublished doctoral dissertation, University of California, Berkeley.

Losey, K. (1997). *Listen to the silences: Mexican American interaction in the composition classroom and the community*. Norwood, NJ: Ablex.

Luria, A. (1983). The development of writing in the child. In M. Marlew (Ed.), *The psychology of written language* (pp. 237–277). New York: John Wiley.

Moll, L., & Whitmore, K. (1993). Vygotsky in classroom practice: Moving from individual transmission to social transaction. In E. Forman, N. Minick, & C.A. Stone (Eds.), *Contexts for learning: Sociocultural dynamics in children's development* (pp. 19–42). New York: Oxford University Press.

Moss, G. (1989). *Un/popular fictions*. London: Virago.

Ninio, A., & Bruner, J. (1978). The achievement and antecedents of labeling. *Journal of Child Language, 5*, 1–15.

Nystrand, M. (with A. Gamoran, R. Kachur, & C. Prendergast). (1996). *Opening dialogue: Understanding the dynamics of language and learning in the English classroom*. New York: Teachers College Press.

Philips, S. (1975). Literacy as a mode of communication on the Warm Springs Indian Reservation. In E.H. Lenneberg & E. Lenneberg (Eds.), *Foundations of language development* (pp. 367–381). New York: Academic Press; Paris: UNESCO.

Read, C. (1986). *Children's creative spelling*. London: Routledge.

Reyes, M. de la Luz. (1991). A process approach to literacy using dialogue journals and literature logs with second language learners. *Research in the Teaching of English, 25*, 291–312.

Ringgold, F. (1992). *Aunt Harriet's underground railroad in the sky*. New York: Crown.

Rogoff, B. (1994). Developing understanding of the idea of communities of learners. *Mind, Culture, and Activity: An International Journal, 1*, 209–229.

Schieffelin, B., & Cochran-Smith, M. (1984). Learning to read culturally: Literacy before schooling. In H. Goelman, A.A. Oberg, & F. Smith (Eds.), *Awakening to literacy* (pp. 3–23). Portsmouth, NH: Heineman.

Sola, M., & Bennett, A. (1985). The struggle for voice: Narrative, literacy, and consciousness in an East Harlem School. *Journal of Education, 167*, 88–110.

Sowers, S. (1982). Reflect, expand, select: Three responses in the writing conference. In T. Newkirk & N. Atwell (Eds.), *Understanding writing: Ways of observing, learning, & teaching* (pp. 47–56). Chelmsford, MA: Northeast Regional Exchange.

Sowers, S. (1985). Learning to write in a workshop: A study in grades one through four. In M.F. Whiteman (Ed.), *Advances in writing research (Vol. 1): Children's early writing development* (pp. 297–342). Norwood, NJ: Ablex.

Sperling, M., & Woodlief, L. (1997). Two classrooms, two writing communities. *Research in the Teaching of English, 31*, 235–239.

Street, B. (1995). *Social literacies: Critical approaches to literacy in development, ethnography, and education.* London: Longman.

Tough, J. (1977). *Teaching and learning.* London: Ward Lock Educational.

Walker, E.V.S. (1992). Falling asleep and failure among African-American students: Rethinking assumptions about process teaching. *Theory Into Practice, 31*, 321–328.

Vasquez, O., Pease-Alvarez, L., & Shannon, S. (1994). *Pushing boundaries: Language and culture in a Mexicano community.* New York: Cambridge University Press.

Vygotsky, L.S. (1962). *Thought and language.* Cambridge, MA: MIT Press.

Vygotsky, L.S. (1978). *Mind in society: The development of higher psychological processes* (M. Cole, V. John-Steiner, S. Scribner, & E. Souberman, Eds. & Trans.). Cambridge, MA: Harvard University Press. (Original work published 1934)

Vygotsky, L.S. (1987). *L.S. Vygotsky, collected works: Volume 1, Problems of general psychology.* New York: Plenum Books.

7

Exploring Vygotskian Perspectives in Education: The Cognitive Value of Peer Interaction

Ellice A. Forman and Courtney B. Cazden

T wo important and related themes in Vygotsky's writings are the social foundations of cognition and the importance of instruction in development:

> An important point to note about Vygotsky's ideas on the social origins of cognition is that it is at this point that he uses the notion of internalization. He is not simply claiming that social interaction leads to the development of the child's abilities in problem-solving, memory, etc.; rather, he is saying that the very means (especially speech) used in social interactions are taken over by the individual child and internalized. Thus, Vygotsky is making a very strong statement here about internalization and the social foundations of cognition. (Wertsch, 1981, p. 146)

> If all the development of a child's mental life takes place in the process of social intercourse, this implies that this intercourse and its most systematized form, the teaching process, forms the development of the child, creates new mental formations, and develops higher processes of mental life. Teaching, which sometimes seems to wait upon development, is in actual fact its decisive motive force.... The assimilation of general human experience in the teaching process is the most important specifically human form of mental development in ontogenesis. This deeply significant proposition defines an essentially new approach to the most important theoretical problem of psychology, the challenge of actively developing the mind. It is in this that the main significance of this aspect of Vygotsky's enquiries lies. (Leontiev & Luria, 1968, p. 365)

In all of Vygotsky's writings with which we are familiar, the social relationship referred to as "teaching" is the one-to-one relationship between one adult

From Wertsch, J.V. (Ed.), *Culture, Communication and Cognition: Vygotskian Perspectives* (pp. 323–347). Copyright © 1986 by Cambridge University Press. Reprinted with permission of the publisher.

and one child. When we try to explore Vygotskian perspectives for education, we immediately confront questions about the role of the student peer group. Even if formal education takes place in a group context only for economic reasons, because no society can afford a teacher for each individual child, the presence of peers should not be ignored or relegated only to discussions of issues in classroom management and control.

We see two separate but related issues concerning the group presence. First, there are the problems posed for the teacher in carrying out direct teaching to a group of students; second, there are the questions raised for the teacher's more indirect planning for the social organization of all work-related talk in the classroom setting, specifically the contribution that peers can make to each other. We focus on the second set of questions in this piece. This is not to underestimate the importance of the first. If teaching is conceived as assistance to the child in the child's zone of proximal development, then teaching to a group of children whose "zones" overlap only in part, or not at all, poses obvious problems. But to state the problem thus seems mainly to give new labels to the familiar problem of within-group variation in any group being taught. We focus instead on the less-discussed problem of the potential contribution of social interactions among the children themselves.

Understanding this contribution has both practical and theoretical significance. Practically, despite the fact that school classrooms are unusually crowded social environments, group work is rarely encouraged (Galton, Simon, & Croll, 1980), perhaps in part because there has been no clear rationale for its value. (See Sharan, 1980, for one review of arguments and evidence.) Theoretically, most developmental research studies in the United States have traditionally focused on the value of peer interactions in the socialization of behavior and personality and have said less about their possible value for cognition and intellectual learning. According to Lawler (1980), until recently the same has been true of most writing on education in the Soviet Union—for example, the work of Makarenko.

Interactions among peers focused on intellectual content can be placed on a continuum, depending on the distribution of knowledge or skill among the children, and therefore on the roles they take toward each other. At one extreme, one child knows more than the others and is expected to act as a peer tutor (or "consultant" in the Soviet work of M.D. Vinogradova and I.B. Pervin, summarized in Lawler [1980]). In the contrasting case, knowledge is equal, or at least not intentionally unequal, and the give and take of equal status collaboration is expected. We present research first on two different forms of peer tutoring and then on collaboration. Because empirical as well as theoretical analysis of peer interactions is at such a beginning stage, we include excerpts from interaction protocols, not only as evidence for our interpretations, but to provide material for alternative interpretations as well.

Peer Tutoring

The report of Vygotsky's pupil, Levina, points to possible cognitive benefits to a tutor from the activity of giving verbal instructions to peers:

> Vygotsky said that speech does not include within itself the magical power to create intellectual functioning. It acquires this capacity only through being used in its instrumental capacity. (Levina, 1981, p. 296)

To the extent that this is true, then what Levina calls the "intellectualization" as well as the internalization of speech should be promoted by the use of instrumental speech to others. Levina suggests exactly that

> what is silently perceived as something unitary and whole is immediately broken up into its component elements in any attempt to make a verbal formulation of it. It is easy to be convinced of this as soon as one tries to introduce the clarity of a verbal characterization into an unconscious impression. What are the motivating forces behind this type of verbal formulation? What is it that compels the child to represent his/her perceptions verbally and to formulate and label his/her actions? In answering this question, Vygotsky laid great stress on factors having to do with the social order. He thought that in labeling an ongoing action, the child initially pays tribute to people in the environment by means of verbal representation. He/she makes this representation accessible to them, as if to clarify it. Vygotsky believed that the very act of labeling arose out of the necessity for giving one's own actions a specialized form comprehensible to others. (Levina, 1981, pp. 288–289)

Levina's examples of labeling stimulated by the need to communicate to another, taken from notes and protocols collected under Vygotsky's supervision, contain only child speech that is directed back to the experimenter. Though the need to communicate to peers is not mentioned, it seems consistent with the Levina–Vygotsky perspective that the need to communicate to a less knowledgeable other—such as a peer—would motivate the identical process at least as strongly. Instruction of peers could, in this respect, be an intermediate step between receptively being directed by the speech of another and productively and covertly directing one's own mental processes via inner speech.

The first analysis of peer tutoring comes from research in an inner-city multigrade primary classroom in San Diego. Twelve peer tutoring sequences called instructional changes (ICs) were videotaped for analysis (Carrasco, Vera, & Cazden, 1981; Cazden et al., 1978; Mehan & Riel, 1982). Briefly, in each IC the teacher (T) taught a lesson to one child who then taught the same lesson to one or more peers. Leola, a black third grader, was asked to learn and then teach a language arts task. At the top of page 166 are the first three items on her worksheet in completed form.

1. new   1. Y ǿ̶l̶o d̶u   2. t̶ý̶é̶o l̶ś̶d   3. m ǿ̶ń̶e
2. no
3. off   You   told   me

Following is a transcription, minus repetitions, corrections, and so on, of the teacher's (T's) direction as she talked to Leola (L) through the first two items on the task:

Item 1

T: Okay, now number one here says *new*. What's the opposite of *new*?

L: Old.

T: *Old*. How would you spell *old*?

L: O-l-d.

T: Okay, in the letters that are on this paper, cross out the letters you just used for spelling *old*.

L: [L does it.]

T: Good. What word is left?

L: Y-o-u.

T: What does it spell?

L: You.

T: Okay, and down here you'll write *you*.

Item 2

T: Okay, now number two there says...

L: No.

T: *No*. What's the opposite of *no*?

L: Yes.

T: Okay, how do you spell *yes*?

L: Y-e-s.

T: All right. Now what are you going...

L: [L crosses out the letters y-e-s] Told.

Note first that the T's questions serve to talk Leola through the task until she can do it herself, as Wertsch (1978) has shown for mothers' help to their preschool children in a puzzle-copying task. That such aid does help Leola work independently is shown by a comparison of T's instructions for the first and second items. The first three questions are repeated, but then a much vaguer and incomplete question, "Now what are you going...," is sufficient, and Leola takes off on her own.

The second noteworthy aspect of this IC from the Levina–Vygotsky perspective is the development of increased articulateness and precision in Leola's verbalizations of the task. If one considers the entire instructional chain as a "discourse imitation test," the T's instructions must be reconstructed by the tutor's cognitive, linguistic, and sociolinguistic system. Whereas T taught with questions, Leola teaches with statements, often "You gotta X." (Mehan & Riel, 1982, show that his contrast in teaching styles was characteristic of all 12 ICs.)

It was not immediately easy for Leola to put the directions for this task into words. When Leola first tried to explain to T, pretask, what she was going to tell the group, she included explicit reference to only one of the four essential components, the idea of having some letters "left":

T: Tell me what you are going to tell them to do.

L: Spell these letters, and then put out that letter, and then have another letter left.

T goes over the instructions again, this time asking Leola specifically to say the word *opposite*. Leola then includes that word, but with the vague verb *do*:

T: You want to cross out the opposite of *new*. You better say that, because it's going to be really important. They are going to read "new," and then what are they going to do?

L: Do the opposite of it.

Leola achieves the clearest explanation in round 3 (without hesitations and self-repairs):

L: The opposite of *off* is *on*, so on number three, you gotta cross *on* off. O-n. And it is *me* left, m-e.

Overall, one is tempted to argue that the changes in Leola's instructions constitute an example of what Wertsch and Stone (1978), following the Soviet psychologists, call microgenesis—that is, development within an observable time period, and it is a kind of development that Leola seemed to need. In the nine lessons analyzed by Mehan (1979), some 3 hours of talk in all, she spoke four times, and only twice more than one word. This is not to say she was in any way nonverbal, but is to suggest that she could benefit from challenges to formulate academic content in words, and that the demands of tutoring, including the need for repeated formulation and for corrections of others, provide that challenge well. If there is any validity to the internalization hypothesis, practice in explicit overt formulation should ultimately aid inner speech as well. Vague, inexplicit speech—or a unitary and unformulated perception, in Levina's words—is not the same as predication and "sense" in inner speech.

Finally, there is an interesting reduction of information in Leola's instruction after round 3. With two exceptions, in all the rounds after 3 Leola is talking out loud, head down, while she does her own work. In the reduced rounds 4–5 and 7–10, the reduction in information is more by alternative formulations of the components than by deletion of them altogether. For example, the critical word *opposite* is spoken only in rounds 1–3, and then when the first item has to be repeated (IR) and round 6. In the other rounds, Leola says only "out is in" (presupposing that *is* means *is the opposite of*) or, even more briefly, simply places the two words in juxtaposition: "west east." In the two exceptions, IR and 6, explicitness returns as Leola corrects her tutees and she notices that they have made a mistake.

Two alternative explanations are possible for the decreased explicitness in the reduced rounds. It may be due either to Leola's understanding that the concept of "opposites" can now be assumed or to the decreased explicitness that characterizes speech to oneself. As Wertsch (1979) points out, the decay of old or "given" information is functionally equivalent in dialogue and private speech.

The second analysis of peer tutoring comes from observations by Kamler (1980) in a second-grade classroom in New Hampshire in which Donald Graves's research team was observing the teaching of writing. The teacher, Egan, held regular conferences with individual children. In addition, she encouraged the children to hold "peer conferences" about their writing with each other. Here is one observer's account of the conferences between two children, Jill and Debbie:

> On March 11, Jill was one of six children scheduled for a writing conference....
> At Egan's direction, Jill and the other conferees went to the language table.
> Egan had requested that Jill first spend time with 7-year-old Debbie going over
> the book to be sure it was ready for a conference....
> Jill began by reading each page aloud to Debbie.... As Jill listened to her
> own words, she made changes on pages 1, 2, and 3 without any prompting or
> comment from Debbie, and on pages 4, 5, and 8 in direct response to questions
> Debbie asked....
> At the conclusion of this half-hour conference, Jill had made six content
> changes which affected the overall meaning of the piece. She had deleted infor-
> mation which made no sense or which she could not support; she added infor-
> mation to clarify or explain. Debbie's presence was crucial to the content
> revisions of the draft. Her physical presence forced Jill to reread the book for
> the first time since composing; Debbie seemed to make the concept of audience
> visible for Jill. Jill also needed an active reader to ask questions....
> [Later] Debbie claimed her time: "O.K., Jill, you help me now!" They re-
> versed roles, returned to the language table to work on Debbie's book *Ice Follies*,
> until Egan was ready to see Jill 20 minutes later.... (Kamler, 1980, pp. 683–685)

Note first that this is a more reciprocal model of peer assistance. The roles of writer and helpful questioner are interchangeable among the children. All the children can learn what to do and say in the questioner role from the teacher's model in the conferences with her, a consistent model of how to ask helpful questions that are focused on the content of writing, not form. The teacher believes that questions focused on content are more helpful than questions about form; they are also the kind of questions that children can understandingly ask of each other. The teacher's model thus makes it possible for the children to take turns performing the teacher's role for each other—to the benefit of each child as author, who can have so many more experiences with a responsive audience, and to the benefit of each child as critic, who can internalize such questions through the process of not only answering them to the teacher, but of asking them of peers as well.

For these benefits to occur, the teacher's model must be learnable by the children. Graves reports (personal communication) that the conference structure of another teacher in the same school was not as learnable by the children, and so there was less of a multiplier effect via peer conferences in his classroom. This comparison suggests that the intellectual value of peer interactions in a classroom will be enhanced when the teacher consistently models a kind of interaction in which the children can learn to speak to each other.

As Kamler points out, the child writer benefits in two different ways from the peer's presence. Most obviously, the peer asks questions, following the adult model but with content appropriate to the writing at hand; some of Jill's changes (pages 4, 5, and 8) were in direct response to Debbie's questions. Less obviously, the peer silently but no less effectively represents the needs of an audience and makes "the concept of audience visible."

We can locate the effect of such a silent audience in the otherwise empty cell created by Wertsch and Stone's (personal communication) separation of the interpsychological/intrapsychological and external/internal dimensions in Vygotsky's analysis. Wertsch and Stone separated the two dimensions in order to make a place for egocentric speech. In Vygotsky's words, "Egocentric speech is internal speech in its psychological function and external speech physiologically" (1956, p. 87)—that is, intrapsychological in function but external in form. We suggest that the changes Jill made in response to Debbie's silent presence are exactly the opposite: internal in form (though recorded in writing) and interpsychological in function, to make the writing more informative to another.

Peer Collaboration

In comparison with peer tutoring, even less is understood about the intellectual value of peer collaboration. This may be partly due to the fact that collaboration requires a work environment that is even further from traditional classroom organization. Peer tutoring tasks tend to resemble common classroom activities: filling in workbooks, reading aloud, editing written assignments, and so forth. In these activities the tutor helps inform, guide, and/or correct the tutee's work. Collaboration requires a mutual task in which the partners work together to produce something that neither could have produced alone. Given the focus on individual achievement in most Western industrial societies, curricula that promote collaboration are rarely found in schools or studied by educators or psychologists.

Research on peer collaboration has thus been sparse. The major exception to this generalization is a body of research conducted by a group of Genevan psychologists (Doise, Mugny, & Perret-Clermont, 1975, 1976; Mugny & Doise, 1978; Perret-Clermont, 1980). They have conducted a series of experiments to examine the effect of peer collaboration on logical reasoning skills associated with the Piagetian stage of concrete operations: perspective-taking, conversation, and so on.

Most of the Genevan research employs a training study design in which subjects are randomly assigned to treatment or control groups in which they are exposed to different social contexts. For example, the subjects in the treatment group may be asked to solve a conservation task in a small peer group composed of conservers and nonconservers, while subjects in the control group are asked to solve the same problem alone. All subjects are individually pretested and posttested on some standard measure of concrete-operational reasoning, and the effect of exposure to peer collaboration is assessed by comparing the pretest-to-posttest gains in concrete-operational reasoning found in each group. The Genevans have employed this same training study design across a number of studies in which the particular reasoning task chosen, the social groups assembled, and the criteria used to evaluate cognitive growth are systematically varied. After reviewing this entire body of research, Perret-Clermont (1980) concludes that peer interaction enhances the development of logical reasoning through a process of active cognitive reorganization induced by cognitive conflict. She claims also that cognitive conflict is most likely to occur in situations where children with moderately discrepant perspectives (e.g., conservers and transitional subjects) are asked to reach a consensus.

Two Russian researchers, Lomov (1978) and Kol'tsova (1978), and two Japanese investigators, Inagaki and Hatano (Inagaki, 1981; Inagaki & Hatano, 1968, 1977), have reached similar conclusions—that peer interaction helps individuals acknowledge and integrate a variety of perspectives on a problem, and that this process of coordination, in turn, produces superior intellectual results. For Kol'tsova, the results are precise, rich, and logically rigorous definitions of a social science concept. For Inagaki and Hatano, the results are generalizable and stable conservation concepts. For Perret-Clermont, the results are increased ability to use concrete operational logic.

In none of these studies were subjects' interactions during collaborative problem solving systematically observed. The studies provide only anecdotal evidence to support the hypothesis that peer interaction is capable of enhancing intellectual performance because it forces individuals to recognize and coordinate conflicting perspectives on a problem. To test this hypothesis, one would need to examine the process of social coordination that occurs during problem solving in order to isolate the social conditions that are the most responsible for cognitive growth. For example, one could observe the interactions that occur while the group is working in order to differentiate those groups in which members work closely together and frequently attempt to coordinate their differing perspectives from those in which members work largely on their own. Then one could examine how these different group interactional patterns affect the problem-solving strategies used. Just this approach is advocated by Perret-Clermont:

> We have also shown that, for the task to have educational value, it is not sufficient for it merely to engage children in joint activity; there must also be confrontation between different points of view. Are all the activities described as "cooperation" by research workers such as to induce real interindividual coordinations which are the source of cognitive conflict? This question can only be answered by the systematic observation which remains to be done. (1980, p. 196)

> In further studies of the psychology of intelligence, we should envisage not solely the effect of interindividual coordination on *judgment* behavior, or on *performance* as an index of development...but also the impact of different types of social interaction, and in particular of partner's strategies, on the *strategy* which the subject adopts in order to carry out the task. (1980, p. 192)

We will describe a recent study (Forman, 1981) in which videotapes of collaborative problem-solving sessions were analyzed for the social interactional patterns used and the problem-solving strategies employed. In addition, individual measures of logical reasoning were collected on this sample of collaborative problem solvers that were compared with similar measures collected on a previous sample of solitary problem solvers.

The research design used by Forman is a modification of the training study design utilized by Perret-Clermont and her colleagues. Instead of providing only one opportunity for children to solve a problem in a collaborative fashion, Forman exposed her subjects to a total of 11 problem-solving sessions. There are several reasons for using a longitudinal design to assess children's problem-solving skills. One can observe the process of cognitive growth directly, rather than having to infer it from pretest-posttest performance, and children can develop stable working relationships. In addition, a longitudinal design was chosen for this study so that the data collected on collaborative problem solving could be compared with similar longitudinal data collected by Kuhn and Ho (1980) on solitary problem solving. (See Kuhn & Phelps, 1979, and Forman, 1981, for a more detailed explanation of the strengths of this kind of longitudinal design.)

Forman's study thus provides two kinds of information about collaboration: how the reasoning strategies of collaborative problem solvers differ from those of solitary problem solvers and how some collaborative partnerships differ from others in both social interactional patterns and cognitive strategy usage. In the following discussion, we will focus on these two kinds of data: comparisons of collaborators with solitary problem solvers and comparisons among different collaborative partnerships. We will then discuss the findings of Forman's study in light of Perret-Clermont's hypothesis and what seems to us the essential and complementary theory of Vygotsky.

Forman's Study

Like Perret-Clermont, Forman asked children to cooperate in the solution of a logical reasoning task. Unlike Perret-Clermont, Forman selected a chemical reaction task that has been used to assess the ability to isolate variables in a multivariate context (Kuhn & Phelps, 1982). In addition, her subjects were older (approximately 9 years of age) than those selected by Perret-Clermont (4–7 years).

In both the study conducted by Forman (1981) and that conducted by Kuhn and Ho (1980) the subjects were fourth- to fifth-grade, middle class children—15 singletons (Kuhn & Ho) and 4 pairs (Forman)—who showed no ability to isolate variables in a multivariate task known as the "simple plant problem." In addition to the pretest used for subject selection, all subjects were given an additional pretest: a combinations problem in which subjects were asked to arrange five kinds of snacks in all possible combinations. The singletons and pairs participated in 11 problem-solving sessions, approximately once a week over a 3-month period. The two pretest measures were readministered as posttests within a week after the final problem-solving session. All pretests and posttests were administered individually.

The chemical reaction problem consisted of a series of seven chemical problems that were ordered in terms of logical complexity. Problem 1, the simplest, requires that subjects identify the one chemical from a set of five odorless, colorless chemicals that is necessary and sufficient for producing a specified color change when mixed with a reagent. In problems 2 and 3, two or three of the five chemicals are capable of producing the color change, either separately or together. In problem 4, two chemicals are capable of producing the change, but only when *both* of them are present, and so forth.

Problem 1, with a different operative chemical each time, was presented for the first four sessions. This procedure ensured that the children were repeatedly exposed to the simplest problem in the series before more difficult problems were introduced. After the fourth session, a new problem in the series was presented whenever the previous problem had been solved once. Thus, progress through the problem series is one measure of the effectiveness of the subjects' problem-solving strategies.

Each of the 11 problem-solving sessions in both studies followed the same format. First, two demonstration experiments were performed by the experimenter. Then, the children were asked a standard set of questions about the demonstration, for example, "What do you think makes a difference in whether it turns purple or not?" Next, the children were invited to set up the experiments they wanted to try in order to determine what chemicals were responsible for the change. No mixing of chemicals was permitted during this setting-up phase of the task. After the experiments were set up and some additional questions about them were posed, the children were permitted to mix together the combinations they had selected. In Forman's study, the dyads were encouraged to work together on setting up and mixing the chemical experiments. Finally, after the results from the experiments had been observed, the experimenter repeated the original set of questions in order to assess whether the correct chemicals had been identified.

Forman analyzed only the part of the sessions devoted to planning and setting up the experiments. Four sessions for each of three subject pairs (George and Bruce: sessions 3, 5, 8, 11; Lisa and Linda: sessions 3, 5, 9, 11; Matt and Mitch: sessions 3, 5, 8, 10)—12 tapes in all—were coded. (The fourth pair had been included only as insurance against illness, etc.) The two coding systems used in the analysis consisted of one set of social interactional categories and one set of experimentation categories. In this piece, we will discuss only one type of social behavior code (procedural interactions) and three types of experimentation strategies (random, variable isolation, and combinatorial).

Procedural interactions occurred during most of the problem-solving sessions coded (a range of 71% to 100% of the available time). They were defined as all activities carried out by one or both children that focus on getting the task accomplished.[1] Examples of procedural interactions were distributing and arranging task materials, choosing chemical experiments, and recording experiments. Three levels of procedural interactions were identified: parallel, associative, and cooperative (adapted from Parten's 1932 study of social interaction). These three levels represent three qualitatively different approaches to the sharing of ideas and the division of labor. During parallel procedural interactions, children share materials and exchange comments about the task. However, they make few if any attempts to monitor the work of the other or to inform the other of their own thoughts and actions. Associative procedural interactions occur when children try to exchange information about some of the combinations each one has selected. However, at the associative level, no attempt is made to coordinate the roles of the two partners. Cooperative interactions require that both children constantly monitor each other's work and play coordinated roles in performing task procedures.

The experimentation strategy codes were adapted from Kuhn and Phelps (1982). Three basic types of experimentation strategies were observed: a random or trial-and-error strategy; an isolation-of-variables strategy; and a combinatorial strategy. The random experiments strategy represents a relatively ineffective, unsystematic approach to experimentation. The variable-isolation strategy is effective for solving the first three problems only. The more advanced problems, 4 through 7, require both experimental isolation and combinatorial strategies. Thus, this experimentation coding system was devised to identify when or if this strategy shift (from only variable isolation to both variable isolation and combinatorial) occurred.

Experimental strategy codes were assigned to a dyad based solely on the type of chemical experiments set up. Neither the type of social organization used to select these experiments nor the kinds of conversations that occurred during the setting-up process affected the assignment of an experimentation code. Thus, the coding of experimentation strategies constituted an assessment of each dyad's behavior that was independent of that obtained by coding their social interactions.

For the comparisons of the problem-solving achievements of collaborators versus singletons, two kinds of data are available: the number of chemical problems solved during the 11 sessions and pretest-to-posttest change scores. The first comparison produced striking differences between collaboration and solitary problem solving. While Kuhn and Ho found that only 4 of the 15 singletons solved problems 1 through 3 in the 11 sessions, all 4 of Forman's dyads solved problems 1 through 4 in the same amount of time. In addition, one dyad (George and Bruce) solved problems 1 through 6 during this three-month period, an achievement approached by none of Kuhn and Ho's subjects.

The pretest-posttest comparison between singletons and dyads produced more mixed results. These results are displayed in Tables 1 and 2 (ignoring for now the initials in parentheses). On the simple plant problem (Table 1), the singletons showed greater progress than the pairs between the pretest and posttest. In contrast, subjects who had worked in pairs seemed to show greater progress on the combinations problem (Table 2) than did the subjects who had worked alone.[2] Thus, while the pairs seemed able to master the series of chemical problems at a much faster rate than did the singletons, they did not show consistently greater pretest-posttest gains.

One clear difference between these two comparisons (progress through the problems versus posttest performance) is that both partners were able to contribute to the solution of each chemical problem presented, but on the pretest-posttest measures the partners were on their own. The relatively sophisticated problem-solving strategies that collaborators were able to display when they could assist each other were not apparent when each partner was asked to work alone on similar problems.

Another reason why collaborators did not always outperform the singletons may lie in difference among the partnerships. Due to the very small number of dyads examined, large differences between dyads may obscure all but massive differences between dyads and singletons. Therefore, we turn to the second set of comparisons: those of dyads. First, we will discuss the types of social interactions that occurred over time in the three collaborative partnerships examined. Second, we will look at the experimentation strategies used by those same dyads. Third, we will reexamine their pretest-posttest data.

TABLE 1
Pretest and Posttest Category Frequencies on the Simple Plant Problem

Group	Predominantly Concrete	Transitional	Predominantly Formal	Total *N*
Pretest				
Singletons	15	0	0	15
Pairs	8	0	0	8
Posttest				
Singletons	4	5	6	15
Pairs	6 M1, L2, M2, G, K1, K2	1 (B)	1 (L1)	8

TABLE 2
Pretest and Posttest Category Frequencies on the Combination Problem

Group	Predominantly Concrete	Transitional	Predominantly Formal	Total *N*
Pretest				
Singletons	15	0	0	15
Pairs	8	0	0	8
Posttest				
Singletons	12	3	0	15
Pairs	5 K2, L1, M1, K1, G	3 L2, M2, B	0	8

The most obvious difference among the social behavior of the three dyads concerned the development of procedural interactions patterns. All procedural interactions were classified as either parallel, associative, or cooperative. Table 3 shows that all three dyads engaged in predominantly parallel and associative interactions during the first session coded (session 3 for all three dyads). Only Lisa and Linda showed any degree of cooperative behavior during this session. However, by sessions 5, 8, and 11, George and Bruce were entirely cooperative. Lisa and Linda retained some associative interaction patterns in session 5, but by sessions 9 and 11 they too were engaging in cooperative interactions. In contrast, Matt and Mitch never cooperated throughout the 3-month period. The interaction pattern that Matt and Mitch seemed to prefer was either predominantly or entirely parallel in nature.

Table 4 summarizes the differences in experimentation strategies used in each pair's last two sessions. All three pairs used similar kinds of experimentation strategies during the earlier sessions. George and Bruce, the dyad who solved the greatest number of problems, used both an isolation of variables and

TABLE 3
Percentage of Procedural Time Spent in Parallel, Associative, and Cooperative Activities

Subject Pair	Type of Procedural Activity (%)		
	Parallel	Associate	Cooperative
George and Bruce			
Session 3	61	39	0
Session 5	0	0	100
Session 8	0	0	100
Session 11	0	0	100
Lisa and Linda			
Session 3	42	26	32
Session 5	0	44	55
Session 9	0	0	100
Session 11	0	0	100
Matt and Mitch			
Session 3	90	10	0
Session 5	85	15	0
Session 8	100	0	0
Session 10	100	0	0

a combinatorial strategy in the later two sessions. Lisa and Linda used only the variable-isolation strategy in session 9 but both strategies by session 11. In contrast, Matt and Mitch produced either random experiments or experiments capable of isolating single variables throughout the study, despite the fact that neither of these strategies was sufficient for solving the advanced problems that were presented to them during sessions 8 and 10.

Returning to the pretest-posttest measures, we find that George and Bruce, who worked so well together, did not maintain this high degree of performance when they were tested individually. The initials on Tables 1 and 2 show the posttest status of the six children whose tapes were analyzed: George (G), Bruce (B), Lisa (L1), Linda (L2), Matt (M1), Mitch (M2), plus the remaining unanalyzed fourth pair (K1 and K2). On the simple plant problem (Table 1), the children receiving the highest scores were Bruce and Lisa; on the combinations problem (Table 2), Bruce, Linda, and Mitch exhibited the most advanced/reasoning skills. Thus, the clear differences among dyads that were apparent on the videotapes of collaborative problem-solving sessions were not reflected in the posttest results.

In summary, when pairs were compared with singletons, the pairs solved the chemical combination problems at a much faster rate. However, the pairs

T A B L E 4
Experimentation Strategies Used in Chemical Problems 4–7

Subject Pair	Random Combinations	Isolation-of-Variables Strategy	Systematic Combinational Strategy
George and Bruce			
Session 8		X	X
Session 11		X	X
Lisa and Linda			
Session 9		X	
Session 11		X	X
Matt and Mitch			
Session 8	X	X	
Session 10		X	

did not do better than the singletons on all of the posttest measures. Singletons appeared to outperform the pairs on the simple plant problem, a test of subject's ability to isolate variables, whereas the pairs seemed to do better on the combinations problem.

When comparisons were made between the pairs, it was found that George and Bruce solved more chemical combination problems than did the other pairs. In addition, George and Bruce were the first pair to switch to an entirely cooperative interaction pattern and to use a combinatorial experimentation strategy. On some of these variables, that is, the degree of cooperation shown and the use of a combinatorial strategy, Lisa and Linda appeared to hold an intermediate position between the two pairs of boys. However, these fairly consistent differences in interactional style and problem-solving strategy use were not reflected in the posttest performance of these children. In general, George and Bruce did not exhibit consistently higher levels of reasoning on their individual posttests than did the other subjects.

Discussion

What can these results tell us about the hypothesis proposed by Perret-Clermont that peer interaction can induce cognitive conflict that, in turn, results in cognitive restructuring and growth? Forman did find an association between high levels of social coordination (cooperative procedural interactions) and the use of certain experimentation strategies (combinatorial strategies). However, she did not devise a measure of cognitive conflict for her study, and her findings thus cannot establish that social coordination results in cognitive conflict, which then affects problem-solving skills.

One reason why cognitive conflict was not assessed was that overt indices of conflict, that is, arguments, were relatively rare during the portion of the problem-solving session examined—the setting-up phase of the task during which experimentation strategies were most apparent. In this portion of the session, hypotheses concerning the experiments could be proposed but not tested. During most of the setting-up time, children were busy working, separately or together, on laying out and sharing task materials and on planning and choosing experiments. Among the children who interacted at a cooperative level, a great deal of mutual support, encouragement, correction, and guidance was exchanged. For example, one child would select chemical combinations while the other checked for duplicates. Instead of conflicting points of view, one saw two people attempting to construct and implement a joint experimentation plan to be tested later on in the task.

Conflicting points of view were apparent later in the problem-solving session, when most or all of the results of the experiments were visible. At that time, one could observe children forming distinct and sometimes opposing conclusions about the problem solution. Just such a conflict occurred in problem-solving session 3 between George and Bruce: Here is a summary of their interaction taken from a videotape record.

> In this session, chemical C alone was the solution to the chemical problem. The two boys set up and mixed the following set of experiments: B, C, BE, CD, CE, DE, BDE, CDF, DEF. In addition, they could examine the results of the two demonstration experiments: BCE, DEF. All the experiments containing chemical C turned purple; the rest remained clear.
>
> After all the experiments were mixed, the experimenter asked both children, "What makes a difference in whether it turns purple?" Bruce initially concluded that the answer was C and E. George expressed his surprise that a single element, for example C, produced the desired color change. In response to the standard prompt from the experimenter, "Can you be sure it's C and E?" Bruce reexamined some experiments and found one that contained E (and not C) that did not change color. Bruce, however, did not conclude at this point that C was the only operative chemical. George then asked Bruce whether all the experiments containing C produced the desired color change. Bruce scanned each experiment containing C and announced that each did change color.
>
> Based on the experimental evidence and some information remembered from previous sessions, George concluded that C was the solution to the problem. Bruce, however, contradicted George by asserting it was F. At this point, they both reexamined the experiments. Afterward, George still concluded it was C and Bruce concluded it was C and F.
>
> The experimenter asked whether they could be sure of their answers. George replied that he was sure of C but not of F. Once again, the evidence was examined. This time, Bruce identified the experiment CDF as indicating that F was an operative chemical. George countered this argument by comparing it with experiment DEF that did not produce the desired reaction. Bruce responded that

D and E were more powerful liquids than F and therefore prevented F from working. George then tried another approach by asking Bruce how he could tell it was F and not C that made the mixture CDF turn purple. Bruce replied by asking George how he could tell it wasn't both C and F that made CDF turn purple. George's concluding remark was an assertion that he just knew it was C alone.

This interchange shows the kinds of activities that conflicting solutions to the problem seemed to induce. The children returned repeatedly to the experimental evidence for supporting data. Because their conclusions differed, they were forced to acknowledge information that refuted their own inferences as well as data that supported them. These data then had to be integrated into a convincing argument in support of their own point of view. Counterarguments to their partner's position also had to be constructed. Bruce, in particular, was forced to revise his conclusions based on the evidence George brought to his attention. Despite his efforts, George was unable to convince Bruce to accept his conclusion. Unfortunately, they had not provided themselves with enough of the appropriate experimental evidence in session 3 to enable them to reach a consensus about the solution.

Collaboration on the chemical reaction task thus seems to involve two different types of social interactive processes. The first process, which occurs during the setting-up or planning stage of the task, involves either separate (parallel) working patterns or closely coordinated cooperative patterns. Cooperation during the setting-up stage consists of mutual guidance, encouragement, and support. Often during this phase of the task, complementary problem-solving roles are assumed.

Later on in the task, when experimental evidence is being examined, the second kind of interactive process occurs. At this time, each child seems to be reaching independent conclusions about the solution of the task that are based on all or only some of the available experimental evidence. After each child comes to a conclusion, he or she may find that his or her partner does not agree. In this circumstance, overt conflicting perspectives on the experimental evidence are expressed in the form of an argument. Arguments capable of producing a consensus seemed to be those that made use of appropriate supporting evidence.

It appears that Perret-Clermont's notion that cognitive conflict is the mediator between peer interaction and cognitive reorganization can be tested best in contexts where overt manifestations of conflict are likely. These contexts seem to occur when children have access to a wealth of empirical evidence, when this evidence is capable of suggesting at least two distinct solutions to the problem, and when a consensual solution is solicited.

Perret-Clermont's hypothesis about the importance of cognitive conflict comes from Piaget's theory concerning the role of social factors in development. Most of the past research on the topic of peer collaboration has been based on Piaget's ideas. Piaget placed more importance on peer interaction than on adult-child interaction, so it is not surprising that the bulk of research on collaboration has shared a Piagetian perspective.

In order to understand the limitations as well as the strengths of this perspective on collaboration, one needs to appreciate the role that peer interaction plays in Piaget's theory. Piaget (1970) identified four factors that he believed are necessary for a theory of cognitive development: maturation, experience with the physical environment, social experiences, and equilibration or self-regulation. In addition, Piaget claimed that equilibration is the most fundamental of the four factors. Peer interaction, and social experiences in general, derive their importance from the influence they can exert on equilibration through the introduction of cognitive conflict. Perret-Clermont shares this view of development when she writes,

> Of course, cognitive conflict of this kind does not create the *forms* of operations, but it brings about the disequilibriums which make cognitive elaboration necessary, and in this way cognitive conflict confers a special role on the social factor as one among other factors leading to mental growth. Social-cognitive conflict may be figuratively likened to the catalyst in a chemical reaction: it is not present at all in the final product, but it is nevertheless indispensible if the reaction is to take place. (Perret-Clermont, 1980, p. 178)

When Piaget looks at peer interaction, therefore, he looks for evidence of disequilibrium, that is, cognitive conflict. He is not interested in describing or explaining social interactional processes as a whole. Piaget's theory is most helpful in explaining those situations where cognitive conflict is clearly and overtly expressed in external social behaviors, for example, arguments. However, in situations where overt conflict is not apparent and where mutual guidance and support are evident, his theory provides few clues concerning the role of social factors in development. Fortunately, Vygotsky's writings on adult-child interaction offer insights into the intellectual value of these kinds of peer interactions.

To illustrate how Vygotsky's ideas shed light on some of the processes involved in peer collaboration, we will discuss another set of observations of George and Bruce. One of the most puzzling findings from Forman's study was the discrepancy between how a dyad functions as a unit and how the partners function separately. George and Bruce were clearly the most successful collaborators, yet they did not show the same consistently high level of functioning when they were posttested separately. This discrepancy between dyadic and individual performance levels was also apparent when subjects who collaborated were compared with those who worked alone. On the posttest measures, which were individually administered, collaborative problem solvers did not do better than solitary problem solvers. Nevertheless, collaborative partners were able to solve many more chemical problems than could solitary problem solvers during the same period of time.

Vygotsky acknowledged that a discrepancy might exist between solitary and social problem solving when he developed his notion of the zone of proximal development. He defined this zone as "the distance between the actual developmental level as determined by independent problem solving and the level of potential development as determined through problem solving under adult guidance or in collaboration with more capable peers" (1934/1978, p. 86). Thus, Vygotsky hypothesized that children would be able to solve problems with assistance from an adult or more capable peer before they could solve them alone. This seemingly obvious observation was then used to reach several original conclusions. One conclusion was that the zone of proximal development could be used to identify those skills most amenable to instruction. Another was that learning consists of the internalization of social interactional processes. According to Vygotsky, development proceeds when interpsychological regulation is transformed into intrapsychological regulation.

Returning to Forman's data, it appears that a similar process of interpsychological to intrapsychological regulation may also occur in collaborative contexts where neither partner can be seen as objectively "more capable," but where the partners may assume separate but complementary social roles. One child may perform an observing, guiding, and correcting role while the other performs the task procedures. This observing partner seems to provide some of the same kinds of assistance that has been called scaffolding by Wood, Bruner, and Ross (1976). Such support from an observing partner seems to enable the two collaborators to solve problems together before they are capable of solving the same problems alone. When collaborators assume complementary roles, they begin to resemble the peer tutors described earlier. For example, the observer/performer roles are functionally similar to the critic/author roles observed in Egan's New Hampshire classroom.

In addition, one can see in Forman's data instances where problem-solving strategies first appear as social interactional procedures and are later internalized. Remember that a combinatorial problem was administered to each child individually at three different times (as a pretest, as an immediate posttest, and as a delayed posttest). In addition, these same children were presented with a similar combinatorial problem in each problem-solving session when they were asked to decide jointly which chemical mixtures to set up. Therefore, a comparison can be made between the combinations generated by each child when he or she worked alone or in pairs.

> Both George and Bruce used an empirical strategy to generate combinations during their pretest—for example, selecting a combination at random and then basing the next combination on the first by adding, subtracting, or substituting one of its elements. The third combination would then be produced by copying, with another minor revision, the second combination. Pairwise checking of each new

combination with each previous combination was the empirical procedure used for guarding against duplications.

In their early collaborative problem-solving sessions, George and Bruce worked in parallel and each used an empirical strategy similar to the one used on the pretest to generate combinations. After about a month of working together, they devised a social procedure for generating combinations empirically by assuming complementary problem-solving roles: One selected chemicals and the other checked their uniqueness.

After two months, they had begun to organize their combinations into groups based on their number of elements. In addition, they had devised a deductive system for generating two-element combinations. This deductive procedure enabled the child who had previously done the checking to prompt, correct, and reinforce the selections of his partner. Higher-order combinations were produced empirically using the familiar social procedure.

At the last session, the boys continued to assume complementary roles but now used the blackboard as a recording device. They produced combinations in a highly organized fashion—singles, two-element combinations, three-element combinations, and so on—and were able to generate almost all of the 31 possible combinations. They used a deductive procedure for generating the two-element combinations but still relied on their empirical procedure for the higher-order combinations.

At the first posttest one week after the last collaborative session, the degree to which each boy had internalized a deductive combinatorial system was assessed by asking them to generate combinations independently. Bruce was able to generate all 10 two-element combinations deductively on his own, but George was not. George used an empirical system to generate combinations. On the second posttest four months later, however, both boys had internalized a deductive procedure for producing two-element combinations.

It appears that these two boys were able to apply a preexisting intrapsychological rule, an empirical combinatorial procedure, to a collaborative context by dividing the procedure into complementary problem-solving roles. With repeated exposure to the problem, these boys were able to progress to a deductive procedure for generating simple, two-element combinations. At first, deductive reasoning was clearly a social activity for George and Bruce. Each time one partner selected a series of combinations, the other guided, prompted, and corrected his selections. Later, one partner was able to demonstrate that he had internalized this deductive procedure by using it to generate all possible two-element combinations on his own. Four months later, both partners were able to generate all possible pairs of five objects deductively by themselves. Thus, for these two boys, deductive combinatorial reasoning first appeared in a collaborative context. Only one of the two boys was initially able to show that he had internalized this procedure when he generated combinations alone. Months later, however, both boys had internalized this deductive process.

In summary, a Piagetian perspective on the role of social factors in development can be useful in understanding situations where overt indices of cognitive conflict are present. However, if one wants to understand the cognitive consequences of other social interactional contexts, Vygotsky's ideas may be more helpful. In tasks where experimental evidence was being generated and where managerial skills were required, by assuming complementary problem-solving roles, peers could perform tasks together before they could perform them alone. The peer observer seemed to provide some of the same kinds of "scaffolding" assistance that others have attributed to the adult in teaching contexts.

Thus, the Vygotskian perspective enables us to see that collaborative tasks requiring data generation, planning, and management can provide another set of valuable experiences for children. In these tasks, a common set of assumptions, procedures, and information needs to be constructed. These tasks require children to integrate their conflicting task conceptions into a mutual plan. One way to achieve a shared task perspective is to assume complementary problem-solving roles. Then each child learns to use speech to guide the actions of her or his partner and, in turn, to be guided by the partner's speech. Exposure to this form of social regulation can enable children to master difficult problems together before they are capable of solving them alone. More important, experience with social forms of regulation can provide children with just the tools they need to master problems on their own. It enables them to observe and reflect on the problem-solving process as a whole and to select those procedures that are the most effective. When they can apply this social understanding to themselves, they can then solve, independently, those tasks that they had previously been able to solve only with assistance.

Thus, collaborative problem solving seems to offer some of the same experiences for children that peer tutoring provides: the need to give verbal instructions to peers, the impetus for self-reflection encouraged by a visible audience, and the need to respond to peer questions and challenges. The reciprocal model of peer assistance that characterized the children in Egan's classroom is even more apparent in collaborative problem-solving contexts, similar to those observed by Forman.

Conclusion

In conclusion, in these analyses we are not talking about a children's culture separate from adults. What Leont'ev and Luria discuss as the "most important specifically human form of mental development"—namely, "the assimilation of general human experience in the teaching process"—must ultimately be grounded in adult-child interactions. But peer (and cross-age) relationships can function as intermediate transforming contexts between social and external adult-child interactions and the individual child's inner speech.

Although such peer interactions take place in home and community as well as at school, they may be especially important in school because of limitations and rigidities characteristic of adult-child interactions in that institutional setting. Cazden (1983) argues for the value to child development of a category of parent-child interactions of which the peek-a-boo game and picture book reading are familiar examples. In interactions such as these, there is a predictable structure in which the mother initially enacts the entire script herself and then the child takes an increasingly active role, eventually speaking all the parts initially spoken by the mother. The contrast between such learning environments and the classroom is striking. In school lessons, teachers give directions and children nonverbally carry them out; teachers ask questions and children answer them, frequently with only a word or a phrase. Most important, these roles are not reversible, at least not within the context of teacher-child interactions. Children never give directions to the teachers, and questions addressed to teachers are rare except for asking permission. The only context in which children can reverse interactional roles with the same intellectual content, giving directions as well as following them, and asking questions as well as answering them, is with their peers.

Acknowledgments

Forman's research was supported, in part, by a grant from Radcliffe College; by a grant to Deanna Kuhn from the Milton Fund, Harvard University; and by NIMH Grant No. 5 T32 MH15786 to the Department of Psychology, Northwestern University. We would like to thank the students, faculty, and principal of the Straton Elementary School, Arlington, Massachusetts, for their generous participation in this research; and Leonard Scinto, Addison Stone, and Jim Wertsch for their helpful comments on earlier drafts of this piece.

Notes

[1] Other social interactional codes were used to identify conversations that served to plan, reflect on, or organize these procedural activities (metaprocedural interactions), task-focused jokes (playful interactions), task-focused observations (shared observations), and off-task behavior.

[2] A second set of posttests was administered to both samples 4 months after the first posttest. The pairs constantly outperformed the singletons on both second posttest measures. However, the interpretation of these findings is problematic due to the fact that this 4-month period occurred during the school year for the pairs but during the summer for the singletons.

References

Carrasco, R.L., Vera, A., & Cazden, C.B. (1981). Aspects of bilingual students' communicative competence in the classroom: A case study. In R. Duran (Ed.), *Latino language and communicative behavior. Discourse processes: Advances in research and theory* (Vol. 6). Norwood, NJ: Ablex.

Cazden, C.B. (1983). Peekaboo as an instructional model: Discourse development at school and at home. In B. Bain (Ed.), *The so-ciogenesis of language and human conduct: A multi-disciplinary book of readings* (pp. 33–58). New York: Plenum.

Cazden, C.B., Cox, M., Dickinson, D., Steinberg, Z., & Stone, C. (1978). "You all gonna hafta listen": Peer teaching in a primary classroom. In W.A. Collins (Ed.), *Children's language and communication* (12th Annual Minnesota Symposium on Child Development, pp. 183–231). Hillsdale, NJ: Erlbaum.

Doise, W., Mugny, G., & Perret-Clermont, A.N. (1975). Social interaction and the development of cognitive operations. *European Journal of Social Psychology*, 5, 367–383.

Doise, W., Mugny, G., & Perret-Clermont, A.N. (1976). Social interaction and cognitive development: Further evidence. *European Journal of Social Psychology*, 6(3), 245–247.

Forman, E.A. (1981). *The role of collaboration in problem-solving in children*. Doctoral dissertation, Harvard University, Cambridge, MA.

Galton, M., Simon, B., & Croll, P. (1980). *Inside the primary classroom*. Boston: Routledge & Kegan Paul.

Inagaki, K. (1981). Facilitation of knowledge integration through classroom discussion. *Quarterly Newsletter of the Laboratory of Comparative Human Cognition*, 3(3), 26–28.

Inagaki, K., & Hatano, G. (1968). Motivational influences on epistemic observation. *Japanese Journal of Educational Psychology*, 6, 191–202.

Inagaki, K., & Hatano, G. (1977). Amplification of cognitive motivation and its effects on epistemic observation. *American Educational Research Journal*, 14, 485–491.

Inhelder, B., & Piaget, J. (1958). *The growth of logical thinking from childhood to adolescence*. New York: Basic Books.

Kamler, B. (1980). One child, one teacher, one classroom: The story of one piece of writing. *Language Arts*, 57, 680–693.

Kol'tsova, V.A. (1978). Experimental study of cognitive activity in communication (with specific reference to concept formation). *Soviet Psychology*, 17, 23–38.

Kuhn, D., & Ho, V. (1980). Self-directed activity and cognitive development. *Journal of Applied Developmental Psychology*, 1(2), 119–133.

Kuhn, D., & Phelps, E. (1979). A methodology for observing development of a formal reasoning strategy. *New Directions for Child Development*, 5, 45–58.

Kuhn, D., & Phelps, E. (1982). The development of problem-solving strategies. In H. Reese (Ed.), *Advances in child development* (Vol. 17). New York: Academic.

Lawler, J. (1980). Collectivity and individuality in Soviet educational theory. *Contemporary Educational Psychology*, 5, 163–174.

Leont'ev, A.N. (1981). The problem of activity in psychology. In J.V. Wertsch (Ed.), *The concept of activity in Soviet psychology* (pp. 37–71). Armonk, NY: Sharpe.

Leontiev, A.N., & Luria, A.R. (1968). The psychological ideas of L.S. Vygotsky. In B. Wolman (Ed.), *Historical roots of contemporary psychology*. New York: HarperCollins.

Levina, R.E. (1981). L.S. Vygotsky's ideas about the planning function of speech in children. In J.V. Wertsch (Ed.), *The concept of activity in Soviet psychology* (pp. 279–299). Armonk, NY: Sharpe.

Lomov, B.F. (1978). Psychological processes and communication. *Soviet Psychology*, 17, 3–22.

Mehan, H. (1979). *Learning lessons*. Cambridge, MA: Harvard University Press.

Mehan, H., & Riel, M.M. (1982). Teachers' and students' instructional strategies. In L. Adler (Ed.), *Cross-cultural research at issue*. New York: Academic.

Mugny, G., & Doise, W. (1978). Socio-cognitive conflict and structure of individual and collective performances. *European Journal of Social Psychology*, 8, 181–192.

Parten, M. (1932). Social participation among preschool children. *Journal of Abnormal and Social Psychology*, 27, 243–269.

Perret-Clermont, A.N. (1980). *Social interaction and cognitive development in children*. New York: Academic.

Piaget, J. (1970). Piaget's theory. In P.H. Mussen (Ed.), *Carmichael's manual of child psychology* (3rd ed., Vol. 1, pp. 703–732). New York: Wiley.

Sharan, S. (1980). Cooperative learning in small groups: Recent methods and effects on achievement, attitudes, and ethnic relations. *Review of Educational Research*, 50, 241–271.

Simon, B. (Ed.). (1957). *Psychology in the Soviet Union*. Stanford, CA: Stanford University Press.

Simon, B., & Simon, J. (Eds.). (1963). *Educational psychology in the USSR*. Stanford, CA: Stanford University Press.

Slavina, L.S. (1957). Specific features of the intellectual work of unsuccessful pupils. In B. Simon (Ed.), *Psychology in the Soviet Union* (pp. 205–212). Stanford, CA: Stanford University Press.

Vygotsky, L.S. (1956). *Izbrannye psikhologicheskie issledovaniya* [Selected psychological research]. Moscow: Izdatel'stzo Akademii Pedagogicheskikh Nauk RFSFR.

Vygotsky, L.S. (1978). *Mind in society: The development of higher psychological processes* (M. Cole, V. John-Steiner, S. Scribner, and E.

Souberman, Eds. & Trans.). Cambridge, MA: Harvard University Press. (Original work published 1934)

Vygotsky, L.S. (1981). The genesis of higher mental functions. In J.V. Wertsch (Ed.), *The concept of activity in Soviet psychology.* Armonk, NY: Sharpe.

Wertsch, J.V. (1978). Adult-child interaction and the roots of metacognition. *Quarterly Newsletter of the Institute for Comparative Human Development, 2*(1), 15–18.

Wertsch, J.V. (1979). The regulation of human action and the given-new organization of private speech. In G. Zivin (Ed.), *The development of self-regulation through private speech* (pp. 79–98). New York: Wiley.

Wertsch, J.V. (Ed.). (1981). *The concept of activity in Soviet psychology.* Armonk, NY: Sharpe.

Wertsch, J.V., & Stone, A.C. (1978). Microgenesis as a tool for developmental analysis. *Quarterly Newsletter of the Laboratory of Comparative Human Development, 1*(1), 8–10.

Wood, D., Bruner, J.S., & Ross, B. (1976). The role of tutoring in problem-solving. *Journal of Child Psychology and Psychiatry, 17,* 89–100.

8

The Children of Trackton's Children: Spoken and Written Language in Social Change

Shirley Brice Heath

The brief finale of *Middlemarch*, the celebrated tale of families in a Victorian community, opens with these lines:

> Every limit is a beginning as well as an ending. Who can quit young lives after being long in company with them, and not desire to know what befell them in their after-years? For the fragment of a life, however typical, is not the sample of an even web.

George Eliot then capsules in a few pages the lives of Middlemarch's young families as they lived them out beyond the period of time covered in the novel's preceding chapters. Eliot's reminder that any novel is reduction and selection pertains, of course, as well to ethnography. We feel the fragmentary nature of such accounts most especially perhaps when they have focused on children, and after we have closed the pages of such works, we cannot easily quit these young lives, knowing that the ethnographic present never remains as it is described, and we wonder what followed in the after-years.

Such curiosity applies especially to the young of groups known to be in the midst of rapid social change when the anthropologist chooses to write a description of their lives. This piece looks in on such a community—southern, black, working class families described initially during the turbulent years of the 1960s and 1970s. *Ways With Words: Language, Life, and Work in Communities and Classrooms* (Health, 1983) gives ethnographic accounts of how the children of two working class communities in the southeastern United States learned to use language at home and school between 1969 and 1977. One community was Roadville, a group of white families steeped for four generations in the life of

From Stigler, J.W., Shweder, R.A., & Herdt, G.S. (Eds.), *Cultural Psychology: Essays on Comparative Human Development* (pp. 496–519). Copyright © 1990 by Cambridge University Press. Reprinted with permission of the publisher.

the textile mills, but set by the end of the 1970s on a path toward suburban living and careers in small businesses, education, and service industries. The other community was Trackton, a collection of black families traditionally bound to farming but seemingly inextricably tied to life in the textile mills by the end of the 1970s. Within five years after the end of the fieldwork in these two communities, neither existed any longer as a geographical entity. Roadville's families had moved into either the largest towns of the region or to the suburbs of cities of the South, and the children of focus in the ethnography were either continuing their education or settling into their first jobs, planning ahead for homes and the beginning of their families. Trackton's families had become scattered, dispersed by the radical upheaval of the economic recession of the early 1980s, with its concomitant severe reduction in the number of textile mills in the Piedmont region of the Southeast. The children of two of the Trackton children introduced in the 1983 ethnography are the subject of this study. We look in on their lives, in one instance, in a high-rise, low-income housing unit in Alabama, and in the other, in temporary housing in what is currently called "a black slum area" across town from the former neighborhood of Trackton.

The epilogue of *Ways With Words* reminded readers that the dramatic and widely varying social changes taking place for blacks in different geographic regions and economic settings following the War on Poverty and Black-Is-Beautiful movements of the 1960s and 1970s made it especially necessary to recognize that research on black culture would increasingly be a study in diversity. There is no single black experience. In the geographic region of Trackton, the 1970s proved a time of apparent economic advancement for those blacks who worked in the textile mills. Both males and females had begun to work in the mills before finishing high school, because the mill offered "good pay." Their parents, often combining work on one shift at the mill with part-time domestic work or local construction jobs, sought to rent better housing, buy a place of their own, or purchase their first car. But the recession of the early 1980s, accompanied by the dissolution of many of the small local textile mills and the closings or consolidations of the mills of several national textile corporations in response to foreign competition, wiped out the mills as the source of a secure economic future. The erosion by inflation of Trackton families' low wages even during periods of employment made saving impossible. The work opportunities available in the early 1970s through community-based employment provisions of the model cities program, and later the Comprehensive Employment and Training Act (CETA), were short-lived, and after 1981 essentially no new public job programs for the young black poor existed. Those who turned to the aid for families with dependent children (AFDC) program found benefits much lower in real terms than they had been a decade earlier; increased stringency rulings forced fathers to remain "absent" members of what had become single-parent households and proscribed help to mothers from their older children living out of the household. In the 1960s and 1970s, Trackton families had chosen to remain independent of "the projects" of public housing and to rent instead small, frame, two-family units from absentee black landlords. By 1984, all of the "old-time" Trackton residents had given up hope of independence: Those with grown children moved about, taking turns staying with each child for short periods; families with young children moved to cheaper temporary housing in the older part of town and put their names on the waiting list for public housing. Women who had in earlier days worked as domestics for some white families found when they inquired about such jobs in the mid-1980s that these families had engaged professional cleaning services and put their preschoolers in cooperative play groups or nursery schools. Men who had previously always been able to "pick up" local seasonal agricultural work found the farms and orchards of past years either closed or dependent on machinery for most harvesting tasks. Trackton's proud independent families, intent on "gettin' on" and full of the ideology of "changin' times" in the 1960s and 1970s, met daily in the mid-1980s poverty and dependency that allowed neither time nor inclination for considering the meaning of black movements, Martin Luther King's dream, or the promise of bygone interracial human relations councils.

It is customarily not the anthropologist, but the policy analyst or sociologist, who speaks of the effects of national policy shifts and global economic directions on the lives of members of sociocultural groups set apart in American society by ethnic, racial, geographic, or class boundaries. In 1987, several public figures who were also social scientists published reports of the resulting failed education, family dissolution, and increased percentage of children in poverty (Coleman & Hoffer, 1987; Edelman, 1987; Lefkowitz, 1987; Moynihan, 1987). The central focus of most of these studies was the dysfunctional nature of families and the impoverishing effects of changed social policies, tax laws, and the inadequacy of minimum-wage employment to sustain even very small families (e.g., in 1987 a full-time, minimum-wage job provided 75% of the amount specified as poverty level for a family of three). These reports and the prediction from many that the major issue of the next presidential term would be social problems—especially the poverty of children—led me to turn again to the work of anthropologists who studied minority cultures in the United States during the 1960s and 1970s. If we look, for example, at the studies of black communities, most reports, including my own (published in 1983 but based on fieldwork carried out between 1969 and 1981), described intact sociocultural groupings whose cultures were not "deficient," but variant and certainly equivalent in their way to the mainstream pattern. Legacies of African norms and social organizational adaptations to slavery had given black communities not only identifiable value systems and socialization processes but also cultural ideologies they believed to be of their own creation and definition and of sufficient strength to enable them to push ahead. Key individuals—both nationally and locally—reinforced the significance (as well as the mystification) of these ideologies by linking them to a continued faith in education, the future of their youth, the centrality of religious conviction, and the power of the bonds of brotherhood and sisterhood among blacks.

But by the late 1980s the image both within and beyond many black communities had become largely one of poverty, dissolution, and strife. Nearly half of all black children lived in poverty, most of these in households headed by a mother under 25 years of age who had neither the education nor self-image to look for or to secure and sustain employment. Nearly 30% of the children entering school in inner cities in the fall of 1987 were born to school dropouts who were themselves still of school age. Moreover, the social scientist/public policy reporters of 1987 argued that although most of the publicity pointed to minority cultures, especially blacks, the trends for blacks foreshadowed those for white; between 1969 and 1984 the white child poverty rate went up two thirds, while the black rate increased only one sixth (Edelman, 1987, pp. 23–33). Relatively few anthropologists have studied closely the everyday-life meanings of these figures and trends among either minority or white communities in the United States. Yet long-term fieldwork in a single region or community builds the basis for continuing ties, and a close look at Trackton families—and especially the young unwed mothers of the late 1980s who were among the children of Trackton in the 1970s—offered me an opportunity to look behind the statistics currently put forward by policymakers to support the agendas for social change of the 21st century (Foster et al., 1979).

This piece takes up three issues. The first is the question of the extent to which the meanings of cultural membership, played out in numerous texts by Trackton adults for and with their children during my earlier fieldwork, were retained and understood by the young sufficiently to be carried into their socialization practices with their own children. The collective shared and public symbols of Trackton seemed in the 1970s to be elaborated and highly interdependent; through nearly a decade of life with community members, I had seen them persevere in their ideas and values and enforce the sharing of ties to the collective identity of their own community and black membership. Their everyday narratives and—of special interest to me—their verbal and nonverbal patterns of language socialization with their young had seemed to fix and stabilize the identity of individuals as members of their own group and as outsiders to others' cultural groups. From their church services and joking rituals to their habits of jointly reading newspapers and retelling stories, they both performed and commented on their performances of crisscrossing and redundant themes, as they alternately insulated themselves against the otherness of communities beyond them and yet admitted sometimes the need to build bridges to outside institutions that could secure predictable connections when they needed public services, commercial exchanges, and education. But in a totally different spatial setting, without family members or national media to replay either public or intimate symbols of community membership and black pride, would the cultural symbols and tests of their childhood be sufficiently sustained for adaptation in the socialization of a new generation?

This query leads to a second: What are the resources for adaptation within different symbols or cultural texts? and What difference does the degree of time spent with local community-created and sustained symbols, as opposed to mass-produced ones, make to the vitality of one's identification as a member of any sociocultural body? Much has been written about the nature of adaptation, and radically different types of evidence have been used to determine whether aspects of human behavior can be interpreted as strategies of individuals to promote their fitness in specific social and cultural contexts (Mulder, 1987). During the 1960s and 1970s, social historians and anthropologists of Afro-America agreed that numerous patterns of language use, male-female relations, and parent-child bonding evolved during the decades of slavery and promoted the preservation of blacks under slavery in the New World (Levine, 1977; Whitten & Szwed, 1970). Considerable disagreement has followed, however, on the extent to which the particular habits that made positive contributions under slavery, and within a society rigidly divided along occupational and educational lines, now serve negative ends. Currently, America's postindustrial society, so highly dependent on literate-based communication, holds to the ideal of the nuclear family and the value of multiplex linkages to institutions beyond the family. In a climate of these values, black oral traditions, extended real and fictive kin linkages, and primary ties beyond the family centering in religious affiliations may well confer disadvantages (Black Family Summit, 1984; Blau, 1981; Ogbu, 1981).

My third concern relates specifically to the comparative differences between the socialization of Trackton's children in the 1970s and the children of those children in the late 1980s. Language socialization is a lifelong process in which individuals learn to communicate competently across contexts and experiences. The rate of change and conditions of change are crucial here. This concern derives from both the current debates over the relative places of orality and literacy and my own efforts to consider the cross-cultural contexts of a dependence on written artifacts for oral performances, often taken to the fundamental forms of cultural knowledge. Perhaps, naively, the epilogue of *Ways With Words* suggested that language socialization patterns lay deeply embedded within certain cultural frames, such as family loyalties, space and time orderings, problem-solving techniques, and preferred patterns of recreation—all resistant to externally imposed social changes. Hence, habits of language socialization were likely to change very slowly and in concert with shifts in these broader activities, values, and organizations.

Language Socialization in Trackton

Any study of language socialization carries the goal of understanding both how language is used to socialize the young to become competent members of their cultures and how youngsters learn to use language as part of the totality of social understandings they must gain. "Language socialization research looks for world view—language connections as expressed through forms and functions of language use. It looks for cultural information not only in the content of discourse but in the organization of discourse as well" (Schieffelin & Ochs, 1986). Talk, as well as talk about talk, nonverbal reinforcements of spoken and written language, written artifacts, and the activities and role regulations that frame all of these become the texts that those who study language socialization attempt to study.

In the years of fieldwork in Trackton, adults of the community talked of their children "comin' up." On the porches of their small two-family units and on the plaza that fronted them, they surrounded their youngsters with the talk and activities of children and adults in the midst of everyday activities. They valued children's early nonverbal displays that indicated they had been watching and learning from life around them. They encouraged independent—sometimes even physically dangerous—ventures by young children. In contrast to the assertions of the bulk of studies of parents interacting with young children acquiring language, they did not simplify their talk to children or even feel the need to address them directly. They did not have special routines of question-and-answer displays or baby-talk games, and they did not offer the labels for items of the environment to their children. Instead, they expected that children would learn to talk "when they need to," and to judge when and to whom to give information and to be "wise" and cautious about answering "foolish" questions. Their philosophy of "what's done is done" seemed to keep them from asking children to recount verbally what they had done or were currently doing, unless adults believed children had information adults needed. The display of knowledge through talking about what was done could invite ridicule or punishment, unless offered as a poetic, clever, entertaining, and quasifictional narrative that could be jointly constructed by initiator and audience. (For some indication of the sharp contrast between these views and those held by mainstream families, see Heath, 1991; Ochs & Schieffelin, 1984.)

As soon as they could toddle, boys became public objects of verbal teasing, and successful verbal retorts could command attention from spectators on several porches. They learned a string of alternative ways of expressing similar meanings as well as alternative ways of performing the same utterance—always a well-formed short sentence with a variety of semantic values and contexts for interpretation. Adults and older children played different roles at different times with toddlers, who were expected to adapt, coperform, and learn that roles did not rest in a single individual, but in widely distributed types of performances across the community. Of children, especially boys, adults said, "Gotta watch hisself by watchin' other folks."

Girl babies entered the same general world as boys of swirling multiparty talk, shifting roles, and widely distributed functions of child caring. As toddlers they did not enter the public stage for the same kind of teasing as boys, although they watched their male peers undergo such public immersions. Carried about on the hips of older girls, they entered their games and banter, talked to themselves replaying conversations about them, and acted out fussin' routines with their dolls and, throughout the preschool years, with younger children. All infants and young children accompanied adults to church services, and as they grew older, the girls took part in junior choirs and summer choir trades arranged among black churches during summer revival meeting times.

As they began to attend school, Trackton boys and girls spent some after-school time outside the community, but the neighborhood worried considerably about the whereabouts of young girls. Although accepted as inevitable, early pregnancies were the reason given for trying to keep young girls close under the watchful eye of adults. Yet the community valued children as children, not as the offspring of a combination of particular individuals; thus, although the pregnancy was protested, the child was not, and from 1969 through 1986, no girl in Trackton completed her teenage years without having at least one baby. The particular father or mother mattered little in the 1970s; the neighborhood seemed glad to have a child. Almost invariably, the baby became part of the family under the full-time care of the mother of the teenager, who returned to high school and the usual social life of other teenage girls.

Two of these teenage mothers provide the cases for discussion here. The first is Zinnia Mae, the middle daughter of a blind diabetic mother. A large girl who was a favorite target of the taunts of peers in the neighborhood and at school, she had her first child at age 14. Trackton judged her situation as especially unfortunate because her mother was not able to keep her baby, and the boy's father's family never took any interest in the baby. The child went to the oldest sister, who lived across town and took the baby into her household to raise and to become her own. Zinnia Mae returned to school, but at 16, the legal age for "quitting" school, she and a girlfriend unknown in Trackton ran away to Atlanta, where Zinnia Mae had three more children, a girl and twin boys, within the next 2 years.

The second case is that of Sissy, the next to the oldest child in a family of five children. Within Trackton, her household, headed by a strong-minded mother held in high respect by the community, served as a collecting place for other children of the neighborhood during the 1970s. Her mother, Lillie Mae, worked intermittently in several textile mills, and her father supplemented his work on a construction crew with second-shift work at one of the mills. In 1981, after failing in repeated attempts to get steady mill work, he left the family, and Lillie Mae had to move to temporary housing and put her name on the waiting list for public housing. The oldest child in the family, Tony, finished 4 years at a small college within the state, and after 2 years of living at home and helping his mother with contributions from the local part-time work he could find, he took a computer training course, found a job within the state government, and left home.

Between 1982 and 1987, Lillie Mae and the four children at home lived on her welfare check, occasional small checks coerced from the children's father when authorities could find him, and, since Tony left home, the few secret supplements he could send from time to time. Local public housing officials explained the delay in her obtaining public housing by telling her that her family was "too big" for their available units. Sissy became pregnant during her junior year in high school, dropped out of school briefly to have the baby, gave over care of the baby boy, Denny, to her mother, returned to graduate from high school, and continued to live at home while attending a local technical school part-time. For a while, she worked part-time at a local fast-food restaurant, but her wages threatened the larger welfare check her mother received, and she was forced to quit. The baby's father and his family took care of the baby on 1 weekend every 6 weeks or so, and they bought him presents and some supplies on these visits.

The Move to Urban Life

The high-rise public housing apartment unit in which Zinnie Mae and her three children live looks like any of thousands of others built in American inner cities in the 1960s. The six-story concrete unit in which she lives is one of eight, each of which covers a city block in a downtown section of Atlanta. The units surround an internal dirt plot on which parts of swings, see-saws, and tire mazes spring from clusters of dry wiry grass and weeds. Two broken wooden benches that once bordered one side of the plot now stand on end facing each other and forming a narrow miniature prison that mocks the taller versions that surround it in the form of the apartment units.

Soon after she turned 16, Zinnia Mae and Gloria Sue, a girlfriend who was 17, caught a ride to Atlanta with some young men they met at a local disco. Once in Atlanta, both girls stayed for a while with Gloria Sue's grandmother, but within a few months, she threw Zinnia Mae out for "sassin" her. Zinnia Mae telephoned her older sister, who had become the virtual mother of the boy Zinnia Mae had when she was 14, asked for bus fare home, and was told there was no money to send. For nearly 3 years, no one in Trackton heard from Zinnia Mae, and those missing months remain a mystery. Her sister heard from her again in early 1985, when she telephoned to say she wanted to see her boy, she was living in Atlanta, she had a little girl who was a year old, and she was expecting twins.

Although her sister had neither money nor inclination to send the boy to Zinnia Mae, she asked me to take pictures of the child to her if I was ever in Atlanta. A series of phone calls to Zinnia Mae opened the way for me to visit her in mid-1985 when her girl, Donna, was 16 months old and her twin boys were 2 months old. When I telephoned, she asked to meet me at a local fast-food restaurant and she took me to her apartment from there. Although 100 pounds heavier than she had been as a teenager, Zinnia Mae still walked the skipping walk she had years earlier, and she smiled as timidly as she had in response to the neighborhood teases. We walked up the six flights of stairs ("the elevator don't work yet"), and in the living room of her apartment, we found a 12-year-old neighbor's child "mindin'" the babies, who left when Zinnia Mae handed her a dollar bill. Zinnia Mae asked about my children, and we settled into talk of old acquaintances. When she asked about her son, I handed her the envelope of photographs. She held each one up to the light, looked at it silently, and gave them back, saying, "He's sure cute, ain't he?" She asked what I had been doing, and when I told her I was still trying to figure out how kids learned to talk, she said she wondered if her little girl would ever learn. While we had been talking, the child had been lying quietly sucking on a pacifier on the mattress on the floor where her child caregiver had left her. I assured Zinnia Mae that she would surely learn, she was young yet, and asked how Zinnia Mae spent her days with her children. She answered, "Well, I ain't havin' no more, that's for sure. I have my tubes tied when the twins came. I've done all I'm doin' for menfolks who just pick up and leave when the music's gone." She paused, looked out the window, and then picked up my earlier question. "My days, you know, I just do what I can, can't get away much, watch some television, try to keep 'em clean, get some groceries now and then." She volunteered that she had tried to get some work back before the twins came, but she could only find part-time dishwashing work at $4.25 an hour, and her welfare check gave her more than that. The babies' father sometimes used to bring formula and diapers and gave her cash for food and makeup.

Before I left that first visit, she mentioned again about wondering if her girl would learn to talk. Trying to reassure her, I bet her that the child had already begun to talk some, but Zinnia Mae just might not notice since there weren't any older children around for her little girl to play with. She laughed and said, "You bet there ain't. I can't haul her up and down those six flights of steps to get her out with them other kids, and the place in here is too cramped as it is; I sure can't have nobody else's babies in here, so me and Donna, we pretty much stay in here with the babies by ourselves 'cept when I get the neighbor girl to come in so I can go get some food for us to eat, 'n' my girlfriends, they come by sometimes, but they don't like to climb them steps either." I suggested that she might hear Donna talk if she tape-recorded some of the hours during the day while she was bathing, dressing, and feeding her. Zinnia Mae agreed this might be a fun idea. I left and returned that afternoon with two tape recorders, several boxes of tapes, and a notebook and pencil. Zinnia Mae agreed to turn the tape recorder on for several hours on several days each week and to write down what she and Donna had been doing while the tape was being made. (For a discussion of this participatory data collection technique used with another dropout mother, see Heath & Branscombe, 1985, 1986.)

Between mid-1985 and mid-1987, Zinnia Mae taped over 400 hours and wrote approximately 1,000 lines of notes about her activities. The two of us met about every 6 months, listened to certain tapes, and talked about what was happening on the tapes and in her notes. During these years, she remained on welfare, stayed in the same apartment, and remained unsuccessful in either obtaining work or getting Donna into a day-care center. She had two hospitalizations, both as a result of falls, and one of the twins had to be hospitalized once for a bronchial infection.

Analysis of Zinnia Mae's data through superimposing portions of the notes and tapes on those collected at similar ages for Trackton's children revealed four primary resources for organizing language socialization: spatial and time allotments, access to coparticipants and audience, availability of props (animate and inanimate), and the affective tone or mood of interactions.

The everyday life of Donna and her twin brothers was played out in the living room, bedroom, and bathroom of Zinnia Mae's apartment. Since the small kitchen opened off the living room, and a table sat at its entry, there was no available space for them in the kitchen. In the bedroom, Donna slept in her mother's bed and the twins on a pallet on the floor; in the living room, all three children played on both the floor—on a small mattress in the corner—and the sofa set before the television set. The six flights of stairs and the lack of either available outdoor space for sitting or easy transportation with three small children were the reasons Zinnia Mae gave for not taking the children out. After Donna could walk well and climb the steps on her own, Zinnia Mae took her to the grocery store with her once or twice a week. They walked the two-and-a-half blocks to the store, Donna sat in the cart, and they walked back—Donna carrying small packages and walking alone, while her mother usually held packages in both arms. The twins remained in the apartment with the teenage neighbor girl. Once every 2 or 3 weeks, she took sheets and towels to the nearby laundromat, and Donna went with her and waited, sitting on the high orange plastic chair in the waiting area.

As preschoolers, Zinnia Mae and her peers had lived primarily on the porches of Trackton's houses and in the dirt plaza out front. They rarely went into the homes of others, and unless the weather was exceptionally bad they spent very few of their daylight hours inside their own family's house. Because there were few cars in Trackton, a trip to the supermarket occurred rarely, and the available shared space in any car making the trip went to adults. A small neighborhood grocery was within walking distance, and adults sent the community's neighborhood children there to buy what was needed. On any of these trips, older children would ask permission to carry toddlers astride their hips, often using some of the money they received for doing the errand to buy candy for the youngster. Infants and toddlers went to church with their families whenever car space was available. Those children whose fathers did not live within Trackton often went to spend weekends with their father's mother or other relatives.

Time allotments for preschool children in Trackton and Zinnia Mae's household seemed on the surface very similar. For the majority of time, the children's mothers did not work outside the home, and when Trackton mothers did, they depended on older children or made reciprocal arrangements with neighbor friends to take care of the youngest ones. Beneath the surface evidence, however, patterns of time usage differed greatly. Trackton mothers seemed "busy." Inside the house they cleaned and washed or got a big washing together to take to the nearby laundromat; each morning they prepared food that sat on the stove available for stand-up meals throughout the day. Once a day at least, clocks in both the bedroom and the living room roused sleepers to get off to their shift work and alerted family members who had moved out onto the front porch to their duty of making sure no one overslept. On the porch, women took whatever work they could bring outside: beans to string, mending to do, magazines to look through, newspapers to read, potatoes to peel, or a cigarette for relaxation. There, even without tasks to keep their hands busy, they always found neighbors who either joined them or walked by, and there were always children in the plaza to watch, tease, and scold. Gossip, quarrels, retold stories, chewed-over newspaper or mail items, and interactions with children on the plaza filled the air with sounds of busyness.

Zinnia Mae, in contrast, never described herself as "busy" but always as "overworked" or "tired." She woke with the children, changed diapers, fixed bottles for the twins and cereal for Donna, ate some toast and smoked a cigarette, closed the bedroom door so the children would stay in the living room, and turned on the television before she sat down on the sofa. She had no clock in the house, but told time by matching television programs to *TV Guide* listings. When any of her girlfriends were not working, and when she had money to keep a telephone, she would call them and talk, often comparing notes on a particular television game show or soap opera. The pace of her life varied not at all for Saturdays or Sundays, except through the occasional extra availability of her girlfriends on the weekends for short visits. Zinnia Mae kept movie and television star magazines her girlfriends sometimes brought, and she would often thumb through these or the free advertisements for department and grocery stores that came to all the apartment mailboxes.

Each day, after she gave the children their morning meal, Zinnia Mae put the children in the living room "to play." Donna centered her activities around the mattress, playing sometimes with utensils or plastic dishes from the kitchen. As the twins got older, she and they made a game of climbing on and off the sofa, hiding under the table at the kitchen entry or under the coffee table on which the television sat. They had no set meal of the day other than their breakfast, but the children called for food whenever they felt hungry or seemed bored. Donna fed herself and the children to break the boredom of daylight hours. Zinnia Mae planned trips to the grocery or laundromat on the basis of need and the availability and mood of the neighbor's teenager, who was not always anxious to sit with the twins. She made the bed, swept the floor, and cleaned the kitchen or bathroom if she knew a girlfriend was coming by, and often on the days when she came home from the laundromat.

Thus her time seemed to flow endlessly with few interruptions, but engagement with or activities carried out directly with her children came rarely. The following episode illustrates the language and social interactional aspects of daily life. The episode took place when Donna was 2;4 and the twins were 1;2.

> [Donna picks up a movie magazine and begins tearing out its pages to place the separate pages around the living room floor. Zinnia Mae sits on the sofa watching a game show and hears the tearing pages.]

> Zinnia Mae: Hey, what do you think you're doing? [sounds of pages rustling and furniture movement]

> Donna: Makin' places, see, here?

> Zinnia Mae: You ain't tearin' up my books; get them playtoys over there. You hear? Shhh, I cain't hear.

> [sound of plastic banging on the floor]

> Zinnia Mae: Now, what you doin'? I told you I cain't hear. Put that thing down, I say.

> [Donna begins to cry.]

This episode characterizes the types of interactions that filled the tapes, that took place on my visits, and that Zinnia Mae wrote of in her notes:

> Monday. Watched television, Donna eat cheers [Cheerios], babies cry and I catch Donna give cheers; she make a house under the chair. [Jan 9, 1986]

In a random selection of 20 hours of the tapes made over the 2 years, approximately 14% of recording sessions included talk between Zinnia Mae and any of her children. During these encounters, she asked direct questions about the children's immediate actions, offered comment on those actions (and her response to them), and gave directions or requested certain actions, usually in exchanges of talk that lasted less than 1 minute. During those sessions that contained more than four contingent exchanges between mother and child, 92% took place when someone else was in the room. A girlfriend or the neighbor girl as audience seemed to provoke talk as performance and invitations for others to comment on the children. Following the episode in which Donna had "set places," Zinnia Mae reported this to a visiting girlfriend (partly as explanation for the torn magazine). Seemingly speaking directly to Donna, she asked, "You think you gonna be a waitress or something?" She then explained to her girlfriend that she and Donna had stopped at a Burger King on the way home from the grocery last week, and Donna had liked the place mats. She then said, "You ate them fries and drank that Coke down." During these exchanges, Donna started several times to tell the girlfriend something that is unintelligible on the tape, but Zinnia Mae explained on hearing the tape several weeks later that Donna wanted to let the girlfriend know that she (Zinnia Mae) had spilled part of her Coke, and it had run down off the table into Donna's lap. The intonational pattern and the length of sustained talk provided evidence that Donna was trying to offer some account of a past event—no doubt, the one her mother remembered as having made a considerable impression on Donna at the time.

The availability of coparticipants and audience, as well as access to props, was limited to girlfriends and neighbor girl, visits to the grocery and laundromat, and the usually traumatic visits to the doctor's office. In a large shoe box near the mattress, Donna had several plastic toys bought at the grocery store, pieces of a blanket, several plastic spoons and food cartons, and a collection of fuzzy animals brought by Zinnia Mae's girlfriends. The twins inherited these toys and acquired in addition a small rubber ball, a roller skate abandoned in the apartment entryway downstairs, and several plastic cars. Zinnia Mae rarely brought anything into the living room, except diaper boxes, food items, or cigarettes. Occasionally, she left the open grocery bags on the living room floor for the children to crawl in and out of.

Zinnia Mae's most frequent words were "I'm so tired." She rarely laughed, except in response to something on television or to a jesting approach from one of her girlfriends. She met the needs her children made known for food, water, clean diapers, relief from pain, and occasional physical help (being lifted onto a sofa, into a chair, etc.). She held and hugged all the children when her mood was good and they approached her; she did not hit at them or push them away roughly. The tapes and her own talk about her notes and the tapes reveal that she waited for the children to address or approach her most of the time. In only 13 instances within the hours of taping did she initiate talk to one of the children that was not designed to give them a brief directive or query their actions or intentions. She once told Donna to come sit beside her to see the puppet on television, twice asked one of the twins to give her a bite of cookie and talked about why she liked that particular kind of cookie, and once she said to Donna that someone on television looked like one of her girlfriends. On nine occasions, she talked to the children as a result of introducing some written artifact to them.

Often while watching television or sitting at the kitchen table smoking a cigarette, she read magazines and advertisements. She sometimes talked with her girlfriends about the magazine materials, commenting on the differences between two stories, changed events in the lives of certain television or movie stars, and certain hairstyles or dress styles she liked or disliked. She read the advertisements to see pictures of hair and clothing styles and to learn about special sales at the only grocery store near enough for her to walk to. Her primary purposes for reading were thus instrumental and social interactional/recreational. She wrote as an aid to memory and occasionally to record financial records related to Medicaid, food stamps, or her welfare payments. On three occasions, she brought Donna's attention to a magazine or paper by pointing to an object foreign to the child (swimming pool, horse, and large helium-filled balloon). She then asked her to look at the picture, named it, and commented on the item ("that's like a big bathtub," "you see one of them on TV," "that'll take you right up into the air"). Four times, she gave Donna a page of advertisements and a pencil and told her to draw; she circled one of the items to demonstrate what she meant. On two other occasions, she showed the children a cartoonlike figure in an advertisement that looked like one of the Saturday morning cartoon figures, saying, "You know him, you seen him on TV." (For further treatment of the influence of literacy artifacts on prompting demonstration-type talk by mothers who do not otherwise point out environmental items and name them for their children, see Heath & Branscombe, 1984; Heath & Thomas, 1984).

In summary, the language socialization resources of Trackton and Zinnia Mae's apartment contrast sharply along nearly every dimension of interaction. The spatial—and resultant social—isolation forced the great majority of interactions with her children to be dyadic rather than multiparty, as was the case in Trackton's open and shifting arena of speakers and listeners and play and work. In the absence of audience, almost no playful and teasing episodes or requested routines or demonstration of physical feats by the children took place. The public dimensions of socialization in Trackton multiplied the number of interlocutors, events, genres, and goals of talking and listening for young and old. Without actors of her preceding generation to socialize her by direct and indirect teaching, and without the actors and props of her own socialization, Zinnia Mae did not assume a key role in enabling her children to learn to use language across a wide variety of genres, styles, and functions. Cut off from the family and community of her childhood, and walled in a transient community of people who remained strangers to her, Zinnia Mae's own language socialization had been brought to a halt. For most of her waking hours each day of the week, she was a passive spectator of television and movie or TV magazines, and a passive listener to the episodes of the worlds her girlfriends frequent. Her active engagement in spoken and written language resided primarily in instrumental exchanges. In her taped exchanges with her girlfriends, they talked nearly 80% of the time, and her contributions centered on queries about the events they told of, changes in welfare check rulings, or problems with Medicaid, apartment tenants, and getting someone to stay with the twins while she shopped. Any talk of the future in her language was of the near future: how to get the papers to the welfare office, when Donna might start talking, whether day-care rulings might change, and what she would do if she could get her hands on the children's father, who stopped sending money shortly after the twins were born. She did not talk of distant future events or accomplishments for the children or herself. The only group she talked of belonging to was "us women," a term she used to signify females without male companions, mothers of young children without fathers, and competitors for welfare resources.

Rarely involved in manipulative activities (such as sewing) for any extended period of time, and engaging in these without talk of the activities while they were in process, Zinnia Mae could provide few occasions for guided or collaborative tasks with her children, few chances for mother and children to co-construct tasks or talk for more than a fleeting minute or so. One exception to this relative absence of opportunities for guided interactions in task accomplishment was sweeping the floor. Once Donna was old enough to stand alone, she leaned on the broom as Zinnia Mae pushed it about, and later one of Donna's favorite activities was to try to sweep by herself. During these events, Zinnia Mae gave directives, sometimes laughed, and offered encouragement or admonishments after Donna initiated talk during the process. For Zinnia Mae, time did not flow between work—or accomplishful activities—and play or leisure. On the few occasions when she went out to interview for a job or tried a job for a few weeks (usually at the instigation of one of her girlfriends), she came back talking about those jobs washing dishes in fast-food restaurants or waitressing as "kids' jobs." She was convinced that employers wouldn't put anyone "as big and fat as me out there shoveling food in front of other people." Zinnia Mae expected the few people she met outside her apartment to hold the same opinions she held; she judged their intentions by the immediate effect of their actions on her.

Staying Home

The climate of despair about American inner cities that developed in the mid-1980s makes it easy to see Zinnia Mae's cultural membership as created (or obliterated) by her particular location and exacerbated by her own physical condition. Without contemporary accounts of the everyday life of other inner-city household units, the uniqueness of her situation is difficult to judge. It is, however, possible to compare the language socialization of her children with that of another young Trackton mother, Sissy, who did not leave home.

When Sissy had her first child at 16, she and her mother, Lillie Mae, and brothers and sisters had moved from Trackton to temporary housing to await placement in public housing. Located on a long street lined with shade trees, the house into which they moved had long been abandoned by the white families who used to live in this area of town. Without paint, running water, or heat, the single-family dwelling offered primarily a roof and four walls when Lillie Mae moved in. Now owned by a black man who lived "up North," the house rented on a short-term basis for $150 a month. Lillie Mae, Tony, and the older children set about clearing the weeds in the front yard, putting the bricks back into the sidewalk, patching holes in the floor, painting, and hounding the landlord to get a gas line run into the house. Sissy's baby, Denny, arrived within a few months of the move and slept in the bed with Lillie Mae and Sissy. From the outset, Lillie Mae and Tony took charge of the baby, carrying him about wherever they sat in the living room to visit or to watch television. They knew no one in the neighborhood, made up primarily of transients waiting to go elsewhere, except Lillie

Mae's cousin who lived several houses down and around the corner on a street of small, well-kept houses owned by black families.

The competitive spirit of the families who came and went on Lillie Mae's street kept any long-term associations from building up. Most of the households consisted of women and children waiting to get into public housing and living on welfare. Those men who maintained close connections with their families usually lived with their mothers and aunts in another part of town, staying away from their own women and children to ensure continuation of AFDC payments. Some worked in other parts of the state on construction sites and came to town only occasionally. Few of the houses had front porches and those that did were usually filled with visiting family and friends who came by car on weekends. On those occasions, a mix across generations talked, teased, prepared to go to special church services, or planned coming weekend events.

Within Lillie Mae's house, Denny had Sissy's three brothers and younger sister to take him with them when they went to the nearby service station/grocery store or on errands to the cousin's house. When Denny was 8 months old, Lillie Mae agreed to tape record half an hour or so several times each week when the baby was awake, and Sissy wrote several lines each week describing the baby's activities and the contexts of the tape recordings. These recordings began in December 1986 and continued through October 1987, when Denny was 18 months old. In addition, I visited about every 2 months. During most of the first 6 months of taping. Denny was a listener and spectator to multiparty interactions primarily in the living room and kitchen and at the cousin's house, where some of the taping was done. Denny's spatial world extended from this house to the corner store and three times to church services. His toys, contributed primarily by the cousin and Tony, stayed in a box in a corner of the living room and included a woolly puppy, large plastic ball, two cast-off hats from older boys, plastic eggs that came in two parts, and a toy gun holster found in the yard. He played with these or howled whenever he was not taken up as a toy himself by one or the other of the older children, who encouraged him to learn to crawl, sit up, walk, kick, and to resist their teasing. They let him play school with them from time to time when they did their homework, and from the time he was 16 months old, they kept him away from their books by giving him crayons and paper bags to draw on while they worked. Major responsibility for Denny rested with Lillie Mae, and in days of tension over no word from the housing authority or threatened cuts in her check, she spoke harshly to Denny and chided Sissy for "doing nutn' to help us out." Sissy spent as much time as possible out of the house at the technical school, where she was taking a "modeling course." She and her girlfriends carpooled to nearby shopping centers, where they told Lillie Mae they had to do "homework." Unlike the days before the textile mills closed, Lillie Mae and her oldest children, Tony and Sissy, found few common work experiences outside the home to talk about. The stuff of shared stories, complaints, and jokes about working in the mill was no more, and a lot of talk at home focused on frustrations, disappointments, and anger over the failure to find work, to hear from the housing authority, or to keep the landlord from raising the rent.

Lillie Mae pored over the papers that came in the mail from various authorities and asked Tony to interpret them and write some kind of answer. Each day she read the local paper as well as the advertising brochures that came in the mail. While doing so, she often held Denny on her lap. She sometimes walked to her cousin's house with the paper, where they read and talked about local events. Her instrumental uses of reading and writing related primarily to keeping track of applications for housing, welfare, and Medicaid, and occasionally writing a letter to relatives up North. She gave up going to church except on rare occasions when an out-of-town relative with a car came to take her. Tony went regularly, read church materials at home, and kept his college books around to read from time to time. Once he started computer training, he was rarely at home, and when he got a full-time job, he took his books and moved out on his own. On his visits, he sometimes helped the younger children with their homework, and Denny was always party to these occasions.

When they had tasks to do in the house or errands to run, Denny went along as well, and as soon as he could stand, he was sent on errands within the household and told to pick up things from the floor. By 13 months, he echoed end bits and pieces of the talk of those around him, usually with no acknowledgment by the adults or older children present. When they initiated talk to him, they asked him to name family members or stop doing something they objected to. At 18 months, his vocabulary consisted of names of family members and two fixed phrases that varied in two moods—happy and angry: "get it" and "open it." He called Lillie Mae "Ma" and all other family members by their given or nicknames. This pattern of language development matches that of Trackton's children, which moved through three stages: (1) a repetition stage, in which they picked up and repeated chunks of phrasal and clausal utterances of speakers around them; (2) a repetition with variation stage in which they manipulated pieces of the conversations they picked up from the discourse around them; and (3) participation, usually reached around 2 years of age, during which they attempt to bring their own talk into that of adult conversation, making themselves part of the ongoing discourse (Heath, 1983, chap. 3).

Interaction time with Sissy differed little in flavor from time with all other members of the family (including the neighbor cousin) except Lillie Mae, who always kept watch over his whereabouts and inclusion in others' activities. On his monthly visits to the home of his father's parents (who called him their "gran"), he went with them to church, choir practices, shopping centers, and the grocery store. The 40 hours of tape and 10 pages of notes collected over 10 months indicate that during approximately 40% of the taped time at least three people were engaged in conversations that surrounded both work and leisure time (visiting, watching television, washing dishes, preparing to go somewhere). Talk consisting of more than a vocative or term of endearment directed specifically to Denny occurred on only 12 occasions, 10 of them bunched in the first few tapings and, no doubt, artificial performances for the benefit of the tape recorder. The two exceptions were teasing exchanges in the seventh and eighth months of taping. On both these occasions, Tony tried to get Denny to wear his hat and Denny kept throwing it on the floor. Tony repeatedly asked Denny who he thought he was, how he was going to the store without a hat, and where his hat was. Denny and Tony played this game on each occasion for more than 5 minutes, Denny interjecting "get it" each time he threw the hat on the floor.

Symbols in Adaptation

Let's return to the question of the extent that Zinnia Mae and Sissy—as young mothers—now demonstrate that they sufficiently understood and retained the narratives, rituals, and everyday rhythm of their socialization as cultural members in Trackton, to adapt them in current circumstances. Although Trackton residents during the 1960s and 1970s saw their time there as temporary and hoped to "move on," they cohered as a group in their waiting. Although respectables separated themselves from the "real" transients and the "no-counts," the community's connections across residents of all ages met in their attempts to get and keep jobs, to enjoy weekends, to keep up on the news, and to keep from being "pulled down" by hard circumstances. The Black-Is-Beautiful spirit of the public media and the prominence given to black concerns through model city, CETA, Head Start, and human relations councils only added vocabulary and slogans for their performances and sometimes instrumental access to goods and services within their power. The intense publicity surrounding the first few years of desegregation, amidst frequent school shifts and openings and closings, gave them a sense of being players in a larger drama than that of their own small neighborhood. They read the local paper, shared news of events and people, and sustained a sense of connection as members to the outside world. Their young heard and felt much from these societal shifts in school, but only Tony, 8 years old when he moved to Trackton, could remember what came before in the slum dwellings across the tracks on the outskirts of town. He intensified his sense of otherness by going to a predominantly white Southern college.

Those just behind him, such as Zinnia Mae and Sissy, remembered nothing before Trackton, and as children they listened to tales of cotton fields, dime-store counter sit-ins, and race riots with less involvement than to tales of last weekend's dance. Today, for Zinnia Mae and Sissy alike, the struggles are of the individuals, not of the group, and the enemies are shifting, faceless, and largely unseeable—rulings, paperwork, neighbors downstairs or down the street who breed cockroaches or report to the welfare worker that Tony brought extra money home to Lillie Mae last week. In earlier days, the black church preached and sang of group struggles and the strength to be gained in comradeship, faith, and perseverance. Neither Zinnia Mae nor Sissy is connected to a black church or any other institution of voluntary membership.

These case studies suggest the power of groups and allegiances beyond the immediate family to give a sustaining ideology of cultural membership. The sense of belonging was punctuated for Trackton's members by the black church (and its affiliated organizations, such as choirs), constant access to several generations and their tales of history, as well as the availability of commentators on the current scene (played by Trackton members who read their newspapers in porch groupings, listened to Trackton's self-appointed "mayor" talk about the human relations council, etc.). Moreover, recent sociological research underscores the importance of such contacts for the academic and mental health of young minorities—especially blacks. In a comparative study of black dropouts and high school graduates in Chicago, those who graduated found support in a system of school and community associations, as well as church attendance; 72% of the graduates reported regular church attendance, whereas only 14% of the dropouts did (Williams, 1987). In a Boston study, positive effects on the academic success of children came with the association of their mothers with organizational ties beyond the family (and with friends who had such ties also), nondenominational religious affiliations, and stability in the labor force over a number of years (Blau, 1981). Acceptance and assimilation within institutions beyond the home for both parent and child provide positive carryovers for mental health, academic retention, and job stability. Alienation from family and community—and subsequently school—appears to play a more critical role in determining whether a student finishes high school than the socioeconomic markers of family income, education level, and so on (Williams, 1987). For Sissy and Zinnia Mae, in the absence of such associations of sustenance and reinforcement of cultural membership, the intimate symbols of connectedness, pride, and perseverance have left them seemingly unable to adapt their own socialization for that of the next generation or to re-create new foundations of togetherness.

But what of the resources for adaptation that might lie within the symbols of the culture of their childhood? Were the porch tales, teasings, newspaper readings, church services, fussings, and other public performances sufficiently identified as theirs for their significance to be maintained? These texts of Trackton carried much of the same significance and ideological weight as similar performances detailed for other black communities (e.g., Baugh, 1983; Folb, 1980; Smitherman, 1977). Persistence, assertive problem solving, and adaptability—especially in human relations—emerge as primary individual and group survival characteristics from these texts. In addition, authoritative—firm but supportive—human bondings stand out as those most desirable (Moses, 1985; Spencer, Brookings, & Allen, 1985; Stack, 1974). However, in all studies reporting the celebration, performance, adaptation, and fitness of these characteristics, the contexts have been relatively free from external influences that cut at the heart of the extended and fictive kin family and the centrality of children to a group's sense of self-perpetuation. Currently, AFDC rulings that encourage fathers to remain outside the household of the mother and children, as well as public housing regulations limiting the number of occupants per unit of space, have cut away the traditional supportive contexts for key performances. Zinnia Mae's children have no entry into the contexts in which they might witness or participate in repetitive collaborative celebrations of persistence or assertive problem solving. Those available to Sissy's son are severely diminished from those of her own childhood, since Lillie Mae and she both find their struggles against individuals in the bureaucracies they encounter unsuitable for translation into verbal performance. Moreover, an absence of shared work and leisure experiences set mother and daughter apart in the shared background fundamental to leisure talk, and Sissy's continued socialization from womanhood and motherhood comes less and less from her own mother, but from other young women as adrift as she from either a past or a future.

Language socialization research currently gives primary attention to the role of social interactions in enabling children to become competent communicators in their sociocultural group. "Mutual tuning-in" (Schutz, 1951) and eventual linguistic and metalinguistic awareness are said to rest in the fast-paced co-constructions of reality that adults and children create in everyday life (Rogoff & Wertsch, 1986; Vygotsky, 1978). In addition, however, linguists increasingly emphasize the subjective and alternative interpretations that children create as a result of their opportunities to constantly conform and inform through verbal and nonverbal means (Heath, 1989a). Children call on numerous perceptual levels—seeing, hearing, touching, tasting—in their creation of representational systems for gaining, storing, and displaying information. The contexts of language socialization for the children of the children of Trackton in the cases offered here hold few opportunities for solidarity; social construction of reality; and guided learning through verbal direction, observation, or apprenticeship. The language socialization of these children holds little promise that they will enter school with the wide range of language uses, varieties of performance, types of genres, and perspectives on self-as-performer that Trackton's children had. Their association with written materials rests primarily in the instrumental and not in the confirmational, social interaction/recreational, or news-related reading of their mother's childhood. (For discussions of the relevance of these ranges of uses of written language in academic achievement and school-defined "critical thinking," see Heath, 1983, 1991.) It is too early to predict the extent to which the pattern of language socialization for Sissy's son and her future children may come to match that of Zinnia Mae's. It is likely that Lillie Mae will be unable to secure public housing as long as Sissy and her son remain with her. If they have to leave Lillie Mae to strike out on their own, Sissy may be forced into the atomization and separation that small-apartment living of public housing imposes.[1]

Recent critiques within anthropology have suggested that those who have written ethnographies may well have made many mistakes of analysis and interpretation. They have been characterized as victims of alienated nostalgia (Clifford, 1983; Clifford & Marcus, 1986), prone to read too much into other people's ways of talking about their experiences and motives (Keesing, 1987), too willing to reveal the private ways of minority groups (Scheper-Hughes, 1987), too ready to focus on solidarity and sharedness (Fernandez, 1986), and unable to avoid championing the underdog (Foster, 1979). The current spirit of confessions and probings of methods of analysis and interpretation by ethnographers will contribute much to the sociology of knowledge and our understanding of the fact that just as those we describe have historically established contexts that define and sustain them, so do our descriptions. The reinterpretations and new considerations they bring can only improve our own understandings of what we do, have done, and can do (e.g., Keesing, 1982).

The task of describing American minorities, especially black Americans, is fraught not only with all the problems these critics have noted, but also with numerous others. It is essential that we see relationships of knowledge and power that both connect those within communities and disconnect them. In an era in which national and state policies strike at the core of intimate family relations—male to female, and grandparent to parent, and parent to child—tracing these connections depends on searching out some sense of covariance for role relations, everyday narratives and metaphors, problem-solving strategies, and a sense of future. We perhaps further our understanding of social change best when we can understand the relative extent of control that individuals both have and believe they have over the actual texts that enter their leisure and work time. We must be able to specify the nature of continuity between situations and the degree to which actors know they are making choices as they live under the rubric of change. Detailed studies will allow us to consider how collectively sustained are social structures, value systems, and other glosses "on the will to power" (Barth, 1981, p. 83).

We must run the risk of demonstrating that fewer and fewer individuals in some minority groups define themselves in terms of webs of significance they themselves spin and many may be caught without understanding, interpreting, or transmitting anything like the cultural patterns into which they themselves were socialized. In addition, interpreting in our own society, we cannot forget that what we have viewed as "normal" or stable contexts for children's socialization into a definable group may be ruled out for many under external policy impositions. The novelist George Eliot has warned that no fragment of a life can be "the sample of an even web." Today's social changes for American minority groups reinforce her message and remind us of both the fragility and the unevenness of the web.

Acknowledgments

I wish to acknowledge the helpful comments of Peggy Miller of the Department of Education, University of Chicago, on this piece.

Note

[1] In the spring of 1988, less than 6 months after this piece was written, Sissy and Denny, as well as Lillie Mae and Sissy's younger brothers and sisters, moved together into a three-bedroom, two-story public housing apartment. Tapes and notes made in the first 3 months following this move illustrate the power of multiparty talk from extended family members on the language socialization of Denny. The full range of challenging language that surrounded toddlers on the plaza of Trackton in Sissy's childhood reappeared for Denny in a housing situation that kept the extended family together and provided numerous spaces for out-of-doors play under the watchful eye of family and neighbors. Language data and analysis that provide an update on the language socialization of Denny appear in Heath (1989b).

References

Barth, F. (1981). *Process and form in social life: Selected essays* (Vol. 1). London: Routledge & Kegan Paul.

Baugh, J. (1983). *Black street speech: Its history, structure, and survival.* Austin: University of Texas Press.

Black Family Summit. (1984). Charge to task force on developing and mobilizing resources for supporting the black family. *The Crisis, 91*(6), 262–302.

Blau, Z.S. (1981). *Black children/white children: Competence, socialization, and social structure.* New York: Free Press.

Clifford, J. (1983). On ethnographic authority. *Representations, 1*(2), 118–146.

Clifford, J., & Marcus, G. (Eds.). (1986). *Writing culture: The poetics and politics of ethnography.* Berkeley: University of California Press.

Coleman, J.S., & Hoffer, T. (1987). *Public and private high schools: The impact of communities.* New York: Basic Books.

Edelman, M.W. (1987). *Families in peril.* Cambridge, MA: Harvard University Press.

Fernandez, J.W. (1986). The argument of images and the experience of returning to the whole. In V.W. Turner & E. Bruner (Eds.), *The anthropology of experience.* Urbana: University of Illinois Press.

Folb, E.A. (1980). *Runnin' down some lines: The language and culture of black teenagers.* Cambridge, MA: Harvard University Press.

Foster, G.M., Scudder, T., Colson, E., & Kemper, R.V. (Eds.). (1979). *Long-term field research in social anthropology.* New York: Academic.

Heath, S.B. (1983). *Ways with words: Language, life, and work in communities and classrooms.* Cambridge, UK: Cambridge University Press.

Heath, S.B. (1989a). The learner as cultural member. In M.L. Rice & R.L. Schiefelbusch (Eds.), *The teachability of language.* Baltimore: Paul H. Brooks.

Heath, S.B. (1989b). Oral and literate traditions among black Americans living in poverty. *American Psychologist, 44*(2), 45–56.

Heath, S.B. (1991). The sense of being literate: Historical and cross-cultural features. In R. Barr, M.L. Kamil, P. Mosenthal, & P.D. Pearson (Eds.), *Handbook of reading research* (Vol. 2, pp. 3–25). White Plains, NY: Longman.

Heath, S.B., & Branscombe, A. (1985). Intelligent writing in an audience community. In S.W. Freedom (Ed.), *The acquisition of written language: Revision and response.* Norwood, NJ: Ablex.

Heath, S.B., & Branscombe, A. (1986). The book as narrative prop in language acquisition. In B.B. Schieffelin & P. Gilmore (Eds.), *The acquisition of literacy: Ethnographic perspectives.* Norwood, NJ: Ablex.

Heath, S.B., & Thomas, C. (1984). The achievement of preschool literacy for mother and child. In H. Goelman, A. Oberg, & F. Smith (Eds.), *Awakening to literacy.* Portsmouth, NH: Heinemann.

Keesing, R.M. (1982). *Kwaio religion.* New York: Columbia University Press.

Keesing, R.M. (1987). Anthropology as interpretive quest. *Current Anthropology*, *28*(2), 161–176.

Lefkowitz, B. (1987). *Tough change: Growing up on your own in America*. New York: Free Press.

Levine, L.W. (1977). *Black culture and black consciousness: Afro-American folk thought from slavery to freedom*. New York: Oxford University Press.

Moses, E.G. (1985). Advantages of being disadvantaged: A paradox. *Journal of Negro Education*, *54*(3), 333–343.

Moynihan, D. (1986). *Family and nation*. San Diego, CA: Harcourt Brace.

Mulder, M.B. (1987). Adaptation and evolutionary approaches to anthropology. *Man*, *22*(1), 25–41.

Ochs, E., & Schieffelin, B.B. (1984). Language acquisition and socialization: Three developmental stories and their implications. In R. Schweder & R. LeVine (Eds.), *Culture theory: Essays on mind, self, and emotion*. New York: Cambridge University Press.

Ogbu, J. (1981). School ethnography: A multilevel approach. *Anthropology and Education Quarterly*, *12*(1), 3–29.

Rogoff, B., & Wertsch, J.V. (Eds.). (1984). *Children's learning in the "zone of proximal development."* San Francisco: Jossey-Bass.

Scheper-Hughes, N. (1987). The best of two worlds, the worst of two worlds: Reflections on culture and fieldwork among the rural Irish and Pueblo Indians. *Comparative Studies in Society and History*, *29*(1), 56–75.

Schieffelin, B., & Ochs, E. (1986). Language socialization. *Annual Review of Anthropology*, *15*, 163–191.

Schutz, A. (1951). Making music together: A study in social relationship. *Social Research*, *18*(1), 76–97.

Smitherman, G. (1977). *Talkin' and testifying: The language of black America*. Boston: Houghton Mifflin.

Spencer, M., Brookins, G., & Allen, W. (Eds.). (1985). *The social and affective development of black children*. Hillsdale, NJ: Erlbaum.

Stack, C.B. (1974). *All our kin: Strategies for survival in a black community*. New York: HarperCollins.

Vygotsky, L.S. (1978). *Mind in society: The development of higher psychological processes* (M. Cole, V. John-Steiner, S. Scribner, & E. Souberman, Eds. & Trans.). Cambridge, MA: Harvard University Press. (Original work published 1934)

Vygotsky, L.S. (1985). *Culture, communication, and cognition: Vygotskian perspectives*. Cambridge, UK: Cambridge University Press.

Whitten, N.E., Jr., & Szwed, J.F. (Eds.). (1970). *Afro-American anthropology: Contemporary perspectives*. New York: Free Press.

Williams, S.B. (1987). A comparative study of black dropouts and black high school graduates in an urban public school system. *Education and Urban Society*, *19*(3), 311–319.

9

Literacy and the Identity Development of Latina/o Students

Robert T. Jiménez

Various national efforts are currently underway to explore, examine, and search for ways to improve the literacy development opportunities of Latina/o students (August & Hakuta, 1997; Secada et al., 1998; Snow, Burns, & Griffin, 1998). Unfortunately, all too often, these efforts have been interpreted as calls to repair presumably defective students, their parents and communities, or their teachers. Macedo (2000) points out the absurd consequences of such an approach by indicating that many mainstream, middle class language practices, which serve as the basis for recommendations made to teachers and parents, are grounded in class and economic assumptions (p. 19). In this article, I present the results of a yearlong research project in which I sought to better understand some of the contextual factors that influenced the literacy development of a group of Latina/o students. In addition, I present some of the ways that these students responded to literacy instruction that was designed and implemented as a component of this research project. The basic premise of this instruction was to identify literate practices and ways of thinking about literacy that had been previously derived from Latina/o students.

The theoretical framework for this research combined critical theoretical, Vygotskian, and poststructural constructs for the purpose of describing, analyzing, and drawing conclusions about the literacy development of the participants. Issues that arose during this research included questioning the role that literacy plays in the lives of students from linguistically diverse communities, in particular the ways that these same students perceived its uses. In addition, my analysis focused on the students' understanding of how key participants influenced their literacy development, their views of the relationship of the Spanish and English languages to literacy, and finally, their evolving sense of identity. The influence that students' understanding of their identity had on their access to and

From *American Educational Research Journal*, *37*(4), 971–1000. Copyright © 2000 by the American Educational Research Association. Reprinted with the permission of the publisher.

stance toward literacy are also discussed. Finally, an instructional component was designed using a Vygotskian conceptual framework to examine the specific interactions between students and their teachers, students and one another, students and their environment, and students and texts.

Latina/o youth currently constitute the largest group of minority students in U.S. schools, calculated at 13.5% of the total (National Center for Education Statistics [NCES], 1998a), and this fact may account for some of the increased public interest in their academic achievement. They continue, however, to demonstrate depressed levels of literacy development in comparison to students from mainstream backgrounds (NCES, 1998b). Valencia (1991) described these low levels of academic achievement as persistent, pervasive, and disproportionate. Previous neglect of this population by researchers and policymakers has resulted in a relatively limited knowledge base of potential usefulness for addressing this situation (García, 2000). For example, a definitive statement describing the relationship of native language literacy to that in a second language has yet to be produced (see Snow, Burns, & Griffin, 1998).

Researchers have issued calls for a multifaceted approach to literacy development, drawing from relevant theoretical and empirical research, that incorporates insights from cognitive, linguistic, and sociocultural perspectives (García, Pearson, & Jiménez, 1994; Weber, 1991). Critical theorists have also raised concerns that key stakeholders such as students, their families, and teachers are too often neglected when instructional and programmatic efforts are designed to address the literacy learning needs of marginalized students (Freire & Macedo, 1987).

This research sought to address the aforementioned concerns and to accomplish two distinct but related goals. The first was better understanding of the literacy instruction provided to Latina/o students in four bilingual classrooms, and the second was to refine and develop an instructional approach for promoting these students' literacy development in those same classrooms. The second goal was designed as a collaborative effort between myself, a university researcher, and four intermediate-grade bilingual teachers. The yearlong project included classroom observations, continuous dialogue between the teachers and the researcher, student interviews that included think-aloud procedures, cognitive strategy instruction, and various means of recording student response to the instruction, such as student writing and recording of instructional interactions. In the next section, relevant research and theory related to promoting the literacy learning of Latina/o students are reviewed.

Theoretical Directions

Teacher-student relationships have been identified as crucial with respect to students' academic achievement. Cummins (1986), for example, stated that students are empowered or disabled as a direct result of their interactions with educators in the schools. In his interactive empowerment theory, Cummins elaborates further on this theme and proposes four propositions to assess the quality of instruction provided to language minority students. These propositions state, in essence, that language minority students will succeed or fail to the extent that their language and culture are incorporated into the school program, to the extent that their parents and their overall community are included as an integral component of their education, and to the extent that the students are provided with instruction designed to allow them to generate their own knowledge through activities such as reading and writing. Cummins also identifies assessment of student ability, and the extent to which educators serve as advocates for students versus explaining learning difficulties by locating problems within the child, as a critical variable for considering the potency of educational programs. His framework thus draws on critical, cultural ecological, and constructivist notions. It includes facets of these theoretical positions while emphasizing language minority student achievement. The scope and emphasis of his framework are largely confined to the level of individual schools, although he does acknowledge societal influences.

Freire and Macedo (1987) also see teacher-student relationships as pivotal, but they identify the political and economic power of the teachers' and students' communities as keys to understanding patterns of academic achievement. They call on teachers, other educators, and researchers to consider literacy development as "the vehicle by which the oppressed are equipped with the necessary tools to reappropriate their history, culture, and language practices" (p. 157). Such a stance, they believe, will result in providing students with "the right to express their thoughts, their right to speak, which corresponds to the educators' duty to listen to them" (p. 40). Both Freire and Macedo (1987; Macedo, 1994) specifically identify the necessity of adopting the language of the student, whether it be the national language or not, as the means of instruction and interpersonal interaction. They argue that under these circumstances, students will be able to develop their voice. Macedo (1994) explains the concept of voice as follows:

> Voice requires struggle and understanding of both its possibilities and limitations. The most educators can do is to create structures that would enable submerged voices to emerge. It is not a gift. Voice is a human right. It is a democratic right. (p. 4)

In other words, Freire and Macedo outline an agenda for accomplishing Cummins's vision of empowering students by having them recognize themselves as learners or, in the authors' words, "to understand that no one knows everything and that no one is ignorant of everything" (p. 40). They claim that the current educational system has been "put in place to ensure that these students pass through school and leave it as illiterates" (p. 121). The authors view literacy as a triggering mechanism that could potentially lead to societal transformation. Such an outcome is their stated goal.

Although Cummins, Freire, and Macedo speak to teachers, particularly in terms of how to interact with children from culturally and linguistically diverse backgrounds, their ideas can be difficult for teachers and their coworkers to transform into a program of literacy instruction. The examples these researchers provide come from contexts such as the African islands of Guinea-Bissau, which have distinct histories, cultures, and sociolinguistic realities. Cummins's framework suggests tantalizing alternatives to the kinds of instructional fare generally offered the majority of language minority students, and his ideas have been well disseminated among bilingual education teachers. Vygotskian scholars, on the other hand, have appealed to a wide range of educators but especially those whose work focuses on literacy development. Insights from the neo-Vygotskian school have influenced educators in terms of the materials presented to students and the types, kinds, and amounts of instructional support they receive. In essence, educators working within the Vygotskian tradition view teachers' interactions with students, and these same students' accomplishments during these supported or scaffolded interactions, as the basis for students' later independent activity. These interactions depend on the social relationships that occur in specific contexts, shaped by historical antecedents, and they are fueled by the raw materials of language and other symbols that mediate human activity. In this view, teachers, and by extension researchers, need to understand how participants, context, and activity combine and influence one another in an ongoing and dynamic fashion. This understanding can then be used to draw conclusions about teaching and learning.

In somewhat different, yet complementary ways, all of these theoretical frameworks place student-teacher interactions at the center of the educational enterprise. Cummins contributes the notion that student learning, particularly for language minority students, depends on a deep understanding and acceptance of the language and culture of the specific community served by a given school. Freire and Macedo ask teachers and researchers to consider literacy as a necessary starting point for the transformation of society. In essence, they urge subversion and resistance to established authority, particularly in terms of its role in subordinating culturally and linguistically diverse groups. Vygotskian scholars identify some of the more salient instructional components involved in literacy development and they provide a convincing rationale for considering the influence that each has on students' learning.

Scholars identified with postmodern theories have added some potentially transformative and conceptually distinct categories to this discussion. For example, the role of identity and its relationship to language learning and literacy has been theorized and empirically explored by McKay and Wong (1996) and Ferdman (1990). McKay and Wong examined the English-language learning of four Chinese American high school students and concluded that their varying levels of English-language learning and academic achievement could be explained in terms of their identity construction. Identity, in their words "is multiple, fluid, and often contradictory" (p. 579). They showed how the students were often negatively positioned by educators in their schools and how the students, in turn, resisted that positioning by employing counterdiscourses. Students in the McKay and Wong study who found fulfillment in activities outside of school, these researchers argued, had less motivation to excel in traditional academic pursuits. Ferdman (1990) theorized that identity is rooted in an individual's membership in particular ethnocultural groups and that this membership has consequences for "becoming and being literate" (p. 182). These consequences include the possibility that one's cultural identity will be either affirmed or negated during literacy events. In Ferdman's view, curriculum, and by extension, instruction, ought to "facilitate the process by which students are permitted to discover and explore ethnic connections" (p. 200).

In addition to identity, the construct of discourse increasingly has been used to guide, describe, and explain the literacy development of various groups of learners. Brodkey (1992) argued that prevalent discourses are the principal means by which worldviews or ideologies are disseminated and, perhaps more important, accepted by individuals as natural, rational, and true. These discourses, and the most important of these for the purpose of this piece is that of educational discourse, serve, perhaps most distressingly, to silence the concerns of children from diverse backgrounds. Educational discourse, she claims, is rooted in middle class ideology. One of her goals as a theoretician and researcher is to provide teachers with the tools to "interrupt" discursive practices that "alienate" students from literacy.

Luke (1995–1996) carefully described the mechanisms through which discourses shape and constrain our views of phenomena such as the academic achievement of culturally and linguistically diverse students. He claims that "discourse in institutional life can be viewed as a means for the naturalization and disguise of power relations that are tied to inequalities in the social production and distribution of symbolic and natural resources" and that the power of discourse is that we, in turn, come to view "facts" like the school achievement of minority groups "as if they are the product of organic, biological, and essential necessity" (p. 12). Luke calls for a "systematic attempt to build on minority discourses in schools, classrooms, and other public places" (p. 39). The goal, then, is a "multicultural, socially critical, and just education" (p. 39). These theorists and researchers, then, have maintained the critical theorists' concern with societal inequities and the exclusion of minority students, but they have shifted their analytical gaze toward identifying and interpreting discourse and its influence on student development of identity.

What is missing from much of the preceding discussion, particularly from the perspective of teachers, are sufficient examples of instructional practices that embody these recommendations and principles. Although the aforementioned scholars eschew instructional prescriptions, teachers and other educators often request classroom-based demonstrations of instruction that are guided by and grounded in theory. I have endeavored to honor the spirit of the theorists' desire to avoid authoritarian mandates while at the same time offering teachers and other educators a detailed description of how I went about implementing some theoretically derived ideas in this research project. In the section that follows, I examine research that focuses on teachers of Latina/o students.

Teachers of Latina/o Students

Two broad domains of inquiry emerge from research conducted on teachers of Latina/o students: their use of language and the instruction they provide their students. Some of the issues dealt with include how they use language, in this case Spanish and English (separately and at the same time); how teachers establish rapport with their students, and how they implement discipline; how they organize their instruction for the purpose of promoting biliteracy; and how they negotiate, subvert, and, at times, acquiesce to institutional constraints, demands, and influences.

Language

Guerra (1998) provided evidence that the adults in immigrant Mexican families possess the necessary oral and literate resources required by their children for full literacy development. He rejects deficit views concerning the linguistic competence of members of the Latina/o community and explicitly questions mainstream perceptions of language use in Latina/o homes. Through the skillful presentation of data collected from a network of families who move back and forth between Chicago and Mexico, and accompanying discussion of relevant poststructural theory, Guerra highlights the distinctive and abundant nature of these families' linguistic abilities. His data provide a unique and viable resource to educators concerned with culturally responsive instruction. Such usefulness, however, has yet to be specified or demonstrated by research, particularly because Guerra did not report much information on the participation of children in these activities (Jiménez & Barrera, 1999).

In accord with the theoretical positions outlined in this report, researchers have identified several of the functions played by Spanish in school settings. For example, Lucas, Henze, and Donato (1990) identified the high value placed on students' language and culture as the first of eight characteristics of high schools in which Latina/o students achieved high levels of academic achievement. They also noted that these schools provided students with a wide selection of advanced placement courses taught in Spanish. Likewise, Carter and Chatfield (1986) reported that an elementary school, recognized for its success with Latina/o students, maintained a commitment to native-language instruction as a pivotal element in its philosophy of instruction. These studies support and confirm Cummins's tenet that language minority students are successful academically to the extent that their language, or at least some dialect of it, is included in the curriculum.

A few research studies have focused directly on some of the ways that teachers of Latina/o students actually use language (Carger, 1996; Ernst-Slavit, 1997; García, 1997; Jiménez, Gersten, & Rivera, 1996; Jiménez & Gersten, 1999; Molt, 1988; Montero-Seiburth & Perez, 1987). Teachers who were successful with their students recognized them as fully competent speakers of a particular variety of Spanish. Such recognition helped avoid many of the difficulties associated with a deficit perspective. In other words, they did not treat their students as linguistic incompetents—or solely as non-English speakers— but rather as individuals involved in the very natural process of second-language development. On the other hand, problems can arise when teachers do not share or value the particular variety of Spanish spoken by their students (Ernst-Slavit, 1997). The following section highlights research findings that reveal important characteristics of the instruction provided to Latina/o students.

Instruction

An intriguing strand of educational research has identified instructional practices that motivate, involve, challenge, and provide successful learning experiences to students from linguistically and culturally diverse backgrounds (Ladson-Billings, 1994; Lipka, 1991; McCarty, Wallace, Lynch, & Benally, 1991; Montero-Sieburth & Perez, 1987). These researchers have documented how students respond in positive ways when their teachers demonstrate sensitivity to their concerns, when they demonstrate knowledge of their language and culture, and when they design instruction to build on culturally familiar activities. For example, Native American and Inuit children, often considered taciturn, were surprisingly voluble when instructional activities paralleled those deemed important within their communities (Lipka, 1991; McCarty, Wallace, Lynch, & Benally, 1991).

Some of the more salient characteristics related to the effective instruction of Latina/o students include a high regard for instruction and instructional innovation, a demand for high student performance, and the provision of a challenging curriculum. Effective teachers of Latina/o students are knowledgeable concerning both more traditional and current conceptualizations of literacy instruction (Gersten & Jiménez, 1994; Goldenberg, 1996; Moll, 1988). For example, in reference to literacy development, a teacher in the Jiménez, Gersten, and Rivera (1996) study stated, "I don't insult them [my students] with books in English that are too easy. They are good Spanish readers" (Jiménez, Gersten, & Rivera, 1996, p. 337).

Lucas, Henze, and Donato (1990) and Carter and Chatfield (1986) indicated that teachers in these studies emphasized and made use of sheltered English instruction, cooperative learning, and reading and writing in the content areas. Both of the previous studies also reported that the continual improvement of instruction was emphasized by the schools as a whole and by individual teachers. In the next section, I briefly explain the results of my colleagues' and my own research working with Latina/o students.

Previous Research on Bilingual Latina/o Readers

The findings from two research projects have shaped my understanding of the reading comprehension of bilingual Latina/o students. In the first project, my colleagues and I described and enumerated the cognitive and metacognitive reading strategies of competent and less-competent bilingual Latina/o readers in grades 6 and 7 (Jiménez, García, & Pearson, 1996). All of the participating students (8 high-achieving and 3 average readers) had been identified on the basis of teacher judgment and their reading test scores (between the 75th and 95th percentile for the competent readers and around the 50th percentile for the less-competent readers). These students were interviewed, and they also engaged extensively in the think-aloud procedure while reading a variety of texts in Spanish and English.

In more recent work (Jiménez, 1997), I examined the responses made by low-literacy Latina/o middle school students to literacy instruction characterized by cognitive strategy instruction, culturally relevant text, and language-sensitive teaching methods. Participating students were selected from two grade 7 classrooms. Three were in a self-contained special education classroom and had been identified as having language-related reading and writing learning disabilities. The other 2 were identified as "at-risk" for referral to special education and were recent arrivals to the United States. All 5 students were identified by their teachers as the students who were experiencing the most difficulty with literacy. Some of the more relevant findings from these two projects are discussed below.

The highest achieving bilingual Latina/o students created multiple connections across and between their two languages. For example, they all verbalized some understanding of cognate vocabulary relationships between Spanish and English. The competent bilingual readers also provided clues that they knew about and used strategies such as transferring and translating. In addition, they made use of questioning, rereading, evaluating, and monitoring of comprehension. In their words, these were activities they could implement whether reading in Spanish or English. The findings from this project convinced me that less-successful readers might benefit from this knowledge.

The less-competent bilingual Latina/o readers were more apt to see bilingualism as problematic than were the competent readers. These readers felt that as second-language learners, knowledge of their first language caused them confusion while reading. For example, another student said that native speakers of English had an advantage over native Spanish speakers and remarked, "I get mixed up because I talk Spanish and English." In general, these readers only occasionally implemented a strategic approach when confronted with problems.

The lowest-performing bilingual readers (Jiménez, 1997) said very little, in general, when interviewed. Their overall perceptions of literacy were that it is an almost complete mystery. Statements such as "reading is something very special," "reading is something you have to learn," and "I don't know what reading is" typified their responses. These students were able to demonstrate deeper processing of text when presented with some of the strategies used by the more successful bilingual readers. These research findings allow for some interesting speculation concerning potentially effective literacy instruction for older Latina/o students.

Because the investigation of bilingual Latina/o students' literacy development in English and Spanish involves understanding of the continuously interacting domains of culture, context, and cognition (Jacob, 1992), I decided to adopt a Vygotskian theoretical framework for the instructional component of the current research project. In the following section, I explore some of the ramifications of this choice for my research design.

Use of Formative Experiments in Research Design

The influences exerted by culture, context, and participants both on one another and on students' learning opportunities and potential are ideally suited to examination through the use of what has been termed a formative experiment. The formative experiment is a modern interpretation of the methods employed by Vygotsky (1962) as he sought empirical verification for his theory. His description of the zone of proximal development, its temporal and culturally conditioned nature, its dependence on the interaction between the learner and a more knowledgeable other, is well suited to being described, recorded, and analyzed using this research design.

One direction taken by neo-Vygotskian scholars has been to include the introduction of culturally or linguistically derived tools and information as part of the research design (Jacob, 1992; Moll, Velez-Ibañez, Greenberg, & Rivera, 1990). These tools and/or this information may already be possessed by the participants or it may be taught during the course of the research to alter the instructional context in such a way that students who might have appeared incompetent under one set of conditions will now be recognized as successful. The work of Moll and colleagues (Moll, Estrada, Díaz, & Lopes, 1980), in which they encouraged Latina/o students to use Spanish in their discussions while reading English text, provides a clear and successful example of how a formative experiment can foster student success. Moll and colleagues reported higher levels of participation, more sophisticated and more extended discourse, and more complex forms of thinking as a result of this change. Their current work has documented and expanded our understanding of the cultural and linguistic capital available to students from working class Latina/o backgrounds (Moll, Amanti, Neff, & González, 1992).

Jacob (1992) focused her description of formative experiments on their usefulness to qualitative researchers who are interested in observing the effects of theoretically driven instructional innovations.

> [S]uch studies are explicitly concerned with improving instruction. To achieve their goals, researchers combine qualitative methods of investigation with interventions in learning situations. Traditional experiments lack ecological validity

and descriptive/observational studies often tell readers about the way things are but fail to provide a vision of the way things could be. Researchers have a specific educational goal in mind and they modify materials or social organization to bring about a desired goal. (Jacob, 1992, pp. 321–322)

The use of a formative experiment provides multiple benefits to researchers with certain goals and objectives but who wish to remain open to the need to modify their interactions with children and teachers as the demands of the classroom become evident (Reinking & Watkins, 1997). Although I wanted to know whether students had benefited from a fairly specific instructional emphasis, I was much more interested in their response during this phase of the study. The former issue can be answered with a *yes* or a *no*, whereas the latter can only be explored through careful examination of students' interactions and discourse during the actual process of instruction. The use of a formative experiment as a guide for conceptualizing the instructional component of the study allowed me to design my data collection in such a way as to tap students' evolving understanding of literacy in two languages.

Methods

Setting

The study was conducted in a midwestern city in a school district that serves approximately 30,000 students, of which about 7,000 are Latina/o. At the time of the study, there were 517 students enrolled in this school; 290 of them were Latina/o and 186 received bilingual education services. Four grade 4–6 classrooms that included many low-performing students participated in the study. One classroom was designated as a bilingual special education classroom (grades 4–6), and the other three were general bilingual classrooms (two grade 4 classrooms and one grade 5 classroom). A total of approximately 85 students and their 4 teachers participated in the research project.

Participants

Participating Students. Student ages ranged from 9 to 12 years old. Their mean length of residence in the United States was 6.6 years; however, the range was from 1 to 12 years of residence. Seventeen of the students had spent 3 or fewer years living in the United States. Thirty of the students had been born in the United States, 1 had been born in Puerto Rico, and the remainder had been born in Mexico. All but 1 of the students indicated that Spanish had been their first language. Their mean length of enrollment in classes designated as providing bilingual instruction was 4.2 years. In essence, all of these students, with 1 exception, were all either recent immigrants or the children of immigrants. As is typical with transitional bilingual educational programs, students served were those with the lowest levels of English proficiency; those with higher levels had already been moved into the all-English, general educational program. Almost as many Latina/o students were enrolled in the latter program as the former. Such a situation is not uncommon in schools and programs designed to serve Latina/o students (Hakuta, 1986).

Participating Teachers. Diana Orozco was of Mexican origin. She had been raised in Chicago but had ties to relatives in northern Mexico. Diana was more comfortable speaking English even though her Spanish-language proficiency was high. She was a second-year teacher when I first met her, and she was teaching in a grade 5 classroom. Diana had a degree in elementary education and she was certified to teach kindergarten through grade 9, with a bilingual credential.

Claudia Contreras was Puerto Rican. While living in Puerto Rico, she was recruited by the district to teach in this midwestern state. Claudia was, therefore, more comfortable speaking Spanish but she also spoke fluent English. She held a special education credential with a bilingual endorsement. She also held both a B.A. in education and an M.A. in special education. Claudia had 28 years of teaching experience, most of it in Puerto Rico, but she was only in her second year of teaching in the participating school. She taught students in a self-contained special education classroom in which students were at grade levels 4–6.

Lee Nelson was Anglo. She was a native speaker of English and a fluent second-language speaker of Spanish. As a result, she was stronger in her English-language fluency. She held a B.A. and a combined master's degree in Spanish literature and linguistics, and education. Lee had 6 years of teaching experience, all of it in the same district. She team-taught with Lynn Middleton in a combined fourth-grade classroom. They worked with approximately 50 students.

Lynn Middleton also had a B.A. and M.A. in education. She was Anglo but had been raised in Honduras. Her English and her Spanish were nativelike but she used more English than Spanish. She also had 6 years of teaching experience.

Data Collection Sources

Data sources included classroom observations of literacy instruction, continuous dialogue between the teachers and me, and student interviews of between 4 and 6 focal students per classroom.

Classroom Observations. Students were observed in each of the four classrooms during times designated as literacy or language arts instruction over a 4-month period on six occasions. These observations entailed in-depth qualitative data-gathering sessions. Data were recorded using handwritten field notes. Each of the observations was between 1.5 and 2 hours in length. Emphasis was placed on capturing the participating students' responses, both verbal and nonverbal, to literacy learning events. The types of literacy tasks students were asked to engage in were recorded for evidence concerning the language or languages used by the students, and the overall level of success, challenge, and instructional support they received while engaging in these tasks.

Teacher Interviews. The participating teachers were interviewed on approximately 12 distinct occasions. These interviews were approximately 1–1.5 hours in length. They included the use of semistructured protocols, but they were primarily informal occasions. The researcher tried to meet with the 4 teachers as a group, but at least 1 teacher was usually absent. On those cases, a follow-up interview was arranged and conducted. Teachers were asked to share their understandings of the participating students, their concerns regarding literacy instruction and student progress, and their input concerning influences on student literacy development in two languages. In addition, teachers were interviewed throughout tile course of the research project on an informal basis.

Think-Aloud Procedures and Student Interviews. Either 5 or 6 focal students from each of the participating classrooms were asked to engage in a think-aloud procedure and interview session both prior to and after the instructional component of the research study. The researcher asked each of the focal students to read selected passages and to answer questions about their knowledge of Spanish and English literacy. The think-aloud sessions involved asking students to stop at predetermined points in a text, usually after each sentence, at which time they were asked to describe their thinking. These sessions were taped, transcribed, and later analyzed for evidence of strategic reading processes. Students were also interviewed using a semistructured interview protocol to determine their understanding of literacy, their knowledge of reading strategies, and their feelings toward literacy in their two languages.

Formative Experiment. Finally, 10 cognitive strategy lessons were included as the culminating field-based component of the research study. The cognitive strategy instruction was considered a formative experiment (Jacob, 1992; Reinking & Watkins, 1997) and data were collected using various means such as collecting students' written responses to the instruction, the recording of field notes, and tape-recording of actual instructional interactions. In the next section, the instructional component of the study is described briefly.

Bilingual Strategic Reading Instruction. The instructional component or formative experiment involved introducing students to various reading strategies. Special emphasis was placed on the following: making inferences, asking questions, dealing with unknown vocabulary items, accessing cognate vocabulary, translating, and transferring information across linguistic boundaries (see Figure 1 for descriptions and examples of these strategies). These sessions were primarily conducted in Spanish, but English was used when deemed appropriate.

FIGURE 1
Strategies Taught During the Formative Experiment

Making Inferences	Students were taught how to supply information not included in the text, usually from prior knowledge, or to establish connections across clauses or sentences. A student-derived example follows:
	And now they have these tiger cubs. I don't know how they get them there because when they get bigger they'll be really protective of their area and they'll probably have to release them in a real open area because it would love to roam around.
Asking Questions	Students were taught to identify obstacles to comprehension and to formulate a question whose answer could help them clarify their understanding.
	That's weird, why would a man need to take care of, I mean why would someone like a man need to be taken care of by someone like a biologist?
Dealing With Unknown Vocabulary	Students were shown how to identify problematic lexical items and to assign at least a tentative meaning to them. Resolution often involved the use of other strategies such as accessing cognate vocabulary knowledge.
	No sé que es la palabra *palidece*. Será que brilla o algo, no sé *palidece*, o sea o quizás, no sé,... (I don't know what the word *palidece* <dims> is. It might be shines or something, I don't know *palidece*, or is it, or maybe, I don't know....)
Accessing Cognates	This was the strategy of consciously drawing upon the lexicon in one language to comprehend, or more fully comprehend, a text that contains cognate or related vocabulary. This strategy required that its user possess at least tacit knowledge of the relationship that exists between the Spanish and English languages.
	Like from the Greek, octopus, eight, eight, like in Spanish ocho pies, octopus. Pus might be pies and octo eight.
Translating	Translating within the context of reading refers to the strategy of paraphrasing parts of a text via the bilingual's other language for the purpose of clarification:
	Y luego acá dice se desaparece y se forma un agujero negro y esas dos palabras se oyen como black hole, como siga, porque agujero it's like a hole and negro is black, and it has to be black hole. (And then it says that it disappears and forms a black hole [agujero negro] and those two words sound like black hole, as it must follow, because argujero it's like a hole and negro is black, and it has to be black hole.)
Transferring	Readers consciously accessed information gained from experience, text, or instruction in one of their languages for use when processing text in their other language:
	Las novas me recuerdan con los libros que leo en inglés, las estrellas. (The novas remind me of the books that I read in English, the stars.)

Adapted from Jiménez, García, and Pearson (1996).

The following sequence describes the approach:

1. *Elicit extended student discourse.* A modified language experience approach was used to generate a computer-printed copy of the students' oral text, which was then used as the basis for teaching students the think-aloud procedure.

2. *Teach students the think-aloud procedure.* The think-aloud procedure was demonstrated by the researcher who silently read a text one line at a time while simultaneously describing text processing (Ericsson & Simon, 1984; Wade, 1990).

3. *Introduce culturally relevant text and demonstrate focal reading strategies.* Next, students were introduced to culturally relevant text, which was used as the basis for teaching strategic reading (Au, 1993; Harris, 1993).

4. *Assist students with word recognition and reading fluency.* When students demonstrated difficulty with word recognition or overall fluency in reading (overly slow, choppy, meaning-altering miscues), they were asked to orally reread specific phrases until they attained a level approximating automaticity in their reading fluency. Often this involved techniques such as choral reading or paired oral reading.

Data Analysis Procedures

The classroom observations, student and teacher interviews, classroom interactional data, and student written responses were transcribed and then analyzed using the qualitative analysis techniques described by Taylor and Bogdan (1984), Patton (1990), and Glesne and Peshkin (1992). These techniques were initiated during data collection, but also involved extensive data coding, which was supplemented by my own insights and interpretation as well as input provided by consultation with the collaborating teachers, a research assistant, and experts in the various relevant fields. These experts included researchers in the fields of special education, critical literacy, English education, bilingual education, and immigrant education. Some of the codes that were developed from the interviews conducted with the students included their views on identity—both its development and its vulnerabilities—understandings of literacy in Spanish and English, involvement of family members with literacy development, and the importance of bilingualism and biliteracy. The comments of one of the participating Latina teachers were particularly useful in terms of helping me stay true to the setting and participants. She engaged in an ongoing e-mail dialogue with me concerning the message of the manuscript, in particular its advocacy-oriented stance. I found her comments quite insightful as I revised and rewrote some of the sections.

I constructed classroom and focal student analytical profiles to synoptically display data from the various sources. These profiles then yielded salient thematic trends in the data, a few of which are described in the next section. The final thematic trends that emerged were used as the basis for constructing an outline that served as the skeletal structure for initial drafts of a final research report. These drafts were more fully fleshed out by a process of continually rereading the data, considering the implications of relevant research and theory, and through dialogue with colleagues. In addition, I presented the results of this manuscript at state and national conferences. Comments that session participants shared helped me to refine and develop conclusions that I drew from the data.

Results

Identity Development in the Cultural Borderlands

Rosaldo (1989) has written that social scientists need to move away from the notion that cultural borderlands are in his terms "annoying exceptions" and move toward viewing them as "central areas for inquiry" (p. 28). The children and some of the teachers who participated in this study were shaped and profoundly influenced by their experiences in what could be described as cultural borderlands. Important aspects of their identity, with subsequent implications for literacy development, were connected to their status as bicultural, bilingual, biliterate persons. Bits and traces of these identities could be identified in the comments of these children and used to construct representations, however silhouette-like they might be. Admittedly, these representations are incomplete, but they differ markedly from those commonly held by society at large and, by extension, the schools in which these students were enrolled (Ferdman, 1990). These are also identities which are too often misunderstood, misinterpreted, and at times, entirely overlooked by those representing mainstream institutions which see and position these children in ways that often serve to distance them from more fully literate identities. I will explore a few of the ways that students' hybridized identities surfaced during the data collection for this research project and discuss their implications for literacy development.

First, on a few occasions, students made direct statements concerning who they were. Their formulations are intriguing for what they reveal concerning the students' awareness of identity and its influence on academic achievement. For example, in the following quote, Petra explained how her status of being born in the United States as the child of immigrants had affected and changed her. Notice how she positioned herself in contradistinction to both native, monolingual English speakers and her own family members. Notice also how my question did not anticipate that Petra would share aspects of her identity with me:

> Interviewer: Bueno, ponte a pensar. ¿Cómo es diferente leer en inglés que leer en español? (Well, think about it. How is it different reading in English than reading in Spanish?)

Petra: Pues, como yo soy, yo nací aquí, y soy de padres mexicanos era dificil para mi aprender el inglés, es una diferencia que nos cambia porque en inglés hay palabras que uno no entiende y en español, como yo soy española, son más así las en español que en inglés. (Well, since I am, I was born here, and I am from Mexican parents it's difficult for me to learn English, it's a difference that changes us because in English there are words that one does not understand, and in Spanish, well, since I am Spanish there are more like that in Spanish than in English.)

Gary's response was similar to that of Petra when I asked him where he was from. Although his comment was much more truncated, it also reveals a blending of identities, a special status unique to these students and one that was probably not fully appreciated. Although born in the United States, Gary still claims to be from Mexico. His perspective is similar to that of many other persons of Mexican origin I have known in the midwest. Perhaps most importantly, Gary and Petra's responses reveal their identity construction as one that straddles two culturally and linguistically distinct zones.

Interviewer: ¿Tú, de dónde eres? (Where are you from?)

Gary: De México, nací en EE.UU. (From Mexico; I was born in the United States.)

Although these comments are perhaps the most direct evidence that these children possessed intriguing and complex identities, there were other indications that they inhabited a place quite unlike that experienced by many mainstream educators. For example, these students, like some of their Latina teachers, made ample and frequent use of their two languages. Their facility in using both languages might be compared to an individual living in a border town who makes frequent trips from one side to the other. At times these crossings, as frequent as they were, led to rather comical outcomes, as if the speaker or traveler met himself or herself coming and going. Saúl, for example, said the following when we initially met and were attempting to negotiate our language of interaction, an activity in and of itself unique to bilingual individuals. Notice that I did not offer two possible outcomes to this negotiation but three.

Interviewer: We can do this in English if you want; would you rather do this in English? Or you can switch back and forth, como quieras.

Saúl: Spanish.

Interviewer: En español está bien, ¿Hay otros?

Saúl: Uh, my dad and my mom.

Lito provided the following example of code-switching while thinking aloud as he read Tomie de Paola's book *The Virgin of Guadalupe* (1980). The type of linguistic behavior that Lito engaged in has been amply studied, cataloged, and defined by sociolinguists (McClure, 1977; Zentella, 1997), and recognized early on as an indication of group membership but only recently interpreted as behavior that reflects the individual's dual, hybridized, and somewhat unique identity construction. It can be inferred that Lito is acquainted with the story and that his dual linguistic rendition of that story makes it uniquely his own while at the same time claiming the spiritual power of the Virgin for his Latina/o community in the cultural borderlands.

Interviewer: ¿Qué piensas despues de leer esa oración (What do you think after reading that sentence?)

Lito: Um, que está...la virgencita le, um, la virgencita told the...la virgencita le dijo al hombre que...um um he could go to the side to get some flowers for he could be on the...and um...she says go to the other side...she says, vayate para el otro lado, y um llevaron las flores y vete and, y, he said okay and he left, dice he went to the village and showed the...the roses, flowers. [Then] she disappeared.... (Um, that there is, the little Virgin [told] him, um the little Virgin told the...the little Virgin told the man that...um, um, he could go to the side to get some flowers for he could on the...and um...she says go to the other side...she says you go to the other side and um, they carried the flowers and go and, and, he said okay and he left, it says he went to the village and showed the roses, flowers. [Then] she disappeared....)

Lito did not simply switch between languages because of a lack of vocabulary nor did he simply translate. Instead, he reiterated some of what he considered to be important information in both Spanish and English. In fact, he appears to have switched into Spanish for the purpose of quoting textual information. Other examples of students' hybridized identity surfaced when they made references to brokering activities (McQuillan & Tse, 1995). Linguistic brokering is an activity often engaged in by immigrant children, but because of the marginalized realities of these students, the stakes were often quite high and, it might be inferred, involved very stressful obligations and responsibilities with which few of their mainstream counterparts would be familiar (see Farr & Guerra, 1995, for a description of some of these transactions). The parents and other adult members of their families depended on these children because of their emerging bilingualism and expected them to translate documents such as lease contracts, income tax forms, billing invoices, and other very complex texts. The literacy demands of such a task, of course, are enormous and are seldom a formal part of the school curriculum. Some of this stress is reflected in Gil's comment and provides a very interesting insight into his view of reading in particular and literacy in general.

Interviewer: Ahora quiero que me lo digas, qué es la lectura? (Now, I want you to tell me, what is reading?)

Gil: Es muy importante...tienen algo que está en el libro y si, este, no sé leer, pues, como le voy a entender...y cuando te dan como así...algo que tienes que pagar...y no tienen numeros y solamente así como en letras...y no vas a saber que vas a pagar. (It's very important...they have something that is in the book and if, uh, I don't know how to read, well, how am I going to understand it...and when they give you something like that...something that you have to pay...and it doesn't have numbers and it only has it like that in letters...and you are not going to know what you are going to pay.)

Laura provided a much more common example of linguistic brokering when I asked her about translating. I wanted to know whether she translated while reading in Spanish or English, but she thought I needed to know how translating was a part of her life. Laura's comment radiates the intensity of the typical translation interaction, the importance of speed, and the rather frantic pace of keeping two participants, who have monolingual mindsets, engaged in something approaching the casualness of any other monolingual interaction. Note that Laura was not performing very well in the classroom. Her bilingual teacher considered her a low-literacy student who struggled greatly with English.

Interviewer: ¿Me puedes decir cuando [traduces], como por ejemplo? (Can you tell me when [you translate], like for example?)

Laura: Como por ejemplo cuando voy a la tienda y voy con mi tía y ella no sabe como decirle y yo debo...yo debo de decirle, y lo que me dice mi tía, le digo...le digo a la señora...mi tía me dice una cosa que le diga...yo se la digo y...y...diciendo lo que me diga la señora se lo digo a mi tía. (Like for example I go to the store and I go with my aunt and she doesn't know how to speak to him/her and I have to...I have to say it to him/her and what my aunt says to me, I say it, I say it to the lady...my aunt says something to me that I say...I say it to her and... and saying whatever the lady says, I say it to my aunt.)

Perhaps one of the conclusions that might be drawn concerning these students' emerging sense and understanding of their identities was that they were a bit unsure and insecure concerning who they were. The fragility of their sense of self surfaced on occasion when students mentioned that English might supplant Spanish and when they hinted that literacy development itself was a language-specific activity, either Spanish or English. Comments like that of Petra indicate a bit of this ambivalence toward both English-language learning and its relationship to literacy. Christopher made the most telling comment in the following excerpt. Forgetting to read in Spanish and forgetting the Spanish language altogether was not only something these children feared, it was a reality that some were observing or had observed in their own families.

Interviewer: When you read in English, Christopher, does it help that you know how to read in Spanish?

Christopher: No.

Interviewer: It doesn't? Not at all? OK. That's possible. Umm, do you think, does it cause problems?

Christopher: It does. You can forget to read in Spanish.

While Christopher worried that his Spanish literacy ability and development were withering and diminishing, Saúl, and probably some of the other students as well, saw first-hand the problems caused by Spanish-language loss. When I asked Saúl if he would describe to me the benefits of literacy, he chose to tell me a short cautionary tale concerning his own 20-something-year-old sister. Saúl and his father were teaching her Spanish. This boy, who had been labeled as having a learning disability, found that in his family, his community, his Spanish-language abilities were valued, appreciated, considered necessary, and worthy of special status.

Saúl: Para aprender porque luego como ya todos vamos a estar más grandes, luego te mandan cartas tu mama o tu papa y vas a saber que era lo que te estaba diciendo. (To learn because later we are all going to grow up, and then your mother and father will send you letters and you are going to know what they are saying to you.)

Interviewer: Háblame. (Talk to me [about that].)

Saúl: Como mi hermana. Le explico así como palabras en español. Es porque estaba tomando una clase de español. Ya se le olvidó casi el español pero, ya, ya se lo sabe más. Cuando tenía tarea de español decía a las palabras, que significaban. Yo y mi papá le decíamos. (Like my sister. I explain to her, like words in Spanish. It's because she was taking a Spanish class. She has already forgotten almost all of her Spanish but now, now she knows a little more. When she had Spanish homework, she said the words, what they meant. I and my father, we tell [this to] her.)

Laura, like Saúl, connected literacy with a specific language, this time English. The association between English learning and literacy development could lead to potentially problematic outcomes if students perceived either as a threat to themselves and their carefully forged identities. These identities are created in the margins with little support from those who usually provide this help to youngsters.

Interviewer: Ahora, yo quiero que tu me digas lo que piensas tu que es la lectura. (Now, I want you to tell me what you think reading is.)

Laura: Es para que aprendas más inglés. (It's so that you learn more English.)

María poignantly described the ambivalence and general apprehension felt by many of the students as they developed their English-language proficiency. The motivation on the part of this student is palpable and her desire to attain higher levels of literacy and English-language proficiency instructive. Educational personnel who are not trained in second-language acquisition, or bilingual and multicultural education, however, seldom treat her fear explicitly. Montero-Sieburth and Pérez (1987) found that a Latina teacher, sensitive to the issues surrounding language learning and the problems faced by recent immigrant high school students, could scaffold her students' entry into a new bicultural and bilingual identity by empathically identifying with the students and by sharing her own experiences with them.

María: Voy a tener que estudiar mucho inglés, voy a tener que saber escribir bien, saber leer bien. (I am going to have to study a lot of English, I am going to have to write well, I am going to have to read well.)

Interviewer: ¿Y que piensas...y como te hace sentir eso? (And what do you think...and how does that make you feel?)

María: A veces me da miedo. No sé, me pongo nerviosa, porque es difícil. (Sometimes it scares me. I don't know, I get nervous, because it's difficult.)

Interviewer: ¿En que sentido es difícil? (How is it difficult?)

María: Es que...es que...quiero tratar de hablar en inglés...lo hablo pero...pero...pero el inglés me da...me da...no sé...no sé. (It's just that, that, I want to try and speak in English, I speak it but, but, but English makes me, makes me, I don't know, I don't know.)

This identity that emerged, for which some common elements across individuals surfaced, shows some of the ways that bilingualism, biculturalism, and biliteracy shaped and influenced the stance taken by the students toward their academic learning. Some other, perhaps equally important facets of their identity were revealed in their comments regarding other family members, particularly their siblings and their fathers. For example, I was genuinely surprised that the students mentioned their fathers so frequently, not because I did not already know the importance of fathers in Latina/o families, but because the majority of these comments were made in reference to literacy learning. The comments concerning siblings were a bit more expected, but they also serve as a means for viewing these students as members of caring, loving, and mutually supportive family situations.

The focal students provided multiple examples and descriptions of how they interacted with siblings on topics related to literacy. The descriptions they provided of their own roles as teachers are very similar to the interactions that Gregory (1996) identified in the literacy learning of Asian immigrant students living in London. Gregory described the pattern as it was used for vocabulary learning:

> Just like Kalchuma and many other emergent bilinguals, Tony is storing up a
> bank of words. Their insistence on hearing words correctly, asking for repeti-
> tion and then repeating them after the teacher show how important lexical clues
> are in the reading process. (p. 58)

This pattern of demonstrate-repetition-practice (p. 43) also seemed to be familiar to the Latina/o students in this study, at least insofar as they were able to describe their interactions with siblings. The following examples provide a sense of the types and kinds of literacy events in Latina/o homes that have yet to receive much research attention.

Interviewer: How is Jose Luis doing in school?

Christopher: Not too good. He doesn't know how to do his homework. I'm teaching him how and I read it. I tell him to read a book and then he reads it and then I read it again.

Interviewer: Si esa hermana tuya viniera y te preguntara—oye Laura yo quiero leer bien, como tu lees, que tengo que hacer—¿qué le dices a ella? (If that sister of yours came and asked you, "Hey, Laura, I want to read well, like you read, what do I have to do?"—what would you say to her?)

Laura: Al menos lo leo yo y despues ella lo va a leer. (At least I would read it and then she would read it.)

Interviewer: ¿Y cómo lo vas a hacer? (And how would you do it?)

Juan: Leyendo un libro y le voy a enseñar las palabras. Le voy a leer el libro y después que él también lo trate de leer. (Reading a book and I'm going to teach the words. I'm going to read the book and then later he also would try to read it.)

The focal students provided many examples of how their parents, primarily their fathers, were involved in their literacy learning. They described how their fathers gave them money to buy books, how they took them to the library after receiving exhortations from their classroom teachers to do so, and they spoke of *consejos* or advice they had received from their fathers in terms of how they should read. The following description, provided by Lito, indicates how intensely involved and concerned some of the fathers had become in their children's literacy learning. The emphasis on approaching decoding as an exercise in syllabification, the bottom-up application of graphophonic information, and the appeal to transfer of skills from Spanish to English literacy mark this exchange as unique.

Lito: I cried because in third grade I couldn't read in English, but then my father showed me if you want to be in fourth grade you better know how to read in English and talk in English and write in English...so my father taught me, also he helped me to talk in English, and then write English.

Interviewer: Do you remember what he told you?

Lito: He told me...at first you got to learn how to do the syllables and then you got to read in English *like you did in Spanish*.

Interviewer: How do you do it in Spanish?

Lito: You put two words together...two letters, like...*c*...this one...and...this one like, for that, you could write *cerdo*, that is like a pig, *cerdo*. He showed me how to do that.

Opportunities to Assume Literate Identities

Unlike many current research studies of students from marginalized communities, I originally designed this work as a collaborative effort between the teachers and myself to foster the literacy development of the participating students. I was very much aware that the formative experiment was only one piece of a much larger literacy environment, which is one of the reasons why data were collected over the course of an entire school year. As is always the case in schools, many other instructional efforts were underway, primarily those of the participating teachers of which I was only partially aware, but also many which, no doubt, were unknown to me and perhaps even to the teachers. The students' comments concerning their own roles as teachers of younger siblings and the instruction they received from their fathers highlight an extremely important and potentially influential source of information. Such being the case, it seemed to me that it was my obligation to report any and all of data indicating that these students were assuming literate identities.

Bilingual, Bicultural, and Biliterate Processors of Text. One possible literate identity that I overtly wanted to make available to the participating students was that of a competent bilingual, bicultural, and biliterate processor of text. This identity was one that my colleagues and I sought to describe and theorize in a study that compared competent Spanish–English biliterate middle school students with less-competent bilingual students and competent monolingual Anglo readers (Jiménez et al., 1996). I made it clear to the participating students and their teachers that this was my goal and they did their best to please me. A substantial amount of data was produced by the students in all three classrooms, attesting to their willingness to try out this particular identity. I want to stress, however, that although I presented this information in a somewhat contrived and prepackaged form, I inductively determined what the ideas, strategic interaction with text, and the particular stance toward text were by making use of data that documented the literate behaviors of bilingual Latina/o readers.

As may already be apparent, a surprisingly large number of the students mentioned letter writing as one of, if not the primary use of and purpose for, literacy. In addition to affirming the importance of this activity, letter writing to relatives in Mexico makes an important statement concerning students' identity as transnational individuals (Guerra, 1998). In addition, the students' concerns for letter writing provide supportive data validating Guerra's description of this activity as vitally important to the adult members involved in his study of the oral and literate practices of an immigrant Mexicano community in Chicago. Guerra, however, did not report the extent of children's participation in this activity. In the following data excerpts, students in the bilingual special education class reported their feelings in writing concerning the importance of literacy for purposes of correspondence.

> Bilingual Special Education Class: Y para hacer cartas./La escritura sirve para mandarnos cartas./La lectura es para mandar cartas a mi tía o mi tío./Se usa para leer muchas cosas y para hacer cartas. (And for making letters./Writing is good for sending us letters./Writing is for sending letters to my aunt or my uncle./It is used for reading a lot of things and for making letters.)

The students also mentioned their bilingualism, their Mexican heritage, and their own unique individuality as important components of their literate identities. Christopher, for example, like many of the other students in this project, described in detail how translating functioned to sharpen and deepen his comprehension as he processed text. As a linguistic behavior, translating was one of the more intriguing communicative and comprehension strategies employed by the students because it represents a very visible manifestation of students' attempts to connect and bridge various aspects of their identity.

> Interviewer: Yeah, ¿qué se puede hacer para entender mejor? (Yeah, what can you do to understand better?)
>
> Christopher: Poder traducirlo. (To be able to translate it.)

Interviewer: Háblame de eso. (Talk to me about that.)

Christopher: Como si usted no entienda algo, y si está en español pues, usted piensa de la palabra, que significará en inglés. (Like if you don't understand something, and it's in Spanish well, you think about the word, what does it mean in English.)

María described her approach to what my colleagues and I termed a *searching for cognates strategy* (Jiménez et al., 1996). Both this strategy and that of translating, which were explicitly taught during the instructional component, were in my opinion, enthusiastically embraced by these students because of their power to affirm and display specific aspects of the students' identities that are so often ignored.

Interviewer: ¿Cuando lees en inglés, cómo te ayuda lo que has aprendido, en español? (When you read in English, how does what you learned in Spanish help you?)

María: Si no entiendo el inglés, tengo que pensar en, en español y así me ayuda...vienen como la "i" de "mi" y "my" y es "i" griega "my," "mi" es con la "i" pequeña. (If you don't understand English, I have to think in, in Spanish and that helps me.... They come with the "i" of "mi" and "my" and it is "y" "my," "mi" is with small "i.")

In all three of the following quotes, it can be inferred that the students are making connections between their lives and the texts presented to them in books. Some of the students such as Gil and Juan are able to describe in detail, as well as in metacognitive terms, how their prior knowledge can be integrated with textual information. Their ability to engage in this type of interaction, of course, is a product of many factors: their instruction, the texts they are reading, the support and prompting provided to them, as well as the overall context of the activity (Lipson & Wixson, 1991). Saúl, it can be observed, has gone quite a bit beyond the text and interpreted the central character, Quetzalcóatl, in almost messianic terms. Note that Quetzalcóatl was, and for some, still is, considered the god of education and culture. Saúl's comments reveal the deep understanding possessed by many of these students concerning their own fragile, unsure, and ever-changing identities.

Interviewer: ¿Qué es lo que tiene uno que hacer para aprender a leer? (What do you have to do to learn how to read?)

Gil: Que...leer cuentos y tratar de ver si te ha pasado a ti...como si...como si está...así comparar el libro y tu vida...para entender mejor el libro...como...también como en el...en la fiesta o en las posadas...que en una fiesta...este...yo veo los dibujos este...te está dando una imagen de como se parece. (That...to read stories and try to see if it has happened to you...like if...as if it is...that way compare the book and your life...to understand better the book...like...also in the...at the party or the "posadas" like in a party, umm...I see the pictures umm, they are giving you an image of what they are like.)

Juan: Que se parece a lo que hacen en mi casa.... Ellos hacen tamales y también nosotros. Casi hacen lo mismo que haces tu...que es casi igual como cuando tu haces las cosas y hablas de ellas, en el libro sale. (That it is similar to what happens at my house.... They make tamales and so do we. They do almost the same thing that you do...that it is almost the same as when you do these things and talk about them, it comes out in the book.)

Saúl: Que hay mucha gente como, de México que viene, que viene así pa' trabajar, pa' tener dinero y allá se están muriendo porque no pueden pasar [aquí]. (That there are many people like, from Mexico that come, that way to work, to have money and there they are dying because they cannot come [here].)

Interviewer: Okay, okay, y cómo sacas eso [de la historia]? (OK, OK, and how do you get that [out of this story]?)

Saúl: Porque dice que tengo que ayudar a mi gente como, así como eso, hacerte ciudadano y arreglarle con papeles, pa' venir pa' acá o visitarlos pa' acá. (Because it says that I have to help my people like, like that, to make yourself a citizen and take care of your papers to come over here or visit over here.)

Perhaps this last insight on the part of the students, that is, the ability to make connections between their lived experience and textual information, hints at some of the most far-reaching potential for altering the relationship between themselves and literacy. The role of prior knowledge, a classic concern of schema theorists (Anderson & Pearson, 1984), is shown here to have potentially transformative power for promoting students' desire to acquire higher levels of literacy and engage in literate behaviors.

Conclusion

For a long time, we have known that many students from linguistically and culturally diverse backgrounds reject behaviors and attitudes generally considered necessary for academic success, particularly when these are intended to replace values recognized by these same communities (Erickson, 1984; Ogbu, 1992; Ogbu & Matute-Bianchi, 1986). This information, although useful for understanding how mainstream curriculum and instructional methods alienate students from diverse backgrounds, has failed to show how this alienation develops and how students might be prevented from adopting this stance. Other research has provided demonstrations of how culturally congruent curriculum and instructional methods involve students from diverse backgrounds in more meaningful and productive ways (Ladson-Billings, 1994; Lipka, 1991; McCarty, Wallace, Lynch, & Benally, 1991; Montero-Sieburth & Perez, 1987).

Demographic descriptions of the teaching force, however, currently indicate that the majority of teachers working with Latina/o students are overwhelmingly European American (de la Rosa, Maw, & Yzaguirre, 1990; National Education Association, 1990; Zimpher, 1989; Zimpher & Yessayan, 1987). In addition, many of the teachers working with Latina/o students are young, inexperienced, and receive little specific training for working with students from culturally and linguistically diverse communities. At present, only a little less than 3% of all teachers are Latina/o (de la Rosa et al., 1990). At the same time, fewer persons from minority backgrounds are enrolling in teacher education programs (Gay, 1993; McCurdy, 1987). One might reasonably conclude that it is unlikely these proportions will change much and that the vast majority of teachers working with Latina/o students will know little concerning culturally responsive instruction, multicultural education, and/or bilingual and sheltered English instruction (Berman et al., 1992). As a result, it is my hope that this research will add to the current U.S. national conversation on Latina/o academic achievement, in particular that of literacy development, by identifying heretofore neglected aspects of students' evolving identities.

The participating students explained some of their fears as well as described facets of their identity that are not frequently included in discussions of Latina/o students. The challenge of learning English and English literacy, their fear of Spanish-language loss and the gaping hole left behind in terms of their identity, and their stories of strength all add to the professional knowledge base available to educators. In addition, the students described the special demands placed on them because of their bilingual and biliterate abilities. Finally, their role as intermediaries for siblings and parents, and how their families served as sources of strength, provided useful information for reconsidering dominant discourses that marginalize and exclude these students from true educational opportunity. Students indicated that literacy learning was a much more appealing activity if viewed as supportive of their Latina/o identity, if it fostered their Spanish-language and literacy development. They also indicated that if literacy were identified with subtractive bilingualism (Lambert & Tucker, 1972), that is, when they perceived it as a threat to their Spanish-language and literacy proficiencies, it induced anxiety and fear accompanied by avoidance behaviors.

Hearing the students' voices on these topics provides at least partial answers to Freire's questions, "Why are the majority of the people silenced today? Why should they have to muffle their own discussion? When they are called upon to read, why do they read only the dominant discourse?" (p. 55).

The instructional component of the study implemented practices that also invited students to display their bilingual and biliterate abilities, knowledge, and experiences. This instruction was derived from and grounded in their community's language and literacy expertise. Moll et al. (1992) demonstrated how such an approach can yield positive results. The formative experiment, then, at its most basic level, sought to provide these students with literate behaviors, instructional practices, and materials that would be familiar, and meaningful, as well as effective in promoting higher levels of engagement with text. In terms of overall literacy development, I determined that there was an increase in the quantity and quality of student-generated discourse dealing with literacy as a distinct domain of human activity; however, I did not fully explore this issue. The findings presented in this piece are exploratory and my conclusions should be considered emergent. Be that as it may, students did demonstrate some increased awareness of literacy, of basic cognitive operations related to processing text, and of the Spanish and English languages and their influences on literacy development. I attributed these increases to the provenance of the content, the cultural relevance, and linguistic sensitivity of the instruction. In a sense, I wanted to provide students with an opportunity to maximize their cultural and linguistic abilities, to further develop their Latina/o literate identities (Ferdman, 1990).

Although the results of this research are admittedly at an early stage of their development, at least a few trends are emerging. Pedagogically, support is emerging for instruction that is characterized by a linguistically sensitive, culturally relevant, and a cognitively challenging approach. Theoretically, the data are providing insight into why some teachers seem to be able to create higher levels of rapport with their students, as well as how aspects of students' Latina/o identity, such as language and oral language styles, influence their ability and desire to participate in literacy learning events. Teachers can facilitate the development of rapport by helping their Latina/o students view their dual-language backgrounds as a strength. Helping students see how to make connections across and between their two languages by accessing cognate vocabulary, by judicious use of translation, and by transferring information learned via their first language is a way to accomplish this goal. Furthermore, teachers can engage in discussion with their students concerning some of the multiple literacies such as translation, language brokering, and teaching younger siblings that were mentioned by students in this research study. Instructional activities might also be designed that require students to demonstrate and implement their bilingual/biliterate skills. One possibility might be to work with a school's central office to produce documents that employ the language or languages understood by community members. This activity could involve the rewriting or translation of official school documents.

Finally, it seems that Rosaldo's (1989) suggestion that researchers place the cultural borderlands at the center of their gaze rather than at the margins is providing fertile ground for producing much-needed information. These borderlands may in fact be the most culturally and linguistically productive spaces in contemporary society. Their ecological counterparts, known as ecotones, have been identified as the most prolific habitats for plants and animals; perhaps an analogous concept may apply to those spaces where the most linguistic and cultural contacts occur. Both spaces are in constant transition; they demand a great deal from their participants and the competition for survival is fierce.

Acknowledgments

This work was supported in part by a grant from the Division of Innovation and Development, Office of Special Education Programs, H023N70037-97. The author wishes to thank Rosalinda B. Barrera, Georgia Earnest García, Arlette I. Willis, and Mark Dressman for their helpful comments on an earlier version of this manuscript.

References

Anderson R.C., & Pearson, P.D. (1984). A schema-theoretic view of basic processes in reading. In P.D. Pearson, R. Barr, M.L. Kamil, & P. Mosenthal (Eds.), *Handbook of reading research* (pp. 255–292). New York: Longman.

Au, K.H. (1993). *Literacy instruction in multicultural settings*. Fort Worth, TX: Harcourt Brace Jovanovich.

August, D., & Hakuta, K. (1997). *Improving schooling for language minority children: A research agenda*. Washington, DC: National Academy Press; New York: Longman.

Berman, P., Chambers, J., Gandara, P., McLaughlin, B., Minicucci, C., Nelson, B., et al. (1992). *Meeting the challenge of language diversity: Volume I, Executive summary*. Berkeley, CA: BW Associates.

Brodkey, L. (1992). Articulating poststructural theory in research on literacy. In R. Beach, J.L. Green, M.L. Kamil, & T. Shanahan (Eds.), *Multidisciplinary perspectives on literacy research* (pp. 293–318). Urbana, IL: National Conference on Research in English/National Council of Teachers of English.

Carger, C.L. (1996). *Of borders and dreams: A Mexican-American experience of urban education*. New York: Teachers College Press.

Carter, T.P., & Chatfield, M.L. (1986). Effective bilingual schools: Implications for policy and practice. *American Journal of Education*, *95*(1), 200–232.

Cummins, J. (1986). Empowering minority students: A framework for intervention. *Harvard Educational Review*, *56*(1), 18–36.

de la Rosa, D., Maw C.E., & Yzaguirre, R. (1990). *Hispanic education: A statistical portrait 1990*. Washington, DC: National Council of La Raza.

de Paola, T. (1986). *Nuestra Señora de Guadalupe (Our Lady of Guadalupe)*. New York: Holiday House.

Erickson, F. (1984). School literacy reasoning and civility: An anthropologist's perspective. *Review of Educational Research*, *54*(4), 525–546.

Ericsson, K.A., & Simon H.A. (1984). *Protocol analysis: Verbal reports as data*. Cambridge, MA: MIT Press.

Ernst-Slavin, G. (1997). Different words, different worlds: Language use, power, and authorized language in a bilingual classroom. *Linguistics and Education*, *9*, 25–48.

Farr, M., & Guerra, J. (1995). Literacy in the community: A study of Mexicano families in Chicago. *Discourse Processes*, *19*(7), 7–19.

Ferdman, B. (1990). Literacy and cultural identity. *Harvard Educational Review*, *60*(2), 181–204.

Freire P., & Macedo, D. (1987). *Literacy: Reading the word and the world.* South Hadley, MA: Bergin and Garvey.

García, E. (1997). Effective instruction for language minority students: The teacher. In A. Darder, R.D. Torres, & H. Gutierrez (Eds.), *Latinos and education: A critical reader* (pp. 362–372). New York: Routledge.

García, G.E. (2000). Bilingual children's reading. In M.L. Kamil, P.B. Mosenthal, P.D. Pearson, & R. Barr (Eds.), *Handbook of reading research* (Vol. 3, pp. 813–834). Mahwah, NJ: Erlbaum.

García, G.E., Pearson, P.D., & Jiménez, R.T. (1994). *The at-risk situation: A synthesis of the reading literature* (Special report). Champaign: University of Illinois, Center for the Study of Reading.

Gay, G. (1993). Ethnic minorities and educational quality. In J.A. Banks & C.A. Banks (Eds.), *Multicultural education* (pp. 171–194). Boston: Allyn & Bacon.

Gersten, R.M., & Jiménez, R.T. (1994). A delicate balance: Enhancing literacy instruction for students of English as a second language. *The Reading Teacher, 47,* 438–449.

Glesne, C., & Peshkin, A. (1992). *Becoming qualitative researchers.* White Plains, NY: Longman.

Goldenberg, C. (1996). The education of language-minority students: Where are we, and where do we need to go. *The Elementary School Journal, 96*(3), 353–361.

Gregory, E. (1996). *Making sense of a new world.* London: Paul Chapman.

Guerra, J.C. (1998). *Close to home: Oral and literate practices in a transnational Mexicano community.* New York: Teachers College Press.

Hakuta, K. (1986). *Mirror of language: The debate on bilingualism.* New York: Basic Books.

Harris, V.J. (1993). *Teaching multicultural literature.* Norwood, MA: Christopher-Gordon.

Jacob, E. (1992). Culture, context, and cognition. In M.D. Lecompte, W.L. Millroy, & J. Preissle (Eds.), *The handbook of qualitative research in education* (pp. 293–335). San Diego, CA: Academic Press.

Jiménez, R.T. (1997). The strategic reading abilities and potential of five low-literacy Latina/o readers in middle school. *Reading Research Quarterly, 32,* 224–243.

Jiménez, R.T., & Barrera, R.B. (1999). Review of close to home: Oral and literate practices in a transnational Mexicano community, by Juan Guerra. *Journal of Literacy Research, 31*(4), 483–490.

Jiménez, R.T., García, G.E., & Pearson, P.D. (1996). The reading strategies of Latina/o students who are successful English readers: Opportunities and obstacles. *Reading Research Quarterly, 31,* 90–112.

Jiménez, R.T., & Gersten, R.M. (1999). Lessons and dilemmas derived from the literacy instruction of two Latina/o teachers. *American Educational Research Journal, 36*(2), 265–301.

Jiménez, R.T., Gersten, R.M., & Rivera, A. (1996). Conversations with a Chicana teacher: Transition from native-to English-language instruction. *The Elementary School Journal, 96*(3), 333–341.

Ladson-Billings, G. (1994). *The dreamkeepers: Successful teachers of African American children.* San Francisco: Jossey-Bass.

Lambert, W.E., & Tucker, G.R. (1972). *Bilingual education of children: The St. Lambert experiment.* Rowley, MA: Newbury House.

Lipka, J. (1991). Toward a culturally-based pedagogy: A case study of one Yup'ik Eskimo teacher. *Anthropology and Education Quarterly, 22,* 203–223.

Lipson, M.Y., & Wixson, K.K. (1991). *Assessment and instruction of reading disability: An interactive approach.* New York: HarperCollins.

Lucas, T., Henze, R., & Donato, R. (1990). Promoting the success of Latino language minority students: An exploratory study of six high schools. *Harvard Educational Review, 60*(3), 315–340.

Luke, A. (1995–1996). Text and discourse in education: An introduction to critical discourse analysis. In M. Apple (Ed.), *Review of research in education* (pp. 3–48). Washington DC: American Educational Research Association.

Macedo, D. (1994). *Literacies of power: What Americans are not allowed to know.* Boulder, CO: Westview.

McCarty, T.L., Wallace, S., Lynch, R.H., & Benally, A. (1991). Classroom inquiry and Navajo learning styles: A call for reassessment. *Anthropology and Education Quarterly, 22,* 42–59.

McClure, E. (1977). Aspects of code-switching in the discourse of bilingual Mexican-American children. In M. Saville-Troike (Eds.), *Linguistics and anthropology. Georgetown University Roundtable on languages and linguistics, 1977* (pp. 93–115).

Washington, DC: Georgetown University Press.

McCurdy, J. (1987, May 27). Teacher-education reforms move ahead, but movement faces skeptics and problems. *The Chronicle of Higher Education*, p. 23.

McKay, S.L., & Wong, S.L.C. (1996). Multiple discourses, multiple identities: Investment and agency in second-language learning among Chinese adolescent immigrant students. *Harvard Educational Review*, 66(3), 577–608.

McQuillan, J., & Tse, L. (1995). Child language brokering in linguistic minority communities: Effects on cultural interaction, cognition, and literacy. *Language and Education*, 9(3), 195–215.

Moll, L.C. (1988). Some key issues in teaching Latino students. *Language Arts*, 65(5), 465–472.

Moll, L.C., Amanti, C., Neff, D., & González, N. (1992). Funds of knowledge for teaching: Using a qualitative approach to connect homes and classrooms. *Theory Into Practice*, 31(1), 132–141.

Moll, L.C., Estrada, E., Díaz, E., & Lopes, L.M. (1980). The organization of bilingual lessons: Implications for schooling. *The Quarterly Newsletter of the Laboratory of Comparative Human Cognition*, 2(3), 53–58.

Moll, L.C., Velez-Ibañez, C., Greenberg, J., & Rivera, C. (1990). *Community knowledge and classroom practice: Combining resources for literacy instruction*. Arlington, VA: Development Associates.

Montero-Seiburth, M., & Perez, M. (1987). Echar Pa'lante, moving onward: The dilemmas and strategies of a bilingual teacher. *Anthropology and Education Quarterly*, 18(3), 180–189.

National Center for Education Statistics. (1998a). *Report in brief. NAEP 1996 trends in academic progress*. Washington, DC: U.S. Department of Education.

National Center for Education Statistics. (1998b). *Mini-digest of education statistics 1997*. U.S. Department of Education.

National Education Association. (1990). *Federal education funding: The cost of excellence*. Washington, DC: National Education Association.

Ogbu, J.U. (1992). Understanding cultural diversity and learning. *Educational Researcher*, 21(8), 5–14.

Ogbu, J.U., & Matute-Bianchi, M.E. (1986). Understanding sociocultural factors: Knowledge, identity, and school adjustment. In *Beyond language: Social and cultural factors in schooling language minority students* (pp. 73–142). Los Angeles: California State Department of Education.

Patton, M.Q. (1990). *Qualitative evaluation and research methods*. Newbury Park, CA: Sage.

Reinking, D., & Watkins, J. (1997, December). *Balancing change and understanding in literacy research through formative experiments*. Paper presented at the annual meeting of the National Reading Conference, Scottsdale, AZ.

Rosaldo R. (1989). *Culture and truth: The remaking of social analysis*. Boston: Beacon Press.

Secada, W.G., Chavez-Chavez, R., García, E., Muñoz, C., Oakes, J., Santiago-Santiago, I., et al. (1998). *No more excuses: The final report of the Hispanic dropout project*. Washington, DC: U.S. Senate (http://www.senate.gov/~bingaman/hdprept.pdf).

Snow, C., Burns, M.S., & Griffin, P. (1998). *Preventing reading difficulties in young children*. Washington, DC: National Academy Press.

Taylor, S.J., & Bogdan, R. (1984). *Introduction to qualitative research methods: The search for meanings*. New York: John Wiley.

Valencia, R.R. (1991). *Chicano school failure and success: Research and policy agendas for the 1990s*. New York: Falmer.

Vygotsky, L.S. (1962). *Thought and language*. Cambridge, MA: MIT Press.

Wade, S.E. (1990). Using think alouds to assess comprehension. *The Reading Teacher*, 43, 442–453.

Weber, R.M. (1991). Linguistic diversity and reading in American society. In R. Barr, M.L. Kamil, P. Mosenthal, & P.D. Pearson (Eds.), *Handbook of reading research* (Vol. 2, pp. 97–119). White Plains, NY: Longman.

Zentella, A.C. (1997). Returned migration, language, and identity: Puerto Rican bilinguals in dos worlds/two mundos. In A. Darder, R.D. Torres, & H. Gutiérrez (Eds.), *Latinos and education: A critical reader*. New York: Routledge.

Zimpher, N.L. (1989). The RATE Project: A profile of teacher education students. *Journal of Teacher Education*, 40(6), 27–30.

Zimpher, N.L., & Yessayan, S. (1987). Recruitment and selection of minority populations into teaching. *Metropolitan Education*, 5, 57–71.

10

Young Bilingual Children and Early Literacy Development

Patton O. Tabors and Catherine E. Snow

Our goal in this piece is to summarize what we know about the early literacy development of young bilingual[1] children in the United States. This is an extensive and complicated topic, and a field of investigation that has generated remarkably little systematic research. Although there has been considerable research on second-language acquisition among young children, there is much less research on early literacy acquisition of bilingual children. Clearly, however, this is an important topic, not only as a theoretical area of inquiry that can illuminate comparative processes of literacy acquisition but also as a topic of compelling practical urgency, as more and more bilingual children are entering school in the United States.[2] And their prospects for literacy achievement, based on the scores of bilingual children in U.S. schools today, are not as good as those of their monolingual English-speaking peers.[3] Knowledge about how young children acquire more than one language and about what effect bilingualism has when these children begin the learning-to-read process is critical for all educators in the present circumstances. A better understanding of the process of literacy acquisition for such children may lead to recommendations for parents about language use in the home, to expanded programmatic options in early childhood and early elementary school programs, and to improved practices to ensure optimal learning in each of these settings.

To arrive at some understandings of the important influences on the literacy acquisition process of young bilingual children, we think it is critical to examine their learning experiences, not only confronting formal reading instruction in the early grades but also prior to their entrance into kindergarten. We know from research on monolingual English speakers that the early childhood period constitutes a critical opportunity for young children to develop language and emergent literacy skills that constitute the foundation for more sophisticated literacy skills (Snow & Tabors, 1993). In longitudinal analyses with a low-income, English-speaking population, the Home-School Study of Language and Literacy

Development, for example, has shown that language input and support for literacy in the prekindergarten time period, at home and in preschool, is predictive of early literacy abilities in kindergarten, which in turn are highly predictive of skill in fourth-grade reading comprehension (Snow, Roach, Tabors, & Dickinson, 2001). Furthermore, we know that skills such as alphabet knowledge (Adams, 1990; Bruck, Genesee, & Caravolas, 1997; Ehri, 1997), phonological awareness (Adams & Bruck, 1993; Juel, 1988; Perfetti & Zhang, 1996), and understanding concepts of print (Clay, 1993; Downing, 1986) predict later literacy outcomes.

What happens to the development of these preliteracy and literacy-related language skills if a child is exposed to a second language during the early childhood period? Are young children capable of developing the full array of language skills in two languages simultaneously? How much exposure is required to ensure that their English level is comparable to that of monolingual speakers at school entry? Does the time needed to acquire English detract from attention to preliteracy skills for such children?

And what happens to the home language? When young children start to acquire a high-prestige societal language—as English is in this society—there is a real threat that they will, at the same time, suspend development in, or even begin to lose use of, their first language (Wong Fillmore, 1991a). Parents and children receive somewhat conflicting messages from educators and the media alike; one is that their home language is without value, irrelevant, or an impediment to learning English and, therefore, to school success, whereas another is that the home language, having been learned first, is robust, so all available learning efforts need to be directed to English. The sociopolitical context in the United States may result in the marginalization of the group to which the bilingual child belongs, leading to low expectations for learner success and failure to attend to maintenance of the first language. What impact does losing a first language have on literacy acquisition in that or another language?

In this piece we discuss bilingual development in three periods: 0 to 3 years old, 3 to 5 years old, and 5 to 8 years old. We have selected a particular focus for each period in order to pinpoint major themes and organize the available research. Throughout the piece we raise questions that still need to be addressed in the future by research on the literacy development of young bilingual children. To simplify an already complex topic, we concentrate on discussing the possible range of experiences that bilingual children born in or brought to the United States at a young age might have. Of course, we recognize that bilingual children can and do, in fact, arrive in a second-language community at any time in their lives and start the second-language learning process at any age, inevitably making their experiences different in many ways from the children who will be the focus of this piece (see Collier & Thomas, 1989, for achievement based on age of arrival; see Valdes, 1998, for a study of middle school students; see Faltis & Wolfe, 1999, for studies of secondary school students).

Zero to Three: Family and Community Language Environments for Bilingual Children

All normally developing children learn a first language in the context of social interaction within their family structure, beginning with the production of babbled syllables at about 6 months, moving on to stable sound sequences used somewhat predictably for communication around 1 year of age, and continuing with the rapid acquisition of words and grammar throughout the early childhood period. For children to be considered native speakers of a particular language, they must have age-appropriate control over all aspects of the language system, including phonology, grammar, vocabulary, discourse, and pragmatics. Developing control of the linguistic system of their native language is a major undertaking of the early childhood period for all children.

Children who develop these skills in a second language as well as a first can be considered bilingual from the time they are exposed to a second language—even before they begin to use the language themselves. For some children this exposure to two languages begins at birth or occurs in infancy or toddlerhood (ages 0–3). Table 1 outlines the complexities of the types of language environments that very young bilingual children may be exposed to and the possible results of that exposure.

Table 1 details four different bilingual environments. The first column refers to an environment in which the home language is used, but the home is situated in the English-language society of the United States. Reading down this column, we see that the defining features of this environment are that family members use the home language exclusively with the child in the context of a community that also uses that language. However, English (as indicated by its parenthetical inclusion under community) is a powerful influence in the United States, particularly through the medium of television and other aspects of the popular culture of the country. It cannot, therefore, be assumed that the child's language exposure excludes English.[4] Although the language outcomes and bilingual status of a child raised in this environment point to the child being *monolingual* in the home language, the societal influence of English continues to be taken into account in the parenthetical comments under "What Happens?" and "Bilingual Status."

In the second column, the environment at home is similar to that in the first column, but community context is more predominantly English speaking. This situation pertains to families that immigrate to neighborhoods in which there is no established community of speakers of their home language, or families that choose to live in English-speaking communities. In this case, the child can be considered an *incipient bilingual* at this time, with grounding in the linguistic system used at home but a good chance of some knowledge of English phonology and even vocabulary from community sources by the age of 3.

TABLE 1
Family and Community Language Environments
for Bilingual Children 0–3 Years Old

	I: Home Language in English-Language Society	II: Home Language in English-Language Community	III: Bilingual Home in Bilingual Community	IV: Bilingual Home in English-Language Community
Bilingual Exposure				
Family Members/ Caretakers Language Use	L1	L1	L1 and English	L1 and English
Community Language Use	L1 (English)	English	L1 and English	English
What Happens?	Child acquires L1; may acquire some English	Child acquires L1: may acquire some English	Child acquires L1 and English	Child acquires L1 and English; may begin to lose L1
Language Outcomes in L1	Strong development of L1	Strong development of L1	Range of development in L1	Range of development in L1
Bilingual Status	Monolingual in L1; incipient bilingual	Incipient bilingual	Emergent bilingual	At-risk bilingual

L1 = any first language other than English.

In neither of the cases just outlined, however, would the child be considered an active bilingual, and, not surprisingly, there is no specific research that targets this early period for children who are being raised as non-English monolinguals or incipient bilinguals in the United States. The assumption would be that their development would parallel and vary in much the same way that any monolingual child's would. The research that has been done at this age has focused, instead, on very young children who are being raised as active bilinguals.

Early bilingual exposure may occur for young children because different members of the household use different languages with the child (see Fantini, 1985; Saunders, 1988; and Taeschner, 1983, for case studies of children raised in the "one-parent, one-language" model), because one language is used by members of the household and another is used by caretakers inside or outside the home (see Hatch, 1978, for case studies of children raised in these circumstances), or because some or all the members of the household are themselves bilingual, using two languages regularly (see Zentella, 1997). In columns three and four in Table 1, we can see how these different bilingual environments may vary for very young children and the differences such variations may generate.

In column three, the environment outlined is one in which a child is being raised bilingually in a bilingual community and, therefore, can be expected to be an *emergent bilingual* with a range of abilities in the two languages. Research with this group of children has focused on questions related to the types of input that they receive and the effect of that input on their emergent bilingualism.

For children growing up in a bilingual household and neighborhood the possible combinations of exposure to and use of two (or more) languages (or dialects) are numerous. In looking at language use at home in a Puerto Rican neighborhood in New York city, for example, Zentella (1997) characterizes six major patterns of language use among the 20 families in her ethnographic study. These patterns consisted of different combinations of who spoke what language to whom, including families in which adults spoke Spanish with other adults but used both Spanish and English with their children; families in which adults used both Spanish and English with each other and their children but children answered in English; families in which adults used only Spanish in the household but children were too young to use any language yet; families in which adults used English with each other but the males used English and the mothers used Spanish and English with the children; and single mothers who were Spanish dominant, one of whom chose to speak Spanish to her children and another who used both Spanish and English. To add to the complications for the children in these homes, many of the adults in this community spoke what Zentella calls "Hispanized English," in which the phonology of Spanish has been transferred to English. In this situation, a young child's first task might well be to figure out that there are actually two languages present in the household, before beginning the process of differentiating and acquiring those two languages.

What do these different types of language use and exposure mean for very young bilingual children? In a study of children being raised bilingually in Miami, Pearson and her colleagues (Pearson & Fernández 1994; Pearson, Fernández, Lewedeg, & Oller, 1997) not only accounted for the words the children knew in each of their languages but also tracked the amount of exposure the children had in their two languages between 8 and 30 months of age. Given the fluidity of the social aspects of bilingual exposure, it is not surprising that the children in this study experienced various amounts of input in their two languages at different times across this time span. Although all 24 families intended to use equal amounts of each language with their children, the exposure of almost all of the children was unbalanced (i.e., more in one language than the other) and/or varied (i.e., one that changed over time). The exposure patterns were related to numbers of words learned in each language at different times during the study, with a lag of about 2 months between a change in the amounts of exposure and a change in vocabulary composition.

Figure 1 graphically displays the effect of the change in one child's language environment. In this case the child experienced a Spanish-dominant (70%) environment until 20 months of age, at which time Spanish input fell to between 40 and 50% for the remainder of the study. At the time of the change, the child's vocabulary in Spanish (SV) was well advanced over English vocabulary (EV). However, when the language environment changed, the child's Spanish word learning plateaued and the child's English vocabulary surged. It would appear that the child was acquiring English words for already known words in Spanish; the total vocabulary (TV; Spanish and English words added together) showed a marked increase after the environmental change, but total conceptual vocabulary (TCV; the number of concepts for which the child had a lexical representation) increased more slowly. Of course, this exposure pattern is only one of many that any one child being raised bilingually might experience before the age of 3.

Returning to Table 1, the final column represents a bilingual home situation similar to that of the child in column three but embedded in a community, including any out-of-home care for the toddler and educational settings of older siblings, which is predominantly English speaking. In this situation the child may be an *at-risk bilingual*. In these circumstances children often choose to maintain receptive abilities in the non-English language but to develop productive use of only one language—English. Once children discover that most significant others in their life also understand or speak the societal language, they often shift rapidly, even at this young age, to operating in a single language. Wong Fillmore (1991b) writes about Mei-Mei, a young Chinese girl who arrived in the United States from Beijing when she was 3 years old. She and her mother had come to

FIGURE 1
The Effect of Change in a Young Bilingual Child's Language Environment

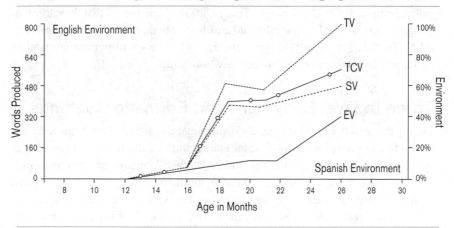

From Pearson and Fernández (1994). Copyright 1994 by Blackwell Publishing. Reprinted with permission.

join her father, who was already in the United States as a student. Over the period of a year, during which Mei-Mei attended an English-language preschool, she began answering in English when addressed in Chinese and then began not to understand what was being said to her in Chinese. When her father asked her to speak Chinese, she would say, "Papa, I can't say it in Chinese. Can I say it in English? English is easier." Sometimes this shift occurs not because the children have made the decision to use only English but because the adults in the family have decided that they need to speak English, even if it is not their stronger language, in order to "help" their children be successful in school (Evans, 1994; Rodriguez, 1983).

By age 3, then, young bilingual children can have already been exposed to a number of home and community factors that will have had an effect on their bilingual language proficiency. A child's bilingual status may fall anywhere along the spectrum from monolingualism in the home language to at risk for becoming monolingual in English. How does any of this relate to literacy development?

Given the link that research has established between language skills and literacy accomplishments (Snow, Burns, & Griffin, 1998), it is certainly of interest to know what linguistic capacity a child has developed, and in what language, by the age of 3. Children with a strong foundation in their home language and continuing support for that language through home activities such as book reading are developing skills that will transfer to English later. Children who are at-risk bilinguals, however, may also be at risk in acquiring English literacy; their parents may have insufficient proficiency in English to support high-level conversations and preliteracy activities in English, but at the same time they may be so focused on English as the language of literacy that they fail to engage in such activities in the home language. This set of decisions leaves these children without the home support for language and literacy development that seems to be crucial in this early period as well as in the preschool period to follow (Dickinson & De Temple, 1998; Dickinson & Tabors, 2001). This means that the early language environment of young bilingual children, whether intentionally constructed by families or merely happenstance, will have an important impact on children's later language and literacy development.

Three to Five: Early Care and Education Settings

During the preschool period (ages 3–5), bilingual children may continue to be exposed to any combination of first language and/or bilingual environments at home and first-language, bilingual, and/or English-language environments outside the home. If they remain in at-home care, their language development will be most strongly influenced by the home-language environment and the language use patterns of caretakers, as it was in the 0–3 period. In this case, their development will most likely continue as outlined in Table 1.

However, this is often the time that children enter some type of out-of-home care for the first time; for bilingual children in the United States, this frequently means their first extensive exposure to an English-language environment. As there is no mandate for bilingual children to be served by bilingual programs at the prekindergarten level in the United States, it is unusual for them to be in a first-language or a bilingual classroom, although these types of settings do exist in some communities. Table 2 details the three main types of early childhood education classrooms that serve bilingual children, the defining features of each, and the expected language outcomes for the children.

In a first-language classroom, as outlined in the first column, all interactions are conducted in the first (other-than-English) language, supporting the development

TABLE 2
Early-Childhood-Education Settings for Bilingual Children 3–5 Years Old

Type of Classroom	I: First-Language Classroom	II: Bilingual Classroom	III: English-Language Classroom
Teachers	Native speakers of L1 (likely bilingual in L1 and English)	Bilingual in L1 and English *or* Native speaker of L1 paired with native speaker of English	Native speakers of English
Children	All native speakers of L1 *or* All bilingual speakers of L1 and English *or* Any combination of the above	All native speakers of L1 *or* All bilingual speakers of L1 and English *or* Any combination of L1 speakers, bilingual speakers, and English speakers	All native speakers of same L1 *or* All native speakers of different L1s *or* Any combination of native speakers of same or different L1s, bilingual speakers of same or different L1s and English, and English speakers
Language of Interaction	All interaction in L1	Interaction split between L1 and English	All interaction in English (except between children with common L1s)
Language Outcomes	Development of L1; no development of English	Maintenance or development of L1, while also developing English	Development of English; little or no maintenance or development of L1

L1 = any first language other than English.
From Tabors (1997, p. 4). Copyright © 1997 by Paul H. Brookes Publishing Co. Reprinted with permission.

of that language while developing conceptual knowledge in the first language of the children. Children who attend this type of classroom may be monolingual in the first language, or they may already be incipient or emergent bilinguals in the first language and English. In fact, some parents might seek out such a classroom because of concern about their children losing their home language. In this type of classroom, bilingual children will continue to develop their linguistic and, therefore, their preliteracy skills in their home language, maintaining the match between home support and the activities in the classroom.

An ethnographic study of a Spanish-language Head Start classroom serving 3-year-old monolingual and bilingual Spanish-speaking children (Tabors, Aceves, Bartolomé, Páez & Wolf, 2000) found that the teachers in the classroom felt strongly that they were in a position to work effectively with the children because they could use the language in which the children were most competent. Sara, the head teacher,

> explained that she had reached most of her social and language objectives for the children during the year precisely because she had been allowed to utilize Spanish. Sara reported that this group of bilingual children, in comparison to other groups she had worked with in the past, was much more verbal, confident, and independent. She attributed the children's quick progress to the use of Spanish in the classroom. (p. 431)

Alicia, the assistant teacher, similarly expressed her opinions about the benefits of Spanish-language use. She argued that second-language learning would be greatly facilitated once the bilingual children had a strong home-language foundation:

> Lo importante es enseñar su primer idioma...no van a tener problemas en aprender inglés—pero vamos a darle una buena base para que ellos sigan construyendo encima de su base. [What is important is to teach them their native language...they won't have problems learning English—but let's give them a good base on which to construct meaning.] (p. 431)

What effect did this classroom have on the children's language proficiency? Unfortunately we do not have measures over time for these children. However, in receptive vocabulary testing at the end of the year in both languages (see Table 3), children who spoke only Spanish or Spanish and English at home scored better, on average, on the Spanish receptive vocabulary test (Test de Vocabulario en Imágenes Peabody [TVIP]; Dunn, Padilla, Lugo, & Dunn, 1986), than on the English receptive vocabulary test (Peabody Picture Vocabulary Test–Revised [PPVT-R]; Dunn & Dunn, 1981), indicating that Spanish was, indeed, the children's stronger language. Further, the children who were exposed to more English at home scored better, on average, on the English receptive vocabulary test than those whose families used Spanish alone, but the range of

TABLE 3
Standardized Scores for the Students in the Spanish-Language Classroom on the Spanish Receptive Vocabulary Test (TVIP) and the English Receptive Vocabulary Test (PPVT-R) by Language(s) Spoken at Home

	Number of Children	Spanish Vocabulary (TVIP) Average Score[a]	Spanish Vocabulary (TVIP) Range	English Vocabulary (PPVT-R) Average Score[b]	English Vocabulary (PPVT-R) Range
Spanish	10	85.6	72–103	45.3	0–66
Spanish–English	5	93.2	86–102	61.2	0–91
English[b] (Spanish)	1	83	n.a.	85	n.a.

A total of 16 children were tested.

From Tabors, Aceves, Bartolomé, Páez, and Wolf (2000). Copyright © 2000 by *NHSA Dialog*. Reprinted with permission.

[a] Standardized scores, normed on a population mean of 100.

[b] This child's mother spoke English and her father was bilingual in Spanish and English.

scores in English indicates widely differing abilities in English vocabulary among this group of children. A tentative conclusion from this study would be that the children's Spanish proficiency had been supported in this classroom, while their English proficiency depended on their exposure to English outside the classroom.

In a bilingual early education classroom, as outlined in column two of Table 2, children could be expected to have their home language supported at the same time that they are beginning to acquire English. The extent to which this happens may depend on the *actual* language use in the classroom setting, however. If the children's first language is used by the teachers only for management purposes rather than for curricular material, then they may well not increase either vocabulary or grammar skills in their first language in the classroom context. If the program has little curricular content and if the children choose to spend most of their time within play groups where the first language is used, then their development in English may not be extensive. A well-balanced program that purposefully presents opportunities for children to be exposed to challenging levels in both languages is necessary if the maximum amount of language learning is to occur in both languages in a bilingual early care and education classroom.

In the comparative ethnographic study discussed previously (Tabors et al., 2000), children were also observed in a bilingual Spanish–English Head Start classroom, where Spanish was used by the teachers in communication with individual children or small groups but English was used as the language of circle time, book reading, and songs. In an interview Brenda, the head teacher, stated that she strongly believed that children should have the choice of speaking their home language at school and that she supported the use of Spanish and English in her classroom. As she said in the interview, "In my classroom everything is done in English and Spanish—this is how children learn." (p. 422)

For analysis purposes it was useful to think of there being four groups of children in this classroom—a group of children from Spanish-speaking homes, a group of children from Spanish-dominant homes in which some English was spoken, a group of children from English-dominant homes in which some Spanish was spoken, and two non-Spanish speakers, one from an English-speaking and one from a Vietnamese-speaking home. Table 4 displays the results of receptive vocabulary tests for the first three of these groups.[5]

The children who spoke Spanish at home and the children who were reported as using primarily Spanish with some English at home (Spanish–English) scored higher on the Spanish vocabulary test than did the children who were reported to speak mostly English at home with some Spanish (English–Spanish). The results of the English vocabulary test, not surprisingly, indicated that the children who were reported to speak mostly English at home with some Spanish did better than the other two groups. The fact that the children who were reported as speaking mostly English at home with some Spanish scored the lowest, as a group, on the Spanish receptive vocabulary test may reflect lack of focus on

TABLE 4

Standardized Scores for the Students in the Bilingual Classroom on the Spanish Receptive Vocabulary Test (TVIP) and the English Receptive Vocabulary Test (PPVT–R) by Language(s) Spoken at Home

Home Language	Number of Children	Spanish Vocabulary (TVIP) Average Score[a]	Spanish Vocabulary (TVIP) Range	Number of Children	English Vocabulary (PPVT) Average Score[a]	English Vocabulary (PPVT) Range
Spanish	9[b]	85.1	59–98	8[c]	42.1	40–57
Spanish–English	3	86.3	77–98	2[d]	59.0	52–66
English–Spanish	3	70.7	63–77	3	66.3	63–73

A total of 16 children were tested.
From Tabors, Aceves, Bartolomé, Páez, and Wolf (2000). Copyright © 2000 by *NHSA Dialog*. Reprinted with permission.
[a] Standardized scores, normed on a population mean of 100.
[b] One child did not pass the practice test.
[c] Two children did not pass the practice test.
[d] One child refused to be tested.

Spanish at home and/or insufficient support for development of Spanish in this particular bilingual preschool context.

In another study, Spanish-speaking children of Mexican descent who attended Spanish–English bilingual preschool classrooms were compared with a control group of similar children who did not attend preschool (Rodríguez, Díaz, Duran, & Espinosa, 1995). This study employed a repeated measures design, assessing receptive vocabulary, sentence comprehension, and story retelling in both languages at the beginning and end of the school year. The results of this study indicated that the children in both groups (preschool and no preschool) increased their proficiency in Spanish, but the children in the bilingual preschool classrooms made greater gains in English. The authors of this study conclude that this faster rate of English development did not have a negative effect on the Spanish development of the children in the bilingual preschool classrooms. One reason for this conclusion might be that these children were growing up in a highly supportive Spanish-speaking community, so their language development in Spanish was being encouraged both inside and outside school at the same time that they were being exposed to greater amounts of English in the classroom.

The final type of early childhood classroom setting for bilingual children, presented in column three of Table 2, is an English-language classroom, by far the most typical experience for bilingual children in the United States. In this type of classroom the teachers communicate primarily in English, a practice that may be dictated by a number of factors: (1) It may be the only language that the teachers know, (2) the teachers may speak the first language of some or all of the children but feel it is more important for the children to begin to learn English, or (3) the teachers are working with children from a variety of first-language backgrounds and English is the "common" language for the classroom.

Research has shown that young children who are exposed to a second language in an out-of-home setting such as an English-language early-childhood classroom move through a specific developmental sequence that includes the following four phases (Tabors, 1997):

1. *Home language use*. Children who come from a monolingual other-than-English home may continue to speak their home language with those who speak that language, but they may also continue to speak their home language with others who do not speak that language. They have not yet discovered that a new language is being used in the new setting. These children may take time to realize that the language they are hearing is, in fact, a different language from the one they hear and use at home.

2. *Nonverbal period in the new language*. When children realize that their home language does not always work, they give up using it with those who do not understand it, but they do not stop communicating. Crying, whimpering, whining, pointing, and miming are all used as nonverbal requests during this period.

These techniques are, of course, most effective with understanding adults. To become full members of the classroom, however, children need strategies for moving beyond the nonverbal period. Most children do this by using the nonverbal period to collect information: They watch and listen intently—spectating—and they talk to themselves—rehearsing—in preparation for using their new language. They also develop receptive understanding of the new language during this period.

3. *Telegraphic and formulaic language*. For most young bilingual children, breaking out of the nonverbal period means using a combination of telegraphic and formulaic language. Telegraphic language use includes naming people and objects, using the alphabet, and counting. Formulaic language use involves employing catch phrases for getting into and out of social situations (no, yes, uh oh, OK, hey!, mine, lookit, bye-bye, excuse me, I don't know). The use of these two types of language helps children get into the flow of the activities in the classroom and begin to sound like members of the group.

4. *Productive use of the new language*. By combining formulaic phrases and the names of objects, young children begin the process of building their own unique sentences to describe their activities ("I do a ice cream"), their ideas ("I got a big"), or their needs ("I want a playdough"). Because they are no longer adopting whole phrases ("Hey, what's going on here?"), it may seem that their language ability has actually decreased; children make many more mistakes ("me's doctor") as they take on the process of figuring out how English works.

This developmental sequence is cumulative and there are individual differences in children's rate of acquisition. As children progress, they move into new phases without giving up earlier ones, except for giving up the use of their home language with those who do not speak it. Researchers have identified at least four factors—motivation, exposure, age, and personality—that may have an impact on how quickly young children acquire a second language. Older children, children with greater exposure to English, children who have higher motivation to communicate in English, and/or those with more outgoing personalities may move more quickly through the developmental sequence.

We present here a transcript (Figure 2) that demonstrates how volatile a young second-language-learning child's control over his new language can be, at times seeming very sophisticated, and at other times very fragile, so that the child needs to fall back on nonverbal communication. This interaction involved the first author and Leandro, a Portuguese-speaking, 5-year-old boy who had arrived from Brazil just before the start of school in the fall. This interaction occurred in the spring while we were working on building a house out of plastic blocks.

In this transcript we can see that Leandro has control over some aspects of English but that there are also areas that are still being developed. Perhaps the most advanced aspect of Leandro's English acquisition, and the one that

FIGURE 2

L: I need help.

P: OK. What do you need help with?

L: To, – to building a house.

P: Well, I have to start with a wall.

L: I make them apart.

P: You're making a what?

L: Part.

P: Apart? You're going to *take* them apart. OK. Let's see if we can get this door here.

L: How?

P: We have to go up to the top here.... We need the...lintel (pushing pieces around).

L: And what is for that [showing me a piece]?

P: That's for the corners.

L: For the what?

P: Corner. To go around a corner.

L: Lot of windows...

P: You need a lot of windows?

L: The house has a lot of windows. [pause] I know what, why have windows.

P: Why?

L: Cuz to we can see outside.

P: That's true.

L: It's tru-u-u-e.

P: You couldn't see outside if you didn't have a window, right? [pause] Do you think it would be very dark inside, Leandro, without a window? I-it would be dark, wouldn't it?

L: Yeah...I think that window, window...

P: Is that one of these windows? One of these corner windows? Let me put it on the corner, huh?

L: Corner...

P: Can you get that one to go the right way?

L: Can you put it?

P: ...There, you can do it. You just had to get those things lined up. [pause] Good. I think you got it...

L: The corner window.

P: Yeah...

L: Corner window. I didn't know it was a corner window. And we have to do it like that [pointing to the picture].

P: Really big?

L: Yeah.

P: We'll have the world's biggest house, huh?

L: Like–[gesturing with his hands like a roof].

P: You mean with a roof?

L: Yeah...

P: OK. That looks like it's going to be hard.

L: Yes. How we going to put it...?

P: I don't know.

L: I think we're going to do it with windows.

P: OK. We'll have a solar roof.

"P" is Patton Tabors; "L" is Leandro, a 5-year-old Portuguese-English bilingual.

From Tabors (1997). Copyright © 1997 by Paul H. Brookes Publishing Co. Reprinted with permission.

cannot be assessed by reading this transcript, is his phonological skill. Other than being a bit singsong, Leandro's English pronunciation at this time was close to native-like, indicating that he had already developed considerable competence in the English phonological system. His pragmatic abilities were also quite advanced. He certainly knew how to carry on a conversation, how to ask for help, and how to ask for further information. In each of these cases, the pragmatic skills that he had developed first in Portuguese, combined with English vocabulary items, made it possible for Leandro to navigate the conversational context in an appropriate fashion.

In this interaction Leandro demonstrates a basic level of vocabulary in English, but there are times in the transcript when he is close but gets it wrong ("I make them apart") and he even acquires a new vocabulary item—"corner"—during the course of the interaction. At the end of the transcript, he needs to fall back on nonverbal communication when he does not know the required item in English—"roof."

English grammar is another area with which Leandro is struggling. Phrases such as "I need help...to building a house," "cuz to we can see outside," "how we going to put it?" show that he does not have complete control over more complex syntactic forms. In other interactions Leandro used overgeneralized past tenses and a negative insert strategy ("you no my mommy") as he worked hard at making sense of the English syntactic system. The use of these problematic forms, along with his rudimentary vocabulary knowledge, did not often impair Leandro's obvious desire to communicate. However, if Leandro had been in a kindergarten or first-grade classroom where the expectation was that he would be beginning to read in English, his inconsistent grasp of English could well have made that task quite challenging.

How much English do bilingual children learn in an English-language classroom? In the comparative ethnographic study presented earlier (Tabors et al., 2000), an English-language Head Start classroom was also studied. In this classroom, both teachers spoke English exclusively, although there were also children from Spanish-speaking and Haitian Kreyol-speaking homes, as well as English-speaking children. Robert, the lead teacher in this classroom, stated in an interview that he felt that children learn English more quickly and easily when they are immersed in the language in the classroom. However, he was also careful to use many supportive techniques in his work with the bilingual children, using lots of gesture and context-embedded speech.

Table 5 displays the receptive vocabulary scores for the children in the English language classroom. The scores for the Spanish-speaking children who had been in this supportive English-language classroom for a school year are similar to the scores of children in the Spanish-language and bilingual classrooms who came from homes in which English was used at least some of the time (see Tables 3 and 4). The children from Haitian Kreyol homes scored higher in

TABLE 5
**Standardized Scores for the Students in the English-Language Classroom
on the English Receptive Vocabulary Test (PPVT–R) by Language Spoken at Home**

Home Language	Number of Children	English Vocabulary (PPVT) Average Score[a]	English Vocabulary (PPVT) Range
Haitian Kreyol	4	75.5	50–100
Spanish	4	60.5	44–75
English	6	92.5	42–109

At the time of the assessment, there were 17 children in the class. One child was absent and one refused to be tested. One child, a Haitian Kreyol speaker, was new to the classroom, spoke almost no English, and did not understand the test; therefore he could not be tested.
From Tabors, Aceves, Bartolomé, Páez, and Wolf (2000). Copyright © 2000 by *NHSA Dialog*. Reprinted with permission.
[a] Standardized scores, normed on a population mean of 100.

English receptive vocabulary, on average, than the Spanish-speaking children, but both groups scored well below the English-speaking children in the classroom. These findings indicate that young children do not miraculously make gains in English simply by being placed in an English-speaking environment for part of each day. Once more, it would be important to know what other influences, at home and in the community, might be having an effect on these children's vocabulary acquisition.

What is the connection between the types of early care and education settings that bilingual children experience and their later literacy development? As foreshadowed in the discussion of the 0–3 period, the preschool period is important for the development, at home and in any out-of-home setting, of all the aspects of the linguistic system that will play a role in learning to read. It is during this period that monolingual children develop sound segmentation and rhyming abilities; expand their vocabularies by an estimated 6 to 10 new words a day; learn to use complex syntactic forms such as past, future, and conditional; and acquire discourse skills in such forms as narrative and explanations. What does all this mean for bilingual children?

If there has been continuity of language development in a child's first language throughout the early childhood period—either because the child has remained at home, has recently arrived in the United States, or has attended a first-language early-care setting—then we can predict that she will follow the course of acquisition outlined earlier for monolingual children with, perhaps, only minor modifications related to living in an English-speaking society. In fact, proponents of first-language preschool classrooms (Wong Fillmore, 1991a) cite this as a major advantage for young children and advocate that these children then enter a bilingual program in which they will acquire literacy in their well-developed first language, as they begin to acquire oral proficiency in English.

However, for children who have been in bilingual circumstances all along or for whom there has been a discontinuity—moving from a home language into a bilingual or monolingual English context—the 3–5 period may be more problematic in terms of developing precursor abilities for literacy. Let us take the example of vocabulary. Considerable evidence suggests that the size of a child's vocabulary—a good proxy for language knowledge in general—is heavily dependent on amount of total input for monolinguals (e.g., Hart & Risley, 1995; Huttenlocher, Haight, Bryk, Seltzer, & Lyons, 1991) and input per language for bilinguals (Pearson & Fernández, 1994; Pearson et al., 1997). For example, when the percentiles of vocabulary development of the 24 children in the Pearson study discussed earlier were collapsed across children over time and compared to a monolingual English-speaking sample (Pearson & Fernández, 1994), word learning *individually* in Spanish and English was well below the monolingual children's level in English, but the Total Vocabulary (Spanish and English added together) was greater than the monolinguals' word level. However, as Pearson (2002) cautions, "Practically speaking...the bilingual has a somewhat restricted vocabulary in each language, and this is something that educators of bilinguals need to take into consideration and work to expand for them."

The following conclusions can be drawn concerning vocabulary development of bilingual children: (1) Variation in the amount of time devoted to each of a child's languages will be reflected in sophistication of knowledge of that language; (2) it is almost inevitable that a bilingual child for whom no planning of the language environment has occurred will be exposed to less input in a given language than a monolingual child, and thus will have a smaller vocabulary in each language during the preschool years; and (3) because vocabulary is an excellent predictor of reading skill, this limitation on a bilingual child's vocabulary skills, along with all the other linguistic skills the child will need, may well have implications for literacy outcomes once the child enters elementary school.

Further, there is certainly an assumption that some preliteracy skills, such as concepts of print, the alphabetic principle (if each language is alphabetic), rhyming, syntactic knowledge, and extended discourse abilities are transferable from one language to another (e.g., Nagy, McClure, & Mir, 1997). However, for these skills to be transferable, they must have been developed in the first place. And if there has been a discontinuity in language environment leading to truncated development of these aspects of preliteracy development in the child's first language, there may be nothing to transfer to the new language, requiring that teachers begin again building these understandings in a language that a child, like Leandro, may not yet have under sufficient control to use in the service of literacy acquisition.

Five to Eight: Bilingualism/Biliteracy in the Early Elementary Grades

When bilingual children enter elementary school programs, again a plethora of programmatic options exists, with an array of possible outcomes depending on the language status of the child and the type of program that the child experiences. It is, of course, during this period that these children will be expected to begin the formal process of learning to read and write. Further complexities are introduced at this time, because decisions are made concerning *in what language or languages* literacy instruction will occur.

Table 6 illustrates some of the programmatic options that may exist for bilingual children in the early elementary grades and the possible outcomes of these programs in terms of language and literacy development. Of course, not all these options will necessarily be available in the community in which a bilingual

TABLE 6
Elementary School Programs for Bilingual Children 5–8 Years Old

Program Type	I: First-Language Program	II: Transitional Bilingual Education	III: Two-Way Bilingual Education	IV: Mainstream Classrooms With or Without ESL Support
Language Use	L1	L1 and English	L1 and English	English only
Language Outcomes in L1	Strong development	Continued development, at risk	Strong development	No development
Literacy Outcomes in L1	Strong development	Emergent, at risk	Emergent	None
English-Language Development	Minimal	Continued development	Strong development	Range of proficiencies
English Literacy Development	Minimal	Emergent	Emergent	Range of proficiencies
Bilingual Language Development	Incipient	English-dominant, at-risk bilingual	Range of bilingual proficiencies	English-dominant, highly at-risk bilingual
Bilingual Literacy Development	Incipient	English dominant, at-risk biliterate	Range of biliterate proficiencies	None

L1 = any first language other than English.

child resides, and, even if they are all available, there may be a variety of constraints on the placement decisions that parents and/or school systems make on behalf of a particular child.

As with programming at the preschool level, a first-language program, as outlined in the first column, is an option that does not exist in many communities. However, there are programs (even transitional bilingual programs) that look very much like first-language programs in the early grades. In these programs, first-language and literacy development is strongly supported and second-language and literacy development, in this case in English, is delayed or only enters the program informally from societal influences. For example, Éxito Para Todos, the Spanish-language version of Success for All, introduces English literacy only after children have achieved a criterial level, approximately end-of-second-grade reading level, in Spanish literacy skills (Slavin & Madden, 1999). The purpose of this type of program is to establish literacy in the child's first—and presumably still stronger—language, before exposing him or her to literacy in the second language. Children participating in this type of program become literate in their first language as a result of literacy instruction but are only incipient biliterates in the early grades because they have not yet received literacy instruction in English. The major questions in this type of program are when and how to introduce oral English and English literacy, and whether or not to continue literacy instruction in the first language after introduction of literacy in English.

In traditional transitional bilingual programs, outlined in column two of Table 6, the emphasis is on beginning bilingual children's schooling experience in their first language but moving as quickly as possible to exit the children into mainstream English-only classrooms. In this situation, an initial effort is often made to instruct children in reading and writing in their first—and presumably still stronger—language, but English literacy instruction may be introduced simultaneously, while the children are still in the early stages of acquiring oral English-language skills. Alternately, English literacy instruction may be postponed until children are deemed to be proficient enough in English. In transitional programs, literacy and all other instruction in the children's first language is discontinued as early as possible, placing the children at risk both as biliterates and as bilinguals.

The following narrative, written by the first author after a follow-up kindergarten visit for one of the Spanish-speaking children who was a participant in the research study of the New England Quality Research Center on Head Start,[6] illustrates this point:

> Although Pamela was originally assigned to the bilingual Spanish kindergarten, she was mainstreamed in January into Ms. Logan's class. When we interviewed Ms. Logan she mentioned that she had the children organized in homogeneous groups and that Pamela was in the top group, despite the fact that she had only arrived in the classroom in January. I asked how the decision to move Pamela had been made. She said that, as part of the "expanded English program" at the

school, all of the bilingual children spent time in the mainstream classrooms for specialist activities and that Pamela had been coming to her class since the fall. The decision to move her had been made in conjunction with the bilingual teacher because Pamela was "eager" and "ready" to join the mainstream class. The only concern that Ms. Logan had was that Pamela had some difficulty with vocabulary on occasion, but, according to Ms. Logan, she was already reading. During the visit there was no mention of any support for Spanish in the classroom and no attempt to make the classroom a venue for multilingualism or multiculturalism. Apparently, being mainstreamed into this classroom meant never having to speak or read Spanish in school again.

In this situation, first-language literacy skills are placed at risk because these skills are still developing and require opportunities to be practiced and consolidated if reading is to become fluent and pleasurable. The risk to first-language skills derives in part from the lack of literacy as an ongoing stimulus to language development. Much of the more sophisticated vocabulary and more complex syntax that adult speakers of a language know comes from exposure to literacy in that language; after about third grade, oral language development derives from and depends on literacy.

The contrasting model to transitional bilingual education is two-way bilingual education, as detailed in column three, a model that includes two groups of children in the same classroom: English-speaking children and children from the same other-than-English-speaking background. In this model, instruction is delivered alternately in the two languages, so that half the time the children are hearing their stronger language and the other half they are in a second-language-learning situation. In this model, literacy is developed in both languages simultaneously, resulting ideally in bilingualism and biliteracy for both groups of children. This type of program requires a group of English-speaking parents who are interested in their children becoming bilingual and biliterate in the other language being offered. Spanish is the most popular of these languages, but there are also two-way programs in the United States in Chinese, French, Korean, Japanese, Navaho, Arabic, Portuguese, and Russian (Center for Applied Linguistics, 1999). A recent evaluation of one of the longest-established programs, the Amigos program, a Spanish-English two-way program in Cambridge, Massachusetts, reported the following:

> [T]he data from these analyses of 8 years of the Amigos program suggest that both the English-Amigos and Spanish-Amigos are moving toward a balanced state of skill in reading both English and Spanish and in using the two languages to solve math problems. The Spanish-Amigos have achieved remarkable proficiency in both English and Spanish. The English-Amigos have maintained high proficiency in English, and although their Spanish achievement may occasionally fall behind that of Spanish speakers, they are clearly achieving a high degree of Spanish proficiency. (Cazabon, Nicoladis, & Lambert, 2000, p. 25)

The final type of classroom setting for bilingual children is a mainstream English classroom, as shown in column four of Table 6. Again, as in the preschool period, this is the most common experience for bilingual children. Although bilingual education is mandated for children who speak a language that is well represented in a given school district, there are a variety of reasons why a bilingual child might be placed in a mainstream classroom, including the fact that the child speaks a language that is not well represented in the school district, that the child is designated by the school system as sufficiently proficient in English to be mainstreamed, or the child's parents have requested that the child be placed in such a classroom. Often bilingual children who are placed in a mainstream classroom are also designated as needing special services from an English as a Second Language (ESL) program (see Ernst, 1994, for a discussion of an exemplary ESL program).

Bilingual children in a mainstream English classroom are faced with the task of learning to understand and speak English, and beginning simultaneously to learn to read and write English, without the benefit of academic instruction in their first language. In this situation, there is no possibility of children becoming literate in their first language in the schooling context, and they are clearly placed at risk for loss of their first language.

Several ethnographic studies have been done to look specifically at how young English-language-learning children respond to literacy instruction in kindergarten and first grade when they are still only beginning the process of developing oral language proficiency in English (Fitzgerald & Noblit, 1999; Weber & Longhi-Chirlin, 2000; Xu, 1996). These studies indicate that young emergent bilingual children can and do engage in a wide variety of literacy-related activities in English, such as developing concepts about print, naming and writing letters of the alphabet, and, in some cases, developing impressive sight word vocabularies. Difficulties arise, however, when more sophisticated linguistic knowledge is required of the children (e.g., when they are asked to demonstrate rhyming abilities but know only a few words with any rhyme-pattern in English or are asked to predict what an unknown word might be from a context they only partially understand). All these case studies suggest that the early accomplishments of the children seem almost language free—centered around recognizing sight words and decoding regular words but not focused on integrating comprehension into early reading processes. Even the children who made the most progress in these case studies did not seem to be taking meaning from the texts they were reading.[7] As Weber cautions, "The risk is that learners' interests in literacy may subside without the meaning of the texts to support their engagement" (p. 35). Further, it does not appear that any of the children in these studies used literacy as an entry point for further development of their oral English abilities, which continued to develop slowly in parallel, drawing primarily from the social context of the classrooms rather than the texts in the reading program.

In the various programmatic models outlined in Table 6 the question of what language to use for initial reading instruction is answered in different ways. In first-language, transitional, and two-way bilingual programs, the assumption typically is made that it is more advantageous to begin literacy instruction in the child's first language (though some two-way programs choose to introduce literacy to all children in both languages simultaneously, and others start with non-English literacy for all students, including English speakers). In mainstream classrooms, the assumption is that young bilingual children can catch up with monolingual English speakers and learn to read in English. Which of these assumptions is correct?

Bilingual education has traditionally been justified on the grounds that children should be taught to read in the language that they know best (Collier & Thomas, 1989). This claim rests on two parallel arguments: (1) that reading is a meaning construction process, and thus it is more difficult, less motivating, and less authentic to learn to read words one does not know; and (2) that literacy skills acquired in a first language transfer rapidly once oral proficiency in the second language has been established. Both these claims may well be true. Nonetheless, we have only a relatively shallow understanding both of how meaning supports literacy development and of how literacy transfer occurs. Can young children read words they do not understand? Can they learn decoding with unknown words? What skills are transferable from a first to a second language? Under what programmatic circumstances? Does the nature of transfer differ with different pairs of languages? Are there age limits on transfer? At what level of first-language literacy does transfer occur? At what level of second-language proficiency?

The National Research Council report *Preventing Reading Difficulties in Young Children* (Snow et al., 1998) concluded that teaching a child to read initially in a second, not yet proficient, language carried with it additional risk of reading problems. Thus, that report did not claim that such instruction would never work; clearly many children in many parts of the world have been successfully taught to read in a second language. Rather, the report concluded that an increment of risk to reading success was introduced for children learning to read initially in a language they did not know reasonably well. If children are to understand that reading is about accessing and constructing meaning, then learning to read in a language in which they cannot yet access meaning is inherently risky. If children are meant to understand and become fluent in applying the alphabetic principle, they should have a grasp of the phonemic distinctions represented graphemically in the target language. If they are meant to be accessing lexical items through processing print, they need to have both stable phonological representations and meanings of those lexical items stored for accessing. If they need lots of practice to become good readers, they need access to texts that are comprehensible and pleasurable, as they are unlikely to persist in reading texts they do not understand.

This general conclusion leaves open, though, many questions about how and when to introduce second-language reading. How early in the process of first-language literacy development is it risk free to introduce second-language reading? Does reaching higher levels of first-language reading facilitate more rapid acquisition of second-language reading? Are there methods of reading instruction that protect children against the risk of being taught literacy initially in a language in which they have low proficiency? How much proficiency in a language is needed to safely introduce initial literacy instruction in that language? How long can one wait for children to develop oral proficiency without disrupting literacy development by having postponed its initiation too long?

Additional questions about initial literacy instruction arise if we consider not the largest subgroup of other language speakers in the United States, namely, Spanish speakers, but the many speakers of other, lower-incidence first languages which may differ more dramatically from English in orthography and in vocabulary, and which may differ as well in not being world languages, richly supplied with literacy materials, as Spanish is. Does it make sense, for instance, to teach a child to read first in Hmong or Haitian Kreyol? There are few literacy materials available in those languages, because writing systems for them have only been developed recently. Furthermore, the parents of children who speak these languages themselves are more likely to be literate, if at all, in Vietnamese or French, respectively. Children's books and initial reading materials are unavailable. Thus, the likelihood that high levels of literacy will be achieved is very low. So how can one best introduce literacy to child speakers of languages such as these?

Conclusion

The purpose of this piece has been to develop a framework for detailing the complexities of the circumstances of young bilingual children in the United States from birth to age 8 and to look at some of the research that has been developed to illuminate these complexities, particularly in the area of literacy acquisition. Clearly, one of the strongest conclusions that can be reached at this point is that there are multiple pathways available to young bilingual children, pathways that are susceptible to a variety of influences, many of which may not be under the child's control or that of his or her parents or educators, but others for which research can inform the decision-making process. As we have seen, some of these pathways involve consistent support for a child's bilingualism and support for literacy acquisition in two languages. Other pathways, however, while leading to acquisition of English-language and literacy skills are, nonetheless, dead ends for bilingualism or biliteracy. Further, some of these pathways, for example, ones that involve parents switching to English when it is not their stronger language or children attending an English-language preschool before their first language is well developed, may even make it more difficult for bilingual children to develop high levels of achievement in literacy in English in the long run. However, many questions remain in each of these areas, particularly related to the factors that may make a difference in each of these situations.

Given that there are many questions still remaining to be answered by research, what can educators do in the meantime in developing programs for young bilingual children?

First, it would clearly be useful if educators would encourage parents to maintain their first language at home and use it—if they are comfortable doing so—for literacy activities (see Nord, Lennon, Liu, & Chandler, 1999, for information about Hispanic and non-English-speaking families' lower incidence of literacy activities at home) as well as everyday conversation throughout the early childhood period. Educators know how important early-childhood interactions are but may not understand that it is the quality of the interaction, not the language that it is carried on in, that is the critical factor.

Second, educators need to find out much more about the language and literacy background of the bilingual children with whom they are working. Detailed language histories could reveal just what types of language exposure a child has had since birth. Asking some simple questions about home literacy experiences and the language associated with them (e.g., the Home Language and Literacy Exposure Index; Páez, De Temple, & Snow, 2000) could provide further critical information.

Finally, educators need to have creative ways of assessing young bilingual children's abilities. Knowing what a child knows—and in what language—is necessary before any informed placement or program decisions can be made. Often, however, assessment—if it occurs at all—only occurs in English, providing no information about possible early literacy strengths that have been developed in the child's first language. Unfortunately, assessment tools for young bilingual children that take into account their abilities in both languages are only just beginning to become available (Munoz-Sandoval, Cummins, Alvarado, & Ruef, 1998) or are still being developed (Iglesias, Pena, Gutierrez-Clellen, Bedore, & Goldstein, 1999), but more informal methods can be used in lieu of normed tests. The crucial point is that young bilingual children, when confronted with the task of learning to read in either or both of the languages to which they have been exposed, will have skills to bring to the process. Educators need to know what those skills are and how to take advantage of them, so that the process of literacy acquisition can be optimized for all young bilingual children.

Acknowledgments

Some of the material in this piece was presented by Patton O. Tabors in an invited address, "Becoming (and Staying) Bilingual in Early Childhood," for the Early Childhood Special Interest Group at the Meetings of the National Association of Bilingual Educators, Dallas, Texas, February 26, 1998.

Notes

[1] The term *bilingual* in this piece is used in the most general sense possible, that is, to refer to individuals who have been exposed to at least two languages, no matter what their level of proficiency in the languages.

[2] In the 1990 Census, about 14% of the total student population of the United States were reported to live in a home in which a language other than English was spoken. Clearly, not all these students could be considered limited English proficient (LEP), however, as estimates of the number of English-language learners in schools at this time ranged from 2.0 to 3.3 million depending on the estimation methods used (Hopstock & Bucaro, 1993). In the 1992–1993 school year, it was reported that around 8% of kindergarten, first graders, and second graders were LEP; the percentages declined throughout the grades to 3.2% in 12th grade (Fleischman & Hopstock, 1993). California had the largest percentage of LEP students (42%) followed by Texas and New York. Nearly three quarters of these students came from Spanish-speaking backgrounds, but schools were given federal support in the form of Title VII funding for students from 198 different language groups in the early 1990s.

[3] National Assessment of Educational Progress (NAEP) results suggest that Hispanic children (of whom some large, but undetermined, percentage are immigrants and/or LEP) score well below Anglo children in reading (Campbell, Hombo, & Hazzeo, 2000). For example, in the most recent NAEP, 64% of Hispanic students were reading below the basic level in fourth grade. States with higher than average numbers of immigrant children also perform poorly on the NAEP and schools with higher than average number of immigrant children, many of whom are bilingual, score poorly within their districts.

[4] We focus here on English-language learners in the United States, but it is worth noting that precisely the same impact of the environmental language has been observed in countries with less "powerful" societal languages, such as the Netherlands (e.g., Vedder, Kook, & Muysken, 1996).

[5] The English-speaking and Vietnamese-speaking children were not included in this testing.

[6] The New England Quality Research Center on Head Start (NEQRC) is directed by David K. Dickinson of the Education Development Center, Newton, Massachusetts. The research consortium also includes the Harvard Graduate School of Education (Catherine E. Snow, Principal Investigator), Boston College (Martha Bronson, Principal Investigator), and the Massachusetts Society for the Prevention of Cruelty to Children (David Robinson, Principal Investigator). Head Start research partners include Community Teamwork, Inc. (CTI) Head Start in Lowell, Massachusetts, Cambridge Head Start (CHS) in Cambridge, Massachusetts, the Community Action Programs in the Inner City (CAPIC) Head Start in Chelsea, Massachusetts, Communities United, Inc. (CUI) Head Start in Waltham, Massachusetts, and Action for Boston Community Development, Inc. (ABCD) Head Start in Boston, Massachusetts.

[7] These observational findings are echoed by results from large-scale quantitative analyses of bilingual children carried out in both Denmark and in the Netherlands, where initial literacy instruction for all children occurs entirely in Danish or Dutch, respectively. In the middle elementary grades, children of immigrant families scored very well on tests of word reading, but well below monolingual comparison groups on measures of comprehension and of vocabulary knowledge (Aarts & Verhoeven, 1999; Appel & Vermeer, 1998; Neilson, 1997, 1998; Verhoeven, 1987).

References

Aarts, R., & Verhoeven, L. (1999). Literacy attainment in a second language submersion context. *Applied Psycholinguistics, 20,* 377–394.

Adams, M.J. (1990). *Beginning to read: Thinking and learning about print.* Cambridge, MA: MIT Press.

Adams, M.J., & Bruck, M. (1993). Word recognition: The interface of educational policies and scientific research. *Reading and Writing, 5,* 113–139.

Appel, R., & Vermeer, A. (1998). Speeding up second language vocabulary acquisition of minority children. *Language and Education, 12,* 159–173.

Bruck, M., Genesee, F., & Caravolas, M. (1997). A cross-linguistic study of early literacy acquisition. In B. Blachman (Ed.), *Foundations of reading acquisition and dyslexia* (pp. 145–162). Mahwah, NJ: Erlbaum.

Campbell, J.R., Hombo, C.M., & Mazzeo, J. (2000). *NAEP 1999 trends in academic progress: Three decades of student performance* (NCES 2000-469). Washington, DC: U.S. Department of Education, Office of Educational Research and Improvement, National Center for Education Statistics. Retrieved August 29, 2000, from http://nces.ed.gov/nationsreportcard/pubs/main1999/2000469.shtml

Cazabon, M.T., Nicoladis, E., & Lambert, W.E. (2000). *Becoming bilingual in the Amigos Two-Way Immersion Program.* Center for Research on Education, Diversity & Excellence. Retrieved August 24, 2000, from http://www.cal.org/crede/pubs/research/rr3.htm

Center for Applied Linguistics. (1999). *Directory of two-way bilingual immersion programs in the U.S.* Retrieved February 2, 2000, from http://www.cal.org/db/2way/tables.htm#table3

Clay, M. (1993). *An observation survey of early literacy achievement.* Portsmouth, NH: Heinemann.

Collier, V., & Thomas, W. (1989). How quickly can immigrants become proficient in school English? *Journal of Educational Issues of Language Minority Students, 5,* 26–38.

Dickinson, D.K., & De Temple, J.M. (1998). Putting parents in the picture: Maternal reports of preschoolers' literacy as a predictor of early reading. *Early Childhood Research Quarterly, 13*(2), 241–261.

Dickinson, D.K., & Tabors, P.O. (Eds.). (2001). *Building literacy with language: Young children learning at home and school.* Baltimore: Brookes.

Downing, J. (1986). Cognitive clarity: A unifying and cross-cultural theory for language awareness phenomena in reading. In Y. Yaden, Jr., & S. Templeton (Eds.), *Metalinguistic awareness and beginning literacy* (pp. 13–29). Portsmouth, NH: Heinemann.

Dunn, L.M., & Dunn L.M. (1981). *Peabody Picture Vocabulary Test—Revised.* Circle Pines, MN: American Guidance Service.

Dunn, L.M., Padilla, E.R., Lugo, D.E., & Dunn, L.M. (1986). *Test de Vocabulario en Imagenes Peabody.* Circle Pines, MN: American Guidance Service.

Ehri, L. (1997). Sight word learning in normal readers and dyslexics In B. Blachman (Ed.), *Foundations of reading acquisition and dyslexia* (pp. 163–190). Mahwah, NJ: Erlbaum.

Ernst, G. (1994). Beyond language: The many dimensions of an ESL program. *Anthropology and Education Quarterly, 25*(3), 317–335.

Evans, C.A. (1994). English only children from bilingual homes: Considering the home–school connection. In C.K. Kinzer & D.J. Leu (Eds.), *Multidimensional aspects of literacy research, theory, and practice* (43rd yearbook of the National Reading Conference, pp. 172–179). Chicago: National Reading Conference.

Faltis, C.J., & Wolfe, P.M. (Eds.). (1999). *So much to say: Adolescents, bilingualism, and ESL in the secondary school.* New York: Teachers College Press.

Fantini, A. (1985). *Language acquisition of a bilingual child.* San Diego, CA: College-Hill Press.

Fitzgerald, J., & Noblit, G.W. (1999). About hopes, aspirations, and uncertainty: First-grade English-language learners' emergent reading. *Journal of Literacy Research, 31*(2), 133–182.

Fleischman, H., & Hopstock, P. (1993). *Descriptive study of services to limited English proficient students.* Washington, DC: Development Associates.

Hart, B., & Risley, T.R. (1995). *Meaningful differences in the everyday experiences of young American children.* Baltimore: Brookes.

Hatch, E.M. (Ed.). (1978). *Second language acquisition: A book of readings.* Rowley, MA: Newbury House.

Hopstock, P., & Bucaro, B. (1993). *A review and analysis of estimates of the LEP student population.* Arlington, VA: Development Associates, Special Issues Analysis Center.

Huttenlocher, J., Haight, W., Bryk, A., Seltzer, M., & Lyons, T. (1991). Early vocabulary growth: Relation to language input and gender. *Developmental Psychology, 27,* 236–248.

Iglesias, A., Peña, E., Gutierrez-Clellen, V.F., Bedore, L., & Goldstein, B. (1999, November). *Development of a language test for bilingual Spanish-English speaking children.* Symposium presented at the annual meeting of the American Speech, Hearing, and Language Association, San Francisco.

Juel, C. (1988). Learning to read and write: A longitudinal study of 54 children from first through fourth grades. *Journal of Educational Psychology, 80*, 437–447.

Muñoz-Sandoval, A.F., Cummins, J., Alvarado, C.G., & Ruef, M.L. (1998). *Bilingual verbal ability tests.* Itasca, IL: Riverside.

Nagy, W., McClure, E., & Mir, M. (1997). Linguistic transfer and the use of context by Spanish–English bilinguals. *Applied Psycholinguistics, 18*, 431–452.

Neilson, J.C. (1997). *Bilingual students' achievement in Danish at the uppermost levels of primary and lower secondary school.* Report from the Danish National Institute for Educational Research, Copenhagen.

Neilson, J.C. (1998). *Bilingual students' language and reading performance in their first and second languages—A study on Turkish-speaking students in Danish schools.* Report from the Danish National Institute for Educational Research, Copenhagen.

Nord, C.W., Lennon, J., Liu, B., & Chandler, K. (1999). *Home literacy activities and signs of children's emerging literacy, 1993 and 1999* (NCES 2000-026). Washington, DC: U.S. Department of Education, Office of Educational Research and Improvement, National Center for Education Statistics. Retrieved August 29, 2000, from http://nces.ed.gov/pubs2000/2000026.pdf

Páez, M.M., De Temple, J.M., & Snow, C.E. (2000). *Home language and literacy exposure index.* Unpublished manuscript, Harvard Graduate School of Education, Cambridge, MA.

Pearson, B.Z. (2002). Bilingual infants: What we know, what we need to know. In M.M. Suárez-Orozco & M.M. Páez (Eds.), *Latinos: Remaking America.* Berkeley: University of California Press; Cambridge, MA: Harvard University Press.

Pearson, B.Z., & Fernández, S.C. (1994). Patterns of interaction in the lexical growth in two languages of bilingual infants and toddlers. *Language Learning, 44*(4), 617–653.

Pearson, B.Z., Fernández, S.C., Lewedeg, V., & Oller, D.K. (1997). The relation of input factors to lexical learning by bilingual infants. *Applied Psycholinguistics, 18*, 41–58.

Perfetti, C., & Zhang, S. (1996). What it means to learn to read, In M.F. Graves, P. van den Broek, & B.M. Taylor (Eds.), *The first R: Every child's right to read.* New York: Teachers College Press; Newark, DE: International Reading Association.

Rodríguez, J., Díaz, R., Duran, D., & Espinosa, L. (1995). The impact of bilingual preschool education on the language development of Spanish-speaking children. *Early Childhood Research Quarterly, 10*, 475–490.

Rodriguez, R. (1983). *Hunger of memory: The education of Richard Rodriguez.* New York: Bantam.

Saunders, G. (1988). *Bilingual children: From birth to teens.* Clevedon, UK, and Philadelphia: Multilingual Matters.

Slavin, R.E., & Madden, N.A. (1999). *Success for All/Roots & Wings: Summary of research on achievement outcomes.* Center for Research on the Education of Students at Risk (CRESPAR), Report No. 41. Retrieved August 24, 2000, from http://www.successforall.net/resource/research/report4lentire.pdf

Snow, C.E, Burns, M.S., & Griffin, P. (Eds.). (1998). *Preventing reading difficulties in young children.* Washington, DC: National Academy Press.

Snow, C.E., Roach, K., Tabors, P.O., & Dickinson, D.K. (2001). Predicting 4th grade reading comprehension: Home and school influences beginning at age three.

Snow, C. E., & Tabors, P. O. (1993). Language skills that relate to literacy development. In B. Spodek & O. Saracho (Eds.), *Yearbook in early childhood education, 4.* New York: Teachers College Press.

Tabors, P.O. (1997). *One child, two languages: A guide for preschool educators of children learning English as a second language.* Baltimore: Brookes.

Tabors, P.O., Aceves, C., Bartolomé, L., Páez M.M., & Wolf, A. (2000). Language development of linguistically diverse children in Head Start classrooms: Three ethnographic portraits. *NHSA Dialog, 3*(3), 409–440.

Taeschner, T. (1983). *The sun is feminine: A study of language acquisition in bilingual children.* New York: Springer-Verlag.

Valdés G. (1998). The world outside and inside schools: Language and immigrant children. *Educational Researcher, 27*(6), 4–18.

Vedder, P., Kook, H., & Muysken, P. (1996). Language choice and functional differentiation of languages in bilingual parent-child reading. *Applied Psycholinguistics, 17*, 461–484.

Verhoeven, L. (1987). *Ethnic minority children acquiring literacy.* Dordrecht, the Netherlands: Foris.

Weber, R.M., & Longhi-Chirlin, T. (2001). Beginning in English: The growth of linguistic and literate abilities in Spanish-speaking first graders. *Reading Research and Instruction, 41*(1), 19–50.

Wong Fillmore, L. (1991a). When learning a second language means losing the first. *Early Childhood Research Quarterly, 6,* 323–346.

Wong Fillmore, L. (1991b). Language and cultural issues in the early education of language minority children. In S. Kagan (Ed.), *The care and education of America's young children: Obstacles and opportunities* (Ninetieth yearbook of the National Society for the Study of Education, Part I, pp. 30–49). Chicago: University of Chicago Press.

Xu, H. (1996). A Filipino ESL kindergartner's successful beginning literacy learning experience in a mainstream classroom. In D.J. Leu, C.K. Kinzer, & K.A. Hinchman (Eds.), *Literacies for the 21st century: Research and practice* (45th yearbook of the National Reading Conference, pp. 219–231). Chicago: National Reading Conference.

Zentella, A.C. (1997). *Growing up bilingual: Puerto Rican children in New York.* Malden, MA: Blackwell.

11

"This Wooden Shack Place": The Logic of an Unconventional Reading

Glynda Hull and Mike Rose

This is a paper about student interpretations of literature that strike the teacher as unusual, a little off, not on the mark. When we teachers enter classrooms with particular poems or stories in hand, we also enter with expectations about the kind of student responses that would be most fruitful, and these expectations have been shaped, for the most part, in literature departments in American universities. We value some readings more than others—even, in our experience, those teachers who advocate a reader's free play. One inevitable result of this situation is that there will be moments of mismatch between what a teacher expects and what students do. What interests us about this mismatch is the possibility that our particular orientations and readings might blind us to the logic of a student's interpretation and the ways that interpretation might be sensibly influenced by the student's history.

The two of us have been involved for several years in a study of remedial writing instruction in American higher education, attempting to integrate social-cultural and cognitive approaches to better understand the institutional and classroom practices that contribute to students being designated remedial (Hull & Rose, 1989). One of the interesting things that has emerged as we've been conducting this research is the place of reading in the remedial writing classroom, particularly at a time when composition professionals are calling for the integration of reading and writing while affirming, as well, the place of literature in remedial instruction (Bartholomae & Petrosky, 1986; Salvatori, 1983). As this integration of reading, and particularly the reading of literature, into the remedial writing classroom continues, composition teachers will increasingly be called on to explore questions of interpretation, expectation, and background knowledge—particularly given the rich

From *College Composition and Communication*, 41(3), 287–298. Copyright © 1990 by the National Council of Teachers of English. Reprinted with permission of the publisher. The poem "And Your Soul Shall Dance" is reprinted from *Yellow Light Poems*, copyright © 1982 by G.K. Hongo. Reprinted with permission of Wesleyan University Press.

mix of class and culture found in most remedial programs. We would like to consider these issues by examining a discussion of a poem that was part of a writing assignment. Specifically, we will analyze a brief stretch of discourse, one in which a student's personal history and cultural background shape a somewhat unconventional reading of a section of a poem. We will note the way the mismatch plays itself out in conversation, the logic of the student's reading and the coherent things it reveals about his history, and the pedagogical implications of conducting a conversation that encourages that logic to unfold.

The stretch of discourse we're going to analyze comes from a conference that immediately followed a classroom discussion of a poem by the contemporary Japanese American writer Garrett Kaoru Hongo. The class is designated as the most remedial composition class at the University of California; it is part of a special program on the Los Angeles campus (the Freshman Preparatory Program) for students determined by test scores to be significantly at risk. (The SAT verbal scores of this particular section, for example, ranged from 220 to 400). Mike Rose taught the class at the time he was collecting data on remedial writing instruction at the university level, and though his class was not the focus of his research, he did keep a teaching log, photocopy all work produced by the class, and collect sociohistorical and process-tracing data on several students and tape-record selected conferences and tutorial sessions with them. For reasons that will shortly be apparent, a student named Robert was one of those Rose followed: He will be the focus of this paper. Let us begin this analysis with the poem Robert and the others in the class read; the discussion took place during the third week of the fall quarter:

And Your Soul Shall Dance
   for Wakako Yamauchi

Walking to school beside fields
of tomatoes and summer squash,
alone and humming a Japanese love song,
you've concealed a copy of *Photoplay*
between your algebra and English texts.
Your knee socks, saddle shoes, plaid dress,
and blouse, long-sleeved and white
with ruffles down the front,
come from a Sears catalogue
and neatly complement your new Toni curls.
All of this sets you apart from the landscape:
flat valley grooved with irrigation ditches,
a tractor grinding through alkaline earth,
the short stands of windbreak eucalyptus
shuttering the desert wind
from a small cluster of wooden shacks
where your mother hangs the wash.

You want to go somewhere.
Somewhere far away from all the dust
and sorting machines and acres of lettuce.
Someplace where you might be kissed
by someone with smooth, artistic hands.
When you turn into the schoolyard,
the flagpole gleams like a knife blade in the sun,
and classmates scatter like chickens,
shooed by the storm brooding on your horizon.

Garrett Kaoru Hongo

The class did pretty well with "And Your Soul Shall Dance." They followed the narrative line, pictured the girl, and understood the tension between her desires (and her dress) and the setting she's in. The ending, with its compressed set of similes and metaphors, understandably gave them some trouble—many at first took it literally, pictured it cinematically. But, collaboratively, the class came to the understanding that the storm meant something powerful and disquieting was brewing, and that the girl—the way she looks, her yearning for a different life—was somehow central to the meaning of the storm. The class was not able, however, to fit all the pieces together into one or more unified readings. And during the discussion—as members of the class focused on particular lines—some students offered observations or answers to questions or responses to classmates that seemed to be a little off the mark, unusual, as though the students weren't reading the lines carefully. Rose wondered if these "misreadings" were keeping the students from a fuller understanding of the way the storm could be integrated into the preceding events of the poem. One of these students was Robert.

A Brief Introduction. Robert is engaging, polite, style-conscious, intellectually curious. His father is from Trinidad, his mother from Jamaica, though he was born in Los Angeles and bears no easily discernible signs of island culture. His parents are divorced, and while he spends time with both, he currently lives with his mother in a well-kept, apartment-dense area on the western edge of central Los Angeles. Robert's family, and many of their neighbors, fall in the lower middle class SES bracket. He was bused to middle and high school in the more affluent San Fernando Valley. His high school GPA was 3.35; his quantitative SAT was 410, and his verbal score was 270. In class he is outgoing and well-spoken—if with a tinge of shyness—and though his demeanor suggests he is a bit unsure of himself, he volunteers answers and responds thoughtfully to his classmates.

During the last half-hour of the class on the Hongo poem, the students began rough drafts of an interpretive essay, and in his paper Robert noted that his "interpretation of this poem is that this girl seems to be want to be different from society." (And later he would tell his teacher that Hongo's poem "talked about change.") Robert clearly had a sense of the poem, was formulating an interpretation, but he, like the others, couldn't unify the poem's elements, and Rose assumed Robert's inability was caused by his misreading of sections of the poem. Here is Rose's entry in his teacher's log:

> Robert was ok on the 1st third of the poem, but seemed to miss the point of the central section. Talk with the tutor—does he need help with close reading?

Rose decided to get a better look, so he moved his regularly scheduled conference with Robert up a week and tape-recorded it. In the 3-minute excerpt from that conference that follows, Robert is discussing the storm at the poem's conclusion—the foreboding he senses—but is having some trouble figuring out exactly what the source of this impending disruption is. Rose asks Robert if—given the contrast between the farming community and the girl's dreams and appearance—he could imagine a possible disruption in her not-too-distant future. We pick up the conversation at this point. To help clarify his own expectations, Rose replayed the stretch of tape as soon as Robert left, trying to recall what he intended in asking each of his questions.

1a. Rose: What do you think...what, you know, on the one hand, what might the reaction of her parents be, if she comes in one day and says, "I, I don't like it here, I want to leave here, I want to be different from this, I want to go to the city and...." [*Expectation*: Robert will say the parents will be resistant, angry—something rooted in the conservative values associated with poor, traditional families.]

1b. Robert: Um, that would basically depend on the wealth of her family. You'd wanna know if her parents are poor...[mumbling]...they might not have enough money, whereas they can't go out and improve, you know.... [Responds with a *qualification* that complicates the question by suggesting we need to know more. This further knowledge concerns the family's economic status, something Rose had assumed was evident.]

2a. Rose: Okay. Okay. [*Acknowledges with hesitation*] From what we see about the background here and the times and the look, what can...can we surmise, can we imagine, do you think her parents are wealthy or poor? [*Focuses* on the poem, asking for a conjecture. *Expectation*: Robert's attention will be drawn to the shacks, the hand laundering, the indications of farm labor.]

2b. Robert: I wouldn't say that they're wealthy but, again, I wouldn't say that they are poor either. [Responds with a *qualification*]

3a. Rose: Okay. [*Acknowledges with hesitation*] And why not? [Requests *elaboration*. *Expectation*: Robert will provide something from the poem, some line that explains the ambiguity in his answer.]

3b. Robert: Because typical farm life, is, you know, that's the way that you see yourself, you know, wear jeans, just some old jeans, you know, some old saddle shoes, boots or something, some old kinda shirt, you know, with some weird design on the shoulder pad... [Responds by creating a *scenario*]

3c. Rose: Uh huh... [*Unsure about direction*, but *acknowledges*]

3d. Robert: ...for the guys. And then girls probably wear some kind of plain cloth skirt, you know, with some weird designs on it and a weird shirt. I couldn't really...you really wouldn't know if they're...whether they were rich or not. 'Cause mainly everyone would dress the same way.... [Continues *scenario* leading to an observation]

4a. Rose: Yeah. [Sees the purpose of the scenario] That's right, so you wouldn't be able to tell what the background is, right? [*Confirms* Robert's observation and *reflects back*] Let's see if there's anything in the poem that helps us out. [pause] "All of this sets you apart..." this is about line 12 in the poem, "All of this sets you apart from the landscape: / flat valley grooved with irrigation ditches, / a tractor grinding through alkaline earth, / the short stands of windbreak eucalyptus / shuttering the desert wind / from a small cluster of wooden shacks / where your mother hangs the wash." [*Focuses* on poem] Now if she lives with her mother in a wooden shack, a shack.... [*Begins line of reasoning*]

4b. Robert: Okay. Okay. Oh! [*interrupts*] Right here—is it saying that she lives with her mother, or that she just goes to this wooden shack place to *hang* her clothes? [*Challenges* teacher's line of reasoning]

4c. Rose: Oh, I see. So you think that it's possible then that her mother... [*Reflects back*]

4d. Robert: [*picks up thought*] ...washes her clothes probably at home somewhere and then walks down to this place where the wind...the wind...so the eucalyptus trees block this wind, you know, from... [*Elaborates*]

4e. Rose: [*picks up thought*] ...so that the clothes can dry.

4f. Robert: Right. [*Confirms*]

5a. Rose: Well, that's certainly possible. That's certainly possible. [*Confirms*] Um, the only thing I would say if I wanted to argue with you on that would be that that's possible, but it's also the only time this writer lets us know anything about where she might live, etc.... [*Begins to explain his interpretation*—an interpretation, we'd argue, that is fairly conventional: that the family is poor, and that poverty is signaled by the shacks, the place, most likely, where the family lives]

Certainly not all of Robert's exchanges—in classroom or conference—are so packed with qualification and interruption and are so much at cross purposes with teacher expectation. Still, this stretch of discourse is representative of the characteristics that make Robert's talk about texts interesting to us. Let us begin by taking a closer look at the reasoning Robert exhibits as he discusses "And Your Soul Shall Dance." To conduct this analysis, we'll be intersecting socioeconomic, cognitive, and textual information, bringing these disparate sources of information together to help us understand Robert's interpretation of sections of "And Your Soul Shall Dance," explicating not the poem, but a particular reading of it in a particular social-textual setting.

A Few Brief Comments on Method. Our data comes from the stretch of discourse we just examined, from other sections of the same conference, from a stimulated-recall session (on an essay Robert was writing for class) conducted 1 week prior to the conference,1 and from a follow-up interview conducted 4 months after the conference to collect further sociohistorical information.

To confirm our sense of what a "conventional" reading of this section of the poem would be, we asked six people to interpret the lines in question. Though our readers represented a mix of ages and cultural backgrounds, all had been socialized in American literature departments: two senior English majors (one of whom is Japanese American); two graduate students (one of whom is African American); and two English professors (one of whom is Mexican American). Regardless of age or cultural background, all quickly offered the same interpretation we will be suggesting is conventional.[2]

Analysis

1a–1b

1a. Rose: What do you think...what, you know, on the other hand what might the reaction of her parents be, if she comes in one day and says, "I, I don't like it here, I want to leave here, I want to be different from this, I want to go to the city and...."

1b. Robert: Um, that would basically depend on the wealth of her family. You'd wanna know if her parents are poor...[mumbling]...they might not have enough money, whereas they can't go out and improve, you know....

Robert claims that the reaction of the girl's parents to "I want to leave here...[and] go to the city..." would "depend on the wealth of her family." This qualification is legitimate, though the reasoning behind it is not quickly discernible. In the follow-up interview Robert elaborates: "[If she goes to the city] she's gonna need support...and if they're on a low budget they won't have that much money to be giving to her all the time to support her." The social context of Robert's reasoning becomes clearer here. He comes from a large family (11 siblings and half-siblings), some members of which have moved (and continue to move) across cultures and, to a degree, across class lines. It is the parents' obligation to help children as they make such moves, and Robert is aware of the strains on finances such movement brings—he is in the middle of such tension himself.

2a–4f

This segment includes Robert's qualified response to "do you think her parents are wealthy or poor?" his farm fashion scenario, and his perception of the "small cluster of wooden shacks." As we've seen, we need to understand Robert's perception of the shacks in order to understand his uncertainty about the parents' economic status, so we'll reverse the order of events on the transcript and deal first with the shacks.

4a. Rose: Yeah. That's right, so you wouldn't be able to tell what the background is, right? Let's see if there's anything in the poem that helps us out. [pause] "All of this sets you apart..." this is about line 12 in the poem, "All of this sets you apart from the landscape: / flat valley grooved with irrigation ditches, / a tractor grinding through alkaline earth, / the short stands of windbreak eucalyptus / shuttering the desert wind / from a small cluster of wooden shacks / where your mother hangs the wash." Now if she lives with her mother in a wooden shack, a shack....

4b. Robert: Okay. Okay. Oh! Right here—is it saying that she lives with her mother, or that she just goes to this wooden shack place to *hang* her clothes?

Those of us educated in a traditional literature curriculum, and especially those of us trained in an English graduate program, are schooled to comprehend the significance of the shacks. We understand, even if we can't readily articulate them, the principles of compression and imagistic resonance that underlie Hongo's presentation of a single image to convey information about economic and historical background. Robert, however, isn't socialized to such conventions, or is only partly socialized, and so he relies on a model of interpretation Rose had seen him rely on in class and in the stimulated-recall session: an almost legalistic model, a careful, qualifying reasoning that defers quick judgment, that demands multiple sources of verification. The kind of reasoning we see here, then, is not inadequate. In fact, it's pretty sophisticated—though it is perhaps inappropriately invoked in a poetic world, as Rose begins to suggest to Robert in 5a. We'll come back to this momentarily, but first we want to address one more issue related to Robert's uncertainty about the income level of the girl's parents.

We would like to raise the possibility that Robert's background makes it unlikely that he is going to respond to "a small cluster of wooden shacks" in quite the same way—with quite the same emotional reaction—as would a conventional (and most likely middle class) reader for whom the shacks might function as a quickly discernible, emblematic literary device. Some of Robert's relatives in Trinidad still live in houses like those described in the poem, and his early housing in Los Angeles—further into central Los Angeles than where he now lives—was quite modest. We would suggest that Robert's "social distance" from the economic reality of poor landscapes isn't as marked as that of the conventional/middle class reader, and this might make certain images less foreign to him, and, therefore, less emotionally striking. This is certainly *not* to say that Robert is naive about his current position in American society, but simply to say that the wooden shacks might not spark the same dramatic response in him as in a conventional/middle class reader. The same holds true for another of Hongo's indicators of economic status—the hanging of the wash—for Robert's mother still "likes to wash her clothes by hand." Paradoxically, familiarity might work against certain kinds of dramatic response to aspects of working class life.

In line with the above assertion, we would like to consider one last indicator of the girl's economic status—the mention of the Sears catalog. The Sears catalog, we believe, cuts two ways in the poem: It suggests lower income-level shopping ("thrifty," as one of our readers put it) and, as well, the importing of another culture's garments. But the catalog also carries with it an ironic twist: It's not likely that conventional readers would consider a Sears catalog to be a source of fashion, so there's a touch of irony—perhaps pity mixed with humor—in this girl fulfilling her romantic dreams via Sears and Roebuck. We suggest that Robert's position in the society makes it difficult for him to see things this way, to comply with this conventional reading. He knows merchandise from Sears is "economical" and "affordable," and, to him, there's nothing ironic, pitiable, or humorous about that. When asked if he sees anything sad or ironic about the girl buying there he responds, "Oh, no, no," pointing out that "some of the items they sell in Sears, they sell in other stores." He then goes on to uncover an interesting problem in the poem. He uses the Sears catalog to support his assertion that the family isn't all that poor (and thus doesn't necessarily live in those shacks): "She couldn't be really poor because she has clothes from the Sears catalog." Robert knows what real poverty is, and he knows that if you have enough money to buy at Sears, you're doing okay. He goes on to speculate—again with his careful, qualifying logic—that if she is as poor as the shacks suggest, then maybe the Sears clothes could be second-hand and sent to her by relatives, in the way his family sends clothes and shoes to his relatives in Trinidad. Hongo's use of the Sears catalog is, in some ways, undercut by other elements in his poem.

> 3b. Robert: Because typical farm life is, you know, that's the way that you see yourself, you know, wear jeans, just some old jeans, you know, some old saddle shoes, boots or something, some old kinda shirt, you know, with some weird design on the shoulder pad...
>
> 3c. Rose: Uh huh...
>
> 3d. Robert: ...for the guys. And then girls probably wear some kind of plain cloth skirt, you know, with some weird designs on it and a weird shirt. I couldn't really...you really wouldn't know if they're...whether they were rich or not. 'Cause mainly everyone would dress the same way....

Now we can turn to the farm fashion scenario. Given that the "small cluster of wooden shacks" doesn't seem to function for Robert as it might for the conventional reader, he is left more to his own devices when asked, "Do you think her parents are wealthy or poor?" What begins as a seeming non sequitur—and a concrete one at that—does reveal its purpose as Robert plays it out. Though Robert has a frame of reference to understand the economics of the scene in "And Your Soul Shall Dance" and the longing of its main character, he is, after all, a city boy, born and raised in central Los Angeles. What he does, then, when asked a question about how one determines the economic background of people moving across a farm landscape is to access what knowledge he does have about farm life—things he's read or heard, images he's gleaned from movies and television shows (e.g., *The Little House on the Prairie*)—and create a scenario, focusing on one indicator of socioeconomic status: fashion. (And fashion is a sensible criterion to use here, given the poem's emblematic use of clothing.) Classroom-observational and stimulated-recall data suggest that Robert makes particularly good use of visual imagery in his thinking—e.g., he draws pictures and charts to help him comprehend difficult readings; he rehearses sentences by visualizing them before he writes them out—and here we see him reasoning through the use of scenario, concluding that in certain kinds of communities, distinctions by readily discernible indicators like dress might not be all that easy to make.

4d. Robert: ...washes her clothes probably at home somewhere and then walks down to this place where the wind...the wind...so the eucalyptus trees block this wind, you know, from...

4e. Rose: ...so that the clothes can dry.

4f. Robert: Right.

This section also involves the wooden shacks, though the concern here is Robert's assertion that the mother doesn't have to live in the shacks to hang the wash there. Robert's reasoning, again, seems inappropriately legalistic. Yes, the mother could walk down to this place to hang her clothes; the poem doesn't specify "that [the girl] lives with her mother, or that [the mother] just goes to this wooden shack place to *hang* her clothes." But to Rose during the conference this seemed like a jurisprudential rather than a poetic reading. In the follow-up interview, however, Robert elaborated in a way that made Rose realize that Robert might have a better imagistic case than his teacher first thought—for Rose missed the full visual particulars of the scene, did not see the importance of the "tractors grinding through alkaline earth." Robert elaborates on "this place where...the eucalyptus trees block this wind." He describes this "little shack area where the clothes can dry without being bothered by the wind and dust...with all this...the tractor grinding through the earth. That brings up dust." Robert had pictured the surrounding landscape—machines stirring up grit and dust—and saw the necessity of trees to break the dust-laden wind so that wash would dry clean in the sun. The conventional reader could point out that such a windbreak would be necessary as well to protect residents, but given Robert's other interpretations, it makes sense, is coherent, to see the shacks—sheds of some kind perhaps or abandoned housing—as part of this eucalyptus-protected place where women hang the wash. What's important to note here is that Robert was able to visualize the scene—animate it, actually—in a way that Rose was not, for Rose was focusing on the dramatic significance of the shacks. Robert's reading may be unconventional and inappropriately jurisprudential, but it is coherent, and it allows us—in these lines—to animate the full landscape in a way that enhances our reading of the poem.

Conclusion

We hope we have demonstrated the logic and coherence of one student's unconventional reading. What we haven't addressed—and it could certainly now be raised—is the pedagogical wisdom of encouraging in a writing classroom the playing out of such unconventional readings. Reviewing the brief stretch of Rose and Robert's discourse, we see how often teacher talk is qualified, challenged, and interrupted (though not harshly), and how rarely teacher expectations are fulfilled. If the teacher's goals are to run an efficient classroom, cover a set body of material, and convey certain conventional reading and writing strategies to students who are on the margin of the academic community, then all these conversational disjunctions are troubling.

What we would like to suggest, though, is that the laudable goal of facilitating underprepared students' entry into the academic community is actually compromised by a conversational pattern that channels students like Robert into a more "efficient" discourse. The desire for efficiency and coverage can cut short numerous possibilities for students to explore issues, articulate concerns, formulate and revise problems—all necessary for good writing to emerge—and can lead to conversational patterns that socialize students into a mode of interaction that will limit rather than enhance their participation in intellectual work.[3] We would further suggest that streamlined conversational patterns (like the Initiation-Comment-Response pattern described by Mehan, 1979) are often reinforced by a set of deficit-oriented assumptions about the linguistic and cognitive abilities of remedial students, assumptions that are much in need of examination (Hull et al., 1989; Rose, 1989).

We would pose instead a pedagogical model that places knowledge-making at its center. The conversational techniques attending such a model are not necessarily that demanding—Robert benefits from simple expressions of encouragement, focusing, and reflecting back—but the difference in assumptions is profound: that the real stuff of belonging to an academic community is dynamic involvement in generating and questioning knowledge, that students desperately need immersion and encouragement to involve themselves in such activity, and that underprepared students are capable—given the right conditions—of engaging in such activity. We would also underscore the fact that Robert's reading (a) does bring to light the problem with the Sears catalog and (b) animates the landscape as his teacher's reading did not do. Finally, we would suggest that engaging in a kind of "social-textual" reading of Robert's reading moves us toward deeper understanding of the social base of literary interpretation (cf. Salvatori, 1989).

In calling for a richer, more transactive model of classroom discourse, we want to acknowledge that such a model removes some of the control of teacher-centered instruction and can create moments of hesitance and uncertainty (as was the case with Rose through the first half of the transcript). But hesitance and uncertainty—as we all know from our own intellectual struggles—are central to knowledge-making. Furthermore, we are not asking teachers to abandon structure, goals, and accountability. A good deal of engineering still goes on in the transactive classroom: the teacher focusing discussion, helping students better articulate their ideas, involving others, pointing out connections, keeping an eye on the clock. Even in conference, Rose's interaction with Robert is clearly goal driven, thus Rose's reliance on focusing and reflecting back. Rose operates with a conventional reading in mind and begins moving toward it in 5a—and does so out loud to reveal to Robert the line of such reasoning. Robert's interpretation, though, will cause his teacher to modify his reading, and the teacher's presentation of his interpretation will help Robert acquire an additional approach to the poem. (In fact, the very tension between academic convention and student experience could then become the focus of discussion.) This, we think, is the way talk and thought should go when a student seems to falter, when readings seem a little off the mark.[4]

Notes

[1] In stimulated recall, a student's writing is videotaped and, upon completion, replayed to cue recall of mental processes occurring during composing. For further discussion of the procedure and its advantages and limitations, see Rose (1984).

[2] Frankly, we had trouble arriving at a way to designate the readings we're calling conventional and unconventional. And we're not satisfied yet. Certain of Robert's responses seem to be influenced by class (e.g., his reaction to the wooden shacks and Sears), and we note that, but with reluctance. We don't want to imply that class is the primary determiner of Robert's reading (versus, say, socialization into an English department—which, we realize, would correlate with class). We also don't want to imply that middle class readers would, by virtue of class, automatically see things in a certain way, would have no trouble understanding particular images and allusions. One of the people who read this paper for us, Dennis Lynch, suggested that we use Wayne Booth's notion of "intended audience"—that Robert is simply not a member of the audience for whom the poem was written, thus he offers a reading that differs from the reading we're calling conventional. The notion of intended audience makes sense here and fits with our discussion of socialization. Hongo, like most younger American poets, honed his craft in an English department and an MFA program, places where one's work is influenced by particular audiences—fellow poets, faculty, journal editors, etc. But, finally, we decided not to use the notion of intended audience, for it carries with it a theoretical framework we're not sure does Robert or Hongo full justice here. We use words like *conventional* and *middle class*, then, with reserve and invite our readers to help us think through this problem.

[3] For two different but compatible perspectives on this claim see Shor (1992) and Tharp and Gallimore (1989).

[4] We would like to thank Linda Flower, Kay Fraser, Marisa Garrett, Jonathan Lovell, Dennis Lynch, Sandra Mano, Cheryl Pfoff, Mariolina Salvatori, Melanie Sperling, and Susan Thompson-Lowry for their comments on this paper. We benefited from a discussion at a meeting of the directors of the California Writing Project, and we would also like to acknowledge three anonymous *CCC* reviewers who gently guided us toward an understanding of the gaps and blunders in the essay. This work has been supported by grants from the McDonnell Foundation Program in Cognitive Studies for Educational Practice and the Research Foundation of the National Council of Teachers of English.

References

Bartholomae, D., & Petrosky, A. (Eds.). (1986). *Facts, counterfacts and artifacts: Theory and method for a reading and writing course.* Upper Montclair, NJ: Boynton.

Hongo, G.K. (1982). And your soul shall dance. *Yellow Light, 69.*

Hull, G., & Rose, M. (1989). Rethinking remediation: Toward a social-cognitive understanding of problematic reading and writing. *Written Communication, 6,* 39–54.

Hull, G., Rose, M., Fraser, K.L., & Garrett, M. (1989, February). *The social construction of remediation.* Paper presented at the Tenth Annual Ethnography in Education Forum, University of Pennsylvania, Philadelphia.

Mehan, H. (1979). *Learning lessons: Social organization in the classroom.* Cambridge, MA: Harvard University Press.

Rose, M. (1984). *Writer's block: The cognitive dimension.* Carbondale: Southern Illinois University Press.

Rose, M. (1989). *Lives on the boundary: The struggles and achievements of America's underprepared*. New York: Free Press.

Salvatori, M. (1983). Reading and writing a text: Correlations between reading and writing patterns. *College English, 45*, 657–666.

Salvatori, M. (1989). Pedagogy: From the periphery to the center. In P. Donahue & E. Quandahl (Eds.), *Reclaiming pedagogy: The rhetoric of the classroom* (pp. 17–34).

Carbondale: Southern Illinois University Press.

Shor, I. (1992). *Empowering education: Critical teaching for social change*. Chicago: University of Chicago Press.

Tharp, R.G., & Gallimore, R. (1989). *Rousing minds to life: Teaching, learning, and schooling in social context*. New York: Oxford University Press.

12

Preschoolers' Developing Ownership of the Literate Register

Beverly E. Cox, Zhihui Fang, and Beverly White Otto

Cohesion concerns the interrelatedness and interpretability of words and sentences in a text. It is one authentic aspect of text making that differs by the context in and for which it is constructed or used (i.e., cohesive choices vary by what is technically called *register*). As a measurable linguistic phenomenon (Jonz, 1987), cohesion has considerable evidence of construct validity as a measure of textual quality (Brandt, 1989; Halliday & Hasan, 1989). Overall, familiarity with how cohesion is used to establish meaning in written-for-others text (i.e., book-like text or what we call *literate register text*) is statistically significantly related to more proficient reading and more comprehensible writing from elementary through adult years (e.g., Kintsch, 1977; Lesgold, 1972).

An extensive research base relating cohesion to literacy, developed largely during the 1970s and early 1980s, was soundly criticized for its persistent view of cohesion as simple counts of specific devices (e.g., noun/pronoun pairs). This view, the critics argued, limited the studies' explanatory power (Hasan, 1984; Mosenthal & Tierney, 1984). Also, questions of ecological validity were raised because these studies often used specially written or very brief texts manipulating the cohesion devices to examine subjects' interpretive expertise.

The present study brings new theoretical perspectives, design, and investigative tools to the study of cohesion and literacy. It merges sociolinguistic (e.g., Halliday, 1978, 1985a) and sociocognitive (e.g., Vygotsky, 1934/1962, 1934/1978) theory to address issues of ecological validity and past inadequacy of analytical tools. Using this broader, more complete theoretical framework and related tools, the study (a) addresses an age group (preschoolers) generally ignored in the earlier work; (b) uses a reconceptualization of cohesion (cohesive harmony) as clause-level redundancies that simultaneously realize textual cueing systems recognized as fundamental to literacy (e.g., Goodman, 1967); (c) uses children's original texts, constructed for a real purpose, rather than specially written texts with experimental manipulations; and (d) brings both quantitative and qualitative indicators, grounded in linguistic theory, to bear on how cohesion is related to emergent literacy. It offers unique, analytical, and authentic insights into important holistic observations by others (e.g., Snow & Ninio, 1986; Sulzby, 1985) concerning young children's emergent use of written language patterns (i.e., literate register options) and reveals authentic, potentially developmental patterns not previously revealed in other research. Before discussing the study further, we will examine its theoretical grounding, the reconceptualization of cohesion, and research studying cohesive harmony and literacy.

Halliday's Linguistic Theory. For Halliday (1978; Halliday & Hasan, 1989) language is a sociosemiotic system—a meaning-driven symbol system with its roots, evolution, and individual development in social interactions and functions. Specific semantic features in the context (e.g., interpersonal relations, oral/written channel, linguistic function) predict the appropriate register (see the discussion of register that follows), which, in turn, foregrounds a corresponding set or system of linguistic options. These could include choices of process or verb categories (e.g., mental or physical actions) and participants/roles (e.g., Ann as actor, Mark as recipient, or friend as speaker). Speakers/writers who code switch (Gumperz, 1971) or change registers (Halliday, 1978) choose from foregrounded options to construct meaning appropriately for a particular context.

Within monologue, oral and written modes alter cohesive options. For example, an author's cohesive choices are necessarily constitutive of the written-for-others message, while oral monologue options may be more ancillary, though not as ancillary as in dialogue (Halliday & Hasan, 1989). An author of a literate register text develops comprehensibility by choosing precise wordings that appropriately specify, repeat, elaborate, and emphasize information intralinguistically for a reader's interpretation. This attention to intralinguistic interpretability increases the text's lexical and cohesive density (Halliday, 1985b) and affects both production and comprehension processes (Hildyard & Hidi, 1985). Differences in oral and literate registers typically require readers/writers to attend to different interpretive sources and interact with a text in ways that are distinct from what is expected of speakers/listeners in a vis-à-vis oral context.

Register. As children use language they develop familiarity with how it varies in different contexts. Halliday described this pragmatic knowledge in terms of registers. *Register* is a technical term denoting a certain conventional pattern or configuration of language that corresponds to a variety of situations or contexts and to which Halliday (1978) equated with "code switching" (p. 68). Further, Halliday suggested the correspondence between certain language choices and a context is related to three aspects that describe that context: (a) field (i.e., the topic), (b) tenor (i.e., interpersonal relations among interlocutors), and (c) mode (i.e., channel of communication affecting availability of feedback).

Cohesive Harmony. Hasan (1984) developed an important reconceptualization of Halliday's cohesion devices, called *cohesive harmony*. Cohesive harmony varies in crucial ways from the earlier conceptualization of cohesion as specific devices used in most earlier research. Specifically, cohesive harmony describes a text-level interweaving of multiple layers and types of clause-level redundancies. It facilitates a rigorous examination of individuals' linguistic choices and does so from within a sociolinguistic system that identifies and accommodates different contexts (see Method for a more technical discussion). As a theory-based analytical tool, cohesive harmony supports in-depth developmental analysis, specification, and categorization of literate (or other) register word/wording choices and clause patterns. Consequently, it can specify and track instances of code switching through register-appropriate cohesive choices. Of particular importance to literacy studies, the components of cohesive harmony address the intertwining and repetition of semantic, syntactic, and pragmatic cueing systems in a text. For example, word/wording choices that compose the cohesive chains realize semantic and syntactic cues (technically, Halliday's lexicogrammar) as well as graphophonemic ones and, when appropriately matched to context also, realize pragmatic cues. Cohesive harmony interactions repeat these cues in clause-level redundancies throughout a text. When carefully referenced to socially and/or culturally defined groups, functions, and contexts, cohesive harmony can yield qualitative insights and quantitative/statistical results for productive generalizations and further testing.

Cohesive Harmony and Literacy Research. Several researchers (e.g., Cox, 1990; Cox, Shanahan, & Sulzby, 1990; Cox, Shanahan, & Tinzmann, 1991; King & Rentel, 1981; Pappas, 1985; Pettegrew, 1981; Rentel & King, 1983a, 1983b) have employed Hasan's text-level and theory-based cohesive harmony. Differences among the studies using cohesive harmony as the analytical tool suggest the cohesive harmony/literacy development relationship is strong and statistically significant. For example, the King and Rentel group (e.g., Pappas, 1985) conducted a longitudinal study (grades 1 through 5) at middle-income suburban and low-income urban schools. They examined the children's developing knowledge of written language as evidenced in their retold, dictated, and handwritten stories; one aspect examined was cohesion. They reported that at entry to first grade the low-income children used more cohesion in their stories, but it was more likely to be appropriate for an oral context. In contrast, the middle-income children tended to use more cohesion in their tales that was appropriate for the written context. However, regardless of income, as the children advanced in school and became readers, they became more proficient at referencing cohesion devices intralinguistically to explicate precise referents for a reader. Furthermore, Pettegrew (1981) reported that increases in reading ability in grade 1 were significantly tied to developing expertise with contextually appropriate cohesive choices.

Related to the income variable studied by King and Rentel (1981), other demographic and sociolinguistic studies agree that many low-income children are overrepresented among those not gaining easy or adequate access to literacy in school (e.g., Bernstein, 1975; Purcell-Gates, McIntyre, & Freppon, 1995). Social, linguistic, and emergent literacy research suggests differences in experience and social function for language play a vital role in this low-income/low-literacy correlation (e.g., Gee, 1990; Heath, 1983; Sulzby, 1985). For example, research reports that preschool children's storybook reading performances realize differences in their home experiences with storybooks read aloud (Sulzby, 1985). Wells (1985) also suggests differences in home literacy experiences subsequently have an impact on children's school literacy achievement. Despite such studies, the low-income/low-literacy relation is often interpreted, especially in folk wisdom, as a deficit and so deserves continuing attention.

Other research using cohesive harmony (e.g., Cox et al., 1990, 1991) looked at third- and fifth-grade children, equally divided between good and poor readers. This research reported that children's greater use of literate register cohesive options in their own narrative and expository texts for others was statistically significantly related to being a better reader, regardless of grade. Finally, another study (Cox & Carpenter, 1996) suggested that some adults who are poor readers also have difficulty code switching to literate register cohesive options as they write texts for others to read. Together, this body of research suggests that among those experiencing difficulty with literacy achievement, code switching from oral to literate register cohesive options remains a significant problem, and neither advancing age nor traditional instruction has much positive impact. This research also raises questions of when and how some children develop crucial knowledge of literate register choices associated with school literacy achievement (e.g., good readers as young as third grade) while others (e.g., poor readers at diverse ages) do not.

The Present Study. The present study examined preschoolers' familiarity with cohesive options (operationalized as cohesive harmony) that differ by the context in which they are used. The body of research and theory reviewed previously supported two hypotheses related to income and literacy development. First, it was predicted on the basis of research with school children that if preschoolers can code switch to the cohesive options of literate register text when the situation requires it, it most likely would be observed among those emergent readers more closely approximating conventional reading. Second, it was expected that middle income would be related to indicators of stronger preschool literacy (e.g., Purcell-

Gates et al., 1995) and use of context-appropriate cohesive options (King & Rentel, 1981; Pettegrew, 1981).

Four questions were asked: (1) Do some preschool children independently, and in response to a verbally described change in context, modify their own oral monologue's cohesive options appropriately to construct a literate register text for others to read? (2) If so, is such sophisticated control over oral/literate register options related to differences in economic factors (i.e., low or middle income) and/or differences in experience indicated by emergent reading performance? (3) What is the impact of other variables naturally present within the sample: age, gender, or assumed, for example, differences in cognitive ability (i.e., being judged average or gifted)? and (4) Are there qualitative differences in the children's use of cohesive choices to develop literate register texts that align with their emergent reading ability?

Method

Participants and Settings

Forty-eight children (twenty-one 4-year-olds, twenty-seven 5-year-olds; 21 females, 27 males) from two preschool sites participated in the study. One site, a university, was wholly middle income and had both a regular and a gifted program for children. The other site, operated by the county, served primarily low-income families (about 70%). These sites were selected because if the same emergent reading categories existed at both sites and children within each category were very similar relative to cohesion knowledge regardless of site, it would suggest that literacy experiences, rather than simply income, underlie this knowledge.

All the children were native speakers of English and nearly all were from European American descent. The Test of Early Language Development (TELD, 1981) and informal observations by the researcher and teachers all indicated that these children were at least average in oral language development. None of the children had received any formal literacy instruction. Other informal data on literacy gathered at all preschools were (a) informal interviews with the children about home read-alouds, favorite books and authors, and favorite readers; (b) observations of the children's book handling; and (c) informal conversations about literacy events and literate behaviors with teachers and/or parents.

The University Preschool Sites. Overall, 20 children attended one of the two preschool programs at the university. Twelve of the children (four 4-year-olds and eight 5-year-olds) attended the university's regular preschool; gender was equally distributed within each age group. All came from homes that were middle income and European American in background. Informal interviews and observations suggested that these children were very familiar with storybooks, were regularly and frequently read to at home, and had favorite storybooks and/or informational books.

Classroom visits also confirmed that the university's regular preschool offered many enriching literacy experiences including planned daily storybook reading times and themed units employing diverse genres. Read-alouds typically encouraged oral interactions, and informal opportunities to talk, draw, write, and dictate were generally available. However, at the time of this study, the preschool's books were not usually available for children to handle.

Eight other children attended a special preschool program at the same university for children identified as gifted. They were included because common sense often suggests that early reading ability reflects higher cognitive ability. However, research (e.g., Gates, 1921) reports only a minimal and statistically nonsignificant relationship between early reading and intellectual ability (IQ). Nevertheless, the relationship between proficient reading and IQ does increase in later grades when reading is examined as higher-level comprehension (e.g., Gates, 1921). Since cohesive choices are related to comprehensibility and comprehension, the relationships among early literacy, cohesive choices, and academic aptitude deserve some revisiting.

Judgments for admission to the gifted program were not consistent. In some instances, admission reflected formal test scores (e.g., standardized intelligence tests); in others, admission reflected simple recommendations by parents or teachers. All the children were of European American descent with the exception of one African American child, and all were from middle-income homes. Again, gender was equally distributed within each age group.

The gifted program in which they were enrolled was quite different from the program at the regular university preschool. The gifted program was highly structured and during this study focused on three content areas: science, fine arts, and mathematics. Typically, the class engaged in teacher-led whole-group discussions and activities. These were well planned, but no activities using books were observed, though one child in the art group told of dramatizing a familiar nursery tale. Furthermore, at least in the sessions observed, books were never available for children's handling. However, informal observations of these children and interviews with them, teachers, and parents clearly suggested that the children had extensive knowledge about and experience with literacy and book handling elsewhere.

The County Preschool. Twenty-eight children from the county-operated preschool (fifteen 4-year-olds and thirteen 5-year-olds) were also participants in the study. Of the fifteen 4-year-olds, 9 were males and 6 were females. Among the thirteen 5-year-olds, 8 were males and 5 were females. Most (24) were European American; 3 were African American, and 1 was Hispanic. The county preschool enrollment was about 70% low income as determined by the preschool's sliding scale fees.

The county preschool was open 24 hours a day. It provided a warm and supportive environment. However, because it also offered overnight care, floor space was needed for portable cots. Consequently, the room had fewer toys and play centers than one expects in a preschool classroom, which probably contributed to the frequent use of teacher-directed whole-group activities (e.g., craft assembly projects). Like the university preschool, only a few books were available for the children to handle, though a good assortment of books was accessible to teachers. At the time of this study, no specific time was scheduled for storybook reading, and purposeful follow-up activities were never observed. Instead, storybooks were used primarily to fill time or to quiet the group (e.g., while lunch was being set out).

Across Preschools. Informal interviews with children and teachers, observations of book handling, and informal classroom visits supported the general assumption that the children at all sites knew how to handle storybooks and had literacy-related experiences at home as well as in the preschool. However, differences in these experiences were also apparent. While nearly all the children reported having favorite stories, the referent for these tales was often quite different. Specifically, in response to questions about favorite books or stories, the children at the university site tended to name books familiar to the researchers (e.g., Golden Book renditions of known tales) or recognized children's classics (e.g., *Cinderella*). In contrast, while many of the children at the county site readily shared a favorite story, its title was often unfamiliar to the researchers. Pursuit of the title often revealed it was a television series or video rather than a book. This suggests a general difference in each group's story-based literacy experiences that may affect general familiarity with the literate register text given priority in schools.

Materials and Procedure

A Measure of Emergent Reading Development. Sulzby's (1985) Storybook Reading Categories were developed based upon a yearlong observation of 24 kindergartners and thirty-two 2- to 4-year-olds pretending to read familiar storybooks. A developmental progression of 11 storybook reading categories, associated with increasing parent/child storybook experiences, was reported across age groups. Sulzby's 11 categories were used to determine each child's emergent reading category in the present study.

Most of Sulzby's categories are labeled descriptively; therefore, their description is minimal. Within Sulzby's categories, two major groups describe what the child attends to primarily while pretend reading, the pictures or the print. Within the *attention-to-pictures* category, Sulzby identified three further subcategories describing the kind of story formed during the pretend reading: (1) *no story formed*, (2) *an oral-like story formed*, and (3) *a written-like story formed*. Each of these subcategories (no story, oral-like, and written-like) comprises further divisions that generally describe the child's pretend reading performance. Within the no story subcategory, a pretend reading may be either simple labeling of pictures or comments that follow the pictured action. An oral-like pretend reading may be either dialogic (using dialogic devices such as voices for characters or making dialogic comments) or monologic (giving a monologue that depends on seeing the book for interpretation, though with reading intonation). Within the written-like subcategory, a pretend reading may be reading/storytelling mixed, providing a story similar to the original text, or developing a story that is or almost is verbatim the original text.

Four subcategories compose the *attention-to-print* group. They describe the child's emerging reading behaviors: (1) *print-related refusal* (a refusal to pretend read because of an awareness that print, not pictures, is read), (2) *aspectual reading* (known textual aspects, such as known words or letter/sound relations, are used to cue reading), (3) *strategies imbalanced* (excessive reliance on one or more strategies, such as saying known words), and (4) *conventional reading* (strategies are in balance and child reads conventionally). (See Sulzby, 1985, for a complete description of this informal tool.)

Evaluation Using Sulzby's Storybook Reading Categories. Children's pretend readings of favorite storybooks were audiotaped, transcribed, and then compared with Sulzby's 11 categories of storybook reading. In the initial comparison, children's pretend readings were assigned to 10 of the 11 subcategories. However, preliminary analyses (*t* tests for independent samples) enabled collapsing of multiple categories because the children within them did not differ significantly from each other in terms of cohesive choices.

First, *t* tests showed that children *within* each of the attention-to-pictures categories did not differ significantly from each other in their use of cohesive options in either their face-to-face oral or literate register attempt texts. Therefore, the divisions within these subcategories were collapsed, leaving the no story, oral-like, and written-like groups for further analyses. Second and rather surprisingly, no statistically significant differences were found between the attention-to-pictures, written-like story children, and the attention-to-print group in terms of their cohesive options. Due to the small cell number ($n = 4$) in the attention-to-print emergent reading category and the lack of a statistically significant difference in terms of cohesion, this category was collapsed into the picture-governed, written-like story group. This left the no story ($n = 11$), oral-like ($n = 21$), and the combined written-like/print-governed ($n = 16$) groups for further statistical analyses.

However, the two conventional readers and each of the other picture-governed emergent reading subcategories (no story, oral-like, and written-like) were kept separate for the qualitative analyses. This decision was made because (a) adult readers felt some qualitative distinctions existed and (b) being a conventional reader represents a major distinction in reading behavior, attending to print as well as actually reading the print.

The distribution of children at each emergent reading category for each preschool follows. At the university preschool, there were 3 no story (1 in the gifted program), 4 oral-like (1 in the gifted program), 9 written-like (3 in the gifted program), 2 print-governed refusal (1 in the gifted program), and 2 conventional readers (both in the gifted program). At the county preschool, 8 children pretend read at the no story category, 17 at the oral-like category, and 3 at the written-like category, and none gave print-governed readings. As predicted by other research (e.g., Purcell-Gates et al., 1995), the largest distribution of emergent readers closest to conventional reading aligned with greater economic resources. However, it is important to note that all picture-governed emergent reading categories (including the written-like) occurred at all sites, suggesting that appropriate experiences with storybooks may dominate cohesion knowledge effects associated with low income at school entry (e.g., King & Rentel, 1981).

Procedure. The adults spent several days in the classrooms as participant observers (Spradley, 1980) prior to the actual study. They talked and played with the children, helped set out materials and lunch, and generally became familiar adult friends. Then, each child was seen individually at two sessions. At these sessions rapport was reestablished; no child seemed intimidated or nervous. Rather, the children were eager to participate. If a child seemed tired or distracted, the session was ended and rescheduled. All sessions were audiotaped and transcribed for later analysis.

The Task. The task was construction of two monologues (i.e., two or more sentences about a topic produced without dialogue support). The first was a face-to-face oral register monologue that emerged as part of an adult/child conversation. The second was a written-attempt (i.e., dictated) or literate register monologue. This was specifically requested by the adult as a retelling of the earlier oral monologue but for others "much like yourself" to read.

These two tasks were selected for four reasons. First, an adult encouraging an oral recounting of an experience is not an unfamiliar occurrence for 4- and 5-year-old children (e.g., McCabe & Peterson, 1991). Second, the sequence of oral to written-for-others experience story allowed the child to (a) use his or her own memorable experiences as the content for a piece of continuous text; (b) move from social/verbal interactions to independent, individual production; and (c) maintain a real, functional use of language. Third, the request for a retelling of the oral story as one written for others defined a new context in terms of tenor (audience) and mode while allowing the field (topic) to be constant and, so, implicitly requested a shift from oral to literate registers (or codes). In order to comply, the child must recognize the change in context, address the difference in audience comprehension needs (albeit intuitively), and be sufficiently familiar with the associated register to make appropriate choices and adaptations to the cohesive structure. Fourth, the adult acting only as a scribe freed the child from mechanical aspects that would likely interfere with his or her address of content- or context-related changes while simultaneously limiting the adult from interfering as a cocomposer. Thus, the task was specifically designed and sequenced to maximize what the child knew intuitively about code switching in terms of appropriate oral and literate register cohesive options.

Session 1. At the first session, the adult engaged the child in conversation, conducted the informal interview about home reading and favorite storybooks, and encouraged a personal experience monologue as described previously. Once the child began an oral monologue, the adult only used nonsubstantive or continuative utterances (e.g., "um," "uh huh," "and" with rising intonation, or repeating the child's last few words) or nonverbal cues such as nods and smiles to encourage extension of the topic. Following completion of the oral monologue, the adult praised the child and requested the child dictate the oral monologue as a story for others "much like yourself." After dictation, the scribe reread the text and invited edits. All edits came strictly from the child.

Session 2. At the second session, after reestablishing rapport, the TELD and Sulzby's (1985) Categories of Storybook Reading were administered. It was necessary for two reasons to use different procedures at the preschools with the Categories of Storybook Reading. First, the preschools differed distinctly in their use of storybook reading. The university's regular preschool provided extensive storybook and informational book experiences. The county and gifted preschool programs, at the time of this study, provided very minimal storybook experiences. All of the preschools strictly limited the children's opportunities to handle storybooks.

Second, the homes from which the university and county preschool children came were very different in terms of economic and family resources. The children's interviews suggested these economic differences had an impact on the children's storybook experiences.

Therefore, in accord with Sulzby's (1985) research-based guidelines, different procedures were instituted. Specifically, Sulzby suggested that whether children choose their own favorite book, select a book from a prescribed but familiar set, or are asked to read a particular one makes very little difference in how their performance is rated with the Storybook Reading Categories. Although this may seem intuitively controversial, other research (e.g., Cox, 1994) has reconfirmed the soundness of Sulzby's observations and guidelines.

At the university's regular/gifted programs, each child was asked to select and bring his or her favorite storybook from home because the preschool setting did not make books available for handling by the children. The children readily responded to this request. Each child was asked individually to pretend read the favorite storybook he or she had brought.

At the county preschool, the researcher selected four books (viz., Burningham's [1973] *Mr. Gumpy's Motor Car*, Flack's [1931] *Angus and the Cat*, Freeman's [1978] *Pocket for Corduroy*, and Sendak's [1963] *Where the Wild Things Are*). The teachers, and later the children, confirmed that with the exception of the Sendak text, these stories were generally unfamiliar to the children. These books all had some pattern repetition, but, as with the books brought to the university preschool programs, this was not a dominant feature. Multiple copies of the four books were placed in the classroom for the children's handling, and the preschool teachers agreed to read each book four to six times over a 2-week period. Although it may be counterintuitive, research (e.g., Otto, 1984/1985; Putnam, 1989) suggests this schedule makes a book sufficiently familiar and generally equivalent to a favorite book for pretend-reading evaluations with Sulzby's Categories of Storybook Reading.

Each child was asked to pretend read two books from the set—his or her favorite and *Mr. Gumpy's Motor Car*. In general, most children seemed to consider the Mr. Gumpy text also a favorite. Two books were used in order to provide a measure of consistency across children with one book and to address potential effects of personal selection. Two trained scorers independently evaluated all audiotaped and transcribed storybook readings. Interscorer agreement was 76%, with all disagreements resolved through discussion.

Data Analyses

The oral and literate register (i.e., dictated) texts were analyzed for their ratios (or indices) of register-appropriate and inappropriate cohesive harmony options. Then, the same texts were examined qualitatively for evidence of code switching from oral to literate patterns.

Cohesive Harmony Analysis. Hasan's (1984) model of cohesion—*cohesive harmony*—identifies clause-level redundancies that chain throughout a whole text. Of particular importance to literacy research (and as previously noted), the semantic and syntactic cues (Halliday's lexicogrammar) considered fundamental to the reading process (e.g., Goodman, 1967) are realized through word/wording choices that make up the text's cohesive chains and clauses. Further, pragmatic cues are realized through context/register-appropriate choices. Thus, cohesive harmony inherently realizes the textual cues used by readers and writers to construct meaning. Such cues also are recognized in research as used in distinctive ways by readers/writers in written and oral texts (e.g., Hildyard & Hidi, 1985). In addition, analyses of picture storybooks reveal they are exceptionally rich in clause-level cohesive harmony redundancies (e.g., Otto, 1992).

To develop cohesive harmony, Hasan recategorized the cohesion devices (Halliday & Hasan, 1976) according to four bonds: identity (i.e., coreference), co-classification (i.e., class membership), coextension (e.g., synonyms, antonyms), and hierarchical (e.g., superordinate/subordinate, part-whole) bonds. These bonds guide the formation of chains of related words (taken from a text). The related words (technically called *tokens*) may function as participants or circumstantials (e.g., nouns, pronouns, adverbs) in the text or be instances of process or verb categories. (See Halliday, 1985a, for a description of seven process categories: material, mental, verbal, behavior, existential, identity, and attributive.)

Consistent with Halliday's theory, membership in any chain (whether participant, circumstantial, or process) has two criteria. First, membership is determined by being clearly interpretable for a given context. For example, in conversation *They won't like it* might be quite clear without *they* and *it* being clearly explicated within the preceding text because the referents are familiar or available in the situation. If so, both pronouns could be included as members of a cohesive chain. In contrast, in a literate register text for readers, *they* and *it* would have to be clearly specified within the preceding text in order to be included in a cohesive chain. Second, chain membership is determined through a semantic bond (i.e., identity, synonymy, antonymy, meronymy, hyponymy) or a process category. The following brief text is used to exemplify the construction of cohesive chains using the preceding criteria. An explanation of the text's scoring for cohesive harmony follows the example.

I have many pets. I have a horse. Her name is Kandy. I have a dog, too.

Participants		Processes	
I	Pets	Attributive	Identity
I* (carrier)	pets* (attribute possessed)	have*	
I* (carrier)	horse* (attribute possessed)	have*	
	(her) name (value)		is
	Kandy (token)		
I* (carrier)	dog* (attribute possessed)	have*	

The use of *I* as author builds an interpretable chain based solely on identity relations. The *pets* chain, however, uses both similarity (e.g., pets, horse, dog) and identity relations (e.g., horse, Kandy). Also, both the *I* and *pets* chains have clauses that use attributive verbs (processes), and so these also form a chain. In contrast, there is only one identity process mentioned, so this cannot form a chain. Single mentions (e.g., the identity process in the example) and difficult-to-interpret words are removed to a noncohesive column as not contributing to a text's overall cohesion.

Hasan also incorporated Halliday's (1985a) implicit assignment (by the process category) of functional roles (e.g., location, actor, goal) to the participants and circumstantials in each clause. In the previous brief example, the participants and processes listed in the chains have been assigned functional roles (in parentheses, below each participant) using Halliday's guidelines. Finally, where members of the same participant chain are assigned the same roles by the process category across two or more clauses, it constitutes a cohesive harmony interaction (indicated by *).

A cohesive harmony interaction is considered maximally cohesive (Hasan, 1984). It echoes the attendant tripartal information complex, both semantic and syntactic (e.g., who in what role does/attributes what to whom or where), increasing that information complex's salience (via its repetition) throughout a text. In effect, these repetitions echo the child's (or a speaker's or adult author's) topic, theme, and its elaboration. Last, the number of interactive tokens (words) can be figured as a ratio or index of the whole text (i.e., all interactive tokens divided by all the tokens in the text). Similarly, the number of noncohesive tokens (i.e., words not clearly interpretable for a given context or single mentions) can be calculated as a ratio of the whole text. Detailed explanations of the scoring along with examples are available elsewhere (e.g., Cox et al., 1990; Hasan, 1984; Rentel & King, 1983a).

The cohesive harmony analysis was completed independently by two trained scorers. Four indices were calculated: two cohesive harmony indices (one for the oral monologue [CHIO], one for the written-attempt or literate register [i.e., dictated] monologue [CHID]) and two noncohesive indices (one for the oral [NCHIO] and one for the dictated [NCHID] monologue). Interscorer agreement was 82%, with 100% resolution of all disagreements through discussion.

Statistical Analysis. SPSS[X] advanced statistics software package was used for the quantitative analyses. Because the four dependent variables (CHIO, NCHIO, CHID, and NCHID) were correlated, multiple analyses of variance (MANOVA) were performed to examine the effects of the independent variables (i.e., income, emergent reading category, age, gender, judgment of academic aptitude) on children's use of cohesive options in both oral- and written-register texts. When MANOVA resulted in statistically significant findings, univariate tests for the individual variables were examined to gain further insights into where between-group differences occurred. Finally, paired *t* tests were conducted to examine whether children successfully code switched from oral to literate registers in terms of their cohesive choices. Statistical significance was set at .05 for all analyses.

Descriptive Analysis. For the descriptive analysis, the children's oral and written-for-others texts, including the cohesive harmony analyses, were reread guided by linguistic theory and research identifying general properties of monologue for either context and register (e.g., Chafe, 1985; Eggins, 1994; Halliday, 1985b;

Hasan, 1984). The properties selected make a text more readily interpretable for a reader (intralinguistically specifying the content and relations among ideas); aid the development of its events, participants, or topic/theme (intralinguistically elaborating content and relations); and/or give it a literary tone (literary-sounding phrases not common to oral language). We believe that children experience these text properties through interactions with adults in storybook reading. The first two properties—intralinguistic specification (i.e., within the written text) and intralinguistic development of elaborative information—are fundamental aspects of the cohesion analysis; the use of literary-sounding phrases is not. Differing from the cohesion analysis, the descriptive one focused on differences in the quality of literate register choices among emergent reading groups, especially ones representing code switching between oral and literate register attempt texts.

Results

Table 1 shows the means and standard deviations for income, age, gender, judged cognitive aptitude, and emergent reading category for contextually appropriate (i.e., cohesive) and inappropriate (i.e., noncohesive) ratios or indices of cohesive harmony in both oral and literate register (i.e., dictated) texts.

MANOVA yielded two statistically significant main effects: income and emergent reading category. In the case of income, the Wilks' lambda was $\Lambda^{(s)} = .80$, $p = .04$. Univariate F tests were statistically significant for the literate register texts' cohesive, $F(1, 46) = 10.34$, $p = .002$, and noncohesive harmony indices, $F(1, 46) = 5.16$, $p = .03$, but not for the oral register texts' cohesive and noncohesive harmony indices. The means (Table 1) reveal that the middle-income children used more literate register cohesive harmony and fewer noncohesive options than did low-income children in their literate register texts. However, the two groups did not differ with statistical significance in their use of cohesive options in the oral monologues. In the case of emergent storybook reading category, the Wilks' lambda was $\Lambda^{(s)} = .68$, $p = .03$. Univariate F tests showed that in their oral monologues, the three emergent reading groups did not differ with statistical significance in their use of cohesive and noncohesive options. With respect to the literate register texts, statistically significant differences were found among the three groups for their cohesive, $F(2, 45) = 7.13$, $p = .002$, and noncohesive harmony indices, $F(2, 45) = 7.09$, $p = .002$. Further multiple comparisons within the three groups using post hoc Student-Newman-Keuls revealed that with statistical significance, the picture-governed, no story and picture-governed, oral-like children had lower cohesive harmony indices and higher noncohesive harmony indices than did the collapsed pictured-governed, written-like, and print-governed children. The multivariate main effects for age, gender, or judged cognitive aptitude were not statistically significant. No statistically significant interaction effects were observed.

TABLE 1
Means and Standard Deviations for Proportional Use of Cohesive Harmony by Income, Age, Gender, Judged Cognitive Aptitude, and Emergent Reading Category for Oral and Literate Register Texts

	Oral Register Monologue		Literate Register Monologue	
	Cohesive Index	Noncohesive Index	Cohesive Index	Noncohesive Index
Income				
Low (county preschool) (*n* = 28)				
M	.65	.14	.55	.22
SD	.19	.11	.20	.15
Middle (university preschools) (*n* = 20)				
M	.73	.09	.72	.13
SD	.18	.08	.15	.11
Age				
4 years (*n* = 21)				
M	.68	.13	.57	.21
SD	.20	.11	.24	.15
5 years (*n* = 27)				
M	.69	.10	.66	.16
SD	.18	.08	.16	.12
Gender				
Female (*n* = 21)				
M	.73	.10	.65	.16
SD	.15	.06	.22	.14
Male (*n* = 27)				
M	.65	.13	.60	.19
SD	.21	.12	.19	.14
Judged Cognitive Aptitude				
Regular (*n* = 40)				
M	.67	.12	.59	.20
SD	.20	.10	.20	.14
Gifted (*n* = 8)				
M	.75	.07	.75	.08
SD	.11	.03	.12	.10
Emergent Reading Category				
Picture-governed, no story (*n* = 11)				
M	.67	.12	.57	.24
SD	.19	.09	.17	.15
Picture-governed, oral-like story (*n* = 21)				
M	.63	.14	.54	.22
SD	.21	.12	.22	.14
Combined picture-governed, written-like/print-governed (*n* = 16)				
M	.76	.07	.76	.09
SD	.14	.06	.10	.07

Taken together, the quantitative analyses indicated that with statistical significance, the children who were from middle-income families or whose emergent storybook reading more closely approximated conventional reading (i.e., picture-governed, written-like/print-governed) used more appropriate cohesive and fewer inappropriate cohesive choices for the literate register text than did the others. Those who used fewer contextually appropriate and more inappropriate cohesive options at a statistically significant level were children from low-income families and whose emergent storybook reading was less like conventional reading (i.e., picture-governed, no story, and oral-like). It is important to note that this income finding generally replicates that of King and Rentel (1981) with first graders.

Overall, it is especially important to note that the statistically significant finding for emergent reading category defines the emergence of an application level of familiarity with literate register cohesive options as significantly associated with written-like emergent reader approximations of conventional reading. Further, the emergent reading data suggest this relationship between the written-like category and an application level of familiarity with literate register cohesion holds despite other factors (income, cognitive aptitude). Finally, the statistically nonsignificant finding for the oral register text's cohesive and noncohesive harmony indices, irrespective of the independent variables (i.e., income, age, gender, judged cognitive aptitude, or emergent reading category), clearly suggests all the children in this study were roughly equivalent in their use of cohesion to produce a readily interpretable face-to-face oral monologue. This finding is important because it (a) supports the informal judgments and TELD results for the children's general oral language development and (b) clearly identifies any statistically significant differences among the children as associated with literate register language.

Code Switching From Oral to Literate Register in Monologue. First, it must be understood that familiarity and experience with various registers affect their successful use (Halliday, 1975). Because the literate register can be presumed less familiar to preschoolers, it would be expected that their literate register attempts would have somewhat lower indices of register-appropriate cohesive harmony than would the oral ones. Using this assumption, if the literate register texts' cohesive harmony indices were statistically significantly lower than the oral ones, it would suggest the children were not able to make the cohesive and wording choice adaptations needed to actually code switch. In contrast, if the literate register texts attained a similar level of cohesion to the oral ones, it would indicate some degree of successful code switching.

Paired t tests showed that, as a group, the 48 children did not code switch from oral to literate registers in their texts. As would be expected if the oral register were more familiar, their oral monologue text's cohesive index, $M = .68$,

$SD = .19$, was statistically significantly higher than their literate register text's cohesive index, $M = .62$, $SD = .20$, $t(47) = 1.98$, $p = .05$. Similarly, their oral monologue noncohesive index, $M = .12$, $SD = .10$, was statistically significantly lower than their literate register attempt, $M = .18$, $SD = .14$, $t(47) = 3.0$, $p = .004$. This means that the children as a group did not make their dictated literate register texts as cohesive as their oral versions.

Examination within income revealed a somewhat different picture (see Table 1 for means and standard deviations). Like the larger group, the low-income children did not code switch. They used statistically significantly more contextually appropriate cohesion in their oral texts than in their literate register attempts, $t(27) = 2.21$, $p = .04$. Low-income children used statistically significantly more noncohesive items in their literate than oral register texts, $t(27) = 2.49$, $p = .02$. This suggests the low-income children's familiarity with oral context cohesive choices continued to dominate their literate register attempts. In contrast, the middle-income group showed no statistically significant differences in cohesive/noncohesive indices between their oral and literate register texts. This means that the middle-income children did successfully code switch because they altered their oral register cohesive choices to accommodate the written context and maintained a similarly high cohesion index for both texts (see Table 1).

For the storybook reading category, the picture was more complex. Between their oral and literate register texts, statistically significant differences existed for the picture-governed, no story group's use of noncohesive options that indicated a continuing dominance of oral register choices in their literate register texts. Specifically, the use of *noncohesive* items in the no story children's literate register texts doubled (see Table 1) in comparison to their oral texts, $t(10) = 2.46$, $p = .03$, clearly showing that they did not successfully code switch.

In important contrast, no statistically significant differences existed within any of the three emergent reading groups' (no story, oral-like, written-like/print-governed) contextually appropriate use of cohesive items for their oral and literate register texts. In other words, statistically, these three emergent reading groups all showed some success in code switching in terms of appropriate adaptations of cohesive choices. However, the means and standard deviations (Table 1) indicated a clear pattern in which the no story and oral-like children tended to use a considerably higher (though statistically nonsignificant) proportion of contextually appropriate cohesive choices in the oral than used in their literate register texts. It is also important that the standard deviations indicated there were considerably more individual variations with respect to code switching in the no story and oral-like groups than there were in the combined written-like/print-governed group. It is impressive that the combined group used exactly the same proportion of appropriate cohesive choices for each context and did so with considerable within-group consistency, thus clearly code switching. Overall, the means and standard deviations suggest developmental differences related to the storybook reading category that may prove statistically significant with a larger sample. Further insights gained from the qualitative analysis relative to code switching follow.

Descriptive Analyses. Our descriptive analysis is limited to the emergent reading variable because (a) it most likely captures the artifacts of income and experience and (b) all emergent reading categories occurred at all sites. In contrast, the middle-income finding suggested it did not merit a separate descriptive treatment. For example, the number of low-income children who pretend read at the written-like category was very small ($n = 3$). In their dictated texts for others, however, these three made appropriate literate register cohesion choices (CHID, $M = .67$, $SD = .09$) and monitored inappropriate ones (NCHID, $M = .09$, $SD = .04$) with mean indices and standard deviations that closely approximated those of the larger written-like/print-governed emergent reader group (see Table 1). Still, the small number warrants caution.

The within-group stability of the statistically significant emergent reading effect for the collapsed picture-governed, written-like/print-governed group's contextually appropriate uses of literate register cohesion is important. This finding remained statistically significant regardless of age, gender, cognitive aptitude, or income factors. It thus suggests that with greater numbers, the income/literacy confound should untangle to privilege the explanatory power of appropriate literacy/storybook experiences. The strength and perseverance of the emergent reading finding also suggests that familiarity with English literate register cohesive options is related to (a) young children's experiences with storybooks and (b) at least one aspect of register—differences in cohesive options—that is fundamental to developing literacy. Therefore, the emergent reading categories were the focus of our descriptive analysis.

The properties selected as general attributes of written-for-others text (i.e., intralinguistic specification of precisely interpretable words, intralinguistic development of elaborative and relational information, and literary-sounding phrases) showed distinctly different trends related to the four emergent reading subcategories (i.e., attention to picture—no story, oral-like, written-like, and attention to print—conventional).

The No Story Emergent Readers. *Miles*, a lively and playful European American 5-year-old, pretend read at the no story category. He lived with his mother, stepfather, and stepsister. It was clear in watching Miles that he liked books. He had considerable book-handling knowledge, orienting books correctly and paging through them with interest. However, he did not readily list favorites and said little about who read to him, or when, at home.

Miles was chosen as exemplary of his emergent reading group because his oral and literate register attempt texts were very similar to other no story emergent readers, regardless of other factors. As with the other no story children, Miles's emergent reading behavior seemed the most clear and relevant predictor of what he knew and used about literate register cohesive and other text-making choices.

Miles's oral register monologue text attempt

I buy a Ninja Turtle. I buyed a sweater from the Easter Bunny. I buyed a new bike, a Ninja Turtle one.

Miles's literate register text attempt

I got a Ghost Buster man. And I bought a new shoe and I bought clothes, too. And I bought me those and I buyed one of those, too. I bought a power car. It's just my size, just like my bike. And that's all.

When Miles's oral and literate register attempts are compared, it is clear that he did not truly code switch when the implicit request prompted him to do so. Though his topic was clear in conversation (shopping at a national chain), he did not respecify this information intralinguistically for a future reader. Further, whether or not he restated his tale at all was unclear; it seems possible he simply continued his oral one. This suggests that Miles, like his cohorts, had not yet developed a concept of story as a stable unit, a concept that emerges with experience.

Only once did Miles attempt to develop a part of his literate register text with elaborative information (when he described his power car). If he repeated particular items, it was in more general terms (e.g., *sweater* may have become *clothes*). Using literate register criteria, Miles's word choices could be considered of lesser quality in his written-attempt text. However, it is worth noting that he used the correct past tense of *buy* (bought) in most of his literate register text, suggesting an emergent recognition of the more precise word choices used in literate register text.

At a clause level of addressing intralinguistic specification and elaboration, Miles also developed very simple cohesive chains in terms of participant/process/role redundancies. For example, his processes are almost wholly material actions and his participants almost wholly *I* as author. Therefore, his chains are dominated by identity relations and actor roles. Possibilities for cohesive chains using similarity relations were attempted by a few in this group but were generally unrealized because of unclear or imprecisely interpretable word choices. Attempts to merge two chains into a complex one (e.g., through use of *we*) were never successfully attempted. Finally, Miles is exemplary of the no story group in never using anything approximating a literary-sounding phrase that would be unusual in oral language.

The Oral-Like Emergent Readers. The oral-like emergent readers' mean use of appropriate and inappropriate cohesive choices was very similar to the no story group. However, qualitatively they revealed a more complex construction of literate register familiarity because a greater variety of differences existed within this group. These differences are exemplified in the three oral-like children presented next.

Nelson, like Miles, was a lively 5-year-old. He was also European American, but Nelson attended the regular university preschool. He sometimes protested composing, stating that his mother said he should not tell stories (his teacher said he was a renowned teller of tall tales). Nelson was familiar with books and handled them appropriately. He had favorite stories and enjoyed being read to; however, videos and television stories were also prominent in his world. Quite often, his oral stories were long, rambling recounts of favorite videos or television shows. Nelson was chosen because his texts are representative of most oral-like children.

Nelson's oral register monologue text attempt

I went rollerskating at Skate Away. In the middle of Skate Away, they played a game called *Go Under*. If you knock the stick down, you can't play. I tried it but I knocked it down.

Nelson's literate register text attempt

I was roller skating fast and then everybody came. And then everybody went home. And then we played and played outside. And then we did, we went home. And then I (inaudible) my jump rope. And I putted my toys away and went inside and ate supper. The end.

Note that, similar to Miles, Nelson did not clearly code switch when asked to dictate his tale for others to read. It seems clear that Nelson either did not repeat his oral tale (simply continuing on with the day's events), or he assumed his future readers already knew about Skate Away and proceeded to attempt a text including others beyond himself.

Nelson never really included more in-depth elaborative information in his literate register text, though he did add more specific actions (e.g., playing, putting toys away, going inside). Despite adding specific actions, Nelson was particularly unsuccessful in specifying participants. His "everybody came and everybody went" is not clearly referenced and is further confused with "we played outside and we went home." Although this might be considered an attempt to form a complex chain merging participants, it does not succeed as literate register text. While such attempts at complex chains were typical of several oral-like emergent readers, it was telling that not a single child succeeded.

At a clause-level consideration of Nelson's text, his participant/process/role redundancy patterns were very simple noun, action verb, actor constructions, again, much like Miles. While this is not inappropriate, it is less literary sounding than others who used more varied structures (see written-like example). With only the author as a clearly interpretable actor, Nelson (like Miles) also developed his cohesive chains using only identity relations. However, his final use of "the end" is clearly one piece of conventional literary language imported from children's storybooks.

Karen was another oral-like emergent reader, also age 5 and European American. In contrast to Nelson, she attended the county preschool and came from a low-income, single-parent family. Karen was vivacious and full of tales. She loved to talk and would ramble on about her life experiences with few prompts from her dialogue partner. Her oral and literate register texts were also typical of other oral-like emergent readers.

Karen's oral register monologue text attempt

I don't have any brother or sisters but I have a friend. I make friends at school and at home. I like to play with them. There's a friend next door. She can come out when I come outside—like chase or play with my doggie. I get her up there. Her gets scared. I like to scare her....

Karen's literate register text attempt

Claudia's my age but she played with me. But I don't like to play with her. I like to make friends but she is my friend. But you know what I do, I play with her and her and the dog chases me. And then, I don't like her chasing me, I get up in the couch and I get scared of her so I put her in the cage.

In comparing Karen's oral/written texts, one notices that she (a) selected just one part of a lengthy conversation to dictate as a story, (b) attempted to code switch, and (c) was at least partly successful. For example, in her literate register text Karen used a specific name (Claudia) to replace "friend next door" in her oral text; she also replaced the deictic "there" with "couch." On the other hand, Claudia was not clarified as her friend until several clauses later (technically, cataphoric reference, which is generally not a literate register preference). Thus, Karen seemed to intuitively recognize the shift in registers and attempted intralinguistic specification for her literate register text, though she was not yet very expert at it. She also elaborated intralinguistically (though not always clearly) on her relationship to Claudia. While her elaboration of what they played with her dog is considerably clearer in her literate register than in her oral text, her referent for the pronoun *her* in "I don't like her chasing me" remains unclear (though it can be implied, again cataphorically). Further, it is noteworthy that Karen clearly did not just add on to her oral text; rather, she attempted to retell a portion of her oral text as a literate register version.

At the level of clause components (i.e., participant/process/role choices), Karen used multiple process types (e.g., the attributive "is," mental "like," and material action "play") and attendant roles, redundantly. Due to this, her literate register cohesion index is surprisingly high (.70) for her group. Despite her fuller use of linguistic resources, however, Karen's text does not readily proclaim the precision of a literate voice, in part because she still used many (.17) noncohesive choices. Further, some phrases (e.g., "you know what I do") are distinctly oral in tone. Overall, her text suggests a continuing reliance on familiar oral language patterns that do not adequately address a reader's needs, though her attempts to be specific and clarify events suggest an intuitive and emerging familiarity with literate register options.

Matt was another oral-like emergent reader. He differed substantively from most others in the group. Matt was a serious 5-year-old who lived alone with his mother. He was of European American descent, and he attended the county preschool. He enjoyed books and talked about his mother reading aloud to him at bedtime. He also enjoyed talking with the adult interviewer, readily regaling her with tales of friends, visitors, and a memorable camping trip. His text suggests an important developmental advance in use of literate register options, which set him apart from most others in his emergent reading group.

> *Matt's oral register monologue text attempt*
>
> A rattlesnake bit me. We were on our vacation last summer. And the, he bit me right here [points]. Then so, we had to put band aids on it. Then, when we took it off, it was still bleeding so I had to go to the hospital.
>
> *Matt's literate register text attempt*
>
> When a little snake came to the camper, I went for a walk. The snake bit me on the knee and I stabbed it. Then it was killed. Then I went to my mom. I yelled for her. She found me and she got me. She saw my knee was hurt and took me to the hospital. She got a little wheel that wasn't flat and put it on the camper. And then, she could drive me to the hospital. That's all.

Matt's code switching, albeit intuitive, to intralinguistically specify and elaborate his oral tale's content for a reader, is impressive. He not only retold the oral tale but selected appropriate and precise words for the literate register version (e.g., replacing the deictic "here" with the precise "knee"). Through his use of diverse process types (e.g., material, verbal actions, attribution), he established varied roles for both his mother and himself. Additionally, and with some distinction in this emergent reading category, Matt appropriately employed a precise choice of temporal relations (e.g., "when," "then," "and") that help specify meaning intralinguistically for a reader. Overall, his text was much like those of the statistically significantly different written-like emergent readers, with one exception. Although Matt established multiple roles for his participants, he failed to establish them as clause-level redundancies with the same consistency as the written-like/print-governed group.

The Written-Like Emergent Readers. *Shirley*, a confident and rather sophisticated 5-year-old of European American descent, attended the regular university preschool. Shirley came from a two-parent home and enjoyed many economic advantages. She enthusiastically told about a trip to England and social events at her home, one of which was the topic of her oral and literate register text excerpts. Shirley loved to hear books read aloud and was familiar with not only picture storybooks but also chapter books that some might consider beyond her years. At the time of the study, her mother was reading C.S. Lewis's *The Lion, the Witch and the Wardrobe* (1970) to Shirley. When asked to pretend read a picture storybook favorite, she eagerly did so with expression and great enjoyment even though she attended mostly to the pictures. However, Shirley was aware that the print was to be read, commenting, "This page doesn't have any words so you just look at it." While she had an excellent memory for the original text, she also freely made up appropriate literate register text using dialogue carriers (e.g., "'Here we are at the house,' said Rudolph").

Shirley's oral register monologue text attempt

And I had an Easter party on Easter. I found a Hershey Kisses and a basket with surprises but the Easter bunny didn't leave the basket, my Mom and Dad did. The basket had thin markers in there for us and lots of candy. I even dumped my Hershey Kisses in my basket. And I got to put on a dress that my Gramma gave me. And I got to put on my pretty shoes and a shirt that I used to wear with the dress. And the guests came and we had an Easter dinner but it wasn't real dinner. It was sort of an Easter lunch with potatoes and meat and crustini. And that's all I can remember.

Shirley's literate register text attempt

We woke up in the morning and I said, "Yippee" and just then Sam woke up and said, "What?" and stuff. We raced to wake up Papa but he wasn't in bed. And we asked Mom where he was and he was downstairs. We went to find the Easter eggs and Hershey Kisses were leading to a trail with different color wrappers like pink, blue, green, silver, and dark pink, and light pink. And then we found our Easter baskets with surprises. And then we went in (the house) and the guests came. And we had the water with the ice and lemon in it. And we went outside and we got out the crustini. And we let out the dogs. And Tony took a piece of crustini, that's my dog, and we smacked him....

When Shirley's oral and literate register texts are compared, it is quite clear that she code switched with considerable expertise (albeit intuitively). She clearly retold her oral tale, but in so doing she eliminated personal comments more appropriate for a familiar audience (e.g., Gramma's dress, pretty shoes). She precisely specified and elaborated her oral text's *I* focus to one on multiple participants that is more literary-like. With the exception of her first *we* and perhaps Sam's *what*, she also consistently used precise word choices readily interpretable by a reader.

Many of Shirley's word choices for her literate register text also have a marked literary quality. For example, Shirley's description of the "Hershey Kisses" and the new role she gave them in her written-for-others text is vivid literary language. It is also reminiscent of parts of the fairy tale *Hansel and Gretel*. The possible importation of such literary language from other texts (beyond story end markers) was first observed within the written-like group. Her attempt at a clarifying appositive, "Tony..., that's my dog...," also suggests an important emergent literary recognition (an audience's needs) and a literary convention (an appositive) to address it. Shirley incorporated other literary conventions (e.g., dialogue carriers) and literary-sounding phrases (e.g., "We raced to wake up Papa") using forms uncommon in oral language. Also, note that she replaced the common word *Dad* (in her oral text) with the less common *Papa* used in some older book tales. This is especially interesting because it again suggests her internalization and importation of such forms from professionally authored texts.

In addition, Shirley developed a family chain that used both identity and similarity relations, a feat that never occurred with the no story group and was very atypical of the oral-like children. She also successfully merged the originally separate cohesive chains of family and guests into a complex one through a clearly interpretable *we* in "And the guests came. And we had the water...." Later, she also successfully separated these two chains. This was a feat accomplished only by the written-like emergent and conventional readers. Further, she typically chose clearly interpretable words to complete participant/process/role clause-level redundancies. For example, Shirley portrayed herself as a doer, behaver, and speaker, repeating roles in ways that realized herself, others, and the event in clear and precise language.

The Conventional Readers. The sample of children who were conventional readers prior to any formal reading instruction was very small ($n = 2$). This strongly dictates against making generalizations. However, this small group is important because it suggests how a developmental model of emergent literacy may continue into conventional reading.

Paul was a small, highly verbal, and vibrantly engaged European American child. At age 5 he read fluently. His father said Paul had been reading the newspaper since he was 3. Paul attended the university's gifted preschool and seemed likely to be truly gifted in terms of literacy. He listed reading as his favorite thing to do, said that he had "hundreds of 'em" (i.e., books), and volunteered that Mark Brown was his favorite author. He also listed *The Beast in the Bathtub* (1987) as a favorite, which he explained was authored by Kathleen Stevens and illustrated by Ray Bowler. He was clearly very experienced with books. When asked where/when he had learned to read, Paul replied, "One day I saw this word and it came to me. And poof, I've been reading ever since."

Paul's oral register monologue text attempt

[commenting while drawing] This beach is in Florida, close to Disneyworld. There is this restaurant and it's like, well, there was a song. It was called, I forget what the name was, but Winnie Pooh was singing, "Humlee, humlee, whatever" and he was at the restaurant we were at. And then the Disney characters were like passing out food. I wanted a hot dog when we went there. We went to this other restaurant and well, it looked like it was run by Pinnochio. It wasn't really run by Pinnochio, it just looked like it because it had all these decorations and stuff and it's so big.

Paul's literate register text attempt: The restaurant mystery

There was a restaurant and it had hundreds of hot dogs. But there was one unusual hot dog. It was a gold and silver one that was very fancy.

A man ordered the special which was the gold and silver and fancy hot dog. And he ate it but when he bited into it, it wasn't cooked. So, he asked the waiter to cook it for him but the waiter said if they cooked it, the gold and silver would melt. So the thing the man did was he tried to cut the gold and silver (off) because he wanted the chunks of gold and silver and he cooked it and ate it. But it still had gold and silver on it. So, he put it back in where the hot dogs went.

And then the next day, the man came back to the restaurant and he saw that it was gone. Who could steal it? And then, (he thought) I know who stole it. It was him. He didn't put it back in the exact spot. He put it where the fries were. He put it where the fries were because then the people who were making them kind of got a little confused. So, well that's it.

Paul was very similar to the other conventional reader, Carl, who was 4 and African American. Both code switched with considerable expertise and also engaged in considerable predictation planning talk. For example, Paul specifically identified not only his vacation experience but a television text as contributing to his eventual tale. He also talked about merging parts of his oral tale into one story. Thus, he explicitly recognized and imported substantive intertextual material, a feat first observed implicitly in the written-like group. In addition, he identified his story as a mystery (commenting that he liked mysteries) and that his tale would be "made up."

In comparing Paul's oral and dictated texts, he clearly displayed a sophisticated intralinguistic reorganization of a vacation event into a "made-up" mystery/fantasy tale with a title. His topic and participants are, for the most part, clearly specified and well elaborated intralinguistically. Note, also, he began his story about a restaurant by introducing a class, *hot dogs*. Across several subsequent sentences, Paul specified a very distinctive and particular hot dog that became a main participant in his tale.

Discussion

This study merged theoretical perspectives from Vygotsky (e.g., 1934/1962, 1934/1978) and Halliday (e.g., 1978, 1985a) to compare preschoolers' face-to-face oral and literate register texts for others. The results clearly answered the researchers' questions. Some preschoolers did code switch, and such sophisticated control of literate register options was statistically significantly related to higher income and emergent reading that most closely approximated or was conventional reading. Qualitative differences in code switching were also evident within and between emergent reading categories. In addition, new or further insights were suggested regarding how cohesion is related to (a) emergent literacy development, (b) differences in income, and (c) connections between reading, writing, and the reading process during the emergent literacy phase. A discussion of the results and how they contribute to the field follows.

Cohesion, Code Switching, and Literacy Development. The cohesion/literacy findings suggest an important and new understanding—that is, when and how intuitive knowledge of cohesive options, literate phrasings, and their contextually appropriate use for oral and written contexts interface with emergent reading development. Although it has been generally assumed that preschool children are not yet able to address issues of audience and code switching, this study documents that this knowledge develops for some but not for others. Further, this developing knowledge about literate register cohesion reached statistical significance during the emergent reading phase when children were still attending to pictures but produced a written-like pretend reading. Rather surprisingly, there appeared to be few quantitative changes in children's familiarity with literate register patterns as they became conventional readers. Although the number of conventional readers in this study was too small for great confidence in this final observation, the written-like data alone suggest that such knowledge may be an authentic precursor (or coordinate) of conventional literacy achievement.

In support of this suggestion, we may recall that other studies consistently reported that familiarity with literate register cohesive harmony was related with statistical significance to more proficient literacy (and the reverse) across elementary ages (grades 1–5) (e.g., Cox et al., 1990; King & Rentel, 1981). Thus, this study suggests familiarity with complex literate register cohesive options is important: (a) It explains one part of what differentiates Sulzby's three attention-to-pictures subcategories of emergent reading, and (b) it is a vital aspect of English literacy development, though one that traditional instruction seems not to foster adequately (e.g., Cox et al., 1990).

Perhaps of most importance to educators, familiarity with literate register options is both incrementally and qualitatively observable in children's own texts as they progress toward becoming conventional readers. Interesting patterns that appear developmental emerged both within and between emergent reading categories. Because this study used only cross-group comparisons, it would be premature to identify these observations as more than potentially developmental insights. Nevertheless, important differences and accomplishments began to emerge during the oral-like category (e.g., Karen's and Matt's differing expertise with precise wordings, attention to clause-level redundancy patterns, or clear elaboration) and generally were brought under consistent and simultaneous control once a child became a written-like emergent reader.

The Income Effect. The statistically significant income effect for greater familiarity with literate register cohesion should be treated with caution. The unequal distribution of other factors within income (e.g., age, gender) at the county site suggests guarding against overinterpretation. However, when examined carefully and qualitatively, the study yields important insights supporting other sociocultural and emergent literacy research related to experience and income.

In emergent literacy research, Sulzby (1985) associated her categories with increasing child-centered, adult-mediated experiences with storybooks. Interviews with the children triangulated with their performance on Sulzby's emergent reading categories suggested this storybook experience assumption was so for these children. Both data sources indicated that the written-like children came from homes providing strong, child-centered book experiences regardless of differences in income, age, gender, or judgments of cognitive aptitude. While the no story and oral-like children also valued and were familiar with books, recall there were also indications that their favorite stories were less likely to come from books. We suggest these differences in experience may have led these children's learning about literate register texts and their cohesive options. This is a view that agrees with other emergent literacy and sociocultural research and with Vygotsky's (1934/1962, 1934/1978) sociocognitive and Halliday's (1975) developmental linguistic theory.

For example, Gee (1990) suggested the functions for which literacy is used vary by socioeconomic and cultural factors often associated with income. Further, these functions and forms often differ from the functions and forms of literacy privileged in schools (e.g., Heath, 1983). Additionally, fewer economic resources may greatly limit both literacy materials available and a parent's time to interact with such materials with a child. Also, low income may be (though not always) related to a parent's own low level of literacy, which, in turn, may severely limit or alter parent/child interactions with book-type literacy materials. Clearly, these were experiential factors involving literacy materials, and differences within the experiences seem a best explanatory fit to the income finding. They accounted simultaneously for (a) the unequal distribution of the more advanced emergent readers at the county and university sites and (b) the presence at all preschool programs of the full range of picture-governed categories (including the statistically significant written-like one).

Reading/Writing Connections and the Reading Process. The study also relates emergent reading to writing in the sense of composition. This is quite distinct from the many studies documenting emergent writers developing their own invented writing systems. In contrast, this study reveals these young children working on complex issues of composition involving more precise and literary-sounding wordings within redundancy patterns, and specifically associated these observations with categories of emergent reading behaviors and strategies.

Furthermore, these young children demonstrated familiarity with literate register text and cohesive options at two levels of ownership related to reading and writing. For example, the picture-governed, written-like children successfully and independently (a) reconstructed a written-like monologue from a familiar storybook (i.e., a pretend reading) and (b) took their own oral monologue based on personal experience and modified it to a literate register for an audience of readers. This is a rather surprising level of expertise and ownership of the literate register among such young children; it suggests an important level of internalization and intuitive automaticity with these two codes.

Of considerable importance, a related analysis of the children's literate register texts revealed this level of ownership was accompanied by a statistically significant increase in the children's emergent metacognitive utterances to regulate their text's content and production. Specifically, the written-like children not only successfully produced original literate register texts but also audibly planned and monitored their text's composition and comprehensibility for a reader with regulatory speech indicating emergent literacy-related metacognition (Cox, 1994).

A further reading/writing process connection was revealed in the literate register cohesive patterns used so well by the written-like children. Recall that earlier discussion related cohesive harmony choices/patterns directly to three of the four cueing systems (semantic, syntactic, pragmatic) recognized as fundamental to the reading process. The statistically significant emergent reading effect for greater use of literate register cohesion suggests an important emerging internalization of how the cueing systems work in literate register text. Such expertise suggests that an intuitive understanding of how and where to direct attention differently (e.g., Hildyard & Hidi, 1985) in order to comprehend or to compose a literate register (as opposed to common oral) text was already developing for these children prior to formal instruction. These are crucial understandings about reading and writing that have been generally assumed to develop during school literacy instruction.

Instructional Implications. The clearest instructional implications concern both the content and timing of beginning reading instruction. Relative to content, it reaffirms that informal, child-centered opportunities to attend to semantic and structural aspects should be given at least equal focus with the traditional and well-recognized emphasis on word-recognition strategies. As to timing, this study suggests familiarity with and appropriate use of literate register cohesive options should be added to a preschool literacy set (Holdaway, 1979) as another important precursor of conventional literacy.

Caution must be raised against interpreting this study's findings as supporting either a stage model of literacy development or a traditional skills model of instruction. Sulzby (1985) clearly stated that her emergent reading categories do not realize sequential developmental stages; rather, they suggest a general and child-centered progression toward conventional reading. This study's grounding in sociolinguistic and sociocognitive theory and literacy research suggests a social constructivist model of instruction based on experience but also one in which knowledgeable teachers can explicitly scaffold children into literacy, when appropriate. This model offers many child-centered, adult- or knowledgeable-peer–mediated experiences with books that merge social interaction with functional use and opportunities to experiment with and explore the literate register privileged in schools. However, as others have argued (e.g., Cazden, 1992; Delpit, 1995), if crucial aspects of literacy are not sufficiently familiar from experience, the model supports explicitly scaffolded instruction by a knowledgeable other. This study identifies two aspects (literate register cohesive/wording options) that appear as likely precursors to conventional literacy. When children may respond best to implicit or explicit instruction, and for whom, are important; these issues remain to be addressed in further research.

Associated with the teacher's mediational role is the need to be familiar with language forms and functions that individual children may bring to school and how they are related to developing literacy. Familiarity with children's linguistic culture and developing knowledge of literate register patterns should help teachers decide whether and when particular supports should be implicit or explicit. This is essential literacy content knowledge if teachers are to build on the language children bring to the classroom in order to open new and different meaning-making potentials.

Research Limitations and Implications. This study, like most, has limitations. However, because of its statistically significant findings, the limitations also suggest further research. Several of these were identified during the discussion. In addition, it seems reasonable that the written-like children in this study are likely to become conventional, and later proficient, readers and writers with ease. This expectation, along with other developmental suggestions, is limited by the study's cross-sectional design. It deserves further exploration in longitudinal work.

Another limitation is the study's fairly small and racially/ethnically homogenous sample. Also limiting are the unequal distributions and sometimes small numbers within certain variables (e.g., the small group of gifted children and the standards by which they were judged). These limits suggest a need for replication, with a more rigorous design employing equal numbers in each cell and extension to more ethnically diverse children, and more children judged as gifted by more consistent and objective means.

A more thorough examination of home experiences could provide useful insights into how familiarity with the literate register may be enhanced in some parent/child exchanges and not in others. Extension into the classroom can address the role of different types of literature and teacher-student interviews in developing familiarity and use of literate register options. For example, how might cohesive differences in simple and more complex patterned books or different genres interact to develop more complete familiarity with the literate register serving diverse functions?

In final summary, this study affirms once more that familiarity with literate register cohesive options is significantly tied to literacy development. However, because this study uses a more thorough concept of cohesion that is text level and sensitive to changes in context and register, it contributes new insights into literacy development, emergent reading/writing connections, and the tie between cohesion and literacy. Equally important, this study's findings can directly inform instructional decisions. Specifically, the findings suggest (a) sufficient familiarity with literate register cohesive and wording patterns (associated with written-like emergent reading) may be one legitimate precursor of conventional reading; and (b) on the way to the written-like category, developmental patterns appear that seem useful in assessing, documenting, and scaffolding young children into literacy.

Acknowledgments

The research reported in this article was assisted by a grant from the Spencer Foundation. The data presented, the statements made, and the views expressed are solely the responsibility of the authors.

References

Bernstein, B. (1975). *Class, codes, and control 3: Towards a theory of educational transmissions*. London: Routledge & Kegan Paul.

Brandt, D. (1989). The message is message. *Written Communication, 6,* 31–44.

Burningham, J. (1973). *Mr. Gumpy's motor car.* London: Penguin.

Cazden, C. (1992). *Whole language plus.* New York: Teachers College Press.

Chafe, W. (1985). Linguistic differences produced by differences between speaking and writing. In D.R. Olson, N. Torrance, & A. Hildyard (Eds.), *Literacy, language, and learning: The nature and consequences of reading and writing* (pp. 105–123). New York: Cambridge University Press.

Cox, B.E. (1990). The effects of structural factors of expository texts on teachers' judgments of writing quality. In J. Zutell & S. McCormick (Eds.), *Literacy theory and research: Analyses from multiple paradigms* (39th yearbook of the National Reading Conference, pp. 137–144). Chicago: National Reading Conference.

Cox, B.E. (1994). Young children's regulatory talk: Evidence of emerging metacognitive control over literary products and processes. In R.B. Ruddell, M.R. Ruddell, & H. Singer (Eds.), Theoretical models and processes of reading (4th ed., pp. 733–756). Newark, DE: International Reading Association.

Cox, B.E., & Carpenter, S. (1996). *Examining at risk adolescent/adult readers' textual knowledge: An exploratory study.* Purdue University, West Lafayette, IN.

Cox, B.E., Shanahan, T., & Sulzby, E. (1990). Good and poor readers' use of cohesion in writing. *Reading Research Quarterly, 25,* 47–65.

Cox, B.E., Shanahan, T., & Tinzmann, M.B. (1991). Children's knowledge of organization, cohesion, and voice in written exposition. *Research in the Teaching of English, 25,* 179–218.

Delpit, L. (1995, December). *Other people's children.* Paper presented at the annual meeting of the National Reading Conference, New Orleans, LA.

Eggins, S. (1994). *An introduction to systemic functional linguistics*. London: St. Martin's Press.

Flack, M. (1931). *Angus and the cat*. New York: Doubleday.

Freeman, D. (1978). *Pocket for Corduroy*. New York: Penguin.

Gates, A.I. (1921). An experimental and statistical study of reading and reading tests (in three parts). *Journal of Educational Psychology, 12,* 303–314, 378–391, 445–465.

Gee, J.P. (1990). *Social linguistics and literacies: Ideology in discourses*. London: Falmer.

Goodman, K. (1967). Reading: A psycholinguistic guessing game. *Journal of the Reading Specialist, 4,* 126–135.

Gumperz, J.J. (1971). *Language in social groups: Essays selected and introduced by Anwar S. Dil*. Stanford, CA: Stanford University Press.

Halliday, M.A.K. (1975). *Learning how to mean: Explorations in the development of language*. London: Edward Arnold.

Halliday, M.A.K. (1978). *Language as social semiotic: The social interpretation of language and meaning*. London: Edward Arnold.

Halliday, M.A.K. (1985a). *An introduction to functional grammar*. London: Edward Arnold.

Halliday, M.A.K. (1985b). *Spoken and written language*. Geelong, Victoria, Australia: Deakin University Press.

Halliday, M.A.K., & Hasan, R. (1976). *Cohesion in English*. London: Longman.

Halliday, M.A.K., & Hasan, R. (1989). *Language, context, and text: Aspects of language in a social-semiotic perspective*. New York: Oxford University Press.

Hasan, R. (1984). Coherence and cohesive harmony. In J. Flood (Ed.), *Understanding reading comprehension* (pp. 181–219). Newark, DE: International Reading Association.

Heath, S.B. (1983). *Ways with words: Language, life and work in communities and classrooms*. Cambridge, UK: Cambridge University Press.

Hildyard, A., & Hidi, S. (1985). Oral-written differences in the production and recall of narratives. In D.R. Olson, N. Torrance, & A. Hildyard (Eds.), *Literacy, language, and learning: The nature and consequences of reading and writing* (pp. 285–306). New York: Cambridge University Press.

Holdaway, D. (1979). *The foundations of literacy*. New York: Scholastic.

Jonz, J. (1987). Textual cohesion and second language comprehension. *Language Learning, 37,* 409–438.

King, M.L., & Rentel, V.M. (1981). How children learn to write: A longitudinal study (RF Project 761861/712383 and 761513/711748, Final Report, June). Columbus: The Ohio State University.

Kintsch, W. (1977). On comprehending stories. In M.A. Just & P.A. Carpenter (Eds.), *Cognitive processes in comprehension* (pp. 33–62). Hillsdale, NJ: Erlbaum.

Lesgold, A.M. (1972). Pronominalization: A device for unifying sentences in memory. *Journal of Verbal Learning and Verbal Behavior, 11,* 316–323.

Lewis, C.S. (1970). *The lion, the witch and the wardrobe*. New York: Collier.

McCabe, A., & Peterson, C. (1991). Linking children's connective use and narrative macrostructure. In A. McCabe & C. Peterson (Eds.), *Developing narrative structure* (pp. 29–54). Hillsdale, NJ: Erlbaum.

Mosenthal, J.H., & Tierney, R.J. (1984). Commentary: Cohesion problems with talking about text. *Reading Research Quarterly, 19,* 240–244.

Otto, B. (1984/1985). *Evidence of emergent reading behaviors in young children's interactions with favorite storybooks*. Unpublished doctoral dissertation, Northwestern University, Evanston, IL.

Otto, B. (1992, April). Evidence of cohesive harmony in reconstructed beginning reader texts and complex trade book texts by emergent readers. Paper presented at the annual meeting of the American Educational Research Association, San Francisco, CA.

Pappas, C.C. (1985). The cohesive harmony and cohesive density of children's oral and written stories. In J.D. Benson & W.S. Greaves (Eds.), *Systemic perspectives on discourse volume 2: Selected applied papers from the 9th international systemic workshop* (pp. 169–186). Norwood, NJ: Ablex.

Pettegrew, B.C. (1981). *Text formation: A comparative study of literate and pre-literate first grade children*. Unpublished doctoral dissertation, The Ohio State University, Columbus.

Purcell-Gates, V., McIntyre, E., & Freppon, P.A. (1995). Learning written storybook language in school: A comparison of low-SES children in skills-based and whole language classrooms. *American Educational Research Journal, 32,* 659–685.

Putnam, L. (1989, November). *Effects of repeat storyreadings and dramatizations on the development of book-specific vocabulary and syntax in three inner city kindergartners.* Paper presented at the annual meeting of the National Council of Teachers of English, Baltimore, MD.

Rentel, V.M., & King, M.L. (1983a). *A longitudinal study of coherence in children's written narratives* (Ed. Rep. No. 327 089). Columbus: The Ohio State University.

Rentel, V.M., & King, M.L. (1983b). Present at the beginning. In P. Mosenthal, L. Tamor, & S.A. Walmsley (Eds.), *Research on writing: Principles and methods* (pp. 139–176). New York: Longman.

Sendak, M. (1963). *Where the wild things are.* New York: HarperCollins.

Snow, C.E., & Ninio, A. (1986). The contracts of literacy: What children learn from learning to read books. In W.H. Teale & E. Sulzby (Eds.), *Emergent literacy: Writing and reading* (pp. 116–138). Norwood, NJ: Ablex.

Spradley, J.P. (1980). *Participant observation.* New York: Holt, Rinehart & Winston.

Stevens, K. (1987). *The beast in the bathtub.* New York: HarperCollins.

Sulzby, E. (1985). Children's emergent readings of favorite storybooks: A developmental study. *Reading Research Quarterly, 20,* 458–481.

Vygotsky, L.S. (1962). *Thought and language* (E. Hanfmann & G. Vakar, Eds. & Trans.). Cambridge, MA: MIT Press. (Original work published 1934)

Vygotsky, L.S. (1978). *Mind in society: The development of higher psychological processes* (M. Cole, V. John-Steiner, S. Scribner, & E. Souberman, Eds. & Trans.). Cambridge, MA: Harvard University Press. (Original work published 1934)

Wells, G. (1985). Preschool literacy-related activities and success in school. In D.R. Olson, N. Torrance, & A. Hildyard (Eds.), *Literacy, language, and learning: The nature and consequences of reading and writing* (pp. 229–255). New York: Cambridge University Press.

13

Learning to Read Words: Linguistic Units and Instructional Strategies

Connie Juel and Cecilia Minden-Cupp

I n preparing the grant proposal for the Center for the Improvement of Early Reading Achievement (CIERA), we asked teachers and administrators what research questions they most needed answered in order to improve primary-grade reading instruction. They raised more questions about how to teach children to read words than any other area in early reading. They expressed concern over which, and how many, strategies for word recognition teachers should model for first-grade children. Should teachers, for example, model either how to sound out unknown words or how to make an analogy to a key word on a word wall? Should teachers focus on what makes sense? Should they model some combination of these (and other) strategies? Or—and under what conditions—should they simply tell a child an unknown word? Should they focus on the visual array of letters by spelling the word? Whatever instructional strategies were or were not emphasized, they wanted to know which unit in the text or word should be the main focus. Should they focus on the meaning of the text to puzzle out an unknown word? Should they focus on the whole word (e.g., *stand*), little words in big ones (e.g., the *and* in *stand*), the onset and rime (e.g., /st/ and /and/), or individual letter sounds in words (e.g., /s/, /t/, /a/, /n/, /d/)? They wanted answers to the nitty-gritty questions involved in word-recognition instruction.

While practitioners raised more questions about how to teach word recognition than other areas in reading instruction, they expressed concern about the amount of time spent on word recognition in their total language arts programs. They were very concerned about the development of both reading and writing and the development of rich vocabularies and world knowledge with which to comprehend decoded texts.

Our approach to the above questions and issues was to examine how reading instruction worked in the complexity of real classrooms. Although there were key elements of instruction we wanted to observe, we did not want to ignore the

From *Reading Research Quarterly*, *35*, 458–492. Copyright © 2000 by the International Reading Association.

context in which this instruction occurred. We reasoned that certain instructional procedures might be more effective if they were delivered both in particular ways and to specific groups of children. Onset and rime instruction, for example, might be most effective for children with some decoding skill and some degree of phonological awareness, while sequential letter-by-letter decoding might be more effective for children with less early literacy knowledge (Bruck & Treiman, 1992; Ehri & Robbins, 1992; Vandervelden & Siegel, 1995). Further, the form of instruction might alter its effectiveness. That is, whether instruction was delivered to large or small instructional groups, the character of those groups, the types of materials, and the form of interactions—among other factors—were all likely to influence the effectiveness of particular types of instruction. We wanted to closely examine the interactions of factors such as the aforementioned and allow room to study unanticipated classroom characteristics that seemed to affect the success of word-recognition instruction.

The current study was a microanalysis of word-recognition instruction in four first-grade classrooms. We considered both the form of word-recognition instruction (e.g., whether it occurred through sorting words into patterns or through writing) and how that instruction was situated in the broader picture of language arts. We studied the linguistic units of words (e.g., syllables, onset and rime, phonemes) that were the focus of instruction as well as the strategies the teacher modeled for children to use to identify unknown words. We also considered how word-recognition instruction was balanced with other aspects of language arts.

In sum, in the current study we examined whether specific forms of instruction might differentially affect students with varying levels of phonological awareness, alphabet knowledge, and other early literacy foundations. Our goal was to begin to identify specific instructional practices that appear to best foster learning to read words for particular profiles of children.

Background

The sheer volume of words that children are expected to read quickly and accurately is daunting. According to Adams (1990) and Carroll, Davies, and Richman (1971), if children successfully negotiate all the texts normally encountered by the end of eighth grade, they will encounter over 80,000 different words. In third grade alone, they will encounter about 25,000 distinct words.

A child is quickly faced with an orthographic avalanche of printed words. Only a few thousand words usually receive direct instruction in the primary grades. It would be impossible to directly teach children all the words they will encounter in print. It is also impossible to directly teach children all the letter–sound correspondences that they will need to be able to sound out novel words. Even the most comprehensive phonics programs rarely provide direct instruction for more than about 90 phonics rules. Yet over 500 different spelling-sound rules are needed to read (Gough & Juel, 1990; Juel, 1994).

Further, it is questionable that what is taught in phonics are the actual units used by the skilled reader. The rules of phonics, at least in most instructional programs currently in use, are explicit, few in number, and slow in application. The identification of spelling-sound patterns by skilled readers, on the other hand, is implicit, requires considerable orthographic knowledge, and works very fast. It is not clear whether the *units* of phonics instruction (e.g., individual letters or letter pairs) or the basic *processes* assumed in phonics instruction (i.e., applying rules to letter sounds and blending these sounds together or decoding by analogy) are involved in skilled word recognition (Gough, Juel, & Griffith, 1992).

While traditional phonics instruction may not reflect the *actual* units and processes used in word recognition by the skilled reader, it may point the child in a useful direction. Phonics instruction may prompt a child to look for the relationship between the letters in a printed word and the sounds she utters as she says the word. Part of the unending controversy surrounding phonics instruction may have to do with the fact that it is not perfect; there may be better ways—or multiple ways—to help children link letters and sounds.

Phonics instruction may also promote awareness of words as sequences of sounds (i.e., phonemic awareness, phonological sensitivity). However, other forms of instruction such as invented spelling or writing for sounds (i.e., as a word is slowly segmented and articulated by a teacher, the child writes the letter sounds he perceives) might also promote both phonological awareness and letter-sound knowledge (Dahl, Scharer, Lawson, & Grogan, 1999). Awareness of the internal phonological structure of words is necessary in learning to read an alphabetic script like printed English. It is an awareness that is more explicit than is ever demanded in listening to and responding to speech (Liberman & Shankweiler, 1985). It is an awareness that is not readily acquired by most children. So what may be most effective about traditional phonics instruction or activities like writing for sounds may not be the actual letter-sound rules that are taught or employed at a given time, but the fact that while the child attempts to represent his speech with letters, he becomes aware of spoken words as sequences of somewhat separable speech units (e.g., the /k/ in *cat*). Armed with this awareness, a child can then go on to induce for himself the multitude of spelling-sound correspondences that are actually required to read.

What needs to be induced will eventually be very complete orthographic representations of individual words. For the skilled reader, spelling and word reading represent nearly synonymous sources of orthographic knowledge (Ehri, 1980, 1991, 1992, 1998). When readers read words, they access information stored about each word from previous encounters with it. This information comes to include complete spellings that are bonded with the word's pronunciation and meaning. As adults refer to dictionaries or computer spellcheckers, they are aware that gaining complete orthographic information is an ongoing task. Complete orthographic representations of common words in print are more likely to be achieved before those of rare words because these words are more frequently seen. As Share and Stanovich (1995) described it, "the process of word recognition will depend primarily on the frequency to which an individual child has been exposed to a particular word together, of course, with the nature and success of item identification" (p. 18).

There is some evidence that relatively few exposures to the same word allow its subsequent identification (Reitsma, 1983, 1990). The problem, of course, is that most words are not commonly seen. Primary-grade children are hit with an avalanche of printed words. While some words are seen a lot, the most meaningful words (the content words) are not. After encountering, for example, *hen* and *haystack* in *Rosie's Walk* (Hutchins, 1968), it will be miles of print before children again encounter *hen*, let alone *haystack*. To be more precise, in 5 million words of running text, the reader is likely to encounter *hen* only 77 times and *haystack* 11 times (Carroll et al., 1971). What children will soon see again are the subword units such as the onsets (i.e., /h/, /st/), the rimes (i.e., /en/, /ay/, and /ack/), and the individual phonemes (i.e., /h/, /a/). It is the act of conscious attention specifically focused on these component units in a word that will likely foster the word's eventual orthographic representation in memory.

Fledgling readers begin identifying (or spelling) words by relying on partial orthographic information such as initial letters. This rudimentary orthographic knowledge soon contains a phonetic component. As children learn letter names or sounds, words are often learned by connecting one or more letters with sounds in pronunciation (Ehri & Wilce, 1985, 1987a, 1987b). In the word *hen*, for example, the letter-name knowledge of /n/ is likely to be applied in spelling or recognizing the printed version. Indeed, a likely invented spelling of *hen* as *n* or *hn* reveals both letter-name knowledge and at least a surface-level understanding that words contain sounds.

According to the self-teaching hypothesis (Share, 1995; Share & Stanovich, 1995; Torgesen & Hecht, 1996), children basically learn to read by developing phonological awareness, learning some basic letter–sound relationships, and phonologically recoding a specific printed word a few times. The phonological recoding process is what ultimately cements the word's orthographic representation in memory. The driving idea behind the self-teaching hypothesis is that when a child is armed with phonological awareness and letter-sound knowledge—and provided a rich exposure to print—the child can ultimately teach herself to read. Indeed, she must do so, as the sheer number of words that are learned far exceed the number that are even explicitly taught. Thus, the critical question may be how teachers can most efficiently help children gain enough skill to successfully enter the world of print so that, in a sense, they can then read enough to become their own teachers.

Linguistic Units

Words are composed of syllables. Most syllables are composed of initial consonants or consonant clusters called *onsets* (e.g., the /k/ in *cat*, the /ch/ in *chat*, or the /spl/ in *splat*) and the vowel and what follows it—the word unit called *rimes* (e.g., the /at/ in *cat* or the /eat/ in *cheat*; Pinker, 1994). Onsets and rimes are themselves composed of sound units called *phonemes* (e.g., *cat* consists of three phonemes, /k/ /a/ /t/, *splat* consists of five phonemes, and *cheat* consists of three phonemes). Learning to read and write involves attending to these sound units and connecting them to spelling patterns (e.g., perceiving the /at/ in *cat* and knowing it is spelled /at/, or that /eat/ is spelled /eat/ in *cheat* but /ete/ in *Pete*). Learning to read and write words involves perceiving the sound units in spoken words and knowing which spelling patterns are linked to them in which words.

There is a developmental progression in how sound units in spoken words become consciously accessible to young children (Goswami, 1995; Treiman, 1992). At about age 4, many children can perceive, segment, and manipulate the rather distinctive syllable units in words. At about ages 4 to 5, onsets and rimes become transparent—which is one reason that, at this age, children seem fond of rhyming games, poems, chants, and even manipulations of linguistic units in the creation of pseudolanguages such as Pig Latin. But awareness of the individual phonemes within rime units often develops only with reading instruction (Perfetti, Beck, Bell, & Hughes, 1987). This is because phonemes are particularly hard to perceive in spoken words, because they are abstract. That is, as we say a word, we begin saying the upcoming phoneme as we are still articulating the one that came before it. So, in *cat* we begin to say the /a/ as we are finishing up the /k/. Thus, it is difficult to pull these units apart, and when teachers try to do so they end up saying something like the letter *k* makes a /kuh/ sound—but, of course, there is no /kuh/ in *cat*.

Because phonemes are difficult to untangle in words, there has been debate over whether initial reading instruction should emphasize them. It has been proposed that initial reading instruction should mirror the accessibility of linguistic units. Thus, after children perceive the fairly accessible syllable units, emphasis should turn to onsets and rimes. In support of this argument is the utility of rime units in reading. Thirty-seven rimes (e.g., *at*, *ack*, *ap*, *ash*, *eat*, *op*, *ing*) appear in over 500 different words that children commonly see in the early grades (Adams, 1990; Wylie & Durrell, 1970). It has been shown that children can make analogies from rime units to read and write new words (Goswami, 1995; Goswami & Bryant, 1992; Goswami & Mead, 1992; Treiman, 1992). That is, once a rime like /at/ is known, students can use their knowledge of onsets and the /at/ rime to write or read a never-before-seen word, perhaps *sat* or *splat*.

Rimes are not only more psychologically accessible to children than are their individual phonemes but also more predictable in their spellings than are smaller linguistic units. Trying to teach rules about how individual letters map to phonemes, for example, can create a problem in traditional phonics programs. While rules at the phoneme level work fairly well for consonants, they do not work well for the vowels in English. In English, it is very difficult to know what sound a vowel will represent without a consideration of subsequent letters. That is, within a rime unit such as /at/ or /ad/ or /ay/ or /ate/, the vowel is fairly predictable; but /a/, on its own, is not. Most phonics rules involving vowels are disturbingly short on accuracy (e.g., the rule "when there are two vowels together, the first one is long and the second one is silent" is true only 45% of the time; Clymer, 1963/1996). Within common rimes, however, there are very stable pronunciation patterns (Adams, 1990; Stahl, 1992).

Although some studies (Goswami, 1995; Treiman, 1992) support a heavy dose of rimes in early reading instruction, other research suggests that rimes may not be so helpful (Bruck & Treiman, 1992; Ehri & Robbins, 1992; Foorman, Francis, Fletcher, Schatschneider, & Mehta, 1998; Gaskins, Ehri, Cress, O'Hara, & Donnelly, 1996/1997; Vandervelden & Siegel, 1995). Some children may need to analyze words at the phoneme level *before* they can successfully make analogies involving rimes. Certainly they need to delete initial consonants to segment the rime. And there is evidence that consonants in spoken English are more salient to young children than are short vowels, as children first attempt to write and read words by depicting or relying on their consonant sounds (e.g., writing *cat* as *kt* or identifying *cat* in print by knowledge of the first and final consonants; Bruck & Treiman, 1992; Henderson, 1981). Thus, the self-generative nature of rime units, such as being able to decode *sat* because the /at/ rime has already been learned in *cat*, may be less than robust for very beginning readers (Gaskins et al., 1996/1997). Further, Foorman et al. (1998) provided evidence that starting at the phoneme level may, in the end, provide the best results. Although a rime like /at/ is easier to perceive in a word than its constituent phonemes, especially the vowel, working toward the phoneme from the start may be more productive in the long run. On the other hand, once some consonant and vowel knowledge is secured, knowledge of rimes may be exactly what helps children chunk and decode unknown words (Bruck & Treiman, 1992). The issue of the best instructional unit, and for which children, is far from complete.

Instructional Strategies

While word-level instruction can differ on what linguistic units receive the focus of attention, it can also differ on the instructional strategies with which children are told to approach these linguistic units in unknown printed words. An instructional strategy is what the teacher instructs the child to do when faced with a word that is not instantly recognized. The teacher may provide a menu of strategies ranging from using the contextual cues provided by illustrations to sounding out and blending individual letter sounds.

There are countless instructional strategies and combinations of strategies possible. We believe that most instructional strategies that are provided in classrooms to help children identify unknown words in texts can be categorized along three dimensions: (a) the degree to which personal or contextual meaning is emphasized, (b) the degree to which attention is directed to phonological decoding, and (c) the extent to which particular linguistic units (i.e., words, syllables, onsets and rimes, phonemes) are privileged. The first dimension is exemplified when a teacher queries a child to consider, concerning an uncertain word identification, "Does it make sense?" An example of the second dimension is the prompt to blend the /a/ and /t/ sounds together. The third dimension is illustrated by a prompt such as, "Is there an /at/ in that word?" There are numerous permutations on the above, as well as overlapping dimensions. For example, a teacher might prompt, "Think, what starts with a /b/ and makes sense?"

Does It Make Sense? Because the goal of reading is sense making, it may seem surprising that fostering a stance of word identification by asking this question has been especially contentious. Perhaps this tension is captured by Pressley's (1998) statement:

> By the conclusion of this book, it will be clear that advising children to attend first and foremost to meaning cues (e.g., to look at picture cues) to decode words is instructional advisement that belongs on the same scrap heap as eye-movement training. (p. 56)

The issue is attending to meaning cues first and foremost. Pressley (1998) immediately went on to state the following:

> Meaning cues are critical, however, in appraising whether decoding was done properly: if the decoding makes no sense given the context, the good reader knows to go back and look at the word again. Context cues also help the skilled reader zero in on the intended meaning of words that have more than one definition. (p. 56)

Pressley (1998) drew from research that has shown that skilled readers are so swift at word recognition that they do not use context to help them identify words (a summary of this research also can be found in Stanovich, 1992). That is, the orthographic representations of words (described by Ehri earlier) are what account for the effortless process of word recognition in skilled reading. Further, the difference between skilled and unskilled young readers lies primarily in their development of these orthographic representations and consequently their ability to rapidly identify words, rather than in their ability to use context to facilitate word recognition.

Children who only have partial orthographic knowledge of a word, however, will likely need to use contextual information to resolve a particular word's pronunciation. If a child is reading *Rosie's Walk* (Hutchins, 1968), for example, and cannot readily identify *hen*, he may need to look at the illustration or recall from previously hearing the story that Rosie is a hen. The critical point in the self-teaching hypothesis of learning to read would be if he then looks at the letters in *hen* as he is placing this pronunciation on it. If he skips over the word *hen* in the text, after identifying it by looking at the illustration, he loses the opportunity to learn about its spelling patterns. He loses information that might be useful in furthering his self-teaching mechanism.

To balance the emphasis of sense making and the development of ortho-graphic knowledge, some instructional strategies encourage the use of multiple cue sources. Clay (1989) suggested these four cue sources:

1. Sense, Meaning: Does it make sense?
2. Visual Cues: Does that look right?
3. Letters/Sound: What would you expect to see?
4. Structure, Grammar: Can we say it that way?

An emphasis is placed on continual self-monitoring for meaning as one reads. There is an emphasis on these four types of cues—any two of which can be cross-checked to confirm whether one's hypothesis about an unknown word is correct.

So, if a child were reading about a bear wearing a funny hat and stumbled over *hat*, the child might be encouraged to ask what makes sense from looking at the illustration. If the child suggested *hat*, then a crosscheck might be made by looking to see that the unknown word did indeed start with the letter *h*.

A concern that has been expressed about this approach is that most teach-ers have children only check on letters in the word when context fails—and even then limit letter checks to as few letters as possible (Tunmer & Chapman, 1993). Tunmer and Chapman stated,

> We believe that when confronted with an unfamiliar word, the child should be en-couraged to look for familiar spelling patterns first and to use context as back up support to confirm hypotheses about what the word might be. Our concern is that in New Zealand children are much more likely to be encouraged to use context to identify unfamiliar words than to engage in word analysis activities. (pp. 3–4)

On the other hand, Pressley (1998), who clearly shared Tunmer and Chapman's (1993) view that use of context should be secondary to letter-sound cues as an instructional strategy, found in observing teachers in Madison, Wisconsin, USA, who follow Clay's (1989) advice, that they do not rely on context first and foremost. He stated,

> The teachers I have been watching are encouraging the students to make use of a variety of cues, consistent with whole language emphases, but, consistent with the

work on decoding, they are encouraging students to rely more on sounding words out, including thorough recognition of word parts for the initial decoding. Context cues are then used to decide if the word as sounded out really makes sense. (p. 146)

Synthetic Phonics: An Emphasis on Letter-by-Letter Phonological Decoding.

Instructional strategies are not isomorphic to instructional methods or materials, although they are certainly related. As described by Beck (1998), for example, phonics is "an umbrella term for a variety of ways of 'showing' (be it explicit or implicit) young learners how the print-to-speech system works" (p. 21). For Beck, the defining features of phonics methods are the text materials and the instructional strategies. The text materials in phonics involve using a vocabulary that is controlled on the basis of letter–sound correspondences. The dominant instructional strategy requires "learners to decode phonologically from the beginning to the end of words" (p. 26).

The linguistic unit that is generally emphasized in phonics is the phoneme, and the instructional strategy is to sound and blend the sequential letter sounds. This is called *synthetic phonics*. Here is an example of what a teacher using this approach might find in a teacher's guide:

> For the word *hat*, write each spelling, touch it, and have the children say each sound. Blend the sounds successively in the following manner: After writing and sounding /h/ /a/ (ha), make the blending motion under the word and have the children blend *hat*. (Adams, Bereiter, Hirshberg, Anderson, & Bernier, 1995, p. 127)

Of course, such instruction would include other exemplars, writing, and the reading of text such as "Matt has a tan hat" (p. 127). It is, in particular, the stringently controlled vocabulary in phonics texts, with its seemingly unappealing nature, that leaves many researchers and practitioners cold.

Beck (1998) was very clear that starting a young reader off in children's literature like *Rosie's Walk* (Hutchins, 1968) is wrongheaded. This is because the lack of controlled vocabulary inherent in such literature affords few attempts to practice sounding and blending the letter sounds that have been taught. There is evidence that if the dominant instructional strategy in the classroom is decoding unknown words letter by letter, children both learn the strategy quicker and go on to induce untaught letter–sound relationships faster if their beginning reading textbooks have vocabulary that is controlled for letter–sound correspondences (Juel & Roper/Schneider, 1985). The issue, however, of the percentage of words that need to appear in such texts is far from clear. Both Beck (1998) and Beck and Juel (1995) suggested that the controlled vocabulary in most phonics texts could be considerably reduced and still achieve the goal of such texts.

Another Form of Phonics: Identifying Unknown Words With Analogy to the Onsets and Rimes in Known Words.

In this approach, children are taught key words that contain common spelling patterns. These key words are frequently printed on cards and placed on the classroom word wall. A child is taught to break an unknown word into its component onsets and rimes and to search a word wall for known words with the same onset or rime. If *hat* were an unknown word, the child might proceed by noticing the /at/, finding the known word *cat* on the word wall, and saying, "If I know *cat* then I know *hat*" (Gaskins et al., 1988).

The stable pronunciation pattern of rimes compared to individual vowels, as well as the comparative accessibility of onset and rime units over individual phonemes, might seem reason enough to focus on these linguistic units in instruction. However, another reason behind the development of perhaps the best-known decoding by analogy approach, that developed by Gaskins and her colleagues at the Benchmark School in Media, Pennsylvania, USA, was the observation that some children seemed unable to benefit from a synthetic phonics approach (Gaskins, Gaskins, Anderson, & Schommer, 1995). With considerable teacher assistance, however, these children could learn by analyzing whole words into their component onsets and rimes.

Indeed, there is evidence that even with extensive phonemic awareness training, some children are not able to perceive phonemes (Torgesen & Davis, 1996). Such children would likely have difficulty learning to read by a synthetic phonics approach that depends upon letter-phoneme analysis. These might be some of the children Gaskins et al. (1995) found at Benchmark School. It also might be that it is easier for some children to remember and blend two sounds (the onset and rime) to decode a syllable rather than hold in mind the accumulated letter-by-letter phonemes in a syllable (Gaskins et al., 1996/1997). This might be particularly true for multisyllabic words.

In their continual evaluations of the Benchmark program, Gaskins et al. (1996/1997) have noted that some children have such difficulty recalling the key words that it prevents success in using them to make analogies. To improve the approach, it was found that key words need to be scrutinized more carefully when they are initially introduced by segmenting them into their component phonemes. This more careful and in-depth analysis of the key words makes them more memorable and retrievable for use in making analogies to other words.

Key Issues and Current Research Questions

There is now evidence that of those children who really struggle with decoding, some profit more from a synthetic phonics approach, while others find an analogy approach easier to use as an instructional strategy (Berninger, 1995; Berninger, Yates, & Lester, 1991; Wise, 1992; Wise, Olson, & Treiman, 1990). The optimal match of instructional strategies and linguistic units used in that instruction, for children with differing levels of word-recognition skill, is far from clear in laboratory settings—let alone in classroom settings. Both the instructional unit (i.e., phoneme or onset and rime) and instructional strategy (i.e., sequential letter-by-letter decoding versus making an analogy to a key word) may differentially affect children. Further, the balance between emphasizing contextual and orthographic information is debated.

Whether a child actually can or does use the instructional strategies suggested by a teacher may also depend on whether the child understands the instruction, has the knowledge to use the instruction, and the overall usefulness of the particular strategies. Success may be related to many factors, including (a) the type of practice provided in reading materials, (b) the types of activities in which the strategies are illustrated (e.g., reading or spelling), (c) how the teacher models the strategy, and (d) the degree of individualization of instruction. Phonics instruction, whether it takes a synthetic or an onset-rime approach, can or cannot be associated with phonics types of controlled vocabulary textbooks. Activities to teach letter–sound relationships can range considerably. A teacher might, for example, include more spelling for sounds or more word card sorts (e.g., where words are compared and contrasted as to their spelling patterns and then sorted into different categories; Bear, Invernizzi, Templeton, & Johnston, 1995). A teacher may or may not frequently model how to segment words into their component phonemes or onset and rime patterns and then show how to sound and blend the derived linguistic units together to figure out an unknown word. And, a teacher may do any of the above with large- or small-class groups.

Given the range of competing hypotheses about the effectiveness of both the linguistic units and the instructional strategies employed during reading instruction, and given the range of activities and materials in which they are embedded, we decided to undertake a systematic yearlong examination of word-recognition instruction as it occurred in a richly described instructional context. We were interested in examining which activities, reading materials, instructional strategies, and linguistic units of instruction seemed to promote word learning in first grade for children with different incoming literacy profiles. Our two basic research questions were the following:

1. Does instruction with an emphasis on different levels of linguistic units (e.g., onsets and rimes, individual phonemes) differentially affect children at various levels of reading development?

2. When and how are which linguistic units and which instructional strategies best taught to children?

Method

Participants and Setting

We began by identifying four first-grade classrooms in two schools in a city in the southeastern United States. The two schools have similar demographics. They are located in nearby neighborhoods in the same school district. In each school, approximately 70% of the children qualify for subsidized lunch, 60% are African American, 36% are Caucasian, and 4% are from other ethnic groups.

Each first-grade classroom had no more than 18 children. By the time we began our assessments in September the population in each classroom was fairly stable: No more than two children moved from each class after this time. Each of the classroom teachers was a female Caucasian who had more than 10 years of teaching experience (at least 5 of which were at the current school). Each was considered a very good teacher by her school principal. The principals' judgments were based on two primary factors. The first consideration was that the level of achievement in these classrooms compared favorably with that of other first-grade classrooms at the school. Because the schools in the district do not administer formal reading assessments in first grade, this evaluation was based on both observations in the classroom and district language arts folders that indicate spelling stage and alphabet knowledge development of each child from the beginning to the end of first grade. The second consideration was classroom management. It was deemed smooth and efficient in each of these classrooms. This consideration was based on classroom observations, disciplinary referrals, and accumulated input from parents. Classrooms 1 and 2 were in one school and Classrooms 3 and 4 at the other school.

Classroom Structures. Language arts instruction generally lasted for 1½ hours in each of the four classrooms. The language arts period in Classroom 3 tended to run longer, however, while Classroom 2 never ran longer because language arts in that room was strictly limited in time by school scheduling of subjects such as music and physical education. Although each classroom had three reading groups, the 90-minute language arts time period was spent somewhat differently. In Classroom 1, about 20 to 30 minutes of language arts time was spent in a whole-class word wall activity before dividing up into reading groups. In Classroom 2, language arts was spent solely in reading groups. In Classroom 3, the morning message was expanded from the 15 minutes that each class spent on this activity to an additional 15 to 20 minutes. In this classroom, the whole-class morning message formed an integral part of language arts instruction. In Classroom 4, language arts instruction was conducted solely in reading groups.

Each classroom had a teacher's assistant. When children were not in direct instruction in a reading group, they were supervised by the assistant in centers or seatwork. Centers included art, book nooks, computers, writing, and listening to taped stories. Each classroom also made weekly visits to the school library, which included listening to a story read by the librarian.

The teachers all had available a basal reading series from 1986. Although this basal had more leveled text by vocabulary control than do many current literature-based basals, it was still considered too difficult for the low groups. The school district had, in recent years, been adding commercial little books (i.e., commercial series of very short books with predictable or easily memorized text) to their classrooms. These books were considered easier than the basal for the children who knew little about letters or texts. In addition to the basal and little books, teachers borrowed from the library or had their own collections of trade books. The teachers had discretion over whether to use the basal and other reading materials: They could choose not to use the basal or other materials.

The school system strongly emphasized the growth of content knowledge. There were daily math lessons and nearly daily science and social studies lessons. In addition, the children rotated through music, art, physical education, and special lessons that might include speech therapy, guidance, enrichment, or other special activities.

Materials and Procedure

Classroom Observations. We conducted weekly classroom observations of language arts instruction throughout the school year. We spent a minimum of an hour each week (frequently 90 minutes) observing the instruction in each classroom. We observed each low group each week and the other two groups in each class at least once every 2 weeks. We also spent time observing the whole-class word wall instruction in Classroom 1 and the expanded morning message in Classroom 3 because these were integral parts of their respective language arts periods.

We used laptop computers to write running narratives of what was going on during language arts. We started the year by developing a coding sheet that would focus these observations on four primary areas: (1) activities, (2) materials, (3) strategies, and (4) linguistic units. Activities included the major focus of instruction or activity (e.g., a read-aloud by the teacher, spelling words, discussion of the meaning of a text, oral vocabulary development, oral phonemic awareness, phonics). Materials included the major materials used in the activities (e.g., a poem on a chart, word cards, word wall, personal journals, trade books, basals). Strategies included what children were told to do or what the teacher modeled doing when encountering an unknown word (e.g., teacher models sounding and blending onset and rime, teacher models sounding and blending phonemes, teacher models use of picture clues and known letter sounds, child told to reread, peers asked to provide clues, child asked if the suggested word makes sense). As we coded and discussed the running narratives, we added items. One teacher, for example, frequently gave children teacher-made little books containing the poem they had read on a chart in a group lesson. So, a code for a material, child copies of poems in a teacher-made little book, was added.

While our focus was on these four areas, we recorded whether instruction was being conducted in small groups or with the whole class. Our observations, and subsequent coding of the observations, were based on the individual experiences of each child. For example, if Tish (pseudonym) was in the low-reading group, then the forms of instruction and interaction in that group were what she was tallied as having experienced, in addition to any whole-class language arts. That is, if Tish was in Classroom 1 or 3, then her language arts instruction was a combination of whole-class and reading-group instruction; if Tish was in Classroom 2 or 4, then her language arts instruction occurred solely in a reading group. When the class was divided into reading groups, we concentrated our coding on what went on in individual reading groups when the teacher was instructing them. Thus, we focused on the experiences Tish had when she was in a reading group with the teacher present, not on what she was doing at her seat when the teacher was working with another reading group.

The procedure we employed was to write a running narrative while in the classroom. We later coded the narrative by listing the four (if that many) primary activities during language arts that each child experienced (e.g., choral reading a little book, listening to a teacher read aloud a trade book, writing in a journal, pair reading of a basal). Similarly, we listed the four (if that many) major reading materials a child experienced during language arts (e.g., trade books, Big Books, phonics worksheets), the major strategies to word identification that were experienced (e.g., use of context, use of initial consonant plus context), and the focal unit of this instruction (e.g., whole word, rime).

We initially intended to record the actual time children spent simply reading. This proved impossible for two reasons. First, children often shared a book (sometimes between a pair, sometimes in a group), making it very hard to determine whose eyes were actually falling on the printed words. Second, even when each child had a copy of the text (e.g., in round-robin reading), it was apparent that many children were not looking at the text.

Each observer was a reading specialist. During the first 2 months of the school year there were often two observers in the same classroom. After the observations, the two observers coded their individual narratives into the top four activities, materials, strategies, and linguistic units that were observed in a particular reading group or during whole-class instruction. We discontinued having two observers in a classroom when they consistently achieved 94% interrater reliability—that is, until the same codes were applied 94% of the time. At the end of the year, all narratives were independently coded by two reading specialists. Interrater reliability was .97. Examples of observations and codes applied from each of the four classrooms appear in the Appendix. These examples were chosen because they are typical of the form of instruction in each classroom.

Assessments. We assessed every child in the four first-grade classrooms in September, December, and May on the individually administered Book Buddies Early Literacy Screening (BBELS—an early literacy screening procedure expanded from that used in Book Buddies; Johnston, Invernizzi, & Juel, 1998). The BBELS assessment includes two parts. Part 1 assesses both early literacy understandings involved in word recognition and word recognition itself. Part 2 assesses ability to read and comprehend passages. Details of test development, from its clinical roots to its current evolution into a statewide assessment, can be found in Invernizzi, Robey, and Moon (1998).

BBELS Part 1 includes assessments of alphabet knowledge, letter-sound awareness (including phonemic awareness and invented spelling), concept of word, and word recognition in isolation. Alphabet knowledge is assessed by having children both name and produce the letters of the alphabet. In the naming task, the letters are printed in lowercase. In the production task, case is not considered in scoring the child's printed letters. Letter-sound awareness is assessed by three tasks: (1) Children sort picture cards under the letter matching the beginning phoneme, (2) children provide a letter sound as the tester points to a letter, and (3) children write words pronounced by the tester. The spellings produced in this third task are later scored by the number of phonemes represented. Concept of word refers to the emergent reader's ability to match spoken to written words as she reads (Morris, 1981; Roberts, 1992). It is assessed by two tasks: (1) Children point to each printed word with their finger as they recite a short memorized text, and (2) they go back and identify target words within a line of the text. Word recognition is assessed by having children read word lists that represent levels from preprimer through third grade. BBELS Part 2 consists of oral reading and comprehension of increasingly difficult passages. The passages range from early preprimer level through third grade. Subtest alpha reliability coefficients range from .78 to .91.

We also assessed every child on the word-reading subtest of the Wide Range Achievement Test (WRAT, 1994) in September, December, and May. This test is individually administered. Children are asked to read from a list of 42 words. The words range in difficulty from *cat* to *terpsichorean*. The test-retest reliability is .98.

In December and May, each child read five decodable words and five sight words that were specific to their reading groups. The purpose of this testing was to see if the children were learning what they had specifically been taught. The sight words had received specific direct instruction in the reading group as whole words (and they generally appeared on a class word wall). Typical sight words in December were *is*, *the*, and *we* for a low group; *get*, *had*, and *put* for a middle group; and *there*, *some*, and *with* for a high group. The decodable words contained elements that had been the object of direct instruction in the group (e.g., initial consonants, rimes, short vowels). Typical decodable words in December were *rat*, *pig*, and *ball* for a low group; *frog*, *that*, and *dig* for a middle group; and *flat*, *smell*, and *drop* for a high group.

In addition to these word lists, we created two stories that had the same pictures but had different degrees of word difficulty (see Johnston et al., 1998, for an example of the form of these short stories). The first story contained words similar to those encountered in the low-reading groups, while the second story contained words that were similar to those encountered in the high-reading groups. The stories contained both decodable and sight words. If children had considerable difficulty with the first story, they were not asked to read the second story. Children's strategies for decoding both words on the word lists and the short stories were assessed in a think-aloud procedure.

Children were assessed individually on reading the words and asked to explain how they figured out how to pronounce each word (whether or not it was correctly pronounced). They were encouraged to make comments as they actually attempted to decode a word. The comments of the children generally fell into the following categories: sound and blend an onset and rime, sound and blend phonemes, look for help from the class word wall, try to figure out what made sense or was a meaningful word, combine the first letter sound with what made sense, state that it "looks like" the word, state that they "had it before" or "just knew" because recognition was automatic.

If a child said she recognized *tan* because it had /t/ and /an/, it was considered a sound and blend onset-rime strategy. If a child, instead, demonstrated sounding and blending each phoneme, as in /t/,/a/,/n/, it was considered a sound and blend phonemes strategy. If a child looked at the word wall for a match, it was considered a word wall strategy. If a child suggested it had to be a color word, and *tan* made sense, it was considered a meaning strategy. If the child said the first sound, /t/, and then tried to figure out what made sense, it was considered a first letter plus sense strategy. If a child said, "It looks like...," it was considered a visual strategy. If a child gave a phonics-like statement such as a reference to a rule or one letter sound it was labeled a phonics statement.

Results

Classroom Instruction

As previously described, the four classrooms had similar demographics and each was organized into three reading groups, with approximately the same number of children per group. An analysis of variance (ANOVA) of September assessments on BBELS and the WRAT showed no statistically significant differences on mean scores among the classrooms. In September, children in all four low-reading groups could not identify all the letters of the alphabet and could print fewer of them, appeared to lack a solid concept of word, demonstrated little phonemic awareness or knowledge of letter sounds, and could not read any words on the WRAT. Children in the middle groups generally knew most or all of the letters of the alphabet, demonstrated some phonemic awareness and some knowledge of letter sounds in their spelling, and could read a couple of words on the WRAT. Children in the high groups were all reading at least early first-grade materials, and some were fluent decoders of almost any late first- or early second-grade–level texts. Classroom 1 had two children in the high group who were especially advanced readers at the beginning of first grade.

The structure of each classroom in terms of overall number of children in the class and in each reading group was nearly identical. Smooth classroom management was observed in each classroom. Our assessments indicated that the spread of literacy profiles of the children in each classroom was very similar. Yet, considerable variation was observed in instructional practices among the four classrooms. In fact, there was as much difference between the two classrooms at the same school as there was across schools.

In some classrooms the types of activities differed considerably between the fall and spring. Phonics, for example, might be a dominant activity during the fall but not in the spring. In the tables that describe each classroom, we attempt to capture this kind of difference by separating the data into September through December and January through May time periods.

As we discussed, of the 1½ hours available for language arts, teachers in Classrooms 1 and 3 devoted some of this time to whole-class instruction while teachers in Classrooms 2 and 4 did not. The tables reflect the percentage of activities that went on during this 1½ hours. Thus, for Classrooms 1 and 3 whole-class instruction is included. The percentage of language arts activities devoted to the word wall in Classroom 1 was 26%, for children in the low-reading group in the fall (Table 1). That is, out of all the language arts activities these children experienced during the 1½ hours of language arts, 26% of them involved the word wall. Most of their experience with the word wall occurred in whole-class instruction, but follow-up might occur in their reading group. Although the percentages listed for activities are quite correlated with time, they are not the same. There is a synonymous nature of many classroom activities. Word wall activities in Classroom 1, for example, involved spelling and writing: A child could be staring at a word on the word wall as he was spelling it out loud.

Classroom 1. Classroom 1 was the most traditional of the classrooms. During both the fall and spring semesters, the class format for language arts was an opening whole-class activity using a word wall, followed by reading-group instruction (Tables 1 and 2). The word wall was the dominant means of introducing words to the class. Its structure was always identical. The sequence was to spell the new word, clapping for each letter, and then to write each word three times and use one new word in a sentence (see Appendix). Approximately five new words were introduced each week. During reading-group time, some of these words might be revisited.

In Classroom 1, reading groups were conducted frequently in a round-robin fashion, especially in the spring (Table 2). Even with the addition of little books to the classroom, this teacher and the other teachers all found a need to create additional text for the low-group children to read. During the fall, Teacher 1 used little books and text she wrote on the board (usually containing word wall words)

TABLE 1
Overall Percentage of Activities and the Specific Forms of Those Activities in Classroom 1, September–December

	Low Group %	Middle Group %	High Group %
Reading Text	38	36	32
How:			
Individual reading	29	21	23
Choral reading	21	21	15
Round-robin reading	29	42	39
Free-choice reading	14	11	15
Rereading	7	5	8
In what:			
Basal readers	6	14	6
Little books	23	17	18
Trade books	12	22	29
Board books	53	43	47
Child-made books	6	4	0
Writing Text	17	11	15
Form:			
Individual text writing	50	50	50
Journal	50	50	50
Word Wall Sight Words[a]	26	19	20
Spelling Words	11	13	13
Phonics	0	3	2
Form:			
Phonics worksheets	0	100	100
Phonemic Awareness	3	2	1
Form:			
Rhyming	100	100	100
Meaning of Text Discussion	0	6	5
Text Grammar/Punctuation	5	10	12

[a] Whole-class activity with occasional group follow-up.

for the low group. The materials for her three reading groups were not that dissimilar in the fall, though the level of little books used differed among the groups (Table 1). The little books employed in the middle and high groups were less predictable and longer than those used in the low group. In the spring, each of the three reading groups read more from the basal than from other types of texts (Table 2). The format of the reading groups, such as a heavy use of round-robin reading, was the same across the groups; only the level of what was read differed.

Topics for writing assignments and time for individual journal writing were the same across the reading groups.

In Classroom 1, most direct word-recognition instruction occurred during the opening language arts activity of the whole-class word wall exercise. This activity constituted about 20% of the language arts activities from September through May for all children (Tables 1 and 2). In general, children in the class frequently focused on the sequential letters in a word, by spelling the word both orally and in writing (see Appendix). In reading groups, the word wall was also consulted. There was practically no phonics instruction; word-recognition development was very tied to the basic word wall activity.

TABLE 2
Overall Percentage of Activities and the Specific Forms of Those Activities in Classroom 1, January–May

	Low Group %	Middle Group %	High Group %
Reading Text	27	24	20
How:			
Choral reading	17	0	0
Round-robin reading	83	71	100
Rereading	0	29	0
In what:			
Basal readers	38	55	71
Little books	25	0	0
Trade books	0	0	29
Board books	37	44	0
Writing Text	17	13	21
Form:			
Individual text writing	100	100	100
Word Wall Sight Words[a]	31	20	32
Spelling Words	17	17	21
Phonics	4	3	0
Form:			
Phonics worksheets	100	100	0
Phonemic Awareness	0	7	0
Form:			
Rhyming	0	100	0
Read-Aloud by Teacher	4	7	5
Meaning of Text Discussion	0	9	0

[a] Whole-class activity with occasional group follow-up.

TABLE 3
Percentage of Units Used in Word-Recognition Instruction and Strategies
Provided to Low-Reading Group Children in Classroom 1

	September–December %	January–May %
Primary Units		
Initial consonants	34	8
Rimes	8	0
Short vowels	0	8
Long vowels	0	17
Initial consonant blend	0	25
Medial consonants	8	0
Final consonant digraph	0	8
Whole word	50	34
Primary Strategies		
Child asked if it makes sense	13	13
Child asked to reread	22	0
Child asked to spell word	20	13
Child given a phonics statement[a]	0	11
Told it is on word wall	11	13
Child told to predict what might be	11	0
Teacher tells child the word	23	50

[a] A statement like "There is a silent letter."

In Classroom 1, word-recognition instruction in the low-reading group was of the same form and duration as that in the middle- and high-reading groups. As described, it occurred primarily in the whole-class word wall activity. No more than 4% of the activities we saw involved phonics instruction, and these activities were solely with phonics worksheets (Tables 1 and 2). Likewise, there was very little phonemic awareness work, and what there was consisted of rhyming words (Tables 1 and 2). There was little attention paid to word units other than initial consonants and whole words (Table 3). The teacher was never observed modeling sounding and blending units within words. If a child came to an unknown word in a text, she was told to consider the meaning of the text, to predict, to reread, to spell the word, or to look on the word wall. Frequently the teacher simply told the child the word (Table 3).

Classroom 2. Classroom 2 was next-door to Classroom 1. The two classrooms were very distinct, however. Children in Classroom 2 spent almost all their language arts time either in a reading group or in reading-group–related assignments. The teacher in Classroom 2 made up for the relatively small number of books for very beginning readers by creating many charts and individual little books.

This practice was especially common during the fall semester for the low- and middle-reading groups. Typically, the teacher had printed a poem on a chart and after a reading group read and discussed the chart, each child was given a copy of the poem in the form of a little book (Appendix; Tables 4 and 5). The poem might

TABLE 4
Overall Percentage of Activities and the Specific Forms of Those Activities in Classroom 2, September–December

	Low Group %	Middle Group %	High Group %
Reading Text	42	39	30
How:			
Individual reading	50	56	0
Choral reading	30	33	33
Round-robin reading	20	11	67
In what:			
Poem on chart	40	35	0
Poem copied for child	20	21	0
Teacher-made chart	0	20	0
Text copied for child	0	6	33
Basal readers	20	0	0
Little books	0	6	0
Magazines	20	6	20
Trade books	0	6	47
Writing Text	4	4	20
Form:			
Individual text writing	100	100	100
Word Wall Sight Words	9	9	10
Phonics	26	27	20
Form:			
Sorting words by pattern	39	20	0
Writing for sounds	17	40	50
Phonics worksheets	17	20	50
Make word with letter cards	17	0	0
Word families on chart	10	20	0
Phonemic Awareness	11	9	10
Form:			
Sorting pictures by sound	75	60	0
Rhyming	25	40	100
Letter Identification/Formation	4	0	0
Meaning of Text Discussion	4	0	0
Text Grammar/Punctuation	0	12	10

TABLE 5
Overall Percentage of Activities and the Specific Forms of Those Activities in Classroom 2, January–May

	Low Group %	Middle Group %	High Group %
Reading Text	32	51	64
How:			
Individual reading	25	29	25
Choral reading	25	29	33
Round-robin reading	50	42	42
In what:			
Poem on chart	0	12	12
Poem copied for child	0	0	0
Teacher-made chart	12	18	19
Text copied for child	11	0	0
Basal readers	11	0	0
Little books	11	29	25
Trade books	11	12	13
Big books	11	12	6
Board books	33	17	25
Writing Text	7	6	2
Form:			
Individual text writing	100	100	100
Word Wall Sight Words	7	3	4
Spelling Words	8	3	4
Phonics	38	19	9
Form:			
Writing for sounds	20	17	0
Phonics worksheets	40	33	100
Word families on chart	40	50	0
Meaning of Text Discussion	0	6	9
Vocabulary Discussion	0	6	4
Text Grammar/Punctuation	7	6	4

differ between the middle- and low-reading groups in response to the children's skill in word recognition. Even when the poems were the same across the two groups, the words singled out for discussion would be different, corresponding to the different word-recognition skill needs. In contrast, during the fall, the high-reading group mainly read from text (not poems) copied on a chart, magazines, or trade books (Table 4). In all three reading groups, the form of reading ranged from round-robin reading to choral reading (where all children simultaneously pointed to words in text as they read the text aloud) to individual text reading (Tables 4 and 5).

In Classroom 2, most direct word-recognition instruction occurred during reading groups. All three reading groups received phonics instruction during the year (Tables 4 and 5). The use of poetry in the low- and middle-reading groups lent itself to a focus on onsets and rimes and making analogies to words with similar units. After reading the chart poem, the students often first choral read and then individually read a little book copy of it. Teacher 2 was fairly insistent that children finger-point to words as they read text. After these readings, the children frequently read teacher-made charts with similar rhyming words, sorted word cards on charts based on their rime unit, worked on worksheets to identify the rimes, and wrote words as they were slowly segmented into onsets and rime units by the teacher (a form of writing for sound activity; Tables 4 and 5). Phonics activities across the groups ranged from 20% to 38% of the language arts period activities (Tables 4 and 5).

Especially during the fall semester, Teacher 2 made considerable use of hands-on materials in phonemic awareness and phonics instruction. Children in the low and middle groups frequently sorted word cards into categories based on orthographic patterns or sorted picture cards on the basis of sounds.

During the fall, children in the low group in Classroom 2 were provided with considerable modeling by their teacher about how to chunk words into their component units (Table 6). They frequently made an analogy between a rime in a key word and lists of unknown words. In the spring, the teacher was especially insistent on combining what made sense in text with known chunks such as rime units. In general, the focal units were onsets and rimes, though other consonant units also were examined (Table 6).

Classroom 3. Students in Classroom 3 were allowed more freedom to move around the room than in the other three classrooms. This was productive movement, with children going to pick out a book to read individually or with a buddy, going to the writing center to write, or moving to their reading group. The general format for language arts was to begin with a relatively long morning message during which various literacy skills were interwoven in writing the news from home, the schedule for the day, or text the teacher had written on the chalkboard. After the morning message, the children frequently were observed reading or writing individually or in pairs.

Classroom 3 was filled with more books than the other three classrooms, especially trade books. During the first semester, Teacher 3 found, as did the teachers in the other classrooms, a dearth of reading materials suitable for the beginning reader. Like Teacher 2, she made frequent use of poetry on charts, as well as other chart text (Table 7). During the spring, many more trade books were used across all reading groups (Table 8). Teacher 3 never used the basal reader.

TABLE 6
**Percentage of Units Used in Word-Recognition Instruction and Strategies
Provided to Low-Reading Group Children in Classroom 2**

	September–December %	January–May %
Primary Units		
Initial consonants	45	20
Rimes	20	36
Initial consonant blends	5	5
Final consonants	10	0
Short vowels	0	13
Initial consonant digraphs	10	0
Long vowels	0	13
Whole word	10	13
Primary Strategies		
Teacher models and helps segment word into chunks[a]	23	0
Teacher models combining what makes sense with known letter sounds	0	16
Finger-pointing and other modeling of text by teacher	15	12
Child told to use first letter(s) and what makes sense	8	0
Child told to sound and blend onset and rime	8	12
Child told to sound and blend letter sounds	0	12
Child asked if it makes sense	8	0
Child asked to put finger under word	8	0
Child told to "get mouth ready"	8	0
Child reminded of word family	8	12
Child asked to reread	0	12
Teacher says, "It rhymes with __."	0	24
Teacher tells child the word	14	0

[a] Generally onset and rime but sometimes syllables or little words in big words.

TABLE 7
Overall Percentage of Activities and the Specific Forms of Those Activities in Classroom 3, September–December

	Low Group %	Middle Group %	High Group %
Reading Text	30	30	44
How:			
Individual reading	20	33	43
Choral reading	60	56	43
Rereading	20	11	14
In what:			
Poem on chart	30	13	27
Teacher-made chart	20	5	9
Little books	10	38	27
Trade books	10	19	10
Big Books	10	10	0
Board books	10	10	18
Overhead	10	5	9
Writing Text	22	14	14
Form:			
Individual text writing	40	0	0
Journal writing	10	0	0
Morning message[a]	50	100	100
Word Wall Sight Words	6	3	7
Spelling Words	18	3	7
Phonics	6	10	0
Form:			
Writing for sounds	100	100	0
Peer Coaching	6	17	7
Concept of Word	6	3	0
Read-Aloud by Teacher	0	3	7
Meaning of Text Discussion	6	14	7
Form:			
Discussion	100	50	100
Expressive reading	0	50	0
Vocabulary Discussion	0	3	0
Text Grammar/Punctuation	0	0	7

[a] Whole-class activity with occasional group follow-up.

TABLE 8
Overall Percentage of Activities and the Specific Forms of Those Activities in Classroom 3, January–May

	Low Group %	Middle Group %	High Group %
Reading Text	24	29	29
How:			
Individual reading	37	43	60
Choral reading	13	33	30
Rereading	24	8	10
Pair reading	13	8	0
Free reading	13	8	0
In what:			
Poem on chart	6	17	7
Teacher-made chart	11	5	7
Little books	17	34	36
Trade books	36	22	29
Big Books	10	5	7
Board books	11	5	7
Child-made book	9	12	7
Writing Text	21	24	14
Form:			
Individual text writing	33	54	57
Journal writing	33	27	29
Language experience	22	9	0
Morning message[a]	12	10	14
Word Wall Sight Words	3	3	3
Spelling Words	5	3	3
Phonics	8	6	9
Form:			
Writing for sounds	0	50	34
Phonics worksheets	100	50	66
Phonemic Awareness	9	0	0
Form:			
Rhyming	100	0	0
Peer Coaching	3	6	6
Read-Aloud by Teacher	8	7	6
Meaning of Text Discussion	11	11	14
Vocabulary Discussion	5	8	10
Text Grammar/Punctuation	3	3	6

[a] Whole-class activity with occasional group follow-up.

There was considerably more modeling of writing (through the morning message) and individual text writing in Classroom 3 than in the other four classrooms (Tables 7 and 8). Children in the low group also engaged in several language-experience type writing activities (i.e., activities in which their sentences were dictated to the teacher on a chart or on the board).

We also observed more discussion of texts in Classroom 3 in the fall, especially in the middle-reading group (Table 7), than we saw in the other three classrooms. In the spring, the amount of text discussion across reading groups was more than what occurred in Classrooms 1 and 2, but less than that in Classroom 4.

During reading groups, Teacher 3 relied on peer coaching to facilitate word recognition. Peer coaching involved other children in the group helping a child who was having difficulty recognizing a word. When a child in a reading group could not identify a word, other children in the group were encouraged to provide a clue (see Appendix). There were suggested clues that had been taught (e.g., reread, sound it out, see if it makes sense, look at the word wall), but the children were encouraged to provide any clues they thought would help. Peer coaching was unique to Classroom 3.

There was relatively little systematic phonics instruction in Classroom 3 (Tables 7 and 8). What phonics there was came as it fell out of the trade books. In other words, there was not a preset phonics curriculum; rather, the teacher took advantage of a word in the morning message, a book, or a chart to highlight an orthographic pattern. This lack of a sequence of instruction can be seen in Table 9. Children in the low group were exposed mostly to initial consonants, long vowels, syllables, and whole words in the fall, though there is a sprinkling of phonics in almost every unit. In the spring, there was slightly more attention placed on initial consonants, but many orthographic units were commented upon. The lack of a sequence, or much time spent in direct word recognition, was purposeful. All children were expected to learn these skills in the context of reading and writing, which were dominant activities in this classroom.

Classroom 4. Teacher 4 was clearly the most phonics-oriented of the four teachers. She was also the most adamant about the behavior of her students (see Appendix). Instruction, however, differed considerably between her reading groups (Tables 10 and 11). During the fall, 39% of the activities in which the low group engaged involved phonics, 11% involved phonemic awareness, and only 17% involved reading of text. In contrast, in the high groups, 42% of the activities involved the reading of text, 8% phonics, and 8% phonemic awareness (Table 10). This differential instruction evened out more in the spring in terms of percentage of activities devoted to particular areas. Systematic phonics instruction was virtually completed in February in the low group; we then observed very similar activities across the low-, middle-, and high-reading groups—activities devoted to vocabulary development—reading text, and discussion of text (Table 11).

TABLE 9
**Percentage of Units Used in Word-Recognition Instruction and Strategies
Provided to Low-Reading Group Children in Classroom 3**

	September–December %	January–May %
Primary Units		
Initial consonants	18	23
Rimes	0	8
Final consonants	9	8
Short vowels	9	15
Long vowels	18	8
Medial consonants	0	8
Syllable	18	15
Whole word	28	15
Primary Strategies[a]		
Teacher models and helps segment word into chunks[b]	17	14
Finger-pointing and other modeling of text by teacher	25	4
Child told to sound and blend onset and rime	0	9
Child told to sound and blend letter sounds	0	9
Child asked if it makes sense	8	10
Child asked to put finger under word	8	4
Child told to "get mouth ready"	0	4
Child reminded of word family	0	4
Child asked to reread	10	4
Child asked to spell word	8	0
Child told to feel sound in mouth	8	4
Child given a phonics statement[c]	0	4
Teacher says, "It rhymes with __."	0	18
Analogy to key word on word wall	8	4
Told it is on word wall	8	4
Teacher tells child the word	0	4

[a] Most of the strategies not designated as teacher given were provided by other children in the context of peer coaching.
[b] Generally onset and rime but sometimes syllables or little words in big words.
[c] A statement like "There is a silent letter."

During the fall, the low groups most frequently read text created on charts (as occurred in all the classrooms) and read from the 1986 basal used in Classrooms 1 and 2, as well as the little books used in all the classrooms (Table 10). Like Teacher 2, this teacher was especially insistent during the fall semester that children finger-point to words as they read.

The middle group spent most of its time reading from little books (Table 10). The high group evenly split time reading from teacher-made charts, the basal, little books, and magazines (Table 10). From January through May, reading teacher-made charts dropped out as reading material in all three groups. The low group read from the basal, little books, and trade books (Table 11). The middle and high groups likewise read from the basal, little books, trade books, and also from Big Books.

TABLE 10
Overall Percentage of Activities and the Specific Forms of Those Activities in Classroom 4, September–December

	Low Group %	Middle Group %	High Group %
Reading Text	17	26	42
How:			
Individual reading	33	20	20
Choral reading	67	60	40
Round-robin reading	0	0	20
Free-choice reading	0	0	20
Rereading	0	20	0
In what:			
Teacher-made chart	50	17	25
Basal readers	25	0	25
Little books	25	66	25
Magazines	0	0	25
Board books	0	17	0
Writing Text	0	0	8
Form:			
Individual text writing	0	0	100
Word Wall Sight Words	11	11	18
Phonics	39	33	8
Form:			
Sorting words by pattern	66	33	0
Writing for sound	17	23	98
Phonics worksheets	17	22	0
Child chalkboard	0	22	2
Phonemic Awareness	11	11	8
Form:			
Sorting pictures by sound	100	100	100
Letter Identification/Formation	11	14	0
Meaning of Text Discussion	0	0	8
Text Grammar/Punctuation	11	5	8

TABLE 11
Overall Percentage of Activities and the Specific Forms of Those Activities in Classroom 4, January–May

	Low Group %	Middle Group %	High Group %
Reading Text	25	21	25
How:			
Individual reading	16	0	40
Choral reading	52	25	20
Round-robin reading	32	75	0
Free-choice reading	0	0	20
Pair reading	0	0	20
In what:			
Basal readers	33	20	43
Little books	33	20	14
Trade books	17	40	29
Big Books	0	20	14
Writing Text	0	0	10
Form:			
Individual text writing	0	0	100
Word Wall Sight Words	4	5	5
Phonics	16	10	10
Form:			
Sorting words by pattern	50	0	15
Writing for sound	25	0	14
Phonics worksheets	25	50	28
Child chalkboard	0	50	43
Read-Aloud by Teacher	13	16	15
Vocabulary Discussion	13	16	20
Meaning of Text Discussion	21	16	10
Text Grammar/Punctuation	8	16	5

Teacher 4 showed the most change in her instructional practices before and after December in each of her reading groups. After December, the children in each group were considerably more involved in vocabulary and text discussions than they had been during the fall. These discussions were based both on text read aloud by the teacher and text read during reading groups (Tables 10 and 11).

As stated, during the fall semester the low group engaged in many phonics activities. The phonics activities were very hands-on. Seventeen percent of the phonics activities involved writing for sounds, sometimes on phonics worksheets as in the sample in the Appendix. Sixty-six percent of the phonics activities involved sorting word cards into categories based on orthographic patterns (e.g., making columns of words that differed in their rimes or short vowels; Table 10). Likewise, phonemic awareness activities always involved the hands-on process of sorting pictures by their component sounds (e.g., put all the initial /b/ pictures, such as the pictures of the bear and the bat, in one column and the initial /s/ pictures, such as the pictures of the sink and the sun, in another column).

There was a preset phonics curriculum in Classroom 4. At the beginning of the year, initial consonants were stressed. The children were encouraged to use the first letter(s) in an unknown word and what made sense to identify an unknown word in text. Rimes were added quickly, and these rimes received heavy emphasis, especially in word sorts (Table 12). During this time, the teacher modeled segmenting words into onset and rime chunks and encouraged children

TABLE 12
Percentage of Units Used in Word-Recognition Instruction and Strategies Provided to Low-Reading Group Children in Classroom 4

	September–December %	January–May[a] %
Primary Units		
Initial consonants	23	0
Rimes	44	50[b]
Initial consonant blends	11	0
Final consonants	11	0
Short vowels	11	50
Primary Strategies		
Teacher models and helps segment word into chunks[c]	18	0
Teacher models and helps sound and blend letter sounds	5	0
Teacher models combining what makes sense with known letter sounds	5	30
Child told to use first letter(s) and what makes sense	17	0
Child told to sound and blend letter sounds	11	20
Child asked if it makes sense	5	20
Child asked if it looks like the word	17	10
Child asked to spell word	11	0
Child asked to put finger under word	11	0
Child told to feel sound in mouth	0	10
Teacher tells child the word	0	10

[a] Direct phonics instruction was completed by the end of February.

[b] Rimes in the fall included many short vowels, such as /an/, while the winter included many long vowel rimes, such as /ain/.

[c] Generally onset and rime but sometimes syllables or little words in big words.

to find these chunks in an unknown word (Table 12). At the same time, however, the rime unit was also broken down into its individual phonemes, especially during the writing for sounds activities (see Appendix). As the year progressed, the teacher increasingly modeled and encouraged children to sound and blend individual letter sounds to recognize a word (Table 12).

As mentioned earlier, systematic phonics instruction in Classroom 4 was completed by the end of February. In January and February, phonics instruction focused on rimes and short vowels. Often, words with long vowel rimes (e.g., /oat/ as in *boat* or *float*) were contrasted with words with short vowel rimes (e.g., /at/ in *bat* or *flat*). Short vowels also received much attention, especially when writing for sounds. During this time, the teacher modeled—and expected children to combine—what made sense with known letter sounds to identify an unknown word in text. She frequently asked a child to sound and blend the individual letter sounds in a word and consider what made sense (Table 12).

Summary of the Four Classrooms. Table 13 highlights the similarities and differences among instructional activities in the four classrooms. The reading and writing of texts was the activity all reading groups engaged in most extensively, except those in Classroom 4. Throughout the school year, about 40% or more of the language arts activities in all reading groups, except those in Classroom 4, involved reading and writing text.

Phonics and phonemic awareness activities were much more common in Classrooms 2 and 4 than in Classrooms 1 and 3. From September through December, 3% of the activities in the low-reading group in Classroom 1 involved

TABLE 13
A Comparison of Percentage of Activities Across Classrooms

Classrooms	1	2	3	4	1	2	3	4	1	2	3	4
	Low Group (%)				Middle Group (%)				High Group (%)			
September Through December												
Reading and writing text	55	46	52	17	47	43	44	26	47	50	58	50
Phonics and phonemic awareness	3	37	6	50	3	36	10	44	3	30	0	16
Word wall and spelling	37	9	24	11	32	9	6	11	33	10	14	18
Vocabulary and text discussion	0	4	6	0	6	0	17	0	5	0	7	8
January Through May												
Reading and writing text	44	39	45	25	37	57	53	21	41	66	43	35
Phonics and phonemic awareness	4	38	17	16	10	19	6	10	0	9	9	10
Word wall and spelling	37	15	8	4	32	6	6	5	33	8	6	5
Vocabulary and text discussion	0	0	16	34	6	12	19	32	5	13	24	30

phonics and, similarly, 6% of the activities in Classroom 3 involved phonics. In sharp contrast, during this same time, 50% of the activities in the low-reading group in Classroom 4 involved phonics as did 37% of the activities in Classroom 2. None of the classrooms used phonics readers. The form of the phonics instruction involved reading teacher-made charts and poems and the extensive use of word and picture sorts. There were some differences between Classrooms 2 and 4 in the phonics instruction, again as described previously in more detail. These differences were (a) although both teachers made use of onsets and rimes, Teacher 4 more frequently broke the rime unit into individual letter sounds, whereas Teacher 2 treated a key rime in a word as a source for analogies to other words; (b) the phonics curriculum was more preset in Classroom 4 than in Classroom 2; and (c) phonics instruction stayed at about the same level in Classroom 2 throughout the year, whereas systematic phonics instruction ceased in Classroom 4 by the end of February.

Teachers in Classrooms 1 and 3 relied on a class word wall and spelling activities to foster word recognition more than they did direct phonics instruction (Table 13). Word wall and spelling activities in these two classrooms emphasized the visual letter strings of words. It should be noted that spelling differs from writing for sounds—the latter is considered a phonics activity. This is because the emphasis in spelling is on memorizing correct spellings, whereas writing for sounds emphasizes translating sounds into letters (see Appendix).

There was relatively little development of oral vocabulary or discussion of the meaning of texts from September through December, except in the middle-reading group in Classroom 3 (Table 13). There was a marked increase in activities involving discussion of vocabulary and text after December, especially in Classrooms 3 and 4 (Table 13). During this second semester, the percentage of language arts activities devoted to vocabulary and text discussion ranged from a low of none in the low groups in Classrooms 1 and 2 to 16% in the low-reading group in Classroom 3 and 34% in the low-reading group in Classroom 4.

The Impact of Instruction on Reading Measures

Overall Reading Differences for the Four Classrooms. The differences in instructional practices among the four classrooms appeared related to growth in reading skill. Despite a lack of significant difference on BBELS or the WRAT in September, an analysis of covariance (ANCOVA) conducted between children in the four different first-grade classrooms at the end of the year revealed statistically significant differences in reading skill. Children's end-of-the-year BBELS assessment (Part 2) passage reading scores, using scores on Part 1 in September as a covariate, indicated a statistically significant difference in reading growth among children from the four classrooms, $F(3, 50) = 6.69$, $p < .001$ (Figure 1). Follow-up pairwise contrasts were conducted using a Bonferroni adjustment to control for Type I errors. These comparisons revealed consistent differences among all the classrooms, which can be summarized succinctly by the ranking $4 > 3 > 2 > 1$. Overall

FIGURE 1

**Mean Words Correctly Read on Graded Passages in September and May
on BBELS Part 2 and Predicted BBELS Part 2 Performance
Based on Early Literacy Skills in September as Assessed by BBELS Part 1**

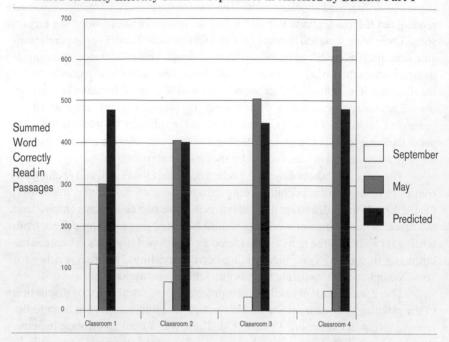

means on the passage reading showed that, in May of first grade, children in Classroom 4 were reading on a late-second-grade level; children in Classroom 3 were reading on a mid-second-grade level; children in Classroom 2 were reading at an end-of-first-grade level; and children in Classroom 1 were reading at a primer level.

The covariate in the above ANCOVA analysis, Part 1 scores on BBELS in September, was used to predict overall scores on Part 2 in May. The predicted scores can be compared with the actual scores on BBELS Part 2 in May (Figure 1). Children in Classrooms 3 and 4 exceeded predictions on reading passages on BBELS Part 2 in May based on their entering literacy levels assessed on BBELS Part 1 in September. Classroom 2 lived up to what was predicted. Classroom 1 fell below. Overall, in three of the four classrooms, the mean reading level on both BBELS and the WRAT was at least an end-of-first grade level—a level that would make many parents, teachers, and administrators happy.

A Reading Group by Classroom Type of Interaction. There was a surprising interaction, however. Children in the low-reading group in Classroom 3 were relatively poor readers at the end of first grade (Table 14; Figure 2). On the other

TABLE 14
Low-Group Word Recognition While Reading Passages

	Classroom 1	Classroom 2	Classroom 3	Classroom 4
December				
Preprimer 1				
M	55.5	83.5	7.6	77.3
SD	32.9	14.9	16.9	10.2
May				
Preprimer 3				
M	92.9	100.0	91.8	100.0
SD	10.6	.0	7.1	.0
Primer				
M	83.0	87.5	80.7	94.0
SD	11.1	16.7	17.1	3.5
End first grade				
M		86.7		91.3
SD		12.7		5.8

The values represent mean percentages of correctly read words on the specified grade-level passages. Children in Classrooms 1 and 3 were not asked to read the end-of-first-grade passages as they were at frustration level on the primer level passages.

FIGURE 2
Growth on WRAT in Low-Reading Groups

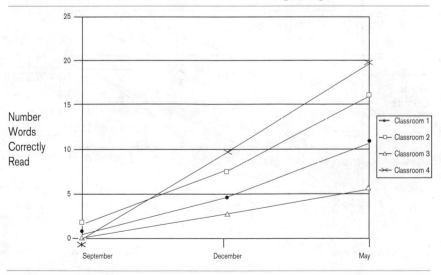

hand, a child in the middle or high group of Classroom 3, who entered with middle-range early literacy skills (e.g., alphabet knowledge, spelling-sound knowledge), was likely to make exceptional growth in reading during the year. In fact, nine children who entered Classroom 3 with literacy skills in the middle range exited with reading skills one standard deviation above the mean. This interaction can be observed by comparing Figure 2 (Growth on WRAT in low-reading groups) with Figure 3 (Growth on WRAT in middle-reading groups) and Figure 4 (Growth on WRAT in high-reading groups).

Children in the low groups in the four classrooms did not differ statistically significantly from one another on any of the BBELS subtests or on the WRAT in September (Figure 2). Of these low-group children, only those in Classrooms 2 and 4 were reading near grade level at the end of first grade (Table 14; Figure 2). Classroom 4 was the only classroom in which almost all the low-group children were reading at an end-of-first-grade level in May, with a mean score of 91.3% word recognition on end-of-year-first-grade passages (Table 14). The very poor development in word recognition of low-group children in Classroom 3 was evident as early as December. In December, these children could barely read at all, with a mean score of 7.6% on a first-level preprimer passage (this is a level of book normally read well before December in first grade).

FIGURE 3
Growth on WRAT in Middle-Reading Groups

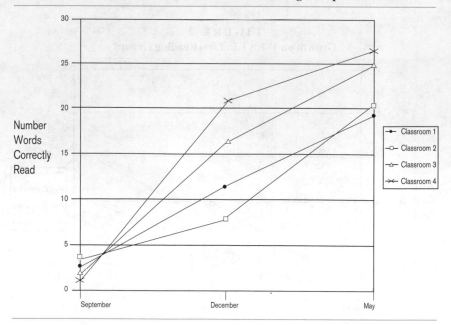

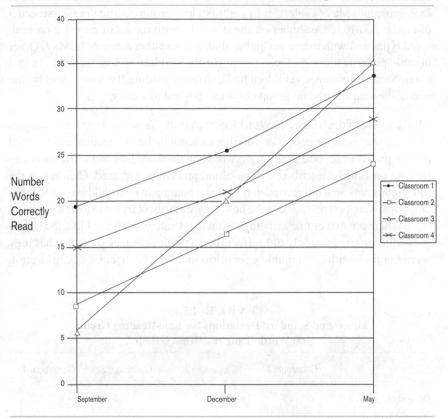

FIGURE 4
Growth on WRAT in High-Reading Groups

Table 14 reports the means and standard deviations for words correctly read during oral reading of graded passages on BBELS Part 2. We did measure comprehension of these passages, but comprehension was limited by the children's ability to read the words in the passages. That is, children could not comprehend passages in which they failed to identify many words. At the first-grade level, reading comprehension is ruled by word-recognition ability (Juel, Griffith, & Gough, 1986).

Performance of Children on Reading Words They Had Been Taught. In terms of being able to read what they specifically had been taught in their reading groups, all children in Classroom 4 did well, with an especially impressive performance by the low-group children. Recall that we had asked the children to read five sight words (usually word wall words) and five decodable words (ones whose spelling patterns had received attention). In Classroom 4, the children had mean scores between 3.8 and 4.5 on both sight and decodable words in December and May (Table 15). In contrast, low-group children in Classroom 3 did quite poorly in December on these words, with means of only 1.2 on both word types and with means no higher than 3.2 on either measure in May. Other notable patterns included those found for the children in Classroom 1. In this classroom the low-group children had difficulty reading the words, and by the end of the year the middle-group children also had difficulty.

Strategies Children Used in Word Recognition. Table 16 shows the strategies (whether they were successful or not) that children in the low-reading groups used as they read both decodable and sight words on the word lists and in the short stories. As previously described, a think-aloud procedure was used. Children in the low groups, whose word recognition was less automatic than children in the higher groups, were best able to describe how they went about trying to identify a word.

There are two primary findings from this strategy analysis. First, the strategies children tried to apply did reflect the strategies (or lack of such) that they were taught—with one notable exception that will be discussed. Children in

TABLE 15
Means and Standard Deviations for Low-Reading Groups
on Words Taught to That Group

	Classroom 1	Classroom 2	Classroom 3	Classroom 4
December				
Decodable words				
M	2.5	3.5	1.2	4.5
SD	1.9	1.9	1.3	1.0
Sight words				
M	1.7	3.5	1.2	3.8
SD	1.8	1.7	.8	1.0
May				
Decodable words				
M	2.1	3.8	2.6	4.0
SD	2.0	1.9	1.8	1.2
Sight words				
M	3.0	3.8	3.2	4.0
SD	1.9	1.9	.8	.0

The values represent the mean number of words correctly read on a list of five words of each type. Decodable words are ones with linguistic units that received instruction in the reading group. Sight words are ones that were taught as whole words in the reading group, generally on the word wall.

TABLE 16
**Percentage of Strategies Tried as Indicated in Think-Alouds
by Low-Reading Group Children**

Classroom 1		Classroom 2		Classroom 3		Classroom 4	
December							
Decodable Words							
Visual	50	S & B phonemes	25	S & B phonemes	20	Meaning	25
Spell	17	S & B onset/rime	25	Visual	60	S & B phonemes	50
Word wall	33	"Had before"	25	Spell	20	Visual	25
		First letter + sense	25				
Sight Words							
Visual	50	Word wall	100	Visual	60	S & B phonemes	25
Spell	17			S & B onset/rime	20	Spell	50
Word wall	33			Meaning	20	Word wall	25
May							
Decodable Words							
S & B phonemes	14	First letter + sense	50	S & B phonemes	20	S & B phonemes	50
S & B onset/rime	14	Word wall	25	S & B onset/rime	20	Visual	25
Visual	29	Just knew (fast)	25	Visual	60	Phonic statement	25
Phonic statement	14						
Word wall	29						
Sight Words							
Visual	29	First letter + sense	20	S & B phonemes	20	Visual	75
Word wall	71	Word wall	40	Visual	80	Phonic statement	25
		Just knew (fast)	20				
		Visual	20				

S & B stands for sound and blend.

Classroom 1 were not taught strategies: The emphasis was on the visual array of letters, memorizing word spellings, and learning words on the word wall. They were not taught orthographic spelling patterns. Their strategies in December reflect this visual orientation; decodable and sight words are approached in the same fashion. Likewise, children in Classroom 3 mainly applied visual strategies throughout the year. Reflecting their instruction, children in Classroom 4 attempted to sound and blend the sequential phonemes represented by letters more than children in the other classrooms.

The second interesting finding reflects the notable exception mentioned above. Children in the low groups had difficulty seeing the chunks in words. Despite the heavy dose of onset and rime instruction in Classroom 2, for example, the low-group children did not recognize many of the rimes to which they had been exposed (as evidenced in their ability to read words with taught onsets and rimes).

They were not quite as successful as children in Classroom 4 in recognizing words they had been taught (Table 15) or words on the WRAT (Figure 2). During September through December, the teachers in Classrooms 2, 3, and 4 all modeled how to chunk words into their component onsets and rimes, chunk words into syllables, or find little words in big ones (Tables 6, 9, and 12). Yet children who had difficulty with word recognition did not regularly employ this strategy (Table 16). In short, poor readers did not seem to readily see the larger orthographic patterns in words.

By the end of the year, poor readers frequently tried to sound and blend by letter/phoneme, but they were not very successful at it, except in Classroom 4, where they received the most practice in the strategy. From this data, it appears that the major strategy of use to children who enter first grade with few reading skills is sounding and blending phonemes. However, it also appears that they cannot use this strategy successfully without considerable instruction, as was provided in Classroom 4.

Peer coaching in Classroom 3 seemed ineffective for children who entered first grade with minimal reading skill. Overall, as noted before, these children had poor word recognition. Despite comparatively little direct instruction in phonics, they still tried to sound and blend letter sounds and onsets and rimes, but they were quite unsuccessful at it. They were not even able to read most of the words that had been the focus of some attention in their reading groups (Table 15). It appears that the assistance provided to struggling readers by equally poor readers is unhelpful and misleading, and we hypothesize that it may damage the self-image of both. Peer coaching seemed to be more effective with children who entered first grade with some reading skill, suggesting that there is a threshold level of competence required before students can benefit from the metacognitive stance this approach seems to involve.

Compared with the poor readers, average and above-average first-grade readers frequently chunked words into patterns. At the end of first grade, the two major word identification problems of most middle- and high-group children were (a) vowel patterns other than long and short vowels and (b) separating words into syllables. These are the decoding problems, however, of children who are on track, or even advanced, in terms of their reading acquisition.

Discussion

Before we venture into a discussion, we want to be clear on the limitations of this study. Although we believe the findings raise provocative questions, and that this type of in-depth analysis is extremely useful, limitations certainly exist.

Limitations of the Current Study

This was not an experimental study, and it only involved four classrooms. The findings are provocative, but they need follow-up. In subsequent discussion of reading groups and differentiated instruction, for example, we urge caution. We did not have controlled conditions with classrooms without reading groups. We further followed these children for only one school year. We do not know whether first-grade reading placements will haunt these children, as suggested in prior research. We do not know if the time spent on word recognition in first grade, and the relatively little time spent on vocabulary development and in discussions of text that would foster world knowledge, are ultimately a good ratio. That is, we do not have a control group where a lot of emphasis was placed on these latter activities; nor are we following these children into the next grade levels.

Of course, issues raised in the current study have captured our attention. We are currently conducting a longitudinal study of a much larger number of classrooms. We remain convinced, however, that microlevel interactions within each classroom are worth capturing. We know we have learned a lot with this intermediate-level view—a view that is neither set on wide frame nor so sharply focused that it loses the background. So with the above limitations strongly evoked, we want to consider what we believe are the most important findings that should be further explored in future research.

Differential Instruction May Be Helpful in First Grade. One of the most provocative findings from this study is the indication that differential instruction may be helpful in first grade. All the teachers used homogenous reading groups. The more time incoming students with comparatively fewer early literacy skills spent in these groups—as opposed to whole-class instruction—the better they did. Further, the two classrooms that were most successful in getting them off to a good start in first grade had the most differentiated word-recognition instruction. That is, word recognition in the low-reading group was different from that in the higher groups. In fact, the classroom (Classroom 4) that had the very highest success both overall and with the low group had considerably different instruction across the groups. As compared with the other low groups, and with the other reading groups within this classroom, the focus of the low group was squarely on phonics—but only through February.

We have a well-deserved history in our field of concern over reading-group placements becoming permanent—that is, once in the low group always in the low group (Barr & Dreeben, 1983; Juel, 1990). Further, differential treatment by teachers of high- and low-reading groups has not always been considered favorable to the low-reading group children. There is evidence of differential treatment by teachers of high- and low-reading groups in praise-giving, number of higher-order questions asked, responses to reading errors, and time spent reading texts (Allington, 1980, 1984; Au, 1980; Collins, 1982; Gambrell, 1984; Hiebert, 1983; Hoffman & Baker, 1981; Pflaum, Pascarella, Boswick, & Auer, 1980). Differential treatment, however, has sometimes not been found (Weinstein, 1976) or has even been interpreted as being appropriate because children who have fewer literacy skills require different types of responses to their errors and instruction than children with more advanced skill in word recognition (West & Anderson, 1976).

At least two interesting questions emerge from the current study about homogeneous first-grade reading groups. First, are low-group children in first grade who are grade-level readers as they enter second grade automatically placed in low-reading groups there? Will, for example, the low-group children in Classroom 4—who were grade-level readers at the end of the year—be assigned to low groups with children who did not learn to read as well in first grade (such as the low groups in Classrooms 1 and 3)? Indeed, past research would suggest they will be; they will not be reshuffled. If this is the case, it might well wipe out the gains they achieved in first grade.

Second, are reading groups needed in other grade levels? That is, is there less of a need to place children in reading groups as they become swift at word recognition? Are reading groups more of a first-grade concern than they are at either earlier or later grade levels?

Phonics Is Critical for Some Children but May Not Be Helpful for Others. Certainly the finding from the current study that appeared the most clear-cut (but still subject to the limitations discussed above) was that children who entered first grade with few literacy skills benefited from a heavy dose of phonics. However, children who possessed middle-range literacy skills on entering first grade benefited from a classroom with more trade book reading and time for writing text. The apparent ability by treatment interaction was that children who entered first grade with some reading ability did exceptionally well in a classroom that included a less-structured phonics curriculum and more reading of trade books and writing of text (Classroom 3; Figures 3 and 4), whereas children who entered with fewer literacy skills benefited from a curriculum with an early word-level focus. Yet—and this needs to be underscored—with a successful early and strong dose of effective phonics and a rapid rise in word-level skill, these low-group children then benefited from the same type of increased vocabulary and text discussions, and reading from a variety of types of materials, as did their peers.

By far the most successful classroom for low-group children was characterized by phonics first and fast (see Anderson, Hiebert, Scott, & Wilkinson, 1985, for a similar recommendation). The teacher in this successful classroom provided a heavy dose of phonics at the beginning of the year for the low group and then moved on to other activities, namely vocabulary and comprehension, by February.

The Form of Phonics Matters and May Encompass Activities Not Traditionally Considered Phonics. Of course, the form of phonics instruction mattered. A structured phonics curriculum that included both onsets/rimes *and* the sound and blending of phonemes within the rimes seemed very effective.

There are two very critical points in the above statement. First, the rime unit had to be further analyzed into its component letter-phoneme correspondences, especially for children who entered first grade with little knowledge of letter sounds. This finding is in line with the research findings of Bruck and Treiman (1992), Ehri and Robbins (1992), Gaskins et al. (1996/1997), and Vandervelden and Siegel (1995)—that using analogies to rimes in key words is not an effective instructional strategy until children have a good grasp of consonant and vowel sounds. Second, it was not an either/or phenomenon of onsets and rime versus sequential letter-sound decoding. The extremely effective teacher in Classroom 4 did both simultaneously. Yet, her poorest readers were especially dependent on the sequential sounding and blending of letter sounds that this teacher modeled for them. We believe that knowledge of rimes may be exactly what ultimately helps children chunk and decode unknown words, but that children do not naturally chunk words into these units until they have been able to independently read enough text to respond fairly automatically to rime patterns.

The teacher in Classroom 4 often emphasized rimes during phonics instruction involving word sorts; but in writing for sounds (see Appendix) the emphasis was on the sequential letter/phonemes in a word. We hypothesize that it is during writing that the relationship between individual letters and phonemes might be the most vivid. That is, a child with pencil in hand as he sounds the phonemes in his mouth and attempts to represent these sounds with letters on paper is likely to reach down to the phoneme level. The literature on invented spelling is certainly supportive of this notion (Henderson, 1981). Notice, however, that Teacher 4 did press for correct spellings. That is, she employed what was taught in rimes in her word-recognition instruction and emphasized the vowel in writing, which appeared to be a winning combination.

The phonics instruction in the two most successful classrooms for low-reading group students was very hands-on and included writing for sounds. The hands-on phonics and phonemic awareness activities frequently involved sorting word cards into columns based on orthographic patterns and sorting picture cards in terms of the onset, rime, or medial vowel sounds. These activities focus children's attention as they either sort the pictures or word cards themselves or respond to where the teacher should place them on a pocket chart. Thus, active decision making and thought are required to compare and contrast sounds and spelling patterns in word-sorting activities (Bear et al., 1995).

Children who entered first grade with minimal reading skill seemed to have greatest success with the following classroom practices:

1. Teachers modeled word recognition strategies by (a) chunking words into component units such as syllables or onset/rimes or finding little words in big ones, as well as modeling and encouraging the sound and

blending of individual letters or phonemes in these chunks, and (b) considering known letter sounds in a word and what makes sense.

2. Children were encouraged to finger-point to words as text was read.

3. Children used hands-on materials (e.g., pocket charts for active sorting of picture cards by sound and word cards by orthographic pattern).

4. Writing for sounds was part of phonics instruction.

5. Instructional groups were small, with word-recognition lesson plans designed to meet the specific needs of children within that group.

Final Thoughts

The current study suggests that the self-teaching hypothesis works for children with some early literacy skills (Share, 1995; Share & Stanovich, 1995; Torgesen & Hecht, 1996). However, some upfront teaching is required regarding how to approach unknown words before self-teaching can manifest itself in children who have few literacy skills on entering first grade. In other words, the development of phonological sensitivity and a lot of reading experience are not sufficient for some children. Rather, phonics instruction on onsets, rimes (including short- and long-vowel rimes), *and* short vowels—coupled with modeling how to approach unknown words—might be enough to set these children into a self-teaching mode, provided they subsequently have sufficient text to read.

We found that our teachers' instruction did not fall neatly into any easily definable method, strategy, or linguistic unit approach to word recognition. Yes, the two teachers most successful with children who entered first grade with few literacy skills could be classified as phonics teachers. However, as described above, this phonics instruction combined reading and writing of words and, in the most successful classroom, combined an onset/rime approach with sequential letter-sound decoding. Further, the phonics instruction reflected knowledge of both the hands-on nature of activities that focus the attention of young children and the active-child decision making involved in compare-and-contrast activities that can facilitate cognitive growth. All of our teachers showed enormous energy in creating materials that were suitable for their children. We thus concur with the statement of Duffy and Hoffman (1999) that "improved reading is linked to teachers who use methods thoughtfully, not methods alone" (p. 15). Teachers need, however, to be knowledgeable about what methods are effective and for what children, and methods have to take on a richer meaning.

Rather than a broad-brush, either/or instructional approach that is applied to all children in a classroom, word-recognition instruction is likely to be most effective if there is an emphasis on different linguistic units at different levels of reading development. Differential instruction requires a knowledgeable teacher.

Acknowledgments

This research was conducted as part of CIERA and supported under the Educational Research and Development Centers Program, PR/Award R305R70004, as administered by the Office of Educational Research and Improvement, U.S. Department of Education. However, the contents of the described report do not necessarily represent the positions or policies of the National Institute on Early Childhood Development or the U.S. Department of Education, and readers should not assume endorsement by the U.S. federal government.

References

Adams, M.J. (1990). *Beginning to read: Thinking and learning about print.* Cambridge, MA: MIT Press.

Adams, M.J., Bereiter, C., Hirshberg, J., Anderson, V., & Bernier, S.A. (1995). *Framework for effective teaching, grade 1: Thinking and learning about print, teacher's guide, Part A.* Chicago: Open Court.

Allington, R.L. (1980). Teacher interruption behaviors during primary-grade oral reading. *Journal of Educational Psychology, 72,* 371–377.

Allington, R.L. (1984). Content coverage and contextual reading in reading groups. *Journal of Reading Behavior, 16,* 85–96.

Anderson, R.C., Hiebert, E.H., Scott, J.A., & Wilkinson, I.A.G. (1985). *Becoming a nation of readers: The report of the Commission on Reading.* Washington, DC: National Institute of Education.

Au, K.H. (1980). *A test of the social organizational hypothesis: Relationships between participation structures and learning to read.* Unpublished doctoral dissertation, University of Illinois, Urbana-Champaign.

Barr, R., & Dreeben, R. (1983). *How schools work.* Chicago: University of Chicago Press.

Bear, D., Invernizzi, M., Templeton, S., & Johnston, F. (1995). *Words their way: A developmental approach to phonics, spelling, and vocabulary instruction.* Columbus, OH: Merrill/Macmillan.

Beck, I.L. (1998). Understanding beginning reading: A journey through teaching and research. In J. Osborn & F. Lehr (Eds.), *Literacy for all: Issues in teaching and learning* (pp. 11–31). New York: Guilford.

Beck, I.L., & Juel, C. (1995). The role of decoding in learning to read. *American Educator, 19*(2), 8, 21–25, 39–42.

Berninger, V.W. (1995). Has the phonological recoding model of reading acquisition and reading disability led us astray? *Issues in Education: Contributions From Educational Psychology, 1,* 59–63.

Berninger, V.W., Yates, C., & Lester, K. (1991). Multiple orthographic codes in reading and writing acquisition. *Reading and Writing: An Interdisciplinary Journal, 3,* 115–149.

Bruck, M., & Treiman, R. (1992). Learning to pronounce words: The limitations of analogies. *Reading Research Quarterly, 27,* 375–388.

Carroll, J.B., Davies, P., & Richman, B. (1971). *Word frequency book.* New York: American Heritage.

Clay, M.M. (1989). *The early detection of reading difficulties* (3rd ed.). Hong Kong: Heinemann.

Clymer, T. (1963/1996). The utility of phonic generalizations in the primary grades. *The Reading Teacher, 50,* 182–187.

Collins, J. (1982). *Differential treatment in reading groups. Final report of school-home ethnography project* (Rep. No. G-78-0082). Washington, DC: National Institute of Education.

Dahl, K.L., Scharer, P.L., Lawson, L.L., & Grogan, P.R. (1999). Phonics instruction and student achievement in whole language first-grade classrooms. *Reading Research Quarterly, 34,* 312–341.

Duffy, G.G., & Hoffman, J.V. (1999). In pursuit of an illusion: The flawed search for a perfect method. *The Reading Teacher, 53,* 10–16.

Ehri, L.C. (1980). The development of orthographic images. In U. Frith (Ed.), *Cognitive processes in spelling* (pp. 311–338). London: Academic Press.

Ehri, L.C. (1991). Development of the ability to read words. In R. Barr, M.L. Kamil, P. Mosenthal, & P.D. Pearson (Eds.), *Handbook of reading research* (Vol. 2, pp. 383–417). White Plains, NY: Longman.

Ehri, L.C. (1992). Reconceptualizing the development of sight word reading and its relationship to recoding. In P.B. Gough, L.C. Ehri, & R. Treiman (Eds.), *Reading acquisition* (pp. 107–143). Hillsdale, NJ: Erlbaum.

Ehri, L.C. (1998). Grapheme-phoneme knowledge is essential for learning to read words in English. In J.L. Metsala & L.C. Ehri (Eds.), *Word recognition in beginning reading* (pp. 3–40). Mahwah, NJ: Erlbaum.

Ehri, L.C., & Robbins, C. (1992). Beginners need some decoding skill to read words by analogy. *Reading Research Quarterly, 27,* 13–26.

Ehri, L.C., & Wilce, L. (1985). Movement into reading: Is the first stage of printed word learning visual or phonetic? *Reading Research Quarterly, 20,* 163–179.

Ehri, L.C., & Wilce, L. (1987a). Cipher versus cue reading: An experiment in decoding acquisition. *Journal of Educational Psychology, 79,* 3–13.

Ehri, L.C., & Wilce, L. (1987b). Does learning to spell help beginners learn to read words? *Reading Research Quarterly, 22,* 47–65.

Foorman, B., Francis, D.J., Fletcher, J.M., Schatschneider, C., & Mehta, P. (1998). The role of instruction in learning to read: Preventing reading failure in at-risk children. *Journal of Educational Psychology, 90,* 37–55.

Gambrell, L. (1984). How much time do children spend reading during teacher-directed reading instruction? In J. Niles & L. Harris (Eds.), *Changing perspectives on research in reading/language processing and instruction* (33rd yearbook of the National Reading Conference, pp. 193–198). New York: National Reading Conference.

Gaskins, I.W., Downer, M., Anderson, R.C., Cunningham, P.M., Gaskins, R.W., Schommer, J., et al. (1988). A metacognitive approach to phonics: Using what you know to decode what you don't know. *Remedial and Special Education, 9,* 36–41, 66.

Gaskins, I.W., Ehri, L.C., Cress, C., O'Hara, C., & Donnelly, K. (1996/1997). Procedures for word learning: Making discoveries about words. *The Reading Teacher, 50,* 312–327.

Gaskins, R.W., Gaskins, I.W., Anderson, R.C., & Schommer, M. (1995). The reciprocal relationship between research and development: An example involving a decoding strand for poor readers. *Journal of Reading Behavior, 27,* 337–377.

Goswami, U. (1995). Phonological development and reading by analogy: What is analogy and what is not? *Journal of Research in Reading, 18,* 139–145.

Goswami, U., & Bryant, P. (1992). Rhyme, analogy, and children's reading. In P.B. Gough, L.C. Ehri, & R. Treiman (Eds.), *Reading acquisition* (pp. 49–63). Hillsdale, NJ: Erlbaum.

Goswami, U., & Mead, F. (1992). Onset and rime awareness and analogies in reading. *Reading Research Quarterly, 27,* 153–162.

Gough, P.B., & Juel, C. (1990, April). *Does phonics teach the cipher?* Paper presented at the annual meeting of the American Educational Research Association, Boston, MA.

Gough, P.B., Juel, C., & Griffith, P.L. (1992). Reading, spelling, and the orthographic cipher. In P.B. Gough, L.C. Ehri, & R. Treiman (Eds.), *Reading acquisition* (pp. 35–48). Hillsdale, NJ: Erlbaum.

Henderson, E.H. (1981). *Learning to read and spell: The child's knowledge of words.* DeKalb: Northern Illinois University Press.

Hiebert, E.H. (1983). An examination of ability grouping for reading instruction. *Reading Research Quarterly, 18,* 231–255.

Hoffman, J.V., & Baker, C. (1981). Characterizing teacher feedback to student miscues during oral reading instruction. *The Reading Teacher, 34,* 907–913.

Hutchins, P. (1968). *Rosie's walk.* New York: Macmillan.

Invernizzi, M.A., Robey, R.R., & Moon, T.R. (1998). *Phonological awareness literacy screening: Technical manual and report.* Charlottesville: University of Virginia and the Virginia Department of Education.

Johnston, F.R., Invernizzi, M., & Juel, C. (1998). *Guidelines for volunteer tutors of emergent and early readers.* New York: Guilford.

Juel, C. (1990). Effects of reading group assignment on reading development in first and second grade. *Journal of Reading Behavior, 22,* 233–254.

Juel, C. (1994). *Learning to read and write in one elementary school.* New York: Springer-Verlag.

Juel, C., Griffith, P., & Gough, P.B. (1986). Acquisition of literacy: A longitudinal study of children in first and second grade. *Journal of Educational Psychology, 78,* 243–255.

Juel, C., & Roper/Schneider, D. (1985). The influence of basal readers on first-grade reading. *Reading Research Quarterly, 18,* 306–327.

Liberman, I.Y., & Shankweiler, D. (1985). Phonology and the problems of learning to read and write. *Remedial and Special Education*, *6*, 8–17.

Morris, D. (1981). Concept of word: A developmental phenomenon in the beginning reading and writing process. *Language Arts*, *58*, 659–668.

Perfetti, C.A., Beck, I., Bell, L., & Hughes, C. (1987). Phonemic knowledge and learning to read are reciprocal: A longitudinal study of first grade children. *Merrill-Palmer Quarterly*, *33*, 283–319.

Pflaum, S.W., Pascarella, E.T., Boswick, M., & Auer, C. (1980). The influence of pupil behavior and pupil status factors on teacher behaviors during oral reading lessons. *Journal of Educational Psychology*, *74*, 99–105.

Pinker, S. (1994). *The language instinct*. New York: HarperPerennial.

Pressley, M. (1998). *Reading instruction that works: The case for balanced teaching*. New York: Guilford.

Reitsma, P. (1983). Printed word learning in beginning readers. *Journal of Experimental Child Psychology*, *75*, 321–339.

Reitsma, P. (1990). Development of orthographic knowledge. In P. Reitsma & L. Verhoeven (Eds.), *Acquisition of reading in Dutch* (pp. 43–64). Dordrecht, the Netherlands: Foris.

Roberts, E. (1992). The evolution of the young child's concept of word in text and written language. *Reading Research Quarterly*, *30*, 958–996.

Share, D.L. (1995). Phonological recoding and self-teaching: Sine qua non of reading acquisition. *Cognition*, *55*, 151–218.

Share, D.L., & Stanovich, K.E. (1995). Cognitive processes in early reading development: Accommodating individual differences into a model of acquisition. *Issues in Education*, *1*, 1–57.

Stahl, S.A. (1992). Saying the "p" word: Nine guidelines for exemplary phonics instruction. *The Reading Teacher*, *45*, 618–625.

Stanovich, K.E. (1992). Speculations on the causes and consequences of individual differences in early reading acquisition. In P.B. Gough, L.C. Ehri, & R. Treiman (Eds.), *Reading acquisition* (pp. 307–342). Hillsdale, NJ: Erlbaum.

Torgesen, J.K., & Davis, C. (1996). Individual difference variables that predict response to training in phonological awareness. *Journal of Experimental Child Psychology*, *63*, 1–21.

Torgesen, J.K., & Hecht, S.A. (1996). Preventing and remediating reading disabilities: Instructional variables that make a difference for special students. In M.F. Graves, P. van den Broek, & B.M. Taylor (Eds.), *The first R: Every child's right to read* (pp. 133–159). New York: Teachers College Press; Newark, DE: International Reading Association.

Treiman, R. (1992). The role of intrasyllabic units in learning to read and spell. In P.B. Gough, L.C. Ehri, & R. Treiman (Eds.), *Reading acquisition* (pp. 65–106). Hillsdale, NJ: Erlbaum.

Tunmer, W.E., & Chapman, J.W. (1993). To guess or not to guess, that is the question: Metacognitive strategy training, phonological recoding skill, and beginning reading. *Reading Forum N.Z.*, *1*, 3–14.

Vandervelden, M.C., & Siegel, L.S. (1995). Phonological recoding and phoneme awareness in early literacy: A developmental approach. *Reading Research Quarterly*, *30*, 854–875.

Weinstein, R.S. (1976). Reading group membership in first grade: Teacher behaviors and pupil experiences over time. *Journal of Educational Psychology*, *68*, 103–116.

West, C.K., & Anderson, T.H. (1976). The question of preponderant causation in teacher expectancy research. *Review of Educational Research*, *68*, 103–116.

Wise, B.W. (1992). Whole words and decoding for short-term learning: Comparisons on a "talking-computer" system. *Journal of Experimental Child Psychology*, *54*, 147–167.

Wise, B.W., Olson, R.K., & Treiman, R. (1990). Subsyllabic units in computerized reading instruction: Onset-rime versus postvowel segmentation. *Journal of Experimental Child Psychology*, *49*, 1–19.

Wylie, R.E., & Durrell, D.D. (1970). Teaching vowels through phonograms. *Elementary English*, *47*, 787–791.

Appendix

Examples of Observations and Codes Applied From Classrooms 1–4

Classroom 1, Low-Reading Group, November 5

The teacher is going over the new word wall words for the week. The words are *come*, *are*, *put*, *with*. The routine is to clap, spell, and chant each word five times. Sometimes an individual child is called upon; most times children do this in unison.

Teacher:	Let's start with the word *are*. Student 1, spell it for us.
Student 1:	*a, r, e*
Teacher:	Everyone
All:	*a,r,e—a,r,e—a,r,e—a,r,e—a,r,e*

This pattern is repeated with each word.

Teacher:	Write each word three times and make a sentence using *are*.

Primary materials: Word wall

Primary activities: Spell words, chant word wall sight words, individual text writing

Primary units: Whole word

Primary strategies: Spell

Classroom 2, Low-Reading Group, October 21

The children first read a poem on a chart. Then they are given an individual copy of the poem. A refrain in the poem is as follows:

> We're scary skeletons
> We're scary skeletons
> Clickety-clack, down our boney backs

Teacher (to all):	Can anyone find *skeletons*?
Student 1:	Yes. [Points to the three instances of the word in the poem.]
Teacher (to Student 2):	Can you find a word that begins with *sc*? The *sc* is the same as /sk/ in skeleton.
Student 2:	[Finds *scary* but doesn't know it.]
Teacher:	It is another word for spooky. It is *scary*. *We're* has an apostrophe and that means it's a contraction. It's a short way to say *we are*. It sounds like *we're*. What sound does *cl* make?

Teacher:	[continues reading poem] What do *clack* and *back* have in common?
Student 3:	/ack/
Teacher:	Yes, they both are the /ack/ family. If I take out *cl* (from *clack*) what is this part?
Student 2:	/ack/
Teacher:	Now, if I put a *b* on this?
Student 4:	*Back.*

They choral-read the poem. Then the teacher gives them an individual copy of the poem. They read it to themselves and are reminded to point to each word. Then each child reads the poem out loud.

A chart with a list of /ack/ words is put up. The first letter is printed in a different color than is the /ack/.

Teacher:	Let's look at the first word. It was in your poem.
Student 5:	*Bones.*
Teacher:	Look at the whole word.
Student 5:	*Back.*
Teacher:	The next word is *pack*. *Back* and *pack* rhyme. What's the next word?
Student 2:	*Sack.*
Teacher:	Tell me how you knew.
Student 2:	They all have /ack/.
Teacher:	Let's see who knows this one.
Student 6:	*Stack.*
Teacher:	[to all] What does *ack* say?
All:	/ack/.
Teacher:	What does the *st* say?
All:	/st/
Teacher:	Let's put it together.
All:	*Stack.*
Teacher:	Look at beginning sounds and then add chunk. That's what good readers do. Let's read back through the list.

Primary materials: Poem on chart, poem copied for child
Primary activities: Choral reading, individual reading, phonics, grammar

Primary units: Initial consonant, initial consonant blend, rime
Primary strategies: Teacher models and helps segment word in chunks, child reminded of word family, child told word rhymes with ___, finger-point to word

Classroom 3, Middle-Reading Group, October 30

They are reading a new Halloween book. Peer coaching is used as they read it.

Student 1:	Can we tell the word?
Teacher (to Student 1):	That doesn't help. He needs a chance to stretch his brain.
Student 2:	On Halloween you can be a... [looks at the teacher] ghost?
Teacher:	What would have to be there for it to be *ghost*?
Student 2:	A *g*.
Teacher:	There's not a *g*.
Student 2:	[Says *an* and tries to sound it out.]
Teacher:	I liked the way you stretched it out. It does have the little word *an* in it. The word is *anything*. Does that make sense?
Student 3:	*Y* like in *Tracy*.
Student 4:	[looking at upcoming word] This is *pat*.
Teacher:	/at/ word family.
Teacher:	[Makes a letter *b* and letter *p* with her hand to distinguish the letters.]
Teacher:	I know you know it but telling her doesn't help. Is that word *bat* or *busy* or *balls*? How do you know?
Student 5:	What do your parents do on Halloween?
Teacher:	That clue makes sense, but it would be hard for her to remember by herself.
Student 6:	[Sounding word out.]
Student 5:	There's an /an/ in it.
Teacher (to Student 6):	Sometimes that helps and sometimes not.
Teacher:	What other things can we do to help her?
All:	Sound it out. Look at the word wall. Go back and reread it. Skip it.
Teacher:	You guys are really working hard.

They continue to read. When Student 1 is stuck on the word *looks*, he goes back and rereads the word and gets it.

Teacher (to Student 1): Good for you!

Student 3: I saw this word in one of the book nook books!

Teacher: Good readers find words in other places, don't they? What do those two say? It rhymes with *books*?

Student 1: *Looks*!

Teacher: Has everyone had a turn? [They choral-read the rest of the book.] The teacher reminds them to sound like a bell, when they read *ding-dong*.

At the end of reading, everyone gets a Halloween stamp.

Primary materials: Trade book
Primary activities: Peer coaching, individual reading, choral reading
Primary units: Initial consonant, rime, whole word
Primary strategies: Child told word rhymes with ___, child reminded of word family, rereading, child asked if it makes sense

Classroom 4, Low-Reading Group, October 30

The children all have phonics worksheets. They are writing names to go with pictures. The pictures depict /at/ words.

Teacher (to Student 1): Where did you learn to write those letters?

Student 1: [Talks to himself as he writes] Straight stick down.

Teacher (to Student 2): What's the next picture? What do you hear at the beginning? /p/ What letter goes with /p/?

Teacher (to Student 3): Don't be playing around, you'll get left behind. Watch me, here is a new way to make a letter. Keep up. We're ready to go. Sleep at home, not in my reading group.

Teacher (to all): Stretch it out. What's in the middle? [She models sound and blending all phonemes.]

Teacher (to Student 4): Trace over mine [printing].

Teacher (to all): What word did we write? /k/-/a/-/t/? [Teacher calls attention to individual phonemes and letters that match each. She then describes how to form those letters.]

Teacher (to Student 3): What is the first sound?

Student 3: *C*

Teacher: I don't want to hear the name of the letter, tell me the
                            sound.

[They do a few more /at/ words like *bat*.]

Teacher: Good job here, guys. Writing is hard now, but you'll
                            get really good at it and speed up.

Primary materials: Phonics worksheet
Primary activities: Writing for sounds, letter formation
Primary units: Initial consonant, short vowel, final consonant
Primary strategies: Teacher models and helps sound and blend letter sounds

14

Phases of Word Learning: Implications for Instruction With Delayed and Disabled Readers

Linnea C. Ehri and Sandra McCormick

During the last 20 years, many researchers have conducted studies to understand how children learn to read. The focus of their research has been on the cognitive and linguistic processes that are central to the development of reading ability rather than on methods of instruction (Adams, 1990; Gough, Ehri, & Treiman, 1992). It is important to distinguish between learner processes and teacher methods because very often these are confused. For example, some educators interpret *phonics* to mean worksheets or skill and drill, in other words, a method of instruction. To other educators, however, this term refers to the graphophonic knowledge and decoding procedures that beginners must acquire to become competent readers. Many methods of instruction besides worksheets and skill and drill can promote the acquisition of these reading processes. The present article explains the processes that students acquire in learning to read and then considers their implications for instruction.

In portraying the course of acquisition of reading processes suggested by research findings, various schemes have been proposed for distinguishing stages or phases of development through which all readers pass on their way from pre-reading to skilled reading (e.g., Chall, 1983; Ehri, 1987, 1991, 1994; Ehri & Wilce, 1985, 1987a; Frith, 1985; Goswami, 1986, 1988; Gough & Hillinger, 1980; Juel, 1983, 1991; Juel, Griffith, & Gough, 1985; Mason, 1980; Soderbergh, 1977; Stuart & Coltheart, 1988). Of interest in the present article are schemes that portray the development of word-reading processes and their instructional implications for students who have word-identification difficulties.

Information about word-learning processes can assist teachers of problem readers in several ways. First, it can help them understand and interpret the word-reading behaviors they see in delayed and disabled readers. Behaviors that might be regarded as bizarre, atypical reactions to print are in most cases just behaviors that typify less-mature readers who are at an earlier phase of development. Information

From *Reading & Writing Quarterly: Overcoming Learning Difficulties*, *14*(2), 135–163. Copyright © 1998 by Taylor & Francis. Reprinted with permission of the publisher.

about development can help to clarify the reading processes used by students in a particular phase and also the constraints that limit their word learning.

Second, information about word-learning processes can clarify the locus of difficulties that students have in learning to read words. Various studies have indicated that some students, called *delayed readers*, take longer to learn to read because of absence from school or lack of adequate instruction. Other students, referred to as *disabled readers*, are thought to possess a processing deficiency that makes it harder to learn to read. These deficits may involve greater difficulty in processing words phonologically or slower processing speeds (Bowers & Wolf, 1993; Wimmer, 1993). Both types impede the word-learning processes described below, making explicit instruction and practice much more important for acquiring reading competence.

Third, information about phases of development can help teachers determine how to support, scaffold, and guide their students to the next phase. Too often, instruction in word identification is unsuccessful with problem readers because it requires capabilities that students have not yet acquired. Taking account of the properties of word-learning processes at each phase helps to ensure that instruction does have utility for learners. Recognizing signs of progress, or lack of it, in learners can help teachers decide whether their teaching techniques are working or whether a different approach might better address a learner's difficulties. Space does not allow us to consider the variety of techniques that teachers might use with problem readers and how these techniques relate to phases of development. However, if teachers understand the processes to be cultivated at each phase, they have a basis for judging whether a teaching technique might work in a particular instance. As teachers gain experience relating their methods of instruction to students' phases of development, they will become more skilled at this trouble shooting, problem-solving approach to reading instruction (Ehri & Williams, 1996).

Ways to Read Words

Before describing the phases of development, it is important to characterize the various ways that words might be read by mature readers (Ehri, 1991, 1994, 1995). A goal of instruction is to enable readers to read words in all of the following ways:

1. Decoding. Words can be read by applying decoding or word-attack strategies. A decoding strategy enables readers to read words that are unfamiliar in print. Decoding involves identifying the sounds of individual letters, holding them in mind, and blending them into pronunciations that are recognized as real words. A more mature form of decoding that requires more alphabetic knowledge is to pronounce and blend familiar

clusters of letters, such as phonograms, common affixes, syllables, and spelling patterns. In English, this strategy works sometimes, but not always. It is more effective when combined with other strategies.

2. Analogy. Another way to attack unfamiliar words is to read them by analogy, that is, by recognizing how the spelling of an unfamiliar word is similar to a word already known. To analogize, readers access the known word in memory and then adjust the pronunciation to accommodate the new word, for example, reading *fountain* by analogy to *mountain* (Gaskins et al., 1988; Goswami, 1986).

3. Prediction. A third way to attack unknown words is to guess what the words might be by using initial letters in the words, preceding and succeeding words in the text, or context cues such as pictures (Goodman, 1976). Prediction, however, does not explain how most words in text are read because most words, particularly content words, cannot be guessed very accurately (Gough & Walsh, 1991).

4. Sight. A very different way to read words is by sight, which involves using memory to read words that have been read before. Sight of the word immediately activates its spelling, pronunciation, and meaning in memory. When sight words are known well enough, readers can recognize their pronunciations and meanings automatically, without expending any attention or effort figuring out the word (LaBerge & Samuels, 1974). This property makes sight-word reading especially valuable for text reading because it allows word-reading processes to operate unobtrusively, with the reader's attention focused on the meaning of print.

It is important to understand what sight-word learning involves because recent findings have challenged traditional views (Ehri, 1992). To account for sight-word learning, we must explain how readers are able to look at printed words they have read before and recognize those specific words while bypassing thousands of other words also stored in memory, including words with very similar spellings or meanings. Moreover, we must explain how readers are able to store and remember new words easily after reading them only a few times. The kind of process we have found to be at the heart of sight-word learning is a *connection-forming process*. Connections are formed that link the written forms of words to their pronunciations and meanings. This information is stored in the reader's mental dictionary or lexicon.

What kinds of connections are formed to store sight words in memory? The traditional view holds that readers memorize connections between the visual shapes of words and their meanings. However, Ehri's (1992) work suggests that this view is incorrect. Her findings indicate that readers learn sight words by forming connections between graphemes in the spellings and phonemes underlying the pronunciations of individual words. The connections are formed out of readers' general knowledge of grapheme–phoneme correspondences that recur in many words. Graphemes are the functional letter units symbolizing phonemes. Phonemes are the smallest units of "sound" in words. Readers look at the spelling of a particular word, pronounce the word, and apply their graphophonic knowledge to analyze how letters symbolize individual phonemes detectable in the word's pronunciation. This secures the sight word in memory.

Figure 1 reveals how beginners might analyze several different words to secure them as sight words in memory. In this figure, uppercase letters designate spellings, lowercase letters between slashes indicate phonemes, and lines linking letters to phonemes indicate connections. To secure sight words in mem-

FIGURE 1
Connections Formed in Memory Between Graphemes and Phonemes
in Specific Words Learned by Sight

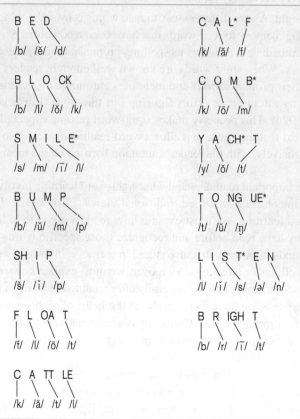

Uppercase letters indicate graphemes, lowercase letters between slashes indicate phonemes, lines indicate graphophonic connections, asterisks indicate unpronounced letters.

ory in this way, readers must possess alphabetic knowledge, including letter shapes, how to segment pronunciations into phonemes, and which graphemes typically symbolize which phonemes (Ehri, 1997).

The process of forming connections allows readers to remember how to read not only words containing conventional letter–sound correspondences but also words that have less regular spellings. Connections that might be formed to remember irregular words are included in Figure 1. Note that the same types of connections are evident. In fact, most of the letters in irregular words conform to grapheme–phoneme conventions. In remembering letters that do not correspond to phonemes, readers may remember them as extra visual forms, or they may flag them as silent in memory, or they may remember a special spelling pronunciation that includes the silent letter—for example, remembering *listen* as "lis-ten" or *chocolate* as "choc-o-late." Or they may see them as part of a larger spelling pattern, for example, the *gh* in -ight.

Spellings of words are like maps that visually lay out their phonological forms. Skilled readers are able to compute these mapping relations very quickly when they read words. Knowledge of letter–sound relations provides a powerful mnemonic system that bonds the written forms of specific words to their pronunciations in memory. When readers acquire working knowledge of the alphabetic spelling system, they can build a lexicon of sight words easily as they encounter new words in their reading (Ehri, 1992).

To explain the development of word-reading ability, we need to take account of these various ways to read practiced and unpracticed words—by decoding, by analogizing, by predicting, and by sight—and to specify how these processes are acquired.

Phases of Word Learning

Researchers have applied different terminology to describe stages or phases of development. In this piece we borrow from Ehri's (1991, 1994, 1995) scheme to distinguish five phases of word learning. Each phase is characterized by learners' understanding and use of the alphabetic system in their word reading. The five phases are (1) the pre-alphabetic phase, (2) the partial-alphabetic phase, (3) the full-alphabetic phase, (4) the consolidated-alphabetic phase, and (5) the automatic-alphabetic phase. We prefer the concept of phase, which is a less-stringent way to characterize periods of development than the concept of stage. One phase may overlap with the next phase, and mastery of one phase may or may not be a prerequisite for movement to the next. Each phase highlights a characteristic of word learning that becomes prominent.

To give an overview, the pre-alphabetic phase characterizes preschoolers and older severely disabled readers who have little working knowledge of the alphabetic system. The partial-alphabetic phase characterizes kindergartners, first graders, and older disabled readers who have rudimentary working knowledge of the alphabetic system but lack full knowledge, particularly vowel knowledge. The full-alphabetic phase characterizes students in first grade and beyond who have working knowledge of the major grapheme–phoneme units in English. The consolidated-alphabetic phase characterizes students, usually in second grade and beyond, who possess working knowledge of the major graphophonic relations, who have used this knowledge to build a sizable sight vocabulary, and who as a result have learned how to decode commonly recurring letter patterns as units. Their reading is faster and more fluent. The automatic-alphabetic phase characterizes mature readers who recognize most words in text automatically by sight and who are facile if not automatic in applying the various strategies to attack unfamiliar words.

Pre-Alphabetic Phase

The first phase is called *pre-alphabetic* because alphabetic knowledge is not used to read words. Children at this phase have very limited knowledge of letters, and they do not understand that letters in written words map onto sounds in oral language. Pre-alphabetic readers are limited to sight-word reading, that is, reading words from memory, and to guessing words from context. They have no ability to decode words or to analogize because they lack any working knowledge of the alphabetic system.

This phase has been called the *selective-cue* stage (Juel, 1991) because children attend to selected cues in remembering how to read words. It has been labeled the *paired-associate* stage (Gough & Hillinger, 1980) to denote that arbitrarily chosen associations are formed to link some feature of a written word to its spoken form or meaning. It has also been termed the *logographic* phase (Ehri, 1991; Frith, 1985) because readers focus on nonalphabetic graphic features of words that have nothing to do with sounds in the words—for example, the length of the word or its shape.

The following word-reading behaviors are in evidence during the pre-alphabetic phase of development (Ehri, 1987, 1991, 1994; Ehri & Wilce, 1985; Gough & Hillinger, 1980; Juel et al., 1985; Soderbergh, 1977):

1. Children may read words that they encounter frequently in their environment, for example, *stop*, *Burger King*, *Pepsi*, *milk*. However, when environmental cues such as logos and distinctive print are removed and the word is presented by itself, children can no longer read it (Mason, 1980). If a trick is played by showing children familiar words in their environment with one letter altered—for example, changing the *p* to an *x* on a can of *Xepsi*—children fail to detect the change and read the print as *Pepsi* (Masonheimer, Drum, & Ehri, 1984). This indicates that children "read the environment" rather than the print. They remember

nonalphabetic visual cues rather than letters. This has been called *visual cue reading* (Ehri & Wilce, 1985).

2. Children have trouble learning to read words that are written without any context clues such as pictures or logos. With practice they may learn some words, but the words are quickly forgotten (Mason, 1980). This is because the associations formed are arbitrary and hard to hold in memory. When students remember how to read words, they use visual cues and rote learning. Bits of the word, such as its length or shape, or other gross cues, are selected rather than the sequence of letters.

3. Students may select meaning-bearing cues in remembering how to read words, for example, remembering the word *look* because it has two "eyes" in the middle. This makes it easier to remember the word. However, because letters are not linked to sounds in memory, the letters do not constrain how the meaning is labeled. As a result, the student may read it as *see* rather than *look*. Another problem is that similarly spelled words, such as *book*, *moon*, and *tool*, may also be mistaken as the same word. Because meaning-bearing cues are absent in most words, this is not effective for building a sight vocabulary. Teachers who have observed delayed and disabled readers produce misreadings such as these, which are way off base, have attributed them to cognitive processing difficulties. However, there is a simpler explanation. The students are pre-alphabetic–phase readers. The only cues they have available for remembering how to read words are nonphonetic, visual cues.

4. Connected text cannot be read independently; however, readers may "pretend read" text that they have heard several times and memorized.

5. The strategy of guessing from context cues is used to read words. For example, students who see a picture of a Ford convertible may read the written word *wheels* printed beneath it as *car*. Letters exert little influence on the word that is guessed because students lack knowledge of letter–sound relations.

The pre-alphabetic phase of word learning is typical in preschool and kindergarten. The most telling sign that students are in this phase is their lack of letter knowledge. Children who know few letter names or sounds are shut off from reading words alphabetically, so by default they process words as strictly visual forms. Another telling sign is lack of awareness of constituent sounds in words.

When behaviors indicative of this phase are present in older students, these learners may be labeled *nonreaders*, *severely delayed readers*, or *severely disabled readers* (McCormick, 1994). Instruction is needed to help them become alphabetic readers of print. Basically, they need to acquire letter knowledge and phonemic awareness, and they need to engage in activities that strengthen this knowledge and incorporate it into their literacy activities.

To ensure that letter use is possible, students need to learn both lowercase and uppercase letters. Practice should include opportunities to print as well as name the letters because this improves letter-recognition learning (Adams, 1990). Accurate, immediate letter-name recognition is one of the best predictors of success in learning to read (Biemiller, 1977/1978; Blachman, 1984; Chall, 1967; Share, Jorm, Maclean, & Matthews, 1984).

Studying letters in words is important. When teachers detect students focusing on unprofitable cues, their focus should be redirected. For example, when Jim says, "I know that word is *look* because it has eyes," the teacher can say, "Yes, it has two letter *o*s in the middle. Now, can you name the letters of this word?" Scott and Ehri (1989) found that having novice beginners count or name letters in words helped them remember how to read the words. Many of the letter names contain relevant sounds (e.g., /s/ in *ess*, /t/ in *tee*, /m/ in *em*, but not /y/ in *wie*), so students who know names can use this knowledge to discover relations between letters they see in spellings of words and sounds they detect in the word pronunciations (Ehri, 1986, 1987).

Teaching phonemic awareness to students, that is, awareness that spoken words are made up of separate sounds, also is important in moving them to the next phase. Phonemic awareness is a crucial precursor to the development of skill in processing grapheme–phoneme relations in words (Juel, Griffith, & Gough, 1986; Share et al., 1984). Many studies have indicated that a deficiency in phonemic awareness is a principal cause of word-identification difficulties (e.g., see Pratt & Brady, 1988). Several tasks to assess the extent of beginners' phonemic awareness have been identified: saying the first and final sounds in words, counting the number of sounds in short words, listening to a sequence of two to three sounds and blending them to form a word, identifying different words with the same initial or final sounds, and removing the first or final sound from a word and saying what remains (e.g., see Stahl & Murray, 1994).

If phonemic awareness is weak in a pre-alphabetic–phase reader, there are many research-based activities that can be used to train students in these important understandings (e.g., Ball & Blachman, 1991; Griffith & Olson, 1992). Gamelike listening and sound manipulation activities can be used to help students segment words into their component syllables or phonemes (analysis activities) or to give students practice in blending sounds to form words (synthesis activities). Students' attention should be directed at articulatory gestures as well as acoustic properties of sounds. Mouth positions and movements involving the lips, tongue, and teeth to produce sounds provide a reliable basis for discovering the sound segments in words, particularly for disabled readers who have phonological segmentation difficulties (Lindamood & Lindamood, 1975). Segmentation as well as blending exercises are important antecedents that prepare learners to process print alphabetically.

Because prevention is the best antidote to disabled reading, it is crucial for kindergarten teachers to offer effective letter instruction and to make sure that all their students master letters by the end of the year before formal reading instruction begins. For students who enter school knowing few letters, a program such as Letterland (Wendon, 1993) can make the task of remembering the shapes and sounds of letters much easier. Mnemonics that help children form memorable links between letters and sounds are used in this program. Letters are drawn to resemble animate characters shaped like the letter with a name whose initial sound is symbolized by that letter—for example, *s* drawn as Sammy Snake, *c* as Clever Cat, *m* as Mike the Munching Monster. Alliteration in the name draws attention to the relevant sound. These names provide a way of referring to the letters that avoids problems arising from conventional letter names that do not always contain relevant sounds.

Exercises that give pre-alphabetic readers practice using their letter knowledge to invent spellings of words directs their attention to letter–sound relations. It also helps them acquire not only letter knowledge but also phonemic awareness (Ehri & Wilce, 1987b). Teachers can help students stretch out the pronunciations of words, listen for initial and final sounds in the words, and select letters for those sounds. With this knowledge, students are equipped to move from the pre-alphabetic to the partial-alphabetic phase of development.

Partial-Alphabetic Phase

Word-reading behaviors in this phase may typify kindergartners, novice first-grade readers, and older problem readers. Students can remember how to read words by sight using partial-alphabetic cues. They can use guessing strategies to read words. However, they are weak at decoding words and reading words by analogy because both of these strategies require more working knowledge of the alphabetic system than they possess.

Mason (1980) called this the *visual recognition* stage because children begin to detect letters in words. This phase has also been labeled the *rudimentary-alphabetic* phase because beginners can match some of the letters in words to sounds in their pronunciations (Ehri, 1991). The following capabilities characterize readers in the partial-alphabetic phase (Ehri, 1991, 1994; Ehri & Wilce, 1985, 1987a; Mason, 1980):

1. Students use partial letters combined with context cues to guess the identities of unfamiliar words (Stahl & Murray, 1998). For example, on seeing a picture of a farm with a word beginning with *b* printed beneath the picture, students might read it as *barn*. This contrasts with the previous phase, in which alphabet letters were ignored in guessing words. Words are often misread as other words having similar letters, for example, *man* for *men*, *this* for *that*, *horse* for *house*.

2. Students who read words backwards—for example, *was* for *saw*—are not seeing them backwards but simply have not acquired a strong left-to-right orientation in their word reading (Vellutino, 1979). One important achievement at this phase involves practicing the reading direction until it becomes automatic.

3. Students can remember how to read words by sight more effectively in this phase than in the previous phase. This is because they have available some alphabetic knowledge to use in forming connections between letters and sounds in words. However, because their knowledge of the system is limited, and because they lack full phonemic segmentation ability, they process only partial letter–sound relations to form connections in learning sight words. For example, in remembering how to read *block*, they might link the initial and final letters *b* and *k* to sounds /b/ and /k/ in the pronunciation of the word. However, other letters and sounds in the word are overlooked. Although it is easier to retain words in memory in this phase than in the previous phase, the problem is that other similarly spelled words, such as *book* and *black*, may be mistaken for *block*. Ehri and Wilce (1985, 1987a, 1987b) have called the use of partial graphophonic cues to read words *phonetic cue reading*.

4. At this phase, readers typically know the sounds of consonants whose letter names contain these sounds: *b, d, f, j, k, 1, m, n, p, r, s, t, v, z*, including the "soft" sounds of *c* (/s/) and *g* (/j/). However, they may not know the hard sounds of *c* (/k/) and *g* (/g/), or the sounds of *h, w*, and *y*, whose names are not informative about sounds and may even mislead (e.g., initial /w/ sound in the name of Y *wie*). Also, they may not know graphemes involving more than one letter to symbolize a phoneme: *sh, wh, th, ch, ck*.

5. Decoding strategies are not available for reading unfamiliar words. Also, analogizing is not operable because sight words are not represented in memory in sufficient detail to recognize that new words have similar spelling patterns to known words. Rather than read new words by analogy, the new words are often misread as the known words because of a partial resemblance between letters (Ehri & Robbins, 1992).

Instructional Implications. The following instructional activities are useful in helping older delayed or disabled readers become full alphabetic readers.

To ensure that readers acquire working knowledge of the major grapheme–phoneme relationships in their word processing, direct instruction is necessary because the graphophonic system is too complicated for most readers, particularly disabled readers, to figure out on their own. Explicit instruction in letter–sound correspondences should be provided in a way that links the correspondences to their occurrence in specific words. Although phonic analysis instruction has historically been the subject of much controversy, careful consideration of research studies addressing this controversy points definitively to the benefits of instruction in phonics when it is carried out appropriately. In a comprehensive review of this research, Adams (1990) summarizes these conclusions:

> The best differentiator between good and poor readers is repeatedly found to be their knowledge of spelling patterns and their proficiency with spelling–sound translations. Phonic mastery is not only highly correlated with phonic coverage, but for low-readiness children—for those who lack it most—it is strongly and directly dependent on it. (p. 290)

Learners in this phase already use letter–sound associations to some extent; however, because their focus is on initial and final letters in words rather than on all the letters, they need to learn to process letters in words more completely. When words contain grapheme–phoneme relations known but overlooked by a student, the teacher should direct attention to these sounds. For example, when a student reads *black* as *back*, the teacher might say, "Yes, this word does begin with the *b* sound and ends with the *k* sound, but here is the letter *l*. What is that sound?" Then, the teacher should model the blending of all the sounds while sliding a finger under each to produce the correct word and have the student copy the procedure immediately.

Knowledge of the vowel spelling system, particularly short vowels, can be promoted by teaching students mnemonics that link the shapes of letters to their sounds in the fashion of alliterative Letterland characters (Wendon, 1991). For example, *a* can be drawn in the shape of an apple and labeled *Annie Apple*, *e* in the shape of an elephant head and trunk labeled *Eddy Elephant*, *i* in the shape of an ink pen labeled *Impy Ink*, *o* in the shape of an octopus labeled *Oscar Octopus*, and *u* in the shape of an umbrella called *Uppy Umbrella*. Ehri, Deffner, and Wilce (1984) found that such mnemonics were effective ways to teach letter–sound associations to beginners; adaptations that are age appropriate can be made for older delayed readers.

It also is helpful for partial-alphabetic readers to engage in writing activities. Dual approaches to writing should be adopted; for example, when students are writing their own stories or other creative pieces, *invented spellings* (also called *temporary spellings*) may be encouraged if correct spellings of words are unknown (Henderson, 1981; Read, 1970). Studies have indicated that teaching students to stretch out the sounds in spoken words and to select letters representing those sounds helps them acquire skills that are useful for reading words (Ehri & Wilce, 1987b). As students analyze words to spell them, teachers can intervene and use the opportunity to scaffold students' learning. The beauty of interacting with students about their invented spellings is that the spellings make visible the difficulties that students are having with the graphophonic system. Teachers can help students find hard-to-detect sound segments such as consonant clusters (e.g., the /l/ in *black*). They can help them identify more conventional letters for the sounds detected, for example, *w* rather than *y* to spell the sound /w/ as in *witch*. Teachers can list other known words spelled with that sound in the initial position to show how common the grapheme–phoneme relation is in words.

If teachers notice students reversing *b*s and *d*s, they can teach them a mnemonic for distinguishing the two letter shapes—for example, by using one's fists and thumbs to form the shape of a bed, with *b* on the left and *d* on the right. (To create this mnemonic, make two fists with your thumbs extended upward; bring the two fists together with knuckles touching to form the shape of a bed that also looks like the word *bed*, with the left *b* hand at the beginning and the right *d* hand at the end of the word.) Students can quickly form this *bed* mnemonic on their own to remind themselves which letter is which.

The aim of guiding students as they invent spellings is to help them use conventional grapheme–phoneme relations to produce phonetically complete spellings. Teaching students to invent spellings is particularly helpful for novice beginning readers (Ehri & Wilce, 1987b) and for older delayed readers (Baron & Treiman, 1980).

The other aspect of the dual approach to writing instruction involves making students aware that each word has a unique, prescribed sequence of letters that constitutes that word's identity and that distinguishes it from similarly spelled words. To this end, the second part of this dual approach is to teach students to write, conventionally, words that have been targeted for their reading instruction. Students can be prompted to write these words conventionally by posting the words on charts in the classroom and by placing an alphabetized word bank on each student's desk. However, it is unrealistic to expect partial-alphabetic readers to remember the correct spellings of words if they cannot make graphophonic sense of letters in the spelling. To be easily remembered, spellings must fall within students' knowledge of the alphabetic system. For this reason, the production of correct spellings of words from memory will not be very common until the next phase of development, when students' knowledge of the alphabetic system is more extensive (Ehri, 1997).

Other ways to heighten students' understanding of the spellings of specific words are to have them engage in gamelike and manipulative activities. For example, students might spell targeted words with magnetic letters; or write words on small handheld chalkboards or Magic Slates; or play word games, such as Hangman, that focus attention on the internal letters in words.

When students analyze the spellings of specific words, they need to recognize how letters match up to sounds in the pronunciation of the words. This helps to establish the words in memory as fully analyzed forms. Teachers at Benchmark School (Gaskins, Ehri, Cress, O'Hara, & Donnelly, 1996/1997) have devised activities to help students do this. Each day, time is set aside for students to practice analyzing words targeted for that week, for example, *tent*, *skate*, and *round*. Several steps are performed to help students learn the words. First, the teacher pronounces the word. Then he or she has children stretch out their pronunciations and segment the word into its sounds. They do this by saying each sound as they raise a finger; for example: "*Skate*: /s/-/k/-/a/-/t/: I hear four sounds." Benchmark teachers found that segmenting had to be done before the spelling of the word was presented to get children to attend to sounds and not to letters. After segmentation, a card showing the spelling is placed on the board, and children state the number of letters they see. The teacher asks why there are five letters but only four sounds, and the students reconcile the discrepancy by replying that very often when final *e* occurs in words, it does not make a separate sound, but rather it makes the preceding vowel say its own name. Students are then prompted to search the list of key words they have already learned to find another word with the same vowel sound. For *skate*, they might find *place*. Students practice writing the words from memory as well. They might stretch out the word with the teacher and write the letters needed for each sound, or they might stretch out the word and insert letters into Elkonin (1973) boxes to show how each letter goes with a sound.

To speed word learning in this phase, it is advisable to teach similarly spelled words in separate sets—for example, *on* and *no*; *what*, *want*, and *that*; *for* and *from*. Otherwise, the words become confused, and learning time is increased (Gough & Hillinger, 1980).

Readers are able to read connected text by applying their sight-word knowledge and guessing strategies. Their reading is bolstered substantially if they have heard or read the text before because they can incorporate their memory for the text into their reading (Sulzby, 1985). In assessing students' independent reading skill, it is important to observe them reading unfamiliar rather than familiar text. In selecting unfamiliar books that are not frustrating for students to read, it is important to assess the match between their sight-word repertoires and words in the books because students have very limited word-attack skills. In this phase it is important for students to be weaned from excessive reliance on text memory in their reading. To develop into independent readers, they must acquire and use their alphabetic knowledge to process graphophonic cues when they read words in text.

In sum, the instruction given to partial-alphabetic readers should be aimed at helping them expand their working knowledge of grapheme–phoneme relations for writing as well as for reading, to make use of this knowledge in building a sight vocabulary, and to use their growing sight vocabulary and prediction strategies to read connected text independently.

Full-Alphabetic Phase

Readers at the full-alphabetic phase of development differ from partial-alphabetic readers in a number of respects (Ehri, 1991, 1994; Frith, 1985). The full-alphabetic phase has also been called the *spelling-sound* stage (Juel, 1991) and the *cipher reading* stage (Gough & Hillinger, 1980) to convey the point that learners acquire and use orderly relationships for associating sounds to the letters they see in words. In terms of development, there is a marked contrast between the previous two phases and this phase. The pre- and partial-alphabetic phases occur inevitably among beginners who lack full knowledge of the alphabetic system and who, as a result, grapple with word reading in ways that are not completely effective. In contrast, the full-alphabetic phase is an essential beginning point that enables beginners to acquire the foundation for attaining mature reading skill in an alphabetic writing system. Mastery of this phase is essential for moving into the next two phases. Beginners who are taught to read words in writing systems whose spelling–sound correspondences are more regular than English—for example, German—and who receive systematic phonics instruction spend little if any time in the pre- and partial-alphabetic phases once they learn how letters symbolize sounds (Wimmer, 1993; Wimmer & Goswami, 1994).

The following word-reading responses characterize students at the full-alphabetic phase (Ehri, 1991, 1994; Gough & Hillinger, 1980; Juel, 1991; Juel et al., 1985; Soderbergh, 1977):

1. Learners possess working knowledge of the major grapheme–phoneme correspondences, including vowels, and they possess phonemic awareness, which enables them to match up phonemes in pronunciations of words to graphemes seen in the conventional spellings of words. This knowledge enables them to decode unfamiliar words, to perform complete graphophonic analyses on words to store them as sight words in memory, and to read unfamiliar words by analogy to familiar words.

2. Early in this phase, decoding operations are executed slowly. The slow, nonfluent reading seen initially has been called *gluing to print* because learners consciously and deliberately sound out and blend letter–sound associations in their word reading (Chall, 1983). Painstaking decoding is a typical, temporary aspect of reading development often traceable to direct instruction in sequential decoding as a means of attacking unfamiliar words (e.g., Barr, 1974/1975; Chall, 1983; Clay, 1967; Monaghan, 1983; Soderbergh, 1977). Beginners become more rapid in applying this strategy as they practice decoding words and as their knowledge of fully analyzed sight words grows. They become familiar with the most frequent sounds symbolized by letters and how these sounds are typically blended in words. Their decoding fluency increases with practice.

3. One very important development at this phase is the sizable growth that occurs in students' sight vocabularies as a result of reading practice. Much of this practice involves reading words in the context of stories. As indicated above, students must possess working knowledge of the

alphabetic system to be able to look at words in text and perform the matching operations linking graphemes to phonemes. Students who have practiced reading new words in this way, perhaps as few as four times (Reitsma, 1983), retain the new words in memory and can read them by sight. As a result, the learner's sight vocabulary grows steadily and rather substantially during the full-alphabetic phase.

4. At this phase, students become able to read unfamiliar words by analogy to familiar words they know by sight, for example, reading *beak* by analogy to *peak*. Goswami (1986, 1988) has shown that beginners can analogize early in their reading development when the analogs are present to prompt word reading. However, for beginners to read new words by analogy to sight words retrieved from memory, they must have some decoding skill (Ehri & Robbins, 1992). This enables them to store the sight words in memory in sufficient letter detail to recognize that the new words resemble but are not identical to the known words and to adapt their knowledge of known words in blending sounds to form new words. Although analogizing becomes possible at this phase, it is more common at the next phase as readers' knowledge of sight words grows and as their decoding skills become easier to execute.

5. Text reading is initially slow and laborious even though students know most grapheme–phoneme relations. How laborious it is depends on how many unfamiliar words the text contains and how accessible its meaning is. According to conventional wisdom based on work by Betts (1954) and others, for text reading to be sufficiently comfortable and productive, students must be able to read most of the words accurately, with comprehension at or above 75%. Texts that students can read independently are those whose words are read at accuracy levels above 95%. Texts at an instructional level are read with about 95% accuracy, allowing teachers to observe students' miscues and fluency, identify difficulties, and provide help. Texts become frustrating when word reading accuracy drops below 95%.

Text reading practice is essential for acquiring reading skill, particularly in English, which involves retaining the specific forms of words in memory to read them effectively (Share & Stanovich, 1995). Students must be exposed to these words to learn how to read them. They must have the decoding and prediction skills to read the unfamiliar words accurately and to activate connection-forming processes that will retain the words in memory as sight words. Because each book they read contains only a few unfamiliar words, they need to read many books for their sight vocabularies to grow.

Instructional Implications. To promote learning in the full-alphabetic phase, and to help students move into the next phase, a number of instructional suggestions can be offered.

To help learners move from slow, deliberate decoding to faster decoding that involves less overt attention to each grapheme–phoneme relation, the key is practice. Beginners must read—a lot. Much practice in analyzing letter–sound associations within words is necessary so that these associations become rapidly executed and automatic.

Accuracy levels in reading words in text can be enhanced by having students read books that they have heard or read before. However, the problem is that if students rely mainly on their memory for the text and do not pay sufficient attention to the print, this form of reading will contribute little to strengthening their text reading fluency or their sight-word acquisition. The alternative is to have students practice reading texts that they have not read before. However, the problem here is that texts must be found in which the words can be read by sight, by decoding, or by prediction with at least 95% accuracy. It is especially hard to find such books for beginners with small sight vocabularies and slow decoding skill.

In this phase the strategy of reading new words by analogy to known words can be strengthened by teaching students to divide words into syllabic and sub-syllabic units. Monosyllabic words can be divided into onsets and rimes (Treiman, 1985). An *onset* is the part of a syllable that comes before a vowel (e.g., the *h* in *hall*), while the *rime* is the rest of the syllable (i.e., the *all* in *hall*). Teachers have often called the rime a *phonogram*. The term *word family* applies to word sets that contain a commonly spelled and pronounced rime, for example, *hall*, *ball*, *tall*, *call*.

Recent findings suggest the importance of helping students recognize and practice reading words using onsets and rimes (e.g., see Treiman, 1985). Students might experiment with the spellings of rimes by substituting alternative onsets in front of the rimes (sometimes called *consonant substitution*) and then reading the product to determine whether it is a recognizable word, or students might be given an assortment of new words that are analogous to words they already know, with the task of identifying the familiar analog and showing how it can be applied to read the new word—for example, using the known word *book* to read the unknown word *cook*. Use of rimes to promote analogizing is considered particularly serviceable because research findings indicate that it is easier for beginners to make an analogy between the ending portions of words than between the beginning portions, for example, *book* ⟶ *cook* versus *hea*t ⟶ *hea*p (Goswami, 1986).

Gaskins and her staff at Benchmark School (Gaskins et al., 1988) have developed a word-identification program that teaches students to read words by analogy. The program was developed to address the word reading problems of children having difficulty learning to read. Students are taught over the course of the first year of instruction to read and spell a set of 93 key words in the way described above, by fully analyzing the graphophonic relations in the words so that they are retained in memory as sight words. The words are selected to exhibit major grapheme–phoneme relations and common rime spellings. As each key word is learned, students are asked to identify its spelling pattern—for example, in *skate*, the letters *ate*—and to think of other words with the same pattern. Students are given much practice using key words to read unfamiliar words, multisyllabic as well as monosyllabic. Students are especially proud when they are successful at decoding "college level" words in this way—for example, reading *temperature* by recognizing the following analogies and stating aloud, "If I know *ten* then I know *tem*, if I know *her* then I know *per*, if I know *fur* then I know *tur*." Lovett et al. (1994) found that this approach helps disabled readers make progress in learning to read.

At this phase, it is important for students to practice reading words in connected text in a way that combines graphophonic processing with comprehension. One characteristic of disabled readers is that they slight graphophonic cues and rely excessively on context for reading words in text. As a result, their sight vocabularies may fail to develop adequately. The antidote to this is to strengthen disabled readers' working knowledge of the alphabetic system sufficiently so that graphophonic connections in words are processed spontaneously during text reading.

In observing students read text orally, teachers should look for signs of the following behaviors. Students should use sight-word memory to read familiar words. They should apply decoding or analogizing strategies mainly to read unfamiliar words. They should use a prediction strategy to confirm the accuracy of the words that are identified by the other strategies. (Failure to do this is evidenced by miscues that do not make sense and that are not self-corrected.) Prediction can also be used to aid in identifying words that are resistant to the other strategies. However, if students rely on prediction as the primary means of identifying words and skip over words so predicted without processing their graphophonic connections, then text reading practice will fall short as a means of building students' word-reading skills.

Consolidated-Alphabetic Phase

The consolidated-alphabetic phase actually begins during the full-alphabetic phase. Its onset is characterized by the consolidation of larger units out of grapheme–phoneme relations that recur in different words. This phase has also been referred to as the *orthographic* phase to indicate that the focus is on spelling patterns (Ehri, 1991; Frith, 1985). Word learning becomes more mature in several respects (Ehri, 1991, 1994; Juel, 1983).

1. The important acquisition at this phase involves learning chunks of letters that recur in different words and how they are pronounced. These
letter chunks might include affixes, root words, onsets, rimes, and syllables. The patterns might be linked to their linguistic origins—Anglo-
Saxon, Greek, and Latin—to clarify the distinctions and regularities
(Henry, 1989). The value of these chunks is that they facilitate word-
decoding accuracy and speed (Juel, 1983) as well as sight-word learning
(Ehri, 1995). Whereas full-alphabetic readers operate primarily with
grapheme–phoneme relations, consolidated-alphabetic readers can operate with larger units as well, hence reducing the total number of units
to be processed in words. For example, the word *interesting* contains
10 graphophonic units (including *ng*, symbolizing one phoneme) but
only 4 graphosyllabic units.

2. Among the first spellings that are likely to become consolidated are
those that occur most frequently in children's texts. These include the
morphemic suffixes *-ed*, *-ing*, *-er*, and *-est* (Bryant, 1997) as well as
spelling patterns that recur in many words and are high-frequency words
themselves: *-it*, *-at*, *-in*, *-an*, *-and*, *-all*.

3. Students' sight vocabularies continue to grow. It is easier to store longer
words in memory because learners can form connections between familiar letter chunks; they are not limited to grapheme–phoneme connections. Readers in the consolidated-alphabetic phase recognize sight
words by remembering connections involving multiletter combinations
as well as single graphemes. When words are learned in this way, they
are seldom confused with other words having similar spellings.

4. Students who learn the strategy of reading words by analogy are assisted in recognizing spelling patterns that recur in different words and in
building neighborhoods of words organized by spelling pattern in memory (Laxon, Coltheart, & Keating, 1988). This facilitates the consolidation of letter sequences into units.

5. To read unfamiliar words, decoding strategies are expanded to include
hierarchical decoding as well as sequential decoding. In hierarchical
decoding, more complex understandings are acquired about the influence of graphemes occurring in one part of the word on the sounds of
graphemes in other parts of the word—for example, the influence of final *-e* on the preceding vowel (e.g., *fine* vs. *fin*, *pane* vs. *pan*, *cone* vs.
con), the influence of *e* and *i* on the preceding consonant *g* or *c* (e.g.,
wage vs. *wag*, *cent* vs. *cant*, *face* vs. *fact*, *city* vs. *cat*), and the influence
of double consonants on a preceding vowel (e.g., *cutter* vs. *cuter*, *latte*
vs. *late*) (Venezky, 1970; Venezky & Johnson, 1973). Students acquire
working knowledge, that is, implicit knowledge, of these relations.

Teaching students explicitly stated rules may promote acquisition of working knowledge, but it is no guarantee (Beck, 1981). Evidence that students have acquired working knowledge is revealed in tasks requiring them to read real words they have never read before (such as *gather*) or nonwords (such as *cibe*) containing the patterns.

Instructional Implications. Signs that average readers are using consolidated units in their reading become apparent typically in second grade (Bowey & Hansen, 1994; Ehri, 1991; Juel, 1983, 1991). Acquisition of more complex relationships may continue to mature through at least the eighth grade (Juel, 1991; Venezky, 1976).

Although the analogy strategy may be taught in the full-alphabetic phase, continued attention is warranted during the consolidated-alphabetic phase. To direct students' attention to common spelling patterns, they can practice dividing written words into onsets and rimes and practice the strategy of reading words by analogy. As this phase progresses, students should be helped to make the transition from (a) analogizing with prompts to (b) analogizing consciously on their own to (c) analogizing unconsciously on their own.

Students should learn to break apart multisyllabic words into separate syllables by locating vowel nuclei and pronouncing each vowel with its adjacent consonants as a separate syllable. Some syllables can be read by analogy to familiar words. As students practice decoding multisyllabic words, they acquire implicit awareness that syllable breaks tend to come between certain letters and not between others. Practice is much more effective for learning this than having students memorize syllabication rules. Segmenting spelling patterns into syllables and pronouncing them can be done not only to decode unfamiliar words but also to analyze the spellings of lengthy words whose identities have already been determined, perhaps from context. This type of analysis should help students form the connections needed to retain the words in memory as sight words.

Additional regularities of the English spelling system will become apparent to students who engage in word-study activities that involve distinguishing the linguistic roots of spellings and then analyzing words with these roots to discover relationships between the meanings of words and the meanings of their parts (Henry, 1989). For example, students can learn to identify and analyze words containing Anglo-Saxon parts, such as *hood*, *ful*, *ness*, *ship*, and *ish*; or Greek parts, such as *tele*, *graph*, *ology*, *phon*, and *auto*; or Latin parts, such as *tion*, *ture*, *scrib*, *struct*, and *rupt*. They can explore whether different words having the same parts bear any similarities in their meanings as a result. Word-study activities such as these can be quite fascinating to students.

Delayed readers may gain control of graphophonic word-identification strategies with carefully planned programs, but their progress is often halted around the fourth grade, when they encounter increasing numbers of multisyllable

words—not just two-syllable words, but words having three, four, and five syllables or more. Orthographic recoding through application of word-pattern analysis,
use of typical word units, and recognition of prefixes and suffixes must receive direct practice for disabled readers to become skillful in identifying these words.
Providing recoding models ("look for affixes, then look for a base word"), teaching students to detect analogies, giving practice dividing words into syllables,
using word sorts designed to point up common syllables, building longer words
from shorter ones, and other activities can develop skill in processing multisyllabic words. (See Cunningham, 1998, for additional specific suggestions.)

Students should engage in much practice using the various knowledge
sources and strategies to read words during text reading so that word reading
becomes automatic and fluent. This is important so that word reading operates
unobtrusively as an integral part of text reading with the reader's attention focused on comprehension.

Automatic Phase

This is the phase of proficient word reading. Chall (1983) termed this the *automatic phase* because of readers' highly developed automaticity and speed in identifying unfamiliar as well as familiar words. The majority of words that readers at
this phase encounter are words in their sight vocabularies, enabling them to read
most words effortlessly in or out of context. On the occasions when an uncommon, technical, or foreign word is met, these readers have several strategies at
their disposal for identifying the word. There is some evidence that when
automatic-phase readers recognize words by sight, the other word-reading strategies are at work as well, though at an unconscious level, and contribute to efficient reading by confirming the identities of words and thus creating redundancy
in the processing of text (Perfetti, 1985). The presence of multiple sources to verify word recognition maintains a high level of reading accuracy. Automatic, fluent
word recognition frees the reader's attention to focus on text meaning.

Conclusion

In this review we have indicated that as readers progress from the earliest phase
of reading to the most proficient phase, they learn to read words by several different means: by using context, by decoding through use of letter–sound associations or spelling patterns, by analogy, and by sight. At each phase, reading
improves as new mechanisms for recognizing words are added to the learner's
repertoire. When readers reach the automatic phase, all of these systems are under their control. It is important for teachers to recognize which systems are operational at each phase and which are beyond reach at that phase.

Knowledge of the characteristics of each phase can provide teachers with a
basis for assessing the strategies available to readers when they respond to print.

As a first step, teachers can examine the list of characteristics typical of each phase and compare them to the predominant responses of a learner. Once the probable phase is identified, a program of word learning can be tailored to capitalize on the student's learning strengths, to avoid instruction that requires processes the learner has not yet acquired, and to provide lessons that will move the student through that phase into the next. In this way, knowledge about the phases of word learning allows teachers of delayed and disabled readers to move beyond generalized prescriptions for word learning. It provides them with a basis for designing lessons that more precisely make contact with each student's word-reading knowledge and strategies.

In the past, a common approach to instruction has been to determine which specific skill needs to be taught to students—for example, developing a larger sight vocabulary, or increasing knowledge of letter–sound relationships, or increasing fluency. Once determined, a rather standard group of activities has typically been used with all students. In contrast, according to phase theory, what is taught depends on a student's phase of development. Although all facets of word learning may need to be addressed in some fashion, the specific type of instruction that facilitates reading for students in one word-learning phase may not advance learning for students in a different phase. Vellutino and Scanlon (1987) provide one example of this disparity. Teachers may expedite breakthroughs into reading during the pre-alphabetic phase of development by giving students immediate access to word names through whole-word instruction. However, this will not contribute to students' development in the next phase. For progress to continue, teachers must provide opportunities for students to develop skill in analyzing words into their sound-symbol constituents. Another example is the teacher who attempts to teach letter–sound decoding to students who lack phonemic awareness or knowledge of all the letter shapes and sounds. This is destined to result in slow and incomplete learning as well as frustration for both teacher and student.

It is important to recognize that, compared to normally developing readers, delayed and disabled readers have more difficulty learning to read words in most of the ways we have described. They are slower to acquire a sight vocabulary (Ehri & Saltmarsh, 1995). They have limited knowledge and use of decoding and analogizing strategies (Rack, Snowling, & Olson, 1992). One reason why multiple word-reading deficiencies are apparent in these students is that the various ways of reading words develop together and are mutually interdependent throughout development, as we have indicated. If one way does not develop adequately, then the other ways will not develop adequately either. Decoding skill is needed to retain fully analyzed sight words in memory. A sight vocabulary is needed to read words by analogy. Familiarity with analogous relations among sight words helps in learning spelling patterns that are useful for more efficient decoding. This means that students having difficulty learning to read need instruction that is thorough in covering all aspects of word reading. Very little can be left to self-discovery or chance. Clues about how growth can be promoted at each phase of development are found in the cognitive and instructional descriptions we offer in this piece. With practice applying this phase theory in their teaching, we hope that teachers can acquire a more refined sense of their students, of how far they have progressed in their ability to read words, and of what types of instruction are most helpful for advancing their development as readers.

References

Adams, M. (1990). *Beginning to read: Thinking and learning about print*. Cambridge, MA: MIT Press.

Ball, E., & Blachman, B. (1991). Does phoneme awareness training in kindergarten make a difference in early word recognition and developmental spelling? *Reading Research Quarterly, 26*, 49–66.

Baron, J., & Treiman, R. (1980). Use of orthography in reading and learning to read. In J. Kavanaugh & R. Venezky (Eds.), *Orthography, reading, and dyslexia* (pp. 155–170). Baltimore: University Park Press.

Barr, R. (1974/1975). The effect of instruction on pupil reading strategies. *Reading Research Quarterly, 10*, 555–582.

Beck, I. (1981). Reading problems and instructional practices. In G. Mackinnon & T. Waller (Eds.), *Reading research: Advances in theory and practice* (Vol. 2, pp. 55–95). New York: Academic Press.

Betts, E. (1954). *Foundations of reading instruction* (3rd ed.). New York: American Book Co.

Biemiller, A. (1977/1978). Relationship between oral reading rates for letters, words, and simple text in the development of reading achievement. *Reading Research Quarterly, 13*, 223–253.

Blachman, B. (1984). Relationship of rapid naming ability and language analysis skills to kindergarten and first-grade reading achievement. *Journal of Educational Psychology, 76*, 610–622.

Bowers, P., & Wolf, M. (1993). Theoretical links among naming speed, precise timing mechanisms and orthographic skill in dyslexia. *Reading and Writing: An Interdisciplinary Journal, 5*, 69–85.

Bowey, J., & Hansen, J. (1994). The development of orthographic rimes as units of word recognition. *Journal of Experimental Child Psychology, 58*, 465–488.

Bryant, P., Nunes, T., & Bindman, M. (1997). Children's understanding of the connection between grammar and spelling. In B. Blachman (Ed.), *Foundations of reading acquisition and dyslexia: Implications for early intervention* (pp. 219–240). Mahwah, NJ: Erlbaum.

Chall, J. (1967). *Learning to read: The great debate*. New York: McGraw-Hill.

Chall, J. (1983). *Stages of reading development*. New York: McGraw-Hill.

Clay, M. (1967). The reading behaviour of five-year-old children: A research report. *New Zealand Journal of Educational Studies, 2*(1), 11–31.

Cunningham, P.M. (1998). The multisyllabic word dilemma: Helping students build meaning, spell, and read "big" words. *Reading & Writing Quarterly, 14*, 191–218.

Ehri, L. (1986). Sources of difficulty in learning to spell and read words. In M. Wolraich & D. Routh (Eds.), *Advances in developmental and behavioral pediatrics* (Vol. 7, pp. 121–195). Greenwich, CT: JAI Press.

Ehri, L. (1987). Learning to read and spell words. *Journal of Reading Behavior, 19*, 5–31.

Ehri, L. (1991). Development of the ability to read words. In R. Barr, M.L. Kamil, P. Mosenthal, & P.D. Pearson (Eds.), *Handbook of reading research* (Vol. 2, pp. 383–417). White Plains, NY: Longman.

Ehri, L. (1992). Reconceptualizing the development of sight word reading and its relationship to recoding. In P. Gough, L. Ehri, & R. Treiman (Eds.), *Reading acquisition* (pp. 107–143). Hillsdale, NJ: Erlbaum.

Ehri, L. (1994). Development of the ability to read words: Update. In R.B. Ruddell, M.R. Ruddell, & H. Singer (Eds.), *Theoretical models and processes of reading* (4th ed., pp. 323–358). Newark, DE: International Reading Association.

Ehri, L. (1995). Phases of development in learning to read words by sight. *Journal of Research in Reading, 18*, 116–125.

Ehri, L. (1997). Learning to read and learning to spell are one and the same, almost. In C. Perfetti, L. Rieben, & M. Fayol (Eds.), *Learning to spell: Research, theory and practice across languages* (pp. 237–269). Mahwah, NJ: Erlbaum.

Ehri, L. (1997). Sight word learning in normal readers and dyslexics. In B. Blachman (Ed.), *Foundations of reading acquisition and dyslexia: Implications for early intervention* (pp. 163–189). Mahwah, NJ: Erlbaum.

Ehri, L., Deffner, N., & Wilce, L. (1984). Pictorial mnemonics for phonics. *Journal of Educational Psychology, 76*, 880–893.

Ehri, L., & Robbins, C. (1992). Beginners need some decoding skill to read words by analogy. *Reading Research Quarterly, 27*, 12–26.

Ehri, L., & Saltmarsh, J. (1995). Beginning readers outperform older disabled readers in learning to read words by sight. *Reading and Writing: An Interdisciplinary Journal, 7*, 295–326.

Ehri, L., & Wilce, L. (1985). Movement into reading: Is the first stage of printed word learning visual or phonetic? *Reading Research Quarterly, 20*, 163–179.

Ehri, L., & Wilce, L. (1987a). Cipher versus cue reading: An experiment in decoding acquisition. *Journal of Educational Psychology, 79*, 3–13.

Ehri, L., & Wilce, L. (1987b). Does learning to spell help beginners learn to read words? *Reading Research Quarterly, 22*, 47–65.

Ehri, L., & Williams, J. (1996). Learning to read and learning to teach reading. In F. Murray (Ed.), *The teacher educator's handbook: Building a knowledge base for the preparation of teachers* (pp. 231–244). San Francisco: Jossey-Bass.

Elkonin, D. (1973). U.S.S.R. In J. Downing (Ed.), *Comparative reading* (pp. 551–579). New York: Macmillan.

Frith, V. (1985). Beneath the surface of developmental dyslexia. In K.E. Patterson, J.C. Marshall, & M. Coltheart (Eds.), *Surface dyslexia: Neuropsychological and cognitive studies of phonological reading* (pp. 301–330). London: Erlbaum.

Gaskins, I., Downer, M., Anderson, R., Cunningham, P., Gaskins, R., Schommer, M., et al. (1988). A metacognitive approach to phonics: Using what you know to decode what you don't know. *Remedial and Special Education, 9*, 36–41.

Gaskins, I., Ehri, L., Cress, C., O'Hara, C., & Donnelly, K. (1996/1997). Procedures for word learning: Making discoveries about words. *The Reading Teacher, 50*, 312–327.

Goodman, K. (1976). Reading: A psycholinguistic guessing game. In H. Singer & R.B. Ruddell (Eds.), *Theoretical models and processes of reading* (2nd ed., pp. 497–508). Newark, DE: International Reading Association.

Goswami, U. (1986). Children's use of analogy in learning to read: A developmental study. *Journal of Experimental Child Psychology, 42*, 73–83.

Goswami, U. (1988). Orthographic analogies and reading development. *Quarterly Journal of Experimental Psychology, 40*, 239–268.

Gough, P., Ehri, L., & Treiman, R. (Eds.). (1992). *Reading acquisition*. Hillsdale, NJ: Erlbaum.

Gough, P., & Hillinger, M. (1980). Learning to read: An unnatural act. *Bulletin of the Orton Society, 30*, 179–196.

Gough, P., & Walsh, S. (1991). Chinese, Phoenicians, and the orthographic cipher of English. In S. Brady & D. Shankweiler (Eds.), *Phonological processes in literacy: A tribute to Isabelle Y. Liberman* (pp. 199–209). Hillsdale, NJ: Erlbaum.

Griffith, P., & Olson, M. (1992). Phonemic awareness helps beginning readers break the code. *The Reading Teacher, 45*, 516–523.

Henderson, E. (1981). *Learning to read and spell: The child's knowledge of words*. DeKalb: Northern Illinois University Press.

Henry, M. (1989). Children's word structure knowledge: Implications for decoding and spelling instruction. *Reading and Writing: An Interdisciplinary Journal, 2*, 135–152.

Juel, C. (1983). The development and use of mediated word identification. *Reading Research Quarterly, 18*, 306–327.

Juel, C. (1991). Beginning reading. In R. Barr, M.L. Kamil, P. Mosenthal, & P.D. Pearson (Eds.), *Handbook of reading research* (Vol. 2, pp. 759–788). White Plains, NY: Longman.

Juel, C., Griffith, P., & Gough, P. (1985). Reading and spelling strategies of first-grade children. In J. Niles & R. Lalik (Eds.), *Issues in literacy: A research perspective* (pp. 306–309). Rochester, NY. National Reading Conference.

Juel, C., Griffith, P., & Gough, P. (1986). Acquisition of literacy: A longitudinal study of children in first and second grade. *Journal of Educational Psychology, 78*, 243–255.

LaBerge, D., & Samuels, J. (1974). Toward a theory of automatic information processing in reading. *Cognitive Psychology, 6*, 293–323.

Laxon, V., Coltheart, V., & Keating, C. (1988). Children find friendly words friendly too: Words with many orthographic neighbours are easier to read and spell. *British Journal of Educational Psychology, 58*, 103–119.

Lindamood, C., & Lindamood, P. (1975). *Auditory discrimination in depth: The ADD program.* Austin, TX: Pro-Ed.

Lovett, M., Borden, S., DeLuca, T., Lacerenza, L., Bensen, N., & Brackstone, D. (1994). Treating the core deficits of developmental dyslexia: Evidence of transfer of learning after phonologically- and strategy-based reading training programs. *Developmental Psychology, 30*, 805–822.

Mason, J. (1980). When do children learn to read? An exploration of four-year-old children's letter and word reading competencies. *Reading Research Quarterly, 15*, 202–227.

Masonheimer, P., Drum, P., & Ehri, L. (1984). Does environmental print identification lead children into word reading? *Journal of Reading Behavior, 16*, 257–272.

McCormick, S. (1994). A nonreader becomes a reader: A case study of literacy acquisition by a severely disabled reader. *Reading Research Quarterly, 29*, 156–177.

Monaghan, J. (1983, April). *A four-year study of the acquisition of letter–sound correspondences.* Paper presented at the annual meeting of the American Educational Research Association, Montreal, Quebec, Canada.

Perfetti, C. (1985). *Reading ability.* New York: Oxford University Press.

Pratt, A., & Brady, S. (1988). Relation of phonological awareness to reading disability in children and adults. *Journal of Educational Psychology, 80*, 319–323.

Rack, J., Snowling, M., & Olson, R. (1992). The nonword reading deficit in developmental dyslexia: A review. *Reading Research Quarterly, 27*, 28–53.

Read, C. (1970). Pre-school children's knowledge of English phonology. *Harvard Educational Review, 41*, 1–34.

Reitsma, P. (1983). Printed word learning in beginning readers. *Journal of Experimental Child Psychology, 75*, 321–339.

Scott, J., & Ehri, L. (1989). Sight word reading in prereaders: Use of logographic vs. alphabetic access routes. *Journal of Reading Behavior, 22*, 149–166.

Share, D., Jorm, A., Maclean, R., & Matthews, R. (1984). Sources of individual differences in reading acquisition. *Journal of Educational Psychology, 76*, 1309–1324.

Share, D., & Stanovich, K. (1995). Cognitive processes in early reading development: Accommodating individual differences into a model of acquisition. *Issues in Education: Contributions From Educational Psychology, 1*, 1–57.

Soderbergh, R. (1977). *Reading in early childhood: A linguistic study of a preschool child's gradual acquisition of reading ability.* Washington, DC: Georgetown University Press.

Stahl, S., & Murray, B. (1994). Defining phonological awareness and its relationship to early reading. *Journal of Educational Psychology, 86*, 221–234.

Stahl, S., & Murray, B. (1998). Issues involved in defining phonological awareness and its relation to early reading. In J.L. Metsala & L.C. Ehri (Eds.), *Word recognition in beginning literacy* (pp. 65–88). Hillsdale, NJ: Erlbaum.

Stuart, M., & Coltheart, M. (1988). Does reading develop in a sequence of stages? *Cognition, 30*, 139–181.

Sulzby, E. (1986). Children's emergent reading of favorite storybooks: A developmental study. *Reading Research Quarterly, 20*, 458–481.

Treiman, R. (1985). Onsets and rimes as units of spoken syllables: Evidence from children. *Journal of Experimental Child Psychology, 39*, 161–181.

Vellutino, F. (1979). *Dyslexia: Theory and research.* Cambridge, MA: MIT Press.

Vellutino, F., & Scanlon, D. (1987). Phonological coding, phonological awareness, and reading ability: Evidence from a longitudinal and experimental study. *Merrill-Palmer Quarterly, 27*, 321–363.

Venezky, R. (1970). *The structure of English orthography.* The Hague, the Netherlands: Mouton.

Venezky, R. (1976). *Theoretical and experimental base for teaching reading.* The Hague, the Netherlands: Mouton.

Venezky, R., & Johnson, D. (1973). Development of two letter–sound patterns in grades one through three. *Journal of Educational Psychology, 64*, 109–115.

Wendon, L. (1991). *First steps in Letterland*. Cambridge, UK: Letterland Ltd.

Wendon, L. (1993). Literacy for early childhood: Learning from the learners. *Early Child Development and Care*, *86*, 11–22.

Wimmer, H. (1993). Characteristics of developmental dyslexia in a regular writing system. *Applied Psycholinguistics*, *14*, 1–33.

Wimmer, H., & Goswami, U. (1994). The influence of orthographic consistency on reading development: Word recognition in English and German children. *Cognition*, *51*, 91–103.

15

The Texts of Beginning Reading Instruction

Elfrieda H. Hiebert and Leigh Ann Martin

Basal readers have been the foundation on which reading instruction has been built (Chall & Squire, 1991). While approaches to reading instruction and the materials used to support this instruction have changed over the years, what has remained constant in U.S. reading instruction is the use of prepackaged materials offered by textbook companies. In 1992, over 85% of schools reported using basal reading programs (Shannon, 1997), and this figure appears to have remained fairly stable since then (Baumann, Hoffman, Duffy-Hester, & Ro, 2000).

Although the ways in which teachers use the same textbook can vary considerably, the contents of textbooks create parameters for teachers and their students. Particularly with children who are on the cusp of acquiring independent reading proficiency, characteristics of texts such as the presence of illustrations, the nature of the language, and the number of words can influence the kinds of experiences children and their teachers can have. Our interest in this review lies with the textbooks intended for beginning readers, especially those whose literacy experiences occur primarily in school. Approximately 40–45% of an American fourth-grade cohort read so slowly that they are unsuccessful with complex literacy tasks (Donahue, Voelkl, Campbell, & Mazzeo, 1999). Aiming to improve students' reading achievement, state officials in two of the three largest states in the United States—California and Texas—have used reading textbooks, primarily those intended for beginning readers, as a foundation for reform in reading achievement. In both states, the use of state monies for textbook purchases is limited to those texts that meet the state's criteria. Both states have mandated substantially different texts for beginning readers from one adoption cycle to another. When mandates have identified high-quality literature as the requisite materials for beginning readers, research has been cited as driving this mandate (California English/Language Arts Committee, 1987; Texas Education Agency, 1990). When mandates have identified decodable text as the requisite materials

From Neuman, S.B., & Dickinson, D.K. (Eds.), *Handbook of Early Literacy Research* (pp. 361–376). Copyright © 2001 by The Guilford Press. Reprinted with permission of the publisher.

for beginning readers, research has been cited as driving this mandate (California English/Language Arts Committee, 2000; Texas Education Agency, 1997).

The purpose of this review is to study the existing research on the effects that particular types of texts have on beginning readers. There were three questions of particular interest. The first considers how reading acquisition is facilitated or hindered by different types of texts. The limited number of existing studies on the effects of texts on children's reading acquisition is not surprising because isolating text effects is difficult. Even so, the policies of Texas and California—particularly those on decodable text—would suggest a much more substantial empirical foundation than currently exists.

The second question addressed in this review was how different types of words are acquired. The literature on how words are learned individually or in phrases or single sentences is fairly extensive. This learning is typically evaluated in research contexts where an individual child interacts with an investigator. Despite the limitations of the texts and contexts of these studies, these studies provide the bulk of the available evidence on how children learn to read.

Third, we examined the research on characteristics of current texts for beginning readers. Texts have changed substantially over the past two decades. Our interest lay in establishing how current texts matched the patterns from text and word-learning studies.

Effects of Particular Text Types on Children's Reading Development

In light of the sizable investments publishers make in reading textbooks and the daily use of these texts in classrooms, it is surprising to find few studies on the effects of texts on beginning reading development. Most existing studies are limited in scope and often flawed in their design. The primary shortcoming is the confounding of text effects with those of instructional method. For example, when Foorman, Francis, Fletcher, Schatschneider, and Mehta (1998) investigated the effects of using a direct code approach, an embedded code approach, and an implicit code approach, each of these approaches had unique text types and instructional activities in addition to their approaches to phonics.

Hiebert (1999) identified three types of texts for beginning readers: high-frequency texts, phonics texts, and literature-based texts. In one group that Hiebert described as high-frequency texts, words such as *here*, *can*, and *he* are overrepresented. Phonics texts support word recognition through a preponderance of decodable vocabulary. Literature-based texts emphasize the meaningfulness of the entire text, one form of which are "predictable" texts which repeat phrases or sentences. Any text can embody any of these supports to varying degrees. However, the swings in reading instruction have tended to categorize texts based on one dimension. Following proposals that predictable texts could serve as the entree to conventional reading (Holdaway, 1979; Martin & Brogan, 1971), predictable texts have dominated the textbook programs available for beginning reading instruction. Despite their dominance over the past 15 years, the effectiveness of predictable texts in supporting reading acquisition is unclear. This review emphasizes predictable text because of the critical role it continues to have in programs for beginning readers.

In the studies of predictable text that have been conducted, the nature of miscues as a function of reading has been a particular focus. Although beginning readers display more fluency with predictable texts than texts from basal reading programs or phonics texts (Gourley, 1984; Rhodes, 1979), this fluency is an artifact of the predictable pattern of the text. When Rhodes (1979) divided each text into quarters, she found that children did well after they mastered the repetitive, patterned portion of the predictable texts. Once the text broke the pattern, children tended to experience difficulty. Similarly, Leu, DeGroff, and Simons, (1986) found that once children had mastered the pattern (but not before), the contextual supports of a predictable text helped poor readers improve their reading rates and comprehension to the level of good readers. But poorer readers were less likely to attend to deviations in the pattern than good readers. Within the context of the predictable text itself, the pattern of the text offers support for beginning and poor readers but only after children have mastered the pattern. Further, these texts appear to encourage an overreliance on the pattern.

The studies of children's miscues fail to indicate how well children remember words that they have read in predictable texts. In Bridge, Winograd, and Haley's (1983) study of the effects of reading predictable or basal texts on measures of target word recognition, the predictable text group learned significantly more target words than the basal group. Although these findings suggest that the use of multiple rereadings and sentence and word activities based on the text may result in superior word learning, the exact contribution of the text to this learning is unclear because instructional activities of the groups differed substantially. The predictable text group engaged in multiple rereadings of texts, sentence and word card activities, and writing of stories, and the basal group engaged in two readings of texts (one silent and one oral) and comprehension checks.

An experiment by Boylin (1998), in which one group of first graders read decodable texts while another group read predictable texts, resulted in no discernible differences between the groups. Boylin, however, observed that the children's reading of the decodable texts occurred only during twice-weekly tutoring sessions. Children's typical fare was the predictable texts that were part of the classroom program rather than the decodable texts.

While not comparing predictable and decodable texts directly, a study by Hoffman, Roser, Patterson, Salas, and Pennington (1999) examined children's reading of seven randomly ordered texts which teachers had leveled for decodability and predictability. Hoffman et al. (1999) found that the decodability of texts significantly correlated with student performance. The combined decodability and predictability index with reading levels from the Qualitative Reading Inventory were the best predictors of student performance on the texts. Although this study does not measure the impact of decodable texts on students' reading development, the results from this study indicate that the decodability and predictability of texts affect beginning readers' fluency, accuracy, and rate.

Reviews of literature typically conclude that phonics-based instruction produces reading achievement superior to approaches that emphasize high-frequency words or meaningful stories (Adams, 1990; Chall, 1995; Foorman et al., 1998), but the relative contribution of particular types of texts—especially texts that consist mainly of highly decodable words—to lessons or writing activities is unclear. One exception is Juel and Roper/Schneider's (1985) examination of the reading development of first graders who received the same phonics lessons but who read in texts from two different basal reading programs. The two basal series differed significantly only in the characteristics of the preprimers, with one preprimer containing easily decodable words while the other preprimer contained mostly high-frequency words. The two factors that contributed most to end-of-the-year reading performance were students' initial knowledge (scores on the Metropolitan Readiness Text) and the basal series. Students who read from the decodable preprimers were more likely to learn letter–sound correspondences early, including ones not explicitly taught, and to use decoding knowledge when encountering unfamiliar words. Use of decodable texts for a particular part of the reading acquisition period seems to help, but this study does not indicate how long this period extends.

Research on Children's Word Learning

Because the research on children's reading acquisition within texts is so limited, we turn to the more extensive research on children's word learning in word lists and phrases. In studies in which word learning individually or in phrases is investigated relative to those in which words are learned in extended texts, researchers can control numerous variables. But, because children's learning is rarely so compartmentalized in the real world of homes and classrooms, the generalizability of findings from laboratory studies of word learning has limitations. Similar findings from numerous studies, however, are suggestive for the design of reading materials and lessons. Children's learning of the three kinds of words that Hiebert (1999) identified as characterizing different text types are reviewed: highly meaningful, highly regular, or phonetically regular words and high-frequency words.

Highly Meaningful Words

Young children's first interest is in words that represent engaging and meaningful concepts. In a yearlong study using children's self-chosen words (see Ashton-Warner, 1963), Hiebert (1983) found that nouns accounted for 98% of the words that young children chose and that half these nouns were proper nouns; words such as *Uncle Dan*, *Magic Marker*, and *Crayolas* were chosen by the young children in that study. Similar to Ashton-Warner's (1963) self-chosen vocabulary, the themes of the beginning reading textbooks from the 1930s through the mid-1980s were chosen to be familiar and relevant to young children (Gray, Monroe, Artley, Arbuthnot, & Gray, 1956). For instance, the theme of a passage in an early text from this period pertains to a child learning to roller-skate. In this passage, the words *roller skate* and *fall down* are never used. The words of interest have been substituted with high-frequency words that ostensibly convey the gist of the passage: "Look, Dick. Dick, Dick. Help Jane."

Texts with this generic vocabulary were replaced in the late 1980s with authentic literature. Rather than repetitive text about a cast of characters, the first passage in a 1993 anthology enumerated things that a young child can do, such as "brush my teeth" and "carry the groceries." The second passage also dealt with things that young children do, but all the activities were new, such as "skate on our roller skates" and "ride our bikes." The emphasis in textbook programs since the late 1980s has been on the engagingness of the text as a whole with less attention given to the repetition of meaningful words.

When many different words are introduced in passage after passage, remembering a core set of words will be difficult for beginning readers. A core set of high-meaning words, however, appears to be critical in reading acquisition. In Ehri's (1994, 1998) model of word learning, the first stage is described as "logographic reading." Children associate visual or quantitative characteristics of words with their spelling or semantic properties. The word *dinosaur*, for example, may be remembered because of the height of the first letter ("The dinosaur has a long neck") and the length of the word ("A dinosaur has a long body"). At this stage, spellings of words represent the meanings of words and are not used as a cipher that represents the sounds of words. This strategy becomes difficult to maintain as children are introduced to more and more words. At this point, they need to use the alphabetic relationships of words. The more refined representations allow children to discriminate and recognize many more words. But these first words to which children attend because of their meaningfulness in their lives (*dinosaur*, *Uncle Dan*) lay the foundation for the next stage in which they attend to alphabetic relationships.

Laing and Hulme (1999) compared beginning readers' learning of words with high and low imagery values. Words with higher imagery values are more concrete than words with low imagery values. For example, *cake* has a higher imagery value than *food*, and *food* has a higher imagery value than *things* or *it*. Laing and Hulme taught target words that varied in imagery values but were similar in familiarity and number of letters and phonemes, as in *cake* and *food*, to children from 4 to 6 years of age. These researchers found that young children learned significantly more highly imageable words than words with low imagery values.

In Metsala's (1999) study, phonological tasks with high-meaning words and words with consistent and common alphabetic relationships (e.g., *cat*, *fat*, and *hat*) were compared with the same tasks using less-meaningful and less-decodable words. Young children performed better on the phonological tasks with words that were meaningful and alphabetic. Although the research base is small for this particular aspect of word learning, the findings support inclusion of at least a core set of meaningful, high-imagery words in beginning texts.

Highly Regular Words

Efficient word recognition in an alphabetic language depends on the beginning reader gaining insight into the alphabetic nature of the written language: that word spellings map onto word pronunciations (Adams, 1990). These mappings can occur at several levels: whole word, syllable, subsyllable, morpheme, and phoneme. For example, the word *cat* may be recognized as a whole (e.g., the sequence of *cat*), as the sequence of three phonemes (e.g., *c*, *a*, and *t*), and as a syllable comprised of an onset *c* and rime *at*. Advanced readers flexibly use any or all of these correspondences, whereas beginning readers usually rely on one mapping or even a partial mapping. Whether beginning readers should be directed in making correspondences at the level of large units (e.g., word or rime) to smaller units (phonemes) or from small units to large units remains a source of debate, but scholars agree that more advanced readers are able to recognize and use both small and large units in reading unfamiliar words (Brown, 1998; Ehri, 1994, 1998; Goswami, 1990, 1998; Thompson, 1999).

Beginning readers benefit from guidance in the alphabetic patterns of written English, but studies of text leave a critical set of questions unanswered. For example, what should the unit of the alphabetic relationship be? Examples of units of the alphabetic relationships are individual grapheme–phonemes such as the letter *t* and sound /t/ or a set of grapheme–phonemes that commonly appears in words such as the *at* (/at/ in *cat*, *fat*, or *hat*). The vowel and the consonant(s) that follow it, as in the example of *at*, are called *rimes*.

The content of the unit is a critical issue in the current political context. The Texas and California mandates both emphasize the phoneme as the unit of learning (California English/Language Arts Committee, 2000; Texas Education Agency, 1997). One of the California criterion for acceptable beginning reading programs is quite explicit: two little books for each of 44 phonemes in both the grade 1 and grade 2 programs. According to this perspective, an individual grapheme–phoneme element becomes known once it has been taught. A word is described as having the potential for accuracy once all its elements have been taught. Take, for example, a beginning text from one of the beginning reading programs on the Texas list (Afflerbach et al., 2000). By the time children begin the first passage in the first-grade texts, these grapheme–phoneme relationships have been taught: *a*, *m*, *t*, *n*, *p*, *b*, *d*, *g*, *w*. These words appear in the first passage:

am, *nap*, *at*, *bat*, *mat*, *cat*, *cap*, *dad*, *wag*. Children should also be able to read *Nat*, *pat*, *bad*, *pad*, *tan*, and *Dan* without further instruction. The criterion of "if taught, then learned" is applied despite evidence that instructional suggestions are many and often superficial in first-grade teachers' guides (Hiebert, Menon, Martin, & Huxley, 2000).

Both the Texas and California mandates present this perspective on the phoneme as the unit of instruction as research based. The research that indicates that children learn individual grapheme–phoneme relationships—especially those children who come to school with little conventional literacy—is less conclusive. To understand the task that confronts beginning readers in becoming fluent in alphabetic relationships, an understanding of the differences between consonants and vowels is useful.

Of the phonemes that Moats (1999) identifies as essential for a teacher of beginning readers to know, 25 are consonants and 18 are vowels. Twenty-one graphemes account for the 25 phonemes that are consonants, while 7 graphemes account for 18 vowel phonemes. Because several alphabet letters (*q*, *x*, *c*) have no unique phonemes associated with them and seven consonants phonemes have several graphemes associated with each (e.g., *f*, *ff*, *sp*, *gh*, and *lf* for /f/), a stance for diversity is useful with consonants. Overall, however, consonants are fairly consistent in their grapheme–phoneme relationships. Treiman, Mullennix, Bijeljac-Babic, and Richmond-Welty (1995) reported that initial consonants are pronounced similarly in 94% of consonant–vowel–consonant (CVC) words, and final consonants are pronounced the same in 92% of CVC words.

The task of associating phonemes with graphemes is quite challenging with vowels where seven graphemes—*a*, *i*, *e*, *o*, *u*, *y*, and *w*—either individually or in combination (*w* always in combination with another grapheme)—account for 15 different phonemes. Further, when the consonant *r* follows the graphemes *a*, *e*, *i*, *o*, and *u*, three more phonemes are produced. Unlike the high percentage of consistency in consonants, vowels have the same pronunciation in only 62% of similarly spelled words (Treiman et al., 1995). When the vowel and the consonant(s) that follows it—the rime—are taken into account, however, consistency increases to 80% in CVC words (Treiman et al., 1995). Wylie and Durrell (1970) report that 272 rimes with stable vowel sounds are contained in 1,437 words and that 37 of these stable rimes occur in 10 or more exemplars, for a total of 500 words.

This stability of particular rimes has led investigators to compare the ease of learning rimes versus the individual grapheme–phoneme. Goswami (1990, 1998), in particular, has argued for analogies to known rime units as the point of departure for beginning readers, with later extension of this knowledge to individual graphemes and phonemes. Goswami (1986, 1988) found that prereaders could make analogies at the level of the rime to read words from a list when a clue word containing the rime was present. But, because the size of the rime analogy effect is small (prereaders identified only 1 word out of 12 in the 1986 experiment), others have investigated the question further (Bowey & Hansen, 1994; Brown, 1998; Savage & Stuart, 1998; Treiman et al., 1995). These studies indicate that facility with rime analogies increases with reading ability and is affected by phonological priming (producing a rhyming response based on the pronunciation of the clue word rather than its orthography) (Bowey & Hansen, 1998; Brown, 1998; Goswami, 1990), the presence of clue words, and the type of prompt given (Goswami, 1986, 1988, 1990; Muter, Hulme, Snowling, & Taylor, 1997; Savage & Stuart, 1998). Beginning readers have also been found to make analogies to the beginnings of words (CV-) as well as the rime units but less often to medial vowels (Bowey & Hansen, 1994; Bruck & Treiman, 1992; Savage & Stuart, 1998). When Bruck and Treiman compared the effectiveness of training beginning readers to make analogies based on rimes, consonant–vowel units, or vowels, children in the rime-based group learned the target words more quickly than did children in the consonant vowel (CV-) or vowel analogy groups, but they performed the poorest on the retention test. Children in the vowel group performed the best on the generalization test. The poor performance of the rime group suggests that training in rime-based analogies may not be as effective as training to make analogies based on the vowel. Because rime-based analogies are easy to make, children who receive rime training may not have fully internalized the rime units. When training does not incorporate a clue word and uses a more rigorous criterion level, children trained to use rime-based analogies perform the same as children trained to make CV-based analogies or to phonologically recode through blending (Levy & Lysynchuk, 1997).

While the ability to phonologically detect onsets and rimes seems to interact with children's use of rime-based analogies (Bruck & Treiman, 1992; Muter et al., 1997), segmentation at the phonemic level and/or knowledge of letter–sound correspondences appears to affect beginning readers' ability to make rime-based analogies (Ehri & Robbins, 1992; Treiman, Goswami, & Bruck, 1990). Sensitivity to the consistency of rimes appears to develop with reading experience (Bowey & Hansen, 1994; Treiman et al., 1990, 1995). Because these studies were based on the frequencies of rimes or the regularity of their pronunciations, the results suggest that it is exposure to the rime, rather than the general development of decoding ability, that enables beginning readers to internalize these units and make use of them. Wylie and Durrell (1970) also found that first graders were more likely to recognize the spellings of high-frequency rimes compared to low-frequency rimes.

A two-part study by Thompson, Cottrell, and Fletcher-Flinn (1996) indicates that the frequency with which particular units appear in words influences children's acquisition of the units. Having established that *b* and *th* in the final position of words occurred significantly less often than *t* and *m*, Thompson et al. (1996) assessed 24 children on CV and VC pseudowords incorporating the target consonants. Words with *b* and *th* in the final position were read with significantly lower accuracy than *m* and *t* in the final position. In a second experiment, Thompson et al. (1996) manipulated the amount of exposure beginning readers had to words containing the consonant *b* in the final position by having children read sentences with a target word that ended in *b* or sentences in which the target words were omitted in the text but supplied orally by the investigator. The former group significantly improved in the accuracy with which pseudowords with *b* in the final position were read, whereas the latter group made no improvement.

In most studies reviewed to this point, words in training and assessment tasks appeared singly or in phrases. In two of Goswami's (1988, 1990) studies, exemplars of rimes were studied within texts. The texts varied in their inclusion of a target word in the title. By having the investigator read the title aloud, children were exposed to the target word. Significantly more words sharing the rime or the CV- unit of the target words than words that shared common letters were read by children who received the "title target word" training than children who did not. Apparently, young children can make analogies while reading text if they have learned the unit that the analogous words share. Conclusions from Goswami's studies need to be interpreted cautiously because participants were almost 7 years old—an age when many children are fluent readers. Within a tutoring intervention of first graders, however, Leslie and Allen (1999) found that when rimes that had been highlighted in instruction occurred in the texts that students read, reading development was positively influenced.

To date, there is no research that supports equal attention to each of 43 or 44 phonemes. There is a research base, however, that provides directions for textbook publishers and researchers. In particular, exposure to words that encourages attention to particular grapheme–phoneme relationships supports reading development. The size of the unit is likely a function of children's existing awareness of graphemes and phonemes. Finally, as Thompson et al. (1996) and Wylie and Durrell (1970) showed, some phonemes have substantial function whereas others appear in significantly fewer words.

High-Frequency Words

One of the problems with an overabundance of instruction on highly decodable words is that much of written text consists of a small group of words—prepositions, connectives, pronouns, and articles. In an analysis of the texts used in grades 3 through 9, Carroll, Davies, and Richman (1971) found that 109 high-frequency words accounted for 50% of the total running words. The issue is muddled by the fact that many high-frequency words have irregular letter–sound relationships. While 29 of the 100 most frequent words have vowel consonant (VC) rimes, a handful of words in the group have a CVC pattern but an atypical pronunciation (e.g., *was*). Among the remaining 67 high-frequency words, 35 are either irregular in their adherence to other patterns (e.g., *have* and *some*) or multisyllabic.

Believing that the irregular or ambiguous pronunciations of these words may confuse beginning readers, publishers of some phonics texts have attempted to restrict the occurrence of high-frequency words (see, e.g., Rasmussen & Goldberg, 1964). But restricting the use of irregular high-frequency words may prevent beginning readers from developing a flexible stance toward reading that can incorporate both regular spelling pronunciations and common variants (Gibson & Levin, 1975).

Readability formulas that were based on high-frequency word counts and sentence length drove textbooks through the late 1980s. Much of the justification for providing an abundance of high-frequency words in beginning texts came from studies in the 1930s. Gates (1930; Gates & Russell, 1938/1939), for example, conducted studies using first-grade materials that varied considerably in the average number of repetitions per word. Gates (1930) interpreted the results of these studies as verification that each word should be repeated an average of 35 times within a basal series.

Several decades later, Reitsma (1983) investigated how frequency of exposure to individual words affects the speed with which midyear first graders and older, reading-disabled students recognized words. Children read sentences with the target word two, four, or six times, followed by posttests that assessed the speed of recognizing individual words. The assessments included homophonic versions of the target words, where spellings differed by only one letter such as *read* and *red* and *to* and *too*. First graders' speed of responding to target words decreased systematically with a leveling off between four and six exposures. Apparently, first graders were recognizing words automatically at around four exposures. Further, because first graders recognized the homophonic variants more slowly, Reitsma concluded that they were internalizing the spellings of the target words. The reading-disabled students showed only a marginally significant increase in the speed of recognizing words that had been practiced four times or the homophonic words and those practiced twice. These findings suggest that the reading-disabled students were not attending to and internalizing the spellings of the words in the same way as the first graders.

Ehri and Wilce (1983) similarly measured the word-identification speed of first- and second-grade readers. Skilled and less-skilled readers were given lists of words to read, some of which were practiced either 6 or 18 times. Word-identification speed increased significantly between pretest and posttest for CVC nonsense words. Skilled readers were able to recognize target words as quickly as they could name digits, an indication that the words had come to be recognized automatically as wholes (Biemiller, 1977/1978). Less-skilled readers' speed increased also, but their word-recognition speed still fell short of their digit naming speed, suggesting that these words had not become a fully automatic part of their sight vocabulary. Similar to Reitsma (1983), Ehri and Wilce (1983) found that additional practice did not appear to significantly increase word-identification speed for familiar words by less-skilled readers.

As a result of the emphasis on the "whole word" that was part of the high-frequency word method, basal readers often incorporated words that were visually dissimilar (Samuels & Jeffrey, 1966). Beginning readers learn dissimilar words more quickly than similar words (Samuels & Jeffrey, 1966). In all likelihood, beginning readers focus on one or two letters that identify a word from other words. Attending to only part of the spellings within visually dissimilar word lists may work initially, but this strategy is not particularly effective as more and more words appear in beginning reading texts.

When children are able to make use of even partial phonological cues, beginning readers acquire phonetically spelled words more quickly and accurately than visually distinct spellings (Ehri & Wilce, 1985). The more beginning readers were able to attend to phonological cues, the faster and more accurate they were at learning target words (Ehri & Wilce, 1987).

Further proof that the kind of exposure students require for words is a function of the type of word comes from Juel and Roper/Schneider's (1985) study of children's strategies as a function of their textbook program. First graders who read a decodable preprimer were more influenced in their word recognition by the decodability of the words than by the number of repetitions. The word recognition of children who read the basal preprimer was most affected by the number of repetitions of the word, particularly if the word contained unusual letter combinations.

Research on Features of Existing Texts

While the features of beginning reading texts have been documented since at least 1930 (Hockett, 1938), features documented in the texts of one copyright are not necessarily generalizable to subsequent copyrights. There was a substantial amount of stability from the 1930s through 1960s (Chall, 1995; Hockett, 1938; Morris & Johns, 1987; Olson, 1965; Perry & Sagan, 1989; Rodenborn & Washburn, 1974), but following Chall's (1995) critique of the mainstream reading programs, vacillations in the texts over each of the subsequent decades have been considerable. Hoffman, McCarthey, et al. (1994) describe substantial changes between the beginning reading texts adopted for use in Texas classrooms in 1987 and in 1993. Whereas texts in 1987 had had controlled vocabularies, the texts in 1993 were recognizable trade book selections. Since then, the 1997 guidelines of Texas, which advocated texts quite different than the 1993 copyrights, have been operationalized in the 2000–2001 copyrights that will be used in Texas classrooms in the fall of 2000. The focus of this review is on the changes in texts over the past decade, describing the changes from California's mandate for literature-based programs in 1987 (California English/Language Arts

Framework Committee, 1987) to the Texas mandate (Texas Education Agency, 1997) for particular percentages of decodable text in first grade.

This review considers the characteristics of current texts on three dimensions that have received attention previously: (1) number of total and unique words in texts; (2) proportion of unique words that are phonetically regular, multisyllabic, and highly frequent; and (3) engagingness. Although researchers have yet to link these dimensions to the ease or difficulty that young children experience in reading acquisition, a compelling case can be made theoretically for each of these dimensions as a factor in reading acquisition.

Number of Total and Unique Words

Historically, the number of total words in a text or set of texts and the number of unique words among those total words have been used as indicators of the demands of reading programs on beginning readers (Chall, 1995; Hockett, 1938; Morris & Johns, 1987; Olson, 1965; Perry & Sagan, 1989; Rodenborn & Washburn, 1974). For children in their first months of formal reading instruction, the number of words that appear on a page in instructional texts can influence their willingness to read. For example, when asked to choose books to read, first-grade readers who were challenged in learning to read identified texts as easy when the number of words on a page was few and difficult when texts had more words per page (Hiebert, Lui, Levin, Huxley, & Chung, 1995).

A product of the mandate for literature-based selections has been to create greater variety across beginning reading programs in the total number of words. The first-grade anthologies of the five major programs that met the Texas guidelines for literature-based, beginning reading programs in 1992–1993 ranged in total words from 6,629 to 17,102, with an average of 12,265 (Hoffman et al., 1994). The range for total words for the 1986–1987 copyrights of these five programs that had controlled vocabulary was small in comparison: 16,865 to 17,319 words, with an average of 17,282 words. The more recent requirement of Texas that the initial texts of grade 1 comply with decodability standards may have leveled differences across programs to some degree. The range of total words for approximately 40% of four first-grade textbook programs (10 passages from the beginning and 10 from the end) is 4,020 to 5,500 with an average of 4,270 (Hiebert, 2000).

The cohort of children who enter school while the 2000–2001 textbooks are used may be exposed to roughly the same number of words, whatever the program chosen by their state, district, or school. Even so, these children will be exposed to considerably more words than their counterparts were exposed to in the decades prior to literature-based programs. An analysis of the copyrights from one textbook program over the past 40 years (from 1960 to 2000) indicates that texts for beginning readers have gotten substantially longer from 1962 to 2000 (Hiebert, 2000). The total number of words of a selection that would provide the instruction during the first quarter of grade 1 increased from 18 words per passage in 1962 to 83 words per passage in the 2000 copyright. The three other programs with 2000–2001 copyrights, similarly, had passages that averaged 76 to 115 words.

The number of total words is a general indicator, at best, of the task posed by texts for beginning readers. For children who are at the beginning stages of reading, every different word in a passage poses an occasion for remembering a known word or, if unknown, figuring out the word. In a historical analysis of the longest published beginning reading program in the United States, Hiebert (2000) found that the total number of words for the first passages reached its highest point in 1983 with an average of 144 words per beginning passage. In its 2000 copyright, the beginning passages averaged 83 words. On the basis of total words, the 2000 passages would be described as easier, but the ratios of unique or different words per 100 running words varied substantially: 5 per 100 in 1983 and 22 per 100 in 2000. With the 1983 copyright, every 20th word that first graders encountered was a unique word. Every fifth word that first graders in classrooms with the 2000 copyright encounter is a unique word. Because 10 high-frequency words account for one third of the total number of words in the sample, the other 177 unique words occur an average of three times each. Even this figure for repetition is misleading because of these 177 unique words, 80 are what Hiebert (2000) has identified as "singletons"—words that occur only once in a set of 10 instructional passages. For beginning readers with the 2000 copyright, 5% of the words are repeated an average of 25 times each, another 43% of the words will appear only over 10 passages, and the other 42% of the words will occur approximately five times each.

Demands for figuring out unique words remain consistent for young readers with the texts from the 2000 copyright, whether they are reading texts from the beginning or end of first grade or second grade: 21 to 22 across 10 selections at each point per 100 words in time (Hiebert, 2000). These figures differ substantially from the ratios of unique to 100 words for equivalent samples of passages from the beginning and end of grade 1 and the end of grade 2 for the 1962 and 1983 copyrights: 10, 9, and 13 for 1962 and 5, 11, and 14 for 1983 (Hiebert, 2000).

The sheer number of words and the infrequency with which all but a small group of high-frequency words appear creates a formidable task for beginning readers. The number of unique words in the 2000 copyright—187—is 10 times the number of unique words that first graders were expected to learn over 10 passages in 1962 and 2.5 times more than in 1983 (Hiebert, 2000). The heavy repetition of high-frequency words in these pre-1993 copyrights and the lack of high-meaning words could create obstacles for beginning readers (Brennan, Bridge, & Winograd, 1986). By the same token, we have been unable to locate evidence that beginning readers can identify dozens of different words after a single exposure or even after four to five exposures.

Decodability of Words

Chall's (1995) observation that basal reading texts did not provide sufficient phonics experiences—either in the lessons or in the children's texts—spurred research into the relationship between the phonics instruction of teachers' editions and the phonics patterns in the words that appear in children's texts. Beck and McCaslin (1978) analyzed the percentages of words in eight series published in the mid-1970s that could be decoded based on previous instruction in all of a word's constituent phonic elements. According to Beck and McCaslin (1978), lessons on the consonants *c*, *t*, and *n* and the short vowel *a* would mean that the words *can*, *cat*, and *Nat* in the text had "potential for accuracy." If *nag* were introduced, however (and a lesson on the consonant *g* had not been provided previously), this word would have only a partial potential for accuracy. After applying this criterion to basal programs, Beck and McCaslin reported that texts from the first third of first grade in four phonics programs contained significantly higher percentages of decodable words (6–100%) compared to the texts from traditional basal programs (0–13%).

"Potential for accuracy" criterion was included in the guidelines for beginning reading textbooks in the most recent Texas textbook adoption (Texas Education Agency, 1997). Stein, Johnson, and Gutlohn (1999) examined the compliance of texts that were presented for the Texas textbook adoption to this criterion. Stein et al. (1998) recognized, however, that many of the high-frequency words that make up much of text are not decodable. Hence, they determined the potential accuracy of a series by adding the percentage of decodable words to the percentage of high-frequency words. Overall, they found that the potential for accuracy within some programs is low, although programs varied considerably from one another. Four programs had potential for accuracy rates that ranged from 79 to 100%.

In analyses of the mid-1990s copyrights of three textbook programs conducted by Menon and Hiebert (2000) and Martin and Hiebert (1999), the opportunities afforded by texts for learning about and applying knowledge of phonics were examined (1) by considering the decodability ratings of words and (2) by establishing the number and repetition of rimes. Decodability of words was established on an 8-point scale where lower points on the scale represented simple vowel patterns such as CV (e.g., *go*) and VC (e.g., *at*) or CVC (*cat*), middle points represented more complex vowel patterns such as CVVC (e.g., *meat* and *meet*) or CVC-e (e.g., *ride*), and higher points on the scale variant vowels (e.g., *bread*) and multisyllabic words (e.g., *tomorrow*). These three programs were chosen because of their differences in perspectives on beginning reading acquisition. One program has literature as its core (Literature Core); the second begins with phonics books but moves to literature by midyear of grade 1 (Phonics/Literature); and the third emphasizes phonics but has added a literary supplement (Phonics Core). Menon and Hiebert (2000) analyzed the features of the anthologies and literary components of these three programs, whereas Martin and Hiebert (1999) analyzed the features of the phonics texts as well as "little book" components that all of the programs had.

Overall, the little books and phonics texts contained higher percentages of words with simpler vowel patterns than the literature anthologies. Further, the little books and, as might be expected, the phonics texts showed a more gradual introduction of words with complex vowel patterns and multisyllabic words, whereas the literature anthologies showed a relatively stable distribution of each type of word in the beginning, middle, and final components of the program. In the literature components, the percentage of unique words that were multisyllabic stayed at a fairly consistent level of 25%, regardless of the philosophy of the program and projected time period (i.e., beginning or end of grade 1).

As has already been summarized in the review of highly regular words, learning to recognize bigger and bigger chunks of words characterizes proficient readers. The "rime" measure used by Martin and Hiebert (1999) and Menon and Hiebert (2000) establishes the opportunity children have to apply knowledge of rimes—the clusters of vowel and their subsequent consonant(s)—across words. The computer program used by these researchers indicates the number of different times as well as the number of "instantiations" of individual times. Instantiations refer to the number of different onsets that appear with the same rime. If the rime *ed* appears exclusively with the onset *r* in a program, the number of instantiations would be one. If the words *bed, sled, Ted, fed*, and *led* appear in addition to *red*, the instantiations would be six.

Within the literature components of all three programs, Menon and Hiebert (2000) found the number of different rimes to be many. The number of different rimes per passage ranged from a high of 62 and 60 (Phonics/Literature and Phonics Core, respectively) and a low of 41 (Literature Core). The number of different rimes per passage was lower for the phonics and little books than for the literature component, an understandable phenomenon because the passages for these texts were considerably shorter. However, the average number of rimes within phonics and little-book text for the Literature Core program and the Phonics Core program were identical: 28. The Phonics/Literature program had a slightly higher average: 34 rimes per text. Rimes were represented, on average, by two instantiations, regardless of program (Literature Core, Phonics/Literature, or Phonics Core) or component within program (i.e., literature, little book, or phonics text). That is, first-grade readers would rarely encounter a rime with more than two onsets, such as *jump, bump, lump*, and *dump*, in a passage.

While texts can be judged as decodable because constituent elements have been presented in lessons in the teachers' edition (Stein et al., 1997), there is a substantial amount of phonics data that beginning readers must be able to navigate to be successful with the texts of beginning reading programs (Martin & Hiebert, 1999; Menon & Hiebert, 2000).

Text Engagingness

Alvermann and Guthrie (1993) proposed engagement as a defining construct in literacy. Wigfield (1997) notes that within the reading literature, most discussions of engagement have been restricted to a consideration of attitudes toward reading and interest in reading. Rarely have features of texts that engage readers, especially young readers, been considered. In this context, the term *text engagingness* describes the potential of a text for creating engagement. This term is distinguished from *text engagement*, which will occur as a result of the interaction between particular readers and particular texts, in specific instructional contexts.

Hoffman, Christian, et al. (1994) have identified three ways in which the potential of a text for engagingness can be measured: design, content, and language. Initially, children are likely to be engaged by the illustrations and the format of the book—design. Once children have begun attending to the text, other factors likely influence their sustaining interest in the text. When the content is unfamiliar, complex, or trivial, a text may not continue to be engaging. Further, if the language of the text is bland, children's interest may not be sustained. We do not intend to suggest that particular texts will be equally engaging to all children, irrespective of their race, class, ethnicity, or personal interests. Nevertheless, it is important to consider whether texts hold promise for engaging at least some of the children within a group for whom texts are being developed or selected.

Hoffman, Christian, et al. (1994) considered the engagingness of first-grade texts from four traditional basal series published in the mid-1980s with texts from five (1993) literature-based series, using these three indices. As well as using scales for the design, content, and language of the texts, these researchers used an overall 5-point holistic rating scale. Their results suggested that the newer literature basals were potentially more engaging than the older, traditional basal texts, both at a holistic level and along the dimensions of content, language, and design. However, as McCarthey et al. (1994) pointed out, while the newer texts on average are potentially more engaging, they only rated an average of 3.2 on the 5-point holistic scale (compared to 2.0 for the older basal texts), suggesting that many of the newer texts are still lacking in their potential engagingness.

Menon and Hiebert (2000) similarly had teachers rate passages from the literature anthologies of three programs, using McCarthey et al.'s (1994) scales of content, language, and design. The texts from the literature-based core program were rated the most highly on all three scales. The texts from the literature/phonics program were rated slightly less appealing, and the literature from the phonics core program was rated the least appealing. Of these differences, however, only the ratings on design between literature-core texts and the phonics-core texts were significantly different. Overall, although many of the texts were highly rated, these findings similarly suggest that there is still room for improvement in the engagingness of new texts offered by basal publishers.

The texts in the Hoffman, McCarthey, et al. (1994) study were also rated by kindergartners and first and second graders. Pairs of texts were read aloud to children who rated each story using a smiley, neutral, or sad face. The children also commented on each story and ranked the stories within each pair. The children's ratings were similar to the researchers' ratings in 7 out of 10 pairs of texts, centering on the content, language, and design of the texts. Children attended to three additional categories: familiarity (author, text, and vocabulary), personal experience, and realism. The children's comments about the familiarity of texts and their ability to read these texts suggest that, for beginning readers, the accessibility of the text may affect its engagingness.

Next Steps

The role that the textbooks serve in beginning reading instruction and the critical role of reading acquisition in the subsequent success in school and beyond for children lead to the expectation that there would be a substantial amount of research on features of effective beginning texts. Our review of the literature indicates that this is simply not so. One of the reasons that research on textbooks has fallen between the cracks is the gulf between the publishing industry and academe. The policies on programs issued by states include the requisite "research base" (e.g., Florida Department of Education, 1999), but these investigations appear to be conducted in house by publishers (and are not available for review by scholars) or consist of reviews of related literature, some of which contains research and some of which does not. The few program evaluations that have been conducted as part of research programs (e.g., Foorman et al., 1998) are difficult to interpret when the effect of materials is confounded with critical components such as staff development. Further, the texts on which research was conducted several decades ago may have little trace in the current copyright of the program (e.g., Englemann, Becker, Carnine, & Gersten, 1988). Unlike the medical and pharmacy industries, there is neither in-house research within publishing companies nor a federal agency that provides consumers with research. Since Gray's (Elson & Gray, 1930) affiliation with Scott Foresman, university-level educators have been involved as consultants (often given the title of "author"), but their work has been in program development and representation, not in research and evaluation.

Publishers and researchers need to collaborate in addressing critical questions on appropriate texts for beginning readers. We describe the most urgent of these questions: (1) the texts for the initial period of independent word recognition and (2) issues related to decodability.

First Books

The intent of the mainstream programs was originally to provide text on familiar, interesting scenarios to young children (Elson & Gray, 1930; Gray et al., 1956).

To increase children's exposure to high-frequency words, however, the words that could be expected to interest young children—words such as *roller skates* and *crash* in a passage on learning to skate—were eliminated. The thousands of little books that now exist contain an overabundance of vocabulary on topics interesting to young children. But the vocabulary changes from book to book, with a core set of high-meaning words rarely found in more than one book in a set of books (Hiebert, 1999). A single set of concepts that is interesting to all children is not possible, but studies of little books with a shared vocabulary of highly meaningful words are needed. For example, rather than include the menagerie of one widely used beginning text—*wren, hen, cony, pony, fox, ox, duck, camel, dog, elephant* (Pikulski et al., 1993)—the set might be *dog, cat, fish*, and *parrot*. Other words would be part of the passages, but the children who have not attained the logographic stage would have the opportunity to begin reading with a group of meaningful words.

Unresolved Decodability Issues

Mandates within Texas specify that the texts for beginning readers that will be accepted in Texas need to contain particular percentages of words that give children the *potential for accuracy*, a term used by Beck and McCaslin (1978) and then by Stein et al. (1999). *Potential for accuracy* is defined as a word where all of the elements have been taught prior to a beginning reader's encountering of that word in a text. This definition, however, begs several critical questions:

1. What should the unit of information be?
2. How many exemplars are needed of a unit?
3. At what speed can beginning readers—especially the ones who depend most on good instruction and materials to become literate—assimilate new information?

Studies that describe the number of repetitions and rate of introduction of high-frequency words have been conducted, but these studies have not considered the viability of particular units of decodability within texts. The studies have been conducted with either lists of words or a single passage. The acquisition of decodable units alongside meaningful words and high-frequency words—some of which at least are necessary to make a somewhat coherent text—has not occurred.

A strictly laboratory approach where individual children are taught from "precise" texts disregards the role of engagingness of concepts, language, and illustrations that are part of texts and the different speeds with which children crack the code. The experiments that would be needed to isolate optimal units, instantiations of units, and the competing units at different points in a beginning reader's development—in the context of texts in which multiple forms of words are present—are sufficiently numerous to be prohibitive. But a large-scale research effort on textbooks that includes a focused number of experiments, classroom-based interventions, and descriptions of best practices is possible.

One of the questions that requires attention in a focused set of experiments has to do with the effects of treatments that give children different exposure to units. One group of children, for example, might be taught through a focused set of rimes (e.g., 8–10, with 2 for each of the 5 short vowels) that are used consistently over time. Their learning would be compared with children in groups that are taught with a more diffuse set of rimes (4 or 5 for each short vowel). Such an experiment would take the form of Cunningham's (1990) study in which a group of kindergartners were randomly assigned to different treatment groups but came from the same classroom. The critical question that would be addressed is how quickly children generalize to other rimes. Does a focus on a particular set of rimes leave children with a limited repertoire and perspective on rimes? Or does an experience with many rimes (as is currently the case in texts that children are given) create a difficulty? Another experiment would consider the percentage of words within texts that comply with the rimes that provide the focus of instruction. Given that there are thousands of classrooms in which different textbook programs are used, it should be possible to establish general program effects as well. Even though many variables are confounded with the use of textbooks, the large-scale use of textbooks allows for establishing at least the general effect of particular programs.

Without systematic research on text features, the vacillation evident in textbooks over the past 20 years (Hiebert, 2000) will continue. The vacillations in philosophy must be negotiated by teachers at a time that they are under pressure to bring students to the high levels of literacy required for full participation in the digital age. It is imperative that the research community join teachers and publishers in ensuring that the children of the digital age are initiated into literacy with the best possible texts and the best possible experiences with those texts.

References

Adams, M. J. (1990). *Beginning to read: Thinking and learning about print.* Cambridge, MA: MIT Press.

Afflerbach, P., Beers, J., Blachowicz, C., Boyd, C. D., Diffily, D., Gaunty-Porter, D., et al. (2000). *Scott Foresman reading.* Glenview, IL: Addison-Wesley.

Alvermann, D., & Guthrie, J. (1993). *Themes and directions of the National Reading Research Center* (National Reading Research Center, Perspectives in Reading Research, No. 1). Athens: University of Georgia, National Reading Research Center.

Ashton-Warner, S. (1963). *Teacher.* New York: Simon & Schuster.

Baumann, J.F., Hoffman, J.V., Duffy-Hester, A.M., & Ro, J.M. (2000). The First R yesterday and today: U.S. elementary reading instruction practices reported by teachers and administrators. *Reading Research Quarterly, 35,* 338–377.

Beck, I.L., & McCaslin, E.S. (1978). *An analysis of dimensions that affect the development of code-breaking ability in eight beginning reading programs* (Report No. 6). Pittsburgh, PA: Learning Research and Development Center.

Biemiller, A. (1977/1978). Relationships between oral reading rates for letters, words, and simple text in the development of reading achievement. *Reading Research Quarterly*, *13*, 223–253.

Bowey, J.A., & Hansen, J. (1994). The development of orthographic rimes as units of word recognition. *Journal of Experimental Child Psychology*, *58*, 465–488.

Boylin, M.C. (1998). *Effects of predictable and decodable texts and strategy instruction on literacy acquisition.* Unpublished doctoral dissertation, University of Virginia, Charlottesville.

Brennan, A., Bridge, C., & Winograd, P. (1986). The effects of structural variation on children's recall of basal reader stories. *Reading Research Quarterly*, *21*, 91–104.

Bridge, C.A., Winograd, P.N., & Haley, D. (1983). Using predictable materials vs. preprimers to teach beginning sight words. *The Reading Teacher*, *36*, 884–891.

Brown, G.D.A. (1998). The endpoint of skilled word recognition: The ROAR model. In J.L. Metsala & L.C. Ehri (Eds.), *Word recognition in beginning literacy* (pp. 121–138). Mahwah, NJ: Erlbaum.

Bruck, M., & Treiman, R. (1992). Learning to pronounce words: The limitations of analogies. *Reading Research Quarterly*, *27*, 374–388.

California English/Language Arts Committee (1987). *English-language arts framework for California public schools (kindergarten through grade twelve).* Sacramento: California Department of Education.

California English/Language Arts Committee. (2000). *English-language arts framework for California public schools (kindergarten through grade twelve).* Sacramento: California Department of Education.

Carroll, J.B., Davies, P., & Richman, B. (1971). *Word frequency book.* Boston: Houghton Mifflin.

Chall, J.S. (1995). *Learning to read: The great debate* (3rd ed.). Fort Worth, TX: Harcourt Brace.

Chall, J.S., & Squire, J.R. (1991). The publishing industry and textbooks. In R. Barr, M.L. Kamil, P. Mosenthal, & P.D. Pearson (Eds.), *Handbook of reading research* (Vol. 2, pp. 120–146). White Plains, NY: Longman.

Cunningham, A.E. (1990). Explicit instruction in phonemic awareness. *Journal of Experimental Child Psychology*, *50*, 429–444.

Donahue, P.L. Voelk, K.E., Campbell, J.R., & Mazzeo, J. (1999). *NAEP 1998 reading report card for the nation and the states.*

Washington, DC: U.S. Government Printing Office.

Ehri, L.C. (1994). Development of the ability to read words: Update. In R.B. Ruddell, M.R. Ruddell, & H. Singer (Eds.), *Theoretical models and processes of reading* (4th ed., pp. 323–358). Newark, DE: International Reading Association.

Ehri, L.C. (1998). Grapheme–phoneme knowledge is essential for learning to read words in English. In J.L. Metsala & L.C. Ehri (Eds.), *Word recognition in beginning literacy* (pp. 3–4). Mahwah, NJ: Erlbaum.

Ehri, L.C., & Robbins, C. (1992). Beginners need some decoding skill to read words by analogy. *Reading Research Quarterly*, *27*, 12–26.

Ehri, L.C., & Wilce, L.S. (1985). Movement into reading: Is the first stage of printed word learning visual or phonetic? *Reading Research Quarterly*, *20*, 163–179.

Ehri, L.C., & Wilce L.S. (1983). Development of word identification speed in skilled and less skilled beginning readers. *Journal of Educational Psychology*, *75*, 3–18.

Ehri, L.C., & Wilce, L.S. (1987). Cipher versus cue reading: An experiment in decoding acquisition. *Journal of Educational Psychology*, *79*, 3–13.

Elson, W.H., & Gray, W.S. (1930). *Elson basic readers.* Chicago: Scott Foresman.

Englemann, S., Becker, W.C., Carnine, D., & Gersten, R. (1988). The direct instruction follow-through model: Design and outcomes. *Education and Treatment of Children*, *11*, 303–317.

Florida Department of Education. (1999). *Instructional materials specifications: Reading grades K–12* (2001–2002 adoption). Tallahassee: Florida Department of Education.

Foorman, B.R., Francis, D.J., Fletcher, J.M., Schatschneider, C., & Mehta, P. (1998). The role of instruction in learning to read: Preventing reading failure in at-risk children. *Journal of Educational Psychology*, *90*, 37–55.

Gates, A.I. (1930). *Interest and ability in reading.* New York: Macmillan.

Gates, A.I., & Russell, D.H. (1938/1939). Types of materials, vocabulary burden, word analysis, and other factors in beginning reading. *The Elementary School Journal*, *39*, 27–35, 119–128.

Gibson, E.J., & Levin, H. (1975). *The psychology of reading*. Cambridge, MA: MIT Press.

Goswami, U. (1986). Children's use of analogy in learning to read: A developmental study. *Journal of Experimental Child Psychology, 42*, 73–83.

Goswami, U. (1988). Orthographic analogies and reading development. *Quarterly Journal of Experimental Psychology, 40A*(2), 239–268.

Goswami, U. (1990). Phonological priming and orthographic analogies in reading. *Journal of Experimental Child Psychology, 49*, 323–340.

Goswami, U. (1998). The role of analogies in the development of word recognition. In J.L. Metsala & L.C. Ehri (Eds.), *Word recognition in beginning literacy* (pp. 41–63). Mahwah, NJ: Erlbaum.

Gourley, J.W. (1984). Discourse structure: Expectations of beginning readers and readability of text. *Journal of Reading Behavior, 16*, 169–188.

Gray, W.S., Monroe, M., Artley, A.S., Arbuthnot, A.H., & Gray, L. (1956). *The new basic readers: Curriculum foundation series*. Chicago: Scott, Foresman.

Hiebert, E.H. (1983). A comparison of young children's self-selected reading words and basal reading words. *Reading Improvement, 20*, 41–44.

Hiebert, E.H. (1999). Text matters in learning to read (Distinguished Educators Series). *The Reading Teacher, 52*, 552–568.

Hiebert, E.H. (2000, April). *The task of the first-grade texts: Have state policies influenced the content?* Paper presented at the symposium The Content of Text for Young Readers in Learning to Read and Reading to Learn, at the annual meeting of the American Educational Research Association, New Orleans, LA.

Hiebert, E.H., Liu, G., Levin, L., Huxley, A., & Chung, K. (1995, November). *First graders reading the new first-grade readers*. Paper presented at the annual meeting of the National Reading Conference, New Orleans, LA.

Hiebert, E.H., Menon, S., Martin, L.A., & Huxley, A. (2000, April). *Teachers' guides and reading instruction: The interactions between teachers, texts, and beginning readers*. Paper presented at the symposium The Content of Text for Young Readers in Learning to Read and Reading to Learn, at the annual meeting of the American Educational Research Association, New Orleans, LA.

Hockett, J.A. (1938). The vocabularies of recent primers and first readers. *The Elementary School Journal, 38*, 112–115.

Hoffman, J.V., Christian, C., Corman, L., Elliott, B., Matherne, D., & Stahle, D. (1994). Engaging the new basal readers. *Reading Research and Instruction, 33*, 233–256.

Hoffman, J.V., McCarthey, S.J., Abbott, J., Christian, C., Corman, L., Curry, C., et al. (1994). So what's new in the new basals? A focus on first grade. *Journal of Reading Behavior, 26*, 47–73.

Hoffman, J.V., Roser, N., Patterson, E., Salas, R., & Pennington, J. (1999, December). *The effects of leveled texts and varying types of support on first graders' reading performance*. Paper presented at the annual meeting of the National Reading Conference, Orlando, FL.

Holdaway, D. (1979). *The foundations of literacy*. Sydney, NSW, Australia: Aston Scholastic.

Juel, C., & Roper/Schneider, D. (1985). The influence of basal readers on first grade reading. *Reading Research Quarterly, 20*, 134–152.

Laing, E., & Hulme, C. (1999). Phonological and semantic processes influence beginning readers' ability to learn to read words. *Journal of Experimental Child Psychology, 73*, 183–207.

Leslie, L., & Allen, L. (1999). Factors that predict success in an early literacy intervention project. *Reading Research Quarterly, 34*, 404–424.

Leu, D.J., Jr., DeGroff, L.J.C., & Simons, H.D. (1986). Predictable texts and interactive–compensatory hypotheses: Evaluating individual differences in reading ability, context use, and comprehension. *Journal of Educational Psychology, 78*(5), 347–352.

Levy, B.A., & Lysynchuk, L. (1997). Beginning word recognition: Benefits of training by segmentation and whole word methods. *Scientific Studies of Reading, 1*(4), 359–387.

Martin, B., & Brogan, P. (1971). *Teacher's guide to the instant readers*. New York: Holt, Rinehart and Winston.

Martin, L.A., & Hiebert, E.H. (1999, April). *Little books and phonics texts: An analysis of the new alternatives to basals*. Paper presented at the annual meeting of the American Educational Research Association, Montreal, Quebec, Canada.

McCarthey, S.J., Hoffman, J.U., Christian, C., Corman, L., Elliott, B., Matherne, D., et al. (1994). Engaging the new basal readers.

Reading Research and Instruction, 33(3), 233–256.

Menon, S., & Hiebert, E.H. (2000). *Literature anthologies: The task for first-grade readers* (CIERA Rep. No. 1–009). Ann Arbor, MI: Center for the Improvement of Early Reading Achievement.

Metsala, J.L. (1999). Young children's phonological awareness and nonword repetition as a function of vocabulary development. *Journal of Educational Psychology, 91,* 3–19.

Moats, L. (1999). *Teaching reading is rocket science: What expert teachers of reading should know and be able to do.* Washington, DC: American Federation of Teachers.

Morris, J.A., & Johns, J.L. (1987). Are 1st grade reading books easier than 20 years ago? *The Reading Teacher, 40,* 486–487.

Muter, V., Hulme, C., Snowling, M., & Taylor, S. (1997). Segmentation, not rhyming, predicts early progress in learning to read. *Journal of Experimental Child Psychology, 65,* 370–396.

Olson, A.V. (1965). An analysis of the vocabulary of seven primary reading programs. *Elementary English, 42,* 261–264.

Perry, L.A., & Sagan, P.S. (1989). Are basal readers becoming too difficult for some children? *Reading Improvement, 26,* 181–185.

Pikulski, J.J., Cooper, J.D., Durr, W.K., Au, K.H., Greenlaw, M.J., Lipson, M.Y., et al. (1993). *The literature experience.* Boston: Houghton Mifflin.

Rasmussen, D., & Goldberg, L. (1964). *The bad fan* (Level A, Basic Reading Series). Chicago: Science Research Associates.

Reitsma, P. (1983). Printed word learning in beginning readers. *Journal of Experimental Child Psychology, 36,* 321–339.

Rhodes, L.K. (1979). Comprehension and predictability: An analysis of beginning reading materials. In J.C. Harste & R.F. Carey (Eds.), *New perspectives on comprehension* (pp. 100–131). Bloomington: Indiana University School of Education.

Rodenborn, L.V., & Washburn, E. (1974). Some implications of the new basal readers. *Elementary English, 51,* 885–893.

Samuels, S.J., & Jeffrey, W.E. (1966). Discriminability of words and letter cues used in learning to read. *Journal of Educational Psychology, 57,* 337–340.

Savage, R., & Stuart, M. (1998). Sublexical inferences in beginning reading: Medial vowel digraphs as functional units of transfer. *Journal of Experimental Child Psychology, 69,* 85–108.

Shannon, P. (1997). Manufacturing dissent: Basal reading and the creation of reading failures. *Reading and Writing Quarterly: Overcoming Learning Difficulties, 13,* 227–245.

Stein, M.L., Johnson, B.J., & Gutlohn, L. (1999). Analyzing beginning reading programs: The relationship between decoding instruction and text. *Remedial and Special Education, 20,* 275–287.

Texas Education Agency. (1990). *Proclamation of the State Board of Education advertising for bids on textbooks* (Proclamation 68). Austin, TX: Author.

Texas Education Agency. (1997). *Proclamation of the state board of education advertising for bids on textbooks.* Austin, TX: Author.

Thompson, G.B. (1999). The processes of learning to identify words. In G.B. Thompson & T. Nicholson (Eds.), *Learning to read: Beyond phonics and whole language* (pp. 25–54). New York: Teachers College Press; Newark, DE: International Reading Association.

Thompson, G.B., Cottrell, D.S., & Fletcher-Flinn, C. M. (1996). Sublexical orthographic–phonological relations early in the acquisition of reading: The knowledge sources account. *Journal of Experimental Child Psychology, 62,* 190–222.

Treiman, R., Goswami, U., & Bruck, M. (1990). Not all nonwords are alike: Implications for reading development and theory. *Memory and Cognition, 18*(6), 559–567.

Treiman, R., Mullennix, J., Bijeljac-Babic, R., & Richmond-Welty, E.D. (1995). The special role of rimes in the description, use, and acquisition of English orthography. *Journal of Experimental Psychology: General, 124,* 107–136.

Wigfield, A. (1997). Children's motivations for reading and reading engagement. In J.T. Guthrie & A. Wigfield (Eds.), *Reading engagement: Motivating readers through integrated instruction* (pp. 14–33). Newark, DE: International Reading Association.

Wylie, R.E., & Durrell, D.D. (1970). Teaching vowels through phonograms. *Elementary English, 47,* 427–451.

16

Fluency:
A Review of Developmental
and Remedial Practices

Melanie R. Kuhn and Steven A. Stahl

The process of becoming literate can be conceptualized as a series of qualitatively different stages through which learners progress as they become increasingly proficient with print (Chall, 1996b; Harris & Sipay, 1990). One of the primary advances in this process involves the shift from dealing with words on a word-by-word basis to a rapid, accurate, and expressive rendering of text. In other words, learners develop such familiarity with print that they achieve fluency in their reading. Fluent reading may underlie or assist in effective engagement with text (LaBerge & Samuels, 1974). The purpose of this article is a review of the literature examining how children move toward fluent reading. It will incorporate both theoretical discussions and practical studies relating to fluency research. Specifically, to accomplish this purpose, we have reviewed the theoretical accounts of reading that include an important role for fluency in the reading process and studies that have attempted to facilitate its development.

Stages of Reading Development

Although a number of stage models have been proposed, we will focus on Chall's (1996b) stages of reading development because they provide a comprehensive view of the reading process as well as a strong theoretical underpinning for the view of fluency that will be presented here. Chall's (1996b) model is a broad one, and it will be useful to focus more specifically on the growth of word recognition as well. As such, the description of stages presented here will be followed by a brief outline of Ehri's (1995, 1998) phases of sight-word learning and the contribution that automatic word recognition makes to fluent reading.

Chall (1996b) proposed six stages through which readers proceed, each of which emphasizes a particular aspect of reading development. The first is an early reading or emergent literacy stage. This period encompasses the literacy behaviors that are developed prior to formal instruction. That is, the learner develops a foundation that will allow for later instruction to proceed in a meaningful manner. For example, children develop insights into the reading process that include concepts about print, phoneme awareness, and book-handling knowledge. Further, they come to recognize that print represents language and carries the story's message. However, it is important to note that the exact nature of what a child learns prior to formal instruction is highly dependent on the sociolinguistic community and culture in which he or she participates. Next comes the initial stage of conventional literacy or the beginning of formal reading instruction. At this stage, the instructional emphasis is on developing learners' recognition of basic sound–symbol correspondences while providing them with sufficient opportunity to establish their decoding ability.

Following this is a period called confirmation and fluency or "ungluing from print" (Chall, 1996b, p. 18) in which readers confirm what is already known to develop their fluency. Having established their accuracy in decoding during the previous stage, learners must now develop their automaticity with print. Further, as their reading becomes increasingly less halting, they develop the ability to represent what is read in ways that imitate natural or conversational tones. In other words, they are able to make use of prosodic features such as appropriate phrasing, stress, and intonation in their reading. Once a learner has established this level of comfort with print, it is easier to construct meaning from a text than when he or she still struggles with word identification. This stage is the focus of this review.

During the next stage, there is a precipitous shift in the amount of expository text with which students are presented. In fact, in the majority of school systems in the United States, students move from reading for enjoyment to reading for instruction. Chall (1996b) called this stage of development "reading for learning the new." The focus of the curriculum shifts to the understanding of content area material, and students are expected to gain proficiency with increasingly complex texts. However, throughout this period, much of the information is presented from a single perspective, often by way of introduction to a subject.

As students acquire a solid base of knowledge in a given area, they are increasingly likely to be exposed to a number of sources on that subject. This stage incorporates what Chall (1996b) referred to as "multiple viewpoints." It is here that readers begin to deal with a variety of viewpoints regarding a given topic, and learners are expected to critically evaluate these sources. The final stage in Chall's (1996b) model is that of "construction and reconstruction." It is during this stage that an individual begins to synthesize the myriad of viewpoints presented in texts to determine his or her own perspective on a given subject, a skill that is essential if a learner is to develop into a critical reader.

Confirmation, Fluency, and Ungluing From Print

According to Chall's (1996b) model, after the learners have established a basic familiarity with sound–symbol correspondences, there is a need for young readers to focus on automatizing their decoding ability. This period of development is not for the learning of new skills, "but for confirming what is already known to the reader" (Chall, 1996b, p. 18). Such practice allows learners to gain comfort with print, thereby enabling the transition from learning to read to reading to learn (Chall, Jacobs, & Baldwin, 1990) to proceed smoothly. Without such automatic processing, students will continue to expend a disproportionately large percentage of their attention on decoding, which in turn leaves them with an inadequate amount for comprehension (Adams, 1990; LaBerge & Samuels, 1974; Stanovich, 1980, 1984). In other words, fluency is a prerequisite if learners are to succeed at the primary purpose of reading: the construction of meaning from text (Allington, 1983; Samuels, 1988; Schreiber, 1980).

Phases of Sight-Word Development

Embedded within the decoding and fluency stages, children seem to go through a series of phases as they develop automaticity of sight-word reading. We are defining *sight words* as did Ehri (1995)—as *all words that have been recognized accurately on several occasions* (i.e., words that are in one's instant recognition repertoire), rather than the more common definitions of either *words with irregular spellings* or *words that are recognized as a result of their visual features or a particular method of instruction*. Ehri (1995) suggested that words become sight words through a thorough analysis of the word's orthographic structure. The resulting mental representation enables a reader to access the word quickly and automatically. She further argued that, on each additional encounter, the sight of such words triggers the memory of these words in the learner. This identification includes information about the word's spelling, pronunciation, and meaning. However, the establishment of a complete representation does not occur immediately. Instead, Ehri proposed that such a full depiction occurs in four distinct phases: pre-alphabetic, partial-alphabetic, full-alphabetic, and consolidated-alphabetic.

The pre-alphabetic phase corresponds to Chall's (1996b) early reading stage. During this phase, beginning readers remember sight words by making connections between certain visual attributes of a word and either its pronunciation or its meaning (e.g., the tail at the end of the word *dog* or the two eyes in the middle of the word *look*). It is considered to be pre-alphabetic because letter–sound relationships are not involved in the recognition process. Although this can be an effective strategy as long as the number of words encountered remains low, it becomes increasingly ineffective as the number of sight words increases.

Following the visual cue phase, there is a shift to the second phase, that of partial-alphabetic recognition. At this point, students begin to read sight words by making the connections between some of the letters in written words, usually the initial and/or final letters because of their salience, and their corresponding sounds. The advantage here is that the alphabetic system is available to aid in word recognition. This phase is enabled both by knowledge of letter names and a certain amount of phonological awareness (Stahl & Murray, 1998). Because readers at this stage lack a full knowledge of the spelling system and the ways in which to segment and match phonemes and graphemes, this form of sight-word recognition remains incomplete.

As learners continue to develop an understanding of the alphabetic system, they move toward full-alphabetic coding. This parallels the initial stage of conventional literacy in Chall's (1996b) model. At this point, readers recognize how most graphemes represent phonemes in conventional spelling. This allows readers to easily recognize different words with similar spellings (e.g., *bat*, *bait*, and *brat*) because each word's representation is sufficiently complete. It further enables them to read new words by determining how the unfamiliar spellings will be pronounced. However, although learners at the full-alphabetic phase can decode words, those words that are encountered sufficiently often become sight words. As such, recognition is immediate. Such immediate recognition also occurs for those words that are phonetically irregular and therefore not decodable using sound–symbol correspondence rules.

During the final phase, the consolidated-alphabetic phase, learners come to recognize letter patterns that occur across different words as units; this becomes part of their generalized knowledge of the orthographic system. This final advance reduces the memory load for readers, makes it easier to learn new words, and speeds up the process of word recognition by increasing their awareness of the ways letters co-occur in the spelling system. This final phase of sight-word development ensures that learners establish automatic and accurate word recognition that is integral to the reading process.

Perfetti (1992) argued that readers may need to proceed through these phases of development with every word to assure that each is processed accurately and automatically. The final phase of word recognition corresponds with the confirmation and fluency stage of Chall's (1996b) model. Such accuracy and automaticity are essential components of fluent reading; however, we will argue that they are necessary but not sufficient conditions for fluency.

Fluency as a Factor in the Reading Process

Given that the ultimate goal of reading is the construction of meaning (Anderson, Hiebert, Wilkinson, & Scott, 1985), it is important to assess the role fluency plays in comprehension. There are two primary theories regarding fluency contribution to a reader's understanding of text, each of which emphasizes one of fluency's component parts. The first and better known of the two theories stresses the contribution of automaticity to fluent reading, whereas the second focuses on the role of prosody.

There seems to be a consensus regarding the primary components of fluency: (a) accuracy in decoding, (b) automaticity in word recognition, and (c) the appropriate use of prosodic features such as stress, pitch, and appropriate text phrasing. When reviewing the theories relating to fluency's role in the overall reading process, it is important to tease out the various ways these components may contribute to a learner's ability to interpret text. There is a rich literature about the contribution of accurate word recognition to reading comprehension (Johns, 1993) and enjoyment of reading (Nell, 1988). This will not be reviewed here. Instead, we will concentrate on the relative importance of automaticity and prosody to comprehension.

Contribution of Automaticity

Proficient readers have certain features in common; they not only read accurately, their recognition of words is automatic. The question is, How does this automaticity contribute to the primary goal of reading, comprehension of text? An individual has a limited amount of attention available for any given cognitive task (LaBerge & Samuels, 1974; Perfetti, 1985; Stanovich, 1980). This being the case, attention expended on one activity is, necessarily, attention unavailable for another.

In the case of reading, an individual is required to perform at least two interdependent tasks: The reader must determine what words compose the text while simultaneously constructing meaning. As such, the greater the amount of attention expended on decoding, the less that is available for comprehension. To ensure that readers have enough attention to understand texts adequately, the argument continues, it is necessary for them to develop decoding to the point where each word is recognized instantaneously. Once this occurs, they will have the necessary attention to focus on the sense or meaning of the text.

According to Stanovich's (1980) interactive-compensatory model, information from multiple sources is available for aiding readers in their construction of meaning. This is true at each stage of development and presumes that learners will make use of information from orthographic, phonological, semantic, and syntactic sources. However, if a reader is less adept at gleaning information from one source, he or she may become overreliant on other sources. It follows that, until readers achieve automaticity in word recognition, they will necessarily depend more on alternative knowledge sources to make sense of what is being read. In other words, they are more likely to rely on context as an aid to word recognition and comprehension than are fluent readers. (This refers only to the use of context as an aid to identifying words already in a child's lexicon, not to the use of context in learning new word meanings. Stanovich [1980] would argue that automatic word recognition allows readers to concentrate on the meaning of text, rather than on identifying words. Thus, automatic word recognition allows one to focus contextual analysis on constructing meaning, rather than decoding [see also Adams, 1990].)

The question then becomes, How do learners make the shift from decoding accurately but deliberately to decoding automatically? According to the automaticity theorists, the best way to ensure this transition is through extensive practice. As with any skill that requires an individual to coordinate a series of smaller actions to create a unified process, it is practice that allows the learner to develop expertise. In terms of reading, this practice consists primarily in providing successive exposures to print. As letters, and later words, become increasingly familiar to the learner, less and less attention needs to be directed toward processing text at the orthographic level. This ability to complete a process without conscious attention fulfills LaBerge and Samuels's (1974) criterion for automaticity. In this way, the automaticity theory accounts for two of the components of fluent reading, accurate decoding at a sufficient rate. It further posits an explanation for automaticity's role in text comprehension. However, there is an important aspect of fluency that this theory does not attend to, that of prosody.

Contribution of Prosody

Although the automaticity theory accounts for the accurate and effortless decoding that fluent readers exhibit, it fails to provide a sufficient explanation for the role prosody plays in the reading process. When an individual provides a fluent rendering of a text, there is a tacit understanding that he or she is doing more than simply reading the words quickly and accurately; he or she is also reading with expression. Implicit in the phrase *reading with expression* is the use of those prosodic features that account for the tonal and rhythmic aspects of language (Dowhower, 1991).

Prosody comprises a series of features including pitch or intonation, stress or loudness, and duration or timing, all of which contribute to an expressive rendering of a text (Allington, 1983; Dowhower, 1991; Schreiber, 1980, 1987, 1991). Additionally, prosodic reading includes appropriately chunking groups of words into phrases or meaningful units in accordance with the syntactic structure of the text. Taken together, these features are classified as *suprasegmental* because they extend over more than one speech sound and contribute to meaning. Given this understanding of what constitutes prosody, it is necessary to determine the role prosody plays in the development of fluency and the ways in which these features contribute to the construction of meaning from a text.

Prosody may provide a link between fluency and comprehension. Chafe (1988) speculated that, to read a sentence with intonation, one must assign syntactic roles to the words in the sentence. The assignment of syntactic roles is a key component of microprocessing, or the mental parsing of a text into hierarchically ordered propositions (Kintsch, 1998). Schreiber (1987) also suggested that the explicit presence of prosodic cues may be one crucial difference between speech and reading and one of the reasons that speech is easier to understand. However, Schreiber (1987) reported that the evidence supporting a link between prosody and microprocessing is weak, with some studies finding links between the use of prosodic features and syntactic comprehension and others failing to find such an effect.

Dowhower (1991) identified six distinct markers that comprise prosodic reading: pausal intrusions, length of phrases, appropriateness of phrases, final phrase lengthening, terminal intonation contours, and stress. From a linguistic perspective, readers who use these markers appropriately are capable of making the connection between written and oral language. In other words, they are able to transfer their knowledge of syntax from speech to text by effectively applying these features to their reading. Such readers can produce a rendering of text that maintains the important features of expressive oral language in addition to reading it accurately and at an appropriate rate.

Children who have not achieved fluency read either in a word-by-word manner or by grouping words in ways that deviate from the type of phrasing that occurs naturally in oral language (Allington, 1983; Chall, 1996b; Clay & Imlach, 1971; Dowhower, 1991; Samuels, 1988). Young children are highly attuned to the use of prosodic features in speech (Dowhower, 1991; Schreiber, 1987; Schreiber & Read, 1980). In fact, research indicates that infants under a year old use prosodic features as a primary cue to the syntactic structure of their language and that their babbling follows the characteristics inherent in the prosody of their primary language. Further, Read and Schreiber (1982) and Schreiber (1987) have determined that children are not only highly attuned to prosodic elements in oral language but that they are actually more reliant on them for determining meaning than are adults.

Given children's sensitivity to prosody in oral language, it seems reasonable to assume that they are equally dependent on these features in determining the meaning of text (Allington, 1983; Dowhower, 1991; Schreiber, 1991). In fact, appropriate phrasing, intonation, and stress are all considered to be indicators that a child has become a fluent reader (Chomsky, 1978; Rasinski, 1990b; Samuels, Schermer, & Reinking, 1992). The reasoning behind this emphasis is that such readings provide clues to an otherwise invisible process; they act as indicators of the reader's comprehension. Given that a fluent reader is one that groups text into syntactically appropriate phrases, this parsing of text signifies that the reader has an understanding of what is being read.

Research on Fluency Instruction

One approach to examining the relative effects of automaticity and prosody to the development of fluency and comprehension is to examine the instructional research. The National Reading Panel (NRP) (National Institute of Child Health and Human Development [NICHD], 2000) conducted an examination of the instructional literature in two areas related to fluency—guided oral reading and independent silent reading. They defined *guided oral reading* as approaches that involve having the student read with guidance and feedback. Included in this definition were common approaches such as repeated reading, impress reading, paired reading, shared reading, and assisted reading. Independent silent reading involved providing time for children to read by themselves, such as sustained silent reading, Drop Everything And Read, and so on. The NRP's thorough examination of the PsycINFO and ERIC databases found 364 unique articles, with 77 articles meeting their methodological criteria. The 14 studies on the effectiveness of independent silent reading did not provide conclusive evidence that the approach improved reading achievement. Krashen (2001), however, criticized the methodology behind this finding, suggesting that there were many studies about independent silent reading that the NRP did not include and was concerned that the NRP overemphasized certain studies in their narrative review.

Consider four groups of studies not included. Anderson, Wilson, and Fielding (1988) had 155 fifth graders keep logs of their out-of-school activities. They found that the amount of time spent reading was the best predictor of gains in reading achievement. Taylor, Frye, and Maruyama (1990) similarly had 195 fifth and sixth graders keep daily logs of their reading in and out of school. They found that reading in school, but not reading at home, contributed significantly to gains in reading achievement. These two studies were correlational and, thus, were not included in the NRP (NICHD, 2000) corpus. Elley (2000) reported a number of studies of "book floods" or giving children large amounts of high-interest texts. He reported that book floods lead to significant gains in English literacy when compared with a control. Although these studies examined English literacy, the participants were non-English speakers, thus making these studies ineligible for inclusion. Another source of support for the effects of reading volume comes from a series of studies conducted by Stanovich, Cunningham, and their colleagues. Cunningham and Stanovich (1991, 1998), for example, used a children's literature Title Recognition Test to assess the amount of exposure that elementary school children had to print. They found that print exposure had significant impacts on children's fluency and other aspects of reading skill, even when general ability is controlled. Again, this study is correlational. Taken together, this body of evidence is strong support for the importance of practice in reading on reading achievement.

The NRP (NICHD, 2000) found an overall effect size of 0.41 for guided oral reading, with effect sizes on individual measures ranging from 0.53 on measures of reading accuracy to 0.44 on measures of reading fluency to 0.35 on measures of reading comprehension, all of which were significantly different from 0. We have reviewed the studies in their corpus and found them to be a mixture of a number of different types of oral-reading practice. In shared reading, a teacher would read a Big Book to a class repeatedly, encouraging the children to take greater responsibility for reading with repetition. In repeated reading, the child reads the passage as a whole, with the teacher monitoring and providing feedback. In other approaches, the child reads the passage once. In one study, the guidance was provided before reading. In short, the studies reviewed by the NRP were so wide ranging that one can only draw the broadest of conclusions about the effectiveness of fluency-oriented instruction from their meta-analysis.

We will restrict our discussion to a few different approaches used to improve children's fluency. Among these are approaches primarily used with clinical populations or children with reading problems, such as repeated reading (Samuels, 1979) and assisted reading (Chomsky, 1978; Heckelman, 1969, 1986), and approaches used with entire classes, such as the oral recitation lesson (Hoffman, 1987) and fluency-oriented reading instruction (Stahl, Heubach, & Cramond, 1997). There have been other studies that attempted to improve children's speed of word recognition in isolation (e.g., Fleisher, Jenkins, & Pany, 1979/1980) and approaches that segmented text to enable children to identify pausal units in the text (e.g., O'Shea & Sindelar, 1993). We will use these studies to inform our knowledge of the issues related to fluency development.

To obtain a large corpus of studies relating to instructional approaches to fluency development, we first undertook a search of both the ERIC and the PsycLIT databases for any articles that referred to reading fluency. As we began to locate these articles, we either read through the abstract or briefly scanned the article to confirm that the contents were appropriate for further review and analysis. In addition, if the article was to be included, the reference list was used as a means of cross-checking references. In this way, we were able to locate a number of articles that were not identified in the initial search. The articles that emerged from this search process fell into four broad categories: theoretical bases of fluency development, research pertaining to the validity of these theories, recommendations for classroom practice, and intervention studies. Given our purpose, we chose to concentrate on intervention studies to determine the overall effectiveness of fluency instruction.

When deciding whether a given article should be included as part of this review, we had both inclusionary and exclusionary criteria. We selected studies that focused on evaluating strategies designed to promote readers' fluency development, such as the development of either the automaticity or prosodic components of fluent reading or some combination of the two. Methods and representative studies are presented for each type of intervention, along with a summarization of the results.

We chose not to consider articles that dealt with either external or self-correction strategies because such studies focus on components of the reading process that lead to more effectively attending to the text rather than on a fluent rendition of the reading (e.g., Mudre & McCormick, 1989). Nor did we include studies that focused exclusively on training accurate word recognition. It is reasonably well established that teaching children to be more accurate at recognizing words leads to improved comprehension (e.g., Chall, 1996a).

We intended to conduct a meta-analysis, but did not, for three reasons. First, we found relatively few studies with control groups. Baseline studies can be submitted to meta-analytic techniques (e.g., Scruggs, 1987), but these studies cannot be combined with control group studies. Two separate analyses are more likely to be confusing than enlightening. Second, the effect sizes we calculated fluctuated widely, from 0.13 to 2.79. High effect sizes are likely because of a lack of variance in the control condition, leading to exaggerated estimates of effect. These few effect sizes over 1.00 would have to be eliminated from the analysis to avoid their having an excessive influence on the calculated effect. Finally, there were a number of different conditions used as controls, from no treatment to having the students spend an equivalent amount of time in nonrepetitive reading. These different control conditions made it difficult to come up with a common metric, as should be done in a meta-analysis. Instead, we used vote-counting procedures to analyze the data, combined with qualitative synthesis of the studies themselves.

Studies

We found 58 studies dealing with assisted reading, repeated reading, or classroom interventions designed to improve fluency. In addition, we found nine studies dealing with segmented text and four studies dealing with speeded isolated word recognition. This is a total of 71 studies.

Segmented text and isolated word-recognition studies were analyzed separately. Our logic in doing so was as follows: If fluency-based instruction affects microprocessing, then we might also expect to find effects in studies using segmented text, that is, text broken up by phrases. If fluency instruction improves comprehension by helping students develop automatic word recognition, then we might see similar effects from studies in which readers' word recognition was speeded up through practice of reading words in isolation (see Table 1).

There are several reasons for the preponderance of studies without control groups. Repeated reading and assisted readings were developed as clinical approaches for working with children with reading problems (e.g., Dahl, 1979).

TABLE 1
Studies With and Without Control Groups

Approach	Control Group	No-Control Group	Total
Repeated Reading	15	18	33
Assisted Reading	7	8	15
Classroom Intervention	4	6	10
Total	26	32	58

Thus, testing their effectiveness with targeted children using baseline or multiple baseline designs is appropriate. In other cases, researchers compared different variations of repeated reading (Rashotte & Torgesen, 1985). In another case, students involved in a pilot study made so much gain as to make a control group seem to be unethical (Stahl et al., 1997).

Authors who used baseline designs did test for statistical significance, but the lack of studies with a control in this literature as a whole is problematic. Baseline designs are useful in evaluating the effectiveness of approaches for children who are in small, heterogeneous populations, such as learning-disabled children or children with reading problems. There is an assumption in such designs of a null hypothesis in which the child would make no growth over the period of instruction. This may be tenable in the case of children with severe reading problems but not tenable with a more average population. Chomsky (1978) illustrated this point. She used a set of taped readings to bring children with reading problems to fluent reading, finding significant improvement over time. But this improvement was equivalent to 6 months over a 10-month school year. Thus, her students, although ahead of where they started, were further behind their classmates. Similarly, in Blum et al.'s (1995) study, although all children made significant progress, only 1 of the 5 children used in the study progressed beyond the preprimer level during the 19 weeks of the intervention. Neither result would be the accelerated progress needed by children who are behind their classmates in reading (Clay, 1993).

Fluency Instruction as Remediation

The studies of fluency instruction were in two overarching categories, those that build on independent learning, or what Dowhower (1989) labeled *unassisted strategies*, and assisted-reading strategies that provide learners with a model of fluent reading behaviors. Further, these studies consist of two types of interventions, those that dealt with fluency training as a means of remediation for individuals and those designed for classrooms. Additionally, researchers looked at a range of indicators to determine reading improvement, including measures of accuracy, rate, prosody, and comprehension. The studies are categorized here, first, according to the type of intervention provided and, second, in terms of whether their reading methods were designed for individual learners, dyads, or groups. We discuss both near transfer, that is, improvement on fluency measures such as increased reading rate on previously unread texts, and far transfer, for example, improvement in comprehension on new material.

Unassisted Repeated Reading

Perhaps the best known of the reading interventions designed to support fluency development is that of repeated reading. This is a strategy that relies on independent practice of text. The basic method of repeated reading was developed by Samuels (1979) and Dahl (1979) in an attempt to apply LaBerge and Samuels's (1974) automaticity theory to practice. Samuels (1979) and Dahl noted that classroom practice often consists of students reading new text on a daily basis in the hope that they will improve their word-recognition skills. However, it struck them that, by increasing the amount of practice on a given passage, students might be able to improve not only their accuracy but their fluency as well. Growth in fluency was to be measured through the establishment of a speed criterion that, if effective, should lead to an increase in reading rate.

They developed a process in which students were required to read a 100-word passage repeatedly until they reached the criterion rate of 100 words per minute (wpm). An initial reading rate of between 35 and 50 wpm was deemed appropriate for the first reading of the passage. Should the learner read outside these initial wpm guidelines, the passage difficulty would be adjusted, and the student would be placed with material at a higher or lower reading level. Similarly, if a student made an excessive number of miscues in a given passage, difficulty levels would likewise be adjusted. Students were expected to read the passage orally to an adult, then reread the passage silently, keeping track of the number of rereadings. On completion of a given number of practices, they were asked to reread the passage orally. Students' accuracy and reading rates were expected to improve until they achieved a predetermined criterion.

Dahl (1979) first tested this approach in a study designed to evaluate three reading strategies: training in the use of hypothesis testing (the active use of context to predict the identity of unknown words), repeated reading, and isolated word recognition. The study consisted of 32 struggling second-grade readers randomly assigned, 4 to a treatment group. Dahl reported that both the hypothesis testing and the repeated-reading conditions, as well as the interaction of the two, produced significant gains on a measure of reading rate and on a traditional cloze test. Additionally, the repeated-readings training significantly reduced the number of miscues made. No significant effects were found favoring the isolated word condition.

Given that Samuels's (1979) and Dahl's (1979) original goal was to develop a procedure that would allow for increases in reading rate as well as in the improvement of learners' accuracy, the method of repeated reading proved successful. In fact, the success of the method led to the recommendation of its use as a remedial reading strategy. Samuels (1979) modified the method so that passages of 50 to 200 words could be used and established a more flexible wpm criterion rate, dependent on the learner's grade level and reading-level placement, while continuing to stress speed over accuracy. He also presented it as an effective strategy for improving not only fluency, here defined as *automaticity in word recognition* (Samuels et al., 1992), but also for comprehension. According to automaticity theory, freeing readers' attention from decoding and allowing focus on the content of the passage should improve the construction of understanding.

Given the initial success of this method, it was used with both average and learning-disabled children. We found a total of 33 comparisons dealing with repeated reading, over half of the total population of studies dealing with fluency reading instruction. These studies are summarized in Table 2. The vast majority dealt with either students at the second- or third-grade level or older children with reading problems who could be presumed to be reading at a primary level. Thus, researchers generally appeared to target their work toward students in Chall's (1996b) confirmation and fluency stage.

Effects of Repeated Reading on Fluency and Comprehension

We found 15 studies that assessed the effects of repeated reading on fluency using a control group. We did a vote count (Light & Pillemer, 1984) of these studies, vote counting in two ways. First, we counted each study once, using the majority of comparisons to assign it depending on whether there was evidence of repeated-reading effectiveness. In six studies, repeated reading produced significantly greater achievement than the control; eight studies had no such an effect, and, in one, repeated reading improved fluency for familiar passages but not for a transfer passage. In the second vote-counting procedure, we counted each individual comparison. This procedure gave added weight to studies with multiple comparisons. In eight comparisons, the repeated-readings group performed significantly higher than the control, whereas 21 comparisons did not. Overall, repeated reading did not produce significantly greater achievement than a control. However, this may be the result of the type of control group involved. In some cases, students were assigned to a no-treatment control group, whereas, in others, students were expected to read equivalent amounts of connected text as the intervention group but not in a repeated manner (e.g., Mathes & Fuchs, 1993; Rashotte & Torgesen, 1985). As will be discussed later in the article, the two types of controls are likely to produce very different outcome measures.

Criteria. The majority of studies had students read each passage a set number of times, usually three readings, rather than using the criterion suggested by Samuels (1979; i.e., 100 wpm). Of the 15 studies with a control group, 2 used criteria. Of these 2, 1 had a significant treatment difference and 1 did not. Of the remaining 13 studies in which students read a set number of times, 3 found significant differences, 9 did not, and 2 studies had mixed findings. Overall, there were too few studies that used a criteria to evaluate its effectiveness.

Difficulty. We also examined the relative difficulty of the passages. It could be argued that having students read and reread relatively easy passages would improve their fluency (e.g., Clay, 1993). It could also be argued that the rereadings

TABLE 2
Repeated-Reading Studies

Study	Criteria (Multiple Readings vs. Criteria)	Grade of Participants	Reading Level of Participants[a]	Initial Fluency of Participants	Material Read	Fluency Results	Microprocessing Comprehension (Results)	General Comprehension	Notes
Bell, Markley, & Yonker (1990)	Set number of readings (3)	2–3	Average	Not given	Instructional level	Improvement over time			No effect on attitudes
Bohlen (1988)	Criterion (until s/he could read the text fluently)	3	Below grade level (2.5–3.4)	Not given	Instructional level	No significant improvement over time			Small *n*, good effect size
Carver & Hoffman (1981)		High school	4th–6th-grade level		2nd–9th-grade level	Improvement over time	Improvement over time	No improvement over time	
Dahl (1979)	Criterion (100 wpm)	2	Below grade level	Disfluent (35–60 wpm)	Difficult	T > C	T > C	T = C	No effect on tahistoscopic recognition of words (automaticity)
Dowhower (1987)	Criterion (100 wpm)	2	Average	Disfluent (less than 50 wpm)	2nd-grade level	Improvement over time	Improvement over time (4/5 groups)		
Hannah (1994)	Criterion	2	Low achieving	Disfluent	Not given	T = C	T = C		
Herman (1985)	Criterion (85 wpm)	4–6	2nd–l/7th percentile	Disfluent (35–50 wpm)	Instructional level	Improvement over time	Improvement over time	T = C; improvement over time	

(continued)

The technique used for all studies was repeated reading. wpm = words per minute; T > C = the treatment produced a significantly higher score than a control on the measure; T = C = the difference between the treatment and a control was not statistically significant; C > T = the control produced a significantly higher score than the treatment on this measure.

[a] Numbers in parentheses refer to the tested level of participants.

[b] The group that read the passage(s) two times read faster than the group that read the passage(s) six times or the control.

TABLE 2 (continued)
Repeated-Reading Studies

Study	Criteria (Multiple Readings vs. Criteria)	Grade of Participants	Reading Level of Participants[a]	Initial Fluency of Participants	Material Read	Fluency Results	Microprocessing Comprehension (Results)	General Comprehension	Notes
Homan, Klesius, & Hite (1993)	Set number of readings (4)	6	Below grade level high 4th-grade, beginner 5th-grade levels	Not given	Instructional level (5th-grade level)	T = C; improvement over time			
Knupp (1988)	Criterion (85 wpm)	4–6	2nd–4th grade (2–4 levels below placement)	Disfluent	45–65 wpm; 4–8 incorrect words per 100; 50–75% comprehension	Improvement over time	Improvement over time		
Koch (1984)	Set number of readings (variable)	2	Low achieving	Not given	Above grade level	T > C			2x group read faster than 6x or control[b]
Koskinen & Blum (1984)	Set amount of time	3	Below average (1.7–4.5)	Disfluent	Grade level	T > C	T > C		
Levy, Barnes, & Martin (1993)	Set number of readings	College	Above average	Probably high	Appropriate	Improvement over time			
Levy, Newell, Snyder, & Timmins (1986)	Set number of readings	College	Above average	Probably high	Appropriate	Improvement over time	Improvement over time		
Mathes & Fuchs (1993)	Set number of readings	4–6	Learning disabled	Not given	Easy	T = C	T = C	T = C	

Study	Criteria (Multiple Readings vs. Criteria)	Grade of Participants	Reading Level of Participants[a]	Initial Fluency of Participants	Material Read	Fluency Results	Microprocessing Comprehension (Results)	General Comprehension	Notes
Mathes & Fuchs (1993)	Set number of readings	4–6	Learning disabled	Not given	Instructional	T = C	T = C	T = C	
O'Shea, Sindelar, & O'Shea (1985)	Set number of readings	3	At or above grade level	Average (70–119 wpm)	Above grade level	Improvement over time	Improvement over time	Improvement over time	
O'Shea, Sindelar, & O'Shea (1987)	Set number of readings	5–8	Learning disabled (3rd-grade level average)	Below average to above average (34–156 wpm)	Above grade level	Improvement over time			
Person & Burke (1984)	Set number of readings (3)	2–4	Not given	Not given	Easy	T = C			
Rashotte & Torgesen (1985)	Set number of readings	2–5	Below average	Disfluent (less than 6.5 wpm)	2nd grade (low overlap)	T = C	T = C		Text with high overlap produced better fluency
Rashotte & Torgesen (1985)	Set number of readings	2–5	Below average	Disfluent (less than 6.5 wpm)	2nd grade (high overlap)	T = C	T = C		
Rasinski (1990a)	Set amount of time	3	Above average	4th grade (above level)	Improvement over time	Improvement over time			
Simmons, Fuchs, Fuchs, Mathes, & Hodge (1995)	3 readings	2–5	Learning disabled and low performing (2nd–3rd grade)	Disfluent (67 correct wpm)	Appropriate	T = C	T > C	T = C	

The technique used for all studies was repeated reading. wpm = words per minute; T > C = the treatment produced a significantly higher score than a control on the measure; T = C = the difference between the treatment and a control was not statistically significant; C > T = the control produced a significantly higher score than the treatment on this measure.

[a] Numbers in parentheses refer to the tested level of participants.

[b] The group that read the passage(s) two times read faster than the group that read the passage(s) six times or the control.

(continued)

TABLE 2 (*continued*)
Repeated-Reading Studies

Study	Criteria (Multiple Readings vs. Criteria)	Grade of Participants	Reading Level of Participants[a]	Initial Fluency of Participants	Material Read	Fluency Results	Microprocessing Comprehension (Results)	General Comprehension	Notes
Stoddard, Valcante, Sindelar, O'Shea, & Algozzine (1993)	Set number of readings (7); measurement at 1st, 3rd, & 7th reading	4–5	Low achieving	Fluent (70 wpm)	Instructional level	Improvement over time			
Tingstrom, Edwards, & Olmi (1995)	Criterion (100 wpm with no errors)	3–4	Low achieving	Disfluent (40–69 wpm)	Instructional level	Improvement over time	Improvement over time		Found that previewing improved repeated reading for 2 out of 3 students
Turpie & Pastore (1995)	Set number of readings (7)	1	Low achieving	Not given	Grade level	Improvement over time	Improvement over time (2 out of 4 students)		
Van Bon, Boksebeld, Font Freide, & Van den Hurk (1991)	Set number of readings (4)	3	Learning disabled		1 year above level	T > C for familiar text, but T = C for transfer text			Compared repeated readings with readings while listening with nonrepeated text
van der Leij (1981), Experiment 1	Set number of readings (5)	5–7	1st grade	Not given		T = C			

Study	Criteria (Multiple Readings vs. Criteria)	Grade of Participants	Reading Level of Participants[a]	Initial Fluency of Participants	Material Read	Fluency Results	Microprocessing Comprehension (Results)	General Comprehension	Notes
van der Leij (1981), Experiment 3	Set number of readings (4)	5–7	1st grade	Not given		C > T; T = C			
Weinstein & Cooke (1992)	Criterion (90 wpm)	2–5 (ages 7 to 10)	Below average (1.0 to 1.3)	Disfluent	1st grade (on level)	Improvement over time	Improvement over time		No difference between criteria
Weinstein & Cooke (1992)	3 successive improvements	2–5 (ages 7 to 10)	Below average (1.0 to 1.3)	Disfluent	1st grade (on level)				
Young, Bowers, & MacKinnon (1996)	Set number of readings (3)	5	Low achieving	Not given	Instructional level	T > C			

The technique used for all studies was repeated reading. wpm = words per minute; T > C = the treatment produced a significantly higher score than a control on the measure; T = C = the difference between the treatment and a control was not statistically significant; C > T = the control produced a significantly higher score than the treatment on this measure.

[a] Numbers in parentheses refer to the tested level of participants.

[b] The group that read the passage(s) two times read faster than the group that read the passage(s) six times or the control.

scaffold children's word-recognition abilities so that they can read more diffi-cult material.

Mathes and Fuchs (1993) compared the use of easy and difficult materials and found no effect for the difficulty of materials. However, they also failed to find a difference between a repeated-reading treatment and a control group. Rashotte and Torgesen (1985) used relatively easy reading materials and also failed to find significant differences between their repeated-readings treatment and a con-trol group. The remainder of the studies used materials at or above the child's in-structional level. Six of the 11 remaining studies found differences favoring the treatment group. Our best guess is that more difficult materials would lead to greater gains in achievement, but more research is needed on this question.

Comprehension. As noted in Table 2, the basic results for comprehension mir-ror those for fluency. Generally, where an increase in fluency was found, there was also an increase in comprehension. The exceptions were in Carver and Hoffman's (1981) study and Dahl's (1979) study, in which there were effects for microcomprehension (generally cloze) measures but not for more general comprehension measures (such as standardized tests). This is consonant with the notion that fluent reading would affect the reader's microcomprehension processes, through the assignment of syntactic relations in sentences, but might not affect macrocomprehension processes, which are more affected by prior knowledge and more global comprehension strategies (see Stahl, Jacobson, Davis, & Davis, 1989). It also may be that the more general measures of com-prehension, such as standardized achievement tests, are more resistant to change.

Other Findings. Dowhower (1987) not only used rate and accuracy as meas-ures of fluency but also found that repeated reading had measurable effects on speech pauses and intonation. Herman (1985) found not only effects on speech pauses and rate for read material but also that repeated-readings treatment trans-ferred to previously unread material.

Rashotte and Torgesen (1985) found that students reading texts with a high overlap of words improved in rate and accuracy better than students reading texts with a low overlap. Although these two groups differed significantly, neither was significantly more fluent than a group engaged in nonrepetitive reading. However, Rashotte and Torgesen limited students to four readings of each text; they might have found stronger effects had they had students read a fluency cri-terion for each text.

Assisted-Reading Strategies

As with the unassisted repeated reading, assisted readings emphasize practice as a means of improving accuracy, automaticity, and prosody as well as the learn-er's understanding of a text. Further, they provide extensive exposure to print. However, unlike traditional repeated reading, assisted-reading methods provide learners with a model of fluent reading (Dowhower, 1989). There is also a greater amount of variation among the different intervention strategies. To maintain a sense of cohesion, we will outline the various methods along with several studies that evaluate the effectiveness of these methods.

We found 15 studies involving assisted reading. Of these, 7 had a control group to evaluate effectiveness of the treatment, and 8 did not. These studies are summarized in Table 3.

Neurological Impress Method or Assisted Reading. Heckelman (1969) suggested the neurological impress method as a remedial strategy for disfluent readers, although the term may go back further. Its name reflects a naiveté about neurology—it was supposed to impress the words directly into the student's "brain." Nowadays, this notion, and the name, seem quaint, at best. However, the underlying method is still used in practice. Currently, it is called *assisted reading* or even *choral reading*, because a tutor and tutee read the same material chorally. The method requires the teacher and student to read simultaneously and at a rapid rate. The student sits in front of the teacher, both hold the book, and the teacher reads into the student's ear. The teacher slides a finger under the words and can vary the pace so that sometimes the reading is louder and faster and sometimes it is slower and softer. This joint reading continues until the teacher notes the student is becoming tired or uncomfortable. Although some of the research followed this exact procedure, other studies varied in their application of the format.

Heckelman (1969) used the technique with 24 seventh through tenth graders, all of whom were at least 3 years behind their grade level in reading. Instructors worked with students using the assisted-reading strategy for 15 minutes a day, 5 days a week, for a maximum of 7.25 hours as part of a remedial summer program. Students selected their own material but were encouraged to use relatively easy material at first before graduating to more difficult selections as they became increasingly fluent. Although not all students made "substantial" (Heckelman, 1969, p. 281) improvements, the mean gain was 1.9 years. That is, the instructional strategy improved the students' oral reading fluency and their comprehension on a standardized measure of reading comprehension. Similar results were found in other case studies (e.g., Langford, Slade, & Burnett, 1974; Mefferd & Pettegrew, 1997).

Although assisted reading is quite successful in improving the reading fluency of struggling readers, Hollingsworth (1970) recognized the time-consuming nature of the procedure. Given the requirement of one-on-one teacher support for the method, it was feasible for assisted reading to be used primarily in tutoring situations but did not provide a viable approach for integration into most traditional classrooms. As such, Hollingsworth (1970) redesigned the procedure so that it could be used with up to 8 students simultaneously. By using a

TABLE 3
Assisted-Reading Studies

Study	Criteria (Multiple Readings vs. Criteria)	Number of Participants	Grade Level	Reading Level of Participants	Initial Fluency of Participants	Material Read	Fluency Results	Microprocessing Comprehension (Results)	General Comprehension	Notes
Carbo (1978)		8	2–6	Learning disabled	Not given	Difficult	Improvement over time			
Chomsky (1978)	Criterion "achieve fluency"	5	3	Below grade level	Disfluent	Difficult	Mean gain lower than expected (.60 in 1 year)		Mean gain lower than expected (.75 in 1 year)	
Dowhower (1987)	Criterion (100 wpm)		2	Average	Disfluent (< 50 wpm)	2nd-grade level	Improvement over time	Improvement over time (2/5 groups)		
Eldredge (1990)	Criterion (until students could read it expressively without teacher assistance)	18	3	Low achieving	Not given	3rd–6th-grade level readability			T > C	Significant effect on Gates-MacGinitie vocabulary
Gardner (1965)			5–8	Below grade level		Unclear			T > C	
Gilbert, Williams, & McLaughlin (1996)	Set number of readings (4)	3	1–2	Learning disabled	Low (28–58 wpm)	Unclear				
Heckelmann (1969)		24	7–10	3 years below grade level		Unclear			Improvement over time	Growth in oral reading accuracy as well

Study	Criteria (Multiple Readings vs. Criteria)	Number of Participants	Grade Level	Reading Level of Participants	Initial Fluency of Participants	Material Read	Fluency Results	Microprocessing Comprehension (Results)	General Comprehension	Notes
Hollingsworth (1970)	Set amount of time	8	4	Average		Varied from 1 year below grade level to 1 year above grade level	T = C	T = C		
Hollingsworth (1978)	Set amount of time	20	4–6	Below average		Varied from 1 year below grade level to 1 year above grade level			T > C	
Langford, Slade, & Burnett (1974)		2	4–6	Below average	Disfluent		Improvement over time			
Mefferd & Pettegrew (1997)	Set number of readings	3	4–5	Developmentally handicapped	Low (14, 48, & 89 wpm)	Above grade level	Improvement over time	Improvement over time		
Rasinski (1990a)	Set amount of time	20	3	Above average		4th (above grade level)	Improvement over time			
Richek & McTeague (1988)	Set number of readings	37	2–3	Chapter 1	Not given	Difficult	T > C		T > C	
Strong & Traynelis-Yurek (1983)	Not given	26	2–6	Not given			T = C			
Young, Bowers, & MacKinnon (1996)	Set number of readings (3)	10	5	Low achieving	Not given	Instructional level	T > C			

wpm = words per minute; T > C = the treatment produced a significantly higher score than a control on the measure; T = C = the difference between the treatment and a control was not statistically significant.

wireless system, children could listen to a tape recording of a text while allowing the teacher to monitor their reading. To test this modification, Hollingsworth (1970) randomly selected 8 fourth graders reading at grade level and 8 controls matched to these students on the basis of their scores on a standardized reading test. There were no significant differences on any measure between the students who participated in the assisted-reading procedure and those who did not. However, none of the students who took part in the study, either as controls or in the intervention group, were considered to be struggling readers. Rather, they were reading on grade level and were, therefore, unlikely to benefit greatly from fluency instruction (Chall, 1996b). In fact, Hollingsworth (1970) considered the students' ability to read at grade level the most likely explanation for the seeming ineffectiveness of the intervention. As such, he decided to replicate the study using a different population.

For his second study, Hollingsworth (1978) selected 20 fourth-, fifth-, and sixth-grade students identified by their school district as remedial readers. The students were randomly selected and assigned to either the assisted-reading or control condition. The wireless system allowed 10 students to listen to taped recordings of the passages simultaneously. Hollingsworth (1978) further increased the number of sessions from 30 to 62. Beyond this difference, the investigation was similar to his first study (Hollingsworth, 1970). This time, however, there was a significant treatment effect on the standardized comprehension test. In real terms, students using the assisted-reading technique made 1 year's growth over the course of a semester, whereas the other students made only 0.04 year's growth during the same period. For students identified as remedial readers, assisted reading was effective in promoting fluency and comprehension development, at least as measured by standardized test scores. However, these gains did not generalize to students who were already fluent readers.

Reading-While-Listening. Chomsky (1978) and Carbo (1981) also used tapes for an assisted-reading approach called *reading-while-listening*. Chomsky worked with 5 eight-year-olds who were identified by their teacher as struggling readers. Although all 5 children, 2 girls and 3 boys, had extensive instruction in decoding strategies, they seemed unable to apply their knowledge to connected text. Each of these children was reading 1 to 2 years below their grade level in January of third grade, and all professed an intense dislike of reading. Chomsky felt that the most important aspect of any successful intervention for these students would, by necessity, expose them to significant amounts of print while making that print accessible to them. To achieve this goal, she made available on tape two dozen books ranging in reading level from second to fifth grade. (The tapes were originally developed to teach English to Japanese students.) The children were asked to listen repeatedly to the books until they were able to render the text fluently. The children selected their own books and set their own pace for the assisted repeated reading. They were instructed first to listen to an entire book or chapter from a book before selecting a portion that they wanted to practice. They were then to read along while repeatedly listening to those parts of the story they wanted to rehearse. In addition, Chomsky and a research assistant worked with each child on a weekly basis both to monitor progress and to engage the learner in further analysis of the text through language games.

Initially the process was slow and the children had some difficulty coordinating their eye movements with the voices on tape. If they lost their place, they were instructed to return to the beginning of the passage, but, as they became increasingly familiar with their texts as well as the process, it became easier for them to keep track of the story. Four of the children took approximately 20 listenings over a month-long period to become fluent with their selection, although 1 child achieved fluency over the course of 2 weeks. Further, each subsequent selection took the learners less time, until by the fourth or fifth book (or for 1 child, the third chapter), students were achieving fluency with their text in approximately 1 week. Perhaps even more telling, however, was the fact that, according to both parents and teachers, the children were reading independently and were willing to engage in writing activities as well. In addition, all students demonstrated growth on the posttest measures administered as part of the study, although averaging only a 6-month gain in fluency and a 7.5-month gain in comprehension over the course of 10 months. This may have been a greater gain than they had made in previous years, but it still is not accelerated progress (Clay, 1993).

Carbo (1978) used a slightly modified approach in a read-along procedure. Her tapes stressed phrases. Children were instructed to slide their fingers along under the words as a form of tactile reinforcement, and each page was cued to minimize the chances that the listeners might lose their place. She worked with 8 learning-disabled children over the course of 3 months using these individualized recordings. During this period, she reported that the students gained 4 to 15 months in word-recognition ability, with the average gain being 8 months.

These two studies differ from Hollingsworth's (1970, 1978) modified assisted-reading approach insofar as there was less direct monitoring from the teacher, and students were responsible for determining the length and frequency of their sessions. One of the primary concerns regarding such read-along techniques is that there was no way to ensure active engagement on the part of the learners. Indeed, in a number of classroom observation studies (e.g., Evans & Carr, 1985; Leinhardt, Zigmond, & Cooley, 1981), time spent listening to tapes in class did not significantly affect achievement. In these reading-while-listening studies, however, students were held responsible for being able to read the text fluently, so that they did actively participate in the process. Further, students seemed both to enjoy the taped stories and to display pride in their abilities and their success.

There were several differences between the Carbo (1978) and Chomsky (1978) studies. First, Carbo (1978) used specially developed tapes in which the stories were read slowly, with cues to turn the page. Chomsky used commercially available taped stories, recorded at ordinary conversational speed. The materials in Carbo's (1978) tapes were chosen to be difficult but not too far away from the child's ability. Chomsky did not measure their difficulty, but her taped stories were probably well above the children's reading level.

Carbo (1978) reported an average gain of 8 months in word recognition in 3 months' time; Chomsky (1978) reported average gains of 6 months in 10 months' time in fluency and 7.5 months in comprehension. Chomsky's results reinforce our caution about accepting results of improvement over time. Although her students made a significant improvement, it was less than ordinarily expected as normal progress. Thus, her students were actually further behind their peers at the end of their treatment than they were before beginning it.

Closed-Caption Television. Rather than designing material that needed to be used in conjunction with a television monitor, Koskinen, Wilson, and Jensema (1985) made use of the closed-caption option available on a number of television programs with remedial readers in an exploratory study. Ten clinicians taught 35 second through sixth graders in a summer reading clinic. Although part of the lessons revolved around making predictions based on plot development and discussions of figurative-language use, students were also expected to practice short portions of the script to develop fluent renderings of the text. Selected programs included *Sesame Street*, *Scooby Doo*, and sitcoms. Because the study was exploratory in nature, no statistical measures were provided. However, many of these "turned off learners" (Koskinen et al., 1985, p. 5) not only enjoyed the lessons but felt they benefited from the strategy. The clinicians considered the lessons effective in promoting the learners' fluency.

Overall, using the same vote-counting procedure as for repeated reading, five of the seven studies, with a control group using assisted reading, had significant treatment differences. When analyzed by number of comparisons, six of the nine comparisons proved significant treatment effects.

Comparisons of Assisted and Unassisted Repeated Reading. Dowhower (1987) and Rasinski (1990b) looked at the effectiveness of both repeated reading and reading-while-listening on the development of reading fluency. Dowhower (1987) examined the effects of repeated reading on second graders at a transitional stage of reading development, that is, learners who were in the process of shifting from accurate but deliberate decoding to fluent reading. In designing the intervention, Dowhower (1987) chose to look at repeated reading and a reading-while-listening procedure to determine the effectiveness of these strategies in promoting fluency on measures of rate, accuracy, comprehension, and prosody. Further, she looked at these measures on both practiced and unpracticed text as well as across a series of passages. Her primary goal was for the students to reread a meaningful passage until their oral production was "fluid, flowing and facile" (Dowhower, 1987, p. 390).

Students were randomly assigned either to the assisted condition in which they worked with a tape-recorded model or to the unassisted condition in which they worked independently but were able to request assistance on difficult words. For the read-along conditions, students were encouraged to practice with the tape until they were comfortable with their reading, after which they were to continue practicing without the tape. Materials consisted of six basal stories with an early second-grade reading level rewritten to maximize equivalency. Students were assessed on rate, accuracy, the number of rereadings necessary to reach a 100 wpm criterion, and their literal comprehension. In addition, a microcomputer was used to determine changes in students' prosody, assessing the following features: pausal intrusions or inappropriate hesitations within words or syntactical units; the length of phrases or number of words between pauses; appropriate phrasing or the use of syntactically and/or phonologically acceptable phrases; phrase final lengthening in which the last stressed syllable is longer than it would be if the word were located elsewhere in a phrase; and intonation or the appropriateness of the rise-fall patterns that occur at phrase boundaries, within the sentence, and at terminal markers.

Both forms of repeated reading produced significant increases in word accuracy and comprehension from the first to the last reading of the first half of the passage. Gains in reading rate also occurred on the second half of all passages and reached significance for three of the five stories. There was also evidence of minimal gains in accuracy from the practiced to the unpracticed portion of the passages; however, this was significant only for one trial in the assisted-reading condition. Additionally, comprehension gains were significant in two of the five trials for the assisted group and four of the five trials for the unassisted groups. Similarly, there were significant gains across readings for both groups on rate, accuracy, and, for the assisted condition, in comprehension scores. Likewise, the number of rereadings it took for students to reach the criterion level significantly decreased across both conditions, and both groups had mean gains in rate and accuracy from the initial to the final test, all of which were significant. Further, the unassisted group's comprehension score had a mean gain as well. It is important to note that there were few shared words among the passages, but 77% of the words on the final test occurred in the stories.

There were slightly different results for the prosodic measures. Pausal intrusions lessened, and length of phrases increased significantly for both groups from the initial to the final readings of the stories as well as across readings. Additionally, the assisted group had significantly fewer inappropriate phrases from the initial to the final reading as well as across readings. Further, the assisted-readings condition group significantly improved their intonation across readings, whereas the unassisted group's intonation improved significantly from the initial to the final readings of the passages. Finally, 8 of the 15 students demonstrated significant change in the lengthening of the final stressed syllable in a phrase. Overall, both forms of repeated reading were effective at improving rate, accuracy, and comprehension, and these gains transferred to similar but unpracticed passages. Further, these improvements increased over a series of passages. Although both strategies appear to be relatively equivalent on rate, accuracy, and comprehension measures, the reading-while-listening intervention had a more facilitative effect on the measures of prosodic development.

Following Dowhower's (1987) work, Rasinski (1990a) compared the effectiveness of repeated reading and reading-while-listening on rate and accuracy. Twenty 3rd-grade students were paired according to both teacher judgment of their reading abilities and their scores on a standardized reading test. As with Dowhower's (1987) research, students had significant gains in both reading speed and accuracy for both strategies, but no significant differences were reported between the two types of intervention. Given these findings, Rasinski (1990a) argued that, because both strategies appear to be equally effective and the reading-while-listening strategy was easier to implement, it may prove to be the more efficient aid in assisting readers' transition to fluency.

It is important to make a distinction between the reading-while-listening used in these studies and listening centers commonly found in classrooms. In these interventions, students had to recite the readings and thus were held responsible for practicing the readings. In listening centers, there are often no criteria for the reading. If students are not held responsible, then they are unlikely to practice and thus unlikely to make gains. We note that classroom observational studies, such as those of Evans and Carr (1985) and Leinhardt et al. (1981), reported no effect on reading achievement for listening center activities.

Classroom Approaches

Two general approaches have been taken when attempting to adapt the principles of fluency instruction to the classroom. First, authors have tried to adapt clinical approaches directly. Assisted-reading approaches, rather than unassisted repeated reading, have been adapted because of the need for social interaction to manage instruction in a classroom setting. Alternatively, authors have used a variety of techniques, such as echo reading, repeated reading, partner reading, and so on, in an integrated lesson plan. Both approaches show promise.

Classroom Extensions of Assisted Reading

Although the assisted-reading approaches outlined previously incorporate models of fluent reading as an aid to reading development, another alternative to the individual repeated reading involves the use of a partner as a means of facilitating fluency development. When the repeated-reading approach is modified so that 2 readers can work together, students are able to receive the type of immediate feedback that is not available when working on unassisted readings or prerecorded models. It is also a technique that can be effectively adopted in traditional classrooms.

Eldredge and Quinn (1988; Eldredge, 1990) examined a modified version of assisted reading (Heckelman, 1969) in which a classmate was chosen to be the lead reader. The struggling reader, known as the "assisted reader," received support and feedback from a partner. Pairs were changed weekly. The lead readers were selected on the basis of their ability to render the chosen texts fluently. They set the pace for the pair, read in phrases, and indicated each word as it was read. Five schools participated in the study, and second-grade classrooms were randomly assigned either to the dyad reading condition or to a control condition that made use of traditional basal reading groups throughout the course of the school year.

The assisted readers in the dyad classrooms read with partners until they reached the point where they could read grade-level material independently. At this point, they began reading on their own. Significant differences were found between the dyad and traditional basal groups on the vocabulary, comprehension, and total reading scores. Twenty-seven of the 32 struggling readers participating in the dyad condition achieved scores at or above grade level, but only 6 of the 32 students (19%) in the traditional basal group did so. As a result of the intervention strategy, students read with assistance material that would have been beyond their instructional level had they been working independently. Eventually, this led to independent reading of grade-level text.

Koskinen and Blum (1984) implemented a procedure that allowed for paired repeated reading of texts with below-average third graders. Students in the repeated-reading condition worked in pairs where they learned to select their own texts, to follow the strategy, and to provide both self-evaluations and evaluations of their partners (the procedure is fully described in Koskinen & Blum, 1986). Students in the repeated-reading condition not only significantly outperformed the students in a study activities condition, they made significantly fewer semantically inappropriate miscues.

Hoskisson and Krohm (1974) provided a transition from assisted readings to partner reading. Second-grade students were presented a series of tape-recorded stories at a read-along center. Tapes were prepared for a number of books; reading levels and pace of narration were adjusted to the individual reading abilities of students to assure that struggling readers did not get lost and better readers would remain engaged in the activity. Additionally, students were provided with weekly opportunities to read one of these stories to a peer. Children were partnered with students both at the same reading level and across reading levels. During this period, students performed the practiced text, and their partners provided any words that were not recognized. The slow readers became more confident in their renderings of a text, their reading rates increased, they made more frequent attempts and were more successful at identifying new words, their listening skills improved, and they appeared to derive more pleasure from their own reading. As with other forms of assisted readings, this version provided students with the opportunity to develop fluent reading behaviors in their presentation of connected text. Their lessons were extended to a home reading program.

Another effective way of encouraging students to read a text repeatedly is by giving them a real purpose for doing so. Such a purpose is provided by the cross-age reading strategy suggested by Labbo and Teale (1990). In this study, the authors invited fifth graders to read aloud to kindergartners from books that were appropriate for the younger participants. Twenty 5th graders experiencing reading difficulties were randomly assigned to one of three groups: cross-age readers, art partners in which the students worked with kindergartners on art projects, or a basal reading group in which students participated in their regular basal activities.

Students in the cross-age reading group were prepared for their reading performances in three ways. They were taught to select appropriate texts for their audience, they were given opportunities to develop fluency with the books, and they determined ways in which they could involve kindergartners in discussions of the texts. According to anecdotal evidence, not only did both the fifth graders and the kindergartners enjoy their experience, 6 of the cross-age readers "were able to break poor oral reading habits" (Labbo & Teale, 1990, p. 365) as a result of their repeated readings. Further, the cross-age readers made significant gains on a standardized reading measure and produced significantly higher scores than the other two groups.

We found two other studies that examined cross-aged tutoring but with less salutary results. Sutton (1991) examined the effects of cross-age tutoring with first and second graders. She reported improvement over time in fluency and the amount of time spent engaged in reading, but she did not have a control group. Ramunda (1994) used above-average second graders as tutors, but she did not find a significant effect on comprehension compared with a control group.

It seems that cross-age tutoring appears to be successful with below-grade-level tutors but does not seem to affect above-grade-level tutors. This may be because the below-grade-level tutors in Labbo and Teale's (1990) study were reading relatively difficult materials, but the above-grade-level tutors in Ramunda's (1994) study were reading relatively easy texts. It could also indicate that the procedure aids fluency development in struggling readers but does not assist readers who are already considered to be fluent.

Integrated Fluency Lessons

Hoffman (1987) developed an oral recitation lesson (ORL) format as an alternative means of presenting a traditional basal reader story. The goal of the ORL was to use oral reading as a means of developing students' prosody, rather than treating it as a form of assessment. In this procedure, the teacher began by reading the basal story aloud. This reading was followed by a group discussion to deal with comprehension prior to the students' oral reading of the text. The teacher then reread the story, paragraph by paragraph, with the children following along and echoing back each paragraph. Next, the students chose or were assigned a portion of the text to master, with the understanding that their reading was to be expressive. They were provided with opportunity to practice this text until they could read it at an adequate rate with few errors (2 errors per 100 words). The final step involved the students reading their passage to the group before going on to the next story. Hoffman reported that the lessons were successful, but he did not present statistical data.

The effectiveness of the ORL was examined in two studies by Reutzel and Hollingsworth (Reutzel & Hollingsworth, 1993; Reutzel, Hollingsworth, & Eldredge, 1994). Both of these studies involved second graders. In the first study (Reutzel & Hollingsworth, 1993), the oral recitation lesson was compared with a traditional round-robin-reading approach. Lessons lasted 30 minutes per day over 4 months, but because the teachers in the round-robin condition divided their classes into three ability groups, they worked directly with each group only 10 minutes per day. As a result, the ORL group may have had more teacher-directed reading time. The ORL was found to be superior on measures of fluency and experimenter-designed measures of comprehension but not on a standardized comprehension test.

For the second study (Reutzel et al., 1994), the ORL was compared with the shared-book experience (Holdaway, 1979). The shared-book experience consisted of the teacher's introduction of a story using a Big Book (a text enlarged so that it can be read by groups of children). This was followed by a discussion of the book and opportunities to reread the text as a group, in pairs, or independently. The lessons lasted 30 minutes a day for a 4-month period. The students in the shared-book experience produced significantly higher scores on the Word Analysis subtest of a standardized achievement test and on an experimenter-developed measure involving answering implicit questions. The ORL group, on the other hand, made significantly fewer oral reading errors. There were no significant differences between the groups on measures of fluency, vocabulary, self-corrections, oral retelling, answering text-explicit questions, or the Comprehension subtest on the Standardized Achievement Test.

Eldredge, Reutzel, and Hollingsworth (1996) also compared the effectiveness of the shared-book experience and a round-robin-reading approach with reading instruction over a 4-month period. The shared-book experience followed the format discussed previously, whereas the round-robin-reading lesson divided a 30-minute period into three components. Ten minutes were spent reading the story in a round-robin manner with the teacher, 10 minutes were spent reading the text independently, and 10 minutes were spent reading it in pairs. In this case, the shared-book-experience group significantly outperformed the round-robin-reading group on every measure of word recognition, fluency, and comprehension.

Morris and Nelson (1992) created a program based on the ORL for a group of struggling second-grade readers. The goal was to incorporate the modeling of fluent reading along with the opportunity for practice into the student's reading lessons. The lessons took place for a 20-minute period, three times a week. On the first day, the teacher read a text aloud to the students and discussed the story with them. This was followed with an echo reading of the text. On the second day, students completed a paired reading of the text. The students then practiced a 100-word passage from the story until they could read it fluently with few errors. On the last day, the students read the passage they selected aloud while the teacher took a running record of the text. The intervention helped the children in one class develop word-recognition skills. However, Morris and Nelson did not use a control group, and whereas the students demonstrated growth on the ITBS, they were not reading at grade level according to that measure.

Rasinski, Padak, Linek, and Sturtevant (1994) used a similar format in their fluency development lesson; but instead of using basal reader stories, they used 50- to 150-word texts. The researchers specifically suggested short texts so that the teachers were able to complete the entire lesson in a 15-minute session. In this way, the lessons could be incorporated into the current reading curriculum. Teachers read each passage aloud, students and teachers discussed the material then read the texts chorally, and students practiced reading in pairs. During the final component, the partners gave each other positive feedback. This intervention took place on a daily basis for a 6-month period; however, the only gains attributable to the treatment were in reading rate. These students were compared with children getting traditional literacy activities. Differences between the experimental treatment and the control in overall reading level, as measured by an informal reading inventory, were not statistically significant.

Another program based on Hoffman's (1987) work is the fluency-oriented reading instruction program (Stahl et al., 1997). This approach is an attempt to use repeated reading in a classroom program to develop fluent and automatic word recognition in second graders. The resulting program had three aspects—a redesigned basal reading lesson, a free-reading period at school, and a home reading program.

The redesigned basal reading lesson used the story from the children's second-grade reading text. This text would be difficult for children reading below grade level. With the support provided by the program, however, children who entered second grade with some basic reading ability could profit from a conventional second-grade text. The teacher began by reading the story aloud to the class and discussing it. This discussion put comprehension right in front, so that children were aware that they were reading for meaning. Following this, the teachers reviewed key vocabulary and did comprehension exercises and other activities around the story itself. Sometimes, this involved echo reading or having the teacher read part of the story and the class or a group echo it back. Other times, it involved having children read and practice part of the story. Then the story was sent home and read with the child's parents or other readers listening. For children who struggled, the story was sent home additional times during the week. Children who did not have difficulty with the story did other reading at home on these days.

The next day, the children reread the story with a partner. One partner would read a page while the other would monitor the reading. Then they would switch roles until the story was finished. Following partner reading, the teacher would do some extension activities and move on to another story.

Although this lesson was an important part of the program, it was not the only reading that children did. Time was set aside for children to read books that they chose each day. The children usually selected easy-to-read books that they read for enjoyment. Children sometimes read with partners during this period as well. The time ranged from 15 minutes in the beginning of the school year to 30 minutes by the end.

This program was carried out by four teachers in two schools during the first year and was expanded to 10 teachers in three schools for the second year. In both years, children gained, on the average, nearly 2 years in reading growth over the course of their second-grade year, as measured by an informal reading inventory. What was more gratifying were the effects that this intensive reading experience had on struggling readers. Over 2 years, all the children but 2 who began the second-grade year reading at a primer level (out of a total of 105) or higher were reading at a second-grade level or higher at the end of the year.

In terms of the vote-count procedure, out of six studies that examined the effects of redesigned lessons designed to increase fluency, only three had a control group. Of the controlled studies, only one found clear evidence that the fluency-oriented lessons produced significantly better achievement than traditional instruction or a shared-book experience (which was commonly used in basal reading programs at the time). The effects of this instruction were suggestive, especially given the large gains reported by Stahl et al. (1997), but these approaches need to be examined in more controlled research.

Discussion

When fluency instruction was compared with the traditional instruction used with a basal reader, fluency instruction improved children's reading fluency and comprehension. When different approaches to fluency instruction were compared, the results were less clear-cut. Overall, these strategies seem, to a greater or lesser degree, effective in assisting readers making the transition to fluent reading. These include normally achieving students at the point where they are making this transition and those who are experiencing difficulties in becoming fluent.

This finding is subject to a caveat. Relatively few studies had conventional experimental or quasi-experimental designs. Many of the studies, from a special education tradition, used single or multiple baseline designs, in which progress is examined over a period of time. These studies can be robust (Neuman & McCormick, 1995), but we find the reliance on this design in an entire body of research to be problematic. Also, in a number of studies in which progress could be compared with a norm, students' progress fell below what would be expected (e.g., Blum et al., 1995; Chomsky, 1978).

Conclusions

Fluency Instruction and the Stage Model. According to Chall's (1996b) stage model presented at the beginning of this article, one would expect that fluency instruction would be most effective for children in the confirmation and fluency stage, from the end of first grade to third grade. This proposition is difficult to test because practically all studies used either normally achieving second graders or older children with reading problems who were reading at the second-grade level. That is, nearly all of the researchers working with fluency instruction implicitly accepted a stage view and acted accordingly. Of the few studies that used populations outside of this range, the results supported the stage model. Hollingsworth (1970) used average fourth graders, who should have been in the learning-the-new stage and not in need of fluency instruction and found that the treatment did not produce significant improvement over a control. Hollingsworth (1978) replicated this study with below-average fourth graders, who would have been predicted to benefit from this training, and found that they did. Stahl et al. (1997) found that their fluency-oriented reading instruction program was highly effective with children reading at a primer level or higher at the beginning of second grade. Nearly all of those students were reading at the second-grade level by the end of the year. With children reading below the primer level, the approach brought only half to that level. Teachers dropped children who were reading at an emergent stage from the program because it did not seem to benefit them at all. Blum et al. (1995) found that only children who entered their assisted-reading treatment with some reading ability (a preprimer level) benefited from the treatment. Both Marseglia (1997) and Turpie and Pastore (1995) found that their repeated-readings treatment seemed to work better for the higher-level first graders that they worked with than with the lower-achieving first graders.

Therefore, the research results are consistent with the stage model. Fluency instruction seems to work best with children from between a late preprimer level and late second-grade level. Beyond or below that level, the results are not as strong. Children need to have some entering knowledge about words to benefit from rereading but not be so fluent that they cannot demonstrate improvements.

Effects of Rereading. We stressed approaches that involved rereading of text through assisted reading, repeated reading, or approaches that integrated a number of activities into a classroom lesson design. Although these approaches all seem to be effective, it is not clear why they are effective. Specifically, it is not clear whether these studies have their effects because of any particular instructional activities or through the general mechanism of increasing the volume of children's reading. Fluency instruction may work only by increasing the amount of reading children do, relative to traditional instruction. If so, then there may be other approaches that work as well or better. We know that increasing the amount of reading children do will improve their achievement (Anderson et al., 1988; Berliner, 1981; Taylor et al., 1990). Repeated reading and assisted readings may enable children to read more difficult material than they might otherwise be able to read or may provide a manageable structure to enable increased amounts of reading.

Several studies compared repeated and nonrepeated reading. Homan, Klesius, and Hite (1993); Mathes and Fuchs (1993); Rashotte and Torgesen (1985); and Van Bon, Boksebeld, Font, Freide, and Van den Hurk (1991) found no difference in effects between repeated reading of a small number of texts and nonrepetitive reading of a larger set of texts. It is not the repetition that leads to the effect but the amount of time spent reading connected text.

We did not review the effects of paired reading, a nonrepeated assisted-reading approach (Topping, 1987; Topping & Whitley, 1990). In paired reading, a more capable reader, usually an adult, works one-on-one with a struggling reader. A paired reading session begins with the tutor and tutee choosing a book together. The book need be only of interest to the tutee. There should be no readability limits (although our experience is that children rarely choose material that is far too difficult). They begin by reading in unison. The child signals the tutor, by touching the tutor or raising a hand or some other prearranged signal, when he or she wants to read solo. This continues until the child makes an error. Errors are corrected by the tutor's provision of the word. The pair then repeat the sentence in unison and continue reading. Paired reading has been used in the classroom and by parents. Morgan and Lyon (1979), for example, examined the effects of paired reading in the home. Over the 12 to 13 weeks during which children read with their parents, students made an average gain of 11.75 months in word recognition and 11.50 months in comprehension, with a range of 10–13 months. Thus, paired reading with parental support can be an effective way of developing the fluency of readers experiencing difficulty with connected text.

Because we did not find studies that directly compared paired reading with assisted reading and we did not have enough information to do a meta-analysis, we cannot say whether paired reading is more or less effective than assisted reading. Because paired reading does not involve repetition, although assisted reading does, this comparison would be useful in teasing out the effects of repetitive reading.

Relative Difficulty of the Text. What level should the text be on? Some have argued that having children read easy text improves fluency (e.g., Clay, 1993), but it seems that the most successful approaches involved children reading instructional-level text or even text at the frustration level with strong support (see Stahl et al., 1997). Mathes and Fuchs (1993), however, used both relatively easy and relatively difficult texts and found no effect for text difficulty. More directed work needs to be done to assess the effects of the relative difficulty of text on learning.

Next, both practice and support are essential to the development of fluent reading and can be provided either through repetition or modeling. Whether this provision comes through the use of taped narrations, another individual, or repetition seems to be less crucial a matter than the fact that it exists, for such support seems to allow learners to work within their zone of proximal development (Vygotsky, 1934/1978), offering the scaffolding that allows learners to successfully move beyond the point at which they are able to work independently.

An Irony

The "method of repeated reading," as discussed by Samuels (1979, 1988; Samuels et al., 1992), was developed as an approach to translate LaBerge and Samuels's (1974) automatic information processing model into an instructional approach. LaBerge and Samuels's model is based on the notion that automatic processing of words will free up attentional resources that can then be devoted to comprehension. Samuels contended that through repeated reading, children would develop automatic word recognition, thus allowing them to be able to improve their comprehension. As shown in this review, repeated reading and other fluency-oriented approaches do improve comprehension. However, the irony is that they do not appear to improve automatic word recognition, as measured by conventional experimental psychology measures. Dahl (1979) failed to find that repeated reading improved tachistoscopic recognition of words, and neither Dowhower (1989) nor McFalls, Schwanenflugel, and Stahl (1996) found that fluency-oriented instruction improved children's response latency to words. Thus, fluency-oriented instruction seems to have salutary effects in a number of areas but not in the area that it was intended for, rapid recognition of isolated words.

Prosody, Automaticity, and Comprehension

Both the assisted and unassisted methods of fluency interventions have been generally effective in facilitating reading rate and accuracy. Given the amount of repetition or practice with print that they require on the part of learners, these results are not surprising. However, they also lead to improvements on measures of learners' comprehension. The following question then arises: Does this understanding develop simply from the amount of practice students undergo with regard to word recognition, or is there something more specific to their reading of connected text and their emerging sense of its relation to oral language that allows for this understanding to develop?

If comprehension were improved only by improved automatic word recognition, then teaching children to identify words faster would have an effect on comprehension. A number of studies have examined teaching children to say words faster (Fleisher et al., 1979/1980; Levy, Abello, & Lysynchuk, 1997; Spring, Blunden, & Gatheral, 1981). Although in all of these studies children's passage reading fluency improved, in none of these studies did their comprehension significantly differ from that of a control group. In these studies, children were taught to say the words in a list that they knew faster. In contrast, preteaching words that children did not know seems to improve comprehension (e.g., Blanchard, 1981; Tan & Nicholson, 1997). Thus, it seems that more than speed of recognition is involved in the effects of repeated and assisted readings on comprehension.

Another source of information is the research on parsing or segmenting texts. Beginning with Cromer (1970), a number of researchers have found that presenting students with text segmented by phrase units seems to produce better comprehension than conventional text. This effect is especially pronounced for children who are slow but accurate readers (Cromer, 1970; O'Shea & Sindelar, 1983). Segmenting the text may provide the same cues to phrasal structure as prosody does in oral language (Schreiber, 1980, 1987). However, nearly all researchers studied the effects of segmenting text with older children, fourth grade and higher, a different population than we are concerned with. O'Shea and Sindelar (1983) were the only researchers we found who worked with primary-grade children. They found that segmented text produced better comprehension than conventional text, as measured by a maze-type cloze test. Being able to segment text by phrasal boundaries may improve comprehension in primary-grade children, but we are reluctant to infer from the results of one study that fluency instructional effects on comprehension are due to their effects on prosody.

Given that assisted and repeated reading and parsing of texts both seem to aid learners' comprehension and speeded recognition of isolated words does not, we would argue that it is more than simply automaticity and accuracy that allow this understanding to develop. Further, the discussion surrounding prosody as a necessary component in children's ability to understand oral language and its role in language acquisition all add to the argument that prosody is equally necessary to developing an understanding of written text. Finally, given that fluent oral reading is considered to be expressive as well as quick and accurate and that prosodic features are, to a large extent, responsible for such expression, it is important to consider a definition of fluency that encompasses more than rate and accuracy.

Directions for Future Research

Fluency instruction seems to be a promising approach to teaching children in the confirmation and fluency stage of reading, especially those in late first and second grades, but also children with reading problems who are disfluent. Although the basic approaches have been around for over 30 years, there are many unanswered questions. We are still not sure of the role of repetitive reading, whether increasing the amount of reading done would have similar effects, what the effects are of reading texts at a range of difficulties, whether fluency instruction works by improving automatic word recognition or whether it affects perception of phrasal boundaries, and how does improved fluency affect comprehension. These are questions worth exploring.

These issues all relate to the larger notion of "practice." It has been argued that practice in reading is vital to develop as a reader (e.g., Berliner, 1981). But what kind of practice is needed? We know that time spent reading is an important variable in learning to read, but time spent reading what? Is reading difficult material more useful than reading easy material? Is reading the same material repeatedly as useful as reading new material? Does repeated reading lead to improved self-monitoring and correction? Are there different effects for oral and silent reading?

From this review, we have come to view fluency instruction as successful in improving the reading achievement of children at a certain point in their reading development. However, we have seen relatively little of this instruction in the schools. To help more readers move from labored decoding to the construction of meaning, we consider it to be important that educators integrate these techniques in the classroom more frequently.

References

Adams, M.J. (1990). *Beginning to read: Thinking and learning about print*. Cambridge, MA: MIT Press.

Allington, R.L. (1983). Fluency: The neglected reading goal. *The Reading Teacher, 37*, 556–561.

Anderson, R.C., Hiebert, E.H., Wilkinson, I.A.G., & Scott, J. (1985). *Becoming a nation of readers: The report of the Commission on Reading*. Washington, DC: National Institute of Education.

Anderson, R.C., Wilson, P.T., & Fielding, L.G. (1988). Growth in reading and how children spend their time outside of school. *Reading Research Quarterly, 23*, 285–303.

Bell, D.M., Markley, B.K., & Yonker, R.J. (1990). *The effect of repeated reading on elementary students' attitude toward reading*. East Lansing, MI: National Center for Research on Teacher Learning. (ERIC Document Reproduction Service No. ED326844)

Berliner, D.C. (1981). Academic learning time and reading achievement. In J.T. Guthrie (Ed.), *Comprehension and teaching: Research reviews* (pp. 203–226). Newark, DE: International Reading Association.

Blanchard, J.S. (1981). A comprehension strategy for disabled readers in the middle school. *Journal of Reading, 24*, 331–336.

Blum, I.H., Koskinen, P.S., Tennant, N., Parker, E.M., Straub, M., & Curry, C. (1995). *Using audiotaped books to extend classroom literacy instruction into the homes of second-language learners* (Reading Research Report No. 39). Athens, GA: National Reading Research Center.

Bohlen, L. (1988). *Building fluency through repeated reading in the third grade*. East Lansing, MI: National Center for Research on Teaching Learning. (ERIC Document Reproduction Service No. ED294158)

Carbo, M. (1978). Teaching reading with talking books. *The Reading Teacher, 32*, 267–273.

Carbo, M. (1981). Making books talk to children. *The Reading Teacher, 35*, 186–189.

Carver, R.P., & Hoffman, J.V. (1981). The effect of practice through repeated reading on gain in reading ability using a computer-based instructional system. *Reading Research Quarterly, 16*, 374–390.

Chafe, W. (1988). Punctuation and the prosody of written language. *Written Communication, 5,* 396–426.

Chall, J.S. (1996a). *Learning to read: The great debate* (3rd ed.). New York: McGraw-Hill.

Chall, J.S. (1996b). *Stages of reading development* (2nd ed.). Fort Worth, TX: Harcourt Brace.

Chall, J.S., Jacobs, V., & Baldwin, L. (1990). *The reading crisis.* Cambridge, MA: Harvard University Press.

Chomsky, C. (1978). When you still can't read in third grade. After decoding, what? In S.J. Samuels (Ed.), *What research has to say about reading instruction* (pp. 13–30). Newark, DE: International Reading Association.

Clay, M.M. (1993). *Reading recovery: A guidebook for teachers in training.* Portsmouth, NH: Heinemann.

Clay, M.M., & Imlach, R.H. (1971). Juncture, pitch, and stress as reading behavior variables. *Journal of Verbal Learning and Verbal Behavior, 10,* 133–139.

Cromer, W. (1970). The difference model: A new explanation for some reading difficulties. *Journal of Educational Psychology, 61,* 471–483.

Cunningham, A.E., & Stanovich, K.E. (1991). Tracking the unique effects of print exposure in children: Associations with vocabulary, general knowledge, and spelling. *Journal of Educational Psychology, 83,* 264–274.

Cunningham, A.E., & Stanovich, K.E. (1998). The impact of print exposure on word recognition. In J.L. Metsala & L.C. Ehri (Eds.), *Word recognition and beginning literacy* (pp. 235–262). Mahwah, NJ: Erlbaum.

Dahl, P. R. (1979). An experimental program for teaching high speed word recognition and comprehension skills. In J.E. Button, T. Lovitt, & T. Rowland (Eds.), *Communications research in learning disabilities and mental retardation* (pp. 33–65). Baltimore: University Park Press.

Dowhower, S.L. (1987). Effects of repeated reading on second-grade transitional readers' fluency and comprehension. *Reading Research Quarterly, 22,* 389–406.

Dowhower, S.L. (1989). Repeated reading: Theory into practice. *The Reading Teacher, 42,* 502–507.

Dowhower, S.L. (1991). Speaking of prosody: Fluency's unattended bedfellow. *Theory Into Practice, 30,* 165–175.

Ehri, L.C. (1995). Phases of development in learning to read words by sight. *Journal of Research in Reading, 18,* 116–125.

Ehri, L.C. (1998). Grapheme–phoneme knowledge is essential for learning to read words in English. In J.L. Metsala & L.C. Ehri (Eds.), *Word recognition in beginning literacy* (pp. 3–40). Mahwah, NJ: Erlbaum.

Eldredge, J.L. (1990). Increasing the performance of poor readers in the third grade with a group-assisted strategy. *Journal of Educational Research, 84,* 69–77.

Eldredge, J.L., & Quinn, D.W. (1988). Increasing reading performance of low-achieving second graders with dyad reading groups. *Journal of Educational Research, 82,* 40–46.

Eldredge, J.L., Reutzel, D.R., & Hollingsworth, P.M. (1996). Comparing the effectiveness of two oral reading practices: Round robin reading and the shared book experience. *Journal of Literacy Research, 28,* 201–225.

Elley, W.B. (2000). The potential of book floods for raising literacy levels. *International Review of Education, 46,* 233–255.

Evans, M.A., & Carr, T.H. (1985). Cognitive abilities, conditions of learning and the early development of reading skill. *Reading Research Quarterly, 20,* 327–350.

Fleisher, L.S., Jenkins, J.R.. & Pany, D. (1979/1980). Effects on poor readers' comprehension of training in rapid decoding. *Reading Research Quarterly, 15,* 30–48.

Gardner, C. (1965). *Experimental use of the impress method of reading rehabilitation.* East Lansing, MI: National Center for Research on Teacher Learning. (ERIC Document Reproduction Service No. ED003838)

Gilbert, L.M., Williams, R.L., & McLaughlin, T.F. (1996). Use of assisted reading to increase correct reading rates and decrease error rates of students with learning disabilities. *Journal of Applied Behavior Analysis, 29,* 255–257.

Hannah, A.M. (1994). *The effects of repeated readings on the reading fluency and comprehension of second-grade, Chapter 1 students.* Unpublished doctoral dissertation, University of Delaware, Newark, DE.

Harris, A.J., & Sipay, E. (1990). *How to increase reading ability* (10th ed.). White Plains, NY: Longman.

Heckelman, R.G. (1969). A neurological-impress method of remedial-reading instruction. *Academic Therapy Quarterly, 4,* 277–282.

Heckelman, R.G. (1986). N.I.M. revisited. *Academic Therapy, 21*, 411–420.

Herman, P.A. (1985). The effect of repeated readings on reading rate, speech pauses, and word recognition accuracy. *Reading Research Quarterly, 20*, 553–565.

Hoffman, J. (1987). Rethinking the role of oral reading. *The Elementary School Journal, 87*, 367–373.

Holdaway, D. (1979). *The foundations of literacy.* Sydney, Australia: Ashton-Scholastic.

Hollingsworth, P.M. (1970). An experiment with the impress method of teaching reading. *The Reading Teacher, 24*, 112–114.

Hollingsworth, P.M. (1978). An experimental approach to the impress method of teaching reading. *The Reading Teacher, 31*, 624–626.

Homan, S., Klesius. P., & Hite, S. (1993). Effects of repeated readings and nonrepetitive strategies on students' fluency and comprehension. *Journal of Educational Research, 87*, 94–99.

Hoskisson, K., & Krohm, B. (1974). Reading by immersion: Assisted reading. *Elementary English, 51*, 832–836.

Johns, J.L. (1993). *Informal reading inventories.* DeKalb, IL: Communitech International.

Kintsch, W. (1998). *Comprehension: A paradigm for cognition.* Cambridge, UK: Cambridge University Press.

Knupp, R. (1988). *Improving oral reading skills of educationally handicapped elementary school-aged students through repeated readings.* East Lansing, MI: National Center for Research on Teacher Learning. (ERIC Document Reproduction Service No. ED297275)

Koch, K.A. (1984). *The effects of oral repeated reading on second grade students' oral reading accuracy, rate, and comprehension.* Unpublished doctoral dissertation, Purdue University, West Lafayette, IN.

Koskinen, P.S., & Blum. I.H. (1984). Repeated oral reading and the acquisition of fluency. In J.A. Niles & L.A. Harris (Eds.), *Changing perspectives on research in reading/language processing and instruction* (33rd yearbook of the National Reading Conference, pp. 183–187). Rochester, NY: National Reading Conference.

Koskinen, P.S., & Blum, I.H. (1986). Paired repeated reading: A classroom strategy for developing fluent reading. *The Reading Teacher, 40*, 70–75.

Koskinen, P.S., Wilson, R.M., & Jensema, C. (1985). Closed-captioned television: A new tool for reading instruction. *Reading World, 24*(4), 1–7.

Krashen, S. (2001). More smoke and mirrors: A critique of the National Reading Panel report on fluency. *Phi Delta Kappan, 83*, 119–123.

Labbo, L.D., & Teale, W.H. (1990). Cross age reading: A strategy for helping poor readers. *The Reading Teacher, 43*, 363–369.

LaBerge, D., & Samuels, S. J. (1974). Toward a theory of automatic information processing in reading. *Cognitive Psychology, 6*, 293–323.

Langford, K., Slade, B., & Burnett, E. (1974). An examination of impress techniques in remedial reading. *Academic Therapy, 9*, 309–319.

Leinhardt, G., Zigmond, N., & Cooley, W. (1981). Reading instruction and its effects. *American Educational Research Journal, 18*, 343–361.

Levy, B.A., Abello, B., & Lysynchuk, L. (1997). Transfer from word training to reading in context: Gains in fluency and comprehension. *Learning Disability Quarterly, 20*, 173–188.

Levy, B.A., Barnes, L., & Martin, L. (1993). Transfer of fluency across repetitions and across texts. *Canadian Journal of Experimental Psychology, 47*, 401–427.

Levy, B.A., Newell, S., Snyder, J., & Timmins, K. (1986). Processing changes across reading encounters. *Journal of Experimental Psychology, 12*, 467–478.

Light, R.J., & Pillemer, D.B. (1984). *Summing up: The science of reviewing research.* Cambridge, MA: Harvard University Press.

Marseglia, P. (1997). *The effect of repeated readings on the fluency of high and low ability readers in a first grade class.* East Lansing, MI: National Center for Research on Teacher Learning. (ERIC Document Reproduction Service No. ED405562)

Mathes, P.G., & Fuchs, L.S. (1993). Peer-mediated reading instruction in special education resource rooms. *Learning Disabilities Research and Practice, 8*, 233–243.

McFalls, E.L., Schwanenflugel, P.J., & Stahl, S.A. (1996). The influence of word meaning on the acquisition of a reading vocabulary in second grade children. *Reading and Writing, 8*, 235–250.

Mefferd, P.E., & Pettegrew, B.S. (1997). Fostering literacy acquisition of students with developmental disabilities: Assisted reading with predictable trade books. *Reading Research and Instruction, 36*, 177–190.

Morgan, R., & Lyon, E. (1979). "Paired reading": A preliminary report on a technique for parental tuition of reading-retarded children. *Journal of Child Psychology and Psychiatry and Allied Disciplines, 20,* 151–160.

Morris, D., & Nelson, L. (1992). Supported oral reading with low achieving second graders. *Reading Research and Instruction, 32,* 49–63.

Mudre, L.H., & McCormick, S. (1989). Effects of meaning-focused cues on underachieving readers' context use, self-corrections. and literal comprehension. *Reading Research Quarterly, 24,* 89–113.

National Institute of Child Health and Human Development. (2000). *Report of the National Reading Panel. Teaching children to read: An evidence-based assessment of the scientific research literature on reading and its implications for reading instruction: Reports of the subgroups* (NIH Publication No. 00-4754). Washington, DC: U.S. Government Printing Office.

Nell, V. (1988). *Lost in a book: The psychology of reading for pleasure.* New Haven, CT: Yale University Press.

Neuman, S.B., & McCormick. S. (1995). *Single-subject experimental research: Applications for literacy.* Newark, DE: International Reading Association.

O'Shea, L.J., & Sindelar, P.T. (1983.). The effects of segmenting written discourse on the reading comprehension of low- and high-performance readers. *Reading Research Quarterly, 18,* 458–465.

O'Shea. L.J., Sindelar, P.T., & O'Shea, D. (1985). The effects of repeated readings and attentional cues on reading fluency and comprehension. *Journal of Reading Behavior, 17,* 129–142.

O'Shea, L.J., Sindelar, P.T., & O'Shea, D. (1987). The effects of repeated readings and attentional cues on the reading fluency and comprehension of learning disabled readers. *Learning Disabilities Research, 2,* 103–109.

Perfetti, C.A. (1985). *Reading ability.* New York: Oxford University Press.

Perfetti. C.A. (1992). The representation problem in reading acquisition. In L.C. Ehri, R. Treiman, & P.B. Gough (Eds.), *Reading acquisition* (pp. 145–174). Hillsdale, NJ: Erlbaum.

Person, M.E., & Burke, D.M. (1984, October). *Oral reading in the classroom.* Paper presented at the annual meeting of the Northern Rocky Mountain Educational Research Association, Jackson Hole, WY. (ERIC Document Reproduction Service No. ED251796)

Ramunda, J.M. (1994). *A cross-age reading program: Building fluency and comprehension.* Unpublished master's thesis, Kean College, Union, NJ. (ERIC Document Reproduction Service No. ED366940)

Rashotte, C.A., & Torgesen, J.K. (1985). Repeated reading and reading fluency in learning-disabled children. *Reading Research Quarterly, 20,* 180–188.

Rasinski, T.V. (1990a). Effects of repeated reading and listening-while-reading on reading fluency. *Journal of Educational Research, 83,* 147–150.

Rasinski, T.V. (1990b). Investigating measures of reading fluency. *Educational Research Quarterly, 14,* 37–44.

Rasinski, T.V., Padak, N., Linek, W., & Sturtevant, B. (1994). Effects of fluency development on urban second-grade readers. *Journal of Educational Research, 87,* 158–165.

Read, C., & Schreiber, P.A. (1982). Why short subjects are harder to find than long ones. In E. Wanner & L. Gleitman (Eds.), *Language acquisition: The state of the art* (pp. 78–101). Cambridge, UK: Cambridge University Press.

Reutzel, D.R., & Hollingsworth, P.M. (1993). Effects of fluency training on second graders' reading comprehension. *Journal of Educational Research, 86,* 325–331.

Reutzel, D.R., Hollingsworth, P.M., & Eldredge, J.L. (1994). Oral reading instruction: The impact on student reading development. *Reading Research Quarterly, 29,* 40–62.

Richek, M.A., & McTeague. B.K. (1988). The "Curious George" strategy for students with reading problems. *The Reading Teacher, 42,* 220–226.

Samuels, S.J. (1979). The method of repeated readings. *The Reading Teacher, 32,* 403–408.

Samuels, S.J. (1988). Decoding and automaticity: Helping poor readers become automatic at word recognition. *The Reading Teacher, 41,* 756–760.

Samuels, S.J., Schermer, N., & Reinking, D. (1992). Reading fluency: Techniques for making decoding automatic. In S.J. Samuels & A.E. Farstrup (Eds.), *What research has to say about reading instruction* (2nd ed., pp. 124–144). Newark, DE: International Reading Association.

Schreiber, P.A. (1980). On the acquisition of reading fluency. *Journal of Reading Behavior, 12,* 177–186.

Schreiber, P.A. (1987). Prosody and structure in children's syntactic processing. In R. Horowitz & S.J. Samuels (Eds.), *Comprehending oral and written language* (pp. 243–270). New York: Academic Press.

Schreiber, P.A. (1991). Understanding prosody's role in reading acquisition. *Theory Into Practice, 30,* 158–164.

Schreiber, P.A., & Read, C. (1980). Children's use of phonetic cues in spelling, parsing, and—maybe—reading. *Bulletin of the Orton Society, 30,* 209–224.

Scruggs, T.E. (1987). The quantitative synthesis of single subject research: Methodology and validation. *Remedial and Special Education, 8,* 24–33.

Simmons, D.C., Fuchs, L.S., Fuchs, D., Mathes, P., & Hodge, J.P. (1995). Effects of explicit teaching and peer tutoring on the reading achievement of learning-disabled and low-performing students in regular classrooms. *The Elementary School Journal, 95,* 387–408.

Spring, C., Blunden, D., & Gatheral, M. (1981). Effect on reading comprehension of training to automaticity in word-reading. *Perceptual and Motor Skills, 53,* 779–786.

Stahl, S., Heubach, K., & Cramond. B. (1997). *Fluency-oriented reading instruction.* Athens, GA: National Reading Research Center; Washington, DC: U.S. Department of Education, Office of Educational Research and Improvement Educational Resources Information Center.

Stahl, S.A., Jacobson, M.G., Davis, C.E., & Davis, R.L. (1989). Prior knowledge and difficult vocabulary in the comprehension of unfamiliar text. *Reading Research Quarterly, 24,* 27–43.

Stahl, S.A., & Murray, B.A. (1998). Issues involved in defining phonological awareness and its relation to early reading. In J.L. Metsala & L.C. Ehri (Eds.), *Word recognition in beginning literacy* (pp. 65–88). Mahwah, NJ: Erlbaum.

Stanovich, K.E. (1980). Effects of explicit teaching and peer tutoring on the reading achievement of learning disabled and low-performing students in regular classrooms. *Reading Research Quarterly, 16,* 32–71.

Stanovich, K.E. (1984). The interactive-compensatory model of reading: A confluence of developmental, experimental, and educational psychology. *Remedial and Special Education, 5*(3), 11–19.

Stoddard, K., Valcante, G., Sindelar, P., O'Shea, L., & Algozzine, P. (1993). Increasing reading rate and comprehension: The effects of repeated readings, sentence segmentation, and intonation training. *Reading Research and Instruction, 32,* 53–65.

Strong, M.W., & Traynelis-Yurek, E. (1983). *Behavioral reinforcement within a perceptual-conditioning program of oral reading.* East Lansing, MI: National Center for Research on Teacher Learning. (ERIC Document Reproduction Service No. ED233328)

Sutton, P.A. (1991). *Strategies to increase oral reading fluency of primary resource students.* East Lansing, MI: National Center for Research on Teacher Learning. (ERIC Document Reproduction Service No. ED335660)

Tan, A., & Nicholson, T. (1997). Flashcards revisited: Training poor readers to read words faster improves their comprehension of text. *Journal of Educational Psychology, 89,* 276–288.

Taylor, B.M., Frye, B.J., & Maruyama, G.M. (1990). Time spent reading and reading growth. *American Educational Research Journal, 27,* 351–362.

Tingstrom, D.H., Edwards, R.P., & Olmi. D.J. (1995). Listening previewing in reading to read: Relative effects on oral reading fluency. *Psychology in the Schools, 32,* 318–327.

Topping, K. (1987). Paired reading: A powerful technique for parent use. *The Reading Teacher, 40,* 608–614.

Topping, K., & Whitley, M. (1990). Participant evaluation of parent-tutored and peer-tutored projects in reading. *Educational Research, 32,* 14–32.

Turpie, J.J., & Paratore, J.R. (1995). Using repeated readings to promote reading success in a heterogeneously grouped first grade. In K.A. Hinchman & D.J. Leu (Eds.), *Perspectives on literacy research and practice* (44th yearbook of the National Reading Conference, pp. 255–264). Chicago: National Reading Conference.

Van Bon, W.H., Boksebeld, L.M., Font Freide, T.A., & Van den Hurk, A.J. (1991). A comparison of three methods of reading-while listening. *Journal of Learning Disabilities, 24,* 471–476.

van der Leij, A. (1981). Remediation of reading-disabled children by presenting text simultaneously to eye and ear. *Bulletin of the Orton Society, 31*, 229–243.

Vygotsky, L.S. (1978). *Mind in society: The development of higher psychological processes* (M. Cole, V. John-Steiner, S. Scribner, & E. Souberman, Eds. & Trans.). Cambridge, MA: Harvard University Press. (Original work published 1934)

Weinstein, G., & Cooke, N.L. (1992). The effects of two repeated reading interventions on generalization of fluency. *Learning Disability Quarterly, 15*, 21–28.

Young, A.R., Bowers, P.G., & MacKinnon, G.E. (1996). Effects of prosodic modeling and repeated reading on poor readers' fluency and comprehension. *Applied Psycholinguistics, 17*, 59–84.

17

Matthew Effects in Reading:
Some Consequences
of Individual Differences
in the Acquisition of Literacy

Keith E. Stanovich

To synthesize the ever-growing body of literature on individual differences in the cognitive skills related to reading is difficult because of the plethora of relationships that have been found. Good and poor readers have been compared on just about every cognitive task that has ever been devised, and group performance differences have been observed on a large number of these tasks (see, for example, Carr, 1981; DeSoto & DeSoto, 1983; Mitchell, 1982; Palmer, MacLeod, Hunt, & Davidson, 1985; Share, Jorm, Maclean, & Matthews, 1984; Singer & Crouse, 1981; Stanovich, 1982a, 1982b, 1986). Mounds of correlations and significant differences have been found. There is, then, at least one sense in which it can be said that we do not lack empirical evidence. The problem is in deciding what it all means.

The aim of this paper is to attempt to clarify the literature by drawing attention to some alternative ways of interpreting relationships between cognitive processes and reading ability. These alternative interpretations have all been discussed before by numerous authors (e.g., Bryant & Bradley, 1985; Byrne, 1986; Chall, 1983; Donaldson, 1978; Ehri, 1979; Morrison & Manis, 1982), but their implications have not been fully explored, nor have they been brought together within a coherent framework. This review presents such a framework and, in addition, a model of the development of individual differences in reading achievement and related cognitive processes that seems to follow logically from it.

Problems With the Existing Evidence

For many years, research on individual differences was plagued by the failure to carry out thorough process analyses on the experimental tasks employed. Thus, it

---

From *Reading Research Quarterly*, *21*, 360–407. Copyright © 1986 by the International Reading Association.

was rarely possible to ascribe any cognitive specificity to an observed group difference. This problem has partially been alleviated due to the general influence of a paradigmatic assumption of cognitive psychology: that performance on any single task is the result of the simultaneous or successive operation of many different information-processing operations. However, it took a long time for reading disability researchers to accept an implication of this assumption: that one could not merely observe a difference on, for example, a perceptual task, and then announce that "visual processing" was the key to reading failure, based on one's introspection about what the task tapped. It was sometimes hard to understand that no matter how large the performance difference observed on a single task, such an outcome represented not the end, but instead the beginning of a careful task analysis that one hoped would reveal the cognitive locus of the difference. The rise and fall of many of the popular hypotheses in the dyslexia literature mirrors this belated realization (see Vellutino, 1979).

Beyond the issue of inferring the appropriate process difference from task performance lies an even more vexing problem: that of inferring causation. After observing a performance difference in a purely correlational study and carrying out the appropriate task analysis, we are still left with the question of whether the processing difference thus isolated causes variation in reading achievement, whether reading achievement itself affects the operation of the cognitive process, or whether the relationship is due to some third variable. Also, there is the possibility of *reciprocal causation*: that there are causal connections running in both directions.

Complicating the picture even further is the possibility that the causal connections between variation in reading achievement and the efficiency of various cognitive processes may change with development. This possibility has been strongly emphasized by some researchers (e.g., Chall, 1983; Satz, Taylor, Friel, & Fletcher, 1978), but has been inadequately reflected in much research on individual differences in the cognitive skills of reading. For example, it is possible that some relationships are *developmentally limited*—that individual differences in a particular cognitive process may be a causal determinant of variation in reading achievement early in development but at some point have no further effects on the level of reading efficiency. In this case, a correlation between reading achievement and the efficiency of a cognitive process may obtain in adults because the efficiency of the cognitive process determined the ease with which the individual traversed earlier stages of the reading process—stages that laid the foundation for the present level of reading ability—but further progress is dependent on the development of processes other than the one in question. A residual correlation between the efficiency of the process and reading level remains as a remnant of a causal connection present during an earlier developmental stage.

The vast literature on individual differences in the cognitive processes of reading will only be fully understood when we are able to determine which performance linkages reflect causal relationships, which are developmentally limited, which are the result of third variables, which enter into relationships of reciprocal causation, and which are consequences of the individual's reading level or reading history. Achieving such a classification will be easier if it is recognized that certain relationships may change status at different levels of reading development. In this review, some tentative classifications for some of the cognitive processes that have received considerable attention in recent research will be hypothesized. In order to provide a context for these hypotheses, I will first present a brief outline of a preliminary (and incomplete) model of the development of individual differences in reading skill.

A Model of the Development of Individual Differences in Reading

Evidence is mounting that the primary specific mechanism that enables early reading success is phonological awareness: conscious access to the phonemic level of the speech stream and some ability to cognitively manipulate representations at this level. Although general indicators of cognitive functioning, such as nonverbal intelligence, vocabulary, and listening comprehension, make significant independent contributions to predicting the ease of initial reading acquisition, phonological awareness stands out as the most potent predictor (Share et al., 1984; Stanovich, Cunningham, & Cramer, 1984; Stanovich, Cunningham, & Feeman, 1984a; Tunmer & Nesdale, 1985). Indeed, phonological awareness tasks often correlate more highly with early reading acquisition than do omnibus measures such as general intelligence tests or reading readiness tests (Mann, 1984; Share et al., 1984; Stanovich, Cunningham, & Cramer, 1984; Stanovich, Cunningham, & Feeman, 1984a; Zifcak, 1981).

Of course, although the strength of these correlations serves to draw attention to phonological awareness, it is not proof that variation in awareness is causally connected to differences in the ease of initial reading acquisition. Proving causation requires much stronger evidence, and this evidence is much less plentiful than the purely correlational data. However, a growing body of data does exist indicating that variation in phonological awareness is causally related to the early development of reading skill. This evidence is of several different types. First, there are several studies showing that measures of phonological awareness predict reading ability even when the former are assessed very early in development (Bradley & Bryant, 1983, 1985; Fox & Routh, 1975; Share et al., 1984; Williams, 1984). Second, Tunmer and Nesdale (1985) reported a contingency analysis of their first-grade data which indicated that phonemic segmentation skill was a necessary, but not sufficient, condition for reading acquisition (see also Perfetti, Beck, & Hughes, 1981). In addition, the results of some recent longitudinal studies where cross-lagged correlational methods and/or structural equation modeling have been employed have led to the conclusion that early skill at phonological awareness leads to superior reading achievement (Perfetti et al., 1981; Torneus, 1984). Evidence supporting this conclusion also comes from reading-level match designs. When 10-year-old disabled readers perform worse on phonological tasks than nondisabled 6-year-old children reading at the same level (e.g., Bradley & Bryant, 1978), it is somewhat more difficult to argue that the latter are superior because they have had more reading experience. Last, and of course most convincing, are the results of several studies where phonological awareness skills were manipulated via training and the manipulation resulted in significant experimental group advantages in reading, word recognition, and spelling (Bradley & Bryant, 1983, 1985; Fox & Routh, 1984; Olofsson & Lundberg, 1985; Torrieus, 1984; Treiman & Baron, 1983).

It should be noted that several of the studies cited above have also supported Ehri's (1979, 1984, 1985) position that reading acquisition itself facilitates phonological awareness (see also Perfetti, 1985; Perfetti et al., 1981; Wagner & Torgesen, 1987), so that the situation appears to be one of reciprocal causation. Such situations of reciprocal causation can have important "bootstrapping" effects, and some of these will be discussed in this review. However, the question in this section is not which direction of causality is dominant. The essential properties of the model being outlined here are dependent only on the fact that a causal link running from phonological awareness to reading acquisition has been established, independent of the status of the opposite causal link.

Many researchers have discussed the reasons phonological awareness is important in early reading acquisition (see Gough & Hillinger, 1980; Liberman, 1982; Perfetti, 1984; Williams, 1984). A beginning reader must at some point discover the alphabetic principle: that units of print map onto units of sound (see Perfetti, 1984). This principle may be induced; it may be acquired through direct instruction; it may be acquired along with or after the build-up of a visually based sight vocabulary—but it must be acquired if a child is to progress successfully in reading. Children must be able to decode independently the many unknown words that will be encountered in the early stages of reading. By acquiring some knowledge of spelling-to-sound mappings, the child will gain the reading independence that eventually leads to the levels of practice that are prerequisites to fluent reading. The research cited above appears to indicate that some minimal level of explicit phonemic awareness is required for the acquisition of the spelling-to-sound knowledge that supports independent decoding.

It is apparently important that the prerequisite phonological awareness and skill at spelling-to-sound mapping be in place *early* in the child's development because their absence can initiate a causal chain of escalating negative side effects. Biemiller (1977/1978; see also Allington, 1980, 1983, 1984) has documented how extremely large differences in reading practice begin to emerge as early as the middle of the first-grade year. In October, the children in the three most able groups in his sample read a mean of 12.2 words per child per reading session, the children in three average ability groups read 11.9 words per child per reading session, and the children in the two least able groups were not reading. By January, the mean for the most able groups was 51.9, for the average ability groups, 25.8, and for the least able groups, 11.5. In April, the respective means were 81.4, 72.3, and 31.6. This, of course, says nothing about differences in home reading, which would probably be at least as large. Thus, soon after experiencing greater difficulty in breaking the spelling-to-sound code, poorer readers begin to be exposed to less text than their peers.

Further exacerbating the situation is the fact that poorer readers often find themselves in materials that are too difficult for them (Allington, 1977, 1983, 1984; Bristow, 1985; Forell, 1985; Gambrell, Wilson, & Gantt, 1981; Jorgenson, 1977). The combination of lack of practice, deficient decoding skills, and difficult materials results in unrewarding early reading experiences that lead to less involvement in reading-related activities. Lack of exposure and practice on the part of the less-skilled reader delays the development of automaticity and speed at the word-recognition level. Slow, capacity-draining word-recognition processes require cognitive resources that should be allocated to higher-level processes of text integration and comprehension (LaBerge & Samuels, 1974; Perfetti, 1985; Stanovich, 1980). Thus, reading for meaning is hindered, unrewarding reading experiences multiply, and practice is avoided or merely tolerated without real cognitive involvement. The downward spiral continues—and has further consequences.

The better reader more rapidly attains a stage of proficiency where decoding skill is no longer the primary determinant of reading level. As word recognition becomes less resource demanding by taking place via relatively automatic processes of visual/orthographic access, more general language skills become the limiting factor on reading ability (Chall, 1983; Sticht, 1979). But the greater reading experience of the better reader has provided an enormous advantage even here. Reading itself is an important contributor to the development of many language/cognitive skills. For example, much vocabulary growth probably takes place through the learning of word meanings from context during reading (Nagy & Anderson, 1984; Nagy, Herman, & Anderson, 1985; Sternberg, 1985). Similarly, much general information and knowledge about more complex syntactic structures probably also takes place through reading itself (Donaldson & Reid, 1982; Mann, 1986; Perfetti, 1985). In short, many things that facilitate further growth in reading comprehension ability—general knowledge, vocabulary, syntactic knowledge—are developed by reading itself. The increased reading experiences of children who crack the spelling-to-sound code early thus have important positive feedback effects. Such feedback effects appear to be potent sources of individual differences in academic achievement (Walberg, Strykowski, Rovai, & Hung, 1984).

Paring Down the Number of Causal Relationships

It will be argued here that these bootstrapping effects of reading experience and other secondary effects have been inadequately considered in the extensive literature on individual differences in the cognitive processes of reading. Although it might seem that a consideration of the effects of these reciprocal relationships would complicate our models, it actually has great potential to clarify reading theory. If only a few of these reciprocal effects control a large portion of the variance in reading ability, we will be able to exercise parsimony elsewhere. Such a consideration will suggest that much of the explanatory power available from all of the variables that have been linked to reading ability in individual difference studies is superfluous; and this should spur us to eliminate some as causal factors accounting for variance in reading achievement.

It is only by trying to pare down the number of potential causal relationships by classifying some as spurious, some as consequences of reading, and some as developmentally limited that any clarity will be brought to the reading literature. In the remainder of this review some specific examples of candidates for possible "paring" will be discussed. A number of hypotheses are also advanced for incorporating reciprocal relationships and feedback effects within a general model of developmental changes in the cognitive processes related to reading. The tentative causal model I have outlined will be elaborated in the course of the discussion. Many of the hypotheses to be advanced are quite tentative, as the empirical evidence relating to several of them is far from definitive. The following discussion was not intended to be exhaustive, and it certainly will not present the final and definitive classification of process linkages, but hopefully it will serve to focus future research efforts.

The easiest processing differences to eliminate as causes of individual differences in reading ability should be those where performance differences arise merely because the individuals are reading at different levels—in short, situations where the efficiency of reading is determining how efficiently the cognitive process operates, rather than the converse. We will turn first to some possible examples of this type of relationship.

Eye Movements: A Consequence of Reading Level

There may be many processes that we are prone to view as causal determinants of reading efficiency but that are, in fact, determined by that efficiency. One might have thought that the classic example of this reverse causal path in reading—individual differences in eye movement patterns—would make us all more cautious about interpreting every one of the enormous number of cognitive performance differences between good and poor readers that are present in, for example, adult readers (e.g., M. Jackson & McClelland, 1975, 1979; Palmer et al., 1985) as if each of the processes were a cause of the current level of reading ability.

The relationship of certain eye movement patterns to reading fluency has repeatedly, and erroneously, been interpreted as indicating that reading ability was determined by the efficiency of the eye movements themselves. For example, researchers have repeatedly found that less-skilled readers make more regressive eye movements, make more fixations per line of text, and have longer fixation durations than skilled readers (Rayner, 1985a, 1985b). The assumption that these particular eye movement characteristics were a cause of reading disability led to the now thoroughly discredited "eye movement training" programs that repeatedly have been advanced as "cures" for reading disabilities. Of course, we now recognize that eye movement patterns represent a perfect example of a causal connection running in the opposite direction. Poor readers do show the inefficient characteristics listed above, but they are also comprehending text more poorly. In fact, we now know that eye movements rather closely reflect the efficiency of ongoing reading—with the number of regressions and fixations per line increasing as the material becomes more difficult and decreasing as reading efficiency increases (Aman & Singh, 1983; Just & Carpenter, 1980; Olson, Kliegl, & Davidson, 1983; Rayner, 1978, 1985a, 1985b; Stanley, Smith, & Howell, 1983; Tinker, 1958)—and this is true for all readers, regardless of their skill level. When skilled readers are forced to read material too difficult for them, their eye movement patterns deteriorate and approximate those usually shown by the less-skilled reader. The eye movement patterns of the latter look more fluent when they are allowed to read easier material. In short, the level of reading determines the nature of the eye movement patterns, not the reverse.

The example of eye movements should illustrate the importance of considering whether individual differences in a particular cognitive process may reflect the reading level of the subject, rather than be a cause of it. We will next consider the less firmly established, and therefore more controversial, case of the effect of context on word recognition.

Context Effects on Word Recognition: A Consequence of Reading Level?

Few areas of reading research are so fraught with confusion as are investigations of context use. One reason for this is that reading researchers have often failed to distinguish between levels in the processing system when discussing contextual effects (Gough, 1983; Mitchell, 1982; Stanovich, 1980, 1982b, 1984). The failure to distinguish the specific processing subsystems that are being affected by a particular experimental manipulation is one of the main reasons why there is still considerable looseness and confusion surrounding the term *context effect* in the reading literature. The point is that there can be many different *types* of context effects.

It will be argued here that the literature on context effects is considerably clarified if care is taken to distinguish the different types of context effects that are discussed in reading research. For example, the claim that variation in the use of context in part determines reading efficiency, and that contextual effects are more implicated in the performance of better readers, has often been made in the reading literature:

> Skill in reading involves not greater precision, but more accurate first guesses based on better sampling techniques, greater control over language structure, broadened experiences and increased conceptual development. (Goodman, 1976, p. 504)

> Guessing in the way I have described it is not just a preferred strategy for beginners and fluent readers alike; it is the most efficient manner in which to read and learn to read. (Smith, 1979, p. 67)

> The more difficulty a reader has with reading, the more he relies on the visual information; this statement applies to both the fluent reader and the beginner. In each case, the cause of the difficulty is inability to make full use of syntactic and semantic redundancy, of nonvisual sources of information. (Smith, 1971, p. 221)

> Less often the possibility is considered that use of context makes better readers. (Smith, 1982, p. 230)

It will be argued here that the truth of this hypothesis—that more fluent readers rely more on context—is critically dependent on the distinction between the use of context as an aid to *word recognition* and its use to aid *comprehension processes*. The claim appears defensible when referring to the latter but appears to be largely incorrect when applied to the word-recognition level of processing.

We must first ask the question: Do less-skilled readers use contextual information to facilitate word recognition when it is available; and if they do, to what extent do they rely on it? Many discrete-trial reaction-time studies of context effects have been conducted to investigate this question. Note that many of these studies have ensured the condition "when it is available" by using materials that were well within the reading capability of the least skilled subjects in the study. (This will become an important consideration in a later discussion.) Most of these studies have used priming paradigms where a context (sometimes a word, sometimes a sentence, and sometimes several sentences or paragraphs) precedes a target word to which the subject must make a naming or lexical decision response. Although this paradigm does not completely isolate the word-recognition level of processing (see Forster, 1979; Seidenberg, Waters, Sanders, & Langer, 1984; Stanovich & West, 1983; West & Stanovich, 1982), it does so more than the other methodologies that have been used in the developmental literature. The finding has consistently been that not only do the poorer readers in these studies use context, but they often show somewhat larger contextual effects than do the better readers (Becker, 1982; Briggs, Austin, & Underwood, 1984; Perfetti, Goldman, & Hogaboam, 1979; Perfetti & Roth, 1981; Schvaneveldt, Ackerman, & Semlear, 1977; Schwantes, 1981, 1982, 1985; Schwantes, Boesl, & Ritz, 1980; Simpson & Foster, 1985; Simpson & Lorsbach, 1983; Simpson, Lorsbach, & Whitehouse, 1983; Stanovich, Nathan, West, & Vala-Rossi, 1985; Stanovich, West, & Feeman, 1981; West & Stanovich, 1978; West, Stanovich, Feeman, & Cunningham, 1983).

Some investigators have employed oral reading error analyses in order to examine individual differences in the use of context to facilitate word recognition. However, the use of the technique for this purpose is problematic. An oral reading error occurs for a variety of complex and interacting reasons (see Kibby, 1979; Leu, 1982; Wixson, 1979). Most critical for the present discussion is the fact that such errors often implicate levels of processing beyond word recognition. For example, hesitations and omissions are probably some complex function of word-recognition and comprehension processes (e.g., Goodman & Gollasch, 1980). Self-corrections in part reflect comprehension monitoring. Nevertheless, analysis of initial substitution errors has been used to throw light on the use of context to aid word recognition, and it is likely that these errors do partially implicate processes operating at the word-recognition level. So it is probably useful to consider this evidence if it is clearly recognized that it does not isolate the word-recognition level of processing as cleanly as the reaction-time studies.

Fortunately, there turns out to be no dilemma because the results of oral reading error studies largely converge with those of the reaction-time studies. When skilled and less-skilled readers are in materials of comparable difficulty (i.e., materials producing similar error rates), the relative reliance on contextual information relative to graphic information is just as great—in many cases greater—for the less-skilled readers (Allington & Fleming, 1978; Batey & Sonnenschein, 1981; Biemiller, 1970, 1979; A.S. Cohen, 1974/1975; Coomber, 1972; Harding, 1984; Juel, 1980; Lesgold & Resnick, 1982; Perfetti & Roth, 1981; Richardson, DiBenedetto, & Adler, 1982; Weber, 1970; Whaley & Kibby, 1981). The findings from other paradigms, such as text disruption manipulations (Allington & Strange, 1977; Ehrlich, 1981; Schwartz & Stanovich, 1981; Siler, 1974; Strange, 1979) and timed text reading (Biemiller, 1977/1978; Doehring, 1976; Stanovich, Cunningham, & Feeman, 1984b) also converge with this conclusion.

Reconciling Differing Views on Context Use

In light of this evidence, it might seem difficult to understand how the claim that poor readers are less reliant on context for word recognition arose and gained popularity. There are several possible explanations, and they are not mutually exclusive. First is the tendency to conflate different levels of processing, discussed earlier. Skilled readers *are* more prone to use context to facilitate comprehension processes (see Stanovich, 1982b), so it is perhaps not surprising that there was a tendency to overgeneralize this relationship to the case of word recognition. Second, the popularity of the hypothesis may also have arisen from understandable confusion surrounding information-processing concepts. For example, theorists proposing top-down models of reading have often defended the position that skilled readers rely less on graphic cues:

> As the child develops reading skill and speed, he uses increasingly fewer graphic cues. (Goodman, 1976, p. 504)

> But if in fact you are not making errors when you read, you are probably not reading efficiently, you are processing more visual information than you need. (Smith, 1979, p. 33)

> The more difficulty a reader has with reading, the more he relies on visual information; this statement applies to both the fluent reader and the beginner. (Smith, 1971, p. 221)

> One difference between the good beginning reader and the one heading for trouble lies in the overreliance on visual information that inefficient—or improperly taught—beginning readers tend to show, at the expense of sense. (Smith, 1973, p. 190)

Smith's (1971) well-known hypothesis is that, because the good reader is sensitive to the redundancy afforded by sentences, he or she develops hypotheses about upcoming words and is then able to confirm the identity of a word by sampling only a few features in the visual display. Good readers should then process words faster because their use of redundancy lightens the load on their stimulus-analysis mechanisms. Despite its surface plausibility, this notion is contradicted by much recent data.

Advances in eye movement technology have quite recently made available a host of powerful techniques for collecting data relevant to this hypothesis. The results of studies employing these new methodologies have consistently indicated that fluent readers rather completely sample the visual array—even when reading fairly predictable words (Balota, Pollatsek, & Rayner, 1985; Ehrlich & Rayner, 1981; Just & Carpenter, 1980; McConkie & Zola, 1981; Rayner & Bertera, 1979; Rayner, Inhoff, Morrison, Slowiaczek, & Bertera, 1981; Zola, 1984). Fluent readers are not engaging in the wholesale skipping of words, nor are they markedly reducing their sampling of visual features from the words fixated. Although Smith's (1973) conclusion that "it is clear that the better reader barely looks at the individual words on the page" (p. 190) could not be evaluated at the time it was made, current research using the latest eye movement technology has rendered it untenable.

It appears that in the top-down models of reading, use of the features in the visual array was conflated with the cognitive resources necessary to process those features. In fact, it is not that the good reader relies less on visual information but that the visual analysis mechanisms of the good reader use less *capacity*. That is, good readers are efficient processors in every sense: They completely sample the visual array *and* use fewer resources to do so. The good reader is not less reliant on the visual information, but the good reader does allocate less capacity to process this information. In short, it is important to note that the attentional resources allocated to graphic processing and the amount of graphic information itself are two different things.

Perhaps a third reason for the popularity of the context-use hypothesis as an explanation of differences in reading ability is that there is considerable confusion about the distinction between the importance of a mechanism as a determinant of a general developmental sequence and as a determinant of individual differences in the developmental sequence (McCall, 1981). The reasoning error involved seems to have been one of taking an idea that was valid in one sphere and extending it into a domain where it was not applicable. The error was not in emphasizing that context use occurs in reading but in generalizing it as a mechanism that could explain individual differences. For example, research cited earlier indicates considerable use of context by early readers. This context use is clear from the reaction-time studies and from the fact that oral reading error studies of first-grade children have found that 70% to 95% of the initial errors are contextually appropriate (Biemiller, 1970, 1979; Weber, 1970). Note, however, that if the variability in context use is low relative to the variability in other factors that determine reading ability (phonological awareness, for example), then context use will not be strongly related to individual differences in reading ability, despite its importance as an underlying factor in every child's reading performance.

This point is similar to cautions researchers have raised about interpreting the effects of heredity and environment on intelligence test performance. It is often pointed out that if the variability in one factor is restricted, then the other will necessarily be more strongly related to individual differences. For example, individual differences between the intelligence scores in identical twins must be entirely due to environmental differences because they share the same genetic background. This, of course, does not mean that the general developmental sequence of identical twins is not partially under genetic control. However, although heredity is contributing to the development of the organism, it cannot be linked to individual differences in this case.

We must raise the question of whether an analogous phenomenon is not occurring in the case of contextual facilitation. All the empirical evidence indicates considerable use of context by first-grade children, and models of first-grade reading acquisition often include at least one stage defined in part by context use. For example, Biemiller's (1970) proposed early reading stages include an initial stage of context dependency, a stage of increasing attention to graphic processing, and a stage where the integration of both graphic and contextual cues occurs. Bissex's (1980) case study can be interpreted within this framework; she particularly emphasizes the importance of the third stage, in which both contextual and graphophonemic information is used in an integrated manner. But even if we accept the importance of a stage of graphic and contextual cue integration, the question arises whether passage into this stage is blocked by the inadequate development of context-use skills or by the failure to develop skills of graphophonemic processing. All children may indeed go through this stage, but is the speed of its attainment actually determined by variation in context-use skills? The research reviewed above suggests that the answer may be *no*: that stages may indeed exist that are defined in part by context use but that the existence of such stages may misleadingly suggest that context use is a source of individual differences. Instead, it appears that compared to other prerequisite skills—such as phonological awareness—the variability in the ability to use context to facilitate word recognition is so relatively low that it may not be a major determinant of individual differences in reading acquisition. The very ubiquity of contextual facilitation—the thing that has led some theorists to single it out as a mechanism for generating ability differences—is precisely the thing that prevents it from being a cause of individual differences.

The hypothesis about context use among readers of differing skill generated from the top-down models thus needs several modifications in order to bring it into congruence with current research evidence. First, it is not that good readers are less reliant on visual information but that they expend less capacity to process visual information fully. Second, the reason that they expend less capacity is not because they rely on context but because their stimulus-analysis mechanisms are so powerful. These modifications are all more completely explicated in Perfetti's (1985) verbal efficiency theory. Once these alterations are made, it possible to see more congruence between some of the insights that were the source of the top-down models and those of more bottom-up models like verbal efficiency theory. For example, both classes of model are in agreement on the necessity of expending processing capacity on higher-level comprehension processes rather than on word recognition. In fact, there are considerable grounds here for a rapprochement between the proponents of various global models of the reading process. Long before most cognitive psychologists became interested in reading, top-down theorists were investigating critical processing issues in the domain of context use. The latter were responsible for the crucial insight that readers need to allocate attentional capacity to comprehension rather than to word recognition in order to become fluent. However, recent work by cognitive and developmental psychologists—some of whom are of a more bottom-up persuasion—has helped to specify accurately the key mechanism that allows capacity to be allocated to comprehension. This mechanism turns out to be efficient decoding rather than context use. Both groups of researchers have thus made important contributions to our current knowledge of the interrelationships between decoding, context use for word recognition, and comprehension.

Compensatory Processing and Decoding Skill

The common finding that the magnitude of contextual facilitation effects is inversely related to the word-recognition skill of the reader has been seen as an example of interactive-compensatory processing (Perfetti & Roth, 1981; Stanovich, 1980, 1984; Stanovich, West, & Feeman, 1981) because it presumably results from the fact that the information-processing system is arranged in such a way that when the bottom-up decoding processes that result in word recognition are deficient, the system compensates by relying more heavily on other knowledge sources (e.g., contextual information). The extent to which the compensatory processing in children is obligatory and the extent to which it is strategic is an issue of much complexity and is currently being debated in the literature (see Briggs, Austin, & Underwood 1984; Simpson & Lorsbach, 1983; Stanovich, Nathan, West, & Vala-Rossi, 1985; Stanovich & West, 1983), but the current evidence appears to indicate that to a considerable extent it is obligatory and automatic. It appears that reading skill is not determined by skill at contextual prediction, but rather that the level of word-recognition skill determines the extent to which contextual information will be relied on to complete the process of lexical access. The slower the word-decoding process, the more the system draws on contextual information. In the interactive-compensatory model, the magnitude of context effects is thus conceived to be largely a consequence of the efficiency of reading—making it analogous to the case of eye movements.

Perfetti (1985) has provided the data that most convincingly demonstrate that the magnitude of contextual facilitation effects (at the word-recognition level) are a function of decoding skill. He has shown that words and individuals are "interchangeable" (p. 149). When the target word in a discrete-trial experiment is visually degraded so that the recognition speed of a good reader is as slow as that of a poor reader, the good reader shows as large a contextual effect as the poor reader. Increased word difficulty appears to operate in the same way (Perfetti et al., 1979; Stanovich, 1984; Stanovich & West, 1981, 1983; Stanovich, West, & Feeman, 1981). Perfetti (1985) has shown that in his data there is a linear relationship between the contextual facilitation effect and the isolated word-recognition time across a wide variety of conditions of word difficulty, visual degradation, and reading skill. He concluded, "In other words, it does not matter whether a word's isolated identification time is measured from a high-ability or low-ability reader or from a degraded or normal word. The context effect simply depends on the basic word-identification time" (p. 149).

Unfortunately, the function relating word-recognition difficulty and the magnitude of the context effect presented by Perfetti (1985) turns out to be a special case rather than a completely generalizable relationship. It applies only under conditions where both the skilled and the less-skilled readers have adequately processed the context. It is restricted to such conditions because the compensatory processing can only occur when the contextual information is available to supplement bottom-up analyses. Availability of context was ensured in the case of the reaction-time studies because materials were used in those studies that were well within the capability of the poorest readers; and it can be crudely controlled in the case of the oral reading error studies by looking at performance in materials where the overall error rates have been equated. However, in classroom reading situations, poorer readers will more often be dealing with materials that are relatively more difficult (Allington, 1977, 1983, 1984; Bristow, 1985; Forell, 1985; Gambrell, Wilson, & Gantt, 1981; Jorgenson, 1977) and in which they may experience decoding problems. These decoding problems will reduce the context available to the poorer reader. Thus, even though both groups may be reading the same materials, the poorer reader will have, in effect, less contextual information to utilize. This could lead such readers to display less contextual facilitation. (There may also be reader-skill differences in general knowledge and semantic memory that could affect contextual processing, but so little is known about this possibility that it will not be considered here.) The point is that we must eventually refine our theories of context use in order to distinguish the nominal context (what is on the page) from the effective context (what is being used by the reader).

Thus, in order to fully trace out the function relating contextual facilitation to the recognition time for the target word in isolation, we must consider another dimension: the difficulty of the material preceding the target word. And this added dimension will interact with reading skill in determining the amount of contextual facilitation observed. For a given target word, in very easy materials (at or below the reading level of the less-skilled readers), poorer readers will show more contextual facilitation (Perfetti, 1985; Stanovich, 1980, 1984). But as the material becomes more difficult, this difference will disappear, and eventually a level of difficulty will be reached where the better readers display larger facilitation effects because the prior text (which forms the context for the word currently being recognized) is simply too difficult for the poorer readers to decode. In short, the relationship between the difficulty of the target word, the difficulty of the contextual material, the ability of the reader, and the amount of contextual facilitation is a complex one. Note, however, that taking the difficulty of the contextual material into account does not change the source of individual differences in contextual facilitation: They are directly determined by the decoding ability of the subject (and the difficulty level of the contextual material and the target word).

Consideration of the difficulty factor may throw light on a question that is often raised in response to the reaction-time and oral reading error studies cited above: If poor readers use context so much, how can we explain the frequently reported description of problem readers as plodding through text, not using context, and understanding little? How should we interpret the performance of such readers? One interpretation that flows from the top-down perspective is that these children have learned inefficient word-recognition strategies:

Excessive stress, in reading instruction and materials, on phonics or word attack skills, will tend to make recoding an end in itself, and may actually distract the child from the real end: decoding written language for meaning. (Goodman, 1968, p. 21)

Trying to sound out words without reference to meaning is a characteristic strategy of poor readers; it is not one that leads to fluency in reading. (Smith, 1982, p. 145)

If you had read the backwards passage aloud, incidentally, you probably would have sounded very much like many of the older "problem readers" at school, who struggle to identify words one at a time in a dreary monotone as if each word had nothing to do with any other. Such children seem to believe—and may well have been taught—that meaning should be their last concern. (Smith, 1978, p. 154)

An alternative conceptualization would view the lack of contextual facilitation shown by such a reader as the result of extremely poor decoding skills. The research reviewed above strongly supports the view that the word recognition of poor readers *is* facilitated by contextual information *when they understand the context*. When poor readers are in difficult materials, their slow and inaccurate word-decoding processes may, in fact, degrade the contextual information that they receive, rendering it unusable (Kibby, 1979). The observation that, under such conditions, poor readers do not rely on context should not—according to this interpretation—be viewed as indicating that they *never* use context to facilitate word recognition.

Using a longitudinal research design, some colleagues and I (Stanovich, Cunningham, & Feeman, 1984b) tested these alternative explanations. In the fall and again in the spring, we assessed the speed and accuracy with which skilled and less-skilled first-grade children read coherent story paragraphs and random word lists. A recognition efficiency score was constructed that reflected the mean number of words read correctly per second. Of course, the skilled readers were better in both types of materials. In the fall, they also displayed more contextual facilitation, but again, they were decoding the passages much better. The question one needs to ask is whether the less-skilled readers displayed as much contextual facilitation as the skilled readers *when at a comparable level of context-free decoding ability*. The data from our study (Stanovich, Cunningham, & Feeman, 1984b) are relevant to this question because the decoding efficiency of the less-skilled readers on the random lists measured in the spring was similar to that displayed by the skilled readers measured in the fall. Thus, by comparing the analogous efficiency scores for the coherent paragraphs, it is possible to address the question of whether these two groups were getting a similar contextual "boost" when at comparable levels of context-free decoding ability. In the data we collected (Stanovich, Cunningham, & Feeman, 1984b; see also Kibby, 1979), the question was answered in the affirmative: The recognition efficiency scores of the less-skilled readers actually displayed somewhat more contextual facilitation than those of the skilled readers.

A final point that emerges from the research on contextual facilitation effects is the importance of differentiating the presence of a knowledge base from the use of that knowledge. For example, Perfetti, Goldman, and Hogaboam (1979) found that the same skilled readers who displayed smaller context effects than less-skilled readers on a word-recognition task were superior on a cloze-like prediction task. Of course, the finding that skilled readers possess superior prediction abilities is nothing new; it merely reconfirms older findings of a relationship between reading ability and cloze performance (Bickley, Ellington, & Bickley, 1970; Ruddell, 1965). What is new—and the important lesson in the Perfetti et al. (1979) results—is that the presence of prediction abilities does not necessarily imply that these abilities are *used* to facilitate ongoing word recognition. In fact, the Perfetti et al. (1979) results suggest just the opposite. Though the better readers possessed superior prediction abilities, they *also* were superior decoders, and the data appear to indicate that the latter is the critical causal mechanism sustaining fluent reading. The context-free decoding efficiency of the better readers is so high that they are less in need of contextual support. They have more knowledge of contextual dependencies but are simultaneously less reliant on this knowledge because they possess other processing advantages that are more important for word recognition—namely, context-free decoding skills.

The Phenomenon of "Word Calling"

This discussion of contextual facilitation effects on word recognition is obviously related to the phenomenon described as "word calling" in the reading literature. Despite the frequency with which this term occurs in reading publications, it is rare to find an author who spells out the clear, operational meaning of the term as it is being used. However, the implicit assumptions behind its use appear to be as follows: (1) Word calling occurs when the words in the text are efficiently decoded into their spoken forms without comprehension of the passage taking place. (2) This is a bad thing, because (3) it means that the child does not understand the true purpose of reading, which is extracting meaning from the text. (4) Children engaging in word calling do so because they have learned inappropriate reading strategies. (5) The strategic difficulty is one of overreliance on phonic strategies. These assumptions can be detected in the following representative quotations:

> Trying to sound out words without reference to meaning is a characteristic strategy of poor readers. (Smith, 1982, p. 145)

> Preoccupation with teaching children to recode may actually short circuit the reading process and divert children from comprehension. It is even possible that children will reach a high level of proficiency in recoding, actually taking graphic input and recasting it as very natural sounding speech, with little or no awareness of the need for decoding for meaning. (Goodman, 1968, p. 20)

> In fact, few children who become remedial readers lack the ability to attack words. (Smith, Goodman, & Meredith, 1976, p. 270)

> Remedial reading classes are filled with youngsters in late elementary and secondary schools who can sound out words but get little meaning from their reading. (Goodman, 1973, p. 491)

The idea of a "word-caller" phenomenon embodying the assumptions outlined above has gained popularity despite the lack of evidence that it applies to an appreciable number of poor readers. There is no research evidence indicating that decoding a word into a phonological form often takes place without meaning extraction, even in poor readers. To the contrary, a substantial body of evidence indicates that even for young children, word decoding automatically leads to semantic activation *when the meaning of the word is adequately established in memory* (Ehri, 1977; Goodman, Haith, Guttentag, & Rao, 1985; Guttentag, 1984; Guttentag & Haith, 1978, 1980; Kraut & Smothergill, 1989; Rosinski, 1977). Inadequate attention has been directed to the possibility that word calling may simply be a consequence of a low level of reading ability. This might occur in a number of different ways. First, reports of word calling rarely definitively establish whether the words that are "called" are even in the child's listening vocabulary. If the child would not understand the meaning of the word or passage when spoken, then overuse of decoding strategies can hardly be blamed if the child does not understand the written words. In short, a minimal requirement for establishing word calling as defined by the assumptions outlined above is the demonstration that the written material being "called" is within the listening comprehension abilities of the child (see Gough & Tunmer, 1986; Hood & Dubert, 1983).

Second, it is necessary to show that the word calling is not a simple consequence of poor decoding. Although reasonably efficient decoding would appear to be an integral part of any meaningful definition of *word calling*, decoding skills are rarely carefully assessed before a child is labeled a *word caller*. Instead, a rough index of decoding accuracy is usually employed, and any child near the normal range on this index is considered a candidate for the label. As other investigators have previously noted (e.g., LaBerge & Samuels, 1974; Perfetti, 1985, 1986), one does not obtain a clear picture of a child's decoding abilities unless speed and automaticity criteria are also employed. It is quite possible for accurate decoding to be so slow and capacity-demanding that it strains available cognitive resources and causes comprehension breakdowns. Such accurate but capacity-demanding decoding with little comprehension should not be considered word calling as defined above. To the contrary, it is a qualitatively different type of phenomenon. Comprehension fails not because of overreliance on decoding but because decoding skill is not developed *enough*.

Consequences of Reading History and Practice

The previous sections have outlined how individual differences in eye movements and context use for word recognition may be considered to be consequences of the reading level of the subject. Because these cognitive processes operate primarily during the act of reading itself, they are most accurately assessed by experimental methodologies that do not depart too far from the real-time processing requirements of reading. These types of processes may represent one class of the consequences of reading: processing differences that arise due to the differential efficiency of ongoing reading in individuals of varying skill.

However, individual differences in other types of cognitive processes may be linked to reading because the processes are affected by the differential behavioral histories of individuals who acquire reading at varying rates. For example, as discussed in the introduction, readers of differing skill soon diverge in the amount of practice they receive at reading and writing activities. They also have different histories of success, failure, and reward in the context of academic tasks. The long-term effects of such differing histories could act to create other cognitive and behavioral differences between readers of varying skill. Consider some possible examples. Many of the motivational differences between good and poor readers that are receiving increasing attention (see Johnston & Winograd, 1985; Oka & Paris, 1986) may well be consequences of the histories of success and failure associated with groups of differing skill. There is already some evidence suggesting that differences in self-esteem, rather than being the cause of achievement variability, are actually consequences of ability and achievement (Bachman & O'Malley, 1977; Maruyama, Rubin, & Kingsbury, 1981).

Ehri's (1984, 1985) work has elegantly demonstrated the effect that experience with print has on knowledge of sound structure and metalinguistic functioning. Others have speculated that the development of the ability to comprehend more complex syntactic structures is in part the result of reading experience (Donaldson & Reid, 1982; Mann, 1986; Perfetti, 1985). The status of the relationship between naming speed and reading ability is currently being debated by researchers, some of whom think that variation in this skill is a cause of reading ability differences, whereas others think it is a consequence of the differential reading histories of the subjects (M. Jackson, 1980; N.E. Jackson & Biemiller, 1985; Perfetti, 1985; Stanovich, 1986; Wolf, 1984).

Torgesen (1985) has raised the interesting possibility that some of the memory performance differences between readers of varying skill might be consequences of reading once-removed. He speculated that, because a good deal of knowledge acquisition takes place via reading, the knowledge base of less-skilled readers may be less developed because of their lack of reading practice. It has also been demonstrated that performance on many memory tasks is affected by the nature of the subject's knowledge base. The poorer reader might therefore display relative inferiority on such tasks due to a lack of reading experience (see Bjorklund & Bernholtz, 1986).

On a broader level, much of the literature on the consequences of literacy (Donaldson, 1978; Goody, 1977; D. Olson, 1977; D. Olson, Torrance, & Hildyard, 1985; Scribner & Cole, 1981) may be viewed as demonstrating the importance of some of the more global consequences of reading. This research also illustrates that it is a mistake to dismiss cognitive differences that are consequences of the reading histories of the individuals as unimportant. Such an unfortunate inference explains why many investigators resist the conclusion that individual differences in the process they are studying are actually caused by variation in reading skill. Surely the literature on the consequences of literacy— speculative and empirically sparse though it is—has at least suggested that the cognitive consequences of the acquisition of literacy may be profound. A few reading theorists have warned that we should be giving increasing attention to these types of effects. For example, Chall (1983) has stated,

> The influence of the development of reading and writing—"literate intelligence"— on general cognitive development has unfortunately been underestimated. Indeed, when reading development is delayed by personal or environmental factors or both, the effects on the person, unless given special help, are too often disastrous. (pp. 2–3)

The Reading-Level Match Design

Because of concern that some of the processing differences that have been attributed as causes of variation in reading ability are instead simple consequences of the overall level of reading or of the reading histories of the subjects, the reading-level match design has grown in popularity (Backman, Mamen, & Ferguson, 1984; Bryant & Goswami, 1986). In this research design, the performance of a group of older disabled readers is compared with that of a younger, nondisabled group reading at the same level. The reading-level match design is often employed in order to rule out differential practice explanations of correlations between cognitive skills and reading ability. When 10-year-old disabled readers are found to perform worse on a cognitive task than normally progressing 6-year-old children (as in Bradley & Bryant, 1978), it is difficult to invoke the differential practice explanation; or at least, the inferior performance of the 10-year-olds is much less likely to be due to relative lack of experience than a performance deficit displayed in comparison to a control group of equal chronological age.

The recent exciting research on individuals with acquired dyslexia and the resulting debate about what these cases tell us about the nature of developmental dyslexia (Coltheart, Masterson, Byng, Prior, & Riddich, 1983; Ellis, 1984; Snowling, 1983) also point to the need for a reading-level match design, which should help to alleviate some of the interpretive problems in this research area. For example, the claim that the acquired dyslexic cases reveal a qualitatively distinct syndrome reflecting the breakdown of a specific mechanism that is the cause of their reading problems will only be sustained when it is demonstrated that the performance patterns observed do not merely reflect a depressed overall level of reading skill—in short, that normal children reading at the same level do not show similar performance patterns (Bryant & Impey, 1986; Prior & McCorriston, 1985).

The results from reading-level match designs also have important implications for developmental lag theories of variation in reading achievement (Beech & Harding, 1984; Fletcher, 1981; Stanovich, Nathan, & Vala-Rossi, 1986; Treiman & Hirsh-Pasek, 1985). These theories posit that the less-skilled reader is traversing the same stages of cognitive development as the skilled reader but at a slower rate. Thus, reading will be commensurately delayed because the prerequisite cognitive subskills are inadequately developed. The strong form of the lag hypothesis posits that the performance profiles of less-skilled readers should be similar to those of younger readers at a similar level of achievement; that is, when older, less-skilled children and younger skilled children are matched on reading level, their performance should not differ on any other reading-related cognitive task (see Fletcher, 1981). However, Bryant and Goswami (1986) have pointed to the ambiguity inherent in null findings obtained with a reading-level match. That is, all processes—like eye movements—that are basically epiphenomena of the efficiency of reading will display precisely the pattern predicted by the developmental lag model. However, unlike the lag model, in which it is assumed that reading level is determined by the lagging cognitive processes, an alternative explanation in terms of the consequences of reading posits that the operation of the process is determined by the reading level.

Developmentally Limited Relationships: Phonological Awareness and Phonological Recoding Ability?

In the tentative causal model previously outlined, it was posited that phonological awareness is an enabling subskill in early reading and that individual differences in this subskill contribute to variance in reading ability. A growing body of evidence appears to indicate that some level of phonological awareness is necessary for the discovery and exploitation of the alphabetic principle (Perfetti, 1984, 1985). The major advantage conferred by the alphabetic principle is that it allows children to recognize words that are in their vocabulary but have not been taught or encountered before in print. It is necessary for the child to make this step toward independent reading, and recognizing unknown words via phonological recoding seems to be the key to it (Ehri & Wilce, 1985; Jorm & Share, 1983). The point of phonological mediation is to provide the child with what Jorm and Share (1983) have termed a *positive learning trial* for an unknown word. Phonological mediation enables the child to associate a visual/orthographic representation of the word with its sound and meaning (Barron, 1986; Ehri, 1984, 1985). Once this early hurdle is cleared, the child will begin to attain the amount of reading practice that leads to other positive cognitive consequences.

However, just because phonological awareness enables word recognition via phonological recoding in beginning reading, it does not follow that this mechanism determines reading ability at all developmental levels. To the contrary, there is mounting evidence indicating that there is a developmental trend away from phonologically mediated word recognition in early reading stages toward direct, nonmediated visual access at more advanced stages of reading (Backman, Bruck, Hebert, & Seidenberg, 1984; Ehri, 1985; Ehri & Wilce, 1985; Juel, 1983; Reitsma, 1984; Waters, Seidenberg, & Bruck, 1984). (The controversy concerning the existence of an initial paired-associate learning stage will not be entered into here; see Ehri & Wilce, 1985; Gough & Hillinger, 1980.) Early development of decoding skill leads to many positive learning trials that provide opportunities for visual/orthographic codes to become established in memory as future access mechanisms for the recognition of words (Barron, 1986; Ehri, 1984, 1985; Henderson, 1982; Jorm & Share, 1983). Of course, the efficiency with which visual/orthographic codes are established may depend upon *more* than just phonological recoding skill. That is, equally proficient phonological decoders may still differ in their ability to form visual/orthographic codes. But this caveat does not change the essential features of the present discussion.

It appears that for fluent adults the vast majority of words that are encountered in print are recognized by direct visual access (Ellis, 1984; Henderson, 1982; Mason, 1978; McCusker, Hillinger, & Bias, 1981; Seidenberg, Waters, Barnes, & Tanenhaus, 1984; Waters et al., 1984). Phonological information appears to be activated prior to lexical access only for low-frequency or very difficult words (McCusker et al., 1981; R. Olson, Kliegl, Davidson, & Foltz, 1985; Perfetti, 1985; Seidenberg, Waters, Barnes, & Tanenhaus, 1984; Waters & Seidenberg, 1985). Reader skill appears to mimic the frequency variable: The less skilled the reader, the more likely it is that phonological information is activated prior to word recognition (Waters et al., 1984). The existing evidence is consistent with a class of models in which phonological codes are automatically activated as a consequence of visual processing, are not under strategic control, and are determined solely by the time course of visual access (Perfetti, 1985; Seidenberg, 1985b; Seidenberg, Waters, Barnes, & Tanenhaus, 1984). Note that, according to these models, phonological information is less implicated in the *lexical access* processes of the fluent reader. They do not claim that phonological information is not implicated in reading at all. Instead, they posit that even in the fluent reader, such information is activated postlexically, where it serves to support comprehension processes operating on the contents of working memory.

The developmental trend toward word recognition via direct visual access suggests that individual differences in phonological awareness and phonological recoding skills observed at advanced stages of reading may be examples of *developmentally limited* relationships: those where individual differences in processes that cause variance in reading ability early in development at some point cease to be causal factors. The suggestion that phonological recoding skill may be involved in a developmentally limited relationship with reading has been advanced previously by Mason (1978). She speculated on the finding that, for adult college students as well as for young children, pseudoword naming (presumably an indicator of phonological decoding skill) is one of the best predictors of reading ability, even though other evidence indicates that adults recognize most words by direct visual access: "I suspect that the nonword decoding task differentiates skilled and less skilled readers because it provides a measure of linguistic awareness that, in turn, determines the ease with which reading *was* acquired in adult readers" (p. 579). Thus, just as when we gaze at the night sky we are actually observing the past history of stars, when we measure differences in phonological decoding skills in adults we may be tapping the mechanisms that earlier in their developmental histories led different individuals to diverge in the rates at which they acquired reading skill but are not currently causing further variation in reading fluency.

Of course, some indicators of phonological skill may be tapping the speed with which phonological information is accessed *postlexically*, and these—unlike the use of phonological information for decoding purposes—may still be a determinant of current reading ability. That is, the availability of the phonological information that follows lexical access in the more advanced reader may be a critical factor in determining reading ability. Because of the integrated nature of orthographic and phonological codes in the fluent reader (Ehri, 1984; Jakimik, Cole, & Rudnicky, 1985; Perin, 1983; Seidenberg & Tanenhaus, 1979), fast visual access rapidly and automatically activates the phonological codes that serve a reference-securing function in working memory which facilitates comprehension (Perfetti, 1985). This is why it is important to note that in this section we are concerned with the use of phonological information at a prelexical stage.

In their study of developmental changes in the use of spelling-sound correspondences, Backman, Bruck, Hebert, and Seidenberg (1984) emphasized the importance of a distinction already discussed: the distinction between the availability of knowledge and the actual use of that knowledge in the word-recognition process. They highlighted two important trends in their data. Older and more skilled readers displayed a greater tendency to recognize words without phonological mediation. They made fewer errors on words with homographic spelling patterns. At the same time, however, the more skilled readers were more rapidly expanding their knowledge of spelling–sound correspondences. This knowledge was indicated by a greater proportion of rule-governed errors and fewer errors on nonwords. These differences between readers of varying skill mirror an earlier developmental hypothesis of Venezky (1976):

> The reliance on letter-sound generalizations in word recognition slowly decreases as word identification ability increases, and the mature reader probably makes little use of them in normal reading. Nevertheless, the ability to apply letter-sound generalizations continues to develop at least through Grade 8. (p. 22)

The conclusion of Backman, Bruck, Hebert, and Seidenberg (1984) that "children's knowledge of spelling-sound correspondences is increasing at the very time they are learning to recognize many words without using it" (p. 131) parallels that of Perfetti et al. (1979) in the domain of context effects on word recognition. The latter investigators found that although good readers were better at contextual prediction, they were less dependent on such prediction for word recognition, demonstrating that the existence of a knowledge base does not necessarily mean that the information from it is used to facilitate word recognition. The studies by Perfetti et al. (1979) and by Backman, Bruck, Hebert, and Seidenberg (1984) both indicate that the operation of rapid visual-access processes short-circuits the use of other information.

Backman, Bruck, Hebert, and Seidenberg (1984) elaborated their conclusions by distinguishing between the pre- and postlexical activation of phonological information. They noted that the finding that less-skilled readers rely more on prelexical phonological information

> does not mean that less skilled readers rely more on phonological information than do good readers, only that they utilize this information more in the *initial decoding* of words.... The confusion in the literature as to whether it is good or poor readers who rely more heavily upon phonological information in reading may be due in part to failing to distinguish between its pre- and postlexical functions. Poor readers may rely more upon this information, derived from spelling-sound knowledge, in word decoding, to their detriment; good readers may be more facile in using phonological information that is accessed postlexically, facilitating text comprehension. (p. 131)

What the findings both of Backman, Bruck, Hebert, and Seidenberg (1984) and of Perfetti et al. (1979) emphasize is that in word recognition there is a developmental trend away from supplementing bottom-up processes of direct visual access with additional knowledge (spelling–sound correspondences and contextual expectancies). It appears that as reading skill develops, the word-recognition process during reading becomes increasingly modular (Fodor, 1983; Forster, 1979; Gough, 1983; Seidenberg, 1985a, 1985b; Seidenberg, Waters, Sanders, & Langer, 1984; Stanovich, Nathan, West, & Vala-Rossi, 1985;

Stanovich & West, 1983). That is, word recognition via direct visual access occurs more autonomously, and other knowledge sources tend to interact only with the *outputs* of completed word recognition, not with the word-recognition process itself. When the task demands it, adults can utilize phonological mediation to name a stimulus (as in pseudoword naming), but ordinarily this mechanism is not used to support their ongoing processes of word recognition.

The hypothesis that adult differences in phonological coding are remnants of an earlier causal relationship suggests many questions that will require investigation. Even if the hypothesis is correct, the developmental change in the linkage between reading ability and individual differences in phonological coding skill will have to be fully traced. An intriguing possibility—already suggested by some research (Barron & Baron, 1977; Kimura & Bryant, 1983; Reitsma, 1983)—is that visual access for most words begins to develop very rapidly (e.g., after only a few exposures), rendering phonological coding differences noncausal relatively early in development. Finally, note that in the case of phonological recoding the term *developmentally limited* may be a slight misnomer. Individual differences in this process may be less implicated in determining reading ability among older readers simply because fewer unknown words are encountered, but it may, in fact, be fully operative on those few occasions when such words occur.

Of course, phonological coding may be only one example of what might turn out to be a host of developmentally limited relationships. One intriguing candidate is individual differences in word-recognition efficiency itself. Although there is some evidence indicating that word-recognition efficiency is a causal determinant of reading skill (e.g., Biemiller, 1970; Blanchard, 1980; Herman, 1985; Lesgold, Resnick, & Hammond, 1985; Lomax, 1983), it has sometimes been difficult to demonstrate a causal connection, particularly in research employing adults and older children as subjects. For example, it has been surprisingly difficult to show that disrupting word-recognition processes diminishes comprehension (Levy, 1981; Masson & Sala, 1978; Wilkinson, Guminski, Stanovich, & West, 1981; but see Bowey, 1982) or that making word recognition more efficient results in better comprehension (Fleisher, Jenkins, & Pany, 1979; but see Blanchard, 1980; Blanchard & McNinch, 1980; Herman, 1985). Thus, the possibility that the causal link between individual differences in word-recognition efficiency and comprehension is developmentally limited deserves further investigation.

Some Variables Display Reciprocal Causation: Vocabulary

As mentioned in the introduction, one of the problems in conceptualizing the literature is that there are too many differences between good and poor readers. These differences lead to a plethora of explanations for reading failure, and in many cases the explanations are incompatible. Each investigator—emotionally wedded to his or her particular task(s)—likes to believe that his or her variable (and associated theory) is the key to understanding reading disability. The possibility that the difference observed is a consequence of the reading level or reading history is often not considered or, at most, is given a footnote or parenthetical comment. Of course, no one would wish to deny that individual differences in reading ability may be a function of the differential efficiency of many cognitive processes. However, the previous discussion was intended to suggest the possibility that the situation may have become overly confused through the indiscriminate application of the stricture "Reading ability is determined by variability in many different processes." In this review, I have suggested that the literature on individual differences in reading could be considerably clarified if the number of potential causal relationships could be pared down by classifying some as consequences and some as having developmental limits.

Classifying relationships as either causes or consequences of reading ability of course does not exhaust the possibilities. Reading ability may be correlated with the efficiency of a certain cognitive process because both are linked to some third variable. For example, it is possible that a maturational lag in the general development of language abilities is what leads to the linkage between reading and phonological skills (Mann, 1984, 1986). Tallal (1980) has speculated on how a basic problem in processing rapidly presented information might serve to link low reading ability, speech disorders, and lack of phonological awareness.

Researchers investigating individual differences in reading have also become increasingly sensitized to the possibility that processes may be interlocked with reading in relationships of *reciprocal causation*: that individual differences in a particular process may cause differential reading efficiency, but that reading itself may in turn cause further individual differences in the process in question. There is mounting evidence that in the early acquisition stages this is precisely the status of phonological awareness and reading (Ehri, 1979, 1984, 1985; Perfetti, 1985; Perfetti, Beck, & Hughes, 1981). Individual differences in certain aspects of phonological awareness appear to be causally linked to variation in the ease of early reading acquisition; but initial success at cracking the spelling-to-sound code further develops phonological awareness and provides the experiences necessary for the acquisition of increasingly differentiated phonological knowledge and the ability to access it consciously. Ehri (1979, 1984, 1985) has provided the most convincing evidence for the effects of orthographic representations on phonological awareness.

However, as hypothesized in the previous section, in the case of phonological awareness there is probably a developmental limit on the time course of the reciprocal relationship. If reading is progressing normally, children may move quickly into stages where direct visual access predominates (Barron & Baron, 1977; Kimura & Bryant, 1983; Reitsma, 1983) and variation in phonological awareness is no longer the primary causal determinant of differences in reading ability. This example illustrates that hypotheses involving the concept of reciprocal causation must be framed developmentally. For example, assume that individual differences in a certain process (call it A) both cause differences in reading acquisition and in turn are also affected by reading. However, suppose that at some point, variation in A no longer causes variation in reading ability. Then, it is important to investigate whether the "kickback" from reading to A occurs early enough for the newly facilitated A to affect subsequent reading acquisition. The research question concerns whether the "bootstrapping" occurs early enough for a true reciprocal relationship to develop, or whether the facilitation of A occurs too late for its extra efficiency to cause further achievement differences in reading. In the case of phonological awareness, evidence from a longitudinal study by Perfetti et al. (1981) suggests that a true reciprocal relationship may be occurring.

Nevertheless, if the conclusion of the previous section is correct, then this bootstrapping involving phonological awareness has some inherent limits. There will be a point when the facilitation of phonological awareness by reading becomes much less important because the level of phonological awareness is no longer determining reading ability. A more powerful reciprocal relationship would be one that was operative throughout reading development. The motivational differences that are associated with variability in reading ability (e.g., Butkowsky & Willows, 1980; Oka & Paris, 1986) may be involved in relationships of this type. In this section we will explore what may be another example of such a potent reciprocal relationship: the association between vocabulary development and individual differences in reading ability.

The correlation between reading ability and vocabulary knowledge is sizeable throughout development (Anderson & Freebody, 1979; Mezynski, 1983; Stanovich, Cunningham, & Feeman, 1984a). Although, as in most areas of reading research, correlational evidence is much more plentiful than experimental evidence (Anderson & Freebody, 1979; Mezynski, 1983), there is a growing body of data indicating that variation in vocabulary knowledge is a causal determinant of differences in reading comprehension ability (Beck, Perfetti, & McKeown, 1982; McKeown, Beck, Omanson, & Perfetti, 1983; Stahl, 1983). It seems probable that like phonological awareness, vocabulary knowledge is involved in a reciprocal relationship with reading ability, but that—unlike the case of phonological awareness—the relationship is one that continues throughout reading development and remains in force for even the most fluent adult readers.

There is considerable agreement that much—probably most—vocabulary growth takes place through the inductive learning of the meanings of unknown words encountered in oral and written language. It appears that the bulk of vocabulary growth does not occur via direct instruction (Nagy & Anderson, 1984; Nagy, Herman, & Anderson, 1985; Jenkins & Dixon, 1983; Jenkins, Stein, & Wysocki, 1984; Sternberg, 1985; Sternberg, Powell, & Kaye, 1982). Also, there is substantial agreement among researchers that reading is a significant contributor to the growth of vocabulary. However, positions on this issue run from the conservative conclusion of Jenkins et al. (1984)—"Because we do not know how many words individuals know, we are seriously limited in accounting for changes in these totals. Whatever the totals, incidental learning from reading could account for some portion of the growth in vocabulary knowledge" (p. 785)—to the stronger position of Nagy and Anderson (1984)—"We judge that beginning in about the third grade, the major determinant of vocabulary growth is amount of free reading" (p. 327).

The role hypothesized for vocabulary in this review will reveal a bias toward the stronger position of Nagy and Anderson (1984). The association between variation in vocabulary knowledge and reading achievement seems a good candidate for a strong reciprocal relationship. Much more evidence on the nature of both causal connections clearly is needed, but recent studies that are methodologically superior to earlier work have provided support for causal mechanisms operating in both directions. Also, some recent theoretical extrapolations support the plausibility of a reciprocal bootstrapping interaction between vocabulary and reading.

Although some earlier studies had failed to verify the relation, recent research has demonstrated a causal connection between vocabulary knowledge and reading comprehension (Beck et al., 1982; McKeown et al., 1983; Stahl, 1983). Regarding the reverse connection, there has also been some research progress. The most recent estimates of children's vocabulary sizes serve to emphasize the futility of expecting major proportions of vocabulary growth to occur via direct instruction; they also serve to reinforce the importance of learning word meanings from encountering words in different contexts during free reading (Nagy & Anderson, 1984). However, until quite recently the evidence for the assumption that much vocabulary growth occurs through inducing the meanings of unknown words from context during reading was virtually nonexistent. This is because, as many investigators have pointed out (e.g., Jenkins et al., 1984; Nagy et al., 1985), most previous studies have focused on the ability to *derive* meanings from context when that was the explicit task set, rather than on the extent to which meanings are naturally learned during reading. However, recent studies by Jenkins et al. (1984) and Nagy et al. (1985) have indicated that learning from context during reading does occur (but see Schatz & Baldwin, 1986). Furthermore, an analysis of the extent of the vocabulary learning in both studies, taken in conjunction with some reasonable estimates of children's reading volume and vocabulary growth, led Nagy et al. (1985) to conclude, "Despite the uncertainties, our analysis suggests that words learned incidentally from context are likely to constitute a substantial portion of children's vocabulary growth" (p. 250).

Matthew Effects in Reading: The Rich Get Richer

If the development of vocabulary knowledge substantially facilitates reading comprehension, and if reading itself is a major mechanism leading to vocabulary growth—which in turn will enable more efficient reading—then we truly have a reciprocal relationship that should continue to drive further growth in reading throughout a person's development. The critical mediating variable that turns this relationship into a strong bootstrapping mechanism that causes major individual differences in the development of reading skill is the volume of reading experience (Fielding, Wilson, & Anderson, 1986; Nagy et al., 1985).

As previously discussed, Biemiller (1977/1978) found large ability differences in exposure to print within the classroom as early as midway through the first-grade year. Convergent results were obtained by Allington (1984). In his first-grade sample, the total number of words read during a week of school reading group sessions ranged from a low of 16 for one of the children in the less-skilled group to a high of 1,933 for one of the children in the skilled reading group. The average skilled reader read approximately three times as many words in the group reading sessions as the average less-skilled reader. Nagy and Anderson (1984) estimated that, as regards in-school reading,

> the least motivated children in the middle grades might read 100,000 words a year while the average children at this level might read 1,000,000. The figure for the voracious middle grade reader might be 10,000,000 or even as high as 50,000,000. If these guesses are anywhere near the mark, there are staggering individual differences in the volume of language experience, and therefore, opportunity to learn new words. (p. 328)

There are also differences in the volume of reading outside the classroom that are linked to reading ability (Fielding et al., 1986), and these probably become increasingly large as schooling progresses.

The effect of reading volume on vocabulary growth, combined with the large skill differences in reading volume, could mean that a "rich-get-richer" or cumulative advantage phenomenon is almost inextricably embedded within the developmental course of reading progress. The very children who are reading well and who have good vocabularies will read more, learn more word meanings, and hence read even better. Children with inadequate vocabularies—who read slowly and without enjoyment—read less and, as a result, have slower development of vocabulary knowledge, which inhibits further growth in reading ability. Walberg (Walberg et al., 1984; Walberg & Tsai, 1983), following Merton (1968), has dubbed those educational sequences where early achievement spawns faster rates of subsequent achievement "Matthew effects," after the Gospel according to Matthew: "For unto every one that hath shall be given, and he shall have abundance: but from him that hath not shall be taken away even that which he hath" (XXV:29).

The concept of Matthew effects springs from findings that individuals who have advantageous early educational experiences are able to utilize new educational experiences more efficiently (Walberg & Tsai, 1983). Walberg et al. (1984) speculated that

> those who did well at the start may have been more often, or more intensively, re-
> warded for their early accomplishments; early intellectual and motivational cap-
> ital may grow for longer periods and at greater rates; and large funds and
> continuing high growth rates of information and motivation may be more in-
> tensely rewarded Thus, rather than the one-way causal directionality usually as-
> sumed in educational research, reverberating or reciprocal states may cause
> self-fulfilling or self-reinforcing causal processes that are highly influential in de-
> termining educational and personal productivity. (p. 92)

In short, Walberg et al. (1984) emphasized that reciprocally facilitating relationships, like the one between vocabulary and reading, can be major causes of large
individual differences in educational achievement.

The facilitation of reading comprehension by vocabulary knowledge illustrates a principle that has been strongly emphasized in much recent research
on cognitive development: the importance of the current knowledge base in acquiring new information (Bjorklund & Weiss, 1985; Chi, Glaser, & Rees, 1982;
Keil, 1984; Larkin, McDermott, Simon, & Simon, 1980). Sternberg (1985) has
articulated the point in the context of vocabulary:

> Thus, vocabulary is not only affected by operations of components, [but] it af-
> fects their operations as well. If one grows up in a household that encourages
> exposure to words, then one's vocabulary may well be greater, which in turn may
> lead to a superior learning and performance on other kinds of tasks that require
> vocabulary. (p. 123)

Thus, one mechanism leading to Matthew effects in education is the facilitation
of further learning by a previously existing knowledge base that is rich and elaborated. A person with more expertise has a larger knowledge base, and the large
knowledge base allows that person to acquire even greater expertise at a faster
rate. An analogous Matthew effect in reading arises from the fact that it is the better readers who have the more developed vocabularies.

There are several factors contributing to Matthew effects in reading development. For example, the research cited above has pointed to reading exposure differences between individuals of different skill levels. This is an example
of the important principal of *organism–environment correlation*: Different types
of organisms are selectively exposed to different types of environments.
Recently, theorists have emphasized the importance of understanding that there
are important organism–environment correlations that result from the child's own
behavior (Lerner & Busch-Rossnagel, 1981; Plomin, DeFries, & Loehlin, 1977;
Scarr & McCartney, 1983; Sternberg, 1985; Wachs & Mariotto, 1978).
Organisms not only are acted on by their environments, but they also select,
shape, and evoke their own environments. Particularly later in development (see
Scarr & McCartney, 1983), a person has partly selected and shaped his or her
own environment (sometimes termed *active organism–environment correla-*

tion) and has been affected by the environment's response to the particular type of organism (sometimes termed *evocative organism–environment correlation*).

The differences in volume of reading between readers of differing skill are partly due to these active and evocative organism–environment correlations. Children who become better readers have selected (e.g., by choosing friends who read or choosing reading as a leisure activity rather than sports or video games), shaped (e.g., by asking for books as presents when young), and evoked (e.g., the child's parents noticed that looking at books was enjoyed or perhaps just that it kept the child quiet) an environment that will be conducive to further growth in reading. Children who lag in reading achievement do not construct such an environment. Anbar (1986) noted the importance of these active and evocative organism–environment correlations in her studies of children who acquired reading before school:

> Once the parents began to interact with their children around the reading activities, the children reciprocated with eagerness. The parents then intuitively seemed to follow the child's learning interests and curiosity, sensitively responding to requests for aid. One could say, therefore that the parents facilitated the child's natural course of development. (p. 77)

However, the vocabulary superiority of the better reader is due to more than just the differential exposure to written language that is the result of active and evocative organism–environment correlations. As Sternberg (1985, pp. 306–308) has emphasized, although the amount of practice and extent of the knowledge base are important factors in acquiring expertise, the sheer amount of experience is less than perfectly correlated with the level of skill attained in a particular domain. This point applies to reading and vocabulary. Although better readers are indeed exposed to more written language, they are also superior at deriving the meanings of unknown words from a passage when differences in the knowledge base are controlled. Sternberg (1985; Sternberg & Powell, 1983; Sternberg, Powell, & Kaye, 1982) found that the ability to derive the meanings of unknown words from unfamiliar passages displayed a correlation of .65 with reading comprehension ability. Interestingly, in the two best controlled studies of learning word meanings from natural reading (Nagy et al., 1985; Jenkins et al., 1984), there was also a tendency for the better readers to learn more word meanings. Thus, there appears to be evidence for several different mechanisms involving vocabulary and reading that operate to create rich-get-richer effects. Better readers are exposed to more written language than poorer readers; the expanded knowledge base that they thus acquire probably facilitates the induction of new word meanings; and finally, better readers appear to learn new words from context with a greater efficiency than do less-able readers, even when differences in the knowledge base are controlled.

Matthew Effects and the Less-Skilled Reader

Because Matthew, or rich-get-richer, effects have been shown to be an important source of achievement variance in many areas of schooling, researchers need to explore more fully the operation of such effects in the domain of reading, Also, of course, the other side of the coin—poor-get-poorer effects—may help to explain certain aspects of reading failure. For example, Matthew effects may arise from conditions other than those described above. In addition to the achievement differences that will occur as a result of the information-processing efficiency of the better reader (e.g., Sternberg, 1985) and the exposure differences resulting from active and evocative organism–environment correlations (e.g., Nagy & Anderson, 1984), there are also *passive organism–environment correlations* that contribute to rich-get-richer and poor-get-poorer effects. A passive organism–environment correlation is a relationship between the type of organism and environmental quality that is not due to the organism's active selection and shaping of the environment. Some of these passive organism–environment effects are unavoidable, such as the passive genotype/environment effects discussed by Scarr and McCartney (1983): The genotypes of a child's parents partially determine both the home environment of the child and the child's genotype. Other passive organism–environment correlations are a function of social structures: Less healthy organisms grow up in impoverished environments. Biologically unlucky individuals are provided with inferior social and educational environments, and the winners of the biological lottery are provided better environments (Rutter & Madge, 1976).

An example of a passive organism–environment correlation that contributes to Matthew effects is provided by the literature on the influence of a school's ability composition on academic achievement. The evidence, as summarized by Rutter (1983), indicates that "quite apart from the individual benefits of above-average intellectual ability, a child of any level of ability is likely to make better progress if taught in a school with a relatively high concentration of pupils with good cognitive performance" (p. 19). But, of course, a child of above-average ability is much more likely to reside in a school with a "concentration of pupils with good cognitive performance" (Jencks, 1972). Such a child is an advantaged organism because of the superior environment and genotype provided by the child's parents. The parents, similarly environmentally and genetically advantaged, are more likely to reside in a community which provides the "concentration of pupils" that, via the independent effects of school composition, will bootstrap the child to further educational advantages. Conversely, disadvantaged children are most often exposed to inferior ability composition in the schools that they attend. Thus, these children are the victims of a particularly perverse "double whammy."

Recently, Share et al. (1984) uncovered some fascinating ability-composition effects that illustrate how passive organism–environment correlations contribute to Matthew effects in the area of reading achievement. They investigated the relationship of 39 cognitive and home environment variables measured at kindergarten entry to reading achievement at the end of kindergarten and of grade 1. (In Australia, the country of these subjects, formal reading instruction begins in kindergarten.) Share et al. (1984) tested over 500 subjects in many different classrooms located in several different schools. Their ability-composition analysis focused on phoneme segmentation ability because it was the single best predictor of reading achievement. Each child was assigned three phoneme segmentation scores. One was the child's own score on the phoneme segmentation test. Next, the mean score of each classroom was calculated and assigned to each child in that room. Finally, the mean score for each school was calculated and assigned to each child in that school. The zero-order correlations confirmed for phonological awareness—a critical determinant of the ease of initial reading acquisition—what is observed for ability in general: Higher-ability students are surrounded by higher ability peers. The correlation between individual and classroom phoneme segmentation ability was .59, and the correlation between individual and school phoneme segmentation ability was .45.

But does being surrounded by better phoneme segmenters make a difference in early reading? Apparently it does. The child's own phoneme segmentation ability at kindergarten entry correlated .65 with that year's reading achievement (correlations were similar for grade 1 reading achievement); the correlations involving the classroom and school means were .64 and .68. After *all* 39 cognitive and home background variables had been entered into a regression equation predicting end-of-kindergarten reading ability (the results were similar when grade 1 ability was the criterion variable), the school ability mean accounted for a statistically significant additional 9% of the variance. After the individual variables were entered, classroom mean accounted for an additional 5% of the variance in individual kindergarten achievement (again, statistically significant). Note that the 39 variables entered first include the child's *own* phoneme segmentation ability.

Although Share et al. (1984) have speculated on the reasons for these ability-composition effects (teacher responsiveness to ability differences, language interactions among the children, etc.), the issue of the precise mechanism involved is beyond the scope of this review. For the present purpose, the importance of the Share et al. findings is in the demonstration of an ability-composition effect—a passive organism—environment correlation that contributes to poor-get-poorer effects in achievement—in the domain of phonological awareness and reading. Unlike some of the unavoidable organism–environment correlations discussed by Scarr and McCartney (1983), this one is partially a function of social policy. It is controllable, perhaps unlike many such correlations that contribute to Matthew effects in education. Rutter (1983) emphasized this point in his conclusion:

Nevertheless, the implication is that there are considerable disadvantages in an educational system that allows such an uneven distribution of children that some schools have intakes with a heavy preponderance of the intellectually less able. There can be no dodging the need to ensure a reasonable balance of intakes among schools, but the best way to do this is not obvious. (p. 20)

This example illustrates the importance of research aimed at uncovering the existence and causes of Matthew effects in reading because a thorough understanding of the causes is a necessary prerequisite to sound social policy in education.

Reconceptualizing the Reading Disability Literature in Terms of Reciprocal Causation and Matthew Effects

A thorough exploration of the possible influence of reciprocal relationships and Matthew effects on observed performance profiles might help to clarify some problematic issues in the area of individual differences in reading ability. For example, reading disabilities would be better understood if some of the observed individual differences could be differentiated as cases of consequences of reading level or history, or as cases of reciprocal causation. Indeed, I will argue in this section that a consideration of the relationships between reading and other cognitive skills in terms of the concepts outlined above can help to resolve some recurrent problems in the area of reading disabilities (or dyslexia; these terms are used interchangeably in the following discussion). Some of these conceptual problems are so serious that they threaten to undermine the entire field if they are not soon resolved. For example, one assumption that is essential to all definitions of reading disability is the "assumption of specificity" (Hall & Humphreys, 1982; Stanovich, 1986). This assumption underlies all discussions of the concept, even if it is not stated explicitly. Simply put, it is the idea that a child with this type of learning disability has a brain/cognitive deficit that is reasonably specific to the reading task. That is, the concept of a specific reading disability requires that the deficits displayed by such children not extend too far into other domains of cognitive functioning. If they did, there would already exist research and educational designations for such children (low intelligence, "slow learner," etc.), and the concept of reading disability would be superfluous.

The assumption of specificity is contained within virtually all psychometric and legal definitions of reading disability, and it is also quite salient in media portrayals of dyslexia. The typical "media dyslexic" is a bright, capable individual with a specific problem in the area of reading (the quintessential example of the white-collar worker who through dictation, secretaries, and various office maneuvers, covers up the fact that he cannot read). In terms of the concepts I have developed in this review, such individuals have remained immune to the negative cascade of interacting skill deficits and Matthew effects surrounding reading. For example, their vocabularies and other language abilities have continued to develop without the benefit of reading, and they have (to some degree) avoided the negative motivational consequences of reading failure. It will be argued here that the number of such individuals—those who truly escape the snowballing consequences of reading failure—is much smaller than is commonly presumed.

A major problem in the area of reading disabilities research is that the literature on individual differences in the cognitive processes related to reading has undermined the assumption of specificity. When researchers went looking for cognitive differences between reading-disabled and nondisabled children, they found them virtually everywhere. The plethora of cognitive differences that has been uncovered threatens to undermine the concept of a reading disability because the existence of such differences calls into question the assumption of specificity and instead suggests that dyslexic children exhibit rather generalized cognitive deficits.

Consider the concatenation of processes that have been found to differentiate disabled from nondisabled readers. Not surprisingly, phonemic awareness and associated spelling-to-sound decoding skills are markedly deficient in disabled readers (Bradley & Bryant, 1978; Gough & Tunmer, 1986; Snowling, 1980, 1981). However, more general aspects of speech perception have been implicated by the findings of Brady, Shankweiler, and Mann (1983) that poor readers make more perceptual errors when listening to speech in noise and the findings of Godfrey, Syrdal-Lasky, Millay, and Knox (1981) that disabled and nondisabled readers differ in the categorical perception of certain speech contrasts. Briggs and Underwood (1982) have presented evidence of a deficit in the speech code that is closer to articulatory in level, and Tallal (1980) has even uncovered processing deficits with nonspeech auditory stimuli. Of course, naming deficits have also long been associated with reading failure (Denckla & Rudel, 1976; Spring & Capps, 1974; Wolf, 1984). Thus, indications are that the speech and auditory processing problems of the disabled reader are multiple and pervasive.

Moreover, language-processing differences have turned up at other levels. Syntactic knowledge and awareness seem to be deficient in disabled readers (Bowey, 1986; Byrne, 1981; Hallahan & Bryan, 1981; McClure, Kalk, & Keenan, 1980; Menyuk & Flood, 1981; Newcomer & Magee, 1977; Semel & Wiig, 1975; Siegel & Ryan, 1984; Stein, Cairns, & Zurif, 1984; Vellutino, 1979; Vogel, 1974). Their performance is relatively low on tests of general listening comprehension and general linguistic awareness (Berger, 1978; Downing, 1980; Kotsonis & Patterson, 1980; Menyuk & Flood, 1981; Newcomer & Magee, 1977; Siegel & Ryan, 1984; Smiley, Oakley, Worthen, Campione, & Brown, 1977). Comprehension strategies that are very general seem to be deficient. Concatenating these findings with those on phonological awareness and speech cited previously, we seem to be uncovering a deficiency in a "specific" area that can only be labeled "language—in all its conceivable aspects." This is not the type of "specific" psychological disability that the originators of the idea of dyslexia had in mind.

Work on short-term memory as a psychological locus of the processing difficulties of disabled readers was originally motivated by the desire to uncover a specific "site" that was the source of reading problems. Although some proportion of the performance difference between normal and disabled readers on short-term memory tasks is almost certainly due to the specific phonological coding problems experienced by the latter (R.L. Cohen, 1982; Jorm, 1983; Torgesen & Houck, 1980), research on individual differences in memory performance soon pushed the mediating cognitive mechanisms far beyond an explanation purely in terms of phonological coding. Cognitive and developmental psychologists have linked many processing strategies to memory performance, and research has shown reading-disabled children to be deficient in their ability and/or willingness to employ virtually every one of these strategies (Bauer, 1977, 1979, 1982; Foster & Gavelek, 1983; Newman & Hagen, 1981; Tarver, Hallahan, Kauffman, & Ball, 1976; Torgesen, 1977a, 1977b, 1978/1979; Torgesen & Goldman, 1977; Wong, Wong, & Foth, 1977). These findings have led to characterizations of the underlying cognitive deficit of learning-disabled children that are strikingly general. For example, Torgesen's (1977a, 1977b) early work on memory functioning led him to characterize the learning-disabled child as an inactive learner, one who fails to apply even cognitive strategies that are within his or her capabilities.

Torgesen's notion is, of course, similar to currently popular ideas regarding the importance of metacognitive or executive functioning. Indeed, recent work on the performance of reading-disabled children has reinforced Torgesen's earlier position and explicitly tied his ideas in with recent views on metacognitive functioning (Baker, 1982; Bos & Filip, 1982; Foster & Gavelek, 1983; Hagen, Barclay, & Newman, 1982; Hallahan & Bryan, 1981; Wong, 1984). However, the tendency to link deficiencies in metacognitive functioning with reading disability will undermine the assumption of specificity. Recent conceptualizations (e.g., Baron, 1978; Campione & Brown, 1978; Sternberg, 1980, 1982, 1985) have stressed that metacognitive awareness of available strategies is a critical aspect of *intelligence*. Thus, further developments along these lines will surely evolve a paradoxical conclusion: that reading-disabled children are deficient in a generalized ability to deal with cognitive tasks of all types (i.e., that they lack metacognitive awareness: a critical aspect of intelligence). This, of course, would be the death knell for the assumption of specificity, and hence the entire rationale for the concept of dyslexia would be undermined.

Escaping the Paradox: Subject Selection

There are at least three ways to escape the dilemma posed by the fact that the literature on individual differences in the cognitive processes of reading threatens to erode the fundamental assumption upon which the concept of dyslexia rests. One is to question the nature of the subject samples employed in the research. It may be that the less-skilled children were not sufficiently disabled: that many studies contained substantial numbers of children who were experiencing only a moderate degree of reading difficulty and whose cognitive performance profiles—unlike those of the truly disabled reader—were characterized by mild but pervasive deficits. To the extent that some investigators have employed primarily school labeling as the criterion for forming subject groups—rather than scores on their own self-administered tests and strictly applied psychometric criteria—this criticism is appropriate.

Since the advent of the concept of a reading disability, it has repeatedly been pointed out that schools do not identify reading-disabled children in accord with the actual definitions of *dyslexia* prevailing in the professional literature (Ames, 1968; Bryan, 1974; Kirk & Elkins, 1975; Miller & Davis, 1982; Norman & Zigmond, 1980). We have come to think of a reading-disabled child—in the view that is certainly the one promoted by parent groups and the media—as a child with normal intelligence. But surveys of school-labeled reading-disabled children have consistently shown that even on nonverbal and performance intelligence tests, the mean score of the children does not approximate 100 but is usually closer to 90 (Anderson, Kaufman, & Kaufman, 1976; Gajar, 1979; Hallahan & Kauffman, 1977; Kirk & Elkins, 1975; Klinge, Rennick, Lennox, & Hart, 1977; Leinhardt, Seewald, & Zigmond, 1982; McLeskey & Rieth, 1982; Norman & Zigmond, 1980; Satz & Friel, 1974; Shepard, Smith, & Vojir, 1983; Smith, Coleman, Dokecki, & Davis, 1977; Tarver, 1982; Valtin, 1978/1979).

Thus, to the extent that school-labeled samples have been used, researchers have been comparing less-skilled readers with mild IQ deficits to the normal control groups, and it is perhaps not surprising that a large number of performance differences have appeared. This problem extends even to research where an attempt has been made to match (or restrict the range of) the reading-disabled and control groups on other environmental variables (Fletcher, Satz, & Scholes, 1981; Hallahan & Kauffman, 1977; Klinge et al., 1977). For example, from a group of 108 learning-disabled children, Klinge et al. (1977) selected 30 children to match 30 controls on sex, race, age, socioeconomic status, and geographic community. Despite the matching, the mean performance intelligence test score of the learning-disabled group (94) was 9 points lower than that of the control group (103).

The problem is pervasive even in research studies that have attempted to match subjects on intelligence test scores. Although these procedures often ensure that the intelligence test scores of the reading-disabled sample approximate 100 and are not significantly different from those of the control group, it is almost invariably the case that the IQs of the disabled group turn out to be lower (Hall & Humphreys, 1982; Stanovich, 1986; Torgesen, 1985). In a formal survey of the research literature, Torgesen and Dice (1980) found that the mean intelligence test scores of the learning-disabled groups averaged 6 points lower than those of the control groups. Wolford and Fowler (1984), in their survey, came to similar conclusions.

A discussion of the IQ matching problem leads naturally to a consideration of some of the statistical problems surrounding the concept of reading disability— statistical complications often unknown to the teachers and practitioners who are using the concept. For example, it is well known that performance on intelligence tests correlates with reading achievement. This correlation is usually in the range of .3 to .5 in the early elementary grades but rises to the range of .6 to .75 in adult samples (see Stanovich, Cunningham, & Feeman, 1984a). An individual with a reading disability is by definition a person for whom this performance linkage does not hold, or at least for whom it is severely attenuated. Such a person has severely depressed performance on one variable (reading) but virtually normal performance on the other (intelligence test score). These individuals are statistical outliers, defined by their deviation from the regression line in a scatterplot of reading achievement scores against intelligence test scores. It is important to realize that because part of the outlier status of this group *must* be the result of measurement error, on a retesting (due to statistical regression) they will score lower on the IQ test (or highly related cognitive measure) and somewhat higher on the reading test (Crowder, 1984; Hall & Humphreys, 1982). Defining reading-disabled children on the basis of a single testing will conceal this fact and thus artificially magnify their outlier status (Shepard, 1980). A reading-disabled classification that partially reflects measurement error will contribute to the plethora of deficits obtained because whatever cognitive tasks are administered become the "second testing" on which these subjects will regress to performance levels below those of their IQ-matched, nondisabled controls.

When we combine the purely statistical artifact of regression with the empirical fact, reviewed above, that the reading-disabled children in the schools and in research reports have mild IQ deficits, we may have a large part of the explanation for the tendency of the research literature to undermine the assumption of specificity. To some extent, the children in these samples *should* have small but pervasive cognitive deficits because on one omnibus index of cognitive functioning (an intelligence test) they show a small deficit. They are not the extreme statistical outliers that the definitions of reading disability imply. Second, the moderate outlier pattern that they do display is, in part, measurement artifact.

The solutions to these statistical problems have clear implications for research and practice. Both practitioners and researchers should adopt a much stricter psychometric criterion for defining a child as reading disabled. A second testing to ensure that the bulk of the performance discrepancy is not measurement artifact is essential for accurate classification (see Shepard, 1980). It is only by isolating the true outliers that researchers can hope to obtain the evidence for specificity that the dyslexia concept requires if it is to be of scientific and practical utility.

The parent groups who have pushed for ever-more-inclusive definitions of dyslexia (estimates from such groups often claim that anywhere from 10% to 30% of the school population should be so labeled) are indirectly undermining the concept. The wider the net that is cast, the greater will be the difficulties in distinguishing dyslexia from other educational designations (e.g., borderline retardation, educable mentally retarded). Lack of restraint in applying the label is in part responsible for the failure of researchers to demonstrate consistently that the performance profiles of disabled subjects differ reliably from those of other poor readers (Algozzine & Ysseldyke, 1983; Bloom, Wagner, Reskin, & Bergman, 1980; Coles, 1978; Gottesman, Croen, & Rotkin, 1982; Taylor, Satz, & Friel, 1979), and it is one of the main reasons why the diagnostic utility of the concept of dyslexia continues to be questioned (Arter & Jenkins, 1979; S. Cohen, 1976; Coles, 1978; Gross & Gottlieb, 1982; Miller & Davis, 1982; Ysseldyke & Algozzine, 1979).

The best existing evidence in favor of demarcating reading disability as a qualitatively distinguishable behavioral concept comes from the epidemiological Isle of Wight study reported by Rutter and Yule (1975; Rutter, 1978; Yule, 1973). Their study contrasts with many others that have failed to distinguish reading-disabled children from other poor readers (Bloom et al., 1980; Coles, 1978; Taylor et al., 1979), and two of its critical features deserve attention. One was the use of regression procedures to define outliers (Horn & O'Donnell, 1984; Shepard, 1980; Wilson & Cone, 1984). But probably most important was their use of a conservative criterion for classifying a case as an outlier; as a result, only 3.7% of the subjects in their sample were classified as "specifics." A conservative criterion like that employed by Rutter and Yule (1975) is probably essential in forming samples that stand a chance of providing evidence consistent with the assumption of specificity. It seems reasonable to speculate that only studies that classify less than 5% of the sampled population as reading disabled will stand a chance of uncovering evidence for specificity. When the proportion gets much above 5%, one will probably observe more generalized deficits.

Escaping the Paradox: Subtypes

A second way of putting the assumption of specificity on a firmer footing—and one that by no means excludes the previous recommendation of a conservative criterion—is suggested by the "subtypes" argument. This is the argument that there may be many subtypes of reading disability, and that if a research sample comprises several subtypes (each with a distinct, but different, single-factor deficit), the overall results from the sample will mistakenly seem to indicate multiple deficits. Although this is a logical possibility, the subtyping literature itself remains confusing (Jorm, 1983; Lundberg, 1985; R. Olson, Kliegl, Davidson, & Foltz, 1985; Perfetti, 1985; Stanovich, 1986; Vellutino, 1979) and has produced no strong evidence implicating subtypes in the wide variety of deficits that have been observed. In fact, most researchers would probably find themselves having to agree that no "tight" subgroupings have been identified (Stanovich, 1986) and to accept Jorm's (1983) statement that "there is no agreed-upon taxonomy of subtypes" (p. 312). However, newer research methodologies for evaluating the subtype hypothesis are just beginning to be evaluated (Doehring, Trites, Patel, & Fiedorowicz, 1981; Lovett, 1984; Torgesen, 1982). Pursuing the subtype hypothesis, in conjunction with using a conservative definition of reading disability, might establish a firmer empirical foundation for the assumption of specificity.

Escaping the Paradox: A Developmental Version of the Specificity Hypothesis

There is, however, a third alternative—again, not exclusive of searching for subtypes and using a conservative criterion—which may be theoretically the most interesting. This alternative is to hypothesize developmental change in the cognitive specificity of the deficits displayed by reading-disabled children, change that is in part a consequence of individual differences in reading acquisition and the reciprocal relationships between reading, other cognitive skills, and motivational factors. This hypothesis follows from the tentative causal model presented earlier.

According to this hypothesis, the performance of reading-disabled children *is* characterized by a relatively high degree of specificity upon entering school (see Jorm, Share, Maclean, & Matthews, 1986). The obvious candidate for the critically deficient process is phonological awareness. Thus, it is hypothesized that due to several incompletely determined—but undoubtedly complex and interacting—genetic and environmental causes (Chall, 1983; S. Cohen, Glass, & Singer, 1973; Duane, 1983; Feitelson & Goldstein, 1986; Guthrie, 1981; Rutter et al., 1974; Stevenson et al., 1985), children who will later be candidates for the label of reading disabled enter school with markedly underdeveloped phonological awareness, but with either mild deficits in other cognitive skills or none at all. Deficient phonological awareness makes it difficult for the child to understand the alphabetic principle and delays the breaking of the spelling-to-sound code. The differences in in-school exposure to text chronicled by Allington (1980, 1983, 1984) and Biemiller (1977/1978) begin to build up by the middle of the first-grade year. These exposure differences compound any out-of-school differences already present and leave reading-disabled children farther behind their peers in the development of the rapid, automatic processes of direct visual recognition. These processes enable the type of reading for comprehension that is more enjoyable than that encumbered by the cognitively demanding conscious process of "sounding out." The resulting motivational differences lead to further increases in the exposure differences between good and poor readers that are then exacerbated by further developments such as the introduction of more difficult reading materials.

Of course, the exact timing of this developmental sequence and of its feed-back effects remains to be worked out. What is critical for the present discussion is the hypothesis that at some point, slower progress at reading acquisition begins to have more *generalized* effects: effects on processes that underlie a broader range of tasks and skills than just reading. That is, the initial specific problem may evolve into a more generalized deficit due to the behavioral/cognitive motivational spinoffs from failure at such a crucial educational task as reading. For example, at some point reading exposure differences begin to result in marked divergences in the vocabularies of skilled and less-skilled readers, and those vocabulary differences have implications for other aspects of language use. The same is probably true of syntactic knowledge and world knowledge.

Perhaps just as important as the cognitive consequences of reading failure are the motivational side effects. These are receiving increasing attention from researchers. Butkowsky and Willows (1980) manipulated success and failure in a reading and a nonreading task. The poor readers in the fifth-grade sample were less likely to attribute success to ability, and more likely to attribute it to luck or to the easiness of the task, than were the better readers. Following failure, however, they were more likely to attribute their performance to ability and less likely to attribute it to luck or task difficulty. The poorer readers also displayed less task persistence than the better readers. Their behavioral and attributional patterns displayed characteristics consistent with the concept of academic learned helplessness, which has been studied in several areas of educational achievement (Diener & Dweck, 1978; Fowler & Peterson, 1981; Johnston & Winograd, 1985; Licht & Dweck, 1984; Torgesen & Licht, 1983). Interestingly, the same behavioral and attributional patterns were displayed on the nonreading task as on the reading task, indicating that by this age, achievement-thwarting motivational and behavioral tendencies were being exhibited on tasks other than reading, even though the disabled group was constituted solely on the basis of lagging reading achievement. Thus, the learned helplessness that may have been the result of reading failure was beginning to influence performance on other cognitive tasks, perhaps eventually leading to an increasingly generalized inability to deal with academic and cognitive tasks of all types. Thus, not only the negative cognitive effects but also the motivational spinoffs of reading failure can lead to increasingly global performance deficits.

Butkowsky and Willows (1980) point to the possibility of a negative Matthew effect in their paper—"These data provide convincing evidence in support of the notion that children with reading difficulties may display an eroding motivation in achievement situations that increases the probability of future failure" (p. 419)—and they suggest one mechanism contributing to this effect. They note that the lower persistence that is part of the learned helplessness pattern is self-defeating:

Children who give up easily in the face of difficulty may never persist long enough at a task to discover that success may, in fact, be possible. Such children may never spontaneously discover that they do possess the capacity to achieve outcomes that exceed their expectations. (p. 419)

Perfetti (1985) has explicated these proliferating Matthew effects and the related motivational problems using the framework of his verbal efficiency theory:

The low-achieving reader starts out behind in terms of some of the linguistic knowledge on which this verbal processing system gets built. He falls farther behind as his reading experiences fail to build the rich and redundant network that the high-achieving reader has. By the time a fifth-grade student is targeted for remediation, the inefficiency (and ineffectiveness) of his (or her) verbal coding system has had a significant history. To expect this to be remedied by a few lessons in decoding practice is like expecting a baseball player of mediocre talent to suddenly become a good hitter following a few days of batting practice. This problem, the need for extended practice, is unfortunately coupled with the problem of motivation. (p. 248)

Evaluating a Developmental Version of the Specificity Hypothesis

The hypothesis entertained here is that there is a developmental trend in the specificity of the disability: A specific cognitive deficit prevents the early acquisition of reading skill. Slow reading acquisition has cognitive, behavioral, and motivational consequences that slow the development of other cognitive skills and inhibit performance on many academic tasks. In short, as reading develops, other cognitive processes linked to it track the level of reading skill. Knowledge bases that are in reciprocal relationships with reading are also inhibited from further development. The longer this developmental sequence is allowed to continue, the more generalized the deficits will become, seeping into more and more areas of cognition and behavior. Or, to put it more simply—and more sadly—in the words of a tearful 9-year-old, already falling frustratingly behind his peers in reading progress, "Reading affects everything you do" (Morris, 1984, p. 19).

The presence of a developmental trend in the specificity of the disability may in part account for why the literature has failed to uncover strong evidence for specificity and instead has augmented the number of possible cognitive deficits: The subjects in many of the studies may have been so developmentally advanced that generalized cognitive deficiencies had begun to appear. This account is certainly true of studies of cognitive differences among adult readers of varying skill.

At present, there is little direct evidence with which to evaluate this developmental variant of the specificity hypothesis. Clearly, we need longitudinal research designs to obtain the most diagnostic data. Also, such a developmental trend may be difficult to detect because the period during which specificity might be observed could be quite short. Perhaps it is only in the very earliest stages of reading acquisition—when the seriously disabled readers may be harder to identify—that considerable cognitive specificity occurs. Again, the need for longitudinal data is obvious.

There are many other methodological, conceptual, and statistical problems in evaluating some of the predictions that follow from the hypothesis. One such prediction is that reading and the cognitive skills related to it should become more interrelated with development. Unfortunately, this predicted trend will probably be confounded with the fact that more complex cognitive processes are engaged mainly at the more advanced levels of reading (Chall, 1983). For example, the more complex types of inferencing skills are necessary only when the material being read attains a certain level of difficulty. Thus, the correlation between reading and these cognitive skills will increase not only because of the consequences of differential reading experience but also because the *task* of reading is changing (Chall, 1983). Separating the operation of these two mechanisms could be extremely difficult.

Additionally, researchers who attempt to evaluate the hypothesis during the developmental stages that are critical—the very earliest reading acquisition stages—will encounter some statistical complications. For example, the reliability of some tasks may increase during this period, necessarily leading to changes in correlations. It is not surprising, given these difficulties, that there is currently little evidence to permit a strong test of the developmental version of the specificity hypothesis. Nevertheless, there are some suggestive trends in the literature that should at least motivate more definitive tests. The hypothesis is worth pursuing because—like the subtypes hypothesis, for which there is arguably little more evidence—it may provide a way of preserving the assumption of specificity (and the concept of dyslexia) in the face of the mounting body of data indicating pervasive cognitive deficiencies.

Developmental studies of multivariate relationships between reading-related cognitive processes have yielded suggestive evidence that the intercorrelation of subskills increases with age. In one study, we (Stanovich, Cunningham, & Feeman, 1984a) found that at the end of first grade, measures of phonological awareness, decoding speed, vocabulary, listening comprehension, and abstract problem-solving were only weakly correlated; but by the fifth grade, performance on these tasks was highly correlated. In the first grade, the mean correlation between tasks tapping different cognitive skills was .24, whereas this correlation rose to .59 in the fifth grade. A similar trend runs through the correlations reported by Curtis (1980). Comparisons of other multivariate studies of reading-related skills in the early grades (e.g., Stevenson, Parker, Wilkinson, Hegion, & Fish, 1976) with adult studies (e.g., M. Jackson & McClelland, 1975, 1979) suggest a similar pattern.

In a test of several components of memory functioning, Brainerd, Kingma, and Howe (1986) found that second-grade learning-disabled children displayed deficits primarily in poststorage-retrieval learning, whereas in the sixth grade, deficits appeared there as well as in storage and in prestorage-retrieval aspects of performance. These results suggest that the memory problems of learning-disabled children become more pervasive as they grow older. R.L. Cohen (1982) presented results suggesting a similar pattern operating at an even earlier stage in development. He found that performance in nonstrategic serial memory tasks measured in kindergarten was related to first-grade reading ability but that performance on a strategic memory task was not. However, when assessed in the first grade, both types of memory tasks were related to reading ability. In an argument similar to the one being developed in this section, R.L. Cohen (1982) speculated that deficits on the nonstrategic and strategic memory (STM) tasks were of two different types, "the former being one manifestation of their basic deficit and the latter being an acquired deficit" because "following academic experience that comprises practice in ineffective reading, these children will not develop the strategies required for successful performance in other STM tasks" (p. 51).

Bishop and Butterworth (1980) have reported one of the few longitudinal studies within the relevant age range, and their data are quite suggestive. They found that performance and verbal IQs assessed at age 4 were equally good predictors ($r = .36$) of reading ability at age 8; however, when assessed concurrently with reading ability at age 8, verbal IQ displayed a stronger relationship. Furthermore, the children in their sample who had reading problems at age 8 appeared to have lower verbal than performance IQ scores at age 8 but did not at age 4. These trends are consistent with the idea that success or failure at the initial stages of reading acquisition has effects on more general aspects of verbal intelligence.

Studies of reading-related cognitive skills in the early grades have consistently indicated that the different cognitive processes are only weakly interrelated. Our (Stanovich, Cunningham, & Feeman, 1984a) mean correlation of .24 is similar to that reported by other researchers, as follows: Blachman (1984), .30; Curtis (1980), .32, .27; Evans and Carr (1985), .39, .18; Share et al. (1984), .38; and Stevenson et al. (1976), .14, .26, .09, and .32. Although low reliabilities may be attenuating some of these correlations, these results do suggest the interesting possibility of considerable dissociation between the cognitive subskills related to reading when a child enters school. Such a relatively loose linkage between cognitive skills in the early grades would allow greater cognitive specificity among younger poor readers.

A similar pattern of relative dissociation appears when one examines the correlations between reading ability and scores on various intelligence tests. Although these correlations cluster in the ranges of .45 to .65 in the middle grades and .60 to .75 among adults, they are more commonly between .30 and .50 in the early elementary grades (see Stanovich, Cunningham, & Feeman, 1984a). Of particular interest is the finding that performance on phonological awareness tasks in kindergarten and first grade often predicts subsequent reading achievement better than intelligence tests that tap a variety of cognitive processes (Bradley & Bryant, 1983, 1985; Goldstein, 1976; Mann, 1984; Share et al., 1984; Stanovich, Cunningham, & Cramer, 1984; Stanovich, Cunningham, & Feeman, 1984a; Torneus, 1984; Tunmer & Nesdale, 1985; Zifcak, 1981). (Of course, it has long been known that letter knowledge prior to entering school is a better predictor of initial reading acquisition than IQ: Chall, 1967; Richek, 1977/1978; Stevenson et al., 1976.)

Additionally, several studies have demonstrated that phonological awareness accounts for a statistically significant and sizable portion of variance in reading ability after the variance associated with standardized intelligence measures has been partialled out (Bradley & Bryant, 1983, 1985; Goldstein, 1976; Stanovich, Cunningham, & Feeman, 1984a; Tunmer & Nesdale, 1985). In short, some suggestive evidence does exist to indicate that, at school entry, phonological awareness is dissociated from other cognitive skills to such an extent that it could be the source of a specific reading disability: one that—according to the hypothesis outlined above—develops into a more generalized cognitive deficit.

Breaking the Cycle of Interacting Skill Deficits

The discussion in several previous sections, emphasizing as it did the cycle of negative Matthew effects set in motion by reading failure, invites speculation on how the cycle is to be broken. Although this discussion has highlighted the importance of breaking the cycle, it has also hinted at the difficulty of doing so. One of the reasons that the cycle will be difficult for educators to break is that some of the Matthew effects are linked to events in the child's out-of-school environment. Also, as a result, certain interpretive problems are often encountered when one is attempting to evaluate the effects of interventions to facilitate reading achievement. In order to better understand these issues, we may find it instructive to consider the interpretive problems in an area with analogous problems—research on schooling effects.

Findings on the effects of schooling on achievement appeared confusing and inconsistent until researchers generally recognized the importance of differentiating those factors that explain the variance in academic performance from those that determine the absolute level of performance (see McCall, 1981; Rutter, 1983). Rutter illustrated this point by pointing to Tizard's (1975) discussion of the fact that in the last 50–60 years, the average height of London children ages 7–12 has increased by 9 centimeters—probably due to better nutrition—yet there has been no change in the variation in height among the children. Current variation is probably just as strongly determined by genetic factors as it always was, even though nutritional changes have raised the overall height of the population.

Understanding the effects of schooling on achievement requires that we understand the distinction drawn in the Tizard example. Although school variables explain very little of the *variance* in achievement (family background being the dominant factor), the *absolute level* of academic achievement is linked to a number of school variables (Rutter, 1983). This distinction provides a context for understanding Matthew effects in education. Raising the population's mean level of performance will not eliminate individual differences. In fact, raising absolute levels of performance might well *increase* performance variance because high achievers will make better use of the new learning opportunities.

One might think that if overall performance levels rise, the lowest readers will eventually reach an acceptable level of achievement, one where they would no longer be considered "disabled." Unfortunately, ever-escalating absolute levels of performance will not necessarily be a panacea for the low-achieving student. Rising absolute levels of performance more often result in increased societal expectations, marketplace adjustments, and higher criteria of acceptable performance on the part of the public and employers (Levine, 1982; Resnick & Resnick, 1977).

In this context, note that researchers and educators who are focusing on the problem of reading disability are in effect aspiring to reduce the variance in reading ability (i.e., to bring up the lowest readers to some reasonable standard). The existence of negative Matthew effects that go beyond the school, and the history of research on the attempts to decrease achievement variability, suggest that educational interventions that represent a "more-of-the-same" approach will probably not be successful. The cycle of escalating achievement deficits must be broken in a more specific way to short-circuit the cascade of negative spinoffs. This suggests that the remedy for the problem must be more of a "surgical strike" (to use a military analogy).

The field of learning disabilities has always implicitly recognized this logic, for its underlying motivation and associated techniques are of specific remediation rather than generalized enrichment. This logic pervades the whole area of perceptual process training in learning disabilities. Although process training is now discredited (Allington, 1982; Arter & Jenkins, 1979; Kavale & Mattson, 1983), it is important to appreciate the reasons why it has fallen into disfavor. Some of these I have outlined previously with regard to reading disability. First, there is the definitional problem. The children studied may not have been identified using a criterion that was stringent enough to select only those with specific deficits. Second, the "processes" that were trained may simply have been the wrong ones. With the hindsight of current research we now know that in some cases this was most certainly true (e.g., the fiasco of poor readers subjected to balance beams and eye movement training). Third, the training may have begun too late, perhaps after the specific deficit had turned into a more generalized learning difficulty. Thus, perhaps the idea that animated the process training attempts was correct, but it was inadequately carried out.

The conclusions drawn in this review will suggest what optimal specific remediation might be. I have hypothesized that if there is a specific cause of reading disability at all, it resides in the area of phonological awareness. Slow development in this area delays early code-breaking progress and initiates the cascade of interacting achievement failures and motivational problems. Fortunately, developmental delays in this ability can be detected fairly early. Several of the tasks used to assess this ability have been employed with preschool and kindergarten children (Bradley & Bryant, 1983; Fox & Routh, 1975; Stanovich, Cunningham, & Cramer, 1984; Williams, 1984). Recently, several studies have reported attempts to facilitate the development of phonological awareness and thus affect the speed of early reading acquisition. The most influential has been the study of Bradley and Bryant (1983, 1985), in which a group of 5- to 6-year-old children who had scored 2 standard deviations below the mean on a phonological awareness task were given 40 sessions of training in sound categorization stretching over a two-year period. A group matched on IQ and phonological ability received equivalent training in conceptual classification. The results indicated that the sound categorization training group was 4 months advanced in reading ability when assessed at age 8 (a group taught sound categorization with the aid of letters displayed a striking 8-month gain). This study provides strong evidence that early identification and subsequent training in phonological awareness can partially overcome the reading deficits displayed by many children whose phonological skills develop slowly.

A critic of the Bradley and Bryant (1983, 1985) study might argue that the achievement difference between the experimental and control groups appeared to be fairly small in magnitude (e.g., Yaden, 1984). However, one inference that follows from the argument presented here is that small achievement differences that appear early can be the genesis of large differences later in development. When viewed in light of possible Matthew effects and reciprocal relationships involving reading, the achievement differences observed by Bradley and Bryant (1983, 1985) can hardly be deemed unimportant. A longitudinal study by Jorm, Share, Maclean, and Matthews (1984) illustrates how phonological skills may generate individual differences in reading acquisition that multiply with development. They formed two groups of kindergarten children who differed on phonological recoding skill but were matched on verbal intelligence and sight-word reading, By the first grade, the group superior in phonological recoding skill was 4 months advanced in reading achievement. Importantly, the two groups tended to diverge with time: The performance difference increased to 9 months by the second grade.

The Bradley and Bryant (1983, 1985) study illustrates an ideal way to attack the problem of snowballing achievement deficits in reading: Identify early, remedy early, and focus on phonological awareness. But what is to be done at later points in development, when negative reciprocal relationships have already begun to depress further achievement? One answer is to aim an attack at a major bootstrapping mechanism: reading practice. A computer-aided reading system developed by McConkie and Zola (1985) exemplifies this approach (a similar system has been developed by R. Olson, Foltz, & Wise, 1986). They explicitly acknowledge that thwarting Matthew effects was one of the motivations for developing their system: "Since there are probably many aspects of reading skill that develop primarily through extended involvement in reading, these people (with reading difficulties) have been essentially blocked from this further development" (p. 9). The logic behind the system rests on some simple facts about individual differences in reading ability. One is that—particularly in the early stages of reading acquisition—poor readers have trouble identifying words (Perfetti, 1985), and this appears to be the primary causal mechanism behind their reading problems. Without efficient mechanisms of word identification, reading is difficult and unsatisfying because comprehension cannot proceed when word meanings are not efficiently extracted (Perfetti, 1985). Reading becomes less and less pleasurable as the poorer reader spends an increasing amount of time in materials beyond his or her capability. He or she avoids reading, and the resultant lack of practice relative to his or her peers widens achievement deficits.

The computer-aided reading system of McConkie and Zola (1985; see also R. Olson, Foltz, & Wise, 1986) is designed to partially eliminate the word-processing problems of the poorer reader. The subject reads text on a color monitor attached to a computer. When the reader encounters a word that cannot be decoded, he or she touches the word on the screen with a light pen. In less than a second the word is "spoken" by an audio unit interfaced with the computer. Preliminary tests of the device indicate that with it children can read material that would have been beyond their capability without the word-identification support provided by the computer. In short, the system prevents the numerous comprehension breakdowns that poor readers experience due to their inefficient word-identification processes. It allows the poor reader to read material appropriate to his or her age level, thus circumventing a problem that increases as schooling proceeds: The poor reader becomes less and less able to read age-appropriate material, an additional factor contributing to the distastefulness of reading.

The computer-aided reading system has at least two major advantages over natural reading, where the child must guess at an unknown word. First, it provides the word faster than does conscious guessing, thus leading to fewer comprehension breakdowns. Second, it provides a positive learning trial (Jorm & Share, 1983) for the child to amalgamate a visual/orthographic representation of the word with its meaning and pronunciation (Ehri, 1984). Initial tests of the system have indicated that for many problem readers it was their first experience of reading without a struggle. Some mentally retarded students and children with severe reading disabilities read passages where they had to touch almost every word, yet they comprehended the passage to some extent and were enjoyably engaged in the activity. The system thus has the potential to address at least partially the problem of the differential reading practice received by readers of differing skill.

The purpose of this section was not to survey techniques for remedying or preventing reading failure but to illustrate two research programs with particular relevance to the model of the development of individual differences in reading ability that has been outlined here. The studies of Bradley and Bryant (1983, 1985) and McConkie and Zola (1985) represent two ways of attacking the problem of early reading deficits that spiral the child into a pattern of ever-increasing scholastic achievement problems. The work of the former investigators represents the strategy of prevention; that of the latter represents the strategy of intervention to attenuate one of the most pervasive causes of Matthew effects on achievement: differential practice.

Conclusions, Speculations, and Caveats

In the foregoing, I have sketched the type of conceptualization of individual differences in reading and related cognitive processes that results from a consideration of the cognitive consequences of reading, reciprocal causation, organism–environment correlation, and developmental change. The review is not so much a complete model of the development of individual differences as an outline to be filled in by future research. It is hoped that this framework might help to clarify aspects of the existing research literature and to focus future experimental efforts. For example, the statement that reading ability is multiply determined has become a cliché. But the number of causal mechanisms may not be as large as is commonly believed. Some of the differences in cognitive processes that are linked with reading ability may actually be the effects of reading efficiency itself. Similarly, some of the individual differences in cognitive processes that are associated with reading ability in the adult (M. Jackson & McClelland, 1979; Palmer et al., 1985) may be remnants of the reading histories of the subjects. This would be especially true if the processes responsible for reading ability variation change several times during development, leaving behind differences in cognitive processes that were causal at earlier stages.

The framework I have outlined may also help to clarify thinking about other issues in reading research. Consider two examples. A moderately popular genre of individual differences research has been the attempt to identify readers who have similar ability but different cognitive profiles. Often researchers have implicitly assumed that when such qualitatively different patterns have been observed among less-skilled readers, they represent differing etiologies of reading failure. This conclusion is a consequence of the "many different types of reading failure" assumption that guides most research. But perhaps more attention should be directed to the possibility that the qualitatively different processing patterns represent alternative ways of *coping* with a reading deficit that had a common cause. This alternative explanation looms larger when older subjects are the focus of the investigation.

A second example is provided by the recent flurry of exciting research on comprehension strategies and cognitive monitoring during reading (e.g., August, Flavell & Clift, 1984). It is often assumed that what is being investigated is a set of cognitive abilities separate from those linked with word-recognition skill. However, as Perfetti (1984; 1985; see also Lovett, 1984) has noted, few such studies have included a comprehensive evaluation of decoding skill. This leaves open the possibility that the reading skill differences in comprehension strategies that are observed may be consequences of differing overall reading levels. The better readers could be decoding words more efficiently and thus have more cognitive resources available to allocate to comprehension. As Underwood (1985) has noted, "It is partly as a consequence of having automatic processes available that reading can be flexible" (p. 173). No doubt this is not the whole story. It is more likely that the comprehension strategy differences observed represent a combination of cognitive monitoring differences and the differential resource availability due to decoding skill variation. The point is that it is important—both practically and theoretically—to separate out the part of the relationship that is a consequence of reading level.

An emphasis on the importance of Matthew effects and reciprocal relationships will also help to highlight the necessity of providing some explanation of the massive individual differences in levels of acquired reading skill. Recall that Allington (1984) observed some skilled first-grade groups to be reading three times as many words a week as some less-skilled groups. The differences among an adult population can be even more startling. Perfetti (1985) has emphasized this point by noting that even among a self-selected and range-restricted group of college students, threefold differences in reading speed occur with regularity. If these large differences are indeed the result of Matthew effects, then research must begin to move beyond the mere chronicling of the achievement differences and begin to specify and evaluate the mechanisms that produce the Matthew effects. Some of the progress already made on this problem has been outlined above. However, one important possible mediator of Matthew effects has so far been omitted because it deserves extended discussion beyond the scope of this review: instruction.

Despite some disagreement, researchers are increasingly uncovering support for Gough and Hillinger's (1980) provocative characterization of reading as an "unnatural act" (Barron, 1986; Byrne, 1984, 1986; Calfee, 1982, 1983;

Donaldson, 1984; Donaldson & Reid, 1982; Ehri & Wilce, 1985; Masonheimer, Drum, & Ehri, 1984). Although it is popular for authors to cite examples of children who have acquired reading on their own—or, more often, have been able to identify some boxtop labels via paired-associate learning or guessing from context (Masonheimer et al., 1984)—for the vast majority of children the initial stages of reading must be traversed with the aid of some type of guided instruction from a teacher (who in the case of early readers may well be a parent; see Anbar, 1986; Durkin, 1982). Thus, because instruction must mediate the initial stages of reading acquisition, it could well interact with the child's initial level of cognitive skill to cause Matthew effects. Some of these effects will result from passive organism–environment correlations: Biologically disadvantaged children must learn in instructional environments (composed of teachers, schools, parents, etc.) that are inferior to those experienced by advantaged children (Rutter & Madge, 1976). Again, some part of this correlation is the result of social structures and is potentially manipulable, and some part of it is not.

Other Matthew effects may arise from evocative organism–environment correlations involving instruction. If Allington (1983) is correct that the reading instruction provided to less-skilled readers is suboptimal in many ways, then a Matthew effect is being created whereby a child who is—for whatever reason— poorly equipped to acquire reading skill may evoke an instructional environment that will further inhibit learning to read. Certainly this was true of many of the ineffective visual training programs, which had the effect of removing from conventional reading instruction the very children who needed practice at actual reading. Calfee (1983) has previously speculated on such a mechanism's operating to cause reading disabilities:

> It is true that dyslexia is associated with many correlates of the individual—being a boy, poor preparation for school, language deficiencies, among others....
> A plausible hypothesis, which cannot be rejected from the available data is that these characteristics serve as markers about what to expect of the child in school and which thereby determine the instructional program in which he or she is placed. (pp. 77–78)

If Matthew effects of this type are an appreciable source of ability variance, it will indeed be fortunate, because they are controllable.

In short, a major problem for future research will be to determine whether instructional differences are a factor in generating Matthew effects. In addition, it will be interesting to investigate whether any of the important consequences of the ease of initial reading acquisition arise indirectly from instructional differences determined by reading ability. Some progress has been made on these problems, as there is an increasing amount of good research appearing on the effects of instructional variations on cognitive processes and achievement (Alegria, Pignot, & Morais, 1982; Anderson, Hiebert, Scott, & Wilkinson, 1985; Anderson, Mason, & Shirey, 1984; Barr, 1974/1975; Duffy, Roehler, & Mason,

1984; Evans & Carr, 1985; Hiebert, 1983; Hoffman & Rutherford, 1984). Several other fruitful research programs would probably arise from attempts to specify the mechanisms that mediate the cognitive consequences of individual differences in reading acquisition.

Acknowledgments

The author wishes to thank Anne Cunningham, Ruth Nathan, and Richard West for their comments on the manuscript.

References

Alegria, J., Pignot, E., & Morais, J. (1982). Phonetic analysis of speech and memory codes in beginning readers. *Memory & Cognition, 10,* 451–456.

Algozzine, B., & Ysseldyke, J. (1983). Learning disabilities as a subset of school failure: The over-sophistication of a concept. *Exceptional Children, 50,* 242–246.

Allington, R.L. (1977). If they don't read much, how they ever gonna get good? *Journal of Reading, 21,* 57–61.

Allington, R.L. (1980). Poor readers don't get to read much in reading groups. *Language Arts, 57,* 872–876.

Allington, R.L. (1982). The persistence of teacher beliefs in facets of the visual perceptual deficit hypothesis. *The Elementary School Journal, 82,* 351–359.

Allington, R.L. (1983). The reading instruction provided readers of differing reading abilities. *The Elementary School Journal, 83,* 548–559.

Allington, R.L. (1984). Content coverage and contextual reading in reading groups. *Journal of Reading Behavior, 16,* 85–96.

Allington, R.L., & Fleming, J.T. (1978). The misreading of high-frequency words. *Journal of Special Education, 12,* 417–421.

Allington, R.L., & Strange, M. (1977). Effects of grapheme substitutions in connected text upon reading behaviors. *Visible Language, 11,* 285–297.

Aman, M., & Singh, N. (1983). Specific reading disorders: Concepts of etiology reconsidered. In K. Gadow & I. Bialer (Eds.), *Advances in learning and behavioral disabilities* (Vol. 2, pp. 1–47). Greenwich, CT: JAI Press.

Ames, L. (1968). A low intelligence quotient often not recognized as the chief cause of many reading difficulties. *Journal of Learning Disabilities, 1,* 45–48.

Anbar, A. (1986). Reading acquisition of preschool children without systematic instruction. *Early Childhood Research Quarterly, 1,* 69–83.

Anderson, M., Kaufman, A., & Kaufman, N. (1976). Use of the WISC-R with a learning disabled population: Some diagnostic implications. *Psychology in the Schools, 13,* 381–386.

Anderson, R.C., & Freebody, P. (1979). *Vocabulary knowledge* (Tech. Rep. No. 136). Urbana-Champaign: University of Illinois, Center for the Study of Reading.

Anderson, R.C., Hiebert, E.H., Scott, J.A., & Wilkinson I.A.G. (1985). *Becoming a nation of readers: The report of the Commission on Reading.* Washington, DC: National Institute of Education.

Anderson, R.C., Mason, J., & Shirey, L. (1984). The reading group: An experimental investigation of a labyrinth. *Reading Research Quarterly, 20,* 6–38.

Arter, I., & Jenkins, J. (1979). Differential diagnosis-prescriptive teaching: A critical appraisal. *Review of Educational Research, 49,* 517–555.

August, D., Flavell, J., & Clift, R. (1984). Comparison of comprehension monitoring of skilled and less skilled readers. *Reading Research Quarterly, 20,* 39–53.

Bachman, J., & O'Malley, P. (1977). Self-esteem in young men: A longitudinal analysis of the impact of educational and occupational attainment. *Journal of Personality and Social Psychology, 35,* 365–380.

Backman, J., Bruck, M., Hebert, M., & Seidenberg, M. (1984). Acquisition and use of spelling-sound correspondences in reading. *Journal of Experimental Child Psychology, 38,* 114–133.

Backman, J., Mamen, M., & Ferguson, H. (1984). Reading level design: Conceptual and methodological issues in reading research. *Psychological Bulletin, 96,* 560–568.

Baker, L. (1982). An evaluation of the role of metacognitive deficits in learning disabilities. *Topics in Learning and Learning Disabilities, 2,* 27–35.

Balota, D., Pollatsek, A., & Rayner, K. (1985). The interaction of contextual constraints and parafoveal visual information in reading. *Cognitive Psychology, 17,* 364–390.

Baron, J. (1978). Intelligence and general strategies. In G. Underwood (Ed.), *Strategies in information processing* (pp. 403–450). London: Academic Press.

Barr, R. (1974/1975). The effect of instruction on pupil reading strategies. *Reading Research Quarterly, 10,* 555–582.

Barron, R. (1986). Word recognition in early reading: A review of the direct and indirect access hypothesis. *Cognition, 24,* 93–119.

Barron, R., & Baron, J. (1977). How children get meaning from printed words. *Child Development, 48,* 587–594.

Batey, O., & Sonnenschein, S. (1981). Reading deficits in learning disabled children. *Journal of Applied Developmental Psychology, 2,* 237–246.

Bauer, R. (1977). Memory processes in children with learning disabilities: Evidence for deficient rehearsal. *Journal of Experimental Child Psychology, 24,* 415–430.

Bauer, R. (1979). Memory, acquisition, and category clustering in learning-disabled children. *Journal of Experimental Child Psychology, 27,* 365–383.

Bauer, R. (1982). Information processing as a way of understanding and diagnosing learning disabilities. *Topics in Learning and Learning Disabilities, 2,* 33–45.

Beck, I.L., Perfetti, C.A., & McKeown, M.G. (1982). Effects of long-term vocabulary instruction on lexical access and reading comprehension. *Journal of Educational Psychology, 74,* 506–521.

Becker, C.A. (1982). The development of semantic context effects: Two processes or two strategies? *Reading Research Quarterly, 17,* 482–502.

Beech, J., & Harding, L. (1984). Phonemic processing and the poor reader from a developmental lag viewpoint. *Reading Research Quarterly, 19,* 357–366.

Berger, N. (1978). Why can't John read? Perhaps he's not a good listener. *Journal of Learning Disabilities, 11,* 633–638.

Bickley, A.C., Ellington, B.J., & Bickley, R.T. (1970). The cloze procedure: A conspectus. *Journal of Reading Behavior, 2,* 232–249.

Biemiller, A. (1970). The development of the use of graphic and contextual information as children learn to read. *Reading Research Quarterly, 6,* 75–96.

Biemiller, A. (1977/1978). Relationships between oral reading rates for letters, words, and simple text in the development of reading achievement. *Reading Research Quarterly, 13,* 223–253.

Biemiller, A. (1979). Changes in the use of graphic and contextual information as functions of passage difficulty and reading achievement level. *Journal of Reading Behavior, 11,* 307–319.

Bishop, D., & Butterworth, G. (1980). Verbal-performance discrepancies: Relationship to both risk and specific reading retardation. *Cortex, 16,* 375–389.

Bissex, G.L. (1980). *Gnys at wrk.* Cambridge, MA: Harvard University Press.

Bjorklund, D., & Bernholtz, J. (1986). The role of knowledge base in the memory performance of good and poor readers. *Journal of Experimental Child Psychology, 41,* 367–393.

Bjorklund, D., & Weiss, S. (1985). Influence of socioeconomic status on children's classification and free recall. *Journal of Educational Psychology, 77,* 119–128.

Blachman, B. (1984). Relationship of rapid naming ability and language analysis skills to kindergarten and first-grade reading achievement. *Journal of Educational Psychology, 76,* 610–622.

Blanchard, J. (1980). Preliminary investigation of transfer between single-word decoding ability and contextual reading comprehension by poor readers in grade six. *Perceptual and Motor Skills, 51,* 1271–1281

Blanchard, J., & McNinch, G. (1980). Commentary: Testing the decoding sufficiency hypothesis: A response to Fleisher, Jenkins, & Pany. *Reading Research Quarterly, 15,* 559–564.

Bloom, A., Wagner, M., Reskin, L., & Bergman, A. (1980). A comparison of intellectually delayed and primary reading disabled children on measures of intelligence and achievement. *Journal of Clinical Psychology, 36,* 788–790.

Bos, C., & Filip, D. (1982). Comprehension monitoring skills in learning disabled and average students. *Topics in Learning and Learning Disabilities, 2,* 79–85.

Bowey, J.A. (1982). Memory limitations in the oral reading comprehension of fourth-grade children. *Journal of Experimental Child Psychology, 34,* 200–216.

Bowey, J.A. (1986). Syntactic awareness in relation to reading skill and ongoing reading comprehension monitoring. *Journal of Experimental Child Psychology, 41,* 282–299.

Bradley, L., & Bryant, P.E. (1978). Difficulties in auditory organization as a possible cause of reading backwardness. *Nature, 271,* 746–747.

Bradley, L., & Bryant, P.E. (1983). Categorizing sounds and learning to read: A causal connection. *Nature, 301,* 419–421.

Bradley, L., & Bryant, P.E. (1985). *Rhyme and reason in reading and spelling.* Ann Arbor: University of Michigan Press.

Brady, S., Shankweiler, D., & Mann, V. (1983). Speech perception and memory coding in relation to reading ability. *Journal of Experimental Child Psychology, 35,* 345–367.

Brainerd, C., Kingma, J., & Howe, M. (1986). Long-term memory development and learning disability: Storage and retrieval loci of disabled/nondisabled differences. In S. Ceci (Ed.), *Handbook of cognitive social, and neuropsychological aspects of learning disabilities* (Vol. 1, pp. 161–184). Hillsdale, NJ: Erlbaum.

Briggs, P., Austin, S., & Underwood, G. (1984). The effects of sentence context in good and poor readers: A test of Stanovich's interactive-compensatory model. *Reading Research Quarterly, 20,* 54–61.

Briggs, P., & Underwood, G. (1982). Phonological coding in good and poor readers. *Journal of Experimental Child Psychology, 34,* 93–112.

Bristow, P.S. (1985). Are poor readers passive readers? Some evidence, possible explanations, and potential solutions. *The Reading Teacher, 39,* 318–325.

Bryan, T. (1974). Learning disabilities: A new stereotype. *Journal of Learning Disabilities, 7,* 46–51.

Bryant, P.E., & Bradley, L. (1985). *Children's reading problems.* Oxford, UK: Basil Blackwell.

Bryant, P.E., & Goswami, U. (1986). The strengths and weaknesses of the reading level design. *Psychological Bulletin, 100,* 101–103.

Bryant, P.E., & Impey, L. (1986). The similarities between normal readers and developmental and acquired dyslexics. *Cognition, 24,* 121–137.

Butkowsky, S., & Willows, D. (1980). Cognitive-motivational characteristics of children varying in reading ability: Evidence for learned helplessness in poor readers. *Journal of Educational Psychology, 72,* 408–422.

Byrne, B. (1981). Deficient syntactic control in poor readers: Is a weak phonetic memory code responsible? *Applied Psycholinguistics, 2,* 201–212.

Byrne, B. (1984). On teaching articulatory phonetics via an orthography. *Memory & Cognition, 12,* 181–189.

Byrne, B. (1986, March). *Learning to read the first few items: Evidence of a nonanalytic acquisition procedure in adults and children.* Paper presented at the Conference on the Process of Reading Acquisition, Center for Cognitive Science, University of Texas, Austin.

Calfee, R. (1982). Literacy and illiteracy: Teaching the nonreader to survive in the modern world. *Annals of Dyslexia, 32,* 71–91.

Calfee, R. (1983). Review of "Dyslexia: Theory and Research." *Applied Psycholinguistics, 4,* 69–79.

Campione, J., & Brown, A. (1978). Toward a theory of intelligence: Contributions from research with retarded children. *Intelligence, 2,* 279–304.

Carr, T. (1981). Building theories of reading ability: On the relation between individual differences in cognitive skills and reading comprehension. *Cognition, 9,* 73–113.

Chall, J. (1967). *Learning to read: The great debate.* New York: McGraw-Hill.

Chall, J. (1983). *Stages of reading development.* New York: McGraw-Hill.

Chi, M., Glaser, R., & Rees, E. (1982). Expertise in problem solving. In R. Sternberg (Ed.). *Advances in the psychology of human intelligence* (Vol. 1). Hillsdale, NJ: Erlbaum.

Cohen, A.S. (1974/1975). Oral reading errors of first-grade children taught by a code emphasis approach. *Reading Research Quarterly, 10,* 615–650.

Cohen, R.L. (1982). Individual differences in short-term memory. In N. Ellis (Ed.), *International review of research in mental retardation* (Vol. 11, pp. 43–77). New York: Academic Press.

Cohen, S. (1976). The fuzziness and the flab: Some solutions to research problems in learning disabilities. *Journal of Special Education*, *10*, 129–136.

Cohen, S., Glass, D.C., & Singer, J.E. (1973). Apartment noise, auditory discrimination, and reading ability in children. *Journal of Experimental Social Psychology*, *9*, 407–422.

Coles, G. (1978). The learning disabilities test battery: Empirical and social issues. *Harvard Educational Review*, *48*, 313–340.

Coltheart, M., Masterson, J., Byng, S., Prior, M., & Riddich, J. (1983). Surface dyslexia. *Quarterly Journal of Experimental Psychology*, *35A*, 469–485.

Coomber, J.E. (1972). *A psycholinguistic analysis of oral reading errors made by good, average, and poor readers* (Tech. Rep. No. 232). Madison: University of Wisconsin, Research and Development Center.

Crowder, R.G. (1984). Is it just reading? *Developmental Review*, *4*, 48–61.

Curtis, M. (1980). Development of components of reading skill. *Journal of Educational Psychology*, *72*, 656–669.

Denckla, M.S., & Rudel, R.G. (1976). Rapid "automatized" naming (R.A.N.): Dyslexia differentiated from other learning disabilities. *Neuropsychologia*, *14*, 471–479.

Desoto, J., & Desoto, C. (1983). Relationship of reading achievement to verbal processing abilities. *Journal of Educational Psychology*, *75*, 116–127.

Diener, C., & Dweck, C. (1978). An analysis of learned helplessness: Continuous changes in performance, strategy, and achievement cognitions following failure. *Journal of Personality and Social Psychology*, *36*, 451–462.

Doehring, D.G. (1976). Acquisition of rapid reading responses. *Monographs of the Society for Research in Child Development*, *41*(2; Serial No. 165).

Doehring, D.G., Trites, R.L., Patel, P.G., & Fiedorowicz, C.A.M. (1981). *Reading disabilities: The interaction of reading, language, and neuropsychological deficits*. New York: Academic Press.

Donaldson, M. (1978). *Children's minds*. London: Fontana/Collins.

Donaldson, M. (1984). Speech and writing and modes of learning. In H. Goelman, A. Oberg, & F. Smith (Eds.), *Awakening to literacy* (pp. 174–184). London: Heinemann.

Donaldson, M., & Reid, J. (1982). Language skills and reading: A developmental perspective. In A. Hendry (Ed.), *Teaching reading: The key issues*. London: Heinemann.

Downing, J. (1980). Learning to read with understanding. In C.M. McCullough (Ed.), *Persistent problems in reading education* (pp. 163–178). Newark, DE: International Reading Association.

Duane, D.D. (1983). Neurobiological correlates of reading disorders. *Journal of Educational Research*, *77*, 5–15.

Duffy, G.G., Roehler, L.R., & Mason, J. (1984). *Comprehension instruction*. New York: Longman.

Durkin, D. (1982). *A study of poor black children who are successful readers* (Reading Education Rep. No. 33). Urbana-Champaign: University of Illinois, Center for the Study of Reading.

Ehri, L. (1977). Do adjectives and functors interfere as much as nouns in naming pictures? *Child Development*, *48*, 697–701.

Ehri, L. (1979). Linguistic insight: Threshold of reading acquisition. In T. Waller & G. MacKinnon (Eds.), *Reading research: Advances in research and theory* (Vol. 1, pp. 63–114). New York: Academic Press.

Ehri, L. (1984). How orthography alters spoken language competencies in children learning to read and spell. In J. Downing & R. Valtin (Eds.), *Language awareness and learning to read* (pp. 119–147). New York: Springer-Verlag.

Ehri, L. (1985). Effects of printed language acquisition on speech. In D. Olson, N. Torrance, & A. Hildyard (Eds.), *Literacy, language, and learning* (pp. 333–367). New York: Cambridge University Press.

Ehri, L., & Wilce, L. (1985). Movement into reading: Is the first stage of printed word learning visual or phonetic? *Reading Research Quarterly*, *20*, 163–179.

Ehrlich, S. (1981). Children's word recognition in prose context. *Visible Language*, *15*, 219–244.

Ehrlich, S., & Rayner, K. (1981). Contextual effects on word perception and eye movements during reading. *Journal of Verbal Learning and Verbal Behavior*, *20*, 641–655.

Ellis, A. (1984). *Reading, writing, and dyslexia: A cognitive analysis*. Hillsdale, NJ: Erlbaum.

Evans, M.A., & Carr, T.H. (1985). Cognitive abilities, conditions of learning, and the early development of reading skill. *Reading Research Quarterly*, *20*, 327–350.

Feitelson, D., & Goldstein, Z. (1986). Patterns of book ownership and reading to young children in Israeli school-oriented and nonschool-oriented families. *The Reading Teacher, 39,* 924–930.

Fielding, L., Wilson, P., & Anderson, R. (1986). A new focus on free reading: The role of trade books in reading instruction. In T. Raphael & R. Reynolds (Eds.), *Contexts of literacy.* New York: Longman.

Fleisher, L.S., Jenkins, J.R., & Pany, D. (1979). Effects on poor readers' comprehension of training in rapid decoding. *Reading Research Quarterly, 15,* 30–48.

Fletcher, J.M. (1981). Linguistic factors in reading acquisition. In F. Pirozzolo & M. Wittrock (Eds.), *Neuropsychology and cognitive processes in reading* (pp. 261–294). New York: Academic Press.

Fletcher, J.M., Satz, P., & Scholes, R. (1981). Developmental changes in the linguistic performance correlates of reading achievement. *Brain and Language, 13,* 78–90.

Fodor, J. (1983). *Modularity of mind.* Cambridge, MA: MIT Press.

Forell, E.R. (1985). The case for conservative reader placement. *The Reading Teacher, 33,* 857–862.

Forster, K.I. (1979). Levels of processing and the structure of the language processor. In W.E. Cooper & E. Walker (Eds.), *Sentence processing: Psycholinguistic studies presented to Merrill Garrett* (pp. 27–85). Hillsdale, NJ: Erlbaum.

Foster, R., & Gavelek, J. (1983). Development of intentional forgetting in normal and reading-delayed children. *Journal of Educational Psychology, 75,* 431–440.

Fowler, J., & Peterson, P. (1981). Increasing reading persistence and altering attributional style of learned helpless children. *Journal of Educational Psychology, 73,* 251–260.

Fox, B., & Routh, D.K. (1975). Analyzing spoken language into words, syllables, and phonemes: A developmental study. *Journal of Psycholinguistic Research, 4,* 331–342.

Fox, B., & Routh, D.K. (1984). Phonemic analysis and synthesis as word attack skills: Revisited. *Journal of Educational Psychology, 76,* 1059–1064.

Gajar, A. (1979). Educable mentally retarded, learning disabled, emotionally disturbed: Similarities and differences. *Exceptional Children, 45,* 470–472.

Gambrell, L.B., Wilson, R.M., & Gantt, W.N. (1981). Classroom observations of task-attending behaviors of good and poor readers.

Journal of Educational Research, 74, 400–404.

Godfrey, J.J., Syrdal-Lasky, A.K., Millay, K.K., & Knox, C.M. (1981). Performance of dyslexic children on speech perception tests. *Journal of Experimental Child Psychology, 32,* 401–424

Goldstein, D. (1976). Cognitive-linguistic functioning and learning to read in preschoolers. *Journal of Educational Psychology, 68,* 680–698.

Goodman, G.S., Haith, M.M., Guttentag, R.E., & Rao, S. (1985). Automatic processing of word meaning: Intralingual and interlingual interference. *Child Development, 56,* 103–118.

Goodman, K.S. (1968). The psycholinguistic nature of the reading process. In K.S. Goodman (Ed.), *The psycholinguistic nature of the reading process* (pp. 13–26). Detroit, MI: Wayne State University Press.

Goodman, K.S. (1973). The 13th easy way to make learning to read difficult: A reaction to Gleitman and Rozin. *Reading Research Quarterly, 8,* 484–493.

Goodman, K.S. (1976). Reading: A psycholinguistic guessing game. In H. Singer & R.B. Ruddell (Eds.), *Theoretical models and processes of reading* (pp. 497–508). Newark, DE: International Reading Association.

Goodman, K.S., & Gollasch, F.V. (1980). Word omissions: Deliberate and non-deliberate. *Reading Research Quarterly, 16,* 6–31.

Goody, J. (1977). *The domestication of the savage mind.* New York: Cambridge University Press.

Gottesman, R., Croen, L., & Rotkin, L. (1982). Urban second grade children: A profile of good and poor readers. *Journal of Learning Disabilities, 15,* 268–272.

Gough, P.B. (1983). Context, form, and interaction. In K. Rayner (Ed.), *Eye movements in reading* (pp. 203–211). New York: Academic Press.

Gough, P.B., & Hillinger, M.L. (1980). Learning to read. An unnatural act. *Bulletin of the Orton Society, 30,* 171–176.

Gough, P.B., & Tunmer, W.E. (1986). Decoding, reading, and reading disability. *Remedial and Special Education, 7,* 6–10.

Gross, J., & Gottlieb, J. (1982). The mildly handicapped: A service distinction for the future? In T. Miller & E. Davis (Eds.), *The mildly handicapped student* (pp. 497–511). New York: Grune & Stratton.

Guthrie, J. (1981). Reading in New Zealand: Achievement and volume. *Reading Research Quarterly*, *17*, 6–27.

Guttentag, R. (1984). Semantic memory organization in second graders and adults. *Journal of General Psychology*, *110*, 81–86.

Guttentag, R., & Haith, M. (1978). Automatic processing as a function of age and reading ability. *Child Development*, *49*, 707–716.

Guttentag, R., & Haith, M. (1980). A longitudinal study of word processing by first grade children. *Journal of Educational Psychology*, *72*, 701–705.

Hagen, J., Barclay, C., & Newman, R. (1982). Metacognition, self-knowledge, and learning disabilities: Some thoughts on knowing and doing. *Topics in Learning and Learning Disabilities*, *2*, 19–26.

Hall, J., & Humphreys, M. (1982). Research on specific learning disabilities: Deficits and re-mediation. *Topics in Learning and Learning Disabilities*, *2*, 68–78.

Hallahan, D., & Bryan, T. (1981). Learning disabilities. In J. Kauffman & D. Hallahan (Eds.), *Handbook of special education* (pp. 141–164). Englewood Cliffs, NJ: Prentice Hall.

Hallahan, D., & Kauffman, J. (1977). Labels, categories, behaviors: ED, LD, and EMR reconsidered. *Journal of Special Education*, *11*, 139–149.

Harding, L.M. (1984). Reading errors and style in children with a specific reading disability. *Journal of Research in Reading*, *7*, 103–112.

Henderson, L. (1982). *Orthography and word recognition in reading*. London: Academic Press.

Herman, P.A. (1985). The effect of repeated reading on reading rate, speech pauses, and word recognition accuracy. *Reading Research Quarterly*, *20*, 553–565.

Hiebert, E.H. (1983). An examination of ability grouping for reading instruction. *Reading Research Quarterly*, *18*, 231–255.

Hoffman, J., & Rutherford, W. (1984). Effective reading programs: A critical review of outlier studies. *Reading Research Quarterly*, *20*, 79–92.

Hood, J., & Dubert, L.A. (1983). Decoding as a component of reading comprehension among secondary students. *Journal of Reading Behavior*, *15*, 51–61.

Horn, W.F., & O'Donnell, J.P. (1984). Early identification of learning disabilities: A comparison of two methods. *Journal of Educational Psychology*, *76*, 1106–1118.

Jackson, M. (1980). Further evidence for a relationship between memory access and reading ability. *Journal of Verbal Learning and Verbal Behavior*, *19*, 683–694.

Jackson, M., & McClelland, J. (1975). Sensory and cognitive determinants of reading speed. *Journal of Verbal Learning and Verbal Behavior*, *14*, 565–574.

Jackson, M., & McClelland, J. (1979). Processing determinants of reading speed. *Journal of Experimental Psychology: General*, *108*, 151–181.

Jackson, N.E., & Biemiller, A.J. (1985). Letter, word, and text reading times of precocious and average readers. *Child Development*, *56*, 196–206.

Jakimik, J., Cole, R.A., & Rudnicky, A.I. (1985). Sound and spelling in spoken word recognition. *Journal of Memory and Language*, *24*, 165–178.

Jencks, C. (1972). *Inequality*. New York: Basic Books.

Jenkins, J., & Dixon, R. (1983). Vocabulary learning. *Contemporary Educational Psychology*, *8*, 237–260.

Jenkins, J., Stein, M., & Wysocki, K. (1984). Learning vocabulary through reading. *American Educational Research Journal*, *21*, 767–787.

Johnston, P.H., & Winograd, P.N. (1985). Passive failure in reading. *Journal of Reading Behavior*, *17*, 279–301.

Jorgenson, G. (1977). Relationship of classroom behavior to the accuracy of the match between material difficulty and student ability. *Journal of Educational Psychology*, *69*, 24–32.

Jorm, A. (1983). Specific reading retardation and working memory: A review. *British Journal of Psychology*, *74*, 311–342.

Jorm, A., & Share, D. (1983). Phonological recoding and reading acquisition. *Applied Psycholinguistics*, *4*, 103–147.

Jorm, A., Share, D., Maclean, R., & Matthews, R. (1984). Phonological recoding skills and learning to read: A longitudinal study. *Applied Psycholinguistics*, *5*, 201–207.

Jorm, A., Share, D., Maclean, R., & Matthews R. (1986). Cognitive factors at school entry predictive of specific reading retardation and general reading backwardness: A research note. *Journal of Child Psychology and Psychiatry*, *27*, 45–54.

Juel, C. (1980). Comparison of word identification strategies with varying context, word type, and reader skill. *Reading Research Quarterly*, *15*, 358–376.

Juel, C. (1983). The development and use of mediated word identification. *Reading Research Quarterly*, *18*, 306–327.

Just, M.A., & Carpenter, P.A. (1980). A theory of reading: From eye fixations to comprehension. *Psychological Review*, *4*, 329–354.

Kavale, K., & Mattson, P. (1983). "One jumped off the balance beam": Meta-analysis of perceptual-motor training. *Journal of Learning Disabilities*, *16*, 165–173.

Keil, F. (1984). Mechanisms of cognitive development and the structure of knowledge. In R. Sternberg (Ed.), *Mechanisms of cognitive development* (pp. 81–99). New York: W.H. Freeman.

Kibby, M.W. (1979). Passage readability affects the oral reading strategies of disabled readers. *The Reading Teacher*, *32*, 390–396.

Kimura, Y., & Bryant, P. (1983). Reading and writing in English and Japanese: A cross-cultural study of young children. *British Journal of Developmental Psychology*, *1*, 143–154.

Kirk, S., & Elkins, J. (1975). Characteristics of children enrolled in the child service demonstration centers. *Journal of Learning Disabilities*, *8*, 630–637.

Klinge, V., Rennick, P., Lennox, K., & Hart, Z. (1977). A matched-subject comparison of underachievers with normals on intellectual, behavioral, and emotional variables. *Journal of Abnormal Child Psychology*, *5*, 61–68.

Kotsonis, M., & Patterson, C. (1980). Comprehension-monitoring skills in learning-disabled children. *Developmental Psychology*, *16*, 541–542.

Kraut, A.G., & Smothergill, D.W. (1980). New method for studying semantic encoding in children. *Developmental Psychology*, *16*, 149–150.

Laberge, D., & Samuels, S.J. (1974). Toward a theory of automatic information processing in reading. *Cognitive Psychology*, *6*, 293–323.

Larkin, J., McDermott, J., Simon, D., & Simon, H. (1980). Expert and novice performance in solving physics problems. *Science*, *208*, 1335–1342.

Leinhardt, G., Seewald, A., & Zigmond, N. (1982). Sex and race differences in learning disabilities classrooms. *Journal of Educational Psychology*, *74*, 835–843.

Lerner, R., & Busch-Rossnagel, N. (1981). *Individuals as producers of their development: A life-span perspective*. New York: Academic Press.

Lesgold, A., & Resnick, L. (1982). How reading difficulties develop: Perspectives from a longitudinal study. In J. Das, R. Mulcahey, & A. Wall (Eds.), *Theory and research in learning disabilities* (pp. 155–187). New York: Plenum.

Lesgold, A., Resnick, L., & Hammond, K. (1985). Learning to read: A longitudinal study of word skill development in two curricula. In G. MacKinnon & T. Walter (Eds.), *Reading research: Advances in theory and practice* (Vol. 4, pp. 107–138). London: Academic Press.

Leu, D. (1982). Oral reading error analysis: A critical review of research and application. *Reading Research Quarterly*, *17*, 420–437.

Levine, K. (1982). Functional literacy: Fond illusions and false economics. *Harvard Educational Review*, *52*, 249–266.

Levy, B.A. (1981). Interactive processes during reading. In A. Lesgold & C. Perfetti (Eds.), *Interactive processes in reading* (pp. 1–35). Hillsdale, NJ: Erlbaum.

Liberman, I. (1982). A language-oriented view of reading and its disabilities. In H. Mykelbust (Ed.), *Progress in learning disabilities* (Vol. 5, pp. 81–101). New York: Grune & Stratton.

Licht, B., & Dweck, C. (1984). Determinants of academic achievement: The interaction of children's achievement orientations with skill area. *Developmental Psychology*, *20*, 628–636.

Lomax, R. (1983). Applying structural modeling to some component processes of reading comprehension development. *Journal of Experimental Education*, *52*, 33–40.

Lovett, M. (1984). A developmental perspective on reading dysfunction: Accuracy and rate criteria in the subtyping of dyslexic children. *Brain and Language*, *22*, 67–91.

Lundberg, I. (1985). Longitudinal studies of reading and reading difficulties in Sweden. In G. MacKinnon & T. Waller (Eds.), *Reading research: Advances in theory and practice* (Vol. 4, pp. 65–105). London: Academic Press.

Mann, V. (1984). Reading skill and language skill. *Developmental Review*, *4*, 1–15.

Mann, V. (1986). Why some children encounter reading problems. In J. Torgesen & B. Wong (Eds.), *Psychological and educational perspectives on learning disabilities* (pp. 133–159). New York: Academic Press.

Maruyama, G., Rubin, R., & Kingsbury, G. (1981). Self-esteem and educational achievement: Independent constructs with a common cause? *Journal of Personality and Social Psychology, 40,* 962–975.

Mason, M. (1978). From print to sound in mature readers as a function of reader ability and two forms of orthographic regularity. *Memory & Cognition, 6,* 568–581.

Masonheimer, P.E., Drum, P.A., & Ehri, L.C. (1984). Does environmental print identification lead children into word reading? *Journal of Reading Behavior, 16,* 257–271.

Masson, E.J., & Sala, L.S. (1978). Interactive processes in sentence comprehension and reading. *Cognitive Psychology, 10,* 244–270.

McCall, R.B. (1981). Nature-nurture and the two realms of development: A proposed integration with respect to mental development. *Child Development, 52,* 1–12.

McClure, J., Kalk, M., & Keenan, V. (1980). Use of grammatical morphemes by beginning readers. *Journal of Learning Disabilities, 13,* 262–267.

McConkie, G.W., & Zola, D. (1981). Language constraints and the functional stimulus in reading. In A.M. Lesgold & C.A. Perfetti (Eds.), *Interactive processes in reading* (pp. 155–175). Hillsdale, NJ: Erlbaum.

McConkie, G.W., & Zola, D. (1985, April). *Computer aided reading: An environment for developmental research.* Paper presented at the meeting of the Society for Research in Child Development, Toronto, Ontario, Canada.

McCusker, L.X., Hillinger, M.L., & Bias, R.G. (1981). Phonological recoding and reading. *Psychological Bulletin, 89,* 217–245.

McKeown, M., Beck, I., Omanson, R., & Perfetti, C. (1983). The effects of long-term vocabulary instruction on reading comprehension: A replication. *Journal of Reading Behavior, 15,* 3–18.

McLeskey, J., & Rieth, H. (1982). Controlling IQ differences between reading disabled and normal children: An empirical example. *Journal of Learning Disabilities, 15,* 481–493.

Menyuk, P., & Flood, J. (1981). Linguistic competence, reading, writing problems, and re-mediation. *Bulletin of the Orton Society, 31,* 13–28.

Merton, R.K. (1968). The Matthew effect in science. *Science, 159*(3810), 56–63.

Mezynski, K. (1983). Issues concerning the acquisition of knowledge: Effects of vocabulary training on reading comprehension. *Review of Educational Research, 53,* 253–279.

Miller, T., & Davis, E. (1982). *The mildly handicapped student.* New York: Grune & Stratton.

Mitchell, D. (1982). *The process of reading: A cognitive analysis of fluent reading and learning to read.* Chichester, UK: John Wiley.

Morris, J. (1984). Children like Frank, deprived of literacy unless.... In D. Dennis (Ed.), *Reading: Meeting children's special needs* (pp. 16–28). London: Heinemann.

Morrison, F.J., & Manis, F.R. (1982). Cognitive processes and reading disability: A critique and proposal. In C. Brainerd & M. Pressley (Eds.), *Verbal processes in children* (pp. 59–93). New York: Springer-Verlag.

Nagy, W.E., & Anderson, R.C. (1984). How many words are there in printed school English? *Reading Research Quarterly, 19,* 304–330.

Nagy, W.E., Herman, P.A., & Anderson, R.C. (1985). Learning words from context. *Reading Research Quarterly, 20,* 233–253.

Newcomer, P., & Magee, P. (1977). The performance of learning (reading) disabled children on a test of spoken language. *The Reading Teacher, 30,* 896–900.

Newman, D.S., & Hagen, J.W. (1981). Memory strategies in children with learning disabilities. *Journal of Applied Developmental Psychology, 1,* 297–312.

Norman, C., & Zigmond, N. (1980). Characteristics of children labeled and served as learning disabled in school systems affiliated with child service demonstration centers. *Journal of Learning Disabilities, 13,* 16–21.

Oka, E., & Paris, S. (1986). Patterns of motivation and reading skills in underachieving children. In S. Ceci (Ed.), *Handbook of cognitive, social, and neuropsychological aspects of learning disabilities* (Vol. 2). Hillsdale, NJ: Erlbaum.

Olofsson, A., & Lundberg, I. (1985). Evaluation of long term effects of phonemic awareness training in kindergarten. *Scandinavian Journal of Psychology, 26,* 21–34.

Olson, D. (1977). From utterance to text: The bias of language in speech and writing. *Harvard Educational Review, 47,* 257–281.

Olson, D., Torrance, N., & Hildyard, A. (1985). *Literacy, language, and learning.* New York: Cambridge University Press.

Olson, R., Foltz, G., & Wise, B. (1986). Reading instruction and remediation with the aid of computer speech. *Behavior Research Methods, Instruments, & Computers, 18*, 93–99.

Olson, R., Kliegl, R., & Davidson, B. (1983). Dyslexic and normal readers' eye movements. *Journal of Experimental Psychology: Human Perception and Performance, 9*, 816–825.

Olson, R., Kliegl, R., Davidson, B., & Foltz, G. (1985). Individual and developmental differences in reading disability. In G. MacKinnon & T. Waller (Eds.), *Reading research: Advances in theory and practice* (Vol. 4, pp. 1–64). London: Academic Press.

Palmer, J., MacLeod, C.M., Hunt, E., & Davidson, J.E. (1985). Information processing correlates of reading. *Journal of Memory and Language, 24*, 59–88.

Perfetti, C.A. (1984). Reading acquisition and beyond: Decoding includes cognition. *American Journal of Education, 92*, 40–60.

Perfetti, C.A. (1985). *Reading ability.* New York: Oxford University Press.

Perfetti, C.A. (1986). Continuities in reading acquisition, reading skill, and reading disability. *Remedial and Special Education, 7*, 11–21.

Perfetti, C.A., Beck, I. & Hughes, C. (1981, March). *Phonemic knowledge and learning to read.* Paper presented at the meeting of the Society for Research in Child Development, Boston, MA.

Perfetti, C.A., Goldman, S., & Hogaboam, T. (1979). Reading skill and the identification of words in discourse context. *Memory & Cognition, 7*, 273–282.

Perfetti, C.A., & Roth, S. (1981). Some of the interactive processes in reading and their role in reading skill. In A. Lesgold & C. Perfetti (Eds.), *Interactive processes in reading* (pp. 269–297). Hillsdale, NJ: Erlbaum.

Perin, D. (1983). Phonemic segmentation and spelling. *British Journal of Psychology, 74*, 129–144.

Plomin, R., DeFries, J., & Loehlin, J. (1977). Genotype-environment interaction and correlation in the analysis of human behavior. *Psychological Bulletin, 84*, 309–322.

Prior, M., & McCorriston, M. (1985). Surface dyslexia: A regression effect? *Brain and Language, 25*, 52–71.

Rayner, K. (1978). Eye movements in reading and information processing. *Psychological Bulletin, 85*, 618–660.

Rayner, K. (1985a). Do faulty eye movements cause dyslexia? *Developmental Neuropsychology, 1*, 3–15.

Rayner, K. (1985b). The role of eye movements in learning to read and reading disability. *Remedial and Special Education, 6*, 53–60.

Rayner, K., & Bertera, J.H. (1979). Reading without a fovea. *Science, 206*, 468–469.

Rayner, K., Inhoff, A.W., Morrison, R.E., Slowiaczek, M.L., & Bertera, J.H. (1981). Masking of foveal and parafoveal vision during eye fixations in reading. *Journal of Experimental Psychology: Human Perception and Performance, 7*, 167–179.

Reitsma, P. (1983). Printed word learning in beginning readers. *Journal of Experimental Child Psychology, 36*, 321–339.

Remma, P. (1984). Sound priming in beginning readers. *Child Development, 55*, 406–423.

Resnick, D.P., & Resnick, L.B. (1977). The nature of literacy: An historical exploration. *Harvard Educational Review, 47*, 370–385.

Richardson, E., DiBenedetto, B., & Adler, A. (1982). Use of the decoding skills test to study differences between good and poor readers. In K. Gadow & I. Bialer (Eds.), *Advances in learning and behavioral disabilities* (Vol. 1, pp. 25–74). Greenwich, CT: JAI Press.

Richek, M. (1977/1978). Readiness skills that predict initial word learning using two different methods of instruction. *Reading Research Quarterly, 13*, 200–222.

Rosinski, R. (1977). Picture-word interference is semantically based. *Child Development, 48*, 643–647.

Ruddell, R. (1965). The effect of similarity of oral and written patterns of language structure on reading comprehension. *Elementary English, 42*, 403–410.

Rutter, M. (1978). Prevalence and types of dyslexia. In A. Benton & D. Pearl (Eds.), *Dyslexia: An appraisal of current knowledge* (pp. 5–28). New York: Oxford University Press.

Rutter, M. (1983). School effects on pupil progress: Research findings and policy implications. *Child Development, 54*, 1–29.

Rutter, M., & Madge, N. (1976). *Cycles of disadvantage.* London: Heinemann.

Rutter, M., Yule, B., Quintin, D., Rowlands, O., Yule, W., & Berger, M. (1974). Attainment and adjustment in two geographical areas: III. Some factors accounting for area differences. *British Journal of Psychiatry, 125*, 520–533.

Rutter, M., & Yule, W. (1975). The concept of specific reading retardation. *Journal of Child Psychology and Psychiatry, 16*, 181–197.

Satz, P., & Friel, J. (1974). Some predictive antecedents of specific reading disability: A preliminary two-year follow-up. *Journal of Learning Disabilities, 7*, 437–444.

Satz, P., Taylor, H., Friel, J., & Fletcher, J. (1978). Some developmental and predictive precursors of reading disabilities: A six year follow-up. In A. Benton & D. Pearl (Eds.), *Dyslexia: An appraisal of current knowledge* (pp. 325–347). New York: Oxford University Press.

Scarr, S., & McCartney, K. (1983). How people make their own environments. *Child Development, 54*, 424–435.

Schatz, E.K., & Baldwin, R.S. (1986). Context clues are unreliable predictors of word meanings. *Reading Research Quarterly, 21*, 439–453.

Schvaneveldt, R., Ackerman, B., & Semlear, T. (1977). The effect of semantic context on children's word recognition. *Child Development, 48*, 612–616.

Schwantes, F.M. (1981). Effect of story context on children's ongoing word recognition. *Journal of Reading Behavior, 13*, 305–311.

Schwantes, F.M. (1982). Text readability level and developmental differences in context effects. *Journal of Reading Behavior, 14*, 5–12.

Schwantes, F.M. (1985). Expectancy, integration,. and interactional processes: Age differences in the nature of words affected by sentence context. *Journal of Experimental Child Psychology, 39*, 212–229.

Schwantes, F.M., Boesl, S., & Ritz, E. (1980). Children's use of context in word recognition: A psycholinguistic guessing game. *Child Development, 51*, 730–736.

Schwartz, R., & Stanovich, K. (1981). Flexibility in the use of graphic and contextual information by good and poor readers. *Journal of Reading Behavior, 13*, 263–269.

Scribner, S., & Cole, M. (1981). *The psychology of literacy*. Cambridge, MA: Harvard University Press.

Seidenberg, M. (1985a). Lexicon as module. *Behavioral and Brain Sciences, 8*, 31–32.

Seidenberg, M. (1985b). The time course of information activation and utilization in visual word recognition. In D. Besner, T. Waller, & G. MacKinnon (Eds.), *Reading research: Advances in theory and practice* (Vol. 5, pp. 199–252). New York: Academic Press.

Seidenberg, M., & Tanenhaus, M. (1979). Orthographic effects on rhyme monitoring. *Journal of Experimental Psychology: Human Learning and Memory, 5*, 546–554.

Seidenberg, M., Waters, G., Barnes, M., & Tanenhaus, M. (1984). When does irregular spelling or pronunciation influence word recognition? *Journal of Verbal Learning and Verbal Behavior, 23*, 383–404.

Seidenberg, M., Waters, G., Sanders, M., & Langer, P. (1984). Pre- and post-lexical loci of contextual effects on word recognition. *Memory & Cognition, 12*, 315–328.

Semel, E., & Wiig, E. (1975). Comprehension of syntactic structures and critical verbal elements by children with learning disabilities. *Journal of Learning Disabilities, 8*, 53–58.

Share, D.L., Jorm, A.F., Maclean, R., & Matthews, R. (1984). Sources of individual differences in reading acquisition. *Journal of Educational Psychology, 76*, 1309–1324.

Shepard, L. (1980). An evaluation of the regression discrepancy method for identifying children with learning disabilities. *Journal of Special Education, 14*, 79–91.

Shepard, L., Smith, M., & Vojir, C. (1983). Characteristics of pupils identified as learning disabled. *American Educational Research Journal, 20*, 309–332.

Siegel, L., & Ryan, E. (1984). Reading disability as a language disorder. *Remedial and Special Education, 5*, 28–33.

Siler, E.R. (1974). The effects of syntactic and semantic constraints on the oral reading performance of second and fourth graders. *Reading Research Quarterly, 9*, 603–621.

Simpson, G., & Foster, M. (1985, April). *Lexical ambiguity and children's word recognition*. Paper presented at the meeting of the Society for Research in Child Development, Toronto.

Simpson, G., & Lorsbach, T. (1983). The development of automatic and conscious components of contextual facilitation. *Child Development, 54*, 760–772.

Simpson, G., Lorsbach, T., & Whitehouse, D. (1983). Encoding and contextual components of word recognition in good and poor readers. *Journal of Experimental Child Psychology, 35*, 161–171.

Singer, M., & Crouse, J. (1981). The relationship of context-use skills to reading: A case for an alternative experimental logic. *Child Development, 52*, 1326–1329.

Smiley, S., Oakley, D., Worthen, D., Campione, J., & Brown, A. (1977). Recall of thematically relevant material by adolescent good and poor readers as a function of written versus oral presentation. *Journal of Educational Psychology, 69*, 381–387.

Smith, E.B., Goodman, K.S., & Meredith, R. (1976). *Language and thinking in school.* New York: Holt, Rinehart & Winston.

Smith, F. (1971). *Understanding reading.* New York: Holt, Rinehart & Winston.

Smith, F. (1973). *Psycholinguistics and reading.* New York: Holt, Rinehart & Winston.

Smith, F. (1978). *Understanding reading* (2nd ed.). New York: Holt, Rinehart & Winston.

Smith, F. (1979). *Reading without nonsense.* New York: Teachers College Press.

Smith, F. (1982). *Understanding reading* (3rd ed.). New York: Holt, Rinehart & Winston.

Smith, M.D., Coleman, J.M., Dokecki, P.R., & Davis, E.E. (1977). Intellectual characteristics of school labeled learning disabled children. *Exceptional Children, 43*, 352–357.

Snowling, M. (1980). The development of grapheme-phoneme correspondence in normal and dyslexic readers. *Journal of Experimental Child Psychology, 29*, 294–305.

Snowling, M. (1981). Phonemic deficits in developmental dyslexia. *Psychological Research, 43*, 219–234.

Snowling, M. (1983). The comparison of acquired and developmental disorders of reading—A discussion. *Cognition, 14*, 105–118.

Spring, C., & Capps, C. (1974). Encoding speed, rehearsal, and probed recall of dyslexic boys. *Journal of Educational Psychology, 66*, 780–786.

Stahl, S. (1983). Differential word knowledge and reading comprehension. *Journal of Reading Behavior, 15*, 33–50.

Stanley, G., Smith, G., & Howell, E. (1983). Eye-movements and sequential tracking in dyslexic and control children. *British Journal of Psychology, 74*, 181–187.

Stanovich, K.E. (1980). Toward an interactive-compensatory model of individual differences in the development of reading fluency. *Reading Research Quarterly, 16*, 32–71.

Stanovich, K.E. (1982a). Individual differences in the cognitive processes of reading: I. Word decoding. *Journal of Learning Disabilities, 15*, 485–493.

Stanovich, K.E. (1982b). Individual differences in the cognitive processes of reading: II. Text-level processes. *Journal of Learning Disabilities, 15*, 549–554.

Stanovich, K.E. (1984). The interactive-compensatory model of reading: A confluence of developmental, experimental, and educational psychology. *Remedial and Special Education, 5*, 11–19.

Stanovich, K.E. (1986). Cognitive processes and the reading problems of learning disabled children: Evaluating the assumption of specificity. In J. Torgesen & B. Wong (Eds.), *Psychological and educational perspectives on learning disabilities* (pp. 87–131). New York: Academic Press.

Stanovich, K.E., Cunningham, A.E., & Cramer, B. (1984). Assessing phonological awareness in kindergarten children: Issues of task comparability. *Journal of Experimental Child Psychology, 38*, 175–190.

Stanovich, K.E., Cunningham, A.E., & Feeman, D.J. (1984a). Intelligence, cognitive skills, and early reading progress. *Reading Research Quarterly, 19*, 278–303.

Stanovich, K.E., Cunningham, A.E., & Feeman, D.J. (1984b). Relation between early reading acquisition and word decoding with and without context: A longitudinal study of first-grade children. *Journal of Educational Psychology, 76*, 668–677.

Stanovich, K.E., Nathan, R.G., & Vala-Rossi, M. (1986). Developmental changes in the cognitive correlates of reading ability and the developmental lag hypothesis. *Reading Research Quarterly, 21*, 267–283.

Stanovich, K.E., Nathan, R.G., West, R.F., & Vala-Rossi, M. (1985). Children's word recognition in context: Spreading activation, expectancy, and modularity. *Child Development, 56*, 1418–1429.

Stanovich, K.E., & West, R.F. (1981). The effect of sentence context on ongoing word recognition: Tests of a two-process theory. *Journal of Experimental Psychology: Human Perception and Performance, 7*, 658–672.

Stanovich, K.E., & West, R.F. (1983). On priming by a sentence context. *Journal of Experimental Psychology: General, 112*, 1–36.

Stanovich, K.E., West, R.F., & Feeman, D.J. (1981). A longitudinal study of sentence context effects in second-grade children: Tests of an interactive-compensatory model. *Journal of Experimental Child Psychology, 32*, 185–199.

Stein, C.L., Cairns, H.S., & Zurif, E.B. (1984). Sentence comprehension limitations related to syntactic deficits in reading-disabled children. *Applied Psycholinguistics, 5*, 305–322.

Sternberg, R. (1980). Sketch of a componential subtheory of human intelligence. *Behavioral and Brain Sciences, 3*, 573–584.

Sternberg, R. (1982). Introduction: Some common themes in contemporary approaches to the training of intelligent performances. In D. Detterman & R. Sternberg (Eds.), *How and how much can intelligence be increased?* (pp. 141–146). Norwood, NJ: Ablex.

Sternberg, R. (1985). *Beyond IQ: A triarchic theory of human intelligence.* New York: Cambridge University Press.

Sternberg, R., & Powell, J. (1983). Comprehending verbal comprehension. *American Psychologist, 38*, 878–893.

Sternberg, R., Powell, J., & Kaye, D. (1982). The nature of verbal comprehension. *Poetics, 11*, 155–187.

Stevenson, H., Parker, T., Wilkinson, A., Hegion, A., & Fish, E. (1976). Longitudinal study of individual differences in cognitive development and scholastic achievement. *Journal of Educational Psychology, 68*, 377–400.

Stevenson, H., Stigler, J., Lee, S., Lucker, G., Kitamura, S., & Hsu, C. (1985). Cognitive performance and academic achievement of Japanese, Chinese, and American children. *Child Development, 56*, 718–734.

Sticht, T. (1979). Applications of the audread model to reading evaluation and instruction. In L.B. Resnick & P. Weaver (Eds.), *Theory and practice of early reading* (pp. 209–226). Hillsdale, NJ: Erlbaum.

Strange, M. (1979). The effect of orthographic anomalies upon reading behavior. *Journal of Reading Behavior, 11*, 153–161.

Tallal, P. (1980). Auditory temporal perception, phonics, and reading disabilities in children. *Brain and Language, 9*, 182–198.

Tarver, S.G. (1982). Characteristics of learning disabilities. In T. Miller & E. Davis (Eds.), *The mildly handicapped student* (pp. 17–36). New York: Grune & Stratton.

Tarver, S.G., Hallahan, D.P., Kauffman, J.M., & Ball, D.W. (1976). Verbal rehearsal and selective attention in children with learning disabilities: A developmental lag. *Journal of Experimental Child Psychology, 22*, 275–285.

Taylor, H.J., Satz, P., & Friel, J. (1979). Developmental dyslexia in relation to other childhood reading disorders: Significance and clinical utility. *Reading Research Quarterly, 15*, 84–101.

Tinker, M. (1958). Recent studies of eye movements in reading. *Psychological Bulletin, 55*, 215–231.

Tizard, J. (1975). Race and IQ: The limits of probability. *New Behaviour, 1*, 6–9.

Torgesen, J. (1977a). Memorization processes in reading-disabled children. *Journal of Educational Psychology, 69*, 571–578.

Torgesen, J. (1977b). The role of nonspecific factors in the task performance of learning disabled children: A theoretical assessment. *Journal of Learning Disabilities, 10*, 27–34.

Torgesen, J. (1978/1979). Performance of reading disabled children on serial memory tasks. *Reading Research Quarterly, 14*, 57–87.

Torgesen, J. (1982). The use of rationally defined subgroups in research on learning disabilities. In J. Das, R. Mulcahey, & A. Wall (Eds.), *Theory and research in learning disabilities* (pp. 111–131). New York: Plenum.

Torgesen, J. (1985). Memory processes in reading disabled children. *Journal of Learning Disabilities, 18*, 350–357.

Torgesen, J., & Dice, C. (1980). Characteristics of research in learning disabilities. *Journal of Learning Disabilities, 13*, 531–535.

Torgesen, J., & Goldman, T. (1977). Verbal rehearsal and short-term memory in reading-disabled children. *Child Development, 48*, 56–60.

Torgesen, J., & Houck, D. (1980). Processing deficiencies of learning-disabled children who perform poorly on the digit span test. *Journal of Educational Psychology, 72*, 141–160.

Torgesen, J., & Licht, B. (1983). The learning disabled child as an inactive learner: Retrospect and prospects. In J. McKinney & L. Feagans (Eds.), *Topics in learning disabilities* (Vol. 1, pp. 100–130). Norwood, NJ: Ablex.

Torneus, M. (1984). Phonological awareness and reading: A chicken and egg problem? *Journal of Educational Psychology, 70*, 1340–1358.

Treiman, R., & Baron, J. (1983). Phonemic-analysis training helps children benefit from spelling-sound rules. *Memory & Cognition, 11*, 382–389.

Treiman, R., & Hirsh-Pasek, K. (1985). Are there qualitative differences in reading behavior between dyslexics and normal readers? *Memory & Cognition, 13*, 357–364.

Tunmer, W.E., & Nesdale, A.R. (1985). Phonemic segmentation skill and beginning reading. *Journal of Educational Psychology*, 77, 417–427.

Underwood, G. (1985). Information processing in skilled readers. In G. MacKinnon & T. Waller (Eds.), *Reading research: Advances in theory and practice* (Vol. 4, pp. 139–181). London: Academic Press.

Valtin, R. (1978/1979). Deficit in reading or deficit in research? *Reading Research Quarterly*, 14, 201–221.

Vellutino, F. (1979). *Dyslexia: Theory and research*. Cambridge, MA: MIT Press.

Venezky, R.L. (1976). *Theoretical and experimental base for reaching reading*. The Hague, the Netherlands: Mouton.

Vogel, S. (1974). Syntactic abilities in normal and dyslexic children. *Journal of Learning Disabilities*, 7, 103–109.

Wachs, T., & Mariotto, M. (1978). Criteria for the assessment of organism–environment correlation in human developmental studies. *Human Development*, 21, 268–288.

Wagner, R.K., & Torgesen, J.K. (1987). The nature of phonological processing and its causal role in the acquisition of reading skills. *Psychological Bulletin*, 102, 192–212.

Walberg, H.J., Strykowski, B.F, Rovai, E., & Hung, S.S. (1984). Exceptional performance. *Review of Educational Research*, 54, 87–112.

Walberg, H.J., & Tsai, S. (1983). Matthew effects in education. *American Educational Research Journal*, 20, 359–373.

Waters, G., & Seidenberg, M. (1985). Spelling-sound effects in reading: Time-course and decision criteria. *Memory & Cognition*, 13, 557–572.

Waters, G., Seidenberg, M., & Bruck, M. (1984). Children's and adults' use of spelling-sound information in three reading tasks. *Memory & Cognition*, 12, 293–305.

Weber, R. (1970). A linguistic analysis of first-grade reading errors. *Reading Research Quarterly*, 5, 427–451.

West, R.F., & Stanovich, K.E. (1978). Automatic contextual facilitation in readers of three ages. *Child Development*, 49, 717–727.

West, R.F., & Stanovich, K.E. (1982). Source of inhibition in experiments on the effect of sentence context on word recognition. *Journal of Experimental Psychology: Learning, Memory, and Cognition*, 8, 385–399.

West, R.F., Stanovich, K.E., Feeman, D.J., & Cunningham, A.E. (1983). The effect of sentence context on word recognition in second-

and sixth-grade children. *Reading Research Quarterly*, 19, 6–15.

Whaley, J., & Kibby, M. (1981). The relative importance of reliance on intraword characteristics and interword constraints for beginning reading achievement. *Journal of Educational Research*, 74, 315–320.

Wilkinson, A.C., Guminski, M., Stanovich, K.E., & West, R.F. (1981). Optional interaction between visual recognition and memory in oral reading. *Journal of Experimental Psychology: Human Learning and Memory*, 7, 111–119.

Williams, J. (1984). Phonemic analysis and how it relates to reading. *Journal of Learning Disabilities*, 17, 240–245.

Wilson, L.R., & Cone, T. (1984). The regression equation method of determining academic discrepancy. *Journal of School Psychology*, 22, 95–110.

Wixson, K. (1979). Miscue analysis: A critical review. *Journal of Reading Behavior*, 11, 163–175.

Wolf, M. (1984). Naming, reading, and the dyslexias: A longitudinal overview. *Annals of Dyslexia*, 34, 87–115.

Wolford, G., & Fowler, C. (1984). Differential use of partial information by good and poor readers. *Developmental Review*, 6, 16–35.

Wong, B. (1984). Metacognition and learning disabilities. In T. Waller, D. Forrest, & G. MacKinnon (Eds.), *Metacognition, cognition, and human performance* (pp. 137–180). New York: Academic Press.

Wong, B., Wong, R., & Foth, D. (1977). Recall and clustering of verbal materials among normal and poor readers. *Bulletin of the Psychonomic Society*, 10, 375–378.

Yaden, D. (1984). Reading research in metalinguistic awareness: Findings, problems, and classroom applications. *Visible Language*, 18, 5–47.

Ysseldyke, J., & Algozzine, B. (1979). Perspectives on assessment of learning disabled students. *Learning Disability Quarterly*, 2, 3–13.

Yule, W. (1973). Differential prognosis of reading backwardness and specific reading retardation. *British Journal of Educational Psychology*, 43, 244–248.

Zifcak, M. (1981). Phonological awareness and reading acquisition. *Contemporary Educational Psychology*, 6, 117–126.

Zola, D. (1984). Redundancy and word perception during reading. *Perception & Psychophysics*, 36, 277–284.

18

A Road Map for Understanding Reading Disability and Other Reading Problems: Origins, Prevention, and Intervention

Louise Spear-Swerling

ew topics in reading have inspired more controversy than have learning disabilities (LDs). Traditionally, LDs, and in particular reading disability (RD), have been viewed as serious learning impairments that require early identification and treatment. However, RD also has been described in very different terms as a social category that justifies school failure (Christensen, 1998), a subjective diagnosis that harms children and public education as a whole (Skrtic, 1999), and even a ruse for obtaining certain educational entitlements (Shalit, 1997).

Although criticisms of RD—both as a construct and as an area of education—often have been warranted, and although I have made more than a few such criticisms myself (Spear-Swerling, 1999; Spear-Swerling & Sternberg, 1996), the concept of RD captures some important truths about a subgroup of children who experience reading failure. Specifically, there are children who have unusual difficulty learning to read and whose reading problems cannot be accounted for by other disabilities, broad intellectual limitations, impoverished home environments, or generally inadequate instruction. Although the number of these children is likely much smaller than the number currently identified in schools as having RD, many of these children do require ongoing, intensive educational support in order to learn to read.

Somewhat ironically, research on prevention, identification, and treatment of RD has provided at least as much insight into typical reading development and poor reading in general as it has into RD. This article begins by considering research-based and educational definitions of RD. I make the argument that an analysis of the overall cognitive profile typical of RD, as well as four specific cognitive patterns within this profile, provides a more educationally relevant and research-based way of conceptualizing RD than do conventional educational definitions. The cognitive profile characteristic of RD also is contrasted with common cognitive profiles found among other poor readers. Although this article makes a distinction between RD and other types of reading problems, it is important to note that all reading difficulties merit timely and effective intervention. Next, I discuss possible causes of RD, including both intrinsic (biological) and extrinsic (experiential or environmental) causes. Many of these causal influences are important to understanding not only RD but also poor reading in general. Third, I review approaches to instruction and intervention. Again, these instructional approaches can be applied to children with a variety of reading problems as well as to those with RD. The article concludes with a consideration of possible future directions for research.

What Is Reading Disability?

Historically, a number of concepts have been central to RD, including the ideas that RD involves intrinsic, presumably biologically based, learning difficulties (as opposed to reading failure associated with poverty, for example), as well as a specific cognitive deficit or set of deficits (as opposed to generalized learning problems). Thus, genuine cases of RD have been viewed as involving "unexpected" reading failure that cannot be accounted for by other disabilities, generalized cognitive–linguistic weaknesses, or obvious environmental causes, including a lack of appropriate instruction.

Educational and Research Definitions of Reading Disability

Many current educational guidelines subsume RD under the umbrella category of LDs. The U.S. federal definition, found in the Individuals With Disabilities Education Act (IDEA) (1997), defines LDs as "a disorder in one or more of the basic psychological processes involved in understanding or in using language, spoken or written" that is not primarily the result of "visual, hearing, or motor disabilities, of mental retardation, of emotional disturbance, or of environmental, cultural, or economic disadvantage" (Code of Federal Regulations, 1997, 300.7, C10). The other disability conditions or environmental factors are termed *exclusionary criteria*. Measures of "psychological processing" used in education can involve a wide variety of tests, including those of visual and auditory processing, memory, and language. Educational guidelines generally also specify that individuals with LDs must have a severe discrepancy between intellectual ability (often measured by intelligence quotient [IQ] tests) and achievement in at least one of seven areas, two of which involve reading: basic reading skill (e.g., word recognition) and reading comprehension. IDEA further stipulates that a child cannot be identified as having a disability if the reason for the child's difficulties involves lack of instruction in reading or limited English proficiency. Individual states typically have their own educational guidelines—strongly influenced by IDEA and previous federal legislation—for identifying LDs.

In the United States, LDs currently constitute by far the largest single category of special education. After a period of rapid growth in the late 1970s and 1980s, the percentage of children classified as learning disabled remained relatively stable from 1990 through at least 2000: approximately 45–46% of all children served in federally supported programs for the disabled and 5–6% of all K–12 children in public schools (National Center for Education Statistics, 2001). By comparison, during the 1990s the next largest category of special education—speech or language impaired—involved 17–21% of all disabled children served, and about 2.3% of all K–12 children. Most children classified as learning disabled have problems in reading or reading-related areas such as spelling and written expression (Moats & Lyon, 1993).

Educational guidelines on LDs, and especially the discrepancy requirement, have met with numerous criticisms from researchers (e.g., Fletcher et al., 1994; Moats & Lyon, 1993; Siegel, 1988, 1989; Spear-Swerling & Sternberg, 1996; Stanovich, 1991; Stanovich & Siegel, 1994). These criticisms include concerns about (a) IQ tests being used as measures of overall "potential" for learning, (b) children who lack discrepancies being excluded from educational services, (c) psychometric problems such as regression effects, (d) lack of consistency in methods of determining discrepancy across districts and states, and (e) the fact that discrepancy criteria make early identification of reading problems difficult. Poor readers who fail to meet discrepancy criteria may be viewed erroneously as lacking the capacity for improvement. Perhaps most important, the discrepancy approach provides little insight into the best way to help children with reading difficulties.

An alternative proposal for defining RD involves the concept of treatment resistance (e.g., Berninger & Abbott, 1994; Fuchs & Fuchs, 1998). This view suggests that children with RD are those who are relatively unresponsive to well-designed, research-based interventions—that is, those who experience persistent reading difficulties over time, despite intervention that is generally effective with most children. The percentage of treatment resisters varies somewhat across studies but frequently involves about 30% of treated research samples. For example, Vellutino and Scanlon (2002) studied a group of first graders identified as severely impaired readers through a combination of teacher ratings and individual testing of word-recognition skills. The children also met exclusionary criteria; that is, those with problems such as serious emotional disorders, broad intellectual disabilities, and socioeconomic disadvantages were excluded from the sample. A semester of daily one-on-one tutoring brought 67% of these children to average or above-average reading levels, with 33% still below average. Similarly, Torgesen, Morgan, and Davis (1992) found that about 30% of kindergartners failed to respond to a short-term intervention involving phonological awareness training. Approaches to and length of intervention undoubtedly influence the percentage of children who are deemed treatment resisters (Blachman, 1994). A longitudinal project involving the use of peer-mediated literacy strategies in kindergarten and first grade classified only 7% of treated children as unresponsive (Al Otaiba, 2001). The peer-mediated strategies involved pairing high- and low-achieving children in dyads to work together on a variety of basic reading activities, with both children in a dyad alternating as "coach" and "player" (Fuchs, Fuchs, Thompson, et al., 2001). The children were supervised closely by the teacher, who provided corrective feedback when necessary.

In a survey of researchers, Speece and Shekitka (2002) found that the majority of them favored defining RD in terms of treatment resistance rather than in terms of an IQ-achievement discrepancy. Most surveyed researchers also favored retaining exclusionary criteria, especially mental retardation, inadequate instruction, and sensory impairment. However, they disagreed about abandoning the discrepancy concept entirely; researchers were almost evenly split on the issue of whether RD should be defined as involving a discrepancy between listening comprehension and reading comprehension, and a significant minority of researchers, 32%, favored the retention of an IQ-achievement discrepancy.

Scruggs and Mastropieri (2002) have argued that criticisms of LD identification would be better addressed by attention to local implementation of educational guidelines (e.g., greater consistency of eligibility criteria across states and greater adherence to existing guidelines) than by elimination of discrepancy criteria. Schools frequently ignore not only discrepancy requirements but also other criteria in determining eligibility for LD services (MacMillan & Speece, 1999). Determination of eligibility often is driven by practical considerations such as the need to provide assistance to struggling students. If special education is, or is perceived to be, the only avenue for extra help, then children tend to be funneled into special education whether or not they meet eligibility guidelines. Moreover, because LD may be perceived as a less-pejorative category compared to others in special education (e.g., emotional disturbance), this phenomenon may be especially likely to occur for children identified with LDs and RD.

Professional development for and prereferral intervention by teachers appear to be promising ways to reduce inappropriate referrals of children for LDs services. For instance, Drame (2002) examined contextual influences on teachers' referral decisions when the teachers were given descriptions of children with academic or behavioral difficulties. Teachers at schools with well-defined prereferral intervention programs, such as those involving multidisciplinary or consultative models, were less likely to recommend children for LDs evaluations than were teachers at schools without such intervention programs. Likewise, teachers' instructional preferences appeared to influence referral decisions; teachers who preferred whole-class groups for teaching reading were more likely to refer children for LDs evaluations than were those who used a combination of grouping methods, perhaps because individual differences are more difficult to accommodate in large groups. Unfortunately, however, many states do not mandate prereferral intervention or do not provide training for professionals who participate in the prereferral process (Buck, Polloway, Smith-Thomas, & Cook, 2003).

In current educational practice, distinguishing genuine cases of RD from more experientially based reading problems often is impossible (Spear-Swerling, 1999). Although it is not yet clear whether treatment-resister models accurately identify genuine cases of RD, these models are more educationally useful than is the discrepancy approach because they are framed in terms of levels of intervention. In addition, an analysis of the specific cognitive patterns typical of children with RD, and of the cognitive profiles found in other poor readers, is extremely helpful for early identification and for planning instruction. An important foundation for interpreting cognitive patterns and profiles involves understanding the development of normally achieving readers.

Abilities Involved in Typical Reading Development

A number of reading development models emphasize the importance of two broad types of abilities in reading: oral language comprehension and word recognition (e.g., Adams, 1990; Chall, 1983b; Hoover & Gough, 1990; Samuels, 1994, see #40 this volume). Each of these two broad areas includes numerous component abilities. For instance, oral language comprehension includes vocabulary knowledge and grammatical understanding, whereas word recognition includes knowledge of letter–sound relationships, the ability to decode unfamiliar words, and automatic as well as accurate recognition of words. Reading text fluently requires not only automatic word recognition but also integration of a range of important subword, word-, and comprehension-level processes (Fuchs, Fuchs, Hosp, & Jenkins, 2001; Good, Simmons, & Kame'enui, 2001; Wolf & Katzir-Cohen, 2001).

One central set of linguistic processes in reading involves phonological processes, which require the use of phonological codes (abstract mental representations of speech sounds), or of actual speech, in a variety of cognitive and linguistic tasks, including memory and oral language as well as written language (Scarborough & Brady, 2002). Phonological processes play a key role in word recognition, especially in an alphabetic language such as English, in which the printed letters primarily correspond to sounds in spoken words. For example, *phonemic awareness*, which involves awareness and manipulation of individual sounds in spoken words (e.g., being able to segment a spoken word such as *fish* into three separate sounds, /f/, /i/, /sh/), greatly facilitates learning to decode printed words. *Phonological awareness* is a more rudimentary level of phonemic awareness that includes the ability to perform tasks such as rhyming and alliteration. *Phonological decoding* (i.e., word decoding or word attack) involves using phonological skills to read unfamiliar words. This ability may be measured by having the individual read out-of-context words that are either pseudowords, such as *frain*, or real words that are unfamiliar to the individual (i.e., not common words recognized by sight).

Other phonological processes play a direct role in comprehension. For instance, *phonological memory* involves the ability to use phonological codes in memory when reading or listening to a text. If phonological memory is faulty or inefficient and the individual cannot hold words in his or her memory long enough to integrate the meaning of the text, then comprehension may be impaired. Considerable evidence suggests that phonological processes are a core problem in RD and often in other cases of poor reading as well (Adams, 1990; Fletcher et al., 1994; Rack, Snowling, & Olson, 1992; Stanovich & Siegel, 1994).

Most models of reading reflect the idea that the importance of various cognitive processes shifts with development. Although many abilities are ultimately important in learning to read, abilities involved in word recognition (such as phonemic awareness and knowledge of letter–sound relationships) tend to be especially important in the early elementary grades when word-recognition skill is developing most rapidly and the comprehension demands of most texts are relatively low. By grade 4, most typically developing children already have acquired reasonably automatic, accurate word recognition, and the comprehension demands of texts escalate substantially, so oral language comprehension begins to account for correspondingly more of the variance in reading comprehension (Chall, 1983b; Rupley, Willson, & Nichols, 1998). Furthermore, in many models (e.g., Chall, 1983b; Ehri, 1991, 1992; Frith, 1985; Gough & Juel, 1991) development is conceptualized as involving a series of phases that nearly all children pass through in the same sequence—though at varying rates—to develop reading proficiency. Within a phase, children's general approaches to most words and reading tasks are similar. Transitions between phases involve changes in children's understanding of reading and in the development of specific cognitive abilities that underlie reading.

A Model of Typical Reading Development

An extensive research base exists on the cognitive processes involved in reading development, and the model I will discuss owes much to the work of other researchers (e.g., Adams, 1990; Carver & David, 2001; Chall, 1983b; Ehri, 1991, 1992; Frith, 1985; Gough & Juel, 1991; LaBerge & Samuels, 1974; Perfetti, 1985; Rupley et al., 1998; Stanovich, 2000). The model was developed collaboratively by me and Robert Sternberg (Spear-Swerling & Sternberg, 1994, 1996) and involves a series of six phases that constitute a "road" to proficient reading. The version of the model presented here, both the part pertaining to typical development and the part involving patterns of RD to be described in the following section, is generally similar to earlier versions. However, this model contains some additions to earlier versions, as well as some changes in terminology and conceptual details, primarily reflecting the ever-expanding research base on reading.

Table 1 displays the phases of typical reading development in the model, which also appear on the left-hand sides of Figures 1 and 2. These phases are

TABLE 1
Phases of Typical Reading Development

Phase	Defining Feature(s)	Additional Features	Approximate Age (Grade)
Visual-Cue Word Recognition	Child uses visual cues (e.g., word shape, color, or a familiar logo) rather than phonetic cues, in word recognition.	Child • lacks understanding of the alphabetic principle; • often lacks phonological awareness and knowledge of letter–sound relationships; • makes very heavy use of context in word recognition; and • has age-appropriate oral language comprehension but extremely weak or nonexistent reading comprehension, primarily because of very limited word recognition.	2–5 years (preschool to early kindergarten)
Phonetic-Cue Word Recognition	Child uses partial phonetic cues (e.g., first and last letter of a word) in word recognition.	Child • grasps the alphabetic principle; • has at least some knowledge of letter–sound relationships and rudimentary phonological awareness; • still relies on context to aid word recognition; and • has age-appropriate oral language comprehension but much lower reading comprehension, primarily because of limitations in word recognition.	5–6 years (kindergarten to first grade)
Controlled Word Recognition*	Child makes full use of phonetic cues in word recognition and is generally accurate, but not automatic, in reading common words.	Child • has more advanced level of phonemic awareness; • may rely on context to speed word recognition; and • has age-appropriate oral language comprehension but lower reading comprehension, primarily because of limitations in word recognition.	Beginning at 6–7 years (later first to second grade)

(continued)

* These phases overlap in time, with students in later phases of reading continuing to acquire controlled recognition of some new words, make refinements in automatization of word recognition, and develop strategic knowledge.

TABLE 1 (*continued*)
Phases of Typical Reading Development

Phase	Defining Feature(s)	Additional Features	Approximate Age (Grade)
Automatic Word Recognition*	Child recognizes common words automatically (without effort) as well as accurately.	Child • does not usually rely on context to aid or speed word recognition; • makes use of larger letter-pattern units in word recognition; • integrates automatic word recognition with comprehension processes for fluent text reading; and • has age-appropriate oral language comprehension, with reading comprehension still somewhat lower than oral comprehension. Limits on reading comprehension now begin to revolve more around factors such as vocabulary, background knowledge and strategy knowledge than word recognition.	Beginning at about 7 to 8 years (second to third grade)
Strategic Reading*	Child routinely uses at least some comprehension strategies (e.g., using context to determine word meanings, summarization, and knowledge of text structure) to aid reading comprehension.	Child • has well-developed, accurate, automatic word-recognition skills • usually does not rely on context for word recognition but frequently uses context to aid comprehension (e.g., to help determine word meanings); • uses reading easily and extensively as a "tool" for gathering information; • gains increasing vocabulary and background knowledge from reading; and • has age-appropriate oral language comprehension, with reading comprehension becoming comparable to oral language comprehension in the middle of this phase. Late in this phase, reading comprehension may surpass oral comprehension for some types of texts (e.g., technical or dense informational texts).	Beginning at about 8 to 9 years (third to fourth grade)

Phase	Defining Feature(s)	Additional Features	Approximate Age (Grade)
Proficient Reading*	Individual has higher-order comprehension skills.	Individual • has highly accurate and automatic word recognition; • uses a wide range of strategies to aid reading comprehension; • evaluates and integrates information across a variety of sources; • reads critically; and • has age-appropriate oral language comprehension, with reading comprehension comparable to oral language comprehension. For some types of texts (e.g., technical or dense informational texts), reading comprehension may surpass oral comprehension.	Beginning in later adolescence (later high school or college)

* These phases overlap in time, with students in later phases of reading continuing to acquire controlled recognition of some new words, make refinements in automatization of word recognition, and develop strategic knowledge.

intended to be specific to English, with the age and grade ranges in the table approximations based on research involving mainly samples of middle class English-speaking children. Research on other alphabetic languages, such as German, Swedish, Spanish, and Portuguese (e.g., Cardoso-Martins, 2001), suggests that children learning a variety of alphabetic languages progress through a series of phases roughly similar to those in Table 1. Furthermore, many of the cognitive processes underlying reading, such as phonemic awareness, appear similar across alphabetic languages (e.g., Durgunoglu & Oney, 2002). However, an important difference among alphabetic languages involves transparency, that is, whether letter–sound relationships are relatively straightforward and consistent (transparent), as in German or Spanish, or more complex (opaque), as in English. For instance, the pronunciation of English vowels can vary substantially depending on the vowel position in a word, the letter that follows the vowel, and so forth. In transparent alphabetic languages, children may advance more rapidly through the initial phases of learning to read than do children learning English (Cardoso-Martins, 2001; Landerl, Wimmer, & Frith, 1997).

Oral language comprehension—including semantic knowledge (e.g., vocabulary), syntactic knowledge (e.g., understanding of grammatically complex sentences), and pragmatic knowledge (e.g., understanding the social uses of language)—develops prior to and simultaneously with word-level reading abilities, beginning during the early preschool years and continuing into adulthood. As noted in the following discussion, oral language comprehension substantially exceeds reading comprehension for most children until about seventh or eighth grade (Biemiller, 1999). Even among typical readers, individual differences in oral language comprehension exist that influence and set limits on reading comprehension, especially after word-recognition skills have developed. Moreover, children's own reading experiences and volume of reading exert important influences on their oral language development. Thus, oral language and reading development interact and are mutually facilitative.

Visual-Cue Word Recognition. This phase of reading, termed *visual-cue word recognition* by Ehri (1991, 1992), is characteristic of very young children, primarily preschoolers. Children do not yet grasp the alphabetic principle—the fundamental insight that written English involves a code in which printed letters map onto speech sounds in spoken words—and also often lack phonological awareness and knowledge of most letter–sound relationships. Instead, young children rely on a salient visual cue, such as a distinctive logo or word shape, to recognize words and are heavily dependent on context in word recognition. For instance, a typical preschooler might recognize the word *stop* on a red, octagonal sign or the word *McDonald's* from the golden arches but would not recognize those words if they were written in ordinary type on a page. Because of their lack of alphabetic insight, visual-cue readers also have been termed *pre-*

alphabetic readers (Ehri, 1997). In this phase, children's oral language comprehension far exceeds their reading comprehension, which is very restricted or nonexistent because of limitations in word recognition.

Phonetic-Cue Word Recognition. Ehri (1991, 1992) uses the term *phonetic-cue word recognition* for a second phase of reading. This phase is typically seen in K–1 children but also may be seen in some preschoolers, especially those who have had extensive exposure to literacy. Phonetic-cue readers can use partial phonetic cues in word recognition because they grasp the alphabetic principle, have at least a rudimentary level of phonological awareness (e.g., recognizing spoken words with similar beginning or ending sounds), and know at least some letter–sound relationships, especially for single consonants such as *m* and *s*. Often, they attend to the first few letters of a word, or to the first and last letters, but not to the middle part of a word. Hence, they may confuse similarly spelled words such as *boat* and *boot*. Because they do not make full use of all the letters in a word, phonetic-cue readers remain dependent on context, such as pictures or sentences, to aid word recognition. Children in this phase also have been termed *partial-alphabetic* readers (Ehri, 1997). They continue to have oral language comprehension that substantially exceeds their reading comprehension, primarily because of inaccuracies in word recognition.

Controlled Word Recognition. Children in this phase of reading development, typically those in late first grade to second grade, can read a variety of common words accurately. They make full use of phonetic cues in word recognition; therefore, this phase has been termed *full alphabetic* (Ehri, 1998). Children with controlled word recognition have more advanced levels of phonemic awareness than do children in previous phases of reading, and they know a wide range of letter–sound relationships, including not only those for single consonants but also those for vowels and common vowel patterns (e.g., *ay*, *ee*, and *oo*), as well as for other common letter patterns (e.g., *sh*, *th*, and *ck*). However, they must expend mental effort to recognize many words, so their word recognition is not automatic. Children in this phase may continue to rely on context cues, especially to speed word recognition. Their reading comprehension still lags behind oral language comprehension, often because the effort they must put into word recognition tends to drain mental resources from comprehension.

Automatic Word Recognition. In this phase, children can recognize a wide range of common words automatically as well as accurately. Automatic recognition of words appears to be facilitated by consolidation and use of larger letter patterns such as prefixes, suffixes, and common rimes (e.g., *ight*). Hence, this phase is roughly analogous to one that has been termed *consolidated alphabetic* (Ehri, 1997). Children in this phase integrate automatic word recognition with a variety of comprehension processes to achieve fluent, and increasingly rapid, reading of text. Children with automatic word recognition, usually second to third graders, depend on context only infrequently to aid their word recognition, which is accurate, fast, and effortless. Although their reading comprehension continues to be lower than their oral language comprehension, limits on their reading comprehension now begin to revolve more around general language abilities and knowledge (e.g., vocabulary, background knowledge, and strategic knowledge) than around word recognition.

Strategic Reading. Strategic readers have the ability to use routinely at least some reading comprehension strategies. Examples include "fix-up" strategies for when comprehension fails, such as rereading part of a text that did not make sense (Anderson, Hiebert, Scott, & Wilkinson, 1985); summarizing what has been read; and using context to determine a word's meaning (as opposed to using context to recognize words). For instance, a strategic reader reading the sentence *Her scarlet cape flashed red in the crowd* would be able to recognize all the words in the sentence accurately and easily, including *scarlet*, but would concurrently use sentence context to figure out that the word *scarlet* means *red*. Children may develop and use some comprehension strategies in listening well before the strategic reading phase. However, what distinguishes strategic reading is children's routine use of strategies in their reading as well as their listening—an achievement facilitated by automatic word recognition, which allows children to focus more of their mental resources on comprehension of the text. Early in this phase, children's reading comprehension is only beginning to approach their oral language comprehension, with the two areas of comprehension generally becoming comparable in about seventh or eighth grade (Biemiller, 1999). Late in this phase, reading comprehension actually may exceed oral language comprehension for certain types of texts, such as dense informational texts or complex narratives, largely because written text can be reread but information presented orally usually cannot be reviewed. Children can now use reading extensively as a tool for gathering information, and their own reading contributes increasingly to development of vocabulary and background knowledge (Cunningham & Stanovich, 1990). Strategic reading typically begins around the middle elementary grades (third to fourth grade) and continues to develop in subsequent grades.

Proficient Reading. The primary distinction between strategic reading and proficient reading involves the development of higher-order comprehension abilities, such as the ability to read critically and reflectively, understand and appreciate more profound literary themes, and evaluate and integrate different kinds of information. For example, a student who is writing a research paper might need to evaluate information from different sources, decide which sources are most credible, reconcile apparent conflicts among sources, and synthesize all this information in a coherent way. Increases in background knowledge fueled in part by reading volume may influence performance on a range of basic information-processing tasks (Ceci, 1990). Although reading volume certainly affects background knowledge in previous phases of reading, its cumulative effects are greatest in this final phase. Thus, over time, reading volume may contribute to growth in verbal intelligence and to overall cognitive development (Stanovich, 2000; Stanovich & Cunningham, 1993). Oral and reading comprehension are comparable, and reading comprehension may even exceed oral comprehension for certain types of texts, as noted previously. Proficient reading typically begins in later adolescence (high school or college) and continues throughout adulthood.

Several general points should be made about the preceding model of typical reading development. First, the term *development* is not intended to imply that learning to read unfolds spontaneously—largely independent of experience or instruction—as does learning to walk, for instance. As I will discuss further in the next section, experience and instruction have substantial influences on both reading development and reading difficulties. Second, although this article's focus is on reading, many of the cognitive processes typical of a given phase of reading also are revealed in children's spelling (see Ehri, 1997, for a detailed discussion).

Third, as Table 1 illustrates, although beginning readers often rely on contextual cues to supplement faulty word recognition, progress in reading is characterized by decreasing reliance on context to aid word recognition. That is, skilled reading involves the development of increasingly accurate and automatic word recognition, which frees mental resources for use in comprehension—not the continued use of multiple cueing systems for recognizing words. It is useful to distinguish the use of context in *word recognition* from its use in *comprehension*, as when determining the meanings of unfamiliar vocabulary words. Good readers use context to aid comprehension and have more mental resources free for doing so because their word recognition is automatized. However, using context to aid word recognition is the hallmark of unskilled, not skilled, reading (see, e.g., Adams, 1998).

Fourth, the various phases in the model are not independent of the words or reading tasks themselves. For instance, a child in the phase of controlled word recognition might recognize automatically a few very common words; a proficient adult reader who recognizes the vast majority of words automatically might use controlled processing for very unusual or technical words, such as unfamiliar science terminology. The phases describe an individual's general approach to *most*, but not necessarily *all*, words and reading tasks within a given phase.

A related point is that some overlap exists among the final four phases in the model. For example, although controlled recognition of most common words is achieved in the third phase of controlled word recognition, readers continue to acquire some new words, especially low-frequency words, in subsequent phases of the model; and although automatic recognition of most common words is achieved in the fourth phase, automatization and text fluency also continue to develop in later phases. Likewise, by the strategic reading phase, children have acquired the ability to use routinely at least some comprehension strategies in reading, but further development in strategy knowledge and strategy application continues into the proficient reading phase.

Cognitive Patterns of Reading Disability

This part of the model (Spear-Swerling & Sternberg, 1994, 1996) conceptualizes RD as involving deviations from the path to proficient reading at one of the first four phases in development. (See Figure 1, which depicts both the model of typical reading development discussed in the previous section and the patterns of RD to be discussed in this section.) Depending on the point at which a reader goes astray, RD may involve four patterns of difficulty, listed in the first four rows of Table 2 and also shown in the center of Figure 1 as four branches off the road to proficient reading. The model incorporates the idea that the further children go off track (e.g., falling increasingly behind their age cohort because of lack of intervention), the harder it is for them to get back on the road to proficient reading. For all four patterns, the negative consequences of reading failure, such as decreased motivation, practice levels, and expectations—shown on the right-hand side of Figure 1—tend to complicate reading difficulties. These complications may begin as early as first grade (Chapman & Tunmer, 1997; Stanovich, 1986, see #17 this volume).

Again, this part of the model has been influenced strongly by the work of many researchers, including Fletcher et al. (1994), Frith (1985), Lovett (1987), Mann and Liberman (1984), Shankweiler, Crain, Brady, and Macaruso (1992), Siegel (1988, 1989), Stanovich (1986, 1990), Stanovich and Siegel (1994), Torgesen, Wagner, and Rashotte (1994), Vellutino and Scanlon (2002), and Wolf and Bowers (1999), to name only a few. The patterns of RD, as with phases of normal reading development, describe those seen in poor readers who speak English. RD appears to be a cross-linguistic phenomenon (Grigorenko, 1999), and there certainly are similarities in patterns of RD across different languages, especially alphabetic languages. However, factors such as the transparency of the language also seem to be important (e.g., Landerl et al., 1997).

As shown in Figure 1 and Table 2, the model conceptualizes RD as involving a specific word-recognition deficit (SWRD) profile rather than generalized oral language problems, with deviations from typical reading development occurring in the early phases pertaining to word recognition. This conceptual emphasis is based on evidence that many children with RD have a core phonological deficit that affects word recognition much more severely than oral language comprehension (e.g., Rack et al., 1992). It also is consistent with traditional views that RD involves unexpected reading failure rather than more generalized cognitive–linguistic difficulties. That is, when children have good oral language comprehension and no

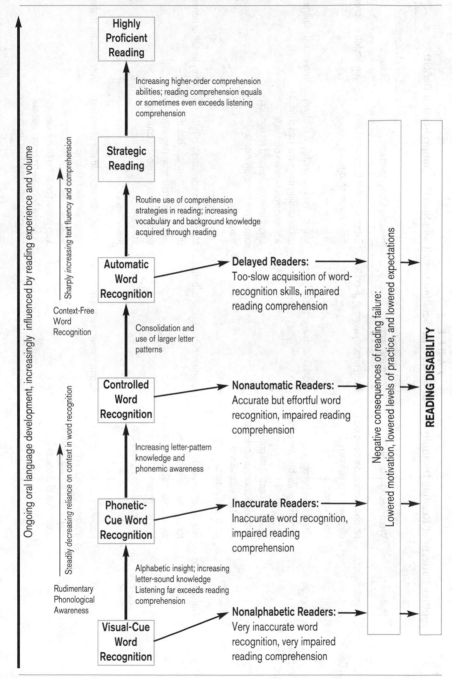

TABLE 2

Cognitive Patterns of Reading Disability (Specific Word-Recognition Deficit and Specific Comprehension Deficit)

Profile	Pattern	Word-Recognition Skills	Oral Language Comprehension	Reading Comprehension	Use of Comprehension Strategies
Specific Word-Recognition Deficit (SWRD)	Nonalphabetic	No phonological decoding skills. Uses visual cues in word recognition.	Approximately average or better	Extremely weak because of very limited word recognition.	Very limited or nonexistent
Traditional Reading Disability/ "Unexpected" Poor Reading	Inaccurate	Has some phonological decoding skills, but these are inaccurate. Relies on contextual cues, such as pictures or sentence context, to supplement weak word recognition.	Approximately average or better	May perform adequately in relatively undemanding materials. Has difficulty when comprehension demands escalate because word recognition consumes too many mental resources.	Very limited or nonexistent
	Nonautomatic	Has accurate word-recognition skills, but these are effortful, not automatic. May rely on sentence context to help speed word recognition.	Approximately average or better	May perform adequately in relatively undemanding materials. Has difficulty when comprehension demands escalate because word recognition consumes too many mental resources.	Very limited or nonexistent
	Delayed	Has accurate and automatic word-recognition skills, but lagged well behind peers in acquisition of those skills.	Approximately average or better	Weak, with impaired use of reading comprehension strategies Child was not "ready" for comprehension instruction at the time it was delivered because he or she was still struggling with basic word recognition.	Very impaired strategy use

Profile	Pattern	Word-Recognition Skills	Oral Language Comprehension	Reading Comprehension	Use of Comprehension Strategies
Specific Comprehension Deficit (SCD)	Nonstrategic	Has reasonably accurate and automatic word-recognition skills, apparently acquired on schedule.	Sometimes below average	Weak, with impaired use of comprehension strategies (but not associated with a history of word-recognition problems)	Very impaired strategy use
	Suboptimal	Has reasonably accurate and automatic word-recognition skills, apparently acquired on schedule.	Sometimes below average	Lacks higher-order comprehension skills, but functions at a somewhat higher level than a nonstrategic reader.	Basic strategy use but may lack higher-level strategies

obvious disabilities such as sensory or broad intellectual impairments, one would not expect them to have reading difficulties. Nevertheless, children with generalized language problems involving both oral language comprehension and word recognition—sometimes termed *garden-variety poor readers* (Gough & Tunmer, 1986)—appear to be on a continuum with children who have a specific phonological deficit (Fletcher et al., 1994; Stanovich & Siegel, 1994).

Nonalphabetic Readers. Nonalphabetic readers experience difficulty early in the process of reading development, in the phase of visual-cue word recognition. Like normally developing readers in this phase, they do not grasp the alphabetic principle and must rely solely on visual cues, such as word shape, to recognize words. Like normally developing readers, they also generally lack phonological awareness and knowledge of letter sounds. Unlike normally developing readers, however, they do not progress beyond this phase but fail to develop alphabetic insight and increased letter-sound knowledge. They may have been resistant to treatments (instructional interventions) that were successful with normally developing readers. Because it is not possible to progress very far in an alphabetic language, such as English, without understanding the alphabetic code and acquiring at least some ability to use phonetic cues, nonalphabetic readers have extremely impaired word recognition and reading comprehension. They are often young children and may be especially likely to be noticed because of the severity of their difficulties. Nevertheless, even adults can be nonalphabetic readers (Byrne, 1992).

Inaccurate Readers. These children go off track in the phase of phonetic-cue word recognition. They have grasped the alphabetic principle, have some knowledge of letter sounds, and perhaps have a rudimentary level of phonological awareness, which enables them to use some phonetic cues in attempting to read words. They are similar to normally developing readers in this phase because they do not make full use of phonetic cues in reading words, and therefore their word recognition is inaccurate. However, unlike normally developing readers, they may remain stuck in this phase because of difficulties in using phonetic cues, which may be related to poor phonemic awareness, insufficient knowledge of letter–sound relationships, or both. Inaccurate readers may continue to rely on context cues, such as pictures or sentences, to aid word recognition. They may achieve good reading comprehension sometimes, especially in relatively easy texts; however, as the text demands escalate in the middle and upper grades, both in terms of comprehension demands and the sheer volume of reading required in school, it will become increasingly difficult for inaccurate readers to compensate effectively for their poor word recognition, and their reading comprehension will likely be impaired.

Nonautomatic Readers. Nonautomatic readers go astray in the phase of controlled word recognition, failing to move forward to other phases. As with normally developing readers in the controlled word-recognition phase, nonautomatic readers generally have accurate but effortful word reading; however, perhaps because nonautomatic readers fail to move on to the use of larger associated letter patterns, their reading speed may remain very slow. Their use of mental resources to speed word recognition (e.g., via use of context cues) tends to impair reading comprehension, especially in more demanding texts. Nonautomatic readers may have underlying deficits in rapid serial naming of letters or digits (e.g., Sunseth & Bowers, 2002; Wolf & Bowers, 1999). However, the interpretation of naming speed deficits, especially whether or not such deficits reflect a core phonological weakness, remains a matter of dispute (Scarborough & Brady, 2002). Adult poor or marginal readers—especially those with a history of childhood reading difficulties—sometimes are nonautomatic readers (Davidson & Strucker, 2002; Fowler & Scarborough, 1993; Sabatini, 2002). For example, college students with RD frequently complain that if they read at a comfortable pace, they have good reading comprehension but cannot keep up with the reading volume required in their classes; if they try to force themselves to read faster, they lose comprehension.

Delayed Readers. Delayed readers have the only pattern of RD with reasonably accurate and automatic word-recognition skills. However, delayed readers have reading comprehension weaknesses, especially in the use of reading comprehension strategies. In the model, this pattern of RD is conceptualized as involving delayed development of word-recognition skills and not poor oral language comprehension (i.e., the "delay" pertains specifically to word recognition, not overall cognitive–linguistic development). In other words, delayed readers have a history of word-recognition difficulties that they eventually overcame, but at a cost: While delayed readers struggled to develop word recognition, they missed out on other kinds of reading experiences and instruction important to the development of reading comprehension. Moreover, the use of comprehension strategies requires a proactive rather than passive stance on the part of the reader (Garner, 1990), in addition to task persistence (Gersten, Fuchs, Williams, & Baker, 2001). Thus, strategic weaknesses in poor readers sometimes may reflect maladaptive attributional patterns, such as learned helplessness or a tendency to give up easily when confronted with challenging reading tasks, not a true inability to develop or use strategic knowledge (Borkowski, Carr, & Pressley, 1987).

Key Points About the Patterns

The model involves an interactive perspective on reading development and RD (Spear-Swerling & Sternberg, 1996). That is, both good and poor reading are viewed as involving an interaction between children's intrinsic characteristics (e.g., innate abilities, temperament, and motivation) and extrinsic factors (e.g., experience, home environment, and instruction). Although the four patterns are described in terms of deviations from the path of typical reading development, children with RD differ from typical younger readers in some important respects. For instance, children with RD may compensate for deficient phonological skills in ways uncharacteristic of younger, normally achieving children matched to them on word-recognition level (Greenberg, Ehri, & Perin, 2002), and they certainly have a host of negative experiences with reading—such as repeated failure—not typical of younger good readers. The road map metaphor and the right-hand box, labeled "negative consequences of reading failure," shown in Figure 1, attempt to capture these distinctions between children with RD and normally achieving but younger readers. Finally, both intrinsic characteristics and extrinsic factors may contribute to some variations within patterns. For example, an inaccurate reader with exceptionally strong oral language comprehension may be better at compensating for weak phonological decoding than is an inaccurate reader with average oral language abilities. Nevertheless, inaccurate reading likely will cause problems for both readers, as the comprehension demands and volume of reading increase across grade levels.

Other Broad Profiles of Poor Reading

The preceding model of RD focuses on children who have (or, in the case of delayed readers, have had in the past) a *specific word-recognition deficit* (SWRD) coupled with approximately average or above-average oral language comprehension. This profile of unexpected reading failure traditionally has been viewed as typical of RD. However, at least two other broad deficit profiles may be possible among poor readers: children with weaknesses in both word recognition and language comprehension—sometimes called *garden-variety poor reading* (GVPR)—and children who have comprehension weaknesses coupled with adequate word recognition. The last profile is sometimes termed a *specific comprehension deficit* (SCD). All three profiles are summarized in Table 3. Research suggests a nontrivial prevalence of each profile (Badian, 1999; Catts, Fey, Zhang, & Tomblin, 1999; Leach, Scarborough, & Rescorla, 2003; Nation & Snowling, 1997; Spear-Swerling, in press; Yuill & Oakhill, 1991), but their relative frequency varies across studies depending on methodology (e.g., whether SCD is defined in relation to reading or listening comprehension, the specific measures used to assess reading and language, and the cutoffs for defining poor performance), as well as on the age of the population studied. In particular, a specific word-recognition deficit (i.e., traditional RD) and GVPR are more likely to be identified in the early grades, whereas SCD typically emerges in the middle or later grades. For example, Leach et al. (2003) found that SCD—defined in terms of *reading comprehension*—constituted only about 6% of reading problems identified in third grade or earlier, whereas SWRD and GVPR involved approximately 49% and 46% of reading difficulties in third grade or earlier, respectively. However, late-identified reading problems were highly heterogeneous, with

TABLE 3
Broad Cognitive Profiles of Poor Reading

Profile	"Unexpected" Poor Reading/ Traditional Reading Disability	Word-Recognition Skills	Oral Language Comprehension	Reading Comprehension
Specific Word-Recognition Deficit (SWRD)	Yes	Deficient word recognition: nonalphabetic, inaccurate, nonautomatic, and/or delayed	Approximately average or better. Child performs well on age-appropriate comprehension tasks presented verbally.	Usually weak, resulting from deficient word recognition. May perform adequately in undemanding materials.
Garden-Variety Poor Reading (GVPR)	No, because GVPR involves generalized language problems as well as word-recognition difficulties. However, GVPR may cause serious problems in school.	Deficient word recognition: nonalphabetic, inaccurate, nonautomatic, and/or delayed	Below average. Child experiences difficulty on age-appropriate comprehension tasks even when they are presented verbally.	Usually weak, resulting from deficient word recognition and below-average oral language comprehension. May perform adequately in undemanding materials.
Specific Comprehension Deficit (SCD)	No, because SCD does not involve specific word-recognition difficulties and may involve generalized language problems. However, SCD may cause serious problems in school, especially at upper grade levels.	Approximately average or better, with apparently normal progress in the early phases of learning to read	Some readers are below average; some are not.	Usually weak. Often results from (1) below-average oral language comprehension and/or (2) lack of knowledge or application of reading comprehension strategies. May perform adequately in undemanding materials.

proportions of SWRD, GVPR, and SCD roughly similar for cases identified after grade 3 (i.e., each profile constituted about one third of the poor reading group).

Similar to children with RD, children with GVPR and SCD also may be understood in relation to the road map metaphor. The basic processes implicated in typical reading development, the overall sequence of development, and an interactive perspective all are relevant to understanding GVPR and SCD as well as RD. Likewise, children with GVPR or SCD are affected by the negative consequences of poor reading, although for the latter profile, these consequences may come somewhat later in the course of formal schooling rather than in the primary grades. Although GVPR and SCD do not constitute RD as traditionally defined by unexpected poor reading or a specific word-recognition deficit, they may seriously impede success in school and adulthood. Thus, all three profiles require timely intervention and remediation.

Garden-Variety Poor Reading. Garden-variety poor readers, like children with RD, experience difficulty in the early phases of reading development, primarily because of poor word recognition and phonological weaknesses. Unless their oral language weaknesses are particularly severe, in the early grades the word-recognition difficulties of garden-variety poor readers may be more obvious than are their comprehension problems, because the comprehension demands of beginning texts often are fairly low (Chall, Jacobs, & Baldwin, 1991) and because reading comprehension cannot even come into play without a basic level of word recognition. However, children with GVPR can be expected to have difficulties in reading comprehension even after their poor word recognition has been remediated because their reading comprehension difficulties relate partially to generalized language comprehension problems. In contrast to children with RD, who generally perform well with material presented verbally (e.g., class discussions of material read aloud by the teacher), children with GVPR may have obvious comprehension difficulties in listening as well as in reading. They may appear to respond to intervention targeting word recognition in the early grades, only to fall behind again in the later grades (e.g., Slavin et al., 1996). Thus, children with GVPR require remediation in both word recognition and language comprehension.

Specific Comprehension Deficit. In contrast to children with GVPR and RD, children with SCD have apparently normal reading development and acquisition of word-recognition skills in the early grades. For instance, Badian (1999) studied a group of late-emerging poor readers who had average word-recognition, phonological, and comprehension skills at grade 2, and who continued to have average phonological skills in grade 6, but whose reading comprehension fell below average in grades 5 through 8. Similarly, the children with SCD studied by Leach et al. (2003) had good word recognition and apparently good reading comprehension in the early grades, but they dropped sharply in reading comprehension after grade 3. This later emergence of comprehension difficulties may relate in part to increases in vocabulary and comprehension demands across grades. For example, Chall et al. (1991) followed a group of low-income children who showed adequate reading progress in the early grades but appeared to lack the more abstract vocabulary important to good reading comprehension in the upper-elementary grades. Children's vocabulary weaknesses started to become apparent in grade 4 but did not begin to have a significant impact on reading comprehension until about grade 6 or 7, with a progressive deterioration in reading comprehension thereafter.

Interestingly, Chall et al. (1991) found that a deceleration in vocabulary scores also was associated with a deceleration in word-recognition and spelling scores in the later grades, perhaps in part because morphemic and vocabulary knowledge become especially important to word recognition and spelling at these advanced levels (Ehri, 1992, 1997). For instance, a pure decoding process can yield an approximation of words such as *capillary* and *esophagus*, but some oral familiarity greatly facilitates accurate recognition and pronunciation of these kinds of words, and print exposure is important for accurate spelling of the words.

In this article, SCD is conceptualized in relation to reading comprehension rather than listening comprehension, similar to the conceptualization of Leach et al. (2003). Oral language comprehension weaknesses (e.g., a poor vocabulary) would be one common reason, but not the only possible reason, for SCD; another common reason would involve lack of knowledge, or lack of application, of reading comprehension strategies (e.g., Anderson et al., 1985; Garner, 1990; Kletzien, 1991). Other factors, such as limited background knowledge, also may underlie SCD. In terms of the model of typical reading development, children with SCD might be conceptualized as progressing normally into the phase of automatic word recognition before they experience difficulties. Then, they might go astray at two points, (1) in the automatic word-recognition phase, becoming nonstrategic readers, or (2) in the strategic reading phase, becoming suboptimal readers. These two patterns of SCD are shown in the top center portion of Figure 2 and in the last two rows of Table 2.

Nonstrategic readers fail to develop routine use of reading comprehension strategies and thus are very impaired with regard to strategy use and comprehension. Suboptimal readers go astray somewhat later in the process of reading acquisition and lack higher-order comprehension abilities; although they have the ability to use at least some reading comprehension strategies, they may lack some higher-level strategies. Thus, the two patterns of SCD differ primarily in onset and degree of reading comprehension impairment, with suboptimal readers somewhat less impaired than are nonstrategic readers. However, at advanced levels of schooling, such as high school and college, suboptimal reading may still create serious difficulties.

FIGURE 2
Patterns Involved in a Specific Comprehension Deficit (SCD) Profile

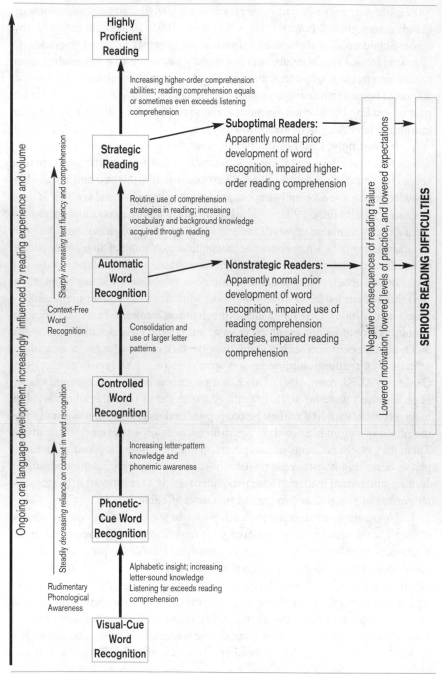

The model differentiates nonstrategic readers from delayed readers, who constitute one of the four patterns of RD. Both types of readers go astray at the same point in reading acquisition but for different reasons. Delayed readers have a delay in acquiring word-recognition skills, which has secondary effects on their acquisition of strategic comprehension skills. Nonstrategic readers make apparently normal progress in the early phases of learning to read but fail to acquire reading comprehension strategies for reasons other than a word-recognition delay. These other reasons could include inadequate comprehension instruction or reading experiences, broad oral language comprehension weaknesses, or lack of engagement or motivation.

Many comprehension strategies—for example, summarization and prediction—can be applied to listening as well as reading. Therefore, students with strategic weaknesses often show impairments in both listening and reading comprehension, especially if the listening measure involves text and tasks highly similar to the reading measure (e.g., Badian, 1999; Nation & Snowling, 1997). However, this is not always the case. For example, the children with SCD studied by Leach et al. (2003) functioned well within average range on a listening comprehension measure and had listening comprehension far above their level of reading comprehension. Furthermore, some children might show impairments on relatively narrow measures of listening comprehension but still have overall oral language comprehension—vocabulary knowledge, syntactic functioning, and pragmatic understanding—that is within average range.

Although the profile often associated with RD involves a specific word-recognition deficit, the elimination of discrepancy criteria would make poor readers with the other two cognitive profiles more likely to be classified as having RD. In order to obtain an SWRD profile, children must have broad language comprehension that is high compared to their word-recognition skill, which makes it more likely that they also will meet IQ-achievement and especially listening comprehension and reading comprehension discrepancy criteria. If these criteria were eliminated completely in favor of a treatment-resister definition of RD, as many researchers appear to favor (Speece & Shekitka, 2002), then children with other profiles of reading difficulty also could be identified as having RD—assuming that they failed to respond to research-based interventions in word recognition or comprehension.

The use of profiles, as well as the specific patterns of RD and SCD explained earlier, can be very helpful in early identification and intervention planning. For example, as shown in Table 3, all three profiles usually are associated with poor reading comprehension. However, children with poor reading comprehension related to a specific word-recognition deficit require a different kind of instructional program than do those whose difficulty involves a specific comprehension deficit. Furthermore, a child whose word recognition is inaccurate will have different instructional needs than will a child with accurate but nonautomatic word recognition. Determining the underlying profile or pattern associated with poor comprehension is essential to designing appropriate intervention.

Possible Causes of Reading Disability

Although cognitive patterns and profiles are very useful educationally, they are at the level of psychological description; by themselves, they do not permit conclusions about the ultimate causation of children's reading problems. For instance, children with SWRD may have intrinsic learning problems—a genuine RD—or they simply may have had inadequate experiences or instruction related to word recognition (Vellutino & Scanlon, 2002). Likewise, SCD may be caused by intrinsic language disorders or insufficient experiences with language. For example, adult, nonnative English speakers sometimes demonstrate a specific comprehension deficit profile in English (Chall, 1994); they may be able to transfer alphabetic skills learned in their native language to English fairly readily but may lack the experience with English vocabulary and broad language skills necessary for higher-level reading comprehension in English.

Knowing about the ultimate causation of individual cases is not necessary for making educational use of cognitive profiles. Poor readers who have deficits in key areas of reading need instruction in those areas, whether their difficulties relate to lack of experience or to intrinsic learning problems. However, knowledge about ultimate causation may have important implications for preventing reading difficulties, improving the effectiveness of intervention, and setting educational policy. Considerable research exists on the possible causes of RD, including both biological and environmental causes, as discussed next. Much of this research is relevant to understanding possible causes of GVPR and SCD as well as RD.

Biological Influences on Reading Disability

Genetic Influences. It has long been recognized that children with a family history of RD are at substantially increased risk of reading failure (Scarborough, 1998). By itself, this increased risk does not provide evidence that RD is genetically based because familial incidence also could be caused by environmental influences such as parents' inability to provide a supportive home literacy environment for their children. However, recent research in behavioral genetics has provided strong evidence for genetic influences in at least some cases of RD. Behavioral-genetic studies typically have used traditional definitions of RD involving unexpected reading failure; thus, children from poverty environments or whose native language is not English would be excluded from the samples. The studies often have focused on families with a history of reading difficulties and have compared the incidence of RD in identical twins, who share identical genes, with the incidence of RD in fraternal twins, who share half their genes on average—the same as other siblings.

The outcomes of these studies consistently suggest a substantial role for genetic factors in word-level reading difficulties (Grigorenko, 1999; Olson, 1999; Olson & Gayan, 2002). (The possible role of genetic factors in comprehension difficulties has received less attention, but studies are beginning to focus on this area as well.) Genes involved in RD are generally believed to affect specific language abilities, such as phonological skills, that in turn affect reading, typically in more profound ways than they affect oral language comprehension (Olson & Gayan, 2002). Genetic influences appear strongest for higher-IQ poor readers and for readers who have a combination of accuracy and speed deficits in word recognition rather than deficits in word accuracy alone (Olson, 1999). Although research sometimes has implicated particular chromosomes as locations for genes involved in RD, specific genes for RD have not yet been identified, and genetic mechanisms may well vary across families (Grigorenko, 1999). Thus, it currently is not possible to perform a genetic test for susceptibility to RD, although it may be possible to do so in the future.

Structural and Functional Brain Differences. Genetic influences may result in differences in early brain development and structure in individuals with RD. Research on structural brain differences has focused on areas of the brain involved in language processing and reading, such as the planum temporale, an area on the surface of each temporal lobe behind the primary auditory cortex. However, research findings on structural brain differences between individuals with and without RD have been inconsistent (Pennington, 1999). Moreover, sometimes these findings have been difficult to interpret because of incomplete knowledge about the range of structural variation in normal individuals and individuals with disorders that may co-occur with RD (such as ADHD).

Shaywitz (2003) maintains that functional, not structural, brain differences characterize individuals with RD. Functional brain differences have been studied using a noninvasive and nonradiological technique, functional magnetic resonance imaging (fMRI). According to Shaywitz (2003), fMRI studies suggest that RD is associated with a "wiring glitch" (p. 82) in posterior brain systems involving phonological aspects of reading and the development of automatic word recognition. Recent work is beginning to examine possible biological antecedents of RD in very young children. For instance, in research using evoked potentials, electroencepholographic (EEG) data are recorded while the participant responds to different stimuli such as flashes of light or spoken words. Because of the noninvasive, nonradiological nature of this technique, like fMRI, it can be used with young children. Researchers interested in RD have even employed the technique with infants. Preliminary studies involving event-related potentials during phoneme discrimination tasks have suggested differences between infants with and without a family history of RD (Leppanen, Pihko, Eklund, & Lyytinen, 1999). In addition, preschool language disorders tend to presage reading problems (Scarborough, 1998), and research is currently underway to examine whether there is a shared genetic etiology between these kinds of early language difficulties and later RD in school-age children (Olson & Gayan, 2002).

Other Biological Influences. Research has implicated some other possible biological influences on reading difficulties, including repeated episodes of otitis media with effusion (middle ear fluid associated with ear infections; Roberts & Burchinal, 2002), very low birthweight due to prematurity or other prenatal problems (Samuelsson, Finnstrom, Leijon, & Mard, 2000), and lead poisoning (Centers for Disease Control and Prevention, 1997). However, many of these influences tend to affect overall language development and cognition; that is, they may be more likely to result in GVPR than in the SWRD profile characteristic of RD. Nevertheless, these kinds of factors are important—and often preventable—causes of reading difficulties.

Some Caveats. As the preceding discussion suggests, there is a biological substrate for some cases of RD. However, biological influences do not render intervention pointless. Many behavioral geneticists have emphasized that genes are expressed only in interaction with the environment; indeed, the same evidence that suggests a substantial role for genetic influences in RD also indicates the importance of shared family environment (Olson, 1999). Even if some cases of RD are related entirely to genetic inheritance, RD is not necessarily inevitable in such individuals. For example, an individual may inherit a strong genetic susceptibility to colon cancer but may be prevented from ever developing the disease through frequent screening and removal of polyps. However, genetic testing in such cases of RD could be an important tool for early identification and intervention. Likewise, structural or functional brain differences do not necessarily mean that an individual is condemned to poor reading because the brain has considerable plasticity, particularly in young children. For instance, fMRI studies indicate that struggling readers who are given effective early reading interventions develop patterns of brain functioning comparable to those of good readers (Shaywitz, 2003). Experience and learning influence the brain, including the actual physical structure of cells as well as their chemical contents (Grigorenko, 1999).

Environmental Influences on Reading Disability

The studies described in the previous section usually focus on a relatively small subset of poor readers whose reading failure seems most likely to relate to intrinsic characteristics (Olson, 1999). Other research using treatment-resister models—in which more diverse groups of poor readers are provided with research-based interventions and reading outcomes are assessed over time—suggests that most cases of reading failure in beginning readers involve experiential or instructional factors rather than intrinsic learning problems (Al Otaiba, 2001; Vellutino & Scanlon, 2002). Of course, even in genuine cases of RD, environmental influences are important. In this section, environmental influences on literacy development in the preschool years will be considered first, followed by influences during formal schooling.

Preschool Influences. Research on early literacy has emphasized the fact that environmental influences on children's reading begin very early in the preschool period. Individual differences in language- and literacy-related knowledge are well established before children enter kindergarten (see, e.g., Neuman & Dickinson, 2002). One very important set of influences during this period is the amount and quality of adult–child interactions involving language. Hart and Risley (1995) studied language development in a group of socioeconomically diverse children, beginning when the children were under 1 year old. Intensive, extended observations of the children's family lives revealed that the most striking difference among families was in the sheer volume of language exposure that children received, with children from the highest socioeconomic group hearing, on average, more than three times as many words per hour as those from the lowest socioeconomic group. Although differences in volume of language were linked to socioeconomic status (SES), amount of language stimulation and the nature of adult–child interactions emerged as more critical factors in children's language development than SES itself. These differences in children's early experiences with language were strongly associated with differences at age 3 in children's vocabulary size and growth rate, as well as to differences in children's school performance at age 9.

Another important set of environmental influences during the preschool period involves children's early experiences with literacy, such as shared book reading, opportunities to write, and exposure to letters and print. Similar to Hart and Risley's (1995) findings for oral language development, global indicators of home literacy, such as SES, appear less effective in predicting children's developmental outcomes than are more direct measures of what adults actually do with children to foster early literacy, such as the amount of shared reading (Burgess, Hecht, & Lonigan, 2002). The two broad areas of early literacy development—oral language and print-related knowledge (e.g., basic print concepts, knowledge about letters, and phonological awareness)—appear to be connected in the preschool period (Dickinson & Sprague, 2002). For example, a threshold level of vocabulary development appears necessary for children to begin to develop phonological awareness (Whitehurst & Lonigan, 2002). However, early literacy experiences are multifaceted and may affect the two domains of development somewhat differently. For instance, reading to children appears to have its primary impact on oral language development, whereas activities involving sounds and letters—such as playing with magnetic letters, rhyming games, and parental attempts to teach the alphabet—may more directly influence print-related knowledge (Burgess et al., 2002; Whitehurst & Lonigan, 2002).

Reading to children appears to be an especially important source of new vocabulary. Hayes and Ahrens (1988) found that preschool children's books were much better sources of sophisticated vocabulary than were educational television shows for preschoolers such as *Sesame Street*; in this age group, books were approximately on par with the everyday language of parents who were college graduates speaking to other adults. As children move into the elementary years, children's books become substantially better sources of new vocabulary than is parental speech, with even comic books surprisingly good sources for exposure to new word meanings (Hayes & Ahrens, 1988).

Influences During Formal Schooling. Once children enter school, variables related to beginning reading instruction are key influences on their reading achievement. Research has focused especially on word-recognition instruction during the early elementary grades because of the importance of skilled word recognition to success in beginning reading and the prevalence of word-recognition difficulties in poor readers. Moreover, word-recognition instruction is especially relevant in considering possible causal influences on RD, because difficulties in this area are central to traditional conceptualizations of RD.

The strategies that beginners use to read words—not only in English (Byrne, 1992; Seymour & Elder, 1986) but also in more transparent languages such as Portuguese (Cardoso-Martins, 2001)—are influenced strongly by methods of instruction. Most beginning readers do not infer the alphabetic principle or letter–sound relationships automatically simply from exposure to print or even from whole-word teaching. Rather, beginning readers in general, and at-risk children in particular, benefit from explicit, systematic instruction in phonemic awareness and phonics (Anderson et al., 1985; National Institute of Child Health and Human Development [NICHD], 2000; Snow, Burns, & Griffin, 1998). *Explicit* means that important letter–sound relationships and patterns are taught directly; *systematic* means that instruction is planful and sequentially organized (e.g., children are not expected to decode long, complex words before they can decode simpler one-syllable words). Manipulative activities—such as sorting word cards with similar letter patterns, building words with letter tiles, and writing letters for sounds—can be very effective ways of teaching phonics to at-risk children (e.g., Juel & Minden-Cupp, 2000, see #13 this volume; McCandliss, Beck, Sandak, & Perfetti, 2003). For many at-risk children, relatively short-term instruction in phonemic awareness and phonics appears to be successful. For instance, the National Reading Panel (NICHD, 2000) concluded that effective phonemic awareness programs often last less than 20 hours in total; Juel and Minden-Cupp (2000) found that at-risk children did especially well with a first-grade teacher who began instruction with a heavy dose of phonics for the initial half of the school year but provided a greater emphasis on vocabulary and comprehension beginning in February.

Another important influence on children's reading development during formal schooling involves the resources available to schools and how those resources are used. Duke (2000) contrasted the print environments of very low-SES and very high-SES first-grade classrooms and found pervasive differences in children's exposure to and experiences with print. On average, relative to children at high-SES schools, those at low-SES schools had fewer books and magazines available in the classroom library, fewer opportunities to use the library, fewer opportunities to choose what they read, and less experience with extended forms of text. These differences are especially disturbing because low-SES children also tend to have fewer print resources at home than do high-SES children. In other words, rather than helping to equalize opportunities to learn for children from different SES groups, formal schooling may sometimes serve to exacerbate those differences.

Scarborough (1998) notes that the relation between SES and reading achievement is more complex than is sometimes realized. Specifically, the relation is much stronger at the level of the school than at the level of individual students' families. In an extensive review, White (1982) found that the average correlation between individual students' SES and their achievement was a modest .23. However, with data aggregated at the level of the school (i.e., average SES of schools correlated with average achievement at the same schools), the correlation was much higher at .68. These findings are consistent with the idea that differences among low- and high-SES schools are important influences on reading achievement.

Other influences connected to formal schooling may affect reading development in older children. For instance, Snow (1991) found that a group of low-income adolescents—including some who were very able students and avid readers—tended to select undemanding materials for independent reading. Many of the adolescents were in relatively unchallenging courses in high school. Snow argues that wide reading outside of school does not substitute for exposure to higher-level reading tasks and rigorous content in school. Like low-SES students, special education students also may experience barriers to content learning, even when they are included in content area courses. Palincsar and her colleagues (Palincsar, Collins, Marano, & Magnusson, 2000; Palincsar, Magnusson, Collins, & Cutter, 2001) studied the participation and learning of special education students, most of whom were identified as learning disabled, in upper-elementary classrooms during guided inquiry science instruction. They found that identified students did not have equal access to participation, even when they had worthwhile ideas during oral discussions, perhaps because of the stigmatizing effects of their reading difficulties or their labels.

Unlike word-recognition instruction, comprehension instruction has been considered less often as a possible causal influence on RD. Children with RD traditionally are defined as having relatively strong oral language abilities, and the assumption generally has been that, with remediation of their word-recognition difficulties, they would progress normally in reading. However, ineffective comprehension instruction certainly may exacerbate or complicate RD. In their study of K–5 resource rooms for children with LDs, one group of researchers (Moody, Vaughn, Hughes, & Fischer, 2000; Vaughn, Moody, & Schumm, 1998) found little or no attention to comprehension occurring during reading instruction. Most comprehension activities involved asking children literal questions about material they had read. Teachers often were overwhelmed with groups so large—as many as 19 children at a time, sometimes spanning four or five grade levels in reading achievement—that individualizing instruction was impossible. No significant gains in reading comprehension were made by students during the term of the study. Lack of attention to comprehension in reading instruction might well compound the difficulties of children with RD, particularly as they advance beyond the elementary grades and the texts used in school become more demanding in terms of comprehension. Of course, many special educators recognize the importance of addressing reading comprehension in instruction. For example, Rankin-Erickson and Pressley (2000), in a study of special education teachers nominated by their supervisors as effective teachers of elementary students with RD, found that these teachers reported teaching comprehension strategies and critical thinking as well as word decoding and basic skills.

Comprehension instruction might be a more direct causal influence on the reading difficulties of garden-variety poor readers and those with SCD. For instance, vocabulary is a critical component of comprehension, and children vary tremendously in their exposure to vocabulary in the preschool years, as Hart and Risley (1995) demonstrated. For children with the lowest levels of language exposure, intensive preschool intervention may be warranted. Other children with vocabulary weaknesses might be helped by attention to vocabulary instruction in the early grades, whereas by the later elementary grades, children's cumulative vocabulary deficits might be very difficult to overcome (Biemiller, 2001). In addition, the observations of Chall et al. (1991) and Snow (1991) suggest that, for some low-SES children who do well in reading in the early grades, insufficient comprehension instruction or reading challenge may contribute to the emergence of SCD in the later grades.

A somewhat different kind of causal influence on children's reading during formal schooling involves influences stemming from individual differences in reading acquisition. Stanovich (1986, see #17 this volume) has termed these "Matthew effects" in reading, after the Biblical phrase about the rich getting richer and the poor getting poorer. For example, children who are initially successful in reading tend to get more practice reading than do poor readers, both in and out of school. Good readers are more likely than poor readers to have a wide array of experiences that further encourage and foster reading, such as reading interesting books, receiving books as gifts, or being commended for their expertise as readers. Children who are poor readers may become aware of their reading problems quite early and quickly lose motivation for reading (Chapman & Tunmer, 1997).

Because reading itself contributes to the development of important linguistic and cognitive abilities, individual differences in learning to read also may have broad effects on background knowledge and language over time. In fact, Stanovich (1991) suggests that some children with RD eventually may develop a garden-variety poor reader profile as their originally circumscribed word-recognition difficulties have a spreading effect on other areas of language and knowledge. (However, a number of studies have failed to find this spreading effect in individuals with RD; see, e.g., Parker, 2003.) Although these kinds of influences are by definition secondary to the original causes of children's reading problems, they may sometimes serve to complicate and intensify children's reading difficulties.

Different Causal Models of Reading Disability

In the cognitive literature on RD, debates about causation often have revolved around the issue of unitary versus multiple deficit models of causation. For example, some investigators (e.g., Shankweiler et al., 1992) have argued that the range of difficulties seen in RD—including poor phonemic awareness, serial naming speed, verbal short-term memory, word decoding, and reading comprehension—can be traced to a single underlying phonological deficit, whereas others (e.g., Sunseth & Bowers, 2002; Wolf & Bowers, 1999) view deficits in naming speed and phonemic awareness as somewhat more separable difficulties that may affect different aspects of reading (and perhaps also spelling). In the latter view, children with deficits in one area—phonemic awareness *or* naming speed—are at increased risk of reading problems, but those with a "double deficit" are at the greatest risk for serious reading difficulties.

Although these debates are important for both theoretical and practical reasons, they do not address *ultimate* causation such as the underlying cause of the phonological deficit. For example, a child might have a phonological deficit because of an underlying genetic vulnerability or lack of instruction in important phonological reading skills. In educational identification of RD, processing measures do not, by themselves, allow educators to determine whether a child has a processing disorder (i.e., an intrinsic learning problem). However, a treatment-resister approach, involving appropriate reading-related measures in conjunction with research-based teaching in deficient areas, might help to rule out instructionally based causes of apparent processing weaknesses.

Interactive models of RD, such as the one discussed here, are by definition multiple-deficit models because even a unitary intrinsic deficit is expressed only in interaction with extrinsic factors. For instance, a child who inherits a genetic vulnerability to RD that is expressed as a unitary phonological deficit might still learn to read well with appropriate intervention and instruction. Therefore, the development of an RD—as well as other cases of poor reading, such as GVPR or SCD—can be understood only by considering both intrinsic and extrinsic causes.

Finally, cognitive researchers interested in RD have observed that, especially in the preschool period, children's oral language deficit profiles may change over time (Scarborough, 2002). Among the youngest preschoolers, syntactic and speech production abilities tend to be most deficient in the children who subsequently go on to develop reading problems, whereas later in the preschool period, vocabulary and phonological awareness problems are more prominent in these children. Children with a history of early language impairment are at increased risk of reading difficulties even if they appear to have caught up to typically developing peers by the time they enter kindergarten. Scarborough (2002) suggests that these observations might be explained by a unitary, underlying language disorder that manifests itself somewhat differently at different points in development. Apparent changes in children's language deficit profiles could relate in part to the fact that preschool language development is not linear but rather involves growth spurts and plateaus. Language deficits may be harder to detect if the deficit area is measured during a period when normally developing children are in a plateau, especially in mild to moderate cases of language impairment. Of course, extrinsic variables, such as early language and literacy experiences, also could affect the manifestation of language deficits in different areas.

Reading Instruction and Intervention

Experience and instruction are powerful influences on children's reading achievement, including the achievement of poor and at-risk readers. Thus, effective general education instruction can play an important role in preventing reading problems, including some cases of RD. Many authorities (e.g., Anderson et al., 1985; NICHD, 2000; Pressley, 1998; Snow et al., 1998) have emphasized the importance of a comprehensive approach that develops a range of abilities known to be important in learning to read, including phonemic awareness, word decoding, oral reading fluency, vocabulary, and comprehension. In addition, the reading curriculum should reflect what is known about the process of reading development rather than putting equal emphasis on the same abilities in every grade. For instance, most children in kindergarten and the beginning of first grade are phonetic-cue readers and will need a much greater emphasis on phonemic awareness and basic letter-sound knowledge than will typical second or third graders. Within a grade, different children also may need different emphases in instruction. For example, unlike typical third graders, a third-grade inaccurate reader still might need work on phonemic awareness and letter-sound knowledge as part of a broader program of reading instruction.

Effective reading instruction requires teachers to have a broad knowledge base about language, literacy, children's development, and individual differences that may affect learning to read. One line of research has focused on professional development aimed at increasing teachers' knowledge about various aspects of reading, including both word decoding and comprehension, with the ultimate goal of improving children's achievement. Usually these studies have involved inservice teachers with some prior preparation and experience in teaching reading. Several investigators (e.g., McCutchen et al., 2002; McCutchen & Berninger, 1999; O'Connor, 1999) have found that developing educators' knowledge base about English word structure and phonemic awareness leads to improvements in their students' phonemic awareness, basic reading ability, and spelling skills. Professional development efforts aimed at comprehension and content learning also can improve student achievement (e.g., Palincsar, Collins, et al., 2000; Palincsar, Magnusson, et al., 2001).

Although effective classroom reading instruction may prevent many cases of reading failure, some children still need more individualized, intensive teaching in order to learn to read. Without intervention, children who experience reading difficulties generally continue to struggle (Juel, 1988), and their reading problems tend to become harder to remediate as the children advance in school. Unfortunately, despite early intervention, some children may continue to need long-term support in reading. Other children's difficulties may not emerge until the later grades, as in the case of SCD, or may reemerge after an earlier intervention that at first appeared to be successful (Scarborough, 2002). Thus, providing both early intervention efforts and services to older poor readers is essential.

In the remainder of this section, I will discuss a variety of instructional methods and interventions for children with RD and other poor readers to develop a range of reading-related abilities. Linkages between instruction in one particular ability and the rest of a child's program are very important. For instance, if children are taught word-decoding skills in one component of the curriculum but are not encouraged to apply those skills in reading text, then the word-decoding instruction may be ineffective. This section concludes with some examples of comprehensive programs for helping poor readers, including both young elementary children and older struggling students.

Early Language and Literacy Skills

Because individual differences in language and early literacy knowledge are well established by the time children begin formal reading instruction, interventions in recent years have focused increasingly on preschool and kindergarten children. These interventions have emphasized developing oral language abilities, phonological awareness, and print-related knowledge (such as basic print concepts and letter knowledge), especially in at-risk children (e.g., Dickinson & Sprague, 2002; Notari-Syverson, O'Connor, & Vadasy, 1998; O'Connor, Notari-Syverson, & Vadasy, 1998a, 1998b; Whitehurst & Lonigan, 2002). Target children have included those at risk because of poverty, as well as those with mild disabilities or weaknesses in phonological and other linguistic abilities. Teacher professional development frequently is a component of these approaches. The kinds of activities used in early literacy interventions—such as shared storybook reading, emergent writing, and rhyming or alliterative games—may be especially helpful to some nonalphabetic readers.

Many experimental studies (see Bus & van IJzendoorn, 1999, for a review) have demonstrated that phonological and phonemic awareness instruction benefits children's basic reading and spelling skills. Phonemic awareness instruction is particularly effective when integrated with teaching of letter–sound correspondences. The meta-analysis of the National Reading Panel (NICHD, 2000) found benefits of phonemic awareness instruction for reading comprehension as well as word reading, and for at-risk and disabled readers as well as typical beginning readers. Effect sizes were especially large at the preschool level (see, e.g., Byrne & Fielding-Barnsley, 1995). Interactive computer programs also show promise as a way to foster phonological awareness in young children (Foster, Erickson, Foster, Brinkman, & Torgesen, 1994).

Overall, research indicates that early literacy interventions can be successful in giving children a better start in reading in kindergarten and first grade. For instance, O'Connor et al. (1998a) demonstrated that their program, Ladders to Literacy, improved the phonological awareness, reading, and spelling skills of both special education and general education children, with benefits sustained over a year after the initial intervention. These kinds of findings are very encouraging given the importance of beginning reading in predicting later reading achievement. However, most early literacy interventions are too new to know whether they prevent reading failure beyond the early grades.

Word-Decoding Accuracy

Development of word-decoding accuracy through phonics instruction is a key need for nonalphabetic and inaccurate readers. Phonics instruction may emphasize synthetic blending strategies at the phoneme level (e.g., sounding out *stack* by blending /s/, /t/, /a/, and /k/), utilize larger subsyllabic units such as onsets and rimes (e.g., sounding out *stack* by blending the onset /st/ with the rime /ack/), or teach decoding by analogy (e.g., decoding *stack* based on its similarity to a known word such as *back*). Integration of phonemic awareness instruction with phonics teaching is important and may require particular emphasis for children with RD, who often have deficits in phonemic awareness. After they can decode simpler words, children need to be taught strategies for decoding multisyllabic words, such as structural analysis and looking within words for morphological units (e.g., *un* in *unwise*, or *know* in *knowledge* and *knowledgeable*). Many of these strategies are useful for building vocabulary and spelling knowledge as well as word-decoding skill.

The meta-analysis of the National Reading Panel (NICHD, 2000) found a clear advantage for explicit, systematic phonics instruction as compared to a variety of unsystematic phonics or no-phonics programs. The panel did not find a significant difference in efficacy between systematic phonics programs emphasizing the blending of individual phonemes and systematic phonics programs emphasizing larger units such as onsets and rimes. Phonics instruction benefited not only children's word decoding but also their spelling and reading comprehension. Benefits were found for beginning readers in general; for younger, at-risk readers, including those at risk because of poverty; and for older children diagnosed with RD based on discrepancy definitions. Interestingly, older children with a garden-variety poor reader profile were not found to derive these same benefits from phonics instruction, perhaps because their poor reading also related to general language limitations. However, the number of studies addressing this population was relatively small, so lack of power to detect a genuine benefit of phonics for garden-variety poor readers also may have been a factor.

Word-building activities with letter cards or tiles may be very effective in phonics instruction. McCandliss et al. (2003) used a word-building activity requiring weak decoders to focus on minimal contrasts in words. In this activity, children used letter cards to form a series of words where each word differed from the preceding word only by a single letter (e.g., *sat* to *sap* to *tap* to *top*). Children in the word-building intervention made significantly greater improvements than a control group in phonemic awareness, word decoding, and reading comprehension. Phonics teaching also can include active discovery of word patterns, as in a "word detectives" approach (see, e.g., Gaskins, Ehri, Cress, O'Hara, & Donnelly, 1996/1997). In this approach, children are encouraged to compare unknown words with known words to analyze and talk about word structure, and to form hypotheses about letter–sound relationships based on their observations of words (e.g., when a vowel is followed by the letter *r*, the vowel sound changes).

Several programs have been developed specifically for children with severe decoding deficits. For instance, the Lindamood Phoneme Sequencing (LiPS) program (Lindamood & Lindamood, 1998) emphasizes the use of articulatory cues (e.g., classifying sounds according to how they are formed with the lips and tongue and whether or not they involve voicing) in developing children's phonemic awareness and word-decoding skills. Several studies have found the LiPS program effective in improving the word-reading skills of children with RD, including some children with very severe reading difficulties (Alexander, Anderson, Heilman, Voeller, & Torgesen, 1991; Torgesen, Wagner, Rashotte, Alexander, & Conway, 1997). Another program, designed for older students and based on the Orton–Gillingham multisensory approach (see, e.g., Gillingham & Stillman, 1997), is the Wilson Reading System (Wilson, 1996). An extensive review of programs for secondary-level struggling readers (Peterson, Caverly, Nicholson, O'Neal, & Cusenbary, 2000) rated the Wilson Reading System as promising for older poor readers with decoding deficits. Instruction involves a 10-part lesson plan that focuses largely on word decoding, spelling, and reading phonetically controlled text, although in the later stages of the program students are expected to read uncontrolled texts.

As compared to younger, normally achieving readers, children with RD often require particularly intensive, structured teaching of phonics and phonemic awareness. It is not yet clear whether these children benefit more from one specific type of systematic phonics approach than from others. Some authorities (e.g., Anderson et al., 1985; Beck & Juel, 1995; Chall, 1983a) have concluded that synthetic blending approaches to phonics are more effective than are analytic (i.e., learning phonics by analyzing whole words) approaches, especially for at-risk populations. However, even for children with RD, the National Reading Panel (NICHD, 2000) did not find an advantage in phonics approaches emphasizing the phoneme level over larger unit approaches. For example, Lovett and her colleagues (Lovett et al., 2000) compared a synthetic phonics program based on Engelmann's (1980) Direct Instruction model—which emphasizes blending individual phonemes into words—with one adapted from the Benchmark program (Gaskins et al., 1988), which emphasizes larger subword units and decoding by analogy. Both approaches were found to be similarly effective in improving the word-reading and comprehension skills of children (ages 6 to 13) with serious reading difficulties. More recently, Lovett, Barron, and Benson (2003) have argued that a combination of synthetic-blending and larger-unit approaches to decoding is more effective than is either approach alone.

The details of phonics teaching in a given approach (e.g., the extent to which individual phoneme–grapheme relationships are taught directly, whether and how phonemic awareness is taught, the amount of time devoted to various aspects of phonics) undoubtedly are important. Also, children may respond differently to a specific approach depending on their underlying profile of abilities and their phase of reading development. Given the key role of phonemic awareness in learning to read an alphabetic language, as well as the utility of phonemic blending strategies in decoding long words, ultimately it seems essential for children to be able to use these kinds of strategies. Nevertheless, phonics approaches emphasizing larger units, taught systematically, appear very effective with some children, including some with serious reading problems. Moreover, given the nature of the English writing system, which requires attention to letter patterns and to individual letters within words, a combination of phonemic-blending and larger-unit strategies may ultimately be most successful, as Lovett et al. (2003) suggest.

Reading Fluency

Nonautomatic readers require an emphasis on developing automatic word recognition and fluent reading. Sufficient reading practice is very important in fluency development. Although poor readers are much less likely than are good readers to read independently, effective teachers can find ways to motivate reading in students from a range of achievement levels (Ruddell, 1995; Ruddell & Unrau, 1994, see #51 this volume). For instance, teachers can allow choices of reading material, increase students' familiarity with favorite authors or book series, and encourage peer recommendations of books (Gambrell, Codling, & Palmer, 1996). Because it is very difficult for children to build fluency in texts that they cannot read accurately, poor readers must have access to independent reading materials at appropriate reading levels, as well as from a range of genres and topics.

Some nonautomatic readers, such as those with naming deficits, appear to have particular problems developing fluency. These children may benefit from more focused fluency-building techniques. Two such techniques involve repeated reading of connected text (e.g., Samuels, 1979) and speed drills on isolated words or phrases presented out of context (e.g., Fischer, 1995). In the former approach, students reread an instructional-level passage until they reach a preestablished criterion for rate, with the procedure repeated for increasingly difficult passages. In the latter approach, students read individual words out of context until they meet a predetermined rate criterion, with different or more difficult words used in subsequent trials. The words may involve common sight vocabulary or irregular words, or they may be selected to represent a phonetically regular pattern (e.g., consonant–vowel–consonant words with the vowel *a*) that children can decode accurately but on which they need to build speed. In both approaches, fluency-training sessions typically are relatively brief, from a couple of minutes for isolated word drills up to 15 or 20 minutes for some approaches using passage rereading.

In a literature review on methods of increasing fluency, Meyer and Felton (1999) conclude that both repeated reading of text and isolated word or phrase drills may be effective in improving fluency. Fluency practice should occur in texts that students can read with at least 90% to 95% accuracy, and texts should be read three or four times for optimal benefit. However, Meyer and Felton found mixed results for transfer of fluency instruction to comprehension. Assessment of gains in comprehension is complicated by (a) the fact that good comprehension draws from many other abilities besides fluency, (b) problems with accurate assessment of reading comprehension, and (c) variables such as children's age and reading development phase.

Several promising programs specifically target children with fluency difficulties. For example, RAVE-O (Retrieval, Accuracy, Vocabulary, Elaboration-Orthography), developed by Wolf and her colleagues (Wolf & Bowers, 1999; Wolf, Miller, & Donnelly, 2000) and used in conjunction with the synthetic phonics program of Lovett and her colleagues (e.g., Lovett et al., 2000), is a comprehensive approach to building fluency. The RAVE component of the program emphasizes multiple meanings of decodable core words (e.g., *bat* meaning something used to hit a ball vs. a winged mammal); the O component emphasizes automatic pattern recognition of word parts, such as common rimes, prefixes, and suffixes, with the idea that reading speed is facilitated by chunking of word parts. RAVE-O also includes the use of computer games, repeated reading of text, and word webs to build vocabulary and comprehension.

The Great Leaps program (Campbell, 1995; Mercer, Campbell, Miller, Mercer, & Lane, 2000) can be used with a wide range of students from the primary grades through adulthood. The program supplements existing reading instruction and can be used in as little as 5 to 7 minutes daily. Instruction is delivered on a one-on-one basis. Students read isolated word and phrase lists, as well as instructional-level passages, in 1- or 2-minute segments. Tutors provide feedback and model fluent reading. In a study using the Great Leaps program with middle school students identified with LDs, Mercer et al. (2000) found that the program significantly improved students' reading rate and instructional reading levels as measured by curriculum-based measures.

There is widespread agreement among authorities (e.g., NICHD, 2000; Samuels, 1979; Snow et al., 1998; Wolf & Katzir-Cohen, 2001) that fluency should be addressed directly in reading instruction, along with other important areas of reading. Because accurate word decoding is necessary (though not sufficient) for the development of fluency, many fluency approaches incorporate a systematic phonics component. Even after developing accurate decoding, some children appear to need a greater instructional emphasis on fluency than do others. However, effective techniques for improving fluency do not necessarily require large amounts of instructional time. Investigators have emphasized that, although fluency development plays an important role in reading comprehension, the development of comprehension abilities may also facilitate fluency. That is, the relation between fluency and comprehension may be a reciprocal one—with causality running in both directions (Meyer & Felton, 1999)—similar to the relation between phonemic awareness and word decoding. This view reinforces the importance of integrating fluency instruction into a more comprehensive program that also addresses vocabulary and comprehension.

Vocabulary and Comprehension

Vocabulary and oral language comprehension are not core problems for children with the traditional cognitive profile of RD involving a specific word-recognition deficit. However, like all children, children with RD need vocabulary and comprehension instruction as part of a broader program of reading development. Moreover, lack of higher-level reading experiences, inadequate comprehension instruction (e.g., Moody et al., 2000; Vaughn et al., 1998), and limited task persistence that may be a long-term consequence of academic failure (Gersten et al., 2001) all may combine to produce reading comprehension weaknesses in children with RD, even though they have good oral comprehension and even when they are reading material that they can decode accurately. This pattern is typical of delayed readers. In contrast, garden-variety poor readers have difficulties in oral as well as reading comprehension; these students require additional instructional emphasis on developing vocabulary and comprehension skills in both listening and reading. In the case of students with SCD, including both nonstrategic and suboptimal readers, it would be important to determine whether their comprehension difficulties are associated with generalized oral language comprehension problems and to provide remediation in this area if needed.

For beginning readers and children with RD, oral language is an especially critical vehicle for building vocabulary and comprehension. Some readers with RD may be able to decode only very simple text, which provides little opportunity for exposure to new vocabulary or higher-level comprehension skills. However, the same children may be quite capable of understanding and discussing age-appropriate texts that the teacher reads to them. Oral and written exposure to a variety of text types, including expository as well as narrative text, also is vital. Sensitivity to text structure, which differs across text types, is important to comprehension, and some of the comprehension difficulties of children with LD relate to poor awareness of text structure (Gersten et al., 2001).

Much of the variance in children's comprehension can be accounted for by individual differences in vocabulary (Stahl, 1999). Some investigators have argued that fostering the ability to infer word meanings from context, during either reading or listening, is a more effective way of developing vocabulary than is trying to teach a large number of specific words (e.g., Sternberg, 1987). However, one problem with learning words from context is that the very children who need to build vocabulary the most may be the least likely to encounter new words through reading (because they do little independent reading) or may be the least skilled at using contextual cues to infer word meanings.

A number of authorities (e.g., Beck, McKeown, & Omanson, 1987; Biemiller, 2001) have found that direct teaching of specific vocabulary words can be highly effective under certain conditions. Beck et al. (1987) suggest that vocabulary development should involve "rich instruction" (p. 149) that requires students to manipulate words in a variety of ways (e.g., relating new words to their own experiences and explaining associations among words), with much discussion of words. As opposed to traditional vocabulary instruction in which students study a set of new words each week from a workbook, rich vocabulary instruction provides students with many encounters with new words and requires them to use words outside vocabulary lessons. Words targeted for rich instruction should be chosen carefully with regard to their general utility and their relation to the overall curriculum. Beck et al. recommend that vocabulary instruction focus on "second tier" words—unusual words that children are unlikely to know but that also have relatively high generalizability across texts. For example, for typical third graders "second tier" words might be *discourage* and *amazement*, as opposed to common "first tier" words such as *house* and *kitchen* or "third tier" words such as *falcon* and *talons* (i.e., unusual words that may be important for understanding a specific text but that lack substantial generalizability across texts). Biemiller (2001) argues that most children can learn vocabulary at normal rates if given the opportunity to do so through systematic teaching of vocabulary beginning in the early grades. He suggests that instruction should emphasize common root words necessary to vocabulary development at various grade levels, as well as focus on deriving word meanings from prefixes, suffixes, and word families.

Another critical aspect of comprehension involves the ability to employ comprehension strategies such as summarization, prediction, inferencing, generating questions, and using graphic and semantic organizers (Pearson & Dole, 1987; Pressley, Harris, & Marks, 1992). Strategy instruction is important for all children, but especially for nonstrategic and delayed readers, who are particularly impaired in this area. For both normally achieving and struggling readers, teaching a combination of strategies appears to be more effective than is relying on a single strategy (Gersten et al., 2001; NICHD, 2000). Teacher modeling, think-alouds, and small interactive groups can be very effective in comprehension strategy instruction. Peterson et al. (2000) provide an excellent review of different approaches to strategy instruction that have been effective with middle school and secondary-level struggling readers.

Gersten et al. (2001) note a shift over several decades from strategy instruction emphasizing structured, explicit teaching of a series of steps (see, e.g., the Strategic Instruction Model described in Peterson et al., 2000) to a more fluid and flexible, but extensive, discussion of text (e.g., Ruddell & Unrau, 1994, see #51 this volume). In the latter approaches, including those such as Questioning the Author (Beck, McKeown, Sandora, Kucan, & Worthy, 1996) and reciprocal teaching (Palincsar & Brown, 1984), strategies such as summarization may be taught, but the emphasis is on careful reading and thoughtful reflection more than on acquisition of specific strategies. In their thorough review of research on comprehension instruction for students with LD, Gersten et al. (2001) conclude that structured, explicit instruction in well-defined strategies appears to be desirable for this population.

However, the optimal approach to comprehension instruction also might vary depending on the underlying cognitive profile of the struggling reader. For instance, students with weak oral language comprehension might require a different approach to reading comprehension instruction than do students with a specific word-recognition deficit but strong oral comprehension abilities. Likewise, students with a specific comprehension deficit who have good oral language comprehension but poor strategy knowledge might benefit from a different approach than do students with SCD who have poor oral language comprehension. Moreover, students whose oral language abilities are weak because of insufficient exposure to vocabulary and language might respond differently, or more rapidly, to instruction than do those with genuine language disorders. Research using a treatment-resister model and differentiation of poor reader profiles, with a focus on comprehension instruction, could help to clarify these issues.

Examples of Comprehensive Approaches for Remediating Reading Difficulties

Many comprehensive programs that address multiple areas of reading (e.g., word decoding, fluency, and comprehension) exist for remediating reading difficulties. Although an extensive review of these programs is beyond the scope of the article, four programs exemplifying a range of approaches for addressing reading problems will be discussed briefly: Success for All, Reading Recovery, READ 180, and LANGUAGE!

Success for All. Success for All (SFA) is an extensive school reform model originally developed by Slavin, Madden, and their colleagues (e.g., Slavin et al., 1996; Slavin, Madden, Dolan, & Wasik, 1996) at Johns Hopkins University in Baltimore, Maryland. The model has been used most commonly in large, economically needy urban school districts with a history of widespread reading failure. SFA has a Spanish as well as an English version. The reading curriculum—called *Roots* in the beginning elementary grades and *Wings* at the upper-elementary level—is highly structured with specific materials, assessments, lesson plans, and time allotments for various activities. Homogeneous grouping, sometimes across grades, is used. Both *Roots* and *Wings* involve a 90-minute reading period in which important reading-related abilities, including oral language comprehension, are addressed, with greater emphasis on phonemic awareness and word decoding in *Roots* and on reading comprehension in *Wings*. One-on-one tutoring is provided for students continuing to experience reading difficulties in the early grades.

The effectiveness of SFA in reducing special education placement and retention rates, as well as in improving children's overall reading achievement relative to control groups of economically needy children, is well documented (e.g., Slavin et al., 1996; Slavin & Madden, 2000). Effect sizes of SFA are particularly large for the lowest quartile of children in a class—the population from which most special education children would come—and SFA has been found to reduce referrals of children for LDs services by one half or more (Slavin & Madden, 2000; Smith, Ross, & Casey, 1994). However, SFA has not been without its critics. One area of criticism has involved the fact that, although SFA children perform significantly better than similar populations of children without treatment, many do not perform at grade-appropriate levels on nationally standardized tests, especially beyond the primary grades (e.g., Venezky, 1994). It appears that SFA is most successful at keeping children on track in reading in the earliest grades, when basic word-recognition skills are being acquired, but may be somewhat less successful in the later grades, when vocabulary, broad language skills, and strategic knowledge become more critical to continuing progress in reading.

Another issue in the implementation of SFA involves teachers' responses to this kind of highly structured and programmed model. For instance, Datnow and

Castellano (2000), who studied two different SFA schools, found that, despite the expectation that teachers would follow prescribed lesson plans and activities closely, almost all teachers made adaptations to the program. Interestingly, despite some dissatisfaction with the constraints of SFA, most teachers supported its continued implementation because they believed (correctly) that it benefited student achievement. However, as Datnow and Castellano (2000) point out, it appears inevitable that teachers will make adaptations to any method. Therefore, it is important to determine which specific features of SFA (or any other program) are most essential to student achievement and how different adaptations may affect student learning.

Reading Recovery. Reading Recovery (RR), originally developed by Clay (1985) in New Zealand but now widely used in the United States and elsewhere, is a first-grade intervention program. RR involves 30- to 40-minute tutorial sessions delivered by teachers trained extensively in the method. Tutorial sessions focus on having the child reread familiar books, do letter- and word-identification activities using plastic letters, reassemble a cut-up story, and read a new story. While writing the story, the child is also encouraged to listen for sounds when attempting to spell unknown words. In each session, the teacher obtains a running record of the child's reading in text for use in instructional decision making. RR is a short-term intervention, approximately 12 to 20 weeks in duration. Children who do not benefit after 20 weeks may be referred for additional help elsewhere, such as to special education or Title I reading programs.

Proponents of the program have reported strong gains in reading by RR children (e.g., Pinnell, Lyons, DeFord, Bryk, & Seltzer, 1994), with 80% or more of treated samples attaining grade-appropriate reading skills. However, RR also has met with criticism from researchers. Some concerns have revolved around methodological issues, for example, that RR does not serve the most impaired readers or that methods of constituting comparison groups tend to bias results in favor of RR (Hiebert, 1994; Shanahan & Barr, 1995). Other concerns have been raised about the cost-effectiveness of the program.

Recent criticisms have focused especially on the instructional activities and theoretical underpinnings of RR. Both Pressley (1998) and Chapman, Tunmer, and Prochnow (2001) point out that RR relies on a multiple-cueing-systems model of reading development. This model is not consistent with research evidence indicating that the development of skilled reading is associated with increasingly accurate and automatic word recognition, not the use of multiple cueing systems for reading words. Although word decoding and phonological skills are addressed to some extent in RR through the plastic letters and writing activities, these skills are not emphasized or taught systematically. In a longitudinal study in New Zealand, Chapman et al. (2001) found that most RR children had deficiencies in phonological skills that were not improved by the program. Reading

Recovery did not significantly increase the reading achievement of these children, who also evidenced the usual negative effects of reading failure, such as a decline in self-concept. Conversely, adaptations of RR that include a strong, systematic phonological component (Hatcher, Hulme, & Ellis, 1994; Iverson & Tunmer, 1993) report substantial increases in the effectiveness of the program.

READ 180. READ 180 is a computer-supported program for struggling readers in grades 4 to 12. It was originally developed by Hasselbring and his colleagues (Hasselbring, Goin, Taylor, Bottge, & Daley, 1997) at Vanderbilt University in Nashville, Tennessee, and has been used in numerous school districts around the United States (see, e.g., Taylor, 2002). It is available in Spanish as well as English. The main components of the program, organized within a 90-minute block period, include the following: whole-group teacher-directed instruction in areas such as vocabulary, word decoding, and reading comprehension; small-group direct instruction; development of background knowledge through video clips on CD-ROM, followed by instructional reading of leveled, content area passages; independent use of software to give students individualized skills practice in areas such as structural analysis of unfamiliar words; modeled reading using audiobooks; and independent reading of leveled novels.

READ 180 is a relatively new program that lacks a research base in peer-reviewed journals. However, the program directly addresses a range of skills known to be important in reading, with substantial use of technology, in a way that appears to be appropriate and motivating for middle school and secondary-level poor readers. It is rated as a promising program for struggling secondary readers by Peterson et al. (2000).

LANGUAGE! LANGUAGE! (Greene, Eberhardt, Whitney, & Moats, 2000) is a comprehensive literacy curriculum designed for struggling readers, including English-language learners, "curriculum casualties" (those for whom previous literacy instruction was problematic), and students with RD. The curriculum includes separate sets of materials for grades 1–5 and 6–12 and is implemented by teachers after considerable training in the method. LANGUAGE! addresses numerous areas important to literacy achievement, including oral language comprehension, phonemic awareness, word decoding, reading fluency, vocabulary, reading comprehension, basic grammar, and both mechanical and content aspects of written expression. Students are grouped homogeneously for instruction, which is very highly structured and sequential. Materials that accompany LANGUAGE! include assessments, teacher guides, phonemic awareness materials, decodable books, and a CD-ROM for selecting supplemental reading materials.

Like READ 180, LANGUAGE! is a relatively new program that does not have an independent research base in peer-reviewed journals. However, Greene (1996) demonstrated that a 6-month intervention using the program was very effective in improving the oral reading fluency, word decoding, spelling, and reading comprehension of a group of adolescents with low literacy who had also been in trouble with the law. The program is especially comprehensive in scope and addresses many important literacy abilities in a highly systematic fashion.

Conclusions and Future Directions

This article has suggested that cognitive profiles provide a more educationally useful way to conceptualize and address reading disability (RD)—and other reading problems—than do educational guidelines involving discrepancy criteria and IQ tests. Identifying reading-related cognitive patterns and profiles does not involve a scattershot administration of processing tests to establish a "processing disorder." Rather, it involves assessment of specific abilities known to be important in learning to read, as well as interpreting patterns of performance in relation to research evidence on typical reading development and difficulties. Researchers have associated RD as it is viewed traditionally—that is, a specific difficulty in learning to read not caused by more generalized learning problems—with a specific word-recognition deficit profile, which typically involves phonological weaknesses. This profile in turn may include four possible patterns of difficulty that were discussed at length in the article. Two other common profiles of poor reading, garden-variety poor reading (GVPR) and a specific comprehension deficit (SCD), including two patterns of SCD, also were discussed. Although GVPR and SCD differ from the profile associated with traditional RD, with some different implications for identification and intervention, all three profiles constitute serious reading difficulties that require prompt intervention and remediation.

The profiling approach, by itself, does not distinguish genuine cases of RD from more experientially or instructionally based reading problems (nor does the use of processing measures or discrepancy criteria). A variety of ultimate causes could underlie any given profile or pattern. Nevertheless, this approach is very useful in early identification because certain kinds of cognitive patterns tend to presage later reading problems, and it provides clear implications for instruction. Furthermore, the use of cognitive profiles is relevant to poor readers in general, not only those with RD. This final section of the article will consider some issues involved in using cognitive profiles in education and some possible future directions for research.

One important issue in the use of profiles has to do with their stability (or lack of it) over time. As discussed previously, language deficit profiles may shift during the preschool years, with children who later become poor readers showing different patterns of deficits at different points in development (Scarborough, 2002). During early elementary school, word-decoding and language comprehension skills become relatively separable (Whitehurst & Lonigan, 2002), with some children showing quite different levels of performance in the two areas. Formal schooling also introduces an important set of variables that may influence whether and how a particular deficit is manifested. For instance, some children may have relatively stable underlying weaknesses in naming speed or oral language comprehension that become more problematic, and hence more noticeable, as the curriculum makes greater demands on reading volume and comprehension. Ultimately, poor reading itself may negatively affect some cognitive and linguistic abilities because these abilities appear to be acquired, in part, through reading (Stanovich & Cunningham, 1993). More optimistically, effective instruction also may alter a child's deficit profile. All these factors may underlie the observation that, even in school-age children, deficit profiles frequently are unstable over time (e.g., Badian, 1999). Although stability over time is not essential for making use of profiles in instruction, further knowledge about the stability and relationship of different profiles could have important educational implications. For example, unraveling the relationship between preschool language deficit profiles and later reading difficulties could increase the success of early intervention, and identification of subtle oral language deficiencies, coupled with effective remediation, might prevent the later emergence of some SCDs in reading.

Current arguments about educational identification of RD often pit discrepancy criteria against treatment-resister models. Discrepancy criteria tend to identify as reading-disabled poor readers with a specific word-recognition deficit, especially if the metric used involves a discrepancy between listening comprehension and reading comprehension. (If an IQ-achievement discrepancy is employed, children with more generalized language problems occasionally may be identified, providing their nonverbal IQs are high.) However, without an analysis of the cognitive patterns involved in children's reading difficulties, the discrepancy approach is not useful educationally, in addition to its numerous other limitations (e.g., Siegel, 1988, 1989; Stanovich, 1991). Moreover, without the incorporation of a treatment-resister component, or at least the use of well-defined prereferral strategies in reading, this approach risks inappropriately classifying as learning disabled many poor readers who have instructionally or experientially based reading problems. A few state guidelines on LD do incorporate extensive prereferral strategies that target specific areas of reading (see, e.g., Connecticut State Department of Education, 1999). Nevertheless, although IDEA stipulates that children should not be identified as having a disability if the reason for their difficulties is lack of instruction in reading, many states do not mandate any kind of prereferral intervention (Buck et al., 2003).

Many researchers appear to favor adoption of a treatment-resister model for identifying RD (Speece & Shekitka, 2002). If discrepancy criteria were abandoned entirely, children with a wide range of cognitive profiles, including those with GVPR and SCD, could be identified as having RD. However, some practical problems exist with using treatment-resister definitions in eligibility guidelines, as a variety of LD organizations pointed out in May 2003, when the

U.S. House of Representatives approved a reauthorization of IDEA allowing—not requiring—states to employ a treatment-resister definition of LD in lieu of discrepancy criteria (e.g., Learning Disabilities Association of America, 2003). Legitimate concerns have been raised about exactly how treatment-resister definitions would be implemented in education (although some specific implementation plans have been proposed, e.g., Horowitz, Lichtenstein, & Roller, 2002) and about the lack of longitudinal research on the efficacy and cost of treatment-resister models. Conceptual and technical problems involved in using treatment-resister models include measurement issues, large-scale implementation, and decisions about whether treatments should be rooted primarily in general education or in more individualized, intensive interventions such as tutoring (Denton, Vaughn, & Fletcher, 2003; Vaughn & Fuchs, 2003). Furthermore, although state education agencies generally appear receptive to treatment-resister views of LD, most current state guidelines are based heavily on discrepancy criteria, and implementing treatment-resister models will require extensive change in classification practices (Reschly, Hosp, & Schmied, 2003).

A considerable research base exists on treatment-resister models (e.g., Al Otaiba, 2001; Fuchs, 2003; Speece, Case, & Molloy, 2003; Torgesen, Alexander, et al., 2001; Vellutino & Scanlon, 2002; Vellutino, Scanlon, & Lyon, 2000), but most treatment-resister studies have focused on young children. Applications of the models to older children and to children with SCD have received much less attention. Research focused on these populations is vital to implementing a treatment-resister approach in education on a large scale. In addition, more research is needed on the different components of comprehension (e.g., vocabulary, listening comprehension, and strategic knowledge) and on how different types of comprehension weaknesses might respond to different approaches to comprehension instruction. Further study of the efficacy of interventions aimed specifically at older poor readers is essential because there is substantial agreement that even the most effective early intervention programs will not prevent reading difficulties in all children and because some serious reading problems do not emerge until the middle grades or later. A profiling approach could be especially helpful with older poor readers, who must cope with high reading demands in the general education curriculum and whose difficulties may involve an especially wide range of patterns. For example, three struggling secondary readers might obtain the same reading comprehension score on a standardized test, but if one has strong oral language comprehension coupled with poor word-decoding accuracy and fluency, the second has the opposite pattern, and the third has fluency problems only, then the interventions for the three students will need to differ in some significant ways.

Longitudinal research addressing the conceptual and technical issues involved in large-scale implementations of treatment-resister models is very important. However, there already is a substantial research consensus on the conceptual, as well as technical and practical, flaws in the discrepancy approach. If the history of the LD field were different and an IQ-achievement discrepancy were proposed as a "new" alternative to determine eligibility, few researchers would embrace that alternative with enthusiasm. Moreover, although the tendency of schools to ignore eligibility criteria is well documented (MacMillan & Speece, 1999; Scruggs & Mastropieri, 2002), schools might be more inclined to adhere to eligibility guidelines and diagnostic approaches that actually are useful educationally. Of course, to implement treatment-resister models appropriately, schools and teachers also require adequate human and material resources. Whether they are general educators, special educators, or reading specialists, even the most caring, competent teachers cannot be effective if they are overwhelmed with large groups of struggling readers spanning many reading levels (Moody et al., 2000; Vaughn et al., 1998).

Finally, implementing both treatment-resister models and the use of cognitive profiles requires that teachers have strong preservice preparation and many opportunities for ongoing professional development. Employing cognitive profiles in diagnosis and instruction entails a broad knowledge base not only about literacy development, the nature of written English, and individual differences that may affect learning to read, but also about how to select and use measures of important reading-related abilities, interpret diagnostic data to plan a comprehensive program of reading instruction, and teach a wide range of reading-related abilities to diverse learners. This kind of approach to teacher education is consistent with the current recommendations of many professional organizations (e.g., Brady & Moats, 1997; International Reading Association, 2000), but it also places high demands on teacher preparation. Furthermore, relatively brief preparation on some topics may not be sufficient for developing the level of knowledge needed for teaching reading effectively, especially to children experiencing difficulties (e.g., Spear-Swerling & Brucker, 2003). Thus, establishing priorities at different levels of professional development—for instance, for preservice teachers, first-year teachers, and more experienced educators—appears crucial.

Encouragingly, a number of studies (McCutchen et al., 2002; McCutchen & Berninger, 1999; O'Connor, 1999; Palincsar, Collins, et al., 2000; Palincsar, Magnusson, et al., 2001) have suggested that developing teachers' knowledge base about language and reading can improve children's achievement. Continued research in this area may offer important insights about which approaches to teacher education are most successful in yielding benefits for children and in attracting and retaining effective teachers. Research designs focused on differences among teachers (e.g., those with more versus less prior preparation or experience), as well as differences among children (e.g., older versus younger struggling readers), can be especially helpful. Studies exploring contextual factors, such as those affecting teachers' willingness to continue to implement research-based programs and their tendency to make adaptations to programs (e.g., Datnow & Castellano, 2000), also are valuable.

Although treatment-resister approaches can help to rule out instructional causes of reading difficulties, at present there is no definitive way for educators to diagnose genuine RD in individual children. Not only do current educational guidelines fail to provide this kind of definitive diagnosis, but those relying on discrepancy criteria also make early identification difficult, may misidentify as "disabled" poor readers whose problems are largely experiential or instructional in nature, and offer little educational insight into reading problems. In contrast, an analysis of the cognitive patterns seen in RD, based on the kinds of abilities that are known to play a role in learning to read, and interpreted in reference to typical reading development is highly relevant to early identification and instructional planning. Moreover, such an approach is useful not only for students with RD but for other poor readers as well.

References

*indicates that article is included on TMPR5 supplementary CD.

Adams, M.J. (1990). *Beginning to read: Thinking and learning about print*. Cambridge, MA: MIT Press.

Adams, M.J. (1998). The three-cueing system. In F. Lehr & J. Osborn (Eds.), *Literacy for all: Issues in teaching and learning* (pp. 73–99). New York: Guilford.

Alexander, A., Anderson, H., Heilman, P.C., Voeller, K.S., & Torgesen, J.K. (1991). Phonological awareness training and remediation of analytic decoding deficits in a group of severe dyslexics. *Annals of Dyslexia, 41*, 193–206.

Al Otaiba, S. (2001). Children who do not respond to early literacy instruction: A longitudinal study across kindergarten and first grade. *Reading Research Quarterly, 36*, 344–346.

Anderson, R.C., Hiebert, E.H., Scott, J.A., & Wilkinson, I.A.G. (1985). *Becoming a nation of readers: The report of the Commission on Reading*. Washington, DC: National Institute of Education.

Badian, N. (1999). Reading disability defined as a discrepancy between listening and reading comprehension: A longitudinal study of stability, gender differences, and prevalence. *Journal of Learning Disabilities, 32*, 138–148.

Beck, I.L., & Juel, C. (1995). The role of decoding in learning to read. *American Educator, 19*(2), 8, 21–25, 39–42.

Beck, I.L., McKeown, M.G., & Omanson, R.C. (1987). The effects and uses of diverse vocabulary instructional techniques. In M.G. McKeown & M.E. Curtis (Eds.), *The nature of vocabulary acquisition* (pp. 147–163). Hillsdale, NJ: Erlbaum.

Beck, I.L., McKeown, M.G., Sandora, C., Kucan, L., & Worthy, J. (1996). Questioning the author: A yearlong classroom implementation to engage students with text. *The Elementary School Journal, 96*(4), 385–414.

Berninger, V.W., & Abbott, R.D. (1994). Redefining learning disabilities: Moving beyond aptitude-achievement discrepancies to failure to respond to validated treatment protocols. In G.R. Lyon (Ed.), *Frames of reference for the assessment of learning disabilities: New views on measurement issues* (pp. 163–183). Baltimore: Brookes.

Biemiller, A. (1999). *Language and reading success* (Reading Research to Practice, Vol. 5). Cambridge, MA: Brookline Books.

Biemiller, A. (2001). Teaching vocabulary: Early, direct, and sequential. *American Educator, 25*, 24–28, 47.

Blachman, B.A. (1994). What we have learned from longitudinal studies of phonological processing and reading, and some unanswered questions: A response to Torgesen, Wagner, and Rashotte. *Journal of Learning Disabilities, 27*, 287–291.

Borkowski, J.G., Carr, M., & Pressley, M. (1987). Spontaneous strategy use: Perspectives from metacognitive theory. *Intelligence, 11*, 61–75.

Brady, S., & Moats, L.C. (1997). *Informed instruction for reading success: Foundations for teacher preparation. A position paper of the International Dyslexia Association.* Baltimore: International Dyslexia Association.

Buck, G.H., Polloway, E.A., Smith-Thomas, A., & Cook, K.W. (2003). Prereferral intervention processes: A survey of state practices. *Exceptional Children, 69*(3), 349–360.

Burgess, S.R., Hecht, S.A., & Lonigan, C.J. (2002). Relations of Home Literacy Environment (HLE) to the development of reading-related abilities: A one-year longitudinal study. *Reading Research Quarterly, 37,* 408–426.

Bus, A.G., & van IJzendoorn, M.H. (1999). Phonological awareness and early reading: A meta-analysis of experimental training studies. *Journal of Educational Psychology, 91*(3), 403–414.

Byrne, B. (1992). Studies in the acquisition procedure for reading: Rationale, hypotheses, and data. In P.B. Gough, L.C. Ehri, & R. Treiman (Eds.), *Reading acquisition* (pp. 1–34). Hillsdale, NJ: Erlbaum.

Byrne, B., & Fielding-Barnsley, R. (1995). Evaluation of a program to teach phonemic awareness to young children: A 2- and 3-year follow-up and a new preschool trial. *Journal of Educational Psychology, 87,* 488–503.

Campbell, K.U. (1995). *Great leaps reading program.* Gainesville, FL: Diarmuid.

Cardoso-Martins, C. (2001). The reading abilities of beginning readers of Brazilian Portuguese: Implications for a theory of reading acquisition. *Scientific Studies of Reading, 5*(4), 289–317.

Carver, R.P., & David, A.H. (2001). Investigating reading achievement using a causal model. *Scientific Studies of Reading, 5*(2), 107–140.

Catts, H.W., Fey, M.E., Zhang, X., & Tomblin, J.B. (1999). Language basis of reading and reading disabilities: Evidence from a longitudinal investigation. *Scientific Studies of Reading, 3*(4), 331–361.

Ceci, S.J. (1990). *On intelligence...more or less: A bio-ecological treatise on intellectual development.* Englewood Cliffs, NJ: Prentice Hall.

Centers for Disease Control and Prevention. (1997). *Screening young children for lead poisoning: Guidance for state and local public health officials.* Atlanta, GA: Author.

Chall, J.S. (1983a). *Learning to read: The great debate* (2nd ed.). New York: McGraw-Hill.

Chall, J.S. (1983b). *Stages of reading development.* New York: McGraw-Hill.

Chall, J.S. (1994). Patterns of adult reading. *Learning Disabilities, 5*(1), 29–33.

Chall, J.S., Jacobs, V.A., & Baldwin, L.E. (1991). *The reading crisis: Why poor children fall behind.* Cambridge, MA: Harvard University Press.

Chapman, J.W., & Tunmer, W.E. (1997). A longitudinal study of beginning reading achievement and reading self-concept. *British Journal of Educational Psychology, 67,* 279–291.

Chapman, J.W., Tunmer, W.E., & Prochnow, J.E. (2001). Does success in the Reading Recovery program depend on developing proficiency in phonological processing skills? A longitudinal study in a whole language instructional context. *Scientific Studies of Reading, 5,* 141–176.

Christensen, C.A. (1998). Learning disability: Issues of representation, power, and the medicalization of school failure. In R.J. Sternberg & L. Spear-Swerling (Eds.), *Perspectives on learning disabilities: Biological, cognitive, contextual* (pp. 227–249). Boulder, CO: Westview.

Clay, M.M. (1985). *The early detection of reading difficulties* (3rd ed.). Auckland, NZ: Heinemann.

Connecticut State Department of Education. (1999). *Guidelines for identifying children with learning disabilities* (2nd ed.). Hartford, CT: Author.

Cunningham, A.E., & Stanovich, K.E. (1990). Tracking the unique effects of print exposure in children: Associations with vocabulary, general knowledge, and spelling. *Journal of Educational Psychology, 83,* 264–274.

Datnow, A., & Castellano, M. (2000). Teachers' responses to Success for All: How beliefs, experiences, and adaptations shape implementation. *American Educational Research Journal, 37*(3), 775–799.

Davidson, R.K., & Strucker, J. (2002). Patterns of word-recognition errors among adult basic education native and nonnative speakers of English. *Scientific Studies of Reading, 6*(3), 299–316.

Denton, C.A., Vaughn, S., & Fletcher, J.M. (2003). Bring research-based practice in reading intervention to scale. *Learning Disabilities Research & Practice, 18,* 201–211.

Dickinson, D.K., & Sprague, K.E. (2002). The nature and impact of early childhood care environments on the language and early literacy development of children from low-income families. In S.B. Neuman & D.K. Dickinson (Eds.), *Handbook of early literacy research* (pp. 263–280). New York: Guilford.

Drame, E.R. (2002). Sociocultural context effects on teachers' readiness to refer for learning disabilities. *Exceptional Children, 69*(1), 41–53.

Duke, N.K. (2000). Print environments and experiences offered to first-grade students in very low- and very high-SES school districts. *Reading Research Quarterly, 35*, 456–457.

Durgunoglu, A.Y., & Oney, B. (2002). Phonological awareness in literacy acquisition: It's not only for children. *Scientific Studies of Reading, 6*(3), 245–266.

Ehri, L.C. (1991). Learning to read and spell words. In L. Rieben & C.A. Perfetti (Eds.), *Learning to read: Basic research and its implications* (pp. 57–73). Hillsdale, NJ: Erlbaum.

Ehri, L.C. (1992). Reconceptualizing the development of sight word reading and its relationship to recoding. In P.B. Gough, L.C. Ehri, & R. Treiman (Eds.), *Reading acquisition* (pp. 107–143). Hillsdale, NJ: Erlbaum.

Ehri, L.C. (1997). Learning to read and learning to spell are one and the same, almost. In C.A. Perfetti, L. Rieben, & M. Fayol (Eds.), *Learning to spell: Research, theory and practice across languages* (pp. 237–269). Mahwah, NJ: Erlbaum.

Engelmann, S. (1980). *Direct instruction.* Englewood Cliffs, NJ: Prentice Hall.

Fischer, P. (1995). *Multi-sequence speed drills for fluency in decoding.* Farmington, ME: Oxton House.

Fletcher, J.M., Shaywitz, S.E., Shankweiler, D.P., Katz, L., Liberman, I.Y., Stuebing, K.K., et al. (1994). Cognitive profiles of reading disability: Comparisons of discrepancy and low achievement profiles. *Journal of Educational Psychology, 86*(1), 6–23.

Foster, K.C., Erickson, G.C., Foster, D.F., Brinkman, D., & Torgesen, J.K. (1994). Computer administered instruction in phonological awareness: Evaluation of the DaisyQuest Program. *Journal of Research and Development in Education, 27*(2), 126–137.

Fowler, A.E., & Scarborough, H.S. (1993). *Should reading-disabled adults be distinguished from other adults seeking literacy instruction? A review of theory and research*

(Tech. Rep. No. TR93-7). University of Pennsylvania, National Center on Adult Literacy.

Frith, U. (1985). Beneath the surface of developmental dyslexia. In K.E. Patterson, J.C. Marshall, & M. Coltheart (Eds.), *Surface dyslexia: Neuropsychological and cognitive analysis of phonological reading* (pp. 301–330). London: Erlbaum.

Fuchs, D., Fuchs, L.S., Thompson, A., Svenson, E., Yen, L., Al Otaiba, S., et al. (2001). Peer-assisted learning strategies in reading: Extensions for kindergarten, first grade, and high school. *Remedial and Special Education, 22*(1), 15–21.

Fuchs, L.S. (2003). Assessing intervention responsiveness: Conceptual and technical issues. *Learning Disabilities Research & Practice, 18*, 172–186.

Fuchs, L.S., & Fuchs, D. (1998). Treatment validity: A unifying concept for reconceptualizing the identification of learning disabilities. *Learning Disabilities Research & Practice, 13*, 204–219.

Fuchs, L.S., Fuchs, D., Hosp, M.K., & Jenkins, J.R. (2001). Oral reading fluency as an indicator of reading competence: A theoretical, empirical, and historical analysis. *Scientific Studies of Reading, 5*(3), 239–256.

Gambrell, L.B., Codling, R.M., & Palmer, B.M. (1996). *Elementary students' motivation to read* (Research Rep. No. 52). Athens, GA: National Reading Research Center.

Garner, R. (1990). When children and adults do not use learning strategies: Toward a theory of settings. *Review of Educational Research, 60*, 517–529.

Gaskins, I.W., Downer, M.A., Anderson, R.C., Cunningham, P.M., Gaskins, R.W., Schommer, M., et al. (1988). A metacognitive approach to phonics: Using what you know to decode what you don't know. *Remedial and Special Education, 9*(1), 36–41.

Gaskins, I.W., Ehri, L.C., Cress, C., O'Hara, C., & Donnelly, K. (1996/1997). Procedures for word learning: Making discoveries about words. *The Reading Teacher, 50*, 312–327.

*Gersten, R., Fuchs, L.S., Williams, J.P., & Baker, S. (2001). Teaching reading comprehension strategies to students with learning disabilities: A review of research. *Review of Educational Research, 71*(2), 279–320.

Gillingham, A., & Stillman, B.W. (1997). *The Gillingham manual: Remedial training for children with specific disability in reading,* spelling, and penmanship (8th ed.). Cambridge, MA: Educators Publishing Service.

Good, R.H., Simmons, D.C., & Kame'enui, E.J. (2001). The importance and decision-making utility of a continuum of fluency-based indicators of foundational reading skills for third-grade high-stakes outcomes. *Scientific Studies of Reading, 5*(3), 257–288.

Gough, P.B., & Juel, C. (1991). The first stages of word recognition. In L. Rieben & C.A. Perfetti (Eds.), *Learning to read: Basic research and its implications* (pp. 47–56). Hillsdale, NJ: Erlbaum.

Gough, P.B., & Tunmer, W.E. (1986). Decoding, reading, and reading disability. *Remedial and Special Education, 7*(1), 6–10.

Greenberg, D., Ehri, L.C., & Perin, D. (2002). Do adult literacy students make the same word-reading and spelling errors as children matched for word-reading age? *Scientific Studies of Reading, 6*(3), 221–243.

Greene, J.F. (1996). Effects of an individualized structured language curriculum for middle and high school students. *Annals of Dyslexia, 46*, 97–121.

Greene, J.F., Eberhardt, N.C., Whitney, A., & Moats, L.C. (2000). *Language! A literacy intervention curriculum.* Longmont, CO: Sopris West.

Grigorenko, E.L. (1999). The biological foundations of developmental dyslexia. In R.J. Sternberg & L. Spear-Swerling (Eds.), *Perspectives on learning disabilities: Biological, cognitive, contextual* (pp. 22–59). Boulder, CO: Westview.

Hart, B., & Risley, T.R. (1995). *Meaningful differences in the everyday experience of young American children.* Baltimore: Brookes.

Hasselbring, T.S., Goin, L., Taylor, R., Bottge, B., & Daley, P. (1997). The computer doesn't embarrass me. *Educational Leadership, 55*(3), 30–33.

Hatcher, P.J., Hulme, C., & Ellis, A.W. (1994). Ameliorating early reading failure by integrating the teaching of reading and phonological skills: The phonological linkage hypothesis. *Child Development, 65*(1), 41–57.

Hayes, D.P., & Ahrens, M.G. (1988). Vocabulary simplifications for children: A special case of "motherese"? *Journal of Child Language, 15*(2), 395–410.

Hiebert, E.H. (1994). Reading Recovery in the United States: What difference does it make to an age cohort? *Educational Researcher, 23*(9), 15–25.

Hoover, W.A., & Gough, P.B. (1990). The simple view of reading. *Reading and Writing: An Interdisciplinary Journal, 2*(2), 127–160.

Horowitz, S.H., Lichtenstein, B., & Roller, C. (2002, February). *An intervention-oriented, multi-tiered approach for identifying and serving students with learning disabilities.* Paper prepared for the Learning Disabilities Roundtable "Finding Common Ground" Initiative, Washington, DC.

Individuals With Disabilities Education Act PL 105-17 of 1997, 20 U.S.C.A§1400 *et seq.*

International Reading Association. (2000). *Excellent reading teachers: A position statement of the International Reading Association.* Newark, DE: Author.

Iverson, S., & Tunmer, W.E. (1993). Phonological processing and the Reading Recovery Program. *Journal of Educational Psychology, 85*, 112–126.

Juel, C. (1988). Learning to read and write: A longitudinal study of fifty-four children from first through fourth grades. *Journal of Educational Psychology, 80*(4), 437–447.

Juel, C., & Minden-Cupp, C. (2000). Learning to read words: Linguistic units and instructional strategies. *Reading Research Quarterly, 35*, 458–492.

Kletzien, S.B. (1991). Strategy use by good and poor comprehenders reading expository text of differing levels. *Reading Research Quarterly, 26*, 67–86.

LaBerge, D., & Samuels, S.J. (1974). Toward a theory of automatic information processing in reading. *Cognitive Psychology, 6*, 293–323.

Landerl, K., Wimmer, H., & Frith, U. (1997). The impact of orthographic consistency on dyslexia: A German-English comparison. *Cognition, 63*(3), 315–334.

Leach, J.M., Scarborough, H.S., & Rescorla, L. (2003). Late-emerging reading disabilities. *Journal of Educational Psychology, 95*(2), 211–224.

Learning Disabilities Association of America. (2003). *LDA points on reauthorization of IDEA.* Pittsburgh, PA: Learning Disabilities Association of America. Retrieved May 22, 2003, from http://www.ldanatl.org

Leppanen, P.H.T., Pihko, E., Eklund, K.M., & Lyytinen, H. (1999). Cortical responses of infants with and without a genetic risk for dyslexia. II. Group effects. *Neuroreport, 10*, 969–973.

Lindamood, P., & Lindamood, P. (1998). *LiPS: The Lindamood phoneme sequencing pro-*

gram for reading, spelling and speech. Austin, TX: Pro-Ed.

Lovett, M.W. (1987). A developmental approach to reading disability: Accuracy and speed criteria of normal and deficient reading skill. *Child Development*, 58(1), 234–260.

Lovett, M.W., Barron, R.W., & Benson, N.J. (2003). Effective remediation of word identification and decoding difficulties in school-age children with reading disabilities. In H.L. Swanson, K.R. Harris, & S. Graham (Eds.), *Handbook of learning disabilities* (pp. 273–292). New York: Guilford.

Lovett, M.W., Lacerenza, L., Borden, S., Frijters, J., Steinbach, K., & DePalma, M. (2000). Components of effective remediation for developmental reading disabilities: Combining phonological and strategy-based instruction to improve outcomes. *Journal of Educational Psychology*, 92(2), 263–283.

MacMillan, D.L., & Speece, D.L. (1999). Utility of current diagnostic categories for research and practice. In R. Gallimore, L.P. Bernheimer, D.L. MacMillan, D.L. Speece, & S. Vaughn (Eds.), *Developmental perspectives on children with high-incidence disabilities* (pp. 111–113). Mahwah, NJ: Erlbaum.

Mann, V.A., & Liberman, I.Y. (1984). Phonological awareness and verbal short-term memory. *Journal of Learning Disabilities*, 17(10), 592–599.

McCandliss, B., Beck, I.L., Sandak, R., & Perfetti, C. (2003). Focusing attention on decoding for children with poor reading skills: A study of the word building intervention. *Scientific Studies of Reading*, 7(1), 75–104.

McCutchen, D., Abbott, R.D., Green, L.B., Beretvas, S.N., Cox, S., Potter, N.S., et al. (2002). Beginning literacy: Links among teacher knowledge, teacher practice, and student learning. *Journal of Learning Disabilities*, 35(1), 69–86.

McCutchen, D., & Berninger, V.W. (1999). Those who know, teach well: Helping teachers master literacy-related subject-matter knowledge. *Learning Disabilities Research & Practice*, 14(4), 215–226.

Mercer, C.D., Campbell, K.U., Miller, M.D., Mercer, K.D., & Lane, H.B. (2000). Effects of a reading fluency intervention for middle schoolers with specific learning disabilities. *Learning Disabilities Research & Practice*, 15(4), 179–189.

Meyer, M.S., & Felton, R.H. (1999). Repeated reading to enhance fluency: Old approaches and new directions. *Annals of Dyslexia, 49*, 283–306.

Moats, L.C., & Lyon, G.R. (1993). Learning disabilities in the United States: Advocacy, science, and the future of the field. *Journal of Learning Disabilities, 26*(5), 282–294.

Moody, S.W., Vaughn, S., Hughes, M.T., & Fischer, M. (2000). Reading instruction in the resource room: Set up for failure. *Exceptional Children, 66*(3), 305–316.

Nation, K., & Snowling, M. (1997). Assessing reading difficulties: The validity and utility of current measures of reading skill. *British Journal of Educational Psychology, 67*, 359–370.

National Center for Education Statistics. (2001). *Digest of education statistics, 2001.* Washington, DC: National Center for Education Statistics. Retrieved June 17, 2003, from http://nces.ed.gov/pubs2002/digest2001/tables/dt052.asp

National Institute of Child Health and Human Development. (2000). *Report of the National Reading Panel. Teaching children to read: An evidence-based assessment of the scientific research literature on reading and its implications for reading instruction* (NIH Publication No. 00-4769). Washington, DC: U.S. Government Printing Office.

Neuman, S.B., & Dickinson, D.K. (Eds.). (2002). *Handbook of early literacy research.* New York: Guilford.

Notari-Syverson, A., O'Connor, R.E., & Vadasy, P.F. (1998). *Ladders to literacy: A preschool activity book.* Baltimore: Brookes.

O'Connor, R.E. (1999). Teachers learning ladders to literacy. *Learning Disabilities Research & Practice, 14*(4), 203–214.

O'Connor, R.E., Notari-Syverson, A., & Vadasy, P. (1998a). First-grade effects of teacher-led phonological activities in kindergarten for children with mild disabilities: A follow-up study. *Learning Disabilities Research & Practice, 13*(1), 43–52.

O'Connor, R.E., Notari-Syverson, A., & Vadasy, P.F. (1998b). *Ladders to literacy: A kindergarten activity book.* Baltimore: Brookes.

Olson, R.K. (1999). Genes, environment, and reading disabilities. In R.J. Sternberg & L. Spear-Swerling (Eds.), *Perspectives on learning disabilities: Biological, cognitive, contextual* (pp. 3–21). Boulder, CO: Westview.

Olson, R.K., & Gayan, J. (2002). Brains, genes, and environment in reading development. In S.B. Neuman & D.K. Dickinson (Eds.),

Handbook of early literacy research (pp. 81–94). New York: Guilford.

Palincsar, A.S., & Brown, A.L. (1984). Reciprocal teaching of comprehension-fostering and comprehension-monitoring activities. *Cognition and Instruction, 1*, 117–175.

Palincsar, A.S., Collins, K.M., Marano, N.L., & Magnusson, S.M. (2000). Investigating the engagement and learning of students with learning disabilities in guided inquiry science teaching. *Language, Speech, and Hearing Services in the Schools, 31*, 240–251.

Palincsar, A.S., Magnusson, S.M., Collins, K.M., & Cutter, J. (2001). Making science accessible for all: Results of a design experiment in inclusive classrooms. *Learning Disabilities Quarterly, 24*, 15–32.

Pearson, P.D., & Dole, J.A. (1987). Explicit comprehension instruction: A review of research and a new conceptualization of instruction. *The Elementary School Journal, 88* (2), 151–165.

Pennington, B.F. (1999). Toward an integrated understanding of dyslexia: Genetic, neurological, and cognitive mechanisms. *Development and Psychopathology, 11* (3), 629–654.

Perfetti, C.A. (1985). *Reading ability.* New York: Oxford University Press.

Peterson, C.L., Caverly, D.C., Nicholson, S.A., O'Neal, S., & Cusenbary, S. (2000). *Building reading proficiency at the secondary level: A guide to resources.* Austin, TX: Southwest Educational Development Laboratory.

Pinnell, G.S., Lyons, C.A., DeFord, D.E., Bryk, A.S., & Seltzer, M. (1994). Comparing instructional models for the literacy education of high-risk first graders. *Reading Research Quarterly, 29*, 8–39.

Pressley, M. (1998). *Reading instruction that works: The case for balanced teaching.* New York: Guilford.

Pressley, M., Harris, K.R., & Marks, M.B. (1992). But good strategy instructors are constructivists! *Educational Psychology Review, 4*, 3–31.

Rack, J.P., Snowling, M.J., & Olson, R.K. (1992). The nonword reading deficit in developmental dyslexia: A review. *Reading Research Quarterly, 27*, 28–53.

Rankin-Erickson, J.L., & Pressley, M. (2000). A survey of instructional practices of special education teachers nominated as effective teachers of literacy. *Learning Disabilities Research & Practice, 15*, 206–225.

Reschly, D.J., Hosp, J.L., & Schmied, C.M. (2003). *And miles to go...: State SLD requirements and authoritative recommendations.* Nashville, TN: National Research Center on Learning Disabilities. Retrieved January 3, 2004, from http://www.nrcld.org

Roberts, J.E., & Burchinal, M.R. (2002). The complex interplay between biology and environment: Otitis media and mediating effects on early literacy development. In S.B. Neuman & D.K. Dickinson (Eds.), *Handbook of early literacy research* (pp. 232–241). New York: Guilford.

Ruddell, R.B. (1995). Those influential literacy teachers: Meaning negotiators and motivation builders. *The Reading Teacher, 48*, 454–463.

Ruddell, R.B., & Unrau, N.J. (1994). Reading as a meaning-construction process: The reader, the text, and the teacher. In R.B. Ruddell, M.R. Ruddell, & H. Singer (Eds.), *Theoretical models and processes of reading* (4th ed., pp. 996–1056). Newark, DE: International Reading Association.

Rupley, W.H., Willson, V.L., & Nichols, W.D. (1998). Exploration of the developmental components contributing to elementary school children's reading comprehension. *Scientific Studies of Reading, 2*, 143–158.

Sabatini, J.P. (2002). Efficiency in word reading of adults: Ability group comparisons. *Scientific Studies of Reading, 6* (3), 267–298.

Samuels, S.J. (1979). The method of repeated readings. *The Reading Teacher, 32*, 403–408.

Samuels, S.J. (1994). Toward a theory of automatic information processing in reading revisited. In R.B. Ruddell, M.R. Ruddell, & H. Singer (Eds.), *Theoretical models and processes of reading* (4th ed., pp. 816–837). Newark, DE: International Reading Association.

Samuelsson, S., Finnstrom, O., Leijon, I., & Mard, S. (2000). Phonological and surface profiles among very low birthweight children: Converging evidence for the developmental lag hypothesis. *Scientific Studies of Reading, 4*(3), 197–217.

Scarborough, H.S. (1998). Early identification of children at risk for reading disabilities: Phonological awareness and some other promising predictors. In B.K. Shapiro, P.J. Accardo, & A.J. Capute (Eds.), *Specific reading disability: A view of the spectrum* (pp. 75–119). Timonium, MD: York Press.

Scarborough, H.S. (2002). Connecting early language and literacy to later reading (dis)abilities: Evidence, theory, and practice. In S.B.

Neuman & D.K. Dickinson (Eds.), *Handbook of early literacy research* (pp. 97–125). New York: Guilford.

Scarborough, H.S., & Brady, S.A. (2002). Toward a common terminology for talking about speech and reading: A glossary of the "phon" words and some related terms. *Journal of Literacy Research, 34,* 299–334.

Scarborough, H.S., & Parker, J.D. (2003). Matthew effects in children with learning disabilities: Development of reading, IQ, and psychosocial problems from grade 2 to grade 8. *Annals of Dyslexia, 53,* 47–71.

Scruggs, T.E., & Mastropieri, M.A. (2002). On babies and bathwater: Addressing the problems of identification of learning disabilities. *Learning Disabilities Quarterly, 25*(3), 155–168.

Seymour, P.H.K., & Elder, L. (1986). Beginning reading without phonology. *Cognitive Neuropsychology, 3,* 1–36.

Shalit, R. (1997, August 25). Defining disability down. *New Republic,* pp. 16–22.

Shanahan, T., & Barr, R. (1995). Reading Recovery: An independent evaluation of the effects of an early instructional intervention for at-risk learners. *Reading Research Quarterly, 30,* 958–996.

Shankweiler, D., Crain, S., Brady, S., & Macaruso, P. (1992). Identifying the causes of reading disability. In P.B. Gough, L.C. Ehri, & R. Treiman (Eds.), *Reading acquisition* (pp. 275–305). Hillsdale, NJ: Erlbaum.

Shaywitz, S. (2003). *Overcoming dyslexia: A new and complete science-based program for reading problems at any level.* New York: Knopf.

Siegel, L.S. (1988). Evidence that IQ scores are irrelevant to the definition and analysis of reading disability. *Canadian Journal of Psychology, 42,* 201–215.

Siegel, L.S. (1989). IQ is irrelevant to the definition of learning disabilities. *Journal of Learning Disabilities, 22*(8), 469–478.

Skrtic, T.M. (1999). Learning disabilities as organizational pathologies. In R.J. Sternberg & L. Spear-Swerling (Eds.), *Perspectives on learning disabilities: Biological, cognitive, contextual* (pp. 193–226). Boulder, CO: Westview.

Slavin, R.E. (Ed.) (with Madden, N.A., Dolan, L.J., & Wasik, B.A.). (1996). *Every child, every school: Success for All.* Thousand Oaks, CA: Corwin.

Slavin, R.E., & Madden, N.A. (2000). Research on achievement outcomes of Success for All: A summary and response to critics. *Phi Delta Kappan, 82*(1), 38–40, 59–66.

Slavin, R.E., Madden, N.A., Dolan, L.J., Wasik, B.A., Ross, S., Smith, L., et al. (1996). Success for All: A summary of research. *Journal of Education for Students Placed at Risk, 1,* 41–76.

Smith, L.J., Ross, S.M., & Casey, J.P. (1994). *Special education analyses for Success for All in four cities.* Memphis, TN: University of Memphis, Center for Research in Educational Policy.

Snow, C.E. (with Hemphill, K., & Barnes, W.S.). (1991). *Unfulfilled expectations: Home and school influences on literacy.* Cambridge, MA: Harvard University Press.

Snow, C.E., Burns, M.S., & Griffin, P. (Eds.). (1998). *Preventing reading difficulties in young children.* Washington, DC: National Academy Press.

Spear-Swerling, L. (1999). Can we get there from here? Learning disabilities and future educational policy. In R.J. Sternberg & L. Spear-Swerling (Eds.), *Perspectives on learning disabilities: Biological, cognitive, contextual* (pp. 250–276). Boulder, CO: Westview.

Spear-Swerling, L. (in press). Fourth-graders' performance on a state-mandated assessment involving two different measures of reading comprehension. *Reading Psychology.*

Spear-Swerling, L., & Brucker, P. (2003). Teachers' acquisition of knowledge about English word structure. *Annals of Dyslexia, 53,* 72–103.

Spear-Swerling, L., & Sternberg, R.J. (1994). The road not taken: An integrative theoretical model of reading disability. *Journal of Learning Disabilities, 27*(2), 91–103, 122.

Spear-Swerling, L., & Sternberg, R.J. (1996). *Off track: When poor readers become "learning disabled."* Boulder, CO: Westview.

Speece, D.L., Case, L.P., & Molloy, D.E. (2003). Responsiveness to general education instruction as the first gate to learning disabilities identification. *Learning Disabilities Research & Practice, 18,* 147–156.

Speece, D.L., & Shekitka, L. (2002). How should reading disabilities be operationalized? A survey of experts. *Learning Disabilities Research & Practice, 17,* 118–123.

Stahl, S.A. (1999). *Vocabulary development.* Cambridge, MA: Brookline Press.

Stanovich, K.E. (1986). Matthew effects in reading: Some consequences of individual differences in the acquisition of literacy. *Reading Research Quarterly, 21,* 360–407.

Stanovich, K.E. (1991). Discrepancy definitions of reading disability: Has intelligence led us astray? *Reading Research Quarterly, 26,* 7–29.

Stanovich, K.E. (2000). *Progress in understanding reading: Scientific foundations and new frontiers.* New York: Guilford.

Stanovich, K.E., & Cunningham, A.E. (1993). Where does knowledge come from? Specific associations between print exposure and information acquisition. *Journal of Educational Psychology, 85*(2), 211–229.

Stanovich, K.E., & Siegel, L.S. (1994). Phenotypic performance profile of children with reading disabilities: A regression-based test of the phonological-core variable-difference model. *Journal of Educational Psychology, 86*(1), 24–53.

Sternberg, R.J. (1987). Most vocabulary is learned from context. In M.G. McKeown & M.E. Curtis (Eds.), *The nature of vocabulary acquisition* (pp. 89–106). Hillsdale, NJ: Erlbaum.

Sunseth, K., & Bowers, P.G. (2002). Rapid naming and phonemic awareness: Contributions to reading, spelling, and orthographic knowledge. *Scientific Studies of Reading, 6,* 401–429.

Taylor, R. (2002). Creating a system that gets results for older, reluctant readers. *Phi Delta Kappan, 84*(1), 85–87.

Torgesen, J.K., Alexander, A.W., Wagner, R.K., Rashotte, C.A., Voeller, K.K., & Conway, T. (2001). Intensive remedial instruction for children with severe reading disabilities: Immediate and long-term outcomes from two instructional approaches. *Journal of Learning Disabilities, 34*(1), 33–58, 78.

Torgesen, J.K., Morgan, S., & Davis, C. (1992). Effects of two types of phonological awareness training on word learning in kindergarten children. *Journal of Educational Psychology, 84*(3), 364–370.

Torgesen, J.K., Wagner, R.K., & Rashotte, C.A. (1994). Longitudinal studies of phonological processing and reading. *Journal of Learning Disabilities, 27*(5), 276–286.

Torgesen, J.K., Wagner, R.K., Rashotte, C.A., Alexander, A.W., & Conway, T. (1997). Preventive and remedial interventions for children with severe reading disabilities. *Learning Disabilities: A Multidisciplinary Journal, 8*(1), 51–61.

Vaughn, S., & Fuchs, L.S. (2003). Redefining learning disabilities as inadequate response to instruction: The promise and potential problems. *Learning Disabilities: Research & Practice, 18,* 137–146.

Vaughn, S., Moody, S.W., & Schumm, J.S. (1998). Broken promises: Reading instruction in the resource room. *Exceptional Children, 64*(2), 211–225.

Vellutino, F.R., & Scanlon, D.M. (2002). Emergent literacy skills, early instruction, and individual differences as determinants of difficulties in learning to read: The case for early intervention. In S.B. Neuman & D.K. Dickinson (Eds.), *Handbook of early literacy research* (pp. 295–321). New York: Guilford.

Vellutino, F.R., Scanlon, D.M., & Lyon, G.R. (2000). Differentiating between difficult-to-remediate and readily remediated poor readers: More evidence against the IQ-achievement discrepancy definition of reading disability. *Journal of Learning Disabilities, 33*(3), 223–238.

Venezky, R. (1994). *An evaluation of Success for All: Final report to the France and Merrick Foundations.* Newark: University of Delaware.

White, K.R. (1982). The relation between socioeconomic status and academic achievement. *Psychological Bulletin, 91*(3), 461–481.

Whitehurst, G.J., & Lonigan, C.J. (2002). Emergent literacy: Development from prereaders to readers. In S.B. Neuman & D.K. Dickinson (Eds.), *Handbook of early literacy research* (pp. 11–29). New York: Guilford.

Wilson, B. (1996). *Wilson reading system.* Millbury, MA: Wilson Language Training.

Wolf, M., & Bowers, P.G. (1999). The double-deficit hypothesis for the developmental dyslexias. *Journal of Educational Psychology, 91*(3), 415–438.

Wolf, M., & Katzir-Cohen, T. (2001). Reading fluency and its intervention. *Scientific Studies of Reading, 5*(3), 211–238.

Wolf, M., Miller, L., & Donnelly, K. (2000). Retrieval, automaticity, vocabulary elaboration, orthography (RAVE-O): A comprehensive fluency-based reading intervention program. *Journal of Learning Disabilities, 33*(4), 375–386.

Yuill, N., & Oakhill, J. (1991). *Children's problems in text comprehension: An experimental investigation.* Cambridge, UK: Cambridge University Press.

19

Vocabulary Processes

William E. Nagy and Judith A. Scott

This piece is about vocabulary processes and, in particular, vocabulary acquisition processes. Our focus is on how schoolchildren add words to
their reading and writing vocabularies and how they learn the meanings
of new words.

There continues to be a strong, if not increasing, interest in vocabulary
among reading researchers, according to extensive reviews of recent research provided by Beck and McKeown (1991) in Volume II of the *Handbook of Reading
Research*, as well as by Baumann and Kameenui (1991) and Ruddell (1994). A
similar concern for vocabulary among second-language researchers is evidenced by
several recent books (e.g., Coady & Huckin, 1997; Schmitt & McCarthy, 1997).
This interest in vocabulary stems in part from the longstanding recognition that
vocabulary knowledge strongly influences reading comprehension (Davis, 1944;
Anderson & Freebody, 1981). Among practitioners, on the other hand, interest in
vocabulary has varied and is currently not especially high. For the last 2 years, the
International Reading Association reported on a survey of "hot topics" in literacy
research (Cassidy & Wenrich, 1997, 1998). In both years, vocabulary was rated as
"cold," the bottom category. This low level of interest reflects an emphasis on instruction that is authentic, meaningful, and integrated, which stands in stark contrast
to most traditional practices associated with vocabulary. To many, the word *vocabulary* may suggest a reductionist perspective in which words are learned by
memorizing short definitions and sentences are understood in a strictly bottom-up
fashion by putting together the meanings of individual words—a picture inconsistent with our current understanding of the reading process.

This piece counters a reductionist perspective on vocabulary in two ways.
In the first section of the piece we discuss the complexity of word knowledge.
In the second section we discuss how children gain information about words from
context, word parts, and definitions, noting the limitations as well as the potential
of each of these sources and emphasizing the role of metalinguistic awareness
in vocabulary learning.

The Complexity of Word Knowledge

Any attempt to understand the processes by which children's vocabularies grow must be based on a recognition of the complexity of word knowledge. Five aspects of this complexity that have long been recognized by vocabulary researchers are (1) incrementality—knowing a word is a matter of degrees, not all-or-nothing; (2) multidimensionality—word knowledge consists of several qualitatively different types of knowledge; (3) polysemy—words often have multiple meanings; (4) interrelatedness—one's knowledge of any given word is not independent of one's knowledge of other words; and (5) heterogeneity—what it means to know a word differs substantially depending on the kind of word. We consider these in turn.

Incrementality

Word learning is incremental—it takes place in many steps. In her classic research on early childhood language development, Eve Clark (1973, 1993) provided a detailed picture of how children's knowledge of word meanings is often initially incomplete but, over time, gradually approximates the adult understanding. Likewise, Susan Carey's (1978) seminal work on children's word learning distinguished between quick mapping (i.e., the initial establishment of a partial representation of a word meaning, sometimes on the basis of a single encounter) and extended mapping (i.e., the process of progressive refinement of word knowledge).

The incremental nature of word learning has sometimes been expressed in terms of a linear scale with several points. Dale (1965) proposed four stages: (1) never saw it before; (2) heard it but doesn't know what it means; (3) recognizes it in context as having something to do with...; and (4) knows it well. A recent variation by Paribakht and Wesche (1997) is similar, but adds a fifth point: (5) can use this word in a sentence.

Although such scales are a great improvement over an all-or-nothing picture of word knowledge, and serve as a useful basis for more sensitive assessments of word knowledge (Paribakht & Wesche, 1997), they are not intended to imply that there are only four or five discrete levels of word knowledge. In a series of experiments, Durso and Shore (1991) found that college undergraduates were able to distinguish between correct and incorrect uses of words, at a rate significantly greater than chance, even for words that they had previously judged not to be real English words at all. These results suggest that even at the lowest levels of word knowledge, within Dale's stage 1, there are measurable differences in word knowledge. At the other end of the scale, in a series of studies of high-quality vocabulary instruction, Beck, McKeown, and their colleagues (Beck, Perfetti, & McKeown, 1982; McKeown, Beck, Omanson, & Perfetti, 1983; McKeown, Beck, Omanson, & Pople, 1985) found that up to 40 instructional encounters with a word (and high-quality instruction at that) do not bring students to a ceiling.

An incremental view of word learning helps explain how a great deal of vocabulary knowledge can be gained incidentally from context, even when individual encounters with words in context are not particularly informative (Schatz & Baldwin, 1986). Several studies have used tests representing multiple levels of word knowledge to measure the amount of word knowledge readers gain when encountering words in natural context (Nagy, Herman, & Anderson, 1985; Schwanenflugel, Stahl, & McFalls, 1997; Stallman, 1991). If incidental learning from context could lead to only vague knowledge of words, one would expect the benefits of reading to be strongest for the most lenient criteria of word knowledge, and weaker or absent for more stringent criteria. However, in all three of these studies, the amount of word learning observed was not significantly different for different levels of word knowledge.

The research is clear in showing that word learning *can* be incremental—that one's knowledge of a word can grow on the basis of almost infinitesimally small steps. Less is known about the extent to which word learning is *necessarily* incremental—that is, what limits may exist on the amount or type of knowledge that a learner can gain about a word on the basis of any single encounter. Although good instruction is unquestionably more efficient than chance incidental encounters for learning a specific set of words, there is still good reason to believe that there are practical, if not theoretical, limits to how much an individual can learn about a word on any given occasion. Even four instructional encounters of high quality do not lead to a level of word knowledge adequate to measurably improve comprehension of text containing the instructed word (McKeown et al., 1985). Other research on word learning (e.g., Gildea, Miller, & Wurtenberg, 1990) suggests that there are significant limitations on learners' ability to integrate information from multiple sources on any given occasion.

Multidimensionality

Discussions of the incremental nature of word learning sometimes appear to assume that word knowledge can be expressed in terms of a single dimension. For some purposes, it may be useful to conceptualize word knowledge in terms of a continuum ranging from "none" to "complete." However, it has long been recognized that word knowledge consists of multiple dimensions (Calfee & Drum, 1986; Cronbach, 1942; Kameenui, Dixon, & Carnine, 1987; Richards, 1976). Nation (1990) offered eight aspects of word knowledge: knowledge of the word's spoken form, written form, grammatical behavior, collocational behavior (what other words does this word commonly occur with?), frequency, stylistic register, conceptual meaning, and associations with others words. Other versions of such a list (e.g., Laufer, 1998) distinguish among different types of relationships between words, such as morphological relationships (prefixation and suffixation) and semantic relationships (antonyms, synonyms), and further subcategorize meaning into referential (denotative) and affective (connotative). Graves (1986) distinguished different kinds of word-learning tasks—learning new concepts, learning new labels for known concepts, and bringing words into students' productive vocabularies.

Various aspects of word knowledge might be reducible to a single continuum if one could show that there were strong implicational relations between them. However, it is unlikely that there are any absolute constraints governing the order in which different aspects of word knowledge are acquired. Everyday observation suggests that different facets of word knowledge are relatively independent: One student might know the definition for a word but not be able to use it properly in a sentence; another may use the word in seemingly appropriate ways and yet have a misunderstanding of its meaning. One person may recognize a word and yet have no understanding at all of what it means, whereas others (as was demonstrated by Durso and Shore, 1991) may not recall having ever seen a word before and yet have a partial understanding of its meaning.

In a recent study of learners of English as a second language, Schmitt (1998) found that one could not predict on the basis of one aspect of word knowledge what the learner's knowledge of another aspect would be. Thus, word knowledge must be characterized in terms of a number of different aspects that are at least partially independent. Furthermore, each of these is itself likely to be best characterized as a matter of degree.

Polysemy

Words often have more than one meaning, and the more frequent a word is in the language, the more meanings it is likely to have. The simple fact that a word can have two or more unrelated meanings (e.g., *bear* meaning "animal" and *bear* meaning "carry") adds substantial cognitive complexity to the task of using a dictionary (Miller & Gildea, 1987). Even more troublesome, at least to the theoretician, is the fact that the multiple meanings of words range from being completely unrelated to being so close that the shade of meaning separating the two may exist only in the mind of a compulsive lexicographer (Anderson & Nagy, 1991). In fact, word meanings are inherently flexible, and always nuanced in some way by the context in which they occur (Green, 1989; Nagy, 1997). The meaning of a word one encounters must be inferred from context, even if the word is already familiar, as in the phrase "a soft distant symphony of rushing wind" (Polacco, 1996, p. 25). In many cases, the required inferences are easy and natural, but figurative language is certainly not without its pitfalls for students (Ortony, Reynolds, & Arter, 1978; Winner, Engel, & Gardner, 1980). If vocabulary instruction is to address this aspect of the complexity of word knowledge, students must not only be taught to choose effectively among the multiple meanings of a word offered in dictionaries, but to expect words to be used with novel shades of meanings.

Interrelatedness

Words are often taught and tested as if they were essentially isolated units of knowledge. Clearly such practice is inconsistent with a constructivist understanding of knowledge that emphasizes the importance of linking what is learned to familiar words and concepts. How well a person knows the meaning of *whale* depends in part on their understanding of *mammal*. A person who already knows the words *hot*, *cold*, and *cool* has already acquired some of the components of the word *warm*, even if the word *warm* has not yet been encountered.

The potential extent of interconnectedness in vocabulary knowledge is underscored by the Landauer and Dumais (1997) simulation of word learning from context. In their simulation, the input was 4.6 million words of text (in samples each about 150 words in length) from an electronic encyclopedia. A multidimensional vector was calculated for each word on the basis of its co-occurrence with other words in the sample texts. The simulation was evaluated by using the knowledge represented in these vectors to take a test of 80 items from the Test of English as a Foreign Language (TOEFL), a test commonly used to measure the English proficiency of international students studying in the United States. Interestingly, the Landauer and Dumais model got a score almost identical to the mean of a large sample of applicants to U.S. colleges from non-English-speaking countries.

One of the most striking findings of this study is the fact that as much as three fourths of the learning that resulted from the input of a segment of text was for words that were not even contained in that segment. At first glance, this finding seems counterintuitive. On the other hand, in the case of words obviously related in meaning, it is not difficult to understand how exposure to a text can contribute to one's knowledge of words not in the text. For example, reading a text about weaving might well increase one's understanding of the words *warp* and *woof* even if these words did not occur in the text. In the Landauer and Dumais (1997) simulation, computationally equivalent to a connectionist network, the information about any given word is represented throughout the entire network, and input about any single word can potentially change the configuration of relationships throughout the network. Although one must be cautious in extrapolating from this simulation to human learning, at very least it raises the possibility that the interconnectedness among words in human memory may be far greater than is commonly assumed, and certainly far greater than is represented in dictionary definitions.

Heterogeneity

Another type of complexity in word knowledge is the fact that what it means to know a word depends on what kind of word one is talking about. For example, knowing function words such as *the* or *if* is quite different from knowing terms such as *hypotenuse* or *ion*. The fact that the different dimensions of word knowledge are at least partially independent of each other also means that the same word can require different types of learning from different types of students, depending on what they already know about a word.

Implications of the Complexity of Word Knowledge

The complex picture of word knowledge we have outlined stands in sharp contrast to some of the traditional vocabulary instruction practices still being used in schools, although most of the points we have made have been acknowledged by vocabulary researchers for decades (e.g., Calfee & Drum, 1986; Cronbach, 1942; Richards, 1976). The knowledge that students have for many words is far more complex than could be attained through instruction that relies primarily on definitions. Not only are there too many words to teach them all to students one by one; there is too much to learn about each word to be covered by anything but exceptionally rich and multifaceted instruction. Hence, the complexity of word knowledge further bolsters the argument that much of students' vocabulary knowledge must be gained through means other than explicit vocabulary instruction. In those cases when students are dependent on instruction to learn a word, if they are to truly gain ownership of that word, the instruction must provide multiple and varied encounters with that word (Stahl & Fairbanks, 1986).

Although we believe it is important to recognize that only a small proportion of words that students learn can be covered in explicit vocabulary instruction, we want to stress an even more basic point: that knowing a word cannot be identified with knowing a definition. This point was argued at length by Anderson and Nagy (1991) in Volume II of the *Handbook of Reading Research*. Here we want to emphasize the point that word knowledge is primarily procedural rather than declarative, a matter of "knowing how" rather than "knowing that." Admittedly, there is a declarative component to at least some types of vocabulary knowledge. This seems especially true in the realm of technical or content-specific vocabulary; for example, if someone is not able to explain what *carbon dioxide* is, it is questionable that he or she knows the meaning of the word. On the other hand, for much nontechnical vocabulary, it may be more useful to conceptualize word knowledge as being primarily procedural. That is, knowing a word means being able to do things with it: to recognize it in connected speech or in print, to access its meaning, to pronounce it—and to be able to do these things within a fraction of a second. None of these processes is anything like remembering a verbal definition. In most cases, knowing a word is more like knowing how to use a tool than it is like being able to state a fact. Word knowledge is applied knowledge: A person who knows a word can recognize it, and use it, in novel contexts, and uses knowledge of the word, in combination with other types of knowledge, to construct a meaning for a text.

Metalinguistic Demands of Word Learning

In traditional vocabulary instruction, students spend much of their time learning definitions (Watts, 1995). Such instruction is inconsistent with current understandings of the learning process. In the previous section of this piece, we have outlined the dimensions of word knowledge that are rarely conveyed adequately in definitions. Another problem with memorizing definitions is the passive nature of the role it assigns to students. Teaching students new words by giving them definitions is the antithesis of a constructivist approach to learning.

If students are to take an active role in word learning, and assume increasing responsibility for their own vocabulary growth, they need at least some information about the nature of word knowledge and the processes by which it is acquired. That is, they need metacognitive and metalinguistic ability in the realm of word learning. In this section of the piece, we describe some of the specific types of metalinguistic abilities that contribute to word learning.

Metalinguistic ability is the ability to reflect on and manipulate the structural features of language (Tunmer, Herriman, & Nesdale, 1988). It can be understood as a subcategory of metacognition, that is, the awareness of and control over one's cognitive processes. Recently, much attention has been devoted to a particular kind of metalinguistic ability, phonemic awareness (i.e., the ability to reflect on and manipulate phonemes, the individual units of sound out of which spoken words are constructed). However, other types of metalinguistic awareness, such as morphological awareness and syntactic awareness, are also believed to play an important role in reading (Carlisle, 1995; Tunmer et al., 1988; Tunmer, Nesdale, & Wright, 1987; Warren-Leubecker, 1987; Willows & Ryan, 1986).

A number of vocabulary researchers (e.g., Anderson & Nagy, 1992; Baumann & Kameenui, 1991; Graves, 1986) have held up the idea of "word awareness" or "word consciousness" as an important goal of vocabulary instruction. However, the exact nature of such awareness has seldom been explicated. We believe that word awareness, like word knowledge, is a complex and multifaceted construct, and that there are many ways in which students' awareness of language impacts their word learning. Understanding the metalinguistic demands of the vocabulary-related tasks students encounter in school provides insight into the surprising difficulties students often experience with these tasks.

Metalinguistic Awareness and Word Parts

The importance of phonemic awareness has been highlighted in a growing body of research on learning to read. In an alphabetic language like English, in which letters generally map onto phonemes, it is crucial that children are able to segment spoken words into phonemes and learn the mappings between these phonemes and the letters that represent them.

Recently, however, the contribution of morphological awareness to reading has drawn the attention of some researchers. Morphemes are meaningful word parts; for example, the word *walks* can be divided into two morphemes, *walk* and *s*. In those places where English orthography deviates from the phonemic principle, it is often in the direction of giving consistent representations to morphemes. For example, *ed* is pronounced differently in the words *helped*, *poured*, and *pleaded*. The less-regular relationship between spelling and sound allows for a more consistent link from spelling to meaning. Only by noticing the shared morpheme in *sign* and *signature* can one make any sense of the spelling of the former. The fact that many of the apparent irregularities in English spelling are motivated by morphological relationships suggests that awareness of these relationships may contribute to spelling and reading ability. And, in fact, it has been found that morphological awareness makes a significant contribution to reading ability, even when phonemic awareness has been taken into account (Carlisle, 1995; Carlisle & Nomanbhoy, 1993). Knowledge of morphology is likewise correlated with reading ability into high school (Nagy, Diakidoy, & Anderson, 1993).

It is hard to overstate the importance of morphology in vocabulary growth. Nagy and Anderson (1984) estimated that about 60% of the new words a student encounters in reading are analyzable into parts that give substantial help in figuring out their meaning. Anglin's (1993) study of children's vocabulary growth showed that between first and fifth grade, the number of root words known by children in his study increased by around 4,000 words. In the same time period, the number of derived (prefixed or suffixed) words known by students increases by about 14,000 words. There is a veritable explosion in children's knowledge of derived words, especially between third and fifth grades. As Anglin noted, the bulk of this increase appears to reflect morphological problem solving, that is, interpreting new words by breaking them down into their component morphemes.

There is reason to believe that effective use of morphology in word learning depends on metalinguistic sophistication that continues to develop through high school. Most children presumably achieve the basic morphological insight—that longer words can often be broken down into shorter words or pieces that give clues to their meanings—before fourth grade (Anglin, 1993; Tyler & Nagy, 1989). However, word structure in English is complex, and there is development in children's knowledge of word formation processes at least through high school (Nagy et al., 1993; Nagy & Scott, 1990; Tyler & Nagy, 1989).

English and Spanish share many cognates—word pairs such as English *tranquil* and Spanish *tranquilo* that are similar in spelling, pronunciation, and meaning. Recognizing such relationships must depend on abilities similar to those required to recognize morphological relationships in English. Many pairs of morphologically related words in English likewise involve changes in spelling and pronunciation as well as shifts in meaning—or example, *divide/division*, *sane/sanity*, *combine/combination*, *respond/responsible*. Hancin-Bhatt and Nagy (1994) found that Spanish–English bilingual students' ability to recognize such relations increased far more dramatically between fourth and eighth grade than did their vocabulary knowledge in either Spanish or English. These results suggest that the ability to see morphological relationships that are partially obscured by changes in spelling and pronunciation may depend on metalinguistic sensitivities that develop, or at least increase substantially, after fourth grade.

It should also be noted that some aspects of morphological knowledge are closely related to syntactic awareness. In particular, learning the meanings of derivational suffixes (e.g., *-tion, -ness, -ly*) requires reflecting on the syntactic role of the suffixed word in the sentence (see Nagy et al., 1993).

Not surprisingly, there are differences of opinion about the contribution of morphological knowledge to reading and vocabulary growth. Some (e.g., Nation, 1990) note the irregularities of English morphology (what does *casualty* have to do with *casual*, or *emergency* with *emerge?*) and suggest that students should only consider morphological clues after they have first used context to make a hypothesis about the meaning of a word. However, the vast majority of words composed of more than one morpheme are semantically transparent—that is, their meanings are largely predictable on the basis of the meanings of their parts (Nagy & Anderson, 1984). The fact that some words (like *casualty*) are irregular indicates not that word parts are useless as clues, but that readers must be strategic and flexible in their use of potential sources of information about words.

Metalinguistic Awareness and Use of Context

Context and morphology (word parts) are the two major sources of information immediately available to a reader who comes across a new word. Effective use of context, like effective use of morphology, requires some level of metalinguistic awareness.

Tunmer and his colleagues (Gough & Tunmer, 1986; Tunmer, 1990; Tunmer et al., 1988) argued that syntactic awareness (i.e., the ability to reflect on and manipulate the order of words in a sentence) contributes to reading ability in at least two ways. First of all, developing one's reading vocabulary depends on both phonological recoding and context, because phonological recoding alone cannot always uniquely determine the pronunciation of a word; context is sometimes necessary to determine which of several possible sounds a letter may represent. Effective use of context is, in turn, hypothesized to rely on syntactic awareness. Second, syntactic awareness may help the reader monitor comprehension.

Gottardo, Stanovich, and Siegel (1996), on the other hand, claimed that syntactic awareness does not make an independent contribution to reading, above and beyond the contribution represented by short-term, phonological memory. That is, correlations between reading difficulty and deficient syntactic awareness may arise as epiphenomena of deficiencies in phonological processing (p. 563). Although not denying the importance of phonological processing in reading difficulties, we believe that several types of evidence suggest a direct link between syntactic awareness and reading comprehension.

First of all, syntactic awareness training has been shown to improve reading comprehension (Kennedy & Weener, 1974; Weaver, 1979). Likewise, training studies in the use of context (e.g., Buikema & Graves, 1993; Jenkins,

Matlock, & Slocum, 1989; see Kuhn & Stahl, 1998, for a review) have resulted in increases in children's ability to learn words. The relative brevity of most such interventions makes it likely that the benefits reflect increased metalinguistic and metacognitive awareness rather than gains in short-term phonological memory.

Second, it could be argued that the verbal working memory task used by Gottardo et al. (1996) includes a component of metalinguistic awareness. Subjects were asked to make true–false judgments about simple statements (e.g., *fish swim in the sky*), and their score on these judgments was incorporated into the verbal working memory score. After listening to a set of sentences, they were asked to recall the final word of each sentence in the set. To do this, subjects must pay attention to the surface form of the sentence, rather than its meaning, a task that requires conscious attention to word order, that is, syntactic awareness.

Third, there is evidence that the contribution of syntactic awareness and other components of metalinguistic awareness to reading comprehension, relative to that of phonological awareness, increases with grade level (Roth, Speece, Cooper, & De la Paz, 1996).

The most convincing evidence that syntactic awareness contributes to effective use of context comes from examining the protocols of students attempting to infer the meanings of novel words from context. In Werner and Kaplan's (1952) classic study of inferring word meanings from context, children were given a series of sentences containing a nonsense word and asked to infer its meaning. Here are the responses from an 11-year-old boy (p. 16; the word *hudray* was intended to mean "grow" or "increase"):

Sentence 1: If you eat well and sleep well you will hudray.

Response: Feel good.

Sentence 2: Mrs. Smith wanted to hudray her family

Response: Mrs. Smith wanted to make her family feel good.

Sentence 3: Jane had to hudray the cloth so that the dress would fit Mary.

Response: Jane makes the dress good to fit Mary so Mary feels good.

These responses show that this child is willing to ignore the syntactic structure of the sentences (especially sentence 3) in order to maintain his original hypothesis about the word's meaning. McKeown's (1985) study of high- and low-ability readers learning from context likewise included examples of responses that appear to reflect lack of attention to the syntactic role of the target word in the sentence.

Does use of context to learn the meanings of new words always require metalinguistic awareness? Presumably not; the rapid vocabulary acquisition of very young children takes place at an age when many aspects of metalinguistic awareness are not measurably present. However, a distinction must be made between incidental learning of word meanings from context and deriving word meanings. The latter process is usually examined by asking students to come up with, or select, an appropriate meaning for an unfamiliar word with the context available. Such a task is likely to be more metacognitively and metalinguistically demanding than incidental word learning. This may account for the fact that studies of truly incidental word learning have often found no significant effects of verbal ability (e.g., Nagy, Anderson, & Herman, 1987; Nagy et al., 1985; Stahl, 1989; Stallman, 1991), whereas studies of deriving word meaning have generally found large ability effects (e.g., Daneman & Green, 1986; Jenkins, Stein, & Wysocki, 1984; McKeown, 1985; Sternberg & Powell, 1983).

The research on learning words from context clearly documents the fact that chances of learning very much about a word from any single encounter with that word in natural context are very slim (Beck, McKeown, & McCaslin, 1983; Nagy et al., 1987; Schatz & Baldwin, 1986). It is extremely important for teachers to recognize that although context may be a "natural" means of word learning, it is not especially effective in the short run. Likewise, it is important for students to have realistic expectations about the amount of information they can gain from context. Training students on artificially helpful contexts may actually decrease their effectiveness at using the contextual clues available in natural text (Kranzer, 1988).

Metalinguistic Awareness and the Use of Definitions

The chief strength of definitions is that they provide explicit information about word meanings that is normally only implicit in context. If you want a student to know what a particular word means, explaining it is unquestionably more effective than waiting for the student to encounter it numerous times in context.

One of the chief weaknesses of definitions is their failure to provide information about usage that is accessible to schoolchildren. Miller and Gildea (1987) studied sentences children generated when given definitions of unfamiliar words and concluded that this widely used task, although it reveals interesting things about children's processing of definitions, is pedagogically useless. Children's difficulty with this task may stem in part from the often convoluted language of definitions, but even clearly written definitions do not guarantee success. McKeown (1993) carefully revised definitions to make them both more accurate and more clear to students and found that the revised definitions were significantly superior to their original dictionary counterparts in terms of students' ability to apply knowledge of their meanings. There was also an effect on usage: Only 25% of the sentences generated from the original definitions were judged acceptable, whereas 50% of the sentences generated from the revised definitions were acceptable. This is a substantial increase, but it is also a striking demonstration of the fact that even definitions of very high quality are often inadequate as sources of information on usage.

Students sometimes have trouble extracting even a general idea of the meaning of a word from a definition (Scott & Nagy, 1997). Some of the difficulty may stem from lack of familiarity with the conventions of traditional definitions, but changing the format and style of definitions does not necessarily increase their usefulness to students (Fischer, 1990, 1994; Scott & Nagy, 1997). A bigger problem appears to be the metacognitive and metalinguistic demands of using definitions.

Scott and Nagy (1997), following up on Miller and Gildea's (1987) study, found that the difficulty experienced by children in interpreting definitions was primarily due to their failure to take the syntax, or structure, of definitions into account. Their errors could be best characterized as selecting a salient fragment of the definition as representing the meaning of the whole word.

There are two metalinguistic dimensions to these errors. One is a lack of sensitivity to syntactic structure. In analyzing think-aloud protocols of children attempting to integrate information from definitions with sentences containing the word defined, Scott (1991) found a common problem was failure to take part of speech into account. It was not clear whether the failure was in the analysis of the sentence or in the analysis of the definition, but lack of attention to syntax was obviously a major factor.

Another aspect of metalinguistic awareness involved in children's understanding of definitions has to do with their concept of definition. Fischer's (1990, 1994) investigation of German high school students' use of bilingual dictionary definitions suggested that the students approached the task with the expectation of finding simple synonyms. It may be natural for students of a second language as similar to their first as English is to German to expect one-to-one mappings between words. Language instruction may contribute to such expectations. However, true synonyms are rare, both within and between languages.

The Concept of Word

We have just described some of the ways that metalinguistic awareness contributes to students' independent word learning—their use of word parts, context, and definitions. However, metalinguistic awareness contributes to vocabulary learning at an even more fundamental level. Almost any conceivable vocabulary activity requires children to talk and think about words and their meanings; that is, it presupposes the metalinguistic concept of word. This concept is more complex and more problematic than is commonly recognized. In fact, research on the acquisition of this concept suggests that, even in the middle elementary grades, it cannot be taken completely for granted.

Roberts (1992) documented the gradual nature of children's development of the concept of word. Five-year-old preschoolers have trouble dissociating a word from its referent; when asked which is the bigger word, *caterpillar* or *dog*, they will usually answer *dog*. In Roberts's study, even third-grade students were not all at ceiling in her measures of their understanding of the concept of word.

Bowey and Tunmer (1984) pointed out that there are three requirements for full awareness of the concept of word: (1) awareness of the word as a unit of language, (2) awareness of the word as an arbitrary phonological label, and (3) comprehension of the metalinguistic term *word*. In a review of research on metalinguistic awareness, Gombert (1992) argued that there is no clear evidence for the existence of these abilities before the age of 7 years (p. 80). Likewise, there is evidence that some of these requirements are not fully present in children up to the age of at least 10. Piaget (1926) claimed that children did not recognize words as a simple sign (i.e., as an arbitrary label) until the age of 9 or 10. Berthoud-Papandropolou (1980; as cited in Gombert, 1992), investigating children's ability to segment sentences into words, concluded that children younger than 11 did not consistently reach 100% accuracy.

Understanding the Function of Vocabulary in Decontextualized Language

The language young children most commonly experience is contextualized—that is, it is language about, and embedded in, a shared context. In a face-to-face conversation, the speakers share a physical context, use gesture and intonation, and make many assumptions about shared knowledge, experiences, and beliefs. They are able to communicate effectively in words that would not necessarily be understood by someone who had access only to a transcript of the conversation. Written language—and especially language written for an audience not present and not personally known to the writer—tends to be decontextualized; that is, the success of the communication relies more heavily on the language itself, and less on shared knowledge or context (Snow, 1991, 1994). What contextualized language accomplishes through gesture, intonation, and allusions to shared knowledge and experiences, decontextualized language must accomplish primarily through precision in choice of words (Chafe & Danielewicz, 1987). This is one of the reasons why written language, which is typically decontextualized, tends to use a far richer vocabulary than oral language, which is typically contextualized (Hayes, 1988).

Not all oral language is contextualized. Storytellers use language to create a world distinct from the here-and-now context, in which the language alone carries most of the communicative burden. But many children, especially if they have not been read to very much, may come to school having had relatively little experience with decontextualized language. Not surprisingly, facility with decontextualized language is related to children's reading ability (Snow, 1991, 1994; Snow, Cancino, Gonzales, & Shriberg, 1989).

Because decontextualized language contains richer vocabulary, exposure to such language is important for children's vocabulary growth. However, we would like to suggest that children's vocabulary growth is benefited not just by exposure to decontextualized language, but by an appreciation of the role that vocabulary plays in such language. Precision of word choice is seldom crucial in everyday conversation, but it is the primary communicative tool of the writer. The motivation to learn the richer vocabulary of decontextualized language may depend on a student's feel for the difference between the communicative strategies of speakers and writers. Scott, working with a group of teacher researchers, found that conscious attention to words and word choice helped students' writing, led to critical analysis of authors' writing, and changed the way teachers taught both reading and writing (Scott, Asselin, Henry, & Butler, 1997; Scott, Blackstone, et al., 1996; Scott, Butler, & Asselin, 1996; Scott & Wells, 1998). Research on the long-term impact of such instruction on students' vocabulary growth is still needed.

Conclusion

Any type of learning, if examined closely enough, looks so complex that one wonders how children can do it at all. In this piece, we have tried to convey some of the complexity of the processes involved in vocabulary acquisition.

For many children, of course, vocabulary growth appears to proceed with astonishing ease and rapidity. Beck and McKeown (1991), comparing previously published figures, estimated that average children learn words at a rate of something like 2,500 to 3,000 words a year. More conservative accounts put the figure at 1,000 words a year (Goulden, Nation, & Read, 1990; D'Anna, Zechmeister, & Hall, 1991). We have argued elsewhere at length (Anderson & Nagy, 1992; Nagy, 1998) why we consider these latter estimates unrealistically low. Anglin (1993) conducted a major study of children's vocabulary growth between first and fifth grade that helped clarify the nature of the differences between conflicting estimates. Given a conservative definition of vocabulary—counting only root words—Anglin found a rate of growth identical to that reported by Goulden et al. (1990) and D'Anna et al. (1991). However, using a more inclusive concept of "psychologically basic vocabulary"—including, for example, idioms and derived words for which there was no evidence that children used morphological analysis—Anglin (1993) arrived at an estimate in the range suggested by Beck and McKeown (1991). In their commentary on Anglin's work, Miller and Wakefield (1993) argued that Anglin's figures should be doubled.

Regardless of exactly where the truth lies within this range of estimates, we are left with a paradox. At least some children learn 2,000 or more new words per year, most of these apart from explicit instruction. Is the complexity and difficulty of the vocabulary acquisition processes presented in this piece illusory?

We believe not. The high rates of vocabulary growth seen in many children occur only through immersion in massive amounts of rich written and oral language. Students who need help most in the area of vocabulary—those whose home experience has not given them a substantial foundation in the vocabulary of literate and academic English—need to acquire words at a pace even faster than that of their peers, but by no means do they always find this process easy or automatic.

Vocabulary researchers concerned with second-language learning have argued that "natural" vocabulary acquisition is simply not efficient enough to produce the desired rates of learning. Natural context is not an especially rich source of information about word meanings. If there are particular words one wants a student to learn, free reading is perhaps the least effective means available. However, presenting students with more concentrated information about words introduces another set of difficulties. We have outlined two major categories of such difficulties in this piece. The first is the complexity of word meanings. Definitions, the traditional means of offering concentrated information about words to students, do not contain the quantity or quality of information that constitutes true word knowledge. Students can gain some word knowledge from definitions, but generally only if they are given other types of information about the word (e.g., examples of how it is used) and opportunities to apply this information in meaningful tasks (Stahl, 1986; Stahl & Fairbanks, 1986). Some types of words (e.g., verbs and abstract nouns) may be more difficult to learn from definitions than others (e.g., concrete nouns).

A second major type of difficulty is the metalinguistic sophistication that is presupposed by most vocabulary-related school tasks. Vocabulary activities at every grade level require metalinguistic abilities and awareness that cannot be taken for granted on the part of students. In the early elementary grades, even fundamental concepts about words as units of form and meaning are still in the process of being consolidated. Independent word learning strategies rely on metalinguistic knowledge that is still developing during the upper elementary grades.

A recent study on the development of phonemic awareness (Scarborough, Ehri, Olson, & Fowler, 1998) shows that this aspect of metalinguistic awareness, which impacts the earliest stages of formal reading instruction, does not appear to reach a ceiling among college students. Given the complex nature of word knowledge, we feel safe in predicting that the various aspects of metalinguistic awareness involved in word learning will not be fully present even in many adults.

We believe that the role of metalinguistic awareness in vocabulary growth offers a promising area for future research. Although there is substantial research support for the broad outlines of the picture of vocabulary processes that we have drawn in this piece, there are also large areas of uncharted territory. Roberts's (1992) article on children's development of the concept of word is one of the few examples of research explicitly addressing the metalinguistic foundations of vocabulary learning in the literature on literacy research. No one, to our knowledge, has addressed the effects of varying levels of metalinguistic awareness on children's ability to profit from different types of vocabulary instruction or from different types of information about words. There is also need for research examining the effects of instruction that fosters word consciousness on students' vocabulary growth.

If students are to become active and independent learners in the area of vocabulary, they need to have some understanding of the territory that they are operating in. Such an understanding depends on explanations by teachers who themselves have some grasp of the complexity of word knowledge. Students' understanding of words and of the word-learning process also depends on the type of vocabulary instruction they experience. A diet of synonyms and short glossary definitions runs the danger of failing to produce usable knowledge of those words and creates simplistic beliefs that can interfere with future word learning. The quality of vocabulary instruction must therefore be judged, not just on whether it produces immediate gains in students' understanding of specific words, but also on whether it communicates an accurate picture of the nature of word knowledge and reasonable expectations about the word-learning process.

References

Anderson, R.C., & Freebody, P. (1981). Vocabulary knowledge. In J. Guthrie (Ed.), *Comprehension and teaching: Research reviews* (pp. 77–117). Newark, DE: International Reading Association.

Anderson, R.C., & Nagy, W. (1991). Word meanings. In R. Barr, M.L. Kamil, P. Mosenthal, & P.D. Pearson (Eds.), *Handbook of reading research* (Vol. 2, pp. 690–724). White Plains, NY: Longman.

Anderson, R.C., & Nagy, W. (1992). The vocabulary conundrum. *American Educator, 16*, 14–18, 44–47.

Anglin, J.M. (1993). Vocabulary development: A morphological analysis. *Monographs of the Society for Research in Child Development, 58*(10, Serial No. 238).

Baumann, J.F., & Kameenui, E.J. (1991). Research on vocabulary: Ode to Voltaire. In J. Flood, J.M. Jensen, D. Lapp, & J.R. Squire (Eds.), *Handbook of research on teaching the English language arts* (pp. 604–632). New York: Macmillan.

Beck, I., & McKeown, M. (1991). Conditions of vocabulary acquisition. In R. Barr, M.L. Kamil, P. Mosenthal, & P.D. Pearson (Eds.), *Handbook of reading research* (Vol. 2, pp. 789–814). White Plains, NY: Longman.

Beck, I., McKeown, M., & McCaslin, E. (1983). All contexts are not created equal. *The Elementary School Journal, 83*, 177–181.

Beck, I., Perfetti, C., & McKeown, M. (1982). Effects of long-term vocabulary instruction on lexical access and reading comprehension. *Journal of Educational Psychology, 74*, 506–521.

Bowey, J., & Tunmer, W.E. (1984). Development of children's understanding of the metalinguistic term *word. Journal of Educational Psychology, 76*(3), 500–512.

Buikema, J., & Graves, M. (1993). Teaching students to use context cues to infer word meanings. *Journal of Reading, 36*, 450–457.

Calfee, R.C., & Drum, P. (1986). Research on teaching reading. In M.C. Wittrock (Ed.), *Handbook of research on teaching* (pp. 804–849). New York: Macmillan.

Carey, S. (1978). The child as word learner. In M. Halle, J. Bresnan, & G. Miller (Eds.), *Linguistic theory and psychological reality* (pp. 264–293). Cambridge, MA: MIT Press.

Carlisle, J. (1995). Morphological awareness and early reading achievement. In L. Feldman (Ed.), *Morphological aspects of language processing* (pp. 189–209). Hillsdale, NJ: Erlbaum.

Carlisle, J., & Nomanbhoy, D. (1993). Phonological and morphological awareness in first graders. *Applied Psycholinguistics, 14,* 177–195.

Cassidy, J., & Wenrich, J. (1997). What's hot, what's not for 1997. *Reading Today, 14*(4), 34.

Cassidy, J., & Wenrich, J. (1998). What's hot, what's not for 1998. *Reading Today, 15*(4), 1, 28.

Chafe, W., & Danielewicz, J. (1987). Properties of spoken and written language. In R. Horowitz & S.J. Samuels (Eds.), *Comprehending oral and written language* (pp. 83–113). San Diego, CA: Academic Press.

Clark, E.V. (1973). What's in a word? On the child's acquisition of semantics in his first language. In T.E. Moore (Ed.), *Cognitive development and the acquisition of language* (pp. 65–110). New York: Academic Press.

Clark, E.V. (1993). *The lexicon in acquisition.* Cambridge, UK: Cambridge University Press.

Coady, J., & Huckin, T. (1997). *Second language vocabulary acquisition.* Cambridge, UK: Cambridge University Press.

Cronbach, L.J. (1942). An analysis of techniques for diagnostic vocabulary testing. *Journal of Educational Research, 36,* 206–217.

Dale, E. (1965). Vocabulary measurement: Techniques and major findings. *Elementary English, 42,* 82–88.

Daneman, M., & Green, I. (1986). Individual differences in comprehending and producing words in context. *Journal of Memory and Language, 25,* 1–18.

D'Anna, C.A., Zechmeister, E.B., & Hall, J.W. (1991). Toward a meaningful definition of vocabulary size. *Journal of Reading Behavior, 23,* 109–122.

Davis, F.B. (1944). Fundamental factors in reading comprehension. *Psychometrika, 9,* 185–197.

Durso, F.T., & Shore, W.J. (1991). Partial knowledge of word meanings. *Journal of Experimental Psychology: General, 120,* 190–202.

Fischer, U. (1990). *How students learn words from a dictionary and in context.* Unpublished doctoral dissertation, Princeton University, Princeton, NJ.

Fischer, U. (1994). Learning words from context and dictionaries: An experimental comparison. *Applied Psycholinguistics, 15,* 551–574.

Gildea, P., Miller, G., & Wurtenberg, C. (1990). Contextual enrichment by videodisk. In D. Nix & R. Spiro (Eds.), *Cognition, education,* *and multimedia: Exploring ideas in high technology* (pp. 1–29). Hillsdale, NJ: Erlbaum.

Gombert, J. (1992). *Metalinguistic development.* Chicago: University of Chicago Press.

Gottardo, A., Stanovich, K., & Siegel, L. (1996). The relationships between phonological sensitivity, syntactic processing, and verbal working memory in the reading performance of third grade children. *Journal of Experimental Child Psychology, 63,* 563–582.

Gough, P., & Tunmer, W.E. (1986). Decoding, reading, and reading ability. *Remedial and Special Education, 7,* 6–10.

Goulden, R., Nation, P., & Read, J. (1990). How large can a receptive vocabulary be? *Applied Linguistics, 11,* 341–363.

Graves, M.F. (1986). Vocabulary learning and instruction. In E.Z. Rothkopf & L.C. Ehri (Eds.), *Review of research in education* (Vol. 13, pp. 49–89). Washington, DC: American Educational Research Association.

Green, G.M. (1989). *Pragmatics and natural language understanding.* Hillsdale, NJ: Erlbaum.

Hancin-Bhatt, B., & Nagy, W. (1994). Lexical transfer and second language morphological development. *Applied Psycholinguistics, 15,* 289–310.

Hayes, D. (1988). Speaking and writing: Distinct patterns of word choice. *Journal of Memory and Language, 27,* 572–585.

Jenkins, J.R., Matlock, B., & Slocum, T.A. (1989). Two approaches to vocabulary instruction: The teaching of individual word meanings and practice in deriving word meaning from context. *Reading Research Quarterly, 24,* 215–235.

Jenkins, J.R., Stein, M.L., & Wysocki, K. (1984). Learning vocabulary through reading. *American Educational Research Journal, 21,* 767–787.

Kameenui, E.J., Dixon, D.W., & Carnine, R.C. (1987). Issues in the design of vocabulary instruction. In M.G. McKeown & M.E. Curtis (Eds.), *The nature of vocabulary acquisition* (pp. 129–145). Hillsdale, NJ: Erlbaum.

Kennedy, D., & Weener, P. (1974). Visual and auditory training with the cloze procedure to improve reading and listening comprehension. *Reading Research Quarterly, 8,* 524–541.

Kranzer, K.G. (1988). *A study of the effects of instruction on incidental word learning and on the ability to derive word meaning from con-*

text. Unpublished doctoral dissertation, University of Delaware, Newark.

Kuhn, M., & Stahl, S. (1998). Teaching children to learn word meanings from context: A synthesis and some questions. *Journal of Literacy Research, 30*, 119–138.

Landauer, T., & Dumais, S. (1997). A solution to Plato's problem: The Latent Semantic Analysis theory of acquisition, induction, and representation of knowledge. *Psychological Review, 104*, 211–240.

Laufer, B. (1998). What's in a word that makes it hard or easy: Some intralexical factors that affect the learning of words. In N. Schmitt & M. McCarthy (Eds.), *Vocabulary: Description, acquisition and pedagogy* (pp. 140–155). Cambridge, UK: Cambridge University Press.

McKeown, M. (1985). The acquisition of word meaning from context by children of high and low ability. *Reading Research Quarterly, 20*, 482–496.

McKeown, M. (1993). Creating definitions for young word learners. *Reading Research Quarterly, 28*, 16–33.

McKeown, M., Beck, I., Omanson, R., & Perfetti, C. (1983). The effects of long-term vocabulary instruction on reading comprehension: A replication. *Journal of Reading Behavior, 15*, 3–18.

McKeown, M., Beck, I., Omanson, R., & Pople, M. (1985). Some effects of the nature and frequency of vocabulary instruction on the knowledge and use of words. *Reading Research Quarterly, 20*, 522–535.

Miller, G., & Gildea, P. (1987). How children learn words. *Scientific American, 257*, 94–99.

Miller, G., & Wakefield, P. (1993). On Anglin's analysis of vocabulary growth. *Monographs of the Society for Research in Child Development, 58*, 167–175.

Nagy, W. (1997). On the role of context in first- and second-language vocabulary learning. In N. Schmitt & M. McCarthy (Eds.), *Vocabulary: Description, acquisition and pedagogy* (pp. 64–83). Cambridge, UK: Cambridge University Press.

Nagy, W., & Anderson, R.C. (1984). How many words are there in printed school English? *Reading Research Quarterly, 19*, 304–330.

Nagy, W., Anderson, R.C., & Herman, P. (1987). Learning word meanings from context during normal reading. *American Educational Research Journal, 24*, 237–270.

Nagy, W., Diakidoy, I., & Anderson, R.C. (1993). The acquisition of morphology:

Learning the contribution of suffixes to the meanings of derivatives. *Journal of Reading Behavior, 25*, 155–170.

Nagy, W., Garcia, G.E., Durgunoglu, A., & Hancin-Bhatt, B. (1993). Spanish-English bilingual students' use of cognates in English reading. *Journal of Reading Behavior, 25*, 241–259.

Nagy, W., Herman, P., & Anderson, R. (1985). Learning words from context. *Reading Research Quarterly, 20*, 233–253.

Nagy, W.E., & Scott, J.A. (1990). Word schemas: Expectations about the form and meaning of new words. *Cognition and Instruction, 7*, 105–127.

Nation, I.S.P. (1990). *Teaching and learning vocabulary*. New York: Newbury House.

Ortony, A., Reynolds, R., & Arter, J. (1978). Metaphor: Theoretical and empirical research. *Psychological Bulletin, 85*, 919–943.

Paribakht, T.S., & Wesche, M. (1997). Vocabulary enhancement activities and reading for meaning in second language vocabulary acquisition. In J. Coady & T. Huckin (Eds.), *Second language vocabulary acquisition* (pp. 174–200). Cambridge, UK: Cambridge University Press.

Piaget, J. (1926). *The language and thought of the child* (M. Worden, Trans.). New York: Harcourt, Brace, & World.

Polacco, P. (1996). *I can hear the sun: A modern myth*. New York: Philomel.

Richards, J. (1976). The role of vocabulary teaching. *TESOL Quarterly, 10*, 77–89.

Roberts, B. (1992). The evolution of the young child's concept of word as a unit of spoken and written language. *Reading Research Quarterly, 27*, 124–138.

Roth, F., Speece, D., Cooper, D., & De la Paz, S. (1996). Unresolved mysteries: How do metalinguistic and narrative skills connect with early reading? *Journal of Special Education, 30*, 257–277.

Ruddell, M.R. (1994). Vocabulary knowledge and comprehension: A comprehension-process view of complex literary relationships. In R.B. Ruddell, M.R. Ruddell, & H. Singer (Eds.), *Theoretical models and processes of reading* (4th ed., pp. 414–447). Newark, DE: International Reading Association.

Scarborough, H., Ehri, L., Olson, R., & Fowler, A. (1998). The fate of phonemic awareness beyond the elementary school years. *Scientific Studies of Reading, 2*, 115–142.

Schatz, E.K., & Baldwin, R.S. (1986). Context clues are unreliable predictors of word meanings. *Reading Research Quarterly, 21,* 439–453.

Schmitt, N. (1998). Tracking the incremental acquisition of second language vocabulary: A longitudinal study. *Language Learning, 48*(2), 281–317.

Schmitt, N., & McCarthy, M. (Eds.). (1997). *Vocabulary: Description, acquisition, and pedagogy.* Cambridge, UK: Cambridge University Press.

Schwanenflugel, P., Stahl, S., & McFalls, E. (1997). Partial word knowledge and vocabulary growth during reading comprehension. *Journal of Literacy Research, 29,* 531–553.

Scott, J. (1991). *Using definitions to understand new words.* Unpublished doctoral dissertation, University of Illinois at Urbana-Champaign.

Scott, J., Asselin, M., Henry, S., & Butler, C. (1997, June). *Making rich language visible: Reports from a multi-dimensional study on word learning.* Paper presented at the annual meeting of the Canadian Society for the Study of Education, Newfoundland.

Scott, J., Blackstone, T., Cross, S., Jones, A., Skobel, B., Wells, J., et al. (1996, May). *The power of language: Creating contexts which enrich children's understanding and use of words.* A microworkshop presented at the 41st annual convention of the International Reading Association, New Orleans, LA.

Scott, J., Butler, C., & Asselin, M. (1996, December). *The effect of mediated assistance in word learning.* Paper presented at the 46th annual meeting of the National Reading Conference, Charleston, SC.

Scott, J., & Nagy, W. (1997). Understanding the definitions of unfamiliar verbs. *Reading Research Quarterly, 32,* 184–200.

Scott, J., & Wells, J. (1998). Readers take responsibility: Literature circles and the growth of critical thinking. In K. Beers & B. Samuels (Eds.), *Into focus: Middle school readers* (pp. 177–197). Norwood, MA: Christopher-Gordon.

Snow, C. (1991). The theoretical basis for relationships between language and literacy development. *Journal of Research in Childhood Education, 6,* 5–10.

Snow, C. (1994). What is so hard about learning to read? A pragmatic analysis. In J. Duchan, L. Hewitt, & R. Sonnenmeier (Eds.), *Pragmatics: From theory to practice* (pp. 164–184). Englewood Cliffs, NJ: Prentice Hall.

Snow, C., Cancino, H., Gonzales, P., & Shriberg, E. (1989). Giving formal definitions: An oral language correlate of school literacy. In D. Bloome (Ed.), *Literacy in classrooms* (pp. 233–249). Norwood, NJ: Ablex.

Stahl, S. (1986). Three principles of effective vocabulary instruction. *Journal of Reading, 29,* 662–668.

Stahl, S. (1989). Task variations and prior knowledge in learning word meanings from context. In S. McCormick & J. Zutell (Eds.), *Cognitive and social perspectives for literacy research and instruction* (38th yearbook of the National Reading conference, pp. 197–204). Chicago: National Reading Conference.

Stahl, S., & Fairbanks, M. (1986). The effects of vocabulary instruction: A model-based meta-analysis. *Review of Educational Research, 56,* 72–110.

Stallman, A. (1991). *Learning vocabulary from context: Effects of focusing attention on individual words during reading.* Unpublished doctoral dissertation, University of Illinois at Urbana-Champaign.

Sternberg, R., & Powell, J.S. (1983). Comprehending verbal comprehension. *American Psychologist, 38,* 878–893.

Tunmer, W.E. (1990). The role of language prediction skills in beginning reading. *New Zealand Journal of Educational Studies, 25,* 95–114.

Tunmer, W.E., Herriman, M., & Nesdale, A. (1988). Metalinguistic abilities and beginning reading. *Reading Research Quarterly, 23,* 134–158.

Tunmer, W.E., Nesdale, A.R., & Wright, A.D. (1987). Syntactic awareness and reading acquisition. *British Journal of Developmental Psychology, 5,* 25–34.

Tyler, A., & Nagy, W. (1989). The acquisition of English derivational morphology. *Journal of Verbal Learning and Verbal Behavior, 14,* 638–647.

Warren-Leubecker, A. (1987). Competence and performance factors in word order awareness and early reading. *Journal of Experimental Child Psychology, 43*(1), 62–80.

Watts, S.M. (1995). Vocabulary instruction during reading lessons in six classrooms. *Journal of Reading Behavior, 27,* 399–424.

Weaver, P. (1979). Improving reading instruction: Effects of sentence organization instruction. *Reading Research Quarterly, 15*, 127–146.

Werner, H., & Kaplan, E. (1952). The acquisition of word meanings: A developmental study. *Monographs of the Society for Research in Child Development, 15*(1, Serial No. 51).

Willows, D., & Ryan, E.B. (1986). The development of grammatical sensitivity and its relationship to early reading achievement. *Reading Research Quarterly, 21*, 253–266.

Winner, E., Engel, M., & Gardner, H. (1980). Misunderstanding metaphor: What's the problem? *Journal of Experimental Child Psychology, 30*, 22–32.

20

Role of the Reader's Schema in Comprehension, Learning, and Memory

Richard C. Anderson

The past several years have witnessed the articulation of a largely new theory of reading, a theory already accepted by the majority of scholars in the field. According to the theory, a reader's *schema*, or organized knowledge of the world, provides much of the basis for comprehending, learning, and remembering the ideas in stories and texts. In this paper I will attempt to explain schema theory, give illustrations of the supporting evidence, and suggest applications to classroom teaching and the design of instructional materials.

A Schema-Theoretic Interpretation of Comprehension

In schema-theoretic terms, a reader comprehends a message when he is able to bring to mind a schema that gives a good account of the objects and events described in the message. Ordinarily, comprehension proceeds so smoothly that we are unaware of the process of "cutting and fitting" a schema in order to achieve a satisfactory account of a message. It is instructive, therefore, to try to understand material that gives us pause, so that we can reflect upon our own minds at work. Consider the following sentence, drawn from the work of Bransford and McCarrell (1974):

> The notes were sour because the seam split.

Notice that all of the words are familiar and that the syntax is straightforward, yet the sentence does not "make sense" to most people. Now notice what happens when the additional clue, "bagpipe," is provided. At this point the sentence does make sense because one is able to interpret all the words in the sentence in terms of certain specific objects and events and their interrelations.

Let us examine another sentence:

The big number 37 smashed the ball over the fence.

This sentence is easy to interpret. *Big Number 37* is a baseball player. The sense of *smash the ball* is to propel it rapidly by hitting it strongly with a bat. The fence is at the boundary of a playing field. The ball was hit hard enough that it flew over the fence.

Suppose a person with absolutely no knowledge of baseball read the Big Number 37 sentence. Such as person could not easily construct an interpretation of the sentence, but with enough mental effort might be able to conceive of large numerals, perhaps made of metal, attached to the front of an apartment building. Further, the person might imagine that the numerals come loose and fall, striking a ball resting on top of, or lodged above, a fence, causing the ball to break. Most people regard this as an improbable interpretation, certainly one that never would have occurred to them, but they readily acknowledge that it is a "good" interpretation. What makes it good? The answer is that the interpretation is complete and consistent. It is complete in the sense that every element in the sentence is interpreted; there are no loose ends left unexplained. The interpretation is consistent in that no part of it does serious violence to knowledge about the physical and social world.

Both interpretations of the Big Number 37 sentence assume a real world. Criteria of consistency are relaxed in fictional worlds in which animals talk or men wearing capes leap tall buildings in a single bound. But there are conventions about what is possible in fictional worlds as well. The knowledgeable reader will be annoyed if these conventions are violated. The less-knowledgeable reader simply will be confused.

It should not be imagined that there is some simple, literal level of comprehension of stories and texts that does not require coming up with a schema. This important point is illustrated in a classic study by Bransford and Johnson (1972) in which subjects read paragraphs, such as the following, written so that most people are unable to construct a schema that will account for the material:

If the balloons popped the sound wouldn't be able to carry since everything would be too far away from the correct floor. A closed window would also prevent the sound from carrying, since most buildings tend to be well insulated. Since the whole operation depends upon a steady flow of electricity, a break in the middle of the wire would also cause problems. Of course, the fellow could shout, but the human voice is not loud enough to carry that far. An additional problem is that a string could break on the instrument. Then there could be no accompaniment to the message. It is clear that the best situation would involve less distance. Then there would be fewer potential problems. With face to face contact, the least number of things could go wrong. (p. 719)

Subjects rated this passage as very difficult to understand, and they were unable to remember much of it. In contrast, subjects shown the drawing on the left side of Figure 1 found the passage more comprehensible and were able to remember a great deal of it. Another group saw the drawing on the right in Figure 1. This group remembered no more than the group that did not receive a drawing. The experiment demonstrates that what is critical for comprehension is a schema accounting for the *relationships* among elements; it is not enough for the elements to be concrete and imageable.

Trick passages, such as the foregoing one about the communication problems of a modern-day Romeo, are useful for illustrating what happens when a reader is completely unable to discover a schema that will fit a passage and, therefore, finds the passage entirely incomprehensible. More typical is the situation in which a reader knows something about a topic, but falls far short of being an expert. Chiesi, Spilich, and Voss (1979) asked people high and low in knowledge of baseball to read and recall a report of a half-inning from a fictitious baseball game. Knowledge of baseball had both qualitative and quantitative effects on performance. High-knowledge subjects were more likely to recall and

FIGURE 1

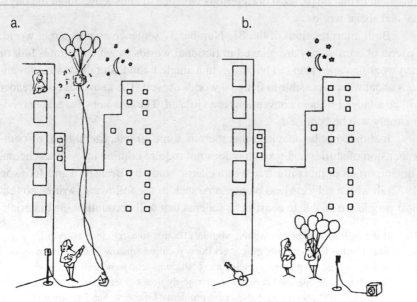

a.   b.

Version "a" represents the appropriate context and version "b" represents the inappropriate context. See text for accompanying passage.

From Bransford, J.D., & Johnson, M.K. (1972). Contextual Prerequisites for Understanding. *Journal of Verbal Learning and Verbal Behavior, 11,* 717–726. Copyright © 1972 by Academic Press, Inc. Reprinted with permission of Elsevier.

embellish upon aspects of strategic significance to the game. Low-knowledge subjects, in contrast, were more likely to include information incidental to the play of the game.

Schema theory highlights the fact that often more than one interpretation of a text is possible. The schema that will be brought to bear on a text depends upon the reader's age, sex, race, religion, nationality, occupation—in short, it depends upon the reader's culture. This point was illustrated in an experiment completed by Anderson, Reynolds, Schallert, and Goetz (1977), who asked people to read the following passage:

> Tony slowly got up from the mat, planning his escape. He hesitated a moment and thought. Things were not going well. What bothered him most was being held, especially since the charge against him had been weak. He considered his present situation. The lock that held him was strong but he thought he could break it. He knew, however, that his timing would have to be perfect. Tony was aware that it was because of his early roughness that he had been penalized so severely—much too severely from his point of view. The situation was becoming frustrating; the pressure had been grinding on him for too long. He was being ridden unmercifully. Tony was getting angry now. He felt he was ready to make his move. He knew that his success or failure would depend on what he did in the next few seconds.

Most people think the foregoing passage is about a convict planning his escape from prison. A special group of people, however, see the passage an entirely different way; these are men who have been involved in the sport of wrestling. They think the passage is about a wrestler caught in the hold of an opponent. Notice how the interpretation of *lock* varies according to perspective. In the one case, it is a piece of hardware that holds a cell door shut; in the other it may be a sweaty arm around a neck. Males enrolled in a weightlifting class and females enrolled in a music education class read the foregoing passage and another passage which most people interpret as about several people playing cards, but which can be interpreted as about a rehearsal session of a woodwind ensemble. The results were as expected. Scores on a multiple-choice test designed to reveal interpretations of the passages showed striking relationships to the subjects' background. Physical education students usually gave a wrestling interpretation to the prison/wrestling passage and a card-playing interpretation to the card/music passage, whereas the reverse was true of the music education students. Similarly, when subjects were asked to recall the passages, theme-revealing distortions appeared, even though the instructions emphasized reproducing the exact words of the original text. For example, a physical education student stated, "Rocky was penalized early in the match for roughness or a dangerous hold," while a music education student wrote, "he was angry that he had been caught and arrested."

The thesis of this section is that comprehension is a matter of activating or constructing a schema that provides a coherent explanation of objects and events mentioned in a discourse. In sharp contrast is the conventional view that comprehension consists of aggregating the meanings of words to form the meanings of clauses, aggregating the meanings of clauses to form the meanings of sentences, aggregating the meaning of sentences to form the meanings of paragraphs, and so on. The illustrations in this section were intended to demonstrate the insufficiency of this conventional view. The meanings of the words cannot be "added up" to give the meaning of the whole. The click of comprehension occurs only when the reader evolves a schema that explains the whole message.

Schema-Based Processes in Learning and Remembering

According to schema theory, reading involves more or less simultaneous analysis at many different levels. The levels include graphophonemic, morphemic, semantic, syntactic, pragmatic, and interpretive. Reading is conceived to be an interactive process. This means that analysis does not proceed in a strict order from the visual information in letters to the overall interpretation of a text. Instead, as a person reads, an interpretation of what a segment of a text might mean is theorized to depend both on analysis of the print and on hypotheses in the person's mind. Processes that flow from the print are called "bottom-up" or "data driven" whereas processes that flow in the other direction are called "top-down" or "hypothesis driven," following Bobrow and Norman (1975). In the passage about Tony, who is either a wrestler or a prisoner, processing the word *lock* has the potential to activate either a piece-of-hardware meaning or a wrestling-hold meaning. The hypothesis the reader has already formulated about the text will tip the scales in the direction of one of the two meanings, usually without the reader's being aware that an alternative meaning is possible. Psychologists are at work developing detailed models of the mechanisms by which information from different levels of analysis is combined during reading (see Just & Carpenter, 1980; Rumelhart & McClelland, 1980).

The reader's schema affects both learning and remembering of the information and ideas in a text. Six functions of schemata that have been proposed (Anderson, 1978; Anderson & Pichert, 1978) are briefly explained.

A schema provides ideational scaffolding for assimilating text information. The idea is that a schema provides a niche, or slot, for certain text information. For instance, there is a slot for the main entree in a dining-at-a-fine-restaurant schema and a slot for the murder weapon in a who-done-it schema. Information that fits slots in the reader's schema is readily learned, perhaps with little mental effort.

A schema facilitates selective allocation of attention. A schema provides part of the basis for determining the important aspects of a text. It is hypothesized that skilled readers use importance as one basis for allocating cognitive resources—that is, for deciding where to pay close attention.

A schema enables inferential elaboration. No text is completely explicit. A reader's schema provides the basis for making inferences that go beyond the information literally stated in a text.

A schema allows orderly searches of memory. A schema can provide the reader with a guide to the types of information that need to be recalled. For instance, a person attempting to recall the food served at a fine meal can review the categories of food typically included in a fine meal: What was the appetizer? What was the soup? Was there a salad? And so on. In other words, by tracing through the schema used to structure the text, the reader is helped to gain access to the particular information learned when the text was read.

A schema facilitates editing and summarizing. Since a schema contains within itself criteria of importance, it enables the reader to produce summaries that include significant propositions and omit trivial ones.

A schema permits inferential reconstruction. When there are gaps in memory, a rememberer's schema, along with the specific text information that can be recalled, helps generate hypotheses about the missing information. For example, suppose a person cannot recall what beverage was served with a fine meal. If he can recall that the entree was fish, he will be able to infer that the beverage may have been white wine.

The foregoing are tentative hypotheses about the functions of a schema in text processing, conceived to provide the broadest possible interpretation of available data. Several of the hypotheses can be regarded as rivals—for instance, the ideational scaffolding hypothesis and the selective attention hypothesis—and it may be that not all of them will turn out to be viable. Researchers are now actively at work developing precise models of schema-based processes and subjecting these models to experimental test.

Evidence for Schema Theory

There is now a really good case that schemata incorporating knowledge of the world play an important role in language comprehension. We are beginning to see research on differentiated functions. In a few years it should be possible to speak in more detail about the specific processing mechanisms in which schemata are involved.

Many of the claims of schema theory are nicely illustrated in a cross-cultural experiment, completed by Steffensen, Joag-Dev, and Anderson (1979), in which Indians (natives of India) and Americans read letters about an Indian and an American wedding. Of course, every adult member of a society has a well-developed marriage schema. There are substantial differences between Indian and American cultures in the nature of marriages. As a consequence, large differences in comprehension, learning, and memory for the letters were expected.

Table 1 summarizes analyses of the recall of the letters by Indian and American subjects. The first row in the table indicates the amount of time subjects spent reading the letters. As can be seen, subjects spent less time reading what for them was the native passage. This was as expected since a familiar schema should speed up and expedite a reader's processing.

The second row in Table 1 presents the number of idea units recalled. The gist measure includes not only propositions recalled verbatim but also acceptable paraphrases. The finding was precisely as expected. Americans recalled more of the American text, whereas Indians recalled more of the Indian passage. Within current formulations of schema theory, there are a couple of reasons for predicting that people would learn and remember more of a text about a marriage in their own culture: a culturally appropriate schema may provide the ideational scaffolding that makes it easy to learn information that fits into that schema, or, it may be that the information, once learned, is more accessible because the schema is a structure that makes it easy to search memory.

The row labeled *Elaborations* in Table 1 contains the frequency of culturally appropriate extensions of the text. The row labeled *Distortions* contains the frequency of culturally inappropriate modifications of the text. Ever since Bartlett's day, elaborations and distortions have provided the intuitively most compelling evidence for the role of schemata. Many fascinating instances appeared in the protocols collected in the present study. A section of the American passage upon which interesting cultural differences surfaced read as follows:

> Did you know that Pam was going to wear her grandmother's wedding dress? That gave her something that was old, and borrowed, too. It was made of lace over satin, with very large puff sleeves and looked absolutely charming on her.

TABLE 1
Mean Performance on Various Measures

| Measure | Nationality | | | |
| | Americans | | Indians | |
	American Passage	Indian Passage	American Passage	Indian Passage
Time (Seconds)	168	213	304	276
Gist Recall	52.4	37.9	27.3	37.6
Elaborations	5.7	.1	.2	5.4
Distortions	.1	7.6	5.5	.3
Other Overt Errors	7.5	5.2	8.0	5.9
Omissions	76.2	76.6	95.5	83.3

From Steffensen, Joag-Dev, and Anderson (1979).

One Indian had this to say about the American bride's dress: "She was looking all right except the dress was too old and out of fashion." Wearing an heirloom wedding dress is a completely acceptable aspect of the pageantry of the American marriage ceremony. This Indian appears to have completely missed this and has inferred that the dress was out of fashion, on the basis that Indians attach importance to displays of social status, manifested in such details as wearing an up-to-date, fashionable sari.

The gifts described in the Indian passage that were given to the groom's family by the bride's, the dowry, and the reference to the concern of the bride's family that a scooter might be requested were a source of confusion for our American subjects. First of all, the "agreement about the gifts to be given to the in-laws" was changed to "the exchange of gifts," a wording which suggests that gifts are flowing in two directions, not one. Another subject identified the gifts given to the in-laws as favors, which are often given in American weddings to the attendants by the bride and groom.

In another facet of the study, different groups of Indians and Americans read the letters and rated the significance of each of the propositions. It was expected that Americans would regard as important propositions conveying information about ritual and ceremony whereas Indians would see as important propositions dealing with financial and social status. Table 2 contains examples of text units that received contrasting ratings of importance from Indians and Americans. Schema theory predicts that text units that are important in the light of the schema are more likely to be learned and, once learned, are more likely to be remembered. This prediction was confirmed. Subjects did recall more text information rated as important by their cultural cohorts, whether recalling what for them was the native or the foreign text.

Of course, it is one thing to show, as Steffensen, Joag-Dev, and Anderson did, that readers from distinctly different national cultures give different interpretations to culturally sensitive materials, and quite another to find the same phenomenon among readers from different but overlapping subcultures within the same country. A critical issue is whether cultural variation within the United States could be a factor in differential reading comprehension. Minority children could have a handicap if stories, texts, and test items presuppose a cultural perspective that the children do not share. An initial exploration of this issue has been completed by Reynolds, Taylor, Steffensen, Shirey, and Anderson (1981), who wrote a passage around an episode involving "sounding." Sounding is an activity predominantly found in the black community in which the participants try to outdo each other in an exchange of insults (Labov, 1972). In two group studies, and one in which subjects were individually interviewed, black teenagers tended to see the episode as involving friendly give-and-take, whereas white teenagers interpreted it as an ugly confrontation, sometimes one involving physical violence. For example, when attempting to recall the incident, a black male

TABLE 2
Examples of Idea Units of Contrasting Importance to Americans and Indians

American Passage		Indian Passage	
Idea Units More Important to Americans	Idea Units More Important to Indians	Idea Units More Important to Americans	Idea Units More Important to Indians
Then on Friday night *they had the rehearsal* at the church *and the rehearsal dinner,* which lasted until almost midnight. *All the attendants wore dresses that were specially designed to go with Pam's.* Her mother wore yellow, which looks great on her with her bleached hair, *and George's mother wore pale green.*	*She'll be lucky if she can even get her daughter married, the way things are going.* Her mother wore yellow, which looks great on her *with her bleached hair,* and George's mother wore pale green. Have you seen the diamond she has? *It must have cost George a fortune because it's almost two carats.*	Prema's husband had to wear a dhoti *for that ceremony and for the wedding the next day.* *There were only the usual essential rituals:* the curtain removal, the parents giving the daughter away, walking seven steps together, etc., *and plenty of smoke from the sacred fire.* There must have been about five hundred people *at the wedding feast. Since only fifty people could be seated at one time, it went on for a long time.*	*Prema's in-laws seem to be nice enough people.* They did not create any problem in the wedding, *even though Prema's husband is their only son.* *Since they did not ask for any dowry,* Prema's parents were a little worried about their asking for a scooter before the wedding, *but they didn't ask for one.* *Prema's parents were very sad when she left.*

Important idea units are in italics.

wrote, "Then everybody tried to get on the person side that joke were the best." A white male wrote, "Soon there was a riot. All the kids were fighting." This research established that when written material has an identifiable cultural loading there is a pronounced effect on comprehension. It remains to be seen how much school reading material is culturally loaded.

In the foregoing research, schemata were manipulated by selecting subjects with different backgrounds. Another approach for getting people to bring different schemata to bear is by selecting different passages. Anderson, Spiro, and Anderson (1978) wrote two closely comparable passages, one about dining at a fancy restaurant, the other about a trip to a supermarket. The same 18 items of food and beverage were mentioned in the two texts, in the same order, and attributed to the same characters. The first hypothesis was that subjects who received the restaurant passage would learn and recall more food and beverage information than subjects who received the supermarket passage. The reasoning was that a dining-at-a-fine-restaurant schema has a more constrained structure than a trip-to-a-supermarket schema. That is to say, fewer food and beverage items will fit the former schema; one could choose soda pop and hot dogs at a supermarket, but these items would not be ordered at a fine restaurant. Moreover there are more cross-connections among items in a restaurant schema. For example, a steak will be accompanied by a baked potato, or maybe french fries. In two experiments, subjects who read the restaurant text recalled more food and beverage items than subjects who read the supermarket text.

The second prediction was that students who read the restaurant text would more often attribute the food and drink items to the correct characters. In a supermarket it does not matter, for instance, who throws the Brussels sprouts into the shopping cart, but in a restaurant it does matter who orders which item. This prediction was confirmed in two experiments.

A third prediction was that order of recall of food and beverages would correspond more closely to order of mention in the text for subjects who read the restaurant story. There is not, or need not be, a prescribed sequence for selecting items in a grocery store, but there is a characteristic order in which items are served in a restaurant. This hypothesis was supported in one experiment and the trend of the data favored it in a second.

Another technique for manipulating readers' schemata is by assigning them different perspectives. Pichert and Anderson (1977) asked people to pretend that they were either burglars or home buyers before reading a story about what two boys did at one of the boys' homes while they were skipping school. The finding was that people learned more of the information to their assigned perspective. For instance, burglars were more likely to learn that three 10-speed bikes were parked in the garage, whereas home buyers were more likely to learn that the house had a leaky roof. Anderson and Pichert (1978; see also Anderson, Pichert, & Shirey, 1979) went on to show that the reader's perspective has independent effects on learning and recall. Subjects who switch perspectives and then recall the story for a second time recall additional, previously unrecalled, information important to their new perspective but unimportant to their original perspective. For example, a person who begins as a home buyer may fail to remember that the story says the side door is kept unlocked, but may later remember this information when told to assume the role of a burglar. Subjects report that previously unrecalled information significant in the light of the new perspective "pops" into their heads.

Recent unpublished research in my laboratory, completed in collaboration with Ralph Reynolds and Paul Wilson, suggests selective allocation of attention to text elements that are important in the light of the reader's schema. We have employed two measures of attention. The first is the amount of time a subject spends reading schema-relevant sentences. The second is time to respond to a probe presented during schema-relevant sentences. The probe is a tone sounded through earphones; the subject responds by pushing a button as fast as possible. The logic of the probe task is that if the mind is occupied with reading, there will be a slight delay in responding to the probe. Our results indicate that people assigned a burglar perspective, for instance, have slightly longer reading times and slightly longer probe times when reading burglar-relevant sentences. Comparable results have been obtained by other investigators (Cirilo & Foss, 1980; Haberlandt, Berian, & Sandson, 1980; Just & Carpenter, 1980).

Implications of Schema Theory for Design of Materials and Classroom Instruction

First, I urge publishers to include teaching suggestions in manuals designed to help children activate relevant knowledge before reading. Children do not spontaneously integrate what they are reading with what they already know (cf. Paris & Lindauer, 1976). This means that special attention should be paid to preparation for reading. Questions should be asked that remind children of relevant experiences of their own and orient them toward the problems faced by story characters.

Second, the teachers' manuals accompanying basal programs and content area texts ought to include suggestions for building prerequisite knowledge when it cannot be safely presupposed. According to schema theory, this practice should promote comprehension. There is direct evidence to support knowledge-building activities. Hayes and Tierney (1980) asked American high school students to read and recall newspaper reports of cricket matches. Performance improved sharply when the students received instruction on the nature of the game of cricket before reading the newspaper reports.

Third, I call for publishers to feature lesson activities that will lead children to meaningfully integrate what they already know with what is presented on the printed page. From the perspective of schema theory, prediction techniques such as the Directed Reading-Thinking Activity (Stauffer, 1969) can be recommended. The DRTA would appear to cause readers to search their store of knowledge and integrate what they already know with what is stated. It must be acknowledged, however, that the empirical evidence for the efficacy of the DRTA is flimsy at present (Tierney & Cunningham, 1984). Recently, Anderson, Mason, and Shirey (1984) have illustrated that under optimum conditions strong benefits can be obtained using a prediction technique. A heterogeneous sample of third graders read sentences such as, "The stupid child ran into the street after the ball." Children in the prediction group read each sentence aloud and then indicated what might happen next. In the case of the sentence above, a frequent prediction was that the child might get hit by a car. A second group read the sentences aloud with an emphasis on accurate decoding. A third and a fourth group listened to the sentences and read them silently. The finding was that the prediction group recalled 72% of the sentences, whereas the average for the other three groups was 43%.

Fourth, I urge publishers to employ devices that will highlight the structure of text material. Schema theory inclines one to endorse the practice of providing advance organizers or structured overviews, along the lines proposed by Ausubel (1968) and Herber (1978). Ausubel, who can be regarded as one of the pioneer schema theorists, has stated that "the principal function of the organizer is to bridge the gap between what the learner already knows and what he needs to know before he can successfully learn the task at hand" (1968, p. 148). There have been dozens of empirical studies of advance organizers over the past 20 years. Thorough reviews of this bulky literature by Mayer (1979) and Luiten, Ames, and Ackerson (1980) point to the conclusion that organizers generally have a facilitative effect. Nevertheless, from within current formulations of schema theory, there is room for reservations about advance organizers. Notably, Ausubel's insistence (cf. 1968, pp. 148, 333) that organizers must be stated at a high level of generality, abstractness, and inclusiveness is puzzling. The problem is that general, abstract language often is difficult to understand. Children, in particular, are more easily reminded of what they know when concrete language is used. As Ausubel himself has acknowledged (e.g., 1968, p. 149), "To be useful…organizers themselves must obviously be learnable and must be stated in familiar terms."

A final implication of schema theory is that minority children may sometimes be counted as failing to comprehend school reading material because their schemata do not match those of the majority culture. Basal reading programs, content area texts, and standardized tests lean heavily on the conventional assumption that meaning is inherent in the words and structure of a text. When prior knowledge is required, it is assumed to be knowledge common to children from every subculture. When new ideas are introduced, these are assumed to be equally accessible to every child. Considering the strong effects that culture has on reading comprehension, the question that naturally arises is whether children from different subcultures can so confidently be assumed to bring a common schema to written material. To be sure, subcultures within the United States do overlap. But is it safe simply to *assume* that when reading the same story, children from every subculture will have the same experience with the setting, ascribe the same goals and motives to characters, imagine the same sequence of actions, predict the same emotional reactions, or expect the same outcomes? This is a question that the research community and the school publishing industry ought to address with renewed vigor.

References

Anderson, R.C. (1978). Schema-directed processes in language comprehension. In A. Lesgold, J. Pellegrino, S. Fokkema, & R. Glaser (Eds.), *Cognitive psychology and instruction*. New York: Plenum.

Anderson, R.C., Mason, J., & Shirey, L.L. (1984). The reading group: An experimental investiga-

tion of a labyrinth. *Reading Research Quarterly*, *20*, 6–38.

Anderson, R.C., & Pichert, J.W. (1978). Recall of previously unrecallable information following a shift in perspective. *Journal of Verbal Learning and Verbal Behavior*, *17*, 1–12.

Anderson, R.C., Pichert, J.W., & Shirey, L.L. (1979, April). *Effects of the reader's schema at different points in time* (Tech. Rep. No. 119). Urbana: University of Illinois, Center for the Study of Reading. (ERIC Document Reproduction Service No. ED169523)

Anderson, R.C., Reynolds, R.E., Schallert, D.L., & Goetz, E.T. (1977). Frameworks for comprehending discourse. *American Educational Research Journal, 14*, 367–382.

Anderson, R.C., Spiro, R.J., & Anderson, M.C. (1978). Schemata as scaffolding for the representation of information in connected discourse. *American Educational Research Journal, 15*, 433–440.

Ausubel, D.P. (1968). *Educational psychology: A cognitive view.* New York: Holt, Rinehart.

Bobrow, D.G., & Norman, D.A. (1975). Some principles of memory schemata. In D.G. Bobrow & A.M. Collins (Eds.), *Representation and understanding: Studies in cognitive science.* New York: Academic.

Bransford, J.D., & Johnson, M.K. (1972). Contextual prerequisites for understanding: Some investigations of comprehension and recall. *Journal of Verbal Learning and Verbal Behavior, 11*, 717–726.

Bransford, J.D., & McCarrell, N.S. (1974). A sketch of a cognitive approach to comprehension. In W.B. Weimer & D.S. Palermo (Eds.), *Cognition and the symbolic process.* Hillsdale, NJ: Erlbaum.

Chiesi, H.L., Spilich, G.J., & Voss, J.F. (1979). Acquisition of domain-related information in relation to high- and low-domain knowledge. *Journal of Verbal Learning and Verbal Behavior, 18*, 257–274.

Cirilo, R.K., & Foss, D.J. (1980). Text structure and reading time for sentences. *Journal of Verbal Learning and Verbal Behavior, 19*, 96–109.

Haberlandt, K., Berian, C., & Sandson, J. (1980). The episode schema in story processing. *Journal of Verbal Learning and Verbal Behavior, 19*, 635–650.

Hayes, D.A., & Tierney, R.J. (1980, October). *Increasing background knowledge through analogy: Its effects upon comprehension and learning* (Tech. Rep. No. 186). Urbana: University of Illinois, Center for the Study of Reading. (ERIC Document Reproduction Service No. ED195953)

Herber, H.L. (1978). *Teaching reading in content areas* (2nd ed.). Englewood Cliffs, NJ: Prentice Hall.

Just, M.A., & Carpenter, P.A. (1980). A theory of reading: From eye fixation to comprehension. *Psychological Review, 87*, 329–354.

Labov, W. (1972). *Language in the inner city: Studies in the black English vernacular.* Washington, DC: Center for Applied Linguistics.

Luiten, J., Ames, W., & Ackerson, G. (1980). A meta-analysis of the effects of advance organizers on learning and retention. *American Educational Research Journal, 17*, 211–218.

Mayer, R.E. (1979). Can advance organizers influence meaningful learning? *Review of Educational Research, 49*, 371–383.

Paris, S.G., & Lindauer, B.K. (1976). The role of inference in children's comprehension and memory. *Cognitive Psychology, 8*, 217–227.

Pichert, J.W., & Anderson, R.C. (1977). Taking different perspectives on a story. *Journal of Educational Psychology, 69*, 309–315.

Reynolds, R.E., Taylor, M.A., Steffensen, M.S., Shirey, L.L., & Anderson, R.C. (1981, April). *Cultural schemata and reading comprehension* (Tech. Rep. No. 201). Urbana: University of Illinois, Center for the Study of Reading.

Rumelhart, D.E., & McClelland, J.L. (1980). *An interactive activation model of the effect of context in perception* (Part 2; CHIP Tech. Rep.). La Jolla, CA: University of California, Center for Human Information Processing.

Stauffer, R.G. (1969). *Teaching reading as a thinking process.* New York: Harper & Row.

Steffensen, M.S., Joag-Dev, C., & Anderson, R.C. (1979). A cross-cultural perspective on reading comprehension. *Reading Research Quarterly, 15*, 10–29.

Tierney, R.J., & Cunningham, J.W. (1984). Research on teaching reading comprehension. In P.D. Pearson, R. Barr, M.L. Kamil, & P. Mosenthal (Eds.), *Handbook of reading research* (pp. 609–655). New York: Longman.

21

Schema Activation and Schema Acquisition: Comments on Richard C. Anderson's Remarks

John D. Bransford

Professor Anderson has done an excellent job of presenting the essentials of schema theory and of highlighting a number of its implications. My comments on his paper are divided into two points. First, I want to reemphasize some of Anderson's major arguments and elaborate on several of their implications. I shall then discuss some potential shortcomings of many versions of schema theory and suggest some modifications that seem relevant to the issue of understanding how people learn from texts.

Several of Anderson's points about schema theory can be reviewed by considering the processes involved in understanding, and later remembering, a simple statement such as the following: "Jane decided not to wear her matching silver necklace, earrings, and belt because she was going to the airport." In order to comprehend this statement, one must go beyond the information that was given and postulate a reason for the connection between airports and Jane's style of dress. People who are familiar with airports—who have a well-developed "airport schema"—might assume that Jane decided not to wear her silver jewelry because of the metal detectors in airports. In Anderson's terminology, their schemata provide a basis for interpreting and elaborating on the information they heard.

Anderson also argued that schemata affect processes at the time of output as well as at input. For example, adults who attempt to recall the original "airport" statement three days later may rely on their knowledge of airports for a selective search of memory and then state that "Jane decided not to wear some metal jewelry because it could cause unnecessary delays at the airport." Note that this type of response reveals the comprehender's assumptions about important elements. It is the fact that the jewelry was metal that was most important and not, for example, that it was expensive or pretty. Anderson also emphasized this

From Anderson, R.C., Osborn, J., & Tierney, R.J. (Eds.), *Learning to Read in American Schools: Basal Readers and Content Texts* (pp. 259–272). Copyright © 1984 by Lawrence Erlbaum Associates. Reprinted with permission of the publisher.

function of schemata: They provide a basis for determining the important elements in a message or text.

Overall, Anderson discussed six functions of schemata. They provide a basis for (1) assimilating text information, (2) making inferential elaborations that fill in the gaps in messages, (3) allocating attention to important text elements, (4) searching memory in an orderly fashion, (5) formulating a summary of information, and (6) making inferences that can enable one to reconstruct an original message despite having forgotten some of the details. It may be possible to add to Professor Anderson's list of "schema functions," but the six functions he cited are sufficient to illustrate why the knowledge possessed by the learner has pervasive effects on performance. I might add that Anderson was not simply arguing that the activation of appropriate knowledge is a useful thing to do; he was asserting that it is a fundamental aspect of the act of comprehending and remembering. One clear implication of this position is that some children may appear to have poor comprehension and memory skills *not* because they have some inherent comprehension or memory "deficits," but because they lack, or fail to activate, the background knowledge that was presupposed by a message or a text.

It is instructive to note that there are many levels at which a child may lack the background knowledge necessary to understand a text. At one extreme, the child may have no information about a concept; he or she may know nothing about airports, for example. At another level, a child may know something about a concept (for example, airports) yet still fail to understand many statements that involve this concept. As an illustration, consider once again the simple statement about Jane's trip to the airport and her decision about her silver jewelry. A child may know that airports are "places where planes take off and land" yet have no knowledge that airports contain metal detectors. The child therefore knows something about airports, but his or her "airport schema" is still less articulated than that of most adults. The child's knowledge may be sufficient for understanding some types of statements about airports (e.g., John went to the airport because his aunt was coming to visit) yet insufficient for others (e.g., the earlier statement about Jane.) The question of what it means for children to be "familiar" with the words used in a story is therefore more complicated than might be apparent at first glance.

Imagine another child who knows that airports are places where planes land and take off, and also knows that airports are often crowded and may be havens for thieves. This child may form the following interpretation of the statement about Jane and the airport: "Jane did not wear her expensive jewelry because she was afraid that someone might take it." This interpretation is quite different from one that focuses on the fact that airports have metal detectors. According to the "crowded airport" interpretation, the important elements are that the jewelry is valuable, visible, and easily accessible, rather than the fact that the jewelry is metal and hence may trigger a security alarm. Relatively subtle differences in people's schemata (in this case their "airport schemata") can therefore have important effects on the interpretations they make.

Consider some of the problems that can arise when two people form different interpretations of the same message. For example, imagine that a teacher forms a "metal detector" interpretation of the statement about Jane and that a child forms a "thief" interpretation. In a one-to-one conversation, these two individuals might well discover their differences in interpretation and agree that both are reasonable. However, extended one-to-one conversations are often impossible in an educational setting. Teachers are frequently forced to use assessment questions in order to evaluate students' comprehension. These questions may be supplied either by the author of a text or by the teacher. In either case, the phrasing of the question may reflect the question asker's initial interpretations of a message. For example, a question such as "Why didn't Jane wear something metal?" may stem from a "metal detector" interpretation, whereas the question "Why didn't Jane wear her expensive jewelry?" tends to reflect a "thief" interpretation. My colleagues and I have found that even relatively subtle mismatches between a learner's initial interpretations and a teacher's or a tester's way of phrasing questions can cause considerable decrements in memory performance (Barclay, Bransford, Franks, McCarrell, & Nitsch, 1974). If my phrasing of a question is not congruent with a child's initial interpretation of an event, I may erroneously conclude that the child did not learn.

Mismatches between the phrasing of questions and a child's initial interpretations affect not only teachers' assessments of children's learning abilities; I am convinced that they also affect children's assumptions about their own abilities. Several years ago, Marcia Johnson and I conducted a study with college students that is relevant to this point (Bransford & Johnson, 1973). We created a passage about a man walking through the woods; nearly all our students interpreted the story as describing a hunter. They did not realize that the passage could also be interpreted from the perspective of an escaping convict. As Anderson noted, the perspective one takes on a story affects one's interpretation of the significance of information. For example, the story included information about it being muddy, hence the man's boots sank in deeply. He then came to a little stream and walked in it for a while. From the perspective of a hunter, this information suggests that the boots may have become caked with mud and that the man tried to clean them by walking in the stream. From the perspective of an escaping convict, however, the same information suggests that the man was leaving footprints and must take precautions in order to avoid being tracked.

We asked one group of college students to read the story I have described but said nothing about the possibility of interpreting it as an escaping convict. They therefore assumed that it was about a hunter, and the story made sense from this point of view. After reading the story, we supplied students with questions and explained that these should help them retrieve the information they had studied. However, the questions were written from the perspective of the escaping convict interpretation. For example, one question was "What was the concern with the trail and what was done to eliminate it?" Not surprisingly, these questions did not help students remember relevant aspects of the story; instead they caused confusion. Many of the students thought about the questions for a considerable amount of time and eventually concluded that they had completely misinterpreted the story. Several apologized for having made such an error. In reality, however, they had not "misinterpreted" the story; their original interpretations had been perfectly reasonable. We eventually told the students this, of course, because it would have been unfair to let them think that they had been in error. The point I want to stress, however, is that these mismatches between initial interpretations and the phrasing of questions can occur inadvertently in almost any situation. Furthermore, learners who do not realize why their performance suffered may mistakenly attribute their difficulties to their own inabilities to learn.

The preceding examples illustrate only a few of many important implications of schema theory, but I now want to consider some possible shortcomings of many versions of this theory. I refer to these as *possible* shortcomings because I am uncertain whether they are shortcomings of the actual theory or shortcomings that stem from my personal interpretation of schema theory (i.e., my "schema theory schema" may be only partially developed). At any rate, I believe that there are some issues concerning schema theory that need to be explored, especially when one begins to ask how teachers and authors might use this theory to help themselves avoid some of the text–student mismatches and question–student mismatches that have been discussed.

One possible approach to the problem of mismatches is to analyze carefully the materials presented to children and then to simplify them so that mismatches are much less likely to occur. There are some obvious merits to this approach, but it involves some potential problems as well. These problems revolve around the issue of what it means to "simplify" texts.

Several years ago, I participated in a conference where the topic of simplifying texts arose during one of the discussion periods. One of the participants at the conference expressed some concerns about the reading materials that his children had received in the elementary grades (see Kavanagh & Strange, 1978, pp. 329–330). He felt that the content of the stories (e.g., about a milkman, mailman, etc.) was extremely dull. When he asked the teachers why the children received such uninteresting materials, he was told that the children were familiar with the "community helpers." The teachers had not read about schema theory, so they did not say, "These stories are written to be congruent with the children's preexisting schemata." Nevertheless, the teachers were emphasizing the importance of providing children with materials that were congruent with the knowledge they already possessed.

The conference participant went on to say that his children did not like to read stories about topics that were extremely familiar; they were much more interested in reading about novel situations. In addition, he asked how theories that emphasize the importance of assimilating information to preexisting knowledge can account for the fact that it is possible to understand stories about novel situations. I think that this is a crucial question to ask schema theorists. It is especially crucial for those schema theorists who argue that comprehension involves the activation of a preexisting schema that provides a coherent account of the givens in a message. Many schema theorists have very little to say about the processes by which novel events are comprehended and new schemata are acquired.

In his presentation, Professor Anderson mentioned two types of situations involving schemata. One involves the activation of preexisting schemata. The second, which he noted was more interesting, involves the construction of new schemata. Since a major goal of education is to help students develop new skills and knowledge—to help them become able to understand things that they could not understand previously—the issue of schema construction or schemata acquisition is extremely important. Nevertheless, nearly all the experiments used to support schema theory involve situations where students are prompted to activate preexisting schemata. For example, students may be prompted to activate a "washing clothes" schema, "prisoner" schema, "fancy restaurant" schema, "home buyer" schema, and so forth. We have seen that these schemata provide important support for both comprehension processes and memory processes. However, experiments involving these schemata "work" only because the students in the experiments have already acquired the necessary schemata. If a person knew nothing about washing clothes, for example, it would do no good to simply tell him or her that this is the topic of the washing clothes passage. Similarly, imagine that a child is told that "Jane did not wear her silver jewelry because she was going somewhere" and is then given the cue, "She is going to the airport." A child who knows only that airports are places where planes take off and land is still going to have difficulty understanding this statement. In situations such as this, we confront the problem of helping students develop new schemata or of helping them refine the structure of schemata that they have already acquired (e.g., Bransford & Nitsch, 1978; Bransford, Nitsch, & Franks, 1977; Brown, 1979).

Imagine that we want to help a child develop a more sophisticated "airport schema." We will assume that the child knows that airports are places where planes take off and land, yet is unaware that there are metal detectors in airports. A basic and time-honored procedure for helping the child acquire this new information is to tell him or her about it. One might therefore supply information such as "There are metal detectors in airports" either prior to the child's reading a text or in the text itself.

There are many reasons why a statement such as "There are metal detectors in airports" may not be helpful to a child. An obvious reason is that a child may not be familiar with the concept of metal detectors. However, assume that our child is familiar with this general concept. He or she may still not benefit from the statement that "There are metal detectors in airports." The child needs to understand what the detectors are for and who uses them. Without this information, the child may assume that there are stores in airports that sell things, and hence conclude that most airports have "metal detector" stores. This is not the interpretation we want the child to make.

It seems clear that effective teachers or writers would do much more than simply state, "There are metal detectors in airports." They would elaborate by helping the child realize that pilots guide planes to particular locations, that someone could try to force a pilot to fly to a different location, that this act may involve a gun or knife, that these objects can be detected by metal detectors, that the detectors at the airport are designed to keep people from taking knives and guns aboard the plane, and so forth. The amount of explanation needed will depend on the preexisting knowledge base of the learner (e.g., a relatively knowledgeable child may need only be told that "There are metal detectors in airports in order to discourage hijacking.") The point I want to emphasize is that the goal of this instruction is to help the child develop a more sophisticated schema rather than simply to activate a schema that already exists. The teacher or author is attempting to help the child activate various preexisting "pockets" of knowledge that previously had been unrelated, and to help the child reassemble these "pockets" of knowledge into an integrated schema. This schema should then provide support for comprehending and remembering subsequent events. For example, the child's interpretation of "the metal-detector repairman received a phone call and rushed to the airport" may now be more likely to involve the assumption that he was rushing to repair a machine rather than rushing to catch a plane or to meet someone arriving by plane.

At a general level, an emphasis on the importance of helping students activate sources of preexisting knowledge that can be reassembled into new schemata is consistent with Ausubel's (1963, 1968) theory of meaningful learning. For example, he advocates the use of "advanced organizers" in order to prepare students for texts. I think it is fair to say, however, that many aspects of this theory need greater articulation; in particular, the guidelines for writing advanced organizers are relatively vague. One of the difficulties of constructing these guidelines is that advanced organizers must differ depending on whether one is dealing with a problem of schema activation or schema construction. An advanced organizer that is relatively general can be effective if learners have already acquired the schemata necessary for understanding a text; these general statements can prime concepts that learners might fail to activate spontaneously. When one is dealing with problems of schema construction or acquisition, however, advanced organizers composed of general statements will not suffice.

Earlier, I emphasized some of the specific elaboration or explanations that may be required to help a child incorporate information about metal detectors into his or her airport schema. It seems valuable to explore this issue further by examining the processes involved in acquiring knowledge about a more complex domain. Imagine, therefore, that someone is familiar with the general terms *vein* and *artery*, yet wants to learn more about them. (This is analogous to knowing something about airports, yet needing additional information.) Assume that the person reads a passage which states that arteries are thick, are elastic, and carry blood that is rich in oxygen from the heart; veins are thinner, are less elastic, and carry blood rich in carbon dioxide back to the heart. To the biological novice, even this relatively simple set of facts can seen arbitrary and confusing. Was it veins or arteries that are thin? Was the thin one or the thick one elastic? Which one carries carbon dioxide from the heart (or was it to the heart)?

Even the biological novice who is familiar with the terms *veins* and *arteries* may have difficulty learning the information in this passage. The problem the learner faces is that the facts and relationships appear arbitrary. It is possible to create an analogous situation by using concepts that are familiar to everyone. For example, imagine reading 10 statements such as those listed below and then answering questions about them from memory:

> The tall man bought the crackers.
>
> The bald man read the newspaper.
>
> The funny man liked the ring.
>
> The hungry man purchased the tie.
>
> The short man used the broom.
>
> The strong man skimmed the book.

College students do quite poorly when they are presented with these statements and are then asked memory questions such as "Which man bought the crackers?" (Stein & Bransford, 1979; Stein, Morris, & Bransford, 1978). The students rate each sentence as comprehensible, yet have difficulty remembering because the relationship between each type of man and the actions performed seem arbitrary. The biological novice is in a similar position because he or she sees no particular reason why an artery should be elastic or nonelastic, thick or thin. Note that to a child, a statement such as "Airports have metal detectors" can also seem arbitrary. The child may therefore have difficulty retaining the new information about airports; hence it will not be available for future use. This problem of retention becomes even more acute if we make the reasonable assumption that children are introduced to a number of new ideas during the course of a day. For example, they may receive new information about airports, fancy restaurants, dinosaurs, countries, and so forth. If these new facts seem arbitrary, it can be difficult to remember which things go with what.

In order to make the facts less arbitrary, we need to give a learner information that can clarify their significance or relevance (see Bransford, Stein,

Shelton, & Owings, 1980). For example, what's the significance of the elasticity of arteries? How does this property relate to the functions that arteries perform? Note that our imaginary passage states that arteries can carry blood from the heart—blood that is pumped in spurts. This provides one clue about the significance of elasticity—arteries may need to expand and contract to accommodate the pumping of blood. It can also be important to understand why veins do *not* need to be elastic. Since veins can carry blood back to the heart, they may have less of a need to accommodate the large changes in pressure resulting from the heart pumping blood in spurts.

The process of clarifying the significance of facts about veins and arteries can be carried further. Since arteries carry blood *from* the heart, there is a problem of directionality. Why doesn't the blood flow back into the heart? This will not be perceived as a problem if one assumes that arterial blood always flows downhill, but let's assume that our passage mentions that there are arteries in the neck and shoulder regions. Arterial blood must therefore flow uphill as well. This information might provide an additional clue about the significance of elasticity. If arteries expand from a spurt of blood and then contract, this might help the blood move in a particular direction. Arteries might therefore perform a function similar to one-way valves.

My colleagues and I have argued that there are at least two important consequences of activities that enable a learner to understand the significance or relevance of new factual content (e.g., Bransford et al., 1980). First, people who understand the significance of facts develop knowledge structures that enable them to deal with novel situations. As an illustration, imagine that a biological novice reads a passage about veins and arteries and is then given the task of designing an artificial artery. Would it have to be elastic? A person who has merely memorized the fact that "arteries are elastic" would have little basis for answering the question. In contrast, the person who understands the significance or relevance of elasticity is in a much better position to approach the problem. For example, this person might realize the possibility of using a relatively nonelastic material that is sufficient to withstand the pressure requirements of spurting blood, plus realize the possibility of equipping the artificial artery with one-way valves that direct the flow of blood. This individual may not be able to specify all the details for creating the artificial artery, of course, but he or she at least has some appreciation of various possibilities and has an idea of the types of additional information that need to be discovered or acquired.

Activities that enable people to understand the significance of new factual content also facilitate memory. Facts that initially had seemed arbitrary and confusing become meaningful; the information is therefore much easier to retain. As an illustration, consider once again the earlier statements about the different types of men. I noted that college students have a difficult time remembering which man did what because the relationship between the type of man and the actions performed seem arbitrary. These same statements become easy to remember if students are supplied with information, or are helped to generate information, that renders these relationships less arbitrary (Stein & Bransford, 1979). For example:

> The tall man purchased the crackers that had been lying on the top shelf.
>
> The bald man read the newspaper in order to look for a hat sale.
>
> The funny man liked the ring that squirted water.
>
> The hungry man purchased the tie so that he could get into the fancy restaurant.
>
> The short man used the broom to operate the light switch.
>
> The strong man skimmed the book about weightlifting.

Elaborations such as these help people understand the significance or relevance of linking a particular type of man to a particular activity. They are therefore able to answer memory questions such as "Which man purchased the tie?" "Which man used the broom?" etc. In a similar manner, people who understand the significance of various properties of veins and arteries (e.g., the significance of the elasticity of arteries) are able to remember which properties go with what, and the child who understands the significance of having metal detectors in airports is better able to remember this fact.

It is important to note, however, that there are constraints on the type of additional information, or elaboration, that will enable students to understand the significance or relevance of new facts. As an example, consider the following list:

> The tall man purchased the crackers from the clerk in the store.
>
> The bald man read the newspaper while eating breakfast.
>
> The funny man liked the ring that he received as a present.
>
> The hungry man purchased the tie that was on sale.
>
> The short man used the broom to sweep the porch.
>
> The strong man skimmed the book before going to sleep.

These statements include elaborations that make sense semantically, but the elaborations do not help one understand why a particular type of man performed a particular activity. College students who receive a list of 10 sentences such as those above do *worse* than students who received the first list (the list *without* any additional elaboration; Stein & Bransford, 1979). My colleagues and I refer to elaborations such as those just noted as *imprecise* elaborations. In contrast, *precise* elaborations (such as those provided earlier) clarify the significance or relevance of facts (Stein & Bransford, 1979; Stein, Morris, & Bransford, 1978). Imprecise elaborations can make sense semantically; that is, they need not be nonsense. Nevertheless, they can actually produce poorer memory than a set of arbitrary statements that receive no elaborations at all. Note that there are many potential elaborations of facts about veins and arteries, airports, etc., that would also be imprecise. For example, a statement such as "Arteries are elastic so that they can stretch" does not help one understand why they need to be elastic, and a statement such as "There are metal detectors in airports that are used to check passengers" does not help one understand what is being checked nor why.

An emphasis on the degree of precision necessary to help people understand the significance of facts is important for analyzing the issue of what it means to "simplify" texts. A text can be composed of relatively simple words and simple syntax yet still seem quite arbitrary. My colleagues and I asked metropolitan Nashville teachers to provide us with samples of some of the passages their elementary school students are asked to read, and found a large number that seem arbitrary. For example, one passage discussed the topic of "American Indian Houses." It consisted of statements such as "The Indians of the Northwest Coast lived in slant-roofed houses made of cedar plank.... Some California Indian tribes lived in simple, earth-covered or brush shelters.... The Plains Indians lived mainly in teepees," etc. The story provided no information about why certain Indians chose certain houses. For example, it said nothing about the relationship between the type of house and the climate of the geographical area, nor about the ease of finding raw materials to build houses depending on the geographical area. Furthermore, the story said nothing about how the style of house was related to the lifestyle of the Indians (e.g., teepees are relatively portable). If students either did not know or failed to activate this extra information, the passage was essentially a list of seemingly arbitrary facts.

Other passages we examined discussed topics such as tools, animals, machines, and so forth. In each case, the passages contained a number of facts, yet frequently failed to provide the information necessary to understand the significance of the facts. For example, a passage describing two types of boomerangs—a returning versus a nonreturning boomerang—provided information about each boomerang's shape, weight, length, function, and so forth. However, it failed to systematically help the reader understand how the structure of each boomerang was related to its function (e.g., how the shape affected whether it returned to the thrower or not, how the weight was a factor in determining whether a boomerang could be used to hunt small versus large game, and so forth). The passages about animals also failed to help students focus on relationships between structure and function. For example, camels have a number of properties that help them adapt to certain aspects of desert life, including desert sandstorms. Facts such as "camels can close their nose passages" and "camels have thick hair around their ear openings" become more significant when one understand how they reduce problems caused by blowing sand. Students who are unable to make these connections on their own experience difficulty because the facts seem arbitrary. They also fail to develop a level of understanding that can provide support for learning subsequent materials. For example, a student who realizes how various properties of camels protect them during sandstorms is in a better position to understand a subsequent story about desert travelers who wear scarves over their faces even though it is hot.

It is important to note that passages such as the ones I have described do not necessarily seem arbitrary to someone who has already developed expertise in these areas. The expert not only already knows the facts but also understands their significance or relevance. Even new facts (e.g., camels can close their nose passages) can seem meaningful to the person whose preexisting schemata provide a basis for understanding their significance (e.g., a person may already know that camels are adapted to survive in desert sandstorms). Adults who construct or evaluate passages for children are usually in a "schema activation" mode, but children who read these passages are usually confronted with the problem of constructing new schemata or of developing more detailed schemata. This is as it should be; the goal of the educator is to help children develop new skills and knowledge. However, we need to recognize that schema activation and schema construction represent two different problems. Our attempts to simplify texts can be self-defeating if we inadvertently omit the kinds of precise elaborations necessary for understanding the significance of the information. Indeed, we may sometimes need to introduce children to relatively sophisticated concepts that can provide a basis for more precise understanding. For example, the general concept of adaptation (of structure–function relationships) provides a powerful schema that supports the comprehension of new facts in a number of domains (e.g., structure–function relationships are important for understanding biological systems such as veins and arteries, tools such as different types of boomerangs, animals and environments such as camels and their desert habitats, and so forth). The careful introduction of core concepts such as this one may facilitate learning to a considerable degree.

Summary and Conclusions

I began by reemphasizing Professor Anderson's arguments about schema theory because they are extremely important. For example, Dr. Anderson's discussion of the six functions of schemata provided a powerful argument for the pervasive effects of students' preexisting knowledge. I elaborated on two implications of his argument. One implication was that students may have developed partial schemata that are sufficient for understanding some types of statements but not for understanding others. We therefore need a more precise analysis of what it means for students to be "familiar" with the words in a text. The second implication was that preexisting schemata affect the interpretation of teachers and authors as well as the interpretation of students, and that a person's interpretation can affect the way that he or she phrases test questions. If there is a mismatch between the phrasing of a question and a student's interpretation of a passage, decrements in performance can occur.

Most of my comments were directed at differences between schema activation and schema construction. Professor Anderson noted that these represented two different (although related) problems. Most of the experiments he discussed dealt with schema activation because this represents the current state of the experimental literature. I emphasized schema construction because a major task for the educator is to help children develop new knowledge and skills.

The concept of precision provided the framework for my discussion of schema construction. To the novice, new facts can seem arbitrary unless they are precisely elaborated in a way that clarifies their significance or relevance. New facts that are not elaborated, or that are imprecisely elaborated, are difficult to remember and hence are not available for future use. In contrast, precisely elaborated facts can be integrated into new schemata that can provide support for the comprehension of subsequent texts. I also noted that texts can be composed of simple words and syntax, yet can still seem arbitrary to the novice; the notion of what it means to "simplify" texts, therefore, warrants careful consideration. Indeed, we may need to introduce children to relatively sophisticated "core concepts" that can provide a basis for understanding the significance of a wide variety of new facts.

The final point I want to emphasize involves an issue which I have not mentioned but which I feel is extremely important. I have noted that texts which are not precisely elaborated can seem arbitrary to the novice, but I do not believe that children's materials should always be elaborated explicitly. The reason is that children must learn to identify situations where they need more information in order to understand precisely, and they must learn to supply their own elaborations. More generally, I believe that they must learn about themselves as learners. This includes an understanding of how different texts and text structures influence their abilities to comprehend new information and to remember it at later points in time.

My colleagues and I have been working with fifth graders who are proficient at decoding but who differ in their abilities to learn from texts. In contrast to the successful learners in our samples, our less-successful learners have very little insight into the factors that make things easy or difficult to comprehend and remember, and they rarely attempt to use information that is potentially available to understand the significance or relevance of new facts. Their ability to learn is therefore impaired. We have created sets of materials that enable these students to experience the effects of their own learning activities and that enable them to learn to modify their activities. We find that these exercises can improve their performance considerably. In order to do this, however, we purposely create materials that are arbitrary, help the students evaluate these materials and experience their effects on memory, and then help them learn what to do to make the same materials significant or relevant. This seems necessary in order to help the students learn to learn on their own. The learning-to-learn issue is beyond the scope of Professor Anderson's paper and mine. I simply wanted to mention the issue at this point in order to emphasize that the procedures necessary to make texts easy to learn are not necessarily identical to those necessary to help children learn to learn on their own.

References

Ausubel, D. (1963). *The psychology of meaningful verbal learning*. New York: Grune and Stratton.

Ausubel, D. (1968). *Educational psychology: A cognitive view*. New York: Holt, Rinehart.

Barclay, J.R., Bransford, J.D., Franks, J.J., McCarrell, N.S., & Nitsch, K. (1974). Comprehension and semantic flexibility. *Journal of Verbal Learning and Verbal Behavior, 13*, 471–481.

Bransford, J.D., & Johnson, M.K. (1973). Considerations of some problems of comprehension. In W. Chase (Ed.), *Visual information processing*. New York: Academic.

Bransford, J.D., & Nitsch, K.E. (1978). Coming to understand things we could not previously understand. In J.F. Kavanagh & W. Strange (Eds.), *Speech and language in the laboratory, school, and clinic*. Cambridge, MA: MIT Press.

Bransford, J.D., Nitsch, K.E., & Franks, J.J. (1977). Schooling and the facilitation of knowing. In R.C. Anderson, R.J. Spiro, & W.E.

Montague (Eds.), *Schooling and the acquisition of knowledge*. Hillsdale, NJ: Erlbaum.

Bransford, J.D., Stein, B.S., Shelton, T.S., & Owings, R.A. (1980). Cognition and adaptation: The importance of learning to learn. In J. Harvey (Ed.), *Cognition, social behavior and the environment*. Hillsdale, NJ: Erlbaum.

Brown, A.L. (1979). Theories of memory and the problems of development: Activity, growth, and knowledge. In L.S. Cermak & F.I.M. Craik (Eds.), *Levels of processing and human memory*. Hillsdale, NJ: Erlbaum.

Kavanagh, J.F., & Strange, W. (Eds.). (1978). *Speech and language in the laboratory, school, and clinic*. Cambridge, MA: MIT Press.

Stein, B.S., & Bransford, J.D. (1979). Constraints on effective elaboration: Effects of precision and subject generation. *Journal of Verbal Learning and Verbal Behavior, 18*, 769–777.

Stein, B.S., Morris, C.D., & Bransford, J.D. (1978). Constraints on effective elaboration. *Journal of Verbal Learning and Verbal Behavior, 17*, 707–714.

22

To Err Is Human: Learning About Language Processes by Analyzing Miscues

Yetta M. Goodman and Kenneth S. Goodman

Everything people do, they do imperfectly. This is not a flaw but an asset. If we always performed perfectly, we could not maintain the tentativeness and flexibility that characterize human learning and the ways we interact with our environment and with one another. This model of imperfection causes us as researchers not to worry about why people fall short of perfection; rather, we are concerned with why people do what they do and with what we can learn about language processes from observing such phenomena.

The power of language users to fill knowledge gaps with missing elements, to infer unstated meanings and underlying structures, and to deal with novel experiences, novel thoughts, and novel emotions derives from the ability to predict, to guess, to make choices, to take risks, to go beyond observable data. We must have the capability of being wrong lest the limits on our functioning be too narrowly constrained. Unlike the computer, people do not exhibit specifically programmed, totally dependable responses time after time. We are tentative, we act impulsively, we make mistakes, and we tolerate our own deviations and the mistakes of others.

If you doubt that perfection in human behavior is the exception rather than the norm, consider how intensely a performer of any kind—athlete, actor, musician, writer, reader—must practice to achieve anything approaching error-free performance. If you doubt our view of how people deal with mistakes, think about the proofreader who skips over errors in a text or the native North Americans who deliberately insert flaws in handicrafts to remind themselves that the crafts are the work of human hands.

Miscues: Unexpected Responses

For more than 25 years we have studied the reading process by analyzing the miscues (or unexpected responses) of children and adults orally reading written texts. Ken Goodman coined this use of the word *miscue* because of the negative connotation and history of the term *error*. The term *miscue* reveals that miscues are unexpected responses cued by readers' linguistic or conceptual cognitive structures.

We started with the assumption that everything that happens during reading is caused, that a person's unexpected responses are produced in the same way and from the same knowledge, experience, and intellectual processes as expected responses. Reading aloud involves continuous oral response by the reader, which allows for comparisons between expected and observed responses. Such comparisons reveal the reader's knowledge, experience, and intellectual processes. Oral readers are engaged in comprehending written language while they produce oral responses. Because an oral response is generated while meaning is being constructed, it not only is a form of linguistic performance but also provides a powerful means of examining readers' process and underlying competence.

Miscue analysis requires several conditions. The written material must be new to the readers and complete with a beginning, middle, and end. The text needs to be long and challenging enough to produce sufficient numbers of miscues for patterns to appear. In addition, readers receive no help and are not interrupted. At most, if readers hesitate for more than 30 seconds, they are urged to guess, and only if hesitation continues are they told to keep reading even if it means skipping a word or phrase. Except that it takes place orally and not silently, the reading during miscue analysis requires as normal a situation as possible.

Depending on the purpose of miscue analysis research, readers often have been provided with more than one reading task. Various fiction and nonfiction reading materials have been used, including stories and articles from basal readers, textbooks, trade books, and magazines. Readers have been drawn from elementary, secondary, and adult populations and from a wide range or proficiency and racial, linguistic, and national backgrounds. Studies have been conducted in many languages other than English and in various writing systems (Goodman, Brown, & Marek, 1993).

Betsy's oral reading of the folk tale "The Man Who Kept House" (from McInnes, Gerrard, & Ryckman, 1964, pp. 282–283) is used throughout for examples (Goodman, Watson, & Burke, 1987). The story has 68 sentences, 711 words. Betsy, a 9-year-old from Toronto, was selected by the teacher as representative of students with reading difficulties. Betsy read the story hesitantly, although in most places she read with appropriate expression. Following are the first 14 sentences (s1–s14) from the story, with the actual printed text on the left and the transcript of Betsy's oral reading on the right.

	Text	*Transcript*
s1	Once upon a time there was a woodman who thought that no one worked as hard as he did.	Once upon a time there was a woodman. He threw...who thought that no one worked as hard as he did.
s2	One evening when he came home from work, he said to his wife, "What do you do all day while I am away cutting wood?"	One evening when he...when he came home from work, he said to his wife, "I want you do all day...what do you do all day when I am always cutting wood?"
s3	"I keep house," replied the wife, "and keeping house is hard work."	"I keep...I keep house," replied the wife, "and keeping...and keeping... and keeping house is and work."
s4	"Hard work!" said the husband.	"Hard work!" said the husband.
s5	"You don't know what hard work is!	"You don't know what hard work is!
s6	You should try cutting wood!"	You should try cutting wood!"
s7	"I'd be glad to," said the wife.	"I'll be glad to," said the wife.
s8	"Why don't you do my work some day?	"Why don't you.... Why don't you do my work so...some day?
s9	I'll stay home and keep house," said the woodman.	I'll start house and keeping house," said the woodman.
s10	"If you stay home to do my work, you'll have to make butter, carry water from the well, wash the clothes, clean the house, and look after the baby," said the wife.	"If you start house.... If you start home to do my work, well you'll have to make bread, carry...carry water from the well, wash the clothes, clean the house, and look after the baby," said the wife.
s11	"I can do all that," replied the husband.	"I can do that.... I can do all that," replied the husband.
s12	"We'll do it tomorrow!"	"Well you do it tomorrow!"
s13	So the next morning the wife went off to the forest.	So the next day the wife went off to the forest.
s14	The husband stayed home and began to do his wife's job.	The husband stayed home and began to do his work.

Betsy's performance reveals her language knowledge. These examples are not unusual; what Betsy does is done by other readers. She processes grapho-phonic information: Most of her miscues show a graphic and phonic relationship between the expected and the observed response. She processes syntactic information: She substitutes noun for noun, verb for verb, noun phrase for noun phrase, verb phrase for verb phrase. She transforms phrases, clauses, and sentences: She omits an intensifier, changes a dependent clause to an independent clause, shifts a *wh* question sentence to a declarative sentence. She draws on her conceptual and linguistic background and struggles toward meaning by regressing, correcting, and reprocessing as necessary. She predicts appropriate structures and monitors her own success based on the degree to which she is making sense. She develops and uses psychosociolinguistic strategies as she reads. There is nothing random about her miscues.

Reading Miscues and Comprehension

Because we understand that the brain is the organ of human information processing, that it is not a prisoner of the senses but controls the sensory organs and selectively uses their input, we should not be surprised that what is said in oral reading is not what the eye has seen but what the brain has generated for the mouth to report. The text is what the brain responds to; the oral output reflects the underlying competence and the psychosociolinguistic processes that have generated it. When expected and observed responses match, we get a little insight into this process. When they do not match and a miscue results, researchers have a window on the reading process.

We have come to believe that the strategies readers use when miscues occur are the same as when there are no miscues. Except for s3, s8, and s9, all of Betsy's miscues produced fully acceptable sentences or were self-corrected. By analyzing whether miscues are semantically acceptable with regard to the whole text or are acceptable only with regard to the prior portion of text, it is possible to infer the strategies readers actively engage in. s2 provides a powerful example. Betsy reads, *I want you do all day*, hesitates, reads slowly, and eventually—after a 23-second pause—reconsiders, probably rereads silently, and self-corrects the initial clause in this sentence. The verb *said* in the sentence portion prior to her miscue and her knowledge about what husbands might say when they come home from work allowed her to predict *I want you....* After she self-corrects the first part of the dialogue, she reads, *when I am always cutting wood* for *while I am away cutting wood* with confidence and continues her reading. These two substitution miscues (*when* for *while* and *always* for *away*) produce a clause that fits with the meaning of the rest of the story. The more proficient the reader, the greater the proportion of semantically acceptable miscues or miscues acceptable with the prior portion of the text that are self-corrected (Goodman & Burke, 1973).

In s12 Betsy produces, *Well you do it tomorrow* instead of *We'll do it tomorrow*. Although it seems that Betsy simply substitutes *well* for *we'll* and inserts *you*, the miscues are shown to be more complex when we examine how the phrase and clauses are affected by the miscues. Betsy substitutes an interjection prior to the subject *you* to substitute for the noun and the beginning of the verb phrase represented by the contraction *we'll*. In addition, Betsy shifts into-nation to indicate that the wife rather than the husband is talking. Apparently Betsy predicted that the wife was going to speak to maintain the pattern of husband–wife conversation that is established by the author in the previous sections (s2 and s11). Although the author's intended meaning is changed, the sentence is semantically acceptable within the story.

A reader's predicting and confirming strategies are evident in miscues that are acceptable with the text portion prior to the miscues. Such miscues often occur at pivotal points in sentences, such as junctures between clauses or phrases. At such points the author may select from a variety of linguistic structures to compose the text; the reader has similar options but may predict a structure that is different than the author's. Consider these examples from Betsy's reading:

Text	*Transcript*
s38 "I'll light a fire in the fireplace and the porridge will be ready in a few minutes."	"I'll light a fire in the fireplace and I'll...and the porridge will be ready in a flash...a few minutes."
s48 Then he was afraid that she would fall off.	Then he was afraid that the...that she would fall off.

Betsy's predictions of *I'll* instead of *the* in the second clause of the first example is logical. Because *and* often connects two parallel items, it is not an un-reasonable prediction that the second clause will begin with the subject of the first. However, when *I'll* does not fit with the second clause, Betsy confidently disconfirms her prediction and immediately self-corrects. The miscue substitu-tion of *the* for *she* in the second example is also at a pivotal point in the sen-tence. Whenever an author uses a pronoun to refer to a previously stated noun phrase, a reader may revert to the original noun phrase. The reverse phenome-non also occurs. When the author chooses a noun for which the referent has been established earlier, the reader may use that pronoun. Choosing a noun for which the referent has been established earlier, the reader may use that pronoun. Betsy was probably predicting *the cow* which *she* refers to. These miscues clear-ly show that Betsy is an active language user as she reads. Ken Goodman has done studies on the control readers have over determiners and pronouns in rela-tion to the cohesion of text (Goodman, 1983; Goodman & Gespass, 1983).

The idea that miscues often occur at specific pivotal points in any text is important enough to provide an example from another reader. An Appalachian reader, while reading the phrase "By the time I got out and over to where they were," inserted *of the water* between *out* and *and*. In the previous paragraph the male character is in the water. The author and the reader have similar options at this point in the grammatical structure. The prepositional phrase *of the water* is understood by the reader though not stated by the author and therefore may be omitted or inserted without changing the meaning. In this case, the reader makes explicit what the author left implicit.

Miscues that result in semantically acceptable structures are confirmed as acceptable to readers and, therefore, are less likely to be corrected than those that are not acceptable or acceptable only with the immediately preceding text. Miscues at pivotal points in the text are often acceptable with regard to the preceding text. Of the 10 semantically acceptable miscues that Betsy produced in the first excerpt, she corrected only 1 (*all* in s11). However, of the 6 miscues that were acceptable only with the prior portion of the text, she corrected 4. Such correction strategies tend to occur when the reader believes they are most needed—when a prediction has been disconfirmed by subsequent language cues.

Insights are gained into the reader's construction of meaning and the process of comprehension when we ask questions such as "Why did the reader make this miscue? Does it make sense in the context of this story or article?" Through such examination, it is possible to see the pattern of comprehending strategies a reader engages in.

We contrast comprehending—what the reader does to understand during the reading of a text—with comprehension—what the reader understands at the end of the reading. Open-ended retellings that always follow the reading during miscue analysis are an index of comprehension. They add to the profile of comprehending, which shows the reader's concern for meaning as expressed through the reading miscues. Retellings also provide an opportunity for the researcher or teacher to gain insight into how concepts and language are actively used and developed throughout a reading event.

Although the concept of retelling is common to present-day research, in the early 1960s when we first used this concept, many questioned the term and the appropriateness of its use in reading research. Rather than asking direct questions that would give cues to the reader about what is significant in the story, we asked for unaided retelling. Information on the readers' understanding of the text emerges from the organization they use in retelling the story, from whether they use the author's language or their own, and from the conceptions or misconceptions they reveal. Here is the first segment of Betsy's retelling:

> Um...it was about this woodman and um...when he...he thought that he um...he had harder work to do than his wife. So he went home and he told his wife, "What have you been doing all day." And then his wife told him. And then, um...and then, he thought that it was easy work. And...so...so his wife, so his wife, so she um...so the wife said, "Well so you have to keep," no...the husband says that you have to go to the woods and cut...and have to go out in the forest and cut wood and I'll stay home. And the next day they did that.

By comparing our interpretation of the story with Betsy's retelling and her miscues, we are able to analyze how much learning has occurred during

Betsy and the author's transaction. For example, although the story frequently uses *woodman* and *to cut wood, forest*, the noun used to refer to setting, is used twice. Not only does Betsy provide evidence in her retelling that she knows that *woods* and *forest* are synonymous, she also indicates that she knows the author's choice is *forest*. The maze she works through suggests her search for the author's language. Her oral language mazes are evidence of her intentions and self-correction patterns. Betsy seems to believe that the teacher is looking for the author's language rather than her own. Additional evidence of Betsy's concern to reproduce the author's language is seen in her use of *woodman* and *husband*. In the story, the woodman is referred to as *woodman* and *husband* eight times each and as *man* four times; the wife is referred to only as *wife*. Otherwise pronouns are used to refer to the husband and wife. In the retelling, Betsy uses *husband* and *woodman* six times and *man* only once; she called the wife only *wife*. Betsy always uses appropriate pronouns in referring to the husband and wife. However, when *cow* was the referent, she substituted *he* for *she* twice. (What does Betsy know about the sex of cattle?)

The linguistic and conceptual schematic background a reader brings to reading not only shows in miscues but also is implicit in the developing conceptions or misconceptions revealed through the reader's retelling. Betsy adds to her conceptual base and builds her control of language as she reads this story, but her ability to do both is limited by what she brings to the task. In the story, the husband has to make butter in a churn. Betsy makes miscues whenever butter-making is mentioned. For example, in s10 she substituted *bread* for *butter*. (Breadmaking is much more common than butter-making as a home activity for North American children.) The next time *butter* appears, in s15, she reads it as expected. However, in s18, *Soon the cream will turn into butter*, Betsy reads *buttermilk* for *butter*. Other references to butter-making include the words *churn* or *cream*. Betsy reads *cream* as expected each time it appears in the text but produces miscues for *churn*. She pauses about 10 seconds at the first appearance of *churn* and finally says it with exaggerated articulation. However, the next two times *churn* appears, Betsy reads *cream*.

Text	*Transcript*
s25 ...he saw a big pig inside, with its nose in the churn.	...he saw a big pig inside, with its nose in the cream.
s28 It bumped into the churn, knocking it over.	It jumped...it bumped into the cream, knocking it over.
s29 The cream splashed all over the room.	The cream shado [nonword miscue]... splashed all over the room.

In the retelling, Betsy provides evidence that her miscues are conceptually based and not mere confusions:

And the husband was sitting down and he poured some buttermilk and um...in a jar. And, and he was making buttermilk, and then he um...heard the baby crying. So he looked all around in the room and um.... And then he saw a big, um...pig. Um...he saw a big pig inside the house. So, he told him to get out and he, the pig, started racing around and um...he di...he um...bumped into the buttermilk and then the buttermilk fell down and then the pig, um...went out.

Betsy, who is growing up in a metropolis, knows little about how butter is made in churns. She knows that there is a relationship between cream and butter, although she does not know the details of that relationship. According to her teacher, she has also taken part in a traditional primary school activity in which sweet cream is poured into a jar, closed up, and shaken until butter and buttermilk are produced. Although Betsy's miscues and retelling suggest that she has only some knowledge about butter-making, the concept is peripheral to comprehending the story. All that she needs to know is that butter-making is one of the wife's many chores that can cause the woodman trouble.

For a long time, teachers have been confused about how a reader can know something in one context but not know it in another. Such confusion comes from the belief that reading is word recognition; on the contrary, words in different syntactic and semantic contexts become different entities for readers, and Betsy's responses to the structure *keep house* is good evidence for this. In s3, where the clauses *I keep house* and *and keeping house* occur the first time, Betsy reads the expected responses but repeats each several times before getting the words right, suggesting that she is grappling with their meanings. In s9 she reads *start house and keeping house* for *stay home and keep house,* and she reads the first phrase in s10 as *If you start home to do my work.* The structure *keep house* is a complex one. To a 9-year-old, *keep* is a verb that means being able to hold on to or take care of something small. *Keeping house* is no longer a common idiom in American or Canadian English. *Stay home* adds complexity to *keep house.* Used with different verbs and different function words, *home* and *house* are sometimes synonyms and sometimes not. The transitive and intransitive nature of *keep* and *stay* as well as the infinitive structure *to keep* and *to stay* add to the complexity of the verb phrase.

In her search for meaning and her transaction with the published text, Betsy continues to develop strategies to handle these complex problems. In s14 she produces *stayed home*; however, in s35 she encounters *keeping house* again and reads, *perhaps keeping house...home and...is hard work.* She is exploring the concept and grammaticality of *keeping house.* She first reads the expected response and then abandons it. In the story *home* appears 7 times and *house* 10 times. Betsy reads them correctly in every context except in the patterns *staying home* and *keeping house.* Yet as she continues to work on these phrases throughout her reading she finally is able to handle the structures and either self-corrects successfully or produces a semantically acceptable sentence. Thus

Betsy's miscues and retelling reveal the dynamic transaction between a reader and written language.

Through careful observation and evaluation, miscue analysis provides evidence of the ways in which the published text teaches the reader (Meek, 1988). Through continuous transactions with the text, Betsy develops as a reader. Our analysis also provides evidence for the published text as a mediator. Betsy is in a continuing zone of proximal development as she works at making sense of this text (Vygotsky, 1934/1978). Because the text is a complete one it mediates Betsy's development.

The Reader: An Intuitive Grammarian

Reading is not simply knowing sounds, words, sentences, and the abstract parts of language that can be studied by linguists. Reading, like listening, consists of processing language and constructing meaning. The reader brings a great deal of information to this complex and active process. A large body of research has been concerned with meaning construction and the understanding of reading processes and has provided supporting evidence to many of the principles we have revealed through miscue analysis. However, there is still too little attention paid to the ability of readers to make use of their knowledge of the syntax of their language as they read.

Readers sometimes cope with texts that they do not understand well by manipulating the language. Their miscues demonstrate this. The work of both Chomsky and Halliday has helped us understand the syntactic transformations that occur as readers transact with texts. Such manipulations are often seen when readers correctly answer questions about material they do not understand. For example, we ask readers to read an article titled "Downhole Heave Compensator" (Kirk, 1974). Most readers claim little comprehension, but they can answer the question "What were the two things destroying the underreamers?" by finding the statement in the text that reads, "We were trying to keep drillships and semisubmersibles from wiping out our underreamers" (p. 88). It is because of such ability to manipulate the syntax of questions that we decided to use open-ended retellings for miscue analysis.

In miscue analysis research, we examine the syntactic nature of the miscues, the points in the text where miscues occur, and the syntactic acceptability of sentences that include miscues. Readers often produce sentences that are syntactically, but not semantically, acceptable. In s10 Betsy finally reads, *If you start home to do my work* for the text phrase *If you stay home to do my work*. Her reading of this phrase is syntactically acceptable in the story but unacceptable semantically because it is important to the story line that the woodman stay home.

We became aware that readers were able to maintain the grammaticality of sentences even if the meaning was not maintained when we examined the phenomenon of nonwords. Such nonsense words give us insight into English-speaking readers' grammatical awareness because sentences with nonwords often retain the grammatical features of English although they lose English meaning. Betsy produces only 2 nonword miscues among the 75 miscues she produces. In s58 Betsy reads, *As for the cow, she hang between the roof and the gorun* instead of the expected response, *She hung between the roof and the ground*. She repeats *and the* prior to *ground* three times and pauses for about 10 seconds between each repetition. She seems to be aware that the word *ground* is not a familiar one in this context, but she maintains a noun intonation for the nonword. This allows her to maintain the grammatical sense of the sentence so that later in the story when the text reads *the cow fell to the ground*, she reads it as expected without hesitation.

Use of intonation also provides evidence for the grammatical similarity between the nonword and the text word. Miscues on the different forms of *to* (as the initial part of an infinitive or as a preposition), *two*, and *too* are easy to clarify by paying attention to intonation patterns. Nonwords most often retain similarities not only in number of syllables, word length, and spelling but also in bound morphemes—the smallest units that carry meaning or grammatical information within a word but cannot stand alone (for example, the *ed* in *carried*). In one of our research studies (Goodman & Burke, 1973), a group of sixth graders read a story that included the following: "Clearly and distinctively Andrew said 'philosophical'" and "A distinct quiver in his voice." The nonword substitutions for each were different depending on the grammatical function of the word. For *distinctly* readers read nonwords that sounded like *distikily, distintly*, and *definely*, while for *distinct* they read *dristic, distink, distet*.

There is abundant evidence in miscues of readers' strong awareness of bound morphemic rules. Our data on readers' word-for-word substitutions, whether nonwords or real words, show that, on average, 80% of the observed responses retain the morphemic markings of the text. For example, if the text word is a noninflected form of a verb, the reader will tend to substitute that form; if the word has a prefix, the reader's substitution will tend to include a prefix. Derivational suffixes will be replaced by derivational suffixes, contractional suffixes by contractional suffixes.

Maintaining the syntactic acceptability of the text allows readers to continue reading and at the same time to maintain the cohesion and coherence of the text. Only a small portion of Betsy's substitution miscues do not retain the same grammatical function as the text word. Analysis of the word-for-word substitutions of fourth and sixth graders showed that their miscues retained the identical grammatical function over 73% of the time for nouns and verbs (Goodman & Burke, 1973). Function words were the same 67% or more of the time, while noun modifiers were retained approximately 60% of the time. In addition, an examination of what kinds of grammatical function were used for substitution when they were not identical indicated that nouns, noun modifiers, and function words are substituted for one another to a much greater degree than they are for verbs. Again this suggests the power of grammaticality on reading. Of 501 substitution miscues produced by fourth graders, only three times was a noun substituted for a verb modifier, and sixth graders made such a substitution only once in 424 miscues.

Evidence from miscues occurring at the beginning of sentences also adds insight into readers' awareness of the grammatical constraints of language. Generally, in prose for children few sentences begin with prepositions, intensifiers, adjectives, or singular common nouns without a preceding determiner. When readers produced miscues on the beginning words of sentences that do not retain the grammatical function of the text, we could not find one miscue that represented any of these unexpected grammatical forms. (One day we will do an article titled "Miscues Readers Don't Make." Some of the strongest evidence comes from all the things readers could do that they do not.) These patterns are so strong that we have been able to detect manufactured examples in some professional texts. The authors have offered examples of errors readers do not make.

Readers' miscues that cross sentence boundaries also provide insight into the readers' grammatical sophistication. It is not uncommon to hear teachers complain that readers read past periods. Closer examination of this phenomenon suggests that when readers do this they are usually making a logical prediction that is based on a linguistic alternative. Although Betsy does this a few times, we will use an example from a story we used with fourth graders: *He still thought it more fun to pretend to be a great scientist, mixing the strange and the unknown* (Goodman & Goodman, 1978). Many readers predict that *strange* and *unknown* are adjectives and intone the sentence accordingly. This means that their voices are left up in the air, so to speak, in anticipation of a noun. The more proficient readers in the study regress at this point and self-correct by shifting to an end-of-sentence intonation pattern. Less-proficient readers either do not correct at all and continue reading sounding surprised or try to regress without producing the appropriate intonation pattern.

Interrelations of All the Cueing Systems

Reading involves the interrelationship of all the language systems. All readers use graphic information to various degrees. Our research (Goodman & Burke, 1973) demonstrates that the least proficient readers we studied in the 6th, 8th, and 10th grades use graphic information more than the most proficient readers. Readers also produce substitution miscues similar to the phonemic patterns of text words. An examination of Betsy's word substitution miscues reveals that she pays more attention to the look-alike quality of the words than to their sound-alike quality. Although attention to graphic features occurs more frequently than attention to the phonemic patterns, readers use both systems to show that they call on their knowledge of the graphophonic system. Yet the use of these systems cannot explain why Betsy would produce a substitution such as *day* for *morning* or *job* for *work* (s13 and s14). She is clearly showing her use of the syntactic system and her ability to retain the grammatical function and morphemic constraints of the expected response. But the graphophonic and syntactic systems together do not explain why Betsy could seemingly understand words such as *house*, *home*, *ground*, and *cream* in certain contexts but not in others. To understand these aspects of reading, one must examine the interrelationship of all the cueing systems.

The integration of all the language systems (grammatical, graphophonic, semantic, and pragmatic) are necessary in order for reading to take place. Miscue analysis provides evidence that readers integrate cueing systems from the earliest initial attempts at reading. Readers sample and make judgments about which cues from each system will provide the most useful information in making predictions that will get them to meaning. All the miscue examples we have cited point to the notion that readers monitor their reading and ask themselves, "Does this sound like language?" (syntactically acceptable) and "Does this make sense in this story?" (semantically acceptable). Finally, if they have to return to the text to check things, they look more closely at the print using their graphophonic knowledge to confirm and self-correct as they read.

As readers make use of their knowledge of all the language cues, they predict, make inferences, select significant features, confirm, and constantly work toward constructing a meaningful text. Not only are they constructing meaning, they are constructing themselves as readers.

Schema-Forming and Schema-Driven Miscues

Our analysis of oral reading miscues began with the foundational assumption that reading is a language process parallel to listening. Everything we have observed among readers from beginners to those with great proficiency supports the validity of this assumption. The analysis of miscues, in turn, has been the basis for the development of a theory and model of the reading process.

What we have learned about miscues in reading has been applied to aspects of language such as spelling, composition, response to literature, and oral language development. Such research, liberated from the "perfection misconception," has demonstrated the linguistic creativity of humans. Errors children make as they develop oral language have provided insight not only into how the young learn language but into the nature of language—how it develops, grows, and changes (Brown, 1973). Children also invent schemata about the nature of written language as they become writers (Ferreiro & Teberosky, 1982; Goodman & Wilde, 1992). Invented punctuation and spelling are especially good examples of the ways in which children learn to control the relationship between the sound system of their dialects and the conventions of the writing system (Read, 1986; Wilde, 1992). Adults develop the craft of writing through making miscues

(Shaughnessy, 1977). Rosenblatt (1978) has long argued for a transactional view of reader response to literature in which all response is seen as a transaction between reader and text which of necessity results in variation among readers as they proceed toward interpretation, evaluation, and criticism. The readers' schemata are vital to the transactions.

What we have learned from the study of oral reading miscues and what we have seen in research on other language processes can help to explain the generation of miscues. The concept of schema is helpful to explore how miscues are necessary to language learning. A schema, as we define the term, is an organized cognitive structure of related knowledge, ideas, emotions, and actions that has been internalized and that guides and controls a person's use of subsequent information and response to experience.

Humans have schemata for everything they know and do. We have linguistic schemata (which we call rules) by which we produce and comprehend language. For example, we know when to expect or produce questions and when a question requires an answer. We have schemata for what language does and how it works. With such schemata, we use language to control the behavior of others. We have conceptual schemata for our ideas, concepts, and knowledge of the world. We may reject a Picasso portrait because it does not meet our expectation or schema of the human face.

Our work has led us to believe that humans also develop overarching schemata for creating new schemata and modifying old ones. These we might call schemata for new schema formation. Chomsky's (1965) concept that the generation of language is controlled by a finite set of transformational rules is a case of a schema for schema formation. The rules determine and limit what syntactic patterns may be accepted as grammatical in a language; these same rules also make it possible for speakers to create new sentences that have never been heard before but will be comprehensible to others.

Conceptual schemata work much the same way, and they are also controlled by overarching schemata. That explains why we often use analogy and metaphor in making connections to well-known words and ideas when we talk about new experiences. An example is the use of the term *docking* for space travel. Conceptual and linguistic schemata are at work simultaneously. The schemata must all be in harmony. If more than one complexity occurs, the result is compounding; the possibility of miscues increases disproportionately.

The earlier discussion about Betsy's miscues relating to the concepts of *to stay home* and *to keep house* is a good example. Her complete retelling after reading indicates good understanding of these concepts. In order to build this kind of understanding, Betsy has to work hard during her reading. She related her own limited knowledge of staying home and keeping house to the meanings she is constructing in transaction with the author. She has to develop control over the syntactic and conceptional complexity of *stay home* and *keep house* and add to her understanding of the relationship of *home* and *house*. She keeps selectively using the available graphophonic cues to produce both expected and unexpected responses. It is important to understand the complexity of thinking that Betsy has to use and that her miscues reflect. Much of children's language learning can be explained in terms of developing control over language schemata. With growing linguistic and conceptual schemata, children use language to predict, process, and monitor expression and comprehension.

Now let's reconsider a concept from miscue analysis: Miscues are produced by the same process and in response to the same cues as expected responses. Putting that together with what we have just said about schema formation and use, we can consider miscues from the perspective of two schema processes: *schema-forming* or *schema-driven* miscues. And because schemata can be forming while we use our existing schemata, both processes can go on at the same time.

Piaget's (1977) concepts of assimilation and accommodation are pertinent here. A schema-forming miscue may be seen as a struggle toward accommodation, while a schema-driven miscue shows assimilation at work. Further, the effect of the miscue on subsequent language processing or intent may result in a disequilibrium, which may lead to reprocessing—that is, self-correction. Schemata may need to be abandoned, modified, or reformed as miscues are corrected.

A *schema-forming* miscue reflects the developmental process of building the rule systems of language and concepts, learning to apply those language rule systems, and delimiting them. For example, Susie responds to the printed name Corn Flakes on a box of cereal by pointing to each line of print successfully while drawing out the word *ceeerrreeeeuuuull* until she finishes moving her finger. Although she has not yet developed the concept that English print is alphabetic, she shows through her unexpected response that she is developing a schema concerning a relationship between the length of print and the length of oral utterance.

The young child's development of the rules of past tense, number, and gender are reflected in the miscues children make in oral language (Brown, 1973). Rebecca, age 3, provides a good example when she says to her aunt, who is waiting to read her a story, "I'll come and get you in a few whiles." She shows her control of the schema for pluralization (*few* take a plural) but she has taken *while*, which functions as a noun in the idiom *wait a little while* and has made it a count noun (*a few whiles*).

In the view of some scholars, a subject's production of language is dependent on whether the subject is dealing with old or new information. A schema-forming miscue is likely to involve new information, either linguistic or conceptual, which may not be easily assimilated. A schema-driven miscue may involve either old (given) information or new information in a predictable context. Furthermore, the schema, as well as the information, may be old or new.

A *schema-driven* miscue is one that results from the use of existing schemata to produce or comprehend language. In our research the concept of prediction has become important. Texts are hard or easy in proportion to how predictable they are for readers. They may use their existing schema to predict and comprehend, but sometimes the organization of the knowledge—that is, the schema on which the predictions are made—is so strong that it overrides the text and miscues occur. In the initial paragraph of a story that many adolescents and adults have read for us, the phrase *the headlamps of the car* occurs. The majority read *headlights* rather than *headlamps*. Many of those who do read *headlamps* indicate that they expected *headlights* and had to reread to accept *headlamps*.

Language variations also show evidence of schema-driven miscues. We shift dialects and registers when we move from formal written language to more information styles or from one regional dialect to another. Tommy was overheard saying to his mother, a Texan, "Mom, Dad wants to know where the bucket is" and then to his father, a Midwesterner, "Here's the pail, Dad." Tommy had learned to switch codes depending on the situation, and his schema-driven responses were appropriate to each parent. Understanding that dialect miscues are driven by schema may help teachers and researchers see them in proper perspective. A rural African American fourth grader in Port Gibson, Mississippi, was reading a story that included the line *the ducks walked in single file*. At this point in the story, mother duck was leading her babies in a proud and haughty manner. The child reading that line produced *the ducks walk signifying*.

The malapropisms that we all exhibit are also evidence of schema-driven miscues at work. We try to use schemata for word formation beyond word-formation limits. These result in miscues in listening as well as speaking. Television's Archie Bunker was upset because of the *alteration* he had had with a boisterous customer. We cannot help relating the concept of schema-driven miscues to Tannen's (1990) work on conversations between men and women and among different ethnic groups. "I make sense of seemingly senseless misunderstandings that haunt our relationships and show that a man and a woman can interpret the same conversation differently, even when there is no apparent misunderstanding," she writes (p. 13). By understanding the reasons that underlie our misunderstandings perhaps we can form schemata that will help us "prevent or relieve some of the frustration" (p. 13).

In many cases it is not easy to separate miscues into schema-forming or schema-driven processes because they often occur simultaneously. At any particular point in time, it is fairly easy to explain the schemata that drive the miscues that occur. Schema formation, on the other hand, is less likely to occur at a single point and be easily discernible in a single miscue. The study of children's writing development allows us one way to observe the process of schema formation. It also reveals how both schema-forming and schema-driven miscues can occur in concert. An example from a story that Jennifer wrote in the first grade illustrates invented spelling that is driven by her linguistic schemata. Jennifer produced past-tense verbs about 20 times. Each reflected her invented phonic rules (and her awareness of the phonological rules of her own speech) because each had the letter *d* or *t* at the end, representing the appropriate phoneme. These spelling miscues included *rapt* (wrapped) and *yeld* (yelled). Her phonic schemata at this point led her to invent consistent spellings of single letters for single sounds. But a year later her spelling represented an awareness of the interrelationship of both the morphophonemic rules (past tense taking one of three forms depending on the preceding consonants) and the orthographic rule that spelling is not determined by sound in a simple one-to-one manner. Of 28 regular past-tense verbs in a story she wrote in the second grade, 25 were spelled conventionally. Jennifer was in a classroom where a lot of writing was encouraged but there was no direct teaching of spelling. During this year, she continually reformed her schemata and moved toward socially conventional ones.

Readers' miscues often can be driven by conceptual schemata, but at the same time readers can be forming new schemata. This is often revealed through the retelling as well as the miscues. In our research, we have had children read a story that has a significant concept represented by an unfamiliar but high-frequency word. One such word was *typical*. Although the children who read this story often reproduced oral substitutions for *typical* in the text (such as *tropical, type-ical*, and *topical*), they usually were able to explain the meaning of the word as it developed in the reading of the text. One Texas youngster said, "Oh, yeah, *tropical* means ordinary, just like all kinds of other babies. But, you know, it could also be a big storm."

Sometimes a new word represents a concept well known to the reader. In this case the reader must assimilate the new term to the old concept. Bilingual students often face this when they begin to read in a second language. We studied Arabic immigrant students who produced miscues on the word *plow* in a story they were reading, substituting *palow, pull, pole, polo, plew*, and *blow*, among other words and nonwords (Goodman & Goodman, 1978). However, they all were able to provide evidence that they had a "plowing" schema. One reader's example is representative:

> Well, it's a thing with two handles and something pointing down. You got to pull it. But they don't push it with a camel. They push it with a cow. When the cow moves, the one who's pushing it got to go push on it so it goes deeper in the underground.

In such a context we see both schema-driving and schema-forming processes taking place in a dynamic way. These fourth-grade Arabic readers are new to English. They use their developing knowledge of English to produce unexpected responses to the word *plow* and their knowledge about plowing to show understanding of the concept (schema-driven). At the same time, they add new knowledge as they encounter the English word for the concept (schema-forming).

The example also indicates that the reader rejected the story element that a camel was used to pull a plow as implausible because of his conceptual schema.

We hope that our discussion of the role miscues play in language learning communicates to teachers and researchers that miscues are the positive effects of linguistic and conceptual processes rather than the failure to communicate or comprehend. If a language user loses meaning, she or he is likely to produce a miscue. If the language user chooses a syntactic schema different from the author's, a miscue will likely result. If a reader or listener interprets in a way different from the meaning intended by the speaker or author, a miscue will result. Miscues reflect readers' abilities to liberate themselves from detailed attention to print as they leap toward meaning. Readers make use of their linguistic and conceptual schemata to reverse, substitute, insert, omit, rearrange, paraphrase, and transform. They do this not only with letters and single words, but also with two-word sequences, phrases, clauses, and sentences. Their own experiences, values, conceptual structures, expectations, dialects, and lifestyles are integral to the process. The meanings they construct can never be a simple reconstruction of the author's conceptual structures because they are dependent on the reader's schemata.

Risk-taking has been recognized as a significant aspect of both language learning and proficient language use. In risk-taking there is a necessary balance between tentativeness and self-confidence. Miscues reflect the degree to which existing schemata fit the existing circumstance and the level of confidence of the language user. In speaking a second language, speakers often show great tentativeness, consciously groping for control of developing schemata. As their confidence grows so does their risk-taking, and their miscues show the influence either of schemata for the first language (schema-driven) or of their developing schemata for the second language (schema-forming). An example of the former cautious type is this sentence from a native Spanish-speaking adult who is asking his English teacher for advice: "Ms. Buck, please, I hope I do not molest you." This oral miscue is driven by the speaker's schema for the Spanish *molestar* (to bother). In her response to the student, the teacher will provide information that will help the student form a schema to provide semantic limits for the English *molest*.

Oral and Silent Reading

We need to say a word about the relationship between oral and silent reading because much of miscue analysis research uses oral reading. The basic mode of reading is silent. Oral reading is special because it requires production of an oral representation concurrently with comprehending. The functions of oral reading are limited. It is a performing art used by teachers, entertainers, politicians, and religious leaders. We have already explained why we use oral reading in miscue analysis. But a basic question remains: Are oral and silent reading similar enough to justify generalizing from studies of oral reading miscues to theories and models of silent reading?

In our view, a single process underlies all reading. The language cueing systems and the strategies of oral and silent reading are essentially the same. The miscues we find in oral reading occur in silent reading as well. We have some research evidence of that. Studies of nonidentical fillers of cloze blanks (responses that do not match the deleted words) show remarkable correspondence to oral reading miscues and indicate that the processes of oral and silent reading are much the same (Anderson, 1982; Cambourne & Rousch, 1979; Chapman, 1981). Still, there are dissimilarities between oral and silent reading. First, oral reading is limited to the speed at which speech can be produced; therefore, it need not be as efficient as rapid silent reading. Next, superficial misarticulations such as *hangaber* for *hamburger* occur in oral reading but are not part of silent reading. Also, oral readers, conscious of their audience, read passages differently from when they read silently. Examples are production of nonword substitutions, persistence with several attempts at problem spots, overt regression to correct miscues already mentally corrected, and deliberate adjustments in ensuing text to cover miscues so that listeners will not notice them. Furthermore, oral readers may take fewer risks than silent readers. This can be seen in the deliberate omission of unfamiliar words, reluctance to attempt correction even though meaning is disrupted, and avoidance of overtly making corrections that have taken place silently to avoid calling attention to miscues. Finally, relatively proficient readers, particularly adults, may become so concerned with superficial fluency that they short-circuit the basic concern for meaning. Professional oral readers (newscasters, for example) seem to suffer from this malady. With these reservations noted, we believe that making sense is the same in oral and silent reading; in construction of meaning, miscues must occur in both.

Parts and Wholes

Too much research on language and language learning is still concerned with isolated sounds, letters, word parts, words, and even sentences. Such fragmentation, although it simplifies research design and the complexity of the phenomena under study, seriously distorts processes, tasks, cue values, interactions, and realities. Many years ago, Kintsch (1974) wrote as follows:

> Psycholinguistics is changing in character.... The 1950s were still dominated by the nonsense syllables...the 1960s were characterized by the use of word lists, while the present decade is witnessing a shift to even more complex learning materials. At present, we have reached the point where lists of sentences are being substituted for word lists in studies of recall recognition. Hopefully, this will not be the endpoint of this development, and we shall soon see psychologists handle effectively the problems posed by the analysis of connected text. (p. 2)

Through miscue analysis we have learned that, other things being equal, short language sequences are harder to comprehend than are long ones. Sentences are easier than words, paragraphs easier than sentences, pages easier than paragraphs, and stories easier than pages. We see two reasons for this. First, it takes some familiarity with the style and general semantic thrust of a text's language for the reader to make successful predictions. Style is largely a matter of an author's syntactic preferences; the semantic context develops over the entire text. Short texts provide limited cues for readers to build a sense of either style or meaning. Second, the disruptive effect of particular miscues on meaning is much greater in short texts. Longer texts offer redundant opportunities to recover and self-correct. This suggests why findings from studies of words, sentences, and short passages produce different results from those that involve whole texts. It also raises a major question about using standardized tests, which employ words, phrases, sentences, and short texts to assess reading proficiency.

Sooner or later all attempts to understand language—its development and its function as the medium of human communication—must confront linguistic reality. Theories, models, grammars, and research paradigms must predict and explain what people do when they use language and what makes it possible for them to do so. Researchers have contrived ingenious ways to make a small bit of linguistic or psycholinguistic reality available for examination. But then what they see is often out of focus, distorted by the design. Miscue analysis research makes fully available the reality of the miscues language users produce as they participate in real speech and literacy events. Huey (1908) said,

> And so to completely analyze what we do when we read would almost be the acme of a psychologist's achievements, for it would be to describe very many of the most intricate workings of the human mind, as well as to unravel the tangled story of the most remarkable specific performance that civilization has learned in all its history. (p. 6)

To this we add that miscues are the windows on language processes at work.

References

Anderson, J. (1982, July). *The writer, the reader, the text*. Paper presented at the 19th annual UKRA Reading Conference, Newcastle-upon-Tyne, United Kingdom.

Brown, R. (1973). *A first language: The early stages*. Cambridge, MA: Harvard University Press.

Cambourne, B., & Rousch, P. (1979). *A psycholinguistic model of the reading process as it relates to proficient, average, and low-ability readers* (Tech. Rep.). Wagga Wagga, NSW, Australia: Riverina College of Advanced Education, Charles Sturt University.

Chapman, J.L. (1981). The reader and the text. In J.L. Chapman (Ed.), *The reader and the text*. London: Heinemann.

Chomsky, N. (1965). *Aspects of the theory of syntax*. Cambridge, MA: MIT Press.

Ferreiro, E., & Teberosky, A. (1982). *Literacy before schooling*. Portsmouth, NH: Heinemann.

Goodman, K.S. (1983, July). *Text features as they relate to miscues: Determiners* (Occasional Paper No. 8). Tucson: Program in Language and Literacy, College of Education, University of Arizona.

Goodman, K.S., Brown, J., & Marek, A. (1993). *Annotated chronological bibliography of miscue analysis* (Occasional Paper No. 16).

Tucson: Program in Language and Literacy, College of Education, University of Arizona.

Goodman, K.S., & Burke, C.L. (1973, April). *Theoretically based studies of patterns of miscues in oral reading performance* (Project No. 9-0375). Washington, DC: U.S. Office of Education.

Goodman, K.S., & Gespass, S. (1983, March). *Text features as they relate to miscues: Pronouns* (Occasional Paper No. 7). Tucson: Program in Language and Literacy, College of Education, University of Arizona.

Goodman, K.S., & Goodman, Y.M. (1978). *Reading of American children whose language is a stable rural dialect of English or a language other than English* (Final Report, Project NIE-C-00-3-0087). Washington DC: U.S. Department of Health, Education and Welfare, National Institute of Education.

Goodman, Y.M., Watson, D., & Burke, C. (1987). *Reading miscue inventory: Alternative procedures*. Katonah, NY: Richard C. Owen.

Goodman, Y.M., & Wilde, S. (1992). *Literacy events in a community of young writers*. New York: Teachers College Press.

Huey, E.B. (1908). *The psychology and pedagogy of reading*. New York: Macmillan.

Kintsch, W. (1974). *The representation of meaning in memory*. Hillsdale, NJ: Erlbaum.

Kirk, S. (1974, June). Downhole heave compensator: A tool designed by hindsight. *Drilling-DCW*, 88.

McInnes, J., Gerrard, M., & Ryckman, J. (Series Eds.). (1964). *Magic and make believe* (Basal Program). Don Mills, ON: Thomas Nelson.

Meek, M. (1988). *How texts teach what readers learn*. Exeter, UK: Thimble.

Piaget, J. (1977). *The development of thought: Equilibration of cognitive structures*. New York: Viking.

Read, C. (1986). *Children's creative spelling*. London: Routledge & Kegan Paul.

Rosenblatt, L. (1978). *The reader, the text, the poem: The transactional theory of the literary work*. Carbondale: Southern Illinois University Press.

Shaughnessy, M.P. (1977). *Errors and expectations: A guide for the teacher of basic writing*. New York: Oxford University Press.

Tannen, D. (1990). *You just don't understand: Women and men in conversation*. New York: Morrow.

Vygotsky, L.S. (1978). *Mind in society: The development of higher psychological processes* (M. Cole, V. John-Steiner, S. Scribner, & E. Souberman, Eds. & Trans.). Cambridge, MA: Harvard University Press. (Original work published 1934)

Wilde, S. (1992). *You kan red this! Spelling and punctuation for whole language classrooms, K–6*. Portsmouth, NH: Heinemann.

23

Cognitive Flexibility Theory: Advanced Knowledge Acquisition in Ill-Structured Domains

Rand J. Spiro, Richard L. Coulson, Paul J. Feltovich, and Daniel K. Anderson

Advanced knowledge acquisition in a subject area is different in many important ways from introductory learning (and from expertise). In this paper we discuss some of the special characteristics of advanced learning of complex conceptual material. We note how these characteristics are often at odds with the goals and tactics of introductory instruction and with psychological biases in learning. We allude to our research in biomedical cognition that has revealed a substantial incidence of misconception attributable to various forms of oversimplification, and we outline the factors that contribute to suboptimal learning at the advanced stage. We then sketch a theoretical orientation for more successful advanced knowledge acquisition in ill-structured domains, cognitive flexibility theory. This orientation emphasizes the use of multiple mental and pedagogical representations; the promotion of multiple alternative systems of linkage among knowledge elements; the promotion of schema assembly (as opposed to the retrieval of prepackaged schemata); the centrality of "cases of application" as a vehicle for engendering functional conceptual understanding; and the need for participatory learning, tutorial guidance, and adjunct support for aiding the management of complexity. A computer hypertext approach that implements cognitive flexibility theory is discussed.

The Goals of Advanced Knowledge Acquisition

In our work we have been interested in "advanced knowledge acquisition"— learning beyond the introductory stage for a subject area but before the achievement

From *Tenth Annual Conference of the Cognitive Science Society Proceedings*. Copyright © 1988 by Cognitive Science Society. Reprinted with permission of the publisher.

of practiced expertise that comes with massive experience. This often neglected intermediate stage is important because the aims and means of advanced knowledge acquisition are different from those of introductory learning. In introductory learning the goal is often mere exposure to content and the establishment of a general orientation to a field; objectives of assessment are likewise confined to the simple effects of exposure (e.g., recognition and recall). At some point in learning about a knowledge domain, the goal must change; at some point, students must "get it right." This is the stage of advanced knowledge acquisition (Feltovich, Spiro, & Coulson, 1989; Spiro, Feltovich, Coulson, & Anderson, 1989; Spiro et al., 1987): The learner must *attain a deeper understanding of content material, reason with it, and apply it flexibly in diverse contexts.* Obstacles to advanced knowledge acquisition include conceptual complexity and the increasing ill-structuredness that comes into play with more advanced approaches to a subject area. By *ill-structuredness* we mean that many concepts (interacting contextually) are pertinent in the typical case of knowledge application, and that their patterns of combination are inconsistent across case applications of the same nominal type. (See Spiro et al., 1987, for a more detailed treatment of the nature and consequences of ill-structuredness.)

The methods of education in introductory and advanced learning seem, in many ways, to be at odds. For example, compartmentalizing knowledge, presenting clear instances (and not the many pertinent exceptions), and employing reproductive memory criteria are often in conflict with the realities of advanced learning—knowledge, which is intertwined and dependent, has significant context-dependent variations and requires the ability to respond flexibly to "messy" application situations. These discrepancies in aims and tactics (along with many others that we have observed) raise the possibility that introductory learning, even when it is "successful," lays foundations in knowledge and in an approach to learning that interfere with advanced acquisition. As we have seen repeatedly demonstrated, that possibility is an actuality (Coulson, Feltovich, & Spiro, 1986; Feltovich et al., 1989; Spiro et al., 1987; Spiro et al., 1989).

Deficiencies in Advanced Knowledge Acquisition

Medical school is an archetype of an advanced knowledge acquisition setting (Feltovich et al., 1989). Medical students have already had introductory exposure to many of the subject areas of biological science that they go on to study in medical school, but they are certainly not yet expert. Furthermore, the goals of medical education are clearly those of advanced knowledge acquisition. Important aspects of conceptual complexity must now be mastered (superficial familiarity with key concepts is no longer sufficient), and the ability to apply knowledge from formal instruction to real-world cases is certainly something that is expected of those studying to be physicians.

In our laboratory we have been studying medical students' learning, understanding, and application of important but difficult biomedical science concepts. This effort has revealed widely held systematic misconceptions among students, despite their having been exposed to appropriate information (Coulson et al., 1986; Feltovich et al., 1989; Spiro et al., 1987; Spiro et al., 1989). Stubborn misconceptions, notwithstanding usual classroom efforts at instruction, have been found for difficult concepts in other areas as well (e.g., physics: Champagne, Gunstone, & Klopfer, 1985; White, 1984).

The biomedical misconceptions that we have identified are of various kinds (Feltovich et al., 1989; Spiro et al., 1989). These include *contentive* errors, often involving overgeneralization—for example, areas of subject matter are seen as being more similar than they really are. Errors attributable to dysfunctional biases in *mental representation* are also observed—for example, dynamic processes are often represented more statically. *Prefigurative "world views"* that underlie learners' understanding processes also cause problems—for example, the presupposition that the world works in such a way that "parts add up to wholes" leads students to decompose complex processes into components that are treated (mistakenly) as independent. Furthermore, at all these levels misconceptions interact in *reciprocally supportive* ways and combine to yield higher-order misconceptions (Coulson et al., 1986; Feltovich et al., 1989). Failures of understanding *compound* themselves, building up durable chains of larger-scale misconception.

Reductive Biases: The Pervasive Role of Oversimplification in the Development of Misconceptions

A predominant share of the misconceptions (and networks of misconception) that we have identified reflect one or another kind of *oversimplification* of complex material—associated with learners' earlier experiences with introductory learning, and even influenced by many experiences with advanced learning. Misconceptions of advanced material result both from interference from earlier, simplified treatments of that material and from a prevailing mode of approaching the learning process in general that fosters simplificational strategies and leaves learners without an appropriate cognitive repertoire for the processing of complexity (Feltovich et al., 1989; Spiro et al., 1987; Spiro et al., 1989).

We have termed the general tendency to reduce important aspects of complexity the *reductive bias*. Several forms of the bias have been identified, selected examples of which follow (see Coulson et al., 1986; Feltovich et al., 1989; Spiro et al., 1989, for *examples of biomedical misconceptions* corresponding to the types of reductive bias listed).

1. Oversimplification of complex and irregular structure. Superficial similarities among related phenomena are treated as unifying characteristics. Interacting components are treated as independent. Incomplete conceptual accounts are presented (or accepted by the learner) as being comprehensive.

Instances that are referred to as belonging to the same generic category are treated in a uniform manner despite their being highly diverse. The irregular is treated as regular, the nonroutine as routine, the disorderly as orderly, the continuous as discrete, the dynamic as static, the multidimensional as unidimensional. (This first reductive bias is the most general one, encompassing many of the specific ones listed below.)

2. Overreliance on a single basis for mental representation. A single, encompassing, representational logic is applied to complex concepts and phenomena that are inadequately covered by that logic—for example, understanding of a new concept is reduced to the features of a (partially) analogous concept. New, highly divergent examples are understood by exclusive reference to a single prototype. A single schema or theory is proffered and preferred, despite the fact that its coverage is significantly incomplete. Complexly multifaceted content has its understanding narrowed to just those aspects covered by a single organizational scheme. And so on.

3. Overreliance on "top down" processing. Understanding and decision-making in knowledge application situations (i.e., cases) rely too exclusively on generic abstractions (i.e., concepts, theories, etc.); detailed knowledge of *case* structure is not used enough (i.e., knowledge of "how cases go," as well as reasoning from specific case precedents).

4. Context-independent conceptual representation. The contexts in which a concept is relevant are treated as having overly uniform characteristics. This promotes the representation of conceptual knowledge in a manner too abstract for effective application (i.e., without sufficient regard for the specifics of application in context). Concepts are insufficiently tailored to their uses; concepts are not recognized as relevant when, in fact, they are; and concepts are mistakenly judged to be relevant in contexts where they are not.

5. Overreliance on precompiled knowledge structures. *Fixed* protocols or rigidly *prepackaged* schemata are presented to learners and used by them as recipes for what to do in new cases.

6. Rigid compartmentalization of knowledge components. Components of knowledge that are in fact interdependent are treated as being separable from each other. Learners develop mistaken beliefs in the independence of the components. Relatedly, where knowledge components do function independently, it may nevertheless be the case that conveying relationships between their conceptual structures would aid understanding; these connections are not drawn. When components are interrelated, there is a tendency to use just one linkage scheme, thereby underrepresenting the richness of interconnection in the system and promoting narrow, doctrinaire viewpoints (see the problem of single representations).

7. Passive transmission of knowledge. Knowledge is preemptively encoded under a scheme determined by external authority (e.g., a textbook) or a scheme that facilitates delivery and use. Knowledge is "handed" to the learner.

The preemptive encoding is passively received by the learner, and useful benefits that result from personalized knowledge representations, derivable from active exploration and involvement in the subject area, do not develop. When active, participatory learning is encouraged, adequate support for the management of increased indeterminacy and cognitive load is not provided (e.g., mentor guidance, memory aids, etc.).

The next section will outline our theoretical approach to *remedying* the problems of advanced knowledge acquisition caused by these reductive biases.

Cognitive Flexibility Theory: Themes of Advanced Knowledge Acquisition

Where has our research on the *problems* of advanced knowledge acquisition led us? To an overall theoretical orientation that in many ways derives its fundamental themes from the specific nature of those learning problems, as the problems relate to the characteristics of ill-structured domains and the special goals of advanced knowledge acquisition (i.e., mastery of conceptual complexity and knowledge application/transfer).

In this section we provide a brief discussion of our most fundamental, theoretically motivated remedies for the problems of advanced knowledge acquisition. The following themes constitute different facets of what we call *cognitive flexibility* (Spiro et al., 1987). The themes are, in a sense, *conditions* for developing mastery of complexity and knowledge transferability. Each of the headlined theoretical commitments has received some form of implementation, either in our experiments or in our theory-based computer hypertext systems (including one prototype that implements the theory's principles of advanced knowledge acquisition in cardiovascular medicine, the Cardioworld Explorer). Given the extreme limitations of space, the themes are discussed schematically and in the abstract; detailed development of theoretical rationales, examples of our concrete instantiations of the themes (in the biomedical domain and others that we have studied), and patterns of empirical support for our claims can be found in our cited papers.

1. Avoidance of oversimplification and overregularization. Because of the strong bias toward oversimplification that we have observed, it is clear that advanced knowledge acquisition must place a high premium on making salient those ways that knowledge is not as simple and orderly as it might first seem in introductory treatments. Where the problem is so often a presumption of simplicity and regularity, the remedy is to take special measures to *demonstrate complexities and irregularities*. It is important to lay bare the limitations of initial, first-pass understandings, to highlight exceptions, to show how the superficially similar is dissimilar and how superficial unities are broken. Where conceptual error frequently occurs from atomistic decomposition of complexly interacting information followed by misguided attempts at "additive" reassembly of the decomposed elements, the remedy is to take pains to *highlight component inter-actions*, to clearly demonstrate the intricate patterns of *conceptual combination*.

This is a very general theme, encompassing many of the others that follow in this list. Cognitive flexibility involves the *selective* use of knowledge to *adaptively fit* the needs of understanding and decision making in a particular situation; the potential for maximally adaptive *knowledge assembly* depends on having available as full a representation of complexity to draw upon as possible.

2. Multiple representations. Single representations (e.g., a single schema, organizational logic, line of argument, prototype, analogy, etc.) will miss important facets of complex concepts. Cognitive flexibility is dependent on having a diversified repertoire of ways of thinking about a conceptual topic. Knowledge that will have to be used in many ways has to be learned, represented, and tried out (in application) in many ways.

The use of multiple representations is important at different levels. For example, we have found multiple analogies to be very useful in understanding complex individual concepts (Spiro et al., 1989; see the example below of force production by muscle fibers; see also Collins & Gentner, 1987; White & Frederiksen, 1987). However, the importance of multiple representations may be even more important for larger units of analysis. For example, we have found that students' understandings of the entire domain of biomedical knowledge are adversely affected by the tendency to use just one way of modeling the various phenomena they encounter, one that comes from the *metaphor of the machine*. This one "lens" leads them to take for granted certain issues related to the nature of explanations, the structure of mental models of functional systems, and so on. These students develop understandings that do not capture important aspects of the biomedical domain (e.g., inherently organic processes). Their understandings would be more complete if they were to augment the selective view that results from their mechanistic bias with other understandings that selectively emerge from the unique aspects of other cognitive "lenses"—for example, from *organicist* metaphors (Feltovich et al., 1989).

The need for multiple representations applies not only to complex concepts, but to cases as well. In an ill-structured domain, cases (examples, occurrences, events—occasions of use of conceptual knowledge) tend to be complex and highly variable one to the next. The complexity of cases requires that they be represented from multiple theoretical/conceptual perspectives; if cases are treated narrowly by characterizing them using a too limited subset of their relevant perspectives, the ability to process future cases will be limited. First, there will be an assumption that cases are simpler than they in fact are, and attempts to deal with new cases will prematurely conclude after they are only *partially* analyzed. Second, there will be insufficient preparedness to deal with the specific patterns of interaction of theoretical/conceptual perspectives within cases. Third, to the extent that performance in future cases will require reasoning from sets of precedent cases (which is always a greater need in ill-structured domains), the likelihood of having case representations available in prior knowledge which are maximally apt in their relation to some new case is lessened to the extent that cases are narrowly represented in memory. This is especially so when there is substantial across-case dissimilarity; the relative novelty of a new case in an ill-structured domain will require more elaborate efforts to find appropriate precedents—the wider the variety that is available, the better the chances of finding a fit.

An example of multiple representations: Integrated multiple analogies for complex concepts. As we have said, our studies of medical students have indicated that one of the most serious contributors to the problems of advanced knowledge acquisition is the use of a single knowledge representation. Complex concepts can rarely be adequately represented using a single schema, theoretical perspective, line of exposition, and so on. Nevertheless, in practice, complex concepts frequently are represented in some single fashion, with substantial consequences.

Our remedy has been to approach learning in all the domains that we have studied with the goal of promoting *multiple representations* (e.g., multiple precedent cases for a new case; multiple organizational schemes for representing the same content material in our computer hypertexts; etc.). Here we will briefly consider just the case of analogy. We have discovered a large number of misconceptions that result from the overextended application of analogies (Spiro et al., 1989). To combat the negative effects of a powerful and seductive single analogy, we employ *sets of integrated multiple analogies*. Whenever a source concept in an analogy is missing important aspects of a target concept or the source concept is in some way misleading about the target concept, we introduce *another* analogy to counteract those specific negative effects of the earlier analogy.

So, where we find that misconceptions about the nature of force production by muscle fibers often develop because of a common analogy to the operation of rowing crews (sarcomere "arms" and "oars" both generate force by a kind of "pulling"), other analogies are introduced to mitigate the negative effects of the limited rowing-crew analogy (Spiro et al., 1989). An analogy to turnbuckles corrects misleading notions about the nature of relative movement and the gross structures within the muscle. An analogy to "finger handcuffs" covers important information missing in the rowing-crew analogy about limits of fiber length (the elastin covering on muscle fiber bundles constricts at long lengths, stopping extension in a manner similar to the cross-hatched finger cuffs when you try to pull a finger out of each end). And so on. A composite imaging technique that helps the user integrate the multiple analogies, so that the correct aspects of each analogy can be selectively instantiated in relevant contexts of use of the target concept, has also been developed. The procedure facilitates the learning of a concept (through the pedagogical benefits of analogy), while maintaining the integrity of the concept's complexities (by using multiple analogies to cover the concept's multifacetedness and to vitiate the force of incorrect aspects of any single analogy) (see also Burnstein, 1983).

Theory-based hypertext systems to implement the themes of advanced knowledge acquisition in ill-structured domains: The importance of revisiting and rearranging in the development of multiple representations. Much of the work on computer hypertext systems has been driven by the power of the technology rather than by a coherent view of the cognitive psychology of nonlinear and multidimensional learning and instruction. In contrast, our hypertext approaches have a basis in cognitive theory—they derive from the themes of cognitive flexibility theory. And their realm of operation is specified; they are especially targeted at advanced knowledge acquisition in ill-structured domains. (There is no point in imposing the extra cognitive load of nonlinearity and multidimensionality if the domain being studied is simple and well structured or if the goals of learning are the more easily attainable ones of introductory treatments). We will briefly characterize our approach to implementing cognitive flexibility theory in computer hypertext systems.

Our hypertext systems build multiple representations in a manner that can be understood using a metaphor of landscape exploration. Deep understanding of a complex landscape will not be obtained from a single traversal. Similarly for a *conceptual* landscape. Rather, *the landscape must be criss-crossed in many directions* to master its complexity and to avoid having the fullness of the domain attenuated (Spiro et al., 1987; Wittgenstein, 1953). The same sites in a landscape (the same cases or concepts in a knowledge domain) should be *revisited* from different directions, thought about from different perspectives, and so on. There is a limit to how much understanding of a complex entity can be achieved in a single treatment, in a single context, for a single purpose. By *repeating* the presentation of the same complex case or concept information in *new contexts*, additional aspects of the multifacetedness of these "landscape sites" are brought out, enabling the kind of rich representations necessary in a complex and ill-structured domain. Thus, cognitive flexibility is fostered by a flexible approach to learning and instruction. The same content material is covered in different ways at different times in order to demonstrate the potential flexibility of use inherent in that content (Spiro & Jehng, 1990; Spiro et al., 1987).

3. Centrality of cases. The more ill structured the domain, the poorer the guidance for knowledge *application* that top-down structures will generally provide. That is, the way abstract concepts (theories, general principles, etc.) should be used to facilitate understanding and to dictate action in naturally occurring cases becomes increasingly indeterminate in ill-structured domains. The application of knowledge to cases in an ill-structured domain (i.e., a domain in which cases are individually multidimensional and irregularly related one to the next) cannot be prescribed in advance by general principles. This is because, in ill-structured domains, there is great variability from case to case regarding which conceptual elements will be relevant and in what pattern of combination. In an ill-structured domain, general principles will not capture enough of the structured dynamics of cases; increased flexibility in responding to highly diverse new cases comes increasingly from reliance on reasoning from precedent cases.

Thus, examples/cases cannot be assigned the ancillary status of merely illustrating abstract principles (and then being discardable); the cases are key—examples are necessary and not just nice (Feltovich et al., 1989; Spiro & Jehng, 1990; Spiro et al., 1987).

4. Conceptual knowledge as knowledge in use. Not only is it more difficult to count on top-down prescriptions for performance in new cases in an ill-structured domain (i.e., abstract concepts/theories inadequately determine responses to new cases), but there is also considerable indeterminateness in defining conditions for *accessing* conceptual structures in the first place, to engage the guidance the conceptual structures *do* offer. It is not that abstract knowledge has no role in ill-structured domains but that its role is highly intertwined with that of case-centered reasoning. Put another way, in an ill-structured domain there will be greatly increased variability across cases in the way the same concept is used or applied. Thus it is harder to get from features of cases to the concepts that might need to be applied to those cases. And it is harder to apply a concept, once assessed, if it has many different kinds of uses across cases—concepts must be *tailored* to their application contexts. The Wittgensteinian dictum that meaning is determined by use clearly applies in ill-structured domains. If a concept's meaning in use cannot be determined universally across cases (as in an ill-structured domain), then one must pay much more attention to the details of how the concept is used—*knowledge in practice*, rather than in the abstract (Spiro & Jehng, 1990; Spiro et al., 1987; Wittgenstein, 1953).

In medical training, this issue of *variability and combination in concept instantiation* has an obvious implication for the traditional difficulty of integrating the biomedical basic science parts of the curriculum with the clinical parts. Physicians' practice would be improved if in problematic situations they could apply the interacting basic biomedical science concepts that underlie the clinical situation that is posing the problem. However, it is very difficult for medical students to learn how to get to the basic science concepts from clinical presenting features, partly because of the great variability across clinical cases in the way those concepts get instantiated. A key feature of our Cardioworld Explorer hypertext is that it permits the learner to selectively examine the full range of uses of any selected basic science concept (or any selected combination of concepts) across cases with differing clinical features, teaching the patterns of concept application and thus facilitating *access* to conceptual information in clinical contexts (as well as fostering an understanding of the different ways that a given concept has to be tailored to be clinically relevant).

Again, in an ill-structured domain the meaning of a concept is intimately connected to its patterns of use. When the uses (instances, cases) of the same concept have a complex and irregular distribution (i.e., the domain is ill structured), adequate prepackaged prescriptions for proper activation of the concept cannot be provided (i.e., *concept instantiation is nonroutine*). Instead, greater weight (than in a well-structured domain) must be given to activating concepts in a new case by examination of family resemblances across the features of *past cases* that have been called (labeled as instances of) that concept.

5. Schema assembly (from rigidity to flexibility). In an ill-structured domain, emphasis must be shifted from *retrieval* of intact, rigid, precompiled knowledge structures to *assembly* of knowledge from different conceptual and precedent case sources to adaptively fit the situation at hand (Spiro, 1980; Spiro et al., 1987). This follows, again, from characteristics of ill-structured domains. Since ill-structuredness implies kinds of complexity and irregularity that militate against the use of knowledge structures that assume routinizability across cases, the role of intact schema retrieval must be diminished—greater across-case differences cause a necessary decline in the ability of any large, single precompilation to fit a wide variety of cases. In complex and ill-structured domains, one cannot have a prepackaged schema for everything. As ill-structuredness increases, the use of *rigid* knowledge structures (i.e., the same precompiled knowledge structure used for many cases) must be replaced by *flexible*, recombinable knowledge structures. For any particular case, many *small* precompiled knowledge structures will need to be used. And there will be relatively little repetition of patterns across case-specific assemblies of these smaller pieces of precompiled knowledge. Accordingly, in knowledge acquisition for cognitive flexibility, the "storage of fixed knowledge is devalued in favor of the *mobilization of potential knowledge*" (Spiro et al., 1987; see also Schank, 1982).

6. Noncompartmentalization of concepts and cases (multiple interconnectedness). Because of the complex and irregular way that abstract conceptual features weave through cases/examples in ill-structured domains, knowledge cannot be neatly compartmentalized. In order to enable the situation-dependent, adaptive schema assembly from disparate knowledge sources that characterizes cognitive flexibility, those multiple sources must be highly interconnected. Concepts cannot be treated as separate "chapters." Retroactive assembly of independently taught, and noninterrelated, constituent conceptual aspects too often fails. Also, although cases have to be focused on separately so that the complexity of case structure is conveyed, they should not be taught in *just* that way—connections across cases must also be established. Rather than relegating concepts or cases to separate compartments, chapters, and so on, our systems strive for *multiple interconnectedness (of cases and concepts) along multiple conceptual and clinical dimensions.*

Our approach to fostering multiple interconnectedness of knowledge representations in our hypertexts is to code case segments with a multidimensional vector indicating the relevance of a variety of thematic/conceptual dimensions to that case segment (Spiro & Jehng, 1990). (Positive values in the vector also point to commentary, providing expert guidance about the nature of the conceptual dimension's instantiation in that particular case segment; this helps with the problem of teaching conceptual knowledge in use, discussed earlier). Then, as the hypertext program guides the learner in criss-crossing the domain's "landscape" by exploring patterns of overlap in the vectors for different case segments, knowledge representations are built up in which parts of cases are connected with many parts of other cases, along many conceptual/theoretical dimensions of case-segment similarity. In that way, many alternative paths are established to get from one part of the overall knowledge base to any other part of the knowledge base that aspects of some future case may signal as relevant. Thus, the potential for flexible, situation-adaptive schema assembly is fostered (along with such other virtues as the establishment of multiple routes for memory access to any node in the system).

So, for example, in the Cardioworld Explorer, segments of clinical cases are encoded with a vector of clinical and basic biomedical science themes that are relevant to each segment. The system can then establish connections between a segment of one case and segments of many other cases, along the various (conceptual and clinical) thematic dimensions represented in the vector. In case-based instruction, it is often true that there are important, instructive relationships between an aspect of one case and aspects of others. Such relationships are rarely brought out. Our hypertext systems capture these many lessons that are missed in strict case-by-case (or problem-by-problem) instruction. In an ill-structured domain, facilitating retrieval of multiple (partial) precedents is important, because understanding what to do in a given case context will usually require reference to more than any single prototype—the case in question will be "kind of like this earlier one, kind of like that one," and so on. Also, understanding of the case in question will require that various concepts be brought to bear and integrated; this, too, is facilitated by the multiple conceptual coding scheme employed in our systems.

There are several other benefits of the multiple-conceptual coding of multiple case segments. A power/efficiency advantage is that it allows the hypertexts to automatically generate large numbers of lessons (many "landscape criss-crossings"). If, for example, each of 20 cases is divided into an average of 10 case segments, each with a value of 15 relevant thematic dimensions, there is a manyfold increase in the number of possible automatizable instructional comparisons and contrasts that results from having 200 case segments (instead of 20 full cases) intertwined by relationships in the 15-slot vector.

Also, the use of case segments prevents the subsumption to a "common denominator" that occurs when larger structural units are used; an interesting local element of a case will tend to get lost if it has features that are not present in other parts of the case (when the monolithic case is the structural unit). Using small case segments (minicases) helps retain the *plurality* of situations.

There is another virtue of the division into case segments and the multi-dimensional coding of the segments that relates to keeping case understanding from being overly simplified. In an ill-structured knowledge domain, by definition, there is sufficient variability across cases (due in part to the interaction of the many factors that make up complex cases) that the set of cases that might be nominally grouped together under some schema or classification will be greatly variable in their particulars. A case, instead of being represented as one kind of thing conveying one kind of "lesson," is instead clearly shown to the learner to be *many things*. Cases of the same nominal type have different segments or scenes that are demonstrated not to be the same, and each of the segments is shown to have multiple significances. Therefore, the common temptation to nest cases uniquely under a single superordinate conceptual category will be resisted, making it less likely that the complex relationships among cases in a domain will be artificially regularized. In an ill-structured domain, cases are related to many different concepts of the domain, and it promotes dysfunctional simplification to nest or "slot" cases hierarchically under single conceptual categories (e.g., "The following cases are examples of x [only]"). When there is considerable across-case variability, as there will be in an ill-structured domain, cognitive flexibility requires that case information be coded conceptually for the many different kinds of use that new situations may require.

The thematic coding scheme and the landscape criss-crossing system of instruction result in a weblike multiple interconnectedness on multiple dimensions that is not subject to the limitations of instruction characterized by a single organizational slant. Instead of a single text with a single organizational scheme and a single sequencing of comparisons and contrasts, our hypertexts allow the same information to be automatically reconfigured according to a huge number of possible organizational schemes determined by using subsets of the multiple thematic coding space; our hypertexts enable the *virtually limitless automatic generation of new text configurations*. Because of the richness of ill-structured domains such as biomedical science, each of these text configurations teaches some case- (experience-) grounded lessons that would not have been taught (or easily seen if taught) from another text's organizational perspective. Such additional experiences and perspectives are always helpful in a complex domain—a physician never learns all that it would be helpful to learn (which is why additional experience is always valued in a physician). Hypertext systems like the Cardioworld Explorer systematically *consolidate the process of acquiring experience.*

Yet another virtue of the multiple interconnectedness along multiple dimensions of the representations that our systems build has to do with the problem of reciprocal-misconception compounding that we have observed in our studies of medical students and physicians (Coulson et al., 1986; Feltovich et al., 1989).

Misconceptions bolster each other and combine to form seductively entrenched *networks of misconception.* Our approach helps forestall the development of misconception networks by developing a kind of *positive reciprocation.* Because *correctly conceived representations with a high degree of multiple interconnectedness are established*, the fresh entry of fallacious knowledge at any node in the weblike network will fire off so many connections that it would be likely to activate some *misconception-disabling correct knowledge.* Before you can go too far wrong, you are likely to touch something that sets you right.

   7. Active participation, tutorial guidance, and adjunct support for the management of complexity. In an ill-structured domain, knowledge cannot just be handed to the learner. A priori codifications of knowledge are likely to misrepresent. (That is part of what ill-structuredness means). Hence the importance, increasingly widely recognized today, of active learner involvement in knowledge acquisition, accompanied by opportunistic guidance by expert mentors (which can be incorporated in a computer program—it does not have to be live, one-to-one guidance). Furthermore, aids must be provided to help the learner manage the added complexity that comes with ill structure. Our hypertext programs allow learners to explore complex conceptual landscapes in many directions with expert guidance and various kinds of cognitive support (e.g., integrated visual displays). When there are limits to the *explicit* transmission of knowledge, learners will need special kinds of help in figuring things out for themselves (see Barrows & Tamblyn, 1980; Collins, Brown, & Newman, 1989; Spiro et el., 1987).

Recapitulation: A Shift From Single to Multiple Representations and From Generic Schema Retrieval to Situation-Specific Knowledge Assembly

In general, we argue that the goals of advanced knowledge acquisition in complex and ill-structured domains can best be attained (and the problems we have identified avoided) by the development of mental representations that support cognitive flexibility. Central to the cultivation of *cognitive flexibility* are approaches to learning, instruction, and knowledge representation that (a) allow an important role for *multiple representations*, (b) view learning as the multidirectional and multiperspectival "criss-crossing" of cases and concepts that make up complex domains' "landscapes" (with resulting interconnectedness along multiple dimensions), and (c) foster the ability to assemble diverse knowledge sources to adaptively fit the needs of a particular knowledge application situation (rather than the search for a precompiled schema that fits the situation). We suggest that theory-based computer hypertext systems can implement the goals and strategies of cognitive flexibility theory, engendering multiple cognitive representations that capture the real-world complexities of the kinds of cases to which abstract conceptual knowledge must be applied.

Acknowledgments

The research reported in this paper was supported by grants from the Army Research Institute (MDA903-86-K-0443), the Office of Naval Research (N00014-88-K-0286, N00014-87-G-0165, N00014-88-K-0077), the Josiah Macy Foundation (B852001), and the Office of Educational Research and Improvement (OEG 0087-C1001). The publication does not necessarily reflect the views of the agencies supporting the research.

The authors would like to acknowledge the contributions of Jane Adami and Joan Feltovich to various aspects of this research.

References

Barrows, H.S., & Tamblyn, R.M. (1980). *Problem-based learning*. New York: Springer.

Burnstein, M. (1983). Concept formation by incremental analogical reasoning and debugging. *Proceedings of the International Machine Learning Workshop*, Champaign, IL.

Champagne, A.B., Gunstone, R.F., & Klopfer, L.E. (1985). Effecting changes in cognitive structures among physics students. In L.H. West & A.L. Pines (Eds.), *Cognitive structure and conceptual change*. Orlando, FL: Academic.

Collins, A., Brown, J.S., & Newman, S.E. (1989). Cognitive apprenticeship: Teaching the crafts of reading, writing, and mathematics. In L.B. Resnick (Ed.), *Knowing, learning, and instruction: Essays in honor of Robert Glaser*. Hillsdale, NJ: Erlbaum.

Collins, A., & Gentner, D. (1987). How people construct mental models. In D. Holland & S. Quinn (Eds.), *Cultural models in thought and language*. Cambridge, UK: Cambridge University Press.

Coulson, R.L., Feltovich, P.J., & Spiro, R.J. (1986). *Foundations of a misunderstanding of the ultrastructural basis of myocardial failure: A reciprocating network of over-simplifications* (Tech. Rep. No. 1). Springfield: Southern Illinois University School of Medicine, Conceptual Knowledge Research Project.

Feltovich, P.J., Spiro, R.J., & Coulson, R.L. (1989). The nature of conceptual understanding in biomedicine: The deep structure of complex ideas and the development of misconceptions. In D.A. Evans & V.L. Patel (Eds.), *The cognitive sciences in medicine: Biomedical modeling*. Cambridge, MA: MIT Press.

Schank, R.C. (1982). *Dynamic memory: A theory of reminding and learning in computers and people*. Cambridge, UK: Cambridge University Press.

Spiro, R.J. (1980). Accommodative reconstruction in prose recall. *Journal of Verbal Learning and Verbal Behavior, 19*, 84–95.

Spiro, R.J., Feltovich, P.J., Coulson, R.L., & Anderson, D.K. (1989). Multiple analogies for complex concepts: Antidotes for analogy-induced misconception in advanced knowledge acquisition. In S. Vosniadou & A. Ortony (Eds.), *Similarity and analogical reasoning*. Cambridge, UK: Cambridge University Press.

Spiro, R.J., & Jehng, J.C. (1990). Cognitive flexibility and hypertext: Theory and technology for the nonlinear and multidimensional traversal of complex subject matter. In D. Nix & R.J. Spiro (Eds.), *Cognition, education, and multimedia: Exploring ideas in high technology*. Hillsdale, NJ: Erlbaum.

Spiro, R.J., Vispoel, W.L., Schmitz, J., Samarapungavan, A., & Boerger, A. (1987). Knowledge acquisition for application: Cognitive flexibility and transfer in complex content domains. In B.C. Britton & S. Glynn (Eds.), *Executive control processes in reading*. Hillsdale, NJ: Erlbaum.

White, B.Y. (1984). Designing computer games to help physics students understand Newton's law of motion. *Cognition and Instruction, 1*, 69–108.

White, B.Y., & Frederiksen, J.R. (1987, November). *Causal model progressions as a foundation for intelligent learning environments* (BBN Rep. No. 6686). Cambridge, MA: Bolt Beranek & Newman.

Wittgenstein, L. (1953). *Philosophical investigations*. New York: Macmillan.

24

Principled Pluralism for Adaptive Flexibility in Teaching and Learning to Read

Rand J. Spiro

I write from the perspective of Cognitive Flexibility Theory (CFT) (Spiro, Coulson, Feltovich, & Anderson, 1994; Spiro & Jehng, 1990; Spiro, Vispoel, Schmitz, Samarapungavan, & Boerger, 1987). In CFT, a successor of schema theories (Anderson, 1977; Anderson, Spiro, & Anderson, 1978; Spiro, 1980), it has been argued for many years that *all* learning, instruction, mental representation, and knowledge application should be governed by a principled utilization of interlocking multiple representations, multiple methodologies, multiple perspectives, multiple case precedents, and multiple analogies (Spiro et al., 1994; Spiro, Feltovich, Coulson, & Anderson, 1989). CFT was designed for learning in ill-structured domains, where cases of knowledge application are characterized *individually* by complexity and *across cases* by considerable variability and irregularity in the conditions of knowledge use. Given the complexity of such domains, single approaches of any kind will be limiting, successful in some contexts and off the mark in many others. This is so whether the domain is a content area like history or biology, a process like reading, or an arena of practical application of knowledge like medicine or teaching.

CFT is intended to prepare people to flexibly and adaptively apply their knowledge to new cases or situations, situations that are often unlike any they have encountered before. Hence the inappropriateness of old-style schema theory, which depends on the retrieval of a prestored schema or template from memory, despite the unlikelihood that one would have a prepackaged schema for everything that might be needed, especially in reading (Spiro & Myers, 1984). CFT argues that, when facing a complex new case or situation, you need to assemble elements of prior knowledge and past experience and tailor those elements to fit the new situation's needs. This situation-sensitive assembly of multiple perspectives from prior knowledge is the part of *pluralism* that the title of this piece refers to that is *principled*—it is not just throwing together any old set of theories, method-ologies, and knowledge elements. Rather, one must assemble just those aspects that will help in the current situation, while discounting those aspects that are less helpful. Further, the assembled elements must be meaningfully related to each other and tailored to the specific content of the case at hand. In a sense, one must build a "schema-of-the-moment" (Spiro et al., 1987, 1994; Spiro & Jehng, 1990). For most domains there are strengths and weaknesses of all the credible approaches, and patterns of combined strength and weakness (across approach-es) are usually determined by features of the teaching or learning situation one is facing. The key question for CFT is which approaches, theories, methods, and content schemas are most appropriate for a new situation, and then how are they to be put together (combined, coordinated, aligned) to fit that new context.

It is hard to imagine a domain where these principles would be more ap-plicable than in learning to read and in the teaching of reading. Therefore, it is heartening to see an increasing tendency toward pluralism in the reading field, to-ward the advocacy of integration of different theoretical and methodological per-spectives (see Flippo, 1999; International Reading Association, 1999; Pearson, 1996). And, of course, it should not be surprising to see the agreements in the Expert Study (Flippo, 1998), of which I was a part, which indicate a belief that many things that are said to be true of reading and learning to read *are* true—in many but not all situations—for some children, at some times, for some teach-ing and learning purposes. Furthermore, it will usually be the case that beliefs and practices in the teaching of reading are best applied in combinations, and these combinations will also shift according to changing contexts. In other words, the only summary statement that applies to all of reading is this: *It all depends*.

The skilled teacher of reading will have a rich repertoire to draw from, and he or she will examine each teaching situation closely—and, based on that close reading, assemble a situation-sensitive approach that draws from different elements of knowledge and different prior-case experiences. Furthermore, this mix will be fluidly changeable as the reading situation evolves and changes. Similarly, the skilled reader will sometimes rely more on the use of knowledge of phonics, sometimes use whole-word approaches; sometimes rely on prior knowl-edge and contextual information, sometimes accept a premise of novelty and rely less on prior knowledge; sometimes read for accuracy, sometimes skim for gist—all depending on characteristics of what is being read, why it is being read, and who is doing the reading. And, of course, sometimes these strategies of reading are used in combination rather than in isolation from each other. In these senses, there is a principled pluralism required at the "micro" level (the act of reading) that mirrors that which has been argued for at the "macro" level of the field of reading research and the theory of the teaching of reading.

I believe that these issues of cognitive flexibility and situation-adaptive as-sembly of multiple perspectives are central to the next generation of educational research, not just in the "reading wars," but also across the spectrum of learning and teaching. The development of principled pluralisms of the mind and of pedagogy are crucial for learning and teaching in *all* complex domains of knowledge acquisition and application—and we are coming to find that more and more domains that we had thought to be relatively simple and orderly actually have crucial properties of complexity and ill structure. Unfortunately, those approaches that work for learning in simple domains are exactly the opposite of the ones that are best for dealing with complexity—what helps for one, hurts for the other. Examples include single versus multiple representations, compartmentalized versus interconnected knowledge, knowledge-centeredness versus case-centeredness, and retrieval from memory of prepackaged prescriptions for how to think and act versus case-sensitive knowledge assembly (Spiro et al., 1987, 1994). Fortunately, we also now possess new theories and theory-based educational technologies to help foster these more difficult kinds of complex learning that have so often resisted our best efforts in the past (see Spiro, Feltovich, Jacobson, & Coulson, 1992a, 1992b).

One of the most important of the next-generation research questions concerns the manner of operation of principled pluralisms. How does situation-adaptive assembly of knowledge and experience occur, and how should it be fostered (in teachers and students)? There are at least two key elements in the answer to these questions. The first is a recognition of the centrality of case experience (Spiro et al., 1994). The organizing nexus for assembling multiple perspectives is the *case* (example, occurrence, actual event in the world). In ill-structured domains of real-world practice (e.g., reading, teaching reading), wide-scope generalizations, abstractions, and schemas do not work. Instead, one must attend to "how the world goes" and learn how to piece together and tailor knowledge to the demands of practice—there is no "formula." So it is the case that becomes the organizing focus for knowledge assembly that provides the guidance for what needs to be part of the schema-of-the-moment and how that assemblage needs to be put together. This contrasts with well-structured domains, where examples or cases are interchangeable illustrations of generic knowledge that spins out in highly routinized ways. In ill-structured domains, the principled basis for adaptive knowledge assembly referred to in the phrase *principled pluralism* is to be found in the landscape of a domain's cases—alignment and coordination of multiple knowledge sources and methods are governed by their fit to the events to which they are being applied and their usefulness in dealing with those events.

An important implication of this shift in emphasis to the situation-adaptive assembly of schemas-of-the-moment out of multiple perspectives is that the structures of prior knowledge must be conceived differently than they were in schema theory. It is no accident that the situated cognition movement has deemphasized and, at times, been antagonistic to earlier views that placed abstract cognitive structures in a central place. Such views were notorious for their failures to account for novel transfer, the ability to apply knowledge to new situations that differ from the conditions of initial learning. The situations of the world are too rich to permit wide-scope application of generic cognitive structures. However, the problem is not with knowledge structures per se, but rather with the kind of knowledge structure that has typically been proffered. What is required is a different kind of knowledge structure, one that works with the jagged and messy contours of situations in the world rather than smoothing them out—open structures to think with, rather than closed structures that dictate thought. The goal of CFT is to foster the learning of such open, situation-sensitive structures (Spiro et al., 1987, 1992a, 1992b, 1994).

The second key element of preparing people to assemble knowledge in situation-adaptive ways is the role of new technologies. Certain uses of case-based hypermedia are designed to promote knowledge assembly skills by modeling them across a range of contexts (Spiro et al., 1994; Spiro & Jehng, 1990). The nonlinear traversal capability of hypermedia, along with the newly expanded ease of dealing with digital video cases, allows real-world examples to be overlaid by shifting constellations of perspectives and then compared and contrasted in varying ways to illustrate the vagaries of situation-adaptive knowledge assembly across diverse contexts. With this technology it is possible to demonstrate and teach principled pluralism in operation, in all its forms.

Finally, perhaps the most important frontier for next-generation research is that of changing students' and teachers' habits of mind, their underlying epistemic stance toward the world, in the direction of ones that are more compatible with the changing circumstances of knowing and doing that characterize our increasingly complex and rapidly evolving modern world of life and work (Feltovich, Spiro, & Coulson, 1989; Spiro, Feltovich, & Coulson, 1996). We often speak of cognitive structures; rarely do we speak of the underlying assumptions and structures that determine the shape of the cognitive structures that get built, the background "lenses" that prefigure the shape of knowledge (Feltovich et al., 1989). It is these prefigurative schemas that I refer to as habits of mind. There is considerable evidence that the predominant habits of mind are overly simple in a variety of ways (see Spiro et al., 1996) and are thus antithetical to the needs of successful performance in complex domains (such as reading and the teaching of reading). Habits of mind suited to dealing with complexity must be developed; finding ways to do this will be a major challenge of the coming years. Progress in the use of principled pluralisms for the cognitively flexible, situation-adaptive assembly of prior knowledge and experience will be slow until we are able to develop corresponding changes in the underlying habits of mind of teachers and students who would greatly prefer that things were simpler.

In summary, it should be clear to the reader by now what led me to indicate agreement to all the items in the final lists of the Expert Study. My research has led me to believe that all credible approaches are useful on some occasions, that none are always useful, and that the relevance of one does not preclude the simultaneous relevance of others with which it might be fruitfully combined. This is an inevitable outcome of advocating for a principled pluralism. In the end, it will all depend on an expert teacher making a judgment about which ensemble of approaches and practices to select for a particular student and context. It is the job of those who prepare teachers of reading to ensure that those future teachers understand the implications of principled pluralism and are able to apply knowledge and methods of various types with adaptive flexibility.

Acknowledgments

The author wishes to acknowledge the many helpful comments and great patience of Rona Flippo. The writing of this piece was supported in part by grant No. DE-P342A99059 from the Office of Educational Research and Improvement of the U.S. Department of Education.

References

Anderson, R.C. (1977). The notion of schemata and the educational enterprise. In R.C. Anderson, R.J. Spiro, & W.E. Montague (Eds.), *Schooling and the acquisition of knowledge* (pp. 415–432). Hillsdale, NJ: Erlbaum.

Anderson, R.C., Spiro, R.J., & Anderson, M.C. (1978). Schemata as scaffolding for the representation of information in discourse. *American Educational Research Journal, 15,* 433–440.

Feltovich, P.J., Spiro, R.J., & Coulson, R.L. (1989). The nature of conceptual understanding in biomedicine: The deep structure of complex ideas and the development of misconceptions. In D.A. Evans & V.L. Patel (Eds.), *The cognitive sciences in medicine: Biomedical modeling* (pp. 113–172). Cambridge, MA: MIT Press.

Flippo, R.F. (1998). Points of agreement: A display of professional unity in our field. *The Reading Teacher, 52,* 30–40.

Flippo, R.F. (1999). Redefining the reading wars: The war against reading researchers. *Educational Leadership, 57,* 38–41.

International Reading Association. (1999). *Using multiple methods of beginning reading instruction: A position statement of the International Reading Association* [Brochure]. Newark, DE: Author.

Pearson, P.D. (1996). Six ideas in search of a champion: What policymakers should know about the teaching and learning of literacy in our schools. *Journal of Literacy Research, 28,* 302–309.

Spiro, R.J. (1980). Constructive processes in prose comprehension and recall. In R.J. Spiro, B.C. Bruce, & W.F. Brewer (Eds.), *Theoretical issues in reading comprehension: Perspectives from cognitive psychology, linguistics, artificial intelligence, and education* (pp. 245–278). Hillsdale, NJ: Erlbaum.

Spiro, R.J., Coulson, R.L., Feltovich, P.J., & Anderson, D.K. (1994). Cognitive flexibility theory: Advanced knowledge acquisition in ill-structured domains. In R.B. Ruddell, M.R. Ruddell, & H. Singer (Eds.), *Theoretical models and processes of reading* (4th ed., pp. 602–615). Newark, DE: International Reading Association.

Spiro, R.J., Feltovich, P.J., & Coulson, R.L. (1996). Two epistemic world views: Prefigurative schemas and learning in complex domains [Special issue on reasoning processes]. *Applied Cognitive Psychology, 10,* 51–61.

Spiro, R.J., Feltovich, P.J., Coulson, R.L., & Anderson, D.K. (1989). Multiple analogies for complex concepts: Antidotes for analogy-induced misconception in advanced knowledge acquisition. In S. Vosniadou & A. Ortony (Eds.), *Similarity and analogical reasoning* (pp. 498–531). Cambridge, UK: Cambridge University Press.

Spiro, R.J., Feltovich, P.J., Jacobson, M.J., & Coulson, R.L. (1992a). Cognitive flexibility, constructivism, and hypertext: Random access instruction for advanced knowledge acquisition in ill-structured domains. In T. Duffy & D. Jonassen (Eds.), *Constructivism and the technology of instruction* (pp. 57–75). Hillsdale, NJ: Erlbaum.

Spiro, R.J., Feltovich, P.J., Jacobson, M.J., & Coulson, R.L. (1992b). Knowledge representation, content specification, and the development of skill in situation-specific knowledge assembly: Some constructivist issues as they relate to cognitive flexibility theory and hypertext. In T. Duffy & D. Jonassen (Eds.), *Constructivism and the technology of instruction* (pp. 121–128). Hillsdale, NJ: Erlbaum.

Spiro, R.J., & Jehng, J.C. (1990). Cognitive flexibility and hypertext: Theory and technology for the nonlinear and multidimensional traversal of complex subject matter. In D. Nix & R.J. Spiro (Eds.), *Cognition, education, and multimedia: Exploring ideas in high technology* (pp. 163–205). Hillsdale, NJ: Erlbaum.

Spiro, R.J., & Myers, A. (1984). Individual differences and underlying cognitive processes in reading. In P.D. Pearson, R. Barr, M.L. Kamil, & P. Mosenthal (Eds.), *Handbook of reading research* (pp. 471–501). New York: Longman.

Spiro, R.J., Vispoel, W.L., Schmitz, J., Samarapungavan, A., & Boerger, A. (1987). Knowledge acquisition for application: Cognitive flexibility and transfer in complex content domains. In B.C. Britton & S. Glynn (Eds.), *Executive control processes in reading* (pp. 177–200). Hillsdale, NJ: Erlbaum.

25

Building Representations of Informational Text: Evidence From Children's Think-Aloud Protocols

Nathalie Coté and Susan R. Goldman

Research during the past decade has revealed a wide range of strategies used by adults and children to comprehend what they read. For example, researchers using think-aloud methods have demonstrated that adults and children who explain and elaborate what they are reading to themselves and who have a flexible approach to solving comprehension problems (i.e., use a variety of strategies) remember text and solve problems better than those who do not (e.g., Chi, deLeeuw, Chiu, & LaVancher, 1994; Goldman, Coté, & Saul, 1994; Goldman & Saul, 1990b; Graesser, Singer, & Trabasso, 1994; Trabasso & Magliano, 1996). In fact, Pressley and Afflerbach (1995) were able to compile an impressive catalog of the wide range of comprehension, monitoring, and evaluation processes that researchers have found in think-aloud protocols of reading, usually in studies of highly skilled adult readers. However, our knowledge of the range of activities that skilled readers may engage in does not yet allow us to understand exactly how readers, especially children, construct coherent representations online as they process text, or which activities are related to constructing different types of representations. This information is particularly lacking for expository text from which readers are to learn and acquire new information, that is, informational or instructional text (e.g., Goldman, 1996; Goldman, Varma, & Coté, 1996; Lorch, 1995).

In common with contemporary discourse theories (e.g., W. Kintsch, 1988; W. Kintsch & van Dijk, 1978; van Dijk & W. Kintsch, 1983), the research reported here is based on several assumptions about the processing involved in constructing cognitive representations of text: (a) information from text is processed sequentially; (b) information from the text and information retrieved from long-term working memory are operated on in working memory and then stored as parts of an evolving representation; (c) readers construct different levels of representation online, such as a propositional representation of the text content as well as a representation of the situation being described in the text; (d) relationships between two units of text information, or between information from the text and information received from long-term memory, can only be detected or generated if the pieces of information are active in working memory at the same time; and (e) the capacity of working memory is limited. (For further discussion of capacity limitations, see Goldman & Varma, 1995.)

It is well established that readers often do not construct coherent propositional or situational representations of text information. One reason for failures to detect or generate the connections necessary for coherent discourse representations is the unavailability of relevant information in working memory. In the process of reading a long text, keeping relevant information active in working memory often requires monitoring the coherence of the evolving representations and strategically using discourse and topic knowledge to identify relevant information in order to reinstate selectively previous text information, retrieve or reinstate information from long-term memory, or both (e.g., Ericsson & W. Kintsch, 1995; Fletcher, 1986; W. Kintsch, 1988; W. Kintsch & van Dijk, 1978).

Earlier work in our lab investigated several of these assumptions about the construction of coherent representations and failures to do so by assessing the reading behaviors and strategies of adult participants as they read difficult informational passages (Coté, Goldman, & Saul, 1993; Goldman & Saul, 1990b). By allowing readers to control the pace of their reading and the order in which they accessed the sentences of a text, Goldman and Saul (1990b) found differences both within and across adults in patterns of where and how much they chose to reread and in what order, indicating that the readers were very flexible in their backtracking or physical reinstatement of sentences. The adults seemed to be applying reading behaviors strategically. This research showed that characterizing readers' strategies based on their reading traces or patterns of movement through text predicted recall performance better than merely measuring the time adults spent processing the sentences. The high frequency with which Goldman and Saul's readers physically reinstated prior text led to a follow-up study to investigate adults' processing more directly by using a think-aloud methodology in conjunction with reading trace information (Goldman & Saul, 1990b, Experiment 3). The adults' verbalizations verified that their patterns of reading and reinstatement behavior were strategic and related to failures to establish local and global coherence as they constructed their mental representations of the text.

The research that we report in this piece is part of a larger study extending our previous work to children. The issue of interest in the present context is how children attempt to generate and update coherent representations of the central concepts and relationships in instructional text. The relationships between children's reading behaviors, their difficulties in establishing and maintaining coherent conceptual understanding, and their choice of strategies were studies using think-aloud protocol methodology and a presentation format that allowed readers to control the pace and direction of their reading behaviors (Goldman & Saul, 1990a). In this piece, we focus our discussion on the cognitive activities occurring during the online processing of the texts.

Think-Aloud Protocol Methodology

The participants were 16 elementary schoolchildren in the sixth grade (ages 11 to 13) who were recruited to participate individually in two reading sessions. The children had the option of refusing to participate, although none did. As part of a larger study, the children whose data are discussed in the current piece read four passages that contained material new to them. Two were on the more-familiar topics of fat and sugar and two were on the less-familiar topics of metabolism and hybrids. Students read two of the texts (on a more-familiar topic and a less-familiar topic) midway through the school year and then read another two texts (on a more-familiar topic and a less-familiar topic) at the end of the school year. At each time point (midyear and end of year), the children began by reading a short training text to practice think-aloud and recall task procedures.

The data reported here focus on the children's processing of the two less-familiar texts, Metabolism and Hybrids (see Appendixes A and B), because these texts are the most revealing of the problems and processes involved in children's construction of a coherent representation. Also, it is commonly accepted that think-aloud protocols provide a more accurate picture of processing when the text being read is not so easy that reading activities are automatic and inaccessible to verbalization (Chi et al., 1994; Ericsson & Simon, 1984/1993; Trabasso, Suh, Payton, & Jain, 1995). Note that the texts were not unreasonably difficult; they were similar to material that children might encounter in school.

The texts were each presented on a computer screen in a format that exposed only one sentence at a time with the words of the other sentences masked. Information such as punctuation and paragraph indentation was not masked (Goldman & Saul, 1990a). This format allowed the students to read and reread sentences in any order for as long as they liked, leaving a computer record of their patterns of reading. The children were asked to verbalize what they were thinking as they tried to understand the passage, what they were doing to understand the passage, what they found easy or hard, and to describe any problems they had and what they were doing about them. The sessions were videotaped.

The students were instructed to read each passage in order to dictate a report on what they read for their peers, a form of recall task. After reading each passage, they dictated a report that the experimenter typed on the computer.

Analyses and Results

The analyses of the children's efforts to build representations for the passages are based on transcripts of the videotapes of the students' verbalizations as well as the computer-recorded trace of their movement through the text. Ambiguities in the transcripts were resolved by consulting the actual videotapes.

Text Analysis

To provide a context for the analysis of the children's processing, it is informative to characterize the passages that they read. The Metabolism text is about factors that affect metabolism or metabolic rate (see Appendix A, page 682). The text gives some explicit information about metabolic rate in separate paragraphs about food, climate, activity, and genetic inheritance. However, to establish a coherent understanding of how metabolic rate is related to energy sources and energy requirements, the reader must integrate information from several text paragraphs as well as from general knowledge about the body. Readers who do not already know very much about the topic of metabolism are heavily dependent on the information explicitly available in the text for making the inferences and connections necessary for a coherent representation. Thus, we expected to find frequent reinstatement of information from the text and from long-term memory in the processing of children who attempted to construct a coherent representation of this text.

The second text was about hybrids and was titled "Improving Mother Nature" (see Appendix B, page 683). Whereas the Metabolism passage implicitly expressed, and thus required readers to infer, a complex relationship among a concept and the factors affecting it, the Hybrids text did not. Rather, the Hybrids passage contains a number of situations and examples of hybrids and how they are helpful. From these examples, readers (who in this case had little knowledge of the topic) must construct an understanding of the central concept, a hybrid. Most of the children found the central concepts of both of these texts to be new and relatively difficult to understand.

In this piece, we report several aspects of our analyses of the think-aloud protocols to address the issue of what students do as they attempt to build representations of instructional texts. The think-aloud protocols were coded for number and type of events. Consistent with Coté, Goldman, and Saul (1998), an event was defined as a comment or set of comments on the same core sentence or group of sentences, as well as the reading behavior associated with those comments. Events can vary in length, ranging from a short utterance focused on one text sentence to several statements and some rereading behavior focused on the sentences of an entire paragraph. We categorized the events in terms of the types of reasoning that they reflected, as described in the next section. We also determined whether the reasoning on a particular focal sentence reflected use of information provided elsewhere in the text or in the student's comments given earlier in the think-aloud protocol.

Types of Events in the Think-Aloud Protocols

The categorical coding and analyses are of interest in terms of the kinds of comprehension and reasoning strategies and processes that they reveal.

Self-Explanations. Coded in this category were statements that elaborated on the focal sentence, interpretations of it in the student's own language, inferences, or implications of the text information, examples, analogies, cause–effect statements, or questions about cause–effect. This kind of reasoning reveals students' efforts to create coherence within the text and with their prior knowledge by using logical relationships and content-relevant knowledge to build causal structures, draw out of the implications of the information in focal sentences, make comparisons and contrasts with what they believe about the world, and so forth. Information in these protocol events came from prior knowledge, elsewhere in the text, or from the focal sentence.

Monitoring. Statements in this category confirmed comprehension (e.g., *I get it*), detected failures to understand (e.g., *I do not get it*), marked new knowledge (e.g., *I didn't know that*), or detected information inconsistent with known information or information that had been presented elsewhere in the text. Monitoring statements indicate evaluations of comprehension in that students are comparing their sense of understanding to some internal criterion of satisfactory meaning or coherence.

Evaluation statements form a subset of the monitoring category. They are similar to the first group of monitoring statements in that they reflect some evaluation of the text. Statements of this type commented on the organization of information in the passage (e.g., *That sentence belongs up there*), indicated affected responses (e.g., *That seems strange*), or suggested information that was missing from the text (e.g., *They should put in < >*).

Paraphrases. Protocol events were placed in this category if students merely reorganized the words in the sentence, repeated a phrase or clause, or substituted synonyms but otherwise preserved the text language. Trabasso et al. (1995) indicated that a primary function of paraphrases is to maintain information in working memory. The repeated processing of the meaning, perhaps with conversion into more familiar vocabulary, not only strengthens the memory trace through repetition but also may make it more likely that the new information is connected to prior knowledge.

Predictions. These were statements that indicated what students expected to find in the next part of the text. In the context of story comprehension, predictions are referred to as forward inferences and have been shown to occur only under constrained circumstances (van den Broek, 1990, 1994). If they are confirmed, predictions are a mechanism for creating coherent connections. In general, due to a greater degree of uncertainty about the content and structure of expository texts, it is often the case that students are not very successful in predicting the information that will come next. In the context of the present study, predictions were infrequent, general, and only rarely confirmed. When they did occur, they were in response to the titles or to the topic sentences in the Metabolism and Hybrid passages. For example, the topic sentence *There are several factors that affect metabolic rate* sometimes led to a general prediction (e.g., "'They' (the text) will go on to tell what those factors are") but rarely led to predictions of the specific content or identity of those factors.

Associations. In this category were statements of connections that seemed to have little bearing on the text (e.g., *I love carrots* when the word *carrots* appeared in the text). These events do not further understanding of the focal sentence but do provide a link between the focal sentence and some aspect of prior experience, albeit unrelated to the passage context.

The distributions of these five types of protocol events are presented in Table 1. Self-explanation and monitoring/evaluation accounted for the majority of the protocol events. The most frequent and universally used source of information for self-explanations was prior knowledge. The focal sentence was the focus of the self-explanation more often in the Hybrids than in the Metabolism passage. In the latter, other parts of the texts were brought in more frequently in the self-explanations. Of the Monitoring statements, 16% for Metabolism and 33% for Hybrids were evaluative statements, primarily affective responses such as "That seems strange." Prediction, paraphrase, and association events were less frequent and tended to be localized in the protocols of smaller subsets of the children. Analyses of the correlations among the proportions of each type of protocol event for each passage showed few statistically reliable relationships. The only

TABLE 1
Mean Proportion of Protocol Events Observed in Think-Aloud Protocols

Category	Metabolism	Hybrids
Mean Total Events Per Protocol	26.13	25.13
Self-Explanations	.41	.48
Monitoring/Evaluation	.44	.38
Predictions	.04	.07
Paraphrases	.10	.05
Associations	.03	.02

meaningful exception was that for both passages, there was a strong negative correlation between self-explanations and monitoring/evaluation events ($r = -.77$, $p < .01$ for Metabolism and $r = -.68$, $p < .05$ for Hybrids).

Reinstatement of Information

The analysis of types of protocol events was intended to capture the children's reasoning and comprehension strategies as they constructed a representation of the text. In a second analysis, we were interested in the degree to which children were making connections among elements in the text and between text elements and prior knowledge. To address this question, we examined the occurrence of reinstatements, which bring into working memory either previously processed text or knowledge elements previously retrieved or generated by the student. Because reinstatements bring elements into working memory contemporaneously, they enable connections that would not be possible otherwise. Using the children's verbalizations as well as the computer record of their patterns of sentence accessing, we categorized reinstatements into three types according to the source of the reinstated information.

Physical Reinstatements. Because the computer presentation allowed us to record the order in which students accessed and read the sentences in the passage, we were able to distinguish between prior text that was physically reinstated as compared with mental reinstatement from memory without reexposing the text information. Consistent with findings in our previous work with adults and children (e.g., Coté et al., 1998; Goldman & Saul, 1990b; Saul, Coté, & Goldman, 1993), the reading traces showed that many of the children spontaneously and selectively reinstated previously read sentences by reexposing them physically. As the data in Table 2 show, in processing the Hybrids text, 50% of the children physically reinstated sentences they had read earlier. In processing the Metabolism text, 37.5% of the children physically reinstated text information.

Mental Reinstatements. In addition to the physical reinstatements, there was evidence in the think-aloud protocols of two types of mental reinstatements. Mental–Text were reinstatements where the reader mentioned information previously presented in the text without physically uncovering the sentence. Mental–Student Generated were reinstatements of information known prior to reading the text, that is, prior knowledge of concepts and ideas related to the text information that the reader had verbalized on earlier focal sentences. When such reinstatements of text or student-generated information from memory are considered in addition to the physical reinstatements, the data in Table 2 show that almost all the children (100% on Metabolism, 87.5% on Hybrids) engaged in at least one instance of reinstatement as they read.

Table 2 also shows the mean number of reinstatements of each type. In both passages, the most frequent type of reinstatement was of information previously

TABLE 2
TABLE 2
Occurrence and Sources of Reinstatements of Information

Type of Information Reinstated	Metabolism		Hybrids	
	% Students[a]	Mean # Reinsts.	% Students[a]	Mean # Reinsts.
Physical–Text	37.50%	1.44	50%	1.63
Mental–Text	100%	3.69	75%	2.44
Mental–Student Generated				
From Prior Knowledge	68.75%	2.06	75%	1.56
(No Reinstatements)	(0%)		(12.5%)	

[a] Percent who reinstated at least once, out of 16 students.

provided in the text. In the Hybrids passage, reinstatements of information students had generated from prior knowledge and physical requirements occurred equally often, but in the Metabolism text, reinstatements of prior knowledge tended to occur more often than physical reinstatements of text information. In addition, somewhat more reinstatements occurred during the processing of the Metabolism passage ($M = 7.19$, $SD = 5.86$) than of the Hybrids passage ($M = 5.63$, $SD = 4.86$), although the variance among the readers was high and a paired t test indicated that the difference between the means was not reliable, $t < 1$. The moderately higher total number of reinstatements in the Metabolism as compared to the Hybrids text indicates that children tried to make more connections among the units of information in the former. We speculate that these data reflect the previously mentioned semantic and structural differences between the texts and suggest that the children were sensitive to them.

Relationships Between Protocol Events and Reinstatements

The process model we described earlier posits that reinstatements are related to attempts to make the connections necessary for constructing a coherent representation of text. As noted in the introduction, these connections may be among text elements themselves or between text elements and elements of prior knowledge. In examining the relationships between reinstatements and the difficult types of protocol events, we expected to find that children who often engaged in self-explanations were strategically reinstating information in their attempts to construct a coherent representation. Reinstatements were not expected to occur as often in the context of other types of protocol events such as monitoring/evaluation, association, or paraphrasing, which seemed to be tied more closely to processing single sentences.

These expectations were supported by positive (although not statistically reliable) correlations between total number of reinstatements and the proportion of protocol events coded as self-explanations ($r = .48$, $p < .07$ for Metabolism and $r = .32$, $p < .25$ for Hybrids). Also, the relationships between total reinstatements and the other types of protocol events were negative or near zero for both passages. A closer look at the relationship between reinstatements and self-explanations revealed a strong and reliable positive correlation between self-explanations and the subtype of reinstatements in which students mentally reinstated information that they had brought in earlier from prior knowledge ($r = .58$, $p < .05$ for Metabolism and $r = .50$, $p < .05$ for Hybrids). The correlations of prior knowledge reinstatement and self-explanations suggest that students were making sense of new information with respect to known information and were creating representations integrated with prior knowledge.

This pattern of correlations suggests that individuals might be differentiated on the basis of their active, constructive efforts after meaning (Bartlett, 1932; Scardamalia & Bereiter, 1991). We pursued this possibility by taking a more holistic approach to the protocols to capture individual differences in the students' general approach to processing each text.

General Approaches to Processing

The pattern of correlations between reinstatements and protocol events suggested that it would be fruitful to examine individual protocols to gain further understanding of the dynamic interplay of the various processing activities and students' attempts to establish coherent representations. Indeed, when we looked at individuals' protocols for a particular passage, it was clear that there were qualitative and emergent properties that were not captured by the correlations over the whole sample. These properties seemed to reflect differences in responding to difficulty establishing coherence, the types of events that co-occurred, the frequency of reinstatements and types of information reinstated, and how much of the passage was involved in a particular event. For example, some students adopted an approach of bringing in prior knowledge to self-explain individual sentences, whereas others made inferences connecting multiple sentences in their self-explanations. Such distinctions are not reflected in the previous correlations and frequency analyses.

To capture the nature of an individual student's processing activities over the whole passage, we developed a set of four categories. The first two categories, as compared to the third, reflect distinctions drawn by Bereiter and Scardamalia (1989) between reasoning that intentionally enhances understanding versus processing that "retells" the presented information.

Successful Knowledge-Building. Students who engaged in this type of processing put a lot of effort into their attempts to construct a coherent model of the central concepts and relations by engaging in a range of activities such as cause–effect explanations, elaborations, and cross-text integrative inferences that identified the macrostructure of the text.

Less-Successful Knowledge-Building. These students also made an effort to understand the central concepts and relations expressed by the text, but their monitoring comments and requests for information indicated that they were less successful in constructing a coherent representation. Frequently, their self-explanations involved questions they wanted the text to answer but that it did not.

Text-Focused Processing. Students who engaged in text-focused processing demonstrated varying degrees of effort through paraphrasing, interpreting, questioning, bringing in examples, making affective evaluative comments, or monitoring, but their activities were primarily in reaction to single sentences rather than attempts to construct a global understanding of the text meaning.

Minimalists. These students gave verbalizations on approximately half or fewer of the text's sentences, resulting in protocols too poor to support a reliable analysis of their processing. For three of the five children in this category, the few comments that they made indicated that understanding the text presented few problems for them and was largely automatic, perhaps because they were familiar with the context. Two others appeared to be rushed and unmotivated, possibly because they read the text in the last days of the school year.

The authors each sorted all 32 of the children's protocols and initially agreed on over 80% of the categorizations. Disagreements were resolved in discussion. The sorting was done holistically; that is, the authors did not categorize a protocol based on a "count" of types of events or reinstatements. Rather, each transcript was read in its entirety to determine the approach to processing reflected by the constellation and pattern of cognitive activities. The numbers of students in each category on each of the passages is provided in Table 3.[1] The

TABLE 3
Number of Children in Each General Approach Protocol Category for Each Text[a]

Category	Metabolism	Hybrids
Successful Knowledge-Builder	4	2
Less-Successful Knowledge-Builder	3	3
Text-Focused Processor	6	8
Minimalist	3	3

[a] Both texts were read by all 16 children. Note that these categories apply to individuals in interaction with particular texts. Eight of the 16 students were in the same category for both texts.

protocols of 8 of the 16 students fell into the same general approach category on both passages. Generally speaking, more evidence of knowledge-building was found in the Metabolism protocols as compared to the Hybrids protocols. Of the 7 students who engaged in knowledge-building (more or less successfully) while reading Metabolism, 4 also took a knowledge-building approach to Hybrids. The other 3 adopted text-focused approach when they read Hybrids. One student engaged in a text-focused processing on Metabolism but was categorized as a Less-Successful Knowledge-Builder on Hybrids. The remaining students were either categorized as Text-Focused Processors or Minimalists on both passages or moved between those two categories.

To verify that our holistic classification of the children's attempts to construct coherent representations of the texts was related to their strategic reinstatement of information and their attempts to explain the text to themselves, we looked at the distribution of protocol measures for the children in each of the general processing approach categories (see Tables 4 and 5). In both passages,

TABLE 4
Means (and Standard Deviations) of Protocol-Based Measures for Each General Approach Category for Metabolism Text

Category	Total Reinstatements	Self-Explan.	Monitor/ Evaluate	Paraphrase
Successful Knowledge-Builder ($n = 4$)	12.25 (8.54)	20.00 (9.35)	8.75 (2.99)	1.00 (.82)
Less-Successful Knowledge-Builder ($n = 3$)	9.00 (5.00)	15.67 (6.81)	9.33 (4.73)	4.33 (3.51)
Text-Focused Processor ($n = 6$)	5.33 (2.88)	8.17 (4.45)	13.83 (7.08)	4.50 (5.86)
Minimalist ($n = 3$)	2.33 (.58)	2.67 (2.08)	7.33 (2.52)	.67 (1.15)

TABLE 5
Means (and Standard Deviations) of Protocol-Based Measures for Each General Approach Category for Hybrids Text

Category	Total Reinstatements	Self-Explan.	Monitor/ Evaluate	Paraphrase
Successful Knowledge-Builder ($n = 2$)	20.50 (3.54)	11.00 (2.83)	0.00	6.00 (4.24)
Less-Successful Knowledge-Builder ($n = 3$)	20.00 (2.65)	13.00 (6.25)	2.33 (1.53)	13.33 (4.93)
Text-Focused Processor ($n = 8$)	11.38 (4.00)	8.25 (5.06)	1.00 (1.85)	4.50 (1.77)
Minimalist ($n = 3$)	3.67 (2.89)	6.00 (2.65)	.33 (.58)	.67 (1.15)

self-explanation events and total number of reinstatements occurred more frequently among the children who took a knowledge-building approach to reading the texts. In contrast, monitoring/evaluation and paraphrase events have more inverted U-shaped distributions across the general approach categories. We followed up with correlation analyses.[2] For both the Hybrids text ($r = .58, p < .05$) and the Metabolism text ($r = .63, p < .01$), the correlations between the children's total number of reinstatements and the level of general processing approach evident in their protocols were positive and statistically reliable. Also, in both texts there was a positive relationship between the children's general processing approach levels and the proportion of their protocol events that were coded as self-explanation ($r = .71, p < .01$ for Metabolism and $r = .53, p < .05$ for Hybrids). A regression model with number of reinstatements and proportion of self-explanation as predictors of general processing approach level showed that the two variables, although intercorrelated, were independent and each was a strong predictor of the children's protocol category for both texts.

The patterns evident in Tables 4 and 5 and in the correlation analyses support the interpretation that the more "knowledge-building-like" children's general approach to constructing a representation of the text, the more likely they were to engage in frequent reinstatement and self-explanation. These reinstatements and self-explanations were often in the service of cognitive activities such as cause–effect reasoning, elaborating with prior knowledge or personal experiences, generating and testing hypotheses, requesting information, and interpreting sentences.

The data presented thus far reflect the types of things children did and, to some degree, the contexts in which they did them as they attempted to build coherent representations of the passages. However, the texture of the thinking and reasoning children were doing and the interplay between the text information and prior knowledge can only be fully appreciated by examining some of the individual think-aloud protocols. In the next section, we present excerpts from the protocols of three children who took different processing approaches: Successful Knowledge-Building, Less-Successful Knowledge-Building, and Text-Focused Processing.

Think-Aloud Protocols Illustrative of Differences in Online Processing

Student 3, Successful Knowledge-Building

Student 3 engaged in Successful Knowledge-Building in her reading of both texts. While reading Metabolism, for example, her protocol shows that she was determined to construct a coherent situational representation of the concepts and relationships presented in the text. She was very persistent, using strategies such as rereading the focal sentence, backtracking to reread previous sentences, making casual inferences, and elaborating the text with examples from prior knowledge until she was satisfied enough with her understanding of the relationship between each factor, energy, and metabolic rate to go to the next paragraph. In the process of reading Metabolism, she physically reinstated sentences she had already read 11 times, reinstated text information from memory 5 times, and reinstated student-generated information, such as concepts she earlier had brought in from prior knowledge, 9 times.

Table 6 contains excerpts from Student 3's Metabolism protocol. This excerpt shows her verbalizations as she read the first three paragraphs of the text. Note that at the very beginning she read the title and checked against her prior knowledge, commenting that she knew nothing about metabolism. Line 4 in the passage gives a definition of metabolism, which she recognized and used as the basis for an inference that updated her understanding of the situation being described in the first few sentences. The child continued in this vein over the next few sentences, making connections among sentences and bringing in examples and inferences based on her general knowledge of when energy is required.

The next paragraph discusses the first factor that affects metabolic rate—food. Here the child engaged in extended effort after meaning that ranged far beyond the information that was explicitly in the text. She used words from the text, like *food* and *carbohydrates*, to activate some information she had learned the day before. She appeared to be using the information to update her evolving representation, as she realized that some of it might not be relevant to her understanding of the current text, but some of it was. As she said after reading lines 9 and 10 a few times, "Like I just said, if you eat Coke or something, it'll make you a little more hyper or something. Have a higher metabolic rate." We interpreted this statement as indicating that she understood that different foods have a different relationship with energy and metabolism. However, she apparently had a little trouble establishing a coherent understanding of the last two sentences in the paragraph. As she reinstated the information in them she made causal inferences until finally she was satisfied that she understood, and she went on to the next paragraph.

Student 2, Less-Successful Knowledge-Building

Like Student 3, Student 2 also tried hard to construct a coherent understanding of Metabolism and Hybrids. As he read Hybrids, for example, he physically reinstated sentences he had already read 11 times, reinstated text information from memory 5 times, and reinstated student-generated information 3 times. However, this student met with less success than Student 3. As he tried to construct an understanding of the central concept of hybrid, which is crucial to building a coherent representation of the text information, he generated and abandoned a number of hypotheses. He also at several points in the text appeared to be aware of gaps in his representation, as he asked questions looking for more information and he noted several vocabulary problems.

TABLE 6
Excerpt From Think-Aloud Protocol of Student 3 Reading Metabolism

(Student's comments are in boldface.)

1 Metabolism. **I don't know anything about Metabolism.**

2 Customers in many pharmacies may soon be seeing the latest in new devices for the health con. . . sish . . ious [conscious]. **Con. . . I don't know that word. Con. . .sish. . .ious. Con. . . I don't know.**

3 A sports physiologist is developing a Tab O Meter [metabometer], a device that he hopes will measure the human body's ability to produce energy efficiently. **OK.**

2 [rereads] **OK.**

3 **So the new device is the sports. . . . Metab -O- Meter.**

4 The rate at which the body produces energy is called metabolism. **Ohh-K. So that's why. So he's going to make an invention that'll hopefully measure how much your body produces energy. OK.**

5 Different people have different metabolic rates that indicate how easily they can produce energy. **OK. That's sort of describing this sentence.** [returns to 4 briefly and then back to 5] **Different people. . . . Ur. . .Helping it more. Not describing.**

6 The same person may have different metabolic rates depending on the circumstances. **The same person. . .OK. So if they're like in a game or something, they may have a higher metabolic rate, and if they're just sitting on a couch watching TV, they might not have as high cause they're not using as much energy.**

7 Different species of animals also have different metabolic rates. **OK. So animals are different from humans, and I am thinking right now that the animals are going to have a little bit maybe higher metabolic rate, cause humans don't always have to run around watching out for predators.**

8 There are several factors that affect the metabolic rate. **OK.**

9 One factor is the type of food a person or animal eats. **OK. So like yesterday when we were talking about Coke, and it gives you sugar and energy** [referring to Sugar text]. **Coke would give you more. . . higher metabolic rate than like a vegetable without sugar or something. I'm not going to say anything, because, like name a certain vegetable, because I didn't know apples had sugar** [referring to Sugar text].

10 For example, some foods are hard to digest, such as complex carbohydrates like rice. **Ooohh. . . Processed sugar and carbohydrates** [referring to Sugar text]. **Processed sugar and rice are both carbohydrates, but that doesn't have anything to do. . . . OK.**

9 [rereads 9, 10, 9, 8, back to 9] **OK. the type of food a person eats. Like I just said,**

10 **if you eat Coke or something, it'll make you a little more hyper or something,**

11 **have a higher metabolic rate.** The body has to work harder to get energy from rice.

10 Some foods are hard to digest. **The body has to work hard to digest rice.**

11 Work harder to get energy. **Probably has to work harder because it's harder to digest.**

12 If a person ate a steady diet of rice, the result would be a higher metabolic rate. If a person ate a steady diet of rice, the result would be a higher metabolic rate.

11 **If they ate. . . The body has to work harder.**

12 **They would get a higher metabolic rate. Because the body is working up more energy maybe.**

11 **Because** the body has to work harder to get energy from rice.

12 If a person ate a steady diet of rice, the result would be a higher metabolic. . . . **But. . . OK. I don't really understand that. If the body has to work harder to get the energy. . . .** If a person ate a steady diet of rice, the result would be a higher metabolic rate.

11 **I'm thinking that maybe if the body has to work harder to get the energy from rice, if they kept eating it, the body might get used to having to work to get the energy.**

[continues reading]

The excerpts in Table 7 show places in the text where Student 2 found information that he used to figure out what a hybrid is. His problems were evident early on in his response to line 4, which defines a hybrid. He said, "I don't get that sentence either. I didn't get this whole paragraph. I don't get this sentence. At all. I don't know what a hybrid is. That's why. It didn't tell you what it is." The next few sentences also contain the word *hybrid* and he repeated that he was still having trouble understanding what it means.

When he reached lines 7 and 8 he generated a hypothesis: "I think a hybrid is something in a plant or a plant...I don't know what. Or something you can eat. It says it adds vitamins." However, subsequent sentences do not bear out this hypothesis, and so later, on line 17, he generated another one: "I think that hybrid is something in a plant that helps it grow and grow faster or something and makes it like stronger roots in a plant or something. I think that's a hybrid." But then he read on and again found information that challenged his hypothesis. Although this child tried very hard to generate and test hypotheses to construct a coherent understanding of the main concept in the text, the window onto his processing provided by his verbal protocol suggests that he did not succeed. Although he tried, failing to understand the central concept made it very unlikely that he was able to generate a coherent representation.

Student 15, Text-Focused Processing

The knowledge-building approach taken by Students 3 and 2, even though they varied in how successful they seemed to be at building a coherent representation, can be contrasted with the text-focused processing of Student 15. This child had a standardized reading comprehension score slightly higher than Student 2, a less-successful knowledge-builder. In the sample as a whole, the standardized reading scores did not predict the children's general approach to reading as identified by their protocol category ($r = .25$, $p > .05$ for Metabolism; $r = .15$, $p > .05$ for Hybrids), as illustrated by the differences between Students 2 and 15.

Student 15 read straight through the sentences sequentially, with no physical reinstatements of prior sentences, only 2 reinstatements of text information from memory, and 3 reinstatements of student-generated information. Table 8 provides excerpts from Student 15's protocol. His verbalizations were short, and most of them were focused on the sentence level. For example, in response to line 3, he pointed to several words and said, "I don't understand that word [*genetically*], that word [*altered*], that word [*era*], and that word [*ushered*]" but he made no further attempt to address the problems. He paraphrased or interpreted several sentences; for example, his response to line 5 was "They mixed up broccoli and cauliflower." These brief comments continued throughout, with little evidence that the child was making connections among text segments or trying to construct, monitor, and update a coherent situational representation of the text.

(Student's comments are in boldface.)

1   Improving Mother Nature. **I think it's going to talk about how they keep the forest clean. No littering or something. And take care of animals and don't pollute and all that.**

2   Produce department and garden shops are brimming with odd new . . . **let's see. . .what's that?. . . I don't know that word.** . . hybrids. . . of some familiar fruits and vegetables. **I'm thinking . . . . what . . . ? . . .What has that got to do with**

1   Mother Nature?

2   **It's talking about the shops and all that.**

3   This year the first genetical. . . genetically. . . . **what's that? . . . I dunno that**. . . . altered tomato went on the market. . . and. . .**what's that**. . . ushered?. . . **I dunno that**. . . in a new area [era]. . . **I don't know that one.** This era in growing crops for food. **I don't know some words in here. I still don't know what's. . .this don't make sense with this.** [returns to title]

3   **I think this should not. . .this should make another title or something because this. . .this sentence right here . . . I don't think goes with this.** [returns to title].

3   **This is talking about markets and foods, and this**

1   **is just Mother Nature.** [returns to 3]

4   A hybrid refers to a plant or animal that has been created by crossing two different plants. **I don't get this sentence either. I didn't get this whole paragraph.** [points to first paragraph] **I don't get this sentence. At all. I don't know what a hybrid is. That's why. It didn't tell you what it is.** [reads a few more sentences]

7   Hybrids are helpful for several reasons. **I'm thinking like. . .like. . .I still don't know what hybrids is. That's why I don't know. . . .**

8   For one thing, plants can be altered so that the hybrid has more vitamins than the original plant did. **I think a hybrid is some sort of plant of some. . . I think it's like, uh, something in a plant or a plant. . . I don't know what. Or something you can eat. It says it adds vitamins. Than the original plant did.**

9   Or if the original plant is high in some un. .de. .sirable substance such as fat or sugar, the amount may be reduced in the hybrid. **Wait a second. I think. . .I don't get this sentence. Well, because it doesn't make sense because it's talking about. . .see it says. . .uh. . .let's see. . .** [clicks on 8 and returns to 9] **I get it. . . Why they. . . I. . .See. . . I don't know. I don't get this. Because they just talk about plants, and the thing about sugar. . .and they have sugar. Why'd they tell us that for?**

10   This type of hybrid is helpful for people who may only have access to a small amount of food such as the people living on a sub. . . submarine. . . Is that submarine? **See. . . wait. . .I'm thinking like. . .I think. . .I think that a hybrid is like some sort of vitamin or something. And it keeps you healthy and if you don't get a lot amount of food, you eat 'em or something. I think that's what they're talking about.**

11   Another reason that hybrids are helpful is that they make a plant stronger and better able to resist environmental threats such as insects or frost. **Now I don't know, because it says hybrids are helpful to make the plant stronger. And to protect. . .See—it says. . now it says uh. . .uh. . . that it can resist. . .it can make plants resist threats such as insects or frost. And I thought it was a vitamin or something. Now I don't know what it is. Because first I thought it was a vitamin because it said all that stuff about it being vitamins. . . had vitamins and all that. Now. . .now it says it can plants resist insects and frost. So I don't know what it is now.** [reads a few more sentences]

17   Finally, hybrids may change the appearance of a plant in some way, perhaps making it easier to grow. **I think hybrid is something in a plant that helps it grow and grow faster and makes it like stronger roots in a plant or something. I think that's a hybrid.** [continues reading]

TABLE 8
Excerpt From Think-Aloud Protocol of Student 15 Reading Hybrids

(Student's comments are in boldface.)
1   Improving Mother Nature. **It's gonna talk about how you can help the world.**
2   Produce departments and garden shops are brimming with odd new hybrids of some familiar fruits and vegetables. **This new hybrids...**
3   This year the first gen...genet...genetically altered...altered tomato went to the market and un... ushered in a new era in growing crops for food. **I don't understand that word** [genetically], **that word** [altered], **and that word** [era] **and that word** [ushered].
4   A hybrid refers to a plant or animal that has been created by crossing two different plants. [experimenter gives neutral prompt] **Like, cross breeding.**
5   For example, the broccoflower is a hybrid of broccoli and cauliflower. **They mixed up broccoli and cauliflower.**
6   Hybrids such as the broccoflower are being created by scientists through a process known as genetic engineering. **It don't make sense...to me.**
7   Hybrids are helpful for several reasons. **They'll tell the reasons what they are.**
[continues reading]

Our quantitative and qualitative analyses of the strategies and reasoning processes used to build coherent representations of instructional text reveal that rather than restricting themselves to a very narrow range of operations, most students are quite flexible in how they use text information and their existing knowledge as they proceed through an informational text. However, when reading material of this type, readers (and especially children) are often in knowledge-lean situations (Coté et al., 1998) and limited in the kind of inferences they can make. The representational coherence that results from the use of strategies such as self-explaining, including cause–effect reasoning and reasoning by analogy, is constrained by both the topic and discourse knowledge the reader brings to the task and by the content and structure of the passage. For example, the self-explanations in the Metabolism and Hybrids passages differed, with those in the Hybrids passage more frequently restricted to thinking just about the focal sentence. This may have been a reflection of the passage differences in that the Hybrids text deals with relatively encapsulated examples of how hybrids are helpful, whereas the Metabolism text deals throughout with relationships among energy needs and energy sources. As well, twice as many self-explanation questions occurred in the Hybrids (31%) as compared to the Metabolism (16%) passage, which reflected students' desires to better understand the reasons why hybrids are helpful. Because instructional texts such as the ones examined here may be structured in a variety of ways (cf. Beck & McKeown, 1992; Britton, 1994; Meyer, 1985), readers need to be sensitive to such differences and appropriately adapt their strategies for achieving coherent representations.

Conclusions and Discussion

Although researchers have identified many strategies in which readers engage, identifying them is not enough; we need to know about relationships between strategies and online processes of representation construction. In the research reported here, reading traces and think-aloud protocols of reading showed a wide range in the approaches of elementary students to reading difficult information-al text. The strategies and meaning construction efforts we have reported are similar to those found when children process story texts (cf. Trabasso et al., 1995). However, the dominant mode of explanation appropriate to understanding stories is causal inferencing; here, prior knowledge limitations and a greater variety of expository content structures constrain the success of efforts to understand not only underlying causal mechanisms but also other types of relationships among concepts in instructional texts.

Indeed, children often find themselves reading in areas where they know little about the topic and where the discourse structure is unfamiliar. One strategic adaptation to this situation is to devote processing resources to the information in the text and relevant prior knowledge for purposes of creating connections among seemingly disparate pieces of information (cf. Chi et al., 1994). Our knowledge-builders provide examples of this type of approach. In about a third of the students, the pattern of online processes seemed to be aimed at knowledge-building, where students often reinstated information, both physically and mentally, as they carried out a variety of processing strategies. These students did not always succeed in constructing a coherent situational representation, but they exhibited a wide range of strategies in their attempts. For example, they made relevant connections to examples from their prior knowledge, generated and checked hypotheses, made inferences to interpret the text and create new knowledge, monitored the mapping between text information and their existing knowledge, monitored the coherence of their evolving representations, and persisted in their attempts to resolve difficulties. These students appeared to be attempting to construct rich situation models for the material. Situation models for expository material reflect the underlying structure of the content domain and are important for performance on reasoning and problem-solving tasks (cf. McNamara, E. Kintsch, Songer, & W. Kintsch, 1996; van Dijk & W. Kintsch, 1983; Zwaan & Brown, 1996). In the two-dimensional framework discussed by Coté et al. (1998), the representations of the successful knowledge-builders would be placed high on the dimension of integration with prior knowledge as well as high on the dimension of textbase quality.

Another adaptation to coping with a text presenting new information on an unfamiliar topic, especially when the purpose for reading is to provide a report from memory, is to focus on the text and create as strong a "veridical" trace as possible. Our text-focused processors took this approach. They tended to direct their processing resources to achieving local understanding of the focal sentence by paraphrasing and bringing in examples or associations from prior knowledge and to monitoring comprehension problems, although they did not persist in attempts to resolve them. They did not attempt to create a coherent, interconnected representation of the underlying message of the text. The pattern of processing strategies in text-focused processing was related to a low level of reinstatement activity. About half the students were classified as engaging in this type of processing. Text-focused processing can produce a reasonably solid textbase, that is, a representation of the information explicitly presented in the text. There are many tasks for which a strong textbase is all that is needed for good performance (e.g., E. Kintsch, 1990; McNamara et al., 1996; Zwaan & Brown, 1996). Thus, as an adaptation to difficult and new material, the strategy of focusing on the text per se can produce a representation that allows adequate performance on at least some tasks. In the two-dimensional framework discussed by Coté et al. (1998), the representations of the text-focused processors might be placed high on the dimension of textbase quality, like those of the successful knowledge-builders. However, their representations would place low on the dimension of integration with prior knowledge.

The children's think-aloud protocols revealed some interesting aspects of monitoring, a skill that is often cited as very important to good comprehension (e.g., Baker & Brown, 1984). Our data indicate that although monitoring is important, unless readers actively apply strategies to resolve the problems they identify, they are likely to end up with fragmentary representations. For example, some students showed evidence of comprehension monitoring by pointing out words they did not know, but their protocols showed no evidence of a strategic response such as attempting to understand the words from the context. In contrast, the students who engaged in knowledge-building often attempted to resolve difficulties by selectively reinstating information and engaging in various strategic activities like rereading and hypothesis checking. In related work (Coté et al., 1998), we reported positive correlations between problem *resolution* and comprehension, with the strongest correlations occurring in more difficult passages, but no correlation between problem *identification* and comprehension. In the process of constructing a coherent representation of a text, readers must not only be aware of gaps and problems in their understanding, but must also bring to bear strategies to resolve the problems in order to build coherent representations.

In accord with several recent publications on think-aloud protocols and comprehension strategies (e.g., Chi et al., 1994; Coté et al., 1998; Long & Bourg, 1996; Pressley & Afflerbach, 1995; Trabasso & Magliano, 1996; Trabasso et al., 1995; Trabasso & Suh, 1993; Zwaan & Brown, 1996), the work reported in this piece supports the utility of think-aloud methodology for studying online processing activities. It extends what we know about the construction of coherent representations by examining comprehension in reading-to-learn situations where students are faced with texts of unpredictable structure containing new concepts and ideas. Focusing on how readers adapt to these kinds of learning situations constitutes an important research area (Coté et al., 1998; Goldman et al., 1996; W. Kintsch et al., 1993; Lorch, 1995). Strategies learners use to capitalize on whatever relevant prior knowledge they do have, how they reason with it and the information in the text, and how they determine what they do and do not understand are all aspects of the online construction of meaning and knowledge acquisition. The patterns of correlations among protocol events and reinstatements plus the illustrative cases suggest that there are prior knowledge and processing constraints that may limit the success of strategies used in online construction of discourse representations. To understand how readers overcome such constraints we need to examine how they allocate resources to different processing strategies and how they capitalize on resources in their learning environments (cf. Goldman, 1997).

Acknowledgments

This piece is based on papers presented at the annual meeting of the Society for Text and Discourse, Albuquerque, New Mexico, July 1995, and at the conference of the European Association for Research on Learning and Instruction, Nijmegen, the Netherlands, August 1995.

Notes

[1] These results are consistent with the distribution we found in an earlier think-aloud protocol study with elementary students reading different expository texts (Goldman et al., 1994), in which about a third of the students took an explanation/reasoning approach, about half mainly paraphrased sentences, and the rest gave very limited protocols.

[2] For the correlation analysis, Minimalists were scored as 1, Text-Focused Processors as 2, Less-Successful Knowledge-Builders as 3, and Successful Knowledge-Builders as 4.

References

Baker, L., & Brown, A.L. (1984). Metacognitive skills and reading. In P.D. Pearson, R. Barr, M.L. Kamil, & P. Mosenthal (Eds.), *Handbook of reading research* (pp. 353–392). New York: Longman.

Bartlett, F.C. (1932). *Remembering: A study in experimental and social psychology.* Cambridge, UK: Cambridge University Press.

Beck, I.L., & McKeown, M.G. (1992). Young students' social studies learning: Going for depth. In M.J. Dreher & W.H. Slater (Eds.), *Elementary school literacy: Critical issues* (pp. 133–156). Norwood, MA: Christopher-Gordon.

Bereiter, C., & Scardamalia, M. (1989). Intentional learning as a goal of instruction. In L.B. Resnick (Ed.), *Knowing, learning, and understanding: Essays in honor of Robert Glaser* (pp. 361–392). Hillsdale, NJ: Erlbaum.

Britton, B.K. (1994). Understanding expository text: Building mental structures to induce insights. In M.A. Gernsbacher (Ed.), *Handbook of psycholinguistics* (pp. 641–674). San Diego, CA: Academic Press.

Chi, M.T.H., deLeeuw, N., Chiu, M., & La-Vancher, C. (1994). Eliciting self-explanations improves understanding. *Cognitive Science, 18,* 439–477.

Coté, N., Goldman, S.R., & Saul, E.U. (1993, November). *Do kids read like adults? A qualitative comparison of the reading behaviors of college and elementary school students.* Invited address to the Vanderbilt University Department of Psychology and Human Development Developmental and Cognitive Psychology Brown Bag Series.

Coté, N., Goldman, S.R., & Saul, E.U. (1998). Students making sense of informational text:

Relations between processing and representation. *Discourse Processes, 25,* 1–53.

Ericsson, K.A., & Kintsch, W. (1995). Long-term working memory. *Psychological Review, 102,* 211–245.

Ericsson, K.A., & Simon, H.A. (1984/1993). *Protocol analysis: Verbal reports as data.* Cambridge, MA: MIT Press.

Fletcher, C.R. (1986). Strategies for the allocation of short-term memory during comprehension. *Journal of Memory and Language, 25,* 43–58.

Goldman, S.R. (1996). Reading, writing, and learning in hypermedia environments. In H. van Oostendorp (Ed.), *Cognitive aspects of electronic text processing* (pp. 7–42). Norwood, NJ: Ablex.

Goldman, S.R. (1997). Learning from text: Reflections on the past and suggestions for the future. *Discourse Processes, 23,* 357–398.

Goldman, S.R., Coté, N., & Saul, E.U. (1994, January). *Children's strategies for making sense of informational text.* Paper presented at the fifth annual Winter Text Conference, Jackson Hole, WY.

Goldman, S.R., & Saul, E.U. (1990a). Applications for tracking reading behavior on the Macintosh. *Behavior Research Methods, Instruments, and Computers, 22,* 526–532.

Goldman, S.R., & Saul, E.U. (1990b). Flexibility in text processing: A strategy competition model. *Learning and Individual Differences, 2,* 181–219.

Goldman, S.R., & Varma, S. (1995). CAPping the construction–integration model of discourse comprehension. In C.A. Weaver, III, S. Mannes, & C.R. Fletcher (Eds.), *Discourse comprehension: Essays in honor of Walter Kintsch* (pp. 337–358). Hillsdale, NJ: Erlbaum.

Goldman, S.R., Varma, S., & Coté, N. (1996). Extending capacity-constrained construction integration: Toward "smarter" and flexible models of text comprehension. In B.K. Britton & A.C. Graesser (Eds.), *Models of understanding text* (pp. 73–113). Mahwah, NJ: Erlbaum.

Graesser, A.C., Singer, M., & Trabasso, T. (1994). Constructing inferences during narrative text comprehension. *Psychological Review, 101,* 371–395.

Kintsch, E. (1990). Macroprocesses and microprocesses in the development of summarization skill. *Cognition and Instruction, 7*(3), 161–195.

Kintsch, W. (1988). The role of knowledge in discourse comprehension: A construction–integration model. *Psychological Review, 95,* 163–182.

Kintsch, W., Britton, B.K., Fletcher, C.R., Kintsch, E., Mannes, S.M., & Nathan, M.J. (1993). A comprehension-based approach to learning and understanding. In D.L. Medin (Ed.), *The psychology of learning and motivation: Advances in research and theory* (Vol. 30, pp. 165–214). San Diego, CA: Academic Press.

Kintsch, W., & van Dijk, T.A. (1978). Toward a model of text comprehension and production. *Psychological Review, 85,* 363–394.

Long, D.L., & Bourg, T. (1996). Thinking aloud: "Telling a story about a story." *Discourse Processes, 21,* 329–339.

Lorch, R.F., Jr. (1995). Integration of topic information during reading. In R. Lorch & E. O'Brien (Eds.), *Sources of coherence in text comprehension* (pp. 279–294). Hillsdale, NJ: Erlbaum.

McNamara, D.S., Kintsch, E., Songer, N.B., & Kintsch, W. (1996). Are good texts always better? Interactions of text coherence, background knowledge, and levels of understanding in learning from text. *Cognition and Instruction, 14,* 1–43.

Meyer, B.J.F. (1985). Prose analysis: Purposes, procedures, and problems. In B.K. Britton & J.B. Black (Eds.), *Understanding expository text: A theoretical and practical handbook for analyzing explanatory text* (pp. 11–64). Hillsdale, NJ: Erlbaum.

Pressley, M., & Afflerbach, P. (1995). *Verbal protocols of reading: The nature of constructively responsive reading.* Hillsdale, NJ: Erlbaum.

Saul, E.U., Coté, N., & Goldman, S.R. (1993, April). *Students' strategies for making text make sense.* Paper presented at the annual meeting of the American Education Research Association, Atlanta, GA.

Scardamalia, M., & Bereiter, C. (1991). Literate expertise. In K.A. Ericsson & J. Smith (Eds.), *Toward a general theory of expertise* (pp. 172–194). Cambridge, UK: Cambridge University Press.

Trabasso, T., & Magliano, J.P. (1996). Conscious understanding during comprehension. *Discourse Processes, 21,* 255–287.

Trabasso, T., & Suh, S. (1993). Understanding text: Achieving explanatory coherence through on-line inferences and mental operations in working memory. *Discourse Processes, 16,* 3–34.

Trabasso, T., Suh, S., Payton, P., & Jain, R. (1995). Explanatory inferences and other strategies during comprehension: Encoding effects on recall. In R. Lorch & E. O'Brien (Eds.), *Sources of coherence in text comprehension* (pp. 219–239). Hillsdale, NJ: Erlbaum.

van den Broek, P. (1990). The causal inference maker: Toward a process model of inference generation in text comprehension. In D.A. Balota, G.B. Flores d'Arcais, & K. Rayner (Eds.), *Comprehension processes in reading* (pp. 423–445). Hillsdale, NJ: Erlbaum.

van den Broek, P. (1994). Comprehension and memory of narrative texts: Inferences and coherence. In M.A. Gernsbacher (Ed.), *Handbook of psycholinguistics* (pp. 539–588). San Diego, CA: Academic Press.

van Dijk, T.A., & Kintsch, W. (1983). *Strategies for discourse comprehension.* New York: Academic Press.

Zwaan, R.A., & Brown, C.A. (1996). The influence of language proficiency and comprehension skill on situation-model construction. *Discourse Processes, 21,* 289–327.

Appendix A: Metabolism Text*

1. Metabolism

2. Customers in many pharmacies may soon be seeing the latest in new devices for the health conscious.

3. A sports physiologist is developing the metabometer, a device that he hopes will measure the human body's ability to produce energy efficiently.

4. The rate at which the body produces energy is called metabolism.

5. Different people have different metabolic rates that indicate how easily they can produce energy.

6. The same person may have different metabolic rates, depending on the circumstances.

7. Different species of animals also have different metabolic rates.

8. There are several factors that affect metabolic rate.

9. One factor is the type of food a person or animal eats.

10. For example, some foods are hard to digest, such as complex carbohydrates like rice.

11. The body has to work harder to get energy from rice.

12. If a person ate a steady diet of rice, the result would be a higher metabolic rate.

13. Another factor affecting metabolism is the climate of the environment.

14. Temperature may cause the metabolism to change.

15. People and animals that live in cold environments need to produce more energy in order to keep warm.

16. Most animals that live in polar regions have high metabolisms.

17. If people move from a warm to a cold climate, their metabolic rates will increase.

18. Metabolic rate also differs depending on activity level.

19. Changing the level of activity may cause the body to change its metabolism because different activities require different amounts of energy.

20. For example, basketball players use more energy than golfers so their metabolic rates are generally higher.

21. To some degree, metabolic rate is influenced by genetic inheritance.

22. Children of parents who have high metabolic rates tend to have high metabolic rates also.

23. This is because the body chemistry of the children is a combination of the body chemistry of the parents.

24. Metabolism is regulated by hormones produced by the thyroid gland, a tiny gland located at the base of the neck.

25. These hormones regulate the behavior of all the cells in the body so that enough energy is produced.

26. The metabometer will work by measuring hormone levels in the blood.

---

*The sentences are on separate numbered lines here for clarity. In the actual experimental text, the sentences ran consecutively within paragraphs and were not numbered.

Appendix B: Hybrids Text*

1. Improving Mother Nature

2. Produce departments and garden shops are brimming with odd new hybrids of some familiar fruits and vegetables.

3. This year, the first genetically altered tomato went on the market and ushered in a new era in growing crops for food.

4. A hybrid refers to a plant or animal that has been created by crossing two different parents.

5. For example, the "broccoflower" is a hybrid of broccoli and cauliflower.

6. Hybrids such as the broccoflower are being created by scientists through a process known as genetic engineering.

7. Hybrids are helpful for several reasons.

8. For one thing, plants can be altered so that the hybrid has more vitamins than the original plant did.

9. Or, if the original plant is high in some undesirable substance, such as fat or sugar, the amount may be reduced in the hybrid.

10. This type of hybrid is helpful to people who may only have access to a small amount of food, such as those people living on a submarine.

11. Another reason that hybrids are helpful is that they may make a plant stronger and better able to resist environmental threats, such as insects or frost.

12. Raising stronger plants helps farmers be assured of a good crop.

13. Hybrids help farmers in another way as well.

14. They allow farmers to adapt plants to new environments.

15. For example, some tomatoes have been designed to grow in unusual environments such as styrofoam containers, or even in space.

16. Plants that would normally only grow in very warm weather may be changed to allow them to grow year-round.

17. Finally, hybrids may change the appearance of a plant in some way, perhaps making it easier to grow.

18. For example, scientists have developed a tiny version of the carrot.

19. The hybrid carrot's smaller size makes it possible to grow it in window boxes in the city, or other places where space is limited.

20. Genetic engineering involves taking the genes of one plant and adding on, or splicing, the genes from another so that the new plant has characteristics of both plants.

21. Scientists can examine the parent plants and decide what traits they wish for the plant to have from each parent.

22. It is a bit like being able to design a human baby so that it has the father's nose, but the mother's eyes, and so on.

---

*The sentences are on separate numbered lines here for clarity. In the actual experimental text, the sentences ran consecutively within paragraphs and were not numbered.

26

Traversing the Topical Landscape: Exploring Students' Self-Directed Reading–Writing–Research Processes

Joyce E. Many, Ronald Fyfe, Geoffrey Lewis, and Evelyn Mitchell

In "Traversing the Topical Landscape: Reading and Writing as Ways of Knowing," McGinley and Tierney (1989) outline a theoretical view and program of research on "students' self-directed engagements in reading and writing to learn" (p. 245). When students direct their own investigation of a topic, they make their own decisions about sources of information, methods of working from text, and uses of reading/writing. Little is known, however, about students' self-directed reading and writing engagements and thinking processes as they undertake to learn and write about a specific topic across an extended period of time (Tierney, Soter, O'Flahavan, & McGinley, 1989).

When investigating a research topic, students need to draw from a complex combination of reading and writing processes. Recent research on collaborative uses of reading and writing has focused on two areas: (1) discourse synthesis and (2) reading and writing to learn. Studies focusing on discourse synthesis have examined how readers/writers select and organize information from sources when writing their own new texts (Spivey & King, 1989). Factors such as reading ability and prior knowledge of a topic (Kennedy, 1985; Nelson & Hayes, 1988; Spivey, 1984; Spivey & King, 1989; Symons & Pressley, 1993), formulating plans or goals for a search (Dreher & Guthrie, 1990; Dreher & Sammons, 1994; Guthrie & Mosenthal, 1987), and task impression (Nelson & Hayes, 1988; Raphael & Boyd, 1991) have been shown to affect students' performances on search and synthesis tasks. McGinley (1992), however, documents the individual variability that is evident in students' composing-from-sources processes, and his

---

From *Reading Research Quarterly*, *31*, 12–35. Copyright © 1996 by the International Reading Association.

work underscores the importance of utilizing multiple-case study methodology in order to avoid overgeneralizations that gloss over important differences.

Studies examining the effects of reading and writing on learning have analyzed various types of writing tasks (note-taking, question answering, personal responses, formal analyses of texts, essay writing, etc.). This research, reviewed by Shanahan and Tierney (1990), documents that more extended responses are linked to greater learning, and that there is some indication that different types of tasks lead to different types of learning. Reading and writing in combination seem to be more effective than reading or writing alone in terms of encouraging students to extend thinking and to consider multiple perspectives (Tierney et al., 1989). It appears that when students engage in a dialectical process of using reading and writing, they tend to be more critical in their thinking (Langer & Applebee, 1987; Newell, 1984; Salvatori, 1985). However, research examining students' use of reading and writing to learn has typically prescribed specific sets of reading and writing activities. Consequently, our understanding of students' dynamic use of reading, writing, and critical thinking in naturally occurring situations is limited (McGinley & Tierney, 1989).

In different areas of the school curriculum children are asked to read texts (both narrative and expository) and then to draw from these sources in their own writing. A major aim of this investigation was to achieve some understanding of how students choose, read, and respond to texts, and of how they write new texts based on gathered information. To retain the dynamics of the complex interaction of factors that might influence processes in a classroom setting, we chose a naturalistic approach (Lincoln & Guba, 1985). Such an approach also allowed for an emergent design; prior to immersion in data collection we could not know the mutually shaping patterns that might exist. We began with an overall interest in how the genre of source texts and the genre of students' own writing might impact their reading and writing processes; but, we were open to issues which might arise during long-term data collection and analysis. The following question became the focus of inquiry and of this article: What patterns are apparent in the reading–writing–research processes used by 11-year-old students as they investigate a topic?

Method

The Participants and Context

The Participants. This study took place in 1992–1993 in Mrs. Longman's (pseudonym) Primary 7 class (27 eleven- and twelve-year-old students) in a school of open-concept design in Aberdeen, Scotland. The children were from primarily middle class, suburban families, and, with the exception of one English girl, all were native born Scots. Classes of similar age students were clustered on wings, and these classes were partially divided from each other by half walls and shared common areas that were used for art or group projects. The general philosophy of the school focused on a student-centered curriculum, with a strong emphasis on peer interaction and self-directed learning.

Mrs. Longman's class was chosen initially because of her emphasis on involving children in writing and because her students would be reading and writing a variety of texts across an extended period of time during the last two terms of the year. Mrs. Longman was a senior teacher in her school. Her expertise was relied on within the school community, and she was described as exemplary by the school administrators.

Students also worked periodically with specialty teachers in the areas of art, drama, music, and home economics and with a preservice teacher who was involved with the class for 4 weeks. In addition, a learning support teacher worked with the regular teacher to give assistance to a small number of students who had learning difficulties in the areas of reading and mathematics.

The Classroom Context. The daily class routine was flexible, but often began with sustained silent reading. Few whole-class teacher-directed lessons were employed. Those that did occur were often in the form of minilessons lasting 5–10 minutes on a strategy or skill or were general discussion sessions. Students were grouped for language, mathematics, and reading although the makeup of these groups differed across areas and was changed periodically. Flowcharts of activities to be addressed were posted each morning, and students were responsible for moving independently from one learning task to the next. Students were also expected to monitor their own progress on long-term assignments. The degree of responsibility for their own learning allocated to students was a major factor influencing the pictures of students' reading and writing engagements that emerged from our data. McGinley and Tierney (1989) note that complex combinations of reading and writing are enabled by instructional settings that promote student initiative and self-direction. The social relations within this class were such that the teacher did not assume the role of expert or dispenser of knowledge; instead, learners routinely engaged in problem solving and in investigation in collaboration with both the teacher and peers. Children commonly sought information from one another, went to other classes for information or as peer tutors, and worked on individual assignments at their own rate.

Evaluation of student progress differed considerably from that commonly seen in U.S. schools. Reports to parents on students' progress occurred in the form of individual conferences twice during the year, with detailed written reports given at the end of the year. There was no reporting/averaging of numerical grades, and no mention was made by the students or the teachers of completing assignments because they were to be graded. The teacher reviewed and gave feedback on student work on a daily basis and conferenced with students periodically on their progress. Students also completed weekly self-assessments.

Personal Research Projects and Project Work. During each of the last two terms of the 1992–1993 school year, these Primary 7 students were involved in personally researching topics related to the projects being studied in the class. Project work is analogous to a unit or thematic work. In Scotland, project work is used to develop knowledge and understanding of both subject matter and learning strategies (Fyfe & Mitchell, 1984). The investigation of reading and writing described in this study was based on the students' efforts to research a self-selected topic related to World War II (the topic for the January to March 12-week term). In the preceding year, students had also conducted a research project in which they had been responsible for researching and reporting on any self-chosen topic.

Learning experiences in language and mathematics were often related to the overall World War II project, although students undertook reading, writing, and other activities that were not project related. Sources of information for the World War II project included informational books, biographical narratives, historical fiction, newspapers, play scripts, teacher-made information sheets, and artifacts such as ration books and identity cards. Students were also exposed to videos (both fictional and informational), computer software, slides, posters, artifacts such as actual gas masks and coins, and audiotapes of short stories. In addition, students were requested to interview parents, relatives, and friends and to either audiotape or write about those accounts and to bring those materials to class. In addition to the personal research task, students were expected to write a piece of historical fiction set during World War II.

Data Collection and Analysis

Data Collection. Data sources included interviews, field notes, videotapes, and photocopies of student work and source texts. In addition, the teacher's curriculum outline of projected activities for the January to March term and notes taken on discussions with the participating teacher and on the meetings of the research team were preserved. Table 1 outlines the data-collection schedule.

This inquiry was the result of collaboration that occurred while the first author, Many, was a Bicentennial Research Fellow in the Language Studies Department at Northern College in Aberdeen, Scotland. All field notes and interview information were collected by Many using a notebook computer. Field notes consisted of (a) descriptions of student behavior, peer interactions, and instructional activities; (b) interview information; and (c) the interpretive reflections and working hypotheses of the data collector. Throughout the inquiry three basic types of interviews were conducted: unstructured, structured, and debriefing.

Unstructured interviews were typically short conversations, often student initiated, which occurred during the class observation. Structured interviews were

TABLE 1
Outline of Data Collection

Dates	Activities
Nov. 16	Initial interviews with school staff and participating teacher.
Nov. 23–25	Classroom observation, unstructured interviews with students.
Dec. 9, 10, 15, 18	Classroom observation, initial interviews with students.
Jan. 6–Mar. 26	Daily observation in the classroom with ongoing student interviews/debriefing. Average of 2½ hours each day was spent in the classroom, alternating from morning to afternoon.
Feb. 18–Mar. 24	In addition to the above, small-group research sessions led by the first author were conducted and videotaped.
Mar. 29–Apr. 9	School holidays—end of term.
Apr. 12–Jun. 22	Two or three half-day visits a week. Continued debriefing/interviews with students, member checks.

held with all students before they started their personal projects, at various points when students were working on their projects, and when projects were completed. In the initial interview, students were asked general questions regarding their reading and writing processes and were asked to complete a sorting activity that indicated their awareness of genre. Throughout the period of investigation, as working hypotheses were generated through inductive analysis of the data, questions were formulated that were then discussed with all students. In the final interview, general questions were asked of all students and student-specific questions were also included to provide member checks on our interpretations of the research processes unique to individuals.

In addition, debriefing interviews began in January as students began working on their individual research projects. Because of the individualization of learning in the classroom, it was possible for debriefing to be ongoing throughout each day without posing an interruption to the classroom routine. Students were individually called (or volunteered to come) to a table in the corner of the classroom. Debriefing took the form of retrospective recall as students discussed in detail their research process. Students described their use of planning, their selection of sources, and their process of working from and writing texts. When their responses revealed they had used multiple sources, students gave a line-by-line analysis of what they had written to help in identifying sources of specific information. Debriefing interviews varied in length from 2–3 minutes to as long as 20 minutes and focused primarily on students who were selected as key informants for the study. Although students' research projects were intended to be completed in March, some students continued working until June. Debriefing continued for these students until the completion of their projects.

With respect to all data sources, the role of the first author as data collector is integral to the data that emerged. Guba and Lincoln (1981) stress that humans are uniquely qualified for naturalistic inquiry, particularly because of their ability to be responsive to the cues in the natural situation, to collect information about multiple factors and across multiple levels, to take a holistic look at situations, to draw from both propositional and tacit knowledge, to process data and generate and test hypotheses immediately, to ask for clarification and elaboration, and to explore idiosyncratic responses. Throughout the data collection and analysis, effort was made to capitalize on these qualities in order to develop a rich perception of the myriad factors influencing the reading and writing engagements of the students as they approached their research task. At the same time we recognize that the data observed and collected were shaped by the first author's values and background including the fact that her perspectives were formed as a U.S. educator viewing a Scottish Primary classroom. Informing Many's perceptions of the students' processes were her 8 years' experience of teaching at the elementary school level and her previous research examining children's responses to literature. The open-concept design of this school and the social, academic, and cultural backgrounds of these Scottish students contrasted sharply to the educational systems, students, and communities in Louisiana and Texas where Many had previously worked. As noted by Dillon (1989) in her ethnographic work as a participant-observer in an unfamiliar context, such a blend of experience and inexperience with teaching and learning in a new cultural context allows a researcher to "make the familiar at first strange and then familiar again (Spindler & Spindler, 1982)" (Dillon, p. 234).

In the first 6 weeks of the students' project work, Many as participant-observer made classroom observations and conducted interviews. During the second half of the January to March term, five research groups were formed based on common interests, and Many also served as participant/discussion facilitator for these groups. Each research group met on two or three occasions with the purpose of helping students make connections among their individual research topics. Group sessions were videotaped and later transcribed.

Students recorded the results of their work in booklets. These booklets and any additional notes were photocopied midterm and on completion of the project. Effort was made to identify the sources of each booklet entry and, when possible, to photocopy the corresponding source texts.

General Data Analysis Procedures. Analysis followed the naturalistic procedures set out by Lincoln and Guba (1985). Data were continually inspected through a search for patterns, and this helped to focus subsequent observations and interviews. Using an emergent sampling design, data collection began through a serial selection of participants. The first author initially touched base with all students, but as we began to glimpse patterns in the way students worked we targeted specific students as key informants for in-depth analysis. Key informants emerged across the data collection based on the degree to which the data provided by a student were recognized as redundant in light of data provided by other participants. As we developed new working hypotheses, all students were periodically tapped, and when a student's reading or writing engagements provided information that contrasted with or filled in the gaps in the information from the cases already selected, that student was added to the targeted key informants. Our concern was to allow for in-depth analysis of individuals as they proceeded with their research, while at the same time to remain comprehensive enough to fully sample the range of approaches employed by students. At the end of the study, detailed data had been collected on the reading and writing processes of 16 students. Because some of these cases were included due to reasons not directly related to the focus of this particular article, the number of key informants for the analysis presented here was further refined to 12 cases. Data collected from all sources were used to construct flowcharts to illustrate the chronology of research processes for each individual informant.

Throughout data collection, working hypotheses were generated through ongoing constant comparative analysis (Glaser & Strauss, 1967) of the data. These hypotheses were used to generate subsequent foci for data collection. For example, early in January Many noted from debriefing interviews that individual students seemed to be approaching the research in different ways. To gain additional information about students' conceptions of their research, all students were subsequently asked, (a) How would you tell a new student who had never done research how to go about doing a personal research project? (b) What makes a good research project? and (c) What do you think the purpose is in doing a research project—why do you think your teacher wants you to do one? Students' responses to such questions and all comments from debriefing sessions related to students' conception of their research were then printed out, examined, and sorted into categories. These categories regarding students' conceptions of what it meant *to do research* were later triangulated with students' actual research processes. Similar procedures were followed as other hypotheses emerged.

Working hypotheses were discussed informally with the classroom teacher. In addition, drafts of the field notes were periodically given to Mrs. Longman for review, and discussions were held regarding the inductive analysis that was taking place. Feedback from the teacher was recorded into the field notes and was used to confirm or disconfirm hypotheses through triangulation with other data sources.

Throughout, collaboration between Many and the other members of the research team served two principal roles. First, peer debriefing occurred to discuss the first author's working hypotheses. Second, additional inductive analysis of the data was conducted and attempts were made to assimilate the patterns that were emerging into a grounded theory (Glaser & Strauss, 1967; Lincoln & Guba, 1985).

The concept of grounded theory is consistent with a pattern model of explanation in that the information from the natural context is used to build a holistic model that describes and explains the system (Lincoln & Guba, 1985). For instance, as patterns became apparent in data relating to students' understanding of doing research and the strategies they used in working from texts, efforts were made to understand the manner in which these factors were related and the influence of contextual and social factors impacting these cognitive processes.

Results

In this section we describe the ways in which different students conducted their research. As outlined in Table 2, three task impressions (Raphael & Boyd, 1991) were identified as characterized by differing emphases on research subtasks. These task impressions were also coupled with strategies students used in working from text. In addition, individual task impressions and strategy use influenced and were influenced by the materials used and the social and instructional context of the classroom. Although we begin with discussion of the students' task impressions, discussion of the strategies used in working from text, of the materials used, and of changes that occurred across time will be interwoven as appropriate to illustrate the interrelationships that existed. We will demonstrate the commonalities, the interindividual differences, and the intraindividual variations.

In the sections that follow, citations from the field notes have been edited for spelling and punctuation and bracketed information has been added to clarify where necessary. Pseudonyms have been substituted for the children's actual names.

TABLE 2
Primary Relationships Between Task Impressions, Research Subtasks, and Strategies Used in Working From Sources

	Task Impressions		
Ways of Working	Accumulating Information	Transferring Information	Transforming Information
Research Subtasks	Finding, recording	Searching, finding, recording	Planning, searching Finding, recording Reviewing, presenting
Strategies Used to Work From Sources	Photocopying Verbatim copying Drawing and labeling	Sentence-by-sentence reworking Read/remember/write	Cut-and-paste synthesis Discourse synthesis

Particular subtasks and strategies were associated with particular task impressions; however, these relationships were also affected by the materials used and immersion in the social and instructional context.

Students' Task Impressions

Students differed considerably in their impressions of the research task. Evidence for this came from their discussion of the purpose of doing research, their description of the tasks involved, how they undertook planning, how they selected their sources, what they thought of as "good" projects, and why they included specific information in their booklets. Three distinct views of the research task emerged: (1) research as accumulation of information, (2) research as transferring information, and (3) research as transforming information. These reflected different understandings of the task itself and were characterized by differing emphases students placed on the subtasks of planning, searching, finding, recording, reviewing, and presenting.

Research as Accumulating Information. Researching a topic inevitably involves accumulating information or materials. However, the rationale underlying why students collected particular information often reflected their perspective on what research entailed. Unsurprisingly, many students chose information that they thought was interesting. For some pupils, however, this was the central purpose guiding their research. Some accepted almost any information associated in some way with World War II, regardless of their specific topic. Two students from this class became key informants for the way in which they dealt with the issues of interest and relevance. For these students, whose task impression we described as "Research as accumulating information," finding and recording interesting information were the focus of their research.

The first pupil, Claudia, carefully lettered the title "Aberdeen at War" across the front of her booklet. For Claudia, however, this title was not regarded as a topic about which information had to be gathered, in that it appeared peripheral to her investigation. This was first evident in her planning web, which contained her title in a central cloud with spokes reaching outward to a wide array of terms indicating topic descriptors. Although it might be possible to relate the war as experienced by those in Aberdeen to some of the descriptors included such as "children, evacuation, gas mask; or soldiers killed, injured," it would be difficult for anyone to focus on "Aberdeen at War" while discussing Anne Frank and the fate of the Jews in concentration camps. Yet these also appeared as descriptors in Claudia's planning web. In discussing the web with Claudia throughout the study (Field notes: January 11, 15; March 26; April 12), it became clear that she chose to include aspects in her web because she felt they were of interest or "good" rather than because they were relevant to her chosen topic.

Claudia's title and the accompanying descriptors on her web rarely drove her search for information. Instead, finding information was the result of serendipity. When Claudia turned in her project at the end of the 12-week school term, only 7 scattered pages in her 21-page research booklet could be clearly related to "Aberdeen at War." Her reasons for incorporating information included the following: (a) She had leafed through books and had seen something that she felt would be good or interesting, (b) information had been shared as part of the overall class project and so she thought she would include it, and (c) her friends had done something like it in their booklets (Field notes: January 15; March 26; April 12). All the information contained in her booklet was the result of her having come across the material rather than having deliberately sought it out. When asked why she included certain items Claudia responded, "I didn't know what else to do," and typically she had to be prompted to elaborate before she offered any additional explanation. Claudia believed the purpose in doing research was to find something interesting, something the teacher might want to read out to other classes. Her presentation of the interesting information she had found primarily involved photocopying the material and gluing it into her project booklet or copying passages verbatim into her booklet. In the end, Claudia was satisfied with her efforts because she believed she accomplished her goal of finding interesting information and because she had filled all the pages in her booklet (Field notes: March 15, Final interview).

A second student, Robert, worked in much the same way as Claudia. He too seemed concerned with collecting interesting material, but in Robert's case it was material that was interesting to him. In addition, he showed some awareness that information included in his booklet should be pertinent to his research topic.

When Robert encountered items that attracted his interest, he did not automatically incorporate them into his booklet without concern for their relevance. Instead, Robert changed his topic, thus maintaining consistency between his topic and the new information. During the first weeks of the project he shifted his focus from weapons and artillery to the RAF (Royal Air Force) to weapons and artillery and the RAF and then to posters. As Robert encountered pictures in books that he would like to draw, or saw aspects of his peers' works he admired, he verbally acknowledged his changing topic as he incorporated the information in his own booklet (Field notes: January 11, 20, 22; Research group transcripts: February 17). The old information remained in his booklet, but he did at times erase the title on his planning web to indicate the topic shift. At the end of the term, his planning web once again held the title "RAF" surrounded by the following descriptors on individual spokes: "jets, bombs, machine guns, pilot, aircraft carrier, parachute, missiles, control deck." The pages of his booklet went beyond these elements, however, containing not only descriptions, drawings, and surveys related to planes, but also two propaganda posters, two pages of text on Pearl Harbor, a survey of which countries his peers felt were damaged most by Germany, and drawings of the flags of countries involved in the war.

Despite the relatively unconstrained nature of his final presentation, Robert indicated a degree of awareness of strategies one might use in conducting a more targeted search for information. For example, in discussions about how one decides what to include in a project, Robert noted, "I looked in a couple of books and I got some ideas about it and put them down. You go back [to your planning web] if you find something else on your project so you add it" (Field notes: January 20). Later in the term he further explained his impression of how to conduct research: "It depends what you are doing in your project, if you want to do something like Churchill you would go in the index for Churchill and you read over it and you put in your own words instead of their words that they tell you..." (Field notes: March 16). Some indication of Robert's understanding of the function of a planning web can be gathered from his statements that new items should be added to a web as new content is added to a booklet. His reference to the use of an index revealed some knowledge of tactics that could be used to conduct a systematic search for material. However, when investigating his own topic, he did not use these tactics, and, furthermore, when talking about his project Robert indicated he was quite satisfied with his work and would change nothing if he did it over again (Field notes: March 16, Final interview).

Both Claudia and Robert worked on their research largely by accumulating material. They used browsing techniques, serendipitously finding information. Decisions to incorporate information into their project booklets were largely based on the fact that they found the material interesting or because peers had done something similar in their booklets (these reasons often overriding concern for relevance). Their research efforts therefore focused mainly on the subtasks of finding and recording. Advance planning and subsequent searching for relevant texts or information had very little influence on their activities.

Research as Transferring Information. Another task impression that emerged reflected both a different awareness of the research process and a different balance of emphasis on subtasks of research. It was characterized by the students' beliefs that research primarily involves searching for and then transferring relevant information and material to their booklets. These students (including those who occasionally copied verbatim) felt that essentially what they were expected to do was to take information from a book and present it in their own words. Two dominant threads ran through the data for those with this perspective on research: (1) These students planned a purposeful search for texts relevant to their topic, and (2) they used a variety of strategies for recording information from texts (although they primarily focused on one source text at a time). In the following sections we will discuss these two aspects, and then we will describe in detail a key informant who viewed research as transferring information but who seemed at first to represent an anomaly in our data in that she relied on oral rather than written sources.

Searching for information. These students' purposeful searches for texts varied in the levels of specificity that were evident. For some pupils it simply involved finding a book with a title similar to the title they had chosen for their topic. Then the students leafed through the book until they found a piece of text that was relevant as well as interesting. Others examined the index or the table of contents to determine if the source contained relevant information to their topic. In addition, students often relied on peer recommendations to locate passages of information on their given topics. Generally, for both types of searches, the students' titles for their topics, not specific descriptors listed in planning webs, were the focus for their searches.

Recording information. After locating a relevant source, these students set out to transfer the information into their booklets. All the students in the class had been enjoined not simply to copy information; rather, they had to express it in their own words. To do this, these students primarily focused on one of two strategies for recording information: (1) sentence-by-sentence reworking or (2) read/remember/write.

In the first of these strategies students paraphrased one sentence at a time (as evidenced in the line-by-line comparisons of research booklets with source texts). For example, the following sentence from a source text, "By the outbreak of World War Two in 1939, almost all the new warplanes were monoplanes," was rewritten into a booklet as, "By the time the outbreak of world war two broke out in 1939, nearly all the new warplanes were monoplanes" (Field notes: January 22). Such transcriptions, described by students as "writing it in your own words," typically involved minor changes such as word substitutions, the elimination of pronominal referents, or the elimination of entire clauses or sentences.

One key informant who used this strategy was Ian. Ian would first copy an entire section verbatim onto a sheet of looseleaf paper, and then he would work laboriously to reword his handwritten copy sentence by sentence (Field notes: February 1, March 9). Toward the end of the term Ian explained, "I look up the person and sometimes I copy it out on a page of paper so I don't have to keep on looking up the page in the book" (Field notes: March 16). Thus rewriting the text verbatim as an initial step was a way for Ian to cope with the frustration caused by having to look through hundreds of pages to relocate the section on which he had been working. His pride in using an adult book and the social recognition he got from his peers for working from such a text (Field notes: February 19; March 1, 9, 16) made the effort worthwhile even though he was aware of shorter texts that covered the same things in simpler language.

Ian also helped us to understand that recording information in such a way did not necessarily imply an understanding of the material. In research group discussions, Ian seemed unable to talk freely concerning the information that he had written down (Research group transcripts: February 18; March 10). He seldom initiated points in the conversation or commented on others' topics without turning to his booklet and reading verbatim from his written text.

Sentence-by-sentence reworking allowed students to choose more difficult texts than they might have been able to use had they been working with a different strategy. Many of the students, like Ian, sought out adult reference books from their local libraries. Reworking such texts sentence by sentence meant that it was not necessary for students to internalize information. The source text itself stored the information, and by marking their place in the paragraph with their finger or a straight edge, students were able to work on small segments of text at a time. In such a way students produced a text written in their own words but which closely matched the author's structuring of the original text. As might be expected, entries written in this manner often exhibited accurate punctuation, spelling, and paragraph indentations, and some were lengthy and syntactically complex sections of text.

Other students who shared this task impression used different strategies to record information. Some read a small portion of text, attempted to remember what was written, and then wrote about it in their booklets. Another key informant, Mhairi, described how she did this:

> I read a paragraph maybe once or twice and I try to remember it all and put it down in my own words and then I go to the next paragraph and do it again.... I'd draw the posters and read the section and put down notes, read and take notes at the same time. If [the paragraph was] short, [I would] read and then write. Take the most important parts and then put it in my own words. (Field notes: February 8)

The resulting entry was generally a synthesis across the sentences in a given paragraph. This recording strategy, which we called read/remember/write, required more internalization of the text, and some pupils took notes to help them placehold bits of information. At the same time the texts produced by the students using this strategy were similar to the texts produced by students using verbatim copying in that there was minimal deviation from the content of the original source. Information was still essentially transferred from the source into the students' booklets.

Regardless of whether these students used sentence-by-sentence reworking or a read/remember/write strategy, they all focused their attention on only one text at a time. Some students used the table of contents of one particular book to create their planning web and then relied heavily on that book throughout their research even though multiple sources of information were available. Others did refer to multiple texts, but they relied on only one text per subarea covered in their booklets, using a different source only when beginning a new subarea. These students considered a particular section of their project completed when they had finished writing in their own words whatever the source text contained on that aspect of their topic. Consequently, while many of these young researchers commented that it was important to use multiple sources of information, this was not demonstrated within specific subareas of their projects but rather through their use of multiple sources across the project research as a whole.

These strategies of working from texts exemplified the processes of the majority of the students whose impression of the research task was to locate a source text and rewrite it in their own words. However one student, Jean, was added to the list of key informants soon after the study began because she seemed to represent an anomaly in the data. Jean's processes will be discussed in detail in the next section.

Searching for and recording information from oral sources. Most of the students in this class focused on written sources of information, and this was particularly true for those whose task impressions centered on transferring information from sources. In contrast, Jean relied heavily on oral sources for information on her project. The following entry made in the field notes during the first days of the project help illustrate how Jean's perspective of the messages being conveyed in the instructional context facilitated her subsequent reliance on oral sources.

> I [J.M.] asked what she [Jean] had written on the other page—she said a recipe. I asked why and she said because they had to cook things and make do with the food they had. I asked her where she got it [the recipe] and she said, "this book but I can't use it any more." [J.M.:] "Why?" [Jean:] "Because I got in trouble— Mrs. Longman said I have to use my own stuff and can't get it from books." She had copied the recipe directly from the booklet. Now the [information] she was putting down about women doing men's job[s] was "her own," she just knew it but didn't know how she knew it. In the folder sitting in front of her was a packet of books—one on women at war which would have had a lot of information on her topic—but she wasn't using [them]. I don't think she truly understands what L. meant about doing her own work. (Field notes: January 11)

Jean had not been told specifically that she should not have copied the recipe (later in the day Mrs. Longman expressed surprise at Jean's interpretation, noting that a recipe would have been an acceptable thing to copy). However, the need to write information in the students' own words was stressed in sharing sessions throughout the term. Jean interpreted the statement that she had to write it in her own words to mean that she could not take material from books, and henceforth she avoided written texts. Instead, she looked to first-hand accounts and class discussions as sources for information. While this may seem a drastic interpretation, it was a sensible alternative for Jean. Jean was one of three students who used the services of a learning support teacher for language and mathematics. Students are rarely retained in Scottish primary schools and, instead, such support teachers come into the classrooms to assist students who have difficulties. Jean's difficulty in reading texts and then writing about their contents without direct copying may have led to the use of oral sources as a workable alternative. The conversation that follows shows not only that Jean prefers oral sources but also that she can use these sources effectively to acquire information:

> Jean: [When asked about the entry titled "How Women Work"] This is about when the men went away to war the women had to [do] their jobs while the men went away.
>
> J.M.: What sort of things did they do?

Jean:	They had to work in factories and farms—just everything and they also had the children to feed at the same time as doing the men's work.
J.M.:	How [do you] know?
Jean:	My grandad told me 'cause I asked him what they did and he just told me.
J.M.:	I am just interested in how students get information—from books or people. What did you do—did you take notes or just listen?
Jean:	Just sat and listened and then wrote it down.
J.M.:	Have you seen any books on that too?
Jean:	There is one over here, one that you brought.
J.M.:	Did you look at it before or after you wrote this?
Jean:	I looked at it too—after.
J.M.:	Do you find it easier when people talk about it or when you read a book for information?
Jean:	Yeah, it is easier to talk to someone 'cause you don't have to wonder like what it is—it's [the book] talking about—so it is easier. Sometimes we share things with each other and get ideas. (Field notes: January 25)

Although Jean relied on oral sources, her overall view of the research task was not inconsistent with that of the others with the transferring information perspective. She searched purposefully for information, and although she relied primarily on oral sources, she often described her intention to find books related to her topic (Field notes: January 25; February 10, 11). In addition, when asked at various times what she planned to do next, she showed some awareness of the purpose of planning by discussing the topic descriptors that she still needed to cover (Field notes: January 25; February 24; March 23, Final interview). Sometimes she not only referred to her web to organize her next steps, she actually followed through by writing entries in her booklet about specific descriptors. In fact, unlike most students with this task impression, Jean's search for information tended to focus more on her topic descriptors (such as "The Blackout," "How to Make Weapons," "Ration Books") than on her overall topic. This may be because Jean's title, "Make Do and Mend," was both relatively abstract and narrowly focused. In addition, it may not have readily engaged the forms of knowledge in which her informants held their information. At times Jean's searches involved finding individuals who could give her specific information. When addressing some descriptors, however, Jean searched her memory of class sessions and previous conversations for relevant information that she could record into her booklet. However, like the others who viewed research as transferring information, Jean primarily focused on one source or conversation per subarea. The only exception to this seemed to occur on an entry on the blackout where she incorporated photocopies and information shared by her teacher across a number of class sessions.

Research as Transforming Information. A third task impression that emerged was that research involved transforming information. Students holding this view approached their research in ways that were different from those of other students. In particular, three aspects played key roles in their work: (1) planning, (2) reviewing the coverage of information, and (3) consideration of audience.

Planning the research. Pupils who viewed research as transforming information saw planning as playing a key role in the process. These students relied heavily on their planning webs, generating a list of specific descriptors that then focused their search for factual information. This is exemplified in the work of one key informant, Mary, who researched "The Holocaust." Before sketching her planning web, Mary located numerous texts and scanned them for information. As she skimmed the various sources, she began taking note of which aspects she might like to pursue in depth, and she created an initial planning web (see Figure 1). After reading various texts and participating in research group discussions, her knowledge of Hitler and the Holocaust grew, and she continually added to this web (Photocopies of Mary's notes: February 12, May 21; Field notes: January 21, March 17, April 21; Research group transcripts: February 18). The planning web served as a guide to subsequent fact finding and Mary used it as a touchstone, crossing off information as she had completed various entries in her booklet (Field notes: April 21). According to Mary planning is a big part of research because "you have got to know where you are going next so you won't make a mess of it" (Field notes: March 17).

For these students, planning was a continuous process throughout the term. When asked about the role planning played in research, one student responded, "Quite a big role, you will have to decide what you are going to do and then what you manage to do. Like you may want to do a lot more and then you have to do quite a lot of replanning as well" (Field notes: March 9).

In following a planned search for information, students with this perspective on research focused on specific aspects of their subtopics, often formulating questions they wanted to answer. This was illustrated in the work of another key informant, Geoff, who decided to do a comparison of biographical data on Hitler and Churchill. One afternoon shortly after the beginning of the project work, Geoff asked for permission to go to the library to get a book that might compare the lives of these two men, and, upon his teacher's recommendation, he also sought information from another teacher on the wing who had previously taught history (Field notes: January 18). Later, he complained that he did not find what he needed. Subsequently, during class share time Mrs. Longman told the class of his interest, inviting other students to suggest books that might be helpful. One student offered

20 shillings = £1
12 pennies = 1 shilling.
To warn people of bombs policemen blew short
whistles Not a lot of Jobs.
A. R. P = Air Raid Prevension

After the surprise attempt to over throw the
existing power Hitler spent 13 pleasent
months in Landburg prison

anything   WW meanings   Hitler   Austria

datebook   why   How

                    Holocaust

datebook Oddette   Germany & Germans
war   Churchill   Anne Frank

            spies   Jews   Soldiers

                    Hiding   army, RAF

        France

                    Holland   Germany,
                                    Austria

a suggestion. The next day Geoff described his plans: "I came up with a brainstorm
and I decided to use two pages, one for Hitler and one for Churchill. I am going to
put different facts and then do a half a page comment on what I think about them"
(Field notes: January 19). The following month Geoff was searching for texts again
and he turned to Ian, a member in Geoff's research group which had been dis-

cussing world leaders. Together the students looked in the indexes of a number of books (Field notes: February 18). In March, although Geoff could discuss information from numerous texts related to Hitler and Churchill, his search was still continuing because he had not found precisely the information he wanted (Field notes: March 1). Simply finding a text related to the topic was not sufficient; Geoff needed quite specific information to answer his questions.

For pupils who worked in this way the greater specificity of their search was accompanied by a conscious monitoring of the suitability of the source texts. Elizabeth, who was looking for information on gas masks for her project on "Wartime Children," explained, "I skimmed through the table of contents or looked at the index and I would skim through them to see if it was what I was looking for and some had a lot of information but it was not what I was wanting because I wanted to write about *children's* gas masks" (Field notes: May 5).

Besides searching for specific information, these students also carefully reviewed their material, thinking about how they would present the information they had found in their project booklet. They were concerned about two things: whether they had covered their topic adequately and accurately and whether they were presenting their information in ways that would appeal to their audience. We will begin by looking at content coverage.

Reviewing the coverage of information. One indication that these pupils were concerned about presentation was the fact that they carefully reviewed the breadth of their coverage of each subarea in their booklet. As one student noted, "If some of them [books] didn't have a lot of information I went and looked up more" (Field notes: January 29). This concern led to the use of multiple sources to find material for any particular entry. Two different strategies were used by students who drew on more than one text to find the information they presented: (1) cut-and-paste synthesis and (2) discourse synthesis. In what follows, we draw primarily from the work of Linda, a key informant, who alternately used both strategies as she covered various subareas in her research on "Children at War."

In investigating one of her subareas, "Jewish Children," Linda used cut-and-paste synthesis. This strategy involved internalizing information from one source, writing about it, and then beginning a second paragraph/section on the same subarea using a second source. For example, Linda's first paragraph was synthesized from an informational text on the lives of children during the war, and the second drew from some notes Linda borrowed from Mary, who was investigating the Holocaust (Field notes: March 8). These two paragraphs were completed by the second month of the term (Photocopies: February 12), and the rest of the page remained half finished for some time. By May, Linda had read *Number the Stars* (Lowry, 1989), and, drawing from that work, she added a third paragraph and four stars of David to the page.

Linda also demonstrated the use of a second and more complex strategy of working from multiple texts, which involved true discourse synthesis. "In discourse synthesis, readers (writers) select, organize, and connect content from source texts as they composed their own new texts" (Spivey & King, 1989, p. 9). For example, in Linda's commentary on her section about "Schools" (see Table 3), she discusses historical fiction, newspaper articles, personal experiences, biographical narratives, and informational texts as her sources. Like Linda, the students who used this approach wrote from what they had learned not only from written texts but also from personal interviews, computer program information, and television documentaries. When writing their entries, these students referred back to source texts or to their notes for accuracy of important information such as names or dates.

These students were not simply concerned with achieving quantity. As Linda's final comments in Table 3 illustrate, these students recognized the importance of ensuring the correctness of information they had included. The use of multiple sources allowed pupils to cross-check the accuracy of material from dif-

TABLE 3
Linda's Project: Research as Transforming Information

Linda's Entry–"Schools"	Linda's Commentary
Despite the problems created by the war, for most children school had to go on as normal as possible. For others it was not so normal.	[I] took the sheet that we did from our research group and my mom said well why don't you set it out before you write—so I scratched out how different children would feel and then I wrote about it.... The language problems of children who were sent to other places like Wales—got from *Carrie's War*. I got the bit about them being more excited than scared—there was an article in the *Evening Express* about the Blitz in Aberdeen and the heading said that the person was more excited than scared. The bits on clothes and nicknames—happened here—like at our schools just now and I can't imagine that it would have been any different then—like if they had been wearing different things the others were bound to say something.... The bit about the gas masks and the air raid practices were from *War Boy* and *Growing Up at War*. [These sections] are more from in my head than from in a book—I thought like, I have heard this and I have to check up on it to see if it is right—a lot of things I have heard but I am not quite sure where—I checked up by looking at books and TV programs—and I read the parts I had on schools.
There were gas mask and air raid practices, the times of schools changed, and the evacuees joined the classes. As a result of this there were a lot of behaviour and playground problems. There was a lot of teasing and bickering. Accents and different clothes were picked up on, and nicknames developed. There were even language problems if children were sent to countries like Wales. It was a very frightening time for children who'd never been away from their mothers before. Of course some children were more excited than scared. New friends, new teachers, new schools, new country! All of these things were exciting.	
All in all, it was a very stressful time for everyone.	

ferent sources and to refine and deepen their understanding in important ways. In the following discussion of her entry on "The Blitz," another key informant, Elizabeth, explains how she had incorporated information from both her grandmother's account and from books she had read:

> I knew that they had bombed cities but Gran told me that it was mainly London and Coventry. She told me it lasted about nine months and that was in the books as well. She told me about the docks and I looked it up later in books, to find out about the docks and who suffered the most, whether it was factories or families. There was lots of families as well but the main thing was factories that they were after. (Field notes: May 5)

The question of accuracy was raised for another student through a discussion with two friends of her family. They indicated that some of the information she had found in a book might not be correct: "I showed them my project and I first told them about my project. He said, 'No, that's not right.' Different bits I got from books, like a Lancaster bomber the book said was a two engine and they said it was a four engine" (Field notes: February 1). Thus the use of multiple sources can enable accuracy checking, even when students do not set out with that intention.

Consideration of audience. These students were also aware of the needs of their perceived audience. Linda's work and her comments gave clear indications that she considered the reading abilities of her audience as she constructed her entries. Regarding the entry she wrote on the evacuation, Linda commented, "I used this portion [pointing] 'cause I thought that was good and I tried to adapt this into something a bit more understandable 'cause this was actually made at wartime" (Field notes: March 8). On the following day she further discussed who she saw as her audience and whether she thought about audience when writing:

> I think people about my age and slightly younger—'cause some of it, the books I have read are very complicated and I have had to change some of the words— 'cause there are some words that I understand and I have to change it and go to the dictionary and put a slightly more understandable word in for someone like age 10 or so. (Field notes: March 9 [structured interview])

A more forceful example of Linda's awareness that she was writing for an audience or for an implied reader is found in Figure 2. Booth (1961) and Iser (1980) describe an implied reader as the reader whom the author has in mind when the text is written. Note in this entry on "Gas Masks" how Linda's notions of the abilities of her audience or an implied reader were evident. Prior to writing this entry Linda had talked about her plans for what she would like to cover (Field notes: March 8). She flipped through the biographical narrative *War Boy* (Foreman, 1989), sharing the information about spitting on the window and laughing about the author's account of making rude noises. After Linda completed her research booklet, the first author compared Linda's "Gas masks" entry with the information in *War Boy*. Although the actions in paragraph four (see Figure 2) were described in *War Boy*, neither the pronunciation of "mica" nor the definition came from *War Boy*. Thus, Linda did not merely mimic the techniques of the author of her primary source. She purposefully constructed her own text, incorporating the pronunciation key and elaboration of word meaning that she projected her audience would find useful. Her writing style gives an initial indication

FIGURE 2
Linda's Entry, "Gas Masks," Showing Her Awareness That She Is Writing for an Audience

GASMASKS

HITLER WON'T SEND NO WARNIN' SO ALWAYS CARRY YOUR GASMASK!

Posters carrying the same message as this little boy are one of the most popular ones that I've seen in books. Cigarette cards also showed how to put on, take off, and adjust your gasmask.

Some people gave up carrying their gasmasks after a while. They thought that the war wasn't going to start, but it did.

One of the roles of the Air Raid Precaution (A.R.P) wardens, was to make sure that every single person in their district had a gasmask that fitted.

MICA WINDOW

People were taught to spit on the inside of the mica (pronounced mika) window, which is the plastic or perspex window which you see out of, to prevent it from misting up. Gasmasks were good for making rude noises, and got fogged up anyway.

BLEAARGHH!!

They were issued inside a cardboard box with some string attached. Lots of children drew pictures, or patterns on their boxes with crayons, or pencils, as my little boy has. (see picture) 8.

that she is conversing with her reader. Her sense of an implied reader is also evident in her use of capitals and punctuation to help the reader hear the rude noises she describes (also not in the original source), and, in doing so, she incorporates her own sense of humor. Finally, she writes, "Lots of children drew pictures, or patterns on their boxes with crayons, or pencils, *as my little boy has* (see picture)." This closing gives a poignant impression of her awareness that she is sharing her own uniquely created work with the person reading.

This purposeful transformation of information in light of an implied audience is in striking contrast to the perceptions of students whose task impressions were of research as transferring information. Students who transferred information could readily identify audiences for their work (including people in their class, children about their age or slightly younger, people who wanted to know about World War II or who didn't know much about World War II). However, unlike the students who viewed the research task as a transformation process, the students focusing on transferring information noted they really did not think about audience while writing. As a student who was working from a transferring perspective in her research on propaganda commented, "For [my] project I don't really think about audience 'cause I write what I think about propaganda and posters" (Field notes: March 16).

In summary, pupils who held the task impression that research involved transformation worked in ways that were markedly different from students described in the two previous sections. This they demonstrated in their use of planning and replanning to guide their investigations, in their concern for thorough coverage of the subareas, in their integration of information from multiple sources, and in their awareness of audience.

Strategies of Working From Sources

The primary data sources for the analysis of the strategies students used to work from consisted of the students' descriptions of how they worked from texts and the line-by-line comparisons of students' entries with their original sources. The strategies identified were duplicating (of words and pictures), drawing/labeling, sentence-by-sentence reworking, read/remember/write, cut-and-paste synthesis, and discourse synthesis. The most prevalent strategies used by pupils in working from written texts were verbatim copying (a duplicating strategy), sentence-by-sentence reworking, and read/remember/write. Read/remember/write was typically used to synthesize across sentences, and some key informants took notes to help them remember information. For some students a single strategy dominated their investigations, whereas others employed multiple strategies to complete even a single entry.

Drawings and photocopies were often used to illustrate content and to decorate students' booklets. Indeed, awareness that the page layout should be "nicely set up" and thus should include well-positioned pictures/illustrations in addition to text was continually stressed by students when they were asked what they thought made a good project. It should be noted, however, that some students duplicated pictures and text (by either photocopying or copying verbatim) as their primary means of presenting information. This tendency was most prevalent in the work of students who viewed research as accumulating information.

Students' strategies were previously discussed in relation to task impressions. At this point, we wish to discuss hidden processes that related to strategy use and to elaborate on the relationship between students' task impressions and their use of strategies.

Strategies and Hidden Processes. Although in general we considered duplicating and sentence-by-sentence reworking to represent less-complex text handling, we found the products did not reliably indicate the detailed nature of the students' thinking. Debriefing interviews showed that even simple drawings with one-word labels sometimes represented very involved thought processes. Dugald, a key informant, was asked to talk about a drawing he had labeled "My ideas for weapons and artillery." Pointing to one of the weapons, he explained,

> There is the hand piece and a back piece and power pack for the laser and you open the little door and you put the power pack in and inside a little bit connects from the gun to the power pack so it can form the laser and there is a telescopic aim in the top and there is a little rectangular shaped window in the top and if you hold down the trigger it will go higher and higher and the little zigzag things and you get more and more power and the laser comes out. The longer you hold down the trigger the bigger the force of the laser. (Field notes: February 11)

After this detailed explanation we learned not to take anything in the students' projects for granted: In this case a simple drawing represented only a fraction of the knowledge upon which it was based.

The triangulation of the field notes detailing classroom behaviors, the debriefing interviews, and the line-by-line comparisons of the research booklets with the source texts proved to be vital in revealing the hidden processes embedded in some students' use of particular strategies. Another key informant, Christine, worked systematically through her source text. She used a straightedge to mark her place as she reworked her source text sentence by sentence into her booklet. At the same time, however, she was very concerned with monitoring her overall understanding of each paragraph and of what she had written. She explained,

> I read a paragraph and then I change that one sentence by sentence, like you have to make certain when you finish a paragraph that it makes sense when you start the next paragraph. So I do it sentence by sentence but after a paragraph I read the whole next paragraph before I start because if the first sentence takes up where the last sentence left off and you change the last sentence, then what you write wouldn't make sense. (Field notes: March 20)

Her final comment indicates a sophisticated concern for coherence. Thus, while for some students a sentence-by-sentence reworking of a source text was accompanied by a difficulty in discussing what had recently been written, for Christine what was apparently the same strategy involved an intense concentration on her own ongoing comprehension and on making sense of her report.

Strategies and Students' Task Impressions. As previously noted, clear links were apparent between students' uses of the complex strategies of cut-and-paste synthesis or discourse synthesis and whether they viewed the research task as a transformation process. It is important to stress, however, that students' abilities to use sophisticated strategies were distinct from their impressions of the research task. Victoria, another key informant, helped us to see that students' impressions of the research task could limit the strategies that were utilized during the project itself.

Victoria held strong beliefs that to do research meant she was to find a text and write about it in her own words. In her initial interview (December 9), she noted a preference for writing nonfiction (such as the research project) because she could look up the information in a book, whereas fiction would be harder because it would be her own thoughts. Her original planning web for her project ("Wartime Children") was taken from the table of contents of a book of the same title, and for much of the term her writing was confined to information from that single source text. Comparisons between her project booklet and the text indicated that she drew heavily from that source not only for information but also for structure. Her initial entries in her booklet were completed through a sentence-by-sentence reworking of text, but in later entries she started to synthesize across paragraphs from the source text (Field notes: January 11, 13). Oddly, at least from an adult point of view, Victoria seemed to feel synthesizing across paragraphs was less desirable because she had not covered everything that was in the source text (Research group transcripts: February 25; Field notes: April 12). Her impression that research meant to transfer information from a source text limited the strategies she employed. Data indicated, however, that Victoria was actively synthesizing information from multiple sources to construct an understanding of her topic. When talking about her project, when discussing subjects in class, and when writing on her historical fiction story, Victoria expanded on the content addressed in her personal project. Her discourse revealed knowledge gleaned from personal sources (accounts from relatives and friends of her family), videos, a computer program, and other informational texts (Field notes: January 13, 15, 25, 27; February 1, 3, 25; March 8, 20). This information, however, was not incorporated into her writing for her project during the first 3 months of her research.

In March, Victoria came to Many expressing that she was "stuck" in her project. When asked what she thought would help her get started again, she replied, "Like if someone just gave me a little help and told me what to do next

I think I could get started again, I just need a little push, a little help" (Field notes: March 8). Talking with Victoria soon revealed the cause of her stalemate, her source—the text she had used for her planning web and for all of her entries thus far—had disappeared. Without her source text, Victoria was indeed stuck.

Across March, ongoing discussions occurred between Many and Victoria regarding her reluctance to continue with her project. Various alternatives were brainstormed to help Victoria resume her work (Field notes: March 8, 17, 20, 23, 24, 26). Specifically, her approach thus far to her project work was discussed, and it was noted that she could choose a new source text or that she could draw from the information she had encountered in books, films, and classroom discussions to address one of her remaining topic descriptors. Often Victoria laughed about her own disinterest in getting started again, and she repeatedly mentioned her inability to relocate her original source.

After the school holiday at the end of the term, Victoria excitedly met with Many to share her recently completed entry on "Jews." The following transcription of that conversation illustrates Victoria's changing views of the research task and reveals the shift in strategy use that accompanied her changing conception:

Victoria: I got this from my head—I did it on holiday—I did it from what we were talking about with [the preservice teacher]—on Jews.

J.M.: That is different from your usual approach of working from a source.

Victoria: I thought I wanted to do some on it—I knew about this from what I learned from [the preservice teacher]. It is just from what I learned.

J.M.: Did you find it easier or harder to do than when writing from a book?

Victoria: (looking over her text as we are talking) I have got to read over it. I found some mistakes in it already. I find it quite easier because when I read it I find in a book it is harder to learn it straight away in my head—so I thought I knew this cause I found it really interesting and I find it easy to learn when I am really interested and I said I will have to do what Prof. Many told me to do and just write what I know about the Jews.

J.M.: Any other reason it was easier?

Victoria: The other I copied it from paragraph to paragraph and I missed two pages and I said oh no I missed two pages but this is quite short cause it came up out of my head—it was easier cause it came out of my mind—like on the other I had to do how many paragraphs that were in that book and squash them on that page.

J.M.: (Directs her to talk about where she obtained the information in her new entry)

Victoria: First sentence was from what [preservice teacher] did on the racism and religion, and then next part was on racism. The Jewish symbols was from the posters that were hanging on the wall so I got that from when I came back after I had been sick. The part about the concentration camp was from the film we watched and the section on why some Jews went into hiding came from the film, and the middle section was from [preservice teacher]. The section on calling Jews up came from Anne Frank. (Field notes: April 12)

Thus, this pupil showed herself to be capable of synthesizing ideas from multiple sources when writing on her research topic, just as she had previously synthesized across sources when participating in other forms of discourse. It had been her understanding of what was legitimate in research that had inhibited her from engaging wholeheartedly in this strategy. After changing her conception of what it meant to do research, Victoria consistently wrote passages in her booklet that revealed meaningful synthesis across sources (Field notes: April 12, 29). A follow-up interview in June revealed Victoria's changed task impression dominated her approach to her subsequent research the next term, and discourse synthesis was prevalent in her work (Field notes: June 12).

In summary, students used a wide range of strategies in working from sources, and in these significant hidden processes were embedded. Strategies were closely linked, although not synonymous with students' task impressions. In addition, strategy use was shaped by immersion in the social and instructional context. Next we will discuss an important element of the instruction, the material available to students.

Materials

A wide variety of materials was available for students' project research. Frequent references were made to these diverse materials, and students were encouraged to make use of a variety of sources for their project work (Field notes: January 7, 11, 15, 22, 27; February 2, 8, 10). Examination of students' booklets and the debriefing interviews, however, indicated that a rather narrow range of sources was actually used. For the most part students' sources of information consisted of written materials. The majority of these were books with expository text structure, although there were indications that students could use narrative texts (both fictional accounts and biographical narratives) as sources for information.

Rarely (except in the case of Jean described earlier), did any students write entries based entirely on interviews with an individual or from other oral sources. Students did talk about such information in research groups and in sharing sessions. They also incorporated such information into other writing such as their historical fiction stories and the booklet relating wartime experiences, which they made for the class library. But, although the majority of students did not base their booklet entries solely on information from oral sources, some students did synthesize information from both oral and written sources.

Students whose research involved transforming information were the ones most likely to not only attend to written material but also incorporate information from oral sources as well. For example, both Linda's work on "Schools" and Victoria's text on the Jews, discussed earlier, made connections between what had been read and information derived from parents and friends, whole-class sessions, research-group sessions, and videos. Consequently, their entries often blended information from both oral and written sources. In contrast, students who accumulated information and the majority of those who focused on transferring information relied primarily on informational books.

Just as there were links between the use of certain types of materials and students' task impressions, the materials that students chose as sources for information were also closely intertwined with the strategies they used to work from the texts. The strategies students used fluctuated in relation to the difficulty of the materials. Students who were capable of drawing information from a source and molding it for their own purposes regressed to less-arduous strategies when faced with difficult texts. Some reverted to copying verbatim, whereas others employed sophisticated coping strategies. For example, in the following conversation, Mary explained the way she worked from a text that was written in "grown up language":

> "I asked my mum what it meant, it didn't have that word [referring to her use of 'money flow problems'], and she told me and I said money flow problems instead." After [Mary] scored out the words and wrote her "own words" above it, she wrote it [the section] out on another sheet rough and checked for spelling mistakes and then she put it in her project book. (Field notes: April 21)

Mary was capable of synthesizing information drawn from multiple sources, but when she encountered this more difficult text, she adjusted by using a sentence-by-sentence reworking strategy, which was less demanding.

Immersion in the Social and Instructional Context of Project Research

Students' task impressions, the materials used, and the strategies students used to work from texts shaped one another. Transactions among these were also affected across time, through social interactions that conveyed formal and informal messages regarding the research project. For example, we have already indicated how Victoria's concept of the research task changed across time resulting in her employing more complex strategies in working from text and in drawing from a wider range of materials.

For other students the stage of their research affected the strategies they chose. Across the term students like Mhairi and Elizabeth, who had begun working from texts by relying on note-taking while reading (prior to writing), found they were able to read/remember/write without relying on notes to placehold important bits of information. Their change of strategy may have reflected increased knowledge of their topics or greater proficiency in composing from sources.

The approaching deadline for the completion of the projects, the end of term, also influenced students' reading and writing engagements. It should be noted that Mrs. Longman allowed students to continue work on their research beyond the end of term if they wished, even though the focus of classwork was to change at the end of March. Most students, however, set out to complete their projects by the due date.

Individuals reacted to the approaching end of the term in different ways. A few, such as Christine and Linda, could describe in depth what they wanted to cover and the ways in which they wanted to present their information. They seemed oblivious to the deadline and worked steadily on following their original plans. For others, like Dugald, the arrival of the end of term simply signaled the time to turn in their projects with whatever had been achieved to date.

Many students, however, were strongly affected by the approaching deadline. They abruptly changed the strategies they had used throughout the previous 11 weeks. The need to shift in strategy use seemed to be exacerbated by the fact that students were initially given research booklets with 15–20 empty pages. For students like Claudia, Robert, Mhairi, and Geoff, successful completion of the research project hinged on filling up the booklets (Field notes: March 23, 24; May 5). Thus, some students began abandoning previous work from sources strategies for ones they found more time efficient. For instance, Geoff, who previously had not used duplicating strategies, began copying passages verbatim. Other students made interesting shifts toward relying on what they had already learned rather than using the sentence-by-sentence reworking or read/remember/write strategies, which had dominated their earlier work. For Mhairi, who researched propaganda, this shift was a positive move. In the resulting work she was more willing to express her personal opinion of wartime issues and to incorporate discourse synthesis across texts. She also applied what she had learned about propaganda in the creation of her own posters and in comparing and contrasting her posters with those of the World War II era (Line-by-line comparisons of research booklet/source texts; Field notes: March 23, 24).

The key informants who shifted strategy in order to fill up their booklets repeatedly expressed satisfaction with their work (regardless of whether they had resorted to verbatim copying or photocopying) because they had finished. Interestingly, Mary, who did not change strategies as the deadline approached, dealt with the tension she felt about filling up the booklet by simply removing all the empty pages before turning in her booklet (Field notes: May 5).

Discussion

This discussion is organized in three parts. In the first part we relate our work to previous research. This replicates our own recursive process in that as patterns emerged and changed in the course of our investigation we worked to situate our findings and interpretations within the context of other research. In the second part we discuss the theoretical position and analogies explored by McGinley and Tierney (1989) in light of our findings. In the third part we consider the implications of our findings for teachers whose students are working on research projects.

Making Connections to Related Research

Research on reading and writing to learn and on discourse synthesis has tended to restrict students' decision making by isolating specific processes, prescribing specific materials, or imposing limited time frames. In contrast, our study explored how students carried out a research task in an everyday classroom situation over an extended period of time. Students in this study experienced a considerable degree of freedom in their selection of a research topic, in their choice of sources of information, and in the way they presented their information. Together these provided a social and instructional context conducive to relatively independent research and allowed us the opportunity to explore what influenced students' engagements in reading–writing–research activities.

Our data confirmed that students' reading and writing engagements were strongly shaped by their impressions of the research task. The effect of students' task impressions on reading/writing tasks has been noted with both older readers in a self-directed task (Nelson & Hayes, 1988) and with elementary-age students completing a prescribed synthesis task (Raphael & Boyd, 1991). It is not surprising that what pupils do is strongly influenced by what they think they have to do (i.e., their task impressions). In this study we were able to look carefully at what pupils actually did, record their comments, examine the materials they were using, and observe the contexts in which they carried out their work. Through these analyses we were able to construct a description of what different pupils seemed to think they had to do. When these task impressions were uncovered, we were better able to appreciate how reasonable the pupils' actions usually were. What pupils thought they had to do explained to some degree why particular subtasks were undertaken in particular ways by particular pupils.

Our data also address the call for additional research on understanding individual variation in students' research processes (McGinley, 1992). Students did indeed differ greatly in their task impressions, and two important findings arose from this. The first was that task impressions related closely to the subtasks on which students chose to concentrate their efforts and, second, that task impressions related to the strategies students used when working from sources. For example, those whose task impression was that they should accumulate material to fill their booklets concentrated on the subtasks of finding and recording and typically used duplicating strategies. At the same time, some of these students were able to describe effective and efficient ways of carrying out other subtasks such as planning and searching. Similarly, Wray and Lewis (1992) noted discrepancies between what primary pupils said they would do to locate sources, search for information, and write up that information, and what the students actually did when involved in a research project.

In an analysis of research on secondary school reading practices, Alvermann and Moore (1991) concluded, "we know more about *what* needs to be done in order to learn from text than *how* teachers and students approach that learning" (p. 974). Consistent with this, previous research on locating information has led to the development of a model of *what needs to be done* in order to conduct an efficient search (Dreher & Guthrie, 1990; Dreher & Sammons, 1994; Guthrie & Mosenthal, 1987). This model consists of the following steps:

> (a) formulating a goal or plan of action, (b) selecting appropriate categories for inspection (e.g. index, table of contents), (c) extracting relevant information from the inspected categories, (d) integrating extracted information, and (e) monitoring the completeness of the answer and recycling through the component processes until the task is completed. (Dreher & Sammons, 1994, p. 303)

While our research subtasks—planning, searching, finding, recording, reviewing, and presenting—fit with this model, our data emerged from an analysis of *how students approach* research, and we suggest that (a) developmental and (b) social dimensions need to be considered.

First, it is a major contention of this article that for students of this age and level of experience, conducting research or inquiry work is so complex that learners may find it difficult if not impossible to work continuously on the totality of any investigation. They may find it difficult to give to each subtask in the inquiry process the balance of attention that it deserves. Their understanding of the nature of the subtasks develops as their grasp of the whole task increases. It may be that full understanding of what is involved in planning and searching cannot be grasped without seeing how it influences and is influenced by the other subtasks. There is, therefore, an important developmental dimension to be considered.

The final outcome of student efforts may often seem inadequate or inefficient. If, however, students try to improve their current level of performance by giving more attention to aspects hitherto neglected or try to incorporate new subtasks or strategies, then they may well put at risk the level of success that they have achieved. Because of this, students may be reluctant to abandon strategies that have given them comparative success. If they are to develop as researchers, however, they have to be willing to put their existing level of success at risk. Only those learners who recognize shortcomings in what they have currently achieved, and who want to attain an apparently higher level, will confront this dilemma. On the other hand, some students may be genuinely satisfied with their current performance. And it should be noted that their level of performance may indeed be high in some respects: high, for example, in terms of information finding and recording but relatively weak, say, in review and presentation. A classroom ethos that encourages autonomy, flexibility, and risk taking will support the development of effective reading-writing-research.

Second, this study has only begun to recognize the critical role played by the social dimension in the instructional context in which students' research is embedded. What children actually learn, and therefore practice and demonstrate, is learned as a result of social processes. "Learning is not just a matter of cognitive processing.... Literacy learning takes place in a social environment through interactional exchanges in which what is to be learnt is to some extent a joint construction of teacher and student" (Cook-Gumperz, 1986, p. 8). This view may be broadened to contend that it is not only teacher/child interactions that shape learning, but that interactions with parents, peers, and researchers collecting data, for example, also have significant influence. The act of learning, in this case learning inquiry and research skills, can be seen as a developing inter-subjectivity between the child and others (MacGillivray, 1994). From this perspective, research or inquiry work is not an objective reality of which a child develops greater understanding. Research as viewed and performed by children and teachers is created within and through a social dynamic, consisting of not only a number of explicit teaching/learning experiences but also a potentially infinite number of other experiences that together create implicit understandings. For instance, in a classroom where pupils are encouraged to select their own subjects for artwork, to have responsibility for storing and retrieving materials, and to carry out a conference independently of the teacher, autonomy is likely to be developed. Not all these experiences relate in obvious ways to student research, yet all contribute to developing a feeling of autonomy that would impact on how students conduct research.

In our study, interactions, tacit understandings, and value assumptions shaped the decisions related to sources of information, the content to be included, the notions of what was valued in project work, and the perceptions of the research task. This is true not only in reference to the students' perspectives and research but also to our own perspectives and research. Our interest in the social dimension was sharpened after data collection had been completed. Consequently, we were unable to fully capitalize on our increasing appreciation of social influences through additional member checking or refocusing data collection. However, the importance of social influences is still clearly evident in the data we have presented. Future studies on students' reading–writing–research processes need to further examine the social dimension.

Traversing the Topical Landscape

McGinley and Tierney (1989) see a topic for investigation as "analogous to a landscape about which knowledge is best acquired by 'traversing' it from a variety of perspectives" (p. 250). If students engage in self-directed reading and writing, then it becomes possible for them to explore multiple ways of viewing and thinking about topics.

Our analysis showed that students traversed the World War II landscape in very different ways. The students who were most likely to consider multiple perspectives were those who viewed research as transforming information. They skimmed, took notes, brainstormed, read, reflected, searched, and read more, and sometimes produced initial outlines or drafts prior to writing their final syntheses. These students used texts of one genre as sources for information for writing in another (e.g., historical fiction texts as sources for expository prose). They were capable of switching strategies when working from texts of different levels of difficulty (e.g., using sentence-by-sentence reworking to record information from a difficult text). They used reading, writing, viewing, listening, discussing, and illustrating as ways of exploring their topics. Their explorations were extensive as well as intensive. Their recursive uses of the research subtasks of planning, searching, finding, recording, reviewing, and presenting exemplify the dynamic interplay of reading and writing McGinley and Tierney (1989) argue is fundamental to thinking critically about a topic. In a similar way, Kennedy (1985) found that fluent undergraduate readers enlisted a repertoire of strategies in order to write with intention and purpose and that they integrated material from their notes and sources with their own thoughts and ideas.

While students who viewed research as transforming information appeared to explore their topic, this did not seem to be the case for students who viewed research as accumulating or transferring information. These students seemed more concerned with completing a product. Their approaches illustrate that students' naturally occurring reading and writing processes are not necessarily dynamic and recursive; students' self-directed reading and writing engagements can also progress in a less flexible, more linear fashion. In some cases students' uses of reading and writing constrained creativity and limited original thought. This was consistent with Tierney's (1990) cautions against overstating the benefits of reading and writing in combination.

In our study, students who viewed research as accumulating or transferring information worked with a rather linear, goal-directed orientation, similar to what McGinley (1992) contends was implied in earlier studies on discourse synthesis. When these students in our study worked on a subarea, they found a source, examined/read it, and then wrote about it utilizing sentence reworking or a read/remember/write strategy. In contrast, students who viewed research as transforming information exemplified what McGinley describes as a "complex orchestration of a variety of reading, writing, and reasoning activities in a nonlinear, dynamic fashion" (p. 23). Thus the interplay of reading and writing for the participants in this study was strongly affected by their perception of what it meant to do research. However, factors other than task impressions also compelled students to adopt a more linear approach.

Reading and writing engagements were also strongly influenced by the difficulty of the texts with which the students were working and the stage of the research project. Thus some of our students, whose processes and strategies at times resembled the fluent readers or higher-ability readers in previous research (Kennedy, 1985; Spivey & King, 1989), at other times exhibited characteristics of the less-fluent or less-able readers from those same studies. They adopted a more linear approach when working from difficult text or when short of time to complete their booklets. These findings underscore the importance of examining factors related not only to the reader but also to the texts (both sources read and the student's written entries), to the context (instructionally and across time), and to interrelationships that may exist among them.

Implications of the Study

The implications of this study are many and various. We will begin this section by discussing the importance of developing an awareness of students' and teachers' task impressions, and then we will address how teachers might develop students' reading–writing–research processes.

In any classroom where reading–writing–research tasks are being undertaken, the task impressions of the students will be different. Our study suggests that teachers need to make a deliberate effort to understand individual task impressions. First, teachers should be aware of the explicit and implicit messages about the nature of research that they themselves convey. For example, in our study an explicit injunction that pupils should write in their own words had unexpected outcomes. In terms of implicit messages, we suspect that the issuing of empty booklets early in the research task implies to some students that filling the booklet has high priority. Messages such as these affect task impressions and the strategies students choose to use. In the same way teachers need to ensure that they convey an appropriate balance of concern for research processes on the one hand and research products on the other. For example, some pupils in our study regarded the approaching deadline for submission as a signal to concentrate on completing the end product.

Second, to understand individual task impressions teachers need to observe pupils' reading–writing–research activities across a range of occasions. How pupils perform at any one time can be affected by powerful situational factors not immediately obvious to the teacher. For example, Victoria's research came to a halt, not as might have been thought because she had run out of ideas, but because someone had taken her book. Victoria's planning web was based solely on the table of contents in that book. Her task impression was that research involved finding a relevant book and transferring its contents into her booklet. Thus, when her selected book was missing, she lost interest and motivation for her research and stopped working. Supporting Victoria's development as a researcher could only begin once the situational factors operating and the nature of her task impression had been recognized.

We turn now to the question of what teachers might do to develop students as researchers. Our study was an in-depth exploration of pupils' reading–writing–research in a particular context. On the basis of our findings, we offer the following hypotheses as to instructional situations that may support the development of student research. It is left to individual readers to make judgments regarding the transferability of our suggestions to their context.

If teachers are concerned with developing pupils' reading–writing–research, they must be concerned with pupils' task impressions. The basic premise on which to proceed is that what students are currently doing is essentially reasonable according to their existing task impressions. Any movement to change what pupils do or to alter their task impression can induce feelings of insecurity and thus inhibit their development.

Increasing the range of subtasks (see Table 2) in which pupils engage broadens their repertoire without challenging what they already do. It may be that pupils who practice finding and recording should be encouraged to undertake search activities, such as discussing what kind of sources might have information relevant to their topic. In this way pupils who principally accumulate information may be coaxed to new understandings of the research task and to begin to engage in a broader range of subtasks. It is possible that some pupils are asked to plan too early in relation to a specific research project. Students with little knowledge of topic produce plans of little benefit in guiding their research process. A recursive process, in which planning and replanning are encouraged throughout the research process, not seen as a necessary (and sometimes restrictive) first step is most beneficial.

Increasing the range of strategies that pupils use may also lead them to form new impressions of the research task. In order for pupils to move from the perspective of research as transferring information to one in which research is seen as transforming information, students must employ more complex strategies for working from text. However, teachers must ensure that students have texts that allow the use of these strategies. With difficult texts students resort to duplicating, sentence-by-sentence reworking, and read/remember/write strategies.

Finally, we suspect that texts have been accorded too high a status in reading–writing–research undertaken by students. Informational texts predominate as sources of information for research work and predominate as the form in which research end products are presented. Using multimedia, including videotapes, audiotapes, drama, oral accounts, and so on, could be beneficial in a number of ways. For instance, it could allow for a closer and richer engagement with ideas. Encouraging students to explore a topic and to present their findings in diverse media could also increase the range of strategies that students employ. In addition, using the media with which individuals feel most comfortable should increase their sense of autonomy, their willingness to take risks, and their feelings of confidence and competence (Dyson, 1993).

In summary, in this study learners were provided with the materials, the time, and the teacher and peer support to carry out relatively self-directed research. In this context students constructed their own perceptions of the task. They moved fluidly between reading and writing, choosing the materials they wished to read and the entries they wished to construct. Students could change strategies as conditions changed, and they could decide how much attention to devote to different subtasks as familiarity with content and with reading–writing–research processes developed. We believe that additional investigation of students' research in naturally occurring contexts is merited. Through further examination of students' reading–writing–research, we can increase our understanding of instructional situations that enable students to become lifelong independent learners.

References

Alvermann, D.E., & Moore, D.W. (1991). Secondary school reading. In R. Barr, M.L. Kamil, P. Mosenthal, & P.D. Pearson (Eds.), *Handbook of reading research* (Vol. 2, pp. 951–983). White Plains, NY: Longman.

Booth, W. (1961). *The rhetoric of fiction.* Chicago: University of Chicago Press.

Cook-Gumperz, J. (Ed.). (1986). *The social construction of literacy.* Cambridge, UK: Cambridge University Press.

Dillon, D.R. (1989). Showing them that I want them to learn and that I care about who they are: A microethnography of the social organization of a secondary low-track English-reading classroom. *American Educational Research Journal, 26,* 227–259.

Dreher, M.J., & Guthrie, J.T. (1990). Cognitive process in textbook chapter search tasks. *Reading Research Quarterly, 25,* 323–339.

Dreher, M.J., & Sammons, R.B. (1994). Fifth graders' search for information in a textbook. *Journal of Reading Behavior, 26,* 301–314.

Dyson, A.H. (1993). *Social worlds of children learning to write in an urban primary school.* New York: Teachers College Press.

Foreman, M. (1989). *War boy: A country childhood.* New York: Arcade.

Fyfe, R., & Mitchell, E. (1984). *Reading in project work: First investigation.* Aberdeen, Scotland: Northern College.

Glaser, B., & Strauss, A. (1967). *The discovery of grounded theory: Strategies for qualitative research.* New York: Aldine.

Guba, E.G., & Lincoln, Y.S. (1981). *Effective evaluation.* San Francisco: Jossey-Bass.

Guthrie, J.T., & Mosenthal, P. (1987). Literacy as multidimensional: Locating information and reading comprehension. *Educational Psychologist, 22,* 279–297.

Iser, W. (1980). Interactions between text and reader. In S.R. Suleiman & I. Crosman (Eds.), *The reader in the text* (pp. 106–119). Princeton, NJ: Princeton University Press.

Kennedy, M.L. (1985). The composing processes of college students writing from sources. *Written Communication, 2,* 434–456.

Langer, J.A., & Applebee, A.N. (1987). *Writing as a means of shaping thought.* Urbana, IL: National Council of Teachers of English.

Lincoln, Y.S., & Guba, E.G. (1985). *Naturalistic inquiry.* Newbury Park, CA: Sage.

Lowry, L. (1989). *Number the stars.* Boston: Houghton Mifflin.

MacGillivray, L. (1994). Tacit shared understandings of a first-grade writing community. *Journal of Reading Behavior, 26,* 245–266.

McGinley, W. (1992). The role of reading and writing while composing from sources. *Reading Research Quarterly, 27,* 226–249.

McGinley, W., & Tierney, R. (1989). Traversing the topical landscape: Reading and writing as ways of knowing. *Written Communication, 6,* 243–269.

Nelson, J., & Hayes, J.R. (1988). *How the writing context shapes college students' strategies for writing from sources* (Tech. Rep. No. 1). Pittsburgh, PA: University of Pittsburgh, Center for the Study of Writing.

Newell, G. (1984). A case study/protocol of learning to write. *Research in the Teaching of English, 18,* 205–287.

Raphael, T.E., & Boyd, F.B. (1991). *Synthesizing information from multiple sources: A descriptive study of elementary students' perceptions and performance of discourse synthesis* (Tech. Rep. Series No. 45). East Lansing: Michigan State University, Center for the Learning and Teaching of Elementary Subjects.

Salvatori, M. (1985). The dialogical nature of basic reading and writing. In D. Bartholomae & A. Petrosky (Eds.), *Facts, artifacts, and counterfacts: Theory and method for a reading and writing course* (pp. 137–166). Upper Montclair, NJ: Boynton/Cook.

Shanahan, T., & Tierney, R.J. (1990). Reading-writing connections: The relations among three perspectives. In J. Zutell & S. McCormick (Eds.), *Literacy theory and research: Analyses from multiple paradigms* (39th yearbook of the National Reading Conference, pp. 13–34). Chicago: National Reading Conference.

Spindler, G., & Spindler, L. (1982). Rodger Harker and Shonhausen: From familiar to strange and back again. In G. Spindler (Ed.), *Doing the ethnography of schooling: Educational anthropology in action* (pp. 20–46). New York: Holt, Rinehart and Winston.

Spivey, N.N. (1984). *Discourse synthesis: Constructing texts in reading and writing* (Outstanding Dissertation Monograph Series). Newark, DE: International Reading Association.

Spivey, N.N., & King, J.R. (1989). Readers as writers composing from sources. *Reading Research Quarterly, 24,* 7–26.

Symons, S., & Pressley, M. (1993). Prior knowledge affects text search success and extraction of information. *Reading Research Quarterly, 28,* 250–261.

Tierney, R.J. (1990). Learning to connect reading and writing: Critical thinking through transactions with one's own subjectivity. In T. Shanahan (Ed.), *Reading and writing together: New perspectives for the classroom* (pp. 131–143). Norwood, MA: Christopher-Gordon.

Tierney, R.J., Soter, A., O'Flahavan, J.F., & McGinley, W. (1989). The effects of reading and writing upon thinking critically. *Reading Research Quarterly, 24,* 134–173.

Wray, D., & Lewis, M. (1992). Primary children's use of information books. *Reading, 26,* 19–24.

27

A Research Agenda
for Improving Reading
Comprehension

RAND Reading Study Group

* * *

Editors' Introduction

In *Reading for Understanding: Toward an R&D Program in Reading Comprehension*, the book in which this piece originally appeared, the RAND Reading Study Group (RRSG) defines reading comprehension in language that would make it accessible to organized research and development. The group defines reading comprehension as "the process of simultaneously extracting and constructing meaning through interaction and involvement with written language" (p. 11). The words *extracting* and *constructing* are used to underscore the essential but limited role of text alone as a determining factor in reading comprehension. The group's working definition includes a framework of core elements situated in a sociocultural context.

Acknowledging the group's use of terms that others have used to define reading comprehension, the RRSG identifies three elements participating in comprehension: a reader comprehending, a text to be comprehended, and an activity contributing to comprehension. These three distinct dimensions contributing to a definition of comprehension are embedded in a sociocultural context. While that context interacts with each embedded element, the reader shapes the context and is shaped by it.

While the RRSG acknowledges that many researchers have contributed to this conception of reading comprehension and provides a chapter elaborating on the elements constituting the group's definition of comprehension, readers can explore the definition's features and implications more fully in other articles in this volume (see, for example, Galda & Beach [#31] and Ruddell & Unrau [#35]). In these pieces, the broad sweep and particular elements of comprehension as defined are more fully described and envisioned.

* * *

n this piece, the RRSG proposes a research agenda that prioritizes three specific domains of reading comprehension for future research: instruction, teacher preparation, and assessment. In making these proposals, the RRSG emphasizes the need for research that builds on what is already known, that will contribute to better theories of reading development, and that will produce knowledge that is usable both in classrooms and in policymaking arenas. To that end, this piece describes what is already known within each of these three domains and describes areas for future work.

Comprehension Instruction

Good instruction is the most powerful means of developing proficient comprehenders and preventing reading comprehension problems. Narrowly defined, comprehension instruction promotes the ability to *learn from text*. More broadly, comprehension instruction gives students access to culturally important domains of knowledge and provides a means of pursuing affective and intellectual goals. A major goal for the research agenda we propose is improving classroom instruction in comprehension, both by exploring how to ensure the broader implementation of instructional strategies known to work and by building a research base to inform the design of new instructional paradigms.

Effective teachers of comprehension enact practices that reflect the orchestration of knowledge about readers, texts, purposeful activity, and contexts for the purpose of advancing students' thoughtful, competent, and motivated reading. Instructional decision making is a dynamic and highly interactive process. To illustrate, chapter 3 in *Reading for Understanding* describes the many reader variables that are integral to proficient reading comprehension. Drawing on this literature, we characterize students along a continuum from "low need" to "high need" in terms of the instructional support they will require to become proficient comprehenders. However, this characterization of the reader must also take into account the nature of the text that the student is reading and the nature of the task that is motivating the reader. We argue that any reader can be considered high-need depending on how challenging the text is (i.e., the text is poorly written, dense, or contains a number of unfamiliar ideas) or depending on the way the reader is to demonstrate his or her understanding of the text (e.g., recall, reasoning, application, or evaluation). Finally, the teacher must consider the broad range of contextual factors that influence instructional opportunities for particular learners.

These contextual factors include, but are not limited to, community- and schoolwide factors, the culture of the classroom, the specific curriculum and instructional activities in which students are engaged, and the nature of the interaction between teacher and students as well as among students. Similarly, a student who appears to be a high-need reader when the reader variables are considered in isolation may, in fact, be very successful in an instructional setting in which the teacher attends to this student's needs while selecting texts, designing tasks for him or her, and deciding how to structure the context to best support the student's participation and learning.

To maximize the possibility that research will yield *usable knowledge*, instructional research, regardless of the method employed, needs to attend to each of these elements of reading comprehension. Careful descriptions of both the texts used in the research and the specific nature of the task(s) for which students are using reading in the specific context of instruction need to accompany careful descriptions of the participants. The context includes, but is not limited to (in the case of classroom-based research), general classroom conditions (reported in Pressley et al., 2001) that set the stage for effective instruction, the specific nature of the instructional activity or activities in which the learner is engaged, and the specific nature of the support that teachers, peers, and instructional tools (e.g., computers) provide.

What We Already Know About Comprehension Instruction

The RAND Reading Study Group's prioritization of comprehension instruction set forth in the agenda presented in this piece is based on a fairly well-articulated knowledge base.

1. *Instruction that is designed to enhance reading fluency leads to fairly significant gains in word recognition and fluency and to moderate gains in comprehension.*

A substantial amount of practice over an extended period of time is required for a reader to acquire fluency. Most fluency instruction consists of the repeated reading of the same text and uses many techniques. Sometimes the repeated reading practice is done independently; sometimes the reader is assisted by a teacher who provides corrective feedback; sometimes the reader listens to the text before practicing or reads along with a teacher or a tape. Some studies have incorporated partner reading in which peers, not a teacher, give feedback.

The National Reading Panel (NRP) (National Institute of Child Health and Human Development [NICHD], 2000) examined the wide-ranging literature on repeated reading. A meta-analysis of 14 studies indicated that the mean weighted effect size of comparisons of one or another of these techniques versus a no-instruction control varied depending on what type of outcome measure was examined. It was largest (.55) when the outcome measure was word recognition, next largest (.44) with a fluency measure, and smallest (.35) with a comprehension outcome measure. The NRP found that repeated reading was effective for normal readers through grade 4 (there were no studies of normal readers beyond grade 4) and for students with reading problems throughout high school.

The NRP also examined three other sets of studies: studies looking at the immediate effect of different programs of repetition and feedback during oral reading on the reading performance of a specific passage (these studies did not attempt to assess transfer to uninstructed passages); studies using small groups of students; and studies that compared the efficacy of two different oral reading procedures. All three sets of studies corroborated the findings of the meta-analysis, indicating the value of repeated reading. No conclusions could be drawn about the relative effectiveness of independent repeated reading and guided oral reading practice or of any other two procedures, such as reading with or without feedback. One exception to this conclusion of no differences comes from a study by Rashotte and Torgesen (1985). They compared passages that either shared or did not share many words with the outcome measures. They noted gains when the passages shared words but no gains when the passages did not share words. This result suggests that very poor readers probably at least learn words from repeated reading (Faulkner & Levy, 1999). Most studies have found that reading interconnected text is necessary for effective fluency instruction, but one recent study (Tan & Nicholson, 1997) has indicated that reading of isolated word lists also leads to increased fluency.

Several studies have indicated that these repeated-reading techniques are feasible for classroom use (Dixon-Krauss, 1995; Rasinski, 1990). No extensive preparation is needed to use these techniques successfully (Reutzel & Hollingsworth, 1993). Studies dealing with readers with learning disabilities have found that peer tutoring can be successfully incorporated into the instruction (Mathes & Fuchs, 1993; Simmons et al., 1994).

Other studies have assessed the effect of simple practice in reading, such as Sustained Silent Reading. However, merely encouraging students to read extensively did not result in improved reading, according to the findings of a meta-analysis (NICHD, 2000). It is thus not clear whether there are conditions under which practice in reading would promote fluency and comprehension.

Another approach to promoting fluency involves ensuring that proficiency and fluency are acquired during instruction in all components of reading, starting with letter knowledge and phonemic awareness and moving to decoding and word recognition (Berninger, Abbott, Billingsley, & Nagy, 2001; Wolf & Katzir-Cohen, 2001). Berninger, Abbott, Brooksher, et al. (2000) and Wolf and Katzir-Cohen (2001) have developed intervention programs that address specific component skills, foster linkages among all relevant systems—orthographic, phonological, semantic, and morphological—and emphasize fluency at each step. These programs are very new, and no data on their success in promoting fluency are currently available.

2. *Instruction can be effective in providing students with a repertoire of strategies that promote comprehension monitoring and foster comprehension.*

Because meaning does not exist in text, but rather must be actively constructed, instruction in how to employ strategies is necessary to improve comprehension.

To construct meaning, students must monitor their understanding and apply strategic effort. We know that students who are good comprehenders read for a purpose and actively monitor whether that purpose is being met. They notice when something they are reading is incongruous with their background knowledge or is unclear; then they take action to clarify their understanding, such as rereading or reading ahead. They may also stop periodically when reading to summarize what they have read as a way to check their understanding.

To further enhance comprehension, good comprehenders also use strategies that help them retain, organize, and evaluate the information they are reading. Among these strategies is a well-defined set that we know, as a result of rigorous investigation and replication, leads to improved comprehension when employed by readers. This set of strategies includes concept mapping, question generating, question answering, summarizing, and story mapping as delineated in the NRP report (NICHD, 2000). Additional strategies investigated in nonexperimental studies that may also prove beneficial to students include mental imagery, knowledge activation, mnemonics, and expository pattern identification.

Judging by the experimental studies reviewed by the NRP (NICHD, 2000), we know that engaging students in identifying the big ideas in a text and in graphically depicting the relationships among these ideas improves their recall and comprehension of text. We also know that in grades 3–5, engaging students in elaborative questioning improves their comprehension of text read during instruction and their comprehension of new text read independently. Similarly, teaching students in grades 3–9 to self-question while reading text enhances their understanding of the text used in the instruction and improves their comprehension of new text. Studies conducted in the upper-elementary grades indicate that learning to paraphrase text, identify the gist of a text, and identify and integrate the big ideas in a text enhance the recall of text and the capacity to understand new text. Teaching students in grades 3–6 to identify and represent story structure improves their comprehension of the story they have read. In the case of this strategy, there was no evidence that the strategy transferred to the reading of new stories and improvement was more marked for low-achieving readers.

3. *The explicitness with which teachers teach comprehension strategies makes a difference in learner outcomes, especially for low-achieving students.*

Understanding the nature of the reading comprehension problems experienced by many students who are low achieving has helped in developing instructional approaches that enhance the comprehension abilities of these students. An important instructional strategy for these learners consists of making instruction very explicit. Explicit instruction provides a clear explanation of the criterion task, encourages students to pay attention, activates prior knowledge, breaks the task into small steps, provides sufficient practice at every step, and incorporates teacher feedback. It is particularly important for the teacher to model the comprehension strategies being taught. Careful and slow fading of the scaffolding is important.

Sometimes this explicit instruction is helpful for low-achieving students but is superfluous for normal readers (Wong & Jones, 1982). Sometimes improvement occurs not because of the specific strategies being taught but because students have been actively interacting with the texts. This active integration triggers the use of strategies that inactive learners possess but do not normally use.

Explicit instruction generates the immediate use of comprehension strategies, but there is less evidence that students continue to use the strategies in the classroom and outside of school after instruction ends (Keeny, Cannizzo, & Flavell, 1967; Ringel & Springer, 1980) or that they transfer the strategies to new situations.

Recent studies have underscored the importance of teacher preparation when the goal is to deliver effective instruction in reading comprehension strategies (Brown et al., 1996; Duffy et al., 1987). This is especially important when the students are low performing. Implementing a direct approach to cognitive strategy instruction in the context of the actual classroom has proven problematic. Proficient reading involves much more than using individual strategies. It involves a constant, ongoing adaptation of many cognitive processes. Successful teachers of reading comprehension must respond flexibly and opportunistically to students' needs for instructive feedback as they read. Lengthy, intensive teacher preparation is effective in helping teachers deliver successful strategy instruction that has improved student outcomes on reading comprehension tests.

4. *There are a number of working hypotheses about the role of instruction in explaining and addressing the problems of poor comprehenders.*

One of the most vexing problems facing middle and secondary school teachers today is that many students come into their classrooms without the requisite knowledge, skills, and dispositions to read the materials placed before them. These students are, for one reason or another, poor comprehenders. Poor comprehenders are students who can neither read nor demonstrate satisfactory understanding of texts appropriate for their grade level. Many teachers are frustrated by what they see as an ever-increasing number of students who are poor comprehenders.

Instructional research with poor comprehenders has been motivated by a particular set of hypotheses about impediments to comprehension. Some of these hypotheses suggest that the problems of poor comprehenders are an outgrowth of differential instruction; that is, these students have been denied the kinds of instruction that advance reading comprehension. This hypothesis is particularly relevant for students who have a history of reading problems (e.g., decoding problems in grades 1 and 2). For example, McDermott and Varenne (1995) documented that teachers working with high-achieving students focused on higher-order thinking with text and communicated clearly that the purpose of reading was understanding. In contrast, these same teachers, when working with low-achieving students, focused on low-level factual reading, interrupted children's reading more frequently than their errors would justify (see also Shake, 1986), and communicated little about comprehension as the goal of reading. A corollary to this hypothesis is that students with a history of reading challenges read less text; hence, they accrue less background knowledge to bring to the reading of new text.

Research has indicated, however, that specific instruction, for example, prereading, can improve poor comprehenders' understanding of a difficult text. Researchers have used instructional scripts that provide students with essential background knowledge, key concepts, and vocabulary (Graves, Cooke, & LaBerge, 1983) or have activated students' background knowledge through extended discussions (Langer, 1984). Researchers have also used such activities as story structures or graphic organizers to provide scaffolding for improved comprehension of a selected text (NICHD, 2000). Pre- and postwriting activities have also been used as effective instructional activities to promote comprehension for low-achieving readers. These instructional activities effectively address the problem of poor comprehension by providing this sort of instructional scaffolding to help low-achieving readers comprehend texts above their independent reading level.

In addition, poor comprehenders can be guided to effectively employ a number of strategies to improve their understanding of text. For example, researchers have helped poor comprehenders draw inferences by using a prereading strategy in which they activate attention and prior knowledge or by using particular strategies in the course of reading, such as restating information from the text (Chan et al., 1987; Idol-Maestas, 1985; Schumaker et al., 1982).

The nature of the strategy taught seems less significant than the role that strategy instruction plays in engaging the reader in active interaction with the text (Chan & Cole, 1986). A synthesis of the research literature on teaching comprehension strategies to students with learning problems (Gersten, Fuchs, Williams, & Baker, 2001) indicates that successful comprehension instruction for the poor comprehender is characterized by explicit modeling by the teacher, additional opportunities for practice with feedback, skillful adjustments to the learner's level, and the reader's mindful engagement with the purposes for reading.

5. The role of vocabulary instruction in enhancing comprehension is complex.

As we describe in *Reading for Understanding*, vocabulary knowledge is strongly linked to reading comprehension (Freebody & Anderson, 1983), and there is reason to believe that vocabulary knowledge is an especially important factor in understanding the reading problems experienced by second-language learners (García, 1991; Laufer & Sim, 1985). However, this relationship between vocabulary knowledge and comprehension is extremely complex, confounded, as it is, by the complexity of relationships among vocabulary knowledge, conceptual and cultural knowledge, and instructional opportunities.

These complexities speak to the unique and significant role that instructional research can play in enhancing the education field's understanding of the role of vocabulary knowledge in comprehension. The NRP (NICHD, 2000) found that direct instruction of vocabulary improved reading comprehension. The effects of extensive reading on vocabulary growth are, however, debatable. The NRP did not find compelling evidence that programs that are designed to increase independent reading, such as Sustained Silent Reading, promoted vocabulary growth. Nevertheless, there is a powerful correlational relationship between the volume of reading and vocabulary growth among first-language learners (Stanovich & Cunningham, 1992), and "book-flood" studies (in which children are provided with numerous books for use at school or at home) with second-language learners have shown powerful effects (Elley, 1991). Further, a wealth of evidence relates children's oral language experiences to subsequent vocabulary growth (Dickinson & Tabors, 2001). Much of this evidence comes from studies of the effects of homes and preschools on language development. Less is known about the effects of school-based oral language activities and vocabulary learning and growth, although Meichenbaum and Biemiller (1998), among others, have argued that the fourth-grade slump is caused, at least in part, by the failure of schools to promote oral language development while children are still working on the mechanics of reading.

Much of the instructional research in vocabulary has been designed to document, or compare, the effectiveness of different methods of teaching individual words. Although some generalizations can be made about the characteristics of effective vocabulary instruction (Stahl & Fairbanks, 1986), the number of studies that have directly examined the effects of vocabulary instruction on reading comprehension is still relatively small. Some of the strongest demonstrations of the effects of vocabulary instruction on reading comprehension— the work of Beck and her colleagues (e.g., Beck, Perfetti, & McKeown, 1982; McKeown, Beck, Omanson, & Pople, 1985)—used rather artificial texts heavily loaded with unfamiliar words. Little, if any, research addresses the question of which conditions—the types of texts, words, readers, and outcomes—can actually improve comprehension.

Effective vocabulary instruction presupposes choosing the right words to teach. This is another area in which more research is needed. How does a teacher choose which words to teach? What are the instructionally relevant subcategories of words? Graves (2000) and others have suggested some distinctions that must be considered, such as the difference between teaching new concepts and teaching new labels for familiar concepts, or the difference between teaching students to recognize in print words already in their oral vocabularies and teaching them words not yet in their reading or oral vocabularies. Nation (1989; Laufer

& Nation, 1999) has offered another instructionally relevant way to categorize words—as high-frequency words, domain-specific technical vocabulary, low-frequency words, or high-utility academic vocabulary. Although such distinctions are undoubtedly crucial in making instructional decisions, there is still little documentation of how well teachers can use such categories or of the actual effect of such categories on the effectiveness of vocabulary instruction.

Some vocabulary researchers (e.g., Laufer & Sim, 1985) have stressed the importance of high-frequency words for learners of English, because a relatively small number of words constitute the bulk of words encountered in text. However, the most effective methodology for teaching high-frequency words still needs to be explored, given that such words are also the most likely to have multiple meanings. Others have stressed the importance of focusing on words intermediate in frequency—not so frequent that they are already known by almost everyone, yet frequent enough to be worth teaching. Much remains to be learned about identifying these words and about the effectiveness of instructional approaches that focus on such words. Another dimension of choosing words for instruction has to do with the relationships among instructed words. Materials for learners of English as a second language often group words on the basis of meaning. However, some evidence suggests that teaching words in groups that are highly similar in meaning is a hindrance, rather than an aid, to learning (Tinkham, 1993; Waring, 1997).

Teaching individual words presupposes some sort of explanation of their meanings, which is most likely to be in the form of a definition. Although some research has explored the effectiveness of different types of definitions (Fischer, 1994; McKeown, 1993; Scott & Nagy, 1997), relatively little is known about this area. To our knowledge, for example, no one has explored the question of whether different types of definitions are appropriate for different types of words or for different stages of word learning (e.g., initial exposure versus consolidation and refinement of word knowledge). Research could help illuminate what knowledge, skills, and abilities best allow learners to benefit from definitions or, more generally, from vocabulary instruction (e.g., dictionary skills, metalinguistic abilities, language proficiency levels). There is little question that one component of proficient comprehension is the ability to cope with any unfamiliar words encountered during reading. Readers need to be able to use the information provided by context, by morphology (word parts), and by dictionaries or other reference materials and to coordinate information from these sources.

In a recent meta-analysis, Fukkink and de Glopper (1998) found that instruction in the use of context improved students' ability to use contextual clues to figure out word meanings. However, on the basis of a similar meta-analysis, Kuhn and Stahl (1998) argued that such instruction was not demonstrably more effective than simple practice. Instruction in the use of morphology and definitions has been less thoroughly investigated than instruction in the use of context.

The possibility of online dictionaries and other word-learning aids opens up additional areas for research.

The effectiveness of context for second-language learners is still a matter of debate. A variety of evidence indicates that second-language learners have more difficulty using context than do native-language learners (e.g., Nagy, McClure, & Montserrat, 1997). However, second-language learners who face the task of simply learning new labels rather than learning new concepts may be at a relative advantage.

Research is also needed on what makes some students more effective independent word learners than others. Some of the contributing factors, such as language proficiency and existing vocabulary and background knowledge, are obvious. Phonological processing ability contributes to vocabulary learning, especially for second-language learners (Eviatar & Ibrahim, 2000; Muter & Diethelm, 2001). It also seems likely that a variety of metalinguistic abilities contribute to vocabulary learning (Nagy & Scott, 2000).

A number of vocabulary researchers have expressed the opinion that "word consciousness" or "word awareness" may be an important element in promoting vocabulary growth (Graves, Watts-Taffe, & Graves, 1998). As yet, no research has measured such a construct, let alone documented its effects on vocabulary learning. One reason that word consciousness and its effects on vocabulary growth are not well understood is that various constructs could fall under this heading but they are not all necessarily related to one another. For example, the concept of words (Roberts, 1992), morphological awareness (Anglin, 1993; Carlisle, 1995), word schemas (Nagy & Scott, 1990), word play, and an appreciation for effective word choice (Scott & Nagy, 1997) could all fall under the term *word consciousness*. Little is known, however, about how these constructs relate to one another or to vocabulary growth.

Various aspects of word consciousness may be crucial to strategies for independent word learning. Morphological awareness is undoubtedly involved in using word parts to make inferences about the meanings of new words. Word schemas—knowledge of what might constitute a possible meaning for a word—could be an important part of making inferences about new words encountered in context (Nagy & Scott, 1990) and may also contribute to the effective use of definitions. For example, Fischer (1994) speculates that one factor limiting the effectiveness of second-language learners' use of bilingual dictionaries is the expectation that there will be one-to-one mappings between the meanings of words in two languages.

For speakers of Spanish who are learning English (or vice versa), a specific type of word awareness—awareness of cognate relationships—may be specifically important. Many words in the vocabulary of literate or academic English are similar in both form and meaning to everyday Spanish words (e.g., *tranquil/tranquilo* and *pensive/pensivo*). Bilingual students differ in their ability to recognize such relationships (Nagy, García, Durgunoglu, & Hancin-Bhatt, 1993; García & Nagy, 1993), and the ability to recognize such relationships appears to be associated with more effective reading strategies (Jiménez, García, & Pearson, 1996).

Each of the four components of a vocabulary curriculum outlined by Graves (2000)—teaching individual words, encouraging wide reading, teaching word-learning strategies, and promoting word consciousness—is likely to make an important contribution to students' long-term vocabulary growth and, hence, to their reading comprehension. However, in addition to our incomplete knowledge about each component, we know extremely little about their relative contribution and how they interact with one another.

6. *Teachers who provide comprehension strategy instruction that is deeply connected within the context of subject matter learning, such as history and science, foster comprehension development.*

As we described earlier in this piece, the NRP evidence suggests that teaching such reading strategies as questioning, summarizing, comprehension monitoring, and using graphic organizers facilitates reading comprehension. Several quasi-experimental investigations show that when the strategy instruction is fully embedded in in-depth learning of content, the strategies are learned to a high level of competence (Guthrie, Van Meter, Hancock, Alao, Anderson, & McCann, 1998). If students learn that strategies are tools for understanding the conceptual content of text, then the strategies become purposeful and integral to reading activities. Connecting cognitive strategies to students' growing knowledge of a content area enables students to both increase their awareness of and deliberately use the strategies as means for learning (Brown, 1997) in microgenetic analyses of instruction. Unless the strategies are closely linked with knowledge and understanding in a content area, students are unlikely to learn the strategies fully, may not perceive the strategies as valuable tools, and are less likely to use them in new learning situations with new text.

Integrating strategy instruction into content domains requires a balance. The priority of instructing for reading comprehension must be balanced with the priority of teaching the content area itself. Teachers can help students learn that gaining new ideas, increased understanding, and literary experience is an aim of reading and that strategies are a powerful way to accomplish that aim. This information helps students use strategies reliably when they are appropriate. If comprehension strategies are taught with an array of content and a range of texts that are too wide, then students will not fully learn them. If strategies are taught with too narrow a base of content or text, then students do not have a chance to learn how to transfer them to new reading situations (Rosenshine & Meister, 1994). The optimal balance enables students to learn that strategies are an important means for understanding but are not the main point of reading activities. The main purposes for reading are gaining meaning and gaining knowledge.

An important aspect of strategy development is to enable students to become self-initiating (Alexander & Murphy, 1998), according to several reviews of empirical literature. Students who spontaneously apply a strategy, such as questioning, when it is sensible will improve their comprehension. Thus, to be effective comprehenders, students must have motivation, self-efficacy, and ownership regarding their purposes for reading and their strategies. Teaching strategies integrated with content enables students to become proficient, self-regulating strategy users.

7. *Using various genres of text (i.e., narrative and informational text) diversifies instructional opportunities, as assessed by teacher and student discourse.*

A knowledge of text structure is an important factor in fostering comprehension. Students with some knowledge of text structure expect texts to unfold in certain ways. Even before they enter school, children have a rudimentary sense of narrative structure. The first texts they are introduced to in school are narrative in structure, which allows an easy transition from oral to written language (Van Dongen & Westby, 1986). In school, children are also introduced to expository text, which is more complex, diverse, and challenging.

Readers who are unaware of structure do not approach a text with any particular plan of action (Meyer, Brandt, & Bluth, 1980). Consequently, they tend to retrieve information in a seemingly random way. Students who are aware of text structure organize the text as they read, and they recognize and retain the important information it contains.

Simple exposure to stories is helpful, but explicit instruction is valuable. Children are taught to ask themselves generic questions that focus on the principal components of a story, which helps them identify the relevant and important information in stories (Mandler & Johnson, 1977; Stein & Glenn, 1979; Williams, 1993). In addition to their value as an organizational guide to the text structure, the questions enhance the active processing of the text, thus qualifying the generic questions as comprehension-monitoring instruction. Such instruction improves students' ability to see relationships in stories, answer comprehension questions, and retell the stories in a focused fashion. The positive effects of an intervention are most likely to accrue on measures closely aligned with the specific instruction provided. The effect of interventions that teach the use of text structure is not as strong on transfer measures. Although stories constitute the bulk of reading material for instruction in the early grades, a case for greater inclusion of other text genres has been made (Duke, 2000; Pappas & Barry, 1997). Such inclusion will allow instruction that more closely matches the demands of reading in later grades.

As readers progress through school, the demands placed on them change. At about grade 4, they are expected to read expository material in content instruction. Because expository text is often dense with information and unfamiliar technical vocabulary, students must perform complex cognitive tasks to extract and synthesize its content (Laff, Flood, & Ranck-Buhr, 1995). Expository text involves relatively long passages, less familiar content, and more complex and varied structures (Armbruster & Anderson, 1984). Explicit teaching about structure enables students to differentiate among common structures and to identify the important information in a text in a coherent, organized way (Armbruster & Armstrong, 1993).

Various instructional techniques have been used to help students comprehend expository text, including teaching them to use generic questions to self-question (Wong & Jones, 1982), to use mapping to analyze the text (Boyle & Weishaar, 1997; Swanson, Kozleski, & Stegink, 1987), to summarize (Nelson, Smith, & Dodd, 1992), and to employ other simple strategies. These interventions were effective.

A body of research exists on methods for adapting or modifying texts (e.g., Beck, McKeown, Sinatra, & Loxterman, 1991) to make them easier to comprehend. This literature is important, but it does not address the issue of helping students understand the texts they may encounter in their content area classes and on high-stakes tests.

8. *Teachers who give students choices, challenging tasks, and collaborative learning structures increase their motivation to read and comprehend text.*

For students from grade 1 to grade 12, classroom activities that enable and encourage them to take responsibility for their reading increase their reading achievement. For example, extensive observations of classroom instruction for primary students show that when teachers provide challenging passages for reading, students exert effort and persistence. And when students have a limited, but meaningful, choice about the learning activity, such as which part of a text to read, they invest greater energy in learning than when the tasks are always prescribed by the teacher (Turner, 1995).

With elementary and middle school students, quasi-experimental and structural equation modeling studies have shown that teachers who provide meaningful choices and autonomy increase students' motivation to read and to expend effort to gain knowledge from text (Reeve, Bolt, & Cai, 1999). The explanation for the benefit of autonomy support for reading comprehension is that students become more-active learners when teachers provide a minimal, but meaningful, choice in the topics, texts, activities, and strategies for learning. For example, when given a choice of two books for a comprehension activity, students will choose the one that interests them. This interest deepens the students' thinking and their use of strategies and background knowledge during reading (see Schiefele, 1999, for a review of experimental evidence). High interest, derived from choice, leads to high comprehension.

The roles of motivation and engagement as links between instruction and achievement have been documented by many investigators (Skinner, Wellborn, & Connell, 1990; see Guthrie & Wigfield, 2000, for a review of empirical research). In brief, the most predictive statistical models show that engagement is a mediator of the effects of instruction on reading achievement. If instruction increases students' engagement, then students' achievement increases. In this literature, engagement refers to a combination of the following: (a) the use of cognitive strategies; (b) the presence of an intrinsic motivation to read; (c) the use of background knowledge to understand text; and (d) the social interchanges in reading, such as discussing the meaning of a paragraph or the theme of a narrative. Therefore, instruction affects reading comprehension outcomes through the avenue of active engagement in frequent, thoughtful reading for understanding.

9. *Effective teachers enact a wide range of instructional practices that they use thoughtfully and dynamically.*

Most people do not realize how complex teaching is. Effective teachers do more than teach specific strategies or make available to students a wide variety of texts. Indeed, effective teachers of reading engage in a diverse array of instructional practices (NICHD, 2000; Pressley et al., 2001; Taylor, Pearson, Clark, & Walpole, 1999). This panoply of practices results in a complex environment in which comprehension can be fostered.

A review of studies of effective teachers reveals some of these important instructional practices and activities. For example, effective teachers establish a complex set of organizational and management routines in their classrooms, which they use to ensure a minimal amount of disruption and a maximal amount of time-on-task. Indeed, almost all the time in the classrooms of effective teachers is spent on instruction. In addition, effective teachers provide an atmosphere of support and encouragement. In their classrooms, readers feel comfortable taking risks and are expected to achieve.

Effective teachers also use a variety of instructional practices that relate more specifically to reading comprehension. For example, effective teachers ask high-level comprehension questions that require students to make inferences and to think beyond the text. Effective teachers help readers make connections between texts they read and their personal lives and experiences. Effective teachers use small-group instruction to meet the individual needs of their readers. Effective teachers provide their readers with practice reading materials at their appropriate reading level. Effective teachers of young readers monitor progress in reading by using informal assessments.

One critically important, but thorny, aspect of teaching reading in general and comprehension in particular is the appropriate balance between teaching skills and using literature. Over the last 20 years, the reading field has vacillated between the two—with fierce opposition between those recommending one or the other. However, the choice does not seem to concern most teachers. In a survey of teacher practices, Baumann, Hoffman, Moon, and Duffy-Hester (1998) reported that teachers believed both to be essential for good teaching. In fact, teachers reported that they taught skills *and* extensively used literature.

10. *Despite the well-developed knowledge base supporting the value of instruction designed to enhance comprehension, comprehension instruction continues to receive inadequate time and attention in typical classroom instruction across the primary and upper-elementary grades.*

In the late 1970s, research revealed that teachers devoted only 2% of the classroom time designated for reading instruction to actually teaching students how to comprehend what they read (Durkin, 1978/1979). Twenty years later not much has changed in the upper-elementary (Pressley, 2000) or primary grades (Taylor et al., 1999). For example, Taylor and colleagues documented the limited opportunities that children in grades K–3 had to develop knowledge and thinking even in the context of schools that were effectively "beating the odds"—that is, schools that were realizing higher early reading achievement gains than would be predicted given the demographics of their student populations. Using survey and classroom observation data, they reported that only 16% of the teachers in the entire sample emphasized comprehension.

Despite the hypothesized role that inexperience with informational text plays in the fourth-grade slump (Chall, Jacobs, & Baldwin, 1990), and despite evidence that some young children prefer to read informational text (Pappas & Barry, 1997), primary-grade classrooms have a significant dearth of informational texts (Duke, 2000). Beginning in grade 4 and throughout their formal education, students will spend the majority of their time reading expository text, yet instruction in grades 1–3 primarily uses narrative text. Recently a plethora of engaging informational texts, written for primary-grade students, has become available. However, these books are not yet in sufficient supply in primary classrooms, and primary-grade teachers have not yet balanced teaching reading for informational and narrative texts.

What We Need to Know About Comprehension Instruction

What specific issues of educational urgency exist, and how can we formulate the most promising research directions for addressing them? We start with four problem statements related to low-achieving students and one concerning second-language readers, then turn to issues of instructional design relevant to the entire student population.

1. *For poor comprehenders in the general education setting, would focusing more time on comprehension instruction while using currently available curricula and instructional strategies generate adequate gains?*

Studies of classroom practice are unanimous in noting the scarcity of time devoted to comprehension instruction. Neither in the primary grades, when the focus of reading instruction is typically word reading, nor in the middle elementary grades do teachers spend much time helping students learn how to approach complex texts strategically. Although the current approaches to teaching comprehension are neither adequately rich nor research based, the possibility exists that they are adequate to address comprehension problems for some learners, if sufficient time is devoted in instruction.

2. *For poor comprehenders in the general education setting, how should time and instructional emphasis be allocated among (a) promoting fluency, (b) teaching vocabulary, (c) instructing students in the use of reading strategies, (d) providing extensive reading of informational and literary text, (e) encouraging writing based on reading, (f) using multimedia to support content learning, and (g) using computer programs to improve reading skills?*

Some evidence supports the efficacy of promoting fluency, teaching vocabulary, teaching strategies, promoting wide reading, and encouraging writing based on reading in promoting comprehension. In contrast, little evidence supports the efficacy of using multimedia for content learning or computer programs for skill development, but these practices are widely implemented. Teachers need guidance, which is totally absent in the available research literature, about how to combine and prioritize these various instructional approaches in the classroom.

3. *How do teachers identified as effective with low achievers create, administer, and use reading assessments that are related to curricular goals and useful for informing instruction across grade levels and across diverse populations of students? Further, how do effective teachers determine the knowledge, skills, and dispositions that diverse readers bring to reading activities?*

Studies of effective teachers have been informative about aspects of instruction that work well to improve comprehension. We know little, though, about effective teachers' selection, use, and interpretation of assessments to inform their practice. Such practice-based wisdom, if it is indeed available, could be useful if verified and disseminated more widely.

4. *For low-achieving students in high-poverty schools, what organization of instructional practices is beneficial: (a) instruction in word recognition and fluency, (b) access to and use of an abundance of content and literary texts, (c) explicit teaching of reading strategies, (d) explicit teaching of vocabulary and use of vocabulary knowledge in reading, (e) out-of-school literacy pursuits to*

enhance reading development, (f) writing based on reading, and (g) opportunities for multimedia links to support reading and writing tasks?

As noted above, little evidence supports the efficacy of giving instruction in word recognition and fluency, teaching vocabulary, teaching strategies, promoting wide reading, and encouraging writing based on reading in promoting comprehension. Also, there is little evidence concerning the efficacy of computer programs for skill development or of out-of-school literacy supports, but these practices seem promising. Teachers working in high-poverty schools need guidance on how to combine and prioritize various instructional approaches in the classroom. In particular, they need to learn how to teach comprehension while attending to the often poor word-reading skills their students bring to the middle and later elementary grades.

5. *For students who are learning English as a second language, how should time and instructional emphasis be allocated among (a) giving instruction in word recognition and fluency, (b) teaching vocabulary, (c) instructing about strategies, (d) providing extensive reading of informational and literary text, (e) encouraging writing based on reading, (f) using multimedia to support content learning, (g) using of out-of-school literacy pursuits to enhance reading development, and (h) using computer programs to improve reading skills?*

Teachers of English-language learners, like teachers of poor comprehenders in the general education setting and teachers working in high-poverty schools, have available a number of instructional techniques and strategies that research has shown to be effective and additional techniques that are endorsed by the wisdom of practice. However, selecting among these various instructional practices for particular students and groups of students and devoting appropriate amounts of time to using the practices remain a challenge. And research offers little guidance.

6. *Under what conditions does instruction about strategies to improve reading comprehension actually lead to students' using the strategic approaches for various texts and tasks in diverse contexts and at different age levels? What specific instructional activities, materials, and practices are related to effective comprehension and to the engagement of students from various cultural and linguistic backgrounds at varying grade levels?*

It is well documented (NICHD, 2000) that students can be taught to use strategies to advance their ability and inclination to independently learn from text.[1] Furthermore, evidence suggests that a relatively small set of strategies appears to be consistently effective across diverse populations of students, with diverse forms of text, and for diverse tasks that the reader is to accomplish. Finally, and perhaps most important, there is evidence that the power of strategy instruction is the extent to which strategies are taught in the service of interpreting text, not as ends in and of themselves. But this robust knowledge base is still incomplete.

7. *How can excellent, direct comprehension instruction be embedded in content instruction that uses inquiry-based methods and authentic reading materials?*

Contemporary national benchmarks in science call for instruction to be inquiry based. The standards in history call for students to learn the practices of historical analysis, including the use of primary documents. Contemporary language arts standards call for students, at all ages, to read authentic literature across genres (e.g., novels, memoirs, interviews) and to write in various genres. Web-based technology affords students the opportunity to access numerous sources of information. All of these opportunities provide potentially powerful contexts in which students can learn to interpret text and can learn how to learn from text. However, with the exception of a few studies (Brown & Campione, 1994; Guthrie et al., 1998) we know little about how these instructional contexts lead to improved reading comprehension or about how specific teacher practices in these contexts can lead to improved comprehension. Specifically,

- What is the role of direct instruction in specific comprehension-monitoring and comprehension-fostering strategies in an inquiry-focused learning environment?
- How can activities that are designed to promote knowledge-building be extended to enhance self-regulated reading?
- What role does experience with a diverse array of texts, used in the context of subject matter learning, play in promoting thoughtful, competent, and motivated readers?

8. *How do we ensure that all children know the vocabulary they will encounter in content area and advanced texts?*

A number of significant researchable issues are related to the role of vocabulary in enhancing comprehension. We focus here on four subsets: (1) selecting the words to teach, (2) teaching strategies for learning words independently, (3) fostering word consciousness, and (4) examining the interplay between different components of a vocabulary curriculum.

9. *How do national, state, and local policies and practices facilitate or impede the efforts of teachers to implement effective comprehension instruction?*

The policy literature and teacher journals are filled with examples of how policy changes improved or undermined educational effectiveness. There are notable examples of successfully implemented policies imposed or encouraged by districts and states that changed instructional practices in the domain of word reading. However, a systematic analysis of the effect of these and other policies on comprehension instruction has not been undertaken.

Teacher Education and Professional Development in Reading Comprehension

An important goal of research on reading comprehension is the larger goal of improving students' reading proficiency. This goal, however, is mediated by at least two critical variables. First, the research must be translated into appropriate *instruction*. Second, *teachers* must enact that instruction. Regardless of the quantity and quality of research-based knowledge about comprehension, unless teachers use that knowledge to improve their instruction, students' reading achievement will not improve. In other words, as Sykes (1999) argued, recent advances in research-based best practices have an effect only to the extent that teachers adopt those practices.

There is reason to question whether teachers use research-based best practices to teach comprehension or other subject areas. Cuban (1993) has argued that, in general, although teachers have made some changes in their classrooms over the last 100 years, the basic forms of instruction have not changed. The Third International Math & Science Study (TIMSS) Videotape Classroom Study (Stigler, Gonzales, Kawanaka, Knoll, & Serrano, 1999) corroborated Cuban's observations and conclusions. In the TIMSS study, researchers found that most U.S. teachers, even those who say they use reform models, still teach using traditional practices. Hiebert and Martin (2001) showed that teachers distort much knowledge about mathematics reform to make it consistent with their existing practices. These researchers found that true changes in teaching practice based on research were rare among U.S. teachers.

Whereas some researchers have questioned the extent to which teachers use research-based best practices in their instruction, other researchers have pointed to teacher quality as one of the most critical variables in student achievement. Teacher quality is defined in many ways, from advanced degrees to deep subject matter knowledge to deep pedagogical knowledge (Shulman, 1986). Whatever way it is defined, it is clear that the expertise of the teacher matters, and it matters a lot. In an extensive review of the research on teacher quality and student achievement, Darling-Hammond (2000) found that teacher quality and expertise consistently and accurately predicted student achievement. Additionally, Sykes (1999) pointed to the rather weak effects of efforts at systemic reform efforts—focused on new assessments, new curriculum frameworks, and teaching standards—are not enough to improve student achievement. Research has demonstrated that these efforts need to be accompanied by strong professional development. More-recent systemic reform efforts have focused squarely on the teacher as the center of reform.

One particularly puzzling aspect of school reform is that despite the key role ascribed to teachers when explaining why reforms fail (Cohen & Ball, 1990; Cremin, 1965; Darling-Hammond, 1990), we continue to craft fairly minimal roles for teachers in conceptualizing and enacting reform. The minimal role of the teacher is also vexing when we consider the findings on factors affecting student achievement. Although 48% of the variance in student achievement is attributable to home and family factors that are largely out of the school system's control, 51% of the variance is attributable to controllable factors, 43% of which can be attributed to teacher quality (Ferguson, 1991). Despite these findings, we seem to have few ideas about how to enlist the support of teachers in reform efforts, how to enhance their capacity to maximally contribute to the reform effort, and how to engage teachers in reshaping reform efforts in response to their experiences in enacting reform.

Fullan (1992) reported that the time spent in deliberating on and enacting new educational policies has generally been three times greater than the average time allotted for planning the initial implementation. One hypothesis for this finding might be that we know very little about how to structure and support such a planning process.

Many policymakers have identified the critical role of the teacher in the reform process. "Teachers are, in one sense, the problem that policy seeks to correct" (Cohen & Ball, 1990, p. 238). Underinvestment in teacher knowledge has killed many a reform movement in the past, especially those that strove toward child-centered forms of education (Darling-Hammond, 1990). Cremin (1965) attributes the past failures of educational reform efforts to teacher capacity. The landmark research reported in the special issue of *Educational Evaluation and Policy Analysis* devoted to teachers' responses to the California mathematics reforms was enormously helpful to our getting a finer sense of the role of the teacher in mediating the change process. The direct study of how innovations affected teaching practices across five elementary teachers' classrooms revealed the varied responses that these teachers made as a function of their knowledge and beliefs. In addition, this research illustrated the ways in which teachers filled in the gaps in their understanding of the policy, creating a melange of practices.

Thus the teacher must be front and center as we discuss how to improve comprehension instruction is schools today. The question becomes, *How can we bring about increased teacher quality and expertise in teaching reading comprehension?* Teachers who exhibit increased teacher quality and expertise have a deep knowledge about the reading process and reading comprehension. They also have the knowledge and skills to implement research-based instructional strategies in their teaching, ideally while also making their practice-based reflections on those instructional strategies available to researchers. In this report, we identify what we know about the answer to this question and raise new questions for additional research.

To answer this question, we look at two bodies of research: one on teacher education and another on professional development. Teacher education or teacher preparation programs refer to four- and five-year programs (both undergraduate and graduate) whose goal is to prepare individuals for teacher certification. Professional development refers to the ongoing education of certified teachers. We limit our discussion to teacher education and professional development that directly relate to learning how to teach reading comprehension, even though we draw from the larger educational research base in order to answer our question. And we acknowledge in advance that the research base on effective teacher education and professional development is disappointingly thin. Nonetheless, we argue that it is sufficient to support doing a better job than we are now doing, even as we pursue research designed to provide enhanced content about excellent comprehension instruction and about improved models for teacher education and professional development.

What We Already Know About Teacher Preparation

A common belief among many Americans is that teaching is something that people can do without much preparation (Darling-Hammond & Green, 1994). The need for teacher preparation programs has always been suspect. In fact, during the 1990s, many alternative teacher education programs were developed to certify teachers without requiring traditional teacher preparation. These programs were based in the belief that individuals with extensive life experiences and expertise in a particular domain—science, history, physics, math—could certainly teach in that domain with minimal preparation.

Although this trend has continued over the past 10 years, a plethora of literature related to teacher preparation programs has become available (for the most recent review of this work, see Sikula, 1996). Most of this literature, however, consists of descriptions and discussions of existing teacher preparation programs, case study analyses of preservice teachers' beliefs and experiences, and recommendations for improving teacher preparation programs that are based on theory, logic, or experience. In addition, the literature is largely descriptive and qualitative (for a recent review of this work applied to reading education, see Fisher, Fox, & Paille, 1996). Although this body of work can be helpful in identifying issues and constructs for future study, it cannot, by itself, be used to make legitimate claims about teacher education programs. In fact, the NRP (NICHD, 2000) found no studies that measured student achievement as a result of teacher education. As Anders and her colleagues (Anders, Hoffman, & Duffy, 2000) stated, "Few...claims [about teacher education and reading] stand on a solid research base" (p. 727).

Nevertheless, we do know a few things about teacher preparation programs. For example, we know that preservice teachers often enter teaching programs with firmly held beliefs about the nature of knowledge and the nature of teaching. These beliefs have been acquired through their own experiences as learners in schools. These beliefs shape how they view the teaching and learning processes and their own teaching and learning. We also know that many preservice teachers enter teaching with the idea that there is "little need to obtain a knowledge base in pedagogy in order to become effective teachers" (Lanier & Little, 1986, p. 11). In the past, these candidate teachers have viewed education courses as weak and easy courses, the "Mickey Mouse" courses of the university. The NRP (NICHD, 2000) found, however, that preservice teacher education programs appear to improve candidate teachers' knowledge about teaching and learning; preservice teachers, in other words, learn what they are taught. Thus it is reasonable to conclude that well-designed teacher education programs have a positive effect on reading outcomes.

What We Need to Know About Teacher Preparation

These claims leave much work to be done before we can better understand the effect of teacher preparation programs on developing expertise in teaching reading comprehension. Several key questions need to be addressed:

- What knowledge base (e.g., in language development, sociolinguistics, multiculturalism, reading development) do teachers need for effective reading comprehension instruction?
- What is the relative power of various instructional delivery systems (e.g., field-based experiences, video-based cases, demonstration teaching, microteaching) for helping teachers acquire the knowledge and skills they need to successfully teach comprehension to students of different ages and in different contexts?
- What do extant national data sets (e.g., NAEP) show about the extent to which teacher preparation experiences relate to teacher practices and student performances on comprehension measures?

What We Already Know About Teacher Professional Development

Conventional wisdom among teacher educators is that preservice teachers are easier to work with than practicing teachers. Although preservice teachers certainly hold prior beliefs about teaching and learning, these teacher educators think that the beliefs of practicing teachers are typically more entrenched. Many believe that practicing teachers, through their teaching experiences and classroom routines, have developed established ways of thinking about and implementing instruction—ways that are often resistant to change. For example, it is very difficult for practicing teachers to learn how to use instructional strategies that are different from the ones with which they are familiar. Joyce and Showers (1996) found that it takes as many as 30 instances of practicing a new routine before teachers can successfully incorporate it into their repertoire of practice.

Other research has corroborated this conventional wisdom. A body of research demonstrates the ineffectiveness of many traditional forms of inservice education for teachers (Cochran-Smith & Lytle, 1999). First, we know that the traditional staff development format is a relatively brief "one shot" workshop in which a presenter presents information to teachers about instructional practices. The effectiveness of these workshops, when evaluated at all, is typically measured through surveys of teacher satisfaction and only rarely by changes in teacher behavior. For the most part, teachers report that they perceive professional development in general to be of little use or value.

What We Need to Know About Teacher Professional Development

But what conditions promote effective professional development experiences? Effective professional development is associated with several characteristics (NICHD, 2000). First, effective programs cover longer periods of time than do less-effective programs. Second, extensive investment of both money and time is needed on a continual basis for effective professional development. Third, effective professional development is content focused and provides teachers with theoretical understandings of subject matter (Darling-Hammond, 2000; Elmore, 1999/2000; Joyce & Showers, 1996). Finally, a wide variety of content, when used for professional development, appears to be successful (NICHD, 2000).

Since most of these claims about professional development in general relate to professional development to improve reading instruction as well, we can use the claims to identify what we do not know about effective professional development that supports high-level reading comprehension instruction. Among the things we need to know are the following:

- What content (declarative and procedural knowledge about readers, text, tasks, and contexts) and sequencing of content lead to effective professional development programs?

- How do various instructional delivery systems for professional development (e.g., in-class coaching, participatory learning, video-based cases, demonstration teaching, collaborative planning, lesson studies) influence the acquisition of knowledge and skills that lead teachers to enact effective instructional practices for students of different ages and in different contexts?

- What are the critical components of professional development that lead to effective instruction and sustained change in teachers' practice?

- How do teachers' existing beliefs and instructional practices influence how teachers use new information about teaching reading when that new information conflicts with what they already believe and do?

- What are the various ways to support teachers so that they are willing to spend the time and cognitive effort and energy necessary to improve their comprehension instruction?

Assessment of Reading Comprehension

Understanding the nature of the problem of reading comprehension requires having available good data identifying which readers can successfully undertake which activities with which texts. Such data are not available, in part because the widely used comprehension assessments are inadequate. Further, the improvement of instruction relies crucially on the availability of information about the effectiveness of instruction. Teachers need reliable and valid assessments tied closely to their curricula so that they can see which students are learning as expected and which need extra help. In addition, schools, districts, and states are increasingly calling for reliable and valid assessments that reflect progress toward general benchmarks of reading, writing, and mathematics ability. For the area of reading comprehension, good assessments that are tied to curriculum as well as good assessments of general comprehension capacity are sorely needed. These assessments need to be constructed in accordance with the many advances in psychometric theory.

What We Already Know About Comprehension Assessments

Currently available assessments in the field of reading comprehension generate persistent complaints that these instruments

- inadequately represent the complexity of the target domain;
- conflate comprehension with vocabulary, domain-specific knowledge, word-reading ability, and other reader capacities involved in comprehension;
- do not rest on an understanding of reading comprehension as a developmental process or as a product of instruction;
- do not examine the assumptions underlying the relationship of successful performance to the dominant group's interests and values;
- are not useful for teachers;
- tend to narrow the curriculum; and
- are unidimensional and method dependent, often failing to address even minimal criteria for reliability and validity.

Indeed, most currently used comprehension assessments reflect the purpose for which they were originally developed—to sort children on a single dimension by using a single method. Even more important, though, is that none of the currently available comprehension assessments is based in a viable or articulated theory of comprehension. And none can give us a detailed or convincing picture of how serious the problem of comprehension achievement in the United States is. These considerations, as well as the thinking about the nature of reading comprehension represented in this document, create a demand for new kinds of assessment strategies and instruments that (a) more robustly reflect the dynamic, developmental nature of comprehension; (b) represent adequately the interactions among the dimensions of reader, activity, text, and context; and (c) satisfy criteria set forth in psychometric theory.

Currently, widely used comprehension assessments are heavily focused on only a few tasks: reading for immediate recall, reading for the gist of the meaning, and reading to infer or disambiguate word meaning. Assessment procedures to evaluate learners' capacities to modify old or build new knowledge structures, to use information acquired while reading to solve a problem, to evaluate texts on particular criteria, or to become absorbed in reading and develop affective or aesthetic responses to text have occasionally been developed for particular research programs but have not influenced standard assessment practices. Because knowledge, application, and engagement are the crucial consequences of reading with comprehension, assessments that reflect all three are needed. Further, the absence of attention to these consequences in widely used reading assessments diminishes the emphasis on them in instructional practices as well.

What We Need in the Area of Comprehension Assessments

The entire research enterprise sketched out in *Reading for Understanding* depends on having a more adequate system of instrumentation for assessing reading comprehension. A satisfactory assessment system is a prerequisite to making progress with all aspects of the research agenda we propose. Thus we argue that investing in improved assessments has very high priority. It is clear that we cannot even sketch the seriousness of the problem of reading comprehension in the United States or the nature of the decline in comprehension outcomes that is the source of much worry until we have an assessment system that can be used across the developmental range of interest and that assesses the same construct across that range.

Assessing the effect of changes in instruction depends on having valid, reliable, and sensitive assessments. The effect of assessment on instruction is a question that constitutes a research agenda of its own, particularly in this highly accountability-oriented era of education reform. But the power of high-stakes assessments over instruction and curriculum can be somewhat mitigated if teachers have available alternative assessment options that give them more useful information.

Any system of reading assessments should reflect the full array of important reading comprehension consequences. We argue that a research program to establish expectable levels of performance for children of different ages and grades on this full array of consequences is necessary. Such a program is a prerequisite to developing performance criteria at different age and grade levels and to pursuing questions about reader differences associated with instructional histories, social class, language, and culture in reading comprehension outcomes.

Although the reading comprehension consequences defined above constitute the basis for designing a comprehension assessment that would reflect success, our view suggests that assessments designed to reflect readers' cognitive, motivational, and linguistic resources as they approach a reading activity are also necessary. For instance, when the outcomes assessment identifies children who are performing below par, process assessments could help indicate why their reading comprehension is poor. Further, diagnostic assessments are crucial in dissecting the effect of particular instructional or intervention practices. Ideally, we would move ultimately toward assessment systems that can also reflect the dynamic nature of comprehension, for example, by assessing increments of knowledge about vocabulary and particular target domains that result from interaction with particular texts.

We see the development of an assessment system for reading comprehension as having a very high priority. Such a system should be based in contemporary approaches to test development and evaluation. We recognize that developing a comprehensive, reliable, and valid assessment system is a long-term project. Crucial for such a system are the criteria for judging performance across the developmental span. Nonetheless, a substantial start could be made in the short run, either by targeting the assessment of outcomes and reader resources as a major task of the research agenda or by encouraging the development of prototype assessments for outcomes and reader resources within other research efforts (such as research focused on instructional efficacy). Such an effort is central to pursuing larger research agendas, such as longitudinal work to create a picture of the development of reading comprehension, a large-scale effort to determine how U.S. children are functioning as readers, or a systematic pursuit of differences in reading comprehension performance related to cultural background, social class, and language status.

The approach to assessment proposed here differs from current approaches to reading assessment in that it would both grow out of and contribute to the development of an appropriately rich and elaborated theory of reading comprehension. Assessment procedures generated by this approach are thus more likely to be influenced and changed by theoretically grounded reading research. Our approach also highly values the utility of assessment for instruction. Of course, comprehensive assessment systems can place high demands of time on students and teachers; thus, we have an obligation to develop assessments that are embedded in and supportive of instruction, rather than limited to serving the needs of researchers.

A comprehensive assessment program reflecting the thinking about reading comprehension presented here would have to satisfy many requirements that have not been addressed by any assessment instruments, while also satisfying the standard psychometric criteria. The minimum requirements for such a system follow:

- *Capacity to reflect authentic outcomes.* Although any particular assessment may not reflect the full array of consequences, the inclusion of a wider array than that currently being tested is crucial. For example, students' beliefs about reading and about themselves as readers may support or obstruct their optimal development as comprehenders; teachers may benefit enormously from having ways to elicit and assess such beliefs.

- *Congruence between assessments and the processes involved in comprehension.* Assessments that target particular operations involved in comprehension must be available, in the interest of revealing inter- and intraindividual differences that might inform our understanding of the comprehension process and of outcome differences. The dimensionality of the instruments in relation to theory should be clearly apparent.

- *Developmental sensitivity.* Any assessment system needs to be sensitive across the full developmental range of interest and to reflect developmentally central phenomena related to comprehension. Assessments of young children's reading tend to focus on word reading rather than on comprehension. Assessments of listening comprehension and of oral language production, both of which are highly related to reading comprehension, are rare and tend not to be included in reading assessment systems despite their clear relevance. The available listening comprehension assessments for young children do not reflect children's rich oral language–processing capacities because they reflect neither the full complexity of their sentence processing nor the domain of discourse skills.

- *Capacity to identify individual children as poor comprehenders.* An effective assessment system should be able to identify individual children as poor comprehenders, not only in terms of prerequisite skills such as fluency in word identification and decoding, but also in terms of cognitive deficits and gaps in relevant knowledge (background, domain specific, etc.) that might adversely affect reading and comprehension, even in children who have adequate word-level skills. It is also critically important that such a system be able to identify early any child who is apt to encounter difficulties in reading comprehension because of limited resources to carry out one or another operation involved in comprehension.

- *Capacity to identify subtypes of poor comprehenders.* Reading comprehension is complexly determined. It therefore follows that comprehension difficulties could come about because of deficiencies in one or another of the components of comprehension specified in the model. Thus, an effective assessment system should be able to identify subtypes of poor comprehenders in terms of the components and desired outcomes of comprehension. It should also be capable of identifying both intra- and inter-individual differences in acquiring the knowledge and skills necessary for becoming a good comprehender.

• *Instructional sensitivity.* Two major purposes for assessments are to inform instruction and to reflect the effect of instruction or intervention. Thus, an effective assessment system should provide not only important information about a child's relative standing in appropriate normative populations (school, state, and national norms groups), but also important information about the child's relative strengths and weaknesses for purposes of educational planning.

• *Openness to intraindividual differences.* Understanding the performance of an individual often requires attending to differences in performance across activities with varying purposes and with a variety of texts and text types.

• *Usefulness for instructional decision making.* Assessments can inform instructional practice if they are designed to identify domains that instruction might target, rather than to provide summary scores useful only for comparison with other learners' scores. Another aspect of utility for instructional decision making is the transparency of the information provided by the test given to teachers without technical training.

• *Adaptability with respect to individual, social, linguistic, and cultural variation.* Good tests of reading comprehension, of listening comprehension, and of oral language production target authentic outcomes and reflect key component processes. If performance on a task reflects differences owing to individual, social, linguistic, or cultural variations that are not directly related to reading comprehension performance, the tests are inadequate for the purposes of the research agenda we propose here.

• *A basis in measurement theory and psychometrics.* This basis should address reliability within scales and over time, as well as multiple components of validity at the item level, concurrently with other measures and predictively relative to the longer-term development of reading proficiency. Studies of the dimensionality of the instruments in relationship to the theory underpinning their construction are particularly important. Test construction and evaluation of instruments are important areas of investigation and are highly relevant to our proposed research agenda.

Clearly, no single assessment would meet all these criteria. Instead, we propose an integrated system of assessments, some of which may be particularly appropriate for particular groups (e.g., emergent or beginning readers, older struggling readers, second-language readers, or readers with a particular interest in dinosaurs). Further, the various assessments included in the system would address different purposes, such as a portmanteau assessment for accountability or screening purposes, diagnostic assessments for guiding intervention, curriculum-linked assessments for guiding instruction, and so on. Given that we are proposing multiple assessments, we believe that studies of their dimensionality and of the interrelations of these dimensions across measures are especially critical.

A sample of issues that would certainly arise in the process of developing a comprehensive assessment system for reading comprehension follows:

- The effect of various response formats on performance
- Variation in performance across types of text
- The effect of nonprint information
- The effect of various formats and accommodations on the test performance of learners of English as a second language
- Variation in performance across a variety of types of discourse and genres, including hypertext
- The effect on performance of specifying different purposes for reading
- The capacity to differentiate domain-specific and reading-general operations
- The need to reflect performance on literacy tasks typical of electronic reading, such as retrieval
- The capacity to explore issues that go outside the traditional rubric of comprehension, such as scanning, intertextuality, domain-specific strategies, and consulting illustrations
- The reliability, validity, and dimensionality of different assessment instruments and approaches

Key Issues the Research Agenda Should Address

The key questions and issues that a research agenda on reading assessment needs to address, and that are closely connected to the RRSG's proposed areas for future instruction research, include the following:

- How can the education community measure strategic, self-regulated reading, including a students' use of such strategies as questioning, comprehension monitoring, and organizing the knowledge gained from text?
- To what extent are performance-based assessments of reading sensitive to a student's competencies in such processes as vocabulary, cognitive strategies, writing ability, oral language (syntax), reading fluency, domain content knowledge of the texts, and such dispositions as motivation and self-efficacy for reading?

- How do we design valid and reliable measures of self-regulated, strategic reading that teachers can administer in the classroom to inform their instructional decisions?

- What informal assessments should teachers use to identify children who may need additional or modified instruction within the classroom to prevent a referral to special education services?

- How do we construct informal assessments to assist teachers in identifying how to help students who have low reading comprehension? For example, how could teachers identify which children need to be taught specific reading strategies or supported in domain knowledge acquisition or motivational development?

- What reading comprehension assessment could be both administered efficiently by all teachers in a school and used across grades to document student growth and guide teacher decisions about the appropriate texts, tasks, contexts, and learning activities for students?

- What available measures of motivation and engagement in reading can be linked to reading competencies, related to growth over time, and used to guide classroom learning activities?

- What measures of reading fluency can be used at the levels of the individual student, the classroom, and the school and can be related to reading comprehension and reading motivation?

- Which measures of reading comprehension are sensitive to specific forms of reading instruction and intervention for all readers?

- What are the dimensions evaluated by different assessments in relation to more traditional assessments and the proposed new approaches to assessment? How well does the dimensionality map onto the theories behind the development of the assessments?

Acknowledgments

The RAND Reading Study Group is comprised as follows:
Chair: Catherine Snow (Harvard University)
Members: Donna Alvermann (University of Georgia), Janice Dole (University of Utah), Jack Fletcher (University of Texas at Houston), Georgia Earnest García (University of Illinois at Urbana-Champaign), Irene Gaskins (The Benchmark School), Arthur Graesser (University of Memphis), John T. Guthrie (University of Maryland), Michael L. Kamil (Stanford University), William Nagy (Seattle Pacific University), Annemarie Sullivan Palincsar (University of Michigan), Dorothy Strickland (Rutgers University), Frank Vellutino (State University of New York at Albany), Joanna Williams (Columbia University)

Note

[1] This statement applies to upper elementary through adult education. We have a much leaner knowledge base regarding strategy instruction in the preschool and primary grades.

References

Alexander, P.A., & Murphy, P.K. (1998). Profiling the differences in students' knowledge, interest, and strategic processing. *Journal of Educational Psychology, 90*(3), 435–447.

Anders, P.L., Hoffman, J.V., & Duffy, G.G. (2000). *Teaching teachers to teach reading: Paradigm shifts, persistent problems, and challenges.* In M.L. Kamil, P.B. Mosenthal, P.D. Pearson, & R. Barr (Eds.), *Handbook of reading research* (Vol. 3, pp. 719–742). Mahwah, NJ: Erlbaum.

Anglin, J.M. (1993). Vocabulary development: A morphological analysis. *Monographs of the Society for Research in Child Development, 58*(10), 1–166.

Armbruster, B.B., & Anderson, T.H. (1984). Structures of explanations in history textbooks or so what if Governor Stanford missed the spike and hit the rail? *Journal of Curriculum Studies, 16*(2), 181–194.

Armbruster, B.B., & Armstrong, J.O. (1993). Locating information in text: A focus on children in the elementary grades. *Contemporary Educational Psychology, 18*(2), 139–161.

Baumann, J., Hoffman, J., Moon, J., & Duffy-Hester, A.M. (1998). Where are teachers' voices in the phonics/whole language debate? Results from a survey of U.S. elementary teachers. *The Reading Teacher, 51*, 636–652.

Beck, I.L., McKeown, M.G., Sinatra, G.M., & Loxterman, J.A. (1991). Revising social studies text from a text-processing perspective: Evidence of improved comprehensibility. *Reading Research Quarterly, 26*, 251–276.

Beck, I.L., Perfetti, C.A., & McKeown, M.G. (1982). Effects of long-term vocabulary instruction on lexical access and reading comprehension. *Journal of Educational Psychology, 74*(4), 506–521.

Berninger, V.W., Abbott, R.D., Billingsley, F., & Nagy, W. (2001). Processes underlying timing and fluency of reading: Efficiency, automaticity, coordination, and morphological awareness. In M. Wolf (Ed.), *Dyslexia, fluency, and the brain.* Timonium, MD: York Press.

Berninger, V.W., Abbott, R.D., Brooksher, R., Lemos, Z., Ogier, S., Zook, D., et al. (2000). A connectionist approach to making the predictability of English orthography explicit to at-risk beginning readers: Evidence for alternative, effective strategies. *Developmental Neuropsychology, 17*, 241–271.

Boyle, J.R., & Weishaar, M. (1997). The effects of expert-generated versus student-generated cognitive organizers on the reading comprehension of students with learning disabilities. *Learning Disabilities Research and Practice, 12*(4), 228–235.

Brown, A.L. (1997). Transforming schools into communities of thinking and learning about serious matters. *American Psychologist, 52*, 399–414.

Brown, A.L., & Campione, J.C. (1994). Guided discovery in a community of learners. In K. McGilly (Ed.), *Classroom lessons: Integrating cognitive theory and classroom practice* (pp. 229–270). Cambridge, MA: MIT Press.

Brown, R., Pressley, M., Van Meter, P., & Schuder, T. (1996). A quasi-experimental validation of transactional strategies instruction with low-achieving second-grade readers. *Journal of Educational Psychology, 88*(1), 18–37.

Carlisle, J.F. (1995). Morphological awareness and early reading achievement. In L.B. Feldman (Ed.), *Morphological aspects of language processing* (pp. 189–209). Hillsdale, NJ: Erlbaum.

Chall, J.S., Jacobs, V.A., & Baldwin, L.E. (1990). *The reading crisis: Why poor children fall behind.* Cambridge, MA: Harvard University Press.

Chan, L.K., & Cole, P.G. (1986). The effects of comprehension monitoring training on the reading competence of learning disabled and regular class students. *RASE: Remedial & Special Education, 7*(4), 33–40.

Chan, L.K., Cole, P.G., & Barfett, S. (1987). Comprehension monitoring: Detection and identification of text inconsistencies by LD and normal students. *Learning Disability Quarterly, 10*(2), 114–124.

Cochran-Smith, M., & Lytle, S. (1999). Relationship of knowledge and practice: Teacher learning in communities. In A. Iran-Nejad & C.D. Pearson (Eds.), *Review of research in education* (Vol. 24, pp. 249–306). Washington, DC: American Educational Research Association.

Cohen, D.K., & Ball, D.L. (1990). Policy and practice: An overview. *Educational Evaluation and Policy Analysis, 12*(3), 347–353.

Cremin, L.A. (1965). *The genius of American education.* Pittsburgh, PA: University of Pittsburgh Press.

Cuban, L. (1993). *How teachers taught: Constancy and change in American*

Classrooms 1890–1990. New York: Teachers College Press.

Darling-Hammond, L. (1990). Achieving our goals: Superficial or structural reforms? *Phi Delta Kappan, 72,* 286–295.

Darling-Hammond, L. (2000). Teacher quality and student achievement: A review of state policy evidence. *Educational Policy Analysis Archives, 8*(1), 1–42.

Darling-Hammond, L., & Green, J. (1994). Teacher quality and equality. In J. Goodlad & P. Keating (Eds.), *Access to knowledge.* New York: College Entrance Examination Board.

Dickinson, D.K., & Tabors, P.O. (Eds.). (2001). *Beginning literacy with language: Young children learning at home and school.* Baltimore: Brookes.

Dixon-Krauss, L.A. (1995). Partner reading and writing: Peer social dialogue and the zone of proximal development. *Journal of Reading Behavior, 27*(1), 45–63.

Duffy, G.G., Roehler, L.R., Sivan, E., Rackliffe, G., Book, C., Meloth, M.S., et al. (1987). Effects of explaining the reasoning associated with using reading strategies. *Reading Research Quarterly, 22,* 347–368.

Duke, N.K. (2000). For the rich it's richer: Print environments and experiences offered to first-grade students in very low- and very high-SES school districts. *American Educational Research Journal, 37,* 456–457.

Durkin, D. (1978/1979). What classroom observations reveal about reading comprehension instruction. *Reading Research Quarterly, 14,* 481–533.

Elley, W.B. (1991). Acquiring literacy in a second language: The effect of book-based programs. *Language Learning, 41*(3), 375–411.

Elmore, R.F. (1999/2000). Building a new structure for school leadership. *American Educator, 23*(4), 6–13.

Eviator, Z., & Ibrahim, R. (2000). Bilingual is as bilingual does: Metalinguistic abilities of Arabic-speaking children. *Applied Psycholinguistics, 21*(4), 451–471.

Faulkner, H.J., & Levy, B.A. (1999). Fluent and nonfluent forms of transfer in reading: Words and their message. *Psychonomic Bulletin & Review, 6*(1), 111–116.

Ferguson, R.F. (1991). Paying for public education: New evidence on how and why money matters. *Harvard Journal of Legislation, 28*(2), 465–498.

Fischer, U. (1994). Learning words from context and dictionaries: An experimental comparison. *Applied Psycholinguistics, 15*(4), 551–574.

Fisher, C.J., Fox, D.I., & Paille, E. (1996). Teacher education research in the English language arts and reading. In J. Sikula, T.J. Buttery, & E. Guyton (Eds.), *Handbook of research on teacher education* (2nd ed., pp. 410–441). New York: Macmillan.

Freebody, P., & Anderson, R.C. (1983). Effects of vocabulary difficulty, text cohesion, and schema variability on reading comprehension. *Reading Research Quarterly, 18,* 277–294.

Fukkink, R.G., & de Glopper, K. (1998). Effects of instruction in deriving word meaning from context: A meta-analysis. *Review of Educational Research, 68*(4), 450–469.

Fullan, M.G. (1992). *Successful school improvement: The implementation perspective and beyond.* Bristol, PA: Open University Press.

García, G.E. (1991). Factors influencing the English reading test performance of Spanish-speaking Hispanic children. *Reading Research Quarterly, 26,* 371–392.

García, G.E., & Nagy, W.E. (1993). Latino students' concept of cognates. In D.J. Leu & C.K. Kinzer (Eds.), *Examining central issues in literacy research, theory, and practice* (42nd yearbook of the National Reading Conference, pp. 367–373).

Gersten, R., Fuchs, L.S., Williams, J.P., & Baker, S. (2001). Teaching reading comprehension strategies to students with learning disabilities: A review of research. *Review of Educational Research, 71*(2), 279–320.

Graves, M.F. (2000). A vocabulary program to complement and bolster a middle-grade comprehension program. In B.M. Taylor, M.F. Graves, & P. van den Broek (Eds.), *Reading for meaning: Fostering comprehension in the middle grades.* New York: Teachers College Press; Newark, DE: International Reading Association.

Graves, M.F., Cooke, C.L., & LaBerge, M.J. (1983). Effects of previewing short stories. *Reading Research Quarterly, 18,* 262–276.

Graves, M.F., Watts-Taffe, S.M., & Graves, B.B. (1998). *Essentials of elementary reading.* Needham Heights, MA: Allyn & Bacon.

Guthrie, J.T., Van Meter, P., Hancock, G.R., Alao, S., Anderson, E., & McCann, A. (1998). Does concept oriented reading instruction increase strategy use and conceptual learning from text? *Journal of Educational Psychology, 90*(2), 261–278.

Guthrie, J.T., & Wigfield, A. (2000). Engagement and motivation in reading. In M.L. Kamil, P.B. Mosenthal, P.D. Pearson, & R. Barr (Eds.), *Handbook of reading research* (Vol. 3, pp. 403–422). Mahwah, NJ: Erlbaum.

Hiebert, E.H., & Martin, L.A. (2001). The texts of beginning reading instruction. In S.B. Neuman & D.K. Dickinson (Eds.), *Handbook of early literacy research* (pp. 361–376). New York: Guilford.

Idol-Maestas, L. (1985). Getting ready to read: Guided probing for poor comprehenders. *Learning Disability Quarterly, 8*(4), 243–254.

Jiménez, R.T., García, G.E., & Pearson, P.D. (1996). The reading strategies of bilingual Latina/o students who are successful English readers: Opportunities and obstacles. *Reading Research Quarterly, 31*, 90–112.

Joyce, B., & Showers, B. (1996). Staff development as a comprehensive service organization. *Journal of Staff Development, 17*(1), 2–6.

Keeny, T.J., Cannizzo, S.R., & Flavell, J.H. (1967). Spontaneous and induced verbal rehearsal in a recall tast. *Child Development, 38*(4), 953–966.

Kuhn, M., & Stahl, S. (1998). Teaching children to learn word meanings from context: A synthesis and some questions. *Journal of Literacy Research, 30*, 119–138.

Langer, J.A. (1984). Examining background knowledge and text comprehension. *Reading Research Quarterly, 19*, 468–481.

Lanier, J.E., & Little, J.W. (1986). Research on teacher education. In M. Wittrock (Ed.), *Handbook of research on teaching* (3rd ed., pp. 527–569). New York: Macmillan.

Lapp, D., Flood, J., & Ranck-Buhr, W. (1995). Using multiple text formats to explore scientific phenomena in middle school classrooms. *Reading & Writing Quarterly: Overcoming Learning Disabilities, 11*(2), 173–186.

Laufer, B., & Nation, P. (1999). A vocabulary-size test of controlled productive ability. *Language Testing, 16*(1), 33–51.

Laufer, B., & Sim, D.D. (1985). Measuring and explaining the reading threshold needed for English for academic purposes texts. *Foreign Language Annals, 18*(5), 405–411.

Mandler, J.M., & Johnson, N.S. (1977). Remembrance of things parsed: Story structure and recall. *Cognitive Psychology, 9*, 111–151.

Mathes, P.G., & Fuchs, L.S. (1993). Peer-mediated reading instruction in special education resource rooms. *Learning Disabilities Research and Practice, 8*(4), 233–243.

McDermott, R., & Varenne, H. (1995). Culture as disability. *Anthropology & Education Quarterly, 26*, 324–348.

McKeown, M.G. (1993). Creating effective definitions for young word learners. *Reading Research Quarterly, 28*, 16–31.

McKeown, M.G., Beck, I.L., Omanson, R.C., & Pople, M.T. (1985). Some effects of the nature and frequency of vocabulary instruction on the knowledge and use of words. *Reading Research Quarterly, 20*, 522–535.

Meichenbaum, D., & Biemiller, A. (1998). *Nurturing independent learners: Helping students take charge of their learning.* Cambridge, MA: Brookline.

Meyer, B.J.F., Brandt, D.M., & Bluth, G.J. (1980). Use of top-level structure in text: Key for reading comprehension of ninth-grade students. *Reading Research Quarterly, 16*, 72–103.

Muter, V., & Diethelm, K. (2001). The contribution of phonological skills and letter knowledge to early reading development in a multilingual population. *Language Learning, 51*(2), 187–219.

Nagy, W., García, G.E., Durgunoglu, A., & Hancin-Bhatt, B. (1993). Spanish-English bilingual students' use of cognates in English reading. *Journal of Reading Behavior, 25*(3), 241–259.

Nagy, W.E., McClure, E.F., & Montserrat, M. (1997). Linguist transfer and the use of context by Spanish-English bilinguals. *Applied Psycholinguistics, 18*(4), 431–452.

Nagy, W.E., & Scott, J.A. (1990). Word schemas: Expectations about the form and meaning of new words. *Cognition & Instruction, 7*(2), 105–127.

Nagy, W.E., & Scott, J.A. (2000). Vocabulary processes. In M.L. Kamil, P.B. Mosenthal, P.D. Pearson, & R. Barr (Eds.), *Handbook of reading research* (Vol. 3, pp. 269–284). Mahwah, NJ: Erlbaum.

Nation, P. (1989). A system of tasks for language learning. In A. Sarinee (Ed.), *Language teaching methodology for the nineties.* Selected papers from the Southeast Asian Ministers of Education Organization (SEAMEO) Regional Language Centre Seminar (1989). Anthology Series 24.

National Institute of Child Health and Human Development. (2000). *Report of the National Reading Panel. Teaching children to read:*

An evidence-based assessment of the scientific research literature on reading and its implications for reading instruction (NIH Publication No. 00-4769). Washington, DC: U.S. Government Printing Office.

Nelson, J.R., Smith, D.J., & Dodd, J.M. (1992). The effects of teaching a summary skills strategy to students identified as learning disabled on their comprehension of science text. *Education & Treatment of Children*, *15*(3), 228–243.

Pappas, C.C., & Barry, A. (1997). Scaffolding urban students' initiations: Transactions in reading information books in the read-aloud curriculum genre. In N.J. Karolides (Ed.), *Reader response in elementary classrooms: Quest and discovery* (pp. 215–236). Hillsdale, NJ: Erlbaum.

Pressley, M. (2000). What should comprehension instruction be the instruction of? In M.L. Kamil, P.B. Mosenthal, P.D. Pearson, & R. Barr (Eds.), *Handbook of reading research* (Vol. 3, pp. 545–562). Mahwah, NJ: Erlbaum.

Pressley, M., Wharton-McDonald, R., Allington, R., Block, C.C., Morrow, L., Tracey, D., et al. (2001). A study of effective first-grade literacy instruction. *Scientific Studies of Reading*, *5*(1), 35–58.

Rashotte, C., & Torgesen, J. (1985). Repeated reading and reading fluency in learning disabled children. *Reading Research Quarterly*, *20*, 180–188.

Rasinski, T.V. (1990). Effects of repeated reading and listening-while-reading on reading fluency. *Journal of Educational Research*, *83*(3), 147–150.

Reeve, J., Bolt, E., & Cai, Y. (1999). Autonomy-supportive teachers: How they teach and motivate students. *Journal of Educational Psychology*, *91*(3), 537–548.

Reutzel, D.R., & Hollingsworth, P.M. (1993). Effects of fluency training on second graders' reading comprehension. *Journal of Educational Research*, *86*(6), 325–331.

Ringel, B.A., & Springer, C.J. (1980). On knowing how well one is remembering: The persistence of strategy use during transfer. *Journal of Experimental Child Psychology*, *29*(2), 322–333.

Roberts, B. (1992). The evolution of the young child's concept of "word" as a unit of spoken and written language. *Reading Research Quarterly*, *27*, 124–138.

Rosenshine, B., & Meister, C. (1994). Reciprocal teaching: A review of the research. *Review of Educational Research*, *64*, 479–530.

Schiefele, U. (1999). Interest and learning from text. *Scientific Studies of Reading*, *3*(3), 257–279.

Schumaker, J.B., Deshler, D.D., Alley, G.R., Varner, M.M., Clark, F.L., & Nolan, S. (1982). Error monitoring: A learning strategy for improving adolescent academic performance. In W.M. Cruickshank & J.W. Lerner (Eds.), *Coming of age: Vol 3. The Best of ACLD* (pp. 170–183). Syracuse, NY: Syracuse University Press.

Scott, J.A., & Nagy, W.E. (1997). Understanding the definitions of unfamiliar verbs. *Reading Research Quarterly*, *32*, 184–200.

Shake, M.C. (1986). Teacher interruptions during oral reading instruction: Self-monitoring as an impetus for change in corrective feedback. *Remedial and Special Education (RASE)*, *7*(5), 18–24.

Shulman, L.S. (1986). Those who understand: Knowledge growth in teaching. *Educational Researcher*, *15*(2), 4–14.

Sikula, J. (1996). *Handbook of research on teacher education* (2nd ed.). New York: Macmillan.

Simmons, D.C., Fuchs, D., Fuchs, L.S., Hodge, J.P., & Mathes, P.G. (1994). Importance of instructional complexity and role reciprocity to classwide peer tutoring. *Learning Disabilities Research and Practice*, *9*(4), 203–212.

Skinner, E.A., Wellborn, J.G., & Connell, J.P. (1990). What it takes to do well in school and whether I've got it: A process model of perceived control and children's engagement and achievement in school. *Journal of Educational Psychology*, *82*(1), 22–32.

Stahl, S.A., & Fairbanks, M.M. (1986). The effects of vocabulary instruction: A model-based meta-analysis. *Review of Educational Research*, *56*(1), 72–110.

Stanovich, K.E., & Cunningham, A.E. (1992). Studying the consequences of literacy within a literate society: The cognitive correlates of print exposure. *Memory & Cognition*, *20*, 51–68.

Stein, N.L., & Glenn, C. (1979). An analysis of story comprehension in elementary school children. In R. Freedle (Ed.), *New directions in discourse processing: Vol. 2. Advances in discourse processing* (pp. 53–120). Norwood, NJ: Ablex.

Stigler, J.W., Gonzales, P., Kawanaka, T., Knoll, S., & Serrano, A. (1999). The TIMSS videotape classroom study: Methods and findings from an exploratory research project on eighth-grade mathematics instruction in Germany, Japan, and the United States. *Education Statistics Quarterly*, *1*(2), 109–112.

Swanson, H.L., Kozleski, E., & Stegink, P. (1987). Disabled readers' processing of prose: Do any processes change because of interventions? *Psychology in the Schools*, *24*(4), 378–384.

Sykes, G. (1999). Teacher and student learning: Strengthening their connection. In L. Darling-Hammond & G. Sykes (Eds.), *Teaching as the learning profession: Handbook of policy and practice* (pp. 151–180). San Francisco: Jossey-Bass.

Tan, A., & Nicholson, T. (1997). Flash cards revisited: Training poor readers to read words faster improves their comprehension of text. *Journal of Educational Psychology*, *89*, 276–288.

Taylor, B.M., Pearson, P.D., Clark, K.F., & Walpole, S. (1999). Effective schools/accomplished teachers. *The Reading Teacher*, *53*, 156–159.

Tinkham, T. (1993). The effect of semantic clustering on the learning of second language vocabulary. *System*, *21*(3), 371–380.

Turner, J.C. (1995). The influence of classroom contexts on young children's motivation for literacy. *Reading Research Quarterly*, *30*, 410–441.

Van Dongen, R., & Westby, C.E. (1986). Building the narrative mode of thought through children's literature. *Topics in Language Disorders*, *7*(1), 70–83.

Waring, R. (1997). The negative effects of learning words in semantic sets: A replication. *System*, *25*(2), 261–274.

Williams, J.P. (1993). Comprehension of students with and without learning disabilities: Identification of narrative themes and idiosyncratic text representations. *Journal of Educational Psychology*, *85*, 631–641.

Wolf, M., & Katzir-Cohen, T. (2001). Reading fluency and its intervention. *Scientific Studies of Reading*, *5*(3), 211–239.

Wong, B.Y.L., & Jones, W. (1982). Increasing metacomprehension in learning disabled and normally achieving students through self-questioning training. *Learning Disability Quarterly*, *5*(3), 228–240

28

Self-Regulated Comprehension During Normal Reading

Douglas J. Hacker

Cognitive psychologists and educational psychologists have not always agreed on the kinds of cognitive processes that should be included under the rubric of comprehension monitoring, nor have they always agreed on a common usage of the term *comprehension monitoring*. In general, cognitive psychologists have used the terminology *metamemory for text*, *calibration of comprehension*, or *metacomprehension* and have restricted the kinds of processes to those that concern prediction of whether text has been or will be understood (e.g., Glenberg & Epstein, 1985; Glenberg, Wilkinson, & Epstein, 1982; Maki & Serra, 1992; Weaver, 1990). The concept underlying these terms often has been operationalized by relating readers' predictions of comprehension with their actual performance on comprehension-type questions. Readers whose predictions and performance are highly correlated are judged to have good calibration of comprehension, whereas readers whose predictions and performance are minimally correlated are judged to have poor metacomprehension.

By contrast, educational psychologists have tended to favor the term *comprehension monitoring* and typically have conceptualized it as a multidimensional process that includes evaluation and regulation (e.g., Baker, 1985; Brown, 1980; Hacker, Plumb, Butterfield, Quathamer, & Heineken, 1994; Palincsar & Brown, 1984; Zabrucky & Ratner, 1992). Evaluation involves monitoring of one's understanding of text material, and regulation involves control of one's reading to resolve problems and increase comprehension. Often, comprehension monitoring has been operationalized through the use of the error-detection paradigm in which readers detect and resolve various kinds of textual errors that have been deliberately planted in texts. Good comprehension monitoring is demonstrated by those readers who detect and resolve all or most of the errors; poor comprehension monitoring is demonstrated by those who fail to detect the errors or who detect the errors but fail to resolve them.

From Hacker, D.J., Dunlosky, J., & Graesser, A.C. (Eds.), *Metacognition in Educational Theory and Practice* (pp. 165–191). Copyright © 1998 by Lawrence Erlbaum Associates. Reprinted with permission of the publisher.

However, there is growing agreement among researchers to view this process called metamemory for text, calibration of comprehension, metacomprehension, comprehension monitoring, or whatever term is favored, as processing that involves both evaluation and regulation of reading comprehension (e.g., Baker, 1989; Markman, 1985; Otero & Companario, 1990; Weaver, 1995; Zabrucky & Moore, 1989). Perhaps this growing agreement has been encouraged by an increasingly shared interest among cognitive psychologists and educational psychologists to examine reading processes during normal reading conditions.

In contrast to reading for the purposes of detecting errors or predicting comprehension, the purpose of normal reading is to construct meaningful interpretations from text that is assumed to be considerate (i.e., consistent, coherent, and written at a level commensurate with the reader's abilities and knowledge). As long as readers are able to construct meaning that is compatible with developing interpretations, reading is likely to proceed uninterrupted. In this case, ongoing evaluation of comprehension provides information to the reader that understanding is occurring and reading can proceed. However, when readers fail to establish consistency or coherence during normal reading, or when constructed meaning fails to fit with their developing interpretations of the text, ongoing evaluation alerts readers to comprehension failures.

Because of the assumption of text considerateness held by most readers during normal reading, readers are likely to look first to themselves as the source of comprehension failure. Is the failure due to gaps in their linguistic or topic knowledge? Is the failure due to lack of perceived coherency, or to an inability to generate an interpretation of the text that is compatible with their own expectations for the text or with their understanding of the author's intended meaning? During or after this search, readers may get a sense that the failure is due not to them but to the text itself, at which point the focus of the search is directed to textual inadequacies.

Whatever the source of the failure, once it is evaluated, readers must resolve it, and further, as reading continues, they must periodically reevaluate whether their resolution continues to establish consistency, coherence, and compatibility with the ongoing interpretation of the text. Thus, when comprehension failures are monitored during normal reading, comprehension monitoring is more than a metacognitive judgment that a failure has occurred. Comprehension monitoring becomes a goal-directed metacognitive process through which the processes of evaluation *and* regulation interplay for the purposes of reestablishing the construction of a text's meaning and developing its interpretation.

One purpose of this piece is first to propose a standardization in the terminology that has been used to describe evaluation and regulation of reading comprehension. Because of the growing agreement among researchers concerning the kinds of processes that are involved in reading, there is a growing need to standardize the terminology used to describe those processes. Developing a common language that strives for precision in its meaning is essential for the communication of scientific knowledge. Therefore, rather than favoring *comprehension monitoring*, which is something of a misnomer in that only part of the overall process appears to be implicated, or any of the other terms that have been used (e.g., *metamemory for text, calibration of comprehension*), which lack precision, I propose the use of the term *self-regulated comprehension*. This term not only connotes both monitoring and control of reading processes, it brings the concept closer to the growing corpus of research that has focused on self-regulated learning.

A second purpose of the piece is to describe a cognitive–metacognitive model of self-regulated comprehension. This model conceptualizes self-regulated comprehension as monitoring and control of cognitive processes by related metacognitive processes. Using this cognitive–metacognitive model, self-regulated comprehension during normal reading will be examined.

Finally, although much research has shown that comprehension can be facilitated by encouraging readers to monitor and control their reading, there may be limits to how much readers can monitor and control their own construction of meaning. The notion of one level of thought monitoring and controlling another level is problematic in that it represents a closed system that can act on itself only to the extent to which its own subjective standards are applied. In other words, it is possible that readers may judge their understanding of text as complete, consistent, and compatible with their prior knowledge even though the text may be inaccurate or inconsistent with standards external to them. To overcome this limitation, readers must monitor and control their reading of text using not only their own internal standards but standards external to them. In an educational context, this can be accomplished by engaging readers in a dialogue about the text.

A Cognitive–Metacognitive Model of Self-Regulated Comprehension

Flavell's (1979) model of cognitive monitoring has been a useful theoretical foundation for researchers interested in the metacognitive aspects of human thinking. According to his model, cognitive monitoring occurs through the actions and interactions among four classes of phenomena: metacognitive knowledge, metacognitive experiences, goals, and strategies. Metacognitive knowledge consists of a person's stored world knowledge that has to do with people, their cognitive tasks, goals and strategies for achieving them, actions, and experiences. Metacognitive experiences are concerned with one's awareness of his or her cognitive or affective processes and whether progress is being made toward the goal of a current process. Metacognitive experiences can add to, delete from, or revise one's metacognitive knowledge. They can cause one to abandon goals and establish new ones, or they can lead to the activation of cognitive or metacognitive strategies. Furthermore, Flavell's model has both declarative and procedural aspects: The former concern understanding strategic demands of tasks and one's limits and strengths as a problem solver; the latter concern monitoring and regulation of ongoing cognition.

Many theorists have amended Flavell's conceptualization of metacognition. Noteworthy among them have been Nelson and Narens (1990). Their model of metacognition integrates the declarative aspects of Flavell's model, called *metacognitive understanding*, with the procedural aspects, called *monitoring* and *control*. Underlying the Nelson and Narens model are three principles: (1) Mental processes are split into two or more specifically interrelated levels, a cognitive level and a metacognitive level; (2) the metacognitive level contains a dynamic model of the cognitive level; and (3) there are two dominance relations called control and monitoring, which are defined in terms of the direction of flow of information between the metacognitive and cognitive levels. A distinction that can be made between cognition and metacognition is that the former involves knowledge of the world and strategies for using that knowledge to solve problems, whereas the latter concerns monitoring, controlling, and understanding one's knowledge and strategies (Butterfield, Albertson, & Johnston, 1995).

Thus, metacognition can be viewed as monitoring and controlling of a lower-level thought process by a higher-level thought process (Broadbent, 1977). This relationship can be characterized as a dynamic interplay between monitoring, in which information regarding the status of knowledge or strategies at a cognitive level is provided to a corresponding metacognitive level, and control, in which understanding at a metacognitive level is used to influence thought at a corresponding cognitive level. Through the interplay of information, a metacognitive level controls or modifies thought at a cognitive level by treating it as the object of thought, and thought at a metacognitive level can in turn be modified by the kinds of information monitored at a cognitive level or by being treated as the object of thought by yet higher levels of thought.

When considering the relation between metacognitive and cognitive processes, it is important to consider that neither one occurs in isolation. The cognitive-level process being controlled must first be monitored, and second, must be contained as a model within the metacognitive level (i.e., there must be a representation of the cognitive-level process for it to be understood and modified; Conant & Ashby, 1970). Thus, control depends on the processes being monitored and how those processes are represented at a metacognitive level, and monitoring depends on the processes that are being controlled or potentially controlled (Butterfield, Albertson, & Johnston, 1995). Therefore, the Nelson and Narens model of metacognition must be considered as a system of interacting thought processes and not as a collection of independent parts.

The Components of Self-Regulated Comprehension

Butterfield, Albertson, and Johnston (1995) argue that many task-specific models of cognition can be conceptualized using this cognitive–metacognitive framework. Thus, as another kind of task-specific cognition, self-related comprehension can be conceptualized as the interaction between two levels of thought, a metacognitive level that monitors and controls a cognitive level (see Figure 1). At the metacognitive level is understanding of both world knowledge and strategies. Understanding at a metacognitive level is made possible through dynamic mental models of the person's cognitive system (Johnson-Laird, 1983; Nelson & Narens, 1990). At the cognitive level are comprehension processes, strategies, standards of text evaluation (e.g., lexical, syntactic, and semantic), and world knowledge. World knowledge, strategies, and standards of evaluation affect comprehension, and, in turn, can be affected by comprehension, and, hence, the relationships among

FIGURE 1
Theoretical Mechanisms of Comprehensive Monitoring

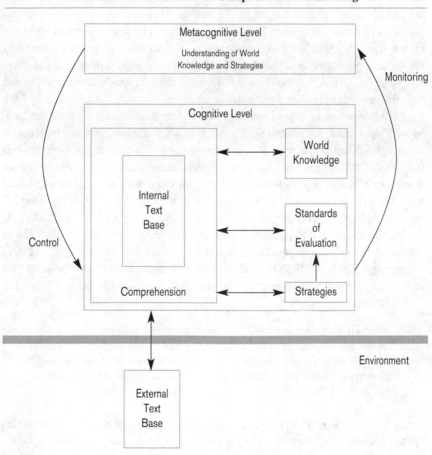

them and comprehension are represented by double-headed arrows. Furthermore, a reader's strategies for increasing comprehension may include using standards of evaluation; therefore, the relation between strategies and standards of evaluation is represented by an arrow directed from the former to the latter.

Theoretical Mechanism of Comprehension Monitoring. Comprehension is the process through which understanding is derived through the construction of an internal representation of a text. It is a process that occurs in parallel at several levels, with a special kind of text representation being associated with each level and with the outputs of each level interacting in important ways (Adams & Collins, 1979; Carpenter & Just, 1989; Graesser, Singer, & Trabasso, 1994; Just & Carpenter, 1992; Kintsch, 1988; Rumelhart & McClelland, 1981). First, there is a verbal representation consisting of words and syntactical units such as phrases, sentences, and paragraphs. Second, the verbal representation is parsed into semantic units called text propositions. Propositions are stored in memory as interrelated chunks of text information forming a representation of the text that can form or modify the reader's world knowledge. The reader's modified world knowledge is another level of representation that in turn can be used to modify his or her representation of the text. Finally, there is a representation of the overall gist of the text, which can be used to modify all previously constructed levels or influence those levels yet to be constructed.

Either before or during reading, people set certain goals for their reading. Most often, readers focus their goals on higher semantic levels of text representation (e.g., to identify the main idea of a paragraph); however, in the event readers fail to meet their goals, they must be prepared to evaluate the monitored failure at all levels of text representation. Is the failure due to a mistakenly identified word? Is it due to the use of poor syntax? Is it due to a lack of topic knowledge? Evaluation at each level of text representation occurs by applying a standard of evaluation specific to that level (Baker, 1985). Readers can consciously select standards to evaluate comprehension failures, or, as Just and Carpenter (1992) suggest, standards may be selected according to implicit allocation policies that readers rely on in the event of excessive demands on comprehension.

Strategies are

> composed of cognitive operations over and above the processes that are a natural consequence of carrying out the task, ranging from one such operation to a sequence of interdependent operations. Strategies achieve cognitive purposes (e.g., comprehending, memorizing) and are potentially conscious and controllable activities. (Pressley, Forrest-Pressley, Elliot-Faust, & Miller, 1985, p. 4)

Strategies provide ways to lessen demands on working memory and therefore facilitate information processing. In the present context, strategies serve to facilitate comprehension. They include both monitoring strategies (e.g., rereading a difficult passage, looking back to prior text, predicting upcoming information, comparing two or more propositions) and control strategies (e.g., summarizing text information, clarifying text information by using reference sources external to the text, correcting incomplete or inaccurate text information).

The remaining element of the model is the external text base, which is any written representation of linguistic input (e.g., a word, sentence, book, one's own writing). The external text base is represented internally within the comprehension process through constructive processing of the external text (e.g., August, Flavell, & Clift, 1984; Bransford & Franks, 1971; Kintsch, 1988; Markman, 1985). The relation between the external text base and the internal processing of the text is represented by a double-headed arrow to denote that the external text base serves as linguistic input to comprehension, and as a result of these processes, the reader (or writer) can in turn modify the external text base.

In addition to placing self-regulated comprehension within a general theory of cognition, the proposed cognitive–metacognitive model offers a coherent interpretation of the existing literature and provides a useful taxonomy for sources of comprehension failure. At a general level, failures to comprehend written discourse can be attributed either to a failure to monitor comprehension or a failure to control comprehension. Each of these general sources can be divided into more specific ones. Table 1 provides a description of each specific source along with examples of research that have investigated it. With the exception of motivation, which can affect the model at all of its components, each source of failure can be identified with a specific component of the proposed model.

Self-Regulated Comprehension in Operation

The cognitive–metacognitive model of self-regulated comprehension indicates that people's understanding of their world knowledge is distributed among mental models at metacognitive levels of their cognitive systems. In the context of reading, metacognitive models include readers' understanding of their prior knowledge and their goals for reading and comprehending, understanding of an author's intent, understanding of text propositions, and understanding of the ways in which knowledge from the text is integrated with their own knowledge (cf. Kintsch's, 1988, situation model of the text). As a person reads a text and constructs an internal representation of it at a cognitive level, any part of that representation can be compared to a model at a related metacognitive level. The basis on which the comparison is made at the metacognitive level is determined by the reader's implicit or explicit application of a standard or standards of evaluation.

Thus, evaluation of comprehension occurs when readers monitor similarities and differences between their cognitive representation of a text and their metacognitive models by applying standards of evaluation. Similarities monitored between the representation at the cognitive level and the models at the metacognitive level serve as indicators that comprehension is occurring and reading can

TABLE 1

Failures to Comprehend Written Discourse Due to Failures to Monitor Comprehension or Failures to Control Comprehension

Source	Failures to Monitor Comprehension	
	Part of Model	Citations
1. Readers lack linguistic or topic knowledge necessary to monitor sources of dissonance.	World knowledge	Hacker et al. (1994); Pressley, El-Dinary, & Brown (1992); Weaver (1995)
2. Readers possess necessary linguistic or topic knowledge but lack monitoring strategies.	Strategies	Armbruster, Anderson, & Ostertag (1987); August, Flavell, & Clift (1984); Baker (1989); Garner & Anderson (1982); Hacker (1996); Hacker et al. (1994); Zabrucky & Ratner (1986)
3. Readers possess strategies but lack metacognitive understanding about where and when to apply them.	Metacognitive understanding	Hansen & Pearson (1983); Palincsar & Brown (1984); Pressley, El-Dinary, & Brown (1992); Pressley et al. (1987); Reder (1987)
4. The standard of standards of evaluation used by readers are inappropriate for the levels of text representation that need to be monitored.	Standards of evaluation	Baker (1985); Garner & Anderson (1982); Glenberg, Wilkinson, & Epstein (1982); Markman (1979); Winograd & Johnston (1982); Zabrucky & Moore (1989)
5. Sources of dissonance are resolved by the inferences readers make during the comprehension process.	Comprehension	August, Flavell, & Clift (1984); Baker (1979); Beal (1990); Vosniadou, Pearson, & Rogers (1988)
6. Comprehension and/or monitoring are too demanding of the reader's resources thereby hindering his or her ability to monitor reading.	Interaction of cognitive with metacognitive level	Baker (1984); Brown et al. (1977); Hacker (1986); Just & Carpenter (1992); Oakhill (1993); Plumb et al. (1994); Vosniadou & Brewer (1987); Vosniadou, Pearson, & Rogers (1988)
7. Although not specifically noted in the model but implicit in all controlled cognitive processes, readers lack motivation to monitor their reading.		

Failures to Control Comprehension

Source	Part of Model	Citations
1. Readers lack linguistic or topic knowledge necessary to control the problems they monitor.	World knowledge	Hacker (1994); Pressley, El-Dinary, & Brown (1992)
2. Readers possess necessary linguistic and topic knowledge but lack strategies to apply their knowledge.	Strategies	Hacker (1994); Otero & Companario (1990); Vosniadou, Pearson, & Roger (1988); Zabrucky & Moore (1989); Zabrucky & Ratner (1986)
3. Readers possess strategies but lack metacognitive understanding about where and when to apply them.	Metacognitive understanding	Palincsar & Brown (1984); Pressley, El-Dinary, & Brown (1992); Pressley et al. (1987); Reder (1987)
4. Comprehension and/or control are too demanding of the reader's resources thereby hindering his or her ability to control reading.	Interaction of cognitive with metacognitive level	Baker (1984); Brown et al. (1977); Hacker (1986); Just & Carpenter (1992); Oakhill (1993); Plumb et al. (1994); Vosniadou & Brewer (1987); Vosniadou, Pearson, & Rogers (1988)
5. Although not specifically noted in the model but implicit in all controlled cognitive processes, readers lack motivation to monitor their reading.		

proceed. Differences monitored are taken as signs that comprehension has failed or textual problems have been encountered. If, however, readers are unaware of either similarities or differences, comprehension at the cognitive level may be occurring, but monitoring has not occurred.

Differences monitored during the constructive processing of a text, regardless of whether their source is comprehension failure or problematic text, can produce a sense of dissonance in the reader—dissonance that has been described on intuitive bases as a sense of confusion, uncertainty, or some similar feeling of not understanding (Flower, Hayes, Carey, Schriver, & Stratman, 1986; Markman, 1979). Such feelings may occur spontaneously, as when an unfamiliar jargon word is encountered (Markman, 1979), or they may result from explicitly questioning underlying assumptions or stating hypotheses and implications clearly and unambiguously (Palincsar & Brown, 1984).

When dissonance is sensed, readers can exert control over subsequent reading to identify and correct the source of dissonance and reestablish a coherent representation of the text. To this end, the reader has linguistic knowledge, topic knowledge, and strategies represented at a metacognitive level (Butterfield, Hacker, & Plumb, 1994) that can be invoked to facilitate further monitoring of the dissonance and ultimate correction of the problem. What knowledge or strategy will be invoked depends on the reader's metacognitive understanding of the source of the dissonance and the possible actions that could be taken to resolve it. If the reader can specify precisely how to change a text so that it is consistent with his or her model of a content domain, the monitored source of dissonance can be attributed to the text (correctly if one's model is correct). However, if the reader cannot specify how to make a text consistent with his or her model of a content domain, the monitored source of dissonance is attributed to one's inability to comprehend (correctly if the text is correct). Whatever the source of dissonance, once it is identified and resolved, the reader must further evaluate whether the resolution of the problem remains compatible with his or her evolving constructions of subsequent text information. If not, the monitored source of failure may need to be revisited.

Self-Regulation of Meaning-Making

In this section, self-regulated comprehension during normal reading is described within the framework of the proposed cognitive–metacognitive model. First is a brief discussion of normal reading and normal reading problems. A discussion follows on the relation between meaning and interpretation during normal reading and how self-regulated comprehension can facilitate that relation. Finally, this section ends with suggestions for future research on self-regulated comprehension during normal reading.

Normal Reading and Normal Reading Problems

Because the majority of comprehension monitoring research has been conducted using texts with planted errors or ambiguities, our knowledge of self-regulated comprehension may be restricted primarily to atypical reading and may have little transfer to normal reading. In fact, because an abundance of research has shown that readers' purposes for reading and the kinds of problems that are encountered during reading strongly affect the kinds of reading in which readers engage (e.g., Baker & Zimlin, 1989; Beal, 1990; Beal, Bonitatibus, & Garrod, 1990; Hacker, 1997; Hacker et al., 1994; Markman, 1985), it is quite possible that much of what is known about self-regulated comprehension during atypical reading does not generalize to the kinds of reading typically encountered in educational contexts. Thus, it is necessary to revisit research on self-regulated comprehension from the standpoint of normal reading.

Before discussing self-regulated comprehension during normal reading, however, a brief look at factors influencing how readers' construct textual representations during normal reading and the kinds of problems they may encounter during this construction is necessary to understand whether and how those problems can be regulated. Most theories of reading involve the notion of internal representation of meaning. Reading is a process during which "a mental representation is constructed of the discourse in memory, using both external and internal types of information, with the goal of interpreting (understanding) the discourse" (van Dijk & Kintsch, 1983, p. 6; see also Bransford & Franks, 1971; Perfetti & McCutchen, 1987). Much research has focused on just how this mental representation is constructed (e.g., Adams & Collins, 1979; Kintsch, 1988; Rumelhart & McClelland, 1981), but for present purposes we need accept only the notion that reading is the generation of an internal representation of the external text base. In the case of normal reading, the internal text representation usually is used by the reader to derive a coherent interpretation of the author's intended meaning. As this interpretation evolves, it also can affect further construction of the reader's mental representation of the text (Otero & Kintsch, 1992).

Each reader's internal representation of a text is likely to be constructed somewhat differently, even for very simple texts. People differ in the kinds and amounts of knowledge they have concerning the topic being read; they differ in the ways they reason about what has been read and in the kinds of inferences they may draw from their reasoning. They also may differ in the goals they have for reading a particular text. Even the meaning ascribed to the same words may differ from one reader to the next. In fact, with all of these potential differences among readers, any agreement on what a text "says" seems remarkable. And yet, even with these differences, careful readers are able to agree on at least the major features of their constructed representations of text (Otero & Kintsch, 1992). Perfetti and McCutchen (1987) argue that any given text will have a range of possible representations, and as long as the reader's constructed representation overlaps in some way with the possible representations, the reader is said to have comprehended the text. Therefore, any number of readers will each construct a given text differently, but as long as those individually constructed text representations share some commonality, the readers will share some common understanding of the text.

Agreement among readers on what a text "says" is in no small part due to the ability of the author to constrain the number of potential representations a text can assume. This can be done by precisely defining words within the text or providing a glossary, organizing chapters around logically sequenced themes, dividing each chapter into headings and subheadings, or illustrating key concepts with graphics. Also, authors can constrain the range of potential text representations by writing for a specific audience. Many studies have shown that attending to audience contributes significantly to writing quality and clarity (e.g., Beal, 1996; Roen & Willey, 1988; Traxler & Gernsbacher, 1993; Wong, Butler, Ficzere, & Kuperis, 1994).

But perhaps more important, readers themselves constrain the construction of text representations. As part of their construction-integration model of reading, van Dijk and Kintsch (1983) propose that during normal reading, readers often use key propositions within a text as organizing principles around which other text information is interpreted. For example, in expository texts, these key propositions, or "macropropositions" (van Dijk & Kintsch, 1983), are often contained within the topic sentence of each paragraph. Identifying the macropropositions that are central to the author's intended meaning and using them as organizing principles can constrain the construction of the text in a way that facilitates comprehension. The use of macropropositions as organizers has been identified as a strategic process typical of what good comprehenders do (Pressley, El-Dinary, & Brown, 1992).

However, if readers believe too strongly in a macroproposition, or if they hold too strongly to prior beliefs or knowledge, "an imbalance between what readers believe and what they actually read" can result that may hinder comprehension (Otero & Kintsch, 1992, p. 229). An exaggerated emphasis on a macroproposition, one's prior beliefs, or one's prior knowledge can cause the reader to ignore or resolve textual information that amends, contradicts, or is inconsistent with the macroproposition, beliefs, or knowledge (Otero & Kintsch, 1992; Vosniadou, Pearson, & Rogers, 1988). Otero and Kintsch propose that many of the failures to detect textual contradictions reported in the comprehension monitoring literature can be explained as a result of this imbalance between what readers believe and what they actually read.

Also, constraints are placed on the construction of internal text representations because readers are occasionally unable to manage excessive demands imposed by reading. Just and Carpenter (1992) have compiled considerable support for their thesis that comprehension is constrained by working memory capacity. Their review of the literature and their own research have led them to conclude that

> constraints on every person's capacity limit the open-ended facets of compre-
> hension, so that a reader or listener cannot generate every possible forward in-
> ference, represent every interpretation of every ambiguity, or take into
> consideration every potentially relevant cue to an interpretation. (p. 135)

Furthermore, these constraints on comprehension are greater for readers with small working memory capacity versus large working memory capacity, which is often a difference between poor comprehenders and good comprehenders, respectively. Thus, during normal reading, readers constrain their representations of text not only as a normal consequence of reading, but as a result of constraints on working memory that may prohibit simultaneous construction or consideration of alternative text representations.

No doubt, constraints that are placed on the construction of a text, both by the author and reader of the text, help to narrow its possible representations so that author and reader can share common meaning. However, even with the narrowing of possible representations, there remains a great deal of uncertainty whether the text representation constructed by the reader overlaps in an appreciable way with the constructions of other readers or with the construction intended by the author. Readers can agree on the major features of texts, but what agreement can be reached on the more subtle or complex aspects? And with words themselves carrying a range of meaning rather than fixed meanings (Rosch, 1973; Wittgenstein, 1958), how much overlap can be achieved between reader's constructed text and author's actual text? "Our understanding of written tradition per se is not such that we can simply presuppose that the meaning we discover in it agrees with what its author intended" (Gadamer, 1993, p. 372). Literary theory, semiotics, and cognitive theory have all moved away from the notion that the actual text has an entirely objective meaning that can be extracted (Hartman, 1994). Meaning "resides either in the reader, in the cultural systems in which the reader resides, or in the transaction of reading" (p. 617). And, as long as meaning resides "outside the text," agreement on what is "in the text" will be in question.

Understanding that a text can have multiple interpretations likely is not developed until later in the elementary school years (Ackerman, 1988; Castell, 1993). Even after this understanding has developed, readers have little reason to consider alternative interpretations during normal reading as long as the interpretation they are generating is consistent and meaningful, and their goals for reading are being satisfied. With the additional demands on working memory, some readers may not have the resources necessary to construct and consider alternative interpretations, and those who do would need to be convinced that additional expenditures of time and effort will pay off. Moreover, for those readers who are convinced, it may be difficult for them to construct alternative interpretations if they have already invested in an interpretation that conforms with their prior knowledge and purposes for reading. Put differently, readers may not question their reading unless some triggering event calls their attention to a comprehension failure (Brown, 1980). The old adage "If it's not broken, don't fix it" in general seems to apply to most reading: If you don't believe comprehension is broken, don't fix it. Unfortunately, though, comprehension is often broken, and it is often broken without the reader's awareness that it is.

Comprehension of a text can become "broken" during normal reading in a variety of ways without the reader's awareness. Normal comprehension problems include failing to amend current understanding of a text in light of newly encountered information, glossing over unfamiliar words, drawing incorrect inferences, failing to compare information with prior knowledge, failing to encode key information, forgetting key information, failing to identify main propositions, and failing to understand information but continuing to read with the expectation that sooner or later understanding will be achieved. Some or all of these failures may occur, and yet readers can come away from reading believing they have comprehended the text; that is, readers are left with "illusions of knowing" (Glenberg, Wilkinson, & Epstein, 1982).

Using the proposed cognitive–metacognitive model of self-regulated comprehension, "illusions of knowing" can be explained in one of two ways. First, readers simply may fail to monitor or control comprehension. In this case, triggering events alerting readers to comprehension failures never occur, and readers come away from the text believing they have comprehended even though one or more comprehension failures may have occurred.

Alternatively, "illusions of knowing" can occur even when readers monitor and control comprehension. Recall that self-regulated comprehension involves monitoring similarities and differences between the cognitive representation of a text and the reader's metacognitive models, which consist of readers' understanding of their prior knowledge, text propositions, goals for reading, and author's intent. When similarities are monitored between what is represented in the text and what is represented in their metacognitive models, readers will believe that comprehension has occurred; when differences are monitored and readers are able to control them in satisfactory ways, they again will believe that comprehension has been achieved. And yet, if the metacognitive models that readers relied on to monitor similarities and differences have no bases in the actual text, readers will have failed to comprehend. In other words, as readers conform their constructions of text to fit their metacognitive models, deviations between what readers believe to be in a text versus what is actually in the text can and often do occur (Bransford & Franks, 1971; Paris, 1975; Paris & Lindauer, 1976; Paris & Mahoney, 1974). Otero (1998) argues that deviations between a reader's understanding of text and the actual text can occur when excessive activation of certain propositions leads to the suppression of other propositions. Excessive activation can occur as a result of the reader's emphasis of specific connections between text information and knowledge recently learned or overlearned. Moreover, Mannes and Kintsch (1987) have shown that readers' memory for text is often more reflective of what readers know about the topic than what is in the text itself.

Thus, in either of these two ways an "illusion of knowing" can occur, but the reasons for each differ. In the first, the "illusion of knowing" occurs because self-regulated comprehension is never engaged. In the second, the "illusion of knowing" occurs not because self-regulation of comprehension fails, but because readers construct a text that conforms with their metacognitive models of the text (i.e., their understanding of what is believed to be in the text) rather than the actual text.

The second explanation of "illusions of knowing" also explains the role that self-regulated comprehension can play when comprehension has not failed and yet differences in meaning-making keep readers apart in their interpretations. In the course of normal reading, a reader can activate relevant knowledge, understand all words and concepts, appropriately represent all text propositions in memory, and make relevant comparisons of related textual information, in other words, comprehend the text, and yet still encounter a comprehension problem if his or her interpretation of the text differs from the author's intentions or from other readers' constructions (Beal, 1996). Problems of interpretation are not at all uncommon and have long been the focus of hermeneutic inquiry. Awareness of the range of possible interpretations a text may have can bring readers together in what a text "says." Therefore, understanding the role that self-regulated comprehension can play in facilitating that awareness is essential to knowing how meaning-making can be shared during normal reading.

Encouraging Self-Regulated Comprehension at the Nexus Between Meaning-Making and Interpretation

Reading comprehension is the nexus between meaning and interpretation (Perfetti & McCutchen, 1987): Readers affix meaning to the words and propositions of a text, build on that meaning within the context of the text, and bring understanding to the contextualized meaning, that is, interpret the text, by melding it with what one already knows. As long as readers affix similar meanings to the words and propositions of a text and share a similar knowledge base, they likely will find agreement in what a text says. By contrast, because of ambiguities in word meaning and differences in knowledge, readers may comprehend a text, but differences in comprehension will arise.

Rarely is a word defined by precise and invariant characteristics. Rather, words are represented by spectrums of meaning (Wittgenstein, 1958). Where within a spectrum a word is temporarily affixed depends on cultural, social, and historical conventions, the writer's intent, the reader's understanding, and the context in which the word is embedded. Despite this ambiguity of meaning, the conveyance of understanding through words is made possible because there are at least some constraints on words. For example, the word *dog* carries with it a spectrum of meaning, and where it is affixed within that spectrum will vary depending on conventions, intent, understanding, and context. But, the word is constrained to that particular spectrum, and it does not carry a meaning that could be confused with the words *horse*, *building*, or *flying*.

Readers build on word meaning within the context of the text by combining word meanings to form propositions, combining propositions to form sentences, and combining sentences to form paragraphs. The resulting mental representation does not carry just any meaning. Rather, as described earlier, the text is constrained by the meaning of the words and propositions and the syntax that governs the ways in which the words and propositions are combined. Similarly, because interpretation depends on word meaning, not just any interpretation can be given to that mental representation. Just as a word represents a spectrum of meaning, the text represents a spectrum of interpretation, but the spectrum is constrained by the meanings ascribed to the words and propositions of the text (Perfetti & McCutchen, 1987).

For example, the meaning of the sentence *The dog ran home* is constrained by the meaning of each word and the syntax of the proposition in which those words appear. Depending on the extent of the reader's knowledge of dogs, running, and home, there will be ambiguity in meaning regarding just what kind of dog, how it was running, and what kind of home or to whose home it was running. Despite this ambiguity, the meaning of the sentence is constrained in that a dog is involved, not a cat, moose, or whale; that the dog was running, not skipping, hopping, or jumping; and that the dog's running was taking it home, not to school, work, or the grocery store. In this case, as with many ordinary texts, interpretation of sentence meaning (i.e., understanding of the contextualized meaning) and knowledge of word meaning are highly overlapping (Perfetti & McCutchen, 1987).

In contrast, consider the sentence "The Vietnam War, in the final analysis, was a contest between the U.S. with its abundantly subsidized, protected surrogate, and a Revolutionary movement whose class roots and ideological foundations gave it enormous resiliency and power" (Kolko, 1985, p. 553). This sentence demonstrates how interpretation, although constrained by meaning of words and propositions, varies greatly depending on the reader's knowledge. Knowledge of Vietnam and its history; knowledge of the United States, its history and its politics during the 1950s through 1970s; knowledge of the author and his political position; and knowledge of China, the U.S.S.R., and France all affect the interpretation of the text's meaning, and depending on differences in knowledge, differences in interpretation are likely to arise. In this case, interpretation of sentence meaning and knowledge of word meaning are not highly overlapping. It is apparent that the interpretation of text depends on meaning and how meaning is built within the context of the text, but interpretation is also strongly influenced by the reader's knowledge. Moreover, the text itself contains information that will likely alter or amend the reader's knowledge. Altered or amended knowledge then provides feedback into further construction of the text representation. Reading, therefore, is a doubly interactive process (Hesse, 1991): The text modifies the reader's knowledge, which then modifies the meaning affixed to the text and the interpretations of the text, which further modify the reader's knowledge.

By encouraging monitoring and control of comprehension at the nexus between meaning-making and interpretation, readers can open up alternative possibilities of text understanding. Increasing awareness of ambiguities in word meaning and differences in knowledge can help readers consider ranges of textual meaning. Greater awareness of what has been learned from the text can serve as self-feedback in the further construction of text. And, self-regulation of reading can help readers gain awareness of the differences in textual construction that arise when interpretation of sentence meaning and knowledge of word meaning are not highly overlapping.

One way of encouraging self-regulation of meaning-making and interpretation is through questioning. "Questioning opens up possibilities of meaning, and thus what is meaningful passes into one's own thinking on the subject" (Gadamer, 1993, p. 375). Questioning provides a means for readers to test their constructions of text against their metacognitive models (i.e., their understandings of text propositions, prior knowledge, goals, and the author's intent). The information generated from these tests is essential for readers to know whether their understanding of the text is actually founded in the text.

Also, understanding of text can be questioned by encouraging readers to monitor and control the inferences and assumptions they make as they read. When inferences and assumptions are not identified, monitoring and controlling discrepancies between a reader's interpretations of a text and the actual text are more difficult (Beal, 1990), as is the reinterpretation of the text when new information is encountered (Ackerman, 1988). By focusing readers' attention on the making of meaning at the inference level, a broader spectrum of interpretation can be encouraged. Consider the following illustration of the role of inference:

> As the fading light of a dying day filtered through the window blinds, Roger stood over his victim with a smoking .45, surprised at the serenity that filled him after pumping six slugs into the bloodless tyrant that had mocked him day after day, and then he shuffled out of the office with one last look back at the shattered computer terminal lying there like a silicon armadillo left to rot on the information highway. (Brill, 1995)

Granted, even though this is not a typical kind of text, it does illustrate very well how inferences can lead the reader to some quite surprising results. Often, an incorrect interpretation of text is constructed because authors are insufficiently explicit (in this case, intentionally) to constrain the possible interpretations (Olson, 1994). Awareness of meaning derived through inference and assumption, therefore, plays a critical role in the interpretation and reinterpretation of text.

These are just a few of the ways that readers can question their under-standing of text (i.e., their metacognitive models), and more will be described in the following section. The point here is that in the quest to create coherent mean-ing from the written word, readers may hold too strongly to their prior beliefs or knowledge and construct an interpretation of the text that differs from the literal or intended meaning (Otero & Kintsch, 1992). If readers are to become aware of interpretive differences, they must learn to question their metacognitive mod-els. By evaluating the answers to their questions and controlling reading and comprehension in light of their answers, readers are better able to set one inter-pretation aside so that another can be considered.

Directions for Research

Hartman (1994) provides an excellent example of the role that self-regulated comprehension can play in the interpretation of text. The purpose of this study was to highlight the online intertextual links that readers make among multiple passages. Hartman argues that

> much of what good readers do while reading is connect and relate ideas to their previous reading experiences over time. The net effect of these connected and ac-cumulated readings is that the reader's understanding transcends that of any single passage. (p. 616)

Readers

> transpose texts into other texts, absorb one text into another, and build a mosaic of intersecting text.... Adopting this intertextual view of reading, then, readers are conceived of as generators of interconnections or "links" between texts, resulting in a web of meaning—an evolving mental web. (p. 617)

Furthermore, readers use their interpretations of a currently read text to revise their interpretations of previously read texts, and their revised interpretations feedback to affect the interpretation of the current text. Thus, the interpretations that readers give to a text depend on the kinds of interpretations they have constructed from other texts and how they have linked those interpretations to the current text.

In Hartman's study, eight high school students, all capable readers, were asked to read a five-passage tableau designed to present a variety of perspec-tives and rhetorical styles. Students were asked to silently read the passages, to report aloud their thoughts while reading, and to mark the text with a pen when-ever they stopped reading and thought aloud. Following reading, students were asked 9 prompting questions designed to encourage insights into the passages and to form links among them, and 14 debriefing questions designed to gather self-descriptive data on what students had done while reading the text and answer-ing the prompting questions.

Analysis of the think-aloud protocols and answers provided abundant evidence of readers metacognitively monitoring and controlling their intertextual linking of texts. Monitoring was demonstrated in many ways. Students consciously and deliberately identified ideas, characters, and settings that served as links not only among the five texts but to previously read texts. They evaluated whether they understood a passage and recognized that understanding of one text "spills over" to the understanding of another. They were aware that their own interest or lack of interest in a passage could affect how they interpreted it. They were aware of the task complexities and of the demands placed on them. They considered the indeterminacy and openness of interpretation, and after generating alternative interpretations and weighing each, they reevaluated the texts according to each. They also linked their own affective feelings to each text by developing a discourse stance and then used the discourse stance as a measure of the texts' content. Finally, they not only sought to clarify the author's intent by evaluating a text from the author's perspective, but they also sought to bring greater breadth of meaning to the texts by evaluating them from multiple perspectives.

Information generated through their monitoring enabled students to exert various kinds of cognitive control over their comprehension. In response to their self-generated questions, readers either continued reading or reread passages flipping back and forth among them to elaborate and revise the meaning and interpretations they had given to them. Acknowledging their lack of interest in a specific passage, readers either consciously directed more attention to the task or they glossed over the passage and directed greater attention to those passages that did interest them. Readers tested alternative interpretations against previously and currently read material. They summarized passages and compared and contrasted summaries to one another and to prior knowledge. Evaluations of the passages from the perspective of the author or another reader often led readers to revise the meaning they had given to earlier passages, which in turn revised the meaning they were giving to those currently read. Finally, to bring greater meaning to the passages and to aid in their interpretation, readers occasionally created metaphors in which their prior knowledge was linked with their current understanding of the passages.

Hartman's research suggests a rich program for research of self-regulated comprehension during normal reading. This paradigm could be used to guide descriptive as well as experimental studies. Descriptive studies could include examinations of intertextual linking in other domains (e.g., science, math, or history), or in similar domains but using less-capable or younger readers versus more-capable or older readers. Experimental studies could include examinations of monitoring and control using texts that differ thematically versus texts that are thematically linked, texts that contain information known to the readers versus novel information, or texts that contain compatible versus incompatible information. I am currently exploring some of these research possibilities. Certainly, how we derive meaning and interpretations from the written word and how knowledge of meaning and interpretation further affect reading are fundamental questions of literacy. The study of self-regulated comprehension can do much to provide answers.

Overcoming the Constraints on Self-Regulated Comprehension Through Dialogue

Much research has shown that the more actively readers monitor and control comprehension during reading, the more likely they are to understand the text and to know that they understand (e.g., Baker, 1984; Brown, 1980; Markman, 1985; Palincsar & Brown, 1984; Pressley, El-Dinary, & Brown, 1992; Raphael, Kirschner, & Englert, 1986). However, apart from obvious constraints such as working memory capacity, insufficient knowledge, reading ability, and ambiguous goals, there may be limits to the extent to which readers can monitor and control their making of meaning from a text. In other words, even capable readers who read for clearly specified goals in content domains familiar to them may encounter still other constraints that prohibit their monitoring and controlling comprehension to the extent they need.

As readers construct an internal representation of text, they integrate the knowledge contained in the text with their prior knowledge. Monitoring this construction and judging that comprehension has failed indicates to readers that they need to control their reading to reestablish comprehension. Monitoring and judging that comprehension is complete, internally consistent, and compatible with prior knowledge indicates that reading can continue. In both cases, self-regulated comprehension has succeeded. However, as was argued earlier, readers can actively monitor and control their comprehension but still fail to comprehend the text if the metacognitive models on which they relied have no bases in the actual text. In this case, even though readers believe they understand, they need to question whether their understanding is actually supported by the text. Questioning during normal reading fosters text comprehension by focusing readers on the ambiguities of word meaning, the role of inference, and differences in interpretation.

There are limits, however, to how much readers can monitor and control their own construction of meaning. The notion of one level of thought monitoring and controlling another level of thought is problematic in that it represents a closed system that can act on itself only to the extent to which its own subjective standards are applied. Readers can question their metacognitive models in an attempt to test their understanding of a text against what is actively in the text, but because what is actually in the text is known only by their mental constructions of it, they ultimately end up testing one kind of mental representation against another kind of mental representation. If compatibility between the mental representations has been achieved, finding further discrepancies in one on the basis of the other is simply attempting to box with one's own shadow (Gadamer, 1993). This does not mean that a more complete understanding of a text cannot be gained through questioning.

What it does mean is that because readers cannot "know" the text but through their own knowing, there are necessarily constraints on the quantity and quality of understandings they can bring to the text through their own subjective standards.

To overcome these other constraints on understanding, readers should be encouraged to monitor and control their comprehension using not only their own subjective standards of evaluation but objective standards as well. Readers can access objective standards in at least two ways. They can go beyond the primary reading source and consult secondary sources. Once a text has been read, readers can read secondary sources in which alternative interpretations of the primary source are provided. By questioning one's understanding of a text against the understanding of others, a deeper comprehension can be gained.

Readers also can engage in a dialogue with other readers. The educational significance of dialogue cannot be overstated (Hacker & Graesser, in press). Among other things, dialogue encourages (a) active construction of knowledge through culturally meaningful activities, (b) generation of questions to guide comprehension, and (c) reflection on the progress of learning throughout the learning event (Daiute & Dalton, 1993). Through question and answer, give and take, talking at cross purposes, and assuming other perspectives, readers actively construct knowledge together and expand on their individual understandings of the text by merging their understandings with others. Meaning and interpretation are no longer constrained by one's knowledge, but rather are negotiated by the group (Pearson & Raphael, 1990). In addition, readers who have difficulty with word meaning and interpretation can receive help from others in the group. No longer constrained by their own constructions of the text, readers can test their understanding of the text against others' understanding of it. Eventual internalization of this dialogue into one's cognitive system can provide additional bases on which to direct future self-regulated comprehension (cf. Vygotsky, 1934/1978).

Thus, it is not only desirable to encourage dialogue in the classroom as a way to facilitate instruction, it is imperative to encourage dialogue as a way for students to expand their understanding of text beyond themselves. The role of dialogue has been identified in many areas of learning as key to development (Goodwin & Heritage, 1990; Roschelle, 1992; Suchman, 1987; Vygotsky, 1934/1978). Certainly, the role it plays in the development of reading can be included among these.

Conclusion

The purpose of this piece was first to propose a standardization in the terminology that has been used to describe evaluation and regulation of reading comprehension. Because of the growing agreement among researchers concerning the kinds of processes that are involved in reading and the growing need to standardize the terminology used to describe those processes, the term *self-regulated comprehension* was proposed. Next, a cognitive–metacognitive model of self-regulated comprehension was described, and a conceptualization of self-regulated comprehension during normal reading was given. Using this model, the relation between meaning and interpretation during normal reading was described and ways in which self-regulated comprehension could facilitate that relation were provided. Suggestions for future research on self-regulated comprehension during normal reading also were given. Finally, ways in which potential limitations of one level of thought monitoring and controlling another level of thought were discussed. The proposed model of self-regulated comprehension suggests that these limitations can be overcome by encouraging readers to apply standards of evaluation that are external to their own cognitive system. This can be done by asking readers to go beyond the primary reading source and consult secondary sources, or by engaging readers in a dialogue with other readers. Both ways have significance for education.

Very little research of self-regulated comprehension has focused on the role that comprehension monitoring plays when comprehension has not failed but differences in meaning-making keep readers apart in their interpretations of text. Believing that one has comprehended a text when in fact one's understanding is not supported by the actual text, or not knowing that one's understanding differs from that of the author or other readers are fundamental problems that can occur during normal reading. Encouraging readers to monitor and control their comprehension at the nexus between meaning-making and interpretation can help readers overcome these problems by focusing them on the ambiguities of word meaning, the role of inference, and differences in interpretation.

Research that attempts to examine the role of self-regulated comprehension during normal reading is more difficult to conduct than research that has relied on texts with planted errors or ambiguities. It is easier to test for comprehension failures than comprehension successes. However, the difficulties of the task should not dissuade researchers from undertaking it. Current research on how readers monitor and control their making of meaning during normal reading has provided insightful views into the ways meaning is constructed; however, much more needs to be done. As a meaning-making process, reading has particular significance to our cultural, historical, social, and psychological understanding of ourselves. It is important, therefore, to know how readers of all ages and abilities engage in it. It is equally important to know how readers of all ages and abilities can consciously and deliberately regulate meaning-making to further increase its usefulness.

References

Ackerman, B.P. (1988). Reason inferences in the story of comprehension of children and adults. *Child Development, 59,* 1426–1442.

Adams, M.J., & Collins, A. (1979). A schema-theoretic view of reading. In R.O. Freedle (Ed.), *Discourse processing: Multidisciplinary*

perspectives (pp. 486–502). Norwood, NJ: Ablex.

August, D.L., Flavell, J.H., & Clift, R. (1984). Comparison of comprehension monitoring of skilled and less skilled readers. *Reading Research Quarterly, 20,* 39–53.

Baker, L. (1984). Children's effective use of multiple standards for evaluating their comprehension. *Journal of Educational Psychology*, *76*, 588–597.

Baker, L. (1985). How do we know when we don't understand? Standards for evaluating text comprehension. In D.L. Forrest-Pressley, G.E. MacKinnon, & T.G. Waller (Eds.), *Metacognition, cognition, and human performance* (pp. 155–205). New York: Academic.

Baker, L. (1989). Metacognition, comprehension monitoring, and the adult reader. *Educational Psychology Review*, *1*, 3–38.

Baker, L., & Zimlin, L. (1989). Instructional effects on children's use of two levels of standards for evaluating their comprehension. *Journal of Educational Psychology*, *81*, 340–346.

Beal, C.R. (1990). The development of text evaluation and revision skills. *Child Development*, *61*, 247–258.

Beal, C.R. (1996). The role of comprehension monitoring in children's revision. *Educational Psychology Review*, *8*, 219–238.

Beal, C.R., Bonitatibus, G.J., & Garrod, A.C. (1990). Fostering children's revision skills through training in comprehension monitoring. *Journal of Educational Psychology*, *82*, 275–280.

Bransford, J.D., & Franks, J.J. (1971). The abstraction of linguistic ideas. *Cognitive Psychology*, *2*, 331–350.

Brill, L. (1995). Winner of the Bulwer-Lytton contest. *San Jose Mercury News*.

Broadbent, D.E. (1977). Levels, hierarchies, and the locus of control. *Quarterly Journal of Experimental Psychology*, *29*, 181–201.

Brown, A.L. (1980). Metacognitive development and reading. In R.J. Spiro, B.C. Bruce, & W.F. Brewer (Eds.), *Theoretical issues in reading comprehension* (pp. 453–481). Hillsdale, NJ: Erlbaum.

Butterfield, E.C., Albertson, L.R., & Johnston, J. (1995). On making cognitive theory more general and developmentally pertinent. In F. Weinert & W. Schneider (Eds.), *Memory performance and competencies: Issues in growth and development*. Hillsdale, NJ: Erlbaum.

Butterfield, E.C., Hacker, D.J., & Plumb, C. (1994). Topic knowledge, linguistic knowledge, and revision skill as determinants of text revision. In E.C. Butterfield (Ed.), *Children's writing: Toward a process theory of the development of skilled writing*. Greenwich, CT: JAI.

Carpenter, P.A., & Just, M.A. (1989). The role of working memory in language comprehension. In D. Klahr & K. Kotovsky (Eds.), *Complex information processing: The impact of Herbert A. Simon* (pp. 31–68). Hillsdale, NJ: Erlbaum.

Casteel, M.A. (1993). Effects of inference necessity and reading goal on children's inferential generation. *Developmental Psychology*, *29*, 346–357.

Conant, R.C., & Ashby, W.R. (1970). Every good regulator of a system must be a model of that system. *International Journal of Systems Science*, *1*, 89–97.

Daiute, C., & Dalton, B. (1993). Collaboration between children learning to write: Can novices be masters? *Cognition and Instruction*, *10*, 281–333.

Flavell, J.H. (1979). Metacognition and cognitive monitoring: A new area of cognitive-developmental inquiry. *American Psychologist*, *34*, 906–911.

Flower, L., Hayes, J.R., Carey, L., Schriver, K., & Stratman, J. (1986). Detection, diagnosis, and the strategies of revision. *College Composition and Communication*, *37*, 16–55.

Gadamer, H.G. (1993). *Truth and method* (2nd ed.). New York: Continuum.

Glenberg, A.M., & Epstein, W. (1985). Calibration of comprehension. *Journal of Experimental Psychology: Learning, Memory, & Cognition*, *11*, 702–718.

Glenberg, A.M., Wilkinson, A.C., & Epstein, W. (1982). The illusion of knowing: Failure in the self-assessment of comprehension. *Memory & Cognition*, *10*, 597–602.

Goodwin, C., & Heritage, J. (1990). Conversational analysis. *Annual Review of Anthropology*, *19*, 283–307.

Graesser, A.C., Singer, M., & Trabasso, T. (1994). Constructing inferences during narrative text comprehension. *Psychological Review*, *101*, 371–395.

Hacker, D.J. (1997). Comprehension monitoring of written discourse across early-to-middle adolescence. *Reading and Writing: An Interdisciplinary Journal*, *9*, 207–240.

Hacker, D.J., & Graesser, A.C. (in press). The role of dialogue in reciprocal teaching and naturalistic tutoring.

Hacker, D.J., Plumb, C., Butterfield, E.C., Quathamer, D., & Heineken, E. (1994). Text revision: Detection and correction of errors.

Journal of Educational Psychology, 86, 65–78.

Hartman, D.K. (1994). The intertextual links of readers using multiple passages: A postmodern/semiotic/cognitive view of meaning making. In R.B. Ruddell, M.R. Ruddell, & H. Singer (Eds.), *Theoretical models and processes of reading* (4th ed., pp. 616–636). Newark, DE: International Reading Association.

Hesse, D. (1991, November). *Strange attractors: Chaos theory and composition studies* (Rep. No. CS213191). Paper presented at the annual meeting of the National Council of Teachers of English. (ERIC Document Reproduction Service No. ED342010)

Johnson-Laird, P.N. (1983). A computational analysis of consciousness. *Cognition and Brain Theory, 6,* 499–508.

Just, M.A., & Carpenter, P.A. (1992). A capacity theory of comprehension: Individual differences in working memory. *Psychological Review, 99,* 122–149.

Kintsch, W. (1988). The role of knowledge in discourse comprehension: A construction–integration model. *Psychological Review, 95,* 163–182.

Kolko, G. (1985). *Anatomy of a war: Vietnam, the United States, and the modern historical experience.* New York: Pantheon Books.

Maki, R.H., & Serra, M. (1992). The basis of test predictions for text material. *Journal of Experimental Psychology: Learning, Memory, & Cognition, 18,* 116–126.

Mannes, S.M., & Kintsch, W. (1987). Knowledge organization and text organization. *Cognition and Instruction, 4,* 91–115.

Markman, E.M. (1979). Realizing that you don't understand: Elementary school children's awareness. *Child Development, 50,* 643–655.

Markman, E.M. (1985). Comprehension monitoring: Developmental and educational issues. In S.F. Chipman, J.W. Segal, & R. Glaser (Eds.), *Thinking and learning skills: Vol. 2 Research and open questions* (pp. 275–291). Hillsdale, NJ: Erlbaum.

Nelson, T.O., & Narens, L. (1990). Metamemory: A theoretical framework and new findings. *The Psychology of Learning and Motivation, 26,* 125–141.

Olson, D.R. (1994). *The world on paper: The conceptual and cognitive implications of writing and reading.* Cambridge, UK: Cambridge University Press.

Otero, J.C. (1998). Influence of knowledge activation and context on comprehension monitoring of science texts. In D.J. Hacker, J. Dunlosky, & A.C. Graesser (Eds.), *Metacognition in educational theory and practice.* Hillsdale, NJ: Erlbaum.

Otero, J.C., & Campanario, J.M. (1990). Comprehension evaluation and regulation in learning from science texts. *Journal of Research in Science Teaching, 27,* 447–460.

Otero, J.C., & Kintsch, W. (1992). Failures to detect contradictions in a text: What readers believe versus what they read. *Psychological Science, 3,* 229–235.

Palincsar, A.S., & Brown, A.L. (1984). Reciprocal teaching of comprehension-fostering and comprehension-monitoring activities. *Cognition & Instruction, 1,* 117–175.

Paris, S.G. (1975). Integration and inference in children's comprehension and memory. In F. Rustle, R. Shiffrin, J. Castellan, H. Lindman, & D. Pisoni (Eds.), *Cognitive theory* (Vol. 1). Hillsdale, NJ: Erlbaum.

Paris, S.G., & Lindauer, B.K. (1976). Constructive processes in children's comprehension and memory. In R.V. Kail & J.W. Hagen (Eds.), *Memory in cognitive development.* Hillsdale, NJ: Erlbaum.

Paris, S.G., & Mahoney, G.J. (1974). Cognitive integration in children's memory for sentences and pictures. *Child Development, 45,* 633–642.

Pearson, P.D., & Raphael, T.E. (1990). Reading comprehension as a dimension of thinking. In B.F. Jones & L. Idol (Eds.), *Dimensions of thinking and cognitive instruction.* Hillsdale, NJ: Erlbaum.

Perfetti, C.A., & McCutchen, D. (1987). Schooled language competence: Linguistic abilities in reading and writing. In S. Rosenberg (Ed.), *Advances in applied psycholinguistics: Vol. 2, Reading, writing, and language learning* (pp. 105–141). New York: Cambridge University Press.

Pressley, M., El-Dinary, P.B., & Brown, R. (1992). Skilled and not-so-skilled reading: Good information processing and not-so-good information processing. In M. Pressley, K.R. Harris, & J.T. Guthrie (Eds.), *Promoting academic competence and literacy in school* (pp. 91–127). San Diego, CA: Academic.

Pressley, M., Forrest-Pressley, D.L., Elliot-Faust, D.J., & Miller, G.E. (1985). Children's use of cognitive strategies, how to teach strategies, and what to do if they can't be taught. In M. Pressley & C.J. Brainerd (Eds.),

Cognitive learning and memory in children (pp. 1–47). New York: Springer-Verlag.

Raphael, T.E., Kirschner, B.W., & Englert, C.S. (1986). *Student's metacognitive knowledge about writing* (Research Series No. 176). East Lansing: Michigan State University, Institute for Research on Teaching.

Roen, D.H., & Willey, R.J. (1988). The effect of audience awareness on drafting and revising. *Research in the Teaching of English, 22,* 75–88.

Rosch, E. (1973). On the internal structure of perceptual and semantic categories. In T.E. Moore (Ed.), *Cognitive development and the acquisition of language* (pp. 111–144). New York: Academic.

Roschelle, J. (1992). Learning by collaboration: Convergent conceptual change. *Journal of the Learning Sciences, 2,* 235–276.

Rumelhart, D.E., & McClelland, J.L. (1981). Interactive processing through spreading activation. In A.M. Lesgold & C.A. Perfetti (Eds.), *Interactive processes in reading* (pp. 37–60). Hillsdale, NJ: Erlbaum.

Suchman, L.A. (1987). *Plans and situated actions: The problem of human–machine communication.* Cambridge, UK: Cambridge University Press.

Traxler, M.J., & Gernsbacher, M.A. (1993). Improving written communication through perspective taking. *Language and Cognitive Processes, 8,* 311–334.

van Dijk, T.A., & Kintsch, W. (1983). *Strategies of discourse comprehension.* New York: Academic.

Vosniadou, S., Pearson, P.D., & Rogers, T. (1988). What causes children's failure to detect inconsistencies in text? Representation versus comparison difficulties. *Journal of Educational Psychology, 80,* 27–39.

Vygotsky, L.S. (1978). *Mind in society: The development of higher psychological processes* (M. Cole, V. John-Steiner, S. Scribner, & E. Souberman, Eds. & Trans.). Cambridge, MA: Harvard University Press. (Original work published 1934)

Weaver, C., III. (1990). Constraining factors in calibration of comprehension. *Journal of Experimental Psychology: Learning, Memory, & Cognition, 16,* 214–222.

Weaver, C.A., III. (1995). Monitoring of comprehension: The role of text difficulty in metamemory for narrative and expository text. *Memory & Cognition, 23,* 12–22.

Wittgenstein, L. (1958). *Philosophical investigations* (2nd ed.). Oxford, UK: Blackwell.

Wong, B.Y.L., Butler, D.L., Ficzere, S.A., & Kuperis, S. (1994). Teaching problem learners revision skills and sensitivity to audience through two instructional modes: Student–teacher vs. student–student interactive dialogues. *Learning Disabilities Research and Practice, 9,* 78–90.

Zabrucky, K., & Moore, D. (1989). Children's ability to use three standards to evaluate their comprehension of text. *Reading Research Quarterly, 24,* 336–352.

Zabrucky, K., & Ratner, H.H. (1992). Effects of passage type on comprehension monitoring and recall in good and poor readers. *Journal of Reading Behavior, 24,* 373–391.

29

Instructing Comprehension-Fostering Activities in Interactive Learning Situations

Ann L. Brown, Annemarie Sullivan Palincsar,
and Bonnie B. Armbruster

Introduction

"Pupils don't learn to comprehend by osmosis" (Cushenbery, 1969). As with any definite statement concerning the acquisition of reading skills, this could be a controversial position, but a main theme of this piece is that, at least for a sizable number of children, the statement is true. It is also argued that children who need extensive instruction in comprehending written materials most are least likely to receive it. The latter part of the piece describes cognitive-skills training studies that have provided extensive practice in comprehension-fostering activities and have resulted in substantial improvements in students' ability to learn from texts.

Resnick (1979) has argued that there are two main biases in reading instruction, namely direct instruction of decoding and informal teaching of comprehension. Those who advocate a heavy emphasis on decoding mechanisms in early reading also tend toward the direct-instruction approach, whereas those who emphasize early attention to language processing, language arts, or comprehension tend also to espouse learner-directed, informal instructional approaches. As Resnick also argued, there is no reason in principle why one cannot have direct instruction in comprehension or (a little harder to envisage) informal instruction in decoding. In this piece, concern is with one of the underpopulated cells, relatively direct or explicit instruction in comprehension. Of particular concern is the explicit instruction of comprehension-fostering skills with children at risk for academic failure precisely because they experience unusual difficulties in this arena.

From Mandl, H., Stein, N.L., & Trabasso, T. (Eds.), *Learning and Comprehension of Text* (pp. 255–286). Copyright © 1984 by Lawrence Erlbaum Associates. Reprinted with permission of the publisher.

Prereading Experiences

Preschool Reading Dyads

Learning to read does not begin when the child enters school; the child brings a history of preschool learning experiences that, to a greater or lesser extent, have prepared the way for a smooth transition. Some of these experiences could clearly be classified as prereading activities; others are more general learning practices with some relevance to reading. Many of these early experiences have taken place in social settings that share pertinent features with common school learning activities. Some children have considerable preschool experience in interactions that are very similar to school reading groups; others have not.

Certain parent-child interactions are ideal practicing grounds for subsequent teacher-child activities that will be of central importance in the early grades. Social settings such as these, where the child interacts with experts in a problem-solving domain, are settings where a great deal of learning occurs in and out of school. Indeed, some would argue that the majority of learning is shaped by social processes (Laboratory of Comparative Human Cognition, 1986; Vygotsky, 1934/1978). From this perspective it is claimed that children first experience a particular set of problem-solving activities in the presence of others and only gradually come to perform these functions for themselves. First, the adult (parent, teacher, etc.) guides the child's activity, doing much of the cognitive work herself, but gradually the adult and child come to share the cognitive functions with the child taking initiative and the adult correcting and guiding where the child falters. Finally, the adult allows the child to take over the major thinking role and adopts the stance of a supportive and sympathetic audience.

This developmental progress from social to individual cognitive processing (other regulation to self-regulation) is nicely illustrated in parent-child learning dyads such as those reported by Wertsch (1978). Of particular interest to the argument here are the interactions of mothers and children as they engage in picture book "reading."

At least in middle class homes, a stable locus of parent-child interactions is the picture book task. Ninio and Bruner (1978) observed one mother-infant dyad longitudinally, starting when the child was only 8 months old and terminating (unfortunately) when he was 18 months old. From the very beginning, their interaction can best be described as a dialogue with the timing of mother's and child's behavior following an almost complete alternation pattern strikingly similar to the turn-taking conventions observed in dialogue. The mother initially is very much in command and seduces the child into the ritual dialogue for picture book reading by accepting any response from the baby as appropriate for his turn in the conversation. Indeed, Ninio and Bruner point out that the mother accepts an astonishing variety of responses as acceptable turn-taking behavior interpreting anything as having a "specific, intelligible content." The "imputation of intent and content" to the child's activities constitutes "an important mechanism by which the child is advanced to more adult-like communicative behavior" (Ninio & Bruner, 1978, p. 8).

A dramatic shift in responsibility comes when the child begins to label pictures for himself. Now the mother acts as if she believes the child has uttered words rather than babble. As the mother's theory of the child changes, so does her part in the dialogue. At first she appears to be content with any vocalization, but as soon as actual words can be produced the mother steps up her demands and asks for a label with the query "What's that?" The mother seems to increase her level of expectation, first "coaxing the child to substitute a vocalization for a non-vocal sign and later a well-formed word for a babbled vocalization." Initially, the mother does all the labeling because she assumes that the child cannot. According to Ninio and Bruner (1978),

> Later, the mother starts a cycle with a label *ONLY* if she thinks that the child will not label the picture himself, either because he does not yet know the correct word or he is not attentive enough to make the effort at labeling. If circumstances seem more favorable for labeling to occur, she will usually start the cycle with a *"What's that?"* question. (p. 14)

Responsibility for labeling is transferred from the mother to the child in response to his increasing store of knowledge, finely monitored by the mother. During the course of the study, the mother constantly updated her inventory of the words the child had previously understood and repeatedly attempted to make contact with his growing knowledge base. For example:

1. You haven't seen one of those; that's a goose.
2. You don't really know what those are, do you? They are mittens; wrong time of year for those.
3. It's a dog; I know you know that one.
4. We'll find you something you know very well.
5. Come on, you've learned "bricks."

DeLoache (1983) has repeated many of these observations in a cross-sectional study of mothers reading to their children. The children ranged from 17–38 months. The mothers of the youngest children point to the objects and label them, sometimes providing some additional information. In the middle age group, the children are much more active. Their mothers ask them to point to and label objects to provide other information about the picture. These children often spontaneously provide labels ("There's a horsie") or ask the mothers for labels ("What's this?"). In the oldest group studies, more complex stories were introduced, and the mothers do much more than simply label objects. They talk about the relation among the objects in the picture and relate them to the child's experience—e.g., "That's right, that's a bee hive. Do you know what bees make? They make honey. They get nectar from flowers and use it to make honey, and then they put the honey in the bee hive." When the child can recognize the pictures and knows something about them, the mother uses the material to provide the child with a great deal of background information only loosely related to the actual pictures. It is not simply that the amount of help changes as the child becomes more competent, but the quality of help is finely geared to the child's current level.

In both the Ninio and Bruner and DeLoache dyads, the mother is seen functioning repeatedly in the child's "region of sensitivity to instruction" (Wood & Middleton, 1975) or "zone of proximal development" (Vygotsky, 1934/1978). As the child advances so does the level of collaboration demanded by the mother. The mother systematically shapes their joint experiences in such a way that the child will be drawn into taking more and more responsibility for the dyad's work. In so doing, the mother not only provides an optimal learning environment, she also models appropriate comprehension-fostering activities such as elaboration, activating appropriate background knowledge, and questioning strategies. These crucial activities are thereby made *overt* and *explicit*.

Inadequate Early Mediated Learning

It has been argued that parent-child interactions such as the social reading experiences just described are important preparations for early school success. It has also been argued that a severe lack of interactive experiences is a primary source of academic retardation. A leading advocate of this position is Feuerstein (1979, 1980), who argues that cognitive growth is very heavily dependent on the quality of *mediated learning* that the child experiences. According to Feuerstein (1979), "Mediated learning is the training given to the human organism by an experienced adult who frames, selects, focuses, and feeds back an environmental experience in such a way to create appropriate learning sets" (p. 6). These mediated-learning experiences are an essential aspect of development beginning when the parent selects significant objects for the infant to focus on and proceeding throughout the development with the adult systematically shaping the child's learning experiences. Feuerstein believes that this is the principal means by which children develop the cognitive operations necessary for learning independently. By interacting with an adult, who models and guides problem-solving activities and structures learning environments, children gradually come to adopt structuring and regulating activities of their own. It is argued that cognitive skills, including those of comprehension fostering and monitoring, develop normally via a process whereby the adult models and prompts their use and the children gradually adopt such activities as part of their own repertoire.

Feuerstein believes that the principal reason for the poor academic performance of many disadvantaged students is the lack of consistent instruction by parental models in their earlier developmental histories because of parental apathy, ignorance, or overcommitment. Quite simply, parents in disadvantaged homes were often themselves disadvantaged children and cannot be expected to teach what they perhaps do not know; large family size and the need for a working mother do not leave a great deal of time for Socratic dialogue games. In addition, interactive styles of continually questioning and extending the limits of knowledge that are typical of middle class social-interaction patterns (Ninio & Bruner, 1978) may even be alien to some cultures (Au, 1979; Bernstein, 1971).

Mediated-learning activities, however, are exactly what occurs in schools, and the middle class child comes well prepared to take part in these rituals. Not only does the disadvantaged child lack sufficient prior exposure, but there is evidence that teachers give less experience in this learning mode to those who, because of their lack of prior experience, need it most.

School Reading Experiences

Teachers as Models of Reading Strategies

Ideally when the child reaches school, teachers take over some of the mediating functions, acting as models and promoters of comprehension-fostering activities. In schools, effective teachers are those who engage in continued prompts to get children to plan and monitor their own reading activities. Effective teachers model many forms of critical thinking for their students (Collins & Stevens, 1982). Thus, Collins and Smith's (1982) recent call for teachers to model comprehension-monitoring activities is timely but not novel. In a recent review of the literature, Bird (1980) traces the history of this idea and points out that it is a recurrent theme in the reading-education literature. For example, Lorge (1957) stressed that the teacher should model active-comprehension processes and direct the child's attention to the thinking and reasoning processes that he or she engages in while reading for meaning. Smith (1961) also called for teachers to ask questions that stimulate the drawing of inferences, the making of predictions and of comparisons, and the use of cause and effect reasoning. This theme was repeated by King (1967) and Gantt (1970), who described programs of teacher-directed questioning by which children are led through the sequence of thinking necessary to understand the passage. Similarly, Schwartz and Scheff (1975) suggested that teachers encourage active reading by demonstrating their own curiosity, posing questions, reasoning, predicting, and verifying inferences and conclusions.

Good teachers do this, of course. Even teachers who refrain from such activities in reading group do demonstrate them in, for example, reading a story to the whole class (Griffin, 1977). In their discussion of why teachers are easier to understand than texts, Schallert and Kleiman (1979) identified four main activities that teachers use to help children understand. They tailor the message to the child's level, activate relevant background knowledge, focus student attention on main points, and force comprehension monitoring by probing and question-asking aimed at testing the degree of understanding.

The main theme of all this work is that the ideal teacher functions as a model of comprehension-fostering and comprehension-monitoring activities largely by activating relevant knowledge and questioning basic assumptions. These are the essential features of the teaching style referred to variously as Socratic, case, or inquiry methods. Collins and Stevens (1982) have examined a variety of teachers and developed a taxonomy of tactics that are commonly used by outstanding teachers, notably the "entrapment ploys" of counterexamples and invidious generalizations, the "extension ploys" that force students to apply their newfound knowledge broadly, and the "debugging ploys" that force students to correct their misconceptions (Collins & Stevens, 1982).

Collins and Stevens point out that a main goal of such dialogues is not to convey the content of a particular domain. If this were the aim, the method would be inefficient due to the low rate of information transfer; more points can be conveyed in a lecture than can be discussed in a Socratic dialogue. If the method is successful, it is because it teaches students to think scientifically, to make predictions, to question and evaluate. An effective aid to knowledge-building and revision is the ploy of forcing learners to make their theories explicit and to defend them to others.

In order for these activities of questioning, predicting, hypothesis generation, testing, and revision to be of service to the child, it is necessary that they are transferred from the teacher to the child in such a way that they form part of the learner's battery of comprehension-fostering skills. A common problem with all these approaches, as pointed out by Jenkinson (1969) and Gall (1970), is that they presuppose that children witnessing these activities will come to employ them on their own. This is the problem of *internalization*, how the child comes to personally use activities that were originally social (Vygotsky, 1934/1978). We return to this point later.

Reading Groups and Reading Status

Not all children are exposed to gifted teachers, and even the same teachers may offer different learning environments to those viewed as good or poor readers (Brown, Palincsar, & Purcell, 1986). The selection of a curriculum is itself the selection of a particular reading environment. Bartlett (1979) claimed that disadvantaged children are most likely to be exposed to early reading programs with a heavy emphasis on decoding such as Distar, whereas middle class children receive earlier exposure to programs that emphasize comprehension such as Open Court. Bartlett goes on to compare the types of questions featured prominently in Distar exercises to those recommended by Open Court. In general, the Distar questions tend to focus on locating and remembering specific information, whereas the Open Court questions promote reflection upon and the questioning of the meaning of the text. Hence, a different type of instruction is aimed at children who enter school differentially prepared for the experience.

Even if the curriculum and classroom placement do not differ, there remains evidence that the reading environment is not equal for all children. For example, detailed observations of reading groups (Allington, 1980; Au, 1980; Cazden, 1979; Collins, 1980; McDermott, 1978) have shown that good and poor readers are not treated equally. Good readers are questioned about the meaning behind what they are reading, and they are asked to evaluate and criticize material frequently. A considerable amount of time in the good reading group is "on task"; i.e., reading-related activities occur, and a sizable amount of the group activities are of an optimal "comprehension-fostering" type. In the good reading group, the teacher adopts the procedure of asking every child to read in turn; but in the poorer reading group, turn-taking is at the teacher's request, and the really poor readers are not called upon to perform to save everyone embarrassment (McDermott, 1978). Precious little time in the poor reading group is spent doing comprehension-fostering activities; the lion's share of activities involve the establishment of such rituals as turn-taking and hand raising. When and if they are required to read, poor readers receive primarily drill in pronunciation and decoding. Rarely are they given practice in qualifying and evaluating their comprehension (Allington, 1980; Collins, 1980). A case could even be made that the poorest readers receive little formal reading comprehension instruction in these groups (McDermott, 1978).

Children who come to school inadequately prepared for reading, for whatever reason, tend to end up in the bottom reading groups and are, therefore, exposed to different reading experiences. The emphasis is clearly on decoding and not on comprehension. If as a result of their initial failure and subsequent treatment these children are singled out for special education, they run the risk of an intensive version of this same treatment; for special education in reading problems has an even heavier emphasis on decoding skills at the expense of reading-comprehension instruction.

A strong emphasis on direct instruction in basic skills permeates resource rooms and special education classrooms, perhaps an understandable reaction to the "lack" of these skills demonstrated by the students. Special education classes are more likely to provide step-by-step instruction for students in basic skills (decoding, etc.) and rarely allow the students to figure out meanings or question their assumptions. Heavily programmed and guided learning of this type may be a practical and efficient means of getting less-successful students to perform better on a particular task, i.e., word recognition. But it is the teacher, not the child, who is making all the learning decisions. Such experience is less likely to be the appropriate procedure for promoting insightful learning. Students may learn something about a particular task, but they are less likely to learn how to learn from reading (Brown, 1982).

Of course we are not arguing against the practice of direct instruction in decoding per se. As Resnick (1979) has pointed out, there is a great deal of evidence to support the success of reading programs that favor early direct instruction of decoding. We do argue, however, that instruction in comprehension can and should be offered in addition (Tharp, 1982), because the current state of affairs is that poor readers, particularly those labeled as learning disabled or mildly retarded, are unlikely in the present system to develop adequate reading-comprehension skills. Decoding is mastered eventually but reading-comprehension scores remain low and possibly permanently and severely depressed. Many factors may be responsible for this typical pattern, but one that is rarely addressed is the simple explanation of practice. Practice makes possible; if so, perhaps we should not be surprised to find a cumulative deficit in comprehension skills in those who are systematically denied extensive experience in comprehension-fostering activities.

In summary, following repeated experience with experts (parents, caretakers, teachers, etc.) who situate, elaborate, evaluate, and extend the limits of their experience, many students develop a battery of school-relevant autocritical skills (Binet, 1909; Brown, 1985) that include comprehension-fostering activities ideally tailored for reading. These skills are essential acquisitions, if students are to learn how to learn independently. If for some reason the child is deprived of a constant history of such interaction in and out of school, the development of an adequate battery of self-regulatory skills for performing independently on academic tasks may be impeded.

Given this argument, an appropriate training experience would be to attempt to mimic naturally occurring interactive-learning settings as a context for instruction. In a subsequent section, a series of experiments is reviewed that may have promise for improving comprehension skills precisely because they attempt to help children adopt for themselves questioning and monitoring activities that they experience initially in interactive settings.

Comprehension-Fostering Activities

Before proceeding to a discussion of instruction, an attempt is made to be somewhat more explicit about the nature of the comprehension processes involved in effective reading. We concentrate on those that promote comprehension and lead to effective comprehension monitoring, i.e., activities engaged in by readers to ensure that comprehension is proceeding smoothly. Although far from a detailed task analysis of reading comprehension, there are several overlapping skills that have been mentioned repeatedly as prime comprehension-fostering activities in a variety of recent theoretical treatments (Baker & Brown, 1984a, 1984b; Brown, 1980; Collins & Smith, 1982; Dansereau, 1980; Markman, 1981). These activities include

1. clarifying the purposes of reading, i.e., understanding the task demands, both explicit and implicit;

2. activating relevant background knowledge;

3. allocating attention so that concentration can be focused on the major content at the expense of trivia;

4. critical evaluation of content for internal consistency and compatibility with prior knowledge and common sense;

5. monitoring ongoing activities to see if comprehension is occurring by engaging in such activities as periodic review and self-interrogation; and

6. drawing and testing inferences of many kinds, including interpretations, predictions, and conclusions.

All of these activities appear as academic tasks in their own right; for example, it is a common practice to call on children to concentrate on the main idea, to think critically about the content of what they are reading, or to summarize or answer questions on a passage. But, in addition, these activities, if engaged in while reading, serve to enhance comprehension and afford an opportunity for the student to check whether it is occurring. That is, they can be both *comprehension-fostering* and *comprehension-monitoring* activities if properly used. Self-directed summarization is an excellent comprehension-fostering and comprehension-monitoring technique (Brown & Day, 1983; Brown, Day, & Jones, 1983; Day, 1980; Linden & Wittrock, 1981). Monitoring one's progress while reading, to test whether one can pinpoint and retain important material, provides a check that comprehension is progressing smoothly. If the reader cannot produce an adequate synopsis of what is being read, this is a clear sign that comprehension is *not* proceeding smoothly and that remedial action is called for.

Similarly, self-directed questioning concerning the meaning of text content leads students to a more active monitoring of their own comprehension (André & Anderson, 1978/1979). Thus, closing one's eyes (metaphorically) and attempting to state the gist of what one has read and asking questions of an *interpretive* and *predictive* nature (Collins & Smith, 1982) are activities that both improve comprehension and permit students to monitor their own understanding. These are also the kinds of active and aggressive interactions with texts that poor readers do not engage in readily; the need for explicit instruction in comprehension-enhancing activities is particularly acute for the slow-learning student (Brown & Palincsar, 1982).

Instructing Reading Comprehension

Teaching Settings and Reading Strategies

In this section a series of successful training studies is described which attempt to combine a knowledge of effective teaching settings and appropriate learning activities in order to improve comprehension (Palincsar & Brown, 1983). We have argued that many students lack sufficient practice in interactive-learning situations where comprehension-fostering activities are modeled and promoted. If this were true, then an obvious compensatory strategy would be to design instruction where practice in the essential skills is embedded within an interactive-learning situation that mimics the idealized mother-child, teacher-child dialogues previously described.

The particular skills selected for training were *summarizing* (self-review), *questioning*, *clarifying*, and *predicting*. There is a large literature connected with each activity. A considerable amount is known about the use or nonuse of the activities in isolation, especially in response to direct instruction. But considerably less is known about the spontaneous orchestration of a battery of such activities in the face of different forms of comprehension failure. For example, high school and junior college students have a great deal of trouble writing adequate synopses of texts (Brown & Day, 1983), although well-designed training can improve these skills (Day, 1980). Very little is known, however, about the use of self-directed paraphrasing as a method of periodic review or as a means of monitoring comprehension when the text gets difficult. Also, young and poor readers have difficulty evaluating texts for clarity, internal consistency, or compatibility with known facts (Markman, 1981), and training helps here too (Markman & Gorin, 1981). But again, little is known about where and when and with what actual processes the reader will engage in such monitoring spontaneously. Similarly, students often fail to generate questions and can be trained to perform better on these skills in isolation (André & Anderson, 1978/1979), but little is known about the spontaneous use of questioning as part of a concerted, personally designed, and coordinated plan of attack in the face of comprehensive difficulties. Therefore, in this series of studies the four activities of self-directed summarizing (review), questioning, clarifying, and predicting are combined in a package of activities with the general aim of enhancing understanding. Each "separate" activity, however, was used in response to a concrete problem of text comprehension. Clarifying occurred only if there were confusions either in the text (unclear referent, etc.) or in the student's interpretation of the text. Summarizing was modeled as an activity of self-review; it was engaged in in order to state to the group what had just happened in the text and as a test that the content had been understood. If an adequate synopsis could not be reached, this fact was regarded *not* as a failure to perform a particular decontextualized skill but as an important source of information that comprehension was not proceeding as it should and remedial action (such as rereading or clarifying) was needed. Questioning, similarly, was not practiced as a teacher-directed isolated activity, but as a concrete task—what question would a teacher or test ask about that section of the text. Students reacted very positively to this concrete detective work, rather than the more typical isolated skills-training approach as we will see.

We embedded these activities within a training procedure that was very similar to the interactive mother-child, teacher-student dyads described earlier.

The procedure was also similar to that of reciprocal questioning. Manzo (1969) introduced a variant of this with his ReQuest procedure. Teachers and small groups of remedial-reading students took turns asking themselves questions about what they were reading. Questions followed every sentence, a procedure that would not encourage synthesis across larger segments of text. And the types of questions modeled and generated were not necessarily optimal. For example, one teacher modeled the question, "What was the third word in the first sentence?" Even so, Manzo reported significant improvement in standardized reading-comprehension scores. Frase and Schwartz (1975) also had college students taking turns generating or answering questions. Regardless of which role the students assumed, they performed better than when engaged in silent reading. Even though training was not extensive and again there was no attempt to ensure adequate quality of questions, the intervention produced a modest but reliable effect. Given these promising precursors, a reciprocal teaching method was adopted where, in addition to question generation, the activities of reciprocal paraphrasing, clarifying, and predicting were added.

Instructing Comprehension-Fostering by Reciprocal Teaching

So far three studies have been completed (Palincsar & Brown, 1983). The first two are laboratory studies with an experimenter (Palincsar) interacting with individual children or with pairs of students. The third study was conducted in the classroom by regular classroom teachers. The students in all three studies were seventh graders with average decoding skills but seriously deficient comprehension scores.[1]

Study 1. In Study 1, four students served as subjects in an extensive training experiment (for full details see Palincsar & Brown, 1983). Each subject served as his or her own control. After completing the decoding and comprehension tests that made them eligible for the study, the students received a period of baseline assessment, on each day of which they read a 500-word expository passage and then attempted to answer 10 comprehension questions independently. This baseline procedure of reading and answering questions on a novel assessment passage each day was also followed during maintenance and long-term follow-up periods. During training periods the students also read and answered questions on a novel assessment passage, but the assessment stage was preceded by interactive training sessions on still different passages. All data reported are percent correct from the daily independent-assessment test, *not* from the interacted-upon texts.

There were 6–8 days of initial baseline, 10 days of reciprocal teaching, followed by 6 days of maintenance and then a further 3 days of reciprocal teaching. Six months later, the students were retested for 8 days—4 days of untreated maintenance followed by 2 days where reciprocal teaching was reintroduced, which was followed in turn by a final 2 days of maintenance.[2]

During the reciprocal-teaching intervention, the investigator and the student engaged in an interactive-learning game that involved taking turns in leading a dialogue concerning each segment of text. If the passage was new, the investigator called the student's attention to the title, asked for predictions based upon the title, and discussed the relationship of the passage to prior knowledge. For example, if the passage were entitled *Ship of the Desert*, the investigator and student would speculate about what the passage might concern and would review what they knew about the characteristics of the desert. If the passage were partially completed, the investigator would ask the student to recall and state the topic of the text and several important points already covered in the passage.

The investigator then assigned a segment of the passage to be read (usually a paragraph) and either indicated that it was her turn to be the teacher or assigned the student to teach that segment. The investigator and student then read the assigned segment silently. After reading the text, the teacher for that segment summarized the content, discussed and clarified any difficulties, asked a question that a teacher or test might ask on the segment, and finally made a prediction about future content. All of these activities were embedded in as natural a dialogue as possible with the teacher and student giving feedback to each other.

Throughout the interventions, the students were explicitly told that these activities were general strategies to help them understand better as they read and that they should try to do something like this when they read silently. It was pointed out that being able to say in your own words what one has just read and being able to guess that the questions will be on a test are sure ways of testing oneself to see if one has understood.

At first the students had difficulty taking their part in the dialogue, experiencing particular difficulties with summarizing and formulating questions. The adult teacher helped with a variety of prompting techniques such as "What question did you think a teacher might ask?" "Remember, a summary is a shortened version; it doesn't include detail" and "If you're having a hard time summarizing, why don't you think of a question first?"

The adult teacher also provided praise and feedback specific to the student's participation: "You asked that question well; it was very clear what information you wanted"; "Excellent prediction; let's see if you're right"; "That was interesting information. It was information that I would call detail in the passage. Can you find the most important information?" After this type of feedback, the adult teacher modeled any activity that continued to need improvement: "A question I would have asked would be..."; "I would summarize by saying..."; "Did you find this statement unclear?"

Initially, then, the experimenter modeled appropriate activities, but the students had great difficulty assuming the role of dialogue leader when their turn came. The experimenter was sometimes forced to resort to constructing paraphrases and questions for the student to mimic. In this initial phase, the experimenter was modeling effective comprehension-monitoring strategies, but the student was a relatively passive observer.

In the intermediate phase, the students became much more capable of playing their role as dialogue leader and by the end of 10 sessions were providing paraphrases and questions of some sophistication. For example, in the initial sessions, 46% of questions produced by the students were judged as nonquestions or as needing clarification. By the end of the sessions only 2% of responses were judged as either needing clarification or nonquestions. Unclear questions drop out and are replaced over time with questions focusing on the main idea of each text segment. Examples of questions judged to be needing clarification, main idea, and detail are shown in Table 1.

A similar improvement was found for summary statements. At the beginning of the session, only 11% of summary statements captured main ideas, whereas at the end 60% of the statements were so classified. Examples of summary statements are shown in Table 2.

With repeated interaction with a model performing appropriate questioning and paraphrasing activities, the students became able to perform these functions on their own. Over time the students' questions became more like the tutor's, being classified as *inventions*, that is, questions and summaries of gist in one's own words, rather than selections, repetitions of words actually occurring in the text (Brown & Day, 1983). For example, an early occurring form of question would be to take verbatim from the text "plans are being made to use nuclear power" and append the question with the inflection "for what?" Later forms of questioning were most likely to be paraphrases of the gist in the students' own words. For example, reading a passage about fossils, one student posed the following question: "When an animal dies, certain parts decay, but what parts are saved?" This question was constructed by integrating information presented across several sentences. Given the steady improvement on the privately read texts, it would appear that students internalize these activities as part of their own repertoire of comprehension-fostering skills. In support of this statement are the data from peer tutoring sessions taken at the termination of the study. Trained tutees faced with naive peers did attempt to model main idea paraphrase and questions (Palincsar & Brown, work in progress).

In addition to the qualitative changes in the students' dialogues, there was a gratifying improvement in the level of performance on the daily assessment question-answering score. The students averaged 15% correct during baseline. After the introduction of the reciprocal teaching, the students reached accuracy levels of 80–90% correct. This level was durable across both the maintenance and brief reintroduction of the intervention. After the 6-month delay, the students averaged 60% correct without help, significant savings over their original level of 15%. After only 1 day of renewed reciprocal teaching, the performance of 2 students returned to 80% and for the remaining students it reached 90% correct; again, the levels were maintained when the intervention was removed.

TABLE 1
Examples of Student-Generated Questions During Reciprocal Teaching

Main-Idea Questions

Why don't people live in the desert?
Why are the grasslands of Australia ideal for grazing?
What does the light on the fish do?
What did these people [the Chinese] invent?
Plans are being made to use nuclear power for what?
What are three main problems with all submarines?
Is there just one kind of explosive?
What are one of the three things people used explosives for?
What are the Philippine officials going to do for the people?

Questions Pertaining to Detail

How far south do the maple trees grow?
What color is the guards' uniforms?
How many years did it take to build the Great Wall?
What are chopsticks made out of?
Tell me where the cats hide?
What was the balloon material made of?
What (on the fish) overlaps like shingles on a roof?
How far can flying fish leap?
What is the temperature along the southern shores of Australia?

Questions Requiring Clarification
(and Suggested Appropriate Questions Regarding the Same Material and Ideas)

What was, uh, some kings were, uh, about the kings? (Why is it that kings did not always make the best judges?)
What were some of the people? (What kinds of people can serve on a jury?)
What was the Manaus built for? Wait a minute. What was the Manaus built for, what certain kinds of thing? Wait a minute. OK. What was the Manaus tree built for? (Why was the city of Manaus built?)
What does it keep the ground? (What effect does snow have on the ground?)
What are the Chinese people doing today, like.... What are they doing? (Why are the Chinese people rewriting their alphabet today?)
There's you know, like, a few answers in here and one of my questions is, uh, anything that burns and explodes can be fast enough to.... See, they got names in here. OK? (Name some explosives.)
In Africa, India, and the Southern Islands where the sun shines what happens to the people? You know, like...? (Why do people who live in Africa, India, and the Southern Islands have dark skin?)

Remember that these scores were obtained on the *privately read* assessment passages, i.e., different texts that the students read independently after their interaction with the instructor. What was learned during the instructional sequence was used independently by the learners.

TABLE 2
Examples of Student-Generated Summary Statements During Reciprocal Teaching

Main-Idea Statements

It says if a man does his job real good, then he will do better in his next life.
I learned that they have different kinds of Gods, not just Brahman, every family has their own.
It tells us about the two kinds of camels, what they are like and where they live.
My summary is that the part of the earth that we live on and see and know is the top layer, the crust.
This paragraph talks about what happens when people perspire or sweat. They lose a large amount of
    salt and they get weakness.

Details Statements

It is a pair of fins which look like legs.
The sea horse always swims head up.
There were large lizards and four eyed fish and 30 foot dandelion.
What I learned is that a submarine went around the world in 84 days.
I learned that Cousteau's first artificial island was in the North Sea.
Professor Charles went 27 miles and rose 2000 feet in his balloon.
They [the aborigines] don't wear much clothes on.
They [Egyptians] made bread a long time ago.

Incomplete Statements and Corresponding Text Segment

They talk about it was the richest island; but it didn't have something, OK, it was the richest island but
    didn't have everything. They didn't have something. (Although this was a very rich land, no people
    lived there.)
If you pick a cherry branch in the winter you will have luck hoping they will bloom early. (If you pick a
    cherry branch in the winter, you will have no luck with it blooming.)
And uranium can be making explosion that equals a skyscraper. (A small amount of uranium can cause
    an explosion as great as a skyscraper full of dynamite.)

Examples of Student-Generated Critical/Evaluative Comments

"Boy, the paragraph sure is a mess. It is all over the place."
"I don't see how they can say 'heat lightning occurs on hot summer days.' How could you see it?"
"It says here 'cloud to cloud' then 'cloud to earth.' Wouldn't that be the same thing?"
"The word *meter* throws me off in this sentence."
"What's the difference between soap and detergent anyway?"
"At first I didn't get this because I thought the word *pumping* was *bumping*."
"I don't know what *omitting* is."
"I have one, what do they mean by 'far away dreams'?"

Generalization to classroom settings. Throughout the study, a series of 5 probes was made in the social studies classroom setting to see if the students would show any improvement on the identical task of answering 10 comprehension questions on a test. The students were not told that these tests, administered by the classroom teacher, had anything to do with the intervention. All seventh graders took the social studies test as part of their regular classroom activity. The experimental students began the study below the 15th percentile on this task compared with the remaining seventh graders in their school. Performance fluctuated widely, which was not surprising as little was done to promote generalization to the classroom; e.g., the classroom teaching did not encourage the use of strategies and the students received no feedback regarding classroom performance. However, the following mean gains in percentile ranks were obtained between the baseline and final probes: Student 1 = 20, Student 2 = 46, Student 3 = 4, and Student 4 = 34.

In summary, students in Study 1 showed a dramatic improvement in their ability to answer comprehension questions on independently read texts. This improvement was durable in the resource room setting and showed some tendency to generalize to the classroom setting. In addition, qualitative improvement in the students' dialogues reflected their increasing tendency to concentrate on questions and summaries of the main idea. The reciprocal-teaching procedure was a powerful intervention for improving comprehension.

Study 2. Encouraged by the success of the initial study, it was decided to replicate the main features of the successful reciprocal-teaching procedure with 6 additional students, in 3 groups of 2. In addition to group size, the second study also differed from the first in that (1) a criterion level of 75% correct on 4 out of 5 consecutive days was established; (2) students received explicit (graphed) knowledge of results; and (3) tests of transfer were included.

The tests of transfer were selected because it was believed that they tapped the skills taught during the reciprocal teaching and, pragmatically, because a considerable body of prior work has established "normal" levels of performance for seventh graders. Two of the four transfer tests were measures of the two most frequently engaged in activities during the reciprocal-teaching sessions, *summarizing* (Brown & Day, 1983) and *predicting questions* that might be asked concerning each segment of text. In addition, two other tests were used as measures of general comprehension monitoring, *error detection* (Harris, Kruithof, Terwogt, & Visser, 1981; Markman, 1981) and *rating importance of segments of narratives* (Brown & Smiley, 1977).

There were 4 phases to the study. As in Study 1, each student was given a daily assessment passage on which he or she answered 10 comprehension questions, and this was all that occurred on baseline and maintenance days. On intervention days, the assessment passage was preceded by the reciprocal-teaching intervention, identical to that described in Study 1. The phases of Study 2 were as follows:

1. *Variable baseline* consisting of 4 days for Group 1, 6 days for Group 2, and 8 days for Group 3

2. *Reciprocal-teaching intervention* consisting of approximately 20 days

3. *Maintenance* consisting of 5 days of testing at the termination of training

4. *Long-term follow-up* that took place 8 weeks later (3 days)

All students were appraised of their progress on a daily basis. They were shown graphs depicting the percentage correct for the previous day's assessment.

The data from the daily assessment passages are shown in Figure 1. The 6 students of Study 2 had baseline accuracy not exceeding 40% correct. They proceeded to make stepwise progression toward means in excess of 75%. Four of the six students reached a stable level of 80% for 5 successive days, taking 12, 11, 11, and 15 days respectively to do it (Students 1, 3, 4, and 6). Student 5 reached criterion of 75% correct in 12 days. Student 2 was the only "failure"; she progressed from a baseline of 12% correct and reached a steady level of 50% correct in 12 days, a significant improvement, but she never approached the criterion level of the remaining 5 students. All students maintained their improved level of performance on both short- and long-term maintenance tests.

A similar improvement in the quality of the dialogues over time was found in Study 1 and Study 2 (see Palincsar & Brown, 1983, for details). At the outset, students required more assistance with the dialogue, asked more unclear and detailed questions, and made more incomplete/incorrect or detailed summaries than they did on the last intervention day. Both main-idea questions and paraphrases increased significantly over time.

Students improved at differential rates. For example, Student 6, a minority student whose Slossen test indicated an IQ of 70, made steady but slow progress as indicated by the dialogue shown in Table 3. The data are taken from Days 1 to 15, the day on which he reached criterion. From a very slow start, this student did achieve an acceptable level of performance both on the dialogues and on his daily assessment passages.

Generalization probes taken in the classroom setting resulted in variable performance but did show clear evidence of improvement. Probes were taken in two settings, social studies and science. At baseline on the social studies probe the range of percentile rankings was .9–43, with four students at or below the 5th percentile. The percentile rankings were typically higher in science with a range of 2–47, four students scoring at or below the 25th percentile. Although performance on these probes was variable, the total mean change in percentile rankings (combined across settings and phases) were Student 1, 47; Student 2, –.5; Student 3, 26; Student 4, 35.5; Student 5, 40.6; and Student 6, 36. Excluding Student 2, at the conclusion of the study, the range of subjects' mean percentile ranks was 49–76. All students, except Student 2, demonstrated considerable generalization to the classroom setting. Student 2 was also the only student who did not reach criterion during the intervention.

Transfer tests were conducted in a pre- and posttest format. It would be impossible to go into all the details of the transfer probes here (see Palincsar &

FIGURE 1
An Example of the Daily Data From Individual Subjects During Baseline, Intervention, Maintenance, and Long-Term Follow-Up

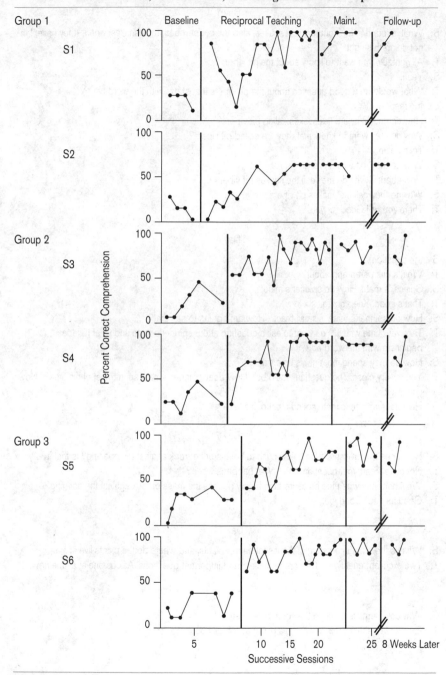

These data are taken from the six experimental subjects of Palincsar and Brown (1983), Study 2.

TABLE 3
The Acquisition of Question-Asking by One Seventh-Grade Student

Day 1

S: What is found in the southeastern snakes, also the copperhead, rattlesnakes, vipers–they have. I'm not doing this right.

T: All right. Do you want to know about the pit vipers?

S: Yeah.

T: What would be a good question about the pit vipers that starts with the word *why*?

S: (no response)

T: How about, "Why are the snakes called pit vipers?"

S: Why do they want to know that they are called pit vipers?

T: Try it again.

S: Why do they, pit vipers in a pit?

T: How about, "Why do they call the snakes pit vipers?"

S: Why do they call the snakes pit vipers?

T: There you go! Good for you.

Day 4

S: (no question)

T: What's this paragraph about?

S: Spinner's mate. How do spinner's mate....

T: That's good. Keep going.

S: How do spinner's mate is small than.... How am I going to say that?

T: Take your time with it. You want to ask a question about spinner's mate and what he does, beginning with the word *how*.

S: How do they spend most of his time sitting?

T: You're very close. The question would be, "How does spinner's mate spent most of his time?" Now you ask it.

S: How does spinner's mate spend most of his time?

Day 7

S: How does the pressure from below push the mass of hot rock against the opening? Is that it?

T: Not quite. Start your question with "What happens when?"

S: What happens when the pressure from below pushes the mass of rock against the opening?

T: Good for you! Good job.

Day 11

S: What is the most interesting of the insect-eating plants, and where do the plants live at?

T: Two excellent questions! They are both clear and important questions. Ask us one at a time now.

Day 15

S: Why do scientists come to the south pole to study?

T: Excellent question. This is what this paragraph is all about.

Brown, 1983, for details). Briefly, three of the four tests showed a significant improvement: writing summaries, designing questions to be asked on a test, and error detection using the Harris et al. (1981) procedure. The students did not improve on the Brown and Smiley (1977) task of rating narratives for variations in importance, although they did improve in their ability to select important elements in their summary writing.[3]

To give only the flavor of the transfer results, we consider one test, the question-prediction task. The ability to generate important and clear questions was a skill that received considerable focus during training. A transfer measure was included to assess the accuracy with which students could identify and construct "teacher-like" questions. The students were given 4 randomly assigned passages, 2 prior and 2 following the study. Students were asked to predict and write 10 questions a classroom teacher might ask if testing the student's knowledge of the passage.

The pre- and posttest scores are shown in Figure 2 for the students of Studies 2 and 3 and also for an untreated control group. The comparison group on the right of the figure represents the level set by average seventh-grade readers on this task. Training brought the level of performance up to that set by the normal comparison group. The graph is designed to illustrate where the improvement was found. Trained students improved in the overall quality of their questions,

FIGURE 2
**An Example of the Transfer Effects Found in Palincsar and Brown (1983),
Studies 2 and 3**

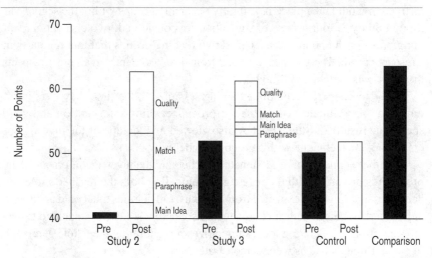

These data are taken from the Question-Prediction Task. The degree and type of posttest improvement of the experimental subjects are detailed.

in the match between their questions and those actually generated by teachers, in their ability to paraphrase rather than lift questions directly from the text, and in their ability to concentrate on the main ideas.

In summary, the main findings of Study 2 were that students diagnosed as experiencing particular problems with reading comprehension improved considerably as a result of taking part in the reciprocal-teaching sessions. All students reached asymptote within 15 days, and for 5 of the 6 the level was at 70–80% correct, comparable to accuracy attained by 13 good comprehenders who acted as control subjects. Only Student 2 failed to reach the normal level, but she did improve from 12 to 50% and maintained that level well. Indeed, all of the students maintained their asymptotic level for at least 8 weeks.

In addition to this dramatic increase on the daily comprehension measures, the students improved their percentile ranking in the classroom, gaining an average of 37 percentile points. The quantitative improvement in the ability to answer comprehension questions on texts read in a variety of settings was accompanied by a qualitative improvement in the students' dialogues. Main-idea statements and summaries came to predominate, and unclear, incomplete, or detail responses dropped out.

There was also encouraging evidence of transfer to new tasks. Reliable improvement was found in the ability to use condensation rules for summarizing, in the ability to predict questions that a teacher might ask concerning a text segment, and in the ability to detect incongruous sentences embedded in prose passages.

Study 3. Given the success of Studies 1 and 2, another replication was attempted, but this time the teacher would be a "real" teacher, not an investigator, and the instruction would take place in naturally occurring groups within the school setting. In Study 3, four groups of students were considered, two classroom reading groups for the poorest readers and two reading groups that met regularly in a resource room. The group size ranged from 4 to 7 students. In all other respects the study was a replica of Study 2.

The teachers received three training sessions. In the first, they were introduced to the rationale behind the reciprocal-teaching intervention and were shown the results of Study 1. They also viewed a videotape of the investigator employing the technique with a group of students.

In the second training session, the teacher and the investigator practiced the procedures privately with the investigator modeling both the teacher's role and behaviors that might be expected from students. Difficulties that could arise were anticipated and discussed, such as situations where a student is unable to generate a question or where a student summarizes by reiterating the whole paragraph in detail. Remedial steps were demonstrated.

In the final session, the teacher and the investigator met with a group of seventh graders who were not taking part in the study and practiced the procedure. The investigator modeled how the procedure would be introduced to the students and modeled the four main activities and the process of feedback. The teachers then assumed responsibility for the group, and as the practice session transpired, the teacher and investigator discussed the proceedings with each other. In addition, the teachers were left with several pages of directions regarding the introduction and daily format of the training sessions. The investigator also checked weekly on the teacher-directed sessions to see if the intervention was being conducted properly. These visits provided further opportunity for discussion and resolution of any difficulties encountered. The students were shown their progress charts on a daily basis during baseline, maintenance, and long-term follow-up, and on a weekly basis during intervention, and their improvement was discussed with them. All reciprocal-teaching sessions were tape-recorded.

The four groups of subjects were subjected to different amounts of baseline (4–10 days); otherwise, they were treated identically. Individually, the students performed in a manner similar to that found in Study 2 (see Palincsar & Brown, 1983, for full details). All of the subjects in Groups 1–3 individually reached criterion within 15 days. In Group 4, all students reached criterion in 5 days. If one considers the group means, two groups reached criterion in 13 days (Groups 1 and 2), one in 9 days (Group 3), and one in 5 days (Group 4). It is interesting to note that in Group 4, 2 of the 4 students were performing quite well on the first day. The resultant group in some sense consisted of three models, the teacher and the 2 good students, and 2 tutees, the remaining two poor students. In this favorable milieu, the poor students rapidly improved, and the entire group reached criterion in 5 days, versus a mean of 12 days for the other groups. Such findings if replicated could have important implications for decisions concerning the composition of the "optimal" reading group. All improvements were maintained over both short- and long-term follow-up sessions.

Quality of dialogue. An improvement in quality of dialogue was found as in Studies 1 and 2 but was less dramatic in Study 3. In the group settings, the teachers decided to call upon the "better students" in the initial sessions and then gradually to introduce the poorer students into the dialogue as they felt they could handle the responsibility, a natural procedure for experienced teachers. This resulted in a level of student responses that was higher initially and did not improve as dramatically over sessions. The trend was still the same, however, with incomplete or unclear questions decreasing from 20% to 4% and main-idea questions increasing from 57% to 70% across the sessions. Similarly, main-idea summaries increased from 68% to 85% of the total produced by the groups.

Transfer Tests

The same pattern of transfer performance occurred in Studies 2 and 3. Reliable improvements were found on three of the four tests: writing summaries, predicting questions, and error detecting. Again training brought the level of performance up to that set by normal seventh-grade readers.

The Palincsar and Brown series of studies can be regarded as successful for six main reasons:

1. The effect was large and reliable; of the 10 subjects included in Studies 1 and 2, 9 improved to the level set by good comprehenders, and all of the subjects in Study 3 met this level.

2. The effect was durable; maintenance probes showed no drop in the level of performance for up to an 8-week period (Studies 2 and 3). Although there was a decline after 6 months (levels dropping from 70–80% to 50–60%), only one session with the reciprocal-teaching procedure was sufficient to raise performance back to the short-term maintenance level (Study 1).

3. The effect generalized to the classroom setting; of the 10 students taking part in Studies 1 and 2, 9 showed a clear pattern of improvement, averaging a 36 percentile-rank increase, thus bringing them up to at least the average level for their age-mates. Given the difficulty reported in obtaining generalization of trained skills across setting (Brown & Campione, 1978; Meichenbaum & Asarnow, 1978), this is an impressive finding.

4. Training resulted in reliable transfer to dissimilar tasks; summarizing, predicting questions, and detecting incongruities all improved. Again this is an impressive finding given prior difficulty with obtaining transfer of cognitive-skills training (Brown & Campione, 1978; Brown, Campione, & Day, 1981).

5. Sizable improvements in standardized comprehension scores were recorded for the majority of subjects.

6. The intervention was no less successful in natural group settings conducted by teachers than it was in the laboratory when conducted by the experimenter.

Training Studies and the Problem of Multiple Determinants

Let us consider some possible reasons for the success of the Palincsar and Brown studies when so many other attempts have failed to find durability, generalization, and transfer of the effects of training. First, the training was extensive. Second, the activities trained were well specified theoretically, and well established empirically as particularly problematic for poor readers. Third, the training was specifically tailored to the needs of these particular students, good decoders but passive comprehenders. Fourth, the skills themselves could reasonably be expected to be trans-situational. Such ubiquitous activities of self-review and self-interrogation are pertinent in a wide variety of knowledge-acquisition tasks.

In addition, a great deal of attention was paid to "metacognitive" variables (Baker & Brown, 1984a): The subjects were fully informed about the reasons why these activities were important; the subjects were given explicit information concerning the generality of the activities and their range of utility; the subjects were trained in self-regulatory activities including the checking and monitoring of their own comprehension; and the skills themselves were general comprehension-monitoring activities applicable in a wide variety of reading/studying tasks.

The reciprocal-teaching mode itself could be responsible for the improvement. The interactive format permits extensive modeling of the target activities in a reasonably natural setting. It also forces the students to participate at whatever level they can so that the teacher can evaluate current states and provide appropriate feedback and assistance (refer to Table 3).

Listing all the good points about the Palincsar and Brown studies leads us to the obvious problem of interpretation. The studies are multiply confounded, and this is true to some extent of all the successful cognitive-training studies to date (Chipman, Segal, & Glaser, 1985). For example, would a single activity rather than the package of paraphrasing, questioning, predicting, and clarifying have been successful? Component analyses studies currently underway in our laboratory suggest that whereas all of the activities engaged in individually result in improvement, the summary component is the most powerful. The combined package, however, is the most effective intervention.

Similarly, the addition of the metacognitive setting variables may or may not be essential and such variables permit of degrees. For example, in a Ph.D. thesis conducted in our laboratory, Day (1980) trained junior college students to apply basic rules of summarization and to check that they were using the rules appropriately. The subjects were remedial students who, although of normal reading ability, were diagnosed as having writing problems. There were three main instructional conditions that varied in how explicit the training was:

1. *Self-management*: The students were given general encouragement to write a good summary, to capture the main ideas, to dispense with trivia and all unnecessary words—but they were not told rules for achieving this end.
2. *Rules*: The students were given explicit instructions and modeling in the use of the rules of deletion, selection, invention, etc.
3. *Control of the rules*: The third and most explicit training condition involved training in the rules and additional explicit training in the control of these rules; i.e., the students were shown how to check that they had a topic sentence for each paragraph, how to check that all redundancies had

been deleted, all trivia erased, etc., and how to check that any lists of items had been replaced with superordinates, etc.

An example of the results is shown in Figure 3, where the data from one of the rules, selection, are shown. The degree of posttest improvement was significantly related to the explicitness of training. Merely telling students to stay on task, be economical, concentrate on main ideas, i.e., the self-management condition, produced significantly less improvement than did direct instruction in using the specific rules, which in turn was less successful than a combined package that involved both practice using the task-appropriate rules *and* direct instruction in monitoring and overseeing their application. In this context it should be noted that in the Palincsar and Brown studies, the students not only received modeling of the appropriate comprehension-fostering activities, they were also explicitly and repeatedly directed to use these activities while reading on their own.

There is growing evidence that the most successful cognitive-skills training packages will include three components: (1) *skills* training, practice in the use of the task-appropriate cognitive skills; (2) *self-control* training, direct instruction in how to orchestrate, oversee, and monitor the effective use of the skills; and (3) *awareness* training, information concerning the reasons why such strategy use improves performance and detailed instruction in when and where the strategies

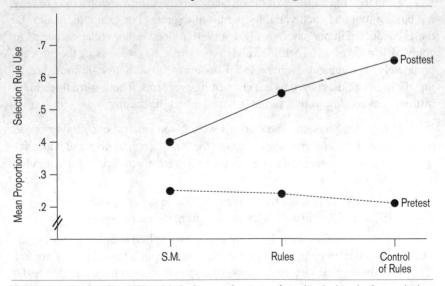

FIGURE 3
An Example of the Type of Improvement Found as a Result of the Explicitness of Training

These data are taken from Day (1980) and depict the pre- and posttest results on the selection rule of summarization.

should be used. For practical reasons, interventions should include all these factors (Brown & Palincsar, 1982), but for theoretical reasons, we need to conduct component analyses of the separate effect of all three forms of metacognitive settings (Brown, Bransford, Ferrara, & Campione, 1983).

The reciprocal-teaching package is also multiply confounded. Would modeling alone, feedback alone, or just explicit instruction be as effective? Such component analyses studies are currently underway in our laboratory. Preliminary evidence again favors the combined package (see also Bird, 1980), but more data are needed.

From a practical standpoint, the results of the required component analyses would be helpful in permitting the streamlining of the training packages into efficient and economical units. From a theoretical perspective, we need considerable further research before we can attribute the success of the intervention appropriately. Of course, it could be that multiply confounded interventions are needed because successful reading comprehension is a multiply determined outcome; i.e., effective comprehension rests on the interaction of a number of "separate" activities. Given the typically limited outcome of restricted cognitive-skills training studies (Brown, Campione, & Day, 1981), we advocate the procedure of *first* obtaining an educationally relevant, sizable, durable, and generalized effect of training and then conducting the necessary investigations to determine the subcomponents that are primarily responsible for the improvement.

The Theoretical and Practical Status of Training Studies

Until the mid-1970s, the prognosis of worthwhile educational gains from cognitive-skills training studies was poor. Although some success had been achieved in obtaining improvement on a particular skill in isolation, this improvement was often slight and fleeting, and there was very little evidence of transfer. Maintenance over time, generalization across settings, and transfer within conceptual domains were rarely found. The more difficulties the learner experienced initially, the more fleeting and bounded were the effects of training (Brown & Campione, 1978, 1981; Meichenbaum & Asarnow, 1978). But the picture has changed in the last few years; the success of the Palincsar and Brown studies is not an isolated phenomenon (Chipman, Segal, & Glaser, 1985). The current outlook is quite optimistic. From a practical point of view, it is clear that we can train instructionally relevant cognitive skills even with subjects who would be regarded as recalcitrant. This training can be carried out under the pressure of normal classroom settings, and it does result in worthwhile and reliable improvements in the Palincsar and Brown studies, bringing students from the very bottom of the distribution of their age peers to the average set by their normal reading classmates. The necessary research needed now consists of extensions across skills and settings and of "clean-up" operations that would permit us to test the limits of these exciting findings and streamline our instructional packages. Cognitive skills can be trained, and such training can be durable and generalizable.

From a theoretical standpoint, training studies are not just exercises in cognitive engineering with immediate applicability to school settings. They are also direct tests of theory involving degrees of experimental manipulation and control in an area where a great deal of data consist of simple one-shot developmental demonstrations (see chapter 9 of *Learning and Comprehension of Text,* 1984, for a detailed discussion of this argument). A great deal of development research is correlational in nature, and there are problems with interpreting such results. To give an example from our own work, in many studies we consider the performance of students who do or do not spontaneously adopt an appropriate text-processing strategy, and this is often the major variable carrying a developmental trend. For example, 5th and 7th graders who make adequate rough drafts when paraphrasing (Brown, Day, & Jones, 1983) or spontaneously underline or take notes of important text elements and so on (Brown & Smiley, 1978) perform as well as the majority of 12th graders, whereas 12th graders who fail to employ these activities perform more like 5th graders. This pattern suggests that it is the strategy that leads to efficiency, and developmental trends showing improvements with age are created by the increased proportion of strategic subjects. This is a reasonable interpretation, but as the data are primarily correlational, the interpretation is not that simple. It could be that the young, spontaneous strategy users are the more efficient children in general and would perform better than their peers on any task and on the particular task in question without the use of strategies. Even partialling out ability factors such as IQ or reading scores does not totally bypass this problem.

The training study is then an important tool for providing convergent evidence of the importance of the strategy under consideration. First, the theorist speculates about the underlying processes involved in reading comprehension. Next is the correlational step; students who read well are also found to perform well on the identified underlying processes, whereas poor readers experience particular difficulty on just these activities (Armbruster, Echols, & Brown, 1982; Baker & Brown, 1984a, 1984b; Brown & Palincsar, 1982). Finally, students who are not using the strategy are given training designed to induce the use of processes theoretically specified as key activities underlying efficiency. Others are not. If the theory is correct (and training adequate) and these are the underlying effective processes, trained students' performances should become more like those of spontaneous users. There are nontrivial problems with interpreting the outcomes of training studies (Brown & Campione, 1978, 1981), but they do provide an important manipulative tool to aid theory development. Thus from the point of view of both theory development and successful cognitive instruction, training studies such as those reported here are valuable tools for enhancing our understanding of the mechanism of reading comprehension.

Acknowledgments

The preparation of this manuscript was supported in part by Grants HD06864 and HD05951 from the National Institute of Child Health and Human Development and in part by NIE-C-400-76-0116 from the National Institute of Education.

Notes

[1] The students were of low-normal intelligence (mean IQ 84) and low socioeconomic status. Their decoding was judged adequate as they could read grade-appropriate texts at a rate of 80–100 wpm with no more than 2 errors per minute. Their standardized reading comprehension scores averaged 3 years delayed.

[2] In Study 1, another group of students received a second intervention, locating information (see Palincsar & Brown, 1983, for details), where they were trained to answer comprehension questions by using the text intelligently. These students did improve from their starting level of 15% to approximately 50%, but they never reached the level of the reciprocal-teaching group, and they failed to maintain this level over time.

[3] In Studies 2 and 3, there were treated and untreated control groups consisting of students matched with the experimental subjects for decoding and comprehension scores, as well as IQ, standardized tests, and class placement. These students demonstrated no significant change on their performance on the baseline, maintenance, and follow-up stages of the study. Neither did they improve their performance on any of the tests of generalization (to the classroom) or transfer (across laboratory tasks). For full details on the control groups included in Studies 1 to 3, see Palincsar and Brown (1983).

References

Allington, R. (1980). Teacher interruption behavior during primary-grade oral reading. *Journal of Educational Psychology, 72*(3), 371–377.

André, M.D.A., & Anderson, T.H. (1978/1979). The development and evaluation of a self-questioning study technique. *Reading Research Quarterly, 14,* 605–623.

Armbruster, B.B., Echols, C.H., & Brown, A.L. (1982). The role of metacognition in reading to learn: A developmental perspective. *Volta Review, 84*(5), 45–56.

Au, K.H. (1979). Using the Experience-Text-Relationship method with minority children. *The Reading Teacher, 32,* 677–679.

Au, K.H. (1980). *A test of the social organizational hypothesis: Relationships between participation structures and learning to read.* Unpublished doctoral dissertation, University of Illinois, Urbana-Champaign.

Baker, L., & Brown, A.L. (1984a). Cognitive monitoring in reading. In J. Flood (Ed.), *Understanding reading comprehension* (pp. 21–44). Newark, DE: International Reading Association.

Baker, L., & Brown, A.L. (1984b). Metacognition and the reading process. In P.D. Pearson, R.

Barr, M.L. Kamil, & P. Mosenthal (Eds.), *Handbook of reading research* (pp. 353–394). New York: Longman.

Bartlett, E.J. (1979). Curriculum, concepts of literacy and social class. In L.B. Resnick & P.A. Weaver (Eds.), *Theory and practice of early reading* (Vol. 2). Hillsdale, NJ: Erlbaum.

Bernstein, B. (1971). *Class codes and control* (Vol. 1). London: Routledge & Kegan Paul.

Binet, A. (1909). *Les idées modernes sur les infants.* Paris: Flammarion.

Bird, M. (1980). *Reading comprehension strategies: A direct teaching approach.* Unpublished doctoral dissertation, University of Toronto, Ontario, Canada.

Brown, A.L. (1980). Metacognitive development and reading. In R.J. Spiro, B. Bruce, & W. Brewer (Eds.), *Theoretical issues in reading comprehension.* Hillsdale, NJ: Erlbaum.

Brown, A.L. (1982). Learning how to learn from reading. In J.A. Langer & M.T. Smith-Burke (Eds.), *Reader meets author/bridging the gap: A psycholinguistic and social linguistic perspective.* Newark, DE: International Reading Association.

Brown, A.L. (1985). Mental orthopedics: A conversation with Alfred Binet. In S. Chipman, J.

Segal, & R. Glaser (Eds.), *Thinking and learning skills: Research and open questions* (Vol. 2). Hillsdale, NJ: Erlbaum.

Brown, A.L., Bransford, J.D., Ferrara, R.A., & Campione, J.C. (1983). Learning, remembering, and understanding. In J.H. Flavell & E.M. Markman (Eds.), *Carmichael's manual of child psychology* (Vol. 1). New York: Wiley.

Brown, A.L., & Campione, J.C. (1978). Permissible inferences from cognitive training studies in developmental research. In W.S. Hall & M. Cole (Eds.), *Quarterly Newsletter of the Institute for Comparative Human Behavior, 2*(3), 46–53.

Brown, A.L., & Campione, J.C. (1981). Inducing flexible thinking: A problem of access. In M. Friedman, J.P. Das, & N. O'Connor (Eds.), *Intelligence and learning*. New York: Plenum.

Brown, A.L., Campione, J.C., & Day, J.D. (1981). Learning to learn: On training students to learn from texts. *Educational Researcher, 10*(2), 14–21.

Brown, A.L., & Day, J.D. (1983). Macro-rules for summarizing texts: The development of expertise. *Journal of Verbal Learning and Verbal Behavior, 22*, 1–14.

Brown, A.L., Day, J.D., & Jones, R.S. (1983). The development of plans for summarizing texts. *Child Development, 54*, 968–979.

Brown, A.L., & Palincsar, A.S. (1982). Inducing strategic learning from texts by means of informed, self-control training. *Topics in Learning and Learning Disabilities, 2*(1), 1–17.

Brown, A.L., Palincsar, A.S., & Purcell, L. (1986). Poor readers: Teach, don't label. In U. Neisser (Ed.), *The school achievement of minority children: New perspectives*. Hillsdale, NJ: Erlbaum.

Brown, A.L., & Smiley, S.S. (1977). Rating the importance of structural units of prose passages: A problem of metacognitive development. *Child Development, 48*, 1–8.

Brown, A.L., & Smiley, S.S. (1978). The development of strategies for studying texts. *Child Development, 49*, 1076–1088.

Cazden, C.B. (1979). Learning to reading in classroom interaction. In L.B. Resnick & P.A. Weaver (Eds.), *Theory and practice of early reading* (Vol. 3). Hillsdale, NJ: Erlbaum.

Chipman, S., Segal, J., & Glaser, R. (Eds.). (1985). *Thinking and learning skills: Research and open questions* (Vol. 2). Hillsdale, NJ: Erlbaum.

Collins, A.M., & Smith, E.E. (1982). Teaching the process of reading comprehension. In

D.K. Detterman & R.J. Sternberg (Eds.), *How and how much can intelligence be increased*. Norwood, NJ: Ablex.

Collins, A.M., & Stevens, A. (1982). Goals and strategies of inquiry teachers. In R. Glaser (Ed.), *Advances in instructional psychology* (Vol. 2). Hillsdale, NJ: Erlbaum.

Collins, J. (1980). Differential treatment in reading groups. In J. Cook-Gumperz (Ed.), *Educational discourse*. London: Heinemann.

Cushenbery, D.C. (1969). Building effective comprehension skills. In J.A. Figurel (Ed.), *Reading and realism* (Proceedings of the 13th Annual Convention of the International Reading Association). Newark, DE: International Reading Association.

Dansereau, D.F. (1980, October). *Learning strategy research*. Paper presented at NIE-LRDC Conference on Thinking and Learning Skills, Pittsburgh, PA.

Day, J.D. (1980). *Training summarization skills: A comparison of teaching methods*. Unpublished doctoral dissertation, University of Illinois, Urbana-Champaign.

DeLoache, J.S. (1983, April). *Mother-child picture book reading as a context for memory training*. Paper presented at the Society for Research in Child Development Meeting, Detroit, MI.

Feuerstein, R. (1979). *The dynamic assessment of retarded performers: The learning-potential assessment device, theory, instruments, and techniques*. Baltimore: University Park Press.

Feuerstein, R. (1980). *Instrumental enrichment: An intervention program for cognitive modifiability*. Baltimore: University Park Press.

Frase, L.T., & Schwartz, B.J. (1975). Effect of question production and answering on prose recall. *Journal of Educational Psychology, 67*, 628–635.

Gall, M.D. (1970). The use of questions in teaching. *Review of Educational Research, 40*, 707–720.

Gantt, W.N. (1970). Questions for thinking: A teaching strategy that makes a difference for disadvantaged learners. *The Reading Teacher, 24*, 12–16, 22.

Griffin, P. (1977). How and when does reading occur in the classroom? *Theory Into Practice, 16*, 376–383.

Harris, P.L., Kruithof, A., Terwogt, M.M., & Visser, P. (1981). Children's detection and awareness of textual anomaly. *Journal of Experimental Child Psychology, 31*, 212–230.

Jenkinson, M.D. (1969). Cognitive processes in reading: Implications for further research and classroom practice. In J.A. Figurel (Ed.), *Reading and realism* (Proceedings of the 13th Annual Convention of the International Reading Association). Newark, DE: International Reading Association.

King, M.L. (1967). New developments in the evaluation of critical reading. *Forging ahead in reading* (International Reading Association Proceedings, *12*), 179–185.

Laboratory of Comparative Human Cognition. (1986). The zone of proximal development: Where culture and cognition create one another. In J.V. Wertsch (Ed.), *Culture, communication, and cognition: Vygotskian perspectives*. New York: Cambridge University Press.

Linden, M., & Wittrock, M.C. (1981). The teaching of reading comprehension according to the model of generative learning. *Reading Research Quarterly, 16*, 44–57.

Lorge, I. (1957). Reading, thinking, and learning. *International Reading Association Proceedings, 2*, 15–18.

Manzo, A.V. (1969). The ReQuest procedure. *Journal of Reading, 13*, 123–126, 163–164.

Markman, E.M. (1981). Comprehension monitoring. In W.P. Dickson (Ed.), *Children's oral-communication skills*. New York: Academic.

Markman, E.M., & Gorin, L. (1981). Children's ability to adjust their standards for evaluating comprehension. *Journal of Educational Psychology, 83*(3), 320–325.

McDermott, R.P. (1978). Kids make sense: An ethnographic account of the interactional management of success and failures in one first-grade classroom (Doctoral dissertation, Stanford University, 1976). *Dissertation Abstracts International, 38*, 1505A.

Meichenbaum, D., & Asarnow, J. (1978). Cognitive-behavioral modification and metacognitive development: Implications for the classroom. In P. Kendall & S. Hollon (Eds.), *Cognitive-behavioral interventions: Theory, research, and procedure*. New York: Academic.

Ninio, A., & Bruner, J.S. (1978). The achievement and antecedents of labeling. *Journal of Child Language, 5*, 1–15.

Palincsar, A.S., & Brown, A.L. (1983). *Reciprocal teaching of comprehension-monitoring activities* (Tech. Rep. No. 269). Champaign: University of Illinois, Center for the Study of Reading.

Resnick, L.B. (1979). Theories and prescriptions for early reading instruction. In L.B. Resnick & P.A. Weaver (Eds.), *Theory and practice of early reading* (Vol. 2). Hillsdale, NJ: Erlbaum.

Schallert, D.L., & Kleiman, G.M. (1979, June). *Some reasons why the teacher is easier to understand than the text book* (Reading Education Rep. No. 9). Champaign: University of Illinois, Center for the Study of Reading. (Eric Document Reproduction Service No. ED172189)

Schwartz, E., & Scheff, A. (1975). Student involvement in questioning for comprehension. *The Reading Teacher, 29*, 150–154.

Smith, N.B. (1961). The good reader thinks critically. *The Reading Teacher, 15*, 162–171.

Tharp, R.G. (1982). The effective instruction of comprehension: Results and description of the Kamehameha Early Education Program. *Reading Research Quarterly, 17*, 503–527.

Vygotsky, L.S. (1978). *Mind in society: The development of higher psychological processes* (M. Cole, V. John-Steiner, S. Scribner, & E. Souberman, Eds. & Trans.). Cambridge, MA: Harvard University Press. (Original work published 1934)

30

Effects of Structure Strategy Training and Signaling on Recall of Text

Bonnie J.F. Meyer and Leonard W. Poon

B oth young and old adults need good reading comprehension skills to maintain functional competence, independence, and quality of life. At the top of the list of strategies identified by Pressley and McCormick (1995) as promoting comprehension and memory of text is using and analyzing text structure to abstract the main ideas. They explained that knowledge of the structure of text helps readers to separate the "wheat from the chaff" as they read. Readers who use such a strategy (the structure strategy; Meyer, 1985a; Meyer, Brandt, & Bluth, 1980) approach reading with the strategic knowledge that authors structure text in predictable ways, and that they can construct an integrated representation of the text by following the hierarchical organization of the text and the relative importance of its conceptual content. The present study addresses mechanisms of the structure strategy on recall of younger and older adults.

Hierarchical text structure refers to the elements of text that provide coherence by emphasizing ideas central to the author's main thesis and deemphasizing peripheral ideas (Meyer & Rice, 1984). When reading a text, a reader builds a mental representation of the information in text (Britton & Graesser 1996; Gernsbacher, Varner, & Faust, 1990; Kintsch, 1998). One important way to build a coherent mental representation for encoding and retrieving information from text is to utilize the structure in text (Grimes, 1975; Mann & Thompson, 1986; Meyer, 1975; Sanders, Spooren, & Noordman, 1992). Because of limited processing capacity (Baddeley, 1992), readers cannot remember and learn everything in a text, so some information more than others must be selected for deeper encoding and more cycles of processing or elaboration.

Focusing on the superordinate or top levels of the structure of text (top-level structure) can help readers select the most important information for thorough encoding. Readers who use the structure strategy tend to remember more of

From *Journal of Educational Psychology*, *93*(1), 141–159. Copyright © 2001 by the American Psychological Association. Reprinted with permission of the publisher.

what they read and to remember more of the important information than do those who do not use the strategy (e.g., Meyer et al., 1980; Meyer, Young, & Bartlett, 1989; Samuels et al., 1988; Taylor & Beach, 1984). Instruction about text structure has yielded positive effects on understanding and remembering information from text with children, young adults, and older adults (e.g., Bartlett, 1978; Cook & Mayer, 1988; Gordon, 1990; Meyer, 1999; Meyer et al., 1989; Paris, Cross, & Lipson, 1984; Polley, 1994; Slater, Graves, & Piche, 1985).

The Aid of Signals in Text to Reading

Authors often convey important ideas and relationships in text through the use of signals. Signals are stylistic writing devices that highlight aspects of semantic content or structural organization in text without communicating additional semantic content (Lorch, 1989; Meyer, 1975, 1985b). Such devices may include headings, preview statements, summary statements, pointer words, or words that explicitly state the relational structure among main propositions of the text (Meyer, 1975, 1985b).

Signaling the organization of text or signaling main ideas yields superior recall of main ideas (e.g., Brooks, Dansereau, Spurlin, & Holley, 1983; Dee-Lucas & DiVesta, 1980; Krug, George, Hannon, & Glover, 1989; Loman & Mayer, 1983; Lorch & Lorch, 1985, 1995, 1996; Mayer, Dyck, & Cook, 1984; Meyer et al., 1980; Meyer & Rice, 1982, 1989). In a number of studies, signaling did not increase the total amount of information recalled under normal reading conditions (Britton, Glynn, Meyer, & Penland, 1982; Meyer, 1975; Rickards, Fajen, Sullivan, & Gillespie, 1997) but did affect recall of the signaled information (Loman & Mayer, 1983; Lorch, Lorch, & Inman, 1993; Meyer & Rice, 1989), organization (Lorch et al., 1993; Meyer et al., 1980), processing speed (Haberlandt, 1982; Millis & Just, 1994), and cued recall (Millis & Just, 1994). Other research points to the magnitude of signaling effects being dependent on the complexity and structure of the text (Lorch & Lorch, 1996; Spyridakis & Standal, 1987) or readers' abilities (Meyer et al., 1980), interests (Meyer, Talbot, Stubblefield, & Poon, 1998), or cognitive styles (Rickards et al., 1997).

How Do Signals Facilitate Prose Processing?

Meyer et al. (1980) proposed a model to explain the interaction of reader strategies and signaling in text (see Figure 1). The two dominant reader strategies summarized in Figure 1 are the structure strategy and the list strategy. Readers who use the list strategy encode text as a list of facts to be learned. As depicted at the bottom of Figure 1, some readers who predominantly use a list strategy switch their strategy to the structure strategy when signals highlight the superordinate organization of the text. Both Meyer (Meyer et al., 1980; Meyer & Rice, 1982, 1989) and Mayer

FIGURE 1
Model Depicting an Interaction of Reader Strategies and Signaling in Text

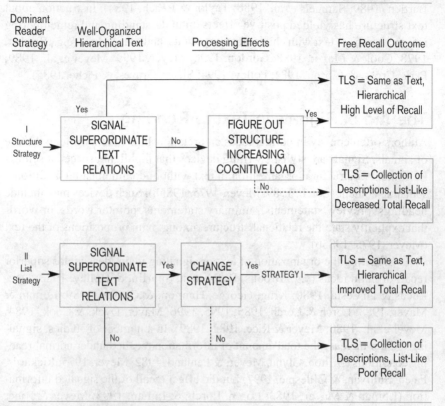

TLS = Top-Level Structure of Retelling.
From "Use of the Top-Level Structure in Text: Key for Reading Comprehension of Ninth Grade Students," by B.J.F. Meyer, D.M. Brandt, and G.J. Bluth, 1980, *Reading Research Quarterly, 16*, 79. Copyright © 1980 by the International Reading Association.

(Loman & Mayer, 1983; Mayer et al., 1984) suggested that signals cause readers to switch their strategies for encoding text information. Lorch and Lorch (1995) labeled this switching of strategies the *strategy switch hypothesis*. That is, readers use a qualitatively different encoding strategy, that of a temporally organized list of facts to be learned, when organizational signals are omitted from text. The strategy switch hypothesis states that readers do not routinely encode a text's overall structure in the absence of signals. Lorch and Lorch (1995) compared signaling effects in a free-recall task with signaling effects in a cued-recall task and concluded that signals impact recall by encouraging the reader to switch to the structure strategy to encode information.

Meyer et al. (1980) found that signaling enabled underachieving ninth-grade students, whose reading comprehension test scores were substantially lower than their vocabulary scores, to switch their strategy to the structure strategy from the list strategy. The performance of these students was compatible with the solid lines shown under the list strategy in Figure 1. However, they found no effect of signaling for ninth graders identified by teachers and standardized tests as exceptionally high in reading comprehension. Most of these skilled readers used the same organization as the author to organize their recall and maintained high levels of recall regardless of the presence of signaling; their performance was compatible with the solid lines shown for the structure strategy, depicted in Figure 1. In addition, Meyer et al. (1980) reported ninth-grade students with poor comprehension and vocabulary scores exhibited the list strategy regardless of signaling (dashed and lowest paths under list strategy in Figure 1).

Another prominent explanation for signaling effects is the common strategy hypothesis, which states that mature readers use the structure strategy for encoding and retrieval (Lorch & Lorch, 1985, 1995; Sanchez, Lorch, & Lorch, 2001). According to the common strategy hypothesis, signals influence recall by increasing accessibility of topic information at retrieval. Signals provide learners with a clearer, more memorable organizational structure that aids access to text ideas (Lorch & Lorch, 1995).

Testing the Connections Between Reader Strategies and Signals

The structure strategy training in the present investigation explicitly taught learners to identify and use signaling in text to aid their encoding and to organize their recall as depicted in Table 1, a centerpiece of the instruction. Nine hours of training involved direct instruction, modeling, and practice, individually as well as with a partner, to teach effective use of text structure for encoding and retrieval with a wide variety of texts. This instruction was designed to change readers' dominant strategy for prose recall tasks to the structure strategy from the list strategy and to produce a group of readers who would follow the solid lines shown at the top of Figure 1. Training in use of the structure strategy was hypothesized to (a) increase the amount of information remembered from text (total recall), (b) increase the amount of important information remembered (gist), (c) change and improve the organization of recall (recall organized more like the top-level structure of the text rather than a list), and (d) increase readers' consistency in their use of the structure strategy over multiple texts (organization of recall matching the text's top-level structure for all of the five texts read). An additive effect of training plus signaling was predicted for consistent use of texts' top-level structures to organize recalls. For readers trained in the structure strategy, signaling was

TABLE 1
Five Basic Organizational Structures and Their Signals

Writing Plan and Definition	Signals
Description Descriptive ideas that give attributes, specifics, or setting information about a topic. The main idea is that attributes of a topic are discussed. For example, newspaper article describing who, where, when, and how.	for example, which was one, this particular, for instance, specifically, such as, attributes of, that is, namely, properties of, characteristics are, qualities are, marks of, in describing, ____
Sequence Ideas grouped on the basis of order or time. The main idea is procedure or history related. For example, recipe procedures, history of Civil War battles, growth from birth to 12 months.	afterward, later, finally, last, early, following, to begin with, to start with, then, as time passed, continuing on, to end, years ago, in the first place, before, after, soon, more recently, ____
Causation Presents causal or cause-and-effect–like relations between ideas. The main idea is organized into cause and effect parts. For example, directions: if you want to take good pictures, then you must...; explanations: the idea explained is the effect and the explanation is its cause.	as a result, because, since, for the purpose of, caused, led to, consequence, thus, in order to, this is why, if/then, the reason, so, in explanation, therefore, _____
Problem/Solution The main ideas are organized into two parts: a *problem* part and a *solution* part that responds to the problem by trying to eliminate it, or a *question* part and an *answer* part that responds to the question by trying to answer it. For example, scientific articles often first raise a question or problem and then seek to give an answer or solution.	problem: problem, question, puzzle, perplexity, enigma, riddle, issue, query, need to prevent, the trouble, _____ solution: solution, answer, response, reply, rejoinder, return, comeback, to satisfy the problem, to set the issue at rest, to solve these problems, _____
Comparison Relates ideas on the basis of differences and similarities. The main idea is organized in parts that provide a comparison, contrast, or alternative perspective on a topic, e.g., political speeches, particularly where one view is clearly favored over the other.	not everyone, but, in contrast, all but, instead, act like, however, in comparison, on the other hand, whereas, in opposition, unlike, alike, have in common, share, resemble, the same as, different, difference, differentiate, compared to, while, although, despite, ____
Listing Can occur with any of the five writing plans. For example, listing can occur when groups of descriptions, causes, problems, solutions, views, and so on are presented.	and, in addition, also, include, moreover, besides, first, second, third, etc., subsequent, furthermore, at the same time, another, ____

Blanks indicate spaces provided for learners to add signaling words found in their everyday reading.
From *Memory Improved: Reading and Memory Enhancement Across the Life Span Through Strategic Text Structures* (pp. 115–116). By B.J.F. Meyer, C.J. Young, and B.J. Bartlett, 1989. Hillsdale, NJ: Erlbaum. Copyright © 1989 by Lawrence Erlbaum Associates, Inc. Reprinted with permission.

hypothesized to aid in the use of the strategy by making the task of figuring out the top-level structure of the text easier (reducing the cognitive load; see Figure 1).

Six stages in the mastery of the structure strategy are summarized in Table 2. For Stages 3, 5, and 6, recall would be organized with the same top-level structure as the text, but readers would vary in their knowledge of the use of the strategy and their ability to use it consistently with a variety of texts. It was hypothesized that both systematic training with the structure strategy and signaling were needed to get most readers to Stage 6—consistent use of the strategy. We hypothesized that adult readers whose dominant reading strategy was the list strategy could often switch to the structure strategy when signaling was provided (the strategy switch hypothesis). However, their mastery of the strategy would be limited and would remain at Stage 3 rather than Stage 6 (consistent use of the strategy; see Table 2). Consistent with past research findings on signaling, we predicted main effects for signaling on signaled information, gist, and top-level structure scores but not on total recall or consistent use of the structure strategy across five passages.

In this investigation, an alternative training, the interest–list strategy training, was designed to yield a group of readers who would enter the prose learning task with the list strategy as their dominant strategy but who would also be as motivated to perform as the structure strategy group. The interest–list strategy group served as contact control group for the structure strategy group, with readers of equivalent abilities (e.g., working memory, vocabulary, and reading comprehension) involved in practice reading and recalling the same instructional texts. Learners in both groups spent equivalent time involved with direct instruction, modeling, and practice, both in pairs and individually. The substance of the training for the interest–list strategy group followed the general suggestions

TABLE 2
Six Operational Levels of Using Text Structure With the Structure Strategy

Stage	Characteristics
1	Readers *do not use* any systematic form of organization in writing their recall.
2	Readers *use different* organization *without knowing* what they have done.
3	Readers *use the same organization* as in the text without knowing what they have done.
4	Readers *use* a different organization *thinking it to be the same* as that of the text.
5	Readers use the same organization as in the text, and *know* that they have done so.
6	Readers *consistently use* the same organization as in the text, and *know* that they have done so, or consciously decide *not* to apply the strategy.

From *Memory Improved: Reading and Memory Enhancement Across the Life Span Through Strategic Text Structures* (p. 83), by B.J.F. Meyer, C.J. Young, and B.J. Bartlett, 1989. Hillsdale, NJ: Erlbaum. Copyright © 1989 by Lawrence Erlbaum Associates, Inc. Reprinted with permission.

for boosting motivation listed in the *Motivated Strategies for Learning Questionnaire Manual* (Pintrich, Smith, Garcia, & McKeachie, 1991), that is, identifying topics that are of interest and those that are not and learning ways to make the uninteresting topics more interesting. The interest–list strategy was also based on research relating interest to prose learning (e.g., Schiefele, 1992; Schraw, Bruning, & Svoboda, 1995).

In addition to providing a control for contact and practice, the interest–list strategy group can aid in ascertaining the dominant reading strategy for adult readers. If a control group (receiving no instruction) does not differ in organization of recall from the interest group using the list strategy but does differ from the structure strategy group, then the dominant learner strategy for the sample of adult readers may be the list strategy or, alternatively, another strategy not focused on text structure. If, however, the control group is more similar to the structure strategy group than to the interest–list group, then the dominant reader strategy in the prose learning settings is more likely to be the structure strategy.

Numerous studies have reported poorer text recall for older adults compared with younger adults (cf. Hartley, 1986, 1988; Hultsch, Hertzog, Dixon, & Small, 1998; Meyer & Rice, 1989). Meyer and Rice (1983, 1989) found older adults with high school education levels and average verbal skills to be deficient in using signaling to aid recall of signaled text information when compared with younger adults with similar abilities; these older adults did not appear to know the function of signaling in text. They also were less able than comparable younger adults to use the structure strategy to organize recall. However, structure strategy training involving similar, high school–educated older adults was effective in teaching how to use signals and the strategy (Meyer et al., 1989).

Older adults can compensate for declines in basic processing (e.g., slowing and working memory deficits; Salthouse, 1985; Salthouse & Babcock, 1991) through expertise in reading (e.g., related to education, reading comprehension, and vocabulary; Hultsch et al., 1998; Johnson et al., 1997; Meyer & Rice, 1983; Meyer & Talbot, 1998). Age differences were not found for high-verbal, college-educated adults in either use of signaling or organization of recall (Meyer & Rice, 1983, 1989). High-verbal older adults appeared to understand the function of signaling as well as younger adults. In fact, with high-verbal readers, Meyer and colleagues (Meyer & Rice, 1989; Meyer et al., 1998) found that older adults showed greater signaling effects than did younger adults. As depicted in Figure 1, the lack of signaling increases processing demands for figuring out the text's structure; this may place a greater burden on older adults who have less processing resources in terms of working memory capacity and processing speed (e.g., Salthouse, 1985). The older sample for this investigation was comprised of highly educated adults; thus, differences in total recall between young and older participants were expected to be minimal. However, an age by signaling interaction was predicted, with signaling affecting the organization of recall and recall of signaled information by older adults more than younger adults. In the present investigation, we also examined the generalizability of the effects of structure strategy instruction found by Meyer et al. (1989) with a more educated sample of older adults.

In addition, we also examined the transfer of the structure strategy training to the recall of other types of everyday materials. Training with the structure strategy taught conditional knowledge about when to use the strategy effectively. The structure strategy was hypothesized to become the dominant strategy when trained participants wanted to understand an author's main points and to remember this information. Thus, it was expected to be useful for prose recall as well as for other situations requiring such understanding and memory. Training in text structures (Cook & Mayer, 1988) and signaling in text (Loman & Mayer, 1983) have been found to improve performance on problem-solving questions that require learners to transfer information from a text by using it in a new way. In the present investigation, two transfer tasks were examined. One involved watching a video about nutrition, similar to an educational television program, and later recalling this information. The other involved a simulated decision-making task where conflicting health information was examined from physicians and research articles and later recalled. The structure strategy was hypothesized to be more useful than the interest–list strategy in encoding and recalling information presented in these everyday contexts.

Hypotheses for the present study clustered around four main issues. The first cluster of hypotheses was compatible with the strategy switch hypothesis rather than the common strategy hypothesis. Training with the structure strategy was expected to switch most readers from using the list strategy to using the structure strategy. Training with the structure strategy was hypothesized to increase (a) total recall, (b) memory for the most important information (gist), and (c) top-level structure scores, measuring the correspondence between the organization of recall and the text's organization. Signaling was expected to facilitate switching to the structure strategy and was hypothesized to increase performance on (d) signaled information, (e) gist, and (f) top-level structure scores but not (g) total recall. The second issue centered around a predicted additive effect of structure strategy instruction and signaling; structure strategy training plus signaling was hypothesized to yield the most consistent use of the structure strategy over the five texts. The third cluster of hypotheses focused on age differences. No age differences were expected for total recall, and structure strategy training was expected to be as effective for older adults as for younger adults. However, a signaling by age group interaction was expected for organization of recall as well as recall of signaled information, particularly for participants who received training with the structure strategy. The final issue dealt with transfer; training with the structure strategy was predicted to transfer to remembering other types of everyday materials.

Method

Participants and Design

Participants were 56 young adults (21 men and 35 women) and 65 older adults (25 men and 40 women) recruited from advertisements in the community and from university courses and affiliated groups. Each participant was paid US$75 for his or her participation in ten 90-minute sessions. In addition to the variable of age, there were two other between-group variables: training condition (structure strategy training, interest–list strategy training, or no training) and signaling (texts with signaling or texts without signaling).

Materials

Materials included tests of vocabulary, working memory, reaction time, cognitive status, and reading comprehension and numerous questionnaires focusing on reading, memory, interests, health, and biographical information. The materials also included summary and recall performance tasks, which followed the reading of texts, and two transfer recall tasks involving (a) an educational video and (b) a simulated decision-making task involving medical information.

Vocabulary. Vocabulary was measured by means of the Quick Word Test (Borgatta & Corsini, 1964). The Quick Word Test is a 100-item multiple-choice (e.g., "heart means beat, draw, core, or vein") test used to measure verbal ability. The correlation between the Quick Word Test and the Wechsler Adult Intelligence Scale vocabulary subtest (Wechsler, 1955) is .83 (Meyer & Rice, 1983).

Working Memory and Processing Speed. Working memory was measured by reading span (RSPAN) and computation span (CSPAN; Babcock & Salthouse, 1990). RSPAN is presented on a computer with multiple-choice questions for each sentence and oral recall of the last word of each sentence in a series. CSPAN is similar but uses simple math problems and numbers. Correlations among RSPAN, CSPAN, and Daneman and Carpenter's (1980) working memory test ranged from .55 to .74 (Meyer, Talbot, & Poon, 1995). Four reaction-time tasks were administered (Johnson et al., 1997; Poon, 1989) and combined for a measure of processing speed.

Cognitive Status. Cognitive status was measured by the Folstein Mini Mental State Exam (MMSE; Folstein, 1983). This test is comprised of questions tapping basic knowledge, processing (e.g., "spell *world* backwards"), and following directions.

Reading Comprehension. Reading comprehension was assessed with the first half of the Davis Reading Test (Form 1B; Davis, 1944). The Davis Reading Test has been found to be a powerful predictor of prose recall (Hartley, 1986, 1988; Johnson et al., 1997). This portion of the Davis Reading Test is made up of 40 multiple-choice questions designed to measure reading comprehension of several short passages. Forty points are possible, with a correction for guessing.

Questionnaires. Questions were asked regarding biographical information, health, interests, and reading and memory habits. Descriptive data taken from these questionnaires can be found in Meyer, Poon, and Talbot's (1999) report. Questions were asked at the final posttest about changes in reading and remembering noted since the beginning of the research project.

Texts and Reading Performance Requested. Because of concerns involved in designing equivalent passages in terms of interest (see Meyer et al., 1998) and difficulty, the same problem/solution texts were read as the first, third, and fifth passages on the pretest and posttest (administered 2½ months after the pretest). The texts read second were organized with a comparison structure (creation vs. evolution set of passages: archaeopteryx or coal mine—129 idea units each; Meyer et al., 1989), as were the texts read fourth (set on transportation: airplanes or railroads—240 idea units each; Meyer, Talbot, et al., 1995). Participants read a different comparison passage on the pretest and posttest, and their presentation was counterbalanced. This interspersion of comparison texts between problem/solution texts was designed to reduce transfer caused by serially reading two texts with identical structures (e.g., Rickards et al., 1997). Only the texts read third and fifth, on schizophrenia and trusts, respectively (191 idea units each; Meyer et al., 1989), had identical structures presenting three problems and a solution with its explanation and description. The first passage (Meyer, 1985a; Meyer et al., 1998) described a problem regarding oil spills from supertankers, their causes, multiple effects, and three major solutions. The average readability level for the passages was high school level (11th grade).

One half of the participants read texts with signaling, whereas the remaining participants read texts without signaling. Signaling (Meyer, 1975) did not vary the content presented, only whether major relationships among main ideas were made explicit and emphasized. Appendix A includes with- and without-signaling versions of the trusts and coal mine passages.

After reading the first passage, participants wrote a brief summary of the passage on six lines and then answered questions about the passage. After reading the second passage, participants wrote another summary and then everything they could remember, but there were no questions. For the remainder of the passages, participants completed all three tasks, a brief summary, recall of everything they could remember, and questions about the passage. Participants were informed of the performance tasks to be completed prior to reading each passage.

Transfer Tasks for Remembering Everyday Information. The first transfer task was a 13-minute nutrition video (Wright, 1998) portraying a man and a woman using a remote control to flip through various nutrition programs on a television and giving their reactions. The video was professionally produced, included a good deal of information about fats and nutrition, and was presented at an average rate of 149 words per minute. The transcript from the video was broken down into 228 scorable idea units following the Meyer (1975, 1985a) approach to text analysis. The materials for the second transfer task concerned breast cancer treatments and were taken from Meyer, Russo, and Talbot's (1995) study. The participants were asked to put themselves in the place of the patient while reading a three-part scenario about an experience with breast cancer. At the end of each part, they were asked to make a treatment decision. In making their final decision, they read conflicting advice from experts and the research literature and were later asked to recall it. This information was analyzed into 148 scorable idea units (Meyer, 1975, 1985a; Meyer, Russo, et al., 1995).

Procedure

First Three Testing Sessions (Pretests). During the first two 90-minute testing sessions, we administered the Quick Word Test, MMSE, the Davis Reading Test, working memory measures, reaction-time tasks, and questionnaires. Then, participants were stratified on the basis of their age group and reading comprehension scores from the Davis Reading Test (categorized as very low, low, average, high, or very high). Through a stratified random assignment procedure, participants were assigned to the training conditions. We wanted more people to receive the structure strategy instruction than the control conditions, so slightly less than half of the total number of participants were randomly assigned to the structure strategy condition, whereas the remainder were randomly assigned to the two control conditions (interest–list strategy training or no-contact control with structure strategy training scheduled after completion of the study). Within each of these groups, participants were again stratified on age group and reading comprehension scores and randomly assigned to signaling and passage order (e.g., railroads or airlines on the pretest) conditions. Finally, the third testing session consisted of a series of reading and recall tasks. Five different passages were read at this session, and recall tasks from them are identified as the pretest.

Participants randomly assigned to training attended six 90-minute sessions, spread over 3 weeks. Participants in both the structure strategy and interest–list strategy groups read and recalled the same materials, received the same number of sessions of equal duration, and were involved in the same amount of cooperative learning in pairs during training. The two training programs were conducted by the same team of instructors and were run in groups of about 10 participants. During the sixth session for both instructional groups, participants were asked to apply what they had learned in their training to remember information typical of everyday learning. The first task involved learning and recalling information from the nutrition video. The second task focused on a long magazine article about osteoporosis; the structure strategy group took notes organized with the article's top-level structure and compared their notes with a model provided by the instructor, whereas the interest–list strategy group read the article and evaluated it with the aid of interest questionnaires. Finally, both groups read and recalled the information presented in the simulated decision-making task about breast cancer.

Structure Strategy Training. Instruction with the structure strategy, identified to the learners as "the plan strategy," followed the teacher and student manuals published in Meyer et al. (1989) with the addition of the sixth session. In training, participants learned to identify and use basic top-level structures to organize their ideas (see Table 1). Participants also learned to recognize these structures in everyday reading materials and to use these structures as a framework for acquiring new information. Guided by the text's structure, participants conducted a systematic memory search to organize and write (or retell to their partners) what they remembered. Performance was monitored closely, and individual feedback was provided.

The structure strategy involves two steps. In reading, the learner finds the overall structure used by the writer and the main idea or ideas organized by that structure. In recalling, the learner uses the same organization as a strategy to improve memory. A key motto of the training program was "choose it, use it, or lose it." To find and choose the organizational structure in text was explained as the key to getting the writer's main ideas or message. Participants were told that this strategy is a good one to use under certain conditions such as when they want to know what a writer is trying to tell them or when they want to tell someone about what they read in an article. However, the structure strategy is not useful merely to find a particular detail or when the reader has no interest in the point the writer is trying to make. Likewise, the structure strategy is probably less useful when reading about very familiar topics, where prior knowledge is available for the assimilation of new information (Meyer, 1984, 1987; Voss & Silfies, 1996).

In the first two sessions of the training program, we used everyday text from advertisements, magazine articles, books, and newspapers that could be clearly classified into one of the five structures identified in Table 1. Appendix B presents two short texts from an exercise used toward the end of Session 2, where participants underlined signaling words and identified the top-level structure. Diagrams of text structure were examined to help students focus on the overall organizational plan of a text. The diagrams pointed out the hierarchy of

FIGURE 2
**Example of Diagrams Used in the Structure Strategy Training
to Explain the Top-Level Structure of Text**

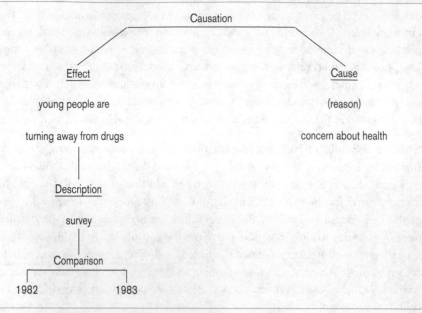

From *Memory Improved: Reading and Memory Enhancement Across the Life Span Through Strategic Text Structures* (p. 119), by B.J.F. Meyer, C.J. Young, and B.J. Bartlett, 1989. Hillsdale, NJ: Erlbaum. Copyright © 1989 by Lawrence Erlbaum Associates, Inc. Reprinted with permission.

major logical relationships in the passages (see Figure 2 for a diagram of the second text in Appendix B).

Instruction stressed the organizational components of various text structures for aiding encoding and retrieval from memory. For example, in the comparison structure, when opposing views are contrasted, they often are compared on the same issues, such as two political candidates' opposing views on abortion, taxes, government spending, and defense. Participants were told that recall could be improved from such a text by remembering that a comparison structure was used and the four particular issues compared. In addition, when reading a problem/ solution text, readers were encouraged to look for possible causes of the problems, descriptions of the effects of these causes, and the problem itself. Readers were encouraged to look for a proposed solution and to check to see whether it could eliminate a cause of the problem. When recalling problem/solution text, readers used this structure to search memory and to organize recall.

Appendix B presents a comparison text and a problem/solution text used in the instruction for Session 4 of the structure strategy training, along with corresponding forms providing feedback. Participants were expected to practice the strategy at home after each day of training. Homework for the second session involved reading 15 magazine articles and sorting them into groups based on the five structures. Also, the homework packet included short magazine articles, and participants identified each article's overall structure and signaling. Other homework activities were less formal and involved finding the five structures in their everyday reading, identifying signaling words, and sharing these materials with others in the class. In the final sessions, the strategy was applied to texts with confusing signaling or less signaling.

Interest–List Strategy Training. Participants learned to evaluate systematically their interest in an article and to use this information to monitor and increase their motivation for reading articles by thinking of others who would find the article interesting. Activities in the first sessions were (a) evaluating the interest of the materials read through use of the Perceived Interest Questionnaire (Schraw et al., 1995) or the Sources of Interest Questionnaire (Schraw et al., 1995), (b) discussing with their partners articles and disagreements of more than 2 points on the questionnaires' 5-point rating scales, and (c) practicing remembering reading materials. Participants were told to practice in class and at home and received homework packets with the same reading materials as the structure strategy group, but with the task of ranking the texts on interest. (Compare the first examples in Appendixes B and C to see the use of the same text in Session 2 for both types of training programs.)

The instructional aim of the fourth session was to provide a rationale for evaluating one's own interest for the purpose of monitoring motivation for learning and remembering information from text (see Figure 3, adapted and drastically simplified from Schiefele's 1992 model). The instruction explained that motivation influences the focusing of attention and understanding as well as enjoyment of a reading activity. Participants were referred to Figure 3, which depicts

FIGURE 3
Explanation of How Interest Influences Recall,
Presented in the Interest Strategy Training Program

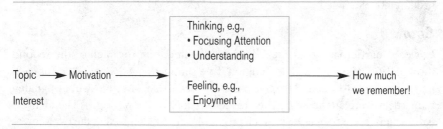

how these factors influence how much is remembered from reading. The program explained that interests produce motivation and that motivation spurs on effort and gives the persistence needed to attend to and work at understanding the text. Participants reflected on some articles they thought were boring but were of interest to their partners. Next, they were informed that it would be helpful when faced with an article of little interest to think of friends or relatives that might be interested in the topic and to create some interest so that they could relay the information to them. This strategy was aimed at providing them with motivation and discipline to increase their learning from texts on uninteresting topics. If, after scanning an article to be read, they determined they had low interest in the topic, they were instructed to think of a person they knew who would be interested in the topic. Examples of activities from the interest–list strategy training are provided in Appendix C, with the same comparison text used in Session 4 of the structure strategy training. Sessions 5 and 6 continued to apply this approach with longer and more complex texts.

Checking Motivation in the Two Programs. Motivation checks were administered at the first and fifth training sessions. All participants indicated at least some interest in improving their ability to remember what they read. There were no significant differences in motivation expressed between the two instructional programs at either time, $\chi^2(2, N = 87) = 1.80, p > .05; \chi^2(2, N = 87) = 3.80, p > .05$.

Posttest. The final testing session was conducted 2 days after completion of training. It was very similar to the pretest, involving reading and recall tasks from five passages, but occurred 2½ months later. At the end of the posttest, participants evaluated any changes in their reading that occurred during the project. After completion of the posttest. the control group received training with the plan strategy. Prior to their first training session, they worked on the two transfer tasks. First, they viewed and recalled the nutrition video. The conditions for testing were similar to those of the structure strategy and interest–list strategy groups (in all conditions, viewing the video was the first scheduled task of each session, and time on the task was controlled by the same videotape). Task demands were different for the control group on the medical decision-making task. Thus, findings from the control group with respect to the medical decision-making task are not examined.

Scoring

For each participant, four recalls were collected, one for each of the second through fifth passages read. In addition, five summaries were collected for each participant, one for each of the five passages read. Also, questions about signaled main ideas were answered by each reader for four of the passages. The identification numbers associated with each protocol were hidden so that the two scorers were blind to membership in a particular age group and experimental condition. Meyer's (1975, 1985a) prose analysis system was used to score total recall, recall of the most important information (gist), and top-level structure (how a protocol was organized; scored from 1 to 9; Meyer, 1985a) for the texts, the video, and the health information from the decision-making task.

Total Recall. Each idea unit in the propositional analysis for each text or script was scored according to the procedures outlined by Meyer (1975, 1985a). A reliability check of a random sample of 10% of the free-recall data indicated high reliability ($r = .96$). The average agreement in scoring the same specific idea units was 94%. Correlations among the total recall scores for the four texts recalled were high (.80 between schizophrenia and railroad/airlines, .67 between trusts and schizophrenia as well as trusts and creation/evolution, .68 between railroad/airlines and creation/evolution, .69 between railroad and trusts, and .70 between creation/evolution and schizophrenia). A principal-components factor analysis yielded only one significant factor, which accounted for 69% of the variance in recall. Although the texts varied in content, length, and idea units, recall from them appeared to reflect the same construct; so to simplify data presentation, recall scores on the texts were converted to z scores and added together and averaged to obtain a single measure for total recall.

Gist. Memory for gist was assessed in a number of ways: (a) production of a summary rated for quality, called *summary quality*; (b) inclusion of ideas in a summary from high in a propositional analysis of the text's structure (Meyer, 1975, 1985a), called *summary main ideas*; (c) free recall of ideas from high in the text's structure, called *recall main ideas*; and (d) questions about signaled main ideas, called *questions*. A reliability check of a random sample of 10% of the summary data also indicated high reliability ($r = .96$ for recall of summaries; $r = .93$ for quality of summaries). The average agreement in scoring the same specific idea units was 99%. Questions were scored for gist, and the reliability coefficient for scoring was .96. The average summary quality on the 4-point scale of quality was the average over the five passages. For the remaining dependent measures, z scores were calculated for each and averaged over the passages.

Top-Level Structure. Top-level structure scores of 6 or greater on the 9-point scale (Meyer, 1985a) indicated use of the structure strategy on a particular text. For example, for the problem/solution texts, scores of 6 through 9 indicated that all the problem information was presented together followed by all the solution information. To receive scores of 6 through 9, the order of recall of the problems followed by the solutions had to match that of the text, but the content of the problems or solutions did not have to match that of the text. A score of 7 indicated that, in addition, the participant used a signaling word to explicitly identify a problem. A score of 8 indicated that a solution had been signaled, and a score of 9 showed that both the problem and solution parts of the problem/solution structure had been explicitly signaled. The interrater reliability coefficient for top-level structure scores on 10% of the summaries and recalls was .88. Top-level structure scores on each of the five passages read (summary for the first text and recall for the others) were averaged for the pretest and again for the posttest to get average measures of the match between protocol organization and structure of the text. Consistency in use of the structure strategy was examined by looking at whether the structure strategy was used for each of the five passages read during a testing session. Scores of 6 and greater counted as use of the structure strategy whereas scores less than 6 did not. Participants who used the structure strategy on each of the five passages were identified as reaching Stage 6 of strategy use (showing consistent use, see Table 2), whereas those who did not use the structure strategy on each of the five passages were classified as not showing consistent use.

Results

Equivalence of Experimental Groups Prior to Instruction and Self-Appraisal of Training

Characteristics of Experimental Groups Prior to Training. Table 3 summarizes some of the individual-differences measures collected on the younger and older adults in the three training groups. A multivariate analysis of variance (MANOVA) examining age group, training condition, and signaling was conducted for age, education, vocabulary (Quick Word Test), reading comprehension (Davis Reading Test), working memory (CSPAN and RSPAN), reaction time, and cognitive functioning (MMSE). The only significant finding was for age group (Wilks's $\Lambda = .02$), $F(8, 100) = 640.33$, $p < .0005$. The younger adults performed significantly better than did the older adults on tests of working memory, reaction time, and cognitive functioning, whereas older adults had more education and higher scores on the vocabulary test (univariate analyses of variance [ANOVAs]; see Table 3). This pattern of higher performance of older adults on vocabulary but lower performance on processing measures is typical in aging research where aspects of crystallized intelligence are stable or increase over the life span but fluid intelligence declines (e.g., Schaie, 1996). Interestingly, for the present investigation of reading, both age groups showed equivalent performance on the Davis Reading Test.

As summarized in the last row of Table 3, the training groups did not differ on average top-level structure scores across the five passages read prior to instruction, $F(2, 109) = .76$, $p = .47$, $MSE = 1.02$. Prior to training, there was a significant main effect for signaling, $F(1, 109) = 5.07$, $p = .026$, $MSE = 1.02$, supporting the strategy switch hypothesis. The average score for the readers receiving signaling was 5.47 ($SD = 1.02$), whereas the average for those reading text without

TABLE 3

Means (and Standard Deviations) for Major Individual-Difference Characteristics of Old and Young Adults in the Three Training Conditions

Variable	Structure Strategy (n = 57)		Interest–List Strategy (n = 30)		No Training (n = 34)	
	Old (n = 31)	Young (n = 26)	Old (n = 16)	Young (n = 14)	Old (n = 18)	Young (n = 16)
Age	69.42 (4.38)	21.00 (2.62)	71.50 (5.35)	20.00 (1.62)	68.59 (3.37)	19.94 (1.53)
Education[a]	16.52 (2.43)	14.65 (1.79)	15.88 (2.96)	14.14 (1.29)	16.92 (2.25)	14.20 (1.42)
Vocabulary[b]	64.23 (13.92)	47.89 (13.74)	58.88 (18.03)	44.50 (9.83)	66.67 (16.27)	45.69 (11.32)
Reading (Davis Reading Test)	18.90 (7.64)	21.12 (8.15)	14.94 (7.36)	17.07 (5.76)	18.29 (7.81)	20.75 (7.57)
Working Memory[c]	3.45 (1.36)	4.17 (1.30)	2.41 (0.66)	4.43 (1.53)	2.72 (1.26)	4.31 (1.24)
Cognitive Status[d]	29.07 (0.81)	29.58 (0.64)	28.75 (0.78)	29.36 (1.01)	29.17 (0.99)	29.69 (0.60)
Pretest Top-Level Structure	5.20 (0.90)	5.33 (1.02)	4.77 (1.03)	5.47 (1.32)	5.34 (1.94)	5.46 (0.97)

CSPAN = computation span; MMSE = Mini Mental State Exam.
[a] Education: $F(1, 107) = 28.79$, $p < .0005$, $MSE = .08$.
[b] Vocabulary: $F(1, 107) = 41.55$, $p < .0005$, $MSE = 204.93$.
[c] CSPAN: $F(1, 107) = 35.87$, $p < .0005$, $MSE = 1.63$.
[d] MMSE: $F(1, 107) = 14.24$, $p < .0005$, $MSE = 4.51$.

signaling was 5.06 (SD = 1.01). The main effect for age group was not significant, $F(1, 109) = 2.48$, $p = .118$, $MSE = 1.02$, and there were no significant interactions among age, training condition, or signaling. The hypothesized age group by signaling interaction was not statistically significant, $F(1, 109) = 2.90$, $p = .09$, $MSE = 1.11$. Contrary to earlier studies, signaling did not influence organization of recall more for older adults than for younger adults; in fact, the pattern of the data was in the opposite direction, with signaling tending to aid the younger adults more than the older adults.

Participants' Appraisal of Changes in Reading After Instruction. Table 4 summarizes data on self-appraisal of changes in reading over the duration of the study by participants in the structure strategy, the interest–list strategy, and control groups along with results from statistical analyses comparing the three groups on questions posed to them. Young adults in both the structure strategy and interest–list strategy groups felt they remembered more on the posttest as compared with the pretest than did those in the control group, and the structure strategy and interest–list strategy groups did not differ significantly, $\chi^2(1, N = 40) = .44$, $p = .91$. As shown in Table 4, most of the older adults in all of the experimental groups felt they had made significant pretest-to-posttest gains. Younger and older readers in the structure strategy and interest–list strategy groups tended to feel that after instruction they remembered more from their everyday reading than did participants in the control group (see the second question in Table 4). For young adults, the structure strategy and interest–list strategy groups did not differ significantly, $\chi^2(1, N = 40) = .84$, $p = .36$, but the old adults in the structure strategy group claimed more everyday reading gains than did those in the interest–list strategy group, $\chi^2(1, N = 47) = 52.49$, $p = .02$. Most participants in all of the groups felt that they remembered different kinds of information on the posttest than they remembered on the pretest (see the third question in Table 4). Young and old participants in the structure strategy group felt that they remembered different kinds of information from their everyday reading since volunteering for the project, whereas this was not the case for participants not receiving any instruction (see the fourth question in Table 4). Although the young adults in the structure strategy and interest–list strategy groups did not differ significantly in this appraisal, $\chi^2(1, N = 40) = .03$, $p = .86$, more older adults from the structure strategy group than the interest–list group claimed changes in the types of information they remembered in everyday life, $\chi^2(1, N = .47) = 4.87$, $p = .027$.

As depicted in the fifth question in Table 4, nearly all participants in the structure strategy group reported trying to figure out how a passage was organized during the posttest, whereas only about half of the control group and three fourths of the interest–list group reported trying to focus on text organization. More participants in the interest–list strategy group than in the other groups reported trying to evaluate their interest in the texts. The readers in the two in-

TABLE 4

Self-Appraisal of Changes in Reading Over the Duration of the Experiment by Young and Old Participants in the Structure Strategy, Interest–List Strategy, and Control (No-Training) Groups (Percentages of Participants Indicating "Yes" to Queries)

Query and Age Group	Percentage Answering "Yes"			$\chi^2(2)$	p
	Plan	Interest	Control		
Do you feel that you remembered more from your reading in this testing session than you did in the last testing session?					
Young	92	86	53	9.41	.009
Old	87	75	75	1.35	ns
Do you feel that you remember more from your reading in everyday life than you did before you volunteered for this project?					
Young	88	71	47	8.39	.015
Old	90	56	53	10.17	.006
Do you feel that you remembered different kinds of information in today's testing session?					
Young	88	71	60	4.52	ns
Old	82	63	59	5.66	ns
Do you feel that you remember different kinds of information from your reading in everyday life than you did before you volunteered for this project?					
Young	65	57	20	8.13	.017
Old	90	56	41	12.83	.002
When you read in this testing session, did you try to figure out how a passage was organized?					
Young	96	79	47	13.66	.001
Old	97	75	56	11.73	.003
When you read in this testing session, did you try to evaluate your interest in the passage?					
Young	65	100	73	6.15	.046
Old	45	87	71	8.06	.018

structional groups were trying to apply the goals of their particular training, a focus on text organization or a focus on interest, during the final posttest.

These data, along with the formative evaluation during training to check motivation, permit the conclusion that the goals for the interest–list strategy training were met. That is, this training served as an excellent contact control group by providing motivation equivalent to the structure strategy training, equivalent practice experiences, and feelings of satisfaction with the training experiences.

Did Training With the Structure Strategy Increase Total Recall?

Tests of Hypotheses Focusing on Total Recall. There were no significant main effects on the pretest for age group, $F(2, 109) = 1.04$, $p = .31$, $MSE = .54$, training condition, $F(2, 109)$ 1.78, $p = .18$, $MSE = .54$, or signaling, $F(1, 109) = 1.63$, $p = .20$, $MSE = .54$, and no significant interactions. The finding of no difference between the age groups on total recall supports the age-related hypothesis for total recall and other studies with highly verbal, college-educated older adults (e.g., Meyer & Rice, 1983). The lack of signaling effects on total recall supports the predictions and is consistent with prior research (e.g., Lorch & Lorch, 1995; Meyer, 1975). There was a significant effect for training condition on the posttest $F(2, 109) = 6.22$, $p = .003$, $MSE = .77$, but no significant effects for age group, $F(1, 109) = 1.19$, $p = .28$, $MSE = .77$, or signaling, $F(1, 109) = 1.76$, $p = .19$, $MSE = .77$ and no significant interactions (age by training condition interaction: $F[2, 109] = .42$, $p = .66$, $MSE = .77$). The means (z scores) on the posttest for older and younger adults in the three training groups are presented in Table 5. The no-training group ($M = .01$, $SD = .76$) did not differ from the interest–list strategy group ($M = -.12$, $SD = .90$, Tukey $a = .84$). However, the participants in the structure strategy group ($M = .49$, $SD = .92$) recalled significantly more information from the text than did participants in both the interest–list strategy group (Tukey $a = .006$) and the no-training group (Tukey $a = .026$).

Thus, the first hypothesis of the investigation was supported in that training in the structure strategy increased the amount of information recalled from reading for both the young and older adults. The findings replicate those of Meyer et al. (1989) with a more educated group of older adults. In addition, two of the age-related hypotheses were supported in that there were no age effects on total recall, and structure strategy training aided both younger and older adults.

Practicality of Findings and Intraindividual Gain. The effect size computed comparing the two training groups on total recall on the posttest was .64. The average reader in the structure strategy group had a total recall score equal to a reader in the interest–list strategy group who scored at the 74th percentile. Thus, the magnitude of the effect of the structure strategy intervention was large enough to make a substantial difference in performance.

As noted in Table 4, all groups of older participants and young adults in both training groups believed they improved from pretest to posttest, suggesting beliefs of self-efficacy on the posttest. As summarized in Table 5, average gain scores for total recall (pretest scores minus posttest scores) were positive for all training conditions. An age group by signaling by training condition ANOVA

TABLE 5

Means (and Standard Deviations) for Old and Young Adults in the Three Training Conditions on the Amount, Organization, and Type of Recall on the Posttest

Variable	Structure Strategy (n = 57)		Interest-List Strategy (n = 30)		No Training (n = 34)	
	Old (n = 31)	Young (n = 26)	Old (n = 16)	Young (n = 14)	Old (n = 18)	Young (n = 16)
Total Recall	.32 (.82)	.69 (.99)	−.19 (.77)	−.04 (1.05)	−.03 (.77)	.05 (.76)
Gains in Total Recall	.48 (.46)	.76 (.54)	.34 (.41)	.26 (.73)	.21 (.48)	.17 (.51)
Top-Level Structure	6.74 (1.22)	7.53 (1.44)	5.35 (1.1)	6.21 (1.47)	5.50 (1.28)	5.45 (1.40)
Gist						
Summary quality	2.23 (57)	2.39 (6)	1.65 (4)	1.84 (.46)	1.94 (62)	1.78 (4)
Summary main ideas	.22 (.62)	.39 (.77)	−.28 (.58)	−.11 (.57)	.03 (.84)	−.12 (.56)
Recall main ideas	.02 (.53)	.18 (.71)	−.40 (.43)	−.14 (.68)	−.12 (.70)	−.11 (.66)
Questions	.37 (.64)	.29 (.76)	−.17 (.78)	.02 (.53)	−.01 (.58)	.19 (.56)

on gains in z scores for total recall yielded only one significant main effect—training condition, $F(2, 109) = 8.24, p < .0005, MSE = .27$—and no significant interactions (e.g., age group by training condition: $F[1, 109] = 1.55, p = .22, MSE = .27$). The structure strategy group had higher gains than did the interest–list strategy group (Tukey $a = .02$) and the control group (Tukey $a = .001$), which did not differ from each other (Tukey $a = .68$). The structure strategy condition yielded significantly more intraindividual gain, an important consideration in training research and aging (e.g., Willis, 1989).

Did Structure Strategy Training and Signaling Increase Recall of the Most Important Information?

Training with the structure strategy was hypothesized not only to boost total recall but also to increase recall of the most important information. There was a significant effect on pretest performance for age group (Wilks's $\Lambda = .84$), $F(4, 106) = 5.04$, $p = .001$, but not for signaling (Wilks's $\Lambda = .95$), $F(4, 106) = 1.41, p = .24$, training condition (Wilks's $\Lambda = .96$), $F(8, 212) .60, p = .78$, or any of their interactions. The only statistically significant univariate F test for age group was on questions where young adults answered more questions correctly, $F(1, 109) = 4.68, p = .03$, $MSE = .41$. The nonsignificant multivariate F for signaling does not replicate previous demonstrations of signaling increasing recall of main ideas and signaled information. However, one of the univariate analyses was significant: Questions about signaled information were answered better from the with-signaling texts than from the without-signaling texts, $F(1, 109) = 5.43, p = .02$.

There was a significant effect for training condition on posttest scores (Wilks's $\Lambda = .73$), $F(8, 212) = 4.06, p < .0005$, but no significant age group effect (Wilks's $\Lambda = .98$), $F(4, 106) = .43, p = .79$, signaling effect (Wilks's $\Lambda = .94$), $F(4, 106) = 1.77, p = .14$, or interaction. As displayed in Table 5, participants in the structure strategy group remembered more of the information from the texts than did participants in the other groups. Univariate tests were statistically significant for summary quality, $F(2, 109) = 15.28, p < .0005, MSE = .27$, summary main ideas, $F(2, 109) = 6.88, p = .002, MSE = .45$, recall main ideas, $F(2, 109) = 4.03, p = .021, MSE = .38$, and questions, $F(2, 109) = 4.34, p = .015, MSE = .43$. The quality of summaries produced by the structure strategy group were superior to those produced by the interest–list strategy group (Tukey $a < .0005$) and the no-training group (Tukey $a = .001$), but the latter two groups did not differ (Tukey $a = .62$). The structure strategy group included more main ideas in their summaries than did the interest–list strategy group (Tukey $a = .004$), recalled more main idea ideas than this group (Tukey $a = .026$), and correctly answered more main idea questions (Tukey $a = .018$). However, neither trained group differed significantly from the no-training group on questions, summary main ideas, or recall main ideas, but the structure strategy group tended to include more main ideas in their summaries than did the no-training group (Tukey $a = .059$). Overall, our hypothesis was supported: Training with the structure strategy increased recall for the most important information in texts.

Again, the multivariate F was not significant for signaling on the posttest, but some of the univariate Fs were significant. On all of the gist variables, the means were higher for the with-signaling versions than for the without-signaling texts (questions: $F[1, 109] = 3.61$, $p = .06$, $MSE = .43$; summary quality: $F[21, 109] = 4.05$, $p = .047$, $MSE = .27$; summary main ideas: $F[1, 109] = 1.72$, $p = .19$, $MSE = .76$; recall main ideas: $F[1, 109] = 4.02$, $p = .047$, $MSE = .38$). There was no clear support for the strategy switch hypothesis for explaining signaling effects from the gist data. Contrary to past research and predictions, signaling did not significantly increase recall of main ideas. However, there was a trend compatible with past findings and the strategy switch hypothesis. The hypothesized interaction between signaling and age group was not supported with any of the pretest or posttest gist measures. In addition, we did not find the predicted interaction among signaling, age group, and training condition on the posttest.

Did Training With the Structure Strategy and Signaling Affect Organization of Recall?

Top-Level Structure Scores. After training, there were statistically significant main effects on average top-level structure scores for age group, $F(1, 109) = 4.40$, $p = .038$, $MSE = 1.58$, training condition, $F(2, 109) = 23.56$, $p < .0005$, $MSE = 1.58$, and signaling, $F(1, 109) = 14.45$, $p < .0005$, $MSE = 1.58$, but no significant interactions. As detailed in Table 5, the younger adults organized their recall by following the text structure more than the older adults. This age group difference was not predicted for this highly educated sample. Similar to the findings for gist, the predicted age by signaling interaction for recall organization was not found.

The no-training group ($M = 5.27$, $SD = 1.24$) did not differ from the interest–list strategy group ($M = 5.31$, $SD = 1.15$, Tukey $a = .59$), but the structure strategy group ($M = 6.86$, $SD = 1.28$) performed significantly better than the interest–list strategy group (Tukey $a < .0005$) and the no-training group (Tukey $a < .0005$). The structure strategy training taught participants to use the structure strategy to organize their recalls. Thus, our hypothesis was supported: Structure strategy training affected the organization of recall.

The differences in organization of recall by the trained structure strategy group and the interest–list strategy group indicate that the former was using the structure strategy on the posttest, whereas the latter was not. The similarity in recall organization between the no-training control group and the interest–list group, rather than the structure strategy group, suggests that the typical reading strategy for this sample of readers was not the structure strategy. These findings are supportive of the strategy switch hypothesis rather than the common strategy hypothesis.

The average top-level structure score for the group reading text without signaling was 5.88 ($SD = 1.52$), whereas the average for the with-signaling group was 6.78 (SD = 1.43), suggesting that most participants reading text with signaling had switched to the structure strategy. The significant signaling effects for top-level structure scores on both the pretest and posttest also lend support to the strategy switch hypothesis.

Thus, in general, the findings concerning gist recall and, particularly, organization of recall support the strategy switch hypothesis as opposed to the common strategy hypothesis. Signaling and structure strategy training increased the correspondence between protocol organization and text organization.

Consistent Use of the Structure Strategy. As shown in Table 6, few participants consistently used the structure strategy on all five passages. There were no statistically significant age differences in consistency of use of the structure strategy (pretest: young = 5% vs. old = 3%, $\chi^2[1, N = 121] = 0.03, p = .93$; posttest: young = 39% vs. old = 25%, $\chi^2[1, N = 121] = 2.36, p = .12$). As noted earlier, there were age differences after training but not before in use of top-level structure. However, this appears to reflect differences in use of signaling words in writing recalls rather than actually organizing the recall to match the structure used by the author, as the older adults' average top-level structure score was over 6 (see Table 5), indicating use of the structure strategy, and the age groups did not vary on consistency of structure strategy use.

On the pretest, the no-training group displayed more consistent use of the structure strategy than did the structure strategy training group (see Table 6), $\chi^2(2, N = 121) = 7.51, p = .02$. In contrast, on the posttest, 47% of the structure strategy group consistently used the structure strategy on all texts, whereas 12% of the no-training group and 23% of the interest–list strategy group demonstrated consistent use, $\chi^2(2, N = 121) = 13.74, p = .001$.

TABLE 6
**Percentages of Readers Consistently Using the Structure Strategy
in the Three Training Groups on the Pretest and Posttest
for the With-Signaling and Without-Signaling Conditions**

	Structure Strategy		Interest–List Strategy		No Training	
	Signals ($n = 31$)	No signals ($n = 26$)	Signals ($n = 16$)	No signals ($n = 14$)	Signals ($n = 18$)	No signals ($n = 16$)
Consistent Use (5/5 texts)						
Pretest[a]	0	0	7	0	12	12
Posttest[b]	65	33	27	18	20	6

[a] $\chi^2(5, N = 121) = 8.35, p = .14.$
[b] $\chi^2(5, N = 121) = 21.64, p = .001.$

Table 6 includes the percentages of participants consistently using the structure strategy when reading with- and without-signaling texts in the three training conditions. On the pretest, there were no significant differences in consistent strategy use between participants reading texts with signaling (5%) and those reading texts without signaling (3%), $\chi^2(1, N = 121) = .01$, $p = .93$. On the posttest, however, signaling affected consistent use of the structure strategy (with signaling: 41% consistent use; without signaling: 22% consistent use), $\chi^2(1, N = 121) = 5.15$, $p = .023$. Evidently, explicitly showing readers how to use signaling was necessary before signaling could affect consistent use of the structure strategy.

It was hypothesized that there would be an additive effect of structure strategy instruction and signaling for consistent use of the structure strategy. As depicted in the second row of Table 6, this hypothesis was supported. The group that received both structure strategy instruction and signaling clearly outperformed the groups that received one or the other. Sixty-five percent of the participants in the structure strategy and with-signaling group appeared to demonstrate the sixth operational level of structure strategy usage outlined in Table 2. With a more lenient requirement of consistent use on at least four out of the five passages, 88% of the structure strategy's with-signaling group and 65% of the structure strategy's without-signaling group attained this level of mastery. We obtained the hypothesized additive effect of structure strategy instruction and signaling for consistent use of the structure strategy over the five texts read.

Structure strategy training increased total recall, recall of the most important information, correspondence between recall and text organization, and consistent use of the structure strategy across five passages. Information in the five passages came from everyday materials found in magazine articles and informative brochures. The next section focuses on whether structure strategy training can aid in the recall of other types of everyday materials.

Did Training in the Structure Strategy Transfer to Remembering Other Types of Everyday Materials?

The structure strategy training helped readers to acquire information from text and systematically organize it at recall. Two transfer tasks were examined to investigate whether these improved skills transferred to other types of everyday learning tasks. The first everyday task involved the recall of a nutrition video with a problem/solution top-level structure discussing problems with fats in the diet and ways to reduce this intake (see Table 7 for means of each training group). There was a statistically significant effect for training condition on free recall, $F(1, 81) = 10.11$, $p = .002$, $MSE = 223.10$, with adults in the structure strategy group recalling an average of 50.16 ideas ($SD = 16.68$) from the video, whereas adults in the interest–list strategy group recalled an average of 39.69 ($SD = 12.21$) ideas. Neither age group nor the interaction between age group and condition was significant. To determine whether the participants in the structure strategy group were using the

TABLE 7
Recall Means (and Standard Deviations) for Plan- and Interest-Strategy Young and Old Adults on Everyday Tasks

Measure	Plan Strategy		Interest Strategy	
	Old	Young	Old	Young
Recall of Nutrition Video				
Total recall	45.63 (16.94)	55.39 (15.03)	41.33 (14.69)	37.93 (9.11)
Top-level structure	6.60 (1.99)	6.96 (2.32)	4.06 (1.81)	4.36 (2.27)
Recall After Breast Cancer Decision-Making Task				
Total recall	19.52 (11.71)	25.04 (13.06)	6.88(5.78)	18.43 (11.88)
Top-level structure	7.19 (2.06)	7.92 (1.38)	4.25 (2.44)	4.86 (1.92)

problem/solution organization of the video to organize their recall more than participants in the interest–list strategy group, an ANOVA was conducted on top-level structure scores for the recall protocols. Again, the only significant finding was experimental condition, $F(1, 82) = 31.15, p < .0005, MSE = 4.13$. Participants in the structure strategy group ($M = 6.77, SD = 2.14$) tended to organize their recalls with the problem/solution structure and to use explicit signaling of this structure in their protocols more than did participants in the interest–list strategy group ($M = 4.20, SD = 1.75$). In fact, only 10% of the adults in the interest–list group organized their recall protocols with a problem section and a solution section, whereas 65% of the adults in the structure strategy group organized their recalls with a problem/solution organization, $\chi^2(1, N = 87) = 21.83, p < .0005$. The structure strategy training appeared to transfer to watching informative videos.

The second transfer task involved making a final treatment decision about breast cancer. Participants read contrasting advice from seven experts and a summary of the relevant research literature (Meyer, Russo, et al., 1995). After making a decision, they were asked to recall everything they could remember from the seven experts and research literature. Both age group, $F(1, 79) = 10.82, p = .002, MSE = 128.7$, and condition, $F(1, 79) = 13.75, p < .0005, MSE = 128.7$, were significant, with no significant interaction (see Table 7). Younger adults ($M = 22.73, SD = 12.91$) recalled more information about the research and experts' views than did older adults ($M = 14.81, SD = 11.62$); this replicates Meyer, Russo, et al.'s (1995) findings for lower-educated adults with this highly educated sample. Participants in the structure strategy group recalled an average of 22.23 ideas ($SD = 12.58$), whereas participants in the interest–list strategy group recalled an average of 12.27 ($SD = 10.72$). In addition, participants in the structure strategy group ($M = 7.55, SD = 1.78$) tended to organize their recalls like the structure of the materials read more than did participants in the interest–list group ($M = 4.53, SD = 2.19$). Training condition was significant, $F(1, 79) = 46.11, p < .0005, MSE = 3.73$, but neither age group nor the interaction was significant. Only 24% of the participants in the interest–list strategy group used the comparative (comparison of alternative views) or problem/solution (alternative solutions for the cancer problem) structures in the reading materials to organize their recall, whereas 77% of the participants in the structure strategy group used such organization, $\chi^2(1, N = 83) = 19.53, p < .0005$. In summary, training in the structure strategy for remembering expository text transferred to the ability to remember conflicting treatment information from various sources on a medical decision task. Thus, the data from both transfer tasks were consistent with the hypothesis that training with the structure strategy transfers to remembering other types of everyday materials.

The interest–list strategy did not increase recall as much as the structure strategy for the texts read in the study. The cognitive strategy had more positive effects than the motivational strategy on reading performance. However, in comparing gain scores of the interest–list strategy group with those of the control group (see Table 5), it is apparent that the interest–list strategy was not detrimental to recall. Thus, it does not appear likely that the interest–list strategy actually interfered with recall on the transfer tasks, causing the disparate performance between the two trained groups.

The no-training group viewed the nutrition video after completion of the study, and these data can provide some insight related to whether differences between the interest–list and structure strategies were due to the facilitative effect of the structure strategy or to the detrimental effect of the interest–list strategy. An ANOVA comparing the three conditions and age groups on information recalled from the nutrition video yielded a statistically significant effect for training condition, $F(2, 112) = 9.52, p < .0005, MSE = 217.68$, and no age effect, $F(1, 112) = .36, p = .55, MSE = 217.68$, or interaction. The structure strategy group recalled more than did the interest–list strategy group (Tukey $a = .010$) and the no-training group (Tukey $a < .0005$; no-training young: $M = 37.65, SD = 15.05$, and no-training old: $M = 36.07, SD = 17.02$, as compared with the means for the other groups; see Table 7). The interest–list strategy group and the no-training group did not differ significantly (Tukey $a = .51$). Thus, the interest–list strategy was not detrimental to recall, but it did not boost recall over the control condition like the structure strategy did. The structure strategy training was useful in facilitating recall on the transfer tasks.

Discussion

Most of the hypothesized effects for structure strategy training, signaling, and aging were supported. Hypotheses clustered around four main issues: (1) the strategy switch hypothesis, (2) an additive effect of structure strategy training and signaling for consistent strategy use, (3) aging, and (4) transfer. Structure strategy training and signaling were hypothesized to facilitate switching from the list strategy to the structure strategy and to increase scores for top-level structure and gist. However, only structure strategy training was hypothesized to increase total recall because it explicitly taught how to use signals, identify top-level structure, and use it during processing for systematic encoding and retrieval. As predicted, training with the structure strategy increased performance on total recall, gist, and top-level structure. Signaling increased top-level structure scores but not most measures of gist. The hypothesized additive effect of training plus signaling was supported for use of the structure strategy consistently over five passages.

Both younger and older adults benefited more from the structure strategy training than from the interest–list strategy training. With this highly educated sample of older adults, there were no age differences in total recall except on the medical decision-making task. Text recall can be maintained particularly well across the life span by adults with high verbal skills (see also Hultsch et al., 1998; Meyer & Rice, 1983). The medical decision-making task involved multiple demands and may have more severely taxed older adults' resources. Alternatively, the older adults may have understood the task demands differently and focused more on the decision and affect surrounding it, rather than trying to learn and recall the information presented. Older adults seek and examine less information than do younger adults in decision-making tasks (e.g., Johnson, 1993; Meyer, Russo, et al., 1995).

The hypothesized interaction between signaling and age group was not supported. Older adults were not more dependent on signaling than were younger adults. This suggests that (a) contrary to the work of Britton et al. (1982), the model in Figure 1 is incorrect with respect to the increased cognitive load required for text without signaling; (b) conceptual short-term memory, reported to be preserved in normal aging (e.g., Wingfield & Tun, 1999), plays a larger role than processing resources in the generation of text-based inferences needed without signaling; or (c) the high reading comprehension and verbal abilities of the older adults enabled them to compensate for their reduced working memory capacities in the more resource-demanding condition without signaling.

A practical, new finding from the present study is the transfer of the structure strategy training with relatively short texts to the recall of more complex everyday information found in an educational video and a medical decision-making task. Both structure strategy and interest–list strategy training groups reported positive changes in reading, but only the structure strategy group increased total recall and organization of recall from different types of texts and an informative video.

The present study has important theoretical and practical implications. Positive effects from instruction about text structure are consistent with Meyer's earlier work with younger and older adults (Meyer et al., 1989) and that of others with young adults and children (e.g., Bartlett, 1978; Cook & Mayer, 1988; Gordon, 1990; Paris et al., 1984; Slater et al., 1985). In examining the findings with regard to the model in Figure 1, the dominant reading strategy for this sample of readers before training was the list strategy, and it followed the paths in the lower half of the model. In fact, on the pretest prior to any training, only 4% of the participants consistently used the structure strategy over the five passages read. Most appeared to approach text by trying to remember a list of ideas without taking advantage of text structure, as has been noted by others (Barnett, 1984; Cook & Mayer, 1988; Samuels et al., 1988; Sanchez et al., in press).

Structure strategy training changed most readers from using the list strategy to using the structure strategy on most passages, regardless of the presence of signaling. That is, the dominant reading strategy on the posttest for most participants who received training with the structure strategy became the structure strategy (see Figure 1). The lack of signaling in passages read by these trained readers appeared to affect them as modeled in the top half of Figure 1. It diminished their ability to demonstrate consistent use of the strategy on all five posttest passages, a feat performed by most participants trained with the structure strategy, who read signaled versions of the passages. More sessions of practice during training focusing on text with little or no signaling may be needed to increase mastery of the strategy when reading text without clear signaling.

Overall, the investigation into the effects of signaling and training supports the strategy switch hypothesis, not the common strategy hypothesis. The strategy switch hypothesis is supported in that signaling increased the correspondence between the organization of recalls and the texts both before and after instruction. However, most readers who did not receive structure strategy instruction did not consistently use the structure strategy across the five different texts. Signaling increased consistent use of the structure strategy on the posttest but not on the pretest. Signaling increased consistent use of the structure strategy only after about half of the participants in the sample had received instruction with the strategy and learned how to use signals in text to better identify and use text structure. Training and practice with the structure strategy are needed to enable students to acquire the cognitive and metacognitive knowledge to use the structure strategy proficiently and consistently, the final stage of strategy use described in Table 2.

Structure strategy training had a much larger impact on performance than signaling. Although they both affected the organization of recall and consistency in use of the structure strategy after instruction, only instruction with the structure strategy substantially increased recall on measures of total and gist recall. Encouraging writers to signal their text appropriately can be helpful, but this aid is limited. In order for readers to utilize signals fully and cope with text without appropriate signaling, it appears necessary to provide readers with instruction about how to identify and use text structure to aid recall and determine what is the important information.

The findings of this investigation are important because they show that readers can be trained with the structure strategy and can use it effectively to boost total recall, regardless of whether an author has provided signaling.

Providing learners with instruction in the structure strategy and conditional knowledge for its use can be extremely valuable because texts encountered in everyday life may lack signals or use them inappropriately (Lorch, Ritchey, & Garrett, 1999). Even learners with some expertise in reading and success in school can benefit substantially from instruction about text structure. Also, we have found substantial beneficial effects of structure strategy instruction for a sample of low-educated, older African American adults (Meyer, Talbot, Poon, & Johnson, 2001). Reading, study, or life-skills programs for adults across the life span may augment their effectiveness by incorporating systematic instruction with the structure strategy. In addition, such instruction with children and adolescents may provide them with a useful strategy to promote comprehension and memory of text throughout their lives.

These findings have practical implications for everyday learning. Reading comprehension is an important skill for adults to use in maintaining functional independence and quality of life. Understanding and remembering written information are useful in health maintenance and management as well as in continued learning in a variety of areas. Reading comprehension also plays an important role in managing finances and enjoying leisure and recreational activities. The structure strategy is an important strategy for younger and older adults to maintain and apply to enhance their reading performance. Further research is needed to investigate the usefulness of the structure strategy with other tasks and materials such as remembering information read on the Internet or clearly organizing and signaling a learner's own writing projects.

Acknowledgments

The research reported in this article was supported in part by National Institute of Aging Grant AG09957. As per American Psychological Association Publication Manual policy, we note that this article is one of a series developed from a large-scale, multiyear, multidisciplinary project on reading comprehension and aging, Bonnie J.F. Meyer, Principal Investigator, and Leonard W. Poon, Co-Principal Investigator. The complexity, magnitude, and scope of the data sets, analyses, and literature necessitate serial publication. We appreciate the assistance of Andrew Talbot, Cathy Hetrick, R. Allen Stubblefield, Kathy Wright, Deana Puskar, Jackie Edmondson, and Steve Shaffer, who contributed as graduate students in the Penn State University laboratory.

References

Babcock, R., & Salthouse, T. A. (1990). Effects of increased processing demands on age differences in working memory. *Psychology and Aging, 5*, 421–428.

Baddeley, A.D. (1992, January). Working memory. *Science, 255*, 556–559.

Barnett, J.E. (1984). Facilitating retention through instruction about text structure. *Journal of Reading Behavior, 16*, 1–13.

Bartlett, B.J. (1978). *Top-level structure as an organizational strategy for recall of classroom text*. Unpublished doctoral dissertation, Arizona State University.

Borgatta, E.F., & Corsini, R.J. (1964). *Manual for the quick word test*. New York: Harcourt, Brace.

Britton, B.K., Glynn, S.M., Meyer, B.J.F., & Penland, M.J. (1982). Effects of text structure on use of cognitive capacity during reading. *Journal of Educational Psychology, 74*, 51–61.

Britton, B.K., & Graesser, A.C. (1996). Five metaphors for text understanding. In B.K. Britton & A.C. Graesser (Eds.), *Models of understanding text* (pp. 341–351). Mahwah, NJ: Erlbaum.

Brooks, L.W., Dansereau, D.F., Spurlin, J.E., & Holley, C.D. (1983). Effects of headings on text processing. *Journal of Educational Psychology*, *75*, 292–302.

Cook, L.K., & Mayer, R.E. (1988). Teaching readers about the structure of scientific text. *Journal of Educational Psychology*, *80*, 448–456.

Daneman, M., & Carpenter, P.A. (1980). Individual differences in working memory and reading. *Journal of Verbal Learning and Verbal Behavior*, *19*, 450–466.

Davis, F.B. (1944). Fundamental factors in reading. *Psychometrica*, *9*, 185–197.

Dee-Lucas, D., & DiVesta, F. (1980). Learner-generated organizational aids: Effects on learning from text. *Journal of Educational Psychology*, *72*, 304–311.

Folstein, M. (1983). The Mini-Mental State Exam. In T. Crook, S. Farris, & R. Bartus (Eds.), *Assessment in geriatric psychopharmacology* (pp. 47–51). New Canaan, CT: Mark Powley.

Gernsbacher, M.A., Varner, K.R., & Faust, M. (1990). Investigating differences in general comprehension skill. *Journal of Experimental Psychology: Learning, Memory, and Cognition*, *16*, 430–445.

Gordon, C.J. (1990). Contexts for expository text structure use. *Reading Research and Instruction*, *29*, 55–72.

Grimes, J.E. (1975). *The thread of discourse.* The Hague, the Netherlands: Mouton.

Haberlandt, K. (1982). Reader expectations in text comprehension. In J.F. Le Ny & W. Kintsch (Eds.), *Language and language comprehension* (pp. 239–249). Amsterdam: North-Holland.

Hartley, J.T. (1986). Reader and text variables as determinants of discourse memory in adulthood. *Psychology and Aging*, *1*, 150–158.

Hartley, J.T. (1988). Aging and individual differences in discourse memory. In L.L. Light & D.M. Burke (Eds.), *Language, memory, and aging* (pp. 36–57). New York: Cambridge University Press.

Hultsch, D.F., Hertzog, C., Dixon, R.A., & Small, B.J. (1998). *Memory change in the aged.* New York: Cambridge University Press.

Johnson, M.M., Elsner, R.J.F., Poon, L.W., Meyer, B.J.F., Yang, B., Smith, G., et al. (1997). Building a model to test the capacity–speed hypotheses. In C.A. Noble & R.J.F. Elsner (Eds.), *An odyssey in aging: Symposia from the 1997 student convention in gerontology and geriatrics* (pp. 123–141). Athens: The University of Georgia Gerontology Center.

Johnson, M.M.S. (1993). Thinking about strategies during, before, and after making a decision. *Psychology and Aging*, *8*, 231–241.

Kintsch, W. (1998). *Comprehension: A paradigm for cognition.* New York: Cambridge University Press.

Krug, D., George, B., Hannon, S.A., & Glover, J.A. (1989). The effect of outlines and headings on readers' recall of text. *Contemporary Educational Psychology*, *14*, 111–123.

Loman, N.L., & Mayer, R.E. (1983). Signaling techniques that increase the understandability of expository prose. *Journal of Educational Psychology*, *75*, 402–412.

Lorch, R.F., Jr. (1989). Text signaling devices and their effects on reading and memory processes. *Educational Psychology Review*, *75*, 402–412.

Lorch, R.F., Jr., & Lorch, E.P. (1985). Topic structure representation and text recall. *Journal of Educational Psychology*, *77*, 137–148.

Lorch, R.F., Jr., & Lorch, E.P. (1995). Effects of organizational signals on text-processing strategies. *Journal of Educational Psychology*, *87*, 537–544.

Lorch, R.F., Jr., & Lorch, E.P. (1996). Effects of headings on text recall and summarization. *Contemporary Educational Psychology*, *21*, 261–278.

Lorch, R.F., Jr., Lorch, E.P., & Inman, W.E. (1993). Effects on signaling topic structure in text recall. *Journal of Educational Psychology*, *85*, 281–290.

Lorch, R.F., Jr., Ritchey, K., & Garrett, R. (1999). *Overdoing it: Extensive signaling of a text's topic structure interferes with recall.* Unpublished manuscript, University of Kentucky at Lexington.

Mann, W.C., & Thompson, S.A. (1986). Relational propositions in discourse. *Discourse Processes*, *9*, 57–90.

Mayer, R.E., Dyck, J.L., & Cook, L.K. (1984). Techniques that help readers build mental models from scientific text: Definitions pretraining and signaling. *Journal of Educational Psychology*, *76*, 1089–1105.

Meyer, B.J.F. (1975). *The organization of prose and its effects on memory*. Amsterdam: North-Holland.

Meyer, B.J.F. (1984). Text dimensions and cognitive processing. In H. Mandl, N. Stein, & T. Trabasso (Eds.), *Learning and understanding texts* (pp. 3–51). Hillsdale, NJ: Erlbaum.

Meyer, B.J.F. (1985a). Prose analysis: Purposes, procedures, and problems. In B.K. Britton & J. Black (Eds.), *Analyzing and understanding expository text* (pp. 11–64, 269–304). Hillsdale, NJ: Erlbaum.

Meyer, B.J.F. (1985b). Signaling the structure of text. In D.H. Jonassen (Ed.), *The technology of text* (pp. 64–89). Englewood Cliffs, NJ: Educational Technology.

Meyer, B.J.F. (1987). Following the author's top-level structure: An important skill for reading comprehension. In R. Tierney, J. Mitchell, & P. Anders (Eds.), *Understanding readers' understanding: Theory and practice* (pp. 59–76). Hillsdale, NJ: Erlbaum.

Meyer, B.J.F. (1999). The importance of text structure in everyday reading. In A. Ram & K. Moorman (Eds.), *Understanding language understanding: Computational models of reading* (pp. 227–252). Cambridge, MA: MIT Press.

Meyer, B.J.F., Brandt, D.M., & Bluth, G.J. (1980). Use of top-level structure in text: Key for reading comprehension of ninth-grade students. *Reading Research Quarterly, 16*, 72–103.

Meyer, B.J.F., Poon, L.W., & Talbot, A.P. (1999). *Minimizing age differences in reading comprehension: An examination of reading strategies, text signals, and learning tasks with various types of adult readers* (Research Rep. No. 9 of the Reading and Aging Series). University Park: The Pennsylvania State University.

Meyer, B.J.F., & Rice, G.E. (1982). The interaction of reader strategies and the organization of text. *Text, Interdisciplinary Journal for the Study of Discourse, 2*, 155–192.

Meyer, B.J.F., & Rice, G.E. (1983). Learning and memory from text across the adult life span. In J. Fine & R.O. Freedle (Eds.), *Developmental studies in discourse* (pp. 291–306). Norwood, NJ: Ablex.

Meyer, B.J.F., & Rice, G.E. (1984). The structure of text. In P.D. Pearson, R. Barr, M.L. Kamil, & P. Mosenthal (Eds.), *Handbook of reading research* (pp. 319–352). New York: Longman.

Meyer, B.J.F., & Rice, G.E. (1989). Prose processing in adulthood:. The text, the reader, and the task. In L.W. Poon, D.C. Rubin, & B.A. Wilson (Eds.), *Everyday cognition in adulthood and later life* (pp. 157–194). New York: Cambridge University Press.

Meyer, B.J.F., Russo, C., & Talbot, A. (1995). Discourse comprehension and problem solving: Decisions about the treatment of breast cancer by women across the life span. *Psychology and Aging, 10*, 84–103.

Meyer, B.J.F., & Talbot, A.P. (1998). Adult age differences in reading and remembering text and using this information to make decisions in everyday life. In M. Cecil Smith & T. Pourchot (Eds.), *Adult learning and development: Perspectives from educational psychology* (pp. 179–200). Hillsdale, NJ: Erlbaum.

Meyer, B.J.F., Talbot, A.P., & Poon, L.W. (1995). *An exploration of the effects of slow and faster computer-paced reading presented sentence by sentence in isolation or with prior context available for review on the reading comprehension and memory of young and old adults trained in the structure strategy and a long-term follow-up of this training strategy* (Research Rep. No. 2 of the Reading and Aging Series). University Park: The Pennsylvania State University.

Meyer, B.J.F., Talbot, A.P., Poon, L.W., & Johnson, M.M. (2001). Effects of structure strategy instruction on text recall in older African American adults. In J.L. Harris, A. Kamhi, & K. Pollock (Eds.), *Communication and literacy in African Americans* (pp. 233–264). Hillsdale, NJ: Erlbaum.

Meyer, B.J.F., Talbot, A.P., Stubblefield, R.A., & Poon, L.W. (1998). Interest and strategies of young and old readers differentially interact with characteristics of texts. *Educational Gerontology, 24*, 747–771.

Meyer, B.J.F., Young, C.J., & Bartlett, B.J. (1989). *Memory improved: Enhanced reading comprehension and memory across the life span through strategic text structure*. Hillsdale, NJ: Erlbaum.

Millis, K.K., & Just, M.A. (1994). The influence of connectives on sentence comprehension. *Journal of Memory and Language, 33*, 128–147.

Paris, S.G., Cross, D.R., & Lipson, M.Y. (1984). Informed strategies for learning: A program to improve children's reading awareness and comprehension. *Journal of Educational Psychology, 76*, 1239–1252.

Pintrich, P.R., Smith, D.A.F., Garcia, T., & McKeachie, W.J. (1991). *A manual for the use of the motivated strategies learning questionnaire (MSLQ)*. Ann Arbor: University of

Michigan, National Center for Research to Improve Postsecondary Teaching and Learning.

Polley, R.R. (1994). *Facilitating recall through awareness of text structure.* Unpublished master's thesis, University of Kentucky at Lexington.

Poon, L.W. (1989). The translation of laboratory findings in cognitive aging to clinical application. In O.C. Gilmore, P. Whitehouse, & M. Wykle (Eds.), *Memory, aging, and dementia: Theory, assessment, and treatment* (pp. 99–111). New York: Springer.

Pressley, M., & McCormick, C.B. (1995). *Advanced educational psychology for educators, researchers, and policymakers.* New York: HarperCollins.

Rickards, J.P., Fajen, B.R., Sullivan, J.F., & Gillespie, G. (1997). Signaling, notetaking, and field independence–dependence in text comprehension and recall. *Journal of Educational Psychology, 89,* 508–517.

Salthouse, T.A. (1985). Speed of behavior and its implications for cognition. In J.E. Birren & K.W. Schaie (Eds.), *Handbook of the psychology of aging* (2nd ed., pp. 400–426). New York: Van Nostrand Reinhold.

Salthouse, T.A., & Babcock, R.L. (1991). Decomposing adult age differences in working memory. *Developmental Psychology, 27,* 763–776,

Samuels, S.J., Tennyson, R., Sax, L., Mulcahy, P., Schermer, N., & Hajovy, H. (1988). Adults' use of text structure in the recall of a scientific journal article. *Journal of Educational Research, 81,* 171–174.

Sanchez, R.P., Lorch, E.P., & Lorch, R.F. (2001). Effects of headings on text processing strategies. *Contemporary Educational Psychology, 26,* 418–428.

Sanders, T.J.M., Spooren, W.P.M., & Noordman, L.G.M. (1992). Towards a taxonomy of coherence relations. *Discourse Processes, 15,* 1–35.

Schaie, K.W. (1996). *Intellectual development in adulthood.* New York: Cambridge University Press.

Schiefele, U. (1992). Topic interest and levels of text comprehension. In A. Renninger, S. Hidi, & A. Krapp (Eds.), *The role of interest in learning and development* (pp. 151–182). Hillsdale, NJ: Erlbaum.

Schraw, G., Bruning, R., & Svoboda, C. (1995). Sources of situational interest. *Journal of Reading Behavior, 27,* 1–17.

Slater, W.H., Graves, M.F., & Piche, G.L. (1985). Effects of structural organizers on ninth-grade students' comprehension and recall of four patterns of expository text. *Reading Research Quarterly, 20,* 189–201.

Spyridakis, J.H., & Standal, T.C. (1987). Signals in expository prose: Effects on reading. *Reading Research Quarterly, 22,* 285–298.

Taylor, B.M., & Beach, R.W. (1984). The effects of text structure instruction on middle-grade students' comprehension and production of expository text. *Reading Research Quarterly, 19,* 134–146.

Voss, J.F., & Silfies, L.N. (1996). Learning from history text: The interaction of knowledge and comprehension skill with text structure. *Cognition and Instruction, 14,* 45–68.

Wechsler, D. (1955). *Manual for the Wechsler Adult Intelligence Scale.* New York: Psychological Corporation.

Willis, S.L. (1989). Improvement with cognitive training: Which old dogs learn what trick? In L.W. Poon, D.C. Rubin, & B.A. Wilson (Eds.), *Everyday cognition in adulthood and later life* (pp. 545–569). New York: Cambridge University Press.

Wingfield, A., & Tun, P.A. (1999). Working memory and spoken language comprehension: The case of age stability in conceptual short-term memory. In S. Kemper & R. Kliegl (Eds.), *Constraints on language: Aging, grammar, and memory* (pp. 29–52). Boston: Kluwer.

Wright, K.J.A. (1998). *Nutrition education for older adults: The use of captions to improve retention of nutrition information.* Unpublished doctoral dissertation, The Pennsylvania State University, University Park.

Appendix A: Signaling Versions of the Trusts and Coal Mine Passages

Trusts Passage

With-Signaling Version. The need to distribute your property while at the same time avoiding court costs is taking form as one of the major financial problems that you must resolve before your death. At your death you want your estate to go to chosen survivors as you desired. As for court costs, avoid the need for a probate court to distribute your estate. Proceedings of a probate court can be expensive. Probate courts distribute legacies, devises of real property, and residuary property to the spouse, descendants, and charities through an attested will made by the deceased in testamentary capacity.

A related problem of equal magnitude is the need to avoid obstacles in U.S. Courts. These obstacles or hurdles in distributing your estate as you desire include delays in time, the management of your estate by the court, and state laws for equal distribution of your wealth. Proceedings of probate court have tied up estates for as long as six years, while the spouse lived without these funds. If you die without a will your estate is distributed to relatives equally.

The trust, a type of will substitute, holds great promise as the solution to these problems. There are a number of reasons why trusts hold the answer to these problems. First, trusts avoid probate court to transfer title of ownership. Trusts avoid court costs and delays. Second, they completely avoid payment to the government at death of gift taxes and estate taxes listed in the Economic Recovery Tax Act. Third, trusts enable you to control your property without legally owning it. In light of these three main assets of trusts, Lloyd Copenbarger, Pep Jackson, and others concerned with estate planning have systematically mounted an effort to distribute pamphlets to educate the public about trusts.

In establishing a trust the trustor divides the property into legal and beneficial ownership. The property transferred into a trust is called by a special term; it is called the corpus of the trust. Legal ownership is held by the trustee and beneficial ownership is held by the beneficiary. The trustee holds the legal title and the beneficiary uses the property. The trust merely divides the legal ownership from the beneficial ownership. The trustor can change the trust with provisions of a revocable living trust. Property is distributed according to the wishes of the trustor. The trustee, such as the trustor's bank, can transfer a deceased trustor's farm, part of the trust's property, to new beneficiaries. The trustor as the former beneficiary would have had the right to all benefits of the property, such as income, and the right to use the property, such as living on the farm. The trustee transfers the beneficiary rights to the farm to the new beneficiaries, such as the deceased trustor's spouse and the deceased trustor's children.

It has been mentioned that trusts avoid court costs and delays. A trust does not have a "life span." Trusts cannot die. Trusts provide transfer of property at your death to chosen individuals without court involvement. Trusts allow you to control the use of your property during your life and after your death.

Without-Signaling Version. You want to distribute your property while at the same time avoid court costs, At your death you want your estate to go to chosen survivors as you desired. As for court costs, avoid the need for a probate court to distribute your estate. Proceedings of a probate court can be expensive. Probate courts distribute legacies, devises of real property, and residuary property to the spouse, descendants, and charities through an attested will made by the deceased in testamentary capacity.

You want to avoid the obstacles in U.S. Courts. These obstacles or hurdles in distributing your estate as you desire include delays in time, the management of your estate by the court, and state laws for the equal distribution of your wealth. Proceedings of probate court have tied up estates for as long as six years. During this time the surviving spouse lived without these funds. If you die without a will your estate is distributed to relatives equally.

The trust is a type of will substitute. Trusts avoid probate court to transfer the title of ownership. Trusts avoid court costs and delays. They completely avoid payment to the government at death of gift taxes and estate taxes listed in the Economic Recovery Tax Act. Trusts enable you to control your property without legally owning it. Lloyd Copenbarger, Pep Jackson, and others concerned with estate planning have systematically mounted an effort to distribute pamphlets to educate the public about trusts.

In establishing a trust the trustor divides the property into legal and beneficial ownership. The property transferred into a trust is called by a special term; it is called the corpus of the trust. Legal ownership is held by the trustee and beneficial ownership is held by the beneficiary. The trustee holds the legal title and the beneficiary uses the property. The trust merely divides the legal ownership from the beneficial ownership. The trustor can change the trust with provisions of a revocable living trust. Property is distributed according to the wishes of the trustor. The trustee can transfer a deceased trustor's farm, part of the trust's property, to new beneficiaries; the trustee can be the bank of the trustor. The trustor as the former beneficiary would have had the right to all benefits of the property, such as income, and the right to use the property, such as living on the farm. The trustee transfers the beneficiary rights to the farm to the new beneficiaries, such as the deceased trustor's spouse and the deceased trustor's children.

Trusts avoid court costs and delays. A trust does not have a "life span." Trusts cannot die. Trusts provide transfer of property at your death to chosen individuals without court involvement. Trusts allow you to control the use of your property during your life and after your death.

Coal Mine Passage

Signaling Version. Different views about a coal mine in Australia result from different beliefs held by scientists supporting the creation model and those supporting the evolution model. Creationists interpret the coal mine as evidence of the catastrophic, Biblical flood. One reason for the creationists' interpretation is that the right pressure conditions and right heat conditions have been shown to make coal in the laboratory in one day. The Yallourn, Australia coal mine has no soil in it or near it; the mine contains 1000 cubic kilometers of brown coal. Pine logs at all angles and fossilized sea creatures are mixed together in the coal mine. The 300 meter thick seam of coal sits on clean clay; this flat layer of white clay underlies the coal. The clay is without fossilized roots. Since the creation model states that fossil graveyards were created rapidly by a worldwide flood in Noah's time, the model can easily account for the coal on top of the clean clay.

In contrast, evolutionists interpret the huge mine as an old swamp that stood at the same spot and existed years ago. However, additional theories are required to deal with the lack of soil and the clean clay bottom. Evolutionists explain that the swamp's soil must have washed away and the clean, white clay must have washed in under the coal. The evolution model states that coal was formed from peat over billions of years. As a result, evolutionists state that change must have occurred over billions of years in both the swamp and the movement of the soil and clay under the coal mine.

Without-Signaling Version. Creationists interpret a coal mine in Australia as evidence of the catastrophic, Biblical flood. The right pressure conditions and right heat conditions have been shown to make coal in the laboratory in one day. The coal mine in Yallourn, Australia has no soil in it or near it; the coal mine contains 1000 cubic kilometers of brown coal. Pine logs at all angles and fossilized sea creatures are mixed together in the coal mine. The 300 meter thick seam of coal sits on clean clay; this flat layer of white clay underlies the coal. The clay is without fossilized roots. The creation model states that fossil graveyards were created rapidly by a worldwide flood in Noah's time. The creation model can easily account for the coal on top of the clean clay.

Evolutionists interpret the huge coal mine as an old swamp that stood at the same spot and existed years ago. Additional theories are required to deal with the lack of soil and the clean clay bottom. The swamp's soil must have washed away and the clean, white clay must have washed in under the coal. The evolution model states that coal was formed from peat over billions of years. The evolutionists state that change must have occurred over billions of years in both the swamp and the movement of the soil and clay under the coal mine.

Appendix B: Sample of Materials From the Structure Strategy Training Program

Two Items From Let's Check 2 in Session 2 (Answers Underlined)

Instructions

For each of the passages underline the signaling words that cue us into the author's plan. Write the name of the plan used in the space provided. Share your answers with your partner as you finish each item.

> Despite the argument that smoking is harmful, not everyone agrees. Certainly, smoking has been related to lung cancer, high blood pressure, and loss of appetite. But, for some people smoking relieves tension.
>
> - - - - comparison - - - - - - Plan

Note. From Memory Improved: Reading and Memory Enhancement Across the Life Span Through Strategic Text Structures (p. 117), by B.J.F. Meyer, C.J. Young, and B.J. Bartlett, 1989, Hillsdale, NJ: Erlbaum. Copyright 1989 by Lawrence Erlbaum Associates, Inc.

> "Youths Turn Off on Drugs" (U.S. News & World Report, Feb. 20, 1984, p. 18). Back at the schoolyard, the young people are turning away from drugs and alcohol. A new survey for the National Institute on Drug Abuse says that the percentage of high-school seniors using marijuana 20 or more times a month dropped to 5.5 percent last year, from 6.3 in 1982. The survey found that daily alcohol use also dipped in 1983—to 5.5 percent, from 5.7 percent in '82. One big reason for the shift to clean living: Concern about health.
>
> - - - - causation - - - - - - Plan

Note. From Memory Improved: Reading and Memory Enhancement Across the Life Span Through Strategic Text Structures (pp. 117–118), by B.J.F. Meyer, C.J. Young, and B.J. Bartlett, 1989, Hillsdale, NJ: Erlbaum. Copyright 1984 by U.S. News & World Report.

Comparison Text and Problem/Solution Text Recalled During Session 4 of the Structure Strategy Training and Feedback Forms

Instructions

Work on your own reading and recalling the next two passages. Use your table (see Table 1 of the present article) with definitions of writing plans and signaling words to help you; if you find other signaling words, add them to your table. After you recall each passage, check your progress with the feedback forms provided.

The Steamboat Passage

Eastern-style steamboats became a financial success in 1807. These one-story boats operated on the Hudson River and other eastern rivers. These rivers were deep and suited perfectly the deep hulls of the eastern steamboat. The cargo was stored in these deep hulls below the main deck. The eastern steamboats used low-pressure engines. Western-style steamboats, however, were different. They churned their way up the shallow waters of the Missouri, Ohio, and Mississippi Rivers. Their hulls were flat, without room for cargo. The cargo was carried on the main deck or on the superstructure, one or two floors above the main deck. More efficient and dangerous high-pressure engines were used and often burned up to 32 cords of wood a day.

Feedback Form for the Steamboat Passage

1. Did you pick out the organization as <u>comparison</u>?

   If so, _____ great!

   If not, _____ did you ask the two questions before reading?

   _____ did you look for the plan? (contrast between eastern and western steamboats)

   _____ did you find the main idea organized by the plan? (differences in the eastern and western steamboats on the following aspects: hull depth, extent of superstructure, cargo location, and type of pressure engine)

2. Did you write the name of the plan at the top of the recall page?

   If so, _____ so far, so good!

   If not, _____ mmmmmmm!

3. Did you write down the main idea as the first sentence?

   If so, _____ keep it up!

   If not, _____ oh no!

4. Did you have two parts in arranging your sentences?

   If so, _____ not far to go now!

   If not, _____ tut, tut!

5. Were the two parts: one for the eastern steamboat and one for the western steamboat?

   If so, _____ I bet you remembered a lot!

   If not, _____ Oh rats!

6. Did you check?

   If so, _____ double smiles!

   If not, _____ don't be so overconfident!

Note. From *Memory Improved: Reading and Memory Enhancement Across the Life Span Through Strategic Text Structures* (pp. 208–209), by B.J.F. Meyer, C.J. Young, and B.J. Bartlett, 1989, Hillsdale, NJ: Erlbaum. Copyright 1989 by Lawrence Erlbaum Associates, Inc.

Rat Allergies Passage

Psychologists who work with rats and mice in experiments often become allergic to these creatures. This is a real hazard for these investigators who spend hours a week running rats in experiments. These allergies are a reaction to the protein in the urine of these small animals.

At a meeting sponsored by the National Institutes of Health, Dr. Andrew J.M. Slovak, a British physician, recommended kindness to rats and mice by the experimenters. Psychologists who pet and talk softly to their rats are less often splattered with urine and the protein that causes the allergic reaction.

Feedback Form for Rat Allergies Text

1. Did you pick out the organization as <u>problem/solution</u>?

   If so, _____ great!

   If not, _____ did you ask the two questions before reading?

   _____ did you look for the plan? (hazard of allergies to rats, evidence about the cause and suggestion to help eliminate exposure to the cause of the problem: protein in the urine)

   _____ did you find the main idea organized by the plan? (the problem of allergies to rats and mice may be solved by kindness to them since kindness reduces exposure to the cause of the problem: protein in urine)

2. Did you write the name of the plan at the top of the recall page?

   If so, _____ so far, so good!

   If not, _____ mmmmmmm!

3. Did you write down the main idea as the first sentence?

   If so, _____ keep it up!

   If not, _____ oh no!

4. Did you have two parts in arranging your sentences?

   If so, _____ not far to go now!

   If not, _____ tut, tut!

5. Were the two parts: one for the problem and one for the solution?

   If so, _____ I bet you remembered a lot!

   If not, _____ Oh rats!

6. Did you check?

   If so, _____ double smiles!

   If not, _____ don't be so overconfident!

Note. From *Memory Improved: Reading and Memory Enhancement Across the Life Span Through Strategic Text Structures* (pp. 192–193), by B.J.F. Meyer, C.J. Young, and B.J. Bartlett, 1989, Hillsdale, NJ: Erlbaum. Copyright 1989 by Lawrence Erlbaum Associates, Inc.

Appendix C: Sample of Materials and Instructions From the Interest–List Strategy Training Program

Example From Session 2

The following instructions were provided for reading the comparison text about smoking (shown in Appendix B) along with 14 other short texts: "Now that you have had practice evaluating and recalling advertisements you will get a chance to use the same procedures with short texts. Again, you will work with your partner. Read the item by yourself, then rate the article on the two items taken from the interest questionnaires you used last session (rating scale listed below). When you are finished with the evaluation, cover the article and have one member of your group tell the other all they can remember about it."

> Despite the argument that smoking is harmful, not everyone agrees. Certainly, smoking has been related to lung cancer, high blood pressure, and loss of appetite. But, for some people smoking relieves tension.

5 = Strongly Agree, 4 = Agree, 3 = Neutral, 2 = Disagree, 1 = Strongly Disagree

_____ 1. I thought the article was very interesting.

_____ 2. The article was easy to remember.

Example From Session 4

Instructions for participants stated, "For the next article, quickly scan it to determine the topic. Then rate your expected overall interest. Circle High Interest, Moderate Interest, or Low (Little to No) Interest. Once you have determined your interest use this information to take one of two steps: (1) If you circled High Interest, approach the article confidently, looking forward to reading and remembering it. (2) If your circled Moderate or Low (Little to No) Interest, try to think of a friend or relative who would be interested in the topic, and while you are reading, think of what you will be able to share with them.

Now scan the article, "The Steamboat" (see Appendix B for the text), to determine the topic. Next, rate it on interest. Circle your interest below.

HIGH INTEREST MODERATE INTEREST LOW INTEREST

Now use this information to take one of our two steps: (1) If you circled High Interest, approach the article confidently, looking forward to reading and remembering it. (2) If you circled Moderate or Low (Little to No) Interest, try to think of a friend or relative who would be interested in the topic, and while you are reading, think of what you will be able to share with them. List the name of the acquaintance you will be thinking of to motivate your thinking and enjoyment of the article. _____

Next, the steamboat article (see Appendix B) was read and recalled. This was followed by the perceived interest questionnaire (Schraw et al., 1995) and a question asking them to compare their initial reaction to the article with their final evaluation. The perceived interest questionnaire uses a 5-point scale to indicate whether a reader agrees, is neutral, or disagrees with 10 statements indicating interest in an article (e.g., "The article was one of the most interesting things I've read in a long time"; Schraw et al., 1995, p. 15).

Did your initial appraisal of the article's interest to you match your appraisal after you read and recalled the article? Please circle YES or NO.

31

Response to Literature as a Cultural Activity

Lee Galda and Richard Beach

A s recent research reviews (Beach & Hynds, 1991; Marshall, 2000; Martinez & Roser, 2002; Sipe, 1999) on response to literature demonstrate, this body of research has expanded exponentially in the past 30 years. What do we know about response and how has this knowledge changed over the years? We actually know a great deal, but the complex nature of response and the development of new theoretical perspectives on language and learning have yielded increasingly sophisticated questions about texts, readers, and contexts for response. Of equal interest is the effect that all of this research has had on what actually occurs in classrooms. How is literature treated in our schools? What insights from research might influence classroom practice in the 21st century? These are some of the questions that we consider here as we briefly review the evolution of relevant research in both response and in the enactment of response-based practices in classrooms.

The Evolution of Research on Response

From the early days of the development of theory and research on response, studies have focused on (a) text, or how various texts affect response; (b) readers, or how experiences and attitudes situated in readers affect response; and (c) the context in which response is generated. These ways of discussing literature and response remain with us today (Galda, Ash, & Cullinan, 2000; Marshall, 2000; Sipe, 1999), but the ways in which we explore texts, readers, and contexts have changed considerably since the 1970s. In this review, we discuss how earlier perceptions of texts, readers, and contexts actually prefigured later redefinitions of response research in the 1990s in sociocultural terms. These redefinitions suggest new ways of integrating literature instruction within the development of students' larger language systems.

From *Reading Research Quarterly*, *36*, 64–73. Copyright © 2001 by the International Reading Association.

Research on Text

Research on text consists primarily of content and literary analyses, including attention to the author in terms of authenticity or stance. In a few cases these analyses are conducted as a way of explaining or exploring responses to particular texts. For example, early studies such as Squire (1964) explored how the structure of text affected the responses of its readers. Responses changed at different points in the text, such as the climax. More recent research on text, such as Nodelman's (1988) study of the narrative art of picture books, uses semiotic analysis to explore how picture books convey a narrative to children who are constructing that narrative as they read. Stephens's (1992) exploration of ideology in children's fiction uses critical linguistics and narrative theory to demonstrate how texts work to situate child readers in both implicit and explicit ideologies.

For example, authors assume a stance toward the ideologies and societal norms that they portray, that is, either assenting to, advocating, or attacking the characters' sociocultural practices (Sutherland, 1985). Readers may then interrogate texts for their authenticity in terms of whether the social norms portrayed actually represent a culture, as well as the author's stance regarding these social norms (Cai, 1997). Readers may also challenge the author's authority to construct these cultural representations, particularly multicultural literature for children and young adults (Cai, 1997; Harris, 1994; Sims, 1984). Interestingly, many, but not all, studies of text and ideology privilege the importance of text features over the reader in the literary transaction. That is, they assume that their own individual constructions of text are definitive, and allow little room for alternative constructions.

Researchers have also examined how readers acquire knowledge of literary conventions that allows them to interpret the symbolic meaning of various text cues (Hunt & Vipond, 1991; Mackey, 1997; Rabinowitz & Smith, 1998). Through extensive reading within a particular literary genre or form, readers acquire knowledge of conventions for (a) understanding meaning of titles, names, beginnings, and endings; (b) predicting story outcomes; or (c) defining how texts cohere around thematic points. The unresolved developmental question is whether readers acquire this interpretive know-how simply through reading or through active participation in formulating interpretations with others in communities whose members share knowledge of these conventions (Svensson, 1990).

Research on Readers

Just as texts are created within and with ideologies that assume discourse contexts that privilege particular roles and social practices, so, too are readers. Research on readers has evolved in much the same fashion as research on text. Early research looked at expectations, attitudes, and practices of readers with little or no regard of how they were developed through participation in communities of practice. For example, Galda (1982) characterized the responses of 3 fifth-grade girls in a way that highlighted their distinctive styles, and Hancock

(1993) explored the response styles of 4 sixth-grade students, but neither explored how those styles might have been developed. Other research goes beyond these studies to situate individual style within social practices. Sims (1983), for example, linked response to culture in her case study of a young African American girl's responses to books by and about African Americans. Sipe (1998) described how 4 first and second graders differed considerably in the responses they offered during story time discussions. One reader was very logical, using close textual analysis and intertextual references to bolster her arguments during read-aloud time; another used texts to generate creative activities. A third reader often talked about themes that he perceived; a fourth used stories as springboards for his own performances. McGinley and Kamberelis (1996) also presented rich descriptions of 2 third- and fourth-grade readers who vary considerably in style in terms of how they use their reading. One used his literary experience to help him understand the community in which he lived, the other to help her imagine her future. Studies such as these are examples of how research has come to explore how response styles might be connected to readers' lives both within and beyond the classroom.

Researchers have also explored how readers' expectations for characters' actions influence their responses. Readers have expectations for how people ought to behave, expectations that are shaped by the cultures in which they live and work. These expectations hold true for characters' behaviors as well, as many readers treat characters as people regardless of the fact that they exist only in the literary transaction (Mellor & Patterson, 2000). Ample research has described how even young children become involved with characters, often comparing character action and feeling with their own (Hancock, 1993; McGee, 1992). Preschool children are more likely to adopt imaginative modes of response in responding to fantasy picture books than in responding to realistic or informational picture books (Shine & Roser, 1999).

However, not all readers respond positively to the characters they are reading about. Early research (Galda, 1982) discovered that readers rejected the actions of characters when those actions did not correspond to their own lived experience. Enciso (1994) connected this type of response to cultural practice when she documented how some readers might resist or reject a text that does not reflect their cultural expectations. Suburban high school students adopted a stance of resistance to multicultural literature given their reluctance to explore issues of racism and white privilege within their suburban culture (Beach, 1997b).

These responses also take the form of resisting the social norms readers perceive operating in a text or classroom. Students may resist invited stances and dominate discourses in ways that lead them to create their own versions of texts (Lewis, 1997). They may affirm or reject an author's or teacher's stance. For example, in responding to multicultural literature, students may adopt a stance of resistance to the assumption that a book such as *Maniac Magee* (Spinelli, 1991) is being used didactically to discuss race issues (Enciso, 1997).

Other research has explored the types of intertextual connections that individual readers make between texts and their life experiences and/or other texts (Bloome & Egan-Robertson, 1993; Cochran-Smith, 1984; Short, 1992; Sipe, 1998; Sumara, 1996). Students make those intertextual connections fostered in the classroom—links defined in terms of shared topics, themes, issues, or stances, which are also connected to the social and cultural practices that surround them.

More recently, researchers have attended to how readers' responses reflect their cultural models or discourses (Beach, 1997b; Gee, 2000). In one such study (Beach, 1995), students in advanced and regular 10th- and 11th-grade classes wrote responses to a story about advanced and regular high school characters. The advanced and regular students differed in their responses to the story, differences reflecting their cultural models of schooling associated with the ability grouping system and student motivation. The advanced students attributed the fact that the story's main character was a regular student to their perception of him as unmotivated, lazy, and lacking social skills. The regular students perceived the regular student character as satisfied with being in the regular class and not having to cope with the challenges of an advanced class. Through their responses, they were reifying their allegiances to their separate ability-grouping worlds in which language or discourses are used for different purposes.

Another study demonstrated how differences in responses can reflect differences in students' sociocultural experiences related to socioeconomic class. In a comparison of working class versus middle class high school students' responses to poetry, Hemphill (1999) found that working class students focused more on speakers' actions and thoughts, while middle class students focused more on thematic meanings consistent with the goals of literature instruction.

The differences in response in these studies (Beach, 1995; Hemphill, 1999) reflect a larger sociocultural participation in class-based communities of practice in which working class adolescents use literacy to report on immediate interpersonal interactions and conflicts while upper middle class adolescents use literacy to judge and categorize others according to institutional norms (Gee & Crawford, 1998). This research suggests interesting connections between the language used to construct text worlds and the language used to construct readers' lived worlds as well, connections that lead beyond readers and texts into an exploration of contexts, large and small.

Research on Contexts

In the past decade, increasing numbers of studies have explored how teaching practice and classroom context shape responses by the sometimes implicit set of rules and expectations that govern how literature is enacted in a particular classroom or culture. Fish (1980) described how the interpretive community in which readers existed shaped the strategies of individual readers. Hickman (1981) documented the influence of classroom context, especially teacher practice, on response. Others, such as Many and Wiseman (1992), O'Flahavan (1989), and Raphael and McMahon (1994), described how instructional practices enacted by the teacher serve to set the agenda for a class, guiding not only how students respond but also how they read. These and other studies reflect the trend toward an exploration of the larger sociocultural contexts that surround reading and responding.

Texts were once considered discrete entities containing an unchanging meaning that a careful reader could discover. Readers were seen as individuals, pursuing individual interests, perspectives, and practices. Contexts were considered immediate: this book club, that classroom. The sociocultural frame has complicated and expanded these notions. Texts, readers, and contexts, each inseparable from the other, are also inseparable from the larger contexts in which they are enacted. This suggests that the research agenda for the next few years will involve exploring the multifaceted sociocultural nature of response and what that means for instruction.

Blurring the Boundaries: Exploring Sociocultural Perspectives on Texts, Readers, and Contexts

Literary response researchers in the 1990s have focused increasingly on response not simply as a transaction between texts and readers but as a construction of text meaning and reader stances and identities within larger sociocultural contexts. Readers, texts, and contexts are studied as constituted by culture and history. These researchers adopt a range of disciplinary perspectives—sociolinguistic (Beach & Phinney, 1998; Bloome & Egan-Robertson, 1993), dialogic (Kamberelis & Scott, 1992; Knoeller, 1998), genre (Hunt, 1994; Kucan & Beck, 1996; Pappas & Pettegrew, 1998), poststructuralist (Mellor & Patterson, 2000), semiotic (Smagorinsky & O'Donnell-Allen, 1998), phenomenological (Mackey, 1997; Sumara, 1996), performance theory (Lewis, 1997), critical discourse analysis (Beach, 1997a), or critical/postcolonial theory (Blake, 1998; Singh & Greenlaw, 1998)—to examine how texts, readers, contexts, and stances are constructed through language, genres, signs, images, or discourses. In doing so, they reflect a key tenet of a sociocultural theory of learning (Cole, 1996; Engeström, 1987; Engeström, Miettinen, & Punamäki, 1999; Leont'ev, 1978) that defines learning as occurring through participation in a joint, collective activity mediated by cultural tools (Wells, 1999; Wenger, 1999; Wertsch, 1998). This implies that students learn to respond to literature as they acquire various social practices, identities, and tools not only through participation in interpretive communities of practice but also through experience in acquiring social practices and tools and in constructing identities within specific cultural worlds (Hynds, 1997; Sumara, 1996; Wilhelm, 1997).

Researchers who are studying changes in students' ability to use language, genres, signs, images, or discourses as tools to represent their experiences with texts need to examine how students acquire interpretive and social practices over time through participation in particular types of communities of practice. Examining research on response across grade levels can begin to help us understand how readers develop these abilities (Svensson, 1990), and how teachers can help students critically reflect on how the language of their own responses reflects not only construction of worlds in a text but also their own lived worlds.

Constructing Texts as Cultural Worlds

In constructing texts as cultural worlds, readers are learning to interpret characters' actions within larger frameworks of worlds or activity systems constituted by cultural or ideological forces (Engeström, 1987). Moving beyond a focus on individual characters to a consideration of the systems that shape the characters, the author's construction of them, and the readers themselves can help readers consider how lives reflect social forces and how individuals can influence these taken-for-granted practices. As Edelsky (1999) noted,

> Studying systems—how they work and to what end—focusing on systems of influence, systems of culture, systems of gender relations...being critical means questioning against the frame of system, seeing individuals as always within systems, as perpetuating or resisting systems. Being noncritical...means seeing individuals as outside of...[and] separate from systems and therefore separate from culture and history. (p. 28)

Given their attentiveness to cues implying narrative conflict (Rabinowitz & Smith, 1998), readers note tensions between status quo systems that serve to protect existing systems and potential systems that emerge out of the creation of new tools or objects that challenge these status quo systems (Beach, 2000). As Bruner (1990) observed, narratives "mediate between the canonical world of culture and the more idiosyncratic work of beliefs, dreams, and hopes" (p. 52). In describing his own response to the novel *Adventures of Huckleberry Finn*, Engeström (1987) perceived Huck as initially operating in a status quo middle class, small-town, racist system associated with the world of Tom Sawyer. When Huck and Jim go down the river on the raft and enter into a world in which slavery still operates, they mutually construct a potential system "of radical moral anarchism [that] makes Huck a personality of entirely different dimensions from that of Tom Sawyer. For Tom, freeing Jim is a safe, imaginary adventure.... For Huck, it is a deadly serious moral and existential struggle" (p. 183). As Huck and Jim acquire new tools—the use of language, parody, and discourses of freedom—they construct an alternative, potential system (Engeström, 1987).

In responding to texts at the level of activity, students learn to go beyond the usual pedagogical focus on inferring characters' acts or dialogue (what is the character doing or saying), beliefs (what do characters believe about each other), and goals and motivations (what is the character trying to accomplish and why) to interpret and contextualize characters' actions or dialogue as involving various social practices within activities (Beach, 2000). These social practices include (a) defining/constructing identities, (b) including/excluding/positioning others, (c) building relationships, (d) influencing others' actions or beliefs, (e) representing/serving institutions/systems, (f) establishing group allegiances/stances, (g) coping with conflicts/differences, (h) engaging in shared rituals, or (i) constructing/sharing knowledge. By inferring these social practices, students are interpreting how characters' dialogue or actions function or serve as social agendas (Mosenthal, 1998) designed to fulfill the objects or motives driving activity systems. As Gee (2000) noted, people (and characters) are recognized as having certain agendas or being certain kinds of persons through their uses of language or discourses. Stephens (1992) suggested that even in the elementary grades, readers should be taught how to assume an interrogative stance toward the texts they read.

To contextualize characters' acts as trees within the larger forest of object-driven activity systems, readers draw on their own experiences with act/object relationships in lived-world activity systems. For example, in responding to a story portraying a high school English teacher's highly personal reaction to a student's essay, a group of English teachers enrolled in a graduate methods course interpreted the teacher and student as caught within a range of competing systems by drawing on their own participation in the worlds of the methods course, their experiences as teachers, and their own families (Beach, 2000).

Readers also contextualize characters' acts by drawing on historical knowledge of past cultural perspectives and models. For example, in responding to the novel *The Great Gatsby* (Fitzgerald, 1953), high school students contextualized Gatsby's actions of acquiring wealth and status in order to woo Daisy away from Tom within the larger rags-to-riches system of accumulating wealth in the U.S. capitalism system, a system at odds with Daisy and Tom's system of inherited wealth (Beach & Phinney, 1998). The students drew on their knowledge of U.S. history and culture to interpret Gatsby's actions as driven by the objects of accumulating new wealth.

Constructing Identities Through Participation in Worlds

A sociocultural perspective also suggests teaching students to perceive characters as constructed through language and discourses (Mellor & Patterson, 2000; Smagorinsky & O'Donnell-Allen, 1998). Students would draw on their own expectations for appropriate lived-world language practices to interpret characters' social practices, expectations that are shaped by the cultures in which they live and work. They also use these cultural expectations to detect violations dramatizing unusual, extraordinary events central to narrative development or a story's tellability or point (Labov, 1972). For example, a student may draw on lived-world experience with language to infer that the fact that a character's consistent bragging about his accomplishments may be seen as a violation of conventions operating in a particular text world as suggested by other characters' reactions to his bragging.

Readers also draw on their own experiences as persons acquiring social practices constituting identities and competence in lived worlds to interpret characters' own development as participants in text worlds (Athanases, 1998; Kamberelis & Scott, 1992). Second-grade readers (Galda, Rayburn, & Stanzi, 2000) used what they knew about their own varied family structures to make inferences about a character's relationship with his father. Adolescents, socialized to adopt certain social practices and discourses constituting participation in the world of romance (Christian-Smith, 1993; Finders, 1997; Willinsky & Hunniford, 1986), use their knowledge of romance as they read and respond to romance novels.

Readers also rely on their participation in text worlds as forms of socialization for participation in lived worlds, for example in reading romance novels (Christian-Smith, 1993; Radway, 1984). In some cases, adolescents resist the romance-world cultural model (Holland & Eisenhart, 1990) by adopting alternative, feminist discourses acquired through participation in different lived worlds (Alvermann, Commeyras, Young, Randall, & Hinson, 1997; Harper, 2000). In one study of early adolescent females' responses to young adult adolescent novels, participants adopted stances of resistance and roles consistent with practices associated with the "bad-" or "good-girl" characters by publicly adopting deviant practices associated with being the bad girl, for example, by walking across the tops of chairs in the school library (Enciso, 1998).

Younger readers do the same. McGinley and Kamberelis (1996) documented how third- and fourth-grade readers use the books they read to better understand their own lived worlds. One third-grade boy used *Maniac Magee* (Spinelli, 1991) to think about his own home community as plagued by the same kinds of social problems depicted in the novel.

Sharing Responses Through Tools

Readers employ language, genres, signs, images, drama, visual art, or discourses as tools to share responses in communities of practice—such as classrooms, computer chat rooms, or book clubs (Eeds & Wells, 1989; Marshall, Smagorinsky, & Smith, 1995; Raphael & McMahon, 1994). Becoming members of these communities of practice entails learning to successfully employ uses of these tools consistently with a community's objects/motives, roles, norms, beliefs, or traditions (Engeström, 1987; Wertsch, 1998).

Because these tools are used for social shared thinking (Rogoff & Toma, 1997), participants collaboratively construct "coherent beliefs" by "reasoning together rather than against one another" (Smithson & Dias, 1996, p. 255).

Shared thinking also involves being open to disagreement, respecting differences of opinion, and verifying the validity of one's tentative passing theories (Kent, 1993) through triangulation with others' passing theories (Alvermann, Young, & Green, 1997; Hunt, 1994).

Through participation in discussions, students acquire the language and genres that enhance their level of participation and their use of response strategies valued in different types of discussions—small-group or whole-class, student- or teacher-led discussions. Research shows that many types of discussion are valuable, depending on the desired outcome. Small-group discussion without the teacher, for example, can allow students to work together to resolve cognitive conflicts (Almasi, 1995) or develop strategies that lead to successful discussions (Vinz, Gordon, Hamilton, LaMontagne, & Lundgren, 2000). Small-group discussion is the key component of the Book Club program developed by Raphael and colleagues (McMahon, Raphael, Goatley, & Pardo, 1997). This research demonstrated the importance of students having the opportunity to control the content and the flow of discussion. Students were responsible for bringing ideas to the discussion and for asking for and providing clarification during discussion. In Book Club, however, there was also a large-group discussion that was led by the teacher as this provided the opportunity to model strategies, raise issues that students did not raise themselves, clear up confusions, and link to thematic content.

One advantage of teacher-led discussions is that teachers can demonstrate the use of language and genre tools within the students' zone of proximal development (Wells, 1999). For example, Eeds and Wells (1989) described how adult members of literature discussion groups can facilitate discussions to turn them into grand conversations about literature by encouraging student responses, highlighting important student-made points, and demonstrating literate talk by using literary labels such as conflict or plot. Other research (McGee, 1992; McGee, Courtney, & Lomax, 1994) shows how teachers facilitate discussion by helping children focus on topics and clarify contributions, nudge children toward new perspectives, and sometimes act as literary curators, often by posing questions that call for interpretation. When teachers did pose such questions, student discussions reflected an increase in interpretive responses. In a yearlong study of literature discussion in a second-grade classroom, Galda et al. (2000) documented the development of response strategies as mediated by teacher demonstration and explicit instruction. From the early years onward, readers' response strategies are shaped by their communities of practice.

Teachers also can model the uses of language and genre tools involved in (a) posing questions or hypotheses; (b) relating these questions/hypotheses to relevant aspects in the text and their own real-world experiences; (c) generating explanations or interpretations; and (d) critiquing characters and their own beliefs or ideologies shaping perceptions of these concerns, dilemmas, or issues. They may also use informal writing as a tool to assist students in formulating these questions or hypotheses prior to or during discussions, writing that is then read aloud to frame the direction of discussion. Sharing writing that discloses students' own conflicted, alternative interpretations as tentative passing theories (Kent, 1993) serves to invite other students to describe similar tensions in their interpretations. By framing their interpretations as tentative, students are implying the need for further verification—agreements or disagreements—from their peers (Smithson & Dias, 1996). In one study, these disagreements around alternative interpretations resulted in extended stretches, that is, a series of turns by different students with a consistent focus on the same topic or issue (Beach, Eddleston, & Philippot, 2001).

Many elementary teachers use literature journals to help their students express their thoughts during or after reading, and most often before discussion, seeing writing as a way to organize for the discussion (Martinez, Roser, Hoffman, & Battle, 1992; McMahon et al., 1997). It seems that elementary-grade students' responses are both organized and broadened by the opportunity to write. Writing serves to help them think through what they want to express, and experience with various writing prompts gives them access to different ways to think and talk about texts.

The teacher's modeling also provides students with a metalinguistic framework for talking about and reflecting on their uses of language and genres (Hunt, 1994; Wells, 1999). Children in elementary school devote a considerable amount of time to metatalk about their own purposes and strategies (Almasi, Anderson, Russell, & Guthrie, 1998; Galda et al., 2000; Raphael & McMahon, 1994). Second-grade students in a teacher-led literature discussion group often commented on their own behavior and language during discussion as well as the language used by characters in the books they were reading (Galda et al., 2000). From research on high school students' literature discussions, Vinz et al. (2000) found that students are more likely to acquire these discussion strategies when they are given responsibility to direct or lead discussions, although studies of younger students highlight the importance of the teacher in the development of these strategies. That these strategies are important and develop through authentic talk about text is, however, clearly documented from the primary grades through high school.

Unfortunately, although research has affirmed the importance of authentic talk about text in the development of sophisticated, engaged readers, practice has lagged. Most classrooms still rely on the repetitive pattern of teacher question, student response, teacher evaluation (Mehan, 1979). In a recent study based on an extensive analysis of many classroom discussions, Nystrand (1999) found that only about 15% of instruction in more than 100 middle and high school classes involved the use of authentic questions with no predetermined answers or following up on students' answers. There was little dialogic interaction:

Dialogic shifts are rare, occurring in less than 7% of all instructional episodes observed. One striking finding is the virtual absence of dialogic shifts among low track classes: There were only 2 dialogic shifts in the 197 instructional episodes we observed, no doubt a result of emphasis on skill development and test

questions about prior reading. Quite simply, lower track students have little opportunity for engaged discussions. This is particularly important in light of our findings that dialogic classroom discourse increases student achievement. (p. 2)

While all of this research on discussion demonstrates that students can
learn to ask and answer important questions, advance their hypotheses, and listen
to and learn from others, having discussions for their own intrinsic sake may not
engage all students (Hynds, 1997; Miller & Legge, 1999). In the elementary
grades this might be called thematic or integrated instruction as teachers and
students work together to develop coherence around a variety of texts and tasks.
Embedding discussion within larger contexts of inquiry about topics, themes, or
issues of concern to students and teachers as co-inquirers provides some larger
purpose for the discussion (Beach & Myers, 2001).

Teachers can participate as co-inquirers by recognizing how students, as
first-time readers, adopt a different stance than teachers, who are responding on
the basis of multiple rereadings of a text and thematic patterns extracted from
those readings (Rabinowitz & Smith, 1998). It also entails "dis-positioning ourselves as learners, teachers, readers—continually learning to un-know what we
believe, what worked for us in the past, and what made sense in other teaching
or learning situations" (Vinz et al., 2000, p. 148). It means being honest and tentative in discussions, responding as a reader as well as a teacher, and being responsive to the ideas of the students. When student responses are central to the
classroom, then every time a text is read it becomes a new text, the unique construction of a particular group of readers.

In addition to learning to use discussion as a tool to think about text, students may also use writing, images, or graphics in drawings, cut-out figures, or
hypermedia computer productions as tools for rewriting texts, parodying texts, or
creating new versions of texts (Enciso, 1994, 1998; McKillop & Myers, 2000;
Pope, 1995; Smagorinsky & O'Donnell-Allen, 1998; Whitin, 1996). For example, in responding to Toni Morrison's (1994) *The Bluest Eye*, high school students reacted negatively to the idea that the African American characters in the
book would be limited to reading Dick and Jane books as cultural models of
white privilege (Beach, Kalnin, & Leer, 2001). They then used images, language,
and narrative as tools to create their own alternative children's books designed for
the main character, Pecola, that portrayed a world more consistent with her experience and needs. Or students construct their own hypertext versions of texts,
including thematic or lexical annotations; intertextual links to other related texts;
or paths and trails to related themes, topics, biographical information, or historical background (Cornis-Pope, 2000). For example, high school students used
images, photos, video clips, or songs to construct Web-based hypertext responses to stories about love, family, and peer relationships (see examples at
www.ed.psu.edu/k-12/teenissues, Beach & Myers, 2001).

Analysis of seventh graders' hypermedia responses to poetry found that students used images, clips, songs, or other texts as iconic signs to simply illustrate the poem's meaning by, for example, selecting an image that illustrated the poem (McKillop & Myers, 2000). In other cases, they selected texts that, when juxtaposed with the poem, created a new third meaning that served to extend or interrogate the poem's meaning. Preservice college students in a Newfoundland university developed Web-based hypermedia projects to interrogate and resist what they perceived as stereotypical portrayals of their province in the novel *The Shipping News* (Proulx, 1993) (see http://lord.educ.mun.ca/educ41421/; Barrell & Hammett, 1999). Primary-grade students encouraged to draw their images of the stories they were reading became quite involved in what they were reading and used their drawings to begin conversations around the texts. All of this points to the ways in which hypermedia texts and images serve as tools for mediating literary interpretation.

Pedagogical Possibilities: Middle School Students' Response to a Young Adult Novel

We have argued that the meaning of students' responses is grounded in cultural and historical worlds, activity systems, and tools, and suggested the value of instruction based on developmentally appropriate inquiry about the worlds or systems portrayed in literature as well as students' own related experiences. To illustrate how this approach plays out in the classroom, we describe activities involved in inquiry projects conducted by a group of 15 seventh-grade females who volunteered to meet in an after-school group called The Girls' Book Club organized by Sarah Gohman, a middle school teacher at Wayzata Middle School, Wayzata, Minnesota (Beach & Myers, 2001). The focus of their inquiry project was the social world of the Middle Ages as portrayed in the Newbery Honor novel *Catherine, Called Birdy* (Cushman, 1994), which portrays the life of an adolescent female, Catherine, whose father wants to marry her off to an older suitor whom she despises.

Organizing Instruction Around Concerns, Issues, and Dilemmas

Much of literature instruction is currently organized around predetermined topics or themes, which students then use to frame their responses to literature. The sociocultural perspective suggests that learning is more likely to occur when students are grappling with the conflicts, tensions, and dilemmas endemic to shifting or competing worlds portrayed in texts (Mosenthal, 1998). As they respond to texts, students may identify concerns, issues, or dilemmas portrayed in texts or derived from students' own experiences. The fact that they are bothered or disturbed by these concerns, issues, or dilemmas operating in worlds or systems enhances their engagement with inquiry about these worlds or systems. To help students understand the worlds portrayed in the novel, the students first studied specific aspects of medieval life—such as the feudal system, the life of lords and peasants, the church, and education. They then read and shared their responses to *Catherine, Called Birdy* in dialogue journal entries.

Many students were concerned with Catherine's treatment as a female by her authoritarian father and his attempting to marry her off against her wishes. One student noted,

> They [women] were not allowed very much freedom at all and could be abused by men. The roles they played were those of not very smart or talented people, although they might have been as smart or smarter than the men, given the chance to learn...they didn't get educated because it was considered a waste because they were women.

They were particularly perplexed by the issue of the role religion played in politics and were baffled that people were physically punished for not believing in Roman Catholicism. They wondered about how people would learn to truly understand the teachings of the Bible if they weren't allowed to question its meaning. Framing their responses in terms of issues meant that they then wanted to explore larger social and political forces shaping characters' lives. They also wanted to connect issues relevant to the medieval period to current issues of the role of the church and religion, gender status, and education.

Contextualizing the World of the Novel

We have argued for the need for students to go beyond inferences about characters' actions to contextualize these acts as social practices within larger cultural worlds. Students contextualized the characters' acts in the novel in terms of purposes, roles, rules, beliefs, and history operating in the worlds of the novel. For example, in responding to Catherine's family world and the conflict between Catherine and her father, they examined how that conflict stemmed from the family's sense of purpose, the roles family members assign to each other, the rules governing decision making in the family, or beliefs about power and privilege in the family. In all of this, they were focusing on more than just individual characters; they were examining the operation of social worlds as systems. For example, the students compared the roles of females in the medieval world with females in the contemporary world. They constructed a comparison chart, listing aspects of the medieval world on one side and paired aspects of the modern world on the other side. These pairings helped them understand that while women were largely subordinated during the medieval period, such subordination continues still in contemporary society. And, in studying the prevailing beliefs of that period, they, as one student reported in a written log, "were appalled that girls were told who they must marry." They were also disturbed by the fact that Catherine's father beat her regularly. They were upset by "the lack of opportunity for women during this time period."

Critiquing and Transforming Worlds

Based on their contextualizing of the medieval world, the students then interrogated the common-sense, taken-for-granted assumptions underlying that world, asking questions about the objects or motives driving that world such as "Why are people doing this?" or "What is the purpose for this practice?" Then to envision ways of transforming their current world, pairs of students each identified a topic related to women in present-day society: single-sex classrooms, women in the military, the Equal Rights Amendment, girls, sports and Title IX, mail-order brides, comparing women in different cultures, historical women, women during war, the media and females, glass ceilings, and super moms. For example, one group studied the role of advertising related to body weight. They gathered data on the use of thin models in advertising to portray an unrealistic perception of body weight, leading to their critique of these ads. The students then presented their findings to a group of sixth-grade females for the purpose of helping transform these sixth graders' beliefs about women's roles in society. Making these presentations served to bolster their own sense of self-efficacy as having expertise about women's roles, itself a transformative practice. Through experiences such as this with literature in schools, students have the opportunity to access their full potential as readers who can create and transform worlds.

Summary

Research has helped practice get to this possibility. Having built on earlier work, research today is well beyond simple notions of texts, readers, and contexts. Researchers today who study response from a sociocultural frame take for granted the complexities of the reader–text transaction that is embedded in multiple worlds. Teachers, too, recognize the care with which this transaction must be negotiated in the classroom—itself a conflicted cultural world. What teachers say and do, the texts they choose and how they choose them, and the tasks they set for their students all affect this transaction. While teachers can help students develop specific tools to use as they read and respond in a particular classroom, the cultural tools that students bring to the classroom remain varied, sometimes closely aligned to those sanctioned by the teacher, sometimes in opposition. By creating opportunities for students to read and respond in the company of others, teachers foster their students' ability to make sense of text worlds and lived worlds. By encouraging 8-year-olds to make connections between their own experiences and experiences of characters in the books they read, or giving 16-year-olds the tools they need to explore how they and the characters they are reading about are constituted by their cultures, teachers make it possible for students to use their responses to school-sanctioned text to construct and critique their worlds.

References

Almasi, J.F. (1995). The nature of fourth graders' sociocognitive conflicts in peer-led and teacher-led discussions of literature. *Reading Research Quarterly, 30,* 314–351.

Almasi, J.F., Anderson, E., Russell, W.S., & Guthrie, J.T. (1998, December). *Scaffold to nowhere? Appropriated voice, metatalk, and personal narrative in third graders' peer discussions of informational text.* Paper presented at the annual meeting of the National Reading Conference, Austin, TX.

Alvermann, D.E., Commeyras, M., Young, J.P., Randall, S., & Hinson, D. (1997). Interrupting gendered discursive practices in classroom talk about texts: Easy to think about, difficult to do. *Journal of Literacy Research, 29,* 73–104.

Alvermann, D.E., Young, J.P., & Green, C. (1997). *Adolescents' negotiations of out-of-school reading discussions.* Athens, GA: National Reading Research Center.

Athanases, S.Z. (1998). Diverse learners, diverse texts: Exploring identity and difference through literary encounters. *Journal of Literacy Research, 30,* 273–296.

Barrell, B., & Hammett, R. (1999). Hypermedia as a medium for textual resistance. *English in Education, 33,* 21–30.

Beach, R. (1995). Constructing cultural models through response to literature. *English Journal, 84,* 87–94.

Beach, R. (1997a). Critical discourse theory and reader response: How discourses constitute reader stances and social contexts. *Reader, 37,* 1–26.

Beach, R. (1997b). Students' resistance to engagement in responding to multicultural literature. In T. Rogers & A.O. Soter (Eds.), *Reading across cultures: Teaching literature in a diverse society* (pp. 69–94). New York: Teachers College Press.

Beach, R. (2000). Reading and responding at the level of activity. *Journal of Literacy Research, 32,* 237–251.

Beach, R., Eddleston, S., & Philippot, R. (2001). *Enhancing large-group literature discussions.* Unpublished manuscript, University of Minnesota, Minneapolis.

Beach, R., & Hynds, S. (1991). Research on response to literature. In R. Barr, M.L. Kamil, P. Mosenthal, & P.D. Pearson (Eds.), *Handbook of reading research* (Vol. 2, pp. 453–491). White Plains, NY: Longman.

Beach, R., Kalnin, J., & Leer, E. (2001). *High school students' construction of literary worlds.* Unpublished manuscript, University of Minnesota, Minneapolis.

Beach, R., & Myers, J. (2001). *Inquiry-based English instruction: Engaging students in life and literature.* New York: Teachers College Press.

Beach, R., & Phinney, M.Y. (1998). Framing literary text worlds through real-world social negotiation. *Linguistics and Education, 9,* 159–198.

Blake, B.E. (1998). "Critical" reader response in an urban classroom: Creating cultural texts to engage diverse readers. *Theory Into Practice, 37,* 238–243.

Bloome, D., & Egan-Robertson, A. (1993). The social construction of intertextuality in a classroom reading and writing lessons. *Reading Research Quarterly, 28,* 304–333.

Bruner, J.S. (1990). *Acts of meaning.* Cambridge, MA: Harvard University Press.

Cai, M. (1997). Reader response theory and the politics of multicultural literature. In T. Rogers & A.O. Soter (Eds.), *Reading across cultures: Teaching literature in a diverse society* (pp. 199–212). New York: Teachers College Press.

Christian-Smith, L.K. (1993). *Texts of desire: Essays on fiction, femininity and schooling.* London: Falmer.

Cochran-Smith, M. (1984). *The making of a reader.* Norwood, NJ: Ablex.

Cole, M. (1996). *Cultural psychology: A once and future discipline.* Cambridge, MA: Harvard University Press.

Cornis-Pope, M. (2000). Hypertextual and networked communication in undergraduate literature classes: Strategies for an interactive critical pedagogy. In D. Hickey & D. Reiss (Eds.), *Learning literature in an era of change: Innovations in teaching* (pp. 152–167). Sterling, VA: Stylus.

Cushman, K. (1994). *Catherine, called Birdy.* New York: HarperCollins.

Edelsky, C. (1999). On critical whole language practices: Why, what, and a bit of how. In C. Edelsky (Ed.), *Making justice our project: Teachers working toward critical whole language practice* (pp. 7–36). Urbana, IL: National Council of Teachers of English.

Eeds, M., & Wells, D. (1989). Grand conversations: An exploration of meaning construction in literature study groups. *Research in the Teaching of English, 23,* 4–29.

Enciso, P.E. (1994). Cultural identity and response to literature. *Language Arts, 71,*
524–533.

Enciso, P.E. (1997). Negotiating the meaning of
difference: Talking back to multicultural literature. In T. Rogers & A.O. Soter (Eds.),
*Reading across cultures: Teaching literature
in a diverse society* (pp. 13–41). New York:
Teachers College Press.

Enciso, P.E. (1998). Good/bad girls read together: Pre-adolescent girls' co-authorship of
feminine subject positions during a shared
event reading. *English Education, 30,* 44–62.

Engeström, Y. (1987). *Learning by expanding:
An activity-theoretical approach to developmental research.* Helsinki: Orienta-Konsultit.

Engeström, Y., Miettinen, R. & Punamäki, R.
(Eds.). (1999). *Perspectives on activity theory.* New York: Cambridge University Press.

Finders, M.J. (1997). *Just girls: Hidden literacies and life in junior high.* New York:
Teachers College Press.

Fish, S. (1980). *Is there a text in this class? The
authority of interpretive communities.*
Cambridge, MA: Harvard University Press.

Fitzgerald, F.S. (1953). *The great Gatsby.* New
York: Scribners.

Galda, L. (1982). Assuming the spectator stance:
An examination of the responses of three
young readers. *Research in the Teaching of
English, 16,* 1–20.

Galda, L., Ash, G.E., & Cullinan, B.E. (2000).
Children's literature. In M.L. Kamil, P.B.
Mosenthal, P.D. Pearson, & R. Barr (Eds.),
Handbook of reading research (Vol. 3, pp.
361–379). Mahwah, NJ: Erlbaum.

Galda, L., Rayburn, J.S., & Stanzi, L.C. (2000).
*Looking through the faraway end: Creating
a literature-based reading curriculum with
second graders.* Newark, DE: International
Reading Association.

Gee, J.P. (2000). Discourse and sociocultural
studies in reading. In M.L. Kamil, P.B.
Mosenthal, P.D. Pearson, & R. Barr (Eds.),
Handbook of reading research (Vol. 3, pp.
195–207). Mahwah, NJ: Erlbaum.

Gee, J.P., & Crawford, V. (1998). Two kinds of
teenagers: Language, identity, and social
class. In D.E. Alvermann, K.A. Hinchman,
D.W. Moore, S.F. Phelps, & D.R. Waff
(Eds.), *Reconceptualizing the literacies in
adolescents' lives* (pp. 225–246). Mahwah,
NJ: Erlbaum.

Hancock, M.R. (1993). Exploring the meaning-
making process through the content of litera-

ture response journals: A case study investigation. *Research in the Teaching of English,
27,* 335–368.

Harper, H. (2000). *Wild words/dangerous desires: High school students and feminist
avant-garde writing.* New York: Peter Lang.

Harris, V.J. (1994). Multiculturalism and children's literature: An evaluation of ideology,
publishing, curricula, and research. In C.K.
Kinzer & D.J. Leu (Eds.), *Multidimensional
aspects of literacy research, theory, and practice* (43rd yearbook of the National Reading
Conference, pp. 15–27). Chicago: National
Reading Conference.

Hemphill, L. (1999). Narrative style, social
class, and response to poetry. *Research in the
Teaching of English, 33,* 275–302.

Hickman, J. (1981). A new perspective on response to literature: Research in an elementary school. *Research in the Teaching of
English, 15,* 343–354.

Holland, D., & Eisenhart, M. (1990). *Educated in
romance: Women, achievement, and college
culture.* Chicago: University of Chicago Press.

Hunt, R.A. (1994). Speech genres, writing genres, school genres, and computer games. In A.
Freedman & P. Medway (Eds.), *Learning and
teaching genre* (pp. 243–262). Portsmouth,
NH: Heinemann.

Hunt, R.A., & Vipond, D. (1991). First, catch the
rabbit: Methodological imperative and the
dramatization of dialogic reading. In R. Beach,
J.L. Green, M.L. Kamil, & T. Shanahan (Eds.),
*Multidisciplinary perspectives on literacy re-
search* (pp. 69–90). Urbana, IL: National
Conference on Research in English/National
Council of Teachers of English.

Hynds, S. (1997). *On the brink: Negotiating lit-
erature and life with adolescents.* New York:
Teachers College Press; Newark, DE:
International Reading Association.

Kamberelis, G., & Scott, K.D. (1992). Other people's voices: The coarticulation of texts and
subjectivities. *Linguistics and Education, 4,*
359–403.

Kent, T. (1993). *Paralogic rhetoric.* London:
Associated University Press.

Knoeller, C. (1998). *Voicing ourselves: Whose
words we use when we talk about books.*
Albany: State University of New York Press.

Kucan, L., & Beck, I.L. (1996). Four fourth
graders thinking aloud: An investigation of
genre effects. *Journal of Literacy Research,
28,* 259–288.

Labov, W. (1972). *Language of the inner city: Studies in the Black English vernacular.* Philadelphia: University of Pennsylvania Press.

Leont'ev, A.N. (1978). *Activity, consciousness, and personality.* Englewood Cliffs, NJ: Prentice-Hall.

Lewis, C. (1997). The social drama of literature discussions in a fifth/sixth grade classroom. *Research in the Teaching of English, 31,* 163–204.

Mackey, M. (1997). Good-enough reading: Momentum and accuracy in the reading of complex fiction. *Research in the Teaching of English, 31,* 428–459.

Many, J.E., & Wiseman, D.L. (1992). The effects of teaching approach on third-grade students' response to literature. *Journal of Reading Behavior, 24,* 265–287.

Marshall, J.D. (2000). Research on response to literature. In M.L. Kamil, P.B. Mosenthal, P.D. Pearson, & R. Barr (Eds.), *Handbook of reading research* (Vol. 3, pp. 381–402). Mahwah, NJ: Erlbaum.

Marshall, J.D., Smagorinsky, P., & Smith, M.W. (1995). *The language of interpretation: Patterns of discourse in discussions of literature.* Urbana, IL: National Council of Teachers of English.

Martinez, M.G., & Roser, N.L. (2002). Children's responses to literature. In J. Flood, J. Jenson, D. Lapp, & J. Squire (Eds.), *Handbook of research on teaching the English language arts* (Vol. 2). Mahwah, NJ: Erlbaum.

Martinez, M.G., Roser, N.L., Hoffman, J.V., & Battle, J. (1992). Fostering better book discussions through response logs and a response framework: A case description. In C.K. Kinzer & D.J. Leu (Eds.), *Literacy research, theory, and practice: Views from many perspectives* (41st yearbook of the National Reading Conference, pp. 303–311). Chicago: National Reading Conference.

McGee. L.M. (1992). An exploration of meaning construction in first graders' grand conversations. In C.K. Kinzer & D.J. Leu (Eds.), *Literacy, research, theory, and practice: Views from many perspectives* (41st yearbook of the National Reading Conference, pp. 177–186). Chicago: National Reading Conference.

McGee, L.M., Courtney, L., & Lomax, R. (1994). Supporting first graders' responses to literature: An analysis of teachers' roles in grand conversations. In C.K. Kinzer & D.J. Leu (Eds.), *Multidimensional aspects of literacy research, theory, and practice* (43rd yearbook of the National Reading Conference, pp. 517–526). Chicago: National Reading Conference.

McGinley, W., & Kamberelis, G. (1996). Maniac Magee and Ragtime Tumpie: Children negotiating self and world through reading and writing. *Research in the Teaching of English, 30,* 75–113.

McKillop, A.M. , & Myers, J. (2000). The pedagogical and electronic contexts of composing in hypermedia. In S.Z. DeWitt & K. Strasma (Eds.), *Contexts, intertexts, and hypertexts* (pp. 65–116). Cresskill, NJ: Hampton Press.

McMahon, S.I., Raphael, T., Goatley, V., & Pardo, L. (1997). *The Book Club connection: Literacy learning and classroom talk.* New York: Teachers College Press; Newark, DE: International Reading Association.

Mehan, H. (1979). *Learning lessons: Social organization in the classroom.* Cambridge, MA: Harvard University Press.

Mellor, B., & Patterson, A. (2000). Critical practice: Teaching "Shakespeare." *Journal of Adolescent and Adult Literacy, 43,* 508–517.

Miller, S.M., & Legge, S. (1999). Supporting possible worlds: Transforming literature teaching and learning through conversation in the narrative mode. *Research in the Teaching of English, 34,* 10–65.

Morrison, T. (1994). *The bluest eye.* New York: Penguin.

Mosenthal, P.B. (1998). Reframing the problems of adolescence and adolescent literacy: A dilemma-management perspective. In D.E. Alvermann, K.A. Hinchman, D.W. Moore, S.F. Phelps, & D.R. Waff (Eds.), *Reconceptualizing the literacies in adolescents' lives* (pp. 325–352). Mahwah, NJ: Erlbaum.

Nodelman, P. (1988). *Words about pictures: The narrative art of children's picture books.* Athens: University of Georgia Press.

Nystrand, M. (1999, Spring). The contexts of learning: Foundations of academic achievement. *English Update: A Newsletter From the Center on English Learning and Achievement,* pp. 2, 8.

O'Flahavan, J.F. (1989). *An exploration of the effects of participant structure upon literacy development in reading group discussion.* Unpublished doctoral dissertation, University of Illinois, Urbana-Champaign.

Pappas, C.C., & Pettegrew, B.S. (1998). The role of genre in the psycholinguistic guessing game of reading. *Language Arts, 75*, 36–44.

Pope, R. (1995). *Textual intervention: Critical and creative strategies for literacy studies.* New York: Routledge.

Proulx, E.A. (1993). *The shipping news.* New York: Macmillan.

Rabinowitz, P.J., & Smith, M.W. (1998). *Authorizing readers: Resistance and respect in the teaching of literature.* New York: Teachers College Press.

Radway, J.A. (1984). *Reading the romance: Women, patriarchy, and popular literature.* Chapel Hill: University of North Carolina Press.

Raphael, T.E., & McMahon, S.I. (1994). Book club: An alternative framework for reading instruction. *The Reading Teacher, 48*, 102–116.

Rogoff, B., & Toma, C. (1997). Shared thinking: Community and institutional variations. *Discourse Processes, 23*, 471–497.

Shine, S., & Roser, N.L. (1999). The role of genre in preschoolers' response to picture books. *Research in the Teaching of English, 34*, 197–251.

Short, K. (1992). Researching intertextuality within collaborative classroom learning environments. *Linguistics and Education, 4*, 313–333.

Sims, R. (1983). Strong black girls: A ten year old responds to fiction about Afro-Americans. *Journal of Research and Development in Education, 16*, 21–28.

Sims, R. (1984). Point of view: A question of perspective. *The Advocate, 4*, 21–23.

Singh, M.G., & Greenlaw, J. (1998). Postcolonial theory in the literature classroom: Contrapuntal readings. *Theory Into Practice, 37*, 193–202.

Sipe, L.R. (1998). Individual literary response styles of first and second graders. In T. Shanahan & F.V. Rodriguez-Brown (Eds.), *47th yearbook of the National Reading Conference* (pp. 76–89). Chicago: National Reading Conference.

Sipe, L.R. (1999, Summer). Children's response to literature: Author, text, reader, context. *Theory Into Practice, 38*, 120–129.

Smagorinsky, P., & O'Donnell-Allen, C. (1998). Reading as mediated and mediating action: Composing meaning for literature through multimedia interpretive texts. *Reading Research Quarterly, 33*, 198–227.

Smithson, J., & Dias, F. (1996). Arguing for a collective voice: Collaborative strategies in problem-oriented conversation. *Text, 16*, 251–268.

Spinelli, J. (1991). *Maniac Magee.* Boston: Little, Brown.

Squire, J. (1964). *The responses of adolescents while reading four short stories.* Urbana, IL: National Council of Teachers of English.

Stephens, J. (1992). *Language and ideology in children's fiction.* New York: Longman.

Sumara, D.J. (1996). *Private readings in public: Schooling in the literary imagination.* New York: Peter Lang.

Sutherland, R. (1985). Hidden persuaders: Political ideologies in literature for children. *Children's Literature in Education, 16*, 143–157.

Svensson, C. (1990). The development of poetic understanding during adolescence. In R. Beach & S. Hynds (Eds.), *Developing discourse practices in adolescence and adulthood* (pp. 136–161). Norwood, NJ: Ablex.

Twain, M. (1999). *Adventures of Huckleberry Finn.* New York: Oxford University Press.

Vinz, R., Gordon, E., Hamilton, G., Lamontagne, J., & Lundgren, B. (2000). *Becoming (other)wise: Enhancing critical reading perspectives.* Portland, ME: Calendar Islands.

Wells, G. (1999). *Dialogic inquiry: Toward a sociocultural practice and theory of education.* New York: Cambridge University Press.

Wenger, E. (1999). *Communities of practice: Learning, meaning, and identity.* New York: Cambridge University Press.

Wertsch, J.V. (1998). *Mind as action.* New York: Oxford University Press.

Whitin, P. (1996). Exploring visual response to literature. *Research in the Teaching of English, 30*, 114–140.

Wilhelm, J.D. (1997). *"You gotta BE the book": Teaching engaged and reflective reading with adolescents.* New York: Teachers College Press.

Willinsky, J., & Hunniford. R. (1986). Reading the romance younger: The mirrors and fears of a preparatory literature. *Reading-Canada-Lecture, 4*, 16–31.

32

Adolescents' Perceptions and Negotiations of Literacy Practices in After-School Read and Talk Clubs

Donna E. Alvermann, Josephine P. Young, Colin Green, and Joseph M. Wisenbaker

Athene: I feel like I'm kind of weird 'cuz I read a lot. I mean, people look at me weird, you know?

Bunny: People who read a lot usually get a title—"nerd" or something. You know, they don't want to be a "geek" or nerd.

Crazy E: I don't think you can say you're a nerd because you read.

Bunny: Me neither.

Buzz: But most people—I bring books to school, and they look at me, like, oh my God, what kind of weirdo are you?

The concern adolescents have for how their peers perceive them is evident from this excerpt taken from an after-school book discussion in one of four Read and Talk (R & T) Clubs1 that met weekly in a public library in a small southeastern town of the United States. It is a concern over what Kinney (1993) has described as the "stigma of being labeled nerds" (p. 21). Being labeled a social outcast by one's peer group because one reads a lot may lead ultimately to an avoidance of reading—or to what Resnick and Goodman (1994) describe as a culture of mediocrity. Although such mediocrity poses a problem for society at large, we viewed these adolescents' concern in a more narrow vein. In particular, we were interested in exploring how peer discussions, such as the one just illustrated, signal the power of discourse to shape young people's perceptions of themselves and their literacy practices.

The purpose of the study was to investigate systematically how adolescents' perceptions and negotiations of after-school talk about a variety of texts in a public library setting were shaped by (and helped to shape) the larger institutional and societal contexts that regularly influence young people's actions and interactions with peers and adults. Because researchers working from an emic perspective generally have tended in the past to ignore how this shaping occurs in situation-specific interactions (Gilbert, 1992), we chose a theoretical framework that enabled us to study the institutionalized nature of language in terms of how it locally inscribes particular literacy practices.[2]

Theoretical Framework

A theme that is central to much of the research on adolescent peer culture is the importance of communal activity—a term used to refer to the interactions that occur as adolescents negotiate, reinvent, and jointly create their lifeworlds with others of their own age and with the adults who share their worlds. Communal activity as a theme is particularly prevalent among researchers who have looked at variations in the socialization of young people in school settings (Everhart, 1983; Finders, 1997; Larkin, 1979; Lesko, 1988). According to Corsaro and Eder (1990) in their review of the literature on peer cultures from early childhood through the teenage years, a limiting factor in the research on communal activity is its almost exclusive attention to adult–child and peer interactions in formal school contexts. Noting this limitation, Corsaro and Eder, along with others (e.g., Fine, Mortimer, & Roberts, 1990; Takanishi, 1993), have called for studies that take into account adolescents' experiences outside of school in community settings where informal groupings offer different opportunities for interacting with peers and adults.

The routines, artifacts, values, and concerns that young people produce and share as they work communally with others of their own age group contribute to the shaping of various peer cultures (Corsaro & Eder, 1990). Adolescents' experiences with family and adult members of community institutions such as schools, libraries, and churches also contribute to the shaping of peer culture (Finders, 1997; Wells, 1996). In the latter instance, however, the culture metaphor works only if one acknowledges the dynamic and permeable boundaries within and across the lifeworlds of adolescents and adults.[3] Drawing on Bakhtin's work to reinforce the notion of the inseparability of adolescent and adult communities, Cintron (1991) noted,

> As Bakhtin (1981) suggests, communities that are in contact interanimate each other. They infect, disrupt, and even discharge their differences during their interaction such that each community's beliefs, values, and language system (including its way of speaking) are exchanged, resulting in ephemeral identities. (p. 24)

This broader notion of peer culture, with its emphasis on the dynamic and permeable boundaries within and across adolescents' various and complex life-worlds, has linkages to some of the more recent work on discourse as institutionally informed social practice (Fairclough, 1995; Freebody, Luke, Gee, & Street, 1998; Gilbert, 1992; Kamberelis, 1995). Conceiving of discourse as social practice rests on the view that language is both a social process and a socially conditioned process (Fairclough, 1989, 1995). This view of language and social process holds that there is more than merely an external relationship between the two entities. For Fairclough (1989), a linguist, the relationship is both internal and dialectical in that "linguistic phenomena *are* social phenomena of a special sort, and social phenomena *are* (in part) linguistic phenomena" (p. 23).

Discourse, then, is more than language. Gee (1990), a sociolinguist, called it an *identity kit*—one's way of seeing, acting, believing, thinking, and speaking so that it is possible to be recognized by (and recognize) others like oneself. This ideological perspective is present in Fairclough's (1995) critical discourse analysis, the analytical framework we used in the present study. According to Fairclough, critical discourse analysis aims to

> systematically explore often opaque relationships of causality and determination between (a) discursive practices, events and texts [spoken or written], and (b) wider social and cultural structures, relations and processes; to investigate how such practices, events and texts arise out of and are ideologically shaped by relations of power and struggles over power. (p. 132)

Fairclough's analysis is termed critical because he focuses on the political—that is, on issues related to power and ideology. Such issues may arise at each of three levels of social organization: the local or situation-specific context, the institutional context, and the larger societal context or "context of culture" (Fairclough, 1995, p. 134). As an example, in the present study, we explored the relations of power and ideological processes inherent in adolescents' literacy practices at the local level (Read and Talk Clubs) for the purpose of tracing how those processes were shaped by (and helped to shape) larger institutional and societal contexts.

Literacy, like discourse, can be thought of as critical social practice. In fact, Freebody et al. (1998) argue that "literacy *is* critical social practice" inasmuch as every statement we make about texts that we read, write, or speak raises "a bristling array of silences—things we could have said instead, aspects of a topic we could have highlighted but chose not to" (p. 1). Reasons behind the choices that we make when speaking out or remaining silent are inherently tied to how we perceive ourselves in relation to others, to what we are willing to reveal about our own interests and desires, and to whether or not we believe we can make a difference by adding our voices to the mix. Keeping this view of literacy in the fore as we worked on the present study served to remind us that we were not standing outside the data but in fact were implicated in them. For example, in our research team meetings, decisions about which R & T Club discussions to videotape—that is, which discussions would count as "appropriate" and "worthwhile"—were never independent of our own historically embedded beliefs and assumptions about adolescent talk.

Finally, it is important to bear in mind that conceptions of literacy as critical social practice do not deny the cognitive or behavioral aspects of reading, writing, and speaking; instead, they portray them as attendant processes in a much larger social context, one that is institutionally located in the political structures of society where power is at stake in people's social interactions on a day-to-day basis. Issues of gender, race, class, age, and other identity markers are historically part of these interactions (Luke & Freebody, 1997).

Review of Literature

Voluntary After-School Reading

Positive attitudes toward reading begin to taper off by the middle grades, and they continue to decline through high school (Cline & Kretke, 1980; McKenna, Kear, & Ellsworth, 1995; Thomson, 1987). Accompanying this decline in attitudes, not surprisingly, is a decrease in the amount of time spent in voluntary after-school reading. For example, findings from a landmark study (Anderson, Wilson, & Fielding, 1988) detailing the relation between 155 fifth-graders' growth in reading and how they spent their time outside of school indicated that the median child read 12.9 minutes per day. This compares to 15 minutes of voluntary after-school reading per day for the 195 fifth and sixth graders in Taylor and Maruyama's (1990) study and 7.2 minutes per day for the median child in Walberg and Tsai's (1984) large-scale study of 13-year-olds, who were part of the 1979–1980 National Assessment of Educational Progress (NAEP). A recent NAEP report (Campbell, Voelkl, & Donahue, 1997) shows that 32% of the nation's 13-year-olds reported reading voluntarily during after-school hours, which was not significantly different from statistics gathered in 1984 on a similar group of 13-year-olds. However, there was a statistically significant decrease in voluntary after-school reading among 17-year-olds for the same time period; only 23% of that group reported reading voluntarily in 1996, compared to 31% in 1984.

Evidence of little time being devoted to voluntary reading outside of school hours is not limited to the United States. In a study of 920 fifth graders from a stratified sampling of 31 Irish primary schools, Greany (1980) found that children's daily diaries revealed an average of 5.4% of available out-of-school time was spent in leisure reading. From the results of a written survey aimed at determining Australian teenagers' reading and television viewing habits, Thomson (1987) reported that the majority watched television for more than 3 hours a night, with only 20% of those surveyed saying they read books regularly.

According to Thomson, these findings are comparable to the results obtained on similar surveys conducted in England nearly 2 decades earlier.

Most of the existing literature is concerned with the frequency of voluntary after-school reading in relation to children's growth in reading proficiency (Anderson, 1995; Anderson, Wilson, & Fielding, 1988; Campbell et al., 1997; Taylor & Maruyama, 1990) or the influence of the environment on leisure reading (Greany, 1980; Greany & Hegarty, 1987; Morrow & Weinstein, 1986; Neuman, 1986). Relatively few researchers have looked at the dynamics of peer culture and other social networks in relation to youngsters' voluntary reading practices, and those who have, more often than not, have studied the phenomenon from within schools. For example, Orellana (1995) examined the gendered aspects of tasks, texts, and talk among children in primary school, Dressman (1997b) observed upper-elementary students' enactments of gender and social class in three school libraries, and Myers (1992) investigated the social contexts of school and personal literacy in an eighth-grade classroom. Only Finders (1997), in her study of junior high school girls' gendered literacy allegiances in the classroom, spent additional time observing the girls as they engaged in some of the same practices outside of school.

Libraries and Adolescents

At one time in history, collections in public libraries were developed solely to attract adults and, in particular, working men. In fact, libraries were even referred to as working men's universities (Garrison, 1979). However, today the picture is quite different. Adolescent literacy services in public libraries are on the rise, no doubt partially due to the fact that a quarter of all public library patrons are adolescents between the ages of 12 and 18 (Farmer, 1992). According to the results of a survey conducted for the Carnegie Corporation's Task Force on Youth Development and Community Programs, young adolescents who were asked what services they would use most during nonschool hours listed, among other things, public libraries, complete with all the latest books and videos that appeal to teenagers (Mathews, 1994).

Although school and public libraries share a common goal in their attempts to entice youngsters into leisure reading habits, public libraries represent qualitatively distinct cultures when compared to libraries in schools (Dressman, 1997a; Worthy & McKool, 1996) and other institutional settings (Cole, 1995). For example, the time spent in public libraries is not regulated by a system of bells designed to signal the passage of students from one class to another. Nor do public libraries attempt to regulate what adolescents read, at least not to the extent that school libraries do. And, it is rare in public libraries to see "no talking" rules posted or dress codes enforced. Teenagers are well aware of the relaxed norms operating in public libraries, especially in those that cater to the adolescent reader through young adult services (Farmer, 1992).

Aside from several brief anecdotal reports of adolescent literacy programs in public libraries (e.g., Davidson, 1988; Farmer, 1992; Mathews, 1994) and a large-scale survey (Dwyer, Danley, Sussman, & Johnson, 1990) that indicated families at the upper end of the socioeconomic scale depend on public libraries for after-school child care significantly more often than do lower SES families, we found little else in the literature that related to our study's purpose. Most of the anecdotal reports on adolescent literacy programs in libraries focused on efforts to address issues of aliteracy and illiteracy. We located no research on young adolescents' involvement in after-school reading clubs in public libraries, although descriptions of a summer beach book club involving 17 high school students (Chandler, 1997) and a juvenile detention center book club (Hill & Van Horn, 1995) have been published in the literacy field's leading practitioner journal.

The present study is important in its bid to inquire into adolescents' literacy experiences in a communal setting where interactions with adults are not governed by the same set of conditions operating in the more formal institution of schooling. Although an institution in itself, the public library is a cultural space quite distinct from that of the school and more particularly the school library (Dressman, 1997a). In public libraries, entry is neither compulsory nor inaccessible during set periods of the working day. Public libraries are also gathering places for families, and some set aside special spaces where adolescents can relax in the company of their peers.

Against this backdrop, then, we set out to explore the following questions: Who would come to the Read and Talk Clubs initially, and, if the same adolescents continued coming for the entire 15 weeks of the project, what would be their perceptions of why they did so? How would the adolescents and adults negotiate the social practices of the R & T Clubs relative to how they positioned themselves (and were positioned by others) within the different groups? What traces from the larger institutional and societal contexts that inform adolescents' and adults' daily lives would be present in the weekly interactions of the R & T Clubs?

Method

Description of the Site

The adolescent wing in a regional library that serves residents of a small town in the southeastern United States was the setting for the study. A modern building situated on a spacious lot adjacent to a large middle school, the library houses an attractive young adult section that features fully stocked shelves, revolving paperback display racks, computer equipment, comfortable furniture, and a number of other resources that teenagers value. The library employs a young adult specialist, a distinction accorded only 11% of all public libraries in the United States (National Center for Education Statistics, 1995). Gaining entry to the site involved preliminary discussions with this specialist and her supervisor, the library's associate director.

The atmosphere of the library is one of openness and trust. For example, we noted that one of the adolescents in our study introduced her 12-year-old friend who was pregnant to the young adult librarian for the purpose of helping her friend locate information on pregnancy and counseling services. Adolescents who live in close proximity to the library frequently use it as a place to hang out after school and during vacations. A good number of parents, too, regardless of socioeconomic status, see it as a venue for after-school child care. Entire families are drawn to the library in search of reading materials, videos, and computer access to the World Wide Web.

Recruitment of Adolescent Participants

The 22 adolescent participants, all of whom were protected by policies governing the researchers' university internal review board, were recruited during an intensive 3-week campaign that began in late August. Fliers describing the nature of participants' involvement and offering a $5.00 weekly incentive for keeping a daily after-school activity log and attending a weekly 30-minute book club discussion were distributed in the town's middle schools and high schools, the local mall, a shopping center parking lot diagonally across the street from the library, and area churches. Fliers were also on display at the help desk in the young adult (YA) section of the library, and the YA specialist arranged a special sign-up day at the library when members of the research team were available to answer questions.

At the end of the recruitment period, a total of 22 adolescents had volunteered to participate in the 15-week project. There were 10 girls (7 European Americans, 2 African Americans, and 1 Black American)[4] and 12 boys (9 European Americans, 1 African American, 1 Black American, and 1 Korean boy who had been in the United States for several years). Two of the girls (1 European American and 1 African American) opted to leave the project after a few weeks for personal reasons related to time and interest. Thus, complete data sets were available for only 20 of the original 22 participants. All analyses were based on the 20 who remained in the project for its entirety (15 weeks). Participants came largely from middle class family backgrounds with the exception of three children who lived at or near the poverty level (2 of whom were European American girls and 1 an African American boy).

Formation of the R & T Clubs

The participants were assigned to specific R & T Clubs with their convenience and grade placement in mind. Using a list of preferred afternoon time slots and days that the adolescents had supplied, the two adult facilitators, Josephine[5] and Colin, divided the participants into four clubs. They tried to group the adolescents by grade level as much as possible. However, exceptions were made. In one instance, the parents of a sibling pair needed to pick up both youngsters at the same time. This resulted in Josephine's Tuesday group having a high school girl mixed in with a middle school group. In another instance, two seventh-grade girls, originally in Colin's Thursday group of middle school students, were moved to Josephine's Thursday group after the first meeting because a ninth-grade girl (who later dropped out of the project) complained about being the only girl in that group. This left Colin with an all-boy group. Finally, an eighth-grade boy was placed in Josephine's Thursday high school group at his own request. Josephine chose to work with the older participants because of her past experience as a high school teacher. Colin preferred to work with the younger ones.

The adolescents in this study chose their own pseudonyms and elected to use them throughout the 15 weeks that the R & T Clubs met. Because two boys chose female names and one girl chose a male name, the names of three participants do not match their pronoun referents. Table 1 provides a listing of the participants in each R & T Club by name, grade, sex, and ethnic group.

TABLE 1
Participants in the Four R & T Clubs

Name	Grade	Sex	Ethnicity
Josephine's Tuesday R & T Club			
BJ	9th	Female	Black American
Christian	6th	Male	Black American
Gaby	7th	Female	European American
Melissa	7th	Male	Korean
Josephine's Thursday R & T Club			
Athene	7th	Female	European American
Bunny	9th	Male	European American
Buzz	9th	Male	European American
Crazy E	8th	Male	European American
Einstein	7th	Female	European American
Flea	9th	Male	European American
Colin's Wednesday R & T Club			
Cleopatra	6th	Female	African American
Jane	7th	Female	European American
Jason	7th	Male	European American
Rhiannon	6th	Female	European American
Rose	6th	Female	European American
Tommy	6th	Male	African American
Colin's Thursday R & T Club			
Death-Hand	7th	Male	European American
Dr. Funk	7th	Male	European American
Joe Smith	7th	Male	European American
Shaft	7th	Male	European American

Researchers' Backgrounds

The three researchers, all of whom were white, were presently part of the middle class; however, Colin and Donna had come from working class backgrounds. All three had been classroom teachers and were well acquainted with the institutionalized practices of schooling and their impact on adolescent peer culture. Josephine and Donna had been members of a research team at a large university for 3 years before the start of this project; Colin had been a graduate student in Donna's class before joining the project.

Josephine. Both a former middle school teacher and an alternative high school English/language arts teacher in the southeastern United States, Josephine brought a variety of experiences to bear on her job as graduate research assistant and facilitator of two Read & Talk Clubs. She also had been a participant observer on two previous research projects involving adolescents and text-based discussions. However, this was her first experience working with adolescents in an after-school book club in a setting apart from the school. The mother of two boys (one of whom was an adolescent but not a participant in the study), Josephine had an easy style about her—one that served her well in recruiting adolescents for the R & T Clubs and then later in facilitating their discussions during club meetings.

Colin. As an international doctoral student, with 8 years of public school teaching experience in Belfast, Northern Ireland, Colin was familiar with young adolescents and book clubs, though not from an American perspective. Culturally, he sometimes found himself at sea, especially when the girls in one of his R & T Clubs alluded to popular adolescent fiction, such as the Sweet Valley High (Pascal, 1993) series, or when the boys took it for granted that he would know the difference between a fullback and a running back. At other times, his different cultural experiences served to bring otherwise quiet students into a discussion, as, for example, when one girl assumed he would resonate with her passion for stories set in medieval England.

Donna. Prior to becoming a professor in literacy education, Donna had taught middle school students for 7 years, after which she had earned a master's degree in library science. Her interest in studying adolescent talk about texts began during the time she was a middle school English/language arts teacher. Then, as now, she questioned certain assumptions underlying adult-led discussions in which adolescents were expected to engage. This study marked the first time Donna did not interact directly with the participants in a project for which she was principal investigator. Instead, she assumed the position of observer, typically visiting the R & T Clubs to take field notes, videotape, and occasionally chat with the adolescents either before or after meetings.

Data Sources

The data came from four primary sources: the adolescents' daily activity logs, the researchers' field notes, the transcripts of audiotaped R & T Club discussions, and the transcripts of audiotaped interviews with the adolescents and their parents. Secondary data sources included one videotaped session from each of the R & T Clubs, notes from pre- and poststudy interviews with the specialist in the young adult section of the library, and notes from a telephone interview with one of the adolescents who attempted to initiate an R & T Club at her middle school after the project ended.

Daily Activity Log. Participants were expected to fill in their daily activity log on a nightly basis, including weekends, for a period of 15 weeks. We opted for daily reporting because research on the accuracy of individuals' retrospective self-reports of their actions has shown that "frequent self-reports of experiences over relatively short time periods will provide more reliable and valid data than that obtained from a few widely spaced assessments" (DeLongis, Hemphill, & Lehman, 1992, p. 90). A common time frame for diary-like recordings, such as the activity log used here, is "once-per-day assessments across a period of several weeks...usually before going to sleep for the night" (DeLongis et al., 1992, pp. 98–99).

The activity log, modeled after one developed by Giles (1994), consisted of six questions concerning types of after-school activities in which the participants engaged, the extent to which they used the library as a source of reading material, the types of materials they opted to read, where they read, the amount of time they spent reading after school, and why they chose to read outside of school. Multiple responses to a single question were acceptable. For example, the item that asked respondents to circle all the activities in which they had participated while out of school that day (until they went to sleep) was followed by 18 possible choices. On the other hand, there were items that required respondents to circle simply *yes* or *no* on their log sheets. (A complete copy of the log may be obtained by writing to the first author of this study.)

Participants were required to turn in their logs on a weekly basis to Josephine and Colin, who in turn scanned each log to determine its completeness before compensating the participant for keeping it. All log responses were entered weekly into a computerized database that allowed sorting on 62 variables. The log data were analyzed twice: once midway through the study and again at the end. The midway check was done to detect possible response bias. None was found, and information gleaned from interviews with parents suggested that the logs were representative of their children's after-school activities.

Field Notes. Josephine and Colin typed their field notes as they listened to the weekly audiotaped discussions in each of their R & Talk Clubs. In all, there were 15 taped discussions for each of the four R & T Clubs. These were shared among Josephine, Colin, and Donna as part of the ongoing analysis described under a later section on analytical procedures.

Adolescent and Parent Interview Guides. Josephine and Colin conducted a total of seven semistructured group interviews with each of the R & T Clubs they facilitated. Semistructured interviews were thought to ensure some consistency in data collection across groups. The questions, which were open ended and grew out of the research team's ongoing weekly analyses of the data, included among others: What do you like about the R & T Club discussions (and what would you change)? What materials that we have read and discussed during club meetings are the most important to you, and why? What is your biggest fear about speaking out in your group? When some people in your group talk, do others get hushed (and why do you think this happens)? What is OK (or not OK) to talk about in your group, and who decides that?

Parent interviews were conducted for the most part in their homes and were dialogical in nature (McGinley & Kamberelis, 1996; Mishler, 1986), meaning that both interviewers and respondents frequently negotiated or reformulated their questions and comments. The questions focused on parents' perceptions of their youngsters' participation in the R & T Clubs—e.g., Did they think their children enjoyed talking about books and other materials after school in the library? Could they give reasons for believing as they did? What role did the library play in their family life? How important was the monetary incentive to their child's willingness to keep a daily log and attend the R & T Club discussions? For the most part, it was the mothers who agreed to be interviewed. On two occasions, both parents participated in the interview, and, in three instances, the fathers were the sole respondents.

All interviews were audiotaped and immediately given to a professional for transcribing. When the transcripts were returned, Josephine and Colin listened to the original tapes as they followed along in the transcripts. If inconsistencies were spotted, Josephine and Colin made corrections on the transcripts, which were then given to the transcriber for retyping. The same procedure was used in supplying the names of respondents in the group interviews with the adolescents. For the parent interviews only, Josephine and Colin wrote brief narratives in which they recorded their impressions of the meetings. The narratives were appended to the parent interview transcripts.

Analyses of Logs and R & T Club Meetings

Descriptive statistical procedures were used in analyzing all responses from the logs of the 20 adolescents who remained active throughout the 15-week study. The analysis proceeded in stages. First, we analyzed all of the log data for each of the six questions to determine the proportion of days that the adolescents, as a group, reported doing any one activity (e.g, reading a book, talking on the phone, etc.). We chose not to calculate simple frequency counts because of the variation in the number of days that each participant completed and turned in his or her log. For instance, one participant turned in a log for only 67 days, while others turned in logs for 104 days. Consequently, we converted each participant's response frequency for any given activity into a proportion and then calculated the median proportion for the group as a whole.

After that we plotted the distribution of the calculated proportions using boxplots. As an example, Figure 1 provides the boxplots for Question 1 on the daily activity log. We used the median, or center of the distribution spread, to mark the 50th percentile. The boxplots illustrate the distribution of the relative

FIGURE 1
Boxplots of Out-of-School-Activity Distributions

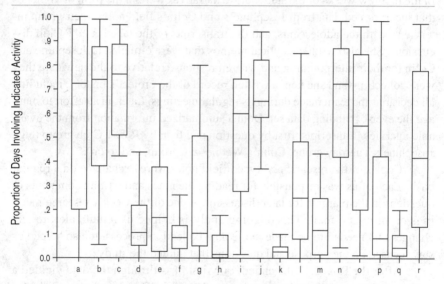

While out of school today until I went to sleep I... (Complete this statement by circling all of the following activities that apply to you for the time period mentioned.)

a. Played with or cared for a pet
b. Did household chores
c. Read a book, magazine, etc.
d. Shopped
e. Played an electronic game
f. Read a set of directions
g. Played or practiced a sport
h. Babysat
i. Visited, talked, or played with a friend

j. Did homework
k. Played with toys or dolls
l. Used a computer
m. Went to a lesson
n. Watched TV
o. Listened to music
p. Rode a bike
q. Had an appointment
r. Talked on the telephone

frequency with which the adolescents selected a given response. The length of a box shows the spread of the distribution—the longer the box, the greater the spread and the shorter the box, the less the spread. The vertical lines drawn outside the box (i.e., the whiskers) represent the more extreme proportions. The top of a box represents the 75th percentile, and the bottom of a box the 25th percentile. The horizontal line within a box represents the median, or 50th percentile.

With the exception of the log data just described, all other data sources were interpreted using Fairclough's (1989, 1995) critical discourse analysis to trace patterns in the R & T Club members' locally mediated talk about texts to the larger institutional and societal structures that constituted such talk and through which it was interpreted. As a research team, we established procedures for ensuring systematicity in simultaneously collecting and analyzing data throughout the 15 weeks of the project. For example, Donna wrote various types of narratives that were shared with Josephine and Colin for their comments and further analysis. In the first few weeks of the study, those narratives were in the form of vignettes that incorporated data from Josephine's and Colin's field notes, their group interviews with the adolescents, and the transcripts of the taped R & T Club discussions. She also wrote analytical memos that were e-mailed to Josephine and Colin for their interpretation and written response relative to the new data they were collecting, and she kept a written record of the project's history, including all decisions the team made during its regular meetings. Later, in an effort to manage the ever-expanding data set, Donna summarized information from the available interview transcripts, first by question and then by R & T Club group (e.g., Josephine's Tuesday group, Colin's Wednesday group, and so on).

Copies of the researchers' typed field notes were exchanged on a regular basis. Each of us was responsible for reading the notes and writing comments or questions in the margins for later discussion at one of the weekly research meetings or through e-mail. This ongoing analysis helped us remain alert to any changes that needed to be made in the data collection process. It also helped us stay focused on the purpose and questions that guided the study.

After the R & T Clubs ended, our first pass through the data yielded a document that was 77 single-spaced pages in length. This document was the focus of numerous research meetings in which we discussed the relative significance and strength of the patterns we were noticing in adolescents' after-school talk about texts. As we started to make connections between the identified patterns and their linkages to the larger institutional and societal contexts described by Fairclough (1989, 1995), we began to write a series of integrative memos that drew from all primary and secondary data sources plus the multiple layered vignettes and analytical memos that we wrote during data collection. Integrative memo writing, according to Roponen (1995), must be grounded not only in the original data sources but also in all other earlier written notes and memoranda. In our case, writing the integrative memos served as a means of keeping the study's purpose and guiding questions in mind while analyzing the findings within the overarching theoretical frame. They also served as preliminary and summary-like narratives that aided in the final write-up of the study's findings.

Discussion of Findings

This section's discussion is organized around the questions that guided the study: (a) Who came to the Read and Talk Clubs initially? (b) For those who remained in the project for the full 15 weeks, what were their perceptions of why they did so? (c) How did the adolescents and adults negotiate the social practices of the R & T Clubs relative to how they positioned themselves (and were positioned by others) within the different groups? (d) What traces from the larger institutional and societal contexts that inform adolescents' and adults' daily lives were present in the weekly interactions of the R & T Clubs?

Who Came?

By far, the vast majority of adolescents who signed up to participate in the R & T Clubs were avid readers. Despite intensive efforts to attract a more diverse group of readers, in the end those who came forward comprised a highly self-selected group of adolescents. As illustrated in Figure 1, half or more of the 20 adolescents who remained in the project for the entire 15-week period reported reading as an after-school pastime on 77% of the days. Doing homework, watching television, taking responsibility for household chores, and playing with or caring for a pet were also frequently reported after-school activities, but reading a book, magazine, and the like stood out amongst the other activities.

As shown in Figure 2, half or more of the adolescents reported reading something they checked out of the library on 67% of the days that they were in the project. Although the library was a source of reading material for a substantial proportion of the days covered by the participants' logs, it certainly was not the only source. As indicated in Figure 3, they also reported reading *TV Guide,* newspapers, something they wrote, directions for accomplishing a task, letters or cards, reference materials, and so on. Books were by far the most popular reading materials, with magazines placing a very poor second. As shown in Figure 3, half or more of the adolescents reported that on the days they chose to read outside of school, they selected books (hardback or paperback) on 84% of those days.

Not surprisingly, half or more of the adolescents reported that on the days they chose to read after school, their bedrooms were their favorite spots for reading on 80% of those days (see Figure 4). No other room in the house came close to rivaling the bedroom in popularity.

When the adolescents in this study read after school, they did so for a substantial amount of time. As shown in Figure 5, half or more of them reported

FIGURE 2
Boxplot of Materials Read From Library

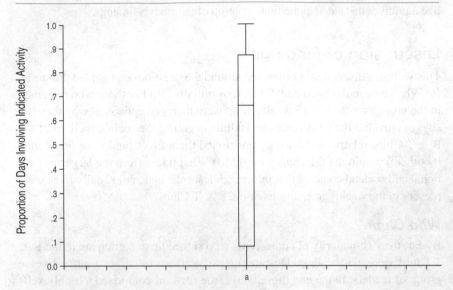

Did you read anything from the time you got out of school today until you went to sleep that you got out of the library?

a. Yes   b. No

reading for 30 minutes on 16% of the days, for 1 hour on 16% of the days, for 1½ hours on 10% of the days, and for 2 hours or more on 8% of the days. As a frame of reference for interpreting these reading times, it is worth noting that only 6% of the eighth graders in the United States who were part of the recent Third International Mathematics and Science Study reported "reading a book for fun" for 3 or more hours after school on what the authors of that study termed "a normal school day" (U.S. Department of Education, 1996, p. 65).

Finally, the adolescents in this study could be described as perceiving themselves to be voluntary readers in almost every sense of the term. As shown in Figure 6, half or more of them reported that, when they read outside of school, they did so "because they wanted to" on 74% of the days that they were part of the study. In addition, half or more reported they read "for their own pleasure/enjoyment" on 54% of the days. No other reasons came close to rivaling those two.

Evidence gathered from analyzing the other primary and secondary data sources puts a face to these statistics compiled from the daily activity logs. This evidence is presented next for each of the four R & T Clubs.

Josephine's Tuesday R & T Club. The Tuesday group met in the young adult section of the library at a table that was reserved for their R & T Club discussions. The table was situated between four tall paperback book carousels and a wall of hardbacks. Library patrons milled around the table as they browsed the revolving paperback carousels. Occasionally a friend or relative walked by, and their presence was briefly acknowledged. Of the four adolescents in the group, two were siblings, and the other two knew each other from school. The sibling pair, BJ (a ninth-grade Black American girl) and her brother Christian (a sixth grader), attended one of the county's private religious academies. BJ usually came to the weekly discussions having read three or four books, mostly about other adolescents. Unlike her brother, who was the youngest member of the group and the most quiet, BJ was eager to talk about the books she had read.

FIGURE 3
Boxplots of Reading Option Distributions

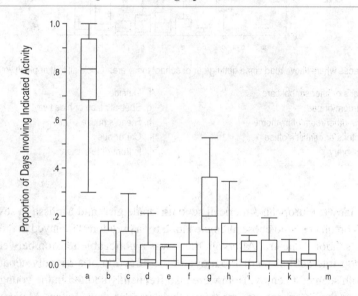

Circle anything listed below that you read from the time you got out of school today to when you went to sleep.

a. Hardback or paperback books
b. Computer program or service
c. Newspaper article or column
d. Letter or card
e. Trading cards (like baseball cards)
f. Reference book (dictionary, encyclopedia, instructions, etc.)
g. Magazine
h. Something you wrote
i. Newspaper comic strips
j. Comic book
k. Set of directions (for example, a recipe book, game directions, car manual, etc.)
l. *TV Guide*
m. Other _____

FIGURE 4
Boxplots of Reading Location Distributions

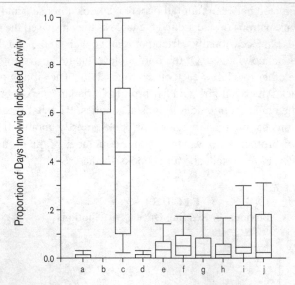

Some places where I have read since getting out of school today are: (Circle all that apply to you.)

a. At sitter's or after-school care
b. In bedroom or bed
c. In some other room of my home
d. At doctor's or dentist's office
e. Public library

f. Outside
g. Special place or hideaway
h. Friend's house
i. Car or bus
j. In front of television

Gaby (a European American seventh-grade girl) and Melissa (a seventh-grade Korean boy who chose a female name for a pseudonym) played in the same middle school orchestra. Although there was a noticeable tension between the two, their interactions tended to move in the direction of a friendly debate that they both seemed to enjoy. Both were also frequently spotted in the young adult section of the library at times other than their meeting days. In fact, Melissa often sat in on (but did not verbally participate in) Colin's Thursday R & T Club discussions. With the exception of BJ, who liked coming-of-age stories, and Melissa, who favored the R.L. Stine series, this group showed no preference for one type of book over another.

Josephine's Thursday R & T Club. The meeting place for this group was a conference room adjacent to the young adult section of the library. Although there were tables and chairs available in the young adult section, Josephine believed that two R & T Clubs meeting simultaneously (Colin's Thursday group met at the same time as Josephine's) would disrupt the normal activity of the library. In retrospect, her hunch proved accurate; the adolescents in her Thursday group were boisterous and liked to engage in friendly arguments among themselves.

The four boys in the group—Flea, Bunny, Buzz (ninth-grade European Americans) and Crazy E (eighth-grade European American)—had attended the same middle school the previous year, and they were all friends outside of school. Bunny and Buzz had made several movies together with help from Shaft (a member of Colin's Thursday group). These movies, which everyone in Josephine's Thursday group had seen, were often referenced during R & T Club discussions.

The other two members of the group, Athene and Einstein (seventh-grade European American girls), knew each other before the study began and were also acquainted with the boys. The two held their own in any group discussion and were not the least bit intimidated by the boys' attempts to interrupt them. In fact, Athene and Einstein often interrupted the boys and were the instigators of some of the group's more rowdy moments.

FIGURE 5
Boxplots of Reading Time Distributions

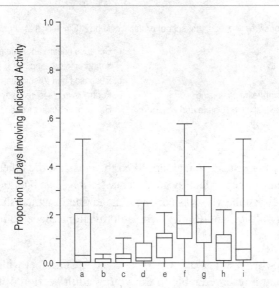

Select the amount of time below that best describes how long you spent reading since getting out of school.

a. None
b. About 1 minute
c. About 5 minutes
d. About 15 minutes
e. About 20 minutes

f. About 30 minutes
g. About 1 hour
h. About 1½ hours
i. For 2 hours or more

FIGURE 6
Boxplots of Selected Reading Reason Distributions

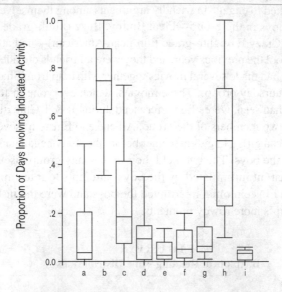

What are some reasons why you read after school or this weekend? (Circle all that apply to you.)

a. I didn't read
b. Because I wanted to
c. To relax/calm down
d. To find out something/learn something
e. Because I didn't have anything else to do/I was bored

f. Because I heard about something that sounded interesting
g. Because I had to/someone made me
h. For my own pleasure/enjoyment
i. Because I couldn't sleep

As for reading tastes, Flea, alone, liked the classics; the others preferred more popular genres, such as fantasy and science fiction. Two budding authors in the group were Einstein, who was editing a magazine in which she expressed her opinions on politics, and Bunny, who sold his homemade comic books to Mainstreet Comics.

Colin's Wednesday R & T Club. On Wednesdays, Colin met with six middle school students at a reserved table in the young adult section of the library. Members of the club included Rhiannon and her friend Rose, both sixth-grade European American girls from a neighboring county that has one of the lowest per capita incomes in the state. Both girls paid Rhiannon's mother $1.00 a week to cover the cost of gas in driving them to the R & T Club meetings. Rhiannon liked to listen to country music and read Sweet Valley High (Pascal, 1993) books. Her tastes in reading were shared by Rose with one exception; according to Rose's mother, Rose also read the Bible daily.

Cleopatra and Tommy were African American sixth graders who attended the same middle school and knew each other from church. Their mothers were also friends. Cleopatra said she sometimes felt self-conscious about contributing to the R & T discussions because she thought Tommy might tell his mom what she had said and that it would get back to her own mom. Tommy protested, saying, "I ain't no snitch!" Cleopatra, the self-identified feminist in the club, was not re-assured and added, "Well, girls worry about those sorts of things." Unlike Tommy, who preferred true stories about sports figures, Cleopatra liked historical fiction, especially if it involved African Americans and strong female characters.

Jane and Jason were seventh-grade European Americans who attended middle schools different from one another and from the other members of their group. Jane, who came from a well-educated and affluent family, read mostly classics when she first joined the club. She confided in her mother that she was appalled at what the other girls read, perhaps deeming her own choice of classics as somehow better than books from the Sweet Valley High series. Jason rarely spoke, although he did become animated when discussions focused on materials that contained forms of humor he appreciated, such as that associated with Monty Python.

Colin's Thursday R & T Club. This group of four seventh-grade European American boys met in a back corner of the young adult section. The area stood out because of its homey atmosphere and large overstuffed chairs, which were arranged in a circle. The group included Dr. Funk, Death Hand, Shaft, and Joe Smith, all of whom attended the same school and who (with the exception of the latter) had been friends for some time—a fact that may have partially explained Joe Smith's reticence to join in discussions. Dr. Funk was the brother of Flea, a member of Josephine's Thursday group. Death Hand and Shaft prided themselves on being, in their words, "a little off the wall at times." By all accounts, Shaft was considered the ringleader of the group and the one most apt to add humor to a discussion. Of all 20 participants in the study, only Shaft boasted that he did not read much. However, he did admit to becoming absorbed in *The Lost World* (Crichton, 1995), saying, "One night I took the book and read three chapters"—a comment that brought on loud cheering and clapping among his peers.

Members of Colin's Thursday group were known to talk animatedly about any texts that pertained to science fiction or horror. They were especially fond of some UFO fact sheets that one of the boys brought in on a regular basis. Unlike the other R & T Club members, the boys in Colin's Thursday group reported spending a lot of time after school playing electronic games or surfing the Web. The group also had the highest number of logged instances in which members checked that they had read nothing outside of school-related assignments for a given day.

Why Adolescents Stayed With the R & T Clubs

Social Outlets for Readers. A likely explanation for much of the sustained interest in the R & T Clubs was that they were perceived to be social outlets for young adolescents, especially for those who liked to read but who, by their own accounts, found that being viewed as a reader could earn one the title of nerd or worse. Even those adolescents who had been spared their peers' ridicule told us that they had no other place to go and talk about what they were reading. Cleopatra, for instance, said she and her mother were the only ones in her family who read books, so she looked forward to club meetings because they gave her a chance to talk with others who read "just for fun." Rhiannon likewise found the meetings personally satisfying. She said she had no one at school with whom she could "talk books" because she read at a higher level than others in her grade. Einstein described her R & T Club as a place where "we talk about books and tease each other.... It means a fun place where I talk about my favorite subject [reading] and see my friends." Similarly, Buzz declared that the R & T Club was a place where he could interact with friends who liked to read and talk about books, while Bunny noted that reading in the public library, unlike in school, was considered "cool."

In interviews with parents, we heard the adolescents' views reiterated. For instance, Cleopatra's mother said, "[The clubs] have been good in that there aren't a lot of kids in our neighborhood who sit down and talk about books.... So it's been a good outlet for her." Similarly, Rhiannon's mother noted that the meetings had given her daughter an opportunity to be with others her age who were "on the same wavelength." And Einstein's mother concluded, "I think she's really enjoying the discussion and the socialization of the reading group.... She looks forward to them [the meetings] and enjoys the social interaction with other avid readers.... It seems to have become a social [occasion]."

An R & T Club was also perceived as a place where new friendships could be struck. Although a majority of the members knew one another before joining the project, for some, such as BJ, a ninth grader who attended a religious academy on the outskirts of town, the club provided an opportunity to make new friends. As the weeks wore on, BJ and Gaby were often observed siding with each other on issues discussed during club meetings. Occasionally, the two girls shared a few private laughs and nodded knowingly at each other across the table. Despite their differences in age and lack of contact outside the club, it appeared that BJ and Gaby had struck up a special kind of friendship, one sparked by common interests in reading and discussing books, magazines, and the like.

Finally, we learned from interviews with the adolescents and their parents that they perceived the library to be a comfortable, family-oriented place where browsing, reading, working with computers, hanging out with friends, and checking out videos were all in the realm of possibility. With the exception of Tommy's mother, who stressed that "the library is like a church—a sacred place [where] you go in and be quiet," others viewed it as a place for sharing information, including talking to others about books. For example, Cleopatra's mother noted that she was pleased to find that her daughter had been exposed to a wide range of books in the library, and she stated that Cleopatra had read some of those discussed by members of her R & T Club.

Monetary Incentive. Although the young adult librarian was fairly convinced that the $5.00 incentive for filling out the daily logs and attending the weekly R & T Club discussions was the primary reason adolescents sustained their interest in the R & T Clubs, we were not so sure. Whereas we did not discount the importance of the $5.00 stipend in motivating the adolescents to take their task seriously—in fact, several parents told us that their children saw the daily activity log as "a job"—we did not believe the stipend fully accounted for their continued attendance and the fact they rarely missed a meeting. They came to meetings even on the days when they had forgotten to bring their logs, or their logs were incomplete, which meant they would not receive the stipend.

On the other hand, it is clear from the data gathered in the adolescent and parent interviews that the $5.00 incentive played an important role in initially attracting the participants to the project. As Gaby's father and several other parents pointed out, a 15-week commitment in the lives of already busy people was not to be taken lightly. In terms of his daughter's decision to participate in the project, Gaby's father believed that money was half the motivation and social gratification the other half. However, as Gaby and several of her peers reminded us, $5.00 was not enough to motivate someone to read who did not already like to do so. A similar observation was made by Mark Dressman, a colleague in the field whom we had asked to read an earlier draft of this report. From Dressman's perspective, the participants in the R & T Clubs

> had already begun a process of self-selection and self-identification of themselves as Readers, a process based...in the positive assertion of identity through *negation*—that is, through discursively defining themselves in opposition to all those others in their schools who are *not* Readers. (M. Dressman, personal communication, July 24, 1996)

The tendency for some members of the R & T Clubs to define themselves in opposition to the nonreader will surface again in a later section of this article. It is an important issue and one that cannot be overlooked in our bid to understand how discursively defined literacy practices at the local level are shaped by, and help to shape, the larger social discourse.

"Real" Discussions. It was clear from our initial interviews with the adolescents that they brought to the project similar ideas of what discussions would entail (the phrase "read and discuss" had figured prominently in the recruitment flier).

Theirs was a definition informed by years of exposure to discussion practices at school, many of which, judging from the research literature at the middle and high school level (e.g., Alvermann, O'Brien, & Dillon, 1990; Moore, 1996; O'Brien, Stewart, & Moje, 1995), resemble recitations more than free-flowing give-and-take discussions. For some, including Rhiannon and Jane, the concept of a Read and Talk Club was completely foreign, which is not surprising given, as Jane noted, that "the only time we discuss books in school is to get what we need to know for the test." However, as the project progressed, an awareness grew among the adolescents that it was possible, as Colin's Thursday group noted, "to mix getting down to business and cutting up." For example, Death Hand's and Dr. Funk's perception of their club's discussion was that it gave them a place to respond to texts in ways that they believed were intellectually honest and socially acceptable. Death Hand noted that in school, if he were to say, "Yuck," in reaction to a book, he would be criticized for speaking his mind. Dr. Funk agreed, adding, "We can get away with saying a lot more in this book club."

Consistently, across groups, the adolescents were forthright in their declarations that R & T Club discussions should not take on the characteristics of the discussions they were accustomed to in school. Although they initially assumed that the discussions in the R & T Clubs would resemble those of school, they admitted to being pleasantly surprised when that turned out not to be so. They were also quick to point out that, had that been the case, they were sure some members of their group would quickly have dropped out of the project. Although the adolescents held various opinions as to what distinguished R & T Club discussions from those they experienced in school, generally their observations came down to two: Club discussions were characterized as being interesting rather than boring, and they were "real" discussions as opposed to talk that is allowed in school. For example, Dr. Funk observed that "here we can interrupt each other, like a real discussion. In school, you can't do that. You got to raise your hand until the teacher allows you to speak. If you don't, you get lunch detention or something." While this observation would certainly not apply to all classroom discussions (nor is it our intent to draw comparisons between two very different contexts), we use Dr. Funk's comment simply to illustrate the perceptions some adolescents had of why they continued coming to the R & T Clubs.

Summary. The public library in this study was a site of communal activity. As such, adolescents' perceptions of what was culturally appropriate conduct in the library ranged from a general understanding that it was "cool" to read there (unlike in school) to a tacit understanding of the rules for engaging in book talk. The discourses associated with adolescence, family, schooling, religion, money, and friendship also made their presence known through the participants' perceptions of what they liked about the R & T Clubs and why they chose to remain a part of them for the entire 15-week period. The adolescents we studied were avid readers to be sure, but, like most of their peers, they liked to socialize. That they perceived the R & T Clubs to be social outlets for talking about books was not lost on the young adult librarian, who told us after the project ended that she was planning a weekly book/movie review club as part of the summer library program. She lamented that it had taken her so long to recognize "how hard [libraries] are trying to make reading attractive to the kids who don't read and not supporting the kids who *do* read" (M.J. Hartel, personal communication, April 16, 1997).

Negotiations of After-School Talk

Negotiations surrounding the types of materials to be read and how they would be discussed in the weekly R & T Clubs led the adolescent and adult members of the clubs to position themselves, and to be positioned by others, differently over the course of the 15-week project. Clashes in discourses and power struggles (sometimes overt, but more often unspoken) over who had the right and/or responsibility to set literacy practices for the group were the issues. Not surprisingly, as Davies (1994) has reminded us, "There is a sense in which we all attempt to *colonise* the world with the discourses we have taken up as our own, and through which we have been constituted" (p. 261). Such was the case in our study.

Positioning Self and Others. The ways that R & T Club members spoke themselves and each other into existence through everyday talk varied in relation to the discourses available to them, especially in terms of who was doing the speaking, from what position, in what context, and with what gain in mind (Davies, 1994). Thus, Colin might speak from his position as an adult member of the club, as a male, as a teacher, as a citizen of Northern Ireland, and so on. Initially, he was unsure as to how he should position himself (or how he would be positioned by the adolescents) in his two R & T Clubs. As time went on, he found that in his Thursday group it was easy to discard any semblance of a teacher persona, given the nature of the participants' interactional styles. In his Wednesday group, however, Colin frequently found himself being positioned as teacher and responding by intervening on the behalf of those individuals who were excluded by the comments and gestures made by other group members.

Colin believed that being a male made it easier for him to establish relationships with the boys in both groups. For example, in the Wednesday group, Tommy's mother told him that her son profited from seeing Colin as a male reader: "He [Tommy] sees you, and he knows he can be a jock and still read." In his Thursday group, composed of all males, Colin believed he came close to being positioned as one of the lads (Willis, 1977). Although the Thursday group came from backgrounds quite dissimilar to those of Willis's lads, Colin found the discursive twists of the group's dialogue reminiscent of interactions he had once had with his peers while growing up in a working class neighborhood of Belfast but attending a predominantly middle class grammar school in a different neighborhood. Often he reported becoming so immersed in the flow of the Thursday R & T Club discussions that he felt the border blurring between what he termed "adult leader" and "adolescent participant." Yet when he or the other club members deemed it necessary, the fluidity of his positioning in the group made it easy to exert some control as the leader.

Josephine's Tuesday R & T Club initially positioned her as teacher. In interviews with club members, she learned that they held her responsible for asking questions, maintaining order, and keeping discussions on track. This was a position Josephine said she would not have chosen for herself, but it was one she had little success in changing. Because Josephine was interested in relations of power, stemming from some courses she had taken in Women's Studies as part of her doctoral program, she was open to exploring her own agency in the group. When she asked Melissa, one of two boys in the Tuesday group, why he expected her to play teacher in an after-school R & T Club, he said that teachers always "keep it [discussion] alive and if it gets kind of boring, they do something...like change the subject or they...ask different questions."

Unlike the Tuesday group, members of the Thursday R & T Club had no intention of positioning Josephine as teacher. In fact, they made it quite clear (in a good-natured way) that if Josephine were to act like a teacher, it would force them to act more out of control than ever. They wanted Josephine to play the part of what they called "a responsible adult"–someone who would pay them for turning in their completed activity logs each week, keep them from starting a riot during discussions, and ensure that they did not, in Buzz's words, "put pennies in the [light] sockets and stuff like that." By positioning Josephine as the responsible adult, the adolescents in her Thursday group freed themselves from taking responsibility for many of their own actions.

The adolescents in Josephine's Thursday group were also adept at positioning one another, especially when it involved negotiating one or more of the R & T Club's discussion practices. For example, when it became evident that Crazy E had not finished reading "Third Configuration," a chapter in *The Lost World* (Crichton, 1995) that was the agreed on stopping place for the group's discussion, Bunny sighed, and Crazy E apologized to him, knowing that his failure to keep up would stop the group from going as far in the discussion as Bunny had hoped. In this moment, Crazy E was positioned as a slow reader, a position he took up as evidenced by the apology he offered Bunny (and by implication, the rest of the group). Josephine and Colin noted many other instances of adolescents positioning one another, sometimes through playful insults, ridicule, humor, and good-natured teasing, but always with the intention of gaining the upper hand in a situation, and typically in relation to what would be read and how it would be discussed.

Choosing Texts and Ways of Discussing Them. At first, Josephine and Colin resisted the adolescents' suggestion that the R & T Clubs abandon the school-sanctioned practice of reading common texts in preparation for group discussions. Concerned about how such discussions would flow (and falling back into their teacher mode), they offered two alternatives. One involved all reading the same book and discussing some aspect of it. The second consisted of reading a book (or other kinds of texts) from a common genre, such as mystery or romance, and then discussing common themes across texts within that genre. Not sold on either of those two options, the members of Josephine's Thursday group came up with a third alternative. They favored reading anything they wanted to, with an eye to discovering common themes as they interacted with one another during club discussions. Curious as to how this would work, Josephine asked, "Should Bunny tell about his book, and then Buzz try to relate to Bunny's book? Is that what you mean?" They agreed she had interpreted them correctly. Soon the idea was adopted by the adolescents in the other clubs as well, with the understanding that any group was free to change its mind at any time. That they did not deviate from the Thursday group's plan, except on one occasion, points to the apparent satisfaction they derived from reading anything they chose in preparation for a common discussion.

The one exception was the time three of the four groups wanted to read *The Lost World* (Crichton, 1995). We purchased individual copies of the book for the two Thursday groups and Josephine's Tuesday group. Despite the popularity of the book and the discussions that surrounded it, when they had finished reading *The Lost World*, the groups went back to their former pattern of reading whatever they wanted and then searching for common threads during club discussions. Only Flea spoke out in favor of reading more books in common. One day, in an attempt to persuade his peers of the value of such a practice, Flea said (following a discussion of *The Lost World*), "I think it's helped our conversation, us having [read] the same book. I want to make a recommendation. I think we should all get like a paperback anthology of short stories.... Do you think it's a good idea?" His suggestion was virtually ignored by everyone except Josephine, who said she liked his idea. However, it was not approved by the group.

All groups stood firm on their preference for reading different materials of their own choice. They told us they liked coming to the discussions to hear about different books and to get ideas about what to read. For instance, when asked what she liked about her R & T Club, Gaby said, "I like the fact that ya'll don't pressure us.... You let us choose our books." Christian added, "I like it because we have our own choice of books and we don't have to read the same thing." Choice was a big factor in Cleopatra's faithful attendance as well. According to her mother, Cleopatra became hooked on reading the summer after she finished second grade when a very special teacher let her choose her own books to read: "The teacher...was wonderful. That was the beginning of it all. I think the first thing that she really got excited about was...the chance to read what she wanted to read."[6]

Wondering About Issues of Authority. In spite of what they were hearing from the adolescents, Josephine and Colin continued to feel some uncertainty about discussions that lacked a common text. Although their uncertainty was more pronounced at the start of the project, it remained an issue throughout. Mainly, their reservations centered on the quality of the adolescents' interactions; in their opinion, the club discussions lacked coherence. At times, they wondered about the wisdom of relinquishing their claim to authority and going along with the adolescents' wishes. Comments such as "If I were a teacher, I would..." appeared in their field notes. But in the discussion groups, the two adults did their best to avoid being positioned as the authority figures. In fact, Josephine recalled writing in her field notes, "I worked really hard not to be a teacher and to let them talk about what they wanted to."

Colin's Wednesday group expected him to maintain a high leadership profile. Rhiannon had let it be known early on that she thought of him as "teacher-like." When he asked other club members if Rhiannon's view was one they also held, they said yes. Puzzled, he asked why. The first to speak, Rhiannon volunteered, "All teacher-like people say everything on the first week or first day." She assured him, however, that "everybody who's in charge does that!" As the weeks wore on, Colin thought he detected a little more willingness on the part of the adolescents to take responsibility for sustaining their own discussions. He attributed this change in part to the fact that they had become better acquainted among themselves and were more aware of one another's expectations—not a small accomplishment given that the group was the most ethnically diverse of the four R & T Clubs and had the greatest range in adolescents' ages and family SES. To the very end of the project, however, Colin found himself stepping in to rescue his Wednesday group from what seemed like endlessly long silences that were embarrassing for everyone. Believing that the situation called for an intervention on his part, Colin would typically resort to a question-and-answer session aimed at restoring what he called "the kids' comfort level."

In Colin's Thursday R & T Club, the issue was one of trying to keep abreast of the group's ever-changing dynamics and knowing when, as the adult in the group, to exert or withhold an appropriate measure of authority. Colin was pleased when the boys picked up on one another's comments and the discussion moved along at a fairly brisk pace, making it possible for him to take a backseat. But just as quickly as a discussion could take off, so too it could falter and sputter. When this occurred, Colin was there to help repair it. He felt his attempts at repair, however, often meant he exerted too high a profile. This had the effect, he believed, of disrupting the flow of talk, as in the following example taken from an interview that focused on what libraries might do to make adolescents want to read more.

Dr. Funk: Well, they could give away books, stuff like that.

Colin: Okay. Anything else. What if...

Shaft:	What I think is like they should have a thing where you have a deadline to read so many books, and then you get a reward.
Colin:	Apart from that?
Death Hand:	Yeah, if you read a certain number of books.
Colin:	Okay, apart from the rewards, what else? We're trying to get you to *want* to read, not *make* you read books, but rather you *wanting* to read them.
Shaft:	As I said, if I was rewarded, I'd want to read a lot.
Colin:	Apart from that...

There was a pattern to Colin's use of the phrase "apart from that." On a number of occasions he used it to indicate dissatisfaction with the direction in which the dialogue was going. By steering the boys' talk in a way he perceived to be more appropriate, he believed he may have prevented some of them from responding candidly, though that seemed not to be the case with Shaft, as just illustrated.

Deciding Who Gets to Talk. Turn-taking, a discussion practice that is widely accepted as part of the discourse of schooling, was a familiar site of negotiation in the R & T Clubs. In school, the expectation is that one person speaks at a time so others may hear and respond. However, as pointed out earlier, the members of Colin's Thursday group believed this practice was too restrictive and not like real discussions. Josephine's Thursday group also spoke in favor of the free-flowing nature of their discussions. They thought it was fine to talk all at once. For example, Buzz said it gave him practice following multiple lines of thought simultaneously. Although Josephine and Colin were less sanguine about the adolescents' overlapping talk and frequent interruptions, both practices are reportedly acceptable in African American dialogue (see Ladson-Billings, 1997; Obidah, 1998) and in the talk that takes place during adult book club discussions (Marshall, Smagorinsky, & Smith, 1995).

Josephine and Colin were mostly concerned about Joe Smith and Crazy E, the two quiet boys in their Thursday groups. Worried that these boys might feel overlooked, Josephine and Colin tried to intervene in subtle ways so that no one would feel excluded. The clubs' more talkative members were adamant, however, in their belief that if someone wanted to say something all he or she had to do was say it. The more talkative adolescents also maintained that individuals were responsible for creating their own time to talk. Joe Smith and Crazy E seemed to agree, at least outwardly, but neither boy made any move throughout the 15-week project to position himself differently in relation to his more boisterous peers. In interviews with both boys' mothers, Josephine and Colin noted that only Joe Smith's mother commented on how much her son enjoyed the club discussions. She told Colin that the biggest motivating factor in her son's participation in the project was the interaction of the group.

Unsure about what contributed to Joe Smith's enjoyment of the discussions, given his low verbal participation, we asked individuals in the group to describe what they liked about interacting with one another. Among those who responded to our question, Shaft volunteered that he liked it when Joe Smith talked and everyone listened to him because he spoke so infrequently—a comment Joe heard but chose not to respond to. We interpreted Joe's silence in several ways. It is possible that Joe perceived his own views were being expressed adequately by the more talkative members of his group, thereby alleviating any need to talk on his own behalf. Alternatively, it is possible that Joe's silence signaled an unwillingness to dispute the other boys' comments. Or, it might be that he had learned to negotiate a way of making his voice heard when it counted—that is, by speaking only when he felt he had something of substance to add to the discussion.

In contrast to the Thursday groups, members of the Tuesday and Wednesday clubs generally were in agreement that talking one at a time was essential for a "good" discussion. Melissa believed that it was Josephine's responsibility as the adult in the group to make sure everyone had an opportunity to talk. His reasoning, seconded by BJ, was that more than one person speaking at a time caused people to lose their train of thought. As to how the adolescents in the Tuesday and Wednesday clubs thought they might help their peers remember when they had held the floor long enough, Rhiannon suggested using body language. She said she could get her message across just by looking bored at the person who was talking.

Finally, tensions stemming from who should talk, and when, were not limited to the adolescents' peer-group interactions. The adults also found themselves negotiating such tensions. For example, one day when Josephine grew impatient with the direction that the Thursday R & T Club's discussion appeared to be headed, she announced with an uncharacteristic ring of authority in her voice, "Okay, wait a minute, wait a minute! We're not going to talk about *this* [gossip about the exclusive private academy Einstein attended] again!" Everyone continued talking over one another, seemingly impervious to her fairly loud interjection. Making a greater effort to be heard, Josephine said, "I have no power. I have none, absolutely none!" In a teasing but rational tone of voice, Buzz said, "You have some; we just don't acknowledge it." To which Flea added, "The world doesn't work on power, it works on the *illusion* of power." Although this exchange could be interpreted as two adolescent males rudely setting the record straight for the female adult in the group, Josephine did not see it that way. Instead, she laughed, partially out of disbelief that 2 ninth graders were engaging in a discourse reminiscent of her Women's Studies class but also out of the realization that her attempts to create a sense of openness in the club's negotiations over whose voices would be heard were apparently paying off.

Summary. In negotiating the various discursive practices associated with being members of the R & T Clubs, the participants called attention to the typically unmarked and invisible ways of displaying (Goffman, 1976) or "doing" (West & Zimmerman, 1987, p. 137) literacy, gender, adolescence, adulthood, and so on that position individuals differently. The negotiation process also called attention to several existing and shifting power relations and the tensions they created relative to what kinds of texts would (or should) be read, how they would (or should) be discussed, and whose voices would (or should) be heard in the weekly R & T Club discussions. By choosing Fairclough's (1989, 1995) critical discourse analysis as a framework for interpreting club members' negotiations of after-school talk about texts, our aim was to make visible how adolescents and adults jointly create and reinvent literacy practices as a communal activity. Although this activity occurred outside the formal context of schooling, club members' practices were shaped by the larger institutional (e.g., school) and societal discourses that constituted them and through which they were interpreted. Reciprocally, members' practices helped to shape the larger contexts in the sense that each time the adolescents and adults drew on available discourse knowledge of how to do literacy, schooling, adolescence, gender, and the like they necessarily inscribed the taken-for-granted or tacit theories of what counts as the normal or right way of thinking, talking, and acting in that discourse (Gee, 1996, p. ix).

Traces That Shape: Identifying Some Contradictions in Adolescent Talk

The adolescents in our study were particularly adept at fashioning new subjectivities[7] as they engaged in positioning themselves and one another in ways that drew attention to existing ambiguities and dissenting voices within the context of the R & T Clubs. In rehearsing their new personas, they often engaged in talk that brought to the surface varying contradictions traceable to the larger institutional and societal contexts that regularly shape (and are shaped by) such talk. This was particularly the case when talk turned to gender-related literacy practices, to low-status books, and to gossip as a means of solidifying group membership in reading.

Gender-Related Literacy Practices. The notion that there is something basic or indispensable to being male or female is at the heart of essentialist talk, or talk that stereotypes on the basis of sex category. Such biological determinism is refuted by constructionists, who view sex differences as being primarily written or spoken into existence through gendered acts of socialization, and by poststructuralists, who seek to disrupt the male/female binary through better understanding the ways in which available positions get taken up and reified (Davies, 1993). In the following example, it is easy to trace Rhiannon's essentialist talk to gendered norms in the larger societal context of which she is a member and to glimpse how such talk can only serve to further inscribe the binary opposition between males and females.

The incident in question involved six participants in Colin's Wednesday R & T Club, four of whom were female, as they discussed elements of their favorite magazines. Noting a reticence on the part of the girls in the group to talk beyond a superficial level about the content of a particular teen zine, Colin inquired why this was so. Rhiannon said that she would never discuss something in the group that had been written specifically for girls for fear of what the boys would say. Then, turning to address the two males, Tommy and Jason, she confidently asserted, "I wouldn't talk about something [girl talk] you boys wouldn't understand." Pressed as to why she felt they would not understand, Rhiannon simply added, "It's a given!" Similar patterns of interaction occurred during discussions of Rhiannon's and Rose's favorite books in the popular Sweet Valley High (Pascal, 1993) series, which is known for its stereotyping of adolescent females. In Rhiannon's words, the series is written "from a girl's point of view." When books in this series were the topic of discussion, Colin wrote in his field notes that questions or comments raised by Tommy, Jason, or himself received scant, if any, consideration from the four female participants.

Rhiannon's reference to "girl talk" as something the males in the group would not understand is a form of female discursive resistance. According to Brodkey (1989), this type of resistance calls for "re-presenting a stereotype as an agent in a discourse [which is] the least committed to preservation of that stereotype—as Toni Morrison does when representing Afro-American women as the agents rather than the victims of events in her novels" (p. 127). In a similar manner, Rhiannon used girl talk (a negative cultural stereotype) to her advantage by demonstrating that a mere mention of the fact that males would not understand her favorite teen zine or Sweet Valley High books could effectively preclude the male point of view from being considered.[8]

Giving agency to girl talk as a form of communication that males reputedly demean (and thus would not understand) is one way of resisting old discourses and opening up new and contradictory ways of thinking about the male/female binary. At the same time, the very act of engaging in essentialist talk, as in Rhiannon's case, served to inscribe still further the stereotypes surrounding male and female preferences in reading materials in larger societal contexts. On only one occasion did we see such essentializing talk challenged. That occasion involved yet another discussion in Colin's Wednesday R & T Club, one in which Rhiannon had commented to the group that "boys spend all their time talking about sports," partly in reference to Tommy's obsession with sport magazines. Jane, who read swimming magazines, strongly disagreed, saying, "me and my friends talk about sports, we're competitive, and we're all girls."

Low-Status Books. Literate practices involved more than doing gender; they also served to mark social class boundaries, as in the case of Jane and her initial disdain for the Sweet Valley High (Pascal, 1993) books—Rose's and Rhiannon's favorite reading fare. Jane was from a comfortable middle class home that was exquisitely furnished with antiques and other period-piece furniture. Jane's mother, who did not work outside the home, spoke at length with Colin about the difficulties of living in "the South." In her words, "We [the two children and their parents] escape to Europe every summer. That keeps us sane."

Rhiannon and Rose, on the other hand, came from families who were living at or near the poverty level in a nearby rural county. In a home interview, Rose's mother told Colin that Rose and Rhiannon "talked about those Sweet Valley High books all the time...and the series known as The Baby-Sitters Club." She added that she generally trusted Rose's sense of what was appropriate for a girl her age to read. Rhiannon's mother also approved of her daughter's reading tastes and let her read books based on a popular television series that the librarian in their rural community thought were too mature for her.

Jane's mother, on the other hand, was not nearly as sanguine about her daughter's sudden liking for such low-status books as those found in the Sweet Valley High series. In an interview with Colin, she shared some doubts she had about the R & T Club's influence on Jane.

Mother: [Initially] Jane did say that some of the kids...read some awful books. And then the next minute she turned around and checked out Sweet Valley High, so I don't know if you all have helped her or if you have led her astray. But she has gone from reading fairly classical work to Sweet Valley High.

Colin: It's interesting because there are two girls who have read everything in the series. I think they have read everything published by...

Mother: I notice that she [Jane] has one, and she even apologized when she checked it out of the library last week because she felt that it was awful. She said, "I'm getting that book there because I think it will put me to sleep at night." And I said, "It probably will."

Certainly there are traces of social class influences filtering into the interviews between Colin and the mothers of three girls in his Wednesday R & T Club. Yet it would be premature to make too much of the seeming connection between low-status books finding general acceptance among two working class mothers and outright rejection by a middle class mother. In Finders's (1996) study of the Social Queens and Tough Cookies, it was the former group of adolescent girls (mostly from middle class families) who read low-status books such as The Baby-Sitters series at home and the Tough Cookies (from working class homes) who read the classics as a way of setting themselves apart from the Social Queens. What seems likely is that low-status books of the Sweet Valley High and The Baby-Sitters series served a different function for Jane than they did for Rose and Rhiannon. For Jane, they were windows into a world she had not bumped into before participating in Colin's Wednesday R & T Club. For Rose and Rhiannon, these series and others like them described experiences with which they could easily identify. And, by identifying and taking on the subject positions available to them, Rose and Rhiannon simultaneously helped to inscribe the very cultural values already at work in a society known to engender social class differences.

Gossip as a Means of Solidifying Group Membership. The R & T Clubs were stages on which the adolescents could try out ways of speaking and acting within relatively safe confines.[9] They performed for one another, often stepping out of character backstage (Goffman, 1959) during a lull in the discussion or as an excuse for digressing from the topic at hand. Traces of the larger institutional and societal contexts that shaped the adolescents' performances were often visible during digressions that took on the semblance of peer group gossip. As a practice, gossip has a history of providing individuals with socially acceptable ways of gaining acceptance and solidifying group membership (Eder, 1995; Eder & Enke, 1991; Leach, 1996). According to Corsaro and Eder (1990), gossip is integral to peer group membership among young adolescents, primarily because "it reaffirms and reveals basic values and beliefs of group members" (p. 214).

In the example that follows, members of Josephine's Thursday R & T Club digress from a discussion on urban myths and cyberpunk literature to gossip about Einstein's (a girl who chose a male name for her pseudonym) peer group at the private academy she attends. Their talk contains traces of varying contradictions, some gender related and some related to their presentation of "selves as readers" in opposition to all the nonreaders at Einstein's school. In the discussion leading up to the exchange below, Athene defends Einstein, saying that Einstein's parents *make* her attend the private academy. Buzz says that everyone at that school brings credit cards to class, and Bunny quips, "I'll trade you my Visa for your Mastercard." Laughter follows, whereupon Einstein adds some gossip of her own.

Einstein: The girls are psychotic. They are like, "Hee, hee, hee, I don't even know what a politician is."

Athene: They haven't one thought worth saying.

Einstein: [Mimicking a girl from her school] "Teacher, teacher, I have to go to the bathroom; I broke a nail."

Bunny: [Feigning a call on his cell phone] "Excuse me, my broker just called; I made another million."

Einstein ends the exchange, saying the boys at her school can think only of football. In her words, the boys are mindless, "Like duhhhh," and Athene agrees, calling them "sexist jocks."

On first brush with the data from this exchange, we were struck by the adolescents' awareness of social class privilege and several markers of gendered normative behavior. However, on closer inspection, we came to question the motivation for their talk and to see the contradictions inherent in it. For instance, we noted that, although the adolescents were critical of their peers who attended a private academy, their attempt to critique certain values associated with privilege and sexist behavior did not preclude their penchant for gossip and stereotyping, which only inscribed further the very social conditions they appeared to deplore.

By engaging in gossip to position others in their larger peer group as sexist individuals who had neither social consciences nor political acumen, the adolescents in Josephine's Thursday R & T Club spoke in a manner that had a decidedly self-righteous ring to it. An alternative and more generous interpretation of their talk might be to argue that these adolescents had merely chosen the relative safety of the club as a stage on which to try out new ways of defending themselves against those who would label them nerds. This interpretation would make sense given that we know the adolescents in Josephine's Thursday group were sensitive about being perceived as social outcasts because they liked to read. It is an interpretation that also resonates with Corsaro and Eder's (1990) sense of gossip as reaffirming, and revealing the basic values and beliefs of a group, passed on as they are through the larger institutional and societal structures that inform adolescents' everyday thinking.

Summary. The gendered discursive practices that we observed in this study were as varied as those known to exist in society at large (Commeyras, Orellana, Bruce, & Neilsen, 1996). Reproduced continually through institutionalized social structures, these practices tend to essentialize differences between males and females. Indeed, research undertaken in English-speaking countries outside the United States has drawn attention to the frequency with which institutional settings are the "sites of varying contradictions, ambiguities and tensions...[related] to sex/gender social relations" (Mac An Ghaill, 1994, p. 8). By studying such conditions as they presented themselves at the local level through the gendered discussions of R & T Club members, we were able to pinpoint some of the constituting forces of the larger institutional and societal discourses that simultaneously regulate adolescents' talk and are informed by it. We were also able to identify certain literate practices that marked social class boundaries and made use of peer gossip to solidify and affirm a group's stance on reading.

Limitations and Conclusions

In exposing our own ideological bent in this study, we have attempted to show that literacy is a critical social practice, one imbued with relations of power that can be traced to larger institutional and social contexts that both shape and are shaped by everyday life. The limitations associated with such exposure are dealt with next. First was the difficult task of representing the adolescents' views in ways that did not position them as the Other—a condition in which researchers effectively communicate to their participant group: "No need to hear your voice when [we] can talk about you better than you can speak about yourself" (hooks, 1990). Although we relied heavily on the adolescents' words to motivate the interpretations we drew, in the end it was our perspective, informed by critical discourse analysis, that framed those interpretations. Second, while the study's design allowed an exploration of the codes of power operating between adolescents and adults as well as among the adolescents themselves, it did not permit us to call the study a critical literacy project per se. To have qualified as such, we would have had to intervene directly in helping the adolescents reflect on how the various negotiations of literacy practices led to their being positioned differently within those practices. The duration of the project and its design simply precluded any such intervention. Third, several manifestations of privilege—as both a racial and class construct—seemed evident to us as the adolescents interacted weekly in the R & T Clubs. Yet, we found no evidence in their talk that they were explicitly aware of such privilege, and our field notes and interview transcripts indicate we did not press the issue. A more culturally diverse research team might have facilitated probing into this aspect of the study. A fourth limitation was the self-selected nature of the participant group. Despite an intensive 3-week campaign to recruit a diverse group of adolescent readers, all were avid readers with the possible exception of three participants.

With these limitations in mind, we offer the following conclusions. As a study site, the public library offered a unique opportunity for adolescents to interact with peers and adults in negotiating and reinventing literacy practices that were themselves traceable to larger social institutions, such as schooling. Specifically, the library afforded a relatively safe niche in which both adolescents and adults felt free to experiment with alternative ways of doing discussion. For example, the adolescents in the R & T Clubs negotiated a discussion genre that differed appreciably from the one reported in a school-based study of Book Club (McMahon & Raphael, 1997), where small groups of students met to discuss a common reading that was later shared in the larger classroom community. In the R & T Clubs, participants opted to discuss something other than a common reading; they negotiated the right to read different materials of their own choosing, with the proviso being that club discussions would focus on discovering common themes across those materials. In reacting to this decision on the part of the R & T Club members, Dressman (personal communication, July 18, 1996) wrote,

> In making this decision, it seems to me that the participants were clearly making a move to emphasize the *social* function of these meetings and to preserve a space where the agenda was very, very tentative—a space inviting social, more than intellectual or literary, experimentation.

Free to question existing arrangements about *what* they would read, the adolescents engaged in a form of communal activity that challenged the status quo of small-group discussions. In doing so, they also made visible the dynamic and permeable boundaries within and across adolescents' and adults' lifeworlds, much as Bakhtin (1981) would have predicted. It is worth noting, however, that most school-sanctioned literacy practices went unchallenged. For example, the practice of waiting for a teacher-like authority figure to signal who was to talk, when, and for how long was so firmly entrenched in two of the R & T Clubs that it became virtually impossible at times to distinguish discussions in those two groups from school-based discussions (Alvermann et al., 1996).

A second conclusion is that the public library provided a climate of acceptance—a liminal space of openings and closings (Foucault, 1986) in which adolescents who liked to read could experience both the welcoming of other readers like themselves and the shutting out of those who would taunt them for being avid readers. Within this welcoming climate, the discourse of the R & T Clubs closely resembled that of adult book clubs (Flood et al., 1994; Marshall et al., 1995). Socializing was central to maintaining club members' interest in participating, and the opportunity to talk about what they read was mentioned by both adolescents and adults as helping them to make new acquaintances and deepen existing friendships.

A third conclusion is that the adolescents in our study, like those described by Heath and McLaughlin (1993), were adept at creating informal out-of-school social networks that served their needs. However, the conditions that made such social networks possible are not easily, if ever, replicated in formal school settings. This creates a tension between what avid adolescent readers desire and what is possible. In many ways, the R & T Club participants' desire for a choice in reading materials and discussion formats bears a close resemblance to Illich's (1973) belief that learners should have "a free choice of what is to be learned and how it is be learned" (p. 16). Yet, as Green (1973) has pointed out, in citing John Dewey,

> The fact that something is desired only raises the *question* of its desirability; it does not settle it. Only a child in the degree of his immaturity thinks to settle the question of desirability by reiterated proclamation: "I want it, I want it, I want it."

Valuing individual choice, making available a variety of textual resources, and working to make an institution such as schooling become more responsive to adolescents are worthy goals. However, as the adult facilitators of the R & T Clubs learned in the present study, the encouragement of adolescent choices produced tensions in terms of whose voices were heard, for how long, and under what conditions. Tensions were also created in working through issues of authority, a point to which we will return in the section on implications.

A final conclusion is that, by identifying traces of the larger institutional and societal discourses that shaped (and were continually being shaped by) local R & T Club interactions, it is possible to demonstrate how relations of power simultaneously reproduced and rendered legitimate the literacy practices of participating members, as well as the perceptions they had of themselves as readers. For example, when those practices consisted of doing gender recurrently in ways that fit the occasion, they left no doubt as to the distinctions between what were considered appropriate male and female tastes in reading materials. That such practices were merely social arrangements whereby socially constituted differences took on appearances of being, "normal and natural" seemed not to matter, for as Marilyn Frye (as cited in West & Zimmerman, 1987, p. 146) noted, "We do become what we practice being."

Implications

Critical discourse analysis is a highly inferential approach. Reading power relations into particular local interactions and relating them to larger institutional and social structures is not without its critics. However, as Gilbert (1992) has reminded us, "Given the contested and deferred nature of meaning, and the inevitable ideological dimension of the processes of production and interpretation, all interpretative research faces this dilemma" (p. 55). Nonetheless, it was a dilemma we could ill afford to ignore when writing up this study's implications. As researchers historically constituted in the same institutional and societal structures we sought to understand, we could not assume that our findings originated separately from the power relations inherent in those larger social structures. Knowing this limited the kinds of implications we were willing to draw for practice.

Implications for Practice

What we can say is that listening to adolescents is a valuable way to begin to understand how they perceive and/or negotiate literacy experiences outside of school in community settings where informal groupings offer a range of opportunities for interacting with peers and adults. Listening can reveal the codes of power that keep some individuals from speaking out in a discussion while persuading others to join in. Like Chandler (1997), we found that by listening carefully to adolescents as they spoke appreciatively about the opportunity to share books in relatively risk-free environments, we were hearing subtle (and sometimes not so subtle) critiques of those same codes of power. Listening can also reveal the extent to which the pedagogization, or schooling, of literacy (Bloome, 1997; Street & Street, 1991) has infiltrated even the most informal of peer-led, small-group discussions in out-of-school settings.

We believe the fact that adolescents valued the social nature of the R & T Clubs is significant and has implications for thinking about different kinds of instruction that can support a developing sense of community among adolescents who are, or have the potential to become, avid readers. For this change in instruction to take root and grow, it may be necessary to rethink what we mean by an authority figure. Writing on the issue of authoritarianism in the classroom over 25 years ago, Armstrong (1973) made a point that we think is as valid today as it was then:

> When first we try to rid ourselves of an authoritarian past, it is hard not to assume that every decision of our pupils is acceptable, if only because we know how deep-seated is our instinct to force them into a "willing" acceptance of our own decisions. Nonetheless the slack permissiveness of this attitude is, in its turn, [equally] authoritarian.... For our refusal as teachers to oppose any decision our pupils make is usually a symptom of our failure to take their experience seriously. To treat another person's experience seriously—as seriously as we treat our own—entails a readiness to challenge it. (p. 53)

Challenging adolescents' choices was something that both Josephine and Colin found difficult to do, especially given the purpose of the study, which was to explore how the various R & T Clubs would negotiate after-school talk about texts in a relaxed setting. Later, in reflecting on her role as the adult facilitator of the Tuesday and Thursday groups, Josephine (Young, 1998) recalled that it was only when she began to question why discussions had to be about the same book, or why talking one at a time was a prerequisite for a "good" discussion, that she was able to release herself (at least temporarily) from thinking about text-based discussions in traditional ways. Only then, she noted, was she able to explore new directions with the adolescents in her R & T Clubs—directions that for her seemed to have potential for better serving the needs and desires of adolescent readers both in and out of school.

A further implication which must be considered in calling for instructional reform that would ostensibly liberate the learner from the institutionalized context of schooling (Illich, 1971; Moffett, 1994) is that there are few, if any, success models on which to rely. As Green (1973) noted in her critique of Illich (1973), "What teacher can seriously accept the idea that each individual has an inalienable right to learn what he likes?" (p. 130). Although we agree with Green's assessment of Illich's proposal from a practical point of view, we also know that teachers are experienced in how to learn from, and live with, tensions of the sort just described. For example, Athene, one of the adolescents in our study, told us, in response to reading Josephine's chapter on "Discussion as a Practice of Carnival" (Young, 1998) which described the Thursday R & T Club, that she recognized a similar practice in one of her classes at school. Athene explained that sometimes her teacher encouraged free and active participation as a way of motivating the students to join in a discussion before expecting them to return to more conventional and school-like interactional patterns of talk. We believe that teachers, such as the one Athene described, are well versed in managing the tension that results from what Green (1973) has acknowledged as two needs: "to guide and to set free" (p. 131).

Implications for Further Research

One implication for further research is the need to recruit a more diverse group of readers in studies conducted outside the normal school day. We believe that if less-avid readers had known more about the R & T Club experience in advance, they might have agreed to participate in the project. Our hunch is that many of the adolescents who received the recruitment flier assumed that the Clubs would be an extension of school-like activities. Initially, this was the impression that most of our 20 participants had, judging from what they told us in subsequent interviews. Four additions to the recruitment strategies described earlier are necessary. First, as researchers, we would personally go into middle and high school English classrooms to explain the project to the students. Second, we would describe the R & T Clubs as spaces where adolescents negotiate their own guidelines for talking about texts. Third, we would define for students our own expanded notion of texts—print, nonprint, classics, pop culture, the Web, and so forth. By doing this, we would be introducing potential participants to the materials available for adolescents in the library. Fourth, we would actively recruit a more ethnically diverse research team.

In addition to expanding the participant pool, we would consider enlarging our concept of community-based literacy projects to include book club discussions that meet in shopping malls. For example, we are aware of at least one such project—a mother–daughter book club at Borders Books in Phoenix, Arizona (Midey, 1998). Research is also needed that takes into account adolescents' acceptance of (or resistance to) formal literacy practices in after-school community activities, especially among populations of disempowered youth (Nieto, 1994).

Implications for further research include how such inquiry might be conceptualized. Within the past few years, the literacy community's approach to studying text-mediated practices has undergone a transformation of sorts, at least in terms of its willingness to consider the broader sociocultural framework for interpreting more individualized notions of the processes involved in reading, writing, speaking, listening, and thinking. Within this broader theoretical orientation, a call has gone out to researchers to look at changing views of meaning: "What meanings *are*, where meanings *come from*, how meanings *get fixed*, what *authorizes* particular meanings; and at changing notions of how we treat or handle texts as far as meanings and meaning-making are concerned" (Gee, as cited in Lankshear, 1997, p. 3). The current study's focus on where meanings associated with particular literacy practices come from and how they get inscribed in larger institutional and social practices is a response to that call. More studies with a similar focus are needed.

Proposing studies—the findings of which may go against the grain of dominant views about literacy—is political work. Relations of power in everyday literacy practices are often not apparent, at least not to those who view reading as a neutral process largely defined through either psychological models or holistic approaches to literacy acquisition. This view of literacy as a neutral process—what Street (1995, p. 133) called the "autonomous model of literacy"—has dominated Western thinking up to the present. Although the autonomous model presumes to "represent itself as though it is not a position located ideologically at all, as though it is just natural" (Street, 1995, pp. 132–133), this is not the case. Like competing models of literacy—for example, literacy as critical social practice—the autonomous model has its own set of assumptions about reading, writing, speaking, and listening that are embedded in relations of power.

Viewing literacy models as competitive in nature and ideologically embedded does not require giving up on the cognitive aspects of various literacy processes. Instead, like Street (1995), we believe these competing models should be viewed as subsuming the autonomous model in their attempt to understand literacy processes "encapsulated within...structures of power" (p. 161). By proposing and carrying out studies framed within one or more of these competing models of literacy, future researchers should not be viewed as attempting to replace an older model with newer ones, but instead, as opening the way for understanding the complexities that undergird conceptions of literacy and discourse as critical social practices. For if history has taught us anything in the field of education research, it is that, without such insight into the complex nature of the problems we choose to investigate, we are destined to replicate what Greer (1973) has labeled "the bloodiness of revolutionary and counterrevolutionary preening and prancing" (p. 84).

Acknowledgments

This study was funded in part by the National Reading Research Center of the Universities of Georgia and Maryland. It was supported under the Educational and Development Centers Program (PR/AWARD No. 117A20007) as administered by the Office of Educational Research and Improvement, U.S. Department of Education. The findings and opinions expressed here do not necessarily reflect the position or policies of the National Reading Research Center, the Office of Educational Research and Improvement, or the U.S. Department of Education.

Notes

[1] Although the Read and Talk Clubs, so named by one of the adolescents in the study, bear a resemblance to Book Club (McMahon & Raphael, 1997; McMahon, Raphael, & Goatley, 1995), they differ in an important way. Unlike Book Clubs, the R & T Clubs were not conceived for instructional purposes; this difference sets them apart, according to McMahon (S. McMahon, personal communication, April 29, 1996). Also, as one of the adolescents in our study pointed out, R & T Clubs were more appropriate because discussions were not limited to books.

[2] Tracing the elements of situation-specific discourse to larger institutional patterns and social structures, Gilbert (1992) acknowledged, is always controversial. As he noted, "Given the contested

and deferred nature of meaning, and the inevitable ideological dimension of the processes of production and interpretation, all interpretive research faces this dilemma, which is not avoided by restricting the focus to a particular exchange or locale" (p. 55).

[3] We thank Margaret Finders of Purdue University for articulating the need to be clear that adolescents do not comprise a subgroup that is distinctly separate from that of adults. We also thank her for directing our attention to the quoted material from Cintron (1991).

[4] Parents of two of the participants preferred the term Black American to the APA convention, African American.

[5] The three researchers are identified by their real names. The adolescents chose their own pseudonyms as explained in the text.

[6] Four grades later and just as enthused, Cleopatra decided to start her own R & T Club after the project ended. She enlisted the help of her school librarian, and it was a go, at least initially. However, in a follow-up telephone interview with Donna a few months later, Cleopatra announced that the school club had not worked out. She said, "I talked with the school librarian, and I thought she understood what I meant, but I guess she didn't." When Donna asked her to explain if she could, Cleopatra added, "The librarian started the club...but she picked the books."

[7] Subjectivity refers to the always changing and always becoming self through relations with others. As Davies (1993) has noted, "unlike identity, subjectivity is not a semi-fixed essence...but is constantly achieved through relations with others (both real and imagined) which are themselves made possible through discourse" (pp. 9–10).

[8] Exclusionary talk of this nature has also been reported by Alvermann, Commeyras, Young, Randall, and Hinson (1997).

[9] We are indebted to Mark Dressman of the University of Houston for suggesting this interpretation.

References

Alvermann, D.E., Commeyras, M., Young, J.P., Randall, S., & Hinson, D. (1997). Interrupting gendered discursive practices in classroom talk about texts: Easy to think about, difficult to do. *Journal of Literacy Research*, *29*, 7–104.

Alvermann, D.E., O'Brien, D.G., & Dillon, D.R. (1990). What teachers do when they say they're having discussions of content reading assignments: A qualitative analysis. *Reading Research Quarterly*, *25*, 296–321.

Alvermann, D.E., Young, J.P., Weaver, D., Hinchman, K., Moore, D.W., Phelps, S.F., et al. (1996). Middle and high school students' perceptions of how they experience text-based discussions: A multicase study. *Reading Research Quarterly*, *31*, 240–267.

Anderson, R.C. (1995). *Research foundations for wide reading.* Unpublished manuscript, University of Illinois at Urbana-Champaign.

Anderson, R.C., Wilson, P.T., & Fielding, L.G. (1988). Growth in reading and how children spend their time outside of school. *Reading Research Quarterly*, *23*, 285–303.

Armstrong, M. (1973). The role of teacher. In P. Buckman (Ed.), *Education without schools* (pp. 494–560). London: Souvenir Press.

Bakhtin, M.M. (1981). *The dialogic imagination.* Austin: University of Texas Press.

Bloome, D. (1997). This is literacy: Three challenges for teachers of reading and writing. *Australian Journal of Language and Literacy*, *20*, 107–115.

Brodkey, L. (1989). On the subjects of class and gender in "The literacy letter." *College English*, *54*, 125–141.

Campbell, J.R., Voelkl, K.E., & Donahue, P.L. (1997). *Report in brief: NAEP 1996 trends in academic progress.* Washington, DC: U.S. Department of Education, National Center for Education Statistics.

Chandler, K. (1997). The beach book club: Literacy in the "lazy days of summer." *Journal of Adolescent & Adult Literacy*, *41*, 104–115.

Cintron, R. (1991). Reading and writing graffiti: A reading. *The Quarterly Newsletter of the Laboratory of Comparative Human Cognition*, *13*, 21–24.

Cline, R.K.J., & Kretke, G.L. (1980). An evaluation of long-term SSR in the junior high school. *Journal of Reading*, *23*, 502–506.

Cole, M. (1995). Fifth Dimension Project. In J.V. Wertsch, P. del Rio, & A. Alvarez (Eds.),

Sociocultural studies of mind (pp. 197–214). Cambridge, UK: Cambridge University Press.

Commeyras, M., Orellana, M.F., Bruce, B.C., & Neilsen, L. (1996). What do feminist theories have to offer to literacy, education, and research? Reading Research Quarterly, 31, 458–468.

Corsaro, W.A., & Eder, D. (1990). Children's peer cultures. Annual Review Sociology, 16, 197–220.

Crichton, M. (1995). The lost world. New York: Knopf.

Davidson, J. (1988, Spring). Adolescent illiteracy: What libraries can do to solve the problem—A report on the research of the Project on Adolescent Literacy. The Bookmark, 46, 180–182.

Davies, B. (1993). Shards of glass. Cresskill, NJ: Hampton Press.

Davies, B. (1994). Poststructural theory and classroom practice. Geelong, VIC, Australia: Deakin University Press.

DeLongis, A., Hemphill, K.J., & Lehman, D.R. (1992). A structured diary methodology for the study of daily events. In F.B. Bryant, J. Edwards, R.S. Tindale, Em J. Posavac, L. Heath, E. Henderson, & Y. Suarez-Balcazar (Eds.), Methodological issues in applied social psychology (pp. 83–109). New York: Plenum.

Dressman, M. (1997a). Congruence, resistance, liminality: Reading and ideology in three school libraries. Curriculum Inquiry, 27, 267–316.

Dressman, M. (1997b). Preference as performance: Doing social class and gender in three school libraries. Journal of Literacy Research, 29, 319–361.

Dwyer, K., Danley, K., Sussman, S., & Johnson, C. (1990). Characteristics of eighth-grade students who initiate self-care in elementary and junior high school. Pediatrics, 86, 448–454.

Eder, D. (1995). School talk: Gender and adolescent culture. New Brunswick, NJ: Rutgers University Press.

Eder, D., & Enke, J. (1991). The structure of gossip: Opportunities and constraints on collective expression among adolescents. American Sociological Review, 56, 495–508.

Everhart, R. (1983). Reading, writing, and resistance: Adolescence and labor in a junior high school. Boston: Routledge.

Fairclough, N. (1989). Language and power. London: Longman.

Fairclough, N. (1995). Critical discourse analysis: The critical study of language. London: Longman.

Farmer, L. (1992). Young adult services in the small library (Small Libraries Publications Series No. 19). Chicago: Library Administration and Management Association & the American Library Association.

Finders, M.J. (1996). "Just girls": Literacy and allegiance in junior high school. Written Communication, 13, 93–129.

Finders, M. J. (1997). Just girls: Hidden literacies and life in junior high. New York: Teachers College Press.

Fine, G.A., Mortimer, J.T., & Roberts, D.F. (1990). Leisure, work, and the mass media. In S. Feldman & G.R. Elliott (Eds.), At the threshold: The developing adolescent (pp. 225–252). Cambridge, MA: Harvard University Press.

Flood, J., Lapp, D., Alvarez, A., Romero, A., Ranck-Buhr, W., Moore, J., et al. (1994). Teacher book clubs: A study of teachers' and student teachers' participation in contemporary multicultural fiction literature discussion groups (Reading Research Rep. No. 22). Athens, GA: National Reading Research Center.

Foucault, M. (1986). Of other spaces. Diacritics, 16, 22–27.

Freebody, P., Luke, A., Gee, J., & Street, B.V. (1998). Literacy as critical social practice. London: Taylor & Francis.

Garrison, D. (1979). Apostles of culture: The public librarian and American society, 1876–1920. New York: Free Press.

Gee, J.P. (1990). Social linguistics and literacies: Ideology in discourses. London: Falmer.

Gee, J.P. (1996). Social linguistics and literacies: Ideology in discourses (2nd ed.). London: Taylor & Francis.

Gilbert, R. (1992). Text and context in qualitative educational research: Discourse analysis and the problem of contextual explanation. Linguistics and Education, 4, 37–57.

Giles, N.D. (1994). Negative and positive reading attitudes as predictors of fourth graders' involuntary out-of-school reading. Unpublished master's thesis, University of West Florida.

Goffman, E. (1959). The presentation of self in everyday life. New York: Doubleday Anchor Books.

Goffman, E. (1976). Gender display. Studies in the Anthropology of Visual Communication, 3, 69–77.

Greany, V. (1980). Factors related to amount and type of leisure time reading. *Reading Research Quarterly, 15*, 337–357.

Greany, V., & Hegarty, M. (1987). Correlates of leisure-time reading. *Journal of Research in Reading, 15*(3), 3–20.

Green, M. (1973). And it still is news. In A. Gartner, C. Greer, & F. Riessman (Eds.), *After deschooling, what?* (pp. 129–136). New York: Harper & Row.

Greer, C. (1973). All schooled up. In A. Gartner, C. Greer, & F. Riessman (Eds.), *After deschooling, what?* (pp. 77–84). New York: Harper & Row.

Heath, S.B., & McLaughlin, M.W. (Eds.). (1993). *Identity and inner-city youth: Beyond ethnicity and gender.* New York: Teachers College Press.

Hill, M.H., & Van Horn, L.V. (1995). Book club goes to jail: Can book clubs replace gangs? *Journal of Adolescent & Adult Literacy, 39*, 180–188.

hooks, b. (1990). *Yearning: Race, gender, and cultural politics.* Boston: South End Press,

Illich, I. (1971). *Deschooling society.* New York: Harper & Row.

Illich, I. (1973). After deschooling, what? In A. Gartner, C. Greer, & F. Riessman (Eds.), *After deschooling, what?* (pp. 1–28). New York: Harper & Row.

Kamberelis, G. (1995). Genre as institutionally informed social practice. *Journal of Contemporary Legal Issues, 6*, 117–171.

Kinney, D.A. (1993). From nerds to normals: The recovery of identity among adolescents from middle school to high school. *Sociology of Education, 66*, 21–40.

Ladson-Billings, G. (1997). For colored girls who have considered suicide when the academy's not enough: Reflections of an African American woman scholar. In A. Neumann & P.L. Peterson (Eds.), *Learning from our lives: Women, research, and autobiography in education* (pp. 52–70). New York: Teachers College Press.

Lankshear, C. (with Gee, J.P., Knobel, M., & Searle, S). (1997). *Changing literacies.* Buckingham, UK: Open University Press.

Larkin, R. (1979). *Suburban youth in cultural crisis.* New York: Oxford University Press.

Leach, M. (1996, April). *Feminist figuration: Gossip as a counter discourse.* Paper presented at the annual meeting of the American Educational Research Association, New York.

Lesko, N. (1988). *Symbolizing society: Stories, rites and structure in Catholic high school.* Philadelphia: Falmer.

Luke, A., & Freebody, P. (1997). Critical literacy and the question of normativity: An introduction. In S. Muspratt, A. Luke, & P. Freebody (Eds.), *Constructing critical literacies* (pp. 1–18). Cresskill, NJ: Hampton Press.

Mac An Ghaill, M. (1994). *The making of men: Masculinities, sexualities and schooling.* Buckingham, UK: Open University Press.

Marshall, J.D., Smagorinsky, P., & Smith, M.W. (1995). *The language of interpretation: Patterns of discourse in discussion of literature.* Urbana, IL: National Council of Teachers of English.

Martin, A.M. (1986). *The baby-sitters club.* New York: Scholastic.

Mathews, V.H. (Ed.). (1994). *Library services for children and youth.* New York: Neal-Schuman.

McGinley, W., & Kamberelis, G. (1996). Maniac Magee and Ragtime Tumpie: Children negotiating self and world through reading and writing. *Research in the Teaching of English, 30*, 1–36.

McKenna, M., Kear, D., & Ellsworth, R. (1995). Children's attitudes toward reading: A national survey. *Reading Research Quarterly, 30*, 934–956.

McMahon, S.I., & Raphael, T.E. (1997). *The book club connection: Literacy teaming and classroom.* New York: Teachers College Press.

McMahon, S.I., Raphael, T.E., & Goatley, V. (1995). Changing the context for classroom reading instruction: The book club project. In J. Brophy (Ed.), *Advances in research on teaching* (pp. 123–166). Greenwich, CT: JAI Press.

Midey, C. (1998, August 18). *Big on books: Clubs bring moms, daughters together.* The Arizona Republic, pp. D1, D3.

Mishler, E.G. (1986). *Research interviewing: Context and narrative.* Cambridge, MA: Harvard University Press.

Moffett, J. (1994). *The universal schoolhouse.* San Francisco: Jossey-Bass.

Moore, D.W. (1996). Contexts for literacy in secondary schools. In D.J. Leu, C.K. Kinzer, & K.A. Hinchman (Eds.), *Literacies for the 21st century: Research and practice* (45th yearbook of the National Reading Conference, pp. 15–46). Chicago: National Reading Conference.

Morrow, L.M., & Weinstein, C.S. (1986). Encouraging voluntary reading: The impact of a literature program on children's use of library centers. *Reading Research Quarterly, 21,* 330–346.

Myers, J. (1992). The social contexts of school and personal literacy. *Reading Research Quarterly, 27,* 297–333.

National Center for Education Statistics. (1995). *Services and resources for children and young adults in public libraries.* Washington, DC: U.S. Department of Education, Office of Educational Research and Improvement.

Neuman, S.B. (1986). The home environment and fifth-grade students' leisure reading. *The Elementary School Journal, 86,* 335–343.

Nieto, S. (1994). Lessons from students on creating a chance to dream. *Harvard Educational Review, 64,* 392–426.

Obidah, J. E. (1998). Black-Mystory: Literate currency in everyday schooling. In D.E. Alvermann, K.A. Hinchman, D.W. Moore, S.F. Phelps, & D.R. Waff (Eds.), *Reconceptualizing the literacies in adolescents' lives* (pp. 51–71). Mahwah, NJ: Erlbaum.

O'Brien, D.G., Stewart, R.A., & Moje, E.B. (1995). Why content literacy is difficult to infuse into the secondary school: Complexities of curriculum, pedagogy, and school culture. *Reading Research Quarterly, 30,* 442–463.

Orellana, M.F. (1995). Literacy as a gendered social practice: Tasks, texts, talk, and take-up. *Reading Research Quarterly, 30,* 674–708.

Pascal, F. (1993). *Sweet Valley High.* New York: Bantam.

Resnick, D.P., & Goodman, M. (1994). American culture and the gifted. In P.O. Ross (Ed.), *National excellence: A case for developing America's talent: An anthology of readings* (pp. 109–121). Washington, DC: U.S. Department of Education, Office of Educational Research and improvement.

Roponen, S. (1995, September). *Writing in computer-assisted qualitative data analysis.* Paper presented at the Conference on Text Analysis and Computers, Mannheim, Germany.

Street, B. (1995). *Social literacies: Critical approaches to literacy in development, ethnography, and education.* New York: Longman.

Street, J., & Street, B. (1991). The schooling of literacy. In D. Barton & R. Ivanic (Eds.), *Writing in the community* (pp. 143–166). London: Sage.

Takanishi, R. (1993). *Adolescence in the 1990s: Risk and opportunity.* New York: Teachers College Press.

Taylor, B.M., & Maruyama, G.M. (1990). Time spent reading and reading growth. *American Educational Research Journal, 27,* 351–362.

Thomson, J. (1987). *Understanding teenagers' reading.* New York: Nichols.

U.S. Department of Education. (1996). *Pursuing excellence* (National Center for Education Statistics Rep. No. 97-198). Washington, DC: U.S. Government Printing Office.

Walberg, H.J., & Tsai, S. (1984). Reading achievement and diminishing returns to time. *Journal of Educational Psychology, 76,* 442–451.

Wells, M.C. (1996). *Literacies lost: When students move from a progressive middle school to a traditional high school.* New York: Teachers College Press.

West, C., & Zimmerman, D.H. (1987). Doing gender. *Gender & Society, 1,* 125–151.

Willis, P. (1977). *Learning to labor: How working class kids get working class jobs.* New York: Columbia University Press.

Worthy, J., & McKool, S.S. (1996). Students who say they hate to read: The importance of opportunity, choice, and access. In D.J. Leu, C.K. Kinzer, & K.A. Hinchman (Eds.), *Literacies for the 21st century: Research and practice* (45th yearbook of the National Reading Conference, pp. 245–254). Chicago: National Reading Conference.

Young, J.P. (1998). Discussion as a practice of carnival. In D.E. Alvermann, K.A. Hinchman, D.W. Moore, S.F. Phelps, & D.R. Waff (Eds.), *Reconceptualizing the literacies in adolescents' lives* (pp. 247–264). Mahwah, NJ: Erlbaum.

33

The Effect of Reader Stance on Students' Personal Understanding of Literature

Joyce E. Many

In her transactional theory of reader response, Rosenblatt (1978, 1985) describes the text as serving as a pattern for the reader, guiding the reader as he or she creates a personal version of the literary work. This uniquely individual literary experience that each reader creates and the factors that influence that personal meaning-making are important to researchers examining students' response to literature.

Reader response theory's emphasis on the role of the reader has resulted in a valuing of individual interpretations. Literature is seen as events to be lived through, offering opportunities for self-knowledge and for understanding others (Cooper, 1985). Consequently, new ways of describing the varying interpretations reached by different readers have evolved which acknowledge the validity of personal understanding (Cox & Many, 1989; Lehr, 1988).

One factor which has been hypothesized to affect a reader's understanding of a work is the reader's stance, or focus of attention (Rosenblatt, 1978, 1985). An *efferent stance* indicates the reader's attention is focused on the information which is to be taken away from the reading and can result in an analysis of or study of the text (Cox & Many, 1989). When assuming the *aesthetic stance*, on the other hand, the reader's focus is upon the lived-through literary experience and the thoughts, feelings, images, and associations which are evoked.

Although Rosenblatt and other reader response theorists, researchers, and teachers have focused on the aesthetic stance and personal understandings of literature as a point of discussion or as an underlying assumption in their works (Corcoran, 1987; Evans, 1987; Probst, 1988, Rosenblatt, 1938, 1978, 1985, 1986), little research has been conducted examining Rosenblatt's concept of stance in response to literature or how stance is related to other factors in stu-

From Zutell, J., & McCormick, S. (Eds.), *Literacy Theory and Research: Analyses From Multiple Paradigms* (39th yearbook of the National Reading Conference, pp. 51–63). Copyright © 1990 by the National Reading Conference. Reprinted with permission of the publisher.

dents' responses. Only one study (Cox & Many, 1989) has investigated the relationship between a reader's stance and level of understanding of literary works. As part of a larger study, Cox and Many examined the free responses of 38 above-level fifth-grade students to four novels. The purposes of their study were (a) to develop data-driven instruments to describe the stances taken in a response and the level of personal understanding reached and (b) to examine the possible relationship between stance, level of understanding, and story preference. Although prior to Cox and Many's study Rosenblatt's use of stance had primarily been used to refer to the focus of attention during the actual reading event, the results indicated stance plays a role in affecting expressed responses as well. A significant positive relationship was found between the mean stance for all four novels and the mean level of understanding reached ($r = .36, p < .0001$).

The purpose of this study was to further explore the variations in stances taken in expressed responses by investigating an older population. Although junior high students' responses to literature have been previously investigated in terms of the objective or subjective formulation of the response (Applebee, 1978), the relationship between reader expectation, comprehension, evaluation, and preference (Cullinan, Harwood, & Galda, 1983), and the elements of the response (Golden, 1979; Purves, 1973, 1981; Rogers, 1988), no research has examined the stances taken in junior high school students' responses or the relationship of aesthetic and efferent stances to personal understanding of a literary work.

Furthermore, Cox and Many's study examined only the relationship between the mean stance and mean level of understanding for all four novels read, leaving unanswered the question of whether the relationship between stance and level of understanding is influenced by text. Although much research has documented the effect of text on students' response to literature (Purves, 1973, 1981), recent research indicates response strategies can be consistent across texts (Beach, 1987). Therefore, this study examined the relationship of stance to level of understanding for three individual short stories to provide information as to whether that relationship is text specific.

Specifically, the purposes of this study were (a) to describe the stances taken in eighth-grade subjects' responses to literature, (b) to analyze the relationship between the reader's stance in a response and the level of understanding reached in the response, and (c) to analyze whether the relationship between reader stance and level of understanding is consistent across individual texts.

Method

Subjects

Subjects for the study were 51 eighth-grade students (26 males and 25 females) in 2 intact classrooms involved in a larger research project (Many, 1989). Two participating schools were chosen, one serving students from a low socioeconomic level and the other serving students from a middle to upper socioeconomic level. One class was randomly selected from the available eighth-grade English classes at each school.

Materials

Three realistic short stories were chosen through a pilot study which used six possible selections. Research indicates realistic stories are preferred reading in the upper-elementary and middle school grades (Golden, 1979; Purves & Beach, 1972), and stories needed to be short enough to allow students to complete the reading in one sitting. Therefore, criteria for the six initial story selections were based on probable interest, appropriate readability, and story length. Using an adapted version of Sword's (1985) "Criteria for Evaluating Picture Story Books," a panel of reading experts rated all six stories as above average on elements of plot unification, plot believability, imaginative plot, main character portrayal, believability of main character, use of vivid imagery, and establishment of mood.

The stories used in this study were those selected for the larger research project based on overall preference by all students participating in the pilot study. The ratings of the three selected stories (1—high, 5—low) by the eighth-grade students in the pilot were "The Dollar's Worth" (Werner, 1979)—2.5, "The Secret of the Aztec Idol" (Bonham, 1976)—3.1 (hereafter referred to as "The Aztec Idol"), and "The Runaway" (Holman, 1976)—3.3.

Procedure

Pilot Study. Two classes at the eighth-grade level from a university lab school participated in the pilot. The students were drawn from the same population as the subjects in the actual study itself. Students were asked to read and respond in writing to one of the six stories and to rate the story on a 1–5 scale. Results from the pilot study were used to determine the stories to be used in the actual study and to refine data collection procedures.

Data Collection. For each of the short stories, subjects were asked to read the selection and then to respond to the prompt "Write anything you want about the story you just read." Data were collected in 3 separate episodes over a 9-week period. The order of the stories was randomized from subject to subject to account for possible influence of story sequence on response.

Data Analysis. Data were analyzed to determine the primary stance of the response as a whole and the level of understanding reached. The instruments used to code the responses are described below.

The reader's stance when responding to the literary work was examined using Cox and Many's (1989) Instrument for Measuring Reader Stance on an

Efferent to Aesthetic Continuum. This instrument was based on Rosenblatt's description (1978, 1985, 1986) of the aesthetic and efferent poles of the reader stance continuum and Corcoran's description (1987) of the types of mental activities involved in an aesthetic reading. Like earlier data-driven methods of classifying response to literature (Applebee, 1978; Galda, 1982; Purves & Rippere, 1968), this rating system emerged from the data analysis of subject responses. Responses rated on one end of the 5-point continuum indicate a primarily efferent stance, while scores on the opposing end indicate a more aesthetic stance. Table 1 gives a brief description of each level on the instrument.

The responses were also classified according to the level of personal understanding reached using An Instrument for Rating a Reader's Level of Personal Understanding (Cox & Many, 1989). The instrument evolved out of Cox and Many's research and is based on Applebee's (1978) levels of meaning and Ricoeur's (1976) interpretation theory. The level of understanding rating indicates the degree to which the response is tied to story events and the level of abstract generalization reached in the response. Table 2 gives a brief description of each level of personal understanding.

It is important to note that the instruments allow for responses demonstrating from low to high levels of understanding at both the efferent and aesthetic poles of the continuum, as shown in the examples below. For instance, the

TABLE 1
Levels of Reader Stance on an Efferent to Aesthetic Continuum

Levels	Description
1. Most efferent response	Analysis of elements according to outside structure (literary elements, realism, what was learned)
2. Primarily efferent response	Retelling (concentration on relating the story line, narrating what the story was about)
3. Elements of aesthetic response	Portions of both efferent analysis and aesthetic experience of work (equal emphasis on both, primary focus using a single stance indeterminable)
4. Primarily aesthetic response	Selection of story events or characters to elaborate preference, judgment, or description (I enjoyed it when..., I thought it was good/funny when...)
5. Most aesthetic response	Focus on the lived-through experience of the literary work (the world created while reading and the emotions or associations resulting from the experience)

TABLE 2
Levels of Understanding

Levels	Description
1	Does not go beyond literal meaning of story
2	Indicates some interpretation of story events
3	Demonstrates understanding of specific story events through analogy to self or world
4	Reaches a generalized belief or understanding about life

following response would be scored at the most efferent stance and would exemplify the highest level of understanding.

Stance Rating 1—Level of Understanding 4

It is a very unusual show. It tells us that we can do anything we want to. It also tells grown-ups a thing or two. One of the things it told grown-ups is: Before you step ahead make sure you've seen all the details.

In contrast, the next example is also written from the most efferent stance, but it would be scored at the lowest level of understanding.

Stance Rating 1—Level of Understanding 1

It was a pretty good story and I enjoyed it. The characters were designed pretty well but I didn't like the way the plot kept skipping time and not telling you what was happening. They picked a good setting for a plot like this one.

At the aesthetic end of the continuum on the stance instrument, responses can also range in the level of understanding demonstrated. The next example shows a response written from the most aesthetic stance which would be rated at the lowest level of understanding.

Stance Rating 5—Level of Understanding 1

I really enjoyed reading the book, it kept me curious throughout. After I was finished I kept going back and thinking about the story. I could picture what was happening.

Finally, as the next response illustrates, aesthetic responses can also demonstrate the highest levels of personal understanding.

Stance Rating 5—Level of Understanding 4

I probably wouldn't have handled it as well as the family in the story did when she died, if my sister or daughter fell out of a tree and died when she was only eleven. The story really made you sit back and think about how unfair life can really be.

The coding of all the data was completed by the researcher. Independent raters, trained in the use of each instrument, coded a random sample of 20% of the data to check for reliability. Interrater reliability was established using the Pearson Product Moment Correlation Coefficient. For the holistic rating of stance the reliability was $r = .79$, and for the holistic rating of level of understanding, $r = .81$.

Results and Discussion

Reader Stance

Analyses of the stances subjects took in their responses revealed responses at all points on the efferent-to-aesthetic continuum. As shown in Table 3, 38% of the total responses were on the efferent end of the continuum (ratings 1 and 2), with 9% of the total responses written from the most efferent stance (rating 1). The efferent responses concentrated for the most part on evaluating the literary elements or on the author's writing style. As shown in the example on the next page and as contended by Rosenblatt (1982), many of the analyses of the literary works tended to be shallow responses.

TABLE 3
Responses at Each Point on the Stance Continuum

| Stance | Stories | | | Total |
	DW	AI	RUN	
1	3	6	4	13
	(6%)	(13%)	(8%)	(9%)
2	16	16	11	43
	(32%)	(34%)	(21%)	(29%)
3	9	9	9	27
	(18%)	(19%)	(18%)	(18%)
4	6	7	3	16
	(12%)	(15%)	(6%)	(11%)
5	16	9	24	49
	(32%)	(19%)	(47%)	(33%)

DW = "The Dollar's Worth"; AI = "The Aztec Idol"; RUN = "The Runaway."

I didn't like the story at all. The story was too confusing. The story didn't tell anything much about the characters. The story didn't share the feelings of the characters. The story was quite boring and I didn't like it. The story didn't explain anything—never got to the point. When people write about stories they want to know a little about the characters and the story.

Martha—"The Aztec Idol"

However, not all responses written from an efferent stance were superficial. Some students searched the stories in an attempt to determine the theme or what the author was trying to say. In the following response to the story "The Runaway," Victoria grapples with that very question.

The Runaway was a story that I really didn't understand. I have my own conclusion about what it meant but I don't think the author's idea is the same as what I think.

I think the author is trying to say (this is my opinion) that home is the best place to be. And that just because things may not go your way or your parents are pressuring you. That your home is the best. Just because things look good on the outside doesn't mean they're good on the inside.

This girl Marcie, thought her friend was so lucky, and that her mother didn't always bug her. But once she went over and found out how it really was she knew that a family's true love is always best. So in this story it was probably made for someone who wants to run away. To try and warn them. Because someone else has always got family problems worse than yours.

This may be what the author had in mind, but it is kind of confusing unless you really sit down and think about it for a while.

I think someone who is experiencing problems would enjoy and understand better than I do.

Rosenblatt (1978) has stressed that often readers fluctuate in their reading between an efferent and an aesthetic stance; such was also the case in 18% of the total responses in which no primary stance (rating 3) could be determined. In many cases, brevity made classification of a primary stance difficult, while in others (as found in the example below) definite efferent and aesthetic elements were mingled in the response.

This story was very good. The author (Herma Werner) did a very good job in giving the characters' personality. Just by reading that story I hate Mr. Watts too. The only thing this story was lacking was a good description of this place. I pictured it out in the country where there isn't much traffic and there aren't many stores. But I don't know. For all I know it could be in New York City. (Except for when it said Mr. Watts went putting along the street at 10 mph.) Other than that, the story was excellent.

Jim—"The Dollar's Worth"

In his response, Jim relates an efferent analysis of the character portrayal and the description of the setting in the story "The Dollar's Worth." He substantiates his evaluative statements by giving us a glimpse of his evocation of the work, the images and feelings which emerged as he pictured the story experience in his mind. Jim's response serves as a reminder that the stance in the reported response may or may not be consistent with the stance taken during the actual reading event. Jim seems to be writing an efferent analysis of the story, based on a very aesthetic reading of the literary work.

Of the total responses, 44% fell at the aesthetic end of the continuum (ratings 4 and 5), with 33% exhibiting the most aesthetic stance (rating 5). Although all of the most aesthetic responses focused on relating the lived-through experience of the stories and the emotions, images, ideas, and associations which were called to mind during the reading and reliving of the story event, the responses themselves were as varied and unique as the individual children who wrote them. The responses below illustrate some of the elements which were found in the primary aesthetic responses: imaging and picturing; relating associations and feelings evoked; and extending, hypothesizing, and retrospecting.

Imaging and Picturing. Aesthetic responses often include a description of a visual image the reader pictured as reading or an account of how the reader imagines it would feel to be one of the characters. Some subjects identify with characters a great deal, as found in the responses of one subject, Amy. In her responses to all three stories, Amy chose to create her own literary works using the voice of the character in the story. The poem below was written in response to "The Dollar's Worth," a story of a young girl who encounters prejudice while working at a gas station.

> The penny-pinching old man in the beat-up old car,
> Drives in, for his dollar's worth of gas.
> His is cold, and mean,
> And his mouth is set in it's downturned frown.
> In disgust, I watch as his wrinkled old finger points,
> His eyes watching me, every step I take.
> I grew to hate him,
> And dread the days he'd come.
> But I learned that he had no-one.
> Almost no-one.
> And he insulted me, simply in a gesture of time gone by,
> and his forgotten past.
> He will be back tomorrow,
> In his beat-up old car,
> Watching me like a hawk,
> Pointing, frowning,
> Shooting Insults,
> And I will give him, his dollars
> worth of gas.

Amy's response illustrates the possibilities for imaginative reading and responding when students focus on living through the story experience. Her identification with the story character, Trish, resulted in her assuming Trish's role and feeling Trish's feelings. Other students identified with story characters also but concentrated more on situations from their own lives which were similar to those experienced by the characters.

Relating Associations and Feelings Evoked. "The Runaway" tells the story of a young girl who feels smothered by her parents' love and runs away to a friend's house, only to find that grass is not always greener on the other side. Forty-seven percent of the eighth-grade responses to this story were written from the most aesthetic stance (as compared to 19% of the responses to "The Aztec Idol" and 32% of the responses to "The Dollar's Worth"). The subject matter of this story seemed to encourage what Cochran-Smith (1984) calls life-to-text connections, in that many of the subjects related to their own problems or their fantasies about or experiences with running away, as illustrated in the responses below.

> I would like to be able to have a family who cares about me, and we could never be split up, and could talk out our family problems, and that I could always go somewhere called home. I feel sorry for Marcie that her and her mother couldn't work things out. Sometimes I think about ways I could runaway and how things would be for me like Marcie.
>
> David

> It was kinda of instering. I mean it was also stupid. I would have killed anybody if they bit me on the leg for no reason. And that chick is going to cry when she runs away! When I ran I was happy. Pluse going over to a friends house. NO WAY! Man ain't gonna help yo out none. Pluse She don't know what trouble is. I been living away from my house for 3½ year. For running, stealing, doing drugs, tresspassing, and vandalizing. She had no reason to go away from home. It was not realistic in some ways. Well there you have it. The end.
>
> Stan

For these students, the story hit close to home and they were able to relate definite associations which came to mind during reading. For David, the story offered a picture of a caring family life which he wished he could share. He saw the story as realistic, although different from his own experience. Stan, while giving evidence which came to mind as he read, eventually rejected the reality of the story world because it did not conform to his own experience.

Hypothesizing, Extending, and Retrospecting. Some students, responding from the primarily aesthetic stance, extended the story line by hypothesizing background information or by continuing the stories to their own end. Others mused over what they were thinking as they read the story. In the following response to "The Dollar's Worth," Victoria explains a character's behavior by imagining what previous life experiences might have resulted in him being the way he was.

> This was a good story. It showed two different sides of people. It showed how the man really felt and how he had to act. Some people don't understand these two sides. You don't really have to know someone, just look at how they act. If someone acts hyper or shows off, they may not be doing it just because they want to, but probably because they want someone's attention.
>
> This man in the story, Mr. Watts, probably wasn't really a mean man, he just wanted someone to talk to or he was just defending himself so people wouldn't feel sorry for him. Maybe he didn't want anyone to know he was poor and lived with his sister because he might have felt ashamed.
>
> He also might not really have been prejudice against girls, but maybe something bad happened, that a girl did to him. He might have even wanted to marry some girl and they wouldn't.
>
> But you can't really be angry with people like that, because if you are a person you should know how people act.

Victoria has taken advantage of what Iser (1980) calls the gaps in the text, filling in the unknown history of a character to rationalize his behavior. In the next response to "The Aztec Idol," a story about two young boys who are conned by an old fisherman when they agree to buy a "secret" from him, Herbert goes beyond extending the story. Imagining himself in the boys' shoes, he reconstructs the personality and motivations of the old fisherman, remaking the character into one that he himself would have believed in and liked.

> If the man was as much as a jerk as the man in this story and if the secrets were so dumb I wouldn't have bought one. That man was so conceited and concerned about himself that I hated him. You could tell from the beginning by the way he talked about welfare, it was the way he said it and what he said about it that made you know he was a jerk. A friendly old guy who enjoyed kids might have had a different approach for selling a secret. He would have been nicer and more interesting. Like an old man who loves to see kids steal peaches off his tree because he likes seeing the kids so joyful and right when the kids got just one peach he runs out of his house and shouts, "You rotten little brats! I'll get you for this!" Even though he really doesn't mean it, he just likes to give the kids a good time and make them feel important.

Like Amy who responded through poetry, Herbert included a creation of a new literary work, a vignette, as he constructed meaning from his literary experience. As well as creating original narrative forms, some students responding from the aesthetic stance referred to stories they had previously read or viewed.

I think one part of the story goes along with the movie with Julie Andrews in it. I also think Marcie should [take] advantage of her parents "loving care." And get rid of that friend Hilda. I think that for an occupation she ought to go into poetry. If she would just try and except her parents "Loving Care" her life would be a lot easier.

Arthur

Arthur's reference to a Julie Andrews movie gives an indication that he has made an intertextual connection as he read, but because he does not elaborate we are left wondering how or if the connection influenced the meaning he made from his evocation of "The Runaway."

Stance and Level of Personal Understanding

To determine the relationship between stance and level of understanding, separate analyses of variances (ANOVAs) were conducted for each story. For the purpose of the ANOVAs, the variable stance was treated as an independent variable and converted to a three-level rating: (1) mostly or primarily efferent, (2) elements of both efferent and aesthetic, and (3) mostly or primarily aesthetic. Separate analyses of variance revealed stance to significantly affect the level of understanding reached for all three stories. Table 4 provides a summary of the ANOVA statistics, and Table 5 lists the means and standard errors for each story and the post-hoc analyses. For all three stories, subjects focusing on the aesthetic stance were significantly more likely to interpret story events, to apply story events to life, and to draw generalizations about the world.

TABLE 4
Summary of ANOVA Results for Each Story

Source	df	MS	F
		"The Dollar's Worth" ($n = 50$)	
Stance	2	4.418	6.33**
Error	47	.698	
		"The Aztec Idol" ($n = 47$)	
Stance	2	4.450	3.76*
Error	44	1.184	
		"The Runaway" ($n = 51$)	
Stance	2	7.301	8.43***
Error	48	.866	

Differences in n across stories due to subject absenteeism.
*$p < .05$; **$p < .01$; ***$p < .001$.

TABLE 5
Means and Standard Errors for Level of Understanding by Stance for Each Story

Stance Level	n	M	Std. Error
		"The Dollar's Worth"	
1	19	2.11_{ab}	.196
2	9	1.56_a	.278
3	22	2.68_b	.178
		"The Aztec Idol"	
1	22	1.68_a	.232
2	9	1.78_a	.363
3	16	2.63_b	.272
		"The Runaway"	
1	15	2.00_a	.240
2	9	2.11_a	.310
3	27	3.11_b	.179

Means with different subscripts differ significantly at $p < .05$.

The relationship between stance and level of understanding proved to be fairly consistent across texts. For all stories, subjects who focused on the lived-through experience of the story had a significantly higher mean level of understanding than subjects who responded with no single primary stance. The aesthetic responses were also higher in level of understanding than the efferent responses, and these differences were significant for two of the three stories. These findings indicate that the relationship between stance and level of understanding is not text specific.

Conclusions

The results of this study are significant in that they provide information as to the range and complexity of stances found in eighth graders' responses and investigate the relationship between stance and level of understanding using junior high school subjects. While the results of studies analyzing written responses are limited since a subject's reported response (and the identifiable stance and level of understanding therein) may not reflect the extent of his or her reading experience, the following conclusions are suggested.

Although the largest percentage of the total responses were written from the most aesthetic stance (33%), in view of the fact that the aesthetic stance is the focus deemed appropriate for the reading of literature (Rosenblatt, 1985) this seems regretfully low. The aesthetic stance, focusing on the evocation of the literary work, was associated with imaginative and creative responses where students found the literacy experience meaningful and relevant. If teachers intend literature to offer unique experiences through which students can live, find pleasure, and reach understanding about themselves and the world, the aesthetic stance needs to be supported and encouraged.

When students are asked to take an efferent approach to literature—for example, in learning about literary elements such as plot, character development, and so forth—they should examine these elements in light of an original aesthetic experience of the literary work. Rosenblatt (1978) has underscored the importance of the reader involved in analyzing literature to "keep his sense of...[his personal evocation] as vividly and fully in mind as possible" (p. 174). This is substantiated by the shallowness and analytical distance found in many of the responses written from the efferent stance in this study. In contrast, some of the responses at stance rating 3, which mingled an efferent analysis of the work with reports of the richness of the lived-through experience or even the lack of such an experience, were much more sophisticated and meaningful.

When examining the relationship between stance and level of personal understanding, responses written from the aesthetic stance were associated with significantly higher levels of understanding. In terms of the classroom, these findings underscore the importance of fostering the aesthetic stance when students respond to literature. When teachers use Ping-Pong questioning techniques, where students parrot back responses to questions listed in the teacher's manual, students may assume the only appropriate focus when reading literature is to analyze the selection and retain important information. Although teachers may use such methods in an attempt to extend literal and inferential comprehension and to develop analytical thinking skills, inviting students to fully relive the literary experience could lead them to greater heights of understanding.

That the results were significant across story selections indicates that stance is a factor affecting response to literature regardless of literary text. While individual texts may vary in their potential for encouraging the aesthetic stance with certain age groups (for example, the story "The Runaway" elicited a large percentage of aesthetic responses focusing on the eighth graders' associations with their life experiences), the occurrence of higher levels of personal understanding in responses written from the aesthetic stance was consistent across all three realistic short stories. Consequently, regardless of the literary works comprising the curriculum, teachers who want to encourage readers to find personal meaning in literature should consider aesthetic teaching strategies which promote and strengthen students' individual evocations. Such strategies would ideally (a) invite open responses, (b) give students time to respond, (c) provide opportunity to talk, (d) encourage personal and intertextual connections, and (e) recognize and encourage the focus of attention on the lived-through experience of the literary evocation.

This research provides empirical support for use of the aesthetic stance, which has long been encouraged in both theoretical and practical essays. Additional research is needed not only on the stance taken in children's responses but also on the reader's stance during the actual reading event, using techniques such as protocol analysis. The stance children take in their response to informational texts as opposed to literary works is another area which needs investigation as well. By understanding how children focus their attention when reading and responding, we can aid them not only in the productive reading of all texts, but also in discovery of how to live through, relate to, and learn from the limitless supply of worlds found in literature.

References

Applebee, A.N. (1978). *The child's concept of story: Ages two to seventeen.* Chicago: University of Chicago Press.

Beach, R. (1987, December). *Applying life to literature: Reader's use of autobiographical experiences to interpret texts.* Paper presented at the annual meeting of the National Reading Conference, St. Petersburg, FL.

Bonham, F. (1976). Secret of the Aztec idol. In A. Diven (Eds.), *The Scribner anthology for young people* (pp. 116–124). New York: Scribner.

Cochran-Smith, M. (1984). *The making of a reader.* Norwood, NJ: Ablex.

Cooper, C.R. (Ed.). (1985). *Researching response to literature and the teaching of literature.* Norwood, NJ: Ablex.

Corcoran, B. (1987). Teachers creating readers. In B. Corcoran & E. Evans (Eds.), *Readers, texts, and teachers* (pp. 41–74). Upper Montclair, NJ: Boynton/Cook.

Cox, C., & Many, J.E. (1989, March). *Reader stance towards a literary work: Applying the transactional theory to children's responses.* Paper presented at the annual meeting of the American Educational Research Association, San Francisco, CA.

Cullinan, B.E., Harwood, K.T., & Galda, L. (1983). The reader and the story: Comprehension and response. *Journal of Research and Development in Education, 16*(3), 29–38.

Evans, E. (1987). Readers recreating texts. In B. Corcoran & E. Evans (Eds.), *Readers, texts, and teachers* (pp. 22–40). Upper Montclair, NJ: Boynton/Cook.

Galda, L. (1982). Assuming the spectator stance: An examination of the responses of three young readers. *Research in the Teaching of English, 16,* 1–20.

Golden, J.M. (1979). A schema for analyzing response to literature applied to the responses of fifth and eighth grade readers to realistic and fantasy short stories (Doctoral dissertation, Ohio State University, 1978). *Dissertation Abstracts International, 39,* 5996A. (University Microfilms No. 7908149)

Holman, F. (1976). The runaway. In A. Diven (Ed.), *The Scribner anthology for young people* (pp. 17–21). New York: Scribner.

Iser, W. (1980). Interaction between text and reader. In S.R. Suleiman & I. Crosman (Eds.), *The reader in the text: Essays on audience and interpretation* (pp. 106–119). Princeton, NJ: Princeton University Press.

Lehr, S. (1988). The child's developing sense of theme as a response to literature. *Reading Research Quarterly, 23,* 337–357.

Many, J.E. (1989). *Age level differences in children's use of an aesthetic stance when responding to literature.* Unpublished doctoral dissertation, Louisiana State University, Baton Rouge.

Probst, R.E. (1988). *Response and analysis: Teaching literature in junior and senior high school.* Portsmouth, NH: Boynton/Cook.

Purves, A.C. (1973). *Literature education in ten countries: An empirical study.* Stockholm: Almqvist & Wiskell.

Purves, A.C. (1981). *Reading and literature: American achievement in international perspective.* Urbana, IL: National Council of Teachers of English.

Purves, A.C., & Beach, R. (1972). *Literature and the reader: Research in response to literature, reading interests, and the teaching of literature*. Urbana, IL: National Council of Teachers of English.

Purves, A.C., & Rippere, V. (1968). *Elements of writing about a literary work*. Urbana, IL: National Council of Teachers of English.

Ricoeur, P. (1976). *Interpretation theory: Discourse and the surplus of meaning*. Fort Worth: Texas Christian University Press.

Rogers, T. (1988, April). *High school students' thematic interpretations of complex short stories*. Paper presented at the annual meeting of the American Educational Research Association, New Orleans, LA.

Rosenblatt, L.M. (1938). *Literature as exploration*. New York: Appleton Century.

Rosenblatt, L.M. (1978). *The reader, the text, the poem: The transactional theory of the literary work*. Carbondale: Southern Illinois University Press.

Rosenblatt, L.M. (1982). The literary transaction: Evocation and response. *Theory Into Practice, 21*, 268–277.

Rosenblatt, L.M. (1985). The transactional theory of the literary work. In C.R. Cooper (Ed.), *Researching response to literature and the teaching of literature* (pp. 33–53). Norwood, NJ: Ablex.

Rosenblatt, L.M. (1986). The aesthetic transaction. *Journal of Aesthetic Education, 20*, 122–128.

Sword, J. (1985). Criteria for evaluating picture story books (CEBSB). In W.T. Fagen, J.M. Jensen, & C.R. Cooper (Eds.), *Measures for research and evaluation in the English language arts* (Vol. 2, pp. 225–227). Urbana, IL: National Council of Teachers of English.

Werner, H. (1979). The dollar's worth. In J. Shapiro (Ed.), *Triple action short stories* (pp. 26–35). New York: Scholastic.

34

Motivational and Cognitive Predictors of Text Comprehension and Reading Amount

John T. Guthrie, Allan Wigfield, Jamie L. Metsala, and Kathleen E. Cox

One goal of the science of reading is prediction. Reading researchers and psychologists attempt to predict educationally or psychologically significant variables such as word recognition or text comprehension from important underlying processes. In the reading research literature, these processes have been primarily cognitive. In this article, we extend our earlier work by examining how motivational and reading amount variables, in concert with cognitive processes, contribute to the prediction of students' text comprehension. By combining motivational and cognitive constructs, we attempt to understand text comprehension more fully.

We refer to *text comprehension* as the capacity of the learner to construct new knowledge or information from written text (Anderson & Pearson, 1984). Two major cognitive predictors of text comprehension are past achievement in text comprehension and prior knowledge. Because of our focus on motivation, we mention this research briefly. Past achievement was shown to predict subsequent text comprehension in many studies conducted with children ranging in age from 6 to 15 (Anderson, Wilson, & Fielding, 1988; Cunningham & Stanovich, 1997; Torgesen, Wagner, Rashotte, Burgess, & Hecht, 1997). Similarly, prior knowledge, often conceptualized as a schema, also predicts subsequent text comprehension (see Alexander, 1997; Dole, Duffy, Roehler, & Pearson, 1991, for further discussion).

Reading Amount Predicts Text Comprehension

Text comprehension is also predictable from the amount and frequency that students read. We use the term *reading amount* to refer to the frequency and time spent reading a range of topics for various purposes. Reading amount is highly similar to the constructs of print exposure (Cunningham & Stanovich, 1997), independent reading (Greaney, 1980), and time spent reading (Anderson et al., 1988). Allen, Cipielewski, and Stanovich (1992) found that the simple correlation of text comprehension and reading amount measured with diaries was .46; the correlation of text comprehension and reading amount using author-recognition tests of print exposure was .50. The correlation of text comprehension and reading amount according to a title-recognition test (TRT) measure of print exposure was .54 in fourth-through sixth-grade students. Similar relations were found in studies using nationally representative samples of National Assessment of Educational Progress data. Campbell, Voelkl, and Donahue (1997) reported that students who read daily for their own enjoyment were 6.7 standard errors higher in reading achievement than students who reported reading yearly or never. Of course, these zero-order correlations do not control for extraneous variables nor permit the inference that one of them explains the other, in any sense of the term. However, controlled and partial correlations were reported in several studies and are discussed next.

Growth of text comprehension as a function of reading amount has been documented. When text comprehension at a given time is predicted by a measure of reading amount taken at the same point in time and the correlation is controlled for the contribution of earlier text comprehension, the inference of growth is permissible (Anderson et al., 1988; Cipielewski & Stanovich, 1992). Using this framework, Anderson et al. (1988) reported that text comprehension in grade 5 was predicted by reading amount (based on time spent reading out of school from diaries), after accounting for prior text comprehension in grade 2. The correlation was .18 between reading amount and growth of text comprehension. Likewise, Cipielewski and Stanovich (1992) reported that reading amount, as measured by the TRT, accounted for 11% of text comprehension in fifth graders after accounting for text comprehension in grade 3. Remarkably, prediction of text comprehension from reading amount across 6 years of schooling has been reported. Cunningham and Stanovich (1997) found that growth of text comprehension from grade 5 to grade 10 was significantly correlated with reading amount, according to a composite of print exposure measured at grade 11. The beta weight for this association was .478, indicating that 23% of the variance in growth of reading from grade 5 to 10 was predictable from reading amount.

Contributions of reading amount to growth in text comprehension, presented in the previous paragraph, have emphasized out-of-school reading and measures of print exposure that are sensitive to reading fiction for enjoyment. However, reading amount in school is also associated with text comprehension. Elley (1992) found that teacher-reported frequency of silent reading in class was significantly associated with a measure of text comprehension. The effect size was .78 between in-school reading amount and text comprehension. In primary schools, Juel (1988) documented the well-known phenomenon that higher-achieving students cover more content than lower achievers. In first grade, good readers encountered 80% more words in their reading instruction than did poor readers (see Biemiller, 1970; Metsala & Ehri, 1998). Good fourth-grade readers encountered 220% more words in text during their instruction to that date than poor readers. Note that the cause–effect directionality cannot be determined in these studies. However, Taylor, Frye, and Maruyama (1990) conducted a true experiment increasing some students' reading time but not others. They observed a significant improvement in text comprehension as a consequence of reading amount. Morrow (1996) confirmed this finding in an experiment with children assigned to increased reading time in classroom book centers. Those students gained more in achievement than control children. Prediction of text comprehension from reading amount, therefore, has been documented for reading within school as well as out-of-school reading.

Motivational Predictors of Reading Amount

Research on motivation is voluminous (for recent reviews of motivation literature, see Eccles, Wigfield, & Schiefele, 1998; Pintrich & Schunk, 1996). Consistent with other researchers, we define *motivation* in terms of characteristics of individuals, such as their goals, competence-related beliefs, and needs that influence their achievement and activities. *Goals* refer to the purposes individuals have for doing different activities. Two broad goal orientations—performance and mastery—received the most research attention (Dweck & Leggett, 1988; Nicholls, Cheung, Lauer, & Patashnick, 1989). A *performance goal orientation* means that focus is on demonstrating that one is capable and can outperform others. A *mastery orientation* refers to attempting to improve one's capabilities and focusing on the task one is doing. Converging evidence suggests that a mastery goal orientation leads to more positive motivational and academic outcomes.

Intrinsic motivation refers to an emphasis on curiosity and interest in the activity one is doing and a mastery orientation toward tasks (see Gottfried, 1990). Empirical research has shown that high levels of intrinsic motivation are associated with a sense of competence (Miller, Behrens, Greene, & Newman, 1993; Skinner, Wellborn, & Connell, 1990), mastery-oriented coping with failure (Lehtinen, Vauras, Saloncn, Olkinuora, & Kinnunen, 1995), and high achievement in text-comprehension tasks (Benware & Deci, 1984).

Extrinsic motivation for learning and reading consists of effort directed toward obtaining external recognition, rewards, or incentives (Deci, Vallerand, Pelletier, & Ryan, 1991). Extrinsically motivated students seek to gain recognition for excellence in reading, win visible rewards, and surpass their peers in publicly acknowledged achievement. Although intrinsic and extrinsic motivation can be contrasted in these ways, it is increasingly clear that many students are motivated to read for both intrinsic and extrinsic reasons (Wigfield & Guthrie, 1977).

In this study, we operationalized *reading motivation* to include several aspects of intrinsic motivation including curiosity (generalized interest in learning about the world through reading), involvement (desire to be immersed and absorbed in reading through a variety of particular texts), and challenge (enjoyment in tackling and learning difficult or complex information). We included also the performance goal and extrinsic motivation aspects of recognition (the goal of receiving rewards or public citation for excellence in reading) and competition (desire to demonstrate excellence through favorable comparison to peers). Reading motivation, then, was not limited to a particular knowledge domain or a particular text; neither was it limited to one kind of motivation. Instead, it was characterized by readers' goals and both intrinsic and extrinsic motivation. We also included readers' self-efficacy, which is discussed later.

Reading motivation and reading amount are correlated. Wigfield and Guthrie (1997) found positive zero-order correlations between reading amount in grades 3 and 5 and several aspects of motivation, including curiosity, involvement, challenge, recognition, and competition. This indicator of reading amount was based on parents' diaries of their children's free reading time over one school year. Another indicator of reading amount was a questionnaire asking children how frequently they read on a range of topics. This latter indicator correlated with children's reported curiosity, involvement, challenge, recognition, and competition; similar correlations also were found by Baker and Wigfield (1999). In the Wigfield and Guthrie study, the differences in reading amount associated with motivation were not trivial. Students who ranked in the top third of the reading motivation scale spent nearly 20 minutes more reading outside of school (29.80 minutes per day) than students in the bottom third on the motivation scales (10.52 minutes per day).

Beyond these correlations, Wigfield and Guthrie (1997) examined the extent to which reading motivation predicted growth in reading amount. Reading motivation predicted reading amount in the spring of an academic year, even when the contribution of reading amount from the previous academic year was entered as a control variable. Also, reading motivation accounted for 7% of the variance in growth of reading amount with time spent from the diaries as the indicator, and reading motivation explained 15% of the variance in growth of reading amount when a questionnaire was the indicator. However, reading motivation in the spring of the academic year did not predict growth of reading amount from fall to spring during the year. Based on this evidence, it appeared that children who reported being highly motivated to read tended to increase their reading amount and breadth over time. It did not appear, however, that children became frequent readers and then at a later point in time reported relatively high levels of reading motivation. One limit of the Wigfield and Guthrie study was that it did not include indicators of text comprehension or reading achievement. Consequently, the present investigation includes all three variables of text comprehension, reading amount, and reading motivation.

Motivational Correlates of Text Comprehension

Researchers have found that reading motivation correlates with text comprehension. Gottfried (1990) reported that academic intrinsic motivation correlated significantly with text comprehension on the Woodcock–Johnson Psycho-Educational Battery–Reading test for 9-year-old students. For younger, 7-year-old students, this correlation did not occur. In a study of urban fifth and sixth graders, Baker and Wigfield (1999) found that some aspects of reading motivation were moderately related to children's achievement on the Gates-MacGinitie Reading test and Comprehensive Test of Basic Skills (CTBS). A positive zero-order correlation between intrinsic motivation and achievement represented as a composite of all CTBS scores was found by Meece, Blumenfeld, and Hoyle (1988).

When teacher-assigned grades or student self-report rather than cognitive tests had been used as the indicator of text comprehension, associations with intrinsic motivation were higher. Gottfried (1990) found that correlations for both 7-year-old and 9-year-old students between reading grades and intrinsic motivations were higher and more frequently significant than between motivation and reading test scores. Corroborating this result, Sweet, Guthrie, and Ng (1998) found that grades in reading for 10-year-olds were substantially correlated with teacher perception of students' intrinsic reading motivations. Also, when students' self-reports of cognitive strategy use or self-regulation were used as indicators of reading, reading motivation variables were highly predictive (Meece & Holt, 1993; Pintrich & DeGroot, 1990). However, for this article, we restrict the indicators of text comprehension to scores on text-comprehension tasks that require cognitive processing and knowledge.

Self-Efficacy Predicts Text Comprehension

Under the broad umbrella of motivation, self-efficacy has been widely researched. Our initial definition of reading motivation subsumed self-efficacy as one of its aspects. Where self-efficacy is indeed a constituent of reading motivation, it has also been distinguished and examined separately. Examining self-efficacy for reading, Schunk and Rice (1993) adopted Bandura's (1986) definition of self-efficacy as "people's judgments of their capabilities to organize and execute courses of action required to attain designated types of performances" (p. 391). Across a range of reading studies, Schunk and Zimmerman (1997) noted that students with high self-efficacy see difficult reading tasks as challenging and work diligently to master them, using their cognitive strategies productively. Schunk and Zimmerman concluded that self-efficacy within a reading task is associated with use of strategies, self-regulation, and text comprehension within the tasks.

A more generalized account was provided by Chapman and Tunmer (1997). They used the phrase *self-concept for reading*, but it was operationalized and measured to make it virtually indistinguishable from the construct presented here as reading efficacy. Their path-analytic data suggested that text comprehension was more likely to contribute significantly to increases in reading efficacy than vice versa for children ages 6 to 7. In beginning reading, reading efficacy seemed to emerge from perceived and actual competence in reading tasks. However, by grade 4, the prediction of text comprehension from reading efficacy was substantial and the prediction increased to grade 7 (Shell, Colvin, & Bruning, 1995). Furthermore, path analyses reported by Kurtz-Costes and Schneider (1994) showed a reciprocal relation between a generalized construct of self-efficacy for achievement in school and grades for students ages 8 and 10. In view of these findings, we incorporated reading efficacy as a separate construct related to motivation, reading amount, and text comprehension.

To build on the work just reviewed, we report the results of two studies. Study 1 included a local sample of third and fifth graders. These age groups were used because they were similar to those used in previous research (Wigfield & Guthrie, 1997) and spanned an important period in terms of the developing relations between motivation and achievement. Study 2 consisted of a national sample of students from grades 8 and 10. These age groups were used because they have not often been included in research on reading motivation; although in the general motivation literature, it has been shown that motivation and achievement relate in these age groups (Stipek, 1996). The constructs of text comprehension, reading amount, reading motivation, and reading efficacy were assessed in both studies, although they were measured differently. Similar regression analyses were conducted on both data sets. Our primary interests were (a) how children's text comprehension was predicted by their reading amount and reading motivation and (b) how children's reading amount was predicted by their reading motivation. The study was organized around the following three questions.

1. To what extent are two types of text comprehension—(a) passage comprehension and (b) conceptual learning from multiple texts—predicted by reading amount when accounting for the contributions of past achievement, prior knowledge, reading motivation, and reading efficacy to text comprehension?

2. To what extent is reading amount predicted by reading motivation when accounting for the contributions of past achievement, prior knowledge, and reading efficacy to reading amount?

3. To what extent is reading amount predicted by intrinsic motivation and extrinsic motivation when analyzed separately and controlling the contributions of each for past reading achievement, prior knowledge, and self-efficacy?

Study 1

Method

Design. Data for this study were drawn from a larger quasi-experimental investigation designed to examine the effects of instructional intervention on reading achievement (Guthrie et al., 1998). The larger study included an assessment administered at the end of the school year, including two measures of text comprehension, prior knowledge relevant to the comprehension measures, reading motivation, reading efficacy, and reading amount. All students in the larger study were included in this analysis.

Participants. Three schools that bordered a large, mid-Atlantic metropolis participated in this study. Each school had a multicultural population consisting of approximately 55% African American, 22% Caucasian, 15% Hispanic, and 7% Asian or other. A total of 271 students participated, with 117 fifth graders in four classrooms completing the standardized test in the fall and the other measures in the spring of the academic year. Also included were 154 third-grade students. These two grades were frequently used in prior research and were of interest to practitioners due to accountability at these levels. The number of students completing the measures varied from 229 to 266 (see Table 1). Boys constituted 47% of the total sample, and girls made up 53%. Two of the schools were designated as Chapter 1. The 10 participating teachers were between 41 and 50 years of age, with 20 to 24 years of teaching experience. They all had bachelor's degrees plus 45 hours of university credit.

TABLE 1

**Means, Standard Deviations, Correlations, and Reliability Estimates
for Motivational and Cognitive Variables in Reading**

	1[a]	2[b]	3[c]	4[d]	5[e]	6[f]	7[g]
1. Passage Comprehension	**.60**						
2. Conceptual Learning	.37**	**.36**					
3. Prior Knowledge	.36**	.37**	**.35**				
4. Past Achievement	.60**	.28**	.25**	**.88**			
5. Reading Motivation	.03	−0.07	−.07	.08	**.85**		
6. Reading Efficiency	.12	0.00	.08	.14*	.64**	**.63**	
7. Reading Amount	.25**	.23**	.15*	.16*	.37**	.24**	**.75**
M	12.02	9.88	3.06	44.12	111.69	12.38	17.82
SD	2.54	6.86	1.05	23.38	17.68	2.70	6.21

Reliability estimates are given on the diagonal in bold.
[a] $n = 242$; [b] $n = 252$; [c] $n = 266$; [d] $n = 239$; [e] $n = 233$; [f] $n = 245$; [g] $n = 229$.
*$p < .05$; **$p < .001$.

Measures. Two measures of text comprehension and measures of reading amount, reading motivation, and reading efficacy were part of a performance assessment administered to all students in April 1996. Measures of past achievement were standardized reading tests given in October 1995.

Passage comprehension. The first measure of text comprehension consisted of a combination of informational text comprehension and narrative comprehension described more fully in Guthrie et al. (1998). Students were randomly assigned to two knowledge domains. Half of the students received questions and accompanying texts that were relevant to life cycles of frogs; the other half received questions and texts relevant to the formation of rivers. In the information-comprehension task, each text was approximately 400 words in length, containing prose, a diagram, and an illustration. Students read this material and answered four questions, which were coded into three levels: no answer or inaccurate answer, simple answer, or elaborated answer. Reliability of this task, as indicated by its correlation with the standardized test of text reading comprehension, was .50 ($p < .001$), which was adequate for this study. For narrative comprehension, students were provided a complete narrative of approximately 1,000 words. Half of the material was relevant to frog life cycles and half was relevant to river formation. Students answered three questions, which were each coded into two levels: no answer or inaccurate answer or reasonable text-based response. Reliability of this task, as indicated by its correlation with the standardized test of reading comprehension, was .60 ($p < .001$), which was adequate for this study.

Conceptual learning from multiple texts. As a second indicator of text comprehension, participants were given the task of independently searching multiple texts for ideas and information about the topic of the assessment. Half of the students were assigned to work on the topic of ponds and deserts, and half were asked to explain the differences between volcanoes and rivers. Each student was given a booklet with 14 sections, and each section contained from one to five pages of information on the assigned topic domain. After reading, students were first asked to draw a picture to show how ponds (volcanoes) are different from deserts (rivers). A six-level coding rubric was used to classify the students' responses on the drawing and writing tasks (see Guthrie et al., 1998, for a detailed description). The correlation of drawing and writing, an estimate of reliability, was .36 ($p < .002$). The conceptual learning from multiple texts construct in the analyses was the writing and drawing combined.

Prior knowledge. At the beginning of the comprehension assessment, students worked independently to write their knowledge of the topic. Students were asked to explain how ponds are different from deserts or how volcanoes were different from rivers. Students were aided in the task by being asked the following:

1. What is a pond like?
2. What is a desert like?

3. How are they different?

4. Explain the differences between volcanoes and rivers.

5. What are their parts?

6. How are they made?

7. How are they different?

All students were given sufficient time to finish their writing. Performance on prior knowledge was rated on the same rubric as writing and drawing. Interrater agreement was examined with the same procedures as used for writing and drawing. For the pond–desert task, exact agreement was 64% and adjacent was 100%. For the volcano–river task, exact agreement was 48% and adjacent was 92%. The correlation of .37 ($p < .001$) for prior knowledge and conceptual learning from multiple texts indicated that the measure had adequate reliability for purposes of this study.

Reading amount. A questionnaire measured reading amount, which assessed the breadth of reading in different topic domains and the frequency of reading in each domain according to student self-report. The questionnaire began with two practice items to acquaint the student with item and response format. All items were administered by reading them aloud with a class of students (see Wigfield & Guthrie, 1997, for more details).

The first section of the questionnaire targeted school reading. Items requested students to report whether they had read a given topic (e.g., literature or science) for school and, if so, how often. The first question asked, "Did you read a science book or science textbook for school last week?" with a response format of *no* or *yes*. Next, students were asked, "If yes, write in the title, author, or specific topic that you read about." Students were awarded one point if they answered *yes* and gave some specific information in the open section. The second question was "How often do you read a science book or science textbook for school?" with a response format of *almost never, about once a month, about once a week,* or *almost every day*. A similar pair of items was given for literature and history, making a total of six items in school reading.

The second set of items requested students to report the topics and frequency of reading for their own enjoyment. The first question was "Did you read a fiction book like a mystery or an adventure last week for your own interest?" with a response format of *no* or *yes*, followed by "If yes, write in the title, author, or specific topic you read about." The next item was "How often do you read a fiction book like a mystery or an adventure for your own interest?" with a response format of *almost never, about once a month, about once a week,* or *almost every day*. The topic domains consisted of fiction, sports, nature, romance, biography, comics, and other, in that order, yielding 14 items. The specific topics were selected and associated with school or enjoyment, based on a previous in-depth interview study of reading motivation and reading amount (Guthrie et al., 1996). To construct a reliable measure of reading amount, we conducted a factor analysis with items from the seven domains of biology, fiction, history, literature, nature, science, and other. In the factor analysis, one factor accounted for 22.9% of the variance, and loadings of the 14 items ranged from .68 to .33. Based on these results, we created a composite measure of reading amount, which had an alpha reliability of .75.

Reading motivation. The Motivation for Reading Questionnaire (MRQ) used in this study was an abbreviated version of the MRQ developed by Wigfield and Guthrie (1997). It contained 31 of the 54 items on the original scale, assessing the following aspects of reading motivation: challenge (5 items), curiosity (6 items), involvement (6 items), recognition (5 items), competition (6 items), and reading efficacy (3 items). The questionnaire consisted of statements such as "I usually learn difficult things by reading." Students responded on a scale from 1 to 4, with choices ranging from 1 (*very different from me*) to 4 (*a lot like me*). As was the case in the Wigfield and Guthrie study, the aspects of motivation correlated moderately, ranging from .30 to .60.

Based on theoretical considerations, we formed an intrinsic motivation–mastery goal composite of items from the MRQ consisting of challenge (Csikszentmihalyi, 1978), curiosity (Alexander, Jetton, & Kulikowich, 1996), and involvement (Schallert & Reed, 1997). We formed an extrinsic motivation–performance goal composite consisting of recognition (Ames & Archer, 1988) and competition (Nicholls et al., 1989). These composites correlated at .64 ($p < .001$), and a factor analysis of all five constructs revealed a strong single-factor solution that accounted for 63% of the variance. Loadings of the five motivation constructs ranged from .84 to .68. Reliability of reading motivation was .85. We selected the single, combined reading motivation construct for the primary analyses in this study because our purpose was not to differentiate among aspects of motivation. Our aim was to examine the role of one robust reading motivation construct in predicting other reading outcomes, consisting of reading amount and text comprehension. However, we conducted follow-up analyses in which each composite was entered as a separate predictor.

Reading efficacy. We defined *reading efficacy* as the student's sense of being able to read, consistent with Schunk and Zimmerman (1997), among others. The measure consisted of three items on the MRQ. One item consisted of the following statement: "I know that I will do well in reading next year." Students answered on a scale of 1 to 4 with the same response format as the reading motivation items. We selected reading efficacy for separate analysis in this study due to its previous strength of association with reading amount (Wigfield & Guthrie, 1997) and its frequent association with reading achievement (Chapman & Tunmer, 1997). The Cronbach's alpha was .63, which was adequate for this study.

Results

Descriptive statistics for all the variables of this study are presented in Table 1. The seven variables in the correlation matrix were used in multiple regressions. Their means, standard deviations, and numbers of students are presented at the bottom of the table. The cognitive variables of passage comprehension, conceptual learning from multiple texts, prior knowledge, and past achievement all correlated with each other significantly at $p < .001$, which was expected. Reading motivation and reading efficacy correlated at .64 ($p < .001$), indicating that two motivational constructs correlated with each other. Reading amount correlated with both the motivational and cognitive variables, and it correlated with passage comprehension at .25 ($p < .001$), conceptual learning from multiple texts at .23 ($p < .001$), prior knowledge at .15 ($p < .05$), past achievement at .16 ($p < .05$), reading motivation at .37 ($p < .001$), and reading efficacy at .24 ($p < .001$). To address the four major questions of the investigation, multiple regressions were conducted.

Question 1a: To what extent is passage comprehension predicted by reading amount when accounting for the contributions of past achievement, prior knowledge, reading motivation, and reading efficacy? To examine this question, we conducted a multiple regression with passage comprehension as the dependent variable. The independent variables consisted of two cognitive constructs—past achievement and prior knowledge—and two motivational constructs—motivation and self-efficacy. We used the forward-entry regression procedure because it is very conservative. Variables in the block are added to the equation one at a time. At each step, the variable not in the equation with the smallest probability of F is entered if the value is smaller than Probability of Going In (PIN; probability of F to enter –.05 as default). The possible contribution of a variable to the prediction is made only after accounting for all the other stronger variables in the set. We also report the final beta, which is the association of the designated independent variable with the dependent variable while controlling for the contributions of all other independent variables. Significance of the final beta was determined by examining the significance of the final F value. Note that this final F was adjusted for design effects present in large samples in Study 2. Missing data were handled with pairwise deletion. The rationale for the forward procedure was that it permitted us to determine the contribution of the independent variable of interest—in this case reading amount—when the potentially competing cognitive and motivational variables were free to enter based on their predictive power. We did not use the forced-entry procedure, as we did not possess a theory to inform the sequence of entry for the variables.

Results of the analysis are shown in the top part of Table 2. With passage comprehension as the dependent variable, past achievement had a multiple correlation of .599, with the squared multiple correlation of .359. The final beta was .526 ($p < .001$), which was significant, $F(1, 179) = 79.46, p < .001$. This final beta

TABLE 2
Regression of Reading Amount and Other Variables
on Two Text Comprehension Variables

Dependent and Independent Variables	R	R^2	ΔR^2	Final F	Final ß
Passage Comprehension					
Past achievement	.599	.359	.359	79.46**	.526**
Prior knowledge	.639	.409	.050	13.31**	.215**
Reading amount	.651	.424	.015	4.77*	.126*
Reading efficacy	NC	NC	NC	ns	ns
Reading motivation	NC	NC	NC	ns	ns
Conceptual Learning From Multiple Texts					
Prior knowledge	.371	.138	.138	19.06 **	.304**
Past achievement	.420	.176	.038	6.82*	.182*
Reading amount	.445	.198	.022	4.84*	.150*
Reading efficacy	NC	NC	NC	ns	ns
Reading motivation	NC	NC	NC	ns	ns

NC = no significant change in the figure from the one preceding it in the column; ns = not significant at $p < .05$.
*$p < .05$; **$p < .001$.

was computed in the last step of this regression analysis, and the F value associated with the final beta is reported. We followed this pattern consistently. Prior knowledge entered the regression next with a multiple correlation of .639 and the squared multiple correlation of .409. The change in R^2 was .05. The final beta was .215, $p < .001$, which was significant, $F(1, 179) = 13.31$, $p < .001$. As Table 2 indicates, reading amount contributed a significant proportion of the variance in passage comprehension. When reading amount was added, the multiple correlation was .651, with the squared multiple correlation of .424. The change in R^2 was .015. The final beta for reading amount was .126 ($p < .05$), which was significant, $F(1, 179) = 4.77$, $p < .05$. In this analysis, reading efficacy did not add significantly to the prediction of passage comprehension, and motivation did not contribute significantly to the prediction of passage comprehension. These results show that reading amount predicted level of passage comprehension even after accounting for previous comprehension levels and prior knowledge of the topic domain. In other words, when controlling for the contributions of past achievement and prior knowledge to passage comprehension, reading amount added significantly to the predictability of conceptual learning from multiple texts.

Question 1b: To what extent is conceptual learning from multiple texts predicted by reading amount when the contributions of past reading achievement, prior knowledge, reading motivation, and reading efficacy to conceptual learning from multiple texts were controlled? To address this question, a multiple regression was conducted with conceptual learning from multiple texts as the dependent variable. The independent variables were entered with the forward-entry procedure identical to the previous analysis. Results are shown in the bottom part of Table 2. Prior knowledge was the strongest predictor of conceptual learning from multiple texts with a multiple correlation of .371 and the squared multiple correlation of .138. The final beta was .304 ($p < .001$), which was significant, $F(1, 179) = 19.06, p < .001$.

Past achievement entered next, producing a multiple correlation of .420 with the squared multiple correlation of .176. The change in R^2 was .038. The final beta for past achievement was .182 ($p < .05$), which was significant, $F(1, 179) = 6.82, p < .05$. With conceptual learning from multiple texts as the dependent variable, reading amount contributed a significant proportion of the total variance accounted for. The multiple correlation was .445 with the squared multiple correlation of .198. The change in R^2 was .022. The final beta for reading amount in the last step of the analysis was .150 ($p < .05$), which was significant, $F(1, 179) = 4.84, p < .05$. Self-efficacy and motivation did not contribute significantly to the prediction of conceptual learning from multiple texts after the variables of prior knowledge, past achievement, and reading amount had been entered in the regression. This pattern of results was similar to the predictions related to paragraph comprehension. That is, reading amount contributed a modest but significant proportion of variance after accounting for prior knowledge and past achievement. One difference in the results is that less variance in conceptual learning from multiple texts was accounted for by the predictor variables than was the case for passage comprehension.

Question 2: To what extent is reading amount predicted by reading motivation when the contributions of past achievement, prior knowledge, and reading efficacy to reading amount were controlled? To address this question, a multiple regression was conducted with reading amount as the dependent variable. The independent variables of reading motivation, prior knowledge, past achievement, and reading efficacy were entered using the forward-entry procedure, identical to the previous analyses. The results of this analysis are presented in the top part of Table 3. Reading motivation predicted reading amount most highly with a multiple correlation of .371 and the squared multiple correlation of .138. The final beta in the last equation was .383 ($p < .001$), which was significant, $F(1, 180) = 31.67, p < .001$. Prior knowledge added to the prediction of reading amount significantly. The multiple correlation was .412 with the squared multiple correlation of .170. This change in R^2 was .032. The final beta was .180 ($p < .05$), which was significant, $F(1, 180) = 7.00, p < .05$. Past achievement did not add significantly to the prediction of reading amount and self-efficacy after accounting for motivation and prior knowledge. Results show that motivation was the strongest predictor of reading amount when considering the variables of past

TABLE 3
**Regression of Motivation and Other Variables
on Reading Amount Dependent Variable**

Independent Variables	R	R^2	ΔR^2	Final F	Final β
Reading Motivation	.371	.138	.138	31.67**	.383**
Prior knowledge	.412	.170	.032	7.00*	.180*
Past achievement	NC	NC	NC	ns	ns
Reading efficacy	NC	NC	NC	ns	ns
Intrinsic Motivation	.327	.107	.107	24.31**	.333**
Prior knowledge	.367	.135	.028	6.05*	.166*
Past achievement	NC	NC	NC	ns	ns
Reading efficacy	NC	NC	NC	ns	ns
Extrinsic Motivation	.352	.124	.124	29.73**	.364**
Prior knowledge	.395	.156	.032	7.18*	.179*
Past achievement	NC	NC	NC	ns	ns
Reading efficacy	NC	NC	NC	ns	ns

NC = no significant change in the figure from the one preceding it in the column; ns = not significant at $p < .05$.
*$p < .05$; **$p < .001$.

achievement, prior knowledge, self-efficacy, and motivation. The final beta of
.383 ($p < .001$) for reading motivation was substantial in view of the robustness
of the two cognitive variables of past achievement and prior knowledge and the
variable of self-efficacy that were recognized in the analysis.

Question 3: To what extent is reading amount predicted by intrinsic motivation and extrinsic motivation when they were analyzed separately, controlling
the contributions of each for past reading achievement, prior knowledge, and
self-efficacy? The multiple regressions used to address this question are reported in the middle and bottom parts of Table 3. As before, a forward-entry procedure was used to examine the role of motivational and cognitive variables in
predicting reading amount. Intrinsic motivation showed a significant contribution. The multiple correlation was .327 with the squared multiple correlation of
.107. The final beta was .333 ($p < .001$), which was significant $F(1, 190) = 24.31$,
$p < .001$. Prior knowledge added significantly to the prediction with the final beta
of .166 ($p < .05$). In the second regression addressing this question, reading amount
was again the dependent variable and extrinsic motivation was used in place of intrinsic motivation in the regressions involving prior knowledge, past achievement,
and self-efficacy. Extrinsic motivation had a final beta of .364 ($p < .001$), which
was significant, $F(1, 190) = 29.73$, $p < .001$. Prior knowledge also contributed
significantly after extrinsic motivation was accounted for, with a final beta of

.179 ($p < .05$). These results show that both intrinsic motivation and extrinsic motivation, taken separately, contribute substantially to the prediction of reading amount. It should be noted that the final beta for the total construct of motivation shown in Table 3 was .383, which is higher than either separate motivation predictor. These findings illustrate that both aspects of motivation contribute to reading amount.

Study 2

Rationale

The purpose of Study 2 was to examine the generalizability of the Study 1 results to an older student population. In Study 1, we found that reading amount significantly predicted reading comprehension after the contributions of past achievement, reading motivation, reading efficacy, and prior knowledge were controlled. Additionally, Study 1 showed that reading motivation predicted reading amount when past achievement, reading efficacy, and prior knowledge were controlled. Study 1 was conducted with students in grades 3 and 5 using measures that were suited to this age group. To examine the generality of these findings in older students and with different measures, Study 2 analyzed data from students in grades 8 and 10, utilizing the same constructs and the same multiple-regression logic as Study 1. Fewer studies on the relation of reading comprehension and reading motivation have been conducted for middle school and high school students than for elementary students (Wigfield, Eccles, & Rodriquez, 1998).

Method

Participants. The population for this investigation was drawn from the National Educational Longitudinal Study (NELS: 88) database. From this public-use database, we selected all the grade 10 students who were included as eighth graders in the base-year sample. There were a total of 17,424 students representing the national sample (see Owings et al., 1994).

Measures. *Passage comprehension*. Reading comprehension was measured with a cognitive test of 21 multiple-choice items. The test contained five short reading passages with three to five questions on each passage that required students to understand word meanings in context, identify figures of speech, interpret authors' perspectives, and evaluate the passage. Items were scaled with item response theory to produce an estimate of the number right, which was equated across the age levels of students in this study.

Reading amount. In the NELS: 88 study, students were given an activity questionnaire that contained the question "How often do you spend time on the following activities outside of school?" Students rated 15 activities, such as visiting with friends, using computers, playing sports, and reading for pleasure.

The response format was 1 (*rarely or never*), 2 (*less than once a week*), 3 (*once or twice a week*), and 4 (*every day or almost every day*). A second question asked, "How much additional reading do you do each week outside of school not in connection with school work?" The response format was 1 (*none*), 2 (*one hour or less per week*), 3 (*two hours per week*), 4 (*three hours per week*), 5 (*four to five hours per week*), and 6 (*six to seven hours per week*). These two items, which correlated at .52 ($p < .0001$), were summed to construct the reading amount variable.

Reading motivation. Students were asked the question "What is the main reason you are taking the following subjects: (1) math, (2) science, (3) English, and (4) history?" with the response format of 1 (*It was required*) and 2 (*I wanted to take it*). A second item asked, "In each of your classes, how often do you try as hard as you can? (1) math, (2) English, (3) history, and (4) science," with the response format of 1 (*never*), 2 (*less than once a week*), 3 (*about once a week*), 4 (*a few times a week*), and 5 (*almost every day*). Responses for English, which correlated at .84 ($p < .0001$), were summed to form the reading motivation construct.

Reading efficacy. Students were asked 25 questions related generally to self-concept. Two asked about English, including "I learn things quickly in English classes," and "English is one of my best subjects." The response format was 1 (*false*), 2 (*mostly false*), 3 (*more false than true*), 4 (*more true than false*), 5 (*mostly true*), and 6 (*true*). Responses to these two items correlated at .86 ($p < .0001$) and were summed to represent reading efficacy.

Socioeconomic status (SES). The composite SES variable available in the data was used. It was composed of mother's education level, father's education level, mother's occupation, father's occupation, and family income based on data from a parent questionnaire. This SES variable was used in Study 2 to control extraneous variance in the large national sample.

TABLE 4
Correlations of All Variables in Study 2

Variable	1	2	3	4	5	6
1. Reading Amount	—	.29*	.22*	.09*	.29*	.07*
2. Reading Motivation		—	.69*	−.01	.59*	.40*
3. Reading Efficacy			—	−.01	.43*	.30*
4. Text Comprehension–Grade 8				—	.20*	.19*
5. Text Comprehension–Grade 10					—	.24*
6. Socioeconomic Status						—

*$p < .0001$.

Results

The correlations of all the variables are provided in Table 4. It is evident that text comprehension in grades 8 and 10 correlated at .20 ($p < .0001$) with each other. Grade 10 reading comprehension also correlated significantly with reading amount, motivation, reading efficacy, and SES.

All the regression analyses were conducted with unweighted data but were adjusted for a design effect, which refers to the ratio of the actual variance to the estimated variance. In large data sets of this type, Johnson and Rust (1992) showed that within-group variances are often underestimated by usual SPSS procedures. Based on the Johnson and Rust report of a design effect of 2.0 for regression analyses in 1988 NAEP data, we reduced the F statistics, dividing them by an estimated design effect of 2.0 (following the suggestion of Owings et al., 1994, for NELS: 88 data). This produced a conservative estimate of the statistical significance of the predictor variables.

To analyze the extent to which passage comprehension was predicted by reading amount, a multiple regression was conducted similar to the multiple regression on passage comprehension in Study 1. The dependent variable was passage comprehension with independent variables of reading amount, past reading comprehension achievement, reading efficacy, reading motivation, and SES. The only differences between this analysis and the analyses in Study 1 were that SES was included in this regression whereas it was not included in Study 1, and prior knowledge was included in Study 1 but was not available for this analysis. The results are shown in the top panel of Table 5. It is evident that passage comprehension was predicted by reading amount (ß = .12, $p < .001$) when past comprehension achievement, SES, reading motivation, and reading efficacy were controlled. The F value adjusted for the design effect was significant, $F(1, 11738) = 116.58$, $p < .001$. Reading motivation also predicted passage comprehension (ß = .42, $p < .001$) when the other variables in the regression were controlled, $F(1, 11738) = 956.16$, $p < .001$). These findings confirm the effects of reading amount on comprehension observed in Study 1. The other variables in the equation (SES, past text comprehension, reading amount, and reading efficacy) also were significant predictors.

To examine the contribution of reading motivation to reading amount in grade 10, a second multiple regression was conducted (see the bottom panel of Table 5). Reading amount was the dependent variable and the independent variables included previous reading achievement, SES, reading efficacy, and reading motivation. The results indicated that reading motivation significantly predicted reading amount (ß = .27, $p < .001$) when accounting for variables of previous achievement, SES, and reading efficacy. The adjusted F was significant, $F(1, 11738) = 302.58$, $p < .001$. Each background and student characteristic in the regression contributed a nonzero amount of variance to reading time. Note that the amount of variance explained by reading motivation was three times higher

TABLE 5
Regression Analyses of Predictors on Reading Amount and Reading Motivation for Tenth-Grade Students

Dependent and Independent Variables	R	R^2	ΔR^2	Final F (Adjusted)	Final β
Text Comprehension					
Reading motivation	.478	.229	.229	956.16**	.419
SES	.535	.286	.057	345.58**	.203
Past achievement	.559	.312	.026	200.80**	.155
Reading amount	.571	.326	.014	116.58**	.122
Reading efficacy	.572	.328	.002	15.62**	.052
Reading Amount					
Reading motivation	.288	.083	.083	302.58**	.266
Past achievement	.304	.092	.009	46.46**	.086
SES	.308	.095	.003	18.97**	.055
Reading efficacy	.310	.096	.001	6.98*	.041

SES = socioeconomic status.
*$p < .01$; **$p < .0001$.

than any other background variable or student characteristic. Consequently, the analysis confirms the finding from Study 1 that reading motivation was a relatively strong predictor of reading amount even when potentially competing variables were included in the analysis.

The findings of Study 2 substantially corroborated the results of Study 1. That is, passage comprehension was significantly predicted by reading amount when accounting for previous achievement, reading efficacy, and reading motivation. A significant contribution of reading motivation to reading amount was found in Study 2, which confirmed the motivation effects in Study 1. As the age of the students and operational procedures for measuring each construct were different in the two studies, the converging findings appear to document the generality of the effects.

Discussion

Our major purpose in this investigation was to examine how reading amount and motivation contribute to text comprehension. The first step in this account was to document that text comprehension was predicted by reading amount. Studies 1 and 2 confirmed the results of previous investigations that showed the effects of reading amount on text comprehension, utilizing a variety of measures of reading amount including print exposure (Cipielewski & Stanovich, 1992;

Cunningham & Stanovich, 1997), children's diaries (Anderson et al., 1988), and self-report questionnaires (Allen et al., 1992; Guthrie, Schafer, Wang, & Afflerbach, 1995; Wigfield & Guthrie, 1997). What the results of Study 1 add to this literature is the control of potentially confounding variables. We found that reading amount predicted text comprehension even when controlling for the background variables of previous achievement, prior knowledge, reading effi- cacy, and reading motivation, all of which have been found to correlate with text comprehension. Study 2 confirmed this controlled correlation for students in grade 10, consistent with the findings of Cunningham and Stanovich.

In Study 1, reading motivation did not correlate significantly with the two indicators of passage comprehension, which is consistent with the findings of Baker and Wigfield (1999). In the research literature, only Gottfried (1990) re- ported correlations of reading motivation and tested reading achievement in third to fifth graders. The frequently reported associations between reading motivation and achievement utilize self-reported strategy use as the indicator of achievement rather than performance on tests of text comprehension (Meece & Holt, 1993). In Study 2, we found that reading motivation did predict text comprehension. This result was likely due to the measure of reading motivation used in Study 2, which was closely linked to effort and learning in English class. It may be also attributed to the increasing role of motivational predictors of achievement as children get older, as found in previous studies (see Eccles et al., 1998).

Reading motivation was a direct predictor of reading amount, in both Studies 1 and 2. Even when recognizing the contributions of previous achievement, pas- sage comprehension, prior knowledge, and reading efficacy, reading motivation accounted for a significant proportion of the variance in reading amount. In Study 1, with third and fifth graders, reading motivation accounted for 14% of the variance, and reading motivation accounted for 8% of the variance after con- trolling statistically for past achievement in text comprehension, reading effica- cy, and socioeconomic status.

Very few studies have attempted to identify variables that explain student reading amount and frequency. Yet, if reading amount predicts achievement in text comprehension as highly as the literature indicates, accounting for reading amount becomes an important theoretical and practical issue for researchers. Our results and those of previous studies suggest that motivation is a preeminent predictor of reading amount. In the Wigfield and Guthrie (1997) study, reading motivation was found to be both antecedent and predictive of reading amount. In that study, reading motivation in the fall of the academic year predicted growth in text comprehension from the fall to the spring. These conditions of antece- dence and prediction are usually suggestive of causal direction. This investigation extended these findings by statistically controlling past comprehension, prior knowledge, and reading efficacy.

Taken together, the results of these investigations point toward the position that reading motivation increases reading amount. This linkage of reading motivation and reading amount is centrally important to understanding the role of motivation in text comprehension. In our view, one of the major contributors of motivation to text comprehension is that motivation increases reading amount, which then increases text comprehension.

This view is compatible with a number of psychological theories in which motivation is an explanatory construct. Most relevant to this investigation is the self-determination theory of Deci and his colleagues (Deci et al., 1991). For example, Skinner et al. (1990) reported a range of evidence that intrinsically motivated students (i.e., students who have motivational goals of curiosity, challenge, and involvement) consistently display behaviors relevant to this motivation (e.g., reading books, working hard in English class, writing frequently). Assuming that reading motivation is a set of goals and purposes for reading (e.g., curiosity, involvement, challenge, recognition, competition), it is likely that students who possess a high number of these motivational goals at high levels of strength will read frequently for substantial amounts of time. Likewise, the motivational construct of self-efficacy for an activity is highly associated with time spent in relevant behaviors (Bandura, 1986). For example, individuals with high self-efficacy in music spend time playing or listening to music; individuals with high self-efficacy in reading spend time in reading activities.

We, and others (Baker & Wigfield, 1999; Wigfield & Guthrie, 1997), showed that different aspects of reading motivation (both intrinsic and extrinsic) predict the reading amount of children and adolescents. In addition, reading amount leads to increases in reading comprehension. How might this occur? One hypothesis is that prior knowledge mediates the effect of reading amount on text comprehension. Students who spend a large amount of time reading gain knowledge about a variety of topics. This knowledge enables them to score highly on tests of reading comprehension. In this investigation, prior knowledge was a controlling variable entering into the regression analyses in Study 1. The effects of reading amount on text comprehension were found even when prior knowledge was entered into the equation. This result raises some doubt about the role of knowledge as the major mediating variable between reading amount and text comprehension.

A second hypothesis was raised by Schunk and Zimmerman (1997), who proposed that reading efficacy is associated with reading amount and reading achievement. In the present investigation, reading efficacy contributed to reading achievement in Study 2 but not in Study 1. In Study 1, reading motivation contributed strongly to text comprehension when reading efficacy was controlled, but the reverse did not occur. It is possible that the three-item measure of reading efficacy used in this study may not have been sufficiently comprehensive to capture this construct.

A third plausible explanation of the effect of reading amount on text comprehension is that cognitive efficacy is a mediator. Students who spend a large amount of time reading will increase in fluency of using such cognitive strategies as applying prior knowledge, finding the main idea, inferencing, and building a causal model of the text. We are not aware of any studies that have measured cognitive efficiency of text comprehension strategies independently of text comprehension itself, and, therefore, we do not have data on which to judge this hypothesis.

A fourth plausible explanation for the effect of reading amount on text comprehension is related to the attunement of student cognitive and motivational goals. This explanation provides a set of hypotheses for possible further study. Reading amount may increase text comprehension by facilitating the coordination of cognitive and motivational goals. Previous research indicated that cognitive goals (e.g., trying to understand the main character's actions, trying to explain the life cycle of a frog) guide attention and processing of information during reading (Lorch & van den Broek, 1997). As mentioned earlier and in parallel to this structure, motivation may also be construed as a set of goals. With both of these cognitive and motivational goal sets in operation, an executive system that enables a person to coordinate them would be valuable (see also Pintrich, Marx, & Boyle, 1993).

The processes of attunement prioritize cognitive goals (e.g., how important it is to understand the main idea of a paragraph completely) based on the strength of the motivational goals operating for the text. For example, a person would persist in reading material that is fulfilling motivational goals and terminate the cognitive activity of reading material that was not fulfilling motivational goals. As Lorch and van den Broek (1997) suggested, "a reader's goals and motivation are likely to influence both the elaboration and coherence of the mental model the reader constructs and the degree to which the mental model is integrated with background knowledge" (p. 231). The level of attunement among the motivational and cognitive goal-attaining activities would improve with successful functioning. This improvement constitutes the effect of reading amount on text comprehension.

This explanation is similar to Greeno and Middle School Mathematics Through Applications Project Group's (1998) account of the acquisition of expertise. They stated that developing a form of expertise, such as reading, can be described as attunement of the cognitive and motivational system to existing constraints and affordances. The accomplishment of both motivational and cognitive goals is fostered by affordances but limited by constraints. One example of a constraint in text comprehension is the lack of curiosity about the topic of the text being read. An example of an affordance for text comprehension is a strong goal, such as challenge and curiosity, for the knowledge domain of the text. A cognitive constraint for text comprehension is lack of reading ability to gain information from a given text. This constraint would lead the reader to shift to a new text if the motivational goal was high but would lead the reader to abandon the topic if the motivational goal was low. Evidence shows that high motivational goals, such as challenge and curiosity, lead to acquisition and use of deep processing strategies for text (Guthrie et al., 1998; Meece & Holt, 1993; Pintrich et al., 1993). However, to perform well on a reading comprehension test, a student must use cognitive strategies for conceptual understanding without high intrinsic motivation. On a test, a person must apply strategies normally used under high intrinsic motivation to perform a task where intrinsic motivation may be low or extrinsic motivation may be high. The good test taker, then, can apply text comprehension strategies under many different motivational conditions.

High reading amount may contribute to attunement in the cognitive–motivational goal system for several reasons. First, a substantial reading amount provides the opportunity for initial learning of the cognitive strategies for text comprehension under high intrinsic motivation. Further, reading widely and frequently provides the opportunity to apply these strategies as needed under low intrinsic (but higher extrinsic) motivation settings, such as finishing homework or taking tests. Finally, As Pressley (1997) observed, "affective–evaluational processes affect text representations" (p. 252). That is, awareness of these affective and motivational aspects of reading may facilitate cognitive self-regulation. In sum, a substantial reading amount may lead to an improvement in the goal attunement of motivational and cognitive goals.

Measurement issues regarding reading amount and motivation are complex. There are multiple indicators of reading amount such as diary measures (Anderson et al., 1988), print exposure (Cunningham & Stanovich, 1997), and questionnaires (Wigfield & Guthrie, 1997). Two limitations of print exposure measures are that they are limited to fiction (because titles of nonfiction books are not easily distinguishable) and that they were not designed to capture school-related reading. Print exposure measures, such as title- and author-recognition tests, appear to have the advantage of not being subject to social desirability effects (Allen et al., 1992). One weakness of measures influenced by social desirability, such as questionnaires, is that they may not possess validity, reliability, or variance to correlate substantially with other measures. However, it appears that print exposure measures and certain types of questionnaires are comparable psychometrically. (Note that the necessary characteristics of such a questionnaire include an adequate number of behavioral questions across a range of situations.) For example, the questionnaire in Study 1 had a reliability of .75, and behavioral questionnaires loaded on the same factor with print exposure in factor analyses (Allen et al., 1992). A second limitation is that such measures may not relate well to outcomes measures. Yet, in this study, such measures did relate to important outcome measures, such as the reading amount and text comprehension measures. These findings help validate the use of self-report measures. Nevertheless, researchers should continue to explore alternative ways to measure reading motivation.

In conclusion, most of the previous research on text comprehension looked at cognitive predictors of text comprehension or examined how children's reading amount relates to their comprehension. We added to this literature by showing that reading motivation increases the reading amount of individuals, thereby facilitating their text comprehension. These findings illustrate that motivation should be included in the scientific study of reading.

Acknowledgments

The work reported herein was supported by the National Reading Research Center of the University of Georgia and University of Maryland in a grant under the Educational Research and Development Centers Program (PR/Award No. 117A20007) as administered by the Office of Educational Research and Improvement, U.S. Department of Education. The findings and opinions expressed do not reflect the position or policies of the National Reading Research Center, the Office of Educational Research and Improvement, or the U.S. Department of Education.

References

Alexander, P.A. (1997). Knowledge seeking and self-schema: A case for the motivational dimensions of exposition. *Educational Psychologist, 32*, 83–95.

Alexander, P.A., Jetton, T.L., & Kulikowich, J.M. (1996). Interrelationships of knowledge, interest, and recall: Assessing a model of domain learning. *Journal of Educational Psychology, 87*, 559–575.

Allen, L., Cipielewski, J., & Stanovich, K.E. (1992). Multiple indicators of children's reading habits and attitudes: Construct validity and cognitive correlates. *Journal of Educational Psychology, 84*, 489–503.

Ames, C., & Archer, J. (1988). Achievement goals in the classroom: Students' learning strategies and motivational processes. *Journal of Educational Psychology, 80*, 260–267.

Anderson, R.C., & Pearson, P.D. (1984). A schema-theoretic view of basic processes in reading. In P.D. Pearson, R. Barr, M.L. Kamil, & P. Mosenthal (Eds.), *Handbook of reading research* (pp. 255–291). New York: Longman.

Anderson, R.C., Wilson, P.T., & Fielding, L.G. (1988). Growth in reading and how children spend their time outside of school. *Reading Research Quarterly, 23*, 285–303.

Baker, L., & Wigfield, A. (1999). Dimensions of children's motivation for reading and their relations to reading activity and reading achievement. *Reading Research Quarterly, 34*, 452–477.

Bandura, A. (1986). *Social foundations of thought and action: A social cognitive theory.* Englewood Cliffs, NJ: Prentice Hall.

Benware, C.A., & Deci, E.L. (1984). Quality of learning with an active versus passive motivational set. *American Educational Research Journal, 21*, 755–765.

Biemiller, A. (1970). The development of the use of graphic and contextual information as children learn to read. *Reading Research Quarterly, 6*, 75–96.

Campbell, J.R., Voelkl, K.E., & Donahue, P.L. (1997). *NAEP 1996 trends in academic progress* (NCES Publication No. 97-985). Washington, DC: U.S. Department of Education.

Chapman, J.W., & Tunmer, W.E. (1997). A longitudinal study of beginning reading achievement and reading self-concept. *British Journal of Educational Psychology, 67*, 279–291.

Cipielewski, J., & Stanovich, K.E. (1992). Predicting growth in reading ability from children's exposure to print. *Journal of Experimental Child Psychology, 54*, 74–89.

Csikszentmihalyi, M. (1978). Intrinsic rewards and emergent motivation. In M. Lepper & D. Green (Eds.), *The hidden costs of reward: New perspectives on the psychology of human motivation* (pp. 205–216). Hillsdale, NJ: Erlbaum.

Cunningham, A.E., & Stanovich, K.E. (1997). Early reading acquisition and its relation to reading experience and ability 10 years later. *Developmental Psychology, 33*, 934–945.

Deci, E.L., Vallerand, R.J., Pelletier, L.G., & Ryan, R.M. (1991). Motivation and education: The self-determination perspective. *Educational Psychologist, 26*, 325–346.

Dole, J.A., Duffy, G.G., Roehler, L.R., & Pearson, P.D. (1991). Moving from the old to the new: Research on reading comprehension instruction. *Review of Educational Research, 61*, 239–264.

Dweck, C.S., & Leggett, E.L. (1988). A social–cognitive approach to motivation and personality. *Psychological Review, 95*, 256–273.

Eccles, J.S., Wigfield, A., & Schiefele, U. (1988). Motivation to succeed. In W. Damon (Series Ed.) & N. Eisenberg (Vol. Ed.), *Handbook of child psychology: Vol. 3. Social, emotional, and personality development* (5th ed., pp. 1017–1095). New York: Wiley.

Elley, W.B. (1992). *How in the world do students read?* Hamburg, Germany: The International Association for the Evaluation of Educational Achievement.

Gottfried, A.E. (1990). Academic intrinsic motivation in young elementary school children. *Journal of Educational Psychology, 82*, 525–538.

Greaney, V. (1980). Factors related to amount and type of leisure-time reading. *Reading Research Quarterly, 15*, 337–357.

Greeno, J.G., & Middle School Mathematics Through Applications Project Group. (1998). The situativity of knowing, learning, and research. *American Psychologist, 53*, 5–26.

Guthrie, J.T., Schafer, W., Wang, Y.Y., & Afflerbach, P. (1995). Relationships of instruction to amount of reading: An exploration of social, cognitive, and instructional connections. *Reading Research Quarterly, 30*, 8–25.

Guthrie, J.T., Van Meter, P., Hancock, G.R., Alao, S., Anderson, E., & McCann, A. (1998). Does Concept-Oriented Reading Instruction increase strategy use and conceptual learning from text? *Journal of Educational Psychology, 90*, 261–278.

Guthrie, J.T., Van Meter, P., McCann, A.D., Wigfield, A., Bennett, L., Poundstone, C.C., et al. (1996). Growth of literacy engagement: Changes in motivations and strategies during Concept-Oriented Reading Instruction. *Reading Research Quarterly, 31*, 306–332.

Johnson, E.G., & Rust, K.F. (1992). Population inferences and variance estimation for NAEP data. *Journal of Educational Statistics, 17*, 175–190.

Juel, C. (1988). Learning to read and write: A longitudinal study of 54 children from first through fourth grades. *Journal of Educational Psychology, 80*, 437–447.

Kurtz-Costes, B.E., & Schneider, W. (1994). Self-concept, attributional beliefs, and school achievement: A longitudinal analysis. *Contemporary Educational Psychology, 19*, 199–216.

Lehtinen, E., Vauras, M., Salonen, P., Olkinuora, E., & Kinnunen, R. (1995). Long-term development of learning activity: Motivational, cognitive, and social interaction. *Educational Psychologist, 30*, 21–35.

Lorch, R.F., & van den Broek, R. (1997). Understanding reading comprehension: Current and future contributions of cognitive science. *Contemporary Educational Psychology, 22*, 213–247.

Meece, J.L., Blumenfeld, P.C., & Hoyle, R.H. (1988). Students' goal orientations and cognitive engagement in classroom activities. *Journal of Educational Psychology, 80*, 514–523.

Meece, J.L., & Holt, K. (1993). A pattern analysis of students' achievement goals. *Journal of Educational Psychology, 85*, 582–590.

Metsala, J.L., & Ehri, L.C. (Eds.). (1998). *Word recognition in beginning literacy.* Mahwah, NJ: Erlbaum.

Miller, R.B., Behrens, J.T., Greene, B.A., & Newman, D. (1993). Goals and perceived ability: Impact on student valuing, self-regulation and persistence. *Contemporary Educational Psychology, 18*, 2–14.

Morrow, L.M. (1996), *Motivating reading and writing in diverse classrooms* (NCTE Research Rep. No. 28). Urbana, IL: National Council of Teachers of English.

Nicholls, J.G., Cheung, P., Lauer, J., & Patashnick, M. (1989). Individual differences in academic motivation: Perceived ability, goals, beliefs, and values. *Learning and Individual Differences, 1*, 63–84.

Owings, J., McMillan, M., Ahmed, S., West, J., Quinn, P., Hausken, E., et al. (1994, April). *A guide to using NELS: 88 data.* Paper presented at the annual meeting of the American Educational Research Association, New Orleans, LA.

Pintrich, P.R., & DeGroot, E.V. (1990). Motivational and self-regulated learning components of classroom academic performance. *Journal of Educational Psychology, 82*, 33–40.

Pintrich, P.R., Marx, R.W., & Boyle, R.A. (1993). Beyond cold conceptual change: The role of motivational beliefs and classroom contextual factors in the process of conceptual change. *Review of Educational Research, 63,* 167–199.

Pintrich, P.R., & Schunk, D.H. (1996). *Motivation in education: Theory, research, and applications.* Englewood Cliffs, NJ: Prentice Hall.

Pressley, M.P. (1997). The cognitive science of reading. *Contemporary Educational Psychology, 22,* 247–260.

Schallert, D.L., & Reed, J.H. (1997). The pull of the text and the process of involvement in reading. In J.T. Guthrie & A. Wigfield (Eds.), *Reading engagement: Motivating readers through integrated instruction* (pp. 68–85). Newark, DE: International Reading Association.

Schunk, D.H., & Rice, M.J. (1993). Strategy fading and progress feedback: Effects on self-efficacy and comprehension among students receiving remedial reading services. *Journal of Special Education, 27,* 257–276.

Schunk, D.H., & Zimmerman, B.J. (1997). Developing self-efficacious readers and writers: The role of social and self-regulatory processes. In J.T. Guthrie & A. Wigfield (Eds.), *Reading engagement: Motivating readers through integrated instruction* (pp. 34–50). Newark, DE: International Reading Association.

Shell, D.F., Colvin, C., & Bruning, R.H. (1995). Self-efficacy, attribution, and outcome expectancy mechanisms in reading and writing achievement: Grade-level and achievement-level differences. *Journal of Educational Psychology, 87,* 386–398.

Skinner, E.A., Wellborn, J.G., & Connell, J.P. (1990). What it takes to do well in school and whether I've got it: A process model of perceived control and children's engagement and achievement in school. *Journal of Educational Psychology, 82,* 22–32.

Stipek, D. (1996). Motivation and instruction. In D.C. Berliner & R.C. Calfee (Eds.), *Handbook of educational psychology* (pp. 85–113). New York: Simon & Schuster/Macmillan.

Sweet, A.P., Guthrie, J.T., & Ng, M.M. (1998). Teacher perceptions and student reading motivation. *Journal of Educational Psychology, 90,* 210–223.

Taylor, B.M., Frye, B.J., & Maruyama, G. (1990). Time spent reading and reading growth. *American Educational Research Journal, 27,* 351–362.

Torgesen, J.K., Wagner, R.K., Rashotte, C.A., Burgess, S., & Hecht, S. (1997). Contributions of phonological awareness and rapid automatic naming ability to the growth of word-reading skills in second- to fifth-grade children. *Scientific Studies of Reading, 1,* 161–185.

Wigfield, A., Eccles, J.S., & Rodriquez, D. (1998). The development of children's motivation in school contexts. In P.D. Pearson & A. Iran-Nejad (Eds.), *Review of research in education* (Vol. 23, pp. 73–118). Washington, DC: American Education Research Association.

Wigfield, A., & Guthrie, J.T. (1997). Relations of children's motivation for reading to the amount and breadth of their reading. *Journal of Educational Psychology, 89,* 420–432.

35

The Role of Responsive Teaching in Focusing Reader Intention and Developing Reader Motivation

Robert B. Ruddell and Norman J. Unrau

Because there can be no responsive, reflective teaching of literacy without a responsive, reflective teacher, we intend in this article to explore the characteristics that such teachers bring to teaching. From the study of influential teachers, their behavior in the classroom, and their impact on students (Ruddell, 1994, 1995; Ruddell, Draheim, & Barnes, 1990; Ruddell & Haggard, 1982), we can garner insights into responsive teachers and ways they promote literacy engagement. Influential teachers may be defined as teachers who have been identified by a former student as having had a significant influence on the student's academic or personal success in school. Influential teachers share characteristics in several areas that include the following:

- They show that they care about their students.
- They help their students to understand and solve their personal and academic problems.
- They manifest excitement and enthusiasm about what they teach.
- They adapt instruction to the individual needs, motives, interests, and aptitudes of their students and have high expectations for them.
- They use motivating and effective strategies when they teach, including clarity in stating problems, use of concrete examples, analysis of abstract concepts, and application of concepts to new contexts.
- They engage students in a process of intellectual discovery.

We also have learned that high-achieving students, those we could suspect are more motivated for learning, can identify at least twice as many influential teachers as lower-achieving students. Whether high or low achieving, these students see their influential teachers as having clear instructional goals, plans, and strategies that contribute to a classroom learning environment that the teacher closely monitors. Further, by emphasizing intrinsic over extrinsic motivation, these influential teachers elicit students' internal motivation by stimulating intellectual curiosity, exploring students' self-understanding, using aesthetic imagery and expression, and focusing on problem solving.

These findings about influential teachers inform our purposes for this article. In it, we tell the story of Ms. Hawthorne, an influential teacher who is striving to redesign her instructional program to promote her students' literacy and learning through an integrated language arts and history curriculum. To better understand Ms. Hawthorne's dilemma and its resolution, we investigate and describe psychological and instructional factors that are critical to the development of both reader and teacher intention and motivation. These psychological and instructional factors form three major categories for both readers and teachers: the developing self, instructional orientation, and task-engagement resources. After presenting a model that represents these features and their influence on the focus of intention, we describe a classroom learning environment that emphasizes meaning negotiation, nourishes the developing self, activates students' instructional orientation, and provides potential for readers to sharpen their focus of intention on reading and meaning construction. We then identify key guidelines for designing literacy-enhancing instruction to develop reader intention and motivation and apply these to Ms. Hawthorne's classroom. We conclude with implications for research.

Ms. Hawthorne's Dilemma

Ms. Hawthorne was discontented with the language arts and history program she had inherited when she began teaching at Taft Junior High School in central Los Angeles, California, 2 years ago. Some of her seventh-grade students read books and completed tasks she assigned, but too many did so halfheartedly, infrequently, or not at all. The program seemed unresponsive, impersonal, and unengaging. She knew that she and her students could do better. With the encouragement of colleagues, a new principal, and faculty at a local university, she decided to investigate what she might do to redesign her program so that more students would become engaged.

She began her action research by collecting as much information as she could about her students to discover who they were—not only as readers but also as people. To get to know individual students better, to understand their motivations and their reading strategies, Ms. Hawthorne decided to conduct a few tutorial sessions once a week after school. Several students responded to this idea; one student, Cynthia, jumped at the opportunity.

At the beginning of the school year, Ms. Hawthorne got the impression that Cynthia was slightly hyperactive and quite social. But, as she got to know Cynthia during the tutorial meetings, she discovered Cynthia was far more complex. The enthusiasm that Cynthia expressed when Ms. Hawthorne offered tutorial help demonstrated some aspects of Cynthia's sense of self and her motivation to learn. At her initial tutoring session, Cynthia told Ms. Hawthorne that she had good memories about school. She said she liked it because she had lots of opportunities to socialize with her friends. Both her parents helped her with schoolwork, her mother in reading and writing and her father in math. In earlier elementary grades, Cynthia often was on the honor role. Like her mother, Cynthia was thinking about becoming a nurse, but she also imagined herself being a story writer, a travel agent, a model, and a fashion designer. She obviously was exploring possibilities for herself.

Cynthia said her favorite subject was history, and she had a passion for books about "old-fashioned" family life and orphans. She told Ms. Hawthorne that she had many of these stories in her head and would much rather write them than complete assigned compositions. During their first meeting, Cynthia told Ms. Hawthorne that two of her goals for the year were to improve her reading and to reduce the number of mistakes she made in her writing.

To get an idea of Cynthia's reading level, Ms. Hawthorne administered an individual reading inventory. She found that Cynthia had an independent reading level of fourth grade, an instructional level of fifth grade, and a frustration level of sixth grade. She also discovered that Cynthia, who said that she understood text that she had read, was unable to answer many literal and interpretive questions about that text. After the assessment, Cynthia complained to Ms. Hawthorne that the last paragraph on the test, one at the seventh-grade level, was unfair because there were words in it that she did not recognize. During the assessment and later in the tutorial, Ms. Hawthorne found that Cynthia had difficulty comprehending what she read and connecting concepts to make meaning. Ms. Hawthorne also observed that Cynthia gave up easily with text she had difficulty understanding and expressed boredom or self-defeat rather than increased effort.

Ms. Hawthorne was impressed with Cynthia's "zest" for writing. Cynthia could construct concept maps or outlines and finish a five-paragraph essay in one period. However, Ms. Hawthorne discovered that Cynthia often misplaced her essays before turning them in. Further, Ms. Hawthorne thought that Cynthia's writing was rudimentary in content and structure. In an essay containing paragraphs with four or five simple sentences, she simply restated the assignment and discussed only the most obvious points, which Ms. Hawthorne described as "conceptually dull" writing. Also, Cynthia's essays contained many grammar and spelling errors, which Cynthia wanted to improve.

As the special tutoring progressed, Ms. Hawthorne discovered that Cynthia's self-projected image of an enthusiastic learner was not always consistent with Cynthia's behavior. Although Cynthia first appeared earnest in seeking help for her literacy needs, Ms. Hawthorne began to think that she was seeking attention and trying to evade standard class work. Ms. Hawthorne also noticed that, although Cynthia wrote enthusiastically, she often did not complete reading assignments, and her written work rarely was turned in when it was due. Inconsistency and irresponsibility marked her performance. In short, while Cynthia showed enthusiasm for improvement, she appeared to have problems with self-regulation in addressing schoolwork.

Cynthia's portrait is similar to that of many middle school students who reveal several selves, including images of the enthusiastic learner, the engaged reader, the fast problem solver, the school socialite, the irresponsible kid, and the budding historian. Cynthia has had opportunities that others in her school have not had available, such as a mother and father she views as supportive, but she is beset with motivational problems that keep her from making the kinds of effort that would result in more success. What moves students, like Cynthia, to read? How might her skills as a reader grow? What kinds of activities might her teachers use in classroom environments to promote literacy engagement?

Factors Critical to Reader and Teacher Motivation

The outcomes of a reader's reading and a teacher's instructional design are quite different. However, the two processes have many features in common. Both reader and teacher have a *developing self* (an identity and self-schema, a sense of self-efficacy and self-worth, expectations, an experiential self, and self-knowledge), an *instructional orientation* (achievement goals, task values, sociocultural values and beliefs, and stances), and *task-engagement resources* (reader text-processing resources or teacher instructional design resources). In the following sections, we describe these features, which are depicted in Figure 1, and show how they are of particular importance to the motivational state of both readers and teachers.

Using an image to help us render and understand reading and instructional design processes, we envision the eye as a metaphor for focusing motivation and intention. In Figure 1, the central, inner circle, the focus of intention, may be seen as the pupil. Factors that influence the focus of intention radiate from the pupil and form a larger concentric circle around it, somewhat like the eye's iris. Perhaps this metaphor will help us understand the complex array of features and processes that affect intentionality.

FIGURE 1
Factors Critical to Developing Reader/Teacher Focus of Intention and Motivation

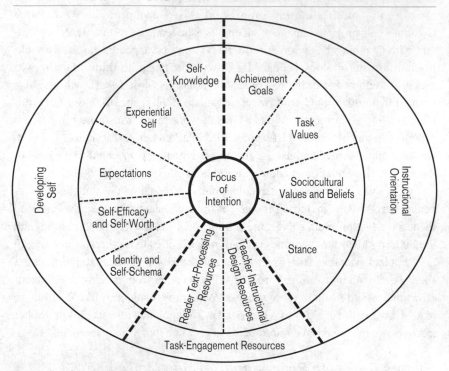

Reader Text-Processing Resources
Knowledge of language
Word analysis
Text-processing strategies
Metacognitive strategies
Knowledge of classroom and social interaction
World knowledge

Teacher Instructional Design Resources
Knowledge of students and their meaning-
    construction process
Knowledge of literature and content areas
Teaching strategies
World knowledge
Metacognitive knowledge

The Focus of Intention

At the center of Figure 1 is the *focus of intention*. It may be compared to the eye's pupil focusing intention not in response to light but in response to the confluence of many motivational factors that influence readers and teachers. This focus is the central point of the mind's intent—of its direction, purpose, and intensity when interacting with a learning environment. We have modified and integrated into our perspective a view of intention that Mathewson (1994, see #50 this volume) developed and built into his model of attitude's influence on reading and learning to read. In that model, intention functions as a mediator between attitude toward reading and reading itself and is defined as a "commitment to a plan for achieving one or more reading purposes at a more or less specified time in the future" (p. 1435 this volume). In the reader/teacher self-system presented in Figure 1, we have extended intention to both reader and teacher. The term *intention* implies not only purpose and goal, but also a self becoming and emerging from a cognitive–affective background. Mathewson refers to these background factors as cornerstone concepts, including values, goals, and self-concepts that are influenced by home and school environments. In light of psychological research on motivation, we have extended these cornerstone concepts to various features that control the focus of intention.

In describing the factors that influence motivation or the focus of intention, we aspire to the ideal of the optimally self-regulated reader or teacher. Self-regulation is essential for self-actualization, the pinnacle of Maslow's (1954) hierarchy of needs that drive motivation.

Developing Self

The developing self comprises those aspects of the reader's or teacher's self-system that shape life's meaning and purpose. As structures in the self-system, they contribute to our focus of intention as readers and learners (Mathewson, 1994). The components of the developing self that govern the focus of intention are arrayed clockwise from the lower left in Figure 1. We will explore each of these constructs and illustrate them with references to Ms. Hawthorne and Cynthia.

Identity and Self-Schema. Both Ms. Hawthorne and Cynthia, as teacher and student, have a sense of who they are—that is, they have an identity. Ms. Hawthorne's identity is far more consolidated in her role as a developing teacher; Cynthia is still exploring what she might become in a stage Erikson (1968) labels identity versus identity confusion. According to Erikson, core identity includes two aspects of self: a sense of self garnered from the integration of many selves or aspects of those selves that have been assumed, played out, rejected, or embraced and a sense of self as an organizing agency that enables self-representation.

The first sense of self in past, present, and future arises from self-schema. Teachers, like their students, access past, present, and future self-schemata (Markus & Nurius, 1986) as facets of their self-system. Those lived, remembered, and possible selves influence each student's and teacher's behavior and motivation. Images of the self shape the choices made, the actions carried out, and the possibilities pursued or resisted.

Cynthia has many images of herself as a young woman in the future. She imagines she could be a nurse, a fashion designer, or a writer. Like students, teachers have self-schemata in the form of possible or potential selves. Ms. Hawthorne often sees herself as a dynamic teacher promoting more engagement with reading than she now witnesses in her classroom. A teacher's activated self-schema provides not only a foundation for the interpretation of students in a learning context, such as the way Ms. Hawthorne interprets Cynthia's behavior, but also an internal context for the interpretation of a specific text, such as a poem.

Garcia and Pintrich (1994) demonstrate how self-schemata contribute to an individual's desire to develop literacy skills or to avoid their development. Cynthia shows both these trends. An individual's schema can generate an identity perceived by ourselves and others that ranges from loathed to loved, failed to fulfilled, incompetent to incomparable.

An example from Moyer (1995) illustrates the self-schema's motivational strength. A poet and teacher who discovered the power of literacy in prison, Jimmy Santiago Baca, eventually won an American Book Award and founded Black Mesa Enterprises, an organization that provides young people with alternatives to violence through a language-centered community. Before becoming a writer, he struggled with a self-schema that profoundly rejected literacy. While in jail, Baca proclaimed,

> Sissies read books. You couldn't do *anything* with a book. You couldn't fix a '57 Chevy with a book. You couldn't take money from some hustler with a book. You couldn't convince or persuade anybody with a book. Books were in the way. And not only that, they were the great enemy. Books were where you found the pain.... So why should I go open a book and give myself all this pain? I didn't *need* that. (pp. 35–36)

However, language and literacy and another possible self caught Baca in what he calls "the fiercest typhoon I have ever been in and from which I have never escaped. I have continually swirled like a leaf" (p. 36).

The second organizing agency of our identity Erikson (1968) refers to as ego-identity, the "actually attained but forever-to-be-revised sense of reality of the self within social reality" (p. 211). Erikson's conception of identity is tied to his theory of identity formation through the life cycle. Students' and teachers' lives can be viewed as psychohistories that, if examined closely, reveal the outcome of the various crises through which they have passed in home, community, and school on their way to manifesting their current role and identity as a student or a teacher.

Seeing a student like Cynthia or a teacher like Ms. Hawthorne as an individual passing through a "forever-to-be-revised sense of reality of the self" provides a perspective that is both practical and theoretically powerful. With the concept of identity as both a capacity to organize selves in a social environment and as a composite of sustainable self-impressions that provides an internal, personal core of reference, we can more clearly appreciate the role of influential teachers in the shaping of both a student's and a teacher's identity. If, as Ruddell and his associates (Ruddell & Greybeck, 1992; Ruddell & Kern, 1986) have demonstrated, influential teachers provide students with models with whom they identify and attempt to emulate, then such influential teachers also may serve as focal images that students and teachers-to-be might use to help themselves organize their ego identities.

The concepts of identity and identification also enable us to understand a teacher's and his or her students' motivation to read at a deeper level. Students may not only decide to enter the field of education because of identification with an influential teacher; they also may be moved to emulate the teaching style of an influential teacher. Responsive teachers, like Ms. Hawthorne, are likely to recognize that their students' identities, and thus their students' motives for learning, are shaped by crises of identity before and during schooling and by identifications with family, community, and cultural figures.

Responsive teachers also recognize that many young people, especially those attending inner-city schools, may see themselves excluded from the school's culture and seek affirmation of an identity and affiliation on the streets (Heath & McLaughlin, 1993). These are often the at-risk students who, by the time they enter middle school, have begun to disidentify with school and become socialized through gang life (Vigil, 1993). Some of these at-risk students may find alternative groups and organizations, such as boys and girls clubs, community organizations, or church groups, in which identities can be found or formed. Some inner-city schools have developed programs, such as cross-age tutoring programs for pregnant teenage girls, to encourage students to find affirmation of their emerging identities in the schools.

Self-Efficacy and Self-Worth. What we believe ourselves capable of doing or learning constitutes our self-efficacy. Cynthia, for example, believes that she knows quite a lot about what she calls "old-fashioned times" in the United States and that she can read stories about people living in those times very well. When Ms. Hawthorne lets her read such stories, Cynthia feels a high sense of self-efficacy and a sharpened focus of intention. As Schunk and Zimmerman point out in *Reading Engagement: Motivating Readers Through Integrated Instruction* (Guthrie & Wigfield, 1997), the self-efficacy of a student will predict his or her motivation for engaging in reading. A student with high self-efficacy will work harder, longer, and more willingly than one with low self-efficacy. Even though Cynthia may encounter challenging vocabulary and difficult narrative, she is likely to be effortful and to work hard to understand.

Schunk (1991, 1994) has shown that teaching students to be more efficacious and persuading them that they are efficacious improves their performance. During her tutorial with Cynthia, Ms. Hawthorne models strategies that she believes will help Cynthia increase her sense of self-efficacy. She shows her how to summarize as she reads, to make predictions, to seek clarification, and to ask questions—strategies that build comprehension and self-regulation (Palincsar & Brown, 1986).

Self-worth may be viewed as a reflection of self-efficacy. According to self-worth theorists, students' highest concern is to protect a sense of ability (Covington, 1992). Accordingly, learners' motivation to engage in school settings frequently depends on their perception of the impact of a learning event on self-esteem. The protection of self-worth may be achieved at the expense of earning low grades if students believe that not studying will preserve esteem more effectively than studying. If students do not engage in reading tasks for school, they may be avoiding them not because they lack motivation but because they are motivated by a paramount concern: the preservation of esteem. By not reading, a student can say to himself (and to his classmates) that he did not expect to perform well because he made no effort to do so. Such a statement would not reflect on the student's ability to compete, which is frequently valued above effort in school cultures.

The concept of self-worth also applies to teachers. Teachers who have low self-esteem are less likely to rise to teaching challenges such as those Ms. Hawthorne is confronting. They may find it more assuring to continue past practices without making efforts and risking failure in planning for future changes in their teaching. What teachers like Ms. Hawthorne judge themselves capable of accomplishing in their classrooms has a determining effect on their motivation and the learning environments they construct.

Expectations. Expectation, a motivational construct related to self-efficacy (Schunk, 1994), often influences focus of intention. Covington (1992) has explored the relations between ability attributions and expectations. He notes that students' personal expectations influence their level of aspiration. That level of aspiration, in turn, may be shaped or limited by the expectations of others, especially teachers.

We know that children like Cynthia achieve at a higher level in classrooms where teachers expect all children to learn (Stipek, 1993). We also know that teachers communicate different expectation messages to students whom the teacher considers to have high or low expectations (Good, 1987). For example, teachers call on high-expectation students more often and wait longer for answers from them but criticize low-expectation students more often for incorrect answers.

It is critical that teachers communicate positive beliefs and attributions to young learners. Ms. Hawthorne knows and does this with Cynthia whenever she can during their work together. Studies of teachers and their students indicate that there is a strong relation between teachers' beliefs about their own efficacy to motivate and to teach students and students' beliefs about their own abilities and chances for success. For example, Midgley, Feldlaufer, & Eccles (1989) found that students who had high-efficacy teachers became significantly more positive (or demonstrated less negative change) compared with students who had low-efficacy teachers and who developed more negative beliefs during the school year. Perhaps responsive teachers like Ms. Hawthorne need to develop and maintain a flexible view of both their self-expectations and their expectations of students; this requires that teachers constantly monitor their own patterns of self-expectation and the patterns of expectation they hold for each student.

Experiential Self. The experiential self is another feature of the developing self-system that controls the focus of intention (Epstein, 1994). The experiential self works parallel to and simultaneously with the other features described but less consciously and less rationally. The features previously described tend to be more verbally coded, such as occurs when Cynthia thinks of herself as "a student who likes history." In contrast, the experiential self processes imagery, narratives, and metaphors to give us a sense of our experience's meaning. In the other structures, reasoning may enable us to make connections between concepts, but in the experiential self there are looser associations among images, stories, and analogies. Truth may not be approached through reason but appears as self-evident; "thinking" tends to lack rational rigor and to leap to stereotypes. While the cognitive structures that we have explored are usually integrated, the experiential self is more likely to reveal dissociation or illogical complexes when, on rare occasions, it appears in consciousness. The experiential self is where seasoned teachers, like Ms. Hawthorne, have stored their teaching stories that contribute to their history and identity as teachers. They refer, almost unconsciously, to these stories to help them make instructional decisions. In their experiential self, students also store their school stories that contribute to their focus of intention.

It is important to emphasize that the nonrational experiential self continually interacts with and influences the more rational structures that compose the developing self-system. Interaction that may occur on unconscious levels can influence the more rational structures, such as identity and self-schema, self-efficacy, self-worth, expectations, goals, and task values. The extent of the influence depends on the power of narratives, imagery, and metaphors contained in the experiential self.

The parallel and interactive aspects of the self-system enable us to understand more comprehensively both the reader's and the teacher's experience of texts that may be represented in long-term memory through words and images. Reading can be explained with the help of schema theory (Rumelhart, 1980), which is more verbally founded, and dual coding theory (Paivio, 1986; Sadoski & Paivio, 1994), which hypothesizes the existence of two means of encoding experience, namely through words and images. Further, the self-system we have postulated enables us to understand not only readers' motivations to seek and engage in literacy events but also their emotional or aesthetic experiences with stories or poetry.

Self-Knowledge. A teacher's or a student's self-knowledge includes all that a teacher or student knows of his or her own self-system, instructional orientation, and task-engagement resources. The assumptions that self-knowledge enables improvements in a teacher's performance and that the inclination to gain self-knowledge should extend throughout a teacher's professional life form the foundation for reflective teaching and the development of more reflective teachers (Schon, 1987; Valli, 1992). We suspect that the more teachers have looked at their own behavior in various settings, especially in classroom interactions, and the more they know about themselves as teachers and how they function, the more they will be able to construct productive learning relationships with their students and learning environments for them.

Students who have begun to gain some degree of self-knowledge often are able to use that knowledge in their reading and discussion of texts to gain more self-understanding. This is especially true if teachers encourage the use of literature to promote self-understanding, as Rosenblatt (1938/1995) has long advocated in works such as *Literature as Exploration*. Through classroom dialogue and reflective writing that allows students to make connections between their own emerging identities and the lives of fictional characters, students may gain deeper personal knowledge.

Both teachers and students can affect their focus of intention through self-knowledge of their own motivational system. Ms. Hawthorne, for example, knows that she is unhappy with her students' level of engagement and that she will continue to be discontent until she modifies her instructional program. She knows that she usually thinks of herself as a confident, capable, and caring teacher, and she tries to envision herself working productively with her students. In addition, she recognizes that what she wants to do involves some risks but is willing to take them in order to evolve in her own development as a teacher. All this self-knowledge will help Ms. Hawthorne understand and sustain herself as she moves through periods of challenge and change.

Summary. The constructs of the developing self-system, including identity and self-schema, self-efficacy and self-worth, expectations, the experiential self, and self-knowledge, are not isolated—they interact as they contribute to teacher or student focus of intention. Although a teacher like Ms. Hawthorne may be conscious of her sense of self as a teacher, of her abilities, and of her expectations, she may be less conscious but nonetheless motivationally influenced by her experiential self, which contains the classroom stories that quietly contribute to the intensity and direction of her focus of intention. Further, the constructs of the developing self interact with features that make up reader or teacher instructional orientation, which is discussed next.

Instructional Orientation

Instructional orientation, or the alignment of teacher or student with a teaching or learning task, affects intention and motivation. The following critical factors make up instructional orientation and regulate the focus of intention.

Achievement Goals. If Ms. Hawthorne asks herself whether an instructional episode is leading toward her becoming a more competent teacher or merely toward the demonstration of her superior skills in classroom instruction, she is, according to Nicholls (1984), questioning achievement goals. Achievement-goal theory stresses the engagement of the learner in selecting, structuring, and making sense of achievement experience. Meece (1994) points out that research has focused on two kinds of achievement goals: mastery or task-oriented goals and performance or ego-oriented goals. Those seeking mastery goals are intrinsically motivated to acquire knowledge and skills that lead to their becoming more competent. The word *mastery* to describe these goals does not mean "mastery learning," "mastery teaching," or a behaviorist perspective of instruction. Ms. Hawthorne, for example, constructs mastery or task-oriented goals for herself as she investigates her students and contemplates redesigning her language arts program. Individuals who are pursuing performance goals are eager to seek opportunities to demonstrate their skills or knowledge in a competitive, public arena. Cynthia would be manifesting performance or ego-oriented goals if she were motivated to read her stories to her classmates primarily to show others her skills as a writer and storyteller.

What might move a teacher, or a reader, toward one or the other goal orientation? Perceptions of personal ability have been shown to be one critical factor that influences patterns of achievement (Meece, 1994). If individuals believe they can become better teachers, or readers, by making an effort, they are more likely embrace a mastery-goal orientation. They see themselves as able to improve over time by making an effort to master challenging tasks. A teacher like Ms. Hawthorne or a student like Cynthia, who acquires knowledge and skills that lead to perceptions of incremental growth in competency, exemplifies a mastery orientation. By making the effort to acquire knowledge and skills, the teacher's or student's feelings of self-worth and competence are likely to increase.

Learners who adopt an ego or performance orientation view their abilities as unchangeable and judge them in comparison to the abilities of others, such as their colleagues, peers, or classmates. If a student must exert more effort to learn a concept, a performance-oriented learner would judge that classmate as having less ability even if both students eventually learn the concept. Performance-oriented learners become preoccupied with ability and see it as basic to success in school performance.

Children's goal orientations appear to result in part from their internalizing parental perspectives, especially the mother's view, of effort and ability in learning (Ames & Archer, 1987). School learning environments also have been found to shape students' goal orientations. Students can be influenced to adopt mastery goals if teachers create environments that accentuate self-improvement, discovery, engagement in meaningful tasks, and practicality while diminishing the importance of competition, demonstration of intellectual skills, and public comparisons of schoolwork (Ames, 1992; Hagen & Weinstein, 1995). We suspect that influential teachers who embrace a mastery or task orientation toward learning will not only create such environments in their classrooms but also will serve as models of learning with whom students can identify as they form their identity as students.

A teacher's expectations influence students, especially in relation to the teacher's degree of emphasis on mastery goals. When examining the differences in students' strategy-use patterns in high- and low-mastery classes, Meece (1994) found significant differences among teachers' expectations for students. In the high-mastery classes, teachers expected students to understand, apply, and make sense of their learning, whereas in low-mastery classes students spent more time memorizing information and had few opportunities to construct meaning or apply their learning in new situations. Such examples illustrate how teachers' expectations can shape students' literacy performance. Teachers can promote literacy engagement by emphasizing a mastery orientation that stresses conceptual understanding, provides for collaborative learning, minimizes social competition, and allows students to participate in curricular decision making.

Task Values. Wigfield (1994) has identified and investigated several interacting components that make up an individual's perception of task values. These components include attainment value (the importance an individual attributes to a task), intrinsic-interest value (the task's subjective interest to an individual), utility value (the usefulness of a task in light of a person's future goals), and the cost of success (the "disadvantages" of accomplishing a task, such as experiencing anxiety). Both students like Cynthia and teachers like Ms. Hawthorne consider a task's values before undertaking it. For instance, Ms. Hawthorne, who is thinking about redesigning her language arts and history curriculum, needs to consider how important the redesign is to her, how interested she is in that redesign, how useful the revised program would be to her goals, and the time and effort necessary to redesign the program.

An additional incentive or purpose that teachers might have for engaging in a teaching task is its intrinsic enjoyment. According to Csikszentmihalyi (1990a, 1990b), motivation is closely related to autotelic experiences that are self-contained and self-rewarding. Autotelic experiences are not pursued for any future purpose or goal but for their intrinsic worth, their enjoyment. Csikszentmihalyi has referred to the autotelic experience as "flow," an optimal psychological experience that puts consciousness on a special level. When teachers experience a sense of flow in their teaching, they are enjoying the process as a self-justifying event. To experience flow, teachers must attain a balance between teaching challenge and teaching ability. Ms. Hawthorne has been frustrated because of her students' lack of engagement in reading and learning. She is seeking an optimum psychological and instructional experience. However, if teaching a particular group of students to engage in a cooperative learning strategy to develop their reading or writing skills becomes too challenging, Ms. Hawthorne will experience anxiety and frustration; if teaching this strategy presents no challenge to her, she may become bored. If she can discover an optimal balance between challenge and ability and engage her students during their literacy activities (Csikszentmihalyi, 1990b), Ms. Hawthorne is likely to enjoy the flow of teaching, and if Cynthia can find books that provide a balance between challenge and boredom, she is more likely to relish the flow of reading.

Sociocultural Values and Beliefs. A teacher's sociocultural values and beliefs have a profound effect on the interpretation of texts, relationships with students, and instructional decision making. Research has shown that students are vulnerable to breakdowns in communication if their sociocultural values and beliefs do not match those of the teacher or if the teacher is not responsive to cultural differences (Erickson, 1979; Hull & Rose, 1994, see #11 this volume; Labov, 1972). For example, culturally diverse readers may enter a learning environment in a monocultural school where specific values and beliefs are essential for success, where achievement depends on the reader's valuing literacy and standard English, and where instructional routines, like turn-taking, are traditional (Mehan, 1979; Phillips, 1970). If teachers hold such values and beliefs that differ vastly from those of their students, students' learning and motivation may be adversely affected.

As Heath (1983) discovered, teachers also can positively affect students who enter school cultures that are divergent from those in which they have grown up. Innovative work by Au and Mason (1981) and by Moll (1994) in understanding the social networks of Hispanic children illustrates how a teacher's awareness of varied sociocultural values and beliefs can enhance students' acquisition of literacy and motivation for learning. Teachers must be prepared to reflect on and examine the sociocultural values and beliefs that they and their students hold. Through reflection and self-exploration, teachers may become more responsive to students' values and beliefs in designing classroom instruction, which will affirm significant aspects of students' cultural and personal identities.

Stance. In literacy studies, stance pertains to the perspective and orientation that a reader adopts toward the reading of a particular text. By guiding the reader's focus of intention, reader's stance influences motivation. While reader's stance refers to the reader's perspective and orientation toward a given text, instructional stance refers to the teacher's perspective and orientation toward the teaching of a text. By guiding the reader's focus of attention and purpose, the teacher's instructional stance also influences a reader's intention to read.

Theorists and researchers (Beach & Hynes, 1990; Langer, 1990; Smith, 1984) have described several different stances that readers and teachers may adopt. Rosenblatt (1978) has strongly influenced the field with her identification and elaboration of two stances—efferent and aesthetic. When adopting an efferent stance, the reader concentrates on taking away information from the text. When taking an aesthetic stance, the reader experiences the text through imagination and feeling. When reading historical stories, Cynthia adopts an aesthetic stance and enters the "old-fashioned" world created in her imagination. We suspect that the experiential self is more deeply engaged during aesthetic readings that draw readers into the flow of narrative and imagery.

These are not either-or stances; rather, they are on a continuum along which the degree of emphasis may change. To varying degrees, the teacher and the reader can control stance. While progressing through a text, the teacher may encourage an instructional stance that guides readers toward the integration of both efferent and aesthetic stances in varied proportions. For example, when reading about Dimmesdale's struggle with Chillingworth in Nathaniel Hawthorne's *The Scarlet Letter*, the reader may be encouraged to focus more attention on the aesthetic stance, but may be instructed to shift to a greater concentration on the efferent stance when trying to analyze Hester Prynne's relationship with her daughter Pearl. According to Rosenblatt (1985), teachers sometimes tend to emphasize an efferent stance at the expense of aesthetic readings; teachers expect students to analyze texts more than they encourage students to live through the experiences depicted in the literature they read. An overemphasis on efferent readings may, in some instances, reduce the value and enjoyment of students' transactions with literature. However, an emphasis on efferent responses may help students develop analytical skills important for critical thinking. Nevertheless, influential teachers tend to emphasize aesthetic responses over efferent ones (Ruddell, 1994).

Summary. Instructional-orientation constructs combined with those of the developing self contribute to creating and sustaining a focus of intention. This focus also may be affected by task-engagement resources.

Task-Engagement Resources

Task-engagement resources refer to information structures that enable a teacher or a reader to undertake a learning task. While most of the features previously discussed contribute directly to motivational states, task-engagement resources provide cognitive tools to accomplish the tasks for which readers or teachers are motivated (see Ruddell & Unrau, 1994, #51 this volume, for a complete review). The reader's text-processing resources include knowledge of language, word analysis, text-processing strategies, metacognitive strategies, knowledge of classroom and social interaction, and world knowledge. Each of these resources helps readers not only focus their intention to read but also interact with texts to construct meanings that can be negotiated through classroom discussion. The teacher's instructional design resources include knowledge of students and their meaning-construction process, knowledge of literature and content areas, teaching strategies, world knowledge, and metacognitive knowledge. With these resources, teachers can create learning environments that nourish the developing self and activate students' instructional orientation. With these task-engagement resources in mind, we present in the following section a model of text interpretation in a classroom context, which provides opportunity for readers to sharpen their focus of intention, heighten their motivation to read, and construct meaning in response to their reading.

Role of Meaning Negotiation in Developing Reader Intention and Motivation

The structures we have explored provide the foundation not only for the meanings that individual readers and teachers construct, but also for meanings negotiated among students during reader-based instruction. In addition, the design and function of the classroom learning environment further affect motivation to engage in literacy events and learning (Marshall, 1992; Unrau & Ruddell, 1995). We can expect readers to engage with reading, interact in the classroom community, and participate in the meaning-negotiation process if they are motivated to read and to learn, if prior knowledge is activated, if tasks are personally relevant, and if they are encouraged to actively construct meanings. As mentioned, the teacher who incorporates features such as these is considered to be mastery-goal oriented and is more likely to witness productive learning among students (Ames, 1992; Covington, 1992).

The classroom meaning-negotiation process is represented in Figure 2. The three overlapping circles in the figure symbolize the interactive nature of the meaning-negotiation process for teachers, readers, and the classroom community. Note, however, that the process overlaps a text (shown by the representation of an open book) on which the dialogue is based. Thus, the text itself is not the sole object carrying meaning; instead, meanings arise from transactions with the text (Rosenblatt, 1978, 1985). During negotiation for meanings related to texts, readers bring their own interpretations to the interaction, teachers bring their understanding of the story and of the reading process, and members of the class interact with the text to shape—and reshape—meanings.

Through this model, we acknowledge that readers like Cynthia and teachers like Ms. Hawthorne read much more than a printed text. In effect, they read several texts—if texts are understood to mean events, situations, behavioral scripts, and other symbolic processes that require interpretation (Bloome & Bailey, 1992). Of course, students and teacher read the text on the page. But students in particular also need to read the task, the authority structure (whose interpretations will count?), the teacher (what are her expectations?), and the sociocultural setting. In addition, they must read the social dynamics of the class, including sociolinguistic rules, such as turn-taking and question-answer response

FIGURE 2
Text and Classroom Context

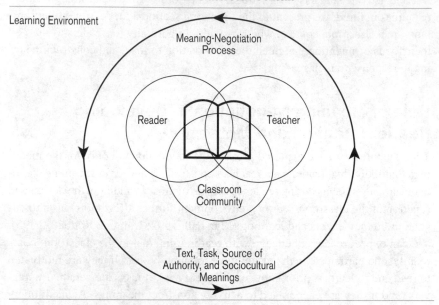

patterns. Responsive teaching entails not only an awareness of this process but also an intention and resources to foster its growth.

If the reader's focus of intention and motivation is to be developed, classroom community negotiation of meaning is imperative. The teacher provides activities that enable readers to shape and share meanings. The sharing of those meanings enables the evolution of an interpretive community that can develop criteria for the validation of interpretations.

Meanings are open—not closed or fixed—though they need to be grounded in the text. Readers and teacher may share common understandings in the interpretive community; however, those understandings or interpretations are not forever fixed. Meanings are shaped and reshaped in the hermeneutic circle (Dilthey, 1900/1976), which is represented by the circle with arrowheads surrounding the meaning-negotiation process in Figure 2. Meaning construction is viewed as a circular and changing process of forming hypotheses and then testing, negotiating, and validating interpretations. As the reader's knowledge changes, as the reader interacts with other readers and with the teacher in a social context, constructed meanings can be expected to change. In a sense, although a text may be fixed, its meanings for the reader are always evolving. The understanding of this process of meaning negotiation is a hallmark of the responsive teacher and enables readers like Cynthia to focus intention and increase motivation.

Guidelines for Designing Literacy-Enhancing Instructional Environments

Given the spectrum of motivational factors that influence the focus of intention, teachers can follow several guidelines that facilitate the creation of an optimal learning environment to promote engagement with literacy. Many of these guidelines operate in the model of text interpretation in classroom contexts that we have explored. However, we can present only in a summary fashion 12 guidelines that teachers might apply in their design of an ideal learning environment to promote both readers' intention and motivation and to cultivate literacy over time.

1. Provide for the exploration of student identity, its roots, and its possibilities; acknowledge that each student has self-schemata that shape behavior and warrant understanding; devise activities and interactions that bolster reflection and self-discovery.

2. Design an environment that intentionally builds student self-worth rather than one that unintentionally threatens it.

3. Promote a climate in which students work toward task-oriented goals that foster a sense of mastery and competency.

4. Develop an atmosphere in which students see that the acquisition of knowledge, skills, and strategies is incremental and proceeds through efforts that become increasingly self-regulated.

5. Activate and extend students' background knowledge to facilitate meaning construction.

6. Model reflectivity and metacognitive processes for students.

7. Design tasks that are perceived as important to students, that involve real-life issues, that have subjective and community-related interest, that are seen as useful in relation to students' future goals, and that provide the chance for the experience of flow.

8. Establish literacy expectations that are appropriate to each student's capacities and provide support for the attainment of those expectations.

9. Encourage the flexibility to view experience from multiple perspectives and to adopt instructional stances that promote literacy engagement; encourage, when appropriate, an aesthetic stance in response to reading in order to engage more of the experiential self and its narrative and imagery.

10. Discover and use students' sociocultural values and beliefs as resources for constructing an environment that reflects students' orientations

while developing understanding of and tolerance for alternative value and belief systems.

11. Allow students to gain a sense of ownership and share authority in the interpretation of texts and criteria for validation of those interpretations.

12. Formulate or select tasks that are suitable to students' task-engagement resources and that allow students to internalize knowledge and skills to become increasingly independent, self-regulating, and self-reliant learners.

These guidelines may be applied in the design of strategies used to construct a learning environment and to maintain that environment. Ms. Hawthorne applied many of these guidelines in redesigning her instructional program in language arts and history.

Ms. Hawthorne's Application of the Guidelines

To improve her instructional program, Ms. Hawthorne decided to take several steps, many of which actualize suggestions provided in the guidelines presented. Her goal was to deepen her students' engagement with literacy tasks including reading assignments in history, to sharpen their focus of intention, and to promote their long-term motivation to read and learn. She decided to shift emphasis from a teacher-centered and -controlled curriculum, designed to develop a learning environment driven by extrinsic rewards and reinforcements, to a student-centered curriculum that would enhance intrinsic motivation. To build intrinsic motives in her students, she used guidelines to move her classroom more toward a community in which students could focus on mastery and competency. She wanted her students to acquire motives and strategies that would lead them toward a higher degree of self-regulation in their reading and learning than she had witnessed.

Ms. Hawthorne used principles of cooperative learning (Slavin, 1995; Slavin et al., 1994) to design her reader response groups. She delegated authority to each group that in turn had to share authority with each of its group members. In mixed-ability groups, members shared responsibilities for learning and were individually accountable for their learning and contributions. She structured the reading response groups so that each team read a different book that Ms. Hawthorne selected on the basis of the team's interests. Cynthia's team, for example, read several historical novels that were set in the time period covered in her history text and that ranged from the fifth- through seventh-grade reading levels. To develop her students' self-understanding and self-knowledge, Ms. Hawthorne used their responses to texts, such as those they wrote in journals, to help them explore their emerging identities (Rosenblatt, 1938/1995). To build vocabulary, she asked each member of a team to keep a journal that included a list of unfamiliar words that students selected.

Ms. Hawthorne also adapted reciprocal reading (Palincsar & Brown, 1986) for use in her reading groups. The modification allowed students to play the role of teacher, to summarize portions of text read, to ask teacher-like questions, and to make predictions. The procedure helped students internalize metacognitive strategies that improved their comprehension during independent reading.

To integrate her history and language arts curriculum while teaching about the Great Depression in the United States during the 1930s, Ms. Hawthorne had her class read Mildred Taylor's *Roll of Thunder, Hear My Cry*, a novel about a young black girl, Cassie Logan, and her family who struggle to survive and maintain their independence in rural Mississippi. Cynthia, who was striving for independence herself, easily identified with Cassie and her struggles. Ms. Hawthorne encouraged teams to develop interpretations of the novel that could be shared and discussed with the whole class. Extending the principle of shared authority over the negotiation of meaning, she talked with her students about what standards should govern the correctness of an interpretation. She also used strategies, such as Directed Reading-Thinking Activities (Stauffer, 1976) to engage her students' background knowledge in the construction of meanings. Before students began reading the novel, she asked them what they thought a book titled *Roll of Thunder, Hear My Cry* would be about. The discussion moved many students to activate background knowledge, formulate hypotheses, and sharpen their focus of intention to read. When the class negotiated interpretations of events in the novel, meanings that teams and individuals constructed were shared in the classroom. While she supported questioning and interaction, Ms. Hawthorne asked teams and individuals to provide evidence from the text to support their interpretations, and she pointed out that historians also must substantiate their interpretations of history with reference to events. Ms. Hawthorne's approach focused the intention and motivation of Cynthia and her peers.

Summary With Implications for Research

If teachers are to become more effective in developing reader intention and motivation, they must carefully reflect on the nature of their teaching. Our discussion of factors critical to responsive teaching highlights the importance of three areas. First, the *developing self* accounts for teacher and student identity and self-schema, self-efficacy and self-worth, expectations, the experiential self, and self-knowledge—all of which underlie and influence a reader's intention to read or a teacher's intention to teach. Second, *instructional orientation* serves to identify and define an individual's goals, task values, sociocultural values and beliefs, and stance. These factors direct teachers' instructional purposes and students' reading purposes. Third, *task-engagement resources* consist of text-processing understandings that enable readers to comprehend various texts and instructional design knowledge that enables teachers to skillfully direct instruction. These three areas, when combined, yield an interactive system of affective and cognitive factors that show how responsive teachers can help readers develop their focus of intention and motivation.

Critical to highly effective and responsive teaching is a clear understanding of the *meaning-negotiation process* that is essential to focusing readers' intention and motivation and engaging students in active learning. Of paramount importance, as we negotiate meanings, is our understanding of text appropriateness and task difficulty for the reader and our willingness to share our interpretive authority with students. We need to incorporate through active discussion the sociocultural meanings and interpretations of our students. This understanding and willingness serve to shift the responsibility for inquiry and learning to the reader, and they focus the reader's intention, commitment, and motivation—as illustrated in Ms. Hawthorne's classroom and in her interaction with Cynthia.

We outlined 12 important instructional guidelines based on our exploration of the factors critical to responsive teaching and the meaning-negotiation process. These guidelines range from exploration and understanding of student identity and self-schema to establishing appropriate literacy expectations for students and adopting an instructional stance that promotes literacy engagement. We encourage teachers to examine carefully these guidelines and use them to reflect on their own teaching.

Although educators have progressed over the last decade in understanding the reader intention and motivation process, many areas still require further exploration for us to comprehend more fully this complex and critically important phenomenon. The following areas of inquiry warrant inclusion in further research.

- How are influential teachers formed? Could teacher preparation programs emphasize the growth of qualities of influential teachers, including their exceptional interpersonal and intrapersonal awareness, so that more students feel that they are understood and that their schooling contributes to the growth of their developing self, their identity, and their self-understanding?

- Which of the factors critical to developing reader and teacher focus of intention are the most effective and enduring motivators, and how do they interact? Further, are there additional factors that explain motivation to read and that would make the focus of intention even more inclusive?

- How can literacy teachers effectively model, transfer to students, and sustain belief in a mastery-goal orientation and the incremental benefits of effortful learning?

- How could we promote literacy engagement through an emphasis on self-regulated learning from the earliest school years? What forms of early school instruction foster metacognition and comprehension? Does student reflection on learning, problem solving, and study strategies promote self-regulation and engagement during reading?

- Knowing that motivation to read, especially to engage in pleasure reading, declines as children progress through school, what kinds of classroom and student–teacher interactions sustain or increase motivation? If responsive teachers in the early school years develop learning environments that encourage the growth of individual competency, mastery, self-regulation, and self-understanding within the classroom community, are students more likely to continue or expand their enjoyment of independent pleasure reading?

- What reader goals, values, and beliefs toward meaning negotiation promote highly productive engagement in the process? What kinds of texts and tasks support a reader's involvement or openness during meaning negotiation?

- We know little about the effects of the teacher's self-system or instructional orientation on motivation. How do narratives from past teaching episodes, which are stored in the experiential self, affect the design of lessons and classroom environments in the present? What contributes to the formation of reflective and responsive teachers, and how could the development of more reflective and responsive teachers be realized?

- How does a teacher's instructional stance affect lesson planning, reader intent, and especially students' motivation to engage in reading?

- What effects does a teacher's orientation toward authority and its role in classroom meaning negotiation have on a reader's comprehension and motivation? For example, do teachers who practice a teacher-directed style have a different impact on meaning negotiation and level of reader engagement from those teachers who consider the classroom community as the center of authority?

By enhancing our knowledge of the critical factors that influence the reader's developing self and the teacher's instructional orientation, we gain important insight into teaching that can lead to gains in the reader's focus of intention. Our understanding of the meaning-negotiation process enables us to create the instructional environment that encourages readers to participate in active learning, share learning responsibility, and experience an increase in reading motivation. The responsive, reflective teacher contributes to the development of focused reader intention and heightened motivation through active literacy engagement.

Acknowledgments

Both Cynthia and Ms. Hawthorne are composites. We wish to thank teachers and graduate students at California State University, Los Angeles, for fieldwork contributing to these portraits.

References

Ames, C. (1992). Classrooms: Goals, structures, and student motivation. *Journal of Educational Psychology, 84*, 261–271.

Ames, C., & Archer, J. (1987). Mothers' beliefs about the role of ability and effort in school learning. *Journal of Educational Psychology, 79*, 409–414.

Au, K.H., & Mason, J.M. (1981). Social organizational factors in learning to read: The balance of rights hypothesis. *Reading Research Quarterly, 17*, 115–152.

Beach, R., & Hynes, S. (1990). *Developing discourse practices in adolescence and adulthood*. Norwood, NJ: Ablex.

Bloome, D., & Bailey, F. (1992). Studying language and literacy through events, particularities, and intertextuality. In R. Beach, J. Green, M. Kamil, & T. Shanahan (Eds.), *Multidisciplinary perspectives on literacy research* (pp. 181–210). Urbana, IL: National Council of Teachers of English.

Covington, M. (1992). *Making the grade: A self-worth perspective on motivation and school reform*. Cambridge, UK: Cambridge University Press.

Csikszentmihalyi, M. (1990a). *Flow: The psychology of optimal experience*. New York: HarperCollins.

Csikszentmihalyi, M. (1990b). Literacy and intrinsic motivation. *Daedalus, 119*(2), 115–140.

Dilthey, W. (1976). The development of hermeneutics. In H. Rickman (Ed. & Trans.), *Selected writings* (pp. 246–263). Cambridge, UK: Cambridge University Press. (Original work published 1900)

Epstein, S. (1994). Integration of cognitive and psychodynamic unconscious. *American Psychologist, 49*, 709–724.

Erickson, F. (1979). Talking down: Some cultural sources of miscommunication in interracial interviews. In A. Wolfgang (Ed.), *Nonverbal behavior: Applications and cross-cultural implications* (pp. 99–126). New York: Academic.

Erikson, E. (1968). *Identity: Youth and crisis*. New York: Norton.

Garcia, T., & Pintrich, P.R. (1994). Regulating motivation and cognition in the classroom: The role of self-schemas and self-regulatory strategies. In D.H. Schunk & B.J. Zimmerman (Eds.), *Self-regulation of learning and performance: Issues and educational applications* (pp. 127–153). Hillsdale, NJ: Erlbaum.

Good, T. (1987). Teacher expectations. In D. Berliner & B. Rosenshine (Eds.), *Talks to teachers* (pp. 159–200). New York: Random House.

Hagen, A.S., & Weinstein, C.E. (1995). Achievement goals, self-regulated learning, and the role of classroom context. In P.R. Pintrich (Ed.), *Understanding self-regulated learning* (pp. 43–55). San Francisco: Jossey-Bass.

Hawthorne, N. (1990). *The scarlet letter*. Oxford, UK: Oxford University Press.

Heath, S.B. (1983). *Ways with words: Language, life and work in communities and classrooms*. Cambridge, UK: Cambridge University Press.

Heath, S.B., & McLaughlin, M.W. (1993). Building identities for inner-city youth. In S.B. Heath & M.W. McLaughlin (Eds.), *Identity and inner-city youth* (pp. 1–12). New York: Teachers College Press.

Hull, G., & Rose, M. (1994). "This wooden shack place": The logic of an unconventional reading. In R.B. Ruddell, M.R. Ruddell, & H. Singer (Eds.), *Theoretical models and processes of reading* (4th ed., pp. 231–243). Newark, DE: International Reading Association.

Labov, W. (1972). *Language in the inner city*. Philadelphia: University of Pennsylvania Press.

Langer, J.A. (1990). The process of understanding: Reading for literary and informative purposes. *Research in the Teaching of English, 24*, 229–260.

Markus, H., & Nurius, P. (1986). Possible selves. *American Psychologist, 41*, 954–969.

Marshall, H. (1992). Associate editor's introduction to centennial articles on classroom learning and motivation. *Journal of Educational Psychology, 84*, 259–260.

Maslow, A.H. (1954). *Motivation and personality*. New York: Harper & Row.

Mathewson, G.C. (1994). Model of attitude influence upon reading and learning to read. In

R.B. Ruddell, M.R. Ruddell, & H. Singer (Eds.), *Theoretical models and processes of reading* (4th ed., pp. 1131–1161). Newark, DE: International Reading Association.

Meece, J.L. (1994). The role of motivation in self-regulated learning. In D.H. Schunk & B.J. Zimmerman (Eds.), *Self-regulation of learning and performance: Issues and educational applications* (pp. 25–44). Hillsdale, NJ: Erlbaum.

Mehan, H. (1979). *Learning lessons.* Cambridge, MA: Harvard University Press.

Midgley, C., Feldlaufer, H., & Eccles, J. (1989). Change in teacher efficacy and student self- and task-related beliefs in mathematics during the transition to junior high school. *Journal of Educational Psychology, 49,* 529–538.

Moll, L.C. (1994). Literacy research in community and classrooms: A sociocultural approach. In R.B. Ruddell, M.R. Ruddell, & H. Singer (Eds.), *Theoretical models and processes of reading* (4th ed., pp. 179–207). Newark, DE: International Reading Association.

Moyer, B. (1995). *The language of life.* New York: Doubleday.

Nicholls, J.G. (1984). Achievement motivation: Conception of ability, subjective experience, task choice, and performance. *Psychological Review, 91,* 328–346.

Paivio, A. (1986). *Mental representations: A dual coding approach.* New York: Oxford University Press.

Palincsar, A.S., & Brown, A.L. (1986). Interactive teaching to promote independent learning from text. *The Reading Teacher, 39,* 771–777.

Phillips, S. (1970). Acquisition of rules for appropriate speech use. In J.E. Alatis (Ed.), *Bilingualism and language contact: Anthropological, linguistic, psychological, and sociological aspects* (Monograph Series on Languages and Linguistics No. 23). Washington, DC: Georgetown University Press.

Rosenblatt, L.M. (1978). *The reader, the text, the poem: The transactional theory of the literary work.* Carbondale: Southern Illinois University Press.

Rosenblatt, L.M. (1985). The transactional theory of the literary work: Implications for research. In C.R. Cooper (Ed.), *Researching response to literature and the teaching of literature* (pp. 33–53). Norwood, NJ: Ablex.

Rosenblatt, L.M. (1995). *Literature as exploration* (5th ed.). New York: Modern Language Association. (Original work published 1938)

Ruddell, R.B. (1994). The development of children's comprehension and motivation during storybook discussion. In R.B. Ruddell, M.R. Ruddell, & H. Singer (Eds.), *Theoretical models and processes of reading* (4th ed., pp. 281–296). Newark, DE: International Reading Association.

Ruddell, R.B. (1995). Those influential literacy teachers: Meaning negotiators and motivation builders. *The Reading Teacher, 48,* 454–463.

Ruddell, R.B., Draheim, M., & Barnes, J. (1990). A comparative study of the teaching effectiveness of influential and non-influential teachers and reading comprehension development. In J. Zutell & S. McCormick (Eds.), *Literacy theory and research: Analyses from multiple paradigms* (39th yearbook of the National Reading Conference, pp. 153–162). Chicago: National Reading Conference.

Ruddell, R.B., & Greybeck, B. (1992, December). *A study of teaching effectiveness of experienced literacy teachers: Connections between self-perceptions, former influential teachers, and observed teaching performance.* Paper presented at the 42nd annual meeting of the National Reading Conference, San Antonio, TX.

Ruddell, R.B., & Haggard, M.R. (1982). Influential teachers: Characteristics and classroom performance. In J.A. Niles & L.A. Harris (Eds.), *New inquiries in reading research and instruction* (31st yearbook of the National Reading Conference, pp. 227–231). Rochester, NY: National Reading Conference.

Ruddell, R.B., & Kern, R.G. (1986). The development of belief systems and teaching effectiveness of influential teachers. In M.P. Douglass (Ed.), *Reading: The quest for meaning* (pp. 133–150). Claremont, CA: Claremont Reading Conference.

Ruddell, R.B., & Unrau, N.J. (1994). Reading as a meaning-construction process: The reader, the text, and the teacher. In R.B. Ruddell, M.R. Ruddell, & H. Singer (Eds.), *Theoretical models and processes of reading* (4th ed., pp. 996–1056). Newark, DE: International Reading Association.

Rumelhart, D.E. (1980). Schemata: The building blocks of cognition. In R.J. Spiro, B.C. Bruce, & W.F. Brewer (Eds.), *Theoretical issues in reading comprehension* (pp. 33–58). Hillsdale, NJ: Erlbaum.

Sadoski, M., & Paivio, A. (1994). A dual coding view of imagery and verbal processes in reading comprehension. In R.B. Ruddell, M.R.

Ruddell, & H. Singer (Eds.), *Theoretical models and processes of reading* (4th ed., pp. 582–601). Newark, DE: International Reading Association.

Schon, D.A. (1987). *Educating the reflective practitioner.* San Francisco: Jossey-Bass.

Schunk, D.H. (1991). Self-efficacy and academic motivation. *Educational Psychologist, 26,* 207–231.

Schunk, D.H. (1994). Self-regulation of self-efficacy and attributions in academic settings. In D.H. Schunk & B.J. Zimmerman (Eds.), *Self-regulation of learning and performance: Issues and educational applications* (pp. 75–99). Hillsdale, NJ: Erlbaum.

Slavin, R.E. (1995). *Cooperative learning* (2nd ed.). Boston: Allyn & Bacon.

Slavin, R.E., Madden, N.A., Karweit, N.L., Dolan, L.J., & Wasik, B.A. (1994). Success for all: Getting reading right the first time. In E.H. Hiebert & B.M. Taylor (Eds.), *Getting reading right from the start* (pp. 125–147). Boston: Allyn & Bacon.

Smith, F. (1984). Reading like a writer. In J.M. Jensen (Ed.), *Composing and comprehending* (pp. 47–56). Urbana, IL: National Council of Teachers of English.

Stauffer, R.B. (1976). *Teaching reading as a thinking process.* New York: Harper.

Stipek, D.J. (1993). *Motivation to learn: From theory to practice* (2nd ed.). Boston: Allyn & Bacon.

Taylor, M.D. (1976). *Roll of thunder, hear my cry.* New York: Dial

Unrau, N.J., & Ruddell, R.B. (1995). Interpreting texts in classroom contexts. *Journal of Adolescent & Adult Literacy, 39,* 16–27.

Valli, L. (Ed.). (1992). *Reflective teacher education: Cases and critiques.* Albany: State University of New York Press.

Vigil, J.D. (1993). Gangs, social control, and ethnicity: Ways to redirect. In S.B. Heath & M.W. McLaughlin (Eds.), *Identity and inner-city youth* (pp. 94–119). New York: Teachers College Press.

Wigfield, A. (1994). The role of children's achievement values in the self-regulation of their learning outcomes. In D.H. Schunk & B.J. Zimmerman (Eds.), *Self-regulation of learning and performance: Issues and educational applications* (pp. 101–124). Hillsdale, NJ: Erlbaum.

36

Researching the Influential Literacy Teacher: Characteristics, Beliefs, Strategies, and New Research Directions

Robert B. Ruddell

The research and related issues presented in this article focus on findings from a set of studies of influential teachers. These are teachers who demonstrate a high level of excellence in literacy teaching. We all recall these special teachers from memory in a vivid and positive way from our academic and personal experiences—kindergarten through college years—and think of them as having had a major influence on our academic and personal lives (Ruddell, 1983, 1994, 1995; Ruddell & Kern, 1986). Literacy in this research is defined in a broad sense as engagement in meaning construction using reading, writing, and oral discourse in the classroom environment. The purpose of this article then is to describe these teachers, their beliefs, their classroom practices, and to offer implications for teaching and future research in the attempt to develop deeper insight into the nature of teaching effectiveness.

Teaching Effectiveness: Current Status

A number of studies have previously served to inform us about the status of literacy teaching nationwide. Notable among these was John Goodlad's (1983) *A Place Called School: Prospects for the Future*. This extensive research, based on observations of some 38 representative schools, 1,000 classrooms, and a survey of some 27,000 teachers across the United States, provided a detailed portrait of teachers in action. Goodlad's findings were somewhat disturbing, however, when we noted that "teacher talk" was by far the most dominant classroom activity. He found that teachers rarely encouraged student-to-student dialogue or afforded opportunities for participation in collaborative or small-group activities that were

From Kinzer, C.K., Hinchman, K.A., & Leu, D.J. (Eds.), *Inquiries in Literacy Theory and Practice* (46th yearbook of the National Reading Conference, pp. 37–53). Copyright © 1997 by the National Reading Conference. Adapted with permission of the publisher.

intellectually engaging. He noted that answers were "right" and answers were "wrong"—but, for the most part, answers were short.

Goodlad's observations revealed that less than 1% of instructional time was devoted to discussions that involved open response reasoning from students and that an extraordinary degree of student passivity characterized the instruction. A surprisingly large number of teachers failed to engage students in active thinking that involved higher-level comprehension processing beyond the factual recall of information.

Similar findings were present in earlier research (Guszak, 1967; Ruddell & Williams, 1972) demonstrating that approximately 70% of teacher questions in kindergarten through sixth-grade classrooms were focused on the factual comprehension level. Durkin's (1979) extensive observational study of teachers using basal readers indicated that most questions that teachers used were of a factual type and served to test and assess children's recall of story content rather than to instruct. She thus characterized the teachers she studied as "interrogators" and "mentioners." These studies also provide evidence that supports Goodlad's (1983) observations that "frontal teaching," in which the teacher stands or sits in front of students and talks, has been the norm in classrooms across a wide range of grade levels.

These findings are discouraging in light of our current knowledge on cognitive processing. Comprehension development relies heavily on the activation of children's background knowledge, and instruction that enhances mental processing and monitoring strategies directed toward a purposeful reading objective (Fielding, Anderson, & Pearson, 1990; Hansen, 1981; Ruddell, 2002; Taba & Elzey, 1964; Unrau & Ruddell, 1995; see also Brown, Pressley, Van Meter, & Schuder, #37, and Langer, #38, this volume). Students' active involvement in teacher and peer interactions that connect prior attitudes and values to reading content also greatly increases their motivation and intention to read (Mathewson, 1994, see #50 this volume; Ruddell & Unrau, 1997, see #35 this volume).

I believe that our future hope for increasing teaching competence in our classrooms is found in three areas: first, improving our understanding of the nature of high-quality teaching—and influential teacher research sheds light in this area; second, increasing the effectiveness of our preservice teacher preparation and inservice graduate programs through partnerships between universities and schools; and third, implementing carefully planned ongoing inservice teacher education programs in our schools that utilize the latest knowledge on literacy development and effective teaching. The report of the National Commission on Teaching and America's Future (1996) revealed that more than half of the teachers who will be teaching in the present decade will be newly hired. In addition, 12% of the new hires enter the classroom without any formal training at all, whereas another 14% reach the classroom without fully meeting state standards. These conditions provide key opportunities for increasing the quality of teacher preparation—both preservice and inservice—and in turn the quality of classroom instruction.

I would now like to turn to the influential teacher research conducted by me and my colleagues and to the insights that this work provides on understanding teaching effectiveness. In the remainder of the article I will, first, establish a brief theoretical base for this work; second, develop a portrait of the influential teacher based on students' perspectives and beliefs held by these teachers; third, explore insights into the genesis of influential teachers and factors that have influenced their teaching effectiveness; fourth, describe strategies used by these master teachers in action; and finally, develop implications for instruction and identify new research directions essential for furthering our understanding teaching effectiveness.

Theoretical Context for Influential Teaching

The theoretical context that provides the basis for understanding and interpreting this influential teacher discussion is found in the sociocognitive reading theory described by Ruddell and Unrau (1994; see #51 this volume). This theory provides a detailed explanation of the meaning-negotiation and meaning-construction process that occurs between teacher and reading in the classroom learning environment. The theory supports the hypothesis that the teacher's prior knowledge and beliefs *about* instruction and knowledge use and control *during* instruction are critical to effective literacy instruction in the classroom. From this perspective, an influential teacher is perceived as an instructional decision maker who develops clear goals and purposes and conducts daily learning through well-formed plans and teaching strategies. These plans and strategies are characterized by the use of higher-level questions, meaning-negotiation strategies, and the successful resolution of instructional episodes in the classroom community of students. In turn, these questions and strategies shape and help direct students' reading purpose and actively engage relevant prior beliefs and knowledge.

The theoretical perspective of this constructivist model also incorporates reader response theory (Rosenblatt, 1985, 1988; see also #48 this volume). It is hypothesized that a teacher who takes a predominant aesthetic instructional stance, using internal reader motivation to enhance reader transaction with the text, will upgrade the emotional importance of the text in the mind of the student (Renouf, 1990; Ruddell & Unrau, 1994, 1997). This stance encourages the reader to become absorbed in a text world of imagination and feeling in which "attention is focused on what [the reader] is living through during the reading event" (Rosenblatt, 1985, p. 38). This effect should in turn (a) influence the student's motivation and intent to read, (b) increase attention, (c) aid in forming mental text representation, and (d) enhance reading comprehension and meaning construction.

I will return to this theoretical perspective later to develop a theory-based interpretation of the meaning-construction process found in the influential teachers' classrooms.

Portrait of the Influential Teacher

The influential teacher in this research is defined as a teacher who has been identified by a former student as having had a major impact on the student's academic or personal achievement (Ruddell, 1994), or who has been selected by a carefully developed nomination process involving former students, peers, and administrators to recognize outstanding teaching effectiveness (Ruddell & Harris, 1989). These studies of influential teachers consist of two data streams and involve a total of 95 such teachers. The first stream consists of longitudinal research that extends from kindergarten through grade 11 (Ruddell, 1994, 2002; Ruddell, Draheim, & Barnes, 1990), and the second, in-depth interviews and classroom observations at the university level (Ruddell & Greybeck, 1992; Ruddell & Harris, 1989; Ruddell & Kern, 1986).

The data using interviews and questionnaire responses from former students of influential teachers (Ruddell, 1995; Ruddell et al., 1990) reveal that these teachers are perceived as individuals who (a) use highly motivating and effective teaching strategies, (b) help students with their personal problems, (c) create a feeling of excitement about the subject matter content or skill area they teach, (d) exhibit a strong sense of personal caring about the student, and (e) demonstrate the ability to adjust instruction to the individual needs of the student.

Further, the research suggests that between kindergarten and grade 11, high-achieving students have, on the average, 3.2 influential teachers, but low achievers have only 1.5 such teachers. Regardless of achievement level, however—and this was a surprising finding—high and low achievers perceive their influential teachers in almost identical ways. These perceptions, corroborated by the observations and video recording analysis, from kindergarten through the university, include the following:

1. Influential teachers use clearly formulated instructional strategies that provide for instructional monitoring and student feedback on their progress.

2. They possess in-depth knowledge of reading and writing processes as well as content knowledge, and they understand how to teach these processes effectively in their classrooms.

3. They frequently tap internal student motivation that stimulates intellectual curiosity, explore students' self-understanding, use aesthetic imagery and expression, and motivate the desire to solve problems.

4. They use sparingly any external student motivation, such as using achievement pressure to "please the teacher." (Ruddell, 1994, 2002; Ruddell & Harris, 1989)

On the basis of in-depth interviews with the influential teachers, from kindergarten through grade 11, and influential teachers at the university level, common features that these teachers believe important to their teaching have been identified. These features are presented in Figure 1.

These teachers view each of these features as having special importance. The personal characteristics feature reflects sensitivity, openness, and a supportive attitude toward students and includes a high performance expectation of self. Understanding of learner potential focuses on the student as an individual who possesses unique abilities, motives, and needs, but also values high performance

FIGURE 1
Shared Beliefs of Influential Teachers About Teaching

1. Personal Characteristics
   * Have energy, commitment, passion
   * Are warm and caring
   * Are flexible
   * Have high expectations of self

2. Understanding of Learner Potential
   * Are sensitive to individual needs, motivations, and aptitudes
   * Understand where students are, developmentally
   * Place high demands on learners

3. Attitude Toward Subject
   * Have enthusiasm
   * Create intellectual excitement
   * Consider alternative points of view

4. Life Adjustment
   * Show concern with students as persons
   * Are attentive to academic problems and personal problems

5. Quality of Instruction
   * Make material personally relevant
   * Stress basic communication: clear writing, comprehension of text, critical thinking
   * Develop logical and strategy-oriented instruction: (a) clear statement of problems, (b) use of familiar concrete examples, (c) extension to more abstract examples, (d) analysis of abstract concepts involved, (e) application of concepts to new contexts
   * Assist in identifying issues that should be considered before conclusions are reached
   * Engage students in the process of intellectual discovery

expectations, in a relative sense, for students. Attitude toward subject emphasizes the importance of high enthusiasm for subject matter and high personal involvement with subject matter content. The life adjustment factor reflects teacher concern with understanding students and helping them solve both academic and personal problems. And finally, the quality of instruction factor emphasizes expertness in the subject and the ability to develop clear explanations and presentations. Collaborative support for many of these features is found in the work of Ladson-Billings (1994), Ayers and Shubert (1994), Perl and Wilson (1986), Beidler (1986), Kridel, Bullough, and Shaker (1996), Sturtevant (1996), Bloome (1982), and Ashton-Warner (1963) (see also Brown & Palincsar, #29; Many, #33; Guthrie, Wigfield, Metsala, & Cox, #34, and Ruddell & Unrau, #35, this volume). Interestingly, however, limited research is available on the study of exceptional teachers. One might speculate that the act of teaching that relies heavily on the oral tradition, and the transitory and demanding nature of teaching, inhibits in-depth analysis and writing about this vitally important educational activity.

It is important to note that not all the influential teachers shared all the features and characteristics that I have described. In order of importance, the teachers ranked the personal characteristics feature as most important with the expressed belief that effective teaching must first establish a bridge of trust and personal contact with students through sensitivity, openness, and a supportive attitude. This feature was followed by quality of instruction, attitude toward subject, understanding of learner potential, and life adjustment. The composite portrait presented here, however, identifies critical features that these influential teachers believe are essential to expert teaching.

As space does not permit full development of the research on the origin of belief systems of these influential teachers, I will make several summary observations. Based on in-depth interviews, their beliefs and teaching effectiveness appear to be shaped by three key influences: (1) their parents and family (Ruddell & Kern, 1986); (2) their own previous influential teachers, both in and out of school (Ruddell & Greybeck, 1992; Ruddell & Kern, 1986); and (3) their self-identity that motivates an intense desire to become a highly effective teacher (Ruddell & Kern, 1986; Ruddell & Unrau, 1997).

Although there were several exceptions, parents of the influential teachers had a distinct impact on their children's perceptions of the value of education and the joy of learning, frequently instilling the belief that their children could accomplish anything they chose to do in life. Often these parents provided children with a psychologically supportive home environment and experiences that encouraged the growth of their children's aesthetic sensitivity.

Former influential teachers had a significant impact on the teachers' belief system and philosophies of teaching. Their former teachers' attitude toward their subject and their understanding of learner potential were critically important factors. Personal characteristics of the former teachers were remembered as a significant factor at the elementary school level but became less important in the students' undergraduate years and graduate education. On the other hand, a former teacher's concern with the quality of instruction and the students' life adjustment became more important in graduate levels of education. Attitude toward subject and understanding of learner potential maintained importance throughout the students' entire academic preparation. The influential teacher professors tended to characterize their former most influential teachers much as they described themselves from the standpoint of teacher characteristics and classroom performance.

A strong sense of self, likely stemming from the influence of both parents and former teachers, was another important factor in the university teachers' self-perception of teaching. The group of professors as a whole shared a high degree of confidence and self-direction. In terms of their own teaching, they rated themselves highest of the following teaching characteristics: personal characteristics, quality of instruction, and attitude toward subject. Their self-rating of classroom performance was highest on use of a problem-solving approach to instruction, classroom communication system, and view of self. The professors' self-ratings and the ratings given to their former most influential teachers were closely allied, both in teacher characteristics and classroom interaction patterns (i.e., teaching performance). The similarity in these ratings provides additional support for the influence of their former teachers on their own teaching belief system.

Although their teaching styles varied widely, all the professors stimulated their students' interest and motivation by demonstrating their own enthusiasm for the material and by engaging students in the thought processes of intellectual inquiry that paralleled that used in their own teaching and research. There was a recurrent concern among these professors for a high standard of intellectual rigor but also a genuine concern and respect for their individual students.

Let me now turn to a description of the meaning-construction process and motivation strategies used by the influential teachers in their classrooms.

Influential Teachers in the Classroom

I will rely on the influential teacher research at the primary grades (Ruddell, 1994; Ruddell et al., 1990) and at the university (Ruddell & Greybeck, 1995; Ruddell & Harris, 1989; Ruddell & Kern, 1986) in highlighting key aspects of their instructional strategy use. These studies provide important insight into how meaning is constructed and negotiated and the nature of the motivational strategies and instructional stance used by these teachers.

Meaning-Construction Strategies

The research at the primary grades (Ruddell, 1994; Ruddell et al., 1990) compared meaning-construction processes and comprehension development strategies used by influential teachers and noninfluential teachers in the same school. The influential teachers had been identified by former students as teachers who had significantly influenced their academic and/or personal lives, whereas noninfluential teachers did not receive such identification. Our analysis of video recordings for the influential teachers and the noninfluential teachers from controlled settings using children's literature revealed statistically significant and qualitative differences favoring the influential teachers in five areas. These areas measured by the Classroom Interaction Scale (Ruddell, 1994; Ruddell et al., 1990) were classroom communication (the extent to which the teacher fosters an open and resolution-seeking pattern as opposed to a closed and defensive one), self-view (the extent to which a teacher demonstrates a secure, strong self-perception or an inferior or weak sense of self), management style (the extent to which cooperation is fostered over authority and reprimand), problem-solving instructional approach (the extent to which a teacher demonstrates high intellectual curiosity and internal motivation or little curiosity and external motivation), and total teaching effectiveness (mean of the four factors described above). These findings served to confirm the hypothesis that the identification of influential teachers by former students was, in fact, related to teaching effectiveness.

Meaning-construction strategies were examined through an analysis of comprehension instruction. This analysis used four thinking-level descriptors for questions used in successful and unsuccessful instructional episodes for the influential and noninfluential teachers. A successful episode was defined as a segment of instruction marked by an opening event, having a coherent or binding purpose, such as a focusing question, a body of discussion involving recall of information or construction of meaning, and an ending, signifying that the instructional purpose had been met (two examples of successful episodes will be presented later in this discussion). Unsuccessful episodes were defined as segments that failed to meet one or more of the above criteria. The thinking-level descriptors consisted of the following:

- *Literal*—recall of text-based information (e.g., "Do you remember the name of the wind-up mouse in the story?");

- *Interpretive*—manipulation of text-based information to infer new meaning (e.g., "Why do you suppose one mouse is smooth and the other one's rough?");

- *Applicative*—transfer and use of text-based and personal knowledge to develop new meaning in a novel situation (e.g., "Well, suppose that at the end of the story you were feeling the way Willy and Alexander were feeling, would you still use those grey colors [as the illustrator did]? Why?"); and

- *Transactive*—empathetic use of text-based and personal knowledge and values to encourage the reader to identify with a character and to enter into and respond to the story more fully (e.g., "Have you ever wanted to be like Alexander at the end of the story? Why?").

The analysis revealed that the influential teachers reached successful initiation, discussion, and resolution in 96% of their episodes. This was in marked contrast to the noninfluential teachers who reached successful resolution in only 57% of their episodes.

Examination of the emphasis placed on different levels of questions used in successful episode completion disclosed distinct differences in the way in which higher-level thinking was developed. The influential teachers were found to use factual-type questions only 22% of the time. In contrast, noninfluential teachers relied on factual-type questions, characterized as text based and teacher directed, 72% of the time.

Also of great interest was the discovery that when the influential teachers did use factual-type questions it was primarily during story initiation (50%); during story development they reduced the use of factual questions substantially (18%) and shifted to higher-order questions at the interpretive (56%), applicative (24%), and transactive (2%) levels. The noninfluential teachers, on the other hand, placed major emphasis on factual-type questions during both story initiation (88%) and story development (70%). These teachers placed minor emphasis on interpretive (27%), applicative (3%), and transactive (0%) level questions during story development.

These results clearly indicate that influential teachers, in contrast to noninfluential teachers, were highly successful in reaching resolution in their classroom discussions, suggesting clear purpose setting, planning and organization, and effective strategy use. They not only place greater emphasis on higher-order questions but also demonstrate much greater flexibility in directing and orchestrating children's thinking processes through the use of factual, interpretive, applicative, and transactive questions. Further insight into orchestration of instruction is evident in the meaning-negotiation strategies used by these teachers.

Meaning-Negotiation Strategies

The meaning-negotiation process using comprehension levels and questioning strategies is illustrated in the following successfully resolved instructional episode for one of the influential teachers and her primary-grade students. This discussion followed the reading and sharing of Leo Lionni's *Alexander and the Wind-Up Mouse* (1969). The story centers around the theme of friendship and caring as Alexander, a real mouse, saves his friend Willy, a toy mouse, with the help of the Garden Lizard and a magic pebble. The teacher and students are examining Lionni's collage-type illustration at the end of the story showing Alexander and Willy. A child asks, "Which one is Willy?"

Teacher: Can't you tell? (Interpretive Level, Focusing Strategy)

Child 1: No.

Teacher: I don't know. It's hard to tell. How could you tell them apart? (Interpretive Level, Focusing Strategy)

Child 1:   Because he's a wind-up mouse.

Teacher: Anything else about them that was different? (Interpretive Level, Extending Strategy)

Child 2:   Yes, he had a key.

Teacher: Yes, anything else? (Interpretive Level, Extending Strategy)

Child 3:   Round—wheels.

Teacher: Yes, maybe.

Child 4:   Kind of like an egg.

Teacher: Sort of.

Child 4:   His ears were like two drops of tears.

Teacher: Well, that's a good description. Can you think of anything else about the way Mr. Lionni *chose* to make the mice? (Interpretive Level, Extending Strategy) Here's Alexander. Here's Willy (shows picture of each). (Wait Time: 5 seconds)

Child 3:   One's rounder.

Child 2:   One of them is smooth and the other one's rough.

Teacher: Why do you suppose one's smooth and one's rough? (Applicative Level, Raising Strategy)

Child 3:   Because one's a toy.

Teacher: Which one would that be, the smooth one or the round one? (Interpretive Level, Clarifying Strategy)

Child 2:   The smooth one.

Teacher: That's probably the one I would choose—because I would think of a toy (interrupted).

Child 4:   Because a real mouse would have fur.

Teacher: And so he wouldn't be very smooth would he? (Interpretive Level, Extending Strategy)

Child 3:   No, he would be rough with hair sticking out.

This interaction illustrates the teacher's ability to negotiate meaning based on the text as she activates children's prior knowledge, encourages the construction of meaning, and incorporates the children's responses as members of a classroom community. She places emphasis on interpretive and applicative levels of thinking that actively engage the children through the skillful use of focusing, extending, clarifying, and raising types of questioning strategies.

The following interchange is representative of discussion episodes used by the noninfluential teachers. This teacher is also in the process of concluding the story discussion, after reading *Alexander and the Wind-Up Mouse* to the children.

Teacher: What did you like about the story? (Interpretive Level, Focusing Strategy)

Child 1: I liked the part where he found the pebble.

Teacher: You like where he found the pebble. Where did he find it, Timmy? (Factual Level, Extending Strategy)

Child 1: By a box.

Teacher: Where? (Factual Level, Extending Strategy)

Child 1: By a box.

Teacher: By a box. What were some of the things that were in the box? (Factual Level, Extending Strategy)

Child 2: Dolls (interruption).

Teacher: There were old toys in that box. Why had they been placed there? (Factual Level, Extending Strategy)

Child 3: Because they were old and couldn't work.

Teacher: And they couldn't work. What did they plan to do with them, Henry? Henry, what did they plan to do with old toys? (Factual Level, Extending Strategy)

This teacher initiates and focuses the discussion using an interpretive-level question that holds potential for active reader response and comprehension development. She might have explored why the first child liked the part "where he found the pebble." The instructional intent, however, immediately shifts to a controlled set of questions based on the teacher's text-based expectations at the factual level.

Almost no opportunity is present in this episode to activate prior knowledge, construct meaning, and encourage reader response based on participation of the classroom community. In fact, the mode of questioning is text based and teacher directed. With the exception of the initial focusing question, factual-level questions are used throughout the discussion and no attempt is made to stimulate thinking through higher-level questions. The teacher-controlled discussion is characterized by a very limited repertoire of questioning strategies, primarily extending.

The study of influential teachers at the university level (Ruddell & Greybeck, 1995; Ruddell & Harris, 1989) shows strikingly similar parallels to the primary-grade influential teachers described previously. Most of the university teachers were found to share the belief that effective teaching is achieved by guiding students through an intellectual discovery process. Although factual questions were asked across all teaching samples, they were used to provide the foundation for higher-order questions. Close examination and analysis of video recordings of their classes reveal a strong emphasis on higher-order questions at the interpretive, applicative, and transactive levels.

A clear meaning-negotiation pattern was evident in large and medium-sized group lectures and in small seminar discussions. This pattern consisted of *posing*, *exploring*, and *resolving* problems that were embedded in meaningful contexts. The three phases of the process were enacted through lecturing as well as question/response and discussion interactions. Teachers' responses to students were generative in nature, in that they clarified understanding, validated students' responses, raised further issues, and used students' responses to explore alternative explanations. Implicit in this, too, was the teachers' apparent monitoring of students' thinking, made explicit through verbal feedback and asking of subsequent questions. These findings and conclusions differ markedly from those reported on teaching that note minimal student–teacher interaction and little or no emphasis on higher-order thinking (Goodlad, 1983; Heath, 1982; Mehan, 1979). This research, however, focused on influential teachers who were identified on the basis of their teaching effectiveness. In addition, the study developed in-depth qualitative analysis of effective instructional strategies used by these influential teachers rather than a quantitative survey of more global teaching behavior.

The influential teachers in this research, regardless of level, appear to be highly sensitive to the use of meaning negotiation as a way of constructing meaning with their students. This process is conceptualized and represented in Figure 2 and is at the heart of the sociocognitive reading theory (Ruddell & Unrau, 1994; see #51 this volume) discussed earlier.

The three overlapping circles symbolize the interactive nature of the meaning-negotiation process for teacher (T), reader (R), and classroom community (CC). Note, however, that process, as illustrated in Figure 2, overlaps a real text (shown in the shaded background representing a printed text) upon which the dialogue is based. Thus, the text itself is not the sole object carrying meaning; instead, meanings arise from transactions with the text. During negotiation for meanings related to texts, readers bring their meanings to the interaction, teachers bring their understanding of the story as well as their understanding of the reading process, and members of the class interact with the text to shape—and reshape—meanings. This process is clearly illustrated in the transcript of the influential teacher episode presented earlier.

This process recognizes that the reader and the teacher read much more than text. In effect, students and teacher read several "texts"—if we take "texts" to mean events, situations, behavioral scripts and other symbolic processes that require interpretation (Bloome & Bailey, 1992). Of course, students and teacher read the text on the page. But students in particular also need to "read" the task, the authority structure (who is in control), the teacher (including the teacher's

FIGURE 2
The Meaning-Negotiation Process: The Text and Classroom Context

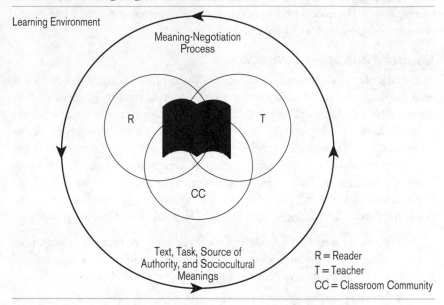

Learning Environment

Meaning-Negotiation Process

R

T

CC

Text, Task, Source of Authority, and Sociocultural Meanings

R = Reader
T = Teacher
CC = Classroom Community

intentions and expectations), and the sociocultural setting. In addition, they must "read" the social dynamics of the group, which includes the group's rules, such as turn-taking and question–answer response patterns. Influential teachers not only appear to be aware of this process, but they also have developed instructional strategies to facilitate meaning negotiation.

Classroom community negotiation of meaning is imperative, even if it does not serve as the ultimate authority for validation of meaning. The readers and the teacher share meanings in the classroom community so that, through dialogue, a community of readers comes to hold a possible range of meanings (Ruddell & Unrau, 1994).

Thus, meanings are negotiated in classrooms among readers and between readers and teacher. Meanings are open—not closed or fixed—though they need to be grounded in text. Classrooms form interpretive communities that may share common understandings; however, those understandings, those interpretations are not then fixed forever. Meanings are shaped and reshaped in the hermeneutic circle (Dilthey, 1900/1976) (represented in Figure 2 by the circle with arrowheads surrounding the meaning-negotiation process). So meaning construction is viewed as a circular and changing process of forming hypotheses and testing, negotiating, and validating meaning. As the reader's knowledge changes, as the reader interacts with other readers and with the teacher in a social context, constructed meanings can be expected to change. In a sense, although a text may be fixed, its meanings for the reader are always becoming (Ruddell & Unrau, 1994). The understanding of this process of meaning negotiation is without question one hallmark of the influential teacher.

Reader Motivation Strategies

The study of reader motivations used the same primary-grade instructional episodes discussed above. This analysis relied on an instructional motivation taxonomy based on the work of Russell (1970), Mathewson (1994; see #50 this volume), Squire (1989), and Ruddell (1992). The taxonomy accounts for seven categories, which were used to identify the teachers' primary motivational intent of each instructional episode. Six of these categories focused on *internal motivations* in the instructional episodes and served to define the teachers' *aesthetic instructional stance*. Examples of books that are highly appropriate for each internal motivation are shown in parentheses. The motivations consisted of

1. *Problem Resolution*, enabling the student to see himself or herself as successful in problem solving or problem resolution (e.g., *Alexander and the Wind-Up Mouse* [Lionni, 1969], *Charlotte's Web* [White, 1952]).

2. *Prestige*, encouraging the child to perceive self as a person of significance, receiving attention and exerting control in his or her life (e.g., *Where the Wild Things Are* [Sendak, 1963], *Henry the Explorer* [Taylor, 1966]).

3. *Aesthetic*, elevating an aesthetic sense, ranging from the appreciation of beauty in nature to the enjoyment of family interaction and harmony (e.g., *On the Banks of Plum Creek* [Wilder, 1953], *When I Was Young in the Mountains* [Rylant, 1982]).

4. *Escape*, enabling the reader to leave the realities of daily existence and travel to far away places doing unfamiliar and exotic things (e.g., *Ramona Forever* [Cleary, 1984], *The Lion, the Witch and the Wardrobe* [Lewis, 1950]).

5. *Intellectual Curiosity*, encouraging the child to discover through the exploration of new concepts and new worlds (e.g., *Sharks* [Berger, 1987], *The Eleventh Hour Curious Mysteries* [Base, 1988]).

6. *Understanding Self*, providing opportunity to understand personal motivations and the motivations of story characters (e.g., *Alexander and the Terrible, Horrible, No Good, Very Bad Day* [Viorst, 1972], *Tales of a Fourth Grade Nothing* [Blume, 1972]).

The seventh motivation accounted for *external motivation* and reflected an *efferent instructional stance*. This motivation was labeled *teacher expectations* and defined as teacher-controlled episodes, using explicit text-based questions and discussion with predetermined answers.

The analysis of reader motivations used in the instructional episodes for the influential and noninfluential teachers revealed distinctly different patterns. Influential teachers relied on internal reader motivations during 89% of their instructional episodes and used external motivation (teacher expectations) in only 11% of their episodes. By contrast, the noninfluential teachers used internal motivations in only 39% of their episodes and external motivations in 61% of their episodes.

The influential teachers relied most heavily on the internal motivation of problem resolution (46%) with decreasing emphasis on aesthetic (14%), intellectual curiosity (14%), understanding self (11%), escape (4%), and prestige (0%). The substantial emphasis on problem resolution may be attributed to the many opportunities present for using this type of motivation in the story *Alexander and the Wind-Up Mouse*. As previously noted, these teachers used the external motivation of teacher expectations in only 11% of their episodes. Although the noninfluential teachers relied predominantly on the external motivation of teacher expectations (61% of the time), the internal motivations used by these teachers, in decreasing order, consisted of problem resolution (21%), intellectual curiosity (14%), and escape (4%), with no use of understanding self, aesthetic, or prestige.

These findings reveal that the dominant stance used in the instructional episodes of the influential teachers was aesthetic, as reflected in their primary reliance on internal reader motivations as they encouraged children to enter into and transact with the text. The stance of the noninfluential teacher was predominantly efferent in nature, with major emphasis on specific story content elicited by teacher-directed questions focusing on factual, text-based information. In short, the influential teachers are highly effective in taking an instructional stance that uses internal reader motivations and incorporates children's prior knowledge, experiences, and beliefs in the meaning-negotiation and -construction process.

Implications for Teaching and Research

This discussion has focused on a composite description, beliefs, and classroom practices of influential teachers that provide insight into the nature of their high-level teaching effectiveness. The research demonstrates that these highly effective teachers are sensitive to individual student needs, motivations, and aptitudes. They possess a unique ability to relate to and use the prior knowledge and beliefs that students bring to their classrooms by making the subject matter content personally relevant. These teachers are strategy oriented and are masters at orchestrating their instruction as they create an instructional flow that provides active participation, cohesion, purposeful direction, and feedback in their learning episodes. They are highly skilled in negotiating meaning by sharing teacher authority and, in turn, creating shared responsibility and ownership for learning with their students. These teachers also provide support to their students in helping them learn how to self-monitor and self-evaluate their own learning. Finally, they not only hold high expectations for self but for their students' achievement as well.

Based on this discussion, 10 key insights emerge and hold implications for increasing our effectiveness as literacy teachers:

1. Develop clear purpose and instructional plans that facilitate successful development and resolution of instructional episodes.

2. Emphasize activation and use of students' prior beliefs, knowledge, and experiences in the construction of meaning.

3. Incorporate higher-level thinking questions, questioning strategies, and sensitivity to students' responses in conducting instruction.

4. Orchestrate instruction using a problem-solving approach to encourage intellectual discovery by posting, exploring, and resolving problems.

5. Monitor students' thinking, use verbal feedback, and ask subsequent questions that encourage active thinking.

6. Understand the importance of text, task, source of authority, and sociocultural meanings in negotiating and constructing meaning.

7. Involve students in meaning negotiation based on the text by encouraging interaction between the students, yourself as teacher, and the classroom community of learners.

8. Share teacher authority in discussions to encourage student thinking, responsibility, interaction, and ownership of ideas in discussion.

9. Understand instructional stance, the role it plays in setting instruction purpose for students, and the importance of using internal reader motivation to enhance student interest and authentic meaning construction.

10. Develop sensitivity to individual student needs, motivations, and aptitudes but hold appropriate and high expectations for learning.

As discussed earlier, research on highly effective teaching and teachers is very limited. Extensive research is needed to more fully understand the nature of teaching effectiveness and the change process that can lead to increasing the quality of our teacher preparation for both preservice and inservice teacher education. The following questions serve to focus our attention on several critical areas that will further our understanding of the nature of teaching effectiveness:

1. What influential teacher characteristics are malleable? For example, what characteristics can be shaped in teacher-preparation and teacher-inservice programs?

2. What teacher goals, values, and beliefs toward meaning negotiation promote highly productive student engagement in the classroom?

3. What effect does a teacher's orientation toward authority and its role in classroom meaning negotiation have on a reader's comprehension and motivation?

4. How does a teacher's instructional stance (e.g., aesthetic, efferent) affect lesson planning, reader intention, and students' motivation to engage in reading, discussion, and text-based meaning construction?

5. How does a teacher's self-system or instructional orientation on motivation affect teaching effectiveness?

6. How do teacher narratives from past teaching episodes affect teaching effectiveness, the design of lessons, and classroom environments in the present?

7. What is the nature of the change process that leads to more reflective and responsive teachers who view meaning negotiation as central to the meaning-construction process?

I close this article with a brief quote from one influential teacher (F. Crews, personal communication, April 26, 1985) that expresses the enthusiasm, vitality, and intellectual curiosity that characterized his classroom:

> For me the main pleasure of teaching resides in coping with the unexpected. Consequently, I try to be well prepared in a way that will leave me both relaxed and alert—looking for fruitful trouble—rather than trying to touch on all the expected points. If there is a philosophy behind this attitude, it is a belief that real teaching occurs not through imparting information but through arousing intellectual passions and presenting an example of thought in action.

The influential teacher enables literacy learning to become an active, exciting, collaborative, and learner-centered process of discovery. Our research challenge then is to continue to work toward an understanding of this learner-centered process to enable us to enhance teaching effectiveness.

Acknowledgments

This paper is adapted from the author's Oscar C. Causey Distinguished Research Award Address at the annual meeting of the National Reading Conference, Charleston, South Carolina, December 6, 1996.

The author would like to thank Gina Palladino for her library research assistance in completing this manuscript.

References

Ashton-Warner, S. (1963). *Teacher*. London: Virgo.

Ayers, W., & Shubert, W.H. (1994). Teacher lore: Learning about teaching from teachers. In T. Shanahan (Ed.), *Teachers thinking, teachers knowing: Reflections on literacy and language education* (pp. 105–121). Urbana, IL: National Council of Teachers of English.

Base, G. (1988). *The eleventh hour curious mystery*. New York: Harry N. Abrams.

Beidler, P.G. (Ed.). (1986). Distinguished teachers on effective teaching. *New Directions for Teaching and Learning, 28*, 3–92.

Berger, G. (1987). *Sharks*. New York: Doubleday.

Bloome, B.S. (1982). The master teachers. *Phi Delta Kappan, 63*, 664–669, 715.

Bloome, D., & Bailey, F. (1992). Studying language and literacy through events, particularities, and intertextuality. In R. Beach, J.L. Green, M.L. Kamil, & T. Shanahan (Eds.), *Multidisciplinary perspectives on literacy research* (pp. 181–210). Urbana, IL: National Council of Teachers of English.

Blume, J. (1972). *Tales of a fourth grade nothing*. Scarsdale, NY: Dutton.

Cleary, B. (1984). *Ramona forever*. New York: Morrow.

Dilthey, W. (1976). The development of hermeneutics. In H. Richman (Ed. & Trans.), *Selected writings*. Cambridge, UK: Cambridge University Press. (Original work published 1900)

Durkin, D. (1979). What classroom observations reveal about reading comprehension instruction. *Reading Research Quarterly, 15*, 481–533.

Fielding, L.G., Anderson, R.C., & Pearson, P.D. (1990). *How discussion questions influence children's story understanding* (Tech. Rep. No. 490). Urbana: University of Illinois, Center for the Study of Reading.

Goodlad, J.I. (1983). *A place called school: Prospects for the future*. New York: McGraw-Hill.

Guszak, F.J. (1967). Teacher questioning and reading. *The Reading Teacher, 21*, 227–234.

Hansen, J. (1981). The effects of inference training and practice on young children's reading comprehension. *Reading Research Quarterly, 16*, 321–417.

Heath, S.B. (1982). What no bedtime story means: Narrative skills at home and school. *Language in Society, 11*, 49–75.

Kridel, C., Bullough, R.V., & Shaker, P. (Eds.). (1996). *Teachers and mentors: Profiles of distinguished twentieth-century professors of education*. New York: Garland.

Ladson-Billings, G. (1994). *The dreamkeepers: Successful teachers of African American children*. San Francisco: Jossey-Bass.

Lewis, C.S. (1950). *The lion, the witch and the wardrobe*. New York: Macmillan.

Lionni, L. (1969). *Alexander and the wind-up mouse*. New York: Knopf.

Mathewson, G. (1994). Model of attitude influence upon reading and learning to read. In R.B. Ruddell, M.R. Ruddell, & H. Singer (Eds.), *Theoretical models and processes of reading* (4th ed., pp. 1131–1161). Newark, DE: International Reading Association.

Mehan, H. (1979). "What time is it, Denise?" Asking known information questions in classroom discourse. *Theory Into Practice, 18*, 285–294.

National Commission on Teaching & America's Future. (1996). *What matters most: Teaching for America's future* (Summary report). New York: Author.

Perl, S., & Wilson, N. (1986). *Through teachers' eyes: Portraits of writing teachers at work*. Portsmouth, NH: Heinemann.

Renouf, G. (1990). *The influence of affect on literary text interpretation*. Unpublished doctoral dissertation, University of California, Berkeley.

Rosenblatt, L.M. (1985). The transactional theory of literary work: Implications for research. In C.R. Cooper (Ed.), *Researching response to literature and the teaching of literature: Points of departure* (pp. 33–53). Norwood, NJ: Ablex.

Rosenblatt, L.M. (1988). *Writing and reading: The transactional theory* (Report No. 13). Berkeley: University of California, Center for the Study of Writing.

Ruddell, R.B. (1983). A study of teaching effectiveness variables of influential teachers. In M.P. Douglas (Ed.), *Reading: The process of creating meaning for senses stimuli* (pp. 57–70). Claremont, CA: Claremont Graduate School Yearbook.

Ruddell, R.B. (1992). A whole language and literature perspective: Creating a meaning making instructional environment. *Language Arts, 69*, 612–620.

Ruddell, R.B. (1994). The development of children's comprehension and motivation during storybook discussion. In R.B. Ruddell, M.R.

Ruddell, & H. Singer (Eds.), *Theoretical models and processes of reading* (4th ed., pp. 281–296). Newark, DE: International Reading Association.

Ruddell, R.B. (1995). Those influential literacy teachers: Meaning negotiators and motivation builders. *The Reading Teacher, 48,* 454–463.

Ruddell, R.B. (2002). *Teaching children to read and write: Becoming an effective teacher.* Boston: Allyn & Bacon.

Ruddell, R.B., Draheim, M., & Barnes, J. (1990). A comparative study of the teaching effectiveness of influential and non-influential teachers and reading comprehension development. In J. Zutell & S. McCormick (Eds.), *Literacy theory and research: Analyses from multiple paradigms* (39th yearbook of the National Reading Conference, pp. 153–162). Chicago: National Reading Conference.

Ruddell, R.B., & Greybeck, B. (1992, December). *An intergenerational study of literacy teaching: Connections between teachers' self perceptions, former influential teachers and observed performance.* Paper presented at the annual meeting of the National Reading Conference, San Antonio, TX.

Ruddell, R.B., & Greybeck, B. (1995, April). *Meaning negotiation and meaning construction strategies used by influential teachers in content area instruction.* Paper presented at the annual meeting of the American Educational Research Association, San Francisco, CA.

Ruddell, R.B., & Harris, P. (1989). A study of the relationship between influential teachers' prior knowledge and beliefs and teaching effectiveness: Developing higher order thinking in content areas. In S. McCormick & J. Zutell (Eds.), *Cognitive and social perspectives for literacy research and instruction* (38th yearbook of the National Reading Conference, pp. 461–472). Chicago: National Reading Conference.

Ruddell, R.B., & Kern, R.B. (1986). The development of belief systems and teaching effectiveness of influential teachers. In M.P. Douglas (Ed.), *Reading: The quest for meaning* (pp. 133–150). Claremont, CA: Claremont Graduate School Yearbook.

Ruddell, R.B., & Unrau, N.J. (1994). Reading as a meaning-construction process: The reader, the text, and the teacher. In R.B. Ruddell, M.R. Ruddell, & H. Singer (Eds.), *Theoretical models and processes of reading* (4th ed., pp. 996–1056). Newark, DE: International Reading Association.

Ruddell, R.B., & Unrau, N.J. (1997). The role of responsive teaching in focusing reader intention and developing reader motivation. In J.T. Guthrie & A. Wigfield (Eds.), *Reading engagement: Motivating readers through integrated instruction* (pp. 102–125). Newark, DE: International Reading Association.

Ruddell, R.B., & Williams, A. (1972). *A research investigation of a literacy teaching model: Project DELTA* (EPDA Project No. 005262). Berkeley, CA: Department of Health, Education and Welfare, Office of Education.

Russell, D.H. (1970). Reading and mental health: Clinical approaches. In R.B. Ruddell (Ed.), *The dynamics of reading* (pp. 207–229). Waltham, MA: Ginn.

Rylant, C. (1982). *When I was young in the mountains.* New York: Dutton.

Sendak, M. (1963). *Where the wild things are.* New York: HarperCollins.

Squire, J.R. (1989). *Research on reader response and the national literature initiative.* Paper presented at the annual convention of the International Reading Association, Atlanta, GA.

Sturtevant, E.G. (1996). Lifetime influences on the literacy-related instructional beliefs of experienced high school history teachers: Two comparative case studies. *Journal of Literacy Research, 28,* 227–257.

Taba, H., & Elzey, F.F. (1964). Teaching strategies and thought processes. *Teachers College Record, 65,* 524–534.

Taylor, M. (1966). *Henry the explorer.* New York: Atheneum.

Unrau, N.J., & Ruddell, R.B. (1995). Interpreting texts in classroom contexts. *Journal of Adolescent & Adult Literacy, 39,* 16–27.

Viorst, J. (1972). *Alexander and the terrible, horrible, no good, very bad day.* New York: Macmillan.

White, E.B. (1952). *Charlotte's web.* New York: HarperCollins.

Wilder, L.I. (1953). *On the banks of plum creek.* New York: HarperCollins.

37

A Quasi-Experimental Validation of Transactional Strategies Instruction With Low-Achieving Second-Grade Readers

Rachel Brown, Michael Pressley, Peggy Van Meter,
and Ted Schuder

Since Durkin's (1978/1979) seminal discovery that American students received little instruction about how to comprehend text, there have been extensive efforts to identify strategies that can be taught to students to increase their understanding of and memory for text. Early strategy research (for reviews, see Dole, Duffy, Roehler, & Pearson, 1991; Pressley, Johnson, Symons, McGoldrick, & Kurita, 1989) tended to focus on instruction of individual strategies and improvements in narrowly defined performances (e.g., improvement on standardized comprehension tests when reading strategies were taught). The typical research tactic taken in these studies was to teach one group of students to use a particular cognitive strategy while reading, often a strategy consistent with a theory of knowledge representation favored by the researcher, with control students left to their own devices to understand text as best they could. Through this approach, a relatively small number of individual strategies were proved effective in increasing elementary students' comprehension of and memory for text (e.g., visualizing ideas in text, summarizing, and self-questioning). What the single-strategy investigations demonstrated was that if students were under exceptionally strong instructional control (i.e., they were told to carry out a particular strategy on a particular occasion), they could carry out strategies that would improve comprehension and learning. Seldom was generalized use of individual instructed strategies observed, nor was there evidence of generalized improvement in reading.

On the basis of what is now known about skilled reading, it is not surprising that improvement in reading has required more than instruction in single

From *Journal of Educational Psychology*, 88(1), 18–37. Copyright © 1996 by the American Psychological Association. Reprinted with permission of the publisher.

strategies. During the late 1970s and early 1980s, a number of analyses of skilled reading were conducted (e.g., Johnston & Afflerbach, 1985; Lytle, 1982; Olshavsky, 1976/1977; Olson, Mack, & Duffy, 1981; see Pressley & Afflerbach, 1995, for a summary). What became apparent was that skilled reading did not involve the use of a single potent strategy but rather orchestration of cognitive processes. This understanding—that skilled readers coordinate a number of strategies while reading—partially fueled researcher efforts to develop instructional interventions that involved teaching of multiple comprehension strategies (Baker & Brown, 1984).

A well-known researcher-designed, multiple-strategies instructional package was Palincsar and Brown's (e.g., 1984) reciprocal teaching. Palincsar and Brown taught students to apply four strategies to expository text as they read (generate predictions, ask questions, seek clarification, and summarize content). The students used these strategies in reading groups, with the adult teacher releasing control of the strategic processing as much as possible to the group. Palincsar and Brown's prediction, consistent with Vygotsky's (e.g., 1934/1978) theory of socially mediated learning, was that participation in reading group discussions that involved predicting, questioning, seeking clarification, and summarizing would lead to internalization of these processes by group members. In fact, a month or two of such instruction produces noticeable improvement in the use of the focal strategies but only modest improvement on standardized reading tests (for a review, see Rosenshine & Meister, 1994).

In addition to the research of Palincsar and Brown (1984), there were other attempts to teach multiple comprehension strategies. Some involved presenting a large number of strategies quickly; these approaches typically failed to produce improvements in elementary-level readers' comprehension (e.g., Paris & Oka, 1986). Other interventions involved more intensive direct explanation and modeling of small repertoires of strategies; these approaches generally were more successful in improving reading (e.g., Bereiter & Bird, 1985; Collins, 1991; Duffy et al., 1987).

Many educators became aware of strategy researchers' instructional successes and began to import strategies instruction into classrooms. What became apparent, however, was that when strategies instruction was successfully deployed in schools, it involved much more than the operations studied in the well-controlled experiments (Pressley, Goodchild, Fleet, Zajchowski, & Evans, 1989). This factor motivated Pressley and his colleagues to study extensively how elementary educators implemented comprehension strategies instruction in schools (see Pressley & El-Dinary, 1993).

After investigating several educator-developed programs, our research group proposed that effective elementary-level comprehension was "transactional" in three senses of the term (Pressley, El-Dinary, et al., 1992), First, readers are encouraged to construct meaning by using strategies that enable the linking of text content to prior knowledge, consistent with Rosenblatt's (1979) use of the term. Second, much of the strategies instruction occurs in reading groups, with group members using strategies to construct meaning together. As such, meaning-making is transactional in the sense that the constructed group understanding differs from the personalized interpretations individuals would have generated on their own, especially if they did not use strategies. This is consistent with the use of the term in organizational psychology (e.g., Hutchins, 1991). Third, the teacher's or group members' actions and reactions cannot be anticipated when the reading group uses strategies to construct interpretations. Rather, the responses of all members of the group (including the teacher) are determined in part by those of others in the group, which is a transactional situation according to social development researchers such as Bell (1968). Thus, group members co-determine each other's thinking about text. Because the strategy instruction the research group observed was so "transactional" in these three senses of the term, this type of instruction was called *transactional strategies instruction* (TSI) (Pressley, El-Dinary, et al., 1992).

The short-term goal of TSI is the joint construction of reasonable interpretations by group members as they apply strategies to texts. The long-term goal is the internalization and consistently adaptive use of strategic processing whenever students encounter demanding text. Both goals are promoted by teaching reading group members to construct text meaning by emulating expert readers' use of comprehension strategies: to emulate how expert readers constructively respond when they need to understand challenging text (e.g., Pressley & Afflerbach, 1995; Wyatt et al., 1993). Expert readers are planful and goal oriented when they read, combine their background knowledge with text cues to create meaning, apply a variety of strategies (e.g., from seeking the important information in text to noting details), monitor their comprehension, attempt to solve their comprehension problems, and evaluate their understanding and performance (e.g., Is the content believable? Is the piece well written? Am I achieving my goals?). The result is a personalized, interpretive understanding of text.

A variety of qualitative methods were used in the previous studies of transactional strategies instruction (see Pressley, El-Dinary, et al., 1992). These included (a) ethnographies; (b) interviews involving questions emanating from Pressley, Goodchild, et al.'s (1989) tentative description of strategies instruction; (c) interviews constructed to illuminate observations made in program classrooms; (d) long-term case studies; and (e) analyses of classroom discourse. Although the TSI programs differed in their particulars, there were a number of common components (Pressley, El-Dinary, et al., 1992):

- Strategy instruction is long-term, with effective strategies instructors offering it in their classroom throughout the school year; the ideal is for high-quality process instruction to occur across school years.

- Teachers explain and model effective comprehension strategies. Typically, a few, powerful strategies are emphasized.

- The teachers coach students to use strategies on an as-needed basis, providing hints to students about potential strategic choices they might make. There are many minilessons about when it is appropriate to use particular strategies.

- Both teachers and students model use of strategies for one another, thinking aloud as they read.

- Throughout instruction, the usefulness of strategies is emphasized, with students reminded frequently about the comprehension gains that accompany strategy use. Information about when and where various strategies can be applied is commonly discussed. Teachers consistently model flexible use of strategies; students explain to one another how they use strategies to process text.

- The strategies are used as a vehicle for coordinating dialogue about text. Thus, a great deal of discussion of text content occurs as teachers interact with students, reacting to students' use of strategies and prompting additional strategic processing (see especially Gaskins, Anderson, Pressley, Cunicelli, & Satlow, 1993). In particular, when students relate text to their prior knowledge, construct summaries of text meaning, visualize relations covered in a text, and predict what might transpire in a story, they engage in personal interpretation of text, with these personal interpretations varying from child to child and from reading group to reading group (Brown & Coy-Ogan, 1993).

Although the qualitative studies provided in-depth understanding of the nature of transactional strategies instruction programs, and a variety of informal data attested to the strengths of these programs (e.g., correlational, nonexperimental, and quasi-experimental comparisons conducted by school-district officials; see Brown & Pressley, 1994), what was lacking until the study reported here was conducted were formal comparisons on a variety of reading measures of students who received transactional strategies instruction versus more conventional instruction. This study begins to fill that gap. There were several important challenges to making such comparisons, however. One challenge was determining what should be measured. Reading strategies instruction has tended to focus on gains on one or a few traditional measures of reading performance (Pressley, El-Dinary, et al., 1992). It became clear on the basis of the qualitative studies that transactional strategies instruction probably affected student cognition in a number of ways, however, with both short-term and long-term impacts (Pressley, Schuder, Teachers in the Students Achieving Independent Learning Program, Bergman, & El-Dinary, 1992).

A second challenge was that many indicators in the qualitative research conducted on transactional strategies instruction suggested that the effects of such an intervention appeared in the long term; that is, at a minimum, only after a semester to an academic year of such instruction (see Marks et al., 1993; Pressley, El-Dinary, et al., 1992; Pressley, Schuder, et al., 1992). A credible evaluation had to be long-term. A constraint was that students often move in and out of schools at a high rate; thus, holding together large groups of students for several years was impractical. Our solution was to evaluate 1 year of transactional strategies instruction, because 1 year of intervention was all we believed could be completed in the participating district with an intact sample of students.

A third challenge resulted in our decision not to assign teachers randomly to conditions. Becoming an effective transactional strategies instruction teacher takes several years (e.g., El-Dinary & Schuder, 1993; Pressley et al., 1991; Pressley, Schuder, et al., 1992). Thus, we felt we could not take any group of teachers and randomly assign them to transactional strategies instruction or control conditions. Moreover, we decided not to assign accomplished transactional strategies instruction teachers randomly to teach strategies versus some other approach. Because the teachers were committed to strategies instruction, we felt it was inappropriate to ask them to alter their teaching for an entire year. Our solution was to use a quasi-experimental design involving accomplished TSI teachers and other teachers in the same district, teachers with reputations as excellent reading educators whose instruction followed the guidelines of the district's regular literacy curriculum.

Before proceeding with a description of the formal methods in our study, we summarize some of the most important features of the Students Achieving Independent Learning (SAIL) program, the specific educator-developed transactional strategies instruction approach evaluated here. A description of SAIL will permit readers to understand our expectations in this quasi-experiment.

The SAIL Comprehension Strategies Instructional Program

The purpose of SAIL is the development of independent, self-regulated meaning-making from text. The program was developed over the course of a decade in one mid-Atlantic school district (see Schuder, 1993, for a history of SAIL and its evolution). SAIL students are taught to adjust their reading to their specific purpose and to text characteristics (Is the material interesting? Does it relate to the reader's prior knowledge?). SAIL students are instructed to predict upcoming events, alter expectations as text unfolds, generate questions and interpretations while reading, visualize represented ideas, summarize periodically, and attend selectively to the most important information. Students are taught to think aloud (e.g., Meichenbaum, 1977) as they practice applying comprehension strategies during reading group instruction. For example, they reveal their thinking to others when they talk about their past experiences in relation to text. All of these reading processes are taught as strategies to students through direct explanations provided by teachers, teacher modeling, coaching, and scaffolded practice, both in reading groups and independently.

Direct explanations and modeling of strategic reasoning are critical components for preparing students to internalize and use strategies adaptively. These core components start the long-term process of helping students become more self-regulated and skillful readers. Direct explanations include providing students with information about the benefits of strategy use, as well as when and where to use strategies. In this dialogue, a SAIL teacher explained what is necessary to make good predictions.

> T: We're going to set a couple of goals. So let's listen carefully and really really try to meet these goals by the end of the lesson. The first thing I want everybody to try to do is to make really good predictions. Can anybody tell me what a prediction is? S8?
>
> S8: When you think what's gonna happen next.
>
> T: When you try to guess what's going to happen next. If you're going to be a good predictor, how do you make good predictions? What do you need to have? S5?
>
> S5: Enough information.
>
> T: You have to have enough information in order for a good prediction to be made. Where can you find your information to get a prediction, where can you find it, S8?
>
> S8: In the book?
>
> T: In the book? You mean like, from what you've already read?
>
> S8: Yeah.
>
> T: S6?
>
> S6: In your head.
>
> T: In your head. Sometimes, a fancy word for that is background knowledge. In other words, knowledge means that you know. If you already know something about foxes, or about what a trot is, you might be able to even make a prediction about what the story is about. But maybe we should read a little bit into it to get a little more information to make sure we can make some good predictions.

Modeling, another critical SAIL component, does not consist solely of showing students how to use a strategy. Instead, SAIL teachers verbally explain their thinking and reasoning as they model appropriate use of strategies. In the following example, a SAIL teacher modeled her use of strategies, verbalizing her thinking as she applied a strategy in response to the demands of the text and her need to understand. However, before modeling, she explained to students why she was going to model: to help them observe how and why she used strategies to comprehend what she was reading.

T: I'm gonna start this morning modeling like I usually do.... This is gonna be a real good opportunity for you to use a lot of your strategies. There are a lot of big words in this story. Okay, so it's going to give us a chance to use some of our "fix-up kit" and it's gonna also give us a chance to use a lot of background knowledge, things that we already know from our own life, to help us understand what this story is about....

The teacher proceeded to read, "Fox was a fine dancer. He could waltz, he could boogie, he could do the stomp." She then modeled her thinking for students.

T: You know what? I'm thinking waltzing, boogieing, doing the stomp. I don't really know what the stomp is. But I'm thinking to myself that the stomp must be a dance because I do know that the waltz is a dance. That's when two people dance together. Because I used to see that on the Lawrence Welk Show. My grandmothers used to watch that a lot. And the boogie, well, I know that was a dance when I was in high school and that's when you move real fast. So, I'm thinking, the word *stomp*, I know that, well you can stomp your foot, and maybe that's what people do when they do the stomp. But I still think it's a dance. So that's what I'm gonna think, that. He could do the stomp, so that's a dance.

The teacher related information from her own experiences to text details. She used her prior knowledge to apply one of the "fix-up" strategies, guessing, when figuring out the meaning of an unknown word (i.e., *stomp*). Later in the same lesson, a student substituted a word when she came to a word she did not know. The teacher reminded students of the strategic reasoning she used when she initially verbalized her thinking. She then explained how readers can select different "fix-up" strategies (i.e., substituting a known word for an unknown one or relying on picture clues) to achieve the same purpose: to understand the gist of a passage.

T: But, back over here, when I first said that there were some big vocabulary that had to do with the kinds of dances...we were talking about the fact that S1 substituted as a strategy and she was able to figure out...[what the word meant]. And then S6 over there gave her the real word, and then we found out that the real word wasn't that important because we could understand. Then I was thinking back to the fact that I didn't know what the stomp was and here I was looking at the picture clue. So, even though S1 was having trouble with the vocabulary, she could still get the gist of the type of dances by looking at the three pictures. There were three types of dances and there were three pictures.

In addition, SAIL students are taught multiple methods for dealing with difficult words, including skipping them, using context clues to determine the meaning of hard-to-decode and unfamiliar words, and rereading for more clues to meaning. Overreliance on any one strategy is discouraged. For example, skipping every unknown word can lead to comprehension failures, particularly if the skipped words are central to the meaning of the text. Instead, students are taught that skipping is just one of several strategies available to them when they encounter unknown words. When students are taught to ignore unknown words judiciously, skipping becomes a powerful problem-solving strategy for those who otherwise might linger too long over an undecodable word. In general, students are taught that getting the overall meaning of text is more important than understanding every word, so that difficult words sometimes can be skipped with little or no loss in meaning.

When SAIL instruction occurs in reading groups, it differs in a number of ways from more conventional reading group instruction: (a) Prereading discussion of vocabulary is eliminated in favor of discussion of vocabulary in the context of reading. (b) The almost universal classroom practice of asking comprehension-check questions as students read in group (e.g., Mehan, 1979) is rarely observed in transactional strategies instruction groups (Gaskins et al., 1993). Instead, a teacher gauges literal comprehension as students think aloud after reading a text segment. (c) There are extended interpretive discussions of text, with these discussions emphasizing student application of strategies to text.

Although reading group is an important SAIL component, the teaching of strategies extends across the school day, during whole-class instruction, and as teachers interact individually with their students. Reading instruction is also an across-the-curriculum activity. (For more detailed descriptions of SAIL, see Bergman & Schuder, 1992; Pressley, El-Dinary, et al., 1992; Schuder, 1993.)

One hypothesis evaluated here was that participating in SAIL would enhance reading comprehension as measured by a standardized test. A second was that there would be clear indications after a year of SAIL instruction of students learning and using strategies. A third was that students would develop deeper, more personalized and interpretive understandings of text after a year of SAIL.

These hypotheses were evaluated with low-achieving second-grade students, a group targeted by SAIL; SAIL was designed originally for introduction to elementary students in either first or second grade who were at risk for reading failure. It is intended as a dramatically richer and more engaging form of instruction than the skill-and-drill approaches so often delivered to at-risk students (Allington, 1991). Thus, the evaluation reported here involved contrasting the achievement of low-achieving second-grade students who participated in SAIL with that of five matched groups of second-grade students receiving high quality, but more conventional. reading instruction.

Method

Participants

Teachers. The five transactional strategies instruction teachers served in the school district that developed the SAIL program; the five teachers in comparison classrooms were from the same school district. This district had garnered numerous national awards for excellence in instruction. Eight of the teachers taught second-grade classes. One SAIL teacher had a first/second-grade combination; one comparison teacher had a second/third-grade combination. All teachers were female. The SAIL teachers had 10.4 years of experience teaching on average; the comparison teachers averaged 23.4 years.[1] The five SAIL teachers exhausted the pool of second-grade teachers in the district with extensive experience teaching in the SAIL program (i.e., 3 or more years; range = 3–6 years). The comparison teachers were recommended by principals and district reading specialists, with nominations of effective second-grade teachers made on the basis of criteria such as the following: (a) They gave students grade-level–appropriate tasks; (b) they provided motivating learning activities; (c) they used classroom management well to avoid discipline problems; (d) they fostered active student involvement in reading; (e) they monitored student understanding and performance; and (f) they fostered academic self-esteem in students.

The comparison teachers were eclectic in their instructional practices, blending the whole language tradition favored in the school district with elements of skill and other traditional forms of conventional reading instruction. For example, a teacher who stressed skills instruction sometimes integrated literature-based activities such as having students write in a response journal or read from a trade book (rather than a basal reader). A teacher who emphasized elements associated with a literature-based approach also taught or reviewed phonics, word attack, and specific comprehension skills before or after reading. Some conventional instructors also taught a few strategies, like skipping unknown words, making predictions, or activating background knowledge. However, they did not teach a flexible repertoire of strategies using explicit, verbal explanations of thinking, elements characteristic of SAIL instruction. The comparison-group teachers had not participated in any SAIL professional development activities.

All participating teachers were administered DeFord's (1985) Theoretical Orientation to Reading Profile (TORP), a 28-item instrument discriminating among teachers identifying with phonics, skills, and whole language orientations. The scoring is such that those favoring phonics-based reading instruction score lower than those favoring skills instruction, who score lower than those identifying with whole language (scores range from 28 to 140). The SAIL teachers' mean score was 113 (SD = 9.7), and the comparison teachers averaged 73 (SD = 7.2), with the SAIL teachers differing significantly from the comparison teachers, dependent $t(4) = 6.24$, $p < .05$. (In the teacher comparisons, teachers were the units of analysis. Each teacher taught a reading group, with each group consisting of six students. SAIL and non-SAIL reading groups were matched on school demographic information. SAIL and non-SAIL students in the matched reading groups were paired on the basis of students' fall standardized test performances, described later in the Method section. As such, a correlated-samples analysis was conducted because SAIL and comparison teachers were matched.) When the particular items of the TORP were examined, it was clear that the SAIL teachers had more of a whole language orientation than the comparison teachers, who endorsed phonics and skills to a greater degree, smallest $|t|(4) = 4.88$, $p < .05$ for any of the three subscales. This finding was as expected because SAIL encourages meaning-making as the goal of reading and discourages teaching of skills in isolation, consistent with whole language. Informal observations of the comparison teachers over the year confirmed that they were more eclectic in their approach to reading instruction than the SAIL teachers, incorporating a balance of whole language, phonics-based, and skills-based instruction. Thus, their more balanced appraisal of the TORP items was consistent with our observations of their teaching.

At the beginning of the study, the 10 participating teachers were also administered a 25-item researcher-constructed questionnaire tapping their beliefs about teaching ($r = .94$; Cronbach's alpha calculated on participating teachers' responses). The questions involved responding to Likert-type statements (i.e., on a *strongly agree* to *strongly disagree* scale). For example, teachers who endorse transactional strategies instruction were expected to respond affirmatively to "The most important message to convey to students is that reading and thinking are inseparably linked," and "During instruction, teachers should ask story-related questions that have no precisely 'right' or 'wrong' answer." It was expected that SAIL teachers would disagree with items such as "Worksheets that enable students to practice comprehension skills can be very useful for low-group students," and "During reading instruction, teachers need to guide students towards one best interpretation of a story." The responses were scored so that consistency with transactional strategies instruction would result in a low score (maximum score = 120; one item was discarded). The scores of the SAIL teachers ranged from 25 to 45 on this scale ($M = 36.8$, $SD = 9.5$), and comparison teachers' scores ranged from 62 to 76 ($M = 70.8$, $SD = 5.3$), a significant difference, dependent $t(4) = -8.84$, $p < .05$. In short, there were multiple indicators at the outset of the study that the SAIL teachers were committed to a different approach to teaching from the conventional teachers and that the SAIL teachers' beliefs about teaching were consistent with a transactional strategies instruction philosophy.

Students. Student participants were assigned to second grade but were reading below a second-grade level at the beginning of the year. They were identified as such through informal testing (teacher assessments involving reading of graded basal passages and word lists), results from assessments administered as part of the Chapter 1 program, and the previous year's grades and reports. Unfortunately, none of the assessments used by the school district to classify readers as weak at the beginning of the year were standardized measurements, although there was converging evidence from the informal measures that all participants experienced at least some difficulty reading beginning-level, second-grade material. Therefore, student mobility patterns, Chapter 1 status, ethnic and minority composition, size and location of schools, and overall performances on standardized tests were used to pair SAIL and comparison classes in the study. Moreover, because we did not have information about students' performance in previous years in any subject area and no formal test data existed for all these students, we administered a standardized achievement test. To attain greater comparability, a standardized achievement test was used to match students in each class as participants. A comprehension subtest of the Stanford Achievement Test (Primary 1, Form J: Grade level 1.5–2.5) was administered in late November or early December (depending on the class) of the school year. Administration of this test occurred at that point because only then did the teachers feel that participating students could function somewhat independently at the 1.5 grade level and thus not perform on the very floor of this measure. Unfortunately, this necessitated that the test be administered after SAIL teachers had introduced SAIL component strategies, so that it is not perfectly accurate to consider this a pretest.

Six students in each of the paired classes (a pair consisted of one SAIL class and one comparison class) were matched on the basis of their reading comprehension scores. All of the children participating in the study spoke and comprehended English. In addition, the sample included no children experiencing severe attentional or behavioral problems. Only 6 students in one SAIL class met the eligibility requirements. Because students were matched on the basis of their standardized comprehension pretest scores, 6 matched pairs were selected for participation. Between the first and second semesters, 1 SAIL student and 2 comparison students in one pair of classrooms left their classrooms. Back-up students were substituted, with no significant difference occurring between the newly constituted groups on the fall reading comprehension subtest.

There were five reading groups for the SAIL condition and five groups for the non-SAIL condition, each consisting of 6 students per group. Thus, in all comparisons between conditions, the reading group mean was the unit of analysis, with each unit consisting of the mean of the 6 designated students in each group.[2] With a maximum raw test score of 40 possible, the SAIL classes in the study averaged 22.20 on this measure ($SD = 6.85$) at the late fall testing, and the comparison classes averaged 22.67 ($SD = 5.89$), a nonsignificant difference (means per class analyzed), $t(4) = -0.59, p > .05$. Although not used for matching, the word skills subtest from the same standardized instrument was also administered (maximum score = 36 for the subtest), SAIL $M = 20.97$ ($SD = 2.76$), and comparison $M = 21.10$ ($SD = 3.40$), $t(4) = -0.10, p > .05$. The comparability of the paired groups is reflected well by considering their means and standard deviations on the fall Stanford Reading Comprehension subtest (see Table 1).

Although the 6 children from each classroom are referred to here as a reading group, their instruction varied through the year. First, reading was most often taught in homogeneous groups, although it also occurred during individualized and whole-class instruction. Second, participants often, but not always, remained members of the same homogeneous group over the course of the year (students who made great progress became members of another group). Because the SAIL program was offered to all children in the SAIL classrooms and the instruction in comparison classrooms did not resemble SAIL instruction, variable grouping did not pose a problem with respect to fidelity of treatment. The 6 participating children in each classroom did meet as a homogenous group for lessons that were formally analyzed, however. Even so, our use of the term *reading group* implies only that the 6 targeted children received either SAIL or conventional instruction daily, always within their classrooms, and frequently in small groups of students.

Design

This was an academic-yearlong quasi-experimental study, carried out in 1991–1992. The reading achievement of 5 reading groups of low-achieving second-grade students receiving SAIL instruction was compared to the reading achievement of 5 groups of low-achieving second-grade students receiving instruction typical of second grades in the district. Each of the 10 reading groups was housed in a different classroom, with each SAIL group matched with a comparison reading group that was close in reading achievement level at the beginning of the study and from a school demographically similar to the school representing the SAIL group. That is, there were five matched pairs of reading groups (6 low-achieving students per reading group), with one SAIL and one comparison reading group per pair.

The present study incorporated a quasi-experimental design in that we did not randomly assign teachers to conditions. Preparing teachers to become

TABLE 1
Stanford Achievement Test Scores: Matched SAIL and Non-SAIL Class Means and Standard Deviations for Word Attack and Reading Comprehension

| | Pretest | | | | | Posttest | | | | |
| | SAIL | | Non-SAIL | | | SAIL | | Non-SAIL | | |
Matched Classes	M	SD	M	SD	t	M	SD	M	SD	t
T1 and T6										
Word Study Skills	19.33	6.35	16.33	3.08		28.00	4.05	22.33	5.75	
Reading Comprehension	20.83	6.94	20.33	7.92		36.83	4.36	26.83	9.28	
T2 and T7										
Word Study Skills	20.83	5.27	19.67	5.65		27.83	4.26	24.67	5.24	
Reading Comprehension	19.67	6.47	20.00	8.07		33.00	6.26	26.67	7.81	
T3 and T8										
Word Study Skills	18.67	4.72	23.33	2.73		23.67	2.80	22.83	6.01	
Reading Comprehension	15.67	4.63	16.83	6.24		30.67	1.63	26.00	9.94	
T4 and T9										
Word Study Skills	20.33	7.42	21.00	4.47		26.50	2.43	24.00	5.73	
Reading Comprehension	21.00	6.23	24.00	6.60		33.67	3.72	29.00	8.12	
T5 and T10										
Word Study Skills	25.67	2.50	25.17	5.04		29.50	5.79	26.17	5.60	
Reading Comprehension	33.83	7.28	32.17	6.88		36.83	2.40	35.17	4.22	
Group Totals										
Word Study Skills	20.97	2.76	21.10	3.40	−0.10	27.10	2.19	24.00	1.53	3.98*
Reading Comprehension	22.20	6.85	22.67	5.89	−0.59	34.20	2.65	28.73	3.77	4.02*

SAIL = Students Achieving Independent Learning.
Maximum possible score on Word Study Skills subtest was 36, and on Reading Comprehension subtest, 40.
SAIL and non-SAIL differences on Word Study Skills and Reading Comprehension pretests tested at $\partial = .05$ (one-tailed).
*$p < .05$ (one-tailed).

competent transactional strategies instructors is a long-term process; therefore, we felt we could not randomly assign teachers, provide professional development, and wait for teachers to become experienced in teaching SAIL in a realistic time frame. Also, the sample incorporated the largest cohort of experienced SAIL teachers in the school system. Therefore, we decided not to take SAIL teachers and randomly assign one group to teach SAIL and one group to teach another method. Even if we had access to a larger pool of SAIL teachers, we would not have asked them to alter for an entire year practices they were committed to.

The fact that SAIL teachers were committed to strategies instruction was not a concern; we felt that effective comparison teachers would be committed to the teaching practices they espoused as well. Although we might have attempted to identify potential comparison teachers in the buildings where SAIL teachers taught and randomly assigned students to teachers, we opted not to do this in favor of seeking the most competent second-grade comparison teachers that we could in the district. Because the comparison second-grade teachers did not serve in the same buildings as the SAIL teachers, random assignment of children to teachers was impossible. We believe the option we selected of matching reading groups taught by SAIL teachers with groups taught by teachers believed by the district administrators and reading consultants to be excellent second-grade reading teachers was a fair test of SAIL relative to highly regarded, more conventional reading instruction. We recognize that the use of a quasi-experimental design invites alternative explanations for results. However, we designed a study that was as close to experimental as possible by instituting as many precautions as we could.

Dependent Measures

The dependent measures are described in the order in which they were administered in the academic year. A summary of the measures appears in Table 2.

Strategies Interview. In October and November (i.e., when SAIL components were being introduced to SAIL students) and in March and April, a strategies interview was administered to all students participating in the study. This interview tapped students' reported awareness of strategies, as measured by the number and types of strategies they claimed to use during reading. We also hoped to assess whether students were aware of where, when, and why to use strategies.

Five open-ended questions (adapted from ones used by Duffy et al., 1987, for their study of strategies instruction with third-grade readers) were administered orally and individually to each participating student:

1. What do good readers do? What makes someone a good reader?
2. What things do you *do* before you start to read a story?
3. What do you *think* about before you read a new story?
4. What do you do when you come to a word you do not know?
5. What do you do when you read something that does not make sense?

These questions were presented in a different order for each student. If initial student responses were unclear or terse, the researcher probed for clarifications and elaborations.

TABLE 2
Description of Data Sources for Students

Data Source	When Given	Why Given	Description
Strategies Interview	October–November March–April	To assess SAIL and non-SAIL classes' awareness of comprehension and problem-solving strategies	Semistructured interview consisting of five base questions that were followed up with nondirective prompts: The questions were administered orally and individually to students.
Retelling Questions	March–April	To assess students' retelling and sequencing of two stories presented by each teacher	Students individually were asked cued and picture-cued retelling questions.
Think-Aloud Task	May–June	To compare SAIL and non-SAIL classes' independent use of strategies during story reading; to determine if students were more text or reader based in their responses to probes	Students were stopped and asked, "What are you thinking?" and other nondirective follow-up probes at four fixed points during story reading; students were questioned individually.
Standardized Subtests of Reading Comprehension and Word Skills	November–December	To form comparable SAIL and non-SAIL reading groups by matching students using Stanford Achievement Test Reading Comprehension scores (fall administration)	Stanford Achievement Test. Primary 1, Form J
	May–June	To compare SAIL and non-SAIL classes on traditional, standardized, and validated measures of reading (fall and spring administration)	Stanford Achievement Test. Primary 1, Form K

SAIL = Students Achieving Independent Learning.

Story Lessons and Retelling Questions. In March or April (depending on class schedule), two stories were read by all participating reading groups. The instruction and interactions that occurred during reading were recorded as these stories were read, and they were analyzed to document differences in instruction in the SAIL and non-SAIL reading groups. (See the Appendix for a description of two SAIL and two non-SAIL lessons serving as a general comparison of SAIL and conventional group instruction.) A descriptive analysis of the lessons revealed that SAIL teachers more often gave explicit explanations, verbalized their thinking, and elaborated explicitly and responsively in reaction to students' comments and actions. Non-SAIL teachers more frequently than SAIL teachers provided information or instruction to students without stating a purpose, gave answers to students when they had difficulty reading or answering questions, drilled students on their learning, and praised and evaluated their performance. Both groups activated students' background knowledge, reviewed previously learned information, and guided students through their difficulties to about the same extent (Brown, 1995a, 1995b).

After the lesson was conducted, each student was asked to retell the story to a researcher, followed by a task requiring students to sequence pictures corresponding to events in the story. The primary purpose of this measure was to assess students' recall of text details, although we thought students might include interpretations in their retellings of story content as well.

All reading groups in the study read the same two illustrated stories. "Fox Trot" was a chapter in a popular children's trade book, *Fox in Love* (Marshall, 1982); "Mushroom in the Rain" (Ginsburg, 1991) was from the Heath Reading Series, Book Level 1. The readability for the 341-word "Fox Trot" was 2.4; the readability for the 512-word "Mushroom in the Rain" was 2.2 (Harris–Jacobson Wide Range Readability Formula, Harris & Sipay, 1985, pp. 656–673).

In "Fox Trot," the main character, Fox, decides to enter a dance contest. He asks two friends to be his dance partner, but they refuse. They suggest that Fox ask Raisin, but Fox is reluctant to do so because Raisin is angry with him. Nevertheless, he asks and she agrees. They practice hard and dance quite well together. On the day of the contest, Raisin gets the mumps. Fox returns home and despondently sits in front of a blank television. Then he decides to teach his sister the dance steps. They rush to the contest and claim second prize.

In "Mushroom in the Rain," an ant seeks shelter from a storm. She squeezes herself into a small mushroom. A butterfly comes by and asks if he can escape the rain as well, with the ant allowing the butterfly to crowd in. Then comes a mouse and a bird, with the crowding in the mushroom increasing. A rabbit then arrives, who is being chased by a fox. The others hide the rabbit in the mushroom. Once the fox leaves and the rain stops, the ant asks the others how they managed to fit under the mushroom. A frog, sitting on top of the mushroom asks, "Don't you know what happens to a mushroom in the rain?" In the version of the story used in the study, the answer was not provided to the children but was left for them to infer.

These stories were selected because they provided ample opportunity for diverse interpretations and personal responses. They were on the school system's approved list and approved by the participating teachers as appropriate for a single lesson for weaker second-grade students in the spring.

All decisions about how to present the stories were made by the teachers. However, they were asked to present each of these stories in one morning lesson that was not to exceed 55 minutes in length. They were consistent with this request, with the mean SAIL lesson lasting 43.40 minutes ($SD = 7.83$) and the mean comparison-group lesson lasting 35.50 minutes ($SD = 13.34$). (Three of the matched pairs of reading groups read "Mushroom in the Rain" first; two pairs read "Fox Trot" first.) Generally, SAIL lessons are lengthier because negotiating interpretations, explaining and modeling strategies, thinking aloud, and selecting and using "fix-up" strategies while reading are time-consuming activities, particularly when they are compared with some activities in conventional reading lessons (e.g., answering skill-and-drill and literal comprehension questions). The lessons were videotaped to allow a manipulation check to ascertain that teaching in the SAIL groups was different as expected from teaching in the comparison reading groups (described in the Results section).

Approximately 2 hours after each lesson was over, each of the 6 students in the reading group was interviewed individually. First, students were asked to retell the story.

> Pretend that you are asked to tell the story to other kids in the class who have never heard the story before. What would you tell them happened in that story? Can you remember anything else? (Adapted from Golden, 1988)

This interview was followed by a cued, picture retelling task. Students were asked to sequence six scrambled pictures taken directly from the story. The students were then informed that sometimes pictures assist in aiding recall of stories, and they were asked to use the pictures to prompt recollection of story content.

Think-Aloud Measure. In May or June, students read a 129-word illustrated Aesop's fable, "The Dog and His Reflection," selected from a trade book (Miller, 1976). The readability for this story was 3.9 (Harris & Sipay, 1985), making it challenging for the students.

In the story, a dog steals a piece of meat from the dinner table. He runs into the woods and starts to cross a bridge. When he chances to look down, he sees his reflection in the water. Thinking his reflection is another dog with a larger cut of meat, he decides to seize the dog's chop. When he opens his mouth, his own piece of meat plunges into the water. Consequently, the dog ends up with nothing at all.

The students met with the researcher individually for this task. Students were stopped at four points in the reading of the Aesop fable and asked to report their thinking. If a student had difficulty reading a segment, the first question posed was "What do you think happened on this page?" Otherwise, the student was asked first, "What are you thinking?" Both questions primarily focused on content, with the "What are you thinking?" probe designed to be open ended enough to elicit interpretive remarks and opinions about the fable, although we expected students to recount story details as well. Thus, the first purpose of the think-aloud task was to supplement the story-recall task. Unlike the recall questions that were designed primarily to assess memory for story details, the more open-ended think-aloud prompt was used to examine students' understandings and interpretations of text.

The other purpose of this measure was to supplement the strategies interview. Although the strategies interview revealed whether students talked about strategies, it did not indicate whether students used them on their own when reading. One limitation of the strategy interview was that students might memorize information repeated by their teachers without being able to translate that knowledge into practice. Therefore, a task was designed to observe whether students actually used comprehension strategies when reading. Our intent was not to have these young students report directly on their thinking processes while reading. Instead, we observed whether students would use comprehension strategies when they were not cued to do so.

When students offered unelaborated responses to initial questions, open-ended follow-ups were asked (see Garner, 1988, p. 70), such as "Can you tell me more?" or "Why do you say that?" Sometimes an unelaborated comment was echoed back to the student in the form of a question. Thus, after a student remarked that a dog stole a piece of meat from his master's table, the researcher asked, "What do you think about the fact that the dog stole a piece of meat from his master's table?" For every text segment, before the student moved on to reading the next segment, the researcher asked, "Is there anything you could say or do before reading on?"

Stanford Achievement Test Subtests. In May or June, students took the Stanford Achievement Test (The Psychological Corporation, 1990), Form K, Reading Comprehension and Word Study Skills subtests. Standardized tests traditionally have been used as measures of reading performance in strategy experiments. Therefore, in addition to the other measures, students were compared on a conventional measure of reading achievement.

The Reading Comprehension subtest consists of two-sentence stories, comprehension questions on short passages, and sentence-completion items that form short stories. The Word Skills subtest includes questions pertaining to structural analysis (e.g., compound words, inflectional endings, contractions) and phonetic analysis (e.g., consonants and vowels). The comprehension test was administered first to all students, followed by the word skills test. The alternate-forms reliability for the full scale scores of Forms J (administered in the fall) and K was .89.

Results

Every hypothesis tested here was one-tailed, and each was an evaluation of whether SAIL instruction produced better performance than the comparison instruction. Most means appeared in only one hypothesis test, and hence, $\partial < .05$ was the Type 1 error probability selected for all hypotheses (Kirk, 1982, for this and all references to statistics). For the standardized test data and strategies interview data, the simple effect of condition within time of testing was evaluated in the fall, as it was in the spring. The Time of Testing $\times$ Condition interaction was also tested. The hypothesis-testing approach taken here was conservative, providing high power for detection of large effects only (Cohen, 1988). For each dependent variable, the same overall Type 1 error probability would have occurred if we had analyzed the data within a 2×2 analysis of variance structure.

All tests were based on the reading group mean as the unit of analysis (i.e., $n = 5$ groups for the SAIL condition, and $n = 5$ groups for the comparison condition, each consisting of 6 students per group), because individual scores within reading groups were not independent (see Endnote 2). Finally, all t tests were dependent t tests that were based on the five matched pairs, with one SAIL and one comparison group to a pair, with pairings determined by demographic information and by the reading groups' fall standardized comprehension performances, as described earlier.

For every dependent t test involving student posttest performance, an exact permutation test was also conducted. In all cases except three, performance in SAIL classes significantly exceeded performance in the comparison classrooms, $p = .03125$ (one-tailed) for the permutation test. In the two exceptions reported in the main text (i.e., the pretest-to-posttest gain on the standardized comprehension measure and the pretest-to-posttest gain on the strategies interview: word attack strategies), the gains for one of the five SAIL and non-SAIL pairs were identical. The SAIL classes exceeded the non-SAIL classes in the other pairs for both measures ($.03 < p < .07$, one-tailed). The third exception was in a supplementary analysis.[3]

In general, the results are reported in the order in which dependent measures were described in the Method section, which parallels the order of data collection in the study.

Fall–Spring Strategies Interview

The interviews were designed to determine whether SAIL and comparison students would differ in their awareness of strategies, operationalized as the number of strategies they claimed to use during reading. Two raters scored 20% of the interviews, with an overall 87% agreement for the strategies named by students. Only one of the two raters scored the remainder of the interviews.

A strategy was scored as mentioned if it was named in response to any of the interview questions. Any strategies mentioned by students were recorded, even if they were not strategies taught in the SAIL program. The comprehension strategies mentioned included the following:

- *Predicting*: Guessing what will happen next
- *Verifying*: Confirming that a prediction was accurate
- *Visualizing*: Constructing a mental picture of the information contained in the text segment
- *Relating prior knowledge or personal experiences to text*: Making an association between information in the text and information in the reader's head
- *Summarizing or retelling*: Saying the most important information (summarizing) or restating in one's own words everything that occurred in the text segment just read
- *Thinking aloud*: Verbalizing thoughts and feelings about text segments just read
- *Monitoring*: Explicitly verbalizing when something just read does not make sense
- *Setting a goal*: Deciding a purpose prior to reading, including decisions about both expository and narrative texts
- *Browsing or previewing*: Flipping through the story, glancing at the pictures, or reading the back cover to get ideas about the story
- *Skipping*: Ignoring a problematic part of text and reading on
- *Substituting or guessing*: Replacing a difficult part of text with something else that appears to make sense and maintains the coherence of the text segment
- *Rereading*: Returning to a problematic segment of text
- *Looking back*: Looking back in the text for information that might help in understanding a difficult-to-understand part of text
- *Clarifying confusions*: Asking a specific question to resolve a comprehension problem
- *Asking someone for help*: Asking another student or the teacher for help with the confusing section of text

The following strategies for attacking unknown or difficult words were mentioned:

- *Skipping*: Ignoring a problematic word and reading on
- *Substituting or guessing*: Replacing an unknown word with another word that appears to make sense or that maintains the coherence of the text segment
- *Rereading*: Returning to a problematic word
- *Looking back*: Looking back in the text for information that might help in understanding a difficult-to-understand word
- *Using picture clues*: Looking at pictures in the story to help determine the meaning of an unknown word or difficult-to-understand piece of text
- *Using word clues*: Relying on the surrounding text to help decide the meaning of an unknown word or difficult-to-understand piece of text
- *Breaking a word into parts*: Seeing if there are recognizable root words, prefixes, or suffixes contained within the larger word
- *Sounding out a word*: Applying knowledge of phonics to the decoding of the word
- *Asking someone for help*: Asking another student or the teacher for help with the confusing word

The comprehension and word-level strategies reports are summarized in Table 3. The means reported in the table are reading group means (i.e., a mean frequency of strategies reported for each reading group in the study was calculated on the basis of individual reading group members' reports, with each of the Table 3 means and standard deviations calculated on the basis of five reading group means). With respect to reports of comprehension strategies, there was no significant advantage for the SAIL students in the fall, shortly after the

TABLE 3
Means and Standard Deviations for Number of Comprehension and Word-Level Strategies Mentioned in the Fall and Spring Strategies Interviews

	Fall					Spring				
	SAIL		Comparison Group			SAIL		Comparison Group		
Strategy	*M*	*SD*	*M*	*SD*	*t*(4)	*M*	*SD*	*M*	*SD*	*t*(4)
Comprehension	0.79	0.45	0.88	0.44	0.58	4.20	0.86	1.25	0.48	9.53
Word Level	2.16	0.79	1.15	0.28	3.52	3.22	0.63	1.68	0.37	4.83

SAIL = Students Achieving Independent Learning.
With the exception of comprehension data in fall interviews, SAIL data were significantly greater than comparison data, *p* < .05, one-tailed.

program had begun. By spring, however, as expected, the SAIL groups reported many more strategies than the comparison-groups. In the spring, only SAIL students reported visualizing, looking back, verifying predictions, thinking aloud, summarizing, setting a goal, or browsing. Although during the spring interview, comparison-group students mentioned predicting, using text or picture clues to clarify confusions, making connections between text and their background knowledge and experiences, asking someone for help, skipping over confusing parts, and rereading, the mean frequency of such reports was always descriptively lower for them compared to the SAIL students. The SAIL and comparison groups mentioned monitoring and guessing approximately equally on the spring interview.

There were qualitative differences in students' responses to the strategy interview questions as well. When asked, "What do good readers do?" SAIL students responded more frequently than non-SAIL students that good readers use comprehension strategies, apply problem-solving strategies, and think. Both groups mentioned that good readers read abundantly, practice frequently, read well, and read for enjoyment. In response to questions about what students do or think before they read a story, students in both groups said they made predictions. However, SAIL students tended to predict what would happen in the story, whereas non-SAIL students predicted whether the story would be too difficult or whether they would like it. When asked, "What do you do when you read something that does not make sense?" students in both groups frequently mentioned they would skip or reread a confusing section; however, SAIL students cited these strategies more frequently.

With respect to word-level strategies, the SAIL students reported more strategies than the comparison-group participants, even during the fall interview (see Table 3). In the fall, SAIL students mentioned skipping words (see Endnote 3), substituting or guessing, using picture or word clues, rereading, and breaking words into parts descriptively more often than did comparison students. There was slightly more mention of sounding out words in the comparison condition in the fall. The introduction to SAIL from the very start of school probably accounts for this fall difference in word-level strategies reports. By the spring, all the word-level strategies were being mentioned by SAIL students. In contrast, the only word-level strategies mentioned consistently by more than 1 student per comparison reading group were skipping an unknown word, sounding out a word, rereading, and asking someone for help.

We also tested whether SAIL students made greater gains in self-reported awareness of strategies over the course of the year. The one-tailed interaction hypothesis test (e.g., fall-to-spring increase in students' strategies scores by condition) was significant, as expected, for both the comprehension strategies, $t(4) = 7.72$, and the word-level strategies, $t(4) = 2.64$.

In general, SAIL students provided more elaborate responses to post-measure questions. For example, this rich spring interview was provided by a student in a SAIL class.

R: What do good readers do?

S: [Good readers have] lots of expression. They do think-alouds.

R: They do think-alouds. Okay. What do you mean by that?

S: Well, they tell people what they think is going on in their own words in the story.

R: Uh huh. What other things do good readers do?

S: Well, I'm an expert reader. And what I do is I skip. But, well, skipping isn't always great because sometimes you need to get the gist of the story. Cause if you always skip, you can't get the meaning of the story.

R: So you can't be skipping everything in the story....

S: [I also do] substituting, and sounding things out is a very good strategy [sic]...and, um, looking back is a good strategy.

R: Looking back.... Why is looking back a good strategy?

S: Because like if I got stuck on a word, like, uh, it might be back on the story.... But sometimes it isn't.

R: Are there any other things good readers do? Are there any other strategies good readers use?

S: Guessing too. Picture clues are very good.... "The Cat and the Canary" has beautiful illustrations, and we think it should have a Caldecott Medal 'cause of the picture clues. I looked there and the word *suddenly* came up because the picture clues just looked like *suddenly*.

R: What things do you *do* before you start to read a story?

S: I look at the title, and I look first at the pictures.

R: Why do you do that?

S: Because that can give me information about what the story is about. But when I make predictions it's not always right. We don't get upset because it's not right. We just know that it's not right and then something goes off in our mind telling us that we should make another one.

R: What do you *think* about before you read a new story?

S: I think about whether it might be good or bad....

R: How would you tell if it were good or bad?

S: If I were alone at home, I would look at the first pictures and start reading the first page and then I get ideas.

R: Okay, then, what might you do after you read the first page and get ideas?

S: I have a think-aloud in my mind that would tell me what the story might be about.

R: What do you do when you come to a word you do not know?

S: I use picture clues, I guess, look back, and sometimes I reread the sentence.

R: What do you do when you read something that does not make sense?

S: I read the sentence very slowly to see if I skipped a word.

R: Hmmm, what else do you do?

S: Sometimes I just skip it and go to the next line.

The following interview is representative of the type of responses given by non-SAIL students to the interview questions. Although some of the same components are apparent (particularly with word-level strategies), the student's responses are less elaborated.

R: What do good readers do?

S: They read a lot of books.

R: Anything else?

S: Nope.

R: What things do you *do* before you start to read a story?

S: Read the title.

R: Read the title. Why do you read the title?

S: Because, when...if you don't read the title you won't know what it's about.

R: What do you *think* about before you read a story?

S: It might be tales.

R: It might be tales...what do you mean? Tell me a little more....

S: Like, it might be funny.

R: Ah, so it might be funny...and how might you find that out? You haven't started reading it yet.

S: You might ask someone who read the story.

R: And what do you do when you come to a word you do not know?

S: You could ask your mother.

R: Is there anything else you could do?

S: I skip and then read the other words and then when you have finished the sentence, you could go back to that letter and you can sound it what it is.

R: What do you do when you read something that does not make sense?

S: You might read the word that you don't know and you're not sure what it is.

R: Anything else?

S: No.

Although the SAIL students mentioned a descriptively greater number of comprehension and problem-solving strategies than non-SAIL students, their responses did not reflect a high degree of complex reasoning about why using strategies is so beneficial. Students exhibited some rudimentary knowledge of when to use strategies appropriately: They were able to respond to questions about what they did or thought before reading and when encountering problems. Also, students were starting to understand that strategies could be used flexibly, especially for problem solving. Mentioning several strategies may have suggested some prerequisite understanding about the adaptive use of strategies. However, students' responses typically did not indicate precise conditions under which certain strategies could be applied effectively.

In summary, by spring the SAIL students definitely reported more comprehension and word-level strategies during the interview than did comparison-group students. That SAIL students were already reporting more word-level strategies in the fall than comparison students probably reflected the effects of the first month or two of instruction in the program. By spring, every strategy except two was mentioned descriptively more often in the SAIL than in the comparison group. The exceptions were sounding it out (which was consistent with the teaching philosophy of the comparison teachers) and asking for help with a word (which is difficult to construe as a strategy associated with independence in reading). Most important, SAIL students learned more about comprehension and word-level strategies over the year than comparison students. However, in general, this information concentrated more on awareness and naming of strategies than on deep understanding of how strategic reasoning works. The results suggest that fully self-regulated thinking is the product of years of development. Perhaps, too, the questions were neither precise nor concrete enough to probe the understanding of young children in an in-depth manner. Furthermore, the students may not have been able to verbalize knowledge of their own strategic processing (Pressley & Afflerbach, 1995).

Spring Story Lessons

Teaching of the Lessons. The March–April lessons were transcribed from the videotape records, with the transcriptions read by four raters who were "blind" to condition.[4] One rater was a SAIL program developer, and the other three were graduate students familiar with transactional strategies instruction and the SAIL program in particular. The program developer correctly classified 9 of the 10 SAIL lessons as consistent with the intent and original vision of the SAIL program; this rater definitely was sensitive to whether teachers explained and modeled strategic processes and encouraged interpretive construction of text meaning by students through use of comprehension strategies. The curriculum developer looked for evidence that the teachers thought aloud in their lessons and coached students to engage text actively (i.e., to relate text content to prior knowledge as well as to apply other strategies as appropriate). He classified all the comparison lessons as not consistent with the SAIL approach and, in fact, not even close to being consistent with SAIL. The three graduate students correctly classified lessons as SAIL or non-SAIL for 59 of the 60 ratings made. Thus, there were clear instructional differences between the SAIL and non-SAIL classrooms during the March–April lessons.

Two raters reviewed the lessons (one rater was "blind" to condition) for evidence of strategies teaching, with interrater agreement of 85% and disagreements resolved by discussion (see Endnote 4). Collapsing across the two lessons observed for each teacher, a mean of 9.20 ($SD = 1.92$) different comprehension strategies were observed in the SAIL lessons compared to a mean of 2.00 ($SD = 0.71$) in the comparison lessons, $t(4) = 7.43$. Predicting, relating text to background knowledge, summarizing, and thinking aloud were observed in all SAIL groups. Only relating to background knowledge was observed in all comparison groups. In no SAIL group were fewer than seven of the comprehension strategies taught; in no comparison group were more than three observed.

On average, again collapsing across each participating reading group's two lessons, 4.80 ($SD = 0.45$) word-level strategies were observed in the SAIL groups, and 4.00 ($SD = 0.71$) were documented in the comparison reading groups, $t(4) = 4.00$. Using semantic context clues and using picture clues were observed in all SAIL groups; using picture clues and sounding words out were observed in all comparison classrooms. The range of word-level strategies was between 4 and 5 in the SAIL groups and between 3 and 5 in the comparison groups. Thus, one important indicator that the instruction in the SAIL groups differed from comparison instruction was that there was more strategies instruction in the SAIL groups. The difference was much more striking with respect to comprehension strategies, however.

Student Recall of Stories Covered in Lessons. The recall protocols were analyzed using a modified analytic induction approach (Goetz & LeCompte, 1984); that is, coding categories emerged from analysis of the data. However, identification of categories also was highly informed by the work of O'Flahavan (1989) and Eeds and Wells (1989). In this study, only the results of the literal and interpretive analyses are presented because only they relate directly to the stated hypotheses.

The full categorization scheme and analysis can be found in the work of Brown (1995a, 1995b). Both "Fox Trot" and "Mushroom in the Rain" were parsed into idea units, a variant of the T unit (Hunt, 1965). Loosely defined, an idea unit is a segment of written or oral discourse that conveys meaning, consisting of a verb form with any associated subject, object, and modifiers. Length or grammatical structure does not determine whether a segment is coded as an idea unit; what counts is whether the unit is meaningful. Interrater agreement was calculated for 20% of the recalled stories (see Endnote 4). It was 89% for classification of the protocols into idea units of various types (e.g., literal, interpretive).

A first issue addressed was whether SAIL students recalled more interpretive idea units than comparison students. These remarks reflected students' relating of background knowledge to text. Interpretive ideas were not explicitly stated in the text or in the pictures but did not contradict information in the text or pictures. For instance, for the Mushroom story, "He wanted to be dry" was scored as an interpretive remark. (The text had said, "One day an ant was caught in the rain. 'Where can I hide?' he wondered. He saw a little mushroom peeking out of the ground in a clearing and he hid under it.") Also, the comment "But they tricked him" was scored as an interpretive unit for the Mushroom story. (The corresponding text was, "'How could a rabbit get in here? Don't you see there isn't any room,' said the ant. The fox turned up his nose. He flicked his tail and ran off.") As a third example, one not corresponding to any specific part of the Mushroom story, the remark "And it was the only place to keep him dry" was coded as an interpretive remark because it was a conclusion that did not contradict anything in the text.

For the Mushroom story, SAIL groups averaged 6.12 interpretive units per student ($SD = 1.54$), which exceeded the corresponding figure of 4.48 in the comparison groups ($SD = 1.70$). $t(4) = 2.99$. For "Fox Trot," SAIL groups averaged 5.58 interpretive units per student ($SD = 1.63$), which exceeded the corresponding figure of 3.84 in the comparison groups ($SD = 1.63$), $t(4) = 2.97$.

In the example below, a SAIL student interjected a personalized interpretation into his retelling of story events. Interpreting occurred even though the task was not designed to elicit such information. The text stated that the frog asked the other animals if they knew what happened to a mushroom when it rained. He then hopped away, laughing. The student recall included the following response.

S: In the story, um um, the frog was just laughing because it was a miracle that came true. And the frog was laughing, the frog was laughing at them. And then really really when he was talking he said, "Don't you know what happens when it rains over a mushroom?" And they didn't know. They thought it was just a miracle, and when it was getting bigger it looked like a sleeping cap. So I think it was going wider and wider, and afterward when the sun came out and the fox was like an evil spirit, it went away. Um, they came, they came right out, and the mushroom was so big they didn't know what happened.

After the retelling was over, the researcher, curious about the origins of the student's interpretation, asked why he thought the fox was an evil spirit. The student replied, "Because it's like you know, the movies. And once there's this evil spirit and it's dark and nothing happens right. And once you kill it, the evil spirit, or if it goes away, and then it turns back into a good life." Thus, the student used his personal knowledge accrued from viewing movies to generate a unique interpretation that entered into his retelling.

In addition to scoring interpretive recall, we evaluated literal recall of ideas represented either in the stories or in the accompanying pictures. For example, one idea unit represented explicitly in the Mushroom story was "He hid under it." If the student recalled this idea unit or a paraphrase of it, the student was scored as having recalled the unit. In "Fox Trot," there was a picture of Carmen and Dexter looking through a window, watching Fox dance. One idea unit was scored as recalled if the student reported something like "His friends were looking at him dance from the window."

For the Mushroom story, SAIL reading groups recalled an average of 17.64 (out of a maximum of 79) literal idea units per student ($SD = 3.95$), which did not exceed literal recall in the comparison groups, who averaged 15.82 units ($SD = 1.31$), $t(4) = 1.10$. For "Fox Trot," however, SAIL recall ($M = 12.26$ out of a maximum of 59 units; $SD = 2.72$) exceeded comparison-group recall ($M = 8.38$, $SD = 2.94$), $t(4) = 2.60$.

In summary, SAIL students were significantly more interpretive in their recalls than comparison students, consistent with our expectations. Even though the questions called for literal recall of story content, SAIL students were more interpretive. This result is consistent with the conclusion that an interpretive propensity is internalized by TSI students. There were no strong expectations about the literal recall of the stories on the basis of condition, for we recognized that the comparison teachers covered the literal content of stories very well in their lessons. Even so, the students in the SAIL groups recalled more literal information than students in the comparison groups, although the difference favoring the SAIL students was significant for only one story.

One explanation of the story-recall results is that the SAIL story lessons were longer on average than the comparison-group lessons. Our impression throughout the conduct of this study was that SAIL students take more time when reading orally, with teachers frequently interjecting explicit explanations, requesting think-alouds, and elaborating responsively. Thus, we believe that at least the increased interpretations in the SAIL condition were due more to how time was spent in the SAIL lesson than to amount of time per se, although the design of this study does not permit a definitive conclusion on this point.

Spring Think-Aloud Analysis. The think-aloud protocols generated by each student in reaction to the Aesop's fable about the dog and his reflection were transcribed and analyzed using an analytic induction approach (Goetz & LeCompte, 1984). Two raters (one rater was "blind" to condition) read through all of the protocols, independently taking notes and identifying potential categories of reported reading processes (see Endnote 4). Through negotiation, a tentative set of process categories was identified, and these were applied by both raters independently to two protocols, one from a SAIL student and one from a comparison-group student. The two raters then met and refined the categories in light of the difficulties experienced scoring these two protocols. The refined categorization was applied to another pair of protocols, again independently by both raters. The refined categorizations captured all the processes represented in these protocols, and thus this set of processes was used to code all the think-aloud protocols.

A response with any indication of comprehension strategy use was coded as "strategy-based." For example, the following dialogue was coded as a strategies-based response.

> [The student read the page about the dog rushing out of the house with the piece of meat. The student then started to talk before the researcher asked an initial probe.]
>
> S: I think my prediction is coming out right. (verifying)
>
> R: Why do you say that?
>
> S: Cuz, cuz I see a bridge over there and water. (using picture clues)
>
> R: Uh huh....
>
> S: And he ran out of the house without anybody seeing him. Like I said before....
>
> R: Okay, so you think your prediction is right and you're using, you were pointing to the pictures.
>
> S: Yep.

The specific strategies used were also coded using the comprehension strategy definitions from the strategies interview, with 89% agreement between two raters on 20% of the protocols on these codings of specific strategies. The mean number of strategies evidenced by SAIL reading group members (averaging across all groups) was 6.93 ($SD = 1.46$). The corresponding comparison-group mean was 3.18 ($SD = 1.06$). The SAIL readers applied significantly more strategies during the think-aloud task than did the comparison-group students, $t(4) = 9.59$, $p < .05$.

In fact, there was no overlap in the group means, with SAIL group means ranging from 5.00 to 8.67 strategies used per student, on average, and corresponding comparison-group means ranging from 2.00 to 4.83. All strategies that were scored, except for one (monitoring), were observed descriptively more frequently in the SAIL than in the comparison protocols. The strategies that occurred in the SAIL condition, from most to least frequent, were as follows: predicting, relating text to prior knowledge, thinking aloud, summarizing, using picture clues, verifying, seeking clarification, monitoring, looking back, visualizing, and setting a goal. The corresponding order for the comparison condition was predicting, using picture clues, verifying, relating text to prior knowledge, monitoring, seeking clarification, thinking aloud, and looking back. No apparent visualizing, summarizing, and setting a goal were observed in the comparison-group think-alouds.

We also examined whether SAIL or comparison groups focused more on text- or reader-based information when they did not respond strategically. Responses not classified as strategies based were coded as either "text-based" or "reader-based" (interrater agreement on 20% of the protocols for classifying text- or reader-based responses was 94%).

Text-based responses contained information explicitly stated or pictured in the story. For example, after reading the first text segment, a student responded to the initial probe.

R: Okay, what are you thinking?

S: The dog stole something.

R: Uh huh...tell me more.

S: He knocked over the table.

R: He knocked over, talk nice and loud...he knocked things off the table... okay.

S: Yeah, and nothing really else.

R: Okay. And what do you think about what the dog did?

S: What do you mean?

R: What do you think about what the dog did?

S: He stole something.

Reader-based responses reflected a connection between the story and a student's prior knowledge, experiences, beliefs, or feelings. In the following example, a student read the segment about the dog stealing a piece of meat from the master's dinner table.

R: What are you thinking about what's happening on this page?

S: Sort of bad because I see that was part of their dinner, but they would not have all the uhm, protein.

R: Okay....

S: The dog ate all that....

Proportions were calculated for each class, indicating the relationship of text- and reader-based responses to the total number of responses that were not coded as strategies based. From these class proportions, SAIL and comparison-group means were computed. The mean for reader-based responding for the SAIL group was .74 (SD = 10). The mean proportion of reader-based responding for the comparison group was .45 (SD = 0.17). Thus, the SAIL group produced more reader-based responses than the comparison group, $t(4)$ = 3.61, $p <$ .05. Without exception, all SAIL classes were proportionally more interpretive than literal in their non–strategies-based responses. In contrast, only 2 of 5 comparison classes were proportionally more interpretive in their responses.

In summary, the SAIL students used strategies on their own more than the comparison students. Although strategy use by itself does not constitute self-regulation, it does suggest that students had begun to apply strategies independently, one aspect of self-regulated reading. Self-regulated readers are not only strategic; they also are goal-oriented, planful, and good comprehension monitors. Because we did not ask students to report directly on their strategic processing while reading, however, we cannot address those aspects.

In addition, the results of the think-aloud analysis supported the results of the recall analyses. For a story in which variable instructional time was not a factor, SAIL students made significantly more reader-based remarks than comparison students. The SAIL students responded more interpretively as well as personally.

Spring Standardized Test Performance

In May–June, the SAIL students outperformed the comparison students on the 40-item comprehension subtest. The reading group raw score mean in the SAIL condition was 34.20 (SD = 2.65); the corresponding comparison-group mean was 28.73 (SD = 3.77), $t(4)$ = 4.02 (see Table 1). The SAIL students also outperformed the comparison students on the 36-item word skills subtest, $t(4)$ = 3.98. The reading group word skills raw score mean in the SAIL condition in the spring was 27.10 (SD = 2.19); the corresponding comparison-group mean was 24.00 (SD = 1.53).

One of the most striking aspects of the spring comprehension standardized test data was the much lower variability among individual students within SAIL reading groups compared to comparison reading groups. (The careful matching of the reading groups in the fall was with respect to both mean performance *and* variability on standardized reading comprehension; thus, there was little difference in SAIL and comparison reading group variabilities in the fall, as reported in the Method section.) Also, with the exception of one pair of classes (T5 and T10), this lower variability among students in SAIL reading groups was evident in the spring word-study skills data. This finding is obvious from examination of the standard deviations for each matched pair of reading groups on the standardized subtests (see Table 1).

We believed that an especially strong demonstration of the efficacy of the SAIL program would be greater gains on standardized measures over the course of the academic year in SAIL versus the comparison condition. Thus, we tested the size of the fall-to-spring increase in raw scores in the SAIL versus the comparison groups. The SAIL group averaged 22.20 on an alternate form of the comprehension subtest ($SD = 6.85$) at the late fall testing, indicating a fall-to-spring gain of 12.00 ($SD = 5.20$) on average, and the comparison classes averaged 22.67 ($SD = 5.89$) in the fall, yielding a fall-to-spring change of 6.07 ($SD = 2.28$) on average. For the word skills subtest the fall SAIL mean was 20.97 ($SD = 2.76$), and the mean fall-to-spring increase was 6.13 ($SD = 1.86$). In the fall, the comparison mean was 21.10 ($SD = 3.40$), and the fall-to-spring mean difference was 2.90 ($SD = 2.70$). The one-tailed interaction hypothesis test was significant, as anticipated for the comprehension subtest, $t(4) = 3.70$. The word skills subtest proved significant as well, $t(4) = 5.41$.

In one of the matched pairs, there were some perfect scores on the comprehension posttest: The SAIL class mean was 36.83 ($SD = 2.40$); the non-SAIL class mean was 35.17 ($SD = 4.22$). For this pair of reading groups, a version of the next level of the Stanford Comprehension subtest (Primary 2, Form J) was then administered. Consistent with the analyses reported in the last two paragraphs, the spring SAIL group mean was greater than the matched comparison-group mean, and the SAIL group standard deviation was lower than the comparison-group standard deviation: SAIL $M = 29.8$, $SD = 5.42$; comparison-group $M = 21.8$, $SD = 10.17$. (The pretest Reading Comprehension subtest mean for the SAIL class was 33.83 [$SD = 7.28$]; the mean for the non-SAIL class was 32.17 [$SD = 6.88$]).

In summary, by academic year's end, the SAIL second-grade students clearly outperformed the comparison-group students on standardized tests, with greater improvement on the standardized measures over the course of the academic year in the SAIL condition. Unfortunately, no additional end-of-year achievement data existed for the students for comparison purposes either in reading or in any other subject area.

On the standardized tests, gains in comprehension were expected because, more than anything else, SAIL is intended to increase students' understanding of text. The effects on students' word skills performance were more of a surprise, albeit a pleasant one, supportive of the SAIL intervention; we knew that all teachers, regardless of condition, taught phonics and word attack skills, although at different times of day (e.g., integrated into various content areas) and in different ways (e.g., covered in the form of worksheets or minilessons).

Discussion

We made many informal and formal observations throughout the 1991–1992 school year indicating that instruction in the SAIL and comparison classes was very different. The differences were apparent in the two lessons that were analyzed in the spring: A SAIL curriculum developer and several graduate students who were familiar with transactional strategies instruction had no difficulty discriminating between transcripts of SAIL and non-SAIL lessons. One important difference highlighted in the analysis of the spring lessons was that discussion of strategies was much more prominent in the SAIL than in the comparison reading groups. That the differences in teaching were so clear bolsters our confidence in this study as a valid assessment of the efficacy of SAIL with at-risk second-grade children.

SAIL had positive short-term and long-term impacts. In the short term, students acquired more information from stories read in reading group and developed a richer, more personalized understanding of the stories. Whether the focus is on the amount of literal information recalled from stories covered in reading group or student interpretations of the texts read, there were indications in these data of superior performance by SAIL students relative to the comparison students. We infer that SAIL students learn more daily from their reading group lessons than do students receiving more conventional second-grade reading instruction.

SAIL had long-term impacts as well. Consistent with our expectations, the SAIL students exhibited greater awareness of strategies by the end of the year than the comparison students. SAIL students also reported use of, or were inferred to use, strategies more than the comparison students: They thought aloud while reading the Aesop's fable at the end of the year. The standardized test performances of the SAIL students also were superior to those of the comparison students at the end of the year. Most critically, there was significantly greater improvement on standardized measures of reading comprehension from fall to spring in the SAIL versus the comparison classrooms. In short, all measurements of student reading achievement reported here converged on the conclusion that a year of SAIL instruction improves the reading of at-risk second-grade students more than does alternative high-quality reading instruction.

This study is the strongest formal evidence to date that transactional strategies instruction improves the reading of elementary-level students. There were many elements taken into consideration in this study that varied freely in more informal comparisons of SAIL and alternative instruction, such as ones generated by the school district that developed the intervention: (a) The student participants were carefully matched in this investigation so that there was no striking difference in their standardized reading achievement at the outset of the study. (b) The teachers were carefully selected. From years of observing and interviewing committed SAIL teachers, we knew that they are excellent teachers in general, who offer rich language arts experiences for their students. Thus, it was imperative that a compelling evaluation of SAIL be in comparison to excellent second-grade instruction. Accordingly, we sought highly regarded comparison teachers. (c) The lessons analyzed in the transactional strategies instruction and comparison groups involved the groups processing the same stories. (d) The same dependent measures were administered by the same tester so that measurement experiences were equivalent for participants.

Another strength of this evaluation was that it did not rely only on standardized assessments but also included assessments of students' reading that were grounded in their typical classroom experiences. The assessments of children's memories for and interpretations of stories read in class reflect better the day-to-day comprehension demands on students than do standardized measures. Although thinking-aloud measures are far from perfect indicators of thinking (Ericsson & Simon, 1980), the assessments of children's thinking as they read the Aesop's fable arguably tapped more directly the thinking processes of the children that SAIL was intended to change than did the standardized assessments.

Are the outcomes reported here generally significant beyond the specifics of the SAIL program? SAIL is a specific instantiation of reading comprehension strategies instruction as adapted by educators. Such instruction may serve as a model for other educators. SAIL provides teachers with a way to blend critical elements of direct teaching and holistic principles of instruction, aspects of instruction that may already exist in conventional reading classrooms. Because many conventional programs already share features with SAIL (e.g., literature-based instruction, teaching of predicting and problem-solving strategies), these programs might be modified to include SAIL components.

As we argued at the beginning of this article, long-term, direct explanation of thinking processes and scaffolded practice of a manageable repertoire of powerful comprehension strategies constitute an approach replicated in a number of settings (see also Pressley & El-Dinary, 1993; Pressley, El-Dinary, et al., 1992, for a number of examples). The practice has raced ahead of the science, however, with the educator-developed adaptations more ambitious in scope, more complex, and ultimately very different from the researcher-validated interventions (e.g., reciprocal teaching) that inspired the educator efforts. There is a real need to evaluate such adaptations, for there is no guarantee that the strategies instruction validated in basic research studies is effective once it is translated and transformed dramatically by educators.

The research reported here contrasts with basic research on strategies instruction in a number of ways. First, the intervention studied here was multicomponential, and this study was not analytical at all with respect to components of the intervention. Typically, basic strategies instruction research has been much more analytical. We can defend this evaluation of an entire transactional strategies instruction package because the whole program is the unit of instruction in the schools we have been studying: When the interest is in whether an instructional package as a whole works, a study evaluating that whole relative to other instruction is definitely defensible, particularly if time spent in direct instructional activities is controlled carefully (e.g., in this study, both groups of students received a year of reading instruction in the context of a full year in the second grade). Moreover, it was not our intent to tease out which aspects of the program were most effective nor to determine which components in combination accounted for student gains, especially because we believe that the complex instruction exemplified by SAIL may be more than the sum of its component parts (Pressley, El-Dinary, et al., 1992).

Second, the program of research that includes this study is a mix of qualitative and quantitative research. In contrast, most basic studies of strategies have been quantitative only. We are certain that the quantitative study reported here would have been impossible without the 3 years of qualitative research leading up to it. At a minimum, that qualitative research affected the selection of dependent measures and the decision to study only accomplished SAIL teachers (see Pressley, Schuder, et al., 1992). More generally, it made obvious to us the scope of an investigation necessary to evaluate transactional strategies instruction so that the treatment would not be compromised by the evaluation.

Third, most basic strategies research is designed and conducted by researchers. When educators have participated in basic studies, it has been as delivery agents only. In the program of transactional strategies instruction research, researchers, program developers, and educators have combined their talents to produce a body of research that realistically depicts transactional strategies instruction and evaluates it fairly. As the study was designed and as it unfolded, school-based educators were consulted frequently about the appropriateness of potential dependent measures and operations of the study. The result has been a much more complete and compelling set of descriptions of transactional strategies instruction and, now, a thorough appraisal of the impact of one transactional strategies instruction program on second-grade, weaker readers.

We do not claim that after 1 year of transactional strategies instruction these students have become self-regulated readers. Pressley and Afflerbach (1995) made the point that truly self-regulated reading is observed only in very mature readers. It has always been suggested that TSI needs to occur over the long term to be effective (Pressley, El-Dinary, et al., 1992). Our hypothesis is that true self-regulation is the product of years of literacy experiences, with TSI intended to get the process off to a good start. One year of such instruction at least gets second-grade readers who are experiencing difficulties in learning to read to improve their reading relative to a year for comparable students in very good conventional classrooms.

Acknowledgments

The work reported in this article was supported in part by the Educational Research and Development Center Program, National Reading Research Center (NRRC, University of Maryland; PR/AWARD No. 117A20007, as administered by the Office of Educational Research and Improvement (OERI), U.S. Department of Education. The findings and opinions do not necessarily reflect the opinions or policies of NRRC, OERI, or the U.S. Department of Education. We are grateful for the input of a number of University of Maryland and school-based collaborators, including Pamela B. El-Dinary, Jan Bergman, Laura Barden, Marsha York, and the 10 teachers who so graciously permitted this research to be conducted in their classrooms during 1991–1992.

Notes

[1] We recognize that some readers may be concerned about the mean difference in years of teaching between the SAIL and non-SAIL teachers. In this study, the SAIL and non-SAIL classes were matched as closely as possible. The primary criteria for matching classes were demographic in nature. To the extent that it was possible, we used student mobility patterns, Chapter 1 status, ethnic and minority composition, size and location of schools, and standardized test performances. At the time, years of teaching experience did not seem to be as critical as some of the other factors. Given our decision, there is no way to separate out the effect that years of experience may have had on the way teachers taught their students. However, readers should bear in mind that the comparison teachers were highly regarded for their teaching abilities by district personnel; therefore, if anything, their greater number of years of experience could be construed as an advantage.

[2] All class means were based on 6 students with the exception of the following, which reduced this number because of either data loss or absence: Strategies interviews: 1 student in two non-SAIL classes (pretest), 1 student in one SAIL class (posttest); retellings: 1 student in one SAIL class ("Mushroom" story), 1 student in one SAIL class ("Fox Trot" story); think-aloud task: 2 students in one SAIL class.

[3] One reviewer strongly felt that the skipping strategy was not as "good" or "useful" as some of the other strategies students reported using. Consequently, we are providing data so that readers can compare the two groups specifically on the skipping strategy. For the fall strategies interview, the SAIL sum of mean frequencies by group for skipping as a word attack strategy was 3.93 (SD = 0.35), and the non-SAIL summed mean was .94 (SD = 0.70), $t(4)$ = 8.20, $p < .05$. For the spring strategies interview, the SAIL summed group mean for skipping as a word attack strategy was 4.33 (SD = 1.10), and the non-SAIL summed mean was 1.47 (SD = 1.55), $t(4)$ = 5.36, $p < .05$. The interaction was $t(4) = -0.36$, $p > .05$. For the fall strategies interview, the SAIL sum of mean frequencies by group for skipping as a *comprehension strategy* (i.e., ignoring a larger segment of text and reading on) was .17 (SD = 0.40), and the non-SAIL summed mean was .57 (SD = 0.50), $t(4)$ = –1.10, $p > .05$. For the spring strategies interview, the SAIL summed group mean frequency was 2.47 (SD = 1.25) and the non-SAIL mean frequency was .83 (SD = 0.80), $t(4)$ = 2.14, $p < .05$. The interaction was also significant, $t(4)$ = 2.20. (The permutation test for the interaction was not significant, however, because of one tie in the data.)

[4] We recognize that to rule out possible alternative explanations of the results, the two raters conducting interrater agreement should be "blind." However, there is a perspective held by some qualitative researchers that the use of blind raters does not do justice to the analysis of data because the blind rater has spent so little time immersed in the experiences that have led to the primary researcher's breadth of understanding. Thus, "expecting another investigator to have the same insight from a limited data base is unrealistic" (Morse, 1994, p. 231). We concurred to some extent with this argument; however, in attempting to reconcile positions, we opted for only one rater to be blind. In that way, the blind rater could lend credibility to the nonblind researcher's interpretations. In attempting to strike a balance, the nonblind researcher often deferred to the blind rater's opinion when a stalemate was reached. Also, when the primary researcher was unsure how to interpret the data in the transcripts and protocols that were not subjected to interrater agreement, the "blind" rater frequently assisted in the coding of the questionable segment or unit.

References

Allington, R.L. (1991). The legacy of "Slow it down and make it concrete." In J. Zutell & S. McCormick (Eds.), *Learner factors/teacher factors: Issues in literacy research and instruction* (40th yearbook of the National Reading Conference, pp. 19–29). Chicago: National Reading Conference.

Baker, L., & Brown. A.L. (1984). Metacognitive skills and reading. In P.D. Pearson, R. Barr, M.L. Kamil, & P. Mosenthal (Eds.), *Handbook of reading research* (pp. 353–394). New York: Longman.

Bell, R.Q. (1968). A reinterpretation of the direction of effects in studies of socialization. *Psychological Review, 75*, 81–95.

Bereiter, C., & Bird, M. (1985). Use of thinking aloud in identification and teaching of reading comprehension strategies. *Cognition and Instruction, 2*, 131–156.

Bergman, J., & Schuder, R.T. (1992). Teaching at-risk elementary school students to read strategically. *Educational Leadership, 50*(4), 19–23.

Brown, R. (1995a). *A quasi-experimental validation study of strategies-based instruction for low-achieving, primary-level readers.* Unpublished doctoral dissertation, University of Maryland at College Park.

Brown, R. (1995b, April). *The teaching practices of strategies-based and non-strategies-based teachers of reading.* Paper presented at the annual meeting of the American Education Research Association, San Francisco, CA.

Brown, R., & Coy-Ogan, L. (1993). The evolution of transactional strategies instruction in one teacher's classroom. *The Elementary School Journal, 94*, 221–233.

Brown, R., & Pressley, M. (1994). Self-regulated reading and getting meaning from text: The transactional strategies instruction model and its ongoing evaluation. In D. Schunk & B. Zimmerman (Eds.), *Self-regulation of learning and performance: Issues and educational applications* (pp. 155–179). Hillsdale, NJ: Erlbaum.

Cohen, J. (1988). *Statistical power analysis for the behavioral sciences* (2nd ed.). Hillsdale, NJ: Erlbaum.

Collins, C. (1991). Reading instruction that increases thinking abilities. *Journal of Reading, 34*, 510–516.

DeFord, D. (1985). Theoretical orientation to reading instruction. *Reading Research Quarterly, 20*, 351–367.

Dole, J.A., Duffy, G.G., Roehler, L.R., & Pearson. P.D. (1991). Moving from the old to the new: Research on reading comprehension instruction. *Review of Educational Research, 61*, 239–264.

Duffy, G.G., Roehler, L.R., Sivan, E., Rackliffe, G., Book, C., Meloth, M.S., et al. (1987). Effects of explaining the reasoning associated with using reading strategies. *Reading Research Quarterly, 22*, 347–368.

Durkin, D. (1978/1979). What classroom observations reveal about reading comprehension instruction. *Reading Research Quarterly, 12*, 481–538.

Eeds, M., & Wells, D. (1989). Grand conversations: An exploration of meaning construction in literature study groups. *Research in the Teaching of English, 23*, 4–29.

El-Dinary, P.B., & Schuder, R.T. (1993). Seven teachers' acceptance of transactional strategies instruction during their first year using it. *The Elementary School Journal, 94*, 207–219.

Ericsson, K.A., & Simon, H.A. (1980). Verbal reports as data. *Psychological Review, 87*, 215–251.

Garner, R. (1988). Verbal report data on cognitive and metacognitive strategies. In C.E. Weinstein, E.T. Goetz, & P.A. Alexander (Eds.), *Learning and study strategies: Issues in assessment, instruction, and evaluation* (pp. 63–76). San Diego, CA: Academic Press.

Gaskins, I.W., Anderson, R.C., Pressley, M., Cunicelli. E.A., & Satlow, E. (1993). Six teachers' dialogue during cognitive process instruction. *The Elementary School Journal, 93*, 277–304.

Ginsburg, M. (1991). Mushroom in the rain. In D. Alvermann, C.A. Bridge, B.A. Schmidt, L.W. Searfoss, P. Winograd, & S.G. Paris (Eds.), *My best bear hug* (pp. 144–154). Lexington, MA: Heath.

Goetz, J.P., & LeCompte, M.D. (1984). *Ethnography and qualitative design in educational research.* San Diego, CA: Academic Press.

Golden, J.M. (1988). The construction of a literary text in a story-reading lesson. In J.L. Green & J.O. Harker (Eds.), *Multiple perspective analyses of classroom discourse* (pp. 71–106). Norwood, NJ: Ablex.

Harris, A.J., & Sipay, E.R. (1985). *How to increase reading ability: A guide to developmental and remedial methods.* New York: Longman.

Hunt, K.W. (1965). *Grammatical structures written at three grade levels* (NCTE Research Report No. 3). Champaign, IL: National Council of the Teachers of English.

Hutchins, E. (1991). The social organization of distributed cognition. In L. Resnick, J.M. Levine, & S.D. Teasley (Eds.), *Perspectives on socially shared cognition* (pp. 283–307). Washington, DC: American Psychological Association.

Johnston, P., & Afflerbach, P. (1985). The process of constructing main ideas from text. *Cognition and Instruction, 2*, 207–232.

Kirk, R.E. (1982). *Experimental design* (2nd ed.). Monterey, CA: Brooks/Cole.

Lytle, S.L. (1982). *Exploring comprehension style: A study of twelfth-grade readers' transactions with text.* Unpublished doctoral dissertation, University of Pennsylvania. (UMI No. 82-27292)

Marks, M.B., Pressley, M., Coley, J.D., Craig, S., Gardner, R., DePinto, T., et al. (1993). Three teachers' adaptations of reciprocal teaching in comparison to traditional reciprocal teaching. *The Elementary School Journal, 94*, 267–283.

Marshall, E. (1982). *Fox in love.* New York: Penguin.

Mehan, H. (1979). *Learning lessons: Social organization in the classroom.* Cambridge, MA: Harvard University Press.

Meichenbaum, D. (1977). *Cognitive-behavior modification: An integrative approach.* New York: Plenum.

Miller, J.P. (1976). *Tales from Aesop.* New York: Random House.

Morse, J.M. (1994). Designing funded qualitative research. In N.K. Denzin & Y.S. Lincoln (Eds.), *Handbook of qualitative research* (pp. 220–235). Thousand Oaks, CA: Sage.

O'Flahavan, J.F. (1989). *Second graders' social, intellectual, and affective development in varied group discussions about literature: An exploration of participation structure.* Unpublished doctoral dissertation, University of Illinois at Urbana-Champaign.

Olshavsky, J.E. (1976/1977). Reading as problem-solving: An investigation of strategies. *Reading Research Quarterly, 12*, 654–674.

Olson, G.M., Mack, R.L., & Duffy, S.A. (1981). Cognitive aspects of genre. *Poetics, 10*, 283–315.

Palincsar, A.S., & Brown, A.L. (1984). Reciprocal teaching of comprehension-fostering and comprehension-monitoring activities. *Cognition and Instruction, 1*, 117–175.

Paris, S., & Oka, E.R. (1986). Children's reading strategies, metacognition, and motivation. *Developmental Review, 6*, 25–56.

Pressley, M., & Afflerbach, P. (1995). *Verbal protocols of reading: The nature of constructively responsive reading.* Hillsdale, NJ: Erlbaum.

Pressley, M., & El-Dinary, P.B. (Guest Eds.). (1993). Special issue on strategy instruction. *The Elementary School Journal, 94*(2).

Pressley, M., El-Dinary, P.B., Gaskins, I., Schuder, T., Bergman, J.L., Almasi, J., et al. (1992). Beyond direct explanation: Transactional instruction of reading comprehension strategies. *The Elementary School Journal, 92*, 513–555.

Pressley, M., Gaskins, I.W., Cunicelli, E.A., Burdick, N.J., Schaub-Matt, M., Lee, D.S., et al. (1991). Strategy instruction at Benchmark School: A faculty interview study. *Learning Disability Quarterly, 14*, 19–48.

Pressley, M., Goodchild, R., Fleet, J., Zajchowski, R., & Evans, E.D. (1989). The challenges of classroom strategy instruction. *The Elementary School Journal, 89*, 301–342.

Pressley, M., Johnson, C.J., Symons, S., McGoldrick, J.A., & Kurita, J.A. (1989). Strategies that improve children's memory and comprehension of text. *The Elementary School Journal, 90*, 3–32.

Pressley, M., Schuder, T., Teachers in the Students Achieving Independent Learning Program, Bergman, J.L., & El-Dinary, P.B. (1992). A researcher–educator collaborative interview study of transactional comprehension strategies instruction. *Journal of Educational Psychology, 84*, 231–246.

The Psychological Corporation. (1990). *Stanford Achievement Test Series: Technical data report* (8th ed.). San Diego, CA: Harcourt Brace Jovanovich.

Rosenblatt, L.M. (1979). *The reader, the text, the poem: The transactional theory of literary work.* Carbondale: Southern Illinois University Press.

Rosenshine, B., & Meister, C. (1994). Reciprocal teaching: A review of the research. *Review of Educational Research, 64*, 479–530.

Schuder, R.T. (1993). The genesis of transactional strategies instruction in a reading program for at-risk students. *The Elementary School Journal, 94*, 183–200.

Vygotsky, L.S. (1978). *Mind in society: The development of higher psychological processes* (M. Cole, V. John-Steiner. S. Scriber, & E. Souberman, Eds. & Trans.). Cambridge, MA: Harvard University Press. (Original work published 1934)

Wyatt, D., Pressley, M., El-Dinary, P.B., Stein, S., Evans, P., & Brown, R. (1993). Comprehension strategies, worth and credibility monitoring, and evaluations: Cold and hot cognition when experts read professional articles that are important to them. *Learning and Individual Differences, 5*, 49–72.

Appendix: Summary of "Mushroom in the Rain" Lessons

SAIL Teachers

Teacher 1. The teacher reviewed what expert readers do. She questioned students about the strategies good readers apply when reading. She augmented their responses, explaining some benefits of strategies use. She reviewed with students what they could do when they came to an unknown word (e.g., use picture clues, guess, skip, look back in text). She also focused on verbalizing thinking, summarizing, and visualizing. She asked students to browse through pages and make predictions. A student predicted that the story might be like "The Mitten," a story the group had read earlier in the year. Students discussed possible connections between the two stories. The teacher directed students to verify their predictions as they read and had them visualize a descriptive segment. Students took turns reading. When they finished reading, students either thought aloud spontaneously or were cued to do so by the teacher. Thinking aloud consisted of summarizing content, voicing an opinion, suggesting an interpretation, making or refining predictions, or relating text content to background knowledge or personal experiences. After the reader thought aloud, other students were encouraged to elaborate, persuade, or counter the interpretation.

Students frequently supported their interpretations with background knowledge or text clues. Students continued to discuss similarities and differences between "Mushroom in the Rain" and "The Mitten." For example, they debated whether the mushroom was growing or stretching. Students practiced sequencing by summarizing story content. During discussions, the teacher restated students' responses, clarified confusions, sought elaborations, and garnered opinions from group members. When students faced a word they did not know, they were urged to use one of their "fix-up" strategies. The teacher generally did not ask specific questions about text details. At the end of the lesson, students verified their predictions and fine-tuned their interpretations using text information and background knowledge. Several students admitted they were confused by aspects of the story. When the teacher asked what they could do about this, a student suggested they reread the story. The teacher replied that a good strategy to clarify confusions was rereading. The lesson ended with a student summarizing the story.

Teacher 2. The teacher reviewed what good readers do. Students described the various strategies and evaluated their usefulness. When students talked about visualizing, the teacher explained a personal use of the strategy. The teacher discussed with students the flexible application of a coordinated set of strategies. She encouraged students to use their strategies during story reading. The teacher told students she would focus on visualizing in the lesson. She read the title and first page, modeling her thinking as she visualized text content and made connections between the story and her experiences. She encouraged students to relate the story to their own experiences. Without prompting, a student predicted that the story would be like "The Mitten," a story the class read earlier in the year. The teacher asked the student to support his claim. Students took turns reading aloud. When they came to an unknown word, they often used strategies without teacher prompting. When they needed help, the teacher cued them to use one of their problem-solving strategies ("fix-it kit"). After reading a page, students would think aloud on their own or be prompted to do so by the teacher. When thinking aloud, students summarized story content, made predictions, or offered interpretations. Other students would then respond to the first student's remarks.

Students continually discussed how "Mushroom in the Rain" was similar to "The Mitten." The group referred to different versions of the story. At one point, a student observed that the animals going under the mushroom were increasing in size. When observations like this one were given by students, the teacher told the group to bear them in mind as they read. Students made and verified predictions frequently and related events to their background knowledge and personal experiences. They elaborated on each other's ideas. During discussions, the teacher did not state her own opinion. Instead, she rephrased students' comments or sought elaboration. When the group thought about what happens to a mushroom in the rain, some students believed the mushroom grew; others countered that the animals stretched it. The teacher allowed students to choose the interpretation they favored. The teacher praised students for their use of strategies, such as making connections between "The Mitten" and "Mushroom in the Rain." She encouraged the group to continue to use strategies in future years because they would help them become better readers.

Comparison Teachers

Teacher 7. The teacher reviewed new words that were presented on cards in the context of sentences. Students were prompted to use the word attack strategies they had been practicing: looking at the first sound, proceeding to the vowel, and then seeing if the word had a suffix. Students took turns reading the story aloud. When students had difficulty, the teacher prompted them to use their word attack strategies and sometimes she gave them the word. After students read, the teacher periodically summarized what had transpired. She drew students' attention to the illustrations. She asked students literal and interpretive comprehension questions about the text, activated their background knowledge, solicited their opinions, and allowed divergence in interpretations (e.g., "Does the ant want to share the mushroom? What does the mushroom remind you of? What do you use in the rain?"). These questions typically did not generate extended discussion. When a student mentioned that the butterfly couldn't fly because his wings were wet, the teacher reminded students of their unit on butterflies. One topic students had been learning about was "persuasion": The teacher related this topic to the way the animals were persuading the ant to let them under the mushroom. After reading a section, the teacher often asked students what they were thinking. The teacher taught new vocabulary in context, relating word meanings to students' background knowledge.

At one point, the teacher drew a mushroom on the board. She asked students to tell her the order of animals that went under the mushroom. She questioned how all the animals fit under the mushroom. She related this story to other stories students had read. One student said the mushroom grew because of the rain. She confirmed that mushrooms grow rapidly in the rain. When students faced unfamiliar words, she directed them to apply their word attack strategies and knowledge of phonics (e.g., "Good boy, it's got that double *p* to keep that *o* short....") After reading one section, she drew students' attention to the quotation marks, colon, commas, and exclamation mark that were on the page. She asked for predictions, without requesting support for students' ideas. Some interpretive discussion occurred around the nature and motives of the fox. When adding the fox to the sequencing on the chalkboard, she said, "When you're making a sequence and you're writing a story or reading it, sometimes it's nice to make an illustration, and then you can add words underneath it to help you organize, get things in, what happened first, second, third, next, and then final." After reading, the teacher frequently drilled students on word skills, using words from the story. Students received a "point" for answering questions correctly. She asked students to find words with suffixes and base words. She frequently provided direct instruction of rules (e.g., making plurals from singular forms; "To keep the *i* short before you add a suffix that begins with a vowel like *-er*, *-ing*, *est*,...*-ious*, we have to make sure there's two consonants, to double the letter."). Periodically, she complimented students on their thinking. After reading, students pretended to touch a mushroom. She asked for descriptive words and similes. At the end of the lesson, the teacher told students to visualize to help them remember the ordering of story events. She informed students that they would retell and illustrate the story the next day.

Teacher 10. The teacher stated the title of the story. She asked the students to read the first three pages silently, looking for words they did not know. As students pointed out unfamiliar words, the teacher helped them with word clues. For example, she said that "one of the ways we can find out what a word is sometimes, if we're not too sure of it, is to see if there are little tiny word clues inside of a big word and that will help sound out the word.... That's a good word attack skill." The teacher then had a student read the first page. She directed the group to look at the illustration. She told them to notice the size of the mushroom and to watch out for what happens. There was little discussion during story reading. However, at one point, a student volunteered that the story was like "The Mitten."

The teacher did not elaborate on the student's comment except to say, "let's see what happens." Toward the end of the story, the teacher asked what happened to the mushroom. One student said the mushroom grew. When the teacher asked why, he answered that it was because "the water came in the soil and made it grow." At the end of the story, the teacher said that the student "found the secret. That was the secret of how they all fit." Others concurred. One student pointed to the picture of the mushroom getting bigger. The teacher elaborated, "All right, so S found out because he was watching the pictures and getting a clue from the pictures." The group talked a little more about plants needing lots of water to grow. The teacher asked students to tell about any character they liked and what they liked about him. Several students gave opinions.

Discussion then centered on the fox's nature. Students used their prior knowledge to state that the fox was smart. The teacher redirected students to a specific page, asking them to look for a clue. The students recognized that the fox was tricked, and they changed their minds. The group spent much time discussing this episode and looking at the picture. The teacher asked students to fold a piece of paper into four sections. She asked them to draw in order what happened to the mushroom, telling them they could refer to the book for help. She guided them through the activity. The teacher then asked students to suggest alternate endings. Several students responded. She asked students to web the character traits of one of the animals. She told them to "go back into your story and see if there are any story clues...and think of some words that would describe that particular character." Students took turns sharing their webs and descriptive words. The teacher asked if they liked the story and whether "it had a nice moral to it. Was it a good lesson about kindness?" Students assented but did not discuss their reasons. She suggested students put new words they learned in their ABC books (i.e., personal word books).

38

Beating the Odds: Teaching Middle and High School Students to Read and Write Well

Judith A. Langer

This is a report of a 5-year study focusing on characteristics of educational practice that accompany student achievement in reading, writing, and English. English classrooms have long been considered places where "high literacy" (Bereiter & Scardamalia, 1987) is learned, where students gain not merely the basic literacy skills to get by, but also the content knowledge, ways of structuring ideas, and ways of communicating with others that are considered the "marks" of an educated person (Graff, 1987). To distinguish this kind of literacy from the more popular notion of literacy as a set of "basic" reading and writing skills, in this work I define the term *high literacy* in an everyday sense to refer to the literacy gained from a well-developed middle and high school English curriculum. Although basic reading and writing skills are included in this definition of high literacy, also included are the ability to use language, content, and reasoning in ways that are appropriate for particular situations and disciplines. Students learn to "read" the social meanings, the rules, and structures, and the linguistic and cognitive routines to make things work in the real world of English-language use, and that knowledge becomes available as options when students confront new situations. This notion of high literacy refers to understanding how reading, writing, language, content, and social appropriateness work together, and using this knowledge in effective ways. It is reflected in students' ability to engage in thoughtful reading, writing, and discussion about content in the classroom, to put their knowledge and skills to use in new situations, and to perform well on reading and writing assessments including high-stakes testing.

From *American Educational Research Journal*, *38*(4), 837–880. Copyright © 2001 by the American Educational Research Association. Reprinted with permission of the publisher.

Theoretical Framework

This work is anchored in a sociocognitive perspective (especially Bakhtin, 1981; Vygotsky, 1987; see Langer, 1986, 1995). From this perspective, learning is seen to be influenced by the values, experiences, and actions that exist within the larger environment. Students' and teachers' voices and experiences, learned within the primary and secondary communities to which they belong (see Gee, 1996), make a contribution to what gets learned and how it is learned. It is largely from these diverse contexts that notions of what counts as appropriate knowledge and effective communication gain their meaning. Bakhtin (1981), in his conceptualization of dialogic thinking and the multivocal nature of language and thought, offers us a way to think about high literacy and its development. Rather than seeing it as composed of independent skills or proficiencies that are called upon at needed moments, he offers us a vision in which the educated individual calls upon a multilayered history of experiences with language and content, cutting across many contexts—assuming that multiple and sometimes competing voices (or ways of interpreting) add richness and depth to emerging ideas. For example, he argues that the discourse of a nation includes an awareness of the special experiences and rhetorics of many subgroups; we recognize and respond differently, he says, to the characteristic prose of doctors, lawyers, or clergy, ways of communication and interpretation that stand in dialogue with one another rather than being reconciled into a single "common" discourse. Such diverse voices also occur both within and across classrooms and subject areas (Applebee, 1996), as students bring the voices of their out-of-school experiences as well as the conversations within their particular academic courses to bear on the topic at hand. Students are enculturated to understand and use these voices (or perspectives) across the grades; their growing proficiency is shaped by the interactions that are fostered in the classrooms in which they participate. It is largely from these diverse contexts that notions of what counts as appropriate knowledge and effective communication gain their meaning. From this perspective, in a learning environment, students and teachers call upon the voices they have already acquired and are given opportunities to gain new voices. They also have opportunities to hone their ability to sift through these multiple sources in understanding purposes and audiences, creating effective ideas and arguments, and entering forms of discourse that help them move forward.

Vygotsky's sociocultural framework (1987) offers a way to conceptualize teacher and student learning as occurring within an environment in which both can participate in thoughtful examination and discourse about language and content because it is an integral part of the social way the educational environment operates and gets work done. The related views of situative theorists (e.g., Brown, Collins, & Daguid, 1989; Greeno, 1997; Greeno & the Middle School Through Applications Group, 1988; Lave & Wenger, 1991) posit that the way in which people learn particular knowledge and skills is reliant on the environment in which the learning takes place; environment is a fundamental part of what gets learned, how it is interpreted, and how it is used. Beginning from this theoretical frame, the present project sought to examine the deeply contextualized nature of both teaching and learning (Dyson, 1993; Myers, 1996; Turner, 1993) in more- and less-successful middle and high school English classrooms.

Related Research

Although there is a long tradition of research examining specific features of writing and literature instruction (cf. Hillocks, 1986; Purves & Beach, 1972), there have been few previous attempts to study the characteristics of more- and less-effective English programs as a whole at the secondary level. One of the earliest was Squire and Applebee's (1968) examination of 158 programs in the 1960s. Although Squire and Applebee had intended to contrast "award winning" with "recommended" programs, they found few differences between their two samples. Their report is useful for its description of best practice, as well as common problems, in the programs they studied. Overall, these programs were marked by the professionalism of the teachers, the availability of resources for instruction, an emphasis on the teaching of literature, and a general lack of attention to the needs of lower-track students.

In a later study that focused on literature instruction, Applebee (1993) surveyed three groups of unusually successful English programs (programs that consistently produced winners in the national Achievement Awards in Writing competition, programs designated as Centers of Excellence by the National Council of Teachers of English, and programs nominated as excellent by administrators and university colleagues) and contrasted them with random samples of private and public English programs. As in the earlier Squire and Applebee study, teachers in the more successful programs tended to be more highly professionalized, to have more adequate resources available, and to enjoy more community support for their efforts. They were also more likely to be influenced by recent reform movements in the teaching of English, emphasizing process-oriented writing instruction, active involvement of students in discussion, and reader-response approaches to literature. Such differences were differences in degree rather than in kind from programs in the random samples of schools, and in general reflect the advantages that flow from better funding rather than from different approaches to curriculum and instruction. Although the 25 years between the Squire and Applebee (1968) and Applebee (1993) studies led to many differences in specific aspects of curriculum and instruction in English, there is no way to link any of these differences to student achievement.

At the elementary level, a number of studies have examined curriculum and instruction in classrooms where students have made unusual progress in reading and writing achievement, in contrast with classrooms where achievement is more typical. Wharton-McDonald, Pressley, and Hampston (1998), for example, studied 9 first-grade teachers in New York state who differed in their effectiveness in promoting literacy. In the most effective classrooms, there was a high level of engagement in challenging literacy activities, a web of interconnections among tasks (so that writing, for example, was often related to what was being read), and skills were taught explicitly but in connection with real reading and writing activities. In a related study, Pressley et al. (1998) studied 30 first-grade classrooms in five states, contrasting typical teachers with outstanding teachers in the same school. The most effective teachers were again characterized by high academic engagement in challenging literacy tasks, explicit teaching of skills, interconnections among activities, and careful matching of tasks and instruction to student competence levels.

Taylor, Pearson, Clark, and Walpole (1999) investigated school and classroom factors related to primary-grade reading achievement in a sample of 14 schools identified as most, moderately, or least effective on several measures of reading achievement. At the school level, important factors included parental support, systematic assessment of student progress, good communication among staff within the building, and a collaborative model for the delivery of reading instruction. At the classroom level, significant factors included more use of small-group instruction, more time for independent reading, high levels of engagement in higher-level literacy tasks, the use of scaffolding to link skill instruction to real reading tasks, and strong links between school and home.

However, no studies have focused on the features of instruction that differentiate English achievement in higher- versus lower-performing middle and high school programs. In the present study, I have examined the educational experiences of both teachers and students, as teachers gain professional knowledge and students achieve higher literacy (as evidenced in reading and writing high-stakes test scores) than their peers in other contexts. In an earlier article (Langer, 2000), I reported on how teachers' professional lives support student achievement. Building from that work, the present article describes features of English instruction that support student achievement, and the kinds of attention given to helping students gain both knowledge and skills in English. My project team and I have been studying these features in order to better understand the various components that make a difference in helping students become more highly literate.

As background, there are six issues at the center of the current educational debate in English and literacy, and that were in turn reflected in differences that emerged (through a process of constant comparison that continued throughout the study) among the classrooms we studied.

Approaches to Skills Instruction

Throughout at least the 20th century, there has been an ongoing debate about the manner in which instruction is delivered, with some scholars positing the effectiveness of skill and concept learning through experience-based instruction (e.g., Dewey, 1938) and others stressing mastery of concepts and skills through decontextualized practice (e.g., Bloom, 1971). This has led to a pedagogical side-taking that continues in English and literacy today. For example, Hirsch (1996) calls for students to remember culturally potent facts, and genre theorists (see Cope & Kalantzis, 1993) call for teaching students the rules of organization underlying written forms, while Goodman and Wilde (1992) and Graves (1983) call for teaching skills and knowledge within the context of authentic literacy activities. Yet, studies of reading and writing instructional practice throughout the century (see Langer & Allington, 1992) indicate that teachers tend to blur distinctions, using what may appear to theorists as a fusion of theoretically dissimilar approaches.

Approaches to Test Preparation

In recent years there has been a widespread call for systemic reform of schools and school systems (e.g., Brown & Campione, 1996; Smith & O'Day, 1991). One part of systemic reform requires that there be alignment between curriculum and assessment. In times such as these, with a widespread focus on achievement scores, how this is done becomes a critical issue. On the other hand, some educators focus primarily on practicing sample test items and helping students become "test wise"; they teach such test-taking skills as ways to select a best answer or how to best respond to a writing task from a reading item. Others advocate teaching the needed literacy abilities throughout the year, as part of the regular grade-level curriculum. In both cases test results are the focus; however, in the first case, improvement in test scores is the primary goal, whereas the second focuses on raising both test scores and student learning by improving the curriculum.

Connecting Learnings

The education literature on learning and instruction is replete with evidence that student learning and recall are more likely to be enhanced when connections can be made to prior knowledge gained from both in- and out-of-school experiences than when the content of instruction is treated as if it is entirely new (see, e.g., Bransford, Brown, & Cocking, 1999; Brown & Campione, 1996). Well-developed knowledge is also linked around important concepts and its relevance to other concepts is well understood. Although many curriculum guides as well as scope and sequence charts have attempted to depict links among specific learnings within and across the grades, too often the connections have been implicit at best, and often in the mind of the teacher or curriculum developer rather than shared with the students (see Applebee, 1996).

Enabling Strategies

During the last 25 or more years, a sizable group of research literature has emphasized the contribution of students' strategic awareness to learning and performance and the importance of teaching students strategies for carrying out reading, writing, and thinking tasks (e.g., Hillocks, 1995; Paris, Wasik, & Turner, 1991; Pressley et al., 1994). This work highlights the importance for students to learn not only content but also intentional ways of thinking and doing. In response, instructional approaches have been developed to help students become aware not only of the content but also of the particular tasks. Although the fields of science and mathematics have always seemed to be natural environments for teaching strategic approaches that enhance student performance (e.g., the scientific method, steps to mathematical solutions), teaching strategies and helping students to be strategic in the ways in which they approach a task (e.g., process approaches to writing, reflective literacy, or reciprocal teaching) are newer to the English language arts.

Conceptions of Learning

What counts as knowing has become a much-used phrase in the educational literature. It is often used as a way to make distinctions among educators who focus on facts and concepts and those who focus on students' abilities to think about and use new knowledge. At one time a student's ability to give definitions, select right answers, and fill deleted information into sentences and charts was considered evidence of learning. But at least two bodies of research changed that: One focused on disciplinary initiation, where the goal became to help students learn to better approximate expert thinking in particular fields, such as thinking like a historian (e.g., Bazerman, 1981), and the other, on critical thinking, where the focus was on higher levels of cognitive manipulation of the material (e.g., Langer & Applebee, 1987; Schallert, 1976). More recently, the issue has turned to engagement (Guthrie & Alvermann, 1999). Here concern goes beyond time on task to student involvement with the material. Although all three bodies of work have had an effect on literacy pedagogy, the National Assessment of Educational Progress (NAEP) (1998) reports that fewer than 7% of students in grades 4, 8, and 12 perform at the "advanced" level, which is the highest of four possible achievement levels in reading. This level represents students' grade-appropriate ability to deal analytically with challenging subject matter and to apply this knowledge to real-world situations.

Classroom Organization

In recent years, a variety of approaches to classroom organization have been proposed to provide students with more opportunities to learn through substantive interaction with one another as well as with the teacher. These approaches include collaborative (Barnes, 1976) and cooperative groups (Slavin, 1983), literature clubs (Raphael & McMahon, 1994), peer writing groups (Graves, 1983), and envisionment-building classrooms (Langer, 1995). These and other similar approaches have been developed in response to both theory and research from a sociocognitive orientation that sees interactive working groups around shared problems to be supportive environments for learning. Bakhtin's (1981) notion of heteroglossia (see also Nystrand & Gamoran, 1997) suggests that all learning is dialogic, reliant on and gaining meaning from the many past and present relevant voices. In dialogic groups students bring their personal, cultural, and academic knowledge to the interaction as they play the multiple roles of learners, teachers, and inquirers, and in thus doing have an opportunity to consider the issue at hand from multiple perspectives. Students can interact as both problem generators and problem solvers. New ideas can be entertained and new ways of thinking modeled as more- and less-expert knowers of the content and those more and less familiar with the task share expertise, provide feedback, and learn from each other. Such contexts emphasize shared cognition, in which the varied contributions of the participants allow the group to achieve more than individuals could on their own. However, several studies have indicated that such groupings are not pervasive in American schools (Applebee, 1993; NAEP, 1998; Nystrand, Gamoran, & Heck, 1992).

These six issues provided a set of lenses through which to understand differences in instructional practices in higher- and lower-performing schools.

The Study

The Excellence in English project examined educational practices in middle and high schools that have been trying to increase students' learning and performance in English language arts. The study focused on the workings of schools, teachers, and classrooms that strive to increase student performance and, despite obstacles and difficulties of serving the poor, beat the odds on standardized tests in reading and writing, that is, gain higher literacy, beyond comparable schools. My research team and I wanted to understand why—to identify features of instruction that make a difference in student learning and to contrast those schools where test scores are higher with demographically comparable schools in which they are not. We asked the following research question: How are the following enacted in school English programs where, when the schools are otherwise comparable, students score higher on high-stakes reading and writing tests than where they do not: approaches to skill instruction, approaches to testing, approaches to connecting learnings, approaches for enabling strategies, conceptions of learning, and classroom organization?

Method

This study took place over a 5-year period, permitting observations and interviews as well as identification and testing of patterns to take place over time. The 5-year period also allowed us to complete data gathering in successive cohorts in four states. Each teacher and school was studied for 2 years, permitting extensive study of how patterns in curriculum and instruction played themselves out in schools and classes across time. The project as a whole focused on both the professional and classroom activities that contribute to the English instruction the students experienced. Results from the study of the professional lives of the teachers have been reported in Langer (2000); the present report focuses on analyses of instructional activities.

Project Sites and Participants

To identify potential sites, recommendations were solicited from university and school communities in four states: Florida, New York, California, and Texas. The states were chosen to include diversity in student populations, educational problems, and approaches to improvement. The schools were nominated by at least three independent sources as places where professionals were working in interesting ways to improve student performance and test scores in English. Test data reported on each state education department's website were checked to identify (a) those schools that were scoring higher than schools with similar student bodies and (b) those schools that were scoring more typically (more like demographically similar schools). In each case, we examined literacy-related test data that carried high stakes for the students, the school, and the district; the relevant data varied from pass rates on Florida Writes! to performance on the Stanford 9 test. Schools whose performance on the high-stakes literacy tests was markedly above that for schools serving demographically similar populations were designated "beating the odds" schools. Schools whose performance did not deviate from that of schools serving demographically similar populations were designated "typically performing" schools. Referencing scores against those from schools serving demographically similar student populations controlled for the overall tendency for "high-performing" schools to be wealthy and suburban (cf. NAEP, 1994). It also means that typically performing schools serving more affluent populations can have higher raw scores than beating the odds schools serving high proportions of children in poverty.

Because we were particularly interested in identifying features of excellence in urban schools, we wished to more heavily sample schools and districts serving poor and culturally diverse students. However, because we also wanted to identify features that marked excellent programs across demographic areas, several suburban and urban fringe schools were also identified. We visited the most promising programs based on a combination of recommendations and test scores, and from these made a final selection based on the teachers' and administrators' willingness to work with us over a 2-year period as well as the school's ability to contribute to the overall diversity in student populations, problems, and locations in our sample. In the end, 25 schools, 44 teachers, and 88 classes were selected to participate in the study, with a focus of 1 class for each of the teachers in each of 2 consecutive years. Fourteen of the 25 participating schools are places where students were beating the odds, performing better on state-administered high-stakes reading and writing tests than schools rated as demographically comparable by statewide criteria. The other 11 schools are also places that came highly recommended, with administrators and teachers who were trying hard to improve student performance, but the school literacy scores were more typical of other schools with similar demographics.

Types of Schools. Selecting schools from Florida, New York, California, and Texas led to great variety in programs and student populations. The Florida sample included schools from the Miami–Dade County area, representing a very diverse student population. The Dade County School District has long been involved in cutting-edge efforts to improve education in English, including in part Pacesetter (sponsored by the College Board), the Zelda Glazer/Dade County Writing Project, the education of all teachers in the education of nonnative English-speaking students, the creation of interdisciplinary teams, and the early development of school-based management.

The New York sample encompassed a large geographic area, with populations ranging from rural to suburban, and middle class to urban poor. It included a number of districts in New York city and the Hudson Valley region that have earned reputations for student-centered and response-based English education; an emphasis on writing and reading across the curriculum; implementation of Goals 2000; and an interdisciplinary approach to math, science, and real-world studies through the English language arts. Two programs we studied (at King Middle School and International High School) focus on high academic competence for English Language Learners.

The California sample included schools from the Los Angeles area, a region with a very diverse student population, which has long been a bellwether for educational innovation and change in English language arts designed to benefit all students. Most recently, in an effort to raise student performance on statewide assessments, a new curriculum, an end to social promotion, a requirement for schools to adopt one of several reform programs, school accountability for student achievement (with schools placed on probation for failure to increase scores), and extra funds for tutoring efforts were put into place.

The Texas schools were in a large urban city district. Both the state and district have been involved in major efforts to improve student performance in literacy achievement including an end to social promotion and a stringent school accountability program to monitor achievement. The district put into place several measures to support improved achievement in literacy, and the state high-stakes tests were being revised at the time of our study. Summary information about the schools is presented in Table 1.

As can be seen in Table 1, schools with poor and diverse student populations predominate in the study. In terms of representation, the schools range from

TABLE 1
School Demographics

School	Student Membership	% Free or Reduced Lunch	Selected Features
Florida			
Reuben Dario Middle School[a, b]	83% Hispanic 12% African American 4% White	80%	Team decision-making councils; reading and language arts across areas
Highland Oaks Middle School[a, b]	47% White 23% African American 27% Hispanic	34%	Interdisciplinary teams; academic wheels; collaborative partnerships
Palm Middle School	60% African American 39% Hispanic 1% White	85%	Media Arts Magnet; tracking; interdisciplinary teams
Hendricks High School	56% Hispanic 43% African American	47%	International Business and Finance Magnet; Jr. ROTC; dropout prevention
Miami Edison High School[b]	92% African American 8% Hispanic	38%	New academies; teams; writing and English in subject areas
Wm. H. Turner Technical Arts High School[a, b]	63% African American 33% Hispanic 4% White	45%	Dual academic and work-related academies; workplace experience; Coalition of Essential Schools
New York			
Henry O. Hudson Middle School[a]	92% White 4% African American	5%	Interdisciplinary teams; active departments
Stockton Middle School	62% White 23% African American 14% Hispanic 1% Asian	76%	Interdisciplinary teams; departments
Abraham S. King Middle School[a]	33% Hispanic 21% African American 43% White	40%	Interdisciplinary teams; active departments; dual language program
Crestwood Middle School	66% White 25% African American 5% Asian 4% Hispanic	62%	Interdisciplinary teams; departments
International High School[a, b]	48 Countries 37 Languages	84%	Academic teams; internships; portfolios; exhibitions
New Westford High School	68% White 22% African American 6% Hispanic 4% Asian	36%	Departments; grade-level teams; arts focus
Tawasentha High School	97% White	12%	Curriculum teams; facilitators

(continued)

TABLE 1 (*continued*)
School Demographics

School	Student Membership	% Free or Reduced Lunch	Selected Features
California			
Rita Dove Middle School	58% Hispanic 41% African American	72%	Literacy coaching; Health/Science Career Magnet; districtwide reform initiative
Charles Drew Middle School[a]	55% Hispanic 32% White 8% African American 4% Asian	57%	Literacy coaching; Strategic Reading Program; districtwide reform initiative
James A. Foshay Learning Center[c] Foshay Middle School[a, b] Foshay High School[a, b]	69% Hispanic 31% African American	86%	USC precollege enrichment; New American School; Urban Learning Center; academies; districtwide reform initiative
Rutherford B. Hayes High School	86% Hispanic 7% Asian 3% Filipino 2% White 2% African American	74%	Humanitas program; teams; Math/Science Magnet; service learning
Springfield High School[a]	63% Hispanic 15% White 10% African American 9% Asian	26%	Foreign Language/International Studies Magnet; UCLA; Career Ed; Bilingual Business/Finance Academy; districtwide reform initiative
Texas			
Parklane Middle School[a]	47% Hispanic 38% White 13% African American 3% Asian	46%	Active English dept.; reading and language arts (double dose)
Ruby Middle School	83% African American 15% Hispanic 2% White	67%	English dept.; reading and language arts (double dose); language arts consortium with Lincoln High School
John H. Kirby Middle School[a]	42% White 34% Hispanic 17% African American 7% Asian	32%	Annenberg Beacon Charter School; Vanguard Magnet; Pre-Int'l Baccalaureate program; school-based center for teacher development; special program for low-motivated students; reading and language arts double dose for sixth grade; interdisciplinary teams
Lincoln High School[a]	78% African American 18% Hispanic 2% White 1% Asian	41%	Active English dept.; Aviation Sciences Magnet; Navy ROTC; Language Arts Consortium with Ruby Middle School

(continued)

TABLE 1 (*continued*)
School Demographics

School	Student Membership	% Free or Reduced Lunch	Selected Features
Lyndon B. Johnson High School[a]	53% Hispanic 23% White 21% African American 2% Asian	37%	Research & Technology Magnet; Int'l Baccalaureate Program; ROTC; departments; grade teams
Sam Rayburn High School	87% Hispanic 7% African American 5% White 1% Asian	58%	Computer technology magnet; Annenberg Challenge Reform Initiative; extensive vocational program; ROTC; double English in grades 9 and 10; departments

Each school's racial/ethnic composition is described using the terminology supplied by the school and/or district. ROTC = Reserve Officer's Training Corps; USC = University of Southern California; UCLA = University of California–Los Angeles.

[a] Denotes schools whose scores on state assessments were above those of demographically comparable schools.

[b] Denotes participants' preference to use real names. In such cases, the actual names of schools, project teachers, and their colleagues are used. For the schools not marked with a superscript b, pseudonyms are used throughout this paper.

[c] We studied both the middle and high school programs at Foshay Learning Center.

a 92% African American study body and no white students in one school, to 86% Hispanic and 2% white students in another, to 97% white students in another, with the other schools populated by students of greater ethnic and racial diversity. The schools also differ in the amount of student poverty, with school records indicating from 86% of the student body to 5% of the study body eligible for free or reduced lunch. We worked closely with one or two teachers at each school (one class each, each year), as well as other teachers and administrators with whom they coplanned, cotaught, or were otherwise engaged (including teams, departments, and other working groups) in the planning and review as well as implementation of instruction. Although we studied each teacher's entire class, 6 students from each class, representing the range of performance in that class as judged by the teacher, acted as key informants, collecting all their work and meeting with us to discuss that work, their classroom activities, and what they were learning.

Teachers Within Schools. The study design allowed us to examine the English teachers within the context of their teams, departments, and districts. Over the years in which we worked in the schools, we came to understand the extent to which the teachers were affected by the larger context in terms of professional growth or malaise, or were achieving unusually good results in spite of the context in which they worked. This led us, eventually, to recognize three broad but distinct patterns within our sample of teachers: (1) exemplary teachers whose work was sustained, perhaps even created, by the supportive district and/or school context; (2) exemplary teachers in more typical schools who achieved their success due to professional contexts unrelated to the school and/or district (often through participation in professional organizations such as local affiliates of the National Council of Teachers of English, the International Reading Association, and writing projects, and collaboration with local colleges and universities); and (3) teachers who were more typical, who did not beat the odds, who were dedicated to their students, but working within a system of traditions and expectations that did not lift them beyond the accomplishments of other comparable schools.

In the first category (beating the odds teachers within beating the odds schools), we found that these unusual teachers were not unusual within the contexts in which they worked; that is, their school and/or district (often both) encouraged all teachers, not just those in our study, to achieve comparable professional goals, and our observations of department meetings and interviews with supervisors and administrators suggested that the instructional approaches of the teachers in our study were widely accepted and carried out in their schools. In working with the second category of teachers (beating the odds in more typical schools) we found that they did not work in contexts that provided students and teachers with consistent and strong curriculum and instructional approaches and development. Thus, while their students may have scored higher than those in other classes in the school, there was no consistent and strong support that sustained student achievement beyond their individual classrooms. We found the third category of teachers (typical teachers in typical schools) in departments and schools that did not support their individual growth and that lacked collective consensus about the most effective approaches to educating their particular student body. Table 2 provides a quick summary of the schools and teachers in the study.

Design

This study involved a nested multicase design with each English program as a case and the class including the teachers and student informants as cases within. This design permitted shifting lenses among the three contexts (program, teacher, and students) as ideas for instructional change and delivery were considered, discussed, and enacted. Field researchers worked with each program, following the teachers' professional as well as classroom activities and interactions, including their interactions with central office staff, to develop an understanding of their roles in instruction. The field researchers each studied one or more programs for 2 years; hence we were able to study the instructional concerns, plans, and enactments over time, with two sets of students. (Case study reports for some of the schools are available at http://cela.albany.edu.) The sample involved 2 years each

TABLE 2
Project Schools and Key Teachers

School	Teacher	Category
Florida		
Reuben Dario Middle School[a]	Karis MacDonnell	1
	Gail Slatko	1
Highland Oaks Middle School[a]	Rita Gold	1
	Susan Gropper	1
Palm Middle School	Nessa Jones	3
Hendricks High School	Elba Rosales	2
	Carol McGuiness	3
Miami Edison High School[a]	Shawn DeNight	2
	Kathy Humphrey	2
Wm. H. Turner Technical	Chris Kirchner	1
Arts High School[a]	Janas Masztal	1
New York		
Henry O. Hudson Middle School	Cathy Starr	1
	Gloria Rosso	1
Stockton Middle School	Helen Ross	3
Abraham S. King Middle School	Pedro Mendez	1
	Donald Silvers	1
Crestwood Middle School	Monica Matthews	3
International High School[a]	Marsha Slater	1
	Aaron Listhaus	1
New Westford High School	Elaine Dinardi	3
	Jack Foley	3
Tawasentha High School	Margaret Weiss	2
	Nicole Scott	3
California		
Rita Dove Middle School	Jonathan Luther	3
	Evangeline Turner	2
Charles Drew Middle School	Alicia Alliston	1
	Tawanda Richardson	1
James A. Foshay Learning Center Middle School[a, b]	Kathryn McFadden-Midby	1
James A. Foshay Learning Center High School[a, b]	Myra LeBendig	1
Rutherford B. Hayes High School	Ron Soja	3
Springfield High School	Celeste Rotondi	1
	Suzanna Matton	1
Texas		
Parklane Middle School	Rachel Kahn	1

(continued)

TABLE 2 (*continued*)
Project Schools and Key Teachers

School	Teacher	Category
	Amy Julien	1
Ruby Middle School	Shaney Young	3
	Erica Walker	3
John H. Kirby Middle School	Cynthia Spencer-Bell	1
	Matt Caldwell	1
Lincoln High School	Viola Collins	1
	Vanessa Justice	1
Lyndon B. Johnson High School	Thelma Moore	1
	Nora Shepherd	1
Sam Rayburn High School	Carol Lussier	2
	Jo Beth Chapin	3

1 = Beating the odds teacher in beating the odds school; 2 = Beating the odds teacher in typically performing school; 3 = Typical teacher in typically performing school.

[a] Denotes participants' preference to use real names. In such cases, the actual names of schools, project teachers, and their colleagues are used. For the schools not marked with a superscript a, pseudonyms are used throughout this paper.

with 44 teachers working in 25 schools and included some 2,640 students and 528 student informants.

None of the schools we studied were dysfunctional, and none of the teachers were considered to be other than good. Fourteen of the 25 schools were performing better than schools serving demographically similar populations, based on score on high-stakes tests, and the teachers in the other schools in which we worked were recommended by district administrators as good, although the overall performance of their schools was more typical. Thus, this is a study of English instruction within both higher-performing and more typically performing schools.

Procedures

Each field researcher spent approximately 5 weeks per year at each site, including a week at the beginning of each year to interview district personnel as well as teachers and students about their goals, plans, and perceptions; to make initial observations of the classes we would be studying; and to plan for the year ahead. This was followed by 2 weeks of additional visits per semester to observe classes, to conduct informal interviews with participating teachers and students, and to shadow the teachers in their professional encounters (i.e., team, department, building, district, and other relevant meetings).

In addition to the on-site visits, we set up e-mail accounts or spoke by phone or in person in order to maintain weekly contact with the teachers and students, during which time we discussed ongoing classroom activities, including examples of student work provided from the student informants (student informants maintained portfolios and their work was collected and mailed to us weekly), reflections on those lessons, as well as future plans.

Data

Parallel sets of qualitative data were gathered at each of the sites. Data consisted of field notes of all meetings, observed classes, and conversations; e-mail messages; artifacts from school and professional experiences; tape recordings and transcripts of all interviews and observed class sessions; and in-process case reports developed by the field researchers. Table 3 summarizes the major types of data collected.

Three types of collaborations contributed to the development of the database within and across cases: full-project team, collaborative dyads, and case study sessions.

Full-Project Team. In addition to meetings with the teacher participants in each state, the teachers and research team interacted in ongoing e-mail discussions about the approaches, activities, and progress in the participating classes and the teacher's experiences in helping students improve their literacy performance.

Collaborative Dyad. Each teacher and field researcher communicated via e-mail approximately once a week to develop, discuss, and reflect on the teacher's professional interactions as well as class sessions and student performance.

Case Study Sessions. The field researchers and I met weekly for case study sessions. During these meetings, the field researchers presented in-process case study reports about the professional networks and instructional activities and offerings at their sites. These sessions offered opportunities for case-related patterns to be discussed, tested, and refined, and for cross-case patterns to be noted for further recursive testing and analysis.

Coding. Coding for this project was used to organize and index the various types of data in ways that permitted us to locate the participants' focus on key areas of concern. For example, where possible, all data were initially coded for the type of community the participants were focusing on or referring to: professional, classroom, or social, as well as for their focus on instruction, curriculum, and assessment. More targeted codes for particular types of knowledge, skills, and processes were also coded. This scheme served as an indexing system that allowed us to later retrieve and more carefully analyze data from one categorical subsection of the data pool, compare it with another, and generate data-driven subcategories for later analysis.

TABLE 3
Data Gathered at Each Site

I. Interviews
    Teacher: Entry and Exit
        Preparation and experience
        Recent coursework and workshops
        Professional memberships and activities
        Instructional goals
        Pedagogical beliefs and teaching concerns
        Topics of instruction
        Content
        Approaches
        Materials
        Activities
        Patterns of discourse
    Chair/Principal/District Supervisor
        School/district reform efforts
        School/district goals
        School/district initiatives
        School/district content
        School/district consultants
        School/district committees

II. Observations
    Baseline (before commitment to the study)
    Entry: 1 week at beginning of school year
    Ongoing: 2 weeks each semester, for 4 semesters
        Topics of instruction
        Content
        Approaches
        Materials
        Activities
        Patterns of discourse
        Student engagement and performance

III. Ongoing Contact
    Weekly, telephone or e-mail
        Assignments, content, instruction, concerns, plans

IV. Student Informants
    Formal and informal discussions of curriculum, instruction, and student work
    Portfolios of all work for English

V. Shadowing (professional lives study)
    Professional meetings
    Curriculum development and other working groups

VI. Documents
    State, district, and school documents, including textbooks and other instructional materials:
        what is available, what is used, and how

Analyses

Data were analyzed by a system of constant comparison, where patterns were identified and tested both within and across cases. For this study, we returned to each coded instance as well as the full data set to qualitatively analyze the conditions under which each existed; this in turn led us to identify the features that differentiated the approaches of the three groups of teachers. Thus, the various data sets were keyed to the individual teacher and classroom, providing multiple views of each instructional context, permitting both in-depth case studies and cross-case perspectives to be developed. In each case, we triangulated the data, drawing on various aspects of the classroom communities for evidence. As key issues began to emerge in the qualitative cross-case analyses, they were checked against the entire sample. Thus, overall ratings of how each teacher dealt with the six features of instruction discussed in the present report are based on the full range of data gathered for each teacher over a 2-year period, including interviews, observations, ongoing conversations (e-mail or telephone), and student reports. Specific categorizations of each teacher's practices were made by the field researcher responsible for data collection at each site, after lengthy discussions with the project team.

Although the findings are limited to the 44 teachers we have studied, the study required the field researchers to shadow and gather data about the teachers, their colleagues, and their school's English language arts programs as the teachers interacted with others at team, departmental, and other meetings and workshops, and as they planned and sometimes cotaught with their colleagues. The field researchers also interviewed the teachers and administrators with whom the participating teachers interacted in order to understand the larger professional and instructional context of each. Thus, although the focus was on one or two teachers in each school, we were able to gain more firsthand "living" knowledge of each school's English program, including the curricular and instructional emphases of the school and district.

In previous studies of effective literature instruction (Langer, 1995), we found that successful instruction was characterized by its adherence to certain underlying principles rather than by any uniformity from teacher to teacher in specific activities or pedagogical routines. The present study thus assumed that currently popular approaches to English and literacy instruction (e.g., process-writing instruction, response-based literature instruction, attention to grammar and mechanics) would be realized in multiple ways by different teachers and students. The notion is related to Sternberg and Horvath's (1995) argument that expert teaching should be viewed in terms of a prototype that allows for considerable variation in the profiles of individual experts, except that our "prototypes" are construed as features within the instructional environment rather than the psychological characteristics (insight, efficiency) that Sternberg and Horvath propose. Thus, the analyses and findings of this study do not focus on the surface content and form of instruction, but rather the underlying principles, beliefs, and approaches that are enacted in different ways in the context of each individual classroom.

Results

I will begin with a brief overview of the results from the cross-case analyses of English instruction in higher and more typically performing schools, and then deal in detail with the six central instructional issues that capture the major differences between these groups.

Although each of the higher-performing schools had its own distinctive emphasis, all were marked by active and engaged students and teachers in academically rich classrooms. Furthermore, they were marked by the professionalism, knowledge, and dedication of the teachers and by collaborative participation of the students in quality, "minds-on" activities. Students were well behaved and remarkably on task almost all the time. Each school managed to create an effective learning environment in which students had opportunities to think with, about, and through English, both as a vehicle for getting things done and as an object of study in its own right. The students in these schools were learning a great deal about high literacy, including the functions and uses of language. The students were learning how language works in context and how to use it to advantage for specific purposes. They were learning grammar, spelling, vocabulary, and organizational structure—sometimes in context but also with carefully planned activities that focused directly on the structure and use of language. We observed a great deal of writing, reading, and oral language as students explored their understanding, prepared presentations, and polished final products. Students in the high-performing schools were beating the odds, as evidenced by higher test scores than in comparable schools.

Both qualitative and quantitative analyses indicate that certain noteworthy features related to the six issues (approaches to skill instruction, approaches to test preparation, approaches to connecting learnings, approaches to enabling strategies, conceptions of learning, and classroom organization) affected the students' experiences with English; these features permeated the environments and provided marked distinctions between higher and more typically performing schools. In each of the six sections below, I present and discuss these results, relating each to one of the educational issues. Table 4 provides a preliminary overview of the six issues along with the ways they differed across instructional contexts.

Approaches to Skill Instruction

Analyses of the approaches to skill instruction in the classrooms in this study identified three distinct approaches that I call *separated*, *simulated*, and *integrated*. Separated instruction is what most educators would consider to be direct

TABLE 4
Issues and Concern and Overview of Findings

Issue	Beating the Odds Schools and Teachers	Typical Schools and Teachers
Approaches to Skills Instruction	Systematic use of separated, simulated, and integrated skills instruction	Instruction dominated by one approach (which varies among schools and teachers)
Test Preparation	Integrated into ongoing goals, curriculum, and regular lessons	Allocated to test prep; separate from ongoing goals, curriculum, and instruction
Connected Learnings	Overt connections made among knowledge, skills, and ideas across lessons, classes and grades, and across in-school and out-of-school applications	Knowledge and skills within lessons, units, and curricula typically treated as discrete entities; connections left implicit even when they do occur
Enabling Strategies	Overt teaching of strategies for planning, organizing, completing, and reflecting on content and activities	Teaching of content or skills without overt attention to strategies for thinking and doing
Conceptions of Learning	When learning goal is met, teacher moves students beyond it to deeper understanding and generativity of ideas	When learning goal is met, teacher moves on to unrelated activity with different goals/content
Classroom Organization	Students work together to develop depth and complexity of understanding in interaction with others	Students work alone, in groups, or with the teacher to get the work done, but do not engage in rich discussion of ideas

instruction of isolated skills and knowledge. Often this takes place separately from the context of a larger activity, primarily as introduction, practice, or review. It can be recognized when the teacher tells students particular rules, conventions, or facts, or when instructional material focuses on listings of vocabulary, spelling, or rules. Sometimes this instruction is used as a way to "cover" the curriculum, other times as a way to help students understand and remember underlying conventions and to learn ways in which they are applied. Teachers use the *separated* activity as a way to highlight a particular skill, item, or rule. It is presented in a lesson that is generally not connected to what is occurring before or after it in class.

In comparison, *simulated* instruction involves the actual application of those concepts and rules within a targeted unit of reading, writing, or oral language. These are often exercises prepared by the teacher or found in teaching materials, where the students are expected to read or write short units of text with the primary purpose of practicing the skill or concept of focus. Often students are asked to find examples of that skill or concept in use in their literature and writing books, as well as in out-of-school activities. They sometimes practice it within the confines of small and limited tasks. I call it *simulated* because the tasks themselves are specially developed for the purpose of practice.

Integrated instruction takes place when students are expected to use their skills and knowledge within the embedded context of a large and purposeful activity, such as writing a letter, report, poem, or play for a particular goal (not merely to practice the skill) or planning, researching, writing, and editing a class newspaper. Here, the focus is on completing a project or activity well, with primary focus on the effectiveness of the work in light of its purpose. This is the time when the skill or knowledge is put to real use as a contributing factor in the success of the work. This becomes a time when the teacher might remind the students of a rule they learned during *separated* or *simulated* activities and how it might be useful in the completion of the activity at hand. If extra help is needed, it is provided by other students or the teacher.

Each of the teachers was rated in terms of how they typically went about introducing new language or literacy skills. The results are summarized in Table 5. As the table indicates, the more successful teachers were more likely to make systematic use of separated, simulated, and integrated skills instruction; two thirds or more of the more successful teachers in both beating the odds and typical schools used all three approaches. In comparison, only 17% of the more typical teachers in typically performing schools made systematic use of all three approaches; their instruction was much more likely to be dominated by a single approach. Although 50% of the typical teachers used separated instruction as their dominant approach, none of the more successful teachers did so.

Although English teachers in the higher-performing schools tended to use all three types of skills instruction, there was great variety in the specific activities they chose to use. For example, in the higher-performing schools, the skills and mechanics of English (grammar, usage, vocabulary) were taught within the context of literature and writing instruction, but there was often a great deal of separate and overt targeted instruction and review in the form of exercises and practice. Gail Slatko and Karis MacDonnell at Reuben Dario Middle School, for instance, had students check each other's grammar even when they did not do peer revision. They, like most of the teachers in the high-performing schools, also engaged in direct teaching of grammar and usage (e.g., sentence structure, punctuation) and used these lessons as models for their students to rely on when responding to each other's as well as their own work.

At Springfield High School, Celeste Rotondi and Suzanna Matton, both teachers who embedded skills and mechanics in long-range activities, always exposed

TABLE 5
Percent of Teachers Using Particular Approaches to Instruction

Dominant Approach	Beating the Odds Teachers in Beating the Odds Schools ($N = 26$)	Beating the Odds Teachers in Typical Schools ($N = 6$)	Typical Teachers in Typical Schools ($N = 12$)
	Percent of Teachers		
Approaches to Skills Instruction			
Separated			50%
Simulated			17%
Integrated	72%	33%	17%
All Three	73%	67%	17%
Approaches to Test Preparation			
Integrated	85%	83%	
Separated			75%
Both	15%	17%	87%
None			17%
Connecting Learnings			
Within Lessons			17%
Across Lessons	12%		
In and Out of School			25%
All Three Connections	88%	100%	
No Connections			58%
Enabling Strategies			
Overtly Taught	100%	100%	17%
Left Implicit			83%
Conceptions of Learning			
Focus on Immediate Goal		100%	
Focus on Deeper Understanding	100%	100%	
Classroom Organization			
Shared Cognition	96%	100%	8%
Individual Thinking	4%		92%

their students to *separated* and *simulated* as well as *integrated* experiences and continually monitored their students' acquisition of new skills, as well as noting where special help was needed. To help her students learn language and comprehension skills, Celeste selected difficult vocabulary words out of context and showed her students how those words could be used in class. She often did this as a *simulated* activity, in the context of the book they were reading, or to incorporate it into their writing practice. Using both *separated* and *simulated* lessons, she also helped her students learn to justify their answers, summarize information, and make connections. However, these new learnings were continually expected to be applied during *integrated* activities, such as literature circles.

Suzanna also used literature circles as activities that call for students' use of the skills and knowledge they were learning. For example, in one instance her students were divided into literature discussion groups and assigned the following roles that changed each week: discussion director, literary illuminary, vocabulary enricher, summarizer, and connector. Each student took responsibility for enriching the group discussion from the vantage point of the assigned role. Because these groups continued throughout the year, each student had many opportunities to practice the skills in context and to see them modeled by the other students. When Suzanna saw that extra help was needed, she either helped the individual or offered a *separated* or *simulated* activity to several students or the entire class, depending on need.

In comparison, one teacher at Hayes High School, a more typical school, responded to the call for greater emphasis on grammar by raiding the book room for a classroom set of *Warriner's English Grammar and Composition*. She said,

> Well, this is how I do it [holding up the book]. I work hard and have no time to read professional journals. I teach five periods and mark papers. I know I have to teach grammar. My students didn't get it before, so I have to teach it. So I use this [*Warriner's*] because it lays out the lessons, and my students can also use it as a reference.

Her skills lesson, through *Warriner's*, were primarily out of context, separate from the rest of her teaching.

Like the Hayes teacher, Carol McGuiness at Hendricks tended to maintain her "old ways" of teaching vocabulary, using a vocabulary workbook in which students did periodic assignments in parsing words to get at Latin and Greek roots. Although she saw this as giving them a tool for encountering new words—a tool to learn how to learn—it was primarily a *separated* activity, and we saw no evidence that she had students use these root word skills elsewhere.

Thus, although teachers in higher-performing schools used a number of well-orchestrated instructional approaches to provide instruction and practice of targeted skills and knowledge in ways that suffused the students' English experiences, more typical schools' approaches to skills development seem to be more restricted and separated from the ongoing activities of the English classroom.

Approaches to Test Preparation

Our analyses of approaches to test preparation found two qualitatively different approaches used by the teachers in this study. One approach treated test preparation as a separated activity, involving test practice and test-taking hints. The second approach integrated test preparation with the regular curriculum by carefully analyzing test demands and reformulating curriculum as necessary to be sure that students would, over time, develop the knowledge and skills necessary for accomplished performance.

Almost all the teachers we studied used both integrated and separated approaches to test preparation some of the time, but there were marked differences in the approaches that received dominant emphasis. Table 5 summarizes the relevant results. As the table indicates, more than 80% of the more successful teachers in both kinds of schools integrated the skills and knowledge that were to be tested into the ongoing curriculum as their dominant approach to test preparation; the others used integrated and separated approaches equally. In comparison, 75% of the more typical teachers used a separated approach to test preparation, primarily teaching test preparation skills and knowledge apart from the ongoing curriculum. The more typical teachers who did not teach test preparation at all were not teaching students who were scheduled to take a high-stakes test that year.

Teachers in the higher-performing schools used the tests as an opportunity to revise and reformulate their literacy curriculum. The primary approach to test preparation involved relevant teachers and administrators in a careful deconstruction and analysis of the test items themselves, which led to a deeper understanding of the literacy skills, strategies, and knowledge needed for students to achieve higher levels of literacy performance. This was followed by a review and revision of both the curriculum and instructional guidelines to ensure that the identified skills and knowledge were incorporated into the ongoing English program the students would experience. Before a test, the format was generally practiced to ensure students' familiarity with it. However, not much teaching time was devoted to this. It was the infusion of the needed skills and knowledge into the curriculum that seems to have made a difference. Students were also taught to become more reflective about their own reading and writing performance, sometimes using rubrics throughout the school year in order to help them gain insight into their better or less well-developed reading and writing performance in response to particular tasks.

Again, however, the specific ways that schools and districts orchestrated the process of understanding and responding to the demands of high-stakes tests varied with their individual situations. Some of this variation will be illustrated in the examples that follow.

At Foshay, Kate McFadden-Midby and Myra LeBendig strove to understand the test demands of Stanford 9 and help their students make connections between their ongoing curriculum and academic real-life situations, including testing. To accomplish this, Kate collaborated with a group of teachers to design a series of lessons that would incorporate the skills tested by the Stanford 9 into their literature curriculum. They identified certain areas in which their students did least well (e.g., vocabulary, spelling, and reading comprehension) and planned lessons that would integrate their use in meaningful ways into the students' everyday experiences. They developed a series of eight lessons as models to be used with a variety of literature. These lessons served as ways for the teachers to create other opportunities to address areas of concern within the regular curriculum.

In higher-performing schools, district-level coordinators often created working groups of teachers, and, together, the coordinates and teachers collaboratively studied the demands of the high-stakes tests their students were taking and used their test item analyses to rethink the curriculum, what to teach, and when to teach it. For example, when the Florida Writes! test was instituted, the Dade County English language arts central office staff and some teachers met to study and understand the exam and the kinds of demands it made on students. Together, they developed an instructional strategy (grade by grade) that would create yearlong experiences in the different types of writing, including the kinds of organization, elaboration, and polishing that were required. This coordination began some years before our study, and the instructional changes that led to greater coherence were very evident in the classrooms we studied. All classes were replete with rich and demanding writing experiences, including direct instruction and help at all stages. In many classes, the teachers spent the first 5 or 10 minutes of each period on an exercise assigned on the board for the students to begin alone or with others as they entered. Sometimes this involved doing analogies or writing their own, or reading a passage and developing multiple-choice questions for others to answer (after studying how the questions were constructed). The student work was always discussed in class and connected to how it might be useful not only on a test but also for their own writing or reading. Connections were made to this activity later in the day, week, or year.

In some schools, teachers selectively used materials and created activities because they knew that their students needed to practice skills and knowledge that would be tapped by the test. For example, Suzanna Matton at Springfield High was constantly aware of enriching her students' vocabulary. She selected words she thought they would need to know, gave them practice, and followed with quizzes every 6 weeks. She also had her students do a great deal of analytic writing throughout the year, helping them become aware of strategic ways to write a well-developed analytic paper in response to the material they read as well as in response to writing prompts. For example, she helped her students trace how a conflict developed and was worked through a story, and how allusion was used and to what affect, and then had them write about it, providing evidence. The students also learned to judge their own and others' writing and gained ability in a variety of writing modes.

Test preparation looked very different in the more typically performing schools. Rather than an opportunity to improve their literacy curriculum, teachers in these schools treated the tests as an additional hurdle, separated from their literacy curriculum. Here, the primary mode of test preparation offered practice on old editions of the test, teacher-made tests, and practice materials, and, sometimes, commercial materials using similar formats and questions to the test at hand. In such cases, if test preparation occurred at all, there was a test-taking practice 1 or 2 weeks (or more) before the exam, or the preparation was sporadic and unconnected across longer periods of time. At Palm Middle School, for example, the Improvement Plan called for 15 test-taking practice assignments to be given to the students across the curriculum during the course of the year, but these assignments, if done at all, were most often inserted into the curriculum as additions rather than integrated. How to take a test, rather than how to gain and use the skills and knowledge tested, seemed to be the focus.

Some readers in typically performing schools seemed to blame the students, or the test, but not themselves. At Hayes, although the principal is a highly motivating personality and told the faculty, "We can do it," there was an underlying belief among the faculty with whom we interacted that the students were not capable of scoring well on the exam. They did not believe they could make a difference. For example, Ron Soja said, "They don't know anything. It's like they never did anything." Ron did not seem to feel personally accountable for ensuring his students possessed the underlying knowledge and skills to do well. He said, "The Stanford test is not a good test to see whether they are achieving in school or not, because up until this year it hasn't meant anything. Half the kids, they think it's a big joke...."

Beginning 2 years hence, students in this district would need to achieve a certain percentile score (not yet determined) on the Stanford 9 test to be eligible for high school graduation. Ron rationalized that the students scored badly on the test because they did not take it seriously (did not understand its implications), rather than focusing on his efforts to prepare them for it.

Practice activities are often developed by states and district or commercial material developers but are not meant to be the sole activity schools use to help students do well. To prepare for the New York State English Regents Exam, which all students must pass to graduate, New Westford High School, a more typically performing school, sent two teachers to a state education department meeting designed to brief them on grading procedures. They, in turn, transmitted what they had learned to their colleagues. The English language arts district supervisor bought sets of guide booklets for Regents practice; Elaine Dinardi bought yet another for additional practice. The books present Regents Exam-like activities for the students to practice. The department faculty also made up grade-level take-home finals that followed the Regents format. Elaine interspersed these practice activities around her usual curriculum until some time in April, when she began to stress Regents practice in her class. This practice became the major class activity—in effect, became the curriculum—for the entire quarter, in preparation for the June exam. Over this time, the practice focused on the kinds of essays the test would require—writing for information, compare and contrast, and critical lens (relating a quote to a work that was read)—presented in the form required by the test. It should be noted that this was the first year that the English Regents Exam was mandated for all students. In prior years, the school's percentage of students passing (based on average grade enrollment) was at or below 50%. Consequently, district educators were very apprehensive about the Regents. Like those at Hayes, teachers in New York Westford did not believe the average student had the capability to perform well on the test.

Administrators of other typically performing schools sometimes purchased professional services or programs that were not integrated into the ongoing program. For example, at Hendricks, an outside consultant was hired to give test-taking strategy workshops to 10th-grade students to help improve their scores. The prepackaged materials exhibited little understanding of the specific test or the needs of the students.

Overall, higher-performing schools seemed to focus on students' overall literacy learning, using the tests to be certain the skills and knowledge that are tested are related to and being learned within the framework of improved language arts instruction. They regarded tests as one of many literacy activities students needed to learn to do well and believed that the underlying skills and knowledge required to do well on tests were related to the underlying skills and knowledge needed to do well in coursework, thus needing to be encompassed within the on-going curriculum. In contrast, the more typical schools viewed test performance as a separate goal, apart from the regular curriculum. Therefore, they saw test preparation as requiring a focus on the tests themselves, with raising test scores, rather than improving students' literacy learning, as the primary goal.

Approaches to Connecting Learnings

Our analyses of instruction in the participating classrooms found that the teachers overtly pointed out connections among three different kinds of student learnings: connections among concepts and experiences within lessons; connections across lessons, classes, and even grades; and connections between in-school and out-of-school knowledge and experiences. Results are summarized in Table 5. As the table indicates, at least 88% of the more successful teachers in both types of schools tended to make all three types of connections with approximately equal focus. In comparison, the more typical teachers tended to make no connections at all, and when they did, they tended to be "real world" connections between school and home. None of the more typical teachers emphasized all three types of connections.

In the higher-performing schools, the teachers worked consciously to weave a web of connections. Thus, at Springfield High School, Suzanna Rotundi planned her lessons with consideration to the ways in which they connected with each other, with test demands, and with the students' growing knowledge. For example, when discussing her goals for the reading of *Invisible Man* by Ralph Ellison, she said,

> My primary goal is to provide them with what I consider a challenging piece of literature that will give them an excellent resource for the AP exam. It fits in well with the works we have studied in that it explores the inner consciousness and makes use of a recurring image/symbol that has been the key to several other literacy works...that of blindness. It allows them to explore the way a symbol can convey meaning in several literary works. Personally, I feel that Ellison's is a monumental literary work. The ramifications in terms of social psychology with the concept of invisibility applies to so many different life experiences. I try to open the students' appreciation of how this work relates to their own world and it introduces them to the question of identity and how the daily interactions are crucial to identify formation.

Thus, her lessons connected texts, tests, and life.

Even in hectic times when the teachers felt the burden of many demands on their instructional time, those in the higher-performing schools and the excellent ones in the more typical schools still tried to weave even unexpected intrusions into more integrated experiences for their students. For example, when his long-range plans were disrupted, Shawn DeKnight, an excellent teacher in a lower-performing school, did what he called "curricular improvising." He said, "If it's possible to bend the disruption so it fits in some way with my instructional plans, then I feel I have triumphed." When a grade-wide project was a field trip to a senior citizens center, his theme was "An Inter-Generational Forum: Senior Citizens and Teens Discuss What It Means to Be Liberal or Conservative." He had planned to teach his students to write character analyses based on their class readings. He decided to use the visit to the senior citizens home as a starter; interviewing the seniors "would force my students to interact with the seniors," he said. But what to do with the interviews? He asked them to write a character sketch. He explained,

> The writing follows a similar format to a persuasive essay, something my kids worked on a couple of months ago. It will also be a nice segue into the character analysis in the sense that both types of writing establish a thesis that a person has a certain character trait, then goes on to provide specific evidence to support the thesis. For the character sketch, the evidence that a person was liberal or conservative or moderate would come from the interviews. With the character analysis, which we will begin in a couple of weeks when we finish *Romeo and Juliet*, the evidence comes from things the character has said or done in the play.

Shawn made connections such as these throughout each day, week, and year, pointing them out to this students so they could recognize ways in which their skills and knowledge were productively used in a range of situations.

Springfield High School, a higher-performing school that was preparing for accreditation, was in the process of revising its mission and approaches to education. Self-study led the teachers to develop a more integrated approach to learning, fostering connections both within school and between school and community. One part of the mission statement focuses on students as effective communicators. Faculty members were collaboratively working on teams to ensure that the skills needed for effective communication would be taught and reinforced across the grades and across the curriculum. This process was followed for the other components of the school's mission as well, and these were coordinated with the statewide standards. The teachers were aware of making these connections. For example, Celeste Rotondi said,

> Standards, as much as they're a kind of pain in the butt when we have these meetings and align the standards and all that stuff, it has helped me.... My curriculum is strong. But once I started really looking at the standards I realized I didn't have a lot of oral writing activities, and so it kind of helped me to conceptualize that a little better and forced me to incorporate that.

It never occurred to Celeste to simply add a few oral activities to her lesson plans. Instead, she rethought ways in which reading, writing, and oral language could be interrelated across the curriculum and across the year in ways that would strengthen her students' oral as well as written communication abilities.

In addition to connectedness of goals, skills, and experiences across the day and year (connections Celeste would plan and make overt to her students when appropriate), she also wanted to ensure that her students could learn to make connections across the literature they were reading as well as connections from literature to life. She wanted her students to learn to read the text and the world. To do this, Celeste organized her literature instruction around thematic units, for example pairing *The Glass Menagerie* and *A Raisin in the Sun* to permit her students to focus on family relationships and ways families deal with the situations they face. For such units, she typically created study guides that provided scaffolding for her students and made overt to both her students and herself the particular connections that were at focus. Comparisons across the pieces helped her students compare and critique aspects of structure, language, and style while they also focused on thematic elements across the pieces and connected (e.g., compared and critiqued) them based on related situations in the world today.

As contrast, in the more typical schools, even when the lessons were integrated within a unit, there was little interweaving across lessons; there were few overt connections made among the content, knowledge (literary or otherwise), and skills that were being taught. Class lessons were often treated as separate wholes—with a particular focus introduced, practiced, discussed, and then put aside. For example, at Hayes High School, Ron Soja said that in his yearlong plans, he moved the students from more subjective to more objective writing tasks. However, we saw no indication he shared this distinction with his students or helped them make other connections among the kinds of writing he assigned.

At Stockton Middle School, Helen Ross asked questions that encouraged her students to make connections, but because discussions were carefully controlled, the connections the students would make were predetermined. For example, when they read *The Diary of Anne Frank* in play form, taking turns reading parts, she asked, "These are real people your age. How would you react in that situation?" "What would you do?" Although these seem open ended, she was actually leading in a particular direction, toward the diary. She steered the discussion with questions and comments until a student came forth with the idea she sought. Then she said, "Her diary. That's how she escapes," marking the conclusion of that day's discussion.

This same pattern of questioning can also be seen in Carol McGuiness's class, at Hendricks High School, as she opened the discussion after reading a chapter of *Anpao: An American Indian Odyssey*.

T: In the Judeo-Christian tradition, do we have animals that converse with God?

S1: No.

T: Only one, and which one is that?

S2: The snake.

T: The snake. Representative of —?

SSS: Satan.

T: Right. Satan. In this case the animals are benevolent. They are not evil. How is humanity according to this legend?

Rather than encouraging her students to make their own connections, or showing them how, Carol guided them to guess the connection she has made. Following this very short pseudodiscussion, Carol had the students sequence 24 events that she had taken from the first chapters of the text. This sequencing activity was disconnected from the discussion that had preceded it and was followed by another disconnected activity the next day, when she planned to have them act out a scene from the text.

The lack of connectedness in the classrooms of Helen and Carol was also reflected in the larger curriculum across the grades; their departments did not foster connectedness. For example, in Helen's district, department chairs in the middle and high schools were eliminated a few years ago in favor of a K–12 English Language Arts Coordinator for the district's schools. He had been trying to foster curriculum coherence and continuity through cross-grade dialogue and within-grade curriculum coordination; however, because of his many responsibilities, he had difficulty accomplishing all his goals. As he told us, "Too many buildings, too many kids, too many teachers. I just can't do what I want anywhere. So I do what I can. You have to keep your sights limited to what you can do."

Although the central office in Carol's district was making monumental efforts to make the language arts program more cohesive, her department chair at Hendricks made little effort to follow through with his teachers. He said that although he gets good ideas and materials from the central office, he just puts the packages in the teachers' mailboxes instead of meeting, discussing, planning, and collaboratively developing ways to incorporate the ideas into the curriculum.

In the more typical schools, when educators gain information from professional encounters, or adopt predeveloped programs or commercial materials, they seem not to use them in the full and integrated ways in which they were intended. Connie McGee, an English Language Arts Supervisor for the Miami–Dade County Schools, calls it the "Key Lime Pie syndrome." She said that even though a set of activities has been planned, demonstrated, and explained within a particular rationale and sequence, with features that build on each other, some teachers choose only the parts that appeal to them. Connie says, "I show them how to make the whole pie, but they make just the meringue or just the filling and wonder why it doesn't taste like key lime pie." The resulting failure of the activities is then blamed on the poor "recipe" or the poor students rather than lack of a coordinated whole.

Approaches to Enabling Strategies

Our analyses of classroom instruction also found considerable differences in the ways teachers went about teaching students strategies to engage in reading and writing activities and to reflect on and monitor their performance. In some of the classrooms, students were overtly taught strategies for thinking and doing; in others, the focus was on new content or skills, without overtly teaching the overarching strategies for planning, organizing, completing, or reflecting on the content or activity. Table 4 summarizes the relevant data. As the table indicates, there were distinct differences in ways the more successful and the more typical teachers approached the teaching of strategies. All of the more successful teachers overtly taught their students strategies for organizing their thoughts and completing tasks, whereas only 17% of the more typical teachers did so. The other 83% of the more typical teachers left such strategies implicit. Examples of the variety of ways in which teachers went about teaching (or not teaching) such strategies follow.

In the higher-performing schools, the teachers often segmented new or difficult tasks, providing their students with guides for ways to accomplish them. However, the help they offered was not merely procedural; rather, it was designed so that the students would understand how to do well. Sometimes the teachers provided models and lists, and sometimes evaluation rubrics. Strategies for how to do the task as well as how to think about the task were discussed and modeled, and reminder sheets were developed for student use. These strategies provided the students with ways to work through the tasks themselves, helping them to understand and meet the task demands. For instance, at Hudson Middle School, Cathy Starr taught her students strategies to use to reflect on their progress as they moved through an activity. After a research activity, the students were to rate themselves on their research and writing using rubrics they had developed.

1. Where do you think you fall for the research [grade yourself]? Did you spend the time trying to find the information? Did you keep going until you had learned enough to write your report?

2. Whether this is a short and informal or longer and more formal piece, you should spend time thinking about the writing. Did you plan what you were going to say? Did you think about it? Did you review it and revise it before putting it in the back?

3. Did you edit? Did you check the spelling and punctuation?

Most of the teachers in the higher-performing schools shared and discussed with students rubrics for evaluating performance; they also incorporated them into their ongoing instructional activities as a way to help their students develop an understanding of the components that contribute to a higher score (more complete, more elaborated, more highly organized response). Use of the rubrics also helped students develop reflection and repair strategies relevant to their reading, writing, and oral presentation activities.

Kate McFadden-Midby at Foshay also provided her students with strategies for completing a task well if she thought it was going to be new or challenging. For example, when her students were learning to do character analyses and to understand different perspectives, she asked them to begin by developing a critical thinking question and then to choose two characters from the book (or books) they had read, in order to compare the characters' viewpoints on that question. The critical thinking questions needed to be ones that anyone could discuss even if they had not read the book (e.g., one student asked, "Why are people so cruel when it comes to revenge?"). Before they met in groups, she provided this outline: (a) Share your critical thinking question with your group; (b) tell your group partners why you chose that particular question and what situation in the book made you think about it; and (c) tell which two characters you have chosen to discuss that question in a miniplay. The students engaged in deep and substantive discussion about their classmates' questions because Kate's strategy list had helped them gain clarity on the goals and process of the task. Discussions were followed, the next day, by a prewriting activity in preparation for writing a description of the characters they chose. Kate instructed them on how to develop a T-chart on which one character's name is placed at the top of one column of the T and the other character's name is placed at the other side. She told them to list characteristics: what their characters were like, experiences they had, opinions, etc. She provided them with strategies to identify characteristics and then ways to compare them across the two characters.

This was followed by group sharing, where the students presented their characters. Here, Kate scaffolded the students' thinking by asking questions about the characters: What kind of person was the mother? What are some adjectives that might describe her? How do you think those things could influence how she feels? Over time, when the students had been helped, through a variety of supportive strategies, to develop deeper understandings of their characters, they were then helped to write a miniplay depicting those same characters involved in the issue raised by their critical thinking question. Although this was a highly complex activity, the students were provided with supportive strategies along the way, gaining insight not merely into the characters themselves, but into ways they could understand characters and differing perspectives when reading and writing on their own.

In the more typical schools, instruction focused on the content or the skill, but not necessarily on providing students with procedural or metacognitive strategies. For example, in the sequencing activity in Carol McGuiness's 10th-grade class at Hendricks mentioned earlier, two of the three groups of students were having some difficulty putting the 24 events in sequence. Rather than eliciting any strategies that might be useful, Carol simply told them, "OK. Divide your slips into thirds. OK? This is research. Start with the beginning, the middle, and the end and put the strips into three different piles. Get this done and you'll have a method." But her guidance did not help the students understand the concept of sequencing any better, nor what it meant to create temporal order from story. Only one group of students seemed to understand what she meant and completed the task. So although Carol wanted her students to practice the skill of sequencing, she provided them with little guidance for doing so, either with her help or on their own.

The English chair at one of the more typically performing schools, speaking about his teachers in general, said, "Incorporating strategies is difficult for most of us because it's hard for us to pull ourselves out of our comfort range. You know, unless we're prepared to teach the strategy, we're inclined to do something the old way."

Conceptions of Learning

When we examined how the teachers in the present study conceived of successful learning, two quite different views emerged. For some of the teachers, learning was seen as successful and complete once students exhibited an initial understanding of the focal skill or concept. For other teachers, such immediate understandings were simply the beginning of the learning process, which continued with related activities to move students toward deeper understandings and generativity of ideas.

Results for the three groups of teachers are summarized in Table 5. Unusually successful and more typical teachers' approaches to student learning were decidedly different. As the table indicates, all the more successful teachers took a generative approach to student learning, going beyond students' acquisition of the skills or knowledge to engage them in deeper understandings. In comparison, all the more typical teachers tended to move on to other goals and activities once they had evidence that the target skills or knowledge had been learned. Examples drawn from more successful and more typical classrooms follow.

Alicia Alliston at Drew Middle School never stopped her literature lessons when she was confident her students had understood the book and developed their own defensible interpretations. Once arriving at this level of expertise, she provided an array of activities that provoked her students to think and learn more. For example when her students were reading and writing about *The Midwife's Apprentice* by Karen Cushman, they also discussed the history, life, and art of the Renaissance. They did research into the life and social patterns of the period and ended with a Renaissance Faire. Celeste Rotondi at Springfield High School had her students work in literature circles where they discussed both the commonalities and differences in the books they read. Literature circle time was her students' opportunity to go beyond the texts they were reading, as more mature discussants and critics. One literature circle involved students in reading the following teacher-selected books: *The Great Gatsby*; *Bless me, Ultima*; *Slaughterhouse Five*; and *Always Running*. At the end of the cycle of discussions the students wrote and performed songs about the books and their deeper meanings and created CD cases with fictional song titles, covers, and artists. The class also read *Night* by Elie Wiesel. To prepare for it, Alicia had her students look at photos from concentration camps and write down words and phrases that were relevant. These were used to create poems. While reading *Night*, the class visited the Museum of Tolerance, completed an assignment while they were there, and wrote letters from three points of view (seven to choose from), all involved with the Holocaust in some way. Thus, the reading of *Night* became not merely an understanding and critique of the work itself (though this was done), but rather an integrated opportunity to contemplate historical, ethical, political, and personal issues raised by the reading.

Gloria Rosso at Hudson Middle School wanted to teach her students research skills using the World Wide Web, hard copy material, and interviews as sources of information. To do this, she engaged her students in a generative activity that would extend their learning of content as well as of the research process. She began with what she called a mini-unit on the students' surnames—

what they meant and their histories—leading to essay writing, the development of coats of arms, and class presentations. In addition to teaching students to access data on genealogies on the Web, she also taught them to develop good questions for interviews with family members, and how to read materials and take notes and citations. Students were invited to explore the use of symbols, as used in coats of arms, as a background to devising their own. While Gloria helped with the research skills, the students discussed what they were learning and ways in which the histories of their names provided a living trail of history. This led into her next and more extensive research unit on African Americans, where once again, the students not only did research and wrote papers but also interacted around the larger implications of the stories of African American experiences and present-day life.

In contrast, in the more typical schools, the learning activity and the thinking about it seemed to stop with the responses sought or the assigned task completed—at a level Vygotsky (1987) calls "pseudo concepts," in which the learning is more a superficial recall of names, definitions, and facts than a deeper and more highly conceptualized learning.

For example, when Jack Foley's class at New Westford High read *To Kill a Mockingbird*, he asked questions about the content and vocabulary. He called on students to provide the answers, and when they did he either added additional comments to their responses or moved on to the next question. Neither the text nor the students' responses were used during the discussion to generate historical, social, or other connections and elaborations.

At Hayes High School, after reading *Romeo and Juliet*, Ron Soja gave his students the following issues and asked them to select the one they most "leaned" toward: Romeo and Juliet are victims of fate, Romeo and Juliet are victims of the society, or Romeo and Juliet are victims of their own passions. The next day they discussed their selections and reasons, then Ron went on to the next topic.

At Hendricks High School, Carol McGuiness ended her lessons when her students provided the answer she was after. Using the example of the sequencing activity again, as soon as the first group finished, Carol asked them to read the strips in sequence. Then the activity was over, even though the other groups were in the midst of struggling with the task. No connection was made either to the chapter as a whole or to the forthcoming chapter, not to sequencing itself as a sometimes useful skill. Even the fact that the teacher was willing to end the task before all but one group had finished was evidence of the lack of value that was attributed to it as a thought-provoking learning experience. Similarly, when her students studied verb tenses, they were given a homework sheet that was a continuation of what they were doing in class. It was more of the same, rather than a generative activity that built upon the new knowledge.

Thus, in the higher-performing schools, students were constantly encouraged to go beyond the basic learning experiences in challenging and enriching ways. In contrast, students in the more typical schools had few opportunities for more creative and critical experiences.

Classroom Organization

The final aspect of instructional approaches that differentiated among the teachers in the present study had to do with the extent to which the classrooms were organized to provide students with a variety of opportunities to learn through substantive interaction with one another as well as with the teacher. In some classrooms, English learning and high literacy (the content as well as the skills) were treated as social activity, with depth and complexity of understanding, and proficiency with conventions growing out of the shared cognition that emerges from interaction with present and imagined others. Other classrooms emphasized individual activity and individual thinking, and students tending to work alone or to interact primarily with the teacher. Even when group work occurred in such classrooms, the activity usually involved answering questions rather than engaging in substantive discussion from multiple perspectives.

The relevant data are summarized in Table 5. As the table indicates, the dominant classroom interaction patterns in the more successful classrooms differed sharply from those in the more typical classrooms. In the higher-performing schools, at least 96% of the teachers helped students engage in the thoughtful dialogue we call *shared cognition*. Teachers expected their students to not merely work together, but to sharpen their understandings with, against, and from each other. In comparison, teachers in the more typical classes focused on individual thinking. Even when their students worked together, the thinking was parallel as opposed to dialogic. Examples of both approaches follow.

In the classes of the higher-performing schools, students not only worked together in physical proximity, but they also gained skill in sharing ideas, reacting to each other, testing out ideas and arguments, and contributing to the intellectual tenor of the class. They engaged in the kind of teamwork that is now so highly prized in business and industry, although sometimes suspect in school settings where solitary work is still too often prized.

All the classes at International High School, including Marsha Slater's, work collaboratively. In Marsha's class, from the first days of school and throughout the year, students are taught to work together, discussing issues and reacting to each others' ideas even as they are gaining a common language through which to communicate. (All students at International are recent immigrants.) During one of the first few weeks of school, Marsha introduced a literature research and writing activity that required group work throughout. The students divided into groups and started planning their strategy. We saw a similar pattern in science, where the students were graphing and mapping on computer the results of their group-accomplished experiments. It is part of the educational philosophy of the school that "The most successful educational programs are those that emphasize high expectations coupled with effective support systems; individuals learn best from each other in collaborative groupings." Throughout our study, Marsha's emphasis was on collaborative and active learning.

Activity guides helped the students in a group work together toward a common goal, but debriefing sessions and conferences provided a time for each student to discuss not only the group's work but also to describe her or his own areas of accomplishment and need. In all the higher-performing schools, such collaborative activities were common. Students worked together to develop the best thinking or best paper (for other product) they collectively could; they helped and learned within the same activity as in life.

In the higher-performing schools, even whole-class activities, particularly discussion, were used to foster similar cognitive collaborations. At Foshay, although her students sometimes worked in groups, Myra LeBendig often favored whole-class discussions. She used discussions as a time for exchanging ideas and stimulating thought, exploration, and explanation. As a whole class, her students were taught to work together, listening to and interacting with one another about the ideas at hand. For example, throughout one whole-class discussion about *The Invisible Man*, her students raised ideas and freely engaged in literary dialogue. One student brought up the issue of how race was treated in the book, and another the symbolism of blindness as ignorance (as portrayed in the book), of not being able to see. One student said he thought Dr. Bledsoe had self-hatred, in response to which a classmate said she didn't think it was self-hatred, but that he [Bledsoe] didn't know where he fit in and didn't know how to connect his two cultural parts. "He hasn't found himself. He's in-between." This generated a discussion that continued for half an hour, with the students in deep discussion about their interpretations of the text and its connection to social issues of identity. Myra explained that she uses such discussions to help students "work through their evolving understandings, ideas, and opinions that will change as they continue reading the book." She explained that early in the year she told her students, "Fight to teach me," meaning she wanted them to disagree with her (and each other) and extend her (and their) thinking with their comments. This is exactly what they did in class discussion.

At the same school, Kate McFadden-Midby's classes often worked in collaborative groups. Group Share was a common activity during which students came up with interesting questions about what they were reading for the group to consider and discuss. When it was group time, the students immediately began interacting in productive ways. They knew what to do and were eager to interact. Kate explained that early in the school year she told students about her expectations, time management, and ways in which their thinking was valued. Her goal was to have her students truly share ideas and stimulate each other's thinking by engaging in real conversations. We have already seen how she orchestrated such activities in the example of her lessons on character analysis presented in the section on strategy instruction. In that example, the students worked together to sharpen their individual and collective understandings of characters in books they had read, even though they had read different books. In turn, the understandings that emerged from those discussions helped the students to develop rich characters in plays of their own. Throughout, they were absorbed in discussion and thought.

Cathy Starr, at Hudson Middle School, used both whole-class and small-group activities; they wove into one another and together supported students' developing thinking. For example, in response to reading assignments, she asked her students to bring three thought-provoking questions to class to stimulate discussion. Students met in groups to discuss these questions and come up with one or two "big" questions for the entire class to discuss. Cathy moved from group to group, modeling questions and comments, and provoking deeper discussion and analysis. After a whole-class discussion, Cathy listed on the board items on which the students had agreed as well as issues that still needed to be resolved. In both small groups and whole-class discussions, the students needed to interact in thoughtful ways; the social activity was critical to moving their understandings forward and doing well. These discussions were interspersed with assignments the students were to complete in groups. For example, while reading *The Giver*, she gave the following assignment:

> Group Task 1—Government [this is one of a set of four]
>
> Form a group of no less than three and no more than five students to complete this task.
>
> Review the chapters we have read. Design a chart that illustrates how the government for this community functions. Include all information you can find about who makes the decisions and who has power in the community. Include the roles of individuals in this structure.

This task required the students not merely to locate information, but to discuss and refine what they meant by "government" and how it functions in the story, as well as the implicit roles the various characters serve. Some of the teachers in this study called such working groups "minds to mind," stressing the thoughtfulness they expected.

In classes in the more typical schools, such collaborative work rarely took place. For example, Monica Matthews at Crestwood Middle School explained that she has tried to have her students work in groups, but "they're unruly." She had them work together in groups minimally "because they talk off task." Similarly, Elba Rosales at Hendricks High School "saved" group work for the honors and advanced placement classes, claiming that the regular students require more lecture and don't handle group work well. Often the group work that was assigned to what she considers her higher-functioning classes required the students to work independently to complete their part of a task, then put the pieces together as final product. For example, after reading *Animal Farm*, each group was to create an Animal Farm Newspaper. However, each group member selected a segment (e.g., obituary, horoscope, cartoon, editorial) and completed it as homework; then the pieces were assembled into a four-page newspaper. While the group effort could be said to reflect what happens at a real news office, the students missed opportunities to work through ideas together for each of the components that was incorporated into the final product.

In other classes, group work often took place, but the students did not "chew ideas" together or challenge each other intellectually. They cooperated in completing the task but did not work conceptualizations through. For example, when Jack Foley's students at New Westford High School worked together doing study guides, they kept the guides in front of them, moving from item to item down the page. As one student called out the answer, the others wrote it onto their worksheets, and together they moved on to the next question.

Thus, there is an essential difference in the way learning activity is carried on in the higher-performing and more typical schools, with the higher-performing teachers treating students as members of dynamic learning communities that rely on social and cognitive interactions to support learning. In contrast, the more typical teachers in more typical schools tend to treat each learner as an individual, with the assumption that interaction will either diminish the thinking or disrupt the discipline. However, because the schools in this study had similar student bodies, it became evident that the students were more actively engaged in their school work more of the time when English and literacy were treated as social activity.

Discussion

This study focused on students' achievement of high literacy as it is taught in English classes and results in scores on high-stakes assessments of reading and writing. We began the work holding a sociocognitive view of instruction, postulating that learning is influenced by the values, experiences, and actions that exist within the educational environment. From this perspective, it is posited that student performance in reading and writing is influenced by the instructional context the students experience, as well as on the larger educational environment that gives rise to what counts as knowing, what gets taught, and how it gets taught. Because educational environments differ in their goals, procedures for arriving at them, and what gets rewarded as success, this view suggests that differing types of environments will result in different approaches to teaching reading, writing, and English, and different types of learning. This study of higher and more typically achieving schools bore out the theoretical expectations and identified the following distinguished features of instruction in the higher-performing schools: (a) Skills and knowledge are taught in multiple types of lessons; (b) tests are deconstructed to inform curriculum and instruction; (c) within curriculum and instruction, connections are made across content and structure to ensure coherence; (d) strategies for thinking and doing are emphasized; (e) generative learning is encouraged; and (f) classrooms are organized to foster collaboration and shared cognition.

These features dominated the higher-achieving English and language arts programs. In contrast, some aspects of these features were present in some of the more typical schools some of the time and other features none of the time. It is the "whole cloth" environment, the multilayered contribution of the full set of these features to the teaching and learning interactions, that distinguished the higher-achieving programs from the others. These features are obviously related to teachers' visions of what counts as knowing and the goals of instruction that guide the teaching and learning process. They shaped the educational experiences of students and teachers in the high-performing schools we studied. All the teachers with whom we worked were aware of concerns about test scores and students' acquisition of skills. Yet in the most successful schools, there was always a belief in students' abilities to be able and enthusiastic learners; they believed all students can learn and that they, as teachers, could make a difference. They therefore took on the hard job of providing rich and challenging instructional contexts in which important discussions about English, language, literature, and writing in all its forms could take place, while using both the direct instruction and contextualized experiences their students' needed for skills and knowledge development. Weaving a web of integrated and interconnected experiences, they ensured that their students would develop the pervasive as well as internalized learning of knowledge, skills, and strategies to use on their own as more mature and more highly literate individuals at school, as well as at home and in their future work.

These findings cut across high-poverty areas in inner cities as well as middle class suburban communities. They occurred in schools that were scoring higher in English and literacy than other schools serving comparable populations of students. They involved concentrated efforts on the part of teachers to offer extremely well-conceived and well-delivered instruction based on identified goals about what is important to be learned, and on an essential understanding of how the particular knowledge and skills identified as learning goals occur and are used in the carrying out of real literacy activities. From these teachers, we have learned that it is not enough to teach to the test, to add additional tutoring sessions or mandated summer school classes, or to add test prep units or extra workbooks on grammar or literary concepts. Although many forms of additional and targeted help were evident as parts of the effort to improve student achievement in the higher-performing schools, these alone were not enough. The overriding contributor to success was the whole-scale attention to students' higher literacy needs and development throughout the curriculum, which shaped what students experienced on a day-to-day basis in their regular classrooms. Such revisioning of both curriculum and instruction requires a careful rethinking of the skills and knowledge that need to be learned; their integration for students' use in broader activities; and continued practice, discussion, and review of them as needed over time. The English and literacy learning goals, at once recognizable and overt, can then permeate a range of direct literacy and literacy-embedded activities.

They are at the heart of the kind of English and language arts teaching and learning across the grades I discussed in the introduction to this article, and underlie the development of the higher literacy and deeper knowledge this entails. Thus, the findings provide us with not merely a vision but also a set of principles and an array of examples to use as guides in revisioning effective instruction.

It is important to emphasize that in the higher-performing schools, the six features worked in conjunction with one another to form a supportive web of related learning. It would be erroneous to assume that the adoption of any one feature, however well orchestrated, without the others could make the broad-based impact needed to effect major change in student learning. Rather, it was the suffusion of the school environment with related and important learnings that were highlighted by the teachers and recognized by the students as making a difference. My earlier article (Langer, 2000) dealt with the principle-led creation of professional contexts in schools that beat the odds; this article adds that next critical dimension, principle-led practice. I hope these reports will be helpful to educators in making decisions about effective paths toward the improvement of student achievement.

Limitations and Next Steps

Because this was an observational study, it cannot prove causality. It does, however, add to our knowledge of the differences between schools and classrooms whose students are attaining higher than expected levels of literacy achievement and those who are not, across a very diverse range of schools and student populations. The schools, teachers, and teaching styles in this study differed in many ways, but they reflected a cohesive set of underlying approaches to curriculum and instruction, despite the many variations in how these general approaches were implemented. Although the approaches were quite consistent across the schools that beat the odds, some also were present in some of the lower-performing schools, but with lesser consistency or pervasiveness. At least two types of follow-up investigation would be helpful. One would focus at a more micro level on teacher and class differences to specify what differences can be tolerated, and to what degree, before achievement is compromised. The second would be an instructional intervention, attempting to put into place the features of beating the odds schools in more typical, lower-performing schools, studying whether these features, when placed in schools that do not already have them, will positively affect student performance, and the kinds of professional and instructional development activities needed for this to occur.

Acknowledgments

This report is based on research supported in part under the Research and Development Centers Program (Award No. R305A60005) as administered by OERI. However, the contents do not necessarily represent the positions or policies of the Department of Education, OERI, or the Institute on Student Achievement. The research was completed with the hard work of an expert team of field researchers: Paola Bonissone, Carla Confer, Gladys Cruz, Ester Helmar-Salasoo, Sally Kahr, Tanya Manning, Eija Rougle, Steven Ostrowski, and Anita Stevens. I offer sincere thanks to the many teachers, students, and schools for their cooperation. It was their commitment to increasing English teachers' knowledge about ways to improve student learning and achievement that motivated each of them to participate. I am grateful.

References

Applebee, A.N. (1993). *Literature in the secondary school.* Urbana, IL: National Council of Teachers of English.

Applebee, A.N. (1996). *Curriculum as conversation: Transforming traditions of teaching and learning.* Chicago: University of Chicago Press.

Bakhtin, M.M. (1981). *The dialogic imagination.* Austin: University of Texas Press.

Barnes, D. (1976). *Communication and the curriculum.* London: Penguin.

Bazerman, C. (1981). What written knowledge does: Three examples of academic discourse. *Philosophy of the Social Sciences, 11*(3), 361–387.

Bereiter, C., & Scardamalia, M. (1987). An attainable version of high literacy: Approaches to teaching higher order skills in reading and writing. *Curriculum Inquiry, 17*(1), 10–30.

Bloom, B.S. (1971). Mastery learning and its implications for curriculum development. In E.W. Eisner (Ed.), *Confronting curriculum reform.* Boston: Little, Brown.

Bransford, J.D., Brown, A.L., & Cocking, R.R. (Eds.). (1999). *How people learn: Brain, mind, experience, and school.* Washington, DC: National Academy Press.

Brown, A.L., & Campione, J. (1996). Psychological theory and the design of innovative learning environments: On procedures, principles, and systems. In L. Schuable & R. Glazer (Eds.), *Innovations in learning: New environments for learning.* Mahwah, NJ: Erlbaum.

Brown, J.S., Collins, A., & Daguid, P. (1989). Situated cognitions and the culture of learning. *Educational Researcher, 18*(1), 32–42.

Cope, B., & Kalantzis, M. (1993). The power of literacy and the literacy of power. In B. Cope & M. Kalantzis (Eds.), *The powers of literacy: A genre approach to writing* (pp. 154–178). Pittsburgh, PA: University of Pittsburgh Press.

Dewey, J. (1938). *Education as experience.* New York: Collier.

Dyson, A. (1993). *Social worlds of children learning to write in an urban primary school.* New York: Teachers College Press.

Gee, J. (1996). *Social linguistics and literacies: Race, writing, and difference.* London: Taylor & Maxwell.

Goodman, Y., & Wilde, S. (1992). *Literacy events in a community of young writers.* New York: Teachers College Press.

Graff, G. (1987). *Professing literature: An institutional history.* Chicago: University of Chicago Press.

Graves, D. (1983). *Writing: Teachers and children at work.* Exeter, NH: Heinemann.

Greeno, J.G. (1997). On claims that answer the wrong questions. *Educational Researcher, 26*(1), 5–17.

Greeno, J.G., & the Middle School Through Applications Project Group. (1998). The situativity of knowing, learning, and research. *American Psychologist, 53,* 5–26.

Guthrie, J.T., & Alvermann, D.E. (Eds.). (1999). *Engaged reading.* New York: Teachers College Press.

Hillocks, G., Jr. (1986). *Research on written composition.* Urbana, IL: National Conference on Research in English.

Hillocks, G.W. (1995). *Teaching writing as reflective practice.* New York: Teachers College Press.

Hirsch, E.D. (1996). *The schools we need and why we don't have them.* New York: Doubleday.

Langer, J.A. (1986). A sociocognitive perspective on literacy. In J. Langer (Ed.), *Language, literacy and culture: Issues of society and schooling* (pp. 1–20). Norwood, NJ: Ablex.

Langer, J.A. (1995). *Envisioning literature: Literary understanding and literature instruction.* New York: Teachers College Press; Newark, DE: International Reading Association.

Langer, J.A. (2000). Excellence in English in middle and high school: How teachers' professional lives support student achievement. *American Educational Research Journal, 37*(2), 397–439.

Langer, J.A., & Allington, R.L. (1992). Curriculum research in writing and reading. In P.W. Jackson (Ed.), *Handbook on research on curriculum* (pp. 687–725). New York: Macmillan.

Langer, J.A., & Applebee, A.N. (1987). *How writing shapes thinking: A study of teaching and learning* (Research Rep. No. 22). Urbana, IL: National Council of Teachers of English.

Lave, J., & Wenger, E. (1991). *Situated learning: Legitimate peripheral participation.* Cambridge, UK: Cambridge University Press.

Myers, M. (1996). *Changing minds.* Urbana, IL: National Council of Teachers of English.

National Assessment of Educational Progress. (1998). *National writing summary data tables for grade 8 teacher data.* Retrieved October 10, 1999, from http://www.nces.ed.gov/nationsreportcard/TABLES/index.shtml

National Assessment of Educational Progress. (1994). *NAEP 1992 Report Card.* Washington, DC: Government Printing Office for the National Center for Education Statistics, U.S. Department of Education.

Nystrand, M., & Gamoran, A. (1997). *Opening dialogue.* New York: Teachers College Press.

Nystrand, M., Gamoran, A., & Heck, M.J. (1992). Using small groups for response to and thinking about literature. *English Journal, 83,* 14–22.

Paris, S.G., Wasik, B.A., & Turner, J.C. (1991). The development of strategic readers. In R. Barr, M.L. Kamil, P. Mosenthal, & P.D. Pearson (Eds.), *Handbook of reading research* (Vol. 2, pp. 609–640). White Plains, NY: Longman.

Pressley, M., Allington, R., Morrow, L., Baker, K., Nelson, E., Wharton-McDonald, et al. (1998). *The nature of effective first-grade reading instruction* (Rep. No. 11007). Albany, NY: Center on English Learning & Achievement.

Pressley, M., El-Dinary, P.B., Brown, R., Schuder, T.L., Pioli, M., Green, K., et al. (1994). Transactional instruction in reading comprehension strategies. *Reading and Writing Quarterly, 10,* 5–19.

Purves, A., & Beach, R. (1972). *Literature and the reader.* Urbana, IL: National Council of Teachers of English.

Raphael, T.E., & McMahon, S.I. (1994). Book club: An alternative framework for reading instruction. *The Reading Teacher, 48,* 102–116.

Schallert, D.L. (1976). Improving memory for prose: The relationship between depth of processing and context. *Journal of Verbal Learning and Verbal Behavior, 15,* 621–632.

Slavin, R.E. (1983). *Cooperative learning.* New York: Longman.

Smith, M., & O'Day, J. (1991). Systemic school reform. In S.H. Fuhrman & B. Malem (Eds.), *The politics of curriculum and testing: The 1990 yearbook of the politics of education association.* London: Falmer.

Squire, J.R., & Applebee, R.K. (1968). *High school English instruction today.* New York: Appleton-Century-Crofts.

Sternberg, R.J., & Horvath, J.A. (1995). A prototype view of expert teaching. *Educational Researcher, 24*(6), 9–17.

Taylor, B., Pearson, P.D., Clark, K.F., & Walpole, S. (1999). *Beating the odds in teaching all children to read* (Rep. No. 2-006). Ann Arbor, MI: Center for the Improvement of Early Reading Achievement.

Turner, J.C. (1993). Situated motivation in literacy instruction. *Reading Research Quarterly, 28,* 288–290.

Vygotsky, L.S. (1987). Thinking and speech. In R. Rieber & A. Carton (Eds.), *The collected words of L. Vygotsky.* New York: Plenum.

Wharton-McDonald, R., Pressley, M., & Hampston, J. (1998). Literacy instruction in nine first-grade classrooms. Teacher characteristics and student achievement. *The Elementary School Journal, 99,* 102–119.

39

Can Minimally Trained College Student Volunteers Help Young At-Risk Children to Read Better?

Jill Fitzgerald

The main purpose of the present study was to investigate at-risk first- and second-grade students' reading growth as they were tutored by minimally trained college students. Also examined were the nature of the growth and the effectiveness of minimally trained college student volunteers on the children's reading growth. The college students in this study were volunteer work-study students who were participating in the recent America Reads initiative sponsored by U.S. President Clinton. The children were first and second graders who were deemed at risk of failure by their classroom teachers and reading specialists in the schools.

In 1996, President Clinton established the America Reads Challenge to mobilize a million work-study college students as reading tutors for children in kindergarten through third grade. The initiative was begun with the understanding that children who do not learn to read well in the early grades usually continue to do poorly in subsequent grades (Clay, 1985; Juel, 1988; Stanovich, 1986), making the early years critical and pivotal in children's academic careers.

The advent of the America Reads initiative immediately provoked controversy in academic and practitioner literacy communities. The majority of prior efforts to provide extra literacy support for children in the early grades have been in-school programs that have involved one-on-one teaching by extensively trained professionals, with Reading Recovery as the prototype of such interventions (Hiebert, 1994; Shanahan, 1998). The popularity of such programs has been fostered by the generally positive results obtained with Reading Recovery (DeFord, Lyons, & Pinnell, 1991). At center stage in the controversy then is the question of whether undergraduate work-study students with no or very little training in teaching reading could significantly impact young children's reading abilities (Wasik, 1998).

From *Reading Research Quarterly*, 36, 28–46. Copyright © 2001 by the International Reading Association.

Two domains of prior theory and research are important to the present study—early reading development and tutoring effectiveness. With regard to research-based reading development theory, two early phases are Literacy Roots, which typically occurs gradually from birth through kindergarten, and Initial Literacy, which typically occurs in first grade (Chall, 1996; Fitzgerald & Shanahan, 2000). The critical kinds of knowledge developed during Literacy Roots are *metaknowledge*, in particular, knowing about functions and purposes of reading and writing; *content knowledge*, about a wide array of subjects; knowledge of particular *text attributes*, especially phonological knowledge and graphemic knowledge; and *procedural knowledge*, or learning what texts are and how to manipulate them (Fitzgerald & Shanahan, 2000). Research has documented that literate knowledge in this period develops concomitantly in reading, writing, listening, and speaking (Teale & Sulzby, 1986). One kind of learning stands out among the others as extremely important during the Literacy Roots phase; that is, development of phonological awareness, or the ability to hear and manipulate separate words, parts in words, and individual sounds in words (Adams, 1990). However, although phonological awareness is critical to literacy development, research indicates that it can develop as a result of reading and writing growth (Adams, 1990; Tunmer & Nesdale, 1985), and that it therefore is not necessarily a precursor to literacy development.

In Chall's words, the essence of the next phase, Initial Literacy, is "learning the arbitrary set of letters and associating these with the corresponding parts of spoken words" (1996, pp. 15–16). *Metaknowledge* continues to be a key, but of a different sort in this stage than in Literacy Roots. Here, students are learning increasingly that readers and writers work together, that is, that each works on the premises of the other (Nystrand, 1989). Further, they learn about self-monitoring of their own meaning and word making. For example, monitoring strategies such as asking, "Does this make sense?" are essential for word reading and production (Clay, 1993). *Content knowledge* continues to grow. Key knowledge about *text attributes* is immeasurably important in this period. During this time, students are continuing to acquire grapheme awareness, and they are learning orthographic or morphological patterns in words. Children also are learning that (a) their knowledge of syntactically acceptable word orders learned previously through oral language applies in reading and writing, and (b) their understandings of acceptable word order can be used to help make sound attempts at new words as they read and write. Finally, they begin to develop *procedural knowledge* such as using strategic searches and learning to select and produce graphic and syntactic cues to read and write words and sentences (Clay, 1993; Schwartz, 1997).

Perhaps most important to the present study with regard to developmental theory about learning to read is that research has affirmed the centrality of word recognition in early reading (Ehri, 1991). Although understanding and response to what is read are always the predominant goals of reading, it is clear that the major work of early reading revolves around recognizing and pronouncing words. During Literacy Roots and Initial Reading, three phases of word recognition occur. In the beginning, word learning is predominantly logographic (Ehri, 1991). That is, children start to remember words using "strictly visual characteristics rather than letter-sound correspondences" (Ehri, 1991, p. 387). Next, children enter an alphabetic phase of phonologically recoding "spellings into pronunciations according to grapheme-phoneme correspondence rules" (Ehri, 1991, p. 396). This typically may begin toward the end of kindergarten or in first grade. Finally, children enter an orthographic phase when they attempt "instant analysis of words into orthographic units without phonological conversion" (Frith, 1985, p. 306).

Tutoring in various subject areas can be an effective strategy for improving student achievement, though the extent of effectiveness varies from program to program and across individuals (Shanahan, 1998). Similarly, it appears that across various subjects, tutors with more training and experience have a greater impact (e.g., Cohen, Kulik, & Kulik, 1982; Shanahan, 1998; Wasik, 1998; Wasik & Slavin, 1993). However, it is clear that not all children benefit from tutoring, with research results suggesting that tutoring is not especially effective with many low-achieving readers (e.g., Mathes & Fuchs, 1994; Shanahan, 1998).

There have been few direct studies of tutor training for reading instruction (Shanahan, 1998; Wasik, 1998). At least two recent studies do suggest that either *long-term training* of college students as tutors (Juel, 1996) or *intense and directed supervision* of community volunteers by graduates in reading education (Invernizzi, Rosemary, Juel, & Richards, 1997) can have an impact on children's reading progress.

In sum, considerable research has accumulated to support a clearly articulated theory of early reading development. Important keys to early reading progress involve development of phonological awareness and word-recognition abilities. However, to date little is known about the extent to which reading tutors who have minimal training can significantly affect children's early reading progress. The complexities involved in helping children to acquire the necessary phonological awareness and word-recognition strategies might lead to the expectation that only teachers with considerable understanding of theory of early reading and of the intricate web of word-recognition mechanisms could suitably nurture early reading. Yet, volunteer tutoring programs are currently plentiful in the United States. America Reads is a costly project with high visibility, but many literacy educators have argued that having work-study students tutor children is not the most effective use of federal monies. Instead, many advocate that the funds might have more impact on children's reading if they were spent in other ways, such as for training reading teachers in school systems.

It seems imperative to research various aspects of volunteer tutoring in reading programs. The present study was designed as a modest step in this direction, an assessment of the effects of one program, involving minimally trained college work-study students, on at-risk children's reading. To my knowledge, this study is among the first involving the America Reads initiative (Gambrell & Dromsky, 1999; Morrow & Woo, 1999).

The present study also is significant in that it provides an example of a unique alternative method for conducting research on field-based programs where traditional control groups may not be possible. This was the case in the present situation because the schools declined the possibility of incorporating control groups into the design. Concern was expressed that teachers of the children in the control group might "look bad," even if they were performing well. Such concern is not unusual in educational programs. In a classic experimental—control comparison, the control group receives none of the experimental treatment. In essence, this is a test of how effective a treatment is compared with none of the treatment. The alternative control group design used in the present study builds on a method demonstrated in research on a volunteer program done by Invernizzi et al. (1997), involving a within-program control group format, where a group of children is compared with a group of similar children in the same program who received identical instruction, but less of it. The alternative design used by Invernizzi et al. (1997) is essentially a test of how effective a treatment is compared to a lesser amount of it, rather than none of it. This alternative within-program control group design is potentially a more stringent test of a treatment than the classic form of comparing something to nothing. If statistically significant outcomes arise, they clearly can be directly attributed to what is happening in the program in conjunction with the amount of treatment that is provided.

Method

Sites and Participants

Schools. Children from four elementary schools and 40 different classrooms were tutored. A representative from each of four University of North Carolina at Chapel Hill Partnership Development School districts chose an elementary school. In each case except one, the school was chosen because it had either the lowest or second-lowest average reading scores in the district on the prior year end-of-grade assessments required by the state. In one case, the school was chosen because it was the closest to the university (approximately 20 minutes away). This school was a designated Title I school, as were the other three.

Tutor and Supervisor Selection and Demographics. Work-study students who were interested in becoming tutors or supervisors under the America Reads initiative were screened through initial interviews with a coordinator responsible for program operations and with Literacy Studies faculty. The coordinator was a Reading Recovery teacher on paid reassignment from a local school district. The purpose of screening interviews was to ensure that all tutors and supervisors were enthusiastic, had a desire to work with young children, were willing to exert the necessary time and effort, would be cooperative, and had no prior criminal record. During the screening the basic tutor and supervisor responsibilities were explained, required appearance and demeanor at the schools were explained, and questions were asked about the students' reasons for wanting to tutor or supervise and about their past experiences with children. Students were asked to sign a pledge regarding prior criminal history and to commit to complete attendance and promptness at training and tutoring sessions. Only one tutor interviewee was turned down.

Forty work-study students were selected as tutors. All except one completed the year. That one dropped out after approximately 2 weeks of training. Five graduate students were selected as supervisors, one of whom graduated midyear. Two additional supervisors were selected for the spring semester. A demographic questionnaire was administered to tutors and supervisors in September.

Tutor Gender and Ethnicity. Thirty-seven of the tutors were female, two were male. There was considerable ethnic diversity. Forty-six percent reported themselves as having African heritage, 40% as Anglo, 5% Native American, 3% Asian, 3% Latino, and 3% Indo.

Tutor College Level and Major. Eight percent were freshman, 45% sophomores, 21% juniors, and 26% seniors. Tutors reported a wide variety of declared or desired majors, including education (21%), communications or journalism (18%), sciences (18%), psychology (15%), sociology (5%), a policy area (5%), English (5%), economics (3%), and history (3%), with 7% undecided. Future plans were also varied, with a full 30% of tutors saying they would like to teach or be involved in education in some way. Twenty-five percent planned to go to graduate school, 17% said something like they "just wanted to get a job," 11% planned to go to a professional school, and 17% were undecided.

Tutor Prior Experience. Many of the tutors (62%) had previous experience with some kind of tutoring. Of those who had tutored before, only one had tutored in reading or writing. Of those who had tutored, nine (39%) had worked with elementary-grade children. Forty-six percent of them had tutored for a year or less, with the remaining having tutored from 2 to 5 years. Aside from tutoring per se, a full 87% of the 39 tutors said they had worked with young children in some form (55% in day-care or baby-sitting situations; 39% in volunteer settings; and 6% in their own family, coaching, or counseling at camp).

Tutors' Reasons for Joining America Reads. It is noteworthy that the majority (67%) of the tutors were interested in becoming a tutor mainly because they wanted to help children in some way. Another 23% were involved because they wanted to teach or help in literacy efforts; and 10% indicated their primary reason was that the pay was good for a work-study student (tutors received approximately US$1.50 more per hour than other work-study students) or that they weren't sure of their reasons.

Supervisor Gender, Ethnicity, and College Major. Five supervisors were female, two male. Three reported having African heritage, three Anglo, and one declined to report. Two were working on a master's in library science, two a master's or Ph.D. in education, two a master's in guidance or school psychology, and one was a Ph.D. student in comparative literature. Two planned to teach in the future, two planned to become library/media specialists, one planned to become a school counselor, and two declined to answer.

Supervisors' Prior Tutoring Experience. Four of the supervisors indicated that they had tutored before in reading, writing, or multiple subjects, with elementary children or with multiple ages. Aside from tutoring, five indicated they had worked with young children, all in situations such as camp counseling or fieldwork for college classes. Only one had ever been a supervisor before. This was in a field component for her college course work.

Supervisors' Reasons for Joining America Reads. Two individuals said they wanted to be supervisors mainly because the experience would be relevant to their field of study, two said they wanted supervisory experience, one said the program looked like a good one to help advance literacy, and the others did not respond.

Child Selection and Demographics. The coordinator met with principals and teachers at each site in August to explain the program and describe the child selection procedures. Teachers were asked to refer children who they thought were among the poorest readers in their classes, but who also were not receiving additional special services such as those provided by Reading Recovery or resource room teachers. First graders were requested, but in some situations first-grade teachers did not refer enough children relative to available tutors, so children from another grade received services.

In all, 144 children received some amount of tutoring, though some of these were children who entered and then left quickly because they moved. One-hundred-thirty-one children were in the program long enough to have received and returned parent permission forms for inclusion in the research study. One-hundred-nineteen permission slips to use data were returned for a 91% return rate. Two parents who returned slips indicated they did not give permission. Of the 117 students whose parents gave permission for their inclusion in analyses, 4 were kindergarten children, 77 were first graders, 32 were second graders, and

4 were third graders. The children were in 40 different classrooms. Nineteen were from school A, 27 from school B, 36 from C, and 35 from D. In 3 schools, 10 children were referred who in fact were not reading below grade as measured by our pretests. The principals or teachers initially did not want any of these 10 children dropped from the program, though some agreed to replacements later in the year.

No child missed more than two sessions while in the America Reads program. However, some children moved away from the school, others moved in and were placed in the tutoring program, and in some schools, children in the tutoring program were shifted in or out of the program by the school principal. In three of the schools, Reading Recovery teachers were working with children who scored the highest among the lowest-scoring 25% of first graders, and these students were not included in the study. A few children attended America Reads tutoring while they were on a waiting list to go to Reading Recovery. After they entered the Reading Recovery program, they typically did not return to the America Reads program. No more than three children who exited from Reading Recovery unsuccessfully were subsequently placed in our tutoring program.

Main analyses were conducted comparing 64 children (47 first and 17 second graders) who received a full complement of sessions (50 sessions, from September through March) to a within-program group of 19 children (15 first and 4 second graders) who received 6 to 12 continuous weeks of tutoring.

Because the targeted instructional group was first and second graders, and because there were very few kindergarten students ($N = 4$) and third graders ($N = 3$), the two latter groups were excluded from any further analyses. All children for whom permission was not granted were also deleted as well as the 10 children who entered the program reading at or above grade level. Following are demographics for the remaining 99 first and second graders. These demographics were obtained from the school with parent permission.

There were 41 females and 58 males. One was Asian; 30 were African American; 60 were Anglo; 5 were Latino; and 3 indicated multiple ethnicities. Information about mother's highest level of education ($N = 55$) and whether the child received free or reduced-cost lunch ($N = 88$) was not available for all children. The available data suggested that although some children receiving services were from very low socioeconomic backgrounds, the majority probably were not. Seven percent of the children's mothers for whom data were available did not have a high school diploma; 25% had completed high school; 38% had some college education; 24% had a bachelor's degree; and 5% had a master's or doctoral degree. Only 28% of the children received free or reduced-cost lunch.

Tutoring Sessions

The Literacy Studies faculty at the University of North Carolina at Chapel Hill (consisting of myself and two others, James W. Cunningham and Dixie Lee

Spiegel) designed the tutoring session format based on assumptions gleaned from previous theory and research as detailed in the introduction to this article. Significant assumptions about children's learning were that (a) children learn to read by reading in meaningful contexts; (b) the ultimate goal of reading is gaining and making meaning with text; (c) the major work of beginning reading is getting words; (d) phonological awareness, or the ability to hear separate words, chunks in words, and separate sounds in words, is an important corollary to early literacy learning; (e) reading and writing develop simultaneously, and learning in one informs learning in the other; and (f) learning to read is facilitated through interaction with a more knowledgeable other.

The tutoring session format was modeled after aspects of Reading Recovery lessons and a format used by Invernizzi et al. (1997). The format was designed to incorporate techniques that have been documented to be effective in research studies. There were four parts as follows: repeated reading of familiar text, word study, writing for sounds, and reading a new book. The first part of the session, rereading, has been shown to facilitate fluency (Samuels, Schermer, & Reinking, 1992), aid automaticity in word recognition (Samuels, 1979), and help comprehension (Dowhower, 1987; Rasinski, 1990).

The word-study portion consisted of various activities and games designed to (a) explicitly teach sight words, (b) explicitly teach several word-getting strategies (using context to get words, structural analysis, and phonics), and (c) provide practice in learning sight words and word-getting strategies. Prior research suggests that *explicitly* helping children to analyze words and learn strategies may be especially beneficial to at-risk readers (e.g., Lysynchuk, Pressley, d'Ailly, Smith, & Cake, 1989; Pearson, 1984, 1985).

In the writing for sounds component, children were asked to write a sentence of their choosing. During this writing, a tutor could use various prompting activities designed to assist the child in developing phonemic awareness and knowledge of letters associated with sounds. Prior research suggests that the segmenting of speech and matching of letters to sounds required of young children as they begin to write short sentences is an excellent activity for developing phonemic awareness (Clay, 1985; cf. Invernizzi et al., 1997).

Last, a new book was presented to the child through guided reading. This part of the format was designed as a way for children to progress through increasingly difficult books using scaffolded instruction. Scaffolding provided by a knowledgeable other in material that has a few, but not too many, unknown words is a beneficial way to move children's learning (cf. Vygotsky, 1934/1978).

Each child received two 40-minute tutoring sessions per week. These sessions were intended to supplement (not replace) classroom reading instruction. Tutors remained with the same child throughout a given child's stay in the program. Tutors were required to maintain brief lesson plans. Books for the sessions were selected from a set of leveled books often used in Reading Recovery (e.g., Wright Group books). Supervisors visited tutoring sessions at least once a week and also held 1-hour group meetings to address questions with their tutors once a month.

Tutor and Supervisor Training

The university work-study office representative interpreted the America Reads guidelines to indicate that a minimal amount of tutor training could be done. Consequently, we held a total of 33 hours of paid training across the fall and spring semesters. Supervisors attended the same sessions as tutors and were provided no additional training. Approximately 10 of the 33 hours were conducted exclusively by the coordinator and dealt primarily with logistical and practical considerations, such as how to talk with teachers and other considerations important to being a university representative working in a school. All tutors and supervisors were required to attend all sessions. Sessions were videotaped, and individuals who missed a session were required to watch the tape.

The three Literacy Studies faculty conducted the remaining training sessions. Twelve hours were held before tutoring began, and the remaining were spaced over the rest of the two semesters. The main components of the sessions were (a) an introduction to principles of emergent literacy; (b) an initial overview of the four parts of the lesson, which included a tape of a Reading Recovery teacher doing a lesson with a first grader; (c) discussion of each of the four parts; and (d) examples of how each of the four parts might be done. Methods of conducting the training sessions included using videotapes, lecture, small-group discussion, and demonstrations. Each session was conducted by pulling from material the three Literacy Studies faculty use in their undergraduate course on teaching reading and writing and then modifying the session for the tutors. Modifications included making sure that all jargon was explained and pared down to essentials, primarily emphasizing the techniques we wanted the tutors to use.

Some examples used in instructing the tutors and supervisors about each of the four lesson parts follow. First, for the session on rereading, the faculty representative talked about what it was, how it functioned in the large picture of what early readers should learn, why it was important, and what research revealed about its importance. Faculty then demonstrated a rereading by asking a student from the class to participate. At the end of the session, tutors met in small groups with their supervisors to select books for rereading for their children and to ask and answer questions.

Second, for the session on word study, four main ways of recognizing words were elicited from the tutors and supervisors by using a short story written with hieroglyphic-like graphemes. The participants read the story as the university professor showed them new words for each page. After the reading, the professor elicited from the class the various strategies and ways that they recognized and remembered the words in the story. She then grouped these ways into four basic mechanisms—sight words, use of context, use of structural analysis, and phonics. Each of the four word-recognition techniques was then studied in turn. Important characteristics of each were discussed (e.g., which words to use, how many to select, when to teach which strategies), and a minilesson for teaching each was demonstrated by asking a small group of students in the class to participate. Handouts were given for minilessons for each of the four techniques. At the end of the sessions tutors met in small groups with their supervisors to plan for implementation of selected minilessons on strategies or techniques of their choice in their word-study sections for lessons in the upcoming week. Finally, the whole group met to ask and answer questions.

Third, in a session on writing for sounds, the faculty representative first discussed the importance of using writing for developing certain reading skills. Then he demonstrated several examples of activities tutors might use with their children, for instance, how tutors might show a child several pictures and ask the child to select one to talk about. The child would then say a sentence about the picture to write. He showed how, if the child had difficulty with a word he or she should be able to write, the tutor could prompt the child to hear certain sounds in the word and think about the correct letter(s) to match the sound. At the end of the session, tutors met in small groups with their supervisors to plan implementation of at least one of the writing-for-sounds techniques demonstrated.

Finally, during the session on reading a new book, a shared reading lesson and a language experience lesson were discussed and demonstrated by asking students in the class to participate. Handouts were given for samples of shared reading and language experience lessons with first graders. Students met in small groups with their supervisors to plan at least one implementation of either a shared reading lesson or a language experience lesson for the following week. The whole group then met to ask and answer questions.

Data Collection

Children's reading level, various reading abilities, and attitude toward reading were measured. Information was also collected from tutors and supervisors. The data about children's reading and information from tutors and supervisors were collected at three time points, at the inception of the program (September), in the middle (December), and at the end (March).

In a 2-hour session, tutors were trained in how to administer all of the assessments. Refresher training took place prior to the midyear assessments and the final assessments. Immediately after each assessment, all protocols were examined by the supervisors and the coordinator for issues such as clarity in miscue marking and whether the tutor had asked the child to advance high enough in the materials. Then I scored and coded all running records, and a trained graduate assistant scored and coded everything else.

Reliability estimates for all measures were obtained by having a second person independently score and categorize a random sample of 20% of the protocols. This person was a clinical research instructor who had recently completed a Ph.D. in special education with a secondary emphasis in literacy. Independent scoring took place after both the graduate assistant and the clinical research instructor were trained about the scoring and categorizing.

Child Measures. Several measures were used with the children, and all were individually administered and repeated at all three time points, except an attitude toward reading measure, which was given only at the beginning and the end. Instructional reading level—including book level, ability to read words in isolation, knowledge of letter names, knowledge of sounds for letters in isolation, knowledge of letters for sounds in context—and attitude toward reading were measured.

Instructional reading level was assessed with the use of passages from the Bader Reading and Language Inventory (Bader & Wiesendanger, 1994), but following procedures outlined by Clay (1993) for running records. The Bader Reading and Language Inventory is an informal reading inventory. It was chosen in part because grade-level equivalents of passages of this published inventory are well established and because, unlike some other inventories, early reading levels are represented in both preprimer and primer passages, providing greater sensitivity to initial reading levels. The child read orally from increasingly difficult passages while the tutor marked the child's miscues (deviations from text) on a second copy of the passage. Then I coded the miscues, and percentage of words read accurately was calculated to help determine instructional level. Inability to successfully pass a preprimer-level passage was assigned a score of "0." A score of ".25" indicated that the child successfully passed the preprimer, but no higher passage. On average, in a normally functioning population, a first grader can read at the preprimer level by the end of November, or about one fourth of the way through the school year. A score of ".50" indicated that the child successfully passed the primer level, but no higher passage. On average, a first grader can read at the primer level by about halfway through the school year. A score of "1" indicated that the child successfully passed the first-grade passage, generally achieved, on average, by the end of the year. A "2" meant the child successfully passed the second-grade passage. Reliability for identifying miscues was .94, and for coding categories, reliability ranged from .88 to .98.

Book level was the Reading Recovery book level being used during tutoring sessions. At the beginning, middle, and end of tutoring, tutors reported these book levels. Levels 3 through 8 are approximately preprimer level; 9 through 12 are approximately primer level; 13 through 16 are typical levels for end of first grade, and 17 through 20 are typical for beginning of second grade (q.v., Modern Curriculum Press, 1996, as cited in Invernizzi et al., 1997).

Ability to read words in isolation was measured by asking children to read words from graded word lists on the San Diego Quick Assessment (LaPray & Ross, 1986). Scores were determined with the use of the test directions, except that as just described for the previous measure, the final score was "0" if the preprimer list was not passed, .25 if the preprimer list was passed, and so on. The reliability estimate for scoring this test was .97.

Knowledge of letter names was measured using part of Clay's (lowercase) (1993) Letter Identification subtest of the Observational Survey. Children looked at individual letters and said the name. The score was given as percentage correct. Reliability was .98.

Knowledge of sounds for letters in isolation was measured by use of a second part of Clay's (1993) Letter Identification subtest of the Observational Survey. The child was shown letters and asked to say a sound the letter could make. The score was given as percentage correct. Reliability was .94.

Knowledge of letters for sounds in context was measured using Clay's (1993) writing dictation task. The child wrote a short sentence as the teacher repeatedly said the sentence slowly. The score was given as the percentage of sounds in words correctly represented. Reliability was .94.

Attitude toward reading was assessed using seven Likert item questions such as "How do you feel when it's time for reading in school?" (see Appendix). The child looked at each question as the examiner read it aloud and then chose and circled one face from a continuum of faces with varying degrees of smiles to frowns. The score was the mean across the items and could range from 1 to 5. Scoring reliability was 1.00.

Tutors' and Supervisors' Questionnaires

At entry and at the end of the year, tutors and supervisors filled out questionnaires that provided demographic information (detailed previously) as well as participants' views on what they would (did) enjoy about their role in the program, what would be (was) most difficult, what strategies would be (were) most important in teaching reading, what materials would be (were) most useful, confidence in their role, and the main reason for confidence in their role. At the end, they were also asked about weaknesses and strengths of tutor training.

Questionnaire responses were coded. Where categories of responses were created, intercoder agreement reliabilities ranged from .70 to 1.00.

Focus Group Interviews

Focus group interviews were conducted at the beginning, middle, and end of the year with 8 to 10 randomly selected tutors. All of the supervisors participated in parallel focus groups at the beginning and end of the year. The interviews gave participants the opportunity to talk in depth about problems they were having, positive events, all aspects of the program, and their training. The interviews were tape-recorded and later transcribed.

Analyses and Results

Preface: Attendance and Treatment Veracity

Tutor attendance at training and tutoring sessions was outstanding. Occasionally a tutor was sick, but all missed sessions were made up at a later date. During assignment to the tutoring program, no child missed more than two sessions.

Supervisors regularly reported that all tutors were using the four-part lesson format, and a reading of selected tutorial transcripts of sessions also supported the belief that the tutors made a good faith effort to carry out the sessions in the prescribed way.

General Indicators of Children's Reading Levels at Various Time Points

It seems important to provide a general picture of the overall progress of the children in the America Reads program in advance of assessing specific research questions. This provides a context or backdrop against which the research questions may be addressed. Fifty-eight percent of the children in the full-term program ($N = 64$) made gains of a half-year or more on instructional reading level (a gain of .50 or better). This is about the gain one would expect in a normally functioning population across a 5- to 6-month period. It is important to keep in mind that the posttests were administered in March, which was the sixth month of a 9- to 10-month school year. Thirty-seven percent made outstanding gains, from 1 year to 4 years' growth over the course of the 6 months. Only 16% showed no gain, while 27% showed an approximate 3-month gain over the 6 months (a gain of .25).

Of the 99 children who met the criteria for inclusion in data analyses, 33% exited the tutoring program reading at or above grade level at the time of their exit. Note that this figure includes the children who received short-term instruction. Of those who were in the program less than the full term, only 24% exited reading at or above grade level.

Table 1 shows figures across time for various reading indicators for the first and second graders with permission for data inclusion. These figures should be taken *only* as general indicators of reading levels for children who were in the program at a particular time point. It is important to remember that each time point does not include the same group of children, and, further, some children at later time points had only recently entered the program. Therefore, one cannot accurately assess actual growth from these figures.

The variable, Book Level, shows the Reading Recovery level of books tutors said they were using with children in their tutoring sessions. Children in the

TABLE 1

Means, Standard Deviations, and Ranges for Selected Reading Measures at Pre-, Mid-, and Posttest for all First and Second Graders With Permissions for Data Inclusion

	Mean			SD			Range		
	Pre(N)	Mid(N)	Post(N)	Pre	Mid	Post	Pre	Mid	Post
Book Level[1]	2.50(76)	6.46(87)	10.48(69)	2.06	3.26	4.88	1–10	1–16	1–22
Instructional Reading Level	.06(92)	.46(93)	1.17(75)	.13	.97	1.33	0–5	0–4	0–4
Attitude Toward Reading[2]	4.23(88)		4.11(74)	.68		.85	2–5		1–5

Numbers of children vary due to differing numbers of children in the program at various times and due to missing data.

[1] Using Reading Recovery levels. Levels 3 through 8 are approximately preprimer, 9 through 12 are approximately primer level, and 13 through 16 are typical levels for end of first grade (cf. publisher Modern Curriculum Press, 1996).

[2] Possible score range, 1–5.

program later in the year were reading at higher levels than those in the program at the beginning of the year, and on average the children in the program at posttest time were reading in primer-level books. Note also that while some children were reading in high levels, some were reading in very beginning levels. A similar picture emerged for reading instructional level except that when reading novel material for the posttest assessment, at the end of the year children were, on average, actually reading at first-grade level, that is, above the level expected in March for a normally functioning population. However, note again the considerable variability, with some children's reading instructional levels very low and others' very high. Finally, children's attitudes toward reading were generally high at both the beginning and ending of the year.

Was the Tutoring Program Effective?

Preliminary Assessments. To test for program effects on achievement level, children who received full-term tutoring were compared to children who received less than full-term tutoring (cf. Invernizzi et al., 1997). In this comparison, children who received less tutoring served as controls for those who received more tutoring. All aspects of the treatment were the same for both groups except for length of treatment.

Children who entered the program at the beginning of the fall semester and stayed in the program throughout the year were designated as receiving high-level treatment. These children ($N = 64$; 47 first graders and 17 second graders) received 25 weeks of tutoring. To ensure distinct groups, those receiving medium amounts of instruction were eliminated. Children ($N = 19$; 15 first graders and 4 second graders) who received 6 to 12 weeks of tutoring were designated as receiving low-level treatment. In the low-level treatment group, 2 children (1 first grader, 1 second grader) received 6 weeks of tutoring, 6 (5 first and 1 second) received 8 weeks, 3 (first) received 10 weeks, and 8 (6 first, 2 second) received 12 weeks. No more than three of the low-level treatment group children had previously received Reading Recovery assistance. Of the 15 tutors who taught children in the low-level treatment group, 12 also taught children in the high-level treatment group. There were six tutors in the high-level group who had previous tutoring experience with elementary-grade children, ranging from 1 to 5 years. Three of the same six tutors also tutored children in the low-level group, and there were no other tutors in the low-level group with prior tutoring experience with elementary-grade children.

To rule out other potential factors that might suggest that any arising statistically significant differences between groups would not indeed be due to the actual tutoring, several analyses were done. First, number of sessions was independent of the pretest measures of instructional reading level, letter-name knowledge, knowledge of sounds for letters in isolation, knowledge of letters for sounds in context, and ability to read words in isolation (correlations = −.01 to

−.19, p = .96 to .09). These results confirm the suitability of using length of tutoring as a basis for defining a within-program control group.

Second, it was possible that the low-sessions group was, by chance, composed of greater numbers of children associated with other risk factors such as poverty. If so, then statistically significant effects would not necessarily be attributable to programmatic treatment. To explore this alternative explanation, correlations were done between treatment group and several other variables: child's ethnicity; child's gender; whether the child received free, reduced-cost, or fully paid lunch; mother's highest level of education; whether the child received additional special services; classroom teacher; and tutor. Only the correlation of gender with treatment group was statistically significant, $\chi^2(N = 83) = .22$, p = .05. There were more boys in the group that received more tutoring. This result would not detract from the legitimacy of statistically significant effects, however, in that generally boys are more at risk for reading difficulty than are girls. Consequently, having more boys in the longer treatment group might be expected to work against greater growth, rather than working to facilitate it. Therefore, with the use of the selected variables, it appeared that the low-level treatment group was not composed of more at-risk children.

Finally, attribution of potential important differences between groups to an end-of-year growth spurt was ruled out. That is, the question was raised as to whether simply being in the program at the end of the year might reflect some sort of typical developmental growth spurt as opposed to an actual effect of tutoring. To address this issue the growth was looked at for five children in the low-level treatment group who were in the program at the end of the year. All entered reading at a .00 or .25 level, and none of these children showed an end-of-year growth spurt; their gain scores in instructional reading level ranged from .00 to .25. Consequently, it did not appear that simply being in the program at the end of the year, regardless of amount of previous tutoring, could account for statistically significant outcomes.

In sum, the within-program control group made an excellent comparison group. The main statistical analyses were repeated measures analyses of variance. Each repeated measures model is described in detail in the following sections. The F ratios were calculated with the use of the multivariate method rather than using the potentially more powerful averaged univariate or mixed model method. That is, the F ratios generated for the models made no assumptions about the variance–covariance matrices as all tests of the variance–covariance matrices required for the mixed model method were significant.

Program Effects on Achievement Level. Two sets of repeated measures analyses of variance were done to examine program effects on achievement level. First, a 2 × 2 repeated measures analysis of variance was conducted with the use of instructional reading level as the outcome, with treatment level (low level and high level) as a between-subjects factor and time of test (pre- and posttest at the time of the child's entry and exit) as a within-subjects factor. There was a statistically significant treatment effect, $MV F(1, 76) = 4.72$, $p = .03$. Overall, high-level treatment children outperformed low-level treatment children in instructional reading level. Table 2 shows the pretest and posttest means and standard deviations and mean gain for each group for pretest and posttest. There was a statistically significant time of test effect, $MV F(1, 76) = 16.72$, $p < .01$. Across both groups, on average, posttest instructional levels were higher than pretest reading instructional levels. Most important, there was a statistically significant interaction between treatment level and time of test, $MV F(1, 76) = 6.27$, $p < .01$. The children receiving more tutoring gained more (1.19) than the group with fewer sessions (.29). The effect size for this gain difference (using the high-level group mean gain minus the low-level group mean gain, divided by

TABLE 2
Number of Complete Cases, Means, and Standard Deviations for Reading Measures at Pre- and Posttest by Treatment Groups

Measure	Number of Cases	Pretest		Posttest		Gain
		M	SD	M	SD	
Instructional Reading Level						
Low-level treatment	15	.08	.12	.37	.76	.29
High-level treatment	63	.04	.12	1.22	1.37	1.19
Total	78	.05	.12	1.06	1.31	1.01
Alphabet Knowledge						
Low-level treatment	16	91.44	8.63	97.38	3.76	5.94
High-level treatment	57	92.51	9.31	98.75	2.24	6.24
Total	73	92.27	9.12	98.45	2.68	6.18
Sounds in Isolation						
Low-level treatment	16	80.50	13.94	92.69	6.79	12.19
High-level treatment	57	75.65	24.82	86.60	20.03	10.95
Total	73	76.71	22.89	87.93	18.12	11.22
Sounds in Context						
Low-level treatment	16	66.06	26.01	87.38	12.76	21.32
High-level treatment	57	56.84	31.06	92.49	8.90	35.65
Total	73	58.86	30.10	91.37	10.00	32.51
Reading Words in Isolation						
Low-level treatment	16	.16	.20	.36	.32	.20
High-level treatment	57	.12	.20	.82	.57	.70
Total	73	.13	.20	.72	.56	.59

*N*s differ due to occasions where there were missing data for selected variables.

the low-group gain standard deviation) was large (1.29). The interaction is shown in Figure 1. This is particularly noteworthy because pretest instructional level reading scores were negatively correlated with number of tutoring sessions. That is, children who had lower pretest instructional levels and more tutoring outperformed those who had higher pretest scores but fewer sessions.

Second, a follow-up 2×2 doubly multivariate repeated measures analysis of variance was done to explore in greater depth possible factors that might account for the instructional-level growth differences between low and high treatment groups. In this analysis, the four outcome measures were letter-name knowledge, knowledge of sounds for letters in isolation, knowledge of letters for sounds in context, and reading words in isolation. Treatment level (low level and high level) was a between-subjects factor, and time of test (pre- and posttest at the time of the child's entry and exit) was a within-subjects factor. All initial multivariate Fs showed statistically significant effects when all four outcome measures were considered at once. There was a statistically significant treatment effect, $MV\ F(4, 68) = 3.20$, $p = .02$. In addition, there was a statistically significant time of test effect, $MV\ F(4, 68) = 31.93$, $p < .01$. There was also a statistically significant interaction between treatment and time of test, $MV\ F(4, 68) = 5.43$, $p < .01$.

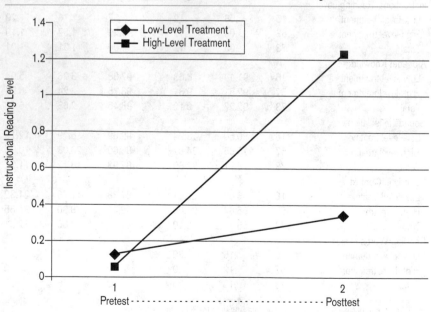

FIGURE 1
Pre- and Posttest Reading Instructional Level
for Low- and High-Level Treatment Groups

The follow-up univariate results shed more light on the multivariate results. (See Table 2 for means and standard deviations.) There were statistically significant time of test effects for each of the four variables. Overall, children's posttest scores were higher than pretest scores for knowledge of letter names, knowledge of sounds for letters in isolation, knowledge of letters for sounds in context, and word recognition.

The remaining statistically significant effects showed that the greatest impact of tutoring was in affecting children's ability to read words. There was a treatment effect for reading words in isolation, $F(1, 71) = 5.09$, $p = .03$. On average, for reading words in isolation, those who received longer treatment had higher word reading abilities overall. Time of test was statistically significant for reading words in isolation, $F(1, 71) = 53.66$, $p < .01$. Posttest scores were higher than pretest scores. Most important, there was a statistically significant interaction of treatment level with time of test, $F(1, 71) = 16.42$, $p < .01$ for reading words in isolation. Children who received tutoring for a longer period made greater gains in reading words in isolation (.70) than did the other children (.20). (See Figure 2.) The effect size for the difference in gains was again large (3.13). This is a particularly noteworthy result because the pretest scores for reading

FIGURE 2
Pre- and Posttest Reading Words in Isolation Scores
for Low- and High-Level Treatment Groups

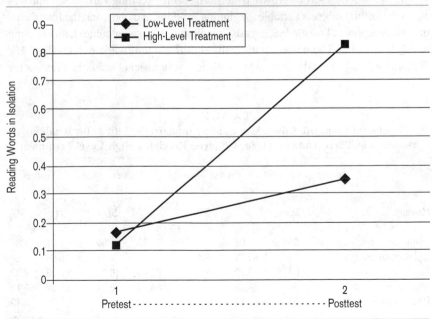

words in isolation were negatively correlated with number of tutoring sessions. Thus, children who had lower pretest word-recognition scores and a higher number of sessions outperformed children who had higher pretest word-recognition scores but a lower number of sessions.

The only other statistically significant univariate effects were for time of test for each of the three other outcomes—letter-name knowledge, knowledge of sounds for letters in isolation, and knowledge of letters for sounds in context. In each case posttest scores were higher than pretest ones, for letter knowledge $F(1, 71) = 21.78$, p < .01; for sounds in isolation $F(1, 71) = 8.55$, $p = .01$; and for sound to letters in context $F(1, 71) = 52.98$, $p < .01$.

What Was Progress Like Over Time for the Long-Term Group as a Whole?

To assess the pattern of progress over time for the group of children who received the program for the entire 6 months, two repeated measures analyses were done for that group, with the use of their scores for the beginning, middle, and end of the program. In the first analysis, the within-subjects variable was time (with three time points) and the outcome measure was instructional reading level. The time effect was statistically significant, $MV F(2, 61) = 24.64, p < .01$, with planned contrasts showing statistically significant growth during the first half of the program, $F(1, 62) = 9.83$, $p = .00$ and again during the second half of the program, $F(1, 62) = 48.03$, $p < .01$. Inspection of the means (see Table 3) showed that the greatest growth occurred in the second half of the program.

In the second analysis, a follow-up doubly repeated measures analysis of variance was done to probe growth patterns in specific reading variables. Time was again the within-subjects variable (beginning, middle, and end), and the four measures were alphabet knowledge, sounds in isolation, sounds in context, and reading words in isolation. There was a statistically significant multivariate time effect, $MV F(8, 46) = 34.24$, $p < .01$. There were statistically significant univariate results for

TABLE 3

Number of Complete Cases, Means, and Standard Deviations for Reading Measures at Three Time Points for Children Receiving High-Level Treatment

Measure	Number of Cases	Pretest		Midtest		Posttest	
		M	SD	M	SD	M	SD
Instructional Reading Level	63	.04	.12	.35	.82	1.21	1.34
Alphabet Knowledge	54	92.37	9.49	96.31	4.18	98.69	2.28
Sounds in Isolation	54	76.22	23.75	87.43	10.06	95.28	7.02
Sounds in Context	54	56.85	30.46	84.39	18.51	92.37	9.12
Reading Words in Isolation	54	.11	.17	.32	.28	.80	.49

time for each of the four measures as well. For alphabet knowledge the effect was $F(2, 106) = 17.68$, $p < .01$; for sounds in isolation, $F(2,106) = 26.29$, $p < .01$; for sounds in context, $F(2, 106) = 74.26$, $p < .01$; and for reading words in isolation, $F(2, 106) = 92.84$, $p < .01$. Planned contrasts showed that for each measure there was statistically significant growth from each time period to the next, range of $Fs(1, 53) = 11.70$ to 102.17, with all $ps < .01$.

Inspection of the means (see Table 3) showed three different patterns of growth. For alphabet knowledge and sounds in isolation, the growth across the first half of the tutoring (from pretest to midtest) was about the same as the growth across the second half (from midtest to posttest). Note, however, that for both of these measures, average scores were quite high at the beginning. These children, on the whole, entered the program with fairly solid knowledge of letter names, and they could say a sound for a letter in isolation quite well. On the other hand, for sounds in context, there appeared to be more growth during the first half of the tutoring as compared to the last half. The pattern for reading words in isolation was reversed, with apparent greater growth during the last half of the tutoring than in the first half.

Taken together, these results suggest that during tutoring the predominant learning was initially in the area of phonological awareness, specifically, in the ability to hear segments in words and in the area of knowing which letters to attach to those sounds. The predominant learning toward the end of tutoring was in the ability to actually read words. These results appear to affirm conclusions from prior research that an optimal level of phonological awareness is a necessary contingency for sight-word development (Adams, 1990).

What Did the Progress of Highest Gain Children Look Like as Compared With the Lowest Gain Children?

To ascertain potential differences in patterns between children who made high gains and those who did not, two repeated measures analysis of variance were done. The data set of the 83 first and second graders who were in the low-level and high-level treatment groups was used to form higher- and lower-gain groups. Those who made no gain or a gain of .25 on instructional reading level comprised the low-gain group ($N = 27$). Those who made a full year or more gain comprised the high-gain group ($N = 22$). Others who made moderate gains were deleted so as to form two distinct groups.

The between-subjects factor was gain group (low, high), the within-subjects factor was time (pretest, midtest, and posttest), and the outcome measure was instructional reading level. There was, of course (because of the selection criteria for the two groups), an overall group effect, $F(1, 47) = 78.81$, $p < .01$. The time effect was statistically significant, $MV F(2, 46) = 123.04$, $p < .01$; for growth from pretest to midtest $F(1, 47) = 11.23$, $p < .01$; for growth from midtest to posttest, $F(1, 47) = 182.44$, $p < .01$. Most important, there was a statistically significant interaction of group with time, $F(2, 46) = 97.11$, $p < .01$. The growth patterns from pretest to midtest and midtest to posttest were different between the low- and high-gains groups. Table 4 shows the means and standard deviations. The high-gains group made strong growth in the first half of the program and phenomenal growth in the second half of the program. In contrast, the low-gains group showed almost no growth throughout the year.

To assess the extent to which the high-gains group's growth might be attributable to children in second versus first grade, I examined the percentage of first graders versus second graders represented in the high-gains group, and the entry instructional reading levels for all 22 children in the high-gains group. Twelve of the 62 first graders (19%) and 10 of the 21 second graders (48%) were in the high-gains group. Thus, proportionately more of the second graders than first graders made gains of 1 year or more. All of the 12 first graders' and half of the second graders' entry instructional reading levels were .00. Only three of the second graders began at level .25, and two began at .50. On the one hand, the five second graders who began at preprimer (.25) and primer (.50) levels were likely to be at more advanced word-recognition phases than the other children. It is also possible that even the remaining five second graders who began at level .00, by virtue of their added year of exposure to reading, had somewhat more

TABLE 4
Number of Complete Cases, Means, and Standard Deviations for Reading Measures at Three Time Points for Children Who Made Low Versus High Gains on Instructional Reading Level

Measure	Number of Cases	Pretest		Midtest		Posttest	
		M	SD	M	SD	M	SD
Instructional Reading Level							
Low gains	27	.04	.09	.05	.10	.19	.16
High gains	22	.08	.16	.82	1.26	2.77	.97
Alphabet Knowledge							
Low gains	22	89.36	13.28	93.73	4.66	97.82	2.68
High gains	20	94.40	5.31	98.10	10.48	99.60	1.23
Sounds in Isolation							
Low gains	22	73.77	28.21	83.45	10.15	93.23	7.81
High gains	20	79.65	20.57	90.10	7.13	97.65	3.80
Sounds in Context							
Low gains	22	47.00	30.96	73.91	23.72	87.27	12.14
High gains	20	70.15	29.02	94.80	7.90	96.35	2.54
Reading Words in Isolation							
Low gains	22	.09	.14	.17	.21	.49	.25
High gains	20	.18	.20	.50	.29	1.18	.54

knowledge about sounds and word patterns than what is reflected in their instructional reading level scores. On the other hand, the relatively small numbers of second graders represented in the entire data set, as well as in this subset, make it difficult to know what to make of the differences between first and second graders' high gains.

To probe specific causes that might underlie the instructional reading level growth, a doubly multivariate repeated measures analysis of variance was done, using the four measures of alphabet knowledge, sounds in isolation, sounds in context, and reading words in isolation. The between-subjects factor was again comprised of low versus high gains on instructional reading level, and the within-subjects factor was time (pretest, midtest, and posttest). There was a statistically significant overall difference between the low- and high-gain groups, $MV\ F(4, 37) = 7.10$, $p < .01$, and in follow-up univariate effects for groups for each of the four measures except sounds in isolation, for alphabet knowledge $F(1, 40) = 8.91$, $p = .01$; for sounds in isolation, $F(1, 40) = 3.40$, $p < .01$; for sounds in context, $F(1, 40)$, $p < .01$; and for reading words in isolation, $F(1, 40) = 29.31$, $p < .01$. Looking at the means for these four variables in Table 4, we see that the high-gains group maintained an edge over the other group at every time point, except on the sounds in isolation measure. Time effect was statistically significant overall, $MV\ F(8, 33) = 29.42$, $p < .01$. The differences held across all four measures, and for each case, there was statistically significant growth from pretest to midtest and then from midtest to posttest, $Fs(2, 80) = 13.01$ to 87.86, $ps < .01$; contrast test $Fs(1, 40)$ ranged from 7.05 to 58.72, ps from $.00$ to $.01$. The low- versus high-gain group by time interaction was also statistically significant, $MV\ F(8, 33) = 5.63$, $p < .01$. Follow-up univariate results showed that the effect was mainly attributable to reading words in isolation, $F(2, 80) = 15.58$, $p < .01$, with both contrasts statistically significant, $Fs(1, 40) = 15.47$ and 16.18, $ps < .01$. That is, the patterns in growth were the same for the two groups for all measures except reading words in isolation (see Table 4). Essentially, for letter knowledge, sounds in isolation, and sounds in context, there was a tendency for each group to make slightly to considerably greater gains in the first half of the year as compared to the second half of the year (although the high-gains group always started higher and ended higher, on average). However, for reading words in isolation, whereas both groups began at similar levels, the high-gains group made more growth in the first half of the year than did the low-gains group. In the second half of the program, the gap widened.

These results continue to support the position that reading words in isolation tends to be dependent on a relatively high development of phonological awareness. The high-gains group tended to be higher on these measures throughout, and their word reading knowledge exploded at the end of the program. The low-gains group tended to be lower on measures that most directly involved phonological awareness, but improved throughout the year. An additional possible interpretation is that the low-gains group might have been traveling the same trajectory as the high-gains group, but that they were moving more slowly.

Tutors' and Supervisors' Perceptions of Aspects of the America Reads Program

We analyzed the focus group interviews using procedures outlined by Coffey and Atkinson (1996) and Glaser and Strauss (1967). Interviews were transcribed and two individuals carefully read them all, making notes in the margins and looking for themes. Thematic categories were created, and instances of support for each theme were compiled. In the next round of analysis, the transcripts were read for nonsupporting examples or competing explanations. Following is a summary of the most salient themes from the focus groups.

Program Benefits. All tutors and supervisors in focus groups felt that the America Reads program was an excellent initiative. At the end of the program, they spoke of the great benefits for children. One tutor put it this way: "I think that being one-on-one with him, it helped him see that he really could do it well. And by the time we were finished, he was reading [level] 18s and 19s and 20s [approximately early second-grade level], when I started him off in the 2s and 3s. I met his father, and he said, 'I really appreciate what you are doing, because I can see it at home.' Even his teacher would come up and say, 'He's doing so much better in class.' That made me feel good, because I was not only helping him with his reading, but with his behavior and even in other parts of his education."

Tutors and supervisors also felt it was a wonderful opportunity for college students to make a difference and give back to the community and children. They felt they had learned a lot about the complexities of learning to read and about the great need for one-on-one tutoring for some children.

Supervisors spoke freely of the strong commitment tutors made. Some talked about tutors who had done a tremendous job, especially those who worked with children who had behavior problems, "turning around" many children. Many tutors, they said, had "gone the extra mile." Supervisors felt that the tutors' positive attitudes were a big factor in the children's progress.

Frustrations and Concerns. In general, tutors and supervisors felt the tutoring "went well," although some frustrations were expressed about some children's behavior, negative attitudes about reading, and fatigue. As the year progressed, however, all tutors in focus groups felt their frustrations eased.

Some tutors sensed that principals and teachers went out of their way to make a special effort to help them to feel welcome and comfortable. In these schools, the tutors thought their children saw and felt this support and that they felt special because they had a reading buddy from the university. Some tutors did not feel as welcomed at their schools, and they tended to think the atmosphere surrounding their visits also affected the children they worked with.

The tutors' biggest concern was that their students would not make progress. As one said, "It would really hurt me if they didn't really get to the levels they need when we leave. That's what I'm most worried about. [I want] to try to make sure that I do make the impact that I'm out to make." All of the tutors in focus groups were very ambitious, wanting to make life-changing differences in their students. Many expressed concern about changing children's attitudes about reading, that is, about helping them to be positive about reading and learning.

Tutor–Supervisor Relationships. Most tutors appreciated their supervisors' help. All remarked that the supervisors were pleasant and easy to talk with. Most liked having their supervisor visit them on site to answer questions and help with behavioral problems or other difficulties. At the end of the program interviews some mentioned that having a supervisor sit with them during tutoring sessions was helpful. Tutors who had supervisors with past experience in teaching reading were extremely positive about their supervisors, more so than tutors who had supervisors with less experience.

Most supervisors felt they had a good relationship with their tutors. However, there were problems and personality conflicts in a few cases. Most of the problems noted in this area were related to logistical concerns, such as turning in paperwork on time and arriving for the carpool on time. Required small-group supervisor–tutor meetings went well for some supervisors, but others said they were "ineffective."

Supervisors nearly unanimously said it was hard to become a supervisor because their role was not clearly defined for them from the outset and because they were about the same age as the tutors.

Training Sessions. For the most part, tutors thought training sessions gave helpful information. They especially liked the sessions that they thought gave them ideas and information they could use with students, such as a training session on games to use for word study and another on how to take and interpret running records.

However, there were aspects of the training sessions that both tutors and supervisors thought should be changed. They thought initial training sessions were too long and repetitive, that there was too much information to absorb in a small amount of time, and that much of the early information did not make sense until they started working with the children.

Suggested Changes. Tutors and supervisors alike suggested several changes for training, including shorter sessions spread out more over the year, starting with just one part of the lesson structure and activities and ideas for the first day, and incorporating the training sessions into the tutoring more. Supervisors also suggested a separate session for them at the outset of the year to focus on their leadership role.

There was consensus about other suggested changes as follows: (a) Find a way to communicate better with teachers and parents, (b) give tutors a list of the kinds of knowledge about reading that their students would be expected to know by the end of the year, (c) ensure quiet places to tutor, (d) have a formal introduction to the principal and teachers at their schools, (e) make sure that tutoring sessions are not scheduled during play times, (f) clarify supervisors' roles from the outset both for them and for the tutors, (g) set consequences for tutors' tardiness and similar problems, and (h) help all teachers and principals to know that the tutors are anxious to help their children, and find ways for all teachers and principals to welcome and support them.

Program Costs

It is difficult to accurately portray program costs because many individuals voluntarily contributed time. However, a rough estimation may be made. Table 5 shows that approximately US$153,746 was spent on the program, and approximately 322 additional in-kind hours were contributed by various university and public school personnel. The approximate dollar cost per student, excluding in-kind contributions, was US$1,068.

TABLE 5
Approximate Program Operations Costs

	In-Kind Hours	Dollar Amount
University Program Operation Funds		US$63,000
Grant Monies Expended		300
Work-Study Monies to Pay Tutors		45,346
Work-Study Monies to Pay Supervisors		37,900
School of Education Monies to Pay Supervisor		7,200
TOTAL		$153,746
Faculty Hours for Planning and Training	120	
Secretarial Time	40	
Principal and Teacher Time	50	
Steering Committee Time	112	
TOTAL	322	
Approximate Dollar Cost Per Student, Excluding In-Kind Contribution (for 144 children)		$1,068

Conclusions and Discussion

The following paragraphs detail the main conclusions of the study.

1. On average, the at-risk first- and second-grade children in this study who were tutored by minimally trained college student volunteers improved their reading achievement. Comparisons using a within-program control group showed that, on average, children made statistically significant gains in instructional reading level that could be attributed to the tutoring. The average gain for children receiving the full term of tutoring was 1.19 grade levels.

2. On average children made positive gains in letter knowledge, knowing sounds in isolation, and knowing letters for sounds in context, but the greatest impact of tutoring was in affecting children's ability to read words. Further, among the children who received the full term of tutoring, most of their instructional reading level growth occurred during the second half of the program. When considering specific underlying reading abilities, the predominant learning during the initial tutoring was in the area of phonemic awareness and correct letter attachment to sound. The predominant learning toward the end of tutoring was in the ability to actually read words.

3. Patterns of growth in instructional reading level were different for low- and high-gains groups of children. The high-gains children, on average, made strong growth in the first half of the program and phenomenal growth in the second half of the program. In contrast, the low-gains children's growth almost flatlined throughout the year. When considering underlying reading abilities, again, growth in reading words was the factor that distinguished the two groups' growth patterns.

4. Finally, tutors and supervisors perceived that the program was beneficial to children and to themselves.

This study provides evidence that minimally trained college student volunteers can help at-risk readers. This is important because, to my knowledge, this is one of the first controlled studies to provide such evidence, particularly in relation to the America Reads initiative (cf. Gambrell & Dromsky, 1999; Morrow & Woo, 1999). Moreover, the 1.19 grade-level gain made by the children receiving the full complement of tutoring is the amount of gain expected for normally functioning children, on average, in a 9- to 10-month school year. Consequently, to achieve this average gain in 6 months with a group of at-risk readers is remarkable.

Further, the effect sizes were very high for low- and high-level treatment group gain differences for instructional reading level and for reading words in isolation (1.29 and 3.13, respectively). These were considerably higher than those reported in other tutorials using paraprofessionals or volunteers, or both, and were comparable to several tutorials using professionally trained teachers (Invernizzi et al., 1997; Slavin, Karweit, & Wasik, 1994).

The results also support the possibility of the effectiveness of a tutorial using a balanced lesson design that aims to develop beginning reading abilities by stressing repeated reading, word study, learning about sounds and sound–letter relationships through writing, and scaffolded learning in increasingly difficult materials.

The pattern of children's progress over the year is consistent with results of prior research on emergent literacy, which suggest that phonological awareness is necessary for word learning (Adams, 1990). Also, the observed pattern for many children of learning more about sounds and letters during the first half of tutoring suggests compatibility with the belief that they were in an alphabetic phase (Ehri, 1991), and their increased actual word recognition abilities during the second half of tutoring suggests the possibility of movement into an orthographic phase (Ehri, 1991).

A related contribution of the present study to the literature is documentation of the importance of long-term tutoring to children's reading development. It is possible that, especially with at-risk early readers, reading development may occur in fits and starts. For example, it appeared in the present study that, on average, phonological awareness development and its concomitants required a rather lengthy early period of instructional support (in the first half of tutoring), but once instantiated, reading words as sight words and acquiring word-reading strategies blossomed (in the second half of tutoring). Consequently, continued tutoring seems critical.

With respect to the phenomenal second-half growth of the high-gains children, due to the relatively small numbers of second graders in the study it was not possible to ascertain the extent to which this growth might have revolved around some sort of optimal entry level related, for example, to being in a particular phase of early reading development. In future research it would be extremely helpful to include more children at the second-grade level in order to more directly assess grade-level effects on as many of the outcome variables and patterns in the data as possible.

Further, because low-gains children displayed a growth pattern different from the high-gains children, we might question whether these children were on the same trajectory, but slower paced, as the high-gains children or whether their developmental path was actually different. Though we cannot know with conviction, there was evidence that their yearlong growth resembled the first half-year growth of the high-gains children, supporting the same trajectory hypothesis.

Another important consideration is the cost of tutoring models such as the one used in the present study. The rough cost per student (US$1,068), excluding approximately 322 hours of in-kind contributions, so far as it could be calculated, appeared in general to be less than other tutorials using highly trained specialists. For example, some have estimated the cost of Reading Recovery to be about US$4,000 per child (Shanahan & Barr, 1995). Reading Recovery is an intensive one-on-one first-grade school reading program conducted by highly trained reading specialists. However, the cost per student in the present program was somewhat higher than that of the Book Buddies program (Invernizzi et al., 1997), a community volunteer program in which former graduate students in reading education assessed each child's needs, wrote daily lessons for tutors, and supervised them. The average cost per student across three cohorts in that program was US$595. When considering the cost-effectiveness of reading tutorial programs, although the program in the present study was more expensive than some other volunteer tutorials have been shown to be, it is important to consider that the effect sizes achieved were more like those attained with programs using trained professionals, who represent a far greater expense to school systems.

It is important to remember that this is just one study, that there are limits to the study that must be considered as well, and that these limits suggest that the results should be interpreted cautiously, especially with regard to future policy decisions about similar initiatives. In one respect, the within-program comparison group provided a more rigorous comparison than some other types of control or comparison groups. In this design, all of the children received identical formats for tutoring. Only one feature distinguished the two groups—amount of tutoring. Thus we know that statistically significant differences between the two groups are due to more tutoring of the sort that was offered. This is a design advantage over a typically used control or comparison in which children from mainstream classrooms are selected (often on a matched basis) for comparison. In a mainstream group comparison design, many other uncontrolled features may exist as competing explanations for statistically significant outcomes.

Also, finding statistically significant effects in a within-program comparison group may be especially important because it may be more difficult to find such significance when comparing a program to itself, so to speak. That is, if the tutoring is effective, then it may be more difficult to produce statistically significant effects when comparing more of it to less of it than when comparing it to a mainstream group of children who received no tutoring.

On the other hand, the design in this study did not reveal anything about the effectiveness of this particular kind of tutoring in comparison to another kind of tutoring, comparing minimally to maximally trained tutors, or comparing tutored groups to those with no tutoring. Further, we cannot know from this study which of the tutoring session components might most account for children's growth.

Other limitations to this study should also be taken into account when considering the meaning and practical significance of the tutorial model used in this study. For instance, long-term effects across more than one academic year are not known for the tutorial model used in this study. Also, the tutoring sessions were designed to address and ensure children's comprehension of what they were reading. However, the major work of beginning reading is getting words, and consequently, the measures used to assess children's progress reflected word learning and its concurrent or preceding factors rather than comprehension. Omission of a measure of reading comprehension may limit the generalizability of the work.

Finally, future research on tutorials such as the one used in the present study is needed to investigate several factors, including the following: (a) Which components of the tutorial contribute to its effectiveness? (b) What roles do social features of the tutorial play in children's progress? For example, does language that suggests a warm and caring tutor disposition tend to positively affect children's development more than on-task, take-charge directive language? (c) Does tutor experience play a role? For example, do children tutored by tutors who continue from year to year tend to do better than others? (d) To what extent does a supervisor's prior knowledge about literacy affect outcomes for children? (e) How do supervisor characteristics interact with tutor characteristics to enhance or detract from children's progress? (f) What is the optimal amount of training and what are the essential characteristics of training that make a difference in student achievement?

References

Adams, M.J. (1990). *Beginning to read: Thinking and learning about print.* Cambridge, MA: MIT Press.

Bader, L.A., & Wiesendanger, K. (1994). *Bader reading and language inventory* (2nd ed.). New York: Merrill.

Chall, J.S. (1996). *Stages of reading development.* Fort Worth, TX: Harcourt Brace.

Clay, M.M. (1985). *The early detection of reading difficulties.* Auckland, New Zealand: Heinemann.

Clay, M.M. (1993). *An observation survey of early literacy achievement.* Portsmouth, NH: Heinemann.

Coffey, A., & Atkinson, P. (1996). *Making sense of qualitative data.* Thousand Oaks, CA: Sage.

Cohen, P.A., Kulik, J.A., & Kulik, C.C. (1982). Educational outcomes of tutoring: A meta-analysis of findings. *American Educational Research Journal, 19,* 237–248.

Deford, D.E., Lyons, C.A., & Pinnell, G.S. (Eds.). (1991). *Bridges to literacy: Learning from Reading Recovery.* Portsmouth, NH: Heinemann.

Dowhower, S.L. (1987). Effects of repeated reading on second grade transitional readers' fluency and comprehension. *Reading Research Quarterly, 22,* 389–406.

Ehri, L.C. (1991). Development of the ability to read words. In R. Barr, M.L. Kamil, P.B. Mosenthal, & P.D. Pearson (Eds.), *Handbook of reading research* (Vol. 2, pp. 383–417). White Plains, NY: Longman.

Fitzgerald, J., & Shanahan, T. (2000). Reading and writing relations and their development. *Educational Psychologist, 35,* 39–51.

Frith, U. (1985). Beneath the surface of developmental dyslexia. In K.W. Patterson, J.C. Marshall, & M. Coltheart (Eds.), *Surface dyslexia* (pp. 301–330). London: Erlbaum.

Gambrell, L.B., & Dromsky, A.J. (May, 1999). *America Reads at the University of Maryland: Practices, evaluation, and implications.* Paper presented at the annual convention of the International Reading Association, San Diego, CA.

Glaser, B.G., & Strauss, A.L. (1967). *The discovery of grounded theory.* Chicago: Aldine.

Hiebert, E.H. (1994). Reading Recovery in the United States: What difference does it make to an age cohort? *Educational Researcher, 23*(9), 15–25.

Invernizzi, M., Rosemary, C., Juel, C., & Richards, H.C. (1997). At-risk readers and community volunteers: A 3-year perspective. *Scientific Studies of Reading, 1,* 277–300.

Juel, C. (1988). Learning to read and write: A longitudinal study of fifty-four children from first through fourth grade. *Journal of Educational Psychology, 80,* 437–447.

Juel, C. (1996). What makes literacy tutoring effective? *Reading Research Quarterly, 31,* 268–289.

Lapray, M., & Ross, R. (1986). The graded word list: Quick gauge of reading ability. In E.E. Ekwall (Ed.), *Ekwall reading inventory* (2nd ed., pp. 171–172). Boston: Allyn & Bacon.

Lysynchuk, L.M., Pressley, M., D'ailly, H., Smith, M., & Cake, H. (1989). A methodological analysis of experimental studies of comprehension strategy instruction. *Reading Research Quarterly, 24*, 458–470.

Mathes, P.G., & Fuchs, L.S. (1994). The efficacy of peer tutoring in reading for students with mild disabilities: A best-evidence synthesis. *School Psychology Review, 23*, 59–80.

Morrow, L.M., & Woo, D.G. (1999, May). *The effect of a volunteer tutoring program on literacy achievement and attitudes of teachers, tutors, and children toward the program.* Paper presented at the annual convention of the International Reading Association, San Diego, CA.

Nystrand, M. (1989). A social-interactive model of writing. *Written Communication, 6*, 66–85.

Pearson, P.D. (1984). Direct explicit teaching of comprehension. In G.G. Duffy, L.R. Roehler, & J. Mason (Eds.), *Comprehension instruction: Perspectives and suggestions* (pp. 223–233). New York: Longman.

Pearson, P.D. (1985). Changing the face of reading comprehension instruction. *The Reading Teacher, 38*, 724–738.

Rasinski, T. (1990). Effects of repeated reading and listening-while-reading on reading fluency. *The Journal of Educational Research, 83*, 147–150.

Samuels, S.J. (1979). The method of repeated readings. *The Reading Teacher, 32*, 403–408.

Samuels, S.J., Schermer, N., & Reinking, D. (1992). Reading fluency: Techniques for making decoding automatic. In S.J. Samuels & A.E. Farstrup (Eds.), *What research has to say about reading instruction* (2nd ed., pp. 124–144). Newark, DE: International Reading Association.

Schwartz, R.M. (1997). Self-monitoring in beginning reading. *The Reading Teacher, 51*, 40–48.

Shanahan, T. (1998). On the effectiveness and limitations of tutoring in reading. In A. Iran-Nejad & D. Pearson (Eds.), *Review of research in education* (Vol. 23, pp. 217–234). Washington, DC: American Educational Research Association.

Shanahan, T., & Barr, R. (1995). Reading Recovery: An independent evaluation of the effects of an early instructional intervention for at-risk learners. *Reading Research Quarterly, 30*, 958–996.

Slavin, R.E., Karweit, N.L., & Wasik, B.A. (1994). *Preventing reading failure: Research, policy, and practice.* Boston: Allyn & Bacon.

Stanovich, K.E. (1986). Matthew effects in reading: Some consequences of individual differences in the acquisition of literacy. *Reading Research Quarterly, 21*, 360–406.

Teale, W.H., & Sulzby, E. (Eds.). (1986). *Emergent literacy: Writing and reading.* Norwood, NJ: Ablex.

Tunmer, W.E., & Nesdale, A.R. (1985). Phonemic segmentation skill and beginning reading. *Journal of Educational Psychology, 77*, 417–427.

Vygotsky, L.S. (1978). *Mind in society: The development of higher psychological processes* (M. Cole, V. John-Steiner, S. Scribner, & E. Souberman, Eds. & Trans.). Cambridge, MA: Harvard University Press. (Original work published 1934)

Wasik, B.A. (1998). Volunteer tutoring programs in reading: A review. *Reading Research Quarterly, 33*, 266–291.

Wasik, B.A., & Slavin, R.E. (1993). Preventing early reading failure with one-to-one tutoring: A review of five programs. *Reading Research Quarterly, 28*, 179–200.

Appendix: Items on the Attitude Toward Reading Measure

How do you feel about going to school?

How do you feel when someone reads you a story?

How do you feel when it's time for reading in school?

How do you feel when you are asked to read out loud?

How do you feel about how well you can read?

How do you think you'll feel about reading when you're older?

How would you feel if someone gave you a book for a present?

Section Three

Models of Reading and Writing Processes

Introduction

What's in a Model of Literacy Processes?

A model represents in ordinary language or graphic form the components of an object or process and explains how those components function and interact with one another. Models are metaphors that help us visualize and understand research and theories that explain components of the reading process. Ranging from the basic to the highly sophisticated, models of reading render specific aspects of the reading process, such as word recognition, or depict more globally an integrated and interacting network of specific components, all of which contribute to the mind making meaning from a text. A model of writing helps us see how components of the writing process, such as planning, use of long-term memory, and revision, function and interact as writers create texts.

We can begin to see a reader's or writer's mind at work with the help of models. They enable us to understand how texts are constructed when a reader reads or a writer writes. Each component depicted in a model, as well as the interaction of components, is based on extensive research and theory that inform the design of a model of reading or writing. Most designers of models draw from their own theory base and research as well as that of others to construct a model. A careful synthesis of components and their functions often brings light to the otherwise dark and mysterious complexities of creating meaning when we read or write.

While some literacy models show complex, interacting systems contributing to comprehension during reading or the construction of text during writing, other models focus on only one component. In either case, our limited capacity to observe, measure, collect information, and describe processes precisely limits the accuracy of a reading or writing model. Furthermore, models of reading or writing, like a snapshot, depict a moment in time described in ordinary language processed linearly, whereas both reading and writing are continuous, recursive, and multileveled processes.

Having clarified the meaning of literacy models, we want to give you a framework for what we plan to accomplish in the rest of this introduction. After describing the benefits of literacy models, we will identify research sources in this volume that inform the design of models presented in this section. We then will describe several oceans of theory and research that have generated specific models of reading and writing.

The Benefits of Reading Models

Everyone who teaches reading has some model of the reading process that influences, perhaps unconsciously, their instructional decision making. We know that teachers understanding the reading process more fully and explicitly contributes to improvements in instructional practice and deeper knowledge of their students' learning (Beck, 1989). Models provide educators with a deeper understanding of reading processes, where breakdowns in comprehension can occur, and what strategies could improve reading processes.

First, with respect to understanding reading, a model integrates research findings, makes theory graphic, and provides us with an explanation of how reading takes place in accord with what we currently know. While taking apart a car's engine helps us see how it works and so discover how to repair it, dismantling the reading process presents us with a very different problem. Although reading is a highly complex and hidden process with no pistons, valves, or crankshafts to pull out for observation, we do have a substantial amount of research and theoretical knowledge about it. What we do know enables us to construct a model to visualize this mysterious, invisible process. Furthermore, once we have begun to make more visible our understanding of reading through models, we tend to move those models toward greater sophistication.

Second, a model of reading will help us detect where breakdowns in comprehension could occur. A model helps us visualize what components may fail to contribute to smooth meaning making while reading. For example, weak or slow word recognition can cause poor comprehension. In short, models help us understand what contributes to a struggling reader's troubles.

Third, a model provides clues about instructional approaches and intervention strategies that could help readers at different stages in reading development. While using a reading model to develop prescriptions for every struggling reader's malady is risky practice, we can use models as resources for good hints. A well-designed model based in solid research can create more opportunities to envision instructional interventions.

From Research to Model

Models of reading and writing picture mental events based on extensive research. Much of the research and theory reported in this and earlier editions of *Theoretical Models and Processes of Reading* has contributed to the models in this section.

The discovery of many intertextual connections awaits readers who have already explored the tributaries flowing from earlier parts of this book into oceans of research from which the models will arise. Among potential interconnections are the following:

- Eras of reading research identified and described by Alexander and Fox (#2)
- Language processes, such as the windows into reading that miscue analysis provides (Goodman & Goodman, #22) or the window into writing that the close observation of young children in classrooms enables (Dyson, #6)

- The social and cultural contexts of literacy, such as reading from a sociocognitive perspective (Gee, #4), the dynamics of peer interaction (Forman & Cazden, #7), or the effects of background knowledge on the interpretation of texts (Hull & Rose, #11)

- Literacy development during early childhood (Cox et al., #12), the development of word recognition (Juel & Minden-Cupp, #13; Ehri & McCormick, #14), and the development of fluency (Kuhn & Stahl, #16; Stanovich, #17)

- Comprehension and comprehension theories and strategies, such as vocabulary development (Nagy & Scott, #19), research on schema theory (Anderson, #20; Bransford, #21; Spiro et al., #23), or inference-making and text representations (Coté & Goldman, #25)

- Extension of comprehension through metacognition, as represented in work on self-regulation during reading (Hacker, #28) or text structure (Meyer & Poon, #30)

- Reader response and engagement, such as readers creating cultural worlds through their response to texts (Galda & Beach, #31), adolescents' engagement with reading in after-school clubs (Alvermann et al., #32), the effects of readers' stance on understanding (Many, #33), and the many factors contributing to both reader and teacher motivational states (Ruddell & Unrau, #35)

- Instructional effects on literacy development appearing in research on influential teachers (Ruddell, #36), the impact of strategy instruction (Brown et al., #37), and collaboration while learning to read and reading to learn (Langer, #38; Fitzgerald, #39)

Many of the models presented in this section rely on these and other research studies, theories that evolved from them, and hypotheses about how features focused on in one study may interact with features of another. For example, hypotheses based on schema theory provide several model builders with an explanation of how background knowledge may affect the reading process. With that theory in mind as an example of how research and theory appear in models of reading, we now provide an overview of the models to come.

Oceans of Theory and Research Generate Model Waves

Several oceans of theory and research serve as resources for the development of models. One of the major oceans of knowledge generating models developed since the 1970s has been fed by rivers of information pouring from research in

cognitive psychology. From research on the mind's cognitive processes, especially studies that related directly to processing information and texts, designers
have created several waves of cognitive processing models, some of which have
crested and diminished in influence while others remain highly influential. Some
waves from the ocean of knowledge on cognitive processes and perspectives contained only one or two models. Other waves included many models, with earlier
models influencing the design of subsequent models within that wave. The waves
begin with bottom-up models, followed by top-down models, and progress to
interactive or bottom-up/top-down designs (Samuels, #40; Rumelhart, #41).
The wave of interactive models was, in turn, followed by important extensions
and elaborations (Just & Carpenter, #43; Adams, #44; Kintsch, #46). One of
these elaborated models accounts for evolving (offline) memory representation
(van den Broek et al., #45).

Several wave-generating oceans of knowledge have been fed by other
sources of research and theory. These sources include Sadoski and Paivio's
Dual Coding Theory (#47) and Rosenblatt's transactional theory (#48). From
research based in cognition during writing, Flower and Hayes made writing
processes more visible in a model that Hayes subsequently revised to achieve
an even clearer depiction (#49). From research and theory on affective dimensions of reading, Mathewson designed an engagement model (#50), a harbinger
to our current era of engagement (Alexander & Fox, #2)

The last wave of cognitive processing models addressed in this volume em-
beds an interactive model within the social context of the classroom where interpretations of texts from students and teacher are shared and meanings are
negotiated (Ruddell & Unrau, #51). Each of the waves arising from work in
cognitive psychology and acknowledged above is described in more detail in
the following paragraphs.

Bottom-Up (Wave 1)

Gough's (1972; see Rumelhart, #41) "one second of reading" model depicted a
process that began with low-level sensory representations (letter input) and proceeded through phonemic and lexical-level representation to deeper structural representation. The flow of information is completely bottom-up with no higher-level
process, such as information held in long-term memory, affecting lower-level
representations. In "One Second of Reading: Postscript," Gough (#42) acknowledges the problems inherent in his model.

Top-Down (Wave 2)

The next (or second) wave of models focused on what readers remembered after reading a text and the discovery that text memory was systematic. The questions guiding the design of that generation was, What do readers remember about
the text they read and what do those memories tell us about the nature of the

memory representations resulting from reading? The theories arising from this wave focused on top-down memory influences, especially that of text structure. Story grammars (Stein & Glenn, 1979), script theory (Schank & Abelson, 1977), and hierarchical theories based on text structure (Meyer, 1975; Meyer & Poon, #30) arose as answers to the question guiding these researchers.

Top-Down (Wave 3)

Nearly synchronous with wave two of theories was a third wave focused on a broader view of what readers bring to a text. Note that the second wave text structure-recall theories described earlier focused only on the connection between the background knowledge that a reader brought to a text and the reader's comprehension of the text (Pearson & Stephens, 1994, see CD 1.4). The new, third wave question became, What influence does a reader's background knowledge have on the meanings constructed when reading? Schema theory (Anderson, #20; Bransford, #21) arose from efforts to answer that question, and the answer constituted a new third wave of reading theory. Schema theory beats at the heart of many models of reading, including several presented in these pages.

Bottom-Up/Top-Down (Wave 4)

A fourth wave of models emerging mostly in the early 1980s favored a focus on a bottom-up plus top-down interaction shaping comprehension. The question for these researchers was, What do readers do as they move through a text? These fourth wave models took into account readers' efforts to construct coherent text representations with respect to that text's referential and causal structure. Different manifestations of the fourth wave appear in Samuels's automatic information processing model (#40), Rumelhart's interactive model (#41), Just and Carpenter's model that accounts for eye fixations (1987, see #43), Adams's processor model (#44), and Kintsch's Construction–Integration model (1988, see #46). Many of these model designers strongly influenced one another, as is the case with Just and Carpenter's influence on Adams's model.

Bottom-Up/Top-Down + Extended Offline Memory Representation (Wave 5)

A fifth wave of models focuses on the complex and bidirectional interaction between comprehension processes and memory representations that are modified continuously. As the reader proceeds through a text, the evolving representations serve as a resource for understanding newly read text. Van den Broek et al. (#45) depict this process of memory representation in a landscape model that shows the interaction between online processing and offline representations. In some ways, this interactive process between knowledge structures parallels Spiro's adaptive flexibility view of schema theory (Spiro et al., #23).

Bottom-Up/Top-Down + Sociocultural Context (Wave 6)

A sixth wave of model building puts the reader with a text in a social and cultural context. That context may be one that shapes and defines the reader (Gee, #4) or influences responses to texts (Alvermann et al., #32). Ruddell and Unrau (#51) present a sociocognitive model of reading as a meaning-construction process depicting a bottom-up/top-down reading process in a classroom context. Readers interpret and negotiate meanings for not only printed texts but also for tasks, sources of authority, and sociocultural factors.

Other Oceans, Other Waves

Another major ocean of knowledge generating models is that fed by Dual Coding Theory (DCT), a theory of general cognition first developed to explain verbal and nonverbal influences on memory. While this ocean has been fed by other theories and studies of cognition, research on DCT, especially the role of imagery in text processing, enabled its extension into the realm of literacy and reading comprehension. Sadoski and Paivio (#47) discuss DCT's explanation of decoding, comprehension, and response to texts. Their DCT model, rich in explanatory power, provides an alternative to reading models based primarily on verbal processes, such as schema theory. Authors of the DCT model also provide compelling evidence for the theory's justification.

From an ocean of multidisciplinary perspectives, including philosophy, comparative literature, aesthetics, linguistics, and sociology that formed early in the 20th century, Louise Rosenblatt (#48) developed a transactional theory and model of both reading and writing. Her model differs in significant ways from cognitive processing models of reading and can be viewed as a wave in an ocean unto itself. However, bottom-up/top-down processes are both implicit and explicit in her transactional model of reading. Rather than thinking of reading as a separate reader taking in a separate text, Rosenblatt views the reader and text as two aspects of a total dynamic situation. Readers do not get meaning from the text where it resides; meaning issues from the transaction between reader and text. Readers, while transacting with a text, form a structure of the text's elements that becomes an object of thought, what she calls the evocation. Readers then respond to emerging evocations while reading and form interpretations that report, analyze, and explain those evocations.

Furthermore, according to Rosenblatt's transactional model, readers adopt a stance toward a text on an efferent–aesthetic continuum. Readers adopt an efferent stance when their purpose for reading is focused on what they extract and retain from a reading event. They adopt the aesthetic stance when they attend to the experience they live through during the reading, the perceptions they have within the text world created through the transaction. Sometimes summed up as "scientific" or "public" for efferent and "artistic" or "private" for aesthetic, these two stances are not binary but mixed in various proportions, depending on the reader's selective attention and intention.

Yet another ocean of theory and research related to cognitive psychology has informed models of writing. An earlier writing model by Flower and Hayes formed a wave arising from this sea of knowledge and was included in the fourth edition of TMPR (1994). In this fifth edition, Hayes significantly revises the earlier Flower–Hayes model and creates what amounts to a new-wave writing model (#49). While the prior model was sociocognitive, this new-wave model is an "individual–environmental" model. In it Hayes emphasizes the role of working memory, includes visual–spatial representation, integrates motivation, and reorganizes the cognitive-processing section.

Finally, from the ocean of research related to literacy engagement arises Mathewson's theoretical model (#50) in which the author explains the roles of attitude and intention in moving readers to read or learn to read. His model reveals how feedback paths influence reading behavior cyclically and provides implications for both instruction and future research. Since the publication of Mathewson's original models in 1976, 1985, and 1994, new waves of research on reader engagement and motivation have established motivation as an essential and critical element of literacy research (Guthrie & Wigfield, 1997; Guthrie et al., #34).

With the discovery of new methods to study reading processes, such as functional magnetic resonance imagery (fMRI) and computer modeling, a new ocean of knowledge and theory is rapidly beginning to form (Keller, Carpenter, & Just, 2001; Shaywitz et al., 2003). From that growing sea of knowledge, waves of new reading models are likely to emerge. In the past few years, researchers have begun to identify brain processes that parallel aspects of text cognition, such as lexical access and syntactic processing, as readers read. Certain regions of the brain, such as the occipital cortex and the amygdala as well as Broca's and Wernicke's areas, become activated as readers respond to words on the page and the need to construct or reconstruct memories while building text representations. Comprehension processes appear to rely on the interaction and collaboration of several cortical regions. Future models of reading, still over the horizon, may be useful in identifying brain patterns of highly effective and skilled readers as well as those of delayed or disabled readers.

Furthermore, research on the origins of language and the genes that contribute to its development has grown over the past decade. Interdisciplinary collaboration in the fields of linguistics, evolutionary biology, cognitive psychology, and neuroscience is producing studies with intriguing theories about the faculty of language, the basis for reading (Hauser, Chomsky, & Fitch, 2002). The contributions to our understanding of language processes and eventually to reading that could flow from the confluence of these lines of research are quite provocative.

We are clearly on a threshold of discoveries that may add enormously to our understanding of reading processes, to the formulation of new theories, and to the creation of innovative models. As outer space is full of unknowns waiting to be discovered if only we had the technologies to do so, so awaits inner space.

Questions for Reflection

1. *An introduction to model building.* Carefully consider how you conceptualize the reading process by reflecting on (a) your personal insights related to your own reading behaviors and interests, (b) your own teaching of reading, and (c) your reading and research on the reading process. First, identify those factors you believe most important in learning to read *or* to becoming an expert reader. Second, attempt to graphically show how these factors are connected or interrelated in the mind of the reader. Third, share your ideas with a classmate or friend. And fourth, revise your model based on this discussion. Then, keep a copy of your model nearby as you examine and explore the models in this section. Add to and revise your model as your reading progresses, and work toward the goal of refining your model to explain the nature of the reading process as completely as possible.

2. Select one of the models (#40 to #51) that has a high level of appeal to you. Find a partner who selects a different model of high interest. Use the following questions to analyze and evaluate the models. Then discuss your findings in detail.

   a. What does the model accomplish?

   b. What assumptions did the designer of the model make about the reader's mind and thinking processes? About the way texts are processed? About the sociocultural context in which the text is embedded?

   c. What research or data sources informed the model's development? How reliable is the research?

   d. From what tradition(s) or discipline(s) does the model arise? What historical developments, including those in research and/or theory, in philosophy, or in the study of literature, shaped the model?

   e. How complete is the explanatory power of the model? When you grasp how the model works, what factors may have been omitted?

f. After formulating predictions the model would appear to support, how could you test the accuracy of those predictions?

g. Is the model internally consistent and externally valid? How could you verify the model's external validity? How well does it apply to readers at different developmental stages and/or different achievement levels?

h. Given the purposes that the model's designer(s) had, what are the model's limitations?

i. How does your understanding of reading (or) writing processes align or misalign with the model of reading (or writing) that you are investigating and evaluating?

j. What diagnostic powers come with the model? How can aspects of the model help to explain reading problems and difficulties?

3. Our introductory discussion used a wave metaphor to describe the gradual development process that characterizes a number of cognitive processing models.

a. Which of the waves involves schema theory and attempts to account for the reader's background knowledge? (#20–Anderson; #21–Bransford; #23–Spiro et al.)

b. Which models incorporate schema theory as a key variable to explain the process of constructing meaning? What specific advantage does this addition offer those models?

c. Which wave incorporates the sociocultural context of the classroom? What does the inclusion of a sociocultural context add to our understanding of reading? (#4–Gee; #32–Alvermann et al.; #33–Many)

d. Which models account for interpreting and negotiating meaning in the sociocultural context of the classroom? What value might be found in accounting for this key variable?

4. Compare the Hayes writing model (#49) with the Ruddell and Unrau reading-as-a-meaning-construction-process model (#51) using the questions found in #2 above. Then, identify the similarities and differences between the two models.

5. Use the Rosenblatt model discussion (#48) to define the following terms: *transaction, evocation, efferent stance, aesthetic stance, validity of interpretation,* and *warranted assertability.* Explain how a predominantly efferent stance *or* a predominantly aesthetic stance

in reading a literature selection might produce a different interpretation of the text and how that interpretation could be justified according to Rosenblatt.

Accompanying CD Selections

CD 3.1 Adams, M.J., & Collins, A. (1985). A schema-theoretic view of reading. In H. Singer & R.B. Ruddell (Eds.), *Theoretical models and processes of reading* (3rd ed., pp. 404–425). Newark, DE: International Reading Association.

CD 3.2 Geyer, J.J. (1970). Models of perceptual processes in reading. In H. Singer & R.B. Ruddell (Eds.), *Theoretical models and processes of reading* (pp. 47–94). Newark, DE: International Reading Association.

CD 3.3 Goodman, K.S. (1976). Behind the eye: What happens in reading. In H. Singer & R.B. Ruddell (Eds.), *Theoretical models and processes of reading* (2nd ed., pp. 470–496). Newark, DE: International Reading Association.

CD 3.4 Goodman, K.S. (1994). Reading, writing, and written texts: A transactional sociopsycholinguistic view. In R.B. Ruddell, M.R. Ruddell, & H. Singer (Eds.), *Theoretical models and processes of reading* (4th ed., pp. 1093–1130). Newark, DE: International Reading Association.

CD 3.5 Ruddell, R.B. (1976). Psycholinguistic implications for a systems of communication model. In H. Singer & R.B. Ruddell (Eds.), *Theoretical models and processes of reading* (2nd ed., pp. 452–469). Newark, DE: International Reading Association.

CD 3.6 Singer, H. (1970). Theoretical models of reading: Implications for teaching and research. In H. Singer & R.B. Ruddell (Eds.), *Theoretical models and processes of reading* (pp. 147–182). Newark, DE: International Reading Association.

CD 3.7 Smagorinsky, P., & O'Donnell-Allen, C. (1998). Reading as mediated and mediating action: Composing meaning for literature through multimedia interpretive texts. *Reading Research Quarterly*, *33*, 198–226.

Additional Recommended Readings

De La Paz, S., Swanson, P.N., & Graham, S. (1998). The contribution of executive control to the revising by students with writing and learning difficulties. *Journal of Educational Psychology*, *90*, 448–460.

Graesser, A.C., Swamer, S.S., Baggett, W.B., & Sell, M.A. (1996). New models of deep comprehension. In B.K. Britton & A.C. Graesser (Eds.), *Models of understanding text* (pp. 1–31). Mahwah, NJ: Erlbaum.

Holmes, J.A. (1970). The substrata-factor theory of reading: Some experimental evidence. In H. Singer & R.B. Ruddell (Eds.), *Theoretical models and processes of reading* (pp. 187–197). Newark, DE: International Reading Association.

Singer, H. (1985). The substrata-factor theory of reading. In H. Singer & R.B. Ruddell (Eds.), *Theoretical models and processes of reading* (3rd ed., pp. 630–660). Newark, DE: International Reading Association.

Van Meter, P. (2001). Drawing construction as a strategy for learning from text. *Journal of Educational Psychology, 93*(1), 129–140.

References

Beck, I.L. (1989). Improving practice through understanding reading. In L.B. Resnick & L.E. Klopfer (Eds.), *Toward the thinking curriculum: Current cognitive research* (1989 ASCD yearbook, pp. 40–58). Alexandria, VA: Association for Supervision and Curriculum Development; Hillsdale, NJ: Erlbaum.

Gough, P.B. (1972). One second of reading. In J.F. Kavanagh & I.G. Mattingly (Eds.), *Language by ear and by eye* (pp. 331–358). Cambridge, MA: MIT Press.

Guthrie, J.T., & Wigfield, A. (1997). *Reading engagement: Motivating readers through integrated instruction.* Newark, DE: International Reading Association.

Hauser, M., Chomsky, N., & Fitch, W.T. (2002). The faculty of language: What is it, who has it, and how did it evolve? *Science, 298*(5598), 1569–1579.

Just, M., & Carpenter, P.A. (1987). *The psychology of reading and language comprehension.* Boston: Allyn & Bacon.

Keller, T.A., Carpenter, P.A., & Just, M.A. (2001). The neural bases of sentence comprehension: A fMRI examination of syntactic and lexical processing. *Cerebral Cortex, 11*(3), 223–237. Available: http://cercor.oupjournals.org/cgi/content/full/11/3/223

Kintsch, W. (1988). The use of knowledge in discourse processing: A construction-integration model. *Psychological Review, 95*(2), 163–182.

Meyer, B. (1975). *The organization of prose and its effect on recall.* Amsterdam: North-Holland.

Schank, R.C., & Abelson, R.P. (1977). *Scripts, plans, goals, and understanding: An inquiry into human knowledge structures.* Hillsdale, NJ: Erlbaum.

Shaywitz, S., Shaywitz, B., Fulbright, R., Skudlarski, P., Mencl, W.E., Constable, R.T., et al. (2003). Neural systems for compensation and persistence: Young adult outcome of childhood reading disability. *Biological Psychiatry, 54*(1), 25–33.

Stein, N.L., & Glenn, C. (1979). An analysis of story comprehension in elementary school children. In R.O. Freedle (Ed.), *New directions in discourse processing* (pp. 53–120). Norwood, NJ: Ablex.

40

Toward a Theory of Automatic Information Processing in Reading, Revisited

S. Jay Samuels

The LaBerge–Samuels (1974) model of automatic information processing in reading is now more than two decades old and has had a long and useful life. In reading methods textbooks, it is the most widely quoted of all the reading theories (Blanchard, Rottenberg, & Jones, 1989). When the model was in its infancy, it attracted the interest of teachers and researchers because it used the concept of automaticity to explain why fluent readers are able to decode and understand text with ease while beginning readers have difficulty. Later the model provided the conceptual groundwork for repeated reading (Samuels, 1979), a method for helping beginning readers become automatic decoders. Researchers have also realized that the concept of automaticity can be extended to any skill in reading. Most recently, it has spurred cognitive psychologists to offer new explanations concerning what happens when one develops a skill to the automatic level. In fact, Logan (1988a) believes the new explanations of automaticity are so important that he stated as follows:

> There is a battle raging in the ivory tower over the concept of automaticity. One faction represents "the old guard," the modal view of the field, and construes automaticity as a way to overcome resource limitations. The other function is revolutionary (or sees itself as such) and construes automaticity as a memory phenomenon reflecting the consequences of running a large database through an efficient retrieval process. The battle may turn out to be a tempest in a teapot, affecting no more than academic promotion and tenure.

In this piece about automaticity theory, I will attempt to do two things:

1. describe automaticity theory and its practical applications
2. explain some of the new ideas about automaticity

From Ruddell, R.B., Ruddell, M.R., & Singer, H. (Eds.), *Theoretical Models and Processes of Reading* (4th ed., pp. 816–837). Copyright © 1994 by the International Reading Association.

The LaBerge–Samuels Model of Automatic Information Processing

A good theoretical model has three characteristics: (1) It summarizes a considerable amount of information discovered in the past; (2) it helps explain and make more understandable what is happening in the present, and (3) it allows one to make predictions about the future. From a scientific viewpoint, the ability to make predictions is most important because the accuracy of the predictions is what allows one to test the model's validity. When the test results fail to support the predictions, then the model has to be revised. The LaBerge–Samuels automaticity model has these three characteristics of summarizing the past, explaining the present, and predicting the future. Many aspects of the model—such as its description of how the eye processes print—were taken from past research on visual processing. Further, the model brings together research findings from a variety of areas in an attempt to explain the present. For example, it explains the crucial differences between beginning and fluent reading so that one can understand why beginning readers have so much difficulty understanding what they read. And finally, over the years a number of tests and revisions have been made of and to the model.

Attention

The LaBerge–Samuels model attempts to identify components in the information-processing system, trace the routes that information takes as it passes through the system, and identify changes in the form of the information as it moves from the surface of the page into the deeper semantic-linguistic centers of the brain. At the heart of the model is *attention*. Attention has two components, internal and external. To the layperson, the external aspects of attention are the more familiar. When a classroom teacher says that a student does not pay attention and therefore is not living up to his or her potential, it is external attention that is being described. Other manifestations of external attention have to do with what may be called *orienting behavior*, the directing of one's sensory organs (such as eyes and ears) in such a way as to maximize information input. If an observer can watch the behavior of another and determine whether that person is paying attention (as a teacher often does), it is the level of external attention that is being determined.

External attention has important implications for learning in general and for learning to read in particular. In fact, most psychologists would agree that it is a prerequisite, that without the external and internal components of attention there can be no learning. Classroom observation has thrown some light on the relationship between external attention and reading. A fairly well-documented finding is that during elementary school years, girls surpass boys in reading achievement. Is this superiority the result of some maturational genetic sex-linked advantage or of cultural forces at work in the classroom? One line of research showed that when boys were put in booths that resemble airplane cockpits for a reading hour, they learned more from texts than did girls, this suggesting a cultural rather than genetic advantage. These booths are not only exciting to boys but also help them focus their attention on the reading by reducing extraneous sources of stimulation. Another line of classroom research found that girls were significantly more attentive during the reading hour than were boys; these same girls were also superior readers. In this classroom study, as external signs of attention (such as looking in books and working on reading assignments) increased in both boys and girls, so did reading scores (Samuels & Turnure, 1974).

Although external aspects of attention are important to learning and comprehension, the internal aspects are even more crucial and represent the core component of the LaBerge–Samuels model. External aspects of attention such as orientation of sensory receptors indicate that internal processing of information is taking place; when a person's eyes are glued to a book, we assume he or she is internally processing the information on the page and trying to construct meaning from it. The internal characteristics of attention are far more difficult to describe. Imagine a laboratory in which an experimental subject is given earphones and told that a male voice will be heard in one ear and a female voice in the other. Our subject is told to remember the information given by the female voice and has no difficulty performing this task. Even if we increase the task difficulty by alternating the ear in which the female voice is transmitted, our subject can successfully direct attention to the appropriate voice. This selection of the appropriate voice to listen to is an example of internal control of attention.

The same ability to process and recall auditory information occurs in natural, real-life settings. Cocktail parties are frequently crowded situations in which many people move about and talk to one another. Imagine talking to a friend at a cocktail party. Both the external and internal components of attention are directed at your friend. Suddenly, from behind, you hear part of an interesting conversation you want to hear more of. Without turning your head away from your friend or giving any outward sign to either your friend or the person behind you, you begin to take in as much of two conversations as you can. This ability to take in parts of several conversations at will by switching attention back and forth without anyone's knowledge has come to be called the "cocktail party phenomenon."

Internal attention has three characteristics, as follows:

1. *Alertness*. Alertness simply refers to the active attempt to come in contact with sources of information. Alertness also can be thought of in terms of vigilance.

2. *Selectivity*. Our environment is such that at any moment under ordinary circumstances, our sensory organs—eyes, ears, nose, skin, tongue— can be bombarded with multiple, competing stimuli. As you read this line, are you aware that the lines above and below are also on your retina? We are generally unaware of this, and the process of selective attention

enables us to choose which line we will process. Similarly, when we go to a party, several conversations usually compete for our attention, yet we are able to select which one we will process at any given moment. Following is a passage that shows how selective attention operates in the visual mode. It contains two different ideas—one written in uppercase and the other in lowercase letters. Read only the text in uppercase letters and be prepared to answer the question at the end:

> WHY the YOU purpose SHOULD of GET the THE investigation SHAFT was A to SHAFT test IS the THE focal MOST attention EFFICIENT hypothesis WAY this TO hypothesis DELIVER suggests POWER that FROM when THE a ENGINE picture TO and THE a REAR word WHEEL are IT presented WILL together NOT the SPRAY student YOU will WITH focus OIL on NOR that WILL part IT of BREAK the AS stimulus EASILY that AS most A readily CHAIN elicits IN a FACT correct A response SHAFT a IS poor ALMOST reader INDESTRUCTIBLE finds AND the BECAUSE picture IT easier IS to ENCLOSED use IN than A the BATH word OF and OIL attends IT to IS the ALMOST picture SILENT
>
> What are the advantages of a drive shaft?

Most people who read this passage have no difficulty selecting the message on which to place their attention. Furthermore, the passage on drive shafts usually is read with a high level of literal comprehension.

3. *Limited capacity.* The human mind, like the fastest computer, has limited capacity to process information. With the human mind, the limitation comes from the limited amount of attention available for information processing. Attention may be thought of as the effort or energy used to process information. When we are learning a complicated skill, the demands of learning that skill use up all our attention resources and we find we can pay attention to only one task at a time. For example, beginning drivers often find that while driving, they dislike experiencing any competing demands on their attention, such as conversation with a passenger. With extensive practice, the attention demands of driving decrease sufficiently so drivers can process multiple sources of information at the same time. Experienced drivers can simultaneously operate the car, engage in conversation, and enjoy music.

One way to think of automaticity is that it represents the ability to perform a task with little attention. The critical test of automaticity is that the task, which at the beginning stage of learning could be performed only by itself, now can be performed along with one or more other tasks. What is the mechanism that allows this transformation from beginner to expert? This question will be addressed in the final section of this piece.

To summarize, attention can be divided into two broad categories, one having to do with external and the other with internal components. The external aspects of attention are directly observable and are generally related to the orientation of one's sensory organs; the internal aspects of attention—alertness, selectivity, and limited capacity—are not directly observable. How do these concepts relate to reading?

Decoding. Internal components of attention are central to the theory of automatic information processing in reading. It is assumed in the theory—as well as by many who study reading—that getting meaning from printed words involves a two-step process: First, the printed words must be decoded; second, the decoded words must be comprehended. *Decoding* in relation to reading is the process of translating printed words into spoken words. It is not necessary for the "spoken words" actually to be uttered aloud.

Comprehension. Even though definitive explanations of the mechanisms underlying comprehension are currently unavailable, it seems reasonably clear that research will find that attention is required for processing an unfamiliar passage for its meaning. With all the practice experienced readers get at processing for meaning, one may wonder why skill development in this area does not reach the point of automaticity. Granted, when a competent adult reader encounters highly familiar words (such as *cat*, *kitchen*, *wheel*, or *milk*) in print, their meaning is in all probability immediately available without the need of attention. The ability to get the meaning of each word in a sentence, however, is not the same as the ability to comprehend a sentence. In comprehending a sentence, one must be able to interrelate and combine the separate meanings of each of its words. From this point of view, comprehension is a constructive process of synthesis and putting word meanings together in special ways, much as individual bricks are combined in the construction of a house. Whereas one may go from print to the meanings of individual words automatically, the acts of integrating, relating, and combining these meanings in the unique ways demanded by sentences are required for comprehension. Even in a passage as simple as "The dog is in the house," attention is necessary to determine, for example, the relationship of the dog to the house. Is the dog on, in, under, or next to the house? An understanding of "The grandmother spanked her grandchild" requires knowledge of what the action is, who the agent is, and who the object of the action is. To understand the relationship of grandmother to grandchild requires complex analysis of such features as how many generations separate the two.

If even simple sentences require a reader's attention in order to determine the relationships that exist among their parts, imagine what happens when more complex sentences on more complex topics are read. When one superimposes the added burdens on attention and memory that occur when a poor reader—who is still using attention to decode—encounters a difficult passage, there is little wonder that comprehension seems to suffer.

Attention Switching in Reading. For many students, learning to read is a difficult task requiring considerable attention. If each student had unlimited quantities of attention to focus on the task there would be no problem, but this is not the case. When a student encounters a task requiring more attention than is available, he or she is faced with a problem. The beginning reader must use attention in order to get the decoding done. Herein lies the dilemma: If the reader's attention is on decoding and if attention can be directed at only one process at a time, the comprehension task is not getting done. Since the end product of reading should be comprehension, the beginning reader is faced with a formidable problem.

Figure 1A shows how beginning readers process text. Because the attention demands of decoding and comprehension exceed their attention capacity, these readers put their attention on the decoding task and then switch attention to comprehension to understand what they have decoded. The process is similar to what happens

FIGURE 1
Attention and Reading

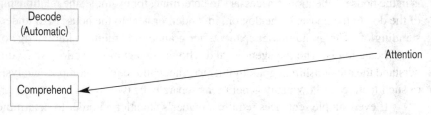

A. Beginning Reading

Decode

Switch

Comprehend

Attention

In beginning reading, attention is switched alternately from decoding to comprehension. Only one task can be done at a time.

B. Fluent Reading

Decode (Automatic)

Attention

Comprehend

In fluent reading, decoding is done automatically and attention remains on comprehension. Both tasks get done at the same time.

at a cocktail party when one tries to take in several conversations by switching attention back and forth among them. A beginning reader often reads a passage several times: first to decode from symbol to spoken words (this puts considerable strain on attention and memory systems) and subsequently to comprehend.

Although the beginning reader *is* able to comprehend by switching attention back and forth in this way, the process is slow, laborious, and frustrating. For those of you who doubt this, can you recall or imagine the difficulty of trying to comprehend a foreign language not yet mastered? To determine meaning, you first have to translate the foreign words and then you must comprehend what has been translated.

In many ways the problem facing the beginning reader is similar to that facing the beginning driver who is trying to drive a car and listen to a passenger's conversation. The beginning driver places attention on the mechanical aspects of driving, such as steering; controlling the accelerator, brake, clutch, and gears; signaling turns; and other operations involved in getting to a destination safely. With attention focused on the mechanical aspects of driving, the driver finds it difficult to process for meaning any ongoing conversation. However, with continued driving practice over considerable time, the beginning driver will become skilled, and a skilled driver can perform the routine mechanical functions of driving with little attention. In fact, skilled drivers who regularly travel the same route often wonder how they arrive at their destination. These drivers are performing the routine, mechanical aspects of driving without attention, and their attention is thus left free to process conversation or think private thoughts.

Thus far, what has been explained is how the beginning reader manages to comprehend by means of attention switching. What is left to explain is how the fluent reader gets the job done.

Attention in Fluent Reading. I recently asked a skilled typist to type what was printed in a newspaper article. My instructions were that she should strive for accuracy and keep up a modest, steady typing pace. While the typist worked, I asked her a number of questions, to which she responded appropriately. Our back-and-forth conversation went on without any noticeable decrease in her typing speed. When she finished the article, we proofed the copy and found it virtually free of errors. The typist was able to perform both tasks—typing and conversing—simultaneously. In a somewhat analogous experimental situation, a skilled piano player was fitted with earphones and given music she had never seen before to sight-read. She was told that she would hear a voice speaking in a conversational manner through the earphones and that she was to repeat aloud what she heard while she played the piece. (In a laboratory procedure, repeating aloud what one hears is called "shadowing.") In order to be sure that the proper notes were played and the correct words were repeated, a tape recorder was set up. When the procedure was completed, we found that the piano player was able to faithfully perform both tasks simultaneously.

There are certain similarities in the experiments. First, in both cases incoming information—visual and aural—had to be processed. Second, the information that came in by ear for the typist (listening to what I said, processing it, and forming an answer) and for the piano player (listening to meaningful speech and then repeating it) required attention so that the subsequent task could be performed. A third similarity is that attention is required at the beginning stages of skill development in both typing and piano playing, but as fluency develops, both tasks can be performed with significantly less attention. Herein lies the answer to the question as to how two tasks, each of which ordinarily requires the services of attention, can be performed simultaneously: As a person develops skill at the task, the skill can be performed with less attention. For example, some years ago I visited a friend who was studying to be a surgeon. To practice his surgical knot tying, he had a small board fitted with tiny pegs on which he would hook the threads and tie the knots. In the beginning stages of skill development, while his fingers were slowly working on the knots, he focused his eyes on his fingers to guide the movements. Any attempt on my part to talk was met with his request to hold off on conversation; he said he could not concentrate on knot tying and talk at the same time. It would appear that his attention was being directed at the knot tying, thus preventing him from processing conversation. After years of practice on the knot-tying board, my friend was able to tie the knots while watching television and conversing.

Automaticity. When a task that formerly required attention for its performance can be performed without attention, the task is being done automatically. Automaticity in information processing, then, simply means that information is processed with little attention. One way to determine if a person is performing a process automatically is to give him or her two tasks to perform at the same time. If the tasks can be performed simultaneously, at least one of them is being done automatically.

With the concept of automaticity in mind, it is now a simple matter to describe how the fluent reader is able to perform the two-step decoding–comprehension process in reading. The decoding is done automatically—and thus attention is available for getting meaning from the printed words. This is shown in Figure 1B.

There are times, however, when skilled readers turn their attention away from getting meaning from the printed words. One such situation arises when unusual words—such as foreign words or scientific terminology—are encountered. The reader must then put attention on decoding in order to translate these verbal symbols. Another such situation occurs when a skilled reader is proofreading. As most experienced writers know, it is a poor idea to read for meaning while trying to locate errors. Proofreading is done most efficiently when one's attention is directed away from meaning and put on possible errors in the text.

Other Components in the LaBerge–Samuels Model

Most information-processing models indicate the components involved and the direction of flow of information through the system. However, these linear models tend to suggest that there is only one way to process information. As any skilled reader who has thought about reading processes knows, there are a variety of ways to read. The LaBerge–Samuels model shows the variety of routes used in going from print to meaning.

Figure 2 shows the LaBerge–Samuels information-processing model with its components. The first component is visual memory (VM), where the visual

FIGURE 2
The LaBerge–Samuels Model

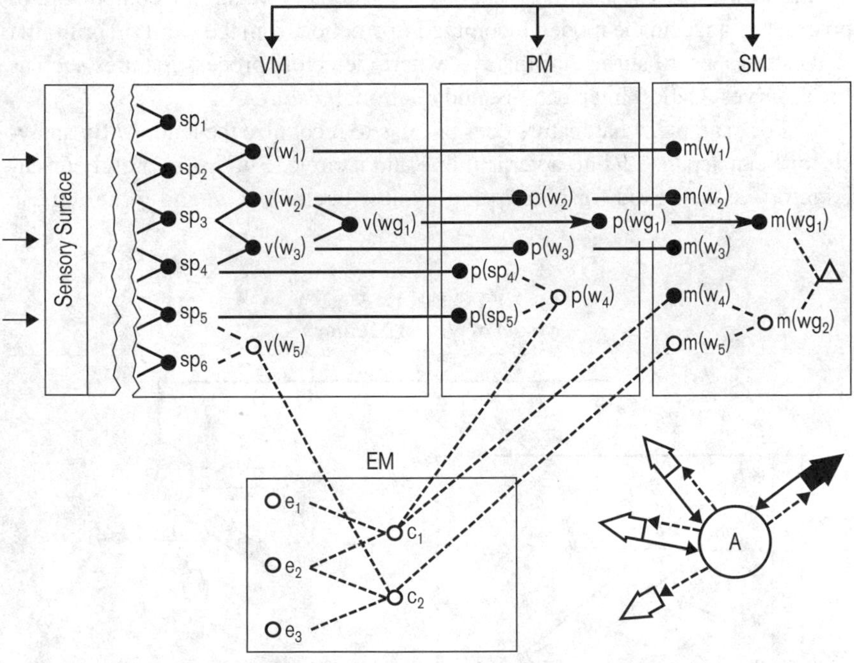

Key

e	temporal-spatial event code	m(w)	word-meaning code
c	episodic code	m(wg)	word group-meaning code
sp	spelling-pattern code	●	code activated without attention
v(w)	visual word code	○	code activated only with attention
v(wg)	visual word-group code	△	code momentarily activated by attention
p(sp)	phonological spelling-pattern code	◀-----	momentary focus of attention
p(w)	phonological word code	——	information flow without attention
p(wg)	phonological word-group code	- - -	information flow only with attention

information from the text is processed. Next, there is phonological memory (PM) where the auditory representations of the visual codes are processed. Because all information arrives in some context, episodic memory (EM) records contextual details pertaining to time and place. In order to process information, attention is required; this is shown as A. Finally, there is semantic memory (SM), where knowledge of all kinds is stored. In order to account for processing of a word through use of the visual information on the page (bottom-up processing) as well as the knowledge stored in semantic memory (top-down processing), the model must allow for an interaction of visual information and knowledge as a basis for word recognition. While some who study our model think of it as bottom up, the feedback loops from semantic memory to phonological memory to visual memory account for top-down processing. For example, if one sees "Father cut the g _ _ _ _ ," the context would suggest the target word is *grass*.

Visual Memory. As seen in Figure 3, visual memory is the first component, or processing stage, in the model. Incoming information from the words in print first strikes the sensory surface of the eye, where detectors process features such as lines, curves, angles, intersections, and relational features.

For example, what feature does one use to recognize the letter *b*? By analysis, one can separate *b* into a vertical line and a circle. But this is entirely unsatisfactory as a method for identifying a letter because *d*, *p*, and *g* share these

FIGURE 3
Model of Visual Memory

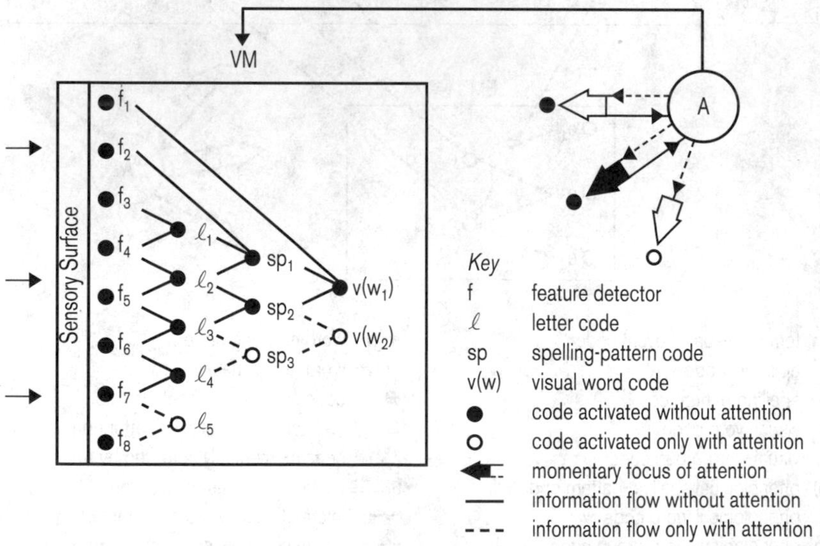

Key	
f	feature detector
ℓ	letter code
sp	spelling-pattern code
v(w)	visual word code
●	code activated without attention
○	code activated only with attention
◀	momentary focus of attention
—	information flow without attention
- - -	information flow only with attention

components. By adding relational features, such as up or down and left or right, we arrive at a set of features uniquely descriptive of *b*—the circle is to the right and at the bottom of the vertical. By contrast, the letter *p* would be described as having the circle to the right and at the top of the vertical. Thus each letter can be described by a set of unique features.

To continue with this explanation of how a perceptual code is learned, as one goes from left to right in the hierarchical model of VM, one notes that different kinds of information get processed. The model shows how the visual information is analyzed by detectors into features, which at the next level are combined to form letters. At the next level in the model, letter combinations such as *sh*, *th*, *bl*, *-ing*, and *anti-* may be combined to form spelling patterns, and the spelling patterns feed into word codes. The use of the term *codes* in the model refers to the form in which information is represented. Thus there may be letter codes, spelling-pattern codes, and word codes.

There are two additional features in this model of VM, labeled f_1 and f_2. Unlike the other features that lead into letters, f_1 and f_2 indicate that features other than letters may be used in the identification of a word. For example, word configuration and length may be used in combination with other sources of textual information in word recognition. Assume that the words we wish to identify are *hippopotamus*, *dog*, and *cat*. It is a simple task to determine which configuration below represents each word:

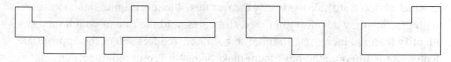

In Figure 3, the various codes are represented by either a filled or empty circle. An empty circle represents a code that is not well learned and consequently can be activated only with attention—for example, codes ℓ_5, sp_3, and $v(w_2)$. A filled circle represents a well-learned code that does not require attention for its activation or processing—for example, codes ℓ_1, sp_1, and $v(w_1)$.

Attention. In Figure 2, the attention center is symbolized by A in a circle. Attention is considered essential in the early stages of learning a perceptual code such as a letter. An individual is free to focus attention at various levels of the VM model—on features, letters, spelling patterns, or whole words. When well-learned codes, symbolized by a filled circle, are activated by stimulation, attention from the attention center is not required for processing. When stimulation of poorly learned codes, symbolized by an empty circle, occurs, attention is required for processing. With continued activation and processing of these poorly learned codes, an individual develops a level of skill such that attention is no longer required for their processing.

It is important to make a distinction between accuracy and automaticity. A student may be accurate without being automatic. At the accurate levels of skill development, attention is required. When asked if two letters are the same, the student may use attention to scan the features to determine the correct answer; with practice, the student will reach automaticity and be able to come up with the correct answer with little attention. In most classrooms the tests that are administered measure response accuracy. We need good tests that measure automatic levels of skill development. Fortunately, there are a number of indicators of automaticity teachers can use. Generally, if a student is automatic, there is a high level of accuracy combined with speed. With reading aloud, for example, automaticity may be indicated by the amount of expression in the student's voice. When a student is familiar with the task of oral reading and decodes automatically, he or she will generally read with expression and comprehend and recall what has been read. Nonautomatic decoders, when asked to read orally, usually read without expression and have difficulty comprehending and recalling what they have read.

Before leaving the hierarchical model of visual memory, it would be useful to outline the probable course of learning to identify a letter. This learning is conceptualized as a two-step process. As explained previously, the first step is to analyze and select the relevant features of the letter. To a large extent, this task of searching for features is similar to the initial stages of a concept-learning task, in which one must identify the relevant attributes of the concept. Generally, the rate at which children are able to identify the features of letters is quite slow. However, with practice they develop improved strategies, and the rate at which they can identify features increases. In order to help new readers select the appropriate features, it is important to have them make same–different judgments among visually similar letters in groups—for example, *huvn*, *mnuv*, *coeu*, *klth*, and *xvzw*. In the next stage of perceptual learning, students must combine these separate features into a single letter code, a process that at first requires attention. With practice, students will unitize the separate features into a single letter code; skilled readers, for example, see *b* and not "l" plus "o." With extended practice at letter identification, students' unitization of the features occurs without attention.

Phonological Memory. Input into the phonological memory (PM) system comes from a variety of sources: visual memory, episodic memory, feedback from semantic memory, and articulatory responses, as well as from direct external acoustic stimulation. Some of these sources of input are shown in Figure 2. It is assumed that the phonological memory system contains units that are related to acoustic and articulatory inputs. Although acoustic input seems logical enough, one might wonder why there would be articulatory input in a phonological system. There is evidence that the kinds of articulatory-muscle responses made in producing a sound may also be involved in perceiving that sound (Liberman et al., 1967). Thus acoustic input from stimulation external to the individual and articulatory input from stimulation internal to the individual are thought to be part of the phonological memory system.

With the rich variety of input flowing into PM, one might be tempted to describe how that input is organized. However, doing so might seriously reduce the effectiveness of the model by attempting to have it explain too much or be overly comprehensive. Therefore, only the organization of acoustic units will be described here. The acoustic units in PM are features, phonemes, syllables, and words. These units in PM are counterparts of the features, letters, spelling patterns, and words found in visual memory. Just as the units in visual memory are arranged in a hierarchy, so too are the units in phonological memory.

Acoustic features are represented by contrasts, such as /pa/–/ga/–/ta/. These differences are represented in the location where the consonant sound is made. The first sound is made with the lips, the second at the back of the throat, and the third at the roof of the mouth. (It is interesting to note that in attempting to describe features we hear, we resort to identifying the place of articulation.) Another difference is the manner in which the sounds are produced. For example, when saying /pa/–/ma/, one observes that both sounds are produced with the lips but that only in the first sound is breath expelled.

The model of visual memory indicates that a letter consists of a set of visual features that uniquely describes it. Similarly, in the model of phonological memory, a phoneme consists of a set of uniquely descriptive acoustic features. A phoneme may be thought of as a sound unit that indicates a change in word meaning, such as the difference between /m/, /p/, and /f/ as in *man, pan, fan*, or the /s/ sound in *cat–cats*. Each of these phonemes signals a change in word meaning. Despite the enormous variety of words found in the English language, approximately 44 phonemes are sufficient to produce the rich variety of words we use.

Similarities Between Visual and Phonological Memory. I described the hierarchy in visual memory as moving from features to letters to spelling patterns and finally to words. The hierarchy in the phonological memory system moves from features to phonemes to syllables and finally to words. In both visual and phonological memory, information processing may move from features up to words or from words down to features. When going from a whole word to features, a decomposition into parts takes place; teachers often call this process "analysis." For example, when a teacher asks students to listen for the difference between /sat/ and /sad/, the process requires a top-down analysis from whole to parts. On the other hand, when students sound out a new word letter-by-letter and blend the sounds to form a word, they are engaging in a bottom-up process of synthesizing a word from its parts to a whole.

Episodic Memory. Episodic memory (EM) is responsible for putting a time, place, and context tag on events and knowledge. When an individual recalls the details of an event that happened in the past, it is episodic memory that is called on. Thus, the organization of knowledge and events in EM may be listed in categories under the *wh* words, such as *when* (time), *where* (place), and *who* (persons). For example, an individual may receive lessons (an event) on how to drive a car. This event may be recalled with details, such as *who* was the instructor, *when* did the instruction occur, and *what* type of vehicle was used. The abstract knowledge of how to drive is the essential information that is retained. This knowledge is stored in semantic memory, while the associated details surrounding the instruction remain in episodic memory where they may eventually be "lost" in time. For example, I have retained the abstract knowledge of how to add, subtract, multiply, and divide, which I learned long ago, but not the names of the teachers who taught me nor of the students who sat next to me.

Semantic Memory and Comprehension. The final component in the automaticity model is semantic memory. It is here that individual word meanings are produced, and it is also here that the comprehension of written messages occurs. Earlier in this article, I distinguished between the attentional processes involved in getting the meaning of a word and comprehending a written passage. When familiar words are decoded by skilled readers, the word meanings may be assessed automatically, without attention. On the other hand, under most conditions comprehension does not occur automatically and therefore requires attention.

In order to get at the underlying meaning in a sentence, attention comes into play in a number of ways during the comprehension process. It is used to organize the words in a sentence into grammatical units, and it is used to determine the relationships in meanings that exist within and between grammatical units. For example, as verbal concepts, the meanings of *fierce* and *dog* may exist separately. When, however, the noun phrase "the fierce dog" is encountered, it has one meaning, and it is in semantic memory that the blending of these two verbal concepts occurs. This example simply illustrates how attention might be used to determine the relationships in meaning within a grammatical unit.

The Role of Attention in Comprehension

Let us now examine how a sentence such as "The fierce dog bit the tall man" is processed for comprehension. (Because the focus of this article is not comprehension, however, the description will be sketchy in the extreme.) When decoding familiar words such as those found in this sentence, a skilled reader assesses the meaning of each word directly, without attention; this is indicated in Figure 4 by the solid lines from V(W1) to M(W1), for example. However, in order for the reader to understand the meaning of the sentence as a whole, the individual word must be grouped into units such as the noun phrase (NP) and verb phrase (VP), and this requires attention. By breaking this sentence into its grammatical units (see Figure 4), the reader determines the agent, the action, and

FIGURE 4
How Attention Is Used to Construct the Meaning of a Sentence

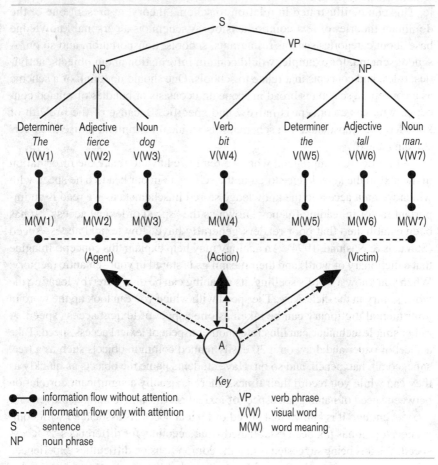

the victim. However, the comprehension process still is not complete. The reader also must decide on the meaning of the sentence as a whole. This combining of meanings is viewed as an active, constructive process that requires attention for its completion.

Automaticity and Comprehension: Application to Schema Theory

When our model was first published, we thought of automaticity in a very limited way. In time, however, we realized that the concept would be extended to include virtually every aspect of reading comprehension—from the metacognitive self-monitoring of comprehension to the actual process of comprehension itself.

While the comprehension process usually is costly in terms of demands on attention, there are subelements within the process that can become automatic. This can be illustrated in relation to schema theory, at present one of the dominant theories of text comprehension. A schema is a personal knowledge base about categories such as restaurants, schools, transportation, and so on. A school schema, for example, would contain information about objects, activities, rules, and concepts that relate to schools. One should not think of a schema as a concept; a schema is broad in scope and consists of bundles of related concepts, whereas a concept is narrow and specific. Because of the breadth of knowledge encapsulated in a schema, it is an ideal instrument to use in understanding a text.

In order to comprehend what we read, we have to relate the information in the text to the knowledge stored in the schemata in our heads. The speed with which we gain access to the knowledge stored in schemata as we read is an important factor in reading fluency known as the "speed of lexical access." It has been established that poor readers generally have slow lexical access speed (Samuels & Naslund, 1994). An analogy may help explain this concept. Imagine that a dictionary of words and their meanings is stored in your semantic memory. When you know a word's spelling, its meaning can be discovered by locating the word's entry in the dictionary. The speed with which you can look up the word in your mental dictionary can be taken as one aspect of lexical access speed. A rather simple technique can illustrate another aspect of lexical access speed. Take a sheet of paper and draw on it 30 easily named common objects such as a tree, shoe, comb, hat, pencil, and so on. Have students name the objects as quickly as they can while you record their times. There is usually a significant correlation between speed of naming, an aspect of lexical access, and reading achievement.

Although it is known that speed of lexical access is associated with comprehension, it has not been established what accounts for differences in access speed. What is being suggested is that the comprehension difficulties experienced by some students may be caused by the fact that the concepts and knowledge stored in the schemata cannot be rapidly and automatically accessed.

The role of schema-based prior knowledge in acquiring comprehension skills is an important issue. Automatic word-decoding skills and prior knowledge of a text's content may interact and strongly affect success in comprehension. It has been observed that skilled readers can efficiently process texts covering unfamiliar materials almost or just as easily as familiar materials, whereas some less skilled readers demonstrate differential success in processing and recalling information from text. Schneider, Körkel, and Weinert (1988) showed such differential performance with materials that were either familiar or unfamiliar to skilled and less-skilled children in a German elementary school. They found that children who knew a great deal about soccer efficiently and accurately comprehended and recalled texts about soccer, regardless of their general mental aptitude (measured with IQ-type tests). In addition, children who had extensive knowledge about soccer but low general mental aptitude recalled significantly more details from soccer texts than did children who had little soccer knowledge and either high or low aptitude. It would appear that a strong relationship exists between reading performance and prior knowledge. When judging the degree of automaticity in readers' decoding skills based on their comprehension and recall of text, familiarity with the subject matter must therefore be taken into account.

This contextual effect in reading also may result from readers' acquisition of internal lexicons and vocabulary through repeated experience. These lexicons may be thought of as particular organizations of vocabulary, with many overlapping entries between lexical categories. A German child who lives for soccer has a soccer lexicon that can be activated more easily and rapidly than could be the soccer lexicon of an American child who lives for baseball. In other words, speed of access is faster for the vocabulary we are most familiar with. Prior knowledge and the lexicon associated with that knowledge can interact with the decoding of words in texts on familiar topics. The process of retrieving lexical information may enhance readers' matching of phoneme combinations with appropriate context-related words. For example, a child who is familiar with soccer might decode a soccer-related word never read before faster than could a child who is unfamiliar with soccer, even if both children are inefficient decoders. The child familiar with the sport may need only to sound out the first few phonemes of *penalty*, for example, to access this word and conclude that it is an appropriate choice to precede the more familiar word *kick*; the child with little knowledge about soccer may struggle with the sounds of *penalty* and not be able to access the meaning of this word very readily. Thus lexical access and knowledge of a subject can compensate somewhat for poor decoding skills.

Optional Word-Recognition Processing Strategies

I have described each of the components of the model of automatic information processing in reading, and in an earlier section I described the different ways to recognize a word. In this section, I will summarize the various options available for processing a word. Referring back to Figure 2, we can trace the information flow for the various options, starting from the top and proceeding downward. (Rather than present the processing options in great detail, I will simply suggest general ways that meaning can be obtained.) Only the symbols in visual memory will be given here. To follow the description, simply start with visual memory and move along the lines in the figure from left to right.

Option 1. The visual word $v(w_1)$ is automatically decoded, and the word meaning $m(w_1)$ is available automatically. This occurs when a skilled reader reads a common word such as *dog* or *car*.

Option 2. The visual $v(w_2)$ is automatically decoded. In turn, the phonological code for the word $p(w_2)$ is automatically activated, which in turn automatically activates the word meaning $m(w_2)$. This occurs when a skilled reader encounters a common word but subvocalizes it.

Option 3. Two different visual words in a visual word group $v(wg_1)$—such as *ice cream*—are decoded automatically. In turn, the phonological code $p(wg_1)$ for the word group is activated automatically. Next, the meaning of the word group $m(wg_1)$ is made available automatically in semantic memory.

Option 4. A visual word such as *digraph* is coded automatically into two spelling patterns—*di* and *graph*—represented by sp_4 and sp_5. Next, the phonological code for these spelling patterns is activated automatically. However, from this point on, attention is used to blend the two spelling patterns into one word, to excite the episodic code, and to access the meaning code for the word. This course of events would occur with a skilled reader who has no difficulty with decoding but is somewhat uncertain about the technical definition of *digraph*.

Option 5. A highly unfamiliar visual word is coded with attention into $v(w_5)$ Attention is used to activate the episodic code, the phonological code, and the meaning code. This sequence of events might occur with a foreign name that is difficult to pronounce easily.

Option 6. There is another route to word meaning that is now shown on the model as depicted in Figure 2. A reader can visually recognize the word as a holistic unit without constructing it from the spelling of individual letters, and then go directly to meaning in semantic memory. A study by Samuels, LaBerge, and Bremer (1978) demonstrated that students who were not automatic decoders did letter-by-letter word recognition, while students who were automatic decoders recognized words as holistic units.

Feedback From Semantic Memory

Before leaving the model of automatic information processing in Figure 2, take note of the arrow leading from semantic memory to visual and phonological memory. This arrow indicates an important function and represents a marked departure from the original automaticity model. The present automaticity model has feedback loops, because what happens in semantic memory may influence processes that occur earlier.

Implications of the Automaticity Model for Diagnosis of Reading Problems and Instruction

Earlier, I mentioned the practicality of a good theory. In this section, a few of the practical implications of the LaBerge–Samuels model are explored.

The automaticity theory helps diagnose certain kinds of common reading problems. Teachers have observed that some students can recognize words accurately but not comprehend them with ease. Teachers call this problem "barking at print." Automaticity theory suggests that one possible reason for the students' problem is that the decoding requires so much attention that it interferes with comprehension. Another common problem is seen when skilled readers, often college students, claim that even though they read the text with care, they cannot remember what they have read. Because the students are skilled readers, the decoding of the words on the page can take place with little attention, thus leaving attention free to be directed elsewhere. Automaticity theory suggests that instead of focusing on deriving meaning from the text and understanding and recalling the author's viewpoints, the students' attention perhaps wanders to matters entirely unrelated to the text.

These problems require quite different remedies. For students whose attention is on decoding rather than comprehension, one solution is to provide texts that are easier to read. Another solution is to suggest that they read the text several times until the meaning becomes clear. This practice is often followed in beginning stages of reading. The first time or two, students read the text, emphasizing decoding; once they are able to decode the words, the students switch their attention to meaning. A third solution lies in the realization that more than accuracy is needed for students to become skilled readers. Readers must go beyond accuracy to reach automaticity. In human activities that require high levels of proficiency, a considerable amount of time must be spent in practicing the skills leading to mastery. Only by spending a great deal of time reading will students develop beyond the level of mere accuracy. Practice may be on important subskills in reading, but it also must include time spent on reading easy, interesting, and meaningful material. At one time, teachers felt guilty about having students spend time on a task at which they had exhibited some minimal level of proficiency; they were afraid of being accused of giving the students busywork. However, since reaching automaticity in reading requires practice, teachers should know that what may appear to be busywork to some is actually "automaticity training."

For students who are skilled readers but have difficulty remembering what they read, it is often helpful to explain that poor recall is due not to a memory deficit but to lack of attention directed on processing the text. Although the mere explanation of the nature of the problem is often helpful to students, additional aid is frequently needed. To help students focus attention on text meaning, they should be taught how to engage in self-testing. Asking themselves, What ideas were expressed on this page? at the end of each page helps students in the areas of comprehension and recall.

The Method of Repeated Readings

An interesting area of inquiry is what can be learned about how to teach reading from areas of human activity that require extraordinarily high levels of skill development, such as music and sports. Both of these areas have training methods that differ from those generally used in reading. In music, for example, the teacher may assign one or two pieces of music and tell the beginning student to practice these pieces for a week. The student's goal is to play the pieces accurately and with fluency, so he practices the same pieces over and over, trying to reduce errors and to blend the notes into a smooth rendition.

A somewhat different situation exists in beginning reading. Although the goals in both music and reading are accuracy and fluency, the beginning reader is seldom encouraged to read and reread a passage until these goals are achieved. Instead, teachers tend to move many students rapidly through the pages in the text before any degree of mastery has been reached. For several years I have been using a technique I call "the method of repeated readings" (Samuels, 1979) with enough resulting improvement in students' comprehension and reading speed to justify suggesting it here. It is used in conjunction with whatever the ongoing method of teaching reading happens to be. Of course, many teachers will probably want to alter this method of repeated readings somewhat to fit particular classroom needs. The technique is as follows:

1. The student selects a passage that is neither so hard that he or she cannot read any of the words nor so easy that all of the words can be read with high accuracy and speed. The selection can be a passage as short as 50 words or as long as 500 words, depending on the reader's skill.

2. The helper—a teacher, teacher's aide, parent, or student tutor—makes a chart for recording word-recognition errors and speed.

3. The student reads the selection aloud to the helper, who counts the number of errors and records the reading time in seconds. These data on errors and speed are put on the chart for each testing.

4. The student rereads the selection independently until called to read aloud again by the helper. It may be necessary to write the words the student cannot read on a sheet of paper and have him or her study them in addition to rereading the selection.

5. The testing–reading cycle is repeated until the student can read the selection with some degree of fluency. It is *not* important to eliminate all word-recognition errors, but it is important to have the student read the selection with fluency. When this goal is reached, a new selection is chosen and the process is repeated. The charts provide feedback to the student to indicate rate of progress.

A useful modification of this technique is to have the helper make a tape recording of the story. While listening to the story on the tape, the student can read along silently. As soon as possible, the student then practices rereading the story silently without the tape recorder. Thus there is a progression from reading with auditory support to reading without support. The practice is continued until the student can read aloud the selection with fluency.

Recent Criticism of the LaBerge–Samuels Automaticity Theory

Publications by Logan (1988a, 1988b) and Stanovich (1990) have called into question some of the basic principles underlying the automaticity theory as put forth by LaBerge and Samuels (1974). As explained earlier in this article, the essence of automaticity theory is that cognitive tasks such as reading expend attentional resources, of which there are only a limited supply available at any instant. Through training and practice, the attentional demands of a particular task decrease to the point where the task is performed automatically and can be completed simultaneously with other tasks. Logan and Stanovich suggest instead that automaticity may be acquired without invoking concepts of resource limitations and attention. What they offer is a view of automaticity as a memory phenomenon:

> The theory assumes that novices begin with a general algorithm that is sufficient to perform the task. As they gain experience, they learn specific solutions to specific problems, which they retrieve when they encounter the same problem again. Then, they can respond with the solution retried from memory or the one computed by the algorithm. At some point, they may gain enough experience to respond with a solution from memory on every trial and abandon the algorithm entirely. At that point, their performance is automatic. Automatization reflects a transition from algorithm-based performance to memory-based performance. (Logan, 1988b)

In this view, there are two routes to a correct response: One is an automatic, direct, and rapid memory retrieval that comes only after a long training period, while the other uses an algorithm acquired during the early stages of learning. At the simplest level, the beginning reader who laboriously sounds out a word is using an algorithm, whereas the reader who has had extended practice can recognize the same word rapidly and automatically as a memory phenomenon.

Anderson (1982) has suggested a model of memory and learning that incorporates ideas about effortful early learning and effortless skilled learning. These ideas are similar to those put forth by Logan and Stanovich. Anderson proposes three phases in learning a skill. During the first or "declarative knowledge" phase, the knowledge is encoded in separate compartments, and execution of the skill requires considerable effort. (One may assume that during the first phase, the execution of the skill is as through an algorithm.) In the second or "compilation" phase, the knowledge is aggregated into larger units. In the third or "procedural knowledge" phase, the knowledge is compiled in large enough units that it allows the task to be performed with little effort from an easily accessed memory. These alternate views of automaticity are a useful addition to work in the field because they explain the mechanism by which attention can be withdrawn from a problem. This does not necessarily make the concept of limited attentional resources a less useful construct, however, since one may assume that when a task has been encapsulated or memorized, less attention is required for its execution.

In closing this article, I am reminded of the story about the college student who went home from school and was asked, "What did you study this term?" The student replied that he had studied theoretical models of reading. "And what did you learn about theoretical models?" the student was asked. "More than I ever wanted to know," he replied. My hope is that this has not been the case for you.

References

Anderson, J.R. (1982). *Cognitive skills and their acquisition*. Hillsdale, NJ: Erlbaum.

Blanchard, J., Rottenberg, C., & Jones, J. (1989). *Foundational literature in elementary reading methodology textbooks*. Tempe: Arizona State University, College of Education.

LaBerge, D., & Samuels, S.J. (1974). Toward a theory of automatic information processing in reading. *Cognitive Psychology, 6*, 293–323.

Liberman, A.M., Cooper, F., Shankweiler, D., & Studdert-Kennedy, M. (1967). Perception of the speech code. *Psychological Review, 74*, 431–461.

Logan, G. (1988a). Automaticity, resources, and memory: Theoretical controversies and practical implications. *Human Factors, 30*, 583–598.

Logan, G. (1988b). Toward an instance theory of automatization. *Psychological Review, 95*, 492–527.

Samuels, S.J. (1979). The method of repeated reading. *The Reading Teacher, 32*, 403–408.

Samuels, S.J., LaBerge, D., & Bremer, C. (1978). Units of word recognition: Evidence for developmental changes. *Journal of Verbal Learning and Verbal Behavior, 17*, 715–720.

Samuels, S.J., & Naslund, J.C. (1994). Individual differences in reading: The case for lexical access. *Reading and Writing Quarterly, 10*(4), 285–296.

Samuels, S.J., & Turnure, J. (1974). Attention and reading achievement in first grade boys and girls. *Journal of Educational Psychology, 66*, 29–32.

Schneider, W., Körkel, J., & Weinert, F.E. (1988, July). *Expert knowledge, general abilities, and text processing*. Paper presented at the Workshop on Interactions Among Aptitudes, Strategies, and Knowledge in Cognitive Performance, Munich, Germany.

Stanovich, K. (1990). Concepts in developmental theories of reading skill: Cognitive resources, automaticity, and modularity. *Developmental Review, 10*, 72–100.

41

Toward an Interactive Model of Reading

David E. Rumelhart

Reading is the process of understanding written language. It begins with a flutter of patterns on the retina and ends (when successful) with a definite idea about the author's intended message. Thus, reading is at once a "perceptual" and a "cognitive" process. It is a process that bridges and blurs these two traditional distinctions. Moreover, a skilled reader must be able to make use of sensory, syntactic, semantic, and pragmatic information to accomplish his task. These various sources of information appear to interact in many complex ways during the process of reading. A theorist faced with the task of accounting for reading must devise a formalism rich enough to represent all of these different kinds of information and their interactions.

The study of reading was a central concern of early psychologists (see Huey, 1908). Now, after years of dormancy, reading has again become a central concern for many psychologists. It would seem that the advent of the information-processing approach to psychology has given both experimentalists and theorists paradigms within which to study the reading process. The formalisms of information processing, the flowcharts, notions of information flow, and so forth have served as useful vehicles for the development of first approximation models of the reading process. Unfortunately, the most familiar information-processing formalisms apply most naturally to models assuming a series of noninteracting stages of processing or (at best) a set of independent parallel processing units. There are many results in the reading literature that appear to call for highly interactive parallel processing units. It is my suspicion that the serial, noninteracting models have been developed not so much because of an abiding belief that interactions do not take place, but rather because the appropriate formalisms have not been available. It is the purpose of this piece to adapt a formalism developed in the context of parallel computation to the specification of a model for reading and then show that such a model can account in a convenient way for those aspects of reading that

From Ruddell, R.B., Ruddell, M.R., & Singer, H. (Eds.), *Theoretical Models and Processes of Reading* (4th ed., pp. 864–894). Copyright © 1994 by the International Reading Association.

appear puzzling in the context of more linear stage-oriented models. No claim is made about the adequacy of the particular model developed. The primary claim is that this richer formalism will allow for the specification of more detailed models. These will be able to characterize aspects of the reading process that are difficult or impossible to characterize within the more familiar information-processing formulations.

First, I will review two recent models of the reading process. Then, I will discuss some of the empirical evidence that is not conveniently accounted for by these models or their natural extensions. Finally, I will develop a reading model that makes use of a formalism allowing highly interactive parallel processing units and then show that this model offers a reasonable account of the problematic results section (see p. 1154).

Current Models of Reading

Gough's Model

Gough (1972) has proposed a model of reading that is remarkable in the degree to which it attempts to give a complete information-processing account of the reading process. Gough attempts to pin down as completely as possible the events that occur during the first second of reading. A schematic diagram representing the flow of information during the reading process is shown in Figure 1. According to Gough's model, graphemic information enters the visual system and is registered in an *icon*, which holds it briefly while it is scanned and operated on by a *pattern-recognition* device. This device identifies the letters of the input string. These letters are then read into a *character register*, which holds them while a *decoder* (with the aid of a *code book*) converts the character strings into their underlying *phonemic* representation. The phonemic representation of the original character strings serves as input to a *librarian*, which matches up these phonemic strings against the *lexicon* and feeds the resulting lexical entries into *primary memory*. The four or five lexical items held in primary memory at any one time serve as input to a magical system (dubbed *Merlin*), which somehow applies its knowledge of the syntax and semantics to determine the deep structure (or perhaps the meaning?) of the input. This deep structure is then forwarded to its final memory register TPWSGWTAU (The Place Where Sentences Go When They Are Understood). When all inputs of the text have found their final resting place in TPWSGWTAU, the text has been read and the reading is complete.

I do not want to discuss the merits or demerits of Gough's particular model at this point. Instead, I point to the general form of the model. For Gough, reading consists of a sequentially ordered set of transformations. The input signal is first registered in the icon and then transformed from a character-level representation to phonemic representation, then lexical-level representation, and finally to

FIGURE 1
Gough's Reading Model

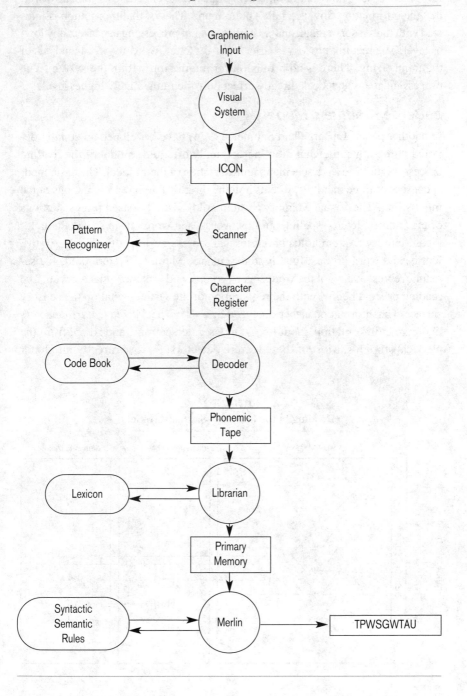

deep structural representation. Thus, the input is sequentially transformed from low-level sensory information into ever higher-level encodings. Note, however, that the information flow is totally "bottom up." That is, the information is initiated with the sensory signal, and no higher level of processing can affect any lower level. The reading process is strict letter-by-letter, word-by-word analysis of the input string. There is no provision for interaction within the system. The processing at any level can directly affect only the immediately higher level.

LaBerge–Samuels Model

In another paper, LaBerge and Samuels (1974) have developed an equally detailed (although somewhat more perceptually oriented) model of the reading process. Figure 2 gives a schematic representation of their model. The basic model consists of three memory systems holding three different representations of the input string. The Visual Memory System holds visually based representations of the features, letters, spelling groups, words, and word clusters. The Phonological Memory System holds phonological representations of spelling groups, words, and word groups. Finally, the Semantic Memory System holds the semantic representation of the words, word groups, and sentences that are read. The reading process begins with the registration of the visual signal on the sensory surface. The information is then analyzed by a set of specialized *feature detectors* that extract information about lines, angles, intersections, and so on, from the physical stimulus. Most of these feature detectors, f_1, feed directly into letter

FIGURE 2
Reading in the LaBerge–Samuels Model

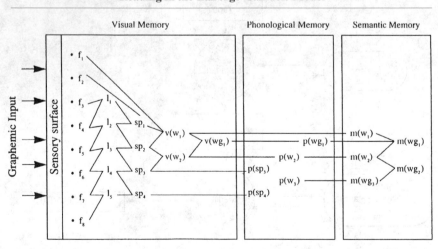

codes, l_1. Thus, the activation of letter codes results naturally from the convergence of a set of feature detectors. These letter codes feed into spelling-pattern codes, sp_1, which in turn feed into visual word codes, $v(w_1)$. Some features (e.g., f_2) map directly into spelling pattern codes and others (f_1) directly into visual word codes. Such features are sensitive to the overall configuration of the words and spelling patterns. There are a number of routes whereby words can be mapped into meanings.

1. Visual word codes can feed directly into word-meaning codes, $m(w_1)$. This route would be necessary for the discrimination of such homophonous word pairs as *pear* and *pair* or *chute* and *shoot*.

2. The visual word codes can pass through a phonological word code, $p(w_1)$, and then into a word-meaning code. This is perhaps the ordinary route of analysis within the LaBerge–Samuels model.

3. The model also allows for word groups, such as *time out*, to be analyzed into visual word-group codes, $v(wg_1)$, from these into phonetic word-group codes, $p(wg_1)$, and finally into group meanings, $m(wg_1)$.

4. When a word has not been learned as a visual stimulus, information can be translated directly from visual spelling patterns into phonological spelling patterns, $p(sp_1)$, from these into phonological word codes, and finally into word-meaning codes. In addition, word-meaning codes feed into word-group–meaning codes.

Ultimately, when the entire set of inputs has been presented, a set of word-group meanings will emerge and the reader will be said to have understood the input.[1]

Again, I do not want to discuss the particular merits or demerits of the LaBerge–Samuels model. Rather, I again point out the general form of the model and suggest that it takes that form, at least to some extent, because of the formalisms used to represent the ideas. The LaBerge–Samuels model, like the Gough model, is a strictly bottom-up process.[2] Although there are alternative routes, the basic sequence is from features to letters, to spelling patterns, to visual word representations, to phonological word representations, to word meanings, to word-group meanings—a series of stages, each corresponding to a level of analysis in which no higher level can in any way modify or change the analysis at a lower level. The LaBerge–Samuels model (unlike the Gough model) does allow certain stages to be bypassed. This allows multiple paths of analysis and alleviates some of the empirical problems of the Gough model. Nevertheless, there are a number of results in the literature that are difficult to account for with either model. I turn now to a discussion of a number of these problems.

Problematic Results

All of the results discussed in this section have one characteristic in common. In each case it appears that the apprehension of information at one level of analysis is partially determined by higher levels of analysis. By and large, such results are very difficult to incorporate in a processing model that assumes that information flows strictly from lower to higher levels. I will begin with a discussion of the effects of orthographic structure on the perception of letters and proceed to a discussion of the effects of syntax on word perception, then to the effects of semantics on word and syntax perception, and finally to the effects of general pragmatic factors on the perception of meanings.[3]

The Perceptions of Letters Often Depend on the Surrounding Letters

The literature on reading abounds with evidence on this point. Perhaps the most difficult of these results for a purely bottom-up model to account for are the well-known context effects illustrated in Figure 3 (after Nash-Weber, 1975). Here we see an ambiguous symbol, *ℓℓ*, which is interpreted as a *w* in one context and interpreted as an *e* followed by a *v* in another context. It would appear that our interpretation of the sentence has determined our perception of the ambiguous symbol.

The problem with results such as these stems from the fact that we appear to have "word-level" or "phrase-level" perceptions determining our perceptions at the letter level, a higher-level perception affecting a lower-level one. These results can be accounted for by bottom-up models but only at some cost. No final decision can be made at the letter level. Either a set of alternative possibilities must be passed on, or the direct feature information must be sent to the higher levels. In either of these cases, the notion that letter perception precedes word perception becomes suspect. Word and letter perception occur simultaneously.

Perhaps the strongest objection to a demonstration such as this one is that it is unusual to find such ambiguous letters and that the norm involves characters that are perfectly discriminable. Although this may be true of printed text, it

FIGURE 3
The Dependence of Letter Perception on Context

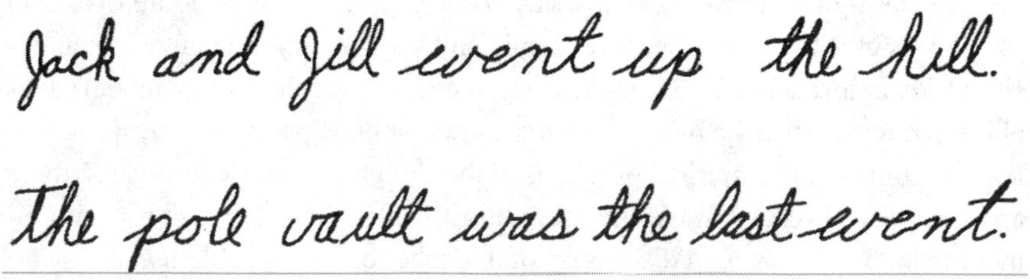

Jack and Jill event up the hill.

The pole vault was the last event.

is not true of handwriting. Characters often can be interpreted only with reference to their context. Yet I would not want to argue that the reading process is essentially different for handwritten than for printed material.

There are many other results that appear to call for this same conclusion. For example, more letters can be apprehended per unit time when a word is presented than when a string of unrelated letters is presented (Huey, 1908/1968). A letter string formed either by deleting a letter of a word or replacing one or two of the letters of the word is often clearly perceived as the original word (Pillsbury, 1897). Even when great care is taken to control for guessing, a letter is more accurately perceived when it is part of a word than when it is among a set of unrelated letters (Reicher, 1969). All of these results appear to argue strongly that letter perceptions are facilitated by being in words. Word-level perceptions affect letter-level perceptions. Here again, the only way that the types of models under consideration can account for these effects is to suppose that partial letter information is somehow preserved and the additional constraints of the word level are brought to bear on the partial letter information.

It is of some interest that these effects can be observed in letter strings that are not words but that are similar to words in important ways. For example, the more the sequential transition probabilities among letters in a string approximate those of English, the more letters can be perceived per unit time (Miller, Bruner, & Postman, 1954). Similarly, even when guessing is controlled (as in the Reicher, 1969, experiment), letters embedded in orthographically regular strings are more accurately perceived than those embedded among orthographically irregular strings (McClelland & Johnston, 1977). Thus, not only is a letter embedded in a word easier to see, but also merely being a part of an orthographically well-formed string aids perception virtually as much. This suggests that orthographic knowledge plays a role nearly as strong as lexical knowledge in the perception of letter strings.

Not only does orthographic structure have a positive effect on the perception of letters embedded in an orthographically regular string, but also our apprehension of orthographically irregular strings often is distorted to allow us to perceive the string as being orthographically regular. This point is nicely illustrated in a recent experiment carried out in our laboratory by Albert Stevens. In this experiment, subjects were presented with letter strings consisting of two consonants (i.e., an initial consonant cluster designated CC_i) followed by two vowels (a vowel cluster, designated VC) followed by two more consonants (a final consonant cluster, CC_f). The initial consonant cluster was constructed from pairs of consonants that can occur at the beginning of English words in only one order (e.g., English words can begin with *pr* but not *rp*). Similarly the vowel clusters used occur as diphthongs in English in one order but not in the other (e.g., *ai* but not *ia*). The final consonant clusters were similarly chosen so that they occur at the end of English words in one order but not the other (e.g., *ck* but not *kc*). Strings were then constructed in which each letter cluster was either in its legal or illegal order. Table 1 illustrates several examples of the various types of letter strings.

Subjects were given tachistoscopic presentations of the various letter strings and asked to name the letters they observed. Of particular interest are the times when they were presented illegal strings but made them legal by transposing the letter pair in their reports. Figure 4 illustrates the comparison of interest. The figure compares the percentage of times an illegally ordered letter cluster is transposed into a legal cluster with the number of times a legal letter cluster is transposed into an illegal one. The results show that although initial consonant clusters are never transposed, illegal vowel clusters are transposed almost 25% of the time as compared to only about 3% transposition for the legal vowel clusters. Similarly, final consonant clusters are transposed almost 14% of the time when they are illegal, but only about 3% of the time when they are legal. These results show clearly the effect that orthographic structure has on our perception of letter strings. The perception of a certain letter in a certain position depends on what we perceive in adjacent positions as well as on the sensory evidence we have available about that position in the string.

To summarize, then, it appears that no model that supposes that we first perceive the letters in a stimulus and then put them together into higher-order units can be correct. However, models such as the Gough model and the LaBerge–Samuels model can survive such results if they assume that partial information is somehow forwarded to the higher levels of analysis and that the final decision as to which letters were present is delayed until this further processing has been accomplished.

Whereas it is not too difficult to see how, say, the LaBerge–Samuels model could account for the effects of orthographic structure on letter perception, it is somewhat more difficult to see how the effects of syntax and semantics can be mediated within such a model. I now turn to evidence for syntactic effects in reading.

TABLE 1
Examples of Legal and Illegal Letter Strings

| | CC_i | | | |
| | Legal VC | | Illegal VC | |
CC_f	Legal	Illegal	Legal	Illegal
Legal	praick	priack	rpaick	rpiack
	stourt	stuort	tsourt	tsuort
Illegal	praikc	priakc	rpaikc	rpiakc
	stoutr	stuotr	tsourtr	tsuotr

FIGURE 4

Transposition as a Function of Letter Location

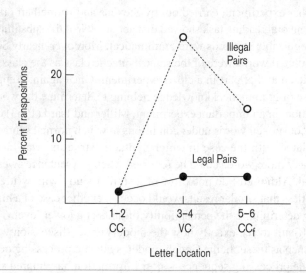

Our Perception of Words Depends on the Syntactic Environment in Which We Encounter the Words

Perhaps the best evidence for syntactic effects on the level of word perception comes from an analysis of oral reading errors. The most common error in oral reading is the substitution error—when an incorrect word is simply substituted for the correct one. If syntax had no effect on word perception, we would expect that reading errors should be determined by visual similarity and not by part of speech. However, there is a strong tendency for a reading error to be of the same part of speech as the word for which it was substituted. Thus, for example, Kolers (1970) reported that nearly 70% of the substitution errors made by adult readers on geometrically transformed text were of the same part of speech as the correct word. By chance, one would expect only about 18% of the errors should be of the correct part of speech.

In another study, Weber (1970) analyzed reading errors by first graders and found that over 90% of the errors made were grammatically consistent with the sentence to the point of the error. Although it is not clear what percentage to expect under assumptions of random guessing, it is obviously much lower than 90% in most texts. One might argue that these results and those of Kolers occur because words in the same syntactic class are more similar to each other than they are to words outside that class. It is interesting to note in this regard that in the

Weber study, the ungrammatical errors were significantly more similar to the correct word than were the grammatical words—at least an indication that this is a syntactic effect and not a visual one.

In another experiment, carried out by Stevens and Rumelhart (1975) with adult readers, an oral reading task showed that about 98% of the substitution errors that were recognizable as words were grammatical. Moreover, nearly 80% of the time the substituted words were of the same syntactic class as the class most frequently predicted at that part in a cloze experiment. Once again, it appears that we have a case of grammatical knowledge helping to determine the word read.

In addition, in an important experiment, Miller and Isard (1963) compared perceptibility of spoken words under conditions in which normal syntactic structure was violated with the case in which syntactic structure was intact. They found that many more words could be reported when the sentences were syntactically normal. Although I do not know of a similar study with written materials, it is doubtless that similar results would occur—another case of a higher level of processing determining the perceptibility of units at a lower level.

It is difficult to see exactly how the models under discussion would deal with results such as these. In the Gough model, syntactic processing occurs only very late in the processing sequence—after information has entered short-term memory. It seems unlikely that he would want to assume that partial information is preserved that far in the process. It is not clear just where syntax should be put in the LaBerge–Samuels model. It is particularly difficult to represent productive syntactic rules of the sort linguists suggest in the LaBerge–Samuels formalism. As I will discuss, it would appear to be essential to be able to represent systems of rules to account for such results.

Our Perception of Words Depends on the Semantic Environment in Which We Encounter the Words

It is even more difficult to incorporate a mechanism for semantic effects on the word-recognition process into a purely bottom-up model than it is to incorporate a mechanism for syntactic effects. There have recently been a number of studies that provide very nice demonstrations of semantic effects on word recognition.

In a series of experiments, Meyer, Schvaneveldt, and Ruddy (Meyer & Schvaneveldt, 1971; Meyer, Schvaneveldt, & Ruddy, 1972, 1974; Ruddy, Meyer, & Schvaneveldt, 1973; Schvaneveldt & Meyer, 1973) have reported convincing evidence of semantic effects on word recognition. The basic procedure in these experiments involved measuring reaction times to come to a lexical decision about a pair of words. The basic result is that the decision can be made much faster when the pair of words are semantically related (such as *bread–butter* or *doctor–nurse*) than when they are unrelated (such as *bread–doctor* and *nurse–butter*). The most plausible account of these results would seem to be that the process of perceiving the first word somehow allows us to process the second word more quickly just in case it is a semantically related word. Thus, we again have the processing at the semantic level modifying our processing at the word level.

In a series of experiments recently carried out in our laboratory, Graboi (1974) demonstrated this same general effect using quite a different method. In one of his experiments Graboi employed a variation of Neisser's search procedure. First, subjects were trained to search for occurrence of any one of five target words among a list of semantically unrelated nontargets. Half of the subjects searched for any one of the words labeled *Experimental Target Set* (see Table 2) scattered among lists constructed from the Unassociated Nontargets. The other half of the subjects searched for the words labeled *Control Target Set* against the same background. Notice that neither target set is semantically related to the nontarget background in which it is searched for. After 14 hours of training, the experimental group was searching their lists at a rate of 182.2 milliseconds (msec) per word. The control group scanned at a rate of 180.0 msec per word. At the 15th hour of practice, the background lists were changed. Both groups now searched for their targets against the Associated Nontarget background. Now the experimental group was searching for its targets against a background of nontargets, all semantically associated with the target set. The control group also was switched, but the Associated Nontargets were not semantically related to the control target set. After the change, we found that the control group scanned against the new

TABLE 2
Alternative Stimuli in the Target and Nontarget Sets

	A. Associated Nontargets	
	WORM CHICK NESTS ROBIN CHIRP WINGS FLY	
Experimental	EAGLE PARROT SONG BLACK GRAY PURPLE	Control
Target	BROWN GOLD BLUE RED YELLOW GREEN PAINT	Target
Set	SAVE SPEND COINS DIME BANK SILVER DOLLAR	Set
	CASH PENNY PEARL BOOKS SCHOOL READ	
	CLASS WRITE TEACH EXAM NOTES GRADE	
	STUDY ORANGE NUTS GRAPE SWEET PLUM	
BIRD:	APPLE PEACH PEAR FRESH LEMON	:ROCK
COLOR:		:CHAIR
MONEY:	B. Unassociated Nontargets	:HOUSE
LEARN:	HUG PEN SLEEP NIGHT BRIDGE STAPLE LAMP	:SPORT
FRUIT:	RULER LEADER ROAR SUNNY PLACE CORNER	:CLOUD
	ALBUM ABOUT RATE WEEK POINT SWITCH	
	ANKLE TOWN DIAL SPOON TOWEL SHEET STOVE	
	CRUST BRUSH GLASS ROAD WHICH AFTER	
	PASS STORY SIGN CHURCH MURAL PHONE	
	BOOTH CARD STREET MOTOR RADIO KNOB	
	PLUG DRIVE LINE TASK PRINT SHIFT	

background at about the same rate as they scanned the old one—179 msec per word scanned. The experimental group, however, scanning through words semantically related to the target set, was slowed to a rate of 197.4 msec per word.

One might suppose that the subjects in the experimental group were just surprised to see related words in the background and a few long pauses accounted for the entire difference. However, on this account one would expect the difference soon to disappear. But this did not happen. Through 5 additional hours of searching (they searched through 2,000 words during a 1-hour session) the difference between the control and experimental subjects remained at about 20 msec per word. It would thus appear that, even when searching for particular words, our expectations are based on meaning as well as visual form.

Using still another experimental procedure, Tulving and Gold (1963) and Tulving, Mandler, and Baumal (1964) found that the prior presentation of a sentence context lowers the threshold at which a tachistoscopically presented word can be recognized.

Again we have a case of a higher level of processing (meaning) apparently affecting our ability to process at a lower level (the word level). Notice, moreover, that semantic relatedness can either make our processing more efficient (as with the Meyer et al., 1974, and Tulving and Gold, 1963, experiments), or it can interfere with our processing (as with the Graboi, 1974, experiment). It is again difficult to see how a strictly bottom-up, stage-by-stage processing model can account for results such as these.

Our Perception of Syntax Depends on the Semantic Context in Which the String Appears

Although neither Gough nor LaBerge and Samuels have attempted to specify their models much beyond the level of words, a complete model of reading must, of course, account for the way semantics affects our apprehension of the syntax of a sentence we are reading. Experiments at this level are few and far between, but there are numerous examples that seem rather compelling on this general point.

Perhaps the most commonly observed effect of this sort involves the semantic disambiguation of syntactically ambiguous sentences. Consider the following sentences:

(1) a. They are eating apples.

b. The children are eating apples.

c. The juicy red ones are eating apples.

At the syntactic level, all three sentences allow for at least two readings:

1. The reading in which the thing referred to by the first noun phrase is performing the act of eating some apples.

2. The reading in which the thing referred to by the first noun phrase is said to be a member of the class of "eating apples."

However, at a semantic level only the first one remains ambiguous—even it would be disambiguated if we had some notion as to the referent of *they*.

Schank (1973) has given a number of similar examples. Consider, for example, the following sentences:

(2) a. I saw the Grand Canyon flying to New York.

   b. I saw the Grand Canyon *while I was* flying to New York.

   c. I saw the Grand Canyon *which was* flying to New York.

Most readers immediately interpret Sentence (2a) as meaning the same as (2b) rather than Sentence (2c) simply on the grounds that it is semantically anomalous to imagine the Grand Canyon actually flying. On the other hand, Sentence (3a) is ordinarily interpreted to mean the same as Sentence (3c) rather than Sentence (3b):

(3) a. I saw the cattle grazing in the field.

   b. I saw the cattle *while I was* grazing in the field.

   c. I saw the cattle *that were* grazing in the field.

In Examples (1), (2), and (3), semantics play the determining role as to which surface structure we apprehend. Thus, just as orthographic structure affects our ability to perceive letters and syntax, and semantics affects our perception of words, so too does semantics affect our apprehension of syntax.

Our Interpretation of the Meaning of What We Read Depends on the General Context in Which We Encounter the Text

Just as the appropriate interpretation of our ambiguous symbol, *ℒℒ*, was determined by the sentence in which it was embedded, so too it often happens that the *meaning* of a word is dependent on the words surrounding it. Consider, for example, the following sentences:

(4) a. The statistician could be certain that the difference was significant *since all of the figures on the right-hand side of the table are larger than any of those on the left.*

   b. The craftsman was certainly justified in charging more for the carvings on the right *since all of the figures on the right-hand side of the table were larger than any of those on the left.*

Here our interpretation of the second clause is thus quite different depending on the nature of the first clause. In Sentence (4a) for example, the term *figure* is readily interpreted as being a number, the term *table* a place for writing numbers, and the relation *larger* can properly be interpreted to mean >. In Sentence (4b) on the other hand, the term *figure* presumably refers to a small statue, the term *table* refers to a physical object with a flat top used for setting things on, and the relation *larger* clearly means something like *of greater volume*. Here we have a case in which no determination about the meaning of these individual words can be made without consideration of the entire sentence. Thus, no decision can be made about the meaning of a word without consideration of the meaning of the entire sentence in which the word appears.

Not only is the interpretation of individual words dependent on the sentential context in which they are found, but the meaning of entire sentences is dependent on the general context in which they appear. The following example from Bransford and Johnson (1973) is a case in point:

(5)

Watching a Peace March from the 40th Floor

The view was breathtaking. From the window one could see the crowd below. Everything looked extremely small from such a distance, but the colorful costumes could still be seen. Everyone seemed to be moving in the same direction in an orderly fashion and there seemed to be little children as well as adults. The landing was gentle, and luckily the atmosphere was such that no special suits had to be worn. At first there was a great deal of activity. Later, when the speeches started, the crowd quieted down. The man with the television camera took many shots of the setting and the crowd. Everyone was very friendly and seemed glad when the music started. (p. 412)

In this passage, the sentence beginning "The landing was gentle..." appears to make no sense. No clear meaning can be assigned to it in this context. As such, when subjects were given the passage and later asked to recall it, very few subjects remembered the anomalous sentence. On the other hand, when the passage was titled "A Space Trip to an Inhabited Planet" the entire passage was given quite a different interpretation. In this case, the anomalous sentence fits into the general interpretation of the paragraph very well. Subjects given the "Space Trip" title recalled the critical sentence three times as often as those given the "Peace March" title. Many other examples could be given. The dependence of meaning on context would appear to be the norm rather than the exception in reading.

To summarize, these results taken together appear to support the view that our apprehension of information at one level of analysis often can depend on our apprehension of information at a higher level. How can this be? Surely we cannot first perceive the meaning of what we read and only later discover what the sentences, words, or letters were that mediated the meaning. To paraphrase a remark attributed to Gough (as cited in Brewer, 1972), it is difficult to "see how the syntax [or semantics, for that matter] can go out and mess around with the print" (p. 360). The problem, I believe, arises from the linear stage formalism that has served so well. The answer, I suspect, comes by presuming that all these knowledge sources apply simultaneously and that our perceptions are the product of the simultaneous interactions among all of them.

An Interactive Model

Perhaps the most natural information-processing representation of the theoretical ideas suggested in the previous section is illustrated in Figure 5. The figure illustrates the assumption that graphemic information enters the system and is registered in a visual information store (VIS). A feature extraction device is then assumed to operate on this information, extracting the critical features from the VIS. These features serve as the sensory input to a pattern synthesizer. In addition to this sensory information, the pattern synthesizer has available nonsensory information about the orthographic structure of the language (including information about the probability of various strings of characters), information about lexical items in the language, information about the syntactic possibilities (and probabilities), information about the semantics of the language, and information about the current contextual situation (pragmatic information). The pattern synthesizer, then, uses all of this information to produce a "most probable interpretation" of the graphemic input. Thus, all of the various sources of knowledge, both sensory and nonsensory, come together at one place, and the

FIGURE 5
A Stage Representation of an Interactive Model of Reading

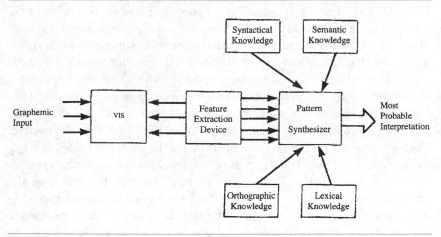

reading process is the product of the simultaneous joint application of all the knowledge sources.

Although the model previously outlined may, in fact, be an accurate representation of the reading process, it is of very little help as a model of reading. It is one thing to suggest that all of these different information sources interact (as many writers have) but quite another to specify a psychologically plausible hypothesis about how they interact. Thus, it is clear why serious theorists who have attempted to develop detailed models of the reading process (e.g., Gough, 1972; LaBerge & Samuels, 1974) have stayed away from a formulation of the sort illustrated in Figure 5. All that is interesting in the model takes place in the box labeled *Pattern Synthesizer*. The flowchart does little more than list the relevant variables. We need a representation for the operation of the pattern synthesizer itself. To represent that, we must develop a means of representing the operation of a set of parallel interacting processes.

Flowcharts are best suited to represent the simple serial flow of information. They are badly suited for the representation of a set of parallel, highly interactive processes. However, with the advent of the parallel computer (at least as a conceptual device), computer scientists have begun to develop formalisms for the representation of parallel processes. It is interesting that the major problem in each case seems to have been the representation of the lines of communication among the otherwise independent processes.

Of the several different systems of communication that have been proposed, two were developed in the context of language processing by computer and seem to be most promising as a formalism for the development of a reading model. One of these was developed by Kaplan (1973) and is called the General Syntactic Processor (GSP). The second was developed by Reddy and his associates at Carnegie Mellon University (see Lesser, Fennell, Erman, & Reddy, 1974) as an environment for a speech understanding program. This system is called HEARSAY II. These two systems have a good deal in common and solve the communication problem in much the same way—namely, both systems consist of sets of totally independent asynchronous processes that communicate by means of a global, highly structured data storage device. In Kaplan's system the communication center is called a *chart*; in the HEARSAY system it is called a *blackboard*. I use the more neutral term *message center* in my development below. This development is most closely related to the HEARSAY system and could well be considered as an application of the HEARSAY model to reading. However, I also draw from aspects of GSP, and the model as I develop it has the Rumelhart and Siple (1974) model of word recognition as a special case.

Following HEARSAY, the model can be characterized as consisting of a set of independent *knowledge sources*. (These knowledge sources correspond to the sources of input to the pattern synthesizer in Figure 5.) Each knowledge source contains specialized knowledge about some aspect of the reading process.

The message center keeps a running list of hypotheses about the nature of the input string. Each knowledge source constantly scans the message center for the appearance of hypotheses relevant to its own sphere of knowledge. Whenever such a hypothesis enters the message center, the knowledge source in question evaluates the hypothesis in light of its own specialized knowledge. As a result of its analysis, the hypothesis may be confirmed, the hypothesis may be disconfirmed and removed from the message center, or a new hypothesis can be added to the message center. This process continues until some decision can be reached. At that point the most probable hypothesis is determined to be the correct one. To facilitate the process, the message center is highly structured so that the knowledge sources know exactly where to find relevant hypotheses and so that dependencies among hypotheses are easily determined.

The Message Center

The message center can be represented as a three-dimensional space: one dimension representing the position along the line of text, one dimension representing the level of the hypothesis (word level, letter level, phrase level, etc.), and one dimension representing alternative hypotheses at the same level. Associated with each hypothesis is a running estimate of the probability that it is the correct hypothesis. Moreover, hypotheses at each level may have pointers to hypotheses at higher or lower levels on which they are dependent. Thus, for example, the hypothesis that the first word in a string is the word *the* is supported by the hypothesis that the first letter of the string is *t* and supports the hypothesis that the string begins with a noun phrase.

Figure 6 illustrates a two-dimensional slice of the message center at some point during the reading of the phrase *the car*.

The figure illustrates hypotheses at five different levels (feature level, letter level, letter-cluster level, lexical level, and syntactic level). The diagram is only a two-dimensional slice inasmuch as no alternative hypotheses are illustrated. In practice, of course, many alternative hypotheses would be considered and evaluated in the course of reading this phrase. It should be pointed out that the tree-like structure should not be taken to mean that the tree was constructed either from a purely bottom-up process (starting with the features, then hypothesizing the letters, then the letter clusters, etc.), nor from a purely top-down analysis (starting with a view that we have a noun phrase and that noun phrases are made up of determiners followed by nouns, etc.). Rather, the hypotheses can be generated at any level. If it is likely that a line begins with a noun phrase, then we postulate a noun phrase and look for evidence. If we see features that suggest a *t* as the first letter, we postulate a *t* in the first position and continue processing. If we later have to reject either or both of these hypotheses, little is lost. The system makes the best guesses and checks out their implications. If these

FIGURE 6
A Two-Dimensional Slice of the Message Center

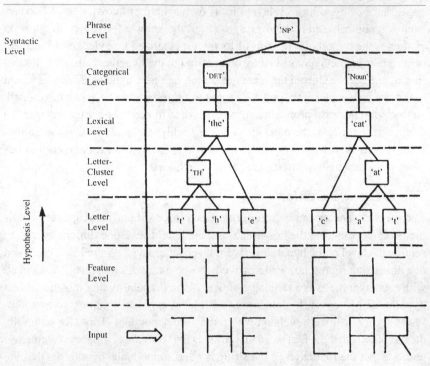

guesses are wrong, it will take a bit longer, but the system will eventually find some hypotheses at some level that it can accept.

An Example. To illustrate the operation of the system, consider the following experimental procedure. A subject is presented with a picture (e.g., Figure 7) and allowed to view it for a few seconds. Then he is given a tachistoscopic presentation of a noun phrase that he knows will refer to one of the objects in the picture. His job is to decide which object was referred to. This experimental procedure is designed to simulate the process of reading a phrase for meaning. (An experimental procedure of this sort is currently under development in our laboratory.) I will illustrate the current model by showing the changes we might expect in the message center as the phrase THE CAR is read after viewing Figure 7.

Figure 8 shows the message center at an early point in the processing of this phrase. The subject knows from the instructions of the experiment that the phrase will refer to some object in the picture. Thus, the semantic-level "object" hypothesis can be entered and assigned a high likelihood value from the start.

FIGURE 7
A Scene

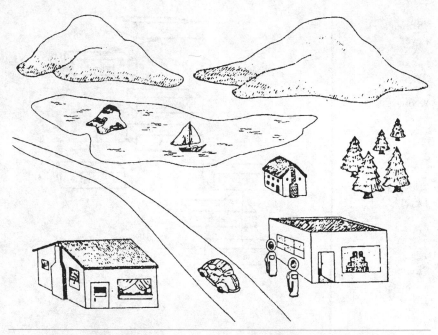

Figure provided by Jean Mandler.

Moreover, through looking at the picture and perceiving certain aspects of it as salient, the subject will develop expectations as to the probable referent of the phrase. In this case, I have assumed that the subject set up special expectations for a phrase referring to *the lake* or to *the Volkswagen*.

Similarly, at the syntactic level, the subject can be quite certain that the input will form a noun phrase. Thus, the hypothesis "NP" is entered into the message center and assigned a high value. Noun phrases have a rather characteristic structure. About 25% of the time they begin with a determiner (DET). Thus, in the example, I have assumed that the hypothesis that the first word was a determiner was entered. Similarly, we can expect the second word of a noun phrase to be a noun about 20% of the time. Thus, I have entered the hypothesis that the second word is a noun. Now, in the case where the first word is a determiner, we could expect it to be the word *the* about 60% of the time and the word *a* about 20%. Thus, I have assumed that these two hypotheses have also been entered.

As all these hypotheses are being entered in top-down fashion, hypotheses at the letter level also are being entered bottom-up on the basis of featural information. In the example, I have assumed that for each of the first five letter

FIGURE 8
The Message Center Shortly After Processing Has Begun on THE CAR

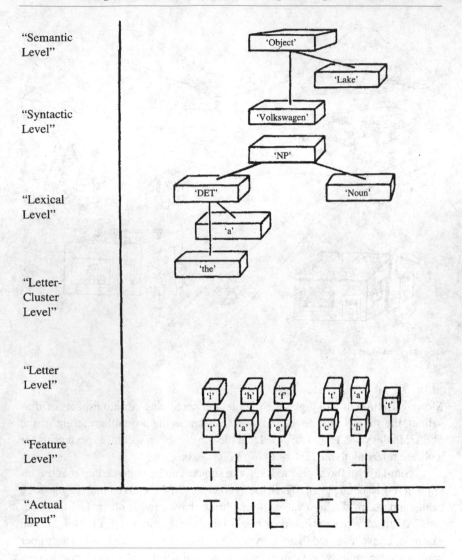

positions the two most promising letter possibilities were entered as hypotheses. For the sixth letter position, which contains very little featural information, I have assumed that only its most likely letter hypothesis has been entered.

Figure 9 illustrates the state of the message center at a later point in the processing. In the meantime, the lexical hypothesis "a" has led to a letter hypothe-

FIGURE 9
The Message Center Slightly Later in the Processing Sequence

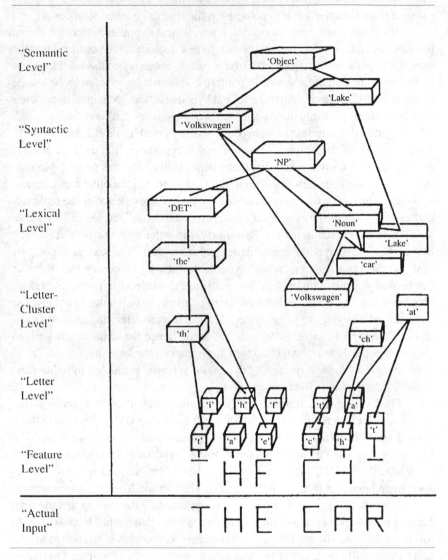

"Semantic Level"

"Syntactic Level"

"Lexical Level"

"Letter-Cluster Level"

"Letter Level"

"Feature Level"

"Actual Input"

sis that was then tested against the featural information and rejected. The hypothesization of an initial "t" has led to the hypothesization of an initial "th" at the letter cluster level—a hypothesis that is given added validity by the possible "h" in the second position. The lexical-level hypothesis of the word "the" also has led to the hypothesization of the letter cluster "th" followed by the letter "e."

The prior existence of these hypotheses generated from the bottom up has led to a mutual strengthening of all of the hypotheses in question and a resultant weakening of the alternative letter hypotheses at the first three letter positions.

While this processing was taking place, lexical hypotheses were generated from the semantic level as possible nouns. In this instance I have assumed that the semantic hypothesis "lake" has led to the lexical hypothesis that the word *lake* was in the string and that the semantic hypothesis "Volkswagen" has led to the lexical hypothesis "Volkswagen" and to the lexical hypothesis "car." Meanwhile, the letter hypotheses have led to alternative letter-cluster hypotheses "ch" and "at."

Figure 10 illustrates the state of the message center at a still later point in the processing of the input. By this point, the hypothesis that the first word is *the* has reached a sufficient value that further processing has ceased. No new hypotheses have been generated about the first word. On the other hand, lexical hypotheses on the second word have proliferated. The existence of the letter hypothesis "c" followed by the letter-cluster hypothesis "at" has led to a hypothesization of the lexical item "cat." Similarly, the letter hypothesis "f" followed by "at" has led to hypothesizing the lexical item "fat." The lexical hypothesis "cat" is consistent with the "noun" hypothesis, thus strengthening the view that the second word is a noun. At the same time, the lexical hypotheses "lake," "Volkswagen," and "car" either have strengthened existing letter hypotheses or have caused new ones to be generated. Notice, in particular, that the prior existence of the letter hypotheses "c" and "a" strengthened the semantically derived lexical hypothesis "car," which in turn strengthened the letter hypothesis "r"— even though the letter hypothesis "r" has not yet been evaluated in light of the featural information in the final position.

Finally, Figure 11 illustrates a state of processing after the letter hypotheses have been tested against the featural information. At this point only three lexical hypotheses for the second word remain—"fat," "cat," and "car." The lexical hypothesis "fat" has led to the syntactic hypothesis that the second word is an adjective (ADJ), and the lexical hypothesis "cat" has led to the semantic-level hypothesis that there should be a cat in the picture. Meanwhile, the semantic hypothesis "Volkswagen" has been strengthened by the finding that the final featural information is consistent with the hypothesis that the last letter is an *r*. At this point the semantic hypothesis "Volkswagen" is probably high enough to lead to a response. If not, a test of the semantic hypothesis "cat" will lead to the rejection of that hypothesis and the consequent strengthening of the "Volkswagen" hypothesis and thus the lexical hypothesis "car" and the letter-level hypotheses "c," "a," and "r."

It should be clear from this example how, in principle at least, one could build a model of reading that actually would employ constraints from all levels concurrently in the process of constructing an interpretation of an input string. Of course, this example is a long way from the specification of such a model. All I

FIGURE 10
The Message Center Well Into the Processing Sequence

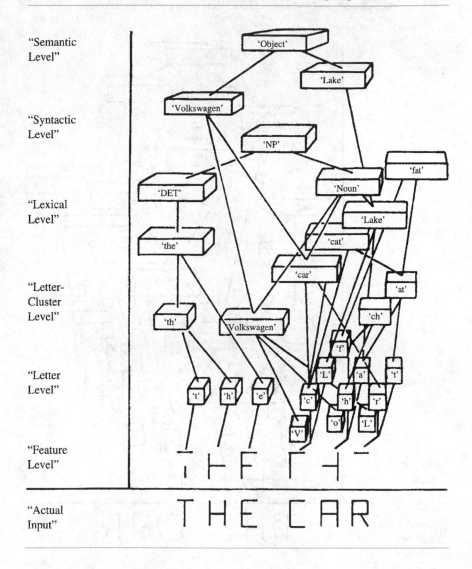

have illustrated here is the nature of the message center and how it is structured to facilitate communication among processes acting at various levels. Before a concrete model of reading can be specified, the nature of the various knowledge sources must be specified as well. I now turn to a brief discussion of the separation of the various knowledge sources.

FIGURE 11

The Message Center Near the End of Processing; at This Point the Semantics of the Input Have Been Pretty Well Determined

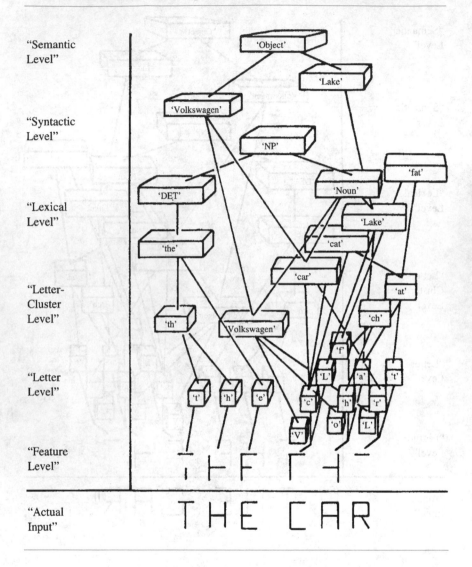

The Knowledge Sources

I do not yet have a detailed model of the operation of all the knowledge sources. However, I do have ideas about a number of them and will now discuss them.

    1. *Featural knowledge.* At this level, I am assuming that features are extracted according to the assumptions of the Rumelhart and Siple (1974) model.

Moreover, I am assuming that these critical features are the basic level of processing. In a tachistoscopic experiment, all decisions must be made with respect to the set of features extracted during and shortly after the exposure. In freereading situations, the reader can go back and get more featural information if no hypothesis gets a sufficiently high rating or if some hypothesis does get a high rating at one point and is later rejected. Such occasions probably account for regressions in eye movements.

2. *Letter-level knowledge.* This knowledge source scans the feature inputs, and whenever it finds a close match to a known letter, it posits a letter hypothesis. In addition, whenever a letter hypothesis appears from a higher level, this knowledge source evaluates that hypothesis against the feature information. In addition to information about letters in various fonts, the letter-level knowledge source presumably takes into account the probabilities of letters in the language. Thus, relatively more featural evidence would be necessary to postulate a "z" or "q" than an "e" or a "t."

3. *Letter-cluster knowledge.* This knowledge source scans the incoming letter-level hypotheses, looking for letter sequences that are likely and form units in the language or for single letters that are frequently followed or preceded by another letter (e.g., as *q* is frequently followed by *u*). In either case a letter cluster is postulated. In the latter case a letter-level hypothesis is also introduced. (That is, if a *q* is found, a *qu* is postulated at the letter-cluster level and a *u* is postulated at the letter level.) The value associated with any of these hypotheses depends on the values of the letter-level information on which it is based and on the frequency of such clusters in the language. In addition, the letter-cluster knowledge source looks for the introduction of letter-cluster hypotheses from the lexical level. Whenever it finds these it evaluates them by proposing the appropriate letter-level hypotheses. For this knowledge source, as with all others, the most probable hypotheses that are unsupported from the following or that support no higher-level hypotheses are evaluated first.

4. *Lexical-level knowledge.* The lexical-level knowledge source operates in exactly the same way as the other knowledge sources. It scans the letter-cluster and letter hypotheses for letter sequences that form lexical items or that are close to lexical items. When it finds such information, it posits the appropriate lexical-level hypotheses and any additional letter-cluster or letter-level hypotheses. When evaluating the goodness of any hypothesis, it takes into account the goodness of the evidence on which it is based and the a priori frequency of that item in the language. In addition, whenever a lexical item is postulated from either the semantic or syntactic levels, this knowledge source evaluates that hypothesis by postulating those letter-cluster and letter hypotheses that are not yet present. Those letter and letter-cluster hypotheses that are present are strengthened due to the convergence of lines of evidence. Other alternatives without such convergent information are relatively weakened.

5. *Syntactic knowledge*. Like all the other knowledge sources, this knowledge source is designed to operate in both a bottom-up and top-down mode. Thus, whenever a lexical hypothesis is suggested, one or more syntactic category hypotheses are entered into the message center. In general, not all syntactic category hypotheses consistent with the lexical form would be expected. Instead, those categories that are most probable, given that lexical item, would be entered first. Similarly, sequences of lexical category hypotheses would be scanned, looking for phrase possibilities, and so on. At the same time, the syntactic knowledge source would have the capacity to operate in a top-down fashion. Thus, for example, whenever a noun-phrase hypothesis were entered, the syntactic knowledge source would establish, say, a determiner, syntactic category hypothesis that in turn might initiate lexical-level hypotheses of determiner words such as *a* and *the*. Following Kaplan's (1973) GSP, I assume that this top-down portion of the syntactic knowledge source would be well represented by an Augmented Transition Network (ATN) parser. (See Stevens and Rumelhart, 1975, for an application of an ATN to reading data.) Like all other levels, the syntactic hypotheses are given values dependent on the goodness of the evidence (or prior probabilities) of the hypotheses on which they are based. Moreover, a convergence of top-down and bottom-up hypotheses strengthens both.

6. *Semantic-level knowledge*. This is perhaps the most difficult level to characterize. Nevertheless, I assume that its operation is essentially the same as the others. Whenever strong lexical hypotheses occur, this knowledge source must have the ability to look for semantic-level correlates to evaluate the plausibility of the hypothesis (at both the lexical and syntactic levels). Moreover, it must be able to develop hypotheses about the content of the input and generate lexical-level hypotheses as possible representations of this. The experimental procedure discussed in the previous section was designed as an attempt to reduce the complexity of the semantic component by supposing a relatively simple referential semantics.

Still, of course, after having outlined the functional characteristics of the various knowledge sources, I am still far from the quantitative model I have in mind. However, it would appear that a HEARSAY-type model such as this offers promise as a framework for the development of serious models of reading that nevertheless assumes a highly interactive parallel processing system.

A Mathematical Model of Hypothesis Evaluation

In this section I will specify in somewhat more detail the nature of the hypothesis-evaluation process I envision. Figure 12 illustrates a simplified version of the message center from the primary example. This figure differs somewhat in format from the previous figures of this type in order to make clearer the sequential dependencies among hypotheses at the same level. Thus, the fact that an "NP" consists of a "DET" and "NOUN" and that the word *cat* consists of

FIGURE 12
**An Illustration of the Relations Among the Hypotheses
in the Message Center**

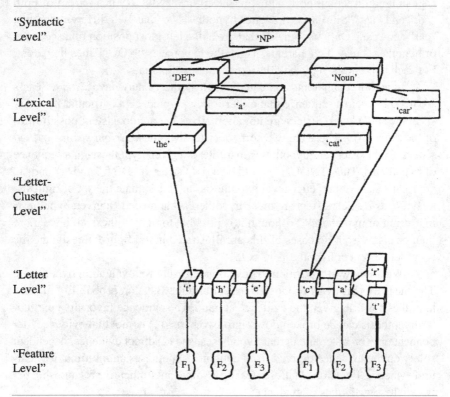

$C + A + T$ is illustrated by the arrows connecting those constituents at the same level. Moreover, the dependency arrows have been drawn to only the left-hand member of such hypothesis sequences. In a sense, as we shall see below, the left-hand member is representing the entire sequence of hypotheses.

There are four different types of dependency relationships among hypotheses in this model. These types are illustrated in the figure. First, a hypothesis may have one or more daughter hypotheses. A daughter hypothesis is one at a lower level that is connected directly to a higher-level hypothesis. In the figure, the hypothesis "DET" has two daughter hypotheses: "the" and "a." The hypothesis "the" has a single daughter, "t." A hypothesis may have any number of daughters. Each daughter is an alternative way in which the higher hypothesis can be realized. Thus, "the" and "a" are alternative ways in which "DET" can be realized. For any hypothesis, h_i, I shall use the symbol D_i to designate its set of daughters.

The reciprocal relationship to daughter is *parent*. Any hypothesis may have one or more parent hypotheses. A parent hypothesis is one to which a hypothesis can lend direct support. Thus, in the figure, "NOUN" is a parent of both "car" and "cat." Similarly, the letter hypothesis "c" has two different parents, "car" and "cat." Only hypotheses that are at the left-most position of a sequence of hypotheses may have parents. Thus, the hypothesis "NOUN" has no parent. For each hypothesis, h_i, I shall designate the set of parents P_i.

In addition to parents and daughters, hypotheses may have *sisters*. Sisters are hypotheses in a sequence that either follow or precede a particular hypothesis at the same level. Sisters are not alternatives but are consistent possibilities of the same level. There are two sorts of sister hypotheses: *right sisters* and *left sisters*. Right sisters are hypotheses that follow a given hypothesis in a sequence of hypotheses. Thus, "NOUN" would be a right sister of "DET," and "r" and "t" are right sisters of the letter-level hypothesis "a." I designate the set of right sisters of h_i as R_i. Left sisters are those hypotheses that precede a given hypothesis in a string of hypotheses. Although it is possible for a hypothesis to have more than one left sister, no cases of this are illustrated in the figure. I designate the set of left sisters of hypothesis h_i as L_i.

We are now in a position to develop a measure for evaluating hypotheses. The measure that I will propose is essentially the Baysian probability that the hypothesis is true given the evidence at hand. The evidence favoring a particular hypothesis can be broken down into two parts: (1) contextual evidence, dependent only on sister and parent hypotheses, and (2) direct evidence, dependent solely on the evidence derived from daughter hypotheses and, ultimately, featural evidence. Equation (1) illustrates the assumed multiplicative relationship between these two kinds of evidence:

(1) $\quad s_i = v_i \bullet \beta_i{}^4$

where s_i is the overall strength of the hypothesis h_i, v_i is a measure of the direct evidence for h_i, and β_i is a measure of the contextual evidence for h_i. Now we can define the values of v_i and β_i in terms of the parents and sisters of h_i. Equation (2) gives the value of the contextual strength of h_i:

(2) $\quad \beta_i = \begin{cases} \Pr(h_i) & P_i = L_i = \phi \\ \Sigma_{s_k} \bullet \dfrac{\Pr(h_i \backslash h_k)}{v_i} & \text{otherwise,} \end{cases}$

where the sum is over all $h_k \in P_i$ or L_i. Thus, when h_i has no parents or left sisters, its contextual strength is given by its a priori probability. Otherwise, its contextual strength is given by the sum, over all of its left sisters and parents of the strength of the left sister or parent, h_k, times the conditional probability of the hypothesis given h_k. The sum is then divided by its own direct strength so that its direct strength will not contribute to its contextual strength (because as we shall see, its own direct strength contributes to the strength of its parents and left sisters and is represented multiplicatively in s_k).

Direct evidence for a hypothesis comes only from its daughters. Equation (3) gives the direct evidence for a hypothesis as a function of a value associated with its daughters:

$$(3) \quad v_i = \begin{cases} \Sigma C_{ik} \cdot \Pr{(h_k \backslash h_i)} & D_i \neq \phi \\ 1 & \text{otherwise,} \end{cases}$$

where the sum is over all $h_k \in D_i$, and where C_{ik} is the *cumulative evidence* for hypothesis h_i associated with the sequence of hypotheses whose left-most member is the daughter h_k. Thus, in the diagram, the direct evidence for "car" is determined jointly by the direct evidence for "c," for "a," and for "r." The value of C_{ik} is given by the following equation:

$$(4) \quad C_{i,\,k} = \begin{cases} vk & R_k \neq \phi \\ \Sigma_j v_k \cdot C_{i,\,j} \cdot \Pr{(h_j \backslash h_i, h_k)} & \text{otherwise,} \end{cases}$$

where the sum is over all $h_j \in R_k$. Thus, the cumulative evidence for hypothesis h_i associated with hypothesis h_k is determined by the product of the direct evidence for h_k and the cumulative evidence for its right sister. If its probable right sisters are very strong, then the cumulative evidence is very strong and thus offers good support to its parent. Otherwise, it offers support against its parent.

Finally, we must give special attention to the first-level hypotheses associated with featural-level inputs. For any letter hypothesis h_i, featural-level inputs have cumulative values of $C_{i,\,F}$ given by:

$$(5) \quad C_{i,\,F} = [\Pr{(F)}]^{-1}$$

where F is the set of features observed in that location. This, in effect, is a normalizer designed to keep the strengths in the 0 to 1 range.

The equations (1) to (5) define a system of evaluation that makes near optimal use of the information available at any given point in time. Whenever a new hypothesis is postulated and a new connection is drawn, new values must be computed for the entire set of hypotheses. Resources can be allotted to the knowledge sources based upon their momentary evaluations. Effort can be focused on generating hypotheses from the top down whenever we have hypotheses with strong contextual strengths and few daughter hypotheses. Effort can be focused on the generation of hypotheses from the bottom up whenever there is strong direct evidence and few parents. Moreover, the strength values can be signals to stop processing and accept a hypothesis. When some criterion strength value is obtained, a hypothesis can be accepted and no further processing need be required. Then resources can be siphoned to other more critical areas.

Of course, specifying equations such as these does not fully specify our model. We must specify all of the knowledge sources and how they postulate hypotheses. They do, I feel, illustrate that the model under consideration can be quantified and can generate specific predictions—in spite of the enormous complexity of a highly interactive system.

Acknowledgments

Research support was provided by grant NS 07454 from the National Institute of Health.

Notes

[1] LaBerge and Samuels were particularly interested in the role of attention and the notion of automaticity in reading. I also have omitted discussion of episodic memory because neither one of these aspects of their model is relevant to my point here.

[2] Actually, the aforementioned attention mechanism of the LaBerge–Samuels model offers some top-down capacity. However, within their model it is limited and serves to speed up certain weak bottom-up paths.

[3] I use the term *perception* rather freely here. In general, it is my opinion that the distinction between the perceptual and conceptual aspects of reading is not that useful. As I will suggest later, there appears to be a continuity between what has been called *perception* and what has been called *comprehension*. My use of the term *perception* in the present context is simply the use of the one term to cover the entire process.

[4] This is the same relationship between these two sorts of evidence assumed by Luce (1959) and which is incorporated into the Rumelhart and Siple (1974) model for word recognition.

References

Bransford, J.D., & Johnson, M.K. (1973). Considerations of some problems of comprehension. In W.G. Chase (Ed.), *Visual information processing*. New York: Academic.

Brewer, W.F. (1972). Is reading a letter-by-letter process? In J.F. Kavanagh & I.G. Mattingly (Eds.), *Language by ear and by eye: The relationships between speech and reading.* Cambridge, MA: MIT Press.

Gough, P.B. (1972). One second of reading. In J.F. Kavanagh & I.G. Mattingly (Eds.), *Language by ear and by eye: The relationships between speech and reading.* Cambridge, MA: MIT Press.

Graboi, D. (1974). *Physical shape, practice and meaning in visual search.* Unpublished doctoral dissertation, University of California, San Diego.

Huey, E.B. (1968). *The psychology and pedagogy of reading.* Cambridge, MA: MIT Press. (Original work published 1908)

Kaplan, R.M. (1973). A general syntactic processor. In R. Rustin (Ed.), *Natural language processing.* New York: Algorithmics.

Kolers, P.A. (1970). Three stages in reading. In H. Levin & J.T. Williams (Eds.), *Basic studies in reading.* New York: Basic.

LaBerge, D., & Samuels, S.J. (1974). Toward a theory of automatic information processing in reading. *Cognitive Psychology, 6,* 293–323.

Lesser, V.R., Fennell, R.D., Erman, L.D., & Reddy, D.R. (1974). *Organization of the*

HEARSAY II speech understanding system (Working Papers in Speech Recognition III). Pittsburgh, PA: Carnegie Mellon University.

Luce, R.D. (1959). *Individual choice behavior.* New York: Wiley.

McClelland, J.L., & Johnston, J.C. (1977). The role of familiar units in perception of words and nonwords. *Perception and Psychophysics, 22,* 249–261.

Meyer, D.E., & Schvaneveldt, R.W. (1971). Facilitation in recognizing pairs of words: Evidence of a dependence between retrieval operations. *Journal of Experimental Psychology, 90,* 227–234.

Meyer, D.E., Schvaneveldt, R.W., & Ruddy, M.G. (1972, November). *Activation of lexical memory.* Paper presented at the meeting of the Psychonomic Society, St. Louis, MO.

Meyer, D.E., Schvaneveldt, R.W., & Ruddy, M.G. (1974). Functions of phonemic and graphemic codes in visual word recognition. *Memory and Cognition, 2,* 309–321.

Miller, G.A., Bruner, J.S., & Postman, L. (1954). Familiarity of letter sequences and tachistoscopic identification. *Journal of Genetic Psychology, 50,* 129–139.

Miller, G.A., & Isard, S. (1963). Some perceptual consequences of linguistic rules. *Journal of Verbal Learning and Verbal Behavior, 2,* 217–228.

Nash-Weber, B. (1975). The role of semantics in automatic speech understanding. In D.B. Bobrow & A. Collins (Eds.), *Representation and understanding.* New York: Academic.

Pillsbury, W.B. (1897). A study in apperception. *American Journal of Psychology, 8,* 315–393.

Reicher, G.M. (1969). Perceptual recognition as a function of meaningfulness of stimulus ma-terial. *Journal of Experimental Psychology, 81,* 274–280.

Ruddy, M.G., Meyer, D.E., & Schvaneveldt, R.W. (1973, May). *Context effects on phonemic encoding in visual word recognition.* Paper presented at the meeting of the Midwestern Psychological Association, Chicago, IL.

Rumelhart, D.E., & Siple, P. (1974). Process of recognizing tachistoscopically presented words. *Psychological Review, 81,* 99–118.

Schank, R.C. (1973). Identification of concep-tualizations underlying natural language. In R.C. Schank & K.M. Colby (Eds.), *Computer models of thought and language.* San Francisco: Freeman.

Schvaneveldt, R.W., & Meyer, D.E. (1973). Retrieval and comparison processes in se-mantic memory. In S. Kornblum (Ed.), *Attention and performance IV.* New York: Academic.

Stevens, A.L., & Rumelhart, D.E. (1975). Errors in reading: Analysis using an augmented net-work model of grammar. In D.A. Norman, D.E. Rumelhart, & the LNR Research Group, *Explorations in cognition.* San Francisco: Freeman.

Tulving, E., & Gold, C. (1963). Stimulus infor-mation and contextual information as deter-minants of tachistoscopic recognition of words. *Journal of Experimental Psychology, 66,* 319–327.

Tulving, E., Mandler, G., & Baumal, R. (1964). Interaction of two sources of information in tachistoscopic word recognition. *Canadian Journal of Psychology, 18,* 62–71.

Weber, R.M. (1970). First graders' use of gram-matical context in reading. In H. Levin & J.T. Williams (Eds.), *Basic studies in reading.* New York: Basic.

42

One Second of Reading: Postscript

Philip B. Gough

his [one-second-of-reading] model is wrong. I take this to be a mark of virtue. It is easy to create a model that is "right"; all you need to do is make one interactive or transactional enough such that everything in reading influences everything else. The result will be "right" because it will be impervious to disprove; it will yield no falsifiable predictions. But my view has always been that such models are not really right; they are simply empty, for a model that cannot be disproved is a model without content.

The purpose of a model is to summarize available knowledge and to lead to new knowledge by yielding novel predictions. It is by this standard that I find this model virtuous, for it embodied several claims that, although now demonstrably false or at least insufficient, have contributed to the growth of our knowledge of reading.

The claim that we read words letter by letter from left to right is one such claim: It is almost certainly wrong. But much, if not most, of what we know about word recognition has been learned in the effort to refute it. Alternative views (e.g., that the unit of word recognition is the visual feature, or the word itself) have not yielded testable predictions. So while I must now concede that my serial assumption was false, I remain committed to the view that the letter mediates word recognition.

The second claim for which this paper is notorious is that word recognition is mediated by phonological recoding. There is clearly a consensus that this, too, is inadequate (see, e.g., McCusker, Hillinger, & Bias, 1981); it is widely agreed that skilled readers have direct or visual access to (at least) high-frequency words. But we have learned much about word recognition in testing predictions derived from the phonological recoding hypothesis (see Gough, 1984). (In contrast, I argue that we have learned nothing from the direct access hypothesis: Because it is nothing but the negation of the phonological recoding hypothesis, it yields no predictions of its own.) Moreover, while high-frequency words account for a considerable fraction of words in print (word tokens), the vast majority of word

From Singer, H., & Ruddell, R.B. (Eds.), *Theoretical Models and Processes of Reading* (3rd ed., pp. 687–688). Copyright © 1985 by the International Reading Association.

types are infrequent. So I still would maintain that most words (i.e., types) are recognized through phonological recoding.

But perhaps the greatest virtue I would claim for the model is that it exemplifies the idea that the skilled reader reads what is on the printed page.

Reading may not be primarily visual; the average sharp-eyed Eskimo cannot read printed English. Psycholinguistic processes beyond word recognition abound in reading, and while my model paid lip service to the problem of sentence comprehension, it clearly gave no heed to the very real and difficult problems of understanding text.

But neither is reading primarily psycholinguistic; the blind can read printed English no better than the Eskimo.

Most scholars resolve this tension by adopting an interactive view, that linguistic knowledge is skillfully combined with visual information to reconstruct the meaning intended by the author. But skilled readers, when seriously reading, not only succeed in extracting meaning from the printed page, they can (and I believe do) also succeed in accurately recognizing virtually every single word on that page (Alford, 1980; Stevens & Rumelhart, 1975). Moreover, eye-movement studies (e.g., Just & Carpenter, 1980) suggest that they do so by successively fixating all but the shortest of those words.

The hallmark of the skilled reader is the ability to recognize, accurately, easily, and swiftly, isolated words (and, even more so, pseudowords). We have argued elsewhere (Gough, 1981, 1983; Gough, Alford, & Holley-Wilcox, 1981) that this skill can be attributed only to the ability to decode, for while highly predictive context can and does facilitate word recognition, proving a strictly "bottom-up" model like mine wrong, most words are not predictable and so can only be read bottom up. A successful model of reading must account for this ability. My model may have failed, but I still believe it pointed in the right direction.

References

Alford, J.A., Jr. (1980). *Lexical and contextual effects on reading time.* Unpublished doctoral dissertation, University of Texas at Austin.

Gough, P.B. (1981). A comment on Kenneth Goodman. In M.L. Kamil (Ed.), *Directions in reading: Research and instruction* (pp. 92–95). Washington, DC: National Reading Conference.

Gough, P.B. (1983). Form, context, and interaction. In K. Rayner (Ed.), *Eye movements in reading: Perceptual and language processes* (pp. 203–211). New York: Academic Press.

Gough, P.B. (1984). Word recognition. In P.D. Pearson, R. Barr, M.L. Kamil, & P. Mosenthal (Eds.), *Handbook of reading research* (pp. 225–253). New York: Longman.

Gough, P.B., Alford, J.A., Jr., & Holley-Wilcox, P. (1981). Words and contexts. In O.L. Tzeng & H. Singer (Eds.), *Perception of print: Reading research in experimental psychology* (pp. 85–102). Hillsdale, NJ: Erlbaum.

Just, M.A., & Carpenter, P.A. (1980). A theory of reading: From eye fixations to comprehension. *Psychological Review, 87,* 329–354.

McCusker, L.X., Hillinger, M.L., & Bias, R.G. (1981). Phonological recoding and reading. *Psychological Bulletin, 89,* 217–245.

Stevens, A.L., & Rumelhart, D.E. (1975). Errors in reading: Analysis using an augmented transition network model of grammar. In D.A. Norman & D.E. Rumelhart (Eds.), *Explorations in cognition* (pp. 136–156). San Francisco: Freeman.

43

A Theory of Reading: From Eye Fixations to Comprehension

Marcel Adam Just and Patricia A. Carpenter

Although readers go through many of the same processes as listeners, there is one striking difference between reading and listening compre-hension—a reader can control the rate of input. Unlike a listener, a read-er can skip over portions of the text, reread sections, or pause on a particular word. A reader can take in information at a pace that matches the internal com-prehension processes. By examining where a reader pauses, it is possible to learn about the comprehension processes themselves. Using this approach, a process model of reading comprehension is developed that accounts for the gaze durations of college students reading scientific passages.

The following display presents an excerpt from the data to illustrate some characteristics of eye fixations that motivate the model. This display presents a protocol of a college student reading the first two sentences of a passage about the properties of flywheels. The reader averages about 200 words per minute on the scientific texts. In this study, the reader was told to read a paragraph with under-standing and then recall its content. Consecutive fixations on the same word have been aggregated into units called *gazes*. The gazes within each sentence have been sequentially numbered above the fixated word with the gaze durations (in milliseconds [msec]) indicated below the sequence number.

1	2	3	4	5	6	7	8	9	1	2
1566	267	400	83	267	617	767	450	450	400	616
Flywheels	are	one	of	the	oldest	mechanical	devices	known	to	man. Every internal-

3	5	4	6	7	8	9	10	11	12	13
517	684	250	317	617	1116	367	467	483	450	383
combustion	engine	contains	a	small	flywheel	that	converts	the	jerky	motion of the pistons into the

14	15	16	17	18	19	20	21
284	383	317	283	533	50	366	566
smooth	flow	of	energy	that	powers	the	drive shaft.

One important aspect of the protocol is that almost every content word is fixated at least once. There is a common misconception that readers do not fixate every word but only some small proportion of the text, perhaps one out of every two or three words. However, the data to be presented in this article (and most of our other data collected in reading experiments) show that during ordinary reading almost all content words are fixated. This applies not only to scientific text but also to narratives written for adult readers. The current data are not novel in this regard. The eye fixation studies from the first part of the century point to the same conclusion (Buswell, 1937, chap. 4; Dearborn, 1906, chap. 4; Judd & Buswell, 1922, chap. 2). When readers are given a text that is appropriate for their age level, they average 1.2 words per fixation. The words that are not always fixated tend to be short function words, such as *the*, *of*, and *a*. The number of words per fixation is even lower if the text is especially difficult or if the reader is poorly educated. Of course, this is not the case when adults are given simple texts such as children's stories; under such circumstances, these same studies show an increase to an average of two words per fixation. Similarly, readers skip more words if they are speed-reading or skimming (Taylor, 1962). These old results and the current results are consistent with the report of McConkie and Rayner (1975; Rayner, 1978) that readers generally cannot determine the meaning of a word that is in peripheral vision. These results have important implications for the present model; since most words of a text are fixated, we can try to account for the total duration of comprehension in terms of the gaze duration on each word.

The protocol also shows that the gaze duration varies considerably from word to word. There is a misconception that individual fixations are all about 250 msec in duration. But this is not true; there is a large variation in the duration of individual fixations as well as the total gaze duration on individual words. As the preceding display shows, some gaze durations are very long, such as the gaze on the word *Flywheels*. The model proposes that gaze durations reflect the time to execute comprehension processes. In this case the longer fixations are attributed to longer processing caused by the word's infrequency and its thematic importance. Also, the fixations at the end of each sentence tend to be long. For example, this reader had gaze durations of 450 and 566 msec on each of the last words of the first two sentences. The sentence terminal pauses will be shown to reflect an integrative process that is evoked at the ends of sentences.

The link between eye fixation data and the theory rests on two assumptions. The first, called the *immediacy assumption*, is that a reader tries to interpret each content word of a text as it is encountered, even at the expense of making guesses that sometimes turn out to be wrong. Interpretation refers to processing at several levels such as encoding the word, choosing one meaning of it, assigning it to its referent, and determining its status in the sentence and in the discourse. The immediacy assumption posits that the interpretations at all levels of processing are not deferred; they occur as soon as possible, a qualification that will be clarified later.

The second assumption, the eye–mind assumption, is that the eye remains fixated on a word as long as the word is being processed. So the time it takes to process a newly fixated word is directly indicated by the gaze duration. Of course, comprehending that word often involves the use of information from preceding parts of the text, without any backward fixations. So the concepts corresponding to two different words may be compared to each other, for example, whereas only the more recently encountered word is fixated. The eye–mind assumption can be contrasted with an alternative view that data acquired from several successive eye fixations are internally buffered before being semantically processed (Bouma & deVoogd, 1974). This alternative view was proposed to explain a reading task in which the phrases of a text were successively presented in the same location. However, the situation was unusual in two ways. First, there were no eye movements involved, so the normal reading processes may not have been used. Second, and more telling, readers could not perform a simple comprehension test after seeing the text this way. By contrast, several studies of more natural situations support the eye–mind assumption that readers pause on words that require more processing (Just & Carpenter, 1978; Carpenter & Daneman, 1980). The eye–mind assumption posits that there is no appreciable lag between what is being fixated and what is being processed. This assumption has also been explored in spatial problem-solving tasks and has been supported in that domain as well as in reading (Just & Carpenter, 1976). The immediacy and eye–mind assumptions are used to interpret gaze duration data in the development of the reading model.

The article has four major sections. The first briefly describes a theoretical framework for the processes and structures in reading. The second section describes the reading task and eye fixation results accounted for by the model. The third section presents the model itself, with subsections describing each component process of the model. The fourth section discusses some implications of the theory for language comprehension and relates this theory of reading to other approaches.

Theoretical Framework

Reading can be construed as the coordinated execution of a number of processing stages such as word encoding, lexical access, assigning semantic roles, and relating the information in a given sentence to previous sentences and previous knowledge. Some of the major stages of the proposed model are depicted schematically in Figure 1. The diagram depicts both processes and structures. The stages of reading in the left-hand column are shown in their usual sequence of execution. The long-term memory on the right-hand side is the storehouse

FIGURE 1
**A Schematic Diagram of the Major Processes and Structures
in Reading Comprehension**

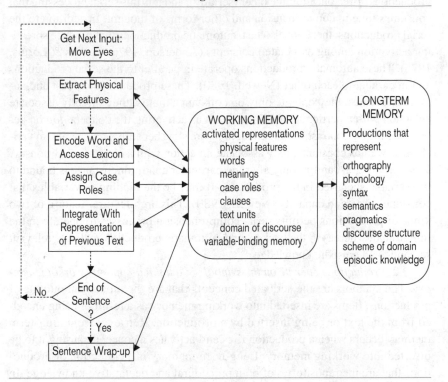

FIGURE 1
**A Schematic Diagram of the Major Processes and Structures
in Reading Comprehension**

Solid lines denote data-flow paths, and dashed lines indicate canonical flow of control.

of knowledge, including the procedural knowledge used in executing the stages on the left. The working memory in the middle mediates the long-term memory and the comprehension processes. Although it is easy to informally agree on the general involvement of these processes in reading, it is more difficult to specify the characteristics of the processes, their interrelations, and their effects on reading performance.

The nature of comprehension processes depends on a larger issue, namely the architecture of the processing system in which they are embedded. Although the human architecture is very far from being known, production systems have been suggested as a possible framework because they have several properties that might plausibly be shared by the human system. Detailed discussions of production systems as models of the human architecture are presented elsewhere (Anderson, 1976; Newell, 1973, 1980). The following three major properties are of particular relevance here:

1. *Structural and procedural knowledge is stored in the form of condition–action rules, such that a given stimulus condition produces a given action.* The productions "fire" one after the other (serially), and it is this serial processing that consumes time in comprehension and other forms of thought. In addition to the serial productions, there are also fast, automatic productions that produce spreading activation among associated concepts (Anderson, 1976; Collins & Loftus, 1975). These automatic productions operate in parallel to the serial productions and in parallel to each other (Newell, 1980). These productions are fast and automatic because they operate only on constants; that is, they directly associate an action with a particular condition (such as activating the concept *dog* on detecting *cat*). By contrast, serial productions are slow because they operate on variables as well as constants; they associate an action with a class of conditions. A serial production can fire only after the particular condition instance is bound to the variable specified in the production. It may be the binding of variables that consumes time and capacity (Newell, 1980). This architectural feature of two kinds of productions permits serial comprehension processes to operate in the foreground, whereas in the background, automatic productions activate relevant semantic and episodic knowledge.

2. *Productions operate on the symbols in a limited-capacity working memory.* The symbols are the activated concepts that are the inputs and outputs of productions. Items are inserted into working memory as a result of being encoded from the text or being inserted by a production. Retrieval from long-term memory occurs when a production fires and activates a concept, causing it to be inserted into working memory. Long-term memory is a collection of productions that are the repositories of both procedural and declarative knowledge. In the case of reading, this knowledge includes orthography, phonology, syntax, and semantics of the language, as well as schemas for particular topics and discourse types (Schank & Abelson, 1977). A new knowledge structure is acquired in long-term memory if a new production is created to encode that structure (Newell, 1980). This occurs if the structure participates in a large number of processing episodes.

One important property of working memory is that its capacity is limited, so that information is sometimes lost. One way in which capacity can be exceeded (causing forgetting) is that the level of activation of an item may decay to some subthreshold level through disuse over time (Collins & Loftus, 1975; Hitch, 1978; Reitman, 1974). A second forgetting mechanism allows for processes and structures to displace each other, within some limits (Case, 1978). Heavy processing requirements in a given task may decrease the amount of information that can be maintained, perhaps by generating too many competing structures or by actively inhibiting the maintenance of preceding information. There is recent evidence to suggest that working memory capacity (as opposed to passive memory span) is strongly correlated with individual differences in reading comprehension performance, presumably because readers with greater capacity can integrate more elements of the text at a given time (Daneman & Carpenter, 1980).

3. *Production systems have a mechanism for adaptive sequencing of processes.* The items in working memory at a given time enable a given production to fire and insert new items, which in turn enable another production, and so on. In this way, the intermediate results of the comprehension process that are placed in working memory can influence or sequence subsequent processing. There is no need for a superordinate controlling program to sequence the mental actions.

The self-sequencing nature of productions is compatible with the model depicted in Figure 1. The composition of each stage is simply a collection of productions that share a common higher-level goal. The productions within a stage have similar enabling conditions and produce actions that serve as conditions for other productions in the same stage. The productions within a stage need not be bound to each other in any other way. Thus, the ordering of stages with a production system is accomplished not by direct control transfer mechanisms but an indirect self-sequencing accomplished by one production helping to create the conditions that enable the "next" production to fire.

This architecture permits stages to be executed not only in canonical orders but also in noncanonical orders. There are occasions when some stages of reading seem to be partially or entirely skipped; some stages seem to be executed out of sequence, and some "later" stages sometimes seem to be able to influence "earlier" stages (Levy, 1981). Stages can be executed earlier than normal if their enabling conditions exist earlier than normal. For example, if a context strongly primes a case role, then the case assignment could precede the lexical access of a word. Having read *John pounded the nail with a* _____, a reader can assign the last word to the instrumental case on the basis of cues provided by the words *pound* and *nail*, before encoding *hammer*. This organization can permit "context effects" in comprehension, where a strong preceding context shortens reading time on a given word or clause. This might occur if a processing stage that is normally intermediate between two others is partially or entirely eliminated. It could be eliminated if the preceding stage plus the context provided sufficient enabling conditions for the later stage. Analogously, a misleading context could lengthen comprehension time by providing elements that enable conflicting processes.

The production system organization can also explain how "later" stages can influence "earlier" stages, so that higher-level schemas can affect word encoding, for example. If the productions of the normally later stage are enabled earlier than usual, then their outputs can serve as inputs to the normally earlier stage. The ordering of stages does not have to be entirely reversed to obtain this top-down influence. It may be sufficient for just a portion of the productions of the "later" stage to fire in order to influence the "earlier" stage.

In this view of processing stages, several stages can be executed cotemporaneously in the sense that firings of productions of two or more stages may be interleaved. Consequently, data and control can be transferred back and forth among different stages, somewhat similarly to computer programs organized into coroutines, which are two or more subprograms that have equal status (i.e., there is no master–slave relationship). When one coroutine obtains control, it executes until it detects a condition indicating it should relinquish control, and then another coroutine executes, and so on. One interesting difference between coroutines and the production system model is that coroutines generally transfer data between each other only along specified paths, used especially for this purpose. By contrast, productions "transfer" data by placing it in the working memory, so that all processes have access to it. In this sense, the working memory serves as a message center, and communication among stages is by means of the items in working memory. This is distinct from one stage feeding its output directly to another stage.

Research

Texts

This section describes the texts that were used in the reading research because their properties, both local and global, have a large influence on the processing. The global organization of a narrative text has been shown to influence how a reader recalls the text (Kintsch & van Dijk, 1978; Mandler & Johnson, 1977; Meyer, 1975; Rumelhart, 1977b; Thorndyke, 1977).

The experiment reported next shows that the organization has at least part of its effect when the text is being read. Scientific texts were selected from *Newsweek* and *Time* because their content and style are typical of what students read to learn about technical topics. The passages discussed a variety of topics that were generally unfamiliar to the readers in the study. When readers were asked to rate their familiarity with the topic of each passage on a 5-point scale, the modal rating was at the "entirely unfamiliar" end of the scale. There were 15 passages averaging 132 words each. Although the texts are moderately well written, they are on the borderline between "fairly difficult" and "difficult" on Flesch's (1951) readability scale, with 17 words per sentence and 1.6 syllables per word. The following is an example of one of the passages:

> Flywheels are one of the oldest mechanical devices known to man. Every internal-combustion engine contains a small flywheel that converts the jerky motion of the pistons into the smooth flow of energy that powers the drive shaft. The greater the mass of a flywheel and the faster it spins, the more energy can be stored in it. But its maximum spinning speed is limited by the strength of the material it is made from. If it spins too fast for its mass, any flywheel will fly apart. One type of flywheel consists of round sandwiches of fiberglass and rubber providing the maximum possible storage of energy when the wheel is

confined in a small space as in an automobile. Another type, the "superfly-wheel," consists of a series of rimless spokes. This flywheel stores the maximum energy when space is unlimited.

The content of the passages was analyzed by segmenting the text into idea units and categorizing these units by means of a simple text grammar. First, all of the 15 passages were segmented into text units called *sectors*, producing 274 sectors. The average sector length was seven words. Each sector was judged to be a single meaningful piece of information, whether it consisted of a word, phrase, clause, or sentence. The general criteria for segmentation into sectors were similar to those used by Meyer and McConkie (1973), who related such text units to recall performance.

A simplified grammar was developed to categorize the sectors of the texts. The grammar (shown schematically in Figure 2) classifies the text units into a structure that is quasi-hierarchical. This abbreviated grammar captures most of the regularities in our short passages (see Vesonder, 1979, for a more complete grammar for longer scientific passages). The initial sentences generally introduced a topic—a scientific development or event. The beginnings of the passage sometimes gave details of the time, place, and people involved with the discovery. Familiar concepts were simply named, whereas unusual concepts were accompanied by an explicit definition. The main topic itself was developed through specific examples or through subtopics that were then expanded with further descriptions, explanations, and concrete examples. Consequences, usually toward the end of the passage, stated the importance of the event for other applications.

FIGURE 2
A Schematic Diagram of the Major Text-Grammatical Categories of Information in the Scientific Paragraphs

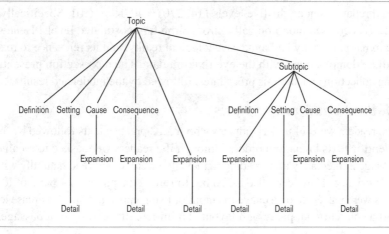

TABLE 1

A Classification of the "Flywheel" Passage Into Text-Grammatical Categories

Category	Sector
Topic	Flywheels are one of the oldest mechanical devices
Topic	known to man
Expansion	Every internal-combustion engine contains a small flywheel
Expansion	that converts the jerky motion of the pistons into the smooth flow of energy
Expansion	that powers the drive shaft
Cause	The greater the mass of a flywheel and the faster it spins,
Consequence	the more energy can be stored in it.
Subtopic	But its maximum spinning speed is limited by the strength of the material
Subtopic	it is made from.
Expansion	If it spins too fast for its mass,
Expansion	any flywheel will fly apart.
Definition	One type of flywheel consists of round sandwiches of fiberglass and rubber
Expansion	providing the maximum possible storage of energy
Expansion	when the wheel is confined in a small space
Detail	as in an automobile.
Definition	Another type, the "superflywheel," consists of a series of rimless spokes.
Expansion	This flywheel stores the maximum energy
Detail	when space is unlimited.

Table 1 shows how each text unit or sector in the "Flywheel" passage was classified according to these categories. Each of the 274 sectors was assigned to one of the five levels of the grammar by one of the authors. The levels of the grammar were further confirmed by a pretest involving 16 subjects who rated the importance of each sector in its passage on a 7-point scale. The mean importance ratings differed reliably among the five levels $F(4, 270) = 40.04, p < .01$. Specifically, the means decreased monotonically through the five postulated levels. Hence, the grammar potentially has some psychological reality, and its relevance to reading will be demonstrated with the eye fixation data. The next section presents the data collection and analysis procedures, followed by the model and results.

Method and Data Analysis

The readers were 14 undergraduates who read 2 practice texts followed by the 15 scientific texts in random order. Although the readers were asked to recall each passage immediately after reading it, they also were told to read naturally without memorizing. They were also asked not to reread the passage or parts of it. The texts were presented on a television monitor using uppercase and lowercase letters and a conventional paragraph layout. To initiate the reading of a passage, the reader had to look at a fixation point (located where the first word of the paragraph would later appear) and press a "ready" button. If the reader's point of regard (as measured by the eye tracker) was within 1° of the fixation point, then exactly 500 msec later the passage appeared in its entirety on the screen. The passage appeared instantaneously (i.e., within one video frame) and remained there until the reader signaled that he had finished reading by pushing a response button.

The reader's pupil and corneal reflections were monitored relatively unobtrusively by a television camera that was 75 cm away. The monitoring system, manufactured by Applied Science Laboratories, computed the reader's point of regard (as opposed to eye or head position) every 16.7 msec. The accuracy of the tracker was verified before and after each passage was read by having the reader look at a fixation point and determining whether the obtained point of regard was within 1° (the size of a three-letter syllable) of that point. This procedure indicated that accuracy was maintained during the reading of 195 of the 210 experimental passages in the entire experiment; the data from the 15 inaccurate trials were discarded.

Data reduction procedures converted the 60 observations per second into fixations and then into gazes on each word. While the data were being acquired, a new "fixation" was scored as having occurred if the point of regard changed by more than 1°. The durations of blinks that were preceded and followed by fixations on the same location were attributed to the reading time on that location. Another program aggregated consecutive fixations on the same word into gazes and computed the duration of gaze on each of the 1,936 words in the 15 passages. Fixations on interword spaces were attributed to the word on the right because the perceptual span is centered to the right of the point of regard, at least for readers of left-to-right languages (McConkie & Rayner, 1976; Schiepers, 1980). The durations of saccades, blinks that occurred between words, regressions, and rereading were not included in the data analysis. Because of the instructions not to reread, these categories account for relatively little of the total reading time, approximately 12% in all. The mean duration of gaze on each word was computed by averaging over readers; these 1,936 mean gaze durations constitute the main dependent measure of interest.

The model presents a number of factors that influence various reading processes; some factors have their effect on individual words and some on larger units such as clauses. The data were fit to the model with a multiple linear regression in which the independent variables were the factors postulated to affect reading time, and the dependent variable was the mean gaze duration on each word. Since the model also applies at the level of clauses and phrases, a second regression analysis was done at the phrase/clause level. The independent variables for the latter analysis were the factors postulated to affect reading time at the clause level, and the independent variable was the mean gaze duration on each of the 274 sectors described previously.

The psychological interpretation of the independent variables in the two regression analyses will be described in detail in the sections that follow. The equation for the analysis of the gaze duration on individual words was

$$GW_i = \sum a_m X_{im} + \epsilon_i$$

where GW_i is the gaze duration on a word i, a_m is the regression weight in msec for independent variable X_m, and X_{im} are the independent variables that code the following seven properties of word i: (a) length, (b) the logarithm of its normative frequency, (c) whether the word occurs at the beginning of a line of text, (d) whether it is a novel word to the reader, (e) its case grammatical role (one of 11 possibilities), (f) whether it is the last word in a sentence, (g) whether it is the last word in a paragraph.

The equation for the analysis of the gaze duration on individual sectors was

$$GS_j = b_o + \sum b_n Z_{jn} + \epsilon_j$$

where GS_j is the gaze duration on sector j, and b_n is the regression weight in msec for independent variable Z_n. The Z_{jn} are the independent variables that code the following eight properties of sector j: (a) its text grammatical level, multiplied by the number of content words; (b) length; (c) the sum of the logarithms of the frequencies of its component words; (d) the number of fine-initial words it contains; (e) the number of novel words it contains; (f) the sum of the case role regression weights of its component words; (g) whether it is the last sector in a sentence; (h) whether it is the last sector in a paragraph.

Results

The mean gaze duration on each word (239 msec) indicated reading rates that are typical for texts of this difficulty. If the 239 msec per word is incremented by 12% to allow for saccades, blinks, and occasional rereading, the reading rate is 225 words per minute. The standard deviation of the 239 msec gaze mean was 168 msec, indicating considerable variability in gaze duration from word to word. The results of the regression analyses are shown in Table 2. The table is divided into three sections, corresponding to the three major processing stages postulated by the model, encoding and lexical access, case role assignment, and interclause integration. The regression weights shown in Table 2 for the word-by-word analysis (above the double line) are derived from a regression equation involving 17 independent variables (11 of which are the case role indicator variables). The standard error of estimate of this model was 88 msec, and the R^2 value was .72. The results of the interclause integration stage make use of both the word-by-word analysis and the sector-by-sector analysis. (The latter analysis will be explained in more detail in the section on interclause integration.) Since the gaze durations on successive words and phrases are time-series data, it is interesting to

TABLE 2
**Application of the Regression Model to the Gaze Duration on Each Word
(Above Double Line) and to Each Sector (Below Double Line)**

Processing Stage	Factor	Regression Weight (msec)
Encoding and Lexical Access	no. of syllables	52**
	log frequency	53**
	beginning of line	30**
	novel word	802**
Case Role Assignment	agent (86)	51**
	instrument (110)	53**
	direct or indirect object (174)	25*
	adverb/manner (35)	29
	place or time (64)	23
	possessive (genitive) (39)	16
	verb (368)	33**
	state/adjective (451)	44**
	rhetorical word (15)	70**
	determiner (243)	26**
	connective (351)	9
Interclause Integration	last word in sentence	71**
	last word in paragraph	157**
	Integration time per content word from regression analysis of data aggregated into sectors	
	topic (22)	72**
	definition/cause/consequence (23)	94**
	subtopic (48)	78**
	expansion (68)	73**
	detail (113)	60**

Frequency of occurrence of cast roles is in parentheses.
$*t = p < 0.05$; $**t = p < .01$.

note that there was no reliable positive serial correlation among the residuals in the word-by-word regression or the sector-by-sector regression.

The Reading Model

The next five subsections describe the major stages shown in Figure 1: get next input, word encoding and lexical access, case role assignment, interclause integration, and sentence wrap-up. Each subsection describes the processes in that stage together with the factors that affect the duration of those processes, and hence the gaze durations.

Get Next Input

This is the first stage of a cycle that finds information, encodes it, and processes it. When the perceptual and semantic stages have done all the requisite processing on a particular word, the eye is directed to land in a new place where it continues to rest until the requisite processing is done, and so forth. The specification of what constitutes "all of the requisite processing" is contained in a list of conditions that must be satisfied before the reader terminates the gaze on the current word and fixates the next one. These conditions include a specification of the goals of normal reading. For instance, one condition may be that a meaning of the word be accessed, and another condition may be that a case role be assigned. These conditions can also reflect more specific reading goals. A reader who is trying to memorize a text may have as a condition that the word or phrase be transferred to long-term memory. By setting the conditions appropriately, the reader can adjust his processes to the situation at hand. When the goal conditions for processing a word are satisfied, the resulting action is get next input.

The command to get next input usually results in a saccade to the next part of the text, one or two words forward. The process that selects the placement of the next forward fixation does not have to be very complex or intelligent. The choice of where to place the next forward fixation appears to depend primarily on the length of the next word or two to the right of the current fixation (McConkie & Rayner, 1975). The length information, which is encoded parafoveally, is then used to program a rightward saccade. However, if only the right margin is visible in the parafovea, then the eye is directed to the first word of the next line, producing a return sweep. In this case the information in peripheral vision is not adequate for accurate targeting. The return sweep is typically too short; the eye often lands on the second word of the new line for a brief amount of time (50 or 75 msec) and then makes a corrective saccade leftward to the first word of the line (Bayle, 1942). On occasion, a comprehension stage may require a review of previously read text to reencode it or process it to deeper levels. In those cases, the get next input stage results in a regressive saccade to the relevant portion of the text.

The duration of the get next input stage is short, consisting of the time for a neural signal to be transmitted to the eye muscles. In monkeys, this takes about 30 msec (Robinson, 1972). This duration must not be confused with the typical 150- to 200-msec latency of a saccade to a visual stimulus that has spatial or temporal uncertainty (Westheimer, 1954). These latencies include stimulus detection, interpretation, and selection of the next fixation target. In normal reading, there is very little uncertainty about direction of the next saccade (it is almost always rightward for forward fixations, except for the return sweeps), nor is there much uncertainty about distance. On the average, the saccade distance may be simply the mean center-to-center distance between words, a distance that does not vary much, relative to the physically possible variation in eye movements. Thus, it is reasonable to suppose that the preprogramming time is very short here, consisting usually of a "go" signal and the time it takes that signal to be translated into a motor movement, about 30 msec (Robinson, 1972). The actual movements, the saccades, constitute about 5%–10% of the total reading time. Recent analyses suggest that the saccade itself may destroy the visual persistence of the information from the preceding fixation so that it does not mask the input from the new fixation (Breitmeyer, 1980). Consequently, it is reasonable to assume that stimulus encoding can commence soon after the eye arrives at a new location.

Word Encoding and Lexical Access

The reading process involves encoding a word into an internal semantic format. It is assumed that prior to this encoding the transduction from the printed word to the visual features has already taken place and that the features have been deposited into the working memory. Perceptual encoding productions use the visual features as conditions; their action is to activate the representation of the word. Once the representation of the word has been sufficiently activated, its corresponding concept is accessed and inserted into working memory. The concept serves as a pointer to a more complete representation of the meaning, which consists of a small semantic network realized as a set of productions. The major nodes of the network are the possible meanings of the word, the semantic and syntactic properties of the meanings, and information about the contexts in which they usually occur (see Rieger, 1979, for a related proposal). The word meanings are represented as abstract predicates, defined by their relations to other predicates.

The productions that encode a word generally trigger on orthographically based subword units such as syllables (Mewhort & Beal, 1977; Spoehr & Smith, 1973; Taft, 1979). However, there are times when alternative codes, including orthographic, phonological, and whole-word codes, are used (Baron, 1977; Kleiman, 1975; LaBerge & Samuels, 1974). Since the syllable-like encoding is believed to be the dominant mode, the data were analyzed in terms of the number of syllables in each word. Encoding time increased by 52 msec for each syllable, as shown in Table 2.

The mechanism underlying lexical access is the activation of a word's meaning representation by various sources. There are three ways that a concept's level of activation can be temporarily increased above its base level. One activation mechanism is perceptual encoding; the encoded representation of a word can activate its meaning. A second source is the parallel productions that produce spreading activation through the semantic and episodic knowledge base of the reader. The third source is activation by the serial productions that do the major computations in all of the stages of processing. When a concept has been activated above some threshold by one or more of these sources, a pointer to its meaning is inserted into working memory. The activation level gradually decays to a subthreshold level unless some process reactivates it. If the word soon reoccurs in the text while the concept is still activated, lexical access will be facilitated because the activation level will still be close to threshold. When the activation level does decrease, it decreases to an asymptote slightly higher than the old base level. In this way, the system can learn from both local and long-term word repetitions. Frequently used words will have a high base level of activation and consequently will require relatively less additional activation to retrieve them. Thus, frequent words should take less time to access than infrequent words (Morton, 1969). Similarly, the various possible interpretations of each word will have different base activation levels, such that the more common interpretations have higher base activation levels. For example, although the word *does* has at least two very different meanings, the "third-person-singular verb" interpretation would have a higher base activation because it is more common than the "female deer" interpretation (Carpenter & Daneman, 1980). The more common interpretation would then be accessed faster since less additional activation would be required to bring the activation level to threshold. This model of lexical access can account for word-frequency effects, priming effects, and repetition effects in reading.

The gaze duration showed both frequency and repetition effects. Frequency was analyzed by relating gaze duration to the logarithm of the normative frequency of each word, based on the Kučera and Francis (1967) norms. It was expected that gaze duration would decrease with the logarithm of the word's frequency; that is, small differences among infrequent words would be as important as much larger differences among frequent words (Mitchell & Green, 1978). For algebraic convenience, the normative frequencies were increased by one (to eliminate the problem of taking the logarithm of zero), and the logarithm was computed and then subtracted from 4.85, the logarithm of the frequency of the most frequent English word. The analysis indicated a clear relation between this measure of frequency and gaze duration. As shown in Table 2, gaze duration increased by 53 msec for each log unit of decrease in word frequency. A moderately frequent word like *water* (with a frequency of 442) was accessed 140 msec faster than a word that did not appear in the norms.

At one extreme of the frequency dimension are words that a reader has never encountered before. In scientific passages, the novel words tend to be technical terms. To read these words, a reader cannot depend on contacting some prior perceptual and semantic representation; neither exists. The reader must construct some perceptual representation (perhaps phonological as well as orthographic), associate this with the semantic and syntactic properties of the concept that can be inferred from the passage, and then possibly construct a lexical entry. These processes seem to take a great deal more time than ordinary encoding and access processes. Two judges identified seven words in the texts (that had zero frequency) as probably entirely novel to the readers. Novelty was coded as an indicator variable, and it was found that these words took an additional 802 msec on average to process, as shown in Table 2. However, there was considerable variability among the words; their gaze durations ranged from 913 msec (for *staphylococci*) to 2,431 msec (for *thermoluminescence*).

Once a word has been encoded and accessed once, it should be easier to access it when it occurs again. Other research has suggested that frequency and repetition have their primary effect on lexical access rather than encoding (Dixon & Rothkopf, 1979; Glanzer & Ehrenreich, 1979; Scarborough, Cortese, & Scarborough, 1977), although the possibility of some small effects on the encoding process does exist. According to the model, repetition effects should occur in reading because the first time a word meaning is accessed, it should temporarily achieve a higher activation level similar to the level of a more frequent word. This mechanism particularly predicts repetition effects for infrequent words, whose activation levels are low to start with, but not for the highly frequent words that occur in natural text. Generally, repetition effects are larger for low-frequency words (Scarborough et al., 1977). "Low frequency" in the Scarborough study was defined as less than 28 occurrences per million, the boundary of 28 emerging from a median split of the frequencies of their stimuli. So the analysis of repetition effects was limited to words with frequencies of 25 occurrences per million or less. There were 346 such instances in the text; 251 were initial occurrences and 95 were repetitions. The repetitions were words with the same morphological stem, disregarding affixes. An analysis of covariance on this subset of the data examined the effects of repetitions covarying out the number of syllables. The adjusted mean gaze durations were 49 msec longer on the initial appearance of these words than on the subsequent appearances, $t(343)$ = 2.21, $p < .03$. Most of this effect (43 msec) was obtained on the second appearance of a word. These results indicate that once an infrequent word appears in a text, processing time on that word is decreased on subsequent appearances.

Lexical access is complicated by the fact that some words have more than one meaning, so the appropriate interpretation must be selected, or at least guessed at. When a polysemous word is accessed, the word representation that is retrieved is a pointer to a semantic network that includes the multiple representations. The interpretation that is selected is the one with the highest activation level, and several factors can affect the activation. First, some interpretations start off with a higher activation level; for instance, the "third-person-singular" interpretation of *does* has a higher base activation level than the "deer" interpretation. Second, the automatic productions that produce spreading activation can contribute selectively to the activation level of one particular interpretation. The spreading activation can emanate from the preceding semantic and syntactic context, from the reader's knowledge of the domain, and from knowledge of the discourse style. Third, the output of other stages operating on the same word may activate a particular interpretation. For example, although *hammer* can be interpreted as a noun or a verb, a sentence context that suggests an instrument to the case role assignment stage (e.g., *John hit the nail with a* _____) may help activate the noun interpretation. Fourth, when a word with many highly related meanings occurs in an impoverished context, there may be no single interpretation with higher activation than the others, and the superordinate concept may be the selected interpretation of the word. This probably occurs for words that have many closely related interpretations, such as *get* and *take*.

The selection of only one interpretation of each word, posited by the immediacy assumption, provides a measure of cognitive economy. Selecting just one interpretation allows the activation of the unselected interpretations to decay, preventing them from activating their associates. Thus, the contextual effects would remain focused in the appropriate semantic domain. This permits a limited-capacity working memory to cope with the information flow in a spreading activation environment that may activate many interpretations and associations for any lexical item. This method of processing also avoids the combinatorial explosion that results from entertaining more than one interpretation for several successive words.

This aspect of the model is consistent with some recent results on lexical access that indicate that although multiple meanings of a word are initially activated, only one meaning remains activated after a few hundred milliseconds. In one experiment, the subjects simultaneously listened to a sentence and pronounced a visually presented word. When an ambiguous word (*rose*) was presented auditorally in a syntactic context (e.g., *They all rose*), the speed of pronouncing a simultaneous visual probe related to either meaning "stood" or "flower" was faster than in a control condition (Tanenhaus, Leiman, & Seidenberg, 1979). In another experiment, the subjects listened to a sentence and performed a lexical decision task on visually presented stimuli. When an ambiguous word (*bug*) was presented in a semantic context (*John saw several spiders, roaches, and bugs*), the speed of a simultaneous lexical decision related to either meaning "insect" or "spy" was faster than a control (Swinney, 1979). In both studies, the facilitation of the inappropriate meaning was obtained only within a few hundred milliseconds of the occurrence of the ambiguous word. If the probe was delayed longer, the inappropriate interpretation was no faster than the control. These results suggest that both meanings are available when an ambiguous word is being accessed, but the inappropriate meaning is lost from working memory after a short time.

As the interpretation of the text is constructed, a corresponding representation of the extensive meaning—the things being talked about—is also being built. If the referents of the words in a passage cannot be determined, the text will be more difficult to understand. One example of this problem is highlighted in a passage from Bransford and Johnson (1973) concerning a procedure that involved arranging "things into groups. Of course, one may be sufficient depending on how much there is" (p. 400). Subjects who were not given the title *Washing Clothes* thought the story was incomprehensible. The referential representation helps the reader disambiguate referents, infer relations, and integrate the text.

The immediacy assumption posits that an attempt to relate each content word to its referent occurs as soon as possible. Sometimes this can be done when the word is first fixated, but sometimes more information is required. For example, although the semantic interpretation of a relative adjective such as *large* can be computed immediately, the extensive meaning depends on the word it modifies (e.g., *large insect* vs. *large building*). The referent of the entire noun phrase can be computed only after both words are processed. The immediacy assumption does not state that the relating is done immediately on each content word, but rather that it occurs as soon as possible. This is an important distinction that will be made again in the discussion on integrative processes.

Assigning Case Roles

Comprehension involves determining the relations among words, the relations among clauses, and the relations among whole units of text. This section describes the first of these processes, that of determining the relations among the words in a clause (or in Schank's, 1972, terms, determining the dependencies among the concepts). These relations can be categorized into semantic cases, such as agent, recipient, location, time, manner, instrument, action, or state (Chafe, 1970; Fillmore, 1968). The case role assignment process usually takes as input a representation of the fixated word, including information about its possible case roles and syntactic properties. For example, hammers tend to be instruments rather than locations or recipients, and information about a word's usual case role can be an important contributor to the assignment process. But this normative information generally is not sufficient to assign its case role in a particular clause. Consequently, the assignment process relies on heuristics that use the word meaning together with information about the prior semantic and syntactic context, as well as language-based inferences. The output of the process is a representation of the word's semantic role with respect to the other constituents in its clause.

Just as certain meanings suggest particular case roles, so, too, can the context prime a particular case role. Consider the sentence *John was interrogated by the* _____. The semantic and syntactic cues suggest that the missing word will be an agent, such as *detective*. The strength of the context becomes evident if the primed case does not occur, for example, *John was interrogated by the window*. The prior semantic context can precede the affected case assignment by more than a few words. In the sentences *The lawyer wanted to know where in the room John had been interrogated* and *Mary told him that John was interrogated by the window*, the thematic focus of the first sentence on a location alters the interpretation of *by* and facilitates a locative case role assignment for *window*.

The specific heuristics that are used in case role assignment have received some attention (see Clark & Clark, 1977, for some examples). Many proposals contain the suggestion that readers use the verb as a pivotal source of information to establish the necessary and possible case roles and then fit the noun phrases into those slots (Schank, 1972). But the immediacy assumption posits that the case role assignment for an item preceding the verb is not postponed in anticipation of the verb. Similar to the lexical access stage, the case assignment stage makes a best guess about a word's case when the word is fixated, rather than making the decision contingent on subsequent words. So, the model would not accord any special status to verbs. Another suggested heuristic (that children appear to use) is to assign a sequence consisting of animate noun–verb–noun to the case roles of agent–action–object (Bever, 1970). Like all heuristics, this one sometimes fails, so young children sometimes misinterpret passive sentences (Fraser, Bellugi, & Brown, 1963). This heuristic may be employed by adults, but in a modified version that conforms to the immediacy assumption. Rather than waiting for the three major constituents before assigning case roles, the reader should assign an animate noun to the agent role as soon as it is encountered, in the absence of contrary prior context.

The immediate assignment of a case role implies that readers will sometimes make errors and have to revise previous decisions. For example, an adult who assigns the role of agent to an animate noun and then encounters a passive verb will have to revise the agent assignment. (Presumably, young children do not make this revision.) The immediacy of the case assignment process is evident in the reading of a sentence such as *Mary loves Jonathan*.... The immediacy assumption suggests that a reader would assign to *Jonathan* the role of recipient; this would in turn result in an incorrect assignment if the sentence continued *Mary loves Jonathan apples*.

Because case roles are assigned within clauses, the assignment process must include a segmentation procedure to determine clause boundaries within sentences. Sentences can sometimes be segmented into clauses on the basis of explicit markers such as a subordinating conjunction (e.g., *because, when*). More often, the reader cannot tell with certainty where one clause ends and another starts until beyond the clause boundary (or potential boundary). A general strategy for dealing with such cases has been suggested, namely to assign a word to the clause being processed, if possible (Frazier & Fodor, 1978). For example, the word *soil* in the sentence *When farmers are plowing the soil...* can continue the initial clause (*When farmers are plowing the soil, it is most fertile*) or start a new one (*When farmers are plowing the soil is most fertile*). The suggested strategy is to continue the initial clause until contrary information is encountered.

Interestingly, the strategy discussed by Frazier and Fodor (1978) presupposes the immediacy assumption; the segmentation decision arises because case roles are assigned as soon as the words are encountered.

There is no direct mapping between particular case roles and the duration of the assignment process. For example, there is no a priori reason to expect that assignment of instruments takes more or less time than locations. The time for a particular assignment might depend more on the context and properties of the word than on the particular case role being assigned. Detailed specification of the process is not within the scope of this article; it probably requires a large-scale simulation model to examine the complex interactions of different levels of processing. Nevertheless, we examined whether, all things being equal, different case role assignments tend to take different amounts of time.

The analysis included the usual case roles just noted (Fillmore, 1968), as well as other categories, such as determiners and adjectives, that are not cases but still play a part in the parsing and assignment process. Each word was classified into 1 of 11 categories: verb, agent, instrument, indirect or direct object, location or time, adverb, adjective or state, connective (preposition or conjunction), possessive, determiner, and rhetorical word (such as *well*). Some cases were pooled (such as location and time) because they were relatively infrequent in the text and because they have some conceptual similarity. The case roles were coded as indicator variables and were all entered into the regression with the intercept forced to zero.

The results of the case role assignment analysis, shown in Table 2, indicate that there are some variations among the cases. As expected, verbs did not take particularly long (33 msec), and in fact, although the time was significantly different from 0, it was not greater than the agent or instrument cases (51 msec and 53 msec, respectively). Four cases had parameters that were not significantly different from 0 connectives (9 msec), adverb/manner (29 msec), place or time (23 msec), and possessives (16 msec). These parameters could reflect some properties of particular word classes, in addition to parsing and case role assignment processes. For example, if a connective (e.g., *and* or *but*) simply takes less time to access than other words, the advantage should appear in this parameter. However, the parameters are not due solely to length or frequency since these variables make a separate contribution to the regression equation. Although this analysis does not examine any of the contextual effects thought to be of some importance in the case assignment process, it does indicate roughly the relative amount of time spent assigning various categories of words to their case roles in a clause. Later theories will have to account for the precise pattern of case assignment durations in terms of specific operations that use prior context and word meanings to assign the various cases.

Interclause Integration

Clauses and sentences must be related to each other by the reader to capture the coherence in the text. As each new clause or sentence is encountered, it must be integrated with the previous information acquired from the text or with the knowledge retrieved from the reader's long-term memory. Integrating the new sentence with the old information consists of representing the relations between the new and the old structures.

Several search strategies may be used to locate old information that is related to the new information. One strategy is to check if the new information is related to the other information that is already in working memory either because it has been repeatedly referred to or because it is recent (Carpenter & Just, 1977a; Kintsch & van Dijk, 1978). Using this strategy implies that adjacency between clauses and sentences will cause a search for a possible relation. For instance, the adjacent sentences *Mary hurt herself* and *John laughed* seem related (John must be a cad) even though there is no explicit mention of the relation. This strategy also entails trying to relate new information to a topic that is active in working memory. This is a good strategy since information in a passage should be related to the topic.

A second strategy is to search for specific connections based on cues in the new sentence itself. Sentences often contain old information as well as new. Sometimes the old information is explicitly marked (as in cleft constructions and relative clauses), but often it is simply some argument repeated from the prior text. The reader can use this old information to search his or her long-term text representation and referential representation for potential points of attachment between the new information and the old (Haviland & Clark, 1974). This second strategy may take more time than the first. In fact, it takes longer to read a sentence that refers to information introduced several sentences earlier than one that refers to recently introduced information (Carpenter & Just, 1977a).

There are two main points at which integration can occur. First, as each ensuing word of the text is encountered, there is an attempt to relate it to previous information (Just & Carpenter, 1978). Second, a running representation of the clause is maintained, with an updating as each word of the clause is read. This running clause representation consists of the configuration of clause elements arranged according to their case relations. This second type of integration involves an attempt to relate the running clause representation to previous information at each update. Integration occurs whenever a linking relation can be computed. Consider the sentence *Although he spoke softly, yesterday's speaker could hear the little boy's question*. The point of this example is not so much that the initial integration of *he* and *speaker* is incorrect, but that the integration is attempted at the earliest opportunity. This model implies that integration time may be distributed over fixations on different parts of a clause. Moreover, the duration of the process may depend on the number of concepts in the clause; as these increase, the number of potential points of contact between the new clause and previous information will increase. There is also evidence for integration triggered by the end of the sentence; this process is discussed next in more detail.

Integration results in the creation of a new structure. The symbol representing that structure is a pointer to the integrated concepts, and this superordinate symbol is then available for further processing. In this way, integration can chunk the incoming text and allows a limited working memory to deal with large segments of prose. The macrorules proposed by Kintsch and van Dijk (1978) can be construed as productions that integrate.

Integration can also lead to forgetting in working memory. As each new chunk is formed, there is a possibility that it will displace some previous information from working memory. Particularly vulnerable are items that are only marginally activated, usually because they were processed much earlier and have not recently participated in a production. For instance, the representation of a clause will decay if it was processed early in a text and was not related to subsequent information. This mechanism can also clear working memory of "lower-level" representations that are no longer necessary. For example, the verbatim representation of a previously read sentence may be displaced by the processes that integrated the sentence with other information (Jarvella, 1971). By contrast, the semantic elements that participate in an integration production obtain an increased activation level. This increases the probability that they will become a permanent part of long-term memory.

The main types of interclause relations in the scientific passages correspond to the text-grammatical categories described previously, such as definitions, causes, consequences, examples, and so forth. Text roles that are usually more important to the text and to the reader's goals, such as topics or definitions, are integrated differently than less-important units such as details. The more central units will initiate more retrievals of relevant previous knowledge of the domain (schematic knowledge) and retrievals of information acquired from the text but no longer resident in the working memory. In addition, more relations will be computed between the semantically central propositions and previous information because centrality inherently entails relations with many other units. By contrast, details are often less important to the reader's goals and to the text. Moreover, when a detail is to be integrated, the process is simpler because details are often concrete instantiations of an immediately preceding statement (at least in these scientific texts), so they can be quickly appended to information still present in the working memory. Thus, higher-level units will take more time to integrate because their integration is usually essential to the reader's goals and because integration of higher-level units involves more relations to be computed and more retrievals to be made.

The nature of the link relating two structures may be explicitly denoted either in the text (with connectives like *because*, *therefore*, and *for instance*), or it may have to be inferred on the basis of schematic knowledge of the domain. For example, the causal relation between the sentences *Cynthia fell off the rocking horse* and *She cried bitter tears* is inferred from the reader's knowledge about the temporal and causal relation between falling and hurting oneself (Charniak, 1972).

The model predicts that the gaze duration on a sector depends on its text-grammatical role and on the number of concepts it contains. Because integration can occur at many points in a sector, the gaze duration associated with integration cannot be localized to a particular word. Thus, to do the clause level of analysis, the gaze durations on the individual words of a sector were cumulated, producing a total of 274 sector gaze durations as the dependent variable. The independent variables were the aggregates of the word-level variables, except for case roles. The independent variable that coded the case role effect for a sector was the sum of the case coefficients (obtained from the word-by-word regression analysis) for each of the words in the sector. A new independent variable coded the text-grammatical role of a sector and its number of content words; it was the interaction of the indicator variables that represented the five text-grammatical levels and the number of content words in the sector, with *content word* defined as in Hockett (1958).

The results indicate that the integration time for a given sector depends on its text-grammatical role. The portion of Table 2 below the double line shows the integration time per content word for each type of sector. Generally, more important or central sectors take longer to integrate. The model describes this effect in terms of the integrative processes initiated by the semantics of the different types of information and their relevance to the reader's goals. An analysis of covariance examined the effect of text roles covarying out the number of syllables. The adjusted mean gaze durations differed reliably, $F(4, 268) = 8.82$, $p < .01$; paired comparisons indicated that details took significantly less time than all other roles, and expansions took significantly less time than topics and definitions/causes/consequences (all $ps < .01$). These results quantitatively and qualitatively replicate those reported previously for a slightly different paradigm (Carpenter & Just, 1981). The previously obtained coefficients for the five text-grammatical categories were 65, 106, 81, 76, and 47 msec per content word, respectively, corresponding to the newly obtained 72, 94, 78, 73, and 60. The model accounts very well for the sector-level data. The R^2 value was .94, and the standard error of estimate was 234. The mean gaze duration on a sector was 1,690 msec, with a standard deviation of 902 msec, and the mean sector length was 4.9 words.[1]

One cost of immediate interpretation, case role assignment, and integration is that some decisions will prove to be incorrect. There must be mechanisms to detect and recover from such errors. The detection of a misinterpretation often occurs when new information to be integrated is inconsistent with previous information. Thus, misinterpretation detection may be construed as inconsistency detection. For example, the sentence *There were tears in her brown dress* causes errors initially because the most frequent interpretation of *tears* is not the appropriate one here, and the initial interpretation is incompatible with *dress*. The eye fixations of subjects reading such garden path sentences clearly indicate that readers do detect inconsistencies, typically at the point at which the inconsistency is first evident (Carpenter & Daneman, 1980). At that point, they use a number of error-recovery heuristics that enable them to reinterpret the text. They do not start reinterpreting the sentence from its beginning. The heuristics point them to the locus of the probable error. Readers start the backtracking with the word that first reveals the inconsistency, in this case, *dress*. If that word cannot be reinterpreted, they make regressions to the site of other words that were initially difficult to interpret, such as ambiguous words on which a best guess about word meaning had to be made. The ability to return directly to the locus of the misinterpretation and to recover from an error makes the immediacy strategy feasible.

Sentence Wrap-Up

A special computational episode occurs when a reader reaches the end of a sentence. This episode, called *sentence wrap-up*, is not a stage of processing defined by its function, but rather by virtue of being executed when the reader reaches the end of a sentence. The processes that occur during sentence wrap-up involve a search for referents that have not been assigned, the construction of interclause relations (with the aid of inferences, if necessary), and an attempt to handle any inconsistencies that could not be resolved within the sentence.

The ends of sentences have two important properties that make them especially good places for integration. First, within-sentence ambiguities are usually clarified by the end of the sentence. For example, if a sentence introduces a new object or person whose identity cannot be inferred from the preceding context, some cue to their identity is generally given by the end of the sentence. For that reason, if readers cannot immediately determine the referent of a particular word, then they can expect to be told the referent or given enough information to infer it by the end of the sentence. Indeed, readers do use the ends of sentences to process inconsistencies that they cannot resolve within the sentence (Carpenter & Daneman, 1980). The second property is that the end of a sentence unambiguously signals the end of one thought and the beginning of a new one. It can be contrasted with weaker cues that signal within-sentence clause boundaries such as commas, relative pronouns, and conjunctions that can signal other things besides the end of a clause. Since ends of sentences are unambiguous, they have the same role across sentences, and they may be processed more uniformly than the cues to within-sentence clause boundaries.

There is ample empirical support for the integrative processing at the ends of sentences. Previous eye fixation studies show that when a lexically based inference must be made to relate a new sentence to some previous portion of the text, there is a strong tendency to pause at the lexical item in question and at the end of the sentence that contains it (Just & Carpenter, 1978). Readers were given paragraphs containing pairs of related sentences; the first noun in the second sentence was the agent or instrument of the verb in the first sentence:

(1a) *It was dark and stormy the night the millionaire was murdered.*

(1b) *The killer left no clues for the police to trace.*

In another condition, the integrating inference was less direct:

(2a) *It was dark and stormy the night the millionaire died.*

(2b) *The killer left no clues for the police to trace.*

It took about 500 msec longer to process Sentence 2b than 1b, presumably due to the more difficult inference linking *killer* to *die*. There were two main places in which the readers paused for those 500 msec, indicating the points at which the inference was being computed. One point was on the word *killer*, and the other was on the end of the sentence containing *killer*. Another eye fixation study showed that integration linking a pronoun to its antecedent can occur either when the pronoun is first encountered or at the end of the sentence containing the pronoun (Carpenter & Just, 1977b).

Reading-time studies also have shown that there is extra processing at the end of a sentence. When subjects self-pace the word-by-word or phrase-by-phrase presentation of a text, they tend to pause longer at the word or phrase that terminates a sentence (Aaronson & Scarborough, 1976; Mitchell & Green, 1978). The pause has been attributed to contextual integration processes, similar to the proposed interclause integration process here. Yet another source of evidence for sentence wrap-up processes is that verbatim memory for recently comprehended text declines after a sentence boundary (Jarvella, 1971; Perfetti & Lesgold, 1977). The model attributes the decline to the interference between sentence wrap-up processes and the maintenance of verbatim information in working memory. Finally, another reason to expect sentence wrap-up processes is that we have observed pauses at sentence terminations in an eye fixation study similar to the one reported here (Carpenter & Just, 1981). However, the current study provides stronger evidence because the text was presented all at once.

The results indicate that readers did pause longer on the last word in a sentence. As Table 2 shows, the duration of the sentence wrap-up period is 71 msec.

It is possible that wrap-up episodes could occur at the ends of text units smaller or larger than a sentence. For example, the data of Aaronson and Scarborough (1976) suggest that there are sometimes wrap-up processes at the ends of clauses. It is also possible that wrap-up could occur under some circumstances at the ends of paragraphs. The decision of when and if to do a wrap-up may be controlled by the desired depth of processing. For example, skimming may require wrap-up only at paragraph terminations, whereas understanding a legal contract may require wrap-up at clause boundaries. In fact, the clause-boundary effects obtained by Aaronson and Scarborough are sensitive to the subjects' reading goals. The current analysis indicated that the final word in the paragraph might also be a wrap-up point; it received an additional 157 msec of fixation. However, since readers also pressed a button to indicate that they had finished reading the passage, this parameter might be influenced by their motor response.

Finally, the model included one other factor that involves a physical property of reading, namely the return sweep of the eyes from the right-hand side of one line of text to the left-hand side of the next line. Return sweeps are often inaccurate, landing to the right of the first word in a line. The inaccuracy is often corrected by a leftward saccade to the first word. As a result of this error and recovery, the first word on a line eventually receives an increased gaze duration, relative to a line-medial word. Almost all readers we have studied display the undershoot, but there are considerable individual differences in whether they compensate for it by making an extra leftward fixation to the first word. In fact, some researchers have associated these corrective leftward movements with poor readers (Bayle, 1942). To test for increased gaze durations on line-initial words, an indicator variable coded whether a word was the first one on a line. As Table 2 shows, these words received an additional 30 msec of fixation.

Fit of the Model

To see how well the model accounts for the data, one can informally compare how closely the estimated gaze durations match the observed gaze durations. The display that follows shows the estimated (in italics) and observed (in msec) gaze durations for two sentences from the "Flywheel" passage. The estimated durations can be computed by an appropriate combination of the weights given in Table 2. These estimates take into account the processes of encoding, lexical access, case role assignment, sentence wrap-up, and the beginning of the line effect; they do not include integration time for text roles since there is no way to distribute this time on a word-by-word basis. In spite of this, the match is satisfactory, and as mentioned earlier, the standard error of estimate was 88 msec overall.

```
 169  215 165   295      290   73  196      504    29  482     0   328     431    51
 165  236  75   409      304   75  249      438    75  413    80   338     349    78
...One type of flywheel consists of round sandwiches of fiberglass and rubber providing the

 369       326   308   22  272   253  128  199  69   336    32 41  267     197  70 164 195
 354       318   297   75  378   138   77  239 128   326    87 102 206     209 112 87 127
maximum possible storage of energy when the wheel is confined in a small space as in an

 340       323   182   72       626        276   46 21  346   60   467     519
 465       334   236   77       513        304   75 102  289   75   361     319
automobile. Another type, the "superflywheel," consists of a series of rimless spokes...
```

Table 3 presents an analogous comparison from the sector-by-sector analysis; this includes integration time. Again, the estimates from the model match the observed data quite well. The standard error of estimate was 234 msec overall.

Another way to evaluate the goodness of fit is to compare the regression results to those of another model that lacks most of the theoretically interesting independent variables and contains only the variable that codes the number of syllables. For the word-by-word analysis, this rudimentary model produces an R^2 of .46, compared to .72 for the complete model. For the sector-by-sector analysis, the rudimentary model accounts for a large portion of the variance between the gaze durations on sectors ($R^2 = .87$). This is not surprising since there is considerable variation in their lengths. The complete sector-by-sector model accounts for 94% of the variance, or 54% of the variance unaccounted for by the reduced model.

The regression equations were also fit to the gaze durations of each of the 14 readers individually. The subjects varied in their reading skill, with self-reported Scholastic Aptitude Test scores ranging from 410 to 660, which were

TABLE 3
Observed and Estimated Gaze Durations (msec) on Each Sector
of the "Flywheel" Passage, According to the
Sector-By-Sector Regression Analysis of the Group Data

Sector	Observed	Estimated
Flywheels are one of the oldest mechanical devices	1,921	1,999
known to man.	478	680
Every internal-combustion engine contains a small flywheel	2,316	2,398
that converts the jerky motion of the pistons into the smooth flow of energy	2,477	2,807
that powers the drive shaft.	1,056	1,264
The greater the mass of a flywheel and the faster it spins,	2,143	2,304
the more energy can be stored in it.	1,270	1,536
But its maximum spinning speed is limited by the strength of the material	2,440	2,553
it is made from.	615	780
If it spins too fast for its mass,	1,414	1,502
any flywheel will fly apart.	1,200	1,304
One type of flywheel consists of round sandwiches of fiberglass and rubber	2,746	3,064
providing the maximum possible storage of energy	1,799	1,870
when the wheel is confined in a small space	1,522	1,448
as in an automobile.	769	718
Another type, the "superflywheel," consists of a series of rimless spokes.	2,938	2,830
This flywheel stores the maximum energy	1,416	1,596
when space is unlimited.	1,289	1,252

correlated with their reading speeds in the experiment, ranging from 186 words per minute to 377 words per minute $r(12) = .54, p < .05$. The mean R^2 of the 14 readers was .36 on the word-by-word analysis and .75 on the sector-by-sector analysis. This indicates substantial noise in each reader's word-by-word data. Some of the regression weights of the readers indicated considerable individual differences with respect to certain processes. For example, 4 of the 14 readers spent no extra time on the last word of a sentence. Another parameter of great variability among readers was the extra time spent on novel words, which ranged from 94 msec to 1,490 msec.

Although the sector-by-sector regression analysis uses an independent variable (the sum of the case role coefficients) that is estimated from the same data, this procedure does not do violence to the results. To estimate the effect of this procedure, the 14 subjects were divided randomly into two subgroups, and the case role coefficients were obtained for each subgroup in a word-by-word analysis. Then these coefficients were aggregated and used as independent variables in a sector-by-sector analysis, such that one subgroup's coefficients were used in the analysis of the other subgroup's sector gaze durations. The results indicated no difference of any importance between the two subanalyses and generally confirmed that using the case role coefficients from the word analysis in the sector analysis was an acceptable procedure.

Some of the variables that were reliable in the word-by-word analysis were not reliable in the sector analysis. For example, sectors that included a line-initial word did not have reliably longer durations, and sectors that included the end of a sentence took 57 msec longer, but the reliability of the effect was marginal ($p < .08$). The sum of the logarithms of the frequencies of the words in a sector did not reliably affect gaze duration on the sector. These differences between the two levels of analysis indicate that some effects that are word specific are not reliable or large enough to be detected when the data are aggregated over groups of words. Nevertheless, some of these effects can be detected at the sector level if the appropriate analysis is done. For example, the reason that the frequency effect was not reliable is that the aggregation of the logarithms smoothes over the differences between infrequent words and frequent words. A regression analysis of the sector data shows a reliable word-frequency effect if the independent variable encodes the number of infrequent words (arbitrarily defined as less than 25 in Kučera & Francis, 1967) occurring for the first time. This latter analysis indicates 82 msec extra spent for each infrequent word and has an R^2 of .94. (Carpenter & Just, 1981, reported a 51-msec effect for this variable.)

Recall Performance

The recall of a given part of a text should depend in part on what happens to the information as it is read. A clause that is thoroughly integrated with the representation of the text should tend to be stored in long-term memory, and therefore should be recalled better. There are two factors that determine how well a clause will be integrated. First, those sectors on which more integration time has been spent, like topics and definitions, should be recalled better. As predicted, the integration parameter for a text role (i.e., the five weights at the bottom of Table 2) reliably affected the probability that a sector would be recalled, $t(271) = 2.01$, $p < .05$. A second factor affecting integration is the number of times an argument of a clause is referred to in the text; each repetition involving that argument may initiate another integration episode that increases its chances of being recalled (Kintsch & van Dijk, 1978). A rough index of this kind of repetition was obtained by counting the number of times the arguments of each sector were repeated in subsequent sectors. The frequency of reference to the arguments did increase the probability of recalling a sector, $t(271) = 5.90$, $p < .01$.

The recall measure just reported was the proportion of the 14 subjects that recalled each of the 274 sectors. Two independent judges assigned 100%, 50%, or 0% credit for the recall of each sector, depending on whether it had been fully, partially, or not at all correctly recalled. Synonyms and paraphrases were given full credit if they were close to the gist of the sector. If only a part of a sector was recalled, then partial credit was given. The two judges were in full agreement about 80% of the time and in partial agreement (i.e., within 50%) on 94% of the judgments; disagreements were resolved by a third judge.

Text units that were higher in the text grammar were generally recalled better, $F(4, 269) = 5.67$, $p < .01$. There was a monotonic increase in the probability of recall as a function of a sector's level in the text grammar. Recall probabilities were lowest for details (.31), then increased for expansions (.34), subtopics (.39), definitions/causes/consequences (.41), and topics (.53). This replicates previous text-role effects observed with other types of texts (Meyer, 1975; Thorndyke, 1977). The model partially explains this result in terms of the processes that occur during comprehension. In addition, retrieval processes may play a role in this effect. For example, there may be many retrieval paths from less-important concepts that lead to topics, but not vice versa. Also, a complete model of recall will have to consider how the recall of particular facts is affected by the reader's previous knowledge. Although the passages were generally unfamiliar, particular facts surely differed in their familiarity, and this could have a powerful effect on recall (Spilich, Vesonder, Chiesi, & Voss, 1979). Finally, there could be response output effects in recall. In summary, the results show that a model of the comprehension processes can be used to partially account for recall performance. To totally explain recall will require a precise account of the role of prior long-term knowledge and the role of retrieval and reconstruction processes in recall.

Discussion

This section discusses three aspects of the theory: first, the implications of the immediacy assumption for language processing in general; second, how variation in reading modes can be handled by the theory; and third, the relation of the current theory to other theories of reading.

The Immediacy Assumption

The model's ability to account for fixation durations in terms of the processes that operate on words provides some validation for the immediacy and eye–mind assumptions. Readers interpret a word while they are fixating it, and they continue to fixate it until they have processed it as far as they can. As mentioned before, this kind of processing eliminates the difficulties caused by the potential ambiguity in language. It avoids the memory load and computational explosion that would result if a reader kept track of several possible meanings, case roles, and referents for each word and computed the final interpretation at the end of a clause or a sentence. This architectural feature also allows a limited-capacity processor to operate on a large semantic network without being bombarded by irrelevant associations. After a single interpretation has been selected, the activation of the unselected meanings can be dampened to their base levels so that they will not activate their semantic associates any further. This minimizes the chances that the reader will be conceptually driven in many directions at the same time.

The cost of this kind of processing is fairly low because the early decisions usually are correct. This is accomplished by taking a large amount of information into account in reaching a decision. The processes have specific heuristics to combine semantic, syntactic, and discourse information. Equally important, the processes operate on a data base that is strongly biased in favor of the common uses of words and phrases, but one that also reflects the effects of local context. The cost is also low because the reader can recover from errors. It would be devastating if there were no way to modify an incorrect interpretation at some later point. However, there are error-recovery heuristics that seem fairly efficient, although the precise mechanisms are only now being explored (Carpenter & Daneman, 1980).

The fact that a reader's heuristics for interpreting the text are good explains why the garden path phenomenon is not the predominant experience in comprehension; it only happens occasionally. Perhaps the most common, everyday garden path experiences occur when reading newspaper headlines, for example, "Carter Views Discussed" and "Judge Admits Two Reporters." The incorrect initial interpretations occur because headlines are stripped of the syntactic and contextual cues that guide the processing of normal text. Similarly, many jokes and puns explicitly rely on the contrast between two interpretations of an ambiguous word or phrase (Schultz & Horibe, 1974). Even garden path sentences sometimes seem funny. The humor in all of these cases resides in the incongruity between the initial interpretation and the ultimate one. Garden path sentences are also infrequent because writers usually try to avoid ambiguities that might encourage or allow incorrect interpretations. These kinds of sentences are useful tools for studying comprehension because they indicate where the usual comprehension strategies fail. But the fact that they are not frequent indicates that a reader's heuristics usually are sufficient.

Variation in Reading

There is no single mode of reading. Reading varies as a function of who is reading, what they are reading, and why they are reading it. The proposed model for the reading of scientific texts in this task is only one point in a multidimensional space of reading models. However, such variation can be accommodated within the framework presented in this article.

The reader's goals are perhaps the most important determinant of the reading process. A reader who skims a passage for the main point reads differently than someone who is trying to memorize a passage or another person who is reading for entertainment. Goals can be represented in several aspects of the theory, but the main way is to require that each goal is satisfied or at least attempted before proceeding on to the next word, clause, or sentence. These goals correspond to the major products of each stage of comprehension and to the specific demands of a particular task. For example, an obvious goal associated with lexical access might be that one interpretation is selected. An added goal associated with the task of memorizing a passage may require rehearsing phrases or constructing explicit mnemonics before going on to the next phrase or sentence. But goals can be deleted as well as added. A speed-reader may well eliminate goals for syntactic coherence because the strategy of skipping over many words will destroy the syntax. Variations in goals can be detected with the current theory and analytic techniques. For example, it is possible to determine how much time is spent integrating different kinds of text roles in different tasks. When readers anticipate a recognition comprehension test, rather than recall, they spend less time integrating details (Carpenter & Just, 1981).

Reading also depends on the text, the topic, and the reader's familiarity with both. A well-written paragraph on a familiar topic will be easier to process at all stages of comprehension. The lexical items will be easier to encode, the concepts will be more easily accessed, the case and text roles will be easier to infer, and the interrelations will be easier to represent. All of these dimensions of variation can be accommodated, measured, and evaluated within the theoretical framework. Moreover, any adequate theory must be sufficiently flexible to encompass such variation.

Even reading of the same text under the same circumstances will vary from person to person. There are several plausible sources of individual differences in the theory. One interesting source is the operational capacity of the working memory. Readers with a large working memory should be able to retain more of the text in the memory while processing new text, so their integration of the information may be more thorough. A promising first exploration of this hypothesis has found a very strong correlation between working memory capacity and various aspects of reading comprehension tests (Daneman & Carpenter, 1980). By contrast, traditional measures of passive short-term memory capacity do not have a strong correlation with reading comprehension. Operational capacity may depend on the automaticity of basic reading processes such as encoding and lexical access. Poor readers may devote more time and attention to these processes (Hunt, Lunneborg, & Lewis, 1975; Perfetti & Lesgold, 1977) and consequently have less capacity for maintaining previous information and integrating the new information (Case, 1978).

Theories of Reading

Previous theories of reading have varied in their choice of dependent measures, the levels of information represented in the theory, and the implementation of top-down effects. It is useful to consider how the current theory compares to these alternative proposals along these three dimensions.

One important feature of the current theory is its attempt to account for reading time on individual words, clauses, and sentences. This approach can be distinguished from research that is more centrally concerned with recall, question answering, and summarizing (e.g., Rumelhart, 1977b). The dependent measure is not an incidental aspect of a theory; it has important implications for which issues the theory addresses. The present focus on processing time has resulted in a theory that accounts for the moment-by-moment, real-time characteristics of reading. By contrast, the theory pays less attention to retrieval and reconstruction, two later-occurring processes that are important to an account of summarization.

Another feature of the theory is the attempt to account for performance at several levels of processing. Previous theories have tended to neglect certain stages. For example, the reading models of LaBerge and Samuels (1974) and Gough (1972) focus on the word-encoding processes, whereas the model of Kintsch and van Dijk (1978) focuses on integration. This is not to say that these models do not acknowledge other aspects of processing, but simply that they describe detailed mechanisms for one aspect of reading and no comparable mechanisms for other stages. The current theory has attempted to span the stages of reading by describing mechanisms for the word-encoding and lexical access stages, as well as the parsing and text integration stages. Moreover, it has attempted to describe some formal similarities by placing them all within the architecture of a production system.

A final but important distinction among reading theories is the manner in which they accommodate top-down and bottom-up factors in reading (see

Rumelhart, 1977a). Some reading theories, particularly those addressed to word encoding, omit mechanisms to account for top-down or contextual effects (e.g., Gough, 1972). At the other extreme, there have been some theories that appear to place a major burden of comprehension on contextual effects. Some of these are recent schema-based theories of language comprehension (Schank & Abelson, 1977). Others are the older top-down models, developed out of analysis-by-synthesis theory; these models suggested that readers form explicit predictions about the next word and fixate it merely to confirm the hypothesis (Goodman & Niles, 1970). The current model falls somewhere between the extremes. It allows for contextual influences and for the interaction among comprehension processes. Knowledge about a topic, syntactic constraints, and semantic associates can all play a role in activating and selecting the appropriate concepts. However, the printed words themselves are usually the best information source that the reader has, and they can seldom be entirely replaced by guesses from the preceding context. Thus the top-down processes can influence the bottom-up ones, but their role is to participate in selecting interpretations rather than to dominate the bottom-up processes. Finally, the production system architecture permits a degree of coordination among different processes, so that any stage can be influenced by any cotemporaneously or previously executed stage.

Future Directions

The current theory suggests two major avenues of reading research. One direction is to construct computer simulations that are driven by reading performance data. The postulated human heuristics can be implemented in a computer program to examine the resulting complex interactions among knowledge sources. Reading-time data may be sufficiently constraining to select among various alternative heuristics. We are currently implementing aspects of the mode presented here as a production system in collaboration with a colleague, Robert Thibadeau, to develop greater specific and more stringent tests of the model.

Although the production system framework is not essential for the interpretation of the empirical results in the present study, it has other benefits. First, it provides an architecture that can accommodate the flexibility and interaction that have been observed among the processes in reading and still express typical or canonical processing. Even though this theoretical framework is minimally specified, it seems sensible to start at this point and allow successive generations of data to constrain it, as Newell (1980) suggests. Finally, when expressed as a computer simulation, the model retains correspondence to postulated human processes and structures. Collections of serial productions may correspond to heuristic processes employed in comprehension. The firing of parallel productions can be identified with spreading activation in long-term memory. The production system's working memory can be identified with the reader's working memory.

Thus, the production system can be viewed as a useful theoretical vehicle, or excess baggage, depending on one's intended destination.

The second avenue includes further empirical research on the real-time characteristics of reading. Eye movement and reading-time methodologies can reveal reading characteristics with other types of texts, tasks, and readers. The useful property of these methodologies is that they can measure reading time on successive units of text. One method is to present the successive words of a sentence one at a time, allowing the reader to control the interword interval (Aaronson & Scarborough, 1976). This procedure is only one end of a continuum defined by what units are presented. Rather than single words, they could be phrases, clauses, sentences, or entire passages (Carpenter & Just, 1977a; Mitchell & Green, 1978; Kieras, 1979). In this way, it will be possible to gain more information about human performance characteristics and then use these data to develop a more complete theory of reading.

Acknowledgments

The research was supported in part by Grant G-79-0119 from the National Institute of Education and Grant MH-29617 from the National Institute of Mental Health. We thank Allen Newell and Robert Thibadeau for their very helpful discussions. The order of authorship was decided by the toss of a coin.

Notes

[1] It might be argued that the variables coding the text-grammatical roles ought to be independent of the number of content words. One might argue that a definition, for example, takes a fixed amount of time to integrate, regardless of the number of content words it contains. Although the model predicts a length-sensitive duration, the analysis can also be done with five simple indicator variables to encode the five levels of the grammar. This analysis produced a fit that was almost as good, ($R^2 = .93$). The weights (assuming a zero intercept) were 250, 341, 257, 214, and 118 msec for the five categories, from topics to details. Although this alternative is not ruled out by the data, we will continue to retain the view that integration time depends on the number of content words involved.

References

Aaronson D., & Scarborough, H.S. (1976). Performance theories for sentence coding: Some quantitative evidence. *Journal of Experimental Psychology: Human Perception and Performance, 2*, 56–70.

Anderson, J.R. (1976). *Language, memory, and thought*. Hillsdale, NJ: Erlbaum.

Baron, J. (1977). Mechanisms for pronouncing printed words: Use and acquisition. In D. LaBerge & S.J. Samuels (Eds.), *Basic processes in reading: Perception and comprehension*. Hillsdale, NJ: Erlbaum.

Bayle, E. (1942). The nature and causes of regressive movements in reading. *Journal of Experimental Education, 11*, 16–36.

Bever, T.G. (1970). The cognitive basis for linguistic structures. In J.R. Hayes (Ed.), *Cognition and the development of language*. New York: Wiley.

Bouma H., & deVoogd, A.H. (1974). On the control of eye saccades in reading. *Vision Research, 14*, 273–284.

Bransford, J.D., & Johnson, M.K. (1973). Considerations of some problems of comprehension. In W.G. Chase (Ed.), *Visual information processing*. New York: Academic Press.

Breitmeyer, B.G. (1980). Unmasking visual masking: A look at the "why" behind the veil of "how." *Psychological Review, 87*, 52–69.

Buswell, G.T. (1937). *How adults read* (Supplementary Educational Monograph 45). Chicago: University of Chicago Press.

Carpenter, P.A., & Daneman, M. (1980). *Lexical access and error recovery in reading: A model based on eye fixations*. Unpublished manuscript, Carnegie Mellon University, Pittsburgh, PA.

Carpenter, P.A., & Just, M.A. (1977a). Integrative processes in comprehension. In D. LaBerge & S.J. Samuels (Eds.), *Basic processes in reading: Perception and comprehension*. Hillsdale, NJ: Erlbaum.

Carpenter, P.A., & Just, M.A. (1977b). Reading comprehension as eyes see it. In M.A. Just & P.A. Carpenter (Eds.), *Cognitive processes in comprehension*. Hillsdale, NJ: Erlbaum.

Carpenter, P.A., & Just, M.A. (1981). Cognitive processes in reading: Models based on readers' eye fixations. In A.M. Lesgold & C.A. Perfetti (Eds.), *Interactive processes in reading*. Hillsdale, NJ: Erlbaum.

Case, R. (1978). Intellectual development from birth to adulthood: A neo-Piagetian interpretation. In R. Siegler (Ed.), *Children's thinking: What develops?* Hillsdale, NJ: Erlbaum.

Chafe, W.L. (1970). *Meaning and the structure of language*. Chicago: University of Chicago Press.

Charniak, E. (1972). *Toward a model of children's story comprehension* (Tech. Rep. No. 266). Cambridge, MA: MIT Artificial Intelligence Laboratory.

Clark, H.H., & Clark, E.V. (1977). *Psychology and language*. New York: Harcourt Brace Jovanovich.

Collins, A.M., & Loftus, E.F. (1975). A spreading activation theory of semantic processing. *Psychological Review, 82*, 407–428.

Daneman, M., & Carpenter, P.A. (1980). Individual differences in working memory and reading. *Journal of Verbal Learning and Verbal Behavior, 19*, 450–466.

Dearborn, W. (1906). *The psychology of reading* (Columbia University contributions to philosophy and psychology). New York: Science Press.

Dixon, P., & Rothkopf, E.Z. (1979). Word repetition, lexical access, and the process of searching words and sentences. *Journal of Verbal Learning and Verbal Behavior, 18*, 629–644.

Fillmore, C.J. (1968). The case for case. In E. Bach & R.T. Harms (Eds.), *Universals in linguistic theory*. New York: Holt, Rinehart & Winston.

Flesch, R.F. (1951). *How to test readability*. New York: Harper.

Fraser, C., Bellugi, U., & Brown, R. (1963). Control of grammar in imitation, comprehension, and production. *Journal of Verbal Learning and Verbal Behavior, 2*, 121–135.

Frazier, L., & Fodor, J. (1978). The sausage machine: A new two-stage parsing model. *Cognition, 6*, 291–325.

Glanzer, M., & Ehrenreich, S.L. (1979). Structure and search for the internal lexicon. *Journal of Verbal Learning and Verbal Behavior, 18*, 381–398.

Goodman, K.S., & Niles, O.S. (1970). *Reading process and program*. Urbana, IL: National Council of Teachers of English.

Gough, P.B. (1972). One second of reading. In J.F. Kavanagh & I.G. Mattingly (Eds.), *Language by eye and ear*. Cambridge, MA: MIT Press.

Haviland, S.E., & Clark, H.H. (1974). What's new? Acquiring new information as a process in comprehension. *Journal of Verbal Learning and Verbal Behavior, 13*, 512–521.

Hitch, G.J. (1978). The role of short-term working memory in mental arithmetic. *Cognitive Psychology, 10*, 302–323.

Hockett, C.F. (1958). *A course in modern linguistics*. New York: Macmillan.

Hunt, E., Lunneborg, C., & Lewis, J. (1975). What does it mean to be high verbal? *Cognitive Psychology, 2*, 194–227.

Jarvella, R.J. (1971). Syntactic processing of connected speech. *Journal of Verbal Learning and Verbal Behavior, 10*, 409–416.

Judd, C.H., & Buswell, G.T. (1922). *Silent reading: A study of the various types* (Supplementary Educational Monograph 23). Chicago: University of Chicago Press.

Just, M.A., & Carpenter, P.A. (1976). Eye fixations and cognitive processes. *Cognitive Psychology, 8*, 441–480.

Just, M.A., & Carpenter, P.A. (1978). Inference processes during reading: Reflections from eye fixations. In J.W. Senders, D.F. Fisher, & R.A. Monty (Eds.), *Eye movements and the higher psychological functions*. Hillsdale, NJ: Erlbaum.

Kieras, D.E. (1979). *Modelling reading times in different reading tasks with a simulation model of comprehension* (Tech. Rep. No. 2). Tucson: University of Arizona.

Kintsch, W., & van Dijk, T.A. (1978). Toward a model of text comprehension and production. *Psychological Review, 85*, 363–394.

Kleiman, G.M. (1975). Speech recoding in reading. *Journal of Verbal Learning and Verbal Behavior, 14*, 323–339.

Kučera H., & Francis, W.N. (1967). *Computational analysis of present-day American English*. Providence, RI: Brown University Press.

LaBerge, D., & Samuels, S.J. (1974). Toward a theory of automatic information processing in reading. *Cognitive Psychology, 6*, 293–323.

Levy, B.A. (1981). Interactive processes during reading. In A.M. Lesgold & C.A. Perfetti (Eds.), *Interactive processes in reading*. Hillsdale, NJ: Erlbaum.

Mandler, J.M., & Johnson, N.S. (1977). Remembrance of things parsed: Story structure and recall. *Cognitive Psychology, 9*, 111–151.

McConkie, G.W., & Rayner, K. (1975). The span of the effective stimulus during a fixation in reading. *Perception & Psychophysics, 17*, 578–586.

McConkie, G.W., & Rayner, K. (1976). Asymmetry of the perceptual span in reading. *Bulletin of the Psychonomic Society, 8*, 365–368.

Mewhort, D., & Beal, A.L. (1977). Mechanisms of word identification. *Journal of Experimental Psychology: Human Perception and Performance, 3*, 629–640.

Meyer, B. (1975). *The organization of prose and its effect on recall*. Amsterdam: North-Holland.

Meyer, B., & McConkie, G.W. (1973). What is recalled after hearing a passage? *Journal of Educational Psychology, 65*, 109–117.

Mitchell, D.C., & Green, D.W. (1978). The effects of context and content on immediate processing in reading. *Quarterly Journal of Experimental Psychology, 30*, 609–636.

Morton, J. (1969). Interaction of information in word recognition. *Psychological Review, 76*, 165–178.

Newell, A. (1973). Production systems: Models of control structures. In W.G. Chase (Ed.), *Visual information processing*. New York: Academic Press.

Newell, A. (1980). Harpy, production systems and human cognition. In R. Cole (Ed.), *Perception and production of fluent speech*. Hillsdale. NJ: Erlbaum.

Perfetti, C.A., & Lesgold, A.M. (1977). Discourse comprehension and sources of individual differences. In M.A. Just & P.A. Carpenter (Eds.), *Cognitive processes in comprehension*. Hillsdale, NJ: Erlbaum.

Rayner, K. (1978). Eye movements in reading and information processing. *Psychological Bulletin, 85*, 618–660.

Reitman, J.S. (1974). Without surreptitious rehearsal, information in short-term memory decays. *Journal of Verbal Learning and Verbal Behavior, 13*, 365–377.

Rieger, C.J. (1979). Five aspects of a full-scale story comprehension model. In N.V. Findler (Ed.), *Associative networks*. New York: Academic Press.

Robinson, D.A. (1972). Eye movements evoked by collicular stimulation in the alert monkey. *Vision Research, 12*, 1795–1808.

Rumelhart, D.E. (1977a). Toward an interactive model of reading. In S. Dornic (Ed.), *Attention and performance VI*. Hillsdale, NJ: Erlbaum.

Rumelhart, D.E. (1977b). Understanding and summarizing brief stories. In D. LaBerge & S.J. Samuels (Eds.), *Basic processes in reading: Perception and comprehension*. Hillsdale, NJ: Erlbaum.

Scarborough, D.L., Cortese, C., & Scarborough, H.S. (1977). Frequency and repetition effects in lexical memory. *Journal of Experimental Psychology: Human Perception and Performance, 3*, 1–17.

Schank, R.C. (1972). Conceptual dependency: A theory of natural language understanding. *Cognitive Psychology, 3*, 552–631.

Schank, R.C., & Abelson, R.P. (1977). *Scripts, plans, goals, and understanding: An inquiry into human knowledge structures*. Hillsdale, NJ: Erlbaum.

Schiepers, C. (1980). Response latency and accuracy in visual word recognition. *Perception & Psychophysics, 27*, 71–81.

Shultz, T., & Horibe, F. (1974). Development of the appreciation of verbal jokes. *Developmental Psychology, 10*, 13–20.

Spilich, G.J., Vesonder, G.T., Chiesi, H.L., & Voss, J.F. (1979). Text processing of domain-related information for individuals with high and low domain knowledge. *Journal of Verbal Learning and Verbal Behavior, 18*, 275–290.

Spoehr, K.T., & Smith, E. (1973). The role of syllables in perceptual processing. *Cognitive Psychology, 5*, 71–89.

Swinney, D.A. (1979). Lexical access during sentence comprehension: (Re)consideration of context effects. *Journal of Verbal Learning and Verbal Behavior, 18*, 645–659.

Taft, M. (1979). Recognition of affixed words and the word frequency effect. *Memory & Cognition, 7,* 263–272.

Tanenhaus, M.K., Leiman, J.M., & Seidenberg, M.S. (1979). Evidence for multiple stages in the processing of ambiguous words in syntactic contexts. *Journal of Verbal Learning and Verbal Behavior, 18*, 427–440.

Taylor, S.E. (1962). *An evaluation of forty-one trainees who had recently completed the "reading dynamics" program* (11th yearbook of the National Reading Conference, pp. 41–55).

Thorndyke, P.W. (1977). Cognitive structures in comprehension and memory of narrative discourse. *Cognitive Psychology, 9*, 77–110.

Vesonder, G.T. (1979). *The role of knowledge in the processing of experimental reports.* Unpublished doctoral dissertation, University of Pittsburgh, Pittsburgh, PA.

Westheimer, G.H. (1954). Eye movement responses to a horizontally moving visual stimulus. *Archives of Ophthalmology, 52,* 932–943.

44

Modeling the Connections Between Word Recognition and Reading

Marilyn Jager Adams

Skillful reading is the product of an amazingly complex array of knowledge and abilities. How is it, then, that so much of the scientific literature on reading is centered on word recognition? One answer is that the field has lacked the scientific sophistication to go much beyond words; another, however, is that until we truly began to understand the relation of words to the rest of the reading process, we were hard pressed to move on.

True, the ability to recognize words is but a tiny component of the larger literacy challenge. Also true, the knowledge and activities involved in visually recognizing individual printed words are useless in and of themselves. And equally true, word recognition is only valuable and, in a strong sense, only possible as it is received and guided by the larger activities of language comprehension and thought.

On the other hand, unless the processes involved in individual-word recognition operate properly, nothing else in the system can either. The purpose of this article is to explore the relationship between word recognition and literacy. It is, moreover, to show how scientific efforts to understand these relationships have brought us ever closer to a larger understanding of the nature of reading.

The Operation of the Reading System

To clarify the relation of word-recognition processes to the rest of the system, an analogy might be useful. Let's say that the system that supports our ability to read is a car. Within this analogy, print is gas. The engine and the mechanics of the car are the perceptual and conceptual machinery that make the system run.

It is obvious that print is essential to reading—no gas, no driving. But print alone is not enough to make the reading car go. Reading cannot begin without

From Ruddell, R.B., Ruddell, M.R., & Singer, H. (Eds.), *Theoretical Models and Processes of Reading* (4th ed., pp. 838–863). Copyright © 1994 by the International Reading Association.

the spark of visual recognition. And just as cars are designed with more than one spark plug, so the reading system is designed to take in the physically separable pieces of print not one at a time, but in intricately coordinated concert. Like the crankshaft in a car, the reader's learned associations among letters and words keep the reading car rolling despite problems that might arise: The occasional letter that is misperceived or even illegible does not stop the reading machine any more than the occasional misfire of a spark plug or impurity in the gas will stop a car. Even so, the engine is only indirectly responsible for making the car go. The engine turns gas into kinetic energy, and the energy turns the wheels. Similarly, the perceptual system turns print to mental energy, such that it can be understood.

Obviously a car *couldn't* be driven without gas, without spark plugs, without a crankshaft, and without a differential and wheels. But it is also important to recognize that a car *wouldn't* be driven if it didn't run well. Imagine that you had to push a button every time you wanted a spark plug to fire. Imagine that the car would only go a couple of miles per hour or that it stalled unpredictably every few moments. You would very likely choose not to drive at all. These problems are analogous to the difficulties that must befall the reader who cannot transform print to language and meaning with reasonable speed and ease. In particular, if a child's word-recognition skills are sufficiently poor, the time and effort involved in reading may well overwhelm its hoped-for rewards. If so, the child is likely to choose not to read at all. And here is the tragedy: To the extent that children do not read, they forfeit the practice and experience needed to make reading easier and more profitable. To the extent that children do not read, they can only continue to have difficulty reading, to fall farther and farther behind their peers in both reading and the conceptual returns it offers (see, especially, Stanovich, 1986, 1993).

Clearly, without gas and without an engine and mechanics in adequate working order, the car will not go. Suppose, however, that your reading system has plenty of print to consume and a fine mechanical system. Are you on your way? No. First, you have to want to go somewhere, and you have to have some idea of how to get there. As you travel, you must monitor and control your path. Periodically, you must assess your whereabouts and progress with respect to your final destination. At the same time, you must attend to the local details of the road and control your car through them. Indeed, the amount of active attention you will have to devote to your immediate progress will necessarily depend on such variables as the navigability of the route—how far you can see ahead and whether the way is bumpy, winding, congested, or unpredictable—and its familiarity.

Similarly, if texts are difficult in wording or structure or unfamiliar in concept, they require the active attention of the reader. But the more one must direct attention to local difficulties of reading, the less attention one has available to support larger understanding. Only to the extent that the ability to recognize and capture the meaning of print is rapid, effortless, and automatic can the reader have available the cognitive energy and resources on which true comprehension depends. Only to that extent can the reader have the perspective and capacity to reflect upon the journey.

As it happens, *everybody* wants to go somewhere. Everybody wants the stimulation of new challenges and the sense of growth and accomplishment that comes with conquering them. Understandably, if reading seems tedious or unproductive, children will seek other ways to spend their time; indeed, they may avoid it altogether. In a recent survey of fourth graders, 40% of the poor readers claimed that they would rather clean their rooms than read. One child stated, "I'd rather clean the mold around the bathtub than read" (Juel, 1988).

Fortunately, for purposes of schooling, most young children will go almost anywhere they are led—so long as they are neither frustrated nor bored. But even as this eases our task as reading educators, it greatly increases our responsibility. It is up to us to lead our children in the right direction.

And it is here that the car analogy breaks down. So apt for describing the operation of the system, it is wholly inappropriate for modeling its acquisition. Building a car is a modular, hierarchical activity. From the bottom up, the discrete and countable parts of the car's subsystems are fastened together; then, one by one, from the inside out and only as each is completed, the subsystems are connected to one another. In contrast, the parts of the reading system are not discrete. We cannot proceed by completing each one in isolation and then fastening it to another. Rather, the parts of the reading system must grow together. They must grow to and from one another.

For the connections and even the connected parts to develop properly, they must be linked in the very course of their acquisition. And this dependency works in both directions. We cannot properly develop the higher-order processes without due attention to the lower; nor can we focus on the lower-order processes without constantly clarifying and exercising their connections to the higher.

The great challenge for reading educators, therefore, is one of understanding the parts of the system and their interrelations. In this article, I will focus on current models of skillful readers. What special kinds of knowledge do skillful readers have? How is it organized and what are the processes that bring it into play? And how does our evolving understanding of skillful readers help us understand the learning process and its difficulties?

What Do Skillful Readers Do?

Perhaps the single most striking characteristic of skillful readers is the speed and effortlessness with which they breeze through text. The rate at which they read typically exceeds five words per second (Rayner & Pollatsek, 1987). Indeed, they appear to recognize whole words at a glance, gleaning their appropriate meaning at once (Cattell, 1885). How do they do so?

Some Questions

Do skillful readers, in fact, recognize words as wholes? In recognizing an individual word, do readers depend on its overall pattern or shape rather than any closer analysis of the letters within it? If so, then doesn't it seem counterproductive to train children to focus on the letter-by-letter spellings of words?

Do skillful readers access the *meaning* of a word directly from seeing it? If so, then doesn't it seem counterproductive to teach children to sound words out?

Do skillful readers use context to anticipate upcoming words so as to reduce the visual detail they need from the text? If so, then in place of rigorous decoding instruction, wouldn't it be better to teach children to use context together with such minimal distinguishing cues of words as first letters and overall length?

Do skillful readers use context to anticipate the words they will see, such that their comprehension consists as much of confirming as of interpreting their meanings? If so, then shouldn't a central focus of beginning reading instruction be one of discouraging children's tendency to pore over the separate words in text and of strengthening their ability to guess the words instead?

Some Answers From Research

Each of these notions has been seriously entertained by researchers at one time or another, and the instructional implications of each are realized prominently in many curricula and classroom practices. Under scrutiny, however, each of these notions has been proved incorrect. More than that, each has been proved incorrect in ways that strongly argue against their instructional translations.

As it turns out, research has long shown that skillful readers are relatively indifferent to the shapes of the words they read (see Woodworth, 1938). Even when the letters that make them up are randomly sampled from a variety of type styles and sizes in both uppercase and lowercase fonts, skillful readers seem to recognize familiar words as wholes (Adams, 1979a). At the same time, skillful readers visually process virtually every letter of every word as they read; this is true whether they are reading isolated words or meaningful, connected text—and, surprise of surprises, it is even true when they are reading cursive handwriting (De Zuniga, Humphreys, & Evett, 1991). To be sure, skillful readers rarely think about individual letters or words as they read. At a conscious level, they may not even notice flagrant misspellings or misprints. But studies show that, conscious or not, letter recognition is integral to the reading process and that even the slightest misprint, tucked deep within a long and highly predictable word, tends to be detected by the visual systems of skillful readers; detection is signaled by readers' eyes flicking back to the misprint to make sure the type was seen correctly (McConkie & Zola, 1981).

Research also negates the notion that skillful readers use contextual guidance to preselect the meanings of the words they will read. Consider the following sentences:

They all rose.

John saw several spiders, roaches, and bugs.

The last word of each of these sentences is, in itself, ambiguous—but would you have noticed if that hadn't been pointed out? Although it feels as though context preselects the appropriate meanings of such words, that is not exactly what happens. Research demonstrates that all the meanings of an ambiguous word are aroused in the course of perception. Very shortly (within tenths of a second) thereafter—too quickly for us to become aware of the confusion—context selects the most appropriate meaning from among the alternatives. (For a review of research in this area, see Seidenberg et al., 1982.)

Finally, research proves that skillful readers habitually translate spellings to sounds as they read (see Barron, 1981a, 1981b; Patterson & Coltheart, 1987). But why? If visually familiar words do indeed activate their meanings directly for readers—and they do—then of what conceivable value are such phonological translations? The answer to this question has come only through many years of work and many research studies: Such spelling-to-sound translations are vital to both fluent reading and its acquisition. To see why, we must look more deeply into the reading system.

Modeling the Reading System: Four Processors

The purpose of models is to combine findings from many studies into a single, coherent system. Because a usefully detailed model lays bare those spots where assumptions are not supported by research, it is an extremely valuable scientific tool. In particular, where the model's pieces seem to fit in more than one way or not to fit at all, the researcher must conclude that some assumption is awry or that some important consideration has been overlooked. Gradually, through the cyclical process of modeling, assessing, and gathering new data, researchers gain an ever more refined and complete image of the parts of a system and how they must work together.

By developing more comprehensive models of the nature of the reading system and the interrelations of its parts, researchers have strived to understand the reading process as a whole. Anchored in psychological research and built through laboratory studies and simulations, contemporary models of reading are complex. However, it is because they have been developed with such analytic care that their instructional implications carry special weight.

Indeed, because they move beyond the boundaries of our field to exploit advances in logical, mathematical, and computational sciences, recent models appear provocatively capable of mimicking the processes of reading and learning to read. These newer models, alternatively known as connectionist, neural net, or parallel distributed processing (PDP) models, are built on the assumption that learning progresses as the learner comes to respond to the relationships among patterns or events. It is, for example, the overlearned relations among its sides that enables recognition of a triangle, just as it is the overlearned relations among its letters that enables recognition of a word. Similarly, it is the relations among the pitch, timing, and quality of its notes that evoke interest in a piece of music, just as it is the relations among the meanings of its words that give texture and meaning to a sentence. (For a description of the logic and dynamics of these models, see Rumelhart & McClelland, 1986; for an exploration of their pertinence to reading, see Adams, 1990, and Seidenberg & McClelland, 1989; for a discussion of their general importance and potential, see Bereiter, 1991).

The power of these models derives from the fact that they are neither top down nor bottom up in nature. Instead, all relevant processes they include are simultaneously active and interactive; all simultaneously issue and accommodate information to and from one another. The key to these models, in other words, is not the dominance of one set of processes over the others, but the coordination and cooperation of all as shaped by the reader's own prior knowledge and experience.

As adapted to the reading situation, the grand logic of these models is schematized in Figure 1 (see Adams, 1990, for a fuller description and discussion). Within each of the "processors," knowledge is represented by many simpler units that have become linked to, connected with, or associated with one another through experience. The oval labeled *orthographic processor,* for example, represents the reader's knowledge of the visual images of words. Within it, individual letters are represented as interconnected bundles of more elementary visual features, while printed words are represented as interconnected sets of letters. Similarly, the meanings of a familiar word are represented in the meaning processor as bundles of simpler meaning elements, just as its pronunciation is represented in the phonological processor as a complex of elementary speech sounds.

I introduced the term "processors" in quotation marks so as to emphasize that it is mostly for descriptive convenience that the different types have been separated one from another. The associations among pieces of knowledge depend not on the "processor" in which each resides, but on the ways in which they have become interrelated or connected through experience. Indeed, the links among any set of representational units are nothing more than a cumulative record of the ways in which those units have been related to one another in a person's experience. The more frequently a pattern of activity has been brought to mind, the stronger and more complete will be the bonds that hold it together. Ultimately it is these bonds, these interrelations—as they pass excitation and inhibition among the elements that they link together—that are responsible for the fluency of the reader and the seeming coherence of the text.

FIGURE 1
Modeling the Reading System: Four Processors

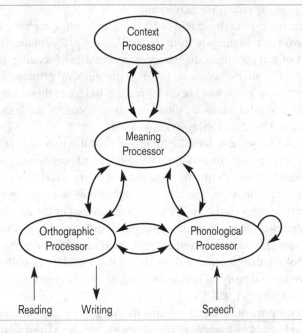

For the skillful reader, as the letters of a word in fixation are recognized, they activate the spelling patterns, pronunciations, and meanings with which they are compatible. At the same time, using its larger knowledge of the text, the context processor swings its own bias among rival candidates so as to maintain the coherence of the message. Meanwhile, as each processor homes in on the word's identity, it relays its progress back to the others such that wherever hypotheses agree among processors, their resolution is speeded and strengthened.

In this way, speed and fluency are seen as an emergent property of the mature reading system. With recognition initiated by the print on the page and hastened by the connectivity both within and between the processors, skillful readers access the spelling, sound, meaning, and contextual role of a familiar word almost automatically and simultaneously. But note: Speed and fluency are not just an outgrowth of skillful reading; they are necessary for its happening. To understand better the knowledge and processes involved, let us examine each of the processors in turn.

The Orthographic Processor

To be fluent and productive, reading depends no more on recognizing words than on astute and flexible consideration of the linguistic and conceptual contexts in which they occur. Indeed, the whole point of the model outlined above is that, in skillful reading, the mind works interactively and in parallel with as many cues and clues as it can recognize as relevant.

Nevertheless, as illustrated in Figure 1, the orthographic processor alone receives information directly from the printed page. By implication, the letters and words of text constitute the basic perceptual data of reading, and this is as it should be. After all, the words on the page are authors' principal means of conveying their message. It will not do for readers to ignore them, nor will guessing suffice: Even skillful adults are unable to guess correctly more than 25% of the time (Gough, Alford, & Holley-Wilcox, 1981).

For skillful readers, meaningful text is read through what is essentially (in English) a left-to-right, line-by-line, word-by-word process. In general, skillful readers visually process virtually each letter of every word they read, translating print to speech as they go. They do so whether they are reading isolated words or meaningful, connected text. They do so regardless of the ease or difficulty of the text, regardless of its semantic, syntactic, or orthographic predictability. There may be no more broadly or diversely replicated set of findings in modern cognitive psychology than those that show that skillful readers visually process nearly every letter and word of text as they read. (For reviews, see Adams, 1990; Patterson & Coltheart, 1987.)

Eye movement research informs us that our eyes do not move smoothly through the lines of text while we read. Instead, they leap from word to word, fixating briefly toward the center of each and then jumping to the next. Occasionally, readers do skip a word, but almost never more than one. Further, the words that are skipped tend rather exclusively to be short function words such as *of*, *a*, and *to*. Many function words and the vast majority of content words receive readers' direct gaze. (For a review, see Just & Carpenter, 1987.)

With normal print, the eye can clearly resolve up to three or so letters to the left of its fixation point and about twice that many to the right during each fixation. With these letters as its basic data, the system goes to work. To see how it proceeds, let us consider two examples. First, suppose the reader's eye lands on the word *the*. Because *the* is a frequently occurring and familiar word, all of its letters should be strongly interconnected within the reader's orthographic memory. As the reader looks at the word, the units corresponding to each of the letters receive visual stimulation from the page. Because the units are so strongly interconnected in the reader's memory, each will pass stimulation to the others, causing all to be recognized nearly at once and to hang together in the reader's mind as a familiar, cohesive spelling pattern.

Now suppose instead that the eye lands upon the nonword *tqe*. Because this string of letters is so similar to the word *the*, the reader's orthographic memory will attempt to process it in the same way. That is, the *t* and *e* units will pass stimulation to each other; they also will pass stimulation to the *h* unit. This time, however, because the *h* receives no direct visual stimulation, it cannot pass any back. At the same time, because *q* is almost always followed by *u* in English, the *q* unit will pass its stimulation to the unit for the absent *u*. As the directly stimulated letter units send their activation inappropriately around the letter network, they end up hurting rather than helping one another's progress. Eventually the direct visual stimulation from the page will bring each of the presented letters to peak stimulation, and the reader will see the string as printed: *tqe*. However, the perception of each letter will have taken longer and will have gelled independently of the others (McClelland & Rumelhart, 1981).

Through experience, the associative network comes to respond not just to next-door neighbors but also to the larger sequences and patterns of letters that represent whole, familiar words. And eventually, through its overlapping representation of many, many different words, it becomes responsive to common spelling patterns independently of the particular words in which they occur. Ultimately, it is the learned associations between and among individual letters that are responsible for the easy, holistic manner in which skillful readers respond to printed words. It is because of them that familiar words and spelling patterns are easier to read than the sum of their parts.

Yet the interletter associations provide other services that are of equal importance to the reader. These services include processing letter order and breaking words into syllables.

Processing Letter Order. Although the visual system is remarkably efficient at extracting information necessary for letter identification, it is quite sloppy about processing letter order. This is a physical limitation, affecting skillful readers as much as unskilled ones (Estes, 1977). Nevertheless, skillful readers almost never make mistakes in reporting the order of the letters in words they read; poor readers, in contrast, may often do so. Although letter-order difficulties were once taken as symptomatic of a basic perceptual deficit, that explanation has been proven incorrect (Liberman et al., 1971). Such difficulties seem instead to reflect insufficient orthographic learning. Specifically, among skillful readers, knowledge about the likely ordering of a string of letters is captured in the learned associations between them. In the very course of perception, therefore, this knowledge serves to corroborate the sensory system's noisy transmission of letter order. In keeping with this view, good readers rarely err in reporting the order of the letters in either real words or regularly spelled nonwords (such as *bome* or *mave*). Yet when faced with orthographically irregular strings such as *gtsi* or *ynrh*, they make just as many ordering errors as do poor readers—even more if they were expecting to see a regularly spelled string (Adams, 1979b).

There are several ways in which readers can conquer the letter-order problem even without well-developed interletter associations. One is to stick with print that is sufficiently large and spaced out so that no two letters will share the same physical input channel; no doubt this is the underlying reason for our time-honored practice of setting primers in large type. Another is for readers to increase the number or duration of their fixations on each word. In keeping with this, note that prolonged and repeated fixations on words are characteristic of young and disabled readers (Just & Carpenter, 1987). In the long run, however, the only efficient and reliable way around this difficulty is for readers to learn more about likely and unlikely sequences of letters in the words of their language. Eventually, this knowledge will come to compensate for the visual system's inherent difficulty with letter order.

Breaking Words Into Syllables. Struggle as they might, poor readers characteristically block on long, polysyllabic words—even when those words are familiar within their oral vocabulary. In contrast, skillful readers rarely experience such difficulty. As an example, try reading the following: *trypsinogen, anfractuosity, prolegomenous, interfascicular.* Although none of these words may be familiar to you, chances are that your attempts to read them were relatively forthcoming as well as correct, or nearly so. Moreover, if you listened carefully to your reading performance, you may have heard yourself producing them in a manner much closer to syllable by syllable than holistically or letter by letter.

It turns out that skillful readers' ability to read long words depends inseparably on their ability to break the words into syllables (Mewhort & Campbell, 1981), and this is true for familiar as well as unfamiliar words. Laboratory studies prove that skillful readers break words into syllables automatically and in the very course of perceiving their letters. The means by which skillful readers do this are again rooted in their overlearned knowledge about likely and unlikely sequences of letters. More specifically, for any language that is basically alphabetic, strings of speech sounds that can be coarticulated tend to be represented by frequent sequences of letters, while those that cannot, are not. As an example, the spoken sequence /dr____/ is a frequent and pronounceable form in English—as in *drag, dress, drip,* and *drove*—while /dn___/ is not. Consistent with this, the letter sequence *dr___* is 40 times more likely to occur in print than the sequence *dn___* (Mayzner & Tresselt, 1965). Through the learned associations in the reader's letter-recognition network, the letters *d* and *r* will automatically boost each other's perceptibility when seen in print, while the letters *d* and *n* will not.

The importance of this difference is that, although unlikely letter sequences such as *dn* cannot occur within the same syllable, they can and do occur at syllable boundaries (for example, *midnight, baldness, kidnap, Sidney*). As the reader processes such words, the likely combinations of letters promote and attract one another, emerging perceptually as a cohesive spelling pattern. At the same time, however, the unlikely pairs inhibit and repel each other, thus pushing separate syllables apart. As a result, the perceived letters are tightly bound to one another within syllables but somewhat detached at the boundaries between syllables. In this way, polysyllabic words are perceived as sequences of spelling patterns corresponding to syllabic units.

At this point, a word of caution is warranted. The knowledge underlying automatic syllabification skills cannot be directly instilled. To ask children to study unlikely letter pairs would be counterproductive: It would serve to increase the strength of the associations between such letters in memory, which is just the opposite of what is needed. Beyond that, one cannot hope to specify spelling patterns corresponding to syllabic units or their boundaries independent of the larger orthographic context in which they occur. That is, one cannot take any given letter string—say, *par*—and proclaim it to be a syllabic unit. Sometimes it will be (*par-tial*, *par-take*), and sometimes it will not (*part-ly*, *pa-rade*). In syllabifying words, the orthographic processor responds to the relative strengths of the interletter associations (Adams, 1981; Seidenberg, 1987). Using knowledge of simple letter sequences as well as larger letter patterns (for example, *fa-ther* versus *fat-head*), it breaks a word into syllables not at predesignated junctures but at the weakest link between letters. It can do so only to the extent that the reader has acquired a broad and deep knowledge of orthography. Meanwhile, there is much to recommend that oft-used technique of helping children penetrate those troublesome long words by uncovering them syllable by syllable as they read.

How to Help

Helping Beginners. Before leaving this section, it is worth reflecting that all the orthographic processor's magic presumes a deep and ready knowledge of the letterwise spellings of words. Quick, holistic word recognition, comfort with grown-up–sized print, automatic syllabification, morphemic sensitivity—all of these depend on such knowledge. At the same time, research indicates that difficulties at the level of letter and word recognition are the single most pervasive and debilitating cause of reading disability (Perfetti, 1985; Stanovich, 1986; Vellutino, 1991; Vernon, 1971).

Fortunately, theory and research also affirm that human memory is well designed for learning about such relations among letters—but only if it is induced to attend to them in the course of perception. Here, then, is a problem. In general, children seem disposed to view words not as ordered and analyzable strings of letters but holistically, rather like pictures (Byrne, 1992; Masonheimer, Drum, & Ehri, 1984). Indeed, given a good visual memory, children have shown themselves able to recognize several thousand words through this approach (Juel, 1991). But can they learn 50,000? And when they find they cannot, how difficult—cognitively and emotionally—will it be to effect repairs?

Beginning reading is quite difficult for some children. One of the reasons is surely that the knowledge to respond instantly, effortlessly, and accurately to frequent words and spelling patterns involves an impressive amount of perceptual learning. Regardless of intelligence, effort, rearing, or desire, this learning settles in more quickly for some children than for others. There are many ways to support this learning—including writing, spelling, and phonics instruction; patience; encouragement; and lots of beneath–frustration-level reading and rereading. However, research argues firmly that there is no substitute for it.

The Context Processor

The context processor is in charge of constructing a coherent, ongoing interpretation of the text. In particular, it is responsible for priming and selecting word meanings that are appropriate to the text. This is important not just for blatantly ambiguous words (such as *soccer ball* versus *inaugural ball*) but, to a lesser extent, for almost any word.

As an example, consider the word *Wyoming*. People in the United States might consider *Wyoming* to have a unique and stable meaning as a proper noun. Nevertheless, its mention brings very different images to mind in a discussion of presidential campaign strategies and electoral college votes than it does in a discussion of beautiful national parks. In fact, both of these images—and many more besides—are part of the total array of meaning that each of us associates with the word *Wyoming*. We are able to follow discussions of Wyoming with understanding because the context processor selectively emphasizes those aspects of a word's total meaning that are relevant to its ongoing interpretation.

In theory, the context processor works by sending its own stimulation to the meanings that it expects. This extra stimulation boosts the contextually appropriate dimensions of a word's meaning, causing them to dominate the reader's interpretation of the text. Yet even while the context processor facilitates the reader's awareness of appropriate words and meanings, it does not prevent stimulation of inappropriate ones. To use an earlier example, given a sentence such as *John saw several spiders, roaches, and bugs*, people very briefly show signs (but not conscious awareness) of having interpreted the last word to mean both "insects" and "spying devices" (Seidenberg et al., 1982). Alternatively, given a sentence such as *At the farmstand, we got tomatoes, squash, and corn on the ___*, the reader may quite automatically—thanks to the context processor—expect the word *cob*. But if the complete sentence turns out, instead, to read, *At the farmstand, we got tomatoes, squash, and corn on the car*, that expectation would be quickly overridden. And, nearly as quickly, the context processor would also revise the reader's understanding of the situation so it meets the text.

For skillful readers, the role of context is not to displace or supplant the information on the page; it is, instead, to help the reader make the most of that information, as quickly and efficiently as possible. To that end, it is necessarily the author's words that must take precedence. Consistent with this, study after study has shown that context significantly affects the speed or accuracy with which skillful readers perceive familiar words *only* when the experimenter has done something to slow or disrupt the orthographic processing of the word (see, e.g., Stanovich, 1980, 1984).

Provided that a text is not too difficult, beginners, like skillful readers, are naturally attuned to its linguistic and semantic flow as they read. Further, as long as the stories are simple and until the processes involved in visual word recognition are fairly well developed, many readers find that they often can guess the identity of a word as accurately and more easily than they can decode it. For these reasons, it has been found that among young and disabled readers, word-recognition performance is especially sensitive to context and contextually appropriate substitution errors are frequent (see, e.g., Biemiller, 1970; Weber, 1970).

Although such sensitivity to context can only be a good sign, its dominance is a symptom that orthographic processing is proceeding neither quickly nor completely enough to do its job. But, one might ask, is this reason for concern? If the children are grasping the meaning of the text well enough to fill in the blanks, then clearly they are reading thoughtfully and strategically. If so, is there any reason to intervene?

As you ponder these questions, I ask you to add the following consideration. As the purpose of classroom texts shifts from one of learning to read to one of reading to learn, children will increasingly encounter words they do not recognize in contexts that do not help. Very often, however, it will be precisely these unknown words—*isosceles*, *circumference*, *photosynthesis*, *Antarctica*, *equator*—that are most central to the point of the lesson.

Research shows that as children move a little further into the reading process—usually toward the end of first grade or the beginning of second—they often turn what seems disproportionate attention to the individual words on the page. Suddenly, they start reading *there* for *three*, *was* for *saw*, and *from* for *form*; the effort they invest in reading a word seems unrelieved by the most obvious of contextual cues; their misreadings, while graphically related to the print on the page, may often be wholly inappropriate in context; and they may develop a tendency to stare at difficult words without responding at all.

For different children, these tendencies may be more or less pronounced and may persist for longer or shorter periods. Nevertheless, as Downing (1979) explains, these tendencies reflect a necessary and highly functional phase in the acquisition of any complex skill. The only way for the visual system to learn about the spellings of words is by devoting attention to them. As the spellings of more and more words are internalized, decoding will become more and more automatic, and only when it becomes automatic can it properly work in concert, rather than in competition, with contextual processing. Meanwhile, the instructional challenge is not to quash this phase but to help children through it as efficiently, effectively, and supportively as possible. To this end, there may be no better means than encouraging a lot of reading and rereading of interesting and beneath–frustration-level text.

C. The Meaning Processor

The inner workings of the meaning processor appear similar to those of the orthographic processor. In particular, the units in the meaning processor apparently do not correspond to whole, familiar words. Instead, just as the spellings of familiar words are represented in the orthographic processor as interassociated sets of letters, their meanings are represented in the meaning processor as interassociated sets of more primitive meaning elements. It is this piecemeal nature of word meanings that allows us to focus on one aspect or another of a word's full meaning as appropriate in context. In addition, it enables us to acquire the meaning of new words gradually by encountering them in context.

1. Learning New Word Meanings From Context. Suppose that, while reading a story, a child encounters a word that he or she has neither seen nor heard before. As usual, the spelling and pronunciation of this word will be shipped automatically to the meaning processor, but because the word is entirely unfamiliar, it cannot in itself evoke any particular meaning. Instead, when the word reaches the meaning processor, all it will find is the pattern of activation provoked by the context processor. This pattern may be more or less diffuse, depending on how tightly the context has anticipated the unknown word. Nevertheless, when the orthographic pattern meets these activated meaning units, a bond will begin to form between them.

The impact of such an incidental learning experience is expected to be small: Context is rarely pointed enough to predict the precise meaning of a word. On the other hand, it's a start. When the same word is encountered again, it will meet whatever was learned from the prior context plus the meaning set off by the new context. Wherever the meaning units of the old and new contexts overlap, they will become more strongly associated with one another and with the orthographic and phonological representations of the word. Given a number of encounters with this word over a variety of different contexts, the units that are reinforced most often will be those that belong to the meaning of the word itself. In this way, the word may eventually be learned well enough to contribute independently and appropriately to the meaning of a text, if not to allow the child to generate a well-articulated dictionary definition.

Although important, such learning from context is inherently gradual and imprecise. The likelihood that a child will learn the meaning of a word from a single exposure in meaningful context ranges from 5% to 20% (Nagy, Anderson, & Herman, 1987). By implication, the extent of such incidental vocabulary acquisition depends strongly on the amount a child reads. The average fifth grader is estimated to read about 1 million words of text per year: 650,000 out of school and the rest in school (Nagy, Herman, & Anderson, 1985). Of these words, roughly 16,000 to 24,000 will be unknown (Anderson & Freebody, 1983). Conservatively assuming a 5% chance of learning each, the result is a vocabulary increase of 800 to 1,200 new words each year through reading. Learning from context accordingly accounts for a substantial fraction of the 3,000 new words that children are, on average, expected to master each year (Miller & Gildea, 1987).

This research sheds light on some of the most striking differences observed in children's conceptual growth. The estimates above are based on the average reader. Some children read millions and millions of words of text each year; their vocabularies are expected to be strong. At the same time, others read practically nothing at all outside of school. Over all, Nagy, Anderson, and Herman (1987) estimate that the 90th percentile student reads about *200 times* more text per year than the 10th percentile student does. Learning begets learning. The amount that children read influences not only their vocabulary growth but also the conceptual and linguistic knowledge that enables that growth and makes it useful.

Direct Vocabulary Instruction. Beyond such learning through reading, direct vocabulary instruction has been shown to result in a general increase in both word knowledge and reading comprehension (Stahl & Fairbanks, 1986). To be most effective, such instruction should include a number of examples of the word's usage in context in addition to definitional information. Research has shown that in direct vocabulary instruction as in incidental learning, the number of times children encounter a word is a strong predictor of how well they learn it. But almost as important as the number of encounters is the richness and variety of the contexts in which the word appears. Of particular interest is the finding that through rich and diverse experiences with a word, children appear to gain a special advantage in understanding its connotations or submeanings in specific contexts and in exploiting its extended meaning in text comprehension (McKeown et al., 1985).

Prefixes, Suffixes, and Roots. The direct link between the orthographic and meaning processors also may be responsible for skillful readers' perceptual sensitivity to the roots and affixes of polysyllabic words (see Fowler, Napps, & Feldman, 1985; Manelis & Tharp, 1977; Taft, 1985; Tyler & Nagy, 1987). Moreover, this link prompts the idea that teaching children about derivational morphologies might be a useful step toward both spelling and vocabulary development.

For example, once one sees that *concurrent* consists of "with" (*con-*) plus *current*, the word is no longer a spelling problem; it must have two *r*s as in *current*, and it can't end in *-ant* or it would mean *with a raisin*. Conversely, knowing the meanings of common roots may qualitatively and profitably change one's understanding of other words in their derivational family. Thus, learning that *fid* means "trust" or "faith" may significantly alter and connect one's understanding of words such as *confidence, fidelity, fiduciary*, and *bonafide*; discovering that *path* means "suffering" may alter and connect one's understanding of words such as *sympathy, psychopath*, and *pathologist*. Moreover, a well-developed sensitivity to morphological clues may be useful for inferring the meanings of new words.

All such advantages notwithstanding, research demonstrates that adult readers of English are surprisingly oblivious to the morphological structure of words (Kaye & Sternberg, 1982), and efforts specifically intended to teach children about the derivational morphologies of words have yielded mixed results (Johnson & Baumann, 1984; Otterman, 1955). Although such lessons have been shown to increase children's proficiency with both the spellings and meanings of the words studied, they have produced little increase in their ability to interpret new derivationally complex words.

In the end, it may be that such morphologically based insights never come automatically but only through deliberate search. Perhaps the wordsmith's advantage is principally strategic; he or she has learned to examine each new word for familiar parts and to think about their implications with respect to the word's usage and meaning. If so, then perhaps the objectives of our lessons on derivationally complex words should be rethought. Perhaps instead of teaching children about any particular sets of roots or affixes, our objective should be one of developing children's *awareness* of word structure and their inclination to look for and think about such relations in new words.

As an inspiring example of the promise of this approach, I refer you to a monograph by O'Rourke (1974). As O'Rourke led his students to make a habit of seeking, comparing, contrasting, and categorizing the meanings and spellings of complex words, their measurable vocabulary scores increased quite dramatically. In addition, showing that these lessons had affected not just their knowledge of particular words but also their thinking about them, the children tended to create new words to suit their expressive needs while writing—for example, *jector* (hurler), *tracted* (pulled, hauled), *audict* (someone who likes to hear records), *intraction* (pulling from within), *solarscope* (sun viewer), *phonomatic* (something that makes sounds by itself), *astrometer* (a device that measures stars). While some of these words are endearingly funny, others are soberingly legitimate.

In any case, it also may be wise to recognize that word roots and syllabic units rarely coincide. In terms of syllables, for example, the word *information* may be parsed into *in-for-ma-tion*; in terms of morphemes, it is *in-form-ation*. Research has demonstrated that the spelling patterns to which children are asked to attend during instruction significantly influence the patterns to which they do attend during word recognition (Juel & Roper/Schneider, 1985). Research also indicates that, for purposes of facilitating word recognition, it is familiarity with patterns that occur in a large variety of words that is most helpful (Juel, 1983). Thus, while appreciation of the *form* in *information* might shed light on its deeper meaning, familiarity with the *for* will help a reader read more words. The suggestion is that even when and if the worth of lessons on derivational morphology is firmly demonstrated, such instruction may nevertheless be best postponed until later years of schooling.

In summary, the most important point of this section is that meaningful experiences with words are important to the acquisition of the words' usage and interpretation as well as their orthography. The best way to foster children's visual vocabulary—as well as their larger literacy growth—is to have them read as frequently, broadly, and thoughtfully as possible. It is not merely that such reading results in vocabulary growth but that, more important, it affords children the conceptual and linguistic experience that at once enable that growth and make it worthwhile.

The Phonological Processor

Intuition suggests that visually familiar words can be recognized immediately and directly by sight, with no need for sounding out at any level. Consistent with this, research affirms that skillful readers do not depend on phonological translations for recognizing familiar words (see Spoehr, 1981). On the other hand, skillful readers automatically and rather irrepressibly seem to produce such translations anyway (Perfetti, Bell, & Delaney, 1988; Tannenhaus, Flanigan, & Seidenberg, 1980; VanOrden, 1991). Far from being unnecessary, the phonological loop provides invaluable support to the reader. First, it provides a redundant processing route—a back-up system—for the orthographic processor. Second, it provides critical support for the comprehension process as it effectively increases the reader's running memory for text. Without the added assistance of the phonological processor, even the most skillful readers would find themselves faltering for fluency and comprehension except with the easiest text.

As with the other processors, the phonological processor is seen to contain a complex network of units. The auditory image of any particular word, syllable, or phoneme corresponds to the activation of a particular, interconnected set of those units (McClelland & Elman, 1986). Figure 1 shows how readers' phonological knowledge and processes are related to the rest of the reading system. Note especially how the phonological processor is connected in both directions to the orthographic processor and the meaning processor. The arrow that runs from the orthographic to the phonological processor indicates that, even as the orthographic processor begins to resolve the image of a string of letters, it relays stimulation to corresponding units in the phonological processor. Meanwhile, the activation of a word's pronunciation will, in turn, pass stimulation to its meaning, as symbolized by the arrow running from the phonological to the meaning processor. In this way, the connections through the phonological processor provide a means for identifying words that, although visually unfamiliar, are in the reader's speaking or listening vocabulary. Yet that is only their most immediate and obvious advantage.

To the extent that any word is both orally and visually familiar, this process ensures that the meaning processor will receive activation from *both* the phonological and the orthographic processor. As these contributions support and interact with one another, they serve to ease and speed recognition of the word. Further, as the response of the meaning processor is strengthened and focused, so too is the activation that it passes back to the other processors—and the stronger the feedback, the greater the learning. Thus, the contributions of the phonological processor act to hasten and consolidate the direct connections between all the processors, and that includes the *direct* connections between sight and meaning.

The connections running from the phonological processor back to the orthographic processor are equally important in supporting visual learning. Specifically, where the efforts of the orthographic processor arouse pronounceable responses in the phonological processor, the phonological processor will reciprocally send excitation right back. In this way, the feedback from the phonological processor provokes the orthographic processor to attend to letters that might otherwise be overlooked, even while helping it glue the whole, correctly ordered string together. The prior knowledge and constraints offered by the phonological processor play an indispensable role in helping young readers organize, consolidate, and remember spelling patterns visually.

Finally, note that there is also an arrow running from the meaning processor to the phonological processor in Figure 1. Because of this connection, the activation of a word's meaning will send stimulation to the phonological units corresponding to its pronunciation. The reader's tendency to translate print to speech is thus doubly stimulated, both from the word's spelling and from its meaning. This is one reason that phonological translation of print is so automatic— and beyond that, it completes the circularity and feedback of the system in both directions. It is this circularity and feedback that ultimately underlies the automaticity of the word-recognition system. Because of this circularity, the responses of all the processors speed and support one another wherever they are consistent; wherever they are inconsistent, they are automatically corrected or flagged for special attention.

The phonological processor has two other features that set it apart from the others. First, like the orthographic processor, the phonological processor accepts information from the outside, although the information it accepts is speech. (The orthographic processor remains the only one to receive information directly from the printed page.) Second—and this turns out to be an important asset in reading—the knowledge represented within the phonological processor can be activated at will. We can speak, subvocalize, or otherwise generate speech images whenever we wish.

Phonological Translation and Fluent Word Recognition. As shown in Figure 1 and supported by our intuitions, phonological translation is not always necessary for word recognition. As reflected by the direct connections between the orthographic and meaning processors, visually familiar words can be recognized and understood with no need of phonological translation. Yet a word can map instantly, effortlessly, and accurately from sight to meaning only to the extent that its unique, ordered sequence of letters has been visually learned and overlearned through experience. The problem is that printed words vary enormously in their frequency and, therefore, in their visual familiarity to a reader.

Analyses of the everyday reading matter of adults reveal that the vast majority of print consists of relatively few, very frequently occurring words (Kučera & Francis, 1967). Because each of these words is highly familiar to the skilled reader, each is recognized quickly and easily. However, these oft-repeated words account for but a small fraction of the number of different words readers encounter. The vast majority of distinct words in print are relatively infrequent—occurring less than once in every million words of running text. Because these words are so rarely seen, the reader's visual familiarity with most of them must be relatively weak and incomplete—often too weak and incomplete to support the perceptual speed and automaticity on which comprehension depends.

Word counts of children's reading materials reveal a similar pattern. Fifty percent of the print they are likely to see, in school and out, is accounted for by only 109 different words, 90% by only 5,000 different words (Carroll, Davies, & Richman, 1971). It is reasonable to suppose that not too far into their schooling, most children will be quick to recognize most of these words by sight. But how are they to cope with the tens of thousands of other words they see? It will not do to skip such words or guess at their identities. Although the coherence of a text depends strongly on its frequent words—*it*, *that*, *this*, *and*, *because*, *when*, *while*, and so on—the information in a text depends on its less-frequent words—*doctor*, *fever*, *infection*, *medicine*, *penicillin*, *Alexander Fleming*, *melon*, *mold*, *poison*, *bacteria*, *antibiotic*, *protect*, *germs*, and *disease*, for example. For skillful readers, automatic phonological translations provide a back-up system for recognizing visually less-familiar words. As a consequence of the alphabetic principle, syllables are represented by frequent spelling patterns. For the skillful reader, therefore, even if a word as a whole is not visually familiar, fragments of its spelling most certainly will be. Because of the reader's spelling–sound associations, these spelling patterns will be translated automatically to their phonological equivalents. If the word is in the reader's speaking or listening vocabulary, its pronunciation will in turn evoke its meaning. In this way, even the occasional never-before-seen word may be read and understood with little or no outward sign or feeling of difficulty.

The automaticity of skillful readers' spelling-to-sound translations ensures that those many words of marginal visual familiarity will be recognized with the ease and speed required for fluent reading comprehension. Further, as the phonological translations serve to turn on both the word's meaning and its spelling, each encounter with the word strengthens direct spelling-to-meaning connections.

2. Phonological Translation and Comprehension. As it turns out, the value of automatic phonological translations extends beyond their service to the word-recognition process. Specifically, the language comprehension system is designed to work with whole, cohesive grammatical units—whole phrases or sentences—at once. Whether in listening or reading, the process through which it does so is much the same (Jarvella, 1971; Kleiman, 1975). In either case, the words of a message are presented and perceived one by one. And although they are tentatively interpreted on the fly, they are fully digested only afterward, when the clause or sentence is complete. In mystical deference to this process, speakers drop their pitch and pause at the end of every sentence; by dropping their pitch, they let their listeners know that it's time to interpret, and by pausing, they afford their listeners time to do so. Mimicking this rhythm, skillful readers are found to march their eyes through all the words of a sentence from beginning to end, and when they reach the period, they pause and think (Just & Carpenter, 1987).

Again, it is during these end-of-sentence pauses that listeners or readers actively construct and reflect on their interpretations, that they work out the collective meaning of the chain of words in memory and that meaning's contribution to their overall understanding of the conversation or text. Yet in order for this interpretive process to succeed, the whole clause or sentence must still exist, more or less intact, in the listener's or reader's memory when she or he is ready to work on it. So what does this have to do with phonological translations? A lot. Whereas the visual system is designed for encoding spatial patterns and transitions, the auditory system is designed for remembering ordered temporal patterns of information. Thus, by thinking or speaking the words to themselves, skillful readers effectively extend the longevity and holding capacity of their verbatim memory. Preventing skillful readers from subvocalizing does not impair their ability to interpret single familiar words or simple sentences; on the other hand, it severely disrupts their ability to remember or comprehend long or complex sentences (Baddeley, 1979; Levy, 1977, 1978; Waters, Caplan, & Hildebrandt, 1987). In keeping with this, you may notice that your own tendency to subvocalize becomes more noticeable when you are trying to read sentences that are especially long and difficult.

Even though this particular advantage of phonological translation has nothing to do with word identification per se, it points up one more reason the speed and effortlessness of the word-recognition process is so important. Auditory memory is highly sensitive to the pace with which information arrives (Dempster, 1981). If it takes a child too long to identify successive words, the beginning of the sentence will fade from memory before the end has been registered. Further, where a child is actively engaged in sounding out individual letters and syllables, the phonological processor is necessarily unavailable for retaining the wording of clauses. (For a discussion of the trade-offs between processing and storage demands in the reading situation, see Daneman & Tardif, 1987; Perfetti, 1985.)

Phonological Translations: A Once-Over. In sum, phonological translations are subservient to both reading and learning to read in a number of different ways. Most obviously, the capacity for phonological translations underlies the ability to "sound out" new words. Less obvious but of equal importance, where the sounding out process is reasonably fast and efficient, it serves powerfully to hasten the word's visual acquisition. Moreover, the benefits of this basic ability are no less valuable for mature readers than they are for beginners. In particular, it ensures that those many, many words of known meaning but limited visual familiarity can be recognized with the ease and speed required for reading with fluency and comprehension.

In this vein, it is worth noting that of the thousands upon thousands of different words that a skillful reader is expected to know, the vast majority are encountered very rarely. The person with an average daily diet of print would be lucky to have seen many of these words even once in a whole year's worth of reading. How many of these words would you lose, how many would fade away or blur together, if you depended on the strength and completeness of your visual memory alone? Finally, research shows that long and complex sentences cannot be understood without the mnemonic support gained through phonological translation.

The capacity for rapid, easy phonological translation has sometimes been dismissed as superfluous, optional, or even as a misguided or dysfunctional diversion of effort. Against these notions, insensitivity to the sounds of speech and difficulties in relating them to letters and spellings are found to be the single most frequent hole in the reading and language abilities of disabled readers of all ages (for reviews, see, e.g., Brady & Shankweiler, 1991; Carr & Levy, 1990; Stanovich, 1986). When given special instruction on breaking words into sounds and relating sounds to spellings, such readers generally do improve—sometimes dramatically (Blachman, 1987; Williams, 1979, 1980). Despite such help, however, Bruck (1992) has shown that, for many dyslexics, a core difficulty with spellings and sounds persists even into adulthood—and alongside, their reading continues to be slow and effortful.

In principle, the letters of an alphabetic script represent the phonemes of its language. Because of this, learning about spelling–sound relationships in a way that is useful for reading depends on phonemic awareness; that is, it depends on a conscious recognition that the sounds of words can be represented by a relatively small set of articulatory gestures, the phonemes.

Phonemic awareness is not natural. Instead, the ease with which people can gain conscious access to their phonological knowledge ranges broadly and appears to be determined, in part, by heredity (Olson et at., 1990). It is because of its difficulty for so many children that solid attention to the development of phonemic awareness is so vital a component of the preschool and primary classroom. Moreover, the pressing issue for the field of dyslexia at this time is the extent to which the elusiveness of its cure derives from the difficulties of trying to turn off or displace an overlearned but self-limiting mode of perceiving text. To what extent would the syndrome go away if we could ensure that all children got off to the right start?

Summary

Relative to the overall literacy challenge, learning to recognize words really is a very small component. Yet it is also wholly necessary. In the end, the print on the page constitutes the basic perceptual data of reading. Rather than diverting efforts in search of meaning, the reader's letter- and word-wise processes supply the text-based information on which comprehension depends. As fluent readers move quickly and easily through the print, literal comprehension automatically unfolds apace.

But neither is literal comprehension the goal of reading. The full interpretation of a complex text may require retrieval of particular facts or events that were presented many pages earlier. It also may require consideration of knowledge and construction of arguments that are entirely extraneous to the text. And it certainly requires the critical and inferential activities necessary for putting such information together.

To be sure, it is this level of interpretation that we think of as true understanding. Yet interpretation at this level is not automatic; it requires active attention and can only be as fruitful as the effort and quality of thought that readers invest in it. But the effort and thought that readers can invest depends, in turn, on the ease and completeness with which they have executed the levels that support it. Deep and ready working knowledge of letters, spelling patterns, and words, and of the phonological translations of all three, is of inescapable importance to both skillful reading and its acquisition—not because it is the be-all or the end-all of the reading process, but because it enables it.

References

Adams, M.J. (1979a). Models of word recognition. *Cognitive Psychology, 11*, 133–176.

Adams, M.J. (1979b). Some differences between good and poor readers. In M.L. Kamil & A.J. Moe (Eds.), *Reading research: Studies and applications* (pp. 140–144). Clemson, SC: National Reading Conference.

Adams, M.J. (1981). What good is orthographic redundancy? In O.J.L. Tzeng & H. Singer (Eds.), *Perception of print* (pp. 197–221). Hillsdale, NJ: Erlbaum.

Adams, M.J. (1990). *Beginning to read: Thinking and learning about print.* Cambridge, MA: MIT Press.

Anderson, R.C., & Freebody, P. (1983). Reading comprehension and the assessment and acquisition of word knowledge. In B. Hutson (Ed.), *Advances in reading/language research* (pp. 231–256). Greenwich, CT: JAI Press.

Baddeley, A.D. (1979). Working memory and reading. In P. Kolers, E. Wrolstad, & H. Bouma (Eds.), *Processing of visible language* (Vol. 1). New York: Plenum.

Barron, R.W. (1981a). Development of visual word recognition: A review. In G.E. MacKinnon & T.G. Waller (Eds.), *Reading research: Advances in theory and practice* (Vol. 3, pp. 119–158). New York: Academic.

Barron, R.W. (1981b). Reading skill and reading strategies. In A.M. Lesgold & C.A. Perfetti (Eds.), *Interactive processes in reading* (pp. 299–328). Hillsdale, NJ: Erlbaum.

Bereiter, C. (1991). Implications of connectionism for thinking about rules. *Educational Researcher, 20*(3), 10–16.

Biemiller, A. (1970). The development of the use of graphic and contextual information as children learn to read. *Reading Research Quarterly, 6,* 75–96.

Blachman, B.A. (1987). An alternative classroom reading program for learning disabled and other low-achieving children. In W. Ellis (Ed.), *Intimacy with language: A forgotten basic in teacher education* (pp. 49–55). Baltimore: Orton Dyslexia Society.

Brady, S.A., & Shankweiler, D.P. (1991). *Phonological processes in literacy.* Hillsdale, NJ: Erlbaum.

Bruck, M. (1992). Persistence of dyslexics' phonological awareness deficits. *Developmental Psychology, 28,* 874–886.

Byrne, B. (1992). Studies in the acquisition procedure for reading: Rationale, hypotheses, and data. In P.B. Gough, L.C. Ehri, & R. Treiman (Eds.), *Reading acquisition* (pp. 1–34). Hillsdale, NJ: Erlbaum.

Carr, T.H., & Levy, B.A. (1990). *Reading and its development.* Hillsdale, NJ: Erlbaum.

Carroll, J.B., Davies, P., & Richman, B. (1971). *Word frequency book.* Boston: Houghton Mifflin.

Cattell, J.M. (1885). Über die Zeit der Erkennung und Benennung von Schriftzeichen, Bildern und Farben [The time it takes to recognize and name letters, pictures, and colors]. *Philosophische Studien, 2,* 635–650.

Daneman, M., & Tardif, T. (1987). Working memory and reading skill re-examined. In M. Coltheart (Ed.), *Attention and performance XII: The psychology of reading* (pp. 491–508). Hillsdale, NJ: Erlbaum.

Dempster, F.N. (1981). Memory span: Sources of individual and developmental differences. *Psychological Bulletin, 89,* 63–100.

De Zuniga, C.M., Humphreys, G.W., & Evett, L.J. (1991). Additive and interactive effects of repetition, degradation, and word frequency in the reading of handwriting. In D. Besner & G.W. Humphreys (Eds.), *Basic processes in reading* (pp. 10–33). Hillsdale, NJ: Erlbaum.

Downing, J. (1979). *Reading and reasoning.* New York: Springer-Verlag.

Estes, W.K. (1977). On the interaction of perception and memory in reading. In D. LaBerge & S.J. Samuels (Eds.), *Basic processes in reading* (pp. 1–25). Hillsdale, NJ: Erlbaum.

Fowler, C.A., Napps, S., & Feldman, L. (1985). Relations among regular and irregular morphologically related words in the lexicon as revealed by repetition priming. *Journal of Experimental Psychology: Learning, Memory, and Cognition, 10,* 241–255.

Gough, P.B., Alford, J.A., & Holley-Wilcox, P. (1981). Words and contexts. In O.J.L. Tzeng & H. Singer (Eds.), *Perception of print* (pp. 85–102). Hillsdale, NJ: Erlbaum.

Jarvella, R. (1971). Syntactic processing of connected speech. *Journal of Verbal Learning and Verbal Behavior, 10,* 409–416.

Johnson, D.D., & Baumann, J.F. (1984). Word identification. In P.D. Pearson, R. Barr, M.L. Kamil, & P. Mosenthal (Eds.), *Handbook of reading research* (pp. 583–608). New York: Longman.

Juel, C. (1983). The development and use of mediated word identification. *Reading Research Quarterly, 18,* 306–327.

Juel, C. (1988). Learning to read and write: A longitudinal study of fifty-four children from first through fourth grade. *Journal of Educational Psychology, 80,* 437 447.

Juel, C. (1991). Beginning reading. In R. Barr, M.L. Kamil, P. Mosenthal, & P.D. Pearson (Eds.), *Handbook of reading research* (Vol. 2, pp. 759–788). White Plains, NY: Longman.

Juel, C., & Roper/Schneider, D. (1985). The influence of basal readers on first grade reading. *Reading Research Quarterly, 20,* 134–152.

Just, M.A., & Carpenter, P.A. (1987). *The psychology of reading and language comprehension.* Boston: Allyn & Bacon.

Kaye, D.B., & Sternberg, R.J. (1982). *The development of lexical decomposition ability.* Unpublished manuscript, Yale University, New Haven, CT.

Kleiman, G.M. (1975). Speech recoding in reading. *Journal of Verbal Learning and Verbal Behavior, 14,* 323–339.

Kučera, H., & Francis, W.N. (1967). *Computational analysis of present-day American English.* Providence, RI: Brown University Press.

Levy, B.A. (1977). Reading: Speech and meaning processes. *Journal of Verbal Learning and Verbal Behavior, 16,* 623–628.

Levy, B.A. (1978). Speech processes during reading. In A.M. Lesgold, S.W. Pellegrino, S.W. Fokkema, & R. Glaser (Eds.), *Cognitive psychology and instruction.* New York: Plenum.

Liberman, I.Y., Shankweiler, D., Orlando, C., Harris, K.S., & Berti, F.B. (1971). Letter confusions and reversals of sequence in the beginning reader: Implications for Orton's theory of developmental dyslexia. *Cortex, 7,* 127–142.

Manelis, L., & Tharp, D. (1977). The processing of affixed words. *Memory and Cognition, 5,* 690–695.

Masonheimer, P.E., Drum, P.A., & Ehri, L.C. (1984). Does environmental print identification lead children into word reading? *Journal of Reading Behavior, 16,* 257–271.

Mayzner, M.S., & Tresselt, M.E. (1965). Tables of single-letter and digram frequency-counts for various word-length and letter position combinations. *Psychonomic Monograph Supplements, 1,* 13–32.

McClelland, J.L., & Elman, J.L. (1986). The TRACE model of speech perception. *Cognitive Psychology, 18,* 1–86.

McClelland, J.L., & Rumelhart, D.E. (1981). An interactive activation model of context effects in letter perception: Part 1, an account of basic findings. *Psychological Review, 88,* 373–407.

McConkie, G.W., & Zola, D. (1981). Language constraints and the functional stimulus in reading. In A.M. Lesgold & C.A. Perfetti (Eds.), *Interactive processes in reading* (pp. 155–175). Hillsdale, NJ: Erlbaum.

McKeown, M.G., Beck, I.L., Omanson, R.C., & Pople, M.T. (1985). Some effects of the nature and frequency of vocabulary instruction on the knowledge and use of words. *Reading Research Quarterly, 20,* 522–535.

Mewhort, D.J.K., & Campbell, A.J. (1981). Toward a model of skilled reading: An analysis of performance in tachistoscopic tasks. In G.E. MacKinnon & T.G. Waller (Eds.), *Reading research: Advances in theory and practice* (Vol. 3, pp. 39–118). New York: Academic.

Miller, G.A., & Gildea, P.M. (1987): How children learn words. *Scientific American, 257*(3), 94–99.

Nagy, W.E., Anderson, R.C., & Herman, P.A. (1987). Learning word meanings from context during normal reading. *American Educational Research Journal, 24,* 237–270.

Nagy, W.E., Herman, P.A., & Anderson, R.C. (1985). Learning words from context. *Reading Research Quarterly, 20,* 233–253.

Olson, R., Wise, B., Conners, F., & Rack, J. (1990). Organization, heritability, and remediation of component word recognition and language skills in disabled readers. In T.H. Carr & B.A. Levy (Eds.), *Reading and its development* (pp. 261–322). Hillsdale, NJ: Erlbaum.

O'Rourke, J.P. (1974). *Toward a science of vocabulary development.* The Hague, the Netherlands: Mouton.

Otterman, L.M. (1955). The value of teaching prefixes and word-roots. *Journal of Educational Research, 48,* 611–616.

Patterson, K.E., & Coltheart, V. (1987). Phonological processes in reading: A tutorial review. In M. Coltheart (Ed.), *Attention and performance XII: The psychology of reading.* Hillsdale, NJ: Erlbaum.

Perfetti, C.A. (1985). *Reading ability.* New York: Oxford University Press.

Perfetti, C.A., Bell, L.C., & Delaney, S.M. (1988). Automatic (prelexical) phonetic activation in silent word reading: Evidence from backward masking. *Journal of Memory and Language, 27,* 1–22.

Rayner, K., & Pollatsek, A. (1987). Eye movements in reading: A tutorial review. In M. Coltheart (Ed.), *Attention and performance XII: The psychology of reading* (pp. 327–362). Hillsdale, NJ: Erlbaum.

Rumelhart, D.E., & McClelland, J.L. (1986). On learning the past tenses of English verbs. In J.L. McClelland & D.E. Rumelhart (Eds.), *Parallel distributed processing, Vol. 2: Psychological and biological models* (pp. 216–271). Cambridge, MA: MIT Press.

Seidenberg, M.S. (1987). Sublexical structures in visual word recognition: Access units or orthographic redundancy. In M. Coltheart (Ed.), *Attention and performance XII: The psychology of reading* (pp. 245–263). Hillsdale, NJ: Erlbaum.

Seidenberg, M.S., & McClelland, J.L. (1989). A distributed, developmental model of word recognition and naming. *Psychological Review, 96,* 523–568.

Seidenberg, M.S., Tannenhaus, M.K., Leiman, J.M., & Bienkowski, M. (1982). Automatic access of the meanings of ambiguous words in context: Some limitations of knowledge-based processing. *Cognitive Psychology, 14,* 489–537.

Spoehr, K.T. (1981). Word recognition in speech and reading: Toward a theory of language processing. In P.D. Eimas & J.L. Miller (Eds.), *Perspectives on the study of speech.* Hillsdale, NJ: Erlbaum.

Stahl, S.A., & Fairbanks, M.M. (1986). The effects of vocabulary instruction: A model-based meta-analysis. *Review of Educational Research, 56*(1), 72–110.

Stanovich, K.E. (1980). Toward an interactive-compensatory model of individual differences in the development of reading fluency. *Reading Research Quarterly, 16*, 32–71.

Stanovich, K.E. (1984). The interactive-compensatory model of reading: A confluence of developmental, experimental, and educational psychology. *Remedial and Special Education, 5*, 11–19.

Stanovich, K.E. (1986). Matthew effects in reading: Some consequences of individual differences in the acquisition of literacy. *Reading Research Quarterly, 21*, 360–406.

Stanovich, K.E. (1993). Does reading make you smarter? Literacy and the development of verbal intelligence. In H. Reese (Ed.), *Advances in child development and behavior* (Vol. 24). New York: Academic.

Taft, M. (1985). The decoding of words in lexical access: A review of the morphographic approach. In D. Besner, T.G. Waller, & G.E. MacKinnon (Eds.), *Reading research: Advances in theory and practice* (Vol. 5). New York: Academic.

Tannenhaus, M.K., Flanigan, H., & Seidenberg, M.S. (1980). Orthographic and phonological code activation in auditory and visual word recognition. *Memory and Cognition, 8*, 513–520.

Tyler, A., & Nagy, W.E. (1987). *Use of derivational morphology during reading.* Unpublished manuscript, University of Illinois, Champaign.

VanOrden, G.C. (1991). Phonologic mediation is fundamental to reading. In D. Besner & G.W. Humphreys (Eds.), *Basic processes in reading* (pp. 77–103). Hillsdale, NJ: Erlbaum.

Vellutino, F.R. (1991). Introduction to three studies on reading acquisition: Convergent findings on theoretical foundations of code-oriented versus whole-language approaches to reading instruction. *Journal of Educational Psychology, 83*, 437–443.

Vernon, M.D. (1971). *Reading and its difficulties.* Cambridge, UK: Cambridge University Press.

Waters, G., Caplan, D., & Hildebrandt, N. (1987). Working memory and written sentence comprehension. In M. Coltheart (Ed.), *Attention and performance XII: The psychology of reading* (pp. 531–555). Hillsdale, NJ: Erlbaum.

Weber, R.M. (1970). First graders' use of grammatical context in reading. In H. Levin & J.P. Williams (Eds.), *Basic studies on reading* (pp. 147–163). New York: Basic.

Williams, J.P. (1979). The ABD's of reading: A program for the learning disabled. In L.A. Resnick & P.A. Weaver (Eds.), *Theory and practice of early reading* (Vol. 3, pp. 227–259). Hillsdale, NJ: Erlbaum.

Williams, J.P. (1980). Teaching decoding with a special emphasis on phoneme analysis and phoneme blending. *Journal of Educational Psychology, 72*, 1–15.

Woodworth, R.A. (1938). *Experimental psychology.* New York: Henry Holt.

45

The Landscape Model of Reading: Inferences and the Online Construction of a Memory Representation

Paul van den Broek, Michael Young, Yuhtsuen Tzeng, and Tracy Linderholm

How do readers construct a memory representation from the texts they read? How does the actual process of going through a text and comprehending individual sentences translate into a mental representation of the text that lingers far after the reader has put down the book? In this piece we present a detailed description of the way in which cognitive processes during reading allow the gradual emergence of a memory representation. Central to this description is the notion that concepts and propositions fluctuate in their activation as the reader progresses through the text. Using core notions from research on human memory and memory access, we show how this landscape of activations results in a memory representation.

In the first section of this piece, we describe the central conceptual properties of the landscape view of reading. In the second section, we illustrate the general model by implementing it in a specific theory of reading comprehension (based on the assumption that readers attempt to maintain coherence) and by empirically testing the implementation's validity. In the third section, we pursue implications of this model by describing how it captures specific phenomena and current issues in the area of discourse processing.

The Landscape Model of Comprehension and Memory for Texts

Three Generations of Cognitive Research in Reading

In the early days of cognitive research on reading, the focus was on what readers remember from the texts that they read. This focus reflected a realization, fueled by anthropological work on the structure of narratives (e.g., Colby, 1973; Propp, 1928), that memory for texts is systematic rather than random. The purpose of this first generation of cognitive research in text comprehension was to determine the defining features of what readers recall and to draw conclusions about the nature of the memory representation that results from reading. One set of models developed in this generation of research emphasized top-down influences on memory, focusing on the role of text elements in the overall structure of the text. Examples include story grammars (e.g., Mandler & Johnson, 1977; Stein & Glenn, 1979) and script theory (Schank & Abelson, 1977) for narrative texts, and hierarchical theories (e.g., Meyer, 1975) for expository texts. A second set of models focused on bottom-up effects, that is, the role that each text element plays in maintaining coherence with other individual elements. These models emphasize that readers attempt to construct mental representations that are coherent in terms of their referential (e.g., Kintsch, 1988; Kintsch & van Dijk, 1978) and causal structure (e.g., Trabasso, Secco, & van den Broek, 1984; see also Goldman & Varnhagen, 1986; Graesser & Clark, 1985).

With the development of methodologies for measuring online activities and activations (eye tracking techniques, probing techniques, etc.) in the mid-1980s, attention shifted from the product of reading, the memory representation, to the actual process of reading itself. The purpose of this second generation of research was to describe and understand what readers do as they proceed through a text. Here, the focus was on the balancing act that the reader must perform: On the one hand the reader needs to make inferences in order to comprehend the text; on the other hand he or she has limited attentional or working memory resources available to do so. Models in this generation describe the cognitive processes that take place online: What are the inferences that readers routinely make (and what are those they do *not* make), how do the conflicting constraints of limited attentional resources and the need for comprehension interact during reading, and so on. Examples of such models are the Current State Strategy (Fletcher & Bloom, 1988), the Causal Inference Maker (van den Broek, 1990a), the Construction–Integration model (Kintsch, 1988), minimalist theories (e.g., McKoon & Ratcliff, 1992), constructionist theories (e.g., Graesser, Singer, & Trabasso, 1994; Singer, Graesser, & Trabasso, 1994), and the Structure Building Framework (Gernsbacher, 1990).

Both generations of research continue to exist, yielding important new insights into reading comprehension and memory. However, in the mid-1990s a third generation of research developed. The purpose of research in this generation is to integrate the online and offline aspects of reading (e.g., Goldman & Varma, 1995; Goldman, Varma, & Coté, 1996; Langston & Trabasso, 1999; van den Broek, Risden, Fletcher, & Thurlow, 1996). Thus, the focus is on comprehension processes *and* memory representation and, most important, on the relation between the two. This relation is complex and bidirectional because not only is the representation constantly modified as the reader encounters and comprehends new text, but the developing representation itself provides an important resource for the reader in understanding subsequent text. Thus, comprehension of new information updates the memory representation, which, in turn, influences subsequent comprehension. The landscape model presented in this piece attempts to capture the online processes and the offline representation as well as their dynamic interaction.

The Reading Process: A Landscape of Fluctuating Activations

As a reader proceeds through a text, he or she activates concepts represented by the text and relations among these concepts. Because attentional resources are very limited, however, a reader can only attend to a subset of all the words, concepts, or relations in the text at any one time (Just & Carpenter, 1992; Kintsch & van Dijk, 1978). What determines which concepts are activated? At each reading cycle (i.e., with each new sentence, proposition, or whatever one takes as the unit of text analysis) there are four potential sources of activation. One source is the text that is currently being processed. A second consists of the immediately preceding reading cycle: As the reader commences a new cycle, information that was activated in the preceding cycle is likely to be, at least in part, carried over and available for processing. Third, readers may reactivate concepts that were processed in even earlier reading cycles (of course, these concepts themselves originally would have been derived from any of the four sources). Fourth, they may access and activate background knowledge.

The role of the current text is obvious, but there is also ample evidence that the other three sources indeed influence activation of concepts during reading. Evidence of carryover from previous cycles is found throughout the memory literature (see Klatzky, 1980, for a review) and has been featured strongly in the study of reading, both in theories (e.g., Fletcher & Bloom, 1988; Kintsch & van Dijk, 1978; van den Broek, 1990a) and in empirical findings (e.g., Fletcher, Hummel, & Marsolek, 1990). Likewise, readers frequently reactivate information that was activated in prior reading cycles either because it is required for comprehension (e.g., Goldman & Saul, 1990; O'Brien, Albrecht, Hakala, & Rizella, 1995; O'Brien, Duffy, & Myers, 1986; Suh & Trabasso, 1993; van den Broek, Rohleder, & Narvaez, 1996; van den Broek & Thurlow, 1990) or because it is strongly associated with information in the current cycle (Albrecht & O'Brien, 1993; McKoon & Ratcliff, 1980; O'Brien & Albrecht, 1992). Such reactivation may involve reinstatement of information that was explicitly mentioned in the prior text or that was originally retrieved from background knowledge (Trabasso & Suh, 1993; van den Broek, 1990a). Finally, there is ample evidence that readers routinely—and often automatically—activate background knowledge that is associated with what they read (e.g., Kintsch, 1988;

McKoon & Ratcliff, 1992; Sharkey & Sharkey, 1992) or that is required for comprehension (Lucas, Tanenhaus, & Carlson, 1990; O'Brien, Shank, Myers, & Rayner, 1988; van den Broek, Rohleder, & Narvaez, 1996).

Thus, it is clear that readers have each of these four sources available to activate concepts as they read. That is not to say that investigators agree on which sources actually are used in a particular instance. Much current research is stimulated by different views on the circumstances in which each source is accessed (e.g., the debate between "minimalists" and "constructionists"; Graesser et al., 1994; McKoon & Ratcliff, 1992; Singer et al., 1994). Here the important point is that most, if not all, researchers agree that readers at various times activate concepts from each of these four sources.

Together, limited attentional capacity and access to these sources of activation cause text elements constantly to fluctuate in activation as the reader proceeds through a text. With each reading cycle, new concepts are activated, some old ones are retained, and others are removed from the focus of attention or working memory (cf. Kintsch & van Dijk, 1978). These fluctuations are central to the proposed model of reading. By simultaneously considering the activation "peaks" and "valleys" for each concept across reading cycles, one obtains a "landscape" of activations (van den Broek, Risden, et al., 1996).[1] Figure 1 provides an example of such a landscape. This particular landscape is derived for the short narrative in Table 1 using certain assumptions about the factors that determine the activations of concepts. We return to these assumptions later in this section, but for the moment we simply illustrate a landscape and its general properties. On the vertical axis is the level of activation (here arbitrarily depicted on a 0–5 scale).

FIGURE 1
Landscape of Activations for the Knight Story

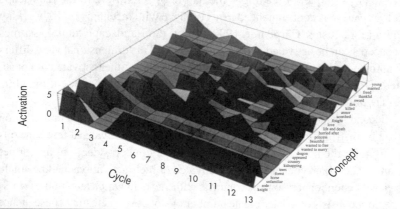

TABLE 1
The Knight Story

1. A young knight rode through the forest.
2. The knight was unfamiliar with the country.
3. Suddenly, a dragon appeared.
4. The dragon was kidnapping a beautiful princess.
5. The knight wanted to free her.
6. The knight wanted to marry her.
7. The knight hurried after the dragon.
8. They fought for life and death.
9. Soon, the knight's armor was completely scorched.
10. At last, the knight killed the dragon.
11. He freed the princess.
12. The princess was very thankful to the knight.
13. She married the knight.

On one horizontal axis are the concepts relevant to the text,[2] and on the other horizontal axis are the reading cycles. A cross-section at a reading cycle shows which concepts are activated during that cycle, whereas a cross-section at a concept captures the concept's activation history over the course of reading. A cross-section at a vertical plane shows which concepts exceed a particular activation threshold and when they do so.[3]

In the current model, the dynamic properties of the shifting landscape are captured in a computational, connectionist model. The technical details of this model have been presented elsewhere (van den Broek, Risden, et al., 1996; van den Broek, Young, & Risden, 1996). Here we focus on the major conceptual aspects of the model.

Levels of Activation and Processing Resources. Central to the Landscape—indeed to any—model of reading is the nature of activation. In the Landscape model, activation is conceptualized in accordance with recent models of working memory (e.g., Just & Carpenter, 1992). First, the Landscape model assumes that concepts can be activated to different degrees. This dimensional view differs from all-or-none views according to which a concept is either activated or not activated. Thus, some concepts can be squarely in the center of attention while others are hovering in the background, still activated but less so.

Second, readers are assumed to have available a limited pool of activation that can be distributed over concepts. Thus, if a reader activates a few concepts very strongly, the pool that is available for other concepts declines and either only a few additional concepts can be activated or their activations will be small. This view of attentional resources contrasts with views in which attention or working memory consists of a determinate number of slots. An interesting consequence of the pool-of-activation feature is that as readers proceed through a text and accumulate more information, they either have to spread the available resources more thinly or more selectively or they have to recruit more resources (e.g., by increasing concentration).[4]

Retrieval From Background Knowledge or From Prior Cycles: Cohort Activation. At times, readers may import concepts that are not mentioned in the current sentence. This occurs when concepts are retrieved from background knowledge or from the reader's emerging representation of the text itself. Such retrieval is likely to happen in two circumstances: (1) when the to-be-imported concepts are strongly associated with concepts in the current processing cycle and (2) when the concepts are retrieved for a specific purpose, for example to allow comprehension of the current sentence. We discuss such specific purposes later. For now, our concern is with the mechanics of retrieval regardless of its origin.

A central feature of the Landscape model is that the processing of a concept is accompanied by *cohort activation*: When a concept is activated, other concepts that are connected to it (i.e., its cohorts) will be somewhat activated as well. This view is closely related to the explicit/implicit focus theory of memory retrieval developed by Garrod and Sanford (1990; see also Ericsson & Kintsch, 1995; Kintsch, 1988; Ratcliff & McKoon, 1988). In the Landscape model, the amount of activation for a secondarily retrieved concept is a function of the strength of its relation to the primarily retrieved concept and of the amount of activation that the primary concept received. Furthermore, it is a function of a cohort-activation parameter that captures the extent to which activation of a primary concept is transferred to members of its cohort. This parameter can range from 0 (no cohort activation) to 1 (activation of cohort concepts is maximal).

As the reader's mental representation for a text emerges during reading, new concepts are added and new associations are formed. Thus, a concept's cohort at one point in the text differs from its cohort at another point and, hence, so will the activations it triggers. In this way, the emerging representation exerts a powerful influence over the online process, which, in turn, influences further changes in the representation.

Carryover From Preceding Cycles and Decay. Part of a concept's cohort is the concept itself. Thus, a concept can maintain its own activation through cohort activation. When the cohort-activation parameter is less than 1.0, concepts exhibit a gradual decrease in activation over subsequent cycles, thus mimicking decay. Like any other member of its cohort, the concept's activation in subsequent cycles is a function of the concept's activation in the preceding cycle and the strength of its self-connection, which we designate its *node strength*. A concept with high node strength is more likely to remain in memory for a while, whereas one with low node strength is more likely to fade quickly after its initial activation.

This description of the activation dynamics for a concept over reading cycles applies to the situation in which the original concept is not reactivated in the subsequent cycles. If the concept is rementioned or for some reason is retrieved from background knowledge or reinstated from preceding cycles, then such reactivation would override the carryover function.

The Sources of Activation and the Landscape Model. The Landscape model in its general form is impartial to the sources of activation. Therefore, it can accommodate any combination of the four sources of activation discussed earlier and, indeed, of any other source of activation one might hypothesize. In this piece, we present an implementation of the model that includes all four sources. Central to such implementations is the notion that the pattern of activations and deactivations is not just a reflection of the text itself. Instead, it is the result of all interaction among the text, the reader's attentional capacities, his or her background knowledge, and the reader's criteria for comprehension and hence for retrieval.[5]

The Reading Product: The Landscape Builds a Mental Structure

The outcome of a successful reading process is a coherent mental representation of the text. Prior research on memory for texts indicates that such representations resemble networks of interrelated concepts (propositions, sentences, etc.). Memory for a particular concept is a function of its individual properties as well as of its relations to other concepts. Among the individual properties, the number of times a concept is mentioned and its salience are important (Kintsch & van Dijk, 1978; Mandler & Johnson, 1977; Miller & Kintsch, 1980; Perfetti & Goldman, 1974; Stein & Glenn, 1979; Trabasso & van den Broek, 1985). With respect to relations, a concept's number of connections to other concepts has been found to be a particularly powerful predictor of memory strength (Fletcher & Bloom, 1988; Graesser & Clark, 1985; O'Brien & Myers, 1987; Trabasso & Suh, 1993; Trabasso & van den Broek, 1985; van den Broek, 1988; van den Broek & Lorch, 1993; van den Broek & Trabasso, 1986).

The Learning Process: Building Nodes and Connections. How do the online activations result in such a memory representation? In the Landscape model, the online activation vectors dynamically and gradually construct the representation. The changes in activation vectors are captured in the mental representation in such a way as to permit storage of a memory for these changes that is as efficient as possible. The emerging representation tries to encode the ordered associations among the story's concepts and their appropriate levels of activation. This encoding is captured by a network of directional connections among the concepts, including the aforementioned self-connections (i.e., node strengths). The construction of connections between concepts allows the model to anticipate and encode the activation of one concept on the basis of the activation of other concepts. These connections, in turn, enable the model to reconstruct the original input during recall. Both encoding and retrieval are probabilistic, so this reconstruction is likely to be approximate only.

In earlier versions of the Landscape model, the accumulation of node and connection strengths at a reading cycle depended only on the activation of the concepts involved. A concept's node strength increased proportional to the amount of its activation. If a concept was highly activated, its salience in the memory representation increased more than when it was weakly activated. Likewise, the increase in connection strength between two coactivated concepts was a multiplicative function of the activation of each. Thus, if both were strongly activated in a cycle, then the increase in their connection strength would be large, whereas if both were weakly activated, the increase in connection strength would be small.

In this (Hebbian) view, each time a reader encounters a concept or pair of concepts of a given activation, the amount of change in node or connection strength is the same. However, this is an unlikely scenario. First, such linear accumulation has no limit: Concepts and concept relations would become stronger ad infinitum, thereby quickly overwhelming the processing system. Second, there is ample evidence of expectancy or surprisingness effects: The first occurrence of an event is likely to bring about a larger change in representation than a subsequent occurrence, other things being equal. For example, imagine that a reader encounters a connection between two concepts, say, between a porcelain vase falling and it breaking, in one of two contexts. In the first context, the reader already has experienced this connection many times. In the second context, the reader has rarely or never experienced this connection. The change in the representation is much larger in the second context than in the first: If one has never seen a porcelain vase fall and break, the change in knowledge status is much larger than if one has already seen that sequence of events take place many times.

The graded effect of multiple experiences is captured in the current version of the model by an *asymptotic (modified Delta) learning rule*. According to this rule, the change in a connection's strength is proportional to the surprisingness of a concept's activation level. If a concept's activation level was perfectly predicted by the existing representation of an ongoing story, there is no reason to change the representation. In contrast, if a concept's activation level was not well anticipated, the network's connectivity needs to change to better capture the dynamics of the story's activation vectors.

A final major effect on the change in connection between two concepts is exerted by the connections of each to other concepts. This is because the concepts "compete" for the privilege of predicting another concept. This *cohort competition* has profound effects on the representation that is constructed with each consecutive reading cycle; it serves to efficiently represent the story dynamics, avoiding redundancies when possible. Cohort competition perhaps is best illustrated by some examples. If a concept has become strongly associated to another concept (i.e., its activation and connections accurately predict activation of the other concept), then there is little room for a third concept to build a connection as well. Consider the story in Table 1. If *knight* always predicted *dragon* early in the story, its connection to *dragon* would approach asymptote. If later in the story *knight* was always paired with *princess* and together they predicted *dragon*, there would be little if any learning of a direct princess → dragon association because it would be redundant. A different form of competition occurs when a group of concepts tends to predict the activation of another concept. In this case, the concepts must share the total associative strength available. In other words, they jointly predict the other concept, but in the absence of other members of the group the prediction would not be as strong.

As a result of the asymptotic learning rule, the connections between two concepts tend to be asymmetrical, with the predictive relation between the two concepts being stronger in one direction than in the other. The resulting asymmetric connectivity matrix contrasts with the symmetric matrices that emerge from the use of Hebbian learning in the earlier version of our model and in other existing models (e.g., Goldman & Varma, 1995; Kintsch, 1988; Landauer & Dumais, 1997; Langston & Trabasso, 1999). The connection asymmetry encodes the ordered relations among the concepts, enabling the model to recall concepts in the order in which they were originally read (cf. Golden, 1994).

Updating the Memory Representation. Together, these three factors—(1) the activation of individual concepts, (2) the asymptotic learning rule, and (3) cohort competition—determine the updating of the strengths of individual concepts and connections at each cycle. Over the entire reading process, the reader gradually learns the various concepts and their interconnections and builds an episodic memory representation of the text.[6] As a result, the representation changes during reading. To illustrate, Figure 2 shows two snapshots of part of the developing network for the Knight story in Table 1 and Figure 1, one after three reading cycles (top panel) and the other after the final cycle (bottom panel). Varying node strengths are represented as circles of different sizes, and connections are represented as links of different thickness. A comparison between the two panels shows that both node strengths and the relative strengths of connections change dynamically as the reader moves through the text.

Several aspects of the updating process are worth highlighting because they may not be immediately obvious from consideration of nodes and connections in isolation. First, the updating process extends beyond the modification of individual nodes and connections. As a result of cohort activation and competition, a change in node strength or connection density of one concept will reverberate

FIGURE 2
Partial Memory Representation of the Knight Story, After Three Reading Cycles
(top panel) and After the Final Cycle (bottom panel)

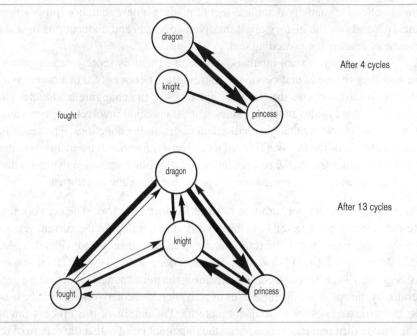

throughout the representation and affect the properties of other concepts. Thus, with each reading cycle, the online activation of concepts results in a restructuring or reconfiguring of the entire representation. One might find that concepts and connections that were prominent at one point had retreated to the middle of the pack in the next cycle, and vice versa. This is illustrated in Figure 2 as well. For example, the predictive connection between *princess* and *dragon* initially was strong, but it declined as the connection between *knight* and *dragon* increased. The fact that restructuring extends beyond individual nodes and connections becomes even clearer when we consider situations in which the updating is more complicated than sheer accumulation of strengths of nodes and connections, for instance when the reader is confronted with information that is inconsistent with information earlier in the text or when the text corrects an earlier statement. In such situations, restructuring is even more extensive. We discuss the model's handling of these situations in a later section.

A second central aspect of the updating process is that the developing representation affects subsequent activation vectors and, hence, the impact that new input has on updating the representation. Again, the three factors of cohort activation, asymptotic learning, and cohort competition are responsible for this.

Cohort activation dictates, in part, what activation vector will result from the new input, whereas asymptotic learning and cohort competition dictate the amount of change that the activation vector achieves. This state of affairs has an important implication, namely that the effect of reading a new sentence (proposition, etc.) depends on the history of all involved concepts and connections over the course of reading the preceding text.

In summary, textual input and developing memory representation interact in updating the node and connection strengths of concepts. The connectivity matrix, in turn, captures the temporal dynamics of the changing landscape. The recursive nature of this process ensures that the updating involves the representation as a whole rather than just individual nodes and connections. The resulting representation of the text can be used as a source for retrieval mechanisms suited for various tasks such as the recapitulation of the original activation dynamics during recall or as a speeded response in a probe-reaction time experiment.

Retrieving Concepts From the Mental Representation. The network representation can be accessed both during and after reading. In the current version of the Landscape model, the retrieval cue is an activation vector (Fletcher, van den Broek, & Arthur, 1996; van den Broek, Young, et al., 1996; cf. Raaijmakers & Shiffrin, 1981). Through cohort activation, the initial pattern of activation generated by the cue will trigger patterns of activation in the network that can be used as the retrieval cues for subsequent patterns. The details of this process can be captured in different mechanisms, but the important point is that the pattern of retrieval depends on (a) the structure (i.e., nodes, node strengths, and connections) of the representation that is completed at the time that the retrieval takes place and (b) the activation vector that is used as the starting point or trigger for retrieval. Exactly what is retrieved and the order in which this happens depend on these two aspects and on their interaction.

Implementing and Testing the Landscape Model

In this section, we implement the Landscape model and test its psychological validity. To do so we must make a final decision, namely what factors determine the actual contents of the activation vectors. As mentioned earlier, this is an important source of differences among theorists' views of the reading process. Most researchers agree that readers access all four sources of activation (i.e., text, carryover, reinstatement from prior cycles, background knowledge) in *some* circumstances, but they differ about what those circumstances are and whether they occur during normal reading. These disagreements are particularly strong with respect to access of background knowledge and reinstatements (e.g., Graesser et al., 1994; McKoon & Ratcliff, 1992; Singer & Ritchot, 1996; cf. van den Broek, Fletcher, & Risden, 1993). In principle, any of these theoretical positions can be implemented in the Landscape model. Indeed, as we discuss later, different implementations can be used to compare the predictive power of each position.

For our implementation, we take a *functional*, coherence-driven view of the reading process (van den Broek, 1990a; van den Broek, Risden, & Husebye-Hartman, 1995). According to this view, readers attempt to maintain a certain level of understanding as they proceed through a text.[7] Whether they retrieve information (from memory for prior cycles or from background knowledge) depends on whether that information is functional in maintaining/attaining comprehension. Readers are relatively unlikely to exert effort to access background information or memory for prior cycles unless that effort is likely to bring them closer to the desired level of coherence. Standards of coherence may vary across individuals as well as within an individual (e.g., as a function of differences in motivation, reading goals, instructions, fatigue), but there is considerable agreement that two standards of coherence are employed by most readers in normal reading situations—(1) *referential* and (2) *causal* (see Singer, 1994; van den Broek, 1994). Referential coherence has been obtained when the reader has clearly identified the reference for the objects, persons, and so forth in the sentence that is currently being read (e.g., Gernsbacher, 1990; Kintsch & van Dijk, 1978; O'Brien, 1987). Thus, the sentence pair *The lady gave the waiter 10 dollars. He returned to give her the change* is referentially coherent if the reader recognizes that *he* refers to the waiter and *her* to the lady. Causal coherence is established when, in the eyes of the reader, the event described in the current sentence has a causally sufficient explanation (Trabasso & van den Broek, 1985; van den Broek, 1990a). In the previous example, the lady's giving the waiter $10 is not causally sufficient for the waiter's returning with change unless one also infers (from background knowledge or prior cycles) that the lady gave too much money to the waiter.

The standards of referential and causal coherence can be incorporated in the implementation of the Landscape model. In essence, this implementation models a reader who steadily moves along, making inferences when they are required for comprehension but not when they are just there to be made. As a result, the vector of activation at each reading cycle is determined by the current text and carryover from the preceding cycle, as well as by retrieval from prior cycles or background knowledge *when such retrieval is required for referential and/or causal coherence* (for methods to determine referential coherence, see Turner & Greene, 1978; for determining causal coherence, see Trabasso, van den Broek, & Suh, 1989; van den Broek, 1990b). The memory representation that results captures the causal and referential contingencies between the concepts in the text. The activation landscape depicted in Figure 1 and the (partial) emerging memory representation in Figure 2 are based on this causal–referential implementation.

As mentioned, the notion that referential and causal coherence determine online activations has considerable support in the research literature. For example, during reading, concepts that are necessary for referential or causal coherence indeed are reactivated from background knowledge or memory for prior cycles (e.g., Casteel, 1993; Gernsbacher, 1990; Myers, 1990; O'Brien, 1987; Trabasso & Suh, 1993; van den Broek, Rohleder, et al., 1996). Likewise, there is ample evidence that causal and referential relations play an important role in readers' memory representations of a text. For example, these relations are strong predictors of frequency of recall, perceived importance, speed of retrieval, and answers to questions (e.g., Goldman, 1985; Goldman & Varnhagen, 1986; Miller & Kintsch, 1980; O'Brien & Myers, 1987; Trabasso & van den Broek, 1985; van den Broek, 1988; van den Broek & Lorch, 1993).

These studies have limited utility as tests of the Landscape model, however. In the online studies, for example, probing occurs at only one or two locations in the text, and only one concept is probed at each location. The Landscape model makes predictions concerning the activation of multiple concepts at all locations in the text. Thus, the real test for a model of the reading process requires assessing activations throughout the text and of all potentially relevant concepts. The offline studies, too, have limitations: The theoretical memory representations that are used to predict task performance are based on a static analysis of the text without consideration of the online process that supposedly yielded the representations. In summary, although bits and pieces of the causal–referential landscape model had been supported in the existing body of literature, the model as a whole remained to be tested.

Two experiments in which the online and offline components of the Landscape model were tested directly are reported in van den Broek, Risden, et al. (1996). The purpose of the first experiment was to investigate online fluctuations in activation. Participants read texts such as the one in Table 1 line by line, at their own pace. After each sentence, they were presented with a list consisting of all concepts related to the text and an equal number of unrelated distractors. For each concept, participants indicated on a 5-point scale how strongly they thought it was activated. Averaging participants' ratings yielded an empirical landscape of activations for all concepts over the course of the text. This landscape was compared to theoretical landscapes based on a simplified version[8] of the causal–referential implementation. The empirical and theoretical landscapes were strongly correlated, $r = .73$ ($p < .01$). To put this correlation in perspective, note that the average correlation between participants' landscapes was .79. Thus, the theoretical model predicted participants' behavior about as well as it possibly could have.

The model's predictions about the mental representation that results from the fluctuating activations during reading were tested in a second experiment. Participants read and recalled the same texts as were used in the first experiment. Recall protocols were compared to the final mental representations produced by the simplified Landscape model. The network properties of concepts were used in hierarchical regression analyses to predict frequency of recall. The empirical and theoretical memory representations were closely related. A concept's node strength strongly predicted frequency of recall, $R^2 = .49$ ($p < .01$). Predictive power was even greater when the strength of the relations that a concept had to other concepts—its connection density—was entered as an additional factor, bringing the total R^2 to .64 (the increase, .15, is significant at $p < .01$).

The theoretical networks not only predicted frequency but also order of free recall. The first text element to be recalled almost inevitably (94%) was the one that had received the largest total of activation across cycles. The conditional probability of subsequent mention was predicted by the strength of relations between concepts, $R^2 = .34$ ($p < .01$): The second element to be recalled usually was the one that had the strongest connection to the first recalled element, the third element was strongly related to the second one, and so on. Node strength had an additional effect, increasing R^2 to .44 (the increase, .10, is significant at $p < .01$): If two or more concepts were equally related to the last-recalled concept, then the strongest of the candidate concepts tended to be recalled next. Thus, it appears that readers first retrieve the concept that is most prominent in strength and relations in the mental representation and then trace their representation along the strongest relational paths to subsequent concepts, using concept strengths as tie-breakers.

These results indicate that the Landscape model captures important aspects of the cognitive processes that take place during reading, and of the mental representation that emerges. These tests are based on a causal–referential implementation and, thus, also provide evidence that much inference-making during reading occurs when such inferences are necessary to establish referential and causal coherence. Other implementations could have been chosen. Indeed, the Landscape model can be used to contrast alternative theoretical accounts of the reading process. Risden (1996), for example, implemented four theories of inference-making in the current Landscape model: (1) constructionist (in which readers are assumed to generate virtually all possible inferences), (2) minimalist (in which readers are assumed to generate inferences only rarely), (3) causal–referential, and (4) order-only (in which no inferences are generated). Of the four implementations, the causal–referential one best predicted online and offline behavior. These results support the causal–referential model and, more important for the present purpose, they show how the Landscape model can be used to compare and test different reading theories.

Implications of the Landscape Model

In the previous section, we illustrated that the model captures general reading phenomena such as concept activation levels and frequency and order of recall. Here we explore specific features of the Landscape model in the context of phenomena that currently are receiving attention in the literature on cognitive processes in reading.

Constructing the Memory Representation

Effects of Input Order. In the Landscape model, the relation between fluctuating activations and episodic representation of the text is reciprocal. At each point during reading, the existing representation is updated on the basis of the current activation vector, but this vector itself is partly influenced by the representation as it has emerged so far. An important implication of this reciprocal relation is the existence of *order effects*. The history of a concept during the reading process affects its properties in the mental representation: Present the same information in different orders and different representations will result. Examples can be found in children's Choose-Your-Own-Adventure books or in Julio Cortazar's (1966) *Hopscotch*. In both cases, the events in the texts can be read in one or more orders, each resulting in a different interpretation of the events, personality traits, how events are connected, and so on.

Resolving Contradictions and Corrections. Texts frequently contain inconsistencies or explicit corrections of earlier information. The Landscape model provides a detailed description of what happens in these situations. According to the model, incompatibilities are noticed by the reader if the two pieces of incompatible information are activated simultaneously. For this to occur, the information in the prior cycle needs to be reactivated. As described earlier, the likelihood of reactivation is a joint function of the memory representation as it has developed so far and the current activation vector. Both influence the likelihood that a contradiction is detected. On the one hand, the more strongly the earlier information is represented in memory (i.e., the greater its node and connection strengths), the more likely it is to be retrieved at a later cycle. Thus, if a concept is repeated or connected to many other concepts through elaboration, its chances of being retrieved later are great.

On the other hand, the more effective the current activation vector is in reactivating the conflicting information, the more likely the two conflicting pieces of information are to be coactivated. In the case of explicit correction, the incompatible information from the earlier cycle is directly restated and hence reactivation is almost guaranteed. In the case of an implicit inconsistency, reactivation of the incompatible information occurs in two circumstances. First, reactivation may occur as part of an effort to establish coherence for the information in the current cycle. In this case, the model stumbles on the inconsistent information as it executes another process. Second, reactivation may result from a passive flow of activation from the current cycle to the preceding concept through cohort activation. Here, the greater and more direct the association between the two pieces of contradictory information is, the more likely they will be activated simultaneously.[9]

Once an inconsistency is detected, the reader needs to restructure the mental representation to reestablish coherence. This process, similar to that observed during wrap-up at the end of a text or sentence, takes time and hence reading slows down. In the case of a correction, the reader knows in what way the representation needs to be revised, whereas in the case of a contradiction the reader needs to resolve the conflict himself or herself. In either case, the new connection enters into the updating process, The old, erroneous connections can be dealt with in one of two ways. They can be deleted through some form of inhibition or suppression, or they can remain in the representation. The Landscape model favors the second possibility: Connections—once established—continue to exist in the representation, although over the course of reading they are likely to lose relative prominence as the correct connections gain in strength. The two possibilities lead to different predictions: In the first scenario, the incorrect (and now deleted) connections should not have an influence on later activations, whereas in the second scenario, the incorrect connections may still surface in later comprehension. The preponderance of evidence supports the second scenario (e.g., Johnson & Seifert, 1994; van Oostendorp & Bonebakker, 1999; Wilkes & Leatherbarrow, 1988). This explains the informal observation that connections, once laid, often are hard to undo. Examples abound in politics and advertising.

Forward Inferences. Forward inferences generally are considered to be less frequent than backward, coherence-building inferences (e.g., McKoon & Ratcliff, 1989; Singer & Ferreira, 1983; van den Broek, 1990a). Although the results of initial studies led researchers to conclude that in the absence of specific reading goals they are not produced at all, it has become clear since then that forward inferences *are* drawn but only when the preceding text provides compelling semantic constraints (Klin & Myers, 1993; van den Broek, 1990a; van den Broek & Huang, 1995; Vonk & Noordman, 1990).

The Landscape model captures the role of constraints in the generation of forward inferences through cohort activation. At a particular reading cycle, the activated concepts spread activation to other concepts to which they are associated (in episodic memory for the text or in background knowledge). If the spreading activation converges on a particular concept, then this event will be activated even if it has not occurred yet (cf. Kintsch, 1988). Examples can be found readily. For example, after reading the first few sentences of the story in Table 1, participants frequently activated concepts such as *fighting*, *killing*, and *marrying the princess* even though none of these concepts had been mentioned yet.

The generation of a forward inference depends not only on the presence but also the timing of adequate constraints. On the one hand, constraints take time to accumulate: Retrieval from episodic memory as well as activation of background knowledge is a slow process (e.g., Balota & Lorch, 1986; Bloom, Fletcher, van den Broek, Reitz, & Shapiro, 1990; Kintsch, 1988; Till, Mross, & Kintsch, 1988). On the other hand, constraints decline when the supporting activation vector dissipates, for example as the time since the last reading cycle increases.

Thus, there may be a small window of opportunity during which all the required constraints are present to allow the forward inference. The results of recent research suggest that this is indeed the case (Keefe & McDaniel, 1993; van den Broek & Huang, 1995). The transient nature of forward inferences has implications not only for theories but also for investigative procedure: Tests of whether a particular inference is made or not are valid only if the inference is probed inside the window of opportunity.

In the Landscape model, a forward inference may influence the generation of backward inferences later in the text. Once generated, the inference becomes part of the new activation vector. As a result, it influences the updating of the developing mental representation and the processing of subsequent text. Imagine a sentence describing someone accidentally dropping a porcelain vase. A reader may well activate background knowledge such as the fragility of porcelain and the forward inference that the vase will break. These inferences will become part of the memory representation. If the text in a later cycle describes an event that begs explanation, for example that the protagonist pays damages to the homeowner, the explanation that the vase broke is readily retrieved. The opposite occurs if the forward inference conflicts with information in a later cycle, for example if the text cycle later mentions that the homeowner sold the vase for a large amount of money. Thus, forward inferences can interact with later backward inferences. The possibility of this interaction has been noted (van den Broek, 1990a; Whitney & Budd, 1996) but has not yet been investigated empirically. Again, this has practical implications as well. Investigations of backward inference generation need to eliminate the possibility that results are confounded by forward inferences.

Top-Down Processing: Activations of Schemas. In the description of cohort activation, we have focused on individual concepts. At times, however, multiple concepts may seem to be activated instantaneously as a unit. This occurs when concepts are interconnected so tightly that activation of one member evokes activation of the others. Such a conglomerate of concepts often consists of knowledge that has been accumulated and generalized over individual experiences, constituting a *schema* (also called *script, generalized knowledge structure*, etc.; see Graesser & Clark, 1985; Mandler, 1984; Schank & Abelson, 1977; Stein & Glenn, 1979). Activation of a schema results in top-down processes, that is, the generation of extensive expectations and inferences. For example, when a reader is told that he or she will read a fairy tale, general knowledge about the content and structure of fairy tales may be activated and influence the interpretation of the text that follows (e.g., McDaniel & Einstein, 1989; Zwaan & Brown, 1996).

In the Landscape model, such knowledge structures are activated in the same way as other groups of concepts are, namely through cohort activation. The activation vector that serves as the starting point or cue for the cohort activation of an abstract knowledge structure may originate before the reading process starts (e.g., from instructions) or once the reading process is on its way (e.g., when the first sentence is *Once upon a time, in a faraway land...*). In either case, the schema will be activated, become part of the new activation vector, and henceforth exert a strong influence on the processing of subsequent text. Thus, the Landscape model parsimoniously captures both top-down and bottom-up processes through the same mechanisms.

Individual Differences in Reading Comprehension

Individuals differ in their attentional capacities, knowledge, and comprehension processes. As a consequence, the same text may be processed, interpreted, and remembered very differently by different individuals. Indeed, even within the same individual, comprehension processes may differ from one reading situation to the next, for example, as a result of different reading goals, motivation, and fatigue (see van den Broek et al., 1993). Here, we illustrate some of the sources for inter- and intra-individual variation. By implementing these variations in the Landscape model, one gains important insights into the reading process in general as well as into the origins of individual differences.

Background Knowledge. One source of individual differences is background knowledge. In the Landscape model, background knowledge is one of the major factors in determining the activation vectors that occur during reading. The more knowledge a reader has, and the more densely interconnected this knowledge is, the more easily and extensively it is accessed through processes such as cohort activation (e.g., Ericsson & Kintsch, 1995). Thus, background knowledge affects the activation vectors that, in turn, affect the eventual memory representation (e.g., Chi, Feltovich, & Glaser, 1981; Chiesi, Spilich, & Voss, 1979; Ericsson & Kintsch, 1995).

Aside from differences in the amount of background knowledge, individuals may differ in the extent to which they tend to access background knowledge. At one extreme would be a reader who attempts to stay as close to the text as possible and to avoid augmenting the memory representation by activating background knowledge, whereas at the other extreme would be a reader who attempts to connect every aspect of the text to his or her background knowledge. The resulting memory representations would be quite different. For the first reader it would consist mainly of the textual units and their direct interconnections, whereas for the second it would contain extensive world knowledge. These representations constitute what are often called the *textbase* and *situation model*, respectively (e.g., van Dijk & Kintsch, 1983). Most readers will likely fall between the two extremes of the continuum, mixing text information with background knowledge (see McNamara & Kintsch, 1996).

Variation in background knowledge use may occur within an individual as well. For example, just as two readers with differences in expertise in an area construct different activation vectors and memory representations, so does a reader at two different stages in the development of his or her knowledge. With respect to textbase and situation model, a reader may sometimes aim to stay close to the text and at other times engage in extensive activation of background knowledge.

Standards for Coherence and Reading Strategies. As described earlier in this piece, the contents of the activation vectors during reading depend, in part, on the reader's standards for coherence. These standards determine when adequate coherence is attained and when additional retrieval from prior reading cycles or from background knowledge is necessary (Lorch, Lorch, & Klusewitz, 1993; van den Broek et al., 1995; see also Goldman & Saul, 1990). If a reader is interested in minimal comprehension (see McKoon & Ratcliff, 1992), the standards for coherence are met relatively easily and little reactivation or background-knowledge retrieval takes place. In contrast, if a reader is interested in attaining a thorough understanding of the text, then the standards for coherence are very demanding: Reading will be relatively slow and involve extensive recruiting of background knowledge or of information from the mental representation that has been constructed so far (e.g., van Oostendorp, 1991). The resulting differences in activation vectors are reflected, in turn, in the updated memory representation and hence in performance in subsequent comprehension and memory tasks. In the implementations of the Landscape model described in this piece, the standards are assumed to be causal and referential coherence. These standards were chosen because they have been found to be shared by individuals and across reading situations. However, there can be little doubt that readers frequently adopt additional standards, particularly in light of a particular task (e.g., exam preparation, literary analysis, trying to identify who's "done it" in detective stories). These additional standards and the relations among standards have not yet been investigated but could easily be implemented in the Landscape model.

A reader's standards for coherence are closely related to his or her reading strategies. On the one hand, a reader's standards determine when the reader feels that comprehension is achieved (which may, of course, differ from what a teacher considers adequate comprehension). On the other hand, a reader's reading strategies and metacognitive skills determine whether he or she can attain the standards for coherence. A reader may realize that a standard of comprehension is not attained but lack the strategies to remedy the problem.

Processing. Readers may differ in various aspects of the processing described by the Landscape model. For example, readers may differ in the amount of attentional resources they have available (e.g., Just & Carpenter, 1992; Singer, Andrusiak, Reisdorf, & Black, 1992; Whitney, Ritchie, & Clark, 1991). As a second example, readers may differ in the extent to which the cohorts of concepts in the current vector are activated. If cohort activation is strong, the textual information will be strongly integrated with all prior information as well as with background knowledge and hence the predictive association between any two concepts will be weak. Conversely, if cohort activation is weak, few connections are built, but those that are will have strong predictive power. As a last example, readers may differ in the slope of their learning curves, attaining the maximum more quickly or more slowly. Activation vectors (and the resulting representation) will be affected by differences in these processing properties.

Retrieval

Retrieval of information from the mental representation can take various forms. It may occur during reading or after reading; it may occur as a general attempt to retrieve the entire text or in an effort to locate specific information. In the Landscape model, the process of retrieval is identical, regardless of timing and purpose, but the outcome is not. The reason is that at any one time retrieval is determined by two factors: (1) the current activation vector and (2) the memory representation. The ease and speed with which one can respond to a task (e.g., a speeded laboratory task, wanting to relate a story to a friend, recalling instructions read in a manual) is influenced by the combination of the two sources. As the memory representation changes (e.g., at different points in the reading process) so does information retrieval. Thus, using *knight* as a prompt, *dragon* is activated more easily after the third cycle in the story than at the end of the story (see connection strengths in Figure 1). Likewise, the activation vector that is the starting point for retrieval influences the ease with which a particular piece of information is retrieved. Thus, the manner in which an activation vector prompts retrieval depends on its content. For example, if the retrieval cue is "Tell me all you can remember about the story about the knight," the network will be accessed in a slightly different way than if the retrieval cue were "Tell me all you can remember about the story about the princess." Even more different outcomes will be observed with retrieval cues that contain two concepts or that elicit entirely different activities (e.g., following directions versus recall of an instruction manual). Evidence that different tasks elicit different retrieval patterns comes from text research (e.g., Trabasso & van den Broek, 1985; van den Broek, 1988) and from general memory research (see Klatzky, 1980).

Retrieval after reading also varies as a function of whether it is immediate or delayed. If retrieval is initiated immediately after reading has been completed, the activation vector for the last cycle is still active and will enter into the equation of the retrieval process, but if recall is delayed it will play no role. These predictions are consistent with findings that, with delay, the influence of overall text structure increases with delay, whereas that of surface properties decreases (e.g., Trabasso et al., 1984; see also Sachs, 1967). Likewise, O'Brien and Myers (1987) observed that retrieval differs as a function of whether the process is started immediately on completion of reading or after a delay.

In summary, retrieval of textual information is a function of the structure of the memory representation that is being accessed as well as of the current activation vector. These two factors, and their interaction, determine both the content and the order of what is retrieved.

Conclusion

In this piece, we have proposed a model of reading comprehension that captures the cognitive processes that take place during reading as well as the memory representation that results. This model exemplifies the third generation of research in reading, in which the insights gained from the first two generations—with a focus on memory representation and online activations, respectively—are combined to yield an integrated theoretical description of process and product in reading comprehension. We have shown that the Landscape model has considerable psychological validity, predicting online activations and both frequency and order of recall. Furthermore, we have illustrated how the model captures specific features of memory and comprehension of text, such as the resolution of contradictions, and generates testable hypotheses on topics ranging from the interaction between forward and backward inferences to the effects of individual differences.

We have illustrated and tested the model by assuming that readers attempt to attain causal and referential coherence as they proceed through a text. This assumption seems a reasonable one, given that it has ample support in the research literature and is embraced by many investigators. It should be pointed out, though, that the Landscape model can be used to implement other assumptions as well. For example, one could model a comprehender who does not care (or have the skills) to attain causal coherence. Or one could add emotional valence of events as a factor in determining online activations. These are just a few examples, but they illustrate how the Landscape model constitutes a general platform for testing and comparing theoretical notions about the sources for activation.

The model is general in another sense as well. In this piece, we have focused on comprehension of narrative texts, but the model has generality that extends beyond narratives. For other types of texts, the factors that determine the content of the vectors and hence the connections that result may differ but the processes of translating the vectors into a memory representation will be the same (cf. Goldman & Varma, 1995; Goldman et al., 1996). Indeed, the Landscape model can be applied to the processing of any type of temporarily distributed information, not just reading. Striking similarities have been observed between processing of narrative texts and that of information presented in television programs (van den Broek, Lorch, & Thurlow, 1996) or movies (Magliano, Dijkstra, & Zwaan, 1996; Sharp, Bransford, Goldman, Risko, Kinzer, & Vye, 1995). Application of the model to these diverse settings will allow us to determine the commonalities and differences in the comprehension skills that people bring to bear in different aspects of their lives (see Gernsbacher, 1990; van den Broek, Lorch, et al., 1996).

Acknowledgments

We thank Susan Goldman, Valerie Gyselink, Herre van Oostendorp, and Sashank Varma for their comments on an earlier version of this piece. The research described in this piece was supported by the Center for Cognitive Sciences at the University of Minnesota through a grant from the National Institute of Child Health and Human Development (HD-07151).

Notes

[1] We are not the first to use a landscape metaphor. In 1890, William James described concept activation during sentence reading in a similar fashion (*Principles of Psychology*, pp. 279–283).

[2] Only concepts directly relevant to the text are included. A complete depiction would include *all* concepts that a person possesses. Most of the additional concepts would, of course, receive zero activation. Those with nonzero activation result in context-dependent learning.

[3] One might speculate, for example, that consciousness consists of those concepts that exceed a certain threshold of activation (Baars, 1988).

[4] In the implementations of the model discussed later, no explicit limits are imposed on the available pool of activation. There are two reasons for this. First, the texts used to illustrate and test the models are simple and unlikely to challenge any limited resources. Second, it allows us to show how the competition learning curve (described in the next section) already considerably constrains the flow of activation.

[5] The comprehension processes themselves can be automatic or strategic.

[6] The focus here is on the construction of an episodic representation of the text. Note, however, that the contents of the reader's semantic memory (i.e., background knowledge) are updated in a similar fashion, for example by comprehension of a text. In light of the asymptotic learning curve, discussed later, the modifications in semantic memory caused by a single text are likely to be small, though, unless a concept or set of concepts receives massive and/or repeated attention.

[7] A reader need not be aware that he or she is engaging in this attempt or that he or she is employing any particular criteria/standards for coherence.

[8] The simplified version did not include cohort activation and used a Hebbian learning rule rather than an asymptotic learning curve.

[9] In this respect, the Landscape model shares many features with the Resonance model (O'Brien & Albrecht, 1992). Unlike the Resonance model, however, the Landscape model explicitly allows for the possibility that reactivation and hence inconsistency detection may take place as a side effect of other processes, such as an effort to comprehend the current sentence.

References

Albrecht, J.E., & O'Brien, E.J. (1993). Updating a mental model: Maintaining both local and global coherence. *Journal of Experimental Psychology: Learning, Memory, and Cognition, 19*, 1061–1070.

Baars, B.J. (1988). *A cognitive theory of consciousness.* New York: Cambridge University Press.

Balota, D.A., & Lorch, R.F. (1986). Depth of automatic spread activation: Mediated priming effects in pronunciation but not in lexical decision. *Journal of Experimental Psychology: Learning, Memory, and Cognition, 12*, 336–345.

Bloom, C.P., Fletcher, C.R., van den Broek, P.W., Reitz, L., & Shapiro, B.P. (1990). An on-line assessment of causal reasoning during text comprehension. *Memory & Cognition, 18*, 65–71.

Casteel, M.A. (1993). Effects of inference necessity and reading goal on children's inferential generation. *Developmental Psychology, 29*, 346–357.

Chi, M.T.H., Feltovich, P.J., & Glaser, R. (1981). Categorization and representation of physics problems by experts and novices. *Cognitive Sciences*, 5, 121–152.

Chiesi, H.L., Spilich, G.J., & Voss, J.F. (1979). Acquisition of domain related information in relation to high and low domain knowledge. *Journal of Verbal Learning and Verbal Behavior*, 18, 257–274.

Colby, B.N. (1973). A partial grammar of Eskimo folktales. *American Anthropologist*, 75, 645–662.

Cortazar, J. (1966). *Hopscotch*. New York: Random House.

Ericsson, K.A., & Kintsch, W. (1995). Long-term working memory. *Psychological Review*, 102, 211–245.

Fletcher, C.R., & Bloom, C.P. (1988). Causal reasoning in the comprehension of simple narrative texts. *Journal of Memory and Language*, 27, 235–244.

Fletcher, C.R., Hummel, J.E., & Marsolek, C.J. (1990). Causality and the allocation of attention during comprehension. *Journal of Experimental Psychology: Learning, Memory, and Cognition*, 16, 233–240.

Fletcher, C.R., van den Broek, P.W., & Arthur, E. (1996). A model of narrative comprehension and recall. In B.K. Britton & A.C. Graesser (Eds.), *Models of understanding text* (pp. 141–163). Hillsdale, NJ: Erlbaum.

Garrod, A., & Sanford, S. (1990). Referential processing in reading: Focusing on roles and individuals. In D.A. Balota, G.B. Flores d'Arcais, & K. Rayner (Eds.), *Comprehension processes in reading* (pp. 465–484). Hillsdale, NJ: Erlbaum.

Gernsbacher, M.A. (1990). *Language comprehension as structure building*. Hillsdale, NJ: Erlbaum.

Golden, R.M. (1994). Analysis of categorical time-series text recall data using a connectionist model. *Journal of Biological Systems*, 2, 283–305.

Goldman, S.R. (1985). Inferential reasoning in and about narrative texts. In A.C. Graesser & J.B. Black (Eds.), *The psychology of questions* (pp. 247–276). Hillsdale, NJ: Erlbaum.

Goldman, S.R., & Saul, E.U. (1990). Flexibility in text processing: A strategy competition model. *Learning and Individual Differences*, 2, 181–219.

Goldman, S.R., & Varma, S. (1995). CAPping the construction-integration model of discourse comprehension. In C.A. Weaver, S. Marines,

& C.R. Fletcher (Eds.), *Discourse comprehension: Essays in honor of Walter Kintsch* (pp. 337–358). Mahwah, NJ: Erlbaum.

Goldman, S.R., Varma, S., & Coté, N. (1996). Extending capacity-constrained construction-integration: Toward "smarter" and flexible models of text comprehension. In B.K. Britton & A.C. Graesser (Eds.), *Models of understanding text* (pp. 73–114). Mahwah, NJ: Erlbaum.

Goldman, S.R., & Varnhagen, C.K. (1986). Memory for embedded and sequential story structures. *Journal of Memory and Language*, 25, 401–418.

Graesser, A.C., & Clark, L.F. (1985). *The structures and procedures of implicit knowledge*. Norwood, NJ: Ablex.

Graesser, A.C., Singer, M., & Trabasso, T. (1994). Constructing inferences during narrative text comprehension. *Psychological Review*, 101, 371–395.

James, W.A. (1890). *Principles of psychology*. New York: Holt.

Johnson, H.M., & Seifert, C.M. (1994). Sources of the continued influence effect: When discredited information in memory affects later inferences. *Journal of Experimental Psychology: Learning, Memory, and Cognition*, 20, 1420–1436.

Just, A.M., & Carpenter, P.A. (1992). A capacity theory of comprehension: Individual differences in working memory. *Psychological Review*, 99, 122–149.

Keefe, D.E., & McDaniel, M.A. (1993). The time course and duration of prediction inferences. *Journal of Memory and Language*, 32, 446–463.

Kintsch, W. (1988). The role of knowledge in discourse comprehension: A construction-integration model. *Psychological Review*, 95, 163–182.

Kintsch, W., & van Dijk, T.A. (1978). Towards a model of text comprehension and production. *Psychological Review*, 85, 363–394.

Klatzky, R.L. (1980). *Human memory structures and processes*. San Francisco: Freeman & Company.

Klin, C.M., & Myers, J.L. (1993). Reinstatement of causal information during reading. *Journal of Experimental Psychology: Learning, Memory, and Cognition*, 19, 554–560.

Landauer, T.K, & Dumais, S.T. (1997). A solution to Plato's problem: The Latent Semantic Analysis theory of acquisition, induction, and representation of knowledge. *Psychological Review, 104,* 211–240.

Langston, M., & Trabasso, T. (1999). Modeling causal integration and availability of information during comprehension of narrative texts. In H. van Oostendorp & S.R. Goldman (Eds.), *The construction of mental representations during reading* (pp. 29–69). Mahwah, NJ: Erlbaum.

Lorch, R.F., Jr., Lorch, E.P., & Klusewitz, M.A. (1993). College students' conditional knowledge about reading. *Journal of Educational Psychology, 85,* 239–252.

Lucas, M.M., Tanenhaus, M.K., & Carlson, G.N. (1990). Levels of representation in the interpretation of anaphoric reference and instrument inference. *Memory & Cognition, 18,* 611–631.

Magliano, J.P., Dijkstra, K., & Zwaan, R.A. (1996). Predictive inferences in movies. *Discourse Processes, 22,* 199–224.

Mandler, J.M. (1984). *Stories, scripts, and scenes: Aspects of schema theory.* Hillsdale, NJ: Erlbaum.

Mandler, J.M., & Johnson, N.S. (1977). Remembrance of things parsed: Story structure and recall. *Cognitive Psychology, 9,* 111–151.

McDaniel, M.A., & Einstein, G.O. (1989). Material appropriate processing: A contextualistic approach to reading and studying strategies. *Educational Psychology Review, 1,* 113–145.

McKoon, G., & Ratcliff, R. (1980). Priming in item recognition: The organization of propositions in memory for text. *Journal of Verbal Learning and Verbal Behavior, 19,* 326–338.

McKoon, G., & Ratcliff, R. (1989). Semantic associations and elaborative inferences. *Journal of Experimental Psychology: Learning, Memory, and Cognition, 15,* 326–338.

McKoon, G., & Ratcliff, R. (1992). Inferences during reading. *Psychological Review, 99,* 440–466.

McNamara, D.S., & Kintsch, W. (1996). Learning from text: Effects of prior knowledge and text coherence. *Discourse Processes, 22,* 247–287.

Meyer, B.J.F. (1975). *The organization of prose and its effects on memory.* Amsterdam: North-Holland.

Miller, J.R., & Kintsch, W. (1980). Readability and recall of short prose passages: A theoretical analysis. *Journal of Experimental Psychology: Human Learning and Memory, 6,* 335–354.

Myers, J.L. (1990). Causal relatedness and text comprehension. In D.A. Balota, G.B. Flores d'Arcais, & K. Rayner (Eds.), *Comprehension processes in reading* (pp. 361–375). Hillsdale, NJ: Erlbaum.

O'Brien, E.J. (1987). Antecedent search processes and the structure of text. *Journal of Experimental Psychology: Learning, Memory, and Cognition, 13,* 278–290.

O'Brien, E.J., & Albrecht, J.E. (1992). Comprehension strategies in the development of a mental model. *Journal of Experimental Psychology: Learning, Memory, and Cognition, 18,* 777–784.

O'Brien, E.J., Albrecht J., Hakala, C., & Rizzella, M. (1995). Activation and suppression of antecedents during reinstatement. *Journal of Experimental Psychology: Learning, Memory, and Cognition, 21,* 626–634.

O'Brien, E.J., Duffy, S.A., & Myers, J.L. (1986). Anaphoric inference during reading. *Journal of Experimental Psychology: Learning, Memory, and Cognition, 12,* 346–352.

O'Brien, E.J., & Myers, J.L. (1987). The role of causal connections in the retrieval of text. *Memory & Cognition, 15,* 419–427.

O'Brien, E.J., Shank, D., Myers, J.L., & Rayner, K. (1988). Elaborative inferences during reading: Do they occur on-line? *Journal of Experimental Psychology: Learning, Memory, and Cognition, 14,* 410–420.

Perfetti, C.A., & Goldman, S.R. (1974). Thematization and sentence retrieval. *Journal of Verbal Learning and Verbal Behavior, 13,* 70–79.

Propp, V. (1928). *Morphology of the folktale.* Austin: University of Texas Press.

Raaijmakers, J.G.W., & Shiffrin, R.M. (1981). Search of associative memory. *Psychological Review, 88,* 93–134.

Ratcliff, R., & McKoon, G. (1988). A retrieval theory of priming. *Psychological Review, 21,* 139–155.

Risden, J. (1996). *Causal inference in narrative text comprehension.* Unpublished doctoral dissertation, University of Minnesota, Minneapolis.

Sachs, J. (1967). Recognition memory for syntactic and semantic aspects of connected discourse. *Perception & Psychophysics, 2,* 437–442.

Schank, R.G., & Abelson, R.P. (1977). *Scripts, plans, goals, and understanding.* Hillsdale, NJ: Erlbaum.

Sharkey A.J.C., & Sharkey, N.E. (1992). Weak contextual constraints in text and word priming. *Journal of Memory and Language, 31,* 543–572.

Sharp, D.L.M., Bransford, J.D., Goldman, S.R., Risko, V.J., Kinzer, C.K., & Vye, N.J. (1995). Dynamic visual support for story comprehension and mental model building by young, at risk children. *Educational Technology Research and Development, 43,* 25–42.

Singer, M. (1994). *Discourse inference processes.* In M.A. Gernsbacher (Ed.), *Handbook of psycholinguistics* (pp. 479–515). New York: Academic Press.

Singer, M., Andrusiak, P., Reisdorf, P., & Black, N.L. (1992). Individual differences in bridging inference processes. *Memory & Cognition, 20,* 539–548.

Singer, M., & Ferreira, F. (1983). Inferring consequences in story comprehension. *Journal of Verbal Learning and Verbal Behavior, 22,* 437–448.

Singer, M., Graesser, A.C., & Trabasso, T. (1994). Minimal or global inference during reading. *Journal of Memory and Language, 33,* 421–441.

Singer, M., & Ritchot, K.F.M. (1996). The role of working memory capacity and knowledge access in text inference processing. *Memory & Cognition, 24,* 733–743.

Stein, N.L., & Glenn, C.G. (1979). An analysis of story comprehension in elementary school children. In R.O. Freedle (Ed.), *New directions in discourse processing* (pp. 53–120). Hillsdale, NJ: Erlbaum.

Suh, S., & Trabasso, T. (1993). Inference during on-line processing: Converging evidence from discourse analysis, talk-aloud protocols, and recognition priming. *Journal of Memory and Language, 32,* 279–301.

Till, R.E., Mross, E.F., & Kintsch, W. (1988). Time course of priming for associate and inference words in a discourse context. *Memory & Cognition, 16,* 283–298.

Trabasso, T., Secco, T., & van den Broek, P.W. (1984). Causal cohesion and story coherence. In H. Mandl, N.L. Stein, & T. Trabasso (Eds.), *Learning and comprehension of text* (pp. 83–111). Hillsdale, NJ: Erlbaum.

Trabasso, T., & Suh, S.Y. (1993). Using talk-aloud protocols to reveal inferences during comprehension of text. *Discourse Processes, 16,* 3–34.

Trabasso, T., & van den Broek, P.W. (1985). Causal thinking and the representation of narrative events. *Journal of Memory and Language, 24,* 612–630.

Trabasso, T., van den Broek, P.W., & Suh, S.Y. (1989). Logical necessity and transitivity of causal relations in stories. *Discourse Processes, 12,* 1–25.

Turner, A., & Greene, E. (1978). Construction and use of a propositional text base. *Journal Supplement Abstract Service Catalogue of Selected Documents in Psychology,* Ms. No. 1713.

van den Broek, P.W. (1988). The effects of causal relations and hierarchical position on the importance of story statements. *Journal of Memory and Language, 27,* 1–22.

van den Broek, P.W. (1990a). The causal inference marker: Towards a process model of inference generation in text comprehension. In D.A. Balota, G.B. Flores d'Arcais, & K. Rayner (Eds.), *Comprehension processes in reading* (pp. 423–446). Hillsdale, NJ: Erlbaum.

van den Broek, P.W. (1990b). Causal inference and the comprehension of narrative text. In A.C. Graesser & G.H. Bower (Eds.), *Inferences and text comprehension* (pp. 175–194). San Diego, CA: Academic Press.

van den Broek, P.W. (1994). Comprehension and memory of narrative texts: Inferences and coherence. In M.A. Gernsbacher (Ed.), *Handbook of psycholinguistics* (pp. 539–588). San Diego, CA: Academic Press.

van den Broek, P.W., Fletcher, C.R., & Risden, K. (1993). Investigation of inferential processes in reading: A theoretical and methodological integration. *Discourse Processes, 12,* 169–180.

van den Broek, P.W., & Huang, Y. (1995). *Forward inferences during text comprehension: The role of causal constraint.* Paper presented at the 36th annual meeting of the Psychonomic Society, Los Angeles, CA.

van den Broek, P.W., & Lorch, R.F., Jr. (1993). Causal relations in memory for narrative text: Evidence from a priming task for network representations. *Discourse Processes, 16,* 75–98.

van den Broek, P.W., Lorch, E.P., & Thurlow, R. (1996). Children's and adults' memory for television stories: The role of causal factors, story-grammar categories, and hierarchical level. *Child Development, 67,* 3010–3028.

van den Broek, P.W., Risden, K., Fletcher, C.R., & Thurlow, R. (1996). A "landscape" view of reading: Fluctuating patterns of activation and the construction of a stable memory representation. In B.K. Britton & A.C. Graesser

(Eds.), *Models of understanding text* (pp. 165–187). Mahwah, NJ: Erlbaum.

van den Broek, P.W., Risden, K., & Husebye-Hartman, E. (1995). The role of readers' standards for coherence in the generation of inferences during reading. In R.F. Lorch, Jr., & E.J. O'Brien (Eds.), *Sources of coherence in reading* (pp. 353–373). Mahwah, NJ: Erlbaum.

van den Broek, P.W., Rohleder, L., & Narvaez, D. (1996). Causal inferences in the comprehension of literary texts. In R.J. Kreuz & M.S. McNealy (Eds.), *The empirical study of literature* (pp. 179–200). Mahwah, NJ: Erlbaum.

van den Broek, P.W., & Thurlow, R. (1990). *Reinstatements and elaborative inferences during the reading of narratives.* Paper presented at the 31st annual meeting of the Psychonomic Society, New Orleans, LA.

van den Broek, P.W., & Trabasso, T. (1986). Causal networks versus goal hierarchies in summarizing text. *Discourse Processes, 9,* 1–15.

van den Broek, P.W., Young, M., & Risden, K. (1996). *The competitive cohort model.* Unpublished manuscript.

van Dijk, T.A., & Kintsch, W. (1983). *Strategies for discourse comprehension.* New York: Academic Press.

van Oostendorp, H. (1991). Inferences and integrations made by readers of script-based texts. *Journal of Research in Reading, 14,* 3–20.

van Oostendorp, H., & Bonebakker, C. (1999). Difficulties in updating mental representations during reading news reports. In H. van Oostendorp & S.R. Goldman (Eds.), *The construction of mental representations during reading* (pp. 319–339). Mahwah, NJ: Erlbaum

Vonk, W., & Noordman, L.G. (1990). On the control of inferences in text understanding. In D.A. Balota, G.B. Flores d'Arcais, & K. Rayner (Eds.), *Comprehension processes in reading* (pp. 447–463). Hillsdale, NJ: Erlbaum.

Whitney, P., & Budd, D. (1996). Think-aloud protocols and the study of comprehension. *Discourse Processes, 21,* 341–351.

Whitney, P., Ritchie, B.G., & Clark, M.B. (1991). Working memory capacity and the use of elaborative inferences in text comprehension. *Discourse Processes, 14,* 133–145.

Wilkes, A.L., & Leatherbarrow, M. (1988). Editing episodic memory following the identification of error. *Quarterly Journal of Experimental Psychology, 40,* 361–387.

Zwaan, R.A., & Brown, C.M. (1996). The influence of language proficiency and comprehension skill on situation-model construction. *Discourse Processes, 21,* 289–327.

46

The Construction–Integration Model of Text Comprehension and Its Implications for Instruction

Walter Kintsch

Comprehension: A Paradigm for Cognition

Understanding and *comprehension* are everyday terms, useful, but imprecise. We know what we mean when we say we understand a text, but understanding is difficult to define precisely: It is not necessary that we repeat the text verbatim, but we ought to be able to come up with the gist; it is not necessary that we think of every implication of what we have read, but we do not understand it if we miss the most obvious ones; it is not necessary that we answer every question that could be asked, but we cannot miss them all. In the laboratory as well as in the classroom, this problem is solved by fiat, operationally: We are willing to say that someone understands a text if he or she passes whatever test we have decided on: provide a summary, answer questions, verify inferences, and so forth. Not all of these operational definitions of understanding are equivalent, nor are they appropriate for all purposes. Much of the discussion in this piece aims at clarifying this situation, empirically, by showing what works where and for what purposes, and theoretically, by providing a framework that allows us to describe the different flavors of comprehension processes and outcomes.

There is, however, also a more technical use of the term *comprehension* that concerns us here. It is the sense in which comprehension is used in the phrase "comprehension as a paradigm for cognition." Cognition ranges from perception on the one hand to analytic thought on the other. Typically, the processes of perception and thinking are conceptualized in different ways. Perception is usually considered as some sort of constraint satisfaction process, where the organism must make sense of a wide variety of sensory inputs involving several modalities, such as solving a puzzle in which the pieces could be assembled in several different ways; the best way is the one that violates the least number of constraints. Thinking or problem solving, in contrast, is a matter of planning, of generating search spaces and using means–end strategies to find a solution path. Reading comprehension shares aspects with both. On the one hand, one normally just reads and understands, much like we understand when we look at a visual scene, without elaborate planning and effortful problem solving. But when this normal process breaks down, the reader (or perceiver) becomes a problem solver who must figure out what it is he reads (or sees). Comprehension in this technical sense is automatic meaning construction via constraint satisfaction, without purposeful, conscious effort. Normal reading involves automatic comprehension, as well as conscious problem solving whenever the pieces of the puzzle do not fit together as they should.

The theory of text comprehension outlined in this piece is a comprehension model in the sense discussed here, but it leaves room for problem solving and planning when that becomes necessary to complement normal reading. This is a matter with considerable educational implications because instruction by its very nature pushes readers beyond what they already know and are comfortable with, requiring active, effortful, resource-demanding problem-solving activities that are difficult to maintain and direct.

Cognition and Representation

Theorists interested in text comprehension talk about the outcome of comprehension in terms of mental representations. Considered most broadly, in the present context, a mental representation is some change in the way the mind views the world as a result of reading a text, that is, some sort of trace of the text read, including indirect effects, cognitive as well as affective ones—perhaps a tendency to act in a certain way or to feel good or bad about something. There is little agreement about mental representations (or the lack thereof) among cognitive scientists at this point, and it would be impossible to do justice to the complex literature in a brief review. But there are a few points that are directly relevant to text comprehension, and that are not overly controversial.

The mind represents different aspects of the world. It is convenient to talk about these as different types or levels of representation. In a reading context, the levels that concern us most directly are perceptual representations, verbal representations, and semantic representations. Perceptual representations may be images of how the words looked on the page or how they sounded when spoken by a particular person. They also may be, however, images of the scene described by the text, constructed by the reader. Verbal or linguistic representations are about the words, sentences, and discourses themselves. Semantic representations refer to the ideas expressed by the words. Obviously, these levels are not cleanly separable. A word has perceptual characteristics as well as meaning, but when we talk about how a word is perceived and remembered, it is useful to keep these different aspects separate because they behave differently. Similar visual forms are confused with each other, as are similar phonemes, but words are more often confused on the basis of semantic similarity; decoding is strongly influenced by word length and word frequency, but semantic relations and conceptual structure are more important for comprehension. Hence, psychologists, as well as educators, do well to differentiate between the various levels of mental representations.

There is one more reason for the distinction among levels of representation. Theorists and model builders can deal quite well with verbal and semantic representations, but so far they have not developed the tools to deal effectively with imagery. Various systems are in use to represent the meaning of words. Feature systems are used widely; for instance, *bachelor* has the features *male* and *unmarried*, plus some others. Alternatively, word meanings are represented by their position in a semantic structure: *Shark* is defined as a member of the category *fish*, with special properties, such as *dangerous*. Or one can define word meanings by their position in a semantic space: *Lion* might be characterized by high values on the dimensions *size* and *ferocity*, whereas *mouse* would have low values. High-dimensional, abstract semantic spaces are especially effective for representing the meaning of words. Propositions are idea units, combining more than one word in a schematic form: *The hiker watches the elk with his binoculars* is a conceptual unit that relates, by means of the predicate *watches*, an agent, object, and an instrument in a meaningful, conventional way. Propositions thus allow the theorist to represent the meaning of sentences, independent of their syntactic structure (e.g., a sentence in passive or active voice would be represented by the same proposition). Furthermore, propositions can be combined to form representations of whole texts, as described in more detail below. The structure of these text representations is of great significance, because it allows the theorist to distinguish important ideas from mere detail, and it predicts how a text is comprehended and remembered.

Propositional structures are useful to represent the meaning of a text because they tend to mimic the properties of how people represent the meaning of a text. As yet we do not have comparable systems to represent mental images. Pictures will not do, for much the same reason that a text is not well represented by the actual words used: The picture does not make explicit the psychologically important aspects of an image. In the auditory domain, phonemic features capture quite well the salient aspects of how people perceive and remember the sounds of a language. However, visual feature systems have been only partially successful and have limited use, for example, in the form of geons (simple, primary shapes, such as bricks, cylinders, cones, and wedges that compose visual images and distinguish one image from another, as in a shoe vs. an ice cream cone) (Biederman, 1987). While propositions provide the theorist with a convenient and workable representation for the meaning of texts, at present there really is no language that we can use to represent the salient features of complex mental images. This deficiency is a major reason why much of the research on text comprehension has focused on the verbal aspects, neglecting the role of mental imagery for all its acknowledged significance. We shall, however, point out that significance wherever possible.

Levels of Text Representation

Texts consist of words, organized into sentences, paragraphs, and higher-order discourse units such as sections or chapters. The mental representation a reader forms thereof often is called the *surface-level memory*—the memory for the actual words and phrases of the text. Surface memory is typically short-lived, especially for instructional texts, where it does not matter much exactly how something is said (Sachs, 1967). Where that matters, as in a poem, joke, or argument, exact wording can be remembered very well, however (W. Kintsch & Bates, 1977).

For many purposes, we are not concerned with exact wording but with the message conveyed. Thus, it is useful to distinguish a semantic level of text representation—the ideas expressed by the text. We shall call this the *propositional level* of representation because propositions are one way of specifying what constitutes an idea in a text.

For present purposes[1] we define an *atomic proposition* as a linguistic unit consisting of a relational term (or predicate) and one or more arguments (which may be concepts or other propositions). Some examples of phrases and their corresponding atomic propositions are as follows:

(1) *Little boy* or *The boy is little* → [LITTLE, BOY]

(2) *The boy chopped the wood* → [CHOP, BOY, WOOD]

Note that this representation does not represent all information in a sentence (e.g., the past tense in (2), which is not important enough in many situations in which such propositional representations are used).

A *complex proposition* is a network of atomic propositions corresponding to a (simple) sentence. Propositions are linked in a network either because they are related referentially, as in (3), or because of propositional embedding (in (4) the arguments of the proposition are themselves atomic propositions).

(3) *The little boy chopped wood* → [CHOP, BOY, WOOD] —— [LITTLE, BOY]

(4) *Although the boy was little, he chopped the wood* →

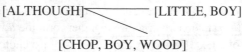

Links may be based on other-than-referential overlap among propositions, for example, on the basis of a causal relationship, as in the following sentence:

(5) *The little boy was tired from chopping wood* →

<pre>
        [TIRED, BOY]‾‾‾‾‾‾‾‾[LITTLE, BOY]

              [CHOP, BOY, WOOD]
</pre>

This form of propositional representation is intentionally crude; its purpose is not to represent the meaning of a text in all its considerable complexity but to make it possible to count idea units in a text in a reasonably principled way (W. Kintsch, 1974; van Dijk & Kintsch, 1983). Both for the purpose of psychological research on text and instructional design, the number of idea units as defined here and their interrelationship are major variables of interest. Usually, we are not interested in how many words someone remembers but in how many and which ideas are remembered. What makes reading difficult is determined not only by sentence length and the familiarity of the words used but also by the number of ideas expressed, their coherence, and their structure (W. Kintsch, 1974). Propositional analysis, therefore, has become a valuable research tool (although it is not a teaching tool). Unfortunately, because it depends on hand coding, it is extremely laborious and not fully objective (a current guide is W. Kintsch, 1998, chap. 3.1.1).

The syntactic information in a sentence largely determines the structure of the propositional network. For instance, the main verb of a sentence is taken to form the superordinate proposition, and modifiers are subordinated to it, as in (3). However, there is more structure in a discourse than the sentence syntax. Discourses are organized globally, often according to conventional rhetorical formats. Thus, the simplest stories are of the form setting-complication-resolution; instructional texts may employ various structures such as a compare-and-contrast schema, or a generalization-plus-examples schema. To distinguish this discourse-level structure from the sentence-level structure, the terms *macrostructure* and *microstructure* are used. The microstructure of a text is the network of propositions that represents the meaning of the text. One can think of it as a translation from the actual words used into an idea-level format. The macrostructure is the global organization of these ideas into higher-order units. Thus, a story may have many propositions, linked in a complex network, but at the macrostructure level these propositions are grouped into the conventional sections: setting, complication, and resolution. However, a writer also could have chosen a different way of telling his story, for example, starting with the resolution and then filling in the setting and complication in the form of a flashback. That approach yields a very different macrostructure, while the microstructure might not be changed very much.

Microstructure and macrostructure together form the *textbase*, the semantic underpinning of a text. However, for purposes of psychological research on text comprehension, as well as for understanding educational practice, it is important to distinguish a further level of text representation, the *situation model*. The situation model represents the information provided by the text, independent of the particular manner in which it was expressed in the text, and integrated with background information from the reader's prior knowledge. What sort of situation model readers construct depends very much on their goals in reading the text, as well as the amount of relevant prior knowledge that they have. Thus, cooperative and attentive readers will more or less form the same textbase micro- and macrostructures, as invited by the author of the text. But depending on their interests, purposes, and background knowledge, they may form widely different situation models. In instruction, it is usually the situation model that the student forms from reading a text that is of interest; the teacher does not care whether the student can recite the text but whether the student understood it correctly and, for future use, was able to integrate the textual information with whatever background knowledge there was.

Situation models are not necessarily verbal. Texts are verbal, and textbases are propositional structures, but to model the situation described by a text, people often resort to imagery. Mental images of maps, diagrams, and pictures are integrated with verbal information in ways not well understood by researchers. Individual preferences in this regard further limit the ability to predict just what sort of a situation model a reader will form from a text.

It is important to ask not only whether a good, correct situation model has been formed by a reader reading a text, but also whether this new model has been integrated with the reader's prior knowledge. It is quite possible that readers may construct adequate textbases but fail to link them with other relevant portions of their prior knowledge. The result is encapsulated knowledge. If readers are reminded of the text from which they have acquired this knowledge, they can remember it and successfully use this knowledge, but it is not part of their generally available knowledge base. Encapsulated knowledge can be retrieved only via the specific episodic text memory; it is not available on occasions when such knowledge may be useful but the episodic retrieval cues are lacking. Thus, students can do their calculus problems at the ends of the chapters in their textbooks, and even on final exams, but have no idea what to do when they are supposed to use their knowledge in an engineering class. To make knowledge acquired from texts usable in novel situations, it must be actively linked to semantic retrieval cues, which is not an automatic process but one that requires strategic action and effort on the part of the reader/learner.

Example: Levels of Representation

"Connected" is a story of about 2,500 words written with the purpose of teaching novice students some basic facts about electricity that are embedded in the story in the form of explanations provided by a father to his daughter, who is trying to solve a puzzle requiring knowledge of these facts. The story has four subheadings: "An important event," "Life on the farm," "How does electricity work?" and "Solving the mystery."

The surface memory for this text refers to whatever sentences and sentence fragments from this text are still available in the reader's memory, and it need not concern us further here.

The macrostructure of the text is shown in Table 1. It is basically a high-level summary, organized according to the classical story schema. It only roughly corresponds to the subheadings of the actual text: The setting comprises the first and part of the second section, the complication corresponds to part of the second and the third sections, and the resolution matches the final section.

An example of the microstructure for this text is given for one brief paragraph in Table 2. The first sentence is represented as two complex propositions, C1 and C2, each consisting of three atomic propositions. C1 and C2 are linked by P4, i.e., the sentence connective *while*. The third and fourth sentences of the paragraph are each represented by a complex proposition, C3 and C4. Note that anaphoric inferences are necessary here: the *she* of the text has to be identified as *Katie*. To understand, a further inference is required: The *appliances* in the last sentence must be identified with the *electric iron*, the *electric lamp*, and the *electric sewing machine* mentioned earlier. For an adult reader, this is an automatic inference, made unconsciously and effortlessly. For a child, however, who does not really know what an appliance is, this may be a major stumbling block, requiring the reader to regress and figure out that the *appliances* are the *lamp* (which makes *light*), the *iron* (which makes *heat*), and the *sewing machine* (whose parts *moved*). What is necessary here is a conscious, strategic process of meaning construction, which is effortful and resource demanding. The reader who avoids this effort still can form a coherent textbase—Katie realizes that appliances make heat and so on—but will be unable to construct an adequate situation model without knowing what *appliances* refers to.

TABLE 1
The Macrostructure of the Story "Connected"

Setting
Location: on a farm
Time: old days
Actors: Katie, Tom, and their parents

Electricity is coming to town.
The children wonder what sort of appliance their parents are going to buy.

Complication
Their father asks them to guess what electricity-using appliance they will get first.
Katie finds out how electricity works and what it is used for.
She finds out that the appliance is not to produce either heat or motion.

Resolution
Because there are two wires on the electric line being installed, the first appliance their parents buy will be a telephone.

TABLE 2
The Microstructure for One Paragraph

*In town, her father filled the Model T's gas tank, while Katie bought a sewing machine belt and browsed in the general store. **She** saw an electric iron, electric lamps, and a sewing machine that no one had to pedal. **She** realized there were **appliances** that made heat and light and those that moved.*

C1	P1	[IN, TOWN, P2]
	P2	[FILL, FATHER, GAS-TANK]
	P3	[HAS-PART, MODEL-T, GAS-TANK]
	P4	[WHILE, P2, P5, P7]
C2	P5	[BUY, KATIE, BELT]
	P6	[HAS-PART, SEWING-MACHINE, BELT]
	P7	[BROWSE, KATIE, GENERAL-STORE]
C3	P8	[SEE, **KATIE**, IRON, LAMPS, SEWING-MACHINE]
	P9	[ELECTRIC, IRON]
	P10	[ELECTRIC, LAMPS]
	P11	[NOT-HAVE, SEWING-MACHINE, PEDAL]
C4	P12	[REALIZE, **KATIE**, P13, P14]
	P13	[MAKE, APPLIANCE, HEAT, LIGHT]
	P14	[MOVE, APPLIANCE]
	INF	[IS, **APPLIANCES**, P9, P10, P11]

For explanation, see page 1276.
C = a complex proposition; P = an atomic proposition.

What sort of situation model might a student construct upon reading this story? The student's reading goal is to learn about electricity. Hence, the situation model we are interested in concerns what the student has learned about electricity; the story is merely there to keep up the students' interest. Skillfully interwoven into our story is a puzzle, the "mystery" Katie must solve for which one needs to know certain elementary facts about electricity. The students are not faced with a list of dry facts about electricity but with information that is significant for the puzzle they—and Katie—are trying to solve. Table 3 lists these facts as the situation model a successful reader will form and link to whatever he or she already knows about electricity.

To construct Table 3, hypothetical prior knowledge for a typical reader has been assumed; any real reader may not know exactly what is listed. What is important is that the reader retrieve such pieces of prior knowledge at the right moment when reading this story so that they can become associated with the new information provided by the text. Thus, suppose a reader already knows that electricity is needed for ironing; now he or she learns that the electric energy generates heat in the process of ironing, and if this new bit of information is linked with what is already known, it successfully becomes a part of the reader's knowledge base, not just an item of information remembered in the context of that particular text.

TABLE 3
The Situation Model

Prior Knowledge	Information Provided by the Text
Electricity needs **wires**.	Electricity comes to you via **wires** (you do not have **to get it like wood to burn in the stove**).
You have to **bring wood in for the stove**.	Electricity is generated from coal or water. Static electricity produces sparks and lightning. Electric current is a form of energy (like water power).

Electricity is needed for **lamps**, **ironing**, **sewing machines**, and **telephones**.	Electric energy is used to
	    make **light** (by heating up the filament in a bulb).
	    make heat (such as for **ironing**).
	    make motion (such as in a **sewing machine** or record player).
	    talk on the **telephone** (which needs extra wire and was invented by Bell).

Links are formed between corresponding items printed in bold.

Surface structure, textbase, and situation model are levels of the mental representation of texts. We next turn to the question of how these representations are constructed.

The Process of Comprehension: Construction and Integration

Most of the research on reading deals with the decoding problem: How do readers translate the written text into words and sentences? In other words, how is the surface representation generated from a written text? This is, of course, an extremely important question with complex answers, but it is not the question that will be addressed here. Instead, we shall assume this level of representation as given and look at the formation of the textbase and the situation model.

Microstructure

Given a text—a structured string of sentences—how are the corresponding idea units derived, and how are they organized? For the most part, the language provides good cues as to the underlying ideas: *The goat ate the grass* unproblematically translates into [EAT, GOAT, GRASS]. However, language is full of ambiguities. We understand both of the following sentences:

(6) *The grade was too steep.*

(7) *His grade was an A.*

And we know who *she* and *he* are in these two sentences:

(8) *The nurse scolded the woman because she had not taken her medicine.*

(9) *The hiker saw the grizzly bear. He was afraid.*

There are two kinds of explanations of how people deal with such ambiguities, top-down theories and bottom-up theories. According to the top-down view, a schema filters out incorrect interpretations: We know we are talking about a hill, or a student, and hence assign the right meaning to *grade*; the nurse–patient schema dictates the referent for *she*; and the grizzly bear schema specifies who has to be afraid. Schema theory is very powerful (e.g., Schank & Abelson, 1977), and schema effects in perception and comprehension are well documented. Nevertheless, schema-as-filter theories of comprehension cannot fully account for comprehension processes and have been replaced by theories that assign a more decisive role to bottom-up processes, such as the Construction–Integration (CI) model (W. Kintsch, 1988, 1998). Instead of trying to construct only the correct meaning of a sentence, the CI model generates several plausible meanings in parallel and only later, when a rich context is available, sorts out which construction is the right one. This sorting out is done by means of an integration or constraint satisfaction process that suppresses those constructions that do not fit in well with the context and strengthens those that do. Specifically, activation is spread around in the propositional network that has been constructed, including the contradictory elements; the activation eventually settles on those nodes of the network that hang together, while outliers and isolated nodes become deactivated. Thus, in (6) and (7) propositions will be constructed initially involving both meanings of *grade*, but the incorrect meaning will become deactivated during the integration phase. For the anaphora identification in (8), the construction process yields

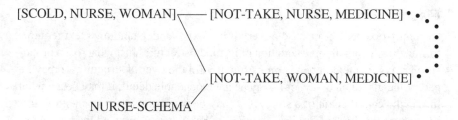

where the dotted line indicates an inhibitory link. In the integration process, the correct proposition will win out because it is connected to prior knowledge about nurses and patients (here labeled the NURSE-SCHEMA). Thus, schemas play a role in the CI model, too, not as filters that control construction but as context that influences the integration process. The inference in (9) is handled similarly: In the construction phase, the model is not sure whether the *hiker* or the *bear* is afraid, but prior knowledge settles that question during the integration phase.

Thus, the CI model uses a bottom-up construction phase in which contradictory assumptions are explored, resulting in an incoherent network that needs to be cleaned up in the integration phase. The computational advantage of such a dual process is that the construction rules do not have to be very smart, because errors can be corrected in the integration phase. Psychological data that suggest that human comprehension processes employ a similar scheme are discussed in a subsequent section on word identification.

To illustrate the construction of a microstructure, let us return to the "Connected" story discussed earlier. The list of propositions in Table 2 corresponds to the network shown in Figure 1. The links in Figure 1 are based on referential overlap between propositions. Two obligatory inferences are required to identify the pronouns for P8 and P12.

The final activation values for the network in Figure 1, once the process of spreading activation has stabilized, are shown in Figure 2. Figure 2 implies that after reading this paragraph, the strongest information in memory should be that Katie bought a belt, browsed in the general store, and saw an electric iron, electric lamps, and a sewing machine. On a recall test, those should be the items most frequently recalled. A large number of studies have borne out such recall predictions (e.g., W. Kintsch, 1974).

Also shown in Figure 2 are the strength values obtained if the reader makes the optional inference [IS-APPLIANCE, IRON, LAMP, SEWING-MACHINE]. This inference changes the picture a great deal by emphasizing the relationship between the (complex) propositions corresponding to the last two sentences of the text. It will be remembered that this was an instructional text supposed to teach about electricity. Note that without this "deep" processing (the inference about appliances) the present paragraph would not contribute much to the goal of learning physics.

Macrostructure

Generally (except for the case of very brief texts), understanding a text requires formulating a mental representation of its macrostructure. Just what role a proposition plays in a text depends on its function in the overall structure: It may be part of the gist of an essay, or it may be an expendable detail; it may be a crucial link in the causal chain of a story, or it may be irrelevant to the main story line. To capture this kind of intuition, van Dijk (1980) has introduced the concept of a macrostructure. The macrostructure of a text consists of those propositions that are globally relevant, that form its gist in everyday language. Macrostructures are frequently but not necessarily schematic; that is, they are based on conventional rhetorical forms. Thus, narratives have a conventional structure in our culture; essays may be in the form of arguments, or definitions-plus-illustrations, and so on (see van Dijk & Kintsch, 1983, chap. 2.9, for a detailed discussion). Van Dijk (1980) has enumerated three rules that describe the formation

FIGURE 1
The CI Network for a Paragraph From the "Connected" Story
(Corresponds to the Proposition List in Table 2)

IN-TOWN	c0	0.1806	(P1)
FILL-GASTANK	c0	0.5027	(P2)
OF-MODEL-T	c0	0.1806	(P3)
WHILE	c0	0.8604	(P4)
BUY-BELT	c0	0.2852	(P5)
FOR-SEWING-MACHINE	c0	0.3566	(P6)
BROWSE-STORE	c0	0.9063	(P7)
SEE	c0	1.0000	(P8)
ELECTRIC-IRON	c0	0.4474	(P9)
ELECTRIC-LAMP	c0	0.4474	(P10)
SEWING-MACH-WITHOUT	c0	0.4474	(P11)
REALIZE	c0	0.8809	(P12)
APPLIANCE-MAKE-LIGHT	c0	0.4474	(P13)
APPLIANCE-MAKE-MOVE	c0	0.4474	(P14)
FATHER	c0	0.1806	(V1)
KATIE	c0	0.7863	(V2)
IS-APPLIANCE	c0	1.0000	(S1)

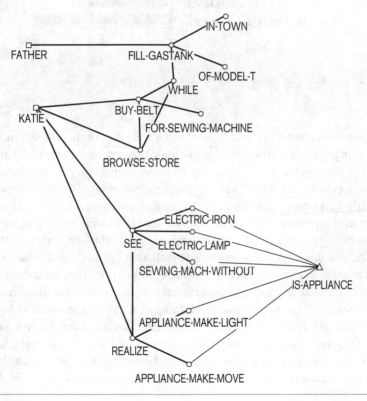

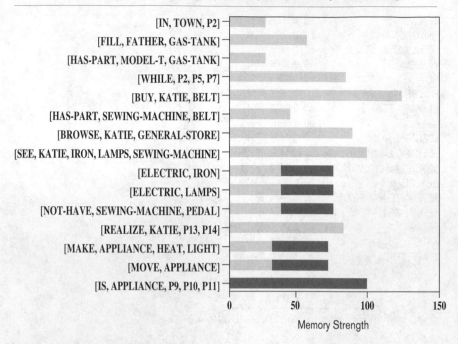

FIGURE 2
The Result of the Integration Process for the Network in Figure 1,
Without the Inference (IS-APPLIANCE) and With It (Darker Bars)

of macrostructures: (1) *Selection* of macrorelevant propositions (and correspondingly the deletion of propositions that are not macrorelevant), (2) *Generalization*, that is, substitution of a superordinate proposition for subordinate propositions; and (3) *Construction*, the substitution of a general proposition describing a whole sequence of interrelated propositions. Given a text and a set of macropropositions, these rules can be used to show how the macropropositions were derived from the text. However, these rules are post-hoc: They describe how macropropositions were derived after the fact, but they are not rules that allow us to generate macropropositions from a text. They do not tell us what is to be deleted or what is to be generalized. In order to use these rules, one must already know what is macrorelevant, what can be subsumed under a construction, and so on. In other words, the macrorules are incomplete because they do not include the conditions for their application. This shortcoming has seriously limited the modeling of macrostructures, which is unfortunate because macrostructures play such an important role in comprehension (e.g., W. Kintsch & van Dijk, 1978).

A logical analysis of the relations linking linguistic units that overcomes some of the limitations of macrorules has been suggested by Le (2002), who distinguishes three types of relations among text units: (1) coordination (either in the form of elaboration or parallelism), (2) subordination, and (3) superordination. After one specifies the relations among text units (sentences or complex propositions), hierarchical structures at levels higher than the sentence can be generated that allow the identification of macropropositions. To illustrate Le's procedure, consider the brief paragraph analyzed in Table 2 that consists of four complex propositions, C1–C4. As shown in Table 4, C1 is subordinated to C2; C2 and C3 are coordinated, C3 being an elaboration of C2. C4 is logically superordinated to C3, because it expresses a generalization based on C3. Thus, Le's analysis identifies C4—the complex proposition at the highest level in the paragraph hierarchy—as the macroproposition for that paragraph.

A different approach to the generation of macrostructures has been taken by W. Kintsch (2002). It is not based on a logical analysis of the relations among text units, but rather on the centrality of the content of the (complex) propositions. Latent Semantic Analysis (LSA; discussed in a later section) allows one to measure the similarity of the content of sentences. The sentence in a paragraph that is most similar to all the other sentences in that paragraph is a good candidate for a macroproposition because it is the most central one. In Table 4, C3 correlates most strongly with the other sentences, as measured by LSA, and hence should be considered as the macroproposition for this paragraph. Note that this is a different result than the one obtained from Le's logical analysis. There is no reason why two so totally different methods should yield identical results; large-scale empirical tests of which predictions correspond best with human judgments have not yet been reported. Note also that in terms of the activation values for complex propositions as shown in Figure 2, the most strongly activated complex

TABLE 4
Determining the Macroproposition for a Paragraph

C1 In town, her father filled the Model T's gas tank,
C2 while Katie bought a sewing machine belt and browsed in the general store.
C3 She saw an electric iron, electric lamps, and a sewing machine that no one had to pedal.
C4 She realized there were appliances that made heat and light and those that moved.

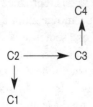

proposition is C2. (Activation values for complex propositions are obtained by adding the activation values of their constituent atomic propositions.)

It has long been known that gist-level—that is, macrostructure—processes, play a decisive role in the comprehension and memory of long texts. That much was shown by W. Kintsch and van Dijk in their 1978 paper. Modeling the generation of macrostructures, however, is still in its infancy, as the earlier discussion illustrates. Worse, there are basic limitations to the approaches of Le (2002) and W. Kintsch (2002): Both models can only select from the propositions in a text, whereas macropropositions often must be constructed by the reader. Macropropositions frequently are inferences that are not stated explicitly in the text. Computational models specifying how new macropropositions are generated do not yet exist. This is an important area for future research, as is the research on the formation of situation models, which is in a similarly underdeveloped state.

Situation Models

The problems faced by the researcher trying to model the formation of situation models are formidable. Textbases at the micro- and macrolevel are tightly constrained by the nature of the text, which a faithful reader must respect. The text, however, is only one factor in the situation model: The reader's goals, interests, beliefs, and prior knowledge also must be taken into account. Generally, these are only incompletely known. Furthermore, even the form that a situation model takes is not fully constrained: Situation models may be imagery based, in which case the propositional formalism currently used by most models fails us. Nevertheless, in well-defined contexts, modeling situation models is quite feasible and will surely be the focus of research on text comprehension in the next decade.[2]

How one might approach this task has been demonstrated by Schmalhofer, McDaniel, and Keefe (2002). The CI model simulates the construction of a textbase: A network of propositions derived from the text is constructed and integrated via a spreading activation constraint satisfaction process. Schmalhofer et al. added to the propositional network two other networks: (1) a surface level, where the nodes are linguistic structures and words, and (2) a situation representation, where the nodes are schemas. Nodes are interconnected at each level, but importantly, there are also links between levels, so that a sentence in the surface structure is connected to the corresponding proposition in the textbase, which in turn is connected to the appropriate schema at the situation model level. Schmalhofer et al. illustrate their model with an example that is reproduced here in simplified form in Figure 3. The text is a story about a movie stunt that results in a fatal accident. For the surface level of analysis, one sentence is shown, with word units L9 to L12 and syntactic units S8 and S9; of course, all this is part of a much larger network with rich interconnections not shown here. The units at the surface level are connected not only to each other but also to the propositional units at the textbase level. The propositions of the textbase are linked, in

FIGURE 3

FIGURE 3
Surface Structure, Textbase, and Situation Model

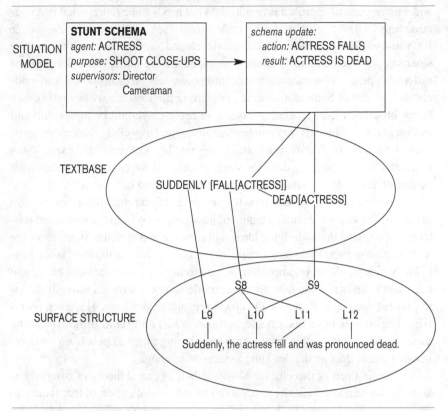

Adapted from Schmalhofer et al. (2002).
L = word units; S = syntactic units.

turn, to the situation model units, which here are schemas. The STUNT-SCHEMA has been partly filled in with information from previous portions of the text, but it is updated now with current information from the sentence being processed: An action and a result slot are filled in. When activation is spread in such a triple network, it is the structure present at each level of analysis that determines which nodes get activated, and complex interactions between levels also occur. This has important consequences, especially for the maintenance of inferences, as Schmalhofer et al. show. A model such as this explains how inferences at the situation model level can become integral parts of text memory, solidly and permanently anchored in the text structure.

The approach to modeling situation models pioneered by Schmalhofer et al. is a very promising one. Still, there are some limitations: The researchers selected their story in such a way that schema units were appropriate to represent the situation model. Not all situation models can be represented by schemas, however, and a more general approach is required. What needs to be represented in a situation model is at least partially understood (see discussion in Zwaan & Radvansky, 1998). Louwerse (2002) has developed a formal language to describe situations, with an emphasis on the coherence among units. His description of different types of coherence relations could potentially be incorporated into models such as that of Schmalhofer et al., extending their generality beyond simple script-based stories. The goal of discourse research should be to develop and evaluate situation models for complex narratives, and especially declarative texts, such as chapters from a science text, at the same level of detail and explicitness as Schmalhofer et al. have done for simple stories. If we understand better what students have to do, we shall be better able to guide and help them.

To summarize the research on the processes of text comprehension, we can say that we have a good understanding of how people go from the words and sentences of a text to the underlying ideas and how the text structure determines the organization of these ideas into a coherent textbase, at least at the local level. Less is known about global organization, or how readers form macrostructures, and even less is known about how situation models are constructed through the interplay between texts, background knowledge, and reader goals. However, promising beginnings have been made in these areas, and rapid progress can be expected now that reading researchers are placing more emphasis on comprehension rather than on the decoding aspects of reading.

The first part of this chapter has described a general theory of comprehension. In the next sections, the focus will be on the application of that theory to important research topics in the area of discourse comprehension: how words are identified in a discourse context, the representation of knowledge, the construction of macrostructures and situation models, the role of inferences and working memory, and the contrast between text memory and learning from text. Of particular interest are the implications of these research results for instruction, which will be emphasized throughout this discussion.

Word Identification

A great deal of research has gone into determining how the letter shapes on a page are turned into meaningful words. The results of this work will not be reviewed here because they have been discussed in other chapters of this volume (see Juel & Minden-Cupp, #13; Ehri & McCormick, #14; Kuhn & Stahl, #16; Nagy & Scott, #19). Instead, a body of research will be introduced here that complements this research in that it is concerned with the question of how readers arrive at the correct sense or meaning of a word[3] when they encounter it in a discourse context. To give a concrete example of what the issue is here, consider the following sentences:

(10) *A beautiful sight in downtown Denver is the mint.*

(11) *A fragrant tea is made with mint.*

How do we know that *mint* is a building in the first sentence but the leaves of a plant in the second? *Mint* is a homonym in English, that is, a word with more than one meaning, and readers obviously and effortlessly find the right meaning when they read (10) and (11). Similarly, when words with only a single meaning are used in different senses, readers readily perceive what is meant:

(12) *The fox ran faster than the hedgehog.*

(13) *The chancellor's decree ran into strong opposition.*

One explanation of how readers identify word meanings in context assumes that all word meanings and word senses are listed in a mental lexicon and that readers must select the right meaning or sense for the given context. There are at least two ways in which this selection could occur:

1. The schema acts as a filter. Suppose that each word meaning/sense in the mental lexicon is associated with a specific context. Thus, *mint* in (10) is associated with *a building-in-which-coins-are-manufactured* schema; reading (10) activates this schema, and the schema selects the proper sense of *mint* from the list of available senses. This is a top-down model, where the schema acts like a filter, admitting only the schema-relevant meaning and not admitting irrelevant meanings. Models of this type have been proposed by, among others, Schank and Abelson (1977).

2. The context suppresses inappropriate meanings. According to this model, all meanings/senses of a word are activated when reading it, but inappropriate meanings are suppressed by the context because they do not fit the contextual constraints. When reading (10), all versions of *mint* in the mental lexicon would be activated initially, but only one—the one associated with *building*, *downtown*, and *Denver*—would be consistent with the sentence context and would survive. Models of this type have been proposed by, among others, Swinney (1979).

Fortunately, it is possible to decide among these alternatives experimentally. Till, Mross, and Kintsch (1988) have reported a relevant experiment using the "lexical decision" method. In this experiment, participants read sentences such as (10) and were then asked to decide as quickly as possible whether a briefly presented string of letters was an English word or not. Four types of test items were used (each participant saw only one of these):

1. a nonword string (e.g., *baher*) for which the correct response was "no"

2. an associate of the target word that was contextually appropriate (e.g., *money*);

3. an associate of the target word that was contextually inappropriate (e.g., *tea*)

4. an unrelated control word (e.g., *baker*)

The correct response for the last three items was "yes," but interesting differences in response speed were observed. When the test item was presented immediately after the sentence, response times for associated items were significantly shorter than response times to unrelated control items, whether or not the association was contextually appropriate. That is, *mint* in (10) primed both *money* and *tea*. When the test item was presented with a 350 millisecond (msec) delay after the sentence, the response time for the contextually appropriate associate was shorter than the response time for either the control word or the inappropriate associate. That is, 350 msec after reading (10), only *money* was primed, not *tea*.

The Till et al. data clearly contradict the schema-as-filter model and support a model that posits a bottom-up activation of all word meanings, followed by a contextual constraint satisfaction process that deactivates inappropriate meaning. Indeed, these data were one of the original inspirations for the CI model (W. Kintsch, 1988). Today there exists a very large and complex literature on this subject, which cannot be reviewed here (but see, e.g., Rayner, Pacht, & Duffy, 1994). Results depend on various boundary conditions, but on the whole they effectively rule out the schema-as-filter model. It appears that, generally, multiple meanings and senses of a word are activated initially but that context-inappropriate meanings and senses are suppressed rapidly.

It is difficult to imagine, however, how such a meaning selection model could work. Just what are the cues that allow the selection of the right meaning or sense among so many alternatives? Furthermore, just what are the alternatives in the mental lexicon? How do we decide how many meanings or senses a word has? People learn to use words in ever-novel ways. Can a mental lexicon in which every use must somehow be explicitly defined do justice to this complexity? What if the different word meanings and senses are not predefined in a mental lexicon but emerge in context? How could such a generative lexicon be constructed? One attempt to do so invokes the idea of semantic elements that can be combined to form all meanings, much like the 100+ chemical elements can be combined to form all the manifold substances in the universe. This approach has not been successful, however, because nobody has been able to come up with a principled list of semantic elements or the rule system that would allow us to construct all meanings from the combination of these elements. An alternative approach that appears promising to achievement of the goal of a generative lexicon is based on some recent developments in statistical semantics. It will be briefly described in the next section.

Knowledge Representation: Latent Semantic Analysis

There exists no complete model of how the totality of human knowledge—including perceptual knowledge, verbal knowledge, action knowledge, and emotional knowledge—is represented in the mind and how it is organized. In the study of reading we are primarily concerned with verbal knowledge. Recently, a model of how human verbal knowledge is represented has been developed which is of considerable use for modeling the use of knowledge in comprehension. The model is called Latent Semantic Analysis (LSA) and provides a good account of the associative basis of human verbal knowledge, although not of analytic, logical thought. Essentially, it allows us to measure the semantic similarity between words, sentences, and whole texts in an objective and automatic way that agrees quite well with human judgments. Full descriptions of LSA are available in Landauer (1998), Landauer and Dumais (1997), and Landauer, Foltz, and Laham (1998).

LSA is a machine learning method that lets a computer induce a semantic structure merely from reading a large amount of text. The computer keeps track of how words are used in many different documents and then uses a mathematical procedure to extract the essential semantic relations among words and texts from this mass of information. The result is a high-dimensional semantic space in which meanings are represented mathematically by vectors.

A good way to think about LSA is in analogy to maps. The data on which maps are based are measurements of various features of the earth: distances, altitudes, and so on. Once we have drawn a map, these features are represented in two dimensions in a conventional way: An inch on the map corresponds to so-and-so many miles on the earth, contour lines indicate altitudes, blue indicates a lake or a sea, and so on. The map is useful because it goes beyond the data: It allows us to compute numerous relations among places that were never directly measured. LSA, analogously, provides a map of meanings. This map, too, is based on a certain set of observations, but it goes beyond the data on which it was based: It allows us to compare the meanings of any points in our map. Meaning relations, however, are much more complex than the relations among points on the surface of the earth and require many more dimensions to represent. In fact, LSA needs about 300 dimensions to satisfactorily map meaning. Thus, meanings are represented not by points but by vectors in a 300-dimensional space. Meaning in LSA is a sequence of 300 numbers, which is meaningful only in comparison to other such meaning sequences. The usual way to measure the distance between vectors is by computing their cosine in the high-dimensional geometric space. A cosine of 1 means identity, and a cosine of 0 means unrelated—much like a correlation coefficient. Here are some examples of cosines between words:

(14)
cop – cops	.78
cop – policeman	.68
buy – bought	.66
high – low	.79
he – his	.97
blackbird – bird	.46
blackbird – black	.04

These examples illustrate both the strength and the limitations of LSA. It is a strength that LSA groups together words that are related in meaning. Note that antonyms are very close semantically, differing only in one—crucial—respect; LSA captures this relation but lacks the analytic power to distinguish between opposites. LSA also neglects syntax, with the consequence that *he* and *his* mean just about the same thing to LSA. Another limitation is illustrated with the *blackbird* example. LSA knows only what is explicit in the texts used to teach it; thus, *blackbird* is a *bird* for LSA, but it is not *black*. (When *blackbird* is used in the training text, it is used in a *bird* context, so LSA makes the necessary inference, but texts do not mention the color of *blackbirds*. We can decompose the word, but LSA cannot.)

The real power of LSA arises because it allows us to compare the meaning of sentences and, indeed, whole texts, as readily as words. Consider the following sentence triplet:

(15)

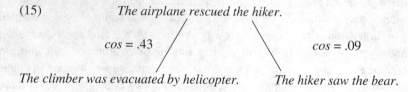

The airplane rescued the hiker.

cos = .43   *cos* = .09

The climber was evacuated by helicopter.   *The hiker saw the bear.*

The sentence pair that is similar in meaning according to our intuition is close in the semantic space (the two sentences have a high cosine), whereas the sentences that appear unrelated to human intuitions are distant in the LSA space (low cosine). Note that this happens in spite of the fact that the semantically related sentence pair does not share any content word, whereas the unrelated pair does. This ability to measure the similarity of texts is the basis for many successful applications of LSA, for example, for grading essays (Landauer, Laham, & Foltz, 2000) and for helping students to write better summaries (E. Kintsch et al., 2000).

Macrostructures and Summaries

Macrostructures are mental representations of text at a global level. They may simply mirror the structure of the text from which they were derived, or they may reflect, to varying degrees, the comprehender's own prior knowledge structure that has been imposed on the text in the creation of a situation model.

Macrostructures as envisaged by van Dijk (1980) and discussed in van Dijk and Kintsch (1983) are hierarchies of propositions. Macropropositions put into words are summary statements at different levels of generality. They subsume what the different sections of a text are about. They are derived from the text by the operations of selection, generalization, and construction, but propositional macrostructures cannot be computed automatically from a text. The macrorules merely help us to explain what can be done, but they are not algorithms or computational procedures that generate macropropositions from a text automatically. A computationally more feasible—but in other ways more limited—alternative for the representation of macrostructures is provided by LSA. Instead of representing the meaning of a sentence by a proposition, the meaning can be represented as a vector in an existing high-dimensional semantic space. For some purposes, such a representation is all that is needed. For example, one can compare new texts, such as summaries students write, with these macrovectors; one can compute the importance or typicality of sentences from the text, and so on.

For other purposes, verbal statements corresponding to macropropositions are needed. W. Kintsch (2002) has described how LSA can be used to select topic sentences from a text and to generate a summary by concatenating these topic sentences. There is more to a summary than just selecting topic sentences, but it is instructive to see what can be achieved in that way—and what is still missing. The text analyzed in W. Kintsch is a chapter titled "Wind Energy," taken from a junior high school science textbook. It is 960 words long and divided by its author into six sections, each with its own subtitles. Thus, the author indicates the intended macrostructure and even provides appropriate macropropositions, in the form of six subtitles. Macrorules can be used to explain where these subtitles come from. Consider the following paragraph (the second subsection of the chapter):

(16) *The history of windmills*

> *Since ancient times, people have harnessed the wind's energy. Over 5,000 years ago, the ancient Egyptians used the wind to sail ships on the Nile River. Later, people built windmills to grind wheat and other grains. The early windmills looked like paddle wheels. Centuries later, the people in Holland improved the windmill. They gave it propeller-type blades. Holland is still famous for its windmills. In this country, the colonists used windmills to grind wheat and corn, to pump water, and to cut wood at sawmills. Today people still sometimes use*

windmills to grind grain and pump water, but they also use new wind machines to make electricity.

The macrorule of construction can be used to compress sentences 2–4 into

People used wind energy in Egypt.

Similarly, the other sentences of the paragraph can be reduced to

People used windmills in Holland.
People used windmills in the colonies.
People use windmills today.

These sentences can be transformed by the macrorule of generalization into

(17) *People used windmills throughout history.*

or

(18) *The history of windmills.*[4]

Thus, macrorules allow us to postdict, or explain, what the author did. But the application of these rules depends on our intuitions about the text and our knowledge about it. By themselves, these rules cannot compute anything.

LSA provides a computational mechanism that can compute macrostructures of a kind. For instance, we can compute a vector in LSA space that is the centroid of all the words in paragraph (16). Such a vector may seem to be totally useless—it is, after all, a list of 300 uninterpretable numbers—but that is not so. It can be quite useful, for instance to decide how appropriate a proposed subtitle is. The cosine between the paragraph vector and the proposed subtitle is a measure of how close the subtitle is to the paragraph as a whole. For instance, (17) and (18) have rather similar cosines with the paragraph—.39 and .48, respectively, high enough to indicate that they are both acceptable summary statements. But suppose we had chosen an ill-considered subtitle for the paragraph, such as "Holland is still famous," or something totally inappropriate such as "Rain douses forest fires." The cosine measure would have allowed us to reject these choices (the cosine is .26 in the first case and only .05 in the second, both much lower than the cosines for (17) and (18)).

There are other uses for vector representation of a macrostructure, too. For instance, we can compute how closely related the sections of a text are to each other. This kind of information can be of interest in various ways. If two sections of a text are very closely related, one might consider combining them. Or if two similar sections are separated by a dissimilar one in the text, one might consider reordering the sections of the text. We also can obtain a measure of how important a section is to the overall text. One way to do this is to compute the cosine between the whole text and each section.

To generate the full range of macropropositions is beyond the scope of LSA; operations such as generalization and construction are not readily modeled within this framework. But we can generate a degenerate macrostructure using only the selection operation. For each section we can find the most typical sentence in the section. For this purpose, we define *most typical* as the sentence with the highest average cosine to all the other sentences in the section. This will not always yield the best result because the ideal macroproposition may involve generalization or construction, but it will serve as a reasonable approximation.

Thus, some progress can be made toward a computational model of macrostructure generation. LSA allows us to generate an abstract vector representation of the macrostructure of a text (at least in those cases where the subsections of the text are clearly indicated, as in the example above). Furthermore, procedures can be devised to select for each section of a text the most typical sentence. However, that does not make a summary yet, and the operations for reducing the selected typical sentence to an essential phrase or fragment depend on more analytic procedures that go beyond LSA.

There are other, more practical uses of LSA's ability to represent the content of a text mathematically and compare it with other texts. For instance, we can express the summary written by a student as a vector and compare it with the vector of the to-be-summarized text. If the cosine between summary and text is high, the summary has much the same content as the original text. On the other hand, if the cosine is low, the summary does not reflect the content of the original text. A system, called *Summary Street*, that employs this method to help students write better summaries has been used with considerable success in some classrooms (E. Kintsch et al., 2000; Wade-Stein & Kintsch, 2003). For instance, students in sixth-grade classes were routinely asked to write summaries of chapters of their science textbooks. The teacher assigned a text to be summarized, say, on energy sources (coal, wind, petroleum, etc.) or Meso-American civilizations (Incan, Mayan, or Aztec). Each text is usually composed of four or five sections, and the teachers wanted the content of each section to be covered in the summary. Furthermore, the teachers required the summary to be of a certain length, say, between 150 and 200 words. The students write their summaries on an interface that is much like a standard word processor and send them to the LSA system for analysis via the Web. The feedback is received almost immediately and involves a number of steps.

Content feedback indicates whether all sections of the text have been covered in the summary. For this purpose, the cosine between the student's summary and each of the sections of a text are computed. If a cosine is below a certain threshold value, the student is told that this section is not adequately covered in the summary. The student then has the option to look at the appropriate section of the text on the computer screen and add some material about this section to the summary. If the threshold is exceeded for all sections, the student is told that he or she has now covered all parts of the text. Because the length of the summaries is restricted to avoid extensive copying from the source texts, students are told how long their summaries are so far and which of their sentences may be redundant or irrelevant.

Summary Street has been shown to be effective in helping students to write better summaries. When summary writing was compared with and without system feedback (Wade-Stein & Kintsch, 2003), the analysis showed that students were willing to work harder and longer when given feedback. Indeed, their time on task more than doubled. Summaries written with content feedback received higher grades from the teachers. This was the case for difficult summaries, for which grades more than doubled, whereas for texts that were easy to summarize anyway, the use of the system had no significant effect. Finally, a transfer effect was observed. Students who had written a summary in the previous week with the help of the system wrote better summaries a week later even when they no longer had access to the feedback the system provided. They had learned something about how summaries should be written.

Inferences and Situation Models[5]

Text comprehension always goes beyond the text. The mental representations that readers construct—their understanding of the text—depend as much on what readers bring to the text, such as their goals, interests, and prior experience, as on the text itself. Readers must make inferences to construct situation models. But not all inferences in comprehension are alike.

Classification of Inferences

A distinction should be made between problem-solving processes on the one hand, where there are premises from which some conclusion is drawn (not necessarily by the rules of logic)—which may be justly called inferences—and knowledge-retrieval processes on the other hand, where a gap in the text is bridged by some piece of preexisting knowledge that has been retrieved (W. Kintsch, 1998). Both inferences proper and knowledge retrieval may be either automatic (and usually unconscious) or controlled (and usually conscious and strategic). This classification results in the 2-by-2 table shown in Table 5.

Retrieval adds preexisting information to a text from long-term memory. Generation, in contrast, produces new information by deriving it from information in the text by some inference procedure. Thus, while the term *inference* is suitable for information-generation processes, it is a misnomer for retrieval processes.

TABLE 5
A Classification System for Inferences in Text Comprehension

	Retrieval A	Generation C
Automatic Processes	bridging inferences, associative elaborations	transitive inferences in a familiar domain
Controlled Processes	B search for bridging knowledge	D logical inferences

Based on Kintsch (1998).

A prototypical example for cell A, the automatic retrieval process that enriches the information in a text, would be the activation of *with a hammer* by *John nailed down a board*, or *cars have doors* by *A car stopped. The door opened*. In both cases sufficient retrieval cues for the information retrieved exist in short-term memory. These cues are linked with pertinent information in long-term memory. Such knowledge use is automatic and rapid, and it places no demands on cognitive resources.

There are two theories that describe automatic knowledge retrieval. One is the long-term working memory theory of Ericsson and Kintsch (1995), which is described in more detail in the next section of this chapter. According to the long-term working memory theory, for well-practiced associations, retrieval cues in short-term memory are linked to contents in long-term memory, which thereby become directly available, thus expanding the capacity of working memory. An alternative model for this kind of knowledge retrieval is the resonance theory of Myers (Myers, O'Brien, Albrecht, & Mason, 1994). According to this model, cues in short-term memory produce a resonance in long-term memory, so that the resonating items become available for further processing in working memory. Thus, either via retrieval structures or resonance, relevant, strongly related items in long-term memory become potential parts of working memory, creating a long-term working memory that is much richer than the severely capacity-restricted short-term working memory. Indeed, it is only this long-term working memory that makes discourse comprehension (or, indeed, any other expert performance) possible. Smooth, efficient functioning would be impossible if we had no way of expanding working memory capacity beyond the rigid limits of short-term memory.

In cell B of Table 5 are cases where automatic retrieval is not possible. That is, the cues present in short-term memory do not retrieve relevant information that bridge whatever gap exists in the text. An extended search of memory is required to yield the needed information. A memory search is a strategic, controlled, resource-demanding process in which the cues available in short-term memory are used to retrieve other likely cues from long-term memory that in turn are capable of retrieving what is needed. Consider the following sentences:

(19) *Danny wanted a new bike. He worked as a waiter.*

Purely automatic, associative elaboration might not retrieve the causal chain from *want-bike* to *buy-bike* to *money* to *work*. However, a directed search for causal connections between the two sentences would easily generate these by-no-means-obscure links. In all probability, genre-specific strategies exist to guide such search processes. In a story, one would look for causal links. In a legal argument, one routinely looks for contradictions. In an algebraic word problem, algebraic formulas guide the search. The difficulty of such procedures, and the resource demands they make, vary widely.

Retrieval processes merely access information available in long-term memory, either automatically or by a resource-demanding search. Generation processes actually compute new information on the basis of the text and relevant background information in long-term memory. They, too, may be either automatic or controlled.

Some generation procedures are fully automatic (cell C of Table 5). For instance, given the sentence

(20) *Three turtles rested on a floating log, and a fish swam beneath them.*

the statement *The turtles are above the fish* is immediately available to a reader. Indeed, readers often are unable to distinguish whether they were explicitly told this information or not (e.g., Bransford, Barclay, & Franks, 1972). Note, however, that this is not merely a question of knowledge retrieval as in *doors are parts of cars*: The statement *the turtles are above the fish* is not something that already exists in long-term memory and is now retrieved, but it is generated during the comprehension process. The reason why it is so highly available in the reader's working memory is, presumably, that the fish-log-and-turtle scene is encoded as an image, and this mental image constitutes a highly effective retrieval structure that provides ready access to all its parts—not just the verbal expression used in its construction.

The information that allows the reader to infer that the turtles are above the fish is, presumably, in the form of a spatial image. It is given directly by the image that serves as the situation model representation of the sentence in question. Indeed, at this level of representation there is no difference between explicit and implicit statements. A difference only exists at the level of the textbase and surface representation, which, however, may not always be effective (as in the experiments of Bransford et al., 1972, in which subjects could not distinguish between explicit and implicit statements, given study and test sentences as in the example discussed here).

However, what happens in cell C of Table 5 should hardly be called an inference either. It is simply a case, in which due to the analog nature of the mental representation involved, more information is generated in forming a situation model than was explicit in the text. The term *inference* really should be reserved for cell D of Table 5. This is the domain of deductive reasoning. It is a domain that extends far beyond text comprehension, although deductive reasoning undoubtedly plays an important role in text comprehension, too. Explicit reasoning comes into play when comprehension proper breaks down. When the network does not integrate, and the gaps in the text cannot be bridged any other way, then reasoning is called for as the ultimate repair procedure.

Inferences (real inferences, as in cell D) require specific inference procedures. It is a matter of considerable controversy in psychology what these inference operations are—whether inference proceeds by rule (Rips, 1994) or mental model (Johnson-Laird, Byrne, & Schaeken, 1992). Inferences in domains where the basic representation is an action or perceptual representation, that is, analog rather than linguistic or abstract, probably involve operations on mental models. Inferences in truly symbolic, abstract domains may be by rule. Inferences in the linguistic domain, where the representation is at the narrative level, may be based on mental models but also could involve purely verbal inference rules.

Inference Generation During Discourse Comprehension

The literature on "inferences" in discourse comprehension is for the most part not concerned with cell D of Table 5. Indeed, it is heavily concentrated on cell A, the processes that are the least inference-like, according to the argument presented here. A major focus of the recent research has been on the question of to what extent inferences are made during normal comprehension. On the one hand, it is clear that if the readers of a story are asked to make inferences and are given sufficient time and incentive, there is almost no limit to what they will produce (Graesser, 1981). On the other hand, there is good evidence that much of the time, and in particular in many psychology experiments, readers are lazy and get away with a minimum of work (e.g., Foertsch & Gernsbacher, 1994). McKoon and Ratcliff (1992, 1995) have elaborated the latter position as the *minimalist hypothesis*, which holds that the only inferences readers normally make are bridging inferences required for the maintenance of local coherence, and knowledge elaboration where there are strong preexisting, multiple associations. Many text researchers (e.g., Graesser & Kreuz, 1993; Graesser, Singer, & Trabasso, 1994; Singer, Graesser, & Trabasso, 1994), however, feel that this minimalist position underestimates the amount of inference-making that occurs during normal reading and would at the least add inferences that are necessary for global coherence to the list (superordinate goal inferences, thematic inferences, and character emotional reactions). While this controversy has contributed a great deal to our understanding of the role of inferences in text comprehension, it also has shown that the question concerning which inferences are necessary for and are normally made during text comprehension has no simple answer. Text characteristics (much of the research is based on stories, mostly ministories), task demands, and individual differences among readers create a complex, though orderly, picture.

Trabasso and Suh (1993) have combined discourse analysis, talk-aloud procedures, and experimental measures, such as recognition priming, reading times, coherence ratings, and story recall, to show that their readers did make causal inferences in reading a story and that these inferences could be predicted by their analysis.

In an illuminating series of studies, O'Brien and his colleagues have shown that causal inferences in story understanding should best be regarded as a passive operation that makes available background and causal antecedents via a resonance-like mechanism (or what I would call a retrieval structure). Such a process contributes to the coherence of the text representation (Garrod, O'Brien, Morris, & Rayner, 1990) but is not predictive. Readers refrain from prediction unless there is absolutely no chance of being discomfirmed (O'Brien, Shank, Myers, & Rayner, 1988). Global automatic goal inferences occur only under limited conditions (Albrecht, O'Brien, Mason, & Myers, 1995), probably because such inferences are as risky as predictions: They are frequently discomfirmed as the later text reveals a different goal. When global goal inferences occur, resonance describes what happens better than the notion of inference. Through resonance, related parts of a text are connected because of preexisting retrieval structures. In contrast, the construction of a full mental model with rich causal connections appears rather as a nonautomatic, controlled process (O'Brien, 1995; Albrecht & O'Brien, 1995).

How much time and resources the reader has strongly determines the amount of inference-making that occurs. Magliano, Baggett, Johnson, and Graesser (1993), using a lexical decision task, found that causal antecedent inferences were not made when texts were presented rapidly at a 250 msec rate, but they were made when the presentation rate was 400 msec. Long, Golding, and Graesser (1992) found that superordinate goal inferences linking various episodes of a story (but not subordinated goal inferences) were made by readers when they were given a lot of time. However, with a rapid presentation rate, only good comprehenders made such inferences, while there was no evidence for goal inferences by poor comprehenders (Long & Golding, 1993).

Readers are much more likely to make antecedent causal inferences than consequent causal inferences (e.g., Magliano et al., 1993). For instance, readers of *The clouds gathered quickly, and it became ominously dark. The downpour only lasted 10 minutes* infer the causal antecedent *the clouds caused the rain*. But given *The clouds gathered quickly, and it became ominously dark*, they do not infer the consequent *the clouds caused rain*. This finding that antecedent, but not consequent causal, inferences are made in text comprehension is readily accounted for by the CI model. Suppose a text describes a situation that is a common cause of some event and then asserts that this event occurred, without mentioning an explicit causal connection between the antecedent and the event. Preexisting retrieval structures causally link the antecedent and the event in the reader's memory, and the causal link will be activated and is likely to become a permanent part of the reader's episodic text memory because it connects two highly activated nodes in the memory structure.

The situation is different for the consequent inferences. The same retrieval structures that made available the causal antecedent will make available the causal consequent, too. But at that point in the reading process, the consequent is a dangling node in the episodic text structure because it is connected to nothing else in the network but the antecedent. Therefore, the consequent will not receive much activation in the integration process and will be excluded from episodic memory. Thus, *The clouds gathered quickly, and it became ominously dark* might make available *the clouds caused rain*, but if nothing else in the text connects to *rain*, this node will become quickly deactivated in the network. When in a later processing cycle other information becomes available that could have linked with *rain*, that node is most likely lost from working memory. Hence, although the retrieval structures in the reader's long-term memory make available both antecedent and consequent information, only the former is likely to survive the integration process and become a stable component of the reader's text memory.

Time Course for Constructing Knowledge-Based Inferences

Of considerable interest is the time course of constructing knowledge-based inferences in text comprehension. We know that it takes about 300–350 msec for word meanings to become fixed in a discourse context. Inferences require more time. In Till, Mross, and Kintsch (1988), no evidence for topic inferences was obtained at a Stimulus Onset Asynchrony (SOA; the time interval between the presentation of the target word and the test word) of 500 msec, but topic inferences were clearly made at an SOA of 1,000 msec (there were no data points in between). In contrast, Magliano et al. (1993) found that antecedent causal inferences required an SOA of only 400 msec. Long, Oppy, and Seely (1994), in a study modeled after Till et al., have used SOAs of 200, 300, 400, 500, 750, and 1,000 msec. Associative effects are already fully apparent in their data at 300 msec. Topic effects develop gradually: They are already apparent at 500 msec but increase in strength up to 750 msec. Because different materials and conditions were used in all these studies, the differences in the results are not surprising. It seems that sentence-level inferences require from 400 to 750 msec, depending on experimental conditions. Thus, sentence meanings take roughly twice as long as word meanings to fixate.

The Construction of Situation Models

Much recent research has been concerned with the construction of situation models (e.g., Glenberg, Kruley, & Langston, 1994; Glenberg & Langston, 1992; Graesser & Zwaan, 1995; Mani & Johnson-Laird, 1982; Trabasso & Suh, 1993; Zwaan, Magliano, & Graesser, 1995). There is no single type of situation model and not a single process for the construction of such models. Situation models are a form of "inference" by definition, and Table 5 is as relevant for situation models as it is for any other "inference" in discourse comprehension. That is, situation models may vary widely in their character. In the simplest case, their construction is automatic. Relevant information is furnished by existing retrieval structures, as in the examples given for cell A in Table 5. Or it may be available simply as a consequence of a particular form of representation, such as imagery. Such situation model inferences do not add new propositions to the memory representation of the text but simply make available information in long-term memory via retrieval structures, or information that is implicit in the mental representation, such as an image (see Fincher-Kiefer, 1993, and Perfetti, 1993, for similar suggestions). On the other hand, situation models can be much more complex and result from extended, resource-demanding, controlled processes. All kinds of representations and constructions may be involved. The process may be shared by a social group or even by a whole culture and extend over prolonged periods of time. Text interpretation is not something that is confined to the laboratory.

Spatial and temporal information are usually important components of a situation model. Perrig and Kintsch (1985) had subjects read descriptions of the spatial layout of a small town. The same town was described in two ways, first by providing route descriptions (*after the church, turn right on Main Street to go to the courthouse*), and second by means of survey descriptions (*the courthouse is north of the church on Main Street*). Subjects were tested both for their ability to recall and recognize the text they had read and to make novel spatial inferences on the basis of that text. The results of their first experiment dramatically illustrated the textbase–situation model distinction: Subjects' recall was excellent and sentence recognition nearly perfect—but their ability to verify inferences was similar to results of random choices. In a second experiment, with a simpler town and more study time, subjects successfully constructed a spatial situation model. They performed well on recall and recognition as well as on inference tasks. Interestingly, the kind of situation model differed, depending on the text they had read: Route texts led to route models, and survey texts led to survey models. When the inference question was in the same form as the text a subject had read, performance was better than when the text was a route description and the question in the survey format or vice versa. The Perrig and Kintsch study shows that situation models are by no means automatic consequences of good textbases and that there may be different types of situation models. Which one is best depends on the reader's purpose.

A study by van der Meer, Beyer, Heinze, and Badel (2002) explored the construction of temporal situation models by presenting events in their chronological order (*fall down–get up*) or in reverse order (*fall down–slip*). Overall, chronologically related information was accessed faster compared with reversely ordered sentences, but processing time made a crucial difference. When there was not enough processing time, neither chronological nor reverse information was integrated into the situation model. When there was a great deal of time for elaboration, both were integrated. In the intermediate condition, however, chronologically ordered events were integrated into the situation model, whereas reverse, past-oriented events were not. Thus, what sort of inferences people make and how elaborate a situation model they construct depend crucially on the amount of processing. If there is time and they are motivated, people will construct rich situation models—but that is a controlled, effortful process, not the kind of automatic knowledge activation discussed earlier. We shall return to the educational implications of this finding in a later section.

The Role of Working Memory in Comprehension[6]

Within the standard working-memory framework, it is not possible to explain how memory is used in many cognitive tasks such as playing chess or text comprehension. The span of immediate memory is seven items plus-or-minus two. People can maintain no more than three or four discrete items in consciousness at the same time. Yet text comprehension requires that people juggle in their working memory large amounts of information: perceptual features, linguistic features, propositional structure, macrostructure, situation model, control structure, goals, lexical knowledge, frames, general knowledge, and episodic memory for prior text. Each of these components by itself would exceed short-term working memory, but each is clearly needed for text understanding, and people have no memory problems in understanding well-written, familiar texts.

Similarly, people can remember well-written, familiar text very well and effortlessly, just as they can remember what they did last night. In the laboratory, on the other hand, it takes people one hour to memorize 100 random words, and from a list of 30 words, college students recall about 12 or 14 after one reading. So why is memory so poor in the lab and so good in (some) everyday situations? Is our psychology of memory irrelevant to real-life memory and comprehension?

The theory of long-term working memory (LTWM) addresses this dilemma. It does so by specifying the conditions under which working memory capacity can become greatly expanded and by describing the mechanisms that are responsible for this expansion of working memory. The theory was first proposed by Ericsson and Kintsch (1995) and further elaborated by W. Kintsch (1998) and W. Kintsch, Patel, and Ericsson (1999).

LTWM is restricted to well-practiced tasks and familiar knowledge domains. With novel tasks and in unfamiliar domains, people must do with short-term working memory, whose capacity is severely restricted. Because the typical laboratory tasks—such as memorizing a list of paired associates—were unfamiliar to the subjects of memory experiments—and the materials used were relatively meaningless—word lists, or, in the extreme case, nonsense syllables—most laboratory studies of memory never involved more than short-term working memory; hence, the ubiquitous findings of severe capacity limitations. However, in some real-life situations in which people perform tasks at which they are highly skilled and well practiced, performance does not suffer from memory limitations. Skilled, expert performance provides many examples of such situations—playing chess or medical diagnosis, for instance. Of course, not everyone playing chess will have a memory advantage. Only the real expert shows exceptional memory in such tasks. Novice chess players can remember briefly presented chess positions no better than the capacity limitations of short-term memory allow them. Only master chess players who have devoted a decade or so to the study of chess will show truly superior memory in these situations. Indeed, part of becoming an expert in a skill consists in the development of superior memory in the expert domain. These memory skills are entirely domain specific, however. The chess master on all memory tasks outside his or her expertise performs no better than people normally do.

Thus, LTWM is an expert skill. There are, however, tasks at which most adults in U.S. society are experts. Text comprehension is an example. As long as the texts to be comprehended are simple, reasonably well written, and about familiar, everyday topics, we are all experts. The reading (or listening) skills involved are highly practiced over a lifetime. The subject matter of many texts often concerns everyday events and human actions and relationships—subjects in which our lifelong experience qualifies us as experts. A text on atomic physics needs a physicist to comprehend, but for a simple story or item in the newspaper, we all have the necessary expertise. Thus, we comprehend such texts readily, retrieve relevant knowledge or personal experiences automatically without special effort, and remember what we read, also without special effort. The LTWM mechanism is responsible for this achievement and explains why our memory is so good in familiar domains and so poor when we read something in an unfamiliar domain or try to acquire a new skill.

The LTWM theory claims that superior memory in expert domains is due to LTWM, whereas in nonexpert domains LTWM can be of no help. Thus, working memory has two components: (1) short-term working memory, which is available under all conditions but is severely limited in its capacity, and (2) LTWM, which is not capacity limited but available only in expert domains. Short-term working memory is what has been studied in most laboratory memory tasks. LTWM is conceived as a subset of long-term memory[7] that is directly retrievable via cues in short-term working memory. Any cue in short-term memory—alternatively we could talk about the contents of consciousness, or items in the focus of attention—that is linked by a stable memory structure to long-term memory nodes makes available these nodes in a single automatic and quick retrieval operation. The retrieval is fast and automatic in that it does not require mental resources (such as an intentional, conscious memory search does). Thus, the contents of short-term memory automatically create LTWM: a zone in long-term memory that is directly linked to these contents and immediately retrievable. The crucial restriction is that the items in short-term working memory and the items in long-term memory are linked by stable, fixed memory structures that permit direct retrieval. This is the case only in very well-practiced domains in which we are experts. Without these expert memory links, retrieval can be a protracted and resource-demanding process and is controlled rather than automatic.

Long-term memory is a relatively permanent system. Additions and modifications occur, as well as forgetting, but the system as a whole changes slowly. Short-term memory, the focus of attention or content of consciousness, on the other hand, changes from moment to moment. Because LTWM is generated dynamically by the cues that are present in short-term memory, LTWM mirrors the changes in short-term memory. A flashlight metaphor often has been used to describe short-term memory: a small beam that lights up three to five nodes in long-term memory. Imagine each of these nodes is linked to nodes in the unlit part of the long-term memory network. The linked nodes form LTWM. Working memory consists of the lit nodes plus the linked nodes in the dark part of long-term memory. The flashlight is able to jump immediately to any of these linked nodes, without external guidance.

The previous description represents the simplest case of LTWM. The links [stable associations or other memory structures such as schemata, frames, etc.] preexist in long-term memory. LTWM in this case involves no more than a set of cues in short-term memory plus the long-term memory nodes to which they are linked in long-term memory. But this is only part of the story because the ongoing cognitive process results in the generation of new nodes, which greatly enrich and complicate LTWM. These nodes are first generated in short-term working memory, but as the focus of attention shifts away, they fade from consciousness. Depending on the nature of these nodes, they may be more or less permanent or subject to forgetting.

Consider what happens in reading comprehension: Comprehension results in the formation of new nodes in memory (propositions derived from the text) that are linked in a complex pattern determined by the nature of the text and the comprehension strategies of the reader. The newly formed links in text comprehension are the result of the reader's comprehension strategies, as specified by the CI model. Some links are strong, some are weak, some nodes are tightly interconnected, and some are sparsely interconnected, depending on how the mental representation of a text has been built up. The structure that supports retrieval is not being formed for the purpose of memory retrieval. Rather, the ability to retrieve is incidental to comprehension: If one comprehends a text properly, a mental structure has been generated that supports memory retrieval via LTWM. What is required for LTWM, therefore, are appropriate comprehension strategies (e.g., as described in van Dijk & Kintsch, 1983) and the knowledge (linguistic knowledge, world knowledge, specific topic knowledge) and skills (language skills) necessary for the use of these strategies.

LTWM is not always incidental. There is a continuum between some processes where LTWM is incidental, as in text comprehension or chess, and other processes where it is intentional, as in the case of the retrieval structures used in mnemonic techniques. Thus, the memory artist studied by Chase and Ericsson (1981) employed a set of specific encoding strategies for digit strings for the sole purpose of memorizing them and used a body of knowledge (about running times) that was needed for the operation of these encoding strategies. Another example is the method of loci, where a complex schema is used over and over again, together with specialized imagery encoding strategies, for the sole purpose of memory retrieval. It is important to realize, however, that the deliberate retrieval structures involved in mnemonic techniques are but one type of structure that supports LTWM. Incidental structures that arise from text comprehension processes or planning moves in a chess game represent quite different cases that are ecologically more important.

Two types of links are involved in LTWM: (1) links among newly formed nodes as a text is being comprehended and (2) links between these newly formed nodes and other nodes in long-term memory. For new nodes and links in text comprehension, the process assumed here is the following: Certain features of a text elicit an appropriate processing strategy; the application of this strategy results in the creation of new memory nodes, links among them, and links among the new nodes and the body of long-term memory. The whole process is automatic. Thus, faced with a particular text, an expert speaker of the language automatically recognizes which comprehension strategies are appropriate, applies them, and generates a network of propositions linked to prior knowledge. A chess player looks at a board and applies appropriate planning strategies, creating a network of representations that enable later recall. A memory artist "sees" a random digit string as a meaningful running time and stores it at a particular place in his reusable retrieval structure. An expert physician recognizes a patient's signs and symptoms, which are stored as a pattern for subsequent decisions about disease, therapy, and management. The performance is quick and effortless in each case but limited to the specific domain in question. In each case, an episodic memory structure is created that supports LTWM. The nature of these strategies, and the resulting structures, is the object of study in psycholinguistics, the psychology of chess, the psychology of clinical reasoning, or mnemonics, respectively, and differs widely between these domains. Although we know something about these strategies and their use, much remains to be learned.

When the text is familiar and the reader is experienced, retrieval structures are thus generated automatically as incidental results of the comprehension process. Student readers, on the other hand, cannot rely on LTWM because they lack the automatic strategies and the background knowledge that makes it possible. The goal of instruction must be to get the student engaged in comprehension processes that are equivalent to the comprehension strategies experts employ that result in retrieval structures and the buildup of LTWM. However, what is automatic and effortless for the expert reader is intentional and effortful for the novice. The theory of LTWM implies that student readers cannot read in the same way as experienced readers, but instead must be taught explicitly to engage in the right kind of comprehension strategies. They have to be induced to be active readers, even though that may be hard work for them, because otherwise their comprehension will be superficial and their memory poor, and their ability to integrate information from a text with their background knowledge remains severely limited. In the next section, the implications of this finding will be explored for learning from text.

Learning From Text[8]

There are important psychological differences between learning from a text and remembering the text. Text memory, that is, the ability to reproduce the text either verbatim, in paraphrase, or by summarizing it, may be achieved on the basis of only superficial understanding. In the extreme case, one can learn to recite a text by rote without understanding it at all. Learning from text, on the other hand, requires deeper understanding. Learning from text is the ability to use the information acquired from the text productively in novel environments. This requires that the text information be integrated with the reader's prior knowledge and become a part of it, so that it can support comprehension and problem solving in new situations. Mere text memory, on the other hand, may remain inert knowledge—reproducible given the right retrieval cues, but not an active component of the reader's knowledge base. Text memory is based on the textbase; learning from text requires the construction of a situation model.

A well-known study by Bransford and Franks (1971) can be characterized as all understanding and no memory. In this study, the texts consisted of four simple sentences such as *The ants were in the kitchen. The ants ate the jelly.* and so on. These ideas also could be expressed in more complex sentences such as *The ants in the kitchen ate the jelly.* Subjects were given several such texts, in either the form of 4 one-idea sentences, 2 two-idea sentences, 1 three-idea sentence and

1 one-idea sentence, or other such combinations. Later, they were given a recognition test consisting of some sentences they had actually read and others they had not seen before. The results of the study were clear: Subjects remembered very well the stories they had read (e.g., they remembered the ants and the jelly and whatever else there was to that text) but did not know which particular sentences they had read. They remembered the meaning of each minitext—a scene or an image, perhaps—but not the way it had been presented verbally. The memory for the actual text they had read was wiped out by heavy interference (the subjects read many sentences, all very similar), but they had no trouble keeping in mind the few simple and distinct situation models they had formed for each of the several texts they had read.

At the other extreme—all memory and little understanding—is a study by Moravcsik and Kintsch (1993). Three factors were varied in their experiment: (1) domain knowledge (high or low), (2) the way the text was written (good, well-organized writing vs. poor, disorganized writing), and (3) reading ability (high or low scores on the comprehension subtest of the Nelson–Denny Reading Test). Domain knowledge was manipulated by using titles that allowed subjects to use their knowledge and to disambiguate the otherwise obscure text.

All three factors—knowledge, writing quality, and reading ability—significantly influenced the amount of reproductive recall. These effects were additive. There was no indication of an interaction and, hence, of compensation (see also Voss & Silfies, 1996). However, there was an interesting difference in the kind of mental representation subjects constructed in the different experimental conditions. Even though high reading skill and good writing enabled low-knowledge readers to form adequate textbases that were capable of supporting reproductive recall, these readers could not form correct situation models to support their elaborative recall.[9] Their elaborations tended to be wrong and fanciful. Only high-knowledge readers were capable of good elaborations. Inadequate situation models did not keep the subjects from elaborating, but their elaborations and inferences were erroneous, whereas the elaborations of readers who could use their knowledge to construct an adequate situation model were appropriate ones.

It is interesting to note the effects of writing quality in this study. All passages were written in two different versions, preserving their content but varying their style. In one version, the language was as helpful as my colleagues and I could make it in signaling discourse importance to the reader. The other version was as unhelpful as my colleagues and I could make it while still writing an English text. Writing quality had a major effect on reproductive recall, facilitating reproduction about as much as domain knowledge did. But it did not help understanding: Whether a text was well written did not have a statistically significant effect on the proportion of erroneous elaborations. Thus, while good writing can help the reader to construct a better textbase, sufficient for recall, it does not by itself guarantee the deeper understanding that is a prerequisite for learning.

Just how low-ability students go about using their domain knowledge to achieve good comprehension results was investigated by Yekovich, Walker, Ogle, and Thompson (1990). One group of their subjects had high knowledge of football, and one had low knowledge. With texts that had nothing to do with football, the two groups performed equivalently. But with a football text, the high-knowledge subjects outperformed the low-knowledge subjects. The questions on which the high-knowledge subjects showed the greatest advantage over low-knowledge subjects were inference questions and integrative summary statements. There was less of a difference on memory and detail questions. This is, of course, exactly what the theory of comprehension would lead one to expect. Even readers with little domain knowledge can understand information that is given explicitly in the text (although they might not remember it because their retrieval structures might not be rich enough). However, inferences and thematic integration that build retrieval structures require knowledge.

The Measurement of Learning

In order to be useful in research, the theoretical distinction between learning from a text and memory for a text requires empirical methods to assess learning separately from memory. However, because learning and memory cannot be separated cleanly even in the theory (textbase and situation model are not two separate structures but are the text-derived and knowledge-derived components of a single structure), measurement procedures are not precisely separable into textbase and situation model measures either. Instead, empirical measures reflect one or the other aspect of the structure to a stronger degree. Thus, one can ask questions that demand a specific detail from the text or that require the integration of textual information and prior knowledge in order to solve a new problem. Even recall reflects both aspects: the textbase, to the extent that the recall is reproductive, and the situation model, to the extent that it is reconstructive. Usually, recall is a mixture of the two, but in some cases it is primarily one or the other.

Text memory is measured through free recall, cued recall, summarization, various types of recognition tests, and text-based questions. Different methods are needed, however, for the measurement of learning. Psychology shares the need for such measures with artificial intelligence (AI), in so far as AI is interested in the construction of knowledge-rich expert systems (e.g., Olson & Biolsi, 1991), and with education, where the assessment of learning is of obvious importance. Education and AI have relied for the most part on direct methods for knowledge assessment, that is, various forms of question asking. That is still by far the most widely used method in psychology too, although more indirect scaling methods also have been developed for purposes of psychological research.

Asking questions is a method for the assessment of knowledge that is fraught with problems. Developers of expert systems rely on this method almost exclusively, but it is difficult to determine the correctness or completeness of the answers that are being elicited. Educationally, the problem is that asking questions is artificial and sometimes yields invalid results. It is an unnatural act when a teacher asks a student for something she knows better than the student. Furthermore, the answers that the students give may indicate much else other than real learning. Students may acquire specific strategies that allow them to generate acceptable answers without deeper understanding. Or questions may be answered correctly or wrongly for various accidental reasons that have nothing to do with the students' understanding. These problems are widely appreciated but not easily avoided.

Instead of direct questions, scaling methods often are employed to assess knowledge indirectly. Scaling methods require a set of keywords or phrases that are characteristic for a certain knowledge domain. (One can ask experts for such words or use more objective methods such as frequency counts of technical terms in relevant scientific publications.) The knowledge of a subject is inferred from the way the subject organizes these keywords. If the structure generated by the subject resembles the structure generated by domain experts, we infer that the subject's knowledge organization is similar to that of the experts. To the extent that the subject structures the set of keywords in ways that differ from the experts, a lack of correct domain knowledge is revealed.

The basic technique for finding out how a subject organizes a set of keywords is to ask the subject for relatedness judgments between all pairs of keywords in the set. A similarity matrix between all keywords is thus obtained, showing the rated closeness between all word pairs. Such a matrix can then be used as the basis for multidimensional scaling (e.g., Bisanz, LaPorte, Vesonder, & Voss, 1978; Henley, 1969). A low-dimensional space is generated in which the keywords are embedded. One can then ask whether the space is the same for the students as for the experts and whether the location of the keywords in this space is similar for students and experts. This method has been used successfully a number of times. For instance, the semantic field of "animal names" has been scaled in this way, yielding a space with the two dimensions of size and ferocity, which account for 59% of the variance of the paired-comparison judgments (Henley, 1969).

However, these scaling methods are of limited usefulness. The pairwise comparison method is laborious for the subject and rapidly becomes impossible to use as the number of keywords increases. Furthermore, multidimensional scaling methods work with group data, but we often need to work with data from individual subjects. Most important, however, it has become apparent that very few knowledge domains (other than animal names) are so regular and simple that they could be described by a space of a few namable dimensions.

A method for indirect knowledge assessment was developed by Ferstl and Kintsch (1999). It was applied to the problem of measuring the amount of learning that occurred from reading a text. If the text had an effect on the reader's memory, knowledge, or both, it should change the way the reader organizes a knowledge domain, and the change should be in the direction of the text organization. A reader's knowledge about a particular domain of interest is first assessed, either by a pairwise comparison of appropriate keywords or by collecting cued associations to these keywords. The reader's knowledge organization can then be inferred from these data either with the hierarchical clustering analysis of Johnson (1967) or the Pathfinder analysis of Schvaneveldt (1990). The reader then studies the to-be-learned text. Afterward, the reader's knowledge organization is reassessed to see whether it changed in accordance with the text organization.

Using Coherent Text to Improve Learning

Learning from text requires that the learner construct a coherent mental representation of the text and that this representation be anchored in the learner's background knowledge. Thus, one reason why students might fail to learn something from reading a text could be that they are unable to form a coherent textbase linked to their prior knowledge. It is easy to see why this might be the case for low-knowledge readers. Not all links either within a text or between the text and the readers' knowledge are always spelled out in a text; they are often left for the reader to fill in, for example, as *bridging inferences*. This is fine and, as we shall see in the next section of this chapter, can be quite advantageous, but it often creates problems for low-knowledge readers. If readers simply do not have the necessary background knowledge to fill in the gaps in the text that an author has left, they will be unable to form a coherent representation of the text or to link it with whatever little they do know. Consider some trivial examples:

> (20) *The heart is connected to the arteries. The blood in the aorta is bright red.*

For a reader who does not know what the relationship between *arteries* and *aorta* is, there will be a coherence problem. Or consider the following example:

> (21) *To stop the North Vietnamese aggressors, the Pentagon decided to bomb Hanoi.*

This sentence may present all kinds of problems to a low-knowledge reader: Namely, what is the *Pentagon* and how does *Hanoi* get into this sentence? A little rewriting of these problem texts that makes the relations between items in the text, or between general knowledge and the text, fully explicit can avoid these problems. Thus, we might define *aorta* for a low-knowledge reader by rewriting (20) as shown at the top of the next page.

(20a) *The heart is connected to the arteries. The blood in the aorta, the artery that carries blood from the heart to the body, is bright red.*

And we can help a low-knowledge reader with (21) by inserting explicit links between the unknown terms and what a reader might be expected to know:

(21a) *To stop the North Vietnamese aggressors, the U.S. Defense Department in the Pentagon decided to bomb Hanoi, the capital of North Vietnam.*

So far we have only considered local coherence problems, but the global coherence of a text often also can be made more explicit. The macrostructure of a text is not always explicitly signaled in the text but may be left for the reader to deduce. This is fine for knowledgeable readers but can be a major source of confusion when the requisite background knowledge is lacking. Thus, most of us need no help to understand the structure of a four-paragraph text, with each paragraph describing the anatomical details of one of the chambers of the heart. However, for a reader who does not know that the heart has four chambers, a title such as *The four chambers of the heart*, plus appropriate subtitles or clearly marked topic sentences for each paragraph, can be of great help.

It is indeed the case that such relatively minor revisions of texts that ensure coherence at both the local and global level facilitate text memory as well as learning for readers who lack background knowledge. A representative study is one by Britton and Gulgoz (1991). The authors used a history text as their learning material that described the U.S. air war in Vietnam. The text was written at the time of the war and presumed considerable prior knowledge on the part of the reader—knowledge that at that time was probably readily available among the population to which the text was addressed. Many years after the war, the people who participated in Britton and Gulgoz's study had very little specific information about the war, and hence found the text hard going. Although they were able to recall quite a bit from the text, and answered more than half of the fact questions correctly, their performance was poor on the inference questions. In fact, they really did not understand the text at all. This conclusion follows from an analysis of the conceptual understanding of the situation as it was assessed by a keyword comparison task.

Britton and Gulgoz selected 12 keywords that were of crucial importance for the understanding of the text and had students give pairwise relatedness judgments for these keywords. They also had the original author of the text plus several other experts on the Vietnam War provide relatedness judgments for the same set of keywords. The author and experts agreed quite well among themselves (average intercorrelation $r = .80$). But the students who had obtained their information from reading the text did not agree with the author or the experts at all (average $r = .08$). Their understanding of the air war in Vietnam on the basis of reading this text was quite different from the one the author had intended (and which the experts achieved from reading the same text). Thus, even though the students recalled a good part of the text and answered questions about it reasonably well, they really did not understand what they were saying. Britton and Gulgoz also report an analysis of the keyword judgment data, which make clear some of the fundamental misconceptions of these readers. For instance, whereas the text emphasized the failure of Operation Rolling Thunder, in the students' judgments *Rolling Thunder* was linked to *success*, instead. Britton likens this result to reading the Bible and concluding the devil was the good guy.

This dismal performance could be improved significantly by some rather simple revisions of the original text that make the text understandable to readers without adequate background knowledge. Britton and Gulgoz located all coherence gaps in the original text that required readers to make a bridging inference. Then they inserted into the text a sentence or phrase making this inference explicit. For instance, if in one sentence *North Vietnam* is mentioned and the next sentence begins with *In response to the American threats, Hanoi decided*, Britton and Gulgoz might have made this sentence pair coherent by revising the second sentence to *The North-Vietnamese government in Hanoi decided....* These revisions were highly effective. Recall increased significantly, as did the performance on inference questions. Readers now understood the text more or less correctly. Their relatedness judgments after reading the revised text correlated reasonably well with those of the experts ($r = .52$), and if one looks at the structure of their judgments as revealed by a Pathfinder analysis, no glaring misunderstandings are apparent, as was the case for the readers of the original version of the text. Hence, making this text locally coherent by filling in the gaps that required bridging inferences yielded a text that readers could understand, even though their background knowledge was lacking.

Several other studies confirm and extend these results (e.g., Beck, McKeown, Sinatra, & Loxterman, 1991; McKeown, Beck, Sinatra, & Loxterman, 1992; McNamara, E. Kintsch, Songer, & W. Kintsch, 1996, Experiment 1). Revising a text for coherence is clearly an effective technique to further understanding and learning. On their own, students without adequate background knowledge cannot fill in gaps in the text that readers with greater familiarity with the domain bridge effortlessly and, in fact, unconsciously. For such readers, providing explicit bridging material in the text, at both the local and global levels, is a prerequisite for understanding and learning.

If this is so, why do authors ever leave gaps in their texts? Why do we not write fully coherent, explicit texts all the time? The answer is that to write such a text is an elusive goal; a writer must always rely on the reader's knowledge to some degree. There is no text comprehension that does not require the reader to apply knowledge: lexical knowledge, syntactic and semantic knowledge, domain knowledge, personal experience, and so on. The printed words on the page, or the sound waves in the air, are but one source of constraints that must be satisfied. The reader's knowledge provides the other. Ideally, a text should contain the new information a reader needs to know, plus just enough old information to allow the reader to link the new information with what is already known. Texts that contain too much that the reader already knows are boring to read and confusing (e.g., legal and insurance documents that leave nothing to be taken for granted). Hence, too much coherence and explication may not necessarily be a good thing.

Improving Learning by Stimulating Active Processing

The contention that if readers possess adequate knowledge, a fully explicit text is not optimal for them, was explored by McNamara et al. (1996). Such readers will remember more and learn better from texts that require them to assume a more active role in comprehension. Specifically, my colleagues and I hypothesized that the results obtained by Britton and Gulgoz, and others described previously, pertain to low-knowledge readers. Readers with good domain knowledge might react in very different ways.

In the McNamara et al. experiment, college students studied a middle school–level encyclopedia article on heart disease. Two versions of the text were used. In one case, the text was maximally coherent and explicit at both the local and global level. For this purpose, potentially ambiguous pronouns were replaced with full noun phrases; elaborations that linked unfamiliar concepts to familiar ones were added, as were missing sentence connectives; and a concept was always referred to in the same way (rather than by a synonym or paraphrase). In addition, titles and subtitles were used to indicate the macrostructure of the text, and explicit macropropositions marked the role of each paragraph in the text. The resulting version was the high-coherence text. The low-coherence version was constructed by deleting all these signals but not otherwise changing the content of the text.

The prior knowledge of the subjects was assessed via a knowledge assessment test consisting of a series of questions on the basic anatomy and functioning of the heart and a recognition test in which subjects were asked to match parts of the heart to a cross-sectional diagram of the heart and its major blood vessels.

After taking this test, subjects read either the high- or the low-coherence text twice and then responded to a series of posttests. First they were asked to recall the text in their own words. Then subjects were given four types of questions: (1) text-based questions, (2) elaboration questions that required relating text information to the reader's background knowledge, (3) bridging inference questions that required connecting two or more separate text segments, and (4) problem-solving questions that required applying text information in a novel situation.

The results of this study reveal a strong interaction between the level of prior knowledge of the students, the coherence of the text, and the method of testing. High-knowledge students always perform better than low-knowledge students. But when tests are used that assess primarily text memory, the high-coherence text is better for all types of students. However, when tests are used that depend on the construction of a good situation model, the low-coherence text actually yields better results for high-knowledge subjects than the high-coherence text. For low-knowledge subjects, on the other hand, the usual superiority of the high-coherence version over the low-coherence version is observed.

It appears that the high-coherence text that spelled out everything these readers already knew quite well induced an illusory feeling of knowing that prevented them from processing the text deeply. They were satisfied with a superficial understanding, which was good enough for recall and answering text-based questions, but they failed to construct an adequate situation model combining their prior knowledge with the information from the text. Hence they learned relatively little from the text that should have been the easiest and most effective.

These results were replicated by McNamara and Kintsch (1996) with the Vietnam War text of Britton and Gulgoz (1991) and a different knowledge manipulation: Half the subjects received a brief lesson about the Vietnam War before studying the text. For untrained, low-knowledge subjects, the original low-coherence text was quite ineffective, as was the revised, high-coherence text for the trained high-knowledge subjects. However, if readers who knew very little about Vietnam were given the coherent, well-written text, their knowledge organization was influenced by the text they had read. Similarly, the better-informed readers clearly learned more from the challenging text, as reflected by the way they sorted the keywords.

These results are paradoxical. Should we start writing incoherent texts and give disorganized lectures so that our better students will benefit from them? The answer to this question seems to be a qualified "yes." Making things too easy for a student may be a significant impediment to learning. However, just messing up a lecture is not a solution. Instead, we need to challenge the student to engage in active, deep processing of a text. This can be done, as we have shown here, by placing impediments in the path of comprehension, but impediments of the right kind and in the right amount. They must be impediments we have reason to think the student can overcome, if he or she tries hard enough, and the activity of overcoming these impediments must be learning relevant. We have shown previously that giving students a text with coherence gaps to study from, for which they do not have adequate background knowledge, is self-defeating. Such students need all the help they can get, and we need to organize and explicate the text for them as well as we can. But, as the literature on generation effects in memory also demonstrates (e.g., McNamara & Healy, 1995), students who are able to perform a task unaided should be encouraged to do so. They will remember better and learn better to the extent that the activity they are engaging in is task relevant. This was certainly the case in the experiments discussed previously in which the incoherent texts forced the high-knowledge students to establish local coherence relations on the basis of their own knowledge, to figure out the macrostructure of the text on their own, and to elaborate the textual material with what they already knew.

The fact that not just any self-generated activity is helpful for text memory has been shown in a series of studies discussed in McDaniel, Blischak, and Einstein (1995). Story recall can be improved by omitting occasional letters from words so that the reader must fill in the missing information from the context. Filling in missing letters forces readers to focus on the details of the stories that readers often disregard in favor of the story line. On the other hand, a different orienting task, such as reordering sentences, has no effect on story recall because readers of a story pay sufficient information to the relational information between sentences, even without the reordering task. These relations are reversed for descriptive texts. The reordering task helps recall by focusing the reader's attention on otherwise neglected order information, but the missing letters task has no effect because readers of essays are quite careful about the details anyway. Thus, simply placing obstacles in the reader's path that force them to expend extra effort does not benefit their learning. Instead, positive effects can be expected only if the extra processing they engage in is task appropriate.

If the effort is task appropriate, however, engaging the reader in active processing can be quite helpful. We have seen this for learning from text in the experiments above. This is also the case for sentence memory. There is a curvilinear relation between the strength of a causal connection between two statements and the memory strength of their connection measured by cued recall, indicating that neither too weak nor too strong links are elaborated as successfully as intermediate links (e.g., Myers, Shinjo, & Duffy, 1987; van den Broek, 1990). Analogous results have been reported by Battig (1979) for paired-associate learning, who reported better retention when the learning was made more difficult through intratask interference. There is also a literature on skill acquisition (Schmidt & Bjork, 1992) that shows that making the learning process too smooth is counterproductive. Learners acquiring a new skill must have the opportunity to face difficulties and learn to repair mistakes.

Mannes and Kintsch (1987) have reported a study that is similar in spirit to the experiments discussed here. In their study, readers were given an advance organizer that either fit perfectly with the target text and, hence, made it easy to read, or that structurally mismatched the target text, so that the readers had to engage in some cognitive effort to relate the advance information and the target text. The target text was a rather long article from a popular science publication about the industrial use of microbes. Because the students knew very little about microbes beforehand, an advance organizer was prepared that told them everything they needed to know about microbes. Two forms of this advance organizer were employed that differed in the order in which the material was presented but, as much as possible, preserved the content of the material. In one case, the general information about microbes occurred in exactly the same order as it was presented in the target text. We called this the congruent advance organizer. In the other version, the material was presented as in the encyclopedia article that we had used as our source. This organization was incongruent with the text.

Participants studied either form of the advanced organizer and took a short test on it, and then they read the target text, which required a certain amount of knowledge about the properties of microbes. After reading the text, they were tested on what they remembered from the text and what they had learned. A dissociation was observed between measures of text memory (correct verifications of old sentences) and measures of learning (correct verifications of inference sentences). When the advance organizer and the content of the text were structurally congruent, subjects readily understood the text and remembered it better than when the advance information and the text were organized differently. The formation of a textbase was presumably facilitated because the macrostructure they had formed for the advanced organizer provided a fitting schema for the text itself. When this was not the case, the textbase was not as perfect, and behavioral measures depending primarily on the textbase were lower. However, the subjects' situation model was enhanced because, in understanding the target text, they had to retrieve and integrate information from the advance organizer that had presented the information in a different context. Therefore, a richer, more interrelated network was constructed, which later helped the readers with inference questions and problem solving.

Thus, it has been demonstrated repeatedly that increasing the difficulty of the learning phase can have beneficial effects. Moreover, these studies are not limited to learning from text but involve other kinds of learning situations as well. Task difficulty can stimulate active processing, with the result that a more elaborate, better-integrated situation model will be constructed. However, this statement must be carefully qualified. The student must possess the necessary skills and knowledge to successfully engage in the required activity, and the activity must be task relevant.

Matching Readers and Texts

Readers without adequate background knowledge have trouble comprehending difficult texts and learn very little from them. On the other hand, the research just discussed shows that readers should be challenged and that making things too easy for students elicits a passive attitude that is not conducive to deep understanding and knowledge building. The problem is to find texts of the right level of difficulty for each student in a classroom where there is typically a broad range of preparation and prior knowledge. Experienced teachers and librarians can do that very well, if they have the time for each individual student. A procedure to do so automatically, proposed by Wolfe et al. (1998), has shown some promise in the laboratory but has not been classroom tested so far.

The procedure employed the ability of LSA to measure automatically how similar two texts are. Wolfe et al. asked students of varying background knowledge to write a brief essay about a medical topic. These essays revealed how much each student knew about the topic: Low-knowledge college students wrote quite different essays than students who happened to know a lot about the topic, and medical students who had studied this topic used a different language yet. Wolfe et al. had four texts, all about the same topic but varying greatly in sophistication, from a popularization for high school students, to college-level texts, to a medical school text. The participants in this study were randomly assigned to one of these instructional texts. How similar the text was to the essay the student wrote was measured by LSA: The cosine between the student's prior essay and the study text he or she was assigned provided a measure of the semantic distance between essay and text. After studying the text they were assigned to, the students were tested (by means of a questionnaire as well as another essay) for how much they had learned. When the cosine between a student's prior essay and the text was low—that is, essay and text were very different in content—there was little learning. When the cosine between essay and test was high—that is, essay and text were similar—there also was very little learning. However, for intermediate cosines (around .5), students learned quite well (30 to 40% improvement in their scores from pretest to posttest).

What Wolfe et al. found was an automatic and easy way to determine the "zone of learning" for individual students. The essay the student writes reveals the student's knowledge level. If the instructional text is too hard for that knowledge level, the student will learn very little from that text; if the text is too easy, there is not much for the student to learn. But if the student is given the right text for his or her level of preparation, learning can be successful. This is an intuitive result, but what makes the Wolfe et al. study interesting is the way they achieved it: Letting students express in their own words what they know about a topic and using LSA to index their knowledge quantitatively may turn out to be a useful practical method for various purposes. Not only can this method be used to match students and texts, as was done in their study, but it also is a useful tool for self-assessment. After reading an instructional text, students could write about what they learned and receive LSA-based feedback about the adequacy of their understanding, such as what content areas they had missed or irrelevancies they had introduced.

Word Problems: From Text to Action

Word problems—in grade school arithmetic, high school algebra, and college physics classes—challenge students because they require not only the correct formal operations but also a correct understanding of the problem. It is useful to view word-problem solving from the standpoint of text comprehension. The student must be able to form the correct situation model before formal operations can be brought to bear on the problem. A second grader may know that $8 - 5 = 3$, but not whether to add or subtract when given

(22) *Joe has 8 red marbles.*

Tom has 5 blue marbles.

How many marbles does Joe have more than Tom?

What makes word problems special is that the usual kind of situation model is insufficient. It is not enough for the student to understand that Tom and Joe have marbles, the marbles are blue and red, and one boy has more marbles than the other; in order to do the arithmetic correctly, a student needs to extract from the text very specific information. The arithmetic set schema specifies what that information is. The text must be used to fill in the empty slots in that schema, resulting in the construction of a problem model. Thus, it takes more than just an informal situation model to determine the appropriate arithmetic operation to solve the problem. A formal arithmetic problem model must be constructed. Normal text comprehension strategies do not support the construction of a formal problem model; special training with arithmetic word problems is required, which is why word problems are so difficult.

Many problems that require formal methods for their solution require this distinction between situation model and problem model. Consider, for instance, a scientist who wants to use a graphics program to design a graph for a manuscript he is writing. His situation model may be a mental image of the graph he wants to construct, specifying its principal features; he could draw such a graph by hand. To use the graphics program, however, the desired image has to be transformed into a formal problem model that takes into account the constraints and requirements of the particular graphics program he is using. In doing so, some details have to be specified that were not considered explicitly in the scientist's situation model (such as font size, precise arrangement of the graph axes, and so on). Only when the scientist's ideas are translated into the format required by the graphics program can action result: In this case, the program designs the desired graph. The second grader is in much the same situation: She must learn just what information in the text is needed for the arithmetic problem model, and in what form it is needed.

Word Arithmetic Problems

W. Kintsch and Greeno (1985; see also W. Kintsch, 1998, chap. 10.1) have formulated a model that simulates the construction of an arithmetic problem model for commonly used word problems in grades 1 to 4. It is based on the set schema, which specifies for a collection of objects their type (e.g., *marbles*), their quantity (e.g., *8*), their specification (*Joe* is the owner), and the relation of this set to other sets (e.g., in [22] the set of Joe's marbles is to be compared with the set of Tom's marbles).

Consider how this simulation would solve a simple word problem such as (23), which is called a *transfer problem*.

(23) *Joe had 3 marbles.*

Then Tom gave him some marbles.

Now Joe has 8 marbles.

How many marbles did Tom give him?

The first sentence provides a cue for making a set S_1:

S_1: Objects: *marbles*

    Quantity: *3*

    Specification: *owner Joe*

    Role: *unknown*

The second sentence cues a second set schema, S_2, and allows the model to determine the relationship between these sets because it knows that transfer problems (*give* is a cue that this problem might be of that type) have a *start-set*, *transfer-set*, and *result-set*.

S_1: Objects: *marbles* S_2: Objects: *marbles*

    Quantity: *3*   Quantity: *unknown*

    Specification: *owner Joe*   Specification: *owner Tom*

    Role: *start-set*   Role: *transfer-set*

The third sentence completes the problem model.

S_1: Objects: *marbles* S_2: Objects: *marbles* S_3: Objects: *marbles*

    Quantity: *3*   Quantity: *unknown*   Quantity: *8*

    Specification: *owner Joe*   Specification: *owner Tom*   Specification: *owner Joe*

    Role: *start-set*   Role: *transfer-set*   Role: *result-set*

With the problem model completed, the model acts: It uses a procedure called Add-On (which is what first and second graders use in this case) to calculate the answer: *Tom gave Joe 5 marbles.*

What good is such a simulation? First, it specifies exactly what information the student must extract from the word problem. That does not mean that the student should be taught to use a set schema—just taught what the needed information is.

Second, the simulation helps us to understand why a child makes certain errors (and hence offers an opportunity for corrective instruction). Consider the following word problem:

(24) *Mark and Sally have 7 trucks altogether.*

Mark has 2 trucks.

How many trucks does Sally have?

The usual answer that the children give (45%, in a study by DeCorte, Verschaffel, & DeWinn, 1985) is 7. The problem is that the children do not know the meaning of *altogether* and parse it as *each*. The number of trucks Mark owns is updated by the second sentence, but they think they already know the answer about how many trucks Sally has when they read the third sentence. When these children are asked to recall problem (24), they recall it the way they understood it as follows, not the way it was actually presented:

(25) *Sally has 7 trucks.*

Mark has 2 trucks.

How many trucks do Mark and Sally have?

What these children are doing is turning a difficult problem that they are unable to solve as stated into an easy problem that they know how to solve—a strategy not only second graders employ.

A third example of how simulations, such as the one by W. Kintsch and Greeno (1985), illuminate the difficulties children have with word problems concerns the role of keywords in problem solving. Consider the following two problems:

(26a) *Tom is 175 cm tall.*   (26b) *Tom is 175 cm tall.*

      Jeff is 12 cm shorter than Tom.   *He is 12 cm taller than Jeff.*

      How tall is Jeff?   *How tall is Jeff?*

Problem (26a) is much easier than (26b) because the keyword *shorter* suggests subtractions, whereas *taller* suggests addition. Therefore, the second sentence of (26a) sets up a bias in favor of subtraction, which is helpful, while the second sentence of (26b) sets up a bias in favor of addition, which interferes with the correct response to the question posed in the last sentence.

Algebraic Schemas

Things get more interesting and more complicated when we consider algebraic word problems, rather than arithmetic word problems, because the importance of situation models in algebraic word-problem solving is at least as great as in arithmetic word-problem solving. In a pioneering study, using extensive protocol analyses, Hall, Kibler, Wenger, and Truxaw (1989) have shown that competent college students reason within the situational context of a story problem to identify the quantitative constraints required for a solution. They use the text to build, elaborate, and verify a situation model from which they derive their solution. A variety of reasoning strategies are used by students to develop these situation models, which are by no means restricted to the algebraically relevant aspects of a problem. Integrating the dual representations of a problem at the situational and mathematical levels appears to be the central aspect of competence according to Hall et al., as indeed it was for children working on arithmetic word problems. However, while there are only a few arithmetic schemas that the theorist must consider, over 1,000 problem types are found in algebra texts (Mayer, 1981).

This complexity, however, is primarily linguistic rather than algebraic. A relatively small number of algebraic schemas can do all the work that is needed for the construction of the necessary formal problem models. The difficulty we encounter is in the construction of the problem model. A broad range of linguistic and general world knowledge is needed for that purpose. The 1,000 algebraic problem types are based on only a few algebraic schemas, however. Four schema types are needed to deal with the largest class of algebra problems—rate problems. Another class of problems involves physics, geometry, and schemas from other domains. This is essentially an open class. Examples are Newton's second law—the sum of all forces for a system in equilibrium must be 0; Ohm's law; the Pythagorean theorem; the formulas for the area and circumference of a circle and other geometric shapes; and so on. Finally, there is a third class of word algebra problems—number problems—which are not schema based but must be constructed from the text directly without the use of a schema.

The four rate schemas are all of the same form:

$$\text{Unit}_1 = \text{rate-of-Unit}_1\text{-per-Unit}_2 \times \text{Unit}_2$$

The units may be amount per time (a boat travels 4 km per hour), cost per unit (a pound of almonds costs \$5.99), portion to total cost (7% of the cost of a car), and amount to amount (5% acid in 3 gallons of solution). These rate schemas are the building blocks of algebraic problem models. The story text usually specifies one or two of the members of a schema (Unit_1, Unit_2, rate). If only one member is missing, it can be computed from the formula above. Algebra problems usually require the instantiation of more than one schema, together with the relation between them. Thus, we might have two kinds of nuts with different costs and mix the two according to certain specifications, requiring three cost-per-unit schemas. To construct a problem model, the problem solver must (a) pick the right schema, which can be done on the basis of textual cues, just as in the case of the arithmetic schemas; (b) specify as many elements for each schema as the text allows; and (c) find or infer from the text the relationships among the schemas used. Once a problem model has been constructed, an equation for the problem can be found by constraint propagation within the problem model.

The problem for the student in all this is to tell whether the formalization that has been constructed adequately represents the problem situation. The real world gives the formalist some feedback as to the adequacy of the formalization: Bridges last for centuries or they collapse; the software is perfect but does not do what the customer imagined. Experienced algebraic word-problem solvers provide their own feedback by checking their answers for reasonableness against their situation model. But that is exactly where students need help; otherwise they come up with negative values for the length of a board and similar absurdities (Paige & Simon, 1966). Because algebra students cannot operate in the real world and receive feedback from it, the next best thing is to supply them with a substitute world in the form of an animation that acts out what is implied by the problem model they have constructed. Nathan, Kintsch, and Young (1992) have built a tutor that shows the student what the implications of a proposed formalization are in the real world. It is not an intelligent tutor because the system does not understand the problem at all. It merely executes an animation as instructed by the student's problem model. (It paints fences, mixes solutions, stacks up piles of money, or lets objects move.) If the right event happens in the animation, the student knows that his solution was correct. If the wrong event happens, the student must figure out how to correct it. If nothing happens because the simulation was not given enough information to execute anything, the student realizes that one or more pieces are missing from his formal model and can try to complete it.

Suppose a student is trying to solve an overtake problem: A plane leaves Denver en route to Chicago with a certain speed; half an hour later, a second plane leaves on the same route with a greater speed. When will the second plane overtake the first plane? The student formulates his problem model and the tutor illustrates what happens according to that model: One plane flies away, then a second one follows and soon overtakes it; or, if the problem model is faulty, the second plane may never leave or may move with a slower speed, and the student realizes that he has done something wrong.

Problem solving often requires an explicit formal problem model. Helping students to construct such a model by providing feedback that allows them to use their everyday understanding of the problem situation can be an effective tutoring tool. The tutoring strategies sketched previously in the context of word problems in arithmetic and algebra have a potentially broad range of application. Making explicit the link between text, formalization, and action could be a powerful instructional tool that deserves further exploration. Problem solvers often understand their problem correctly in everyday terms but have trouble constructing the right formalization for it, which is necessary for the use of powerful, formal solution methods. If an animation can show them whether their problem model actually corresponds to the intended situation or not, they can use their correct situational understanding to repair their formal model.

Research on Reading Comprehension and the Teaching of Reading Comprehension

Research on reading has been an active field in the last few decades. Relatively large sums of money have been made available by federal agencies such as the National Institute of Mental Health (NIMH) to support this field. However, the focus of this research effort has been squarely on early reading instruction—on the study of decoding processes, rather than comprehension. To focus research on decoding was a perfectly defensible and successful strategy: We now have a fairly good understanding of the cognitive bases of decoding processes in reading and about reading instruction in the early grades. Surely, there remain problems to be resolved, but there exists an underlying consensus today about early reading instruction in the United States, as exemplified by the National Research Council report *Preventing Reading Difficulties in Young Children* (Snow, Burns, & Griffin, 1998). Educators know what to do, even if getting it done in schools on a national scale is still another matter.

There also is agreement among reading researchers today that research on reading comprehension lags far behind research on decoding processes and early reading instruction, and that it is time to shift the research focus onto reading comprehension beyond the early years. Recent assessments of research needs by the RAND Reading Study Group (RAND, 2002) and the Strategic Education Research Partnership report of the National Research Council's Panel on Learning and Instruction (Donovan, Wigdor, & Snow, 2003) agree on the need for a better understanding of the processes of text comprehension as well as instructional methods to improve comprehension.

My goal in this chapter has been to show that there exists a solid basis for further research in reading comprehension. We do not have to start from zero; there is a sparse but solid database, as well as a theoretical framework, that can serve at least as a good starting point for further research on reading comprehension. Throughout this chapter, open research questions have been pointed out, most pressingly about the formation of situation models and the modeling of macrostructures. There is much to be learned, but we also have already learned quite a bit about comprehension. This chapter was not intended as a general review of research on comprehension, but rather as a description of one particular research program and theoretical approach. A broader discussion would certainly have provided further evidence of the considerable progress made in the study of reading comprehension in recent years.

The explicit goal of the comprehension research presented here is to inform instructional practice. As yet, this link is weak because there are so many unanswered questions and limited, conditional answers, but there is no reason to suppose that a focused research effort in this area would not yield results that achieve this goal.

Theories of discourse comprehension such as the one presented here are based on data from proficient readers. Indeed, these readers, as long as they read familiar material, can be considered to be comprehension experts. Comprehension for them is fluent, automatic, and easy. Well-established knowledge structures and skills are the basis for this automaticity. The goal of instruction is to help students become such expert readers. Paradoxically, however, comprehension instruction requires students to behave in very different ways than experienced readers. Because for student readers comprehension is not the automatic, fluent process that it is for mature readers, students need to engage in active problem solving, knowledge construction, self-explanation, and monitoring—activities very different from the automatic, fluent comprehension of experts. For the expert reader, comprehension is easy; to become an expert, comprehension must be hard work. Research on comprehension, therefore, has two quite distinct goals: (1) to describe expert comprehension with all its components and (2) to determine the training sequence that leads to this expert performance. What the student needs to do in training is quite different from how the expert operates. This is not a problem peculiar to comprehension training. Take, for example, ski instruction. Watching the instructor glide down a steep slope with elegant turns is not helpful to the novice skier. The novice must learn by doing things quite differently, and with much more effort, and the instructor must gradually, via a carefully thought out training sequence, bring the novice to the point where he can begin skiing like an expert, that is, when he is no longer a novice. Thus, if it is to be relevant for instruction, comprehension theory must pay attention not only to the final automatic comprehension that characterizes expert readers in familiar domains, but also to the strategies that support comprehension for the beginner, or for the expert who is faced with materials outside his or her domain of expertise.

Assessment plays a central role in gaining expertise in reading comprehension. This chapter has stressed how nontrivial comprehension assessment is. The levels of comprehension range from the superficial to the deep, from surface features to the textbase to the situation model. Assessing comprehension at these different levels is tricky because quite different tests are required. To teach comprehension, we need a thorough understanding of the different levels of comprehension and the tests that assess comprehension at these different levels. Richer comprehension tests need to be developed and evaluated that adequately assess the different aspects of comprehension. Furthermore, not only must teachers be able to tell how well students understood something, but the students themselves also must have tools to assess their comprehension or lack thereof. People are notoriously bad at this task, and one of the goals of comprehension research must be to find better, and more practical, ways to assess comprehension.

Research on comprehension will probably see a big boost in the next decades. To fulfill its potential it will have to find the right balance between observation, experiment, and theory. Careful studies of the basic cognitive processes in comprehension are needed, together with research on instructional practices and tools that support effective comprehension. Our goal should be a comprehensive theory of comprehension that allows us to understand how people, novices as well as experts, will react in novel situations. We cannot always perform a new experiment for every new question; instead, we need a broad theoretical framework that provides reasonably good answers to these questions. Educational researchers need a reliable theory to navigate by, much as engineers do in other fields, when they only occasionally resort to experiment because they know they can rely on their computations, except for special problems.

Notes

[1] The term *proposition* was borrowed from logic, where it is used quite differently.

[2] The distinction between textbase and situation model is made for the convenience of the theorist; mental representation integrates aspects of both.

[3] Different word *meanings* are unrelated, as in *bank-(of river)* and *bank-(financial institution)*; different word senses are related, as in *chill-(bodily coldness with shivering)* and *chill-(moderate coldness)*.

[4] For comparison, the auto-summary computed by MS Word is "Later, people built windmills to grind wheat and other grains."

[5] Based in part on W. Kintsch (1998, chap. 6).

[6] Based in part on W. Kintsch, Patel, & Ericsson (1999).

[7] The term *long-term memory* is used broadly here; it includes personal experiences as well as general knowledge.

[8] The section is based in part on W. Kintsch (1998, chap. 9).

[9] Elaborative recall is that portion of a recall protocol that is left over when verbatim or paraphrased reproductions of the text are deleted.

References

Albrecht, J.E., & O'Brien, E.J. (1995). Goal processing and the maintenance of global coherence. In R.F. Lorch & E.J. O'Brien (Eds.), *Sources of coherence in reading* (pp. 263–278). Hillsdale, NJ: Erlbaum.

Albrecht, J.E., O'Brien, E.J., Mason, R.A., & Myers, J.L. (1995). The role of perspective in the accessibility of goals during reading. *Journal of Experimental Psychology: Learning, Memory, and Cognition, 21*, 364–372.

Battig, W.F. (1979). The flexibility of human memory. In L.S. Cermak & F.I.M. Craik (Eds.), *Levels of processing in human memory* (pp. 23–44). Hillsdale, NJ: Erlbaum.

Beck, I.L., McKeown, M.G., Sinatra, G.M., & Loxterman, J.A. (1991). Revising social studies texts from a text-processing perspective: Evidence of improved comprehensibility. *Reading Research Quarterly, 26*, 251–276.

Biederman, I. (1987). Recognition by components: A theory of human image understanding. *Psychological Review, 94*(2), 115–147.

Bisanz, G.L., LaPorte, R.E., Vesonder, G.T., & Voss, J.F. (1978). Contextual prerequisites for understanding: Some investigations of comprehension and recall. *Journal of Verbal Learning and Verbal Behavior, 17,* 337–357.

Bransford, J.D., Barclay, J.R., & Franks, J.J. (1972). Sentence memory: A constructive versus interpretive approach. *Cognitive Psychology, 3,* 193–209.

Bransford, J.D., & Franks, J.J. (1971). The abstraction of linguistic ideas. *Cognitive Psychology, 2,* 331–350.

Britton, B.K., & Gulgoz, S. (1991). Using Kintsch's computational model to improve instructional text: Effects of repairing inference calls on recall and cognitive structures. *Journal of Educational Psychology, 83*(3), 329–345.

Chase, W.G., & Ericsson, K.A. (1981). Skilled memory. In J.R. Anderson (Ed.), *Cognitive skills and their acquisition* (pp. 141–189). Hillsdale, NJ: Erlbaum.

DeCorte, E., Verschaffel, L., & DeWinn, L. (1985). The influence of rewording verbal problems on children's problem representation and solutions. *Journal of Educational Psychology, 77,* 460–470.

Donovan, M.S., Wigdor, A.K., & Snow, C.E. (Eds.). (2003). *Strategic Education Research Partnership.* Washington, DC: National Academy Press.

Ericsson, K.A., & Kintsch, W. (1995). Long-term working memory. *Psychological Review, 102*(2), 211–245.

Ferstl, E., & Kintsch, W. (1999). Learning from text: Structural knowledge assessment in the study of discourse comprehension. In H. van Oostendorp & S.R. Goldman (Eds.), *The construction of mental representations during reading* (pp. 247–278). Mahwah, NJ: Erlbaum.

Fincher-Kiefer, R.H. (1993). The role of predictive inferences in situation model construction. *Discourse Processes, 16*(1), 99–124.

Foertsch, J., & Gernsbacher, M.A. (1994). In search of complete comprehension: Getting "minimalists" to work. *Discourse Processes, 18*(3), 271–296.

Garrod, S., O'Brien, E.J., Morris, R.K., & Rayner, K. (1990). Elaborative inferencing as an active or passive process. *Journal of Experimental Psychology: Learning, Memory, and Cognition, 16,* 250–257.

Glenberg, A.M., Kruley, P., & Langston, W.E. (1994). Analogical processes in comprehension: Simulation of a mental model. In M.A. Gernsbacher (Ed.), *Handbook of psycho-linguistics* (pp. 609–640). San Diego, CA: Academic Press.

Graesser, A.C. (1981). *Prose comprehension beyond the word.* New York: Springer.

Graesser, A.C., & Kreuz, R.J. (1993). A theory of inference generation during text comprehension. *Discourse Processes, 16*(1/2), 145–160.

Graesser, A.C., Singer, M., & Trabasso, T. (1994). Constructing inferences during narrative text comprehension. *Psychological Review, 101*(3), 371–395.

Graesser, A.C., & Zwaan, R.A. (1995). Inference generation and the construction of situation models. In C.A. Weaver, S. Mannes, & C.R. Fletcher (Eds.), *Discourse comprehension: Essays in honor of Walter Kintsch* (pp. 117–139). Hillsdale, NJ: Erlbaum.

Hall, R., Kibler, D., Wenger, E., & Truxaw, C. (1989). Exploring the episodic structure of algebra story problem solving. *Cognition and Instruction, 6,* 223–283.

Henley, N.M. (1969). A psychological study of the semantics of animal terms. *Journal of Verbal Learning and Verbal Behavior, 8,* 176–184.

Johnson, C.S. (1967). Hierarchical clustering schemes. *Psychometrika, 32*(3), 241–254.

Johnson-Laird, P.N., Byrne, R.M.J., & Schaeken, W. (1992). Propositional reasoning by model. *Psychological Review, 99*(3), 418–439.

Kintsch, E., Steinhart, D., Stahl, G., Matthews, C., Lamb, R., & LSA Research Group. (2000). Developing summarization skills through the use of LSA-backed feedback. *Interactive Learning Environments, 8*(2), 87–109.

Kintsch, W. (1974). *The representation of meaning in memory.* Hillsdale, NJ: Erlbaum.

Kintsch, W. (1988). The use of knowledge in discourse processing: A construction-integration model. *Psychological Review, 95,* 163–182.

Kintsch, W. (1998). *Comprehension: A paradigm for cognition.* New York: Cambridge University Press.

Kintsch, W. (2002). On the notion of theme and topic in psychological process models of text comprehension. In M. Louwerse & W. van Peer (Eds.), *Thematics: Interdisciplinary studies* (pp. 157–170). Amsterdam: John Benjamins.

Kintsch, W., & Bates, E. (1977). Recognition memory for statements from a classroom lecture. *Journal of Experimental Psychology: Human Learning and Memory, 3,* 150–159.

Kintsch, W., & Greeno, J.G. (1985). Understanding and solving word arithmetic problems. *Psychological Review, 92*(1), 109–129.

Kintsch, W., Patel, V.L., & Ericsson, K.A. (1999). The role of long-term working memory in text comprehension. *Psychologia, 42,* 186–198.

Kintsch, W., & van Dijk, T.A. (1978). Towards a model of text comprehension and production. *Psychological Review, 85,* 363–394.

Landauer, T.K. (1998). Learning and representing verbal meaning: Latent Semantic Analysis theory. *Current Directions in Psychological Science, 7,* 161–164.

Landauer, T.K., & Dumais, S.T. (1997). A solution to Plato's problem: The Latent Semantic Analysis theory of acquisition, induction and representation of knowledge. *Psychological Review, 104*(2), 211–240.

Landauer, T.K., Foltz, P.W., & Laham, D. (1998). An introduction to Latent Semantic Analysis. *Discourse Processes, 25,* 259–284.

Landauer, T.K., Laham, D., & Foltz, P.W. (2000). The Intelligent Essay Assessor. *IEEE Intelligent Systems,* 27–31.

Le, E. (2002). Themes and hierarchical structures of written text. In M. Louwerse & W. van Peer (Eds.), *Thematics: Interdisciplinary studies* (pp. 171–188). Amsterdam: John Benjamins.

Long, D.L., & Golding, J.M. (1993). Superordinate goal inferences: Are they automatically generated during reading? *Discourse Processes, 16*(1/2), 55–73.

Long, D.L., Golding, J.M., & Graesser, A.C. (1992). A test of the on-line status of goal-related inferences. *Journal of Memory and Language, 31,* 634–647.

Long, D.L., Oppy, B.J., & Seely, M.R. (1994). Individual differences in the time course of differential processing. *Journal of Experimental Psychology: Learning, Memory, and Cognition, 20,* 1456–1470.

Louwerse, M. (2002). Computational retrieval of texts. In M. Louwerse & W. van Peer (Eds.), *Thematics: Interdisciplinary studies* (pp. 189–216). Amsterdam: John Benjamins.

Magliano, J.P., Baggett, W.B., Johnson, B.K., & Graesser, A.C. (1993). The time course of generating causal antecedent and causal consequence inferences. *Discourse Processes, 16*(1/2), 35–53.

Mani, K., & Johnson-Laird, P.N. (1982). The mental representation of spatial descriptions. *Memory & Cognition, 10*(2), 181–187.

Mannes, S.M., & Kintsch, W. (1987). Knowledge organization and text organization. *Cognition and Instruction, 4,* 91–115.

Mayer, R.E. (1981). Frequency norms and structural analysis of algebra story problems into families, categories, and templates. *Instructional Science, 10,* 135–175.

McDaniel, M.A., Blischak, D., & Einstein, G.I. (1995). Understanding the special mnemonic characteristics of fairy tales. In C.A. Weaver, S. Mannes, & C.R. Fletcher (Eds.), *Discourse comprehension: Essays in honor of Walter Kintsch* (pp. 157–176). Hillsdale, NJ: Erlbaum.

McKeown, M.G., Beck, I.L., Sinatra, G.M., & Loxterman, J.A. (1992). The contribution of prior knowledge and coherent text to comprehension. *Reading Research Quarterly, 27,* 78–93.

McKoon, G., & Ratcliff, R. (1992). Inference during reading. *Psychological Review, 99*(3), 440–466.

McKoon, G., & Ratcliff, R. (1995). The minimalist hypothesis: Directions for research. In C.A. Weaver, S. Mannes, & C.R. Fletcher (Eds.), *Discourse comprehension: Essays in honor of Walter Kintsch* (pp. 97–116). Hillsdale, NJ: Erlbaum.

McNamara, D.S., & Healy, A.F. (1995). A generation advantage for multiplication skill and nonword vocabulary acquisition. In A.F. Healy & L.E. Bourne (Eds.), *Learning and memory of knowledge and skills: Durability and specificity* (pp. 132–169). Newbury Park, CA: Sage.

McNamara, D.S., Kintsch, E., Songer, N.B., & Kintsch, W. (1996). Are good texts always better? Interactions of text coherence, background knowledge, and levels of understanding in learning from text. *Cognition and Instruction, 14*(1), 1–43.

McNamara, D.S., & Kintsch, W. (1996). Learning from text: Effect of prior knowledge and text coherence. *Discourse Processes, 22,* 247–288.

Miller, J.R., & Kintsch, W. (1980). Readability and recall for short passages: A theoretical analysis. *Journal of Experimental Psychology: Human Learning and Memory, 6,* 335–354.

Moravcsik, J.E., & Kintsch, W. (1993). Writing quality, reading skills, and domain knowledge as factors in text comprehension. *Canadian Journal of Experimental Psychology, 47*(2), 360–374.

Myers, J.L., O'Brien, E.J., Albrecht, J.E., & Mason, R.A. (1994). Maintaining global coherence during reading. *Journal of Experimental Psychology: Learning, Memory, and Cognition, 20*, 876–886.

Myers, J.L., Shinjo, M., & Duffy, S.A. (1987). Degree of causal relatedness and memory. *Journal of Memory and Language, 26*, 453–465.

Nathan, M.J., Kintsch, W., & Young, E. (1992). A theory of word algebra problem comprehension and its implications for the design of learning environments. *Cognition and Instruction, 9*, 329–389.

O'Brien, E.J. (1995). Automatic components of discourse comprehension. In R.F. Lorch & E.J. O'Brien (Eds.), *Sources of coherence in reading* (pp. 159–176). Hillsdale, NJ: Erlbaum.

O'Brien, E.J., Shank, D.M., Myers, J.L., & Rayner, K. (1988). Elaborative inferences during reading: Do they occur on-line? *Journal of Experimental Psychology: Learning, Memory, and Cognition, 14*(3), 410–420.

Olson, J.R., & Biolsi, K.J. (1991). Techniques for representing expert knowledge. In K.A. Ericsson & J. Smith (Eds.), *Toward a general theory of expertise: Prospects and limits* (pp. 240–285). Cambridge, UK: Cambridge University Press.

Paige, J.M., & Simon, H.A. (1966). Cognitive processes in solving algebra word problems. In B. Kleinmuntz (Ed.), *Problem solving: Research, method, and theory*. New York: Wiley.

Perfetti, C.A. (1993). Why inferences might be restricted. *Discourse Processes, 16*(1/2), 181–192.

Perrig, W., & Kintsch, W. (1985). Propositional and situational representations of text. *Journal of Memory and Language, 24*, 503–518.

RAND Reading Study Group. (2002). *Reading for understanding: Toward an R&D program in reading comprehension*. Santa Monica, CA: RAND.

Rayner, K., Pacht, J.M., & Duffy, S.A. (1994). Effects of prior encounter and global discourse bias on the processing of lexically ambiguous words: Evidence from eye fixations. *Journal of Memory and Language, 33*, 527–544.

Rips, L.J. (1994). *The psychology of proof: Deductive reasoning in human thinking*. Cambridge, MA: MIT Press.

Sachs, J.S. (1967). Recognition memory for syntactic and semantic aspects of connected discourse. *Perception and Psychophysics, 2*, 437–442.

Schank, R.C., & Abelson, R.P. (1977). *Scripts, plans, goals, and understanding: An inquiry into human knowledge structures*. Hillsdale, NJ: Erlbaum.

Schmalhofer, F., McDaniel, M.A., & Keefe, D. (2002). A unified model for predictive and bridging inferences. *Discourse Processes, 33*, 105–132.

Schmidt, R.A., & Bjork, R.A. (1992). New conceptualizations of practice: Common principles in three paradigms suggest new concepts for training. *Psychological Science, 3*, 207–217.

Schvaneveldt, R.W. (Ed.). (1990). *Pathfinder associative networks: Studies in knowledge organization*. Norwood NJ: Ablex.

Singer, M., Graesser, A.C., & Trabasso, T. (1994). Minimal or global inference during reading. *Journal of Memory and Language, 33*, 421–441.

Snow, C.E., Burns, M.S., & Griffin, P. (Eds.). (1998). *Preventing reading difficulties in young children*. Washington, DC: National Academy Press.

Swinney, D.A. (1979). Lexical access during sentence comprehension: (Re)consideration of context effects. *Journal of Verbal Learning and Verbal Behavior, 18*, 645–659.

Till, R.E., Mross, E.F., & Kintsch, W. (1988). Time course of priming for associate and inference words in a discourse context. *Memory & Cognition, 16*(4), 283–298.

Trabasso, T., & Suh, S. (1993). Understanding text: Achieving explanatory coherence through on-line inferences and mental operations in working memory. *Discourse Processes, 16*(1/2), 3–34.

van den Broek, P.W. (1990). Causal inferences in the comprehension of narrative texts. In A.C. Graesser & G.H. Bower (Eds.), *Inferences and text comprehension* (Psychology of learning and motivation, Vol. 25, pp. 175–194). San Diego: Academic Press.

van der Meer, E., Beyer, R., Heinze, B., & Badel, I. (2002). Temporal order relations in language comprehension. *Journal of Experimental Psychology: Learning, Memory, and Cognition, 28*(4), 770–779.

van Dijk, T.A. (1980). *Macrostructures: An interdisciplinary study of global structures in discourse, interaction, and cognition*. Hillsdale, NJ: Erlbaum.

van Dijk, T.A., & Kintsch, W. (1983). *Strategies of discourse comprehension*. New York: Academic Press.

Voss, J.F., & Silfies, L.N. (1996). Learning from history text: The interaction of knowledge and comprehension skill with text structure. *Cognition and Instruction, 14*(1), 45–68.

Wade-Stein, D., & Kintsch, E. (2003). *Summary Street: Interactive computer support for writing.* Manuscript submitted for publication.

Wolfe, M.B., Schreiner, M.E., Rehder, R., Laham, D., Foltz, P.W., Landauer, T.K., et al. (1998). Learning from text: Matching reader and text by Latent Semantic Analysis. *Discourse Processes, 25*(2/3), 309–336.

Yekovich, F.R., Walker, C.H., Ogle, L.T., & Thompson, M.A. (1990). The influence of domain knowledge on inferencing in low-aptitude individuals. In A.C. Graesser & G.H. Bower (Eds.), *Inferences and text comprehension* (Psychology of learning and motivation, Vol. 25, pp. 259–278). New York: Academic Press.

Zwaan, R.A., Magliano, J.P., & Graesser, A.C. (1995). Dimensions of situation model construction in narrative comprehension. *Journal of Experimental Psychology: Learning, Memory, and Cognition, 21,* 386–397.

Zwaan, R.A., & Radvansky, G.A. (1998). Situation models in language comprehension and memory. *Psychological Bulletin, 123*(2), 162–185.

47

A Dual Coding Theoretical Model of Reading

Mark Sadoski and Allan Paivio

Dual Coding Theory (DCT) is an established theory of general cognition that has been directly applied to literacy. This theory was originally developed to account for verbal and nonverbal influences on memory, and it has been extended to many other areas of cognition through a systematic program of research over many years (Paivio, 1971, 1986, 1991). DCT has been extended to literacy as an account of reading comprehension (Sadoski & Paivio, 1994; Sadoski, Paivio, & Goetz, 1991), as an account of written composition (Sadoski, 1992), and as a unified theory of reading and writing (Sadoski & Paivio, 2001). For the fullest understanding of the theory, these references and the specific studies they cite should be consulted. This article briefly discusses the DCT account of certain basic processes in reading, including decoding, comprehension, and response.

The value of explaining reading under the aegis of a theory of general cognition is compelling. Reading is a cognitive act, but there is nothing about reading that does not occur in other cognitive acts that do not involve reading. We perceive, recognize, interpret, comprehend, appreciate, and remember information that is not in text form as well as information that is in text form. Cognition in reading is a special case of general cognition that involves written language. Theories specific to reading must eventually conform to broader theories of general cognition for scientific progress to advance. DCT provides one vehicle for that advancement.

Another value offered by DCT is that it provides a combined account of decoding, comprehension, and response. Theories of reading often focus on one or another of these aspects of reading but not all. As we shall see, the same basic DCT principles apply to grapheme–phoneme correspondences, word meaning, grammar, the construction of mental models of text episodes, and even imaginative responses to text. In this article, we will briefly explain the theory's basic assumptions; provide accounts of decoding, comprehension, and response; compare and contrast DCT with other theories of reading; and discuss its implications for research and practice.

Basic Assumptions

A basic premise of DCT is that all mental representations retain some of the concrete qualities of the external experiences from which they derive. These experiences can be linguistic or nonlinguistic. Their differing characteristics develop into two separate mental systems or codes: one specialized for representing and processing language (the verbal code) and one for processing nonlinguistic objects and events (the nonverbal code). The latter is frequently referred to as the imagery system or code because its functions include the generation, analysis, and transformation of mental images. Each code has its own characteristic units and hierarchical organization. Together, the two codes account for knowledge of language and knowledge of the world.

The two mental codes and our five senses are orthogonal in DCT. This means that the two codes each have subsets of mental representations that are qualitatively different because of the different sensory experiences from which they originated. Because sensory systems are linked to motor response systems in perception (e.g., eye movements, listening attitudes, active touch), these subsets have sensorimotor qualities. We develop visual representations in the verbal code for language units we have seen, such as letters, words, or phrases (e.g., *baseball bat*). But we also develop visual representations in the nonverbal code for nonlinguistic forms that we have seen, such as common objects or scenes (e.g., a wooden or aluminum baseball bat). Likewise, we develop auditory representations in the verbal code for speech units we have heard, such as phonemes and their combinations (e.g., the phoneme /b/, the rime /-at/, the word /bat/), and auditory representations in the nonverbal code for nonlinguistic environmental sounds we have heard (e.g., the crack of a wooden bat or the clink of an aluminum bat hitting a ball). Likewise, we develop haptic (i.e., kinesthetic or tactile) representations in the verbal code for linguistic motor acts (e.g., pronouncing /b/ or writing the letter *b* or touching the Braille sign for *b*), and we develop haptic representations in the nonverbal code for the active "feel" of objects, textures, and movements (e.g., the heft and swing of a baseball bat). We do not represent language in the chemical sense modalities (smell and taste), but we have nonverbal representations for them (e.g., the smell and taste of a juicy hot dog at a baseball game). Images in these modalities are typically less vivid for most people. (Table 1 provides a diagram of this orthogonal relationship.) To these modalities might be added affect—emotional feelings and reactions. These are nonverbal by definition, although we have many names for emotional states. We also have imagery for such states, and it forms an important component of meaning. We might imagine the excitement of an enthusiastic fan at a baseball game, for example.

Understanding these "codes and modes" is basic to understanding the DCT interpretation of reading. The overall system can be imagined as a set of modality-

TABLE 1
Orthogonal Relationship Between Mental Codes and Sense Modalities

	Mental Codes	
Sense Modality	Verbal	Nonverbal
Visual	Visual language (writing)	Visual objects
Auditory	Auditory language (speech)	Environmental sounds
Haptic	Braille, handwriting	"Feel" of objects
Gustatory	—	Taste memories
Olfactory	—	Smell memories

Empty cells indicate the absence of verbal representations in these modalities.

and code-specific subsystems that are laced with interconnections. These subsystems are independent and appear to be specialized in certain, sometimes multiple, areas of the brain. For example, some persons with alexia cannot read the phrase *baseball bat* but can recognize the phrase when it is spoken and even write it, providing evidence of independent, modality-specific representations within the verbal code. Some persons with anomia can recognize a baseball bat but not be able to name it, providing evidence of a general independence between nonverbal and verbal codes. For relevant neuropsychological evidence see Paivio (1986, 1991) and West, O'Rourke, and Holcomb (1998). Sacks (2002) provides a readable case study of neuropathology affecting only certain aspects of reading. A misunderstanding of the distinction between mental codes and sensory modalities has sometimes led to the inaccurate characterization of DCT as being about the verbal and visual codes. The correct distinctions are between verbal and nonverbal (imagery) codes, and between the visual modality and the other sensory modalities.

A common manifestation of the modular nature of our representational subsystems is seen in the phenomenon of modality-specific interference, the limited ability to do two things in the same modality at once. For example, it is difficult to listen to two conversations at once—our verbal, auditory capacity is quickly overcome and we must "shuttle" between the two. This ability has been called the "cocktail-party phenomenon" (Harris & Hodges, 1995, p. 33). In reading, it is somewhat difficult to visually process the print and extensively visualize its semantic content at the same time, particularly for the unskilled reader. Either the reader tends to slow down or the number of oral reading miscues increases (Denis, 1982; Eddy & Glass, 1981; Hodes, 1994; Sadoski, 1983, 1985). More discussion of this phenomenon and its implications will appear later. Next, we will discuss the basic units that compose each system, their organization in each system, and the kinds of interconnections and processing operations that occur to them.

Basic Units

Cognitive theories usually specify basic units or "building blocks" of cognition. The basic units in the verbal system are *logogens*, and the basic units in the non-verbal system are *imagens*. These terms are merely jargon for the way the brain represents different types of information, but DCT assumes that they are concrete, as opposed to being abstract and amodal. The terms are not meant to imply static units. Although memory representations have some permanence, they are better thought of as evolving and flexible, such as the way our vocabulary knowledge is constantly enriched by experiencing words in different contexts or the way images are often of novel scenes comprised of familiar elements.

A logogen is anything learned as a unit of language in some sense modality. Language units vary in size, although some sizes are more familiar than others (e.g., words). Hence, we have visual logogens for written letters, words, and phrases; auditory logogens for phonemes and word and phrase pronunciations; and haptic logogens for pronouncing, writing, or signing these language units. In speech, phonemic logogens may be represented in closely associated auditory–motor form. That is, a phoneme may be represented as a physical articulation of the speech organs as well as an auditory sound (Liberman & Mattingly, 1985).

Logogens are derived from the perception of language and influence its perception. A charming example is the child learning to say the alphabet who perceives the spoken sequence "l, m, n, o" as "elemeno." The letter-name sequence initially is perceived as one auditory–motor unit; with more learning it will be perceived as four separate units. Similarly, words can be learned before their individual letters or phonemes are learned, and words can be identified as rapidly, or more rapidly, than their individual letters or phonemes after they are learned.

Imagens are modality specific and vary in size as well, and they tend to be perceived in nested sets. That is, mental images are often embedded in larger mental images. Hence, we can visually imagine a baseball bat, the bat in the hands of a batter, and the batter at home plate in a crowded stadium. In the auditory modality, we can imagine the crack of the bat, or the crack of the bat over the noise of the crowd. These perceptions may be associated into an auditory–visual mental episode that may be transformed into a sequence of the bat being swung, the crack of the bat and roar of the crowd, and the batter running to base as the ball speeds away. That is, while the imagens remain modality specific, they can be incorporated into a larger mental structure that reflects the multisensory nature of physical reality.

Both types of representations can be activated in various ways. Logogens can be activated by direct sensory input such as seeing printed language, or imagens can be activated by seeing familiar objects. However, both types of mental representation can be activated indirectly, as when we spontaneously form images to words or name objects. Both internal and external contexts also can prime language or imagery. Seeing the word *baseball* can indirectly activate an internal, associated neighborhood of logogens such as *bat*, *glove*, *game*, *cap*, and so on. All these words could in turn activate related imagens. External contexts would serve to limit the activated set to the most relevant members. Therefore, both bottom-up and top-down inputs can activate mental representations in interactive ways. When enough input is received from any one source or a combination of sources, the representation is activated. What constitutes enough activation is a matter of the strength of the inputs or how often or how recently a representation has been excited. Many of these assumptions are common to most network theories of cognition, but DCT is unique in its emphasis on the modality-specific verbal and nonverbal distinctions in mental representation. More discussion of processing operations follows the next section.

Unit- and System-Level Organization

Logogens and the verbal system into which they are organized are characterized by sequential constraints. In all languages, units are combined into certain conventional sequences at all levels. Hence, the letters *b*, *a*, and *t* are sequenced as *bat* or *tab* but not *bta*; the words *a*, *baseball*, and *bat* are sequenced as *a baseball bat* or *bat a baseball* but not *baseball a bat*, and so on. A hierarchy characterizes the verbal system such that smaller units can be synthesized sequentially into larger units (e.g., letters to words) or larger units can be analyzed sequentially into smaller units (e.g., words to letters). However, units at each level retain a degree of independence such that a spoken word, for example, can be recognized without necessarily analyzing its phonemic structure. The developmental basis of this organization is thought to be the temporally sequential nature of speech or the linear nature of print that we experience in encounters with language. A common example is that it is easier to spell a long word forward than backward from memory; the logogen is constrained by our left-to-right conventional experience (the principle is reversed in languages that are read and written right to left).

The hierarchical organization of the nonverbal system is qualitatively different. Imagens are represented and organized in a more continuous, integrated way and cannot be separated as easily into discrete elements comparable to phonemes, letters, or words. The developmental basis for this system is the generally more holistic nature of nonverbal perceptions that occur as clusters of units available simultaneously in different senses. An example is the baseball episode given earlier. We can synthesize images of smaller units (a baseball bat) into embedded or nested units (a bat in the hands of a batter) to still larger sets (the batter in a stadium with a roaring crowd), or we can analyze the scene in reverse. In the visual modality, this often takes a cinematic form in which we "zoom" in or out or "cut" to a wide angle or a close-up. Dynamic, multimodal imagery sequences also can be represented, as the episode of the batter hitting the ball with a loud crack and running to first base as the crowd roars.

Therefore, both the verbal and nonverbal systems have modality-specific units of various size that are organized hierarchically, but the respective units and their hierarchies are qualitatively different. Logogens and their verbal hierarchy are heavily sequentially constrained, whereas imagens and their nonverbal hierarchy are more holistic and simultaneous. This combination provides great flexibility to cognition.

Processing Operations

Three distinct dimensions, or "levels," of processing are theorized in DCT: (1) representational processing, (2) associative processing, and (3) referential processing. The levels metaphor is only partly useful because associative and referential processing can be seen as spreading activation at the same "level" but involving different codes. In DCT, processing involves both the degree and kind of elaboration.

Representational processing is the initial activation of logogens or imagens. This level is analogous to simply recognizing something as familiar and does not necessarily imply meaningful comprehension. The activation of a representation depends on the stimulus situation and individual differences. In reading text, the stimulus would be the text characteristics, and individual differences would include reading ability, background knowledge, instructions, and so on. Therefore, the activation of a visual logogen for a printed word would involve the legibility of the printed form, the reader's familiarity with the word's visual features and configuration, and any priming effects of context. If the visually recognized word also were familiar from speech, its associated auditory–motor phonological logogen usually would be activated rapidly in turn (e.g., *baseball*). All this would be carried out in milliseconds and perhaps without conscious attention. If the visual word were not familiar, visual and phonological logogens at lower levels, such as letter combinations, would be activated, requiring more time and attention (e.g., *base—ball*). This degree of activation may implicate higher-order processes in the word's recognition, as will be seen later. On the other hand, whole familiar phrases can be recognized and named at a glance by the skilled reader (e.g., *baseball bat*).

Associative processing involves spreading activation within a code that is typically associated with meaningful comprehension. The association between a visual word logogen and an auditory–motor word logogen (i.e., phonological recoding) is an example of associative processing that does not necessarily involve meaning and is usually relegated to the representational level. However, the phonological recoding of a visual word may involve its comprehension in some cases. Heteronyms have one spelling but different meanings and respective pronunciations, and their phonological recoding depends on which meaning is implied by context (e.g., *bass* drum, largemouth *bass*). Unfamiliar and grapho-phonemically irregular words may implicate meaning as well because representational processing is slowed.

Meaningful associative processing within the verbal code involves the activation of logogens of at least the morpheme level by previously activated logogens. For example, the word *single* has many verbal associations, but only a subset will be activated in a given context. In a baseball game, the word *single* would activate verbal associations such as *hit*, *first base*, *advance a runner*, and so on. In other contexts, the word *single* could activate very different verbal associates such as *one-dollar bill*, *unmarried*, *hotel room*, and so on. Meaning is both constrained and elaborated by the set of verbal associates activated.

Referential processing involves the spreading of activation between the codes that is associated with meaningful comprehension. In reading, this means that activated logogens in turn activate imagens in the same way they activate other logogens. The phrase *baseball bat* can activate mental images of a wooden or aluminum baseball bat; *single* can activate an entire dynamic, nested set of images of a batter hitting a baseball and running to first base in a stadium. That is, there is not a one-to-one referential correspondence between logogens and imagens. Some logogens might referentially activate few imagens, while other logogens might activate many. Some logogens might activate no imagens at all. This is particularly true of language that is highly abstract; it is difficult to form images of *basic idea*, for example. Without the context of a concrete situation, such phrases lack any referential meaning and can be defined only verbally. This implies that concrete language generally should be better understood, a consistent finding in research.

Once activated logogens spread their activation referentially to one or more imagens in the nonverbal system, associative processing may occur within that system and, in turn, refer back to the verbal system. For example, the set of imagens referentially activated by the logogen *single* might be associatively elaborated in the nonverbal system to include a batter running to first base in a crowded stadium of cheering fans. These imagens might, in return, referentially activate logogens such as *stadium*, *crowd*, or *cheers*. In this way, spreading activation between and within codes defines and elaborates the meaning of language. Further, it supplies inferred information to the interpretation. Mental imagery plays an invaluable role in adding concrete sensory substance to the meaning; taken literally, this is what "making sense" in reading is all about.

Figure 1 shows a theoretical model of these units and processes. Verbal and nonverbal stimuli are perceived by the sensory systems, and logogens and imagens are activated. The verbal system is illustrated as a hierarchical, sequenced arrangement of logogens. These units are modality specific and occur in different sizes so that smaller logogens may be representations for graphemes or phonemes, larger logogens may be visual words or their auditory–motor pronunciations, and so on. The associative relationships illustrated by the arrows

FIGURE 1
General Model of Dual Coding Theory

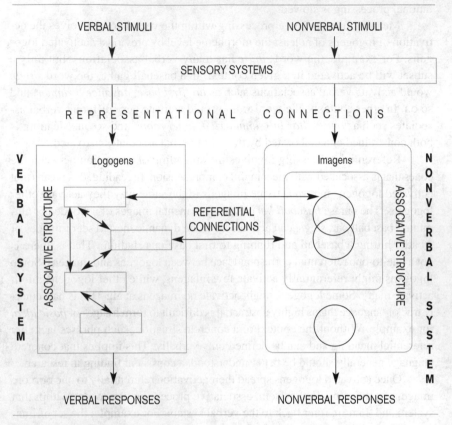

are of many kinds: graphophonemic associations (*b-*/b/), compound word associations (e.g., *base-ball*), common sequences (e.g., *first, second, third, home*), hierarchical associations (e.g., *organized activities, sports, baseball*), synonym or antonym associations (e.g., *batter–hitter*; *safe–out*), and so on. The nonverbal system is illustrated as a series of overlapping and nested sets of imagens (e.g., a baseball bat being swung by a batter in a crowded stadium of cheering fans) or other imagens not associated with a given set. Referential connections are illustrated as arrows running between the coding systems. Verbal and nonverbal responses are shown as output of the respective systems.

Figure 1 illustrates some of the most basic assumptions of DCT, but the illustration is necessarily simple. In actuality, a model for reading even a simple text would be interlaced with connections and abuzz with activity. Further discussion can be found in Sadoski and Paivio (2001).

Explaining the Reading Process

The discussion in the preceding section provided an overview of the basic assumptions of DCT in reading-relevant terms. The reading process can be better explained through an extended example that involves decoding, comprehension, and response in reading a simple sentence. We will deviate briefly to elaborate on decoding, comprehension, and response in turn. We use a single sentence here, but the reader should keep in mind that such sentences are more realistically read in much richer, extended contexts.

Consider the skilled reading and in-depth comprehension of the sentence *The batter singled to center in the first*. The process begins as the eyes fixate on the printed forms, probably *The batter* in the first fixation (eye movement studies indicate an average span of about nine characters per fixation). Visual logogens for the familiar words *The* and *batter* are activated at the representational level and immediately associated with their auditory–motor logogens. *The batter* may be experienced as inner speech, recoded in phonological form. Perhaps equally quickly, the words are syntactically associated as a simple noun phrase. Spreading activation to semantic associations also occurs rapidly, with the different associates of *batter* activated as options. Common verbal associates of *batter* could be *baseball player*, *cake mixture*, or *strike repeatedly*, and nonverbal referential connections could be images of the same. However, in the present context the word *batter* has been used in connection with other baseball terms, and context effects would prime the former option and inhibit the latter ones. Also, *The* preceding *batter* signals a noun usage of *batter*, syntactically inhibiting the verb option *strike repeatedly*. Within perhaps 500 milliseconds (an estimate from electroencephalographic studies), the words *The batter* are phonologically recoded and provisionally comprehended in both verbal and nonverbal form as a baseball player at bat.

A word is needed here about decoding. In reading, this term is theoretically imprecise. The term *recoding* often is preferred because it indicates converting the printed form to the spoken form without necessarily comprehending, as the general definition of decoding implies (i.e., to decode a message). Conformably, DCT assumes that in reading, the activation of logogens at the representational level involves their phonological associations but not necessarily their semantic associates and referents. For highly familiar words this happens without conscious effort, hence the term *automatic*. Very familiar phrases such as *The batter* may be recoded as a single unit similar to *hot dog*. However, less-familiar, phonologically ambiguous, or graphophonemically irregular words may require more grapheme–phoneme-level processing, more conscious effort, and possibly some semantic and syntactic processing. Thus, DCT accommodates multiple-route models of phonology in word reading (e.g., Coltheart, Curtis, Atkins, & Haller, 1993).

Returning to our example, the next fixation falls on the word *singled*, perhaps already noticed in the parafovea of the first fixation. This word appears after the noun phrase and is marked as a verb by the *-ed* suffix. Associative processing syntactically connects *The batter* with *singled*, and the familiar subject–verb syntactic pattern is recognized.

A word is needed here about grammar. Extensive grammatical parsing is not often conscious, and it may be less complex than is commonly assumed. The verb here may be comprehended simply as a modifier of the noun phrase. That is, a mental model of the sentence thus far may be forming in which the batter is imagined in action, hitting the ball and running to first base. This emerging mental model takes the form of a verbal–nonverbal, syntactic and semantic episode in short-term memory. For those readers less familiar with baseball terms, the word *singled* may need to be syntactically paraphrased to *hit a single* for clarification, but the result would be the same. In this sense, grammar need not involve abstract deep-structure propositions or transformational rules. Simple word sequences that evoke a comprehensible image can account for much. This is the DCT view of deep structure; more will be discussed later.

The next fixation includes *to center*. The various associates and referents of *to center* (e.g., *between left field and right field*, *to balance*) are part of the spreading activation, with context inhibiting less-appropriate ones. Again, a less-familiar reader may verbally elaborate this elliptical phrase into *to center field*. The words *The batter singled to center (field)* may then be syntactically parsed as the familiar subject–verb–modifier pattern, recoded phonologically as inner speech, and imagined to now include the ball speeding to the middle outfield as the batter runs to first base.

The final fixation falls on *in the first*. Familiar verbal elaborations of *in the first*, such as *in the first inning* or *in the first place*, may be associatively activated, with context inhibiting the latter. The phrase will be recognized as a modifier by association with the syntax established so far and the entire sentence parsed and cumulatively recoded as inner speech. However, *in the first* probably would add little to the imaginal mental model of the episode except possible time cues such as the fresh uniforms and unscuffed baselines of the early innings of a baseball game. However, it might involve another nonverbal aspect of comprehension—an affective response. More on this topic will be discussed later.

As described so far, the processing of the simple sentence *The batter singled to center in the first* would take about two seconds at a typical reading rate of 250 wpm (longer for readers unfamiliar with baseball). For a skilled reader reading for full comprehension and recall, the result probably would include the sentence recoded as inner speech and comprehended as a verbal–nonverbal mental model of the episode. Note that neither is necessarily experienced consciously, or perhaps only barely so, and both may be rehearsed in memory after the last fixation. These responses differ with readers and situations. However, considerable experimental data, including neuropsychological data, support this scenario (Lucas, 1999; West et al., 1998).

A word is needed here about meaning, comprehension, and mental models. As noted in the present example, the text would be mentally represented in two codes and in at least two different modalities: (1) an auditory–motor representation probably experienced as inner speech and (2) a visuo-spatial representation probably experienced as mental imagery. Both might be elaborated in various ways. As noted, the word *center* may be mentally elaborated to *center field*, and *in the first* may be elaborated to *in the first inning*. Beyond this, verbal elaboration may take the form of a related set of activated associations in the verbal system such as *baseball, pitcher, swing, hit, fly, grounder, outfield, run, first base, safe, stadium, crowd*, and so on. The imagery representation might be in modalities other than the visual, depending on the degree of elaboration. A more fully elaborated image might include the crack of the bat and the roar of the crowd, for example. Associative connections and referential connections between the verbal associates and the nonverbal associates form an internally consistent network that is the basis of meaning, comprehension, and the mental model.

Meaning in this instance consists of this coherent network of activated verbal and nonverbal representations. The richer the elaboration of activated mental representations and their defining interconnections, the more "meaningful" our response. *Comprehension* is the relative equilibrium in the network. The set of verbal associations and the set of nonverbal associations correspond to and restrict each other sufficiently well to produce closure rather than a random-search activation without coherence. The term *mental model*, as used here, applies to the total verbal–nonverbal correspondence aggregate. The mental model *is* the restricted set of activated representations and the associative and referential connections between them. The term does not imply any theoretical construct beyond what already has been explained. A mental model in DCT is not an abstraction; the modality-specific units activated and connected retain some of their original sensory properties, similar to pebbles in an aggregate or particles in a suspension.

However, the discussion of our example does not end here. Consider the inferences that may occur as a mental model is formed for the sentence *The batter singled to center in the first*. The sentence does not specify if the hit was a fly ball or ground ball. It does not specify if the game was a professional baseball game or a Little League game. It does not specify if the stadium was opened or closed or if there was a stadium and spectators at all. It does not specify if the game was at night or during the day. Yet our mental models are often specific on such points. Many of these inferences can be attributed to mental imagery— imagining in concrete specifics the general situation described by the language. Imagery forms an invaluable companion to language in fleshing out language's skeleton.

None of these inferences is obligatory; all are probabilistic in varying degree. Readers read with varying degrees of depth and elaboration based on purposes and individual differences. Comprehension is not an all-or-none process; it occurs in degrees from simple recognition to strategic elaboration. In many cases our comprehension is superficial because there is no time, need, or inclination to elaborate as deeply as we might. In other cases, our comprehension is deeper, richer, and more precise.

This leads us back to the subject of response. In many ways, this term implies the formation of a mental model, a coherent and elaborate rendition of the text. A reader may fully experience even a simple text such as *The batter singled to center in the first* by imagining the event as described. In a still more elaborate response, one might "feel" oneself as the batter, haptically sensing the heft of the bat and the jolt as it connects. But response often implies more than sensory imagery or a mental model. We noted earlier that the phrase *in the first* adds a time cue to the sentence. This simple time cue may evoke an evaluative and mildly affective response. A single *in the first* is not as critical as a single *in the bottom of the ninth with the game tied*. That is, there is a different emotional significance to the two time settings. This introduces a nonverbal, emotional–evaluative dimension to the response. In full and complete narrative texts, such as stories, such emotional responses are an important aspect of experiencing the text (e.g., Sadoski, Goetz, & Kangiser, 1988).

In other contexts, response may take a more logical or rational form. Analyzing an exposition or an argument may introduce a verbal monitoring of the text experienced in inner expressions such as "I don't get this," "Now I see," or "But you haven't considered...." Our critical and evaluative powers also are exercised here, and the experience also may be emotional. We are impressed with a well-argued position with which we are forced to agree. We are disappointed by sloganeering that dismisses a difficult problem with a one-syllable solution. In its fullest sense, response involves the reader as a part of the authoring, a partner who stands toe-to-toe with the author and answers back. This may take the reading beyond what the text language may have included or what the author may have ever intended.

A question sometimes raised about DCT is how readers comprehend and respond to highly abstract language. The answer is that the encoding of abstract language is primarily a matter of verbal associations. Consider the abstract sentence *The basic idea remained vague*. As with a more concrete sentence, this sentence can be phonologically recoded, grammatically parsed, and associated with other language units (e.g., *basic idea = main thought, remained vague = stayed unclear*). But beyond such mental parsing and paraphrasing, there is little substance to the sentence. Without a concrete contextual referent to concretize the abstract, it remains a verbalism with unrealized potential. Such sentences may be integrated as verbal units and achieve a degree of meaning at the associative level, but their fuller meaning and response awaits a more concrete context.

Empirical Evidence

The constellation of predictions derived from the DCT model of reading has been only partially developed and tested, but relevant evidence is available on several research fronts. Next, we will review certain empirical evidence in the areas of decoding, comprehension, and response.

Decoding

Printed words usually are recoded promptly into an auditory–motor (phonemic) form. In DCT, this involves activation of verbal–associative connections between visual logogens and auditory–motor logogens. As discussed previously, these connections generally are assumed to occur at the representational level because they usually can be achieved before a syntactic or semantic interpretation is generated. However, this does involve associative processing, and the time required for this processing will presumably vary with word familiarity, grapheme–phoneme consistency, and other factors. Therefore, spreading activation could theoretically reach and activate still other representations during this time. These representations include imagens, possibly implicating imagery as a semantic factor in word recognition.

In fact, word imageability is one of the best predictors of oral reading performance in beginning reading or in certain acquired disorders of reading. Beginning readers read concrete, imageable words more accurately than abstract words, with these effects more prominent for poor readers (Coltheart, Laxon, & Keating, 1988; Jorm, 1977; Juel & Holmes, 1981). Neurological patients with severe phonological deficits, whose reading ability is assumed to rely mainly on direct access from orthography to semantic interpretations, often are markedly more successful in reading concrete, imageable words than abstract words (e.g., Coltheart, Patterson, & Marshall, 1980; Funnell & Allport, 1987; Plaut & Shallice, 1993). This evidence is supportive of multiple-route models of the oral reading of words (Coltheart, Rastle, Perry, Langdon, & Ziegler, 2001).

If a word's concreteness can influence the process of naming it, this influence might be seen mainly on words in which orthographic-to-phonological recoding is slowed by their low-frequency, their irregular spelling–sound correspondences, or both. Strain, Patterson, and Seidenberg (1995) tested this prediction. They found that, controlling for word familiarity and linguistic variables (i.e., initial phoneme, word length, positional bigram frequency), adults were slower and more error prone when naming abstract irregular words (e.g., *scarce*) than when naming abstract regular words (e.g., *scribe*) or imageable irregular words (e.g., *sword*). That is, irregular concrete words were named sooner and more accurately than irregular abstract words because the spelling–sound processing time was sufficient to allow for the activation of corresponding imagens. However, when the words were regular, the associations between spelling and naming were rapidly achieved whether the words were concrete or abstract, so the activation of imagens for the concrete words did not have time to produce a similar effect in naming. Overall, they found that imageability especially facilitated the naming of low-frequency irregular words.

This study has been subject to considerable replication and scrutiny. It was replicated and extended by Strain and Herdman (1999), who found the same interaction between frequency, regularity, and imageability in word naming. They found an even stronger effect for imageability in the naming of low-frequency regular words, although this was still less than for low-frequency irregular words. They also found that the more skilled in decoding participants were, the less strongly imageability influenced word naming, although the effect was still present even for highly skilled decoders. Overall, Strain and Herdman interpreted their findings to mean that imageability plays a role in naming words when the connections between orthography and phonology are weak, whether this is due to irregular spelling–sound correspondences or low decoding skill.

Monaghan and Ellis (2002) replicated the original study and again found the interaction between regularity and imageability. However, they attributed it to age of acquisition of the word because when this variable was covaried the interaction was nonsignificant. They argued that irregular words and low-frequency words would be acquired later and this would largely account for the effect. However, Strain, Patterson, and Seidenberg (2002) questioned the use of age of acquisition because when they reanalyzed their original data with age of acquisition as a covariate the interaction of regularity and imageability persisted. Furthermore, they presented new data confirming the interaction when age of acquisition was controlled. Ellis and Monaghan (2002) rejoined on methodological grounds but presented no new data. Overall, these results suggest a persistent but qualified interaction between imageability and regularity in word naming.

The theoretical point becomes clearer in different orthographies. Printed languages differ in the degree to which they represent spoken language. In Persian, words are sometimes written with consonant letters only (opaque words) and sometimes with full vowels (transparent words). The opaque words, therefore, present more decoding difficulties. A significant imageability effect was found by Baluch and Besner (2001) in naming both high- and low-frequency opaque words in Persian, while the effect was not present for matched transparent words. These findings have been extended to Turkish, a perfectly transparent orthography in which each of its 29 letters corresponds to only one spoken sound invariantly and independent of context. Raman, Baluch, and Besner (1997) found no significant effects of imageability on word naming of Turkish high- and low-frequency words, consistent with the prediction. However, Raman and Baluch (2001) additionally investigated reading skill and found that skilled readers in Turkish named imageable, low-frequency words faster than matched abstract low-frequency words, similar to what Strain and Herdman (1999) found in English and also consistent with prediction. Less-skilled readers did not name imageable, low-frequency words faster than matched abstract, low-frequency words, a result different from Strain and Herdman, but this was attributed to differences in reading Turkish and English. Janyan and Andonova (2003) still found independent effects of imageability and frequency in naming words in Bulgarian, an orthography with more graphophonemic consistency than English but less than Turkish. Furthermore, these researchers found that imageability was more associated with right-hemispheric brain activation, consistent with a neuropsychological account of encoding differences.

In sum, these studies indicate that imageability plays a role in naming words when the connections between orthography and phonology are labored, whether this is due to irregular spelling–sound correspondences or low word frequency (i.e., unfamiliarity). The effect of decoding skill also interacts with these factors differently in different orthographies. These results are theoretically consistent with the interactive DCT model of reading presented previously, as well as with multiple-route decoding models.

Specifically, visual logogens activated by printed concrete words spread their activation to both auditory–motor naming logogens and imagens for referential meaning. The activated imagens can contribute significantly to the activation of the naming logogens when the route between the visual logogens and the naming logogens is slow. The effect is predictably differential across orthographies, a script-specific phenomenon. The effect is also complex, predicting at least a triple interaction. As Strain et al. (2002) conclude, "almost all of the factors in the domain of word familiarity and meaningfulness are correlated with one another, and it is a brave experimenter who attempts to establish the prominence of one while denying any impact for the others" (p. 212; cf. Venezky & Massaro, 1987). Multiple factors influence word decoding, of which imageability is one, under theoretically predictable conditions. These observations are compatible with DCT but incompatible with theories that posit modality-independent word units, concept nodes, or abstract propositions. Moreover, these observations have implications for sight-vocabulary learning as discussed later.

Comprehension

In DCT, a key factor in reading comprehension is language concreteness. This is mainly because concrete language can referentially activate mental images as well as associatively activate mental language, whereas abstract language has relatively less access to the imagery code. Hence, concrete language, such as *baseball bat*, should be easier to understand than abstract language, such as *basic idea*, because concrete language can be dually encoded. In DCT, the two codes are assumed to be independent and additive in their effects, predicting that concrete language should be nearly twice as comprehensible and memorable as abstract language, other factors being equal. The empirical record over the last 30 years has shown just this. Concrete words, phrases, sentences, paragraphs, and longer texts have been consistently shown to be more than twice as comprehensible and memorable as abstract language units matched for readability, familiarity, and other variables. The evidence relevant to reading has been reviewed extensively (Sadoski & Paivio, 2001). Here we will focus on how predictions made by DCT in the area of comprehension and recall have prevailed in experimental tests against the predictions of other theories.

A case in point involves the competing predictions of DCT and context availability theory (Kieras, 1978). Rather than assuming separate verbal and nonverbal codes, context availability theory assumes that all language, whether abstract or concrete, is comprehended and remembered by incorporation into a network of abstract, amodal propositions. Moreover, this theory assumes that concrete language is easier to comprehend and remember because it can be associated more readily with other propositions in the network—it simply has more connections. But this advantage can be offset when abstract language deals with highly familiar information or when abstract language is presented in a supportive context because the connections are then enhanced for the reader. The differing assumptions of DCT and the context availability model present a situation all too rare in reading research: two rival theories that are sufficiently well articulated to make testable predictions that are contradictory.

A test of these competing predictions was performed by Sadoski, Goetz, and Avila (1995). They used four factual paragraphs about historical figures (Michelangelo and James Madison) that were matched for number of sentences, words, and syllables; sentence length; information density; text cohesion; and rated comprehensibility. In one set, two paragraphs were rated equal in familiarity, but one paragraph was rated more concrete than the other. In this case, DCT predicted that the concrete paragraph should be recalled better than the abstract paragraph because of the additional integrating medium provided by imagery, whereas the context availability model predicted that they should be recalled equally because the abstract language was equally familiar and presented in context. In the other set, the paragraphs differed in both familiarity and concreteness, with the abstract paragraph being the more familiar of the two. In this case, DCT predicted that the familiar abstract paragraph should be recalled about as well as the unfamiliar concrete paragraph (i.e., the advantage of concreteness would be offset by lower familiarity), whereas the context availability model predicted that the abstract paragraph would be recalled better than the concrete paragraph (i.e., the disadvantage of abstractness would be offset by higher familiarity).

In the case in which the concrete and abstract paragraphs were equally familiar, study participants recalled the concrete paragraph nearly twice as well. In the case in which the abstract paragraph was more familiar, study participants recalled the paragraphs equally well. These results were consistent with DCT but inconsistent with context availability theory. Other experimental findings using different methods and materials have confirmed these results (e.g., Holcomb, Kounios, Anderson, & West, 1999; Kounios & Holcomb, 1994; Nelson & Schreiber, 1992; Sadoski, Goetz, & Fritz, 1993; Sadoski, Goetz, & Rodriguez, 2000).

Another case of competing predictions between DCT and another theory involved the relational–distinctiveness model of Marschark and Hunt (1989) in explaining the integration of abstract text. Abstract sentences, such as *The basic idea remained vague*, sometimes can be encoded as integrated verbal units as well as concrete sentences, even though concrete sentences enjoy more comprehensible and memorable content. These questions about the DCT explanation of the integration and recall of abstract text were first raised by Marschark and Paivio (1977). The authors studied the cued recall of concrete and abstract sentences and found that, whereas recall was higher for concrete sentences, the two types of sentences did not differ in the extent to which recall was integrated as measured by the retrieval effectiveness of verbal cues that were related to the whole sentence or to only one content word in the sentence. The higher recall for concrete sentences was consistent with the DCT assumption that dually encoded information is more memorable, but the equal integration effect was inconsistent with the assumption that imagery is a superior integrating medium.

Marschark and Paivio (1977) concluded that dual coding accounted for the higher recall of concrete sentences but that some other explanation was needed to explain the equivalent integration effects. Verbal associative processes were a likely DCT candidate because these processes apply equally to concrete and abstract language. An alternative theory was posed by Marschark and Hunt (1989). This theory assumed that distinctiveness and relatedness are different forms of mental processing that act as partners. Mental imagery evoked by concrete language increases the distinction from or contrast of concrete language to abstract language rather than providing a separate memory code, but this distinctiveness is dependent on an established relationship between the language units. Hence, this theory, like context availability theory, predicts that familiar, contextually associated abstract language should be integrated as well as concrete language.

A resolution to the issue was obtained by Paivio, Walsh, and Bons (1994). Their experimental results showed that strong verbal associations are *necessary* to produce integration of abstract word pairs, whereas imagery is *sufficient* to produce integration of concrete word pairs even when verbal associations are not present. The results were not consistent with the relational–distinctiveness view because integration still occurred for concrete word pairs where the pair members were not related. These findings provide a DCT explanation for the integration of abstract language, but they further offer a possible explanation for the integration of even weakly related concrete language.

For example, consider again the abstract sentence *The basic idea remained vague* and the concrete sentence *The batter singled to center in the first*. The former sentence might be integrated grammatically because the predicate adjective *vague* links directly back to the subject noun *idea*; the modifier is part of the sentence kernel and binds the subject and the predicate closely together. In the latter sentence, the kernel is *The batter singled*; this is followed by two independent modifying phrases in a loose construction. This sentence might be integrated more through its imagery, with *singled to center* and *in the first* adding imaginal and verbal elaboration as discussed previously. Stated differently, the integrative mental model of the abstract sentence may be more verbal–associative, and the integrative mental model of the concrete sentence may be more nonverbal–imaginal. Hence, both concrete and abstract sentences might be encoded as integrated units but for theoretically different reasons. However, this interpretation is speculative, and further research is needed.

In sum, DCT can provide a coherent account of the critical role played by language concreteness in reading comprehension. The evidence cited poses problems for theories that propose that all language is mentally encoded in abstract, propositional form. Furthermore, DCT can provide experimental predictions about the comprehension and recall of concrete and abstract text, and about the integration of both concrete and abstract text, in a theoretically consistent and parsimonious way.

Response

Mental imagery and its correlate, emotional response, are vital to aesthetic response to text. Imaginative and affective processes are how a text is "realized," "lived through," or "brought to life." As discussed earlier, some aspects of response may be contemporaneous with the formation of a mental model of the text, so that the distinction between comprehension and response is somewhat fuzzy. Response can take more objective forms as well, such as critical evaluation against some standard as in rating the importance of a text segment relative to the whole.

The empirical evidence for the relationship between imaginative and affective processes in responding to text was reviewed by Goetz and Sadoski (1996). A program of research carried out over 10 years revealed that imagery and affective response to text can be measured reliably and validly using conventional methods. Both the strength of response, as measured by quantitative ratings, and the nature of response, as measured by qualitative reports, were investigated in this research program.

The core of this research program was a set of complementary studies using literary short stories. In one study (Sadoski & Goetz, 1985), participants read and later rated each paragraph in an adventure story for either the degree of imagery experienced, the degree of emotional response experienced, or the relative importance to the story as a whole. The alpha reliabilities of these ratings, for this story as well as other similar stories, were regularly found to exceed .90 (Goetz, Sadoski, Stowe, Fetsco, & Kemp, 1993; Sadoski et al., 1988). In all these studies, imagery ratings, affect ratings, and importance ratings were moderately to strongly correlated with each other in an overall response aggregate. The correlation between imagery ratings and affect ratings persisted even after controlling for paragraph length and the importance ratings. However, the relationship between either imagery ratings or affect ratings and importance ratings was considerably attenuated when the effects of paragraph length and the remaining rating were partialed. This means that imagery and affective response can generally be seen as a related but qualitatively different form of response from evaluating importance.

Qualitative reports were the focus of another related study (Sadoski, Goetz, Olivarez, Lee, & Roberts, 1990). Using the same story as Sadoski and Goetz (1985), participants read and then produced written recalls and imagery reports. With the most extensive coding system for imagery reports yet devised, imagery was coded into categories such as (a) directly related to a paragraph, (b) a synthesis of information from two or more paragraphs, (c) distortion of story information, (d) an importation consistent with the story, or (e) an importation inconsistent with the story. The imagery reports also were categorized according to modality (e.g., visual, auditory, tactile, affective). Recall protocols were similarly coded in categories including (a) gist, (b) synthesis from across text units, (c) distortion, (d) an importation consistent with the story, or (e) an importation inconsistent with the story. Reliability between independent raters ranged from .84 to .95 for all codings. A factor analysis of the imagery and recall categories revealed four underlying factors, dominated respectively by visual imagery, affective imagery (i.e., imagining the feelings of the characters), imported imagery consistent with the story, and distortion recall. Verbal recall categories loaded on these factors as well but were consistently lower. Hence, story response could be seen as primarily experienced in the form of mental imagery and affect and somewhat less in the form of verbal recall.

A subsequent study used the ratings from Sadoski and Goetz (1985) as predictors of the imagery reports of Sadoski et al. (1990). Goetz, Sadoski, and Olivarez (1991) employed hierarchical regression analyses that first removed between-subjects variance and variance due to surface-level text factors and found that the paragraph-level imagery ratings of the first group of readers were highly significant predictors of the respective paragraph-level imagery reports of the second, independent group of readers. Another finding using the same methodology was that importance ratings and surface-level text factors were better predictors of verbal recalls than of imagery ratings. Hence, the evaluation of importance can again be seen as qualitatively different from imaginative response, although they remain correlated in the overall response.

In sum, this program of research has shown that imaginative responses are central to reading literary stories and that they can be defined, measured, and interpreted reliably and validly using conventional research methods. Imagery and emotional response are moderately to strongly correlated in story response. Further, they are both related to more objective, text-based responses such as evaluations of plot importance. As Sadoski et al. (1988) note, "these three response types often occurred simultaneously, in what may be an overall response comprising both comprehension of plot salience, and vicarious, emotionally infused, and fully perceived experiences of story events" (p. 333). Together, these response types form an overall response that involves both the intellect and the emotions.

Comparison Between DCT and Other Theories of Reading

In an earlier section we compared DCT with context availability theory and distinctiveness–relational processing theory in making predictions about reading. DCT also has been extensively compared with schema theory as an explanation of reading comprehension (Sadoski & Paivio, 1994, 2001; Sadoski et al., 1991). Further, DCT has also been compared extensively with the theories of Rumelhart (1977) and Kintsch (1988) (see Sadoski and Paivio, 2001). An updated version of Kintsch's theory (Kintsch, 1998) also has been addressed from a DCT perspective (Sadoski, 1999). We will summarize and comment on those comparisons here.

These theories of reading have much in common with DCT. A major similarity is that they all are interactive theories in which reading is served by bottom-up and top-down processes working in combination. All these theories are similar in assuming a prominent place for prior knowledge structures in reading. Another similarity is that they allow, to different degrees, for the representation of knowledge in more than one form.

However, a basic distinction between DCT and these other theories is that they assume that most knowledge in memory is abstract and amodal, existing in a state that has no objective reality and is associated with no sensory modality. How any knowledge that is not innate becomes divorced from sensory input is an important theoretical and epistemological question that has not been well explained. These theories propose no apparent answer to this question; rather, they simply assume the existence of abstract, amodal knowledge. One apparent reason for this is so that these theories can be modeled by artificial intelligence and subjected to computer simulations.

Rumelhart's (1977) parallel distributed processing model is one example. The parallel sources of knowledge in this theory are letter-feature knowledge, letter knowledge, letter-cluster knowledge, lexical knowledge, syntactic knowledge, and semantic knowledge. The forms that these different knowledge sources take are not specified, but examples provided suggest that they are ultimately all in an identically computational form. For example, a series of equations is presented in Rumelhart (1977) that determines the Baysian probability of testing a set of multilevel hypotheses for the recognition and comprehension of a phrase against letter-feature data. Several computer programs are cited for the source of these formalisms including Kaplan's (1973) General Syntactic Parser and the

HEARSAY speech recognition program (Lesser, Fennel, Erman, & Reddy, 1975). That is, whatever the source of the original input (e.g., visual features of letters), all information is theoretically converted to, and processed in, a common computational form. As a result, this theory does not discuss the roles of phonological recoding, inner speech, or mental imagery in any form. This would call for at least some differences in internal representation modalities. Rumelhart's (1977) model has since evolved into a connectionist theory that similarly assumes abstract, computational representations (cf. Rumelhart & McClelland, 1986).

Kintsch's (1998) Construction–Integration model is another example. This model assumes three codes or forms of knowledge representation: (1) verbatim information, (2) the propositional textbase, and (3) the mental model. Verbatim information is surface structure information, including specific words and syntactic arrangements. The propositional code is an abstract, deep structure code formed when abstract proposition-schemata are instantiated with surface structure information and the surface structure is quickly lost. Individual propositions are then connected into a propositional textbase. The mental model is either a well-integrated propositional textbase or a mental image of a situation that is somehow derived from the textbase. Hence, this theory can be seen as a triple-coding theory that assumes that verbal language and mental imagery may be inputs and outputs but the central processing unit is propositional in nature. Hence, it is primarily a single-code theory (see Sadoski, 1999, for more discussion).

Recent modifications of this theory have made it still more amenable to computer programming. Rather than thinking of concepts or propositions as abstract nodes in a knowledge network, the theory now treats propositions as vectors of numbers in a multidimensional statistical space, with each number indicating the strength with which the proposition is linked to another proposition (i.e., Latent Semantic Analysis). This brings the theory closer to DCT on the one hand because associational strength between individual mental representations is critical, but further away on the other hand because the entire system is based in computational formalism. As with Rumelhart (1977), this theory does not discuss the role of phonological recoding or inner speech, and it treats mental imagery as an afterthought.

Whether the formalisms of artificial intelligence as posed by these theories are useful in advancing our understanding of cognition in reading remains to be seen. Computer-implemented models that coincide with human data are interesting exercises, but the name of the game in theory is to know why. Such exercises run the risk of reification—the fallacy of explaining something and then treating the explanation as real rather than the thing being explained. In any event, it is useful to remember that abstractions, such as schemata, propositions, and abstract concept nodes, are difficult to operationalize and empirically test with human data. Their interpretive power lies largely in the assumption that they exist in the first place, mentally analogous to computer programs. As an alternative, DCT relies on constructs that may be experienced consciously to some degree and for which plausible human assessments can be devised: natural language, mental imagery, and their associations.

Directions for Further Research

Although it is one of the better-established theories of general cognition, DCT is a relative newcomer to the scene of reading theory. Despite a strong empirical record over the last several decades in accounting for verbal behavior, much more research is needed. In this section, we will pose certain issues deserving of further research in decoding, comprehension, and response.

Decoding

Considerable evidence now exists that the concreteness or imageability of written language is a factor in its phonological recoding. This evidence is consistent with the interactive nature of reading, where top-down semantic and syntactic factors and bottom-up decoding factors interact at all levels. This evidence also reinforces the assertion that there may be more to the phenomena of phonological recoding and inner speech than providing us with a strategy for lexical access—meaning may precede phonology more than we realize. While much phonological recoding may occur at a deep, cortical level, its more conscious manifestation is inner speech.

Despite the pervasiveness of inner speech in reading, too little is known about this phenomenon. Huey (1908/1968) devotes a chapter to it, regarding inner speech as a ubiquitous short-term memory phenomenon. In a landmark study in which subvocalization was measured by surgically inserting electrodes into the speech musculature, Edfeldt (1960) found that (a) all readers appear to engage in inner speech to varying degrees, especially as reading becomes increasingly difficult; (b) inner speech has no detrimental effect on reading; and (c) good readers engage in less inner speech than poor readers. Both Huey and Edfeldt point out that inner speech is not inevitable in reading. Later research reviews by Gibson and Levin (1975) and Rayner and Pollatsek (1989) arrived at the same general conclusions: Inner speech seems to be a useful but not obligatory vehicle for recoding text in short-term memory in order to parse sentences, associate words contextually, and inwardly express a spoken interpretation.

But these explanations raise unanswered questions. If inner speech is not strictly necessary, why not simply an "inner semantics" that operates directly on print input, at least for good readers past the early developmental stages of reading? Speed reading courses have long advocated "breaking the sound barrier" and reading purely visually to increase rate and improve comprehension and retention (Frank, 1994). However, Carver (1982) empirically determined that for skilled readers the optimal rate of comprehending prose while reading was identical to the optimal rate of comprehending prose while listening. This rate was about 300 wpm—about the maximum rate at which speech can be produced comfortably. What accounts for the pervasiveness of inner speech, its increase as text difficulty increases, and its convergence with rate of comprehension if it is unnecessary?

The DCT approach to these issues might pose inner speech as mental imagery in the auditory–motor modality being used to retain the surface form of a sentence while higher-order comprehension processes occur. Recoding printed language from the visual modality to auditory–motor form is needed because the visual modality can be overloaded if it has to simultaneously (a) hold sentence segments already seen in visual memory, (b) process upcoming print, and (c) construct visual mental images as needed or preferred. Earlier in the article we discussed the concept of modality-specific interference, the difficulty of trying to perform different tasks in the same sensory modality. The principle may apply strongly here: There is too much activity in reading for the visual pathways in the brain to handle alone. Recoding to the auditory–motor modality allows nonvisual rehearsal and speech-like parsing to occur while new text is visually processed and a semantic interpretation, including visual images, is constructed. Of course, inner speech may serve other functions as well, such as strategically "sounding out" unfamiliar words or "hearing" vocal phrasings, intonations, or other forms of expressive interpretation. It also may serve as an internal surrogate for the original and most common form of comprehended language, oral speech.

In short, inner speech may serve a needed rehearsal function in an alternative modality without which reading could not optimally occur. Educationally, this implies that inner speech should be encouraged and taught when, in fact, many instructional programs have been introduced to eliminate it. Theoretically, this implies still more problems for propositional theories. If the surface form of the text is immediately converted to abstract, amodal propositions and the surface structure lost, what theoretical purpose could inner speech possibly serve and why should it be so common?

Comprehension

An issue in need of renewed research from the viewpoint of all cognitive theories is that of the nature of grammar and its role in comprehending text. Over the years, grammars of various kinds have been formulated, including traditional grammar, structural grammar, case grammar, and transformational grammar. The similarities and differences between these grammars are more complex than is usually assumed. Chomsky's (1957) transformational grammar, which shared much with traditional grammar and was contrasted with the descriptive patterns of structural grammar, enjoyed considerable popularity during the second half of the 20th century. However, its explanation of sentence comprehension has become heavily strained and has not met with empirical support.

According to the transformational view, all mental activity is rule governed and verbal. Complex sentences are mentally broken down into their deep-structure kernels and understood in terms of transformational rules that are basically innate and universal. Therefore, sentence comprehension is a function of transformational complexity, or the number and nature of transformations that separate a sentence from its underlying structure. However, empirical research has found that after controlling for sentence length and implied changes in meaning, transformations had little effect on processing time (reviewed in Williams, 1998). That is, neither deep structures nor transformations appeared to have any psychological reality. However, studies of sentence transformation consistently showed that word meaning plays a crucial role in comprehension, even overriding syntactic information at times (reviewed in Paivio, 1971). Paivio suggests that imagery might play a substantial role in sentence grammar, particularly in the case of concrete sentences.

Semantic word attributes invited attention to case grammars. These grammars described sentences as relationships between cases such as agent, object, instrument, and so on (e.g., Fillmore, 1968). Early versions of these grammars, modified by developments in artificial intelligence and by some psychological evidence, were used as the basis of various propositional approaches to cognition and language (e.g., Kintsch, 1998). However, Fillmore (1976, 1984) revised his case grammar theory by putting special emphasis on the perceptual, or imagined, scenes and perspectives to which sentences refer. Case grammar with these modifications met with more empirical support than transformational grammar. For example, Black, Turner, and Bower (1979) had subjects read sentences with a single vantage point, such as *Terry finished working in the yard and went into the house,* and sentences with a changing vantage point, such as *Terry finished working in the yard and came into the house*. Sentences with changing vantage points took longer to comprehend, were rated harder to understand, and were likely to be recalled from a single vantage point. Such evidence provides more support for the view that both verbal and nonverbal processes are involved in grammar and comprehension.

More recent developments are still more consistent with the DCT view. Connectionist views have produced a form of grammar called *cognitive grammar* (Langacker, 1987, 1991). Cognitive grammar simplifies the field by rejecting the rule-governed model of mind and language and replacing it with an associational model. In this model, networks of association evolve with the experience of the individual, including linguistic associations. No innate or intrinsic rules are involved; language is governed by patterns of regularity that develop from childhood. The number of common syntactic patterns in a language is relatively small (e.g., the subject–verb–object pattern in English). All sentences are variations on a few patterns that may be represented as exemplars and varied by analogy. Descriptive, structural grammar is best suited to this explanation of grammar, and word meaning plays a more important role.

More significant from the DCT point of view, cognition is not seen as essentially verbal. Cognitive grammar assumes that mental representations can be imagistic. Language processing is a matter of matching words with mental representations and mental models of reality that may be in the form of imagery. Imagery is therefore an important substratum of language in the form of experience-based knowledge of the world to which language refers, rather than a propositional deep structure with innate origins.

In sum, cognitive grammar offers an elegant, empirically verifiable approach that capitalizes on verbal and nonverbal mental representations and syntactic patterns that are experienced readily and do not require the burdensome and unverified assumptions of transformational grammar. The consistency of DCT with these explanations is strong, and future research in this area holds promise for understanding the nature and role of grammar in reading.

Response

Considerable progress has been made in linking theories of literary interpretation to scientific theories of cognition with empirical verification, a situation little entertained as recently as 25 years ago (Kruez & MacNealy, 1996). Indeed, the study of reader response to literature has become one of the more popular subjects in reading research. Mental imagery and affect obviously are crucial to literary response because the sensuous realization of setting, episode, character, and conflict is central to the "lived through" experience of a literary text. If evidence is needed to support this point, Miall and Kuiken (1995) factor analyzed a questionnaire of 68 items covering a broad spectrum of literary responses and found factors for imagery and empathy. They grouped these into a higher-order factor they called *experiencing*, the dimension of being absorbed in a literary work. Conformably, much research from the DCT perspective has shown that imagery and emotional response are persistently related in responding to literature. This research was reviewed by Goetz and Sadoski (1996) and was summarized earlier.

An issue that deserves attention is the challenge posed by this research for some reader-response theories. Rosenblatt's (1994, see #48 this volume) transactional theory has enjoyed considerable attention in recent years as an explanation for the way readers approach texts with different stances in mind. Specifically, this theory proposes that the reading transaction exists on a continuum between efferent reading and aesthetic reading. In the efferent stance, the reader is mainly concerned with information to be extracted and retained after the reading event. In the aesthetic stance, the reader is mainly concerned with the evocation of sensations, images, and scenes as they unfold in the moment. The reader may vary stances so that, for example, poetry could be read as a source of historical information, or a historical exposition could be read to imagine the sights, sounds, and emotions of the historical events. Moreover, readers can slide along the continuum from moment to moment within a reading so that no reading is probably ever purely efferent or aesthetic.

The challenge involved is that considerable evidence shows that what is most imaged and felt in a reading is what is most retained over the long term. For example, Sadoski and Quast (1990) had their participants read and then rate the paragraphs in three feature journalism stories for the imagery experienced, the emotions experienced, or the importance to the story as a whole. Readers were assigned to read the articles as they would normally read an article about current events and people, not for testing. Sixteen days later, the readers were given a surprise recall task: They were asked to write down whatever they most remembered about the stories. What was recalled was overwhelmingly associated with the emotions and imagery experienced during the reading as determined by the readers' own statements and earlier ratings. What was rated as important was recalled poorly. That is, what was retained long after the reading event was the subjective, aesthetic experience.

This result seems inconsistent with the postulation of an efferent–aesthetic continuum. If this continuum works as a true continuum, it follows that as the reader moves toward one pole, he or she must move away from the other. If efferent reading is determined by what is retained, then the aesthetic aspects of the reading, including images and emotions, should have been recalled poorly, and information seen as important should have been recalled better. But these results indicate that what was carried away from the reading was aesthetic. That is, the transactional theory of reader response does not appear to sufficiently take into account the nature of memory for what is read, whatever the reader's stance may be. We do not necessarily remember what we read for information unless we make efforts to memorize or otherwise record the information. Mental imagery and its frequent correlate, emotional response, can be evoked even when reading for superficial information. For example, Sadoski et al. (1990) found that students who were assigned to read to find typographical errors intentionally inserted in the text of a literary story reported as much imagery and affect as students assigned to read the story normally for pleasure. In short, stance may be less consequential than is assumed; a good story is captivating even if we intend to read for other purposes.

Directions for Practice

DCT provides rich implications for instruction in decoding, comprehension, and response. A growing body of empirical support for DCT principles in each of these areas of teaching reading has been identified and synthesized, and more research is forthcoming. We will briefly review highlights.

Decoding

Recently, decodable texts have been used extensively in beginning reading. Decodable texts use a high proportion of graphophonemically regular words that are intended to assist students in learning to decode and gain a sight vocabulary. However, word imageability also has been found to strongly affect sight-word learning. That is, decodability may not be enough.

Hargis and Gickling (1978) taught kindergartners a set of concrete sight words and a set of abstract sight words that were matched for length and frequency. All the words were familiar words that were initially unknown to the children by sight. During training, the children (a) were shown the words on flash cards, (b) heard each word pronounced, (c) heard each word used in a sentence, (d) used the word in a sentence of their own, and (e) repeated the word. Two days later, more than three times as many concrete words were named correctly. Ten days later, more than four times as many concrete words were named correctly. These results were later replicated with both kindergartners of normal ability and older mentally retarded children (Gickling, Hargis, & Alexander, 1981).

Kolker and Terwilliger (1981) also taught first- and second-grade children concrete and abstract sight words. The words were initially unknown by sight but were familiar in speech. The words were presented for one second on a flash card and pronounced for the child. The child then repeated the words, and corrections were provided as necessary. This continued until a learning criterion was reached. The first graders took about 60% more trials to learn to correctly name the abstract words than the concrete words. The difference for the second graders was less (about 8% more trials for abstract words) but still statistically significant. Terwilliger and Kolker (1982) replicated their results while manipulating word confusability (i.e., same or different initial consonants). Similar results were obtained with kindergartners and beginning first graders by van der Veur (1975) and Wolpert (1972).

Hargis, Terhaar-Yonkers, Williams, and Reed (1988) extended this research to middle-grade children with reading problems. In addition to manipulating word concreteness, the experiment included manipulations for word decodability and word presentation in story context or in isolation. Results determined that (a) concrete words were learned about 12% faster than abstract words, (b) words presented in story contexts were learned about 12% faster than words presented in isolation, and (c) decodable words were learned about 6% faster than nondecodable words. An interaction between these factors indicated that abstract words presented in isolation took the longest to learn regardless of decodability, whereas concrete, decodable words were learned fastest regardless of context.

The results of these studies are very consistent with DCT and suggest that beginning reading materials and lessons emphasize concreteness as well as decodability and context in learning sight vocabulary. Overall, concrete words are learned faster even without the benefit of context, especially if decodable. Abstract words that vary in decodability are learned more slowly and are learned better in context. These results are compatible with similar findings regarding word recognition by adults, as discussed earlier (e.g., Strain & Herdman, 1999; Strain et al., 1995, 2002).

Comprehension

Throughout history, DCT principles have been extensively applied—often intuitively—to teaching reading comprehension. Sadoski and Paivio (2001) reviewed the history of teaching text comprehension from ancient to modern times and found an alternation between emphasis on the abstract and the verbal (e.g., outlines, epitomes) and the concrete and the imaginal (e.g., object lessons, imagery training). Clark and Paivio (1991) reviewed decades of empirical studies relevant to DCT in education and determined that mental imagery, concreteness, and verbal associative processes play major roles in the representation and comprehension of knowledge, learning and memory of school material, effective instruction, individual differences, and motivation. Ruddell (1997, see #36 this volume), in his summary of his research program on influential teachers of reading, found that such teachers used highly effective strategies, including the use of concrete examples, their extension to more abstract examples, and the analysis of abstract concepts in concrete terms.

The use of induced mental imagery to enhance student understanding and learning has gained an increasing record of acceptance (see reviews by Gambrell & Koskinen, 2002; Sadoski & Paivio, 2001). The general conclusion of both of these reviews is that instructions to form mental images significantly enhance the reading comprehension and memory of both children and adults in various ways. Numerous studies have shown, for example, that elementary-grade students know how to induce mental imagery and that only brief training and teacher scaffolding are necessary for most children to effectively use mental imagery as a reading comprehension strategy.

For example, Gambrell (1982) had first and third graders read short stories in sections. Before each section, the experimental group was told to make pictures in their minds to help remember, whereas the control group was told to think about what they read in order to remember. After reading each section, the participants were asked a prediction question, "What do you think is going to happen next?" Their responses were scored for factual accuracy and the number of accurate predictions. Third graders in the imagery group reported twice as many facts and made twice as many accurate predictions as the control group members. First graders in the imagery group also tended to outperform control group members on both measures, but the differences were not statistically significant. This study indicates that even with minimal inducement, children can use mental imagery to comprehend factual material and make accurate inferential predictions.

Mental imagery also has been used as a remediation technique for poor comprehenders. One example is a technique developed by Bell (1986) that is based on DCT principles. Instruction involves requiring students to form images in increasing detail to progressively larger units of language, including words, phrases, sentences, and texts. This technique was experimentally tested against reciprocal teaching as a comprehension development strategy (clarify, summarize, question, and predict) and a no-strategy control condition (Johnson-Glenberg, 2000). A variety of comprehension measures were used, including prediction, recall, explicit questions, implicit questions, and a standardized reading comprehension test. While many of the between-group contrasts did not significantly differ, both experimental treatments outperformed the control condition on answering implicit questions. The reciprocal teaching group outperformed the imagery training group only on answering explicit questions. The researcher concluded that both forms of strategy training were generally valuable in improving the comprehension of students with problems in this area. Further research in this area would be useful.

Response

Teaching reader response is an area fraught with controversy. Miall (1996), based on his extensive research into reader response, questions whether response can or should be taught at all. He bemoans the status of teaching literary response in many classrooms:

> I am aware of literature classes in schools and universities that, although often well-intentioned, are laying waste to students' experiences of literature. Like the loggers in one of our northern forests, there are teachers in too many classes whose work succeeds only in clear cutting every shoot of literary interest, leaving hardly a stump behind, mainly for the sake of that giant pulp mill, the testing and examining of students. (pp. 463–464)

There is no easy solution to this problem. Images and feelings are deeply personal, and instruction in *what* to imagine and feel is surely less appropriate *than* to imagine and feel. The basis of an effective literary education is in nurturing response but also in disciplining it so that it is not simply a flight of the imagination or an exercise in the affective fallacy. Finding a way to do this is a pressing problem for researchers and educators. One educationally valid method from a reading viewpoint might involve the avoidance of didactically explaining the effects of a literary work, instead investigating how authors achieve whatever effects they cause in readers.

Sadoski (2002) discusses how DCT principles might explain the way poets use imagery and language in collaboration or contention to obtain effects on readers. Several commonly taught poems are presented, showing that the mental images evoked by the poem are sometimes in contrast with the language of the poem. For example, John Masefield's poem "Sea Fever" (Masefield, 1951) deals with a sailor's yearning to go back to sea, although the reasons for not doing so are unclear. Images are evoked of tall sailing ships, the kick of the wheel, the song of the wind, and the clouds flying by. But the rhythm of the poem alternates between rollicking, fast-paced lines and slower, languorous lines. The images are all of freedom, but the lines constrain the reader every time the poem gets going again. The language, therefore, is inconsistent with the images evoked, and the contrast is provocative. Does this mean that the sailor is somehow incapacitated and either spiritually or physically unable to go back to sea? No explicit meaning can be assigned because it is all inferred and ambiguous. Rather, the effects caused in the readers are discussed in a disciplined way without acceptance or rejection. This approach may be more appropriate for some poems than others, but as a general approach, the scrutiny of the effects produced by language and imagery in collaboration or in contrast may be one useful solution to how to best deal with reader response in education.

Conclusion

DCT is a theory of general cognition that addresses reading in all its psychological aspects. Few theories offer this scope and have achieved its broad base of empirical support. Comprehensive cognitive theories of reading with established programs of scientific testing are young, little more than 30 years old. They may be compared to the first comprehensive theory of gravitation that dates back more than 300 years or to the first comprehensive theory of evolution that dates back nearly 150 years. New theories are subject to change as evidence accumulates, and they can be expected to make few clear and unambiguous predictions (a statement that applies to all the theories in this volume). However, DCT specifies to a considerable extent constructs of mind that have been of interest since ancient times and will undoubtedly continue to be of interest in the future. Both language and mental imagery in its various forms are among these constructs. The predictions of DCT have held up favorably against other theories to date, and its future in advancing the knowledge of reading is promising.

References

Baluch, B., & Besner, D. (2001). Basic processes in reading: Semantics affects speeded naming of high frequency words in an alphabetic script. *Canadian Journal of Experimental Psychology, 55*(1), 63–69.

Bell, N. (1986). *Visualizing and verbalizing for language comprehension and thinking.* Paso Robles, CA: Academy of Reading Publications.

Black, J.B., Turner, T.J., & Bower, G.H. (1979). Spatial reference points in language comprehension. *Journal of Verbal Learning and Verbal Behavior, 18,* 187–198.

Carver, R.P. (1982). Optimal rate of reading prose. *Reading Research Quarterly, 18,* 56–88.

Chomsky, N. (1957). *Syntactic structures.* The Hague, the Netherlands: Mouton.

Clark, J.M., & Paivio, A. (1991). Dual coding theory and education. *Educational Psychology Review, 3,* 149–210.

Coltheart, M., Curtis, B., Atkins, P., & Haller, M. (1993). Models of reading aloud: Dual-route and parallel-distributed-processing approaches. *Psychological Review, 100,* 589–608.

Coltheart, M., Laxton, V.J., & Keating, C. (1988). Effects of word imageability and age of acquisition on children's reading. *British Journal of Psychology, 79,* 1–12.

Coltheart, M., Patterson, K., & Marshall, J.C. (Eds.). (1980). *Deep dyslexia.* London: Routledge & Kegan Paul.

Coltheart, M., Rastle, K., Perry, C., Langdon, R., & Ziegler, J. (2001). DRC: A dual route cascaded model of visual word recognition and reading aloud. *Psychological Review*, *108*(1), 204–256.

Denis, M. (1982). Imaging while reading text: A study of individual differences. *Memory & Cognition*, *10*, 540–545.

Eddy, J.K., & Glass, A.L. (1981). Reading and listening to high and low imagery sentences. *Journal of Verbal Learning and Verbal Behavior*, *20*(3), 333–345.

Edfeldt, A.W. (1960). *Silent speech and silent reading.* Chicago: University of Chicago Press.

Ellis, A.W., & Monaghan, J. (2002). Reply to Strain, Patterson, and Seidenberg (2002). *Journal of Experimental Psychology: Learning, Memory, and Cognition*, *28*, 215–220.

Fillmore, C.J. (1968). The case for case. In E. Bach & R.T. Harms (Eds.), *Universals in linguistic theory* (pp. 1–88). New York: Holt, Rinehart & Winston.

Fillmore, C.J. (1976). The case for case reopened. In P. Cole (Ed.), *Syntax and semantics: Grammatical relations* (pp. 59–81). New York: Academic Press.

Fillmore, C.J. (1984). Lexical semantics and text semantics. In J.E. Copeland (Ed.), *New directions in linguistics and semiotics* (pp. 123–147). College Station: Texas A&M University Press.

Frank, S.D. (1994). *The Evelyn Wood seven-day speed reading and learning program.* New York: Barnes & Noble.

Funnell, E., & Allport, A. (1987). *Non-linguistic cognition and word meanings: Neuropsychological exploration of common mechanisms.* In A.A. Allport, D.G. MacKay, W. Prinz, & E. Scheerer (Eds.), *Language perception and production: Relationships between listening, speaking, reading, and writing* (pp. 367–400). New York: Academic Press.

Gambrell, L.B. (1982). Induced mental imagery and the text prediction performance of first and third graders. In J.A. Niles & L.A. Harris (Eds.), *New inquiries in reading research and instruction* (31st yearbook of the National Reading Conference, pp. 131–135). Rochester, NY: National Reading Conference.

Gambrell, L.B., & Koskinen, P.S. (2002). Imagery: A strategy for enhancing comprehension. In C.C. Block & M. Pressley (Eds.), *Comprehension instruction: Research-based best practices.* New York: Guilford.

Gibson, E.J., & Levin, H. (1975). *The psychology of reading.* Cambridge, MA: MIT Press.

Gickling, E.E., Hargis, C.H., & Alexander, D.R. (1981). The function of imagery in sight word recognition among retarded and nonretarded children. *Education and Training of the Mentally Retarded*, *16*(4), 259–263.

Goetz, E.T., & Sadoski, M. (1996). Imaginative processes in literary comprehension. In R.J. Kreuz & M.S. MacNealy (Eds.), *Empirical approaches to literature and aesthetics* (pp. 221–240). Norwood, NJ: Ablex.

Goetz, E.T., Sadoski, M., & Olivarez, A., Jr. (1991). Getting a reading on reader response: Relationships between imagery, affect, and importance ratings, recall and imagery reports. *Reading Psychology*, *12*(1), 13–26.

Goetz, E.T., Sadoski, M., Stowe, M.L., Fetsco, T.G., & Kemp, S.G. (1993). Imagery and emotional response in reading literary text. *Poetics*, *22*, 35–49.

Hargis, C.H., & Gickling, E.E. (1978). The function of imagery in word recognition development. *The Reading Teacher*, *31*, 870–874.

Hargis, C.H., Terhaar-Yonkers, M., Williams, P.C., & Reed, M.T. (1988). Repetition requirements for word recognition. *Journal of Reading*, *31*, 320–327.

Harris, T.L., & Hodges, R.E. (1995). *The literacy dictionary: The vocabulary of reading and writing.* Newark, DE: International Reading Association.

Hodes, C.L. (1994). The role of visual mental imagery in the speed-accuracy tradeoff: A preliminary investigation. *Journal of Educational Technology Systems*, *23*(1), 53–61.

Holcomb, P.J., Kounios, J., Anderson, J.E., & West, W.C. (1999). Dual-coding, context-availability, and concreteness effects in sentence comprehension: An electrophysiological investigation. *Journal of Experimental Psychology: Learning, Memory, and Cognition*, *25*(3), 721–742.

Huey, E.B. (1968). *The psychology and pedagogy of reading.* Cambridge, MA: MIT Press. (Original work published 1908)

Janyan, A., & Andonova, E. (2003). Visual field differences in word naming. In F. Schmalhofer, R.M. Young, & G. Katz (Eds.), *Proceedings of Eurocogsci 03* (pp. 187–192). Mahwah, NJ: Erlbaum.

Johnson-Glenberg, M.C. (2000). Training reading comprehension in adequate decoders/poor comprehenders: Verbal versus visual strategies. *Journal of Educational Psychology*, *92*(4), 772–782.

Jorm, A.F. (1977). Effect of word imagery on reading performance as a function of reader ability. *Journal of Educational Psychology*, *69*(1), 46–54.

Juel, C., & Holmes, B. (1981). Oral and silent reading of sentences. *Reading Research Quarterly*, *16*, 545–568.

Kaplan, R.M. (1973). A general syntactic processor. In R. Rustin (Ed.), *Natural language processing* (Courant Computer Science, Symposium 8). New York: Algorithmics.

Kieras, D. (1978). Beyond pictures and words: Alternative information-processing models for imagery effects in verbal memory. *Psychological Bulletin*, *85*, 532–554.

Kintsch, W. (1988). The role of knowledge in discourse comprehension: A construction-integration model. *Psychological Review*, *95*(2), 163–182.

Kintsch, W. (1998). *Comprehension: A paradigm for cognition*. Cambridge, UK: Cambridge University Press.

Kolker, B., & Terwilliger, P.N. (1981). Sight vocabulary learning of first and second graders. *Reading World*, *20*(4), 251–258.

Kounios, J., & Holcomb, P.J. (1994). Concreteness effects in semantic processing: ERP evidence supporting dual-coding theory. *Journal of Experimental Psychology: Learning, Memory, and Cognition*, *20*, 804–823.

Kreuz, R.J., & MacNealy, M.S. (Eds.). (1996). *Empirical approaches to literature and aesthetics*. Norwood, NJ: Ablex.

Langacker, R.W. (1987). *Foundations of cognitive grammar: Vol. I, Theoretical prerequisites*. Stanford, CA: Stanford University Press.

Langacker, R.W. (1991). *Concept, image, and symbol: The cognitive basis of grammar*. New York: du Gruyter.

Lesser, V.R., Fennell, R.D., Erman, L.D., & Reddy, D.R. (1975). Organization of the Hearsay-II speech understanding system. *IEEE Transactions on Acoustics, Speech, and Signal Processing*, *23*(1), 11–23.

Liberman, A.M., & Mattingly, I.G. (1985). The motor theory of speech perception revisited. *Cognition*, *21*(1), 1–36.

Lucas, M. (1999). Context effects in lexical access: A meta-analysis. *Memory & Cognition*, *27*, 385–398.

Marschark, M., & Hunt, R.R. (1989). A reexamination of the role of imagery in learning and memory. *Journal of Experimental Psychology:*

Learning, Memory, and Cognition, *15*(4), 710–720.

Marschark, M., & Paivio, A. (1977). Integrative processing of concrete and abstract sentences. *Journal of Verbal Learning and Verbal Behavior*, *16*, 217–231.

Masefield, J. (1951). *Poems*. New York: Macmillan.

Miall, D.S. (1996). Empowering the reader: Literary response and classroom learning. In R.J. Kreuz & M.S. MacNealy (Eds.), *Empirical approaches to literature and aesthetics* (pp. 463–478). Norwood, NJ: Ablex.

Miall, D.S., & Kuiken, D. (1995). Aspects of literary response: A new questionnaire. *Research in the Teaching of English*, *29*(1), 37–58.

Monaghan, J., & Ellis, A.W. (2002). What exactly interacts with spelling-sound consistency in word naming? *Journal of Experimental Psychology: Learning, Memory, and Cognition*, *28*, 183–206.

Nelson, D.L., & Schreiber, T.A. (1992). Word concreteness and word structure as independent determinants of recall. *Journal of Memory and Language*, *31*, 237–260.

Paivio, A. (1971). *Imagery and verbal processes*. New York: Holt, Rinehart, and Winston.

Paivio, A. (1986). *Mental representations: A dual coding approach*. New York: Oxford University Press.

Paivio, A. (1991). Dual coding theory: Retrospect and current status. *Canadian Journal of Psychology*, *45*, 255–287.

Paivio, A., Walsh, M., & Bons, T. (1994). Concreteness effects in memory: When and why? *Journal of Experimental Psychology: Learning, Memory, and Cognition*, *20*, 1196–1204.

Plaut, D.C., & Shallice, T. (1993). Deep dyslexia: A case study of connectionist neuropsychology. *Cognitive Neuropsychology*, *10*, 377–500.

Raman, I., & Baluch, B. (2001). Semantic effects as a function of reading skill in word naming of a transparent orthography. *Reading and Writing*, *14*(7/8), 599–614.

Raman, I., Baluch, B., & Besner, D. (1997). *Imageability and frequency effects on visual word recognition: Evidence from a transparent orthography*. Paper presented at the Fifth European Congress of Psychology, Dublin, Ireland.

Rayner, K., & Pollatsek, A. (1989). *The psychology of reading*. Englewood Cliffs, NJ: Prentice Hall.

Rosenblatt, L.M. (1994). The transactional theory of reading and writing. In R.B. Ruddell, M.R. Ruddell, & H. Singer (Eds.), *Theoretical models and processes of reading* (4th ed., pp. 1057–1092). Newark, DE: International Reading Association.

Ruddell, R.B. (1997). Researching the influential literacy teacher: Characteristics, beliefs, strategies, and new research directions. In C.K. Kinzer, K.A. Hinchman, & D.J. Leu (Eds.), *Inquiries in literacy theory and practice* (46th yearbook of the National Reading Conference, pp. 37–53). Chicago: National Reading Conference.

Rumelhart, D.E. (1977). Toward an interactive model of reading. In S. Dornic (Ed.), *Attention and performance* (pp. 573–603). New York: Academic Press.

Rumelhart, D.E., & McClelland, J.L. (1986). *Parallel distributed processing*. Cambridge, MA: MIT Press.

Sacks, O. (2002, October 7). The case of Anna H. *The New Yorker*, 62–73.

Sadoski, M. (1983). An exploratory study of the relationships between reported imagery and the comprehension and recall of a story. *Reading Research Quarterly, 19*, 110–123.

Sadoski, M. (1985). The natural use of imagery in story comprehension and recall: Replication and extension. *Reading Research Quarterly, 20*, 658–667.

Sadoski, M. (1992). Imagination, cognition, and persona. *Rhetoric Review, 10*, 266–278.

Sadoski, M. (1999). Comprehending comprehension [Essay review of the book *Comprehension: A paradigm for cognition*]. *Reading Research Quarterly, 34*, 493–500.

Sadoski, M. (2002). Dual coding theory and reading poetic text. *Journal of the Imagination in Language Learning and Teaching, 7*, 78–83.

Sadoski, M., & Goetz, E.T. (1985). Relationships between affect, imagery, and importance ratings for segments of a story. In J.A. Niles & R. Lalik (Eds.), *Issues in literacy: A research perspective* (34th yearbook of the National Reading Conference, pp. 180–185). Washington, DC: National Reading Conference.

Sadoski, M., Goetz, E.T., & Avila, E. (1995). Concreteness effects in text recall: Dual coding or context availability? *Reading Research Quarterly, 30*, 278–288.

Sadoski, M., Goetz, E.T., & Fritz, J. (1993). Impact of concreteness on comprehensibility, interest, and memory for text: Implications for dual coding theory and text design. *Journal of Educational Psychology, 85*, 291–304.

Sadoski, M., Goetz, E.T., & Kangiser, S. (1988). Imagination in story response: Relationships between imagery, affect, and structural importance. *Reading Research Quarterly, 23*, 320–336.

Sadoski, M., Goetz, E.T., Olivarez, A., Lee, S., & Roberts, N.M. (1990). Imagination in story reading: The role of imagery, verbal recall, story analysis, and processing levels. *Journal of Reading Behavior, 22*, 55–70.

Sadoski, M., Goetz, E.T., & Rodriguez, M. (2000). Engaging texts: Effects of concreteness on comprehensibility, interest, and recall in four text types. *Journal of Educational Psychology, 92*, 85–95.

Sadoski, M., & Paivio, A. (1994). A dual coding view of imagery and verbal processes in reading comprehension. In R.B. Ruddell, M.R. Ruddell, & H. Singer (Eds.), *Theoretical models and processes of reading* (4th ed., pp. 582–601). Newark, DE: International Reading Association.

Sadoski, M., & Paivio, A. (2001). *Imagery and text: A dual coding theory of reading and writing*. Mahwah, NJ: Erlbaum.

Sadoski, M., Paivio, A., & Goetz, E.T. (1991). A critique of schema theory in reading and a dual coding alternative. *Reading Research Quarterly, 26*, 463–484.

Sadoski, M., & Quast, Z. (1990). Reader response and long-term recall for journalistic text: The roles of imagery, affect, and importance. *Reading Research Quarterly, 25*, 256–272.

Strain, E., & Herdman, C.M. (1999). Imageability effects in word naming: An individual differences analysis. *Canadian Journal of Experimental Psychology, 53*, 347–359.

Strain, E., Patterson, K., & Seidenberg, M.S. (1995). Semantic effects in single-word naming. *Journal of Experimental Psychology: Learning, Memory, and Cognition, 21*, 1140–1154.

Strain, E., Patterson, K., & Seidenberg, M.S. (2002). Theories of word naming interact with spelling-sound consistency. *Journal of Experimental Psychology: Learning, Memory, and Cognition, 28*, 207–214.

Terwilliger, P.N., & Kolker, B.S. (1982). The effects of learning confusable words on subsequent learning of high or low imagery words. *Reading World, 21*, 286–292.

van der Veur, B.W. (1975). Imagery rating of 1,000 frequently used words. *Journal of Educational Psychology, 67*, 44–56.

Venezky, R.L., & Massaro, D.W. (1987). Orthographic structure and spelling-sound regularity in reading English words. In A.A. Allport, D.G. MacKay, W. Prinz, & E. Scheerer (Eds.), *Language perception and production: Relationships between listening, speaking, reading, and writing* (pp. 159–179). New York: Academic Press.

West, W.C., O'Rourke, T.B., & Holcomb, P.J. (1998). Event-related brain potentials and language comprehension: A cognitive neuroscience approach to the study of intellectual functioning. In S. Soraci & W.J. McIlvane (Eds.), *Perspectives on fundamental processes in intellectual functioning* (pp. 131–168). Stamford, CT: Ablex.

Williams, J.D. (1998). *Preparing to teach writing: Research, theory, and practice* (2nd ed.). Mahwah, NJ: Erlbaum.

Wolpert, E.M. (1972). Length, imagery values, and word recognition. *The Reading Teacher*, *26*, 180–186.

48

The Transactional Theory of Reading and Writing

Louise M. Rosenblatt

Terms such as *the reader* are somewhat misleading, though convenient, fictions. There is no such thing as a generic reader or a generic literary work; there are in reality only the potential millions of individual readers of individual literary works.... The reading of any work of literature is, of necessity, an individual and unique occurrence involving the mind and emotions of some particular reader. (Rosenblatt, 1938/1983)

That statement, first published in *Literature as Exploration* in 1938, seems especially important to reiterate at the beginning of a presentation of a "theoretical model" of the reading process. A theoretical model by definition is an abstraction, or a generalized pattern devised in order to think about a subject. Hence, it is essential to recognize that, as I concluded, we may generalize about similarities among such events, but we cannot evade the realization that there are actually only innumerable separate transactions between readers and texts.

As I sought to understand how we make the meanings called novels, poems, or plays, I discovered that I had developed a theoretical model that covers all modes of reading. Ten years of teaching courses in literature and composition had preceded the writing of that statement. This had made possible observation of readers encountering a wide range of "literary" and "nonliterary" texts, discussing them, keeping journals while reading them, and writing spontaneous reactions and reflective essays. And decades more of such observation preceded the publication of *The Reader, the Text, the Poem* (Rosenblatt, 1978), the fullest presentation of the theory and its implications for criticism.

Thus, the theory emerges from a process highly appropriate to the pragmatist philosophy it embodies. The problem arose in the context of a practical classroom situation. Observations of relevant episodes led to the hypotheses that constitute the theory of the reading process, and these have in turn been applied, tested, confirmed, or revised in the light of further observation.

From Ruddell, R.B., Ruddell, M.R., & Singer, H. (Eds.), *Theoretical Models and Processes of Reading* (4th ed., pp. 1057–1092). Copyright © 1994 by the International Reading Association.

Fortunately, while specializing in English and comparative literature, I was in touch with the thinking on the forefront of various disciplines. The interpretation of these observations of readers' reading drew on a number of different perspectives—literary and social history, philosophy, aesthetics, linguistics, psychology, and sociology. Training in anthropology provided an especially important point of view. Ideas were developed that in some instances have only recently become established. It seems necessary, therefore, to begin by setting forth some of the basic assumptions and concepts that undergird the transactional theory of the reading process. This in turn will involve presentation of the transactional view of the writing process and the relationship between author and reader.

The Transactional Paradigm

Transaction

The terms *transaction* and *transactional* are consonant with a philosophic position increasingly accepted in the 20th century. A new paradigm in science (Kuhn, 1970) has required a change in our habits of thinking about our relationship to the world around us. For 300 years, Descartes' dualistic view of the self as distinct from nature sufficed, for example, for the Newtonian paradigm in physics. The self, or "subject," was separate from the "object" perceived. "Objective" facts, completely free of subjectivity, were sought, and a direct, immediate perception of "reality" was deemed possible. Einstein's theory and the developments in subatomic physics revealed the need to acknowledge that, as Neils Bohr (1959) explained, the observer is part of the observation—human beings are part of nature. Even the physicists' facts depend to some extent on the interests, hypotheses, and technologies of the observer. The human organism, it became apparent, is ultimately the mediator in any perception of the world or any sense of "reality."

John Dewey's pragmatist epistemology fitted the new paradigm. Hence, Dewey joined with Arthur F. Bentley to work out a new terminology in *Knowing and the Known* (1949). They believed the term *interaction* was too much associated with the old positivistic paradigm, with each element or unit being predefined as separate, as "thing balanced against thing," and their "interaction" studied. Instead, they chose *transaction* to imply "unfractured observation" of the whole situation. Systems of description and naming "are employed to deal with aspects and phases of action, without final attribution to 'elements' or presumptively detachable or independent 'entities,' 'essences,' or 'realities'" (p. 108). The knower, the knowing, and the known are seen as aspects of "one process." Each element conditions and is conditioned by the other in a mutually constituted situation (cf. Rosenblatt, 1985b).

The new paradigm requires a break with entrenched habits of thinking. The old stimulus–response, subject–object, individual–social dualisms give way to recognition of transactional relationships. The human being is seen as part of nature, continuously in transaction with an environment—each one conditions the other. The transactional mode of thinking has perhaps been most clearly assimilated in ecology. Human activities and relationships are seen as transactions in which the individual and social elements fuse with cultural and natural elements. Many current philosophy writers may differ on metaphysical implications but find it necessary to come to terms with the new paradigm.[1]

Language

The transactional concept has profound implications for understanding language. Traditionally, language has been viewed as primarily a self-contained system or code, a set of arbitrary rules and conventions that is manipulated as a tool by speakers and writers or imprints itself on the minds of listeners and readers. Even when the transactional approach has been accepted, this deeply ingrained way of thinking continues to function, tacitly or explicitly, in much theory, research, and teaching involving texts.[2]

The view of language basic to the transactional model of reading owes much to the philosopher John Dewey but even more to his contemporary Charles Sanders Peirce, who is recognized as the U.S. founder of the field of semiotics or semiology, the study of verbal and nonverbal signs. Peirce provided concepts that differentiate the transactional view of language and reading from structuralist and poststructuralist (especially deconstructionist) theories. These reflect the influence of another great semiotician, the French linguist Ferdinand de Saussure (Culler, 1982).

Saussure (1972) differentiated actual speech (*parole*) from the abstractions of the linguists (*langue*), but he stressed the arbitrary nature of signs and minimized the referential aspect. Even more important was his dyadic formulation of the relationship between "signifier and signified," or between words and concept. These emphases fostered a view of language as an autonomous, self-contained system (Rosenblatt, 1993).

In contrast, Peirce (1933, 1935) offered a triadic formulation. "A sign," Peirce wrote, "is in conjoint relation to the thing denoted and to the mind...." The "sign is related to its object only in consequence of a mental association, and depends on habit" (Vol. 3, para. 360). The triad constitutes a symbol. Peirce repeatedly refers to the human context of meaning. Because he evidently did not want to reinforce the notion of "mind" as an entity, he typically phrased the "conjoint" linkage as among sign, object, and "interpretant," which should be understood as mental operation rather than an entity (6.347). Peirce's triadic model firmly grounds language in the transactions of individual human beings with their world.

Recent descriptions of the working of the brain by neurologists and other scientists seem very Peircean. Although they are dealing with a level not essential to our theoretical purposes, they provide an interesting reinforcement. "Many leading scientists, including Dr. Francis Crick, think that the brain creates unified circuits by oscillating distant components at a shared frequency" (Appenzeller, 1990, pp. 6–7). Neurologists speak of "a third-party convergence zone [which seems to be a neurological term for Peirce's interpretant] that mediates between word and concept convergence zones" (Damasio, 1989, pp. 123–132). Studies of children's acquisition of language support the Peircean triad, concluding that a vocalization or sign becomes a word, a verbal symbol, when the sign and its object or referent are linked with the same "organismic state" (Werner & Kaplan, 1962, p. 18).

Though language is usually defined as a socially generated system of communication—the very bloodstream of any society—the triadic concept reminds us that language is always internalized by a human being transacting with a particular environment. Vygotsky's recognition of the social context did not prevent his affirming the individual's role: The "sense of a word" is

> the sum of all the psychological events aroused in our consciousness by the word. It is a dynamic, fluid, complex whole, which has several zones of unequal stability. Meaning [i.e., reference] is only one of the zones of sense, the most stable and precise zone. A word acquires its sense from the context in which it appears; in different contexts, it changes its sense. (1962, p. 46)

Vygotsky postulated "the existence of a dynamic system of meaning, in which the affective and the intellectual unite." The earliest utterances of children evidently represent a fusion of "processes which later will branch off into referential, emotive, and associative part processes" (Rommetveit, 1968, pp. 147, 167). The child learns to sort out the various aspects of "sense" associated with a sign, decontextualize it, and recognize the public aspect of language, the collective language system. This does not, however, eliminate the other dimensions of sense. A language act cannot be thought of as totally affective or cognitive, or as totally public or private (Bates, 1979, pp. 65–66).

Bates provides the useful metaphor of an iceberg for the total sense of a word to its user: The visible tip represents what I term the public aspect of meaning, resting on the submerged base of private meaning. *Public* designates usages or meanings that dictionaries list. Multiple meanings indicated for the same word reflect the fact that the same sign takes on different meanings at different times and in different linguistic or different personal, cultural, or social contexts. In short, *public* refers to usages that some groups of people have developed and that the individual shares.

Note that *public* and *private* are not synonymous with *cognitive* and *affective*. Words may have publicly shared affective connotations. The individual's private associations with a word may or may not agree with its connotations for the group, although these connotations must also be individually acquired. Words necessarily involve for each person a mix of both public and private elements, the base as well as the tip of the semantic iceberg.

For the individual, then, the language is that part, or set of features, of the public system that has been internalized through that person's experiences with words in life situations. "Lexical concepts must be shared by speakers of a common language...yet there is room for considerable individual difference in the details of any concept" (Miller & Johnson-Laird, 1976, p. 700). The residue of the individual's past transactions—in particular, natural and social contexts—constitutes what can be termed a linguistic–experiential reservoir. William James especially suggests the presence of such a cumulative experiential aura of language.

Embodying funded assumptions, attitudes, and expectations about language and about the world, this inner capital is all that each of us has to draw on in speaking, listening, writing, or reading. We "make sense" of a new situation or transaction and make new meanings by applying, reorganizing, revising, or extending public and private elements selected from our personal linguistic–experiential reservoirs.

Linguistic Transactions

Face-to-face communication—such as a conversation in which a speaker is explaining something to another person—can provide a simplified example of the transactional nature of all linguistic activities. A conversation is a temporal activity, a back-and-forth process. Each person has come to the transaction with an individual history, manifested in what has been termed a linguistic–experiential reservoir. The verbal signs are the vibrations in the air caused by a speaker. Both speaker and addressee contribute throughout to the spoken text (even if the listener remains silent) and to the interpretations that it calls forth as it progresses. Each must construct some sense of the other person. Each draws on a particular linguistic–experiential reservoir. The specific situation, which may be social and personal, and the setting and occasion for the conversation in themselves provide clues or limitations as to the general subject or framework and hence to the references and implications of the verbal signs. The speaker and addressee both produce further delimiting cues through facial expressions, tones of voice, and gestures. In addition to such nonverbal indications of an ongoing mutual interpretation of the text, the listener may offer questions and comments. The speaker thus is constantly being helped to gauge and to confirm, revise, or expand the text. Hence, the text is shaped transactionally by both speaker and addressee.

The opening words of a conversation, far from being static, by the end of the interchange may have taken on a different meaning. And the attitudes, the state of mind, even the manifest personality traits, may have undergone change. Moreover, the spoken text may be interpreted differently by each of the conversationalists.

But how can we apply the conversation model of transaction to the relationship between writers and readers, when so many of the elements that contribute to the spoken transaction are missing—physical presence, timing, actual setting, nonverbal behaviors, tones of voice, and so on? The signs on the page are all that the writer and the reader have to make up for the absence of these other elements. The reader focuses attention on and transacts with an element in the environment, namely the signs on the page, the text.

Despite all the important differences noted above, speech, writing, and reading share the same basic process—transacting through a text. In any linguistic event, speakers and listeners and writers and readers have only their linguistic–experiential reservoirs as the basis for interpretation. Any interpretations or new meanings are restructurings or extensions of the stock of experiences of language, spoken and written, brought to the task. In Peircean terms, past linkages of sign, object, and interpretant must provide the basis for new linkages, or new structures of meaning. Instead of an interaction, such as billiard balls colliding, there has been a transaction, thought of rather in terms of reverberations, rapid oscillations, blendings, and mutual conditionings.

Selective Attention

William James's concept of "selective attention" provides an important insight into this process. During the first half of this century, a combination of behaviorism and positivism led to neglect of the concept, but since the 1970s psychologists have reasserted its importance (Blumenthal, 1977; Myers, 1986). James (1890) tells us that we are constantly engaged in a "choosing activity," which he terms "selective attention" (I.284). We are constantly selecting out of the stream, or field, of consciousness "by the reinforcing and inhibiting agency of attention" (I.288). This activity is sometimes termed "the cocktail party phenomenon": In a crowded room where many conversations are in progress, we focus our attention on only one of them at a time, and the others become a background hum. We can turn our selective attention toward a broader or narrower area of the field. Thus, while language activity implies an intermingled kinesthetic, cognitive, affective, associational matrix, what is pushed into the background or suppressed and what is brought into awareness and organized into meaning depend on where selective attention is focused.

The transactional concept will prevent our falling into the error of envisaging selective attention as a mechanical choosing among an array of fixed entities rather than as a dynamic centering on areas or aspects of the contents of consciousness. The linguistic reservoir should not be seen as encompassing verbal signs linked to fixed meanings, but as a fluid pool of potential triadic symbolizations. Such residual linkages of sign, signifier, and organic state, it will be seen, become actual symbolizations as selective attention functions under the shaping influence of particular times and circumstances.

In the linguistic event, any process also will be affected by the physical and emotional state of the individual, for example, by fatigue or stress. Attention may be controlled or wandering, intense or superficial. In the discussion that follows, it will be assumed that such factors enter into the transaction and affect the quality of the process under consideration.

The paradoxical situation is that the reader has only the black marks on the page as the means of arriving at a meaning—and that meaning can be constructed only by drawing on the reader's own personal linguistic and life experiences. Because a text must be produced by a writer before it can be read, logic might seem to dictate beginning with a discussion of the writing process. It is true that the writer seeks to express something, but the purpose is to communicate with a reader (even if it is only the writer wishing to preserve some thought or experience for future reference). Typically, the text is intended for others. Some sense of a reader or at least of the fact that the text will function in a reading process thus is implicit in the writing process. Hence, I shall discuss the reading process first, then the writing process. Then, I shall broach the problems of communication and validity of interpretation before considering implications for teaching and research.

The Reading Process

Transacting With the Text

The concepts of transaction, the transactional nature of language, and selective attention now can be applied to analysis of the reading process. Every reading act is an event, or a transaction involving a particular reader and a particular pattern of signs, a text, and occurring at a particular time in a particular context. Instead of two fixed entities acting on one another, the reader and the text are two aspects of a total dynamic situation. The "meaning" does not reside ready-made "in" the text or "in" the reader but happens or comes into being during the transaction between reader and text.

The term *text* in this analysis denotes, then, a set of signs capable of being interpreted as verbal symbols. Far from already possessing a meaning that can be imposed on all readers, the text actually remains simply marks on paper, an object in the environment, until some reader transacts with it. The term *reader* implies a transaction with a text; the term *text* implies a transaction with a reader. "Meaning" is what happens during the transaction; hence, the fallacy of thinking of them as separate and distinct entities instead of factors in a total situation.

The notion that the marks in themselves possess meaning is hard to dispel. For example, *pain* for a French reader will link up with the concept of bread and for an English reader with the concept of bodily or mental suffering. A sentence that Noam Chomsky (1968, p. 27) made famous can help us realize that not even the syntax is inherent in the signs of the text but depends on the results of particular transactions: *Flying planes can be dangerous.*

Actually, only after we have selected a meaning can we infer a syntax from it. Usually, factors entering into the total transaction, such as the context and reader's purpose, will determine the reader's choice of meaning. Even if the reader recognizes the alternative syntactic possibilities, these factors still prevail. This casts doubt on the belief that the syntactical level, because it is lower or less complex, necessarily always precedes the semantic in the reading process. The transactional situation suggests that meaning implies syntax and that a reciprocal process is going on in which the broader aspects guiding choices are actively involved.

Here we see the difference between the physical text, defined as a pattern of signs, and what is usually called "the text," a syntactically patterned set of verbal symbols. This actually comes into being during the transaction with the signs on the page.

When we see a set of such marks on a page, we believe that it should give rise to some more or less coherent meaning. We bring our funded experience to bear. Multiple inner alternatives resonate to the signs. Not only the triadic linkages with the signs but also certain organismic states, or certain ranges of feeling, are stirred up in the linguistic–experiential reservoir. From these activated areas, selective attention—conditioned, as we have seen, by multiple physical, personal, social, and cultural factors entering into the situation—picks out elements that will be organized and synthesized into what constitutes "meaning." Choices have in effect probably been made simultaneously, as the various "levels" transact, conditioning one another, so to speak.

Reading is, to use James's phrase, a "choosing activity." From the very beginning, and often even before, some expectation, some tentative feeling, idea, or purpose, no matter how vague at first, starts the reading process and develops into the constantly self-revising impulse that guides selection, synthesis, and organization. The linguistic–experiential reservoir reflects the reader's cultural, social, and personal history. Past experience with language and with texts provides expectations. Other factors are the reader's present situation and interests. Perusing the unfolding text in the light of past syntactic and semantic experience, the reader seeks cues on which to base expectations about what is forthcoming. The text as a verbal pattern, we have seen, is part of what is being constructed. Possibilities open up concerning the general kind of meaning that may be developing, affecting choices in diction, syntax, and linguistic and literary conventions.

As the reader's eyes move along the page, the newly evoked symbolizations are tested for whether they can be fitted into the tentative meanings already constructed for the preceding portion of the text. Each additional choice will signal certain options and exclude others, so that even as the meaning evolves, the selecting, synthesizing impulse is itself constantly shaped and tested. If the marks on the page evoke elements that cannot be assimilated into the emerging synthesis, the guiding principle or framework is revised; if necessary, it is discarded and a complete rereading occurs. New tentative guidelines, new bases for a hypothetical structure, may then present themselves. Reader and text are involved in a complex, nonlinear, recursive, self-correcting transaction. The arousal and fulfillment—or frustration and revision—of expectations contribute to the construction of a cumulative meaning. From a to-and-fro interplay between reader, text, and context emerges a synthesis or organization, more or less coherent and complete. This meaning, this "evocation," is felt to correspond to the text.

Precisely because for experienced readers so much of the reading process is, or should be, automatic, aspects of the reading process tend to be described in impersonal, mechanistic terms. Psychologists are rightfully concerned with learning as much as possible about what goes on between the reader's first visual contact with the marks on the page and the completion of what is considered an interpretation of them. A number of different levels, systems, and strategies have been analytically designated, and research has been directed at clarifying their nature. These can be useful, but from a transactional point of view, it is important to recognize their potentialities and their limitations. A mechanistic analogy or metaphor lends itself especially to analyses of literal reading of simple texts. Results need to be cautiously interpreted. Recognizing the essential nature of both reader and text, the transactional theory requires an underlying metaphor of organic activity and reciprocity.

The optical studies of Adelbert Ames (1955) and the Ames–Cantril "transactional psychology" (Cantril & Livingston, 1963), which also derived its name from Dewey and Bentley's *Knowing and the Known* (1949), deserve first mention in this regard. These experiments demonstrated that perception depends much on the viewer's selection and organization of visual cues according to past experience, expectations, needs, and interests. The perception may be revised through continued transactions between the perceiver and the perceived object.

F.C. Bartlett's theory of *Remembering* (1932) (which I regret having discovered even later than did his fellow scientists) and his term *schema* are often called on to explain psychological processes even broader than his special field. It is not clear, however, that those who so readily invoke his schema concept are heeding his fears about a narrow, static usage of the term. Rejecting the image of a warehouse of unchanging items as the metaphor for schemata, he emphasized rather "active, developing patterns"—"constituents of living, momentary settings belonging to the organism" (Bartlett, 1932, p. 201). His description of the "constructive character of remembering," his rejection of a simple mechanical linear process, and his concepts of the development and continuing revision of schemata all have parallels in the transactional theory of linguistic events. His recognition of the influence of both the interests of the individual and the social context on all levels of the process also seems decidedly transactional.

The Reader's Stance

The broad outline of the reading process sketched thus far requires further elaboration. An important distinction must be made between the operations that produce the meaning, say, of a scientific report and the operations that evoke a literary work of art. Neither contemporary reading theory nor literary theory has done justice to such readings, nor to the fact that they are to be understood as representing a continuum rather than an opposition. The tendency generally has been to assume that such a distinction depends entirely on the texts involved. The character of the "work" has been held to inhere entirely in the text. But we cannot look simply at the text and predict the nature of the work. We cannot assume, for instance, that a poem rather than an argument about fences will be evoked from the text of Frost's *Mending Wall* or that a novel rather than sociological facts about Victorian England will be evoked from Dickens's *Great Expectations*. Advertisements and newspaper reports have been read as poems. Each alternative represents a different kind of selective activity, a different kind of relationship, between the reader and the text.

Essential to any reading is the reader's adoption, conscious or unconscious, of what I have termed a *stance* guiding the "choosing activity" in the stream of consciousness. Recall that any linguistic event carries both public and private aspects. As the transaction with the printed text stirs up elements of the linguistic–experiential reservoir, the reader adopts a selective attitude or stance, bringing certain aspects into the center of attention and pushing others into the fringes of consciousness. A stance reflects the reader's purpose. The situation, the purpose, and the linguistic–experiential equipment of the reader as well as the signs on the page enter into the transaction and affect the extent to which public and private meanings and associations will be attended to.

The Efferent–Aesthetic Continuum

The reading event must fall somewhere in a continuum, determined by whether the reader adopts what I term a *predominantly aesthetic* stance or a *predominantly efferent* stance. A particular stance determines the proportion or mix of public and private elements of sense that fall within the scope of the reader's selective attention. Or, to recall Bates's metaphor, a stance results from the degree and scope of attention paid respectively to the tip and to the base of the iceberg. Such differences can be represented only by a continuum, which I term the *efferent–aesthetic continuum*.

The Efferent Stance

The term *efferent* (from the Latin *efferre*, to carry away) designates the kind of reading in which attention is centered predominantly on what is to be extracted and retained after the reading event. An extreme example is a man who has accidentally swallowed a poisonous liquid and is rapidly reading the label on the bottle to learn the antidote. Here, surely, we see an illustration of James's point about selective attention and our capacity to push into the periphery of awareness or ignore those elements that do not serve our present interests. The man's attention is focused on learning what is to be done as soon as the reading ends. He concentrates on what the words point to, ignoring anything other than their barest public referents, constructing as quickly as possible the directions for future action. These structured ideas are the evocation felt to correspond to the text.

Reading a newspaper, textbook, or legal brief would usually provide a similar, though less extreme, instance of the predominantly efferent stance. In efferent reading, then, we focus attention mainly on the public "tip of the iceberg" of sense. Meaning results from abstracting out and analytically structuring the ideas, information, directions, or conclusions to be retained, used, or acted on after the reading event.

The Aesthetic Stance

The predominantly aesthetic stance covers the other half of the continuum. In this kind of reading, the reader adopts an attitude of readiness to focus attention on what is being lived through during the reading event. The term *aesthetic* was chosen because its Greek source suggested perception through the senses, feelings, and intuitions. Welcomed into awareness are not only the public referents of the verbal signs but also the private part of the "iceberg" of meaning: the sensations, images, feelings, and ideas that are the residue of past psychological events involving those words and their referents. Attention may include the sounds and rhythms of the words themselves, heard in "the inner ear" as the signs are perceived.

The aesthetic reader pays attention to—savors—the qualities of the feelings, ideas, situations, scenes, personalities, and emotions that are called forth and participates in the tensions, conflicts, and resolutions of the images, ideas, and scenes as they unfold. The lived-through meaning is felt to correspond to the text. This meaning, shaped and experienced during the aesthetic transaction, constitutes "the literary work," the poem, story, or play. This "evocation," and not the text, is the object of the reader's "response" and "interpretation," both during and after the reading event.

Confusion about the matter of stance results from the entrenched habit of thinking of the *text* as efferent or aesthetic, expository or poetic, literary or non-literary, and so on. Those who apply these terms to texts should realize that they actually are reporting their interpretation of the writer's intention as to what kind of reading the text should be given. The reader is free, however, to adopt either predominant stance toward any text. *Efferent* and *aesthetic* apply, then, to the writer's and the reader's selective attitude toward their own streams of consciousness during their respective linguistic events.

To recognize the essential nature of stance does not minimize the importance of the text in the transaction. Various verbal elements—metaphor, stylistic conventions or divergence from linguistic or semantic norms, even certain kinds of content—have been said to constitute the "poeticity" or "literariness" of a text. Such verbal elements, actually, do often serve as cues to the experienced reader to adopt an aesthetic stance. Yet it is possible to cite acknowledged literary works that lack one or all these elements. Neither reading theorists nor literary theorists have given due credit to the fact that none of these or any other arrangements of words could make their "literary" or "poetic" contribution without the reader's prior shift of attention toward mainly the qualitative or experiential contents of consciousness, namely, the aesthetic stance.

The Continuum

The metaphorical nature of the term *the stream of consciousness* can be called on further to clarify the efferent–aesthetic continuum. We can image consciousness as a stream flowing through the darkness. Stance, then, can be represented as a mechanism lighting up—directing the attention to—different parts of the stream, selecting out objects that have floated to the surface in those areas and leaving the rest in shadow. Stance, in other words, provides the guiding orientation toward activating particular areas and elements of consciousness, that is, particular proportions of public and private aspects of meaning, leaving the rest at the dim periphery of attention. Some such play of attention over the contents of what emerges into consciousness must be involved in the reader's multifold choices from the linguistic–experiential reservoir.

Efferent and aesthetic reflect the two main ways of looking at the world, often summed up as "scientific" and "artistic." My redundant usage of "predominantly" aesthetic or efferent underlines rejection of the traditional, binary, either–or tendency to see them as in opposition. The efferent stance pays more attention to the cognitive, the referential, the factual, the analytic, the logical, the quantitative aspects of meaning. And the aesthetic stance pays more attention to the sensuous, the affective, the emotive, the qualitative. But nowhere can we find on the one hand the purely public and on the other hand the purely private. Both of these aspects of meaning are attended to in different proportions in any linguistic event. One of the earliest and most important steps in any reading event, therefore, is the selection of either a predominantly efferent or a predominantly aesthetic stance toward the transaction with a text. Figure 1 indicates different readings by the same reader of the same text at different points on the efferent–aesthetic continuum. Other readers would probably produce readings that fall at other points on the continuum.

Although many readings may fall near the extremes, many others, perhaps most, may fall nearer the center of the continuum. Where both parts of the iceberg of meaning are more evenly balanced, confusion as to dominant stance is more likely and more counterproductive. It is possible to read efferently and assume one has evoked a poem, or to read aesthetically and assume one is arriving at logical conclusions to an argument.

FIGURE 1
The Efferent–Aesthetic Continuum

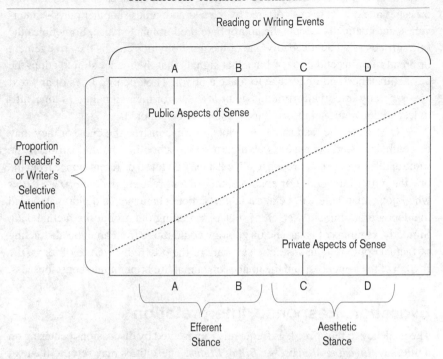

Any linguistic activity has both public (lexical, analytic, abstracting) and private (experiential, affective, associational) components. Stance is determined by the proportion of each component admitted into the scope of selective attention. The efferent stance draws mainly on the public aspect of sense; the aesthetic stance includes proportionally more of the experiential, private aspect.

Reading or writing events A and B fall into the efferent part of the continuum, with B admitting more private elements. Reading or writing events C and D both represent the aesthetic stance, with C according a higher proportion of attention to the public aspects of sense.

Also, it is necessary to emphasize that a predominant stance does not rule out fluctuations. Within a particular aesthetic reading, attention may at times turn from the experiential synthesis to efferent analysis, as the reader recognizes some technical strategy or passes a critical judgment. Similarly, in an efferent reading, a general idea may be illustrated or reinforced by an aesthetically lived through illustration or example. Despite the mix of private and public aspects of meaning in each stance, the two dominant stances are clearly distinguishable. No two readings, even by the same person, are identical. Still, someone else can read a text efferently and paraphrase it for us in such a way as to satisfy our efferent purpose. But no one else can read aesthetically—that is, experience the evocation of—a literary work of art for us.

Because each reading is an event in particular circumstances, the same text may be read either efferently or aesthetically. The experienced reader usually approaches a text alert to cues offered by the text and, unless another purpose intervenes, automatically adopts the appropriate predominant stance. Sometimes the title suffices as a cue. Probably one of the most obvious cues is the arrangement of broad margins and uneven lines that signals that the reader should adopt the aesthetic stance and undertake to make a poem. The opening lines of any text are especially important from this point of view, for their signaling of tone, attitude, and conventional indications of stance to be adopted.

Of course, the reader may overlook or misconstrue the cues, or they may be confusing. And the reader's own purpose, or schooling that indoctrinates the same undifferentiated approach to all texts, may dictate a different stance from the one the writer intended. For example, the student reading *A Tale of Two Cities* who knows that there will be a test on facts about characters and plot may be led to adopt a predominantly efferent stance, screening out all but the factual data. Similarly, readings of an article on zoology could range from analytic abstracting of factual content to an aesthetic savoring of the ordered structure of ideas, the rhythm of the sentences, and the images of animal life brought into consciousness.

Evocation, Response, Interpretation

The tendency to reify words is frequently represented by discussions centering on a title, say, *Invisible Man* or *The Bill of Rights*. These titles may refer to the text, as we have been using the word, that is, to the pattern of inscribed signs to be found in physical written or printed form. More often, however, the intended reference is to "the work." But the work—ideas and experiences linked with the text—can be found only in individual readers' reflections on the reading event, the evocation and responses to it during and after the reading event.

Evocation

Thus far, we have focused on the aspects of the reading process centered on organizing a structure of elements of consciousness construed as the meaning of the text. I term this *the evocation* to cover both efferent and aesthetic transactions. The evocation, the work, is not a physical "object," but, given another sense of that word, the evocation can be an object of thought.

The Second Stream of Response

We must recognize during the reading event a concurrent stream of reactions to, and transactions with, the emerging evocation. Even as we are generating the evocation, we are reacting to it; this may in turn affect our choices as we proceed with the reading. Such responses may be momentary, peripheral, or felt simply as a general state, for example, an ambiance of acceptance or perhaps of confirmation of ideas and attitudes brought to the reading. Sometimes something unexpected or contrary to prior knowledge or assumptions may trigger conscious reflection. Something not prepared for by the preceding organization of elements may cause a rereading. The attention may shift from the evocation to the formal or technical traits of the text. The range of potential reactions and the gamut of degrees of intensity and articulateness depend on the interplay among the character of the signs on the page (the text), what the individual reader brings to it, and the circumstances of the transaction.

The various strands of response, especially in the middle ranges of the efferent–aesthetic continuum, are sometimes simultaneous, interacting, and interwoven. They may seem actually woven into the texture of the evocation itself. Hence, one of the problems of critical reading is differentiation of the evocation corresponding to the text from the concurrent responses, which may be projections from the reader's a priori assumptions. Drawing the line between them is easier in theory than in the practice of any actual reading. The reader needs to learn to handle such elements of the reading experience. The problem takes on different forms in efferent and aesthetic reading.

Expressed Response

"Response" to the evocation often is designed as subsequent to the reading event. Actually, the basis is laid during the reading, in the concurrent second stream of reactions. The reader may recapture the general effect of this after the event and may seek to express it and to recall what in the evocation led to the response. Reflection on "the meaning" of even a simple text involves the recall, the reactivation of some aspects of the process carried on during the reading. "Interpretation" tends to be a continuation of this effort to clarify the evocation.

The account of the reading process thus far has indicated an organizing, synthesizing activity, the creation of tentative meanings, and their modification as new elements enter into the focus of attention. In some instances, the reader at some point simply registers a sense of having completed a sequential activity and moves on to other concerns. Sometimes a sense of the whole structure crystallizes by the close of the reading.

Expressed Interpretation

Actually, the process of interpretation that includes arriving at a sense of the whole has not been given enough attention in theories of reading, perhaps because reading research has typically dealt with simple reading events. For the term *interpret*, dictionaries list, among others, several relevant meanings. One is "to set forth the meaning of; to elucidate, to explain." Another is "to construe, or understand in a particular way." A third is "to bring out the meaning of by performance (as in music)." These tend to reflect the traditional notion of "the meaning" as inherent in the text.

The transactional theory requires that we draw on all three of these usages to cover the way in which the term should be applied to the reading process. The evocation of meaning in transaction with a text is indeed interpretation in the sense of performance, and transactional theory merges this with the idea of interpretation as individual construal. The evocation then becomes the object of interpretation in the sense of elucidating or explaining. The expressed interpretation draws on all these aspects of the total transaction.

Interpretation can be understood as the effort to report, analyze, and explain the evocation. The reader recalls the sensed, felt, thought evocation while at the same time applying some frame of reference or method of abstracting in order to characterize it, to find the assumptions or organizing ideas that relate the parts to the whole. The second stream of reactions will be recalled, and the reasons for them sought, in the evoked work or in prior assumptions and knowledge. The evocation and the concurrent streams of reaction may be related through stressing, for example, the logic of the structure of ideas in an efferent evocation or the assumptions about people or society underlying the lived through experience of the aesthetic reading.

Usually, interpretation is expressed in the efferent mode, stressing underlying general ideas that link the signs of the text. Interpretation can take an aesthetic form, however, such as a poem, a painting, music, dramatization, or dance.

Interpretation brings with it the question of whether the reader has produced a meaning that is consonant with the author's probable intention. Here we find ourselves moving from the reader–text transaction to the relationship between author and reader. The process that produces the text will be considered before dealing with such matters as communication, validity of interpretation, and the implications of the transactional theory for teaching and research.

The Writing Process

The Writing Transaction

Writers facing a blank page, like readers approaching a text, have only their individual linguistic capital to draw on. For the writer, too, the residue of past experiences of language in particular situations provides the material from which the text will be constructed. As with the reader, any new meanings are restructurings or extensions of the stock of experiences the writer brings to the task. There is a continuing to-and-fro or transactional process as the writer looks at the page and adds to the text in the light of what has been written thus far.

An important difference between readers and writers should not be minimized, however. In the triadic sign–object–interpretant relationship, the reader has the physical pattern of signs to which to relate the symbolizations. The writer facing a blank page may start with only an organismic state, vague feelings and ideas that require further triadic definition before a symbolic configuration—a verbal text—can take shape.

Writing is always an event in time, occurring at a particular moment in the writer's biography, in particular circumstances, under particular external as well as internal pressures. In short, the writer is always transacting with a personal, social, and cultural environment. Thus, the writing process must be seen as always embodying both personal and social, or individual and environmental, factors.

Given the Peircean triadic view of the verbal symbol, the more accessible the fund of organismically linked words and referents, the more fluent the writing. This helps us place in perspective an activity such as free writing. Instead of treating it as a prescriptive "stage" of the writing process, as some seem to do, it should be seen as a technique for tapping the linguistic reservoir without being hampered by anxieties about acceptability of subject, sequence, or mechanics. Especially for those inhibited by unfortunate past writing experiences, this can be liberating, a warm-up exercise for starting the juices flowing, so to speak, and permitting elements of the experiential stream, verbal components of memory, and present concerns to rise to consciousness. The essential point is that the individual linguistic reservoir must be activated.

No matter how free and uninhibited the writing may be, the stream of images, ideas, memories, and words is not entirely random; William James reminds us that the "choosing activity" of selective attention operates to some degree. Like the reader, the writer needs to bring the selective process actively into play, to move toward a sense of some tentative focus for choice and synthesis (Emig, 1983).

This directedness will be fostered by the writer's awareness of the transactional situation: the context that initiates the need to write and the potential reader or readers to whom the text will presumably be addressed. Often in trial-and-error fashion, and through various freely flowing drafts, the writer's sensitivity to such factors translates itself into an increasingly clear impulse that guides selective attention and integration. For the experienced writer, the habit of such awareness, monitoring the multifold decisions or choices that make up the writing event, is more important than any explicit preliminary statement of goals or purpose.

The Writer's Stance

The concept of stance presented earlier in relation to reading is equally important for writing. A major aspect of the delimitation of purpose in writing is the adoption of a stance that falls at some point in the efferent–aesthetic continuum. The attitude toward what is activated in the linguistic–experiential reservoir manifests itself in the range and character of the verbal symbols that will "come to mind," and to which the writer will apply selective attention. The dominant stance determines the proportion of public and private aspects of sense that will be included in the scope of the writer's attention (see Figure 1).

In actual life, the selection of a predominant stance is not arbitrary but is a function of the circumstances, the writer's motives, the subject, and the relation between writer and prospective reader or readers. For example, someone who had been involved in an automobile collision would need to adopt very different stances in writing an account of the event for an insurance company and in describing it in a letter to a friend. The first would activate an efferent selective process, bringing into the center of consciousness and onto the page the public aspects, such as statements that could be verified by witnesses or by investigation of the terrain. In the letter to the friend, the purpose would be to share an experience. An aesthetic stance would bring within the scope of the writer's attention the same basic facts, together with feelings, sensations, tensions, images, and sounds lived through during this brush with death. The selective process would favor words that matched the writer's inner sense of the felt event and that also would activate in the prospective reader symbolic linkages evoking a similar experience. Given different purposes, other accounts might fall at other points of the efferent–aesthetic continuum.

Purpose or intention should emerge from, or be capable of constructively engaging, the writer's actual experiential and linguistic resources. Past experience need not be the limit of the writer's scope, but the writer faced with a blank page needs "live" ideas—that is, ideas having a strongly energizing linkage with the linguistic–experiential reservoir. Purposes or ideas that lack the capacity to connect with the writer's funded experience and present concerns cannot fully activate the linguistic reservoir and provide an impetus to thinking and writing.

A personally grounded purpose develops and impels movement forward. Live ideas growing out of situations, activities, discussions, problems, or needs provide the basis for an actively selective and synthesizing process of making meaning. The quickened fund of images, ideas, emotions, attitudes, and tendencies to act offers the means of making new connections, for discovering new facets of the world of objects and events, in short, for thinking and writing creatively.

Writing About Texts

When a reader describes, responds to, or interprets a work—that is, speaks or writes about a transaction with a text—a new text is being produced. The implications of this fact in terms of process should be more fully understood. When the reader becomes a writer about a work, the starting point is no longer the physical text, the marks on the page, but the meaning or the state of mind felt to correspond to that text. The reader may return to the original text to recapture how it entered into the transaction but must "find words" for explaining the evocation and the interpretation.

The reader-turned-writer must once again face the problem of choice of stance. In general, the choice seems to be the efferent stance. The purpose is mainly to explain, analyze, summarize, and categorize the evocation. This is usually true even when the reading has been predominantly aesthetic and a literary work of art is being discussed. However, the aesthetic stance might be adopted in order to communicate an experience expressing the response or the interpretation. An efferent reading of, for example, the U.S. Declaration of Independence might lead to a poem or a story. An aesthetic reading of the text of a poem might also lead, not to an efferently written critical essay, but to another poem, a painting, or a musical composition.

The translator of a poem is a clear example of the reader-turned-writer, being first a reader who evokes an experience through a transaction in one language and then a writer who seeks to express that experience through a writing transaction in another language. The experiential qualities generated in a transaction with one language must now be communicated to—evoked by—readers who have a different linguistic–experiential reservoir, acquired in a different culture.

Authorial Reading

Thus far, we have been developing parallels between the ways in which readers and writers select and synthesize elements from the personal linguistic reservoir, adopt stances that guide selective attention, and build a developing selective purpose. Emphasis has fallen mainly on similarities in composing structures of meaning related to texts. If readers arc in that sense also writers, it is equally— and perhaps more obviously—true that writers also must be readers. At this point, however, some differences within the parallelisms begin to appear.

The writer, it is generally recognized, is the first reader of the text. Note an obvious, though neglected, difference: While readers transact with a writer's finished text, writers first read the text as it is being inscribed. Because both reading and writing are recursive processes carried on over a period of time, their very real similarities have masked a basic difference. The writer will often reread the total finished text, but, perhaps more important, the writer first reads and carries on a spiral, transactional relationship with the very text emerging on the page. This is a different kind of reading. It is authorial—a writer's reading. It should be seen as an integral part of the composing process. In fact, it is necessary to see that writing, or composing, a text involves *two* kinds of authorial reading, which I term *expression oriented* and *reception oriented*.

Expression-Oriented Authorial Reading

As a reader's eyes move along a printed text, the reader develops an organizing principle or framework. The newly evoked symbolizations are tested for whether they can be fitted into the tentative meanings already constructed for the preceding portion of the text. If the new signs create a problem, this may lead to a revision of the framework or even to a complete rereading of the text and restructuring of the attributed meaning.

The writer, like readers of another's text, peruses the succession of verbal signs being inscribed on the page to see whether the new words fit the preceding text. But this is a different, expression-oriented reading, which should be seen as an integral part of the composing process. As the new words appear on the page, they must be tested, not simply for how they make sense with the preceding text but also against an inner gauge—the intention, or purpose. The emerging meaning, even if it makes sense, must be judged as to whether it serves or hinders the purpose, however nebulous and inarticulate, that is the motive power in the writing. Expression-oriented authorial reading leads to revision even during the earlier phases of the writing process.

The Inner Gauge

Most writers will recall a situation that may illustrate the operation of an "inner gauge." A word comes to mind or flows from the pen and, even if it makes sense, is felt not to be right. One word after another may be brought into consciousness and still not satisfy. Sometimes the writer understands what is wrong with the word on the page—perhaps that it is ambiguous or does not suit the tone. But often the writer cannot articulate the reason for dissatisfaction. The tension simply disappears when "the right word" presents itself. When it does, a match between inner state and verbal sign has happened.

Such an episode manifests the process of testing against an inner touchstone. The French writer Gustave Flaubert with his search for *le mot juste*, the exact word, offers the analogy of the violinist who tries to make his fingers "reproduce precisely those sounds of which he has the inward sense" (1926, pp. 11, 47). The inner gauge may be an organic state, a mood, an idea, perhaps even a consciously constituted set of guidelines.

For the experienced writer, this kind of completely inner-oriented reading, which is integral to the composing process, depends on and nourishes an increasingly clear though often tacit sense of purpose, whether efferent or aesthetic. The writer tries to satisfy a personal conception while also refining it. Such transactional reading and revision can go on throughout the writing event. There are indeed times when this is the *only* reading component—when one writes for oneself alone, to express or record an experience in a diary or journal, or perhaps to analyze a situation or the pros and cons of a decision.

Reception-Oriented Authorial Reading

Usually, however, writing is felt to be part of a potential transaction with other readers. At some point, the writer dissociates from the text and reads it through the eyes of potential readers; the writer tries to judge the meaning *they* would make in transaction with that pattern of signs. But the writer does not simply adopt the "eyes" of the potential reader. Again, a twofold operation is involved. The emerg-

ing text is read to sense what others might make of it. But this hypothetical interpretation must also be checked against the writer's own inner sense of purpose.

The tendency has been to focus on writing with an eye on the anticipated
reader. My concern is to show the interplay between the two kinds of authorial
reading and the need, consciously or automatically, to decide the degree of emphasis on one or the other. The problem always is to find verbal signs likely to activate linkages in prospective readers' linguistic reservoirs matching those of
the writer. A poet may be faced with the choice between a personally savored exotic metaphor and one more likely to be within the experience of prospective
readers. Or a science writer may have to decide whether highly detailed precision
may be too complex for the general reader.

Writers must already have some hold on the first, expression-oriented
kind of inner awareness if they are to benefit from the second reading through the
eyes of others. The first becomes a criterion for the second. The experienced
writer will probably engage in a synthesis, or rapid alternation, of the two kinds
of authorial reading to guide the selective attention that filters out the verbal elements coming to mind. When communication is the aim, revision should be
based on such double criteria in the rereading of the text.

Communication Between Author and Readers

The reader's to-and-fro process of building an interpretation becomes a form of
transaction with an author persona sensed through and behind the text. The implied relationship is sometimes even termed "a contract" with the author. The
closer their linguistic–experiential equipment, the more likely the reader's interpretation will fulfill the writer's intention. Sharing at least versions of the same
language is so basic that it often is simply assumed. Other positive factors affecting communication are contemporary membership in the same social and cultural group, the same educational level, and membership in the same discourse
community, such as academic, legal, athletic, literary, scientific, or theological.
Given such similarities, the reader is more likely to bring to the text the prior
knowledge, acquaintance with linguistic and literary conventions, and assumptions about social situations required for understanding implications or allusions
and noting nuances of tone and thought.

Yet, because each individual's experience is unique, differences due to
social, ethnic, educational, and personal factors exist, even with contemporaries.
The reading of works written in another period bespeaks an inevitable difference in linguistic, social, or cultural context. Here, especially, readers may agree
on interpretations without necessarily assuming that their evocations from the
text fit the author's intention (Rosenblatt, 1978, p. 109ff).

Differences as to the author's intention often lead to consultation of extra-
textual sources. For works of the past especially, scholars call on systematic

methods of philological, biographical, and historical research to discover the personal, social, and literary forces that shaped the writer's intention. The contemporary reception of the work also provides clues. Such evidence, even if it includes an author's stated intention, still yields hypothetical results and cannot dictate our interpretation. We must still read the text to decide whether it supports the hypothetical intention. The reader is constantly faced with the responsibility of deciding whether an interpretation is acceptable. The question of validity of interpretation must be faced before considering implications for teaching and research.

Validity of Interpretation

The problem of validity of interpretation has not received much attention in reading theory or educational methodology. Despite the extraordinary extent of the reliance on testing in our schools, there seems to be little interest in clarifying the criteria that enter into evaluation of "comprehension." Actual practice in the teaching of reading and in the instruments for testing of reading ability has evidently been tacitly based on, or at least has indoctrinated, the traditional assumption that there is a single determinate "correct" meaning attributable to each text. The stance factor, the efferent–aesthetic continuum, has especially been neglected; operationally, the emphasis has been on the efferent, even when "literature" was involved.

The polysemous character of language invalidates any simplistic approach to meaning, creating the problem of the relationship between the reader's interpretation and the author's intention. The impossibility of finding a single absolute meaning for a text or of expecting any interpretation absolutely to reflect the writer's intention is becoming generally recognized by contemporary theorists. "Intention" itself is not absolutely definable or delimitable even by the writer. The word *absolute*, the notion of a single "correct" meaning inherent "in" the text, is the stumbling block. The same text takes on different meanings in transactions with different readers or even with the same reader in different contexts or times.

Warranted Assertibility

The problem of the validity of any interpretation is part of the broader philosophical problem cited at the beginning of this piece. Perception of the world is always through the medium of individual human beings transacting with their worlds. In recent decades, some literary theorists, deriving their arguments from poststructuralist Continental writers and taking a Saussurean view of language as an autonomous system, have arrived at an extreme relativist position. They have developed a reading method that assumes all texts can be "deconstructed" to reveal inner contradictions. Moreover, the language system and literary conventions are said to completely dominate author and reader, and agreement concerning interpretation simply reflects the particular "interpretive community" in which we find ourselves (Fish, 1980; Rosenblatt, 1991).

Such extreme relativism is not, however, a necessary conclusion from the premise that absolutely determinate meaning is impossible. By agreeing on criteria of evaluation of interpretations, we can accept the possibility of alternative interpretations yet decide that some are more acceptable than others.

John Dewey, accepting the nonfoundationalist epistemological premises and foregoing the quest for absolutes, solved the scientists' problem by his idea of "warranted assertibility" as the end of controlled inquiry (1938, pp. 9, 345). Given shared criteria concerning methods of investigation and kinds of evidence there can be agreement concerning the decision as to what is a sound interpretation of the evidence, or "a warranted assertion." This is not set forth as permanent, absolute truth, but leaves open the possibility that alternative explanations for the same facts may be found, that new evidence may be discovered, or that different criteria or paradigms may be developed.

Although Dewey used primarily scientific interpretation or knowledge of the world based on scientific methods to illustrate warranted assertibility, he saw the concept as encompassing the arts and all human concerns. It can be applied to the problem of all linguistic interpretation (Rosenblatt, 1978, chap. 7; 1983, p. 151ff). Given a shared cultural milieu and shared criteria of validity of interpretation, we can, without claiming to have the single "correct" meaning of a text, agree on an interpretation. Especially in aesthetic reading, we may find that alternative interpretations meet our minimum criteria, and we can still be free to consider some interpretations superior to others.

In contrast to the notion of readers locked into a narrow "interpretive community," the emphasis on making underlying or tacit criteria explicit provides the basis not only for agreement but also for understanding tacit sources of disagreement. This creates the possibility of change in interpretation, acceptance of alternative sets of criteria, or revision of criteria. Such self-awareness on the part of readers can foster communication across social, cultural, and historical differences between author and readers, as well as among readers (Rosenblatt, 1983).

In short, the concept of warranted assertibility, or shared criteria of validity of interpretation in a particular social context, recognizes that some readings may satisfy the criteria more fully than others. Basic criteria might be (1) that the context and purpose of the reading event, or the total transaction, be considered; (2) that the interpretation not be contradicted by, or not fail to cover, the full text, the signs on the page; and (3) that the interpretation not project meanings which cannot be related to signs on the page. Beyond these items arise criteria for interpretation and evaluation growing out of the whole structure of shared cultural, social, linguistic, and rhetorical assumptions.

Thus, we can be open to alternative readings of the text of *Hamlet*, but we also can consider some readings as superior to others according to certain explicit criteria, for example, complexity of intellectual and affective elements and nature of implicit value system. Such considerations permit comparison and "negotiation" among different readers of the same text as well as clarification of differences in assumptions concerning what constitutes a valid interpretation (Rosenblatt, 1978, 1983). On the efferent side of the continuum, current discussions of alternative criteria for interpretation of the U.S. Constitution provide another complex example.

Criteria for the Efferent–Aesthetic Continuum

Precisely because, as Figure 1 indicates, both public and private elements are present in all reading, the criteria of validity of interpretation differ for readings at various points on the efferent–aesthetic continuum. Because the predominantly efferent interpretation must be publicly verifiable or justifiable, the criteria of validity rest primarily on the public, referential aspects of meaning and require that any affective and associational aspects not dominate. The criteria for the predominantly aesthetic reading call for attention to the referential, cognitive aspects but only as they are interwoven and colored by the private, affective, or experiential aspects generated by the author's patterns of signs. Especially in the middle ranges of the efferent–aesthetic continuum, it becomes important for writers to provide clear indications as to stance and for readers to be sensitive to the writer's purpose and the need to apply relevant criteria.

"Literary" Aspects of Efferent Reading

In recent decades, in one scientific field after another, the opposition between scientific and "literary" writing has been found to be illusory. Writers in the natural and social sciences have become aware of the extent to which they engage in semantic and syntactic practices that have usually been considered "literary" and that they, too, have been using narrative, metaphor, and other rhetorical devices. Examples are the importance of metaphor in writings about economics or the idea that the historian writes narrative and that he can never be completely objective in selecting his facts. Sensitivity to sexist and racist tropes has increased awareness of the extent to which metaphor permeates all kinds of texts and, indeed, all language. Sometimes the efferent–aesthetic distinction seems to be completely erased (for example, the historian is sometimes said to write "fiction").

It becomes necessary to recall that the stance reflecting the aesthetic or efferent purpose, not the syntactic and semantic devices alone, determines the appropriate criteria. For example, in a treatise on economics or a history of the frontier, the criteria of validity of interpretation appropriate to their disciplines, which involve primarily verifiability and logic, would still apply. When an economist remarks that "the scientists had better devise good metaphors and tell good stories" (McCloskey, 1985), the concept of a dominant stance becomes all the more essential. The criteria for "good" should be not only how vivid and appealing the stories are but also how they gibe with logic and facts and what value systems are implied.

The relevance of the efferent–aesthetic continuum (Figure 1) may be illustrated by the example of metaphor: The scientist speaks of the "wave" theory of light, and we focus on the technical concept at the extreme efferent end of the continuum. Shakespeare writes, "Like as the wave makes toward the pebbled shore / So do our minutes hasten to their end," and our aesthetic attention to the feeling of inevitability of the succeeding waves enhances the feeling of the inevitability of the passage of time in our lives. A political analysis suggested surrendering to the inevitability of fascism by calling it "the wave of the future.... There is no fighting it" (Lindbergh, 1940, p. 934). Despite the vividness of the metaphor, efferent attention should have remained dominant, applying the efferent criterion. Did logic and factual evidence support the persuasive appeal?

Implications for Teaching

Reading and Writing: Parallelisms and Differences

Parallelisms between reading and writing processes have raised questions concerning their connections, especially in the classroom. The reading and writing processes both overlap and differ. Both reader and writer engage in constituting symbolic structures of meaning in a to-and-fro, spiral transaction with the text. They follow similar patterns of thinking and call on similar linguistic habits. Both processes depend on the individual's past experiences with language in particular life situations. Both reader and writer therefore are drawing on past linkages of signs, signifiers, and organic states in order to create new symbolizations, new linkages, and new organic states. Both reader and writer develop a framework, principle, or purpose, however nebulous or explicit, that guides the selective attention and the synthesizing, organizing activities that constitute meaning. Moreover, every reading and writing act can be understood as falling somewhere on the efferent–aesthetic continuum and as being predominantly efferent or aesthetic.

The parallels should not mask the basic differences—the transaction that starts with a text produced by someone else is not the same as a transaction that starts with the individual facing a blank page. To an observer, two people perusing a typed page may seem to be doing the same thing (namely, "reading"). But if one of them is in the process of writing that text, different activities will be going on. The writer will be engaged in either expression-oriented or reception-oriented authorial reading. Moreover, because both reading and writing are rooted in mutually conditioning transactions between individuals and their particular environments, a person may have very different experiences with the two activities, may differ in attitudes toward them, and may be more proficient in one or the other. Writing and reading are sufficiently different to defeat the assumption that they are mirror images: The reader does not simply reenact the author's process. Hence, it cannot be assumed that the teaching of one activity automatically improves the student's competence in the other.

Still, the parallels in the reading and writing processes described above and the nature of the transaction between author and reader make it reasonable to expect that the teaching of one can affect the student's operations in the other. Reading, essential to anyone for intellectual and emotional enrichment, provides the writer with a sense of the potentialities of language. Writing deepens the reader's understanding of the importance of paying attention to diction, syntactic positions, emphasis, imagery, and conventions of genre. The fact that the sign–interpretant–object triad is, as Peirce said, dependent on habit indicates an even more important level of influence. Cross-fertilization will result from reinforcement of linguistic habits and thinking patterns resulting from shared transactional processes of purposive selective attention and synthesis. How fruitful the interplay between the individual student's writing and reading will be depends largely on the nature of the teaching and the educational context.

The Total Context

Here we return to our basic concept that human beings are always in transaction and in a reciprocal relationship with an environment, a context, a total situation. The classroom environment, or the atmosphere created by the teacher and students transacting with one another and the school setting, broadens out to include the whole institutional, social, and cultural context. These aspects of the transaction are crucial in thinking about education and especially the "literacy problem." Because each individual's linguistic–experiential reservoir is the residue of past transactions with the environment, such factors condition the sense of possibilities, or the potential organizing frameworks or schema and the knowledge and assumptions about the world, society, human nature, that each brings to the transactions. Socioeconomic and ethnic factors, for example, influence patterns of behavior, ways of carrying out tasks, even understanding of such concepts as "story" (Heath, 1983). Such elements also affect the individual's attitude toward self, toward the reading or writing activity, and toward the purpose for which it is being carried on.[3]

The transactional concept of the text always in relation either to author or reader in specific situations makes it untenable to treat the text as an isolated entity or to overemphasize either author or reader. Recognizing that language is not a self-contained system or static code on the one hand avoids the traditional obsession with the product—with skills, techniques, and conventions, essential though they are—and, on the other, prevents a pendulum swing to overemphasis on process or on the personal aspects.

Treatment of either reading or writing as a dissociated set of skills (though both require skills) or as primarily the acquisition of codes and conventions (though both involve them) inhibits sensitivity to the organic linkages of verbal signs and their objects. Manipulating syntactic units without a sense of a context that connects them into a meaningful relationship may in the long run be counterproductive.

Nor can the transactional view of the reading and writing processes be turned into a set of stages to be rigidly followed. The writer's drafts and final texts—or the reader's tentative interpretations, final evocation, and reflections—should be viewed as stopping points in a journey, as the outward and visible signs of a continuing process in the passage from one point to the other. A "good" product, whether a well-written paper or a sound textual interpretation, should not be an end in itself—a terminus—but should be the result of a process that builds the strengths for further journeys or, to change the metaphor, for further growth. "Product" and "process" become interlocking concerns in nurturing growth.

Hence, the teaching of reading and writing at any developmental level should have as its first concern the creation of environments and activities in which students are motivated and encouraged to draw on their own resources to make "live" meanings. With this as the fundamental criterion, emphasis falls on strengthening the basic processes that we have seen to be shared by reading and writing. The teaching of one can then reinforce linguistic habits and semantic approaches useful in the other. Such teaching, concerned with the ability of the individual to generate meaning, will permit constructive cross-fertilization of the reading and writing (and speech) processes.

Enriching the individual's linguistic–experiential reservoir becomes an underlying educational aim broader than the particular concern with either reading or writing. Especially in the early years, the linkage between verbal sign and experiential base is essential. The danger is that many current teaching practices may counteract the very processes presumably being taught. The organization of instruction, the atmosphere in the classroom, the kinds of questions asked, the ways of phrasing assignments, and the types of tests administered should be scrutinized from this point of view.

The importance of a sense of purpose, of a guiding principle of selection and organization in both writing and reading, is being increasingly recognized. The creation of contexts that permit purposive writing and reading can enable the student to build on past experience of life and language, to adopt the appropriate stance for selective attention, and to develop inner gauges or frameworks for choice and synthesis that produce new structures of live meaning.

Collaborative Interchange

In a favorable educational environment, speech is a vital ingredient of transactional pedagogy. Its importance in the individual's acquisition of a linguistic–experiential capital is clear. It can be an extremely important medium in the classroom. Dialogue between teacher and students and interchange among students can foster growth and cross-fertilization in both the reading and writing processes. Such discussion can help students develop insights concerning transactions with texts as well as metalinguistic understanding of skills and conventions in meaningful contexts.

Students' achievement of insight into their own reading and writing processes can be seen as the long-term justification for various curricular and teaching strategies. For example, writers at all levels can be helped to understand their transactional relationship to their readers by peer reading and discussion of texts. Their fellow students' questions, varied interpretations, and misunderstandings dramatize the necessity of the writer's providing verbal signs that will help readers gain required facts, share relevant sensations or attitudes, or make logical transitions. Such insights make possible the second, reader-oriented authorial reading.

Similarly, group interchange about readers' evocations from texts, whether of their peers or adult authors, can in general be a powerful means of stimulating growth in reading ability and critical acumen. Readers become aware of the need to pay attention to the author's words in order to avoid preconceptions and misinterpretations. When students share responses to transactions with the same text, they can learn how their evocations from the same signs differ, can return to the text to discover their own habits of selection and synthesis, and can become aware of, and critical of, their own processes as readers. Interchange about the problems of interpretation that a particular group of readers encounters and a collaborative movement toward self-critical interpretation of the text can lead to the development of critical concepts and interpretive criteria. Such metalinguistic awareness is valuable to students as both readers and writers.

The teacher in such a classroom is no longer simply a conveyor of ready-made teaching materials and recorder of results of ready-made tests or a dispenser of ready-made interpretations. Teaching becomes constructive, facilitating interchange, helping students to make their spontaneous responses the basis for raising questions and growing in the ability to handle increasingly complex reading transactions (Rosenblatt, 1983).[4]

The Student's Efferent–Aesthetic Repertory

The efferent–aesthetic continuum, or the two basic ways of looking at the world, should be part of the student's repertory from the earliest years. Because both stances involve cognitive and affective as well as public and private elements, students need to learn to differentiate the circumstances that call for one or the other stance. Unfortunately, much current practice is counterproductive, either failing to encourage a definite stance or implicitly requiring an inappropriate one. Favorite illustrations are the third-grade workbook that prefaced its first poem with the question "What facts does this poem teach you?" and the boy who complained that he wanted information about dinosaurs, but his teacher only gave him "storybooks." Small wonder that graduates of our schools (and colleges) often read poems and novels efferently or respond to political statements and advertisements with an aesthetic stance.

Despite the overemphasis on the efferent in our schools, failure to understand the matter of the public–private "mix" has prevented successful teaching even of efferent reading and writing. Teaching practices and curriculums, from the very beginning, should include both efferent and aesthetic linguistic activity and should build a sense of the different purposes involved. Instruction should foster the habits of selective attention and synthesis that draw on relevant elements in the semantic reservoir and should nourish the ability to handle the mix of private and public aspects appropriate to a particular transaction.

Especially in the early years, this should be done largely indirectly, through, for example, choice of texts, contexts for generating writing and reading, or implications concerning stance in the questions asked. In this way, texts can serve dynamically as sources from which to assimilate a sense of the potentialities of the English sentence and an awareness of strategies for organizing meaning and expressing feeling. Emphasis on analysis of the evocations, or terminology for categorizing and describing them, has no value if they overshadow or substitute for the evoked work. Such activities acquire meaning and value when, for example, they answer a writer's own problems in expression or explain for a reader the role of the author's verbal strategies in producing a certain felt response.

The developmental sequence suggested here is especially important in aesthetic reading. Much teaching of poetry at every level, including high school and college, at present takes on a continuously repeated remedial character because of the continued confusion about stance through emphasis on efferent analysis of the "literary" work. Students need to be helped to have unimpeded aesthetic experiences. Very young children's delight in the sound and rhythms of words, their interest in stories, and their ability to move easily from verbal to other modes of expression too often fade. They need to be helped to hold on to the experiential aspect. When this can be taken for granted, efferent, analytical discussions of form or background will not be substitutes for the literary work but become a means of enhancing it. Discussion then can become the basis for assimilating criteria of sound interpretation and evaluation appropriate to the various points on the continuum and to the student's developmental status.

Implications for Research

Research based on the transactional model has a long history (Applebee, 1974; Farrell & Squire, 1990). Until fairly recently, it has generated research mainly by those concerned with the teaching of literature in high schools and colleges, rather than by those concerned with reading per se in the elementary school (Beach & Hynds, 1990; Flood et al., 1991; Purves & Beach, 1972). It is not possible here to survey this already considerable body of research, much of it exploring aspects of response to literature; nor does space allow discussion of recent volumes dealing with applications of transactional theory in elementary school, high school, and college (Clifford, 1991; Cox & Many, 1992; Hungerford, Holland, & Ernst, 1993; Karolides, 1992). I shall instead suggest some general considerations concerning research topics and theoretical and methodological pitfalls.

The transactional model of reading, writing, and teaching that has been presented constitutes, in a sense, a body of hypotheses to be investigated. The shift it represents from the Cartesian to the post-Einsteinian paradigm calls for removal of the limitations on research imposed by the dominance of positivistic behaviorism. Instead of mainly treating reading as a compendium of separate skills or as an isolated autonomous activity, research on any aspect should center on the human being speaking, writing, reading, and continuously transacting with a specific environment in its broadening circles of context. And as Bartlett (1932) reminds us, any secondary theoretical frameworks, such as schemata or strategies, are not stable entities but configurations in a dynamic, changing process. Although the focus here will be on reading research, the interrelationship among the linguistic modes, especially reading and writing, broadens the potential scope of problems mentioned.

The view of language as a dynamic system of meaning in which the affective and the cognitive unite raises questions about the emphasis of past research. Researchers' preoccupation with the efferent is exemplified by their focus on Piaget's work on the child's development of mathematical and logical concepts and the continuing neglect of the affective by behaviorist, cognitive, and artificial intelligence psychologists. This is slowly being counterbalanced by growing interest in the affective and the qualitative (e.g., Deese, 1973; Eisner & Peshkin, 1990; Izard, 1977). We need to understand more fully the child's growth in capacity for selective attention to, and synthesis of, the various components of meaning.

Research in reading should draw on a number of interrelated disciplines, such as physiology, sociology, and anthropology, and should converge with the general study of human development. The transactional theory especially raises questions that involve such broad connections. Also, the diverse subcultures and ethnic backgrounds represented by the student population and the many strands that contribute to a democratic culture present a wide range of questions for research about reading, teaching, and curriculum.

Developmental Processes

The adult capacity to engage in the tremendously complex process of reading depends ultimately on the individual's long developmental process, starting with "learning how to mean" (Halliday, 1975; Rosenblatt, 1985b). How does the child move from the earliest, undifferentiated state of the world to "the referential, emotive and associative part processes" (Rommetveit, 1968, p. 167)? Developmental research can throw light on the relation of cognitive and emotional aspects in the growth of the ability to evoke meaning in transactions with texts.

Research is needed to accumulate systematic understanding of the positive environmental and educational factors that do justice to the essential nature of both efferent and aesthetic linguistic behavior, and to the role of the affective or private aspects of meaning in both stances. How can children's sensorimotor explorations of their worlds be reinforced, their sensitivity to the sounds and qualitative overtones of language be maintained? In short, what can foster their capacity to apprehend in order to comprehend, or construct, the poem, story, or play? Much also remains to be understood about development of the ability to infer, or make logical connections, or, in short, to read efferently and critically.

How early in the child's development should the context of the transaction with the text create a purpose for one or the other dominant stance, or help the reader learn to adopt a stance appropriate to the situation? At different developmental stages, what should be the role or roles of reflection on the reading experience through spoken comments, writing, and the use of other media?

An overarching question is this: How can skills be assimilated in a context that fosters understanding of their relevance to the production of meaning? How can the young reader acquire the knowledge, intellectual frameworks, and sense of values that provide the connecting links for turning discrete verbal signs into meaningful constructs? The traditional methods of teaching and testing recognize the important functions of the symbolic system, the alphabetic and phonological elements (the "code"), and linguistic conventions by fragmenting processes into small quantifiable units. These are quantitatively and hence economically assessable. But do such methods set up habits and attitudes toward the written word that inhibit the process of inferring meaning, or organizing and synthesizing, that enters into even simple reading tasks? How can we prepare the way for increasingly rich and demanding transactions with texts?

Performance

Assessment of performance level is usually required as a means of assuring the accountability of the school. Whether standardized tests accurately measure the student's ability is currently being called into question. Research on correlation of reading ability with factors such as age, gender, ethnic and socioeconomic background, and so on has confirmed the expectation that they are active factors. However, such research reports a state of affairs that is interpreted according to varying assumptions, not all conducive to the development of mature readers and writers. The transactional emphasis on the total context of the reading act reinforces the democratic concern with literacy and supports the call for vigorous political and social reform of negative environmental factors. At the same time teachers must recognize that the application of quantitatively based group labels to individual students may unfairly create erroneous expectations that become self-fulfilling prophecies.

Teaching Methods

In the current transition away from traditional teaching methods, there is the danger that inappropriate research designs may be invoked to evaluate particular teaching methods. What criteria of successful teaching and what assumptions about the nature of linguistic processes underlie the research design and the methods of measurement? Any interpretations of results should take into account the various considerations concerning reader, text, and context set forth in the transactional model.

Results of research assessing different teaching methods raise an important question: Did the actual teaching conform to the formulaic labels attached to the methods being compared? The vagueness of a term such as *reader-response method* can illustrate the importance of more precise understanding of the actual teaching processes being tested in a particular piece of research. The same term has been applied to teachers who, after eliciting student responses to a story, fall back on habitual methods of demonstrating the "correct" interpretation and to teachers who make the responses the beginning of a process of helping students grow in their ability to arrive at sound, self-critical interpretations.

Much remains to be done to develop operational descriptions of the approaches being compared. Studies are needed of how teachers lead, or facilitate, without dominating or dictating. Ethnographic study of classroom dynamics, records of interchange among teacher and students, videotapes of classrooms, and analyses of text give substance to test results.

Response

Students' empirical responses to a text (mainly written protocols) form the basis of much of the research on methods generally referred to as reader response or transactional. (The term *response* should be understood to cover multiple activities.) Protocols provide indirect evidence about the students' evocation, the work as experienced, and reactions to it. Such research requires a coherent system of analysis of students' written or oral reports. What evidence, for example, is there that the reading of a story has been predominantly aesthetic?

The problem of empirical assessment of the student's aesthetic reading of a text offers particular difficulties, especially because no single "correct" interpretation or evaluation is posited. This requires setting up criteria of interpretation that reflect not only the presence of personal feelings and associations, which are only one component, but also their relationship to the other cognitive and attitudinal components. In short, the assessment must be based on clearly articulated criteria as to signs of growing maturity in handling personal response, relating to the evoked text, and use of personal and intertextual experience vis-à-vis the responses of others.

In order to provide a basis for statistical correlation, content analysis of protocols has been used largely to determine the components or aspects of response. The purpose is to distinguish personal feelings and attitudes from, for example, efferent, analytic references to the sonnet form. This requires a systematic set of categories, such as *The Elements of Writing About a Literary Work* (Purves & Rippere, 1968), which has provided a common basis for a large number of studies. As the emphasis on process has increased, refinements or alternatives have been devised. The need is to provide for study of the relationship among the various aspects of response, or the processes of selecting and synthesizing activities by which readers arrive at evocations and interpretations (Rosenblatt, 1985a). Qualitative methods of research at least should supplement, or perhaps should become the foundation for, any quantitative methods of assessing transactions with the written word.

Experimental designs that seek to deal with the development of the ability to handle some aspect of literary art should avoid methodologies and experimental tasks that instead serve to test efferent metalinguistic capacities. For example, levels of ability to elucidate metaphor or to retell stories may not reflect children's actual sensing or experiencing of metaphors or stories so much as their capacity to efferently abstract or categorize (Verbrugge, 1979).

The dependence on single instances of reading in assessing an individual's abilities is currently being called into question. The previous reminder that we are dealing with points in a continuing and changing developmental process is especially relevant. Habits are acquired and change slowly; it may be found that the effects of a change, for example, from traditional to response methods of teaching literature, cannot be assessed without allowing for a period of transition from earlier approaches and the continuation of the new approaches over time.

Basal readers have in the past offered especially clear examples of questions and exercises tacitly calling for an efferent stance toward texts labeled stories and poems. There has been little to help students assimilate and make automatic the aesthetic mode of relating to a text. Here, preparations for reading, the teacher's questions both before and after reading, and the mode of assessment, which powerfully influences teaching, should be scrutinized.

Studies that seek to generalize about the development of abilities by simultaneous testing of the different age levels have the problem of taking into account the factor of schooling. To what extent do changes in children's ability to retell or comment on the grammar of a story reflect schooling in the appropriate way to talk about a story? Similarly, to what extent are reported changing literary interests in the middle years not a reflection of personality changes but of too narrow definitions of *literary*?

Research Methodologies

The preceding discussion has centered on suggesting problems for research implied by the transactional model. Research methods or designs have been mentioned mainly in reference to their potentialities and limitations for providing kinds of information needed and to criteria for interpretation of data. Quantitatively based generalizations about groups are usually called for, but currently there is interest in clarifying the potentialities and limitations of both quantitative and qualitative research. Empirical experimental designs are being supplemented or checked by other research approaches, such as the case study (Birnbaum & Emig, 1991), the use of journals, interviews during or after the linguistic event, portfolios, and recordings in various media. Because the single episode test has various limitations, research in which researcher and teacher collaborate—or carefully planned research carried on by the teacher—provides the opportunity for extended studies. The transactional model especially indicates the value of ethnographic or naturalistic research because it deals with problems in the context of the ongoing life of individuals and groups in a particular cultural, social, and educational environment (Kantor, Kirby, & Goetz, 1981; Zaharlick & Green, 1991). The developmental emphasis also supports the call for longitudinal studies (Tierney, 1991). Interdisciplinary collaboration, desirable at any time, seems especially so for longitudinal studies. Research will need to be sufficiently complex, varied, and interlocking to do justice to the fact that reading is at once an intensely individual and an intensely social activity, an activity that from the earliest years involves the whole spectrum of ways of looking at the world.

Acknowledgments

I want to thank June Carroll Birnbaum and Roselmina Indrisano for reading this manuscript, and Nicholas Karolides and Sandra Murphy for reading earlier versions.

Notes

[1] The 1949 volume marks Dewey's choice of *transaction* to designate a concept present in his work since 1896. My own use of the term after 1950 applied to an approach developed from 1938 on.

[2] By 1981, *transactional theory*, *efferent stance*, and *aesthetic stance* were sufficiently current to be listed and were attributed to me in *A Dictionary of Reading and Related Terms* (Harris & Hodges, 1981). But the often confused usage of the terms led me to write "Viewpoints: Transaction Versus Interaction—A Terminological Rescue Operation" (1985).

[3] The transactional model of reading presented here covers the whole range of similarities and differences among readers and between author and reader. Always in the transaction between reader and text, activation of the reader's linguistic–experiential reservoir must be the basis for the construction of new meanings and new experiences; hence, the applicability to bilingual instruction and the reading of texts produced in other cultures.

[4] *Literature as Exploration* emphasizes the instructional process that can be built on the basis of personal evocation and response. Illustrations of classroom discussions and chapters such as "Broadening the Framework," "Some Basic Social Concepts," and "Emotion and Reason" indicate how the teacher can democratically moderate discussion and help students toward growth not only in ability to handle increasingly complex texts but also in personal, social, and cultural understanding.

References

Ames, A. (1955). *The nature of our perceptions, prehensions, and behavior*. Princeton, NJ: Princeton University Press.

Appenzeller, T. (1990, November/December). Undivided attention. *The Sciences*.

Applebee, A.N. (1974). *Tradition and reform in the teaching of English*. Urbana, IL: National Council of Teachers of English.

Bartlett, F.C. (1932). *Remembering: A study in experimental and social psychology*. London: Cambridge University Press.

Bates, E. (1979). *The emergence of symbols*. New York: Academic.

Beach, R., & Hynds, S. (1990). Research on response to literature. In E. Farrell & J.R. Squire (Eds.), *Transactions with literature* (pp. 131–205). Urbana, IL: National Council of Teachers of English.

Birnbaum, J., & Emig, J. (1991). Case study. In J. Flood, J.M. Jensen, D. Lapp, & J.R. Squire (Eds.), *Handbook of research on teaching the English language arts* (pp. 195–204). New York: Macmillan.

Blumenthal, A.L. (1977). *The process of cognition*. Englewood Cliffs, NJ: Prentice Hall.

Bohr, N. (1959). Discussion with Einstein. In P.A. Schilpp (Ed.), *Albert Einstein, Philosopher-Scientist* (p. 210). New York: HarperCollins.

Cantril, H., & Livingston, W.K. (1963). The concept of transaction in psychology and neurology. *Journal of Individual Psychology, 19,* 3–16.

Chomsky, N. (1968). *Language and mind*. New York: Harcourt Brace.

Clifford, J. (Ed.). (1991). *The experience of reading: Louise Rosenblatt and reader response theory*. Portsmouth, NH: Boynton/Cook.

Cox, C., & Many, J.E. (Eds.). (1992). *Reader's stance and literary understanding*. Norwood, NJ: Ablex.

Culler, J. (1982). *On deconstruction*. Ithaca, NY: Cornell University Press.

Damasio, A.R. (1989). The brain binds entities by multilingual activities for convergence zones. *Neural Computation, 1.*

Deese, J. (1973). Cognitive structure and affect in language. In P. Pliner & T. Alloway (Eds.), *Communication and affect*. New York: Academic.

Dewey, J. (1938). *Logic: The theory of inquiry*. New York: Henry Holt.

Dewey, J., & Bentley, A.F. (1949). *Knowing and the known*. Boston: Beacon.

Eisner, E.W., & Peshkin, A. (1990). *Qualitative inquiry in education: The continuing debate*. New York: Teachers College Press.

Emig, J. (1983). *The web of meaning*. Portsmouth, NH: Boynton/Cook.

Farrell, E., & Squire, J.R. (Eds.). (1990). *Transactions with literature*. Urbana, IL: National Council of Teachers of English.

Fish, S. (1980). *Is there a text in this class?* Cambridge, MA: Harvard University Press.

Flaubert, G. (1926). *Correspondance* (Vol. 2). Paris: Louis Conard.

Flood, J., Jensen, J.M., Lapp, D., & Squire, J.R. (Eds.). (1991). *Handbook of research on teaching the English language arts*. New York: Macmillan.

Halliday, M.A.K. (1975). *Learning how to mean*. New York: Elsevier.

Harris, T.L., & Hodges, R.E. (Eds.). (1981). *A dictionary of reading and related terms*. Newark, DE: International Reading Association.

Heath, S.B. (1983). *Ways with words: Language, life, and work in communities and classrooms*. Cambridge, UK: Cambridge University Press.

Hungerford, R., Holland, K., & Ernst, S. (Eds.). (1993). *Journeying: Children responding to literature*. Portsmouth, NH: Heinemann.

Izard, C.E. (1977). *Human emotions*. New York: Plenum.

James, W. (1890). *The principles of psychology* (2 vols.). New York: Henry Holt.

Kantor, K.J., Kirby, D.R., & Goetz, J.P. (1981). Research in context: Ethnographic studies in English education. *Research in the Teaching of English, 15*(4), 293–309.

Karolides, N.J. (Ed.). (1992). *Reader response in the classroom: Evoking and interpreting meaning in literature*. White Plains, NY: Longman.

Kuhn, T. (1970). *The structure of scientific revolutions* (2nd ed.). Chicago: University of Chicago Press.

Lindbergh, A.M. (1940). *The wave of the future*. New York: Harcourt Brace.

McCloskey, D. (1985). *The rhetoric of economics*. Madison: University of Wisconsin Press.

Miller, G.A., & Johnson-Laird, P.N. (1976). *Language and perception*. Cambridge, MA: Harvard University Press.

Myers, G. (1986). *William James: His life and thought*. New Haven, CT: Yale University Press.

Peirce, C.S. (1933, 1935). *Collected papers* (Vol. 3, Vol. 6) (P. Weiss & C. Hartshorne, Eds.). Cambridge, MA: Harvard University Press.

Purves, A.C., & Beach, R. (1972). *Literature and the reader: Research in response to literature*. Urbana, IL: National Council of Teachers of English.

Purves, A.C., & Rippere, V. (1968). *Elements of writing about a literary work: A study of response to literature*. Urbana, IL: National Council of Teachers of English.

Rommetveit, R. (1968). *Words, meanings, and messages*. New York: Academic.

Rosenblatt, L.M. (1978). *The reader, the text, the poem: The transactional theory of the literary work*. Carbondale: Southern Illinois University Press.

Rosenblatt, L.M. (1983). *Literature as exploration* (4th ed.). New York: Modern Language Association. (Original work published 1938)

Rosenblatt, L.M. (1985a). The transactional theory of the literary work: Implications for research. In C. Cooper (Ed.), *Researching response to literature and the teaching of literature*. Norwood, NJ: Ablex.

Rosenblatt, L.M. (1985b). Viewpoints: Transaction versus interaction—A terminological rescue operation. *Research in the Teaching of English, 19*, 96–107.

Rosenblatt, L.M. (1991). Literary theory. In J. Flood, J.M. Jensen, D. Lapp, & J.R. Squire (Eds.), *Handbook of research on teaching the English language arts* (pp. 57–62). New York: Macmillan.

Rosenblatt, L.M. (1993). The transactional theory: Against dualisms. *College English, 55*(4), 377–386.

Saussure, F. (1972). *Cours de linguistique générale*. Paris: Payot.

Tierney, R.J. (1991). Studies of reading and writing growth: Longitudinal research on literacy development. In J. Flood, J.M. Jensen, D. Lapp, & J.R. Squire (Eds.), *Handbook of research on teaching the English language arts* (pp. 176–194). New York: Macmillan.

Verbrugge, R.R. (1979). The primacy of metaphor in development. In E. Winner & H. Gardner (Eds.), *Fact, fiction, and fantasy in childhood*. San Francisco: Jossey-Bass.

Vygotsky, L.S. (1962). *Thought and language* (F. Hanmann & G. Vakar, Eds. & Trans.). Cambridge, MA: MIT Press.

Werner, H., & Kaplan, B. (1962). *Symbol formation*. New York: Wiley.

Zaharlick, A., & Green, J. (1991). Ethnographic research. In J. Flood, J.M. Jensen, D. Lapp, & J.R. Squire (Eds.), *Handbook of research on teaching the English language arts* (pp. 205–223). New York: Macmillan.

49

A New Framework for Understanding Cognition and Affect in Writing

John R. Hayes

Alan Newell (1990) described science as a process of approximation. One theory will replace another if it is seen as providing a better description of currently available data (pp. 13–14). Since the Hayes–Flower model of the writing process first appeared in 1980, a great many studies relevant to writing have been carried out and there has been considerable discussion about what a model of writing should include. My purpose here is to present a new framework for the study of writing—a framework that can provide a better description of current empirical findings than the 1980 model, and one that can, I hope, be useful for interpreting a wider range of writing activities than was encompassed in the 1980 model.

This writing framework is not intended to describe all major aspects of writing in detail. Rather, it is like a building that is being designed and constructed at the same time. Some parts have begun to take definite shape and are beginning to be usable. Other parts are actively being designed and still others have barely been sketched. The relations among the parts—the flow of traffic, the centers of activity—although essential to the successful functioning of the whole building, are not yet clearly envisioned. In the same way, the new framework includes parts that are fairly well developed—a model of revision that has already been successfully applied, as well as clearly structured models of planning and of text production. At the same time, other parts (such as the social and physical environments), though recognized as essential, are described only through incomplete and unorganized lists of observations and phenomena—the materials from which specific models may eventually be constructed.

My objective in presenting this framework is to provide a structure that can be useful for suggesting lines of research and for relating writing phenomena one to another. The framework is intended to be added to and modified as more is learned.

The 1980 Model

The original Hayes–Flower (1980) writing model owes a great deal to cognitive psychology and, in particular, to Herbert Simon. Simon's influence was quite direct. At the time Flower and I began our work on composition, I had been collaborating with Simon on a series of protocol studies exploring the processes by which people come to understand written problem texts. This research produced cognitive process models of two aspects of written text comprehension. The first, called UNDERSTAND, described the processes by which people build representations when reading a text (Hayes & Simon, 1974; Simon & Hayes, 1976), and the second, called ATTEND, characterized the processes by which people decide what is most important in the text (Hayes, Waterman, & Robinson, 1977). It was natural to extend the use of the protocol analysis technique and cognitive process models to written composition.

Figure 1 shows the Hayes–Flower model as it was originally proposed (Hayes & Flower, 1980). Figure 2 is a redrawing of the original model for purposes of graphic clarity. It is intended to better depict the intended relations in the original rather than as a substantive modification. In the redrawing, memory has been moved to indicate that it interacts with all three cognitive writing processes (*planning*, *translating*, and *revision*) and not just with planning—as some

FIGURE 1
The Hayes–Flower Model Proposed in 1980

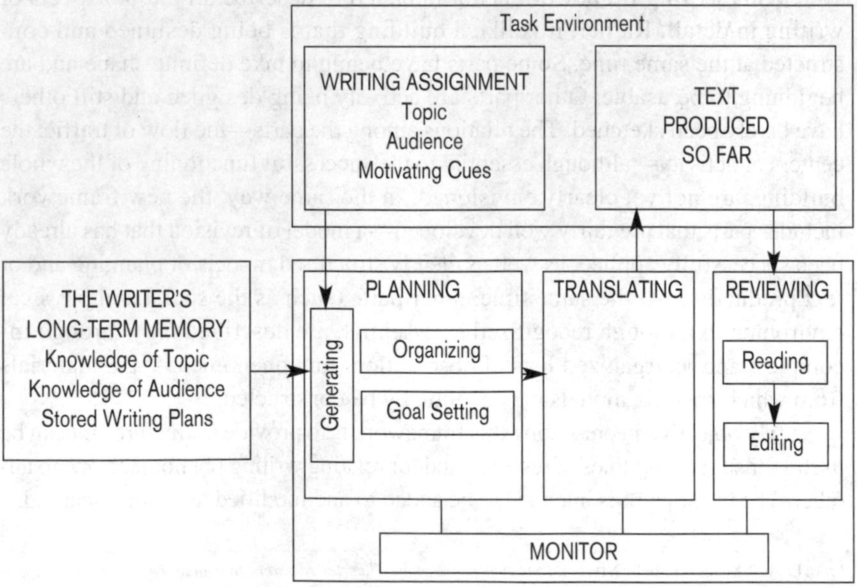

FIGURE 2
The Hayes–Flower Model (1980) Redrawn for Clarification

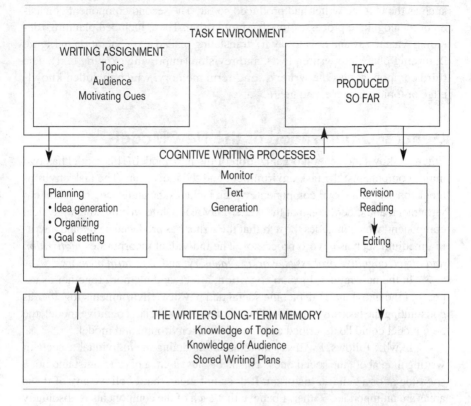

readers were led to believe. The names of the writing processes have been changed to those in more current use. Certain graphic conventions have been clarified. The boxes have been resized to avoid any unintended implication of differences in the relative importance of the processes. Arrows indicate the transfer of information. The process–subprocess relation has been indicated by including subprocesses within superprocesses. In the 1980 model, this convention for designating subprocesses was not consistently followed. In particular, in the original version, the monitor appeared as a box parallel in status to the three writing process boxes. Its relation to each process box was symbolized by undirected lines connecting it to the process boxes. As is apparent in the 1980 paper (pp. 19–20), the monitor was viewed as a process controlling the subprocesses: planning, sentence generation, and revising. Thus, in Figure 2, the monitor is shown as containing the writing subprocesses.

The model, as Figures 1 and 2 indicate, had three major components. First is the *task environment*; it includes all those factors influencing the writing task that lie outside the writer's skin. We saw the task environment as including both social factors, such as a teacher's writing assignment, as well as physical ones such as the text the writer had produced so far. The second component consisted of the cognitive processes involved in writing. These included planning (deciding what to say and how to say it), translating (called text generation in Figure 2, turning plans into written text), and revision (improving existing text). The third component was the writer's long-term memory, which included knowledge of topic, audience, and genre.

General Organization of the New Model

Figure 3 shows the general organization of the new model. This model has two major components: the task environment and the individual. The task environment consists of a social component, which includes the audience, the social environment, and other texts that the writer may read while writing, and a physical component, which includes the text that the writer has produced so far and a writing medium such as a word processor. The individual incorporates *motivation and affect*, *cognitive processes*, *working memory*, and *long-term memory*.

In the new model, I group cognition, affect, and memory together as aspects of the individual; I depict the social and physical environments together as constituting the task environment. Thus, rather than a social–cognitive model, the new model could be described as an individual–environmental model.

In what follows, I will say more about modeling the individual aspects of writing than about the social ones. This is because I am a psychologist and not a sociologist or a cultural historian. It does not mean that I believe any of these areas are unimportant. Rather, I believe that each of the components is absolutely essential for the full understanding of writing. Indeed, writing depends on an appropriate combination of cognitive, affective, social, and physical conditions if it is to happen at all. Writing is a communicative act that requires a social context and a medium. It is a generative activity requiring motivation, and it is an intellectual activity requiring cognitive processes and memory. No theory can be complete that does not include all of these components.

There are four major differences between the old model and the new. First, and most important, is the emphasis on the central role of working memory in writing. Second, the model includes visual–spatial as well as linguistic representations. Scientific journals, schoolbooks, magazines, newspapers, ads, and instruction manuals often include graphs, tables, or pictures that are essential for understanding the message of the text. If we want to understand many of the texts that we encounter every day, it is essential to understand their visual and spatial features. Third, a significant place is reserved for motivation and affect in the framework. As I will show, there is ample evidence that motivation and affect play central roles in writing processes. Finally, the cognitive process section of the model has undergone a major reorganization. Revision has been replaced by text interpretation; planning has been subsumed under the more general category, reflection; translation has been subsumed under a more general text production process.

FIGURE 3
The General Organization of the New Model

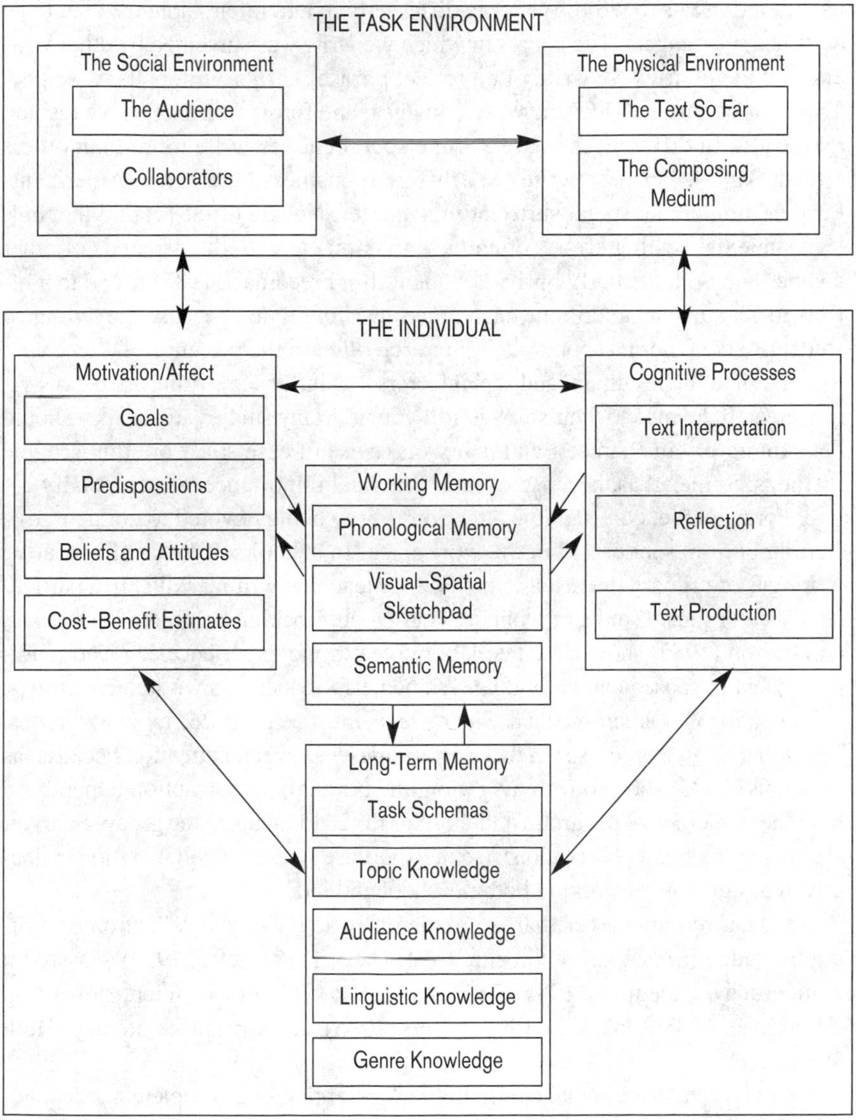

The Task Environment

The Social Environment

Writing is primarily a social activity. We write mostly to communicate with other humans. But the act of writing is not social just because of its communicative purpose. It is also social because it is a social artifact that is carried out in a social setting. What we write, how we write, and who we write to is shaped by social convention and by our history of social interaction. Our schools and our friends require us to write. We write differently to a familiar audience than to an audience of strangers. The genres in which we write were invented by other writers, and the phrases we write often reflect phrases earlier writers have written. Thus, our culture provides the words, images, and forms from which we fashion text. Cultural differences matter. Some social classes write more than others (Heath, 1983). Japanese write very different business letters than Americans. Further, immediate social surroundings matter. Nelson (1988) found that college students' writing efforts often have to compete with the demands of other courses and with the hurly burly of student life. Freedman (1987) found that efforts to get students to critique each others' writing failed because they violated students' social norms about criticizing each other in the presence of a teacher.

Although the cultural and social factors that influence writing are pervasive, the research devoted to their study is still young. Many studies are, as they should be, exploratory in character and many make use of case study or ethnographic methods. Some areas, because of their practical importance, are especially active. For example, considerable attention is now being devoted to collaborative writing both in school and in the workplace. In school settings, collaborative writing is of primary interest as a method for teaching writing skills. In a particularly well-designed study, O'Donnell, Dansereau, Rocklin, Lambiote, Hythecker, and Larson (1985) showed that collaborative writing experience can lead to improvement in subsequent individual writing performances. In workplace settings, collaboration is of interest because many texts must be produced by work groups. The collaborative processes in these groups deserve special attention because, as Hutchins (1995) showed for navigation, the output of group action depends on both the properties of the group and those of the individuals in the group. Schriver (1996) made similar observations in extensive case studies of collaboration in document design groups working both in school and industry.

Other research areas that are particularly active are socialization of writing in academic disciplines (Greene, 1991; Haas, 1987; Velez, 1994), classroom ethnography (Freedman, 1987; Sperling, 1991), sociology of scientific writing (Bazerman, 1988; Blakeslee, 1992; Myers, 1985), and workplace literacy (Hull, 1993).

Research on the social environment is essential for a complete understanding of writing. I hope that the current enthusiasm for investigating social factors in writing will lead to a strong empirical research tradition parallel to those in speech communication and social psychology. It would be regrettable if anti-empirical sentiments expressed in some quarters had the effect of curtailing progress in this area.

The Physical Environment

In the 1980 model, we noted that a very important part of the task environment is the text the writer has produced so far. During the composition of any but the shortest passages, writers will reread what they have written apparently to help shape what they write next. Thus, writing modifies its own task environment. However, writing is not the only task that reshapes its task environment. Other creative tasks that produce an integrated product cumulatively such as graphic design, computer programming, and painting have this property as well.

Since 1980, increasing attention has been devoted to the writing medium as an important part of the task environment. In large part, this is the result of computer-based innovations in communication such as word processing, e-mail, the World Wide Web, and so on. Studies comparing writing using pen and paper to writing using a word processor have revealed effects of the medium on writing processes such as planning and editing. For example, Gould and Grischowsky (1984) found that writers were less effective at editing when that activity was carried out using a word processor rather than hard copy. Haas and Hayes (1986) found searching for information online was strongly influenced by screen size. Haas (1987) found that undergraduate writers planned less before writing when they used a word processor rather than pen and paper.

Variations in the composing medium often lead to changes in the ease of accessing some of the processes that support writing. For example, on the one hand, when we are writing with a word processor, including crude sketches in the text or drawing arrows from one part of the text to another is more difficult than it would be if we were writing with pencil and paper. On the other hand, word processors make it much easier to move blocks of text from one place to another, or experiment with fonts and check spelling. The point is not that one medium is better than another, although perhaps such a case could be made, but rather that writing processes are influenced, and sometimes strongly influenced, by the writing medium itself.

As already noted, when writers are composing with pen and paper, they frequently review the first part of the sentence they are composing before writing the rest of the sentence (Kaufer, Hayes, & Flower, 1986). However, when writers are composing with a dictating machine, the process of reviewing the current sentence is much less frequent (Schilperoord, 1996). It is plausible to believe that the difference in frequency is due to the difference in the difficulty of reviewing a sentence in the two media. When writing with pen and paper, reviewing involves little more than an eye movement. When composing with a dictating machine, however, reviewing requires stopping the machine, rewinding it to find the beginning of the sentence, and then replaying the appropriate part.

The writing medium can influence more than cognitive processes. Studies of e-mail communication have revealed interesting social consequences of the media used. For example, Sproull and Kiesler (1986) suggested that marked lapses in politeness occurring in some e-mail messages (called flaming) may be attributed to the relative anonymity the medium provides the communicator.

Such studies remind us that we can gain a broader perspective on writing processes by exploring other writing media and other ways of creating messages (such as dictation, sign language, and telegraphy) that do not directly involve making marks on paper. By observing differences in process due to variations in the media we can better understand writing processes in general.

The Individual

In this section I discuss the components of the model that I have represented as aspects of the individual writer: working memory, motivation and affect, cognitive processes, and long-term memory. I will attend to both visual and verbal modes of communication.

Working Memory

The 1980 model devoted relatively little attention to working memory. The present model assumes that all of the processes have access to working memory and carry out all nonautomated activities in working memory. The central location of working memory in Figure 3 is intended to symbolize its central importance in the activity of writing. To describe working memory in writing, I draw heavily on Baddeley's (1986) general model of working memory. In Baddeley's model, working memory is a limited resource that is drawn on both for storing information and for carrying out cognitive processes. Structurally, working memory consists of a central executive together with two specialized memories: a "phonological loop" and a visual–spatial "sketchpad." The phonological loop stores phonologically coded information, and the sketchpad stores visually or spatially coded information. Baddeley and Lewis (1981) likened the phonological loop to an inner voice that continually repeats the information to be retained (e.g., telephone numbers of the digits in a memory span test). The central executive serves such cognitive tasks as mental arithmetic, logical reasoning, and semantic verification. In Baddeley's (1986) model, the central executive also performs a number of control functions in addition to its storage and processing functions. These functions include retrieving information from long-term memory and managing tasks not fully automated or that require problem solving or decision making. In the writing model, I represent planning and decision making as part of the reflection process rather than as part of working memory. Further, I specifically include a semantic store in working memory because, as I discuss later, it is useful for describing text generation. Otherwise, working memory in the writing model is identical to Baddeley's model of working memory.

Useful experimental techniques have been developed for identifying the nature of the representations active in working memory. In particular, tasks that make use of phonologic representations such as the memory span task are seriously interfered with when the individual is required to repeat an arbitrary syllable (e.g., la, la, la, etc.). This procedure is called *articulatory suppression*. Similarly, tasks that make use of visual–spatial representation such as interpreting spatial direction are interfered with when the individual is required to engage in spatial tracking tasks (e.g., monitoring the position of a visual or auditory target). These techniques could be useful for identifying the roles of visual and phonological representations in reading and writing tasks.

Motivation

Few doubt that motivation is important in writing. However, motivation does not have a comfortable place in current social–cognitive models. The relatively low salience of motivational concerns in cognitive theorizing is in striking contrast to earlier behaviorist thinking, which provided an explicit and prominent theoretical role to motivation (see, e.g., Hull, 1943). Hilgard (1987) believed that cognitive theorists have not attended to motivation because their information-processing models are not formulated in terms of physiological processes. It is these processes that give rise to the basic drives.

I find this explanation unconvincing for the following reason: Cognitive psychologists have been interested in human performance in areas such as reading, problem solving, and memory. The motivations underlying such performances have never been adequately accounted for by the behaviorists or by anyone else in terms of basic drives. Cognitive psychology's failure to account fully for motivation in these complex areas of human behavior is not unique.

Actually, cognitive psychologists, following the lead of the Gestalt psychologists, took an important step in accounting for the effects of motivation by recognizing that much activity is goal directed. Powerful problem-solving mechanisms such as means–ends analysis and hill climbing are built on this recognition (see Hayes, 1989, chap. 2). Despite the success of such mechanisms in providing insight into a number of important behaviors, much more needs to be understood about motivation and affect. In the following section, I discuss four areas that I believe are of special importance for writing.

1. The Nature of Motivation in Writing. Motivation is manifest not only in relatively short-term responses to immediate goals but also in long-term predispositions to engage in certain types of activities. For example, Finn and Cox (1992) found that teachers' ratings of fourth-grade students for engagement in educational activities correlated strongly with the achievement scores of those students in the first three grades. Hayes, Schriver, Hill, and Hatch (1990) found that students who had been admitted to college as "basic" writers engaged much less in a computer-based activity designed to improve their writing skills than did "average" and "honors" students. In particular, the basic students attended fewer training sessions than did the average and honors students. Further, when basic students did attend training sessions, they spent less time attending to the instructional materials than did the average and honors students.

Research by Dweck (1986) suggests that the individual's beliefs about the causes of successful performance are one source of such long-term predispositions. Dweck compared students who believed that successful performance depended on innate and unchangeable intelligence with those who believed that successful performance depended on acquirable skills. She found that these two groups of students responded very differently to failure. The first group tended to hide failure and to avoid those situations in which failure was experienced. In contrast, the second group responded to failure by asking for help and by working harder. One can imagine that if students believe that writing is a gift and experience failure, they might well form a long-term negative disposition to avoid writing.

Palmquist and Young (1992) explored in college students the relation between the belief that writing is a gift, on the one hand, and the presence of writing anxiety, on the other. They found that students who believed strongly that writing is a gift had significantly higher levels of writing anxiety and significantly lower self-assessments of their ability as writers than other students.

2. Interaction Among Goals. Activities that are successfully characterized by means–end analysis typically have a single dominant goal. In writing there are many situations, however, that involve multiple goals that interact with each other to determine the course of action. For example, the college students described by Nelson (1988) had goals to write papers for their classes, but often those goals were set aside because of competition with other goals. If a writer has a goal, that does not mean the goal will necessarily lead to action.

Writers typically have more than one goal when they write (Flower & Hayes, 1980). For example, they may want both to convey content and also to create a good impression of themselves, or they may want to convey information clearly but not to write a text that is too long, or they may want to satisfy a first audience but not offend a second. Van der Mast (1996) studied experts writing policy documents for the Dutch government. He found that writers employ explicit linguistic strategies for creating texts that are ambiguous about issues on which members of the audience have conflicting interests. In all these cases, the text will be shaped by the writer's need to achieve a balance among competing goals.

3. Choice Among Methods. Even for situations in which the goals are specified, motivational factors can additionally influence action by influencing strategy selection. If a person wants to get from one place to another or to compute the answer to an arithmetic problem, the person can still make choices about what strategies should be used to reach that goal. Siegler, Adolph, and Lemaire (1995) studied strategy choice in a variety of situations. In one situation, infants who had just learned to walk were trying to reach their mothers on the other side of a ramp. To reach their mothers, the infants could traverse the ramp by walking, or by crawling forward or backward, prone or supine. Siegler et al. found that experienced infants chose their strategy on the basis of the steepness of the slope, choosing to walk when the slope was small but choosing other strategies when the slope was large.

In a second study, Siegler et al. studied the choice of strategy for solving arithmetic problems among elderly people. Participants could solve problems by retrieving the answers from memory, by pencil-and-paper calculation, or by calculator. Siegler et al. found that the choice of strategy depended on the difficulty of the problem. The more difficult the problem, the more likely it was that the participants would use the calculator.

Thus, motivation may be seen as shaping the course of action through a kind of cost–benefit mechanism. Even when the overall goal of an activity is fixed, individuals will select the means that, in the current environment, is least costly or least likely to lead to error. This mechanism appears to shape overt as well as reflective actions. In a study by Kenton O'Hara (1996) at the University of Cardiff, participants were asked to solve a puzzle using a computer interface. The experimenter manipulated the interface so that it was either easy or difficult to make moves. At first, individuals using the difficult interface spent more time between trials than those using the easier interface. However, with practice, those using the difficult interface rapidly decreased their time between trials until they were responding more quickly than those with the easy interface.

In another study, O'Hara compared two groups who had practiced for five trials either on the difficult or the easy interface. Both groups were then transferred to a third interface. Those trained on the difficult interface solved problems in fewer steps and with shorter solution times than those trained on the easy interface. O'Hara's results suggest that

- people who use the difficult interface reflect more before making a move about what move is most likely to lead to solution,
- they do so because the cost of reflection is more likely to be outweighed by its benefits—a reduction in the number of steps to solution—when the cost of each step is high, and
- increased reflection leads to increased learning and improved performance in solving the problems.

The studies of Siegler et al. (1995) and O'Hara (1996) indicate that changes in the task environment can have significant impact on the costs of both overt and reflective activities and can thereby influence the way in which tasks are carried out. In the case of writing, changes in the writing media such as those already discussed can influence the cognitive processes involved in carrying out writing tasks. Designers of word-processing systems and other writing media should understand that system characteristics can have significant impact on writing processes.

4. Affective Responses in Reading and Writing. Earlier, I mentioned that students who believe both that they are poor writers and that writing is a gift are likely to experience writing anxiety. Reading and writing have a number of other affective consequences as well.

Schriver (1995) studied reader's affective responses to manuals for consumer electronic products such as videocassette recorders and telephone answering machines. In a first study, she asked 201 consumer electronic customers where they placed the blame when they had difficulty understanding the instructions for electronic products they bought: on the manual, on the machine, on the manufacturer, or on themselves. Across both genders and across all age groups (from under 20 to over 60), readers blamed themselves for more than half of the problems they experienced. In a second study, Schriver collected thinking-aloud protocols from 35 participants as they were using manuals to help them carry out typical tasks with consumer electronics products. Analysis of the comments that the participants made as they worked indicated again that they blamed themselves for their difficulties in more than half of the cases (52%).

Schriver found that people were right in about a third of the cases in which people blamed themselves. They had misread or misused the manual. However, in two thirds of the cases, the manual was clearly at fault. The information was either unintelligible, missing, or incorrectly indexed. The tendency of people to blame themselves when they read poorly designed instructional texts may well lead them to believe they are not competent readers of such materials and therefore make them reluctant to read those texts. We should very seriously consider whether a comparable problem exists in students reading school texts.

Note that people respond effectively not just to the linguistic aspects of a text but to the graphic features as well. Wright, Creighton, and Threlfall (1982), Redish (1993), and Schriver (1996) all noted that if a text is unappealing in appearance then people frequently decide not to read it.

A developing body of research indicates that the act of writing about stress-related topics can have important affective consequences. A number of researchers in the field of health psychology have conducted studies on the use of writing to reduce stress. In a typical study, a group of people subject to stress (e.g., unemployed people, students entering college) are divided at random into experimental and control groups. Both groups are asked to write for about 20 minutes on each of 3 to 5 days. The experimental group is asked to write about a stress-related topic, for example, "Getting laid off" or "Coming to college." The control group is asked to write on a neutral topic such as "What I did today." Then the groups are compared on some stress-related variables such as doctor visits, immune levels, or symptoms of depression. Pennebaker and Beall (1986) found that participants asked to write about traumatic experiences showed a significant drop in health center visits as compared to control groups. Greenberg and Stone (1992) found similar results. Pennebaker, Kiecolt-Glaser, and Glaser (1988) found that experimental participants showed enhanced immune function after the last day of writing compared to controls.

These results are still controversial. Some researchers have failed to find positive effects of writing on mental health. Further, when writing is compared with face-to-face discussion, the effects of discussion are usually found to be more powerful.

Cognitive Processes

There is a fairly popular view in the field of literacy studies in the United States that social/cultural studies are "in" and cognitive studies are "out." Many feel it is no longer appropriate to do cognitive analyses of writing. Comments such as "We've done cognition" are pronounced with a certain finality.

There are two reasonable arguments that might lead to abandoning cognitive studies of writing. First, one might argue that all there is to know has already been learned about the relation of writing to topic knowledge, to language structure, to working memory capacity, and so on, and, therefore, no further investigations are necessary. However, this argument would not be easy to defend. Second, one might argue that all the issues that can be investigated through cognitive measures such as working memory capacity or reading level are better or more conveniently studied through social factors such as race, class, or gender. The validity of this position certainly has not been demonstrated nor is it likely to be.

The real reason for the current rejection of cognitive methods is an unfortunate tendency to faddishness that has plagued English studies in the United States, the locus of much research on writing, though certainly not all or necessarily the best work. It is a sort of professional "7-year itch," a kind of collective attention deficit that has nothing to do with scientific progress. Just as we would think a carpenter foolish who said, "Now that I have discovered the hammer, I am never going to use my saw again" so we should regard a literacy researcher who says, "Now that I have discovered social methods, I am never going to use cognitive ones again." Our research problems are difficult. We need all available tools, both social and cognitive. Let's not hobble ourselves by following a misguided fad.

In this model, I propose that the primary cognitive functions involved in writing are text interpretation, reflection, and text production. *Text interpretation* is a function that creates internal representations from linguistic and graphic inputs. Cognitive processes that accomplish this function include reading, listening, and scanning graphics. *Reflection* is an activity that operates on internal representations to produce other internal representations. Cognitive processes that accomplish reflection include problem solving, decision making, and inferencing. *Text production* is a function that takes internal representations in the context of the task environment and produces written, spoken, or graphic output. It was important to include spoken language in a writing model because spoken language can provide useful inputs to the writing process in the form of content information and editorial comment. In the case of dictation, speech is the output medium for the composing process. Further, for many writers, the process of planning written sentences appears to be carried out, either vocally or subvocally, in the medium of speech.

I assume that the cognitive processes involved in writing are not bound solely to writing but are shared with other activities. For example, I assume that the text-interpreting activities involved in writing overlap with those involved in reading novels and understanding maps, that the reflective activities involved in writing overlap with those involved in solving mystery stories and arithmetic puzzles, and that the text-producing activities involved in writing overlap those used in ordinary conversation and drawing. In addition, I assume that working memory and long-term memory resources are freely shared among both cognitive and motivational processes involved in writing.

Replacing Revision With Reading

Hayes, Flower, Schriver, Stratman, and Carey (1987) reported an extensive series of studies of revision in expert and not-so-expert adults. These studies led to the model of revision shown in Figure 4. Central to this model is the evaluation function—a process that is responsible for the detection and diagnosis of text problems. We postulated that this evaluation function was similar to the process of reading comprehension as described by Just and Carpenter (1980).

Figure 5 shows an adaptation of the Just–Carpenter model for our tasks. The important feature of this model is that it shows reading comprehension as a process of constructing a representation of the text's meaning by integrating many sources of knowledge—from knowledge of word patterns and grammatical structures to factual knowledge and beliefs about the writer's intent. Also represented in Figure 5 is the observation that when we read to comprehend, we do not attend much to text problems. That is, we try to form a clear internal representation of the text's message, but we are rarely concerned with stylistic issues. When we have problems in comprehending a text, we try to solve those problems and then, most usually, forget them. Consequently, when readers are reading for comprehension, their retrospective reports about text difficulty tend to be very incomplete. However, when we read to revise, we treat the text quite differently.

FIGURE 4
The Revision Process

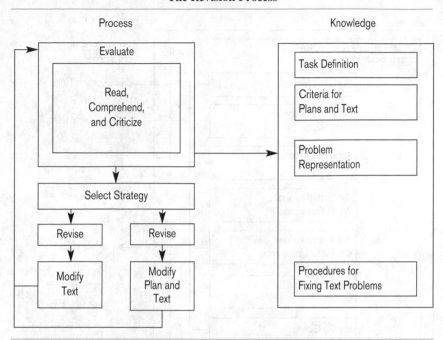

From Hayes et al. (1987). Reprinted with permission of Cambridge University Press.

We are still concerned with the text's message, but now we are also concerned with bad diction, wordiness, and poor organization—features of the text that we may not have attended to when we were reading for comprehension. In revision tasks, people read not only to represent the text's meaning, but, more important, they read to identify text problems. With the extra goal of detecting problems, the reviser reads quite differently than does the reader who is simply reading for comprehension, seeing not only problems in the text but also opportunities for improvement that do not necessarily stem from problems. Our model for reading to evaluate a text is shown in Figure 6.

Our model of revision, then, had a form of reading built in. Before it was constructed, I was concerned that revision did not seem to fit comfortably as a basic process in the writing model. Recognizing that the revision model included reading as a subpart suggested that revision would more naturally be thought of as a composite of more basic processes, in particular, a composite of text interpretation, reflection, and text production.

To understand revision, it is not enough to identify the underlying processes involved. It also is necessary to understand the control structure that determines

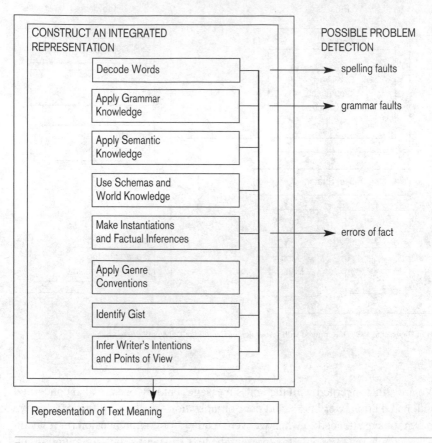

FIGURE 5
Cognitive Processes in Reading to Comprehend Text

CONSTRUCT AN INTEGRATED
REPRESENTATION

POSSIBLE PROBLEM
DETECTION

Decode Words → spelling faults

Apply Grammar
Knowledge → grammar faults

Apply Semantic
Knowledge

Use Schemas and
World Knowledge

Make Instantiations
and Factual Inferences → errors of fact

Apply Genre
Conventions

Identify Gist

Infer Writer's Intentions
and Points of View

Representation of Text Meaning

From Hayes et al. (1987). Reprinted with permission of Cambridge University Press.

how these processes are invoked and sequenced. I propose the following provisional model for that control structure. First, the control structure for revision is a task schema. By task schema I mean a package of knowledge, acquired through practice, that is useful for performing the task and is retrieved as a unit when cues indicating the relevance of the schema are perceived. This package of knowledge might be thought of as a set of productions—that is, condition–action rules—that mutually activate each other. People's knowledge of arithmetic shows evidence of being organized in task schemas for solving particular classes of problems. A person may hear just the first few words of a problem (e.g., "A river boat...") and be able to retrieve the problem category ("river current" problems),

FIGURE 6
Cognitive Processes in Reading to Evaluate Text

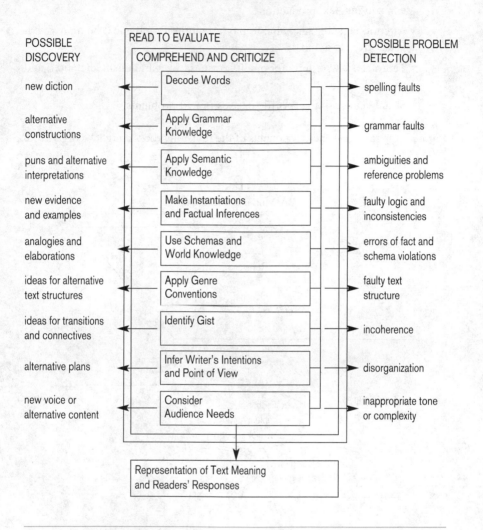

From Hayes et al. (1987). Reprinted with permission of Cambridge University Press.

the nature of the information to be provided (the speed of the boat upstream and downstream), the question to be asked (What would the boat's speed be in still water?), and the kinds of mathematical procedures needed to find the answer.

The control structure for revision is a task schema that might include some or all of the following:

- A goal: to improve the text
- An expected set of activities to be performed: evaluative reading, problem solving, text production
- Attentional subgoals: what to pay attention to in the text being revised, what errors to avoid
- Templates and criteria for quality: criteria for parallelism, dictation, and so on
- Strategies for fixing specific classes of text problems

Figure 7 suggests how the components of the revision process might be organized.

FIGURE 7
A Model of Revision

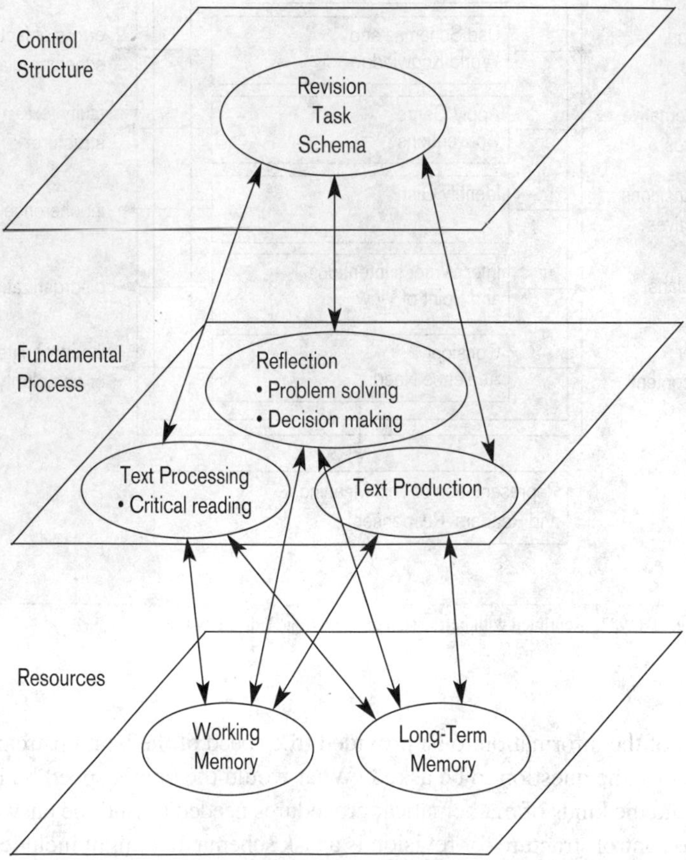

The following example illustrates how this model may be applied. In a protocol study Hayes et al. (1987) observed that college freshmen tended to focus their revision activities on problems at or below the sentence level but that more experienced writers attended both to local and global problems. There are a number of reasons one might propose to account for this failure to revise globally. First, the writer's basic revision processes may be inadequate. For example, the reading process may fail to detect global problems. Second, as Bereiter and Scardamalia (1987) suggested, the writer may lack sufficient working memory to coordinate the basic revision processes. For example, the writer may see the global problems in the text but may be unable to keep the problems in focus while trying to fix them. Third, the writer's task schema may be at fault. For example, as Wallace and Hayes (1991) hypothesized, the control structures of freshman writers simply may not include the goal to attend to global problems.

To test the control structure hypothesis, Wallace and Hayes (1991) designed 8 minutes of instruction that demonstrated the difference between global and local revision, and urged students to revise both globally and locally. The authors reasoned that 8 minutes of instruction might modify the control structure by changing students' definition of the revision task but would be unlikely to cause changes in the basic revision processes or in the functioning of working memory. Wallace and Hayes (1991) then compared revisions produced by a group of freshmen who had received the instruction, the experimental group, with those of a control group that had been instructed simply to make the original text better. The experimental group outperformed the control group both in number of global revisions and in the holistically assessed quality of the revision. These results suggest two conclusions: First, the control structure for revision can be modified by a brief instructional prompt. Second, the control structure plays an important role in determining the nature and quality of revision performance.

Reading as a Central Process in Writing

As discussed previously, reading to evaluate the text is a central component of revision. Poor text evaluation skills, such as Hayes et al. (1987) report, must surely lead to poor revisions. In addition to reading to evaluate, two other kinds of reading play important roles in writing: *reading source texts* and *reading to define tasks*.

Reading Source Texts. Usually, we think of source texts as providing writers with content, that is, with topic information that any competent reader would infer from the source text. However, if writers are not competent readers, if they oversimplify or misunderstand the source texts, their own texts that interpret or summarize those source texts are likely to suffer. For example, Zasloff (1984) studied a group of student writers who were asked to summarize an essay with the form "Others hold Position A but I hold Position B." Some of the students misread the essay to mean that the author held Position A. As a result, these students received very poor grades for their written summaries. Spivey (1984) found that students who wrote more-adequate summaries tended to score better on reading tests than did students who wrote less-adequate summaries. Chenoweth (1995) found that nonnative speakers of English had particular difficulty in identifying the main points of an essay, suggesting that these students may not be responding appropriately to textual cues that indicate the relative importance of information.

However, the reading of source texts is not simply an activity that provides readers with topic knowledge. Readers may form at lease three different representations when they read: a representation of the topic discussed, a representation of the writer's persona, and a representation of the text as a spatial display.

Representations of the Writer's Persona. In addition to forming a representation of the topic of the text, readers also may form another quite different representation as they read—a representation of the writer's personality. Hatch, Hill, and Hayes (1993) asked judges to read college application essays and to identify personality traits of the authors. They found that the judges showed substantial agreement in the personality traits they attributed to the authors. In a second study, Hatch et al. (1993) found that these personality judgments predicted whether or not college admission personnel would vote to admit the author of the application essay to college. Thus, for these texts at least, the reader's representation of the author appeared to play an important role in the functioning of the text, Finally, Hatch et al. (1993) showed that readers' judgments of the writer's personality could be influenced in predictable ways by modifying the style of the text in ways that left the content substantially unchanged. For example, in one of the texts, a student described a play that she and her friends had produced. When that text was modified by replacing the word *we* with the word *I*, there was a sharp reduction in judgments of the author as "likable" and "sensitive to others."

Hill (1992) asked undergraduates to rate the personality traits of writers who would write pro or con essays on a controversial topic (legalization of drugs). He found that the ratings were far more positive for the writer who agreed with the rater's own position than for the writer who did not. Schriver, Hayes, and Steffy (1994) asked primary and secondary school students to make judgments about the text, the graphics, and the author of drug education brochures. They found that the students often perceived the writers as people who would not be credible communicators. For example, students characterized the writers as people who got their information from books rather than from experience, and as people who were different from themselves in age and social class.

These results suggest that the reader's representation of the author can play an important role in the way readers respond to a text. Indeed, in some cases, the acceptance of a writer's argument may depend more on how the writer comes across as a person than on the logical quality of the argument itself.

Representations of the Text as a Spatial Display. Even when texts consist simply of sequences of sentences without any obvious graphic features such as pictures, tables, and graphs, they still have important spatial features. For example, Rothkopf (1971) found that individuals reading from multiple printed texts showed significant incidental memory for the spatial location in the text of information they read. Readers showed better than chance recall of where the information was located both on the page and within the text. Haas and Hayes (1986) found that readers formed a less-precise spatial image of the text when they read one page at a time from a computer screen than from a two-page spread in hard copy. In addition, they provided evidence linking readers' spatial images of the text to their success in searching for information in the text.

Bond and Hayes (1984) asked readers to paragraph text passages from which the original paragraphing marks had been removed. In one condition, the original texts were otherwise unchanged; in other conditions, the original texts were degraded by replacing categories of words (e.g., nouns) with Xs. In the most extreme condition, all the words were replaced with Xs. The result was that readers showed greatest agreement in paragraphing with the undegraded texts. However, they still showed significant agreement even when all the words had been replaced by Xs. To account for their data, Bond and Hayes (1984) proposed a model of paragraphing that included both linguistic and spatial features of the text.

Reading to Understand the Task. Reading to understand the writing task is another important function that reading serves for the writer. It is a specialized reading genre that shapes writers' interpretation of writing tasks in school and at work. Success in carrying out this activity in school seems to depend on skill in interpreting terms such as *describe*, *argue*, and *interpret*. In many school writing tasks, and possibly in other writing tasks as well, a text is judged inadequate because the writer has done the wrong task. For example, when assigned to analyze an article, students often respond by summarizing it. Chenoweth (1995) reported a study of this sort of reading in which students were shown exam questions together with an answer a student had written in response to the question. The task was to select one of four items of advice about how to improve the answer. Teachers and students differed systematically in the answers they chose. Students tended to prefer the suggestion to improve the mechanics. In contrast, teachers preferred the suggestion to make the answer more responsive to the question.

Reading, then, takes on a central role in the new model. It is seen as contributing to writing performance in three distinct ways: reading for comprehension, reading to define the writing task, and reading to revise. The quality of writers' texts often depends on their ability to read in these three ways.

From Planning to Reflection

In the 1980 model, planning played a prominent role in our thinking about writing and about writing pedagogy. Indeed, planning was the only reflective process that was explicitly included in that model. Since that time, consideration of the available data has convinced me that other reflective processes should be included in the model and that they are organized as follows: problem solving (including planning), decision making, and inferencing.

Problem Solving. People engage in problem solving when they want to achieve a goal but do not know as yet what steps will achieve it. Problem solving is an activity of putting together a sequence of steps to reach a goal. In writing, problem solving constitutes a substantial part of any but the most routine composing activities. It may take the form of chaining together a sequence of phrases to form a sentence or of claims to form an argument. It may involve constructing a graph to make a point or it may involve creating a plan for an essay or a book.

In cognitive science, planning is treated as one of several problem-solving methods (see Hayes, 1989). In chapter 2 of *The Science of Writing* (Levy & Randsell, 1996), Hayes and Nash present a theoretical treatment of planning processes in adults together with a taxonomy of these planning processes and a critical review of some of the literature on planning in writing. The most important conclusion we drew from this review was that although several studies showed strong positive correlations between the time spent planning and the quality of the texts, these correlations were confounded with time on task. When time on task was taken into account, the correlations between planning and text quality were generally nonsignificant. These observations do not suggest that planning is unimportant, but they do suggest that we placed too much emphasis on planning in the 1980 model.

Writers, especially student writers, are often required to do writing tasks for which they do not yet have a fully adequate task schema. When this occurs, writers must rely on their general problem-solving and decision-making skills to manage the writing task. It is in such cases that writers engage in process planning described by Hayes and Nash (1996).

Decision Making. People engage in decision making when they evaluate alternatives to choose among them. Like problem solving, decision making also is an important component of all but the most routine writing tasks. Many writing tasks are ill-defined problems. That is, they are problems that cannot be solved unless the writer makes a number of *gap-filling* decisions (Reitman, 1964). For example, if students are asked to write an essay on a controversial topic, they will have to make decisions about what perspective to take, what sources to read, what points to emphasize, how to order those points, how to deal with conflicting views, and so on. In fact, the writers have so many gap-filling decisions to make in writing such an essay that if two students were to submit the same essay, there would be a strong presumption of plagiarism.

If gap-filling decisions are especially important for creating first drafts, evaluative decisions are especially important for revision. When revising, writers must decide whether or not the text is adequate on a variety of dimensions including diction, tone, clarity, effect on audience, and so on. For example, they must answer questions such as "Is this graph clear?" "Is this language appropriate for teenagers?" and "Is this phrase better than that one?"

Difficult writing tasks often require writers to do a substantial amount of problem solving or decision making. Document design tasks may require the designer to produce alternative designs that satisfy complex sets of spatial and linguistic constraints and then to evaluate the relative merits of the designs. As yet, though, relatively little research has been devoted to the complex problem-solving and decision-making processes that go on in writing.

Inferencing. Inferencing is a process by which new information is derived from old. It may or may not be goal directed, and it may be conscious or unconscious. Inferencing is important in both reading and writing. For example, as Braddock (1992) pointed out, readers often infer the main point of a paragraph when that point is not explicitly stated in the text. Similarly, writers often make inferences about the knowledge and interests of their audiences. Clearly, inferencing is an important process that allows readers and writers to make useful extensions of available information. However, in some cases, readers may extend given information in surprising ways. For example, Stein (1992), studying a phenomenon of "elaboration," found that readers may draw inferences from reading that are both idiosyncratic and consequential.

Stein asked readers to imagine themselves as jurors, to read transcripts of a murder trial, and to make judgments as to the degree of guilt of the defendant in the trial. The case involved a fight in which a victim was stabbed to death by the defendant after the victim had threatened the defendant with a razor. In debriefing, participants revealed that their decisions had been influenced by idiosyncratic representations of the crime situation. For example, one participant, who voted for acquittal on the basis of self-defense, had represented the defendant as being unable to avoid the victim because his escape routes were cut off by brick walls. In fact, the trial transcript said nothing about walls. Another participant, who voted for first-degree murder, thought that stabbing was far too strong a response to being threatened with a razor. When asked to draw the razor, she represented a small disposable safety razor, a type that might cause a nick but certainly not a fatal wound.

Notice that there appears to be a strong visual–spatial component in these representations. The fact that the first participant was making inferences about spatial locations of people and objects suggests that his representation included a mental image of the scene. Similarly, the second participant's description of the size and shape of the razor also suggests a mental image. The presence of a visual–spatial component is consistent with the reports of a number of the other participants in Stein's study. For example, one participant reported that the bar mentioned in the transcript (but not described) looked like one with which he was familiar.

If visual representations play an important role in reflecting about texts, as Stein's observations suggest, we need to be alert to the functional properties of these representations. Studies by Paivio (1971) and Bower (1972) indicate that visual and verbal inputs are represented in different ways in memory. Further, studies indicate that these differences in representation can influence the way in which people use the inputs in making inferences and in solving problems. For example, Santa (1977) showed participants a display and asked them to say whether or not it had the same elements as a display they had studied earlier. In some cases, the displays showed an array of geometrical figures and in other cases, an array of names of geometrical figures. Santa found that some matching problems were easier with visual–spatial input but that others were easier with verbal input, indicating that the visual and verbal representations were being processed differently. In a study of physics problem solving, Larkin and Simon (1987) found that visual–spatial inputs were sometimes better than verbal inputs because the visual inputs supported powerful visual inference procedures but the verbal inputs did not. Clearly, if we are to understand how tests are understood and how they are best designed, we have to attend both their verbal and their visual features.

Although reflective processes may be carried on for extended periods without input or output, they are often interleaved with input and output processes. For example, in library research, individuals may alternate between reading paragraphs and summarizing them, and, in brainstorming, individuals may alternate between generating ideas and writing them down.

Text Production

Kaufer, Hayes, and Flower (1986) conducted a series of studies of competent and advanced adult writers that provided several insights into the processes involved in text generation. Protocol data revealed that writers produce text not in whole sentences but, rather, in sentence parts. Sentence parts were identified either by a pause of two or more seconds or by a grammatical discontinuity indicating that the current language represents a revision of earlier language. On average, writers produced about three sentence parts for each sentence of the final text. The average length of these parts was 7.3 words for competent writers and 11.2 words for advanced writers. However, variability in the size of sentence parts was large. In some cases, a sentence part might consist of a single word. In other cases, the same writer might produce a sentence part that consisted of several clauses or a whole sentence.

Generally, sentences were composed from left to right with more than 90% of sentence parts being added at the leading edge of the sentence, that is, the word farthest from the beginning of the sentence that has been produced so far. Writers frequently reread the sentence produced so far, prior to adding a sentence part to an incomplete sentence. About a third of the sentence parts ended at clause boundaries, which is more than would be expected by chance. When sentence parts are produced, they are evaluated and may be rejected either for semantic or syntactic problems. When a sentence part is accepted, writers often appear to search for an appropriate meaning for the next part in the sentence. Thus, the content of the sentence may not be fully determined before the writer begins to produce syntactically complete sentence parts. Kaufer et al. also provided evidence indicating that sentence production was about equally facilitated by prior knowledge of a sentence's meaning and prior knowledge of its grammatical structure. Further, they found that these two facilitative effects, knowledge of syntax and semantics, were independent of each other.

In what follows, I propose a provisional model of text production that draws heavily on the theoretical ideas and empirical results of Kaufer et al. According to this model, text is produced as follows: Cues from the writing plan and from the text produced so far are used to retrieve a package of semantic content. This content is stored in working memory but not in the articulatory buffer. (This may correspond to what Garrett, 1976, described as the "message level" in his model of speech production.) A surface form to express this content then is constructed and stored in the articulatory buffer. Garrett's (1980) observations on "word exchange" errors (e.g., "the room to my door" for "the door to my room") suggest that the construction process may sometimes operate on more than one clause at a time (p. 193). When all the content is expressed or when the capacity limit of the articulatory buffer is reached, the sentence part is articulated either vocally or subvocally. If all the current content has been expressed, then the writer may show evidence of searching for new content. If the articulated sentence part is positively evaluated, then it is written down and the process is repeated. If it is rejected, a new sentence part is constructed and evaluated.

As studies of pausing during composing have indicated (Matsuhashi, 1981; Schilperoord, 1996), working memory demands are especially high following clause boundaries. Thus, the limit of the articulatory buffer is more likely to be exceeded at clause boundaries than at other places. For this reason, the model predicts that sentence parts also will be somewhat more likely to end at clause boundaries than at other places. In addition, experience in writing and, more generally, experience with language should reduce the amount of memory required for constructing sentence parts from content. Therefore, writers who have more language and writing experience should write longer sentence parts than other writers.

The following hypotheses may be derived from this model:

1. Secondary tasks that involve the phonological loop, such as the continuous repetition of a syllable string, should interfere seriously with text production. In particular, such secondary tasks will reduce the rate at which text is produced, the average length of the sentence parts produced, and the cohesion of the text that is produced.

2. The length of sentence parts produced should increase as the writer's experience with the language increases. For example, writers who are learning a new language would be expected to produce short sentence parts. (Observations by Friedlander, 1987, on Chinese students writing in English provide some support for this hypothesis.)

Long-Term Memory

Writing simply would not be possible if writers did not have long-term memories in which to store their knowledge of vocabulary grammar, genre, topic, audience, and so on. I will discuss three topics: task schemas, knowledge of audience, and the impact of extended practice as they relate to long-term memory.

Task Schemas. Task schemas, such as the schema for revision already discussed, are packages of information stored in long-term memory that specify how to carry out a particular task. Typically, task schemas will include information about the goals of the task, the processes to be used in accomplishing the task, the sequencing of those processes, and criteria for evaluating the success of the task. Adults may be expected to have schemas for tasks such as reading graphs, writing business letters, reading a textbook, editing, and so on.

Task schemas are usually activated by environmental stimuli. For example, the editing schema may be triggered by a misspelled word. However, schemas may also be activated by reflection. For example, thinking about a topic may remind us that we have failed to credit the work of a colleague in a paper and thus trigger revision.

Knowledge of Audience. When people are writing to friends or acquaintances, they can draw on a history of personal interaction to decide what to say and how to say it. However, when writers address audiences they do not know personally, they have no such experience to rely on. Writers are sometimes urged to role-play the audience, that is "get inside the skin" of the audience and to try to experience the message as the audience would. To do so would be quite a complex representational act. Protocols of people who are writing for an audience of strangers rarely reveal this sort of complex representation of the audience. Rather, what one sees are not very frequent occasions in which the writer considers whether or not a particular text feature is appropriate for the audience. For example, the writer may say of a teenage audiences, "I wonder if this is too racy for them?" or of a child audience, "Will they know this word?" When writers show evidence of considering the audience at all, they appear to consider them in a limited and one-dimensional way.

Observations such as these, together with the traditional belief that experts have difficulty writing for novices, led Hayes, Schriver, Spilka, and Blaustein (1986) to hypothesize that writers may use themselves as their primary model for the audience. That is, for example, they will judge a text unclear for the audience if and only if it is unclear for them.

To explore this hypothesis, Hayes et al. (1986) asked participants to read a difficult text and to underline parts of the text that would be unclear to another reader. Participants in the experimental condition were given information immediately prior to making judgments of difficulty that clarified a number of points in the text. Participants in the control condition were not given this information. The result was that compared to participants in the control condition, the experimental participants were significantly less likely to identify those points that had been clarified for them as being unclear for others. The participants, then, did appear to be using themselves as models for the imagined reader.

If writers do use themselves as models for the audience, it is easy to understand why experts have trouble writing clear instructions for novices. Writing clear instructions has been a major practical problem for the consumer electronics industry where engineers often write user manuals. Swaney, Janik, Bond, & Hayes (1991) showed that the clarity of instruction manuals could be improved significantly by providing writers with think-aloud protocols of real users trying to use the manuals. This technique, called Protocol-Aided Revision, allowed writers to supplement the knowledge that they would ordinarily use to model the audience with data reflecting the responses of audience members.

Schriver (1987) showed that exposure to user protocols can provide writers with knowledge about readers that is generalizable to new readers and new genres. Schriver constructed a sequence of 10 lessons in which readers first predicted reader difficulties with a passage from a computer manual and then read a protocol of a person trying to use the manual. Using a pre–post paradigm, she showed that students who completed these lessons were significantly better at anticipating readers' difficulties with popular science texts than were controls who received traditional training in anticipating audiences' needs.

The Impact of Extensive Practice. In addition to topic knowledge and audience knowledge, writing practice provides people with other sorts of knowledge that are useful in writing. For example, with increased experience, writers may acquire more effective writing strategies, more refined standards for evaluating text, more facility with specific genres, and so on. Indeed, writing experience is widely assumed to be essential for the development of high levels of writing skills.

The literature on expert performance provides some useful insights into the relation of practice and writing skill. In a landmark study, Chase and Simon (1973) provided evidence that skill in chess depends on a very large store of knowledge of chess patterns. They estimated that a grand master chess player had at least 50,000 chess patterns stored in memory. They noted that chess players typically take 10 years or more to acquire such chess knowledge. Following this lead, Hayes (1985) conducted biographic studies to determine if famous composers also required long periods of practice before they began to produce the works for which they were famous. He examined the lives of 76 composers to determine when each had begun the serious practice of music. He then determined how long after this beginning date each of the composers' major works had been written. (A major work was defined as one for which at least five independent recordings were available.)

Hayes found that almost none of the major works were written in the first 10 years after the beginning of practice. From about 10 to 20 years after the beginning of practice, there was a rapid increase in the production of major works. From 20 years to about 45 years, productivity remained fairly stable at about one work every 3 years. Hayes then carried out a parallel study in which he examined the lives of 131 painters. In this case, the criterion of a major work was inclusion in one of a set of general histories of art. The results for the painters were quite similar to those for the composers. Wishbow (1988) conducted a parallel study of 66 English and American poets, defining a major work as one included in the *Norton Anthology of Poetry*. Her results closely paralleled those found for composers and painters.

These three studies indicate that even very talented individuals require a long period of practice before they can produce notable works of music, art, or poetry. Many years of practice also may be required to attain expert performance in any of the genres of writing.

Conclusions

The new writing framework I have presented here is intended to provide a more accurate and more comprehensive description of available observation than was provided by the Hayes–Flower (1980) model. The major changes in focus in the new framework are greater attention to the role of working memory in writing, inclusion of the visual–spatial dimension, the integration of motivation and affect with the cognitive processes, and a reorganization of the cognitive processes that places greater emphasis on the function of text interpretation processes in writing. In addition, the new framework includes new and more specific models of planning, text production, and revision and proposes a number of testable hypotheses about writing processes.

I hope that the new framework provides a clearer and more comprehensive description of writing processes than did the earlier model. However, it will have served its function if it stimulates new research and discussion.

Acknowledgments

The author wishes to express thanks to Karen A. Schriver for her many critical readings of this manuscript and for her extensive help in its preparation. The author is also greatly indebted to Michael Levy, Sarah Ransdell, Gert Rijlaarsdam, and Eliza Beth Littleton for many helpful comments. In addition, the author would like to recognize the stimulating discussions and collegial support provided by his many friends at the Center for Language and Communication, University of Utrecht, where much of this manuscript was written.

References

Baddeley, A.D. (1986). *Working memory*. Oxford, UK: Oxford University Press.

Baddeley, A.D., & Lewis, V.J. (1981). Inner active processing in reading: The inner voice, the inner ear and the inner eye. In A.M. Lesgold & C.A. Perfetti (Eds.), *Interactive processes in reading* (pp. 107–129). Hillsdale, NJ: Erlbaum.

Bazerman, C. (1988). *Shaping written knowledge: The genre and activity of the experimental article in science*. Madison: University of Wisconsin Press.

Bereiter, C., & Scardamalia, M. (1987). *The psychology of written composition*. Hillsdale, NJ: Erlbaum.

Blakeslee, A.M. (1992). *Investing scientific discourse: Dimensions of rhetorical knowledge in physics*. Unpublished doctoral dissertation, Carnegie Mellon University, Pittsburgh, PA.

Bond, S., & Hayes, J.R. (1984). Cues people use to paragraph text. *Research in the Teaching of English*, *18*, 147–167.

Bower, G.H. (1972). Mental imagery and associative learning. In L. Gregg (Ed.), *Cognition in learning and memory*. New York: Wiley.

Braddock, R. (1992). The frequency and placement of topic sentences in expository prose. *Research in the Teaching of English*, *8*, 287–302.

Chase, W., & Simon, H.A. (1973). Perception in chess. *Cognitive Psychology*, *4*, 55–81.

Chenoweth, A. (1995, March). *Recognizing the role of reading in writing*. Paper presented at the College Composition and Communication Conference, Washington, DC.

Dweck, C. (1986). Motivational processes affecting learning. *American Psychologist*, *41*, 1040–1048.

Finn, J.D., & Cox, D. (1992). Participation and withdrawal among fourth-grade pupils. *American Educational Research Journal*, *29*(1), 141–162.

Flower, L.S., & Hayes, J.R. (1980a). The cognition of discovery: Defining a rhetorical problem. *College Composition and Communication*, *31*, 21–32.

Flower, L.S., & Hayes J.R. (1980b). The dynamics of composing: Making plans and juggling constraints. In L.W. Gregg & E.R. Steinberg (Eds.), *Cognitive processes in writing* (pp. 31–50). Hillsdale, NJ: Erlbaum.

Freedman, S.W. (1987). *Peer response groups in two ninth-grade classrooms* (Tech. Rep. No. 12). Berkeley: University of California, Center for the Study of Writing.

Friedlander, A. (1987). *The writer stumbles: Constraints on composing in English as a second language*. Unpublished doctoral dissertation, Carnegie Mellon University, Pittsburgh, PA.

Garrett, M.F. (1976). Syntactic processes in sentence production. In R.J. Wales & E. Walker (Eds.), *New approaches to language mechanisms* (pp. 231–255). Amsterdam: North-Holland.

Garrett, M.F. (1980). Levels of processing in sentence production. In B. Butterworth (Ed.), *Language production: Vol. 2. Speech and talk*. New York: Academic Press.

Gould, J.D., & Grischkowsky, N. (1984). Doing the same work with hard copy and with CRT terminals. *Human Factors, 26*, 323–337.

Greenberg, M.A., & Stone, A.A. (1992). Writing about disclosed versus undisclosed traumas: Immediate and long-term effects on mood and health. *Journal of Personality and Social Psychology, 63*, 75–84.

Greene, S. (1991). *Writing from sources: Authority in text and task* (Tech. Rep. No. 55). Berkeley: University of California, Center for the Study of Writing.

Haas, C. (1987). *How the writing medium shapes the writing process: Studies of writers composing with pen and paper and with word processing.* Unpublished doctoral dissertation, Carnegie Mellon University, Pittsburgh, PA.

Haas, C., & Hayes, J.R. (1986). What did I just say? Reading problems in writing with the machine. *Research in the Teaching of English, 20*, 22–35.

Hatch, J., Hill, C., & Hayes, J.R. (1993). When the messenger is the message: Readers' impressions of writers. *Written Communication, 10*(4), 569–598.

Hayes, J.R. (1985). Three problems in teaching general skills. In S. Chipman, J. Segal, & R. Glaser (Eds.), *Thinking and learning skills.* Hillsdale, NJ: Erlbaum.

Hayes, J.R. (1989). *The complete problem solver* (2nd ed.). Hillsdale, NJ: Erlbaum.

Hayes, J.R., & Flower, L.S. (1980). Identifying the organization of writing processes. In L. Gregg & E.R. Steinberg (Eds.), *Cognitive processes in writing* (pp. 3–30). Hillsdale, NJ: Erlbaum.

Hayes, J.R., Flower, L.S., Schriver, K.A., Stratman, J., & Carey, L. (1987). Cognitive processes in revision. In S. Rosenberg (Ed.), *Advances in applied psycholinguistics: Vol. 2. Reading, writing, and language processing* (pp. 176–240). New York: Cambridge University Press.

Hayes, J.R., & Nash, J.G. (1996). On the value of planning in writing. In C.M. Levy & S.E. Ransdell (Eds.), *The science of writing: Theories, methods, individual differences, and applications.* Mahwah, NJ: Erlbaum.

Hayes, J.R., Schriver, K.A., Hill, C., & Hatch, J. (1990). *Seeing problems with text: How students' engagement makes a difference* (Final report of Project 3, Study 17). Pittsburgh, PA: Center for the Study of Writing, Carnegie Mellon University.

Hayes, J.R., Schriver, K.A., Spilka, R., & Blaustein, A. (1986). *If it's clear to me, it must be clear to them.* Paper presented at the College Composition and Communication Conference, New Orleans, LA.

Hayes, J.R., & Simon, H.A. (1974). Understanding written problem instructions. In L.W. Gregg (Ed.), *Knowledge and cognition.* Hillsdale, NJ: Erlbaum.

Hayes, J.R., Waterman, D., & Robinson, S. (1977). Identifying the relevant aspects of a problem text. *Cognitive Science, 1*, 297–313.

Heath, S.B. (1983). *Ways with words: Language, life, and work in communities and classrooms.* New York: Cambridge University Press.

Hilgard, E.R. (1987). *Psychology in America: A historical survey.* New York: Harcourt Brace Jovanovich.

Hill, C. (1992). *Thinking through controversy: The effect of writing on the argument evaluation process of first-year college students.* Unpublished doctoral dissertation, Carnegie Mellon University, Pittsburgh, PA.

Hull, C.L. (1943). *Principles of behavior.* New York: Appleton Century Crofts.

Hull, G. (1993). Hearing other voices: A critical assessment of popular views on literacy and work. *Harvard Educational Review, 63*(1), 20–49.

Hutchins, E. (1995). *Cognition in the wild.* Cambridge, MA: MIT Press.

Just, M.A., & Carpenter, P.A. (1980). A theory of reading: From eye fixations to comprehension. *Psychological Review, 87*, 329–354.

Kaufer, D.S., Hayes, J.R., & Flower, L.S. (1986). Composing written sentences. *Research in the Teaching of English, 20*, 121–140.

Larkin, J.E., & Simon, H.A. (1987). Why a diagram is (sometimes) worth ten thousand words. *Cognitive Science, 11*, 65–99.

Matsuhashi, A. (1981). Pausing and planning: The tempo of written discourse production. *Research in the Teaching of English, 15*, 113–134.

Myers, G. (1985a). The social construction of two biologists' proposals. *Written Communication, 2*, 219–245.

Myers, G. (1985b). Text as knowledge claims: The social construction of two biologists' proposals. *Written Communication, 2*, 219–245.

Nelson, J. (1988). *Examining the practices that shape student writing: Two studies of college freshmen writing across disciplines*. Unpublished doctoral dissertation, Carnegie Mellon University, Pittsburgh, PA.

Newell, A. (1990). *United theories of cognition*. Cambridge, MA: Harvard University Press.

O'Donnell, A.M., Dansereau, D.F., Rocklin, T., Lambiote, J.G., Hythecker, V.I., & Larson, C.O. (1985). Cooperative writing: Direct effects and transfer. *Written Communication*, *2*(3), 307–315.

O'Hara, K. (1996). *Cost of operations affects planfulness of problem-solving.*

Paivio, A. (1971). *Imagery and verbal processes*. New York: Holt, Rinehart and Winston.

Palmquist, M., & Young, R. (1992). The notion of giftedness and student expectations about writing. *Written Communication*, *9*(1), 137–168.

Pennebaker, J.W., & Beall, S.K. (1986). Confronting a traumatic event: Toward an understanding of inhibition and disease. *Journal of Abnormal Psychology*, *95*(3), 274–281.

Pennebaker, J.W., Kiecolt-Glaser, R. (1988). Disclosure of traumas and immune function: Health implications for psychotherapy. *Journal of Consulting and Clinical Psychology*, *56*, 239–245.

Redish, J. (1993). Understanding readers. In C.M. Barnum & S. Carliner (Eds.), *Techniques for technical communicators* (pp. 14–41). New York: Macmillan.

Reitman, W.R. (1964). Heuristic decision procedures, open constraints, and the structure of ill-defined problems. In M.W. Shelley & G.L. Bryan (Eds.), *Human judgment and optimality*. New York: Wiley.

Rothkopf, E.Z. (1971). Incidental memory for location of information in text. *Journal of Verbal Learning and Verbal Behavior*, *10*, 608–613.

Santa, J.L. (1977). Spatial transformations of words and pictures. *Journal of Experimental Psychology: Human Learning and Memory*, *3*, 418–427.

Schilperoord, J. (1996). *It's about time: Temporal aspects of cognitive processes in text production*. Unpublished doctoral dissertation, Carnegie Mellon University, Pittsburgh, PA.

Schriver, K.A. (1987). *Teaching writers to anticipate the reader's needs: Empirically based instruction*. Unpublished doctoral dissertation, Carnegie Mellon University, Pittsburgh, PA.

Schriver, K.A. (1995, June). *Document design as*

rhetorical action. Belle van Zuylen Lecture Series, the Netherlands: University of Utrecht (available from Faculteitsbureau, Kromme Nieuwegracht 46, 3512 H.J. Utrecht).

Schriver, K.A. (1996). *Dynamics in document design*. New York: Wiley.

Schriver, K.A., Hayes, J.R., & Steffy, A. (1994). Designing drug education literature: A real audience speaks back. *Briefs on Writing*, *1*(1), 1–4. Berkeley: University of California, National Center for Study of Writing and Literacy.

Siegler, R.S., Adolph, K., & Lemaire, P. (1995). *Strategy choices across the lifespan*. Paper presented at the Carnegie Symposium on Cognition: Implicit Memory and Metacognition.

Simon, H.A., & Hayes, J.R. (1976). The understanding process: Problem isomorphs. *Cognitive Psychology*, *8*, 165–190.

Sperling, M. (1991). *High school English and the teacher-student writing conference: Fine tuned duets in the ensemble of the classroom*. (Occasional Paper No. 26). Berkeley: University of California, Center for the Study of Writing.

Spivey, N.N. (1984). *Discourse synthesis: Constructing texts in reading and writing* (Outstanding Dissertation Monograph Series). Newark, DE: International Reading Association

Sproull, L., & Kiesler, S. (1986). Reducing social context cues: Electronic mail in organization communication. *Management Science*, *32*, 1492–1512.

Stein, V. (1992). *How we begin to remember: Elaboration, task and the transformation of knowledge*. Unpublished doctoral dissertation, Carnegie Mellon University, Pittsburgh, PA.

Swaney, J., Janik C., Bond, S., & Hayes J.R. (1991). Editing for comprehension: Improving the process through reading protocols. In E.R. Steinberg (Ed.), *Plain language: Principles and practice*. Detroit, MI: Wayne State University Press.

van der Mast, N.P. (1996). Adjusting target figures downwards: On the collaborative writing of policy documents in the Dutch government. In M. Sharples & T. van der Geest (Eds.), *The new writing environment: Writers at work in a world of technology*. London: Springer-Verlag.

Velez, L. (1994). *Interpreting and writing in the laboratory: A study of novice biologists as novice rhetors*. Unpublished doctoral dissertation, Carnegie Mellon University, Pittsburgh, PA.

Wallace, D.L., & Hayes, J.R. (1991). Redefining revision for freshmen. *Research in the Teaching of English, 25, 54–66.*

Wishbow, N. (1988). *Studies of creativity in poets.* Unpublished doctoral dissertation, Carnegie Mellon University, Pittsburgh, PA.

Wright, P., Creighton, P., & Threlfall, S.M. (1982). Some factors determining when instructions will be read. *Ergonomics, 25,* 225–237.

Zasloff, T. (1984). *Diagnosing student writing: Problems encountered by college freshmen.* Unpublished doctoral dissertation, Carnegie Mellon University, Pittsburgh, PA.

50

Model of Attitude Influence
Upon Reading and Learning
to Read

Grover C. Mathewson

fter analyzing the content of articles published in *The Reading Teacher* from 1948 to 1991, Dillon et al. (1992) concluded that the topics of attitude, habit, and interest had "maintained their popularity over the years" (p. 365). This finding is consistent with Prawat's (1985) conclusion that affective factors are of great interest to teachers. However, affective influences on reading do not appear to have stimulated similar interest among researchers recently. For example, a reading conference yearbook (Zutell & McCormick, 1991), a reading research handbook (Barr, Kamil, Mosenthal, & Pearson, 1991), and a survey of research implications for reading instruction (Samuels & Farstrup, 1992) lack any paper or chapter titles that reflect traditional affective topics such as attitude, motivation, and interest.

A possible explanation for the lack of focus on affect is the difficulty of researching affective variables; another is a recent strong and exclusive emphasis on cognitive variables. Anderson (1980) and Simon and Kaplan (1989) have pointed out that investigators such as Chomsky (1965) in psycholinguistics, Newell and Simon (1972) in artificial intelligence, and Hebb (1949) in neurophysiology provided foundations for cognitive research. The ascendance of the computer as a model of thinking appears to have reinforced a cognitive approach. The scientific study of affect has been so impoverished that Sorrentino and Higgins (1986) described their own affective interest, motivation, as "flat on its back" (p. 6) by the early 1970s. Much the same could be said for the empirical study of affect in reading research.

Although the study of affect has been quiescent, a number of investigators in social psychology have noted that attitude is beginning to attract attention again (see, e.g., Ajzen, 1989; Breckler & Wiggins, 1989; Chaiken & Stangor, 1987;

From Ruddell, R.B., Ruddell, M.R., & Singer, H. (Eds.), *Theoretical Models and Processes of Reading* (4th ed., pp. 1131–1161). Copyright © 1994 by the International Reading Association.

Petty & Cacioppo, 1986). In view of this resurgence of interest, it is appropriate to revisit the relationships between attitude and reading.

This reinvestigation begins with issues raised by two theoretical models (Mathewson, 1976, 1985) developed to serve as heuristic devices for generating predictions and guiding practice in reading. The 1976 model was intended to clarify relationships between attitude and reading using a small set of variables: attitude, motivation, attention, and comprehension. Other variables were added to the 1985 model in an effort to widen its scope. Research and reflection have shown that although the two models fulfilled their heuristic purposes to some extent, both had shortcomings. The model presented here is intended to correct those shortcomings and to provide directions for future research and practice.

The first section of this article resolves fundamental issues raised by the earlier models and applies these resolutions to construction of subassemblies for the new model. The second section integrates the subassemblies to form the new model and explores its characteristics. Finally, the third section describes the new model's implications for research and instruction.

Issues Raised by the 1976 and 1985 Models

Following the publication of the 1976 and 1985 models, several fundamental issues were identified concerning the relationships of attitude to reading. Some of these issues were conceptual in nature, while others arose from experimental findings. The conceptual issues were identified through evaluation of the strength of the models' individual components and the internal consistency among them. A primary issue was whether attitude, a pivotal construct in the two models, deserved its central role.

Why Is Attitude Central?

In the 1976 model, attitude was chosen as central because it has long played a major role in psychological research. G.W. Allport (1966) called attitude "the most distinctive and indispensable concept in contemporary American social psychology" (p. 15). As mentioned previously, however, attention to the importance of attitude as a scientific concept has diminished in favor of cognitive variables. The study of attitude may also have declined because it failed in many instances to predict specific behaviors (Ajzen, 1989). Applied to reading, this finding means that positive attitude does not always predict such behaviors as attention to and comprehension of reading selections.

The failure of attitude to provide reliable behavioral predictions might be viewed as a justification for abandoning research into attitude–reading relationships. Fazio and Zanna (1981), however, pointed out that the inconsistent relationships obtained between attitude and behavior could be better understood if researchers asked, "Under what conditions do what kinds of attitudes held by what kinds of individuals predict what kinds of behavior?" (p. 165). More specifically, Fazio (1986) indicated that social psychology now has a "'catalog' of variables known to moderate the attitude-behavior relation" (p. 206). This catalog includes normative constraints and inducements, personality factors, level of moral reasoning, and self-monitoring. Specifically concerning reading, extrinsic motivation has been suggested as a moderator variable (Mathewson, 1979). McGuire (1989) listed involvement, publicity of the behavior, and salience of past behavior. More recently, Fortner and Henk (1991) added ego involvement, prior knowledge, and purpose to the list of moderator variables affecting attitude–reading relationships.

The new model should represent the most significant of the widespread variables that moderate attitude–reading relationships. Representing moderating variables is important because researchers seeking to test the effects of attitude on reading must know what conditions permit effects to appear. Similarly, teachers must be aware of the conditions under which readers' internalized attitudes sustain reading as opposed to the conditions under which external influences, such as teacher-provided purpose or incentive, are responsible for reading behavior.

Previously ignored moderating variables may be added to the model either by inserting new components or by modifying the model's underlying theory. Of these approaches, it is preferable to modify underlying theory because the number of components in the model will be minimized. However, components representing important, distinct, and theoretically unitary processes require separate representation. In the following section, the attitude concept is analyzed in detail in order to eliminate the need for some additional components and to clarify attitude's role in reading. Following this analysis, intention to read is proposed as the central component mediating the attitude–reading relationship, and two primary influences affecting intention development are identified.

Defining Attitude

An examination of the literature shows that definitions of attitude emphasize evaluation, action, or feeling, depending on the investigator. Emphasizing evaluation, Beck (1983) defined attitude as "a positive or negative evaluation of some person, object, or thing" (p. 302). Emphasizing action, Ajzen (1989) defined attitude as "an individual's disposition to respond favorably or unfavorably to an object, person, institution, or event, or to any other discriminable aspect of the individual's world" (p. 241). Emphasizing feeling, Petty and Cacioppo (1981) defined attitude as "a general and enduring positive or negative feeling about some person, object, or issue" (p. 7). Each of these definitions contributes important understanding to the attitude concept.

Many attitude theorists now choose to emphasize only the evaluative aspect of attitude (see, e.g., Petty & Cacioppo, 1986), but this minimalist approach may not be best because much of the richness of the attitude concept is lost. A more inclusive option with strong roots in social psychology is the adoption of a tricomponent view of attitude with evaluation as the cognitive component, feeling as the affective component, and action readiness as the conative component. The tricomponent approach has strong precedent in Indo-European thought (McGuire, 1989), and the philosopher Kant (1790/1951) believed that there are three irreducible components of mind: "the faculty of knowledge, the feeling of pleasure and pain, and the faculty of desire" (p. 13). In social psychology, cognitive, affective, and conative aspects have been used extensively to characterize attitude (Kretch & Crutchfield, 1948; Rosenberg et al., 1960), and the unity of the three aspects within a single attitude has been confirmed by strong correlations among them (Ostrom, 1969). F.H. Allport (1924) pointed out the practical power of the tricomponent approach when describing Othello as "wrought upon by the persistent artifices of Iago until an attitude of infuriated vengeance toward Desdemona was developed" (p. 245). Here, Othello's attitude toward Desdemona includes an evaluation that she acted wrongly, a furious feeling toward her, and a plan of action to achieve vengeance. This literary example shows how an attitude concept including evaluative beliefs (cognitions), feelings (affect), and action readiness (conation) provides a richer description of Othello's mental disposition regarding Desdemona than would a narrower conception of attitude.

McGuire (1989) speculated that the three-component model of attitude will continue to be popular but that it might become a more productive research tool if open-ended responses were used in its measurement. This suggestion has strong implications for the place of qualitative research designs in investigating attitude–reading relationships when the tricomponent view of attitude is adopted. A qualitative approach to attitude–reading relationships will be described in the research implications section of this article.

Intention: Mediator Between Attitude and Reading

Fishbein and Ajzen (1975; see also Ajzen, 1989; Ajzen & Fishbein, 1980) made a persuasive case that attitudes do not affect behavior directly but are mediated by intention. This viewpoint implies that attitude toward reading gives rise to an intention to read, which then leads to reading itself. For example, if a person waiting in a doctor's office had a favorable attitude toward reading about current events in *Time* magazine, the person might form an intention to read the particular issue lying on a table. Actually picking up the magazine and reading an article would represent realization of the intention.

In contrast to the Fishbein–Ajzen approach, the 1976 model had no intermediate component between attitude and reading. The 1985 model moved in the Fishbein–Ajzen direction by interpolating decision to read between attitude and reading, although the model still allowed direct connection between attitude and reading through a "short circuit" bypassing the decision component. It now appears justifiable to abandon this short circuit and to replace *decision* with *intention* as the sole mediator between attitude toward reading and reading itself. There are at least three reasons for selecting intention instead of decision to read as the mediator. First, intention is a more inclusive concept than decision. Decisions may be represented as firm, well-defined intentions, but weak intentions also exist although they are not decisions. Second, G.W. Allport (1961) emphasized that intentionality is a basic human characteristic. People are always considering doing or becoming something in the future, and reading appears to be the kind of deliberate activity that people develop intentions to do before actually starting. Finally, Allport's characterization of intention as combining an emotional want with a cognitive plan fits the new model well because feeling and cognition are thereby represented in intention, as they are in attitude. A model subassembly using intention as a mediator between attitude and reading appears in Figure 1.

As a model component, intention may be defined as commitment to a plan for achieving one or more reading purposes at a more or less specified time in the future. Schuman and Kalton (1985) found that intention is closely related to behavior when the planned behavior is well defined and when time between forming the intention and carrying it out is relatively short.

The firmness of an intention may be measured by "the person's subjective probability that he will perform the behavior in question" (Fishbein & Ajzen, 1975, p. 12). For example, the firmness of a person's intention to read tomorrow's newspaper could be measured on a scale ranging from "definitely" (a firm intention) to "unsure" (not committed) to "definitely not" (resistance to forming an intention).

Figure 1 shows the core of the new model. The three aspects of attitude toward reading form a whole attitude that influences intention to read; intention to

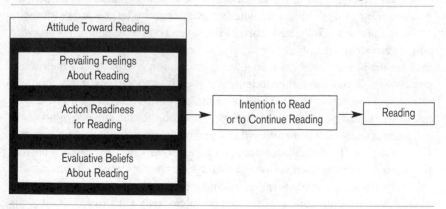

FIGURE 1
Relationships Among Attitude, Intention, and Reading

read in turn influences reading behavior. Intention formation always precedes reading, although at times intentions may be brief and unverbalized. The rationale for omitting a direct route from attitude to reading is that a positive attitude only results in reading if other influences favoring formation of positive intentions to read are present. An appropriate setting and a calm state of mind might, for example, favor development of an intention to read, but absence of these influences would not necessarily mean that attitude toward reading had become negative.

External Motivators and Internal Emotional State

In addition to attitude, external motivators and internal emotional state influence intention to read. External motivators have less intrinsic relationship to reading than does attitude. Attitude toward reading includes evaluations of content and purpose, feelings about engaging in a particular kind of reading, and action readiness for initiating or sustaining reading activity. External motivators are incentives, purposes, norms, and settings outside of readers that influence their intention to engage in reading activity.

Incentives and purposes for reading are similar in that both offer objectives to readers. Incentives energize and direct reading by offering personally desirable objectives such as gold stars, good grades, pizza parties, or success in later life. Purposes, on the other hand, provide objectives such as reading to discover how a character solves a problem or to find the main idea of a text selection.

Norms, often called *subjective norms* in social psychology, are behavioral expectations provided by other people. As does attitude, subjective norms and settings influence intention to read, and intention to read in turn influences reading behavior. Together, subjective norms and settings determine if reading is judged to be an appropriate thing to do regardless of whether one enjoys reading. For example, at a dinner party, even enthusiastic readers normally do not read because social interchange is expected. On the other hand, even those with neutral or negative attitudes toward reading might read at a library because others expect reading to occur there. The social expectations inherent in dinner party and library settings moderate whether existing attitudes toward reading are expressed in action. Subjective norms also depend on the reference groups with which individuals identify. For example, junior high school students in a library may not read because they perceive that conversation is expected by their reference group. In this case, the students are attending to a peer subjective norm rather than the one advocated by librarians. It is not necessary for those with particular subjective norms to be present in a setting for the subjective norms to influence intentions. The memory that a person or group holds certain expectations may be sufficient. Students alone in their rooms may experience normative influences to read their textbooks although no teachers or parents are present.

By including a component representing external motivators, the new model takes into account social influences not previously considered. Attitude is viewed as affecting reading only if readers believe that their social and physical surroundings are compatible with reading activity. The earlier models neither recognized that these compatibilities were important nor that other people sometimes make conscious attempts to influence readers through purposes and incentives for reading.

Whether externally provided incentives are effective in evoking more than transitory activity has been a subject of debate and research. The well-known Lepper and Greene (1975) study suggests that external incentives may suppress children's interest in activities that they previously liked. However, in spite of the potential for external incentives to be perceived as outside control or bribery, it also appears possible that behaviors sustained by external incentives might eventually become intrinsically rewarding. This idea is conveyed in G.W. Allport's (1961) concept of functional autonomy, which he viewed as "self-sustaining, contemporary systems, growing out of antecedent systems, but functionally independent of them" (p. 299). From Allport's perspective, reading behavior initiated by external incentives would have a chance to become functionally autonomous and personally rewarding with the passage of time.

The second primary influence on intention formation, internal emotional state, is important because reading requires close attention to the flow of ideas being reconstructed from the printed page. Reconstructing meaning and making subsequent associations depend on the reader's focusing attention to the exclusion of potentially intruding, incompatible emotions. On the other hand, emotions may facilitate reading if the construction of meaning during reading is accompanied by a simultaneous construction of supportive emotion. The mutual construction of meaning and emotion is related to Mandler's (1985) idea that emotions are constructed experiences based on "cognitive analysis and physiological (autonomic nervous system) response" (p. 114). Given this view of emotions, it is not hard to imagine that readers reconstruct not only authors' meanings but also their feelings.

The subassembly shown in Figure 2 represents the influences upon intention to read described up to this point. External motivators take the place of the extrinsic motivation proposed in Mathewson (1979). Fortner and Henk's (1991) concept of ego involvement is not shown as a separate component but is present as the subjective importance of attitude toward reading. Equating subjective importance with ego involvement is based on Judd and Krosnick's (1989) assessment that there is little difference between these two concepts, and also on the observation that subjective importance does not imply Freudian psychodynamics to the same extent as does ego involvement.

Influences on intention formation not shown in Figure 2 are *internalized purposes*. These purposes are part of intention to read, a complex involving an internalized purpose, a plan, and a time frame for beginning or continuing reading. In contrast, *external purposes* arise from outside sources. Readers weigh

FIGURE 2
Direct Influences Upon Intention to Read

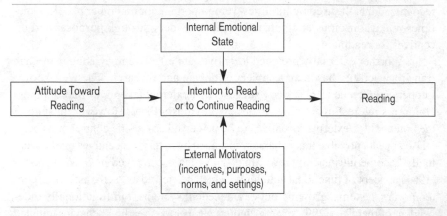

these purposes to determine the advisability of accepting them. If a reader accepts externally provided purposes, they become part of the reader's intentions and thus influence reading. Although not shown in Figure 2, acceptance of external purposes may also change readers' attitudes toward reading. The path for this change will be described when the impact of persuasion on reading attitude is considered in a later section.

In Quest of a Motivational Perspective

Up to this point, motivation has been considered with respect to the activation effects of attitudes, external motivators, and emotional states. In both the 1976 and 1985 models, however, reading motivation was explained by reference to particular motives advocated by psychologists, such as motive to self-actualize (Maslow, 1970), achievement motive (Atkinson & Feather, 1966; McClelland et al., 1953), and curiosity motive (Berlyne, 1960, 1966). These motives were described as providing both energy and direction to the reading process. In the 1976 model, optimum reading was viewed as occurring when specific motives to read along with positive attitudes toward reading were mobilized. However, reviews have questioned aspects of some of the theories of motivation. For example, it is not clear that Maslow's list of motives is hierarchical (the lower motives must be satisfied before the higher ones become active) or that his categorization of motives is accurate (Ewen, 1988). Other motivational theories also may have weaknesses, may overlap, or may be incompatible with one another. Thus, by including so many divergent motivational theories, the two earlier affective models of reading rested on foundations that may have been weak and self-contradictory. Ewen's comment in evaluating Maslow's theory is appropriately applied to the motivational components of the 1976 and 1985 models: "Eclecticism requires more than merely accepting under one theoretical roof all those constructs of other theorists that one likes. The various ideas must also be integrated into a meaningful and noncontradictory whole" (p. 416). Unfortunately, deciding the validity and compatibility of the various motivational theories is a daunting task, seemingly impossible because it is so extensive.

The problem of deciding among motivational theories may be avoided if the inherently motivational nature of attitude and intention is emphasized and reliance on the various theories put forward by motivational psychologists is eliminated. In this approach, motivation may be defined as development of conditions promoting intention to read. In terms of the model subassembly presented in Figure 2, motivation may be enhanced by favorable attitudes toward reading, external motivators, and internal emotional states. Elements of attitude, such as the evaluative belief that reading will bring pleasure, or externally provided incentives, such as a grade on a test, could be regarded as contributing to motivation to read.

Defining motivation in terms of intention has the advantage of creating a theoretically unified view. If a teacher says that John is motivated to read, the teacher means that John has developed firm intentions to read for any of a variety of reasons. One would hope that John's reasons did not depend entirely upon external motivators, for if they did, John's reading would not be sustained if the external motivators were lost. If, however, John's motivation to read was based upon favorable evaluative beliefs, feelings, and action readiness concerning content, his reading would be sustained as long as he found appropriate materials and his energy did not flag.

The model's new view of the motivational functions of attitude and intention to some extent meets Downing and Leong's (1982) criticism that the 1976 model may not have needed a separate motivational component. Attitude in the new model is regarded as dynamic in that it fosters development of intention to read; intention then provides proximal influence on reading behavior. This view of the energizing nature of attitude is somewhat different from that proposed by G.W. Allport (1966) but is more in the spirit of what Downing and Leong appear to have had in mind.

Inconsistent Experimental Findings Now Explicable

Incongruous findings based on the earlier models may be examined from the new perspective. For example, in Mathewson (1985), I predicted specifically that experimentally created positive attitudes toward content should improve attention to and comprehension of text. This hypothesis was tested by Hollingsworth and Reutzel (1990), who induced positive, neutral, or negative attitudes toward a fictitious country called "Titubia" in 3 groups of randomly assigned sixth-grade students. After the attitude induction, the students were given a multiple-choice and a free-recall test on an attitudinally neutral reading selection on Titubia.

Analysis of the data showed no difference in recall among the groups with induced positive, neutral, and negative attitudes toward Titubia. Hollingsworth and Reutzel concluded that their own and others' failures to find an effect of attitude "seems to bear out the fact that content attitudes do not play a major role in the seeking, acceptance, encoding, storage, or retrieval of topical information in text measured immediately after reading" (p. 199). Their findings were replicated in Reutzel and Hollingsworth (1991) and are consistent with findings of Henk and Holmes (1988) and Fortner and Henk (1991), who found no relationship between preexisting attitudes and literal recall.

An alternate explanation of Hollingsworth and Reutzel's (1990) failure to find the expected attitude–recall relationship is suggested by the Figure 2 subassembly. In Figure 2, attitude influences intention to read, and intention to read in turn influences reading. If intention to read in the Hollingsworth and Reutzel study was sustained by an influence other than attitude, this other influence may have accounted for the recall across all groups. An analysis of the method employed in the study indicates that the students knew they would be tested on their reading. Their desire to perform well on the test could have led them to form an intention to comprehend regardless of whether their attitudes toward Titubia were positive, neutral, or negative.

The explanation that an external incentive could produce an intention to read in the presence of neutral or negative attitudes toward content is easy to exemplify. Often students read assignments carefully although they lack favorable attitudes toward the content. Externally provided incentives in the form of grades on tests and report cards frequently sustain intention to read, regardless of whether attitude toward content is positive or negative (Mathewson, 1979).

Another possible explanation of Hollingsworth and Reutzel's (1990) results involves the difference between using attitude toward content and using attitude toward reading to predict reading behavior. In the study, the fictional country of Titubia appeared to be "an island wonderland" to the favorable group and "a most unpleasant and uninviting habitat" (p. 196) to the unfavorable group. The question is whether attitude toward particular content—Titubia in this case—is the same as attitude toward reading *about* that content. If the two are the same, attitude toward content should correlate exactly with intent to read. For example, if readers do not like cats, they will fail to develop intentions to read about cats; if they like cats, they will develop intentions to read about them and follow through with these intentions. The principle seems sensible, but it does not explain why people sometimes read unpleasant content about such things as income tax. Clearly it is not true that people read about income tax because they like income tax.

People's willingness to read disliked content may be understood through this adaptation of a formula proposed by Fishbein and Ajzen (1975, pp. 223–224):

EBT (evaluative belief total) = $\Sigma\ b_i e_i$

Applied to reading, this formula means that the strength of each salient belief about reading (b_i) is multiplied by the evaluation of that belief (e_i) to obtain an evaluative belief score ($b_i e_i$). The evaluative belief scores are then summed (Σ) to obtain the evaluative belief total (EBT). EBT represents the aggregate of the evaluative beliefs about reading. Fishbein and Ajzen originally intended the formula to calculate attitude itself, but EBT has been substituted in this discussion because the formula encompasses only attitude's cognitive component and fails to take into consideration either feeling or action readiness.

Applying the EBT formula to a book about income tax yields interesting insights. Table 1 represents a hypothetical instance in which evaluative belief scores are calculated and summed for four salient beliefs characterizing such a book. The numerical values in this table are for demonstration only and fall on a +3 to –3 scale. Most of the salient beliefs are accompanied by positive evaluations, but Belief 3, "The book is about income tax," has a negative evaluation of –3, resulting in a negative evaluative belief product of –9. However, the EBT of +12 indicates that the aggregate of evaluative beliefs about reading the book is positive in spite of the single negative evaluative belief concerning income-tax content. The EBT of +12 predicts that the reader will read the book if this and the other two components of attitude (feelings and action readiness) lead to development of an intention to read and if expression of the intention is not blocked.

The adaptation of Fishbein and Ajzen's (1975) formula helps show how attitude toward reading may be different from evaluation of content. In the case of the Hollingsworth and Reutzel (1990) study, students in the unfavorable-attitude group held negative evaluative beliefs concerning Titubia but might also have held positive evaluative beliefs counterbalancing the negative ones. For example, although Titubia was judged to be a bad place, reading about Titubians may have been judged good in the light of a possible evaluative belief that "Titubians face difficult problems," presuming that it is interesting to read about people trying to overcome adversity. A positive EBT might therefore have resulted despite the negative evaluative belief that Titubia was uninviting.

TABLE 1
Evaluative Beliefs About a Book on Income Tax

Salient Beliefs	b_i	e_i	$b_i e_i$
1. The book is accurate.	+3	+2	+6
2. The book is comprehensible.	+2	+3	+6
3. The book is about income tax.	+3	–3	–9
4. The book's content is useful.	+3	+3	+9

EBT = $\Sigma \, b_i e_i$ = +12

The evaluative belief concept is useful not only in numerical analyses but in nonnumeric or qualitative descriptions of the model's operations. In the non-numeric sense, evaluative beliefs are those beliefs about reading that carry positive or negative connotations for a given person. For example, a child's belief that Jack London's *Call of the Wild* contains violence would be designated as a negative evaluative belief about the book for a child who regards violence as bad. This negative evaluative belief might become the salient determiner of the child's attitude toward reading *Call of the Wild* unless other salient evaluative beliefs, such as a positive evaluative belief that the book is about a dog, provide counterbalance and prompt an overall favorable attitude toward reading.

In summary, it may be concluded that Hollingsworth and Reutzel's (1990) study and other studies intended to test relationships between attitude and reading may have failed because (1) external motivators to read during testing masked the effects of attitude or (2) a single evaluative belief about content was used as the independent variable instead of total attitude toward reading (the aggregate of evaluative beliefs, prevailing feelings, and action readiness). Ways to correct these problems using the framework of the model are described in detail in the research implications section of this paper.

Objects of Attitudes Toward Reading

When research focuses on overall attitude toward reading rather than specific evaluative beliefs about content or style, an interesting and difficult question arises concerning the nature of the attitude object. If the researcher asks people if they like to read, they are likely to think that they are being asked whether there are frequent occasions during which they enjoy the kinds of reading that they generally do. However, a person's stating that he or she likes to read does not predict whether he or she enjoys reading topics or genres outside of ordinary routines. For example, most people who say they like reading probably would not enjoy a technical book on quantum mechanics. Their response to the suggestion that they read such a book might be "Well, I like to read, but not this!"

Researchers sometimes forget about the need for specificity in defining the attitude objects when performing experiments. Ajzen (1989) states that "broad attitude measures are found to be poor predictors of specific behaviors. This is perhaps the most important lesson to be learned from the prolonged controversy concerning the attitude-behavior relation, but also perhaps the most difficult to accept" (p. 255). Applied to reading, Ajzen's comment means that researchers cannot necessarily expect that general attitude toward reading will predict liking reading of specific types or that teaching students to enjoy one type of reading will influence enjoyment of other types. Instead, attitude measures must be specific to the purposes in question. People's attitudes toward reading about baseball would be expected to predict whether they will develop voluntary intentions to read baseball books, and a classroom project involving reading about baseball would be expected to improve attitude toward reading about baseball but not necessarily about other content.

Projects intended to enhance general attitude toward reading focus on two objectives: (1) improvement of attitudes toward reading a variety of contents and genres and (2) enhancement of the overall reading abilities of students. An example of this type of study was reported by Shapiro and White (1991), who tested attitudes of children from grades 1 through 6 at 2 schools. One of the schools used a traditional basal approach; the other used an individualized approach with 2 periods per day of library time, cross-age tutoring, cross-grade themes, and no regular basal instruction. Using the *Snoopy Reading Attitude Survey* (an informal instrument used previously in one of the schools) and *A Survey of Reading Attitudes* (Wallbrown, Brown, & Engin, 1977), Shapiro and White found that the individualized approach promoted more favorable reading attitudes than did the traditional approach.

From the point of view of the Figure 2 subassembly, the Wallbrown et al. (1977) attitude survey measured all three influences upon intention to read. The Reading as Enjoyment and The Reading Anxiety scales appear to have measured the internal emotional state component. The Expressed Reading Difficulty scale appears to have measured evaluative beliefs about difficulty of reading materials. Finally, the Reading as Direct Reinforcement and Reading Group scales appear to have measured students' responses to incentives and norms.

Although Shapiro and White (1991) probably measured the effects of all three of Figure 2's influences on intention to read, significant differences favoring the individualized treatment emerged on all dimensions of the survey instruments. These findings confirm the high coherence expected among attitude and its related components. However, in view of Ajzen's (1989) caution concerning broad attitude measures, it should also be noted that the attitude objects rated by the two groups of students in Shapiro and White's study were probably different. Reading for the traditional group may have meant reading basals, but reading for the individualized group may have meant reading various self-selected library books. Therefore it may be more appropriate to conclude that children's attitudes toward reading self-selected library books are more favorable than their attitudes toward reading stories and doing work in basals. The attitudes in both cases include feelings, evaluative beliefs, and action readiness with respect to the two different types of reading. General attitude toward reading may not have been measured in the Shapiro and White study, although what appear to be general attitude scales were used. However, the fact that attitudes toward two different types of reading may have been measured does not detract from the findings of the study. The caution is that the objects of attitude measurement should be precisely identified.

Interest and Attention

The need to use language precisely in describing constructs in the model extends to the term *interest*. In the 1976 model, interest was defined as "a favorable attitude with a strong action orientation" (p. 656). In the present model, it is similarly defined as a favorable attitude with high action readiness. Thus, favorable attitudes toward reading particular content would imply an interest if high readiness for action could be demonstrated. For example, observations or reports that readers frequently borrowed or bought books about the U.S. Civil War, spent time reading them on a daily basis, and perhaps even supplemented their reading with searches for original documents would suggest high action readiness and hence an interest in reading about this topic. Interest in the Civil War does not necessarily imply interest in reading about it, however. The probability of reading about the Civil War certainly appears to improve if positive attitudes toward the content are present, but undeveloped reading ability could prevent Civil War buffs from translating their content interests into reading interests. Conversely, reading such content does not necessarily imply favorable attitudes toward the Civil War. External motivators such as grades may give rise to reading although the attitude toward content is neutral or even negative.

As with affect in general, there has not been extensive research into the concept of interest (Wade & Adams, 1990). Much of the research has been done by relating interest in short text segments to ability to recall them. Shirey and Reynolds (1988), for example, found that children attended more to interesting sentences and learned them better than they did uninteresting sentences. This is predicted by the Figure 2 subassembly because increased firmness of intention to read interesting sentences would lead to higher attention, better strategy use, and deeper comprehension.

The Shirey and Reynolds (1988) experiment found a contrast between children's and adults' reading of interesting sentences. Children spent more time on interesting sentences and learned them better; adult readers also learned interesting sentences better but showed no increases in time spent reading them. One explanation for this finding is that adult readers have previous background concerning text that they find interesting and thus can comprehend such text with less allocation of attention. Children, on the other hand, must allocate more time to reading text they find interesting because their background ideas have not yet developed sufficiently to allow quick concept reconstruction.

Background Ideas, Feeling, and Attitude Influence

Although not taken into consideration explicitly in the 1976 and 1985 models, the concept of background ideas is important in the development of the new attitude model. The new model must be able to show that favorable attitude toward reading influences intention to read, that intention to read influences reading, and that the results of reading are ideas and feelings. The model must also show that prior ideas are used in reconstructing meaning from text. These relationships are portrayed in the subassembly presented in Figure 3.

In Figure 3, "Ideas Reconstructed From or Related to Reading Selection" include not only prior ideas relevant to the reconstruction of meaning but also the new ideas resulting from reading. This component therefore represents the unified knowledge network contributing to and resulting from reading processes. Ideas previously in readers' heads are brought to bear on the reconstruction of meaning from text, and reconstructed meaning continually suggests further related ideas.

Ideas reconstructed from or related to reading also give rise to specific feelings in the upper-right component of Figure 3. For example, the idea of Charlotte's death at the end of E.B. White's *Charlotte's Web* may stimulate sad feelings. These sad feelings may in turn lead to new, related ideas. Therefore, the right side of Figure 3 can be viewed as a triangle with reading, feeling, and idea components interacting dynamically during the reading process.

The specific feelings in the component at the top right in Figure 3 are not the same as the prevailing feelings about reading within attitude (see Figure 1) or the internal emotional state of the reader (see Figure 2). Specific feelings are brief responses to particular words and sentences in text. These may cumulatively affect internal emotional state and, if they are significantly strong and representative, may also affect the prevailing feelings that are part of readers' attitudes toward reading.

FIGURE 3
Articulation of the Reading Process

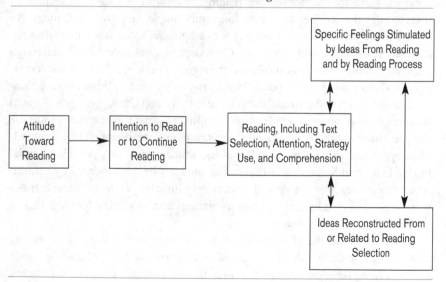

The subassembly in Figure 3 shows that a favorable attitude ultimately results in the development of ideas related to that attitude. For example, a reader with a favorable content-related attitude toward birds would be likely to develop intentions to read bird books, actually read bird books, and learn new information about birds. Under normal circumstances, therefore, it is expected that mature readers with favorable attitudes toward topics also possess more ideas about those topics through selective exposure to reading materials.

It should be noted that attempting to determine the effects of attitude upon comprehension while holding prior knowledge constant is not defensible. Doing so is similar to trying to assess the height of a tree's branches while controlling for the depth of its roots. As are roots and branches, positive attitude and background ideas are mutually facilitative and would be expected to develop concurrently.

Persuasion and Cornerstone Concepts

All of the new model's influences have been defined at this point, except for persuasion and a class of personal commitments I call *cornerstone concepts*. Both persuasion and cornerstone concepts are important because they directly affect students' attitudes toward reading.

The first of the direct influences, persuasion, affects attitude either through central or peripheral routes (Petty & Cacioppo, 1986). Central-route persuasion relies on cognitive processing of the content of a persuasive communication. For example, if a teacher tries to persuade students to read a chapter because its content would allow them greater participation in democratic society, the teacher is attempting to establish a favorable attitude through the central route. Students in the class would be expected to reason that because participation in democratic society is good, the chapter is worth reading. In contrast, persuasive communications through the peripheral route are frequently simple cues evoking feelings. An attractive picture on a book's cover, for example, may lead students to develop a favorable attitude toward the book. Compared to attitudes established through the central route, attitudes established through the peripheral route lack permanence. Mitnick and McGinnies (1958) showed that time to think about a communication improved attitude stability, and Petty and Cacioppo demonstrated that weighing of an argument's issues resulted in greater resistance to attitude change. However, there may be good reasons to mix the peripheral- and central-route approaches. Peripheral approaches to attitude change may provide an initial bridge to favorable reading attitudes that can later be consolidated by central-route approaches. For example, a teacher may initially persuade students that a story is good to read by emphasizing its pictures and later bring forward the fact that the story teaches important lessons.

Research into the effectiveness of persuasive communications on reading attitude is particularly needed because there are important types of reading—such as the reading of science text—that may inspire neutral or negative attitudes.

Central- or peripheral-route persuasive communications may help improve attitudes toward science reading and thus the probability that such reading will occur.

In addition to persuasion, cornerstone concepts have direct influence on attitude. Cornerstone concepts include various superordinate concepts that guide (or fail to guide) formation of people's attitudes and ultimately their intentions and behaviors. Included as cornerstone concepts are values, goals, and self-concepts.

Research has shown that values may influence attitudes (Feather, 1982; Kristiansen & Zanna, 1991; Rokeach, 1968, 1973). Ostrom and Brock (1968) found that attitudes based on values were resistant to change, although the influence of relevant values on attitudes depended on the nature of the reader. The values held by nonreflective people who rely primarily on situational cues have little impact on attitudes. On the other hand, the values held by thoughtful people who attend to their own internal orientations do influence attitudes (Snyder, 1974). Therefore, helping students think reflectively about the interrelationships among their values, attitudes, and intentions may help them to strengthen their clarity of purpose in reading. The topic of values is an extensive one requiring further discussion. The relationships of religious values to reading religious content, for example, would be an interesting focus for research.

Goals, the second of the cornerstone concepts, are outcomes desired by a person. People develop personal goals for a variety of reasons, including their own values and purposes suggested by others. It cannot be assumed, however, that externally suggested purposes are always sufficiently accepted to become personal goals. In the new model, attitude toward reading becomes more favorable if the particular reading is perceived to move readers closer to their own personal goals.

Self-concepts represent conceptualizations and evaluations of the self, either present or possible. Present selves are obviously concepts of the self in the present, but possible selves "represent the potential for change in the self, for better or worse, from the present to the future" (Cantor et al., 1986, p. 99). They are cognitive images of what individuals may become. Both present selves and possible selves are expected to influence readers' attitudes toward reading. Readers who visualize themselves as environmental activists, for example, are expected to have positive attitudes toward reading about the environment. Readers who wish to become environmental activists but who have not yet achieved that status are also expected to have favorable attitudes toward such reading. The extent to which knowledge gained from the reading reinforces either present or possible self-concepts is positively related to attitude toward further reading.

Cantor et al. (1986) emphasize that

> the self-concept includes within its scope a diverse collection of images and cognitions about the self—the good selves (the ones we remember fondly), the bad selves (the ones we would like to forget), the hoped for selves, the feared selves, the not-me selves, and the ideal selves, the ought selves. (p. 102)

All these types of self-concepts have potential for influencing reading attitudes. Even negative self-concepts may result in positive attitudes toward reading if the reading holds promise of eliminating those self-concepts.

The cornerstone concepts mentioned up to this point—values, goals, and self-concepts—are interrelated, top-level determiners of attitude. However, readers do not always appear to consult cornerstone concepts when they develop favorable attitudes toward reading. Many times their reading preferences seem to develop on the basis of peripheral cues such as interesting pictures or thrilling events described in text. However, it seems likely that the most enduring reading interests are based upon cornerstone concepts. Elementary school students fascinated by stories of powerful animals, junior high students entranced by books describing political triumphs, and college students engaged in the serious study of medicine all appear to have consulted their values, goals, and self-concepts in forming their reading attitudes. Research is needed to determine the *extent* to which cornerstone concepts guide reading preferences.

The cornerstone concepts constitute the final components of the new model. With these concepts identified, it is appropriate to explore the full model and discuss the interaction of its components.

The Model of Attitude Influence Upon Reading

The model in Figure 4 integrates the components presented up to this point and adds feedback paths. The influence and feedback connections represent only the major dynamics of the attitude–reading process. Because all psychological processes potentially affect all other processes, the new model cannot portray all possible paths of influence. Also not explicitly represented in the model are attitudes toward things other than reading. These attitudes bridge the idea and feeling components at the right side of the model, have action readiness of their own, and may bias idea development and acceptance during reading.

The various feedback paths add a dynamic, cyclical character to the new model. Cornerstone concepts and persuasive communications influence attitude toward reading, attitude influences intention, intention influences reading, and reading gives rise to ideas, feelings, and internal emotions. To perpetuate the cycle, satisfaction with ideas, feelings, and emotional states that result from reading provides feedback influencing the initial attitude toward reading. Favorable attitudes toward reading thus sustain intention to read and reading as long as readers continue to be satisfied with reading outcomes.

At the upper right of the model, specific feelings resulting from reading affect internal emotional state. Accumulation of specific humorous ideas expressed in text, for example, may precipitate a humorous mood in the reader. In contrast, an accumulation of uncorrected meaning-disrupting miscues may

FIGURE 4

Model of Attitude Influence Upon Reading and Learning to Read

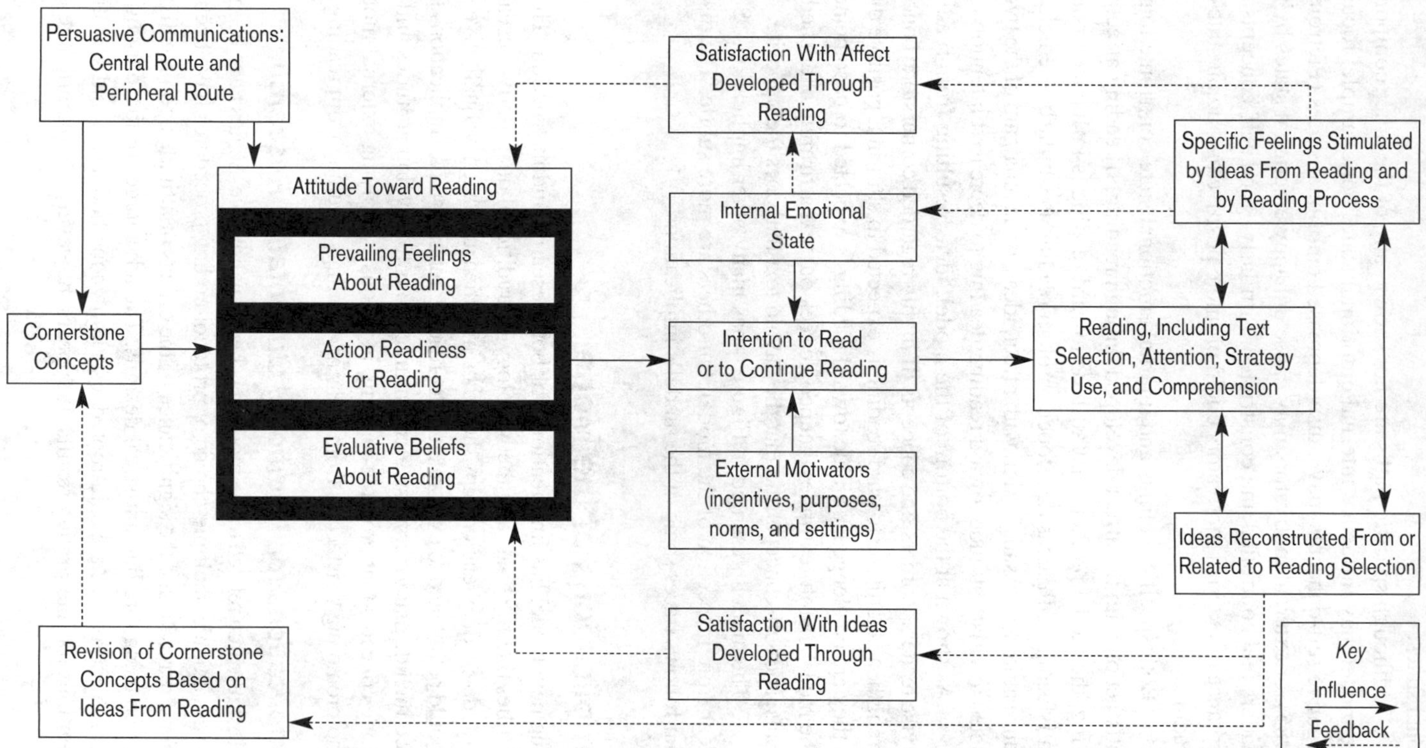

Persuasive Communications: Central Route and Peripheral Route

Cornerstone Concepts

Attitude Toward Reading

Prevailing Feelings About Reading

Action Readiness for Reading

Evaluative Beliefs About Reading

Satisfaction With Affect Developed Through Reading

Internal Emotional State

Intention to Read or to Continue Reading

External Motivators (incentives, purposes, norms, and settings)

Satisfaction With Ideas Developed Through Reading

Revision of Cornerstone Concepts Based on Ideas From Reading

Specific Feelings Stimulated by Ideas From Reading and by Reading Process

Reading, Including Text Selection, Attention, Strategy Use, and Comprehension

Ideas Reconstructed From or Related to Reading Selection

Key

Influence

Feedback

engender unfavorable feelings and result in angry or depressed internal emotional states.

Although specific paths are not shown, any of the other components in the model may influence internal emotional state. For example, focusing on negative self-concepts may cause depressed emotional states (Pietromonaco, 1985), or external motivators may cause unhappy emotional states by making readers feel controlled and constricted. Similarly, good self-concepts and acceptance of external motivators could promote positive emotional states during reading.

Both specific feelings and internal emotional state contribute to readers' satisfaction with the affect developed through reading. If reading affect is satisfying, the model predicts that attitude toward reading is influenced positively. Satisfaction with ideas developed through reading is similarly predicted to enhance attitude. Dissatisfaction with affect, ideas, or an amalgam of the two is predicted to vitiate attitude toward reading, leading to decreased intention to read.

As shown at the bottom of the model, ideas resulting from reading may revise readers' cornerstone concepts. If highly regarded cornerstone concepts are strengthened, attitude toward reading is expected to shift in a positive direction. If they are challenged, attitude toward reading is expected to become negative. The model therefore implies that people seek out text affirming cherished values, goals, and self-concepts and that they avoid text that does the opposite.

The model presented in Figure 4 has many other implications. Some are clear from inspection of the model, but others are more subtle. The discussion that follows traces some of the model's implications.

Implications of the Model

The new model has implications for both research and instruction. The model implies that the goals and methodology of traditional quantitative research into attitude–reading relationships should be modified and that new qualitative research should be initiated to explore attitude–reading relationships. Implications for practice include using persuasive communications to develop attitudes and cornerstone concepts that promote reading, judiciously applying external motivators, and promoting satisfaction from ideas and feelings resulting from reading.

Implications for Traditional Quantitative Research

Most research related to the model has been quantitative. Scales have been used to assess attitude, multiple-choice or protocol-coding procedures have been used to measure recall, and the significance of the effects of attitude upon recall has been tested using familiar statistical designs. The advantages of these traditional research approaches are data-rootedness, known methodology, and scientific conventions for interpreting results. It appears, however, that quantitative research ignores powerful variables moderating the attitude–reading relationship, neglects to measure all aspects of attitude, and fails to define attitude objects adequately. The new model is helpful in solving these problems.

First, the problem of failing to take into account variables that moderate the attitude–reading relationship is addressed by the model's separate external-motivator component. The model shows that external motivators may sustain intention to read even if attitude toward reading is neutral or negative. At least three methods of controlling for external motivators are possible. The first is to reduce or eliminate external incentives and purposes so that the effects of attitude may be revealed. For example, students may be asked to read in order to see how much they like selections or to pass time instead of being asked to read for a test. This procedure may reduce the possibility that external incentives will maintain comprehension regardless of attitude toward reading, as appears to have happened in most studies that have tested the attitude–reading relationship.

The second method to control external motivators is to modify the experimental environment so that school norms and settings do not support intention to read in spite of negative attitude toward reading. Instead of in classrooms, experiments could be conducted in informal environments less likely to be associated with school norms. Examples of these settings are waiting rooms, community centers, and laboratories with home-like furnishings. In these settings, reading should be more sensitive to variations in attitude.

Finally, the third method to control external motivators is implied by a finding of Fortner and Henk (1991). After reading an article about nuclear power, students with neutral attitudes toward this topic scored about the same on multiple-choice questions as did students with unfavorable attitudes, as is expected when external motivation to read is present. However, on open-ended questions about the article, the neutral students "tended overall to give positive, optimistic answers; the antinuclear subjects, by contrast, were more pessimistic" (p. 13). Fortner and Henk attributed the attitude sensitivity of open-ended items to their relative resistance to the leveling influence of extrinsic motivation. It should be noted, however, that Hollingsworth and Reutzel (1990) found no recall differences on their free-recall measure. Thus, while open-ended tests may not cancel the effect of external motivation to read, they may better reveal the ways readers' prior attitudes affect their interpretations and elaborations of textual content.

The second problem, neglecting to measure all aspects of attitude, may be resolved by collecting data on the three components of attitude represented in the model: evaluative beliefs, prevailing feelings, and action readiness. Quantifying all three of these aspects not only ensures that attitudes toward reading have been measured fully but also allows estimation of their subjective importance. If the three aspects are all positive, then an attitude is likely to have subjective importance for an individual. However, if evaluative beliefs are positive but feelings and action readiness are neutral or even negative, then an attitude is unlikely to have subjective importance because it lacks affective and conative involvement. The distinction is important because only attitudes with favorable evaluative beliefs, positive feelings, and high action readiness are predicted to lead to the development of intentions to read.

The third problem, failure to adequately define attitude objects, suggests that investigators should assess attitudes toward specific kinds of reading behavior rather than attitudes toward isolated content or topics. Specific attitudes toward reading may be assessed through the use of sentence completion or other open-ended formats, such as "Reading adventure stories about horses is _____." This constitutes a better measure than does an item evaluating attitudes toward horses themselves because it focuses on reading behavior, not only on content. The distinction between liking something and liking reading about something is crucial to testing the model.

Because feedback from ideas and feelings developed during reading retroflexively influences attitude, quantitative research on the attitude–reading relationship may also be improved if measures are taken after reading as well as before. If readers thought that a selection was appropriately difficult, its style engaging, its topic suitable, and its point of view proper, they would probably be satisfied with the affect and ideas resulting from their reading. Hence measures of attitude and satisfaction taken *after* reading would be expected to correlate more closely with attention, comprehension, and recall than would attitude assessed prior to reading.

In addition to its implications for fine-tuning current quantitative research methods, the model also has implications for extending quantitative research into new attitude-related areas. The first area, persuasion, has been extensively researched in social psychology, but no classroom research seems to have been done investigating the relationships among persuasive communications, intention to read, reading, and satisfaction with reading. The model indicates that persuasive communications, whether through the central or peripheral routes, can influence attitude toward reading both directly and indirectly through the mediation of cornerstone concepts. Research has found that direct, rational approaches to attitude influence may be best for analytical, involved, and well-educated adults (Cacioppo, Petty, & Morris, 1983) but that the attitudes of children may be best influenced by affect-oriented persuasion techniques (Edwards, 1990). Research is needed to test the possibility that peripheral- followed by central-route persuasion more strongly establishes children's favorable attitudes toward reading than does peripheral-route persuasion alone. Also needed are comparisons of effects of various types and styles of persuasion on attitude.

The second area needing research is the effect of cornerstone concepts on attitudes toward reading. Values, the first of the cornerstone concepts, invite investigation not only into the nature of relationships between values and attitudes but also into the various ways reading-related values may be developed in the classroom. If teachers successfully promote values of exploration and discovery, reading that extends the horizons of the individual should stimulate positive attitudes. If teachers successfully promote aesthetic values, appreciation of the beauty of language should find realization in positive attitudes toward poetry, plays, stories, and other literary forms. There appear to be an unlimited number of possibilities.

Goals are the second of the cornerstone concepts identified in the new model. Goals are dynamic, supercategorical identifiers of desired end states achieved through reading behavior. These end states may be cognitive or affective. Many studies have shown that goals are effective in directing behavior, but little research has focused on the effects of internalized, personal goals on attitude toward specific types of reading.

Self-concepts, the third of the cornerstone concepts, have strong implications for reading attitudes. Both a general self-concept of oneself as a reader and content-related self-concepts (such as viewing oneself as a "young scientist," for example) appear to be important in developing positive attitudes toward reading.

Qualitative Research and the Model

At this point, it may seem that the quantitative research necessary to explore the model's many components and relationships will be difficult. Operationalizing the components of the model with simultaneously administered valid and reliable tests appears nearly impossible. In fact, qualitative case study methods may be better for testing the model. While quantitative research seeks to describe phenomena in numbers, qualitative research uses words to describe people, their characteristics, their environments, and their behaviors. Data are gathered from observations, interviews, and documents of various kinds. The primary instruments for data collection are researchers themselves, who may be called research participants (Gans, 1982) because they combine the roles of observer and performer in social situations. These research participants require training to be effective (Patton, 1980). Their attention may be guided by conceptual frameworks such as the new model of attitude in the reading process.

Research participants gather data relating to hypotheses and questions in the natural settings of classrooms and other locations. They collect information in the form of audiotapes of interviews, notes on expressed reading intentions, logs of book selections, reading recalls, reports of feelings, evidence of cornerstone concepts, ratings of reading satisfaction, and portfolios of student products. Influences of external motivators are also noted. Research participants synthesize these data into indexed notes, charts, graphs, and other summary formats. Coherent patterns apparent in the summaries are compared with expectations from the model.

Bringing various sources of data together and drawing conclusions is an approach called "triangulation" (Denzin, 1970). A fit between the model's predictions and observations of various data sources would support the model, but lack of fit would cause a researcher to seek explanations either within or outside of the model. If the most likely explanations lay outside the model's framework, the model itself might need to be reinterpreted, expanded, or reformulated. The method of analytic induction (Katz, 1983) may be used to test the model progressively through a series of qualitative case studies.

Qualitative methods require that researchers strive more consistently for objectivity than do quantitative methods. The benefits of qualitative methods, however, may be worth their risks. The subtlety and diversity of attitudes; the complex nature of interactions; the expressions of intentions; the nature of attention, strategy use, and comprehension; and the satisfaction with constructed meaning and feeling can all be captured in rich descriptions beyond the scope of numeric data analysis. These descriptions support the model in ways impossible through the restricted perspectives of quantitative research.

Although no qualitative research has yet been conducted on the 1976 or 1985 models, the new model provides a basis for hypotheses to be tested and questions to be answered through qualitative case studies in classrooms, with small groups of students, or with individual students. The model's various components are expected to have orderly interrelationships. The degree to which these relationships can be documented through analysis of qualitative data should help determine the model's adequacy.

Although qualitative research has advantages, its limitations are significant enough that it cannot replace quantitative research. Qualitative studies are time-consuming because research participants must observe and interact with readers for extended periods to identify important variables and causal relationships. The close, extended contact inevitably introduces the danger of exaggeration or oversimplification in reporting results (Guba & Lincoln, 1981). Finally, there are questions of reliability, validity, and generalizability: If one case observed in detail supports the model, will other cases do likewise? Johnston (1985) noted that "cognitive scientists in the field of reading have not accepted case studies as sources of data for expanding theory and practice" (p. 155). However, as indicated earlier, a difficulty of using quantitative research methods exclusively is their narrowness of vision and tendency to ignore moderating variables. It is possible that an active interchange of results between quantitative and qualitative research will bring much-needed diversity, richness, detail, and humanity to research in reading.

Instructional Implications

While many questions remain open, the pragmatic validity of the model may be determined by its applicability in classrooms. Below are 10 implications for instruction derived from the model. Reports detailing the extent to which these and other suggestions are useful should help in evaluating the model.

1. *Foster cornerstone concepts underlying attitude toward reading.* Teachers can help students establish personal values, goals, and self-concepts leading to positive attitudes toward reading. For example, promoting explo-

ration as an important human value and helping students conceptualize themselves as explorers may stimulate reading about adventurers and other explorers. Teachers may also link students' previously held values, goals, and self-concepts to reading. Doing this requires that teachers learn about students through conversations, interviews, observations, compositions, free book selections, and other approaches.

2. *Persuade students that various content, genres, and authors are worth reading.* Teachers can experiment with various persuasive methods and record those that work best. The two general approaches are peripheral-route appeals to students' feelings and central-route appeals to their critical thinking processes. For example, teachers might generate excitement about reading Margery Williams's *The Velveteen Rabbit* by showing and discussing a collection of stuffed toy animals (peripheral-route appeal); they might establish confidence in the accuracy of Sally Ride's *Voyager: An Adventure to the Edge of the Solar System* by describing the scientist–author's expertise in space exploration (central-route appeal). In many instances, peripheral- and central-route appeals may be combined to form strongly persuasive cases for reading books, articles, or other materials.

3. *Establish classroom settings and norms that support favorable reading intentions and values.* Settings that influence reading intentions include well-stocked library shelves, magazine storage boxes, reading tables, comfortable chairs, card catalogs, and book-news bulletin boards. Norms for behavior that influence reading intentions include teacher-communicated expectations of sustained reading, respect for other students during reading time, and shared discussion following reading.

Reading settings and the norms communicated within these settings may not only enhance students' intentions to read but also serve as peripheral-route persuaders that contribute to formation of long-term literacy values, goals, and self-concepts. This could occur if students begin to view reading settings as their proper dwelling places and the rules pertaining to these settings as their own rules.

4. *Use minimum external incentive to justify reading.* If students receive strong external incentive to read, they may develop the evaluative belief that reading is done for teachers, not for themselves. This evaluative belief may lead to unfavorable feelings and action readiness for reading. Teachers who use minimum external incentive build students' belief that they are their own sources of energy and direction for reading. This belief can sustain reading not only inside the classroom but also in locations where teachers are not present.

5. *Encourage students to read materials that stimulate satisfying feelings and ideas.* The model indicates that satisfaction with feelings and ideas from reading influences reading attitude through feedback loops. Satisfaction may be based on content or other characteristics of reading. For example, reading horse stories may satisfy students who like horses, while reading poetry may satisfy

students who enjoy aesthetically pleasing unions of language form and meaning. Teachers may therefore wish to consider how each new reading experience satisfies different students in their classes. Using free book selection as opposed to fixed assignments allows students to guide their own reading progress and encourages formation of positive attitudes toward reading.

6. *Develop action readiness for reading.* The best method for developing action readiness for reading is to encourage students to read large amounts of satisfying text. Interesting reading done on an ongoing basis breaks down barriers to initiating reading activity and forms desirable habits. Scheduling frequent reading sessions during the school day and encouraging students to read at home are important strategies for enhancing the action readiness component of reading attitude.

7. *Help students read text of suitable difficulty.* The model shows that reading satisfaction comes from ideas and feelings gained from reading. Some of those feelings may come from the reading process itself. If students have difficulty eliciting meaning from text, dissatisfaction and ultimately negative attitudes toward reading will result. Therefore, in order to prevent the development of negative attitudes, teachers should guide students to read at their "independent" or fluent reading level. Gaskins (1988) reported that at one school, "most teachers have discovered that keeping students at so-called easy levels does not lessen achievement gains during a year" (p. 148). A relaxed pace may increase amounts of reading, enhance action readiness, and lead to better progress than does forcing students to slog through difficult text. This point of view does not imply that students should not occasionally attempt difficult reading, only that such reading should not be the norm. It also implies that development of key vocabulary, background ideas, and specific abilities prior to reading assignments should be accomplished with care.

8. *Teach students abilities that underlie successful reading.* The successful reconstruction of meaning is prerequisite to reading satisfaction. Therefore, abilities in print–sound mapping, word recognition, vocabulary understanding, sentence microstructure use, text macrostructure navigation, and metacognitive strategy application are important for developing favorable reading attitudes. Teaching these abilities, however, requires maintaining students' favorable attitudes toward reading by emphasizing satisfying overall meaning construction during practice sessions. If subsidiary abilities are treated in isolation, they should be brought back into broader and more meaningful contexts as soon as possible.

9. *Apply the model to the early learning of reading.* The model has at least three implications for early reading instruction. First, the model implies that children who develop reading-promoting cornerstone concepts through exposure to parents' and teachers' persuasive communications (central and peripheral) benefit in learning to read. Children's cornerstone concepts positively influence their reading attitudes, and these attitudes promote development of intentions to read

books and other materials. Second, the model implies that if early reading experiences are affectively and cognitively satisfying, children will develop attitudes and intentions that support reading. Satisfaction with early reading is fundamental to the development of reading ability because it provides an important precondition for sustained practice. On the other hand, repetitive drills or isolated subskill exercises may easily lead to the evaluative belief that reading is meaningless, to negative feelings about reading, and to resistance to reading practice. Third, the model's view of physical settings suggests that if young children's surroundings contain reading-related objects, they will be more likely to form intentions to read than if their surroundings do not contain these objects. This expectation has been confirmed by Neuman and Roskos (1992), who found that carefully designed addition of such objects as books, magazines, pencils, and paper to preschool children's play areas increased instances of early reading and other literacy behaviors. In words consistent with the model, Neuman and Roskos stated that the children with the enriched literacy environment "were more internally driven, with action subordinated to the children's intentions" (p. 218).

10. *Develop favorable attitudes toward content to stimulate content area reading.* The new model predicts that content area reading is encouraged by maintaining favorable attitude toward content, but it also indicates that this is only one influence. Cornerstone concepts, internal emotional states, external motivators, available reading strategies, and other influence may also affect intention to engage in content area reading.

Because there are many influences, content area reading may be facilitated in many ways. However, relying on external motivation without fostering favorable attitude toward content risks creating readers who read only if stimulated by outside pressure. It is unlikely that such externally motivated readers learn information in depth or form enduring interests leading to selection of content-related careers. The model implies that successful content area teachers use various approaches to foster positive attitudes both toward the content being taught and toward the reading of that content. If these approaches are successful, students may voluntarily continue to read content area articles and books in the years following their initial classes.

Summary

One implication of the new model is that research testing its predictions should use qualitative case study methods in addition to traditional experimental designs. The rationale for doing case studies arises from the complexity of the model. With so many components in simultaneous operation, isolating single variables for testing ignores other important sources of influence. Qualitative case study methods, on the other hand, provide opportunities for researchers to collect data on many aspects of individual or group behavior within the same research project to determine whether complex predictions of the model can be verified.

An interesting consequence of emphasizing case studies is the convergence of implications for research and for instruction. Classrooms become naturalistic settings in which research participants seek to answer questions and test hypotheses generated by the model. For example, the model predicts that students' values can underlie intentions to read and reading. A teacher who has been successful in promoting the value of protecting the environment might collect information concerning students' attitudes toward reading about the environment, their intentions to do such reading, and the cognitive and affective outcomes of the reading. Interpretations of these data would be expected to support the model if its paths of influence accurately map students' reading processes.

Testing the new model will not be easy. Its many components are intended to describe a variety of mental constructs, processes, and paths of influence. Just as all cell assemblies of the human brain potentially affect all other cell assemblies, all components of the model potentially affect all other components. However, the model also follows brain organization by identifying primary paths of influence. These primary paths are the ones shown in Figure 4.

The development of the new model of attitude influence upon reading and learning to read is one step in the long and difficult effort to clarify the roles of affect and cognition in reading. The model is not and cannot be only affective because cognition and affect are indissolubly linked in reading as they are in all other human endeavors. One major purpose of the model is therefore to bring affect back from the epiphenomenal realm to which much contemporary reading research has consigned it and to reestablish its dynamic interrelationships with cognition.

References

Ajzen, I. (1989). Attitude structure and behavior. In A.R. Pratkanis, S.J. Breckler, & A.G. Greenwald (Eds.), *Attitude structure and function* (pp. 241–274). Hillsdale, NJ: Erlbaum.

Ajzen, I., & Fishbein, M. (1980). *Understanding attitudes and predicting social behavior.* Englewood Cliffs, NJ: Prentice Hall.

Allport, F.H. (1924). *Social psychology.* Boston: Houghton Mifflin.

Allport, G.W. (1961). *Pattern and growth in personality.* New York: Holt, Rinehart.

Allport, G.W. (1966). Attitudes in the history of social psychology. In M. Jahoda & N. Warren (Eds.), *Attitudes.* Harmondsworth, Middlesex, UK: Penguin.

Anderson, J.R. (1980). *Cognitive psychology and its implications.* San Francisco: Freeman.

Atkinson, J.W., & Feather, N.T. (1966). *A theory of achievement motivation.* New York: Wiley.

Barr, R., Kamil, M.L., Mosenthal, P., & Pearson, P.D. (Eds.). (1991). *Handbook of reading research* (Vol. 2). White Plains, NY: Longman.

Beck, R.C. (1983). *Motivation: Theories and principles.* Englewood Cliffs, NJ: Prentice Hall.

Berlyne, D.E. (1960). *Conflict, arousal, and curiosity.* New York: McGraw-Hill.

Berlyne, D.E. (1966). Curiosity and exploration. *Science, 153,* 25–33.

Breckler, S.J., & Wiggins, E.C. (1989). On defining attitude and attitude theory: Once more with feeling. In A.R. Pratkanis, S.J. Breckler, & A.G. Greenwald (Eds.), *Attitude structure* and function (pp. 407–427). Hillsdale, NJ: Erlbaum.

Cacioppo, J.T., Petty, R.E., & Morris, K.J. (1993). Effects of need for cognition on message evaluation, recall, and persuasion. *Journal of Personality and Social Psychology, 45,* 805–918.

Cantor, N., Markus, H., Niedenthal, P., & Nurius, P. (1986). On motivation and the self-concept. In R.M. Sorrentino & E.T. Higgins (Eds.), *Handbook of motivation and cognition* (Vol. 1, pp. 96–121). New York: Guilford.

Chaiken, S., & Stangor, C. (1987). Attitudes and attitude change. *Annual Review of Psychology, 38,* 575–630.

Chomsky, N. (1965). *Aspects of the theory of syntax.* Cambridge, MA: MIT Press.

Denzin, N.K. (1970). *The research act: A theoretical introduction to sociological methods.* Chicago: Aldine.

Dillon, D.R., O'Brien, D.G., Hopkins, C.J., Baumann, J.F., Humphrey, J.W., Pickle, J.M., et al. (1992). Article content and authorship trends in *The Reading Teacher* 1948–1991. *The Reading Teacher, 45,* 362–365.

Downing, J., & Leong, C.K. (1982). *Psychology of reading.* New York: Macmillan.

Edwards, K. (1990). The interplay of affect and cognition in attitude formation and change. *Journal of Personality and Social Psychology, 59*(2), 202–216.

Ewen, R.B. (1988). *Art introduction to theories of personality* (3rd ed.). Hillsdale, NJ: Erlbaum.

Fazio, R.H. (1986). How do attitudes guide behavior? In R.M. Sorrentino & E.T. Higgins (Eds.), *Handbook of motivation and cognition* (Vol. 1, pp. 204–243). New York: Guilford.

Fazio, R.H., & Zanna, M.P. (1981). Direct experience and attitude-behavior consistency. In L. Berkowitz (Ed.), *Advances in experimental social psychology* (Vol. 14, pp. 161–202). New York: Academic.

Feather, N.T. (1982). Human values and the prediction of action: An expectancy-valence analysis. In N.T. Feather (Ed.), *Expectations and actions: Expectancy-value models in psychology* (pp. 263–289). Hillsdale, NJ: Erlbaum.

Fishbein, M., & Ajzen, I. (1975). *Belief, attitude, intention, and behavior: An introduction to theory and research.* Reading, MA: Addison-Wesley.

Fortner, B.H., & Henk, W.A. (1991). Effects of issue-related attitude on readers' comprehension and judgments of unbiased text. *Reading Research and Instruction, 30,* 1–16.

Gans, H.J. (1982). The participant observer as a human being: Observations on the personal aspects of fieldwork. In R.G. Burgess (Ed.), *Field research: A sourcebook and a field manual.* London: Allen & Unwin.

Gaskins, I. (1988). Helping teachers adapt to the needs of students with learning problems. In S.J. Samuels & P.D. Pearson (Eds.), *Changing school reading programs: Principles and case studies* (pp. 143–159). Newark, DE: International Reading Association.

Guba, E.G., & Lincoln, Y.S. (1981). *Effective evaluation.* San Francisco: Jossey-Bass.

Hebb, D.O. (1949). *The organization of behavior.* New York: Wiley.

Henk, W.A., & Holmes, B.C. (1988). Effects of content-related attitude on the comprehension and retention of expository text. *Reading Psychology, 9*(3), 203–225.

Hollingsworth, P.M., & Reutzel, D.R. (1990). Prior knowledge, content-related attitude, reading comprehension: Testing Mathewson's affective model of reading. *Journal of Educational Research, 83,* 194–199.

Johnston, P.H. (1985). Understanding reading disability: A case study approach. *Harvard Educational Review, 55,* 153–177.

Judd, C.M., & Krosnick, J.A. (1989). The structural bases of consistency among political attitudes: Effects of political expertise and attitude importance. In A.R. Pratkanis, S.J. Breckler, & A.G. Greenwald (Eds.), *Attitude structure and function* (pp. 99–128). Hillsdale, NJ: Erlbaum.

Kant, I. (1951). *Critique of judgment* (J.H. Bernard, Trans.). New York: Hafner. (Original work published 1790)

Katz, J. (1983). A theory of qualitative methodology: The social science system of analytic fieldwork. In R.M. Emerson (Ed.), *Contemporary field research.* Boston: Little, Brown.

Kretch, D., & Crutchfield, R.S. (1948). *Theory and problems of social psychology.* New York: McGraw-Hill.

Kristiansen, C.M., & Zanna, M.P. (1991). Value relevance and the value-attitude relation: Value expressiveness versus halo effects.

Basic and Applied Social Psychology, 12, 471–483.

Lepper, M., & Greene, D. (1975). Turning play into work: Effects of adult surveillance and extrinsic rewards on children's intrinsic motivation. *Journal of Personality and Social Psychology, 31*, 479–486.

Mandler, G. (1985). *Cognitive psychology: An essay in cognitive science.* Hillsdale, NJ: Erlbaum.

Maslow, A.H. (1970). *Motivation and personality* (2nd ed.). New York: Harper.

Mathewson, G.C. (1976). The function of attitude in the reading process. In H. Singer & R.B. Ruddell (Eds.), *Theoretical models and processes of reading* (2nd ed., pp. 655–676). Newark, DE: International Reading Association.

Mathewson, G.C. (1979). The moderating effect of extrinsic motivation upon the attitude/comprehension relationship in reading. In C. Pennock (Ed.), *Reading comprehension at four linguistic levels* (pp. 8–20). Newark, DE: International Reading Association.

Mathewson, G.C. (1985). Toward a comprehensive model of affect in the reading process. In H. Singer & R.B. Ruddell (Eds.), *Theoretical models and processes of reading* (3rd ed., pp. 841–856). Newark, DE: International Reading Association.

McClelland, D.C., Atkinson, R.A., Clark, R.A., & Lowell, E.L. (1953). *The achievement motive.* New York: Appleton-Century-Crofts.

McGuire, W.J. (1989). The structure of individual attitudes and attitude systems. In A.R. Pratkanis, S.J. Breckler, & A.G. Greenwald (Eds.), *Attitude structure and function* (pp. 37–69). Hillsdale, NJ: Erlbaum.

Mitnick, L., & McGinnies, E. (1958). Influencing ethnocentrism in small discussion groups through a film communication. *Journal of Abnormal and Social Psychology, 56*, 82–92.

Neuman, S.B., & Roskos, K. (1992). Literacy objects as cultural tools: Effects on children's literacy behaviors in play. *Reading Research Quarterly, 27*, 203–225.

Newell, A., & Simon, H.A. (1972). *Human problem solving.* Englewood Cliffs, NJ: Prentice Hall.

Ostrom, T.M. (1969). The relationship between the affective, behavioral, and cognitive components of attitude. *Journal of Experimental Social Psychology, 5*, 12–30.

Ostrom, T.M., & Brock, T.C. (1968). A cognitive model of attitudinal involvement. In R. Ableson et al. (Eds.), *Theories of cognitive consistency: A sourcebook.* Chicago: Rand-McNally.

Patton, M.Q. (1980). *Qualitative evaluation methods.* Newbury Park, CA: Sage.

Petty, R.E., & Cacioppo, J.T. (1981). *Attitudes and persuasion: Classic and contemporary approaches.* Dubuque, IA: William C. Brown.

Petty, R.E., & Cacioppo, J.T. (1986). *Communication and persuasion: Central and peripheral routes to attitude change.* New York: Springer-Verlag.

Pietromonaco, P. (1985). The influence of affect on self-perception in depression. *Social Cognition, 3*, 121–134.

Prawat, R.S. (1985). Affective versus cognitive goal orientations in elementary teachers. *American Educational Research Journal, 22*, 587–604.

Reutzel, D.R., & Hollingsworth, P.M. (1991). Investigating topic-related attitude: Effect on reading and remembering text. *Journal of Educational Research, 84*, 334–344.

Rokeach, M. (1968). *Beliefs, attitudes, and values.* San Francisco: Jossey-Bass.

Rokeach, M. (1973). *The nature of human values.* New York: Free Press.

Rosenberg, M.J., Hovland, C.I., McGuire, W.J., Abelson, R.P., & Brehm, J.W. (1960). *Attitude organization and change: An analysis of consistency among attitude components.* New Haven, CT: Yale University Press.

Samuels, S.J., & Farstrup, A.E. (1992). *What research has to say about reading instruction* (2nd ed.). Newark, DE: International Reading Association.

Schuman, H., & Kalton, G. (1985). Survey methods. In G. Lindzey & E. Aronson (Eds.), *The handbook of social psychology: Volume 1, Theory and method* (pp. 635–697). New York: Random House.

Shapiro, J., & White, W. (1991). Reading attitudes and perceptions in traditional and nontraditional reading programs. *Reading Research and Instruction, 30*, 52–66.

Shirey, L.L., & Reynolds, R.E. (1988). Effect of interest on attention and learning. *Journal of Educational Psychology, 80*, 159–166.

Simon, H.A., & Kaplan, C.A. (1989). Foundations of cognitive science. In M.I.

Posner (Ed.), *Foundations of cognitive science*. Cambridge, MA: MIT Press.

Snyder, M. (1974). The self-monitoring of expressive behavior. *Journal of Personality and Social Psychology, 30,* 526–537.

Sorrentino, R.M., & Higgins, E.T. (1986). Motivation and cognition: Warming up to synergism. In R.M. Sorrentino & E.T. Higgins (Eds.), *Handbook of motivation and cognition* (Vol. 1, pp. 3–19). New York: Guilford.

Wade, S.E., & Adams, R.B. (1990). Effects of importance and interest on recall of biographical text. *Journal of Reading Behavior, 22,* 331–353.

Wallbrown, F.H., Brown, D.H., & Engin, A.W. (1977). *A survey of reading attitudes.* Unpublished paper, Kent State University, Kent, OH.

Zutell, J., & McCormick, S. (Eds.). (1991). *Learner factors/teacher factors: Issues in literacy research and instruction* (40th yearbook of the National Reading Conference). Chicago: National Reading Conference.

51

Reading as a Meaning-Construction Process: The Reader, the Text, and the Teacher

Robert B. Ruddell and Norman J. Unrau

R eading is indeed a meaning-construction process that enables us to create carefully reasoned as well as imaginary worlds filled with new concepts, creatures, and characters. The complexity of the process, however, is largely hidden from our view, and over the centuries it has taken on the aura of the magical and mysterious. A central goal of our model is to provide insight into the nature of the process that Huey (1908/1968) described early in the 20th century as the "most remarkable specific performance that civilization has learned in all its history" (p. 6).

The challenge, then, is to explain what we do when we read and comprehend language. This challenge is complicated by our belief that such an explanation needs to account for how the process is acquired and used not only from the perspective of the reader but also from the perspective of the teacher. It is the teacher who frequently assumes major responsibility for meaning negotiation within the social environment of the classroom.

Our first goal and a major emphasis of this discussion is to provide an explanation of how the reading process occurs in the classroom context involving reader, text, and teacher. A second goal is to create a model that is productive, that will provide explanations and predictions useful to both teachers and researchers. Our third goal is to develop a model that has utility not only in connecting current and past research but also in charting future research directions.

The construction of an abstract representation of reading and language processing is really an attempt to create a metaphor that resembles or suggests the

Adapted from Ruddell, R.B., Ruddell, M.R., & Singer, H. (Eds.), *Theoretical Models and Processes of Reading* (4th ed., pp. 996–1056). Copyright © 1994 by the International Reading Association. The poem "The Red Wheelbarrow" is by William Carlos Williams, from *Collected Poems: 1909–1939,* Volume 1. Copyright © 1938 by New Directions Publishing Corp. Reprinted with permission of the publisher.

nature of the process. However, there is still much to learn about the nature of reading and its representation in a sociocognitive model. This is especially true if we are to take into account the complex roles of reader, text and classroom context, and teacher.

Our explanation of the reading process has evolved over the years as new knowledge has accrued from various disciplines. Readers who are familiar with the earlier models (Ruddell, 1974; Ruddell & Kern, 1986; Ruddell & Speaker, 1985) will recognize the influence of work in many fields ranging from anthropology and sociolinguistics to cognitive psychology and literary theory. In effect, the creation of this model has relied on what Beach (1992) refers to as "adopting multiple stances." Because of our interest in incorporating the reader, the text and classroom context, and the teacher into the model, it has been necessary to draw on research that accounts for textual, social, cultural, and field/disciplinary stances. We have been especially sensitized to the importance of the social context of the classroom and the influence of the teacher on the reading process through our research on teaching effectiveness (R.B. Ruddell, 1994; R.B. Ruddell & Boyle, 1989; R.B. Ruddell, Draheim, & Barnes, 1990; R.B. Ruddell & Harris, 1989; R.B. Ruddell & M.R. Ruddell, 1994; Unrau, 1989, 1991, 1992, 1993), classroom observations, and direct teaching of students at a variety of levels.

Several key assumptions underlie the model. These are implicit in the research supporting the model's components and the interactions between and among components. They are as follows:

1. Readers—even beginning readers—are active theory builders and hypothesis testers.

2. Language and reading performance is directly related to the reader's environment.

3. The driving force behind language performance and reading growth is the reader's need to obtain meaning.

4. Oral and written language development, which affect the thinking process, contribute directly to the development of reading ability.

5. Readers construct meanings not only of printed manuscripts but also of events, speech, and behaviors as they "read" gestures, images, symbols, signs, and signals that are embedded in a social and cultural environment.

6. Texts are constantly reinvented as readers construct different understandings for them in a hermeneutic circle. Meanings for texts are dynamic, not static, as individuals, texts, and contexts change and interact.

7. The role of the teacher is critical in negotiating and facilitating meaning construction in the text and social context of the classroom.

The remainder of our discussion will be devoted to four areas designed to illuminate the nature of the model:

1. a brief overview of the three major components of the model,

2. a detailed discussion of the rationale and research foundation underlying each of the three major components,

3. a discussion of the model components illustrating strategy-based instruction and meaning negotiation in the classroom, and

4. our conclusion, with implications for practice and new research directions.

The Reader, the Text, and the Teacher: A Brief Overview

For our sociocognitive interactive model, reading is conceptualized as a meaning-construction process in the instructional context of the classroom. A brief survey of the model reveals three major components (as depicted in Figure 1). These consist of the *reader*, *text and classroom context*, and the *teacher*. As the reading process occurs, these three components are in a state of dynamic change and interchange while meaning negotiation and meaning construction take place.

The *reader*, the first major model component as shown on the left side of Figure 1, conceptualizes the student's previous life experiences as prior beliefs and knowledge. This reader component consists of two major interrelated parts. The first, *affective conditions*, includes a range of factors extending from the motivation to read to personal sociocultural values and beliefs about reading and schooling. The second, *cognitive conditions*, accounts for such areas as background knowledge of language, word-analysis skills, text-processing strategies, and understanding of classroom and social interaction.

The reader's ability to construct, monitor, and represent meaning defines *knowledge use and control*. As the *knowledge-construction* process proceeds, it is guided by purpose and plan while drawing on the reader's reservoir of prior beliefs and knowledge. A *text representation* begins to form in the reader's mind; it reflects the reader's meaning interpretation based on the text and is influenced by other factors, such as discussion with peers and the teacher. This representation is overseen and monitored by the *reader executive and monitor*. Prior beliefs and knowledge are used to help confirm, reject, or suspend judgments of new interpretations.

The *outcomes of meaning construction* demonstrate the kinds of understanding that have been created in the reader's mind through the text and classroom interaction. These outcomes may take a variety of forms, ranging from new semantic or lexical knowledge to interpretation of texts to changes in attitudes, values, and beliefs.

FIGURE 1

Reading as a Meaning-Construction Process: The Reader, the Text, and the Teacher

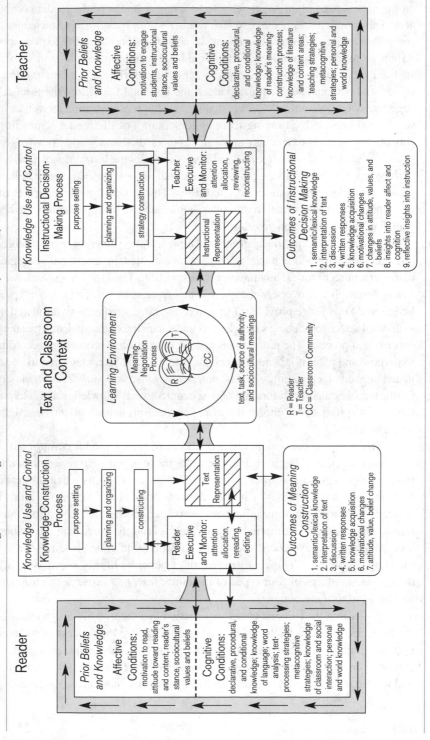

At first glance the *teacher*, the second major model component as shown on the right side of Figure 1, appears to be a mirror image of the reader component. This is only partially the case. The teacher's prior beliefs and knowledge account for previous affective and cognitive conditions based on life experiences. Affective conditions include instructional beliefs and philosophy and involve such things as motivation to engage students, appropriateness of instructional stance, and personal sociocultural values and beliefs. In addition, the teacher's cognitive conditions include conceptual knowledge representation as well as instructional knowledge ranging from understanding of the reader's meaning-construction process to teaching strategies and personal and world knowledge.

The teacher's *knowledge use and control* includes the *instructional decision-making process* that forms a general instructional purpose based on prior beliefs, prior knowledge, and concurrent conditions. This general purpose directs the flow and conduct of instruction through specific purpose setting, planning and organizing, and strategy construction.

As teaching begins, the *instructional representation* emerges in the teacher's mind and reflects such features as classroom activities, instructional strategies, management techniques, and meaning construction. The *teacher executive and monitor* controls and oversees the purpose and representation. The teacher's prior beliefs and knowledge provide information that ranges from motivation and instructional stance to teaching strategies and understanding of the student's meaning-construction process. The process continues if instruction is proceeding according to purpose and plan; if it is not, the original purpose and plan may need to be adjusted or even changed entirely. The *outcomes of instructional decision making* for the teacher range from forming new semantic/lexical knowledge and interpretation of text to insights into reader affect and cognition and reflective insights into instruction.

The *text and classroom context*, the third major model component, is shown in the center of Figure 1. It accounts for the *learning environment* in which the *meaning-negotiation process* occurs. This process begins when the reader first interacts with the text (symbolized by the book at the center of Figure 1) and represents a fusion of meaning between reader, teacher, and classroom community. Here we are attempting to describe the reading process in the responsive classroom context where teacher and students build understandings through meaning negotiation. This requires that the teacher be highly sensitive to student understandings of four types of meaning: *text*, *task*, *source of authority*, and *sociocultural meanings*.

It is within the text and classroom context that the true orchestration of instruction occurs. Here, both student and teacher initiate the process of meaning construction. They negotiate purpose and plans (*knowledge use and control*) and draw on background knowledge (*prior beliefs and knowledge*) to form text and instructional representations while simultaneously monitoring the meaning-construction process. This meaning negotiation directly influences outcomes of meaning construction for the reader and outcomes of instructional decision making for the teacher.

Our detailed discussion of the model begins with the reader component, for the reader is at the very center of meaning construction. We then examine the teacher component as instructional decision making proceeds. Next, we discuss the text and classroom context as we explore the meaning-negotiation process that occurs when reader, teacher, and classroom community interact. We then apply this process to a high school English class as students negotiate and construct meaning of a short story. We conclude with selected implications for research and practice.

The Reader

As we consider various factors that contribute to the reader's meaning-construction process, we should keep in mind that these factors function in a simultaneous and integrated manner. This is reflected in the circular flow of arrows surrounding prior beliefs and knowledge in Figure 2, and in the two-way arrows connecting various reader components.

Prior Beliefs and Knowledge

Prior beliefs and knowledge consist of preexisting factors, both *affective* and *cognitive*, that influence the reader's comprehension and construction of meaning. Beliefs include opinions, assumptions, and convictions—some of which may be thoroughly grounded in reason, and some of which may be based on the reader's life experience but are wholly unexamined. Nevertheless, these beliefs constitute part of the foundation the reader uses to construct meaning through interaction with text. Furthermore, beliefs influence and shape affective conditions critical to the reader's meaning-construction process. These conditions consist of *motivation to read, attitude toward reading and content, reader's stance,* and *sociocultural values and beliefs.*

Knowledge is commonly conceived to be justified belief; however, in the model we interpret knowledge to include concepts, procedures, and even unconscious or unattended knowledge forms that influence the meaning-construction process. Some forms of knowledge are acquired in a deliberate and purposeful manner. For example, we come to know that E.B. White created the delightful story *Charlotte's Web* based on his farm experiences and observations in rural Maine, USA. Our personal interpretation of the story characters leads to an understanding of Charlotte's nurturing and protective nature and Wilbur's childlike attitude toward life as the two become friends. But other forms of knowledge related to reading may not be consciously learned, as is the case with the reader's potential syntactic knowledge, which may be innate and activated through

FIGURE 2
The Reader

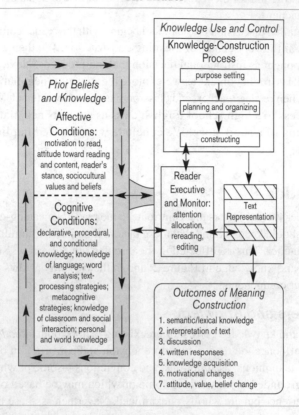

interaction with other language users early in life. Knowledge in our model exerts strong influence on the cognitive conditions, the *declarative*, *procedural*, and *conditional* knowledge forms. These include our mental representation of concepts, language, word analysis, text-processing strategies, metacognitive strategies, classroom and social interaction procedures, and personal and world knowledge.

Our discussion begins with specific affective conditions, followed by consideration of cognitive conditions, which together constitute the reader's prior beliefs and knowledge. We must emphasize, however, that while we describe and explore affective and cognitive conditions separately, these two sets of conditions are interconnected, interdependent, and interactive. For example, the reader's motivation, attitude toward content, and values will most certainly influence the acquisition of new concepts, text interpretation, and use of text-processing and metacognitive strategies.

Affective Conditions. Affective conditions directly influence the reader's decision to read. This decision is shaped by the reason for reading, what is to be read, and how the reading will occur. Motivation and attitude toward reading and content shape the direction and intensity of the reader's interest in reading. As the reader engages the text, one of several stances may be adopted that will have a formative effect on focus of attention, reading purpose, and level of understanding (Many, 1990; see #33 this volume; Rosenblatt, #48 this volume). Focus may be directed toward gathering information, becoming enmeshed in the narrative, grasping a writer's situation and intention, or some combination of these. The reader's sociocultural values and beliefs, which have their origins in the reader's family, community, and to some degree the school, influence both the decision to read and the reading goals.

Inclination to read precedes engagement in the reading process. *Motivation to read* is thus defined as the "development of conditions promoting intention to read" (Mathewson, 1994). If children—or adults—are not moved by the need or desire to read, reading will be put off for other more impelling pursuits. The *NAEP 1992 Reading Report Card for the Nation and the States* (Mullis, Campbell, & Farstrup, 1993) reaffirms that U.S. students spend much more of their personal time watching television than they do reading. Until the last decade of 20th century, the domain of motivation in reading was, according to Athey (1985), relatively uncharted territory. However, attention to literacy motivation has expanded. According to Alexander and Fox (#2 this volume), we have passed through several phases of reading research and practice during the past half century and are now in an "Era of Engaged Learning." Interest in research on motivation emerged into the field of literacy (Guthrie & Wigfield, 1997, 2000). An example of that blending of motivation and literacy appeared during the 1990s in research conducted through the National Reading Research Center (NRRC) where many aspects of literacy engagement were explored.

Research on motivation at NRRC was grounded in an engagement perspective integrating cognitive, motivational, and social aspects of reading, with achievement motivation theory, which includes readers' competence and efficacy beliefs, intrinsic and extrinsic motivation, and purposes for achievement (see Guthrie et al., #34 this volume). We (Ruddell & Unrau, #35 this volume) drew from and synthesized similar research, including that generated through NRRC, to construct an integrated vision of motivation to read. We envisioned an array of factors shaping the intention to read and reading engagement. Our motivational model, which reveals parallels between a reader's motives to read and a teacher's motives to design instruction, depicts the motivational system of an optimally self-regulated reader.

While a reader's reading and a teacher's instructional planning yield different outcomes, they share three major motivational components:

- a *developing self* that includes an identity and self-schema, a sense of self-efficacy and self-worth, expectations, an experiental self, and self knowledge;
- an *instructional orientation* that includes achievement goals, task values, sociocultural values and beliefs, and stances; and
- *task-engagement resources* that include text-processing resources for readers or instructional design resources for teachers.

We use the metaphor of an eye to house these components. Factors influencing motivation radiate like an iris that surrounds the eye's pupil that is the focus of reader intention.

Although an extensive discussion of the components can be found elsewhere in this volume (see Ruddell & Unrau, #35), we focus specifically in the following discussion on the reader's attitude toward reading and text content, reader's stance, and sociocultural values and beliefs.

The reader's *attitude toward reading and text content* plays a critical role in the reading process by influencing intention to read. Mathewson (1994) views attitude as being shaped by reader values and self-concept. Attitude is defined by three elements: (1) prevailing feelings about reading, (2) action readiness toward reading, and (3) evaluative beliefs about reading. These interacting elements directly influence the intention to read. The reader's intention to read and to continue reading is further influenced by such factors as the reader's internal emotional state and external purpose, incentives, and norms, as well as by the instructional setting provided by the teacher.

It is important to note that our earlier discussion of motivation to read is closely connected to attitude toward reading through intention. In effect, motivation is designed to enhance a positive attitude toward reading and, in turn, increase the reader's intention to read and to continue reading. Readers will persevere with and comprehend text that is above their instructional reading level if they have high interest in its content (Shnayer, 1969). We are also aware that several text variables affect the reader's prevailing feelings, action orientation, and evaluative beliefs toward reading. The format of a text, for example, will influence the reader's decision to read and continue reading. This may include the presence or absence of pictures (Samuels, 1970; Samuels, Biesbrock, & Terry, 1974), print size and style (Mathewson, 1976), and even binding in paperback or hardcover (Lowery & Grafft, 1968). The author's writing style also appears to affect the reader's interest, acceptance, and comprehension of the text (Mathewson, 1974).

The reader's intention to continue reading is also influenced by the reader's time expectations and the real or perceived processing time (R.B. Ruddell & Speaker, 1985). The skilled reader is more effective in projecting the real time required for reading a given text. For the less-skilled reader whose attention and purpose are focused primarily on word recognition and oral reading, the time spent with text frequently exceeds expectations. As a result, the reader tends to become discouraged, shift intention, and stop reading (Adams, 1990; Canney & Winograd, 1979; Myers & Paris, 1978). In severe cases, the learner's intention becomes avoidance of reading whenever possible.

Reader's stance refers to the reader's perspective and orientation toward a given text. It serves to direct the reader's focus of attention and purpose in reading (Rosenblatt, 1978) and thus influences motivation, attitude, and intention to read. The reader's perspective and orientation are influenced by the nature of the text and the desired interaction with the text. The stance assumed in directing attention is, to varying degrees, under the reader's control and can be influenced by the teacher in the classroom context.

Rosenblatt (1938, 1978, 1985, 1988, 1994, see #48 this volume) develops the view that readers experience texts through two stances: efferent and aesthetic. In efferent reading, the reader focuses on ideas and concepts to be taken away from the text; in aesthetic reading, the reader becomes absorbed in a text world of imagination and feelings in which "attention is focused on what [the reader] is living through during the reading-event" (Rosenblatt, 1985, p. 38). While the reader may decide to adopt a particular stance during reading, the alternate stance may also be taken at times. Thus, the efferent and aesthetic stances are integrated in varied proportions and may change while the reader progresses through a text (Rosenblatt, 1988). For example, with Fitzgerald's *The Great Gatsby* the reader may focus more attention on the aesthetic stance when reading of Gatsby's absorption in Daisy's first walk through his mansion but shift to the efferent stance when analyzing Gatsby to discover what may have driven him to seek his dream and his "greatness." Rosenblatt (1985) has observed that school-based reading tends to emphasize efferent reading at the expense of aesthetic reading. Students are expected to take away facts from their reading—even of poems—rather than to transact aesthetically with the text by synthesizing "ideas, sensations, feelings, and images from [their] past linguistic, literary, and life experiences" to form a new experience (p. 40). The overemphasis on an efferent stance may diminish the value and enjoyment of transactions with literature.

The reader may also draw on other stances, such as the four fundamental stances (social, textual, institutional, and field) identified by Beach and Hynds (1990; see also Galda & Beach, #31 this volume). When the reader adopts a social stance, ideas are negotiated in collaboration with others or with reference to acquired social knowledge and practices. The reader who understands accepted social practices is better equipped to arrive at inferences about literary texts and related symbolic implications. By adopting a textual stance, the reader focuses attention on features and conventions of the text. In reading a laboratory report, for example, the student may search for aspects of the text that are most important for understanding it. When adopting an institutional stance, the reader may interpret concepts and assume roles that fit with institutional expectations. For example, an institutional stance toward an article on healthcare might assume a business perspective and consider healthcare's impact on the economy; a political perspective might result in the reader's gauging healthcare's effect on government policy. In adopting a field stance, the reader interprets ideas within the framework of specific academic disciplines or fields of expertise. The expert reader, for example, taking the perspective of the literary critic, might examine the text from several perspectives, such as psychoanalytic, feminist, poststructuralist, or semiotic.

With both literary and nonliterary texts, Langer (1990) found that readers can use four stances that offer a range of meaning-making choices to develop understandings. First, the reader can be outside but step into an envisionment as he or she attempts to form a context for meaning-making. Second, the reader can be inside an envisionment and move through it to further build meaning. Third, the reader can step back and reflect on what is known. And fourth, the reader can step outside the text and objectify the reading experience, a stance often taken on completion of a reading as the reader judges or comments on it.

The reader can also assume the stance of the writer (Smith, 1984). Reading and writing share a number of meaning-construction features such as planning, constructing, revising, and monitoring (Kucer, 1985; Tierney & Shanahan, 1991). To adopt the stance of reader as writer, the reader must understand and utilize the purposes and problems that writers have when creating and constructing texts. As Beach and Hynds (1990) emphasize, students need to be capable of adopting various stances or combinations of stances in different situations and to become sensitive to engaging them in appropriate circumstances.

The *sociocultural values and beliefs* that the reader acquires through family, peer group, and community interaction have a profound and pervasive effect on school success in general and reading development in particular. These values and beliefs place the reader in a highly vulnerable position if they do not match those of the teacher. The work of Au and Mason (1981), Coulthard and Sinclair (1975), Erickson (1982a), Hull and Rose (1990, see #11 this volume), and Labov (1972) have demonstrated that sociocultural differences in expectations between students and teachers contribute to communication breakdowns and impede school learning. For example, the reader may experience a monocultural school environment where specific values and beliefs are critical to success, and where achievement is dependent on the reader's view that literacy is important, that standard English is the proper language, and that instructional routines—such as turn-taking—are to be followed (McHoul, 1978; Mehan, 1980; Sacks, Schegloff, & Jefferson, 1974). This effect is closely connected to low performance in literacy achievement. Phillips (1970) found that American Indian children were hesitant to talk in classrooms because their culturally shaped language use acceptable in home learning situations was markedly different from that expected in learning situations in school. The children perceived participation as requiring individual performance under the control of the classroom teacher.

The influence of family and cultural values on schooling is also clearly depicted in Heath's research (1983; see also #8 this volume). She describes literacy development in three communities: Trackton (a black mill community), Roadville (a white mill community), and Gateway (a "mainstream" urban community). Trackton children experienced a social environment in which the community shared in teaching and in uniting the youngsters with the community. Children, especially boys, were expected to respond creatively to challenging questions. Stories they created were designed to exaggerate "truth," glorify self, and entertain the listener. Few children's books or book-reading activities were found in the homes. Roadville children were reared in an environment where parents talked with their babies, modified their language to involve their children, and used interactional patterns that included answering questions, labeling, and naming objects. The children were expected to accept the power of print through association with alphabet letters and workbook-like activities. Stories were characterized by truthfulness and carried a moral message. In Gateway, a high value was placed on schools and schooling for both black and white children. From an early age, families nurtured their children's interest in books. Parents frequently asked their children information-type questions and developed book-sharing routines. The children often saw parents and siblings reading for a variety of purposes. Heath concluded that the Gateway children acquired values about reading and writing that the Trackton and Roadville children found strange. The Gateway children were not only familiar with book-reading routines but with comprehension strategies as well. The discourse and literacy practices of the Trackton and Roadville children needed to be bridged by the school.

In his study, Ogbu (1990) explained why some minority groups experience more success at becoming literate in U.S. schools than do others. He categorizes minorities into two groups: voluntary and involuntary. While voluntary minorities came to the United States seeking to improve their lives, involuntary minorities were brought by slavery or conquest. Ogbu observed that individuals from voluntary minorities generally prosper in literacy acquisition, but those from involuntary minorities often develop values and beliefs that conflict with the learning environments and expectations encountered in U.S. schools.

In an attempt to bridge school and community, Au and her colleagues (Au, 1980; Au & Mason, 1981) found "talk stories," a form of joint performance in Hawaiian culture, useful as a vehicle for reading instruction. The talk story pattern asks a question and encourages four or five children to participate jointly in forming an answer. As a group, the children respond to one another's answers, interact, and build a complete answer. Au found that this strategy influenced cognitive outcomes and reading comprehension for these children. This creative approach to developing sociocultural compatibility between talk stories and speech events in the Hawaiian community is in distinct contrast to the conventional classroom teacher-dominated recitation pattern.

The importance of social networks and information exchange in the literacy achievement of Hispanic children is clearly demonstrated in the work of Moll (1992). One of the critical factors in school success appears to reside in integrating familiar home and community experiences into the classroom (see Jimenez, #9 this volume).

Sociocultural values and beliefs constitute an important aspect of the reader's affective conditions for learning. As we will see later in this discussion, the teacher must exercise understanding and sensitivity to these values and beliefs if the reader's potential for success is to be enhanced.

Cognitive Conditions. The reader's cognitive conditions play a vital role in the reading process. Again, however, we must emphasize that in meaning construction the cognitive conditions constantly interact with the affective conditions just discussed.

We now turn to cognitive conditions and the role of declarative, procedural, and conditional knowledge in the meaning-construction process. Declarative knowledge includes the reader's "what" knowledge of facts, objects, events, language, concepts, and theories about the world. The reader's procedural knowledge consists of how-to skills and strategies for using and applying knowledge, ranging from using a context strategy in identifying a new word to the use of a text-organization strategy in reading a chapter. Conditional knowledge accounts for the reader's awareness of knowledge use. This may be viewed as "when" and "why" knowledge, which provides for application of declarative and procedural knowledge forms. Conditional knowledge thus accounts for understanding the social context in which reading is taking place and for the reader's intent (Paris, Lipson, & Wixson, 1983).

The reader's declarative, procedural, and conditional knowledge forms are stored and represented in memory and include a variety of knowledge essential to meaning construction. As noted in Figure 2, they include knowledge of language, word-analysis skills, text-processing strategies, metacognitive strategies, classroom and social interaction, and self and world. Before discussing the specific knowledge forms, we will first briefly examine how these forms are represented in memory. In the model we assume that the reader's declarative, procedural, and conditional knowledge forms are stored in knowledge structures known as schemata. These memory structures can be thought of as information packets or knowledge modules, each of which is used to organize a particular class of concepts formed from our experience (Adams & Collins, 1985). As described in work by Rumelhart and his associates (Rumelhart, 1980, 1981; Rumelhart & Ortony, 1977), schemata may be seen as generic patterns or abstract representations of knowledge. These knowledge structures are composed of "slots" to be filled with specific information when a problem is to be solved or a text is to be processed. As knowledge is stored in memory, these structures set up expectations for the reader when new information is encountered for interpretation. If new information fits the "slots" of an existing schema so that it becomes filled with concrete instances—a condition called *instantiation*—that schema may exert control over the reader's meaning-construction process (Anderson, 1975; see also #20 this volume; Rumelhart, 1980). The reader may ignore important information because it does not fit the expected conditions or distort information so that it does fit those expected "slots."

The explanatory power of schema theory is found in the idea that the first level of any schema provides for an abstraction and conceptual framework for all of the particular events that fall below it but are within its domain. For example, a schema such as "going to the grocery store" may represent an overarching knowledge module that a grocery store is a business establishment where one purchases food to take home to use in meal preparation. Below this global concept are more specific schemata such as going to a large food market or to a small corner store.

Schemata have a number of important meaning-construction functions. They aid in memory searches, provide for inference-making, allow text content to be reorganized and reconstructed, and are valuable in summarizing content (Anderson & Pearson, 1984). A reader's schema appears to function by using the following properties: (1) procedural information that allows the schema to become activated and instantiated by interaction with the text; (2) inheritance, which simply means that a subschema may acquire knowledge from a higher-level schema; (3) default values that provide for inferences based on the text; and (4) a hierarchical organizational structure, such as that exemplified by the previous example of the "going to the grocery store" schema.

However, the power of schemata to shape the meaning-making process during reading can also lead to the loss of important meanings or to misinterpretations of text. For example, when reading Mark Twain's *The Adventures of Huckleberry Finn*, some readers may activate a schema that leads them to expect simply a series of adventures and proceed to fill in the "slots" with Huck's experiences. With those expectations in place, these readers may have considerable difficulty seeing Twain's novel as a satire about religion, superstition, law, parenthood, morality, or human gullibility. They may create a consistent interpretation of the novel, but that representation may not be as rich as possible because a particular schema has restricted potential understandings. Some readers initially resist the idea that the novel could be read as a satire—until meanings of different readers are discussed in the classroom community and students are encouraged to build additional meanings.

The view of schemata as monolithic, rigid knowledge structures used to direct the comprehension of texts has been expanded to include an alternative perspective that views schemata as knowledge resources for the building of new knowledge structures (Spiro, 1988; see also #23 and #24 this volume). In this less linear and mechanistic, more organic and flexible perspective, the reader does not fill slots but takes chunks of knowledge from existing knowledge structures and assembles new meanings to represent a text far more complex than any one hierarchically designed knowledge structure. The reader takes pieces of knowledge from several different hierarchically designed but in some way related knowledge structures and assembles them to form a novel representation of the complex text. The newly constructed and "purpose-sensitive" schema allows for more elaborate interconnections than does any one hierarchical schema. This "purpose-sensitive" schema accounts for more effective problem solving and meaning construction than does the hierarchical schema that provides for a sole meaning representation, as was the case for those readers who read *The Adventures of Huckleberry Finn* only as an adventure but not a satire.

Several researchers (Alba & Hasher, 1983; Sadoski & Paivio, 1994, see #47 this volume; Sadoski, Paivio, & Goetz, 1991) have challenged the schema theory perspective of knowledge representation in memory, posing instead a dual-coding theory of a verbal and nonverbal knowledge representation. The nonverbal imagery system, which is separate but connectable to the verbal system, includes all sensory modes, such as sight, smell, and sound, and has the capacity to evoke in the reader strong emotion and meaning through images. As William Carlos Williams wrote in his poem "The Red Wheelbarrow,"

> so much depends
> upon
> a red wheel
> barrow
> glazed with rain
> water
> beside the white
> chickens

Such imagery often contributes to the aesthetic and thematic dimensions of our response to literature—for example, as Hester Prynne's *A* in *The Scarlet Letter* acts as an image that carries her anguish and consolidates meaning for many readers. Furthermore, research suggests that imagery plays an important role in the comprehension and long-term recall of both narrative and expository texts. At this time, however, schema theory provides strong explanatory power in accounting for the reader's knowledge representation and the role of this knowledge in the meaning-construction process.

In the model, schemata hold the key to explaining the top-down perspective of reading as an interactive process. The reader's schemata are probably best understood as networks of associated knowledge that are activated and instantiated or as knowledge clusters that can be tapped for pieces of information that the reader reassembles to form new schemata. However, reliance on the use of monolithic, hierarchical schemata for a text representation may be less productive for the reader than the active assembly or construction of multiple representations by interconnecting knowledge from many related schemata. Thus, a more web-like representation can be built by the reader rather than a fixed formula of slots that the reader fills, or tries to fill. We now turn to specific knowledge forms critical to the reader's meaning-construction process.

Reading is a linguistically based process that requires *language knowledge* if the reader is to construct meaning. The reader's language knowledge consists of schemata that represent orthographic, phonological, syntactical, and lexical knowledge. These knowledge forms are well developed for most children long before the start of formal schooling (Cox, Fang, & Otto, #12 this volume; Harste, Burke, & Woodward, 1982; Heath, 1983). The syntactical and lexical features, however, continue to increase in complexity throughout the school years (Juel & Minden-Cupp, #13 this volume; R.B. Ruddell & M.R. Ruddell, 1994).

Phonological knowledge is represented in children's phonological rule systems by about age 4 (Gibson & Levin, 1975; Whorf, 1956). Children at this age choose words that conform to English phonology in contrast to sound clusters that do not follow these phonological rules—*klec* versus *dlek*, for example (Menyuk, 1968; Messer, 1967; Morehead, 1971). Upon entry into kindergarten or first grade, this system is near completion (Ervin & Miller, 1963; McCarthy, 1954; Templin, 1957).

Syntactical knowledge is also well developed before children begin to read. The fundamental capacity to understand and generate language is innate (N. Chomsky, 1959, 1965) but requires a social support system for development. In Bruner's terms (1983, 1986), the Language Acquisition Device (LAD) with which we are born requires a Language Acquisition Support System (LASS) provided by the social world. This support system may develop in many different social settings (Slobin, 1979; Vygotsky, 1986). But it appears that if young children do not get early social interaction and language stimulation (as occurs in rare cases of childhood isolation), normal language development does not occur (Curtiss, 1977; Rymer, 1992a, 1992b). Without language interaction, the capacity to achieve syntactic sophistication and to understand and form grammatical sentences fails to develop. Therefore, the child's innate language capacity must be stimulated and supported.

The development of syntactic knowledge previous to and during school years is well documented. Scollon (1979) discerned subtle syntactic forms before children begin to speak in two-word utterances, while Dore (1979) demonstrated that preschoolers have a significant command of conversational skills and what can be done with language. C. Chomsky's research (1969, 1972) examining the relationship between children's comprehension of oral sentences and exposure to reading revealed that stages of language development were related to early reading acquisition. This acquisition was positively related to the difficulty level of books used in the home. Loban's (1976) longitudinal research demonstrated that children's syntactical knowledge complexity continues to develop throughout the elementary grades. The close connection between syntactical complexity and reading comprehension has also been established (R.B. Ruddell, 1965). Together, these studies demonstrate that potential for developing syntactic knowledge appears to be inborn, that its manifestations begin early in the socially stimulated language environment, and that it directly affects the ability to read.

Lexical knowledge refers to the reader's knowledge of words and word meanings. This knowledge is closely related to the reader's personal and world knowledge and enables the reader to represent this knowledge in schemata. Words representing concepts are clustered in categories that are hierarchically arranged (Johnson, Toms-Bronowski, & Pittelman, 1981). These categories are, in turn, connected to other concept structures.

Lexical knowledge is also directly related to comprehension and meaning construction as demonstrated by a range of vocabulary research (Anderson & Freebody, 1981; Beck & McKeown, 1991). Estimates indicate that children expand their vocabulary at the rate of 2,700 to 3,000 words per year—or about 7 words a day (Beck & McKeown, 1991; Just & Carpenter, 1987; see also Nagy & Scott, #19 this volume). The reader's intellectual curiosity and the social nature and use of language are important motivations in vocabulary acquisition. In her study of conditions that affect independent word learning, Haggard (1980) found four specific social and language conditions for word use: words that sounded adult or appealing, occurred in an emotional incident that involved mispronunciation and embarrassment, had immediate usefulness in the school setting, or were common in a peer group. Peer usage was found to be the most frequent motive for discovering the meaning of a new word, while classroom instruction rarely motivated such acquisition.

That vocabulary and reading comprehension are positively related is not surprising (see Kuhn & Stahl, #16 this volume; Stanovich, #17 this volume). Efficient meaning construction requires a knowledge of concepts, and the reader must rely on the internal mental dictionary as the primary and immediate resource. The larger the lexicon, the larger will be the reader's capacity to comprehend what is read. Furthermore, the reader's speed of access to lexical knowledge is related to processing efficiency and meaning construction. Poor readers usually have slower lexical access speeds than good readers (Samuels & Naslund, 1994). This is explained by the rapid and nearly automatic access of concept knowledge stored in the schemata of the skilled reader.

Knowledge of *word analysis* provides information that enables the reader to transform visual symbols in print to representational forms in the mind for meaning construction. This knowledge base expands from preschool experiences with print and invented spelling to the later grades where such skills are used in the conscious analysis of new words and in automatic processing of known words (Ehri, 1987, 1988; Samuels, 1994). In the early grades, the reader extends understanding of the relationship between print and its oral language counterpart. The beginning reader must develop and refine the idea that print represents language and, in turn, meaning (Strickland & Feeley, 1991). This concept enables the reader to make print predictions using language knowledge already possessed. The beginning reader of English must also come to understand that print is arranged from left to right on the page, that words are represented by printed letters and separated by blank spaces between them, and that print in fact represents meaning (Clay, 1972, 1985). For many children, experiences writing with invented spelling prior to entering school have already provided beginning awareness of the oral language and print connection (Harste, Burke, & Woodward, 1982).

There is strong support for the idea that the reader progresses through several developmental phases in acquiring word-analysis knowledge (Frith, 1985; Mason, Herman, & Au, 1991), regardless of the instructional methodology used. Ehri's extensive research review (1991, 1994; see also Ehri & McCormick, #14 this volume) posits four such phases:

1. Logographic, which uses cues relying on visual, contextual, or graphic features to read words—for example, reading a word such as *monkey* by remembering the "tail" on the word. Many kindergartners and entering first-grade children rely on this system.

2. Transition from logographic to beginning alphabetic, in which, for example, the "two sticks" in the middle of the word *yellow* become associated with the "el" sound in the word. This stage starts to connect the printed letters to sounds and pronunciation and is also typical of kindergarten and first-grade children.

3. Alphabetic, which is characterized by the ability to use letter–sound relationships to read words—*dog*, for example, is read as /dŏg/. This phase involves phonologically recoding the word spelling in order to access the word from the mental lexicon. Some children will be at this stage when they enter first grade while others will not develop control of the alphabetic stage until second or even third grade.

4. Orthographic, which uses alphabetic principles but also predictable letter patterns and groups in "orthographic neighborhoods" that form patterns larger than sound–letter correspondences—for example, *made*, *wade*, *fade*. In this stage, the reader also develops the ability to use analogy to read new words—for example, *-ain* in *rain* is used to read the new

word *train*. These patterns and groups are established in memory just as the letter–sound units are during the alphabetic stage. Such larger letter units help in decoding multisyllabic words, reduce the number of units needed in memory, and speed up the process of recognizing words (Juel, 1983; Venezky & Massaro, 1979). Sensitivity to rhyming patterns in print emerges for most children in first grade, but the ability to use analogy may extend as late as fourth or fifth grade for some children.

These developmental phases account for children's gradual use of larger perceptual patterns that possess a high degree of predictability in specific "orthographic neighborhoods."

Thus, as the reader becomes more skilled in word analysis, progress is made from learning how the spelling system symbolizes phonemes in speech to orthographic pattern processing and eventually to the automatic recognition of many words. The word-analysis knowledge acquired consists of alphabetic and orthographic principles that enable the reader to recode unfamiliar word spellings phonologically. This recoding in turn provides for access to the meaning of words in the mental lexicon.

As the reader progresses developmentally and automatically recognizes many words, phonologically recoded information may not need to be activated. The spelling of specific words in memory may thus serve to represent pronunciation, and, if the word is recognized, the mental lexicon is accessed directly (Ehri, 1991, 1994; Samuels, 1985, 1994). When a word is not recognized, conscious processing using alphabetic and orthographic knowledge and phonological recoding is required to provide for lexical access. The development and use of word-analysis knowledge in meaningful contexts enables the discovery of correct word meaning.

The preceding perspective would hold that orthographic, phonological, and semantic processing are integrated, parallel processes that occur simultaneously and in coordinated networks (J.L. McClelland, Rumelhart, & Hinton, 1986; J.L. McClelland, Rumelhart, & PDP Research Group, 1986). It would seem that for skilled readers, letter, sound, and meaning are interdependent and interacting events in the reading process. While this explanation for the acquisition of word analysis knowledge is most appropriate for our model, contrasting explanations have been developed by other theorists (Adams, 1990; Seidenberg & McClelland, 1989; Stanovich, 1991). These carefully reasoned explanations, however, appear to be extrapolated from the use of word-analysis knowledge by the expert reader rather than the beginning reader.

The role of *text-processing strategies* in the model is critical as the reader responds to and interprets narrative or expository text. These strategies are stored in the form of mental schemata and hold the key to understanding text-pattern organization. Narrative text structure, often referred to as "story grammar," accounts for setting, characters, plot structure, climax, and resolution. Schemata for expository writing account for structures such as comparison-contrast, cause-effect, problem-solution, thesis-support, or enumeration of ideas. The concept of flexible knowledge assembly posited by Spiro (1988) can be used to extend this text-processing view. Spiro's concept, as previously discussed, calls for a "purpose-sensitive" schema that provides for interconnections between schemata and the assembly of new meanings that go beyond a single hierarchical text schema.

At the preschool and kindergarten levels, children develop an understanding of story construction that moves through several stages, from picture-governed attempts in which the story is not formed to print-governed reading in which the story closely follows the print (Sulzby, 1985). For beginning readers, the development of a concept of story structure evolves from unorganized lists of events to full narrative forms (Applebee, 1978). This progression culminates in the understanding that the printed text is the critical source of meaning and that stories follow an organizational pattern (see Hiebert & Martin, #15 this volume).

Through experience with narrative reading, the reader develops a sense of story pattern that provides for expectations and predictions useful in constructing meaning. There is evidence that direct instruction in narrative structures can lead to improved understanding and recall of story information for readers at various levels (Bower, 1976; Gordon, 1980; Thorndyke, 1977). The more-important information, such as setting, initiating events, and consequences, is more likely to be recalled than less-important information, such as a character's response or reaction (Nezworski, Stein, & Trabasso, 1982). The understanding of these text patterns, in effect, enables the reader to form a plan for reading. The plan for narrative text structures enables the reader to direct attention in making inferences and memory searches using prior knowledge (Anderson & Pearson, 1984; Rumelhart, 1975, 1980). Furthermore, such a plan, or "cognitive template," permits the reader to predict text features useful in the comprehension process (Rumelhart & Ortony, 1977).

Expository reading also relies on the reader's awareness of text organization. The identification and use of the organizational plan used in the text leads to more-effective understanding (Meyer, 1984). For example, the reader encountering a text that explores cause–effect relationships reads and comprehends the text better by using a cause–effect text schema. The research evidence suggests that instruction can assist students in identifying organizational structures in expository text and in using these structures to more effectively construct meaning (Bartlett, 1978; Meyer, Brandt, & Bluth, 1980; Meyer & Freedle, 1979; see also Meyer & Poon, #30 this volume).

Although both narrative and expository text organization schemata can set up expectations for readers that lead to misreadings of text (Garner, 1987; Rumelhart, 1980), knowledge of text organization also enables highly efficient top-down text processing in the meaning-construction process. More-skilled readers are highly effective in using text structure strategies in immediate and delayed recall of text information. Poorer readers appear not to have developed these important meaning-construction strategies or are unable to apply them in the comprehension of text (Britton, Meyer, Hodge, & Glynn, 1980; Britton, Meyer, Simpson, Holdredge, & Curry, 1979; Hiebert, Englert, & Brennan, 1983; McGee, 1982; Whaley, 1982).

In the model, the reader's *metacognitive strategies* provide for the self-monitoring and self-correcting routines used in the meaning-construction process (see Hacker, #28 this volume). Strategy use is directed by the reader executive and monitor. The executive directs interactive processing as needed, drawing on prior knowledge forms such as language, word-analysis skills, and text-processing strategies (Garner, 1987). In addition, strategy use is also influenced by the reader's motivation to read and attitude toward reading and content. These influences take the form of the reader's intent to construct meaning based on a given text and to persist in this effort (Mathewson, 1994; Paris, Lipson, & Wixson, 1983).

The emergence of the reader's metacognitive control appears to take place in the preschool years. Several researchers have noted that literacy-related metacognitive strategies such as planning, monitoring, checking, evaluating, and revising are found in the utterances of 4- and 5-year-olds in pretend reading of favorite storybooks (Cox, 1994; Cox & Sulzby, 1982; Rowe, 1989). Earlier research (Baker & Brown, 1984; A. Brown, 1980, 1982; R.B. Ruddell & Speaker, 1985) indicates that skilled readers, in contrast to poor readers, are more aware of the meaning-construction process and the need to take corrective action when meaning difficulties are encountered. Differences in the self-correction of oral reading miscues also indicate that good readers use self-monitoring during reading (K.S. Goodman, 1973; Y.M. Goodman & K.S. Goodman, 1994).

There is some evidence to suggest that less-skilled readers use the same metacognitive decision-making strategies as do more-skilled readers but that the strategies are used less often and less efficiently (Goetz, Palmer, & Haensly, 1983). Poorer readers appear to have more difficulty identifying the sources or causes of problems while reading more-complex text (McGee, 1982). This may be attributed, in part, to attention allocation during word analysis. The ability to use text structure in recall protocols appears to improve with age and reading ability. These findings suggest that less-skilled readers, who possess knowledge and strategies to make metacognitive decisions, are unable to use them effectively.

Metacognitive decisions made by readers have been studied through eye movement research. Carpenter and Just (1981; see also Just & Carpenter, #43 this volume) found that readers allocate additional processing time at the end of a sentence or other syntactically important juncture. If the decision is made by the reader that a portion of text is important, additional time is allocated for comprehension processing. Other researchers have reached similar conclusions (Cirilo & Foss, 1980; Goetz, Schallert, Reynolds, & Radin, 1983).

While metacognitive strategies appear to be initiated in the preschool years, they continue to develop as the reader gains experience in comprehending text. As these strategies are applied, attention is allocated on the basis of reading purpose, interest, and motivation. The detection of meaning "breakdowns" is central to the application of "fix-up" and other metacognitive strategies.

In order to effectively use text in the classroom, the reader must have *knowledge of classroom and social interaction* patterns. As Dyson (1984) and Gee (#4 this volume) have emphasized, literacy is centered in social activity and is much more than skills and strategies. Interaction patterns used in the classroom are largely under the control of the teacher (Green & Harker, 1982). Features of these patterns include message form, message content, addressor, addressee, audience, outcomes, tone, and manner (Hymes, 1974). The reader must internalize these features of classroom dialogue if appropriate and meaningful interaction is to occur.

The reader's classroom and social interaction strategies are closely linked to sociocultural values and beliefs. As we have previously noted, mismatches between the reader's home and community culture and that of the school can produce major obstacles in classroom interaction.

The reader must acquire the communicative competence that provides for successful classroom interaction (see Forman & Cazden, #7 this volume). This includes not only the ability to respond to texts (Mosenthal & Na, 1980) and to teachers (DeStefano, Pepinsky, & Sanders, 1982) but also to the complex social network of the classroom community (Moll, 1992; Santa Barbara Classroom Discourse Group, 1992). As will be discussed later, the teacher must be aware of and sensitive to the reader's understanding of language functions that are critical to classroom discussion and interaction.

Personal and world knowledge includes schemata representing a wide range of experiences and understandings that have been acquired both in school and out. This knowledge includes declarative forms (exemplified by historical information acquired during a field trip to the local museum, for example), procedural forms (such as how to activate a self-directed museum display), and conditional forms (illustrated by understanding the appropriate time to pose questions to the docent). Personal knowledge is stored in the reader's episodic memory as images of personal experience (Tulving, 1983, 1986). These events are bound by time and location. They may range from remembering what one had for breakfast to one's earliest childhood memories centered on a grandmother's chocolate chip cookies. World knowledge is represented in schemata formed from the reader's life experiences and includes facts and assumptions, actions and procedures, and understanding of appropriate conditions for knowledge use. Activation of schemata from world knowledge directly affects the interpretation of a text. Two readers with different world knowledge schemata may read an ambiguous text and provide very different interpretations (Anderson & Pichert, 1978; Hull & Rose, #11 this volume;

Pichert & Anderson, 1977). Thus, the reader's background knowledge schemata are directly related to meaning construction and text interpretation. As Carrell and Eisterhold (1983) point out, "much of the meaning understood from a text is really not actually in the text, per se, but in the reader, in the background knowledge or schematic knowledge of the reader" (p. 559).

Intertextual references frequently influence the meanings that readers construct as they read (Hartman, 1990, 1991). Intertextuality is the process of connecting current texts with past texts to construct meaning (de Beaugrande, 1980). Those past texts are part of the reader's world knowledge. In the model, the meaning of text is expanded to include not only printed texts but also the text of events, communication, and cultures (Bloome & Bailey, 1992). These "texts" range from art and music to ritual and gesture. Intertextuality is thus more broadly conceived as the acknowledged interaction between the text being read and the "texts" based on our experiences. These texts have an important influence on the reader's construction of meaning. For example, students who have read Twain's *The Adventures of Tom Sawyer* will have a richer text representation and fuller understanding of the characters Huck Finn and Tom Sawyer as they connect the characters to *The Adventures of Huckleberry Finn*.

The use of personal and world knowledge has a strong influence on the meaning-construction and comprehension process. The reader who has a rich knowledge base and flexible access to that base can more effectively assemble a coherent and meaningful text representation. The reader's intertextual links to "texts" outside the primary text also facilitate and enrich the meaning-construction process.

Knowledge Use and Control

The knowledge use and control component of the model directs the reader's meaning-construction process. As noted in Figure 2, this component is linked to and interactive with the reader's prior knowledge and beliefs. Knowledge use and control consists of three components: the knowledge-construction process, text representation, and reader executive and monitor.

Knowledge-Construction Process. The reader's knowledge-construction process serves to set the purpose for reading and to integrate prior beliefs and knowledge through planning and organizing and constructing of meaning. We will show later in the discussion that, as meaning is formed, it is reflected in text representation. The reading executive and monitor oversees this entire process based on the original purpose and, if necessary, prompts reconstruction of purpose and meaning.

Purpose setting is initiated as the reader creates a goal or, more commonly, multiple goals when the text is encountered. This aspect of the process reflects the reader's motivation or intent and is influenced by the affective and cognitive conditions noted in Figure 2. For example, the reader's stance may be aesthetic and reflect the intent of savoring the pleasure of constructing and entering an imaginary world of romance, intrigue, or interstellar space, or the reader may take a predominantly efferent stance to learn more about dinosaurs, jellyfish, or electromagnets. The reader may also adopt multiple stances to experience a text from many different perspectives (Beach, 1992; see also Galda & Beach, #31 this volume).

The learning environment created by the teacher will also have a strong influence on the purpose setting of the reader (see Alvermann, Young, Green, & Wisenbaker, #32 this volume). Assignments may be given that request the student to read efferently and attend to particular aspects of a text, such as imagery used to evoke a certain mood or the claims used to support a thesis. By contrast, the teacher may focus attention on pleasure reading designed to encourage an aesthetic transaction with the text and to evoke the reader's feelings and attitudes toward key characters (see Many, #33 this volume).

As the reader's original goals are realized, subsequent goals may take their place as the focus of attention. Thus, purpose setting for the reader is usually in flux as goals, both conscious and unconscious, are made and met.

As the reading purpose is established, a simultaneous process of *planning and organizing* takes place. The plans readers make as they interact with text are of at least two types: (1) a structured text plan of events, concepts, or claims in the form of a text pattern and (2) a path of action, or strategies and approaches, used to meet a goal.

The reader begins to form a text-structure plan and a plan of action to achieve the reading purpose. The reader's text-structure plans may have a top-down or expectation-driven influence on the text-construction process as textual schemata become activated and influence or shape meaning construction. For example, a narrative text-structure plan may be used to integrate story features, or a cause–effect plan may be invoked in reading and interpreting a science experiment. While the beginning reader has fewer and less well-developed textual plans to bring to life, the more experienced reader may instantiate several elaborate textual schemata before eliminating those that do not work and confirming those that do. However, not every text activates textual schemata that might influence comprehension in a top-down fashion. Some texts, especially technical prose, are far better constructed and understood from the bottom up, a process that will be examined when we address text construction in the next section. Frequently, the reader builds meaning in a simultaneous and interactive manner using both top-down and bottom-up processing.

Meanwhile, the plan of action will draw upon more detailed aspects of prior knowledge to assist the reader. This may take the form of procedural and conditional knowledge that enables decision making about using various reading rates to process texts for different purposes, using context clues to infer meanings, and using reference resources to understand unfamiliar words, such as *zygote* in a science reading assignment.

The reader's awareness of text organizational structures plays an important planning and organizing role in creating meaning. Bruner (1986) has postulated two separate ways to order experience and construct meaning. The first, the narrative mode, creates imaginative worlds through stories. Its "truth" is wrung from its imitation of reality—in effect, its likeness to real-life experience. The second, the paradigmatic, is scientific and relies on logical proof and evidence for verification of claims. As the reader interacts with texts, experience in reading both modes will assist in understanding which mode the author has used to order the experience and which must be used to reconstruct the meaning the text embodies.

Reading is a process of *constructing*, of knowledge integration, of building meaning. The goals that the reader forms, the plans adopted or created, and the organizing that occurs as text is processed and interpreted contribute to the text-constructing process. For some kinds of texts (especially narrative), the reader often constructs meaning as schemata are activated and instantiated. But that top-down process is often not sufficient, especially for complex narrative forms.

Text construction may also be a knowledge-assembly process for the reader. Pieces of knowledge from schemata are put together (Spiro, 1988) or an associative net of propositions and concepts is formed, edited, and integrated in order to produce a textbase. Kintsch and his colleagues (Kintsch, 1986, 1988; Kintsch & van Dijk, 1978; van Dijk & Kintsch, 1985) have developed formal propositional representations to stand for the content of a text. In bottom-up fashion, the reader constructs and integrates these text-generated propositions that share related features to form networks or associative nets. These nets enable the reader to produce a textbase—accompanied by a reader's integrated background knowledge—that provides a coherent meaning.

In summary, the constructing process draws on the reader's prior beliefs and knowledge for information essential to both the analysis and synthesis of text. Declarative, procedural, and conditional knowledge of language, reading plans, and the world are brought to life when appropriately aroused by the reader's processing of text. This procedure is often interactive using bottom-up and top-down strategic processing. Meaning construction thus involves the weaving together of threads of many kinds: purposes and goals, language knowledge, text-structure plans and plans of action, intertextual knowledge, propositions clustered into macrostructures, and "gists."

Text Representation. The reader begins to construct a text representation as the interaction with text is initiated. Text representation in the model is conceived of as a "text world" that represents the text meaning structure and a record of text processing (de Beaugrande, 1981; Craik & Tulving, 1975; R.B. Ruddell &

Speaker, 1985). However, only a portion of the text representation remains consciously active because of the reader's limited cognitive capacity for conscious processing. If the reader needs to reactivate information in the text representation to build inferences or evaluate previous inferences, stored portions of the earlier representation may be brought into conscious attention.

The exact nature of text representation—whether a network of concepts, a set of propositions, an image, or some combination—remains in question (see Coté & Goldman, #25 this volume; Kintsch, 1988; see Kintsch, #46 this volume; Sadoski, Paivio, & Goetz, 1991). Although imagery may be part of the symbolic text-in-the-head representation of the text on the page, it seems likely that the bulk of text representation is in the form of propositions that have been "chunked" into a coherent textbase used in ongoing meaning construction.

Reading Executive and Monitor. Managing and overseeing the meaning-construction process is the reader executive and monitor. As shown in Figure 2, it is linked by two-way arrows with knowledge use and control, text representation, and prior knowledge and beliefs. It coordinates such functions as purpose setting, planning and organizing, reading- strategy selection, attention allocation, and "fix-up" routines during construction of text representation. These functions are carried out by drawing on affective and cognitive conditions in prior beliefs and knowledge. The conditions range from establishing motivation and intent to read and the stance to be taken on the one hand, to selecting text-processing strategies and metacognitive strategies to be used on the other. Time allocated to reading the text is also determined by this component. Skilled readers, for example, have been shown to adjust their reading rates and time allocation in relation to the reading purpose (Reynolds, Standiford, & Anderson, 1979; Rothkopf & Billington, 1979) and comprehension difficulty of the text (Wagner & Sternberg, 1987).

The reader executive and monitor evaluates the ongoing process of meaning construction as text representation is formed. This self-monitoring draws on metacognitive strategies in prior knowledge and beliefs and evaluates the "fit" between purpose and the meaning constructed in text representation. The monitor and executive, as part of the evaluative function, may intervene to fix up meaning breakdowns when they are detected. This may require the search for and accessing of additional information in prior knowledge and beliefs, shifts of attention to reread parts of the text, shifts in reading stance, or even altering the reading purpose.

During class discussions, the reader interacts not only with the text but also with the teacher's discourse and classmates' responses. Under these conditions, more cognitive functions are activated and more attention management is required than during individual text reading. Because of the range of tasks, the reader's executive and monitor must make decisions about which cognitive tasks—or distractions—will be given most priority. As text meaning construction is represented in the mind of the reader, that representation undergoes a reviewing process that is under the control of the reading executive and monitor. The reader's text representation may be reviewed depending on the difficulty of the text, and that review may result in further planning, organizing, and reconstructing until the reader creates a text representation that is coherent and meaningful.

In summary, the knowledge use and control component of the model has as its central task the construction of meaning. The reader uses the knowledge-construction process to set purposes, activate and construct plans, organize knowledge, and formulate a text representation. While the knowledge-construction process progresses, the reader executive and monitor manages the process, evaluates the text representation based on purpose, and assists in editing and reconstructing meaning when misunderstandings arise.

Outcomes of Meaning Construction

During and after reading, the reader develops a number of text-related outcomes. These outcomes are identified in Figure 2.

While reading, the reader employs word-analysis and language knowledge to develop *semantic and lexical knowledge*, which includes the learning of new words, their range of meanings, and their use. Often context assists the reader in deciding which meanings are appropriate for the text being read. *Interpretation of text* based on prior knowledge and beliefs may be the central goal for the reader. Most readings of text in classroom settings will lead to *discussion* of the text. Certainly, discussion is a valuable outcome for teacher and readers as they explore responses to the text and expand their understanding and knowledge base. *Written response* offers the reader an opportunity to understand, synthesize, and clarify what has been learned from the text reading and discussion. A wide range of written responses to text is possible, extending from expression of the reader's feelings and emotions to the creation of new works that expand on the reader's understanding. *Knowledge acquisition* includes specific domain knowledge, such as categories, concepts, and processes. While readers learn to read, they read to learn. *Motivational changes* can influence the reader's attitude toward reading and the reader's intention to continue to read. If the reader reads because of an internally driven desire or if meaningful learning accompanies reading, *motivation* to read—and to learn—is likely to increase. However, motivation can diminish if enjoyment and expectations are not fulfilled. The final outcome of the meaning-construction process shown in the model is the reader's *attitude, value, and belief change*. Rich and rewarding personal experiences with books can change the way a reader feels, acts, and perceives the world. Through reading, students can experience new and enchanting narrative worlds, discover new and tantalizing subjects, and gain new knowledge of themselves and others.

The Reader: A Summing Up

In our attempt to explain the mysterious process that enables the reader to construct meaning, we have identified a number of interacting components, as shown in Figure 2. Prior beliefs and knowledge include affective and cognitive conditions that influence and shape meaning construction. Knowledge use and control are at the heart of the knowledge-construction process through purpose setting, planning and organizing, and constructing meaning in the form of text representation. The meaning-construction process is directed by the reader executive and monitor and guided by purpose as attention is allocated and rereading, reconstruction, and editing occur. While the mystery of the process is far from solved, we have explored a number of critical clues that begin to help us understand it. However, much remains to be discovered about this process as we turn to the role of the teacher in facilitating the reader's construction of meaning.

The Teacher

Interest in how skillful teachers function in the learning environment is not new. Five centuries before the birth of Christ, Confucius (as cited in Muller, 1885) observed that when we know the causes that make instruction successful and those that have no effect, we can become successful teachers: "Opening the way and not conducting to the end makes [the learner] thoughtful." Socrates emphasized that a teacher does not "teach" in the sense of transferring knowledge to the pupil; rather, the teacher serves as a mediator to assist the student in becoming consciously aware of knowledge already possessed.

What is common to these thinkers and teachers is the belief that the skillful teacher does not "conduct to the end," as a performer. Rather, the teacher engages the student in a collaborative process of inquiry and self-improvement in which both teacher and student seek to refine respective skills and knowledge. The goal of teaching, then, is not to provide the student with definitive answers but to model thought in action and allow the student to discover answers for himself or herself (R.B. Ruddell & Kern, 1986; Unrau, 1997).

Teachers who have been influential in the academic and personal lives of students (see R.B. Ruddell, #36 this volume; R.B. Ruddell, Draheim, & Barnes, 1990; R.B. Ruddell & Harris, 1989) possess a number of common characteristics. These teachers consistently use clearly formulated instructional strategies that embody focused goals, plans, and monitoring for student feedback. They possess in-depth knowledge of reading and literacy processes as well as content knowledge, and they understand how to teach these processes effectively to students in their classrooms. They also frequently tap internal student motivation, stimulate intellectual curiosity, explore students' self-understanding, use aesthetic imagery and expression, and encourage engagement in problem solving. But these influential teachers reveal something else about their instruction that promoted motivation to learn: They have many personal characteristics that shape their teaching. They are warm, caring, and flexible, while having high expectations of themselves and their students. Furthermore, they are concerned about their students as individuals in the social context of the classroom.

The teacher orchestrates instruction and the meaning-construction process, as shown in Figure 3. The teacher components of the model parallel those of the reader components. As noted earlier, the teacher's prior knowledge and beliefs extend far beyond those of the reader, accounting for more extensive life experience, academic and professional preparation, and teaching experience. The teacher's knowledge use and control draw on prior knowledge and beliefs in the instructional decision-making process as purpose, plan, and strategy construction are created with the goal of involving students in active meaning construction. As

FIGURE 3
The Teacher

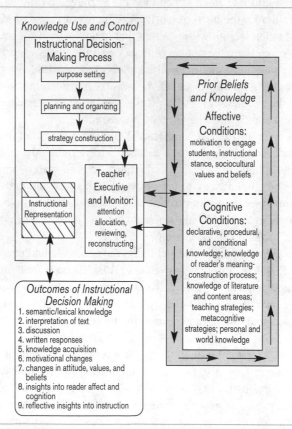

instruction is initiated, an instructional representation begins to form in the teacher's mind. The teacher executive and monitor serves to direct the instructional process based on the instructional purpose setting. These processes directly influence and shape the outcomes of instructional decision making, ranging from text interpretation to attitude, value, and belief changes. In the following sections, we briefly explore these teacher components.

Prior Knowledge and Beliefs

The teacher's prior knowledge and beliefs consist of affective and cognitive conditions based on and shaped by a wide range of life experiences. These conditions have a strong influence on knowledge use and control, instructional decision making, and instructional outcomes in the learning environment.

Affective Conditions. The teacher, like the reader, holds beliefs based on opinions, assumptions, and convictions. Teacher beliefs, however, have a direct impact on the affective conditions that influence and shape the teacher's instructional purpose, plan, and strategy construction. The teacher's *motivation to engage students* is shaped by the same three components that influence a reader's intention to engage in reading: a developing self, an instructional orientation, and task-engagement resources. The teacher's purpose in accounting for these motivation factors is driven by the desire to create an optimal learning environment where students will participate fully and persist in meaning construction. In this process the "fit" between text content, text difficulty, and the student's interests and reading ability is of central importance. Although an extensive discussion of a teacher's motivation to engage students can be found elsewhere in this volume (see Ruddell & Unrau, #35), in the following discussion we focus specifically on a teacher's instructional stance and sociocultural values and beliefs.

Instructional stance is closely connected to instructional purpose and reader motivation. As discussed earlier, the instructional stance selected influences the teacher's instructional objective and pedagogical approach, which, in turn, shapes the reader's purpose and attention focus. For example, an efferent stance may focus predominantly on specific concepts and ideas to be developed and learned in science or social studies material, while an aesthetic stance may emphasize discussion of the reader's response to the feelings and images created while reading and transacting with a poem (Rosenblatt, 1985). Reading may also take social, textual, institution, and field stances (Beach & Hynds, 1990), or the reader may assume the stance of writer (Smith, 1984).

The teacher's *sociocultural values and beliefs* are acquired through life experiences and influence the teacher's attitude toward and expectations of the reader. Our previous discussion emphasized the influence of sociocultural background differences between teacher and reader on school learning and classroom discussion; these effects range from communication breakdowns and limited participation in group discussions to teacher stereotyping and expectations for low achievement. Innovative efforts such as the "talk stories" of Au and her associates (Au, 1979; Au & Mason, 1981) and the work of Moll (1992) in understanding the social networks of Hispanic children illustrate how the teacher's awareness of varied sociocultural values and beliefs can be used to enhance the reader's meaning-construction process. The teacher must examine and understand the sociocultural values and beliefs held within the self and the reader. Only then can the teacher be sensitive to and incorporate the reader's values and beliefs into classroom meaning negotiation and construction.

Cognitive Conditions. The teacher's cognitive conditions are specific knowledge forms stored as *declarative knowledge* ("what"), *procedural knowledge* ("how to"), and *conditional knowledge* ("when" and "why"). These cognitive knowledge forms are highly interactive with one another and with the affective conditions, as illustrated by the broken line separating them in Figure 3. The cognitive conditions consist of knowledge of the reader's meaning-construction process, literature and content areas, teaching strategies, metacognitive strategies, and personal and world knowledge.

The teacher's *knowledge of the reader's meaning-construction process* is essential to instruction and instructional decision making. We assume the teacher constructs meaning from text by relying on the same processes. This knowledge is discussed in depth in our earlier exploration of the reader component. That discussion assumes a constructivist perspective that views the creation of meaning as an active comprehension process in the social context of the classroom. This active comprehension process must account for the reader's prior knowledge and beliefs as knowledge construction occurs and text representation is formed under the control of the reader's executive and monitor. Meaning negotiation in the classroom social context among teacher, reader, and classroom community is an important part of this meaning-construction process, as we shall see in our later discussion.

Knowledge of literature and content areas constitutes a store of information critical to instruction. This knowledge, largely declarative in nature, is acquired through academic experiences and enriched through personal and world knowledge. Knowledge of this type ranges from familiarity with the accepted literary canon to an understanding of important concepts in science, mathematics, and the social sciences. It also includes an understanding of the organization of both narrative and expository text and related text-processing strategies. The teacher selects literary works that are likely to engage students and to move them progressively toward deeper understanding of various literary forms and techniques (Moffett, 1968). Expository or technical prose that the teacher chooses also provides students opportunities for optimum growth in understanding discourse structures commonly used in particular content areas, such as history or biology (M.R. Ruddell, 1993).

Knowledge of teaching strategies is critical to the teacher's instructional decision making and helps implement the selected instructional purpose. Teaching-strategy knowledge may consist of understanding that provides for general problem solving or of strategies that can be used in reaching specific instructional goals. Such strategies are illustrated by the following: the Directed Reading–Thinking Activity or DRTA (Stauffer, 1976), designed to establish reader predictions, confirmations, and conclusions in narratives; the Prereading Plan or PREP (Langer, 1981), which serves to activate and assess reader background knowledge before reading narrative or expository material; the Question–Answer Relationships strategy or QARS (Raphael, 1982), which serves to assist the reader in connecting reading purpose to text and to personal information sources; the Group Mapping Activity or GMA (Davidson, 1978), in which the reader develops a visual representation of the text to integrate and synthesize information; the Reciprocal Questioning Strategy or ReQuest (Manzo, 1969; Manzo & Manzo, 1990), which develops students' ability to create questions, construct meaning, and monitor responses; the Reciprocal Teaching strategy (see Brown, Palincsar, & Armbruster, #29 this volume), which uses teacher modeling to develop student predictions, generate questions, and clarify and summarize meaning; the Vocabulary Self-Collection Strategy or VSS (Haggard, 1982; M.R. Ruddell, 1993), which provides for high personal motivation in vocabulary learning by emphasizing children's selection of personally important words from text; and Students Achieving Independent Learning (SAIL) (Brown et al., #37 this volume), which provides low-achieving second graders with multiple-strategies instruction. Knowledge of and ability to use strategies such as these in a near automatic fashion are critical to effective instruction so the teacher can free attention for the major task of directing meaning synthesis and construction (Duffy & Ball, 1986; McNair & Joyce, 1979).

An important part of the teacher's strategy knowledge resides in understanding and using informal observations and assessments of the reader during instruction. Such information provides not only immediate feedback to the reader but also insight into the reader's meaning-construction process that can be used in planning follow-up instruction.

Metacognitive strategies provide a system for self-monitoring and self-correction of meaning construction during and after instruction. This system is used by the teacher executor and monitor, is guided by the instructional purpose, and is interactive with other cognitive and affective conditions. While little research has been conducted on metacognitive strategy use during instruction, we believe this is an important model component. For example, as instruction proceeds the teacher must allocate attention to a wide range of factors including student responses, content of the lesson, instructional strategies employed, time constraints, and use of text and materials (McNair & Joyce, 1979). The teacher must also be aware of communication breakdowns and possible ways to clarify meaning and alter instructional strategies to improve the meaning-negotiation process. This requires the ability to detect meaning difficulties, shift attention to understand the problem, and draw on specific strategies to correct the problem during instruction.

The teacher also learns what is working for students by reflecting on classroom interaction after instruction. Research has shown that by mentally replaying events, keeping a journal, or videotaping, the experienced teacher is able to reflect on the quality and productivity of the learning relationship with students. This reflection represents an attempt to discover what could be changed to improve instruction (Borko, Shavelson, & Stern, 1981).

The teacher's *personal and world knowledge* represents those experiences acquired through life outside of school and academic experiences. Personal knowledge, formed from these experiences and bound by time and situation, is stored in episodic memory; world knowledge is represented by schemata in semantic memory.

The teacher's personal and world knowledge directly affect the construction of meaning and interpretation of text, as with the reader. However, the teacher's knowledge base may have developed over a longer time or from a wider range of personal and world experiences.

As we noted earlier, the meaning of text as used in the model is expanded through the concept of intertextuality to include the "texts" from areas such as art, music, and cultural rituals. In this sense, the teacher's personal and world knowledge provide for interaction between the "texts" based on experience and the text being read. The extensive intertextual knowledge often held by the teacher can provide an important resource in instructional decision making and assist the reader to negotiate and construct meaning.

Knowledge Use and Control

The teacher's knowledge use and control component directs the instructional decision-making process, provides a mental instructional representation, and evaluates instructional purpose through the teacher executive and monitor. This component is closely connected to and interactive with prior knowledge and beliefs, as shown in Figure 3.

Instructional Decision-Making Process. The instructional decision-making process establishes *purpose setting* for instruction that reflects the teacher's instructional intent. The affective and cognitive conditions, as shown under prior knowledge and beliefs in Figure 3, help influence and shape this intent. For example, the teacher's purpose may be to elicit students' responses in the form of feelings and attitudes toward a main character. This decision, in turn, may result in the rise of a predominantly aesthetic instructional stance.

The *planning and organizing* to support this aesthetic stance draws on the teacher's knowledge of literature and content areas and of the reader's meaning-construction process. This may be reflected in the teacher's selection of a story or novel appropriate to the reader's interest and achievement level. The teacher's expectations will, of course, influence decisions relevant to planning and organizing (Ames, 1992).

Strategy constructing accounts for decisions made about teaching strategies designed to implement the selected instructional stance. For example, if stance toward a text is to be aesthetic and designed to focus reader responses on personal feelings and attitudes, question prompts will need to be more open-ended than would be the case with an efferent stance—for example, "How would you have felt and reacted had you been the first person to see the words *Some Pig* written in Charlotte's web in the barnyard that foggy morning?" In addition, the use of a reader response journal would provide opportunities for the students to record their responses and to share their ideas and reactions in small-group discussions. The teacher's personal and world knowledge may be drawn on in such discussions to provide intertextual personal experiences to illuminate understandings related to the text.

Instructional Representation. An instructional representation is created in the teacher's mind during instructional planning as the lesson's purpose, organization, and strategies are considered. As instruction is initiated with the students, the original representation begins to unfold and change with the ongoing instructional process. This representation is conceived of as an "instructional world" that reflects the meaning structure and record of the instructional interaction with the students (de Beaugrande, 1981; R.B. Ruddell & Speaker, 1985). As is the case with the reader's text representation, only a portion of the instructional representation is consciously active because of limited cognitive capacity for conscious processing. The teacher can reactivate information in instructional representation in order to build inferences and make connections to previous inferences from the instructional interactions.

Teacher Executive and Monitor. The teacher executive and monitor provides for managing and overseeing the instructional decision-making process and meaning construction. As noted in Figure 3, it is in a central position and linked to instructional representation, instructional decision making, and prior knowledge and beliefs.

The executive and monitor controls *attention allocation* during instruction, *review* of interactions and content discussed, and guidance for *reconstructing* of inferences and conclusions. In effect, the executive and monitor evaluates the ongoing instructional process reflected in instructional representation. This teacher-monitoring process draws on metacognitive strategies to evaluate the relationship between the original instructional purpose, plan, strategy use, and the meaning construction reflected in instructional representation. Assuming the classroom interaction and meaning-negotiation process are successful and aligned with the original purpose and plan, instruction proceeds; if they are not, a shift in plan and strategy may be necessary to achieve the original purpose more effectively.

Outcomes of Instructional Decision Making

Based on the instructional plan, the teacher often has expectations that students will acquire knowledge or have experiences of a particular kind (Ames, 1992). The nature of the meaning-negotiation process, shaped by the teacher, will also strongly influence instructional outcomes, as we shall see later in our discussion. The teacher will often obtain two kinds of outcomes arising from instruction. The first includes the teacher's perceptions of the readers' understandings, and the second consists of the teacher's own understandings and insights.

During instruction, the teacher gains an understanding of the *semantic and lexical knowledge* that readers acquire. The teacher learns of the readers' new word knowledge through direct instruction, meaning negotiation in large- and small-group discussions, student self-directed use of classroom resources, or text-based contextual inference. The teacher recognizes that this knowledge may be of short-term duration exemplified by key concepts introduced to understand a specific story, or of long-term duration, as is the case when a new concept is connected to a schema in the reader's prior knowledge. The teacher's semantic and lexical knowledge may also be refined and extended.

The reader's *interpretation of text* depends heavily on the instructional stance and strategies used by the teacher. Certainly, the teacher recognizes that the reader's prior beliefs and knowledge exert a strong influence on the text interpretation that is constructed (see Hull & Rose, #11 this volume). The teacher's interpretation of text may also shift as a result of interaction in the classroom community.

During classroom *discussion* the reader's personal response and understandings of the text are expressed. The discussion may also alter the teacher's response to the text based on insights derived from the reader's and the classroom community's perspective.

Written responses to text provide the teacher with an understanding of the reader's text representation and interpretation. Responses range from straightforward summaries and syntheses to response journal writing that reveals the reader's underlying beliefs and emotions evoked by the text. Again, the teacher's understanding of the text may be enhanced through reflection on the reader's written responses.

The reader's *knowledge acquisition* is evident to the teacher through the reader's use of new concepts and fresh insights as new knowledge is connected to previously established schemata. This acquisition will be heavily influenced by engagement of the reader's interests and motivation through active comprehension. The teacher's acquisition of new knowledge will be influenced in a similar manner.

While the teacher expects to observe *motivational changes* in the reader, these expectations may not always be realized. The teacher's knowledge of the reader's key interests and internal motivations, such as intellectual curiosity or self-understanding, makes possible the connection of the reader with high-interest text. In addition, the teacher may derive new insights into motivation to engage students based on reader response during instruction.

The teacher may recognize the reader's *attitude, value, and belief change* through the reader's discourse involving text interpretations, discussions, and written responses. These activities enable the reader to examine closely held attitudes, values, and beliefs. In addition, the teacher may experience attitude, value, and belief change related to the text content based on the social interaction with students. The teacher's attitude toward readers may also change as a result of reader responses in the instructional setting.

A key instructional outcome for the teacher is found in *insight into reader affect and cognition*. Direct classroom observation of the reader as he or she constructs meaning provides "a window on the mind" that can lead to important insights. These may range from understanding of personal motivations and interests to conceptual knowledge and text-processing strategies.

Closely connected to these reader insights is the outcome of *reflective insight into instruction*. As the teacher gains understanding of the reader in the context of instruction, reflective insight can provide opportunities for refining instruction. This may include use of specific reader motivation and interests, employment of a variety of active comprehension strategies, or incorporation of an instructional stance that recognizes the importance of active reader response.

Text and Classroom Context

Our model takes a constructivist perspective of learning in which the teacher creates a learning environment that engages the reader in active comprehension through confronting and solving authentic problems in a social context. In the text and classroom context, shown in Figure 4, this environment includes a meaning-negotiation process that accounts for text, task, source of authority, and sociocultural meanings.

The Learning Environment

The learning environment has a powerful influence on students' motivation to engage in learning (see Langer, #38 this volume; Marshall, 1992). How teachers structure text-related tasks, who carries the power of authority, and concern for sociocultural meanings can make major differences in the goals that readers

FIGURE 4
The Text and Classroom Context

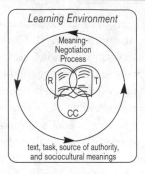

R = Reader
T = Teacher
CC = Classroom Community

attempt to achieve and the way readers feel about themselves, their classmates, and their accomplishments (see Alvermann et al., #32 this volume).

The learning environment influences not only the reader's decision to engage with a text but also the ways in which the text is engaged. We can expect the reader's engagement with reading, interaction with teacher and peers, and participation in the meaning-negotiation process if the reader is motivated to read and to learn, if prior beliefs and knowledge are activated, if tasks are personally relevant, and if active meaning construction is involved. The teacher who incorporates these features in the learning environment is considered to be mastery goal oriented (not to be confused with mastery learning) and is much more likely to produce productive learning in students (Ames, 1992; Covington, 1992; Maehr, 1984; Pintrich & De Groot, 1990).

Furthermore, the reader's motivation to achieve is enhanced if social goals and a constructivist view of learning have been integrated into the learning environment (Blumenfeld, 1992). These social goals include the influence of teachers and parents on children and the impact of cultural expectations on learning.

In their search for optimum conditions that contribute to learning in the literacy-sensitive classroom, Cambourne and his colleagues (H. Brown & Cambourne, 1987; Cambourne & Turbill, 1987) identify several key factors. Among these are useful feedback to students, meaningful demonstrations of language in action to engage students, and the development of learner responsibility for independence and self-direction. These conditions also parallel those described in a mastery orientation toward learning and an optimum learning environment.

The Meaning-Negotiation Process. As shown in Figure 4, the meaning-negotiation process involves interaction between text (shown in the shaded background representing a printed text), the reader (R), the teacher (T), and the classroom community (CC). During negotiation for meanings related to texts, readers bring their own meanings to the interaction, teachers bring their understanding of the story as well as their understanding of the reading process, and members of the class interact with the text to shape—and reshape—meanings. This process recognizes that students and the teacher read much more than the written text. In effect students and teacher read several "texts"—if we take "texts" to mean events, situations, behavioral scripts, and other symbolic processes that require interpretation (Bloome & Bailey, 1992). Of course, students and teacher read the text on the page, but students in particular also need to "read" the task, the authority structure, the teacher (including the teacher's intentions and expectations), and the sociocultural setting; in addition, they must "read" the social dynamics of the group, which include the group's rules, such as turn-taking and question–answer response patterns (Mehan, 1980).

While some critics and theorists have taken the position that the meaning of a text is located in the text itself and that the text is an object that can be objectively described, others (Bleich, 1980; Culler, 1980; Fish, 1980; Iser, 1980; Rosenblatt, 1978, 1994, see #48 this volume) have argued that the meaning of a text is a more subjective construct. This construct is to be found in the reader's mind, perhaps to be authorized by the interpretive community but certainly not by an objective text. We hold, in the model, that meaning results from the reader's meaning-construction process. That meaning is not entirely in either the text or the reader but is created as a result of the interactions among reader, text, teacher, and classroom community.

But, given the multitude of interpretations that readers construct for a particular text, which one is to be accepted as correct or valid? The work of both students and teachers is to confirm that interpretations are grounded in the actual text and in the readers' response to textual features. This does not mean that the ultimate meaning is only in the text but that interpretations should be reasonably supportable with reference to events, statements, or claims that occur there and in relation to concepts or impressions evoked in the reader's mind. As Rosenblatt has observed,

> Fundamentally, the process of understanding the work implies a recreation of it, an attempt to grasp completely the structured sensations and concepts through which the author seeks to convey the quality of his sense of life. Each must make a new synthesis of these elements with his own nature, but it is essential that he evoke these components of experience to which the text actually refers. (1938/1976, p. 113)

The authority of a classroom community has also been taken as a standard for validity (Fish, 1980). In this case, the meaning that is constructed as students and teacher interact in the classroom is the only meaning that counts. Intersubjective negotiation without adherence to textual content becomes paramount in such classrooms. While this view certainly frees readers from adherence to an objective standard—namely, the text—it creates other problems. First, how is one's membership in an interpretive community to be confirmed? And second, how does an independent evaluator identify which text has been interpreted? These problems are of such a magnitude that, in spite of efforts to solve them, we find Rosenblatt's constraint upon interpretations through the principle of "warranted assertability" most tenable for our model—that is, interpretation should be grounded in experiences "to which the text actually refers."

Nevertheless, classroom community negotiation of meaning is imperative, even if that negotiated meaning does not always reside as the ultimate authority for validation. The readers and the teacher share meanings in the classroom community so that, through dialogue, a community of readers comes to hold a possible range of meanings. In Figure 4, the three overlapping circles symbolize the interactive nature of the meaning-negotiation process for teacher (T), reader (R), and classroom community (CC). However, that process overlaps the real text upon which the dialogue is based. Thus, the text itself is not the sole object carrying meaning; instead, meanings arise from transactions with the text.

It is also important to note that in Figure 4, the circle with arrowheads that surrounds the meaning-negotiation process symbolizes that texts and their interpretations exist in a hermeneutic circle. Thus, meaning construction and negotiation are viewed as fundamentally circular. While the meanings we create for whole texts influence the construction of parts, our understanding of parts influences understandings of wholes (Dilthey, 1900/1976). Furthermore, as readers and teacher voice their views about the meaning of the text, a circle of hypothesizing and validation proceeds. In reading and discussing literature, students should discover that interpretations need not be seen as ultimate or final but as constantly reinvented as discourse, dialogue, disagreement, and debate continue. In the words of Ricoeur, "It is always possible to argue for or against an interpretation, to confront interpretations, to arbitrate between them, and to seek for an agreement, even if this agreement remains beyond our reach" (1979, p. 91).

Thus, meanings are negotiated in classrooms among readers and between readers and teacher. Meanings are open, not closed or fixed, though they need to be grounded in text. Classrooms form interpretive communities that may share common understandings; however, those understandings are not then fixed forever. Meanings are shaped and reshaped in the hermeneutic circle. As the reader's knowledge changes, as the reader interacts with other readers and with the teacher in a social context, constructed meanings can be expected to change. In a sense, while a text may be fixed, its meanings for the reader are always becoming.

In the model's learning environment, the meaning-negotiation process involves interplay across text, task, source of authority, and sociocultural meanings. We will briefly examine the role each of these plays in meaning construction.

Text meanings arise from the reader's meaning-construction process described earlier. Because the teacher and student bring different affective and cognitive conditions to the construction of a text representation, we must expect different interpretations for a text. For this reason, the classroom necessarily becomes a forum for the articulation and negotiation of meanings. These meanings are negotiated and negotiable in the hermeneutic circle. Those meanings shared by the entire class become part of the classroom community's intersubjective understanding of a text. However, even those shared meanings are also open for reinterpretation as the meaning-negotiation process continues in the context of classroom interaction.

Task meanings, the interpretations assigned to tasks, have both an academic and social content (Erickson, 1982b; Harris, 1989). Academic meanings include understanding the goals for an activity, knowledge of subject matter, text structure, instructions, and knowing what will count as a completed task. Social meanings consist of understanding the relationship between teacher and reader and understanding what rules will guide participation.

The interpretation of tasks, those structured activities designed or selected by the teacher and related to the text, may differ between teacher and reader. Interpretation differences are closely connected to children's success in the classroom (Dyson, 1984; Harris, 1989; Murphy, 1988). The negotiation and interpretation of task meanings are important aspects of instruction.

Flower (1987) found that college students frequently interpret an assignment quite differently from one another and from the teacher. She discovered that the process was more problematic and perplexing for students than teachers thought. What teachers, as established members of a discourse community, may not realize is that forms of response that may be instructionally transparent to them—such as asking students to analyze their responses to a story—may be very difficult for students to construe. If a task is complex and less well known to the reader, it may require elaborate interpretation to provide structure and meaning. For example, some tasks, such as writing a summary after reading, are represented automatically if the reader has a well-structured summary schema in cognitive conditions. If the reader lacks such a schema, the task may require elaborate interpretation to give it structure. It is thus important that the reader and the teacher construct and negotiate task meanings and also monitor those meanings.

Source of authority meanings refers to a negotiated understanding of where and in whom authority for constructed meanings resides. These sources of authority may reside in the text, the teacher, the reader, the classroom community, or in the interaction between various sources in the meaning-construction process.

Some teachers and readers, because of prior beliefs and knowledge, assume that meaning lies only in the text or only in an understanding of the author's intentions expressed in the text. Such an assumption may invalidate any text representation that does not correspond with the teacher's or the reader's perceived interpretation of the author. Readers, however, construct a text representation through the engagement of their prior knowledge and beliefs that may contribute to unique yet still valid readings.

Readers who think that the teacher is the only participant able to verify a meaning will tend to use the teacher as a bellwether for the "truth" of text interpretation. When this occurs, the students' interpretation is subject to the teacher's approval or stamp of certified correctness. In such environments, meaning negotiation will be very limited.

At the other extreme are readers who assume that their personal meaning is the only meaning that counts in the classroom. With such readers and readings, what the teacher or other readers think is viewed as irrelevant. With such a radical assumption of reader infallibility, meaning negotiation is not likely to be productive.

For some theorists (Fish, 1980), the classroom community, as we discussed earlier, holds the authority for validation of interpretations. Shared meanings for a text find their grounding in the intersubjective negotiation that occurs during discussion and the shaping of meaning. Much negotiation over meaning is likely in classroom communities operating under this assumption, but grounding in texts may be quite limited.

The perspective taken on the source of meaning authority in our model is that meaning should emerge from negotiation based on the text, the teacher, the reader, and the classroom community. From the interaction of these four sources, which are embedded in the hermeneutic circle, meaning should emerge. The continuing conversation grounded in the text contributes to the meanings created. Meanings under such conditions are not fixed in the text, the teacher, the reader, or the classroom community but are subject to change through dialogue and discussion.

Sociocultural meanings are influenced by the school and community ethos as well as the unique conglomeration of attitudes and values that arise in classrooms. The student and the teacher not only bring their own sociocultural values from prior beliefs and knowledge into the classroom, they also interpret the social life and culture they find there. Furthermore, each student and teacher may "read" various aspects of that sociocultural setting differently. While some students may believe that the culture of their school is supportive of their growth and development, other students—even ones in the same class—may be convinced that the school's culture is suffocating them and their identities. Teachers, like their students, may also have a range of sociocultural interpretations. In addition, some understandings of the social and cultural life of a school or classroom may be shared by most, if not all, participants.

In summary, the meaning-negotiation process involves a matrix of meanings that influences meaning construction. Meanings for the text, the task, the source of authority, and sociocultural setting are brought to the negotiation process by both reader and teacher. Furthermore, the classroom community negotiates and acquires group meanings that become influential in confirming validity upon interpretations. The teacher, meanwhile, assumes a critical role in the orchestration and negotiation of meaning in the text and classroom context.

We will now examine the meaning-negotiation process as we apply these model-based concepts to the reality of instruction in a high school English class where students come to read and understand a short story.

Meaning Negotiation in the Classroom Context: An Example

A class of 11th graders taught by Norman Unrau had read J.D. Salinger's *Catcher in the Rye* and was about to begin reading a short story entitled "The Laughing Man," also by Salinger. To gather data on the process, Unrau maintained a teaching log, detailed observational notes, and photocopies of students' log entries over several days of instruction. The learning environment was shaped in part by the instructional decision-making process used by Unrau. One of these decisions was his selection of the text, "The Laughing Man." The meaning-negotiation process for reader, teacher, and classroom community included not only text but also task, source of authority, and sociocultural meanings.

Tasks for the readers included a prediction strategy (similar to Stauffer's Directed Reading–Thinking Activity) designed to activate background knowledge and arouse expectations. As an initial task to activate knowledge and heighten motivation, readers were asked to predict the story's content based on its title. They were then asked to read the story with the intent of forming a text representation that would become part of the meaning-negotiation process. Subsequent tasks for the students called for writing first meanings in their response logs, sharing these in small groups, participating in whole-class discussions, and then writing about newly negotiated meanings in their logs.

The source of authority for the validity of text interpretations was distributed among class members—including Unrau. Authority was structured with the intent of placing a large portion of responsibility on students for sharing and shaping meanings while Unrau tried to nurture the expression of those meanings that students had constructed.

The sociocultural meaning for the setting could be described as that of a mainstream English class composed mostly of college-bound students—some English as a second language, some with learning disabilities, some from minority cultures—embedded in the broader culture of a suburban U.S. academic high school with high expectations for reading and writing. While the teacher and even the majority of the classroom community might view the sociocultural backdrop in this way, an individual reader might "read" it quite differently, perhaps as an externally imposed experience through which he or she must suffer until finally released after graduation, or as a useless exercise in a consumption-crazed, class-conscious, cliquish, and conforming culture. Whatever their understanding of the sociocultural setting, participants in the learning enterprise were affected directly or indirectly by it.

The following brief summary of "The Laughing Man" provides a story context essential for understanding the meaning-negotiation process used in the classroom:

> John Gedsudski, the central character, is a shy, rather short law student who goes to New York University and who chaperons and coaches the Comanches—a group of young, energetic boys, about 9 or 10 years of age. One of the Comanches, now perhaps 35, tells the story as he remembers John Gedsudski, whom the boys considered to be very nearly heroic.
>
> John, known to the boys as Chief, took the Comanches to various parks where they could play baseball. As they traveled to and from parks in an old bus, the boys were frequently entranced by the Chief's exciting stories about a mysterious character called the Laughing Man.
>
> The Laughing Man had been disfigured as a boy when Chinese bandits put his head in a vice because his missionary parents failed to pay a ransom. He grew up among the bandits but was so ugly he would only be tolerated if he wore a mask over his face. Though shunned by people, he befriended animals in the forest. He imitated the bandits' style, soon surpassed them in crime, and aroused their jealousy to such an extent that they longed to kill him.
>
> Before long, the Laughing Man accumulated a fortune. Although he gave most of it to a monastery, he was pursued by an internationally famous detective, Dufarge. He evaded Dufarge with his four friends: a wolf, a dwarf, a Mongolian giant, and a beautiful Eurasian girl. But he was never seen without his mask.
>
> These story installments continued each time the Chief drove the boys for their baseball outings. One day he stopped the bus on the way to a park to pick up a girl, Mary Hudson. She was, in the boy's eyes, a beauty, but when she asked to play baseball with them, she got a "this-isn't-a-girl's-thing" response. She insisted and eventually took centerfield. Her fielding was terrible, but she got a hit every time she was at bat. For over a month, she joined the team a couple of days each week.
>
> One day on the bus as the Comanches waited for Mary to arrive, the Chief told another episode about the Laughing Man. In this episode, through Dufarge's cheap trickery, Laughing Man was captured. He removed his mask, stunning his captors. But Dufarge, who had a coughing fit at the moment of the unveiling, didn't look at the horrific face. Covering his eyes, he emptied his gun at the sound of the Laughing Man's heavy breathing. There the episode ended, but Mary Hudson still hadn't arrived.
>
> Without Mary, the Chief drove the bus to the park. During the middle of the game, she arrived but refused to play ball. The narrator of the story, who was 9 at

this time, explains that he was unaware of what was going on between the Chief and Mary but that he knew she wouldn't play again. She was crying on a distant bench. When the game was called because of darkness, John went over and held the sleeve of Mary's coat. She broke from him and began running away. He didn't follow.

Back on the bus, the Comanches heard what was to be the final episode of the Laughing Man. Four of Dufarge's bullets hit the Laughing Man. As Dufarge approached him, however, the Laughing Man spit out the bullets, a feat that burst Dufarge's heart. But the Laughing Man continued to bleed day after day. The animals in the forest soon summoned the Laughing Man's friend, the dwarf, who came with a fresh supply of eagle's blood, a vital food for the Laughing Man. But when the Laughing Man heard that Dufarge had killed the wolf, Black Wing, he crushed the vial of eagle's blood in his hand and, dying, he removed his mask.

As the story concluded, one of the Comanches was crying and the narrator's knees were shaking with emotion.

A conventional interpretation of "The Laughing Man" establishes a parallel between the events in the Chief's relationship with Mary Hudson and the story episodes that the Chief shares with the Comanches. Often, the Laughing Man is viewed as a persona for the Chief. As the Chief's relationship with Mary dies, so does the beloved masked bandit. The end of the Chief's affair with Mary is transformed through a creative process into the Laughing Man's demise. Although no one in the class predicted that "The Laughing Man" would be a love story or a story about the creative process, in several ways, under its mask, it is both.

To begin the meaning-negotiation process, Unrau asked his students, "Knowing what you know about Salinger's writing, what do you think a story entitled 'The Laughing Man' is going to be about?" Several students responded.

Eric: I think it'll be about a crazy person in a mental hospital. He thinks everything's hysterical.

Sally: Maybe it's about the death of a comedian or a clown.

Margaret: I'd expect it to be ironic. Maybe about someone who's depressed and unhappy with their life but puts on a facade by laughing all the time to make people happy.

These student predictions were creative, often seemed to reflect what students had learned about Salinger's characters, and showed that students' prior beliefs and knowledge shaped their thinking. Actually, Margaret was not too far off in her early prediction.

After reading the story, the students were asked to write in their response logs and discuss what the story meant to them, or if they were—in the words of some students—"totally clueless," to write a summary of it. The responses of Mira and Emily exemplify what happens in many classrooms as meanings are negotiated.

Mira, a student who said she "didn't really have an understanding when I first read the story," wrote the following summary in her log:

> The story is about a young boy who is reflecting back on his childhood when he was in a boys' group called the Comanches. He is telling us how the "Chief" was adored and loved by all. Even though he wasn't very handsome, the boys still thought of him as gorgeous, and he was their hero. He would take them to the park on weekends to play ball. Then, after the game on the way home, he would tell them an installment of the Laughing Man. The Laughing Man was a disfigured man who stole and murdered, but he did it for good. The boys all looked up to him. Once the Chief had a girlfriend whom the boys adored, but she left suddenly one day. That day the boys saw the fall of two of their favorite heroes, for that was the day the Chief also killed the Laughing Man.

The summaries that students like Mira wrote represented their understanding of "The Laughing Man" prior to interacting with other readers. However, other students wrote their initial interpretations, rather than summaries of the story, before discussion. Emily was one of those students. In her log she wrote as follows:

> There is a lesson in this short story. Don't judge a book by its cover. The Laughing Man is a made up creative character. He is hideously ugly so he keeps his face hidden. However, the Laughing Man has a beautiful inside. He means well and has a loving soul.... When a human saw Laughing Man's face, they were frightened. However, the animals didn't know Laughing Man was ugly. They didn't know the difference between it, so the animals loved Laughing Man. They reached further down than just skin to realize how wonderful Laughing Man was. J.D. Salinger I believe wants us to be mature enough not to judge people by their outside appearance.

Emily's interpretation is one of many different meanings that students initially attributed to the story.

After the students had read the story and written their initial interpretations or summaries of it in their logs, they gathered in groups of three to read and discuss one another's summaries and interpretations. Each team selected a recorder to write down ideas and a reporter to communicate those ideas to the entire class after the small-group discussions. The remaining group member was asked to be a prompter, to keep the group on task, to ask questions that would keep the conversation moving toward the goal of collecting ideas about the meaning of the story.

During the interactions among peers that occurred in small groups, meanings for the story were often significantly changed as a result of reading and then discussing what others had written. For example, Kirk, who initially wrote in his log, "I cannot figure out what the story means, and its significance, so I will summarize it," commented that Susan "brought all my thoughts and understanding together" in the peer discussion. In her journal, Susan had written,

> I think the story is about a broken heart. The story inside the story was parallel.... When the Chief and Mary broke up, the Laughing Man died over the death of his wolf. He died of a broken heart at the same time as the death of the love of Mary and the Chief.

Several students reported that reading such commentaries and discussing various interpretations made them think in new ways about the story's significance.

After reading and discussion in small groups, the reporters presented ideas to the whole class. As groups reported, Unrau encouraged the expression and elaboration of meanings, not only of each group within the classroom community but also of the individual meanings of readers within those groups. Concern was also given not only to meanings for the whole story but also meanings for specific objects in the story. For example, during the discussion several students expressed different interpretations of the vial of eagle's blood that the Laughing Man crushes before he dies:

Erica: We thought it represented his love for Mary Hudson.

Unrau: How would that work out?

Erica: When their relationship was going well, the Laughing Man survived by drinking the blood. But, when Mary and the Chief broke up, the Laughing Man crushed the vial, and he died along with his love for Mary.

Unrau: Sort of his life blood being crushed?

Erica: Yeah, something like that.

Unrau: What other explanations for the crushed vial came up in your small-group discussions?

Mark: I thought it stood for children in the Comanche Club.

Unrau: How does that work?

Mark: I don't know. Just seems that way.

Unrau: But we need to tie the meaning to something. Events in the story. Ideas you had when reading it. Something so it makes sense.

Mark: Seemed to me that the children of the Comanche tribe were keeping the Laughing Man alive.

Alison: I thought it was the baseball game.

Katie: Someone in our group said it stood for a false lifestyle.

Unrau: Does anyone want to explain how those meanings would make sense in the context of the story?

Katie:	I don't know about baseball, but I thought there was something false about how the Chief was living or about his relationship with Mary and that when the truth was out, the relationship died.
John:	I'm not absolutely sure what the vial is, but, if it has a deep meaning, I'm sure it isn't baseball or the kids because they are not really deep issues. I can see the false lifestyle, but there are inconsistencies in the story because the Chief doesn't have a false life but a different life than the kids see. The mask would be more appropriate.
Unrau:	So what do you think the vial represents?
John:	I'd have to agree with Erica. The vial would be Mary and the Chief's love.

Unrau explored these and other meanings with the students. He frequently asked them to explain how an interpretation could be grounded in the text and how it made sense in relation to the whole story. But he tried not to impose his own "reading" of the story on the students, favoring interaction among them and with the text. The whole-class discussion gave students an opportunity to create a classroom community meaning for the story or parts of it. One student wrote, "The discussion changed my view of the story completely. I never saw any link between the Coach's life and his bizarre stories. I didn't understand that the Laughing Man's death meant anything."

A few days after the small-group discussions, students were asked to write their current understanding of the story and describe how and why their interpretation changed, if it had. Most students reported that they had formed or reformed the meanings they had given to the story during or after the small-group and class discussions. Mira, whose initial response was shown earlier, arrived at a meaning that went significantly beyond that initial summary. She wrote as follows:

> I think that the story of the Laughing Man that the chief would tell the Comanches was in a sense the way he saw himself. The Laughing Man was an alter ego of John Gedsudski, the Chief. Both were not handsome and shunned by the society and peers. Both had a band of loyal followers who looked up to them. For the Chief, it was the kids; for the Laughing Man, it was a dwarf, a Mongolian, and a beautiful Eurasian girl. At around the time that the Laughing Man is held captive by Dufarge, the Chief is having problems with Mary Hudson. When the Laughing Man gets shot, it is at the same time the Chief and Mary break up. This just enforces my theory that the Chief and Laughing Man are one in the same. The Chief takes the installments from his own day to day life, but he enhances them and makes them more exciting.

Students like Mira contributed to what became a classroom community meaning for the relationship between the Chief and the Laughing Man—that is, the two paralleled each other in many ways. As for the vial of eagle's blood that could have saved the Laughing Man, Mira wrote that it "represents the Chief's love for Mary."

Emily, whose initial and rather stock response to the story was "You can't judge a book by its cover," later wrote that the story was "tragic." She thought that the Chief was so hurt and depressed by the break-up of his relationship with Mary that he "took it out on the players." She wrote as follows:

> That night, driving home on the bus, John began telling the story of the Laughing Man once again. In this final story, John killed the Laughing Man because Mary left him, and because his love was taken away from him, he did the same to the Comanches. They loved the Laughing Man so John took him away from them.

Although Emily interprets the meaning of Laughing Man's death quite differently from Mira, she wrote that the vial of eagle's blood, that might have saved Laughing Man, represented John's crushed love for Mary.

In summary, many readers—the initially "clueless" as well as those who offered early interpretations—began to share a community interpretation of the story. Almost everyone agreed that a close correspondence existed between the Chief's life and that of Laughing Man. Many came to think that the trouble the Chief was having in his relationship with Mary translated into the death of Laughing Man. Nevertheless, many readers still held divergent meanings about several aspects of the story.

Being in an environment that allowed alternative or unconventional readings was important to several students. As one student, Sarah, wrote,

> Too many teachers think that their understanding is the only correct one.... Now I understand that a story can mean so many things, and as long as you can back it with at least some good thought, it's right for yourself. Now I feel I can just put more of my thoughts out there even if other people don't agree. I basically think that's the way my interpretation of "The Laughing Man" has changed. I think I have a little more freedom to say what I think.

What is important about "The Laughing Man" example for our discussion is not only the divergent readings of the story by different readers but also the dialogue, the meaning-negotiation process, that occurred among students and teacher. The meaning-negotiation process enabled readers of the story to engage their prior beliefs and knowledge in the meaning-construction process to develop a text representation of "The Laughing Man." This representation was strongly influenced by the negotiation of text, task, source of authority, and sociocultural meanings.

While this example is from the high school level, the key model components can also be readily applied to the elementary school learning environment (R.B. Ruddell et al., 1990) as well as to that of the college classroom (Hull & Rose, #11 this volume).

Our model thus takes a constructivist perspective of learning. The teacher creates an instructional environment in which students are involved in active comprehension as they confront and solve authentic problems. This environment places an emphasis on meaningful dialogue, negotiated meaning, and understanding.

Implications for Practice and New Research Directions

The major focus of our discussion and our first goal in this chapter centered on an explanation of the reading process within the classroom context involving the reader, the text and classroom context, and the teacher. It is our belief that this explanation has enabled us to achieve our second goal, that of developing a productive model that can serve researchers and teachers in better understanding the nature of the meaning-construction process. Our third goal, that of utility, is achieved by providing the following implications for practice and new research directions based on the review of a wide body of discipline-based research.

Our explanation of reading as a meaning-construction process is a reality-based, classroom-centered model and accounts for interactions that involve the reader, the text and classroom context, and the teacher. Specific instructional implications that derive from the model include the following:

1. Activation of the reader's prior beliefs and knowledge relative to the text is of central importance to effective meaning construction.

2. Mobilization of reader attitudes, values, and beliefs related to the text content is critical to attention focus, persistence, and the comprehension process.

3. Creation of a purpose to guide meaning construction provides for higher interest in the reading comprehension process.

4. Recognition that meaning construction is a purposeful, interactive, and strategic process contributes significantly to the effective comprehension of narrative and expository texts.

5. Utilization of metacognitive strategies that assist in monitoring, rereading, and checking meaning construction is essential to the comprehension process.

6. Awareness of the most appropriate reader stance and teacher stance relative to the text and reading purpose develops higher levels of motivation and comprehension.

7. Understanding and using varied classroom community sociocultural values and beliefs by reader and teacher will provide greater opportunity for active meaning negotiation in the classroom.

8. Sharing authority in the meaning-negotiation process allows readers to seek verification or validity for their interpretation within the classroom community as a whole rather than depending upon the sole authority of the teacher.

9. Encouraging readers to accept the premise that meanings evolve for both teacher and reader facilitates active meaning construction in the classroom.

10. Engaging readers in understanding and reflecting upon divergent meanings will increase the richness of interpretation within the classroom community.

11. Designing instructional activities that foster comprehension, discussion, and inclusion builds readers' perceptions that they are part of a classroom community.

12. Helping readers understand that they construct meanings not only of printed text but also of tasks, sources of authority, and their sociocultural environment furthers the creation of a context for learning that actively involves the reader and classroom community.

Our earlier example of meaning negotiation in the classroom context using Salinger's short story illustrates the application of many of these implications in action.

While reflecting on the formulation of our model of reading as a meaning-construction process, a number of specific research implications have emerged. These implications are intended to contribute to a fuller understanding of the processes that involve the reader, the teacher, and meaning negotiation in the text and classroom context. We will briefly sample these research implications for each of the three major areas of the model.

Our discussion of the reader's prior knowledge and beliefs demonstrates that further research is needed to enable us to better understand the affective conditions that influence the reading process. We know, for example, that motivation to read changes as children progress through the grades, usually resulting in less independent pleasure reading in older children. But what motivational constellation or set of factors is the most potent or enduring motivator? For example, with respect to the issue of extrinsic and intrinsic motivation, how do young readers develop pleasure or find value in reading that results in a desire to read more and encounter progressively more complex works? We have discussed the importance of reader stance in shaping what readers attend to and comprehend, but how are different reader stances developed and to what degree can readers come to control the stances they take toward texts? Which stances are most productive for which purposes? Sociocultural background has been found to shape classroom discourse, but how do differences in sociocultural values and beliefs shape interpretations of texts? We also believe that imagery plays a significant role in reader response and see the need for further research exploring the role it plays in comprehension and meaning negotiation.

Several compelling issues are related to the reader's cognitive conditions and need further research. Schema theory offers a powerful explanatory force for cognitive processing. However, can schema theory be extended to help explain and understand affective conditions, such as motivation, attitude, and reader stance? Implications for research in cognitive conditions also arise from differing views of text processing. For example, to what degree can text-processing strategies improve comprehension of reading across content areas? There is also significant need for further research on metacognition, especially in meaning construction for early readers.

Research on processes that occur in the reader's knowledge use and control is also needed. For example, what effect on reading comprehension and discussion do self-selected purposes have in comparison to teacher-selected purposes? Do some purposes have a more powerful influence on reading comprehension than others? Do conscious and deliberate plans of action change reading outcomes? A number of intriguing issues need exploration to better understand the reader's executive and monitor. For instance, are all functions and resources engaged during knowledge construction under the direct control of an executive? Or do most functions and processes occur automatically? Or do these functions and processes appear to occur automatically to the reader's conscious mind while, in fact, they are controlled at levels beneath consciousness? There are neurological correlates for the psychological processes described in our model. We thus ask, what is the relationship between the psychological description of knowledge construction while reading and the underlying neurological processes?

Future research pertaining to the reader's outcomes of meaning construction needs to explore and explain the way in which reading can significantly change value or belief systems. In particular, what impact do certain literary works and their discussion have on moral values and moral development? Further study is needed to explore the impact of different kinds of writing, such as summary and analysis, on text comprehension and interpretation.

Implications for research arising from our representation of the teacher component are clearly present. In regard to the teacher's prior beliefs and knowledge, future research needs to further define the role of affective conditions in instruction. The most pressing work needs to address the influence of instructional stance on the teacher's instructional decision-making process. What kinds of stances do teachers encourage readers to adopt? And what kinds of stances do teachers take toward instructional programs and instructional design? In regard to cognitive conditions, the influence of teacher-created, expectation-driven schemata on the reader's comprehension needs to be explored. Do teachers' schemata lead to misinterpretations or "misreadings" of students, responses, and patterns of interaction in the classroom context?

The teacher's knowledge use and control constitute an important area also needing further exploration. For example, how do teachers make decisions about creating an instructional lesson or an entire program? How do novice and expert teachers differ in creating instructional plans, in selecting instructional strategies, and in making "in-flight" instructional decisions?

Several areas of research would augment our understanding of the teacher's use of outcomes of instructional decision making. What, for example, do novice and expert teachers gain from observing the outcomes of the knowledge-construction process in the reader? How can practicing teachers be encouraged to become more reflective? What kinds of teacher observation and feedback would encourage the development of reflective teaching for preservice and for practicing teachers?

Many research issues emerge from the text and classroom context in our model. The issue of meaning negotiation is central among these. For example, what reader attitude or stance toward meaning negotiation promotes highly successful engagement in the process? What kinds of texts and tasks support a reader's involvement or openness during meaning negotiation? Do different instructional stances and different sources of authority have a differential impact on the negotiation process? For example, do "authoritative teachers" have a different impact on meaning negotiation than those teachers oriented toward the classroom community as the locus of authority? How is the sociocultural meaning of readers, their concept of the classroom context, related to the meaning-negotiation process? Additional knowledge related to questions like these holds high potential for better understanding the role of meaning negotiation in the meaning-construction process.

In conclusion, our model of reading as a meaning-construction process draws on and integrates knowledge from a wide range of disciplines. Central to our discussion, however, is the role of the social context of the classroom and the influence of the teacher on the reader's meaning negotiation. Our understanding of this negotiation is of vital importance if we are to meet the challenge set forth by Huey (1908) early in the 20th century—that of understanding how the reader constructs meaning.

References

Adams, M.J. (1990). *Beginning to read: Thinking and learning about print*. Cambridge, MA: MIT Press.

Adams, M.J., & Collins, A. (1985). A schema-theoretic view of reading. In H. Singer & R.B. Ruddell (Eds.), *Theoretical models and processes of reading* (3rd ed., pp. 404–425). Newark, DE: International Reading Association.

Alba, J.W., & Hasher, L. (1983). Is memory schematic? *Psychological Bulletin, 93*, 203–231.

Ames, C. (1992). Classrooms: Goals, structures,

and student motivation. *Journal of Educational Psychology, 84*(3), 261–271.

Anderson, R.C. (1975). The notion of schemata and the educational enterprise: General discussion of the conference. In R.C. Anderson, J. Osborn, & R.J. Tierney (Eds.), *Schooling and the acquisition of knowledge* (pp. 415–431). Hillsdale, NJ: Erlbaum.

Anderson, R.C., & Freebody, P. (1981). Vocabulary knowledge. In J.T. Guthrie (Ed.), *Comprehension and teaching: Research reviews* (pp. 77–117). Newark, DE: International Reading Association.

Anderson, R.C., & Pearson, P.D. (1984). A schema-theoretic view of basic processes in reading comprehension. In P.D. Pearson, R. Barr, M.L. Kamil, & P. Mosenthal (Eds.), *Handbook of reading research* (pp. 255–291). New York: Longman.

Anderson, R.C., & Pichert, J.W. (1978). Recall of previously unrecallable information following a shift in perspective. *Journal of Verbal Learning and Verbal Behavior, 17,* 1–12.

Applebee, A. (1978). *The child's concept of story: Ages two to seventeen.* Chicago: University of Chicago Press.

Athey, I. (1985). Reading research in the affective domain. In H. Singer & R.B. Ruddell (Eds.), *Theoretical models and processes of reading* (3rd ed., pp. 527–557). Newark, DE: International Reading Association.

Au, K.H. (1990). Participation structures in reading lessons: Analysis of a culturally appropriate instructional event. *Anthropology and Education Quarterly, 11,* 91–115.

Au, K.H., & Mason, J.M. (1981). Social organizational factors in learning to read. *Reading Research Quarterly, 17,* 115–152.

Baker, L., & Brown, A.L. (1984). Metacognitive skills and reading. In P.D. Pearson, R. Barr, M.L. Kamil, & P. Mosenthal (Eds.), *Handbook of reading research* (pp. 353–394). New York: Longman.

Bartlett, B.J. (1978). *Top-level structure as an organizational strategy for recall of classroom text.* Unpublished doctoral dissertation, Arizona State University, Tempe.

Beach, R. (1992). Adopting multiple stances in conducting literacy research. In R. Beach, J. Green, M. Kamil, & T. Shanahan (Eds.), *Multidisciplinary perspectives on literacy research* (pp. 91–110). Urbana, IL: National Council of Teachers of English.

Beach, R., & Hynds, S. (1990). *Developing discourse practices in adolescence and adulthood.* Norwood, NJ: Ablex.

Beck, I., & McKeown, M. (1991). Conditions of vocabulary acquisition. In R. Barr, M.L. Kamil, P. Mosenthal, & P.D. Pearson (Eds.), *Handbook of reading research* (Vol. 2, pp. 787–814). White Plains, NY: Longman.

Bleich, D. (1980). Epistemological assumptions in the study of response. In J.P. Tompkins (Ed.), *Reader-response criticism: From formalism to post-structuralism* (pp. 134–163). Baltimore: Johns Hopkins University Press.

Bloome, D., & Bailey, F. (1992). Studying language and literacy through events, particularities, and intertextuality. In R. Beach, J. Green, M. Kamil, & T. Shanahan (Eds.), *Multidisciplinary perspectives on literacy research* (pp. 181–210). Urbana, IL: National Council of Teachers of English.

Blumenfeld, P.C. (1992). Classroom learning and motivation: Clarifying and expanding goal theory. *Journal of Educational Psychology, 84*(3), 272–281.

Borko, H., Shavelson, R.J., & Stern, P. (1981). Teachers' decisions in the planning of reading instruction. *Reading Research Quarterly, 3,* 449–466.

Bower, G.H. (1976). Experiments on story understanding and recall. *Quarterly Journal of Experimental Psychology, 28,* 511–534.

Britton, B.K., Meyer, B.J.F., Hodge, M.H., & Glynn, S.M. (1980). Effects of the organization of text on memory: Tests of the retrieval and response criterion hypotheses. *Journal of Experimental Psychology: Human Learning and Memory, 6,* 611–629.

Britton, B.K., Meyer, B.J.F, Simpson, R., Holdredge, T.S., & Curry, C. (1979). Effects of the organization of text on memory: Tests of two implications of a selective attention hypothesis. *Journal of Experimental Psychology: Human Learning and Memory, 5,* 496–506.

Brown, A. (1980). Metacognitive development and reading. In R. Spiro, B. Bruce, & W. Brewer (Eds.), *Theoretical issues in reading comprehension* (pp. 453–481). Hillsdale, NJ: Erlbaum.

Brown, A. (1982). Learning how to learn from reading. In J.A. Langer & M.T. Smith-Burke (Eds.), *Reader meets author/bridging the gap: A psycholinguistic and sociolinguistic perspective* (pp. 26–54). Newark, DE: International Reading Association.

Brown, H., & Cambourne, B. (1987). *Read and retell*. Portsmouth, NH: Heinemann.

Bruner, J. (1983). *Child's talk*. New York: Norton.

Bruner, J. (1986). *Actual minds, possible worlds*. Cambridge, MA: Harvard University Press.

Cambourne, B., & Turbill, J. (1987). *Coping with chaos*. Portsmouth, NH: Heinemann.

Canney, G., & Winograd, P. (1979). *Schemata for reading and reading comprehension performance* (Tech. Rep. No. 120). Champaign: University of Illinois, Center for the Study of Reading.

Carpenter, P.A., & Just, M.A. (1981). Cognitive processes in reading: Models based on readers' eye fixations. In A. Lesgold & C.A. Perfetti (Eds.), *Interactive processes in reading* (pp. 177–213). Hillsdale, NJ: Erlbaum.

Carrell, P.L., & Eisterhold, J.C. (1983). Schema theory and ESL reading pedagogy. *TESOL Quarterly*, *17*(4), 553–573.

Chomsky, C. (1969). *The acquisition of syntax in children from 5 to 10*. Cambridge, MA: MIT Press.

Chomsky, C. (1972). Stages in language development and reading exposure. *Harvard Educational Review*, *42*, 1–33.

Chomsky, N. (1959). A review of B.F. Skinner's *Verbal Behavior*. *Language*, *35*(1), 26–58.

Chomsky, N. (1965). *Aspects of the theory of syntax*. Cambridge, MA: MIT Press.

Cirilo, R.K., & Foss, D.J. (1980). Text structure and reading time for sentences. *Journal of Reading Behavior*, *19*, 96–109.

Clay, M.M. (1972). *Reading: The patterning of complex behavior*. Portsmouth, NH: Heinemann.

Clay, M.M. (1985). *The early detection of reading difficulties* (3rd ed.). Portsmouth, NH: Heinemann.

Confucius. (1885). Hsio Ki or record on the subject of education. In F.M. Muller (Ed.), *The sacred books of the East*. Oxford, UK: Clarendon Press.

Coulthard, R.M., & Sinclair, J.M. (1975). *Towards an analysis of English used by teachers and pupils*. London: Oxford University Press.

Cox, B.E. (1994). Young children's regulatory talk: Evidence of emerging metacognitive control over literary products and processes. In R.B. Ruddell, M.R. Ruddell, & H. Singer (Eds.), *Theoretical models and processes of reading* (4th ed., pp. 733–756). Newark, DE: International Reading Association.

Cox, B.E., & Sulzby, E. (1982). Evidence of planning in dialogue and monologue by five-year-old emergent readers. In J.A. Niles & L.A. Harris (Eds.), *New inquiries in reading research and instruction* (31st yearbook of the National Reading Conference, pp. 124–130). Rochester, NY: National Reading Conference.

Craik, F.I.M., & Tulving, E. (1975). Depth of processing and the retention of words in episodic memory. *Journal of Experimental Psychology: General*, *104*, 268–294.

Culler, J. (1980). Literary competence. In J.P. Tompkins (Ed.), *Reader-response criticism: From formalism to post-structuralism* (pp. 101–117). Baltimore: Johns Hopkins University Press.

Curtiss, S. (1977). *Genie: A psycholinguistic study of a modern-day "wild child."* New York: Academic.

Davidson, J.L. (1978). The group mapping activity for instruction in reading and thinking. *Journal of Reading*, *26*, 52–56.

de Beaugrande, R. (1980). *Text, discourse, and process*. Norwood, NJ: Ablex.

de Beaugrande, R. (1981). Design criteria for process models of reading. *Reading Research Quarterly*, *16*, 261–315.

DeStefano, J., Pepinsky, H., & Sanders, T. (1982). Discourse rules for literacy learning in classrooms. In L. Wilkinson (Ed.), *Communicating in the classroom* (pp. 101–130). New York: Academic.

Dilthey, W. (1976). The development of hermeneutics. In H. Rickman (Ed. & Trans.), *Selected writings*. Cambridge, UK: Cambridge University Press. (Original work published 1900)

Dore, J. (1979). Conversation and preschool language development. In P. Fletcher & M. Garman (Eds.), *Language acquisition* (pp. 337–361). Cambridge, UK: Cambridge University Press.

Duffy, G.G., & Ball, D.L. (1986). Instructional decision making and reading teacher effectiveness. In J.V. Hoffman (Ed.), *Effective teaching of reading: Research and practice* (pp. 163–180). Newark, DE: International Reading Association.

Dyson, A.H. (1984). Learning to write/learning to do school: Emergent writers' interpretations of school literacy tasks. *Research in the Teaching of English*, *18*, 233–265.

Ehri, L.C. (1987). Learning to read and spell words. *Journal of Reading Behavior*, *19*, 5–31.

Ehri, L.C. (1988). Movement into word reading and spelling: How spelling contributes to reading. In J.M. Mason (Ed.), *Reading and writing connections* (pp. 65–81). Boston: Allyn & Bacon.

Ehri, L.C. (1991). Development of the ability to read words. In R. Barr, M.L. Kamil, P. Mosenthal, & P.D. Pearson (Eds.), *Handbook of reading research* (Vol. 2, pp. 383–417). White Plains, NY: Longman.

Ehri, L.C. (1994). Development of the ability to read words: Update. In R.B. Ruddell, M.R. Ruddell, & H. Singer (Eds.), *Theoretical models and processes of reading* (4th ed., pp. 323–358). Newark, DE: International Reading Association.

Erickson, F. (1982a). Talking down: Some cultural sources of miscommunication in interracial interviews. In A. Wolfgang (Ed.), *Research in nonverbal communication*. New York: Academic.

Erickson, F. (1982b). Taught cognitive learning in its immediate learning development. *Education & Anthropology Quarterly, 13*, 148–180.

Ervin, S.M., & Miller, W.R. (1963). Language development. In H. Stevenson (Ed.), *Child psychology* (62nd yearbook of the National Society for the Study of Education, pp. 108–143). Chicago: University of Chicago Press.

Fish, S. (1980). *Is there a text in this class? The authority of interpretive communities*. Cambridge, MA: Harvard University Press.

Flower, L. (1987). *The role of task representation in reading to write* (Tech. Rep. No. 6). Berkeley, CA: Center for the Study of Writing.

Frith, U. (1985). Beneath the surface of developmental dyslexia. In K.E. Patterson, J.C. Marshall, & M. Coltheart (Eds.), *Surface dyslexia* (pp. 301–330). Hillsdale, NJ: Erlbaum.

Gallimore, R., Boggs, J.W., & Jorden, C. (1974). *Culture, behavior, and education: A study of Hawaiian-Americans*. Beverly Hills, CA: Sage.

Garner, R. (1987). *Metacognition and reading comprehension*. Norwood, NJ: Ablex.

Gibson, E.J., & Levin, H. (1985). *The psychology of reading*. Cambridge, MA: MIT Press.

Goetz, E.T., Palmer, D.J., & Haensly, P.A. (1983). Metacognitive awareness of text variables in good and poor readers. In J.A. Niles & L.A. Harris (Eds.), *Searches for meaning in reading, languages processing, and instruc-tion* (32nd yearbook of the National Reading Conference, pp. 129–134). Chicago: National Reading Conference.

Goetz, E.T., Schallert, D.L., Reynolds, R.E., & Radin, D.I. (1983). Reading in perspective: What real cops and pretend burglars look for in a story. *Journal of Educational Psychology, 75*, 500–510.

Goodman, K.S. (1973). Miscues: Windows on the reading process. In K.S. Goodman (Ed.), *Miscue analysis: Applications to reading instruction*. Urbana, IL: National Council of Teachers of English.

Goodman, Y.M., & Goodman, K.S. (1994). To err is human: Learning about language processes by analyzing miscues. In R.B. Ruddell, M.R. Ruddell, & H. Singer (Eds.), *Theoretical models and processes of reading* (4th ed., pp. 104–123). Newark, DE: International Reading Association.

Gordon, C.J. (1980). *The effects of instruction in metacomprehension and inferencing on children's comprehension abilities*. Unpublished doctoral dissertation, University of Minnesota, Minneapolis.

Green, J.L., & Harker, J.O. (1982). Reading to children: A communicative process. In J.A. Langer & M.T. Smith-Burke (Eds.), *Reader meets author/bridging the gap: A psycholinguistic and sociolinguistic perspective* (pp. 196–221). Newark, DE: International Reading Association.

Guthrie, J.T., & Wigfield, A. (1997). *Reading engagement: Motivating readers through integrated instruction*. Newark, DE: International Reading Association.

Guthrie, J.T., & Wigfield, A. (2000). Engagement and motivation in reading. In M.L. Kamil, P.B. Mosenthal, P.D. Pearson, & R. Barr (Eds.), *Handbook of reading research* (Vol. 3, pp. 403–422). Mahwah, NJ: Erlbaum.

Haggard, M.R. (1980). Vocabulary acquisition during elementary and post-elementary years: A preliminary report. *Reading Horizons, 21*, 61–69.

Haggard, M.R. (1982). The vocabulary self-collection strategy: An active approach to word learning. *Journal of Reading, 26*, 203–207.

Harris, P.J. (1989). *First grade children's constructs of teacher-assigned reading tasks in a whole language classroom*. Unpublished doctoral dissertation, University of California, Berkeley.

Harste, J.C., Burke, C.L., & Woodward, V.A. (1982). Children's language and world: Initial encounters with print. In J.A. Langer & M.T. Smith-Burke (Eds.), *Reader meets author/bridging the gap: A psycholinguistic and sociolinguistic perspective* (pp. 105–131). Newark, DE: International Reading Association.

Hartman, D. (1990). *8 readers reading: The intertextual links of able readers using multiple passages*. Unpublished doctoral dissertation, University of Illinois, Urbana-Champaign.

Hartman, D.K. (1991). The intertextual links of readers using multiple passages: A postmodern/semiotic/cognitive view of meaning making. In J. Zutell & S. McCormick (Eds.), *Learner factors/teacher factors: Issues in literacy research and instruction* (40th yearbook of the National Reading Conference). Chicago: National Reading Conference.

Heath, S.B. (1983). *Ways with words.* Cambridge, UK: Cambridge University Press.

Hiebert, E.H., Englert, C.S., & Brennan, S. (1983). Awareness of text structure on recognition and production of expository discourse. *Journal of Reading Behavior, 15,* 63–79.

Huey, E.B. (1968). *The psychology and pedagogy of reading.* Cambridge, MA: MIT Press. (Original work published 1908)

Hull, G., & Rose, M. (1990). "This wooden shack place": The logic of an unconventional reading. *College Composition and Communication, 41,* 287–298.

Hymes, D. (1974). *Foundations in sociolinguistics: An ethnographic approach.* Philadelphia: University of Pennsylvania Press.

Iser, W. (1980). The reading process: A phenomenological approach. In J.P. Tompkins (Ed.), *Reader-response criticism: From formalism to post-structuralism* (pp. 50–69). Baltimore: Johns Hopkins University Press.

Johnson, D.D., Toms-Bronowski, S., & Pittelman, S.D. (1981). *A review of trends in vocabulary research and the effects of prior knowledge on instructional strategies for vocabulary acquisition.* Madison: Wisconsin Center for Educational Research.

Juel, C. (1983). The development and use of mediated word identification. *Reading Research Quarterly, 18,* 306–327.

Just, M.A., & Carpenter, P.A. (1987). *The psychology of reading and language comprehension.* Boston: Allyn & Bacon.

Kintsch, W. (1986). Learning from text. *Cognition and Instruction, 3,* 87–108.

Kintsch, W. (1988). The role of knowledge in discourse comprehension: A construction-integration model. *Psychological Review, 95,* 163–182.

Kintsch, W., & van Dijk, T.A. (1978). Toward a model of text comprehension and production. *Psychological Review, 85,* 363–394.

Kucer, S.L. (1985). The making of meaning: Reading and writing as parallel processes. *Written Communication, 2*(3), 317–336.

Labov, W. (1972). *Language in the inner city.* Philadelphia: University of Pennsylvania Press.

Labov, W. (1982). Competing value systems in the inner-city schools. In P. Gilmore & A.A. Glatthorn (Eds.), *Children in and out of school.* Washington, DC: Center for Applied Linguistics.

Langer, J.A. (1981). From theory to practice: A prereading plan. *Journal of Reading, 25,* 2.

Langer, J.A. (1982). Facilitating text processing: The elaboration of prior knowledge. In J.A. Langer & M.T. Smith-Burke (Eds.), *Reader meets author/bridging the gap: A psycholinguistic and sociolinguistic perspective* (pp. 149–162). Newark, DE: International Reading Association.

Langer, J.A. (1990). The process of understanding: Reading for literary and informative purposes. *Research in the Teaching of English, 24*(3), 229–260.

Loban, W. (1976). *Language development: Kindergarten through grade twelve.* Urbana, IL: National Council of Teachers of English.

Lowery, L.F., & Grafft, W. (1968). Paperback books and reading attitudes. *The Reading Teacher, 21,* 618–623.

Maehr, M.L. (1984). Meaning and motivation: Toward a theory of personal investment. In R. Ames & C. Ames (Eds.), *Research on motivation in education* (Vol. 1, pp. 39–73). San Diego, CA: Academic.

Many, J.E. (1990). The effect of reader stance on students' personal understanding of literature. In J. Zutell & S. McCormick (Eds.), *Literacy theory and research: Analyses from multiple paradigms* (39th yearbook of the National Reading Conference, pp. 51–63). Chicago: National Reading Conference.

Manzo, A.V. (1969). The ReQuest procedure. *Journal of Reading, 13,* 123–126.

Manzo, A.V., & Manzo, U. (1990). *Content area reading: A heuristic approach.* Columbus, OH: Merrill.

Marshall, H. (1992). Associate editor's introduction to centennial articles on classroom learning and motivation. *Journal of Educational Psychology, 84*(3), 259–260.

Mason, J.M., Herman, P.A., & Au, K.H. (1991). Children's developing knowledge of words. In J. Flood, J.M. Jensen, D. Lapp, & J.R. Squire (Eds.), *Handbook of research on teaching the English language arts* (pp. 721–731). New York: Macmillan.

Mathewson, G.C. (1974). Relationship between ethnic group attitudes toward dialect and comprehension of dialect folktales. *Journal of Educational Research, 68*, 15–18.

Mathewson, G.C. (1976). The function of attitude in the reading process. In H. Singer & R.B. Ruddell (Eds.), *Theoretical models and processes of reading* (2nd ed., pp. 655–676). Newark, DE: International Reading Association.

Mathewson, G.C. (1994). Model of attitude influence upon reading and learning to read. In R.B. Ruddell, M.R. Ruddell, & H. Singer (Eds.), *Theoretical models and processes of reading* (4th ed., pp. 1131–1161). Newark, DE: International Reading Association.

McCarthy, D.A. (1954). Language development in children. In L. Carmichael (Ed.), *Manual of child psychology* (pp. 492–630). New York: Wiley.

McClelland, J.L., Rumelhart, D.E., & Hinton, G.E. (1986). The appeal of parallel distributed processing. In D.E. Rumelhart, J.L. McClelland, & PDP Research Group (Eds.), *Parallel distributed processing: Exploration in the microstructures of cognition, Volume 1: Foundations* (pp. 3–44). Cambridge, MA: MIT Press.

McClelland, J.L., Rumelhart, D.E., & PDP Research Group. (Eds.). (1986). *Parallel distributed processing: Exploration in the microstructures of cognition, Volume 2: Psychological and biological models*. Cambridge, MA: MIT Press.

McGee, L.M. (1982). Awareness of text structure: Effects on children's recall of expository text. *Reading Research Quarterly, 17*, 581–590.

McHoul, A. (1978). The organization of turns at formal talk in the classroom. *Language in Society, 7*, 183–213.

McNair, K., & Joyce, B. (1979). *Teachers' thoughts while teaching: The South Bay study, part II* (Research Series No. 58). East Lansing: Institute for Research on Teaching, Michigan State University.

Mehan, H. (1980). The competent student. *Anthropology and Education Quarterly, 12*, 3–28.

Menyuk, P. (1968). Children's learning and production of grammatical and non-grammatical phonological sequences. *Child Development, 39*, 849–859.

Messer, S. (1967). Implicit phonology in children. *Journal of Verbal Learning and Verbal Behavior, 6*, 609–613.

Meyer, B.J.F. (1984). Organizational aspects of text: Effects on reading comprehension and applications for the classroom. In J. Flood (Ed.), *Promoting reading comprehension* (pp. 113–138). Newark, DE: International Reading Association.

Meyer, B.J.F., Brandt, D.M., & Bluth, G.J. (1980). Use of top-level structure in text: Key for reading comprehension of ninth grade students. *Reading Research Quarterly, 16*, 72–103.

Meyer, B.J.F., & Freedle, R. (1979). *The effects of different discourse types on recall*. Princeton, NJ: Educational Testing Service.

Moffett, J. (1968). *A student-centered language arts curriculum, grades K–13: A handbook for teachers*. Boston: Houghton Mifflin.

Moll, L.C. (1992). Literacy research in community and classrooms: A sociocultural approach. In R. Beach, J. Green, M. Kamil, & T. Shanahan (Eds.), *Multidisciplinary perspectives on literacy research* (pp. 211–244). Urbana, IL: National Council of Teachers of English.

Morehead, D.M. (1971). Processing of phonological sequences by young children and adults. *Child Development, 42*, 279–289.

Mosenthal, P., & Na, T. (1980). Quality of text recall as a function of children's classroom competence. *Journal of Experimental Child Psychology, 30*, 1–21.

Mullis, I.V.S., Campbell, J.R., & Farstrup, A.E. (1993). *NAEP 1992: Reading report card for the nation and states*. Washington, DC: Office of Educational Research and Improvement, U.S. Department of Education.

Murphy, S. (1988). *Making sense of school: An ecological examination of students' definitions of reading tasks*. Unpublished dissertation, Virginia Polytechnic Institute & State University, Blacksburg.

Myers, M., & Paris, S.G. (1978). Children's meta-cognitive knowledge about reading. *Journal of Educational Psychology, 70,* 680–690.

Nezworski, T., Stein, N.L., & Trabasso, T. (1982). Story structure versus content in children's recall. *Journal of Verbal Learning and Verbal Behavior, 21,* 196–206.

Ogbu, J.U. (1990). Minority status and literacy in comparative perspective. *Daedalus, 119*(2), 141–168.

Paris, S.G., Lipson, M.Y., & Wixson, K.K. (1983). Becoming a strategic reader. *Contemporary Educational Psychology, 8,* 293–316.

Phillips, S. (1970). Acquisition of rules for appropriate speech use. In J.E. Alatis (Ed.), *Bilingualism and language contact: Anthropological, linguistic, psychological, and sociological aspects* (Monograph Series on Languages and Linguistics, No. 23). Washington, DC: Georgetown University Press.

Pichert, J.W., & Anderson, R.C. (1977). Taking different perspectives on a story. *Journal of Educational Psychology, 69,* 309–315.

Pintrich, P.R., & De Groot, E.V. (1990). Motivational and self-regulated learning components of classroom academic performance. *Journal of Educational Psychology, 82,* 31–63.

Raphael, T.E. (1982). Question-answer strategies for children. *The Reading Teacher, 36,* 186–190.

Reynolds, R.E., Standiford, S.N., & Anderson, R.C. (1979). Distribution of reading time when questions are asked about a restricted category of text information. *Journal of Educational Psychology, 71,* 183–190.

Ricoeur, P. (1979). The model of a text: Meaningful action considered as a text. In P. Rabinow & W. Sullivan (Eds.), *Interpretive social science: A reader* (pp. 73–101). Berkeley: University of California Press.

Rist, R.C. (1970). Student social class and teacher expectations. *Harvard Educational Review, 39,* 411–415.

Rosenblatt, L.M. (1938). *Literature as exploration.* New York: Appleton-Century. (Reprinted 1976, 1983)

Rosenblatt, L.M. (1978). *The reader, the text, the poem: The transactional theory of the literary work.* Carbondale: Southern Illinois University Press.

Rosenblatt, L.M. (1985). The transactional theory of the literary work: Implications for research. In C.R. Cooper (Ed.), *Researching response to literature and the teaching of literature* (pp. 33–53). Norwood, NJ: Ablex.

Rosenblatt, L.M. (1988). *Writing and reading: The transactional theory* (Tech. Rep. No. 13). Berkeley: University of California, Center for the Study of Writing.

Rosenblatt, L.M. (1994). The transactional theory of reading and writing. In R.B. Ruddell, M.R. Ruddell, & H. Singer (Eds.), *Theoretical models and processes of reading* (4th ed., pp.1057–1092). Newark, DE: International Reading Association.

Rothkopf, E.Z., & Billington, M.J. (1979). Goal guided learning from text: Inferring a descriptive processing model from inspection times and eye movements. *Journal of Educational Psychology, 71,* 310–327.

Rowe, D.W. (1989). Preschoolers' use of metacognitive knowledge and strategies in self-selected literacy events. In S. McCormick & J. Zutell (Eds.), *Cognitive and social perspectives for literacy research and instruction* (38th yearbook of the National Reading Conference, pp. 65–76). Chicago: National Reading Conference.

Ruddell, M.R. (1993). *Teaching content reading and writing.* Boston: Allyn & Bacon.

Ruddell, R.B. (1965). Effect of the similarity of oral and written language structure on reading comprehension. *Elementary English, 42,* 403–410.

Ruddell, R.B. (1974). *Reading-language instruction: Innovative practices.* Englewood Cliffs, NJ: Prentice Hall.

Ruddell, R.B. (1994). The development of children's comprehension and motivation during storybook discussion. In R.B. Ruddell, M.R. Ruddell, and H. Singer (Eds.), *Theoretical models and processes of reading* (4th ed., pp. 281–296). Newark, DE: International Reading Association.

Ruddell, R.B., & Boyle, O.F. (1989). A study of cognitive mapping as a means to improve summarization and comprehension of expository text. *Reading Research and Instruction, 29,* 12–22.

Ruddell, R.B., Draheim, M., & Barnes, J. (1990). A comparative study of the teaching effectiveness of influential and non-influential teachers and reading comprehension development. In J. Zutell & S. McCormick (Eds.), *Literacy theory and research: Analyses from multiple paradigms* (pp. 153–162). Chicago: National Reading Conference.

Ruddell, R.B., & Harris, P. (1989). A study of the relationship between influential teachers' prior knowledge and beliefs and teaching effectiveness: Developing higher order thinking in content areas. In S. McCormick & J. Zutell (Eds.), *Cognitive and social perspectives for literacy research and instruction* (pp. 461–472). Chicago: National Reading Conference.

Ruddell, R.B., & Kern, R.G. (1986). The development of belief systems and teaching effectiveness of influential teachers. In M.P. Douglas (Ed.), *Reading: The quest for meaning* (pp. 133–150). Claremont, CA: Claremont Graduate School Yearbook.

Ruddell, R.B., & Ruddell, M.R. (1994). Language acquisition and literacy processes. In R.B. Ruddell, M.R. Ruddell, and H. Singer (Eds.), *Theoretical models and processes of reading* (4th ed., pp. 83–103). Newark, DE: International Reading Association.

Ruddell, R.B., & Speaker, R.B. (1985). The interactive reading process: A model. In H. Singer & R.B. Ruddell (Eds.), *Theoretical models and processes of reading* (3rd ed., pp. 751–793). Newark, DE: International Reading Association.

Rumelhart, D.E. (1975). Notes on a schema for stories. In D.G. Bobrow & A.M. Collins (Eds.), *Representations and understanding*. New York: Academic.

Rumelhart, D.E. (1980). *An introduction to human information processing*. New York: Wiley.

Rumelhart, D.E. (1981). Schemata: The building blocks of cognition. In J.T. Guthrie (Ed.), *Comprehension and teaching: Research reviews* (pp. 3–26). Newark, DE: International Reading Association.

Rumelhart, D.E., & Ortony, A. (1977). The representation of knowledge in memory. In R.C. Anderson, R.J. Spiro, & W.E. Montague (Eds.), *Schooling and the acquisition of knowledge* (pp. 99–136). Hillsdale, NJ: Erlbaum.

Rymer, R. (1992a, April 13). A silent childhood—Part I. *New Yorker*, 41–81.

Rymer, R. (1992b, April 20). A silent childhood—Part II. *New Yorker*, 43–77.

Sacks, H., Schegloff, E., & Jefferson, G. (1974). A simplest systematic for the organization of turn-taking for conversation. *Language, 50*, 696–735.

Sadoski, M., Paivio, A., & Goetz, E.T. (1991). A critique of schema theory in reading and a dual coding alternative. *Reading Research Quarterly, 26*, 463–484.

Samuels, S.J. (1970). Effects of pictures on learning to read, comprehension, and attitudes. *Review of Educational Research, 40*, 397–407.

Samuels, S.J. (1985). Word recognition. In H. Singer & R.B. Ruddell (Eds.), *Theoretical models and processes of reading* (3rd ed., pp. 256–275). Newark, DE: International Reading Association.

Samuels, S.J. (1994). Toward a theory of automatic information processing in reading, revisited. In R.B. Ruddell, M.R. Ruddell, & H. Singer (Eds.), *Theoretical models and processes of reading* (4th ed., pp. 816–837). Newark, DE: International Reading Association.

Samuels, S.J., Biesbrock, E., & Terry, P.R. (1974). The effect of pictures on children's attitudes toward presented stories. *Journal of Educational Research, 67*, 243–246.

Samuels, S.J., & Naslund, J. (1994). Individual differences in reading: The case for lexical access. *Reading and Writing Quarterly, 10*, 285–296.

Santa Barbara Classroom Discourse Group. (1992). Constructing literacy in classrooms: Literate action as social accomplishment. In H. Marshall (Ed.), *Redefining learning: Roots of educational reform* (pp. 119–150). Norwood, NJ: Ablex.

Scollon, R. (1979). A real early stage. In E. Ochs & B.B. Schieffelin (Eds.), *Developmental pragmatics* (pp. 215–227). New York: Academic.

Seidenberg, M., & McClelland, J. (1989). A distributed, developmental model of word recognition and naming. *Psychological Review, 96*, 523–568.

Shnayer, S.W. (1969). Relationships between reading interests and reading comprehension. In J.A. Figurel (Ed.), *Reading and realism* (pp. 698–702). Newark, DE: International Reading Association.

Slavin, R.E. (1991). *Educational psychology* (3rd ed.). Englewood Cliffs, NJ: Prentice Hall.

Slobin, D.I. (1979). *Psycholinguistics*. Glenview, IL: Scott, Foresman.

Smith, F. (1984). Reading like a writer. In J.M. Jensen (Ed.), *Composing and comprehending* (pp. 47–56). Urbana, IL: National Council of Teachers of English.

Spiro, R.J. (1988). *Cognitive flexibility theory: Advanced knowledge acquisition in ill-structured domains* (Tech. Rep. No. 441). Champaign:

University of Illinois, Center for the Study of Reading.

Stanovich, K.E. (1991). Word recognition: Changing perspectives. In R. Barr, M.L. Kamil, P. Mosenthal, & P.D. Pearson (Eds.), *Handbook of reading research* (Vol. 2, pp. 418–452). White Plains, NY: Longman.

Stauffer, R.B. (1976). *Teaching reading as a thinking process*. New York: Harper.

Strickland, D.S., & Feeley, J.T. (1991). The learner develops: Development in the elementary school years. In J. Flood, J.M. Jensen, D. Lapp, & J.R. Squire (Eds.), *Handbook of research on teaching the English language arts* (pp. 286–302). New York: Macmillan.

Sulzby, E. (1985). Children's emergent reading of favorite storybooks: A developmental study. *Reading Research Quarterly*, *20*, 458–481.

Templin, M.C. (1957). *Certain language skills in children* (University of Minnesota Institute of Child Welfare Monographs). Minneapolis: University of Minnesota Press.

Thorndyke, P.W. (1977). Cognitive structures in comprehension and memory of narrative discourse. *Cognitive Psychology*, *9*, 77–110.

Tierney, R.J., & Shanahan, T. (1991). Research on the reading-writing relationship: Interactions, transactions, and outcomes. In R. Barr, M.L. Kamil, P. Mosenthal, & P.D. Pearson (Eds.), *Handbook of reading research* (Vol. 2, pp. 246–280). White Plains, NY: Longman.

Tulving, E. (1983). *Elements of episodic memory*. Oxford, UK: Oxford University Press.

Tulving, E. (1986). What kind of hypothesis is the distinction between episodic and semantic memory? *Journal of Experimental Psychology: Learning, Memory, and Cognition*, *12*, 307–311.

Unrau, N. (1989). *The TASK of reading and writing: A study of the effects of a procedural facilitator on the construction of arguments*. Unpublished doctoral dissertation,

University of California, Berkeley. (UMI No. 9028702)

Unrau, N. (1991). *The effects of explicit instruction on critical reading and argumentative writing: The TASK of reading and writing*. Paper presented at the annual meeting of the American Educational Research Association, Chicago, IL. (ERIC Document Reproduction Service No. ED336737)

Unrau, N. (1992). The TASK of reading (and writing) arguments: A guide to building critical literacy. *Journal of Reading, 35*, 436–442.

Unrau, N. (1993). A transitional phase: From corporate executive to school teacher. *English Education, 25*(2), 100–119.

Unrau, N. (1997). *Thoughtful teachers, thoughtful learners: A guide to helping adolescents think critically*. Scarborough, ON: Pippin.

van Dijk, T.A., & Kintsch, W. (1985). Cognitive psychology and discourse: Recalling and summarizing stories. In H. Singer & R.B. Ruddell (Eds.), *Theoretical models and processes of reading* (3rd ed., pp. 794–812). Newark, DE: International Reading Association.

Venezky, R.L., & Massaro, D.W. (1979). The role of orthographic regularity in word recognition. In L. Resnick & P. Weaver (Eds.), *Theory and practice of early reading* (pp. 85–107). Hillsdale, NJ: Erlbaum.

Vygotsky, L.S. (1986). *Thought and language*. Cambridge, MA: MIT Press. (Original work published 1962)

Wagner, R.K., & Sternberg, R.J. (1987). Executive control in reading comprehension. In B.K. Britton & S.M. Glynn (Eds.), *Executive control processes in reading* (pp. 1–22). Hillsdale, NJ: Erlbaum.

Whaley, J.F. (1982). Readers' expectations for story structures. *Reading Research Quarterly*, *1*, 90–114.

Whorf, B.L. (1956). Linguistics as an exact science. In J.B. Carroll (Ed.), *Language, thought, and reality* (pp. 220–232). Cambridge, MA: MIT Press.

Literacy's New Horizons: An Emerging Agenda for Tomorrow's Research and Practice

Introduction

A s the title suggests, we seek in this last section to catch a glimpse of tomorrow's literacy perspectives, practices, policies, and promises. At the beginning of this 21st century, many literacy researchers experience troubling tensions between paradigms and principles that should guide research and confirm what constitutes scientific research.

In the first article of this section, "Literacy Research in the Next Millennium: From Paradigms to Pragmatism and Practicality" (#52), Deborah Dillon, David O'Brien, and Elizabeth Heilman try to convince readers to move beyond consuming paradigm conflicts to pragmatism and the practical when methods of investigation into literacy topics must be chosen. The authors argue that literacy researchers often have been less effective than they could be. They reflect on their own research histories and wonder what would have become of their careers if they had adopted a less centrist research paradigm than that grounded in cognitive science and positivism, perhaps one based on anthropological theories and methods.

While narrow political agendas have captured public attention with an emphasis on standards, accountability, rigor, and the future of our children, the literacy research community has been divided by arguments about paradigms, research methods, and instructional practices. To regain our vision and commitment to social progress and justice, Dillon and her colleagues recommend pragmatism, a practical philosophy and methodology motivated by the need to solve pressing, pertinent problems rather than defend one's theory about knowledge and the knowable. The authors offer pragmatic approaches to free us from the quagmire of paradigm debates and to refocus our attention on how problems for inquiry are selected, on those with whom research is done, and on how research is conducted. Wider concepts of pragmatism than the one used here have been forged and promulgated (Menand, 2001), including the Jamesian notion that ideas and beliefs always serve interests (James, 1907/1995). However, the particular pragmatism these authors recommend we practice might well serve to pursue the sensible, sturdy objectives they seek, transcending the dilemma of intractable debate over principles.

As the influence and powers of policymakers expand, Dillon and her colleagues emphasize that literacy researchers are challenged to confront and transcend the risk of paradigmatic paralysis that could grip and stifle knowledge growth, transmission, and implementation in our field. Creative investigation in many literacy domains must be nurtured and findings must be shared with shapers of educational policy and institutions supporting literacy's growth.

To develop a fruitful literacy research program, we must shape a purposeful research agenda (see RAND Reading Study Group, #27). The second article in this section, "Strategies for Developing a Research Program on Reading Comprehension" (#53), authored by the RAND Reading Study Group (RRSG), responds to that call for purpose by targeting a critical domain of literacy: reading comprehension. After demonstrating that many questions surround our conception and understanding of comprehension, its growth, and its measurement, the authors encourage us to immediately undertake a comprehensive investigation of comprehension. The authors recommend that we prioritize domains of research on comprehension (such as assessment, instruction, or teacher development), build on our strengths, expand the perceived value of educational research, and select appropriate methods to carry out a dynamic research program.

In their consideration of methodologies appropriate to the task of finding answers for a broad spectrum of research questions about comprehension, the RRSG agreed that a wide range of methods was both necessary and essential. Useful methods that the group identified as those enabling rigorous inquiry included experimental and quasi-experimental designs, structural equation modeling, hierarchical linear modeling, meta-analysis in experimental research, discourse analysis, video analysis, classroom observational analysis, and verbal protocol analysis. The RRSG hopes that the program of research the group proposes could become a model for the selection and application of diverse methods.

To achieve the research goals envisioned by the RRSG, an infrastructure made vital through leadership, coordination, and sustained support will be essential. The RRSG sketched a blueprint; with it, we can build on what they envisioned. Even more important in the long run, their approach to problem identification and solution in the literacy field serves as a model for collaboration that we might emulate as we approach other literacy problems calling for inquiry.

Tomorrow will convey even more electronic information reflecting ourselves and our literacies than even today. As they move "Toward a Theory of New Literacies Emerging From the Internet and Other Information and Communication Technologies" (#54), Donald Leu, Charles Kinzer, Julie Coiro, and Dana Cammack show us what technological innovations we can expect to see and what impact electronic communication is likely to have on literacy and literacy practices. The authors' purpose is to describe a New Literacies Perspective that can provide a window on an electronic communications future. The authors explore emerging theoretical perspectives that enable us to understand our rapidly changing Information Age and provide a set of principles informing a New Literacies Perspective.

The authors recognize that literacy is protean. It never stays put. It is always transforming itself. While pointing out that literacy has always taken on new identities, they demonstrate that electronic information today and the skills to create and use it tomorrow will define an engaged life and learner in an age of communication. What is fast will get faster. In a competitive global economy, those without ever-emerging electronic literacy skills will fall further behind. The authors envision an ever-new horizon of instant global communication and power that requires new literacies and new educational methods to acquire them. New forms of critical literacy and new strategic knowledge, often socially constructed, will be essential for optimum learning.

Many educators nationwide feel the weight of assessment on a daily basis. Accountability has had a wide range of receptions across the United States. In some schools, assessment dominates the learning culture. In others, it is an organic, natural part of the year's academic cycle. While some are hounded by accountability, others herald it. In her article, "The Role of Assessment in a Learning Culture" (#55), Lorrie Shepard presents a historical framework for behaviorist or scientific measurement and a contrasting social-constructivist framework for assessment. She then elaborates on the ways assessment practices should change to be consistent with and support social-constructivist pedagogy. To accomplish that transformation of paradigms, students' thinking and problem solving should be assessed continuously across the disciplines, for example through analysis of student work, and the outcome of those assessments used to promote the process of learning in a learning culture. Shepard, too, calls for a program of research "embedded in the dilemmas of practice," an agenda that would contribute to policymakers and parents grasping the important differences between massive, externally imposed standardized testing programs and internal, locally designed assessments to help students self-regulate and improve their learning.

In the last of this section's horizon-defining pieces, Claude Goldenberg provides an important (pro)vision for children today and tomorrow. In "Literacy for All Children in the Increasingly Diverse Schools of the United States" (#56), he clarifies the challenges we and our schools face and then identifies programs and research that suggest how we can meet and succeed in those challenges. It is a vision of educational equality in the century ahead, a vision of literacy for low-income children that, through school readiness, school success, and parent involvement, will provide schools that work for all children.

The panorama of research and theory presented in this section, together with earlier sections focused on literacy processes and models, displays the richness of literacy studies past and the potential of those to come. This plethora of potential and harvest of opportunity awaits us as students of literacy. Whether a seasoned researcher or newly sprung practitioner, each of us can identify a goal on the horizon that can guide our inquiries, enrich our understanding, and contribute to the growth of knowledge about literacy and learning.

Questions for Reflection

1. What do Dillon and her colleagues mean when they talk about "the quagmire of paradigm debates"? Can you provide an example of a paradigm debate? How do you interpret their proposed "pragmatism solution"? Do you believe that solution is an effective approach to reading research? Why or why not? (#52—Dillon et al.)

2. What methodological approaches are recommended by the RAND Reading Study Group? What connection is there between *research question* and *methodology*? How does the RRSG believe its research goals can best be achieved? Do you agree with the group's proposal? Why or why not? (#53—RAND Reading Study Group)

3. Leu and his colleagues provide a set of principles to inform a New Literacies Perspective—principles designed to address an electronic communications future. Do you agree with their principles? Why or why not? What do they mean when they state that "literacy is protean"? What do you believe are the "new literacies and educational methods" that will enable students to engage in the ever-new horizon of instant global communication and power? (#54—Leu et al.)

4. Shepard's piece presents two contrasting views of accountability: the behaviorist or scientific measurement viewpoint and the social-constructivist framework. She presents an argument to support the latter based on the belief that student thinking and problem solving should be assessed continuously based on their work and those assessment outcomes should be used to guide instructional practice. Do you agree or disagree with her position? Why or why not? (#55—Shepard)

5. Goldenberg reviews important research and programs that offer promise in meeting the challenge to provide literacy for low-income children. His strong advocacy for educational equality based on schools that work for all children focuses our attention on the critical need to support "a social and political agenda aimed at providing adequate financial, material, and social supports known to influence children's academic and, more generally, development outcomes." Do you agree with his assessment of the challenges we face in America's diverse schools? Why or why not? How can such

a social and political agenda be created? Based on your reading of research and theory, what items would you want to see on this agenda? How can such an agenda be implemented? (#56– Goldenberg)

Accompanying CD Selections

CD 4.1 Athey, I. (1985). Developmental processes and reading processes: Invalid inferences from the former to the latter. In H. Singer & R.B. Ruddell (Eds.), *Theoretical models and processes of reading* (3rd ed., pp. 908–919). Newark, DE: International Reading Association.

CD 4.2 Beach, R. (1994). Adopting multiple stances in conducting literacy research. In R.B. Ruddell, M.R. Ruddell, & H. Singer (Eds.), *Theoretical models and processes of reading* (4th ed., pp. 1203–1219). Newark, DE: International Reading Association.

CD 4.3 Durrant, C., & Green, B. (2001). Literacy and the new technologies in school education: Meeting the L(IT)eracy challenge? In H. Fehring & P. Green (Eds.), *Critical literacy: A collection of articles from the Australian Literacy Educators' Association* (pp. 142–164). Newark, DE: International Reading Association.

CD 4.4 Farr, R. (1992). Putting it all together: Solving the reading assessment puzzle. *The Reading Teacher, 46,* 26–37.

CD 4.5 Harste, J.C. (1994). Literacy as curricular conversations about knowledge, inquiry, and morality. In R.B. Ruddell, M.R. Ruddell, & H. Singer (Eds.), *Theoretical models and processes of reading* (4th ed., pp. 1220–1242). Newark, DE: International Reading Association.

CD 4.6 Karchmer, R.A. (2001). The journey ahead: Thirteen teachers report how the Internet influences literacy and literacy instruction in their K–12 classrooms. *Reading Research Quarterly, 36,* 442–466.

CD 4.7 Reinking, D., & Watkins, J. (2000). A formative experiment investigating the use of multimedia book reviews to increase elementary students' independent reading. *Reading Research Quarterly, 35,* 384–419.

CD 4.8 Singer, H. (1985). Hypotheses on reading comprehension in search of classroom validation. In H. Singer & R.B. Ruddell (Eds.), *Theoretical models and processes of reading* (3rd ed., pp. 920–942). Newark, DE: International Reading Association.

Additional Recommended Reading

Reinking, D. (2002). Multimedia and engaged reading in a digital world. In L. Verhoeven & C.E. Snow (Eds.), *Literacy and motivation: Reading engagement in individuals and groups* (pp. 195–221). Mahwah, NJ: Erlbaum.

References

James, W. (1995). *Pragmatism*. New York: Dover. (Original work published 1907)

Menand, L. (2001). *The metaphysical club: A story of ideas in America*. New York: Farrar, Straus & Giroux.

52

Literacy Research in the Next Millennium: From Paradigms to Pragmatism and Practicality

Deborah R. Dillon, David G. O'Brien, and Elizabeth E. Heilman

I t is a daunting (some would say foolhardy) task to attempt to predict what will happen to literacy research in the next decade, let alone in the next millennium. Artist Mary Engelbreit stated in a recent interview (1998), "So the millennium is just around the corner—get over it; get on with it." Engelbreit noted that we might place too much stock in calendar benchmarks, particularly those that end in zero. Her message is well taken. Nonetheless, the approaching triple-zero date provides an opportunity to pause, reflect, and review what we have learned about the conduct of our inquiry and to consider future directions for literacy research. We had four goals in writing this article: (1) to examine broadly how inquiry paradigms have been defined, (2) to critique how paradigms are used in inquiry in literacy and to question their usefulness, (3) to consider pragmatism as a perspective that may be more useful in helping us decide what we study and how we engage in inquiry, and (4) to discuss the future of literacy inquiry.

In literacy research, as in the broader arena of educational research, there are three classes of scholars. The first group tries to anticipate the newest research topic, methodology, and paradigm. These individuals look intently ahead with little attention to historical grounding for a simple reason: In higher education, where most of the research is supported and conducted, researchers are rewarded for carving out new directions, generating articles and grant proposals, and positioning themselves as leaders in the field. To invent new genres, coin new terms, set directions for others to follow, and create new paradigms is to cement one's reputation as a scholar. In contrast, less glamour is associated with grounding one's work solidly on others' research or refining and improving upon existing ideas.

The second group of researchers achieves credibility and enjoys career-long success by introducing a single groundbreaking idea, mapping out a portion of

Reprinted from *Reading Research Quarterly*, *35*, 10–26. Copyright © 2000 by the International Reading Association.

some new territory, or working consistently on a set of problems within a given paradigm over time. In examining types of black intellectuals, Cornel West (1993) described these scholars as the "bourgeois model" who are "prone to adopt uncritically prevailing paradigms predominant in the bourgeois academy" (p. 76).

The third group of scholars is motivated by a position or an issue and is philosophically and ethically driven to find an answer. These researchers focus on collaboratively identifying a problem with participants in a community and working together over time to generate theories and explanations that can be used in local settings.

Researchers in all three groups have generated valuable literacy research findings. Nevertheless, endless debates challenge the credibility of various paradigms (e.g., quantitative versus qualitative, cognitive vs. socially constructed) in which research questions have been grounded and critique the appropriateness of questions posed for inquiry as well as the impact of inquiry on practice.

Paradigms and Inquiry

In this article we posit that the political affiliation with paradigms and the continued preoccupation with debates have resulted in literacy research that has made less difference than it could in practice. We offer pragmatism, and the discourse from which it is constructed, as a promising stance for moving us beyond paradigm affiliations and debates. We conjecture that the field of literacy, like the broader field of education, has not embraced pragmatism because it has been misunderstood and ill-defined. Researchers have characterized pragmatists as individuals who fail to take a firm stance one way or the other on a given issue. We will discuss this further in a later section of the article. An example from within literacy research and practice is the term *balanced or eclectic approach*, which has been associated with "a little of this and a little of that" (Graves, 1998, p. 16), or "two very distinct, parallel approaches coexisting in a single classroom in the name of 'playing it safe'" (Strickland, 1996, p. 32). However, as Graves (1998) stated, "The purpose of creating balanced programs is to provide students with the best possible experiences for becoming competent and eager readers [and quality instruction] goes beyond a simple concept of balance [to] balancing instruction across a number of dimensions" (p. 16).

Graves and Strickland, who take a pragmatic stance, both noted that there are dimensions that undergird balance but that there "is not one specific Balanced Approach" (Strickland, 1996, p. 32). Both imply, however, that the selection and articulation of the dimensions are important for progress to occur and that our guiding principle should be the end in view—students' learning.

In the next section we define paradigms and critique their usefulness in literacy inquiry. The following questions organize the discussion: What are paradigms? What do paradigms mean to inquiry in literacy? Has the multiplicity of paradigms we draw from helped or hindered our inquiry? What paradigms could make a difference in our inquiry and why? Following this discussion we present pragmatism as an alternative to paradigmatic perspectives.

Paradigms: A Plethora of Perspectives

The term *paradigm* is used in so many ways that it is meaningless to talk about it without selecting a definition prior to discussing its usefulness. For example, Patton (1990), a research methodologist, defined a paradigm as a "worldview, a general perspective, a way of breaking down the complexity of the real world" (p. 37). The term has been used to refer to a philosophical position, a research tradition or theoretical framework, and a methodology perspective.

Scholars across the disciplines have looked to philosophers of science for help in defining the term *paradigm*. Like other researchers who have struggled with the term during the last 20 years, we perused Kuhn's (1970) postpositivist position on inquiry in science and scientific revolutions, realizing that Kuhn also proliferated multiple meanings for the term in his classic work. Drawing from Kuhn's work, we defined a paradigm to be a conceptual system, clearly separate from other conceptual systems, with a self-sustaining, internal logic, constituted as a set of epistemological rules directed at solving problems matched to the logic and rules.

Kuhnian perspectives often focus on paradigm shifts. Shifts involve a process in which researchers, in the act of doing normal science (the day-to-day pursuit of problems within a chosen paradigm), are confronted with problems they cannot solve or assimilate, and thus adopt new paradigms following a period of crisis. Kuhn has characterized these shifts as developmental processes. A new paradigm, perhaps more technical or esoteric than the last, is viewed as a sign of scholarly maturity and development in a field. Yet, a certain amount of snobbery accompanies membership in the community aligned with a new paradigm. As new paradigms are accepted, old paradigms are rejected by the dominant research faction (e.g., Mosenthal, 1985).

Polkinghorne (1983) characterized Kuhn's notion of paradigm shifts as an "irrational, discontinuous jump, not an evolutionary or developmental change" (p. 113). Polkinghorne believes that research, when practiced day to day *within* a paradigm, can lead to progress, albeit progress constrained by the constitutive rules and questions permitted within the paradigm. Hence, progress in research not only is made by shifting to *better*, more comprehensive paradigms but also is made within the conduct of normal science (Kuhn, 1970). That is, cumulative progress means continuing to do research within existing paradigms by choosing problems that are solvable, that the community agrees are worth solving, and that the community encourages its members to undertake. However, members of a paradigm may insulate themselves culturally and politically from other paradigmatic communities (Mosenthal, 1985), satisfied to make progress within a paradigm and to buttress it against other paradigms.

In its broadest sense a paradigm refers to a fully realized worldview that suggests not only a research methodology but also a value system or axiology, and ontological and epistemological premises. For example, paradigms as diverse as empiricism, behaviorism, progressivism, existentialism, capitalism, Marxism, feminism, romanticism, and postmodernism can be considered to be philosophical worldviews. Philosophical worldviews offer fully realized theoretical systems for understanding the world. Traditions, however, are distinct from philosophical worldviews. Traditions are disciplines from which we glean theories that guide our research methodologies (often referred to as theoretical frameworks). These traditions often reflect a worldview as well as a methodology, though the dominant worldviews and methodologies are subject to change as the research tradition or discipline changes. For example, anthropology is a discipline within which social and cultural theoretical frameworks are used to guide research; social psychology traditions are linked with symbolic interactionism; from psychology comes cognitive psychology and constructivism; and from theology, philosophy, and literary criticism comes hermeneutics. Both traditions and theoretical worldviews guide methodologies and yet commonly are referred to as paradigms; they are important philosophical choices in research.

For instance, researchers who want to study the social organizations in classrooms and how these affect learning and teaching could draw upon the discipline of anthropology, the theoretical perspectives of cultural and social theories, and the methodology of ethnography. The methodology chosen would dictate the types of data collected and how these data are analyzed. The assumptions undergirding the selected theoretical perspectives would affect the interpretation of the analysis, which also would be heavily influenced by a researcher's philosophical worldviews. Research typically involves many layers of paradigms including a philosophical worldview, a tradition or discipline, and a methodology. Further, each of these paradigms typically makes or implies ontological, epistemological, and axiological claims. The nature of these claims and the meaning of these terms, drawn from several sources (Hitchcock & Hughes, 1989; Lincoln & Guba, 1985; Scheurich & Young, 1997), are elaborated as follows:

- *Ontology*: the nature of reality (what is understood to be real). Ontological assumptions get at what people believe and understand to be the case—the nature of the social world or the subject matter that forms the focus of our research. Ontological beliefs give rise to beliefs about epistemology.

- *Epistemology*: ways of knowing reality (what is true). Epistemological assumptions are those that people hold about the basis of knowledge, the form it takes, and the way in which knowledge may be communicated to others. Scheurich and Young (1997) related that these assumptions arise out of the social history of specific groups and that our typical epistemologies are often biased (e.g., racially). Epistemological assumptions have methodological implications.

- *Axiology*: basic beliefs that form the foundation of conceptual or theoretical systems; the idea that the truth of propositions generated from inquiry depends on shared values between the researcher and participants. These beliefs include what is good or the disputational contours of right and wrong or morality and values (e.g., the need for shared information about knowledge generated during a study and protection for the participants from knowledge generated about them being used against them).

- *Methodology*: ways of undertaking research including frames of reference (e.g., theoretical frameworks), models, concepts (e.g., conceptual frameworks), methods, and ideas that shape the selection of a particular set of data-collection techniques and analysis strategies.

A more narrow interpretation of a paradigm may focus on one or more of the dimensions above. For example, literacy researchers may work primarily from a methodological paradigm and may not feel that a philosophical worldview, complete with ethical or ontological concerns, is necessary. Other researchers, such as postmodern and poststructuralist inquirers, eschew the very authority of scientism that supports assumptions, preferring to work unbound by these perceived constraints. Alternatively, one could argue that any research suggests ontological, epistemological, and axiological concerns, even if researchers do not explicitly acknowledge these assumptions.

Critical, then, to understanding the nature of paradigms is knowing the assumptions, values, shared beliefs, and practices held by communities of inquirers. Literacy researchers seldom address these ontological, epistemological, or axiological assumptions explicitly (if at all) in their writings or their research practices, although methodologies are addressed. Yet many researchers embrace the paradigmatic assumptions as crucial to an internally cohesive, quality research project. Others argue that specific philosophical paradigmatic allegiance, grounded in the assumptions, is neither critical nor even necessary; in fact, opponents argue that philosophical debates over such esoteric matters keep us from the real work we should be doing (e.g., Patton, 1990). The latter group of individuals is more interested in finding new ways to solve problems or in recreating and subsequently shifting the field in the direction of new paradigms. When discussing methodological issues, Patton (1990) noted,

> [Paradigms are] deeply embedded in the socialization of adherents and practitioners: Paradigms tell them what is important, legitimate, and reasonable. Paradigms are also normative, telling the practitioner what to do without the

necessity of long existential or epistemological consideration. But it is this aspect of paradigms that constitutes both their strength and weakness—their strength in that it makes action possible, their weakness in that the very reason for action is hidden in the unquestioned assumptions of the paradigm. (p. 37)

Patton is concerned that "too much research, evaluation, and policy analysis is based on habit rather than situational responsiveness and attention to methodological appropriateness" (p. 38). He reminds us that paradigmatic blinders constrain methodological flexibility and creativity: Instead of being concerned about shifting from one paradigm to another, we may adhere rigidly to the tenets of a paradigm, perhaps because of philosophical arguments about adherence to assumptions underlying our worldview, rather than adjust the paradigm to meet the challenges of new issues and problems we encounter in research.

We have cited Patton throughout our discussion of paradigms because he is a self-proclaimed pragmatist. His stance is that researchers do not need to shift to a new paradigm when the existing one is not broad enough for researchers' needs; nor do they need to stay trapped within the philosophical constraints of a particular worldview. Instead, researchers work to "increase the options available to evaluators, not to replace one limited paradigm with another limited, but different paradigm" (Patton, 1990, p. 38). He differs from Polkinghorne (1983), who suggested that one should work within an existing paradigm and adjust research questions within it. Rather, Patton suggested that researchers work within a paradigm but bring in new frameworks, methods, and tools—whatever is needed—to better address the research questions at hand. In the next section we discuss the use and usefulness of paradigmatic reasoning to literacy inquiry.

Paradigms in Literacy Inquiry: Have They Been Useful?

Recent research in literacy has been influenced by broad shifts in approaches to both natural and social science research. Earlier educational research can be characterized by the use of classical empirical scientific paradigms, which were grounded in a nearly utopian belief in the possibilities of science. Scientific methods were understood to be capable of capturing truth about reality and phenomena that were not available through ordinary discourse and observation. Research was driven by epistemological concerns. A scientific epistemology was thought to reveal ontological certainty upon which actions should be based. For example, the scientific positivist study of literacy was thought to reveal unequivocal universal truths about learners and learning that would allow for the unequivocally scientific application of teaching.

Researchers in both natural and social sciences, however, have become increasingly aware of the role of context, subjectivity, interpretation, and social values in all aspects of what was earlier understood to be an objective research process. What is observed and the meaning that is made of inquiry both are understood to be deeply influenced by the theoretical assumptions of researchers. This recognition has underscored the value of research approaches that shed light on the complexity of learners, researchers, and research settings. This includes paradigms such as sociolinguistics, various qualitative approaches, and phenomenological and hermeneutical interpretations as well as the critical and postmodern. These paradigms are increasingly being pursued not only because of their intrinsic capacity to help clarify complexity, or, in the case of critical theory, to champion the perceptions of the oppressed and underserved, but also because of their popularity in some settings.

A historical glance shows clearly that the field of literacy is not one that has evolved through the adoption, adaptation, and rejection of successive paradigms generated from within. Rather, paradigms in literacy research have been borrowed from various fields that have richly informed research topics and methods, albeit with arguments both supporting and criticizing the multiplicity of paradigms.

A Variety of Paradigms Can Enrich Literacy Inquiry

The diversity of fields and their accompanying paradigms that have informed literacy research can be viewed as enriching our perspectives and methods of inquiry (Beach, 1994; Beach, Green, Kamil, & Shanahan, 1992; Harris, 1969; Pearson & Stephens, 1994; Ruddell, 1998). Pearson and Stephens noted that about 30 years ago scholarship in the field of reading consisted primarily of the study of perceptual processes. They stated that the field was transformed suddenly in the mid- to late-1960s not because of paradigm shifts from within the community of reading researchers but because scholars in other fields (e.g., linguistics, psycholinguistics, cognitive psychology, sociolinguistics) had become interested in reading. Each of these fields defined the reading process using descriptive and operational definitions, constitutive rules, and research methods that fit their individual paradigms. The field of reading (and indeed the broader field of literacy as we define it) is what Pearson and Stephens (1994) referred to as a transdisciplinary field that permits scholars to solve myriad problems using a variety of perspectives.

Pearson and Stephens's (1994) retrospect is validated by Harris (1969), who summarized the field of reading as he saw it at the time. In his chapter called "Reading" in the fourth edition of the *Encyclopedia of Educational Research*, he viewed reading research as a mirror image of research in the broader educational community, a field he characterized as being influenced by other disciplines. Harris traced reading research in this century from an early focus on perception (1910); to case studies (1920s); to evaluation and behaviorism (1930s); to reading comprehension defined by psychometrics and factor analysis (1940s); to experimental research with accompanying hypothesis testing and statistical tests (1950s, 1960s); to the most current work by scholars in other disciplines including psychology, linguistics, sociology, and medicine "who bring conceptual and experimental tools to bear on reading phenomena" (p. 1069). Harris took the perspective that researchers in the reading field should try to mirror the quality of the research being conducted in the multiplicity of fields informing the education field. He positioned the research methodology affecting reading research from outside the field proper as a standard to attain.

A Variety of Paradigms Can Hamper Literacy Inquiry

The notion of paradigm incommensurability (Donmoyer, 1996), if taken literally, means that fields such as literacy, informed by a range of disciplines, remain a set of subcommunities with incompatible assumptions and methodologies and little common language. The pragmatic stance, which we will discuss later, allows for compatibility. But we will explore the literal argument that the field has been hampered in its progress because of the multiplicity of voices emanating from incompatible paradigms (Clay, 1994; Mosenthal, 1985, 1999; Weintraub & Farr, 1976).

Mosenthal, who drew partly from Kuhn's (1970) work on paradigms, discussed the progress of educational research in general (1985) and reading research in particular (1987). He explored three different approaches to defining progress in research: (1) *literal approaches* in which researchers work diligently within a chosen paradigm to refine existing theories, find new features and examples compatible with the theory's higher-order features (normal science), or discover anomalies leading to the creation of recombinant theories more inclusive than that developed within the paradigm supported by normal science (extraordinary science); (2) *interpretive approaches* in which researchers abandon the preoccupation with the fit between empirical definitions and reality in favor of the belief that reality is constructed; and (3) *evaluative approaches* in which ideological implications of inquiry for society are central to the researcher's work. After careful discussion of these idealized ways of making progress, Mosenthal stressed that each group of researchers, or speech communities, embraces and advances members' respective beliefs and abides by the rules that support definitions, cementing members' solidarity with discursive practices that promote each definition as the normative one. Hence, progress, he contended, is defined not by a systematic testing and reconceptualizing of theoretical perspectives but by political dominance and power of one speech community over others (Mosenthal, 1999). This is a less-optimistic view of multiple paradigms and transdisciplinary research perspectives.

We can demonstrate further the negative side of positioning and repositioning of paradigms in literacy by drawing on multiple sources in which scholars synthesized research and discussed trends in the field. Almost 25 years ago, Weintraub and Farr (1976) noted that research in reading was being conducted using the classical empirical design because of what they referred to as "methodological incarceration." They contended that the model was used even though it was inappropriate for some of the research questions posed in the field. Weintraub and Farr also posited that reading researchers adhered to this paradigm to prove to allied professions, particularly psychology, that reading researchers could conduct quality research in that era of classical experimental studies. Although literacy research conducted within this paradigm has been valuable and moved the field forward, one could argue that the self-imposed methodological incarceration did limit methodological vision.

Paradigms That Could Have Made a Difference But Did Not

The field of literacy is one microcosm illustrating the systematic positioning and repositioning of paradigms and their inherent communities. For example, in the first three editions of *Theoretical Models and Processes of Reading* (Singer & Ruddell, 1970, 1976, 1985), each table of contents maps out the dominant research communities. Not surprisingly, the contents of these texts include mostly psychological studies of processes of reading wherein authors have attached operational definitions of various systems such as phonological systems, lexical systems, decoding, recoding, and visual perceptual span. The section on models in the second edition (1976) is divided into four types of models (types based on substantive theories in psychology), tested against theories using methodology grounded in positivist science. Editors Singer and Ruddell hoped that the volume would enhance further theorizing and research productivity, resulting in better reading instruction in the United States.

Embedded within the predominantly psychological perspectives in the 1976 volume is a piece written by Ray McDermott in a section called "Cultural Interaction." In his chapter, McDermott drew on anthropological theories and methods to look at the social reproduction of minority-community pariah status among poor children in school, and how this pariah/host (black children/white teacher) relationship plays out in the social organization of reading instruction. At the time most literacy researchers first acquired the second edition of *Theoretical Models*, they were interested in the dominant psychological paradigm. Few individuals seem to have noticed the unobtrusive McDermott piece, which fell clearly outside the dominant paradigm. In today's current context of interpretive research, significantly influenced by anthropological theories and methods, we can historically situate McDermott as a scholar who was ahead of his time.

In reviewing our own literacy research careers (Dillon & O'Brien), we wonder what would have happened if we had embraced McDermott's 1976 work instead of the dominant psychological paradigm. Might we have engaged in research at the beginning of our careers (in the early 1980s) that would be retroactively viewed as groundbreaking? However, like most of our colleagues, we overlooked McDermott because the dominant paradigm in the early 1980s was reading comprehension research, grounded in cognitive science using positivist and postpositivist methodologies. And even though we both studied qualitative research methodology and conducted such research starting in 1982, it was not readily embraced by our research community at conferences or by journal editors until years later. Hence, paradigms, although useful if considered in their broadest sense, have restricted the potential of research by limiting vision and polarizing competing research communities. Pragmatism, we contend, is a viable alternative.

Implications for the Future: Pragmatism and Practical Discourse

To meet the challenges that literacy researchers and practitioners will face in the new millennium, we look outside the field of literacy to a broader perspective in education—pragmatism (Dewey, 1916, 1919/1993b; Rorty, 1982, 1991). In the following section we define pragmatism and discuss why it is a useful alternative to paradigmatic reasoning.

What Is Pragmatism?

Pragmatism, a branch of philosophy, is 100 years old and is currently undergoing a revival (Dickstein, 1998) as a new way of approaching old problems in several diverse fields (e.g., law, social thought, literary theory). William James introduced pragmatism in his published lectures (1907/1991), but he built his arguments largely on the work of Charles S. Peirce. In its inception, pragmatism was considered highly controversial, but it interested many scholars because

> like modernism, it reflects the break-up of cultural and religious authority, the turn away from any simple or stable truth [truth is provisional, grounded in history and experience or context, not fixed in the nature of things], the shift from totalizing systems and unified narratives to a more fragmented plurality of perspectives. (Dickstein, 1998, pp. 4–5)

In 1917 pragmatism was sharply criticized, and the downfall of this perspective was initiated:

> Dewey's pragmatic justification for America's entry into World War I, which shocked many of his followers, [and] showed up his concern with technique and efficiency at the expense of consistent values...it was a narrowly expedient philosophy of "adaptation" and "adjustment" bereft of ultimate goals. (Dickstein, 1998, p. 8)

Critics were dismayed that a pragmatic approach could be used to support such repugnant ends. Conservatives and Marxists as well as cultural critics rejected pragmatism. After World War II the rejection of pragmatism became even more pronounced because of new influences in thought including existentialism, psychoanalysis, European modernism, and a cultural conservatism linked with a fear of communism (cf. Morton White's 1949 text *Social Thought in America: The Revolt Against Formalism*).

The label *pragmatism*, like other vague terms, has been avoided by leading educational philosophers and researchers because it is overused and misconstrued and a "terminological lightning rod" (Boisvert, 1998, p. 11). Even Dewey, who considered himself a pragmatist, left the term out of his texts, noting, "Perhaps the word lends itself to misconception...so much misunderstanding and relatively futile controversy have gathered about the word that it seemed advisable to avoid its use" (as cited in Boisvert, 1998, p. 11).

In this article we use pragmatism to support what Bernstein (1983) called "radical critiques of the intellectually imperialistic claims made in the name of method" (p. xi). In calling for pragmatism we are not advocating the approach of one or another theorist who is identifiable as a pragmatist; instead, we are advocating the spirit of the pragmatic tradition, which asserts that conducting inquiry to useful ends takes precedence over finding ways to defend one's epistemology. It is important to remember, as Dewey noted, that pragmatism does not mean "if it works then it's true" (Boisvert, 1998, p. 31), even though the term had been so cast. Paradigmatic critiques of research, when played out in the community, especially the popular media, show that researchers are often more concerned about their theoretical positions than about answering important questions. However, pragmatists are not simply persons who push philosophical arguments—particularly metaphysical ones—aside to get research done. Nor are they wishy-washy inquirers who do not know which epistemology to support or individuals who have neglected worldviews to which their work is linked. Rather, they have decided, after careful consideration of the effort and involvement, that the broader epistemological arguments, particularly those based in foundational epistemology, can never be solved because meaning is inseparable from human experience and needs and is contingent upon context. This perspective in some ways prefigures the postmodern worldview.

The value of inquiry using the "pragmatic method" (James, 1907/1991, p. 23) is in looking at the practical consequences of a notion (a method or perspective of inquiry) before deciding to employ it. James argued that when comparing alternative views of science, one must examine the differences these views would make in the world if each were true. If the world is unchanged across alternative views, then discussing them is insignificant. The pragmatic method is not a way to get certain results but, rather, an "attitude of orientation" that looks beyond principles (metaphysics) toward consequences and "facts" (p. 27). Within this stance, ideas, which are based in our experiences, are true only insofar as they help us relate to other facets of our experience and to achieve our goals. As Misak (1998) explained, "The pragmatist argues, were we to forever achieve all of our local aims in inquiry, were we to get a belief which would be as good as it could be, that would be a true belief" (p. 410). Paradigms, or theories developed within paradigms, each may contribute something useful, but ultimately the usefulness in summarizing or synthesizing existing ideas that lead to new ideas (rather than the theoretical purity) is what is important.

Similarly, Dewey (1938/1981) noted that the value of scientific research must be considered in terms of the projected consequences of activities—the end in view. Dewey identified genuine problems that were part of actual social situations as those researchers should address. These problems (from practice), stated Dewey, should be identified and carefully defined before inquiry is undertaken. In fact, this latter point—the need to convert a problematic situation into a set of conditions forming a definite problem—was recognized by Dewey as a weakness of much inquiry (i.e., researchers selected a set of methods without a clear understanding of the problem). After the problem or subject matter (the phenomenon under study) was identified and the dimensions clearly defined, Dewey recommended that the issue be investigated from various perspectives, depending on the purpose or objective of the inquiry. Finally, as Dewey stated, "the ultimate end and test of all inquiry is the transformation of a problematic situation (which involves confusion and conflict) into a unified one" (p. 401).

The usefulness of pragmatic inquiry, however, as conceived by Dewey, also should be considered in terms of its capacity to contribute to a democratic life, broadly defined. Dewey observed that democracy "has not been adequately realized in any time" (as cited in Boisvert, 1998, p. 299), and the goal of democracy is the "creation of a freer and...more humane experience in which all contribute" (Dewey, 1939/1993a, p. 245). Similarly, Rorty (1982) stated,

> Our identification with our community—our society, our political tradition, our intellectual heritage—is heightened when we see this community as ours rather than nature's, shaped rather than found, one among many which men have made. In the end, the pragmatists tell us what matters is our loyalty to other human beings, clinging together against the dark, not our hope of getting things right. (p. 166)

Because the problems that pragmatists address are to contribute to a more democratic way of life characterized by the creation of a freer and more humane experience, the identification of problems for inquiry is particularly important. Democracy is not simply a set of political institutions. For Dewey, democracy is most centrally a way of life, and also a way of inquiry. Dewey wrote, "Apart from the social medium, the individual would never 'know himself'; he would never become acquainted with his needs and capacities" (1908/1982, p. 388) and "Apart from the ties that bind him to others, he is nothing" (1932/1987a, p. 323). Dewey emphasized the inherently social nature of all problem posing, and he believed that people cannot understand themselves, or develop their practical reasoning, in isolation from others. This ontological assumption is consistent with Hegel and, more recently, Charles Taylor's (1994) argument that our very psychology is collectively, situationally constructed. According to this understanding, a crucial feature of human life is its fundamentally dialogical character. As Taylor explained,

> We become fully human agents, capable of understanding ourselves, and hence of defining our identity, through our acquisition of rich human languages of expression...we learn these modes of expression through exchanges with others... the genesis of the human mind is in this sense not monological, not something each person accomplishes on his or her own, but dialogical. (p. 32)

Therefore, problems need to be socially situated and identified to be legitimate foci of inquiry. Dewey believed that all inquiry is "natural, situational, grounded in problems, interrogations of theory and practice and evaluative." Further, "The integration of particular nonexpert experience, fostered by the establishment of interaction and discussion, enables the community to better use the insights" (Campbell, 1995, p. 199).

The inquiry process suggested by a pragmatic stance is quite different from traditional inquiry in which a researcher establishes a question or problem and proceeds without the integration of nonexpert opinion. In fact, for some researchers the integration of nonexpert opinion, which was key to Dewey, is understood as a sign of methodological weakness. The importance of dialogue and listening in inquiry requires new roles for researchers and also for the community of learners and practitioners, or what traditional research would call the subjects of research.

Another issue, which has been pointed out by critics of pragmatism, focuses on the practical challenge of using a method that requires the identification of problems. For example, Thompson (1997) noted, "The contextual, problem-centered character (of pragmatism) limits its ability to identify and analyze structural problems" (p. 426). For those living under hegemonic power structures, the deep structural problems of inequality may not be perceived as such, or for those who benefit from inequity, power structures would not necessarily be considered problematic. Bernstein (1991) described Rorty's pragmatism as failing to engage in radical democratic critique and becoming "an apologia for the status quo—the very type of liberalism that Dewey judged to be 'irrelevant and doomed'" (p. 233). Therefore, Thompson (1997) recommended political pragmatism, which recognizes "systemic conflict between social groups" and "understands experience under such conditions as itself political" (p. 428). We believe that a researcher's biggest challenge within this stance will be working with diverse groups of stakeholders to identify and define the dimensions of problems, resisting the temptation to become fixated on methods yet employing empirical, ethical tools and strategies that yield insightful albeit sometimes unsettling answers to real problems, and writing up the findings to illuminate both the processes and results of inquiry. The following section further explores the implications of these issues for literacy inquirers.

Using a Pragmatic Stance for Literacy Inquiry in the New Millennium

Scrutiny from within and outside the field of literacy has forced internal examination of our research and the ways that we engage in inquiry. As Chall (1998) noted in a recent article, the public "seems to place less confidence now than in the past in the power of research and analysis to find better solutions" (pp. 21–22). And although we have a proliferation of research that informs practice, "it has also contributed to the loss of faith in its use. Perhaps it is too vast and confusing and not sufficiently interpreted and synthesized" (pp. 21–22). Chall commented on the unorganized plethora of research findings that seem to have little impact on pedagogy or on solving current literacy problems, whereas Marty Ruddell (1998) emphasized that, in a time when our theoretical frameworks and methods are more diverse than at any time in our scholarly history in literacy, policymakers, politicians, and others who inform them have marginalized important forms of inquiry. This marginalization has occurred because research does not conform to the accepted, albeit narrow, politically correct paradigm. Moreover, Ruddell contended that the denial of a multiplicity of inquiry paradigms by politically visible national panels and policymakers is an attempt to force compliance to a "party line" (p. 8). The party line requires us to disavow our allegiance to paradigms outside of the canon of research rooted in developmental psychology and traditional scientism. Specifically, researchers who address questions generated in local settings and use interpretive methods to understand how particular teachers and students work together to support learning are positioned as being less scientific and, hence, less credible in terms of their processes and results.

Alternatively, literacy researchers who have conducted research projects that would be characterized by their peers as "scientific" (e.g., use large samples of children in multiple settings with experimental designs to measure growth or impact of programs or strategies) also feel marginalized in the literacy research community, hence the formation of a new organization, the Society for the Scientific Study of Reading (SSSR). Accepted by those in power in governmental agencies (e.g., national boards created to study why we have low reading scores in the United States), these researchers are often positioned even further away from their colleagues whose research is not deemed scientific enough.

Thus, political entities in government and elsewhere, the struggle for resources (grant monies) and jobs (tenure and promotion at universities), and a human need to feel that one has made a mark in the field all have contributed to a preoccupation with paradigm debates resulting in literacy research that has not made the difference it could in practice. Clearly, we need to regroup as a research community and consider the value of pooling our considerable intellectual resources. Difficult questions must be asked about why we engage in inquiry and who benefits from or is affected by the results of our efforts.

Dimensions of Literacy Inquiry for the Future

Although it is difficult to change particular large systems or structures (e.g., university systems, government agencies) and their value systems, we can begin to make changes as individuals and as a research community. We believe that a pragmatic perspective offers literacy researchers a way to approach inquiry that will enable us to agree to disagree, to get over it—ego involvement—and to get on with it—the important work of defining the literacy problems we need to solve, determining how best to solve these problems, and ensuring that the results inform practice (Mosenthal, 1999). In the next section we move in this direction by presenting dimensions of literacy inquiry that we believe must be defined, articulated, put into practice, and evaluated.

Dimension #1: Building Communities of Inquiry

Dewey reminded us that from a pragmatic perspective it is critical that we reconceptualize how inquiry is conducted, who we involve in the inquiry process, and the roles various participants assume within the process.

Community Partnerships. A 1999 Kellogg Commission publication by the National Association of State Universities and Land-Grant Colleges (NASULGC) presents a key issue relating to the reconceptualization of how inquiry is conducted. The report challenges university personnel to work toward organizing staff and resources to better serve local and national needs in meaningful and coherent ways. The Kellogg Commission noted that university personnel must go beyond traditional notions of outreach and service to what is termed engagement. This concept disrupts traditional notions of a one-way distribution of services (e.g., the expert at the university reaches out to the community and transfers knowledge) to promote the creation of partnerships (e.g., among university staff, K–12 teachers and administrators, parents, students, and members of the community) in which all parties come together with resources and expertise. Mutual respect is crucial, and individuals glean valuable information for specified purposes through collaboration. Engagement among partners involves seven key elements:

1. *Responsiveness*: the need to listen to community members and ask appropriate questions to identify public problems;

2. *Respect for partners*: the need to jointly identify problems, solutions, and definitions of success;

3. *Academic neutrality*: the need for activities that involve contentious issues that have profound social, economic, and political consequences and a change in the role university faculty assume in these issues;

4. *Accessibility*: the need to ensure that community members are aware of and can access resources that may be useful in solving problems;

5. *Integration*: the need for faculty members to seek new ways to integrate their outreach/service missions with their teaching and scholarship while also committing to interdisciplinary work;

6. *Coordination*: the need for overall coordination of engagement efforts across the university and community and the assessment and communication of these efforts; and

7. *Resources partnerships*: the need for adequate resources (time, effort, funding) to be committed to the tasks identified by all members of the partnership.

The idea of engagement is consonant with Dewey's pragmatic conception of social inquiry. Clearly, a commitment to engagement is necessary in forming partnerships. Strong leadership, coupled with support by administrators, promotion and tenure committees, and funding agencies, is also necessary. Communities must be open to diverse solutions to problems and varying roles of persons involved in partnerships. Challenges to this new concept of engagement and social inquiry revolve around logistical and accountability issues: How will communities of inquiry come together and function? Who will ultimately be responsible for the success or failure of partnerships? Will personnel be supported and rewarded for their efforts in both the short and long term? How do we know that people in communities of inquiry have the critical skills needed to deliberate problems? How will we mediate power and get along?

These challenges of pragmatism highlight what Bernstein (1983) understood to be a "paradox of praxis": "The type of solidarity, communicative interaction, dialogue, and judgement required for the concrete realization of praxis already presupposes incipient forms of community life that such praxis seeks to foster" (p. 175). Similarly, Dewey (1927/1993c) observed, "A class of experts is inevitably so removed from common interests as to become a class with private interests and private knowledge, which in social matters is not knowledge at all" (p. 187). It is difficult to conduct pragmatic inquiry that relies on communication and dialogue when teachers, community members, and researchers are not accustomed to working together; when literacy researchers are often separated by paradigmatic boundaries reinforced by power interests; and when researchers are similarly unaccustomed to communicative dialogue and interaction across disciplines both within education and across the academy.

Dewey (1916) envisioned communities of inquiry as communities that internally reflect "numerous and varied interests" and "full and free interplay with other forms of association" (p. 83). This conception is opposite our usual conception of independent research or academic communities in which interests and memberships are explicitly narrow. As Foucault (1975/1977, 1980) delineated, disciplinary practices with distinct types of knowledge and knowledge makers are disciplined and understood as systems of power and authority. The suggestion of a more inclusive notion of research participants and academic communities through pragmatism implicates deeply entrenched notions of power and authority.

Partners as Advocates for Learners. A desire to work collaboratively to identify and solve problems is key to the formation of partnerships between school-based personnel, literacy researchers, and community members. This stance requires a form of advocacy by members of the partnership, what Rorty (1982) called "loyalty to other human beings" (p. 162) in order to promote "the creation of a freer and more humane experience" (Dewey, 1939/1993a, p. 245). For instance, partners might take up the cause of students who have been tracked using limited assessment measures. To give an example of the dynamics of such advocacy, and to present a stark contrast to education, we turn to medical research. The following example shows how a pragmatic perspective, with participants in the role of advocate for themselves and others, influences research and practice.

The National Breast Cancer Coalition (NBCC), whose members have demanded a significant role in the scientific research designed to find a cure for their disease, advocate strongly for scientific research that asks the right questions, that is designed in credible ways, and that will yield answers that are appropriate and adequately translated for the public. An article in a recent newsletter ("Science and Research: Call to Action," 1999, January/February) of the NBCC links science and advocacy:

> Science is supposed to be pure, based on data, and objective observation. So how can advocacy give us anything but bad science? Scientists are individuals with their own perspectives and biases. Individuals, who design protocols, determine which questions to ask and decide how to frame issues. The perspective of trained breast cancer activists can enrich the scientific process and through collaboration we can end up with better science and more meaningful answers. (p. 10)

During the design of high-stakes clinical research comparing the use of the drugs tamoxifen and raloxifene for women at high risk of breast cancer, advocates questioned the need for requiring control groups and placebos as well as large numbers of women in the study. Researchers refused to approve a placebo component, claiming that it would be unethical. NBCC advocates questioned what was ethical in the long term. It is crucial to a pragmatic view of research to define what is ethical within the community in which the research is conducted. As a result of many conversations, NBCC advocates are creating partnerships with industry and government as they design new therapies. These partnerships ensure that the participants (and later recipients of the therapies) are able to play a role in the design, implementation, and dissemination of results from clinical trials; the advocates also serve on peer review teams for funding agencies. This advocacy has resulted in what is referred to as a new paradigm for breast cancer research, with collaborative efforts resulting in answers about whether new therapies are effective much sooner than in previous years.

This medical example is interesting in comparison to advocacy efforts of researchers and educators in K–12 education settings. It presents a marked contrast to educators' advocacy for themselves and their students. A challenging question for educators is why we see little need for advocacy with such a large number of stakeholders, including researchers, teachers, parents, students, and citizens.

The NBCC advocates believe that advocacy and science must be paired if shared goals are to be achieved—goals like life itself and quality of life. Do stakeholders in education have shared goals for learners that we believe are so critical that they must be achieved to foster a high quality of life? Could it be that, because education is not a life-or-death enterprise that clearly links actions and accountability, we feel much less urgency toward learners than physicians, medical researchers, and patients feel in their medical endeavors? An alternative response is that we lack practice in working from a moral position to identify social problems and collectively find solutions.

Pragmatists would seek to develop partnerships where engagement is central to the work, where university- and school-based educators as well as students and community members bring their respective expertise to bear during deliberations, and where all stakeholders advocate for themselves to identify educational problems and inquiry designs. Ultimately, all stakeholders would be advocates for student learning.

Dimension #2: Moral Obligation in the Selection of Research Problems

Currently, many educational researchers are stepping back from their inquiry projects and the philosophical debates about the conduct of research to ask themselves these questions: Why do I engage in educational research? How meaningful is my research? and Who benefits from my work? Chall (1998) posed a similar question to her peers in literacy research: "What is the responsibility of scholars? Is it toward searching for new knowledge about the reading process? Or should it also include the responsibility of helping to solve the grave literacy problems facing us today?" (pp. 23–24). Dewey (1938/1981) would urge literacy researchers to consider problems we face in light of the institutional, social, political, and contextual influences surrounding the problems.

The Formulation of Research Problems. As we construct research agendas with participants and think about the ends we hope to influence, we must take more time than we have in the past to identify carefully and then outline the actual problem and its dimensions. Too often, we quickly pose research questions, spending most of our time on elegant designs or intensive analyses. As Dewey (1929/1987b) warned in *The Quest for Certainty*, "The natural tendency of man is to do something at once, there is an impatience with suspense, and lust for immediate action" (p. 178). From a pragmatic perspective, more time must be spent talking about the problem with participants and other constituents, defining the contours and the ways that addressing one feature of a problem may contribute to understanding another, and thinking about the concerns and implications associated with our decisions. This stage is what Dewey characterized as "enjoying the doubtful" (p. 182). The effort at the inception of the study can result in stronger, richer efforts along the way.

Particular discernment for identifying what might be a useful focus of inquiry or a problem to solve usually rests with the researcher, or what Dewey called the expert. Campbell (1995) summarized Dewey's ideas about the role of experts: "To solve problems in our complex modern world requires us to think differently and those members of society with special experience or with special expertise may be particularly helpful in formulating problems and suggesting possible solutions" (p. 149). A pragmatic perspective requires that researchers share this power with participants; researchers come to the table with expertise, but other stakeholders also bring their knowledge and experience. Within this context, researchers are charged with teaching community members about methodological options available to understanding and solving problems. The sort of democratic dialogue Dewey envisioned in such a setting helps foster both understanding and community. Dewey (1927/1993c) observed that "the essential need...is the improvement in methods and conditions of debate, discussion, and persuasion" (p. 187). Such dialogue is an important skill, which is equally appropriate for citizens, researchers, and students. Matthew Lipman (1998) described dialogue as moving in the direction of two kinds of wholeness:

> On the one hand the mental acts form logical connections with one another. On the other hand, those who perform such acts form social relationships with one another. The first kind of wholeness is a completeness of meaning. The second kind, the interpersonal kind, moves toward a communal solidarity. (p. 208)

Within this process researchers lose some freedom in the formulation of problems, the way problems are addressed, and what is reported from the research. However, sharing of power is worthwhile when inquiry is viewed as responsive, meaningful, and credible to all participants.

Developing Multiple, Connected Research Initiatives. Along with broadening the collective of persons associated with inquiry and redefining the roles persons might assume within this process, there is a need to reconsider how we develop research agendas, identify problems, and craft studies. We propose a literacy inquiry agenda spanning three foci: (1) developing a set of critical problems, generated by a diverse group of stakeholders, that are foundational to large-scale research projects with multiple sites and community inquiry teams; (2) developing a set of critical problems generated at the local level by community inquiry teams; and (3) collectively identifying problems that interest individual researchers and that can be parsed into various facets to be addressed by individual expertise. Consistent with a pragmatic stance, we believe that on an international, national, local, and personal level researchers should consider Dewey's vision of inquiry as collectively generating research problems from actual social situations (practices) as identified by all stakeholders through practical discourse.

Researchers themselves pose the biggest challenge to taking a pragmatic stance in developing multiple, interconnected research foci. Wolcott (1992) in his discussion "Posturing in Qualitative Research" (positioning oneself strategically) illuminates the struggle researchers have when attempting to meet several, often competing, agendas, including powerful interests of their own:

> [P]osturing is not only a matter of identifying a strategy and capitalizing on research talents, it is also a personal matter influenced by the kinds of information and kinds of memberships...available to and valued by academicians individually. Prior professional commitments...and future professional aspirations...also exert an influence and extract a corresponding commitment over the problems we select.... These commitments consciously or unconsciously influence our identification of problems or lead us to redefinition of problems that make them amenable to study in some particular way rather than in others. (pp. 41–42)

To Wolcott, research is ultimately a personal matter; we research things we enjoy, believe in, or feel passionately about. Nevertheless, the problems literacy researchers typically pose and the methods they select for solving these problems are almost always mediated by the trends highlighted in professional communities such as the National Reading Conference (NRC), the Society for the Scientific Study of Reading (SSSR), the International Reading Association (IRA), and the American Educational Research Association (AERA). Individual researchers want to position themselves professionally, socially, and culturally— they want their work to fit into acknowledged trends and to be acknowledged by respectable communities. Dewey and other pragmatists oppose the perspective of research as a personal matter, noting that research agendas should be public and socially grounded in intent and process. Inquiry not so grounded fails to serve the purpose of democratic reconstruction.

Embedded within the challenge of public vs. personal research agendas is the question of how the nature of research is influenced by the way researchers are positioned by the social, cultural, and historical contexts in which they conduct inquiry. Colleagues and administrators in the university system, K–12 school-based colleagues, and local, state, and national policymakers define these contexts. For example, researchers are valued in university settings for the innovative knowledge they generate and, like it or not, productivity in the form of quantity of articles in prestigious journals. Add to this narrow conceptualization of productivity the current institutional pressures to reform teacher education programs and a situation is created in which scholars actually have little time to be scholarly. In such a climate, research is often quickly conceived; data are collected, analyzed, and interpreted in a cursory manner; and reports of research are written in bits and pieces when time permits in outlets that university promotion and tenure committees find acceptable (but persons engaged in practice may not read). Thus, much of this research may have little effect on the practices of K–12 educators or on learners' lives. There is evidence that this institutional culture is changing, but it remains a formidable force that affects the character and quality of literacy inquiry.

Literacy research agendas and designs also are shaped by commitments researchers make to commercial publishers when they sign as authors. These scholars/authors often try to balance commitments to the profession with the economic interests of their publishers/employers. Finally, many researchers have strong commitments to addressing broad issues in education (e.g., tracking, assessment, busing) that sometimes displace more immediate subtle contextual issues that uniquely inform research from site to site. Researchers, who are pulled in many different directions as they engage in their work, can disenfranchise the very practitioners and students who are at the heart of the most crucial problems that need to be addressed.

In sum, neither literacy scholars nor prospective advocates of scholarship have clearly identified a broad set of issues that deserve unified, convergent efforts, although policymakers and funding agencies have done so. Further, literacy researchers and other stakeholders currently lack a coherent plan, a process, or the leadership to initiate such efforts. Despite the identified need for a shared research agenda, most literacy researchers also believe that opportunities must be provided for innovative, unconventional research that advances the field. This tension between large-scale and local research agendas, shared and individual agendas, and the role of research paradigms can be managed productively with considerable thought, effort, dialogue, and organization. A pragmatic stance to the formation of multiple yet connected research agendas could facilitate this effort.

Keeping the End in View When Designing Research. In maintaining a pragmatic stance, the selection and design of studies in the literacy field should be developed with the end in view. Traditionally, this end in view is a post hoc entity we call implications or recommendations rather than an a priori design issue. Pragmatic research conversations would begin with these questions: What do we hope to achieve at the conclusion of the study? Why is this end important for learners? The conversation about the end result could help participants better define problems and improve the design of studies, and this conversation could help participants focus on the specific social, cultural, and other contextual aspects that affect a particular inquiry.

Despite its apparent usefulness, an end-in-view perspective, grounded in social responsibility and democratic purposes, presents a new challenge in conducting research. In beginning a study, researchers typically review related research, carefully crafting hypotheses or guiding research questions, developing a design that best addresses questions, collecting and analyzing data, theorizing, and interpreting the results. It is possible that the end-in-view fixation may cause researchers to lose sight of the research process, including methodological possibilities, or of certain structural considerations as a project unfolds (Thompson, 1997).

Dimension #3: Reconsidering Traditions, Methodologies, and How We Communicate Findings

The knowledge we hold and the beliefs we subscribe to dictate what research questions we ask and for whom. Polkinghorne (1983) noted that our scholarship is defined as much by the self-interrogation about why we engage in inquiry as it is in the actual conduct of research. This self-inquiry promotes the use of a broad range of designs and methods but requires that we carefully articulate the assumptions undergirding various approaches and traditions that are the basis of our inquiry.

The Use of Multiple Traditions Within a Study. Technical expertise and theoretical and methodological purity have been the hallmarks of quality in paradigmatically driven research. Researchers believe that if they attend to these elements, more credible findings will result. By contrast, a pragmatic stance values communities engaged in literacy research that focus on solving problems; the selection of the theoretical frameworks and methodologies is tailored to the complexity of the problem and the promise of useful findings rather than discrete technical standards.

That said, we are not promoting the use of a-little-bit-of-this and a-little-bit-of-that inquiry. Particular frameworks or traditions and methodologies *do* have underlying assumptions, some of which are congruent with one another and some of which are not (see Jacob, 1987, for an in-depth discussion of this issue). But is it possible for literacy researchers to employ research traditions with incompatible assumptions in an attempt to explore multiple facets of a problem, to test or add depth to a primary analysis, or to offer additional, compelling evidence that appeals to wider groups of stakeholders who might then also find other less-acceptable forms of data credible? We address this question in the next two sections.

The Purity of Traditions and Methodologies vs. Quality of Use. A pragmatic stance promotes the examination of all assumptions underlying various traditions and encourages collaborative discussion about which could be adopted and which should be rejected. But researchers, in addressing problems, understand, select, employ, and discuss the various traditions and methodologies they use to design and engage in useful research rather than taking political positions aligned with paradigms.

Pitman and Maxwell (1992) discussed the pervasiveness of paradigm wars in spite of a substantial scholarly base offering many options and broad perspectives on inquiry. They contended that philosophical debates in research have become increasingly detached from the actual conduct of research. To address this detachment, they asked researchers to reflect on their *practice* and to critique the various approaches they use within a perspective or methodology (e.g., researchers would examine the quality of research practices used within educational ethnography). In actuality, we rarely systematically critique the quality of one another's use of traditions and methodologies.

From a pragmatic stance, using a variety of methodologies can either strengthen a study or lead to its downfall. The use of multimethodologies can add breadth and depth and numerical, pictorial, and narrative data to support themes, assertions, or findings. But these studies must still evidence the tenets of quality research. Many researchers are careful to ground their work in substantive theories from the field of literacy; nevertheless, these same scholars can sometimes be criticized for neglecting to use and exhibit understanding about the theoretical frameworks undergirding their methodologies. A classic example in literacy research is the popularity of qualitative or interpretive research, specifically educational ethnography. Wolcott (1992), writing about the newly embraced qualitative research methodologies in education, observed, "Qualitative studies completed today often fail to show evidence of the disciplinary lineages that spawned them...the innovative process in educational practice tends toward adaptation rather than adoption" (p. 38). Although Wolcott acknowledged that adaptations developed by educational researchers might have admirable traits despite their hybrid nature, to adopt a methodology, he contended, one must have studied its disciplinary lineage well. Educational researchers must strengthen their theoretical knowledge base in the disciplines that inform the methodologies they wish to draw upon and articulate this knowledge in both their practice and writings. These methodologies and frameworks might include not only ideas from across educational disciplines but also frameworks from outside the current boundaries of education such as those grounded in policy studies, political theories, literacy theories, philosophy, or even biology.

Although the title Doctor of Philosophy is reminiscent of the days in which a broad education was more valued, academe, as already noted, currently does not support the development of broadly educated researchers. Neither does the academy support the development of inquiry communities with school and community collaborators, or with the potentially diverse groups of colleagues that pragmatic inquiry needs to thrive. Again, Foucault (1975/1977, 1980) reminded us that the ways in which we structure knowledge in academe serve to create regimes of truth and structures of power and authority. Thus, a pragmatic turn in inquiry provides us with compelling challenges not only to the ways in which ideas are conceived and pursued but also to the ways in which power and authority are structured among intellectuals, and society in general. The change we suggest has both philosophical and political ramifications.

Considering New Traditions and Methodologies. Concurrent with the need for new knowledge is an awareness of what knowledge bases we draw upon and which ones we inadvertently overlook. For example, we believe that literacy researchers should consider Scheurich and Young's (1997) discussion of race-based paradigms constructed via cultural and historical contexts. The authors argued that all current epistemologies and accompanying tensions (e.g., issues of qualitative vs. quantitative methodologies, objective vs. subjective reality, validity and paradigmatic issues in general) rise out of the social history of the dominant white race, thus reflecting and reinforcing that social history and racial group. This white dominance has negative results for people of color and, in particular, scholars of color (cf. Collins, 1991). We need to extend paradigms to address "epistemological racism," recognizing that dominant and subordinate racial groups "do not think and interpret realities in the same way as White people because of their divergent structural positions, histories, and cultures" (Stanfield, 1985, p. 400). Scheurich and Young (1997) argued that even critical approaches (critical theory, feminism, lesbian/gay orientations, and critical postmodernism), where racism has been a focus, have been racially biased. A pragmatic perspective beckons literacy researchers to attend to how various racial groups select issues for inquiry, conceptualize research, interpret phenomena, and record results. This is a new epistemological issue that is critical to understanding literacy events in the next millennium.

Communicating the Findings of Research. We must consider how we relate the findings from our inquiry to other communities of inquirers, researchers within and across paradigmatic lines and disciplines, and individuals outside the research context (e.g., policymakers and the general public). Writing for multiple audiences and writing about ideas that others find useful (keeping the end in mind as one constructs a study) are important goals. Chall (1998) pointed out that literacy research is becoming more and more technical and complex, making it more difficult to translate findings in a written form that is understandable to practitioners and other researchers. From a pragmatic stance, we believe that the typical article format for sharing work should change to better illuminate complex concepts for a range of readers and to meet the needs of policymakers in terms of brevity (e.g., through the use of executive summaries), clarity, and elimination of jargon.

A shift in the expectations of journal editors and editorial review boards also will be needed to promote the publication of concise research reports while also recognizing the value of longer articles that detail theory and methodology. A pragmatic stance requires that we more carefully consider the audiences that we hope to inform with our inquiry—audiences that span far beyond our universities and research communities to local schools, communities, and state and federal agencies.

Technology also holds promise for offering new forms of representation that will display and explicate concepts that heretofore have been represented with flat text. For example, David Wray, of the University of Warwick, announced the formation of a new journal that would provide a series of abstracts of published research and other materials relating to literacy (post to the National Reading Conference listserv, February 1999). This journal, and others like it, would provide concise and accurate information for researchers and practitioners alike. Published accounts of research in new concise formats have the potential to reach a larger audience and inform practice, policy, and future inquiry efforts.

Conclusions

Many complex questions relating to how learners become and remain literate and how teachers can support this process remain uninvestigated. However, our past practices in selecting questions and formulating inquiry approaches must be adapted for the new millennium. An individual researcher's beliefs and expertise no longer can be the sole rationale for the research questions selected and pursued. Instead, the complexity of problems and social situations that affect practice and concern local constituents must be key to the creation of shared research agendas.

We have proposed the adoption of pragmatism as a new stance for academics and communities of inquirers. Pragmatism is not a paradigm adapted from those that are currently popular; rather, it is a revolutionary break in our thinking and practice relating to inquiry. As a literacy community, we need to challenge ourselves to step back and think collectively and individually about the inquiry in which we are engaged. Is our research meaningful, credible, and prone to making a difference in students' learning and teachers' pedagogy? Does our inquiry work toward concrete alternatives for students and teachers? As Rorty explained, "For the pragmatists, the pattern of all inquiry—scientific as well as moral—is deliberation concerning the relative attractions of various concrete alternatives" (1982, p. 164). We see the goal of research at its best as practical rationality serving moral concerns. Pragmatic research for the new millennium can be a practical and hopeful inquiry, which avoids the arrogance of modernist empiricism and the angst of postmodern deconstructions. We can accomplish this new goal.

References

Beach, R. (1994). Adopting multiple stances in conducting literacy research. In R.B. Ruddell, M.R. Ruddell, & H. Singer (Eds.), *Theoretical models and processes of reading* (4th ed., pp. 1203–1219). Newark, DE: International Reading Association.

Beach, R., Green, J., Kamil, M.L., & Shanahan, T. (Eds.). (1992). *Multidisciplinary perspectives on literacy research*. Urbana, IL: National Conference on Research in English and National Council of Teachers of English.

Bernstein, R. (1983). *Beyond objectivism and relativism: Science, hermeneutics and practice*. Philadelphia: University of Pennsylvania Press.

Bernstein, R. (1991). *The new constellation*. Cambridge, MA: Polity Press.

Boisvert, R.D. (1998). *John Dewey: Rethinking our time*. Albany: State University of New York Press.

Campbell, J. (1995). *Understanding John Dewey*. Chicago: Open Court.

Chall, J.S. (1998). My life in reading. In E.G. Sturtevant, J.A. Dugan, P. Linder, & W.M. Linek (Eds.), *Literacy and community* (pp. 12–24). Commerce, TX: College Reading Association.

Clay, M.M. (1994). Foreword. In R.B. Ruddell, M.R. Ruddell, & H. Singer (Eds.), *Theoretical models and processes of reading* (4th ed., pp. ix–xiii). Newark, DE: International Reading Association.

Collins, P.H. (1991). *Black feminist thought: Knowledge, consciousness, and the politics of empowerment*. New York: Routledge.

Dewey, J. (1916). *Democracy and education: An introduction to the philosophy of education*. New York: Macmillan.

Dewey, J. (1981). Social inquiry. In J.J. McDermott (Ed.), *The philosophy of John Dewey* (pp. 397–420). Chicago: University of Chicago Press. (Original work published 1938)

Dewey, J. (1982). Ethics. In J.A. Boydson (Ed.), *The middle works of John Dewey, 1925–1953* (Vol. 5). Carbondale: Southern Illinois University Press. (Original work published 1908)

Dewey, J. (1987a). Ethics revisited. In J.A. Boydson (Ed.), *The later works of John Dewey, 1925–1953* (Vol. 7). Carbondale: Southern Illinois University Press. (Original work published 1932)

Dewey, J. (1987b). The quest for certainty. In J.A. Boydson (Ed.), *The later works of John Dewey, 1925–1953* (Vol. 4). Carbondale: Southern Illinois University Press. (Original work published 1929)

Dewey, J. (1993a). Creative democracy—The task before us. In D. Morris & I. Shapiro (Eds.), *John Dewey: The political writings* (pp. 240–245). Indianapolis, IN: Hackett. (Original work published 1939)

Dewey, J. (1993b). Philosophy and democracy. In D. Morris & I. Shapiro (Eds.), *John Dewey: The political writings* (pp. 38–47).

Indianapolis, IN: Hackett. (Original work published 1919)

Dewey, J. (1993c). The public and its problems. In D. Morris & I. Shapiro (Eds.), *John Dewey: The political writings* (pp. 173–191). Indianapolis, IN: Hackett. Original work published 1927)

Dickstein, M. (Ed.). (1998). *The revival of pragmatism*. Durham, NC: Duke University Press.

Donmoyer, R. (1996). Educational research in an era of paradigm proliferation: What's a journal editor to do? *Educational Researcher, 25*(2), 19–25.

Engelbreit, M. (1998, December 25–27). So the millennium is just around the corner—Get over it; get on with it. *USA Today*, cover page.

Foucault, M. (1977). *Discipline and punish: The birth of the prison* (A. Sheridan, Trans.). New York: Pantheon. (Original work published 1975)

Foucault, M. (1980). Truth and power. In C. Gordon (Ed.), *Power/knowledge: Selected interviews & other writings, 1972–77* (pp. 109–133). New York: Pantheon.

Graves, M.F. (1998, October/November). Beyond balance. *Reading Today*, p. 16.

Harris, T.L. (1969). Reading. In R.L. Ebel (Ed.), *Encyclopedia of educational research: A project of the American Educational Research Association* (4th ed., pp. 1069–1108). Toronto: Macmillan and the American Educational Research Association.

Hitchcock, G., & Hughes, D. (1989). *Research and the teacher: A qualitative introduction to school-based research*. New York: Routledge.

Jacob, E. (1987). Qualitative traditions: A review. *Review of Educational Research, 37*, 1–50.

James, W. (1991). *Pragmatism*. Buffalo, NY: Prometheus. (Reprinted from *Pragmatism: A new name for some old ways of thinking* by W. James, 1907, Cambridge, MA: Harvard University Press).

Kellogg Commission on the Future of State and Land-Grant Universities. (1999, February). *Returning to our roots: The engaged institution*. Washington, DC: National Association of State Universities and Land-Grant Colleges.

Kuhn, T. (1970). *The structure of scientific revolutions* (2nd ed.). Chicago: University of Chicago Press.

Lincoln, Y.S., & Guba, E.G. (1985). *Naturalistic inquiry*. Newbury Park, CA: Sage.

Lipman, M. (1998, May/June). Teaching students to think reasonably: Some findings of the philosophy for children's programs. *Clearing House, 71*, 277–281.

McDermott, R.P. (1976). Achieving school failure: An anthropological approach to illiteracy and social stratification. In H. Singer & R.B. Ruddell (Eds.), *Theoretical models and processes of reading* (2nd ed., pp. 389–428). Newark, DE: International Reading Association.

Misak, C. (1998). Deflating truth: Pragmatism vs. minimalism. *Monist, 81*, 407–426.

Mosenthal, P.B. (1985). Defining progress in educational research. *Educational Researcher, 14*(9), 3–9.

Mosenthal, P.B. (1987). Research views: Defining progress in reading research and practice. *The Reading Teacher, 40*, 472–475.

Mosenthal, P.B. (1999). Critical issues: Forging conceptual unum in the literacy field of pluribus: An agenda-analytic perspective. *Journal of Literacy Research, 31*, 213–254.

Patton, M.Q. (1990). *Qualitative evaluation and research methods* (2nd ed.). Newbury Park, CA: Sage.

Pearson, P.D., & Stephens, D. (1994). Learning about literacy: A 30-year journey. In R.B. Ruddell, M.R. Ruddell, & H. Singer (Eds.), *Theoretical models and processes of reading* (4th ed., pp. 22–42). Newark, DE: International Reading Association.

Pitman, M.A., & Maxwell, J.A. (1992). Qualitative approaches to evaluation: Models and methods. In M.D. LeCompte, W.L. Millroy, & J. Preissle (Eds.), *The handbook of qualitative research in education* (pp. 729–770). New York: Academic Press.

Polkinghorne, D. (1983). *Methodology for the human sciences*. Albany: State University of New York Press.

Rorty, R. (1982). *Consequences of pragmatism*. Minneapolis: University of Minnesota Press.

Rorty, R. (1991). *Objectivity, relativism, and truth*. New York: Cambridge University Press.

Ruddell, M.R. (1998, December). *Of stand-up comics, statisticians, storytellers, and small girls walking backward: A new look at the discourses of literacy research*. Presidential address presented at the annual meeting of the National Reading Conference, Austin, TX.

Scheurich, J.J., & Young, M.D. (1997). Coloring epistemologies: Are our research epistemologies racially biased? *Educational Researcher, 26*(4), 4–16.

Science and research: Call to action. (1999, January/ February). *The Quarterly Newsletter of the National Breast Cancer Coalition, 5*(1), 10.

Singer, H., & Ruddell, R.B. (Eds.). (1970). *Theoretical models and processes of reading*. Newark, DE: International Reading Association.

Singer, H., & Ruddell, R.B. (Eds.). (1976). *Theoretical models and processes of reading* (2nd ed.). Newark, DE: International Reading Association.

Singer, H., & Ruddell, R.B. (Eds.). (1985). *Theoretical models and processes of reading* (3rd ed.). Newark, DE: International Reading Association.

Stanfield, J.H., II. (1985). The ethnocentric basis of social science knowledge production. *Review of Research in Education, 12*, 387–415.

Strickland, D.S. (1996, October/November). In search of balance: Restructuring our literacy programs. *Reading Today*, p. 32.

Taylor, C. (1994). The politics of recognition. In C. Taylor & A. Gutman (Eds.), *Multiculturalism: The politics of recognition* (pp. 25–73). Princeton, NJ: University of Princeton Press.

Thompson, A. (1997). Political pragmatism and educational inquiry. In F. Margonis (Ed.), *Philosophy of education* (pp. 425–434). Urbana, IL: Philosophy of Education Society.

Weintraub, S., & Farr, R. (1976). Introduction. In R. Farr, S. Weintraub, & B. Tone (Eds.), *Improving reading research* (pp. 1–7). Newark, DE: International Reading Association.

West, C. (1993). *Keeping faith*. New York: Routledge.

White, M. (1949). *Social thought in America: The revolt against formalism*. Boston: Beacon Press.

Wolcott, H. (1992). Posturing in qualitative research. In M.D. LeCompte, W.L. Millroy, & J. Preissle (Eds.), *The handbook of qualitative research in education* (pp. 3–52). New York: Academic.

53

Strategies for Developing a Research Program on Reading Comprehension

RAND Reading Study Group

H aving a purposeful research agenda is only one prerequisite to developing a research program in any domain. In addition to formulating an array of desirable research activities, the education field will need to determine priorities—which aspects of the agenda to begin with and how to sequence the necessary research activities. Further, issues about the required infrastructure for the research effort must be addressed, as well as questions about how to sustain and steer the effort once it is underway so that knowledge can accumulate and its usability can be optimized. Considerations of the research methods are crucial, as are issues of funding levels and funding sources and collaboration among various potential funding agencies. We discuss these various issues in the following sections.

Prerequisites to Establishing an Excellent Educational Research Program

This report makes clear that although the knowledge base in the area of reading comprehension encompasses a very large territory, it is extensive in some areas but limited in others. The RAND Reading Study Group (RRSG) has mapped the various domains of knowledge to help decision makers identify new research that will have the most effect on comprehension instruction and reading outcomes. In so doing, a number of prerequisites for the establishment of a successful and effective reading comprehension research program were identified. Those prerequisites include (1) establishing priorities, (2) building on strengths, (3) improving the status of education research, and (4) choosing methods appropriate to the task.

Establishing Priorities

The usability of knowledge now becomes the major criterion in establishing priorities—usability of knowledge in classrooms and in establishing policies. A research program should be judged not just on its methodological rigor but also on its capacity to generate improvements in classroom practice, enhance curricula, enrich teacher preparation, and facilitate more informative assessments.

1. *Criteria.* We suggest that an educational research effort that focuses only on reading comprehension as a field of research will be insufficient. The effort must also focus within reading comprehension on the highest-utility research topics. We have presented three domains of research within reading comprehension that we argue are of high priority—research on instruction, on teacher preparation, and on assessment. Even within those broad topics, further prioritizing is needed. Consulting with the research community will be key in developing likely priorities; at some point, though, decisive leadership will be needed.

Topics that are of high priority in the program of research on reading comprehension should be judged on the following criteria:

- How much knowledge has already been accumulated about the relevant aspects of comprehension?
- How significantly will expanding the knowledge base in the way proposed affect theory development?
- How important will exploring the instructional applications that might emerge from the research be to improving outcomes?
- To what extent will relevant applications enhance, extend, and expand current practice, rather than represent minor modifications to it?

2. *Tensions.* Any proposed research program represents a compromise between focus and breadth. Establishing priorities is not a formulaic procedure, but one that requires wisdom in weighing various criteria. It may be helpful to note a number of points that arose in our deliberations as we tried to establish priorities.

- *Tension between focusing on a specific age range versus a wider age range.* We discussed at some length the value of focusing our questions more specifically on a particular age range, for example, on kindergarten through grade 3, where most current reading reform efforts are targeted, or on the middle and high school grades, where practitioners are most concerned with effective reading comprehension instruction. We chose not to limit the age range of interest for a number of reasons. First, we did not wish to suggest that reading comprehension should be ignored in reading instruction in the primary grades; many accomplishments of kindergarten, grade 1, and grade 2 readers are directly relevant to current and future comprehension success, as are accomplishments in language even of preschool-age children. Second, in recognizing the practical challenges facing the content area teacher in middle and secondary school classes and the degree to which those challenges are intricately related to reading comprehension, we did not wish to downplay the importance of research on this age range. Third, our conceptualization of reading comprehension is inherently developmental, encompassing precursors that develop in the preschool and primary school years as well as outcomes displayed in secondary school. This conception precludes restricting the age range of interest.

• *Tension between priorities derived from our analysis of research and practice and priorities determined by other factors.* We recognize that competing priorities exist within any research program. For example, priorities are derived from political realities, are associated with the availability of fiscal and human resources, are limited by the practicalities of certain kinds of research undertakings, and are related to the likelihood that results will actually be used to change practice. The group that produced this report limited itself to thinking about what the education community needs to know. Obviously, the ultimately selected research agenda will also need to incorporate the effects of other factors in selecting research targets.

• *Tension between research that is well embedded in existing knowledge and theory and research that is truly innovative.* Researchers want to generate novel conceptualizations and revolutionary findings. Practice is often better served by smaller increments to our knowledge, such as knowing whether a student's comprehension of a text read in English is enhanced or impeded by discussing the meaning in the student's first language or deciding whether vocabulary instruction should incorporate writing sentences with the new words. Since the utility of knowledge is a major criterion, we obviously endorse research efforts that will generate modest increments to the quality of practice. At the same time, research efforts laying down the basis for future improvements in practice in domains that are not yet close to practical utility should not be ignored.

• *Tension between immediate payoff and longer-term research efforts.* Although research priorities tend to be attached to questions or problems, planning a research effort requires thinking about a packet of activities that fit together and address practical as well as intellectual issues. Thus, we suggest that those conducting the research planning effort consider a strategy for soliciting short-term and long-term projects simultaneously. Short-term projects, such as evaluating well-founded instructional interventions, could generate useful outcomes relatively quickly. Long-term undertakings could be designed to underpin future improvements in practice by expanding the education community's basic understanding of reading comprehension. For example, a multi-site, large-scale longitudinal study of reading comprehension development would be a long-term project. The entire research effort needs to be strategic and orchestrated. Although some of its components will have no immediate payoff, an understanding of how they might contribute ultimately to improving practice should always be required.

- *Tension between preplanned and emergent research priorities.* The RRSG achieved a remarkable degree of consensus on the formulation of issues in reading comprehension. It did not conclude, though, that its report should be an unfiltered basis for soliciting research proposals, in part because we agreed on the need to let the quality of research proposed partly determine the research priorities. Bad research on an extremely important topic is not likely to advance the field as much as excellent research on a slightly less pressing topic. Thus, we suggest that any solicitation of proposals be formulated with enough flexibility to allow the field to demonstrate what it can do well, while maintaining sufficient focus so that a coherent research program develops.

Building on Strengths

The quality of reading instruction in the primary grades in U.S. schools has benefited from the products of a 25-year program of research focused on understanding the development of word reading and on formulating interventions for children experiencing difficulties in word reading. We propose a focus on reading comprehension in part to build on these improvements in educational practice and in part to build a stronger research base for improving practice in preschool settings. It is clear that the benefits to reading outcomes that accrue from improved instruction in word reading will be limited if children do not also have access to improved instruction in vocabulary, oral language production, writing, text analysis, and other factors that contribute to comprehension. Such instruction is crucial even in the preschool years for children whose oral language skills are limited, and improved instruction needs to continue throughout the school years. Thus, the focus on reading comprehension we propose complements the currently funded research agenda on word reading, while benefiting from the advances the current research has made possible.

Improving the Status of Educational Research

Before an educational research program can demand support, it must address widespread doubts concerning the quality, relevance, and usefulness of its research. Therefore, educational funders should base their funding decisions not only on the intellectual credibility of a program but also on its practical utility. We suggest that the field of reading research take at least three steps to promote that effort.

1. *Ensure programmatic efforts.* High-utility research efforts are planned as long-term and cumulative undertakings. Changes in practice should not depend on the results of a single study or an attractive new idea; they should be based on well-replicated findings consistent with broader theoretical understandings. This presupposes a process to ensure that the research builds on previous findings and that the results of the various related research efforts are systematically accumulated, reviewed, and analyzed. These cumulative analyses should then become the subject of dissemination and the basis for changes in practice. Of course, the likelihood that research efforts will build on and inform one another is greatly enhanced if efforts are taken to build a collaborative community of researchers.

2. *Develop a community of researchers.* Research relevant to reading comprehension has been carried out within a variety of disciplines (linguistics, sociolinguistics, discourse processing, anthropology, psychology, and cognitive science) and by individuals working in quite distinct fields. In addition, the field of reading itself is sociologically somewhat complex, as emblematized by the existence of several organizations of reading researchers (International Reading Association, National Reading Conference, Society for the Scientific Study of Reading) with only partially overlapping membership and by strong constituencies of reading researchers within other organizations (American Educational Research Association, Society for Text and Discourse, Society for Research in Child Development). Making progress in reading comprehension research will require creating links across the one distinct subfields and subgroups. We suggest below that well-designed proposal review procedures can contribute substantially to forming a community of reading researchers linked by their common intellectual focus.

3. *Make both research- and practice-based knowledge optimally usable for all.* The challenge of improving reading comprehension is intrinsically a practical challenge, and reflective practitioners constitute a source of knowledge that is insufficiently represented in journals or in research proposals. If work on reading comprehension is to affect practice within our lifetimes, the concerns of practitioners need to be incorporated from the beginning. The work must be seen as operating in Pasteur's quadrant[1] rather than as being exported to schools after the research papers are published. Mechanisms for distinguishing excellent from mediocre practice, for reviewing and accumulating the knowledge of effective practitioners, and for incorporating practitioner expertise into the research process need to be developed and nurtured.

Methods Appropriate to the Task

The RRSG considered at length the issue of methodologies that are necessary to address the research questions identified by the committee. There was consensus among the members that a range of methodologies was not only necessary but also essential to ensuring rigorous responses to the various research questions. Further, the field of educational research possesses a diverse array of well-formulated, widely used methods for the conduct of rigorous research. Methods that have proven useful to advancing educational research include (1) experimental and quasi-experimental designs (Pedhazur & Schmelkin, 1991); (2) structural equation modeling (Nevitt & Hancock, 2000); (3) hierarchical linear modeling (Lee, 2000); (4) meta-analysis in experimental research (Schafer, 1999); (5) discourse analysis (Cazden, 1988); (6) video analysis (Stigler, Gallimore, & Hiebert, 2000); (7) classroom observational analysis (Turner & Meyer, 2000); and (8) verbal protocol analysis (Pressley & Afflerbach, 1995).

The body of knowledge about instruction in reading comprehension has been informed by a wide range of research methods. The power of this diversity is that converging evidence now exists for a substantial majority of the claims previously presented regarding the principles of instructional practice. The principle that explicit strategy instruction increases comprehension is supported by two quite different forms of empirical studies. For example, the National Reading Panel (NRP) (NICHD, 2000) summarized experiments showing the effects of instruction on the learning of strategies and on reading comprehension. To complement that evidence, case studies of teachers nominated as outstanding also report that these exemplary teachers provide explicit strategy instruction within the classroom context (Pressley et al., 2001). However, these examples do not imply that our knowledge is completely formed on this principle. For example, the conditions for the use of strategies are not fully explicated in either the experimental literature or the case study literature. However, this convergence does suggest that strategy instruction is a promising starting point for new research on reading comprehension instruction.

Statistical modeling has been advanced to permit the examination of critical aspects of complex problems such as reading comprehension instruction. For instance, structural equation modeling (SEM) allows investigators to study latent variables. Such variables represent the shared variance (e.g., the essential overlap in measurement) between two measured constructs. This is especially useful in reading comprehension research because valid and reliable measures of instructional variables, such as strategy instruction or autonomy support, are in the process of being developed. Further, SEM permits the study of mediation among classroom constructs, student characteristics, and student achievement outcomes. Hierarchical linear modeling (HLM) increases our capacity to study the effects of instruction on reading comprehension by permitting the investigator to eliminate variance in achievement attributable to unwanted sources (Lee, 2000). Especially with large data sets, or with quasi-experimental designs, variance in outcome variables that is not experimentally controlled can be statistically removed from the classroom instructional effects that are of theoretical importance. Both SEM and HLM permit investigators to form growth variables reflecting the slope and curvature of student improvement in reading comprehension or allied variables, such as reading motivation or content knowledge gained from reading.

To complement strong statistical modeling, in-depth analysis techniques permit investigators to examine the cognitive processes of readers through verbal protocol analysis (Pressley & Afflerbach, 1995). In this procedure, students think aloud while reading, and their verbal reports are examined for the qualities of their cognitive self-regulation and other higher-order thinking activities. As procedures for analyzing videotapes have advanced, widely shared guidelines for collecting, transcribing, interpreting, coding, and analyzing data have become available (Erickson, 1992; Stigler et al., 1999). These data are multivariate and interactionist. They can convey the complexity of classroom instruction. However, videotapes are necessarily limited to a few classrooms. When such data are linked to national (or state) probability samples, they can reveal generalizable patterns of instruction. Such patterns represent both the depth of classroom instruction and the breadth of generalization for the findings. Thus, methodological tools that are readily accessible to all investigators permit a diversity of approaches to research, as required in the multifaceted field of reading comprehension instruction.

Further, any substantial research effort will likely need to involve a combination of different approaches and different types of data requiring adherence to multiple evidentiary standards. In the interest of rigor, it is imperative that the methodology selected to address a research question be driven by the question itself and not by arbitrary judgments that some methods are stronger than others. For that matter, it is also not possible to make clear-cut divisions across types of methodologies, for a number of reasons:

- Classes of methodologies overlap to a large extent.
- There is no intrinsic ranking of values associated with any particular methodology.
- High levels of rigor can be defined for any form of disciplined inquiry, whether classified as qualitative or quantitative.
- Methodologies can be assessed only with reference to the research questions they are being used to answer.

Among quantitatively oriented studies, true experiments, of course, represent an ideal methodology for assessing the effect of instruction or intervention. True experiments are sometimes not feasible, though, since their successful implementation requires a set of conditions that cannot always be met in educational settings. In these cases, well-controlled quasi-experiments provide a standard of evidence that, although not as high as that of true experiments, is acceptable. Quantitative studies, including program evaluations, are typically enriched by the inclusion of methods that simultaneously provide descriptive and correlational data on, for example, the interaction of learner characteristics and response to intervention. Similarly, some methodologies that are qualitative and observational may have strong quantitative components, such as the observation and coding of classroom teaching behaviors in a time-by-activity framework essential to evaluating the effects of instructional strategies on student achievement.

Some questions call for ethnographic methods. For example, how do teachers and principals respond to the introduction of a new reading comprehension intervention into a school? Qualitative methods are often the most appropriate ones when the goal is discovery. For example, in-depth qualitative studies on bilingual students' use of metacognitive and cognitive strategies while reading in two languages have generated information on their reading that would have been otherwise difficult to obtain. Qualitative methods are also highly desirable when in-depth information is needed about important components of an intervention's functioning. Such information may illuminate, for example, whether the intervention is likely to be undermined or supported within a school. In addition, qualitative methods are useful for providing a cultural perspective on why certain groups respond the way they do to instruction, or for describing how teachers' practices differentially affect students' reading engagement and performance.

Thus, scientifically rigorous research studies use methods appropriate to the research questions of interest. In many instances, multiple methodologies blend descriptive, correlational, and experimental methods in the more quantitative area with a range of qualitative methods essential to addressing the questions of interest. It is also possible that the appropriate methodology of interest will be predominantly one or another type, although there is substantial variability in the characteristics of a single methodology that defies simple lumping methods into categories.

When multiple types of evidence can be cited in support of a particular conclusion, a greater capacity exists for building consensus, ensuring the translation of research to practice, and supporting the sustainability of research-based practices. We hope that one aspect of this research agenda will be to increase the receptivity of educational thinking to the value of rigorous research and to stimulate the active discussion of research methods and their appropriate application. A program of research, especially one structured across several years, is ideally characterized by procedures to guide selection of questions through a process of setting research priorities. Such a program also ensures that findings can be replicated, deepens understanding, charts progress, and assesses the degree of convergence across studies and research methods. The research program on reading comprehension that we propose here should be a model for effectively choosing and using appropriate and diverse methods.

The Research Infrastructure: Organizing for Programmatic Research on Reading Comprehension

Procedures for getting from here to there also need to be in place. These procedures should at least encompass decisions about how Requests for Applications (RFAs) will be researched and written, who should serve on review panels, and how the accumulation of research findings will be monitored to serve as input to later RFAs.

To ensure that a long-term, large-scale initiative in reading comprehension research is successful, several infrastructure issues must be addressed. Concerns about the quality of educational research and the oversight of projects in the field are widespread. Efforts to extend these resources by collaborations across research entities have enhanced the educational research mission and reflect the judicious use of resources by all the agencies involved in these efforts. Such efforts should be extended, no matter what changes in the organizational structure for education research funding might be undertaken.

1. *Leadership and professionalism.* For this initiative to be successful, the RRSG recommends the following steps to ensure intellectual leadership and long-term planning:

> a. A director should be named to oversee this initiative and related reading research projects.
>
> b. The director should interact and collaborate with individuals across the various federal research entities involved with reading research.
>
> c. The director should interact with the field, help develop proposals, and help synthesize the knowledge base that will emanate from this and other federally sponsored reading research initiatives.
>
> d. The director should not be responsible for review.

As part of this implementation, criteria for evaluating research proposals and procedures for training reviewers and evaluating the quality of reviews need to be developed. A standing review panel with staggered, long-term appointments should be established. Panel members should have expertise that reflects the diversity of the research projects and the methodologies that this initiative is likely to attract. Creating this panel will help to establish continuity in review as well as to possibly provide an advisory component to the reading research program proposed here. This approach to review will provide considerable feedback to investigators in the field, thus contributing to enhanced research expertise. By virtue of the diversity of expertise on the panel, collaborations among researchers with different perspectives will be encouraged. Ultimately, such collaborations will lead to the integration of knowledge across subdisciplines that is essential to advancing our knowledge about reading and instruction. Individuals with limited independent research experience should not be placed on the panel. No reviewer should be appointed to this panel without training and a trial period on the panel, and procedures for terminating reviewers who fail to discharge their responsibilities should be established.

2. *Coordination.* There is an urgent need to coordinate across current efforts, while letting agencies build on their comparative advantages and develop

their own ecological niches. Each federal agency involved in educational research works with its own set of priorities and constraints. The National Institutes of Health (NIH), for example, are well positioned to fund intervention trials but not to fund curriculum development. The National Science Foundation (NSF) has funded Research on Learning Environments and other valuable demonstration projects, but these have so far had limited effect on schools or curricula. The Office of Educational Research and Improvement (OERI) has historically funded a wide array of efforts, including basic research, demonstrations, training, development, technical assistance, and dissemination projects; the payoff from OERI's flexibility has been undermined, though, by its traditionally low funding levels and its failure to focus on particular research topics. At present, funding for R&D activities devoted to reading comprehension is lacking among federal agencies that support education research.

3. *Sustainability*. A fleeting, intermittent, underfunded, or token approach to research on reading comprehension will be a wasted effort. This problem needs sustained attention, support, and funding that cut across administrations and political constituencies. In our view, the size and scope of the effort and the depth of the commitment must be on a scale equal to federal efforts to cure cancer or to develop a network of communications satellites. A number of specific steps will support sustainability.

> a. *Regular syntheses*. Procedures for accumulating, reviewing, and synthesizing knowledge developed through the funded research could be built into the funding effort. The review panel, or perhaps a panel of advisors to the entire research undertaking, might oversee these regular synthesis efforts.

> b. *Talent development*. Sustaining the effort also depends on developing a cadre of well-trained investigators. Much of what we know today about reading comprehension comes from work carried out at the Center for the Study of Reading, which received funding in the late 1970s to mid-1980s. Many researchers active in the field today received their training at this center. A new generation of comprehension researchers is needed, however. To develop a cadre of investigators capable of high-quality research, the RRSG specifically recommends designing research training fellowships and developmental grant programs for young investigators, modeled perhaps on NIH's clinical- and young-investigator postdoctoral awards programs. The optimal training environments for young investigators would give them access to senior researchers from a variety of disciplines and would integrate access to first-rate research training with opportunities to learn about schools and classrooms in an authentic way.

c. *Coordinated solicitations.* Once a reading comprehension agenda is established, research should be solicited in a variety of formats, guided by the nature of the problems under investigation. Solicitations should reflect a long-term plan that incorporates a mix of short-term, medium-term, and long-term goals. The crafting of these solicitations should exhibit continuity, reflecting, for example, feedback on the success of earlier solicitations and the knowledge accumulated about the research agenda. The solicitations should reflect an attempt to coordinate across the efforts of various agencies and initiatives. Although field-initiated research should continue to receive support, it is critical that high-quality reading comprehension research be facilitated through carefully crafted initiatives that reflect the priorities identified in this report and the body of knowledge about reading comprehension that will emerge from this initiative. Different types of grants should be supported, including grants that support multiple connected projects around coherent central themes with collaborations among investigators that are of sufficient scale to address the complex issues involved in research on reading comprehension.

d. *Development work.* To sustain and extend the research effort, a systematic procedure for fostering the development of curricula, software, and instructional programs also needs to be in place. Often the practices that rest on research fail to receive prompt distribution because publishers have not yet rewritten their textbooks to reflect those practices or because the professional development efforts for bringing them to scale are inadequate. Attention to publishing, to software development, and to procedures for influencing teacher educational and professional development is needed from the beginning of the research planning.

e. *Sufficient funding.* The effort described in this report requires a significantly greater level of funding than is currently available for educational research. Improving reading comprehension outcomes in a systematic, research-based way will demand a substantial increase in basic knowledge about comprehension processes and large-scale efforts to implement and evaluate improved instructional, teacher preparation, and professional development programs. Urgent national priorities cannot be addressed without adequate resources. Significant federal funding has been appropriated to address such priorities as establishing satellite communications networks, fighting AIDS, curing cancer, and developing stealth bombers. Our view is that failures in reading comprehension are equally as urgent and equally as complicated; we cannot expect the educational equivalent of radar or the polio vaccine. Nor can we expect to make significant progress without a sum of money comparable to what is available for addressing other urgent national priorities. The U.S. government investment in R&D is between 2% and 3% of all national expenditures (gross domestic product). For example, in the areas of health, energy, and transportation, the United States invests between 2% and 3% of the budgeted dollars in R&D. In contrast, only 0.3% of the expenditures focused on K–12 education are spent on R&D (Office of Science and Technology, 1998). If, as a nation, we committed the same level of research-dollar funding to education research as we currently commit to other areas, reading comprehension outcomes could be substantially improved in the next 20 years.

Acknowledgments

The RAND Reading Study Group is comprised as follows:
Chair: Catherine Snow (Harvard University)
Members: Donna Alvermann (University of Georgia), Janice Dole (University of Utah), Jack Fletcher (University of Texas at Houston), Georgia Earnest García (University of Illinois at Urbana-Champaign), Irene Gaskins (The Benchmark School), Arthur Graesser (University of Memphis), John T. Guthrie (University of Maryland), Michael L. Kamil (Stanford University), William Nagy (Seattle Pacific University), Annemarie Sullivan Palincsar (University of Michigan), Dorothy Strickland (Rutgers University), Frank Vellutino (State University of New York at Albany), Joanna Williams (Columbia University)

Notes

[1] Pasteur's quadrant refers to the quadrant of research defined by simultaneous contribution to basic and applied problems. Pasteur's contributions to the understanding of infection and contamination constituted theoretical breakthroughs at the same time that they also formed a basis for fighting disease and promoting public health.

References

Cazden, C. (1988). *Classroom discourse: The language of teaching and learning.* Portsmouth, NH: Heinemann.

Erickson, F. (1992). Ethnographic microanalysis of interaction. In M.D. LeCompte, W.L. Millroy, & J. Preissle (Eds.), *The handbook of qualitative research in education* (pp. 201–225). London: Academic.

Lee, V.E. (2000). Using hierarchical linear modeling to study social contexts: The case of school effects. *Educational Psychologist, 35*(2), 125–141.

National Institute of Child Health and Human Development. (2000). *Report of the National Reading Panel. Teaching children to read: An evidence-based assessment of the scientific research literature on reading and its implications for reading instruction* (NIH Publication No. 00-4769). Washington, DC: U.S. Government Printing Office.

Nevitt, J., & Hancock, G.R. (2000). Improving the root mean square error of approximation for nonnormal conditions in structural equation modeling. *Journal of Experimental Education, 68*(3), 251–268.

Office of Science and Technology Policy. (1998). *Investing in our future: A national research initiative for America's children for the 21st century.* Washington, DC: The White House.

Pedhazur, E.J., & Schmelkin, L.P. (1991). *Measurement, design, and analysis: An integrated approach.* Hillsdale, NJ: Erlbaum.

Pressley, M., & Afflerbach, P. (1995). *Verbal protocols of reading: The nature of constructively responsive reading*. Hillsdale, NJ: Erlbaum.

Pressley, M., Wharton-McDonald, R., Allington, R., Block, C.C., Morrow, L., Tracey, D., et al. (2001). A study of effective first-grade literacy instruction. *Scientific Studies of Reading, 5*(1), 35–58.

Schafer, W.D. (1999). An overview of meta-analysis. *Measurement and Evaluation in Counseling and Development, 32*(1), 43–61.

Stigler, J.W., Gallimore, R., & Hiebert, J. (2000). Using video surveys to compare classrooms and teaching across cultures: Examples and lessons from the TIMSS video studies. *Educational Psychologist, 35*(2), 87–100.

Stigler, J.W., Gonzales, P., Kawanaka, T., Knoll, S., & Serrano, A. (1999). The TIMSS videotape classroom study: Methods and findings from an exploratory research project on eighth-grade mathematics instruction in Germany, Japan, and the United States. *Education Statistics Quarterly, 1*(2), 109–112.

Turner, J.C., & Meyer, D.K. (2000). Studying and understanding the instructional contexts of classrooms: Using our past to forge our future. *Educational Psychologist, 35*(2), 69–85.

54

Toward a Theory of New Literacies Emerging From the Internet and Other Information and Communication Technologies

Donald J. Leu, Jr., Charles K. Kinzer, Julie L. Coiro, and Dana W. Cammack

The essence of both reading and reading instruction is change. Reading a book changes us forever as we return from the worlds we inhabit during our reading journeys with new insights about our surroundings and ourselves. Teaching a student to read is also a transforming experience. It opens new windows to the world and creates a lifetime of opportunities. Change defines our work as both literacy educators and researchers—by teaching a student to read, we change the world.

Today, reading, reading instruction, and more broadly conceived notions of literacy and literacy instruction are being defined by change in even more profound ways as new technologies require new literacies to effectively exploit their potentials (Coiro, 2003; Kinzer & Leander, 2003; Lankshear & Knobel, 2003; Leu, 2000a; Smolin & Lawless, 2003). These include technologies such as gaming software (Gee, 2003), video technologies (O'Brien, 2001), technologies that establish communities on the Internet (Chandler-Olcott & Mahar, 2003), search engines (Jansen, Spink, & Saracevic, 2000), webpages, and many more yet to emerge.

Moreover, these new literacies change regularly as technology opens new possibilities for communication and information. We see this happening today as people redefine literacy practices while they communicate on a chatboard associated with a website, talk to one another using a video cam, or participate in virtual reality role-playing games (Cammack, 2002; King & O'Brien, 2002;

Adapted from Leu, D.J., Jr., & Kinzer, C.K. (2000). The convergence of literacy instruction with networked technologies for information and communication. *Reading Research Quarterly, 35,* 108–127. Copyright © 2000 by the International Reading Association.

Kinzer, 2003; Lewis & Fabos, 1999). The ability to linguistically manipulate identity as well as the norms of conversation to fit these new electronic spaces has implications for both the development of language and conceptions of the role of technology (Crystal, 2001).

All of these practices impact our conceptions of literacy and, ultimately, influence the definitions of literacies in classrooms, at home, and at work. As more and more individuals use new technologies to communicate, these linguistic activities come to shape the ways in which we view and use language and literacy. Most important, new literacies, whether intentionally or unintentionally, impact literacy instruction in classrooms (Hagood, Stevens, & Reinking, 2003; Lankshear & Knobel, 2003; Lewis & Finders, 2002).

Consider, for example, the changes experienced by students who graduate from secondary school this year. Their story teaches us an important lesson about our literacy future. Many graduates started their school career with the literacies of paper, pencil, and book technologies but will finish having encountered the literacies demanded by a wide variety of information and communication technologies (ICTs): Web logs (blogs), word processors, video editors, World Wide Web browsers, Web editors, e-mail, spreadsheets, presentation software, instant messaging, plug-ins for Web resources, listservs, bulletin boards, avatars, virtual worlds, and many others. These students experienced new literacies at the end of their schooling unimagined at the beginning. Given the increasingly rapid pace of change in the technologies of literacy, it is likely that students who begin school this year will experience even more profound changes during their own literacy journeys. Moreover, this story will be repeated again and again as new generations of students encounter yet unimagined ICTs as they move through school and develop currently unenvisioned new literacies.

While it is clear that many new literacies are emerging rapidly, we believe the most essential ones for schools to consider cluster around the Internet and allow students to exploit the extensive ICTs that become available in an online, networked environment. In an information age, we believe it becomes essential to prepare students for these new literacies because they are central to the use of information and the acquisition of knowledge. Traditional definitions of literacy and literacy instruction will be insufficient if we seek to provide students with the futures they deserve.

Precisely what are the new literacies of the Internet and other ICTs? Any realistic analysis of what we know about new literacies from the traditional research literature must recognize that we actually know very little. Far too little research has been conducted in this area for far too long. This is, perhaps, the most troublesome observation that results from any analysis of research in this area (Lankshear & Knobel, 2003; Leu, 2000a).

Another important problem is that we lack a precise definition of what new literacies are. This makes theory development as well as systematic investigation impossible. In order to move forward in this area, we have begun to frame a conception of new literacies around the following definition:

> The new literacies of the Internet and other ICTs include the skills, strategies, and dispositions necessary to successfully use and adapt to the rapidly changing information and communication technologies and contexts that continuously emerge in our world and influence all areas of our personal and professional lives. These new literacies allow us to use the Internet and other ICTs to identify important questions, locate information, critically evaluate the usefulness of that information, synthesize information to answer those questions, and then communicate the answers to others.

A more precise definition of these new literacies may never be possible to achieve because their most important characteristic is that they change regularly; as new technologies for information and communication continually appear, still newer literacies emerge (Bruce, 1997a; Leu, 2000a; Reinking, 1998). The continuous nature of these profound changes requires new theories to help us understand them and also to direct the important research agenda that lies ahead. We argue that new theoretical perspectives must emerge from the new literacies engendered by the requirements and possibilities of new technologies.

The purpose of this chapter is to explore promising lines of theoretical work and to show how a New Literacies Perspective, a theoretical perspective that has informed much of our own work, can provide important insights into the important changes taking place to literacy as the Internet and other ICTs enter our world. We begin by considering the social contexts throughout history that have shaped both the function and form of literate behavior. Next, we discuss literacy within today's social context and explain how this has produced new ICTs, such as the Internet, and the new literacies that these technologies demand. Third, we explore several theoretical perspectives that are emerging and argue why we believe a New Literacies Perspective is especially useful to understand changes taking place to the nature of reading as well as more broadly conceived notions of literacy. Then, we identify a list of 10 principles that inform a New Literacies Perspective. We conclude by considering the implications of this perspective for both research and practice.

Literacy Within Social and Historical Contexts

The forms and functions of literacy, as well as literacy instruction itself, are largely determined by the continuously changing social forces at work within any society and the technologies these forces often produce (Boyarin, 1993; Diringer, 1968; Gee, 1996; Illera, 1997; Manguel, 1996; Mathews, 1966; Smith, 1965). Historically, the social forces affecting the nature of literacy have had diverse origins. The need to record business transactions in societies moving out of a subsistence economy, the forces of oppression and resistance, the dissemination of religious dogma, the emergence of democratic institutions, and many other disparate forces all have influenced the nature of literacy in different eras.

Often, we lose sight of these historic roots. We need to remember that social forces and the technologies they often produce define the changing nature of literacy today just as much as they have in the past. Briefly identifying previous historical contexts will remind us of how important it is to understand this point before we explore the changing nature of literacy within our contemporary context.

The manner in which social forces define the nature of literacy can be seen at the beginning of written language, which most believe took place in Sumerian society during the fourth century B.C. As agricultural technologies improved, allowing this civilization to expand, it became necessary to record business transactions and tax records. This social necessity prompted the development of the first writing technology, cuneiform tablets that were used throughout Mesopotamia to initially record economic exchanges and tax obligations (Boyarin, 1993; Diringer, 1968; Manguel, 1996).

In other cultural contexts, literacy became a way to communicate common experiences among the oppressed, often using a special symbolic system. In 11th-century Japan, the women at court developed a separate language system and Lady Murasaki used this to write the first novel, *The Tale of the Genji* (Manguel, 1996; Morris, 1964). The language system she used allowed this novel and other writing to be shared only among the women at court who could understand it.

Responses to oppression also shaped the nature of literacy in Czarist Russia among radical members of society. Revolutionaries developed *samizdat*, a secretive system for the self-publication of texts and literature prohibited by the government. From this clandestine form of writing and reading emerged a set of symbolic representations for revolution and resistance, many of which made their way past unknowing censors into officially published works of literature (Teras, 1994).

At other times, the need to spread religious dogma has shaped the form and function of literacy. In medieval Europe, for example, the Christian church used literacy as a vehicle to enforce a common religion in a world with competing religious viewpoints. A literate priesthood was used to faithfully copy, read, and interpret common religious texts. Holding literacy, the technologies of literacy, and the central texts of Christianity so tightly within a priesthood enabled this religion to survive across enormous distances, cultures, and time, while it also enforced inequities in power.

Forces of resistance inevitably emerged, however, largely due to the belief that individuals, not priests, should be responsible for their own salvation. In postreformation Europe, literacy became much more widespread as Martin Luther argued the need for individuals to read and directly access religious texts on their own. Simultaneous with this resistance, printing technologies and new book literacies emerged to enable this more individual definition of salvation and a more distributed definition of literacy.

The printing of books and the emergence of a more widely distributed literacy posed an important political threat to autocratic governments. In England and her colonies, the royal government carefully restricted printing presses. Until 1695, when the Licensing Act of 1662 expired, printing was confined to London, York, and the universities at Oxford and Cambridge (Ford, 2001). Printing was completely forbidden in the royal colony of Virginia until 1730. As one Governor of Virginia, Sir William Berkeley (1642–1652 and 1660–1677) put it, "But, I thank God, there are no free schools nor printing...for learning has brought disobedience, and heresy, and sects into the world, and printing has divulged them, and libels against the best government. God keep us from both" (Ford, 2001, p. 6).

In the United States and other countries, the development of democracy, based on informed citizens making reasoned decisions at the ballot box, led to an even more widely distributed definition of literacy, one that included debate within a free press. The development of democracy also led to the establishment of public schools charged with developing citizens who were literate, and in their literacy might be thoughtfully informed about important national affairs in which many were expected to participate (Kaestle, Damon-Moore, Stedmen, Tinsley, & Trollinger, 1993; Mathews, 1966).

It is clear that social contexts profoundly shape the changing nature of literacy. It is also true that social contexts influence the changing nature of literacy instruction. Nila Banton Smith (1965) demonstrated how social forces at work within the United States regularly altered the nature of literacy instruction:

> The story of American reading is a fascinating one to pursue.... It is a story which reflects the changing religious, economic, and political institutions of a growing and progressive country.... This evolutionary progress in reading has been marked by a series of emphases, each of which has been so fundamental in nature as to have controlled, to a large extent, both the method and content of reading instruction during the period of its greatest intensity. (p. 1)

Smith went on to describe different periods of reading instruction and how each was shaped by the most powerful social forces of its time. These included periods during which reading instruction was influenced by religion (1607–1776), nation building and morality (1776–1840), the education of an intelligent citizenry (1840–1880), the view of reading as a cultural asset (1880–1910), the scientific investigation of reading (1910–1935), international conflict (1935–1950), and culminating, in a prescient analysis, with a period of expanding knowledge and technological revolution (1950 to the present).

Throughout history, literacy and literacy instruction have changed regularly as a result of changing social contexts and the technologies they often prompt. Clearly, the social forces in the present context will exert similar changes. Thus, any attempt to develop a theoretical framework around newly emerging technologies and new literacies must begin by exploring the important social forces at work today. Such an exploration provides the foundation for the New Literacies Perspective.

Literacy in Today's Social Context

What are the important social forces at work today that frame the changes to literacy that we are experiencing? We believe these social forces include the following:

- global economic competition within economies based increasingly on the effective use of information and communication
- the rapid emergence of the Internet as a powerful new technology for information and communication
- public policy initiatives by governments around the world to ensure higher levels of literacy achievement including the use of the Internet and other ICTs

Global Economic Competition Within Economies Based Increasingly on the Effective Use of Information and Communication

The world of work is undergoing fundamental transformation (Bruce, 1997b; Drucker, 1994; Gilster, 1997; Mikulecky & Kirkley, 1998; The New London Group, 2000). Indeed, it is this social context that prompts many of the changes to ICTs and to literacy that we are experiencing, making the effective use of the Internet a necessary component of the literacy curriculum.

In some historical contexts, the nature of work has been defined by one's access to land, labor, or financial capital. Analyses by Bell (1977), Burton-Jones (1999), Reich (1992), and others indicate this definition has changed fundamentally within nations developing postindustrial economies. Increasingly, it is access to information and the ability to use information effectively that enables individuals to seize life's opportunities. More and more frequently, work is characterized by the effective use of information to solve important problems within a globally competitive economy. Moreover, as networked, digital technologies provide increasingly greater access to larger amounts of information, the efficient use of information skills in competitive workplace contexts becomes even more important (Gilster, 1997; Harrison & Stephen, 1996).

Because trade barriers are falling and international trade is expanding, many workplaces are undergoing a radical transformation (Bruce, 1997a; Drucker, 1994; Gilster, 1997; Mikulecky & Kirkley, 1998). In a global economy in which competition is more intense because competing organizations are more numerous and markets are more extensive, workplaces must seek more productive ways of performing if they hope to survive. Often, they seek to transform themselves into high-performance workplaces that are more productive and more responsive to the needs of their customers.

Traditionally, industrial-age organizations were organized in a vertical, top-down fashion. Most decisions were made at the highest levels and then communicated to lower levels, thus wasting much of the intellectual capital within an organization by using tight command and control structures. Information-age organizations seeking to achieve greater productivity are organized horizontally, with teams within lower levels of the organization empowered to make important decisions related to their functioning. Members of these teams must quickly identify important problems, locate useful information related to the problems they identify, critically evaluate the information they find, synthesize this information to solve the problems, and then quickly communicate the solutions to others so that everyone within an organization is informed. These high-performance workplaces seek more fully to utilize the intellectual capital among every employee. This change has had a fundamental effect on the nature of literacy within these organizations.

Each element of change that characterizes the workplace today has important implications for the nature of literacy instruction. First, the change to a high-performance workplace requires organizations to place a premium on people who possess effective problem-solving skills. As collaborative teams seek more effective ways of working, they are expected to identify problems important to their unit and seek appropriate solutions. This has important consequences for schools that will need to provide students with greater preparation in identifying important problems and then solving them, often in collaborative situations.

Having identified important problems, members of high-performance workplace teams must then locate useful information related to those problems. Knowing how, when, and where to locate useful information on the Internet, or on an Intranet, will become an increasingly important component of the literacy curriculum, especially because the availability of information resources and search technologies is expanding rapidly, increasing the importance of effective search strategies.

Having acquired information resources, members of high-performance workplace teams must then know how to critically evaluate that information, sorting out accurate information from inaccurate information, essential information from less-essential information, and biased information from unbiased information. These critical literacies and analytic skills also will become increasingly important elements in the literacy curriculum because they are essential to the careful evaluation of any information one obtains, something that is essential in an informational space such as the Internet where anyone may publish anything.

The ability to synthesize information that one has gathered also will become increasingly important because the ability to use information to solve problems is the essential qualification of successful performance in a globally competitive information economy. We will need to pay increasing importance to informational synthesis in schools to support this important skill.

Finally, members of high-performance workplace teams need to rapidly and clearly communicate their solutions to colleagues in other organizational units. A decentralized workplace requires collaboration and communication skills so that the best decisions get made at every level in an organization and so that changes at one level are clearly communicated to other levels. Because each unit is empowered to identify and solve problems, one must keep others informed of changes that are taking place and negotiate these changes with others who might be affected by them. We need to support the development of effective collaboration and communication skills using new communication technologies if we wish to prepare children for their futures in a world where these skills are so important.

It is not surprising that the Internet and other ICTs have appeared and become such a prominent part of our lives during the transition from an industrial to a postindustrial society. These new information and communication tools allow us to identify important problems, quickly gather information, critically evaluate the information we locate, synthesize that information into a solution, and then communicate the solution to others. The new literacies required to effectively use ICTs to accomplish these functions are central to success in an information age.

It is important, however, to recognize that new literacies do not simply create more productive workers and workplaces. Just as important, the new literacies of the Internet and other ICTs provide individuals with opportunities to make their personal lives more productive and fulfilling. This might happen while refinancing a home, selecting a university, advocating for social justice, purchasing books, or any one of hundreds of other tasks important to daily life. In addition, we are beginning to see that the new literacies of the Internet and other ICTs permit greater civic engagement in democratic institutions. Increasingly, national and local politics are changing as more citizens discover important information about candidates, participate online in campaign efforts, organize online communities to support various political agendas, and communicate more frequently with their representatives via e-mail. Expertise in the new literacies of the Internet and other ICTs helps individuals have more satisfying personal lives, more engaged civic lives, as well as more productive professional lives.

The Rapid Emergence of the Internet as a Powerful New Technology for Information and Communication

The appearance of the Internet is not a spontaneous, arbitrary event. It has appeared and become a central part of our lives because the nature of the workplace and other social institutions is changing.

In the workplace, survey data from the United States show recent rapid increases in Internet use, revealing changes taking place from the restructuring process described in the previous section. In just one year (August 2000 to September 2001), use of the Internet at work among all employed adults 25 years of age and older increased by nearly 60%, from 26.1% of the workforce to 41.7% (U.S. Department of Commerce, 2002). If this rate of increase continues, nearly everyone in the workforce will be using the Internet at work within just a few years. Currently, workers in positions with the highest levels of education report the highest levels of Internet use in the United States. In managerial positions with some professional specialty, 80.5% of workers report using the Internet. But even in technical, sales, and administrative support positions, 70.5% of workers report using the Internet (U.S. Department of Commerce, 2002). Clearly the Internet is rapidly becoming central to full participation in the workplace.

Statistics on Internet usage at home in the United States parallel these changes in the workplace. Nearly 60% of all households report that they had Internet access in 2002. Among those who had not previously used the Internet, 47% report that they are somewhat likely or very likely to go online during 2003 (Lebo, 2003). Moreover, the percentage of U.S. households with broadband Internet access has been doubling each year from 1998 to 2001, an adoption rate in households exceeding that of any previous technology including telephones, color televisions, videocassette recorders, cellular phones, and pagers (U.S. Department of Commerce, 2002). Most interesting, perhaps, is that Internet users report an increase in time they spend on the Internet and a decrease in the time they spend viewing television (Lebo, 2003). Internet users report watching about 10% fewer hours of television per week in 2002 (11.2 hours per week) compared to 2001 (12.3 hours per week). This pattern also holds true for U.S. children: Nearly 33% of children reported in 2002 that they are viewing less television than before they started using the Internet; this frequency is up nearly 50% from just one year earlier (Lebo, 2003).

The Internet also is appearing in school classrooms in the United States and other countries at a rate that parallels its appearance in the workplace and at home. In only eight years (1994 to 2002), the percentage of classrooms in the United States possessing at least one computer with Internet access has gone from 3% to 92% (National Center for Education Statistics [NCES], 2003a). This is an adoption rate that is unprecedented in schools for any previous technology including televisions, radios, telephones, videocassette recorders, and even books. The availability of Internet access has had a demonstrated impact on students. In 2001, 94% of children ages 12–17 who had Internet access said that they used the Internet for school-related research (Lenhart, Simon, & Graziano, 2001).

The quality of Internet access in schools has also undergone a rapid transformation. In 1996, three quarters of U.S. public schools with Internet connections reported using phone modem access (Heaviside, Riggins, & Farris, 1997), while in 2002, 94% of schools reported having broadband access (NCES, 2003a), permitting faster access to richer, more memory intensive media. The rate at which schools have moved from phone modem access to broadband access in the United States is even faster than this same migration in homes (cf. Lebo, 2003).

Thus, it is clear that the Internet is rapidly finding its way to a central location in the workplace as well as in home and school contexts. We believe that the appearance of the Internet in the workplace as well as in home and school contexts is one of the most powerful social revolutions taking place today. At the heart of this revolution are the new literacy skills and strategies demanded by the Internet and other ICTs.

Public Policy Initiatives by Governments Around the World to Ensure Higher Levels of Literacy Achievement

Governments around the world are keenly aware of the consequences of global economic competition for their citizens. They have responded by implementing public policies to raise literacy achievement in an attempt to better prepare their children for the challenges that lie ahead. Simultaneously, they have responded with initiatives that provide new ICTs resources to schools in an effort to prepare children for the new literacies of their future. These simultaneous steps by nations around the world are the beginning of a convergence we anticipate for literacy instruction with networked technologies for information and communication (Leu & Kinzer, 2000).

In the United Kingdom, for example, education has been identified as a top priority of the Labour government. The first white paper of this government, *Excellence in Schools*, explains in detail how higher standards for literacy are to be developed and achieved in England, Wales, and Northern Ireland (U.K. Secretary of State for Education and Skills, 1997). The reason for this is clearly linked to global competition in an information age and the implications of a restructured economy: "We are talking about investing in the human capital in the age of knowledge. To compete in a global economy...we will have to unlock the potential of every young person" (p. 3).

The U.K. Department for Education and Skills (formerly Department of Education and Employment) has published other papers such as this at "The Standards Site" (www.standards.dfee.gov.uk). Both the national standards and the new national curriculum have included ICTs for the first time (U.K. Department for Education and Skills, 1998). Finally, a National Grid for Learning (www.ngfl.gov.uk) was launched in 1998 to provide an online national portal for teacher and student learning.

Similar policy initiatives are taking place in Finland, one of the first nations to begin this work. The Finnish government appointed an expert committee in 1994 to prepare a national strategy for education, training, and research in an information society. This report, *Education, Training and Research in the Information Society: A National Strategy* (Finland Ministry of Education, 1995), outlines the important role the educational system can play in helping Finland to compete in a global information economy. The report served as the impetus for a number of initiatives from the Ministry of Education, including a three-year program launched in 1996 to teach students effective use of ICTs in schools. This program included developing new teaching methods for the use of ICTs, connecting all schools to the Internet before the year 2000, and providing new computers to schools. Most important, the program also provides every teacher with five weeks of paid release time for professional development in the instructional use of new information technologies (Finland Ministry of Education, 1998; R. Svedlin, personal communication, January 8, 1998).

Ireland, like many other nations, also launched two policy initiatives: a National Reading Initiative and a Schools IT 2000 initiative. The National Reading Initiative included the appointment of a national coordinator, provision for remedial services in every school, a tripling of adult literacy funding, increased funding for remedial teachers, and a program of development for literacy-related software (Ireland Department of Education and Science, 1998).

The Schools IT 2000 initiative (Ireland Department of Education and Science, 1998) was implemented because "knowledge and familiarity with new technologies will be an important dimension of employability in the information society" (Ireland Department of Education and Science, 1998). Schools IT 2000 encompassed a number of policy initiatives intended to prepare children for a competitive, global, information economy. These included (a) a Technology Integration Initiative to provide more than 15,000 computers and Internet connections in 1998 with additional funds available during subsequent years; (b) a Teacher Skills Initiative to provide training in ICTs for more than 8,000 teachers; (c) a Schools Support Initiative to develop ScoilNet (www.scoilnet.ie), an Internet portal site to provide information and support for educators; and (d) a School Integration Project to provide funding for at least 40 model schools that will demonstrate the effective use of ICTs in the classroom.

Important policy initiatives also are underway in Australia. In April 1999, the federal government approved *The Adelaide Declaration on National Goals for Schooling in the Twenty-First Century* (Australia Department of Education, Science and Training, 2004), which included an emphasis on both literacy and IT. In particular, the goals noted that "When students leave school, they should...be confident, creative and productive users of new technologies, particularly information and communication technologies." Moreover, the federal government has developed *A Strategic Framework for the Information Economy: Identifying Priorities for Action* (Australia National Office for the Information Economy, 1999), which outlines a national strategy and 10 action priorities for becoming more competitive in a global information economy. The second priority focuses on the role of schools in preparing children in information technology: "Deliver the education and skills Australians need to participate in the information economy."

Finally, the federal government along with commonwealth, state, and territory education departments has developed an online Internet portal, Education Network Australia (www.edna.edu.au). This extensive resource provides a range of information resources for children, teachers, professors, researchers, and policymakers.

New Zealand is also beginning public policy initiatives to raise literacy achievement and to integrate ICTs into the curriculum. At the end of 1998, the government announced that it intended to develop a National Literacy and Numeracy Strategy to enable every 9-year-old to become proficient in reading, writing, and mathematics by 2005 (Literacy Strategy Underway, 1999). As part of this effort, the government appointed a National Literacy Taskforce to assist in developing this strategy. In addition to the need to be competitive in the global economy, the impetus for this is the need to close the gap between good and poor readers (Literacy Strategy Underway, 1999).

Simultaneous with these initiatives in literacy education, the New Zealand national government released a policy paper titled *Interactive Education: An Information and Communication Technologies (ICTs) Strategy for Schools* (New Zealand Ministry of Education, 1998) which describes strategies for supporting the use of ICTs in the nation's schools. This document defines the focus for national initiatives in ICTs: building infrastructure and improving the capability of schools to use ICTs effectively in the curriculum. It describes several new initiatives the national government took in 1999: developing an online portal site for schools, teachers, and children (*Te Kete Ipurangi*, available at www.tki.org.nz/e/tki); providing support for professional development so schools can plan for and implement the use of ICTs more effectively; and supporting model ICTs professional development schools. The reason for these initiatives again was related to global economic competition: "New Zealand schools aim to create a learning environment that enables students to develop the attitudes, knowledge, understandings, and skills to enable them...to succeed in the modern competitive economy" (New Zealand Ministry of Education, 1998, Introduction).

The United States has a long history of state and local control over educational policies and a recent past characterized by intense partisanship at the federal level over educational issues. As a result, national policy initiatives have been difficult to implement in education. Prior to 2002, most of the public policy initiatives for raising literacy achievement took place at the state level. Many states established standards or benchmarks, often in conjunction with new statewide assessment instruments. Many states also initiated polices to infuse more IT and ICTs in the classroom.

At the federal level, educational policy initiatives had been more diffuse in origin, and many were implemented only after bitter partisan debates. Nevertheless, several important initiatives at the federal level have focused on literacy issues. These initiatives produced legislation such as The Reading Excellence

Act, the appointment of a National Reading Panel, and the development of Standards for the English Language Arts (International Reading Association [IRA] & National Council of Teachers of English [NCTE],1996). Each of these initiatives, designed to improve reading achievement, was marked by substantial controversy. The controversy has continued with the passage of the No Child Left Behind Act in 2002.

The No Child Left Behind Act enacts an extensive list of public policy initiatives, many of which are also designed to increase student achievement in reading. These provisions include several requirements: that all students are proficient in reading and math within 12 years; that assessment in both reading and math be conducted annually for all students in grades 3–8 and be conducted at least once in grades 10–12; that reading programs be funded only if they are based on scientifically based reading research; and that all teachers be highly qualified, with state certification.

Similar to other nations, this major policy initiative in reading also contains a technology component. Title II, Section D, of the No Child Left Behind Act is devoted to technology with the stated goal, "To assist every student in crossing the digital divide by ensuring that every student is technologically literate by the time the student finishes the eighth grade, regardless of the student's race, ethnicity, gender, family income, geographic location, or disability." In order to promote the goals of this section, the U.S. federal government plans to provide $1 million each year, most of which will go for state and local technology grants. States must provide a long-range plan for implementing this initiative, and all local units must devote a minimum of 25% of the funds to professional development in the instructional use of the Internet and other ICTs. In addition, the Secretary of Education is charged with developing a national educational technology plan.

In addition to the No Child Left Behind Act, a major policy initiative has been the establishment of the Universal Service Support Mechanism for Schools and Libraries, a policy initiative known informally as the "E-rate program." This program is funded by Congress under the Telecommunications Act of 1996 and is administered by the Schools and Libraries Division (SLD) of the Universal Service Administrative Company (www.sl.universalservice.org), a nonprofit organization established by the Federal Communications Commission for this purpose. Starting in 1998, the program began to annually distribute up to $2.25 billion in financial support to schools and libraries for Internet access based on indicators of financial need. This program has contributed in important ways to the rapid infusion of Internet-connected computers within the K–12 classrooms of the United States.

In summary, many nations around the world, aware of the need to prepare students for the challenges of a competitive global economy, are developing public policy initiatives to raise literacy standards and infuse ICTs into the curriculum. While each nation approaches the issue in its own fashion, what is striking is the common effort in this direction. Especially salient is the federal response from those nations, like Australia and the United States, with a long tradition of local control and little previous history of federal intervention. Even these countries are beginning to develop important national initiatives to raise literacy levels and prepare children in the use of ICTs.

The Importance of an Expanded Definition of Literacy: Emerging Theoretical Perspectives[1]

We have seen how three important social forces in today's world are shaping both the forms and functions of literacy:

1. global economic competition within economies based increasingly on the effective use of information and communication

2. the rapid emergence of the Internet as a powerful new technology for information and communication

3. public policy initiatives by governments around the world to ensure higher levels of literacy achievement, including the use of the Internet and other ICTs

It is clear that the nature of literacy is changing rapidly as new ICTs appear, requiring new literacies to fully exploit their potential in what Reinking (1998) has called our "post-typographic" world. These changes make it increasingly impossible to function in the worlds of research, theory, and practice if we define literacy in ways that ignore the reality of the new literacies of the Internet and other ICTs. Questions and issues about types of texts, types of literacies, assessment, curriculum, and teacher education, and how these are impacted by present and emerging technologies, must be addressed if we are to shape theories and pedagogies of literacy that dynamically respond to social and technological change.

Yet to address these issues in a cogent manner, we must begin to develop an adequate definition of what it means to be literate. To develop such a definition, one must ask whether *literacy* as a term presupposes print, whether it presupposes text. Does literacy mean comprehension of print or comprehension of a message that has permanence in ways that a nonrecorded oral message does not? Does reading children's literature presuppose a printed children's book, or can children's literature exist on a CD-ROM or website? Does text presuppose only print, or does it include all aspects in an author's toolbox, which allows meaning to be preserved for later reading and response by an audience?

In addition, definitions and theories of literacy also must consider the rapid changes we are experiencing today as new ICTs regularly emerge. We have argued that the definition of literacy has always changed over historical periods but that it is changing today at a pace we have never before experienced as new technologies for information and communication appear rapidly and continuously

(Leu, 2000a; Leu & Kinzer, 2000). Literacy, therefore, may be thought of as a moving target, continually changing its meaning depending on what society expects literate individuals to do. As societal expectations for literacy change, and as the demands on literate functions in a society change, so too must definitions of literacy change to reflect this moving target.

Current definitions of literacy have moved well beyond earlier definitions of literacy as the ability to sound out words and/or copy accurately what is dictated. Definitions of reading, for example, have moved far beyond Flesch's (1955, 1981) views that "[we should teach the child] letter-by-letter and sound-by-sound until he knows it—and when he knows it, he knows how to read" (1955, p. 121) and "learning to read is like learning to drive a car.... The child learns the mechanics of reading, and when he's through, he can read" (1981, p. 3). Definitions by Dechant (1982), Goodman (1976), Rumelhart (1994; see #41 this volume), and others include one's interaction between the text and the reader and include comprehension of the message in addition to decoding the printed page. These authors recognized that the ability to communicate, to present one's message, and to understand and evaluate another's message is part of reading, and that an interaction and transaction into one's experiences as well as personal response and meaning-making is part of the goal for literacy instruction (Harste, 1990; Rosenblatt, 1994, see #48 this volume; Shanahan, 1990). Yet all these definitions come from a perspective of print and owe their historical roots and conceptions of literacy to a largely print-based world.

Of course, these definitions can be applied to literacy in technological environments to the extent that the symbol systems available to readers and writers when the definitions were conceptualized also exist in electronic environments. However, to the extent that there are additional demands and capabilities of literacy in electronic environments beyond those available at the times respective definitions were conceptualized, current definitions may be less applicable. And, perhaps, the greatest shortcomings of current definitions can be seen in the requirements of interactions between traditionally available literacy resources and new ones, and in the demands on readers and writers that were previously not required for authorship, comprehension, and response to occur. We argue that, as the medium of the message changes, comprehension processes, decoding processes, and what "counts" as literacy activities must change to reflect readers' and authors' present-day strategies for comprehension and response.

Clearly, definitions of literacy must change to include electronic environments. In some ways, however, incorporating technology into definitions of literacy becomes less an argument about whether or not such changes are needed or are effective and more a recognition that schools must incorporate technology or be viewed as out of touch or even irrelevant (see, e.g., Hagood, Stevens, & Reinking, 2003; Lewis & Finders, 2002). Even though many are calling for more research on the efficacy of technology in learning, there is increasing recognition that technology is here to stay; the demand from businesses, parents, and society at large is such that technology will continue to appear in schools even before research outcomes are known.

In sum, the significance of the increasing availability of technology within and beyond schools relates to their situated use in literacy practice, and perhaps relates just as much to the symbolic capital (Bourdieu, 1991) of the technologies in relation to the social spaces of schooling (Bromley & Apple, 1998; Bruce, 1997a). Technology availability in schools both changes literate signifying practices and signifies change in and of itself. The material and ideological meanings of the computer, as with any tool (Cole, 1996), are deeply intertwined. While this double relation of meaning is true across the subject areas of schooling, it may be particularly true for language arts given the significant construction of a discourse on *technological* knowledge as a form of literacy. In this sense, *literacy* might index a very broad range of knowledge and practice (e.g., having technical skill across programs and platforms, knowing how to install and upgrade software) with developing technologies.

Within such a web of practice and representation, schools and districts lacking technology could well be imagined as only "partially literate" spaces. This, of course, is not an argument for the proliferation of technology in schooling. Rather, it is an argument that, in many ways, the meaning of schooled literacy has already been (and will continue to be) articulated with the availability and meaning of technology. As Cammack (2003) points out in her review of Alvermann's (2002) edited volume, "differences in technology use and perceptions of value between teachers and students can effectively act to block change in the integration and use of technology in literacy pedagogy."

Definitions of literacy must move beyond being located in only paper-printed media. Children's literature cannot be limited only to the pages in a paper-based book of printed pages, but must include books in electronic formats as well. The added information and capabilities that electronic formats provide for authors and readers necessitate an expanded view of literacy, what it means to be literate, and what it means to be a teacher (and learner) in the language arts.

Consider, for example, that "decoding" in a print context involves decoding the alphabetic characters as well as any pictures, charts, maps, and graphs that are included on the page. In this sense, the decoding and interpretation of graphics and other forms of media as literacy practice is certainly not a new development, and over the last decade or so researchers have been giving increasing attention to the significance of images, television, drama, and other forms of media in the literate lives of children (Alvermann, Hinchman, Moore, Phelps, & Waff, 1998; Dyson, 1999; Flood & Lapp, 1995). Such work provides an important research base from which to analyze literacy practices in the multimedia environment of the Internet.

At the same time, the nature and relationships of Internet multimedia also pose unique problems that the study of offline multimedia forms cannot address adequately. For example, forms of decoding are developing that were either relatively minor or simply not possible offline. In an electronic environment, decoding for comprehension includes decoding the strategic use of color; various clues that indicate hyperlinked texts and graphics; the possible actions of meaning-bearing icons and animations; and pictures, maps, charts, and graphs that are not static, but that can change to address questions that an interactive reader can pose to informational text during the reading act. Although definitions of literacy still must include concepts of composition, decoding, comprehension, and response, in order to understand how each of these definitional factors play out in electronic environments we must take into account current uses as indicators of current definitions of literacy.

With personal computers' and the Internet's graphical interfaces, it is no longer possible to position the print text as the focal text in all instances, with images serving only a supporting role in meaning construction. As many webpages are overwhelmingly an assemblage of images, understanding reading across these images significantly decenters print-based reading (Flood & Lapp, 1995). Hypermedia reading practices have at least as much to do with the multiple relations between images as they do with the paths among segments of print text. Importantly, the nature of images also permits writers and readers to link them in ways other than paper-based texts. For instance, while typically a term or phrase of text is linked in linear sequence, an image may be divided into an "image map" in which diverse topological parts of the image are linked to other various images, text, video, or media objects. Running a mouse pointer over an image, for example, often "pops up" text without the mouse being clicked, or causes expansion of an image or graphic. Part of a pie chart might expand with new information when the pointer is moved over its slices, yet no overt clue exists that this would occur, presenting a serendipitous and differential experience across readers who might or might not have moved the mouse pointer over the image.

Perhaps more significant, changing definitions must acknowledge the expanded presence of multimedia, which has led to a proliferation of new combinations of authoring (e.g., voice-annotated websites, video clips with hypertextual analysis). Lemke (1998), from a semiotic perspective, argues convincingly that a central problem is that meanings are not fixed and additive, but multiplicative. That is, in the electronic environment what must be interpreted is not a complementary relation of separately developed texts but the expansive signification of an entire sign system. The literacies necessary to understand multiple, interdependent meanings index the need for complex understandings of literacy "toolkits" (Gee, 1990; Wertsch, 1991) for interpreting and producing meaning in hypermedia that includes but extends traditional texts.

Despite all these changes, our understanding of the new literacies required by ICTs is not well advanced. No single theoretical perspective has yet to explain the full range of the changes to literacy brought about by the Internet and other

ICTs. Nevertheless, several useful perspectives are beginning to evolve from various quarters. These include perspectives that focus on critical literacies (Luke, 1997; Muspratt, Luke, & Freebody, 1998), multiliteracies (The New London Group, 2000), media literacy (Tyner, 1998), and others that provide us with insights about the new literacies of ICTs.

Some, for example, have argued that a literacy curriculum during an age of information needs to include new, critical literacies that enable children to adequately evaluate messages from individuals and corporations that shape the information they provide (Muspratt et al., 1998). These authors argue that it is impossible to discuss literacy without considering who is using it and for what purposes. They describe the essential need to understand the stance of the person producing a message, the motive behind the message, and the need to critically evaluate these messages. They foreground the important need to develop critical literacies as an essential element of any instructional program because new media forms, globalization, and economic pressures engender messages that increasingly attempt to persuade individuals to act in ways beneficial to an economic or political unit but not necessarily beneficial to the individual. During an age of information, any theoretical perspective that seeks to capture the changes taking place to literacy must include these essential critical literacies. As the Internet quickly becomes both an important source for information and an important commercial and political context, critical literacies become even more important to our lives.

A second heuristic that is useful comes from the work of The New London Group (2000). Emerging from sociolinguistic traditions, the group uses the construct *multiliteracies* to capture changes taking place in two dimensions central to literacy: (1) the multiple modalities of communication in a world where many new communication technologies have appeared and (2) the growing diversity of culture and language within an increasingly global community. Instead of defining literacy as a unitary construct, this group recognizes the inherent diversity that constructs literacy in a world defined by new technologies of communication and new cultural and linguistic contexts that become more visible with globalization. Within this type of theoretical framework, one might view reading, writing, and communication on the Internet as including a set of multiliteracies, emerging as individuals from different cultural contexts encounter one another within different communication technologies.

Still others (Silverblatt, Ferry, & Finan, 1999; Tyner, 1998) take a media literacy perspective, which focuses on the new literacies required from new media forms. Media literacy perspectives often are closely aligned with critical literacy perspectives, though they focus more on media forms beyond text such as video and the images that often drive a culture. Like those who take a critical literacy perspective, proponents of a media literacy perspective stress the importance of analyzing an author's stance and motives as well as the need for a critical evaluation of the message itself. This perspective is important to include when considering literacy within Internet technologies because these technologies make possible a panoply of media forms within a single message, thus increasing the importance of understanding how each may be used by an author to shape a reader's interpretation. And, because locations on the Internet often are populated with commercial, political, and economic motives, it becomes essential to be able to carefully evaluate these while gathering information (Kinzer & Leander, 2003).

Other theoretical orientations, too, are possible when considering new literacies appearing on the Internet. These include feminist perspectives (Hawisher & Selfe, 1999), perspectives that draw from postmodernist interpretations of popular culture (Alvermann, Moon, & Hagood, 1999), or perspectives that come from work in cultural transformations (Warschauer, 1999). Each has important insights to contribute to understanding the changes that are taking place.

Although each of these perspectives provides essential insights, we believe they are limited for at least two reasons. First, they fail to place the Internet and other ICTs at the center of their perspective. Instead of emerging from the new literacies of the Internet and other ICTs, these theoretical perspectives have evolved from other contexts and have then been applied to the ICTs landscape. We believe the new literacies of the Internet, because they are more encompassing and because they change more rapidly and in more profound ways than traditional print literacies, require their own theoretical framework in order to adequately understand them and the role they should play in a literacy curriculum.

A second limitation also exists. Other theoretical orientations frequently suffer from a narrower theoretical grounding, often because each has emerged from a more limited tradition of inquiry. For example, while a multiliteracies perspective is a most useful one, its sociolinguistic grounding somewhat limits its ability to predict any of the more cognitive and ontological aspects of new literacies that students must develop in order to become literate with the Internet and other ICTs (Lankshear & Knobel, 2003). We believe that any theory must bring multiple perspectives (Labbo & Reinking, 1999) to bear on framing the totality of the new literacies emerging from the Internet and other ICTs if it is to be useful in informing the complex teaching and learning issues within school contexts.

In short, we believe that a theoretical framework for the new literacies of the Internet and other ICTs needs to be grounded in these technologies themselves, taking advantage of the insights that a variety of different perspectives might bring to understanding the complete picture of the new literacies emerging from these technologies.

Identifying Central Principles of New Literacies Emerging From the Internet and Other ICTs

Although it is too early to define a comprehensive theory of new literacies emerging from these technologies, we are convinced that it is time to begin this process by identifying the central principles on which this theory should be built. Our work is pointing us to these principles of a New Literacies Perspective:

1. The Internet and other ICTs are central technologies for literacy within a global community in an information age.
2. The Internet and other ICTs require new literacies to fully access their potential.
3. New literacies are deictic.
4. The relationship between literacy and technology is transactional.
5. New literacies are multiple in nature.
6. Critical literacies are central to the new literacies.
7. New forms of strategic knowledge are central to the new literacies.
8. Speed counts in important ways within the new literacies.
9. Learning often is socially constructed within new literacies.
10. Teachers become more important, though their role changes, within new literacy classrooms.

The Internet and Other ICTs Are Central Technologies for Literacy Within a Global Community in an Information Age

From a sociolinguistic perspective, Gee (1996) and The New London Group (2000) have argued that literacy is embedded in and develops out of the social practices of a culture. We agree and, from a historical perspective, have demonstrated how different literacies have emerged from different social contexts and the technologies they often prompt.

For the past 500 years, literacy has emerged from a variety of social contexts but has been shaped largely by the technologies of the book and the printing press. Today, both the social context and the technologies of our age are rapidly changing. We believe the Internet and other ICTs are quickly becoming the central technologies of literacy for a global community in an information age. As a result, these technologies are quickly defining the new literacies that will increasingly be a part of our future. Literacy theory, research, and practice must begin to recognize this important fact.

Looking briefly at how reading comprehension takes place on the Internet will illustrate how we need to rethink our assumptions about literacy. Traditionally, reading comprehension has often been defined by the construction of meaning from a fixed body of text. On the Internet, reading comprehension takes on a very different and broader definition. New skills and strategies are required in this context to successfully comprehend information such as how to search for appropriate information; how to comprehend search engine results; how to make correct inferences about information that will be found at any hyperlink; how to determine the extent to which authors "shape" information presented on a webpage; how to coordinate and synthesize vast amounts of information, presented in multiple media formats, from a nearly unlimited set of sources; and how to know which informational elements require attention and which ones may be ignored. Perhaps we can best recognize this fundamentally different conception of reading comprehension when we understand that two students, with an identical goal, will construct meaning differently, not only because they bring different background knowledge to the task but also because they will use very different search strategies, follow very different informational paths, read very different sets of information, draw very different critical conclusions about what they have read, and attend to very different informational elements. Reading comprehension has a very different meaning on the Internet (Coiro, 2003).

The Internet and Other ICTs Require New Literacies to Fully Access Their Potential

New literacies include the skills, strategies, and disposition that allow us to use the Internet and other ICTs effectively to identify important questions, locate information, critically evaluate the usefulness of that information, synthesize information to answer those questions, and then communicate the answers to others. We encounter new literacies nearly every time we try to read, write, and communicate with the Internet and other ICTs. Examples of new literacies include

- using a search engine effectively to locate information;
- evaluating the accuracy and utility of information that is located on a webpage in relation to one's purpose;
- using a word processor effectively, including using functions such as checking spelling accuracy, inserting graphics, and formatting text;
- participating effectively in bulletin board or listserv discussions to get needed information;
- knowing how to use e-mail to communicate effectively; and
- inferring correctly the information that may be found at a hyperlink on a webpage.

It is essential, however, to keep in mind that new literacies, such as these, almost always build on foundational literacies rather than replace them. Foundational literacies include those traditional elements of literacy that have defined almost all our previous efforts in both research and practice. These include skill sets such as phonemic awareness, word recognition, decoding knowledge, vocabulary knowledge, comprehension, inferential reasoning, the writing process, spelling, response to literature, and others required for the literacies of the book and other printed material. Foundational literacies will continue to be important within the new literacies of the Internet and other ICTs. In fact, it could be argued that they will become even more essential because reading and writing become more important in an information age. While foundational literacies become more important, they also will be insufficient if one is to fully utilize the Internet and other ICTs (Coiro, 2003; IRA, 2002; Leu, 2000b; RAND Reading Study Group, 2002; Spires & Estes, 2002; Sutherland-Smith, 2002). Reading, writing, and communication will assume new forms as text is combined with new media resources and linked within complex information networks requiring new literacies for their effective use.

New Literacies Are Deictic

Leu (1997a, 2000a) and Leu and Kinzer (2000) have argued that we are entering a period of literacy as technological deixis. During this period, the forms and functions of literacy change rapidly as new technologies for information and communication emerge and as individuals construct new envisionments for their use.

The term *deixis* (dike-sis) is a word used by linguists and others (Fillmore, 1972; Murphy, 1986) for words such as *now*, *today*, *here*, *there*, *go*, and *come*. These are words whose meanings change quickly depending on the time or space in which they are uttered. If we say "now" as we write this draft, it means our current moment during the spring of 2003. If you say "now" when you encounter this example, it means the moment in time when you read these lines. While to Gertrude Stein "A rose is a rose, is a rose," *now* is not *now*, is not *now*. Rather, its meaning depends on the temporal context when it is uttered or written.

Literacy also is deictic (dike-tic). We have seen how both the forms and functions of literacy have changed regularly over time, but because technological change happened slowly, the changes to literacy occurred over extended historical periods. Today, technological change happens so rapidly that the changes to literacy are limited not by technology but rather by our ability to adapt and acquire the new literacies that emerge. Deixis is a defining quality of the new literacies of the Internet and other ICTs. This will continue into the future but at a much faster pace as new technologies repeatedly appear, requiring new skills and new strategies for their effective use. As literacy increasingly becomes deictic, the changing constructions of literacy within new technologies will require all of us to keep up with these changes and to prepare students for a vastly different conception of what it means to become literate.

There are three sources for the deictic nature of literacy: (1) transformations of literacy because of technological change, (2) envisionments of new literacy potentials within new technologies, and (3) the use of increasingly efficient technologies of communication that rapidly spread new literacies. Each source contributes to the fundamental changes taking place in the nature of literacy.

The rapid transformations in the nature of literacy caused by technological change are a primary source for the deictic nature of literacy. New technologies regularly and repeatedly transform previous literacies, regularly redefining what it means to become literate. Consider, for example, the new writing skills required to effectively use a word processor like Microsoft Word. Each time one upgrades to a new version (Word 6, Word 2001, Word 2003, etc.) one must develop new composing and communication skills to take full advantage of the new potentials within each new version. While one might have needed the ability to save documents in different formats in an early version of this program, later versions require additional composing skills such as inserting photographic images from one's photo files or editing a graphic image that is placed within a document. Subsequent generations of this single program will require even newer literacies as new technologies generate new communication and information potentials.

The deictic nature of literacy also is caused by the envisionments we construct as we use new technologies for literate acts. Individuals who use new technologies often envision new ways of using them and, in their envisionments, change the nature of literacy (Leu, Karchmer, & Leu, 1999). Envisionments take place when individuals imagine new possibilities for literacy and learning, transform existing technologies to construct this vision, and then share their work with others. This happens regularly within technologies that permit users to create new visions for their use, something that defines the Internet and most other ICTs.

Consider a person who wishes to send a specially designed and formatted message via e-mail, but she has an e-mail program containing very limited design and format tools. This person might think to use a word processor with more powerful design tools to compose the message, knowing that she could then paste the formatted message into the e-mail message window. Thus, a word processor can be transformed into a tool for composing e-mail messages, a purpose for which it was not designed, but a function it fills admirably. This potential only comes to life when a person envisions a new function for a technology and enacts this envisionment. In essence, we can say that she envisioned how to repurpose a technology for a new and different function. Envisionments such as this happen regularly as individuals encounter new problems and seek solutions in new and creative uses of existing technologies. They contribute to the deictic nature of literacy.

The third factor that prompts the deictic nature of literacy is the use of increasingly efficient technologies of communication that rapidly distribute new literacies. The Internet and other ICTs not only change themselves, but they also provide the central vehicle for exchanging new technologies for information and communication. Increasingly, for example, we simply download new technologies from the Internet when these appear rather than receive a CD or other storage medium through the traditional mail system. Because we can now immediately download a new technology from the Internet or send it to millions of individuals with just a keystroke, the changes to literacy derived from new technologies now happen at a faster pace than ever before. This increases the already rapid pace of change in the forms and functions of literacy, increasing the complexity of the challenges we face as we consider how best to prepare students for their literacy futures. Thus, the rapid pace of change in the forms and functions of literacy are exacerbated by the speed with which new technologies and new envisionments are communicated (Leu, 2000a).

In summary, we believe that the deictic nature of literacy will increase in the years ahead, limited only by our own ability to adapt to the new literacies that emerge. People, not technology, will limit the speed with which new literacies appear.

The Relationship Between Technology and Literacy Is Transactional

Technology transforms the forms and functions of literacy (Reinking, 1998), but literacy also transforms the forms and functions of technology. Thus, the relationship between literacy and technology is transactional. We have argued above, and most would agree, that new technologies for information and communication require new literacies to fully exploit their potential. It is important to recognize, however, that when we use technology in new ways, we also transform the technology itself, creating additional new literacies in the process.

The most common mechanism by which users transform a technology through their literate behavior is what we have referred to earlier as an envisionment. When individuals imagine new possibilities for literacy, transform the function or the structure of existing technologies to construct this vision, and then share their work with others, an envisionment has occurred.

In addition, though, technology is transformed through instructional practices in literacy classrooms. This happens every day on the Internet when educators construct new curricular resources with Internet technologies and then share their work with others (Leu et al., 1999). Examples include the following:

- Harriet Tubman & The Underground Railroad (www2.lhric.org/pocantico/tubman/tubman.html), a site developed by Patty Taverna, Terry Hongell, and Patty's second-grade class at Pocantico Hills School in Sleepy Hollow, New York

- Earth Day Groceries Project (www.earthdaybags.org), an environmental project developed by Mark Ahlness, a third-grade teacher in Seattle, Washington

- SCORE Cyberguides (www.sdcoe.k12.ca.us/score/cyberguide.html), a collection of Internet resources for individual works of literature contributed by teachers and coordinated by the San Diego schools

- Book Rap (http://rite.ed.qut.edu.au/old_oz-teachernet/projects/book-rap), literature discussion groups run over the Internet from Australia

While these new instructional tools, and thousands of others that are appearing, provide important resources for the literacy classroom, each also requires additional new literacies for their effective use.

New Literacies Are Multiple in Nature

A New Literacies Perspective recognizes that a singular label, literacy, fails to capture the complexity of the changes that can only be captured by a plural label. Increasingly, scholars are beginning to recognize that changes taking place result in multiple new literacies required in different social contexts. For example, The New London Group (2000) defines *multiliteracies* as a set of open-ended and flexible multiple literacies required to function in diverse contexts and communities. We believe the same multiplicity of literacy is emerging because of multiple technological contexts. We believe that the Internet and other ICTs require that we develop a systematic understanding of the multiple literacies that exist within these many different contexts. This multiplicity of new literacies is apparent on at least three different levels.

The first level of multiplicity that characterizes the new literacies of Internet technologies is that meaning is typically represented with multiple media forms. Unlike traditional text forms that typically include a combination of two types of media—print and two-dimensional graphics—Internet texts integrate a range of symbols and multiple-media formats including icons, animated symbols, audio, video, interactive tables, virtual reality environments, and many more (Brunner & Tally, 1999; Lemke, 1998). Also, Web designers often use nontraditional combinations of font size and color, with little uniformity in style and design from one website to another (Ciolek, 1996). As a result, we confront new forms and combinations of texts and images that challenge our traditional understandings of how information is represented and shared with others. The multiplicative effects of these unique combinations of multiple-media forms (Lemke, 1998) demand that students "understand how various literacies and various cultural traditions combine these different semiotic modalities to make meanings that are more than the sum of what each could mean separately" (p. 288). For traditional language arts curriculums that tend to focus on the process of making meaning from text as opposed to critically analyzing and interpreting the messages within images, Internet technologies require literacy educators to broaden their definitions of literacy to encompass these new, complex, and multiple forms of Internet literacies.

The second level of multiplicity is that the Internet and other ICTs offer multiple tools for constructing multiple forms of communication. Literate individuals will be those who can effectively assess their individual purposes for using the Internet and then seek out, from the Internet's many offerings, the particular tool and form that best meet their needs. For example, when seeking particular information, readers will need to know procedures for using keywords within the most appropriate type of search engine while those hoping to browse online resources for the sake of open-ended exploration should be familiar with the hierarchical categories of information indexed by many search engines. Similarly, when hoping to communicate asynchronously with others, Internet users should be literate in tools such as e-mail, listservs, and discussion boards. When seeking more real-time interactive forms of information, Internet users need to have an understanding of how to access instant messaging technologies, communicate effectively with video conference technologies, participate in chat rooms, and enter virtual environments. A New Literacies Perspective assumes that proficient users of the Internet also will understand how to construct, design, manipulate, and upload their own information to add to the constantly growing and changing body of knowledge that defines the Internet.

A final level of multiplicity that characterizes the new literacies of Internet technologies consists of the new skills demanded by our students as they more frequently encounter information from individuals in different social contexts. In schools, at home, and in the workplace, the Internet provides opportunities for individuals to meet and exchange ideas, yet it is important to realize that each of these ideas is not an isolated piece of information but, rather, is shaped by the social and cultural contexts in which each of us exists. Typically, students are accustomed to exchanging information with others within their own classroom, school, or neighborhood and usually are not surprised by what they learn through these exchanges. However, the global sharing of information permitted by the Internet introduces new challenges for students now expected to interpret and respond to information from multiple social and cultural contexts that share profoundly different assumptions about our world. These multiple contexts for new literacies have important implications for educators preparing students to critically understand and interpret the meaning of text and images they find on the Internet.

Critical Literacies Are Central to the New Literacies

Another central principle of the new literacies is that they demand new forms of critical literacy and additional dependence on critical thinking and analysis as one encounters information. Open networks such as the Internet permit anyone to publish anything; this is one of the opportunities this technology presents. However, this open access also is one of the Internet's limitations; information is much more widely available from people who have strong political, economic, religious, or ideological stances that profoundly influence the nature of the information they present to others. As a result, we must assist students in becoming more critical consumers of the information they encounter (Alvermann et al., 1999; Muspratt et al., 1998). Although the literacy curriculum (and assessment programs) have always included items such as critical thinking and separating fact from propaganda, richer and more complex analysis skills will need to be included in classrooms where the Internet and other ICTs begin to play a more prominent role.

As we begin to study the new literacies of the Internet we will depend greatly on work from the communities of critical literacy and media literacy and will be informed by research that targets higher-order thinking about what is being communicated. Multiple, critical literacies populate the new literacies of the Internet, requiring new skills, strategies, and insights to successfully exploit the rapidly changing information and media technologies continuously emerging in our world.

New Forms of Strategic Knowledge Are Central to the New Literacies

Mayer (1997) has reminded us that each technology contains different contexts and resources for constructing meanings and requires somewhat different strategies for doing so. New technologies for networked information and communication are complex and require many new strategies for their effective use. Hypertext technologies, for example, embedded with multiple forms of media and unlimited freedoms of multiple navigational pathways, present opportunities that may seduce some readers away from important content unless they have developed strategies to deal with these seductions (Lawless & Kulikowich, 1996; Lawless, Mills, & Brown, 2002). Other cognitive and aesthetic changes to text on the Internet present new challenges to comprehension (Coiro, 2003; Spires & Estes, 2002), inquiry (Eagleton, 2001), and information seeking (Sutherland-Smith, 2002) as well. Moreover, as we have argued, the technologies of the Internet will continue to change regularly and rapidly, presenting us with even newer technologies of literacy that demand more (and more sophisticated) strategies to effectively exploit them. Thus, the new literacies will be largely defined around the strategic knowledge central to the effective use of information within rich and complexly networked environments.

There will be many types of strategic knowledge important to the new literacies. We can be certain, though, that they will include the new forms of strategic knowledge necessary to locate, evaluate, and effectively use the extensive resources available within the Internet. The extent and complexity of this information is staggering. Moreover, these already extensive resources increase each day as new computers are connected to networks and as people create new information and publish it for others to use. They require new forms of strategic knowledge in order to exploit them effectively. How do we best search for information in these complex worlds? How do we design a webpage to be useful to people who are likely to visit? How do we communicate effectively with videoconference technologies? How do we function in the virtual worlds that are being developed as social learning environments? What are the rules for participating on listservs, chatrooms, bulletin boards, and other electronic communication environments? These questions highlight the central role that strategic knowledge will play for people who communicate using the new literacies of the Internet and other ICTs.

Speed Counts in Important Ways Within the New Literacies

In a world of vast information resources, the new literacies of the Internet will be defined in important ways around the rate at which one can read, write, and communicate. Within competitive information economies where problem identification and solution are critical, the rate at which one can acquire, evaluate, and use information to solve important problems becomes central to success. The speed it takes to acquire information will become an important measure of success within various technologies. Quickly finding, evaluating, using, and communicating information will become central instructional issues.

As speed becomes essential for the effective use of the new literacies of the Internet and other ICTs, it will be critical to solve the equity issues that result from children who process and communicate information at different rates. Slow readers and writers are challenged within traditional literacies; within the new literacies of the Internet these individuals will be left far behind. The gap between highly literate and literacy challenged individuals will be exacerbated by the new literacies of the Internet. Highly literate individuals will skim webpages, link to other webpages, and generally sift through large amounts of information in a short time. Individuals who read slowly and haltingly will still be evaluating the first screen of information by the time a more rapid reader has already completed the informational task. If we truly seek to enable every student to succeed in a society defined by information and the speed with which it may be accessed, we will need to devote substantial resources to discover solutions to this important issue.

Learning Often Is Socially Constructed Within New Literacies

We expect that social learning strategies will be central to literacy instruction in the future, and here we highlight two dimensions that are important to recognize within our current framework of a New Literacies Perspective.

First, social learning plays an important role in the exchange of new skills and strategies needed to interact within increasingly complex and continually changing technologies for information and communication. Models of literacy instruction often have focused on an adult whose role is to teach the skills he or she possesses to a group of students who do not know those skills. This is no longer possible, or even appropriate, within a world of multiple new literacies framed by the Internet and other ICTs. In fact, today, many young students possess higher levels of knowledge about some of these new literacies than most adults. It is simply impossible for one person to know all the new literacies and teach these directly to others. Each of us, however, will know something unique and useful to others.

Consequently, effective learning experiences will be increasingly dependent on social learning strategies and the ability of a teacher to orchestrate literacy learning opportunities between and among students who know different new literacies. This will distribute knowledge about literacy throughout the classroom, especially as students move above the stages of foundational literacy. One student, for example, may know how to edit digital video scenes in the hope of including these within a webpage, but another may know how best to compress the video so that it can function optimally in a Web-based environment. In a student-centered, social learning environment, this knowledge can be exchanged, ironically, in a classroom where the teacher may not know either of these skills as well as the students. By orchestrating opportunities for the exchange of new literacies, both teachers and students may enhance their literacy skills and their potential for effective communication and information use. This social learning ability may not come naturally to all students, however, and many will need to be supported in learning how to learn about literacy from one another (Labbo, 1996; Labbo & Kuhn, 1998).

If, as we believe, literacy learning becomes increasingly dependent on social learning strategies, socially skilled learners will be advantaged while "monastic learners," children who rely solely on independent learning strategies, may be disadvantaged. This will be an important change in many classrooms because individual learning often has been the norm, privileging children who learn well independently. In classrooms where the acquisition of new literacies is important, children who are better at independent learning experiences will be disadvantaged. Increasingly, we must support children who are unfamiliar or ineffective with social learning strategies.

On a second dimension, social learning is not only important for how information is learned, but it also plays a vital role in how information is constructed within the technologies themselves. Much of the Internet is built on the social knowledge constructions of others (e.g., telecollaborative learning projects, threaded discussions, interactive chats, and collaborative databases). Every day, many new websites are developed and serve to expand the global knowledge base shared through Internet technologies. In both the workplace and at home, the new technologies of literacy allow us to take advantage of the intellectual capital that resides in others, enabling us to collaboratively construct solutions to important problems by drawing from the expertise that lies outside ourselves.

Thus, the construction of knowledge will increasingly be a collaborative venture within the learning spaces defined by the Internet and other ICTs. These new technologies will introduce important new instructional challenges for educators, especially with content area contexts. As the Internet and other ICTs bring us closer together, students will need to be prepared for the important, collaborative co-construction of new information and the learning that results (Jonassen, in press; Jonassen, Howland, Moore, & Marra, 2003).

Teachers Become More Important, Though Their Role Changes, Within New Literacy Classrooms

The appearance of the Internet and other ICTs in school classrooms will increase, not decrease, the central role that teachers play in orchestrating learning experiences for students. Teachers will be challenged to thoughtfully guide students' learning within information environments that are richer and more complex than traditional print media, presenting richer and more complex learning opportunities for both themselves and their students. Moreover, in a world of literacy as deixis, new literacies will continuously emerge from even newer technologies, requiring teachers to be (a) aware of emerging technologies for information and communication, (b) capable of identifying the most important new literacies that each requires, and (c) proficient in knowing how to support their development in the classroom.

The teacher's central role will change in a fundamental way, however. Teachers will increasingly need to orchestrate complex contexts for literacy and learning rather than simply dispense literacy skills, since they will no longer always be the most literate person in the classroom. Increasingly, students are coming to school more literate in the new literacies of ICTs than their teachers (Chandler-Olcott & Mahar, 2003). This is a historic change. As a result, roles between student and teacher will sometimes be reversed. Skilled teachers will take advantage of this by constructing contexts for learning in which students who possess new literacies are valued and are supported in sharing their expertise with others. Instead of being the single source for all literacy knowledge, teachers will become orchestrators of literacy learning environments, where members of a classroom community exchange new literacies that each has discovered.

Students with teachers who make thoughtful decisions about what needs to be learned and how it should be learned in new literacies will be privileged; those with teachers who have not yet figured these things out will be disadvantaged, perhaps even more so than with foundational literacies. Because teachers become even more important to the development of literacy in a world of new literacies, greater attention will need to be placed on teacher education and professional development.

A New Literacies Perspective: Implications for Research and Practice

A New Literacies Perspective tells us that the Internet and other continuously emerging ICTs will be central to literacy in both our personal and professional lives and that these technologies require new literacies in order to effectively exploit their potential (IRA, 2002; Kinzer & Leander, 2003; Leu, 2002). It also tells us that it is essential to begin to integrate these new literacies into classrooms if we hope to prepare all students for the literacy futures they deserve (Leu & Kinzer, 2000). In addition, this theoretical perspective suggests that complexity and change define the new literacies of the Internet and other ICTs (Cammack, 2003; Coiro, 2003). Most important, it suggests that the literacy curriculum and assessment practices have not begun to recognize the important new literacies these technologies require (Leu, 2000a; Leu & Ataya, 2002). What is clear from a New Literacies Perspective is that there are important aspects to the literacy curriculum that require our immediate attention for both research and practice.

As we begin to consider the implications of a New Literacies Perspective, we want to make three important points. First, it is important to understand that simply using technology in the classroom does not assure that students are acquiring the new literacies they require. Using technologies such as Accelerated Reader (Topping & Paul, 1999) or other software packages designed to support the acquisition of foundational literacies will not prepare students for the new literacies of the Internet and other ICTs. Using these instructional technologies does nothing to develop the essential skills, strategies, and dispositions that define the new literacies. This type of thinking has been one reason why the field has not moved faster at integrating new literacies into classroom instruction; using software programs to teach foundational literacies is the only vision many have for integrating literacy and technology in classrooms.

Second, a central challenge for both research and practice emerges from the inherently deictic nature of any new literacy. Because new literacies continuously change as even newer technologies require even newer literacies, we require new epistemologies and new instructional practices that keep up with the rapid changes we anticipate. How, for example, can we keep up with new ideas about what to teach within research and dissemination paradigms that require four years or more between the conception of a research problem and the wide dissemination of results through research journals that rely on printed volumes? How can we keep up with new ideas about how to teach with these technologies when the technologies themselves regularly change? How can we assess students on their ability to use the Internet and other ICTs when the very skills we assess will change as soon as new technologies appear? While a New Literacies Perspective does not provide complete answers to these questions, it does suggest that these are critical questions for both research and practice.

Third, and most important, we believe that implementing a New Literacies Perspective in classrooms is essential if we hope to avoid societies in which economic advantage is sustained by the wealthy and denied to the poor. Because of the compounding effect of differences in reading achievement and access to Internet resources by advantaged members of society, we are in danger of developing two classes of citizens: one that is largely poor, minority, and challenged by the new literacies required for reading and learning on the Internet and another that is largely advantaged, white, and excels with the new literacies required for reading and learning on the Internet. Such a development presents fundamental challenges to any society that professes egalitarian ideals and equal opportunities for all its citizens.

According to data from the National Assessment of Educational Progress (NAEP), reading comprehension in the United States has been generally resistant to efforts at improvement (NCES, 2003b). Of particular concern, white fourth-grade students scored at or above the "basic" level of reading at nearly twice the rate as many minority groups (NCES, 2003b). Just as troubling, economically advantaged students at the fourth-grade level scored at or above the "basic" level of reading at nearly twice the rate compared to disadvantaged students (NCES, 2003b). Most troublesome of all, the achievement gap is increasing between high- and low-performing students. Since 1992, NAEP average reading scores for high-performing students have increased, while those for low-performing students have dropped (NCES, 2003b). Given the powerful connection between reading comprehension ability and learning (Alexander & Jetton, 2000; Bransford, Brown, & Cocking, 2000), it is clear that the United States is developing two classes of learners.

As challenging a picture as the NAEP data present, they do not yet reflect students' ability to read and comprehend within the complex, networked, informational spaces of the Internet. The Internet requires new literacies to achieve high levels of reading comprehension in this context, but we know very little about what these literacies are or how best to teach them. The report of the RAND Reading Study Group (2002), *Reading for Understanding: Toward an R&D Program in Reading Comprehension*, captures the essence of the problem: "Accessing the Internet makes large demands on individuals' literacy skills; in some cases, this new technology requires readers to have novel literacy skills, and little is known about how to analyze or teach those skills" (p. 4).

The Internet is also a reading context where digital divide issues abound (Solomon, 2002). It is clear that advantaged and white students have far greater Internet access at home than disadvantaged and minority students (Lebo, 2003). Because the skills necessary to achieve high levels of reading comprehension on the Internet are seldom taught in schools (Padron & Waxman, 1996; Warschauer, 2003; Wenglinski, 1998), the skills are more often acquired at home by those economically advantaged members of society who have the greatest access to the Internet and more extensive learning opportunities (Warschauer, 2003).

Before we can expect all students to be prepared to read and comprehend at high levels on the Internet, we must provide scientific data to demonstrate what these skills are, how to assess them, and how best to teach them (Coiro, 2003; RAND Reading Study Group, 2002). Despite the perceived importance of the Internet as a context for teaching and learning (Web-Based Education Commission, 2000; U.S. Department of Education, 1999), relatively little research exists on the new literacies the Internet requires for achieving high levels of reading comprehension (National Institute of Child Health and Human Development, 2000). This situation must change.

Issues of What Should Be Taught and Learned Within a Context of Continuous Change

A New Literacies Perspective suggests that an aggressive agenda of research must be launched immediately in order to better understand the new skills, strategies, and dispositions required to effectively use the Internet and other ICTs. Little work, especially by the literacy research community, has been conducted in this area. And, it is the literacy research community that needs to bring powerful insights about literacy, instruction, and learning to these issues. The task is so large, involves literacy in such profound ways, and must be accomplished so quickly that it is not possible to vest the responsibility for this work solely in the hands of those who have traditionally explored issues of technology or even literacy and technology. Each of us must bring our special area of expertise to the study of literacy within the new worlds of the Internet and other ICTs.

Scholars who study reading comprehension, for example, need to examine the various components of meaning construction to help us understand the extent to which comprehension processes are similar or different within the multimedia, hyperlinked contexts of the Internet and other ICTs (Coiro, 2003). Reading comprehension is likely to be a major area of investigation because the Internet and other ICTs focus so much on information and learning from text. However, given recent models (RAND Reading Study Group, 2002) that define reading comprehension in terms of reader, text, and task, the parameters of reading comprehension on the Internet are likely to expand to include problem identification, search strategies, analysis, synthesis, and the meaning construction required in e-mail messages and other communication technologies. Many questions await investigation: What new aspects of comprehension are required when reading information on the Internet? Are inferential processes and strategies similar or different on the Internet? How do other aspects of the comprehension process change? Reading comprehension strategies within this context are likely to be especially important, and we need to know what these are.

Scholars doing work in early literacy must bring their special insights to help us understand when and in what ways young children should begin to read, write, and communicate with ICTs. We have always viewed the early years as critical to literacy development. These scholars must now turn their attention to the new literacies emerging from new technologies, helping us to understand how best to teach these new literacies in ways that answer the call for technology use that is developmentally appropriate, equitable, and integrated into the regular literacy learning environment of young children (National Association for the Education of Young Children, 1996).

Media literacy scholars, too, need to bring their understanding of critical literacies to the study of what students need to learn within the new literacies of the Internet and other ICTs. Earlier we argued that critical literacies are essential to reading on the Internet because issues of stance, information shaping, and information validity become so important within an information space where anyone may publish anything. Consequently, there is new sense of urgency in ensuring that students develop an awareness of the diverse perspectives around any question they investigate. Literacy educators will need to incorporate more strategies like those suggested by Brunner and Tally (1999) to foster deeper student insight into the various ways of looking at the same event, for example, viewing a historical event from the perspective of the different people involved (e.g., viewing a Civil War video series while "looking for evidence of the way average soldiers, in contrast to generals, or men in contrast to women, or white in contrast to blacks, experienced the war" [p. 46]).

Scholars in the areas of composition and communication also have much to contribute to this work. They must bring their powerful lenses to bear on issues of e-mail communication, webpage and multimedia composition, and the many other important issues we need to understand in these areas. Clear, rapid, and effective communication that takes advantage of the networked information contexts of ICTs will be central to our students' success. We need to know how to support students in achieving these abilities.

Although many of us have not yet recognized it, insights from multicultural and cross-cultural education also are going to be especially critical to our effective use of ICTs (Leu, 1997b). We need the finest minds in this area to help us understand the important experiences taking place as classrooms link to other classrooms from different cultural contexts, engaging in cooperative projects and seeking to understand one another's cultural context. As we engage in this important work, enormous potential exists to understand the advantages that diversity bestows by bringing multiple perspectives to bear on important problems that face us all. The Internet permits us to construct new definitions of multicultural education and broadens the definition of diversity in the classroom to global dimensions. If we take full advantage of these new opportunities the Internet will allow us to construct a truly global village among classrooms that shows students how to take full advantage of the many benefits that diversity bestows.

A central challenge for each of us is how to use these new technologies to support students with special needs. It is quite possible that the gap between proficient readers and less-proficient readers will increase within the world of rich, complexly structured information networks as the effects of differences in reading rate and accuracy become magnified. If we do not wish to leave a single child behind, we must focus on the issue of how best to support students with special needs with the powerful new technologies that are available to us.

Our colleagues who conduct research on teacher education also have an enormous agenda ahead. They need to apply their finest heuristics, helping us to better understand how to prepare new and experienced teachers to support children in the new literacies of ICTs in the classroom. Increasingly the challenge for classrooms is one that is changing from access to the thoughtful use of powerful new technologies for literacy. We need important new models and clear data to direct us in this area.

Scholars exploring important agendas in adolescent literacy and content area literacy may have the most to contribute. Research in these areas can help us to better understand ways to support information acquisition, develop the critical evaluation skills essential to effective use of Internet resources, and develop strategies for the effective use of information to solve important problems.

Scholars in the area of teacher research also have important work ahead of them. We know that some exceptional teachers are developing new insights and new models of instruction on the Internet (Karchmer, 2001). We need to know how to take advantage of these learning experiences and use the insights developed by these exceptional teachers to support our work in teacher education and staff development.

We also need to invite scholars in the areas of adult literacy to the research table. We cannot afford to abandon adults who have not had the advantage of being prepared for the new literacies required of an information economy. It may be a special challenge to broaden the literacy skills of this population because they do not have the advantage of growing up in a rich multimedia and technology world the way many children have. But, if we succeed in involving adults, it will provide us with special opportunities to take advantage of their many years of experience. Intellectual capital is important to all of us in a networked information context. We cannot afford to lose any of it.

Family literacy scholars are essential, as well, to the research that must be done. Networked information resources provide special opportunities to connect schools with families. How can we best take advantage of information networks to support a collaborative effort in students' education? How can we ensure access to ICTs in the home? We need answers to these questions if we seek to provide the best learning environment possible for every child.

Additionally, scholars in the areas of children's and adolescent literature have much to contribute. New forms of literature, written by students themselves, are beginning to emerge as the Internet makes possible new publishing opportunities. We need to know how best to support the integration of these new opportunities for literacy and learning into school classrooms.

Finally, while considering the contributions we require in all these areas, we also may wish to consider the important consequences resulting from a deictic vision of new literacies for what students need to learn. The continuously changing technologies of literacy mean that we must help children "learn how to learn" new technologies of literacy. In fact, the ability to learn continuously changing technologies for literacy may be a more critical target than learning any particular technology of literacy itself.

In this section, we have presented just some of the areas that require the attention of our brightest minds, our most talented scholars, and all our teachers. The work ahead is immense and requires us to pool all our talents if we are to understand the new skills, strategies, and dispositions that students must acquire in the new literacies of the Internet and other ICTs.

Issues of How to Teach Within a Context of Continuous Change

As we consider issues related to how to teach and learn the new literacies of the Internet and other ICTs, it is likely that our focus will turn to understanding the social and constructivist nature of learning strategies that new literacies demand. We indicated earlier that social and constructive perspectives would be important to the construction of new information within the technologies themselves. Both of these areas are important to research and practice within a New Literacies Perspective. We need to study how best to support the development of new literacies within classrooms where students will know more than teachers about some new literacies and seek new ways in which to organize and orchestrate classroom learning to take advantage of the new literacy knowledge others are acquiring. In short, we need to determine the most effective ways to manage learning experiences in the new literacies when these literacies are distributed throughout a classroom. As we do this, we also need to understand how best to collaboratively construct new information with the Internet and other ICTs, a potential that is at the very heart of most new literacies.

The lessons that classroom teachers are acquiring about both of these issues are important to understand. In fact, we believe that teachers who integrate the Internet and other ICTs into their classrooms will contribute as much—and perhaps more—than traditional researchers to understanding the most effective instructional practices for supporting the development of new literacies. The Internet and other ICTs permit teachers to rapidly connect with other teachers to share successes and exchange insights about how best to teach the new literacies (Karchmer, 2001) and it will be important to study how classroom teachers connect with others, exchange information, and construct new visions of best practices. Resources such as RTEACHER (see www.reading.org), a listserv sponsored by the International Reading Association, where teachers and others can exchange ideas about successful practices, are just the beginning of new epistemologies that will be required to keep up with the rapidly changing nature of information about instructional practice that is a part of the changing nature of the new literacies.

What seems certain is that Internet resources will increase the central role that teachers play in orchestrating learning experiences for students as literacy instruction converges with Internet technologies. Teachers will be challenged to thoughtfully guide students' learning within information environments that are richer and more complex than traditional print media, presenting richer and more complex learning opportunities for both themselves and their students. This alone should make teacher education and professional development issues important priorities. In addition, however, we must recognize that as the new literacies continually change, new professional development and teacher education needs will emerge. It is safe to say that our educational systems have never before faced the professional development needs that will occur in our future. The Internet, however, provides us with new opportunities to rapidly disseminate new models of effective instruction. Models of dissemination that take advantage of the communication potential in these new technologies, such as those developed by the Case Technologies to Enhance Literacy Learning (CTELL) group (Teale, Leu, Labbo, & Kinzer, 2002), may become increasingly important.

Issues of Assessment Within a Context of Continuous Change

A fundamental challenge to the integration of new literacies into the curriculum, at least in the United States, is that we currently do not include these important literacy skills on national and state assessments. Given the evidence that teachers emphasize literacy skills appearing on important assessments (Linn, Graue, & Sanders, 1990), there is little incentive for teachers to make new literacies a central part of the curriculum until these are included in state and national standards and on literacy assessments.

The best evidence that educational systems ignore the new literacies of Internet technologies, at least in the United States, can be seen in the state assessment programs that evaluate children's performance in reading and writing. New literacies, such as reading on the Internet or within other ICTs, are not included on any state assessments, and most states have no immediate plans to include these within literacy assessments (Leu & Ataya, 2002). Moreover, most states have seen the assessment of new literacies, such as comprehending text on the Internet, composing e-mail messages, or writing with a word processor, as a technology assessment issue, not a reading or writing assessment issue. This continues to occur even though the ability to locate, read, and evaluate information on the Internet is increasingly a part of our daily lives (Lebo, 2003). In addition, not a single state permits any student who prefers to use a word processor to do so during state writing assessments, unless this is formally specified in a special education student's Individualized Educational Plan. This continues to occur despite evidence that nearly 20% more students are able to pass the

Massachusetts state writing assessment when permitted to use word processors (Russell & Plati, 2000).

There are other challenges we face in the assessment of new literacies. The most prominent one, perhaps, is that literacy assessments, to date, are always assessments of an individual working alone. Given the importance of social learning and collaborative meaning construction on the Internet and other ICTs, we will need to begin to assess how well students can learn new literacies from others and how well they can co-construct meaning and collaborate in constructing written information with others. As we have pointed out, learning how to learn from others and learning how to collaboratively construct meaning will be increasingly important. It seems clear that new technologies will require new approaches to both what is assessed and how we go about the assessment (Pellegrino, Chudowsky, & Glaser, 2001).

Concluding Thoughts About a New Literacies Perspective

Change increasingly defines the nature of literacy and the nature of literacy learning. New technologies generate new literacies that become important to our lives in a global information age. We believe that we are on the cusp of a new era in literacy research, one in which the nature of reading, writing, and communication is being fundamentally transformed. To inform this journey, we have defined a New Literacies Perspective, which provides a useful starting point to inquiry in this area. We have explained how literacy has changed regularly throughout time, influenced by important social forces and technologies. We explored the social context of the current period including global economic competition, the rise of the Internet and other ICTs, and educational policies from nations around the world that emphasize higher achievement in literacy and the effective use of information technologies. Then, we reviewed emerging theoretical perspectives in this area and explained why we believe a New Literacies Perspective is especially useful to understand the changes that are taking place. Finally, we presented a set of principles that inform our research in this area and discussed some of their more challenging implications to both research and practice.

It will be up to each of us to recognize the continually changing nature of literacy and to develop a rich understanding of these changes. We hope that you will bring your own expertise to the important work that lies ahead as we all seek to prepare students for the new literacies of the Internet and other ICTs that define their future. They deserve nothing less.

Note

[1] Portions of this section are an expansion of work that appeared originally in Kinzer and Leander (2003), and quotations from this section should reference that work.

References

*indicates that article is included on TMPR5 supplementary CD.

Alexander, P.A., & Jetton, T.L. (2000). Learning from text: A multidimensional and developmental perspective. In M.L. Kamil, P.B. Mosenthal, P.D. Pearson, & R. Barr (Eds.), *Handbook of reading research* (Vol. 3, pp. 285–310). Mahwah, NJ: Erlbaum.

Alvermann, D.E. (Ed.). (2002). *Adolescents and literacies in a digital world*. New York: Peter Lang.

Alvermann, D.E., Hinchman, K.A., Moore, D.W., Phelps, S.F., & Waff, D.R. (Eds.). (1998). *Reconceptualizing the literacies in adolescents' lives*. Mahwah, NJ: Erlbaum.

Alvermann, D.E., Moon, J.S., & Hagood, M.C. (1999). *Popular culture in the classroom: Teaching and researching critical media literacy*. Newark, DE: International Reading Association; Chicago: National Reading Conference.

Australia Department of Education, Science and Training. (2004). *The Adelaide declaration on national goals for schooling in the twenty-first century*. Canberra, Australia: Author. Retrieved March 7, 2004, from http://www.dest.gov.au/schools/adelaide/adelaide.htm

Australia National Office for the Information Economy. (1999). *A strategic framework for the information economy: Identifying priorities for action*. Canberra, Australia: Author. Retrieved January 30, 1999, from http://noie.gov.au/projects/framework/reports/dec98_strategy.htm

Bell, D. (1977). *The coming of post-industrial society*. New York: Basic Books.

Bourdieu, P. (1991). *Language and symbolic power* (G. Raymond & M. Adamson, Trans.). Cambridge, MA: Harvard University Press.

Boyarin, J. (Ed.). (1993). *The ethnography of reading*. Berkeley: University of California Press.

Bransford, J.D., Brown, A.L., & Cocking, R.R. (Eds.). (2000). *How people learn: Brain, mind, experience, and school* (Expanded ed.). Washington, DC: National Academy Press.

Bromley, H., & Apple, M.W. (1998). *Education, technology, power: Educational computing as a social practice*. Albany: State University of New York Press.

Bruce, B.C. (1997a). Current issues and future directions. In J. Flood, S.B. Heath, & D. Lapp (Eds.), *Handbook of research on teaching literacy through the communicative and visual arts* (pp. 875–884). New York: Simon & Schuster Macmillan.

Bruce, B.C. (1997b). Literacy technologies: What stance should we take? *Journal of Literacy Research, 29*, 289–309.

Brunner, C.B., & Tally, W. (1999). *The new media literacy handbook: An educator's guide to bringing new media into the classroom*. New York: Anchor Books.

Burton-Jones, A. (1999). *Knowledge capitalism: Business, work and learning in the new economy*. Oxford, UK: Oxford University Press.

Cammack, D. (2002). Literacy, technology, and a room of her own: Analyzing adolescent girls' online conversations from historical and technological literacy perspectives. In D.L. Shallert, C.M. Fairbanks, J. Worthy, B. Maloch, & J.V. Hoffman (Eds.), *51st yearbook of the National Reading Conference* (pp. 129–141). Oak Creek, WI: National Reading Conference.

Cammack, D. (2003). Book review: *Adolescents and literacies in a digital world*. *Reading Online, 6*(10). Retrieved December 15, 2003, from http://www.readingonline.org/electronic/elec_index.asp?HREF=cammack/index.html

Chandler-Olcott, K., & Mahar, D. (2003). "Tech-savviness" meets multiliteracies: Exploring adolescent girls' technology-related literacy practices. *Reading Research Quarterly, 38*, 356–385.

Ciolek, T.M. (1996). The six quests for the electronic grail: Current approaches to information quality in WWW resources. *Review Informatique et Statistique dans les Sciences Humaines (RISSH), 1–4*, 45–71. Retrieved March 15, 2003, from http://www.ciolek.com/PAPERS/six-quests1996.html

Coiro, J. (2003). Reading comprehension on the Internet: Expanding our understanding of reading comprehension to encompass new literacies. *The Reading Teacher, 56*, 458–464.

Cole, M. (1996). *Cultural psychology: A once and future discipline*. Cambridge, MA: Belknap Press of Harvard University Press.

Crystal, D. (2001). *Language and the Internet*. Cambridge, UK: Cambridge University Press.

Dechant, E. (1982). *Improving the teaching of reading* (3rd ed.). Englewood Cliffs, NJ: Prentice Hall.

Diringer, D. (1968). *The alphabet: A key to the history of mankind*. New York: Funk and Wagnalls.

Drucker, P.F. (1994). The age of social transformation. *Atlantic Monthly, 278*(5), 53–80.

* Dyson, A.H. (1999). Coach Bombay's kids learn to write: Children's appropriation of media material for school literacy. *Research in the Teaching of English, 33*(4), 367–402.

Eagleton, M. (2001, December). *Factors that influence Internet inquiry strategies: Case studies of middle school students with and without learning disabilities*. Paper presented at the annual meeting of the National Reading Conference, San Antonio, TX.

Fillmore, C.J. (1972). How to know whether you're coming or going. In K. Huldgaard-Jensen (Ed.), *Linguistik 1971* (pp. 369–379). Amsterdam: Athemaiim.

Finland Ministry of Education. (1995). *Education, training and research in the information society: A national strategy*. Helsinki, Finland: Author. Retrieved January 1, 1999, from http://www.minedu.fi/infostrategy.html

Finland Ministry of Education. (1998). *The information strategies of the Ministry of Education and their implementation*. Helsinki, Finland: Author. Retrieved December 15, 2003, from http://www.minedu.fi/eopm/strategi/alku.html

Flesch, R. (1955). *Why Johnny can't read*. New York: Harper & Brothers.

Flesch, R. (1981). *Why Johnny still can't read*. New York: Harper & Row.

Flood, J., & Lapp, D. (1995). Broadening the lens: Toward an expanded conception of literacy. In K.A. Hinchman, D.J. Leu, & C.K. Kinzer (Eds.), *Perspectives on literacy research and practice* (44th yearbook of the National Reading Conference, pp. 1–16). Chicago: National Reading Conference.

Ford, T.K. (Ed.). (2001). *The printer in eighteenth-century Williamsburg*. Williamsburg, VA: Colonial Williamsburg.

Gee, J.P. (1990). *Social linguistics and literacies*. London: Falmer.

Gee, J.P. (1996). *Social linguistics and literacies: Ideology in discourses*. London: Taylor & Francis.

Gee, J.P. (2003). *What video games have to teach us about learning and literacy*. New York: Palgrave Macmillan.

Gilster, P. (1997). *Digital literacy*. New York: John Wiley.

* Goodman, K.S. (1976). Reading: A psycholinguistic guessing game. In H. Singer & R.B.

Ruddell (Eds.), *Theoretical models and processes of reading* (2nd ed., pp. 497–508). Newark, DE: International Reading Association.

Hagood, M.C., Stevens, L.P., & Reinking, D. (2003). What do THEY have to teach US? Talkin' 'cross generations! In D. Alvermann (Ed.), *Adolescents and literacies in a digital world* (pp. 68–83). New York: Peter Lang.

Harrison, T.M., & Stephen, T. (Eds.). (1996). *Computer networking and scholarly communication in the twenty-first-century university*. Albany: State University of New York Press.

Harste, J.C. (1990). Jerry Harste speaks on reading and writing. *The Reading Teacher, 43*, 316–318.

Hawisher, G.E., & Selfe, C.L. (Eds.). (1999). *Passions, pedagogies and 21st century technologies*. Logan: Utah State University Press.

Heaviside, S., Riggins, T., & Farris, E. (1997). *Advanced telecommunications in U.S. public elementary and secondary schools, Fall 1996* (NCES No. 97–944). Washington, DC: U.S. Department of Education.

Illera, J.L.R. (1997). De la lectura en papel a la lectura multimedia. In Fundalectura (Ed.), *Lectura y nuevas tecnologías: 3er congresso nacional de lectura* (pp. 69–88). Bogotá, Colombia: Fundación para el Fomento de la Lectura.

International Reading Association. (2002). *Integrating literacy and technology in the curriculum: A position statement of the International Reading Association*. Newark, DE: Author.

International Reading Association & National Council of Teachers of English. (1996). *Standards for the English language arts*. Newark, DE: International Reading Association; Urbana, IL: National Council of Teachers of English.

Ireland Department of Education and Science. (1998). *Schools IT 2000*. Retrieved January 1, 1999, from http://195.7.52.179/overview/it2k.htm

Jansen, B.J., Spink, A., & Saracevic, T. (2000). Real life, real users, and real needs: A study and analysis of user queries on the web. *Information Processing and Management, 36*, 207–227.

Jonassen, D.H. (Ed.). (in press). *Handbook of research for educational communications and technology* (2nd ed.). Mahwah, NJ: Erlbaum.

Jonassen, D.H., Howland, J., Moore, J., & Marra, R.M. (2003). *Learning to solve prob-*

lems with technology: A constructivist perspective (2nd ed.). Columbus, OH: Merrill/Prentice Hall.

Kaestle, K., Damon-Moore, H., Stedmen, L.C., Tinsley, K., & Trollinger, W.V., Jr. (1993). *Literacy in the United States: Readers and reading since 1880*. New Haven, CT: Yale University Press.

* Karchmer, R.A. (2001). The journey ahead: Thirteen teachers report how the Internet influences literacy and literacy instruction in their K–12 classrooms. *Reading Research Quarterly, 36*, 442–466.

King, J., & O'Brien, D. (2002). Adolescents' multiliteracies and their teachers' needs to know: Toward a digital detente. In D.E. Alvermann (Ed.), *Adolescents and literacies in a digital world* (pp. 40–50). New York: Peter Lang.

Kinzer, C.K. (2003). *The importance of recognizing the expanding boundaries of literacy*. Reading Online, *6*(10). Retrieved December 13, 2003, from http://www.readingonline.org/electronic/elec_index.asp?HREF=/electronic/kinzer/index.html

Kinzer, C.K., & Leander, K. (2003). Technology and the language arts: Implications of an expanded definition of literacy. In J. Flood, D. Lapp, J.R. Squire, & J.M. Jensen (Eds.), *Handbook of research on teaching the English language arts* (2nd ed., pp. 546–566). Mahwah, NJ: Erlbaum.

Labbo, L.D. (1996). A semiotic analysis of young children's symbol making in a classroom computer center. *Reading Research Quarterly, 31*, 356–385.

Labbo, L.D., & Kuhn, M. (1998). Electronic symbol making: Young children's computer-related emerging concepts about literacy. In D. Reinking, M. McKenna, L.D. Labbo, & R.D. Kieffer (Eds.), *Handbook of literacy and technology: Transformations in a post-typographic world* (pp. 79–92). Mahwah, NJ: Erlbaum.

Labbo, L.D., & Reinking, D. (1999). Negotiating the multiple realities of technology in literacy research and instruction. *Reading Research Quarterly, 34*, 478–492.

Lankshear, C., & Knobel, M. (2003). *New literacies: Changing knowledge in the classroom*. Buckingham, UK: Open University Press.

Lawless, K.A., & Kulikowich, J.M. (1996). Understanding hypertext navigation through cluster analysis. *Journal of Educational Computing Research, 14*, 385–399.

Lawless, K.A., Mills, R., & Brown, S.W. (2002). Children's hypermedia navigational strategies. *Journal of Research on Computing in Education, 34*(3), 274–284.

Lebo, H. (2003). *The UCLA Internet report: Surveying the digital future, year three*. Los Angeles: UCLA Center for Communication Policy. Retrieved December 15, 2003, from http://www.ccp.ucla.edu/pdf/UCLA-Internet-Report-Year-Three.pdf

Lemke, J.L. (1998). Metamedia literacy: Transforming meanings and media. In D. Reinking, M.C. McKenna, L.D. Labbo, & R.D. Kieffer (Eds.), *Handbook of literacy and technology: Transformations in a post-typographic world* (pp. 283–301). Mahwah, NJ: Erlbaum.

Lenhart, A., Simon, M., & Graziano, M. (2001). *The Internet and education: Findings of the Pew Internet & American life project*. Retrieved December 13, 2003, from http://www.pewinternet.org/reports/toc.asp?Report=39

Leu, D.J., Jr. (1997a). Caity's question: Literacy as deixis on the Internet. *The Reading Teacher, 51*, 62–67.

Leu, D.J., Jr. (1997b). Internet en el aula: Nuevas oportunidades para la educación, el aprendizaje y la enseñanza. In Fundalectura (Ed.), *Lectura y nuevas tecnologías: 3er congresso nacional de lectura* (pp. 47–68). Bogotá, Colombia: Fundación para el Fomento de la Lectura.

Leu, D.J., Jr. (2000a). Literacy and technology: Deictic consequences for literacy education in an information age. In M.L. Kamil, P.B. Mosenthal, P.D. Pearson, & R. Barr (Eds.), *Handbook of reading research* (Vol. 3, pp. 743–770). Mahwah, NJ: Erlbaum.

Leu, D.J., Jr. (2000b). Our children's future: Changing the focus of literacy and literacy instruction. *The Reading Teacher, 53*, 424–431.

Leu, D.J., Jr. (2002). The new literacies: Research on reading instruction with the Internet and other digital technologies. In A.E. Farstrup & S.J. Samuels (Eds.), *What research has to say about reading instruction* (3rd ed., pp. 310–337). Newark, DE: International Reading Association.

Leu, D.J., Jr., & Ataya, R. (2002, December). *Assessing assessment strategies among the 50 states: Evaluating the literacies of our past or the literacies of our future?* Paper presented at the annual meeting of the National Reading Conference, Miami, FL.

Leu, D.J., Jr., Karchmer, R., & Leu, D.D. (1999). The Miss Rumphius effect: Envisionments for literacy and learning that transform the Internet. *The Reading Teacher, 52,* 636–642.

Leu, D.J., Jr., & Kinzer, C.K. (2000). The convergence of literacy instruction and networked technologies for information and communication. *Reading Research Quarterly, 35,* 108–127.

Lewis, C., & Fabos, B. (1999). *Chatting on-line: Uses of Instant Messenger among adolescent girls.* Paper presented at the annual meeting of the National Reading Conference, Orlando, FL.

Lewis, C., & Finders, M. (2002). Implied adolescents and implied teachers: A generation gap for new times. In D.E. Alvermann (Ed.), *Adolescents and literacies in a digital world* (pp. 101–113). New York: Peter Lang.

Linn, R.L., Graue, M.E., & Sanders, N.M. (1990). Comparing state and district results to national norms: The validity of the claims that "everyone is above average." *Educational Measurement: Issues and Practice, 9*(3), 5–14.

Literacy Strategy Underway. (1999). *New Zealand Education Gazette, 78*(1). Retrieved January 1, 1999, from http://www.edgazette. govt.nz/articles/show_articles.cgi?id=5024

Luke, C. (1997). Media literacy and cultural studies. In S. Muspratt, A. Luke, & P. Freebody (Eds.), *Constructing critical literacies: Teaching and learning textual practice* (pp. 19–49). Cresskill, NJ: Hampton.

Manguel, A. (1996). *A history of reading.* New York: Viking.

Mathews, M. (1966). *Teaching to read: Historically considered.* Chicago: University of Chicago Press.

Mayer, R.E. (1997). Multimedia learning: Are we asking the right questions? *Educational Psychologist, 32,* 1–19.

Mikulecky, L., & Kirkley, J.R. (1998). Changing workplaces, changing classes: The new role of technology in workplace literacy. In D. Reinking, M.C. McKenna, L.D. Labbo, & R.D. Kieffer (Eds.), *Handbook of literacy and technology: Transformations in a post-typographic world* (pp. 303–320). Mahwah, NJ: Erlbaum.

Morris, I. (1964). *The world of the shining prince: Court life in ancient Japan.* London: Oxford Press.

Murphy, S.M. (1986). Children's comprehension of deictic categories in oral and written language. *Reading Research Quarterly, 21,* 118–131.

Muspratt, A., Luke, A., & Freebody, P. (Eds.). (1998). *Constructing critical literacies: Teaching and learning textual practice.* Cresskill, NJ: Hampton.

National Association for the Education of Young Children. (1996). *Position statement: Technology and young children.* Retrieved December 15, 2003, from http://www.naeyc. org/resources/position_statements/pstech98. htm

National Center for Education Statistics. (2003a). *Internet access in public schools and classrooms: 1994–2002.* Retrieved December 15, 2003, from http://nces.ed.gov/surveys/ frss/publications/2004011

National Center for Education Statistics. (2003b). *The nation's report card: Reading highlights 2003.* Washington, DC: U.S. Department of Education. Retrieved March 7, 2004, from http://nces.ed.gov/pubsearch/pubs info.asp?pubid=2004452.

National Institute of Child Health and Human Development. (2000). *Report of the National Reading Panel. Teaching children to read: An evidence-based assessment of the scientific research literature on reading and its implications for reading instruction* (NIH Publication No. 00-4769). Washington, DC: U.S. Government Printing Office.

New London Group, The. (2000). A pedagogy of multiliteracies: Designing social futures. In B. Cope & M. Kalantzis (Eds.), *Multiliteracies: Literacy learning and the design of social futures* (pp. 9–38). London: Routledge.

New Zealand Ministry of Education. (1998). *Interactive education: An information and communication technologies (ICTs) strategy for schools.* Wellington, NZ: Author. Retrieved January 1, 1999, from http://www.tki.org.nz/r/ ict/curriculum/stdoc_e.php

O'Brien, D. (2001, June). "At-risk" adolescents: Redefining competence through the multiliteracies of intermediality, visual arts, and representation. *Reading Online, 4*(11). Retrieved December 15, 2003, from http://www.reading online.org/newliteracies/lit_index.asp?HREF =/newliteracies/obrien/index.html

Padron, Y., & Waxman, H. (1996). Improving the teaching and learning of English language learners through instructional technology.

International Journal of Instructional Media, 23(4), 341–354.

Pellegrino, J.W., Chudowsky, N., & Glaser, R. (Eds.). (2001). *Knowing what students know: The science and design of educational assessment.* Washington, DC: National Academy Press.

RAND Reading Study Group. (2002). *Reading for understanding: Toward an R&D program in reading comprehension.* Santa Monica, CA: RAND.

Reich, R. (1992). *The work of nations.* New York: Vintage Books.

Reinking, D. (1998). Synthesizing technological transformations of literacy in a post-typographic world. In D. Reinking, M.C. McKenna, L.D. Labbo, & R.D. Kieffer (Eds.), *Handbook of literacy and technology: Transformations in a post-typographic world* (pp. xi–xxx). Mahwah, NJ: Erlbaum.

Rosenblatt, L.M. (1994). The transactional theory of reading and writing. In R.B. Ruddell, M.R. Ruddell, & H. Singer (Eds.), *Theoretical models and processes of reading* (4th ed., pp. 1057–1092). Newark, DE: International Reading Association.

Rumelhart, D.E. (1994). Toward an interactive model of reading. In R.B. Ruddell, M.R. Ruddell, & H. Singer (Eds.), *Theoretical models and processes of reading* (4th ed., pp. 864–894). Newark, DE: International Reading Association.

Russell, M., & Plati, T. (2000). *Mode of administration effects on MCAS composition performance for grades four, eight, and ten.* Retrieved February 1, 2001, from http://www.bc.edu/research/nbetpp/statements/WE052200.pdf

Shanahan, T. (1990). Reading and writing together: What does it really mean? In T. Shanahan (Ed.), *Reading and writing together: New perspectives for the classroom* (pp. 1–18). Norwood, MA: Christopher-Gordon.

Silverblatt, A., Ferry, J., & Finan, B. (1999). *Approaches to media literacy: A handbook.* Armonk, NY: Sharpe.

Smith, N.B. (1965). *American reading instruction.* Newark, DE: International Reading Association.

Smolin, L.I., & Lawless, K.A. (2003). Becoming literate in the technological age: New responsibilities and tools for teachers. *The Reading Teacher, 56,* 570–577.

Solomon, G. (2002). Digital equity: It's not just about access anymore. *Technology and Learning, 22*(9), 18–26.

Spires, H.A., & Estes, T.H. (2002). Reading in Web-based learning environments. In C.C. Block & M. Pressley (Eds.), *Comprehension instruction: Research-based best practices* (pp. 115–125). New York: Guilford.

Sutherland-Smith, W. (2002). Weaving the literacy Web: Changes in reading from page to screen. *The Reading Teacher, 55,* 662–669.

Teale, W.H., Leu, D.J., Labbo, L.D., & Kinzer, C. (2002). The CTELL project: New ways technology can help educate tomorrow's reading teachers. *The Reading Teacher, 55,* 654–659.

Teras, V. (1994). *A history of Russian literature.* New Haven, CT: Yale University Press.

Topping, K.J., & Paul, T.D. (1999). Computer-assisted assessment of practice at reading: A large scale survey using Accelerated Reader. *Reading & Writing Quarterly, 15,* 213–231.

Tyner, K. (1998). *Literacy in a digital world: Teaching and learning in the age of information.* Mahwah, NJ: Erlbaum.

U.K. Department for Education and Skills. (1998). *The standards site: Welcome to schemes of work.* Retrieved January 1, 1999, from http://www.standards.dfee.gov.uk/schemes3/?view=get

U.K. Secretary of State for Education and Skills. (1997). *Excellence in schools.* Suffolk, UK: Author.

U.S. Department of Commerce, National Telecommunications and Information Administration. (2002). *A nation online: How Americans are expanding their use of the Internet.* Washington, DC: U.S. Department of Commerce.

U.S. Department of Education. (1999). *Getting America's students ready for the 21st century: Meeting the technology literacy challenge.* Retrieved January 30, 1999, from http://www.ed.gov/about/offices/list/os/technology/plan/national/index.html

Warschauer, M. (1999). *Electronic literacies: Language, culture, and power in online education.* Mahwah, NJ: Erlbaum.

Warschauer, M. (2003). *Technology and social inclusion: Rethinking the digital divide.* Cambridge, MA: MIT Press.

Web-Based Education Commission. (2000). *The power of the Internet for learning: Moving from promise to practice: The report of the Web-Based Education Commission.*

Washington, DC: U.S. Government Printing Office. Retrieved December 15, 2003, from http://interact.hpcnet.org/webcommission/index.htm

Wenglinski, H. (1998). *Does it compute? The relationship between educational technology and student achievement in mathematics.*

Princeton, NJ: Educational Testing Service. (ERIC Document Reproduction Service No. ED425191)

Wertsch, J.V. (1991). *Voices of the mind: A sociocultural approach to mediated action.* Cambridge, MA: Harvard University Press.

55

The Role of Assessment in a Learning Culture

Lorrie A. Shepard

This article is about classroom assessment—not the kind of assessments used to give grades or to satisfy the accountability demands of an external authority, but rather the kind of assessment that can be used as a part of instruction to support and enhance learning. On this topic, I am especially interested in engaging the very large number of educational researchers who participate, in one way or another, in teacher education. The transformation of assessment practices cannot be accomplished in separate tests and measurement courses, but rather should be a central concern in teaching methods courses.

The article is organized in three parts. First, I present a historical framework highlighting the key tenets of social efficiency curricula, behaviorist learning theories, and "scientific measurement." Next, I offer a contrasting social-constructivist conceptual framework that blends key ideas from cognitive, constructivist, and sociocultural theories. In the third part, I elaborate on the ways that assessment practices should change to be consistent with and support social-constructivist pedagogy.

The impetus for my development of a historical framework was the observation by Beth Graue (1993) that "assessment and instruction are often conceived as *curiously separate* [italics added] in both time and purpose" (p. 291). As Graue notes, the measurement approach to classroom assessment, "exemplified by standardized tests and teacher-made emulations of those tests," presents a barrier to the implementation of more constructivist approaches to instruction.

To understand the origins of Graue's picture of separation and to help explain its continuing power over present-day practice, I drew the chronology in Figure 1. A longer-term span of history helps us see that those measurement perspectives, now felt to be incompatible with instruction, came from an earlier, highly consistent theoretical framework (on the left) in which conceptions of "scientific measurement" were closely aligned with traditional curricula and beliefs about learning. To the right is an emergent, constructivist paradigm in which

FIGURE 1
**A Historical Overview Illustrating How Changing Conceptions of Curriculum,
Learning Theory, and Measurement Explain the Current Incompatibility
Between New Views of Instruction and Traditional Views of Testing**

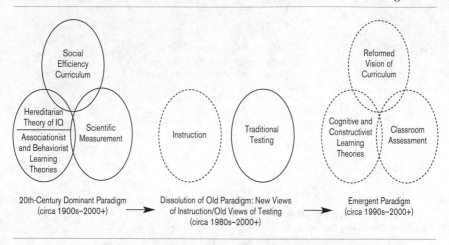

teachers' close assessment of students' understandings, feedback from peers, and student self-assessments would be a central part of the social processes that mediate the development of intellectual abilities, construction of knowledge, and formation of students' identities. The best way to understand dissonant current practices, shown in the middle of the figure, is to realize that instruction (at least in its ideal form) is drawn from the emergent paradigm, while testing is held over from the past.

Historical Perspectives: Curriculum, Psychology, and Measurement

The historical framework I present here is familiar to you. Yet, it is important to remind ourselves where traditional views of testing came from and to appreciate how tightly entwined these views of testing are with past models of curriculum and instruction—because dominant theories of the past continue to operate as the default framework affecting and driving current practices and perspectives. Belief systems of teachers, parents, and policymakers derive from these old theories.

A more elaborated version of the paradigm that has predominated throughout the 20th century can be shown as a set of interlocking circles (Figure 2). The central ideas of social efficiency and scientific management in the curriculum circle were closely linked, respectively, to hereditarian theories of individual

FIGURE 2

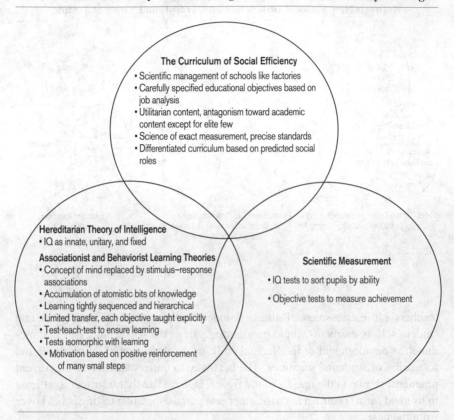

differences and to associationist and behaviorist learning theories. These psychological theories were, in turn, served by scientific measurement of ability and achievement.

In the early 1900s, the social efficiency movement grew out of the belief that science could be used to solve the problems of industrialization and urbanization. According to social efficiency theory, modern principles of scientific management, intended to maximize the efficiency of factories, could be applied with equal success to schools. This meant taking F.W. Taylor's example of a detailed analysis of the movements performed by expert bricklayers and applying similar analyses to every vocation for which students were being prepared (Kleibard, 1995). Then, given the new associationist or connectionist psychology with its emphasis on fundamental building blocks, every step would have to be taught specifically. Precise standards of measurement were required to ensure that each skill was mastered at the desired level. And because it was not possible to teach every student the skills of every vocation, scientific measures of ability were also needed to predict one's future role in life and thereby determine who was best suited for each endeavor. For John Franklin Bobbitt, a leader in the social efficiency movement, a primary goal of curriculum design was the elimination of waste (1912), and it was wasteful to teach people things they would never use. Bobbitt's most telling principle was that each individual should be educated "according to his capabilities." These views led to a highly differentiated curriculum and a largely utilitarian one that disdained academic subjects for any but college preparatory students.

Alongside these curriculum theories, Edward Thorndike's (1922) associationism and the behaviorism of Hull (1943), Skinner (1938, 1954), and Gagne (1965) conceived of learning as the accumulation of stimulus–response associations. The following quotation from B.F. Skinner is illustrative:

> The whole process of becoming competent in any field must be divided into a very large number of very small steps, and reinforcement must be contingent upon the accomplishment of each step. This solution to the problem of creating a complex repertoire of behavior also solves the problem of maintaining the behavior in strength.... By making each successive step as small as possible, the frequency of reinforcement can be raised to a maximum, while the possibly aversive consequences of being wrong are reduced to a minimum. (Skinner, 1954, p. 94)

Note that this viewpoint promotes a theory of motivation as well as one of cognitive development.

Several key assumptions of the behavioristic model had consequences for ensuing conceptualizations of teaching and testing:

1. Learning occurs by accumulating atomized bits of knowledge.

2. Learning is tightly sequenced and hierarchical.

3. Transfer is limited, so each objective must be explicitly taught.

4. Tests should be used frequently to ensure mastery before proceeding to the next objective.

5. Tests are isomorphic with learning (tests = learning).

6. Motivation is external and based on positive reinforcement of many small steps.

It is no coincidence that Thorndike was both the originator of associationist learning theory and the "father" of "scientific measurement," a name given him by Ayers in 1918. Thorndike and his students fostered the development and dominance of the "objective" test, which has been the single most striking feature of achievement testing in the United States from the beginning of the century to the present day. Recognizing the common paternity of behaviorist learning theory and objective testing helps us to understand the continued intellectual kinship between one-skill-at-a-time test items and instructional practices aimed at mastery of constituent elements.

Looking at any collection of tests from early in the century, as shown in Figure 3, one is immediately struck by how much the questions emphasized rote recall. To be fair, at the time, this was not a distortion of subject matter caused by the adoption of objective-item formats. One hundred years ago, various recall, completion, matching, and multiple-choice test types, along with some essay questions, fit closely with what was deemed important to learn. However, once curriculum became encapsulated and represented by these types of items,

FIGURE 3
Examples From Some of the Earliest 20th-Century "Standard" Tests and Objective-Type Classroom Tests

New Stone Reasoning Tests in Arithmetic (1908)

1. James had 5 cents. He earned 13 cents more and then bought a top for 10 cents. How much money did he have left?

Answer: _____

Sones–Harry High School Achievement Test, Part II (1929)

1. Write "25% of" as "a decimal times." _____
2. Write in figures: one thousand seven and four hundredths _____

The Modern School Achievement Tests, Language Usage

1. I borrowed a pen
   a. off
   b. off of   my brother. _____
   c. from

The Barrett–Ryan Literature Test: Silas Marner

1. Dolly Winthrop is:
a. an ambitious society woman.   c. a haughty lady.
b. a frivolous girl.   d. a kind, helpful neighbor.

Examples of True–False Objective Test (Ruch, 1929)

1. Tetnus (lockjaw) germs usually enter the body through open wounds.   *True   False*

American History Examination, East High School (Sam Everett and Effey Riley, 1928)

I. Below is a list of statements. Indicate by a cross (X) after it, each statement that expresses a social heritage of the present-day American nation.
Place a (0) after each statement that is not a present-day social heritage of the American nation.
1. Americans believe in the ideal of religious toleration.   _____
2. Property in land should be inherited by a man's eldest son.   _____
3. Citizens should have the right to say what taxes should be put upon them.   _____

II. To test your ability to see how an intelligent knowledge of past events helps us to understand present-day situations and tendencies.
(Note: Write your answer in essay form on a separate sheet of paper.)

State your reasons for every position assumed.

4. Take some *economic* fact or group of facts in American history about which we have studied and briefly show what seems to you to be the actual significance of this fact in the past, present and future of America.
5. Show this same *three-fold relationship* using some *political* fact or facts.
6. Show this same *three-fold relationship* using a *religious* fact or facts.

The first four examples are borrowed from Ross (1941); the last two, including the Everett–Riley American History Examination, appeared in Ruch (1929).

it is reasonable to say that these formats locked in a particular and outdated conception of subject matter.

The dominance of objective tests in classroom practice has affected more than the form of subject matter knowledge. It has also shaped beliefs about the nature of evidence and principles of fairness. In a recent assessment project, for example, both teachers and researchers were surprised to find that despite our shared enthusiasm for developing alternatives to standardized tests we nonetheless operated from different assumptions about how "standardized" assessments needed to be in classrooms. More surprising still, it was teachers who held beliefs more consistent with traditional principles of scientific measurement. From the perspective of our teacher colleagues, assessment needed to be an official event, separate from instruction (Bliem & Davinroy, 1997). To ensure fairness, teachers believed that assessments had to be *uniformly* administered, so they were reluctant to conduct more intensive individualized assessments with only below-grade-level readers. Because of the belief that assessments had to be targeted to a specific instructional goal, teachers felt more comfortable using two separate assessments for separate goals, running records to assess fluency and written summaries to assess comprehension rather than, say, asking students to retell the gist of a story in conjunction with running records. Most significant, teachers wanted their assessments to be "objective." They worried often about the subjectivity involved in making more holistic evaluations of student work and preferred formula-based methods, such as counting miscues, because these techniques were more "impartial."

Any attempt to change the form and purpose of classroom assessment to make it more fundamentally a part of the learning process must acknowledge the power of these enduring and hidden beliefs.

Conceptual Framework: New Theories of Curriculum, Learning, and Assessment

To consider how classroom assessment practices might be reconceptualized to be more effective in moving forward the teaching and learning process, I elaborated the principles of a "social-constructivist" conceptual framework, borrowing from cognitive, constructivist, and sociocultural theories.[1] (Though these camps are sometimes warring with each other, I predict that it will be something like this merged, middle-ground theory that will eventually be accepted as common wisdom and carried into practice.) The three-part figure (Figure 4) was developed in parallel to the three-part historical paradigm to highlight, respectively, changes in curriculum, learning theory, and assessment. In some cases, principles in the new paradigm are the direct antitheses of principles in the old. The interlocking circles again are intended to show the coherence and interrelatedness of these ideas taken together.

FIGURE 4

**Shared Principles of Curriculum Theories, Psychological Theories
and Assessment Theory Characterizing an Emergent, Constructivist Paradigm**

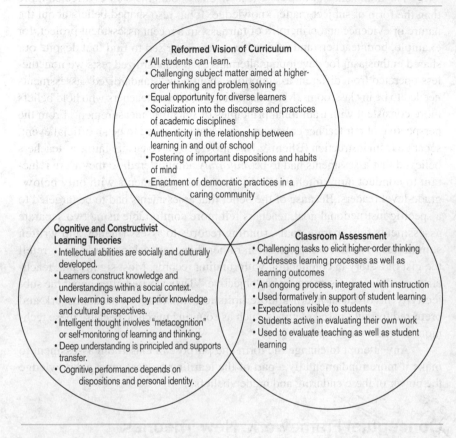

Reformed Vision of Curriculum
- All students can learn.
- Challenging subject matter aimed at higher-order thinking and problem solving
- Equal opportunity for diverse learners
- Socialization into the discourse and practices of academic disciplines
- Authenticity in the relationship between learning in and out of school
- Fostering of important dispositions and habits of mind
- Enactment of democratic practices in a caring community

Cognitive and Constructivist Learning Theories
- Intellectual abilities are socially and culturally developed.
- Learners construct knowledge and understandings within a social context.
- New learning is shaped by prior knowledge and cultural perspectives.
- Intelligent thought involves "metacognition" or self-monitoring of learning and thinking.
- Deep understanding is principled and supports transfer.
- Cognitive performance depends on dispositions and personal identity.

Classroom Assessment
- Challenging tasks to elicit higher-order thinking
- Addresses learning processes as well as learning outcomes
- An ongoing process, integrated with instruction
- Used formatively in support of student learning
- Expectations visible to students
- Students active in evaluating their own work
- Used to evaluate teaching as well as student learning

The cognitive revolution reintroduced the concept of mind. In contrast to past, mechanistic theories of knowledge acquisition, we now understand that learning is an active process of mental construction and sense making. From cognitive theory we have also learned that existing knowledge structures and beliefs work to enable or impede new learning, that intelligent thought involves self-monitoring and awareness about when and how to use skills, and that "expertise" develops in a field of study as a principled and coherent way of thinking and representing problems, not just an accumulation of information.

At the same time, rediscovery of Vygotsky (1934/1978) and the work of other Soviet psychologists led to the realization that what is taken into the mind is socially and culturally determined. Fixed, largely hereditarian theories of intelligence have been replaced with a new understanding that cognitive abilities are "developed" through socially supported interactions. Although Vygotsky was initially interested in how children learn to think, over time the ideas of social mediation have been applied equally to the development of intelligence, expertise in academic disciplines, and metacognitive skills, and to the formation of identity. Indeed, a singularly important idea in this new paradigm is that both development and learning are primarily social processes.

These insights from learning theory then lead to a set of principles for curriculum reform. The slogan that "all students can learn" is intended to refute past beliefs that only an elite group of students could master challenging subject matter. A commitment to equal opportunity for diverse learners means providing genuine opportunities for high-quality instruction and "ways into" academic curricula that are consistent with language and interaction patterns of home and community (Au & Jordan, 1981; Brown, 1994; Heath, 1983; Tharp & Gallimore, 1988). Classroom routines and the ways that teachers and students talk with each other should help students gain experience with the ways of thinking and speaking in academic disciplines. School learning should be authentic and connected to the world outside of school not only to make learning more interesting and motivating to students but also to develop the ability to use knowledge in real-world settings. In addition to the development of cognitive abilities, classroom expectations and social norms should foster the development of important dispositions, such as students' willingness to persist in trying to solve difficult problems.

To be compatible with and to support this social-constructivist model of teaching and learning, classroom assessment must change in two fundamentally important ways. First, its form and content must be changed to better represent important thinking and problem-solving skills in each of the disciplines. Second, the way that assessment is used in classrooms and how it is regarded by teachers and students must change. Furthermore, to enable this latter set of changes within classrooms, I argue that teachers need help in fending off the distorting and demotivating effects of external assessments.

Improving the Content and Form of Assessments

The content of assessments should match challenging subject matter standards and serve to instantiate what it means to know and learn in each of the disciplines. Therefore, a broader range of assessment tools is needed to capture important learning goals and processes and to more directly connect assessment to ongoing instruction. The most obvious reform has been to devise more open-ended performance tasks to ensure that students are able to reason critically, to solve complex problems, and to apply their knowledge in real-world contexts. In addition, if instructional goals include developing students' metacognitive abilities, fostering important dispositions, and socializing students into the discourse and practices of academic disciplines, then it is essential that classroom routines and corresponding assessments reflect these goals as well. This means expanding the armamentarium for data gathering to include observations, clinical interviews, reflective journals, projects, demonstrations, collections of student work, and students' self-evaluations, and it means that teachers must engage in systematic analysis of the available evidence.

In this article, I do not elaborate further on needed changes in the content and form of assessment primarily because this aspect of reform has received the most attention to date. Although I cannot claim that common practice has moved significantly beyond the end-of-chapter test, there are nonetheless already promising models being developed and used in literacy, mathematics, science, history, and so forth. For example, Pat Thompson (1995) provided the set of questions in Figure 5 to illustrate how nonalgorithmic problems can help students "see" a mathematical idea. Two additional open-ended tasks are shown in Figure 6 and serve to illustrate the point that good assessment tasks are interchangeable with good instructional tasks.

Protecting Classroom Assessment From the Negative Effects of High-Stakes Accountability Testing

The arguments advanced thus far—in support of social-constructivist learning theory, challenging curriculum for all students, and imaginative new forms of assessment—follow closely the rhetoric of standards-based reform. I have avoided using that term, however, because, from the beginning, standards-based reform has additionally placed great faith in externally imposed standards and "tests worth teaching to." More recently, the standards movement has been corrupted, in many instances, into a heavy-handed system of rewards and punishments without the capacity building and professional development originally proposed as part of the vision (McLaughlin & Shepard, 1995). Although both large-scale, system-monitoring assessments and classroom assessments could benefit from the same kinds of substantive reform and alignment of content with important learning goals, there is more at stake here than reform of assessment format. If we wish to pursue seriously the use of assessment *for* learning, which I consider in the next section, it is important to recognize the pervasive negative effects of accountability tests and the extent to which externally imposed testing programs prevent and drive out thoughtful classroom practices. In presenting these ideas to an audience of educational researchers and teacher educators, I used the image of Darth Vader and the Death Star (from the popular Star Wars movies) to convey the overshadowing effects of accountability testing.

The negative effects of high-stakes testing on teaching and learning are well known (e.g., Madaus, West, Harmon, Lomax, & Viator, 1992). Under in-

FIGURE 5

An Example of a Set of Questions Designed to Help Students Visualize Part–Whole Relationships as a Way to Understand Fractions

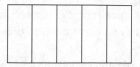

a) Can you see 3/5 of something?
b) Can you see 5/3 of something?
c) Can you see 5/3 of 3/5?
d) Can you see 2/3 of 3/5?
e) Can you see 1 ÷ 3/5?
f) Can you see 5/4 ÷ 3/4?

From Thompson (1995).

FIGURE 6

Examples of Open-Ended Assessment Tasks Intended to Engage Students in Thinking and Reasoning About Important Content

Grade 4 Mathematics Problem Set
(Mathematical Science Education Board, 1993)

All of the bridges in this part are built with yellow rods for spans and red rods for supports, like the one shown here. This is a 2-span bridge like the one you just built. Note that the yellow rods are 5 cm long.

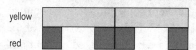

yellow

red

1. Now, build a 3-span bridge.
   a. How many yellow rods did you use? _____
   b. How long is your bridge? _____
   c. How many red rods did you use? _____
   d. How many rods did you use altogether? _____

2. Try to answer these questions without building a 5-span bridge.
   If you want, build a 5-span bridge to check your answers.
   a. How many yellow rods would you need for a 5-span bridge? _____
   b. How long would your bridge be? _____
   c. How many red rods would you need? _____
   d. How many rods would you need altogether? _____

3. Write a rule for figuring out the total number of rods you would need to build a bridge if you knew how many spans the bridge had.

Grade 5 Science Tasks
(California Learning Assessment System, 1994)

Fossils

You are a paleontologist (a scientist who studies past life forms). You were digging and just discovered a large group of fossils.

Directions:

Open BAG A and spread the fossils on the table. Use the hand lens to carefully observe each fossil. Sort your fossils into groups. You may make as many groups as you like.

Write answers to these questions in your journal.

1. Draw your groups. Circle and number each group.
2. How many groups do you have?
3. List the number of each group and tell why you sorted your fossils into these groups.

BAG B has a fossil that was found in the area near where you were digging.

Directions:

Open BAG B.

Take out the new fossil and compare it with the other fossils on the table.

4. Does this new fossil fit into one of your groups? If YES, how are they alike?
5. If the new fossil does not fit into any of your groups, describe a new group in which this fossil would fit.
6. Choose one of the fossils and draw a picture of it.
7. In what kind of habitat (environment) do you think this fossil might have once lived? Why?

tense political pressure, test scores are likely to go up without a corresponding improvement in student learning. In fact, distortions in what and how students are taught may actually decrease students' conceptual understanding. While some had imagined that teaching to good tests would be an improvement over low-level basic-skills curricula, more recent experiences remind us that all tests can be corrupted. And all can have a corrupting influence on teaching (Whitford & Jones, 2000).

Moreover, as Darling-Hammond (1988), McNeil (1988), and others have pointed out, external accountability testing leads to the deskilling and deprofes-sionalization of teachers, even—in my own state recently—to the denigration of teaching. High-stakes accountability teaches students that effort in school should be in response to externally administered rewards and punishment rather than the excitement of ideas. And accountability-testing mandates warn teachers to comply or get out (or move, if they can, to schools with higher-scoring students).

Again, these ideas are not new. It is likely that teacher educators say something about this litany of complaints in teacher preparation courses. But, what do diatribes against testing teach candidates about more meaningful forms of assessment? Given their own personal histories, our students are able to hate standardized testing and at the same time reproduce it faithfully in their own pre- and posttesting routines, if they are not given the opportunity to develop and try out other meaningful forms of assessment situated in practice. So we must teach them how to do assessment well.

Also, teacher candidates need to find support and a way of protecting their own developing understandings of constructivist assessment practices from the onslaught of test-driven curricula. I have in mind here something like the double-entry teaching that teachers had invented in Linda McNeil's (1988) study of the *Contradictions of Control*. In contrast to teachers who trivialized content and taught defensively as a means to control and win compliance from students, McNeil found that excited and engaging teachers in the magnet schools she studied found ways to resist and hold off the pernicious effects of proficiency testing on their curriculum. Specifically, they helped students keep parallel sets of notes, one set for the real knowledge and one for the knowledge they would need for the test. They did this rather than give over the entire course to the "fragments and facts" required on the test.

This is only one example of a strategy for resistance. As I continue next to describe productive ways to use assessment in classrooms, I emphasize the need sometimes to "mark" informal assessment occasions for students as they occur within the normal flow of classroom discourse—because this helps students become self-aware about how assessment can help learning. Similarly, I believe we should explicitly address with our teacher education students how they might cope with the contesting forces of good and evil assessment as they compete in classrooms to control curriculum, time, and student attitudes about learning.

Using Assessment in the Process of Learning

A Learning Culture

Improving the content of assessments is important but not sufficient to ensure that assessment will be used to enhance learning. In this section, I consider the changes in classroom practices that are also needed to make it possible for assessment to be used as part of the learning process. How might the culture of classrooms be shifted so that students no longer feign competence or work to perform well on the test as an end separate from real learning? Could we create a learning culture where students and teachers would have a shared expectation that finding out what makes sense and what doesn't is a joint and worthwhile project, essential to taking the next steps in learning?

I believe that our international colleagues are ahead of us in thinking about the difficulties of making these cultural changes. Sadler (1998) in Australia, for example, writes about "the long-term exposure of students to defective patterns of formative[2] assessment" (p. 77). Perrenoud in Switzerland (1991) notes that there are always certain students in a class who are willing to work harder to learn more and who, therefore, go along with formative assessment. But other children and adolescents are "imprisoned in the identity of a bad pupil and an opponent" (p. 92). According to Perrenoud, "every teacher who wants to practice formative assessment must reconstruct the teaching contract so as to counteract the habits acquired by his pupils" (p. 92). Tunstall and Gipps (1996) have studied classrooms in Great Britain where teachers have developed more interactive ways of discussing work and criteria with students as a means to redistribute power and establish more collaborative relationships with students.

To accomplish the kind of transformation envisioned, we not only have to make assessment more informative, more insightfully tied to learning steps, but at the same time we must change the social meaning of evaluation. Our aim should be to change our cultural practices so that students and teachers look to assessment as a source of insight and help instead of an occasion for meting out rewards and punishments. In the paragraphs that follow, I summarize briefly several specific assessment strategies: dynamic assessment, assessment of prior knowledge, the use of feedback, teaching for transfer, explicit criteria, student self-assessment, and evaluation of teaching. Each of these strategies serves a social, motivational purpose as well as a cognitive, informational one. None of these strategies by themselves will be effective if they are not part of a more fundamental shift in classroom practices and expectations about learning.

Dynamic, Ongoing Assessment

In order for assessment to play a more useful role in helping students learn, it should be moved into the middle of the teaching and learning process instead of being postponed as only the endpoint of instruction. Dynamic assessment—

finding out what a student is able to do independently as well as what can be done with adult guidance—is integral to Vygotsky's idea of a zone of proximal development. This type of interactive assessment, which allows teachers to provide assistance as part of assessment, does more than help teachers gain valuable insights about how understanding might be extended. It also creates perfectly targeted occasions to teach and provides the means to scaffold next steps. Although formal dynamic assessments are assumed to involve an adult working with only one child, these ideas about social mediation of learning can be extended to groups, especially if students are socialized into the ways of talking in a community of practice and become accustomed to explaining their reasoning and offering and receiving feedback about their developing competence as part of a social group.

Note that these ideas, based on activity theory and Lave and Wenger's (1991) concept of legitimate peripheral participation, provide a profoundly different view of motivation from behaviorist reinforcement and create no separation between cognitive and motivational goals. According to Lave and Wenger's theory, learning and development of an identity of mastery occur together as a newcomer becomes increasingly adept at participating in a community of practice. If one's identity is tied to group membership, then it is natural to work to become a more competent and full-fledged member of the group.

Prior Knowledge

Prior knowledge and feedback are two well-established ideas, the meaning of which may have to be reexamined as learning theories are changed to take better account of social and cultural contexts. For example, assessing my prior knowledge using a checklist or pretest version of the intended end-of-unit test may not be very accurate unless I already have sophisticated experience with the teacher's measures and conceptual categories. Open discussion or "instructional conversations" (Tharp & Gallimore, 1988) are more likely to elicit a more coherent version of students' reasoning and relevant experiences and can be a much more productive way for novice teachers to learn about the resources brought by students from diverse communities.

In my own experience working in schools, I have noticed two divergent sets of teaching practices that address students' prior knowledge. First, many teachers rely on a traditional, pretest–posttest design to document student progress but then do not use information from the pretest in instruction. At the same time, a significant number of teachers, especially in reading and language arts, use prior knowledge activation techniques, such as Ogle's (1986) K-W-L strategy (what I know, what I want to learn, what I have learned) but without necessarily attending to the assessment insights provided.

We have a great deal of work to do to develop and model effective assessment strategies, for starting points as well as for other stages of learning. One question we may want to consider is whether assessment should become so much a part of normal classroom discourse patterns that scaffolding and ongoing checks for understanding are embedded (and therefore disguised). Or whether assessment steps should be marked and made visible to students as an essential step in learning. In our efforts to change the culture of the classroom, it may be helpful, at least in the short term, to label prior knowledge activation techniques as instances of "assessment." What safer time to admit what you do not know than at the start of an instructional activity?

Feedback

We take it for granted that providing feedback to the learner about performance will lead to self-correction and improvement. For the most part, however, the existing literature on feedback will be of limited value to us in reconceptualizing assessment from a constructivist perspective because the great majority of existing studies are based on behaviorist assumptions. Typically, the outcome measures are narrowly defined, feedback consists of reporting of right and wrong answers to the learner, and the end-of-study test may differ only slightly from the prior measure and from instructional materials.

More promising are studies of scaffolding and naturalistic studies of expert tutoring—but these studies also reveal how much we have to learn about effective use of feedback. For example, Lepper, Drake, and O'Donnell-Johnson (1997) found that the most effective tutors do not routinely correct student errors directly. Instead they *ignore* errors when they are inconsequential to the solution process and *forestall* errors that the student has made previously by offering hints or asking leading questions. Only when the forestalling tactic fails do expert tutors *intervene* with a direct question intended to force the student to self-correct, or they may engage in *debugging*, using a series of increasingly direct questions to guide the student through the solution process. According to Lepper et al.'s analysis, the tendency of expert tutors to use indirect forms of feedback when possible was influenced by their desire to maintain student motivation and self-confidence while not ignoring student errors. This is a balancing act that new teachers must learn to perform as well.

Transfer

There is a close relationship between truly *understanding* a concept and being able to *transfer* knowledge and use it in new situations. In contrast to memorization—and in contrast to the behaviorist assumption that each application must be taught as a separate learning objective—true understanding is flexible, connected, and generalizable. Not surprising, research studies demonstrate that learning is more likely to transfer if students have the opportunity to practice with a variety of applications while learning (Bransford, 1979). Although there appears to be disagreement between cognitivists and situativists regarding knowledge generalization (Anderson, Reder, & Simon, 1996), in fact, both groups of researchers acknowledge the importance of being able to use what one has learned in new situations (Bransford, Brown, & Cocking, 1999). Cognitivists focus more on cognitive structures, abstract representations, and generalized principles that enable knowledge use in new situations, while situativists are concerned about "learning to participate in interactions in ways that succeed over a broad range of situations" (Greeno, 1996, p. 3).

In working with preservice teachers, I have suggested that a goal of teaching should be to help students develop "robust" understandings (Shepard, 1997). The term was prompted by Marilyn Burns's (1993) reference to children's understandings as being "fragile"—they appear to know a concept in one context but not to know it when asked in another way or in another setting. Sometimes this fragility occurs because students are still in the process of learning and sometimes because the framing of the problem, clues, and other supports available in the familiar context are not available in another. All too often, however, mastery appears pat and certain but does not travel to new situations because students have mastered classroom routines and not the underlying concepts. To support generalization and ensure transfer, that is, to support robust understandings, "Good teaching constantly asks about old understandings in new ways, calls for new applications, and draws new connections" (Shepard, 1997, p. 27). And good assessment does the same. We should not, for example, agree to a contract with our students that says that the only fair test is one with familiar and well-rehearsed problems.

Explicit Criteria

Frederiksen and Collins (1989) used the term *transparency* to express the idea that students must have a clear understanding of the criteria by which their work will be assessed. In fact, the features of excellent performance should be so transparent that students can learn to evaluate their own work in the same way that their teachers would. According to Frederiksen and Collins,

> The assessment system (should) provide a basis for developing a metacognitive awareness of what are important characteristics of good problem solving, good writing, good experimentation, good historical analysis, and so on. Moreover, such an assessment can address not only the product one is trying to achieve, but also the process of achieving it, that is, the habits of mind that contribute to successful writing, painting, and problem solving (Wiggins, 1989). (p. 30)

Having access to evaluation criteria satisfies a basic fairness principle (we should know the rules for how our work will be judged). More important, however, giving students the opportunity to get good at what it is that the standards require speaks to a different and even more fundamental sense of fairness, which is what Wolf and Reardon (1996) had in mind when they talked about "making thinking visible" and "making excellence attainable."

Self-Assessment

Student self-assessment serves cognitive purposes, then, but it also promises to increase students' responsibility for their own learning and to make the relationship between teachers and students more collaborative. As Caroline Gipps (1999) has suggested, this does not mean that the teacher gives up responsibility but that rather, by sharing it, she gains greater student ownership, less distrust, and more appreciation that standards are not capricious or arbitrary. In case studies of student self-evaluation practices in both an Australian and English site, Klenowski (1995) found that students participating in self-evaluation became more interested in the criteria and substantive feedback than in their grade per se. Students also reported that they had to be more honest about their own work as well as being fair with other students, and they had to be prepared to defend their opinions in terms of the evidence. Klenowski's (1995) data support Wiggins's (1992) earlier assertion that involving students in analyzing their own work builds ownership of the evaluation process and "makes it possible to hold students to higher standards because the criteria are clear and reasonable" (p. 30).

Evaluation of Teaching

In addition to using assessment to monitor and promote individual students' learning, classroom assessment should also be used to examine and improve teaching practices. This includes both ongoing, informal assessments of students' understandings to adjust lessons and teaching plans as well as more formal and critical action-research studies. As I have suggested with other assessment strategies, here again I believe it will be helpful for teachers to make their investigations of teaching visible to students, for example, by discussing with them decisions to redirect instruction, stop for a minilesson, and so forth. This seems to be fundamentally important to the idea of transforming the culture of the classroom. If we want to develop a community of learners—where students naturally seek feedback and critique their own work—then it is reasonable that teachers would model this same commitment to using data systematically as it applies to their own role in the teaching and learning process.

Conclusion

In conclusion, let me acknowledge that this social-constructivist view of classroom assessment is an idealization. The new ideas and perspectives underlying it have a basis in theory and empirical studies, but how they will work in practice and on a larger scale is not known. Clearly, the abilities needed to implement a reformed vision of curriculum and classroom assessment are daunting. Being able to ask the right questions at the right time, anticipate conceptual pitfalls, and have at the ready a repertoire of tasks that will help students take the next steps requires deep knowledge of subject matter. Teachers will also need help in learning to use assessment in new ways. They will need a theory of motivation and a sense of how to develop a classroom culture with learning at its center. Given that new ideas about the role of assessment are likely to be at odds with prevailing beliefs, teachers will need assistance to reflect on their own beliefs as well as those of students, colleagues, parents, and school administrators.

I am reminded of Linda Darling-Hammond's (1996) acknowledgment in her presidential address that John Dewey anticipated all of these ideas 100 years ago. But as Cremin (1961) explained, the successes of progressive education reforms never spread widely because such practice required "infinitely skilled teachers" who were never prepared in sufficient numbers to sustain these complex forms of teaching and schooling.

So, we are asking a lot of ourselves and others. Nonetheless, we must try again. This vision should be pursued because it holds the most promise for using assessment to improve teaching and learning. To do otherwise means that day-to-day instructional practices will continue to reinforce and reproduce the status quo. Our goal should be to find ways to fend off the negative effects of externally imposed tests and to develop instead classroom assessment practices that can be trusted to help students take the next steps in learning.

Epilogue

I would be remiss if I did not take this opportunity to provide at least a brief sketch of what we might do concretely to work toward a proposed vision of assessment in the service of learning. Happily for an organization of researchers, I suggest more research—but research of a particular kind embedded in the dilemmas of practice. I also suggest that we develop and pursue an agenda of public education to help policymakers and the general citizenry understand the differences between large-scale, system monitoring tests and what we hope for from teachers on a daily basis.

A Program of Research

To develop effective practices based on social-constructivist perspectives, it will be important to conduct studies in classrooms where instruction and assessment strategies are consonant with this model. In many cases this will mean "starting over again" and not assuming that findings from previous research studies can be generalized across paradigms. For example, as suggested earlier, there are hundreds of studies on feedback but nearly all conform to behaviorist assumptions—instruction is of short duration, posttests closely resemble pretests, feedback is in the form of being told the correct answers, and so forth. New studies will be needed to further our understandings of feedback provided in ways that reflect constructivist principles, for example, as part of instructional scaffolding, assessment conversations, and other interactive means of helping students self-correct and improve. Similarly, the research literature on motivation makes sweeping claims about the risks of evaluating students, especially when they are tackling difficult problems. Yet, these findings are based on students' experiences with traditional, inauthentic, and normative forms of assessment, where students took little responsibility for their own learning, and criteria remained mysterious. If the classroom culture were to be shifted dramatically, consistent with social-constructivist learning perspectives, then the effects of assessing students on difficult problems would have to be reexamined. Thus we face the challenge of trying to find out what works at the same time that we are attempting to create new contexts and new cultural expectations that will fundamentally alter the very relations we are trying to study.

We also need to study what makes sense in terms of teacher development and change. Many of the most exciting current assessment projects are being conducted in classrooms but still have researchers at the helm, taking central responsibility for the development of curriculum, assessment tasks, and technology-based delivery systems. We know that for teachers to make meaningful changes in pedagogical beliefs and accompanying practices, they themselves will need to try out and reflect on new approaches in the context of their own classrooms (Putnam & Borko, 1997). In deference to the enormous constraints on teachers' time, we should also look for ways to introduce new practices incrementally, for example, to develop a portfolio for one subject area or one curriculum unit before trying to do it in all subject areas. To consider how particular classroom assessment strategies might be used to create a learning culture as well as improve achievement, teams of teachers in schools might undertake projects aimed at any one of the assessment elements. For example, one team might want to introduce self-assessment and conference with students about how (or whether) self-assessment helps them learn. Another team of teachers might agree to meet regularly to share examples of "assessment insights," that is, specific occasions when assessment data from a student, written or oral, helped the teacher intervene in a better way because she understood what the student was thinking. And another group of teachers might focus on using feedback explicitly to help students make their work better.

When I say that our research efforts should be embedded in the dilemmas of practice, I am echoing the call for more collaborative forms of research advanced in recent reports by the National Research Council (1999) and National Academy of Education (1999) as well as by Alan Schoenfeld (1999) in his presidential address to the American Educational Research Association. In contrast to a traditional, linear progression from research to development and dissemination, these authors argue for investing in research projects that would advance fundamental understandings at the same time that they would work to solve practical problems in real-world settings. If researchers and professional educators share responsibility for improving educational outcomes, it is hoped that research will lead to continuous improvement of practice and not require a separate translation phase to be useful. In the context of an agenda for improving classroom assessment, this model for research would mean conducting studies aimed at general explanatory principles regarding prior knowledge, self-assessment, and the like, at the same time that practical issues are addressed such as the initial obstacles of negative student attitudes, time seemingly stolen from instruction, and the inevitable demand for better materials and instructional tasks that elicit the kind of thinking and dialogue envisioned.

A Public Education Agenda

Researchers in the United States have engaged policymakers and the public on the topic of testing but have focused almost exclusively on the features of state and district accountability testing programs—what the content should be, whether there should be high-stakes consequences, and so forth. In contrast, we have much to learn from assessment experts in the United Kingdom who have pursued a fundamentally different course of action emphasizing the key role of formative assessment in effective teaching. Beginning in 1989, researchers representing England, Northern Ireland, Scotland, and Wales met as a Task Group of the British Educational Research Association and ultimately established themselves as the Assessment Reform Group. The group is concerned with policy issues and has attempted to have a dialogue with policymakers. Although members of the group have been involved with either the development or evaluation of the National Assessment Programme, they "have become more and more convinced of the crucial link between assessment, as carried out in the classroom, and learning and teaching" (Assessment Reform Group, 1999, p. 1). They commissioned a major review of research examining the impact of assessment of students' learning (Black & William, 1998a), and they have issued two policy-oriented "little books" summarizing the important tenets of *assessment for learning* and urging government policies that would give more than lip service to the importance of improving formative assessment (Assessment Reform Group, 1999; Black & William, 1998b). They have argued for (a) reframing of bureaucratic requirements, such as standards for teacher education and school inspections, to ensure that teachers are skilled assessors of students' learning; (b) increased funding, especially for teacher professional development; and (c) reducing obstacles, especially the influence of external tests that dominate teachers' work.

Assessment experts in the United States should consider whether a similar public education endeavor would be worthwhile and what message we would choose to convey. At a minimum, we should try to get beyond the currently popular sound bite of "instructionally relevant assessment" because, unfortunately, legislators and school board members have taken up this slogan with the intention that once-per-year accountability testing can be used to diagnose individual student needs. Yes, end-of-year tests can be used to evaluate instruction and even tell us something about individual students, but such exams are like shopping mall medical screenings compared to the in-depth and ongoing assessments needed to genuinely increase learning. By pursuing a public education agenda like that undertaken in the United Kingdom we could help policymakers understand the limits to what can be accomplished with accountability tests (and thereby fend off their negative effects) and at the same time garner the support and flexibility that teachers and researchers will need to develop powerful examples and to enact more pervasive shifts in classroom practices.

Acknowledgments

The work reported herein was supported in part by grants from the Office of Educational Research and Improvement, U.S. Department of Education, to the Center for Research on Evaluation, Standards, and Student Testing (CRESST) (Award No. R305B60002) and to the Center for Research on Evaluation, Diversity and Excellence (CREDE) (Award No. R306A60001). The findings and opinions expressed in this article do not reflect the positions or policies of the Office of Educational Research and Improvement or the U.S. Department of Education.

Notes

[1] A more detailed discussion of this framework and supporting literature review are provided in Shepard (2001).

[2] Sadler (1998) uses the term *formative assessment* to mean assessment "that is specifically intended to provide feedback on performance to improve and accelerate learning" (p. 77). He acknowledges that teachers may have difficulty using feedback in positive ways because of students' negative coping strategies developed in response to past practices.

References

Anderson, J.R., Reder, L.M., & Simon, H.A. (1996). Situated learning and education. *Educational Researcher*, 25(4), 5–11.

Assessment Reform Group. (1999). *Assessment for learning: Beyond the black box*. Cambridge, UK: University of Cambridge School of Education.

Au, K.H., & Jordan, C. (1981). Teaching reading to Hawaiian children: Finding a culturally appropriate solution. In H. Trueba, G.P. Guthrie, & K.H. Au (Eds.), *Culture in the bilingual classroom: Studies in classroom ethnography* (pp. 139–152). Rowley, MA: Newbury House.

Ayers, L.P. (1918). *History and present status of educational measurements* (17th Yearbook of the National Society for the Study of Education, Part II, pp. 9–15) Chicago: University of Chicago Press.

Black, P., & William, D. (1998a). Assessment and classroom learning. *Assessment in Education: Principles, Policy, and Practice*, 5(1), 7–74.

Black, P., & William, D. (1998b). *Inside the black box: Raising standards through classroom assessment*. London: School of Education, King's College.

Bliem, C.L., & Davinroy, K.H. (1997). *Teachers' beliefs about assessment and instruction in literacy*. Unpublished manuscript, University of Colorado at Boulder.

Bobbitt, F. (1912). The elimination of waste in education. *The Elementary School Teacher*, 12, 259–271.

Bransford, J.D. (1979). *Human cognition: Learning, understanding, and remembering*. Belmont, CA: Wadsworth.

Bransford, J.D., Brown, A.L., & Cocking, R.R. (1999). *How people learn: Brain, mind, experience, and school*. Washington, DC: National Academy Press.

Brown, A.L. (1994). The advancement of learning. *Educational Researcher*, 23(8), 4–12.

Burns, M. (1993). *Mathematics: Assessing understanding*. White Plains, NY: Cuisenaire Company of America.

California Learning Assessment System. (1994). *A sampler of science assessment—elementary*. Sacramento: California Department of Education.

Cremin, L. (1961). *The transformation of the school: Progressivism in American education, 1876–1957*. New York: Vintage Books.

Darling-Hammond, L. (1988). Accountability and teacher professionalism. *American Educator, 12*, 8–13.

Darling-Hammond, L. (1996). The right to learn and the advancement of teaching: Research, policy, and practice for democratic education. *Educational Researcher, 25*(6), 5–17.

Frederiksen, J.R., & Collins, A. (1989). A systems approach to educational testing. *Educational Researcher, 18*(9), 27–32.

Gagne, R.M. (1965). *The conditions of learning*. New York: Rinehart & Winston.

Gipps, C.V. (1999). Socio-cultural aspects of assessment. In P.D. Pearson & A. Iran-Nejad (Eds.), *Review of research in education* (Vol. 24, pp. 355–392). Washington, DC: American Educational Research Association.

Graue, M.E. (1993). Integrating theory and practice through instructional assessment. *Educational Assessment, 1*, 293–309.

Greeno, J.G. (1996, July). *On claims that answer the wrong questions*. Stanford, CA: Institute for Research on Learning.

Heath, S.B. (1983). *Ways with words: Language, life, and work in communities and classrooms*. Cambridge, UK: Cambridge University Press.

Hull, C.L. (1943). *Principles of behavior: An introduction to behavior theory*. New York: Appleton-Century.

Klenowski, V. (1995). Student self-evaluation process in student-centered teaching and learning contexts of Australia and England. *Assessment in Education, 2*, 145–163.

Kliebard, H.M. (1995). *The struggle for the American curriculum: 1893–1958* (2nd ed.). New York: Routledge.

Lave, J., & Wenger, E. (1991). *Situated learning: Legitimate peripheral participation*. Cambridge, UK: Cambridge University Press.

Lepper, M.R., Drake, M.F., O'Donnell-Johnson, T. (1997). Scaffolding techniques of expert human tutors. In K. Hogan & M. Pressley (Eds.), *Scaffolding student learning: Instructional approaches & issues*. Cambridge, MA: Brookline Books.

Madaus, G.F., West, M.M., Harmon, M.C., Lomax, R.G., & Viator, K.A. (1992). *The influence of testing on teaching math and science in grades 4–12*. Chestnut Hill, MA: Center of Study of Testing, Evaluation, and Educational Policy, Boston College.

Mathematical Sciences Education Board. (1993). *Measuring up: Prototypes for mathematics assessment*. Washington, DC: National Academy Press.

McLaughlin, M.W., & Shepard, L.A. (1995). *Improving education through standards-based reform: A report of the National Academy of Education panel on standards-based educational reform*. Stanford, CA: National Academy of Education.

McNeil, L.M. (1988). *Contradictions of control: School structure and school knowledge*. New York: Routledge.

National Academy of Education. (1999, March). *Recommendations regarding research priorities: An advisory report to the National Educational Research Policy and Priorities Board*. New York: New York University.

National Research Council. (1999). *Improving student learning: A strategic plan for education research and its utilization*. Washington, DC: National Academy Press.

Ogle, D.M. (1986). K-W-L: A teaching model that develops active reading of expository text. *The Reading Teacher, 39*, 564–570.

Perrenoud, P. (1991). Towards a pragmatic approach to formative evaluation. In P. Weston (Ed.), *Assessment of pupils' achievement: Motivation and school success* (pp. 77–101). Amsterdam: Swets and Zeitlinger.

Putnam, R.T., & Borko, H. (1997). Teacher learning: Implications of new views of cognition. In B.J. Biddle, T.L. Good, & I.F. Goodson (Eds.), *International handbook of teachers and teaching* (Vol. 2, pp. 1223–1296). Dordecht, the Netherlands: Kluwer.

Ross, C.C. (1941). *Measurement in today's schools*. New York: Prentice-Hall.

Ruch, G.M. (1929). *The objective or new-type examination*. Chicago: Scott Foresman.

Sadler, D.R. (1998). Formative assessment: Revisiting the territory. *Assessment in Education: Principles, Policy and Practice, 5*, 77–84.

Schoenfeld, A.H. (1999). Looking toward the 21st century: Challenges of educational theory and practice. *Educational Researcher, 28*(7), 4–14.

Shepard, L.A. (1997). *Measuring achievement: What does it mean to test for robust under-*

standing? Princeton, NJ: Policy Information Center, Educational Testing Service.

Shepard, L.A. (2001). The role of classroom assessment in teaching and learning. In V. Richardson (Ed.), *Handbook of research on teaching* (4th ed). Washington, DC: American Educational Research Association.

Skinner, B.F. (1938). *The behavior of organisms: An experimental analysis.* New York: Appleton-Century-Crofts.

Skinner, B.F. (1954). The science of learning and the art of teaching. *Harvard Educational Review, 24,* 86–97.

Tharp, R.G., & Gallimore, R. (1988). *Rousing minds to life: Teaching, learning, and schooling in social context.* New York: Cambridge University Press.

Thompson, P.W. (1995). Notation, convention, and quantity in elementary mathematics. In J.T. Sowder & B.P. Schappelle (Eds.), *Providing a foundation for teaching mathematics in the middle grades* (pp. 199–221). Albany: State University of New York Press.

Thorndike, E.L. (1922). *The psychology of arithmetic.* New York: Macmillan.

Tunstall, P., & Gipps, C. (1996). Teacher feedback to young children in formative assessment: A typology. *British Educational Research Journal, 22,* 389–404.

Vygotsky, L.S. (1978). *Mind in society: The development of higher psychological processes* (M. Cole, V. John-Steiner, S. Scribner, & E. Souberman, Eds. & Trans.). Cambridge, MA: Harvard University Press. (Original work published 1934)

Whitford, B.L., & Jones, K. (2000). Kentucky lesson: How high stakes school accountability undermines a performance-based curriculum vision. In B.L. Whitford & K. Jones (Eds.), *Accountability, assessment, and teacher commitment: Lessons from Kentucky's reform efforts.* Albany: State University of New York Press.

Wiggins, G. (1989). A true test: Toward more authentic and equitable assessment. *Phi Delta Kappan, 70,* 703–713.

Wiggins, G. (1992). Creating tests worth taking. *Educational Leadership, 49*(8), 26–33.

Wolf, D.P., & Reardon, S.F. (1996). Access to excellence through new forms of student assessment. In J.B. Baron & D.P. Wolf (Eds.), *Performance-based student assessment: Challenges and possibilities* (pp. 1–31). Chicago: University of Chicago Press.

56

Literacy for All Children in the Increasingly Diverse Schools of the United States

Claude Goldenberg

Background: Education Goals and Shortcomings

In the final decade of the 20th century, the United States committed itself to eight ambitious education goals for the year 2000 (National Education Goals Panel, 1997). Three of these goals are at the heart of this chapter:

1. All children will begin school "ready to learn" (goal 1).

2. All students will leave grade 4 (and grades 8 and 12) demonstrating competency over challenging subject matter (goal 3).

3. Every school will promote parent involvement to support the social, emotional, and academic growth of children (goal 8).

These goals are highly interrelated. School readiness predicts school success, and parent involvement is deeply implicated in both. The literacy experiences, skills, and knowledge with which a child begins school will influence literacy development, and parents are an important influence at all points in this development. Parents influence how much experience children have with books and other reading materials; their familiarity with letters and sounds; the vocabulary they develop; and the reading and writing habits, opportunities, and experiences they have in and out of school. All these factors influence literacy development. None of this is to suggest that factors intrinsic to the child—for example, motivation and interest, intelligence, and phonemic sensitivity—are irrelevant. The focus of this chapter, however, is on environmental factors: the sorts of experiences schools and families can provide that will enhance literacy development for all children.

Each of the three goals—school readiness, school success, and parent involvement—shines a light on a distinct facet of children's academic and liter-

Adapted from the author's chapter in Neuman, S.B., & Dickinson, D.K. (Eds.), *Handbook of Early Literacy Research* (pp. 211–231). Copyright © 2001 by The Guilford Press. Adapted with permission of the publisher.

acy development. All children must start school ready to benefit from the learning experiences they will have there; all children, once they begin school, must develop academic competencies required for later success in school and in life; and every school must engage parents as partners in an educational process that will help advance the goals of school readiness and school success.

These are tall orders, to be sure. *All* children and *every* school mean a lot of children and many schools. As the 20th century ended, there were nearly 19 million children under age 5 in the United States; nearly 40 million more were between the ages of 5 and 14 (U.S. Census Bureau, 2000a). The U.S. Census Bureaus predicts that by the end of the 21st century these numbers will nearly double to 36 million and 72 million, respectively (U.S. Census Bureau, 2000b). Moreover, in the final school year of the 20th century, over 38 million children (U.S. Department of Education, 2002) attended nearly 96,000 pre-K to grade 8 public and private schools (U.S. Department of Education, 2001a), including combined elementary and middle schools. These numbers will, of course, continue to grow as the population of children grows.

Now that we are well into the 21st century, we must look back and ask whether the United States reached its national goals by the year 2000. The short answer is no. The fact is the country has a way to go, and for some children—particularly those who are poor and members of certain cultural and linguistic groups—the country has an even longer way to go. National-level data from the closing years of the 20th century reveal the disparities between the rhetoric of goals and the reality of schools, families, and children (see Table). Some child well-being indicators that have implications for educational outcomes showed positive trends in the last years of the 20th century; for example, U.S. poverty rates decreased from 22% to 16% between 1993 and 2000 (Federal Interagency Forum on Child and Family Statistics, 2002). Nonetheless, the challenge of making national education goals a reality for all U.S. students is likely to increase as we see increases in the numbers of children and schools as well as increases in the social, economic, and linguistic diversity of the country's populace (Federal Interagency Forum on Child and Family Statistics, 2002).

Attaining these education goals is essential if we are to make schools work for all students. How do we do this for children from low-income families who are linguistically and culturally different from the U.S. mainstream? Each year these children and their families make up a greater percentage of the U.S. population. How do we make schools work for them so that *all* children get off to a good start on the road to literacy? Not surprising, there are no simple answers. The answers depend on a wide range of considerations having to do with the nature of early literacy and how best to promote it; the influence of SES, language, and culture on children's formal schooling; and what parent involvement (home–school connections or partnerships) can and should be. Each of these topics will be discussed in turn.

National Education Goals: The Rhetoric-to-Reality Gap

GOAL 1: All students will begin school ready to learn.		
% of 3- and 5-yr-olds (not in kindergarten) attending early childhood care and education programs[1]		**56**
Association With Parent Education	• % whose mothers are college graduates	70
	• % whose mothers have less than high school diploma	38
Association With Ethnicity	• % white, non-Hispanic children	59
	• % Hispanic children	40
	• % black children	65
Association With Poverty	• % children in families at or above the poverty line	59
	• % children in families in poverty	47
% of 3- to 5-yr-olds read to every day[1]		**58**
Association With Parent Education	• % whose mothers are college graduates	73
	• % whose mothers have less than high school diploma	42
Association With Ethnicity	• % white, non-Hispanic children	64
	• % Hispanic children	42
	• % black children	48
Association With Poverty	• % children in families at or above the poverty line	61
	• % children in families in poverty	48
% of beginning kindergartners who...recognize letters[2]		**66**
Association With Parent Education	• % whose mothers are college graduates	86
	• % whose mothers have less than high school diploma	38
...recognize beginning sounds[2]		**29**
Association With Parent Education	• % whose mothers are college graduates	50
	• % whose mothers have less than high school diploma	9
...often/very often persist at tasks (teacher report)[2]		**71**
Association With Parent Education	• % whose mothers are college graduates	79
	• % whose mothers have less than high school diploma	61
GOAL 3: All students will demonstrate competency over challenging subject matter.		
% of fourth graders reading at least at "basic" level[3]		**63**
% of fourth graders writing at least at "basic" level[4]		**84**
% of fourth graders reading at "proficient" level[3]		**32**
% of fourth graders writing at "proficient" level[4]		**23**
Association With Income	• % non–low-income fourth graders who are "proficient" readers	41
	• % low-income fourth graders who are "proficient" readers	14

(continued)

Association With Parent Education	• % fourth graders with college graduate parent who are "proficient" writers	27
	• % fourth graders with non–high school graduate parent who are "proficient" writers	12
Association With Ethnicity	• % white fourth graders who are "proficient" readers/writers	40/29
	• % Asian/Pacific Islander fourth graders who are "proficient" readers/writers	46/36
	• % Hispanic fourth graders who are "proficient" readers/writers	16/10
	• % black fourth graders who are "proficient" readers/writers	12/8
	• % American Indian fourth graders who are "proficient" readers/writers	17/11

GOAL 8: All schools will promote parent involvement to support children's social, emotional, and academic growth.

% of elementary schools having these parent involvement activities:

Parent conferences, arts events, open houses, or back-to-school nights[5]	92–97
Providing information about school test performance, student progress, or school goals/objectives[6]	83–85
Providing information about how to promote learning at home (e.g., helping with homework, study skills) and to inform parents about child-rearing issues (e.g., discipline)[5]	82–89
Parent advisory group or policy council[5]	79
Providing information about improvements in children's performance[6]	72
Providing examples of student work meeting high standards[5]	60

% elementary schools reporting most or all parents attend[5]

Open house or back-to-school night	49
Parent–teacher conferences	57
Performing arts events	36
Science fairs or academic events	19

Association With % High-Poverty School Population	• % of schools with < 25% high-poverty students reporting high parent turnout	72
	• % of schools with > 50% high-poverty students reporting high parent turnout	28
Association With % Minority School Population	• % of schools with < 20% minority enrollment reporting high parent turnout	60
	• % of schools with > 50% minority enrollment reporting high parent turnout	30

[1] Federal Interagency Forum on Child and Family Statistics (2002).
[2] Federal Interagency Forum on Child and Family Statistics (2000); from Early Childhood Longitudinal Study, Kindergarten Class of 1998–1999 (Available at http://nces.ed.gov/ecls/).
[3] U.S. Department of Education (2001b).
[4] U.S. Department of Education (1999).
[5] U.S. Department of Education (1996).
[6] U.S. Department of Education (1998).

The Challenges of Promoting Early Literacy for All Children

The challenge of making schools work for all children, regardless of income level, is formidable for many reasons. One is the nature of learning to read and the many uncertainties and controversies surrounding this critical accomplishment. Another reason concerns issues of poverty and cultural and linguistic diversity.

Learning to Read: Controversies and Emerging Consensus

One of the most controversial topics in education centers on questions of what early literacy is and how children learn to read. These questions are central to the three U.S. national goals of school readiness, academic competence, and parent involvement. Questions related to what literacy is and how best to promote it color our thinking about how to accomplish the education goals the United States has set for all children. Children from low-income families are more dependent on school experiences for their academic literacy development than are middle class children (Alexander & Entwisle, 1996; Snow, Barnes, Chandler, Goodman, & Hemphill, 1991). It is not that low-income children have no literacy experiences at home; this is a harmful misconception that is flatly untrue (see, e.g., Anderson & Stokes, 1984; Clark, 1983; Goldenberg & Gallimore, 1995; Goldenberg, Reese, & Gallimore, 1992; Paratore, Melzi, & Krol-Sinclair, 1999; Taylor & Dorsey-Gaines, 1988; Teale, 1986). However, the literacy experiences and accomplishments of low-income children do tend to be limited compared to those of more affluent peers (Baker, Serpell, & Sonnenschein, 1995; Whitehurst & Lonigan, 1998), and therefore the school's responsibility is particularly great. Disagreements over how best to promote early and continued literacy growth and what parents ought to be doing to promote literacy for their children take on added significance for children who face greater risk for underachievement.

A key dimension in this controversy is the classic question of how much to emphasize letters and sounds and how they combine to form words. The historic significance of this controversy (see Chall, 1983) was acknowledged once again when *Reading Research Quarterly* reprinted the classic "First-Grade Studies," which demonstrated the importance of "code" emphasis in beginning reading instruction (Readence & Barone, 1997).

Over the past two decades, an analogous controversy about the preschool years has emerged and become an important component in discussions of what it means to be ready to start school. Researchers in the 1980s discovered that *phonological awareness* is an important precursor of learning to read (Stanovich, 1987). Phonological awareness refers to the understanding that spoken speech can be broken down into discreet units of sound at the subword level: syllables, onsets (initial consonant or consonant cluster in a syllable), rimes (what follows the consonant or consonant cluster in a syllable), and phonemes. Phonological awareness training, particularly when coupled with training on letters and corresponding sounds, promotes early decoding and word reading, which in turn promote reading development (Snow, Burns, & Griffin, 1998; Troia, 1999).

Although there is fairly wide agreement that phonological awareness is an important aspect of being ready to learn to read (e.g., Ehri, Nunes, Willows, Schuster, Yaghoub-Zadeh, & Shanahan, 2001; Ralph, Ellis, & Medina, 1998; Snow et al., 1998; Troia, 1999; Yopp, Yopp, Harris, & Stapleton, 1998), there is less agreement about what this means practically. Should children receive direct instruction and training (e.g., Ball & Blachman, 1988, 1991)? Or should teachers promote phonological awareness by using natural language activities, such as poems, chants, and songs (Ralph et al., 1998)? How do teachers attain the right balance between authentic tasks and skill practice (Schickedanz, 1998) when helping children develop phonological awareness?

Practical recommendations differ for what should be done to help all children, particularly those at risk for poor reading achievement, begin school ready to learn, depending on what educators view as critical components of learning to read and what needs to be emphasized to promote early reading success. Proponents of strong phonics and phonological awareness training will recommend a different set of practices than those who emphasize more contextualized uses of literacy. A *sociocultural, developmentalist* perspective on literacy (Neuman, 1998) emphasizes the importance of meaningful and functional literacy experiences. Neuman and Roskos (1993, 1997), for example, have shown that low-income preschoolers can learn important information about print (e.g., identifying a calendar or a telephone book; pretending to take an order at a restaurant by scribbling on a pad) when classroom environments are structured so that they engage with these kinds of literacy activities and materials. In contrast, a *cognitive–linguistic* perspective emphasizes the critical role of phonological knowledge in learning to read. Brady, Fowler, Stone, and Winbury (1994) have shown that inner-city preschoolers can be taught important phonologically related skills, such as generating rhymes and segmenting phonemes.

These perspectives appear to be sharply contrasting. But reading educators are attempting to forge a broad consensus about what literacy is and how best to promote it that incorporates different emphases on literacy development (e.g., National Institute of Child Health and Human Development [NICHD], 2000; Pressley, 1998; Snow et al., 1998). The broad outlines of this consensus suggest that productive early literacy experiences and effective literacy instruction must address comprehensively several distinguishable, yet ultimately interrelated, aspects of literacy (see Snow et al., 1998). No one component alone is sufficient for adequate literacy development; all are needed to one degree or another, although the following components are particularly critical at particular points or stages in the process of learning to read and write:

- understanding and using print functionally (reading and writing for communication, expression, etc.)
- understanding and using the alphabetic principle (phonological awareness, letter names and sounds, efficient and automatic decoding [i.e., reading] and encoding [i.e., writing])
- motivation and interest in using print for a variety of purposes
- language, cognitive skills, and knowledge necessary for comprehension and communication

Although there is no widespread agreement about how much of each aspect should be stressed, a successful literacy program will address each of these in sufficient depth and breadth to promote literacy growth in the earliest and later years. "Optimal" will probably vary by learner and stage of literacy development, but the basic ingredients of a healthy literacy diet are probably the same for all children (and adults) learning to read an alphabetic language (Snow et al., 1998). At the prereading (emergent), early, and beginning stages of reading, phonological processes (e.g., hearing the sounds in words) and insight into the alphabetic principle (letters represent sounds in a predictable system, and words comprise patterns of letters and corresponding sounds) are especially critical for learning to read. Effective literacy practices and programs, particularly for children who do not enjoy a wide range of literacy experiences outside of school, must include adequate amounts of instruction specifically targeted at helping them acquire these understandings and skills, such as how letters and sounds map onto each other and form written and spoken words (Ehri, Nunes, Stahl, & Willows, 2001). But children also must have literacy and oral language experiences that promote vocabulary and language development, build background knowledge and familiarity with stories, and provide opportunities to see and engage in meaningful literacy activities (NICHD, 2000; Snow et al., 1998). Such experiences, both early and later, become increasingly important as children advance in their literacy development.

Effective instructional practices to promote emergent and beginning literacy for all children include the following:

- literate environments where print is used for diverse and interesting purposes, including opportunities for student choice and ample time for looking at books and reading or "pretend reading"
- direct, explicit, systematic instruction in specific skills (e.g., phonological awareness, letter names and sounds, decoding, comprehension strategies), with sufficient practice in successful use of skills in order to promote transfer and automaticity

- discussions and conversations about materials children read or that are read to them

- focus on word-recognition skills and strategies (direct instruction, but also use of techniques such as word walls and making words)

- strategically sequenced instruction and curriculum materials to maintain optimal challenge (instructional or independent, as appropriate)

- organizational and classroom management strategies to maximize academic engagement and appropriate use of materials

- an explicit focus on language (including vocabulary) development

- valid and frequent assessments, using multiple measures as needed and appropriate, to allow teachers to gauge developing skills and target instruction appropriately

- a home–school connection component that links the school's efforts with children's home experiences and enlists parents in supporting their children's academic development

This emerging consensus might provide a foundation for U.S. national efforts to make schools work for all children. Later in this chapter I will describe programs that embody one or more of these practices and have been successful in helping improve literacy development among low-income children.

The Influence of Socioeconomic Status, Language, and Culture on Learning to Read

The complex picture of learning to read becomes further complicated when we factor in socioeconomic status (SES) and issues of language and culture. Low-income children and children from some cultural and linguistic groups have traditionally done poorly in U.S. schools (Natriello, McDill, & Pallas, 1990). As discussed previously, we are further from accomplishing our education goals with poor and minority children than we are with nonpoor, nonminority children. There is a high correlation between SES and cultural and linguistic group membership in the United States, so as a practical matter it is extremely difficult to talk about one without the other. The picture becomes highly complex, with several interrelated factors bearing on children's literacy development.

Socioeconomic Status. Socioeconomic issues are obviously central to discussions of how schools can meet the needs of low-income students and their families. Baker et al. (1995) found that compared to children from middle-income homes, low-income children had fewer opportunities for interactions involving literacy, for example, food preparation, shopping, storybook reading, pretend play, and activities with educational toys. Middle-income parents reported significantly more play with print and more independent reading by children, although only slightly more joint book reading, than did low-income families. Ninety percent of the middle class families in Baker's study reported that their child visited the library at least once a month, whereas only 43% of the low-income families reported this to be so. Once children entered kindergarten, low-income parents (particularly African Americans) reported more reading skills practice and homework (e.g., flash cards, letter practice) than did middle-income parents.

Low-income children also have less exposure to literacy and opportunities to interact with literacy in their communities. Neuman and Celano (2001) report striking contrasts in the print resources available to children in low-income versus moderate-income neighborhoods. For example, the researchers report that in the two moderate-income neighborhoods, they counted 1,600 and 16,000 children's titles, respectively, in stores, but in the two low-income neighborhoods they counted only 55 and less than 400 titles. Similar contrasts were found for signage, public spaces for reading, and other environmental and contextual indicators of literacy materials and opportunities.

Upon entrance to school, low-income children appear to be "less ready," as Whitehurst and Lonigan (1998) point out. They have had less experience with books, writing, hearing stories, learning and reciting rhymes, and many other types of experiences that promote literacy learning. The likely impact on early literacy skills and knowledge is illustrated in Goal 1 of the Table: Children whose parents are more highly educated begin kindergarten with more understanding of important literacy concepts (Federal Interagency Forum on Child and Family Statistics, 2000). Goldenberg and Gallimore (1995) found that, on average, low-income Spanish-speaking children (tested in Spanish) had relatively few emergent literacy skills. Presented with 10 of the most frequently used letters, the average number recognized was 1 lowercase and 1.5 uppercase. Two thirds of the children could not name or recognize a single letter. More than three fifths could write no letters at all. The majority also could write no words, either correctly or attempted. Fewer than half pointed somewhere in the print when asked where the tester should read; one fourth indicated that print was read from left to right; fewer than one fourth could point to the first and last parts of text on a page.

In contrast, children from higher-income families have more text-based literacy experiences and opportunities at home. They arrive in kindergarten able to recognize more letters; they can write letters, words, and even phrases. They have more invented spelling and engage in more scribble writing. They have more concepts about print, such as where in the page the printed text is and that text is read from left to right. Some of these children are even readers in a more conventional sense, although this is less common (Adams, 1990; Chall, 1983; Clay, 1993; Mason, 1977).

There is obviously wide variability within any social group or economic level, yet in general, low-income children begin school with fewer literacy experiences and less literacy knowledge. Once they begin first grade, they then tend to fall further behind more affluent peers. During school months the rate of low-income children's academic progress is equivalent to that of higher-income children, but during summers the academic gap widens (Alexander & Entwisle, 1996).

There are two important qualifications to the economic status–achievement connection, however: (1) Family socioeconomic effects on achievement, at the individual level, are in fact modest, and (2) effective school programs will help more children achieve, regardless of their economic class.

The association between SES and early reading achievement is quite weak when measured at the individual family level. However, socioeconomic influence on achievement is much stronger when measured at the school or community level. In other words, the effects of economic status on achievement are largely the result of living in communities and attending school with large numbers of children from a particular social class, not the result of a single family's socioeconomic characteristics. Average correlations between family SES and measures of academic achievement are a modest .2–.3 (Walberg & Tsai, 1985; White, 1982). In contrast, when SES is measured at the level of the school or community, the correlation with achievement is nearly .7 (White, 1982). So, for example, a low-SES child attending a low-income school and living in a low-income community is at far greater risk for reading difficulties than is the same child attending and living in a middle- or high-income school and community.

One reason for the weak link between family economic status and learning to read is that there is a great deal of variability in family practices and student achievement within any economic stratum. We must therefore avoid deterministic assumptions about the effects of economic status on literacy development. Children's preliteracy skills and knowledge (e.g., phonological awareness, letter knowledge, and concepts of print) are far better predictors of reading achievement than is family SES (Scarborough, 1998; Snow et al., 1998). What children know and can do are variable within economic class and more closely related to literacy outcomes than economic class. Among low-income families, there are those in which children experience relatively high levels of literacy, academic learning, and encouragement (Anderson & Stokes, 1984; Clark, 1983; Goldenberg & Gallimore, 1995; Goldenberg et al., 1992; Heath, 1983; Paratore et al., 1999; Taylor & Dorsey-Gaines, 1988; Teale, 1986). One of the most pernicious and persistent assumptions among many educators is that low-income families, particularly those from cultural groups that typically have done poorly in U.S. schools, barely survive in a culture of poverty and have little time, inclination, or ability to provide their children with learning opportunities to benefit academic achievement (e.g., Grossman, 1984).

Furthermore, as Baker et al. (1995) and Goldenberg et al. (1992) have shown, once children begin school, the amount of literacy in the homes of low-income children increases, suggesting that families are responsive to children's school experiences and support changes in children's home activities to reflect a more academic focus. Indeed, perhaps in part due to families' responsiveness, effective school and classroom practices have been shown to improve the achievement of students from diverse socioeconomic, cultural, and linguistic backgrounds. This is the second qualification we must bear in mind: Effective school and classroom programs will make a difference, no matter children's SES. The extent to which effective programs can completely counter the influence of economic status, however, is an open question. I will return to these issues later in the chapter.

Language. In the United States, socioeconomic factors are often conflated with language and culture because disproportionate numbers of children from certain ethnolinguistic groups are from low-income households. August and Hakuta (1997) report that 77% of English learners qualify for free or reduced-price lunches in contrast to only 38% of the overall student population in the same schools. Latin American immigrants, who constitute by far the largest immigrant group and whose children constitute the largest group of English learners in California and the United States, come to the United States with low levels of education and few material resources (Goldenberg, 1996). Mexican and Central American immigrants tend to have relatively little formal education and are more likely than native-born U.S. residents or immigrants from other countries to be living in poverty. African American, native Hawaiian, and American Indian students are among those groups with disproportionately high numbers of low-SES families (Federal Interagency Forum on Child and Family Statistics, 2000; Tharp, 1989; Tharp & Gallimore, 1988).

Language is perhaps the most controversial of the three demographic dimensions considered in this chapter; most debate has centered on whether children for whom English is not the primary language should be taught to read first in their home language or if they should be immersed in English from the outset of their school careers. The language-of-instruction question has almost completely dominated research and discussions about the education of limited English proficient (LEP) students, now commonly referred to as *English language learners* (August & Hakuta, 1997). Yet cognitive, affective, instructional, curricular, and school-based factors that are important for English speakers learning to read in English, as outlined previously, are also important for English learners learning to read. Indeed, there is considerable evidence that reading and learning to read in one's native language are in many ways like reading and learning to read in a second language (Chiappe & Siegel, 1999; Fitzgerald, 1995). Nonetheless, there are differences that teachers must take into account, such as the more limited vocabulary of English learners and the different experiential base from which English learners can draw in order to make sense of academic instruction. All these considerations are relevant to discussions of how best to promote high levels of academic literacy attainment in early elementary school.

What is the proper role of the primary language in the academic instruction of LEP children? Primary language advocates on one extreme say that the longer, more intensively, and more effectively students learn literacy and academic skills in their home language, the better their eventual academic attainment will be *in English* (Thomas & Collier, 1997, 2002). The theoretical rationale is that we learn best in the language we know best, and that once basic concepts and skills are learned in the primary language, they transfer readily to a second language. In diametric opposition, advocates of English-only instruction say that early, sustained, and effective use of English in the classroom leads to superior attainment in English (Rossell & Baker, 1996). These people cite a different rationale: The more time spent learning and practicing a language, the greater the eventual attainment in that language.

Studies point policy in opposite directions. Rossell and Baker's (1996) review of research concludes that students should be immersed in English as soon as possible and as intensively as possible. But two quantitative syntheses have concluded precisely the opposite: Use of students' primary language produces superior achievement results in English when compared to immersion in English (Greene, 1997; Willig, 1985). One prominent demonstration of the superiority of primary language instruction in the early stages of reading was provided in a nationwide study by Ramírez, Yuen, Ramey, and Merino (1986). The researchers found that kindergarten and first-grade students who received academic instruction *in Spanish* had higher achievement in beginning reading *in English* than did comparable students who received academic instruction in English (there were no significant differences in language and mathematics). At the preschool level, some studies have shown that Spanish-language classrooms for Spanish speakers are also associated with higher levels of language and early literacy attainment in both Spanish and English (e.g., Campos & Keatinge, 1988).

A different rationale for using the primary language as an instructional vehicle has to do with the intrinsic advantages of knowing two languages. Whatever the controversy over the role of primary language (e.g., Spanish) in second-language (e.g., English) attainment, there is no controversy over the facts that (a) primary-language instruction leads to primary-language maintenance without blocking second-language acquisition, in other words a greater chance of bilingualism, and (b) bilingualism confers cognitive, cultural, and economic benefits (August & Hakuta, 1997; Crawford, 1991; Rossell & Baker, 1996). Of course a key question is whether school programs that promote primary-language maintenance and bilingual development sacrifice some degree of English acquisition. The answer would appear to be no, but this is part of the complex debate over the role of the home language in the education of

English learners. Unfortunately, knowing two languages has attracted little attention in the U.S. debate over improving schools; certainly it is not among the country's national education goals. Consequently, the advantages of bilingualism—which are beyond dispute—have played virtually no role in informing research and policy discussions. This is indeed unfortunate and can only serve to heighten the perception of U.S. cultural and linguistic insularity (Simon, 1980).

We also must keep the language issue in perspective and understand that language of instruction per se is only one of several issues educators face in teaching English learners (August & Hakuta, 1997; National Educational Research Policy and Priorities Board, 1999). Other important issues have to do with the sorts and quality of literacy experiences and instruction children receive, as discussed previously.

Culture. Culture and cultural differences also have played a role in discussions and research on the education of historically disadvantaged groups. By definition, the most distinguishing characteristic of English learners is their lack of English proficiency. However, English learners are also members of diverse ethnocultural groups, which itself might have implications for learning to become literate (Tharp, 1989). Socioeconomic and sociopolitical issues also might be relevant, particularly for Spanish-origin English learners in the United States, who historically have been victims of discrimination and economic disadvantage.

As with language, the issue of culture is complex and difficult to disentangle from ideological or philosophical considerations that go far beyond empirical questions and matters of curriculum and instruction. Cultural diversity is increasingly a fact of life in U.S. schools, particularly in border states, such as California, Arizona, and Texas, and states that traditionally or more recently have been destinations of successive waves of immigrants, such as New York, Illinois, and Washington. Yet culture means different things to different people. Even among anthropologists there is no universal, agreed-upon definition. Is culture defined by how people dress? The food they eat? The language they speak? How they think? Behave? What motivates them? Is it all of these? Are some factors more important to cultural identity than others? Culture has many dimensions and no one dimension can be said to define any group of people. Moreover, there is considerable disagreement over whether and how the distinct cultural experiences of different people should inform school programs (Schlesinger, 1991).

Why does culture matter in the early reading development of culturally diverse students, and therefore what is its relevance to a discussion of U.S. national education goals? There are several possibilities. One is that members of different cultural groups might socialize their children differently and have different behavioral expectations for children and that some of these differences might have a negative impact on children's schooling experiences. Valdés (1996) provides an illustration. She shows how children of Mexican immigrants are socialized not to be assertive around adults or engage in displays of information. Yet U.S. teachers often expect a certain amount of assertiveness, even aggressiveness, from students. They expect students to be eager to show off what they know. Children in the kindergarten and first-grade class Valdés studied "had to be ready to perform and indeed outperform their peers" (1996, p. 147). Otherwise, teachers assumed that things had not yet "clicked" (p. 146). In the case of the Mexican-origin children who did not display expected behaviors, teachers lowered their academic expectations for them and placed them in lower reading groups. Valdés suggests this was the beginning of a downward spiral of failure for these students.

Research suggests that certain types of cultural accommodations to behavioral or interactional styles improve students' academic engagement and participation. Au and Mason (1981), reporting data collected as part of the Kamehameha Early Education Project (KEEP), found that when a teacher engaged Hawaiian children in small-group discussions that were similar to the sorts of free-flowing interactions children were used to at home, children were more engaged and participated at a higher cognitive level. When the teacher employed a more controlled turn-taking discussion style that was dissimilar to what students were used to, children participated less and their contributions to the discussion were at a lower academic level. As important as this and other studies of cultural accommodation are (see Tharp, 1989), however, there is actually very little evidence that cultural accommodation per se produces measured gains in achievement (Fueyo & Bechtol, 1999; Goldenberg & Gallimore, 1989). Even when teachers and students are matched by race/ethnicity, there is no difference in student achievement in comparison to students with teachers who are dissimilar racially or ethnically (Vierra, 1984).

The most compelling argument that cultural accommodation produces improvements in student learning and other outcomes has been provided by Allen and Boykin (1992) in their review of laboratory and classroom studies involving African American children. The authors argue that African American children learn best from prescriptive pedagogy because of their interactional and socialization experiences at home. The hypothesis that cultural accommodation can lead to improved student outcomes is important. However, teachers must realize that the evidence for its effects—and therefore its significance to classroom practice—is not as strong as many might assume.

KEEP is cited widely as illustrating the power of culturally accommodated instruction to improve early literacy attainment (Tharp & Gallimore, 1988). Hawaiian children received literacy instruction and classroom experiences that contained elements compatible with their natal culture. For example, they worked in small, peer-oriented collaborative groups in which children were free to interact around academic tasks, compatible with the peer-oriented child culture Hawaiian children experience, with relatively little adult supervision. KEEP teachers also used a more free-flowing discussion style during reading comprehension lessons, which paralleled the overlapping discourse patterns (dubbed "talk-story") that native Hawaiian children and adults engage in naturally. KEEP students at the original demonstration site and at remote sites when the program was exported to other schools demonstrated significant improvement in early reading achievement compared to control and comparison groups (Tharp, 1982).

The KEEP instructional program, however, also contained many elements found to be effective universally, that is, not necessarily accommodated to any particular group (Goldenberg & Gallimore, 1989). For example, KEEP employed active, direct teaching of reading comprehension; collaborative learning; well-run and organized classrooms; a good balance of word-recognition (including phonics) skills instruction and comprehension instruction; and ongoing and substantive professional development for teachers. It is impossible to disentangle the effects of culturally accommodated instruction from the effects of more general or universal principles of effective curriculum and teaching (Goldenberg & Gallimore, 1989). A plausible hypothesis is that both sets of factors—universal principles and culturally accommodated instruction—made contributions to the improvements in achievement.

There are other compelling reasons for teachers to know about cultural facets of children's learning, aside from their possible influence on measured outcomes and on accomplishing national education goals. If nothing else, different cultural groups have different norms of behaving and interacting; teachers should understand and be sensitive to these because doing so can only help students and families feel more comfortable and welcomed in what might seem a very foreign institution. Moreover, educated professionals—particularly those who work with children—must know about the varieties of human experiences, even if that knowledge does not translate neatly into educational prescriptions. But teachers also should understand that there is no consistent set of factors that has yet been discovered that takes cultural understandings and turns them into effective educational interventions.

It is also worthwhile to note, particularly in light of the following section on home–school connections, that parents are skeptical of the idea that their children's teachers must come from similar backgrounds in order to be effective. A *Los Angeles Times* poll asked residents in the Los Angeles Unified School District whether they thought students learned better when teachers and administrators were the same race/ethnicity as the students. An overwhelming majority of parents—85%—responded that race/ethnicity did not matter. Latino and black respondents felt just as strongly as did white respondents that race/ethnicity did not influence their children's academic achievement (*Los Angeles Times* Poll, 1999).

Examples of Efforts to Help Children At Risk: Prospects and Limits

At least since the 1960s educators have been exploring numerous avenues to improve outcomes, among the most important being literacy outcomes, for low-income children. By and large, U.S. schools and society as a whole have not done an exemplary job, although it is probably not for lack of trying. We can cite some successes, but the rhetoric-to-reality gap surrounding U.S. national education goals suggests how much further we must go. In this section I will discuss several types of programs and interventions undertaken to try and address the literacy achievement gap between low- and higher-income students. This will in no way be a comprehensive catalog but instead will illustrate the types of initiatives undertaken and their success and limitations. (A more comprehensive treatment of programs for students at risk can be found in Slavin, Karweit, & Madden, 1989, and Slavin, Karweit, & Wasik, 1994.)

Parent Involvement and Parent Training

Researchers have investigated scores of links between home and school, and a clear consensus has emerged: Children's experiences at home profoundly influence their chances for school success (see, e.g., Epstein, 1992, 1996; Goldenberg, 1993; Hess & Holloway, 1984). Advocates of parent involvement argue that schools should actively seek ways to collaborate with parents for children's academic benefit.

Yet our research base presents a dilemma: On the one hand, we have evidence of low-income and minority parents' willingness and ability to help their children succeed academically, and there are also cases of apparently successful parent involvement or parent education programs. But on the other hand, the evidence for the effectiveness of parent involvement efforts on children's achievement is surprisingly thin. Two meta-analyses that have appeared over the past decade challenge the notion that parent involvement programs have demonstrable effects on student outcomes (Mattingly, Prislin, McKenzie, Rodriguez, & Kayzar, 2002; White, Taylor, & Moss, 1992). Mattingly et al., for example, argue that the strongest claims for effectiveness come from studies with the weakest designs, that is, absence of suitable control groups. Many studies have found improvements in various student outcomes, but in the absence of control or comparison groups, it is impossible to rule out alternative explanations for these improvements.

The concerns raised by these two meta-analyses are important. They signal that we have failed to pay sufficient attention to documenting the outcomes of parent involvement efforts and their impact on important student outcomes. The commendable U.S. national goal notwithstanding, we do not have a firm grasp on what the likely outcome would be of widespread efforts to involve parents as envisioned by the framers of the goal. We do have considerable evidence that parents are positively disposed toward these sorts of activities. Even among low-income, minority families—often assumed to be unable or unwilling to respond to school efforts to involve them in their children's education—parents are willing and able, either on their own or in collaboration with schools, to help children succeed academically (Chavkin, 1989; Epstein, 1992, 1996; Goldenberg, 1993; Moles, 1996; Neuman, Hagedorn, Celano, & Daly, 1995). This is perhaps especially true in the area of early literacy, in which most parents possess the attitudes and at least sufficient early literacy skills and knowledge to help their children get on the road to literacy.

Goldenberg and Arzubiaga (1994) found that teachers' parent involvement efforts were related both to Spanish-speaking kindergarten parents' satisfaction with the child's school experience and to children's early literacy attainment: The more teachers attempted to involve parents in children's academic learning, the more satisfied parents were. Similarly, Campbell and Ramey (1995) report that low-income African American parents were very positive about a home–school academic contact program, with more than 90% of the parents reporting completing home activities with their children. Parents gave 83% of the activities positive ratings (Campbell & Ramey, 1995).

These and other data suggest that parent training should be a viable means for enhancing parent involvement in children's learning. But again, the empirical record is disappointing. Parent involvement programs that involve on-site parent activities necessarily deal with a select group of parents. In one well-known effort in northern California, Ada (1988) met with parents monthly to discuss children's literature and to show them how to read with their elementary-age children. From a total district student population of 14,500, the monthly meetings drew 60–100 parents. Clearly the vast majority of parents were excluded. In another well-regarded and apparently successful parent education program aimed at low-income Latino parents (Owen, Li, Rodriguez-Brown, & Shanahan, 1993), 94% of participants at the beginning of the program—that is, before training—reported reading to their preschool children; more than 70% reported taking their child to the library. This contrasts with much lower figures reported elsewhere for the general population of Latino parents (Ramírez et al., 1986; Teale, 1986). Clearly the Owen et al. study did not draw from the general population at the school.

Given that parent training programs will necessarily include a relatively select group of parents, what happens with the other families? If parent involvement efforts are open only to those parents who can or will go to training sessions, we will invariably exclude substantial numbers of families, perhaps those with the greatest need. This is one of the major issues we must confront as we continue to explore parent involvement as a means for helping close the gap between low- and higher-income students.

Tutoring

Tutoring, in its ideal form, is the ultimate in focused, targeted instruction—one teacher, one student. Individual student needs can be addressed clearly and systematically with no interference from the needs of other students, which can be very disparate from one another. Tutoring is actually a very old form of teaching, its history dating back 2,500 years, far longer than the group-based schooling now considered the norm (Gordon & Gordon, 1990). Contemporary interest in tutoring as a means of helping bridge the gap between low- and high-achieving students probably stems from different sources. Perhaps the most important is an article written by Benjamin Bloom (1984) in which he casts effective tutoring as determining the upper limit of what teachers could accomplish with students. Tutoring, Bloom suggests, is the maximally effective instructional arrangement. He estimates that compared to regular classroom instruction involving one teacher and approximately 30 students, effective tutoring boosts student achievement by 2 standard deviations. In other words the average student, when tutored, could achieve at the 98th percentile (two standard deviations above the 50th percentile, which is considered average achievement) in relation to students instructed conventionally. Because in most circumstances widespread tutoring is impossible, Bloom's challenge to educators was to devise instructional strategies that, in concert with each other, would produce effects on student achievement comparable to the effects of tutoring. This became what Bloom called the "2 sigma problem" (1984, p. 4).

Aside from Bloom's article, which did not stipulate a particular tutoring program but rather key principles of effective teaching delivered in a tutoring context, numerous educators and researchers have become intrigued by the possibility of using tutoring to boost the attainment of students either doing poorly or at risk of doing poorly. Perhaps the most famous tutoring program in the literacy domain has been Reading Recovery (Clay, 1985), which has enjoyed great popularity in the English-speaking world and has been translated into various foreign languages. Other tutoring programs have since made their appearance, such as the Howard Street model (Morris, Shaw, & Perney, 1990) and Book Buddies (Invernizzi, Rosemary, Juel, & Richards, 1997). Although some of these models require a certain amount of training, other researchers have investigated minimum-training models (Fitzgerald, 2001, see #39 this volume). Many tutoring models and programs show at least some evidence of success (see Invernizzi, 2001, for a useful review).

Elbaum, Vaughn, Hughes, and Moody (2000) conducted a meta-analysis of experimental and quasi-experimental studies of tutoring. Although they found that tutoring had a positive effect on students' reading outcomes, it was, overall, far more modest than what Bloom had predicted. In contrast to the very large "2 sigma" effect size[1] cited by Bloom (1984), the average weighted effect size (that is, adjusted for sample size differences) Elbaum et al. found was .41. (The unweighted effect size was .67—still more modest than Bloom's.) An effect size of .40 translates to average achievement at the 66th percentile (not the 98th percentile as Bloom predicted) in relation to a population that is achieving, on average, at the 50th percentile. In other words, the average student in the tutoring condition achieved at the 66th percentile while the average student who did not receive tutoring scored at the 50th percentile.

Despite the more modest overall effects of tutoring that Elbaum et al. (2000) found, the range was enormous. Some tutoring programs obtained incredible effect sizes greater than 4. Elbaum et al. attributed this to various measurement artifacts and either discarded the studies altogether or else truncated the effect sizes by setting an upper limit to what an acceptable effect size could be, in this case 3.45. Some programs obtained *negative* effect sizes, indicating that students in the tutoring condition did worse than those in the control or comparison condition. Nonetheless, the overall effect was positive even if moderate. If we include effect sizes eliminated or truncated as "outliers" by Elbaum et al., we would undoubtedly get a stronger average effect size. Yet the fact remains that only a minority of the studies could be used to support Bloom's claim that tutoring can help the average student achieve at the 98th percentile; as a general rule, effects were not of this magnitude. Yet as part of a set of educational tools to help bridge the achievement gap among sectors of our populace, tutoring might well have a place.

One further aspect of the Elbaum et al. review is worth mentioning. The authors report two studies that compared the effects of tutoring (in both cases, Reading Recovery was being used) to small-group instruction. In one of the studies, the small-group instruction was based on the Orton–Gillingham method, which emphasizes phonics; in the other study, small-group instruction was based on Reading Recovery principles, as applied to small groups. The effects of the tutoring in these two studies were zero, meaning that the small-group intervention (which served 3–4 times the number of students) was just as effective. Although additional research comparing tutoring to small-group instruction would be helpful, the two studies included in the Elbaum et al. meta-analysis suggest that small-group instruction can be as effective as one-to-one instruction— and of course far more cost effective.

Comprehensive School-Based Efforts

At the opposite end from tutoring are comprehensive programs that attempt to influence numerous aspects of the child's environment simultaneously. Some of these models also incorporate tutoring as one of the components. Over the past few years, a number of programs and demonstration projects have emerged that hold promise for helping attain the U.S. national education goals set forth at the beginning of this chapter. Space does not permit a full description of any, but several examples will illustrate.

A prime example of a comprehensive, schoolwide reading program that has many of the components identified in Snow et al. (1998) and described earlier in this chapter is Success for All (SFA) (Slavin, Madden, Dolan, & Wasik, 1996). The original program was intended for low-income English-speaking students and has since been adapted for English learners. There is now a Spanish version (*Exito para todos*) and an English version that uses instructional strategies specifically suited for English learners learning to read and write in English (Slavin & Madden, 1999). SFA is more than simply a reading program; it has comprehensive organizational, management, and home–school connection components. Indeed, it is among the most successful and effective whole-school reform models to emerge in the 1990s (Bodily, 1998). SFA uses a structured and explicit program of reading and writing skill development, beginning in kindergarten and continuing through third grade. Students are in heterogeneous classrooms but are regrouped homogeneously across classrooms for 90 minutes of daily reading instruction. The program uses well-known instructional strategies such as direct instruction, cooperative learning, writing as a process, and frequent assessment. Regular home–school contacts are a key feature, particularly for children experiencing difficulty.

Despite its admirable record of success, however, SFA is not successful with *all* students, as Slavin and colleagues acknowledge. Slavin, Madden, Karweit, Dolan, and Wasik (1994), for example, report that only 46% of third-grade children in SFA schools were on or above grade level in reading, in contrast to 26% of children in control schools. This is equivalent to an effect size of about .5—only slightly higher than the estimated mean effect size of tutoring alone. The effect of SFA on the lowest 25% of students was stronger: In SFA schools, the lowest 25% were, on average, close to the third-grade reading level. In the comparison schools, the lowest 25% of readers were on average a little above the second-grade level; the effect size for this lowest quarter only was a substantial .99. These are clearly meaningful effects and they demonstrate success for many more students than would otherwise be successful, even if SFA's results are still short of success for *all*.

Another well-known and important effort to promote early literacy development for low-income children is the Carolina Abecedarian Project (Campbell & Ramey, 1995; Ramey & Campbell, 1984). Ramey and Campbell report short- and long-term intervention effects on cognitive (reading and math tests) and school-based (special education placement, grade retention) measures. One of the reasons this study is so important is because it used a fully randomized design to examine the combined and separate effects of two interventions on low-income African American children's early academic performance. The preschool intervention comprised a number of curricular and instructional programs, including preliteracy and prephonics curricula emphasizing phoneme identification (Campbell & Ramey, 1995). A school-age follow-up consisted of a home–school resource teacher providing parents with activities designed to "reinforce the basic reading and mathematics concepts being taught at school" (Campbell & Ramey, 1995, p. 751).

In third grade, the group of children that received both the preschool and school-age intervention substantially outperformed other groups (no intervention or only the preschool or only the school-age intervention). The mean third-grade standard score of this group of children on the Woodcock–Johnson reading cluster (letter–word identification, word attack, passage comprehension) was 96, still below the national mean, but substantially higher than the no-intervention controls (83). The effects of the school-age intervention alone, which consisted of the home–school resource teacher, was negligible. The preschool intervention alone had a substantial effect, although not as great as that of the combined preschool and school-age interventions.

An as-yet-unanswered question is whether even these comprehensive efforts can completely overcome the effects of low SES. Miller (1995) concludes, "there is little evidence that any existing strategy can close more than a fraction of the overall achievement gap between high- and low-SES children" (p. 334). Using SFA as a telling example—because it is the most successful of the current school reform models designed to improve reading achievement in Title I schools—Miller points out that the program can raise overall achievement levels from approximately the 30th to the 46th percentile, an effect size of approximately .4. These are noteworthy gains to be sure, as I have already pointed out. But the level of attainment is still "below middle-class and upper-middle-class performance norms" (Miller, 1995, p. 331), which are typically well above the 50th percentile on nationally normed tests.

Despite the influence of SES and the difficulty of schools' making up for SES-based disadvantages, the important point is that effective teaching, schools, and programs influence student achievement. There is no longer any doubt about this. It matters whether a school's overall achievement level is at the 30th or 46th percentile, and at a minimum it is well within educators' grasp to effect this level of influence. Many argue that even this is a gross underestimate of what educators could truly accomplish. In any case, a strong, effective academic program will produce better results on student outcomes than a weak and ineffective program. *This is so whether students are of low or high SES and despite their cultural and linguistic background.* Low SES cannot be used as an excuse for failing to increase substantially the number of low-income and culturally and linguistically diverse students meeting U.S. national education goals.

Implications and Future Directions

The U.S. commitment to high levels of student achievement is on display in the form of national education goals. But at the moment, the goals remain distant visions. What must we do if they are ever to be within our reach?

Practice

First, and most obvious, we must put into practice instruction and intervention programs that we have reason to believe "work." Despite gaps in our knowledge, there are many effective practices for which we have good research evidence but which are not finding their way into enough schools and classrooms. Tutoring and comprehensive programs, such as SFA, suggest productive areas for more widespread utilization. One obvious obstacle is cost, because both types of programs are extremely expensive. Moreover, comparisons of tutoring and small-group instruction suggest the latter might be as effective and cost a fraction as much. Nonetheless, the research base suggests that tutoring and comprehensive and structured approaches such as SFA warrant close attention. In contrast, and despite nearly universal popularity, parent involvement programs seem to lack as solid a research base as tutoring and comprehensive interventions aimed at improving achievement directly. Although it would be extreme and unjustified to say that educators should no longer explore parent involvement to improve student achievement, at the moment the research base is not very firm.

Aside from particular programs, there are effective classroom instructional practices that should be more prevalent than they are. These practices and their research bases are described in publications such as *Preventing Reading Difficulties in Young Children* (Snow et al., 1998), *Report of the National Reading Panel* (NICHD, 2000), and the many sources cited therein. *At a minimum*, all educators must be familiar with these reports and how to carry out instruction based on their conclusions. There is no excuse for teachers, administrators, and teacher educators—anyone who has professional responsibility for assuring that children learn to read well—not to be thoroughly versed in their implications. For example, children benefit from phonological awareness and systematic phonics instruction. The evidence is overwhelming that instruction explicitly and systematically directed at helping children learn and apply the alphabetic principle—that letters represent sounds and sounds can be represented as letters—makes a positive contribution to literacy development. However, different children probably need different amounts of instruction, so teachers must be continually monitoring progress to determine what is necessary. A child who has already begun to decode and has clearly mastered the alphabetic principle does not need phonological awareness instruction.

More generally, neither phonological awareness instruction nor phonics instruction is a panacea. As important as they are, they should not constitute the sum and substance of a reading program. The National Reading Panel (NICHD, 2000) concluded that programs spending less than 20 hours—far less than the total amount of reading instruction time available throughout a school year—on phonological awareness instruction had the strongest effects on reading acquisition. The panel withheld recommendations for how much time should be spent on phonological training, saying that it probably depended on child and situational factors. Similarly, although the case for systematic instruction in phonics is irrefutable, its impact on reading development is moderate. The panel concluded that the overall effect size is .44, which translates roughly into an impact of about 16 or 17 percentile points, depending on students' level of achievement. This is a substantial and meaningful effect, but other factors must come into play. Otherwise, systematic phonics instruction by itself would spell the difference between learning to read and not learning to read. Clearly this is not the case. As a further indication, the panel found that phonics instruction for low achievers in grades 2 through 6 had no significant impact on reading performance. The panel offered no definitive interpretation for these findings, concluding instead that further research is needed.

Other language and literacy experiences are also key to literacy development and must find their way into classrooms. For example, promoting reading fluency and providing comprehension instruction are extremely important; so are instruction and other noninstructional activities that build background knowledge, which is important in its own right as well as essential for reading comprehension. The National Reading Panel (NICHD, 2000) found that guided repeated oral reading had significant impact on various measures of reading outcomes, from comprehension (effect size = .35) to reading accuracy (effect size = .55). Comprehension-oriented instruction, such as teaching vocabulary and various text comprehending strategies, also helps promote reading development. The panel identified no fewer than eight comprehension strategies (or groups of strategies) for which we have firm evidence of impact on reading development: comprehension monitoring, cooperative learning, graphic and semantic organizers, instruction in story structure, question answering, question generation, summarization, and multiple-strategy instruction designed to help readers use different strategies flexibly and appropriately. Many of these strategies show strong effects.

The larger point is this: We have a firm research base that recommends the use of numerous instructional strategies to promote literacy development. One way to make progress toward U.S. national education goals is to aim for widespread dissemination and implementation of this knowledge base. This is, of course, easier said than done, as the school change literature makes painfully clear (e.g., Fullan, 1991, 1993, 1999; Goldenberg, 2004). Nonetheless, we have potential avenues for influencing the knowledge and skill base of practicing educators. Professional development for teachers and other educators is one such potential avenue (Roller, 2001). Moreover, some intervention programs, such as SFA, have well-developed technologies for effective implementation, which takes a comprehensive view of professional development and schoolwide change (Bodilly, 1998). SFA is not the norm, however.

Finally, educators must realize that the impact of socioeconomic, language, and cultural factors on children's literacy attainment is more complex and problematic than generally recognized. For example, the impact of individual children's or families' SES on reading achievement is actually quite small, smaller than the various strategies and interventions that have been described previously. However, at the aggregate level, SES has a substantial impact on achievement. In other words, when children live in low-SES communities or attend schools that are largely low SES, their achievement is likely to suffer; conversely, children living in high-SES communities and attending high-SES schools will benefit. The relationship is not perfect, of course, because there are many instances of high-achieving children (and some high-achieving schools) in low-SES contexts and low-achieving children in high-SES contexts. But in general, SES—when defined in terms of a community or an entire school, not in terms of an individual student—has a moderate to strong effect on achievement.

Similarly, the impact on reading acquisition of coming from a non-English-speaking home is likely to depend on the type of school program a child experiences. Programs that utilize children's primary language during instruction appear to have at least a modest positive effect on achievement in English (Greene, 1997); other nonlanguage instructional factors (reviewed previously) also influence these children's achievement. The knowledge base for promoting literacy among English learners is contradictory and confusing, to say the least, yet there is evidence that these children do better in some programs than others (August & Hakuta, 1997). Although being limited in English proficiency is a risk factor, it is more of a risk factor in some instructional contexts than others. The role of the home culture in the educational process is even more uncertain. Many studies have pointed to potential areas of incompatibility between the home cultures of minority students and the school and classrooms they attend. However, little, if any, direct evidence exists that eliminating or diminishing these discontinuities promotes higher levels of student achievement.

Research

Beyond implementation of practices and programs with high probabilities of success, there is just as obviously the ubiquitous need for additional research. Unquestionably we have made progress in understanding what contributes to early literacy development, what puts children at risk for reading problems, and what schools and families can do to promote literacy growth and minimize literacy difficulties. But many challenges still lie ahead. Preeminent among them is how to accelerate the literacy growth of far more low-income children than we are now succeeding in helping achieve high levels of literacy. Successful implementation of effective programs and practices would take us in this direction, but clearly this is not sufficient. Effect sizes are generally moderate, and even in successful programs such as SFA or the Abecedarian Project, there are still too many children who do not do well enough. A clear challenge for the 21st century, therefore, is to continue to refine and bolster these programs in order to find even more effective ways to help all children, regardless of socioeconomic level or linguistic and cultural background.

There are many instructional issues that remain unresolved, and a full catalog is beyond the scope of this chapter (see NICHD, 2000; Snow et al., 1998, for more comprehensive treatments). Clearly these issues constitute a compelling research agenda. A preeminent issue is whether there is some optimal balance of reading instruction that should be provided. There is wide consensus that children need instruction in alphabetics (phonological awareness, decoding), fluency, and comprehension. They also need opportunities and experiences designed to motivate functional and meaningful uses of print (Snow et al., 1998). What should the mix be? How much of what should be emphasized and when? Should alphabetics receive the lion's share of attention in the early stages, gradually shifting to higher-level processes such as comprehension and functional uses of print, as in "learn to read then read to learn"? Or should children all proceed more or less together from the outset, perhaps emphasizing alphabetics due to its foundational importance but never straying too far from comprehension, meaning, and functional uses for literacy?

Having identified many of the critical components for literacy development, the task is now trying to figure out how the pieces best fit together—if indeed there is a best fit, either for all students, individual students, or groups of students. For example, it might be that students who come to school with fewer literacy experiences require more direct and explicit instruction in order to help them acquire key understandings that underlie literacy development. If true, the instructional balance for these students is likely to be different from the instructional balance for students who come from homes that provide a wealth of literacy experiences.

Parent involvement is another area in great need of additional research. Many readers will be surprised to learn how inadequate the empirical base is. This thin research base does not suggest abandoning parent involvement as a potentially productive venue (although some might argue that it does); instead it argues for renewing our efforts to study parent involvement rigorously so we can determine what its effects really are. The same can be said for efforts to improve minority children's reading attainment by accommodating to the home culture. Allen and Boykin (1992), Tharp (1989), and others have argued that instructional practices in schools must be changed to fit the home and cultural experiences of diverse students. If this hypothesis is correct, it would have very important implications for the education of large numbers of children. At the moment, however, there is insufficient evidence to form a strong basis for policy or practice. Current and future research might well change this, however (see Demmert & Towner, 2003).

Conclusion: Rhetoric and Reality Redux

Kameenui (1998) has identified a chasm that sooner or later we must confront: the rhetoric of all but the reality of some. U.S. national goals are a case in point: As a nation, the United States has committed itself to all children beginning school ready to learn, all students demonstrating competency over challenging subject matter, and every school promoting parent involvement that helps children succeed. These pronouncements remain rhetoric; reality in the schools is far different. But of course the challenges educators face in achieving national education goals for all children go far beyond finding more effective ways of teaching reading and writing in school and involving parents in children's education. Far too many children attend school under circumstances likely to influence academic processes and outcomes adversely. As a group, low-income children are more likely to have to endure a wide range of disadvantages associated with poverty—single parent families, poor access to quality healthcare, poor diets, unhealthy environments, dangerous neighborhoods, behavioral and social-adaptational challenges, and numerous other challenges. Although we can find examples of children who have succeeded in the face of formidable environmental challenges, and therefore we know that poor outcomes for children at risk are not a foregone conclusion (Werner & Smith, 1982), why should children have to struggle against the odds? The issue is one of social justice, not simply of improving reading scores. Ultimately, our solutions must go beyond educational interventions, as important as they might be. Solutions also must focus on integration of programs, policies, and services, the school being but one of many agencies implicated. As Schorr (1994) has argued, "We need bold and comprehensive strategies. Incrementalism will not do it. There are chasms you cannot cross one small step at a time" (p. 237).

Efforts to improve educational outcomes for all children must be part of a broader social and political agenda aimed at providing adequate financial, material, and social supports known to influence children's academic and, more generally, developmental outcomes (Shonkoff & Phillips, 2000). Without such a broad strategy it is difficult to imagine meaningfully addressing the chasm between national rhetoric and children's reality. If we implement well those things we have reason to believe make a difference in children's literacy, and if we vigorously pursue research and political agendas aimed at further breaking down barriers to access, perhaps there is a chance that a future generation will not peer out from the first years of the next century, once again staring into this dark chasm.

Acknowledgments

This chapter was made possible by grants from the Spencer Foundation and the U.S. Department of Education, Office of Educational Research and Improvement (now the Institute for Education Sciences).

Note

[1] An *effect size* is a measure of the impact of some procedure or program. It is the amount of increase or decrease in achievement that can be attributed to the procedure or program. Effect sizes are expressed as portions of a standard deviation, so that an effect size of .5 means an effect of one half of a standard deviation. Generally speaking, an effect size around .2 is considered small, .5 is moderate, and .8 is large (NICHD, 2000).

References

Ada, A.F. (1988). The Pajaro Valley experience: Working with Spanish-speaking parents to develop children's reading and writing skills through the use of children's literature. In T. Skutnabb-Kangas & J. Cummins (Eds.), *Minority education: From shame to struggle* (pp. 223–238). Clevedon, UK: Multilingual Matters.

Adams, M.J. (1990). *Beginning to read: Thinking and learning about print*. Cambridge, MA: MIT Press.

Alexander, K., & Entwisle, D. (1996). Schools and children at risk. In A. Booth and J. Dunn (Eds.), *Family–school links: How do they affect educational outcomes?* (pp. 67–88). Mahwah, NJ: Erlbaum.

Allen, B.A., & Boykin, A.W. (1992). African American children and the educational process: Alleviating cultural discontinuity through prescriptive pedagogy. *School Psychology Review, 21*(4), 586–596.

Anderson, A.B., & Stokes, S.J. (1984). Social and institutional influences on the development and practice of literacy. In H. Goelman, A. Oberg, & F. Smith (Eds.), *Awakening to literacy* (pp. 24–37). Portsmouth, NH: Heinemann.

Au, K.H., & Mason, J.M. (1981). Social organizational factors in learning to read: The balance of rights hypothesis. *Reading Research Quarterly, 17*, 115–152.

August, D., & Hakuta, K. (Eds.). (1997). *Improving schooling for language-minority children: A research agenda*. Washington, DC: National Academy Press.

Baker, L., Serpell, R., & Sonnenschein, S. (1995). Opportunities for literacy learning in the homes of urban preschoolers. In L.M. Morrow (Ed.), *Family literacy connections in schools and communities* (pp. 236–252). Newark, DE: International Reading Association.

Ball, E.W., & Blachman, B.A. (1988). Phoneme segmentation training: Effect on reading readiness. *Annals of Dyslexia, 38*, 208–225.

Ball, E.W., & Blachman, B.A. (1991). Does phoneme awareness training in kindergarten make a difference in early word recognition and developmental spelling? *Reading Research Quarterly, 26*, 49–66.

Bloom, B.S. (1984). The 2 sigma problem: The search for methods of group instruction as effective as one-to-one tutoring. *Educational Researcher, 13*(6), 4–16.

Bodilly, S. (1998). *Lessons from New American Schools' scale-up phase: Prospects for bringing designs to multiple schools*. Santa Monica, CA: RAND.

Brady, S., Fowler, A., Stone, B., & Winbury, N. (1994). Training phonological awareness: A study with inner-city kindergarten children. *Annals of Dyslexia, 44*, 27–59.

Campbell, F.A., & Ramey, C.T. (1995). Cognitive and school outcomes for high-risk African-American students at middle adolescence: Positive effects of early intervention. *American Educational Research Journal, 32*, 743–772.

Campos, J., & Keatinge, H. (1988). The Carpinteria language minority student experience: From theory, to practice, to success. In T. Skutnabb-Kangas & J. Cummins (Eds.), *Minority education: From shame to struggle* (pp. 299–308). Clevedon, UK: Multilingual Matters.

Chall, J.S. (1983). *Learning to read: The great debate* (Updated ed.). New York: McGraw-Hill.

Chavkin, N.F. (1989). Debunking the myth about minority parents. *Educational Horizons, 67*(4), 119–123.

Chiappe, P., & Siegel, L.S. (1999). Phonological awareness and reading acquisition in English- and Punjabi-speaking Canadian children. *Journal of Educational Psychology, 91*(1), 20–28.

Clark, R.M. (1983). *Family life and school achievement: Why poor black children succeed or fail*. Chicago: University of Chicago Press.

Clay, M.M. (1985). *The early detection of reading difficulties* (3rd ed.). Portsmouth, NH: Heinemann.

Clay, M.M. (1993). *An observation survey of early literacy achievement*. Portsmouth, NH: Heinemann.

Crawford, J. (1991). *Bilingual education: History, politics, theory, and practice* (2nd ed.). Los Angeles: Bilingual Education Services.

Demmert, W.G., Jr., & Towner, J.C. (2003). *A review of the research literature on the influences of culturally based education on the academic performance of Native American students*. Portland, OR: Northwest Regional Educational Laboratory. Retrieved December 1, 2003, from http://www.nwrel.org/indianed/cbe

Ehri, L.C., Nunes, S.R., Stahl, S.A., & Willows, D.M. (2001). Systematic phonics instruction helps students learn to read: Evidence from the National Reading Panel's meta-analysis. *Review of Educational Research, 71*(3), 393–447.

Ehri, L.C., Nunes, S.R., Willows, D.M., Schuster, B.V., Yaghoub-Zadeh, Z., & Shanahan, T. (2001). Phonemic awareness instruction helps children learn to read: Evidence from the National Reading Panel's meta-analysis. *Reading Research Quarterly, 36,* 250–287.

Elbaum, B., Vaughn, S., Hughes, M.T., & Moody, S.W. (2000). How effective are one-to-one tutoring programs in reading for elementary students at risk for reading failure? A meta-analysis of the intervention research. *Journal of Educational Psychology, 92*(4), 605–619.

Epstein, J. (1992). School and family partnerships. In M.C. Alkin (Ed.), *Encyclopedia of educational research* (6th ed., pp. 1139–1152). New York: Macmillan.

Epstein, J. (1996). Perspectives and previews on research and policy for school, family, and community partnerships. In A. Booth & J. Dunn (Eds.), *Family–school links: How do they affect educational outcomes?* (pp. 209–246). Mahwah, NJ: Erlbaum.

Federal Interagency Forum on Child and Family Statistics. (2000). *America's children: Key national indicators of well-being, 2000.* Washington, DC: U.S. Government Printing Office. Retrieved December 1, 2003, from http://www.childstats.gov

Federal Interagency Forum on Child and Family Statistics. (2002). *America's children: Key national indicators of well-being, 2002.* Washington, DC: U.S. Government Printing Office. Retrieved December 1, 2003, from http://www.childstats.gov

Fitzgerald, J. (1995). English-as-a-second-language learners' cognitive reading processes: A review of research in the United States. *Review of Educational Research, 65*(2), 145–190.

Fitzgerald, J. (2001). Can minimally trained college student volunteers help young at-risk children read better? *Reading Research Quarterly, 36,* 28–47.

Fueyo, V., & Bechtol, S. (1999). Those who can, teach: Reflecting on teaching diverse populations. *Teacher Education Quarterly, 26*(3), 25–36.

Fullan, M.G. (1991). *The new meaning of educational change* (2nd ed.). New York: Teachers College Press.

Fullan, M.G. (1993). *Change forces: Probing the depths of educational reform* (School Development and Management of Change, No. 10). London: Falmer.

Fullan, M.G. (1999). *Change forces: The sequel* (Educational Change and Development Series). London: Falmer.

Goldenberg, C. (1993). The home-school connection in bilingual education. In M.B. Arias & U. Casanova (Eds.), *Bilingual education: Politics, research, and practice* (92nd yearbook of the National Society for the Study of Education, Part 2, pp. 225–250). Chicago: University of Chicago Press.

Goldenberg, C. (1996). Latin American immigration and U.S. schools. *Social Policy Report of the Society for Research in Child Development, 10*(1), 1–29.

Goldenberg, C. (2004). *Successful school change: Creating settings to improve teaching and learning.* New York: Teachers College Press.

Goldenberg, C., & Arzubiaga, A. (1994, April). *The effects of teachers' attempts to involve Latino parents in children's early reading development.* Paper presented at the annual meeting of the American Educational Research Association, New Orleans, LA.

Goldenberg, C., & Gallimore, R. (1989). Teaching California's diverse student population: The common ground between educational and cultural research. *California Public Schools Forum, 3,* 41–56.

Goldenberg, C., & Gallimore, R. (1995). Immigrant Latino parents' values and beliefs about their children's education: Continuities and discontinuities across cultures and generations. In P.R. Pintrich & M. Maehr (Eds.), *Advances in motivation and achievement: Culture, ethnicity, and motivation* (Vol. 9, pp. 183–228). Greenwich, CT: JAI Press.

Goldenberg, C., Reese, L., & Gallimore, R. (1992). Effects of school literacy materials on Latino children's home experiences and early reading achievement. *American Journal of Education, 100,* 497–536.

Gordon, E.E., & Gordon, E.H. (1990). *Centuries of tutoring.* Lanham, MD: University Press of America.

Greene, J.P. (1997). A meta-analysis of the Rossell and Baker review of bilingual education research. *Bilingual Research Journal, 21,* 103–122.

Grossman, H. (1984). *Educating Hispanic students: Cultural implications for instruction, classroom management, counseling and assessment.* Springfield, IL: Charles C. Thomas.

Heath, S.B. (1983). *Ways with words: Language, life, and work in communities and classrooms.* Cambridge, UK: Cambridge University Press.

Hess, R.D., & Holloway, S.D. (1984). Family and school as educational institutions. In R.D. Parke (Ed.), *Review of Child Development Research 7: The family* (pp. 179–222). Chicago: University of Chicago Press.

Invernizzi, M.A. (2001). The complex world of one-on-one tutoring. In S.B. Neuman & D.K. Dickinson (Eds.), *Handbook of early literacy research* (pp. 459–470). New York: Guilford.

Invernizzi, M.A., Rosemary, C.A., Juel, C., & Richards, H.C. (1997). At-risk readers and community volunteers: A 3-year perspective. *Scientific Studies of Reading, 1*(3), 277–300.

Kameenui, E.J. (1998). The rhetoric of all, the reality of some, and the unmistakable smell of mortality. In J. Osborn & F. Lehr (Eds.), *Literacy for all: Issues in teaching and learning* (pp. 319–338). New York: Guilford.

Los Angeles Times Poll. (1999). *March 20–27— Study #424.* April 3. Retrieved December 1, 2003, from http://www.latimes.com

Mason, J.M. (1977). *Reading readiness: A definition and skills hierarchy from preschoolers' developing conceptions of print* (Tech. Rep. No. 59). Champaign: University of Illinois at Urbana-Champaign, Center for the Study of Reading.

Mattingly, D.J., Prislin, R., McKenzie, T.L., Rodriguez, J.L., & Kayzar, B. (2002). Evaluating evaluations: The case of parent involvement programs. *Review of Educational Research, 72*(4), 549–576.

Miller, L.S. (1995). *An American imperative: Accelerating minority educational advancement.* New Haven, CT: Yale University Press.

Moles, O. (1996). New national directions in research and policy. In A. Booth & J. Dunn (Eds.), *Family–school links: How do they affect educational outcomes?* (pp. 247–254). Mahwah, NJ: Erlbaum.

Morris, D., Shaw, B., & Perney, J. (1990). Helping low readers in grades 2 and 3: An after-school volunteer tutoring program. *The Elementary School Journal, 91*(2), 133–150.

National Education Goals Panel. (1997). *The National Education Goals report: Building a nation of learners, 1997.* Washington, DC: Superintendent of Documents. Retrieved December 1, 2003, from http://www.negp.gov

National Educational Research Policy and Priorities Board. (1999). *Improving the education of English language learners: Best practices.* Washington, DC: Office of Educational Research and Improvement.

National Institute of Child Health and Human Development. (2000). *Report of the National Reading Panel. Teaching children to read: An evidence-based assessment of the scientific research literature on reading and its implications for reading instruction* (NIH Publication No. 00-4769). Washington, DC: U.S. Government Printing Office. Available: http://www.nichd.nih.gov/publications/nrp/report.htm

Natriello, G., McDill, E.L., & Pallas, A.M. (1990). *Schooling disadvantaged children: Racing against catastrophe.* New York: Teachers College Press.

Neuman, S.B. (1998). How can we enable all children to achieve. In S.B. Neuman & K. Roskos (Eds.), *Children achieving: Best practices in early literacy* (pp. 5–10). Newark, DE: International Reading Association.

Neuman, S.B., & Celano, D. (2001). Access to print in low-income and middle-income communities: An ecological study of four neighborhoods. *Reading Research Quarterly, 36*, 8–26.

Neuman, S.B., Hagedorn, T., Celano, D., & Daly, P. (1995). Toward a collaborative approach to parent involvement in early education: A study of teenage mothers in an African-American community. *American Educational Research Journal, 32*, 801–827.

Neuman, S.B., & Roskos, K. (1993). Access to print for children of poverty: Differential effects of adult mediation and literacy-enriched play settings on environmental and functional print tasks. *American Education Research Journal, 30*, 95–122.

Neuman, S.B. & Roskos, K. (1997). Literacy knowledge in practice: Contexts of participation for young writers and readers. *Reading Research Quarterly, 32*, 10–32.

Owen, V., Li, R., Rodriguez-Brown, F., & Shanahan, T. (1993, April). *Parent attitudes: Critical perspectives of the changing nature of parents' pedagogical theories.* Paper presented at the annual meeting of the American Educational Research Association, Atlanta, GA.

Paratore, J.R., Melzi, G., & Krol-Sinclair, B. (1999). *What should we expect of family literacy? Experiences of Latino children whose parents participate in an intergenerational* literacy project. Newark, DE: International Reading Association; Chicago: National Reading Conference.

Pressley, M. (1998). *Reading instruction that works: The case for balanced teaching*. New York: Guilford.

Ralph, K., Ellis, J., & Medina, T. (1998). Developing phonemic awareness through poetry, song, word play, and literature. In C. Cox (Ed.), *Research and practice: "a-m+" reading requirements* (pp. 31–40). Los Angeles: Los Angeles County Office of Education.

Ramey, C.T., & Campbell, F.A. (1984). Preventive education for high-risk children: Cognitive consequences of the Carolina Abecedarian Project. *American Journal of Mental Deficiency, 88*, 515–523.

Ramírez, J.D., Yuen, S.D., Ramey, D.R., & Merino, B. (1986). *First year report: Longitudinal study of immersion programs for language-minority children*. San Mateo, CA: Aguirre International.

Readence, J.E., & Barone, D.M. (Eds.). (1997). *Reading Research Quarterly*. [Entire issue.] *32*(4).

Roller, C.M. (Ed.). (2001). *Learning to teach reading: Setting the research agenda*. Newark, DE: International Reading Association.

Rossell, C.H., & Baker, K. (1996). The educational effectiveness of bilingual education. *Research in the Teaching of English, 30*(1), 7–74.

Scarborough, H. (1998). Early identification of children at risk for reading disabilities: Phonological awareness and some other promising predictors. In B.K. Shapiro, P.J. Accardo, & A.J. Capute (Eds.), *Specific reading disability: A view of the spectrum* (pp. 75–119). Timonium, MD: York Press.

Schickedanz, J.A. (1998). What is developmentally appropriate practice in early literacy? Considering the alphabet. In S.B. Neuman & K.A. Roskos (Eds.), *Children achieving: Best practices in early literacy* (pp. 20–37). Newark, DE: International Reading Association.

Schlesinger, A.M., Jr. (1991). *The disuniting of America: Reflections on a multicultural society*. New York: Norton.

Schorr, L. (1994). Looking ahead: Integrating urban policies to meet educational demands. In K. Wong & M.C. Wang (Eds.), *Rethinking policy for at-risk students* (pp. 221–238). Berkeley, CA: McCutchan.

Shonkoff, J.P., & Phillips, D.A. (Eds.). (2000). *From neurons to neighborhoods: The science of early childhood development*. Washington, DC: National Academy Press.

Simon, P. (1980). *The tongue-tied American: Confronting the foreign language crisis*. New York: Continuum.

Slavin, R.E., Karweit, N.L., & Madden, N.A. (1989). *Effective programs for students at risk*. Needham Heights, MA: Allyn & Bacon.

Slavin, R.E., Karweit, N.L., & Wasik, B.A. (1994). *Preventing early school failure: Research, policy, and practice*. Needham Heights, MA: Allyn & Bacon.

Slavin, R.E., & Madden, N.A. (1999). *Effects of bilingual and English as a second language adaptations of Success for All on the reading achievement of students acquiring English*. Unpublished manuscript.

Slavin, R.E., Madden, N.A., Dolan, L., & Wasik, B.A. (1996). *Every child, every school: Success for All*. Thousand Oaks, CA: Corwin Press.

Slavin, R.E., Madden, N.A., Karweit, N.L., Dolan, L., & Wasik, B.A. (1994). Success for All: A comprehensive approach to prevention and early intervention. In R.E. Slavin, N.L. Karweit, & B.A. Wasik (Eds.), *Preventing early school failure: Research, policy, and practice* (pp. 175–205). Needham Heights, MA: Allyn & Bacon.

Snow, C.E., Barnes, W.S., Chandler, J., Goodman, I., & Hemphill, L. (1991). *Unfulfilled expectations: Home and school influences on literacy*. Cambridge, MA: Harvard University Press.

Snow, C.E., Burns, M.S., & Griffin, P. (Eds.). (1998). *Preventing reading difficulties in young children*. Washington, DC: National Academy Press.

Stanovich, K. (Ed.). (1987). Children's reading the development of phonological awareness. [Entire issue] *Merrill-Palmer Quarterly, 33*(3).

Taylor, D., & Dorsey-Gaines, C. (1988). *Growing up literate: Learning from inner-city families*. Portsmouth, NH: Heinemann.

Teale, W. (1986). Home background and young children's literacy development. In W.H. Teale & E. Sulzby (Eds.), *Emergent literacy: Writing and reading* (pp. 173–206). Norwood, NJ: Ablex.

Tharp, R.G. (1982). The effective instruction of comprehension: Results and description of the Kamehameha Early Education Program. *Reading Research Quarterly, 17*, 503–527.

Tharp, R.G. (1989). Psychocultural variables and constants: Effects on teaching and learning in schools. *American Psychologist, 44*, 349–359.

Tharp, R.G., & Gallimore, R.G. (1988). *Rousing minds to life: Teaching, learning and schooling in social context.* Cambridge, UK: Cambridge University Press.

Thomas, W.P., & Collier, V.P. (1997). *School effectiveness for language minority students.* Washington, DC: National Clearinghouse for Bilingual Education. Retrieved December 1, 2003, from http://www.ncbe.gwu.edu/ncbe pubs/resource/effectiveness/

Thomas, W.P., & Collier, V.P. (2002). *A national study of school effectiveness for language minority students' long-term academic achievement* (Final report, Project 1.1). Santa Cruz, CA: Center for Research on Education, Diversity & Excellence. Retrieved December 1, 2003, from http://www.crede.ucsc.edu/research/llaa/1.1_final.html

Troia, G.A. (1999). Phonological awareness intervention research: A critical review of the experimental methodology. *Reading Research Quarterly, 34*, 28–52.

U.S. Census Bureau. (2000a). *Projections of the total resident population by 5-year age groups, and sex with special age categories: Middle Series, 2001 to 2005.* Retrieved December 1, 2003, from http://www.census.gov/population/projections/nation/summary/np-t3-b.pdf

U.S. Census Bureau. (2000b). *Projections of the total resident population by 5-year age groups, and sex with special age categories: Middle Series, 2075 to 2100.* Retrieved December 1, 2003, from http://www.census.gov/population/projections/nation/summary/np-t3-h.pdf

U.S. Department of Education. (1996). *Statistics in brief: Parents and schools: Partners in student learning* (NCES Rep. No. 96-913). Washington, DC: U.S. Government Printing Office.

U.S. Department of Education. (1998). *Parent involvement in children's education: Efforts by public elementary schools* (NCES Rep. No. 98-032). Washington, DC: U.S. Government Printing Office. Retrieved December 1, 2003, from http://nces.ed.gov/pubs98/98032.html

U.S. Department of Education. (1999). *NAEP 1998 writing report card for the nation and the states* (NCES Rep. No. 1999-462). Washington, DC: U.S. Government Printing Office. Retrieved December 1, 2003, from http://nces.ed.gov/nationsreportcard/pubs/main1998/1999462.pdf

U.S. Department of Education. (2001a). *Digest of education statistics* (Table 5: Educational institutions, by level and control of institution: 1980–81 to 1999–2000). Retrieved December 1, 2003, from http://nces.ed.gov/pubs2002/digest2001/tables/dt005.asp

U.S. Department of Education. (2001b). *The nation's report card: Fourth-grade reading 2000* (NCES Rep. No. 2001-499). Retrieved December 1, 2003, from http://nces.ed.gov/nationsreportcard/pdf/main2000/2001499.pdf

U.S. Department of Education. (2002). *Digest of education statistics* (Table 3: Enrollment in educational institutions, by level and control of institution: 1869–70 to fall 2011). Retrieved December 1, 2003, from http://nces.ed.gov/pubs2002/digest2001/tables/dt003.asp

Valdés, G. (1996). *Con respeto: Bridging the distances between culturally diverse families and schools: An ethnographic portrait.* New York: Teachers College Press.

Vierra, A. (1984). The relationship between Chicano children's achievement and their teachers' ethnicity. *Hispanic Journal of Behavioral Sciences, 6*, 285–290.

Walberg, H.J., & Tsai, S. (1985). Correlates of reading achievement and attitude: A national assessment study. *Journal of Educational Research, 78*(3), 159–167.

Werner, E.E., & Smith, R.S. (1982). *Vulnerable but invincible: A longitudinal study of resilient children and youth.* New York: McGraw-Hill.

White, K. (1982). The relation between SES and academic achievement. *Psychological Bulletin, 91*, 461–481.

White, K.R., Taylor, M., & Moss, V. (1992). Does research support claims about the benefits of involving parents in early intervention programs? *Review of Educational Research, 62*(1), 91–125.

Whitehurst, G.J., & Lonigan, C.J. (1998). Child development and emergent literacy. *Child Development, 69*(3), 848–872.

Willig, A.C. (1985). A meta-analysis of selected studies on the effectiveness of bilingual education. *Review of Educational Research, 55*(3), 269–317.

Yopp, H., Yopp, R., Harris, P., & Stapleton, L. (1998). Phonemic awareness. In C. Cox (Ed.), *Research and practice: "a-m+" reading requirements* (pp. 41–54). Los Angeles: Los Angeles County Office of Education.

Author Index

References followed by *t* or *f* indicate tables or figures, respectively. Those followed by *n* indicate notes. Page spans in italics indicate an author's contribution to this volume.

ENGIN, A.W., 1443
ENGLEMANN, S., 406
ENGLERT, C.S., 774, 1482
ENKE, J., 902
ENTWISLE, D., 27–28, 1640, 1645
EPSTEIN, J., 1651, 1652
EPSTEIN, S., 963
EPSTEIN, W., 755, 762t, 768
ERICKSON, F., 235, 967, 1472, 1501, 1563
ERICKSON, G.C., 552
ERICSSON, K.A., 37, 42, 223, 661, 662, 1031, 1249, 1261, 1295, 1302, 1304, 1324n6
ERIKSON, E., 959, 960
ERMAN, L.D., 1164, 1349
ERNST, G., 260
ERNST, S., 1392
ERNST-SLAVIN, G., 216
ERVIN, S.M., 1477
ESPINOSA, L., 251
ESTES, T.H., 1591, 1596
ESTES, W.K., 1227
ESTRADA, E., 218
EVANS, C.A., 246
EVANS, E.D., 43, 914, 999
EVANS, M.A., 435, 438, 496, 504
EVERETT, S., 1618f
EVERHART, R., 871
EVETT, L.J., 1222
EVIATOR, Z., 729
EWEN, R.B., 1438

F
FABOS, B., 1571
FAIRBANKS, C.M., 69, 588
FAIRBANKS, M.M., 727, 1233
FAIRCLOUGH, N., 872, 882, 899
FAJEN, B.R., 811
FALTIS, C.J., 241
FANG, Z., 98, 281–312, 1477
FANTINI, A., 243
FARMER, L., 874
FARR, M., 40, 226
FARR, R., 1528, 1537
FARRELL, E., 1391
FARRIS, E., 1578
FARSTRUP, A.E., 1431, 1469
FAULKNER, H.J., 723
FAUST, M., 810
FAZIO, R.H., 1432, 1433
FEATHER, N.T., 1438, 1447

FECHO, B., 111
FEDERAL INTERAGENCY FORUM ON CHILD AND FAMILY STATISTICS, 1637, 1638t– 1639t, 1644, 1646
FEELEY, J.T., 1479
FEEMAN, D.J., 456, 462, 466, 468, 479, 490, 495–497
FEITELSON, D., 492
FELDLAUFER, H., 962
FELDMAN, L., 1233
FELTON, R.H., 555, 556
FELTOVICH, P., 42, 48, 640– 653, 641, 642, 645, 648, 651, 654, 656–659, 1261
FENNELL, R.D., 1164, 1349
FERDMAN, B., 213, 214, 224, 236
FERGUSON, H., 472
FERGUSON, M.C., 79
FERGUSON, R.F., 739
FERGUSON-HESSLER, M.G.M., 47
FERNANDEZ, J.W., 207
FERNÁNDEZ, S.C., 244, 245f, 256
FERRARA, R.A., 805
FERREIRA, F., 1259
FERREIRO, E., 148, 631
FERRY, J., 1587
FERSTL, E., 1309
FETSCO, T.G., 1346
FEUERSTEIN, R., 783
FEY, M.E., 536
FICZERE, S.A., 766
FIEDOROWICZ, C.A.M., 492
FIELDING, L.G., 46, 419, 481, 873, 874, 929, 980
FIELDING-BARNSLEY, R., 552
FILIP, D., 488
FILLMORE, C.J., 1199, 1201, 1352, 1591
FINAN, B., 1587
FINCHER-KIEFER, R.H., 1300
FINDERS, M.J., 859, 871, 874, 901, 1571, 1584
FINE, G.A., 871
FINLAND MINISTRY OF EDUCATION, 1579, 1580
FINN, C.E., 12
FINN, J.D., 1407
FINNSTROM, O., 544
FISCHER, M., 548
FISCHER, P., 555

FISCHER, U., 585, 728, 729
FISH, E., 495
FISH, S., 44, 855, 1384, 1499, 1502
FISHBEIN, M., 1434, 1440, 1441
FISHER, C.J., 740
FITCH, W.T., 1122, 1126
FITZGERALD, F.S., 858, 1471
FITZGERALD, J., 113, 260, 1083–1113, 1084, 1118, 1646, 1653
FLACK, M., 291
FLANIGAN, H., 1235
FLAUBERT, G., 1382
FLAVELL, J.H., 43, 502, 725, 757, 761, 762t
FLEET, J., 43, 999
FLEISCHMAN, H., 264n2
FLEISHER, L.S., 420, 447, 477
FLEMING, J.T., 462
FLESCH, R.F., 7, 34, 1188, 1584
FLETCHER, C.R., 661, 1245– 1246, 1250, 1254, 1259
FLETCHER, J.M., 15, 55, 318, 391, 455, 473, 489, 519, 522, 530, 534, 564
FLETCHER-FLINN, C.M., 397
FLIPPO, R.F., 654, 655
FLODEN, R.E., 80
FLOOD, J., 487, 732, 905, 1391, 1585, 1586
FLORIDA DEPARTMENT OF EDUCATION, 406
FLOWER, L.S., 764, 1119, 1122, 1400, 1405, 1408, 1412, 1422, 1426–1428, 1501
FODOR, J.A., 40, 476, 1200– 1201
FOERTSCH, J., 1297
FOLB, E.A., 205
FOLSTEIN, M., 818
FOLTZ, G., 474, 491, 500
FOLTZ, P.W., 1289, 1290
FONT FREIDE, T.A., 428t, 445
FOORMAN, B., 55, 318, 391, 393, 406
FORD, T.K., 1574
FORELL, E.R., 458, 467
FOREMAN, M., 703
FORESMAN, S., 406
FORMAN, E.A., 95, 163–186, 171, 172, 172–177, 180, 181, 1118, 1483
FORREST-PRESSLEY, D.L., 760

GOETZ, E.T., 34, 42, 43, 52, 597, 1329, 1340, 1344–1347, 1353, 1476, 1482, 1487

GOETZ, J.P., 1023, 1026, 1396

GOFFMAN, E., 154, 899, 902

GOIN, L., 561

GOLD, C., 1160

GOLDBERG, L., 399

GOLDEN, J.M., 915, 916

GOLDEN, R.M., 1252

GOLDENBERG, C., 113, 216, 1526, *1636–1666,* 1640, 1644–1646, 1649–1652, 1658

GOLDING, J.M., 1298

GOLDMAN, S.R., 52, 103, 462, 469, 660, *660–683,* 661–663, 666, 679, 679n1, 1118, 1244–1246, 1250, 1252, 1256, 1262, 1264, 1487

GOLDMAN, T., 488

GOLDSTEIN, B., 263

GOLDSTEIN, D., 497

GOLDSTEIN, Z., 492

GOLLASCH, F.V., 462

GOMBERT, J., 586

GOMEZ, E., 13

GONZALES, P., 586, 738

GONZÁLEZ, N., 218, 236

GOOD, R.H., 521

GOOD, T., 962

GOODCHILD, F., 43

GOODCHILD, R., 999, 1000

GOODLAD, J.I., 979, 980, 990

GOODMAN, G.S., 470

GOODMAN, I., 1640

GOODMAN, K.S., 19, 38–40, 52, 57, 100, 102, 281, 291, 367, 461–463, 468–470, *620–639,* 621, 623, 624, 629–631, 635, 1117, 1125, 1214, 1482, 1584

GOODMAN, M., 870

GOODMAN, Y.M., 38–40, 52, 102, *620–639,* 630, 635, 1044, 1117, 1482

GOODWIN, C., 775

GOODWIN, J., 85

GOODY, J., 472

GORDON, C.J., 811, 838, 1481

GORDON, E., 860

GORDON, E.E., 1653

GORDON, E.H., 1653

GORIN, L., 789

GOSWAMI, U., 317, 318, 365, 367, 378–380, 395–398, 473

GOTTARDO, A., 582, 583

GOTTESMAN, R., 491

GOTTFRIED, A.E., 931, 933, 947

GOTTLIEB, J., 491

GOUGH, P.B., 315, 349, 365, 367, 370, 372, 377, 378, 457, 460, 470, 474, 476, 487, 502, 521, 522, 534, 582, 1119, 1126, 1150, 1151f, 1164, 1180, *1180–1181,* 1181, 1213, 1214, 1226

GOULD, J.D., 1405

GOULDEN, R., 587

GOURLEY, J.W., 392

GRABOI, D., 1159, 1160

GRAESSER, A.C., 660, 755, 760, 775, 810, 1125, 1245, 1247, 1250, 1254, 1260, 1297–1298, 1300

GRAFF, G., 1040

GRAFFT, W., 1470

GRAHAM, S., 52, 53, 1125

GRAUE, M.E., 1606, 1614

GRAVES, B.B., 729

GRAVES, D.H., 143n2, 147, 150, 169, 1044, 1045

GRAVES, M.F., 576–577, 580, 582, 726, 727, 729, 811, 1531

GRAY, B., 151

GRAY, L., 394

GRAY, W.S., 34, 394, 406

GRAZIANO, M., 1578

GREANEY, V., 930

GREANY, V., 873, 874

GREEN, B., 1528

GREEN, C., 860, *870–913,* 1485

GREEN, D.W., 1196, 1206, 1215

GREEN, G.M., 577

GREEN, I., 584

GREEN, J., 44, 740, 1396, 1536

GREEN, J.L., 1483

GREEN, M., 905, 907, 908

GREENBERG, D., 536

GREENBERG, J., 218

GREENBERG, M.A., 1411

GREENE, B.A., 931

GREENE, D., 1437

GREENE, E., 1255

GREENE, J.F., 561

GREENE, J.P., 1647, 1659

GREENE, S., 47, 1404

GREENFIELD, E., 159

GREENLAW, J., 856

GREENO, J.G., 48, 49, 949, 1041, 1317, 1319, 1628

GREER, C., 909

GREGORY, E., 230

GREYBECK, B., 960, 982, 984, 985, 989

GRIFFIN, P., 14, 116, 130, 210, 211, 246, 349, 546, 550, 556, 784, 1322, 1641

GRIFFITH, P.L., 315, 365, 372

GRIGORENKO, E.L., 530, 543, 544

GRIMES, J.E., 810

GRISCHKOWSKY, N., 1405

GRISSMER, D.W., 11

GRITSAVAGE, M.M., 97

GROGAN, P.R., 315

GROSS, J., 491

GROSSMAN, H., 1645

GUBA, E.G., 685, 689–691, 1454, 1533

GUERRA, J.C., 215, 226, 232, 236

GUICE, S., 13, 20

GULGOZ, S., 1310, 1311, 1313

GUMINSKI, M., 477

GUMPERZ, J.J., 282

GUNSTONE, R.F., 642

GUSZAK, F.J., 980

GUTHRIE, J., 50–54, 109, 112, 405, 492, 684, 713, 730, 733, 737, 861, *929–953,* 931–938, 947–950, 954, 961, 984, 1045, 1122, 1126, 1469

GUTIERREZ, K., 153

GUTIERREZ-CLELLEN, V.F., 263

GUTLOHN, L., 403

GUTTENTAG, R., 470

GUZZETTI, B., 47, 97

H

HAAS, C., 1404–1405, 1419

HAAS, N.S., 12, 75

HABERLANDT, K., 604, 811

HACKER, D.J., 106, 755, *755–779,* 762t, 763t, 764, 765, 775, 1118, 1482

HAENSLY, P.A., 1482

HAGEDORN, T., 1652
HAGÈGE, C., 143n3
HAGEN, A.S., 966
HAGEN, J.W., 488
HAGGARD, M.R., 954, 1478, 1493
HAGOOD, M.C., 1571, 1584, 1588
HAIGHT, W., 256
HAITH, M.M., 470
HAKALA, C., 1246
HAKUTA, K., 210, 220, 1646–1648, 1659
HALADYNA, T.H., 12, 75
HALEY, D., 392
HALL, J.W., 486, 489–490, 587
HALL, R., 1320
HALLAHAN, D.P., 487–489
HALLER, M., 1337
HALLIDAY, M.A.K., 39, 94, 117, *133–145*, 141–143, 143n4, 144nn6–7, 147, 281, 282, 291–293, 296, 305, 307, 1392
HAMILTON, G., 860
HAMILTON, L.S., 75
HAMMETT, R., 863
HAMMOND, K., 477
HAMPSTON, J.M., 115, 1043
HAMSTON, J., 97
HANCIN-BHATT, B., 581, 730
HANCOCK, G.R., 730, 1562
HANCOCK, M.R., 854
HANEY, W., 71
HANKS, W.F., 119
HANNAH, A.M., 425t
HANNON, S.A., 811
HANSEN, J., 43, 383, 397, 762t, 980
HANSIS, R., 47
HARDENBROOK, M., 97
HARDING, L.M., 462, 473
HARE, V.C., 47
HARGIS, C.H., 1355
HARKER, J.O., 1483
HARKNESS, S., 125
HARMON, M.C., 1622
HARPER, H., 859
HARRIS, A.J., 412, 1013, 1014
HARRIS, K.R., 45, 52, 53, 558
HARRIS, P., 982, 983, 985, 989, 1641
HARRIS, P.J., 1463, 1489, 1501
HARRIS, P.L., 795, 799

HARRIS, T.L., 1331, 1396n2, 1536, 1537
HARRIS, V.J., 223, 853
HARRISON, T.M., 1575
HARSTE, J.C., 39, 1477, 1479, 1528, 1584
HART, B., 256, 545, 548
HART, Z., 489
HARTEL, M.J., 893
HARTLEY, J.T., 816, 819
HARTMAN, D.K., 105, 767, 772, 1484
HARTY, K.R., 101
HARWOOD, K.T., 915
HASAN, R., 39, 143, 281–283, 291, 293, 294
HASHER, L., 1476
HASSELBRING, T.S., 561
HATANO, G., 170
HATCH, E.M., 243
HATCH, J., 1408, 1418
HATCHER, P.J., 561
HAUSER, M., 1122, 1126
HAUSER, R., 11
HAVILAND, S.E., 1202
HAWISHER, G.E., 1588
HAWTHORNE, N., 968
HAYES, D., 586
HAYES, D.A., 44, 604
HAYES, D.P., 545, 546
HAYES, J.R., 95, 684, 712, 764, 1119, 1122, *1399–1430*, 1400, 1405, 1407–1408, 1412, 1413f–1415f, 1417–1420, 1422, 1425–1429
HAZZEO, 264n3
HEALY, A.F., 1313
HEATH, S.B., 44, 46, 95, 151, 154, 187, *187–209*, 192, 195, 200, 203, 206, 208n1, 284, 307, 905, 961, 967, 990, 1388, 1404, 1473, 1477, 1621, 1645
HEATON, R.M., 49, 76
HEAVISIDE, S., 1578
HEBB, D.O., 1431
HEBERT, M., 474–476
HECHT, S.A., 316, 356, 545, 929
HECK, M.J., 1046
HECKELMAN, R.G., 420, 431, 432t, 439
HEGARTY, M., 874
HEGION, A., 495

HEILMAN, E.E., 1524, *1530–1556*
HEILMAN, P.C., 553
HEINEKEN, E., 755
HEINZE, B., 1301
HELLER, C., 157
HEMPHILL, K.J., 879
HEMPHILL, L., 855, 1640
HENDERSON, E.H., 318, 355, 375, 474
HENK, W.A., 1433, 1437, 1440, 1451
HENLEY, N.M., 1308
HENRY, M., 382, 383
HENRY, S., 587
HENZE, R., 215, 216
HERBER, H.L., 4, 605
HERDMAN, C.M., 1342, 1343, 1355
HERDT, G., 187
HERITAGE, J., 775
HERMAN, P.A., 425t, 430, 458, 477, 479, 576, 584, 1232, 1233, 1479
HERRIMAN, M., 580
HERTZOG, C., 816
HERZOG, M., 25
HESS, R.D., 1651
HESSE, D., 771
HEUBACH, K., 420
HEUBERT, J., 11
HICKMAN, J., 856
HIDI, S., 51, 282, 291, 308
HIEBERT, E.H., 12, 50, 98, 353, 354, *390–411*, 391, 393, 396, 401–405, 407, 408, 415, 503, 504, 528, 560, 738, 1083, 1481, 1482
HIEBERT, J., 1562
HIGGINS, E.T., 1431
HILDEBRANDT, N., 1238
HILDYARD, A., 282, 291, 308, 472
HILGARD, E.R., 1407
HILL, C., 1408, 1418
HILL, H.C., 79
HILL, M.H., 875
HILLINGER, M.L., 365, 370, 377, 378, 457, 474, 502, 1180
HILLOCKS, G., JR., 1042, 1045
HINCHMAN, K.A., 979, 1585
HINSON, D., 50, 859, 910n8
HINTON, G.E., 1480

MANN, V.A., 456, 458, 471, 478, 487, 497, 530
MANN, W.C., 810
MANNES, S.M., 768, 1314
MANY, J.E., 44, 103, 109, *684–719,* 856, 914, *914–928,* 915–917, 984, 1118, 1392, 1469, 1485
MANY, J.L., 105
MANZO, A.V., 790, 1493
MANZO, U., 1493
MARANO, N.L., 547
MARCUS, G., 207
MARD, S., 544
MAREK, A., 621
MARIOTTO, M., 482
MARKLEY, B.K., 425t
MARKMAN, E.M., 756, 761, 762t, 764, 765, 774, 787, 789, 795
MARKS, M.B., 558, 1002
MARKUS, H., 959
MARRA, R.M., 1598
MARSCHARK, M., 1345
MARSEGLIA, P., 444
MARSHALL, E., 1013
MARSHALL, H., 969, 1497
MARSHALL, J.C., 1341
MARSHALL, J.D., 852, 859, 897, 905
MARSOLEK, C.J., 1246
MARTIN, J.R., 121, 143n1
MARTIN, L., 426t
MARTIN, L.A., 98, *390–411,* 392, 396, 403, 404, 738, 1481
MARTINEZ, M.G., 852, 861
MARUYAMA, G., 419, 471, 873, 874, 931
MARX, R.W., 949
MASEFIELD, J., 1357
MASLOW, A.H., 959, 1438
MASON, J., 365, 370, 371, 373, 503, 604
MASON, J.M., 967, 1472, 1473, 1479, 1492, 1644, 1649
MASON, M., 474, 475
MASON, R.A., 1295, 1298
MASONHEIMER, P., 370, 503, 1229
MASSARO, D.W., 1343, 1480
MASSON, E.J., 477
MASTERSON, J., 472
MASTROPIERI, M.A., 520, 565

MATHEMATICAL SCIENCES EDUCATION BOARD, 1623f
MATHES, P.G., 114, 424, 426t, 427t, 430, 445, 446, 723, 1085
MATHESIUS, V., 144n7
MATHEWS, J., 26
MATHEWS, M., 1572, 1574
MATHEWS, V.H., 874
MATHEWSON, G., 958, 980, 992, 1119, 1122, *1431–1461,* 1432, 1433, 1437, 1439, 1440, 1469–1470, 1482
MATLOCK, B., 583
MATSUHASHI, A., 1423
MATTHEWS, M.R., 48, 49
MATTHEWS, R., 372, 454, 481, 484, 492, 499
MATTINGLY, D.J., 1651
MATTINGLY, I.G., 1332
MATTSON, P., 498
MATUTE-BIANCHI, M.E., 235
MAW, C.E., 235
MAXWELL, J.A., 1552
MAYER, D.P., 76
MAYER, R.E., 605, 811, 812f, 817, 838, 839, 1320, 1596
MAYZNER, M.S., 1228
MAZMANIAN, D., 74
MAZZEO, J., 390
MCCABE, A., 289
MCCAFFREY, D.F., 75
MCCALL, R.B., 464, 497
MCCANDLISS, B., 546, 553
MCCANN, A., 730
MCCARRELL, N.S., 594, 609
MCCARTHEY, S.J., 400, 405, 406
MCCARTHY, D.A., 1477
MCCARTHY, M., 574
MCCARTHY, S.J., 20, 76
MCCARTNEY, K., 482–484, 485
MCCARTY, T.L., 216, 235
MCCASLIN, E., 403, 407, 584
MCCLELLAND, D.C., 1438
MCCLELLAND, J.L., 460, 495, 501, 598, 760, 765, 1155, 1224, 1227, 1235, 1349, 1480
MCCLOSKEY, D., 1386
MCCLURE, E.F., 226, 256, 729
MCCLURE, J., 487

MCCONKIE, G.W., 463, 500, 501, 1189, 1191, 1194, 1222
MCCORMICK, C.B., 810
MCCORMICK, S., 98, 100, 105, *365–389,* 371, 420, 444, 914, 1118, 1286, 1431, 1479
MCCORRISTON, M., 473
MCCULLOUGH, C.M., 4
MCCURDY, J., 235
MCCUSKER, L.X., 474, 1180
MCCUTCHEN, D., 551, 565, 765, 769, 770
MCDANIEL, M.A., 1260, 1284, 1314
MCDERMOTT, J., 482
MCDERMOTT, R.P., 725, 785, 786, 1538
MCDILL, E.L., 1643
MCDONNELL, L., 86
MCFALLS, E., 446, 576
MCGEE, C., 1067
MCGEE, L.M., 854, 860, 1482
MCGILL-FRANZEN, A.M., *5–32,* 7, 8, 12, 14–19, 21, 34, 70, 75, 77
MCGINLEY, W., 44, 684–686, 712, 715, 854, 859, 880
MCGINNIES, E., 1446
MCGOLDRICK, J.A., 998
MCGOUGH, K., 53
MCGUIRE, W.J., 1433–1434
MCHOUL, A., 1472
MCINNES, J., 621
MCINTYRE, E., 17, 284
MCIVER, M.C., 88
MCKAY, S.L., 213, 214
MCKEACHIE, W.J., 816
MCKENNA, M., 51, 111, 873
MCKENZIE, T.L., 1651
MCKEOWN, M., 51, 479, 480, 557, 558, 574–576, 583, 584, 587, 676, 727, 728, 732, 1233, 1311, 1478
MCKILLOP, A.M., 862, 863
MCKOOL, S.S., 874
MCKOON, G., 1245–1247, 1249, 1254, 1259, 1262, 1297
MCLAREN, P., 46
MCLAUGHLIN, B., 235
MCLAUGHLIN, M.W., 69, 70, 74, 905, 961, 1622
MCLAUGHLIN, T.F., 432t
MCLEAN, R.S., 54

PHILLIPS, S., 967, 1472
PHINNEY, M.Y., 856, 858
PIAGET, J., 180, 183, 586, 633, 1392
PICHE, G.L., 811
PICHERT, J.W., 42, 598, 603, 1483–1484
PIETROMONACO, P., 1450
PIGNOT, E., 503
PIGOTT, T.D., 50
PIHKO, E., 543
PIKULSKI, J.J., 407
PILLEMER, D.B., 424
PILLSBURY, W.B., 1155
PINNELL, G.S., 560, 1083
PINTRICH, P.R., 51, 816, 931, 933, 949–950, 960, 1498
PITMAN, M.A., 1552
PITTELMAN, S.D., 1478
PLATI, T., 1607
PLAUT, D.C., 1341
PLOMIN, R., 482
PLUMB, C., 755, 762t, 763t, 764
POLACCO, P., 577
POLKINGHORNE, D., 1532, 1535, 1551
POLLATSEK, A., 463, 1221, 1350
POLLEY, R.R., 811
POLLOWAY, E.A., 521
POON, L.W., 810–851, 811, 818, 819, 840, 1118, 1120, 1481
POPE, R., 862
POPLE, M., 575, 727
PORCHE, M.V., 114
POSTMAN, L., 1155
POSTMAN, N., 54
POWELL, J., 479, 483
POWELL, J.S., 584
PRATT, A., 372
PRAWAT, R.S., 47, 49, 108, 1431
PRESSLEY, M., 13, 15, 43, 53, 114, 115, 319, 320, 535, 548, 550, 558, 560, 660, 678, 684, 722, 733, 734, 760, 762t, 763t, 766, 774, 810, 980, 998, 998–1039, 999–1002, 1005, 1022, 1031, 1032, 1043, 1045, 1090, 1562, 1563, 1641
PRESSLEY, M.P., 950
PRIOR, M., 472, 473

PRISLIN, R., 1651
PROBST, R.E., 914
PROCHNOW, J.E., 560
PROPP, V., 1245
PROULX, E.A., 863
THE PSYCHOLOGICAL CORPORATION, 1015
PSYCHOLOGICAL REVIEW, 1182
PUGH, K.R., 55
PUNAMÄKI, R., 117, 856
PURCELL, L., 785
PURCELL-GATES, V., 17, 100, 284–285, 289
PURVES, A., 915–917, 1042, 1391, 1394
PUTNAM, L., 291
PUTNAM, R.T., 49, 1631

Q
QIU, S., 134
QUAST, Z., 1354
QUATHAMER, D., 755
QUINN, D.W., 439
QUINN, N., 125

R
RAAIJMAKERS, J.G.W., 1254
RABINOWITZ, P.J., 853, 857, 862
RACK, J., 385
RACK, J.P., 522, 530
RACKLIFFE, G., 18
RADIN, D.I., 1482
RADVANSKY, G.A., 1286
RADWAY, J.A., 859
RALPH, K., 1641
RAMAN, I., 1342
RAMEY, C.T., 1652, 1655–1656
RAMEY, D.R., 1647, 1652
RAMÍREZ, J.D., 1647, 1652
RAMUNDA, J.M., 440
RANCK-BUHR, W., 732
RANDALL, S., 50, 859, 910n8
RAND READING STUDY GROUP, 51, 53, 54, 103, 720, 720–754, 1322, 1525, 1557, 1557–1569, 1591, 1601, 1602
RANKIN-ERICKSON, J.L., 548
RANSDELL, S., 1399, 1420
RAO, S., 470
RAPHAEL, T., 21, 43, 684, 691, 712, 774, 775, 856, 859,

860, 861, 904, 909n1, 1045, 1493
RASHOTTE, C., 422, 424, 427t, 430, 445, 530, 553, 723, 929
RASINSKI, T., 418, 427t, 433t, 436, 438, 442, 723, 1090
RASMUSSEN, D., 399
RASTLE, K., 1341
RATCLIFF, R., 1245–1247, 1249, 1254, 1259, 1262, 1297
RATNER, H.H., 755, 762t, 763t
RAYBURN, J.S., 859
RAYNER, K., 460, 463, 1183, 1191, 1194, 1221, 1247, 1288, 1298, 1350
READ, C., 148, 375, 418, 631
READ, J., 587
READENCE, J.E., 42, 43, 1640
READING RESEARCH QUARTERLY, 5, 281, 313, 454, 684, 852, 1083, 1530, 1640
READING & WRITING QUARTERLY: OVERCOMING LEARNING DIFFICULTIES, 365
REARDON, S.F., 1628
REDDY, D.R., 1164, 1349
REDER, L.M., 45, 762t, 1627
REDISH, J., 1410
REED, J.H., 52, 938
REED, M.T., 1355
REES, E., 482
REESE, L., 1640, 1645
REEVE, J., 732
REICH, R., 1575
REICHER, G.M., 1155
REID, J., 458, 503
REINKING, D., 51, 52, 54, 219, 221, 418, 1090, 1528, 1529, 1571, 1572, 1583, 1584, 1588, 1593
REISDORF, P., 1262
REITMAN, J.S., 1186
REITMAN, W.R., 1420
REITSMA, P., 316, 379, 399, 474, 477, 478
REITZ, L., 1259
REMILLARD, J., 49
RENNICK, P., 489
RENOUF, G., 981
RENTEL, V.M., 283–285, 289, 293, 296, 306
RESCHLY, D.J., 564
RESCORLA, L., 536

Subject Index

References followed by *t* or *f* indicate tables or figures, respectively. Those followed by *n* indicate notes. Page spans in italics indicate an author's contribution to this volume.

CONTENT: attitude toward, 1457, 1467; imputation of, 781–782; review of, 1496
CONTENT AREA READING, 1457
CONTENT AREAS, 1492–1493
CONTENT KNOWLEDGE, 1084
CONTENTIVE ERRORS, 642
CONTEXT: classroom, 686–687, 1464, 1466, 1497–1503, 1498*f*; and comprehension processes, 461; of culture, 872; decontextualized language, 586–587; differing views on use of, 462–465; general, 1161–1163; learning new word meanings from, 1232–1233; and letter perception, 1154, 1154*f*; letter sounds in, 1094, 1098–1100, 1099*t*, 1102, 1102*t*, 1103–1106, 1104*t*; and metalinguistic awareness, 582–584; quality of teaching and learning in, 77, 78*f*; research on, 855–856; semantic, 1160–1161; sociocultural, 856–863, 1121; total, 1388–1389; and word recognition, 460–470
CONTEXT CUES, 319, 371
CONTEXT PROCESSOR, 1230–1231
CONTEXT-FREE DECODING, 468
CONTEXT-INDEPENDENT CONCEPTUAL REPRESENTATION, 643
CONTEXTUALIZING, 864
CONTRADICTIONS, 1258–1259
CONTRERAS, CLAUDIA, 220
CONTROL, 758
CONTROLLED WORD RECOGNITION, 523*t*, 531*f*
CONVENTIONAL READERS, 288, 304–305
CONVERSATION: evolution of, 139–140; ongoing, 144*n*9
COOPERATIVE ACTIVITY, 175, 176*t*
COORDINATION, 1545, 1565–1567
COPING WITH READING DEFICITS, 502
CORNERSTONE CONCEPTS, 1446–1448, 1454–1455
CORRECTIONS, 1258–1259
COSTS, 1108*t*
COUNTY PRESCHOOLS, 286–287
CPRE. *See* Consortium for Policy Research in Education
CREATIVITY MODEL, 133
CRITICAL DISCOURSE ANALYSIS, 872
CRITICAL PRACTICES, 154, 156–157
CRITICAL THINKING, 206; questions for, 1071–1072
CRITIQUING AND TRANSFORMING WORLDS, 865
CSPAN. *See* computation span
CTBS. *See* Comprehensive Test of Basic Skills
CTI. *See* Community Teamwork, Inc.

CUEING SYSTEMS, 630–631
CUES, 320–321; context, 319, 371; graphic, 463; meaning, 319; miscues, 620–639; multiple, 560–561; phonetic, 374, 523*t*, 527, 531*f*; Reading Recovery (RR) program, 560–561; selective-cue word learning, 370; sources for, 320; visual, 370–371, 523*t*, 526–527, 531*f*
CUI. *See* Communities United, Inc.
CULTURAL ACTIVITIES, 852–869
CULTURAL BORDERLANDS, 224–231
CULTURAL DIFFERENCES, 1404
CULTURAL INTERACTION PARADIGM, 1538–1539
CULTURAL MODELS, 125, 126*f*
CULTURALLY RELEVANT TEXT(S), 223
CULTURE: constructing identities through participation in, 858–859; constructing texts as, 857–858; context of, 872; contextualizing, 864; critiquing and transforming, 865; effects on learning to read, 1643, 1648–1650; learning, 1614–1635; of mediocrity, 865
CUNNINGHAM, JAMES W., 1089–1090
CURIOSITY, 992
CURRICULUM: casualties, 561; historical perspective on, 1615*f*, 1615–1619; improvising, 1067; Internet resources, 1593; new theories of, 1619–1621; reformed vision of, 1620*f*; of social efficiency, 1616*f*
CVC WORDS. *See* consonant–vowel–consonant words

D

DADE COUNTY (FLORIDA), 1064
DAILY ACTIVITY LOGS, 879, 880–883, 881*f*
DANISH LITERACY INSTRUCTION, 264*n*7
DAVIS READING TEST, 819, 820
DCT. *See* Dual Coding Theory
DEBUGGING, 1627
DECISION MAKING, 1420–1421; instructional, 1466, 1494–1497; and reading, 1435
DECLARATIVE KNOWLEDGE, 1468, 1492
DECODABILITY: unresolved issues, 407–408; of words, 403–404
DECODERS, 1150
DECODING, 366–367, 1131, 1585; accuracy of, 552–554; compensatory processing and, 463–469; context-free, 468; directions for further research, 1350–1351; directions for practice, 1354–1355; empirical evidence for, 1341–1343; gluing to print, 378; in partial-alphabetic phase, 374; phonological, 321,

growth model of, 133; settings for bilingual children 3–5 years old, 246–256; significance of dialogue for, 775; Vygotskian perspectives in, 163–186

EDUCATION OF HANDICAPPED CHILDREN ACT OF 1975, 9

EDUCATION POLICY, 22

EDUCATIONAL RESEARCH: criteria for, 1557; improving, 1560–1561; prerequisites for, 1557–1561; priorities for, 1557–1560; programmatic efforts, 1561. *See also* research

EFFECT SIZE, 1662n1

EFFECTIVENESS: of literacy teachers, 994; teaching, 994–995

EFFERENT READING, 1386–1387

EFFERENT STANCE, 914, 992, 1372–1373, 1396n2

ELABORATION, 600, 600t, 1421; inferential, 599; precise vs. imprecise, 615–616

ELEMENTARY AND SECONDARY EDUCATION ACT OF 1965 (ESEA), 8–10; Title I, 9, 10–11, 77

ELEMENTARY SCHOOL: bilingualism/biliteracy in, 257–262; early, 257–262; programs for bilingual children 5–8 years old, 257t, 257–258

EMERGENT BILINGUALS, 244

EMERGENT READING: attention-to-pictures, 287–288; attention-to-print, 288; conventional, 304–305; descriptive analysis, 298; income and, 294–296, 295t; measurement of, 287–289; no-story, 287–288, 298–299; oral-like, 287–288, 299–302; print-related refusal, 288; written-like, 287–288, 302–304

EMOTIONAL STATE, 1436–1438

ENABLING STRATEGIES, 1044–1045, 1059t, 1061t, 1070–1072

ENCODING, 1195–1199

ENGAGED LEARNING, 733; Era of Engaged Learning (1996–present), 50–55, 109; rival views, 54–55

ENGAGEMENT, 108–112; task-engagement resources, 957, 968–969, 973–974; text, 405

ENGAGINGNESS, 405–406

ENGLISH: acquisition of, 1647; Excellence in English project, 1046–1058; Hispanized, 244; receptive vocabulary tests, 248–249, 249t; as second language, 577, 635, 729, 736; secondary-level programs, 1042–1046; sheltered instruction in, 216; social languages, 116; Spanish cognates, 581–582

ENGLISH AS A SECOND LANGUAGE (ESL) PROGRAMS, 260

ENGLISH-LANGUAGE CLASSROOMS, 251, 254; developmental sequence in, 251–252; features and expected outcomes of, 247t, 248; mainstream, 258–260; standardized scores for students in, 254–255, 255t

ENGLISH-LANGUAGE LEARNERS, 264n2, 1646, 1659

ENGLISH-LANGUAGE LEARNING: ambivalence toward, 228, 229; of Chinese Americans, 213; and literacy development, 229

ENJOYMENT, 1443

ENVIRONMENTS: influences of, 544–549; learning, 1497–1503; physical, 1405–1406; Research on Learning Environments, 1566; social, 1404–1405; task, 1401f, 1401–1402, 1404–1406

EPISODIC MEMORY, 1139–1140

EPISTEMOLOGICAL RACISM, 1553

EPISTEMOLOGY, 1533–1534

ERA OF CONDITIONED LEARNING (1950–1965), 34–37

ERA OF ENGAGED LEARNING (1996–), 50–55, 109

ERA OF INFORMATION PROCESSING (1976–1985), 41–45, 57

ERA OF NATURAL LEARNING (1966–1975), 37–41

ERA OF SOCIOCULTURAL LEARNING (1986–1995), 45–50

E-RATE PROGRAM, 1582

ERIC DATABASE, 419

ERRORS: contentive, 642; detection of, 795; word exchange, 1423

ESCAPE, 992

ESEA. *See* Elementary and Secondary Education Act of 1965

ESL PROGRAMS. *See* English as a Second Language programs

ESSENTIAL GOALS AND OBJECTIVES IN READING (MICHIGAN), 80, 81

ETHNICITY, 1638t, 1639t

EUROPEAN AMERICANS, 159

EVALUATION, 1412–1413, 1415f

EVALUATIVE BELIEF TOTAL (EBT), 1440–1441

EVALUATIVE BELIEFS, 1441t

EVENTS: classroom events, 152–154; community participation in, 151–154; learning within, 151–152; literacy events, 151; unofficial, 154–156

EVOCATION, 1376

I

IBM: Write to Read program, 23

ICONS, 1150

ICs. *See* instructional changes

ICTs. *See* information and communication technologies

IDEA. *See* Individuals with Disabilities Education Act

IDEA UNITS, 601, 602*t*

IDEATIONAL SCAFFOLDING, 598

IDENTITY, 959–961; constructing, 858–859; in cultural borderlands, 224–231; development of, 211–215, 224–229, 232–234; of Latina/o students, 210–239; literate, 231–234

IDENTITY KITS, 94, 124, 872

ILLITERACY, 8

ILL-STRUCTURED DOMAINS, 640–653

ILLUSIONS OF KNOWING, 768–769

IMAGE MAPS, 1586

IMAGENS, 1332

IMAGERY, 1347, 1356–1357

IMAGING, 921–922

IMMEDIACY ASSUMPTION, 1183–1184, 1211–1212

IMPROVEMENT PLAN, 1065

INCENTIVES, 1455

INCIPIENT BILINGUALS, 242

INCOME: emergent reading and, 294–296, 295*t*; national education goals and, 1638*t*

INCOME EFFECT, 307

INDIANS, 601, 602*t*

INDIVIDUAL DIFFERENCES: in literacy acquisition, 454–516; in reading, 456–458; in reading comprehension, 1261–1263; research on, 454–456; in writing, 1406–1411

INDIVIDUALS WITH DISABILITIES EDUCATION ACT (IDEA), 518, 564

INFERENCES, 771, 1244–1269, 1294, 1297; bridging, 1309; classification of, 1294–1297, 1295*t*; forward, 1259–1260; generation during discourse comprehension, 1297–1299; knowledge-based, 1298–1299; making, 222*f*, 1421–1422; reconstruction of, 599, 1495; and situation models, 1294–1301; situation models as, 1300; theories of making, 1257

INFLUENTIAL TEACHERS, 954, 979–997; beliefs about teaching, 983, 983*f*; in classroom, 985–993; example, 955–969, 972–973; further areas of inquiry, 974–975; implications for teaching and research, 993–995; key influences on, 984; perceptions of,

982–983; portrait, 982–985; theoretical context for, 981–982

INFORMAL KNOWLEDGE, 47

INFORMATION: accumulating, 692–694; basic form of, 139; meaning in form of, 137; from oral sources, 697–699; recording, 695–699; reinstatement of, 666–668, 667*t*; retrieval of, 1263–1264; reviewing coverage of, 701–703; searching for, 694–695, 697–699; transferring, 694–699; transforming, 699–705, 702*t*

INFORMATION AGE, 1589–1590

INFORMATION AND COMMUNICATION TECHNOLOGIES (ICTs): economies based on, 1575–1576; Internet, 1577–1579, 1585–1586, 1589–1590, 1593; new literacies of, 1570–1613

INFORMATION PROCESSING, 57; automatic, 1127–1148; differences in, 671–676; Era of Information Processing (1976–1985), 41–45; general approaches to, 668–671, 669*t*; rival views, 43–44; text-focused, 669, 669*t*, 670*t*, 674–676

INFORMATIONAL TEXT, 660–683

INITIAL LITERACY, 1084, 1085

INITIATE–REPLAY–EVALUATE (IRE) PATTERN, 20–21

INITIATION–COMMENT–RESPONSE PATTERNS, 278

INNER GAUGE, 1382

INNER SEMANTICS, 1350

INPUT ORDER, 1258

INQUIRY METHODS, 785

INSTANTIATION, 1475

INSTRUCTION, 502; anchored, 48; around concerns, issues, and dilemmas, 863–864; attitude and, 1454–1457; automaticity model and, 1144–1147; bilingual strategic, 221–223; classroom, 604–605; classroom activities, 344, 344*t*; comprehension, 721–737, 747; comprehension strategy, 724–725, 730–731; comprehension-fostering, 790–801, 797*f*, 801–802; with consolidated-alphabetic phase readers, 383–384; decision-making outcomes and processes, 1466, 1494–1497; with delayed and disabled readers, 365; design resources, 958*f*; differential, 353–354; direct, 18, 1233; dyadic encounters, 151; effective, 112–113, 1642–1643; explicit, 724–725; in first grade, 353–354; fluency, 418–438, 444, 447–448; for full-alphabetic phase readers, 380–381; in higher-performing schools, 1078;

integrated, 1058, 1060–1062, 1061*t*; of Latina/o students, 216; literacy development and, 112–115; literature, 863–864; for low-reading group children, 332, 332*t*, 335, 336*t*, 339, 340*t*, 343*t*, 343–344; new views of, 1615*f*; organization of practices, 735–736; orientation of, 957, 964–968, 973; for partial-alphabetic phase readers, 374–377; phonics, 315, 323; preschooler literate register ownership and, 308–309; reading, 221–223, 222*f*, 550–562, 734; reading as meaning-construction process and, 1510–1511; reading measures and, 345–352; reflect insight into, 1497; schema theory and, 604–605; sensitivity of, 747; separated, 1058–1062, 1061*t*; simulated, 1058–1062, 1061*t*; skills, 1043–1044, 1058–1062, 1061*t*; strategies, 998–1039; testing and, 1615*f*; time designated for, 734; vocabulary, 726–730, 737, 1233; word-recognition, 314–356
INSTRUCTIONAL CHANGES (ICs), 165–167
INSTRUCTIONAL CONVERSATIONS, 1626
INSTRUCTIONAL ENVIRONMENTS, 971–972
INSTRUCTIONAL READING LEVELS, 1093; in America Reads program, 1095–1097, 1096*t*, 1098–1102, 1099*t*, 1100*f*, 1102*t*, 1103–1106, 1104*t*
INSTRUCTIONAL REPRESENTATIONS, 1466, 1495
INSTRUCTIONAL STANCE, 1491; efferent, 992
INTEGRATED INSTRUCTION, 1058, 1060–1062, 1061*t*; fluency lessons, 440–443
INTEGRATED MULTIPLE ANALOGIES, 646
INTEGRATION, 1545; in comprehension, 1278–1286; connecting learnings, 1044; construction and, 1278–1286; construction–integration model of text comprehension, 1270–1328; interclause, 1202–1205
INTELLECTUAL CURIOSITY, 992
INTELLECTUALIZATION, 165
INTELLIGENCE, 488; assessment of, 496; hereditarian theory of, 1616*f*; IQ matching problem, 490; literate, 472; mild IQ deficits, 489; quotient of (IQ), 518; verbal, 496
INTELLIGENCE QUOTIENT (IQ), 518; assessment of, 496; IQ matching problem, 490; mild deficits, 489
INTENDED AUDIENCE, 279*n*2
INTENTION, 959; direct influences on, 1437–1438, 1438*f*; focus of, 958*f*, 958–959; imputation of, 781–782; as mediator between attitude and reading, 1434–1436, 1435*f*; reader, 954–978; of writers, 1384

INTERACTIONS, 1364; classroom and social, 1483; cultural, 1538–1539; reading group by classroom type, 346–349; review of, 1496
INTERACTIVE LEARNING SITUATIONS, 780–809
INTERACTIVE MODEL, 1163*f*, 1163–1171
INTERCLAUSE INTEGRATION, 1202–1205
INTEREST: and attention, 1444; effects on recall, 823, 823*f*
INTEREST-LIST STRATEGY TRAINING, 823*f*, 823–824; consistent use of structure strategy with, 834*t*, 834–835; reading changes after, 828–830, 829*t*; and recall, 830–832, 831*t*; and recall of everyday materials, 835–836, 836*t*; sample program materials and instructions, 850–851
INTERNAL ATTENTION, 1129–1130
INTERNAL EMOTIONAL STATE, 1436–1438
INTERNALIZATION, 785
INTERNALIZED PURPOSES, 1437–1438
INTERNATIONAL HIGH SCHOOL (NEW YORK), 1049*t*, 1053*t*, 1075–1076
INTERNATIONAL READING ASSOCIATION (IRA), 33, 574, 1052, 1549, 1561; 2003 Albert Harris Award, 112; RTEACHER listserv, 1605
INTERNET, 1577–1579, 1585–1586; as central for literacy, 1589–1590; curricular resources, 1593; new literacies of, 1570–1613
INTERPRETATION, 1376, 1488, 1496; expressed, 1377–1378; nexus between meaning-making and, 769–772; social base of, 278; student, 268–280; unconventional, 268–280; validity of, 1384
INTERPRETIVE COMMUNITY, 1384
INTERVENTION, 550–562, 1627
INTERVIEW GUIDES, 880
INTERVIEWS: focus group, 1094–1095; strategies, 1011, 1012*t*, 1016–1022, 1018*t*
INTONATION, 144*n*8
INTRINSIC MOTIVATION, 931; and reading amount, 942*t*, 942–943
INTUITIVE GRAMMAR, 628–630
INUITS, 216
INVENTED SPELLINGS, 375
INVENTIONS, 792
IQ (INTELLIGENCE QUOTIENT), 518; assessment of, 496; IQ matching problem, 490; mild deficits, 489
IRA. *See* International Reading Association
IRE PATTERN. *See* initiate–replay–evaluate pattern
IRELAND, 1580

in think-alouds, 350, 351*t*; word recognition while reading, 346–348, 347*t*; word-recognition instruction strategies provided to, 332, 332*t*, 335, 336*t*, 339, 340*t*, 343*t*, 343–344

LSA. *See* Latent Semantic Analysis

LTWM. *See* long-term working memory

M

MacDonnell, Karis, 1053*t*, 1060

MACROPROPOSITIONS, 1283*t*

MACROSTRUCTURES, 1274, 1276*t*, 1280–1284, 1291–1294

Madison, Wisconsin, 320–321

MAPPING: Group Mapping Activity (GMA), 1493; image maps, 1586

Massachusetts Society for the Prevention of Cruelty to Children, 264*n*6

MASTERY LEARNING, 965

MASTERY ORIENTATION, 931

MASTERY TEACHING, 965

Masztal, Janas, 1053*t*

MATERIALS: design of, 604–605; schema theory and, 604–605; for student research projects, 709–710

MATHEMATICAL MODELS, 1174–1178

MATHEMATICS: California reforms, 739; open-ended assessment tasks, 1623*f*; TIMSS Videotape Classroom Study, 738

MATHETIC UTTERANCES, 138

Matthew effects, 99, 548; breaking the cycle of, 497–501; in education, 482, 486; and less-skilled readers, 484–486; proliferating, 494; in reading, 480–483, 497–502; reconceptualizing reading disability literature in terms of, 486–494; in vocabulary, 482

McFadden-Midby, Kathryn, 1053*t*, 1063–1064, 1071–1072, 1076–1077

MEANING, 118, 1339, 1369, 1370; activity of, 136–137; correct, 1384; discussion activities, 329–335, 330*t*, 331*t*, 333*t*, 334*t*, 337*t*, 338*t*, 340, 341, 341*t*, 342*t*; in form of information, 137; highly meaningful words, 393–395; interpretation of, 1161–1163; learning from context, 1232–1233; private, 1366; public, 1366; as social phenomenon, 133; sociocultural, 1466; types of, 1466; word meanings, 1222, 1232–1233, 1324*n*3

MEANING CONSTRUCTION, 319–321; attention in, 1140–1141, 1141*f*; children's, 133–145; dialogic, 137–143; and general context, 1161–1163; mapping, 1153; nexus between

interpretation and, 769–772; outcomes of, 1464, 1488, 1497; personal, 926; process of, 1462–1521, 1465*f*; self-regulation of, 764–774; strategies for, 985–987; systematic, 135

MEANING CUES, 319

MEANING NEGOTIATION, 969–970, 974, 1466; in classroom context, 1503–1510; process of, 990–992, 991*f*, 1499–1503; strategies for, 987–992

MEANING PROCESSOR, 1232–1235

MEASUREMENT: historical perspective on, 1615*f*, 1615–1619; scientific, 1614, 1616*f*

MEDIA DYSLEXICS, 486–487

MEDIATED LEARNING, 783; early, 783–784

MEDICAID, 199

MEMORY, 599; episodic, 1139–1140; of everyday materials, 835–837; extended offline, 1120; Landscape model of, 1244–1254; long-term, 1324*n*7, 1402, 1424–1426; metamemory for text, 755, 757; phonological, 522, 1138–1139, 1152–1153, 1406; primary, 1150; recall of letters, 600, 600*t*; schema in, 594–606; semantic, 1140, 1144, 1152–1153; strategic, 496; surface-level, 1272; visual, 1136*f*, 1139, 1152–1153; visual–spatial sketchpad, 1406; working, 818, 1186–1187, 1301–1305, 1402, 1406–1411

MEMORY REPRESENTATION: constructing, 1258–1261; online construction of, 1244–1269; updating, 1252–1254, 1253*f*

MENTAL CODES, 1330–1331, 1331*t*

MENTAL IMAGERY, 1356–1357

MENTAL MODELS, 1339

MENTAL REINSTATEMENTS OF INFORMATION, 666–667, 667*t*

MENTAL REPRESENTATION, 642; modalities of, 1339; overreliance on single basis for, 643; retrieval of information from, 1263–1264; retrieving concepts from, 1254

MENTAL STRUCTURES, 1250–1254

MENTALISM, 37

MERLIN, 1150

MESSAGE CENTERS, 1164, 1165–1171, 1166*f*; example, 1166–1171, 1167*f*–1169*f*, 1171*f*, 1172*f*; relations among hypotheses in, 1174–1175, 1175*f*

MESSAGE LEVEL OF SPEECH PRODUCTION, 1423

METACOGNITION, 106–108

METACOGNITIVE STRATEGIES, 1482, 1493–1494

METACOGNITIVE UNDERSTANDING, 758

METACOMPREHENSION, 755

METAKNOWLEDGE, 1084

METALINGUISTIC AWARENESS: and context, 582–584; and definitions, 584–585; and word parts, 580–582

METAMEMORY, 755, 757

METAPHORS: of machine, 645; organicist, 645

METHODOLOGY, 1534

METROPOLITAN READINESS TEXT, 393

MEXICAN AMERICANS, 215, 251, 1646, 1649; identity development of, 224–226, 232, 233–234

MIAMI EDISON HIGH SCHOOL (FLORIDA), 1049*t*, 1053*t*

MICHIGAN: case study, 79, 80–84; Essential Goals and Objectives in Reading, 80, 81; literacy policy, 80, 81; Public Act 25 (PA 25) of 1990, 80–81

MICHIGAN READING ASSOCIATION (MRA), 80

MICROGENESIS, 167

MICROSTRUCTURE, 1274, 1277*t*, 1278–1280

MIDDLE CLASS, 279*n*2

MIDDLE SCHOOL STUDENTS, 1040–1082; Excellence in English project, 1046–1058; related research, 1042–1046; responses to young adult novels, 863–865

MIDDLE-READING GROUP CHILDREN: growth on WRAT, 346–348, 348*f*; observations of, 362–363

MIDDLETON, LYNN, 220

MINI MENTAL STATE EXAM (MMSE), 818, 820, 826

MINIMALISM, 1297

MINIMALISTS, 669, 669*t*, 670*t*

MINIMALLY TRAINED COLLEGE STUDENT VOLUNTEERS, 1083–1113

MISCONCEPTIONS: biomedical, 642; development of, 642–644; networks of, 652

MISCUES, 621–623; and comprehension, 623–628; examples, 621–622, 624–627; and language processes, 620–639; and oral reading, 636–637; reading, 623–628; schema-driven, 633–634; schema-forming, 633; and silent reading, 636–637

MMSE. *See* Mini Mental State Exam

MODELING, 1003–1004; hierarchical linear, 1562; reading system, 1223–1225; structural equation, 1562; of word recognition and reading connections, 1219–1243

MODELS: bottom-up, 1119; bottom-up/top-down, 1120; bottom-up/top-down + extended memory offline representation, 1120; bottom-up/top-down + sociocultural context, 1121; of literacy, 1116; of reading

and writing, 1115–1521; situation model, 1261; top-down, 1119–1120; waves of, 1118–1123

THE MODERN SCHOOL ACHIEVEMENT TESTS, LANGUAGE USAGE, 1618*f*

MONASTIC LEARNERS, 1598

MONETARY INCENTIVES, 891

MONITORING, 1017; comprehension, 755, 757–759, 759*f*, 760–761, 788; in think-aloud protocols, 664, 665*t*

MONOLOGUE, 296–298

MONOSYLLABIC WORDS, 380

MOODS, 137–138

MORAL IMPERATIVE, 76–77; in selection of research problems, 1547–1551

MORPHOLOGY, 582

MOTIVATION, 108–112, 931, 1402; changes, 1488, 1497; checking, 824; to engage students, 1491; external, 992, 1436–1438; extrinsic, 931, 942*t*, 942–943; intrinsic, 931, 942*t*, 942–943; perspective of, 1438–1439; problems with, 494; reader, 932, 938, 944, 946*t*, 945–946, 954–978, 992–993, 1467, 1469, 1488; and reading amount, 931–932, 942*t*, 942–943, 945–946, 946*t*; reading variables, 935, 935*t*; teacher, 957, 958*f*; text comprehension correlates, 933; in writing, 1407

MOTIVATION FOR READING QUESTIONNAIRE (MRQ), 938

MRA. *See* Michigan Reading Association

MRQ. *See* Motivation for Reading Questionnaire

MULTILITERACIES, 1587, 1594

MULTIPLE ANALOGIES, 646

MULTIPLE INTERCONNECTEDNESS, 649–652

MULTIPLE REPRESENTATIONS, 645–647, 652–653

MULTIPLE STANCES, 1463

MULTIPLE TEXTS, 936, 939–941, 940*t*

MULTIPLE VIEWPOINTS, 413

MULTIPLE-CUEING, 560–561

"MUSHROOM IN THE RAIN" LESSON, 1036–1039

MUTUAL TUNING-IN, 206

N

NAEP. *See* National Assessment of Educational Progress

NAEYC. *See* National Association for the Education of Young Children

NAMING, 144*n*7

NARRATIVES: joint construction of, 140; rating importance of segments of, 795

OBSERVATIONS, 360–364

OERI. *See* Office of Educational Research and Improvement

OFFICE OF ECONOMIC OPPORTUNITY, 9

OFFICE OF EDUCATIONAL RESEARCH AND IMPROVEMENT (OERI), 1566

ONE-SECOND-OF-READING MODEL, 1180–1181

ONLINE PROCESSING: construction of memory representation, 1244–1269; differences in, 671–676

ONSETS, 380; analogy to, 321–322

ONTOLOGY, 1533

OPEN COURT PROGRAM, 785–786

ORAL LANGUAGE, 146–162. *See also* language

ORAL READING: guided, 419; miscues and, 636–637

ORAL RECITATION LESSON (ORL) FORMAT, 440–441

ORAL REGISTER, 296–305

ORAL REGISTER MONOLOGUE TEXTS, 299–305

ORAL SOURCES, 697–699

ORAL-LIKE EMERGENT READERS, 287–288, 299–302

ORDER EFFECTS, 1258

ORDERING BEHAVIOR, 1128

ORGANISM–ENVIRONMENT CORRELATION, 482–483

ORGANIZATION, 1485, 1495; for programmatic research on reading comprehension, 1564–1568

ORGANIZATIONAL STRUCTURES, 813, 814*t*

ORL FORMAT. *See* oral recitation lesson format

OROZCO, DIANA, 220

ORTHOGRAPHIC KNOWLEDGE, 320, 1479–1480

ORTHOGRAPHIC PHASE, 381

ORTHOGRAPHIC PROCESSOR, 1224, 1225*f*, 1225–1230

ORTHOGRAPHY, 555–556

OVERREGULARIZATION, 644–645

OVERSIMPLIFICATION: avoidance of, 644–645; of complex and irregular structure, 642–643; in development of misconceptions, 642–644

P

PACESETTER, 1048

PAIRED-ASSOCIATE STAGE, 370

PARADIGMS, 1532; constructivist, 1620*f*; of cultural interaction, 1538–1539; and literacy inquiry, 1531–1539; usefulness of, 1535–1536

PARALLEL ACTIVITIES, 175, 176*t*

PARALLEL DISTRIBUTED PROCESSING (PDP), 1224

PARAPHRASES, 664; in think-aloud protocols, 665*t*

PARENT EDUCATION, 1638*t*, 1639*t*

PARENT INTERVIEW GUIDES, 880

PARENT INVOLVEMENT, 1636–1637, 1639*t*; example programs, 1651–1652; in literacy learning, 231

PARENT TRAINING PROGRAMS, 1651–1652

PARTIAL LETTERS, 373

PARTIAL-ALPHABETIC PHASE, 373–377, 414–415, 527; characteristic capabilities in, 373–374; instructional implications, 374–377

PARTNERSHIP FOR READING, 53

PARTNERSHIPS: community, 1544–1546; partners as advocates for learners, 1546–1547; resources, 1545; respect for partners, 1544

PASSAGE COMPREHENSION, 936, 939–941, 940*t*, 943

PATTERN RECOGNITION, 1150

PATTERN SYNTHESIZERS, 1164

PDP. *See* parallel distributed processing

PEABODY PICTURE VOCABULARY TEST–REVISED (PPVT-R), 248; scores for students in bilingual classrooms, 250*t*, 250–251; scores for students in English-language classrooms, 254–255, 255*t*; scores for students in Spanish-language classrooms, 248–249, 249*t*

PEARSON PRODUCT MOMENT CORRELATION COEFFICIENT, 919

PEER COACHING, 335, 337*t*, 338*t*

PEER COLLABORATION, 169–183

PEER CONFERENCES, 168

PEER CULTURE, 872

PEER GROUPS, 902–903

PEER INTERACTIONS, 163–186

PEER TUTORING, 165–169

PEER TUTORS, 164

PERCEIVED INTEREST QUESTIONNAIRE, 823

PERCEPTION, 1178*n*3

PERFORMANCE, 1393; high-stakes test scores, 75; recall, 600*t*, 1209–1210; requested, 819–820

PERFORMANCE GOAL ORIENTATION, 931

PERSONAL EXPERIENCES, 1017

PERSONAL GROWTH MODEL, 133

PERSONAL KNOWLEDGE, 1483–1484, 1494

PERSONAL MEANING-MAKING, 926

PERSONAL UNDERSTANDING OF LITERATURE: example responses, 919*t*, 919–924; levels of, 918*t*, 918–919, 924*t*, 924–925, 925*t*; reader stance and, 914–928

1386; and level of personal understanding, 924*t*, 924–925, 925*t*; levels of, 917*t*, 918–919; responses to literary works and, 919*t*, 919–920

motivation, 931–932, 942*t*, 942–943, 945–
946, 946*t*; and text comprehension, 929–
931, 939–941, 940*t*
THE READING ANXIETY SCALE, 1443
READING AS DIRECT REINFORCEMENT SCALE,
1443
READING AS ENJOYMENT SCALE, 1443
READING ASSESSMENT: instruction and, 345–352.
See also assessment
READING COMPREHENSION, 446–447, 529, 536,
1131–1132; attention in, 1140–1141, 1141*f*;
authentic outcomes, 746; automaticity and,
1141–1143; calibration of, 755, 757;
cognitive processes in, 1412–1413, 1414*f*;
context and, 461; control failures, 761, 763*t*;
development from words to worlds, 101–
106; with disability, 556–558; extension
through metacognition, 106–108; failures,
761, 762*t*–763*t*; fostering, 787–788, 790–
801; general context and, 1161–1163;
individual differences in, 1261–1263;
Landscape model of, 1244–1254; major
processes and structures in, 1184–1185,
1185*f*; major properties of, 1185–1187;
metacomprehension, 755; miscues and, 623–
628; monitoring, 755, 757, 759*f*, 759–761,
762*t*, 788; motivation for, 732–733; passage
comprehension, 936, 939–941, 940*t*, 943; vs.
perception, 1178*n*3; phonological translation
and, 1238; professional development in,
738–742; programmatic research on, 1564–
1568; with repeated reading, 424–430;
research agenda for, 720–754; research on,
1322–1324; research program development
strategies, 1557–1569; schema-theoretic
interpretation of, 594–598, 596*f*; semantic
memory and, 1140; specific comprehension
deficit (SCD), 533*t*, 536–542, 537*t*, 540*f*;
Stanford Achievement Test subtest, 1010*t*,
1012*t*, 1015–1016, 1029; strategies for,
723–724, 760, 788–802, 998–1002, 1017,
1018, 1018*t*; teacher education in, 738–742;
teaching, 724–725, 788–802, 1322–1324;
vocabulary instruction and, 726–730. *See
also* text comprehension
READING COMPREHENSION ASSESSMENT, 555,
743–749, 819; demands for, 744;
developmental issues, 748; developmental
sensitivity of, 746–747; key complaints,
743; minimum requirements for, 746–747;
what we already know about, 743–744; what
we need in the area of, 744–748

READING COMPREHENSION INSTRUCTION,
721–737, 788–802; direct, 737; effective,
733–735; explicit, 724–725, 737;
organization of practices, 735–736; for poor
comprehenders, 725–726, 735; proposed
areas for future research, 748–749; by
reciprocal teaching, 790–801, 797*f*;
sensitivity of, 747; time designated for, 734,
735; transactional, 998–1002; transfer tests
of, 801–802; what we already know about,
722–734; what we need to know about,
734–737
READING DIFFICULTY, 1443
READING DISABILITY, 518–542; 2003 Albert
Harris Award, 112; as behavioral concept,
491; biological influences on, 542–544;
broad cognitive profiles of, 536–542, 537*t*;
causes of, 503, 542–550; cognitive patterns
of, 530–535, 532*t*–533*t*; coping with, 502;
definition of, 486; educational definition of,
518–521; environmental influences on, 544–
549; future directions, 562–566; generalized
effects, 493; genetic influences on, 542–543;
patterns of, 530, 531*f*, 535–536;
reconceptualizing, 486–494; research
definition of, 518–521; specificity of, 492–
497; subtypes of, 491–492; traditional, 532*t*
THE READING EXCELLENCE ACT, 1581–1582
READING GROUP SCALE, 1443
READING GROUPS, 785–787, 1593; by classroom
type of interactions, 346–349; literature
circles, 1073; SAIL program, 1009
READING HISTORY, 471–472
READING INSTRUCTION, 550–562; beginning,
390–411; bilingual strategic, 221–223; to
enhance fluency, 722–723; strategies taught
during, 222*f*; texts of, 390–411; time
designated for, 734
READING INTERVENTION, 550–562
READING LEVELS, 472–473, 1093; in America
Reads program, 1095–1106, 1096*t*, 1099*t*,
1100*f*, 1102*t*, 1104*t*; and context effects on
word recognition, 460–470; and eye
movements, 459–460; of first and second
graders, 1095–1097, 1096*t*; indicators of,
1095–1097
READING MATERIALS, 1455–1456
READING MODELS, 1115–1521; benefits of,
1116–1117; current, 1150–1153; dual
coding theoretical model, 1329–1362;
Gough's model, 1150–1151, 1151*f*;
interactive model, 1163*f*, 1163–1171;

LaBerge–Samuels model, 1128–1147, 1152*f*, 1152–1153; Landscape model, 1244–1269, 1247*f*, 1248*t*; one-second-of-reading model, 1180–1181; problematic results, 1154–1163; Resonance model, 1265*n*9; theoretical, 1193–1215

READING PRACTICE, 471–472

READING PROBLEMS, 517–573; comprehensive approaches to, 559–562; diagnosis of, 1144–1147; normal, 765–769

READING PRODUCT, 1250–1254

READING RECOVERY (RR), 19, 560–561, 1083, 1091, 1653, 1654

READING RESEARCH, 1188–1193, 1536–1537; emergent premises, 55–59; future directions, 1214–1215; historical perspective on, 33–68; lessons, 55–59; method and data analysis, 1190–1192; results, 1192–1193, 1193*t*; texts used, 1188–1190, 1189*f*, 1190*t*. *See also* research; *specific topics*

READING SOURCE TEXTS, 1417–1418

READING SPAN (RSPAN), 818, 826

READING SYSTEM: modeling, 1223–1225; operation of, 1219–1221

READING TEXT. *See* text

READING WARS, 656

READING WITH PHONICS, 34

RECALL, 600*t*, 1209–1210; of everyday materials, 835–837; gist, 600, 600*t*; interest and, 823, 823*f*; of most important information, 832–833; organization of, 833–835; stimulated, 279*n*1; of stories in lessons, 1023–1028; structure strategy training and, 830–832, 831*t*; of text, 810–850; total, 825, 830–832; written, 1347

RECALL MAIN IDEAS, 825

RECEPTION-ORIENTED AUTHORIAL READING, 1381, 1382–1383

RECIPROCAL CAUSATION, 455, 478, 486–494

RECIPROCAL QUESTIONING STRATEGY (REQUEST), 1493

RECIPROCAL TEACHING: instructing comprehension-fostering by, 790–801, 797*f*; student-generated questions during, 792, 793*t*; student-generated summary statements during, 792, 794*t*

RECITATION, 440–441

RECODING, 1337, 1351; phonological, 473–477

RECOGNITION PHASE, 523*t*. *See also* word-recognition instruction

RECONDITIONING, 54

RECORDING INFORMATION, 695–697

REDUCTIVE BIASES, 642–644

REFERENTIAL COHERENCE, 1255

REFLECTION, 1412, 1420–1422

REFLECTIVE BEHAVIOR: in instruction, 1497; scaffolding, 149–151

REGISTERS, 281, 282–283; code switching from oral to literate register in monologue, 296–305; literate, 281–312; literate register text, 281; preschooler development of ownership of, 281–312

REINFORCEMENT, 1443

REINSTATEMENT OF INFORMATION, 666–668, 667*t*

REMEDIAL PRACTICES, 412–453

REMEDIATION, 559–562

REMEMBERING: schema-based processes in, 598–599. *See also* memory; recall

REPEATED READING: assisted vs. unassisted, 436–438; comprehension with, 430; difficulty of passages read, 424–430; effects on fluency and comprehension, 424–430; findings, 430; methods of, 446, 1145–1147; rereading, 444–445; studies on, 421, 421*t*, 424, 425*t*–429*t*; technique for, 1146; unassisted, 422–424

REPRESENTATIONS: cognition and, 1271–1272; of informational text, 660–683; instructional, 1466, 1495; knowledge, 1289–1290, 1349; levels of, 1275–1278; memory, 1244–1269, 1253*f*, 1258–1261; mental, 1254, 1263–1264, 1339; propositional level of, 1272; of text, 1272–1278, 1464; of writer's persona, 1418

REQUEST. *See* Reciprocal Questioning Strategy

REQUESTS FOR APPLICATIONS (RFAs), 1564–1565

REREADING, 444–445, 1017, 1018

RESEARCH: as accumulating information, 692–694; adolescent literacy practices and, 908–909; agenda for, 1523–1666; approaches to defining progress in, 1537; assisted-reading studies, 431, 432*t*–433*t*; balanced or eclectic approach, 1531; on bilingual Latina/o students, 217–218; on children's word learning, 393–400; cognitive, 1244–1246; on collaborative uses of reading and writing, 684; communicating findings of, 1553–1554; communities of inquiry, 1544–1547; communities of researchers, 1561; on contexts, 855–856; criteria for, 1557; current questions, 322–323; data analysis procedures, 223–224;

RULES, 803; control of, 803–804
RUSSIAN, 259

S

SAIL PROGRAM. *See* Students Achieving
Independent Learning program
SCAFFOLDING, 95, 150, 1072; ideational, 598; of
reflective behavior, 149–151
SCHEMA THEORY, 43, 101–102, 607–619; and
automaticity and comprehension, 1141–
1143; and classroom instruction, 604–605;
and design of materials, 604–605; evidence
for, 599–604
SCHEMA-DRIVEN MISCUES, 633–634
SCHEMA-FORMING MISCUES, 633
SCHEMAS, 594–606, 1260, 1371; acquisition of,
607–619; activation of, 617, 1260–1261;
algebraic, 1320–1322; assembly of, 649; as
filter, 1287; functional properties of, 1475–
1476; functions of, 608, 617; "of the
moment," 655; prepackaged, 643; purpose-
sensitive, 1476; retrieval of, 652–653; self-
schema, 959–961
SCHOOL READINESS, 1636–1637, 1638*t*
SCHOOL REFORM, 738–739
SCHOOL SUCCESS, 1636–1637, 1638*t*–1639*t*
SCHOOLS: America Reads study, 1086;
comprehensive efforts for children at risk,
1654; diverse, 1636–1666; Excellence in
English project, 1048–1051, 1049*t*–1051*t*;
formal schooling, 546–549; higher-
performing, 1078; historically, 6; in-school
reading, 481; reading experiences in, 784–
788. *See also specific schools*
SCHOOLS IT 2000, 1580
SCIENTIFIC CONCEPTS, 47
SCIENTIFIC MEASUREMENT, 1614, 1616*f*
SCIENTIFIC RESEARCH, 1543
SCIENTIFIC STUDIES OF READING, 6
SCOILNET, 1580
SCORE CYBERGUIDES, 1593
SCRIPTS, 1260
SEA OF TALK, 146–162. *See also* sea of voices
SEA OF VOICES, 157–160; solidification of,
147–154; writing and, 146–162
SEARCHING FOR COGNATES STRATEGY, 232
SEARS AND ROEBUCK, 275
SECOND GRADERS, 1095–1097, 1096*t*
SECOND TESTING, 490
SECONDARY-LEVEL PROGRAMS: research,
1042–1046
SECOND-LANGUAGE LEARNERS, 252–254, 253*f*
SECOND-LANGUAGE LITERACY, 261

SEEGER, PETE, 158
SELECTION, 1282
SELECTIVE ATTENTION, 1368–1369
SELECTIVE-CUE STAGE, 370
SELECTIVITY, 1129–1130
SELF: developing, 957, 959–964, 973;
experiential, 963
SELF-ASSESSMENT, 1629
SELF-CONCEPT, 1447–1448; for reading,
933–934
SELF-CONTROL TRAINING, 804
SELF-DIRECTED READING–WRITING–RESEARCH
PROCESSES, 684, 685–718, 691*t*
SELF-EFFICACY, 961–962; and text
comprehension, 933–934
SELF-EXPLANATIONS, 664; in think-aloud
protocols, 665*t*
SELF-KNOWLEDGE, 963–964
SELF-MANAGEMENT, 803
SELF-REGULATED COMPREHENSION, 775–776;
cognitive–metacognitive model of, 757–764;
components of, 758–761; encouraging,
769–772; in operation, 761–764;
overcoming constraints on, 774–775; during
reading, 755–779; research directions, 772–
774
SELF-REGULATION, 764–774
SELF-REGULATORY SPEECH, 148
SELF-REGULATORY TALK, 148, 149–150
SELF-SCHEMA, 959–961
SELF-TEACHING HYPOTHESIS, 356
SELF-UNDERSTANDING, 992
SELF-WORTH, 961–962
SEM. *See* structural equation modeling
SEMANTIC KNOWLEDGE, 1488, 1496
SEMANTIC MEMORY, 1140, 1144, 1152–1153
SEMANTIC-LEVEL KNOWLEDGE, 1174
SEMANTICS: inner, 1350; Latent Semantic
Analysis (LSA), 1283*t*, 1289–1293;
perception of syntax and, 1160–1161;
perception of words and, 1158–1160, 1159*t*
SENSE MAKING, 319–321. *See also* meaning
construction
SENSE MODALITIES, 1330–1331, 1331*t*
SENTENCE WRAP-UP, 1205–1207
SENTENCES: constructing meaning of, 1140–
1141, 1141*f*; TPWSGWTAU (The Place
Where Sentences Go When They Are
Understood), 1150
SEPARATED INSTRUCTION, 1058–1062, 1061*t*
SES. *See* socioeconomic status

SPECIFIC WORD-RECOGNITION DEFICIT (SWRD), 530, 532*t*, 536; broad cognitive profile of, 536–538, 537*t*

SPECIFICITY HYPOTHESIS, 492–494; developmental version of, 494–497

SPEECH: message level of, 1423; self-regulatory, 149–150; volitional, 148

SPEED, 1597; of lexical access, 1142

SPELLING: classroom activities, 329–331, 330*t*, 331*t*, 332–335, 334*t*, 337*t*, 338*t*, 344*t*, 344–345; invented, 375; temporary, 375

SPELLING-SOUND STAGE, 377–378

SPIEGEL, DIXIE LEE, 1089–1090

SPOKEN LANGUAGE, 187–209

SPONTANEOUS CONCEPTS, 47

SPSS^X SOFTWARE, 293

SSSR. *See* Society for the Scientific Study of Reading

STAGE MODEL, 444

STANCE: aesthetic, 914, 992, 1372, 1373–1374, 1396*n*2; effects of, 914–928; efferent, 914, 992, 1372–1373, 1396*n*2; efferent–aesthetic continuum of, 1372, 1374–1376, 1375*f*, 1386; instructional, 1491; multiple stances, 1463; reader's, 915–925, 1372, 1467, 1471–1472; teacher's, 967–968; writer's, 1379–1380

STANDARDIZED ACHIEVEMENT TEST (SAT), 441

STANDARDIZED ASSESSMENTS, 1619; SAIL vs. non-SAIL scores, 1009, 1010*t*, 1012*t*, 1015–1016; spring performance, 1028–1029

STANDARDS FOR THE ENGLISH LANGUAGE ARTS, 1582

"THE STANDARDS SITE," 1579

STANFORD ACHIEVEMENT TEST: Reading Comprehension subtest, 1009, 1010*t*, 1012*t*, 1015–1016, 1029; Word Skills subtest, 1009, 1010*t*, 1012*t*, 1015–1016

STATUS: low-status books, 900–902; socioeconomic status, 545, 547, 944, 1643–1646, 1658–1659

STAYING HOME, 201–204

STIMULATED RECALL, 279*n*1

STIMULUS ONSET ASYNCHRONY (SOA), 1298

STORY GRAMMAR, 1480–1481

STORY LESSONS, 1011–1014; spring, 1022–1028; student recall of stories in, 1023–1028; teaching, 1022–1023

STORYBOOK READING: attention-to-pictures, 287–288; attention-to-print, 288; conventional, 304–305; no-story, 287–288; no-story emergent readers, 298–299; oral-like, 287–288; oral-like emergent readers, 299–302; print-related refusal, 288; written-like, 287–288; written-like emergent readers, 302–304

STORYBOOK READING CATEGORIES, 287, 288–289

STORYTELLING, 1014

STRATEGIC EDUCATION RESEARCH PARTNERSHIP REPORT (NATIONAL RESEARCH COUNCIL), 1322

STRATEGIC KNOWLEDGE, 1596

STRATEGIC MEMORY (STM) TASK DEFICITS, 496

STRATEGIC READING, 524*t*, 528, 531*f*

STRATEGIC READING INSTRUCTION: bilingual, 221–223; enabling strategies, 1044–1045, 1059*t*, 1061*t*, 1070–1072; transactional, 998–1039

STRATEGIES INTERVIEWS, 1011, 1012*t*; examples, 1019–1022; fall–spring, 1016–1022, 1018*t*; SAIL program, 1019–1021

STRATEGIES-IMBALANCED READING, 288

STRATEGY CONSTRUCTING, 1495

STRATEGY SWITCH HYPOTHESIS, 811–812

STRINGFIELD, KRISTIN, 157

STRUCTURAL EQUATION MODELING (SEM), 1562

STRUCTURAL KNOWLEDGE, 1186

STRUCTURE STRATEGY: consistent use of, 834*t*, 834–835; effects on recall of text, 810–850; operational levels or stages, 815, 815*t*

STRUCTURE STRATEGY TRAINING, 813, 818–837; characteristics prior to, 826–828, 827*t*; diagrams for, 821–822, 822*f*; effects of, 837–840; hypothetical benefits, 817; materials for, 818–820; and organization of recall, 833–835; reading changes after, 828–830, 829*t*; and recall of everyday materials, 835–837; and recall of most important information, 832–833; sample program materials, 847–850; self-appraisal of, 826–830; and total recall, 830–832, 831*t*

STRUCTUREDNESS, 48–49

STRUCTURES: macrostructure, 1274, 1276*t*, 1280–1284, 1291–1294; microstructure, 1274, 1277*t*, 1278–1280; organizational, 813, 814*t*

STUDENT DISCOURSE: extended, 223

STUDENT INTERVIEWS, 221

STUDENT-GENERATED QUESTIONS, 792, 793*t*

STUDENT-GENERATED SUMMARY STATEMENTS, 792, 794*t*

STUDENTS: advocates for, 1546–1547; bilingual, 217–218, 229, 231–234, 240–267, 245*f*,

581–582, 585, 729–730; consideration of audience, 703–705, 704*f*; data sources for, 1011–1016, 1012*t*; dialogic interactions with, 861–862; efferent–aesthetic repertory of, 1390–1391; high school, 1040–1082; Latina/o, 210–239, 1652; middle school, 863–865, 1040–1082; minimally trained college student volunteers, 1083–1113; personal understanding of literature, 914–928; reader stance of, 914–928; research approach, 713; research projects, materials for, 709–710; research strategies used by, 691, 691*t*; research task impressions, 691, 691*t*, 692–705; research topics for, 715–716; SAIL program, 1008–1009; seventh-grade, 796, 798*t*; task impressions, 691, 691*t*, 692–705, 707–709; 10th-grade, 945–946, 946*t*; unconventional interpretations of literature, 268–280; young at-risk children, 1083–1113. *See also* adolescents; children; readers

STUDENTS ACHIEVING INDEPENDENT LEARNING (SAIL) PROGRAM, 112, 1002–1006, 1029–1032; example story recall, 1024–1025; example strategies interview, 1019–1021; instruction in groups, 1005; "Mushroom in the Rain" lessons, 1036–1037; reading groups, 1009; spring standardized test performance, 1028–1029; Stanford Achievement Test subtest scores, 1009, 1010*t*, 1012*t*, 1015–1016; students, 1008–1009; teachers, 1006–1008

SUBJECT SELECTION, 488–491

SUBJECTIVE NORMS, 1436

SUBJECTIVITY, 910*n*7

SUBSTITUTING, 1017, 1018

SUCCESS FOR ALL (SFA) PROGRAM, 23, 25, 559–560, 1655, 1656, 1658; *Éxito Para Todos* (Spanish-language version), 258, 1655

SUFFIXES, 1233–1235

SUMMARIES, 1291–1294

SUMMARIZING, 599, 789, 795, 1017

SUMMARY MAIN IDEAS, 825

SUMMARY QUALITY, 825

SUMMARY STATEMENTS, 792, 794*t*

SUMMARY STREET, 1293, 1294

SUPERVISORS: America Reads program, 1087, 1088; training, 1091–1092

SURFACE STRUCTURE, 1285*f*

SURFACE-LEVEL MEMORY, 1272

SUSTAINABILITY, 1566–1568

SWEDISH, 526

SWEET VALLEY HIGH SERIES, 900, 901

SWITZERLAND, 1625

SWRD. *See* specific word-recognition deficit

SYLLABLES, 1228–1229

SYMBOLIC CONSTRUCTION, 135

SYMBOLS: in adaptation, 204–207; processing of, 1186–1187

SYNTACTIC AWARENESS TRAINING, 583

SYNTACTIC KNOWLEDGE, 1174

SYNTAGMATIC SEQUENCES, 138

SYNTAX: perception of, 1160–1161; perception of words and, 1157–1158

SYNTHETIC PHONICS, 321

T

TALENT DEVELOPMENT, 1566

TALK: adolescent, 899–903; after-school, 893–899; child, 147–149; functions of, 147–149; sea of, 146–162; self-regulatory, 148, 149–150; teacher, 277, 278; volitional, 148; of young children, 147–149. *See also* discussion

TALK STORIES, 1473–1474, 1492, 1650

TASK ENVIRONMENT, 1401*f*, 1401–1402, 1404–1406

TASK IMPRESSIONS, 707–709

TASK MEANINGS, 1466, 1501

TASK SCHEMAS, 1424

TASK VALUES, 966–967

TASK-ENGAGEMENT RESOURCES, 957, 968–969, 973–974

TASS. *See* Texas Assessment of Academic Skills

TAVERNA, PATTY, 1593

TE KETE IPURANGI, 1581

TEACHER EXECUTIVE AND MONITOR, 1466

TEACHER EXPRESSION, 1495–1496

TEACHER INTERVIEWS, 221

TEACHER TALK, 277, 278

TEACHERS, 1466, 1489–1497, 1490*f*; achievement goals, 965–966; beating-the-odds, 112–113; as collaborators, 155; education in reading comprehension, 738–742; effective, 733–735, 994; Excellence in English project, 1051–1052, 1053*t*–1054*t*; expectations of, 992–993; importance of, 1599; influential, 954, 955–969, 972–973, 979–997, 983*f*; as interrogators, 980; Joan of Arc teachers, 19; knowledge use and control, 1466; of Latina/o students, 215–216; as mentioners, 980; minimally trained college student volunteers, 1083–1113; as models of reading strategies, 784–785, 860–861; motivation of, 957, 958*f*; overview of, 1464–1467; preparation of, 740–741; prior knowledge and beliefs of, 1491–1494; professional development for, 741–742; SAIL program, 1006–1008; sociocultural values and beliefs of, 967; stance of, 967–968; study participants, 220

TEACHING: in 21st century, 5–32; abilities that underlie successful reading, 1456; adaptive flexibility in, 654–659; aesthetic strategies, 926; beliefs of influential teachers about, 983*f*; conversation about, 5–32; effectiveness of, 979–981, 994–995; evaluation of, 1629; Excellence in English project, 1046–1080; frontal, 980; future directions, 20–28; history of, 5–20; mastery of, 965; methods of, 1393–1394; of middle and high school students, 1040–1082; new literacies issues, 1605–1606; quality of, 74, 74*f*, 77, 78*f*; reader-response method, 1394; of reading comprehension, 724–725, 788–802, 1322–1324; settings for, 788–802; reciprocal, 790–801; responsive, 954–978; social relationship of, 163–164; Socratic, 785; of story lessons, 1022–1023; of strategies, 1493; tactics used by outstanding teachers, 785; theoretical framework for, 1041–1042; of think-aloud procedures, 223; transactional theory and, 1387–1391; what should be taught, 1602–1605

TECHNOLOGICAL LITERACY, 1585
TECHNOLOGY: new literacies of, 1570–1613
TECHNOLOGY INTEGRATION INITIATIVE, 1580
TELD. *See* Test of Early Language Development
TELECOMMUNICATIONS ACT, 1582
TELEGRAPHIC LANGUAGE, 252
TELEVISION: closed-caption, 436
TEMPORARY SPELLINGS, 375
10TH-GRADE STUDENTS, 945–946, 946*t*
TEST DE VOCABULARIO EN IMÁGENES PEABODY (TVIP), 248; scores for students in bilingual classrooms, 250*t*, 250–251; scores for students in Spanish-language classrooms, 248–249, 249*t*
TEST OF EARLY LANGUAGE DEVELOPMENT (TELD), 285
TEST OF ENGLISH AS A FOREIGN LANGUAGE (TOEFL), 578

TEST PREPARATION, 1059*t*; approaches to, 1044, 1061*t*, 1062–1066
TEST SCORES, 75
TESTING: accountability, 1622–1624; classroom, 1618*f*; instruction and, 1615*f*; standard, 1618*f*; traditional, 1615*f. See also* assessment
TEXAS, 71, 396, 400, 403, 1648; Excellence in English project, 1048, 1050*t*–1051*t*, 1053*t*–1054*t*; LEP students, 264*n*2
TEXAS ASSESSMENT OF ACADEMIC SKILLS (TASS), 75
TEXT, 819–820, 1466; analysis in think-alouds, 663–664; assimilation of, 598; attitude toward, 1470–1471; attributes of, 1084; for beginning reading instruction, 390–411; bilingual, bicultural, and biliterate processors of, 231–234; and classroom content, 969–970, 980*f*, 990, 991*f*; and classroom context, 1497–1503, 1498*f*; cognitive representations of, 660–661; coherent, 1309–1312; as cultural worlds, 857–858; culturally relevant, 223; deconstruction of, 1384; difficulty of, 445–446; discussion of, 344*t*, 344–345, 894–895, 1488; engagement with, 405; engagingness of, 405–406; features of, 400–406; first books, 406–407; genres, 731–732; grammar/punctuation activities, 330*t*, 332–335, 333*t*, 334*t*, 337*t*, 338*t*, 340, 341, 341*t*, 342*t*; high-frequency, 391–392; informational, 660–683; interpretation of, 1488, 1496; learning from, 1305–1316; literary, 1363; literate register, 281; literature-based, 391–392; matching readers and, 1315–1316; meanings of, 1501; memory for, 1244–1254; metamemory for, 755, 757; nonlinear, 50; nonliterary, 1363; overview of, 1464–1467; phonics, 391–392; predictable, 391–392; production of, 1412, 1422–1424; and reading development, 391–393; reading for evaluation of, 1412–1413, 1415*f*; reading in full-alphabet phase, 379; recall of, 810–850; relating prior knowledge or personal experiences to, 1017; research on, 400–406, 853; resources for processing, 958*f*; response to, 1346–1348; selection of, 894–895; signaling in, 811–812, 812*f*; simplifying, 610, 618; sociocultural perspectives on, 856–863; strategies for processing, 1480–1481; student interpretations of, 268–280; of suitable

difficulty, 1456; top-level structure of, 821–822, 822*f*, 825–826, 833–834; transacting with, 1369–1371; as type of meaning, 1466; types of, 391–393; writing about, 1380–1381. *See also* literature

TEXT COMPREHENSION, 929–953; classification of inferences in, 1294–1297, 1295*t*; cognitive processes in reading for, 1412–1413, 1414*f*; construction–integration model of, 1270–1328; motivational correlates, 933; predictors of, 929–953, 935*t*, 940*t*, 944*t*, 946*t*; reading amount and, 929–931, 939–941, 940*t*; self-efficacy and, 933–934. *See also* reading comprehension

TEXT REPRESENTATIONS, 1464, 1486–1487; levels of, 1272–1278; mental, 1339; as spatial display, 1419

TEXT UNITS, 1283

TEXTBASE, 1261, 1274, 1285*f*

TEXT-FOCUSED PROCESSING, 669, 669*t*, 670*t*, 674–676

TEXT-ROLE EFFECTS, 1210

THEORETICAL MODEL, 1193–1215

THEORETICAL ORIENTATION TO READING PROFILE (TORP), 1007

THEORIES OF READING, 1213–1214

THINK-ALOUD TASKS, 1012*t*; examples, 1026, 1027; measures of, 1014–1015; spring, 1026–1028

THINK-ALOUDS, 221; analyses and results, 663–671; events and reinstatements in, 667–668; evidence of building representations of informational text in, 660–683; excerpts, 673*t*, 675*t*, 676*t*; experimental texts for, 682, 683; illustrative of differences in online processing, 671–676; methodology of, 662; strategies tried by low-reading group children in, 350, 351*t*; teaching, 223; text analysis in, 663–664; types of events in, 664–666, 665*t*

THINKING ALOUD, 1017

THINKING-LEVEL DESCRIPTORS, 986

THIRD INTERNATIONAL MATH & SCIENCE STUDY (TIMSS) VIDEOTAPE CLASSROOM STUDY, 738

THORNDIKE, E.L., 6

TIME SPENT READING, 883, 887*f*

TIMSS STUDY. *See* Third International Math & Science Study Videotape Classroom Study

TITLE VII, 264*n*2

TITLE-RECOGNITION TEST (TRT), 419, 930

TOEFL. *See* Test of English as a Foreign Language

TOKENS, 292

"TOP-DOWN" PROCESSING, 643

TOP-LEVEL STRUCTURE: explanation of, 821–822, 822*f*; scoring, 825–826, 833–834

TORP. *See* Theoretical Orientation to Reading Profile

TOTAL RECALL: scoring, 825; structure strategy training and, 830–832, 831*t*; tests of hypotheses, 830

TOTAL WORDS, 401–402

TPWSGWTAU (THE PLACE WHERE SENTENCES GO WHEN THEY ARE UNDERSTOOD), 1150

TRACKTON, 95, 188–191, 1473; children of, 187–209; daily life in, 198; language development patterns in, 203; language socialization in, 191–194, 206

TRADITIONAL QUANTITATIVE RESEARCH, 1450–1453

TRAINING: awareness, 804; cognitive-skills, 804–805; of college students as tutors, 1085; explicitness of, 804, 804*f*; interest-list strategy, 823*f*, 823–824; self-control, 804; skills, 804; structure strategy, 813, 817, 821–823, 822*f*; syntactic awareness, 583; tutor and supervisor, 1091–1092

TRAINING STUDIES: and multiple determinants, 802–805; theoretical and practice status of, 805–806

TRANSACTIONAL PARADIGM, 1364–1369; technology and literacy, 1593–1594

TRANSACTIONAL PSYCHOLOGY, 1371

TRANSACTIONAL STRATEGIES INSTRUCTION, 998–1002, 1006–1032; common components of, 1000–1001; examples, 1003, 1004–1005; previous studies of, 1000; quasi-experimental validation of, 998–1039; spring think-aloud analysis, 1026–1028; summary of lessons, 1036–1039

TRANSACTIONAL THEORY, 1396*n*2; implications for research, 1391–1396; implications for teaching, 1387–1391; of reading and writing, 1363–1398

TRANSACTIONS, 1364–1365; linguistic, 1367–1368; with text, 1369–1371; writing, 1378–1379

TRANSFER EFFECTS, 799, 799*f*

TRANSFER OF KNOWLEDGE, 1627–1628; passive transmission, 643–644

TRANSFER PROBLEMS, 1318

for accuracy, 407; pre-alphabetic reading of, 370–371; processing of, 1592; reading, 366–369; reading in isolation, 1094, 1098–1100, 1099*t*, 1101*f*, 1101–1102, 1102*t*, 1103–1106, 1104*t*; second-tier vs. first-tier words, 557–558; sense of, 1366; singletons, 402; sounding out, 1018; strategies for attacking, 1018; total, 401–402; unique, 401–402

WORDS TAUGHT, 349–350, 350*t*

WORKING MEMORY, 1186–1187, 1402; components of, 1302; in comprehension, 1301–1305; long-term, 1301–1305; measurement of, 818; in writing, 1406–1411

WORKSHOPS, 88

WORLD KNOWLEDGE, 1483–1484, 1494

WORLD VIEWS, 642

WRAT. *See* Wide Range Achievement Test

WRIGHT GROUP BOOKS, 1091

WRITE TO READ PROGRAM (IBM), 23

WRITERS: inner gauge of, 1382; intention of, 1384

WRITER'S PERSONA, 1418

WRITER'S STANCE, 1379–1380

WRITING: Achievement Awards in Writing competition, 1042; affective responses in, 1410–1411; classroom activities, 329–335, 330*t*, 331*t*, 333*t*, 334*t*, 337*t*, 338*t*, 340, 341, 341*t*, 342*t*, 344*t*, 344–345; cognition and affect in, 1399–1430; collaborative uses of, 684; Excellence in English project, 1046–1058; extensive practice, 1425–1426; goals of, 1408; Hayes–Flower model of, 1400*f*,

1400–1403, 1401*f*, 1403*f*, 1426–1427; individual aspects of, 1406–1411; methods of, 1409–1410; models of, 1115–1521; motivation in, 1407–1408; oral language in, around, and about, 146–162; process of, 1378–1381; and reading, 307–308, 1387–1388; reading as central process in, 1417–1419; reading to understand the task, 1419; and sea of voices, 146–162; self-directed, 684–719; in social change, 187–209; teaching middle and high school students, 1040–1082; about texts, 1380–1381; transactional theory of, 1363–1398; Zelda Glazer/Dade County Writing Project, 1048

WRITING CONFERENCES, 150

WRITING TRANSACTION, 1378–1379

WRITTEN RECALL, 1347

WRITTEN RESPONSE, 1488, 1496

WRITTEN-LIKE EMERGENT READERS, 287–288, 302–304; example, 302–304

Y

YOUNG ADULT NOVELS: contextualizing, 864; middle school student responses to, 863–865

YOUNG BILINGUAL CHILDREN, 245, 245*f*

YOUNG CHILDREN: at-risk, 1083–1113; bilingual, 240–267; talk of, 147–149

Z

ZELDA GLAZER/DADE COUNTY WRITING PROJECT, 1048

ZONE OF LEARNING, 1316

ZONE OF PROXIMAL DEVELOPMENT, 95, 150, 164, 783